THE
WORLD BOOK
ENCYCLOPEDIA

P

Volume 15

FIELD ENTERPRISES EDUCATIONAL CORPORATION
CHICAGO LONDON ROME SYDNEY TORONTO

THE WORLD BOOK ENCYCLOPEDIA

COPYRIGHT © 1970, U.S.A.

by FIELD ENTERPRISES EDUCATIONAL CORPORATION

Copyright not claimed on pages 29 to 76

All rights reserved. This volume may not be reproduced in whole or in part in any form without written permission from the publishers.

"WORLD BOOK" Reg. U.S. Pat. Off.   Marca Registrada

Copyright © 1969, 1968, 1967, 1966, 1965, 1964, 1963, 1962, 1961, 1960, 1959, 1958, 1957 by Field Enterprises Educational Corporation. Copyright © 1957, 1956, 1955, 1954, 1953, 1952, 1951, 1950, 1949, 1948 by Field Enterprises, Inc. Copyright 1948, 1947, 1946, 1945, 1944, 1943, 1942, 1941, 1940, 1939, 1938 by The Quarrie Corporation. Copyright 1937, 1936, 1935, 1934, 1933, 1931, 1930, 1929 by W. F. Quarrie & Company. THE WORLD BOOK, Copyright 1928, 1927, 1926, 1925, 1923, 1922, 1921, 1919, 1918, 1917 by W. F. Quarrie & Company. Copyrights renewed 1969, 1968, 1967, 1966, 1965, 1964, 1963, 1962, 1961, 1960, 1958 by Field Enterprises Educational Corporation. Copyrights renewed 1957, 1956, 1955, 1954, 1953, 1952, 1950 by Field Enterprises, Inc.

International Copyright © 1970, 1969, 1968, 1967, 1966, 1965, 1964, 1963, 1962, 1961, 1960, 1959, 1958, 1957 by Field Enterprises Educational Corporation. International Copyright © 1957, 1956, 1955, 1954, 1953, 1952, 1951, 1950, 1949, 1948 by Field Enterprises, Inc. International Copyright 1948, 1947 by The Quarrie Corporation.

Printed in the United States of America

LIBRARY OF CONGRESS CATALOG CARD NUMBER 70-79247

Pp

P is the 16th letter of our alphabet. It was also a letter in the alphabet used by the Semites, who once lived in Syria and Palestine. They named it *pe*, their word for *mouth*, and adapted an Egyptian *hieroglyphic*, or picture symbol, for *mouth* to represent it. The ancient Greeks took the letter into their own alphabet and called it *pi*. When the Romans adopted the Greek alphabet, they developed the letter form that we use today. See ALPHABET.

Uses. *P* or *p* is about the 18th most frequently used letter in books, newspapers, and other printed material in English. In chemistry, *P* stands for *phosphorus*. *P* is used as an abbreviation for *post*, as in *P.S.* for *postscript*. Post comes from the Latin word for *after*, and we also use it in *P.M.*, or *post meridiem*, for afternoon. In bibliographies, *p* stands for *page;* in money, *p* stands for *penny* and for *peso*, a unit of currency in Spanish-speaking countries. In grammar, *p* represents *past* and *participle*. In music, it stands for *piano*, an Italian word that means *softly*.

Pronunciation. In English, a person pronounces *p* by closing his lips and his velum, or soft palate, and temporarily stopping his breath passage. The vocal cords are apart, and do not vibrate. The typical sound of *p* occurs in such words as *pie* and *pen*. The combination *ph* is often sounded as *f* in such words as *physics* and *photograph*. *P* is silent in such words as *pneumonia* and *raspberry*. The letter has always had much the same sound. See PRONUNCIATION.   I. J. GELB and J. M. WELLS

The 16th letter took its shape from an ancient Egyptian symbol for mouth. Its sound, as we use it today, is much the same as that used by the Greeks and Romans.

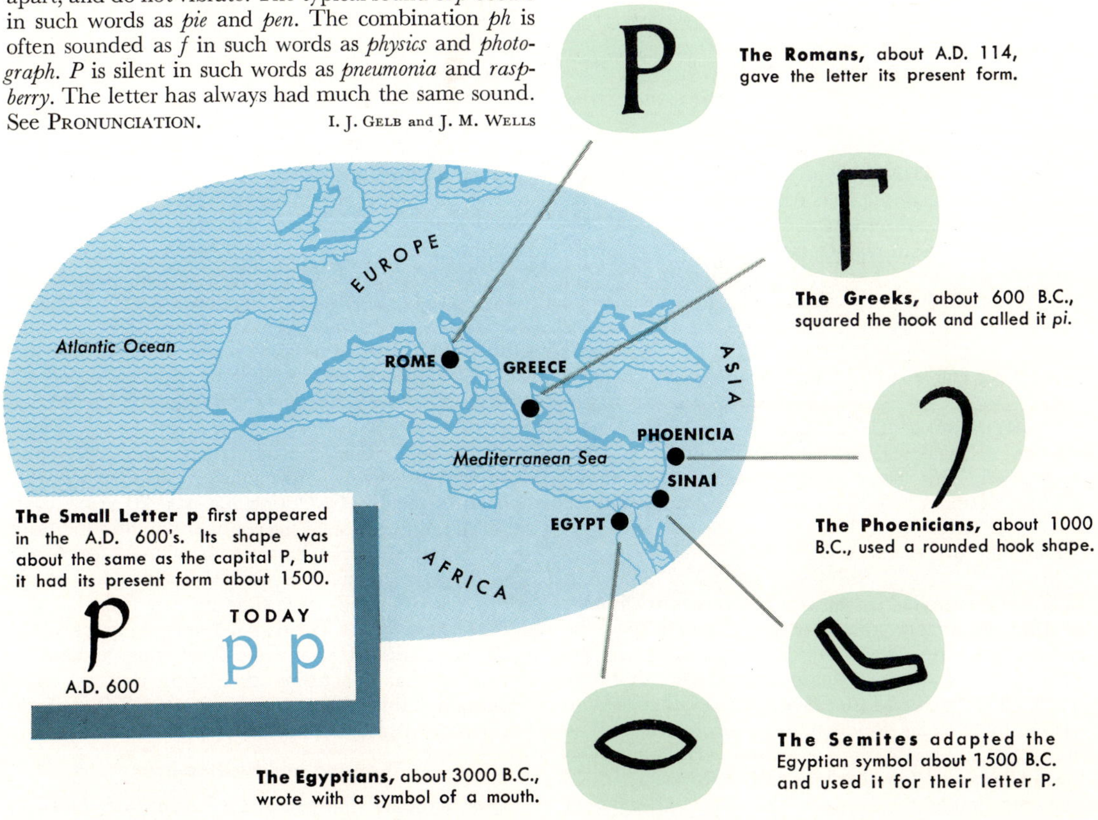

The Romans, about A.D. 114, gave the letter its present form.

The Greeks, about 600 B.C., squared the hook and called it *pi*.

The Phoenicians, about 1000 B.C., used a rounded hook shape.

EUROPE

Atlantic Ocean

ROME

GREECE

PHOENICIA

SINAI

ASIA

Mediterranean Sea

EGYPT

AFRICA

The Small Letter p first appeared in the A.D. 600's. Its shape was about the same as the capital P, but it had its present form about 1500.

A.D. 600

TODAY

p p

The Semites adapted the Egyptian symbol about 1500 B.C. and used it for their letter P.

The Egyptians, about 3000 B.C., wrote with a symbol of a mouth.

PACA, *PAY kuh,* **WILLIAM** (1740-1799), a Maryland signer of the Declaration of Independence, took part in many American political movements from 1771 until his death. He served in the Continental Congress from 1774 to 1779, and was governor of Maryland from 1782 to 1785. President George Washington appointed him judge of the Court for Maryland in 1789, a post he held until death. Born near Abingdon, Md., he attended what is now the University of Pennsylvania, and studied law at Annapolis and in London.   RICHARD B. MORRIS

PACE. See HORSE (Gaits).

PACE COLLEGE is a privately controlled school located in New York City. Courses in liberal arts, accounting, business administration and teacher education lead to B.A., B.B.A., and M.B.A. degrees. Pace was founded in 1906. For enrollment, see UNIVERSITIES AND COLLEGES (table).

PACELLI, EUGENIO. See PIUS (XII).

PACHER, MICHAEL. See SCULPTURE (Medieval; color picture: St. Wolfgang's Altar).

PACHMANN, *PAHK mun,* **VLADIMIR DE** (1848-1933), was a Russian pianist. He won fame for his sensitive interpretations of the music of Frédéric Chopin, arfd for his odd habit of talking to his audiences as he played. Pachmann made his debut in Odessa, his birthplace, in 1869. Dissatisfied, he retired for 10 years of intensive study before finally beginning his concert career.   ROBERT U. NELSON

PACHYDERM, *PACK ih durm,* is one of the *pachydermata,* a zoological classification which has been abandoned. This group included such noncud-chewing, hoofed mammals as the elephant, hippopotamus, and rhinoceros.

PACIFIC, UNIVERSITY OF THE, is a privately controlled coeducational liberal arts school at Stockton, Calif. It is controlled by the United Methodist Church. In 1851, it became the state's first university to be chartered. Besides liberal arts, it has schools of music, education, pharmacy, engineering, and graduate studies. The Pacific Marine Station is at Dillon Beach. Also notable is the Summer Repertory Theatre. The university was originally chartered as California Wesleyan University. For enrollment, see UNIVERSITIES AND COLLEGES (table).   ALICE SAECKER

PACIFIC COAST STATES of Washington, Oregon, and California lie along the Pacific Ocean. They make up a region that extends about 1,300 miles from Canada to Mexico, stretching inland between 150 and 350 miles. The Pacific Coast States have an area of 323,866 square miles, or about a tenth of the United States. About 1 of every 9 persons in the nation lives in these three states.

Juan Rodríguez Cabrillo, a Portuguese navigator, was probably the first white man to see the region. He landed at San Diego Bay in 1542. Several Spanish explorers visited the coast during the 1600's and 1700's, and Spain began to establish missions in the region in 1769. Spanish architecture and place names are still common. Fur traders from Russia, Great Britain, and the United States built trading posts along the northern Pacific Coast in the early 1800's. Britain disputed Spain's claim to the northern part of the region, and claimed all the Pacific Northwest because George Vancouver and other Englishmen had explored it. The Lewis and Clark Expedition of 1804-1806 helped strengthen the United States' claim to the area.

Ownership of the entire Pacific Coast region was settled in the 1840's. The Oregon Treaty, signed by the United States and Great Britain in 1846, gave the United States present-day Oregon and Washington. The Treaty of Guadalupe Hidalgo, which ended the Mexican War in 1848, gave California to the United States.

The Oregon Trail, winding more than 2,000 miles from Independence, Mo., to the Pacific Northwest, opened in the 1840's. During the next 20 years, thousands of families crossed the continent on this and other trails to settle the rich farm lands of the West Coast. The discovery of gold in California in 1848 brought additional thousands of fortune hunters from all parts of the United States. The region developed quickly, and agriculture, mining, commerce, lumbering, and fishing flourished. Manufacturing developed into the most important industry between 1920 and 1950, and the population tripled during this period.

The Land and Its Resources

Land Regions. Thirteen main land regions make up

PACIFIC COAST STATES

Oregon State Highway Commission

The Three Pacific Coast States—Washington, Oregon, and California—stretch along the Pacific Ocean for about 1,300 miles.

the Pacific Coast States. Two of these regions form a great chain of mountains that extends from Canada almost to Mexico. Dry plateaus and valleys stretch eastward from the mountains, and lowland plains and lower mountain ranges lie to the west.

The Cascade Mountains run through central Washington and west-central Oregon, and form a small part of north-central California. This region is a worn lava plateau crowned by volcanic peaks which include some of the highest mountains in North America. Dense forests of evergreens and conifers cover the Cascades.

The Sierra Nevada region lies south of the Cascade Mountains, and extends through California almost to the Los Angeles area. This massive mountain range has several peaks that tower above 14,000 feet. The highest, Mt. Whitney, rises 14,495 feet above sea level. Rushing rivers have cut deep canyons in the western part of the mountains, including famous Yosemite Valley.

The Rocky Mountains region covers northeastern Washington. Gold, lead, magnesite, silver, zinc, and other minerals occur in these forested mountains.

The Columbia Plateau, the largest lava plateau in the world, covers southeastern Washington and most of eastern Oregon. Several rivers, including the Columbia, the Deschutes, and the John Day, have cut canyons through highlands that surround fertile valleys. The Snake River has carved famous Hells Canyon, more than 7,900 feet deep in some places, along the Oregon-Idaho border. Farmers grow hay, grain, and other crops in the valleys, and use the mountain slopes as summer pastures for livestock.

The Basin and Range Region occupies part of south-central and southeastern Oregon, the corner of northeastern California, and a great region along California's eastern border. Much of this area is a semidesert, because the mountains to the west cut off moisture-bearing winds. Occasional low mountains rise above the basin. Death Valley, the lowest point in North America (282 feet below sea level), stretches along the California-Nevada border. Irrigation has made many once dry valleys, such as the Imperial and Coachella valleys, suitable for farming.

The Olympic Mountains region makes up northwestern Washington. The rugged, snow-capped Olympic Mountains have many areas still unexplored. Logging in the foothills ranks as the chief industry.

The Puget Lowland is a heavily populated plain around Puget Sound and the Chehalis River. More than two thirds of the people of Washington live in Seattle, Tacoma, and elsewhere in this region. It is a great shipbuilding, fishing, and shipping center.

The Willamette Lowland lies west of the Cascade Mountains in northwestern Oregon. Rich soil, a favorable climate, nearby water transportation, and the manufacturing cities of Portland and Salem make it Oregon's greatest industrial and farming area.

The Coast Range region makes up part of the coastal area of each of the Pacific Coast States. In Washington, it forms the southwestern corner of the state. Logging and lumber milling are the most important industries in this area. In Oregon, the Coast Range region is a narrow strip of land along the northern two thirds of the coast. Thick evergreen forests cover most of the region. In California, the Coast Range region extends in a narrow strip two thirds of the way down the coast. Beautiful valleys with ranches, vineyards, and truck gardens separate the area's mountain ranges. San Francisco lies on a great landlocked harbor halfway down the California coast.

The Klamath Mountains rise in southwestern Oregon and northwestern California. Heavy timber covers the 6,000- to 8,000-foot-high mountains. Deep canyons break the ranges. The mountains have deposits of copper, gold, and chromite.

The Central Valley lies in California between the Coast Range region and the Sierra Nevada. This lowland, about 450 miles long with an average width of 40 miles, is really two valleys. The Sacramento River flows through one, and the San Joaquin River drains the other. The Central Valley, with three fifths of California's farm land, forms the largest and most important agricultural region west of the Rockies. Farmers here raise almost every kind of crop. The southern part of the valley has oil and gas fields.

The Los Angeles Ranges region extends along California's southern coast almost to Mexico. Farmers in

3

PACIFIC COAST STATES

the valleys grow oranges, lemons, and other fruits. Los Angeles, the largest city in the Pacific Coast States, is in this region. Nearby petroleum and natural-gas fields rank among the most productive in the world.

The San Diego Ranges region covers the southwestern corner of California. Many resorts lie among the area's dry, brush-covered mountains.

Climate. Areas west of the Cascade and Sierra Nevada mountains have a mild, cool, moist climate. Areas to the east receive less rainfall, and are colder in winter and hotter in summer. Average January temperatures west of the mountains include 41°F. at Seattle and 55°F. at Los Angeles. East of the mountains, annual January temperatures vary between 25°F. at Spokane and 46°F. at Barstow, Calif. Seattle has an average July temperature of 66°F., and Los Angeles 73°F. The average July reading in Spokane is 70°F., and in Barstow 84°F. The average annual rainfall in the west varies between 15 inches at Los Angeles and 140 inches in the Olympic Mountains. Hanford, in eastern Washington, receives about six inches of rain a year. The dry regions of eastern California, such as Death Valley, average about two inches yearly. The average annual snowfall varies from none along the middle and southern California coast to over 500 inches on the high slopes of Mt. Rainier.

Activities of the People

The People. The Pacific Coast States had a population of 20,339,105 in 1960. About three-fourths of the people live in California. Los Angeles, San Francisco, San Diego, Seattle, Oakland, and Portland are the largest cities. About four-fifths of all the people live in cities.

The Spaniards who founded missions in California during the 1700's were the first white settlers in the region. Rapid settlement began during the mid-1800's after the discovery of gold in California and the establishment of Oregon as a territory, both in 1848. Between 1850 and 1900, the region's population increased almost 24 times, from 105,891 to 2,416,692. During the 1900's, the Pacific Coast States have gained in population faster than any other major area of the United States. The mild climate, expanding industry, and beautiful scenery attract people from throughout the United States. Most of the newcomers settle in California.

Manufacturing and Processing. Plants and mills employ about one-fourth of the workers in the Pacific Coast States. The most valuable industry is the manufacture of transportation equipment. Factories at Seattle

Outdoor Sports flourish in the Pacific Coast States. Thousands of skiing enthusiasts try the slopes of Mt. Hood every year.

Ray Atkeson

Fishing is one of the largest industries in the Pacific Coast States. Smelt fishing along the shore is a popular sport.

Ray Atkeson

PACIFIC COAST STATES

Barren Areas
Above Timber

Evergreen Trees

Mixed Evergreen and
Deciduous Trees

Deciduous Trees

Shrub

Grass

Barren Arid Areas

Below Sea Level
No Vegetation Shown

✳ Capitals   ● Cities

Railroads

1 inch = 127 Statute Miles

Miles 0   25   50   75   100   125

Lambert Conformal Conic Projection

Pacific Ocean

CANADA
UNITED STATES

WATERTON GLACIER
INTERNATIONAL
PEACE PARK

Vancouver
Bellingham
Victoria
CAPE FLATTERY
Strait of Juan de Fuca
OLYMPIC NAT'L PARK
OLYMPIC MTS.
Tacoma
OLYMPIA
Aberdeen
CAPE DISAPPOINTMENT

Seattle
Wenatchee
WASHINGTON
MT. RAINIER NAT'L PARK
+ MT. RAINIER 14,410 FT.
Cowlitz R.
Yakima
Longview
Walla Walla
COLUMBIA BASIN
Spokane
Coeur d'Alene
Pend Oreille Lake
Lewiston
KETTLE RIVER RANGE
Columbia River
Okanogan River
Kootenai Lake
Trail

MONTANA
Milk River
Great Falls
Missouri River

Portland
SALEM
MT. HOOD 11,245 FT.
The Dalles
Pendleton
Baker
Eugene
Bend
OREGON
BLUE MOUNTAINS
Deschutes River
John Day R.
Snake River
Clearwater R.
Salmon River
SALMON MTS.
Boise
IDAHO

YELLOWSTONE
Yellowstone Lake
NAT'L PARK
GRAND TETON NAT'L PARK
WYOMING
Snake River

Roseburg
KLAMATH MTS.
CRATER LAKE NAT'L PARK
Medford
Rogue River
Klamath Falls
Upper Klamath Lake
Summer Lake
Lake Abert
Malheur Lake
GREAT BASIN
Owyhee River

CAPE BLANCO

LAVA BEDS NAT'L MON.
Eureka
CAPE MENDOCINO
Shasta Lake
LASSEN VOLCANIC NAT'L PARK
Pit River
Clear Lake
PT. ARENA

Winnemucca
Humboldt River
Elko
Great Salt Lake
GREAT SALT LAKE DESERT
Ogden
Salt Lake City
Utah L.
Provo
UTAH
Bear Lake

Pyramid L.
Reno
Lake Tahoe
Carson City
Walker Lake
Mono Lake
SIERRA NEVADA
NEVADA
SHOSHONE MTS.
Reese R.
Humboldt River
Ely
Sevier Lake

SACRAMENTO
Stockton
San Francisco
San Jose
Monterey Bay
PT. PINOS
PT. SUR
Mokelumne R.
YOSEMITE NAT'L PARK
Tuolumne R.
San Joaquin River
CALIFORNIA
Fresno
Kings River
KINGS CANYON NAT'L PARK
SEQUOIA NAT'L PARK
MT. WHITNEY 14,495 FT.
BOUNDARY PK. 13,145 FT.
Tonopah
DEATH VALLEY NAT'L MON.
DEATH VALLEY
282 FT. BELOW SEA LEVEL
Kern R.
Salinas River
Cuyama River
PT. BUCHON
Santa Barbara
PT. CONCEPTION
San Bernardino
MOJAVE DESERT
JOSHUA TREE NAT'L MON.
Los Angeles
Long Beach
Gulf of Santa Catalina
San Diego
Salton Sea
Las Vegas
Lake Mead
LAKE MEAD NAT'L REC. AREA
Colorado River
Virgin River
ZION NAT'L PARK
Cedar City
BRYCE CANYON NAT'L PARK
COLORADO PLATEAU
GRAND CANYON NAT'L MON.
GRAND CANYON NAT'L PARK
COCONINO PLATEAU
HUMPHREYS PK. 12,670 FT. +
Flagstaff
ARIZONA
Phoenix
Gila River
U.S.
MEXICO
Yuma

Pacific Ocean

ON TERRAIN PACIFIC COAST STATES
COPYRIGHT BY
RAND MCNALLY & COMPANY
MADE IN U.S.A.

Longitude West of Greenwich

Especially created for World Book Encyclopedia by Rand McNally and World Book editors

PACIFIC COAST STATES

and Renton, Wash., make large multiengine jet planes. California aircraft centers include Burbank, Glendale, Long Beach, San Diego, and Santa Monica. The Los Angeles area and San Jose-Fremont area manufacture enough cars to make California one of the leading states in automobile production. Giant shipyards operate in coastal cities in all three states. The next most important manufactures include processed foods, lumber and forest products, metal products, machinery, primary metals, and chemicals.

Agriculture. The Pacific Coast States form the greatest fruitgrowing region in North America. About nine-tenths of the pears, a fourth of the cherries, half of the peaches, and almost a third of the apples marketed in the United States come from the three states. Washington leads the states in apple production. California produces all of the country's raisins, almost all the table grapes, and one-fifth of the oranges. California and Washington raise more than nine-tenths of the nation's wine grapes. Most of the country's lemons, prunes, olives, dates, filberts, English walnuts, hops, and apricots come from the Pacific Coast States. Farmers also grow large vegetable crops.

The favorable climate and efficient cultivating methods have helped California become one of the leading cotton-producing states. About one-third of the country's sugar-beet crop comes from the irrigated lands of eastern Washington and Oregon, and from California's Central Valley. Hay and forage crops support large dairy- and beef-cattle industries.

Mining. Petroleum and natural gas, chiefly from California, account for more than two-thirds of the value of the region's mineral production. California has about 13 per cent of the country's petroleum reserves. It ranks as one of the leading states in petroleum production, and stands high in natural gas.

James W. Marshall, a lumberman, began the mineral industry in the Pacific Coast States in 1848 when he found gold along the American River in California. His discovery started the greatest gold rush in history. Since 1850, California has produced more than a third of the gold mined in the United States. Other minerals found in the three states include sand and gravel, lead, zinc, silver, copper, magnesium, and mercury.

Tourist Industry. More than 6 million tourists visit the Pacific Coast States every year. The sunny, mild climate of southern California is world famous, as is the beautiful coastal and mountain scenery of all three states. Many persons visit the area's seven national parks, and the many historic sites, forts, and trading posts.

Forest Products. Nearly 100 million acres of forests, including more than half of the standing commercial timber of the United States, lie throughout the Pacific Coast States. The most important timber trees include the Douglas fir, spruce, hemlock, cedar, pine, and redwood. Important products are wood pulp, paper, shingles, boxes and crates, plywood, veneer, and poles.

Fishing Industry. California leads all the states in the value of its fishery products. San Pedro, Calif., ranks as the nation's chief fishing port. The region's most important fish include sardines, tuna, salmon, anchovies, mackerel, and halibut. Fishermen also take oysters, crabs, shrimps, and clams from the coastal waters. California stands first among the states in the catch of sardines and tuna. Washington fishermen take large quantities of salmon from the ocean.

Electric Power. California ranks first among the states in the production of electric power generated by all types of energy. Washington also ranks among the leaders. Many swift rivers rushing through deep mountain canyons have been dammed throughout the Pacific Coast States to convert their energy into power. The region produces about 45 per cent of the nation's hydroelectric power. The three states are among the leaders in the production of hydroelectric power.

Transportation. During the 1800's, the mountains, deserts, and hostile Indians discouraged travel to and

Great Scientific Research Centers are clustered along the Pacific Coast. The Ernest O. Lawrence Radiation Laboratory at Berkeley, Calif., *below,* is one of the world's leading research laboratories. Experiments in high-energy physics are conducted there.

University of California

from the Pacific Coast States. Many travelers and most of the freight made the long voyage in ships that sailed around South America. In 1869, the first transcontinental railroad connected the region to the East. The opening of the Panama Canal in 1914 greatly improved water transportation between the Atlantic and Pacific coasts.

Today, the Pacific Coast States have about 16,000 miles of railroads, and about 260,000 miles of roads and highways. A system of modern freeways speeds traffic in and out of the chief cities. Airlines operate from the major cities. San Francisco, Los Angeles, San Diego, Portland, and Seattle are the chief ports.

Regional Cooperation. Each of the Pacific Coast States has special departments to manage and conserve natural resources. Experts teach farmers what crops to plant and how best to plant them. The West Coast Lumbermen's Association and the Western Pine Association encourage conservation among private lumber companies. The Keep America Green movement (for forest-fire prevention) and the American Tree Farm System (for scientific planting and cutting) both originated in Washington. Salmon fishermen operate under the regulations of the International Pacific Salmon Commission, in order to prevent salmon from being killed off. A similar agency regulates halibut fishing. State and federal conservation laws control mining throughout the region.

Federal, state, and regional agencies regulate the water resources of the Pacific Coast States in order to prevent waste, floods, and pollution, and to provide fair distribution. The United States Bureau of Reclamation controls the development of water resources in the Columbia Basin and in California's Central Valley. Huge dams, such as Grand Coulee and Shasta, have been built to store water for irrigation and power.   HOWARD J. CRITCHFIELD

Related Articles. For additional information on the Pacific Coast States, see the separate article on each state in this region with its list of Related Articles. Other related articles in WORLD BOOK include:

HISTORY AND GOVERNMENT

Astor	Mexican War
City and Local Governments	Oregon Trail
Compromise of 1850	Pioneer Life in America
Drake, Sir Francis	Pony Express
Fifty-Four Forty or Fight	Puget, Peter
Forty-Niner	State Government
Frémont, John C.	Trails of Early Days
Gold Rush	United States,
Guadalupe Hidalgo, Treaty of	History of
Indian, American	Vancouver, George
Lewis and Clark Expedition	Western Frontier Life
Metropolitan Area	Westward Movement

PHYSICAL FEATURES

Cascade Range	National Park
Coast Range	Olympic Mountains
Colorado River	Pacific Northwest
Columbia River	Puget Sound
Dam	Sacramento River
Death Valley	Salton Sea
Grand Coulee Dam	San Joaquin River
Great Basin	Shasta Dam
Imperial Valley	Sierra Nevada
Juan de Fuca, Strait of	Snake River
Mojave	Willamette River

PACIFIC COMMUNITY

Outline

I. The Land and Its Resources
    A. Land Regions   B. Climate

II. Activities of the People
    A. The People   F. Forest Products
    B. Manufacturing and   G. Fishing Industry
       Processing   H. Electric Power
    C. Agriculture   I. Transportation
    D. Mining   J. Regional Cooperation
    E. Tourist Industry

Questions

What two treaties determined the ownership of the entire Pacific Coast region?

What two events led to the rapid settlement of the Pacific Coast States?

Who was probably the first white man to visit the region?

How many major land regions make up the Pacific Coast States?

Which is the largest of the Pacific Coast States?

What causes two distinct climates in the Pacific Coast States?

When was the Pacific Coast linked to the East by a transcontinental railroad?

What part of the Pacific Coast States has the most productive petroleum and natural-gas fields?

What are the most valuable manufactures of the Pacific Coast States?

What city in the Pacific Coast States ranks as the nation's chief fishing port?

Who began the mineral industry in the Pacific Coast States? When?

What two minerals account for more than two-thirds of the value of the Pacific Coast States' mineral production?

In what agricultural specialty does the Pacific Coast States lead all other regions of North America?

PACIFIC COLLEGE. See UNIVERSITIES AND COLLEGES (table).

PACIFIC COMMUNITY is a loosely defined geographical and political division of the earth. Geographically, it includes Australia, the islands of the Pacific Ocean, and regions bordering the Pacific, such as the western parts of the Americas, the eastern parts of Asia, and the Pacific side of Antarctica. Politically, it includes all nations and states in the area that are concerned with the welfare of peoples in the Pacific community.

These lands and their common ocean cover more than two-thirds of the surface of the earth. More than 1,800,000,000 people live in the Pacific community.

Lands of the Occidental Pacific (the Americas) and of the Oriental Pacific (Asia) lie far apart, and only recently has this huge, loosely knit community been regarded as a division of the globe.

Many young nations of the Pacific community are busy setting up their own institutions and furthering the economic welfare of their people. But science and technology are helping to shatter barriers of distance. This in turn encourages mutual understanding and respect for the cultures and aims of the Pacific community.   PAUL R. HANNA

Related Articles in WORLD BOOK include:

Antarctica	Pacific Coast States
Australia	Pacific Islands
Central America	Pacific Ocean
China	Russia
Japan	South America
New Zealand	Southeast Asia
North America	Treaty Organization

5

Russ Ogg

PACIFIC ISLANDS

Graceful Coconut Palms line the shores of this Samoan island in western Polynesia. Islanders, such as the young man *above*, climb the trees for coconuts which are dried to make copra.

PACIFIC ISLANDS. More than 30,000 islands lie scattered throughout the Pacific Ocean. Most of them are located in the southwestern Pacific where the ocean bed is cut by high ridges and deep troughs. Many islands lie in rows or archipelagoes (groups lying in a curve). A few are isolated peaks, rising abruptly thousands of feet from the ocean floor. The northeastern Pacific is more uniformly deep, and has few islands. For location, see the *color map* with this article.

Most of the Pacific Islands are grouped together under the name *Oceania* (pronounced OH she AN ih uh). Geographers divide Oceania into three main groups: (1) *Melanesia* (pronounced MEHL uh NEE zhuh), (2) *Micronesia* (pronounced MY kroh NEE zhuh), and (3) *Polynesia* (PAHL uh NEE zhuh). This division is based partly on the types of islands, and partly on the kinds of people who live there. Islands in the southwest make up *Melanesia*. Those of the northwest are called *Micro-*

The American Museum of Natural History

The Micronesian has black hair, which may be either straight or curly.

The Melanesian is stocky, and has protruding features and frizzy hair.

The Polynesian, tallest of the Pacific islanders, has light-brown skin.

nesia. All islands east of the International Date Line, and a few islands west of it, form part of *Polynesia* (see INTERNATIONAL DATE LINE).

Geographers generally do not include the continent of Australia and several island groups as part of Oceania. These groups are Indonesia, Formosa, the Philippines, Japan, and such islands as the Kuril and Ryukyu islands near Japan. *Indonesia* consists of Java, Sumatra, Borneo, Celebes, and smaller islands west of New Guinea. Geographers sometimes group Tasmania, Australia, and a few adjoining islands under the term *Australasia*.

People live on most of the far-flung islands. Some historians believe that the first people to enter the Pacific Islands crossed land bridges from Asia to Indonesia. Hundreds of years later, groups from Indonesia pushed east and south. They were skilled navigators, and sailed in canoes steadied by outriggers (see OUTRIGGER BOAT). Later voyagers traveled thousands of miles and settled on islands in the central and eastern Pacific.

Few large animals live on the Pacific Islands except cattle and pigs which were brought by man. The principal wildlife includes birds, insects, and land mollusks (see MOLLUSK).

The vegetation on the Pacific Islands depends upon latitude, rainfall, soil, and altitude. Limited plant life grows on the hot, low coral islets. The higher islands have more rainfall and richer vegetation. Mangrove swamps line the shores of most of these islands, gradually spreading into the shallow water (see MAN-

Edwin H. Bryan, Jr., the contributor of this article, is Manager of the Pacific Scientific Information Center at the Bishop Museum in Honolulu and a consultant on Pacific geography. The article has been critically reviewed by James A. Michener, the author of Tales of the South Pacific, *and winner of the Pulitzer prize for fiction in 1948.*

GROVE). Patches of plants such as taro and sugar cane grow along valley streams. Tropical jungles which thrive in the lowlands may spread upward, covering steep slopes. The useful coconut palm flourishes near the sea. This plant furnishes food, fiber, shells, and *copra* (dried coconut meat) which is valuable for its oil. At high altitudes where the air is cooler, orchids, ferns, and vines grow in the forests.

Rainfall on the islands varies from a few inches to several hundred inches a year. Clear skies and brilliant sunshine often follow violent downpours. *Typhoons* (tropical cyclones) often hit the western Pacific, especially the Caroline, Philippine, and Ryukyu islands, with terrific fury between May and December (see TYPHOON).

Some Pacific Islands are mere mounds of sand on a reef. Some of these sand islets lie along reefs which surround a shallow lagoon. These islands are called *atolls* (see ATOLL). Most of these islands have rough limestone surfaces, with little productive soil. Thick, low forests and tangles of vines may cover caves and depressions. Rain water quickly seeps down through the limestone, so there are no surface streams.

Many islands have been formed by flow upon flow of volcanic lava and ash, and have sharp peaks or rolling hills. Several large islands have many mountains and valleys, covered with rich soil and thick jungles. See VOLCANO.

Islands in the Southwest Pacific are made up of ancient rock. Some geologists believe that they are all that remain of the "Melanesian continent" which once extended far out from Asia, to the north of Australia, as far as Fiji. As centuries passed, erosion and more violent earth forces destroyed parts of the continent. Higher scattered peaks became islands after the rest of the land was flooded.

The islands of the South Seas have inspired artists and writers ever since the white man discovered them. Paul Gauguin painted many of his best-known canvases while living in Polynesia. Thrilling stories of adventure about these exotic lands include *Typee* and *Omoo* by Herman Melville, and *Mutiny on the Bounty* by Charles Nordhoff and James N. Hall. The American novelist James Michener wrote *Tales of the South Pacific*. The popular musical *South Pacific*, by Richard

PACIFIC ISLANDS

ISLANDS IN POLYNESIA

Index (key)	Name	Status	Area (sq. mi.)	Population	Capital
J10	BOUNTY ISLAND	New Zealand Terr.	0.5	0	
G11	CANTON and ENDERBURY ISLANDS	British, U.S. Condominium	27	320	Canton Island
I11	CHATHAM ISLANDS	New Zealand Terr.	372	520	
H12	COOK ISLANDS	New Zealand Terr.	93	21,000	Avarua
	(Aitutaki, Atiu, Rarotonga)				
H15	EASTER ISLAND	Chilean Possession	63	1,200	Hangaroa
G10	ELLICE ISLANDS	British Colony	10	5,444	Tarawa
H13	FRENCH POLYNESIA	French Overseas Terr.	1,544	106,000	Papeete
	(Austral Islands, Gambier Islands, Marquesas Islands, Rapa Island, Society Islands, Tuamotu Islands)				
E12	HAWAIIAN ISLANDS	U.S. State	6,450	744,000	Honolulu
	(Hawaii, Kahoolawe, Kauai, Lanai, Maui, Molokai, Niihau, Oahu)				
E11	JOHNSTON ISLAND	U.S. Possession	0.38	0	
I11	KERMADEC ISLAND	New Zealand Terr.	13	9	
F12; G12	LINE ISLANDS	U.S., British Terr.	262	1,371	
	(Caroline, Christmas, Fanning, Flint, Jarvis, Kingman Reef, Malden, Palmyra, Starbuck, Vostok, Washington)				
E11	MIDWAY ISLAND	U.S. Possession	2	2,356	
I10	NEW ZEALAND	Independent	103,736	2,876,000	Wellington
	(North Island, South Island, Stewart Island)				
G11	PHOENIX ISLANDS	British Colony	7	1,018	
H14	PITCAIRN ISLAND	British Colony	2	92	Adamstown
G11	SAMOA, AMERICAN	U.S. Terr.	76	36,000	Pago Pago
G11	SAMOA, WESTERN	Independent	1,097	148,000	Apia
	(Savai'i, Upolu)				
G11	TOKELAU ISLANDS	New Zealand Terr.	4	1,900	
H11	TONGA ISLANDS	British Protectorate	270	88,000	Nukualofa
G11	WALLIS-FUTUNA ISLANDS	French Overseas Terr.	106	9,900	Mata-Utu

ISLANDS IN MELANESIA

Index (key)	Name	Status	Area (sq. mi.)	Population	Capital
G8	BISMARCK ARCHIPELAGO	Australian Trust Terr.	18,700	224,964	Port Moresby
	(Admiralty Islands, Lavongai, New Britain, New Ireland)				
G9	BOUGAINVILLE	Australian Trust Terr.	3,880	72,490	Port Moresby
G9	D'ENTRECASTEAUX ISLANDS	Australian Dependency	1,280	32,000	Port Moresby
H11	FIJI ISLANDS	British Colony	7,055	537,000	Suva
	(Vanua Levu, Viti Levu)				
G9	LOUISIADE ARCHIPELAGO	Australian Dependency	690	11,300	Port Moresby
H9, 10	NEW CALEDONIA	French Overseas Terr.	7,336	100,000	Nouméa
	(Chesterfield Islands, Huon Islands, Isle of Pines, Loyalty Islands, New Caledonia)				
G8, 9	NEW GUINEA		311,796	2,602,396	
	(West Irian;	Indonesian Province;			
	Territory of New Guinea;	Australian Trust Terr.;			
	Territory of Papua)	Australian Dependency			
H10	NEW HEBRIDES	British and French Condominium	5,700	90,000	Vila
	(Efate, Espiritu Santo)				
G8	SCHOUTEN ISLANDS	Indonesian Possession	1,236	36,793	Sukarnapura
G9	SOLOMON ISLANDS	British Protectorate	11,500	153,000	Honiara
	(Guadalcanal, New Georgia Islands, Santa Cruz Islands)				
G9	TROBRIAND ISLANDS	Australian Dependency	210	12,600	Port Moresby

ISLANDS IN MICRONESIA

Index (key)	Name	Status	Area (sq. mi.)	Population	Capital
F8, 9	CAROLINE ISLANDS	U.S. Trust Terr.	447	59,735	Saipan
	(Kusaie group, Palau group, Ponape group, Truk group, Yap group)				
F10	GILBERT ISLANDS (Makin, Tarawa)	British Colony	102	37,973	Tarawa
F8	GUAM	U.S. Possession	212	119,000	Agana
E8	MARIANA ISLANDS (Excluding Guam)	U.S. Trust Terr.	184	10,275	Saipan
F9, 10	MARSHALL ISLANDS	U.S. Trust Terr.	70	18,205	Saipan
	(Bikini Atoll, Eniwetok Atoll, Kwajalein Atoll)				

8b

Index (key)	Name	Status	Area (sq. mi.)	Population	Capital
G10	NAURU ISLAND	Independent	8	7,000	
E8	VOLCANO ISLANDS (Iwo Jima, Kita-lō-jima, Minami-lō-jima)	Part of Japan	11	0	
E10	WAKE ISLAND	U.S. Possession	3	1,097	

— **OTHER ISLANDS IN THE PACIFIC** —

Index (key)	Name	Status	Area (sq. mi.)	Population	Capital
C11	ALEUTIAN ISLANDS	Part of Alaska	6,777	5,000	Juneau
E8	BONIN ISLANDS (Bailey Islands, Beechey Islands, Parry Islands)	Part of Japan	40	205	
E7	FORMOSA (TAIWAN)	Independent	13,885	14,361,000	Taipei
G16	GALAPAGOS ISLANDS	Ecuadorian Province	2,869	2,934	Puerto Baquerizo
E6	HAINAN ISLAND	Chinese Possession	13,425	3,000,000	
G6	INDONESIAN ISLANDS	Independent	735,272	119,137,000	Djakarta
D8	JAPANESE ISLANDS	Independent	142,727	102,948,000	Tokyo
I17	JUAN FERNÁNDEZ ISLANDS	Chilean Possession	56	615	
C9	KURIL ISLANDS	Russian Possession	6,023	15,000	
H10	NORFOLK ISLAND	Australian Territory	13	1,000	Kingston
F7	PHILIPPINE ISLANDS	Independent	115,830	38,424,000	Quezon City
E7	RYUKYU ISLANDS	U.S. Administration	848	984,000	Naha
		Japanese Administration	512	199,085	Naha

— **INDEX OF PHYSICAL FEATURES** —

C11	Aleutian Trench	F8	Challenger Deep (−36,198 feet)	H11	Horizon Deep (−35,430 feet)	G17	Point Pariñas	
G7	Arafura Sea					D8	Ramapo Deep (−34,038 feet)	
H18	Atacama Trench	G9	Coral Sea	D8	Japan Trench			
G7	Banda Sea	E7	East China Sea	G6	Java Sea	D7	Sea of Japan	
I8	Bass Strait	H15	East Pacific Ridge	H11	Kermadec Tonga Trench	C8	Sea of Okhotsk	
C10	Bering Sea	F7	Galathea Deep (−34,578 feet)	C8	Kuril Trench	J10	South Cape	
G9	Bougainville Trench			F8	Mariana Trench	F6	South China Sea	
C12	Bristol Bay	I7	Great Australian Bight	F7	Mindanao Trench	I8	South East Cape	
I9	Cape Howe	H8	Great Barrier Reef	I10	North Cape	F7	Sulu Sea	
I6	Cape Leeuwin	C13	Gulf of Alaska	H6	North West Cape	G6	Sunda Trench	
C9	Cape Lopatka	E15	Gulf of California	J14	Pacific-Antarctic Ridge	I9	Tasman Sea	
E15	Cape San Lucas	G8	Gulf of Carpentaria			G7	Timor Sea	
G8	Cape York	F5	Gulf of Siam	E7	Philippine Sea	D7	Yellow Sea	
F7	Celebes Sea							

Populations are latest census figures or official estimates.

Rodgers and Oscar Hammerstein II, was based on this book.

Melanesia

Melanesia has more than 380,000 square miles of land. It includes New Guinea and adjoining islands, as well as Fiji, New Caledonia, the New Hebrides Islands, the Solomon Islands, and other island groups. New Guinea is the largest of all the Pacific Islands. It covers 311,796 square miles, an area almost twice the size of the state of California. Melanesia means *black islands*. This name was given to the group because of the black skin of the islanders.

Location and Description. The islands of Melanesia lie north and northeast of Australia, and cover a large part of the Southwest Pacific. A few are atolls surrounded by coral reefs (see CORAL). Most of the islands have hot, wet, heavily forested lowlands, with limited farming land. Mountains on New Guinea rise to peaks as high as 16,000 feet above sea level. Island temperatures in the lowlands range from about 70° F. to 83° F., and the rainy season lasts from January to March. Tropical cyclones bring torrents of rain, sometimes as

much as 10 inches within 24 hours. Such pounding rain and wind may cause deaths and property damage.

The People. Melanesia is a region of cultural extremes. Differences in speech and custom occur not only from island to island, but also from community to community. Most Melanesians have dark skin, Negroid features, and are moderately tall, stocky, and frizzy-haired. On some Melanesian islands, ancestry is counted through the clan of the father (see CLAN). On other islands, descent is considered through the mother. The people speak many dialects of the Austronesian language, and many of them know some English.

Settlements. Most Melanesians live in small, isolated settlements. In many areas in New Guinea, houses are either grouped around a central open space or strung along a ridge, probably for protection. In most island groups, the people build houses of thatch. They erect these houses on the ground or on built-up stone or earth platforms. Beehive-shaped huts were once common throughout New Caledonia, but these islanders now build wooden houses like those in the Western world.

Clothing and Ornaments. In remote areas in New Guinea, the Solomons, and the New Hebrides, Melane-

Ewing Galloway

A Solomon Islands Headhunter Displays His Weapons.

sians wear clothing made of dyed bark cloth, grass, or woven fibers. People in a few isolated forest regions wear no clothing. Melanesians may tattoo their bodies (see TATTOOING). Both men and women may arrange their hair in elaborate styles.

Religion. Most Fijians and New Caledonians are Christians. The tribal religions of many Melanesians revolve around the spirits of the dead who are believed to influence the living. Rites are performed to please the spirits. These rites include sacrificing chickens, pigs, or water buffaloes.

Recreation. Many Melanesians like to gather for what is known in pidgin English as a *sing-sing*, in which they chant and dance for hours or days. In Fiji and the New Hebrides, they refresh themselves by drinking *kava*, made from a peppery root (see KAVA). On islands farther west, Melanesians chew *areca* nuts wrapped in *betel* leaves which color the teeth (see BETEL). Many Melanesian men have secret societies. Initiation ceremonies, which involve dancing and singing, may be long and hard. The men wear masks and headdresses during initiation dances.

Work of the People. Some Melanesian farmers grow taro as a staple food (see TARO). Others prefer yams to taro. Some islanders raise pigs and chickens for food. On New Guinea, the islanders make flour from the sago palm. Many New Guineans raise or hunt cassowary birds which provide food, bones for weapons, and feathers for decoration (see CASSOWARY). People living in forested areas earn their living by hunting or by gathering such forest products as gums and resins. They hunt with spears, bows and arrows, or clubs.

Many New Caledonians work on large coffee plantations owned by Europeans. Some tend herds of cattle on the dry uplands of the islands. In the Fiji Islands,

A Gilbert Islander, *Left Below,* Stands Ready for Battle. Fiji Islanders, *Right Below,* Dance at Suva.

The American Museum of Natural History

Fijians, Indians, and Europeans raise sugar, rice, cacao, coffee, citrus fruits, cotton, and rubber.

People living along the New Guinea coast and on offshore islands fish for a living. They trade dried or salted fish with tribes living inland. Melanesians mine nickel, chromite, copper, gold, lead, zinc, or cobalt on many of the islands. New Caledonia has a mountain of iron ore, as well as antimony and mercury deposits.

Micronesia

Micronesia means *little islands*. It includes the Caroline, Gilbert, Mariana, and Marshall islands, as well as those of Nauru, Volcano, and Wake. The land area covers about 1,100 square miles.

Location and Description. The 2,500 islands of Micronesia lie scattered from Palau, 500 miles east of the Philippines, eastward to the International Date Line. Most islands are low coral atolls, such as the Gilberts and the Marshalls. The Marianas and some Caroline islands are high, with rocks of volcanic origin.

Each year, an average of 180 inches of rain falls on the fertile hills and valleys of Ponape, the wettest of the Micronesian islands. Micronesia is tropical, and has uniformly warm temperatures that average from 70° F. to 80° F. The rainy season lasts from May to December. Typhoons often cause considerable damage to farmland and buildings.

The People. The islanders in eastern Micronesia resemble the Polynesians, who are tall, with light-brown skin. Those in western Micronesia have more Mongoloid features. Most islands are sparsely settled, but a few low, sandy islets have as many as 1,000 persons living on every square mile, especially in the Gilberts.

A man's importance in parts of Micronesia depends on his wealth, not on his descent or clan. Micronesians

Gendreau

speak languages of the Malayo-Polynesian language group.

Houses. The people generally live in wood-frame rectangular houses with fiber walls. They use thatch for roofing. Some houses have corrugated-iron roofs.

One of the most mysterious ruins in all the South Seas is *Nan Matal* on Ponape. This ruin may date back hundreds of years. Its thick walls indicate that it once might have been a fortified town.

Clothing and Ornaments. Most Micronesians wear European- or American-style clothing. Women used to dress in knee-length skirts made from fiber or split coconut leaves, or in loom-woven kilts. Men wore cloth or fiber garments. Both men and women may wear wooden combs in their hair, and necklaces of coconut or shell rings around their necks on ceremonial occasions.

Festivals. Micronesians gather for feasting, dancing, and singing on many occasions, such as births or marriages. They play games and tell stories during celebrations.

Religion. As a result of missionary activities, most Micronesians are now Christians. Others practice traditional tribal religions. For example, some worship the soil, the forests, and the sea.

Work of the People. Most Micronesians depend on fish and other sea food for their livelihood. The men are skillful sailors, especially on the eastern and southern islands. They make a specialty of designing outrigger canoes. Triangular sails help the boats travel swiftly in the wind.

Most Micronesians living inland are farmers. Their crops include yams, taros, breadfruit, bananas, and coconuts. People on the low islands eat *pandanus* (screw pine) fruit. Many islanders sell copra, the only commercial resource (see COPRA). In the Gilbert Islands, this is done through cooperatives.

Polynesia

Polynesia, which means *many islands*, is made up of the most far-flung islands of the Pacific. It includes the Austral, Cook, Ellice, Gambier, Hawaiian, Kermadec, Line, Marquesas, Phoenix, Samoa, Society, Tokelau, Tonga, and Tuamotu island groups. New Zealand, and Easter, Niue, Pitcairn, Wallis, and Futuna islands are also part of this group. New Zealand and the Hawaiian Islands have the largest cities in Oceania. These cities are modern, with well-developed trade and industry, and institutions of higher learning. Hawaii became the 50th state of the United States in 1959.

Location and Description. The islands of Polynesia lie inside an area shaped like a triangle, with sides about 5,000 miles long. Most islands are the small tops of volcanic mountains. Some are blocks of raised reef, and others are atolls. Both limestone and lava rocks cover a number of the islands. In places, wind and rain have weathered the lava rock to rich soil which supports tropical forests. Year-round temperatures at sea level average about 77° F. Rainfall varies from island to island and from year to year. The wettest months are from December to March.

The People. The Polynesians are tall, with superb physiques. They have the lightest coloring of all

PACIFIC ISLANDS

Pacific Islanders, with black hair, either straight or curly. The chief Polynesian peoples are the Hawaiians, Samoans, Tongans, Tahitians, and the Maoris of New Zealand (see MAORI).

Polynesian descent, unlike that of the clan culture of Melanesia, is counted through both the father and the mother. Women have considerable social standing, and many become chiefs of their groups.

Most Polynesians speak various dialects of the Polynesian language, a branch of the Austronesian. The people are known for their athletic grace and skill. They particularly enjoy water sports, such as swimming, diving, and surfboard riding.

Houses. Polynesians in many areas still build homes on stone or earth platforms, to keep out moisture and mud after rain. They thatch their wood-frame houses with coconut palm or pandanus leaves. Houses may have either sharp-peaked or low pitched roofs. Sides may be open or walled.

Clothing. The simplest garment for both men and women is the cotton waistcloth, called *lavalava* or *pareu*. This may be ankle length. In Samoa and Tonga, women still make *tapa cloth* by beating the inner bark of the paper mulberry tree. The bark is first stripped, then soaked, and beaten with four-sided, grooved clubs. Hawaiian women turned the long, loose, cotton *Mother Hubbard* (*muumuu*), introduced by Christian missionaries, into a *holomuu* (a fitted muumuu). Maori men of New Zealand perform dances in kilts made of stems from a flaxlike plant.

Religion. Before most Polynesians became Christians, they worshiped the spirits of their ancestors. On some islands, offerings often included human sacrifices. The ancient Polynesian religion centered around the ideas of *mana* and *tapu*. *Mana* means *power*, and is the force that inhabits all things in nature. *Tapu* means *prohibited*. Some persons and things were considered *tapu* because they possessed powers that the islanders could not explain.

Work of the People. Polynesians are skillful seafarers. They use outrigger boats to fish and to travel. The people harvest coconuts for their food, drink, material for shelter and fiberwork, and household utensils. Copra, or dried coconut meat, is a chief export of many islands.

Food plants grown by people living on the high islands include bananas, breadfruit, taro, yams, sweet potatoes, and cassava. On the low islands the food plants include coconuts and pandanus.

Both men and women are skilled at crafts. They sell articles such as baskets which they make by interweaving leaves from the coconut palm. Hawaiian women make *leis* (wreaths and neckpieces) from the brilliantly colored flowers that grow abundantly in the islands.

History

Most scholars believe that the people of the southwest Pacific Islands probably settled there before the time of written history. They probably came from southern and southeastern Asia. The Melanesians may have traveled eastward from Indonesia, south of the equator. The Micronesians probably spread across the western Pacific, north of the equator. The Polynesians may have been Caucasians who migrated eastward from Asia in prehistoric times. They probably moved eastward from island to island, mixing with other islanders, until they finally reached their present homes.

Discovery. The Pacific Ocean remained unknown to the Europeans until Marco Polo sailed from China to Europe in the 1290's. The Spanish explorer Vasco Núñez de Balboa sighted the Pacific at Panama in 1513. Ferdinand Magellan started around the world with a Spanish expedition six years later. Going west, he

PACIFIC ISLAND GROUPS

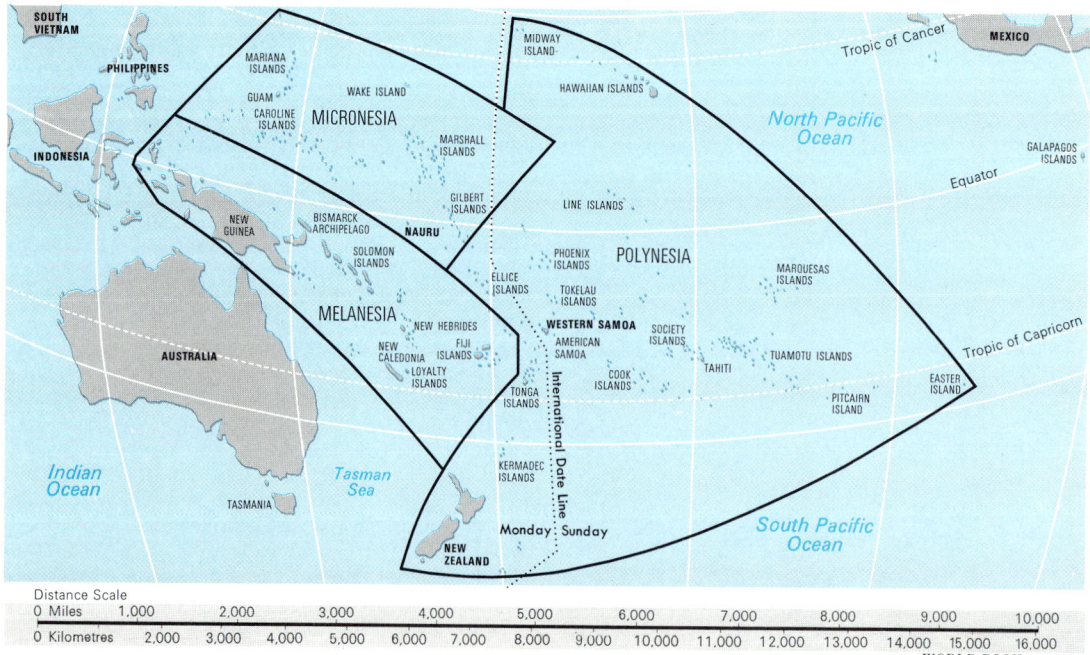

Distance Scale

| 0 Miles | 1,000 | 2,000 | 3,000 | 4,000 | 5,000 | 6,000 | 7,000 | 8,000 | 9,000 | 10,000 |

| 0 Kilometres | 2,000 | 3,000 | 4,000 | 5,000 | 6,000 | 7,000 | 8,000 | 9,000 | 10,000 | 11,000 | 12,000 | 13,000 | 14,000 | 15,000 | 16,000 |

WORLD BOOK map-GJa

crossed the ocean which he named *Pacific* (meaning *peaceful*). See BALBOA, VASCO NÚÑEZ DE; MAGELLAN, FERDINAND; POLO, MARCO.

During the 1600's, many European countries sent men to find and claim the Pacific Islands. On Captain James Cook's historic voyages in the late 1700's, the great English explorer charted the coasts of Australia, New Zealand, and New Guinea. He discovered New Caledonia and the Hawaiian Islands. See COOK, JAMES.

Trade. Yankee traders in clipper ships in the China trade added their discoveries during the early 1800's. Islands such as Baker and Fanning were named for Yankee skippers who discovered them.

By 1850, little of the great Pacific remained unknown. The islanders came into frequent contact with the *sailing gods*, as they first called the white men. Trading ships took sandalwood and other products from the South Seas to sell in the outside world. Christian missionaries converted many islanders.

The *sailing gods* also brought great suffering to the islands. The islanders had no resistance to the diseases brought by the white men, and they died by the thousands. Even ailments such as measles and the common cold took many lives. Within a few years, the populations of many islands had almost disappeared. The Queensland and other *blackbirders*, or slave traders, came to the Pacific to look for islanders to work on plantations in Australia and South America. The islanders did not want to leave their homes, and the traders tried to take them by force. The islanders resisted this cruel treatment, and many whites and islanders were killed during the struggles. Although white men did much harm, medical missionaries and government doctors helped the people and fought the spread of disease.

The Early 1900's. As time went by, the little-known Pacific region was opened to the world. Certain islands became fueling stations for ships making long voyages across the ocean. In the early 1900's, the world began to realize the commercial opportunities in the area. Large coconut, coffee, pineapple, and sugar plantations soon covered portions of the islands. Money and labor from outside the islands began to develop the mineral wealth that had never been touched.

Mainly on the basis of discovery, many countries claimed the islands in the Pacific. These included Spain, Japan, Great Britain, France, The Netherlands, Germany, and the United States. Spain lost many of its Pacific holdings after its defeat in the Spanish-American War of 1898. It ceded Guam to the United States, and sold the other Marianas to Germany. By treaty, Germany acquired other islands extending from the Marianas to Samoa. Before World War I, the United States held some of the Pacific land area, including the Hawaiian Islands, some islands of Samoa, Guam, and the Philippines (also ceded by Spain after the Spanish-American War).

After World War I, Germany lost its Pacific colonies. Japan acquired those north of the equator. Great Britain received those south of the equator, and put them under the control of New Zealand and Australia. Great Britain, France, and The Netherlands were satisfied with the possessions they already had in the Pacific. The United States arranged in 1934 to give independence to the Philippines by 1946. Most countries left the governing of their Pacific territories to island leaders. Commissioners looked after the islanders' health, education, and economic development.

World War II. The military importance of the Pacific Islands became apparent during World War II. In December, 1941, Japan attacked Pearl Harbor in Hawaii, and declared war on the United States, Great Britain, and The Netherlands. In a few months, Japan conquered the Philippines and Netherlands Indies, and occupied many of the Pacific Islands as far southeast as the Solomons. Then the Allies started to drive the Japanese north and west, out of one island group after another. The Allies built air and sea bases with excellent communication systems across the Pacific. They turned island trails into modern roads, and set up ports and radio stations. In August, 1945, Japan surrendered to the Allies and lost its Pacific Island empire. After the war, the United States and Britain became the controlling powers in the Pacific. See WORLD WAR II (The War in Asia and the Pacific).

Recent Developments. After World War II, the United States began testing atomic bombs in the South Pacific. A number of bombs have been exploded on isolated atolls, mainly on Bikini and Eniwetok (see BIKINI ATOLL; ENIWETOK). In 1948, the United States, Great Britain, Australia, New Zealand, France, and The Netherlands set up a South Pacific Commission to promote the economic and social welfare and advancement of the nonself-governing territories in the South Pacific. By the 1960's, many islanders had assumed technical and administrative posts under the commission's supervision. Schools, hospitals, and hotels and other tourist accommodations were built. Farming methods and industrial techniques were improved. The Netherlands withdrew from the commission in 1962. Western Samoa became independent in 1962 and joined the commission in 1964. In 1968, Nauru gained independence from Australia, and the United States returned the Bonin and Volcano islands, which it captured during World War II, to Japan. EDWIN H. BRYAN, JR.

Critically reviewed by JAMES A. MICHENER

Related Articles in WORLD BOOK include:

ISLANDS OF THE PACIFIC

Admiralty Islands	D'Entrecasteaux
Aleutian Islands	Islands
Anatahan	Easter Island
Attu Island	Ellice Islands
Auckland Islands	Eniwetok
Austral Islands	Espíritu Santo
Baker Island	Farallon Islands
Biak Island	Fiji Islands
Bikini Atoll	Formosa
Bismarck Archipelago	Galapagos Islands
Bonin Islands	Gambier Islands
Borneo	Gilbert Islands
Bougainville	Guadalcanal Island
Canton and Enderbury	Guam
Islands	Hawaii
Caroline Islands	Hokkaido
Catalina Island	Hong Kong
Chesterfield Islands	Howland Island
Chichagof Island	Indonesia
Christmas Island	Iwo Jima
Clipperton Island	Japan
Commander Islands	Jarvis
Cook Islands	Johnston Island
Corregidor	Juan Fernández

PACIFIC ISLANDS, TRUST TERRITORY OF THE

Kermadec Islands
Kodiak
Krakatoa
Kuril Islands
Kusaie
Kwajalein
Line Islands
Lord Howe Island
Louisiade Archipelago
Loyalty Islands
Malay Archipelago
Marcus Island
Mariana Islands
Marquesas Islands
Marshall Islands
Midway Island
Moluccas
Nauru
New Britain
New Caledonia
New Guinea
New Hebrides
  Islands
New Ireland
New Zealand
Niue Island
Norfolk Island
Ocean Island
Okinawa
Pagan
Palau Islands
Palmyra
Peleliu
Pescadores Islands
Philippines
Phoenix Islands

Pitcairn Island
Ponape
Pribilof Islands
Queen Charlotte Islands
Quemoy
Rapa Island
Rota
Ryukyu Islands
Saipan
Sakhalin
Samoa
Santa Cruz Islands
Schouten Islands
Singapore
Society Islands
Solomon Islands
Starbuck Island
Swains Island
Tachen Islands
Tahiti
Tarawa
Tasmania
Timor
Tinian
Tokelau Islands
Tonga Islands
Trobriand Islands
Truk Islands
Tuamotu Islands
Vancouver Island
Volcano Islands
Vostok Island
Wake Island
Wallis and Futuna Islands
Western Samoa
Yap

OTHER RELATED ARTICLES

Atoll
Atomic Bomb
Coconut Palm
Copra
Coral

Pacific Islands, Trust
  Territory of the
Pacific Ocean
Races of Man

Sculpture (Pa-
  cific Islands)
Typhoon
Volcano
World War II

Outline

I. Melanesia
II. Micronesia

III. Polynesia
IV. History

Questions

What are the three chief groups of islands in Oceania?
How may the first people have reached the Pacific Islands?
How did the white men affect the islanders?
Who was the first white man to visit the islands?
By what name is one of the most mysterious ruins in the South Pacific called? Where is it?
What countries own or control most Pacific Islands?
What are common foods of Pacific islanders?
What is the largest of all the Pacific Islands?
What famous explorer discovered New Caledonia and the Hawaiian Islands?
What Pacific island has a mountain of iron ore?

PACIFIC ISLANDS, TRUST TERRITORY OF THE, includes about 2,100 islands and atolls, including all the Marshall, Caroline, and Mariana islands except Guam. The United States Department of the Interior is responsible to the United Nations for the administration of the territory. The trust islands were taken from Japan during World War II. Japan had taken them from Germany during World War I. Guam is a United States territory.

The trust territory is divided into six administrative districts. They are Palau, Yap, Truk, Ponape, the Marshall Islands, and the Mariana Islands. Each district has a district officer and staff.

An administration, headed by a high commissioner, has its headquarters on Saipan. It directs finance, communications, education, public health, agriculture, fisheries, and legal problems. The United States Congress grants about $20 million yearly for the administration of these islands. Local government is conducted largely by the Micronesian people themselves. They advise the district administrators. Interdistrict conferences of Micronesian leaders advise the high commissioner. The islanders also elect a legislature that is receiving increased authority.

The islands lie scattered over an area nearly as large as the United States, although the land area measures only 701 square miles. About 88,215 Micronesians live in the territory. The people speak nine different languages. Many of the islands are low and sandy, without good soil for agriculture. Copra ranks as the chief product. Industries include fishing, handicrafts and trading companies.

Teachers receive training on Ponape. English is taught in all of the schools, and it will eventually become the official language of the territory. About 300 Micronesian students receive higher education on other Pacific Islands or on the United States mainland each year.   EDWIN H. BRYAN, JR.

See also CAROLINE ISLANDS; GUAM; MARIANA ISLANDS; MARSHALL ISLANDS; PACIFIC ISLANDS.

PACIFIC LUTHERAN UNIVERSITY. See UNIVERSITIES AND COLLEGES (table).

PACIFIC MISSILE RANGE is operated by the United States Navy at Point Mugu, Calif. The range is the launching site for guided missiles and space satellites developed by the U.S. armed forces and government agencies such as the National Aeronautics and Space Administration and the Atomic Energy Commission. A U.S. naval air station and the U.S. Naval Missile Center are also located there.

The range covers 27,000 acres of land. It includes the San Nicolas and San Miguel islands and the main facilities on a 4,460-acre site at Point Mugu, about 50 miles west of Los Angeles. A sea test strip extends hundreds of miles into the Pacific Ocean. The base was originally established as the Naval Missile Test Center in 1946.   JOHN A. OUDINE

PACIFIC NORTHWEST includes all of Oregon, Washington, and Idaho, and western Montana. The region varies greatly. Part of the Rocky Mountain system stands in the east, in Montana, Idaho, and Washington. The well-populated Willamette Valley of Oregon and the Puget Lowland of Washington lie to the west. They separate the Cascades of Washington and Oregon from the Coast Range and the Olympic Mountains. In the middle lies the Columbia Plateau of Idaho, Oregon, and Washington. The Snake River has cut a mile-deep canyon there. The Columbia River and its branches drain most of the area.   SAMUEL N. DICKEN

Related Articles in WORLD BOOK include:
Cascade Range
Columbia River
Olympic Mountains

Pacific Coast States
Rocky Mountain
  States

Rocky Moun-
  tains
Snake River

PACIFIC OAKS COLLEGE. See UNIVERSITIES AND COLLEGES (table).

PACIFIC OCEAN is the largest and deepest body of water. If all the continents were placed in the Pacific, there would still be room for another the size of Asia, the largest continent. The Pacific covers more than a third of the surface of the world. It stretches from the frozen north to the frozen south, and laps the shores of warm islands in the tropics. Its waters wash the coasts of Hawaii, the Philippines, New Zealand, and Japan.

The Portuguese explorer Ferdinand Magellan looked upon this great ocean and named it *Pacific*, which means peaceful. He sailed for weeks, driven by soft winds. He watched the flying fishes and the porpoises play in its warm, quiet waters. But the mighty Pacific is not always so peaceful. It can rise to heights of wrath. Out of its great spaces blow some of the most destructive storms on earth. Its typhoons have wrecked fleets of ships, and leveled island cities. Earthquakes and volcanic eruptions deep in the sea have caused destructive *tsunamis* (pronounced *tsoo NAH meez*), or tidal waves. These waves sometimes reach heights of 100 feet and roll completely over islands in their paths. A tsunami in 1883 drowned more than 35,000 persons along the Strait of Sunda (see KRAKATOA).

Because the earth's crust under the Pacific is weak, earthquakes occur frequently and thousands of volcanoes rise from the ocean bed. More than 300 of these volcanoes still erupt. Volcanic action formed many Pacific islands. Some of these islands are so high and mountainous that even in the tropics they are sometimes capped with snow. The Hawaiian Islands consist of a chain of such volcanic peaks. Some other islands consist of nothing but thin coral reefs rising only a few feet above the ocean surface. There are few islands in the eastern and northern Pacific. But large groups of islands lie near Asia and Australia. Hundreds of small scattered islands dot the central and southern Pacific.

This article deals with the ocean itself, its physical characteristics, marine life, and climate. For a discussion of the islands and the people of the Pacific, see PACIFIC ISLANDS.

Location and Size. North and South America form the eastern boundaries of the Pacific Ocean. Asia and Australia lie to the west. The *Color Map* shows that the Bering Strait joins the Pacific to the Arctic Ocean on the north. The Antarctic Ocean lies to the south.

The Pacific reaches its greatest width near the equator, between Panama and the Malay Peninsula. Here it measures about 11,000 miles, almost half of the distance around the world. The ocean has a total area of about 63,800,000 square miles. Geographers often divide the Pacific at the equator into the North Pacific and the South Pacific.

Shoreline and Coastal Waters. The Pacific coasts of North and South America are relatively smooth. The Gulf of California forms the only large inlet, and few islands lie offshore. The western Pacific has uneven shores. The coastal inlets include the China Sea, the Sea of Japan, the Yellow Sea, the Sea of Okhotsk, and numerous gulfs and bays. Many islands and the continent of Australia are located in the western Pacific.

The Ocean Floor. The Pacific has an average depth of about 14,000 feet. The depth varies greatly because of the many ridges, deep trenches, plateaus, and sea mountains (*guyots*). A guyot is a flat-topped mountain that does not reach the surface.

Two great ridges cross the ocean floor. One extends from Central America toward Antarctica. This vast, underwater mountain range rises perhaps 10,000 feet above the ocean floor and extends nearly 1,000 miles. Few islands rise from this ridge. A second ridge extends through the western Pacific. Many of the most important Pacific islands lie along it, including the Aleutians, Japan, the Philippines, and New Zealand.

Trenches called *deeps* are located along the eastern side of this western ridge (see DEEP). Four of these trenches have depths of more than six miles. The deepest is the Mariana Trench about 200 miles southwest of Guam, with a depth of 36,198 feet. The three other deeps are the Ramapo Trench southeast of Japan, the Mindanao Trench in the Philippines, and the Tuscarora Trench off the east coast of Japan.

A continental shelf extends along the shores of each continent bordering the Pacific. Here the water is seldom more than 600 feet deep. This shelf is relatively narrow along North and South America, but broad along the coasts of Asia and Australia.

Currents and Tides. The main currents of the Pacific follow a circular pattern, clockwise in the Northern Hemisphere and counterclockwise in the Southern Hemisphere. These currents greatly influence the climate of the land bordering the Pacific. The Japanese Current, for example, sweeps northward from the warm tropics, warming the Japanese islands. The North Pacific drift maintains some of its warmth across the Pacific, and helps moderate the climate of southern Alaska and western Canada.

The cold Peru Current washes the western coast of South America. Winds off this current tend to be cold and dry, making a desert of much of the west coastal area of South America. The Peru Current has brought some advantages as well as disadvantages to this area. Many fishes thrive in its cool waters, and countless birds feed on the fishes. Birds nest on desert islands off Peru, where their waste matter makes a valuable fertilizer called *guano* (see GUANO). Thus, the island birds play an important role in the economy of the area.

A warm current from the north called *El Niño* (The Child) often displaces the Peru Current in December. This current received its name because it frequently arrives about Christmas time, but is nonetheless an unwelcome visitor. Its warm waters sharply reduce the supply of fish along the coast, forcing the birds to migrate to find food. This current also brings warm, moist air. When the air strikes the cool land, torrential rains fall on the deserts, sometimes producing disastrous floods. See OCEAN (How the Ocean Moves).

The tides of the Pacific vary greatly, but not so much as those in the Atlantic. The tide rises 7 feet at Seattle, Wash., but only 11 inches at Midway Island.

Ocean Life in the Pacific ranges from microscopic plankton to whales more than 100 feet long (see PLANKTON). The cold waters of the northern Pacific are among man's greatest fishing grounds. They provide cod, halibut, herring, sardines, salmon, and tuna. Even the shark, of which 30 species live in the Pacific, has value to man. Shark livers produce an oil rich in vitamins.

Tropical fishes have little commercial importance, but they provide food for the island people. Their

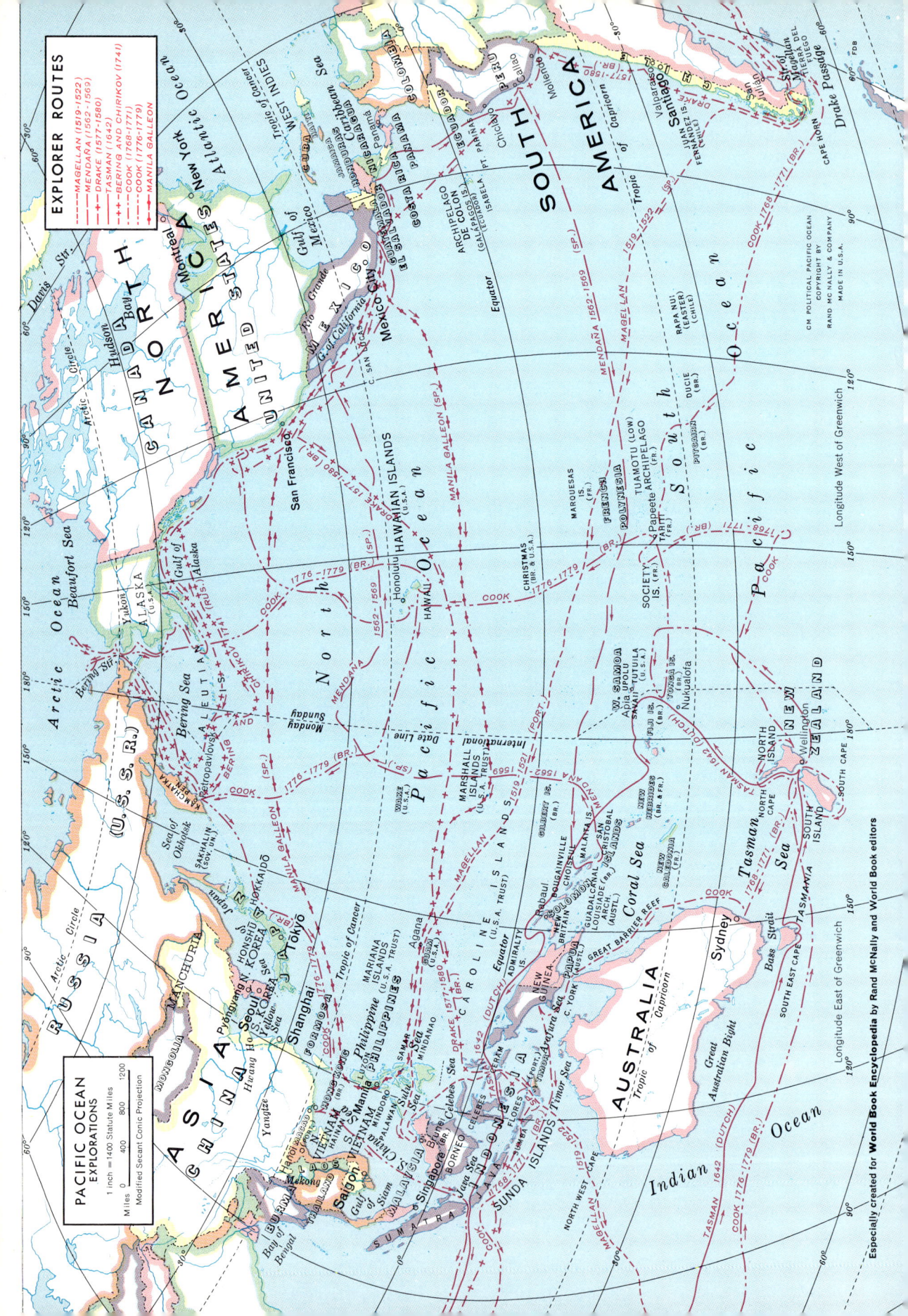

PACIFIC OCEAN
EXPLORATIONS

1 inch = 1400 Statute Miles

Miles 0   400   800   1200

Modified Secant Conic Projection

EXPLORER ROUTES

MAGELLAN (1519-1522)
MENDAÑA (1562-1569)
DRAKE (1577-1580)
TASMAN (1642)
BERING AND CHIRIKOV (1741)
COOK (1768-1771)
COOK (1776-1779)
MANILA GALLEON

Especially created for World Book Encyclopedia by Rand McNally and World Book editors

CM POLITICAL PACIFIC OCEAN
COPYRIGHT BY
RAND McNALLY & COMPANY
MADE IN U.S.A.

brilliant colors make them desirable for aquariums. Flying fish skim over the waters of the tropical Pacific.

Sea lions live on the Pacific Coast of North America and in the South Pacific. Fur-bearing seals, which actually are sea lions, were once more common than today. The only large sea-lion herds inhabit the fog-bound Pribilof Islands in the Bering Sea.

The Pacific abounds with shellfish, with shells of beautiful shapes and colors. One unusual shellfish is a giant clam that measures three feet across. Pearl oysters occur in some of the warmer waters. Coral may be found in shallow areas in the tropical Pacific. People of the Pacific area eat some kinds of seaweed.

Climate. The North Pacific has long, cold winters and short, cool summers. The Aleutian Islands are foggy and wind-swept. Along the equator, the climate stays hot all year. The only seasons are the rainy season and the dry season.

Farther south in the Pacific, the summers are cool and the winters mild. New Zealand, for example, seldom has snow or frost except in the mountains, and rainfall is abundant. The southernmost Pacific, near the Antarctic Ocean, has an extremely cold climate. In the summer, there is much floating ice that has broken away from Antarctic glaciers.

Wind Belts. Four great wind belts cross the Pacific. The trade winds blow steadily along each side of the equator, from the northeast and from the southeast. Heat at the equator causes the air to expand, rise, and flow off at high altitude toward the poles. The trade winds carry cooler air coming in at lower altitude to replace the air that has risen. Seamen once used the northeast trade winds to sail from North America to Asia. See TRADE WIND.

North and south of the trade belts, the westerly winds blow between the latitudes of 30° and 60°. The rotation of the earth causes these winds. The westerly winds in the North Pacific provided a sailing route from Asia to North America. The westerlies in the Southern Hemisphere are sometimes called the "Roaring Forties," because of their strength.

Monsoons blow during the summer from the cool ocean across the warmer coasts and islands of southeastern Asia. These moisture-laden "wet monsoons" bring the rainy season. The monsoons blow in the opposite direction in winter. As "dry monsoons," they blow from the cooler land toward the ocean. See MONSOON.

Typhoons and Hurricanes. Tropical cyclones cause much of the rainfall in the Pacific area. These great circular winds do not usually cause damage, and they may bring needed rain to dry areas. But occasionally, these cyclones become extremely violent. When they reach the velocity of 75 miles an hour, they are called typhoons or hurricanes. The most destructive of these storms howl down on the China Sea between May and November. They strike off the coast of Central America and Mexico between August and October. They hit the North Pacific between January and March. These dangerous storms are called typhoons in the Far East, and hurricanes in the southern and eastern Pacific. Under either name, they can be extremely dangerous both at sea and ashore. Velocities near the center, or "eye," of the storm sometimes reach 150 miles an hour. Such winds can snap off the trunks of palm trees, rip banana groves to shreds, and demolish buildings. At

sea, they produce mountainous waves. They have wrecked large, modern ships. Low islands have been completely swamped by the gigantic waves lashed up by such winds. See HURRICANE; TYPHOON.

Discovery and Exploration. The first European to see the Pacific Ocean was probably Marco Polo, an Italian traveler of the Middle Ages. Polo traveled extensively in China during the late 1200's and saw the Pacific Ocean from its western shores. Vasco Núñez de Balboa, a Spanish explorer, crossed the Isthmus of Panama in 1513 and viewed the Pacific from the east. Balboa is credited as its discoverer, because he recognized the Pacific as a great unknown sea. Ferdinand Magellan, who named the ocean, sailed across it in 1520-1521. Captain James Cook of the British Navy explored more of the Pacific than any other man. He made three long voyages across the ocean, exploring it from east to west and from south to north. Cook produced the first reliable map of the South Pacific. He discovered many of the Pacific islands, among them the Hawaiian and the Society islands.

The great size of the Pacific made it the last ocean to be crossed by ship and airplane. Hugh Herndon and Clyde Pangborn first flew the Pacific nonstop in 1931. Four years later, the first transpacific airline started operations. During World War II, man's knowledge of the Pacific increased greatly. Thousands of ships and airplanes covered its vast area. Many servicemen lived for years on islands they had never even heard of before the war. After the war, the air lanes and sea lanes of the Pacific again became busy with the trade and commerce of the world.

NEAL M. BOWERS

Related Articles in WORLD BOOK include:

Outline

I. Location and Size
II. Currents and Tides
III. Ocean Life
IV. Climate
V. Discovery and Exploration

Questions

Who named the Pacific Ocean? Why may this name be misleading?

About what fraction of the earth's surface does the Pacific Ocean cover?

What is believed to be the deepest place in the Pacific Ocean?

Where is the widest part of the Pacific Ocean? How wide is it there?

Why were Pacific trade winds important to early commerce?

Who explored more of the Pacific than any other man?

How are Pacific currents partly responsible for the desert area along South America's western coast?

What are three examples showing how ocean currents influence the life of people?

Do tropical cyclones have any value? Explain.

Who was probably the first European to see the Pacific Ocean?

PACIFIC TIME. See TIME; STANDARD TIME.

PACIFIC UNION COLLEGE

PACIFIC UNION COLLEGE is a coeducational school at Angwin, Calif. The school is operated by the Seventh-Day Adventist Church. Courses lead to bachelor's and master's degrees. Pacific Union was founded in 1882. For enrollment, see UNIVERSITIES AND COLLEGES (table).

PACIFIC UNIVERSITY. See UNIVERSITIES AND COLLEGES (table).

PACIFISM, *PASS uh fiz'm,* is the doctrine that only peaceful methods ought to be used for settling disagreements. Pacifism would replace physical force with the force of reason, of spirit, and of example as the means of persuasion. A consistent pacifist not only rejects the use of physical force himself, but also refuses to engage in any activities that support wars. He will not help to provide others with physical weapons or with the time with which to commit violent deeds. Persons whose beliefs forbid them to bear arms are called *conscientious objectors.* Such persons may serve in noncombatant assignments, such as the medical corps.

A pacifist may reject physical force either because he believes no one is ever convinced against his will, or because he believes in the sanctity and dignity of human life. In the latter case, if he is a Christian, he may interpret the command "Thou shalt not kill" and the injunction to "turn the other cheek" to be taken literally. Mahatma Gandhi of India, a non-Christian, was perhaps the outstanding pacifist of the 1900's. Some religious denominations advocate pacific means for settling debates, although individual members of these groups have fought in wars.   LOUIS O. KATTSOFF

PACK RAT, also called WOOD RAT, is a native of North and Central America. It looks much like the house rat, but has softer fur and a hairy, instead of a naked, scaly, tail. The pack rat also has cleaner habits. It will not live in sewers and garbage dumps. Some western pack rats live in the mountains and build their nests on rock ledges. Others live on the deserts in clumps of cactus and scrubby growth. They make their nests in piles of sticks and cactus. A female has one or two litters (3 to 6 young) a season.

Pack rats are curious about everything that goes on around them. They pick up and hide or carry home small articles that catch their fancy, such as silverware, nails, buckles, or even brightly colored stones. This is why they got the name *pack rats.* Sometimes the animal

The Desert Pack Rat Fortifies Its Nest With Cactus.
George M. Bradt

will drop and leave behind something he is carrying, in order to "pack off" a more attractive article. This accounts for his being called *trade rat.*

Scientific Classification. The pack rat belongs to the family *Cricetidae.* It is genus *Neotoma,* species *N. floridana, N. cinerea,* or *N. fuscipes.*   THEODORE H. EATON, JR.

See also RAT.

PACKAGING means the wrapping, boxing, or bottling of consumers' goods by the manufacturer or distributors. The purposes of packaging may be to protect a product and to promote its sales.

Packaging may have a great effect on a product's popularity. Phonograph records are one example. Phonographs and records have reached their greatest popularity only since 1938. Records which were formerly sold single and in paper envelopes are now sold in series and in colorful folios, called albums. In at least one case, one month's sales of a recording in a colorful album were as high as the entire sales of that same recording for the previous 11 years. In the field of cosmetics and perfumes, packaging is all-important for advertising and promotion. Artists are constantly at work designing bottles for perfumes, jars for face creams, and attractive containers for face powders. Often the pretty bottle attracts the buyer more than the perfume it holds.

But packaging is also important in keeping certain products fresh and clean. Some cereal manufacturers now offer individual servings of their products in miniature boxes. The small boxes attract the shopper and the variety advertises several products at one time.

Cigarettes and chewing gum are usually packaged first in tinfoil or in paper treated with a waxy substance. This keeps both dampness and dry heat from the product. A second wrapping bears an artistic design and the name of the product. And over this the manufacturer often wraps cellophane, to protect the product still further. Ice cream and butter cartons are coated with a waxy substance, both to protect the contents and to keep them from soaking through the carton.

Sometimes clever packaging helps the consumer in other ways too. The simple sliding metal spout on a salt container keeps the salt fresh and clean when it is closed. When it is open, the user can pour out just the right amount without spilling.

Sometimes packaging helps in transportation of goods. During World War II, a flexible plastic material was sprayed from a gun over airplanes and other large war machinery. This covering protected the airplane from water or weather damage during the long trip over the ocean. The plastic coating then was simply peeled off at the destination. This type of packaging may in time replace the heavy crates in which farm and home implements are now shipped.

Related Articles in WORLD BOOK include:

Cellophane	Plastics (Transparent
Food, Frozen (Packaging)	Plastics)
Glass (Glass Industry Today)	Saran
Industrial Design	Tin Can
Paper Bag	

PACKING HOUSE is an industrial plant where cattle, hogs, and sheep are killed and their meat is prepared for sale. Plants that pack fruit, vegetables, and other perishable foods are also sometimes referred to as packing houses.

Meat packing houses vary greatly in size. They

range from those that can process 500 hogs and 150 cattle in an hour to those that process 100 animals, or fewer, in a week. Packing houses sell wholesale cuts of meat to retail food stores. They also produce and sell sausage, luncheon meats, canned and frozen meats, lard, and cured meats, such as hams and bacon. The inedible parts of meat animals are sent to other factories for use in making leather, soap, fertilizer, animal feeds, and other products.   E. L. HECKLER

See also MEAT PACKING.

PACOIMA DAM. See REAGAN DAM.

PADDLEFISH lives in the rivers of the Mississippi Valley. It has sharklike fins and an oarlike snout that sticks out over its mouth. This snout gives the fish its name. The only other living member of its family inhabits the big rivers of China. The American paddlefish is usually about 3 feet long, but old paddlefish as heavy as 160 pounds have been caught.

The paddlelike blade is a sense organ, probably used in locating the tiny living things on which this fish feeds. A good quality of caviar is made from the roe

The Paddlefish feeds entirely on small forms of marine life. It catches food by straining water through its gills.

Chicago Natural History Museum

(eggs) of the paddlefish. The paddlefish is also known as the *spoon-billed catfish*.

Scientific Classification. The American paddlefish belongs to the family *Polyodontidae*. It is genus *Polyodon*, species *spathula*.   CARL L. HUBBS

PADDY. See RICE (The Rice Field).

PADDYBIRD. See RICE (Enemies).

PADEREWSKI, *pah deh REF skee*, **IGNACE JAN** (1860-1941), was a Polish pianist, composer, and statesman. During World War I, he abandoned his career as a musician to devote his energies to the cause of Polish freedom. At the close of the war, Poland again became an independent nation, largely because of the efforts of Paderewski.

Child Prodigy. Paderewski was born on Nov. 6, 1860, in Podolia, now a part of the Ukraine in Russia. His father was an administrator of large estates. His mother was the daughter of a university professor. He began his piano lessons at the age of six. When he was 12, he entered the Warsaw Conservatory and six years later was appointed a professor there.

Paderewski became a pupil of Theodor Leschetizky in Vienna in 1884. Three years later, he began a brilliant career as a concert pianist, playing to enthusiastic audiences in Europe and America. American audiences heard him for the first time in 1891 in New York City. Within 90 days he gave 117 recitals. In 1897 Paderewski

bought an estate in Morges, Switzerland, overlooking Lake Geneva. He lived there during his later years.

Polish Patriot. Paderewski's devotion to Poland is now a part of history. During World War I he gave concerts to raise relief funds, and he helped enlist men for the Polish Army. He represented his country at the Versailles Peace Conference and at the League of Nations. He served as premier, as well as minister of foreign affairs, in the Polish republic. But political disputes arose, and Paderewski and his cabinet remained in power for only 10 months.

Later Career. In 1922, Paderewski resumed his concerts. His first postwar tour, which included 60 concerts, is said to have earned him about $460,000. He had given away most of the money he had previously earned to help Poland. The first volume of his life story, *The Paderewski Memoirs*, appeared in 1938.

He made his last American tour in 1939 at the age of 78. After suffering a mild heart attack, he returned to Switzerland. A few months later, Germany invaded Poland, and World War II began. Once more Paderewski devoted himself to the cause of Poland. He was named president of the new Polish Parliament in exile, later called the Polish National Council. Late in 1940, he returned to the United States to make his home on a ranch in California. He died in New York City.

Paderewski's compositions include the opera *Manru, Sonata in A minor* for violin and piano, six humoresques for piano, and "Polish Fantasy" and *Concerto in A minor* for piano and orchestra. His last composition, *Symphony in B minor*, is a musical picture of the tragic history of Poland.   ROBERT U. NELSON

Ignace Paderewski won fame and fortune as one of the greatest concert pianists of all time. As a Polish statesman, he helped his country regain its independence after World War I.

Culver

PADRE ISLAND, *PAD ree,* stretches for about 100 miles along the Texas coast. Laguna Madre, a long shallow lagoon, separates Padre Island from the mainland. For location, see TEXAS (physical map). Causeways give easy access to nearby Corpus Christi and Brownsville. The island serves as a recreational center. In addition, air force and naval units use a gunnery and bombing range there. The island takes its name from Padre (Father) Nicolás Balli, a Spanish priest who started a ranch there about 1800. In 1962, a national seashore was authorized for Padre Island. See also TEXAS (color picture).   H. BAILEY CARROLL

PADUA, *PAD yoo uh* (pop. 205,057; alt. 43 ft.), stands on the Bacchiglione River, 22 miles southwest of Venice (see ITALY [political map]). It is the oldest city in northern Italy, and its history is rich in architecture, art, and famous men. Many of Padua's narrow, crooked streets are lined with arcades, and several high Roman bridges cross the various arms of the river. The city has many medieval palaces and churches.

Padua's art treasures include works by such well-known masters as Giotto, Donatello, and Fra Filippo Lippi. The Roman historian Livy was born in Padua, and at one time Dante lived there. Galileo lectured for 18 years in Padua's famous university, which was founded in 1222 by Emperor Frederick II. A celebrated botanical garden, the oldest in Europe, is connected with the university.

Today Padua manufactures automobile parts, refrigerators, and other machinery. It has a prosperous trade in fruit, grain, wine, and cattle.   SHEPARD B. CLOUGH

PADUCAH, *puh DOO kuh,* Ky. (pop. 34,479; alt. 345 ft.), the seat of McCracken County, lies on the southern bank of the Ohio River where the Ohio and Tennessee rivers meet (see KENTUCKY [political map]).

The city is the metropolitan center of the Jackson Purchase area of western Kentucky. Its products include hosiery, chemicals, textiles, and leather goods. A uranium-separation plant opened nearby in 1954. Paducah was founded in 1827 and chartered in 1856. It has a council-manager government.   THOMAS D. CLARK

PAGAN, *pah GAHN,* is a volcanic island in the Pacific Ocean. It is one of the northern Mariana Islands, and lies about 175 miles north of Saipan. Pagan has an area of 19 square miles. The island is steep, and has several dormant volcanoes. Mt. Pagan is 1,870 feet high. The island is part of the Trust Territory of the Pacific Islands administered by the United States. About 50 persons live there.   EDWIN H. BRYAN, JR.

PAGANINI, *PAG uh NEE nee,* **NICCOLÒ** (1782-1840), became one of the greatest violinists of all time. It was said that "he looked like a magician and his playing justified his looks." Paganini was 9 years old when he made his concert debut in Genoa, Italy. From the age of 13, he enjoyed one triumphant concert tour after another. He played quiet melodies so beautifully that his audiences often burst into tears. But he could also perform with such force and speed that a fantastic story began to circulate that the great violinist was in league with the Devil, who guided his bow.

Once Paganini established his fame, his life became a combination of artistic triumphs and extravagant living. At one time he pawned his violin to pay a

gambling debt. A French merchant gave him one made by Giuseppe Guarnieri, so that Paganini could play a concert. Paganini left this violin to the city of Genoa, where it is kept in a museum.

At the age of 13, Paganini began to compose pieces for the violin. His works include 24 caprices for violin; two concertos for violin and orchestra, in *D major* and *B minor;* and *Moto Perpetuo (Perpetual Motion).* Paganini was born in Genoa, Italy, on Oct. 27, 1782.   DOROTHY DeLAY

Brown Bros.
Niccolò Paganini

PAGE. See KNIGHTS AND KNIGHTHOOD.

PAGE, WALTER HINES (1855-1918), was an American editor and diplomat. He served as United States ambassador to Great Britain during World War I. Page was born at Cary, N.C., and was educated at Randolph-Macon College and Johns Hopkins University. In 1899 he became a partner in the publishing firm of Doubleday, Page and Company. In 1900 he founded the magazine *The World's Work,* which he edited until 1913.   KENNETH N. STEWART

PAGE, WILLIAM TYLER (1868-1942), wrote *The American's Creed,* which the U.S. House of Representatives adopted in 1918 (see AMERICAN'S CREED). In 1881, he became a page (messenger) in the House of Representatives, and then made a career of rising through the ranks of House employees. He held the honored position of clerk of the House from 1919 to 1931. Page was born in Frederick, Md.   EDWIN H. CADY

PAGEANT, *PAJ unt,* is a spectacular show. The term comes from the Latin word *pagina,* meaning *platform.* In England by the 1500's the word had become *pageant.* Then it meant a movable platform which was wheeled to the public square to present mystery plays and other dramas.

Today, the word means the dramatic production itself. Most pageants are plays of special significance, such as a drama portraying the growth of a city or the development of medicine. A pageant does not have to be a play. The annual Tournament of Roses parade in Pasadena, Calif., is a pageant.   GLENN HUGHES

PAGEANT OF THE PACIFIC. See GOLDEN GATE INTERNATIONAL EXPOSITION.

PAGLIACCI, I. See OPERA (I Pagliacci).

PAGO PAGO. See SAMOA.

PAGODA, *puh GO duh,* is a towerlike building with many stories. Pagodas are common in India, China, Thailand, Burma, Japan, and other countries of Asia. The pagodas of India are connected with honor given to Buddha. They are often elaborate in design. The pagoda of India may be an addition to a temple, or it may be a temple itself.

In China the pagoda is often a memorial building. The typical Chinese pagoda has eight sides and many stories. Each story has an odd roof which curves upward. The Chinese use brick, glazed tile, or porcelain to build their pagodas, and decorate them with ivory, bone, and stonework. Chinese pagodas are less elaborate than those of India. In some parts of China, the pagoda is as common as the windmill is in The Netherlands. Japanese pagodas are usually built of wood. The pagodas of Thailand and Burma are often round instead of many-sided. HOWARD M. DAVIS

See also BURMA (The Arts); CHINA (color picture: Eight-Sided Pagodas); NANKING (picture); TEMPLE.

PAHANG. See MALAYSIA.

PAIGE, SATCHEL (1904?-   ), was one of the greatest pitchers in baseball history. He pitched for touring Negro teams and teams in Negro minor leagues for almost 30 years at a time when Negroes could not play in the major leagues. He once struck out Rogers Hornsby, one of baseball's greatest hitters, five times in an exhibition game. In 1937, Yankee star Joe DiMaggio called Paige the greatest pitcher he ever faced.

Paige was past his peak when the major leagues ended their ban on Negro players. He was in his 40's when he joined the Cleveland Indians and became the first Negro pitcher in the American League in 1948. Yet, he helped Cleveland win the American League pennant that year. Paige pitched for the St. Louis Browns from 1951 to 1953. In 1968, he joined the Atlanta Braves as a pitcher and coach, but he did not pitch in any regular season games. In 1969, Paige became a trainer for the Atlanta club. LeRoy Robert Paige was born in Mobile, Ala. HERMAN WEISKOPF

PAIN is a sensation that results when body tissue is damaged at a rapid rate. It may be caused by a burn, a blow, or the swelling and stretching of blood vessels that occurs in some types of headaches. Lack of oxygen may cause painful muscle cramps. Nerves carry pain impulses to the brain. Nerves react to stimuli, including electricity, pressure, extreme heat and cold, and many chemicals. Injury also causes the release of chemical substances in the tissues that make the nerve endings easier to stimulate, or more sensitive.

Pain protects a person by causing him to avoid further contact with dangerous objects. For example, after a person has been burned by fire, he tries to avoid touching a flame again. The body's reaction to pain may limit the effect of an injury. A person with a broken leg avoids moving it because movement causes pain.

The least intensity of stimulation that causes pain is the *pain threshold*. Some pain-relieving drugs raise the pain threshold. Others correct the disorder that causes the pain. But most drugs help relieve pain by changing the patient's moods so that he feels pain with less alarm and anxiety. HAROLD G. WOLFF

See also ANALGESIC; ANODYNE; SENSES.

PAINE, ROBERT TREAT (1731-1814), a Massachusetts signer of the Declaration of Independence, served as the first attorney general of his state from 1777 to 1790. He helped write the state constitution of 1780.

In 1790, he became a justice of the state supreme court, where he served until his retirement in 1804. Paine had been active in the prelude to the American Revolution, and had served in the Continental Congress. He was born in Boston, and was graduated from Harvard in 1749. Paine then studied law and became a lawyer in 1757. He helped found the American Academy of Arts and Sciences. CLARENCE L. VER STEEG

PAINE, THOMAS

PAINE, THOMAS (1737-1809), was a famous pamphleteer, agitator, and writer on politics and religion. His writings greatly influenced the political thinking of the leaders of the Revolutionary War in America, and he became a famous figure in Paris during the French Revolution. He has been described as an "Englishman by birth, French citizen by decree, and American by adoption." Paine's opinions and personality aroused strong feelings in those around him. Some admired him greatly, but others hated him fiercely. Many historians regard Paine as a patriot who did much for his adopted country and asked nothing in return. He stated clearly and concisely political ideas that other men accepted and supported, if necessary, to the point of death. Yet he died a social outcast.

Early Life. Paine was born in Thetford, England, on Jan. 29, 1737. His family was poor, and he received little schooling. He began working at the age of 13. At 19, he went to sea for a time. Later, he served as a customs collector in London, but was discharged. His first wife died, and he was separated legally from his second wife. Paine was alone and poor in 1774. But he gained the friendship of Benjamin Franklin, then in London, who advised him to go to America.

American Revolutionary. Paine arrived in America with letters of recommendation from Franklin. He soon became contributing editor to the *Pennsylvania Magazine*, and began working for the freedom cause. In 1776, he published his pamphlet *Common Sense*, a brilliant statement of the colonists' cause. It demanded complete independence from England and the establish-

ment of a strong federal union. George Washington, Thomas Jefferson, and other colonial leaders read it with approval. In December, 1776, Paine followed *Common Sense* with a series of pamphlets called *The Crisis*. The first of these began, "These are the times that try men's souls. The summer soldier and the sunshine patriot will, in this crisis shrink from the service of their country. . . . Tyranny, like hell, is not easily conquered." Washington had the pamphlet read aloud to his soldiers. Paine's bold, clear words encouraged the Continental Army during the darkest days of the war.

Paine served as a soldier in 1776. In April, 1777, he became secretary to the Congressional Committee of Foreign Affairs. His honesty in exposing questionable actions by Silas Deane, American commissioner to France, made him enemies, and Paine was forced to resign from his position.

Paine in Poverty. Paine then lived on the charity of his friends. He received an appointment as clerk of the Pennsylvania Assembly, but gave much of the money he earned by his writings to the revolutionary cause. He continued his *Crisis* pamphlets. Several years after the Revolutionary War, the state of Pennsylvania gave him about $2,500, the New York legislature gave him a house and farm near New Rochelle, and Congress voted him $3,000. But he was soon poor again.

Paine went to France in 1787 and then to England. While in England in 1791 and 1792, he published his famous *Rights of Man*, which ably replied to Edmund Burke's attack on the French Revolution (see BURKE, EDMUND). William Pitt's government suppressed this work, and Paine was tried for treason and outlawed in December, 1792. But he had returned to France.

French Revolutionary. The National Assembly of France made Paine a French citizen on Aug. 26, 1792. He became a member of the National Convention, but he could not sympathize with all the bloodshed and violence of the French Revolution. His lack of tact again brought him enemies, and he was expelled from the convention, deprived of his French citizenship, and imprisoned for more than 10 months. The American minister, James Monroe, claimed him as an American citizen and obtained his release.

While in prison, Paine worked on *Age of Reason*. It stated his views on religion, and many people called it the "atheist's bible." It began: "I believe in one God, and no more; and I hope for happiness beyond this life." Although Paine believed in God, he disagreed with many accepted church teachings. His unorthodox views on religion made him one of the most hated men of his time.

Dies Neglected. In 1802, President Thomas Jefferson arranged for Paine's safe return to the United States. Paine found that people remembered him more for his opinions on religion than for his Revolutionary War services. During his last years, Paine was poor, ill, and a social outcast. He was buried on his farm in New Rochelle, but 10 years later his body was removed to England. MERLE CURTI

PAINE COLLEGE is a coeducational liberal arts school, primarily for Negroes, in Augusta, Ga. It is affiliated with the United Methodist Church and the Christian Methodist Episcopal Church. It grants A.B. and B.S. in Ed. degrees. It was founded in 1882. For enrollment, see UNIVERSITIES AND COLLEGES (table).

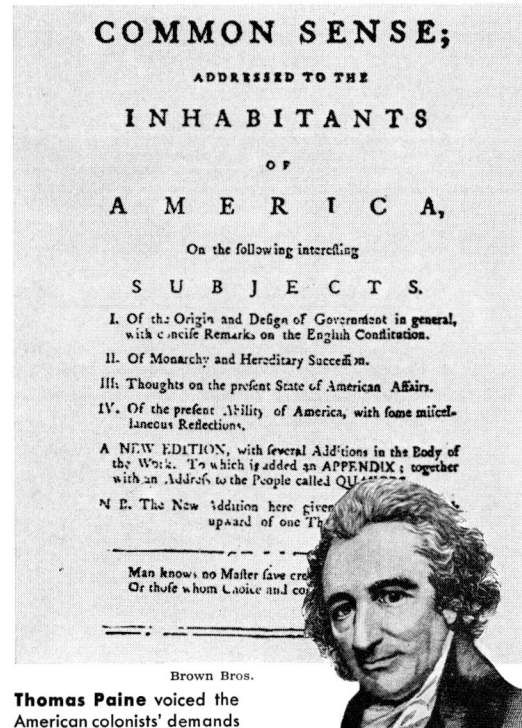

COMMON SENSE;

ADDRESSED TO THE

INHABITANTS

OF

AMERICA,

On the following interesting

SUBJECTS.

I. Of the Origin and Design of Government in general, with concise Remarks on the English Constitution.

II. Of Monarchy and Hereditary Succession.

III. Thoughts on the present State of American Affairs.

IV. Of the present Ability of America, with some miscellaneous Reflections.

A NEW EDITION, with several Additions in the Body of the Work. To which is added an APPENDIX; together with an Address to the People called QUAKERS.

N.B. The New Addition here given upward of one Th...

Man knows no Master save creating HEAVEN, Or those whom Choice and co...

Brown Bros.

Thomas Paine voiced the American colonists' demands for freedom with his famous pamphlet *Common Sense*.

Gaily Colored Paints brighten homes and other buildings indoors and protect outdoor surfaces from the weather.
H. Armstrong Roberts;
Monsanto Chemical Co.

PAINT makes our homes attractive and protects them from the weather. Paint adds color to rooms in schools, offices, and factories. It makes fire-alarm boxes red and mailboxes red, white, and blue. Gaily painted automobiles speed along streets marked by white-painted safety lanes and yellow-painted no-parking areas. Works of art painted by artists add beauty to homes, offices, and public buildings.

Paint protects buildings from wind, rain, and the heat of the sun. It helps ships travel rapidly through the water, because paint protects their hulls from rust and barnacles. Hospital rooms painted in bright colors cheer patients and speed their recovery. A white or cream-painted radiator gives off as much as one fifth more heat than a dark-colored one. Some clocks and watches glow in the dark because the numbers and hands are covered with luminous, or glowing, paint.

Paint manufacturers in the United States sell more than 635,000,000 gallons of paint a year. This amount of paint would cover more than 11,400 square miles, or an area larger than the state of Maryland.

What Is Paint?

Paint is a mixture of a liquid and one or more colored powders. The colored powder is called a *pigment*. The liquid that carries the pigment and makes it easy to spread is called a *vehicle*, or *binder*, and may include a *solvent*, or *thinner*.

Pigments are divided into two chief types: (1) prime and (2) inert. *Prime pigments*, such as white lead, red lead, and chrome green, give paint its color. *Inert pigments* are materials such as talc, mica, or clay, that make the paint last longer. See CHROME; RED LEAD; TALC; WHITE LEAD.

Vehicles may be oils, varnishes, or resins. An *alkyd resin* is an artificially made varnish vehicle. When the vehicle contacts the air, it dries and hardens. This causes paint to become a hard film that holds the pigment on the painted surface. See OIL (Fixed Oils); RESIN; VARNISH.

Solvents, or thinners, often are added to paint to make it more liquid. Turpentine and water are the most common thinners.

Kinds of Paint

Different kinds of paint have different pigments and vehicles. The nine basic kinds of paint are: (1) oil-based, (2) rubber-based, (3) casein and calcimine ("water"), (4) fire-retardant, (5) heat-resistant, (6) cement water, (7) metal, (8) wood and plaster primers, and (9) enamels.

Oil-Based Paints include outside paints, metal-protective paints, flat wall paints, and floor paints.

Outside Paint covers houses, barns, and other buildings. It usually has a vehicle made of vegetable drying oils, such as linseed oil or soybean oil. White lead, zinc oxide, titanium dioxide, and iron oxides are the most widely used prime pigments in outside paints.

Metal-Protective Paint is used both indoors and outdoors on bridges, ships, farm and factory machinery, and other metal surfaces. These paints generally have varnish vehicles, although sometimes they contain oil vehicles. Prime pigments of red lead or zinc chromate help prevent rust and corrosion.

21

MAKING PAINT

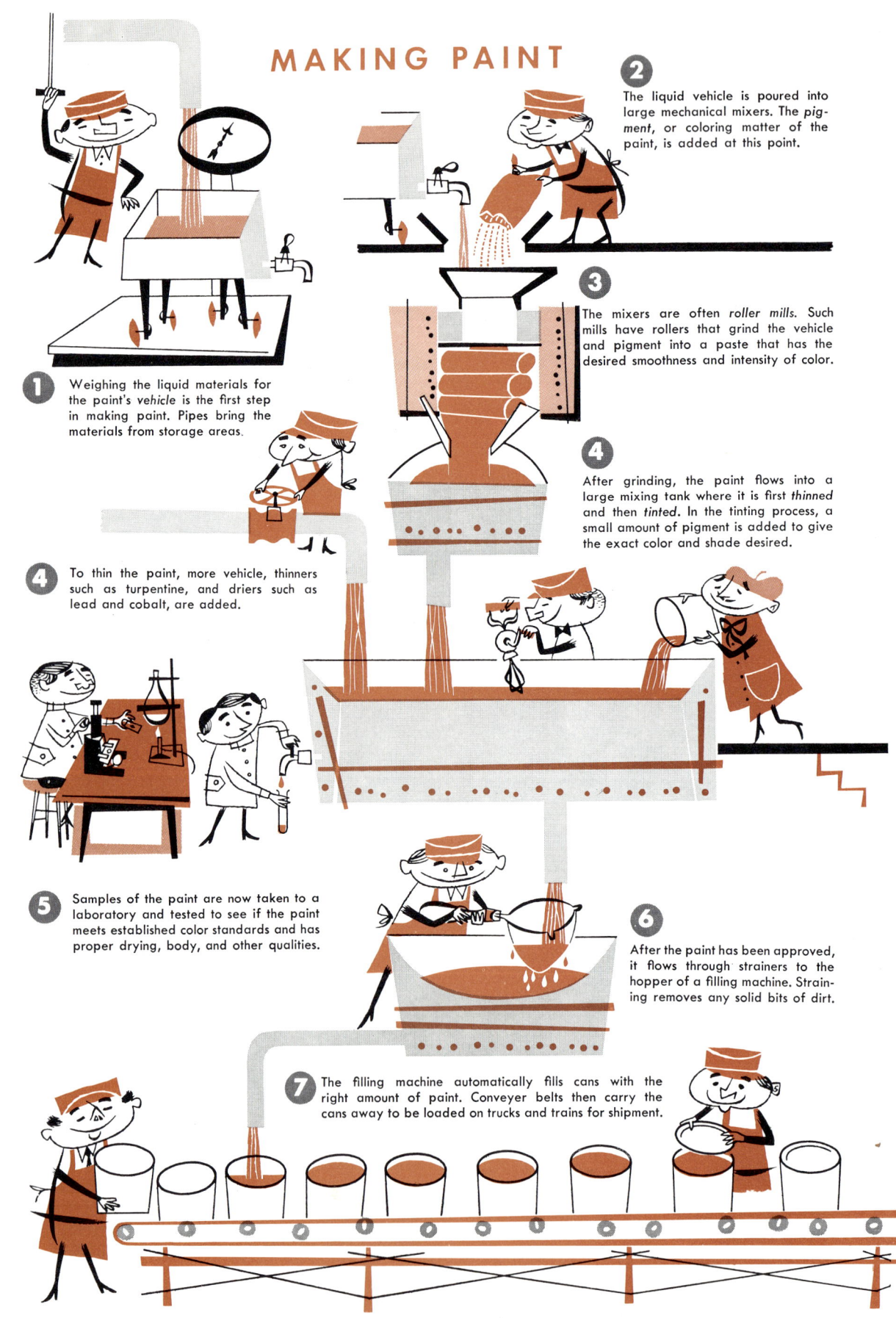

2 The liquid vehicle is poured into large mechanical mixers. The *pigment*, or coloring matter of the paint, is added at this point.

1 Weighing the liquid materials for the paint's *vehicle* is the first step in making paint. Pipes bring the materials from storage areas.

3 The mixers are often *roller mills*. Such mills have rollers that grind the vehicle and pigment into a paste that has the desired smoothness and intensity of color.

4 After grinding, the paint flows into a large mixing tank where it is first *thinned* and then *tinted*. In the tinting process, a small amount of pigment is added to give the exact color and shade desired.

4 To thin the paint, more vehicle, thinners such as turpentine, and driers such as lead and cobalt, are added.

5 Samples of the paint are now taken to a laboratory and tested to see if the paint meets established color standards and has proper drying, body, and other qualities.

6 After the paint has been approved, it flows through strainers to the hopper of a filling machine. Straining removes any solid bits of dirt.

7 The filling machine automatically fills cans with the right amount of paint. Conveyer belts then carry the cans away to be loaded on trucks and trains for shipment.

Flat Wall Paint is used inside homes, offices, schools, and other buildings. It contains an oil-resin-varnish vehicle or an alkyd-resin vehicle. Large amounts of prime pigments give these paints a flat, or dull, gloss or sheen.

Floor Paint covers floors and porches. It has a varnish or alkyd-resin vehicle. Floor paints contain inert pigments such as talc, mica, or clay to make them wear.

Rubber-Based Paints, also called *latex* paints, include wall paints, masonry paints, and chemical-resistant paints. Some rubber-based paints have a vehicle of chlorinated synthetic or natural rubber or styrene-butadiene resin. These paints are *solvent-thinned.* That is, solvents such as xylol are used to thin them at the factory. *Water-thinned,* rubber-based paints have a vehicle of acrylic or polyvinyl resins suspended in water. This suspension is called an *emulsion,* and such paints are often called *emulsion paints.*

Rubber-Based Wall Paint may be used on either inside or outside walls. Most rubber-based wall paints are emulsion paints. They contain both prime and inert pigments.

Rubber-Based Masonry Paint may be used on bricks, concrete blocks, and concrete walls. Some masonry paints are made of solvent-thinned, synthetic-rubber resins. The solvent evaporates, leaving the paint as a hard film that resists the alkali on the masonry surface (see ALKALI). Many modern masonry paints are made with polyvinyl acetate or acrylic emulsions, and are water-thinned. They are easier to apply, and also resist the alkali in concrete. Both types of paint contain both prime and inert pigments.

Rubber-Based Chemical-Resistant Paint is often used to cover laboratory table tops in schools and chemical factories. It has a solvent-thinned rubber base. The synthetic rubber makes these paints acidproof. Prime pigments give them color.

Casein and Calcimine Paints, often called "water paints," are used to cover inside walls of homes. Stores usually sell these paints in powdered form. Water must be added to the powder before painting. The vehicle for casein paints is casein made from milk (see CASEIN). Calcimine paints contain calcium carbonate and prime pigments, and have a vehicle of glue (see CALCIMINE).

Fire-Retardant Paints protect buildings against fire damage. These paints can catch fire and burn, but the blazing paint can be snuffed out when the igniting flame is removed. Good fire-retardant paint contains nitrogen chemicals that make it puff up. The blister forms a thick insulating barrier between the flame and the surface. These paints have prime pigments and either oil or oil-resin vehicles. There is no such thing as a completely fireproof paint.

Heat-Resisting Paints are used to cover warm and hot surfaces. Alkyd-resin vehicles are used in paints for moderately hot surfaces, such as cylinder heads of aircraft engines. Paints with silicone-resin vehicles last longer on hot surfaces, such as ovens. Boilers that become quite hot may be covered with paints containing metallic pigments such as aluminum, and thin vehicles such as varnish. The vehicle burns out and the metal pigment becomes part of the hot surface.

Cement Water Paints add color to sidewalks, cement blocks, basement floors, and cement porches. To make these paints, cement is mixed with prime pigments and inert materials, such as clay or talc. The painter adds water to the paint before using it. The cement and water form the vehicle.

Metallic Paints are made with aluminum or bronze powder. They have many uses, such as on storage tanks and bridges. These paints usually have a prime pigment made of aluminum powder. The powder is made so that the leafy flakes float to the top of the paint. This gives the painted surface a metallic shine. Other metals may be used in the paint to make it dry to a gold color. Metal paints contain oil-resin vehicles.

Wood and Plaster Primers are used for first coats on plaster and wood walls. They fill the tiny openings in the wood and plaster, so that other paints will stick to the surface and not sink into it. Plaster and wood primers have varnish vehicles and prime and inert pigments.

Enamels may be used to cover the inside and outside walls of houses and other buildings, or for bicycles and automobiles. They have varnish or alkyd vehicles and contain only small amounts of prime pigments. The low pigment content makes the paint dry with a high gloss or shine. It is often used in bathrooms and kitchens. *Baking Enamels* used on metal are prepared with synthetic resin-varnish vehicles that dry by baking or heating.

How to Use Paint

The surface to be painted must be clean and free of dust, dirt, grease, oil, moisture, or wax. Otherwise, even the most expensive paint will not stick to the surface properly, and in a short time will peel and chip off. Before painting a surface, old paint should be removed if it is chipped or cracked. This can be done by brushing the surface with a wire brush or scraping it. Most hardware stores and paint shops sell wire brushes and paint scrapers. The rough edges left after scraping should be smoothed down with sandpaper and the surface should then be dusted with a dry brush or washed off to remove loose particles of paint, sand, and dirt. Holes and cracks in the surface should be filled with patching plaster. Hardware and paint stores sell small amounts of special plasters developed for this purpose.

Paint must be stirred and sometimes thinned before it is used. Labels on paint cans have directions for thinning.

Brushes, sprayers, or rollers may be used to apply paint. Flat surfaces such as walls can be painted faster with a roller than with a brush. A brush or sprayer is best for painting small objects and uneven surfaces. Brushes and sprayers can paint small cracks and narrow corners which rollers miss. Brushes, sprayers, and rollers should be cleaned immediately after use with solvents similar to the solvent in the paint. Turpentine, naphtha, and water are generally used for cleaning brushes and rollers. Sprayers can be washed with cleaners such as methyl alcohol or benzene.

The amount of paint needed to cover a surface depends on the kind of paint used and the type of surface. For example, a gallon of an oil-base white paint covers about 300 square feet on an outside wall of a home. But a gallon of rubber-base white paint covers about 200 square feet of an inside wall. A primer should be used as the first coat on any new surface being painted.

23

PAINTING INDOORS

READY THE ROOM

Move out or cover all furniture.

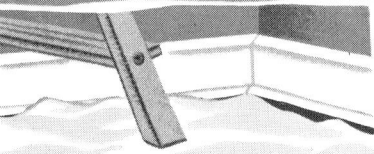

Protect the floor with dropcloths.

Remove fixtures on surface to be painted such as doorknobs and plates over outlets.

ASSEMBLE MATERIALS

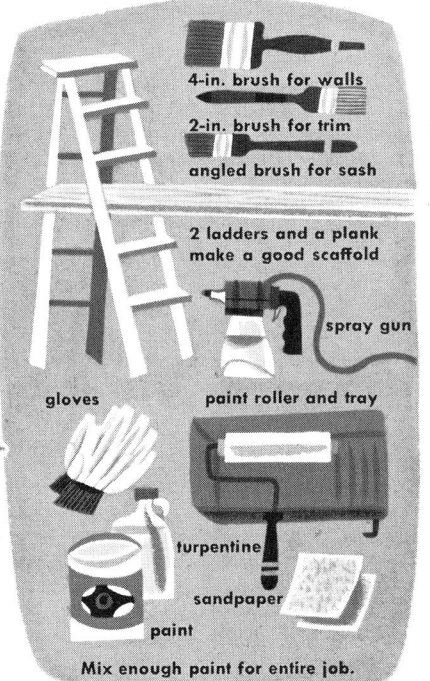

4-in. brush for walls

2-in. brush for trim

angled brush for sash

2 ladders and a plank make a good scaffold

spray gun

gloves

paint roller and tray

turpentine

sandpaper

paint

Mix enough paint for entire job.

PREPARE SURFACES

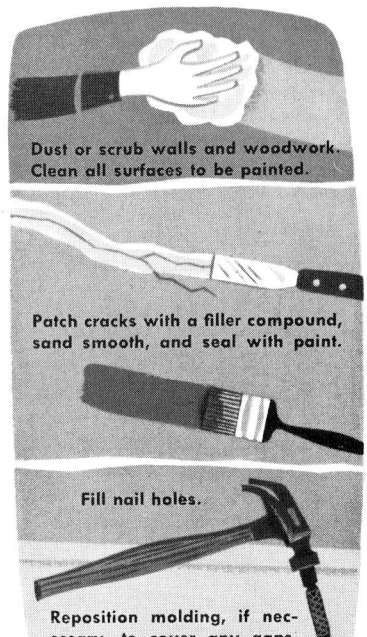

Dust or scrub walls and woodwork. Clean all surfaces to be painted.

Patch cracks with a filler compound, sand smooth, and seal with paint.

Fill nail holes.

Reposition molding, if necessary, to cover any gaps.

Paint ceilings first. Start in a corner and work across narrowest width. Paint in small strips. Use slightly curved strokes, lifting brush as stroke ends.

When painting with a roller, first use a brush to paint corners and along edges the roller cannot reach. Roll up and down on walls and then horizontally to finish. Roll in two directions on ceilings.

Start painting walls in a corner at the top. Paint in 2- or 3-foot-wide strips from ceiling to baseboard. Fan out brush bristles to paint corners and edges.

Paint windows in the order of the numbers, *left*. Do the crosspieces first. Next, do the sash, and then the frames.

Paint door surfaces in the numbered order, *left*. Inset panels should be painted first, then the vertical and horizontal surfaces.

Protect baseboards with masking tape and newspapers. Also protect other wood trim with masking tape.

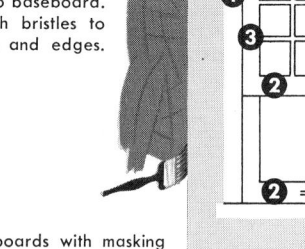

To get paint on the brush, dip bristles halfway into paint. Slap bristles lightly against the inside of the pail to remove excess paint.

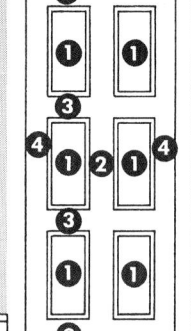

Use cardboard guards, *right*, to protect floors and walls, when painting baseboards and molding.

Rollers vary in width from 2 to 12 inches. They are made of short or long fibers called *naps*. Short naps are used chiefly for enamel. Enamels spread easily with short nap rollers, because they are thinner than most paints. Rollers with long naps are used for thicker paints to assure even coats.

Paint to be applied with a roller is poured into a tray. The painter dips the roller into the paint and lets the excess paint roll out of the fiber onto the base of the tray. He uses crisscross and up-and-down strokes to spread the paint on the wall. To avoid streaks, each rolled strip of paint should extend into the wet edge of the previous strip painted.

Brushes must have hog bristles or synthetic fibers. The bristles should be properly split on the ends, and curved to hold paint. The painter dips the brush into the paint can. He uses a fanlike motion to brush the paint onto a surface. He applies each brushful to a dry part of the surface, and brushes toward the wet area already covered. This prevents streaking. See BRUSH.

Spray Guns force thinned paint into tiny drops under pressure. The painter holds the spray gun about a foot away from the surface to be painted. He regulates the distance so that only a thin film will cover the surface. The paint should overlap the last area covered.

How Paint Is Made

Mixing. The paint maker puts a small amount of the vehicle into a large mechanical mixer at the paint plant. He gradually adds the powdered pigment. The slowly rotating blades of the mixer make a heavy paste out of the pigment and vehicle.

Grinding. A workman puts the paste into a *mill*, or grinder, to break up the pigment particles and scatter them throughout the vehicle. *Ball* or *pebble mills* are large, steel-lined cylinders that contain pebbles or steel balls. As the cylinders rotate, the balls or pebbles spin and hit against each other, grinding the paint. A *roller mill* has steel cylinders that rotate against each other to grind and mix the pigment.

Thinning and Drying. Another worker pours the ground paste into a tank, where it is mechanically mixed with more vehicle, solvents, and driers. Solvents such as naphtha or water thin the paste. Lead, cobalt, and manganese salts are added to make the paint dry quickly. The paint is mixed until it is almost thin enough to use.

Tinting. A workman called a *tinter* adds a small amount of pigment to give the paint the exact color and shade desired. The tinter sends a sample of the new paint to the company's control laboratory, which tests the color and quality. Color and quality standards are set by paint companies and by the National Bureau of Standards (see NATIONAL BUREAU OF STANDARDS).

Straining and Packaging. The paint is strained through a felt bag, or some other type of filter, to remove any solid bits of dust or dirt. Then it is poured into a filling tank, and finally into the metal cans in which it is sold. Stores usually sell paint in half-pint, pint, quart, gallon, and five-gallon containers.

History

Early Paint. Prehistoric men made paints by grinding colored materials such as plants and clay into powder, and adding water. They used it for decoration in their

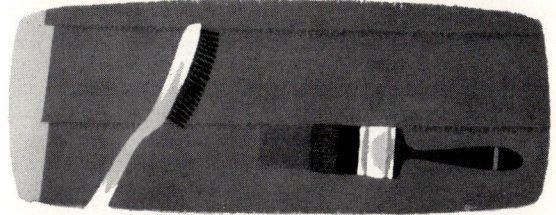

Prepare Outdoor Surfaces by removing loose paint with a wire brush or scraper. Polish rust spots from metal. Put a primer coat of paint on spots where bare wood or metal is exposed.

Clean corners and horizontal surfaces by dusting. A painter's round dusting brush is best for this purpose.

Remove Loose Putty from the windows. Coat the bare wood with a linseed-oil primer and then apply new putty.

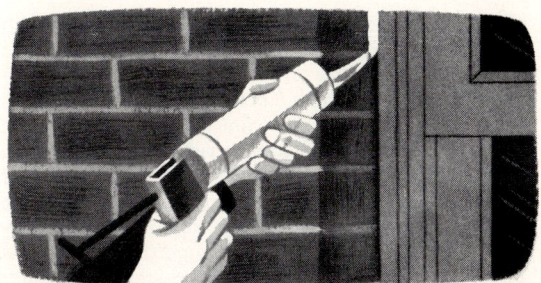

Caulk Loose Joints where door frames, window frames, and porches join the main part of a building. Caulking is especially important to seal seams between masonry walls and wood frames.

Paint Wood Siding by laying a new brushful of paint on two or three spots. Then brush out these spots, doing the edges first. Use only the flat side of the brush. Start at the top, painting several boards across the house, before moving down.

Paint Test Farms research the lasting power of paints by exposing hundreds of samples of paint outdoors for long periods of time.

DuPont

caves and tombs, and on their bodies. Caves with painted walls, dating back 50,000 years, have been found in Europe.

Historians believe that 8,000 years ago the Egyptians became the first people to paint with a wide variety of colors. The Egyptians at first made their paints from materials found in the earth of their own country and in neighboring areas. They also learned how to make crude brushes with which to apply the paint. By 1500 B.C., the Egyptians were importing indigo and madder plants from India to make additional colors (see INDIGO; MADDER). A deep blue color can be made from indigo and different shades of red, violet, and brown from madder. These plants are still used today in various parts of the world to make colors and dyes. Painting and paint making had also become known in Crete and Greece by 1500 B.C.

The Romans learned the skills of making paint from the Egyptians. Examples of the Roman paints and painting can be seen in the ruins of Pompeii. The Romans, in the 400's B.C., were also probably the first to use white lead as a pigment. After the collapse of the Roman Empire in the A.D. 400's, the art of making paints became lost until the English began making paints near the end of the Middle Ages. The English used the paints chiefly on churches at first, then later on public buildings and the homes of wealthy persons. During the 1400's and 1500's, Italian artists made pigments and vehicles for paints. Each artist or craftsman developed his own paint-making processes. Unfortunately they kept the formulas for their paints a secret. The

formula used to produce a paint died with its inventor.

Paint Manufacturing. A few persons went into the business of making paints in the United States and Europe in the 1700's. These early manufacturers ground their pigments and oils on a stone table with a round stone. American colonists also made their own paints. They used materials such as eggs, coffee grounds, and skimmed milk, and thinned the paints with water. In the late 1700's and early 1800's, paint manufacturers began using power-driven machinery to make paint. These first manufacturers, however, only made the materials for paint. They supplied the materials to the painter, who had to do his own mixing. In 1867, manufacturers put the first prepared paints on the market. The development of new machines to grind and mix paints in the late 1800's also enabled paint manufacturers to produce large amounts of paint.

Recent Developments. Chemists developed new pigments and synthetic resins during World Wars I and II. These pigments and vehicles replaced many ingredients of paint, such as linseed oil, which was needed for military purposes. Research projects conducted by chemists and engineers have become a major activity of paint manufacturing. During the late 1950's, chemists developed better finishes for outside house paints, new types of enamels for automobile finishes, and drip-proof paints for inside and outside surfaces. During the 1960's, continued research with synthetic resins improved paint resistance against chemicals and gases. Fluorescent paints also became common in the 1960's.   E. M. FISHER

Related Articles in WORLD BOOK include:

Outline

I. What Is Paint?
    A. Pigments   B. Vehicles   C. Solvents

II. Kinds of Paint
    A. Oil-Based Paints   F. Cement Water Paints
    B. Rubber-Based Paints   G. Metallic Paints
    C. Casein and Calcimine   H. Wood and Plaster
       Paints   Primers
    D. Fire-Retardant Paints   I. Enamels
    E. Heat-Resisting Paints

III. How to Use Paint
    A. Rollers   B. Brushes   C. Spray Guns

IV. How Paint Is Made
    A. Mixing   D. Tinting
    B. Grinding   E. Straining and
    C. Thinning and Drying   Packaging

V. History

Questions

In what ways is paint of great importance to man?

Why must a different paint be used on a barn than on a bedroom wall?

What are the basic ingredients of paint?

What is a pigment? A vehicle? A thinner? A drier?

Why does paint dry to a hard film?

What are fire-retarding paints? How do they differ from heat-resisting paints?

What may cause paint to chip and peel from a surface?

How did ancient men make paints?

What are three ways of applying paint?

What must be done to a surface before it is painted?

National Park Service

The Painted Desert's brilliant coloring appears in terrace, mesa, and hill formations. The desert covers a vast area along the Little Colorado River in north-central Arizona.

PAINTED DESERT is a brilliantly colored region extending about 200 miles along the Little Colorado River in north-central Arizona. For location, see ARIZONA (physical map).

The desert received its name from early Spanish explorers, who called it *El Desierto Pintado*, meaning *The Painted Desert*. It is a fantastic wasteland, with buttes, mesas, pinnacles, and valleys formed by ages of wind and rain cutting into shalelike volcanic ash. The pastel colors of the desert add to its beauty, especially because heat, light, and dust often seem to change the colors from blue, amethyst, and yellow to russet, lilac, and red. The Painted Desert is particularly beautiful at sunrise and sunset, when the colors are the most brilliant and the shadows the deepest. The bright reds and yellows of the desert come from iron oxides—hematite (red) and limonite (yellow).

Several national monuments are in the Painted Desert. These include the Sunset Crater and Wupatki national monuments. ALICE B. GOOD

PAINTED-TONGUE, or SALPIGLOSSIS, is a beautiful garden flower related to the petunia. Like the petunia, it has trumpet-shaped blossoms, but they are much more handsomely colored. The colors cover a wide range, including deep red, pink, purple, brownish orange, salmon, yellow, and white. The petals have a rich velvety sheen, and are often streaked with yellow and other colors. The painted-tongue is an annual plant and must be planted from seed each year. It grows about 18 inches high, and has several flowers near the top of each stalk.

Scientific Classification. The painted-tongue belongs to the nightshade family, *Solanaceae*. It is genus *Salpiglossis*, species *S. sinuata*. ALFRED C. HOTTES

PAINTER refers to the artist who paints pictures, and also to the skilled workman in the building trades. Painters on construction projects work on both the outside and the inside of a structure. There are other opportunities for the skilled painter. If he has a talent for color and design, he may become an interior decorator. Many painters go into business for themselves.

For biographies of artists who are painters, see the Related Articles at the end of the PAINTING article.

PAINTER'S COLIC, which is sometimes called *lead colic*, is a severe pain in the abdomen due to lead poisoning. White and red lead in paints can enter the body through the skin, and lead vapors may be breathed in through the lungs. Besides the colic, lead poisoning brings on weakness, anemia, constipation, and trembling. J. F. A. McMANUS

See also LEAD POISONING.

Trumpet-Shaped Blossoms in a wide range of brilliant colors make the painted-tongue a favorite garden flower.
J. Horace McFarland

27

Super Anscochrome, Ansco

PAINTING

Allen S. Weller, the contributor of this article, is Dean of the College of Fine and Applied Arts at the University of Illinois and author of Art: U.S.A.: Now.

PAINTING is one of the oldest and most important of man's arts. An artist makes a painting by arranging lines and colors on a surface in some interesting way. He puts the paint on the surface with a brush or some other tool. He may try to paint a picture that looks like a scene in nature or like something else that exists. Then anyone who looks at the painting can also imagine that he is looking at the scene or subject itself. The picture is said to *represent* the scene or subject. Or the painter may paint something he imagines.

A painter usually does more than make an exact copy of what he sees. He selects and emphasizes details and qualities that interest him. One painter may be most interested in colors, another in shapes, and a third in movement. The artist may leave out details, and re-arrange what he has chosen into some new form or design. In this way, he expresses his own ideas and feelings, and interprets his subject in a personal way.

If a picture looks very much like its subject, it is said to *represent* the subject, and is called a *realistic* painting. If it contains little or no representation, it is called an *abstract* or *nonobjective* painting.

How to Look at a Painting

There is no one *right* way to look at a painting. But a person who does not understand some of the fine points of painting will miss much that is interesting. In the same way, a person who does not understand base-ball would miss a great deal while watching a game.

Jan Vermeer's painting, *The Artist in His Studio*, shown on the opposite page, is interesting in two main ways: *representation*, or what it shows, and *design*, or how

shapes and colors are arranged. We see an artist looking closely at his model in a room filled with interesting things—Dutch clothing of the 1600's, a wall map, and so on. But, to appreciate the picture fully as represen-tation, we should realize how real Vermeer makes the objects appear. We have the vivid sensation of looking into an actual studio.

We are only vaguely aware of the heavy curtain at the left, because our eyes are drawn to the well-lighted figure of the girl. Light from an unseen window makes objects in the room appear solid by casting highlights and shadows. The objects range in zigzag order from the curtain and chair on the left to the artist on the right, left again to the girl, then right to the map behind her. Vermeer increases the three-dimensional effect by showing how sunlight falls more or less brightly in dif-ferent parts of the room. We cannot find the separate brush strokes that make the slight differences in bright-ness and hue. We forget that the picture is painted, and see instead details of skin, hair, cloth, and wood.

A painter increases the unity of his work by using a strong design. Vermeer builds his design with rec-tangles (the floor tiles, table, and map) and curves (the curtain, chandelier, and figures). He adds to it by re-peating and varying his colors. The major color is blue, but red, black, and green also appear. The girl's pale yellow book is so intense in hue that it attracts and holds our attention. Duller spots of yellow lead our eyes away from it and back again. It is hard to make such colors seem part of the objects in the room. To do so, as Vermeer does, helps make the design seem a part of the scene itself.

Frank Cassidy

Painting Is Popular with mil-lions of "Sunday painters." They find it a pleasant form of re-laxation. At outdoor art fairs, painters display their works.

28

Kunsthistorisches Museum, Vienna, Austria

The Artist in His Studio by Jan Vermeer

THE PAINTER'S MATERIALS

OIL PAINT

Oil paints come in pure colors, and can be mixed to produce special shades and tints. The artist puts his canvas on an adjustable easel.

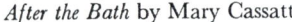

Easel

Brushes

Canvas

Oil

Turpentine

Paint in Tube

Palette

Paint

The Metropolitan Museum of Art, New York, Bequest of Mrs. H. O. Havemeyer, 1929, The H. O. Havemeyer Collection

Boating by Edouard Manet

The tools and materials of painting are fairly simple and easy to use. Anyone, even a young child, can paint. But it is not easy to paint *well*. Anyone can throw a ball, but a big-league pitcher can do it better than a child. To paint well, a person must understand the nature of his materials and the effects they will give.

Paint consists mainly of a pigment and a vehicle. The *pigment,* or coloring material, is usually a powder, produced by a chemical process or by grinding up some kind of earth, stone, or mineral. The *vehicle* is a substance such as oil or water that holds the pigment in a form that can be spread over the surface until it dries. *Tempera* painting uses egg yolks and whites for its vehicle, *casein* uses the curd of milk, and *encaustic* uses

After the Bath by Mary Cassatt

The Cleveland Museum of Art, Cleveland, Ohio, J. H. Wade Collection

PASTEL

Pastel sticks are like hard chalk. The artist sprays fixative over the drawing so that it will not rub off.

Paper

Pencils

Fixative

Pastel Sticks

melted wax. Pigment is sometimes hardened into a cake, as in water colors and Chinese ink. The painter rubs a wet brush on it to dissolve it.

Painters can mix *oil paints* into a great variety of tints and shades. They can put them on side by side or spread them in one thin film over another. Painters can produce rich textures and make them resemble many substances. Painters apply *water-color paints* in thin, almost transparent films. The surface usually shows through and gives a light, delicate texture. Or these paints may be used in a thicker, opaque form called *gouache*. Oil- and water-color paints may flake and crumble when dry, unless they are held on by a thin film of *fixative*, such as clear varnish or glue. See PAINT.

Surfaces. Most artists put oil paintings on sheets of canvas stretched tightly over wooden frames. Smaller canvases are often called *easel* paintings. Larger ones may be mounted on walls as *murals*. In *fresco* paintings, the surface is the damp plaster of the wall itself. The paint soaks in and stays fixed after the plaster dries. Most water-color paintings are made on paper. Paintings can also be made on composition board, wood, glass, or other materials. These surfaces must be specially treated. *Gesso*, a kind of plaster, is used to cover wood and hold the paint without cracking.

.The artist may treat the surface in some special way. He may make a *collage* by putting scraps of paper or other material into it. Or, for emphasis, he may build up thick layers of paint into an *impasto*.

Tools. Brushes are by far the favorite tools for painting. They are made of short hairs fastened to a handle. They may be pointed or broad, stiff and short or soft and flexible. Some artists use an *airbrush*, actually a spray, to make a soft, strokeless film. Others spread paint with a *palette knife* to make rough, heavy strokes. Painters mix their paints on a *palette*, a thin wooden board with a thumbhole, on some other flat surface, such as glass, or on a pieplate.

The Baltimore Museum of Art, Baltimore, Md.,
The Saidie A. May Collection

Le Haras du Pin by Raoul Dufy

WATER COLOR

Water colors come in hard cakes, or in tubes, like oils. The artist may first sketch his work in pencil.

Brushes

Water

Sponge

Color in Tube

Paper

Dry Color

FRESCO Fresco paints are dissolved in water and applied to fresh plaster. Colors do not mix well. José Clemente Orozco, *below*, was one of the masters of this medium.

The Museum of Modern Art, New York

Painting in the National Preparatory School, Mexico City.
Courtesy the National Autonomous University of Mexico

Franciscan Father and Indian by JOSÉ CLEMENTE OROZCO

The Art Institute of Chicago, Mr. and Mrs. Martin A. Ryerson Collection

Old St. Lazare Station, Paris by Claude Monet

Museum of Fine Arts, Boston, Maria Antoinette Evans Fund

The Five-Colored Parakeet and poem
by the Emperor Hui-tsung

Henry VIII by Hans Holbein the Younger

Courtesy the Thyssen Collection, Castagnola, Switzerland

WHAT DO PAINTERS PAINT?

It would be hard to find a subject that someone has not painted or tried to paint. Most painters choose things they can see, such as animals or trees, or things they imagine, such as gods and dragons. A painter may try to suggest something he cannot see, such as a feeling of joy or sorrow. He may do this indirectly, by showing people smiling or weeping. He can try to suggest the song of a bird by rising and falling lines, or a gloomy mood by dark colors. Many artists have been most interested in showing how things look to them.

Most paintings represent the kinds of things we see around us: human beings, birds and animals, plants and flowers, houses, and tools. The paintings on these pages show some of the subjects that painters paint. Some painters choose large outdoor *landscapes*, such as Claude Monet's *Old St. Lazare Station, Paris*. Others show *still-life* arrangements of objects indoors, such as Jean Baptiste Chardin's *Still Life with Clay Pipe*.

When a painter represents things that we can see around us, in the way they appear in normal conditions, he is said to paint in a naturalistic style. But he may choose subjects from the world of *dreams*, as Marc Chagall did in *The Juggler*. His work would be called *fantastic* if it showed details of fairies or demons, life on Mars, or life in the future. A picture of some real but unusual subject, such as life under the sea, may seem fantastic.

Still Life with Clay Pipe by Jean Baptiste Chardin

The Louvre, Paris

The 3rd of May, 1808,
in Madrid: *The Executions
in the Principe Pío Mountain*
by Francisco Goya

The Prado, Madrid

A picture can be partly imagined even if it deals with an ordinary subject from *everyday life*, such as George Bellows' *Stag at Sharkey's*. If the artist paints a picture from memory in his studio, he has to use his imagination. Few artists like to paint exactly what they see without changing it in some way.

Most persons are interested in seeing pictures of other persons, especially some loved relative or friend, or some famous man or woman. Many kings used *portraits* of themselves to impress others with their wealth and power. They usually wanted the artist to make them look as strong, handsome, and heroic as possible. In painting the portrait of *Henry VIII*, Hans Holbein emphasized characteristic facial features, rather than wealth. Other painters are interested in human *figures*, such as the ones George Bellows showed in *Stag at Sharkey's*. Others showed the figures of *animals*, as Hui-tsung did in *The Five-Colored Parakeet*.

Artists often paint scenes from *religion* or *mythology*, such as *The Entombment of Christ* by Titian. They make devils as horrible as possible, or try to show supernatural power and beauty, as Leonardo da Vinci did in *The Last Supper* (shown in color in the JESUS CHRIST article). Painters of *historical scenes* usually arrange their figures in dramatic poses, as Francisco Goya did in "The 3rd of May." Whatever his subject, a creative artist treats it in some personal, original way.

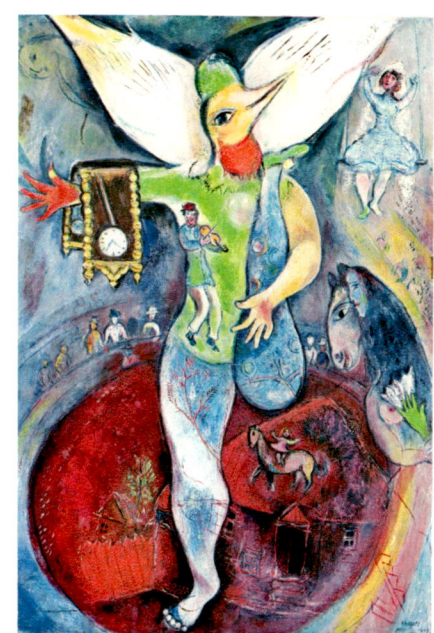

Courtesy of Mrs. Gilbert W. Chapman, New York

The Juggler by Marc Chagall

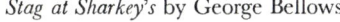

Stag at Sharkey's by George Bellows

The Cleveland Museum of Art, Cleveland, Ohio, Hinman B. Hurlbut Fund

The Entombment of Christ by Titian

The Louvre, Paris

Reproduced by courtesy of the Trustees, The National Gallery, London

The Hay-Wain by John Constable

The Cleveland Museum of Art, Cleveland, Ohio,
John L. Severance Fund

The Poet Lin P'u Wandering in the Moonlight by Tu Chin

34

LANDSCAPES

Views of nature on land or sea have long been among the most popular subjects for both professional and amateur painters. Many persons enjoy sketching as they take a walk. They train themselves to observe carefully and to remember what they see. Many also like to have landscape paintings on their walls.

By choosing a *viewpoint*, as a photographer points a camera, the painter opens an imaginary vista into deep space. He can arrange his lines, shapes, and colors to give the illusion of perspective, as many Western painters have done, or flatten things out as on a screen, as the Japanese painter Korin did (see page P-63). The painter is free to rearrange things and to change his lights and colors, showing any time of day or season of the year.

Pure landscape, without human figures, was rare in Europe before the 1600's. People liked it as a background for figures, as in the *Mona Lisa* on the next page, but not just landscape alone. Some later artists, such as Camille Corot, preferred classical Greek and Roman landscapes, which look like carefully tended parks. Many persons feared scenes in nature as the homes of evil spirits. But, in the 1600's, Dutch painters such as Jacob van Ruisdael showed that nature can be dramatic and beautiful in its own way. Painters today often choose scenes in cities, called *cityscapes*.

The Louvre, Paris

The Jewish Cemetery
by Jacob van Ruisdael

Staatliche Kunstsammlungen, Dresden, Germany, Gemäldegalerie Alte Meister

Reproduced by courtesy of the Trustees, The National Gallery, London

*The Fighting Téméraire
tugged to her last berth
to be broken up, 1838*
by Joseph M. W. Turner

Dance of the Nymphs
by Camille Corot

Staatliche Museen, Berlin-Dahlem, Gemäldegalerie

Hieronymus Holzschuher by Albrecht Dürer

The Louvre, Paris

Mona Lisa (also called *La Gioconda*)
by Leonardo da Vinci

Madame Rivière
by
Jean Auguste Ingres

The Louvre, Paris

Young Girl in Pink by Amedeo Modigliani

From a private collection, Cambridge, Mass.

PORTRAITS

For human beings, what is more interesting than a human face? All through life we study faces, trying to guess what sort of person lies behind them. Some artists are more attracted by faces than by any other subject. Great portraits show us a fascinating gallery of faces in which each artist emphasizes the qualities that especially interest him.

Most artists, like most people, enjoy young and pretty faces. But they also enjoy older faces that show the marks of character, as in Albrecht Dürer's portrait of another painter, *Hieronymus Holzschuher*. Many persons like faces such as the *Mona Lisa* that have unusual expressions, hinting at some unusual personality behind them. Some portrait painters, including Hans Holbein, try to bring out the most distinctive characteristics of each face, as in the portrait on page P-32, without exaggerating them to the point of caricature. Frans Hals fully modeled the features of his subjects with light and shade, in delicate or heavy brush strokes, as in *Malle Babbe*.

Other things besides the face can be worth noticing in a portrait. The person's hands are often expressive and characteristic, as in the *Mona Lisa*. The artist may include interesting costumes and accessories, as in

Charles I
by
Anton Van Dyck

Malle Babbe
by
Frans Hals

The Louvre, Paris

Staatliche Museen, Berlin-Dahlem, Gemäldegalerie

Anton Van Dyck's picture of *Charles I* of England with his horse. In his portrait of *Madame Rivière,* Jean Auguste Ingres created a complex design of graceful lines and colors. Amadeo Modigliani, a painter of the 1900's, liked to repeat a narrow, elliptical shape and the long, flat curves that form parts of an ellipse. He used many variations of these curves in the portrait of the *Young Girl in Pink.*

FIGURES

The whole human body, clothed or nude, has also been a favorite subject for painters since ancient times. Sometimes a painter shows a single figure, or he may show a group of figures against a landscape or some architectural background. The Greeks, who were fond of athletics, liked to represent healthy and graceful bodies in art. Early Christian and medieval artists seldom represented the nude figure. Renaissance painters revived the nude as part of the movements called

humanism and *naturalism:* a return to the Greek and Roman interest in human life and nature on earth, rather than in heaven or hell.

Sandro Botticelli's *La Primavera* illustrates these movements in Renaissance painting as it developed in Italy during the 1400's and 1500's. He painted an allegory of spring, adapting his figures from the stories of Greek and Roman mythology—Mercury, the three Graces, Venus, Flora, and Zephyrus, the west wind. He built up a complex design from the repeated and varied curves of the figures as they stand or dance in the somewhat unreal grove of trees. But his details of flowers are all accurate, even though the landscape seems unreal.

The human body is very flexible, and can be arranged in many shapes and attitudes to create a design. Botticelli contrasted it with the straight lines of trees. He chose graceful poses for his figures, but other painters show rugged violence. George Bellows (page P-33) was more interested in real men, portrayed in strenuous action, than in graceful, classical beauty.

Uffizi Gallery, Florence, Italy

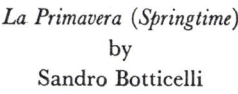

La Primavera (Springtime)
by
Sandro Botticelli

Courtesy Mr. William J. Williams, Cincinnati, Ohio

The Old Violin by William M. Harnett

STILL LIFES

Many artists enjoy painting groups of objects that do not move, rather than asking a model to pose for a long time. Flowers are among the most popular subjects for still-life paintings, but artists also portray such things as food, plants, or pots and pans. They usually choose something closely related to human life. They may pick objects that suggest some particular human interests and activities, such as the musical instruments and sheet music shown in William Harnett's painting and Georges Braque's collage. Or they may choose objects that resemble human forms, such as guitars and bottles.

People often like to look at pictures of familiar objects, like the pipe, box, and cup in Jean Baptiste Chardin's *Still Life with Clay Pipe* on page P-32. By selecting ornate objects made of precious materials, the artist can suggest aristocratic life. Or he can paint peasant tools and dishes to show simplicity.

Many artists and critics today are more interested in the visual form of the picture—the arrangement of shapes and colors—than they are in the objects in it. They admire a still life by Chardin or Paul Cézanne (page P-70), because the artist has organized his objects into a firm, complex design. Realistic painters such as Chardin and Harnett liked to make their objects look solid, with accurate surface textures. Braque deliberately flattened out and simplified the forms of things, and Cézanne changed them in other ways.

Guitar and Clarinet (also called *Musical Forms*) by Georges Braque

Philadelphia Museum of Art, The Louise and Walter Arensberg Collection

Sauve Qui Peut
(*Everyone for Himself*, sometimes
called *Pheasants and Dog*)
by John James Audubon

Collection of the Racquet and Tennis Club, New York, N.Y.
(WORLD BOOK photo by Robert Crandall)

ANIMALS

The oldest paintings known are of animals, the ones made by men in the caves of Spain and southern France thousands of years ago (see page P-60). Artists of almost every time and place have liked to draw and paint animals. Animals appear in many pictures in this article, even when the main subject is something else. They are shown in many different activities and styles of painting. John James Audubon and Peter Paul Rubens showed wild animals in the paintings on this page. Diego Velázquez showed a tame animal in the painting on page P-67. Edward Hicks, in *The Peaceable Kingdom* on page P-47, painted animals that are usually wild, but in a peaceful mood. Some animals are fantastic, as in *The Nine Dragons* on page P-62. Some painters show wild animals in their natural surroundings, as Henri Rousseau did in *The Waterfall* on page P-70, Winslow Homer in *The Gulf Stream* on page P-73, and Hui-tsung in *The Five-Colored Parakeet* on page P-32.

Rubens was especially skillful at showing wild animals in violent, swirling action. Other painters use animals in other designs. Paolo Uccello's horses in the painting on the next page are stiff, like hobby horses, but they help create a decorative design. Many painters use the curving lines of animal bodies as variations from the human body, and paint fur, feathers, and scales for contrasting surface textures.

The Lion Hunt by Peter Paul Rubens

Alte Pinakothek, Munich,
Bayerische Staatsgemäldesammlungen

Reproduced by courtesy of the Trustees, The National Gallery, London

The Battle of San Romano by Paolo Uccello

SCENES FROM HISTORY

Historical paintings can be exciting or dull, depending in some cases on the events they portray. Many Americans are interested in Benjamin West's scene of William Penn making a treaty with the Indians. Italians, looking at Paolo Uccello's work, may envision a battle in 1432 when an army from Florence defeated one from Siena. Some scenes have become world famous. Giovanni Battista Tiepolo and many others have painted the meeting of Antony and Cleopatra (see page P-69).

Whether the picture is dull or exciting depends also on the skill and imagination of the artist. Persons who take part in an event usually want their portraits to show prominently. As a result, some historical paintings are monotonous rows of standing or seated figures, with little variety or action. Painters avoid dullness by introducing some active gestures, by arranging the figures in groups, by contrasting light and dark, and by emphasizing some figures more than others. Goya used all these methods with dramatic results in "The 3rd of May," on page P-33. In many cases, if the event took place long ago and no exact records are available, the artist must imagine how it looked, and he can arrange the figures to make a pleasing design. But he usually has to show great leaders in a somewhat idealized way, as Giovanni Tiepolo did in *The Meeting of Antony and Cleopatra,* on page P-69.

Penn's Treaty with the Indians
by Benjamin West

Pennsylvania Academy of the Fine Arts, Philadelphia

RELIGION AND MYTHOLOGY

Most of the world's religions have used painting and other arts to aid in worship, to instruct children, and to inspire feelings of devotion. Some religions have also used the arts to try to impress and convert nonbelievers. In some religions, the people have practiced *idolatry* by worshiping only sacred images. In other religions, they revered the images only as symbols. The early sacred writings of Judaism and Islam discouraged pictures and statues of God, human beings, or animals, on the grounds that people might worship them. Some other groups, such as the Quakers, avoided elaborate art as a kind of worldly display that would distract from a religious attitude. But religion has usually considered art as one of its most valuable means of expression.

The Art Institute of Chicago, Gift of Kate S. Buckingham

Buddha and Two Attendants by an unknown Japanese artist of the Kamakura period

The Descent from the Cross by Giotto

Museo Civico, Padua, Italy

The Metropolitan Museum of Art, New York, Rogers Fund, 1927

Krishna Overcoming the Naga Demon, Kaliya by an unknown Indian artist
of the Rajput school

And art has been greatly inspired by religious ideas. Much of the world's art has to do with religion.

Artists have been encouraged and have often been employed to express ideas about religion in pictorial form. In turn, great artists such as Phidias in Greece and Giotto, Raphael, and Michelangelo in Italy have influenced people to imagine religious figures in certain visible forms. Many religions have taught that a god or spirit may sometimes assume human or other visible form. He may be distinguished from human beings by a halo or wings, or in some other way. Some peoples have portrayed their gods as part human and part animal, as the ancient Egyptians did. A sacred personage may be indicated by a symbol, rather than a picture. For exam-

ple, Buddha is sometimes symbolized by his footprints.

People tend to place a special value on pictures that deal with their own religions in ways they approve. But, from the standpoint of art, there are things to admire in all religious paintings by capable artists. Religious art is also a clue to the development of civilization in all parts of the world. It shows what ideas of deity people have. It shows their ideals of physical and spiritual perfection in men and women, as they represent them in supernatural beings. Sometimes it also personifies ideas of sins and evils to avoid. For example, artists of many religions show evil as a serpent.

Artists have been fascinated by the stories told about these good and evil characters. Some of these stories tell

42

National Gallery of Art, Washington, D.C., Samuel H. Kress Collection

The Adoration of the Shepherds by Giorgione

Religious Allegory (also called
Allegory of Souls in Purgatory)
by Giovanni Bellini

Uffizi Gallery, Florence, Italy

of dramatic miracles, exciting battles with monsters and demons, and legends of early kings and heroes. In myths, early men tried to explain the nature and origin of things, often in poetic forms. Many of these myths became popular as subjects for paintings. In the Western world, Greek and Roman myths were often painted during and after the Renaissance.

Religion has also influenced painting in another way. For some artists, the work of creating a painting is an act of worship in itself. Fra Angelico, a deeply religious man, painted in this way (see page P-49). This attitude was particularly important during the Middle Ages, and at other times when men were more concerned with the next world than with this one.

43

The Art Institute of Chicago, The Joseph Winterbotham Collection

In the Circus Fernando: The Ringmaster *by Henri de Toulouse-Lautrec*

EVERYDAY LIFE

For many years, persons who were wealthy enough to order and pay for expensive paintings preferred "noble" subjects. They thought that the life of common people was not worthy to be the subject of important painting, sculpture, drama, or poetry. As the middle classes grew in importance and power, they became interested in pictures of their own way of life. In The Netherlands, during the 1600's, painting came to deal more and more with people of the middle and lower classes—a sign of growing democracy.

But painters have always been interested in life around them. As early as the 1400's, Pol de Limbourg showed farm workers near a nobleman's castle in a series of miniatures for a *book of hours,* or religious calendar, for the Duc de Berry. Later, especially after the French Revolution, painters showed common people in greater and greater variety. They painted men and women at simple and humble tasks, living their own lives. Their works on these subjects are sometimes called *genre* paintings. Everyday life provided authors, as well as painters, with a new world of subject matter.

Changes in form and style followed the change in subject. Painters selected casual, everyday poses, instead of striving for symmetrical and monumental compositions. Rather than idealizing faces, bodies, and clothing, they painted people more realistically.

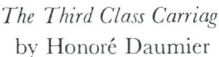

The Third Class Carriage
by Honoré Daumier

The Metropolitan Museum of Art, New York. Bequest of
Mrs. H. O. Havemeyer, 1929, The H. O. Havemeyer Collection

The Hackley Art Gallery, Muskegon, Mich.

Tornado Over Kansas
by John Steuart Curry

June, from the Duc de Berry's
Book of Hours,
by Pol de Limbourg

Handball by Ben Shahn

The Museum of Modern Art, New York,
Abby Aldrich-Rockefeller Fund

Musée Condé, Chantilly, France

The Louvre, Paris

*Peasant Family
in an Interior*
by Louis Le Nain

45

Fear by Yves Tanguy

Collection of the Whitney Museum of American Art, New York

DREAMS

There are many kinds of dreams: clear and distinct, or vague and mysterious; consistent and logical, or disconnected and jumpy. Artists have tried to paint all these dreams, and many more. An artist may dream of a situation that is much like real life, and express it realistically in a picture. It would be hard for us to know that the idea came to him in a dream unless he told us. But if his scene is impossible or unlikely, and suggests the strange, irrational, or mysterious, we call it a fantasy or dream picture. The artist does not have to get such an idea from a dream.

Certain artists have liked to paint fantastic pictures. Outstanding among them are Hieronymus Bosch, Pieter Breughel, William Blake, and Albert Ryder. But these men did not all paint the same kinds of dreams. Ryder liked scenes of dark, mysterious shadow, as in *Toilers of the Sea* (on page P-73). In contrast, Yves Tanguy's *Fear* seems at first sight to be a brightly lighted landscape full of clear-cut objects. But we soon realize that they do not represent anything we can recognize. The empty space in the center seems lonely and a little frightening. Paul Klee's *Fish Magic* appears at first like a child's drawing. But the way Klee arranged the little gesturing man, the fish, the flowers, and other details seems to hint at a hidden meaning or mood that lies beneath the surface.

Some dream pictures have more obvious meanings. Bosch's *The Ship of Fools* represents an imaginary scene aboard a ship where the passengers and crew swim or play games or drink, and no one pays any attention to where the ship is going. We are not surprised when such a ship has a tree for a mast. Edward Hicks, in *The Peaceable Kingdom*, is not so far from everyday life. He shows animals and children with a fair amount of realism. His fantasy comes in the happy dream of a time when the lion and the lamb shall lie down together under the influence of universal love and kindness.

The Louvre, Paris

The Ship of Fools by Hieronymus Bosch

Albright-Knox Art Gallery, Buffalo, N.Y., James G. Forsyth Fund

The Peaceable Kingdom by Edward Hicks

Fish Magic by Paul Klee

Philadelphia Museum of Art, The Louise and Walter Arensberg Collection

HOW DO PAINTERS PAINT?

A quick answer to this question is that most painters touch the end of a brush to some coloring material and apply it to a surface. But of course this tells only a small part of the story. It is like saying that a violinist plays by pulling his bow over the strings. In both cases, what anyone can see from the outside is only part of the result. What distinguishes a good artist is his understanding. Even artists themselves do not understand what makes up *creative imagination,* the chief difference between a genius and a mere imitator.

Various artists work and think in various ways. Some are quite calm, and like to think things out in advance and analyze works of art theoretically. Others create on the spur of the moment, following sudden impulses. Some of the Oriental painters whose works appear in this article took a long time to get themselves into the right frame of mind, with harmonious feelings and no sense of anxiety. They tried to imagine in advance what the picture was to be, and then painted quickly. (See, for example, Hui-tsung's *Five-Colored Parakeet* on page P-32 and Sesshu's *Haboku Landscape* on page P-59.)

In spite of many differences, all artists must go through some of the same steps and processes. Whether they paint, compose music, or write poetry, they must all learn to handle the tools and materials of their art. Knowledge of the medium and skill in using it make up what is called *technique.*

The mental processes by which an artist creates are more obscure than technique, and take a longer time to learn. One of them is sometimes called "storing the well." The artist spends years observing and thinking about what he sees and hears, storing his mind with images and ideas. Then, to the creative artist, there may come a sudden flash of inspiration, an idea for a work of art. He may put it down quickly as a rough sketch. Afterward comes the slow process of developing, correcting, and perfecting it. Some creative artists do not have sudden inspirations, but gradually think out their ideas as they work.

One way a painter may begin a painting is to observe and picture something that already exists in the outside world. He can have a model pose for him, as Vermeer did in *The Artist in His Studio* (on page P-29). He can arrange a still life on a table. Or he can walk through the woods and fields as John Constable did, seeking a scene that seems like a good subject for a picture such as *The Hay-Wain* (on page P-34).

Instead of beginning with something he can see, the painter can start with an imaginary picture from a dream or a story he has read. Sometimes he begins with some framework or pattern, such as a pyramid, or the series of arches in *The School of Athens* by Raphael (on page P-54). Then he must fit the desired figures or objects into the framework. Fresco painters sometimes find that the walls they use form a pattern. José Clemente Orozco had an arched area to fill when he painted *Franciscan Father and Indian.* He followed the curving form in his painting (on page P-31).

No matter how the painter starts, he must constantly decide, as he completes the details and organizes the finished work, what to include and what to leave out; what to emphasize and what to subordinate; how to combine small details into larger groups; and how to organize the whole picture in some unified way.

A finished painting has *form,* a particular arrangement of its parts and qualities. Many paintings have

The Museum of Modern Art, New York, Acquired through the Lillie P. Bliss Bequest

The Starry Night
by Vincent van Gogh

The Louvre, Paris

The Coronation of the Virgin by **Fra Angelico**

complex forms. We can study them for a long time without noticing all the subtle ways in which the artist has selected and arranged things. To look carefully at such details and relationships is to analyze the form into its elements and see how they are put together. The main elements of painting are line, color, texture, light and dark, and space, mass, and perspective.

Line is usually the principal way in which an artist builds up form in a picture. He can make his lines in many ways. For example, he can draw or paint a narrow streak of black or some other color as an outline. By combining lines of different lengths and directions, he can make a complete picture without using colors, but it would be a drawing rather than a painting. The painter can also make lines as the boundaries between two different areas of color. Either kind of line can be sharp and clear, or rough and blurred. In *The Corona-*

tion of the Virgin, Fra Angelico made most of his lines so clear that we can see the most delicate details on the throne. We almost need a magnifying glass to see all the tiny details in the miniature paintings at the bottom. Every object has its own distinct outline in this *linear* style. Vincent van Gogh, on the contrary, made his lines thick, rough, and blurred in *The Starry Night.* He was extremely interested in color, and this kind of painting is called *coloristic* or *painterly* because it emphasizes color more than line drawing. Van Gogh's lines are powerful in suggesting energy and movement. We can see them in the many thick streaks of blue and white that make up the swirling clouds, and also in the wavy shape of the cypress trees against the sky.

Color is actually made up of three different kinds of qualities. One is called *hue,* and in this respect things differ in being red, yellow, blue, green, and so on.

49

The Luncheon of the Boating Party
by Pierre Auguste Renoir

The Baltimore Museum of Art, Baltimore, Md., The Cone Collection

The Purple Robe by Henri Matisse

Pierre Auguste Renoir used many hues in *The Luncheon of the Boating Party*. A second quality of color is *lightness* or *value*, the way in which colors range from very light to very dark, with many intermediate grays. Goya's "The Third of May" (on page P-33) covers a wide range of values. The third quality of color is *saturation* or *chroma*. In this respect, each hue can be pure, strong, and vivid, or it can be mixed with some other hue, or with white. Henri Matisse made use of many strong, intense hues in *The Purple Robe*. See also COLOR.

Matisse did not use his colors to give a realistic impression of sunlight and shadow, even though he used many contrasts of hue, saturation, and lightness. He was more concerned with creating an interesting flat design. Renoir, on the other hand, gives the impression of sunlight and reflected light. He was one of a group of painters called *Impressionists* who emphasized reflections of sunlight on colored objects outdoors.

The Phillips Collection, Washington, D.C.

Matisse often applied his colors in broad, uniform areas, while Renoir preferred to mix them into richer textures by putting small brush strokes of different colors close together. This technique helps represent the shimmering effect of sunlight. Another French painter, Georges Seurat, carried this technique still further into *pointillism*, in which he used tiny dots of pure colors placed side by side (see page P-53).

Texture is another way of describing the appearance

of a surface: it can be plain and uniform, or it can be varied from one point to another by slight differences in line, hue, lightness, saturation, or some other quality. In making his flat patterns, Matisse used some plain textures, some striped ones, some figured, and some dotted. Renoir liked to show the surface qualities of materials, such as cloth, fruit, glass, silver, straw, the hair of a dog, and various tints of human flesh. He used some "warm" colors, such as red and yellow, and

51

The Metropolitan Museum of Art, New York. Bequest of Mrs. H. O. Havemeyer, 1929, The H. O. Havemeyer Collection

View of Toledo by El Greco

some "cool" ones, such as blue and green. By combining and varying his colors and textures, he created extremely natural-looking scenes.

Light and Dark, used together, are sometimes considered as an element separate from color. A black-and-white photograph may have many variations of light and dark, but no variation in hue. Many painters have used the same bright, vivid colors that Renoir and Matisse used, and have used light and dark naturalistically. A black-and-white photograph of Renoir's painting would show some naturally dark areas—a man's hat and coat, a dog's fur, and the wine in a bottle—and such light areas as white shirts and tablecloths. But some painters have used light and dark for dramatic effects, as well as naturalistic ones. In *View of Toledo,* El Greco used many variations of light and dark, but not so many of hue, which is mostly green. He combined and contrasted light and dark areas to look like reflections and shadows from some special lighting effect. This technique is called *chiaroscuro,* which comes from Italian words that mean *light* and *dark.* Many other painters have used chiaroscuro with great effect, including Jacob van Ruisdael (on page P-35) and Tintoretto (on page P-56).

Space. By arranging lines, light and dark areas, and hues properly, the painter can make an object look either flat or solid, and either near or far in space. A sculptor actually makes his forms in three dimensions.

52

The Art Institute of Chicago. Helen Birch Bartlett Memorial Collection

Sunday Afternoon on the Island of La Grande Jatte by Georges Seurat

But a painter works on a flat surface, and can give only the illusion of solidity and depth. He does this in a number of ways: by making distant things smaller in proportion to close ones, by having nearby things overlap the distant ones and partly conceal them from view, and by arranging lights and darks to suggest a highlight or reflection on one side of a solid object and a shadow on the other. Painters sometimes choose warm colors to make an object seem nearer, or cool ones to make it seem farther away.

Many persons consider *mass* or *solidity* as one of the elements of painting, along with *perspective*, or the illusion of deep space. *Space composition* is arranging objects so that they seem to be at different positions and distances in space. Seurat created a complex design in this respect in *La Grande Jatte* (actually titled *Sunday Afternoon on the Island of La Grande Jatte*). He used all the

elements with great skill to place his figures at definite distances in space, as well as to make an interesting design. Some ancient Roman painters also reached a high level in this respect, as in *Ulysses in the Land of the Lestrygonians* on page P-61.

Both Raphael and Pieter Breughel the Elder emphasized the third dimension. Raphael, in *The School of Athens,* used detailed perspective to give the illusion of space. He put the figures of Plato and Aristotle close to the center of his painting, and grouped other Greek philosophers around them. His high arches above, and floor and steps below, lead back toward what seems to be a high, distant step, focusing our attention on the two philosophers. But, to keep the painting from looking too deep, Raphael grouped all the figures on the top step into a horizontal band. In Breughel's painting, we seem to be looking down from a hilltop. Instead of

Vatican Museums

The School of Athens by Raphael

making the center of the painting seem the farthest away, Breughel directs our attention from the returning hunters at the lower left to the hills at the upper right. Many diagonal lines in the painting lead from upper left to lower right, emphasizing the great distance between the hunters and the hill.

Not all painters have wanted to express the feeling of depth and distance. During many periods of history, no one wanted to do so. We must not suppose that, when an artist makes objects look flat, it is because he cannot make them look round. There is comparatively little depth or solidity in the Egyptian painting *Vintage Scene* (on page P-60), in the Byzantine *Enthroned Madonna and Child* (page P-64), in the Persian *King Darius and Herdsmen* (on the following page), in Pablo Picasso's *The Three Musicians* (on page P-57), or in Matisse's *The Purple Robe* (on page P-50). Many painters have used mass and perspective for some effects, and flat, decorative forms for other effects. Because a painting is made on a flat surface, it lends itself to either kind of form. Each can be interesting in its own way, for qualities lacking in the other.

Modes of Composition. Artists have many ways of combining the elements of painting. Scholars often call these ways *modes of composition*. One important mode is *representation*. A painting is representational if the painter arranges its details to look somewhat like an object or a scene. It helps give an observer the illusion that he is looking at an actual object or scene, not just at a painted surface. But the picture does not have to look exactly like what it represents. In painting a still life, the painter may change or leave out some details of the actual apples he is painting to make the finished work look more like some special kind of apple.

Another major mode of composition is *design*. It is built up by repeating and varying lines and spots of colors as themes, and arranging them in decorative ways. Many painters, particularly Oriental ones, have emphasized design rather than strict representation. The Persian painter who created *King Darius and Herdsmen* (on the next page) made flat figures placed one above another, as well as one behind another, as many Western painters would have done. He also used brighter colors than we usually find in nature. But we can easily recognize the king, the herdsmen, and the landscape around them. Many pictures have both representation and design factors. In Picasso's *The Three Musicians* (on page P-57), we can easily see the decorative design, but it is harder to recognize the three musicians by their eyes, a sheet of music, a bow, a clarinet, and a few other details. Much of the representation has been omitted.

Kunsthistorisches Museum, Vienna, Austria

Return of the Hunters by Pieter Breughel the Elder

The Metropolitan Museum of Art, New York, Hewitt Fund, 1911

King Darius and Herdsmen by an unknown
Persian painter of the Bukhara school

Wassily Kandinsky's painting *Panel (4)* has no representation at all. This picture does not look much like any particular thing, although it may vaguely suggest clouds. Such paintings have been called *abstract* or *nonobjective,* but the two terms do not mean exactly the same thing. Many painters begin by making or imagining a realistic picture of an object. But then they leave out more and more of the details that would help us recognize it. Instead, they concentrate on creating a pleasing or exciting design. This process involves abstracting, or taking away details. Other painters do not begin with any particular natural object. They simply try to arrange lines and colors in an interesting way. Then they create nonobjective paintings. A work such as Picasso's musicians, which omits part of the representation, may be called *semiabstract*.

What can an abstract picture do to hold our interest, if it leaves out all representation of things we might like to look at? Many persons feel that it can do the same kind of thing that music does. Most instrumental music does not sound like anything in nature, but we enjoy listening to it because it creates beautiful designs of sounds and because it expresses emotions. Kandinsky was interested in making irregular, expressive designs of free-flowing lines and rich colors. Many painters today, including Willem de Kooning, have become more interested in expressing emotions. Their work is called *abstract expressionism.* De Kooning's *Woman, I,* on page P-76, is semiabstract and very expressive.

Since the Renaissance, many persons have come to enjoy and expect fairly realistic representation in paintings. They miss it when it is absent, especially if they have not learned to see and enjoy design or expression.

The Last Supper by Tintoretto

Basilica of San Giorgio Maggiore, Venice, Italy

56

Conservative critics once thought that a painter did not know how to paint correctly if he distorted or changed the natural appearance of things. Today, more and more persons enjoy paintings that have little or no exact representation. They have learned to appreciate the other kinds of values that paintings offer. They have also learned that many painters, especially ancient, medieval, and Oriental ones, emphasize design and expression.

Two other ways to look at the problem of composing a picture are *utility* and *exposition*. Like music and poetry, paintings can be adapted for some practical use, such as selling products or influencing people's minds. In the Middle Ages, most important paintings told a story or explained religious or ethical ideas with pictorial symbols. Today, as a fine art, painting does not emphasize exposition. But pictures are still used to explain abstract ideas, especially in illustrations.

The more we learn about the history of art, the more we realize that there are many ways of painting and many excellent kinds of pictures. Each great artist and each important period of art has one or more distinctive *styles* of painting. We become more interested in painting and enjoy it more as we learn to tell the difference between a painting by Seurat and one by Renoir, or between a Persian painting and a Japanese one. By comparing styles, we can see how each painter learned from artists before him, and how he influenced those who came after him.

What makes one style differ from another? The answer to this question is largely a matter of the elements and ways of combining them that the painter selects and emphasizes. One style stresses a certain kind of line, another light and dark, another certain hues, another solid mass or deep space. One emphasizes representation, another design. We can learn to recognize styles by asking ourselves, while looking at a picture, what the artist has selected for emphasis and what he has left out or subordinated. We can then learn how each painter paints.

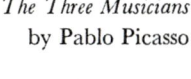

Panel (4) (also called *Spring*)
by Wassily Kandinsky

The Museum of Modern Art, New York,
Mrs. Simon Guggenheim Fund

The Three Musicians
by Pablo Picasso

Philadelphia Museum of Art, A. E. Gallatin Collection

The Night Watch (actually titled *The Company of Captain Franz Banning Cocq and Lieutenant Willem van Ruytenburch*) by Rembrandt van Rijn

The Rijksmuseum, Amsterdam

Haboku Landscape by Sesshu

The Cleveland Museum of Art, Cleveland, Ohio
Gift of the Norweb Foundation

WHAT MAKES A PAINTING GREAT?

To call a painting "great" means that it is not only good, but also one of the most important that has ever been created. A great painting may be hard to understand at first, but, as we study it, we tend to admire and enjoy it more and more. Mere popularity does not make any work of art great. A painting may be admired by millions of persons one year and almost forgotten the next. A truly great work of art may be enjoyed for hundreds of years, perhaps not by huge crowds, but by persons of sensitive and educated taste in all parts of the world.

Authorities on art disagree widely on what pictures, painters, or styles are the greatest. It would be difficult, if not impossible, to compile a list, in order of greatness, that all authorities would agree upon. The works illustrated in this article have been chosen as important examples of various kinds of painting. They illustrate the styles of many artists, countries, and periods. Many of them are generally regarded as among the world's greatest paintings.

What qualities can make a work survive through the ages? What standards of value can we use to judge greatness? Here, again, critics disagree. Many persons once supposed that there were definite laws of beauty and rules of good art. They based these laws and rules mainly on styles in Greek art. Art students learned to follow these rules, and critics used them in judging the value of art. But some of them, such as "unity in variety," were so vague that anyone could interpret them as he liked.

Critics now believe that there are many kinds of values, and that they are hard to express as simple, fixed rules. Basically, the value of a work of art can be judged by its power to produce worthwhile experience in the observer. The work of art does so especially by stimulating the person's sight or hearing, and also by communicating the important ideas, feelings, and attitudes that make up our cultural heritage. This can be done in many ways, and artists constantly invent new ones.

To be ranked as great, a work of art must have values that are broadly human, not limited to any one time or place. It must deal with subjects of lasting, not merely passing, interest. At the same time, great works usually sum up much of the culture of some particular group and period. An important subject is not enough, because a work may deal with profound ideas, but in a dull and imitative way. The subject may even be trivial, like *Cézanne's* apples, Chardin's pipe, or Hui-tsung's bird on a branch. And yet the picture can be considered great, because it makes us feel the reality of this common subject as never before.

The artist can add to the world's artistic heritage by some new way of imagining or looking at things. He can use the materials of art to provide some valuable new experience of visible form and color. *Cézanne* is credited with originating a new way to organize rich, impressionist colors into a solid, strong kind of form.

Rembrandt's *The Night Watch* is regarded as one of the world's greatest paintings. It shows Captain Frans Banning Cocq and his Company of the Civic Guard marching out of Amsterdam. Critics admire the masterly way in which Rembrandt organized his lights and shadows, bringing out some of the faces and figures more than others. He added glints of light here and there on bits of armor and clothing to bring out deep, soft colors from the background, instead of using simple black shadows and bright highlights. As a result, he created an experience in organized light and color that is unsurpassed. He painted a group portrait full of variety and movement, yet balanced and unified as a composition. *The Night Watch* sums up a great deal of the pictorial art that went before it.

Sesshu's *Haboku Landscape* has only a few rough, apparently accidental streaks and smudges of ink. But, if we learn to interpret this kind of painting, it can suggest a whole spacious landscape. In painting and poetry, the Japanese admire extreme simplicity and economy. They have often tried to convey a single image in as few words or brush strokes as possible.

Both Rembrandt and Sesshu achieve excellence, but in different ways. In each case, the artist has employed the painter's means with perfect control to achieve a unified form that can stimulate a valuable kind of visual experience for the observer.

HISTORY

Cave painting
from the Hall of Bulls,
Lascaux, France,
by an unknown
prehistoric painter

Département des Monuments Historiques, Paris

Prehistoric Painting. Many thousands of years ago, men painted pictures of animals on the walls of caves in present-day Spain and southern France. Some of the figures were blurred and crude, but others were amazingly skillful and are still in good condition. Some had been painted over earlier ones. The painters had not arranged the animals in any particular order, although some seemed to be grouped together as in a herd. Much primitive drawing, even when made thousands of years later, consists of only a few "stick figures." But the best cave paintings, like the ones at Lascaux, France, and Altamira, Spain, showed the forms and movements of animals in an accurate, realistic way, simplified only enough to emphasize the main outlines. The painters suggested the solid shapes of the animals and even their natural colors. These paintings have been discovered only in the last hundred years. Scholars believe that prehistoric men made them for magical purposes, perhaps to increase the food supply and ensure successful hunting. See PREHISTORIC MAN.

Ancient Civilizations produced many beautiful paintings, beginning about 3000 B.C. in Egypt, Asia Minor, and northwestern India. Most of these early works of art have been lost or destroyed. But scholars have discovered some excellent examples of large works on the walls of buried temples and palaces, and smaller paintings on vases, manuscripts, and furniture. We know the names of only a few of the artists.

In most early civilizations, paintings were used to glorify the gods, kings, and nobles. Artists decorated buildings for them, and idealized what they looked like. Painters showed them conquering enemies, ruling and judging, directing agriculture or industry, or leading armies. Farmers, hunters, craftsmen, dancers, musicians, and slaves served the kings and nobles. An Egyptian painter showed grape-pickers and wine-pressers at work in *Vintage Scene*. Egyptian artists often gave important figures larger bodies than they gave workers and slaves (see EGYPT, ANCIENT [color pictures, Life Along the Nile]). Thousands of years later, Maya artists used a similar flat-patterned effect of perspective, with farther objects shown higher, and nearer objects lower. They painted *A Raided Village* in the Temple of the Warriors at Chichén Itzá, Yucatán.

Ancient peoples imagined their gods as somewhat like their kings, but with supernatural powers. Often

From the tomb of Ipy, Thebes, Egypt. Reproduction from
Ancient Egyptian Paintings by Davies-Gardiner, courtesy
The Oriental Institute, University of Chicago

Vintage Scene by an unknown Egyptian artist

The Players of Astragali
by Alexander Atheniensis

Museo Nazionale, Naples, Italy

Ulysses in the Land of the Lestrygonians from the *Odyssey* series, by an unknown Roman artist

Biblioteca Apostolica Vaticana

The Heraclion Museum, Crete

Priest King
from a wall-painting at Knossos
by an unknown Minoan artist

the king was also the chief priest, as in the picture of a *Priest King* from the Minoan city of Knossos, in Crete. Paintings gave moral and religious instruction to the people by showing how the wicked were punished and the good rewarded in this life and after death. Legends about famous heroes who obeyed the gods also taught moral and patriotic lessons while entertaining the people with tales of great adventures. A Roman artist painted *Ulysses in the Land of the Lestrygonians* to illustrate a scene from Homer's *Odyssey*.

These ancient paintings show great variations in style. The Egyptian and Maya works come from a more primitive stage in painting than the Roman, even though Maya civilization did not develop until long after the Roman Empire had fallen. But the Roman paintings in the *Odyssey* series show the most advanced stage that ancient painters ever reached, as far as we know. They are almost like European paintings of the 1600's in their realistic drawing and modeling of human figures in action. They are highly advanced in their use of delicately varied coloring to represent sunlight and atmosphere, and in arranging many figures within a deep landscape.

A Raided Village a detail from a wall painting
in the Temple of the Warriors at Chichén Itzá by an unknown Maya artist

From a reconstruction by Ann Axtell Morris, The Peabody Museum, Harvard University, Cambridge, Mass.

Museum of Fine Arts, Boston, Francis Gardner Curtis Fund

The Nine Dragons (detail) by Ch'en Jung

Oriental Civilizations. The history of civilized art in China goes back thousands of years, and comes down to the present day. Many empires and many styles of art have flourished there. Buddhism, one of the most important influences on Chinese art, actually originated in India. It produced many carved and painted temples before it died out in that country. The finest Indian Buddhist paintings are those in the caves of Ajanta, northeast of Bombay. They show the life of Buddha and other stories in colorful imagery. The graceful figures are gently rounded, and each scene has its own perspective.

As Buddhism was carried into Tibet, China, Korea, and Japan, it mingled with other schools of thought, including Confucianism, Taoism, and Shinto. New sects arose, with new beliefs and attitudes toward life, and artists expressed them in new styles. Painters represented their ideas about the universe and its spirits in fantasies of gods and demons, miracle-working saints, and the terrible dragons that Ch'en Jung painted in his scroll painting *The Nine Dragons.*

One of Buddhism's teachings was that men should love nature. Wise men preached that men should regard themselves as part of nature. Busy city officials liked to go to their country estates for relaxation. Some painted calm, spacious landscapes there, such as the Sung scroll *Flight of Geese.* They usually painted on silk scrolls. Sometimes they and their friends wrote poems about the subjects of the paintings on the scrolls. In Japan, a country of exquisite gardens, love of nature was expressed along with brilliant decoration in *Chrysanthemums by a Stream* by Korin, and by Hokusai's *Ducks in a Stream.*

On the whole, Chinese and Japanese art and civilization became more naturalistic and less mystical than those of India. The Chinese and Japanese respected traditional, conservative codes of behavior. A few fine examples of Chinese figure painting are preserved from

Flight of Geese hanging scroll
by an unknown Chinese artist of the Sung Dynasty

The Art Institute
of Chicago, Gift
of the Orientals

"The Toilet Scene"
a detail from
*Admonitions
of the Instructress
in the Palace*
by Ku K'ai-chih

Reproduced by courtesy of the Trustees, The British Museum, London

Hūman, Brother of Piran, Battling Bizhan
miniature by an
unknown
Persian painter

The Art Institute of Chicago,
Lucy Maud Buckingham Collection

as early as the Han Dynasty, at the time of Christ. "The Toilet Scene" by Ku K'ai-chih, a few hundred years later, is part of a scroll showing figures of the royal court in various scenes that teach correct behavior. The painting is gracefully linear, with light and dark areas. The painter did not use landscape backgrounds or illusions of deep space, which developed still later. Oriental painters were not much interested in highlights and cast shadows. They did not try to represent nature exactly, but usually did so in a simplified way, to bring out the main characteristics of the object and their attitudes toward it.

Islamic art spread westward from Asia Minor through North Africa into Spain, and eastward from Asia Minor through Persia into northern India. Some Moslems did not approve of representing God, human beings, or animals in art. Islamic art in the West was mostly abstract, geometrical, and brilliantly decorative. But Moslems in Persia and India did not follow this rule strictly. There, Islamic paintings combined brilliant decoration with storytelling pictures. Artists told stories from history and legend in fine manuscript writing, and illustrated them in bright

Reproduced by courtesy of the Trustees, The British Museum, London

Ducks in a Stream by Hokusai

Chrysanthemums by a Stream by Ogata Korin

The Cleveland Museum of Art, Cleveland, Ohio,
Gift of Hanna Fund

colors and gold, with intricate ornamental margins. *Rajput* painting developed in parts of India that followed Hinduism. Rajput works were sometimes less fine in detail than Persian ones, but they often had bolder designs. Some of them tell stories in the life of Krishna and illustrate various kinds of music (see page P-42).

Throughout the Orient, there has always been a great interest in *calligraphy*, or beautiful writing, usually with brush and ink. Often the same artist wrote the words and painted the pictures. Words and pictures often have the same qualities of graceful, expressive line. The line expresses various moods with changes in breadth and darkness. Some Chinese calligraphy appears at the right of "The Toilet Scene," and Persian writing appears at the top of *Hūman, Brother of Piran, Battling Bizhan.*

63

National Gallery of Art, Washington, D.C.,
Andrew Mellon Collection

Enthroned Madonna and Child
by an unknown Byzantine
artist of the 1200's

The Pierpont Morgan Library, New York

*Angels Restrain
the Four Winds*
from a manuscript Commentary on
The Apocalypse by Beatus of
Liebana, illustrated by an unknown
Spanish artist of the 900's

The Middle Ages in Europe brought new developments in painting. In Byzantium (later Constantinople and then Istanbul), the capital of the Eastern Roman Empire, ornate and brilliant arts became popular, emphasizing gold and precious stones. Byzantine artists gave up the realistic style that had developed in Greece and Rome. They showed stiff, formal gestures and drapery folds, with flat colors and little or no modeling by shadows, against gold backgrounds.

In western Europe, monks copied books by hand, adding beautiful *illuminations* or illustrations. Spanish, Carolingian, and Irish books became famous for decorative miniature paintings. The Gothic style of miniature spread toward the end of the Middle Ages. Gothic artists painted fairly realistic faces and figures with gold and bright, jewel-like colors, as in Pol de Limbourg's miniature on page P-45.

The Renaissance in Southern Europe was one of the greatest periods in art history. One genius after another appeared in quick succession, first in Florence and central Italy, then in Venice and northern Italy. Some, such as Leonardo da Vinci and Michelangelo, were masters of several arts. This was an age of individualism, when men developed and expressed their own ideas and personal styles. It was also an age of naturalism, when artists turned to the sights and sounds of this world, rather than the next. They studied anatomy and perspective as well as realistic lighting and coloring, to show lifelike figures in deep space.

The Renaissance was given its name, meaning *rebirth*, because of the revival of Greek and Roman ideas and styles of art, including humanism. Individualism and naturalism came together in portraiture, bringing out the distinctive characteristics of the person portrayed. Individual men and women again became the favorite subjects of art. They were often treated in an idealistic way, recalling the beauties of Greek sculpture. Artists used increasingly natural lines and colors in painting scenes from mythology and from the life of Christ. They still painted Old and New Testament subjects, especially for church decoration, but often treated them in the new spirit, with figures derived from classical art.

Before about 1300, the favorite style of painting in Italy was still the Byzantine. Then Giovanni Cimabue and Giotto began the revolutionary changes that introduced the Renaissance. They made their figures a little more solid-looking,

Basilica of San Francesco, Arezzo, Italy

*Concert of the Angels
and the Nativity*
by Matthias Grünewald

Musée d'Unterlinden, Colmar, France

with more lifelike colors and gestures. They deepened the imaginary space in their paintings, with bits of landscape and architecture in the background instead of flat gold, as Giotto did in *The Descent from the Cross* (on page P-41). Masaccio carried the changes still further, with softer, more realistic light and shade and even more natural poses, as in *The Tribute Money*. During the 1400's, painters in Florence developed more complex designs of stately but rather hard, statue-like figures, as in Michelangelo's frescoes for the Sistine Chapel, such as *The Creation of Adam,* on the next page.

In the 1500's, the leadership passed to Venice. Venetian painters emphasized landscape backgrounds, the pageantry of gorgeous costumes, and rich, soft coloring, like that of a summer afternoon. Giovanni Bellini (page P-43), Giorgione (page P-43), Titian (page P-33), and Tintoretto (page P-56) were the leaders here.

The Renaissance in Northern Europe. Flanders was another early center for the Renaissance in painting. Jan and Hubert van Eyck were painting in oils in the early 1400's, when tempera and fresco were still

Basilica di Santa Maria del Carmine, Florence, Italy

The Tribute Money
(detail) by Masaccio ▶

The Legend of the Cross:
◀ *The Queen of Sheba at
the Sacred Bridge* (detail)
by Piero della Francesca

Vatican Museums

The Creation of Adam by Michelangelo

The frescoes Michelangelo painted in the Sistine Chapel include some of the world's greatest paintings. But at first he did not want to work on them. He considered himself a sculptor, not a painter, and had already quarreled with the Pope over commissions and fees. His fellow citizens in Florence, fearing trouble with the Pope, forced him to accept the commission. He worked on the ceiling from 1508 to 1512, lying on his back and reaching up with either hand to paint. Pope Julius II often climbed up to hurry him. The results are ranked among the finest examples of Italian Renaissance painting. In The Creation of Adam, Michelangelo showed God giving Adam the spark of life. The detail, above, is about one fifth the size of the original, and the whole panel, left, is about 17 feet wide. For a picture of the whole chapel, see MICHELANGELO.

66

Reproduced by courtesy of the Trustees, The National Gallery, London

The Marriage of Giovanni (?) Arnolfini and Giovanna Cenami (?) by Jan van Eyck

The Prado, Madrid

Las Meninas (The Maids of Honor) by Diego Velázquez

The Mother
by
Pieter de Hooch

Staatliche Museen, Berlin-Dahlem, Gemäldegalerie

Reproduced by permission of The Trustees of The Wallace Collection, London

Reproduced by courtesy of the Trustees, The National Gallery, London

Seaport: The Embarkation of the Queen of Sheba
by Claude

The Swing by Jean Honoré Fragonard

68

The Art Institute of Chicago, A. A. Munger Collection

St. John on Patmos by Nicolas Poussin

The Louvre, Paris

Pilgrimage to the Island of Cythera (also called
The Embarkation for Cythera) by Antoine Watteau

the favorite materials in Italy. This new medium quickly became popular in all parts of Europe. Early Flemish painters had a sharp, fine style, as in Gothic miniatures, but on a larger scale and with more realism of light, color, and perspective. They showed individual details with great clarity, as in Jan van Eyck's wedding portrait of a man named Arnolfini (page 67). Hieronymus Bosch and Pieter Breughel carried on the Gothic love of fantastic scenes (page P-46). Breughel also painted realistic landscapes (page P-55).

For some time, German painters retained medieval gold backgrounds along with new, realistic figures. Matthias Grünewald and Albrecht Dürer were powerful artists who combined Gothic and classic qualities. Grünewald's masterpiece is the Isenheim altarpiece, containing a terrifying *Crucifixion* and a joyous *Nativity* (on page P-65). Both panels are tense with energy and glowing with color. Dürer, like Leonardo da Vinci, had a scientist's keen eye for observing nature.

Baroque Painting flourished from the late 1500's through the early 1700's, a period of great wealth and brilliance. Painters emphasized swirling figures, contrasts of light and shadow, and irregular compositions rather than evenly balanced ones. They used large S-shaped curves and diagonal lines, rather than quiet verticals and horizontals. Tintoretto's *The Last Supper* shows some of these features (see page P-56). Peter Paul Rubens in Flanders and El Greco in Spain derived rich colors from the Venetians and applied them in broad strokes (see pages P-39 and P-52). They often blurred the outlines of things, instead of making sharp lines. French painters continued the classical tradition in the statuesque figures and parklike landscapes of Nicolas Poussin and Claude, Rembrandt and other Dutch painters turned to everyday subjects (see page P-58). Diego Velázquez portrayed the Spanish court with marvelous realism of color and texture in *The Maids of Honor* on page P-67. El Greco expressed the intense religious mysticism of his day.

In the 1700's, an age of luxury and refinement, rather than of power and majesty, *rococo* paintings became popular. Rococo was originally the name of a kind of ornamentation. It is lighter and daintier in line and color than the Baroque. The S-shaped curves in Jean Honoré Fragonard's *The Swing* flutter like ribbons. Antoine Watteau and Fragonard in France,

Reproduced by courtesy of the Trustees, The National Gallery, London

The Shrimp Girl
by William Hogarth

The Meeting of Antony and Cleopatra
by Giovanni Battista Tiepolo

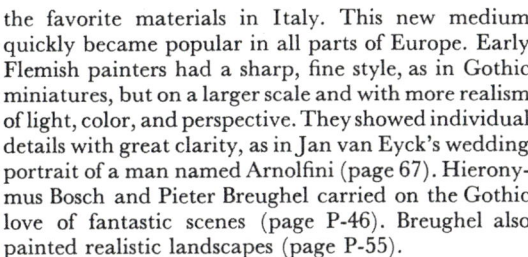

From a private collection, Paris

The Waterfall
by Henri Rousseau

The Art Institute of Chicago, Helen Birch Bartlett Memorial Collection

The Big Apples
by Paul Cézanne

G. Embiricos, Lausanne, Switzerland

Pilgrimage to Canterbury by William Blake

Courtesy of The Trustees, Estate of Sir John Sterling Maxwell, Glasgow, Scotland

The Metropolitan Museum of Art, New York. Alfred N. Punnett Fund and gift of George D. Pratt, 1934

Max Schmitt in a Single Scull by Thomas Eakins

Madame X by John Singer Sargent

Thomas Gainsborough in England, and Giovanni Tiepolo in Italy painted flattering portraits of nobles and rich men. But a few artists, including Jean Baptiste Chardin in France and William Hogarth in England, preferred a more solid, realistic style.

In the 1800's, five important styles followed each other in popular taste. First came *neoclassicism,* during and shortly after the reign of Napoleon I. Its leaders, Jacques Louis David and Jean Auguste Ingres, opposed the luxurious ornamentation of the rococo period. They stressed a severe, hard, linear style derived from Roman sculpture, as in Ingres' portrait of *Madame Rivière* on page P-36. David tried to express the stern military virtue of the ancient Romans.

Romanticism, led by Eugène Delacroix, followed neo-classicism. Romantic painters revived the rich coloring that the Venetian painters and Rubens had used, and shared Rubens' love of swirling movement and violent action. Artists became interested in the colorful, sensuous life of romantic, far-away times.

Naturalism, the third style, was led by Gustave Courbet, who felt that both classicism and romanticism were unreal and artificial. He wanted each painter to use his eyes and paint the everyday life around him, as Honoré Daumier did in *The Third Class Carriage* on page P-44. Most art after the Renaissance has been somewhat naturalistic, but Courbet's was intensely so.

Impressionism. Careful observation of nature became popular in the 1860's and 1870's as people became interested in science. Painters tried to analyze light and color by the laws of physics. They wanted to represent the visual qualities of sunlight at various times of the day and seasons of the year. They put small colored strokes side by side, so that at a little distance the hues

The Metropolitan Museum of Art, New York,
Arthur H. Hearn Fund, 1916

The Art Institute of Chicago, Potter Palmer Collection

On the Stage
by
Edgar Degas

seemed to blend and shimmer, with reflections of color even in the shadows. Leading the Impressionist movement were Edouard Manet (page P-30), Claude Monet (page P-32), Pierre Auguste Renoir (pages P-50-51), Alfred Sisley, and Camille Pissarro. See IMPRESSIONISM.

Post-Impressionism came at the end of the 1800's. It included a number of individual styles. Artists felt increasingly free to experiment with form, design, and expression. Because of photography, painters no longer felt obliged to represent nature realistically. They chose to disregard many of the rules set up for classical painting and sculpture. Paul Cézanne, Renoir, and Georges Seurat led the trend toward combining Impressionist color with clear, solid shapes and deep space. Paul Gauguin became known as a *primitivist,* because he adapted the qualities of life in the Pacific island of Tahiti in such paintings as *Ta Matete* (page P-74). Vincent van Gogh used unnaturally intense colors and swirling, jagged strokes to express his personality in *The Starry Night* (on page P-48).

Other individualists stayed somewhat outside these movements. Edgar Degas painted ballet dancers and race horses with rich pastel colors. Henri de Toulouse-Lautrec created vivid posters and graphic scenes of Paris cafés and theaters. Henri Rousseau designed fantastic jungle scenes. In general, painters chose more everyday subjects, and fewer religious or aristocratic ones. They also worked increasingly on visual form and design, rather than on subject matter.

American painting developed slowly as the United States grew. Keen realists such as Thomas Eakins and Winslow Homer showed flesh-and-blood people in the American scene. Most other Americans chose fairly realistic styles. An occasional dreamer such as Albert Ryder led the imagination into mysterious visions.

After 1900, three main trends dominated painting, all of them carried over from the 1800's. One is that of increasing freedom and variety in experiments. Many leaders started new movements such as cubism, futurism, and surrealism. Each movement quickly died out,

Old Battersea Bridge:
Nocturne—Blue and Gold
by James A. M. Whistler

The Metropolitan Museum of Art, New York,
George A. Hearn Fund, 1915

Toilers of the Sea
by Albert Pinkham Ryder

By Courtesy of The Trustees of The Tate Gallery, London

The Gulf Stream by Winslow Homer

The Metropolitan Museum of Art, New York, Wolfe Fund, 1906

Museum of Art,
Carnegie Institute, Pittsburgh

The Old King
by Georges Rouault

Ta Matete (*The Market*) by Paul Gauguin

Kunstmuseum Basel, Switzerland

Sun and Grey Sea by John Marin

The Denver Art Museum, Denver, Colo., The Helen Dill Collection

but each added something to the variety and rapid pace of contemporary art. Some movements concentrated on one or only a few elements in painting, such as line or flat color. Some, including cubism and futurism, tried to show the same object from several points of view (cubism), or at several moments in time (futurism). See CUBISM; FUTURISM; SURREALISM.

The second main trend is that of increasing emphasis on purely visual form at the expense of representation and storytelling. Some artists have been interested only in designs of line and color. Others have concentrated on emotional expression or the aesthetic ideas that an abstract form may suggest. Many painters went on from distorting nature, as they had done in the early 1900's, to the point where they left out all or almost all resemblance to nature. They specialized in semiabstract, abstract, or nonobjective painting. Surrealist painters went so far as to combine realistic details into unreal fantasies, as in the dream pictures of Giorgio de Chirico and Salvador Dali.

City Art Museum of St. Louis, anonymous gift

The Transformed Dream by Giorgio de Chirico

Men in the City by Fernand Léger

Courtesy of Peggy Guggenheim

74

The Museum of Modern Art, New York, Mrs. Simon Guggenheim Fund

Dutch Interior I
by Joan Miró

Collection of the Whitney Museum of American Art, New York

Early Sunday Morning by Edward Hopper

The third main trend has been continued borrowing from primitive or Oriental art. Manet and J. A. M. Whistler had adapted features from Japanese prints in the 1800's, and Gauguin had taken ideas from the arts of Tahiti. During the early 1900's, Pablo Picasso took some of the qualities of African Negro sculpture and applied them to painting. Then he borrowed from ancient Greek and Byzantine styles. Such borrowing may be purely imitative, or it can be creative. Instead of copying an entire painting, an artist selects one quality, such as flat design, and combines it with other qualities to create something new. Matisse combined Persian miniature qualities with impressionist light and color.

Picasso is in many ways the most typical painter of the 1900's. He experimented along many specialized lines, changing his style radically every few years. Many critics regard his work as almost a summary of the many experimental movements of our time.

The most influential abstractionist was Wassily Kan-

Collection of the Stedelijk Museum, Amsterdam

Composition in Red, Yellow, and Blue
by Piet Mondrian

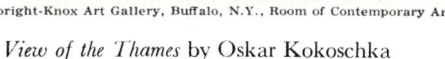
Albright-Knox Art Gallery, Buffalo, N.Y., Room of Contemporary Art Fund

View of the Thames by Oskar Kokoschka

Mr. and Mrs. Samuel M. Kootz, New York

Yellow Burst by Hans Hofmann

Collection of Julian J. and
Joachim Jean Aberbach, New York

Red Figure on a Predella
by Francis Bacon

Courtesy of The Art Institute of Chicago,
Friends of American Art Collection

American Gothic
by
Grant Wood

The Museum of Modern Art, New York

Woman, I by Willem de Kooning

Gangster Funeral by Jack Levine

Collection of the Whitney Museum of American Art, New York

Collection of the Whitney Museum of American Art, New York

Number 27 by Jackson Pollock

dinsky. He began in the early 1900's as a member of the *Fauves* (wild beasts). This group, which included Henri Matisse, emphasized bright colors and rough shapes. Kandinsky went on to abstract painting and became the leading European abstract painter between World War I and World War II. Other leading abstract painters during this period were Joan Miró and Piet Mondrian. Miró, a Spanish artist, painted in a lively, animated style. Mondrian, a Dutch painter, painted in a strict geometric style.

From the mid-1940's through the early 1960's, the most influential group of painters lived in the United States. They were usually called *abstract expressionists*, but they were sometimes called *action painters* or the *New York school*. Abstract expressionism was a general term that covered a wide variety of styles. One group believed that the spontaneous act of creating a picture was the most important part of painting. Painters such as Jackson Pollock created their paintings by splashing, throwing, or dripping paint onto the canvas.

Other painters, including Hans Hofmann, Willem de Kooning, and Philip Guston, emphasized broad, slashing brush strokes and violent color. Franz Kline and Mark Tobey painted mostly in black and white and showed the influence of calligraphy (see CALLIGRAPHY). Painters such as Josef Albers, Ad Reinhardt, and Barnett Newman used strict geometric forms in composing their pictures. Mark Rothko emphasized formless shapes of pure color in his huge paintings. Other U.S. abstract expressionists with individual styles included Adolph Gottlieb, Arshile Gorky, William Baziotes, Robert Motherwell, and Clyfford Still.

National differences in painting disap-

Collection of the Whitney Museum of American Art, New York, gift of an anonymous foundation

Four Men by David Park

Christina's World by Andrew Wyeth

The Museum of Modern Art, New York

peared as abstract art became a dominant style in other countries after World War II. Leading abstract painters included Jean-Paul Riopelle of Canada, Ben Nicholson of England, Matta (Roberto Matta Echaurren) of Chile, and Georges Mathieu of France.

Realistic painters were also active during this time. Ben Shahn and Edward Hopper, who won recognition in the United States in the 1930's, continued to paint pictures of a strong national character. Andrew Wyeth achieved recognition for his realistic pictures that convey a sense of loneliness and mystery. Francis Bacon in England, Jean Dubuffet in France, and Ivan Albright in the United States gained international reputations for figure paintings that show the moral and physical decay of the subjects.

In the early 1960's, a new style developed in the United States that was in direct contrast to abstract painting. This style, usually called *pop art*, often resembled the *dada* school of the early 1900's in its use of shock and humor. Pop artists such as Robert Rauschenberg chose subjects from everyday life. Some of their pictures were merely enlarged reproductions of grocery labels. In the mid-1960's, a geometric style called *optical art* or *op art* developed in many countries. The style was based on scientific theories of optics. The paintings consisted of specially arranged patterns of line and color that seemed to change shape as the spectator looked at the picture.　　　　　ALLEN S. WELLER

Collection of Walter Read Hovey, Pittsburgh

The Phases of the Night by Max Ernst

The Art Institute of Chicago, The Joseph Winterbotham Collection

November 1956 (Pistoia) by Ben Nicholson

Tracer by Robert Rauschenberg

Collection of Mr. and Mrs. Frank Titelman,
Altoona, Pennsylvania

Three People and a Bird by Rufino Tamayo

Courtesy M. Knoedler & Co., Inc., New York

76b

GREAT PAINTERS AND FAMOUS PAINTINGS

The 117 great paintings reproduced in color exclusively for this WORLD BOOK article are listed below. A panel of leading museum directors, art historians, and directors of art education for children helped guide the selection. The museums where the paintings may be seen are indicated in the credit lines for each painting. THE WORLD BOOK has a biography of each painter listed.

Painter	Nationality	Painting	Date	Size in Inches
Alexander Atheniensis	Greek	*The Players of Astragali* (page 60)	99 B.C.-1 B.C.	16½ x 15¾
Audubon, John James	American	*Sauve Qui Peut* (page 39)	1827	55½ x 91
Bacon, Francis	British	*Red Figure on a Predella* (page 76)	1962	78 x 55¾
Bellini, Giovanni	Italian	*Religious Allegory* (page 43)	before 1516	28¾ x 46⅞
Bellows, George Wesley	American	*Stag at Sharkey's* (page 33)	1907	36¼ x 48¼
Blake, William	British	*Pilgrimage to Canterbury* (page 70)	1808	18¼ x 53¾
Bosch, Hieronymus	Flemish	*The Ship of Fools* (page 46)	c. 1480-1510	22¾ x 12¾
Botticelli, Sandro	Italian	*La Primavera* (page 37)	1477-1478	80 x 123¾
Braque, Georges	French	*Guitar and Clarinet* (page 38)	1918	30⅜ x 37⅝
Breughel, Pieter, the Elder	Flemish	*Return of the Hunters* (page 55)	1565	46⅛ x 63¾
Cassatt, Mary	American	*After the Bath* (page 30)	c. 1901	25¾ x 39¼
Cézanne, Paul	French	*The Big Apples* (page 70)	1890-1894	18 x 21¼
Chagall, Marc	Russian-born	*The Juggler* (page 33)	1943	52 x 39½
Chardin, Jean Baptiste	French	*Still Life with Clay Pipe* (page 32)	mid-1700's	12⅝ x 16½
Ch'en Jung	Chinese	*The Nine Dragons* (page 62)	1244	18¼ in. x 36 ft.
Chirico, Giorgio de	Italian	*The Transformed Dream* (page 74)	1908	24¾ x 59⅞
Claude	French	*Seaport: The Embarkation of the Queen of Sheba* (page 68)	1648	58½ x 76¼
Constable, John	British	*The Hay-Wain* (page 34)	1821	51¼ x 73
Corot, Camille	French	*Dance of the Nymphs* (page 35)	c. 1860-1865	19¼ x 30½
Curry, John Steuart	American	*Tornado Over Kansas* (page 44)	1929	46¼ x 60
Daumier, Honoré	French	*The Third Class Carriage* (page 44)	c. 1862	25¾ x 35½
Da Vinci, Leonardo	Italian	*Mona Lisa* (page 36)	1503-1506?	30⅜ x 20⅞
Degas, Edgar	French	*On the Stage* (page 72)	c. 1880	22½ x 16
De Hooch, Pieter	Flemish	*The Mother* (page 68)	c. 1659-1660	36¼ x 39⅜
De Kooning, Willem	American	*Woman, I* (page 76)	1950-1952	75⅞ x 58
Dufy, Raoul	French	*Le Haras du Pin* (page 31)	c. 1932	19¼ x 25
Dürer, Albrecht	German	*Hieronymus Holzschuher* (page 36)	1526	18⅛ x 14⅛
Eakins, Thomas	American	*Max Schmitt in a Single Scull* (page 71)	1871	32¼ x 46¼
Ernst, Max	German	*The Phases of the Night* (page 76b)	1946	36 x 64
Fra Angelico	Italian	*The Coronation of the Virgin* (page 49)	c. 1435	83⅞ x 82
Fragonard, Jean Honoré	French	*The Swing* (page 68)	1768-1769?	32⅝ x 26
Gauguin, Paul	French	*Ta Matete* (page 74)	1892	28¾ x 36
Giorgione	Italian	*The Adoration of the Shepherds* (page 43)	c. 1510	35¾ x 43½
Giotto	Italian	*The Descent from the Cross* (page 41)	1306-1309?	76⅞ x 82¾
Goya, Francisco	Spanish	*The Executions in the Principe Pío Mountain* (page 33)	1814	105 x 136
Greco, El	Spanish	*View of Toledo* (page 52)	1604-1614?	47¾ x 42¾
Grünewald, Matthias	German	*Concert of the Angels and The Nativity* (page 65)	1505-1515	117⅜ x 129¼
Hals, Frans	Dutch	*Malle Babbe* (page 37)	1630-1633	28¾ x 23
Harnett, William M.	American	*The Old Violin* (page 38)	1886	38 x 24
Hicks, Edward	American	*The Peaceable Kingdom* (page 47)	c. 1833	24 x 32
Hofmann, Hans	German-born	*Yellow Burst* (page 75)	1956	52 x 60
Hogarth, William	British	*The Shrimp Girl* (page 69)	before 1764	25 x 20¾
Hokusai Katsushika	Japanese	*Ducks in a Stream* (page 63)	1847	43¾ x 15¾
Holbein, Hans, the Younger	German	*Henry VIII* (page 32)	1537	10¾ x 7¾
Homer, Winslow	American	*The Gulf Stream* (page 73)	1899	28⅛ x 49⅛
Hopper, Edward	American	*Early Sunday Morning* (page 75)	1930	35 x 60
Hui-tsung	Chinese	*The Five-Colored Parakeet* (page 32)	before 1135	21 x 40¼
Ingres, Jean Auguste	French	*Madame Rivière* (page 36)	1805	45⅞ x 32¼
Kandinsky, Wassily	Russian-born	*Panel (4)* (page 57)	1914	64 x 31½
Klee, Paul	Swiss	*Fish Magic* (page 47)	1925	30½ x 38¾
Kokoschka, Oskar	Austrian	*View of the Thames* (page 75)	1925-1926	35⅜ x 51¼
Korin Ogata	Japanese	*Chrysanthemums by a Stream* (pp. 62-63)	before 1716	67 x 148
Ku K'ai-chih	Chinese	"The Toilet Scene" (page 62)	before 405	9¾ x 12
Léger, Fernand	French	*Men in the City* (page 74)	1919	57 x 44
Le Nain, Louis	French	*Peasant Family in an Interior* (page 45)	c. 1643	44½ x 62⅝
Levine, Jack	American	*Gangster Funeral* (page 76)	1952-1953	63 x 72
Limbourg, Pol de	French	*June* (page 45)	c. 1410	8½ x 5¾
Manet, Edouard	French	*Boating* (page 30)	1874	38¼ x 51¼
Marin, John	American	*Sun and Grey Sea* (page 74)	1928	16¾ x 21¾
Masaccio	Italian	*The Tribute Money* (page 65)	1427	100⅜ x 235½

Continued on next page

GREAT PAINTERS AND FAMOUS PAINTINGS (continued)

Painter	Nationality	Painting	Date	Size in Inches
Matisse, Henri	French	*The Purple Robe* (page 50)	1937	$28\frac{3}{4}$ x $23\frac{3}{4}$
Michelangelo	Italian	*The Creation of Adam* (page 66)	1508-1512	c. 124 x 218
Miró, Joan	Spanish	*Dutch Interior I* (page 75)	1928	$36\frac{1}{8}$ x $28\frac{3}{4}$
Modigliani, Amedeo	Italian	*Young Girl in Pink* (page 36)	1917	$23\frac{1}{2}$ x $17\frac{1}{2}$
Mondrian, Piet	Dutch	*Composition in Red, Yellow, and Blue* (p. 75)	1920	$20\frac{1}{4}$ x 24
Monet, Claude	French	*Old St. Lazare Station, Paris* (page 32)	1877	$23\frac{1}{2}$ x $32\frac{1}{2}$
Nicholson, Ben	British	*November 1956 (Pistoia)* (page 76b)	1956	48 x 84
Orozco, José Clemente	Mexican	*Franciscan Father and Indian* (page 31)	1920	$116\frac{1}{4}$ x $98\frac{1}{2}$
Park, David	American	*Four Men* (page 76a)	1958	57 x 92
Picasso, Pablo	Spanish	*The Three Musicians* (page 57)	1921	80 x 74
Piero della Francesca	Italian	*The Legend of the Cross: The Queen of Sheba at the Sacred Bridge* (page 64)	1452-c. 1464	$157\frac{1}{2}$ inches high
Pollock, Jackson	American	*Number 27* (page 76a)	1950	49 x 106
Poussin, Nicolas	French	*St. John on Patmos* (page 69)	1645-1650	40 x $53\frac{1}{2}$
Raphael	Italian	*The School of Athens* (page 54)	1510-1511	$227\frac{1}{4}$ x $416\frac{7}{8}$
Rauschenberg, Robert	American	*Tracer* (page 76b)	1963	84 x 60
Rembrandt van Rijn	Dutch	*The Night Watch* (page 58)	1642	$141\frac{3}{8}$ x $172\frac{1}{2}$
Renoir, Pierre Auguste	French	*The Luncheon of the Boating Party* (pp. 50-51)	1881	51 x 68
Rouault, Georges	French	*The Old King* (page 74)	1916-1938	$30\frac{1}{4}$ x $21\frac{1}{4}$
Rousseau, Henri	French	*The Waterfall* (page 70)	1910	$45\frac{5}{8}$ x 59
Rubens, Peter Paul	Flemish	*The Lion Hunt* (page 39)	c. 1617	$96\frac{7}{8}$ x $147\frac{3}{8}$
Ruisdael, Jacob van	Dutch	*The Jewish Cemetery* (page 35)	after 1670	$33\frac{1}{8}$ x $37\frac{3}{8}$
Ryder, Albert Pinkham	American	*Toilers of the Sea* (page 73)	c. 1880	$11\frac{1}{2}$ x 12
Sargent, John Singer	American	*Madame X* (page 71)	1884	$82\frac{1}{8}$ x $43\frac{1}{4}$
Sesshu	Japanese	*Haboku Landscape* (page 59)	before 1506	$28\frac{1}{4}$ x $10\frac{1}{2}$
Seurat, Georges	French	*Sunday Afternoon on the Island of La Grande Jatte* (page 53)	1884-1886	81 x $120\frac{3}{8}$
Shahn, Ben	American	*Handball* (page 45)	1939	$22\frac{3}{4}$ x $31\frac{1}{4}$
Tamayo, Rufino	Mexican	*Three People and a Bird* (page 76b)	1962	$51\frac{1}{4}$ x $76\frac{3}{4}$
Tanguy, Yves	French	*Fear* (page 46)	1949	60 x 40
Tiepolo, Giovanni Battista	Italian	*The Meeting of Antony and Cleopatra* (p. 69)	c. 1747	$18\frac{1}{2}$ x $26\frac{3}{8}$
Tintoretto	Italian	*The Last Supper* (page 56)	1591	$157\frac{5}{8}$ x $236\frac{3}{8}$
Titian	Italian	*The Entombment of Christ* (page 33)	c. 1525	$58\frac{1}{4}$ x $80\frac{3}{4}$
Toulouse-Lautrec, Henri de	French	*In the Circus Fernando: The Ringmaster* (p. 44)	1888	$39\frac{1}{2}$ x $63\frac{1}{2}$
Tu Chin	Chinese	*The Poet Lin P'u Wandering in the Moonlight* (page 34)	c. 1465-1487	$61\frac{5}{8}$ x $28\frac{1}{2}$
Turner, Joseph M. W.	British	*The Fighting Téméraire* (page 35)	1838?	$35\frac{3}{4}$ x 48
Uccello, Paolo	Italian	*The Battle of San Romano* (page 40)	before 1492	72 x $125\frac{3}{4}$
Van Dyck, Anton	Flemish	*Charles I* (page 37)	c. 1635	$107\frac{1}{8}$ x $83\frac{1}{2}$
Van Eyck, Jan	Flemish	*The Marriage of Giovanni (?) Arnolfini and Giovanna Cenami (?)* (page 67)	1434	$32\frac{1}{4}$ x $23\frac{1}{2}$
Van Gogh, Vincent	Dutch	*The Starry Night* (page 48)	1889	29 x $36\frac{1}{4}$
Velázquez, Diego	Spanish	*Las Meninas* (page 67)	1656	$125\frac{1}{4}$ x $108\frac{5}{8}$
Vermeer, Jan	Dutch	*The Artist in His Studio* (page 29)	c. 1665	$47\frac{1}{4}$ x $39\frac{3}{8}$
Watteau, Antoine	French	*Pilgrimage to the Island of Cythera* (page 69)	1717	$50\frac{3}{8}$ x 76
West, Benjamin	American	*Penn's Treaty with the Indians* (page 40)	1771	$75\frac{1}{2}$ x $108\frac{3}{4}$
Whistler, James A. M.	American	*Old Battersea Bridge: Nocturne—Blue and Gold* (page 73)	c. 1865	$26\frac{1}{4}$ x $19\frac{3}{4}$
Wood, Grant	American	*American Gothic* (page 76)	1930	$29\frac{7}{8}$ x $24\frac{7}{8}$
Wyeth, Andrew	American	*Christina's World* (page 76a)	1948	$32\frac{1}{4}$ x $47\frac{3}{4}$
Unknown	Prehistoric	The Hall of the Bulls, Lascaux Cave (p. 60)	c. 15,000 B.C.-10,000 B.C.	
Unknown	Egyptian	*Vintage Scene* (page 60)	1292-1225 B.C.	$17\frac{3}{4}$ x 26
Unknown	Minoan	*Priest King* (page 61)	1600 B.C.	$86\frac{1}{2}$ in. high
Unknown	Roman	*Ulysses in the Land of the Lestrygonians* (page 61)	c. 100 B.C.	5 ft. x $7\frac{3}{4}$ ft.
Unknown	Spanish	*Angels Restrain the Four Winds* (page 64)	900's	11 x 8
Unknown	Maya	*A Raided Village* (page 61)	1200's-1300's	140 x 81
Unknown	Chinese	*Flight of Geese* (page 62)	1100's-1200's	$27\frac{1}{2}$ x 15
Unknown	Japanese	*Buddha and Two Attendants* (page 41)	1100's-1300's	54 x $19\frac{3}{4}$
Unknown	Byzantine	*Enthroned Madonna and Child* (page 64)	1200's	$32\frac{1}{8}$ x $19\frac{3}{8}$
Unknown	Persian	*Hūman, Brother of Piran, Battling Bīzhan* (page 63)	1500's?	$10\frac{1}{4}$ x $6\frac{7}{8}$
Unknown	Persian	*King Darius and Herdsmen* (page 56)	1522-1523	$11\frac{1}{2}$ x $7\frac{3}{4}$
Unknown	Indian	*Krishna Overcoming the Naga Demon, Kaliya* (page 42)	1750-1800	$7\frac{3}{8}$ x $10\frac{3}{8}$

Related Articles. See CANADA (Arts); UNITED STATES (Arts); also the Arts sections of many other country articles, such as INDIA (Arts). See also the following articles:

BIOGRAPHIES

There is a separate biography in WORLD BOOK for every painter listed in the *table* with this article. See also the following:

EUROPEAN PAINTERS

Apelles	Laurencin, Marie
Bonheur, Rosa	Lippi (family)
Bonington, Richard	Lochner, Stephen
Bonnard, Pierre	Mantegna, Andrea
Breton, Jules A.	Massys, Quentin
Brouwer, Adriaen	Memling, Hans
Caravaggio, Michelangelo	Millais, Sir John E.
Cimabue, Giovanni	Millet, Jean F.
Correggio	Munch, Edvard
Courbet, Gustave	Murillo, Bartolomé E.
Cranach, Lucas, the Elder	Pissarro, Camille
Dali, Salvador F. J.	Pollaiuolo, Antonio del
David, Jacques L.	Polygnotus
Delacroix, Ferdinand V. E.	Raeburn, Sir Henry
Del Sarto, Andrea	Reynolds, Sir Joshua
Doré, Gustave	Ribera, Jusepe de
Duccio di Buoninsegna	Rossetti, Dante Gabriel
Duchamp, Marcel	Schongauer, Martin
Ensor, James	Signorelli, Luca
Fabius (Caius F. P.)	Sisley, Alfred
Gainsborough, Thomas	Tiepolo, Giovanni B.
Géricault, Théodore	Utrillo, Maurice de
Ghirlandajo, Domenico	Van der Goes, Hugo
Goyen, Jan van	Van der Weyden, Roger
Greuze, Jean B.	Van Leyden, Lucas
Gris, Juan	Veronese, Paolo
Grosz, George	Verrocchio, Andrea del
Hobbema, Meindert	Vlaminck, Maurice de
John, Augustus E.	Zorn, Anders L.
Kollwitz, Käthe	Zubarán, Francisco

NORTH AMERICAN PAINTERS

Albers, Joseph	Kent, Rockwell
Albright, Ivan	Kline, Franz
Allston, Washington	La Farge, John
Benton, Thomas Hart	Lawson, Ernest
Bierstadt, Albert	Leutze, Emanuel G.
Bingham, George C.	MacDonald, James E. H.
Burchfield, Charles E.	Marsh, Reginald
Catlin, George	Morse, Samuel F. B.
Cole, Thomas	Moses, Grandma
Copley, John S.	O'Keefe, Georgia
Covarrubias, Miguel	Peale (family)
Davies, Arthur B.	Prendergast, Maurice B.
Davis, Stuart	Rattner, Abraham
Demuth, Charles	Remington, Frederic
Dove, Arthur	Rivera, Diego
Earl, Ralph	Rivers, Larry
Eilshemius, Louis M.	Russell, Charles M.
Feininger, Lyonel	Sheeler, Charles
Feke, Robert	Shinn, Everett
Glackens, William J.	Sloan, John
Gorky, Arshile	Stuart, Gilbert C.
Graves, Morris	Sully, Thomas
Guston, Philip	Thomson, Tom
Harris, Robert	Tobey, Mark
Hartley, Marsden	Tomlin, Bradley W.
Henri, Robert	Trumbull (John)
Inness, George	Warhol, Andy
Jackson, Alexander Y.	Watson, Homer
Kane, Paul	Weber, Max

ORIENTAL PAINTERS

Bihzad, Kamal ad-Din	Kao K'o-kung	Wang Wei
	Ma Yüan	Wu Tao-tzu
Hiroshige Ando	Sharaku Toshusai	

PAKENHAM, SIR EDWARD MICHAEL

STYLES

Barbizon School	Expressionism	Impressionism
Baroque	Fauves	Renaissance
Classicism	Futurism	Rococo
Cubism	Geometric Style	Romanticism
Dadaism	Gothic Art	Surrealism

OTHER RELATED ARTICLES

Art and the Arts	Fresco	Mural Painting
Caricature	Gesso	Paint
Cartoon	Gouache	Pastel
Collage	Icon	Perspective
Design	Illustration	Sand Painting
Drawing	Japanese Print	Stained Glass
Fine Arts	Moiré Pattern	Tempera
Finger Painting	Mosaic	Water Color

Outline

I. **How to Look at a Painting**
II. **The Painter's Materials**
III. **What Do Painters Paint?**
IV. **How Do Painters Paint?**
V. **What Makes a Painting Great?**
VI. **History**

Questions

What are four elements of painting?
Why does a painter make changes in what he sees as he makes a picture?
What qualities should a painting have to be considered great?
What can we learn from analyzing a painting?
Why do many painters use perspective?
What is a *realistic* painting? An *abstract* painting? A *pop* painting? An *op* painting?
Why is there no "right way" to look at a painting?

Books for Young Readers

CHASE, ALICE E. *Famous Paintings: An Introduction to Art for Young People.* Rev. ed. Platt, 1962. *Famous Artists of the Past.* 1964.
HAWKINSON, JOHN. *Collect, Print and Paint from Nature.* Whitman, 1963. *More to Collect and Paint from Nature.* 1964.
JANSON, HORST W. and DORA J. *Story of Painting for Young People.* Abrams, 1952.
MOORE, LAMONT. *The First Book of Paintings: An Introduction to the Appreciation of Pictures.* Watts, 1960.
RUSKIN, ARIANE. *The Pantheon Story of Art for Young People.* Pantheon Books, 1964.
SPILKA, ARNOLD. *Paint All Kinds of Pictures.* Walck, 1963.

Books for Older Readers

GOMBRICH, E. H. *The Story of Art.* 11th ed. Phaidon, 1965.
KIELTY, BERNARDINE. *Masters of Painting: Their Works, Their Lives, Their Times.* Doubleday, 1964.
MACAGY, DOUGLAS and ELIZABETH. *Going For a Walk with a Line; A Step into The World of Modern Art.* Doubleday, 1959.
MUNRO, ELEANOR C. *The Golden Encyclopedia of Art.* Golden Press, 1961.

PAISLEY, *PAYZ lee* (pop. 95,808; alt. 30 ft.), is a city in western Scotland, about seven miles west of Glasgow. It is one of the world's largest centers for making cotton thread. Paisley-pattern shawls were important products in the 1800's. For location, see GREAT BRITAIN (political map).

PAISLEY PATTERN is a printed or woven design that imitates the Paisley shawls made in the 1800's.

PAKENHAM, SIR EDWARD MICHAEL. See WAR OF 1812 ("The Needless Battle").

Hal Linker, Black Star

Houseboats on the Ganges River serve as permanent homes for many Pakistani families. The boats lie near the city of Dacca, the capital and largest city of East Pakistan.

PAKISTAN, *PACK ih STAN,* or *PAH kih STAHN,* is an independent country in the Commonwealth of Nations. The country's official name is THE ISLAMIC REPUBLIC OF PAKISTAN. Islāmābād is the capital.

The country is unusual in that it is divided into two parts more than 900 miles apart. India lies between these two sections. Pakistan depends on airplanes and radio for fast transportation and communication between its two regions.

Pakistan has a short history as an independent country. It was created Aug. 14, 1947, when the subcontinent of India was *partitioned* (divided) along religious lines between Moslems and Hindus. Pakistan became the largest Moslem nation in the world. The Hindus continued to call their country India.

Pakistan has about half as many people as the United States. It is one of the least developed major countries in the world. About eight out of every ten persons in Pakistan depend upon farming for a living.

The Land and Its Resources

Location, Size, and Surface Features. West Pakistan is bordered on the west by Iran, on the north by Afghanistan, on the northeast by Kashmir, on the southeast by India, and on the south by the Arabian Sea. It is about as large as Texas and Oklahoma combined.

The *Color Map* shows that East Pakistan is bounded on the south by the Bay of Bengal, on the southeast by Burma, and on the west, north, and east by India. East Pakistan is only a little larger than Arkansas. The entire country covers 365,529 square miles.

FACTS IN BRIEF

Form of Government: Independent republic, and a member of the Commonwealth of Nations.

Capital: Islāmābād.

Divisions: Two provinces, West and East Pakistan.

Languages: Bengali, English, Urdu.

Head of State: President.

National Assembly: 156 elected members.

Area: 365,529 square miles (West Pakistan, 310,403 square miles; East Pakistan, 55,126 square miles). *Coastline*—965 miles.

Elevation: *Highest*—Godwin Austen, 28,250 feet above sea level (located in Kashmir); *Lowest*—sea level.

Population: *1961 Census*—93,720,613; distribution, 86 per cent rural, 14 per cent urban. *Estimated 1970 Population*—114,158,000; density, 312 persons to the square mile. *Estimated 1975 Population*—126,659,000.

Chief Products: *Agriculture*—cotton, fruit, hides and skins, jute, millet, oil seeds, rice, sugar cane, wheat. *Manufacturing and Processing*—blankets, carpets, cotton textiles, glass, jute bagging, paper, processed fruits, rugs, silk, sports goods, sugar, surgical instruments, tea. *Mining*—coal, petroleum.

Flag: A white crescent and a star stand on a green field, symbolizing the Moslem faith. A white stripe at the left stands for minorities. See FLAG (color picture: Flags of Asia).

National Anthem: "Qaumi Tarana" ("National Anthem").

Money: *Basic Unit*—Pakistani rupee. One hundred paisas equal one rupee. For the value of the rupee in dollars, see MONEY (table: Values).

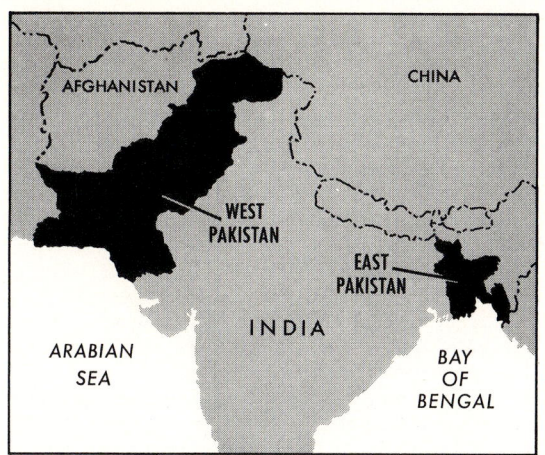

Pakistan (Shown in Black) Is Divided in Two Parts.

The famous Khyber Pass and the mighty ranges of the Hindu Kush and Sulaimān mountains lie on the northwest frontier of West Pakistan. This region was the scene of many of Rudyard Kipling's poems and stories about British army life in the 1800's. To the northeast lie the Himalaya (mountain range). The Indus River flows from the mountains. With its branches, it waters the fertile plains of the Punjab region and empties into

Robert I. Crane, the contributor of this article, is Professor of History at Duke University and the author of Aspects of Economic Development in South Asia.

the Arabian Sea. West Pakistan has snow-covered peaks, dry salt ranges, fertile plains, and a desert area ringed with craggy uplands of rich color. Much of West Pakistan is mountainous or on a high plateau.

East Pakistan is a much different sort of land. Most

Verona, Black Star

A Farmer and His Camel bring a load of cotton to market. Camels are an important means of transportation in Pakistan.

A Policeman Directs Traffic in Rāwalpindi, a manufacturing center. Rāwalpindi was once Pakistan's capital.

Pan Asia, Black Star

79

of it lies near sea level. It is a flat plain covered with groves of bamboo, mango, and coconut palm. It is semitropical country, with heavy rains. Large marshes are filled with malaria-carrying mosquitoes, while forests contain tigers, leopards, and bears. East Pakistan has two major rivers, the Ganges and the Brahmaputra. These rivers and their branches are used for transportation as well as irrigation. More than half of a 2,600-mile system of dikes on the Ganges River delta has been completed. The dikes will protect the land from seawater and allow cultivation of almost 3 million acres of land. Use of this land, which was formerly swamp, is expected to greatly increase Pakistan's agricultural production.

Natural Resources. The major resource of Pakistan is its fertile soil. Almost 60 million acres of land are cultivated. About two-fifths of this land depends upon canal or well water for irrigation.

The Mangla Dam on the Jhelum River was completed in 1967. The dam provides irrigation, as well as flood control and power. About two miles long, it is one of the largest dams in the world. Mangla Dam is part of the Indus River Treaty. The treaty assures equal distribution of water between India and Pakistan through construction of a series of dams.

Pakistan's other natural resources include animals, fish, forests, and minerals.

Climate. The climate in West Pakistan ranges from hot, dry desert to snow-covered mountains. East Pakistan is generally warm and humid throughout. Temperatures in Karāchi, West Pakistan, and in Chittagong, East Pakistan, average about 66° F. in January and 83° F. in July. Both cities stand at low elevations near the sea. Rainfall varies greatly. In Karāchi, it totals about 5 inches a year, and in Chittagong it totals almost 100 inches. Damaging tropical storms often occur in East Pakistan.

The People and Their Work

The People of Pakistan come from many races. The northwest frontier always has been the avenue for the invasion of India, and thus peoples from Siberia, Central Asia, Iran, Turkey, and Arabia have settled in Pakistan. The result has been many differences in languages, food habits, customs, and physical types. East Pakistan has only a seventh of the area of Pakistan. But about one-half of the people live there.

Way of Life. Most people of Pakistan are farmers, struggling to make a bare living from tiny plots of land. They lack money, seldom have good seed, and rarely use fertilizer on their land. Poverty and debt are ever present, while illiteracy, disease, and a sense of helplessness are common. These people live in small villages from birth to death. Few of them ever visit a large town.

Clothing is simple. Women wear a one-piece *sari* or a loose blouse with *shulvar* (trousers similar to pajamas). The men wear a *tahbun* (wrap-around cotton cloth), or a *kameez* (shirt and pajama-like trousers).

The family is bound closely together. It is not unusual for more than one generation to live in the same dwelling. New ideas are not easily accepted in a society so bound by tradition as Pakistan. Most of the people cannot read, and the old ways seem satisfactory to them. The past twenty years have, however, brought new trends and contacts that are producing new ideas. The growth of big cities has done its part to break down the old unity of the small village.

Language. Pakistan has several languages and dialects. Of these, the most important are Urdu, Bengali, Pushtu, Sindhi, and Punjabi. Urdu and Bengali are the national languages. The constitution provides that English may be used for official purposes until 1972, when

PAKISTAN MAP INDEX

Cities and Towns

Abbottābād	31,036	B 8
Ahmadpur East	32,423	E 7
Ārifwāla	18,558	D 8
Bāgherhāt	16,398	L 16
Bahāwalnagar	36,290	E 8
Bahāwalpur	84,377	E 7
Bannu	31,623	C 7
Barisāl	69,936	L 17
Bhairab Bāzār	31,749	K 17
Bhakkar	21,749	D 7
Bhera	17,992	C 8
Bogra	33,784	K 16
Brāhmanbāria	44,784	L 17
Campbellpore	19,041	C 8
Chakwāl	16,843	C 8
Chāndpur	34,837	L 17
Chārsadda*	37,396	B 7
Chīchāwatni*	21,380	D 8
Chiniot	47,099	D 8
Chishtiān Mandi	26,041	E 8
Chittagong	364,205	L 17
Comilla	54,504	L 17
Dacca	556,712	L 17
Dādu	19,142	F 5
Daska*	20,406	C 9
Dāūd Khel	17,524	C 7
Dera Ghāzi Khān	47,105	D 7
Dera Ismāīl Khān	46,140	D 7
Dinājpur	37,711	K 16
Farīdpur	28,333	L 16
Gaibānda	17,738	K 16
Gojra	29,665	D 8
Gujrānwāla	196,154	C 9
Gujrāt	59,608	C 9
Hāfizābād	34,576	C 8
Hārūnābād	22,575	E 8
Hyderābād	434,537	G 6
Islāmābād	50,000	C 8
Jacobābād	35,278	E 6
Jalālpur	16,988	C 9
Jamālpur	37,988	K 16
Jarānwāla*	26,953	D 8
Jessore	46,366	L 16
Jhang Maghiāna	94,971	D 8
Jhelum	52,585	C 8
Kahror Pakka	16,870	E 7
Kamālia	35,248	D 8
Kambar	12,090	F 6
Kāmoke*	25,124	D 9
Kandhkot*	12,253	E 6
Karāchi	1,912,598	G 5
Kasūr	74,546	D 9
Khairpur	34,144	F 6
Khānewāl	49,093	D 7
Khānpur	31,465	E 7
Khulna	127,970	L 16
Khushāb	24,851	C 8
Kishorganj	24,031	K 17
Kohāt	49,854	C 7
Kotri	20,262	G 6
Kushtia	24,952	L 16
Lahore	1,296,477	D 9
Lāla Mūsa	22,633	C 8
Lālmanir Hāt	22,001	K 16
Lārkāna	48,008	F 6
Leiah	19,608	D 7
Lyallpur	425,248	D 8
Mādārīpur	25,328	L 17
Mandi Bahāuddīn*	22,295	C 8
Mandi Burewāla	34,237	D 8
Mardān	77,932	B 8
Miān Channūn*	19,888	D 8
Miānwāli	31,398	C 7
Mīrpur Khās	60,861	G 6
Mitha Tiwāna*	16,046	C 8
Multān	358,201	D 7
Mymensingh	53,256	K 17
Nankāna Sāhib*	17,140	D 8
Naogaon	20,276	K 16
Nārāyanganj	162,054	L 17
Nārowāl	16,127	C 9
Nawābganj	29,725	K 16
Nawābshāh	45,651	F 6
Netrakona	17,008	K 17
Noākhāli	19,874	L 17
Nowshera	43,757	C 7
Okāra	68,299	D 8
Pābna	40,792	K 16
Pākpattan	27,974	D 8
Pārachinār	22,953	C 7
Pārbatipur	27,188	K 16
Peshāwar	218,691	C 7
Pirojpur	15,754	L 16
Quetta	106,633	D 5
Rahīmyār Khān	43,548	E 7
Rājbāri	16,044	L 16
Rājshāhi	56,885	K 16
Rangpur	40,634	K 16
Rāwalpindi	340,175	C 8
Rohri	19,072	F 6
Sādiqābad	16,007	E 7
Saidpur	60,628	K 16
Saidu	15,920	B 8
Sahiwal	75,180	D 8
Sargodha	129,291	C 8
Sātkhira	20,169	L 16
Shāhdādkot	15,043	F 5
Shāhdādpur	21,537	G 6
Shekhūpura	41,635	D 9
Sherpur	24,924	K 16
Shikārpur	53,910	F 6
Shujāābād	16,815	E 7
Siālkot	164,346	C 9
Sirājganj	47,152	K 16
Sukkur	103,216	F 6
Swābi	17,542	B 8
Sylhet	37,740	K 17
Tando Ādam	31,246	G 6
Tando Allāhyār	17,273	G 6
Tando Muhammad Khān	15,536	G 6
Tangail*	23,688	K 16
Toba Tek Singh	17,847	D 8
Vihāri	15,410	D 8
Wah*	37,035	C 8
Wazīrābād*	29,399	C 9

Physical Features

Baluchistan (region)	F 4
Brahmaputra River	J 17
Cape Jaddi	G 3
Cape Jīwani	G 2
Cape Nūh	G 3
Central Makrān Range	F 4
Chāgai Hills	E 3
Chenāb River	D 8
Dasht River	G 3
Ganges River	K 15
Hab River	F 5
Himalaya (Mountains)	C 9
Indus River	D 7
Jammu and Kashmir (region)	B 9
Jamuna River	K 16
Jhelum River	C 8
Khyber Pass	B 7
Kīrthar Range	F 5
Kunar River	B 7
Kundar River	D 6
Makrān Coast Range	G 3
Mangla Dam	C 8
Māshkel River	F 2
Mouths of the Ganges	M 16
Mouths of the Indus	H 5
Nāl River	F 4
Nanga Parbat (Mountain)	B 9
Nāra Canal	F 6
Nihing River	F 3
Pishīn Lora River	E 4
Punjab (region)	D 8
Rakaposhi (Mountain)	A 9
Ravi River	D 8
Rohri Canal	F 6
Siāhān Range	F 3
Sind (region)	G 5
Sonmiāni Bay	G 5
Sulaimān Range	E 6
Sutlej River	E 8
Thar (Indian) Desert	F 7
Tirich Mir (Mt.)	A 7
Tozghi (Mountain)	E 3
Zhob River	D 6

*Name does not appear on map; key gives general location.
Sources: Latest census figures (1961) and official estimate (1967) for Islāmābād

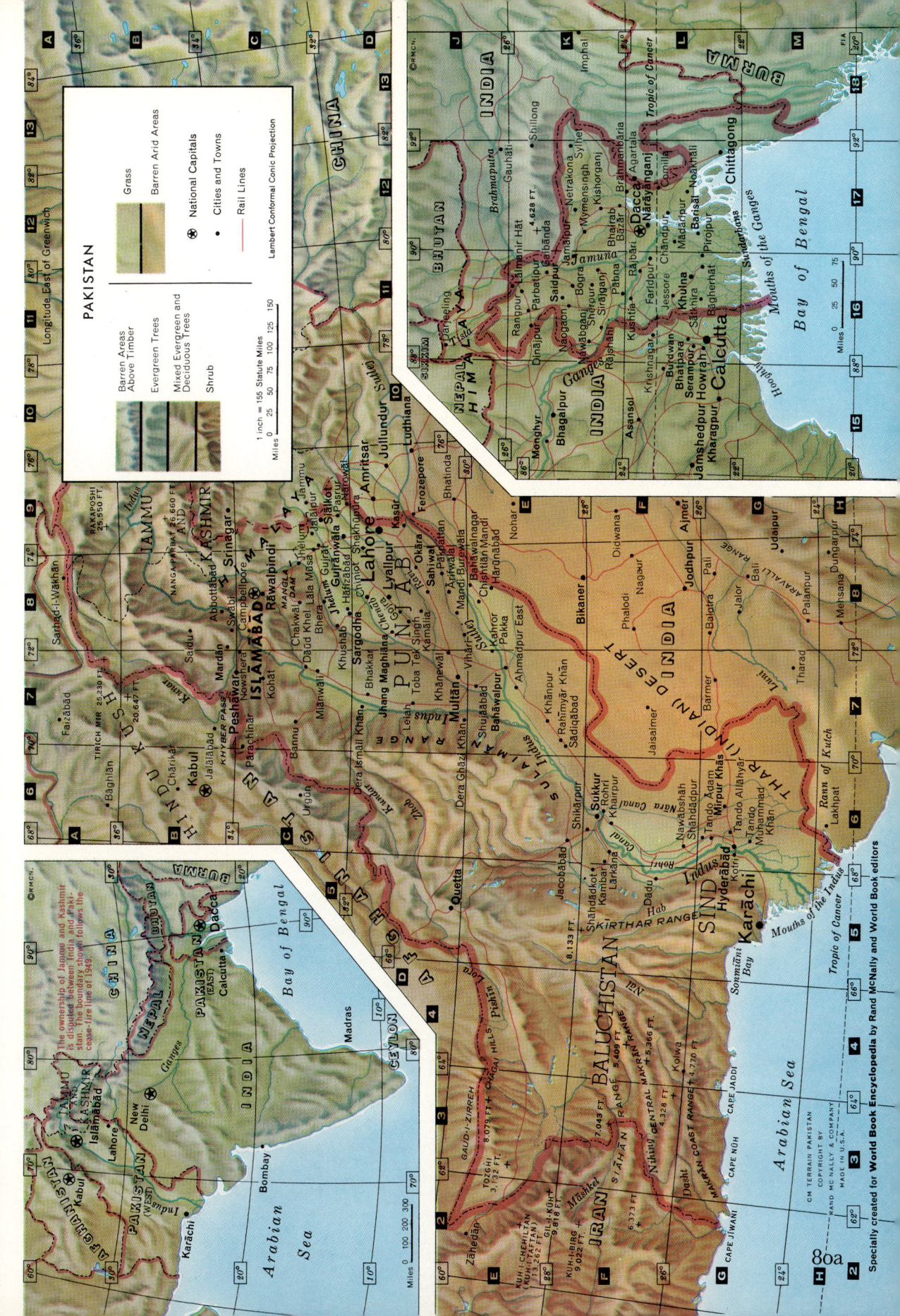

PAKISTAN

Grass

Barren Arid Areas

Barren Areas
Above Timber

Evergreen Trees

Mixed Evergreen and
Deciduous Trees

Shrub

⊛ National Capitals

⊙ Cities and Towns

— Rail Lines

Lambert Conformal Conic Projection

1 inch = 155 Statute Miles

Miles 0 25 50 75 100 125 150

Embassy of Pakistan, Washington, D.C.

Karāchi's Merewether Tower stands at a downtown inter-
section. Sir William Merewether, a British army officer, played an
important part in the British conquest of the Sind region in the
1840's. Karāchi is one of the region's chief cities.

a Presidential commission will consider replacing English with another language.

Cities. Islāmābād is the capital and Karāchi is the
largest city of Pakistan. Lahore is the capital of West
Pakistan. Dacca is the capital of East Pakistan. See the
list of articles on cities in the *Related Articles* section.

Agriculture. One-half of the land under cultivation is planted in wheat or rice. Rice is the major
crop in East Pakistan. It demands careful and intensive
farming on tiny plots of flooded land. Jute, a plant
used in making burlap, is also grown widely. In West
Pakistan, wheat and cotton are major crops. Other
crops include millet, corn, barley, sugar cane, and oil
seeds. Tobacco and tea also are grown, along with a
wide variety of fruits such as plums, quinces, pomegranates, peaches, figs, melons, and mulberries. Pakistan ordinarily grows enough food to feed its own people.

About 80 per cent of the world's jute supply is grown
in East Pakistan. The country also grows and exports
cotton.

Almost all the farming or fruit growing of Pakistan
is done by hand or with the simplest tools. The farmer
with his wooden plow hitched behind an ox is a typical
sight. Sowing and harvesting are done by hand.

Minerals. Pakistan produces small amounts of several
minerals. About 600,000 tons of coal are mined each
year, while smaller quantities of chromite, gypsum,
limestone, and fire clay are produced. The country
produces more than 55 million gallons of petroleum

Dickason, Ewing Galloway

Wind Scoops on Roofs provide natural air conditioning
for the buildings of Hyderābād,
a large city in West Pakistan's
Sind region. The scoops catch
cooling winds and lead the air
down into the buildings.

80b

each year, as well as small amounts of iron ore. Natural gas has been found at Sui, Baluchistan. However, Pakistan has to import many important minerals.

Manufactures. There is a marked contrast between Pakistan's resources and its lack of development industrially. Fewer than ten persons out of a thousand work in organized industry. Although Pakistan produces most of the world's raw jute, it was not until the 1950's that processing began, after the first jute mill was built. Pakistan grows good cotton, and produces enough cotton textiles for the country's needs and for export to Middle Eastern countries. Pakistan also produces other raw materials such as hides and skins, wool, sugar cane, and tobacco, but much of the production is exported in the raw or semifinished state. Pakistan built its first paper mill in 1953.

Transportation. Pakistan is weak in modern transportation. There are only about 7,000 miles of railway tracks, 9,000 miles of surfaced highways, and 50,000 miles of unsurfaced dirt roads.

East Pakistan has a good internal-waterways system, with almost 4,600 miles of rivers and canals that are navigable for small and medium-sized boats and ships.

Transportation between West and East Pakistan is by airplane, or by ship around the tip of India. East Pakistan is faced with scarcities in many goods, including food, and so a great deal of shipping has to take place between the two parts of the country.

Social and Cultural Achievements

Education. Only about 19 of every 100 persons in Pakistan can read and write. There is a serious shortage of schools. About 7 million children are enrolled in the primary grades. About 8,500 secondary schools enroll about $2\frac{1}{2}$ million students. Half the teachers in the secondary schools have little training.

There are about 430 arts and science colleges in Pakistan, with 268,000 students enrolled. The country has 16 colleges of medicine, 13 of law, and 5 of engineering. Pakistan has 13 universities. Among the oldest and largest are the University of Punjab in Lahore, Dacca in Dacca, and Karāchi in Karāchi.

Arts and Crafts. The craftsmen of Pakistan long have been famous for their delicate work. Fine inlaid brasses, beautiful rugs and shawls, lovely carved ivory, and gold-threaded fabrics have been produced in the region for hundreds of years.

For many years, the Moslem architecture of what is now Pakistan has continued the classic forms of Arabic-Moslem building famous in other parts of the world. Recently, however, Pakistani artists and architects have been experimenting with modern functional structures. Another school of architects has returned to the style of the Mogul Era of the 1500's and the 1600's.

The music of Pakistan retains much that is classical and traditional. It is a mixture of the older Hindu music and the music brought into India by the early Arab and Turki invaders. A new popular music that is similar, in some ways, to Western orchestral music has developed with the motion picture.

The Urdu literature of modern Pakistan is passing through a period of stormy change. The supporters of ancient literary style now have to compete with those who have been influenced by Western style and content. As yet there is no single major trend. Realism and religious nationalism are strong factors in Urdu literature.

The most famous literary figure of Pakistan is the poet Sir Mohammed Iqbal. In 1930, Iqbal popularized the idea of making a Moslem homeland out of part of India.

Religion and Philosophy. Religion was the major reason Pakistan came into being, and therefore matters of Moslem religion and philosophy are of considerable importance in the country. Some of the people argue about how large a part the Moslem religion should play in the public life of the country. Moslems today are concerned with the problem of adapting their ancient religion to fit new conditions. This is particularly true because the Moslem faith holds that religion is at the very center of man's life and affects his daily actions in great detail. About 86 out of 100 of the people of Pakistan are Moslems. Most of the rest are Hindus. Less than one person out of 100 is a Christian. However, Pakistan has complete religious freedom.

Recreation. The people of West Pakistan always have been a sturdy and energetic race. Physical ability is prized and hardiness is stressed. The government is building gymnasiums, sports centers, and other athletic

Pictorial Parade

Bales of Jute are Unloaded from boats called *sampans* in Dacca, East Pakistan. Jute is used to make rope, burlap bags, and canvas. Pakistan is the world's leading jute producer.

Sawders, Cushing

In Crowded Open-Air Bazaars in Peshāwar, traders from Europe and Asia have exchanged goods for hundreds of years. Peshāwar lies in Pakistan's northwest frontier region.

facilities. Among the most popular games are soccer, cricket, tennis, and polo.

Social Welfare and Health is one of the most difficult problems facing Pakistan. A shortage of doctors, nurses, and hospitals makes it difficult to control disease. There often are cholera and smallpox epidemics. Tuberculosis is widespread. Leprosy is also an old problem in the area. Malaria kills many persons each year, especially in East Pakistan. In all Pakistan, there are fewer than 200 maternity and child-welfare clinics.

Government and History

The first Moslems to come to India were the Arabs who, in the A.D. 700's, invaded the northwest area of what is now Pakistan. Other invaders had adopted Hindu ways and customs, but the Moslems maintained their separate culture. Under the British government of

A Pakistani Couple sit on straw mats in a market place, waiting for someone to buy the cotton they have grown and spun.
Three Lions

India in the 1800's and early 1900's, the Hindus took advantage of new educational opportunities to gain better jobs. For further information on Pakistan's early history, see INDIA.

In the 1930's, Moslems began a movement to create a country of their own in the subcontinent of India. Moslem students in Great Britain made up the name *Pakistan* in 1933, by taking the first letters of Punjab, Afghan (the North-West Frontier Province), Kashmir, and Sind, and adding the ending *stan* which means *land*. In the Urdu language, *pahk* means *pure* or *clean*, so that Pakistan also means *land of the pure*.

Mohammed Ali Jinnah, president of the Moslem League of India, headed the movement for a free Pakistan. He is known as the founder of Pakistan.

The Dominion of Pakistan was created on Aug. 14, 1947. Jinnah became the first governor general.

Thousands of people were killed in religious riots after the division of India, and thousands died while migrating between India and Pakistan. About 6 million Hindus and Sikhs fled from Pakistan to India, and about 7 million Moslems from India to Pakistan.

Difficulties between Pakistan and India arose over the status of Kashmir. After armed clashes in 1948 between Pakistan and India, the United Nations (UN) was asked to set up the truce line. The line left a large part of Kashmir in control of pro-Indian factions. In 1957, a new constitution established this section as a part of India. See KASHMIR.

In the 1950's, aided by the United Nations and the United States, Pakistan began work on a long-range program to modernize its agriculture and industry. But the country had grave economic problems and food continued to be relatively scarce.

Pakistan became a member of the Southeast Asia Treaty Organization (SEATO) in 1954. The next year, Pakistan joined the Baghdad Pact (now Central Treaty Organization) defense agreement with Turkey, Iraq, and Great Britain, and became one of the strong supporters of the Western powers in the Middle East.

The Republic. In 1956, Pakistan changed its status in the British Commonwealth from a dominion to a republic (see COMMONWEALTH OF NATIONS).

The government adopted a new constitution which stressed the country's belief in Moslem teachings. The constitution called for a Moslem president as head of state. The president was to be elected by the members of the National Assembly and the provincial assemblies. Actual political leadership was to be vested in a prime minister and a Cabinet, all appointed by the president. All citizens over the age of 21 can vote.

Under the constitution, Pakistan's federal government was somewhat like that of the United States. The country was divided into the two provinces of West Pakistan and East Pakistan, each with a governor, ministry, and legislature. Certain powers were reserved to the national government and others belonged to the provincial governments. Local government was administered by elected district boards and municipal boards.

Major General Iskander Mirza was elected the first president. Pakistan's first five-year plan for economic development began in 1956. Ismail Ibrahim Chundrigar became prime minister of Pakistan in 1957. He resigned a few months later and was succeeded by Malik Firoz Khan Noon. In 1958, the sultan of Muscat and Oman peacefully turned over the city of Gwadar to Pakistan, which had claimed it for many years.

On Oct. 7, 1958, President Mirza abolished the constitution and dismissed the national and provincial governments. General Mohammad Ayub Khan succeeded Mirza as president several weeks later. Rāwalpindi replaced Karāchi as the capital in 1960.

President Ayub Khan ruled under martial law until a new constitution became effective in 1962. Under this constitution, *electoral colleges* elect the president and legislature. The people elect the electoral college members. The constitution abolished the office of prime minister. In 1962, Pakistan and Communist China signed trade and border agreements. In the same year, Pakistan and India resumed negotiations over Kashmir. During the mid-1960's, Pakistan built a new capital at Islāmābād. The president lives there, but the National Assembly meets in Rāwalpindi or in Dacca. Ayub Khan began a second term as president in 1965.

In August, 1965, disputes over Kashmir set off heavy fighting between Pakistan and India. The UN secured a cease-fire in September. In January, 1966, Russian premier Aleksei Kosygin invited Ayub Khan and Indian prime minister Lal Bahadur Shastri to hold a peace meeting in Tashkent, Russia. In Tashkent, the leaders agreed to try to settle the dispute peacefully.

In March, 1969, Ayub Khan resigned as president of Pakistan in the face of widespread antigovernment demonstrations. He was replaced by General Yahya Khan, commander in chief of the Pakistan Army, who declared martial law in the country.   ROBERT I. CRANE

Related Articles in WORLD BOOK include:

CITIES

Chittagong	Hyderābād	Lahore	Rāwalpindi
Dacca	Islāmābād	Lyallpur	Sialkot
Gujrānwāla	Karāchi	Multān	

HISTORY

Ayub Khan, Mohammad	Colombo Plan India	Jinnah, Mohammed A. Southeast Asia
Central Treaty Organization	Iqbal, Sir Muhammad	Treaty Organization

PHYSICAL FEATURES

Arabian Sea	Ganges River	Khyber Pass
Bay of Bengal	Hindu Kush	Sutlej River
Brahmaputra River	Indus River	Thar Desert

REGIONS

Baluchistan	Bengal	Kashmir	Punjab

PRODUCTS

For Pakistan's rank in production, see the following:

Banana	Cattle	Cotton	Rice	Sugar Cane

OTHER RELATED ARTICLES

Islam	Jute	Moslems	Shalimar Gardens	Sikhs

Outline

I. The Land and Its Resources
  A. Location, Size, and Surface Features
  B. Natural Resources
  C. Climate
II. The People and Their Work
  A. The People
  B. Way of Life
  C. Language
  D. Cities
  E. Agriculture
  F. Minerals
  G. Manufactures
  H. Transportation
III. Social and Cultural Achievements
  A. Education
  B. Arts and Crafts
  C. Religion and Philosophy
  D. Recreation
  E. Social Welfare and Health
IV. Government and History

European

Pakistani Nurses attend a class in child care on the roof of a clinic in Lahore, the second largest city in Pakistan. In the background are the cupolas and minarets of Badshahi Mosque. Such classes in up-to-date health practices are taught by instructors from the World Health Organization.

Questions

What is unusual about the division of Pakistan?
What countries border Pakistan?
What is Pakistan's chief natural resource?
What are the leading languages in Pakistan?
What kind of clothing do the people wear?
How do most of the people earn their living?
Who is Pakistan's most famous writer?
Why did Pakistan become a separate nation?
When was the Dominion of Pakistan created?
What brought about the India-Pakistan conflict of 1948?

PALACE usually refers to the official residence of kings or emperors. Most palaces are large and ornate. WORLD BOOK has many separate articles and pictures of famous palaces. See the following articles.

Alhambra	Kremlin
Borghese Palace	Pitti Palace
Buckingham Palace	Quirinal Palace
Doge (picture)	Seraglio
Escorial	Tuileries
Holyrood	Uffizi Palace
Japan (picture)	Versailles
Knossos	Windsor Castle

PALAEOLOGUS was the family name of several rulers of the Byzantine Empire. See BYZANTINE EMPIRE (Final Decline).

PALAMEDES. See ULYSSES.

PALANQUIN, *PAL un KEEN,* a device like a litter, was used for many years by Chinese and Japanese, much as Americans use taxis. The passenger sat or lay on the box-shaped palanquin, which was about 8 feet long, 4 feet wide, and 4 feet high. The sides and ends of the palanquin were usually protected by blinds and shutters that could be lowered or raised. In the side of the palanquin was a door. The structure hung from two poles carried by four men.   FRANKLIN M. RECK

PALATE

PALATE is the roof of the mouth. The palate has two parts, the *hard palate*, in front, and the *soft palate*, behind. The hard palate is composed of the *palatine* bones and parts of the *maxillary* bones. It is covered with a *mucous membrane.*

The soft palate is a fold of muscular tissue covered by a mucous membrane. The palate separates the mouth and the nasal cavity. During swallowing, the soft palate rises and blocks off the entrance to the rear nasal passage. A projection called the *uvula* hangs from the middle of the soft palate.

Only mammals and crocodiles have a palate like

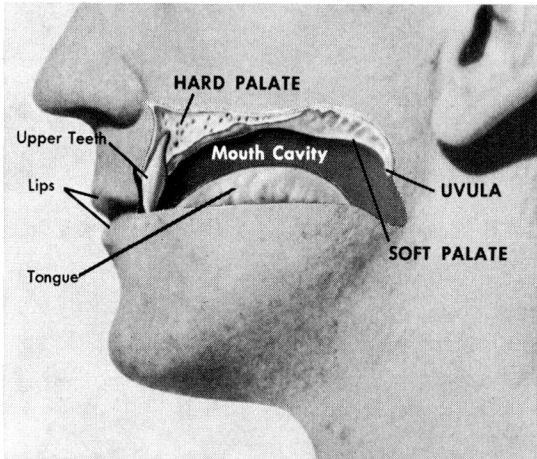

The Hard and Soft Palates Are Shown in This Diagram.

man's. In other animals, the base of the skull serves as the roof of the mouth. Fishes, amphibians, and reptiles may have teeth growing on the palate. Amphibians use the palate to aid in breathing.   WILLIAM V. MAYER

See also CLEFT PALATE; MOUTH; TONSIL (picture).

PALATINATE, *puh LAT uh nayt,* was the name of two little countries of the old German Empire. The two Palatinates were one political unit until 1620. One was called the Upper Palatinate. The other was called the Lower, or Rhenish, Palatinate. The name *Palatinate* once referred to a castle of the German emperor.

The Upper Palatinate is now part of Bavaria, joined with Regensburg to make a single province. The Lower Palatinate is part of Rhineland Palatinate.

The Lower Palatinate region has long been famous for its fertile soil. It produces good crops of potatoes, tobacco, hemp, flax, wheat, rye, and barley. It has always been noted for its wine.   JAMES K. POLLOCK

See also BAVARIA.

PALATINE HILL. See ROME (The City Today).

PALAU ISLANDS, *pah LOU* (pop. about 10,628), is the name of a group of islands in the Western Pacific. They are a part of the Caroline group in the area known as Micronesia. The islands lie about 500 miles east of the large island of Mindanao in the southern Philippines. The Palau group consists of a ragged chain of islands surrounded by a coral reef. They extend about 100 miles from north to south, and about 20 miles from east to west. They cover 179 square miles of land.

The northern islands, including the largest, Babelthuap (129 square miles), are of volcanic origin. These islands are fertile and have many trees. Many kinds of tropical fruits and vegetables are grown. Ancient ruins suggest that man has lived there a long time. The southern islands are formed of upraised coral reef. Some of them are too rugged for people to live on. Angaur and Peleliu, at the southern end, are famous for their phosphate deposits.

The Palau Islands belonged to Germany before World War I. The Allies turned them over to Japan after the Treaty of Versailles. Under Japanese control the islands became headquarters for all Micronesia. The Japanese built roads and concrete piers, developed modern harbors, and brought in Japanese settlers. The Palaus and all the Japanese-mandated islands were closed to foreigners in 1935.

United States forces drove the Japanese from the southern Palaus in 1944. After World War II the Japanese settlers were sent back to Japan. The U.S. government controls the Palau Islands under a United Nations trusteeship.   EDWIN H. BRYAN, JR.

See also CAROLINE ISLANDS; PACIFIC ISLANDS (Micronesia); PACIFIC ISLANDS, TRUST TERRITORY OF THE; PELELIU.

PALAWAN. See PHILIPPINES (The Islands).

PALEMBANG, *PAH lem BAHNG* (pop. 474,971; alt. 5 ft.), is one of Sumatra's chief ports and largest cities. It stands on the Musi River, and is a trading center for petroleum and rubber industries. Palembang's industries include iron foundries, machine shops, and shipyards. For location, see INDONESIA (color map).

PALEOBOTANY. See PALEONTOLOGY.

PALEOCENE EPOCH. See EARTH (table: Outline of Earth History).

PALEOGEOGRAPHY. See PALEONTOLOGY; GEOLOGY (table).

PALEOGRAPHY, *PAY lee OG ruh fih,* is the study of ancient handwriting. By carefully examining the letter forms and abbreviations formerly used in each kind of writing, the paleographer learns to read old manuscripts. He can often make a good guess as to where and when unsigned and undated documents were written. In this way, he can sometimes detect forgeries. *Epigraphy,* a special branch of paleography, is the study of writing cut in permanent material, such as stone or metal. See also MANUSCRIPT; WRITING.   ARTHUR E. GORDON

PALEOLITHIC PERIOD. See STONE AGE; PREHISTORIC MAN (color diagram).

PALEONTOLOGY, *PAY lee ahn TAHL uh jee,* is the science of the study of fossils. Fossil remains of animals and plants occur in layers of *sedimentary rocks* (rocks formed when mineral matter settled out of air, ice, or water). The animals and plants that are now fossils lived when the rocks were formed. They were buried and preserved as the layers of rock piled up.

By studying fossils, paleontologists learn what kind of life existed during various periods of the earth's history. The oldest known fossils are one-celled plants that lived at least 3,100,000,000 years ago. The fossil record shows a gradual increase in the complexity of animals and plants. This gradual change in body form is called *evolution.*

Paleontology is important in the study of geology. The age of rocks may be determined by the fossils in them. Fossils also tell whether rocks were formed under the ocean or on land. Most rocks that contain marine shell fossils were formed under the ocean. Most rocks that contain land animal and land plant fossils were formed on land. The knowledge of which rocks were formed under the ocean helps scientists map the world as it was millions of years ago. Such scientists are called *paleogeographers*.

Paleontology aids in the location of oil. Oil is often found in rocks that contain certain fossils. Oil companies use such fossils as a clue to where to find oil.

There are three main branches of paleontology. (1) *Invertebrate paleontology* deals chiefly with fossil insects and shells. (2) *Vertebrate paleontology* is the branch that is concerned with extinct fishes, amphibians, reptiles, birds, and mammals. (3) *Paleobotany* is the study of fossil plants.   SAMUEL PAUL WELLES

See also FOSSIL.

PALEOZOIC ERA. See EARTH (The Paleozoic Era).

PALERMO, *puh LUR moh* (pop. 622,646; alt. 46 ft.), is the capital and chief seaport of Sicily, an Italian island and political region. The city lies on the northwestern coast, beside the Gulf of Palermo. See ITALY (color map). The city has important fisheries. Tropical fruits, oils, and wine are exported. Palermo is one of the oldest seaports on the Mediterranean. It is a transportation and industrial center. Its factories manufacture steel, glass, furniture, textiles, and canned goods.

The Phoenicians founded Palermo between the 600's and 500's B.C. Several countries held Palermo before it became part of Italy in 1860.   BENJAMIN WEBB WHEELER

PALESTINE, *PAL es tine*, is one of the most famous lands in the world. It is the Holy Land of the Bible. It has been known in history for at least 5,000 years. Palestine is sacred to three great religions: Judaism, Christianity, and Islam. Judaism and Christianity were born here. Most of the events described in the Bible took place in Palestine.

Historic Palestine covers an area of 10,434 square miles along the eastern end of the Mediterranean Sea, between Egypt and Syria. It is a little larger than the state of Vermont. More than 8,000 square miles of Palestine now belongs to Israel, and the rest to Jordan, Lebanon, and Syria.

People lived in Palestine at least 200,000 years ago, during the Old Stone Age. Archaeologists have dug up relics which date back to that time. They have also found rich remains from the New Stone Age, about 12,000 years ago.

The Land of Canaan. By 3000 B.C., Palestine, or *Canaan*, was inhabited by a people called Canaanites. For 1,500 years, the Canaanites developed their civilization. Their arts and industries were much like those of the Egyptians, and they wrote in special signs called *cuneiform* as the Babylonians did. See CANAANITE; CUNEIFORM.

Sometime around the 1900's B.C., the Hebrew patriarch Abraham and his tribesmen came across the Arabian Desert from Mesopotamia and settled in Canaan. The Hebrews made their homes in the area, and traded with their neighbors. Later, perhaps in the 1300's B.C., the Egyptians enslaved many of them. In the 1200's B.C., Moses led the Hebrews out of Egypt, and they returned to Palestine. This was the beginning of a great Hebrew civilization in Palestine.

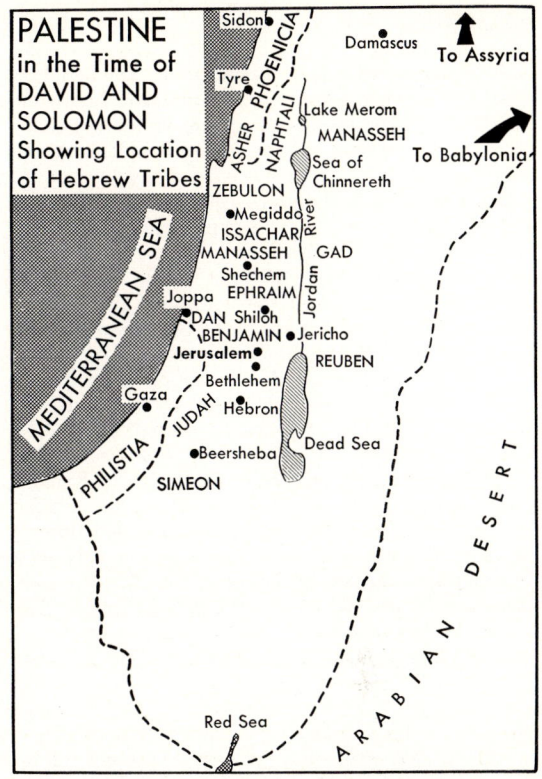

PALESTINE in the Time of DAVID AND SOLOMON Showing Location of Hebrew Tribes

The Hebrews had been simple shepherds. But they soon adopted much of the Canaanite civilization. Many of them began to leave their tents and to live in houses. They also intermarried with the Canaanites.

These changes took place faster in the fertile valleys and towns of northern Palestine than in the southern desert. Differences between the settled Hebrews of the north and the wandering, or *nomadic*, Hebrews of the south divided the people for many years. See NOMAD.

The Israelites had a different religion from the peoples around them. These other peoples worshiped many gods made of wood and stone. But the Israelites worshiped One Invisible God. See JEHOVAH.

The Monarchy. By 1100 B.C. the Israelites had conquered most of the hill country of Palestine. At about this time the Philistines migrated from the Aegean Islands and formed a highly civilized and warlike nation called *Philistia* in southwest Palestine.

The Israelites were loosely organized into twelve tribes. Warfare with the Canaanite and Philistine peoples in Palestine forced these tribes to rally closer together. They established a monarchy under King Saul (1010-970 B.C.). After Saul came David, the first great national king of the Hebrews. David made the Israelites into a strong, united people. He established Jerusalem as the capital of the nation. His son, King Solomon, built the first Temple in Jerusalem.

On Solomon's death, the kingdom split in two. The northern kingdom was called Israel, and the southern kingdom was called Judah. The people of Judah were called Judeans, or *Jews*. Eventually, all the Hebrews came to be called Jews. In 721 B.C., Israel was conquered by the Assyrian Empire. Many of its people were captured and sent to distant lands. The people of these northern tribes lost their identity as Hebrews and mixed with other peoples. They are sometimes called "the Ten Lost Tribes of Israel." The Babylonians conquered Judah in 587 B.C., enslaving many Jews.

The Return from Babylon. After about fifty years, a Persian king called Cyrus conquered Babylonia. He allowed the Judean exiles to return to their homeland. Under Zerubbabel they rebuilt the Temple. During this period, the religious and social code of the Hebrew people, and most of the writings which form the Old Testament, took their final form. See OLD TESTAMENT.

About 170 B.C. the Greek rulers of Syria conquered Palestine. The Hebrews successfully revolted and won back their independence under Judas Maccabeus, who founded a dynasty which lasted a hundred years.

The Beginning of Christianity. In 63 B.C. the Romans conquered Palestine. Their harshness led to constant quarrels with the Jews. During this troubled time of Roman oppression, Jesus of Nazareth began teaching a new religion and philosophy of life in Palestine. He was put to death, but the Gospel of Jesus spread. The hundred years of strife in Palestine ended in a general Jewish revolt against the Roman Empire. But after six years of bitter fighting, the Romans crushed Jewish resistance. In A.D. 70 the Romans destroyed Jerusalem. Most of the Jews went to other lands throughout the world. For 500 years Palestine was under the rule of Rome, and of the Byzantine Empire that followed it.

Arab Conquest. In the A.D. 600's, the Arabs, fresh and zealous converts to Islam, swept out of the Arabian Desert. They seized Palestine in their great campaign of conquests. In Iraq, Egypt, and other countries, great centers of Moslem civilization arose. But Palestine remained in the background. The Arab Empire lasted about 400 years. Then Palestine, together with the other Arab provinces, fell to the Seljuk Turks. Later, the Turks lost most of Palestine to the Christian Crusaders, who came from Europe to free the Holy Land from the Moslems. (See CRUSADES.) The Crusaders were driven out by the Mamelukes of Egypt. In 1517 Palestine was conquered by the Ottoman Turks.

The long series of conquests and increasing neglect turned Palestine into a wasteland. Cities crumbled, and swamps formed over rich soil. The population was mostly Arabs. There was also a small number of Jews. All of them were miserably poor. In 1882 the first group of Jews from Europe came to settle in Palestine. That was the start of the Zionist pioneering movement that led to the creation of the State of Israel. See ZIONISM.

World War I and After. World War I again turned Palestine into a battlefield. In 1918 British troops drove out the Turks and occupied the land. Some of the Jews of Palestine helped the British. In 1917 the great British scientist-statesman and Zionist, Chaim Weizmann, persuaded the British Government to issue a statement favoring the establishment of a Jewish national home in Palestine. This statement was called the Balfour Declaration. After the war, the League of Nations ratified, or approved, the Balfour Declaration. In 1922 it appointed the British to rule the country as a League mandate (see MANDATED TERRITORY).

Many thousands of Jews came to settle in Palestine from different countries. Zionist pioneers drained swamps and built up cities. The country began to flourish. But a feeling of nationalism was awakening among the Arabs of Palestine. They did not want Palestine to become a Jewish national home. They wanted it to become an Arab state. Arab riots broke out against the Jews. Meanwhile the Nazi terror in Germany drove large numbers of German Jews to find a refuge in Palestine.

In 1936 the Arabs started guerrilla fighting against the Jews in Palestine. The British seemed unable to stop it. It lasted for three years. In 1939 the British finally yielded to a large part of the Arab demands. They decided practically to stop Jewish immigration into Palestine. To the Jews, this would have meant the end of the Jewish national home, and they bitterly opposed the British policy. Many Jewish immigrants were brought into Palestine illegally. Trouble between the Jews and the British became steadily worse.

World War II and the Partition Plan. When World War II broke out, the Jews of Palestine joined the Allies. When the war was over they resumed their struggle against the British policy in Palestine.

In 1947 the British Government asked the United Nations to solve the problem of Palestine. After full investigations, the United Nations decided to divide Palestine into two independent states, a Jewish state and an Arab state. It also decided that the city of Jerusalem should be internationalized.

The Jews accepted this partition plan, but the Arabs refused to accept it. Wide-scale Arab attacks broke out against the Jews. Bands of Arabs from the neighboring countries joined the Palestine Arabs. In May, 1948, the British mandate over Palestine came to an end and the Zionists in Palestine proclaimed the new State of Israel.   YEHUDA HARRY LEVIN and WINFRED E. GARRISON

Related Articles. For the land, people, and later history of Palestine, see ISRAEL. See also the following articles in WORLD BOOK:

PALESTRINA, *PAL us TREE nuh,* or *PAH lay STREE nuh,* **GIOVANNI** (1525?-1594), an Italian composer of church music, is known as the master of *polyphonic,* or many-voiced, music for choruses unaccompanied by instruments. In 1564, Pope Pius IV appointed a commission of eight cardinals to undertake the reform of Italian church music. Palestrina took part in this reform by submitting three masses to the commission. These included the *Mass of Pope Marcellus II,* which is now considered his greatest masterpiece and a model for all Roman Catholic masses. It is generally agreed that Palestrina saved church music by writing a noble and spiritual composition at a time when the heads of the church were about to keep only the chants of the mass

Brown Bros.
Giovanni Palestrina

as part of church ritual. In 1576, Pope Gregory XIII asked Palestrina to undertake a complete revision of the plain song, the chant melody of the church service. The fact that the pope entrusted this monumental task to Palestrina shows the esteem in which the church held him.

Palestrina composed about 950 pieces, including 93 masses and over 500 motets. He also wrote many madrigals and songs for at least two voices which are sung without instrumental accompaniment.

Palestrina was born GIOVANNI PIERLUIGI, and took his last name from his birthplace, a small town near Rome. Little is known of his early musical training. As a small boy, he went to Rome, where he spent most of his life. There he held many important posts as a singer and a director of music in various churches. He finally became master of the Sistine Chapel. WARREN S. FREEMAN

PALETTE. See PAINTING (Tools).

PALEY, WILLIAM (1743-1805), was a British theologian and philosopher. His influential *Principles of Moral and Political Philosophy* are based on the assumption that God desires the happiness of His creatures, and rewards and punishes them after death. Paley also published *Natural Theology, or Evidences of the Existence and Attributes of the Deity Collected from the Appearances of Nature* (1802). He also wrote an essay urging the abolition of the slave trade. Paley was born in Peterborough, England. WALTER KAUFMANN

PALGRAVE, FRANCIS TURNER (1824-1897), gained fame as an English critic and poet. He edited the *Golden Treasury of English Verse* (1861), his greatest contribution to literature. Palgrave selected this anthology with good taste and critical judgment. He also wrote criticisms of art and literature, and published a number of poems and hymns. He served as a government educational official from 1855 to 1884 and as professor of poetry at Oxford University from 1885 to 1895. Palgrave was born in Yarmouth, England. LIONEL STEVENSON

PALIMPSEST. See MANUSCRIPT (Parchment Manuscripts).

PALINDROME, *PAL in drohm,* is a word, sentence, or verse that is spelled the same from right to left as from left to right. The word comes from the Greek *palindromos,* meaning *running back again.* The names *Ada, Eve, Hannah,* and *Otto,* and the words *boob, did, gag, noon, peep,* and *radar* are palindromes. Napoleon is credited with "*Able was I ere I saw Elba.*" Another palindrome is "*Madam, I'm Adam.*" WALTER H. HOLZE

PALIO is a famous horse race. See SIENA.

PALISADES are any series of cliffs that rise above the earth like tall pillars, or columns. But when Americans speak of *The Palisades* they generally mean the palisades on the lower Hudson River. These cliffs are formed of basaltic rock, arranged like massive columns. About 51,200 acres of land, surrounding the Palisades on the west bank of the Hudson, have been set aside as Palisades Interstate Park. The park is partly in New Jersey

and partly in New York. It extends north to Bear Mountain and Storm King, two of the most picturesque points on the river. The park is controlled by the Palisades Interstate Park Commission. It has been developed and maintained by funds from both states and by gifts from private individuals. ELDRED D. WILSON

PALISSY, *PAH LEE SEE,* **BERNARD** (1510?-1589), a French potter and enameler, discovered certain fine glaze colors and techniques for decorating pottery. He skillfully blended colors on pottery which he decorated with molded reproductions of shells, leaves, snakes, fish, and other subjects from nature. He also wrote books on art, and was active in science and philosophy.

Palissy began his experiments in ceramics about 1540 in the town of Saintes. For many years, he and his family endured poverty before he became a success. Later in life he suffered religious persecution as a Huguenot (see HUGUENOTS). He died in the Bastille, where he was imprisoned for his beliefs. Palissy was born in Chapelle Biron, France. EUGENE F. BUNKER, JR.

PALL-MALL, *pell mell,* is a game similar to croquet, played with a wooden ball and a mallet. It received its name from the Italian words *palla,* meaning ball, and *maglio,* meaning mallet. Pall-mall was a popular game in Italy and other European countries in the 1600's.

PALLADIO, *pah LAH dyoh,* **ANDREA** (1508-1580), an Italian architect, gained fame for his elegant style and for standardizing classical architecture. His design for the arcades of the Basilica in Vicenza, Italy, established the Palladian motif or arch. This is now the name for any arched opening supported on columns flanked by narrow square-headed openings the same height as the columns. See ARCHITECTURE (Renaissance [color picture]).

His secular work in Vicenza, such as the much-copied *Villa Capra,* is more significant than his great Venetian churches *S. Giorgi Maggiori* and *Il Redentore.* He was the first to conceive of buildings as part of the landscape. In his designs, he tried to unite the gravity of Rome with the sunny breadth of Northern Italy where he was born. RICHARD M. BENNETT

PALLADIUM is a soft, white metal. It is one of six platinum metals. Palladium is often used in place of platinum because it is cheaper, harder, and lighter than platinum. It is found with deposits of other platinum metals, with nickel-copper ores, and sometimes with mercury.

Like platinum, palladium can be shaped and worked in many ways. It can be drawn into fine wire or hammered into thin sheets. It is often mixed with gold to make "white gold" jewelry. It can also be made into thin leaves. It is also used in making surgical instruments and electrical contacts.

Finely divided palladium called *palladium black* can be used as a *catalyst* which brings about chemical changes such as in hydrogenation (see HYDROGENATION). Palladium is able to absorb large volumes of hydrogen during chemical reactions.

The English chemist William H. Wollaston discovered palladium in 1803. It has the chemical symbol Pd, the atomic number 46, and the atomic weight 106.4. It melts at 1552° C. and boils at 2927° C. ALAN DAVISON

See also PLATINUM.

PALLADIUM

PALLADIUM, *puh LAY dee um,* is the name of a statue of Pallas Athena. The Greek myths say it was sent from heaven by Zeus to Ilus the founder of Troy. As long as Troy kept it, the city was safe. In the Trojan War, the Greek hero Ulysses and his companion Diomedes stole the statue, and Troy fell. See ULYSSES.

In modern usage, *palladium* refers to anything that affords protection or guarantees security. For example, trial by jury is considered a *palladium* of civil rights.

PALLAS, or PALLAS ATHENA, was a Greek goddess. The Romans called her Minerva. See MINERVA.

PALLOR. See BLUSHING.

PALM, *pahm,* is a group of trees and shrubs that grow in warm climates, especially in the tropics. Palms are important in tropical regions because they provide food, clothing, and building materials for the people. Palms are most common in Southeast Asia, the Pacific islands, and in tropical America. They grow wild as far north as the coast of North Carolina, Arizona, and the deserts of southern California, and as far south as Uruguay, central Argentina, and central Chile.

Palms are an ancient group of plants. *Fossils* (buried remains) of palm leaves have been found that date from the Age of Dinosaurs. Palms once grew in all parts of the world, and palm fossils have been found as far north as Greenland.

Kinds of Palms. There are more than 2,600 kinds of palms, and they vary greatly in size and the kind of flowers, leaves, and fruits they produce.

Most palms grow straight and tall, but a few do not. The trunks of some palms may lie on the ground. Some types have most of the trunk buried in the soil. The rattan palms that are found in the jungles of Southeast Asia have slender, vinelike stems that are from 10 to 250 feet long. The stems may trail along the jungle floor or climb high in the trees. Most palms have a single trunk, or stem. Many have clustered trunks, however, that grow from the same root base.

The Trunk is usually straight and round and from 4 to 24 inches thick. But some palms have trunks that are no thicker than a pencil, while others have trunks that are 5 feet thick. The trunk may range from a few inches to well over 100 feet tall. It may have rough or smooth bark, and some have sharp, needlelike thorns. Only a few palms have branches growing out from the trunk. A few kinds have a strawlike "skirt" of dead leaves that hangs down along the trunk. But most palms have their fanlike or featherlike leaves clustered at the top of the trunk.

The Leaves vary greatly in size and appearance. Some are only a few inches long. Most of the fanlike leaves are from 2 to 4 feet wide, and the featherlike types may be 20 feet long and from 1 to 4 feet wide. Two types of palms produce the largest leaves known. The talipot palm has fanshaped leaves that may be 15 feet wide. The raffia palm has leaves that may be 50 feet long and 8 feet wide.

The Fruits differ greatly in size and shape. Some fruits are no larger than a pea. The huge fruit of the double coconut palm may become 2 feet in diameter. The fruit of the palm contains from one to seven seeds. The flesh of the fruit may be soft as in the date, or firm and threadlike, as in the coconut. The seed may be hard, as in the date. Only rarely is it soft, or even hollow and filled with "milk," as in the coconut. The double coconut and the true coconut have the largest of all known seeds. In many palms the male and female flowers are on different trees. These palms depend on man or insects for fertilization of their flowers.

Products of Palms. Palms provide shade, building materials (both timbers and thatch), and fuel. Fibers for making ropes and brooms and for *caulking* (making watertight) ships are made from the palm. Strips of leaves are woven into mats, hats, and baskets. Oil for food and light comes from the tree. The sugary sap of such palms as the palmyra palm can be made into food, sweet drinks, and intoxicating beverages such as arrack. The starch of the plant is used for food. The seeds are made into buttons and carvings.

The palm is most important to the people who live in the tropics. But those of us who live in other parts of the world also depend on palms for many useful products. The dried oily meat of the coconut is used to add flavor to cakes. Its rich oil is used in making soap, salad oils,

The Licuala Palm has fan-shaped leaves that grow close to the ground.
Gatteri, The Palm Society

The Petticoat Palm leaves hang on after they die, forming the plant's "petticoat."
Gatteri, The Palm Society

The Fan Palm with its spreading leaves well deserves its descriptive name.
Devereux Butcher

PALM

The Coconut Tree is one of the most graceful of the palms. It has a long slender trunk and a tuft of swaying fronds.

Trunks of Royal Palms are their most striking feature. They resemble pillars molded from concrete.

The Date Palm is topped with a well-rounded group of fronds.

Louis C. Williams; Devereux Butcher; *Nature* Magazine

The Branchlike Top of this queen palm will turn into a new frond shortly.

Fan Palms are sometimes sheathed with old fronds.

cooking fats, and margarine. Dates are a familiar product of the palm. Sago is a starch taken from palm trunks.

Many of our baskets and chair bottoms are woven from strips of palm leaves. The stems of the rattan palm are used in making some of our furniture. Raffia is made of thin layers of cells stripped from the leaves of a Madagascar palm. It is used by gardeners, and children also use it in basketmaking at school. We use the wax from the leaves of the carnauba palm of Brazil in shoe polish and in phonograph records.

Scientific Classification. Palms belong to the palm family, *Palmae*. HAROLD E. MOORE, JR.

Related Articles in WORLD BOOK include:

PALM PRODUCTS

| Carnauba Wax | Palm Oil | Raffia | Rattan | Sago |

TYPES OF PALM TREES

Betel	Date and Date	Ivory Palm
Cabbage Palm	Palm	Palmetto
Coconut Palm	Doum Palm	Palmyra Palm

PALM OIL is a thick, yellowish oil obtained from the fruit pulp of the oil palm of West Africa. The oil is about as thick as butter and has a dark orange color when it is cool. Its odor is so pleasant that the people of Ghana use it for butter, although it is in liquid form in that climate. Palm oil is imported into the United States to make soap and candles, and for oiling machinery. It is also widely used in cosmetics.

The fruit of the oil palm is about the same size as a date. It has a deep-red fleshy portion, outside a stony kernel. A fully grown tree bears about 10 clusters, each containing about 200 nuts. When the fleshy part of the nut is boiled, it gives off the palm oil. The kernels that are left are shipped to Europe or America and crushed in hydraulic presses. The white fat from the kernels is widely used to make margarine. GEORGE R. GREENBANK

PALM SUNDAY is the last Sunday before Easter. It is the beginning of Holy Week. The services of Palm Sunday honor Jesus' triumphant entry into Jerusalem. According to John 12:12-15, Jesus rode into the city on an ass, and the people spread palm branches in His path.

Palm Sunday was first celebrated in the 300's by the Christian Church in Jerusalem. A joyous procession started at the Mount of Olives. The bishop took the part of Jesus and rode on an ass. Children sang and waved palm branches. The Roman Catholic celebration became a solemn processional and a Mass during which the Gospel story of the Crucifixion is chanted solemnly. In the Greek Church, Palm Sunday is a day of rejoicing. Palms are blessed and held, but there is no procession. Protestant churches in general have very simple Palm Sunday services. In many places laurel, olive, willow, and other branches are used instead of the palm. ALBERT E. AVEY and FULTON J. SHEEN

PALMER, A. MITCHELL (1872-1936), served as U.S. attorney general from 1919 to 1921, in President Woodrow Wilson's Administration. Palmer is best known for the *Palmer Raids* of January, 1920, in which thousands of so-called anarchists and Communists were jailed with little regard for their constitutional rights. Many historians believe that Palmer hoped to win the 1920 Democratic presidential nomination by capi-

talizing on the antiradical feelings that many Americans held at that time.

ALEXANDER MITCHELL PALMER was born in Moosehead, Pa. He served in the U.S. House of Representatives from 1908 to 1915. He lost in a bid for the Senate in 1914. As a member of the Democratic national committee in 1912, Palmer helped Woodrow Wilson win the presidential nomination. DAVID A. SHANNON

PALMER, ALICE ELVIRA FREEMAN (1855-1902), gained fame as an American educator. In 1879, at the age of 24, she became head of the history department at Wellesley College. Three years later, she became president of Wellesley, one of the youngest college presidents in history. She resigned in 1887 after her marriage to George Herbert Palmer, a Harvard professor. But she continued in educational work, and served as dean of women at the University of Chicago from 1892 to 1895.

Alice Freeman Palmer also helped organize the group which later became the American Association of University Women. In 1920 she was elected to the Hall of Fame at New York University. She was born at Colesville, N.Y. HELEN E. MARSHALL

PALMER, ARNOLD DANIEL (1929-   ), of the United States, became one of the world's greatest golfers. He was the first to win the Masters tournament four times—in 1958, 1960, 1962, and 1964. He won the United States Open golf tournament in 1960, and the British Open tournament in 1961 and 1962. He was born in Latrobe, Pa., where his father was a golf professional. PAT HARMON

PALMER, JOEL (1810-1881), won fame as a negotiator of important Indian treaties of 1854 and 1855. As superintendent of Indian affairs for the Oregon Territory from 1853 to 1857, he removed warring Indian tribes from the areas of white settlement. He gave the Indians new lands with liberal hunting and farming privileges. He was removed from office because many white men believed he was too considerate of the Indians. Palmer's *Journal of Travels Over the Rocky Mountains* (1847) became a guidebook for overland travelers. It gives an excellent description of a trip on the Oregon Trail. Palmer was born in Ontario, Canada. JESSE L. GILMORE

PALMER, NATHANIEL BROWN (1799-1877), was a U.S. sea captain. He is believed to be the first explorer to sight Antarctica. In 1820, while searching for new seal-fishing grounds, he took his 45-ton sloop, the *Hero*, south from Yankee Harbor in the South Shetland Islands. He sighted land that is now called the *Antarctic Peninsula*, a long arm of the Antarctic continent extending north toward South America. Palmer believed it to be only an island. He was born in Stonington, Conn. FRANKLIN L. FORD

PALMER, POTTER (1826-1902), a merchant and real estate promoter, revolutionized the selling methods of his day. His store in Chicago allowed customers to take home merchandise and inspect it, and to make exchanges or get refunds. About 1865, Marshall Field and Levi Z. Leiter became partners in the business, and in 1881 it became Marshall Field and Company. Palmer built the Palmer House, a famous Chicago hotel, and was a leader in developing Chicago's State Street as one of the world's major retail centers. Palmer was born in Albany County, New York. PAUL M. ANGLE

PALMER PENINSULA. See ANTARCTICA (West Antarctica; color map).

PALMERSTON, PAHM er stun, VISCOUNT (1784-1865),

Chicago Historical Society
Viscount Palmerston

HENRY JOHN TEMPLE, an English statesman, served with distinction as a foreign secretary and a prime minister. He became secretary of state for foreign affairs in 1830 and, except for a short interval, held the post until 1841. After a five-year absence, he returned to the foreign office in the cabinet of Lord John Russell. He established friendly relations with France, helped Belgium gain independence, and supported Turkey against Russia. Russell dismissed him in 1851. Without consulting his cabinet colleagues or Queen Victoria, he had approved the seizure of power in France by Napoleon III.

Palmerston's aggressive foreign policy was popular in England, though often criticized abroad and in Parliament. He had a high conception of Britain's place in the world, and demanded respect for his country from other nations. In one of his speeches, he reminded his listeners that a citizen of ancient Rome was safe anywhere in the Roman Empire, and declared that Great Britain would also protect its subjects the world over.

Palmerston became prime minister in 1855. He saw the Crimean War to a successful end, but resigned in 1858 over criticism of his policy in China. He again became prime minister in 1859 and served until his death.

Palmerston was born at Broadlands, Hampshire, England. He won election to the House of Commons in 1807, and two years later became secretary at war. He held this office for 19 years.   JAMES L. GODFREY

PALMETTO, pal MET oh, is the name given to several kinds of fan-leaved palm trees. The best-known palmetto is the *cabbage palm.* The palmetto is the state tree of South Carolina. Among other kinds of palmettos are the *dwarf*, *blue*, and *saw* palmettos. They grow in low regions along the United States coast, particularly in the southeastern part of the country, and in the West Indies. Some of these trees may grow 50 feet high, but the dwarf variety is low. Wharves are made from wood of the cabbage palm.

Scientific Classification. The palmetto belongs to the palm family, *Palmae*. Palmettos make up the genus *Sabal*.   HAROLD E. MOORE, JR.

See also CABBAGE PALM; SOUTH CAROLINA (pictures).

PALMETTO STATE. See SOUTH CAROLINA.

PALMISTRY is the very ancient practice of reading character and personal futures from the lines, size, and shape of the hand. It is sometimes called *chiromancy*. It is a combination of astrology and handreading. It is a pseudoscience, and, along with the others, it has lost favor with scientific-minded people. But palm readers still flourish in the Orient, and there are many believers in palmistry in the Western world.

In palmistry, the fleshy parts of the palm at the base of the thumb and fingers, and side of the hand from the little finger to the wrist, are called *mounts*. The wrinkles are called *lines*. The mounts and lines are supposed to tell all about a person's character, the kind of life he has had, and what the future will bring him. These mounts are named for the planets Venus, Jupiter, Saturn, Mercury, and Mars; the moon; and Apollo. The thin flesh where the thumb curves to join the first finger is called the plain of Mars. If any of the mounts are well-developed, or fleshy, they are supposed to show that the person has the characteristics of the planet of that mount. A strong mount of Jupiter shows pride and ambition.

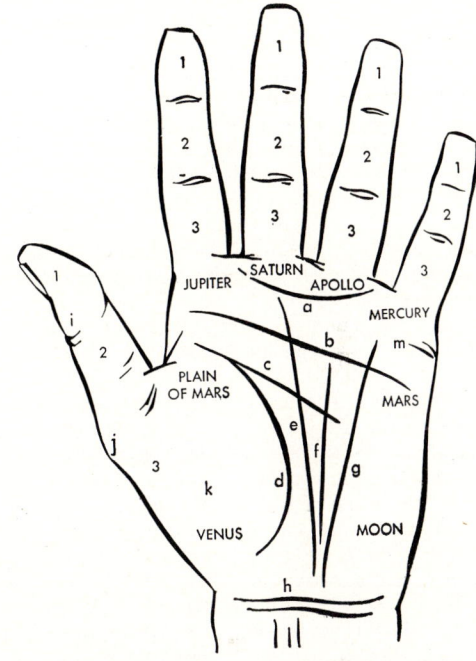

Lines and Parts of the Hand in Palmistry

(a) Ring of Venus	(g) Line of health
(b) Line of heart	(h) Bracelets
(c) Line of head	(i) Will
(d) Line of life	(j) Reason
(e) Line of fate	(k) Love
(f) Line of fortune	(m) Line of marriage

The numbers 1, 2, 3 refer to the mounts of the joints in fingers and thumbs.

Apollo denotes art and riches. Saturn means fatality. Mercury means science and wit. Venus means love and music, and Mars means cruelty and courage.

The curved line of life surrounds the thumb. If it is long, it is supposed to indicate a long life. If it is not continuous, but broken, the person will not live to old age. The line from the outside of the palm beneath the fingers is the line of the heart. If it is long, distinct, and well-colored, the owner has an affectionate disposition. A strongly marked line of the head is supposed to show superior intelligence, and imagination if the line stretches to the mount of the moon.

These are the basic principles on which palmistry is founded. The arguments for it are often clever, but there is no scientific proof for it.   JOHN MULHOLLAND

See also FORTUNETELLING.

PALMITIC ACID. See FAT.

PALMITIN

PALMITIN. See LARD.

PALMYRA was an ancient Syrian city, about midway between the eastern coast of the Mediterranean Sea and the Euphrates River. Palmyra was built around a desert *oasis* (fertile place with water) on an important trade route between the Roman and Persian empires. Caravans traveling across the desert stopped at Palmyra, bringing great riches and a variety of individuals and cultures to the city. The temple of Palmyra's chief god, Bel, is typical of the city's mixture of cultures. Although Bel was an eastern god, the temple's architecture is Roman.

By the A.D. 160's, Palmyra had come under Roman control. Camel troops from Palmyra served in the Roman army. Roman garrison troops helped protect Palmyra. But when Persia invaded Syria about 260, Rome had no troops to spare for Syria's defense. Septimius Odenathus, a Palmyrene prince, commanded Palmyrene cavalry and archers that turned back the invading Persians. In 262, he became Rome's supreme military commander on the eastern frontier. Odenathus died in 267 and his widow Zenobia succeeded him.

Zenobia, a vigorous and able ruler, tried to extend her rule over Egypt and all Asia Minor. Her troops seized land from the Roman emperors. But the Roman emperor Aurelian defeated and captured Zenobia in 274, and destroyed Palmyra. The emperor Diocletian, who ruled from 284 to 305, rebuilt the city, but Moslems destroyed it again in the 600's.　　RAMSAY MACMULLEN

PALMYRA is one of the Line Islands, 1,100 miles south of Honolulu. It is an atoll with only four square miles of dry land on its reef platform. The island was annexed by the Kingdom of Hawaii in 1862, and by Great Britain in 1889. Although part of the Hawaiian chain, the island is not in the state of Hawaii. Palmyra is privately owned, and is administered by the U.S. Department of the Interior.　　EDWIN H. BRYAN, JR.

PALMYRA PALM is a kind of palm that grows throughout India and nearby islands in other hot countries. It is one of the most useful plants known. The wood is used for building houses. The leaves are made into thatch, baskets, mats, hats, fans, and umbrellas. The fiber of the plant is used for twine and rope. The fruit, seeds, and young stalks are eaten. In the northern part of Ceylon, the palmyra palm is almost the sole source of livelihood for thousands of the people.

The ancient Hindu scholars used strips from the leaves of the palmyra and talipot palms for writing material. Some of the oldest existing Hindu manuscripts are preserved in curious books, one to two feet long and never more than two inches wide, made of strips from the leaves of these palms.

The plant grows from 20 to 70 feet high. Its leaves are four feet long. The fruit is large and angular shaped.

Scientific Classification. Palmyra palms belong to the palm family, *Palmae*. They are genus *Borassus*, species *B. flabellifer*.　　IVAN MURRAY JOHNSTON

PALO ALTO, *PAL oh AL toe*, Calif. (pop. 52,287; alt. 65 ft.), lies between San Francisco Bay and the Pacific Coast Range, 32 miles south of San Francisco (see CALIFORNIA [political map]). Palo Alto means *tall tree* in Spanish. This refers to a tall redwood, a landmark at the northwest entrance to the city. Palo Alto is one

of the nation's leading educational, electronics, medical, and research centers. Stanford University is nearby. Palo Alto has a council-manager form of government.　　GEORGE SHAFTEL

PALO ALTO, BATTLE OF. See MEXICAN WAR (Principal Battles).

PALOMAR OBSERVATORY houses the largest telescope in the world—the 200-inch Hale reflector. The observatory is located 5,600 feet above sea level on Palomar Mountain, 40 miles northeast of San Diego, Calif. It is operated jointly by the Carnegie Institution of Washington, D.C., and the California Institute of Technology at Pasadena, as part of the Mount Wilson and Palomar Observatories (see MOUNT WILSON OBSERVATORY).

The work of the Palomar Observatory includes the study of (1) distant galaxies and their motions; (2) the physical and chemical characteristics of stars; and (3) the origin and evolution of stars in our own galaxy and in other stellar systems.

The Hale Telescope is named for George Ellery Hale (1868-1938), an American astronomer who suggested its construction in 1928. The main mirror of the Hale telescope is a concave disk 200 inches in diameter. This is as wide as the length of an average passenger car. It is made of 14.5 tons of Pyrex glass. There is a hole 40 inches in diameter in the center of the mirror to permit the use of the telescope with the Cassegrain arrangement (see TELESCOPE). Astronomers also make observations from a cage at the upper end of the telescope. The telescope collects 360,000 times as much light as the human eye. But, the Hale telescope is largely used to photograph celestial bodies or their spectra, or to measure their brightness. A photographic plate can record much fainter images than those the eye of the astronomer can see. The telescope can photograph objects at a distance of several billion light-years. A *light-year* is about six trillion miles.

The Hale telescope took more than 20 years to plan and build. It was financed by a gift of $6,550,000 from the Rockefeller Foundation. The Hale telescope was

Through the Hale Telescope in Palomar Observatory, astronomers can photograph distant celestial bodies.

Mount Wilson and Palomar Observatories

tested for the first time on Dec. 21, 1947. After two years of adjustment and final polishing, the Hale telescope began operating on a regular basis during the fall of 1949.

The Schmidt Telescope. The work of the Hale telescope is aided by a 48-inch wide-angle reflecting telescope of a type designed by a German optician, Bernhard Schmidt (1879-1935). The Schmidt telescope is used to map the sky and to locate objects for detailed observation by the Hale telescope. The Schmidt telescope can photograph on one plate a portion of the heavens more than 800 times as large as that seen by the Hale telescope. But the Hale telescope can see many times farther out into space. The Schmidt telescope photographed all of the northern skies and half of the southern skies in seven years. The Hale telescope would have required 10,000 years to photograph the same area.   Critically reviewed by MOUNT WILSON OBSERVATORY

PALOMINO HORSE. See HORSE (Color; color picture).

PALOVERDE, *PAH loh VAIR day,* is a thorny little tree that grows in the dry regions of the southwestern United States. The paloverde grows along the sides of desert canyons and dry ditches in south and central Arizona, southeastern California, and northwestern Mexico. It is the state tree of Arizona.

The paloverde grows from 15 to 30 feet tall and its trunk may be up to 20 inches in diameter. It has green bark and leaves about an inch long that unfold in late March or April. The leaves fall almost as soon as they are full grown, and the tree is usually bare by late summer. In late April and May, the tree is covered with small yellow flowers.

The paloverde produces seed pods 2 to 3 inches long. Each pod contains two or three large seeds. Paloverde seeds were once an important source of food. Indians dried them and ground them into meal or ate them like lima beans. The tree has little commercial value. But the roots help to hold the loose desert soil together and slow *erosion* (wearing away) of the soil.

Scientific Classification. Paloverdes belong to the pea family, *Leguminosae.* They are genus *Cercidium.* One common species is *C. floridium.*

PALSY is a name given to paralysis of certain types. Some kinds of palsy are caused by continued pressure on a nerve. Shaking palsy, an involuntary tremor of the muscles, is a symptom of Parkinson's disease (*paralysis agitans*). *Chemopallidectomy* is an operation for this uncontrollable tremor.

See also CEREBRAL PALSY.

PALYNOLOGY. See ARCHAEOLOGY (Relative Chronology).

PAMELA. See RICHARDSON, SAMUEL.

PAMIRS, *puh MEERZ,* **THE,** is a huge region, where the Himalaya, Hindu Kush, Kunlun, and Tien Shan mountains meet. It is one of the highest plateaus of the world. This "Pamir Knot" is called *Bam i Dunya,* which means *roof of the world.* The Pamirs lie in central Asia on the frontiers of five important countries—Russia, China, India, Pakistan, and Afghanistan. The Pamirs cover 36,000 square miles, at an average height of 13,000 to 15,000 feet above sea level.

Most of the region is treeless, with either grass or bare rock. Rugged mountains are cut by deep canyons. In summer the native Kirghiz find pasture for their cattle on the gentler slopes of The Pamirs, along the few lakes

and the *Amu Darya* (Oxus River). Snow covers the mountains and blocks the passes for more than half of each year. High winds blow across the barren mountains in the summer.   J. E. SPENCER

See also ASIA (Natural Features); HINDU KUSH.

PAMPA, *PAHM pah,* is a Spanish word that means *plain.* Geographers use the word *pampas* for several great plains of South America. But it is most commonly used for the huge, grass-covered plain in central Argentina. This plain stretches out between the Salado River on the north and the Negro River on the south, and joins the steppes of Patagonia. During the wet season, the Pampa has a thick growth of grass, which makes excellent pasture for sheep and cattle. Recently, Argentine farmers have devoted more and more of the region to farming.   ERNEST L. THURSTON

See also ARGENTINA (Land Regions; Natural Resources); LLANOS.

PAMPHLET is a short published work of topical interest. It is usually bound in paper covers. Pamphlets originally consisted of manuscripts bound in covers. The word comes from *Pamphilus, seu de Amore,* a Latin poem published in this form in the 1100's. Most early pamphlets discussed religious questions. In the 1600's and 1700's, they discussed politics. Today, most contain information or propaganda.   VAN ALLEN BRADLEY

PAN was the great god of the forests and meadows in Greek mythology, and the son of Hermes (called Mercury by the Romans). Shepherds especially worshiped Pan because he protected flocks and herds. Pan constantly wandered in the woods, playing and dancing with the nymphs. He was half man and half goat, and had the gift of prophecy.

Pan loved many nymphs. One of them, Syrinx, became frightened and fled from Pan when he pursued her. When Pan was about to catch her, she prayed to her sisters for help. They changed her into some reeds.

Pan sighed in disappointment, and noticed that the reeds gave forth a musical sound. He cut a number of them into unequal lengths and tied them together. These are called a *syrinx* (the pipes of Pan).

Pan was worshiped first in Arcadia (Arcady), an area in the southern Greek peninsula. Then the religion spread throughout ancient Greece.

Pan is usually shown with goat feet, curly hair, short horns, and a beard. He carries either a shepherd's crook or his syrinx. He could inspire great and sudden fear by his strange appearance, and thus the word *panic* comes from his name.   NATHAN DANE II

See also FAUN; MERCURY; SATYR.

Alinari

Pan Showing a Youth How to Play upon the Pipes. This Greek sculpture of the rural god is called *Pan and Olympus.* It is now in the National Museum in Naples, Italy.

PAN-AFRICANISM

PAN-AFRICANISM. See AFRICA (Today).

PAN AMERICAN COLLEGE is a state-controlled co-educational school in Edinburg, Tex. It includes schools of arts and sciences, technology, and education. Courses leading to bachelor's degrees are conducted in both the English and Spanish languages. The college owns the second largest telescope and observatory in Texas. Founded in 1927, it became a four-year college in 1952. For enrollment, see UNIVERSITIES AND COLLEGES (table).   RALPH SCHILLING

PAN-AMERICAN CONFERENCES bring together delegates from the American republics. They are also called *Inter-American Conferences*. For many years, the United States and the countries of Latin America have worked together to establish friendly economic, cultural, and political relations with one another.

Simón Bolívar, the South American statesman, took the first steps toward setting up an arrangement among American republics (see BOLÍVAR, SIMÓN). Through his efforts, the independent American countries held their first conference in 1826 in Panama. Other conferences were held at Lima in 1847, at Santiago in 1856, at Lima in 1864 and 1877, and at Montevideo in 1888. Until 1864, discussions were mostly political. After 1864, delegates tried to simplify rules of international law.

Early Days. The First International Conference of American States (better known as the *Pan American Conference*) met in Washington, D.C., in 1889 and 1890. This conference was the first to include all the independent countries of the Western Hemisphere. The delegates established the International Union of American Republics, with the Commercial Bureau of American Republics as its central office. In 1910, the bureau became the Pan American Union (see PAN AMERICAN UNION). The five conferences between 1889 and 1933 met under a cloud of fear of the United States. During this time, the United States interfered in the affairs of several Latin American countries, often by force.

"Good Neighbor" Policy. President Woodrow Wilson, and later President Herbert Hoover, realized the need for better Latin-American relations. But President Franklin D. Roosevelt made the first real progress toward that goal by starting the Good Neighbor Policy. The seventh Pan-American Conference at Montevideo in 1933 agreed that no country had the right to intervene in the affairs of another. In 1936, at the Inter-American Conference for the Maintenance of Peace, held in Buenos Aires, the American republics agreed to cooperate in solving quarrels among themselves.

The eighth Pan-American Conference met in Lima in 1938. This conference declared that any threat to "the peace, security, or territorial integrity of any American republic" was the concern of all. Meetings in accordance with the Declaration of Lima were held in Panama in 1939, Havana in 1940, and Rio de Janeiro in 1942. A regular Inter-American Conference was held in 1948.

Stronger Ties. Representatives at a Mexico City meeting in 1945 realized that the Inter-American system needed strength. They developed it in 1948 at the ninth Inter-American Conference at Bogotá, by forming the Organization of American States. The Inter-American Conference became the supreme organ for the OAS. Meanwhile, in a 1947 conference at Rio de Janeiro, representatives drew up the Inter-American Treaty of Reciprocal Assistance, or *Rio Pact*, which declared that an armed attack on one member is an attack against all. In 1954, the 10th Inter-American Conference adopted an anticommunist resolution at the urging of the United States. In 1960, 19 American countries approved the Act of Bogotá, agreeing to work for the social and economic advancement of Latin-American nations. Also in 1960, the OAS took its first collective action against another country. It imposed diplomatic sanctions against the Dominican Republic, then under the control of dictator Rafael Trujillo. In 1961, the Alliance for Progress charter was signed. It called for a 10-year, $20 billion investment in Latin-American development projects. Countries throughout the world, as well as Latin America, offered funds. In 1962, the OAS unanimously supported a United States naval quarantine to prevent Russian offensive weapons from entering Cuba. CHARLES P. SCHLEICHER

See also ALLIANCE FOR PROGRESS; ORGANIZATION OF AMERICAN STATES; PAN AMERICAN HIGHWAY; PAN AMERICANISM.

PAN AMERICAN DAY is observed yearly on April 14 in 21 American republics. This is the date when the resolution creating the Pan American Union was adopted at the First International Conference of American States in 1889. Pan American Day has been observed since 1931. It was set aside to remind us of the independence of the American nations, and of their cooperation with one another.   ELIZABETH HOUGH SECHRIST

PAN AMERICAN EXPOSITION celebrated the intellectual and scientific progress made by North and South America during the 1800's. The exposition was held in Buffalo, N.Y., in 1901. Its purpose was to promote better unity and understanding.

PAN AMERICAN GAMES are a series of athletic contests, patterned after the Olympic Games and sponsored by 29 Western Hemisphere nations. They are held once every four years, usually during the summer before the Olympic Games (see OLYMPIC GAMES).

The Pan American Games were inaugurated after World War II by the Pan American Sports Congress as a way to increase good will among the countries of the Americas. The game sites have been Buenos Aires, Argentina (1951), Mexico City (1955), Chicago (1959), São Paulo, Brazil (1963), and Winnipeg, Man., Canada (1967).   T. K. CURETON, JR.

PAN AMERICAN HIGHWAY is really a system of highways that extends from the United States-Mexican border to southern Chile. It also connects the east and west coasts of South America, and links the capitals of 17 Latin-American countries. The 29,525-mile system benefits Latin America's economy. It provides a route for raw materials and agricultural products through much of Latin America.

The Pan American Highway is sometimes described as running through the western United States and Canada up into Alaska. But neither country has officially named any highway as part of the Pan American Highway system.

Route. The Pan American Highway has four major terminals in the United States: Nogales, Ariz.; and Eagle Pass, El Paso, and Laredo, Tex. The highway runs through Mexico, Guatemala, El Salvador, Honduras, Nicaragua, and Costa Rica, and into Panama. The

U.S. Bureau of Public Roads

The Pan American Highway begins at four points along the U.S.-Mexican border. Motorists leaving Laredo, Tex., *above*, pass under a building that divides the United States and Mexico, *background*. These motorists can follow the Pan American Highway to many parts of Latin America, including 17 capital cities.

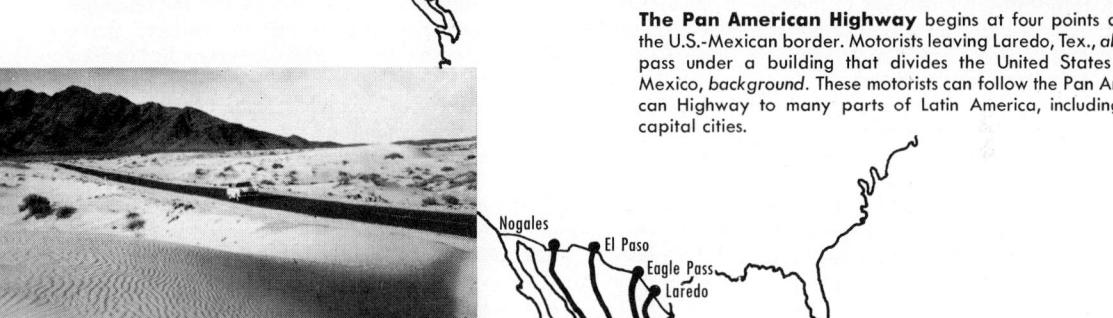

William Aplin

In Northern Mexico, the road becomes a black ribbon of asphalt surrounded by sand dunes.

In South America, a complex clover-leaf section serves traffic from the section in Caracas, Venezuela. This section joins the main highway at Bogotá, Colombia.

Hamilton Wright Organization

95

PAN AMERICAN UNION

Darién Gap, a stretch of over 500 miles of jungle, blocks the highway at Chepo, Panama. Motorists usually ship their cars from either Cristóbal or Balboa, Panama, to Colombia or Venezuela. A road across this area is being planned. South of the Darién Gap, the Pan American Highway follows the western coastline of South America to Puerto Montt, Chile.

At Santiago, Chile, about 660 miles north of Puerto Montt, a major branch of the highway cuts eastward across the Andes Mountains to Buenos Aires, Argentina. From Buenos Aires, it follows the east coast north to Rio de Janeiro, Brazil, then turns inland to Brasília, the capital of Brazil. Other branches lead to the capitals of Bolivia (La Paz and Sucre), Paraguay (Asunción), and Venezuela (Caracas).

Development. The idea to link North and South America dates from the late 1800's, when men talked of building a Pan American railway. But it was not until 1923, at the Fifth International Conference of American States, that a highway was seriously considered. This conference led to the First Pan American Highway Congress at Buenos Aires in 1925.

Organization of the system started in the late 1920's. By 1940, over 60 per cent of the highway between the United States and Panama had been completed. By the early 1950's, most of the project was open to travel in South America. An important link in the system was opened in 1962, when the Thatcher Ferry Bridge was completed over the Panama Canal at Balboa. The mile-long bridge is one of the longest steel arch bridges in the world.

Each South American country has financed the building of the highways within its own borders. In 1930, the United States began giving financial support to speed the building of the Pan American Highway between Panama and Texas. This section is also called the Inter-American Highway. The United States has contributed two-thirds of the cost of building this part of the highway. Only Mexico has not used United States financial aid in building the system.

The Pan American Highway Congress, sponsored by the Organization of American States, meets every three years to discuss the development and progress of the highway system. The congress has headquarters in the Pan American Union, Washington, D.C. 20006.

Critically reviewed by the PAN AMERICAN UNION

See also COSTA RICA (picture: A Huge Costa Rican Coffee Plantation); PANAMA (pictures: The Pan American Highway, Thatcher Ferry Bridge); SOUTH AMERICA (Transportation [picture]).

PAN AMERICAN UNION is an organization of 23 republics of North, Central, and South America. The First International Conference of American States in 1890 created the International Union of the American Republics, with the Commercial Bureau of American Republics as its central office. This bureau was renamed the Pan American Union in 1910.

In 1948, the nations belonging to the Pan American Union created the Organization of American States (OAS). The Pan American Union then became the permanent and central organ of the OAS. The Secretary-General of the OAS was placed in charge of the Pan American Union.

The Pan American Union is the permanent body of the International Conferences of American States, also called the Inter-American Conferences. It prepares the program and regulations of the conferences, helps to get treaties and other agreements ratified, and carries out conference resolutions.

The Pan American Union contributes in many other ways to better understanding and cooperation between American republics. It keeps records of the latest developments in art, literature, and education among member nations. This information is available to interested persons. The Union publishes a monthly *Bulletin* written in English, Spanish, and Portuguese. Other Pan American Union pamphlets deal with reports on North and South American cities and countries, and other subjects.

The Pan American Union has brought many benefits to the peoples of American republics. The Pan American Postal Union grew out of friendly inter-American discussion. The famous Inter-American Highway now links the United States with Mexico and the republics of Central America. Radio agreements have made possible an exchange of ideas among the various American republics.

The Pan American Union has headquarters in Washington, D.C. A beautiful building, donated by Andrew Carnegie in 1910, houses the organization.   TOM B. JONES

See also FLAG (color picture: Flags of World Organizations); ORGANIZATION OF AMERICAN STATES; PAN-AMERICAN CONFERENCES.

PAN AMERICAN WORLD AIRWAYS. See AIRLINE; AVIATION (World Airways).

PAN AMERICANISM means the common ideals among the countries of North and South America. It includes the practical, cooperative steps taken to realize these ideals. The movement began in the early 1800's during the Latin American struggle for independence. Such leaders as Simón Bolívar saw the need for inter-American cooperation. In 1826, representatives of the independent American countries held their first meeting in Panama. But the United States showed little interest in this and other early conferences.

The modern Pan American movement dates from the First International Conference of American States, held in Washington, D.C., in 1889 and 1890. The conference had only one concrete achievement: it established the International Union of the American Republics, with the Commercial Bureau as the central office. The bureau became the Pan American Union in 1910.

The real spirit of Pan Americanism flowed only after the United States adopted the "Good Neighbor" policy in the 1930's (see ROOSEVELT, FRANKLIN DELANO [Good Neighbor Policy]). During World War II, the American republics cooperated to fight the Axis nations. After the war ended in 1945, the members took steps to improve their organization (see PAN-AMERICAN CONFERENCES).

Today, Pan Americanism is based on the principles of (1) nonintervention by American countries in each other's internal or external affairs, (2) disapproval of any territorial conquest by forceful means, (3) legal equality of all American countries, and (4) collective defense of the Americas from internal or external attack. It stresses cooperation among all American countries toward common ends.   CHARLES P. SCHLEICHEI

Wide World

Bananas are Panama's Leading Export. A Choco Indian, *above*, delivers a load of bananas.

Herbert Lanks, Pix

by Rand McNally for WORLD BOOK

The Pan American Highway cuts through Panama. It lies only a few miles from rivers where dugout canoes are still used for transportation.

PANAMA, *PAN uh maw*, is the youngest republic in the Western Hemisphere. It was founded in 1903. This southernmost Central American country has low mountain ranges, thick jungles, and fertile green valleys and plains. The name of the country in Spanish, the official language, is REPÚBLICA DE PANAMÁ, meaning REPUBLIC OF PANAMA. The city of Panamá is the capital.

The Republic of Panama is only a little smaller than South Carolina, and has more than half as many people as that state. About three of every five Panamanians live on small farms and in country villages.

Panamanians call their nation the *Crossroads of the World.* It lies on trade routes between North and South America, and on the route between the Atlantic and Pacific oceans. The Panama Canal runs through the Canal Zone, a strip of land that lies across the center of the country. By a treaty with Panama in 1903, the United States obtained the right to build and operate the canal and to govern the Canal Zone. See PANAMA CANAL; PANAMA CANAL ZONE.

For the relationship of Panama to other nations, see CENTRAL AMERICA; LATIN AMERICA; ORGANIZATION OF AMERICAN STATES; PAN AMERICAN UNION.

The Land and Its Resources

Location and Size. Panama has the shape of a giant "S" lying on its side. The *Color Map* shows that the Caribbean Sea (a part of the Atlantic Ocean) lies to the north of Panama. Colombia lies to the east, the Pacific Ocean to the south, and Costa Rica to the west.

Land Regions. Wooded hills and low mountain ranges cover most of Panama. The country's highest

John and Mavis Biesanz, contributors of this article, are co-authors of The People of Panama. *He is Professor of Anthropology at Wayne State University.*

───────────── FACTS IN BRIEF ─────────────

Form of Government: Republic.

Capital: Panamá.

Official Language: Spanish.

Area: 29,209 square miles (not including the 553 square miles of the Panama Canal Zone). *Greatest Distances*— (east-west) 450 miles; (north-south) 130 miles. *Coastline*—Atlantic Ocean, 426 miles; Pacific Ocean, 767 miles.

Population: *1960 Census*—1,075,541; distribution, 59 per cent rural, 41 per cent urban. *Estimated 1970 Population*—1,465,000; density, 50 persons to the square mile. *Estimated 1975 Population*—1,723,000.

Chief Products: *Agriculture*—abacá, animal hides, bananas, cacao, coconuts, coffee, corn, herbs, livestock, rice, sugar cane. *Fishing Industry*—pearl oysters, shrimp.

Manufacturing and Processing—beverages, cement, clothing, furniture, pottery, processed foods, shoes, soap. *Forest Products*—hardwoods, rubber. *Mining*—gold.

Flag: The white upper left quarter has a blue star. The upper right quarter is red and the lower left quarter is blue. The white lower right quarter has a red star. Blue stands for the Conservative party and red for the Liberal party of 1903. White stands for peace, and the stars symbolize faith and strength. See FLAG (color picture: Flags of the Americas).

National Anthem: "L'Hymn Nacional de Panama."

National Holiday: Independence Day, November 3.

Money: *Basic Unit*—balboa. One hundred centesimos equal one balboa. For the value of the balboa in dollars, see MONEY (table: Values). See also BALBOA.

PANAMA

peak, 11,410-foot Mount Chiriquí, rises near the western border. The mountains slope from this peak to a region of low hills near the center of the country. The Panama Canal runs through this hilly region. East of the canal, the mountains gradually rise to more than 7,000 feet near the Colombian border. Fertile plains and valleys lie between the mountains and the coasts. Most of the people live in western Panama between the canal and the border of Costa Rica. Thick jungles cover much of eastern Panama.

Coastline. The Caribbean coast extends 426 miles. The Pacific coast is 767 miles long. The chief gulfs are Mosquitos on the Caribbean coast, and Chiriquí and Panama on the Pacific coast. Several small islands lie off Panama's coasts.

Rivers. The 125-mile-long Tuíra River flows through eastern Panama near the Colombian border. The Chepo and the Chagres rivers are both in central Panama.

Natural Resources. The fertile soil of the valleys and plains is the country's chief natural resource. Rich forests cover about seven-tenths of the country. Most of the

forests lie in eastern Panama. Shrimp, pearl oysters, and several types of fish live in the coastal waters. The mountains of eastern Panama contain small deposits of gold. Other minerals include manganese, silver, and copper.

Climate. Most of Panama has a hot climate with almost no seasonal changes in temperature. Temperatures in the lowland areas average about 80° F. throughout the year. Mountain temperatures average 66° F., but sometimes drop to 50° F. The Atlantic side of the country receives about 130 inches of rain a year. About 68 inches of rain falls on the Pacific side annually.

Life of the People

The People. Most Panamanians are of mixed white, Indian, and Negro ancestry. The first white men in Panama were Spaniards who arrived in the 1500's and 1600's. The Spaniards brought some Negro slaves to Panama from Africa, but the largest group of Negroes to come to Panama were West Indians who came to build the Panama Railroad and the Panama Canal. The Indians were the original inhabitants of the country. Today, about 62,000 Indians live in isolated tribes in the remote regions of eastern Panama, and on the San Blas Islands in the Caribbean.

Language. Most Panamanians speak Spanish. Many also speak English, mainly because they work in the American-governed Panama Canal Zone. The various Indian tribes have their own languages.

Family Life. Most farmers live in one-story, thatch-roofed houses with walls of bamboo or dried sugar cane. The houses have dirt floors and bamboo ceilings. Most farmers are poor and have little furniture. They sleep on wooden cots and often use boxes or tree stumps for tables and chairs. City people live in houses and apartment buildings made of wood or concrete, with roofs of clay tile or corrugated iron.

Rice is the chief food in Panama. The people eat it plain or mixed with meat and vegetables. They also eat

Panama Is 125 Times Smaller Than the United States.

1 INCH = 1,200 MILES

PANAMA MAP INDEX

---

*Does not appear on the map; key shows general location.   Source: Latest census figures and official estimates.

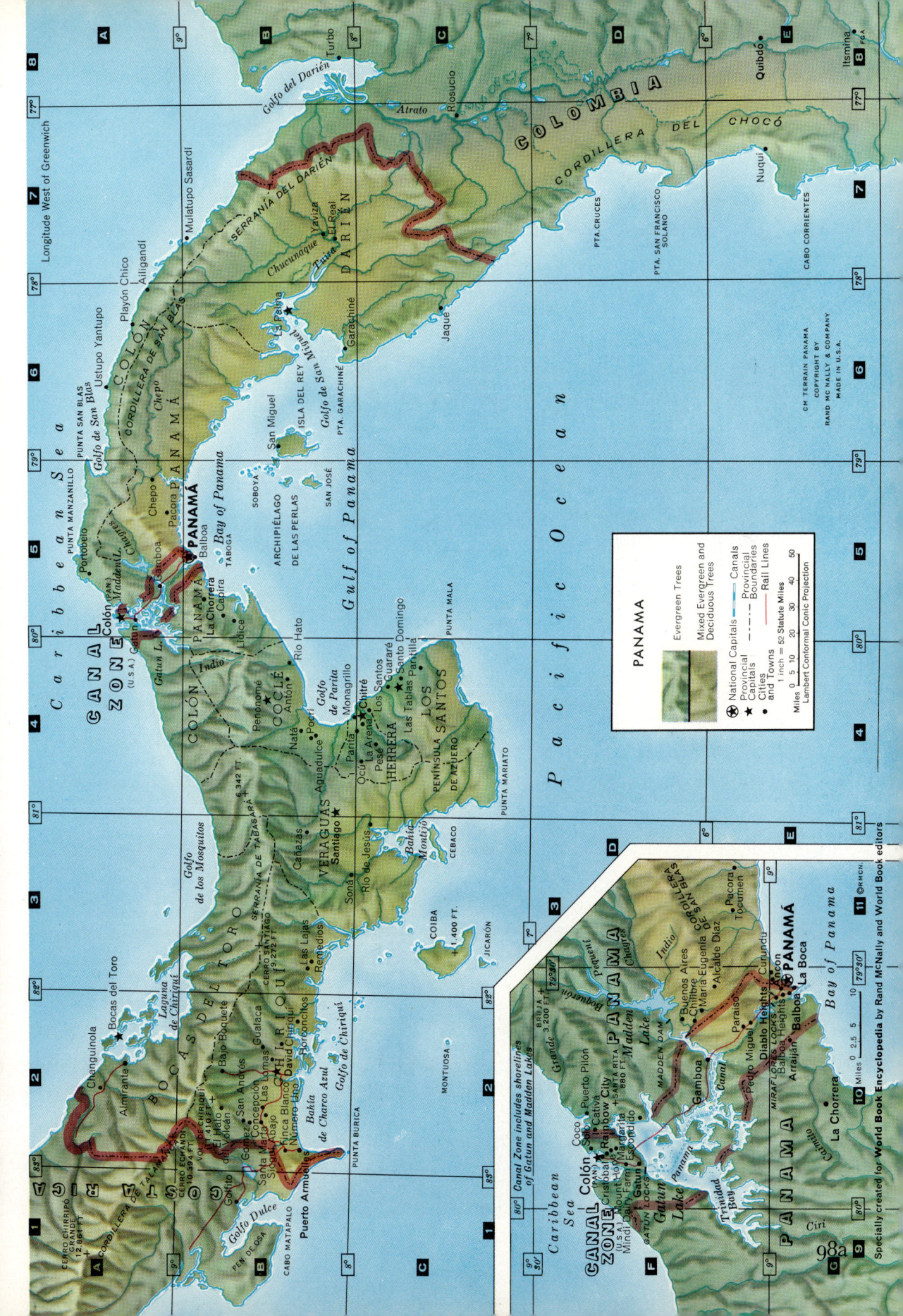

The University of Panama, founded in 1935 as the National University, has modern buildings on its campus. The statue called *Towards the Light* symbolizes the Panamanians' deep wish for higher learning. Almost all university classes are held in the evening because most students work at daytime jobs.

Herbert Lanks, Pix

Wide World

Thatcher Ferry Bridge spans the Panama Canal at Balboa in the Canal Zone. Completed in 1962, the mile-long bridge is an important link between the capital city of Panamá and Panama's western provinces. The United States government built the $20,000,-000 bridge, and named it for Maurice Thatcher, who was civil administrator in the Canal Zone from 1910 to 1912.

much corn and beans. The women grind the corn into a paste from which they make *tortillas*, a type of pancake. Coffee is the chief beverage.

Most people wear light, loose clothing similar to that worn in the United States during the summer. The people dress in their national costume on *fiestas* (feast days) and other special occasions. The women's *pollera* is a long, full dress made of many folds of fine white cotton. Delicate lace and embroidery decorate the pollera. Men wear the *montuno*, a costume made of coarse white cotton. It includes a loose, long-sleeved, embroidered shirt worn over short, fringed trousers.

Panama's chief sports include baseball, horse racing, boxing, swimming, fishing, and hunting. About 93 of every 100 persons are Roman Catholics. Almost every town and village holds a gay fiesta every year to honor its patron saint. City people hold carnivals during the four days preceding Ash Wednesday. During this period, they take part in dances, parties, and parades.

Town and City Life. Panamá, the capital, is the only city with more than 100,000 people. One other city, Colón, has more than 60,000 persons. The cities and towns serve mainly as trading and commercial centers. Panamá and Colón have a few factories and food-processing plants. These cities also have modern government and commercial buildings that line the boulevards and plazas (public squares). For separate articles on Panamanian cities and towns, see COLÓN; PANAMÁ; PORTOBELO.

Country Life. The farmers' houses stand in the fields or in small villages. A Panamanian village usually stands along a single dusty street or around a grass-covered plaza. The people shop in small, thatch-roofed general stores. The children go to one-room country schools. Most villages have churches. Public health nurses provide medical care in some larger rural communities, but most villages do not have doctors.

Work of the People

About 55 of every 100 Panamanians make their living in agriculture, stock raising, and fishing. About 38 of every 100 work in such fields as business, manufacturing, public administration, transportation, and communication. The Panama Canal is the most important factor in Panama's economic life. About 7 of every 100 Panamanians work for the United States government agencies that operate the Panama Canal and govern the Canal Zone. These agencies and the people of the zone buy many goods and services from Panamanian businessmen. Panamanian companies also sell food and other supplies to the ships that pass through the canal.

Agriculture. Most Panamanian farmers cultivate one or two acres of land with simple tools. Since World War II, large landowners have increased farm production by means of modern farm machinery.

Rice, the chief crop, grows on about 35 of every 100 acres of farm land. Tropical fruits such as mangos and bananas grow in the lowlands. Panama ranks high among the banana-producing countries. Other important farm products include coconuts, cacao beans (used to make chocolate), and abacá (a plant whose fibers are used to make rope). Many farmers grow sugar cane, corn, beans, yams, yuccas, and coffee. They raise livestock for meat, milk, and hides.

Fishing Industry. Fishermen catch about 1,800 tons

De Cou, Sawders
Ruins of an Old Church built in 1537 stand in Panamá. Henry Morgan, the pirate, destroyed the church in 1671.

San Blas Indian Women wear nose rings, metal ear discs, and necklaces of coins and beads. They paint black lines on their noses to make them seem longer.

Ewing Galloway

of shrimp a year off the coasts of Panama. Divers gather pearl oysters in the Bay of Panama. Other ocean products include tuna, mackerel, red snappers, and sponges.

Manufacturing and Processing. Rice mills, sugar refineries, and other food-processing plants operate in the cities of Panamá and Colón, the chief industrial centers. Small factories and shops produce cement, pottery, clothing, furniture, shoes, soap, soft drinks, and alcoholic beverages. People in country areas use wood, leather, gourds, and woven fibers to make useful articles such as saddles, mats, baskets, and kitchen utensils and containers.

The chief woven products are hats. These are not the hats that people in other countries call *Panama hats*. The people of Ecuador make those hats. The hats received their name because men found them for sale in Panama as they traveled across the country toward California during the gold rush of 1849. They are still sold in Panama. Hats woven in Panama are called *sombreros de Penonomé*, or hats of Penonomé (a country town). Woven designs or stripes decorate these hats. Panama hats that are made in Ecuador have no decorations.

Forest Products. The rich forests of western Panama provide about 5 million board feet of mahogany and other hardwoods every year for export. Other forest products include sarsaparilla, a flavoring from the roots of the smilax plant, and rotenone, an insect poison made from the root of the cube plant. See ROTENONE.

Trade. The chief exports of Panama are bananas, shrimp, cacao, and abacá. Imports include manufactured goods, food, beverages, and small amounts of raw materials. The United States buys more than nine-tenths of Panama's exports, and supplies more than six-tenths of the country's imports. Panama usually im-

Ewing Galloway

Panamá, the Capital City, sprawls along the Bay of Panama at the entrance of the Panama Canal. Vasco Núñez de Balboa, *right,* sighted the Pacific when he crossed Panama in 1513.

ports much more than it exports. But the money that tourists and the people of the Canal Zone spend there makes up the difference between exports and imports.

Transportation. Several airlines serve the country. A government-owned railway 106 miles long links the chief cities of western Panama. The Panama Railroad, which is owned by the United States, runs through the Canal Zone between the cities of Panamá and Colón. Panama has the beginnings of a fine highway system, but the country still needs many roads to bring farm products to market. Trucks, buses, and automobiles travel on more than 1,400 miles of public roads. The 50-mile-long highway between Panamá and Colón has been called the world's shortest transcontinental highway. The Pan American Highway enters Panama at the southwestern border and extends about 340 miles to Chepo. Thatcher Ferry Bridge, one of the world's longest steel arch bridges, spans the Panama Canal. It links Balboa and the city of Panamá.

Panama's merchant marine is one of the largest in the world. About 700 ships fly the Panamanian flag. Shipping lines of other countries own most of Panama's ships. These companies register their vessels in Panama, because the country allows them to pay lower wages and collect lower taxes than do most other nations. Cristobal and Balboa are Panama's chief ports.

Communication. Panama has several daily newspapers. The three most important newspapers print both English and Spanish editions. Panama also has several book and magazine publishers, and about 40 radio stations.

Activities of the People

Education is free in Panama. By law, all children between the ages of 7 and 15 must attend school. However, about one-third of the school-age children, especially in thinly populated country areas, do not go to school. About one-fourth of the people cannot read or write. The government operates free elementary and high schools and a teachers college. The University of

Panama, founded in 1935, has a beautiful campus in the city of Panamá.

The Arts. Panama has a rich folk art. The people enjoy ballads sung to the music of homemade drums, violins, and guitars. They also enjoy folk dances such as the gay, graceful *tamborito.* In the tamborito, a man and woman dance together in the center of a circle.

Government

President. The people elect the president, a first vice-president, and a second vice-president by direct popular vote for four-year terms. The constitution states that the president cannot be re-elected within eight years after the end of his term. In case the president dies while in office, the first vice-president succeeds to the presidency. A cabinet similar to that of the United States assists the president (see CABINET).

National Assembly. The people elect the 53 deputies of the National Assembly for four-year terms. Each deputy represents about 15,000 persons.

Courts. The president appoints the five judges of the Supreme Court for 10-year terms. The judges of each court appoint the judges of the next lower court. For example, the Supreme Court judges appoint the judges of the Superior Courts.

Local Government. Panama is divided into nine provinces. These are subdivided into municipal districts. The president appoints the provincial governors for indefinite terms. The people elect the mayors and councils of the municipal districts.

Politics. Citizens 20 years old or older may vote in national and local elections. The chief political party is the National Patriotic Coalition.

History

Early Days. Scholars know little about the history of the Indians who lived in Panama before the first Europeans arrived. In 1501, a Spanish explorer, Rodrigo de Bastidas (1460?- ?), became the first white man to visit Panama. In 1509, Spain sent colonists to

Panama. After fierce struggles with the Indians, the Spaniards established settlements along the Atlantic Coast. The Spaniards called the colony Castilla del Oro, or *Golden Castile*, after one of the Spanish kingdoms. In 1513, Vasco Núñez de Balboa, governor of the colony, became the first white man to see the eastern shore of the Pacific Ocean.

In 1519, the Spaniards founded the city of Panamá on the site of an Indian fishing village. The name *Panamá* comes from an Indian word meaning *fishermen*, or *plenty of fish*. For about 200 years, the city was the starting point for Spanish expeditions to Peru. Gold, silver, and Inca Indian treasures were carried to the town of Portobelo on the Caribbean Sea and then shipped to Spain. The colony's commercial importance declined in the 1700's, when ships carrying Peruvian treasures sailed around the tip of South America to avoid pirates in the Caribbean.

Independence. Colombia revolted against Spain in 1819. Two years later, Panama also broke away from Spain and became a province of Colombia. But Colombia misgoverned Panama. Panamanians tried to break away in 1830, 1831, and 1840. Between 1850 and 1902, they staged over 50 uprisings against Colombia. On Nov. 3, 1903, Panama gained its independence.

Panama's first constitution went into effect in 1904. Revolutionary leader Manuel Amador Guerrero (1833-1909) became the nation's first president.

Progress as a Nation. The construction of the Panama Canal brought prosperity to Panama in the early 1900's. Political unrest grew during the early 1930's. It was caused by government corruption and the effects of the world-wide economic depression. In 1931, a nationalist group overthrew President Florencio Harmodio Arosemena (1873-1945). Harmodio Arias (1886-1962), a nationalist, became president in 1932.

Panama declared war on the Axis nations in 1941, but Panamanian troops did no fighting during World War II. The country became a charter member of the United Nations in 1945. A new, more liberal constitution went into effect in 1946. It gave women the right to vote.

Recent Developments. Panamanians elected former chief of the national police José Remón as president in 1952. Assassins killed Remón in 1955. The first vice-president, José Ramón Guizado, then became president. But the National Assembly impeached Guizado and convicted him of taking part in Remón's killing. He was freed in 1957 on the basis of new evidence. The people elected Ernesto de la Guardia as president in 1956. Roberto F. Chiari succeeded him in 1960.

In the late 1950's, Panamanians grew increasingly unhappy over U.S. control in the Canal Zone. They wanted more sovereignty. When riots broke out in 1959, the United States agreed that the U.S. and Panamanian flags would fly side by side in one place in the zone as a symbol of Panama's sovereignty. After more riots in 1962, the United States agreed to let both flags fly side by side throughout the zone. The United States also gave Panamanians employed by the Panama Canal Company equal job opportunities and wages, and encouraged more sales to Panamanians in the Canal Zone.

Riots broke out again early in 1964 when U.S. high school students tried to raise a flag over their school. The United States and Panama had modified their agreement so that both flags would fly only at certain places

and no flags would fly elsewhere in the zone. Four U.S. soldiers and about 20 Panamanians died in the fighting. Panama broke diplomatic relations, charging the United States with brutality. President Chiari also asked that the canal treaty be redrawn. But diplomatic ties were resumed later. The two countries agreed to discuss the causes of the problems existing between them.

In June, 1964, the International Commission of Jurists decided that the United States was not guilty of Panama's charges of brutality in putting down the riots. But the commission said that both countries were guilty of a lack of judgment. In December, 1964, President Lyndon B. Johnson said the U.S. would negotiate a new treaty for the canal. Marco Aurelio Robles was elected president of Panama in 1964. In 1968, Arnulfo Arias succeeded him. But a military group overthrew Arias that same year.   JOHN BIESANZ and MAVIS BIESANZ

Related Articles in WORLD BOOK include:

Outline

I. The Land and Its Resources
- A. Location and Size
- B. Land Regions
- C. Coastline
- D. Rivers
- E. Natural Resources
- F. Climate

II. Life of the People
- A. The People
- B. Language
- C. Family Life
- D. Town and City Life
- E. Country Life

III. Work of the People
- A. Agriculture
- B. Fishing Industry
- C. Manufacturing and Processing
- D. Forest Products
- E. Trade
- F. Transportation
- G. Communication

IV. Activities of the People
V. Government
VI. History

Questions

Why is Panama called the *Crossroads of the World*?

How does the Panama Canal affect Panama's economy?

What is the *tamborito*?

How is Panama's government similar to those of the United States and Canada? How is it different?

What is a *pollera*? A *montuno*?

Why does Panama have a large merchant marine?

How long has Panama been an independent nation?

PANAMÁ (pop. 358,559; alt. 40 ft.) is the capital and largest city of the Republic of Panama. Panamá lies at the Pacific end of the Panama Canal. It is 22 miles east of Colón, which is at the Atlantic end (see PANAMA [color map]). Panamá was founded in 1519 by a Spaniard, Pedro Arias de Avila.

Today, the Panama Canal gives the city of Panamá its importance. The harbor of Panamá is shallow, but the United States has built excellent docks at Balboa, 3 miles away.   JOHN BIESANZ and MAVIS BIESANZ

PANAMA, ISTHMUS OF, is a narrow strip of land that connects the North American continent and the South American continent. The Isthmus of Panama is about 480 miles long and from 28 to 120 miles wide. The Panama Canal cuts across, forming a passageway between the Atlantic and Pacific oceans.   JOHN BIESANZ

PANAMA CANAL

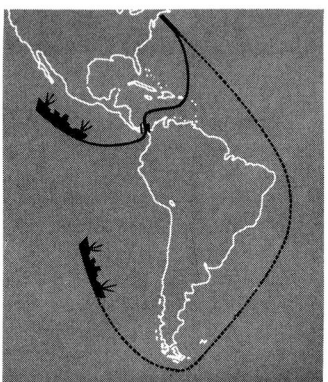

The Panama Canal fulfilled man's dreams of a short route from Atlantic Ocean ports to Pacific ports. The canal across Central America allows ships to enter the Pacific Ocean without traveling entirely around South America.

Panama Canal Co.

PANAMA CANAL ranks as one of man's greatest engineering achievements. It crosses Central America to connect the Atlantic and Pacific oceans. Before the Panama Canal was built, a ship sailing from New York City to San Francisco had to travel more than 13,000 miles around the tip of South America. The Canal shortened the journey to about 5,200 miles.

The United States built the 50.72-mile-long Canal during the early 1900's. Thousands of men labored many years to construct the waterway. They had to move 211 million cubic yards of earth and rock. The builders of the Canal used steam shovels and dredges to cut through jungles, hills, and swamps. They conquered tropical diseases that took the lives of many workmen. Construction of the Panama Canal cost the United States about $380 million.

The Panama Canal has three sets of *locks*, or water-filled chambers, that raise and lower ships from one level to another. The locks of the Canal were built in pairs to allow ships to pass through in both directions at the same time. Each lock has a usable length of 1,000 feet, a width of 110 feet, and a depth of about 70 feet. The dimensions of the locks limit the size of ships that can use the Canal. For example, the United States Navy's supercarriers are too wide to pass through the Canal.

The Panama Canal crosses the Isthmus of Panama in Central America. The Isthmus is the long, narrow strip of land that links North America and South America. The Canal lies almost directly south of Miami, Fla. It extends from Limón Bay on the Atlantic side to the Bay of Panama on the Pacific side. The *Color Map* with the PANAMA article shows that the Canal runs from northwest to southeast across the Isthmus. A ship sailing from the Atlantic to the Pacific actually leaves the Canal 27 miles *east* of where it entered.

The Canal lies in the Panama Canal Zone. A treaty with Panama in 1903 gave the United States the permanent right to govern the Canal Zone and to operate the Canal. However, the Panamanians regard the Canal Zone as part of their country. See PANAMA CANAL ZONE.

A Trip Through the Canal

Entering the Canal. A ship sailing from the Atlantic Ocean enters the Canal by way of Limón Bay, the harbor of the town of Cristóbal, Canal Zone. While the ship is still in deep water, a Canal pilot comes on board from a small boat. The pilot has complete charge of the ship during its trip through the Canal. After passing through the breakwater at the entrance to the bay, the ship heads south along the 7-mile-long channel that leads to the Gatún Locks. The shipyards, docks, and fueling stations of Cristóbal line the eastern shore of the bay.

The Gatún Locks (*guh TOON*) look like giant steps. They consist of three pairs of concrete chambers that lift ships about 85 feet from sea level to Gatún Lake. Small electric locomotives called *mules* run on tracks along both sides of the locks. They pull ships through the locks. The locomotives run up an incline at the end of each chamber to reach the next higher level. This allows the same set of locomotives to pull vessels through the entire length of the Gatún Locks. Four to 12 locomotives are used for each ship, depending on its size.

As the ship approaches the first chamber, its engines are shut off. Canal workers fasten the ends of the locomotives' towing cables to the vessel. The locomotives then pull the ship into the first chamber. Huge steel gates close silently behind the vessel. Canal workers open valves that allow water from Gatún Lake to flow into the chamber through openings in the bottom of the lock. During the next 8 to 15 minutes, the rising water slowly raises the ship. When the level of the water is the same as that in the second chamber, the gates in front of the ship swing outward. The locomotives pull the vessel into the second chamber. Again the water level is raised. This process is repeated until the third chamber of the locks raises the ship to the level of Gatún Lake.

Gatún Lake. The canal workers release the cables, and the ship sails out of the locks under its own power. As it heads south across the quiet water of Gatún Lake, it passes the huge Gatún Dam to the west of the locks. This 23,000,000-cubic-yard earth dam is one of the largest in the world. Gatún Dam created 163-square-mile Gatún Lake by holding back the waters of the Chagres River, which flows into the Atlantic Ocean near the end of the canal. The ship steams across the lake from Gatún Locks to Gamboa, following the 22-mile channel that was once the Chagres River Valley. The tops of trees and hills jut above the water. They were almost completely covered by water when engineers flooded the valley to create Gatún Lake. The violet flowers and green leaves of water hyacinths float on the surface of the lake. The long, coarse stems of these plants can become tangled in the propellers of ships and endanger navigation. A special hyacinth patrol destroys more than 42,000,000 of these plants every year to keep the channel clear.

The Gaillard *(gill YARD)* **Cut.** When the ship reaches the southeastern end of Gatún Lake it enters the 8-mile-long, 500-foot-wide Gaillard Cut, which has a minimum depth of 42 feet. *Cut* is an engineering term for a man-made passageway or channel. The Gaillard Cut runs between Gold Hill on the east and Contractor's Hill on the west. The Gaillard Cut was originally called the *Culebra Cut*. In 1913, it was renamed in honor of David DuBose Gaillard (1859-1913), the engineer in charge of digging between the hills. Dredgers work constantly to keep the channel clear of earthslides. In some years, the dredgers in the Gaillard Cut remove as much as 1,000,000 cubic yards of earth.

The Pedro Miguel and Miraflores Locks. After the ship steams out of the Gaillard Cut, electric locomotives pull it into the Pedro Miguel Locks. These locks lower the vessel 31 feet in one step to man-made Miraflores Lake. The ship sails $1\frac{1}{2}$ miles across the lake to the Miraflores Locks. Here, two chambers lower the vessel to the level of the Pacific Ocean. The distances these chambers must lower the ship depend on the height of the tide in the Pacific. Tides at the Pacific end of the Canal rise and fall about $12\frac{1}{2}$ feet a day. Tides on the Atlantic side change only about 2 feet daily.

Out of the locks, the ship heads down the 8-mile-long channel between the Miraflores Locks and the end of the Canal. It passes the houses and buildings of the towns of Balboa, Balboa Heights, and La Boca that stand on the shore of the channel. The ship also passes under the $20,000,000 Thatcher Ferry Bridge, an important link in the Pan American Highway. After the pilot leaves, the vessel enters the Bay of Panama and steams toward the open sea. The ship has traveled a

Underwood & Underwood

Theodore Roosevelt visited the canal in November, 1906, during his term as President. He wrote to his son about the Culebra Cut (now called the Gaillard Cut), saying "They are eating steadily into the mountain, cutting it down and down."

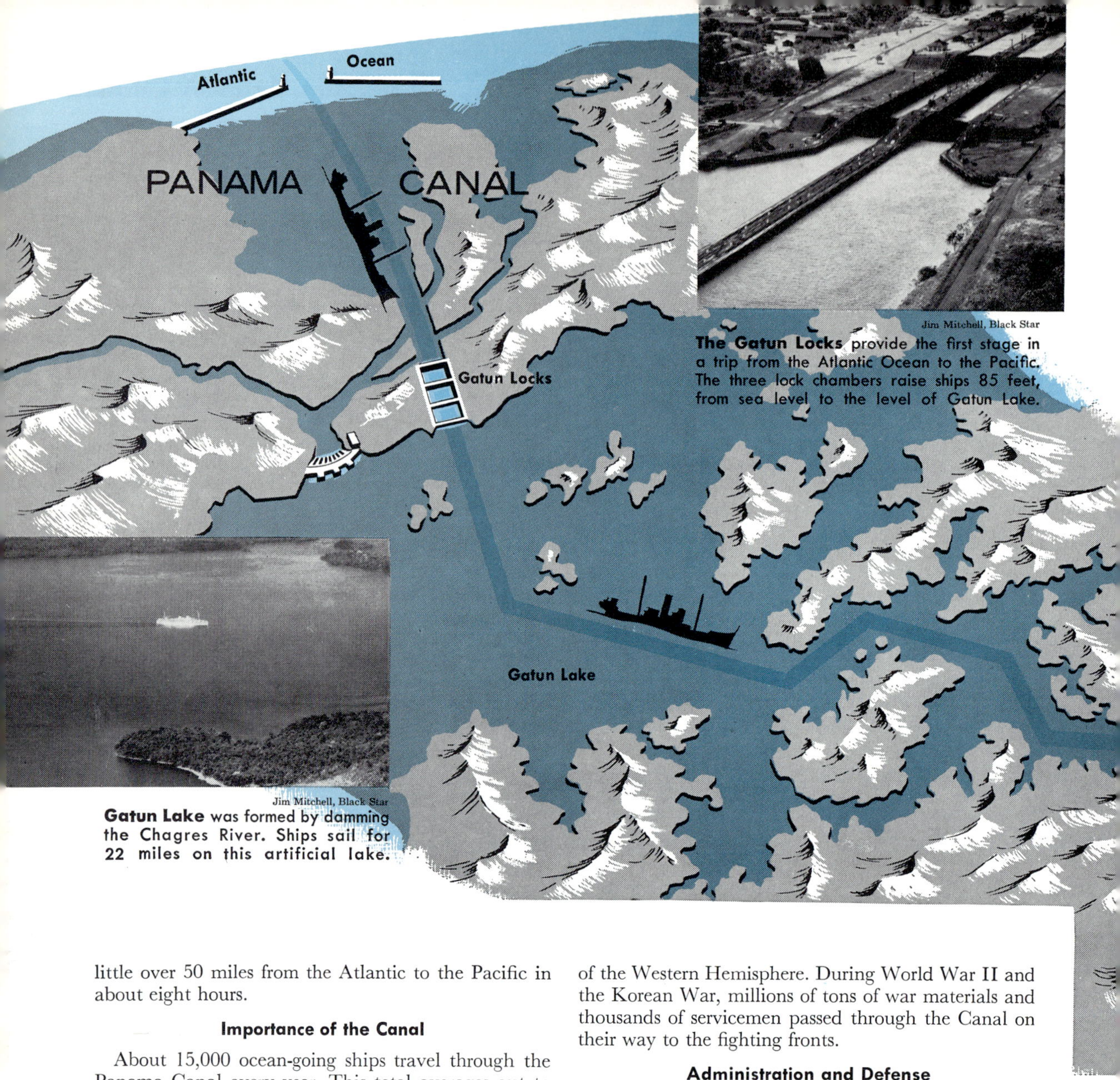

PANAMA CANAL

Atlantic Ocean

Gatun Locks

The Gatun Locks provide the first stage in a trip from the Atlantic Ocean to the Pacific. The three lock chambers raise ships 85 feet, from sea level to the level of Gatun Lake.

Jim Mitchell, Black Star

Gatun Lake

Gatun Lake was formed by damming the Chagres River. Ships sail for 22 miles on this artificial lake.

Jim Mitchell, Black Star

little over 50 miles from the Atlantic to the Pacific in about eight hours.

Importance of the Canal

About 15,000 ocean-going ships travel through the Panama Canal every year. This total averages out to more than 40 ships a day. About one-eighth of the ships fly the United States flag. Great Britain, Japan, Liberia, Norway, and West Germany are other leading users of the canal. By connecting the Atlantic and Pacific oceans, the Panama Canal provides an important link for world commerce. About 118,203,000 tons of cargo pass through the canal locks each year.

The Panama Canal forms a vital link in the defense

of the Western Hemisphere. During World War II and the Korean War, millions of tons of war materials and thousands of servicemen passed through the Canal on their way to the fighting fronts.

Administration and Defense

The Panama Canal Company operates and maintains the Panama Canal. This company is a United States government corporation. It operates harbor facilities in the Canal Zone towns of Balboa and Cristóbal, a steamship that runs between New Orleans and Panama, and a railroad that crosses the Isthmus within the Canal Zone. The company owns all the houses and apartments in the Canal Zone and rents them to Canal

Engineers Building the Panama Canal had to complete three major projects. One was construction of the locks, another was the damming of the Chagres River to form Gatun Lake, and the third, digging of the Gaillard Cut to cross land not flooded by Gatun Lake.

Atlantic Ocean   Gatun Locks   Gatun Lake

employees. It also operates the Zone's telephone, electric-power, and water systems, as well as stores for the people who live in the Canal Zone. The President of the United States appoints the president of the company and the 9 to 13 members of the company's board of directors. The president of the company also serves as governor of the Canal Zone.

Finances. United States federal law requires that the Panama Canal Company be self supporting. Tolls collected from ships that use the Canal provide the chief income of the company. The Panama Canal Company collects an average of $55 million in tolls every year. The toll paid by a merchant vessel depends on its size and the amount of space it has available for carrying cargo. Ocean-going vessels pay an average of $5,200 in tolls.

In 1962, the U.S. supertanker *Orion Hunter* paid the highest toll in the Canal's history, $30,446. Warships, including those of the United States, pay tolls based on their size. The battleship U.S.S. *Missouri* paid the largest toll for a military vessel, $28,838.

Defense. International law requires that the United States allow commercial and military vessels of all nations to pass through the Canal in peacetime. If the United States goes to war, or is in danger of going to war, it can restrict the use of the Canal. The United States maintains army, navy, and air force bases throughout the Canal Zone for the defense of the Canal.

History

Early Efforts. Hundreds of years before the Panama Canal was completed, men of many lands dreamed of building a canal across Central America. As early as 1517, Vasco Nuñez de Balboa, the first European to reach the Pacific, saw the possibility of a canal connecting the Atlantic and Pacific oceans.

Throughout most of the 1800's, Nicaragua was the chief center of efforts to build a canal. Both the United States and Great Britain considered a canal across Nicaragua (see NICARAGUA CANAL). During the 1840's, the

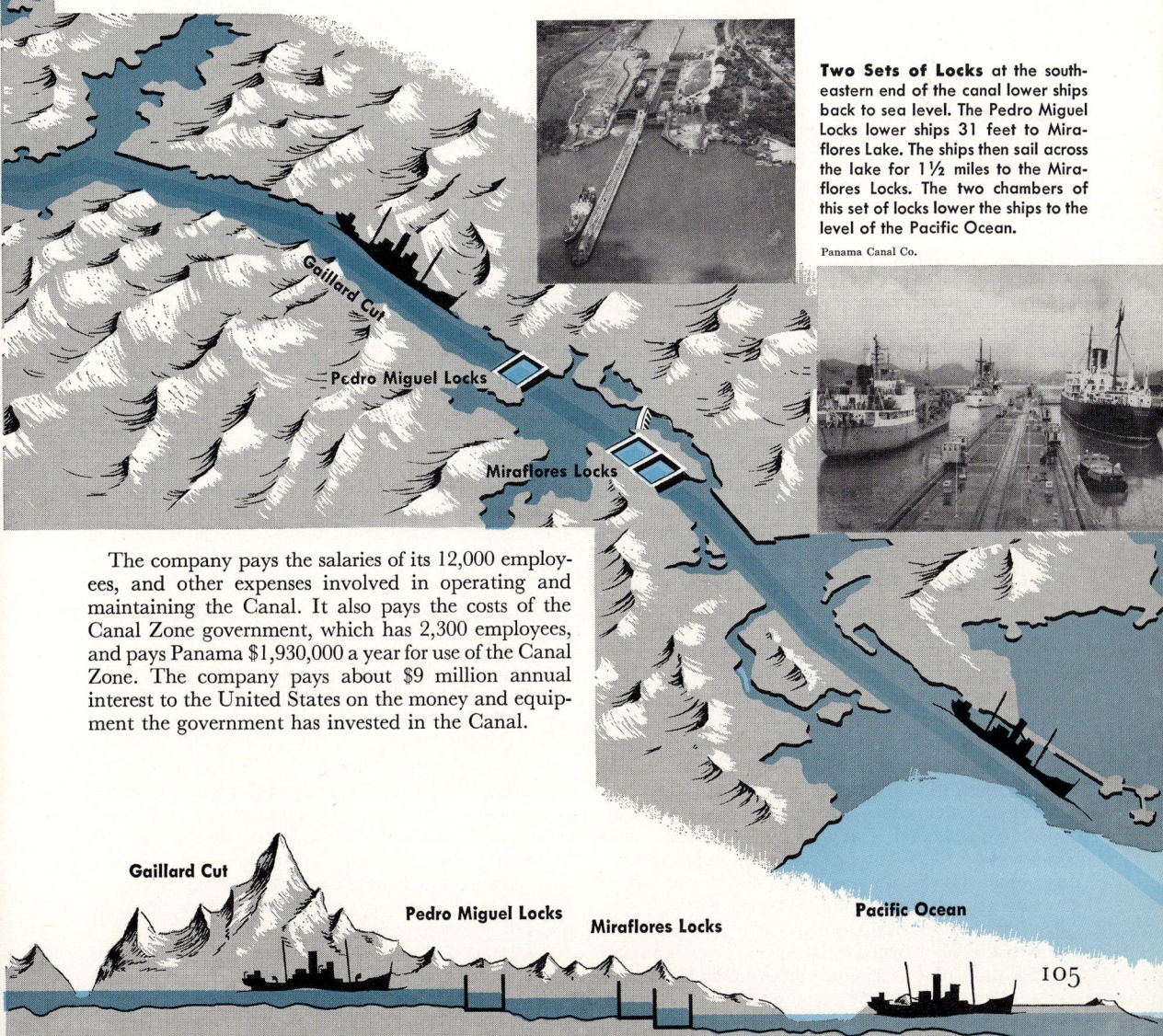

Two Sets of Locks at the southeastern end of the canal lower ships back to sea level. The Pedro Miguel Locks lower ships 31 feet to Miraflores Lake. The ships then sail across the lake for 1½ miles to the Miraflores Locks. The two chambers of this set of locks lower the ships to the level of the Pacific Ocean.

Panama Canal Co.

Gaillard Cut

Pedro Miguel Locks

Miraflores Locks

The company pays the salaries of its 12,000 employees, and other expenses involved in operating and maintaining the Canal. It also pays the costs of the Canal Zone government, which has 2,300 employees, and pays Panama $1,930,000 a year for use of the Canal Zone. The company pays about $9 million annual interest to the United States on the money and equipment the government has invested in the Canal.

Gaillard Cut

Pedro Miguel Locks

Miraflores Locks

Pacific Ocean

105

two nations almost went to war because of disputes over which one would control the proposed canal. In 1850, in the Clayton-Bulwer Treaty, they agreed on joint control of a canal to be built somewhere across the Central American isthmus. See CLAYTON-BULWER TREATY.

During that period, present-day Panama was a province of Colombia. Colombia feared that Great Britain would try to seize Panama for use as a canal site. Colombia signed a treaty with the United States in 1846. The United States agreed to guard all trade routes across Panama and to preserve Panama's neutrality.

The Panama Railroad. During the California gold rush that began in 1849, the Isthmus of Panama became an important route between the eastern United States and California. Many prospectors sailed from Atlantic Coast ports to Panama, crossed the Isthmus by boat, on mules, and on foot, and then took another ship for California. In 1850, Colombia permitted a group of businessmen from New York City to build a railroad across the Isthmus. The line was completed in 1855 at a cost of $8,000,000. It linked Colón on the Atlantic side and the city of Panamá on the Pacific side.

The French Failure. In 1878, Colombia granted a French adventurer, Lucien Napoleon Bonaparte Wyse (1844-1895), a franchise that gave him the right to build a canal across Panama (see FRANCHISE). He sold the franchise to a French company headed by Ferdinand Marie de Lesseps, who had directed the construction of the Suez Canal. The French also bought control of the Panama Railroad for $20,000,000. The company began digging in 1882. The French planned a canal that would run at sea level between the Atlantic and Pacific, and so would need no locks. In 1886, the problems of building a sea-level canal forced the French to decide on a canal similar to the present one. De Lesseps and his assistants planned most of the project carefully, and carried out some of it efficiently. However, the French wasted great quantities of material and effort. A group of dishonest politicians who backed De Lesseps stole much money from the canal company. The French engineers lacked the proper tools to complete such a huge digging job. Scientists did not know how to fight the epidemics of tropical diseases that hit the workmen.

De Lesseps' company went bankrupt in 1889, after digging out some 76,000,000 cubic yards of earth. A second French firm, the New Panama Canal Company, took over the property and franchise of the bankrupt company in 1894. But the new company made only half-hearted efforts to continue digging, in order to keep the franchise until a buyer could be found.

The United States and the Canal. A group of United States businessmen began working on a canal across Nicaragua in 1889. But they ran out of money soon after beginning the work. Both the American and French groups tried to sell their rights and property to the United States government. But American railroads opposed construction of any Central American canal because they feared competition from shipping lines that would use the waterway. So, the United States government took no action on either project.

During the Spanish-American War in 1898, the United States Navy sent the battleship *Oregon* from San Francisco to Cuba to reinforce the Atlantic Fleet. The

Oregon had to sail nearly 13,000 miles around the tip of South America. The trip would have been only about 4,600 miles long through a canal. This helped convince the United States Congress that a Central American canal was essential for the defense of the country.

In 1899, Congress authorized a commission to survey possible canal routes. The commission favored Nicaragua, because a canal there would require less digging than one across Panama. But the French company offered to sell its Panama rights and property and the Panama Railroad for $40,000,000. Philippe Bunau-Varilla, of the French company, persuaded leading Americans that Nicaragua's volcanoes presented the danger of earthquakes, and that Panama was safer. In 1902, Congress gave President Theodore Roosevelt permission to accept the French offer if Colombia would give the United States permanent use of a canal zone. Congress acted after the United States and Great Britain had replaced the Clayton-Bulwer Treaty with the Hay-Pauncefote Treaty. This treaty gave the United States sole right to build and operate a canal across Central America. See HAY-PAUNCEFOTE TREATY.

In 1903, Secretary of State John Hay signed a canal treaty with a Colombian representative, Tomás Herrán. The treaty provided that the United States would give Colombia an initial payment of $10,000,000, plus $250,000 annual rent for the use of the zone. But the Colombian legislature refused to approve the treaty, because it felt that this was not enough money.

A group of Panamanians feared that Panama would lose the commercial benefits of a canal across the isthmus. The French company worried about losing the sale of its property to the United States. The Panamanians, with the help of the French and some encouragement from the United States, revolted against Colombia on Nov. 3, 1903, and declared Panama independent. In accordance with its 1846 treaty with Colombia, the United States sent ships to Panama to protect the Panama Railroad. Marines landed in Colón, and prevented Colombian troops from marching to the city of Panamá, the center of the revolution. On Nov. 6, 1903, the United States recognized the Republic of Panama. Less than two weeks later, Panama and the United States signed the Hay-Bunau-Varilla Treaty. This treaty gave the United States permanent, exclusive use and control of a 10-mile-wide canal zone. In return for the use of the Zone, the United States gave Panama an initial payment of $10,000,000, plus $250,-000 a year, beginning in 1913. The United States also guaranteed Panama's independence. The United States took over the French property in May, 1904.

Victory Over Disease. The greatest obstacle to building the Canal was disease. The Isthmus of Panama was one of the most disease-ridden areas in the world. In 1904, Colonel William C. Gorgas took charge of improving sanitary conditions in the Canal Zone. Gorgas, a physician, had gained fame by wiping out yellow fever in Havana, Cuba, after the Spanish-American War.

Gorgas began a campaign to destroy the types of mosquitoes that carried malaria and yellow fever. The first two years of canal building were devoted largely to clearing brush, draining swamps, and cutting out large areas of grass where the mosquitoes swarmed.

By 1906, Gorgas had wiped out yellow fever and eliminated the rats that carried bubonic plague in the

Canal Zone. By 1913, he had also reduced the rate of deaths caused by malaria.

Cutting Through the Isthmus. President Roosevelt appointed a civilian commission to head the Canal project. In 1906, Congress decided to build a canal with locks, rather than the sea-level canal that the French had originally planned. Engineers believed that a canal with locks would be cheaper and faster to build. They also felt that a canal with locks would control the flood waters of the Chagres River better than a sea-level canal. The work progressed slowly, chiefly because of disagreements among the commission members. In 1907, Roosevelt put Colonel George W. Goethals, an army engineer, in charge of the project and the Canal Zone.

The construction task involved three major engineering projects. The builders had to excavate the Gaillard Cut, build a dam across the Chagres River to create Gatún Lake, and construct the Canal's locks. The biggest job was digging the Gaillard Cut. The hills through which the Cut runs consist of a soft volcanic material, and digging into them was much like digging into a pile of grain. As soon as workers dug a hole, more rock and earth would slide into the space, or push up from below. The engineers originally estimated that they would remove about 95 million cubic yards of earth and rock to build the Canal. Engineers actually dug out about 211 million cubic yards before they finished the Canal. Some of this was used later to build Gatún Dam.

At the height of the work in 1913, more than 43,400 persons worked on the Canal. Three-fourths of the laborers were Negroes from the British West Indies. The rest of the laborers came mostly from Italy and Spain. Most of the more highly paid clerical and skilled workers came from the United States.

The Oceans United. The main work of building the Panama Canal was completed in 1914. On August 15, 1914, a passenger-cargo ship owned by the Panama Railroad Company, the S.S. *Ancon*, made the first complete trip through the Canal. It sailed from the Atlantic to the Pacific and made the words on the official seal of the Canal Zone a reality—"The Land Divided, the World United." A giant landslide in the Gaillard Cut closed the Canal for several months in 1915 and 1916. It was the last major interruption in the operation of the Panama Canal. President Woodrow Wilson proclaimed the official opening of the Canal on July 12, 1920.

The Canal cost the United States about $380 million. This included the $40 million paid to the French company, the $10 million paid to Panama, and $20 million for sanitation. The remaining $310 million was spent for the actual construction work.

The Canal Since 1920. The Madden Dam, completed in 1935, was the first major improvement on the Panama Canal. The dam lies across the Chagres River, east of the Canal. It created 22-square-mile Madden Lake, which stores water for use in Gatún Lake. The dam also holds back the floodwaters of the Chagres River during the rainy season.

In 1939, a new Canal treaty went into effect between the United States and Panama. It increased the annual payments to $430,000. The pact ended America's guarantee of the independence of Panama, and also covered defense measures and the control of highways, radio stations, and air fields.

Congress changed the administration of the Canal

Zone and the Canal in 1951. The Panama Canal had been an independent government agency that managed the Canal and the Canal Zone. The Panama Railroad Company operated various enterprises in addition to running the railroad. Congress changed the name of the Panama Railroad Company to the Panama Canal Company, and gave it control of the Canal and several business activities in the Canal Zone. Congress also established the Canal Zone government, the independent agency that administers the Zone's civil government.

The United States signed another Canal treaty with Panama in 1955. This pact raised the annual payments to $1,930,000. The United States government also agreed to ask Congress for laws that would allow federal agencies to pay Panamanian workers in the Canal Zone the same wages that Americans earn there for the same type of work. Previously, Americans had received higher wages. In return, the Panamanian government permitted the United States to use and control a military-training area on Panamanian soil.

In the 1960's, the Panama Canal Company began paying Panamanian workers on the same scale with U.S. citizens. More Panamanians also got jobs on the Canal.

Engineers widened the Gaillard Cut from 300 to 500 feet in the 1960's. They also installed lights on the Canal banks for better night passages, and tried electric towing locomotives.

Riots broke out in the Canal Zone early in 1964 (see PANAMA [History]). In December, 1964, President Lyndon B. Johnson proposed that the United States build a new sea-level canal across Panama, Colombia, or Nicaragua. He also said the U.S. would negotiate a new treaty on the present canal.   JOHN BIESANZ and MAVIS BIESANZ

Related Articles in WORLD BOOK include:

Balboa Heights	Gorgas (William C.)
Canal	Hay-Pauncefote Treaty
Chagres River	Nicaragua Canal
Clayton-Bulwer Treaty	Panama, Isthmus of
De Lesseps, Ferdinand M.	Panama Canal Zone
Fort Amador	Roosevelt, Theodore
Gatún Lake	(Foreign Policy)
Goethals, George W.	

Outline

I. **A Trip Through the Canal**
II. **Importance of the Canal**
III. **Administration and Defense**
IV. **History**

Questions

What limits the size of ships that can use the canal?

Why is the Panama Canal important?

Who operates the Panama Canal?

What were the three major engineering jobs necessary to dig the Canal?

What was the greatest obstacle to building the Canal? How was it overcome?

What part did the Spanish-American War play in the history of the Canal?

In what direction does a ship travel when passing through the Canal from the Atlantic to the Pacific?

Who was Ferdinand de Lesseps? George W. Goethals? William C. Gorgas?

How long does it take a ship to pass through the Canal? How was Gatún Lake formed?

PANAMA CANAL COMPANY. See PANAMA CANAL (Administration).

PANAMA CANAL ZONE

PANAMA CANAL ZONE, or CANAL ZONE, is a strip of land that lies across the Republic of Panama in Central America. The Panama Canal runs through the center of the zone. The United States and Panama signed a treaty in 1903 establishing the Canal Zone. This pact gave the United States the right to build and operate the Panama Canal and to govern the zone. The United States pays Panama $1,930,000 a year for the use of the zone. Balboa Heights is the administrative center of the Panama Canal Zone.

The zone covers 553 square miles, including 191 square miles of water. The 1903 agreement gave the United States control over a 10-mile-wide strip of land that extends 40 miles from the Atlantic to the Pacific. Later agreements added Madden Lake, northeast of the Canal, and Trinidad Bay, which lies to the southwest.

The United States has no control over the cities of Panamá and Colón, although they lie at the ends of the Canal. Panama did not want to lose its chief cities. The color map with the PANAMA article shows the borders of the Canal Zone. For the history of the zone and a description of the Panama Canal, see PANAMA CANAL.

The People of the Canal Zone. The Canal Zone has a population of 61,000. There are about 110 persons to the square mile. About 6 out of 10 persons are United States citizens, and 3 out of 10 are Panamanians. About 35,000 persons there are civilians. The rest are members of the U.S. armed forces stationed in the zone.

Almost all the civilians work for the United States Army, the Canal Zone government, or the Panama Canal Company. The company is a United States government corporation which operates the canal and its supporting services. Most professional, skilled, or supervisory jobs are filled by Americans. Most of the Panamanians and West Indians in the Zone are laborers and semiskilled workers. Many live in Panamá and Colón.

The civilians live, eat, and dress much as do people in the United States. They rent their houses and apartments from the Panama Canal Company. They shop in company-owned stores and use company-operated recreation centers. The company also owns and operates the 48-mile-long Panama Railroad that runs through the zone between Cristóbal and Balboa. The Boyd-Roosevelt Trans-Isthmian Highway runs between Panamá and Colón, but most of the highway lies outside the zone. United States military men and their families live on bases throughout the zone.

The Canal Zone Government is an independent agency of the United States government. It administers the civil government of the Canal Zone. The President of the United States appoints the governor of the Canal Zone for a four-year term. In time of war, the highest-ranking United States Army officer in the Canal Zone takes charge of the zone and the canal.

The Canal Zone government operates the zone's police and fire departments, and its health and sanitation facilities. It also operates free schools for the children in the zone. These schools are divided into two groups. One follows a U.S. course of study for U.S. children. The other group follows the Panamanian teaching program, and has instruction in Spanish.

Officials appointed by Congress and the President run the Canal Zone. The people send no representatives to Congress. Many U.S. citizens there vote by absentee ballot. Panamanians rioted in 1959, demanding the right to fly their flag in the zone. In 1962, Panama and the United States agreed to fly their flags side by side in civilian areas of the zone. The United States also granted greater rights and better wages to Panamanians in the zone. But in January, 1964, serious riots broke out in the Canal Zone (see PANAMA [History]). In late 1964, President Lyndon B. Johnson said the U.S. would negotiate a new treaty with Panama for the canal. He also proposed building a new sea-level canal in Central America.   JOHN BIESANZ and MAVIS BIESANZ

See also ALBROOK AIR FORCE BASE; BALBOA; BALBOA HEIGHTS; CRISTÓBAL; FORT AMADOR.

PANAMA HAT. See HAT; PANAMA (Manufacturing).

PANAMA-PACIFIC INTERNATIONAL EXPOSITION celebrated the completion of the Panama Canal. It was held in San Francisco in 1915. The exposition attempted to gather together all things that represented civilization as it was in that year. Its purpose was to create a sample world of 1915 from which scientists of the future could reconstruct the period.

PANAMINT MOUNTAINS. See DEATH VALLEY.

PANAY. See PHILIPPINES (The Islands).

PANCAKE TUESDAY. See ENGLAND (Way of Life); SHROVE TUESDAY.

PANCHATANTRA. See STORYTELLING (India).

PANCHEN LAMA served as spiritual ruler of Tibet from 1959 to 1965. He and the other Grand Lama, the Dalai Lama, are regarded as reincarnations of Buddha. The Dalai Lamas ruled Tibet for hundreds of years. In 1959, the Chinese Communists forced the 14th Dalai Lama to flee to India, and installed the Panchen Lama as their puppet ruler. The Communists stripped the Panchen Lama of his powers in 1965.   THEODORE H. E. CHEN

PANCREAS, *PAN kree us,* is a body organ found in man and all animals with backbones. It produces a digestive juice and the hormone *insulin.*

In man, the pancreas is a pinkish-yellow gland about 6 to 8 inches long, 1½ inches wide, and an inch thick. It

The Pancreas Plays an Important Part in Digestion.

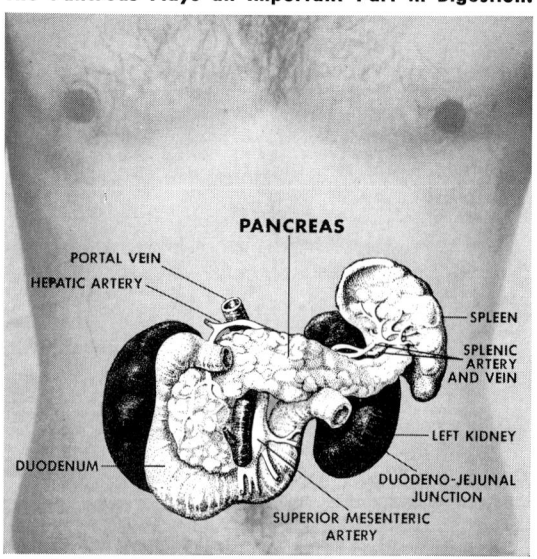

PANCREAS

PORTAL VEIN
HEPATIC ARTERY

SPLEEN

SPLENIC ARTERY AND VEIN

LEFT KIDNEY

DUODENUM

DUODENO-JEJUNAL JUNCTION

SUPERIOR MESENTERIC ARTERY

lies crosswise, behind the stomach. The first part of the small intestine, called the *duodenum*, loops around the pancreas. Digestive juice formed by the pancreas flows through a duct into the duodenum. The juice contains enzymes and salts that help digest proteins, starches, sugars, and fats.

Small islands of special tissue called the *islets* (or *islands*) of *Langerhans* are scattered throughout the pancreas. They secrete insulin directly into the blood stream, which carries it to cells throughout the body. The cells need insulin to help them use *glucose*, the sugar that is their main fuel. The cells cannot work properly if the pancreas secretes too little insulin, because they cannot use glucose normally. Unused glucose accumulates in the blood and body tissues. It is carried out of the body in urine. Sugar in the urine is one of the main symptoms of *diabetes mellitus*. Doctors treat this disease with insulin which is prepared from the pancreases of animals.

TERENCE A. ROGERS

Related Articles. See the Trans-Vision three-dimensional color picture with HUMAN BODY. See also:

Bile (picture)	Digestion	Pancreatin
Diabetes	Insulin	Sweetbread

PANCREATIC JUICE. See DIGESTION; PANCREAS.

PANCREATIN, *PAN kree uh tin* or *PANG kree uh tin,* is a cream-colored powder that is used as a medicine. It is a mixture of enzymes obtained from the fresh pancreas of hogs and oxen. Doctors sometimes prescribe pancreatin to persons with stomach disorders that involve the stopping of the hydrochloric-acid flow. They also prescribe it to relieve some intestinal disorders, and to aid in the digestion of milk and some other foods.

Pancreatin contains three chief enzymes. (1) *Pancreatic amylase*, or *amylopsin*, digests starch into sugar. (2) *Pancreatic lipase* changes fats into the chemical glycerol and fatty acids. (3) *Trypsin* digests proteins into amino acids.

WILLIAM B. YOUMANS

See also PANCREAS.

PANDA is one of two kinds of rare animals that live in mountainous areas of Tibet and southern China. The two kinds are not related. Both kinds feed mainly on bamboo shoots.

The Giant Panda has small, round black ears and black patches around its eyes. Its playful nature makes it popular at the zoo.

Ylla, Rapho Guillumette

The *giant panda* has a white, chubby body with black legs and shoulders. Its face is white with a round, black spot at each eye. The giant panda is difficult to find. Scientists in Europe considered them a myth until the middle 1800's. A live giant panda was first brought to the United States in 1936.

The *lesser panda*, sometimes called the *Himalayan raccoon*, is about the size of a cat. Its body is more or less raccoon-shaped, and is reddish-brown with white face markings. Its long tail has alternating reddish-brown and yellow rings.

Scientific Classification. Giant pandas belong to the bear family, *Ursidae*. They are genus *Ailuropoda*, species *A. melanoleuca*. Lesser pandas belong to the raccoon family, *Procyonidae*, and are genus *Ailurus*, species *A. fulgens.*

E. LENDELL COCKRUM

See also ANIMAL (color picture: Animals of the Mountains); RACCOON.

PANDEMIC. See EPIDEMIC.

PANDIT, VIJAYA LAKSHMI (1900-   ), one of India's most famous women, is distinguished for her work in government and for her interest in the women's movement. Madame Pandit was appointed ambassador to Russia in 1947, and ambassador to the United States in 1949. From 1953 to 1954, she served as the first woman president of the United Nations General Assembly. She then became Indian high commissioner in Great Britain. Madame Pandit became ambassador to Ireland in 1955 and ambassador to Spain in 1958. She held both posts until 1961. Madame Pandit was governor of the Indian state of Maharashtra from 1963 to 1965, and later entered the Parliament.

United Press Int.

Vijaya Lakshmi Pandit

Madame Pandit was born in Allahabad. Like her father and brother, Motilal and Jawaharlal Nehru, she took a prominent part in India's struggle for independence, and was jailed several times. RICHARD L. PARK

See also NEHRU.

PANDORA, *pan DOH ruh,* was the first woman on earth, according to Greek mythology. Zeus (Jupiter) had become angry because Prometheus stole fire from the gods to give to men. He ordered Hephaestus (Vulcan) to create an evil being whom all men would desire. Hephaestus created a woman from earth and water. All the gods gave her gifts, and hence her name, Pandora, meaning *all-gift*. Athena (Minerva) gave her knowledge in the arts, and Aphrodite (Venus) made her beautiful. Hermes (Mercury) gave her cunning and flattery, and the Graces clothed her.

The new creation was presented to Epimetheus, who accepted her in spite of warnings from his brother, Prometheus. Pandora had brought with her a box or vase which the gods warned her never to open. But she could not resist her curiosity, and finally raised the lid. All the world's vices, sins, diseases, and troubles in-

PANEL DISCUSSION

stantly flew out. Pandora shut the lid quickly, but only Hope, man's last comfort, was left.   O. M. PEARL

See also PROMETHEUS; VULCAN.

PANEL DISCUSSION is a method of talking over a problem or subject before an audience. There are usually from four to eight persons in the *panel*. The members of the panel sit at a table before the audience. The chairman sits with the group. He guides the discussion and takes an active part in the informal "give and take" of the talks. The subject or problem is developed by conversation among the members. Each *panelist* may ask questions, make statements, or restate and interpret what the others have said. However, the panel discussion is aimed at the audience. Its purpose is to stimulate and inform the members of the audience about the matter being discussed, so that they will want to take part in a question-and-answer period. No one makes a speech in a panel discussion.

The panel tries to cover the subject in an organized way. This helps both those talking and those listening to understand what the discussion is about. The discussion plan most often used follows the questions below.

What is the problem?
What are the issues in the problem?
What are the possible solutions?
Which is the better solution?
How can we test or evaluate the apparent solution?

The panel part of the program usually lasts 20 to 30 minutes. Then the discussion is opened to questions by members of the audience.   J. V. GARLAND

See also SYMPOSIUM.

PANGOLIN, *pang GO lin.* The pangolins are the only known members of the order *Pholidota.* They bear a resemblance to both the anteater and the armadillo. Pangolins live in southeastern Asia, Indonesia, and parts of Africa south of the Sahara. Like the American anteaters, the pangolins are toothless. They have long, narrow snouts, long tails, and sticky, ropelike tongues which they can thrust far out to catch the ants on which they live. Pangolins have coats of mail formed by overlapping horny scales, instead of the coarse hair of the American anteaters. The scales are various shades of brown.

Pangolins can roll themselves into tight balls so heavily armored that few enemies can harm them. They are inoffensive animals, but when captured they may lash out with their scaled tails.

Pangolins vary in length from 3 to 5 feet, depending on the species. The black-bellied pangolin of West Africa has a very long tail, which is about two-thirds of its total length. This pangolin lives in trees. All pangolins have large, strong claws on their forefeet, which they use to rip open the nests of ants and termites.

Pangolins are much hunted for their excellent meat. But because they are shy and look for food only at night, they have been saved from extermination.

Scientific Classification. Pangolins belong to the scaly anteater family, *Manidae.* All pangolins are classified in the genus *Manis.*   THEODORE H. EATON, JR.

See also ANTEATER.

PANHANDLE. See the Land Regions section of the ALASKA; IDAHO; OKLAHOMA; TEXAS; and WEST VIRGINIA articles.

PANIC OF 1837. See VAN BUREN, MARTIN (The Panic of 1837); WILDCAT BANK.

PANIC OF 1873. See GRANT, ULYSSES SIMPSON (The Panic of 1873); BLACK FRIDAY.

PANICLE. See INFLORESCENCE.

PANKHURST, EMMELINE GOULDEN (1858-1928), led the fight for women's voting rights in England. With her husband, Richard M. Pankhurst, she helped form the Women's Franchise League in 1889. In 1903, she helped organize the National Women's Social and Political Union, with the slogan "Votes for Women." In their bold program, Mrs. Pankhurst's followers differed from older "suffragettes." They staged parades and engaged in such violence as window-breaking to gain attention. She and her followers suffered rough handling and imprisonment. During World War I, they turned to patriotic work. Women received equal voting privileges in England the year of Mrs. Pankhurst's death. She was born in Manchester, England.   LOUIS FILLER

PANMUNJOM, *pahn moon jum,* North Korea, became famous as the site of the truce talks that ended the Korean War. For location, see KOREA (color map). Communist and UN forces signed a truce there on July 27, 1953.   CHARLES Y. HU

See also KOREAN WAR.

PANNONIA. See GOTH.

The Pangolin, or Scaly Anteater, looks like a cross between the anteater and the armadillo.

Rolled into a Ball, the pangolin is protected by its tough scales.

American Museum of Natural History

Large, Showy Pansies make an attractive border around flower gardens. They vary in color from brilliant purples to brown.

H. Armstrong Roberts

PANSY, *PAN zih,* the "flower with a face," is a cultivated kind of violet. The beautiful flowers of the pansy may be purple, violet, blue, yellow, white, brown, or any mixtures of these colors. Like the violet, the pansy is a low-growing flower. Pansies are so hardy they can be easily grown in the home garden. They require plenty of water and not too much sun. Some pansies live only one season. Others are perennials. *Pansy* comes from the French *pensée,* which means *thought.*

Pansies are also called *jump-up-and-kiss-me, heartsease, three-faces-under-a-hood,* and *love-in-idleness.*

Scientific Classification. The pansy belongs to the violet family, *Violaceae.* It is classified as genus *Viola,* species *V. tricolor.*   MARCUS MAXON

PANTAGRUEL. See GARGANTUA AND PANTAGRUEL.

PANTELLERIA, *PAHN tayl lay REE ah* (pop. 9,601), is a small Italian island in the Mediterranean Sea. It lies about midway between Tunisia and the island of Sicily, and covers about 32 square miles. For location, see ITALY (physical map). The extinct crater of Magna Grande rises to a height of 2,743 feet there. The fertile soil of Pantelleria produces cotton, figs, grains, and grapes. The city of Pantelleria is the island's port. It exports dried figs and sweet wines.   SHEPARD B. CLOUGH

PANTHEISM, *PAN thee iz'm,* is the belief that God and the whole universe are one and the same thing and that God does not exist as a separate spirit. Pantheism teaches that God is the whole universe, the human mind, the seasons, and all things and ideas that exist. The word *pantheism* comes from two Greek words meaning *all* and *god.* Poets who wrote about nature often were believers in pantheism. A good example of this belief is William Wordsworth's poem, "Tintern Abbey." See also DEISM; SPINOZA, BARUCH.   A. EUSTACE HAYDON

PANTHÉON. See PARIS (Famous Buildings).

PANTHEON, *PAN thee ahn,* is an architectural masterpiece of ancient Rome. This well preserved structure is now a national shrine and the burial place of King Victor Emmanuel I, King Humbert I, the painter Raphael, and other famous Italians. The Pantheon was completed in A.D. 126, during the reign of Emperor Hadrian, who may have helped design it. The building was used as a church by Christians between the early 600's and 1885.

The Pantheon is a circular building topped by a dome. A 100-foot-long rectangular porch stretches across the front. Over the porch is a triangular roof supported by 16 Corinthian columns of granite, each $42\frac{1}{2}$ feet high. The entrance to the temple still has its original bronze doors. For a picture of the outside of the Pantheon, see ROME (Ancient Rome).

The Pantheon was the first Roman building that emphasized interior space, rather than exterior form. The inside of the temple is a circular chamber 144 feet in diameter. The dome, supported by eight large *piers* (rectangular supports), is 144 feet above the floor at its *apex* (highest point). The only natural light comes in through the *oculus,* an opening 30 feet in diameter at the apex. Colored marble designs on the floor and walls and Corinthian columns and *pilasters* (flat columns) decorate the chamber. Scholars believe that statues of the seven gods of the heavens once stood in recesses in the wall of the chamber and that the dome represented the sky. For a picture of the interior of the Pantheon, see ARCHITECTURE (Roman).   WILLIAM P. DONOVAN

See also DOME (picture).

PANTHER is a name used loosely for certain members of the cat family. It is given to the *leopard,* which is a native of Asia and Africa. The *puma* of North America, also known as the *cougar* and the *mountain lion,* is sometimes called a panther, particularly in the eastern United States. A few authorities apply the name only to large leopards.   ERNEST S. BOOTH

See also LEOPARD.

PANTOGRAPH. See ELECTRIC RAILROAD.

PANTOGRAPH is the name of a mechanical drawing instrument which copies, traces, or cuts in duplicate a design, map outline, or drawing. It is made of four bars or rods held together by adjustable pins. One end of the pantograph is held stationary. One tracing point is moved over the design to be copied, following its outlines. Another point will then move in unison with this point, copying or cutting a duplicate outline. The pantograph can be set, by using adjustable pins, to copy in any size.   HARRY MUIR KURTZWORTH

See also MAP (picture: The Pantograph Router).

By Using a Pantograph, the artist finds it easy to enlarge a smaller design with speed and accuracy.

Press Syndicate

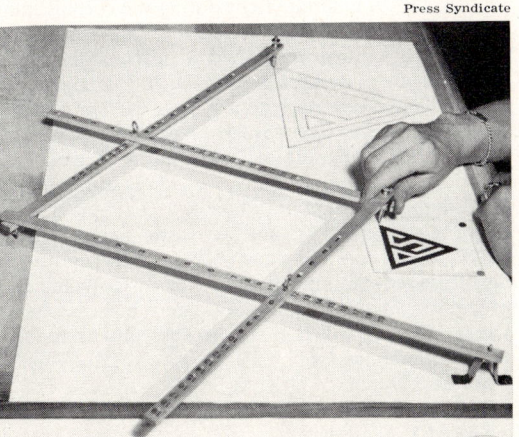

The Story of Cinderella Is Told in Pantomime. Here Cinderella, on her way to the ball, sits in the coach provided

Hans Wild, *Life*

by her fairy godmother. Stories of this kind are frequently acted out in this colorful, but wordless, way.

PANTOMIME, *PAN toh mime*, is acting without words. The word comes from the Greek words meaning *all mimic*. Pantomime usually refers to a short play in which no words are spoken. The actors tell their story by means of gestures. This was a popular form of entertainment in the 1700's and 1800's.

All actors use a certain amount of pantomime when they use gestures instead of words to convey ideas. Many plays have silent passages in which only the movements of the actor's arms, legs, or face express ideas. Modern ballet also has passages that are not strictly dancing, in which the dancer uses expressive movements of parts of the body other than the legs. An opera uses some pantomime, along with singing, instrumental music, and dancing.

No one knows just when pantomime began. It was a popular form of entertainment during the early Roman Empire. The actors wore masks with three compartments. Each compartment had a different face.

Pantomime plays became popular in England in the 1700's. They owed much to a type of Italian comedy, the *commedia dell' arte*. Stock characters included a clown, called Harlequin, a lovable father, called Pantaloon, and a gay daughter, called Columbine (see COLUMBINE; HARLEQUIN; PIERROT). The plays combined music, dancing, and acrobatic acts, and had elaborate scenery and stage effects. The traditional Christmas entertainment in Great Britain includes stage productions of fairy tales and nursery stories. These shows are called *pantos* because they were originally pantomimes.   GLENN HUGHES

See also DANCING (Oriental).

PANZA, SANCHO. See DON QUIXOTE.

PAPACY. See POPE.

PAPAIN. See PAPAYA.

PAPAL BULL. See CONCORDAT.

PAPAL CHAMBERLAIN is the title of several different palace officials in the pope's court in Rome. The Privy Chamberlains to His Holiness and the Chamberlains of Honor of the Purple Habit assist at different Vatican functions and ceremonies. The Chamberlains of Honor *extra Urbem* are chosen from among the clergy of places outside Rome, and have the title of Very Reverend Monsignor.

The Privy Chamberlains of Sword and Cape and Chamberlains of Honor of Sword and Cape have responsibility for many of the secular duties of the papal household.   FULTON J. SHEEN

PAPAL INFALLIBILITY. See VATICAN COUNCIL; POPE (The Powers of the Pope).

PAPAL STATES is a term that refers to the land in Italy over which the Roman Catholic Church formerly had *temporal* (civil) power. Today the Church has temporal power only over the city of the Vatican.

From 756 to 1870 the popes had direct control of several provinces and cities, including Rome, in central Italy. This area was called the Papal States. Pepin the Short, King of the Franks, had given part of the territory to Pope Stephen II. Pepin's successor Charlemagne added to it. In return, Pope Leo III crowned him emperor and gave him the support of the Church in his campaign for power in Western Europe. After the Reformation, the political power of the Pope gradually declined. In 1860, the Papal States became subject to Victor Emmanuel II, who became King of Italy in 1861. Only the land immediately around Rome remained under church control. In 1870, Victor Emmanuel took Rome by force and asked its citizens to vote on whether or not the city should become the capital of a united Italy. The people voted to accept the Italian monarchy. Thereupon Pope Pius IX shut himself up in the Vatican and regarded himself as a prisoner.

The popes after him followed the same policy for nearly 60 years. Then an independent Papal State was created in 1929 through an agreement between Pius XI and the Italian government. The agreement was called the Treaty of the Lateran. Its main parts are as follows:

The treaty reaffirms the principle contained in the first article of the Constitution of the Italian kingdom, by which the Catholic Apostolic Roman religion is the only state religion in Italy.

The treaty recognizes the full property and exclusive dominion and sovereign jurisdiction of the Holy See over the Vatican as at present constituted.

For this purpose, the City of the Vatican is created, and in its territory no interference by the Italian government will be possible, for there will be no authority but the authority of the Holy See.

The Vatican territory will always be considered neutral and inviolable.

The Italian government accepts the canon law in cases of marriage, separation, and other matters over

USDA

Papaya Fruit Has Pulpy Flesh and a thick rind. It is ordinarily eaten raw, but may be cooked or preserved.

The Papal States Before 1870 were large and important tracts of land in the heart of Italy. Today the Holy See has temporal power only over the Vatican City in Rome.

which the Church has jurisdiction.

The Holy See, as a definite settlement of all its financial relations with Italy in consequence of the fall of temporal power, accepts 750,000,000 lire cash (about $37,500,000) and 1,000,000,000 lire (about $50,000,000) in Italian state consols (bonds) at the rate of 5 per cent.   FULTON J. SHEEN

See also ITALY (History); VATICAN CITY.

PAPANICOLAOU SMEAR TEST. See CANCER (How Cancer Is Diagnosed).

PAPAW. See PAPAYA; PAWPAW.

PAPAYA, *puh PIE uh,* is a fruit grown in tropical countries. It has an important place in the diet of the people of these countries. Papaya is eaten raw as a breakfast fruit. Ripe papaya may also be eaten in salads, pies, and sherbets. Because the papaya grows readily from seed, it spread at an early date from its home in Central America to most hot countries. Persons in English-speaking countries often call the papaya *papaw,* or *pawpaw.* This tends to confuse it with the pawpaw of the southeastern United States (see PAWPAW).

The papaya grows on a giant plant which looks like a small palm. The fruit is round to oblong in shape. Sometimes it weighs as much as 10 or 12 pounds. It varies from yellow to dark orange in color. The papaya cannot be shipped long distances because the large hollow cavity in its middle causes the fruit to break down easily when it is ripe and soft. Many black seeds the size of peas are attached to the walls of this cavity. The fruit is mildly sweet, with a slight musky tang.

The plant is normally *dioecious.* That is, the staminate, or male, flowers are borne on one individual, the pistillate, or female, flowers on another. But all sorts of combinations can be found. Sometimes the flowers are perfect, and have the reproductive organs of both sexes.

In addition to the papaya's value as a fruit, it is the source of the drug *papain.* This drug is an enzyme, similar to pepsin, that helps to digest food. It is used as a remedy for dyspepsia and similar ailments, and also as a tenderizer for tough meats before they are cooked.

Scientific Classification. The papaya is a member of the family *Caricaceae.* It is classified as genus *Carica,* species *C. papaya.*   JULIAN C. CRANE

See also PLANT (color picture, Fruits Unknown to Our Forefathers).

PAPEETE. See SOCIETY ISLANDS; TAHITI.

PAPER

PAPER is often called the *handmaiden of civilization*. It is important in the field of knowledge as a keeper of records because it is the material on which manuscripts, books, magazines, and newspapers are printed. The tools of the financial system are paper money, checks, drafts, notes, and stocks and bonds. Communication, industry, and government would be unable to operate without paper. There are about 7,000 different kinds of paper.

Paper consumption per person is often considered a reliable index to the standard of living. The higher the standard of living and the greater the national wealth, the greater the amount of paper used. The United States consumes over 430 pounds of paper and paperboard per person every year. It produces about 44,328,000 tons of paper and paperboard each year.

Chemical engineers have found many ways of treating paper to make it strong, fireproof, and resistant to liquids and acids. As a result, it can replace such materials as wood, cloth, glass, and metals.

All paper is formed into sheets from cellulose fibers. Cellulose is a substance that is found in all plants. Plants that are especially used for papermaking include various kinds of trees, cotton plants, rice, and wheat straws, cornstalks, and such grasses as hemp, jute, and esparto. About nine out of every ten pounds of paper produced in the United States are made from the wood pulp obtained from trees. The pulp of one tree can be used to make hundreds of kinds of paper. From the same shipment of wood, the papermakers can turn out such varied paper products as coarse newsprint, tough greaseproof wrapping paper, and the transparent glassine which covers boxed flowers and candy. The kind of finished paper depends entirely on the manufacturing and chemical processes to which it is subjected. A film similar to paper has even been made from bentonite clay. Particles of this clay mix together, after soaking in water, to form a fireproof, acidproof fabric.

How Paper Is Made

The Raw Materials. For hundreds of years rags were the principal raw material for paper. Today most ordinary paper and many of the finer grades are made from wood pulp. Rag paper is used chiefly for documents that must be kept for many years. High-grade writing paper is generally obtained from cotton rags.

Wood pulp commonly comes from spruce, fir, hemlock, poplar, pine, tamarack, and many hardwood trees. Most of this wood comes from Canada and the northeastern, northwestern, and southern U.S. Canada produces more than a sixth of the world's wood pulp. Europe produces most paper pulp coming from hemp, straw, and esparto.

The Processes. Most pulpwood is made by the mechanical or ground-wood process, and chemical processes.

The *mechanical process* is used chiefly for the production of *newsprint* (paper on which newspapers are printed) and other cheap papers. The logs are held against grindstones, while a spray of water is placed against the stones to prevent charring.

The major *chemical processes* for making pulp from wood are the sulfite, sulfate, and soda processes.

For all of these, the wood is first prepared by being thoroughly washed with water and then cut into chips measuring from five-eighths of an inch to seven-eighths of an inch in length. This is done in a chipping machine which has a revolving steel disk with four or more sharp steel knives mounted on it.

In the *sulfite process* the wood chips are cooked in a closed tank called a *digester*. The chips cook in a solution of calcium bisulfite under steam pressure until the wood forms a pulp.

In the *sulfate process* the wood is cooked in a solution of caustic soda and sodium sulfide.

In the *soda process* the wood chips are cooked with

LEADING PAPER MANUFACTURING COUNTRIES

Tons of paper and paperboard manufactured in 1966

United States 44,328,000	🗞🗞🗞🗞🗞🗞🗞🗞🗞
Canada 11,714,000	🗞🗞🗞
Japan 9,031,000	🗞🗞
Russia 5,737,000	🗞
Great Britain 4,981,000	🗞
Germany (West) 4,780,000	🗞
Finland 3,814,000	🗞
France 3,803,000	🗞
Sweden 3,507,000	🗞
China (Mainland) *3,306,000	🗞

* 1965 estimate, latest information available

Source: Food and Agriculture Organization.

LEADING PAPER MANUFACTURING STATES AND PROVINCES

Tons of paper and paperboard manufactured in 1966

State/Province	
Quebec *4,657,000	🗞🗞🗞🗞🗞🗞🗞🗞🗞
Georgia 3,482,000	🗞🗞🗞🗞🗞🗞🗞
Wisconsin 2,920,000	🗞🗞🗞🗞🗞🗞
Ontario *2,819,000	🗞🗞🗞🗞🗞🗞
Louisiana 2,551,000	🗞🗞🗞🗞🗞🗞
Washington 2,518,000	🗞🗞🗞🗞🗞🗞
Michigan 2,380,000	🗞🗞🗞🗞🗞
Florida 2,344,000	🗞🗞🗞🗞🗞
Maine 2,233,000	🗞🗞🗞🗞🗞
Alabama 2,198,000	🗞🗞🗞🗞🗞

* 1965, latest information available

Sources: Bureau of the Census; Dominion Bureau of Statistics.

HOW PAPER IS MADE FROM WOOD

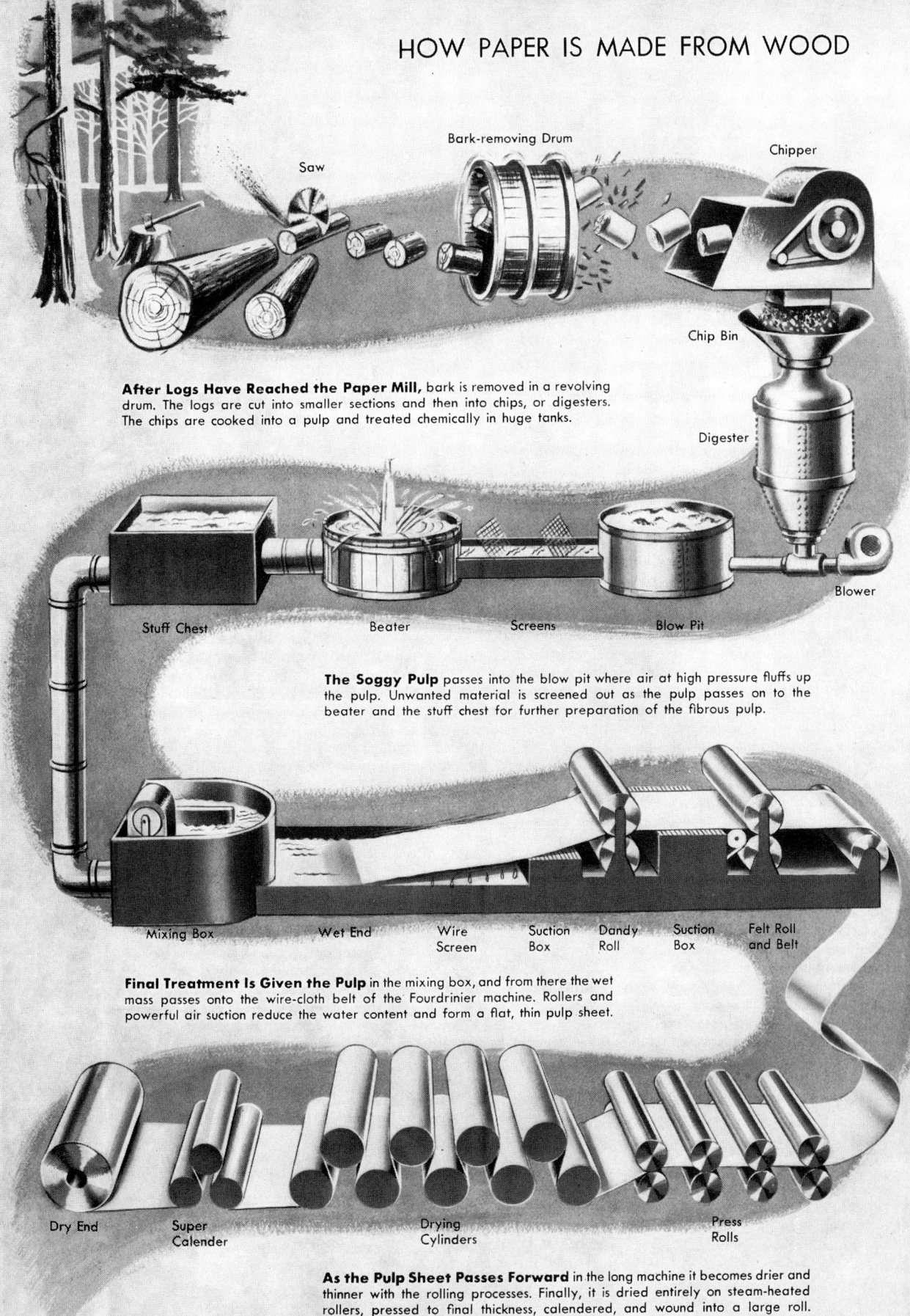

Saw

Bark-removing Drum

Chipper

Chip Bin

Digester

Blower

After Logs Have Reached the Paper Mill, bark is removed in a revolving drum. The logs are cut into smaller sections and then into chips, or digesters. The chips are cooked into a pulp and treated chemically in huge tanks.

Stuff Chest

Beater

Screens

Blow Pit

The Soggy Pulp passes into the blow pit where air at high pressure fluffs up the pulp. Unwanted material is screened out as the pulp passes on to the beater and the stuff chest for further preparation of the fibrous pulp.

Mixing Box   Wet End   Wire Screen   Suction Box   Dandy Roll   Suction Box   Felt Roll and Belt

Final Treatment Is Given the Pulp in the mixing box, and from there the wet mass passes onto the wire-cloth belt of the Fourdrinier machine. Rollers and powerful air suction reduce the water content and form a flat, thin pulp sheet.

Dry End   Super Calender   Drying Cylinders   Press Rolls

As the Pulp Sheet Passes Forward in the long machine it becomes drier and thinner with the rolling processes. Finally, it is dried entirely on steam-heated rollers, pressed to final thickness, calendered, and wound into a large roll.

From "A Pictorial History of Paper" by Stephen Goerl, © Bulkley, Dunton Pulp Co., Inc.

The First Real Paper, made from wood, was invented by the Chinese.

Paper Was First Brought to Europe during the Crusades, some time in the late 1100's.

The Invention of Printing greatly increased the demand for paper.

caustic soda solution to dissolve the materials which hold the cellulose, or papermaking fibers.

Many modifications of the cooking processes have been developed to permit the use of more kinds of wood. These new processes are generally called *semi-chemical* cooking.

The wood pulp made by any of the chemical processes is then washed to free it from the chemical. Then it is passed through a series of screens which remove all knots, cinders, and other foreign material. The pulp is then drained of most of its water to form a thick mass. Next it is bleached in a solution of chlorine and hypochlorite. The pulp is thoroughly washed again and is ready to be put through a process called *beating*.

The *beater* is a large oval-shaped vat, or tub, equipped with many bars which rub and press the cellulose fibers as the wood pulp passes through.

The *Jordan machine* is the next step in the pulp processing. This machine brushes the fibers and cuts them to the proper length.

The *Fourdrinier machine* forms the wet mass of fibers into a sheet. Some of these machines are 300 feet long. The first part, called the *wet end*, is made up of a wire-cloth belt on which the fibers are allowed to mat, or felt, into the form of a sheet. The sheet is dried by being passed over a number of suction boxes which drain out most of the water. The sheet then is squeezed between heavy press rolls and passed over a number of steam-heated drier cylinders. Finally the paper passes through calender presses, where a smooth surface is put on the sheet. It is then wound into large paper rolls.

The *cylinder machine* is used to make heavy paper and paperboard. Wire-covered cylinders, or molds, form the paper. These cylinders are partially immersed in a diluted suspension of paper fibers. The cylinders are rotated. Weights of paper are built up by increasing layers of paper fibers.

Special Kinds of Paper

A blend of pulp is used in making many special papers. Newsprint, for example, is a blend of one part sulfite pulp and three parts of mechanical, or ground wood. Rag pulp, sulfite pulp, and soda pulp are combined to make some writing papers. In addition to the pulp blends, sizing materials, such as clay, rosin size, starch, and alum, may be added to the mixture.

Glue or starch is sometimes added to give the paper a smooth surface for writing or printing ink. Most paper is made water resistant by mixing rosin and alum with the fiber. The fibers may be colored by adding dyes.

The paper sheet is covered with clay and other fine mineral materials when a very smooth surface is desired, as in fine book or magazine paper. The clay is added to the surface of the sheet either by brushes or by rolls. Many paper mills use processes and equipment that permit them to coat high-grade book paper and magazine paper in one continuous operation.

Absorbent papers include such papers as blotting paper, facial tissue, filter paper, matrix paper, toweling, and toilet paper. Such papers are usually made entirely of cotton rag pulp or sulfite pulp, although kraft, or sulfate pulp, may be used for toweling and facial tissues.

Tissue is a lightweight paper made from rags, kraft, sulfite, and soda pulp. It is used for carbon copies of manuscripts and correspondence, stereotyping tissue, insulation, napkins, and paper table cloths.

Paperboard is usually made of kraft pulp or old papers, and of straw pulp. The waste papers consist of old newspapers, cartons, and similar discarded papers. More than 8,500,000 tons of such papers are used by paper mills every year. Paperboard is used chiefly for cartons and containers.

Building papers include roofing felt, wallboard, and asbestos papers. Roofing felt is usually made from old rags and semichemical pulp. It is treated with asphalt to make it fireproof and covered with slate dust and other mineral products to make it wear well.

Wrapping papers and paper bags are usually made of sulfite pulp, kraft pulp, jute, or manila hemp. Manila hemp is especially used for envelopes and tags. Paper used for wrapping articles for overseas shipment is made by laminating a lightweight sheet and a heavier sheet together with asphalt. Vegetable parchment is paper which has been chemically treated with sulfuric acid. It is much like animal-skin parchment in quality (see PARCHMENT).

Writing papers are usually made of rags or of sulfite pulp, or of mixtures of these two. Bond papers are gen-

116

From *A Pictorial History of Paper* by Stephen Goerl. © Bulkley, Dunton Pulp Co., Inc.

The First Paper Mill in America was built at Germantown, Pa., in 1690.

Ground Wood for making paper pulp was first used by the Germans in 1840.

The Sulfite Process of papermaking was invented in 1867.

erally used for business letterheads. A heavy bond is called a *ledger paper*, and is used for keeping records. Sometimes bond papers contain what is called a *watermark*. This is produced by a wire-mesh design which is pressed against the wet pulp sheet before it is fully formed on the Fourdrinier machine. See WATERMARK.

A paper which seems to have a gridiron appearance is called a *laid paper*. One with a plain surface is called a *wove surface*. Among the papers in this group are drawing papers, photographic papers, onionskin papers, Bristol board, and bank-check paper.

Leading Paper Companies

International Paper Company ranks as the largest paper company in the United States. It manufactures kraft pulps and papers for bags and wrappings, and is the leading American producer of newsprint. Crown Zellerbach Corporation is the second largest American paper company. Its chief products include newsprint, wrapping and bag paper, tissues, kraft board, packing materials, and shipping containers.

Other leading paper manufacturing companies, in order of rank, include Weyerhaeuser Company, St. Regis Paper Company, Kimberly-Clark Corporation, The Mead Corporation, and Container Corporation of America. For the sales, assets, and number of employees of each company, see FOREST AND FOREST PRODUCTS (table, 10 Largest Forest Products Companies).

History

Paper gets its name from *papyrus*, a reed which the ancient Egyptians used for making a writing material. The Egyptians cut papyrus stalks into thin slices and pressed them into sheets.

Paper as we know it was invented in China in A.D. 105. It was discovered by Ts'ai Lun, the Emperor Ho-Ti's minister of public works. Ts'ai Lun was dissatisfied with the silk and bamboo that were being used for writing materials, and set out to find something better. He found that the inner bark of the mulberry tree could be broken into fibers and pounded or matted into a sheet. The Chinese later found that good paper could be made by pounding rags, hemp, and old fish nets.

The Chinese art of papermaking spread to other parts of the world after several Chinese papermakers were captured in battles fought between the Arabs and the Chinese in Russian Turkestan. The Chinese prisoners were urged to continue their art and teach it to the Moors at Samarkand. The paper industry was established in Baghdad in A.D. 795. As a result of the Crusades and the Moorish conquest of Northern Africa and Spain, papermaking spread to Europe.

For several hundred years all paper was made by hand from the rag pulp. The process was slow, but there was little demand for paper. In 1750, however, a machine was invented in Holland which reduced the time necessary to break down the rags to fiber. In 1798, Nicholas Louis Robert, a Frenchman, invented a machine to make paper in continuous rolls rather than in small batches. The Fourdrinier brothers financed improvements in this machine in 1803.

In 1840 a German named Keller invented a process for grinding logs into a fibrous pulp. In 1867 an American named Tilghman found that the fibers in wood could be separated if the wood was dissolved in a solution of sulfurous acid. Various European chemists improved on this process so that by 1882 wood pulp was made by processes similar to those in modern paper mills. RONALD G. MACDONALD

Related Articles in WORLD BOOK include:

Cardboard	Lignin	Papyrus
Cellulose	Manuscript	Parchment
Chemurgy	Microcrystalline Wax	Printing
Esparto	Paper Bag	Tall Oil
Foolscap	Paperwork, Decorative	Watermark
Ink	Papier-Mâché	

PAPER BAG is one of our most useful items. It may vary in size from a small candy wrapper to a huge shopping bag. Yet, about a hundred years ago, the paper bag was unknown. In the 1850's, manufacturers shipped most commodities such as flour and sugar to storekeepers in bulk. If the customer did not bring a container, a clerk would make a *cornucopia*, or a twist from paper. As trade developed, many merchants began pasting such containers together in advance. They turned up the end to form a "package" ready for quick use. Several machines for making paper bags were invented in the United States by the early 1860's.

S. E. Pettee built the best known of these machines. He began licensing his apparatus to printers in 1865. He collected a royalty for their use. Pettee's success spurred other inventors to creative effort, but these early attempts did not create the industry. The paper bag industry was born in 1869 when the best features of all types of machinery were purchased and put together in one machine by the Union Company of Pennsylvania.

The swift success of the concerns that started paper bag manufacture caused the Union Company to go into business itself in 1875 as the Union Bag and Paper Company. In the first year it made 606 million bags. This was a fabulous number in those days, and the industry was established. The mass production cut costs to retailers so much that ever since, every shop in the United States has made a paper bag a free part of each purchase for which it is necessary. Today, factories in the United States make more than 1,200,000 tons of these convenient paper containers each year.

Manufacturers produce four main types of paper bags: The *flat bag* is a flat tube sealed at one end, such as a small candy bag. The *square bag* has tucks at the sides to give more space. A popcorn bag is an example. The *satchel-bottom bag* has a large bottom section so that it will stand upright when filled. The *automatic bag* has a rectangle-shaped bottom and tucks in the side, so it can be opened easily with a snap of the hand.

Specialty bags include bags with slick linings to prevent snagging fragile items. Others may be greaseproof, mothproof, or heat-sealed.   STUART LITTLE

PAPER NAUTILUS. See ARGONAUT (mollusk).

PAPERMAKERS AND PAPERWORKERS, UNITED, is an international union that represents Canadian and American workers in the pulp, paper, and paper-products industries. It has about 750 local unions, and is a member of the AFL-CIO. The union was formed in March, 1957, with the merger of the International Brotherhood of Paper Makers, founded in 1893, and the United Paperworkers of America, founded in 1937. Headquarters are at 712-718 N. Pearl Street, Albany, N.Y. 12201. For membership, see LABOR (table).

Critically reviewed by the UNITED PAPERMAKERS AND PAPERWORKERS

PAPERWORK, DECORATIVE. People have designed and used decorative paper for several hundred years. Decorative papers can be divided into several categories, including end papers, lining papers, wallpaper, wrapping paper, and paper handicrafts.

End Papers date back to early printed books. Printers pasted these papers on the inside covers of the books. Most end papers were made of *marbled* paper, printed to resemble the lined and mottled effect characteristic of marble. Craftsmen also used other simple designs.

Lining Papers often have gay floral designs with a recurrent bird pattern. They may also consist of small, repeated landscapes in an informal setting or as an inset in a well-designed framework. People use lining papers to line drawers and to cover cupboards and shelves. These papers lined the coach boxes of the 1800's, and the inside and outside of hatboxes.

Wallpaper has been used for hundreds of years in such countries as France, England, and the United States. Paper hangers of earlier times did not remove the old papers before applying new ones. Decorators have found interesting examples of wallpaper by peeling off layers of paper from the walls of old houses.

Artists of the 1700's designed wallpaper with formal landscape scenes. Such paper was made only for the wealthy. People used it in France and England, and imported it into the United States. The Lee Mansion in Marblehead, Mass., has a beautifully preserved example of this type of paper. Chinese objects and patterns, called *Chinoiserie*, enjoyed great popularity during the 1700's. Merchants imported wallpaper from China.

Several noted artists have designed wallpaper, and have given it originality, interesting appearance, and new uses in interior decoration. See WALLPAPER.

Wrapping Paper. Much decorative paperwork of today comes in the form of wrapping paper. Attractive patterns make it suitable for special objects and events, such as holidays and birthdays. *Packaging*, a form of wrapping, is the art of presenting an object in an attractive way so as to sell it. See PACKAGING.

Paper Handicrafts were a fashionable pastime as early as the 1600's. Samuel Pepys mentioned in his famous diary a paper basket made by his sister. In the United States, people use paper to make decorations and favors for parties and other events. Crepe paper, a colored paper crinkled to resemble crepe cloth, is widely used for such objects as flowers, costumes, accessories, and holiday novelties, including Christmas tree ornaments. People in other countries also find many uses for decorative paper. The Japanese have developed a kind of paper sculpture called *origami* in which they fold paper to make birds and flowers.

Technical processes used to print decorative papers include wood and linoleum blocks.   ARTHUR ZAIDENBERG

PAPIAMENTO. See NETHERLANDS ANTILLES.

PAPIER-MÂCHÉ, *PAY pur muh SHAY*, is a French term meaning *pulped paper*. Papier-mâché can be made by churning ordinary newspaper in water until the fibers are well separated. The excess water is then squeezed out, glue is added, and the soft material is molded into any desired form. It later hardens and becomes fairly durable. Papier-mâché is often used for making relief maps. It takes paint well, so the maps can be colored to give a better picture of mountains and valleys.

Papier-mâché pulp can be mixed with clay, sand, lime, salt, or borax to give it body. Sodium phosphate makes it fireproof. Halloween masks, doll heads, toy helmets, and picnic plates are a few of the many things made of papier-mâché. When pressed and waterproofed, it is used for making such things as water buckets.

An important use of papier-mâché is in casting printing plates. When paper fibers are mixed with a heat-resisting material and pressed upon printing type, they will take an impression of the metal with great exactness. This paper mat is dried, and then, carrying the impression of the type, it is placed in a casting device and molten metal is poured in. Castings made in this way are the printing surfaces for the high-speed printing presses used to print newspapers.   GEORGE L. BUSH

PAPILIONOIDEAE. See LEGUME.

PAPILLA. See HAIR; SKIN; TONGUE.

PAPILLON, *PAP uh lahn*, is a small breed of dogs. They usually weigh between 5 and 11 pounds. Papillon is French for *butterfly*, and refers to the odd, butterfly-like shape of the dog's ears. The papillon has a long, silky coat which may vary in color. Its bushy tail is

DECORATIVE PAPERWORK MAY BE:

Expanded

Bent

Curled

Scored

Pleated

Fasten identical shapes of paper through the center and spread them apart for a three-dimensional effect.

Bend partially cut-out sections of paper outward for a sculptured effect.

Decorate finished figures with pieces of colored paper or paint.

MATERIALS

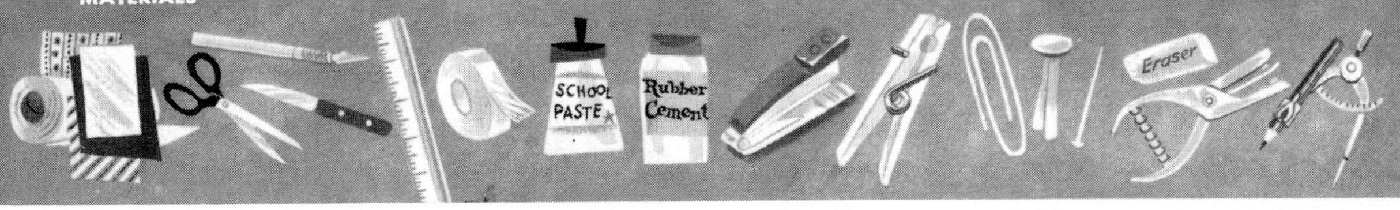

SCHOOL PASTE

Rubber Cement

Eraser

Decorative Paperwork makes gay and colorful place cards, favors, and other party decorations, *above*. The "distinguished" official, *right*, was fashioned from colored construction paper.

Papier-Mâché can be modeled into figures of almost any size or shape, *below*. A pulp mixture works well for small figures. Strips applied to a basic frame formed the arched cat, *right*.

Photos: Dept. of Art, University of Illinois

MATERIALS FOR PAPIER-MÂCHÉ

PASTE   PAINT

Roll and tie newspaper to make foundations for larger forms. Then apply papier-mâché.

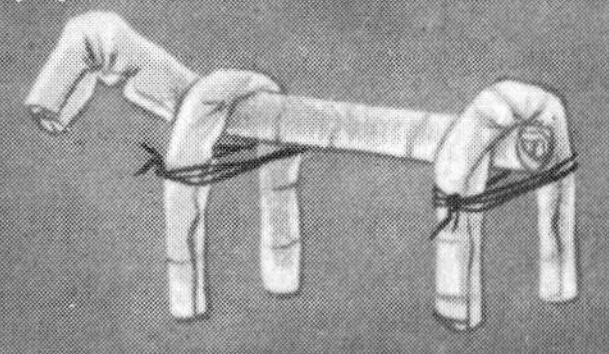

MODELING WITH PULP

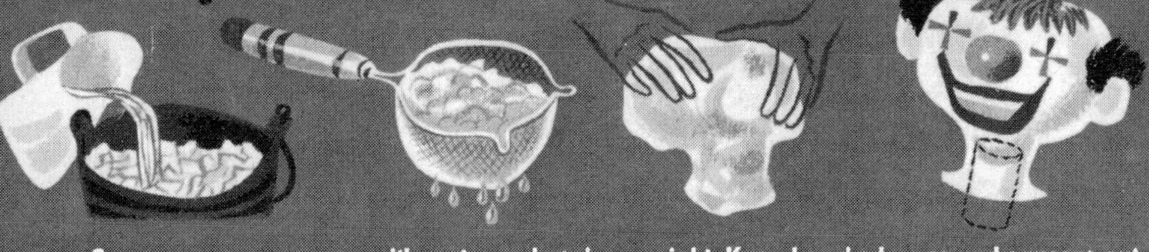

Cover newspaper scraps with water and soak overnight. Knead soaked mass and squeeze out excess water by straining through a sieve. Add paste to hold the mixture together and model it like clay. Decorate the figure after drying. A head modeled over a tube can be used as a puppet.

MODELING WITH STRIPS

Soak 1" x 6" newspaper strips in water for 15 minutes. Grease a gourd and cover it with 6 to 10 layers of paper and paste. When dry, cut through covering and remove gourd core. Fit halves together, cover the joint, and then decorate.

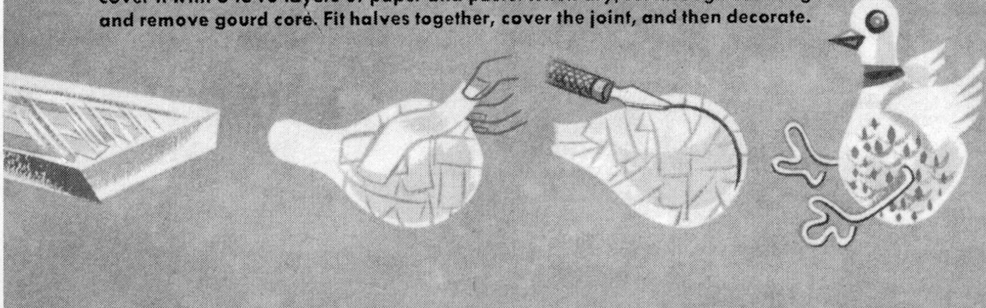

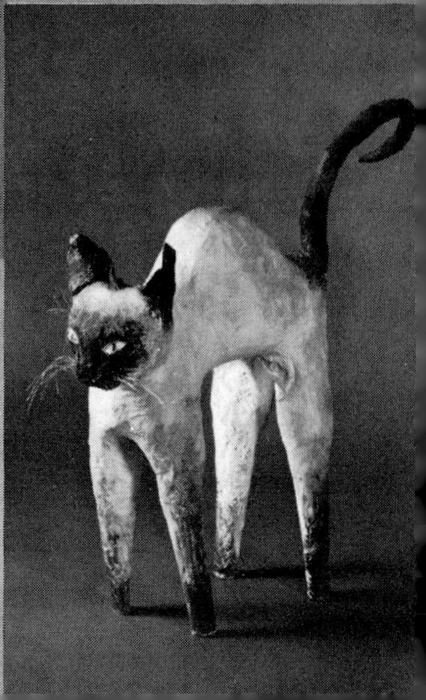

Papillons Were Originally Called Dwarf Spaniels.

Mary Eleanor Browning—Photo Researchers

PAPOOSE is a term sometimes used for a North American Indian baby. Women of some tribes carried their papooses on cradleboards slung on their backs.

PAPRIKA, *puh PREE kuh,* is a favorite household seasoning. It is prepared from the pods of a cultivated pepper plant called *capsicum* (see CAPSICUM). After the seeds have been removed, the pods are dried and powdered. Paprika has a bright-red color, but is less biting than red or cayenne pepper, and has a sweeter taste. See also PEPPER. HAROLD NORMAN MOLDENKE

PAPUA, *PAH pooh uh,* is an Australian territory in the southeastern part of New Guinea. For location, see NEW GUINEA (map). It covers 86,100 square miles and has about 685,000 persons. Port Moresby is the capital of the territory. The British colony of Queensland in Australia annexed the southeast section of New Guinea in 1883. Britain recognized Queensland's claim in 1884 and made the area a protectorate. In 1906, Britain renamed the area Papua and transferred it to the Commonwealth of Australia. See also PORT MORESBY.

PAPYRUS, *pah PIE ruhs,* is an Egyptian water plant whose fibers were used by the ancients as a writing material. It served also as a material for mats, sandals, and sailcloth for light skiffs. The brownish flowers were made into garlands for the shrines of the Egyptian gods. Many people think the little ark in which the mother of Moses hid her son was made of papyrus. Some scholars believe different species of papyrus were used for these purposes, and that all were called by one name.

The plant still grows in the valley of the Upper Nile. It looks like a reed. It has large, straight stems, which grow from 3 to 10 feet in height and bear no foliage. The coarse, sharp-edged leaves spring directly from the rootstock. The flowers are surrounded by bristles.

curved up over its back. This breed was developed in Spain in the 1500's, and is believed to be a relative of the chihuahua. JOSEPHINE Z. RINE

See also CHIHUAHUA; TOY DOG.

PAPINEAU, *PAHP uh no,* or *PAH PEE NO,* **LOUIS JOSEPH** (1786-1871), led the French-Canadian radicals after 1815 in their demands for reform in Canada's government. Papineau had to flee from Canada after the unsuccessful rebellion of 1837. After the amnesty of 1845, he returned and served as a member of the Canadian parliament until 1854. Papineau was born in Montreal. See also CANADA, HISTORY OF (Lord Durham's Report). W. R. WILLOUGHBY

Papyrus, a rough but durable substance, has preserved the records written by Egyptians thousands of years ago.

From *A Pictorial History of Paper* by Stephen Goerl, © Bulkley, Dunton Pulp Co., Inc.

The Papyrus Plant of Egypt was the source of man's first writing paper. The plant is comparatively rare today.

Pomona Quartermaster Depot

A Bulgarian Peasant Woman Strings Pepper Pods.
When dried, the pods will be ground into paprika.

The papyrus of the Egyptians was made of strips of the stem. They were laid in layers, and then placed under pressure. The crushed strips matted into a loose-textured, porous, white paper. Time has turned surviving papyrus manuscripts brown and has made them brittle. Papyrus first appeared in the shape of long, rectangular sheets in different sizes. The sheets were at first rolled and tied with a string. Later they were bound together like the modern books.

Until the 100's B.C., Egypt guarded the monopoly of preparing the paper. Then papyrus was gradually replaced by the more durable parchment.

Scientific Classification. The papyrus plant belongs to the sedge family, *Cyperaceae*. It is classified as genus *Cyperus*, species *C. papyrus*.   FRANK THONE

See also PAPER (History); SCROLL.

PAR. See INVESTMENT (Terms); GOLF.

PARA, *pah RAH*, is a standard coin of Yugoslavia. A hundred paras equal one Yugoslavian dinar. For the value of the dinar, see MONEY (table: Values).

PARÁ NUT. See BRAZIL NUT.

PARABLE, *PAR uh b'l*, is a brief story. It uses events and facts of everyday life. These happenings illustrate a moral or spiritual truth contained in the story. Greek and Latin writers used the parable, but the best examples of the parable are found in the Bible.

One of the best-known parables comes from the Old Testament. Nathan told David a parable about a rich man who seized and killed a poor man's only sheep. The rich man used the excuse that he wanted to feed a traveler who called at his door. David became angry at the story of the man's cruelty. Then Nathan turned on David, saying, "Thou art the man" (II Sam. 12: 1-7).

Jesus used many parables in His teachings. *The Good*

Samaritan (Luke 10: 30-37) tells of a wayfarer who helped a stranger. The stranger had been beaten and robbed by thieves. This parable shows the virtue of neighborliness.

Several parables in Matthew 13 show the growth of the Kingdom of God among men. One is the story of the sower who planted seeds in different kinds of soil. Another tells of the mustard seed that grew into a great tree. Still another is the parable of the leaven that made the whole loaf light. Three parables in Luke 15 picture the joy felt in heaven over a wanderer's return to the Kingdom. These parables are called *The Lost Sheep*, *The Lost Coin*, and *The Prodigal Son*.   FULTON J. SHEEN

See also ALLEGORY.

PARABOLA, *puh RAB oh luh*, is one of the curves most used in science. If a ballplayer hits a high fly, the path of the ball is nearly a parabola. Any point on a parabola is the same distance from a line *AB* as it is from point *C*. Line *AB* is the *directrix* and point *C* is the *focus*. The solid line through point *C*, which bisects the parabola, is called the *axis*.

A parabola revolved about its axis generates a *para-*

The **Parabola**, *right*, is a common curve. The graph, *below*, shows the nearly parabolic paths of balls thrown at different angles. Numbers show height and distance in feet.

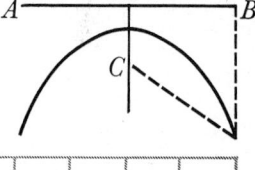

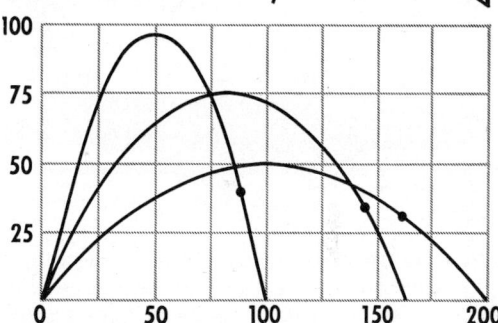

bolic surface. A light at the focus of a mirror with this shape would cause the light rays that hit the mirror to reflect parallel to the axis. Scientists use this principle of the parabolic surface in producing headlight and searchlight reflectors.   ROTHWELL STEPHENS

PARACELSUS, *PAR uh SELL sus*, **PHILIPPUS AUREOLUS** (1493?-1541), a Swiss physician, pioneered in the application of chemistry to medicine and introduced the use of many drugs. He sharply attacked the foundations of ancient medicine, but everywhere he went he met opposition to his theories. However, some of his theories foreshadowed modern medical practices. Paracelsus was the first to point out the relation between goiter in the parent and a condition called *cretinism* in the child (see CRETINISM).

Paracelsus was born near Einsiedeln, Switzerland. His real name was THEOPHRASTUS BOMBASTUS VON HOHENHEIM. He received his early education from his father, a physician and chemist.   CAROLINE A. CHANDLER

See also CHEMISTRY (Chemistry in Medicine; picture: Famous Men of Chemistry); MEDICINE (History).

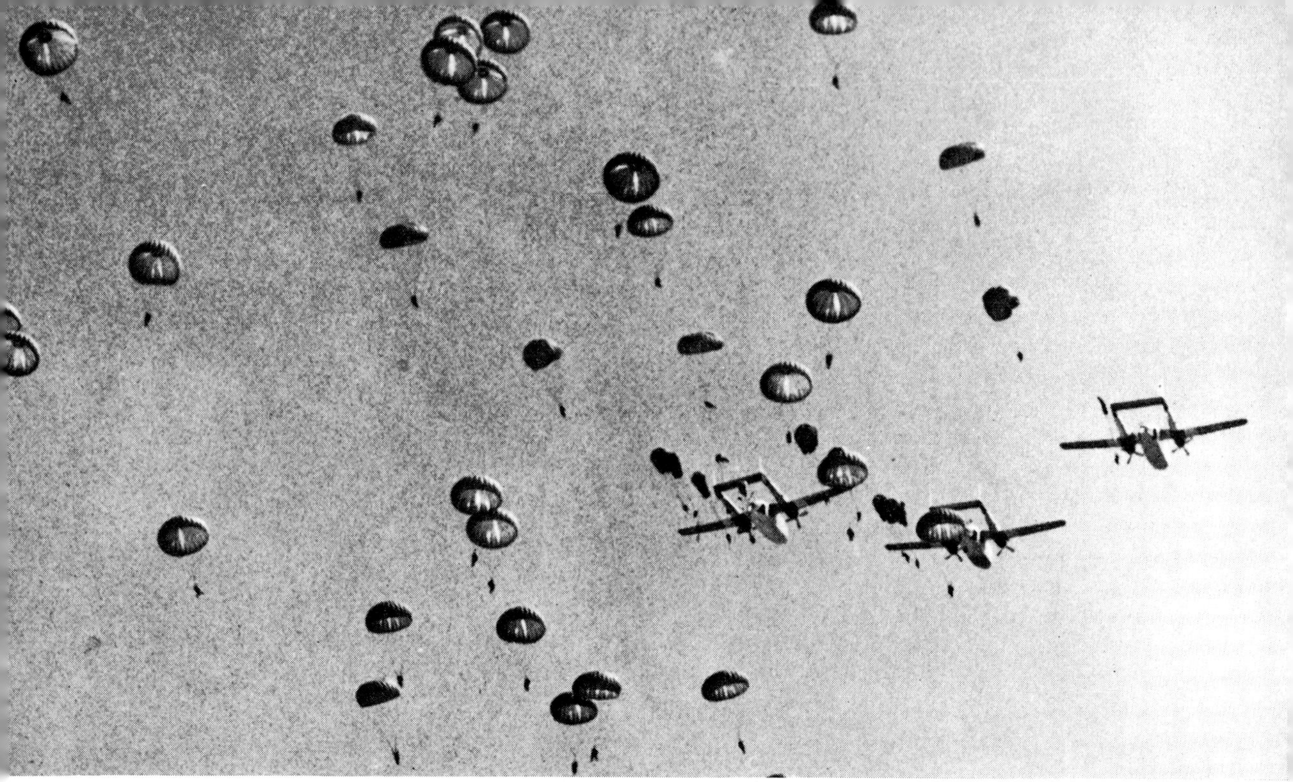

Pegasus Magazine

Paratroopers first fought in World War II. They dropped behind enemy lines to launch sudden surprise attacks.

High-Speed Military Planes often use "drag parachutes," *left,* to slow them down while they are landing.

Pioneer Parachute Co., Inc.

PARACHUTE, *PAR uh shoot*, looks somewhat like a large umbrella. It is used to slow down the fall of a person or an object from aircraft or from any other great height. The operation of the parachute is based on simple principles. There are two forces that act on any falling object—air resistance and gravity. Gravity pulls the object quickly toward the earth. But air resists the object's movement. Because the pull of gravity is much stronger than the resistance of the air, the air can only slow down the speed of the falling object. Large, flat surfaces offer a greater area of resistance to the air than do thin, sharp surfaces. Therefore, an object shaped like a saucer falls more slowly than one shaped like a needle.

Uses of Parachutes. One of the early uses for parachutes was to allow descent from gas-filled balloons. In modern times, parachutes are used for emergency jumps from aircraft. They are also used to deliver cargo. Airplanes and helicopters drop food and medicine by parachute to places that cannot be reached easily by other means. Special military uses were developed during the 1930's. Both the Allies and Germans used *paratroops*, or parachute troops, during World War II. Some jet planes use parachutes as brakes in landing. They are also used for recovering experimental guided missiles and radio-controlled flying targets.

How Parachutes Are Made. For many years parachutes were made of silk. But nylon, which is stronger and cheaper, is used more generally today. Those designed for human use are about 24 to 28 feet across when extended. Parachutes used for cargo are sometimes 100 feet across. The most commonly worn parachute is the *seat pack*. Others attach to the wearer's chest or back.

Parachutes are worn on a *harness*, that consists of a series of straps fitting around the shoulders and legs of the parachutist. The harness acts as a support during descent. Special straps, called *risers*, are attached to the shoulder portion of the harness. They hold the lines, or *shrouds*, which are attached to the *canopy*, the umbrella-like part of the parachute. Also attached to one of the harness straps is a ring for pulling the *rip cord*. When this cord is pulled, the parachute springs out of the pack and the air forces it open. As soon as the canopy opens, the air slows the descent so quickly that the parachutist jerks sharply. To reduce the force of this opening shock, manufacturers have designed a special *ribbon* parachute. This type has holes or slots in the canopy that allow some of the air to flow through, thus reducing the area of resistance. These openings also reduce the amount of swaying during the descent of the parachute.

Manufacturers have developed still another type of parachute called the *vortex ring* parachute. It has four cloth sections that rotate during descent. The rotating sections function much like the rotating wings of a helicopter and allow better control of the parachute. See HELICOPTER.

Parachute Jumping. Parachutes descend at the rate of about 15 feet a second or slightly faster, depending on the weight of the parachutist. Parachute jumps from less than 500 feet above the ground are dangerous because this height does not allow enough distance for the parachute to open.

Parachutists land with such force that they can sprain their ankles or break some bones. This is particularly true if they land on rough ground. Wind also creates a hazard because it adds sideways speed to the speed of the fall. It is as if the parachutist had jumped from a moving car. Therefore, it is important for the parachutist to have some control over his parachute. He must also be able to judge wind speed, altitude, and direction. Parachute jumping has become a sport that has gained many followers in Europe and America.

History. The first successful parachute jump was made from a tower in 1783 by the French physicist

Leonardo da Vinci drew a sketch, *left*, of a parachute he designed in 1495. He called it a "tent roof."

An Early Parachute illustration, *right*, was made in 1617 to accompany an article by an Italian experimenter.

U.S. National Air Museum

Sebastien Lenormand (1757-1839). In 1797, another Frenchman, André Jacques Garnerin, made the first parachute jump from a balloon (see GARNERIN, ANDRÉ JACQUES). ARCHIBALD BLACK

See also AIRBORNE TROOPS; SKYDIVING.

PARADE is a public march or procession honoring a particular occasion. The mood of a parade may vary from joyous excitement to solemn dignity. Members of the armed forces often parade on holidays to show off their strength, condition, equipment, and skill. Many parades are colorful events, with floats, band music, brightly dressed marchers, and trained animals.

Parades in the form of religious processions go back

to about 3000 B.C. Ancient cities often had special, elaborately constructed streets whose main function was to provide a place for processions. The Romans enjoyed parades, especially the processions of the performers at the circus. They also had frequent military parades, called *triumphs*, during the time of the empire (see TRIUMPH). Parades to honor particular feasts became popular in the early Christian church, and remain so today. Political parades were especially popular in the United States in the 1880's and 1890's. See also FEASTS AND FESTIVALS (picture).

PARADISE is a name for heaven. It was originally a Persian word used for the amusement parks of Persian kings. The Greeks borrowed the word from the Persians. Translators of the Old Testament used the word to mean the Garden of Eden (Gen. 2: 8). But the early Christians used the name to mean the future home of the blessed dead. Jesus used the word in this sense when He spoke to the dying thief upon the cross. See also HEAVEN. MERVIN MONROE DEEMS and FULTON J. SHEEN

PARADISE LOST is a long epic poem written by John Milton "to justify the ways of God to man." Based on the Bible, it tells the story of the creation, the revolt of Satan, and his temptation of man. The poem ends as Adam and Eve are expelled from the Garden of Eden. But the Archangel Michael has promised that a Messiah will redeem mankind. Milton, then totally blind, dictated the poem to his daughters. As a result, his blank verse sounds like formal oratory and is frequently compared with organ music. GEORGE A. WICKES

See also EPIC; MILTON, JOHN.

PARAFFIN, *PAIR uh fin,* is a white, partly clear, waxy solid that has no odor or taste. Paraffin forms a moisture-proof film, and is used to make waterproof cardboard containers such as milk cartons. It is also the major ingredient in candles.

Paraffin is made from a mixture of high-boiling petroleum *fractions* (products separated from petroleum). The fractions are chilled and pressed through a filter to remove heavy oil. The remaining solid is paraffin wax.

Ordinary paraffin wax melts at 90° to 150° F. (32° to 66° C.) *Micro-crystalline wax* is composed of larger *hydrocarbons* (a substance containing hydrogen and carbon) than ordinary wax. It melts at 150° to 185° F. (66° to 85° C.) CLARENCE KARR, JR.

See also WAX.

PARAGLIDER. See SPACE TRAVEL (Getting into Space and Back).

PARAGRAPH is a division of written work, consisting of one or more sentences, all related to the same idea. Usually the first line of a paragraph is indented. That is, the first sentence begins a few spaces to the right of the left-hand margin of writing. In some business letters, paragraphs are not indented and a line is left blank between paragraphs. Both methods are designed to help the reader follow the written material.

The paragraph has special forms in newspaper stories and in written conversation. In a news story, the first paragraph is often a single sentence. Paragraphs are not usually directly connected to each other, and so the end of the story may be cut at any point. In writing conversation, a new paragraph is used every time a different person speaks. PAUL ROBERTS

Three Lions

Asunción Is Paraguay's Capital and Chief Port. It Lies on the Paraguay River.

PARAGUAY, *PAR uh gwy*, or *PAR uh gway*, is a small landlocked republic in the heart of South America. The name of the country in Spanish is REPÚBLICA DEL PARAGUAY, meaning REPUBLIC OF PARAGUAY. It is the only country with a flag whose front and back differ. Asunción is the capital and largest city.

Paraguay has about the same area as Kansas and Nebraska, but has only about half as many people. Farmers raise crops in the rich soil. Cattle graze on rolling green pastures. Western Paraguay is the world's chief source of quebracho trees. The bark of quebracho trees is used to make tannin, a leather-tanning material. Orange trees cover many slopes of eastern Paraguay, and line the streets of the cities. The western plains contain oil and other mineral deposits.

Even with its resources, Paraguay is one of the world's poorest countries. Most of the people are farmers, but they raise only enough food for their families. The small population, the lack of a seaport, and unstable governments have hindered the nation's growth. For information about Paraguay's relations with neighboring countries, see LATIN AMERICA; SOUTH AMERICA.

The Land and Its Resources

Location and Size. Paraguay is bordered by Bolivia on the north, Brazil on the east, and Argentina on the south and west. It covers 157,048 square miles.

Land Regions. The Paraguay River divides Paraguay into the eastern region and the Chaco region.

The Eastern Region. Highlands extend from Brazil and rise about 1,600 feet in eastern Paraguay. Rolling foothills spread south, east, and west of the highlands. The

John Tate Lanning, the contributor of this article, is Professor of History at Duke University, and former managing editor of Hispanic American Historical Review.

--- **FACTS IN BRIEF** ---

Form of Government: Republic.

Capital: Asunción.

Official Language: Spanish.

Area: 157,048 square miles. *Greatest Distances*—(north-south) 575 miles; (east-west) 410 miles.

Population: *1962 Census*—1,851,890; distribution, 64 per cent rural, 36 per cent urban. *Estimated 1970 Population*—2,368,000; density, 15 persons to the square mile. *Estimated 1975 Population*—2,759,000.

Chief Products: *Agriculture*—cattle, citrus fruits, corn, cotton, rice, sugar cane, tobacco. *Forest Products*—lumber, petitgrain oil, quebracho extract, yerba maté. *Manufacturing and Processing*—canned meats, leather goods, processed fruits, vegetable oils.

Flag: The red, white, and blue horizontal stripes are believed to honor French ideals. The national coat of arms is centered on the front of the flag. The treasury seal with a lion and liberty cap appears on the back. See FLAG (color picture: Flags of the Americas).

National Anthem: "Himno Nacional del Paraguay" ("National Anthem of Paraguay").

National Holiday: Independence Day, May 14.

Money: *Basic Unit*—guaraní. One hundred céntimos are equal to one guaraní. For the value of the guaraní in United States dollars, see MONEY (table: Values).

124

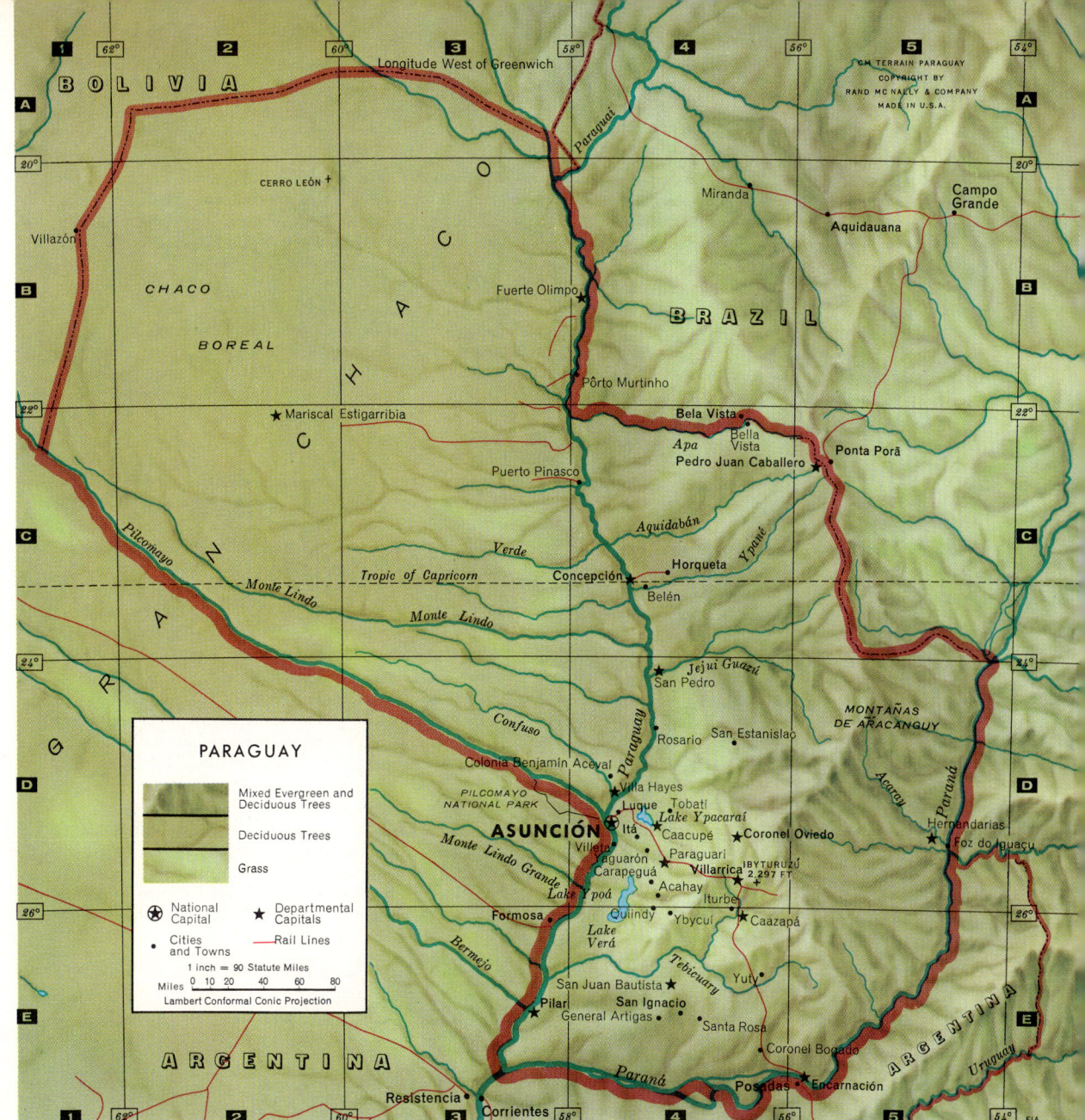

Specially created for **World Book Encyclopedia** by Rand McNally and World Book editors

Departments*

ALTO PARANÁ	26,680	D 5
AMAMBAY	33,782	C 5
ASUNCIÓN, D.C.**	305,160	D 4
BOQUERÓN	42,223	B 2
CAAGUAZÚ	123,590	D 5
CAAZAPÁ	91,807	E 5
CENTRAL	204,719	D 4
CONCEPCIÓN	86,336	C 4
CORDILLERA	189,041	D 4
GUAIRÁ	114,297	D 4
ITAPÚA	151,035	E 5
MISIONES	59,454	E 4
ÑEEMBUCÚ	58,621	E 4
OLIMPO	3,362	B 3
PARAGUARÍ	204,220	D 4
PRESIDENTE HAYES	31,572	C 3
SAN PEDRO	90,991	C 4

Cities and Towns

Acahay	2,502	D 4
Areguá*	3,734	D 4
Asunción	305,160	D 4
Belén	2,523	C 4
Bella Vista	2,292	C 4
Caacupé	4,329	D 4
Caazapá	3,588	E 4
Carapeguá	2,645	D 4
Colonia Benjamín Aceval	3,115	D 4
Colonia Nueva Italia*	2,155	D 4
Concepción	18,232	C 4
Coronel Bogado	3,839	E 4
Coronel Oviedo	9,503	D 4
Encarnación	18,504	E 5
Eusebio Ayala*	2,268	D 4
Fernando de la Mora*	8,638	D 4
Fuerte Olimpo	1,666	B 4
General Artigas	3,106	E 4
Guarambaré*	3,779	D 4
Hernandarias	2,311	D 5
Horqueta	5,095	C 4
Itá	6,223	D 4
Itacurubí*	2,154	D 4
Itauguá*	3,053	D 4
Iturbe	3,239	E 4
Luque	10,834	D 4
Mariscal Estigarribia	1,508	C 2
Paraguarí	4,968	D 4
Pedro Juan Caballero	10,187	C 5
Pilar	7,478	E 3
Pirayú*	2,733	D 4
Piribebuy*	3,769	D 4
Puerto Pinasco	4,495	C 4
Quiindy	2,732	E 4
Rosario	4,580	D 4
San Antonio*	2,889	D 4
San Estanislao	2,894	D 4
San Ignacio	5,344	E 4
San José*	2,418	D 4
San Juan Bautista	5,351	E 4
San Lorenzo*	7,620	D 4
San Pedro	3,317	D 4
Santa Rosa	2,630	E 4
Sapucai*	2,298	D 4
Tobatí	2,397	D 4
Villa Hayes	4,330	D 4
Villarrica	16,739	D 4
Villeta	2,904	D 4
Yaguarón	2,784	D 4
Ybycuí	3,072	E 4
Ypacaraí*	5,330	D 4
Yuty	2,403	E 4

Physical Features

Acaray River		D 5
Apa River		C 4
Aquidabán River		C 4
Cerro León (Mountain)		B 2
Chaco Boreal (Plain)		B 2
Confuso River		D 3
Gran Chaco (Plain)		C 2
Jejuí Guazú River		D 4
Lake Verá		E 4
Lake Ypacaraí		D 4
Lake Ypoá		D 4
Montañas de Aracanguy (Mountains)		D 5
Monte Lindo River		C 3
Paraguay River		D 4
Paraná River		D 5
Pilcomayo River		C 2
Tebicuary River		E 4
Verde River		C 3
Ypané River		C 4

*Does not appear on the map; key shows general location.   **A separate territorial division.   Source: Latest census figures (1962).

125

PARAGUAY

land gradually becomes lower and flatter as it stretches west to the Paraguay River, and south and east to the Paraná River. Most of the people live in the low, marshy region along the Paraguay River. In southern Paraguay, near the Paraná River, the land lies only a few hundred feet above sea level. Marshes and evergreen forests cover this area.

The Chaco Region. The vast, flat Chaco region lies west of the Paraguay River. This area of lowlands, plains, and scattered forests covers about two-thirds of the country. It is part of the region called the Gran Chaco, which extends into southwestern Brazil, eastern Bolivia, and northern Argentina. In the Chaco region, the ground rises gradually from the Paraguay River to the western border of the country, where it reaches about 1,000 feet. Less than 40 of every 100 Paraguayans live in the Chaco. The region has poor transportation, and the land in the region is not as rich as that of eastern Paraguay.

Rivers, Waterfalls, and Lakes. The Paraná River forms the southeastern boundary and provides the country's only outlet to the sea. It joins the Río de la Plata, which flows into the Atlantic Ocean. Waterfalls and rapids stretch for almost 100 miles along the Paraná where it separates Paraguay and Brazil. The Paraguay River links Asunción, the main port, with the Paraná. The Pilcomayo River flows through the Chaco, forming Paraguay's southwestern boundary. The country's two largest lakes are Lake Ypoá and Lake Ypacarai.

Natural Resources. Rich pastures and fertile soil cover the rolling hills of eastern Paraguay. Quebracho trees grow in the Chaco region. The land contains deposits of iron, manganese, copper, limestone, salt, and kaolin. The Chaco region has petroleum deposits.

Climate. Paraguay has a climate similar to that of Florida. Temperatures average 50° F. in winter and 85° F. in summer. Thunderstorms occur frequently in summer, but there is no rainy season. The heaviest rains fall in the east. They often total as much as 60 inches a year.

Life of the People

Most Paraguayans are *mestizos* (people of mixed white and Indian ancestry). The Guaraní Indians were the first people to live in Paraguay, but war and intermarriage with the Spaniards have reduced the number of pure-blooded Guaraní to about 17,000. Most of them live in farm areas, as do most other people in Paraguay. About two-thirds of the country's population live in agricultural districts. The rest live in cities.

Almost every Paraguayan belongs to the Roman Catholic Church, the state church. The government supports the church, but the constitution guarantees freedom to all religions.

Language. Paraguay is the only American nation in which an Indian language is spoken as much as the official language. Spanish and *Guaraní* (the language of the Indians) are spoken to almost the same degree, but school children are taught only in Spanish. Government forms and newspapers are published in both Spanish and Guaraní.

Way of Life. On the average, Paraguayan families have about five children. The father usually farms the land, while the mother cooks, manages the home, and cares for the children. The mother and children often work in the fields with the men.

Shelter. Most people in the cities live in small one-story houses made of brick and plastered on the outside. Many homes have pale-colored fronts, red tiled roofs, and iron grillwork on the windows. Vines cover many of the houses, and trees, roses, and flowering shrubs often surround them.

Most farm families live in one-room houses that have earthen floors, mud walls, and thatch roofs.

Food. The people eat much meat (particularly beef), many kinds of vegetables, and citrus fruits (especially oranges). Meat stews, such as *puchero*, make up an important part of the diet. Paraguayans also enjoy *yerba maté*, a South American tea.

Clothing. People in the cities wear clothes similar to those worn in the United States and Canada. In country areas, men and women often go barefoot. The women wear knee-length cotton dresses and cotton *mantas*. The manta is a scarf arranged to form both a headdress and a wrapping for the shoulders. The men usually wear shirts and trousers made of cotton.

Recreation. Sportsmen from many countries hunt jaguars, wild hogs, deer, crocodiles, and game birds in the Chaco region. The people also enjoy such sports as soccer, golf, tennis, and swimming. They hold religious festivals on Paraguay's many holy days.

City Life. Asunción is Paraguay's largest city. Other cities include Concepción, Encarnación, and Villarrica. Most Paraguayan cities have few public buildings less than 100 years old. City streets are often lined with trees and flowers. A large rural population usually lives near the major cities of Paraguay. See ASUNCIÓN.

Country Life. In the small towns, the buildings cluster around a whitewashed Roman Catholic church in the village square. Most families live in small mud huts and raise only their own food. Less than half the farm people own or even rent their land. Most families simply

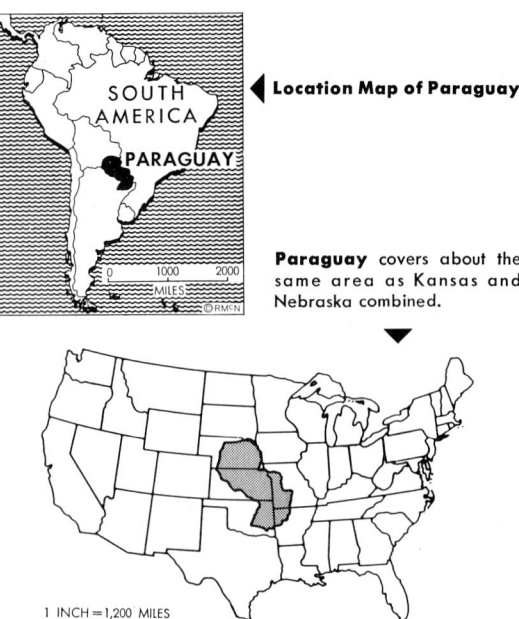

Location Map of Paraguay

Paraguay covers about the same area as Kansas and Nebraska combined.

Three Lions

A Country Town in Paraguay Centers Around the Grass-Covered Town Square.

move to new plots of ground whenever the soil on their farms becomes unproductive.

Work of the People

About 70 of every 100 Paraguayans work in agriculture. Most of the rest make their living by cutting down trees for lumber, or by working in lumber mills. On the average, workers earn about $300 a year.

Agriculture. Although most of the people are farmers, they cultivate only about 3 per cent of the land. This is because the farmers usually raise only enough crops to feed their own families. Primitive tools and inefficient farming methods also keep the people from cultivating as much land as could be farmed. A Paraguayan-United States agricultural mission promotes education and technical training among farmers.

Most farms lie along the banks of the Paraguay River, where the land is well watered and the river can be used for transportation. Cotton is the chief crop, but farmers also raise sugar cane, tobacco, rice, and other grains. Oranges and other fruits grow with little cultivation. Cattle breeding provides one of the chief sources of income, but most farmers own less than 50 cattle. About a dozen large ranches in eastern Paraguay raise more than 20,000 cattle each.

Forest Products. Paraguay's forests provide quebracho, a hard wood from which tannin is obtained. Quebracho makes good railroad ties, and has often been used to pave streets. Paraguay is also the world's largest producer of petitgrain oil, the oil from the leaves and shoots of the bitter orange tree. This oil is used in the manufacture of perfumes and marmalade. Holly trees grow near the Paraná River. Many South Americans use holly-tree leaves to make *yerba maté* (see MATÉ).

Manufacturing and Processing. Poor transportation, scarce power, and lack of technicians have slowed the development of industry. For example, cotton is one of Paraguay's main farm products, but the country has to import cotton clothing and fabrics. Preparing and packaging foods and drinks accounts for about half the manufacturing activity. Small workshops in the cities produce such items as pottery, tools, and leather goods.

Electric Power. The many waterfalls on the Paraná River could provide much more power. But Paraguay has not developed the power because there are not enough people who can use it to justify the expense. Wood-burning plants produce nearly all the nation's electric power.

Trade. Paraguay exports about the same value of goods that it imports. The chief exports include cotton, yerba maté, meats, hides, timber, tobacco, quebracho extract, and vegetable oils. Imports include automobiles, chemicals, cotton goods, farm tools, food, machinery, paper, and petroleum. Meat-packing plants import cattle. Paraguay trades mostly with the United States; western European countries; and member nations of the Latin-American Free Trade Association, a common market formed in 1961 (see COMMON MARKET).

Transportation. Paraguay's rivers provide the chief means of transportation. Asunción, the main port, lies on the Paraguay River, about 1,000 miles from the Atlantic Ocean. To reach the ocean, small river steamers from Asunción must travel down the Paraguay River to the Paraná, and then to the Río de la Plata, which flows into the Atlantic. An 1,800-foot-long concrete bridge across the Paraná River opened in 1965. It

PARAGUAY

links Asunción with a highway leading to the Atlantic port of Paranaguá, Brazil.

Ox-drawn carts often carry goods from the rivers into the interior. Paraguay has about 4,000 miles of roads, but only about 800 miles are suitable for automobiles. More than 700 miles of railroads link the major cities. Airlines provide service throughout the country.

Communication. The country's seven newspapers are published in Asunción. The capital also has several magazine and book publishers. Most of Paraguay's telephones are in Asunción. Telegraph, radio-telegraph, and radio-telephone services connect the cities.

Education

More than 70 of every 100 Paraguayans can read and write. Education is free and the law requires all children to go to school. But a shortage of schools prevents many youngsters from attending. In addition, children often must work on the farms to help support their families. The National University at Asunción has more than 3,000 students.

The Arts

Much of Paraguay's earliest art stemmed from the art schools of the Jesuits, members of a Roman Catholic order. In the 1600's and 1700's, Indian students in Jesuit missions decorated their churches with beautiful statues and pictures. Two outstanding painters, Pablo Alborno (1877-1965) and Juan Samudio (1878-1936), founded the National Academy of Fine Arts in Asunción in the early 1900's. Most of Paraguay's

early writers, such as Antonio Molas and Blas Garay (1873-1899), wrote of the history of Paraguay. People throughout South America enjoy the poetry of Alejandro Guanes and Eloy Fariña Núñez. Juan Natalicio González was a modern historian. Paraguayans play folk music on guitars, and enjoy dances such as the *Santa Fe*, which resembles the Virginia reel.

The women make some of the world's finest lace, called *ñandutí*, the Guaraní word for *spider web*. They often weave designs of flowers or animals into the lace. Craftsmen produce small elaborate silver bowls in which the people serve yerba maté.

What to See and Do in Paraguay

Asunción, with its flowers and tree-lined streets, provides some of Paraguay's main attractions for visitors. The botanical gardens in Trinidad, a suburb of Asunción, display many kinds of plants and flowers.

A pleasure resort on Lake Ypacarai, near Asunción, is a favorite vacation spot. Excursions from the city of Encarnación visit the ruins of Jesuit missions that were built during the 1600's and 1700's. Hunters from many countries shoot wild game in the Chaco.

Government

The constitution of 1967 gives the principal governing powers to the national government, chiefly to the president. The president is head of the government and is Paraguay's strongest political leader.

The President is elected to a five-year term. He must be a citizen of Paraguay, who was born in the country. He must also be more than 40 years old and a Roman Catholic.

Asunción, the Capital of Paraguay, is also the country's cultural center. The city is the home of the National University, National Library, and a museum. The Pantheon of Heroes, *below*, contains tombs of several famous Paraguayans.

Pan American Union

The president chooses a Cabinet of at least five ministers to help him administer the government. The president may choose as many ministers as he wishes. In the late 1960's, there were 11 Cabinet ministers.

The president receives advice from the Council of State. The council includes the Cabinet members, the rector of the National University, the archbishop of Paraguay, the chairman of the Central Bank of Paraguay, and representatives of agriculture, commerce, industry, the army, and the navy.

The Legislature has a 30-member Senate and a 60-member House of Representatives. Members of both houses serve five-year terms. The number of representatives that the voters in each *department* (administrative district) elect is based on the department's population. Senators are elected *at large* (by all the country's voters). Voters also elect 18 alternates to the Senate and 36 alternates to the House of Representatives without regard to political districts. Alternates replace those legislators who die, become ill, or resign. They serve five-year terms.

The Courts. The Supreme Court rules in all cases that are appealed from any lower courts. It has a chief justice and four associate justices. The president appoints the justices to serve five-year terms. Special appeals courts handle criminal, civil, and labor cases. Civil courts handle commercial cases. Justices of the peace decide minor cases.

Local Government. Paraguay is divided into 16 departments. Representatives of the president called *delegados* govern 14 departments. The army has charge of Boquerón and Olimpo. The departments are divided into *municipios*, the municipios into *partidos*, and the partidos into *compañías*. Voters elect councils to govern the municipios. Police chiefs, appointed by the national government, maintain law and order in the partidos and compañías.

Politics. The Colorado Party is the strongest political party in Paraguay. It has controlled the government since 1948. The government did not permit any opposition to the Colorado Party until the 1960's. Between 1962 and 1966, it recognized three other political parties: the Liberal Party, the Radical Liberal Party, and the Revolutionary February Party. These three parties have played a gradually increasing role in Paraguay's political life.

The law requires all citizens over 18 years of age to vote, except policemen and enlisted men in the armed forces. They may not vote. The government believes these groups should stay out of politics. Women voted for the first time in the 1963 presidential elections.

Armed Forces. Paraguay's army has about 9,000 men, the navy has 2,000, and the air force 1,000. The navy has six river patrol boats. The air force has transport planes, but no fighting planes. Men are drafted into the armed forces at 18 years of age and serve from one to two years.

History

Early Days. Guaraní Indians, Paraguay's first inhabitants, lived by farming, fishing, and hunting. Their main villages were in the area that is now Asunción.

Aleixo Garcia (? -1526), a Portuguese explorer, was the first white man to enter Paraguay. He traveled across the country in 1524, hoping to find silver. The

Three Lions

An Oxcart Loaded with Hides for export passes through a village on the way to a river. Steamers carry goods to the ocean.

Spanish navigator Sebastian Cabot sailed up the Río de la Plata in 1526, and explored the Paraná River. In 1537, Domingo Martínez de Irala (1487-1557) became governor of all Spanish territory in southern South America. Irala founded Asunción and made his headquarters there. Governors at Asunción ruled southeastern South America until 1617. Then Buenos Aires replaced it as the capital.

The Jesuits established their first Paraguayan mission in 1609. Within 100 years, they had built 40 flourishing missions. During the 1700's, the Jesuits converted 150,000 Guaraní Indians to Roman Catholicism. The missions exported surplus farm products, creating competition that angered other settlers. The priests raised a 7,000-man army to protect the missions.

The Jesuits' empire within an empire alarmed the Spanish king, Charles III. In 1767, the king issued a sweeping decree that banished the Jesuits from the entire Spanish empire. Soon after this decree, most of them sailed from Paraguay to Italy. When the Jesuits left, the civilization they had built began to decline.

Independence. In 1776, Spain made Paraguay a part of the Viceroyalty of the Río de la Plata. Paraguay deposed the local Spanish governor in 1811, declared its independence, and set up an assembly to rule the country. In 1816, the assembly gave José Gaspar Rodríguez de Francia (1766?-1840), one of the few educated men in Paraguay, absolute control of the country for life. He feared that persons from other countries would exploit Paraguay and undermine his power. He prohibited immigration and trade with other nations. Despite its isolation, Paraguay prospered.

Francia died in 1840, and an assembly appointed Carlos Antonio López (1790-1862) to govern the country. López, a wealthy rancher, was Francia's nephew.

Colvin, Monkmeyer

Spider-Web Lace, called *ñandutí*, is made on stretched cotton cloth. When the lace is finished, the rest of the cloth is cut away.

In 1844, another assembly drew up a constitution and named López president. López reversed Francia's policies. He encouraged trade and immigration, made education free and required by law, and freed the Negro slaves owned by white ranchers. He built roads and brought technicians from other countries. López also built one of the most powerful armies in South America. He amended the constitution so that his son Francisco Solano López (1827-1870) would become president upon his death.

Military Ruin. The younger López took office in 1862. Three years later, Brazilian troops intervened in a revolution in Uruguay. López immediately declared war on Brazil, partly because he feared Brazil was trying to increase its power, but also because he sought military conquests. Argentina refused to let López' troops cross Argentine territory to reach Uruguay, so López also declared war on Argentina. The revolution in Uruguay ended in 1865, and Uruguay joined Argentina and Brazil to form a Triple Alliance.

The Alliance fought Paraguay from 1865 until 1870, when López was killed and Paraguay surrendered. Paraguay's land was devastated, and more than three-fourths of its men killed in the war. The population fell from 1,000,000 to 221,000 during this five-year period. Paraguay has never recovered from the damage it suffered in this war. The country adopted a new constitution in 1870, but struggles for power, mainly among rival army groups, have hampered progress.

The discovery of oil in the Chaco region brought Paraguay into war with Bolivia in 1932. The three-year war began because of a boundary dispute. A final settlement in 1938 gave Paraguay 91,800 square miles of new Chaco land.

Recent Developments. During most of World War II, Paraguay maintained friendly relations with both the Allies and the Axis. The government declared war on the Axis Powers in 1945, but no Paraguayan troops went into battle. Paraguay became a charter member of the United Nations that same year.

Civil war raged in Paraguay in 1947 when rebel forces rose against President Higinio Morínigo (1897-), who had ruled as a dictator since 1940. The rebels were defeated, but the Colorados, who supported Morínigo, split into two rival groups. Army officers in the group that opposed Morínigo forced him to leave the country. Their candidate, Natalicio González (1897-1966), appeared alone on the ballot in the 1948 election.

After a number of uprisings, the rival Colorado group, led by Federico Chaves, seized power in 1950. Chaves, the only candidate on the ballot, was elected president in 1953. The next year, the section of the Colorado Party that originally supported Morínigo was backed by the army, and forced Chaves to resign through a revolt. General Alfredo Stroessner (1912-), leader of the revolt and the Colorado candidate in the 1954 election, was elected president without opposition.

Paraguay took important steps in 1955 to improve its standard of living. The government started a $5 million road-building program. Asunción began to modernize its water-supply system. An aluminum plant opened at Asunción, and a new power plant began operations in Concepción. Paraguay signed a contract in 1956 to buy surplus United States farm products to ease its food shortage. In 1957, the government adopted suggestions of the International Monetary Fund to stabilize Paraguay's money and improve its trade. Paraguay's voters re-elected Stroessner to five-year terms as president in 1958, 1963, and 1968.   JOHN TATE LANNING

Related Articles in WORLD BOOK include:

Asunción	Paraguay River	Quebracho
Gran Chaco	Paraná River	Tupí-Guaraní
Maté	Petitgrain Oil	Indians

Outline

I. **The Land and Its Resources**
  A. Location and Size   D. Natural Resources
  B. Land Regions   E. Climate
  C. Rivers, Waterfalls, and Lakes
II. **Life of the People**
  A. Language   C. City Life
  B. Way of Life   D. Country Life
III. **Work of the People**
  A. Agriculture   D. Electric Power
  B. Forest Products   E. Trade
  C. Manufacturing and   F. Transportation
    Processing   G. Communication
IV. **Education**
V. **The Arts**
VI. **What to See and Do in Paraguay**
VII. **Government**
VIII. **History**

Questions

What has hindered the growth of industry in Paraguay?
What is unusual about Paraguay's main port?
How do the two land regions of Paraguay differ?
What are some of Paraguay's main exports? Imports?
How did the war with the Triple Alliance affect Paraguay's development?
What is unusual about Paraguay's flag?
Why is Paraguay one of the poorest countries in the world?
How many houses does the national legislature have?
Why can some Paraguayans neither read nor write, although the law requires children to attend school?

PARAGUAY RIVER is a 1,500-mile stream that flows southward through Paraguay, cutting the country in two. It is a branch of the Paraná River, and rises in south-central Brazil. From there it flows southward to join the Paraná River at the Argentine boundary.

The Paraguay is a good river for navigation, except for channel shifts. Large steamboats go up the Paraná and continue on the Paraguay to Asunción, the capital of Paraguay. The channel of the Paraguay shifts position, so that settlements on the banks of the river are often left far from the main channel.   MARGUERITE UTTLEY

See also RIVER (chart, Longest Rivers).

PARAGUAY TEA. See MATÉ.

PARAKEET, *PAR uh keet*, is a small member of the parrot family. Parakeets are brightly colored, with green, red, blue, orange, yellow, or purple feathers. Their tails are either short and square, or long and pointed. The name also is spelled *parrakeet*, or *paroquet*.

You can tell the sex of the adult parakeet by the color of the skin at the nostrils. In the male the color is purplish-blue, while in the female it is brownish.

Parakeets usually are affectionate and clever pets. They are natural acrobats, and can do many interesting tricks on toy ladders and seesaws. You can train a parakeet to talk. It is best to start when the parakeet is only a few weeks old. Say the same word or group of words over and over until the parakeet also repeats the word or words. A parakeet may learn many words. Both the male and the female can be taught to talk. Some bird trainers believe the male learns faster.

Many people enjoy the hobby of parakeet breeding. Amateur parakeet breeders often find the hobby both fun and profitable. The best time of the year for breeding is in the spring. Birds hatched in the spring will benefit from the sun and warmth of the summer. Special housing for the birds is necessary, because the space for one bird is naturally inadequate for two. The female bird lays an average of five eggs. The eggs hatch in about 18 to 20 days. A parakeet may live about 10 years.

Seeds and fruit are the chief parakeet foods. Wild parakeets nest in trees and are swift fliers. Many species live in warm parts of the world. The *ground parakeet* of Australia and Tasmania makes its home in bushes rather than in trees. Another Australian parakeet is the *budgerygah, budgereegah,* or *shell parakeet*, sometimes called the *budgie*. It lives well in captivity and becomes very tame. An African parakeet, called the *lovebird*, makes a great show of affection. The best-known Indian bird is the *rose-ringed parakeet*. The *bat parakeet* sleeps hanging from a tree branch.

The *Carolina parakeet* once was common in the United States, ranging northward to New York and Illinois. Its head was orange and yellow, and its body green. These parakeets have disappeared. Many were killed because milliners wanted their feathers for hat trimming. The last flock of Carolina parakeets was seen in the Florida Everglades in 1904.

Scientific Classification. Parakeets belong to the parrot family, *Psittacidae*. The Carolina parakeet is genus *Conuropis*, species *carolinensis*. Bat parakeets are genus *Loriculus;* Indian parakeets and lovebirds are *Agapornis;* shell parakeets are *Melopsittacus* and ground parakeets are *Pezoporus*.   RODOLPHE MEYER deSCHAUENSEE

See also BIRD (color picture, Family Pets); LOVEBIRD.

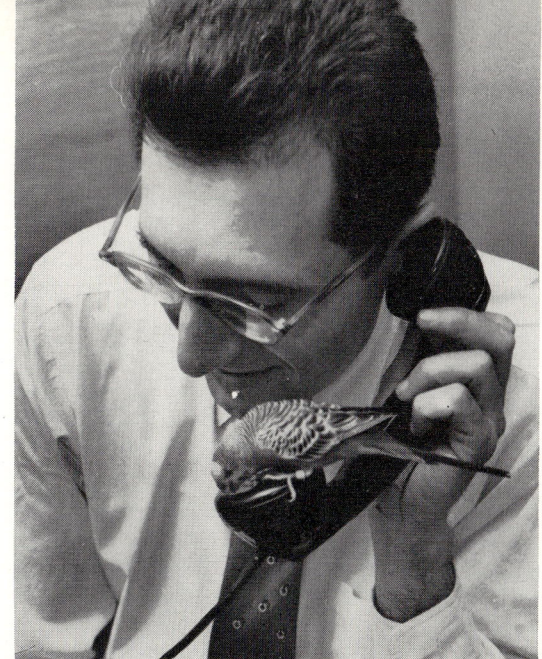

An Australian Shell Parakeet, or Budgie, becomes quite tame in captivity. Any household object fascinates him.

A Playpen for Parakeets includes everything from a ferris wheel to dumbbells, ladders, swings, bells, and rocking horses. The birds amuse themselves for hours with such toys.

Parakeets Are Playful and unusually affectionate pets. They like to climb furniture and to perch on people and friendly animals.

Nina Leen, *Life,* © 1953 Time, Inc.

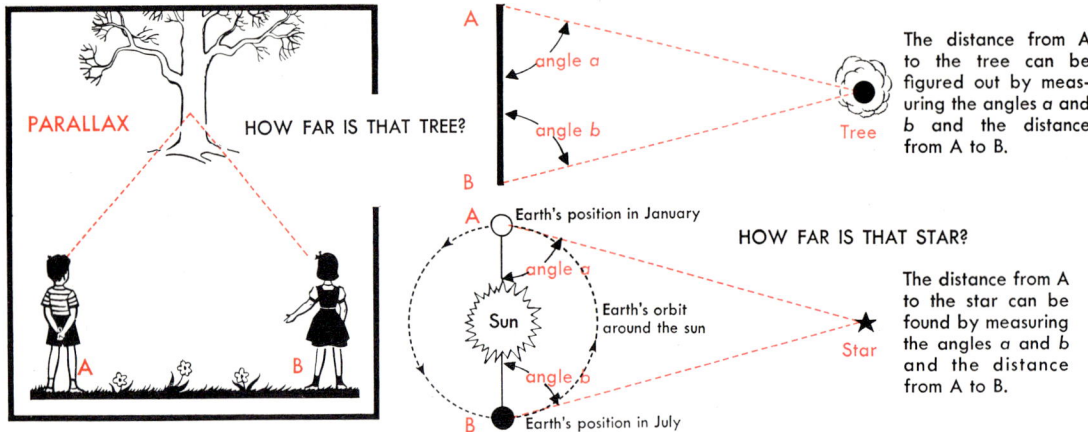

PARALLAX

HOW FAR IS THAT TREE?

angle a

angle b

A

B

Tree

The distance from A to the tree can be figured out by measuring the angles *a* and *b* and the distance from A to B.

Earth's position in January

A

angle a

Sun

Earth's orbit around the sun

angle b

B

Earth's position in July

HOW FAR IS THAT STAR?

Star

The distance from A to the star can be found by measuring the angles *a* and *b* and the distance from A to B.

PARALLAX, *PAR uh lax,* is the difference in direction of an object when seen from two positions which are not in a direct line with each other and the object. Hold up one finger. Look at it first with one eye and then with the other. Notice how the finger seems to change position in relation to more distant objects when seen with one eye and then with the other.

When you look with two eyes, each eye sees nearby things from a slightly different direction. Your mind solves a parallax problem when you look at nearby objects, and you tell how far away they are. A person blind in one eye has no parallax vision, and may have difficulty judging the distance of nearby objects.

Parallax is used in surveying to tell how far away a distant object is. A base line of known length is laid off, the far-off object is viewed from each end of this base line, and the two angles with the base line are noted. Knowing the length of the base line and the number of degrees in the angles at each end, the height of the triangle can be solved by trigonometry.

Parallax is used in astronomy for finding the distance to the stars. But the stars are so far away that a base line across the entire orbit of the earth, 186,000,000 miles long, is big enough to get the parallax only of some of the nearer stars.   R. WILLIAM SHAW

See also ASTRONOMY (Measuring Distances in Space); PHOTOGRAPHY (Accessories [Special Lenses]).

PARALLEL. See MAP (Geographic Grids).

PARALLEL CIRCUIT. See ELECTRIC CURRENT.

PARALLEL FORCES are forces acting on an object in the same direction, as when two horses pull a wagon. Pillars in a building also act along lines of parallel force.

PARALLELOGRAM. See QUADRILATERAL.

PARALLELOGRAM OF FORCES. See FORCE (Composition of Forces).

PARALYSIS, *puh RAL uh sis,* is loss of the power of voluntary movement. Muscular motion is produced by the stimulation of certain nerve cells in the brain and spinal cord. When certain areas of the nervous system are not working properly, muscular movement is not normal. The seat of disorder may be in the cells of the brain or the spinal cord, in their connecting pathways, or in the nerves leading to the muscles. Trouble in the right side of the brain causes paralysis on the left side of the body, and vice versa.

There are two types of paralysis. In *spastic paralysis,* the muscles are weak, but tense and rigid. In this case it is the nerve cells in the brain which are disturbed. *Flaccid paralysis* produces weak and flabby muscles. Here, the disease is in those nerves which connect directly with the muscle. *Polio* is of this type.

Paralysis may also be caused by skull injuries affecting the brain, or by brain abscesses, tumors, and blood-vessel disturbance. If the spinal cord is injured, the nerves below the point of injury can no longer move the muscles they control. There are also certain diseases of the spinal cord which cause loss of muscular movement. *Spinal meningitis* is one of these. Occasionally, a muscle may not move because it, and not the nervous system, is defective. Another type of paralysis, called *paraplegia,* paralyzes the legs and the lower part of the body. Paraplegia can be caused by disease or injury of the spinal cord. It may result from inflammations or infections. Emotional excitement may also bring on muscular weakness, the so-called "hysterical paralysis."

Treatment of paralysis depends upon the disease or injury which caused it. Exercises, massages, electrical treatments, and the use of splints or other apparatus are some of the treatments.   LOUIS D. BOSHES

Related Articles in WORLD BOOK include:

Apoplexy	Palsy	Poliomyelitis
Cerebral Palsy	Paresis	Spastic Paralysis
Meningitis	Physical Therapy	

PARAMARIBO, *PAR uh MAR uh boh* (pop. 122,634; alt. 20 ft.), is the capital and center of trade of Surinam (Dutch Guiana) in South America. For location, see SURINAM (map). The city has attractive modern dwellings. Fort Zeelandia, the residence of the crown representative, and Fort Amsterdam protect the large harbor. Sugar, rum, molasses, bauxite, rice, and rubber are exported.   ARTHUR P. WHITAKER

PARAMECIUM, *PAR uh ME shih um,* is a tiny one-celled animal that can hardly be seen without the microscope. This type of animal is a *protozoan.* Paramecia live in almost all bodies of fresh water, such as pools and streams.

Like the ameba, this animal is made up of the watery material called *protoplasm.* The paramecium is clear on the surface, and granular inside. There are two special cell structures inside it. They are the nuclei, and one spot is smaller than the other.

The paramecium has more special structures than the ameba. A stiffer layer on the outside gives it a permanent shape, unlike the ameba. The paramecium also has a front and rear end. It looks like the bottom of a shoe, and is often called the *slipper animalcule*. The animal is covered with fine hairs called *cilia*. It swims rapidly by beating its cilia. A network of threads below the surface connects the cilia. This network of threads probably shows the beginnings of a nervous system.

Food enters the animal through a hollow in one side called the *oral groove*, which leads to a tube called the *gullet*. Food in the gullet forms a ball which passes into the protoplasm as a food *vacuole*. The food is digested as the vacuole passes through the animal, and the waste is passed out from a special place called the *anal pore*.

Two star-shaped spots which seem to appear and disappear in the animal are the *contractile vacuoles*. They collect excess water, and pass it to the outside.

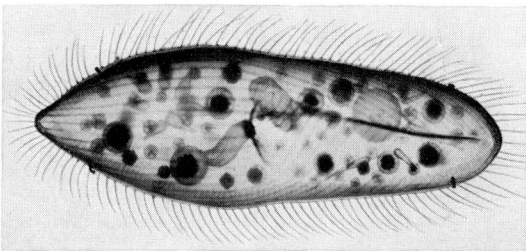

American Museum of Natural History
A Glass Model Shows the Paramecium's Structure.

Paramecia may reproduce by dividing in two across the middle. The nuclei divide, the rear half develops a new gullet, and the front half grows a new anal pore. Then the paramecium breaks into two animals. Paramecia also show the beginnings of sexual reproduction. Two animals may come together and exchange parts of their nuclei. This process is called *conjugation*. Then they separate and divide several times. See Conjugation.

The paramecium shows a *trial-and-error behavior*. It swims until it bumps into something. Then it backs up, changes its direction slightly, and moves ahead again.

Scientific Classification. Paramecia belong to the phylum *Protozoa* and the class *Ciliata*.   Ralph Buchsbaum

See also Protozoan.

PARANÁ, *pah rah NAH* (pop. 124,898; alt. 185 ft.), is the capital of the province of Entre Ríos in east-central Argentina. The city lies on the Paraná River and is a trading center for the products of nearby farmlands. It also serves as an industrial and educational center. For location, see Argentina (political map).

PARANÁ RIVER is the second longest river in South America, with a length of 2,450 miles. It is formed in southern Brazil, where the Rio Grande and Paranaíba rivers meet. From there it flows in a general southerly direction through Brazil and along the boundary between Brazil and Paraguay. Then it makes a boundary between Paraguay and Argentina, and travels through Argentina. It empties into the Atlantic Ocean through the estuary known as the Plata River (Río de la Plata). Ocean vessels can travel through the estuary and up the Paraná as far as Rosario, Argentina, 400 miles from the Atlantic. The Paraguay River is the main branch of the Paraná River.   Marguerite Uttley

See also Paraguay River; Río de la Plata; River (chart: Longest Rivers).

PARANOIA. See Mental Illness (Kinds).
PARAPLEGIA. See Paralysis.
PARAPSYCHOLOGY is a branch of psychology that deals with finding evidence for such phenomena as telepathy, clairvoyance, thought transference, and extrasensory perception. See Clairvoyance; Extrasensory Perception; Psychical Research; Telepathy.

PARASITE is a plant or an animal that feeds and lives on or in another plant or animal. The plants and animals on which parasites feed are called *hosts*. Some authorities point out that all animals are parasites because they must rely on other living things for food. But in a stricter sense, parasites usually live on plants and animals bigger than they are. They only feed on small amounts of the host's tissue or the host's food at a time.

Parasites have varying effects on the body of their host. Experts believe that most parasites cause little or no harm to their host. For example, one type of ameba lives in human intestines. It feeds on partly digested food and other intestinal parasites without causing any obvious ill effects. Other types of parasites may cause great harm. For example, the *protozoans* (one-celled animals) that cause malaria are parasites in the red blood cells of human beings.

Animal Parasites. Many protozoans are parasites. For example, one type of ameba destroys the lining of the intestines of humans. This produces the painful disease called amebic dysentery. Other protozoans may invade the blood of mammals and cause diseases such as malaria and Texas cattle fever. Blood-sucking insects and ticks pick up parasites from infected animals and pass them on to other animals and humans.

Parasitic flatworms and roundworms cause serious damage and often kill their hosts. One group of flatworms, called flukes, live in the intestines, liver, lungs, or blood of animals. Another group, the tapeworms, mature in the intestines of animals. They attach themselves to the intestinal wall with suckers or hooks. The tapeworms then absorb digested food, depriving the host of nourishment. Hookworms are the most harmful group of roundworms. They live in intestines and feed on the blood of their host.

Parasitic insects, ticks, and mites usually attack the skin. Their bites are irritating, but the diseases these tiny animals spread are far more serious. Certain ticks transmit Rocky Mountain spotted fever to man. One type of mosquito spreads yellow fever and another type carries malaria. The tsetse fly transmits African sleeping sickness. Humans may also get typhus fever from a body louse.

Insects, ticks, and mites may be parasitic only during particular periods of life. For example, only adult fleas are parasites. Red bugs and screwworms, a type of fly, are parasites only in their *larval* (infant) stage.

Some animal parasites live on plants and may kill them. *Aphids* (plant lice), scale insects, and threadworms are examples.

Plant Parasites cause many serious diseases in plants, animals, and humans. Parasitic fungi cause wheat and bean rust, potato and tomato blight, apple scab, and downy mildew of grapes. Mistletoe, a parasite of forest trees, is called a *partial parasite* because it

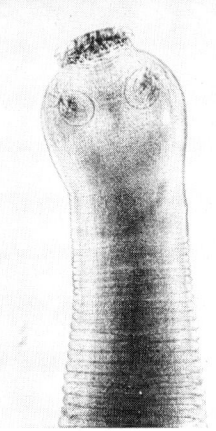

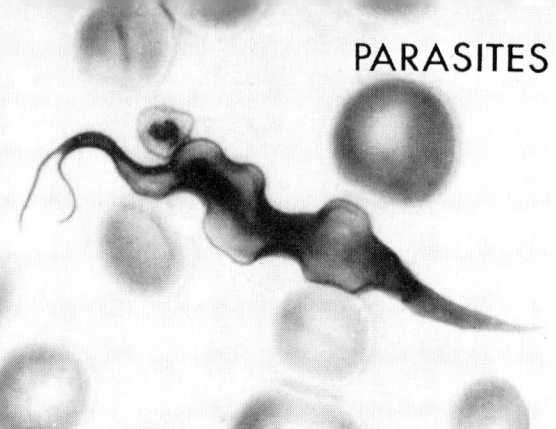

Tapeworms live in the intestinal tract.

The Sheep Tick is a harmful insect that lives on sheep.

Trypanosomes taken from the blood of a rat are the cause of deadly sleeping sickness. Tsetse flies are the carriers.

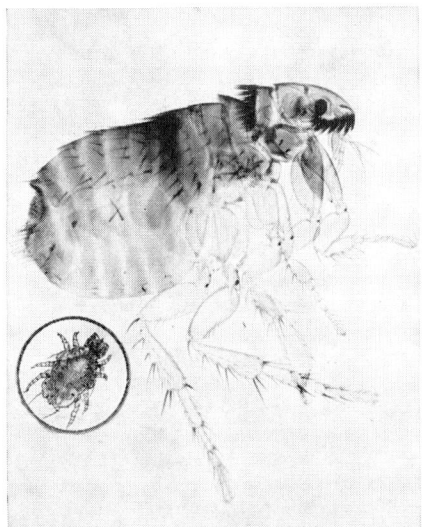

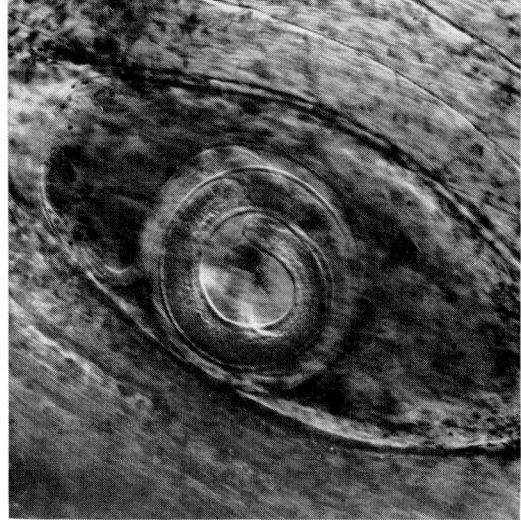

The Smaller Flea was taken from the back of the larger flea, which lived on a cat.

Mistletoe is a parasite on various trees.

The Trichina Worm lodges in the muscles of hogs and humans. It causes the painful disease called *trichinosis*.

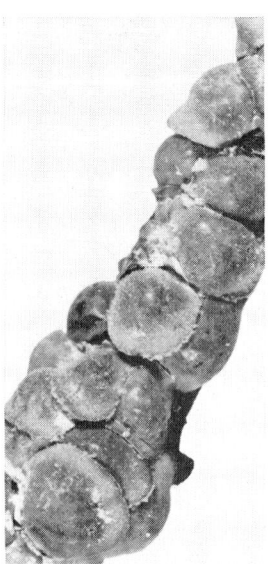

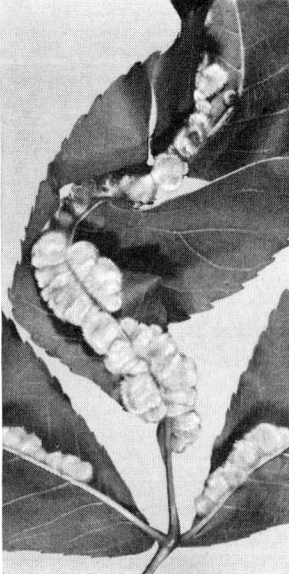

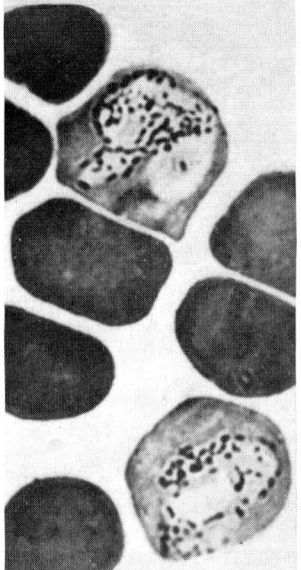

General Biological Supply House; E. O. Essig; Allue, Black Star; J. Horace McFarland; H. Bade; Davey Tree Expert Co.; Army Medical Museum; Ralph Buchsbaum

Magnolia Scale is an insect that looks like a group of tiny mushrooms.

Cockscomb Gall attacks and withers the foliage of trees and other plants that it feeds on.

Plasmodium Vivax is one of the tiny parasites which cause malaria, a serious disease of human beings.

Phylloxera Galls are tiny lice that destroy the leaves and roots of plants.

makes some of its own food. Fungi cause lumpy jaw, a disease that injures the jaws of cattle and hogs. Ringworm is a fungus infection in man. Experts estimate that plant parasites destroy about $3 billion worth of crops in the United States each year.

Most *bacteria* (one-celled organisms) are parasites. Bacterial diseases, such as tuberculosis and pneumonia, are usually considered apart from those caused by other parasites.   R. P. HALL

Related Articles in WORLD BOOK include:

PARASITIC ANIMALS

Ameba	Flea	Louse	Roundworm
Aphid	Fluke	Mite	Tapeworm
Cattle Tick	Hair Snake	Mosquito	Tick
Chigger	Hookworm	Pinworm	Trichina

PARASITIC PLANTS

Dodder	Mildew	Rust	Witchweed
Fungi	Mistletoe	Smut	Yeast

OTHER RELATED ARTICLES

Bacteria (Bacteria and Disease)	Fungus Disease Lumpy Jaw	Saprophyte Symbiosis

PARASOL. See UMBRELLA.

PARASOL ANT. See ANT (Leafcutter Ants).

PARASYMPATHETIC NERVOUS SYSTEM. See NERVOUS SYSTEM (The Peripheral Nervous System).

PARATHION, *PAR uh THY un*, is a brown or yellow insecticide with an onionlike odor. It has the chemical formula $C_{10}H_{14}NO_5PS$. It quickly kills aphids, spider mites, and other insect pests. Parathion may not be effective at temperatures below 60° F.

PARATHYROID GLAND, *PAR uh THY roid*, is any one of four ductless glands located on the thyroid gland, or sometimes in it. Each is about the size of a pea. These glands produce parathormone, a hormone. Parathormone makes bone dissolve to release calcium and phosphate into the blood. It also makes the kidney release more phosphate. When the concentration of calcium in the blood is too low, the parathyroid glands begin to work. If not enough parathormone is produced, a person becomes nervous and has muscle spasms. See also GLAND (The Endocrine Glands).   T. B. SCHWARTZ

PARATROOPS. See AIRBORNE TROOPS.

PARATYPHOID FEVER, *PAR uh TIE foid*, is an acute infection of the intestines. It gets its name because the symptoms often resemble those of typhoid fever (see TYPHOID FEVER). Microscopic organisms called *Salmonella* cause paratyphoid fever. These infective organisms usually enter a person's body in food. Paratyphoid fever can be prevented if food is properly cleaned and cooked. There is no specific drug that will cure this disease.   H. WORLEY KENDELL

PARAVANE is a torpedo-shaped device used by ships in mined areas to sever the moorings of the mines. Paravanes are designed to stream at an angle on each side of a ship at some distance from its sides. The paravane looks like a small airplane, or kite, and is designed so that water forces it away from the ship and downward. If the mooring cable of a mine is struck by the towing cable of the paravane, the mine is guided down the towing cable into a saw-toothed knife on the paravane. This edge cuts the mine adrift from its anchor, allowing the mine to rise to the surface where it can be destroyed by gunfire.   THEODORE ROPP

See also MINE, MILITARY (Mine Detection).

PARCEL POST is a service provided by the post office for sending packages of certain sizes and weights through the mails. The governments of the United States, Canada, and most other countries carry parcels as part of their regular postal services.

The United States established its parcel post service in 1913. The United States Post Office divides all mail into four classes. Parcel post makes up the fourth class, and includes all mailable merchandise that weighs 16 ounces or more. Almost any kind of merchandise may be mailed through parcel post, including such things as day-old live poultry, baby alligators, and bees. However, parcel post cannot be used to send merchandise that might prove dangerous in handling, such as explosives and flammable materials.

Special Services. Parcel post includes a number of special services. Parcels sent *special delivery* are handled and carried in the same manner and with the same speed as first-class mail. Special delivery parcels are given immediate delivery during certain hours. Parcels sent *special handling* are given the fastest handling and land transportation available, but they are delivered on regularly scheduled trips as parcel post is ordinarily delivered.

Parcels sent *air parcel post* are carried by air and by the fastest connecting land transportation. Air parcel post is delivered on regularly scheduled trips, unless a special delivery fee is paid in addition to the air-mail postage. Parcels may be sent as *registered mail* upon payment of postage at the first-class or air-mail rate, in addition to the registry fees. The person to whom the package is sent must sign a postal receipt before the parcel is delivered to him. Parcels may be *insured* against loss, theft, or damage for amounts up to $200.

Parcels may be sent *collect on delivery* (C.O.D.) upon payment of a fee in addition to postage. The person receiving the package pays the postman, and the post office returns the money collected to the sender by a postal money order. The limit on C.O.D. packages is $200.

When registered or C.O.D. parcels or parcels insured for over $15 are delivered, the postman obtains a receipt as evidence of delivery. All other parcels are delivered without obtaining a receipt.

Parcel Post Rates. The post office determines parcel post charges according to the weight of a package and the zone distance it is being shipped. All fractions of a pound are counted as a full pound. The zone distance between two post offices is the same as the distance between their *sectional center facilities*. These are large central post offices that serve the smaller post offices in a given area. All incoming and outgoing mail for an area is routed through the sectional center facility. There are over 500 such postal sectional centers in the United States.

A local zone rate applies to parcels mailed from a post office or one of its rural routes for delivery at that same post office or on one of its rural routes. All other distances are included in one of eight zones. The first zone includes distances up to 50 miles. But rates for zone one are the same as those for zone two, which includes distances up to 150 miles.

PARCEL POST

The Post Office Department publishes postal zone charts for post offices within each sectional center. These charts list the *prefix* (first three numbers) of the ZIP codes of all post offices. The applicable zone is listed to the right of the prefix. Parcel post rates have changed several times. Therefore, a parcel sender should consult his local post office for the most recent information. The table included in this article gives the rates on parcels that became effective in October, 1968.

Congress has established a special library rate and a special fourth-class rate for books and other specified items mailed under certain conditions. The current library rate is 5¢ for the first pound and 2¢ for each additional pound. The special fourth-class rate is 12¢ for the first pound and 6¢ for each additional pound. These rates apply to all zone distances.

Size and Weight Limits on parcels sent through the mails have been established by Congress. The size of a parcel is determined by adding the length of its longest side and the distance around the parcel at the thickest part. Size and weight limits vary according to the classes of post offices involved and the distances over which the parcels are sent. The sender should consult his local post office for current size and weight limits.

Critically reviewed by the POST OFFICE DEPARTMENT

PARCHMENT is material made from the skins of sheep, goats, and other animals. It is used mainly as a fine writing material for important documents. Parchment is made by removing the hair or wool from the skin of the animal, and placing this skin in lime to rid it of its fat. The skin is then stretched on a frame and shaved with knives and scrapers. Powdered chalk is rubbed on with pumice stone, to smooth and soften the skin.

Fine Parchment is often called *vellum*. It is made from the skins of calves, kids, and lambs. This high-quality parchment is used for important writings such as charters, university diplomas, and wills.

Heavy Parchment is made from the skins of donkeys, calves, wolves, and goats. Heavy parchment is used for drumheads.

Parchment Paper, or *Vegetable Parchment*, is made by dipping pure, unsized paper into a cooled mixture of sulfuric acid and water, and then washing and drying it under pressure. This process makes the paper partly transparent and much stronger than ordinary paper. Vegetable parchment is used for legal documents and for maps, and to connect laboratory implements. It is

POSTAL ZONES

WEIGHT NOT EXCEEDING — POUNDS	LOCAL	FIRST-SECOND UP TO 150 MILES	THIRD 150 TO 300 MILES	FOURTH 300 TO 600 MILES	FIFTH 600 TO 1,000 MILES	SIXTH 1,000 TO 1,400 MILES	SEVENTH 1,400 TO 1,800 MILES	EIGHTH OVER 1,800 MILES
2 lbs.	$0.50	$0.60	$0.60	$0.65	$0.70	$0.80	$0.85	$0.90
3 lbs.	.50	.65	.70	.75	.85	.95	1.05	1.15
4 lbs.	.55	.70	.75	.85	.95	1.10	1.20	1.35
5 lbs.	.55	.75	.80	.90	1.05	1.25	1.40	1.60
6 lbs.	.55	.80	.90	1.00	1.15	1.40	1.55	1.75
7 lbs.	.60	.90	.95	1.10	1.30	1.50	1.75	1.95
8 lbs.	.60	.95	1.00	1.15	1.40	1.65	1.90	2.15
9 lbs.	.65	1.00	1.05	1.25	1.50	1.80	2.05	2.35
10 lbs.	.65	1.05	1.15	1.35	1.65	1.90	2.25	2.55
11 lbs.	.65	1.10	1.20	1.40	1.75	2.00	2.40	2.75
12 lbs.	.70	1.15	1.25	1.50	1.85	2.15	2.55	2.90
13 lbs.	.70	1.20	1.35	1.55	1.95	2.25	2.70	3.10
14 lbs.	.75	1.25	1.40	1.65	2.05	2.40	2.85	3.25
15 lbs.	.75	1.30	1.45	1.75	2.15	2.50	3.00	3.45
16 lbs.	.75	1.35	1.55	1.80	2.25	2.60	3.15	3.60
17 lbs.	.80	1.40	1.60	1.90	2.35	2.75	3.30	3.80
18 lbs.	.80	1.45	1.65	1.95	2.45	2.85	3.45	4.00
19 lbs.	.85	1.50	1.75	2.05	2.55	2.95	3.60	4.15
20 lbs.	.85	1.55	1.80	2.10	2.65	3.10	3.75	4.35
21 lbs.	.85	1.60	1.85	2.15	2.75	3.20	3.90	4.50
22 lbs.	.90	1.65	1.90	2.25	2.80	3.30	4.05	4.70
23 lbs.	.90	1.70	1.95	2.30	2.90	3.40	4.20	4.85
24 lbs.	.95	1.75	2.00	2.35	3.00	3.55	4.35	5.00
25 lbs.	.95	1.75	2.05	2.45	3.05	3.65	4.50	5.20
26 lbs.	.95	1.80	2.05	2.50	3.15	3.75	4.65	5.35
27 lbs.	1.00	1.85	2.10	2.55	3.25	3.90	4.80	5.55
28 lbs.	1.00	1.90	2.15	2.60	3.35	4.00	4.90	5.70
29 lbs.	1.05	1.90	2.20	2.70	3.40	4.10	5.05	5.90
30 lbs.	1.05	1.95	2.25	2.75	3.50	4.20	5.20	6.05

U.S. Post Office Dept.

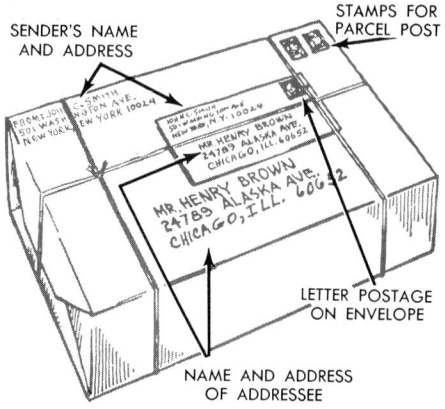

Parcel Post Packages in a large post office travel down a chute to a lower floor where they are separated for mailing.

SENDER'S NAME AND ADDRESS

STAMPS FOR PARCEL POST

LETTER POSTAGE ON ENVELOPE

NAME AND ADDRESS OF ADDRESSEE

From *A Pictorial History of Paper* by Stephen Goerl. © Bulkley, Dunton Pulp Co., Inc.

Parchment Replaced Papyrus as a Writing Material. The thin animal skin is still used for long-lasting documents.

also used as a sanitary covering for many foodstuffs.

History. The word parchment comes from *Pergamum*, a city in the kingdom of the same name in Asia Minor. About 190 B.C., persons in Pergamum began experimenting with parchment. Eumenes II, ruler of Pergamum, ordered these experiments because an Egyptian *pharaoh* (ruler) had prohibited the use of papyrus, a writing material of that time. The pharaoh feared that the library at Pergamum would become greater than the library of Alexandria, Egypt. This marked the first extensive use of parchment. It was commonly used by the Greeks and Romans. RONALD G. MACDONALD

See also LIBRARY (Libraries of Animal Skins); MANUSCRIPT; PAPYRUS.

PARDEE DAM is the principal structure of a water-supply project on the Mokelumne River, a tributary of the San Joaquin River. The dam is about 100 miles northeast of Oakland, Calif. Pardee Dam was built to furnish water to nine cities on the east shore of San Francisco Bay. It is 358 feet high, with a crest length of 1,350 feet. The reservoir has a total capacity of 222,000 acre-feet of water. It was built by the East Bay Municipal Water District of Oakland at a cost of more than $16,000,000. See also DAM. T. W. MERMEL

PARDON is a form of release of a convicted person from custody. Pardons are granted by chief executives, such as kings, presidents, and governors. The executive sometimes acts on a recommendation made by a board, a commission, or a single official. But the right to pardon belongs to the chief executive alone. It is one of the oldest rights of rulers.

Pardons differ from paroles. A person on parole must report from time to time to an individual named by the board. But a person who receives a pardon is entirely free. He is not regarded as a criminal, because the pardon has the effect of wiping out the conviction. The pardon is an important part of the machinery of justice. It is ordinarily used only to free persons whose innocence is established after they have been convicted.

A *commutation of sentence* differs from a pardon in that it merely lessens the terms of punishment. FRED E. INBAU

See also AMNESTY; PAROLE.

PARÉ, *pah RAY,* **AMBROISE** (1510?-1590), became one of the greatest surgeons in the history of medicine. His formal education was sketchy, but he learned on the battlefield as a surgeon in the French Army. Paré stopped treating gunshot and surgical wounds with boiling oil, which was the practice, and learned to rely on the power of nature to heal. He also revived the practice of tying off blood vessels in amputations. In 1552, Paré became surgeon to Henry II, and continued as court surgeon to the three succeeding French kings.

Paré was born the son of a barber at Bourg-Hersent, near Laval, France. In his day, doctors considered surgery beneath their dignity, and most operations were performed by barber-surgeons. Paré's work helped to raise the standing of surgery. GEORGE ROSEN

PAREGORIC is a medicine that acts as an intestinal sedative. Doctors sometimes use it to treat diarrhea. Pharmacists prepare paregoric from powdered opium, anise oil, benzoic acid, and camphor. Chemists first made the drug in the 1700's.

PARENT refers to the father or mother of a person. In the days of the early Romans, a man had the power of life and death not only over his own children, but even over his grandchildren. Since that time, a great change has taken place in the public attitude toward the relationship between parent and child. The law no longer considers children the property of their parents. Today the welfare of the child is considered as important as the legal right of his parents to control him.

Some of this change in thought came about early enough to be expressed in the English common law, which is part of the legal structure of both Canada and the United States. There are also many statutes, or state and provincial laws, that provide for the duties and responsibilities of the parent.

The father of a family, or the mother, if she is its legal head, must support the children and educate them. In most states, if the parent fails to provide food, clothing, and shelter for his children, he is held responsible for any debts the children contract for these things. Parents may correct and punish their children when necessary. But parents may be punished if they are cruel and abuse their children. The state may take a child away from the guardianship of his parents, if such action is necessary for the child's welfare because of the parent's complete unfitness. The parent is entitled to his child's earnings and services. But if the child has been freed from his parents' control by their consent or neglect, or if he has made a valid marriage, this right no longer exists.

A person who takes over the duties of a parent, either temporarily or permanently, is said by the law to be *in loco parentis* (in place of the parent). Teachers and guardians act *in loco parentis*. JOHN W. WADE

Related Articles in WORLD BOOK include:

Aid to Dependent Children	Children's Bureau
Baby	Family
Child	Guardian
Child Labor	Mother
Children, Societies for	Parent Education

PARENT EDUCATION

PARENT EDUCATION aims at a satisfying family life that provides a healthy personality development in children. Through parent education, fathers and mothers gain an understanding of the importance of family relationships, a greater acceptance of themselves, and the ability to meet problems that arise with growing children. Parent education helps parents make their children's early years a firm foundation for future growth.

Parent Education in Action

Subjects studied by parent-education groups vary widely. They include emotional problems of children, family relationships, health, manners, safety, play activities, and spiritual guidance. Men and women who assist these groups include physicians, nurses, psychiatrists, teachers, social workers, judges, ministers, and many others.

Methods also vary. They include panel discussions, lectures, question-and-answer sessions, and dramatic sketches or films. The discussion-group method is most widely used. It permits sharing information and solutions to problems, and stimulates members of the group to try new methods. Parents usually find reassurance when they realize they are not alone in facing problems with children.

In addition to parent-education groups, magazines, books, pamphlets, radio, and television help to bring much information on children and their problems into almost every home.

History

The 1800's. Education for parents in the United States goes back to 1800. The wives of missionaries and clergymen organized study groups of mothers called *maternal associations*. These groups emphasized Bible study and prayer as a means of training children. A number of publications for parents appeared in the 1800's. These publications included *Mother's Magazine* (1832), *Mother's Assistant* (1841), and *Parent's Magazine* (1840-1850). During this period, the kindergarten and nursery school movements aided parent education (see KINDERGARTEN; NURSERY SCHOOL).

In general, organized parent education started in 1888. In this year, a group of women in New York City organized The Society for the Study of Child-Nature. This and other similar groups later formed the Child Study Association of America (see CHILD STUDY ASSOCIATION OF AMERICA). Another group formed at the same time, the American Association of University Women, took an interest in parent education (see AMERICAN ASSOCIATION OF UNIVERSITY WOMEN). In 1897, a number of groups founded the National Congress of Mothers in Washington, D.C. It became the National Congress of Parents and Teachers (see PARENTS AND TEACHERS, NATIONAL CONGRESS OF). One of its original purposes was the education of parents in child development.

The 1900's. From 1900 to 1920, the federal government began to aid parent education. The Children's Bureau, created by Congress in 1912, published the first of its popular child-care pamphlets, *Infant Care*, in 1914 (see CHILDREN'S BUREAU). The Department of Agriculture, through the Smith-Lever Act of 1914, began

instruction that included child care (see AGRICULTURAL EDUCATION). The Office of Education, through the Smith-Hughes Act of 1917, aided vocational training in home economics and promoted education in child care and nutrition (see SMITH-HUGHES ACT). The Public Health Service in 1918 began a program of parent education concerned with the health of children (see PUBLIC HEALTH SERVICE).

The same period brought the development of child study centers at universities; foundation of the National Committee on Mental Hygiene; appearance of the first cooperative nursery schools; and the organization of the Committee on Marriage and the Home of the Federal Council of Churches of Christ in America.

The 1920's and 1930's saw a tremendous growth in parent education carried on by private organizations and churches. Colleges, state departments of education, public and private schools, social agencies, and child-guidance clinics developed parent-education programs. For example, the state departments of education in both California and New York began programs. The Laura Spelman Rockefeller Memorial Fund aided professional work in parent education. It aided research in child-study centers, training programs in colleges, and made grants to national organizations. The Fund also supported the National Council of Parent Education (1925-1938). Many members of this group formed the National Committee on Parent Education, which became part of the National Council on Family Relations in 1953. The Association for Family Living was established as the Chicago Association for Child Study in 1925.

The National Council on Family Relations, first organized in 1938, brought together in one organization the leaders in research, teaching, and professional services in the field of marriage and the family. It now has about 40 regional, state, or local affiliates, and publishes *Marriage and Family Living*, a quarterly containing articles for parents and professional workers.

Recent Developments include a far-reaching leadership program for parents organized by the National Congress of Parents and Teachers. Leadership training courses, led by professionals, cover methods of leadership in parent education. The parent leader forms a local group for instruction, and may call upon professionals for advice and assistance. The Child Study Association publishes the *Parent Education Exchange Bulletin* and holds an annual Institute for Workers in Parent Education. A number of national parent-education organizations have become international. For example, the National Congress of Parents and Teachers has a European Congress for American parents and teachers. The University of Chicago began a parent-education project, *Parenthood in a Free Nation*, in 1953. It has organized parent study groups in the United States and Canada. Agencies of the Family Service Association of America have developed family life education programs.   FREDA S. KEHM

See also BABY; CHILD; TEEN AGE.

PARENTHESIS, *puh REN thee sis*, is a word, phrase, or sentence added to another sentence for the purpose of extra explanation, information, or comment. The word *parenthesis* comes from the Greek, meaning to *put in* or to *place in*. In writing, a parenthesis is often set off in *parenthetical marks* ( ), called *parentheses*. See also ALGEBRA (Symbols in Algebra).

National Congress of Parents and Teachers

PARENTS AND TEACHERS, NATIONAL CONGRESS OF (PTA),

is a volunteer organization that unites the forces of home, school, and community on behalf of children and youth. It is noncommercial, nonsectarian, and nonpartisan. Its educational program is developed through conferences, committees, and projects at national, state, and community levels. Local parent-teacher associations are known as PTA's. They encourage cooperation between home and school. The PTA's interpret the school to the community and the community to the school. They develop study-discussion groups in family life education and other areas of adult education. They also strive to improve the child's environment in home, school, and community. The National Congress cooperates with other organizations and agencies in projects of common interest.

Objectives

Purposes are stated in the following *Objects:*

1. To promote the welfare of children and youth in home, school, church, and community.

2. To raise the standards of home life.

3. To secure adequate laws for the care and protection of children and youth.

4. To bring into closer relation the home and the school, that parents and teachers may cooperate intelligently in the training of the child.

5. To develop between educators and the general public such united efforts as will secure for every child the highest advantages in physical, mental, social, and spiritual education.

Program. The National Congress carries out its program through national, state, and local activities. It now works through more than 25 national standing committees that specialize in such fields as health, safety, citizenship, cooperation with colleges, the exceptional child, high school service, parent and family life education, library service, and school education.

Special committees work on various projects. For example, one committee studies ways to provide children

Parent-Teacher Association Meetings sometimes are broken down into small discussion groups called *buzz sessions*. Members talk over such topics as teaching problems, playground needs, and proposed school legislation.

with wholesome material from comics, motion pictures, radio, and television. The National Congress has set up standards for judging these media both as entertainment and as educational tools, and has encouraged state and local programs for their improvement.

Nearly all of the state congresses offer teacher training scholarships to encourage young people to become teachers, librarians, or guidance counselors. Through an annual legislation program, the National Congress supports legislation aimed at improving the health, safety, and education of children. It urges adequate appropriations for such federal agencies as the Children's Bureau and the Office of Education.

The PTA publishes the monthlies *National PTA Bulletin* and *The PTA Magazine*, the annual *Proceedings*, and pamphlets used by local units.

Local PTA units throughout the United States have initiated such programs as drawing up teen-age codes of conduct and providing clinics for reading assistance. Others have sponsored effective safety education programs and helped solve school traffic problems. Members' work has sometimes resulted in better streets around schools and improved traffic supervision. In some areas, PTA's have worked to keep schools open after hours as social centers. In others, they have helped local health authorities with polio vaccination programs and other types of health services.

The congress encourages its members to become fully informed and to take an active interest in their school program. It does not, however, try to control school administrative activities and policies.

Organization

Government. Bylaws that govern the National Congress provide for a Board of Managers consisting of 91 members, 15 of whom serve on an Executive Com-

PARENTS AND TEACHERS

mittee. Annual conventions of the congress are open to all members, but voting is limited to the accredited state delegates and members of the National Board of Managers. Officers are elected for three-year terms.

State Branches. Each state Congress of Parents and Teachers has a board of managers that handles the affairs within that state branch. Some state branches are divided into districts. In many states, there are also city and county councils. The state branches are responsible for action within the state. They carry out the program of the National PTA, and develop programs that meet particular state needs.

Local Units are formed in each school. A local parent-teacher association develops programs to fit the needs of its school and community. Local associations conduct monthly meetings, study groups, workshops, and programs of community service. A person who joins the local PTA automatically becomes a member of the state and national organizations.

Membership is open to "any person interested in the Objects of the National Congress who is willing to uphold its basic policies and subscribe to its Bylaws." The PTA has over $10\frac{1}{2}$ million members. Its headquarters are at 700 N. Rush St., Chicago, Ill. 60611.

History

The PTA organization was founded as the National Congress of Mothers. It first met in Washington, D.C.,

on Feb. 17, 1897. Alice McLellan Birney and Phoebe Apperson Hearst were the cofounders.

The first local units organized by the congress devoted themselves to child study. Very early in its history, the National Congress urged parents to study the curriculums of the schools their children attended. It also suggested reading courses to give both fathers and mothers information about children and schools.

One of the first large-scale projects the PTA undertook was to extend the kindergarten. In those days, kindergartens were still in the experimental stage. The congress has repeatedly sponsored projects to meet recognized community needs, such as playgrounds and school lunches, until school or government authorities could take over their management. It initiated the famed Summer Round-Up of the Children, a health program for discovering and correcting physical defects of children about to enter school. In recent years, it has adopted a broader program for continuous health supervision of children from birth through high school. It also has begun a long-range program to strengthen community resources for safeguarding the emotional health of children.

The first state congress was organized in New York in 1897. There is now a branch in every state and one in the District of Columbia. There is also a branch in Europe representing schools for American dependents living on military bases there.

Critically reviewed by NATIONAL CONGRESS OF PARENTS AND TEACHERS

See also EDUCATION; PARENT EDUCATION; SCHOOL.

United Press Int.

Local PTA's sponsor such projects as a bicycle safety check to help protect the lives of children in the community. PTA members promote cooperation in home, school, and community for the welfare of children.

PARESIS, *puh REE sis,* is partial paralysis of a muscle or a group of muscles that affects the ability to move. It may result from damage to a nerve, as in spinal cord disease or nerve inflammation. It may also result from such muscle disorders as muscular dystrophy or muscle inflammation. *General paresis* is a disease of the entire body that results from syphilis. In the final stages of syphilis, the brain may become so badly damaged that it no longer functions properly, and some paralysis may result. BENJAMIN BOSHES

PARETO, *pah REH toe,* **VILFREDO** (1848-1923), an Italian nobleman, won recognition as a leading economist and sociologist after a successful career in industry. He helped develop the theory of universal economic interdependence and studied the distribution of income. In his sociological book *Mind and Society* (1916), Pareto stressed the unreasoning elements in social life and emphasized the role of leading groups in society. He criticized democracy and saw history as a succession of aristocracies. Because of his antidemocratic attitude, he is considered an intellectual forerunner of fascism. Pareto was born in Paris, France. H. W. SPIEGEL

PARHELION. See HALO.

PARI-MUTUEL. See HORSE RACING (Betting).

PARIAH. See CASTE.

PARÍCUTIN, *pah REE koo teen,* is the first volcano to form in the Western Hemisphere since 1770. It appeared on Feb. 20, 1943, after two weeks of violent earthquakes. The eruption occurred in a cornfield 180 miles west of Mexico City. For location, see MEXICO (map).

At the start of the eruption, a crack opened in the ground. Sulfur gas and steam oozed from the crack for half an hour. Then explosions began, sending black clouds of gas and ash 4 miles into the air. A cone of cinder and ash was built around the vent. In six days, the cone grew to a height of 550 feet. In seven months, it was 1,200 feet high. Lava flows covered 7 square miles and destroyed the villages of Parícutin and San Juan. The eruption ended on Mar. 4, 1952. The volcano's summit is now 1,345 feet above its base and 9,213 feet above sea level. GORDON A. MACDONALD

PARIETAL BONES. See HEAD.

PARIS, in Greek mythology, was the son of Priam, king of Troy. His mother Hecuba dreamed that her unborn son was a torch that set the country on fire, and a soothsayer said the dream meant the child would cause the destruction of Troy. Priam gave Paris to a slave and ordered him to kill the child. The slave left him to die, but a shepherd saved him and raised him as his own son. He married the nymph Oenone.

One day messengers came from Priam to take a bull as a prize for a wrestling contest. They took Paris' favorite bull, so he entered the contest and won it back. His sister Cassandra recognized him, and Priam accepted him, disregarding Hecuba's dream.

Zeus, the king of the gods, had Paris judge a contest over the Apple of Discord, which bore the words "To the fairest." Aphrodite promised him the most beautiful woman in the world, so he chose her over Hera and Athena. The other goddesses hated him after that.

Paris fell in love with Helen, wife of Menelaus, and took her to Troy with him. Menelaus led the Greeks in the Trojan War to get her back. Paris fought bravely, but craftily. He killed the hero Achilles in the temple of Apollo. Philoctetes later killed him. PADRAIC COLUM

Ewing Galloway

Smoke and Lava Erupted from Parícutin as the Western Hemisphere's newest volcano rapidly built its cone. During its first year of activity, it built a cone more than 1,000 feet high and covered many miles with lava. Parícutin became inactive in 1952.

141

Design Photographers International

Beautiful Paris, the capital of France, is divided by the Seine River. The white Basilica of the Sacré Coeur, a famous church, rises above the horizon in this air view looking northeast.

Bernard G. Silberstein, Rapho-Guillumette

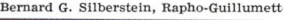

The Eiffel Tower, on the Left Bank of the Seine River, is a symbol of Paris to millions of persons throughout the world.

PARIS

PARIS is the capital and largest city of France. It is one of the most beautiful cities in the world. Lovely gardens and parks and historic squares lie throughout Paris, and chestnut trees line the city's famous avenues. At night, floodlights shine on Paris' many magnificent palaces and monuments. The gleaming beauty of Paris has given it the nickname *City of Light*.

Every year, more than two million tourists come to Paris from other parts of the world. The most popular

David F. Schoenbrun, the contributor of this article, is a radio and television commentator, and the author of As France Goes *and* The Three Lives of Charles de Gaulle.

142

tourist attraction is the Eiffel Tower. This huge structure is known throughout the world as the symbol of Paris. Tourists flock to the Louvre, one of the world's largest art museums, and visit the soaring Cathedral of Notre Dame. The city is also famous for its many restaurants, theaters, and nightclubs.

Paris has long been a world center of the arts and education. For hundreds of years, important styles in painting and literature have developed there. About two-thirds of France's artists and writers live in Paris. The University of Paris, one of the world's largest universities, is more than 800 years old.

The city is also a great industrial center. About a fourth of France's labor force lives in the crowded Paris area. Paris factories turn out a variety of products, including most of France's automobiles. The city is best known for such luxury products as jewelry, perfume, and women's high-fashion clothing. Famous designers of women's clothing create Paris fashions that are copied in many other countries.

The history of Paris goes back more than 2,000 years. In 52 B.C., soldiers of ancient Rome found a tribe of fishermen living in the area. The Romans established a colony there. During the Middle Ages, Paris grew rapidly and became a major center of culture and government. In Paris, in 1792, France became one of the first nations to overthrow its king and set up a republic. The execution of noblemen became a familiar sight during the French Revolution. In World War I, Paris cabdrivers helped win the First Battle of the Marne by speeding French troops to the front in their taxis. German forces occupied Paris during World War II.

Two thousand years ago, the Roman general Julius Caesar described the people of what is now Paris as "clever, inventive, and given to quarreling among themselves." This description is still considered true of Parisians today. They are known for their creative arts and crafts, and their strong political feelings lead to many bitter quarrels. The similarities among the people of Paris through thousands of years help prove a French saying: "The more things change, the more they stay the same." Today, dramatic changes are taking place in Paris. Skyscrapers, modern housing projects, and expressways are being built in a huge government construction program. Beautiful old buildings and monuments are being restored. Paris is staying young while preserving the treasures of its past.

--- **FACTS IN BRIEF** ---

Population: 2,790,091; metropolitan area, 7,735,342.

Area: 41 square miles; metropolitan area, 185 square miles.

Altitude: 250 feet above sea level.

Climate: *Average temperature*—January, 28° F.; July, 68° F. *Average annual precipitation* (rainfall, melted snow, and other forms of moisture)—22 inches.

Government: *Chief executive*—prefect (appointed by the national government). *Legislature*—City Council of 90 members (six-year terms).

Founded: 52 B.C.

PARIS

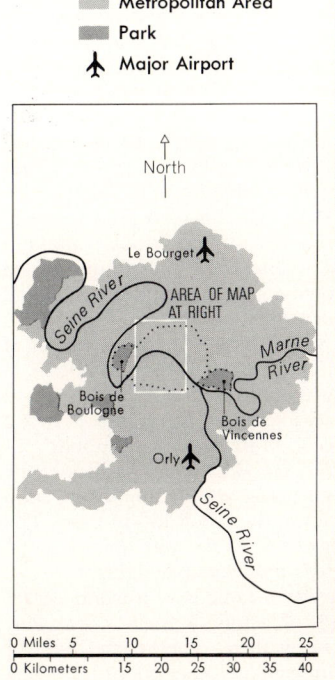

····· City Limits

▓ Metropolitan Area

■ Park

✈ Major Airport

North

Le Bourget ✈

AREA OF MAP AT RIGHT

Seine River

Marne River

Bois de Boulogne

Bois de Vincennes

Orly ✈

Seine River

0 Miles   5   10   15   20   25
0 Kilometers   15   20   25   30   35   40

INNER PARIS

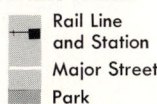

Rail Line and Station

Major Street

Park

Arc de Triomphe
　de l'Étoile............2
Army Museum........17
Bibliothèque Nationale..10
Bourbon Palace........18
Canadian Embassy.....3
Champ de Mars......15
Comédie-Française.....11
École des Beaux-Arts....19
Eiffel Tower..........14
Élysée Palace.......5
Hôtel de Ville........25
Hôtel des Invalides.....16
Louvre Palace
　and Museum........12
Luxembourg Palace
　and Gardens........20
Notre Dame,
　Cathedral of.......22
Opéra.................9
Palace of Justice.......21
Panthéon............24
Place de la Concorde....7
Radio House..........13
Rond-Point............4
Sacré Coeur,
　Basilica of the.......1
Sorbonne.............23
Tuileries Gardens......8
U.S. Embassy..........6

WORLD BOOK map-FGA

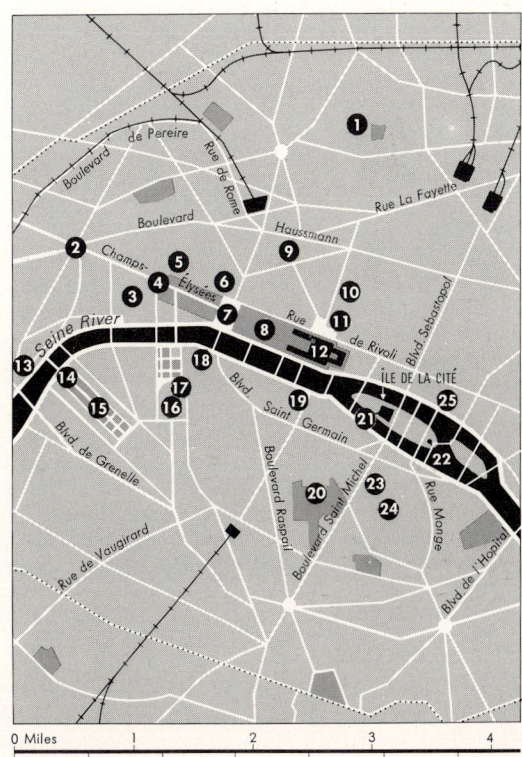

0 Miles   1   2   3   4
0 Kilometers   2   3   4   5   6

143

Paris lies 107 miles southeast of the English Channel. It is in the heart of a fertile, heavily populated lowland called the *Paris Basin*. Paris has more than 2,790,000 persons, and is one of the world's most crowded cities. It has an average of about a hundred persons to the acre. See FRANCE (map: Paris and Suburbs).

The Seine River curves through Paris for about eight miles from east to west. The section of Paris north of the river is called the *Right Bank*. Busy offices, small manufacturing plants, and fashionable shops are on the Right Bank. The *Left Bank*, the section south of the Seine, is a famous center of artist and student life.

Paris is laid out according to plans that developed through hundreds of years. An island in the Seine, the *Île de la Cité* (Island of the City), is the heart of Paris. The city was founded on this island more than 2,000 years ago. Paris soon spread out on both banks of the river. About 1200, a fortified wall was built around the city. Paris continued to grow, and new walls were built in a series of widening circles. Today, there are boulevards where the walls once stood.

Gardens, Squares, and Parks. Paris has been described as being like a woman with flowers in her hair. This description comes from the many beautiful gardens and parks throughout the city. The Tuileries Gardens, on the Right Bank, are one of the finest formal French gardens. Neat flower beds and beautiful statues line a long path through the Tuileries. Children sail toy boats in two round fountains along the broad path. They also sail boats in the central pool of the Luxembourg Gardens, on the Left Bank. This lovely park offers Punch and Judy puppet shows, a great favorite with Paris youngsters. See TUILERIES.

The *Champs-Élysées* (Elysian Fields) is Paris' most famous avenue. It is lined with beautiful gardens and rows of chestnut trees. Along its route is the Rond-Point. This landscaped circle has magnificent fountains, and formal flower beds trimmed to look like a huge bouquet. At the western end of the Champs-Élysées stands the *Arc de Triomphe de l'Étoile* (Arch of Triumph of the Star). Emperor Napoleon I started to build this huge stone arch in 1806, and it was completed in 1836. The arch rises in the *Place de l'Étoile* (Square of the Star), one of more than 130 public squares in Paris. Broad avenues extend from the Étoile in 12 directions. See ARC DE TRIOMPHE DE L'ÉTOILE.

At the eastern end of the Champs-Élysées is the *Place de la Concorde* (Square of Peace). This square was built during the 1700's. Within it are eight huge statues, two fountains, and the 75-foot-high Obelisk of Luxor, a four-sided stone pillar from Egypt (see OBELISK [picture]). During the French Revolution (1789-1799), a *guillotine* (beheading machine) stood in the square. Hundreds of persons, including King Louis XVI and Marie Antoinette, were executed on it. Other important squares in Paris include Carrousel, Nation, République, Saint Michel, Vendôme, and Vosges.

The *Champ de Mars* (Field of Mars) is a beautiful park that was once a military training ground. Among its gardens and tree-lined lawns are many attractions for children, including miniature automobile speed-

ways, merry-go-rounds, puppet shows, and donkey rides. In the Champ de Mars stands the 984-foot-high Eiffel Tower, the world-famous symbol of Paris. For many years, this wrought-iron tower was the world's tallest structure. Visitors can dine in restaurants on various platforms in the tower and enjoy spectacular views of Paris. See EIFFEL TOWER.

Paris' largest parks are the *Bois de Boulogne* (Forest of Boulogne) and the *Bois de Vincennes* (Forest of Vincennes). These parks, each covering more than 2,000 acres, have several lakes for boating. They also have horse-racing tracks, restaurants, theaters, and zoos.

Famous Buildings. The Louvre Palace, one of the largest palaces in the world, extends a half mile along the Seine. Most of the palace houses the Louvre Museum, one of the world's largest art museums. The palace also includes offices of the French Ministry of Finance. The Louvre dates from about 1200, when it was built as a royal fort. It was rebuilt during the 1500's as the royal palace. From then on, many French rulers expanded the Louvre. Napoleon III began to build the last addition in 1852. See LOUVRE.

Many other historic buildings of Paris also house government offices. The main house of Parliament, the National Assembly, meets in the Bourbon Palace, completed in 1728. The Luxembourg Palace is the meeting place of the Senate, the advisory house of France's Parliament. The palace was built during the early 1600's. The president of France lives in the Élysée Palace, built in 1718. The Palace of Justice stands where the ancient Roman governors and early French kings lived on the Île de la Cité. Today, high French courts meet there. The *Hôtel de Ville* (City Hall) stands where Paris' first town hall was built in 1357.

The domed Panthéon is a monument to French heroes and other great men. It was originally a church named for Sainte Geneviève, the patron saint of Paris. In A.D. 451, she organized the city's defenses against a threatened attack by Attila the Hun. It is believed that her prayers prevented the attack and saved the city. In 1791, the church was named the Panthéon, and became a burial place. Jean Moulin, a hero of World War II, was buried there in 1965. After German troops occupied France in 1940, Moulin organized forces to fight them. The Germans captured Moulin and tortured him to make him name his friends. Moulin tried to kill himself so he would not weaken and betray them. He later died from the torture.

The Cathedral of Notre Dame, the most famous of Paris' many beautiful churches, stands on the Île de la Cité. The cathedral was completed in the 1300's, and is known for its majesty and stone carvings (see NOTRE DAME, CATHEDRAL OF). Many Roman Catholic pilgrims visit the *Basilica of the Sacré Coeur* (Basilica of the Sacred Heart). This gleaming white church rises atop 423-foot-high Montmartre, the tallest hill in Paris. The basilica, with its huge bell tower and onion-shaped dome, is one of the city's most familiar sights.

Arts. Paris has long been famous as a world center of the arts. Thousands of actors, musicians, painters, and writers work or study there. They come from all parts of France and from many other countries. They

Boulevards of Paris, where walls once stood to defend the city against attack, are crowded with automobiles, buses, and taxis. The traffic is especially heavy at the Place de l'Opéra, one of Paris' more than 130 public squares. There, the Boulevard des Capucines connects with several major streets. The busy area has business offices, fashionable shops, restaurants, sidewalk cafes, and theaters.

Fred Bond, Publix

are attracted by Paris' special atmosphere of freedom in the arts, in which new styles can develop easily.

Painters and sculptors show their work at exhibitions called *salons,* and in the city's many art galleries. Outstanding painters and sculptors who lived in Paris include Constantin Brancusi, Georges Braque, Pablo Picasso, Pierre Auguste Renoir, and Auguste Rodin. Famous Paris novelists and playwrights include Albert Camus, André Gide, Victor Hugo, Marcel Proust, and Jean-Paul Sartre.

Paris has about 60 theaters, not counting motion-picture theaters. The Comédie-Française, Paris' most famous theater, offers classics of French drama. The Opéra is one of the world's largest opera and ballet theaters. Paris also has several symphony orchestras.

Museums and Art Galleries of Paris are storehouses of many priceless art treasures. The works of painters and sculptors of the late 1800's and the 1900's are displayed in the National Museum of Modern Art. Works considered to be of lasting greatness are housed in the Louvre Museum. This famous museum has such art masterpieces as Leonardo da Vinci's painting *Mona Lisa* and the Greek statue *Venus de Milo.* The huge Louvre Palace also houses the Museum of Decorative Art. This smaller museum has a fine collection of antique French furniture.

The Army Museum is one of the largest military museums in the world. It has outstanding collections of historical weapons and armor. Nearby is the tomb of Napoleon I. The Army Museum and the tomb stand on the grounds of the *Hôtel des Invalides* (Home for Disabled Soldiers), completed in 1676. The Cluny Museum, a house built in the 1400's, has art works and other objects of the Middle Ages. The Carnavalet Museum, a house dating from the 1500's, has displays that tell the history of Paris.

Schools and Libraries. The University of Paris, which dates from about 1150, has more than 85,000 students. The Sorbonne, its college of arts and sciences, is world famous (see SORBONNE). The university area, on the Left Bank, has been called the *Latin Quarter* since the Middle Ages. At that time, the students and teachers who lived there spoke to one another in Latin.

Another world-famous school in Paris is *École des Beaux-Arts* (School of Fine Arts). It offers courses in architecture, painting, sculpture, and similar subjects (see ÉCOLE DES BEAUX-ARTS). Other Paris schools include the College of France and the Polytechnical School.

The Bibliothèque Nationale, France's national library, is one of the largest libraries in Western Europe. It has more than six million books (see BIBLIOTHÈQUE NATIONALE). Other important Paris libraries include the Mazarine Library of the Institute of France, the nation's major learned society, and libraries of the University of Paris.

Economy. The Paris area is the major manufacturing center of France. Most of the country's great automobile industry is based there. Other important Paris industries include book publishing and the manufacture of chemicals, dyes, electronic machinery, furniture, leather goods, and railroad and airplane equipment. Paris has long been a world center of such luxury goods as jewelry, perfume, and women's high-fashion clothing. These famous *articles de Paris* are produced in many small plants in the heart of the city. They are sold in fashionable shops on the Right Bank.

Paris is the transportation center of France. The national railroad network forms a cobweb pattern, with most lines extending from Paris in all directions. Orly Airport, near Paris, is France's largest airport. Its huge new terminal, opened in 1961, can handle eight million passengers a year. The Paris subway, called the *Métro,* has over a hundred miles of track.

Paris has more than 10 daily newspapers. They account for about a third of the circulation of all French dailies. The largest Paris paper, *France-Soir,* has a daily circulation of more than a million copies. A government-owned broadcasting system operates three radio networks and two television networks in Paris.

Government. Paris is governed by a *prefect* appointed by the national government. A City Council of 90 members, elected by the voters to six-year terms, aids the prefect. The council members elect a council president, who performs such duties as welcoming important visitors to the City Hall and supervising the mayors of Paris' 20 *arrondissements* (wards).

Robert Capa, Magnum

The Freeing of Paris in World War II began when soldiers of the secret French Forces of the Interior joined with the people of Paris and rose against the German conquerors. Fighting in the city lasted about a week in August, 1944. Allied armies reached Paris on August 24, and freed the city the next day.

PARIS/History

Early Years. In ancient times, a Celtic tribe of fishermen called the *Parisii* lived in what is now Paris. The Parisii occupied an island in the Seine River. The island is now called the Île de la Cité. In 52 B.C., Roman invaders established a colony there and called it *Lutetia*. The town soon spread out on both banks of the river. It became known as Paris about A.D. 300.

Clovis, the first ruler of the great Frankish kingdom, made Paris his capital in 507. Hugh Capet, the count of Paris and duke of the surrounding region, became king of France in 987. As the French kings became more powerful, the capital grew in importance and population. Philip II, who ruled from 1180 to 1223, developed Paris as a great center of culture, government, and learning.

The Renaissance. The French kings further developed the culture and beauty of Paris during the Renaissance (see RENAISSANCE). The men they hired to design the new boulevards, palaces, and squares looked

to ancient Greece and Rome for models. The Louvre, a fortress dating from about 1200, was rebuilt as the royal palace during the 1500's. Many French rulers later built additions to the Louvre, and made it the largest palace in the world.

Paris was the center of the bloody French Revolution (1789-1799). Parisians became accustomed to the sight of carts carrying persons through the streets to their death on the guillotine. See FRENCH REVOLUTION.

The 1800's. During the early 1800's, Napoleon Bonaparte built many new buildings, laid out public gardens, and made other improvements in Paris. Napoleon III, emperor from 1852 to 1870, did much to give Paris its present appearance. He built banks, hospitals, railroad stations, theaters, and wide, straight avenues.

During the Franco-Prussian War (1870-1871), Paris surrendered to Prussian troops after a hard siege in which the city's food supplies were cut off. The starving Parisians ate cats, dogs, and rats. See FRANCO-PRUSSIAN WAR.

The 1900's. The Germans did some damage to Paris with long-range guns during World War I (1914-1918), but did not capture the city. In September, 1914, the Germans pushed French troops back to the Marne River, about 15 miles from Paris. The French held their ground, and taxicabs from Paris brought out fresh troops. This "taxicab army" helped win the First Battle of the Marne, which ended Germany's chances for a quick victory.

German troops occupied Paris during World War II (1939-1945). They broke through the French defenses in June, 1940, and pushed quickly to Paris. To save Paris from destruction, the French government declared it an *open city*, an undefended city opened to the enemy. German troops entered Paris without a fight, and marched triumphantly down the Champs-Élysées. Paris became a center of a French underground resistance movement. In mid-1944, Allied troops began driving the Germans from France. The Allies freed Paris in August, 1944.

Paris Today is in the early stages of a vast renewal program. The program was drawn up in 1960, and is scheduled to be completed by the year 2000. At that time, the Paris metropolitan area is expected to have a population of more than 12 million. Old buildings and other facilities that will not be able to serve the future population are being replaced. But old monuments, palaces, and other buildings valuable for their beauty are being restored. A 1961 amendment required all building owners to sandblast and wash the front of their property. By the mid-1960's, Paris was a gleaming city.

During the 1960's, much new construction was started throughout Paris. A law prohibiting skyscrapers was amended in 1955, and high-rise office buildings and modern housing projects have gone up. The new housing is especially important because about half the city's apartments do not have private bathrooms.

One of the old facilities being replaced was Les Halles, the central food market of Paris. Its narrow streets and old buildings, in which about 30,000 persons worked, could no longer serve the city. In addition, movement to and from Les Halles tied up Paris traffic. During the mid-1960's, the marketing operations were transferred to Rungis, a suburb six miles south of Paris.

146

By the late 1960's, much of a new 22-mile-long expressway around Paris had been completed. North-south and east-west expressways also were begun or scheduled. A high-speed subway was being built to a new international exhibition hall west of Paris. Similar subways linking eastern and western suburbs were also underway. The new subway trains will speed through Paris at about 60 miles an hour. DAVID F. SCHOENBRUN

PARIS/Study Aids

Related Articles in WORLD BOOK include:

Arc de Triomphe de l'Étoile
Bastille
Bibliothèque Nationale
École des Beaux-Arts
Eiffel Tower
France (pictures)
French Revolution
Hôtel des Invalides
Louvre
Notre Dame, Cathedral of

Obelisk (picture)
Quai d'Orsay
Radium Institute
Seine River
Sorbonne
Trocadéro
Tuileries
Zoo (picture: Pleasant Retreats)

Outline

I. The City Today
  A. Gardens, Squares, and Parks
  B. Famous Buildings
  C. Arts
  D. Museums and Art Galleries
  E. Schools and Libraries
  F. Economy
  G. Government

II. History

Questions

Why is Paris called the *City of Light?*
Where in Paris is the Cathedral of Notre Dame?
What is the largest palace in the world?
What official heads the government of Paris?
What are the Left Bank and the Right Bank of Paris?
What did the ancient Romans call the Paris area?
When did Paris receive its present name?
What is Paris' highest hill? What is atop the hill?
What is the Eiffel Tower? Panthéon? Champs-Élysées?
How did the Latin Quarter receive its name?
How was Paris saved from damage in World War II?

French Embassy Press & Information Div.

France's Radio-Television Center, completed in 1963, represents the new construction going up in Paris. The gleaming white building, covering nearly 10 acres, is one of the largest buildings in Europe. It stands near the Eiffel Tower, *upper right,* from which France's first national radio program was broadcast in 1923.

PARIS, COMTE DE (1838-1894), LOUIS PHILIPPE ALBERT D'ORLÉANS, a claimant to the French throne, became heir apparent on the death of his father in 1842. But he lost his rights when his grandfather, King Louis Philippe, was driven from the throne in the Revolution of 1848.

The count served briefly as a captain of volunteers in the Union Army during the American Civil War. After the fall of Napoleon III in 1870, he returned to France. He became the candidate of the *royalists,* those who favored a return to government by kings. But the suspicious French Republicans passed an Act of Expulsion in 1886, which forced the count into permanent exile in England. The count was born in Paris, and was educated in England. E. J. KNAPTON

PARIS, PACT OF. See KELLOGG PEACE PACT.

PARIS, TREATIES OF. Many treaties of historical importance were signed in Paris, France. Some of the more important ones are described below.

The Treaty of 1763 was signed on Feb. 10, 1763. It ended the Seven Years' War in Europe and the French

and Indian War in America. This treaty doomed French hopes for an empire in North America. Great Britain became the controlling power there and in India.

According to the terms of the Treaty of 1763, France gave all of what is now Canada to Great Britain. France received the islands of St. Pierre and Miquelon, and kept fishing rights off Newfoundland. Great Britain also received all French territories east of the Mississippi River except New Orleans, and France's trading centers in India.

The Treaty of 1783 ended the Revolutionary War in America. John Adams, Benjamin Franklin, and John Jay signed for the United States, and David Hartley signed for Great Britain on September 3. The treaty established peace between Great Britain and the United States and formally recognized the United States.

The United States gained all the lands west to the Mississippi River, measuring from a point west of Lake of the Woods down to 31° north latitude. The treaty of 1783 also set the northern border for the United States territory. The United States received fishing rights in Newfoundland and in the Gulf of Saint Lawrence. Both Great Britain and the United States received the right to use the Mississippi River. The United States government agreed to recommend to the various states that they take measures to restore to the British Loyalists the lands taken from them during the war.

The Treaty of 1814 marked the end of Napoleon's long domination of Europe. It was signed on May 30, after his first abdication. France was reduced to its 1792 boundaries, but otherwise it was treated mildly. It was not occupied or forced to disarm or pay war damages.

The Treaty of 1815 followed the final defeat of Napoleon at Waterloo. It was signed on November 20. This time France was reduced to its boundaries in 1790, and had to pay war damages of 700 million francs.

The Treaty of 1856, signed on March 30, ended the Crimean War. Russia fought this war against France, Great Britain, the Ottoman Empire (now Turkey), and Sardinia. The treaty provided that the Black Sea would be opened to the merchant vessels of all nations, but would be forever closed to warships. The treaty opened the Danube River to free navigation for all nations, and set up an international commission to control the river. The powers agreed to guarantee the independence of the Ottoman Empire.

The Treaty of 1898 ended the Spanish-American War. It was signed on December 10. Cuba gained independence. Spain surrendered Puerto Rico, Guam, and the Philippine Islands to the United States. The United States then paid Spain $20 million for the Philippines. See SPANISH-AMERICAN WAR (The Peace Treaty).

The Treaty of 1919 included all the treaties signed between the Central Powers and the Allies at the end of World War I. All were made legal and binding at Paris. The most important was the Treaty of Versailles, signed between the Allies and Germany on June 28, 1919. See VERSAILLES, TREATY OF. ROBERT G. L. WAITE

PARIS, UNIVERSITY OF. See PARIS (Schools and Libraries).

PARIS CONFERENCES. Many international conferences have met in Paris, France. But the term Paris Conference usually refers either to the Paris Peace Conference of 1919 or to the Paris Conference of 1946.

Representatives of 32 Allied nations met in Paris in January, 1919, to draw up terms of peace with Germany and its allies. German representatives were not allowed to participate in the conference. They were called to Paris in June to sign the treaty in the Palace of Versailles. See WORLD WAR I (Peace Aims). In July, 1946, delegates from 21 nations met in Luxembourg Palace in Paris to consider draft peace treaties with Italy, Hungary, Bulgaria, Romania, and Finland. See WORLD WAR II (The Peace Treaties). NORMAN D. PALMER

PARIS GREEN is a bright green powder, prepared from arsenic acid and copper acetate. It is valued chiefly as a wet or dry spray to kill worms, grasshoppers, potato bugs, and other insects that eat the leaves of plants. Paris green is almost insoluble in water, but is usually mixed with it for wet spraying. Such a preparation must be stirred continually, or the poison sinks to the bottom, leaving the top liquid harmless, and the rest so strong that it can injure plants. Other preparations have largely replaced Paris green. HENRY T. NORTHEN

PARIS OF AMERICA. See BUENOS AIRES; NEW ORLEANS (History).

PARIS OF THE ORIENT. See SAIGON.

PARISH. See LOUISIANA (Local Government).

PARISII. See PARIS (History).

PARITY, in physics, concerns the symmetry between an event and its reflection in a mirror. The idea of parity is a useful tool in quantum mechanics. Physicists say that *parity is conserved* when an event and its mirror image both satisfy laws of nature. In this case, an observer cannot tell whether he is looking at the event or at its reflection. The same laws apply to the event and its image, and give the observer no clue by which to identify one or the other. Parity is conserved in all ordinary mechanical and electrical systems.

Physicists once believed that the conservation of parity was a natural law that applied to all events. But in 1956, two Chinese-born physicists, Tsung Dao Lee and Chen Ning Yang, suggested a number of experiments which proved otherwise. The experiments showed that parity was not conserved in a type of nuclear event called a *weak interaction*. An example of such an event is the emission of an electron by a radioactive nucleus.

The first such experiment was performed at the United States National Bureau of Standards by C. S. Wu of Columbia University and E. Ambler, R. W. Hayward, D. D. Hoppes, and R. P. Hudson of the Bureau who used atoms of the radioactive cobalt-60. The result of their experiment showed that parity conservation is not a universal law of nature. CHEN NING YANG

PARITY, in economics, measures equality of purchasing power of two different currencies, or of the price of goods during two different periods. In the United States the word is usually applied to the price of certain farm products. The parity price for a particular farm product is that price which gives a farmer the same purchasing power that he had during a specified period of time called the *base period*. The most commonly used base period is 1910 to 1914. So, if a farmer could buy a pair of shoes in 1910 for the same price at which he sold two bushels of corn, he should be able to do so today.

Since the 1920's, "agricultural equality"—the idea that the farmer should have a fair share of the national income—has received much attention. The Agricultural Adjustment Act of 1933 introduced parity as a method of measuring agricultural equality, and a program of price supports in order to achieve it. The law provided for an index of prices for things farmers sell, and one for things they buy. The *index number* of prices received for any particular year is found by mathematically comparing the sum of the prices of crops during that year with the sum of the prices of crops during the base period. The index number of prices paid is found the same way. If the index number of prices received equals the index number of prices paid, prices are "at parity."

In 1940, Congress introduced a change in computing parity. The Secretary of Agriculture now must use a "10-year moving average" in computing parity if it gives a higher support price than would be obtained by using the average of the period from 1910 to 1914.

Some persons criticize the parity program because it is based on a period in the past which may not be appropriate under present conditions. JOHN H. FREDERICK

See also DISTRIBUTION.

Ewing Galloway

Central Park in New York City includes 840 acres of green woodland and lakes. Ringed by tall buildings in the heart of the city, Central Park has many playgrounds, an excellent zoo, and many other recreational facilities.

PARK. A park may be only a tiny bit of green in a large city, with a few flowers, trees, and benches. Or it may be a natural wilderness larger than some states. But no matter what its size and facilities, a park today is meant for the enjoyment of all.

A park had an entirely different purpose only a little more than two hundred years ago. The first parks were preserved for royalty and the nobility. They were called *preserves*, and were set aside as hunting areas for the wealthy and the wellborn. The earliest of such parks were set aside in ancient Egypt and ancient Rome.

In England and Scotland during the 1700's, thousands of small farmers and sheepherders were driven from their homes so that nobility could create deer preserves. Any commoner who was caught stealing or killing an animal in these preserves was liable to be hanged or cruelly punished.

The first city parks of London were open only to persons of certain classes, or admission was charged to them. Free public parks later were established in the great cities of Europe, but they were generally located in the central or better residential sections of the city. There was no attempt to provide parks for every community.

Today, the provision of parks for public recreation and enjoyment is a recognized responsibility of city, state, and national governments. Cities carefully plan their parks, public squares, and winding parkways to provide enjoyment for all their citizens. State governments preserve wilderness areas and sites of special historic interest so that all the citizens of the states may enjoy them. State governments also provide convenient picnic areas along state highways. Great national parks occupy thousands of square miles all over North America, and preserve some of nature's most marvelous creations.

City Parks

Probably the first city park in the United States was Boston Common, set aside in 1634 as community ground. Like most of the New England commons, Boston Common at first was used as pasture ground for sheep. Later, such public squares were used as bowling greens.

During the 1850's, parks were established in most of the larger cities. But most of them were formal affairs, designed principally for quiet strolling or relaxing upon benches. During the 1900's, however, city planners saw that a park could accomplish many other things besides providing beauty. The recreational facilities of parks began to be increased.

Today, city planners and recreational experts are pretty well agreed on what makes up the ideal city park. There should be at least one acre of park land for every hundred inhabitants of the city or community. The recreational program of the well-rounded park should provide group activities in the arts, handicrafts, sports, and nature study. Park sports may include such highly organized games as basketball, softball, football, volleyball, soccer, track and field, tennis, archery, badminton, boxing, wrestling, swimming, gymnastics, and outdoor winter sports. Lakeside parks, or parks with artificial lakes or lagoons, can provide interesting water sports such as swimming, canoeing, boating, and sailing. Art and handicraft activities are designed to attract the largest number of enthusiasts from the ranks of boys and girls of grammar school and high school ages. But

149

Colorado Dept. of Public Relations

National Parks cover thousands of acres of scenic land in the United States. Many of them provide picnic and camping grounds.

many adults also show a great interest in such projects. Craft clubs or classes of instruction may be conducted in such arts as wood carving, clay modeling, leather-craft, jewelry making, sewing, rug weaving, and painting. A park is an ideal place for holding contests such as model-airplane tournaments and kite-flying meets.

Classes of instruction may be held in such subjects as dramatic art, voice culture, dancing, choral group work, and the playing of musical instruments. These club groups may offer public performances of dramas, operettas, musical comedies, community concerts, and other events.

Some of the larger park systems also offer professional entertainment, such as performances of outstanding symphony orchestras and concert bands.

The operation and supervision of city parks is usually carried on by a separate department of the city government. A park commissioner, or park superintendent, is directly responsible for the operation of the system. He may be advised by a park board, or park commission. Serving the executive are recreational and sports instructors, playground supervisors, landscape architects and park ground workers, and various other employees. Park systems are supported by taxes, and usually are allotted a definite proportion of each tax dollar collected for general purposes.

Since the early 1900's, there has been a trend away from the formal landscape type of park, and toward the park with a natural setting. Most modern park systems are connected throughout the city system by parkways running alongside paved boulevards.

The largest community park system in the United States is that of Chicago. It covers about 7,000 acres and includes about 440 parks, 225 field houses, and 28 miles of lakefront. The real estate held by the Chicago Park District is valued at many millions of dollars. New York City, Boston, Baltimore, Philadelphia, Kansas City, and St. Louis are other examples of cities with exceptional park systems.

There are more than 805,000 acres of parks and recreation areas in American cities. There are more than 2,700 municipalities that have recreation programs or parks.

State and County Parks

All the states have established parks in scenic areas or sites of special historical interest. There are more than 3,200 of these parks, covering a total of about 7,352,000 acres. One of the largest of these is Palisades Interstate Park, a chain of park areas along the west bank of the Hudson River beginning at Fort Lee in New Jersey and ending at Newburgh, N.Y. This park, covering more than 51,000 acres, is administered by the states of New York and New Jersey. It provides recreation for thousands in the New York City area.

Parks operated by county units of government are more frequent in the eastern states than in the western and southern states. Among the most noted of these systems is the Westchester County Park of New York.

National Parks

The first national park to be set aside in the world was created when Congress passed the Yellowstone Act in 1872. Since the establishment of Yellowstone National Park, 35 other national parks have been established in the United States and its territories. These parks contain great virgin forests, majestic mountains, sprawling glaciers, geysers, volcanoes, and all the animal and plant life natural to wilderness regions.

Parks of Other Lands

Canada has a large number of national and provincial parks (see CANADA [National Parks]). In South America, Argentina and Chile have set aside large national preserves. The older and smaller countries of Europe have been unable to develop national and state parks on a scale to compare with those of the Western Hemisphere, because they do not have the space. The oldest and largest of the European national parks are in Germany, Poland, and Czechoslovakia. After World War I (1914-1918), Soviet Russia established many national, provincial, and city parks. Moscow parks are noted for their cultural and recreational facilities. Denmark and Sweden have been active in establishing parks. In Great Britain, there were few public parks outside London and the other large cities until 1932. In that year, the British Parliament adopted the Town and Country Planning Act, to increase the number of national and local parks.   PHILIP L. SEMAN

See also NATIONAL PARK; PLAYGROUND; RECREATION; and the various city articles, such as CHICAGO.

PARK, DAVID (1911-1960), was an influential American painter and art teacher. His painting *Four Men* appears in color in the PAINTING article. Park painted and taught in California from the mid-1940's until his death. During this period, many American artists painted in an *abstract* or *non-representational* style, with no recognizable subject matter. But Park painted powerful human figures in a representational style which influenced many younger artists. Park was head of the art department of the Winsor School in Boston from 1936 to 1941. Later, he taught at the California School of Fine Arts in San Francisco and at the University of California. Park was born in Boston.   ALLEN S. WELLER

PARK, MUNGO. See EXPLORATION AND DISCOVERY (table: Explorers of Africa).

PARK, NATIONAL. See NATIONAL PARK.

PARK, ROBERT E. See SOCIOLOGY (Modern Sociology).

PARK COLLEGE. See UNIVERSITIES AND COLLEGES (table).

PARKA, *PAHR kuh,* is a hooded coat that is popular in cold regions. Alaskan Eskimos and the Siberians made it from the skins of animals. The long coat is now made from heavy cloth in many colors as well as from fur. Both men and women wear parkas.

PARKER, ALTON BROOKS (1852-1926), an American judge and politician, won the Democratic party nomination for United States President in 1904. He opposed Theodore Roosevelt, who was running for reelection. The party leaders hoped that Parker, a highly respected conservative, would win the votes of many who were opposed to Roosevelt's progressivism. But Roosevelt's great popularity decisively defeated Parker.

Parker began his career by practicing law in Kingston, N.Y. From 1897 to 1904, he served as chief justice of the court of appeals, the highest judicial office of the state. Parker was born in Cortland, N.Y., and was graduated from Albany Law School.   NELSON M. BLAKE

PARKER, CHARLIE (1920-1955), an alto saxophonist and composer, ranks among the most influential musicians in jazz history. Parker and trumpeter Dizzy Gillespie were responsible for the rise of *bebop,* a complex rhythmic, melodic, and harmonic form of jazz that developed in the 1940's. His many recordings illustrate his amazing technique and the richness of his musical ideas. Several of his compositions, including "Ornithology" and "Confirmation," became jazz standards.

CHARLES CHRISTOPHER PARKER, JR., was born in Kansas City, Kans. He was nicknamed "Bird." He worked in the bands of Jay McShann, Earl Hines, and Billy Eckstine before forming his own small groups in the 1940's. From his youth, Parker was addicted to heroin. As a result, he suffered from many physical and emotional ills during his last years. LEONARD FEATHER

See also JAZZ (Bop and Cool Jazz).

PARKER, DOROTHY (1893-1967), an American short-story writer and poet, became one of the great humorists of her generation. Her satirical verse was so popular that her books of poetry became best sellers. Her conversation was as clever as her writing, and she was often given credit for clever remarks that she did not actually make.

Her books of poems include *Death and Taxes* (1931) and *Not so Deep as a Well* (1936). To these she added a solid body of short stories. Perhaps the best known of these is *Big Blonde,* which won the O. Henry Memorial Award in 1929. Her collections of short stories include *Laments for the Living* (1930) and *Here Lies* (1939). Mrs. Parker had strong, liberal political opinions, which were reflected in her writings. Much of her verse is satire on the manners and thought of modern America.

Dorothy Parker was born in West End, N.J. Her

Dorothy Parker
Lofman, Pix

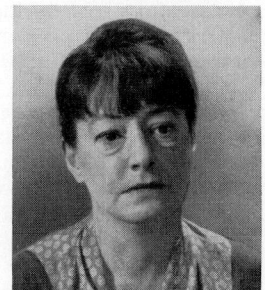

maiden name was DOROTHY ROTHSCHILD, but she wrote under the name of her first husband, Edwin Pond Parker. She worked for magazines until her first volume of verse, entitled *Enough Rope* (1927), became successful.   ARTHUR MIZENER

PARKER, FRANCIS WAYLAND (1837-1902), an American educator, exerted great influence on modern educational practice. He urged that classrooms be informal and free from old-time strict discipline, and that the child be made the center of the educational process. Parker also developed strong programs of science and geography in the elementary schools. In 1883, he became head of the Cook County (Chicago) Normal School and began teaching his new methods to teachers. In 1899, he founded the Chicago Institute. When this school became the University of Chicago's department of education, Parker became its director.

Chicago Teachers College
Francis Parker

Parker was born in Bedford Township, N.H. He taught in New Hampshire and Illinois and, in 1872, went to Germany to study experiments in education.   GALEN SAYLOR

PARKER, SIR GILBERT (1862-1932), gained fame as a Canadian novelist and short-story writer. Such novels as *The Seats of the Mighty* (1896) brought him an international audience because of their sense of romance and high adventure. The short-story collection *Pierre and His People* (1892) is a series of stories about French Canadians who live in the wilderness of northern Canada.

Most of his tales were set in distant times and remote places. He wrote short stories, novels, and two books of verse.

Parker was born in Camden, Ont., and studied at Trinity University. He began his career as a journalist in Australia in 1885. He went to England in 1889, and combined writing with politics. He served in the House of Commons from 1900 to 1918. During the first two years of World War I, he directed British publicity in the United States.   DESMOND PACEY

PARKER, JOHN. See REVOLUTIONARY WAR IN AMERICA (Lexington and Concord).

PARKER DAM is a federal power and water-supply project on the Colorado River about 145 miles south of Hoover Dam. It lies on the boundary between southern California and western Arizona. Parker Dam is 320 feet high and 856 feet long. Its reservoir has a capacity of 717,000 acre-feet of water. The dam was built to supply water and electric power to southern California cities. It was completed in 1938 at a cost of about $13 million. It is a concrete-arch type dam. The bed had to be excavated 235 feet, making it the deepest underwater dam in the world. For the location of Parker Dam, see ARIZONA (physical map).   T. W. MERMEL

PARKES, ALEXANDER. See PLASTICS (The Invention of Celluloid).

PARKING

Parallel Parking, *below*, leaves more street space for moving traffic than angle parking, *below right.* But angle parking allows more cars to park along a single block. Off-street parking in private or municipal parking lots, *right,* relieves much congestion on busy city streets, especially in business sections.

Hedrich-Blessing

Parallel

Angle

Loading Zones provide parking space for trucks making deliveries.

PARKING is the storage of vehicles at the curb of a street, or in a lot or garage. The millions of automobiles, trucks, and buses that crowd the streets of the nation's cities are in use only a fraction of the time. While motorists shop, and buses and trucks load or unload, they must have parking space. But their parking must not hamper the movement of other vehicles.

Proper parking space is especially important in a business district. Where inadequate space is provided, customers may seek business areas where better parking conditions exist. A major problem for most cities is the lack of sufficient curb space for the number of vehicles that normally enter a business district each day. As a means of getting an efficient turnover of parking spaces, short-time limits are established. These are usually one hour in the heart of the business district and longer periods on streets located a short distance away. This eliminates all-day parking, especially by employees or owners of business establishments. Parking limits are generally regulated by police officers on motorcycles who mark tires every period of the alloted time limit. Another means of enforcement is the parking meter (see PARKING METER).

Angle Parking. Because of the demand for more parking space at the curb, many cities established parking at an angle to the curb. This allows more automobiles to park in a given block. For every 100 feet of curb space, 11 cars can park at a 60 degree angle to the curb, but only 5 can park parallel to the curb. However, angle parking takes an additional moving lane out of service in the street and therefore causes congestion. Many accidents are caused by vehicles backing out into the street from angle positions. Consequently, this type of parking is not recommended for major streets in business districts. It is used on minor streets, wide thoroughfares, and in parking lots and garages.

Loading Zones. Business districts require parking spaces for trucks making deliveries to stores and offices. If no space is available at the rear of buildings or at the curb, vehicles making deliveries will "double park," or stand in the lane next to a parked vehicle. This causes congestion and has a bad effect on the health of a business district. One way to correct this is to post signs marking off designated areas at the curb in front of the building for the loading and unloading of vehicles only.

Taxi Zones are also necessary to accommodate taxis waiting for passengers in busy areas of the business district. Usually, two or three parking spaces will be allotted at the curb near intersections or establishments such as hotels or office buildings.

Bus Zones. Buses loading and unloading passengers require at least three parking spaces. These are set aside and signs are erected indicating the bus zones.

Off-the-Street Parking. The many special zones at the curb and the large numbers of vehicles in the business districts make additional parking necessary. Private parking lots and garage operators in the downtown area help relieve the congestion. Cities often maintain their own parking lots or multiple-deck garages. Some businessmen also help by providing free parking for their customers. MATTHEW C. SIELSKI

See also PARKING METER; TRAFFIC.

Rockwell Manufacturing Co.

Automatic Parking Meters provide additional city revenue and help traffic police enforce time-limit regulations.

PARKING METER is a device that indicates the length of time a vehicle parks in a particular parking space. It consists of a time clock that is set in motion by a coin deposited by the person who is parking his vehicle. The person pays for using the parking space for a certain length of time. When this time has passed, a red flag or disc appears on the meter. If the vehicle remains in the parking space and a police officer sees the red indicator, he issues a violation ticket for overparking.

There is one meter for each parking space in the limited-time parking area. The parking meter has been found to be effective in restricting all-day parking. Revenue from parking meters is often used to construct off-street parking lots. MATTHEW C. SIELSKI

PARKINSON'S DISEASE. See PALSY.

PARKMAN, FRANCIS (1823-1893), one of America's greatest historians, wrote vivid accounts of the role of the Indians in North American history. He made a famous journey on the Oregon Trail in 1846, and lived with the Indians for months to gather material for a book. Published in 1849 as *The California and Oregon Trail*, this book later became famous as *The Oregon Trail*.

His *France and England in the New World* gave the whole history of the struggle between France and Great Britain for control of North America, and the part the Indians played in it. Parkman opened with the end of the period and worked backward, instead of starting at the beginning. His books did not include the economic elements of history that are now considered important, but they were so realistically written that they are still read with great pleasure.

Parkman made a thorough and untiring study that included five trips to Europe for material before he published his first book, *History of the Conspiracy of Pontiac* (1851). He also wrote *Pioneers of France in the New World* (1865), *The Jesuits in North America* (1867), *LaSalle and the Discovery of the Great West* (1869), and *Montcalm and Wolfe* (1884).

Brown Bros.

Francis Parkman

Parkman's health, already poor, was further damaged by the hardships of his trip on the Oregon Trail. He wrote with great difficulty, and on some days he could write only half a dozen lines. He was almost blind, but continued his work with the help of a reader. Parkman studied horticulture as a hobby during one of his periods of convalescence, and raised flowers. Parkman was so successful in this occupation that he became a professor of horticulture at Harvard University in 1871.

Parkman was born in Boston, the son of a Unitarian clergyman. He was graduated from Harvard, and later studied law there. He was elected to the Hall of Fame in 1915. MERLE CURTI

PARLEMENT, *PAR luh MAWNG*, was a French high court of justice. About a dozen parlements existed throughout France from the late Middle Ages to the time of the French Revolution.

The Parlement of Paris was the oldest and most important parlement. It came to have the privilege of recording royal decrees before they could become law. Sometimes, the Parlement of Paris even refused to register new decrees. It judged these orders to be in conflict with existing laws. In 1648, the Parlement defied young King Louis XIV and his chief minister, Cardinal Mazarin. However, the Parlement soon was forced to back down.

The parlements probably had their greatest power during the 1600's and early 1700's. They were abolished during the French Revolution, along with other royal institutions. EDWIN J. WESTERMANN

United Press Int.

The Majestic Houses of Parliament cover eight acres along the River Thames. The side facing the river is 940 feet long. The House of Lords sits at the south end, on the left. On the right side of the structure is the House of Commons. Victoria Tower in the foreground is 340 feet high. Big Ben, the world's most famous bell, is in the Clock Tower in the background. Eleven courtyards dot the enclosed grounds. The buildings themselves have 100 stairways, 1,100 apartments, and two miles of passageways.

PARLIAMENT is the highest lawmaking assembly of the United Kingdom of Great Britain and Northern Ireland. The term is also used for the lawmaking bodies of Canada, South Africa, and Australia.

Among the earliest forms of society, there was always a council of elders to give advice to the tribal chief. When a group of tribes united to form a confederacy, there was again a council to advise the king. The Anglo-Saxon tribes that overran Britain also formed advisory councils, and it is from these primitive councils that the modern Parliament grew and developed.

In early times, there were three lawmaking powers in England—the king, the lords, and the commons. The king, acting with advice from his lords, could enact all laws. Many years went by before the common people were able to elect representatives to take part in state councils. The first assembly that can be compared with the modern Parliament met in 1265.

During the reign of Edward III, Parliament was for the first time divided into two houses, the House of Commons and the House of Lords. After a long struggle, the House of Commons became the most important lawmaking power in Great Britain. The Bill of Rights, passed in 1689, took away most of the power of the House of Lords and left the Crown with no legislative authority. The common saying in Great Britain now is, "The king (or queen) reigns, but does not rule." He or she has the right to be present in the House of Lords without taking part in debate, but no sovereign has exercised this right for over two hundred years.

The development of Parliament brought forth one of England's most important contributions to the science of politics. This is the so-called "Cabinet system" of government, by which actual control of the government is in the hands of a group of the more important ministers, who are all members of Parliament. Chief of the Cabinet is the prime minister, who is appointed by the Crown. The other members of the Cabinet are selected by the prime minister with the approval of the Crown. Cabinet government developed in the 1700's, when monarchy was weak in England and the leaders of the Whig Party were very strong. They believed that the Parliament and not the Crown should be the controlling force and the ultimate ruler of the nation.

The House of Commons was once made up of 670 members—495 from England and Wales, 72 from Scotland, and 103 from Ireland. From 1885 to 1922 there were many changes. In 1955, the number was finally set at 630 members—511 from England, 36 from Wales, 71 from Scotland, and 12 from Northern Ireland.

The Commons is the real governing body of the nation, and it has truly come to represent the common people. It has control over all financial legislation.

Before 1702, Cabinet Ministers carried out the wishes of the Crown. Since that time they have become dependent on the House of Commons and must resign when they lose its support on important measures.

The House of Commons is an elected body. Each member represents a *constituency*, or district. The average constituency has about 60,000 voters. Clergymen of the Church of England, the Church of Scotland, or the Roman Catholic Church cannot become members of the House of Commons. Sheriffs and certain other officers of the Crown are also barred from sitting in Parliament. A candidate for a seat in the House does not have to live in the constituency he hopes to represent.

The term of a Parliament is five years, unless it is dissolved before that time. Parliament usually sits from

November to August or September. Members formerly served without pay. But now members of the House of Lords are given traveling expenses if they attend Parliament regularly. Members of the House of Commons have received a salary since 1911. At present, their salary is £3,250, or about $7,800.

Parliaments have met on the site of the House of Commons since 1547. St. Stephen's Chapel, where the Commons met for 500 years, stood there. In May, 1941, the 90-year-old chamber of the Commons was struck by a bomb and practically demolished. Rebuilding was completed in 1950 at a cost of more than £1,800,000. The woodwork is of English oak, cut from trees two and three hundred years old. The various nations of the British Commonwealth contributed most of the new chamber's furnishings. The king or queen is not permitted to enter the House of Commons, but there is a special room for other members of the royal family, from which they may watch and hear the proceedings.

The House of Lords is the upper house of the British Parliament, and consists of about 1,000 members. High members of the Church, legal experts called *law lords*, and certain *peers* (noblemen) make up the body. All the peers of the United Kingdom and all the peers of England are entitled to seats in the House of Lords. But only a few Scottish peers have seats in Parliament.

Although the House of Lords is called the upper house of Parliament, it may in no way be compared with the upper house of the United States Congress. The importance of the House of Lords gradually declined as the Commons grew in power and influence. Today, the Lords may not defeat any measures passed by the House of Commons, although they may cause some delay in the enforcement of new laws. The Parliamentary Acts of 1911 and 1949 considerably weakened the declining power of the House of Lords. Since the 1911 act, any money bill which passes the House of Commons becomes law within one month of its being sent to the Lords, whether they approve it or not. Since the 1949 act, any nonmoney bill passed by the Commons in two consecutive sessions of Parliament becomes law even if the Lords do not approve it.

The Crown may create new peers at any time. In 1958, women were admitted to the House of Lords for the first time.

Larry Burrows, *Life* Magazine
The Chamber of the House of Commons was rebuilt after a German air raid destroyed it in 1941. It is the heart of the British government. Finished in 1950, the new chamber is like the old, but has modern conveniences such as air conditioning and loudspeakers. The Government sits at left, the Opposition at right.

Parliaments in Other Lands. The *Althing* of Iceland ranks as the world's oldest parliament. It was set up in A.D. 930. Spain established the first parliamentary organization on the mainland of Europe. The kingdom of Castile organized the *Cortes* in 1188 with representatives of the nobility, church, and middle class. The two-house parliament of France in its present form began in the early 1800's. The parliament of the French Fifth Republic was set up under the constitution adopted in 1958. It consists of a national assembly and a senate. The German parliament had its basis in the national parliament that convened in 1848 after the revolution of that year. India's parliament had its origin in the Charter Act of 1853. The parliament of Japan is called the *Diet*. It dates from 1867, although as a national legislative assembly it was not created until 1889. The parliaments of Australia, Canada, New Zealand, and South Africa are modeled after the British Parliament. New Zealand calls its legislature the *General Assembly*. But *parliament* is the official title of the legislature in the other countries.   PAYSON S. WILD

Related Articles in WORLD BOOK include:

Visual Education Service
Two Intricately Carved Thrones at the head of the chamber add dignity to the impressive House of Lords.

PARLIAMENTARY PROCEDURE

PARLIAMENTARY PROCEDURE is a way to conduct a meeting in an orderly manner. Whenever people hold a meeting, they need rules to help them accomplish their purpose. The rules of parliamentary procedure help the chairman keep order during a meeting. The procedure is called *parliamentary* because it comes from the rules and customs of the British Parliament. Parliamentary procedure is also known as *parliamentary law, parliamentary practice,* and *rules of order.*

All groups do not use the same rules of order. Lawmaking bodies such as the British Parliament or the Congress of the United States use complicated forms of parliamentary procedure. Social clubs, student councils, church organizations, and community associations follow simpler rules of order. These organizations usually have fewer members and deal with less complicated problems than those of lawmaking bodies. But no matter how simple the rules may be, they are necessary for the group to conduct its business in an orderly manner. Unless all the members understand and follow the rules, a meeting can easily become confused.

Any system of parliamentary procedure should be (1) democratic and (2) efficient. To be democratic, the system must enable each member of the group to express his opinion on a question, then let the majority make the decision. To be efficient, the procedure must help the group meet with little confusion or delay.

Any group that conducts its meetings according to parliamentary rules will face questions about proper procedure in unusual situations. To answer such questions, the group should consult a standard authority on parliamentary procedure. All such books have the same basic purpose, but they differ on various specific points. As a result, an organization should use only one of them. The most commonly used books on the subject include *Robert's Rules of Order, Revised* by Henry M. Robert; *Essentials of Parliamentary Procedure* by J. Jeffery Auer; *Parliamentary Law for the Layman* by Joseph F. O'Brien; and *Sturgis Standard Code of Parliamentary Procedure* by Alice F. Sturgis.

Forming an Organization

A group that wishes to form an organization or club first calls a meeting of those who may be interested. At the meeting, the group sets up a temporary organization and chooses an acting chairman. The acting chairman appoints an acting secretary, who begins keeping a record of the business conducted by the group. Next, the members elect a temporary chairman and a temporary secretary. These two officers serve until the club establishes a permanent organization and elects permanent officers.

Constitution and Bylaws. Before a group becomes a permanent organization, it should have (1) a constitution and (2) a set of bylaws. Members may elect a committee to draw up these documents. Or the chairman may appoint a committee for this purpose. The group may adopt the constitution and bylaws as written by the committee. Or the members can make changes in the documents.

The *constitution* states the basic principles and general structure of the organization. It is the highest law of the organization. The *bylaws* tell the members how to carry out the provisions of the constitution. A debating club might have a constitution that says: "All students of University High School interested in the public discussion of current affairs shall be eligible for membership in the Thomas Jefferson Society." The club bylaws would list special conditions for membership. These might require applicants for membership to be (1) recommended by two present members, (2) approved by the club sponsor, and (3) accepted by a vote of at least two-thirds of the members present at any regular meeting. See BYLAW.

The constitutions and bylaws of most organizations cover the following subjects:

I. Name of the Organization
II. Purpose of the Organization
    A. A general statement of purpose
    B. How the purpose is to be achieved
III. Membership
    A. Qualifications for membership
    B. How members are selected
    C. Membership dues
IV. Officers
    A. Titles and description of duties
    B. Length of terms of office
    C. How officers are elected
V. Committees
    A. Names and duties of standing committees
    B. Procedure for creating special committees
    C. How committee members and chairmen are chosen
VI. Meetings
    A. When regular meetings are held
    B. How special meetings are called
    C. Selection of an authoritative book on parliamentary procedure
    D. Special rules governing meetings
VII. Amendments
    A. How the constitution and bylaws are amended
    B. The vote required to adopt amendments

Officers. The essential officers for any organized group are a president and a secretary. If the members pay dues or raise money for the organization in any way, a treasurer is also necessary. Some groups have an officer who serves as both secretary and treasurer.

The President (1) presides over all meetings, (2) supervises the work of other officers and committees, (3) represents the organization, and (4) appoints committees if the constitution or bylaws give him the power to do so.

The Secretary (1) notifies members of scheduled meetings, (2) keeps and reads the minutes, (3) files copies of committee reports, and (4) handles correspondence.

The Treasurer (1) handles all the organization's finances, (2) keeps a record of income and expenses, (3) prepares financial reports, and (4) helps prepare the annual budget.

Other Officers. Many organizations, especially if they are large or carry on extensive activities, have additional officers. These usually include a *vice-president,* who aids the president and takes his place when he is unable to perform his duties. Some groups have two or more vice-presidents. An organization may divide the secretary's job between a *recording secretary,* who keeps the minutes and other records, and a *corresponding secretary,* who handles all letter-writing. Some clubs elect a *historian,* who keeps a permanent record of activities and members, and a *sergeant at arms,* who maintains order during meetings. A club might also have a *parliamentarian,* who advises the president on matters of procedure.

Electing Officers. Most organizations elect officers once a year. There are two methods of nominating officers. Under the first method, the group chooses a nominating committee to propose one or more candidates for each office. After the committee makes its nominations, other candidates may be nominated *from the floor* (by the members attending the meeting). Under the second method, the presiding officer declares that "nominations are in order." He then accepts nominations from the floor for each office.

A vote for officers, like votes on other business matters, may be held (1) by a show of hands or (2) by secret ballot. There are fewer risks of embarrassing any of the candidates when the members vote by secret ballot. In addition, the candidates do not have to leave the room during the voting. If only two candidates are nominated for an office, one must receive a majority of the votes to win. Usually, if three or more are nominated, the one who receives a *plurality* (the most votes) wins. But the constitution may require that a candidate must receive a majority vote to be elected. In such cases, the winner would be chosen in a run-off election between the two candidates with the most votes.

Committees handle many duties that a group's officers do not or cannot perform. Committees also do jobs that cannot be done by the entire membership at regular meetings. Most organizations have two types of committees: (1) standing committees and (2) special committees.

Standing committees deal with regular and continuing matters such as membership and finance. These committees are usually selected after each annual election, and they *stand* (remain active) through the year.

Special committees may be selected at any time to deal with specific matters. A special committee might be appointed to plan a social event, to revise the group's constitution, or to nominate new officers. The special committee ceases to exist after it completes its job.

Constitutions and bylaws usually state whether standing committees shall be appointed or elected. If they are appointed, the president names the members of each committee. The president usually creates special committees and appoints their members. Organization members can also create special committees by voting

to do so. Each committee should have an odd number of members, in order to avoid tie votes on committee decisions. The president usually selects one of the committee members to be chairman. Committees do not have to follow all the rules of parliamentary procedure. Their meetings are usually informal discussions.

Holding Meetings

A business meeting officially begins when the presiding officer calls the group to order. He does this when a quorum is present. A *quorum* is the minimum number of members who must be present in order to transact business. In most organizations, a majority of the membership must be present for a quorum. But a group's constitution and bylaws can name any part of the total membership as a quorum. See QUORUM.

Order of Business. In a well-organized meeting, a standard series of steps follows the call to order. (1) The secretary reads the minutes of the last meeting. They must be approved by a majority vote. (2) Standing and special committees give their reports. (3) Members take up any unfinished business left over from previous meetings. (4) Members introduce new business. (5) Members introduce miscellaneous matters, such as announcements or requests, that require no formal action by the group. (6) The meeting is adjourned by a majority vote.

Sometimes the members want to devote an entire meeting to some special matter. The meeting would then follow a *special order of business*. After the minutes have been read and approved, the other items in the usual order of business would be dropped, and the special matter would be taken up.

Minutes. The secretary's minutes should be an accurate record of all the organization's actions. At the start of each meeting, the secretary reads the minutes of the previous meeting so the members can recall the actions taken. The secretary keeps a running account of all business matters the club discusses and all actions it takes. The minutes do not summarize the discussions that take place during the meeting. They simply state the actions proposed, and what the organization decided to do about each one.

TERMS USED IN PARLIAMENTARY PROCEDURE

Adjourn means to end a meeting.

Agenda is a list of items to be considered at a meeting.

Amendment is a change proposed or made in a motion, a constitution, or a set of bylaws.

Appeal is a request for a majority vote to overrule a decision of the presiding officer.

Chairman Pro Tempore is the temporary chairman.

Close Debate refers to ending discussion on a motion by passing another motion to vote immediately.

Decorum in Debate, *duh KOH ruhm*, refers to the observance of normal rules of courtesy and proper procedure while discussing motions.

Dilatory Motion, *DIL uh TOH ree*, is a meaningless motion. The presiding officer must rule it out of order.

Division is a count of votes by a show of hands.

Gavel is a small wooden hammer. The presiding officer of an organization uses it to call meetings to order and to quiet disturbances.

Majority is one more than half of those voting.

Order of Business is the series of steps covered in a meeting, from the call to order through adjournment.

Pending Question is any motion open to debate.

Plurality is the largest number of votes received by any candidate in an election involving three or more candidates.

Point of Order is an objection raised by a member because of improper procedure or annoying remarks. It must be ruled upon immediately by the presiding officer.

Previous Question is a motion to end debate on a pending motion and vote immediately.

Privileged Question is a request made by a member who asks the presiding officer to deal with an emergency, disorder in the assembly, or other matters of general welfare.

Quorum, *KWOH ruhm*, is the number of members necessary to transact business. Usually it is a majority of the total membership.

Ratify refers to a motion to approve an action already taken, such as a ruling by the president.

Recess is a temporary interruption of a meeting.

Unanimous Consent refers to a request by the presiding officer on matters where differences of opinion are not expected. He might ask for the unanimous consent of the members on such a matter as approving minutes.

The following motions are listed in order of their rank. When a group is considering any one of them, you may not introduce another that is listed below it. But you may introduce another that is listed above it.

To Do This	You Say This	May You Interrupt Speaker?	Second Needed?	Motion Debatable?	Motion Amendable?	Vote Needed
PRIVILEGED MOTIONS deal with the welfare of the group, rather than with any specific proposal. They must be disposed of before the group can consider any other type of motion.						
Adjourn the meeting	"I move that we adjourn."	no	yes	no	no	majority
Recess the meeting	"I move we recess until ____"	no	yes	no	yes	majority
Complain about noise, room temperature, etc.	"Point of privilege"	yes	no	no	no	none, chairman rules
SUBSIDIARY MOTIONS provide various ways of modifying or disposing of main motions. They must be acted upon before all other motions except privileged motions.						
Suspend debate on a matter without calling for a vote	"I move we table the matter."	no	yes	no	no	majority
End debate	"I move the previous question."	no	yes	no	no	⅔ majority
Limit length of debate	"I move debate on this matter be limited to ____"	no	yes	no	yes	⅔ majority
Ask for a vote by actual count, to verify a voice vote	"I call for a division of the house."	no	no	no	no	none*
Postpone consideration of a matter to a specific time	"I move we postpone this matter until ____"	no	yes	yes	yes	majority
Have a matter studied further	"I move we refer this matter to a committee."	no	yes	yes	yes	majority
Consider a matter informally	"I move that the question be considered informally."	no	yes	yes	no	majority
Amend a motion	"I move that this motion be amended by ____"	no	yes	yes	yes	majority
Reject a main motion without voting on the motion itself	"I move the question be postponed indefinitely."	no	yes	yes	no	majority
INCIDENTAL MOTIONS grow out of other business that the group is considering. They must be decided before the group can return to the question that brought them up.						
Correct an error in parliamentary procedure	"Point of order"	yes	no	no	no	none, chairman rules
Object to a ruling by the chairman	"I appeal the chair's decision."	yes	yes	yes	no	majority
Consider a matter that violates normal procedure, but does not violate the constitution or bylaws	"I move we suspend the rules that interfere with ____"	no	yes	no	no	⅔ majority
Object to considering some matter	"I object to the consideration of this matter."	yes	no	no	no	⅔ majority
Obtain advice on proper procedure	"I raise a parliamentary inquiry."	yes	no	no	no	none, chairman rules
Request information	"Point of information"	yes	no	no	no	none
Withdraw a motion	"I request leave to withdraw the motion."	no	no	no	no	majority
MAIN MOTIONS are the tools used to introduce new business.						
Introduce business	"I move that ____"	no	yes	yes	yes	majority
Take up a matter previously tabled	"I move we take from the table ____"	no	yes	no	no	majority
Reconsider a matter already disposed of	"I move we reconsider our action relative to ____"	no	yes	yes†	no	majority
Strike out a motion previously passed	"I move we rescind the motion calling for ____"	no	yes	yes	yes	majority
Consider a matter out of its scheduled order	"I move we suspend the rules and consider ____"	no	yes	no	no	⅔ majority

* But majority vote if someone objects.

† If original action was debatable.

In most organizations, the secretary keeps the minutes in a permanent record book. Each set of minutes begins with the date and place of the meeting, the time the meeting began, and the name of the presiding officer. Some organizations call the roll at the beginning of each meeting, and include a list of the members present in the minutes. The secretary arranges the minutes in the same order as the members take up items of business.

After the secretary has read the minutes, the president asks whether any member wants to make any corrections or additions. If so, the group must vote on each correction or addition. The president then asks for approval of the minutes. In some organizations, a member must propose that the group approve the minutes. But the simplest way is for the president to state that if there are no objections, the minutes will be considered approved. The secretary notes the approval and the date at the end of the minutes.

Motions. A motion is a brief, precise statement of a proposed action. A member can make a motion only when he *has the floor* (has been given permission to speak by the presiding officer). Before any motion can be discussed by the group, another member must *second* it (state that he supports it). This rule prevents the group from spending time on matters that interest only one member. After a motion has been made and seconded, the presiding officer usually restates it. Or he may ask the secretary to read the motion from the minutes. The members then debate the motion. Perhaps the members want to *amend* (change) the motion in some way. If so, they must propose and *pass* (approve) a new motion amending the original motion. They must then debate the original motion *as amended*. Debate on a motion usually continues until each member who wants to speak has done so. But the members can end the debate at any time by passing a specific motion to have the group vote immediately. The members can also pass a motion to set a time limit on the debate. See CLOTURE.

Each motion must be disposed of in some way before the group can take up another item of business. If the members want to postpone action on a motion, they may vote to "table the motion" or "lay the motion on the table." The presiding officer or the group may dispose of a motion temporarily by referring it to a committee. The committee investigates the matter and presents a report at a later meeting. The group then decides what action it wants to take. Eventually, all motions must be either approved or disapproved by a majority of the membership.

Every motion can be classified as one of four types: (1) privileged, (2) subsidiary, (3) incidental, and (4) main. These motions are explained in the table with this article.

Voting on Motions takes place when there are no more requests to speak on a motion, or after debate has ended. First, the presiding officer restates the motion or has the secretary read it. Then he calls for a *voice vote*. All those in favor of the motion say "aye." Then all those opposed say "nay." If the president cannot tell which side has the majority, he may ask the members to revote by raising their hands. If any member questions the results of a voice vote as announced by the president, a revote by a show of hands is required. The constitution may require a *roll-call vote* on certain types of motions.

The presiding officer usually votes only when his vote would change the result of a vote by the members. He may vote to break a tie vote. Or if the "nay" votes total one less than the "aye" votes, he may vote "nay" to create a tie and thus defeat the motion.

History

In Lawmaking Bodies. No one knows who first used parliamentary rules. But historians believe that some such rules must have guided even the oldest governing bodies. By the 400's B.C., the Greeks in Athens were holding regular meetings of the *ecclesia* (assembly of free citizens). Such a group needed rules of order to accomplish its work. In the senate of the Roman Republic, parliamentary law was further refined. The word *parliament* comes from the French word *parler*, which means *to speak*.

Much of parliamentary procedure as we know it developed in the British Parliament. By the end of the 1600's, the broad principles had become well established. As actual procedures developed, they became the basis for deciding later questions of parliamentary law. Many early questions of parliamentary law were collected and published in 1776 and 1781 by John Hatsell, a clerk of the House of Commons. They are known today as *Hatsell's Precedents*.

When the American colonists established legislatures in the 1600's, they patterned their rules for conducting business after those of the British Parliament. The first United States Senate, which met in 1789, was governed by a set of 16 parliamentary rules. These included rules for making motions, for questions of order, and for priority of speaking. When Thomas Jefferson, as Vice-President, became the presiding officer of the Senate in 1797, he drew up his *Manual of Parliamentary Practice*. This detailed set of parliamentary rules is still used in both the Senate and the House of Representatives. In the preface to his book, Jefferson wrote that his aim was to ensure "accuracy in business, economy of time, order, uniformity, and impartiality."

In Organizations. In 1844, Luther Cushing, an American lawyer, wrote a brief manual that stressed the basic principles governing parliamentary questions. Cushing realized that detailed works on parliamentary law were too complicated to be used easily and quickly. He prepared his manual for use by lawmaking bodies. Its simplicity made it a convenient reference work for all types of organizations.

In 1876, Major Henry M. Robert, a U.S. Army engineer, wrote what became the most popular book on parliamentary procedure, *Robert's Rules of Order*. Robert became interested in the subject after presiding over several business meetings of his church. His book was based upon parliamentary law as practiced in lawmaking bodies. He adapted the rules for private groups. The book became the official parliamentary authority specified in the constitutions of many organizations.

Later authorities have produced books of parliamentary rules that are not based on the practices of lawmaking bodies. These books contain only the essential parliamentary procedures necessary to handle an organization's business as democratically and efficiently as possible.   J. JEFFERY AUER

PARMA

PARMA, *PAHR muh* (pop. 155,132; alt. 187 ft.), is a city in northern Italy. It lies about 75 miles southeast of Milan (see ITALY [political map]). Parma dates from the period of the Roman republic, and is the home of many art treasures. The cathedral, built in the form of a Latin cross, dates from the 1000's. It is an example of Lombard-Romanesque architecture. Its cupola has a fresco, *Assumption of the Virgin,* by the artist Correggio (see CORREGGIO). The University of Parma was founded in 1502.   SHEPARD B. CLOUGH

PARMA, Ohio (pop. 82,845; alt. 862 ft.), is a residential and manufacturing suburb southwest of Cleveland. It covers about 20 square miles, and has over 300 acres of parks. Automotive parts plants form its largest industry. Parma also produces tools, dies, and metal stampings. The village was incorporated in 1924, and became a city in 1932. It has a mayor-council government. See also OHIO (political map).   RUSSELL W. KANE

PARMENIDES, *par MEN ih deez,* was a Greek philosopher who lived about 500 B.C. He played an important part in developing pre-Socratic philosophy. Before Parmenides, philosophers generally tried to explain the origin and nature of the universe in terms of one material substance, such as air. Parmenides used logical arguments to show that what exists is one, eternal, indivisible, motionless, finite, and spherical. Therefore, it cannot become something else and other things cannot be explained by reference to its changing states. Change and *plurality* (reality consisting of many substances) are illusions, or as Parmenides put it, "mere names."

Parmenides was born in Elea, a Greek colony in southern Italy. He was one of the first Greek philosophers to express his thought in poetry. His poem, *On Nature,* is divided into two parts. What is probably most of the first part has survived.   JOSIAH B. GOULD

See also PRE-SOCRATIC PHILOSOPHY.

PARNAÍBA RIVER, *PAHR nuh EE buh,* rises in the Tabatinga Mountains near the border of the state of Goiás, Brazil. It flows 850 miles northeast to the Atlantic Ocean (see BRAZIL [color map]). The river forms the border between the states of Maranhão and Piauí. Its chief tributaries include the Balsas, Gurgueia, Caninde, Poti, and Longa rivers. Ships carry carnauba wax, cotton, rice, and tobacco about 300 miles from Floriano to the city of Parnaíba on the Atlantic coast.   MANOEL CARDOZO

PARNASSUS, *pahr NASS us,* is a mountain in Phocis in Greece. Its twin peaks, rising over 8,000 feet, are snow-covered most of the year.

The ancient Greeks believed Parnassus was one of the most sacred Greek mountains. They believed it was the favorite place of Apollo and the Muses, Dionysus, and Pan. Two spots on Parnassus were especially holy. One was the fountain of Castalia. Its water was supposed to enable those who drank it to write poetry. The other spot sacred to the ancient Greeks was the oracle of Delphi (see DELPHI).   PADRAIC COLUM

See also MOUNTAIN (picture chart).

PARNELL, CHARLES STEWART (1846-1891), an Irish Nationalist leader, almost obtained *home rule* (self-government) for Ireland by constitutional means (see HOME RULE). But scandal ruined his career.

Parnell entered the British House of Commons in 1875 as a member for County Meath. He united the Home Rule party, and tried to make it powerful by obstructing all other legislation until Irish demands were met. To unite Ireland, Parnell came to terms with Irish revolutionaries, and supported the Land League. The league wanted land reforms that would end with tenant farmers owning their farms.

In 1879, Parnell visited the United States and collected large amounts of money for the Land League. When he returned to Ireland, he suggested *boycotting* the landlords in order to force land reform (see BOYCOTT). For this policy and for trying to obstruct legislative proceedings, Parnell was arrested and imprisoned for six months. From prison, he urged tenant farmers not to pay rent. This advice added bitterness to the situation. After his release in 1882, Parnell returned to Parliament and tried again to force home rule. For a time he seemed about to succeed. In 1886, Parliament passed the Tenant's Relief Bill, which improved farmers' conditions.

Brown Bros.

Charles Parnell

But the next year, Parnell had to defend himself against charges that he was involved in the Phoenix Park murders. Irish terrorists had committed these murders in 1882. Parnell proved that letters which seemed to implicate him were forgeries.

In 1889, just as Parliament was about to meet, a political supporter of Parnell named Captain William O'Shea filed divorce proceedings against his wife because of her relationship with Parnell. The charges were proved, and Parnell's reputation and influence were shattered. Parnell later married Mrs. O'Shea after the divorce.

Parnell was born on his family's estate of Avondale in County Wicklow. He was educated at Magdalene College of Cambridge University.   JAMES L. GODFREY

PAROCHIAL SCHOOL, *puh ROH kih ul,* refers to a private school conducted and supervised by a religious group, especially one conducted by the Roman Catholic Church. Technically, parochial schools are elementary schools, but the term *parochial* sometimes includes high schools, colleges, and universities.

In the Roman Catholic system, a superintendent appointed by the bishop directs the parish schools. The joint action of several different parishes directs and supports some of the high schools. A religious order, for example, the Society of Jesus, usually owns and directs colleges and private academies. In a general way, the pope directs the Catholic University of America, but the cardinals and archbishops of the United States supervise it more directly.

The Roman Catholic parochial school system developed rapidly in the 1800's and 1900's. It has had a tremendous growth in the United States, and is the largest private church-related school system in the world. In 1900, the Roman Catholic school enrollment was 854,000 students, about 5 per cent of the total

Parochial Schools include religious education as part of their course of study. The pupils in this Roman Catholic parochial school in Milwaukee, Wis., are being taught by a member of a religious order.

Catholic School Journal

school enrollment at that time. In 1900, the public elementary and high school enrollment was 15,500,000. In the late 1960's, Roman Catholic elementary schools enrolled about 4,400,000 students and Roman Catholic high schools enrolled over 1,100,000, a total of about 5,500,000. This represented about 11 per cent of the school children in the United States. The public elementary and high school enrollment totaled about 44,-000,000. In other words, while the public school enrollment increased about $2\frac{3}{4}$ times, the Roman Catholic enrollment increased $6\frac{1}{2}$ times.

The increase in parochial school enrollments has led some bishops to suggest that parochial schools be recognized as an integral part of the United States school system. Some Roman Catholic spokesmen have proposed that parochial school children share in the benefits provided by state funds for public school children. These benefits include free transportation to school, free textbooks, free lunches, and free health and welfare services. Some persons have suggested that parents of parochial school students be given subsidies from public tax funds, or be allowed tax credits. Others oppose using tax money for these purposes. They believe it would violate the principle of separation between church and state. A few Roman Catholic educators have suggested that the Church give up either its primary or secondary schools because the burden of maintaining both without tax funds is too great.

The United States has about 1,700 Lutheran elementary and secondary schools with about 200,000 pupils. The Protestant Episcopal Church, some Jewish congregations, Seventh-day Adventists, and other groups also maintain parochial elementary schools.   R. FREEMAN BUTTS

See also SCHOOL (Private and Parochial Schools).

PARODY, *PAR oh dih*, is a comic imitation of any serious writing. The subject is usually different, but its manner and form must suggest the original work. The first known parody is the *Battle of the Frogs and Mice*, which dates from the 400's B.C. *Don Quixote* parodies the exaggerated romances of chivalry. Students often write parodies of poems, keeping the same verse form but using a less serious subject.   J. N. HOOK

PAROLE, *puh ROLL*, in criminal law, means release of a convicted criminal from prison before he has served his full sentence. A parole is usually granted to a prisoner as a reward for good conduct. A paroled convict is a free man, but he is under the supervision of a parole officer or some other person until the end of the term of his sentence. The paroled convict reports regularly to the parole officer. He can be sent back to prison if his conduct is not satisfactory.

Parole differs from both *probation* and *pardon*. Instead of sending a wrongdoer to prison, a judge may put him on *probation* for a certain period of time. During the period of probation, the wrongdoer is free to go about his business, but his conduct is carefully supervised. If he violates the conditions of probation, he will be sent to jail or fined for the crime he committed. If the state releases a convict and completely forgives him, this is called a *pardon*. See PARDON.

Parole is also a military term. A prisoner of war may give his word of honor that he will not fight against his captors again if he is released. This pledge made by a prisoner of war is called a *parole*. Paroles are rarely granted to war prisoners today. A parole is also a military watchword used to obtain an accurate identification of military personnel.

A *parol contract* is an oral contract. The term is also used to mean a contract not under seal. *Parol evidence* is evidence that is given verbally by witnesses in a courtroom.   FRED E. INBAU and JOHN W. WADE

PAROQUET. See PARAKEET.

PÁROS, *PAH raws*, or *PAIR us*, is one of the Cyclades islands of Greece in the Aegean Sea. It covers 75 square miles and has about 7,800 people. It is 12 miles long and 10 miles wide. Sculptors have used white Parian marble from the island since the 500's B.C. The chief town of the island is also called Páros. For location, see GREECE (color map).

PAROTID GLAND. See SALIVA.

PARQUET FLOOR. See FLOORING.

PARR, CATHERINE. See HENRY (VIII) of England.

PARRAKEET. See PARAKEET.

PARRINGTON, *PAR ing tun*, **VERNON LOUIS** (1871-1929), an American educator and historian, won a 1928 Pulitzer prize in history for his three-volume *Main Currents in American Thought*. This work showed how social and economic ideas affected the writings of American authors. He was born in Aurora, Ill., and attended the College of Emporia (Kans.) and Harvard University. He served as professor of English at the University of Washington from 1912 until his death.   EDWIN H. CADY

PARRIS ISLAND MARINE CORPS RECRUIT DEPOT, S.C., trains most U.S. Marine Corps recruits east of the Mississippi River. It also trains women marines. It covers 7,800 acres, and lies about six miles south of Beaufort. Horse Island Bridge and causeways connect the island to the mainland. The depot includes schools and a recruit training command. Alexander Parris, public treasurer of South Carolina in the 1700's, once owned the island. The marines established their first post there in 1891.   JOHN A. OUDINE

PARRISH, ANNE (1888-1957), an American novelist and writer for children, won a Harper prize for her novel *The Perennial Bachelor* (1925). Her other works include *All Kneeling* (1928), *A Clouded Star* (1948), and *And Have Not Love* (1954). She wrote such children's books as *Floating Island* (1930), which she also illustrated, and *The Story of Appleby Capple* (1950). With the help of her

Arni

Anne Parrish

brother, Dillwyn Parrish, she wrote and illustrated several other children's books, including *The Dream Coach* (1924). Her other works include *Tomorrow Morning* (1926), *Loads of Love* (1932), *Sea Level* (1934), *Golden Wedding* (1936), *Pray For Tomorrow* (1941), *Poor Child* (1945), and *Lucky One* (1958). She was born in Colorado Springs, Colo., and studied in schools in Pennsylvania and Colorado.   ARTHUR MIZENER

PARRISH, MAXFIELD (1870-1966), an American painter and illustrator, portrayed a world of rich color and poetic fancy. His travels in Italy and his later life among the New Hampshire mountains developed his love for romantic, idealized natural beauty. The towering peak of Ascutney, within sight of his home, is suggested in many of his works. An unusual shade of blue, which Parrish used in many of his pictures, came to be known as "Maxfield Parrish blue."

Posters, magazine covers, murals, and other decorations demonstrate his skillful draftsmanship and distinctively elegant style. The many books he illustrated include *Mother Goose in Prose*, *Knickerbocker's History of New York*, *The Arabian Nights*, *Wonder Book*, *Poems of Childhood*, *Golden Age*, and

Maxfield Parrish

Keystone

Dream Days. The rich and glowing colors Parrish used attracted many admirers.

Parrish was born in Philadelphia of Quaker parents. He was graduated from Haverford College, and later studied at the Pennsylvania Academy of the Fine Arts, and under Howard Pyle at Drexel Institute of Art, Science and Industry (now known as Drexel Institute of Technology).   NORMAN RICE

PARROT is a large family of colorful birds. Parrots are found chiefly in the warm, tropical regions. They are popular as pets, because they become affectionate and tame and can be taught to talk. Parrots may be from about 3 inches to over 3 feet long. They are so alike in general build that they are easily recognized as parrots no matter what color they are. Most parrots are brightly colored and have thick, hooked bills.

Parrots are noisy, sociable birds that live chiefly in forested regions both in lowlands and mountains. Some are found in *savannas* (lightly wooded plains) and dry regions.

Kinds of Parrots. There are about 315 species of parrots. About half of these are found in Central and South America. One kind, the *thick-billed parrot*, sometimes wanders as far north as southern Arizona and New Mexico. The *macaws* of Central and South America are the largest parrots. They have long, pointed tails and brightly colored feathers. Most of the *cockatoos* of Australia are white and have *crests* (tufts of long feathers) on their heads. *True parrots* are chunky and have square tails. The *lories* of Australia have red or orange bills and bright feathers. *Parakeets* are small and most of them have pointed tails and green feathers.

Some parrots are very unusual. New Zealand's *owl parrot*, which cannot fly, has an owllike face and olive green feathers. The *kea parrot*, also of New Zealand, will occasionally attack sheep and eat the fat surrounding the sheep's kidneys. Southeastern Asia has tiny *hanging parrots* which sleep hanging upside down like bats. New Guinea's *pygmy parrots* creep up tree trunks, using their stiff tails for support.

Most parrots live on a diet of buds, fruits, nuts, and seeds. The kea and *kaka* of New Zealand also eat grubs and worms. Lories eat the nectar and pollen they collect with their tongues. They have furry, rough tongues specially suited to this task. All parrots lay round, white eggs in holes in trees, on the ground, in cracks in rocks, or in holes dug in termite nests.

Parrots in Captivity should be kept in cages large enough so that they can exercise. The cages should be clean and warm. Parrots need water, fresh air, and wholesome food to stay healthy. The African gray parrot, gray with a red tail, and the green Amazon parrot of South America learn to talk easily. Patience is necessary to teach a bird to talk, because the words must be repeated many times. Avoid distraction while teaching the bird.

Parrots may carry the virus disease *psittacosis*, or *ornithosis*. This disease is sometimes called "parrot fever." It affects all kinds of birds and can be transmitted to human beings. Because of this disease, severe restrictions have been placed on the importation of parrots. All parrots must be examined by a health officer before being shipped to the United States.

Scientific Classification. Parrots make up the parrot family, *Psittacidae*.   RODOLPHE MEYER DE SCHAUENSEE

Related Articles in WORLD BOOK include:

Bird (color picture: Family Pets)	Lovebird
Cockatoo	Macaw
Florida (Places to Visit)	Parakeet
Kea	Psittacosis
Lory	

PARROT

Scarlet Macaw
Ara macao
Found from Mexico to Bolivia
(⅓ life size)

Rainbow Lorikeet
Trichoglossus haematodus
Found from East Indies
and Australia east to New Hebrides
(⅓ life size)

Yellow-Headed Amazon
Amazona ochrocephala
Found from Mexico
to Ecuador and Brazil
(¼ life size)

Sulfur-Crested Cockatoo
Cacatua galerita
Found in Australia and New Guinea
(⅓ life size)

WORLD BOOK illustrations by Walter Linsenmaier

PARROT FEVER. See Psittacosis.

PARRSBORO SHORE. See Nova Scotia (Places to Visit).

PARRY, SIR WILLIAM EDWARD (1790-1855), a British naval officer and Arctic explorer, led expeditions in 1819, 1821, and 1824, in search of the Northwest Passage. Parry discovered Melville Island on one of these voyages (see Melville Island).

In 1827, Parry sailed on his ship *Hecla* in an attempt to reach the North Pole by way of Spitsbergen (now Svalbard). At Trurenberg Bay, he and his party left the ship and started north. The 28 members of the expedition took two boats and enough supplies for about 70 days. Steel runners attached to the boats enabled them to travel on the ice as well as to sail on the water.

Parry's expedition reached 82°45′ north latitude. It came within 500 miles of the North Pole, the farthest north any explorer had gone up to that time.

Parry wrote of his experiences in *Voyages for the Northwest Passage* (1821) and *Narrative of an Attempt to Reach the North Pole in Boats* (1828). Parry was born in Bath, England, and entered the British Navy as a midshipman. JAMES G. ALLEN

PARSEC, *PAHR seck*, is a unit used in astronomy to measure the distance between stars. It is 3.26 light-years, or 19,200,000,000,000 miles, in length. The word parsec is a combination of the words *parallax* and *second*. A parsec is equal to a distance having a parallax of one second of arc (see Parallax).

PARSIFAL. See Opera (Some of the Famous Operas [Parsifal]).

PARSING, *PAHRS ing*, is a form of recitation involving the analysis of each word in a sentence. The term *parsing* comes from the Latin *pars*, meaning *part*. Schools formerly used parsing in teaching Latin, Greek, and English, but it is not common today.

In parsing a sentence like *The boy found a dime*, a student might say: (1) *Boy* is a common noun, third person, singular number, masculine gender, nominative case, and subject of the verb *found*. (2) *Found* is a transitive, finite, predicating verb, third person, singular number, active voice, indicative mood, and past tense. (3) *Dime* is a common noun, third person, singular number, neuter gender, objective case, and object of the verb *found*.

Much of this recitation is unnecessary, and some of it is misleading. For example, it may be meaningful to say that *boy* is a common noun, but not that it is third person, because all nouns are third person. The word *boy* is singular in number and masculine in gender, but it is not in the nominative case, because English nouns do not distinguish between nominative and objective cases. In order to indicate the case of boy, one would call it *common* case (see Case).

Many scholars believe that parsing is based on faulty or unworkable analysis, and has little bearing on language problems. Most schools have abandoned it as a method of teaching, replacing it with sentence diagraming (see Sentence [Diagram of a Sentence]). But some teachers feel that parsing serves a purpose in grammar drill if the terminology is modified and simplified. PAUL ROBERTS

See also Parts of Speech.

PARSIS, *PAHR seez*, or Parsees, belong to a Zoroastrian religious group located mainly in the Bombay district of India. The name comes from the old Persian province of Parsa. The Parsis came to India from Persia in the early A.D. 700's in order to escape Moslem persecutions.

The Parsis practice Zoroaster's teachings of justice, good deeds, and practical living. Cleanliness is a law of the group, and life in the sunshine guards their health. Their sacred writings are found in the *Zend-Avesta*. Their temples are often called *fire temples*, because they keep a fire burning there as a symbol of the divine light that burns in the soul of man. The Parsis believe that the person who does not love to study is no longer a servant of God. They maintain a school in every temple. GEORGE NOEL MAYHEW

See also Tower of Silence; Zoroaster; Zoroastrians.

PARSLEY, *PAHRS lih*, is a biennial vegetable, sometimes considered as an herb. It is closely related to caraway. The most popular variety produces a low-growing rosette of finely curled and crumpled green leaves. Another variety of parsley produces plain leaves. The fresh leaves are used mainly to decorate meat dishes and salads. The leaves of parsley can also be dried and used in soups.

A special kind of parsley raised in Germany, and occasionally in America, is called Hamburg parsley.

J. Horace McFarland

Sprigs of Parsley Are Used to Decorate Meat Dishes.

This plant produces a long parsniplike root that may be stored for winter use. It is used as a soup flavoring.

Parsley is an excellent source of vitamins A and C, and is rich in minerals, especially iron. But it is usually eaten in such small quantities that it has little effect on a person's health.

Parsley seed is sown in greenhouses, hotbeds, or open beds. It sends up leaves slowly and unevenly. The plants are moved to the garden about a week before the last spring frost. From six to 10 plants are enough for a family. A few leaves at a time are picked off the plant. Sometimes parsley plants are potted and grown indoors in a sunny window during winter.

Parsley was first grown in Sardinia and southern Italy. Early Romans used parsley to fashion garlands to crown military and athletic heroes. Sprigs of parsley were passed during funeral orations and nibbled on by the audience.

Scientific Classification. Parsley belongs to the parsley family, *Umbelliferae*. It is classified as genus *Petroselinum*, species *P. crispum*. S. H. WITTWER

PARSNIP is a biennial vegetable with many deeply and finely lobed leaves. The edible part is the long tapering white root. Parsnips are a common plant in home gardens, but have little commercial importance. They are related to carrots and dill.

The parsnip grows best in a deep rich soil. The seeds must be sown in early spring. The plants come up slowly and unevenly. A few radish seeds are usually mixed with the parsnip seeds. The radishes come up quickly and mark the rows of parsnips so they can be cultivated. If parsnips are neglected they can become troublesome weeds, as wild parsnips are. Parsnip roots grow slowly until the cool weather of fall. Then they grow rapidly. Parsnip roots are not injured by freezing, and are often left in the garden over winter.

Parsnips are usually free from insect enemies and suffer from few diseases. The parsnip is a source of vitamins A and C. It yields considerable energy and contains 380 calories per pound.

The parsnip is native to the Rhine Valley in Europe. It was known and probably used as food early in the Christian Era. It was cultivated in England in 1592 and was grown in New York by 1806.

Scientific Classification. The parsnip belongs to the parsley family, *Umbelliferae*. It is classified as genus *Pastinaca*, species, *P. sativa*.   JOHN H. MACGILLIVRAY

The Long Tapering Root of the parsnip is rich in starches and sugars that make it a healthful food.
Chicago Natural History Museum

PARSONS, CHARLES A. See SHIP AND SHIPPING (Power and Speed); TURBINE (Early Days).

PARSONS, ROBERT (1546-1610), an English Jesuit, risked his life to serve English Roman Catholics during their persecution under Queen Elizabeth I. He became a Jesuit in Rome, but returned to England disguised as

a soldier in 1580. Parsons secretly printed Catholic answers to charges against the church, and supported Spanish attempts to dethrone Elizabeth. He was born in Somerset, England.   JAMES A. CORBETT and FULTON J. SHEEN

PARSONS, TALCOTT. See SOCIOLOGY (Modern Sociology).

PARSON'S CAUSE. See HENRY, PATRICK (Early Life).

PARTCH, VIRGIL FRANKLIN II. See CARTOON (Leading Cartoonists).

PARTHENOGENESIS. See REPRODUCTION.

PARTHENON, *PAHR the nahn*, is an ancient Greek temple that stands on the Acropolis in Athens. It is an excellent example of the Doric *order* (style) of architecture. Today it is generally considered the finest building built in Ancient Greece.

The Greeks built this temple in honor of Athena Parthenos, the patron goddess of Athens. Ictinus and Callicrates designed it, and Phidias, the famous Greek sculptor, directed its decoration. The builders used white *Pentelic marble* (marble from Mount Pentelikon) in building the Parthenon.

The building was 237 feet long, 110 feet wide, and 60 feet high. The outer columns were 34 feet high. Eight of them stood along each end and 17 along each side. The *cella* (inner space) had a porch at each end fronted by six columns. Doric columns stood all around the temple. The cella contained two rooms. A great gold and ivory statue of Athena, done by Phidias, stood in the east room. The west room served as a treasury. Construction of the Parthenon began in 447 B.C. By 438 B.C., it was ready to house the statue.

The Parthenon became a Christian church in the A.D. 500's. When the Turks captured Athens in the 1400's, they used the temple as a mosque and added a minaret. The building was well preserved until the Venetians tried to conquer Athens in 1687. At that time, the Turks were using the Parthenon as a powder house. When the powder exploded, the central part of the building was wrecked. Many of the sculptures were afterward taken to London (see ELGIN MARBLES). Others were dug up when the Greeks cleared the building of rubbish in 1833. They were placed in the Acropolis Museum, which had been built for them. The work of preserving and studying the temple is still going on.

The sculptures of the Parthenon are valued among the greatest works of art ever made by man. Phidias probably designed them all. The *frieze* (decorated band) in low relief that ran around the cella's outer wall was one of the most beautiful features of the building (see RELIEF [picture]). This frieze showed Athenians moving in procession at a festival honoring the birthday of their goddess, Athena. In the festival walked Athenian officials, old men leaning on staves, and priests with animals for sacrifice. Young men rode on horses. Maidens carried the newly woven garment for Athena, while a group of gods watched.

In *metopes* (square spaces) above the outer columns, sculptured panels showed legendary battles, including the struggles of men with *centaurs* (mythological creatures that were half man, half horse).

Sculptures once also filled the *pediments* (gables) at each end of the roof. The sculpture in the eastern pedi-

PARTHIA

ment showed the birth of Athena from the head of Zeus. In the western pediment, Athena struggled with Poseidon for control of Athens.   WILLIAM P. DONOVAN

See also GREECE, ANCIENT (color picture: The Parthenon in Athens); PHIDIAS; TENNESSEE (Places to Visit).

PARTHIA, *PAHR thih uh,* was an ancient kingdom southeast of the Caspian Sea, in Asia. Parthians lived a simple life and were noted as warriors.

The Parthians were independent until the 500's B.C., when Cyrus the Great of Persia conquered them. Alexander the Great also conquered Parthia, and it later became part of the Seleucid kingdom. By 235 B.C., Parthia had regained its independence, and it soon ruled a large empire in the East.

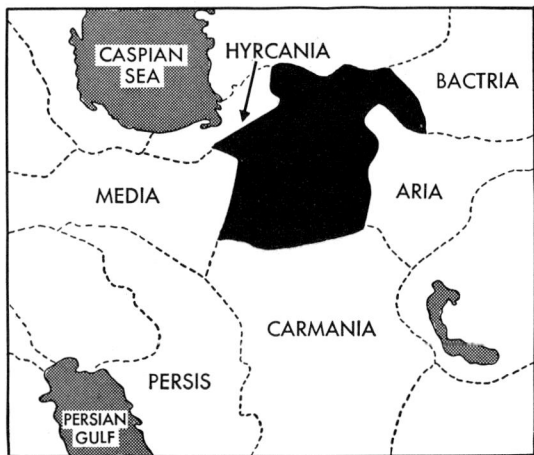

Parthia Is Shown in Black.

Parthia fought several wars against the Romans, defeating Crassus in 53 B.C. and Mark Antony in 36 B.C. and losing to Trajan in A.D. 116. A Persian revolt overthrew the Parthian rulers about 225, and Parthia later became a part of the Sassanian Empire founded by Ardashir I.   THOMAS W. AFRICA

PARTICIPLE is either of two verb forms that partake of the nature of an adjective without losing their character as verbs. The word *participle* comes from the Latin for *partake*. The participle may have an object or an adverbial modifier. It is classed as a *verbal*, like the infinitive.

A verb has two participles in the active voice. The present participle, *drawing*, expresses action in progress. The past participle, *drawn*, expresses finished action. A modified form is the perfect participle, *having drawn*. The passive participle forms are *being drawn* for the present, *drawn* for the past, and *having been drawn* for the perfect.

The Participle Is Used as an Adjective in, "A towering statue known as *Liberty Enlightening the World* stands at the entrance to New York harbor." The word *towering* looks like a participle but is an adjective used only to describe. *Enlightening* is a participle. It is an adjective by nature because it modifies *liberty*. But it also takes an object, *world*, thus showing its verbal nature. *Known* is a past participle used as an adjective to modify *statue*. *Known* is also modified by an adverbial phrase.

The Present Participle Is Used as a Noun in four ways. It may be the subject, object, or complement of a verb, or the object of a preposition. In "Doing nothing is doing ill," the first *doing* is the subject, and the second *doing*, the predicate noun. The participle in certain of its noun uses is called a *gerund*, or sometimes *verbal noun*, *verb noun*, and *noun verbal*.

The Present Participle Is Used Independently when it belongs to the sentence as a whole without modifying any word. Examples are, "*Granting* all that, the mistake seems excusable." This is sometimes called the "absolute construction." The participle may also be used independently in exclamations such as, "*Coming* today!"

The Chief Error in the use of the participle is that of the "dangling participle." An example is, "*Walking* up a hill, a church came into view." The first phrase "dangles" without modifying anything. We should say, "Walking up a hill, we came within sight of a church." The possessive form of a noun or pronoun must be used before a gerund. "Think of *him going* home," should be, "Think of *his going* home."   CLARENCE STRATTON

PARTICLE ACCELERATOR. See CYCLOTRON.

PARTISANS, *PART uh zunz,* work behind enemy lines in wartime to undermine the opponent's hold on their homeland, and to support the military operations of their allies. Partisans perform reconnaissance and sabotage, and disturb enemy movements as much as they possibly can. These fighters do not belong to the regular army, but they usually operate under a professional military commander or under the orders of a regular military force.   STEFAN T. POSSONY

See also GUERRILLA; UNDERGROUND.

PARTITION. See HOUSE (Interior Construction).

PARTNERSHIP is an association formed by two or more persons to carry on a business. The persons usually agree either in writing or verbally to become partners. But people who run a business together and split up the profits are usually considered partners, even if they do not intend to be.

Rights and Responsibilities of Partners. All partners have equal rights in running the business, unless they have agreed on another arrangement. Any disagreement that arises among them is decided by majority vote. Each partner is an *agent* for the other partners. Ordinarily, therefore, anything he does that seems to be carrying on the business in the usual way is binding on the other partners.

All partners share in the profits of the business, but they do not necessarily share equally. The size of each partner's share is agreed upon when the partnership is set up. It depends on how much money or property each contributes to get the business started, and on the kind and amount of work each is to do. Every partner is expected to devote his time to the business in return for his share of the profits. If one does more work than the others, his partners may agree to pay him a salary in addition to his share of the profits.

All the partners must be faithful to one another in their business dealings. No partner may enter into a transaction in the same line of business as the partnership without sharing the profits with his partners. Neither may any partner use the funds or property of the partnership as his own.

All partners are liable for any debts acquired in running the business. These debts are normally paid out of funds or property belonging to the business. If they cannot be paid in this way, any other property belonging to a partner can be taken by the persons to whom the debt is owed. A person can lose a great deal of money by belonging to a partnership that fails. To avoid such loss, many states allow *limited partnerships*. A *limited partner* may not take an active part in running the business, but he is liable only for the amount of money he has invested in the business. If a person wants to take an active part in running a business and still not risk losing more than he has invested, he must form a corporation. See CORPORATION.

Changing or Ending a Partnership. No new partner may be taken into the partnership without the consent of all the members. If a new partner is taken in, a new agreement must be made, stating what he must contribute to the business and what will be his share of the profits. When a person wishes to leave the business, he can agree with his partners on a price for buying him out. If they cannot agree, he may have the business closed out and the property sold. He may then take his share in cash. When a partner dies, the persons named to handle and dispose of his estate have the same rights.

Under the law, all partners are co-owners of the property belonging to the business. The Uniform Partnership Act, which is in force in most states, permits a partner to sell his interest in the whole business, but not in a particular piece of property. Similarly, persons to whom a partner owes money may seize his interest in the whole business, but not in any one piece of property. When a partner sells his interest, or when his creditors seize it, the buyer or creditors can collect his share of the profits, but they cannot help run the business. ROBERT E. RODES, JR.

PARTRIDGE, *PAHR trij*, is the bird that people in the northern and western states call *quail*, or *bobwhite*. It is known to many southerners as partridge. New Englanders use the term *partridge* for the ruffed grouse. Canadians, in turn, call the Canada spruce grouse the *swamp* partridge, or *spruce* partridge.

There is, however, a group of birds in the Eastern Hemisphere that scientists consider true partridges.

The Chukar Partridge, common in Southeast Asia, is also a favorite game bird in the Pacific Northwest of the United States.
William L. & Irene Finley

There are about 150 different kinds of these birds. The bird that sportsmen call the *Hungarian* partridge is typical of this group. It has been imported into America in large numbers for breeding purposes. It is also known as the *European* partridge. This bird lives throughout Europe and in northern Africa and western Asia.

The largest of these birds is about a foot long. The bird is ashy gray on the upper parts of the body, with brown and black markings. Often there is a distinct crescent-shaped spot of deep chestnut on the breast. The bird eats waste grains, tender shoots of plants, and insects. It builds its nest on the ground. The female lays from eight to 20 eggs. The Hungarian partridge is an important game bird in the northwestern part of the United States and in the prairie provinces of Canada. The *chukar*, native to parts of Asia and Europe, is also an important game bird in the northwestern United States.

Scientific Classification. True partridges belong to the partridge family, *Phasianidae*. The gray, or Hungarian, partridge is genus *Perdix*, species *P. perdix*. The chukar is *Alectoris graeca*. JOSEPH J. HICKEY

See also FRANCOLIN.

PARTRIDGE PEA, also called "sensitive pea," is a wild plant of eastern and central United States and of Mexico. Like the common pea, it bears its seeds in pods, which develop from clusters of yellow flowers. The leaves are made up of many small leaflets, which are somewhat sensitive to the touch, and tend to fold together when roughly handled.

Scientific Classification. The partridge pea belongs to the pea family, *Leguminosae*. It is genus *Cassia*, species *C. fasciculata*. EDMUND C. JAEGER

See also CASSIA; FLOWER (color picture: Flowers of Roadside, Field, and Prairie).

PARTS OF SPEECH are the word classes of a language. Words belong to the same class if they occur in the same or similar contexts in sentences. In *Let's play* or *Let's go*, each word following *let's* is a verb. Sometimes more than one word class can be used in the same context. For example, in *It was John* and *It was good*, *was* can be followed by either a noun (*John*) or an adjective (*good*). The same word may belong to more than one class, depending on its use in a sentence. In *He fell down*, *down* is an adverb. But *down* is a verb in *The center tried to down the guard*.

Scholars differ on how to describe parts of speech. The traditional description lists eight classes: nouns, pronouns, verbs, adjectives, adverbs, prepositions, conjunctions, and interjections. Some scholars believe that this arrangement is logically unsound and contains contradictions. It classes unlike words together, and separates like words. Some scholars prefer to distinguish *form classes*—nouns, verbs, adjectives, and adverbs—from *function words*—prepositions, determiners, auxiliaries, and conjunctions. Others distinguish *inflected classes*—nouns, pronouns, verbs, and adjectives—from all other words, called *particles*. PAUL ROBERTS

See the separate articles in WORLD BOOK for each part of speech, such as NOUN. See also ARTICLE; PARSING.

PARTY, POLITICAL. See POLITICAL PARTY.

PARTY GAMES. See GAME (Parlor Games; Party Games).

PAS, THE. See MANITOBA (Places to Visit).

PASADENA

PASADENA, Calif. (pop. 116,407; alt. 830 ft.), is an attractive residential city. It is nationally famous as the home of the Rose Bowl, where two leading college football teams play every New Year's Day. The Tournament of Roses also includes a colorful parade, with flower-covered floats and pretty girls (see CALIFORNIA [color picture: New Year's Day Rose Parade]).

Pasadena lies in the foothills of the Sierra Madre Mountains, overlooking the beautiful San Gabriel Valley. The city is about 10 miles north of Los Angeles. For location, see CALIFORNIA (political map).

The city is the home of the California Institute of Technology, one of the leading colleges of its kind in the world, and the Pasadena Playhouse College of Theatre Arts. It also has two junior colleges. Mount Wilson Observatory is nearby. Pasadena is a center for scientific research laboratories, precision-instrument manufacturing, and gifts and ceramics manufacturing.

The site of Pasadena was once part of the San Gabriel Mission, established by Spanish priests in 1771. In 1873, the land was purchased by the California Colony of Indiana, an organization founded by Thomas B. Elliott of Indianapolis. The original name, "Indiana Colony," was changed in 1875 to *Pasadena,* an Indian word meaning *valley between the hills.* Pasadena was incorporated in 1886 and chartered as a city in 1901. It has a council-manager government.   GEORGE SHAFTEL

PASADENA, Tex. (pop. 58,737; alt. 35 ft.), is a rapidly growing suburb southeast of Houston. It lies in a thriving industrial area along the Houston Ship Channel. Pasadena was founded in 1895 and incorporated in 1928. It has a commission government. For location, see TEXAS (political map).

PASADENA COLLEGE. See UNIVERSITIES AND COLLEGES (table).

PASADENA PLAYHOUSE COLLEGE OF THEATRE ARTS. See UNIVERSITIES AND COLLEGES (table).

PASAY, *PAH sye,* or RIZAL (pop. 157,800; alt. 16 ft.), is a trading center for a large agricultural area in the Philippines. The city lies on Manila Bay, south of the city of Manila (see PHILIPPINES [color map]). Fort Bonafacio—called Fort McKinley when it was a U.S. Army reservation—is east of the city. The United States returned it to the Philippines in 1947. A military cemetery for World War II dead is also in Pasay.

PASCAL, BLAISE (1623-1662), was a French religious philosopher, mathematician, and scientist. Today he is noted mainly for his scientific accomplishments.

His work on the pressure of liquids was of great importance. The principle that liquid in a vessel carries pressures equally in all directions is called *Pascal's Law* after him. This principle is used in hydraulic presses, hydraulic elevators, hydraulic jacks, vacuum pumps, and air compressors. In these devices the pressure on the fluid in them is increased at one point, and the fluid carries the pressure increase to all other points on the machine. See PASCAL'S LAW.

Pascal was born in Clermont-Ferrand. His father took charge of his education and taught him only those subjects which he wanted to know. These were mostly ancient languages, and Pascal's father refused to teach him any of the sciences until he found that at the age of 12 the boy had discovered geometry and

taught it to himself. Pascal attracted the attention of the great mathematician, René Descartes, by writing a book now lost, *The Geometry of Conics,* at the age of 16. His father finally allowed him to continue his work in physics and mathematics.

With Pierre de Fermat, Pascal invented the theory of probability and discussed some of its applications to card games. He also invented a calculating machine which may still be viewed in a French museum.

Through his sister, Pascal became interested in Jansenism, which was one of the Roman Catholic heresies (see JANSEN, CORNELIUS). Religion became more important to him than his scientific pursuits. In 1654, at Port Royal, he became a monk in a Jansenist convent. Pascal kept up his scientific work in the convent, and also began to write religious treatises. From 1656 to 1657 he published his *Provincial Letters,* 18 masterpieces of irony. These letters were a reply to the Jesuits, who had condemned Antoine Arnauld, one of the Jansenist leaders, for heresy.

Eight years after Pascal's death, his *Pensées,* or *Thoughts on Religion and Other Subjects,* was published. This book, subtitled *An Apology for the Christian Religion,* was a defense of Jansenism. It maintained that the only perfect knowledge came through Christian revelation. Pascal believed that faith was a sounder guide than reason. Reason can go only so far, he said, but faith has no limits.   PHILLIP S. JONES

See also CALCULATING MACHINE; FRENCH LITERATURE (Classical Prose); PERMUTATIONS AND COMBINATIONS (History); TRANSPORTATION (Red-Letter Dates [1662]).

PASCAL'S LAW describes the effect of applying pressure on a liquid in a closed container. It states that whenever the pressure in a confined liquid is increased or decreased at any point, the change in pressure takes place equally throughout the liquid. It explains why a thin bottle filled with water will break when the cork is pushed down.   IRA M. FREEMAN

See also HYDROSTATICS; PASCAL, BLAISE.

PASCHAL, *PASS kul,* was the name of two popes of the Roman Catholic Church. Both tried to defend the papacy against imperial power. Their reigns were:

Paschal I, Saint   (817-824)
Paschal II   (1099-1118)

Saint Paschal I and Emperor Louis the Pious agreed to have free papal elections. But the emperor reserved the right to decide disputed elections.

Paschal II proposed that churchmen surrender their feudal possessions, such as taxes and estates, to the emperor. In return, the emperor would surrender his right to nominate and invest clergymen, and free the church from lay control. Powerful bishops opposed the idea and the pope died before an agreement was reached.   THOMAS P. NEILL and FULTON J. SHEEN

PASCHAL CANDLE, *PASS kul,* is a large candle used in Roman Catholic services at Eastertide to symbolize Jesus Christ risen from the dead as the light of the world. It is blessed, engraved with symbols of Christ, and studded with five grains of incense at the ceremonies on Holy Saturday, the eve of Easter. It stands at the left side of the altar from Easter Sunday to Ascension Thursday, and is lit on Sundays and great feast days. The word *paschal* comes from the Greek name for the Jewish Passover, the season of the first Easter.   FRANCIS L. FILAS

PASHTO, or PUSHTU. See AFGHANISTAN (Language); PAKISTAN (Language).

PASIG RIVER. See MANILA.

PASQUEFLOWER, *PASK flou er*, is the name of two small plants with large flowers that open early in the spring. The name pasqueflower means *Easter flower.* Pasqueflowers grow in Europe and North America. The American pasqueflower (Prairie Crocus), is the state flower of South Dakota and the provincial flower of Manitoba. The plant grows throughout the midwestern plains of North America. The flowers range in color from lavender to deep purple and have yellow centers. The blossoms form on very short stems that grow longer as the seeds ripen. The fuzzy leaves have many leaflets that spread out like the fingers of a hand.

Scientific Classification. Pasqueflowers belong to the crowfoot family, *Ranunculaceae.* The American pasqueflower is classified as genus *Anemone,* species *A. patens;* the European is *A. pulsatilla.*   MARCUS MAXON

See also FLOWER (color picture: Flowers of Roadside, Field, and Prairie).

PASS. See MOUNTAIN PASS; JETTY.

PASSAIC, *puh SAY ihk,* N.J. (pop. 53,963; alt. 60 ft.), is a city on the Passaic River in the heart of a great industrial region. *Passaic* is an Indian word for *peaceful valley.* The city is about 10 miles west of New York City. With Paterson and Clifton, N.J., it forms a metropolitan area that has a population of 1,186,873. For the location of Passaic, see NEW JERSEY (political map).

The manufacture of textiles and mechanical rubber goods are the leading industries of Passaic. Thousands of handkerchiefs are made every day in the city's factories. Other industries include the manufacture of radio and telegraph equipment, railroad cars, brakes, leather products, chemicals, paper products, and biscuits. A wide variety of products is shipped from Passaic.

Three railroad lines and many bus lines connect the city with nearby cities and states. The Passaic River has a deep channel so that freighters and tankers can sail between Passaic, New York City, Newark, and other ocean ports.

Dutch traders settled the area in 1676. They named the town *Acquackanonk.* German and Irish families followed. The growth of industry in the 1800's brought newcomers from Central Europe. The name of the town was changed to Passaic in 1854. The city was chartered in 1873. Passaic has a council-manager form of government.

PASSAIC RIVER. See NEW JERSEY (Rivers and Lakes).

PASSAMAQUODDY BAY is a part of the Bay of Fundy between Maine and New Brunswick, Canada. It cuts inland for about 15 miles, and averages about 10 miles in width. For location, see MAINE (physical map). The tides on the rocky Maine coast of Passamaquoddy sometimes rise as much as 27 feet. In 1935 the United States government began the Passamaquoddy Bay Tidal Power Project, designed to use the ocean tides to create electric power. The original project was to have cost $37 million. But Congress refused to appropriate more than the $7 million given for the project in 1935. Only four small dams were completed.

The chief towns in Maine on Passamaquoddy Bay are Eastport and Lubec. The chief towns in New Brunswick are St. Andrews and St. George. Campobello and

Deer islands lie in the bay, and Grand Manan Island is located near the entrance to the bay. Important fisheries along the bay include herring, pollack, sardine, and lobster.   JOSEPH M. TREFETHEN

PASSAU, TREATY OF. See SCHMALKALDIC LEAGUE.

PASSENGER PIGEON was a wild pigeon, about 17 inches long. It had delicately pinkish-tinted dark gray feathers and a long tail. The passenger pigeon was found in large numbers in eastern North America until the end of the 1800's. This beautiful bird does not exist today because of the hunters' greed and foolish waste. What is believed to have been the last passenger pigeon in the United States died in 1914, in the Zoological Gardens of Cincinnati.

The stories that scientists tell us about the once vast numbers of these pigeons seem unbelievable now. Alexander Wilson saw a large flock in Kentucky in 1808. He believed that there were more than 2,230,000,000 birds in this group. In 1813 Audubon watched a flock of passenger pigeons pass in a stream that lasted for three days. The flock was so thick that it darkened the sun. Their wings sounded like thunder. The nesting colonies of these pigeons covered thousands of acres. Every large tree was loaded with dozens of nests. The pigeons left little food for other creatures in their nesting area. The birds were strong fliers. They often traveled as far as a hundred miles a day looking for food.

Hunters came to their nesting places each year. They blinded the birds with lights at night and knocked them off trees with poles. They also choked them with burning sulfur. Sometimes, they cut down the bird's roosting places. The birds were shot after they had been caught in one of these ways. The hunters ate or preserved some of the pigeons they killed. Most, however, were sold. During the nesting season, many carloads were shipped each day to market. The birds sold in New York City and Chicago for one and two cents each.

Scientific Classification. The passenger pigeon belongs to the pigeon and dove family, *Columbidae.* It is genus *Ectopistes,* species *E. migratorius.*   HERBERT FRIEDMANN

PASSEPIED. See DANCING (During the 1600's).

PASSION MUSIC is dramatic vocal music that tells the Gospel story of the suffering of Jesus Christ. It is a kind of *oratorio* (sacred opera) and is usually sung during Holy Week. Scholars believe that passion music was first sung in the A.D. 300's. *The Passion According to St. Matthew* by Johann Sebastian Bach is one of the greatest Passions ever composed.

PASSION PLAY is a dramatic performance representing the suffering and death of Jesus Christ. The most famous Passion Play is given by the people of the village of Oberammergau, Bavaria, in southern Germany. It is performed as a result of a vow that the villagers made in 1633. At that time, a plague raged in the neighborhood of Oberammergau. When the plague ended, the people gratefully promised to honor the Passion of Christ by giving a play. They have kept that vow by performing the play every ten years. The performance was delayed for two years, from 1920 to 1922, during the aftermath of World War I. It was held up again in 1940 because of World War II, but was resumed in 1950. The play lasts eight hours and includes more than 1,200 performers.

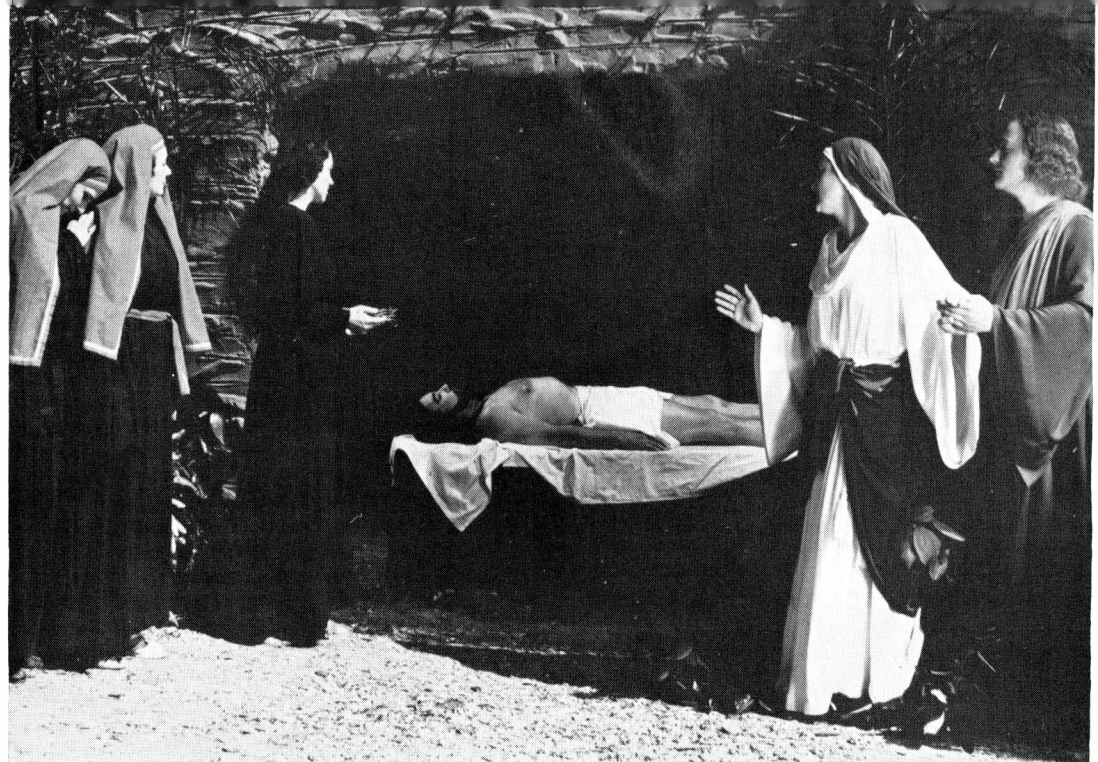

The Black Hills Passion Play is given every summer at Spearfish, S. Dak. This famous play originated in the Cappenburg

Dept. of Highways, South Dakota

Monastery at Lunen, Germany, in 1242. It was presented first in America in 1932, and has been given each year since 1938.

Other German towns, including Freiburg and Regensburg, have given similar, but less famous, plays for hundreds of years. Since 1938, German settlers in South Dakota have given a yearly Passion Play at Spearfish, in the Black Hills. GLENN HUGHES

See also MIRACLE PLAY; OBERAMMERGAU.

PASSION WEEK is the week in the Western Christian church that begins on Passion Sunday, the fifth Sunday in Lent. It is the week before Holy Week. Passion Sunday marks the beginning of the yearly remembrance of Christ's passion, or final sufferings. Beginning with Passion Week, the Roman Catholic Church veils all sacred pictures, crucifixes, and statues. It does this to show the sorrow of the church. The Episcopal Church also veils its sacred ornaments during Lent. See also HOLY WEEK; LENT. ALBERT E. AVEY and FULTON J. SHEEN

PASSIONFLOWER is a group of plants whose elaborate flower parts are said to represent Christ's crucifixion. According to legend, early Roman Catholic missionaries named these plants. They thought the 10 colored petals represented the 10 apostles present at the crucifixion. Inside the flower, colored filaments form a showy crown, which was thought to represent the crown of thorns. The five pollen-bearing anthers suggested Christ's wounds. The divisions of the pistil represented the nails of the cross. The bladelike leaf was symbolic of the spear that pierced His side. The coiling tendrils suggested whips and cords.

Although a few species grow in Malaya, China, and Australia, passionflowers are native chiefly in the tropical and semitropical regions of North and South America. The familiar passionflower of the southern United States is a trailing or climbing woody vine. It bears an edible yellow fruit, called *maypop*, which has a

distinct, slightly acid flavor. Several tropical species of passionflowers have edible fruits.

A greenish-flowered variety that bears small berries grows in moist thickets in Pennsylvania and southward. A Brazilian passionflower is widely cultivated in greenhouses for its beautiful blue, white, or rose-colored blossoms.

Scientific Classification. Passionflowers belong to the passionflower family, *Passifloraceae*. The plants of the southern United States are genus *Passiflora*, species *P. incarnata*. The Pennsylvania species is *P. lutea*. The passionflower of Brazil is *P. caerulea*. ROBERT W. SCHERY

The Passionflower reminded early Roman Catholic missionaries in America of Christ's Passion, and they gave it this name.

W. H. Hodge

PASSIONISTS. See PAUL OF THE CROSS, SAINT; RELIGIOUS ORDERS.

PASSIVE VOICE. See VOICE (in grammar).

PASSOVER is the Jewish festival of freedom. It celebrates the exodus from Egypt, when the Israelites became free men. It begins on the 15th day of the Hebrew month of Nisan, and lasts eight days. Jews in Israel and Reform Jews celebrate it for seven days.

The name *Passover* comes from the Biblical story of the tenth plague that God brought on Egypt (Ex. 12: 3-40). A destroying angel killed the first-born in every Egyptian home, but *passed over* the Israelite houses. The name also refers to the passing over of the Israelites from slavery to freedom. The Hebrew name for Passover is *Pesah*. The festival is sometimes called the *Feast of Unleavened Bread* because the Israelites hastily baked unleavened breads called *matzahs* before they left Egypt (see MATZAH). Traditional Jews eat matzahs instead of bread during the entire festival.

Jews celebrate Passover at home at a feast called the *Seder*. The head of the family reads aloud the story of Passover from the *Haggadah*. LOUIS L. MANN

Seder Meal, which was painted by Moritz Oppenheim during the 1800's, shows a family gathered for the traditional Passover dinner.
Frank Darmstaedter, the Jewish Museum, N.Y.

PASSPORT is a travel document that identifies the holder as a citizen of the country by which it is issued. A passport also requests other countries to give the holder safe passage and all lawful aid and protection. Sometimes a passport must have a *visa* (official endorsement) from the country a person desires to visit before entry into that country is permitted (see VISA).

The Department of State issues passports in the United States. Department of State officials in the following major cities may also issue passports: Boston, Chicago, Honolulu, Los Angeles, Miami, New Orleans, New York, San Francisco, and Seattle. Applications may also be made before a clerk of a federal or state court authorized by law to naturalize aliens. Many American diplomatic and consular officers can issue passports to American citizens overseas. In Canada, passports are issued by the Department of External Affairs at Ottawa.

The United States issues three types of passports: (1) *diplomatic*, for persons going abroad on important government assignments; (2) *official*, for other government employees; and (3) *regular*, for persons traveling overseas for personal reasons.

Many countries do not require citizens of certain other countries to have passports. United States citizens do not need passports to enter Bermuda, Canada, Mexico, and most of the West Indies. TELFORD TAYLOR

PASTA. See ITALY (Food).

PASTE. See PORCELAIN (Kinds).

PASTEL, *pass TELL,* is a chalklike crayon painting. Its colors are soft and durable. Pastels can be made more quickly than oil or water-color paintings. But the paintings soil easily and should be kept under glass. Pastel is also the name for the crayons with which the pictures are drawn or painted. Pastels are made of chalk and pigment mixed with gum water and dried in the form of crayons. They can be applied with a sharp point or edge of the crayon to make a thin line, or with the side of the crayon to make a broad line. Charcoal crayons are used mostly for drawing faces and the human figure. THOMAS MUNRO

PASTERNAK, BORIS LEONIDOVICH (1890-1960), a Russian novelist and poet, won the 1958 Nobel prize in literature. He rejected the award because of pressure from the Russian government. His novel *Doctor Zhivago* is critical of Communism and defends the individual's right to live his own life. It was not published in Russia, but appeared in translation in western Europe and the United States. His poetry includes *My Sister, Life* (1922). He was born in Moscow. ERNEST J. SIMMONS

PASTEUR, *pahs TOOR,* **LOUIS** (1822-1895), of France, was one of the world's greatest scientists. He made major contributions to chemistry, medicine, and industry that have greatly benefited mankind. His discovery that bacteria spread diseases saved countless lives. He was a great theoretical scientist who applied his abstract discoveries to important practical problems in industry and medicine.

His Work in Chemistry brought him his first recognition. His work with the structure of crystals made him famous by the time he was 26. But Pasteur soon started probing the mysteries of *bacteriology* (the study of bacteria). Others saw bacteria before Pasteur did. But he was the first to show that living things come only from living things. Before that, many scientists believed in *spontaneous generation*, a theory that life could come from things that are not alive, such as dirt. Pasteur also showed that although bacteria live almost everywhere, their spread can be controlled. See BACTERIA; SPONTANEOUS GENERATION.

His Work in Industry. Pasteur is credited with saving the silk industry and wine industry in France. In 1864, he noted that wine turns bitter because of *microbes* (germs) that enter the wine while it is being made. He suggested that microbes can be killed by applying controlled heat. This use of heat as a means to kill germs became known as *pasteurization*. Pasteur also used this method to preserve milk and beer, and to preserve food. See PASTEURIZATION.

In 1865, Pasteur set out to help the silk industry. A disease called *pebrine* was killing great numbers of silkworms. He worked several years to prove that a microbe that attacks silkworm eggs causes the disease. He showed that the disease would be wiped out by eliminating this germ in silkworm nurseries.

His Work in Medicine. Pasteur proved that many diseases are caused by other types of germs that multiply in the body. He also proved that if microbes are weakened in a laboratory and then placed in an animal's body, the animal develops an *immunity* (resistance) to the microbe. He called this method of fighting off microbes *vaccination*. He proved its value by vaccinating sheep against a disease called anthrax. He also showed that vaccination prevents chicken cholera and other animal diseases.

Historical Pictures Service
Louis Pasteur

Pasteur began in 1882 to study rabies, a deadly disease spread by the bite of rabies infected animals. He spent endless hours in his laboratory seeking a vaccine to prevent the disease. His tireless work slowly wore down his health. One day in 1885, a small boy named Joseph Meister was bitten by a rabid dog. The boy's parents begged Pasteur to save their son. Pasteur hesitated to use his new vaccine on a human, but he finally agreed. After several anxious weeks of treatment, the vaccine proved successful. The boy did not get rabies. See RABIES.

His Life. Pasteur was born the son of a tanner in Dôle, France. The family soon moved to Arbois, where he received his early education. Pasteur was a slow but careful student who showed a talent for art. He later studied chemistry at the École Normale and the Sorbonne in Paris. In 1849, he became a science professor in Strasbourg, France, where he began studying *fermentation*, a type of chemical breakdown of substances by microbes (see FERMENTATION). His work brought such improvements in brewing and winemaking that some say France was able to save enough money to pay its Franco-Prussian War debt. In 1868, a brain stroke partially paralyzed him. Despite his poor health, he continued his work. Pasteur was one of the few scientists to achieve fame while still alive. The Pasteur Institute in Paris, a world center for the study, prevention, and treatment of disease, was founded in 1888 in gratitude to him. Pasteur is buried in a magnificent tomb in the building.   RENÉ DUBOS

PASTEURIZATION is a method of preserving food by heat and cold. It is most commonly used for milk, but may also be used for cheese, beer, and other foods. Louis Pasteur, a French chemist, invented the process. It consists of heating milk to at least 145° F. for not less than 30 minutes, then chilling it quickly to 50° F. or less. Modern dairies use a faster, high-temperature method in which the milk is heated to at least 161° F. for at least 15 seconds, then cooled. In either method, the milk must be kept cold until used. Pasteurization keeps harmful germs from multiplying rapidly, but

does not greatly affect the flavor of milk or food.

Pasteur discovered that bacteria in food multiply rapidly and cause the food to spoil. Ordinary boiling will kill all bacteria, but the heat of boiling destroys the flavor of milk. Pasteur found that boiling the milk is not necessary, that most of the bacteria are killed with less heat than boiling, and if the milk is chilled after being heated, the bacteria do not multiply again rapidly. Nathan Straus was a pioneer in the campaign for pasteurization laws in the United States.

See also MILK (Pasteurization).

PASTORAL LITERATURE, *PASS toh rul*, refers to poems, dramas, or novels that portray the life of shepherds, or country life. It usually describes idealized, simple rustic life. Pastoral literature was popular in England from the 1500's to the 1700's. *Pastoral music* is lyrical and melodious, and often inspired by scenes of nature.

PASTORE, JOHN ORLANDO (1907-   ), became the first person of Italian descent to win election as a state governor and then as a United States Senator. A Democrat, Pastore served as governor of Rhode Island from 1945 to 1950. He was elected to fill a vacancy in the United States Senate in 1950, and won re-election in 1952, 1958, and 1964. A colorful orator, he gave the keynote address at the 1964 Democratic National Convention. He was born in Providence.   WILLIAM D. METZ

PASTORIUS, *pass TOE rih us*, **FRANCIS DANIEL** (1651-1719?), a German lawyer and scholar, founded Germantown, now a part of Philadelphia. He became interested in the Society of Friends, or Quakers, at about the time that William Penn founded the colony of Pennsylvania. Pastorius bought 15,000 acres of land from Penn in 1683, and laid out the settlement of Germantown for German Quakers and Mennonites. Pastorius was born in the town of Sommerhausen, Germany, near Würzburg. He understood seven languages, and published many books.   IAN C. C. GRAHAM

PASTRY is baked from a stiff, short dough composed basically of flour, salt, shortening, and water. This dough is baked into plain, flaky, or puff pastries.

Different countries are noted for special kinds of pastry. French pastry is made from a puffy dough like that used for éclairs and cream puffs, or from a cake mixture cut into small shapes and decorated elaborately with frostings and flower petals, mint leaves, glazed fruits, jellies, or nuts. Danish people make pastries of flaky yeast dough into which generous amounts of butter have been folded. German pastries usually have a cookie dough base, to which fruits and spices are added.

Americans have adopted the pastries of many countries, especially France and Denmark. Pie is the best-known typically American pastry.   HELEN MARLEY CALAWAY

PASTURE is land from which cattle, horses, sheep, and other livestock get their food by grazing. Such food usually costs farmers less than rations of hay, grain, and other harvested crops. In regions of rich grassland, animals may get all their food from pastures. Many sheep and cattle have been raised in this way on western ranges. But most livestock thrive better when fed other and richer foods in addition to pasturage.

The world has many great pasture areas. The best pastures are usually found in those parts of the temperate regions where the rainfall is moderate. About six-tenths of the land area of the United States is used for pasture during part of every year. Other countries with large pasture areas include Argentina, Australia, Brazil, China, South Africa, and Russia. Grassland areas may be known by such names as *velds*, *savannas*, *steppes*, and *pampas*. The principal plants used as pasturage are grasses, clovers, and related plants. Many farmers improve their pastures by fertilizing and seeding them, or create artificial pastures from tilled fields or open forest land. CARL D. DUNCAN

See also GRASSLAND; PAMPA; SAVANNA; STEPPE.

PATAGONIA, *PAT uh GOHN yuh,* is the name of a territory near the southern tip of South America. A large part of the region is desert. The Portuguese navigator Ferdinand Magellan discovered the region in 1520.

The name Patagonia comes from the Spanish word *patagones,* which means *big feet.* The Indians were tall, and wore large boots stuffed with grass.

In 1865, Welsh settlers came into Patagonia. Welsh is still spoken in some of the towns. The area was in controversy until 1907, when it was divided between Chile and Argentina, under the 1881 treaty.

The Argentine section of Patagonia includes the territories east of the Andes Mountains. Chile controls the Patagonian territory on the west side of the mountains.

Large tracts of the country are used for sheep raising. Coal is found in northern Patagonia. The area had an oil boom, and a big iron ore deposit was found along the coast, in the 1960's. E. TAYLOR PARKS

See also ARGENTINA (Land Regions); RACES OF MAN (picture: The Americas); SOUTH AMERICA (Land Regions; color map).

PATAPSCO RIVER. See BALTIMORE (Location).

PATCH, ALEXANDER McCARRELL, JR. (1889-1945), led United States armies in the Pacific and European theaters during World War II. General Patch commanded U.S. forces at Guadalcanal in the South Pacific in 1942. In 1944, he commanded the Seventh Army in the Allied invasion of southern France. Patch was born in Fort Huachuca, Ariz. He was graduated from the U.S. Military Academy in 1913. PAUL HUBBARD

PATCH TEST. See ALLERGY (Search for Allergic Causes).

PATCHOULI, *PATCH oo lih,* is a brown oil used in making perfumes. It has a rich, spicy, woody scent. Perfume makers add patchouli to perfumes because of its long-lasting fragrance. Many lotions used by men contain patchouli. The oil comes from leaves of the patchouli plant, a member of the mint family. The leaves are picked, partially fermented, and dried. Steam is passed through them to remove the oil. Patchouli is produced in Indonesia, Malaya, the Malagasy Republic, and other countries. PAUL Z. BEDOUKIAN

PÂTÉ DE FOIE GRAS. See GOOSE (Domestic Geese).

PATELLA. See KNEECAP.

PATENT is an official paper issued by a national government to indicate ownership of property. The term *letters patent,* or simply *patent,* refers to the right to control the manufacture and sale of a product. This monopoly, limited in time and type, is given to the inventor of a device or a process to reward him for his genius. The right is represented by a document which, if held to be valid when it is challenged in court, protects the inventor by giving him this monopoly for a certain number of years. In the United States, the title to each tract of real estate goes back to a "patent" issued by the federal government. But a patent can be obtained on personal property as well as on real estate.

Patentable Items. A person entitled to a patent is one who has invented or discovered some new and useful machine, product, substance, or method. A patent may also be granted for some new and useful improvement on something already invented. A person who has invented, discovered, or reproduced any distinct and new variety of plant, other than plants grown from tubers, may secure a patent. For example, varieties of roses have been patented. A patent may also be granted for a new, original, or ornamental design for an article of manufacture. A process, or new method of doing some useful thing, may be patentable. Court rulings carefully define the things which can be patented. They must be "new in the art"—not something described in scientific or popular literature either of this country or others. A machine is not patentable if it differs only in size or shape from another machine which does the same work. Nor can it be considered patentable because it arranges the parts of an old machine differently. A new *principle* must be present. The device must be an *invention* to get a patent. But not every invention can be patented. A patent will not be granted for some change in a device that would occur to any skilled mechanic. The true test of an invention is originality. An article that has been patented must be so marked. Damages may be recovered in the case of patent *infringement,* when a person innocently or purposely uses, sells, or makes an invention patented by another.

United States Patent Laws. The Constitution of the United States places all patent control in Congress. No state may pass a patent law. When a patent is granted, the inventor has the sole right "to make, use, and sell" his invention for 17 years. No person, even for his own use alone, may make an article that another person has patented, without violating the patent laws. A fee of $65 is required when requesting a patent, and another fee of $100 must be paid when the patent is issued. If a patent expires, it can be extended only by a special act of Congress. Such acts allowed veterans of World War I and World War II to have patents extended. Information about securing patents may be obtained from the Commissioner of Patents, United States Department of Commerce, Washington, D.C. 20025.

The United States adopted its first patent laws in 1790. On July 31 of that year, it issued the first patent to Samuel Hopkins of Vermont for a process for "making pot and pearl ashes." Congress established the Patent Office in 1802 within the Department of State. In 1849, it transferred the office to the Department of the Interior, and in 1925 to the Department of Commerce. In 1870, all the patent laws were revised.

In the next 80 years, the rulings of the Patent Office became as archaic as the laws themselves. The Patent Office refused to grant patents unless a person showed that he had developed the invention in a "flash of inventive genius." As a result, a brilliant scientist who worked logically and painstakingly in developing an idea often could not patent it, while an ignorant man who accidentally stumbled onto an idea or a device could patent it.

Widespread criticism of the entire patent system

caused Congress to adopt a new Patent Code, which became law in 1952. The code provides that an inventor may now patent a new "use" of an old device. The "flash of inventive genius" test is no longer required.

The procedure involved in securing a patent is precise. Applications and drawings must conform to strict legal requirements. The wording of patent claims is difficult and technical, requiring the assistance of a skilled patent attorney.

In 1940 and 1941, laws were written to assure secrecy of all inventions important to national defense. All patents controlled by enemy countries were seized and kept as government property. A new permanent statute in 1952 replaced these laws. This law limits such an order for seizure to one year or, if hostilities are then in progress, to one year after the end of hostilities. The order is subject to review by the federal courts.

Canadian Patent Laws. The British North America Act (Confederation Act) of 1867 grants Canada's Parliament full control of patent laws. Patent laws had been passed in parts of Canada before confederation, but the first law after confederation was passed in 1869. The present Patent Act was passed in 1935. Canadian patents are granted for 17 years. A $40 fee is required when requesting a patent and a $70 fee must be paid when the patent is issued. The Commissioner of Patents decides whether an invention deserves a patent. The inventor may appeal a refusal of patent. Information about Canadian patents may be obtained by writing to the Commissioner of Patents, Ottawa, Ont.

In Europe, the patent laws vary from one country to another. In Germany, the general principles for patent rules were set up in the Zollverein Convention in 1842. The basic idea of the German patent law is to use that law as a bargain between the inventor and society. This principle is followed by the Scandinavian countries, The Netherlands, Austria, and Hungary. France adopted its first patent legislation in 1791. It believes that patent laws should be based on the idea that the inventor's right is a natural right.

In England, during the Middle Ages, only the king had the right to grant special privileges, called *letters patent.* This custom was often abused, and resulted in aiding the king's friends and oppressing the rest of the people. The system was so unfair that it was abolished in 1624, during the reign of James I. The only patents left were those on new manufactures in the kingdom, similar to modern patents. Since then, Great Britain has built its patent laws upon the theory that a patent is a monopoly, since it gives the inventor exclusive rights to manufacture the article.   JOHN ALAN APPLEMAN

See also COPYRIGHT; INVENTION (Patents for Inventions); PATENT OFFICE; TRADEMARK.

PATENT LEATHER. See LEATHER (Final Finishing).

PATENT MEDICINE refers to certain medicinal products sold directly to the public. It is a misleading term, because medicines actually are not patented. Drug firms protect some medicines by trademarking their names (see TRADEMARK). Some are protected by patenting new medicinal chemicals, new manufacturing processes, or new applications for known chemicals. Before the Federal Food, Drugs, and Cosmetics Act was adopted, the formulas of most patent medicines were kept secret by the companies owning them. Now there is no such secrecy for drugs sold in interstate commerce, because under the act the ingredients must be declared on the label. Usually the trade name is registered, but if a patent medicine becomes so popular that its trade name becomes identified with the chemical, then the trade name may no longer be claimed as the owner's exclusive property, and becomes instead the common name, as, *aspirin.*

Among the most widely used types of patent medicine are the highly advertised mouthwashes, nose sprays, foot remedies, pain relievers, and cough medicines. The Federal Food, Drugs, and Cosmetics Act requires all patent-medicine companies to list the active drugs in their medicine on the labels of the bottles. It also prohibits companies from marketing any preparation that may have injurious ingredients.

Patent medicines are also called *proprietary medicines,* since these ready-made medicinal products have some "proprietary" or "private" phase to them, such as a secret process or trademark. This distinguishes patent medicines from medicinal products listed and described in the accepted legal standards for drugs and medicines.   SOLOMON GARB

For more information about medicines, see the DRUG article with its list of Related Articles. See also PURE FOOD AND DRUG LAWS.

PATENT OFFICE is the agency of the United States government that grants patents for inventions and discoveries. It also registers trademarks.

This office publishes the weekly *Official Gazette of the Patent Office,* which indexes patents and trademarks. It maintains an extensive scientific library and a search room where the public can examine United States patents and their records. The Commissioner of Patents administers the Patent Office, which was established in 1802. The Patent Office became a part of the Department of Commerce in 1925.   JOHN C. BOLLENS

See also PATENT; TRADEMARK.

PATER, *PAY ter,* **WALTER HORATIO** (1839-1894), an English essayist and critic, won fame for his interpretation of the art and literature of the Renaissance, and for his excellent style. His *Studies in the History of the Renaissance* (1873) includes essays on great masters of art. A work of fiction, *Marius the Epicurean* (1885), was considered to be his masterpiece. It took six years to write. His other works include *Imaginary Portraits* (1887), *Plato and Platonism* (1893), and *The Child in the House* (1894). *Greek Studies* was published in 1895 after his death. Pater was born at Shadwell, near London, and attended Queen's College, Oxford. As a tutor at Oxford, he had a strong influence on his students.   LIONEL STEVENSON

PATERSON, *PAT er s'n,* N.J. (pop. 143,663; alt. 100 ft.), is an important manufacturing center on the Passaic River, 17 miles northwest of New York City (see NEW JERSEY [political map]). Paterson, Clifton, and Passaic form a metropolitan area that has a population of 1,186,873. The Society for Establishing Useful Manufactures, founded in 1791 by Alexander Hamilton, selected the site of Paterson. The water power of the Passaic Falls influenced the choice. The city was named for William Paterson, once governor of New Jersey.

Silk manufacture was introduced in 1840 by John Ryle, an Englishman, and Paterson came to be known as the *Silk City*. At one time Paterson produced more silk products than any other American city. Seventy-five per cent of Paterson's industry was formerly devoted to the weaving and dyeing of silk and rayon. Now these industries make up only about 30 per cent of the total. Steam locomotives and Colt revolvers were early products of Paterson's factories. Other industries include the manufacture of machinery, machine tools, clothing, and chemicals.

Most of the city lies within a large curve of the Passaic River. Paterson covers more than 8 square miles of high ground just northeast of Garret Mountain. The rolling hills around the city provide natural recreation areas.

Outstanding buildings in Paterson include the Paterson Museum, the Danforth Memorial Library, and Lambert's Castle in the Garret Mountain Park Reservation.

Paterson was incorporated in 1851, and since 1907 has operated under a mayor-council form of municipal government. RICHARD P. MCCORMICK

PATERSON, WILLIAM (1658-1719), a British economist and financier, helped found the Bank of England in 1694 and developed its early operations. Paterson attempted to establish a Scottish colony in Darien, Central America, now in Panama. In 1698, he led an expedition of 1,200 colonists to Darien. Many of them, including his wife, died, and Paterson and other survivors returned to Great Britain. Paterson was born in Dumfriesshire, Scotland. He was elected to Parliament in 1707. JOHN B. MCFERRIN

PATERSON, WILLIAM (1745-1806), an American lawyer and jurist, was a signer of the U.S. Constitution. He was a member of the New Jersey Constitutional Convention in 1776, and a delegate to the federal Constitutional Convention in 1787. He served as a U.S. senator from New Jersey from 1789 to 1790, and as governor from 1790 to 1793. In 1793, he was appointed a justice of the Supreme Court of the United States, where he served until his death. Paterson was born in County Antrim, Ireland. KENNETH R. ROSSMAN

PATERSON STATE COLLEGE. See UNIVERSITIES AND COLLEGES (table).

PATHAN, *puh TAHN*, is an Indian term for a member of the major tribal group of Afghanistan. Members of this group call themselves *Pushtuns*. There are also colonies of Pushtuns in parts of India and Pakistan. Most Pushtuns are Moslems. They speak an Aryan language called Pushtu.

PATHET LAO. See LAOS (History).

PATHFINDERS OF AMERICA is an organization to help the young people of the United States. Its membership includes about 20,000 persons of grade- and high-school age.

The purpose of the Pathfinders is to reduce juvenile delinquency and crime by giving young people character training. The organization also works in prisons to fit prisoners for life after they are released. The Pathfinders of America was founded in 1914.

PATHOLOGY, *puh THAHL oh jih*, is the study of disease, or any condition that limits the power, length, or enjoyment of life. *Comparative pathology* compares human diseases with those of various animals. *Plant pathology* studies the diseases of plants. *Human pathology* is a branch of medicine. The pathologist uses modern instruments and methods, such as electron microscopy, to help him recognize the changes caused by disease in the tissues and organs of the body. He tries to explain why a diseased body acts differently from a normal body.

The pathologist uses his knowledge of diseased tissues and body fluids to aid the physician. Pathological tests help physicians diagnose a disease and the extent of its attack. These tests may include examination of the blood, urine, and tissues. The use of laboratory tests to diagnose disease is called *clinical pathology*.

The pathologist also studies diseased parts removed by surgery. He may examine corpses to learn the exact cause of death. This examination is called an *autopsy*, or *post-mortem examination*.

Special kinds of pathology study diseases of separate organ systems. For example, *neuropathology* concerns diseases of the nerves. J. F. A. MCMANUS

See also NEUROPATHOLOGY; GNOTOBIOTICS.

PATINA. See SCULPTURE (Sculptors Today); COPPER (Resistance to Corrosion).

PATIO. See ARCHITECTURE (Architectural Terms); MEXICO (City Life).

PATMOS, *PAT mus*, is a small volcanic island in the Aegean Sea, off the southwest coast of Asia Minor. It is one of the South Sporades, or Dodecanese Islands. For location, see GREECE (color map). It was on Patmos, according to the Book of Revelations, that Saint John saw his prophetic visions. The island covers about 13 square miles and has about 2,500 people. Most of the people make their living by fishing. They are famous for their skill as sailors.

Patmos was ruled by Turkey from 1537 to 1912, when Italy gained control. It was formally given to Italy by the Treaty of Lausanne (1923). After World War II, it was given to Greece. BENJAMIN WEBB WHEELER

PATRI, *PAH tree*, **ANGELO** (1877-1965), an American educator, won fame for his writings on child training and for his experiments in teaching. His rare insight into children's problems brought him national eminence. An advocate of learning by doing, Patri wrote such books as *A School Master of the Great City* (1917), *Pinocchio in America* (1928), and *How to Help Your Child Grow Up* (1948). Patri originated a syndicated newspaper column called *Our Children*. He was born in Italy. From 1898 to 1944, he taught in New York City public schools. JOHN S. BRUBACHER

PATRIARCH, *PAY tree ark*, was the father or ruler of a family or tribe in ancient times. Abraham, Isaac, and Jacob were the patriarchs of the Hebrew nation. In later Jewish history, the president of the *Sanhedrin*, the highest governing council of the Jews, held the title of patriarch.

The early Christians used the title to honor the bishops of the largest and most important churches. The bishops of Rome, Alexandria, and Antioch were recognized as patriarchs in the early 300's. By the early 500's, the bishops of Jerusalem and Constantinople had come to be called patriarchs. In the Roman Catholic Church, the pope has the title *patriarch of the West*. Roman Catholic archbishops in some cities still hold the honorary title of patriarch. The heads of some Eastern Orthodox churches are called patriarchs. All Eastern Orthodox churches regard the patriarch of Con-

Life Magazine

The Patriarch of Romania is the official head of that country's independent branch of the Eastern Orthodox Churches.

stantinople, called the *Ecumenical Patriarch*, as their spiritual leader. R. PIERCE BEAVER and FULTON J. SHEEN

See also EASTERN ORTHODOX CHURCHES; FAMILY (Home Life).

PATRIARCHAL CROSS. See CROSS (picture).

PATRICIAN, *puh TRISH un*, was an aristocrat of the early Roman Republic (509-264 B.C.). The word comes from the Latin word *pater* (father), which was used to describe members of the Roman Senate. Patricians belonged to wealthy families and were proud of their distinguished ancestors. They controlled the government, the army, and the state religion. They resisted the attempts of the *plebeians* (commoners) to share their power. Until 445 B.C., a plebeian could not marry a patrician.

The two classes struggled for power for more than 200 years. During this time, the plebeians increased in numbers and in wealth, and the number of patricians grew smaller. The patricians were forced to allow plebeians to hold more and higher positions. By 287 B.C., the plebeians could hold almost any civil or religious office, and could pass laws that affected everyone. The patricians and wealthy plebeians then joined to a form a new nobility, based on descent from high state officials.

Many patrician families died out during the late Republic (265-27 B.C.). Many emperors created new patricians, but the title was only an honor and carried no privileges. HERBERT M. HOWE

See also PLEBEIAN.

PATRICK, LYNN and **MURRAY.** See HOCKEY (Famous Hockey Players).

PATRICK, *PAT rick*, **SAINT** (about 389-461), is the patron of Ireland and a saint of the Roman Catholic Church. He was born at Bannavem which may have been in England near the Severn estuary, or in Scotland near the modern city of Dumbarton.

The saint's British name is said to have been Sucat. Patrick is the English form of his Latin name, *Patricius*.

Saint Patrick had a romantic life, full of adventures. He was captured by pirates from Ireland at the age of 16. They carried him back there, and set him to tending the flocks of a chieftain in Ulster. Six years of slavery made him a devoted Christian. He escaped to France and became a monk. In 432, a vision led him to return to Ireland as a missionary bishop. He worked zealously in various parts of the island for the rest of his life. His labors were so successful that he came to be known as one who "found Ireland all heathen and left it all Christian." Saint Patrick founded over 300 churches and baptized more than 120,000 persons.

Many legends grew up about this popular saint. One of the best known is that he charmed the snakes of Ireland down to the seashore so that they were driven into the water and drowned. Much else that is told of Saint Patrick is little more than legendary. He left a sort of autobiography in his *Confession*, written in crude Latin.

Many relics of this saint were held sacred for a thousand years, but some of them were destroyed during the Reformation. A four-sided iron bell, said to be his, is in the Museum of Arts and Sciences in Dublin. An ancient stone chair is on the Rock of Cashel. Much study has been given to Saint Patrick, but little that goes beyond

Saint Patrick converted the Irish people to Christianity and became Ireland's patron saint. His feast day is March 17.

the testimony of his own writings can be accepted as certain. Irish people throughout the world celebrate St. Patrick's Day on March 17. FULTON J. SHEEN

See also SAINT PATRICK'S DAY.

PATRICK AIR FORCE BASE, Fla., is the home of the U.S. Air Force Missile Test Center that tests long-range ballistic and guided missiles. The base lies next to Cape Kennedy, 12 miles southeast of Cocoa. It operates a 10,000-mile missile range. The range extends from Cape Kennedy over the Atlantic Ocean and Africa into the Indian Ocean. Merritt Island, a part of the base's aerospace complex, will be a site for manned satellite launchings to the moon. The base was established as a naval air station in 1940. The Air Force later took control of the base and named it for Major General Mason M. Patrick, chief of the U.S. Army Air Service (1921 to 1926), and chief of the Army Air Corps (1926 and 1927). RICHARD M. SKINNER

See also CAPE KENNEDY.

PATRIOTISM is the love and loyal support of a person for his country. Patriotism includes attachment to a country's land and people, admiration for its customs and traditions, and devotion to its welfare. The term suggests a feeling of oneness and membership in the nation.

Patriotism is a normal attitude or feeling. It has existed in all ages and among all peoples, from the most ancient to those of today. Evidence of this universal feeling can be found in the prominence the literature of many countries gives to patriotism. Outstanding literary works praise loyalty to country and willingness to suffer even death in defense of a country's freedom and good name. In times of war, patriotic songs and slogans have helped unite citizens in support of their country.

Schools help develop patriotism in order to create an appreciation for common memories, hopes, and traditions. Through the study of history, for example, many students learn to love their country and admire its great heroes. Patriotic organizations maintain and promote such symbols of patriotism and national glory as the national flag, and national shrines and monuments. Leading patriotic organizations in the United States include the Daughters of the American Revolution, the American Legion, and the Veterans of Foreign Wars. WORLD BOOK has separate articles on these and many other patriotic organizations. See VETERANS' ORGANIZATIONS with its list of Related Articles.

Patriotism requires public service and responsibility of all citizens. Most persons agree that the patriotic citizen has a duty to keep informed on public issues, to take part in civic affairs, and to contribute to the welfare of his country to the best of his ability. President John F. Kennedy stressed public service in his inaugural address of 1961. He told Americans: "Ask not what your country can do for you—ask what you can do for your country."

Most persons agree that patriotism involves serving one's country, but many disagree on how they can best perform such service. Some say that the national government speaks for the country, and that citizens should therefore actively support all government policies and actions. Others argue that a true patriot will speak out if he is convinced that his country is following an unjust or unwise course of action.

Development of Patriotism. The word *patriotism* comes from the Greek word *patris*, which means *fatherland*. Throughout most of history, love of fatherland or homeland was a simple idea with no special political involvement. It was a love for the physical features of the land, including mountains, plains, and rivers.

The idea of patriotism became more complicated after new means of transportation and communication developed. In the 1800's, for example, the railroad and the steamship permitted large numbers of people to move long distances more quickly and easily than ever before. As a result, people were less likely to remain in the hometowns or countries of their forefathers throughout their lives. New means of communication, such as the telegraph, kept persons informed of happenings far away from their communities. The development of tanks, machine guns, and other weapons enabled nations to gain control over greater areas than ever before.

These developments raised some basic questions about patriotism and loyalty. Some men asked whether they were to love the land of their fathers, the land of their birth, or the country in which they were presently living. Others asked how patriotism could mean love of country when most persons had never seen most of the territory in it.

Some answers to these questions were provided by two political forces that were taking shape—*democracy* and *nationalism*. The democratic ideal was that people should have the right to govern themselves. One of the ideals of nationalism was that people with a common language, culture, and tradition should form one nation with their own independent government. Patriotism became entangled with these new forces. Along with love of one's own region, or country, patriotism came to mean supreme loyalty to the nation. Patriots were expected to willingly give their lives, if necessary, to defend the nation. See DEMOCRACY; NATIONALISM.

Abuses of Patriotism. "Patriotism," wrote the English critic Samuel Johnson, "is the last refuge of a scoundrel." He was pointing out that patriotism, like other emotional attitudes, sometimes becomes exaggerated or distorted. Persons with an excessive attachment for a certain group or country are sometimes called *superpatriots*. An unreasoning enthusiasm for the military superiority and glory of one's country is often called *chauvinism* or *jingoism* (see JINGO).

Exaggerated or distorted forms of patriotism have existed at different times in almost all nations. In the late 1800's, the French and English believed they had a moral responsibility to establish colonies in Asia and Africa, and thus bring the benefits of their culture to their "inferior brothers." In the 1900's, the Germans under Adolf Hitler and the Italians under Benito Mussolini became convinced their nations had a patriotic mission to extend their territorial boundaries.

Demands for open and public demonstration of loyalty are often heard in times of national crisis. During World War I, for example, the loyalty of Americans of German ancestry was questioned in the United States. During World War II, thousands of patriotic Japanese-Americans were placed in detention camps because of unreasonable fears that they might be loyal to Japan rather than to the United States. FRANK TACHAU

PATRIOTS' DAY

PATRIOTS' DAY commemorates the Battle of Lexington and Concord, fought on April 19, 1775. The battle between the British troops and American patriots began the Revolutionary War in America. Ralph Waldo Emerson's poem "Concord Hymn" contains these famous lines:

"Here once the embattled farmers stood
And fired the shot heard round the world."

Patriots' Day is a legal holiday in Maine and Massachusetts.　　　　　　　　　　　　RAYMOND HOYT JAHN

PATROCLUS. See ILIAD.

PATROL, SCHOOL SAFETY. See SAFETY (Instruction).

PATRONAGE in politics is the power to name appointees to government jobs. In the United States, the President and various state and local officials can appoint persons to certain positions. Appointments are usually suggested by individual legislators and the local and national political committees. Politicians often use patronage to reward those who worked for them in political campaigns. Such a use of patronage is called the *spoils system* (see SPOILS SYSTEM). Patronage also includes the awarding of favors or contracts to individuals or companies.　　　　　　　IRVING G. WILLIAMS

PATRONS OF HUSBANDRY. See GRANGE, NATIONAL.

PATROON SYSTEM, *puh TROON*, was a plan set up by the Dutch West India Company in 1629. It was used for the colonization of New Netherland, in what are now the states of New York, New Jersey, Delaware, and Connecticut. Any member of the company who brought over 50 families of settlers at his own expense could have an extensive tract of land. The *patroon* (owner of the land) became a kind of feudal lord.

The system did not succeed because Netherlanders would not leave their country to settle in America unless they were free. Five patroonships were granted, but only the Van Renssalaer grant prospered. In 1640, The Netherlands government encouraged immigration to New Netherland by offering Netherlanders some of the freedom that other colonists had.

But many early New York families were granted large estates by the Dutch and later by the English governments. In 1846, the state of New York passed laws to end the landed aristocracy.　　　MARSHALL SMELSER

See also ANTIRENTER; NEW YORK (Exploration).

PATTERNMAKER is a skilled craftsman who makes the patterns used to prepare molds for casting metal. Sand is tamped around the pattern. When the pattern is withdrawn, a mold is left in the sand into which molten metal is poured. See CAST AND CASTING.

PATTI, *PAT ee*, **ADELINA** (1843-1919), a coloratura soprano, won fame as one of the world's greatest operatic singers. Her career was almost without parallel in the history of the operatic stage.

After a tour of the West Indies with the pianist Louis Moreau Gottschalk, she made a sensational New York debut as Lucia in 1859. Her debuts in London in 1861 and in Paris in 1862 were no less brilliant. She sang in Covent Garden, London, each year for 23 years. Her repertoire included about 40 coloratura roles. She was born in Madrid, Spain, of an Italian father and a Spanish mother, both singers.　　　SCOTT GOLDTHWAITE

PATTON, GEORGE SMITH, JR. (1885-1945), was one of the most colorful American generals of World War II. His dramatic manner, outspoken comments on military and political affairs, and reckless behavior won him both applause and criticism. His toughness and rough speech earned him the nickname "Old Blood and Guts."

African Invasion. In November, 1942, Patton led the Western Task Force ashore in Morocco in the Allied invasion of North Africa. In March, 1943, he took command of the Second U.S. Army Corps and won one of the first major U.S. victories of the war at El Guettar. Before the Tunisian campaign ended, Patton took command of the Seventh Army for the invasion of Sicily in July, 1943. In 39 days, his army and the British Eighth Army captured the island. But an event soon after that nearly wrecked Patton's career. While inspecting army hospitals, he slapped two soldiers who were suffering from battle neurosis. One of the soldiers also had malaria. Patton explained that he thought the soldiers were only pretending. General Dwight D. Eisenhower forced Patton to apologize, and Congress temporarily held up his permanent promotion to major general.

United Press Int.

George S. Patton, Jr.

Victory in France. In January, 1944, Patton became commander of the Third Army for the French campaign. When the First Army broke through at Saint Lô, Patton's forces poured through the opening in the first of an amazing series of advances. They went so far ahead of their supplies that they had to be provisioned by plane. His forces crossed France, reaching Metz by autumn, and fought in the Battle of the Bulge near Bastogne, Belgium, in December, 1944.

As Germany collapsed, the Third Army drove across southwestern Germany into Czechoslovakia and Austria. When the Germans surrendered, Patton's army held a large part of what became the American occupation zone. Patton became a general. After May, 1945, he took command of the occupation troops in the American zone. But, in talking with newsmen, he compared the Nazis to the losers in an American political election. Eisenhower transferred him to the command of the Fifteenth Army, a headquarters set up to interview captured German generals and prepare materials for the official history of the war. In December, 1945, Patton died of injuries he received in an automobile accident. He was buried in a Third Army cemetery in Luxembourg.

Early Life. Patton was born on Nov. 11, 1885, in San Gabriel, Calif. He was graduated from the U.S. Military Academy in 1909. An excellent athlete, he placed fifth in the 1912 Olympic pentathlon. Patton entered the cavalry after graduation, and served in the 1916 Mexican expedition. In World War I, he commanded a tank brigade in France.　LADISLAS FARAGO

PATUXENT RIVER NAVAL AIR TEST CENTER is a U.S. Navy installation at Patuxent River, Md., where pilots test and evaluate aircraft and aircraft parts to determine if they meet requirements. The center covers

8,000 acres and is located 65 miles southeast of Washington, D.C. The center was commissioned in 1943.

JOHN A. OUDINE

PAUL was the name of six popes of the Roman Catholic Church. Their reigns were:

Paul I, Saint	(757-767)	Paul IV	(1555-1559)
Paul II	(1464-1471)	Paul V	(1605-1621)
Paul III	(1534-1549)	Paul VI	(1963-)

Paul III (1468-1549) began the important reform movement in the Roman Catholic Church that occurred during the 1500's. In 1545, he summoned the Council of Trent, which had been postponed several times because of wars between King Francis I of France and Emperor Charles V (see TRENT, COUNCIL OF). Paul also restored the Inquisition, excommunicated King Henry VIII of England, and made Michelangelo chief architect of the Vatican and of Saint Peter's Church.

Born in Italy, Paul became a master of humanistic studies (see HUMANISM). He was made a cardinal in 1493. He had led a scandalous life before becoming a priest, but afterward he devoted himself to reform.

Paul IV (1476-1559) had led an austere life before his election to the papacy in 1555. A cofounder of the Theatine order, he ruthlessly set about reforming other religious orders after he was chosen pope. He refused to reconvene the Council of Trent because he believed he could effect reforms himself. He reorganized the Inquisition, established a censorship of books, aided the poor, and demanded a stricter administration of justice. Paul was born near Benevento, Italy.

Paul V (1550-1621) was a trained lawyer who ruled the church justly and sternly. He put the Republic of Venice under the interdict when the republic refused to repeal some anticlerical ordinances, including exemption from trials by civil courts. Paul encouraged religious orders to do missionary work in Persia, and acted to correct abuses among missionaries in the Americas. He was born in Rome.

Paul VI Became Pope in 1963, Succeeding John XXIII.
Karsh, Ottawa

Paul VI (1897-   ) became pope in 1963, succeeding John XXIII. Paul continued the Second Vatican Council, which Pope John had begun (see VATICAN COUNCIL). Paul traveled more than any other pope. In 1964, he became the first pope to visit the Holy Land. He became the first pope to visit the United States when he spoke before the United Nations in New York City in 1965. In 1968, Paul wrote *Humanae Vitae*, an *encyclical* (letter to his bishops) reaffirming the Roman Catholic Church's stand against artificial birth control.

Paul was born on Sept. 26, 1897, in Concesio, near Brescia, Italy. His full name was GIOVANNI BATTISTA MONTINI. He was the second of three sons of a prominent newspaper editor and political leader.

Montini was ordained a priest in 1920 and entered the diplomatic service of the Vatican in 1922. He served in the *Nunciature* (papal delegation) to Warsaw, as a moderator for the Italian Federation of Catholic University Students, and in other posts.

Montini was appointed Vatican pro-secretary of state for ordinary affairs in 1952. He became archbishop of Milan in 1954 and a cardinal in 1958. See also POPE (picture).

THOMAS P. NEILL and FULTON J. SHEEN

PAUL I (1901-1964) was king of Greece from 1947 to 1964. He succeeded to the throne during a civil war with the Communists. With his wife, Queen Frederika, Paul tried to make the Greek monarchy a bulwark of democracy and a benefactor of all classes of Greek society. From 1917 to 1920, Paul lived in exile with his father, King Constantine. From 1923 to 1935 and from 1941 to 1946, he lived in exile again with his brother, King George II. Paul was born in Athens, and was trained as a naval officer. His son Constantine succeeded him. See also CONSTANTINE of Greece; GEORGE of Greece.

Royal Greek Embassy
Paul I

R. V. BURKS

PAUL, SAINT, was known as the *Apostle to the Gentiles*, though he was not one of the original 12 apostles. He was one of the greatest preachers and organizers of the early Christian Church, and had much to do with spreading the new religion.

Early Years and Conversion. Before his conversion, Paul was named *Saul*. His parents were wealthy Jews of Tarsus, a city in Cilicia. Paul was born a Roman citizen (Acts 22: 28). He was sent to Jerusalem to be educated by a great rabbi, Gamaliel. His training was according to the strict Jewish faith and traditions. All boys in his country were taught a trade, so Paul learned tentmaking. Later he supported himself by making tents while he preached in various towns.

Paul was associated with the members of the *Sanhedrin* (high council) at Jerusalem. They asked him to help in suppressing the Christians after Stephen, the first Christian martyr, had been stoned to death. Paul was still doing this work when he was converted to Christianity, on the road to Damascus. His whole life

Statue of Saint Paul was made by the Danish sculptor Bertel Thorvaldsen. It stands in a museum in Copenhagen.

was changed (Acts 9). He astonished the Jews by beginning to preach the gospel of Christ in their synagogues. He was so successful in making converts that he had to flee secretly from the city (II Cor. 11: 32-33).

First Christian Work. Paul went to Arabia and then returned to Tarsus, his native town. After several years he went with Barnabas to Antioch. There they worked for a year among the Gentiles who had started a Christian church in that city. They made many converts and helped to organize the church. It was the disciples in Antioch who were first called "Christians."

Missionary Journeys. About A.D. 47, Paul began his great work of bringing Christianity to the pagan world. The church at Antioch sent him with Barnabas on the first of three missionary journeys. They crossed to the island of Cyprus, the home of Barnabas, and went to Paphos, its western port. Then they sailed to Asia Minor. They worked their way north to Antioch of Pisidia, the chief city of the Roman province of Galatia. There Paul made the great speech reported in Acts 13: 16-41. He had been asked to do so by the rulers of the synagogues. But the important people of the city became angry, and Paul and Barnabas turned to the Gentiles, or non-Jews, for converts. After a short journey eastward, they returned over the same road to strengthen the churches they had founded.

Several of Paul's followers went with him on his second missionary journey. He visited Phrygia and Galatia, then went to Macedonia. On this trip he founded the church at Philippi, and thus brought Christianity to Europe. From Philippi, Paul went west to Thessalonica (now Salonika) and Beroea in Syria. Then he traveled south to Athens and Corinth, where he stayed 18 months. His famous speech to the philosophers of Athens is given in Acts 17. In Corinth he was arrested and put on trial before Gallio, the brother of Seneca, the Stoic philosopher. Gallio released him, and he returned to Antioch. He left behind him one of his most important churches.

In A.D. 52, Paul started on his third and last missionary journey. He passed through Phrygia and Galatia, and arrived at Ephesus, an important and wealthy city. He stayed there for three years and was very successful.

Later Years. Paul left Ephesus and returned to Jerusalem, in spite of the warnings of his friends. There, a mob threatened him. Lysias, the commander of the Roman garrison, saved him and carried him off as a prisoner. Later, Paul was sent to Felix, the governor, to be tried in Caesarea (Palestine). He was still in prison two years later, when Porcius Festus became governor. Festus wanted to please the people by sending him to Jerusalem for trial, but Paul demanded his right as a Roman citizen to be heard by Caesar. He defended himself in a speech before King Agrippa (Acts 26: 1-23). Then he was sent to Rome, where he was a prisoner for at least two more years. His friends worked for his release. It is believed that he was freed and resumed his missionary labors, but was rearrested and beheaded about A.D. 67. This was at the time when Emperor Nero was ordering one of the first great persecutions of the Christians.

Paul's Epistles. Paul's Epistles are letters that he wrote or was supposed to have written to his friends and to various churches. They form a large part of the New Testament. He was on his second missionary journey when he wrote First and Second Thessalonians. Galatians, First and Second Corinthians, and Romans were written while he was on his third journey. Colossians, Philemon, and Philippians were set down while he was in prison in Rome. He is supposed to have written Titus and First and Second Timothy after he was released. He may also have written Ephesians. Most of these letters speak of the truths of Christianity and the ways people should follow them.   FULTON J. SHEEN

Related Articles in WORLD BOOK include:

Colossians, Epistle to the
Corinthians, Epistles to the
Ephesians, Epistle to the
Galatians, Epistle to the
Philemon, Epistle to

Philippians, Epistle to the
Romans, Epistle to the
Thessalonians, Epistles to the
Timothy
Titus

PAUL, SAINT VINCENT DE. See SISTER OF CHARITY.

PAUL BUNYAN. See BUNYAN, PAUL.

PAUL OF THE CROSS, SAINT (1694-1775), founded the Passionist Order, or the Congregation of the Discalced Clerks of the Most Holy Cross and Passion of Our Lord Jesus Christ. Paul had a vision urging him to establish a new order, and in 1725 he received approval for the Passionists. The order grew rapidly and now works in every continent except Africa. The Passionists practice strict poverty. Paul was born in Ovada, Italy. He was canonized, or made a saint, in 1867 by Pope Pius IX.   MATTHEW A. FITZSIMONS and FULTON J. SHEEN

PAUL REVERE'S RIDE. See REVERE, PAUL; REVOLUTIONARY WAR IN AMERICA (Lexington and Concord).

PAULI, WOLFGANG (1900-1958), an Austrian theoretical physicist, won the 1945 Nobel prize in physics for his discovery of the *Pauli exclusion principle*. This principle states that no two electrons in an atom can occupy exactly the same position.

In 1913, the Danish physicist Niels Bohr published his theory which correctly predicted the behavior of the hydrogen atom (see BOHR, NIELS). The periodic table of chemical elements could then be pictured in terms of atomic structure (see ELEMENT, CHEMICAL). A problem with atoms with more than two electrons was how the electrons were arranged about the nucleus. Experiments showed that they could not all be the same distance from the nucleus. Pauli's principle provided a way of assigning positions to the electrons of each atom in the periodic table. Problems of atomic structure and behavior could not have been solved without Pauli's principle.

Brown Bros.

Wolfgang Pauli

Pauli's theory of the hydrogen molecule ion, written in 1921, is still a standard text on the subject. He also worked out the electron theory of metals, important today in designing transistors. He proposed the existence of the *neutrino*, now a known subatomic particle, to account for the mysterious disappearance of energy in atom-smashing experiments. See ATOM.

Pauli was born in Vienna, Austria. He served as a visiting professor at the Institute for Advanced Study at Princeton, N.J., from 1935 to 1954.   SIDNEY ROSEN

PAULING, LINUS CARL (1901-   ), an American chemist, won the 1954 Nobel prize in chemistry and the 1962 Nobel peace prize. He and Marie Curie are the only persons to win two Nobel awards.

Pauling won the chemistry prize for his work on the nature of matter, particularly protein matter. During the 1930's, he became interested in the arrangement of atoms in crystals, and in the forces that hold atoms together. He determined the size and shape of organic molecules. From exact measurements of atoms, he built accurate molecular models. These were essential to understand the arrangement of still larger molecules such as *hemoglobin*, a protein in red blood cells.

In 1958, Pauling presented a petition to ban atom bomb tests to the Secretary-General of the United Nations. He stated in part: "Each added amount of radiation causes damage to the health of human beings all over the world." The petition was signed by over 9,000 scientists from 44 countries. Pauling won the Nobel peace prize for trying to effect a ban on nuclear testing.

Pauling was born in Portland, Ore., on Feb. 28, 1901. He joined the faculty of the California Institute of Technology in 1922.   HERBERT S. RHINESMITH

PAULIST is a member of a Roman Catholic religious community of men. The order's official name is THE MISSIONARY SOCIETY OF SAINT PAUL THE APOSTLE. It was founded in New York City in 1858 by Father Isaac Thomas Hecker (1819-1888). The order was the first men's religious society to originate in the United States.

The Paulists preach missions, especially to non-Catholics. They also promote Catholic radio programs. Since 1865 they have published the *Catholic World* and religious pamphlets. They conduct Newman Apostolates in secular colleges, and they also maintain boys' choirs.   FULTON J. SHEEN

PAUNCEFOTE, *PAWNS foot,* **JULIAN** (1828-1902), BARON PAUNCEFOTE OF PRESTON, a British diplomat, helped establish the Permanent Court of Arbitration at The Hague. After experience in both colonial and foreign offices, Pauncefote served as minister to the United States in 1889 and became ambassador in 1893. Pauncefote negotiated the Hay-Pauncefote treaty regarding the Panama Canal (see HAY-PAUNCEFOTE TREATY). He was born in Munich.   JAMES L. GODFREY

PAUPERISM is a condition of permanent or chronic poverty. Legally, a pauper is a person who must depend on public or private charity for support.

PAVAN. See DANCING (The Renaissance).

PAVEMENT. See ROADS AND HIGHWAYS (Surfacing); STREET (pictures).

PAVIA, *pah VEE ah,* Italy (pop. 74,962; alt. 253 ft.), is the seat of a university founded in 1361. In the days of the ancient Romans, the city was known as Ticinum, and was a place of considerable importance. Pavia was plundered by Napoleon in 1796.

Modern Pavia is situated on the Ticino River, near the place where it meets the Po, 18 miles south of Milan (see ITALY [political map]). It still looks like a city of olden times. The Church of San Michele is the oldest of the many interesting churches.

In the cathedral Church of San Martino, there is a tomb that has the ashes of Saint Augustine. The Certosa di Pavia, a famous monastery, lies north of the city. Modern Pavia manufactures textiles, sewing machines, and farm machinery. It is known for its trade in wines, silk, oil, and cheese.   SHEPARD B. CLOUGH

PAVLOV, IVAN PETROVICH (1849-1936), a Russian physiologist, won the 1904 Nobel prize in physiology and medicine for his research on digestion and the nervous system. He showed how nerves control the flow of digestive juices of the stomach and pancreas.

For the next 30 years, Pavlov studied brain functions. He found that, by repeated association, an artificial stimulus (such as a bell) could be substituted for a natural stimulus (food) to cause a physiological reaction (salivation). He called this a *conditioned reflex*. Pavlov believed that all acquired habits, and even higher mental activity, depend on chains of conditioned reflexes (see REFLEX ACTION). Pavlov was born at Ryazan', Russia. He was educated in Russia and Germany.   MORDECAI L. GABRIEL

See also NOBEL PRIZES (picture: The Physiology Prize).

PAVLOVA, *pav LOH vah,* **ANNA** (1881-1931), a Russian ballerina, became the most famous dancer of her generation. Anna Pavlova was a small, delicate woman whose style was lovely and graceful. She was best known for "The Dying Swan," a three-minute solo that she performed in many parts of the world. It often moved audiences to tears.

Anna Pavlova was born in St. Petersburg (now Leningrad). She graduated from the Imperial Ballet School

Anna Pavlova, Russian Ballerina, performed with a lightness and grace that few ballet dancers have ever attained.

Bettmann Archive

in 1899 and joined the Imperial Ballet Company. In 1906, she became prima ballerina of the company. She left Russia permanently in 1913 and settled in London. During World War I she formed her own company and took it on world tours from that time until her death in The Hague in The Netherlands.   P. W. MANCHESTER

PAWNBROKER is a person who lends small sums of money on articles of clothing, watches, jewelry, and other personal belongings that are left with him as security. The articles left with him are *pawned*. The pawnbroker has the right to sell the article left with him, if the loan is not repaid with interest and charges within a certain time after the debt becomes due.

The pawnbroker usually limits his loan to the amount that he could get by selling the article. This sum is

The Historic Sign of the Pawnbrokers is the same as the three golden balls on the coat of arms of the Medici family.

Ewing Galloway

generally less than the article is worth to the borrower. For this reason, a pawnshop customer does not usually regard his transaction as a sale of his goods. In most cases he pays back the loan and redeems his property. The pawnbroker is sometimes called the poor man's banker. He makes it possible for a person to obtain credit quickly, even in a strange city, though often at high interest rates.

Pawnbroking dates back to the time when there were no banks. Many American cities had pawnshops as early as 1800. But the business was not generally recognized throughout the United States by law until late in the 1800's. Then laws were passed by states and cities to curb abuses, such as unfair charges. In most cases, a state law assures uniform practices by pawnbrokers.

In general, regulations require the pawnbroker to keep a record book. It contains a description of every article received. This book must be submitted upon request to the police or other officers who have authority to demand it, and who may be looking for stolen goods. The pawnbroker is not allowed to receive goods from anyone under the influence of liquor, or from anyone under a specified age.

Three golden balls, an old trade sign of the pawnbroker, usually hang outside the pawnshop. They originated with the moneylenders of Lombardy in Italy, who were important bankers in medieval England. The three golden balls were also the coat of arms of the Medici family. Members of this family were the richest merchants and moneylenders of Florence.   G. L. BACH

PAWNEE INDIANS, *paw NEE*, hunted buffalo on the plains of North America. They once roamed through what is now the state of Nebraska. When not hunting, they lived in villages of earth-covered houses, and raised corn, beans, and squash. They dressed in animal skins, and shaved their heads except for one scalp lock. They stiffened this lock with grease so it stood up like a horn.

The Pawnee had many elaborate tribal ceremonies. Some ceremonies were supposed to bring better crops. Other rituals and dances involved war. The Pawnee were one of the few North American Indian tribes that practiced human sacrifice. A famous chief, Petalesharo, stopped this custom in the 1800's (see INDIAN, AMERICAN [Ceremonies]).

The Pawnee were great fighters and raiders. They wandered as far south as New Mexico, where they terrified Spanish ranchers and the merchants who carried goods along the Santa Fe Trail. They sold white captives as slaves, and sometimes met the same fate themselves. The word *Pawnee* came to mean *slave* among the pioneers.

The Pawnee never fought against the United States. Many acted as scouts in the nation's wars with other Indians. The Pawnee made a series of treaties with the federal government between 1818 and 1876. The last treaty removed the remaining Pawnee Indians to a reservation in Oklahoma. Most of the tribe still lives on the reservation.   JOHN C. EWERS

PAWPAW is a small tree or shrub native to North America. The tree produces a fruit, also called *pawpaw*, that looks somewhat like a thick, short banana. The plant is found in the southern United States, and as far north as Kansas, Michigan, New Jersey, and western New York. Its leaves spread out in umbrellalike whorls, as do those of some species of the magnolia.

USDA

The Pawpaw Tree bears small greenish-brown fruit on slender branches. The yellow pulp of the fruit has a banana flavor.

However, when the leaves are bruised they give off a disagreeable odor.

The pawpaw grows to a height of from 10 to 40 feet, and bears fruit 2 to 6 inches long. The fruit has a greenish-brown skin. The yellow pulp is soft and sweet, but does not have enough taste to make it popular as a table fruit. The wood of the tree is too soft and coarse to be valuable. The thin fibrous bark may be used in making fish nets.

Another tree called *pawpaw, papaw,* or *papaya,* is grown in the tropics for its edible fruit. In Florida, it is cultivated for the local market. See PAPAYA.

Scientific Classification. The American pawpaw belongs to the custard apple family, *Annonaceae.* It is genus *Asimina*, species *A. triloba.* The tropical species belongs to the pawpaw family, *Caricaceae.*   J. J. LEVISON

PAWTUCKET, *paw TUCK et,* R.I. (pop. 77,538; alt. 90 ft.), is the third largest city in Rhode Island. Its name is an Indian word meaning *falls at the mouth of a river.* The city lies at the head of Narragansett Bay, about 5 miles northeast of Providence and about 40 miles southwest of Boston. Pawtucket spreads over nearly 6 square miles on either side of the Blackstone River. Pawtucket and Providence, R.I., form a metropolitan area that has a population of 821,101. For location, see RHODE ISLAND (political map).

Samuel Slater established the first cotton-spinning mill driven by water power in the United States at Pawtucket in 1793. Today Pawtucket has one of the largest cotton-thread plants in the nation. There are other factories for bleaching and dyeing cotton, and for weaving silk and rayon goods. Many machine shops in the city produce rolled steel, machine tools, pressed-metal products, nuts, bolts, hardware, and insulated wire. Other manufactured products include silk, lace, shirts, collars, hosiery, braid, jewelry, chemicals, cement, paper and wood products, sports equipment, and dentists' supplies.

The original village was founded in 1670 by Joseph Jenks, Jr., an ironworker. The part of the city which lies on the east bank of the river once belonged to Seekonk, Mass. It became Rhode Island territory in 1862. The section on the west bank was part of North Providence until 1874. The two villages became the town of Pawtucket. A city charter was granted in 1885. It has a mayor-council government. CLARKSON A. COLLINS III

PAX ROMANA. See ROMAN EMPIRE (History).

PAXTON, SIR JOSEPH. See ARCHITECTURE (The 1800's).

"PAXTON BOYS." See WESTWARD MOVEMENT (Regional Conflicts).

PAYEE is a person to whom money is to be paid or has been paid. See BILL OF EXCHANGE; CHECK.

PAYNE, DAVID L. See OKLAHOMA (The Great Land Rushes).

PAYNE, JOHN HOWARD (1791-1852), an American actor, playwright, and diplomat, wrote the lyrics for the song "Home, Sweet Home." He wrote the words as part of an opera he adapted from the play *Clari, or The Maid of Milan.* Sir Henry R. Bishop (1786-1855) composed the music. *Clari* was first produced at Covent Garden in London in 1823. Payne received very little money for the opera or the song.

Payne was born in New York City. He became an actor when he was 16. In 1820, he went to London. There, one of Payne's theatrical enterprises failed,

Chicago Historical Society
John Howard Payne

and he was put in prison for debt. He later wrote several other plays, but none except *Clari* had any success. From 1842 to 1845 and again from 1851 until his death, he served as United States consul at Tunis, Tunisia.

In 1883, Payne's body was brought to the United States and buried in Washington, D.C. During the ceremony, a choir of a thousand voices sang "Home, Sweet Home." The Eastman School of Music at Rochester, N.Y., owns the original manuscript of the song.   THEODORE M. FINNEY

See also HOME, SWEET HOME.

PAYNE-ALDRICH TARIFF. See TAFT, WILLIAM HOWARD (Legislative Defeats).

PAYSANDÚ, *PYE sahn DOO* (pop. 51,645; alt. 157 ft.), is the third largest city in Uruguay. This important railroad and meat-packing center lies on the east bank of the Uruguay River, about 300 miles northwest of Montevideo. For location, see URUGUAY (map). Steamships sail up the Uruguay River to Paysandú, and some of Uruguay's meat and wool exports go through this port. The city's chief products include meat, soap, and shoes.   JOHN TATE LANNING

PEA is any of several plants belonging to the *pea* or *pulse* family. This family also includes beans, alfalfa, clover, and many other plants. The small, round pea is one of the most nourishing of all vegetables. The seeds, which are the part we eat, grow in long green pods. There are several seeds in each pod. The pods grow on vines with beautiful white flowers. Some kinds of peas

J. Horace McFarland

Pods of Peas need not be opened to determine if the peas are ripe. A gardener can tell by feeling the pods. When fully ripe, the pods shrivel, and the seeds become small, wrinkled, and dry.

have flowers so lovely and fragrant that they are grown as ornamental garden flowers. These include the sweet pea, the chick pea, and the everlasting pea.

All peas are believed to be descended from wild plants that come from southern Europe and southwestern Asia. They were known and used by the Chinese in 2000 B.C., and the Bible mentions peas. But in England, during the late 1600's, green peas seem to have been considered a very low form of food. As one writer of the time remarked, "It is a frightful thing to see persons so sensual as to purchase and eat green peas." Peas were brought to America about 1800.

The pea grows rapidly. It is a hardy, cool-season crop, but cannot stand much summer heat. The oblong green

LEADING PEA GROWING STATES AND PROVINCES

Tons of shelled commercial green peas grown in 1967

Wisconsin
155,600 tons

Washington
146,000 tons

Minnesota
78,620 tons

Oregon
51,700 tons

Ontario
32,710 tons

Sources: U.S. Department of Agriculture; Dominion Bureau of Statistics

pods have from three to nine seeds. The seeds may be eaten about 65 to 70 days after planting.

The vines of low-growing bush peas grow from 12 to 36 inches long. Climbing pea vines are from 60 to 65 inches long. Some varieties have smooth seeds, but the seeds of others are wrinkled. Most home garden and cannery peas are the bushy form, and most dry peas are the climbing type.

Peas may be planted as soon as the ground can be worked in spring, usually about three weeks before the last frost. In home gardens, the seeds are sown in rows from 18 to 24 inches apart. Peas should be harvested just as the seeds reach full size, or just before. After reaching full size, they lose their flavor. Dry peas are ripened on the vines, then harvested.

Peas have almost as much protein and energy value as meat. They are an excellent source of vitamins A and C. Dry peas have 1,655 calories per pound, and green peas have 465 calories. Pea vines and pods are by-products of the canning industry. They are made into a valuable food for dairy cows and sheep.

Scientific Classification. Peas belong to the pea family, *Leguminosae*. Garden, or canning, peas are genus *Pisum*, species *P. sativum*. Dry peas are *P. sativum*, variety *arvense*.   ARTHUR J. PRATT

See also COWPEA; LEGUME; PARTRIDGE PEA.

PEA RIDGE NATIONAL MILITARY PARK. See NATIONAL PARK (National Military Parks).

PEABODY, GEORGE (1795-1869), a merchant and financier, became one of the foremost philanthropists of his time. His gifts for southern education, construction of model low-cost housing, and support of scientific and cultural institutions set a pattern for later philanthropists. After making a fortune in the dry-goods business in Baltimore, Peabody opened a successful investment banking house in London. After his death, this company was reorganized and became J. P. Morgan and Company. Peabody was born in South Danvers (now Peabody), Mass.   ROBERT H. BREMNER

PEABODY COLLEGE. See GEORGE PEABODY COLLEGE FOR TEACHERS.

PEABODY CONSERVATORY OF MUSIC. See PEABODY INSTITUTE OF THE CITY OF BALTIMORE.

PEABODY EDUCATION FUND was a trust created in 1867 by George Peabody, an American merchant and banker. Peabody made four gifts to the fund, totaling $3,484,000. He wanted to counteract Civil War destruction by encouraging education in the Southern and Southwestern States.

In 1875, the fund's trustees set up a college, which later became the George Peabody College for Teachers. The remainder of the fund was combined with the John F. Slater Fund in 1914. In 1937, these funds became part of the Southern Education Foundation.   J. C. DIXON

See also GEORGE PEABODY COLLEGE FOR TEACHERS; SOUTHERN EDUCATION FOUNDATION.

PEABODY INSTITUTE OF THE CITY OF BALTIMORE consists of the Peabody Conservatory of Music and a music library. The conservatory is a coeducational, private school that grants bachelor's, master's, and doctor's degrees in music. It also operates a *preparatory school* (private grade school and high school) that offers music courses. The institute was founded by George Peabody in 1857. For the conservatory's enrollment, see UNIVERSITIES AND COLLEGES (table).   DEAN BOAL

PEACE is freedom from disturbance, a state of being calm and quiet. When we say that a person is at peace, we mean that his mind is at ease. Sometimes we call this *peace of mind*. When we say that a nation is at peace, we mean that it is free from war or revolution.

Today most discussions of peace concern political and military peace, or the absence of war. For thousands of years, periods of war have alternated with periods of peace. Through the years, human beings have probably spent at least as much time at war as at peace. Some nations, however, have known long periods of unbroken peace. Switzerland has not gone to war with any neighbor for about 150 years. Other countries, although they have engaged in foreign wars, have enjoyed domestic peace for a long time. They have not fought civil wars or been invaded. The United States, for example, has known domestic peace since 1865.

In some periods of history, war has seemed the normal state of affairs. Near the end of the Middle Ages, France and England, for instance, engaged in the Hundred Years' War (1337-1453). Most of Europe was involved in the Thirty Years' War during the 1600's. For the whole civilized world to be at peace for a considerable time is rare in history. Probably the best example of this is the *Pax Romana*, or Roman Peace. See WAR with its list of Related Articles.

Views on Peace and War

Although most philosophers have advocated peace, there have also been defenders of war in both the ancient and modern world. The advocates of peace argue that mankind naturally longs for security and tranquillity, and that civilization flourishes in peacetime. The defenders of war, or at least those advocating preparation for war, argue that in times of peace people tend to become decadent. They say that war develops strong characters and manliness. A warlike state of mind prevailed among some of the most powerful peoples in the history of civilization, including the Persians, the Spartans, and the Romans. Among later writers, Friedrich Nietzsche, the German philosopher, was the chief defender of the virtues of war. The German idealist Georg W. F. Hegel said that war is a positive necessity for the moral development of any country, while peace makes it decay.

The Stoic philosophers taught that all men are brothers. Similar ideas had appeared earlier among the Buddhists. According to these doctrines, peace ought to be observed among communities and nations, just as within families, because all people are spiritual brothers and sisters, as children of God. The Judeo-Christian concept of peace is based on the commandment "Thou shalt not kill." Since the beginning of Christianity, peace has been the ideal of most writers and leaders, even though more often in theory than in reality. The principle of "peace on earth, good will toward men" has spread throughout most parts of the world since the time of Jesus Christ.

Maintaining Peace

Until recent times, schemes for securing general peace were closely linked to religious beliefs, because people felt that those with a common religious faith ought not to fight one another. The earliest well-known attempt of this type was the Amphictyonic League of the Greeks,

which seems to have originated in very ancient times. It met at the sacred Greek town of Delphi, and was connected with the cult of the god Apollo. This league forbade its members to engage in atrocities against one another. For instance, they might not destroy any city sharing in their worship, or cut off its supply of water. The league ceased to function after Greece came under the domination of Macedonia.

The Pax Romana maintained peace under Roman domination for about 200 years, from 27 B.C. to A.D. 180. Under the Roman emperors, the central authority at Rome kept down disturbances within the empire by an elaborate system of courts and military garrisons, and protected the civilized world by frontier defenses. From the time of Trajan to that of Marcus Aurelius, the known world was wholly at peace, except on some frontiers. Roman rulers were strongly influenced by Stoic teachings on peace, justice, and brotherhood. But, when the Roman Empire declined, Europe fell into anarchy and almost incessant war for several hundred years. See ROMAN EMPIRE (The Pax Romana).

The Christian Church became the chief influence for keeping the peace as medieval Europe emerged from the confusion of the Dark Ages. The clergy constantly preached peace to the warlike nobles and common people of the Middle Ages, with varying success. In theory, the Holy Roman Emperors, whose power centered in the German states or in Italy, wielded the temporal authority for maintaining peace, and the papacy held the spiritual authority. But the Holy Roman Emperors never exercised the power of the ancient Roman emperors, and much of Europe lay outside their jurisdiction.

The Church did succeed in softening the military tendencies of Europe. One means was the "Truce of God," proclaimed by the clergy, which prohibited warfare on Sundays and holy days. At the same time, the Church did not forbid war in defense of the Christian religion or of one's own country or rights. The popes preached the Crusades to the Holy Land as a means of defending the Christian faith against the Moslems.

Early in the 1300's, the Italian poet Dante pleaded for a general peace, to be maintained by the just authority of the emperors. Instead, Europe sank rapidly into fierce international and civil struggles.

As medieval civilization gave way to the Renaissance, and as the vast power of the medieval church broke up during the Reformation and Counter-Reformation, new means had to be found for seeking peace. In the early 1600's, King Henry IV of France and his minister the Duc de Sully developed a "Grand Design" for European peace. It consisted of an international European council, supported by troops of member states, which would enforce peace. But it never took effect, and, instead, most of Europe engaged in fierce religious wars.

But the Grand Design made a deep impression on European thinkers. It gave rise to other plans, including one of the Abbé de Saint-Pierre, published in 1713 under the title *Project for Perpetual Peace*. Voltaire criticized this project because most of the states it proposed to unify were absolute monarchies. Voltaire believed that there could be no universal peace until all states had become democratic.

PEACE, BREACH OF THE

International Law. As pope and emperor ceased to have general authority, philosophers and statesmen developed a new doctrine of peace. It was not directly connected with religious beliefs, although still influenced by Christian ideas. This doctrine was best expressed in Hugo Grotius' book *On the Law of War and Peace* (1625), a basis for the idea of international law.

The Balance of Power. The Peace of Westphalia (1648), ending the Thirty Years' War, tried to provide for peace through a "balance of power." The statesmen who wrote the treaty believed that injustice among nations led to war. They tried to prevent a new outbreak of hostilities by arranging a just peace, followed by the creation of a balance of great nations. Under this system, the majority of states would join together to resist any power that attacked another member.

International Movements for peace began in the late 1800's. Many liberal political leaders believed that war was obsolete and that it would soon be outlawed by international agreement. Statesmen arranged the Hague Conferences, in 1899 and 1907, to promote peace through the limitation of armaments. The conferences did not succeed, but they did set up The Hague Tribunal, an international court. The world's hopes for peace were shattered by World War I, which President Woodrow Wilson proclaimed to be "a war to end war."

The League of Nations, established at the end of the war, set out to guide the nations of the world toward lasting peace. But the League began to falter in the 1930's, and was destroyed by World War II.

Atomic weapons, first used during World War II, made war more destructive than ever before. The liberal optimism of the 1800's and early 1900's has given way to a search for new means of preventing or restricting war. Statesmen created a new international organization, the United Nations, after World War II. It has had some success, but did not prevent hostilities in Asia and the Middle East. The Cold War between two groups of nations—Russia and its satellites and the Western democracies—has menaced the uneasy peace (see COLD WAR). Western leaders believe peace is vital, but that it must be peace with freedom.

Related Articles in WORLD BOOK include:

Arbitration	International Law
Atoms for Peace Award	International Relations
Balance of Power	Kellogg Peace Pact
Carnegie Endowment for	League of Nations
International Peace	Nobel Prizes
Collective Security	Pacifism
Disarmament	Paris Conferences
Hague, The	United Nations

PEACE, BREACH OF THE. See BREACH OF THE PEACE.

PEACE BRIDGE is a symbol of the years of friendship between the peoples of the United States and Canada. It extends across the Niagara River from Fort Potter, in Buffalo, N.Y., to Fort Erie, Ontario. Five granite-covered concrete piers support the 3,575-foot-long steel bridge. A company with 9 Canadian and 16 American directors owns the bridge. It was formally opened on Aug. 7, 1927.   ALVIN F. HARLOW

See also BUFFALO, N.Y. (picture).

PEACE CONFERENCES. See INTERNATIONAL RELATIONS; PEACE.

PEACE CORPS is an organization of men and women working to raise the levels of living in various parts of the world. The corps, set up in 1961 as an agency of the United States government, accepts volunteers to work for two years in other countries. The corpsmen provide skilled manpower for nations in Asia, Africa, and Latin America. For example, they help farmers with their crops in Chile, teach school in the Philippines, and work as nurses in Tunisia. The Peace Corps establishes projects at the request of the governments of other countries. The nations that receive corpsmen are called *host countries*.

Choosing the Volunteers. Any American citizen 18 years old or older may qualify for service. The corps has no upper age limit. Nor does it require that most applicants have any college training, except for its teaching projects. A man of draft age may be deferred from military service if the corps accepts him, but he may still be liable for military training at a later date. Married couples may volunteer if they have no children under age 18 and if both husband and wife have skills the corps can use in the same country.

All applicants must fill out a detailed form, called a *Peace Corps Questionnaire*. The questionnaire asks the applicant to list his educational and work background, special interests, skills, and hobbies. Questionnaires may be obtained by writing to the Peace Corps, Washington, D.C. 20525. Applicants must also. take a noncompetitive *placement test* which is given in cities and towns throughout the United States. The test measures general aptitude and ability to learn languages. Corps headquarters then picks volunteers to train for specific projects. It bases its choice of trainees on information given in the questionnaire, placement test scores, and references from friends and employers.

Volunteers picked for a project spend 8 to 12 weeks training together at a college or university in the United States. For 10 or 12 hours a day, six days a week, the trainees study the language, history, and culture of the country in which they will serve. They also study United States history and the traditions of American democracy. They receive technical training, physical training, and instruction in health practices for the specific country where they will work. The Peace Corps has permanent training centers in Puerto Rico and Hawaii for advanced field instruction. When the training program is over, a selection board meets to evaluate each individual and to advise Peace Corps headquarters on the suitability of each trainee. The Peace Corps itself makes the final selections. Those Peace Corps members finally chosen for overseas service sometimes receive further training in the host country before they begin work.

How the Volunteers Live. Peace Corps members serve wherever they are needed in their host countries. They live and work side by side with citizens of the host countries. They operate within local institutions, rather than setting up new agencies under American auspices. The most important part of a volunteer's work is not in performing the job itself, but rather in helping to train host country citizens to fill the job. For example, a Peace Corps teacher works with teachers as well as students. A Peace Corps laborer teaches the building trades as he works.

PEACE CORPS

Greeting New Corpsmen, ▶
Sargent Shriver, first director
of the Peace Corps, discusses
the aims of the group going to
Colombia. The trainees studied
at Rutgers University.

United Press Int.

United Press Int.

Scherman, Peace Corps

◀ **Taking the Examination**
is the first step for all applicants. The tough tests, on many
subjects, last two hours.

Learning the Language ▶
and customs of their host
country, Peace Corps trainees
at the University of California
at Berkeley study Twi, a language spoken in Ghana.

Helping Farmers on Cyprus, a young Californian
supervises three women who are planting corn on a
government-operated experimental farm. This volunteer was a farmer before joining the Peace Corps.

Paul Conklin, Pix from Publix

Paul Conklin, Pix from Publix

Teaching Nepalese Children to Read,
a former English teacher from Michigan introduces the alphabet to many youngsters who
normally would never receive any education.

Peace Corps members receive small allowances for living costs and incidental expenses. After corpsmen return to the United States, they receive a lump-sum readjustment allowance of $75 a month for the length of their Peace Corps service.

Organization. The Peace Corps is a semi-independent agency within the Department of State. The President appoints the director, with the approval of the Senate. The director has the status of an assistant secretary of state, and reports directly to the secretary.

Corps headquarters sets policies and standards for all corpsmen. It works with the governments of other countries in deciding what projects to undertake. It works with colleges and universities in the United States in planning how corps members should be trained. And, in planning its operations, it sometimes works with private groups that have had long experience overseas. It may also help in the work of other U.S. government agencies and the United Nations. In every case, the host country must invite the corps to work.

The Vice-President of the United States is chairman of a national advisory council for the Peace Corps. The council, composed of outstanding leaders in national and world affairs, provides guidance for the corps.

History. The idea of an army to work for peace was more than 50 years old when President John F. Kennedy set up the Peace Corps in 1961. In a speech in Boston in 1904, the American philosopher William James suggested forming a youth peace army to tackle important but dangerous civilian projects.

In the years after World War II, many private groups set up international work camps. Others sent young Americans to share their skills with students, farmers, and workers in other lands. They followed the example set by the American Friends Service Committee, a Quaker organization. It started its first international projects as early as 1917.

In January, 1960, Congressman Henry S. Reuss of Wisconsin and Senator Richard Neuberger of Oregon asked Congress to study the possibilities for a youth corps program. Later that year, Senator Hubert Humphrey of Minnesota asked Congress to create a peace corps. Kennedy then used the peace corps proposal as one of the campaign issues in the 1960 presidential election. He pointed out that "There is not enough money in all America to relieve the misery of the underdeveloped world in a giant and endless soup kitchen. But there are enough know-how and knowledgeable people to help those nations help themselves."

On March 1, 1961, soon after his inauguration, Kennedy set up the Peace Corps. Later that year, Congress made it permanent. The first volunteers trained at Rutgers University, New Brunswick, N.J., in 1961. They helped develop communities and improve farming in Colombia. Sargent Shriver, the first director of the Peace Corps, served until January, 1966. He was succeeded by Jack H. Vaughn. Joseph H. Blatchford became director in 1969.

By the late 1960's, Peace Corps volunteers were serving in about 60 countries. Many had completed their two-year period of service. Congress had approved funds allowing the corps to increase its membership to 14,000. The United States also supported the efforts of other nations to set up similar organizations to work for world peace through world development.

Other Service Programs similar to the Peace Corps have been set up by Argentina, Australia, Belgium, Canada, Denmark, France, Great Britain, Italy, Japan, Liechtenstein, The Netherlands, New Zealand, Norway, Switzerland, and West Germany. These corps vary in name, size, length of service, and other ways. But all of them, like the Peace Corps, enlist volunteers from among their own citizens to serve in other lands.

Several less developed nations have also announced plans for national volunteer corps to work within their own countries. In some of these nations, national corpsmen work in cooperation with United States Peace Corps volunteers.   SARGENT SHRIVER

See also SHRIVER, SARGENT; LATIN AMERICA (Relations with the United States).

PEACE DEMOCRAT. See COPPERHEAD.

PEACE DOLLAR. See DOLLAR (picture: The "Peace Dollar").

PEACE GARDEN, INTERNATIONAL. See FLOWER (Famous Flower Gardens).

PEACE OF_____. See key word for special peace agreements. Example: UTRECHT, PEACE OF.

PEACE PALACE. See HAGUE, THE.

PEACE PIPE, or CALUMET, *KAL yoo met*, was a ceremonial tobacco pipe which North American Indians smoked as a sign of peace and friendship. They passed it from one person to another. Among the Indians of the Great Lakes, Mississippi Valley, and Great Plains, this pipe had a stone bowl and a long wooden stem elaborately decorated with feathers. Early French explorers called the pipe and the dance held in its honor the *calumet*, from their word for the reed.

Most Indian pipes were not peace pipes. Men of many tribes smoked solely for pleasure. Other pipes were used only in religious ceremonies.   JOHN C. EWERS

See also INDIAN, AMERICAN (color picture: Hunters of the Plains).

PEACE RIVER, in western Canada, is the largest branch of the Mackenzie River. It is 1,050 miles long, including the length of its main branch, the Finlay. For location, see CANADA (physical map). It drains the Peace River district, a fertile farming area in northwestern Alberta and eastern British Columbia.

The Peace River is formed where the Finlay and Parsnip rivers join in central British Columbia. It cuts through the Rocky Mountains and flows in a general easterly direction for 300 miles, dropping about two and a half feet in each mile. At the town of Peace River in Alberta, where the Smoky River joins it, the river turns and flows north through steep sandstone cliffs. The river bed then widens and becomes more shallow until the stream enters the Slave River 815 miles from its source at Finlay Forks.

The railway built from Edmonton, Alta., after World War I opened up the Peace River district. Grande Prairie, Alta., is now the center of this area, which produces some of the world's finest hard northern wheat.

Vast pools of oil and natural gas lie beneath the Peace River district. Pipelines transport these minerals to Edmonton, Alta., and on to Vancouver, B.C. Natural gas refined at Taylor Flats is sent through a 650-mile pipeline to southern British Columbia and the United States.   J. BRIAN BIRD

PEACH is a roundish, yellow, edible fruit. It has a hard, deeply pitted stone. Its flesh may be soft or quite firm. The peach is second only to the apple in distribution throughout the world. Peach trees grow in most temperate regions. Scientists believe that China is the native home of peach trees. They believe the trees grew there at least 4,000 years ago. No one knows when the peach tree was brought to Europe. But it was brought to the United States by the colonists who settled Virginia. They planted peach trees there before 1629. More peaches are grown in the United States than in all other countries combined. Many are planted in commercial orchards and some are cultivated in gardens as ornamentals.

The peach tree grows 15 to 25 feet high. Its long, slender leaves have toothed edges. Flowers appear before the leaves do. The delicate pink blossoms may be large and showy, but sometimes are quite small. They appear early in the spring and therefore can be injured by late frosts. Most commercial peach orchards are located in regions where there are few late frosts. Clear, hot weather during the growing season is best for peaches. They are grown southward from the Great Lakes region of the Middle West into the deep South, and along the Atlantic and Pacific coasts.

Growing Peach Trees. Peach trees are grown from seed. Growers plant the pits, or seeds, late in the summer. Germination takes place the following spring. Late in summer, the young seedlings serve as rootstocks for buds of desired varieties of peaches. Buds and roots lie dormant until the next spring, when the buds are forced into growth. The age of a peach tree is determined by the age of the bud even though the rootstock is one year older.

Cultivation. Growers plant standard-sized trees about 18 to 25 feet apart in the orchard. But those trees grown on dwarfing rootstocks are planted 12 to 15 feet apart. The best soil is one of medium texture, such as a sandy loam. It must be well drained. A peach orchard begins to bear large crops about 3 or 4 years after it is planted. If the trees are healthy, they live about 20 years. But they reach the peak of their production when they are 8 to 12 years old. A single tree may produce from 4 to 10 bushels of peaches.

Peach trees must be watered regularly. The amount

These Georgia Peaches would be perfect for that time-honored and delicious American dish, peaches and cream.

J. Horace McFarland

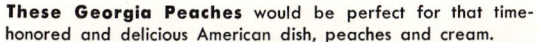

H. Armstrong Roberts

Baskets of Golden Ripe Peaches appear in stores from midsummer to fall. Peaches bruise easily and must be handled carefully.

of water required varies with climate, texture and depth of soil, and depth of the root system. Enough water must be used to wet the entire root system. Cultivation of the orchard is necessary to destroy weeds, which compete with the tree roots for water and food in the soil. Chemical sprays are often used to control weeds.

Peach trees need various chemical elements for normal growth. Most of these occur in sufficient quantity in the soil. But usually nitrogen must be added. Special fertilizers are used to supply this element.

Pruning is essential for good fruit production. Peach trees are pruned more heavily than most other fruit trees. Growers keep their trees pruned low to make spraying and picking easier. Because the fruit is produced on shoots of the previous season's growth, about $\frac{1}{3}$ of the last year's growth is kept. All the rest is cut off. The trees produce so many peaches that the fruit must be thinned. Growers remove some of the peaches early in the season. This increases the size and improves the quality of the fruit that remains. Tree-ripened peaches have the best flavor. They are harvested when ripe but still firm.

Varieties. There are many varieties of peaches. They ripen from early summer to fall—some as late as October. Peaches are called *freestone* or *clingstone*, according to how difficult it is to remove the pit from the fruit. The fruit of freestone peaches is usually softer than that of clingstones. But some varieties of clingstones are very mellow, with fine aroma and excellent texture.

Perhaps the best-known peach variety is Elberta, a freestone. It originated in 1870 in Marshallville, Ga. Other well-known freestone varieties are J. H. Hale, Redhaven, Hiley, Halehaven, July Elberta, and Golden Jubilee. Important clingstone varieties include Fortuna, Paloro, Johnson, Gaume, and Sims. Nectarines are similar to peaches. The two fruits are essentially

LEADING PEACH GROWING STATES

Bushels (48 pounds) of peaches grown each year

California
40,409,000 bu. 🍑🍑🍑🍑🍑🍑🍑🍑🍑🍑🍑🍑🍑

South Carolina
4,664,000 bu. 🍑🍑

Georgia
2,904,000 bu. 🍑

Michigan
1,944,000 bu. 🍑

New Jersey
1,883,000 bu. 🍑

Based on a 4-year average, 1964-1967

Source: U.S. Department of Agriculture

alike except for the skins, and the trees are identical (see NECTARINE).

Uses. Fresh peaches are a delicacy. But many fruits are canned, principally those of the clingstone varieties. Some are frozen for commercial use, and a few are dried. Pastries and preserves can be made from peaches. Distillers sometimes make brandy from them.

Diseases. A number of diseases attack the peach. *Brown rot*, a fungus, causes serious damage. It rots the fruit and prevents the flowers from opening. *Peach leaf curl* is very troublesome. To prevent it, growers spray the tree early in spring before the leaves emerge. Other fungi cause *mildew*, *rust*, and *blight*. To control these, growers use sprays of lime sulfur, Bordeaux mixture, and sulfur dusts.

Peach trees are susceptible to many virus diseases. Among the serious ones are *peach yellows*, *X-disease*, *Western X-disease*, *ring spot*, and *peach mosaic*. Trees infected with these diseases must be uprooted.

Insects. Several insects damage peach trees. The *peach twig borer*, the larva of a moth, may bore into the fruit. But usually it bores into the trunk and branches, sometimes killing the tree. The Oriental fruit moth larva destroys twigs and fruit. Many other moth larvae and beetles prey on the foliage, as do several kinds of caterpillars. Sprays made of miscible oil, lime sulfur, lead arsenate, malathion, parathion, and DDT are used to control insects. Chemicals for disease and insect sprays may be combined.

Production. Peaches are grown throughout the United States, but in some states only in home gardens. They are grown commercially in about 35 states. California leads all states in peach production. It produces about two-thirds of the peaches grown in the United States. South Carolina, Georgia, Michigan, and New Jersey are other leading peach-growing states. The rate of production varies little in California. But weather conditions affect production greatly in states east of the Rocky Mountains. Clingstone varieties make up about three-fourths of California's peach crop.

Scientific Classification. The peach tree belongs to the rose family, *Rosaceae*. It is classified as genus *Prunus*, species *P. persica*.   REID M. BROOKS

See also PLANT (color picture: Some Members of the Rose Family); TREE (color picture: Ornamental Trees).

PEACH MOTH, or ORIENTAL FRUIT MOTH, is a small, mottled brown moth. It is one of the most serious pests of peaches. The peach moth winters as a larva in a cocoon under loose bark or trash. The adults emerge when peaches are blooming. They lay their eggs on leaves, and the eggs hatch into larvae. From 4 to 7 generations of larvae appear every year. The first generation eats tender twigs. The later generations feed upon the fruit.

The peach moth also attacks apples, pears, quinces, cherries, and plums. Parasitic wasps and flies, including some imported from abroad, provide aid in controlling the moth. However, the best control is 2 pounds of DDT powder for every 100 gallons of spray, applied 2 or 3 times after the petals fall.

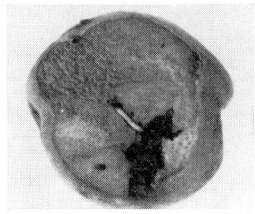

USDA

Peach Moth Larvae burrow into the fruit and spoil it.

Scientific Classification. The peach moth belongs to the olethreutid moth family, *Olethreutidae*. It is classified as genus *Grapholitha*, species *G. molesta*.   ALEXANDER B. KLOTS

See also CODLING MOTH.

PEACH STATE. See GEORGIA.

PEACOCK is one of the showiest of all birds because of its great size and the beauty of its train. Its name is really *peafowl*. The male bird is called a peacock. It is about as large as a turkey. It has a metallic greenish-blue neck and breast, purplish-blue underparts, and a long train of greenish feathers brilliantly marked with bold spots that look like eyes. These feathers, which grow from the back (*not* the tail), are spread into a gorgeous fan as the male bird parades slowly and majestically in front of the female. No one, except perhaps the peacock, knows if it is really proud of its great beauty, but the expression "proud as a peacock" usually means extremely proud. The female bird, called a *peahen*, is smaller, less vividly colored, and has no train.

The description above refers to the best-known species, the Indian peafowl. It is the national bird of India. These peacocks live wild in India and Ceylon, and can be seen in city parks and on country estates. The dark green, broken coloration may have protective value in the midst of colorful tropical foliage. These birds eat snails, frogs, and insects, as well as grain, juicy grasses, and bulbs. They often destroy crops. Varieties with white plumage are sometimes found in captivity. The green peafowl, found in Burma, Malaysia, and Java, has a golden-green neck and breast.

Tame peacocks may be found in all parts of the world. The young cannot stand the changeable weather of temperate climates very well, and are hard to raise. The hen makes its nest in a protected spot on the ground. It lays 10 or more brownish eggs.

In ancient times, the peacock was carried to all parts of the world as a great treasure. During the reign of Solomon, "once in three years came the navy of Tharshish, bringing gold and silver, ivory, and apes, and peacocks" (I Kings 10:22). The peacock is mentioned in *The Birds*, a play by Aristophanes, written in Greece during the 400's B.C. Pliny speaks of it as common in his day in Rome, where the peacock was considered a great delicacy as a roast, served in its own feathers.

The Handsome Peacock spreads its feathers into a gorgeous fan when it courts the female bird, or *peahen*. The feathers in a peacock's colorful tail are almost five times as long as its body.

Anita Este, National Audubon Society

Scientific Classification. Peacocks belong to the partridge, pheasant, and quail family, *Phasianidae*. The Indian peafowl is genus *Pavo*, species *P. cristatus*. The green peafowl is *P. muticus*. JOSEPH J. HICKEY

See also ARGUS; BIRD (Bird Courtship; color picture: Birds of Other Lands); POULTRY (Kinds).

PEACOCK THRONE. See IRAN (History).

PEALE was a family of famous American artists. At least 20 members of the family, covering three generations, were artists. CHARLES WILLSON PEALE (1741-1827), the kind and enthusiastic family patriarch, be-

Charles Willson Peale painted this picture of his family after he returned from London, where he studied under Benjamin West.
New York Historical Society

lieved anyone could learn to paint. He taught many of his 17 children and also his brother JAMES PEALE (1749-1831). James in turn taught his own six children. James painted portraits, figure compositions, landscapes, and still lifes. They were done with the directness and charm that mark the best work of the family.

RAPHAELLE PEALE (1774-1825) and REMBRANDT PEALE (1778-1860) are the best known of Charles Willson Peale's artist sons. Raphaelle is noted for his still lifes and miniatures. Rembrandt painted hundreds of portraits. SARAH MIRIAM PEALE (1800-1885), a daughter of James, was probably the first professional woman portrait painter in America.

Charles Willson Peale gave up painting in middle age to devote full time to his natural history museum in Philadelphia. His finest painting, *The Staircase Group* (1795), contains life-size portraits of his sons Titian and Raphaelle. See also WASHINGTON, GEORGE (color picture: Colonel of the Militia). EDWARD H. DWIGHT

PEALE, NORMAN VINCENT (1898-), an American clergyman, won fame for his writings and his radio and television programs. His combined weekly audience is estimated to be several million persons. Believing that one of the main tasks of religion is to help people, Peale wrote several books on the topic. They include *The Power of Positive Thinking* (1952) and *The Tough-Minded Optimist* (1961). He edits a magazine, *Guideposts*, and a newspaper column "Confident Living."

Peale was born in Bowersville, Ohio. He became a minister of the Methodist Episcopal Church in 1922. In 1932, he became pastor of the Marble Collegiate Reformed Church in New York City. L. J. TRINTERUD

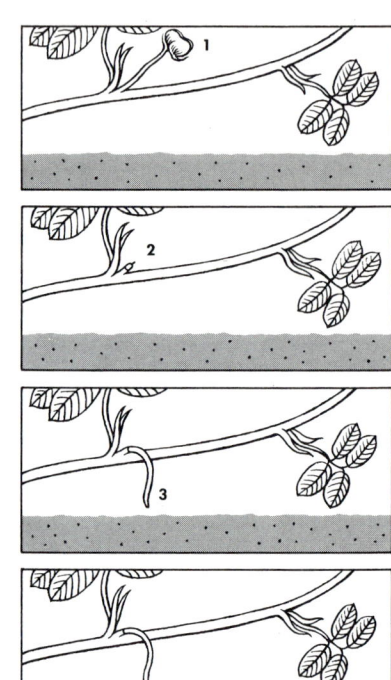

WORLD BOOK illustrations by James Teason

Peanuts Grow Underground. Flowers open at dawn (1), wither, and finally fall off (2). The base of each fertilized flower then begins to grow (3), forming a *peg* (stalklike stem). The peg pushes down into the ground. Its tip then swells and grows into a peanut pod (4).

PEANUT is a fruit of the peanut plant. The peanut is a kind of pea, not a nut. Like other peas, peanuts bear seeds in containers called *pods* (shells). There are two peanuts in most peanut shells. These tiny, tasty peanuts are a favorite food, whether eaten alone or mixed into candy, cookies, or pies. Peanut butter, made from peanuts, is also a popular food. Peanuts also have industrial uses.

The peanut plant is unusual because its pods develop underground. For this reason, peanuts are often called *groundnuts*. Other names for peanuts include *goobers*, *goober peas*, *groundpeas*, and *pindas*.

Peanuts are an important crop, especially in the warm regions of the world. Farmers harvest between 15 million and 18 million tons of peanuts a year. African and Asian farmers grow more than two-thirds of the world's peanuts. Leading peanut-growing countries include India, China, Nigeria, the United States, and Senegal. The leading peanut-growing states are Georgia, North Carolina, Texas, Virginia, Alabama, Oklahoma, and Florida.

Peanuts are a healthful food. One pound of roasted

Ray O. Hammons, the contributor of this article, is a research geneticist with the U.S. Department of Agriculture at the Coastal Plain Experiment Station, Tifton, Ga.

LEADING PEANUT GROWING STATES
Tons of peanuts grown in 1967

Georgia
487,560 tons

North Carolina
173,680 tons

Texas
166,725 tons

Virginia
127,755 tons

Alabama
117,920 tons

Oklahoma
104,550 tons

Florida
39,445 tons

Source: *Field and Seed Crops, By States, 1966-1967*, U.S. Department of Agriculture

peanuts or peanut butter contains more energy-giving Calories than a pound of beefsteak.

Uses of Peanuts

As Food. Most peanuts are used as food. Manufacturers roast peanuts inside the shells and sell them as whole *roasted-in-shell* peanuts. They also remove the shells and roast and sell only the nuts. Peanuts are usually salted to improve their flavor.

Manufacturers make *peanut butter* by grinding roasted, salted peanuts into a thick pasty substance. Peanut butter is a favorite food, eaten alone and in sandwiches. About half of the peanuts consumed in the United States are made into peanut butter. About a fourth are sold as roasted peanuts.

Roasted peanuts are eaten alone, or mixed into candies, cookies, pies, and other bakery products. Some ice cream is flavored with peanut butter. *Peanut bread* is made from ground peanuts. It is rich in proteins and low in starch.

Peanuts are rich in oil. Manufacturers obtain the oil by crushing the nuts in hydraulic presses, or by using chemicals to dissolve the oil out of the nuts. Peanut oil is used to fry foods. It smokes only at high temperatures and does not absorb odors easily. Many salad oils and dressings, margarine, and other vegetable shortenings also contain peanut oil.

In Industry. Low grades of peanut oil are used to oil machinery, and as an ingredient in soaps, face powders, shaving creams, shampoos, and paints. They are also used in making *nitroglycerin*, an explosive.

The solid that remains after the oil is removed from peanuts is a high-protein livestock feed. Peanut protein can also be used to make a kind of textile fiber called *Ardil*.

Even peanut shells have uses. Manufacturers grind the shells into powder. Peanut-shell powder is an ingredient in plastics, cork substitutes, wallboard, and abrasives.

On Farms. A soil conditioner made from peanut shells may be added to fertilizers. Peanut plants make good hay. But most farmers return the harvested plants to the ground so the plants will fertilize the soil.

Growing Peanuts

The Peanut Plant is an annual that grows in warm climates. It grows up to $2\frac{1}{2}$ feet high and from 3 to 4 feet across. There are two main types of peanut plants,

bunch and *runner*. The bunch type grows upright. The runner type spreads out on or near the ground as it grows. Intermediate types also exist. Growers group peanut plants into four market types: (1) large-seeded Virginias; (2) smaller-seeded Virginias, called *Runners;* (3) Spanish; and (4) Valencia. Both the large-seeded and the smaller-seeded Virginias include bunch

PEANUT PRODUCTS

Food for man

Grant Heilman
Livestock feed

Cooking fats and oils

Cosmetics

Wallboard

Plastic filler

Paints

WORLD BOOK photos by E. F. Hoppe
Explosives

FOOD VALUE OF THE PEANUT
Raw peanut with skins

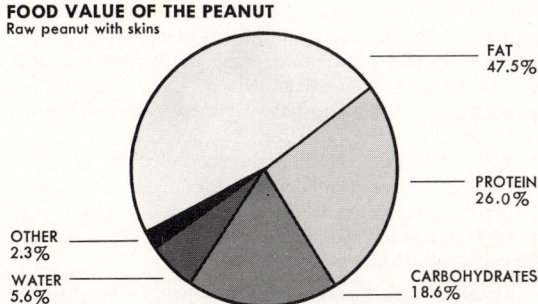

FAT 47.5%

PROTEIN 26.0%

OTHER 2.3%

WATER 5.6%

CARBOHYDRATES 18.6%

Source: *Composition of Foods*, Agriculture Handbook No. 8, Bernice K. Watt and Annabel L. Merrill, U. S. Department of Agriculture, 1963

Farmers Harvest Peanuts
with a *peanut combine*. The combine digs up the plants. Then it strips the nuts from the plants and places the picked pods in a large collecting bin.

National Peanut Council

and runner plants. Spanish and Valencia types are bunch.

Peanut plants bear many small, yellow, pealike flowers where the leaves are attached to the stems. The plants blossom continuously for two to three months. Flower buds open at sunrise. Fertilization takes place during the morning and the flowers usually wither and die about noon. Within a few days, the *pegs* (stalklike stems of the pods) begin to grow. They grow slowly at first, but gradually grow more rapidly.

The pegs grow downward and push into the soil to a depth of 1 to 3 inches. The grown pegs may be 6 or 7 inches long. The tips of the pegs contain the developing seeds. They swell and mature into peanut pods. Most pods contain two seeds, but some may contain only one or as many as five seeds.

Cultivation. Peanut plants grow best in light, well-drained, sandy soil. They need much sunshine, warm temperatures, moderate rainfall, and a frost-free growing period of four or five months.

Farmers prepare the soil by plowing it deeply and thoroughly. Loose soil is important so that the pegs can penetrate the soil easily. Workers plant peanut seeds 2 to 3 inches deep at intervals of 3 to 6 inches, and in rows 24 to 36 inches apart.

Farmers must harvest peanuts at exactly the right time. If they harvest their crops too early, many pods will not have ripened. If they harvest them too late, the pegs may snap, and many pods will be left in the soil. Most pods ripen 120 to 150 days after the seeds are planted.

At harvest time, farmers use digging plows to slice through the main root of each plant below soil level. The plants, with pods attached, are lifted from the soil and left to dry in the sun. The pods are sometimes collected when they are half dry and dried artificially. Machines called *combines* remove the pods from the dried plants. The pods are then cleaned and graded before they are shelled.

Processing Peanuts

Large, unshelled peanuts are cleaned, polished, and whitened before they are marketed. Manufacturers treat them to remove the skins and to produce a whiter color. Then they roast the peanuts to a rich, brownish color and salt them. Some peanuts are salted and roasted in the shell. They are soaked in salt water under pressure, and then dried and roasted.

Peanuts contain more edible oil than most other commercially grown crops. Manufacturers clean the peanuts before removing the oil. Then the peanuts are passed through rollers that grind them into tiny particles. To extract the oil, workers either place the peanut particles in presses that squeeze out the oil or they add a chemical *solvent* that dissolves the oil. The solvent is removed from the oil by distillation. The oil is then bleached to remove impurities.

History

Peanuts are native to South America. South American Indians were growing peanuts at least 1,000 years ago. Early North American settlers grew peanuts, but no one knows whether peanuts were cultivated in North America before the settlers arrived. Early colonists fed peanuts to hogs. Peanut growing increased rapidly during and after the Civil War. But peanuts did not become an important commercial crop until about 1917.

George Washington Carver made an extensive study of peanuts. Carver is credited with having found more than 300 uses for the plant and its fruit. See CARVER, GEORGE WASHINGTON.

Scientific Classification. Peanuts belong to the pea family, *Leguminosae*. Cultivated peanuts are genus *Arachis*, species *A. hypogaea*.   RAY O. HAMMONS

Tasty Pears from the Rogue River Valley in Oregon are sent to all parts of the world. The region's mild climate makes fruit growing profitable. Workers pick the fruit by hand to prevent bruising.

Oregon State Highway Dept.

PEAR is a fleshy, cone-shaped fruit. Pears are large and round at the blossom end and taper inward toward the stem. However, some may be almost completely round, like an apple, and others may be as small as a cherry. The pear tree is closely related to the apple and the quince trees. It grows in temperate regions throughout the world. The *common*, or *European*, pear is native to southern Europe and Asia. The *Japanese* or *Chinese* pears, often called *oriental* pears, are descended from the wild *sand* pear of central and western China. Many hundreds of varieties have been developed.

The fruit is covered with a smooth, thin skin, which may be yellow, russet, or red. Its juicy flesh is sweet and mellow. It is also tender, although tiny, hard grit cells make the flesh taste sandy. European pears contain only a few of these cells. But fruits of other kinds of pear trees may have large numbers of them. Enclosed in the center of the fleshy portion is a core much like the core of an apple. This core may contain as many as 10 seeds. Pears from different varieties vary in shape,

size, color, texture, flavor, aroma, time of ripening, and keeping qualities.

The common pear tree may grow 45 feet high and be 25 feet wide. It sometimes lives to be quite old, often more than 75 years. Its leaves are almost oval but have a sharply pointed tip. They usually have toothed edges and rather prominent veins. The white flowers grow in clusters of 4 to 12 blossoms.

How Pears Are Grown. Pears, like most other fruit trees, are grown by grafting the desired variety on a rootstock. Seedlings of European pears are usually used for planting. They are called French pear seedlings, even though the seeds are no longer imported from France. Seedlings of oriental pears have been used because of their resistance to certain diseases. But the fruit produced was often inedible. However, resistant trunks and branches may be developed from inedible varieties. These varieties are grafted to quince trees and allowed to produce the trunk and main scaffold branches of the tree. Then the desired edible variety is grafted to the branches. If disease attacks a branch, it will be stopped when it reaches the scaffolding branches. Thus, it often is possible to save part of a tree.

Quince rootstock is used to produce dwarf pear trees. But some European pear varieties will not grow on quince. Then the grower uses an intermediate stock. To do this, he first grafts the intermediate stock, which will grow on the quince. When the intermediate stock shoots are long enough, the European variety wanted is grafted to the shoot. Then the grower cuts off all side growth except that on the last graft.

Growers plant standard-sized trees about 18 to 25 feet apart. They plant dwarf trees about 10 to 15 feet apart. Pear trees grow well in soils heavier and wetter than those in which peach trees will grow. Sometimes nitrogen fertilizers are added to the soil to increase the growth of the tree. In some regions, certain varieties may not need cross-pollination to bear fruit. But in other regions the same varieties may need to be cross-polli-

LEADING PEAR GROWING STATES AND PROVINCES

Bushels (50 pounds) of pears grown each year

California	𝄢𝄢𝄢𝄢𝄢𝄢𝄢𝄢𝄢𝄢𝄢𝄢	11,060,000 bu.
Oregon	𝄢𝄢𝄢𝄢𝄢𝄢𝄢	5,973,000 bu.
Washington	𝄢𝄢𝄢𝄢𝄢	4,622,000 bu.
Michigan	𝄢	1,217,000 bu.
Ontario	𝄢	991,000 bu.

Based on a 4-year average, 1964-67.

Sources: U.S. Department of Agriculture; Dominion Bureau of Statistics

191

J. Horace McFarland
A Cluster of Fruit and Foliage of the Seckel Pear

nated. Some varieties of pears always need cross-pollination.

Growers prune pear trees as they do other orchard fruit trees. They cut off unnecessary branches so light can reach all parts of the tree. They also keep the tree quite low to make it easier to spray and pick the fruit.

Some pear trees seem able to withstand very cold weather. Therefore, certain varieties can be grown in regions that have severe winters. However, many pears thrive in hot, dry areas. These varieties are grown in many of the Pacific Coast states. Hybrids produced from common and Japanese pears are quite hardy.

Varieties. From the common, or European, pear have come such familiar varieties as Bartlett, Comice, Anjou, Bosc, Dana Hovey, Hardy, Seckel, and Winter Nelis. Because of their gritty fruit, which is objectionable, oriental pears have been crossed with the common pear. From this cross-breeding come the varieties Kieffer, LeConte, and Garber.

Bartlett pears ripen in summer, but most other varieties ripen later, usually in late fall. Pears ripen to perfection only when they are removed from the tree. Therefore, pears are picked while they are still green and hard. The fruit will ripen in a cool place where the temperature does not exceed 75° F. Many varieties, such as Winter Nelis and Forelle, can be kept in cold storage all winter. Temperatures range between 32° and 40° F. Most other pears, such as Comice and Anjou, must be removed from storage by midwinter.

Uses. Pears are used extensively as a dessert fruit. Most of them are eaten fresh. But many are canned either alone or in combinations with other fruits. Quite a few pears are dried. European people use many pears for pear cider, called *perry*.

Food Value. Fresh pears contain about 14.1 per cent carbohydrates and a small amount of protein and fats. They also contain calcium, phosphorus, iron, vitamin A, thiamine, riboflavin, niacin, and ascorbic acid. Pears have as many calories as apples, more than peaches, but less than plums and cherries.

Diseases. Perhaps the greatest limiting factor in growing the common pear is the occurrence of *fire blight*. This disease is often called *pear blight* because pears are so susceptible to it. Fire blight is a destructive disease that spreads rapidly in warm, humid weather. It is caused by bacteria that attack blossoms, young twigs, and branches, killing them and turning them black, as if they had been burned by fire. The bacteria live from year to year in cankers on the tree trunk and limbs. Insects carry them from tree to tree. Rain, dripping through the tree, carries them from branch to branch. Growers prune all the diseased parts as soon as they are noticed. The growers also spray the tree with a copper solution, or with solutions containing antibiotics such as terramycin and streptomycin.

Two fungus diseases, *scab* and *leaf spot*, damage fruit and leaves. Sprays of lime sulfur and Bordeaux mixture help to control these.

Insects. The *codling moth* is a serious pest. It causes wormy fruit. *Pear psyalla* affects the skin of the fruit and the tree's foliage. *Pear-leaf blister mite* and various other mites cause brownish blisters on the undersides of the leaves. They also cause the fruit to be small and to fall. *Pear thrips* attack the buds early in spring, causing them to shrivel and turn brown. Growers use lime sulfur, oil emulsions, lead arsenates, DDT, malathion, and parathion to control the insects.

Industry. Pears are grown commercially in 11 states. Together, they produce about $24\frac{1}{2}$ million bushels each year. About 85 per cent of the total yearly crop is produced on the Pacific Coast. Bartlett pears constitute more than two-thirds of the total crop. California is the leading producer, averaging about 11 million bushels each year. Oregon and Washington are also leading producers. Michigan and New York produce mostly Bartlett and Kieffer pears.

History. No one knows when pears were first found. The Greek poet Homer, who lived in about the 800's B.C., mentioned this fruit in his works. So did the Roman, Publilius Syrus.

The pear has been grown in America since the earliest colonists arrived. In 1630, John Endecott (or Endicott) of Massachusetts is supposed to have planted the *Endicott pear*, which is famous in the history of horticulture. Most pears in colonial America came from France, which was at that time the center of European pear growing. One of the world's largest pear trees once grew in the Mississippi Valley, near the French settlement of Cahokia. Pear growing spread throughout the United States. Pears are grown in home gardens and farms in almost every state. However, the pear has never become as popular as the apple.

Scientific Classification. The pear tree belongs to the rose family, *Rosaceae*. The common, or European, pear is genus *Pyrus*, species *P. communis*. Most oriental pears are *P. pyrifolia*. Others are the Ussurian pear, *P. ussuriensis*, and the Callery pear, *P. calleryana*.   REID M. BROOKS

See also BLIGHT; PLANT (color picture: Some Members of the Rose Family).

PEARL

Gendreau; Authenticated News

A Fortune in Natural Pearls, *left,* came from pearl beds off the western coast of Australia. Japanese pearl divers, *above,* collect oyster shells from the ocean floor in nets and then unload them into wooden tubs. Cultured pearls come from these oysters grown in commercial beds.

PEARL is one of the most valuable gems. Large, perfectly shaped pearls rank in value with the most precious stones. But pearls differ from other gems. Most gems are minerals that are mined from beneath the earth. But pearls are formed inside the shells of oysters. Mineral gems are hard and usually reflect light. But pearls are rather soft, and absorb, as well as reflect, light.

How Pearls Are Formed

Oysters and other shell-forming mollusks make a special substance, called *nacre* (pronounced *NAY kur*), that lines the insides of their shells. This smooth lining is called the *nacreous layer,* or *pearly layer,* and is often lustrous. It is formed by certain cells in the body of the animal. When a foreign substance, such as a grain of sand or a tiny parasite, enters the body of the mollusk, the nacre-forming cells begin to work. They cover the invading substance with thin sheets of nacre. Gradually they build successive circular layers of nacre until the foreign body is completely enclosed in the shell-like substance, forming the pearl. The pearl has the same luster and color as the lining of the shell of the mollusk. But few pearl-forming mollusks produce the beautifully colored nacre that is essential for valuable pearls. Only

the sea pearl oyster, which lies in tropical seas, produces the precious type of pearls. Edible clams and oysters have dull shells, so their pearls are without luster. As a result, they have no value.

Characteristics of Pearls

When a pearl is cut in two and examined under a microscope, the layers can be seen. Because the layers are *concentric* (formed in a complete circle around the central substance), the cut pearl looks like a sliced onion. The layers are made up of little crystals of a mineral substance called *aragonite.* They are held in position by a cartilage-like material known as *conchiolin* (pronounced *kahng KY oh lin*). The tiny mineral crystals overlap, and break up any light that falls on them into little rainbows of color. This gives pearls their iridescence, which jewelers call *orient.* Conchs, clams, and most edible oysters usually do not make pretty pearls because their aragonite crystals are too large. Even though the pearls may be of beautiful pink, white, or purple color, they lack iridescence.

Color. Oriental pearls, which are not named because they come from the East but because they are iridescent, may also have color. They may be "black," pink,

A Pearl forms inside the shell of an oyster, *left,* when a piece of foreign matter enters the shell, *right.* An epithelium sac then circles this particle and it becomes coated by many thin sheets of pearl. After several years, the particle is completely covered and a lustrous pearl has been formed.

American Museum of Natural History

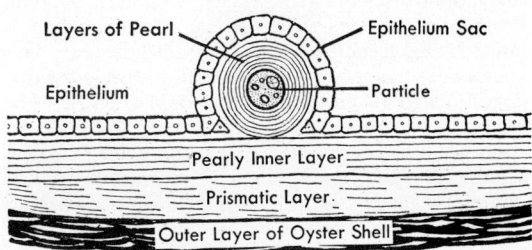

Layers of Pearl — Epithelium Sac

Epithelium — Particle

Pearly Inner Layer
Prismatic Layer
Outer Layer of Oyster Shell

Authenticated News

Skilled Japanese Workers Arrange Pearls for graduated pearl necklaces according to size in special grooved boxes.

orange, gold, cream, or white. "Black" pearls are really a dark, shiny gray. They are among the most valuable.

Shape of a pearl is as important as its color. Round pearls, suitable for necklaces, are the most sought. Next in value are the button-shaped and drop-shaped pearls. These are often used for earrings. Matched pairs of these pearls are even more valuable than pairs of unmatched single ones. Pearls with irregular shapes are called *baroques*. They are of little value in comparison with the others. Abalone pearls have wonderful color and luster but are almost never symmetrical.

Blemishes. Perfect pearls, or pearls with only one blemish, are the most valuable. Sometimes pearl blemishes can be removed if the flaw is not too deep. Specially trained men, called *peelers*, carefully scrape away the blemished layers. When they remove the flaw, the pearl is smaller, but perfect. Such a pearl is worth more than the original large, but blemished, pearl.

Matching Pearls. The matching of pearls to make a pair or a string makes the finished piece more expensive than the total cost of the individual pearls. Each added pearl must be like all the others in color and orient. Often it must be of the same size as the others. It must have no more than one tiny blemish. (One blemish is acceptable because the pearl can be drilled for mounting at the blemish.) It may take many years to fill a necklace of matched pearls.

Weight. Pearls are sold by weight, which is called *grains* by jewelers. Four grains equal 1 carat (see CARAT). Perhaps the most familiar use of the term carat is in connection with the weight of diamonds.

Kinds of Pearls

Natural Pearls. The chief pearl-oyster beds form a ring around an island in the Persian Gulf, near Bahrein. Pearls from this area are never large, for the fishery is limited. One section is fished every seventh year. This allows only time enough for the young oysters to grow large enough to produce moderate-sized pearls. The islands of the South Pacific and those off the northern coast of Australia are other important sources. There the oysters are large and fishing is uncontrolled. Shells from these oysters are also commercially important, for they furnish material for buttons and mother-of-pearl. Pink fresh-water pearls are sometimes found in

waters of the Mississippi River and its tributaries.

Cultured Pearls are real pearls made by oysters. They usually can be distinguished from natural ones only by laboratory tests. The cultured pearl has a larger central body around which the layers of nacre form. It also has fewer and thicker layers of nacre.

Cultured pearls are produced by inserting in an oyster a bead made of mother-of-pearl. The process was developed by Kokichi Mikimoto (1858?-1954) of Japan in the early 1900's. So successful was this process that the cultured-pearl business is much larger than the trade in natural pearls.

To produce cultured pearls, young oysters are planted in carefully selected oyster beds. When the oysters are 3 years old, they are taken from the beds to special plants. There, trained persons open the young oysters' shells and insert tiny pellets made from mussel shells taken from the Mississippi River. The workers then place the oysters in wire cages that will protect them from enemies. The cages are suspended from rafts and lowered into calm, protected waters near the shore. Twice a year attendants raise the cages and remove seaweed and barnacles from the oysters. Progress of the oyster and the care given it are recorded on small metal tags attached to the cage. When the oyster is 7 years old it is removed from the cage and its shell is opened. There is a valuable pearl in about 1 out of every 20 oysters opened. The pearl is washed, graded, and polished before it is sent to the market. About 70 per cent of all the cultured pearls in the world are sold in the United States.

Imitation Pearls are made by man. Usually, manufacturers coat glass beads with a substance known as *pearl essence*. This substance, sometimes known by its French name *essence d'orient*, is a creamy liquid extracted from fish scales. Herring scales usually furnish the main ingredient. Imitation pearls can be recognized by the little loose flaps of dried pearl essence surrounding the hole. Here one also can often see a little of the glass bead which the pearl essence has failed to cover.

Mother-of-Pearl is formed by the nacre secreted by certain inedible clams and oysters. It is the same substance that forms the pearl. The mother-of-pearl of commerce is taken from the lining of the oyster shell. It has the same quality and character as the natural pearl, but is formed in flat layers. Mother-of-pearl is used to make buttons and to decorate small items such as pillboxes and knife handles. See MOTHER-OF-PEARL.

Care of Pearls

Because pearls are soft, they are easily scratched by such hard gems as diamonds. Pearls should always be put away carefully, out of contact with other jewelry. Pearls contain an organic material, conchiolin. This material dries out in time, or can be destroyed by unduly high temperatures. One of the substances from which oysters form pearls is calcium carbonate, which dissolves very quickly in acid. Perspiration sometimes contains an acid that can be harmful. Therefore, necklaces made of pearls should be washed and dried gently after they are worn.   FREDERICK H. POUGH

Related Articles in WORLD BOOK include:

PEARL HARBOR NAVAL BASE, Hawaii, is the hub of United States naval power in the Pacific Ocean. It covers 22,000 acres, and lies five miles west of Honolulu on the southern coast of Oahu Island. Most of the Navy's major commands in the Pacific have headquarters at the base. These include the Pacific Fleet and its fleet marine, service, and submarine forces; an anti-submarine warfare force; Fleet Air Hawaii; Fourteenth Naval District; a Navy shipyard; supply center; and an ammunition storage depot. It supports the operations of the Seventh Fleet.

Pearl Harbor is one of the largest and best-sheltered naval anchorages in the world. It is formed by two mouths of the narrow Pearl Stream. The harbor occupies about 10 square miles of navigable water, and has three *lochs* (nearly landlocked lakes). Its name came from the pearl oysters that once grew there.

In 1887, King Kalakaua of Hawaii gave the United States the right to develop a coaling station at Pearl Harbor. The Navy made its first attempt to deepen the channel through the reef outside the harbor in 1902. But the first dry dock was not completed until 1919.

A surprise attack on Pearl Harbor by Japanese forces on Dec. 7, 1941, forced the United States into World War II. Vice-Adm. Chuichi Nagumo led a 33-ship Japanese striking force that steamed under the cover of darkness to within 200 miles north of Oahu. His carriers launched about 360 airplanes against the Pacific

Fleet, under Adm. Husband E. Kimmel, and the Hawaiian ground troops, under Lt. Gen. Walter C. Short. The first bombs fell on Pearl Harbor about 7:55 A.M. The chief targets were the eight American battleships among the 92 naval vessels anchored in the harbor. The United States had 18 ships sunk or severely damaged, about 170 planes destroyed, and about 3,700 casualties. Kimmel and Short were criticized for the U.S. losses. Several investigations were held following the attack. "Remember Pearl Harbor!" became the rallying cry for the United States in World War II. See WORLD WAR II (The Attack on Pearl Harbor).   JOHN A. OUDINE

PEARL MOSQUE. See DELHI (History).

PEARL OF THE ANTILLES. See CUBA.

PEARL RIVER. See MISSISSIPPI (Rivers and Lakes; physical map).

PEARL SPAR. See DOLOMITE.

PEARSON, KARL (1857-1936), a British geneticist, became known as the founder of the science of statistics. He applied his statistical methods to biological data especially. In 1884, Pearson became professor of mathematics at the University of London. There he wrote his famous *Grammar of Science* (1892), a general textbook on scientific method. Later, Pearson became interested in biology and the new science of eugenics. He was born in London.   DUDLEY DILLARD

Pearl Harbor Tribute, the U.S.S. *Arizona* Memorial, stands above the partly submerged battleship. The memorial honors those who died in the surprise Japanese attack on Dec. 7, 1941. More than a thousand men are entombed aboard the *Arizona*.

Wide World

Canada had 10 provinces when Lester B. Pearson took office as prime minister.

DIEFENBAKER
1957-1963

PEARSON
1963-1968

TRUDEAU
1968-

LESTER B. PEARSON
Prime Minister of Canada
1963—1968

Philippe Halsman

PEARSON, LESTER BOWLES (1897-   ), a former Olympic hockey player and university professor, served as prime minister of Canada from 1963 to 1968. He succeeded John G. Diefenbaker, whose Conservative government fell during a dispute between Canada and the United States. Diefenbaker had refused to allow atomic warheads on defense missiles provided by the United States. Pearson, a Liberal, believed that Canada had agreed to accept the warheads and should do so. Pearson resigned as prime minister in 1968. He was succeeded by Liberal Party leader Pierre E. Trudeau.

Long before taking office as prime minister, Pearson had won fame as an international statesman. He was the first Canadian to receive the Nobel peace prize. As Canada's secretary of state for external affairs, Pearson had helped establish the North Atlantic Treaty Organization (NATO), a military alliance of 15 Western nations. He also served on a United Nations commission that drew up cease-fire plans in the Korean War. Pearson then became president of the UN General Assembly. He later played a leading role in ending a war in Egypt over control of the Suez Canal.

At the UN and NATO, Pearson showed great ability at working behind the scenes to put ideas into action. He could work with men of any temperament. He eased many tense moments with a well-chosen remark. The public became familiar with Pearson's sporty bow ties and his nickname, "Mike." But he had a deep personal reserve that people found hard to penetrate.

When Pearson became leader of the Liberal Party in 1958, one newspaper described him "as eloquent as a professor of algebra." Pearson admitted that he lacked

the ability to inspire audiences with speeches. He spoke with a slight lisp, which hurt his efforts to impress his listeners. He worked hard to make himself a better public speaker, but did not enjoy making speeches.

"There are some things in politics I don't like, never have liked, and never will like," Pearson said. "The hoopla, the circus part of it, all that sort of thing. It still makes me blush."

Early Life

Boyhood. Lester Bowles Pearson was born on April 23, 1897, in Toronto, Ont. He was the son of Edwin Arthur Pearson, a Methodist minister, and Annie Sarah Bowles Pearson. His father's father also had been a minister. Lester had an older brother, Marmaduke, and a younger brother, Vaughan. Edwin Pearson had a great interest in sports, especially baseball, and passed his enthusiasm on to Lester. The boy became a star athlete. He also was an excellent student.

Education and War Service. In 1913, Pearson entered the University of Toronto. He majored in history. World War I began in August, 1914. The following March, at the age of 17, Pearson enlisted in the Canadian Army as a private. In September, 1915, he was assigned to the British forces in Egypt. A month later he was among the first British troops stationed at Salonika, Greece. He served in the Balkan area of southeastern Europe for a year and a half.

Late in 1915, Pearson was sent as a stretcher-bearer to the Gallipoli Peninsula of Turkey. Some wounded British soldiers called the youth "Mike" because he looked Irish, and the nickname stayed with him. In

1917, Pearson received a lieutenant's commission in the infantry. That same year, he transferred to the British Royal Flying Corps as a pilot with the rank of flight lieutenant. Canada had no air corps at the time. Pearson returned to Canada in April, 1918, because of injuries from a training flight accident. He served for the rest of the war as a ground instructor at a Canadian base of the Royal Flying Corps.

After World War I ended in November, 1918, Pearson returned to the University of Toronto. He was graduated with honors in 1919. He then studied law for several weeks in Toronto. Next, Pearson took a job stuffing sausages in the Hamilton, Ont., plant of Armour and Company, a meat packing firm. During this period he played semiprofessional baseball. He then worked as a clerk in Armour's Chicago plant.

In 1921, Pearson received a scholarship from the Massey Foundation, which sent Canadians overseas to study. He studied history at Oxford University in England from 1922 to 1924. Pearson starred on Oxford's hockey team, and played on the British Olympic team. He received a bachelor's degree and a master's degree from Oxford. From 1924 to 1928 he taught history as a lecturer and then as an assistant professor at the University of Toronto.

On Aug. 22, 1925, Pearson married Maryon Elspeth Moody (1902-   ) of Winnipeg, Man. She had been one of his students at the university. The Pearsons had two children—Geoffrey Arthur Holland Pearson, who became a Canadian foreign service officer, and Patricia Lillian Pearson, the wife of Walter Hannah, a Toronto physician. Maryon Pearson disliked public life, but she played an active role in her husband's election campaigns. Pearson once declared: "I couldn't have carried on without her."

Public Career

Early Diplomatic Service. A great turning point in Pearson's life came in 1928. He entered the diplomatic service during the administration of Liberal Prime Minister W. L. Mackenzie King, and served as a first secretary in the department of external affairs. From 1930 to 1935, under Conservative Prime Minister Richard B. Bennett, Pearson took part in many international conferences. Bennett particularly praised Pearson for his work on two Canadian economic commissions. Pearson received the Order of the British Empire, an award for public service, from King George V.

Mackenzie King returned to power as prime minister in 1935. For six years, Pearson served as first secretary in the Canadian high commissioner's office in London. He returned to Ottawa in 1941 and for two years was assistant undersecretary of state for external affairs. In 1942, King assigned him to the staff of the Canadian embassy in Washington, D.C. Pearson headed a United Nations commission on food and agriculture in 1943. As chairman of another UN committee that year, he helped organize the UN Relief and Rehabilitation Administration (UNRRA). Pearson represented Canada at UNRRA meetings in 1944, 1945, and 1946. In January, 1945, King appointed him Canadian ambassador to the United States. Pearson held this post until September, 1946, when he returned to Ottawa as undersecretary of state for external affairs.

Pearson served as senior adviser of the Canadian dele-

gation to the San Francisco conference that signed the United Nations Charter in June, 1945. The Western nations favored him to be the first UN secretary-general, but Russia vetoed him. Pearson played a prominent part in setting up the UN Food and Agriculture Organization in 1945.

Secretary of State for External Affairs. In September, 1948, Pearson was appointed secretary of state for external affairs. Canadian Cabinet members must be members of Parliament, so Pearson ran for office the following month. The district of Algoma East in Ontario elected him to the House of Commons, and he won re-election in succeeding elections through the years. As Canada's chief foreign minister, Pearson headed his country's delegations to the UN General Assembly from 1948 to 1956. Prime Minister King retired in November, 1948, and Louis St. Laurent succeeded him.

In April, 1949, Pearson represented Canada at ceremonies setting up NATO. He had been one of the principal architects of the alliance. Pearson emphasized that NATO, although established to ward off Communism, must work for social, economic, and political progress. "Our treaty," he declared, "is . . . the point from which we start for yet one more attack on all those evil forces which block our way to justice and peace."

In 1949, Pearson represented Prime Minister St. Laurent at a meeting of Commonwealth prime ministers in London. He led Canada's delegates at a Commonwealth foreign affairs meeting in Ceylon in 1950, and at the Japanese peace treaty conference in San Francisco in 1951. In December, 1950, and January, 1951, Pearson served on a three-man UN commission that drew up cease-fire plans in the Korean War. Communist China rejected the plans, but they helped lay the groundwork for the eventual armistice. In September, 1951, Pearson became chairman for a year of the North Atlantic Council, the chief policy-making body of NATO. He served as president of the UN General Assembly in 1952 and 1953.

In October, 1956, France, Great Britain, and Israel invaded Egypt, which had seized the Suez Canal. The UN accepted Pearson's proposal to set up an emergency military force to end the fighting and supervise a cease-fire. The UN troops quickly restored peace before the fighting could turn into a major war.

On Oct. 14, 1957, Pearson became the first Canadian to receive the Nobel peace prize.

Liberal Party Leader. In 1957, St. Laurent's government fell to the Conservatives, led by John G. Diefenbaker. After resigning as prime minister, St. Laurent also stepped down as Liberal Party leader. Pearson disliked the political spotlight, and his wife did not want him to take the post. But Pearson decided to run for party leader. Although some Liberals considered him too inexperienced in domestic affairs, his fame as a statesman and his popularity in Parliament brought him victory. The Liberal Party chose Pearson as its leader by a large majority in January, 1958.

"No one ever started off worse than I did," Pearson said later. His advisers persuaded him to seek a parliamentary vote of no confidence in the new Conservative government. Pearson demanded that Prime Minister Diefenbaker return the government to the Liberals

HIGHLIGHTS OF PEARSON'S CAREER

United Press Int.

As Ambassador to the U.S., Pearson, *left*, visited the White House with U.S. official George Summerlin in 1945.

As President of the UN General Assembly, Pearson

United Press Int.

As President of the UN General Assembly, Pearson worked closely in 1953 with Dag Hammarskjöld, *left*, secretary-general of the United Nations. Andrew Cordier, *right*, was Hammarskjöld's executive assistant.

United Press Int.

The Nobel Peace Prize was presented to Pearson, *left*, in 1957 by Gunnar Jahn, president of the Nobel Committee.

UN Troops, sent to Egypt on Pearson's recommendation, restored peace quickly during the 1956 Suez Canal crisis.

by Donald M. Taka for WORLD BOOK

IMPORTANT DATES IN PEARSON'S LIFE

1897 (April 23) Born in Toronto, Ont.
1925 (Aug. 22) Married Maryon Elspeth Moody.
1928 Entered Canadian diplomatic service.
1945 Became ambassador to United States.
1945 Attended San Francisco conference on UN charter.
1948 Became secretary of state for external affairs.
1948 Elected to Canadian House of Commons.
1949 Represented Canada at signing of NATO pact.
1951 Elected chairman of NATO Council.
1952 Elected president of UN General Assembly.
1956 Helped end Suez Canal crisis.
1957 Received Nobel peace prize.
1958 Elected leader of Liberal Party.
1963 (April 22) Became prime minister of Canada.
1968 (April 21) Resigned as prime minister of Canada.

without an election. This demand gave Diefenbaker, a master of parliamentary maneuvering, a chance to attack Pearson and the Liberals. Diefenbaker then dissolved Parliament and called an election in March, 1958. Under Pearson, the Liberals went down to their worst defeat in history. They won only 49 of the 265 seats in the House of Commons.

During his first year as Liberal Party leader, Pearson did not seem to put much effort into his job. Some of his associates noticed that he appeared tired and dis-

satisfied. Eventually, several party backers demanded that Pearson either become more energetic or resign. They promised him enough funds to strengthen the party, and he decided to meet the challenge.

In 1959, Canadians began to notice a "new" Pearson. One newspaper said he had changed from "Pearson the Statesman" to "Fighting Mike." Pearson became tougher with the Conservatives in Parliament. He acquainted himself thoroughly with Canada's domestic problems and turned for advice to a "brain trust" of professors and businessmen. Pearson also developed plans to solve unemployment, defense, and urban problems.

As a result of Pearson's vigorous leadership, the Liberals more than doubled their parliamentary strength in the June, 1962, elections. The Conservatives fell short of an absolute majority in Parliament, but they still had more seats than any other party.

Prime Minister. Early in 1963, a dispute over defense policy strained relations between Canada and the United States. The question was whether Canada had agreed in 1959 to accept atomic warheads for missiles supplied by the United States. Pearson and the Liberals contended that Prime Minister Diefenbaker should accept the warheads, but Diefenbaker refused to do so. The Conservative government was overthrown by a vote of no confidence taken in February, 1963.

In the elections of April, 1963, the Liberals won 129 seats in the House of Commons, four short of an absolute majority. However, the small opposition parties promised to support Pearson. The Progressive Conservatives won only 95 seats, and Diefenbaker resigned. Pearson was sworn in as prime minister on April 22, 1963.

In May, 1963, Pearson went to London for a meeting with British Prime Minister Harold Macmillan. The two leaders dealt chiefly with trade problems. Later in the month, Pearson met with President John F. Kennedy in Hyannis Port, Mass. Pearson told Kennedy that Canada would accept the atomic warheads from the United States.

Pearson faced serious domestic problems when he became prime minister. Disputes between French-speaking and English-speaking Canadians threatened national unity. Many French Canadians complained that they did not have equal opportunities and rights. One organization, the Quebec Liberation Front, demanded independence from Canada for the province of Quebec. This secret terrorist group used bombings and other forms of violence against the national government.

Canada also had a major unemployment problem. Early in 1963, about 7 of every 100 Canadian workers could not find jobs. Pearson planned to increase employment by expanding Canada's production and trade. Among other steps, he proposed a new government department to promote industrial development.

In 1965, Pearson called a national election because he wanted an absolute Liberal majority in the House of Commons. He kept control of the government, but the Liberals failed to win a majority.

In April, 1968, at the age of 71, Pearson resigned as prime minister and as head of the Liberal Party. Pierre E. Trudeau succeeded Pearson. In August, 1968, Pearson became head of a World Bank commission that was set up to assist the economic progress of underdeveloped countries.　　　　　　　J. M. BECK

See also CANADA, HISTORY OF.

As Candidate for Liberal Leader, Pearson ran against Paul Martin, *right*, in 1958. Louis St. Laurent, *center*, was the retiring Liberal Party leader. The Liberals elected Pearson by a large majority.

Wide World

On the Campaign Trail, Pearson worked vigorously for the Liberal Party in Canada's general election of 1963.

Horst Ehricht for *Business Week*, by special permission

United Press Int.

As Prime Minister, Pearson met with President John F. Kennedy in Hyannis Port, Mass., soon after taking office.

Pearson's Wife, Maryon, took an active part in her husband's election campaigns despite her dislike of politics.

Wide World

into the interior of Greenland. This experience interested him in undertaking further expeditions to explore the uncharted Arctic regions.

When Peary returned to the United States in 1886, he drew the attention of the Philadelphia Academy of Natural Sciences to the need for Arctic exploration. Five years later, the Academy put him in charge of an expedition to northern Greenland. The most important geographical knowledge gained from his explorations on this trip was proof that Greenland is an island. Other expeditions between 1893 and 1897 resulted in important scientific discoveries about the nature of the polar regions. Peary published an account of all these journeys in 1898 in *Northward over the Great Ice*.

North Pole Journeys. In 1897, Peary was granted a five-year leave of absence from the navy to continue his exploration of the Arctic. The following year, he set out in his ship *Windward* on a voyage that he hoped would result in discovery of the North Pole. He was gone for four years, but he did not succeed in his main purpose. Still, he made other important discoveries. His party surveyed the northern coast of Greenland and reached a latitude of 84° 17′ 27″, about 390 miles south of the North Pole. This was the farthest north that anyone had then gone in the American Arctic.

In 1905, Peary again set out to reach the North Pole. He sailed in the *Roosevelt*, a ship that had been especially built to sail among *floes* (masses of moving ice). His party left the ship on the north coast of Ellesmere Island while they pushed northward on sledges over the ice fields of the Arctic Ocean. They reached latitude 87° 6′ and made a new "farthest north" record. But hardships forced Peary to turn back about 200 miles from the pole. His book *Nearest the Pole* (1907) tells of this journey. In 1948, a U.S.-Canadian task force found documents Peary left at Ellesmere Island in 1905.

In 1908, Peary again set out over the ice from Ellesmere Island for the North Pole. One after another of the group turned back because of shortage of supplies. Only four Eskimos and one Negro servant, Matthew Henson, were with Peary when, on April 6, 1909, he reached latitude 89° 57′. He was within sight of the pole, but he was too worn out to go farther. After sleeping for a few hours, however, he pushed on and reached his goal the same day. He took soundings proving that the sea around the North Pole is not a shallow body of water, as scientists had believed.

The news of Peary's discovery was not received so enthusiastically as it might have been. Another American explorer, Frederick A. Cook, had announced, just a week before Peary's return, that he had reached the pole in April, 1908, a year before Peary (see COOK, FREDERICK A.). But the Congress of the United States investigated Cook's claims, and finally gave Peary credit for the discovery. Peary wrote an account of his history-making trip in *The North Pole*, published in 1910.

Official Posts. Peary served as president of the American Geographical Society from 1901 to 1906. He retired from the Navy in 1911 with the rank of rear admiral. In the same year, he was a delegate to the International Polar Commission in Rome. In 1917, during World War I, Peary was appointed chairman of the National Aerial Patrol Commission.   JOHN E. CASWELL

See also BARTLETT, ROBERT A.; CAPE YORK; HENSON, MATTHEW A.

Admiral Robert E. Peary first explored Greenland in 1886. On later trips, he made important scientific discoveries in the polar regions.

Historical Pictures Service

Peary wrote numerous books about his explorations, including an account of his history-making trip to the North Pole.

PEARY, *PEER ih,* **ROBERT EDWIN** (1856-1920), an American Arctic explorer, became famous as the discoverer of the North Pole. He was born on May 6, 1856, in Cresson, Pa., and was graduated from Bowdoin College. From 1879 to 1881, he served as a draftsman for the United States Coast and Geodetic Survey in Washington, D.C. Then he became a civil engineer in the United States Navy.

First Explorations. From 1884 to 1885 and from 1887 to 1888, Peary worked on surveys for a canal across Nicaragua, which was then planned. He was assistant engineer during the first period, and chief engineer during the second. In 1886, he made a trip

PEASANTS' REVOLT. See WAT TYLER'S REBELLION.

PEASANTS' WAR refers to the rebellion of German peasants against their lords in 1524 and 1525. This was the greatest mass uprising in German history. The rebellion broke out late in 1524 at Stühlingen in the Black Forest and spread northward like wildfire. Soon all Germany, except Bavaria, felt the impact of the revolt.

The peasants stormed the castles and forced the nobles to grant their demands. Their flag, called the *Bundschuh*, was a black, white, and red cloth with a picture of a peasant's shoe.

The peasants had grumbled over the ever-increasing dues and services demanded by the princes for 50 years. The teachings of Martin Luther affected the peasants as sparks in a barrel of gunpowder. The peasants hoped for and needed Luther's support of their uprising. But he rejected their charter of liberties. Luther urged the peasants to lay down their arms. When they did not do so, he summoned the lords in a pamphlet to strike down and stab the rebels "like mad dogs."

The nobility drowned the rebellion in blood, and utterly eliminated the peasantry as a political factor for the next 300 years.　　　　　WILLIAM H. MAEHL

PEASE, HOWARD (1894-　　), is an American author of stories for young people. He became best known for his mystery and adventure stories, and sea tales. His works include *Thunderbolt House* (1944), *Heart of Danger* (1946), *Captain of the Araby* (1953), and *Shipwreck* (1957). Pease was born in Stockton, Calif. He was graduated from Stanford University, and later taught at the University of San Francisco.　　　　　CHARLEMAE ROLLINS

PEAT, *peet*, is partly decayed plant matter that has collected in swamps and marshes over long periods of time. It is generally the first stage in the formation of coal. Dried peat varies from a light yellow-brown substance resembling tangled hay, to deeper layers of dark brown, compact material that looks like brown coal.

Peat forms in layers. The pale upper layers contain the remains of plants, herbs, and moss that died and rotted in the shallow, acid water. They are compressed by the weight of water and other plants to form peat. The lower layers of peat contain about 90 per cent water, and look like mud.

Peat is found throughout the world, but Canada, Finland, and Russia have the largest deposits. Russia is the largest peat producer. Ireland, Germany, and other countries produce smaller amounts. The largest peat deposits in the United States are located in Minnesota. There are also other peat *bogs* (marshes) in the United States, such as the Dismal Swamp in Virginia (see DISMAL SWAMP).

In Ireland and some other countries, workers dig and stack peat by hand. Big machines are used to dig, chop, and mix the peat in Russia, Germany, and some other countries. These machines form large amounts of peat into blocks, and spread the blocks on the ground for drying.

Dried peat is used mainly as a fuel in places where coal and oil are scarce. It is used to heat houses in Ireland. Dried peat is also used as fuel in some electric power plants in Russia. Peat is not used as a fuel in the United States because of the high cost of drying it. Black peat is used as a fertilizer. Fluffy brown peat is used as a packing material, and as bedding for farm animals.　　　　　CLARENCE KARR, JR.

See also COAL (How Coal Was Formed); PEAT MOSS; MOSS; HEATH.

PEAT MOSS is any of the several kinds of mosses from which peat is formed. The most important kind is *sphagnum* moss. There are more than 350 species of sphagnum moss, common in swamps in many parts of the North Temperate Zone. Sphagnum or peat moss forms dense mats of light green, and sometimes grows a foot or more high. It is soft and spongy, and has no true roots, but draws water through the walls of its stems and leaves. These organs have the power to store large quantities of water for long periods. For this reason, peat moss is valuable in greenhouses and gardens. Many rare plants, such as orchids and pitcher plants, are potted in peat moss to keep them from drying out. Certain kinds of seeds are also sprouted on beds of chopped peat moss. The moss is often spread on the surface of the ground as a mulch in hot, dry weather.

A Kind of Peat Moss, called *Sphagnum,* is used as an absorbent in shipping flowers and other perishable goods.
William M. Harlow

Scientific Classification. The peat mosses belong to the peat moss family, *Sphagnaceae*. They are all classified in the genus *Sphagnum*.　　　　　A. J. GROUT

PEATTIE, DONALD CULROSS (1898-1964), an American author and botanist, became well known for his popular books of natural history. He wrote with a lyrical beauty about nature. His works include *Singing in the Wilderness* (1935), *Green Laurels* (1936), and *Journey into America* (1943). *The Road of a Naturalist* (1941) is his autobiography. He also wrote scientific papers and books for children. Peattie was born in Chicago and attended Harvard University.　　　　　GEORGE E. BUTLER

PEBBLE. See BOULDER.

Peat Bogs furnish much of the fuel used on the Island of Skye, west of Scotland. Women stack the peat before hauling it home.
Authenticated News

Ross E. Hutchins

The Wide-Spreading Ornamental Pecan Tree has golden yellow leaves in autumn. It produces a delicious, edible nut.

PECAN, *pea CAN*, or *pea KAHN*, is a North American tree valuable for its fruit, the pecan nut. The pecan is a type of hickory. It grows naturally in the Mississippi Valley region from Iowa southward, and in the river valleys of Oklahoma, Texas, and northern Mexico. But pecan orchards are planted throughout the southern states as far north as Virginia, and in California.

Pecan raising is an important industry, especially in the South. Production varies, but about 205 million pounds of nuts are produced in an average year. About four-fifths of the pecans are marketed as shelled nuts. Some trees produce 400 to 500 pounds of nuts each year. But the trees do not begin to bear nuts until they are about five or six years old. For another five years,

A Cluster of Pecans on the Branch. The husks enclosing the shells are much like those of walnuts and hickory nuts.

J. Horace McFarland

LEADING PECAN GROWING STATES

Tons of pecans in the shell grown each year

Georgia
21,000 tons

Texas
19,900 tons

Oklahoma
17,400 tons

Alabama
12,100 tons

Louisiana
12,100 tons

Based on a 4-year average, 1964-67

Source: U.S. Department of Agriculture

they do not bear enough nuts to make them profitable. Only after the trees are about 20 years old does the owner receive full return on his investment.

Although the pecan is chiefly valuable for its fruit, its wood is used in large amounts for flooring, furniture, boxes, and crates. Sometimes the wood is also used as fuel and for smoking meats.

Pecan trees may grow 180 feet high. Their trunks are sometimes 4 to 6 feet in diameter near the ground. The light brown or gray bark is deeply furrowed and cracked. Pecan leaves are 12 to 20 inches long. They are made up of from 9 to 17 lance-shaped leaflets.

Pecan orchard trees are usually grown by placing branch buds from trees that bear fine quality nuts on seedling stocks. Pecan flowers are pollinated by the wind. However, many varieties cannot be pollinated by their own kind, so most pecan orchards contain several different kinds of pecan trees. The thin-shelled pecans, called *papershell*, are the most popular because their shells can be cracked between the fingers.

Growers usually harvest the pecans after they fall to the ground. However, it is sometimes necessary to "thresh" the nuts from the trees by tapping the branches with light poles. The nuts are taken to processing centers where they are cleaned, graded, and packaged for shipment. If the nuts are to be shelled before marketing, they are cracked by machines, but the meat is removed by hand.

Scientific Classification. Pecans belong to the walnut family, *Juglandaceae*. They are classified as genus *Carya*, species *C. illinoensis*. THEODORE W. BRETZ

See also TEXAS (color picture: The State Tree).

A Pecan in Its Shell is seen at the left. At the center, the shell has been broken away to show the kernel. At the right, one-half of the kernel has been removed.

Arthur H. Fisher

Western Ways

The Collared Peccary lives in the Southwestern United States and many parts of South America. It usually has twin offspring.

PECCARY, *PECK uh rih,* is a hoofed forest animal related to the wild hog. There are two kinds of peccaries. The *collared* peccary lives in many sections of South America and as far north as Texas and southern New Mexico and Arizona. The *white-lipped* peccary lives in an area from central Mexico south to Paraguay.

The peccary looks much like a slender, active hog. The collared peccary stands about 21 inches high at the shoulder. It has a coarse, grizzled, blackish-gray coat with a gray collar. The white-lipped peccary is larger and darker. It is marked by white patches that extend from the mouth along the side of its face. Each peccary has a large gland on its arched back, about 8 inches in front of its tail. When the animal is excited, the gland gives off a small amount of very strong musk. For this reason, peccaries are sometimes called *musk hogs.* In the Southwestern States, the name *javelina* (pronounced *HAH vuh LEE nah*) is often used.

The mother usually gives birth to twins, which are about the size of rabbits. They have reddish coats with a black stripe down their backs. If captured when small, they make interesting and affectionate pets.

Peccaries are primarily rooting animals, but sometimes they prey on small animals. They travel in bands that may range from a few to several hundred individuals. They are shy, timid creatures, and will flee from danger whenever possible. But if cornered, peccaries defend themselves viciously with their sharp teeth. Their most common natural enemy is the jaguar. Fine pigskin jackets and gloves are made from the thin, tough hides of peccaries. The skin can be recognized because the hair roots leave a pattern of three holes in evenly distributed groups.

Scientific Classification. Peccaries make up the peccary family, *Tayassuidae.* The collared peccary is genus *Tayassu,* species *T. tajacu.* The white-lipped peccary is *T. pecari.*   VICTOR H. CAHALANE

PECK is a unit of dry measure that equals 8 quarts or a quarter of a bushel. Dry foods, such as potatoes and beans, are measured by the peck. See also WEIGHTS AND MEASURES (Dry Capacity Measure—United States).

PECK, JAMES. See IMPEACHMENT.

PECKHAM, RUFUS W. (1838-1909), was an associate justice of the Supreme Court of the United States. Peck-

ham believed in as little government interference with business as possible, and opposed many reform and welfare measures. Peckham is noted for his opinion in the 1905 *Lochner v. New York* case, in which he voted with a majority of the court to overrule a law limiting bakers to a 60-hour work week (see LOCHNER V. NEW YORK).

Peckham was born in Albany, N.Y. He began to practice law in New York in 1857. He was elected to the New York Supreme Court in 1883. Later, in 1886, Peckham was elected to the State Court of Appeals. President Grover Cleveland named him to the Supreme Court of the United States in 1895, and he served from 1896 until his death in 1909.   STANLEY I. KUTLER

PECOS BILL, *PAY kohs,* an American folklore character, is a mythical super-cowboy. He is the legendary inventor of roping and other cowboy skills.

According to the tall tales, he was born in eastern Texas and took his name from the Pecos River after falling into it from the family wagon on the way west. There were so many other children that Bill was not missed for several days, and then it was too late to turn back for him. Raised by coyotes, he thought he was one of them until he found out that he had no tail.

Pecos Bill then became a cowboy. He rode a mean, pitching horse named Widow Maker because it threw everyone else who tried to ride it. One day, Bill roped and saddled a mountain lion and, whipping it with a rattlesnake, rode into a camp of bad men. They were so scared that they made him boss of their outfit, the toughest in the world.

The only time Pecos Bill was thrown was when he rode a Kansas cyclone, and it "rained out" from under him in Arizona. This rain washed out the Grand Canyon. During a dry spell, he dug the Rio Grande River to get water from the Gulf of Mexico. Some say Bill died of indigestion caused by the rusting of fishhooks that he added to his liquor.   B. A. BOTKIN

PECOS NATIONAL MONUMENT, in north-central New Mexico, contains the ruins of an Indian village and a Spanish mission. The Spanish explorer Coronado discovered the site in 1540, and it became a landmark for other Spanish explorers. The 340.90-acre site became a national monument in 1965.

PECOS RIVER is the largest branch of the Rio Grande. The Pecos starts near Santa Fe, N.Mex., near the foot of Baldy Peak. For most of its 800-mile course, the Pecos flows in a southeasterly direction. It runs beside the palisade of Llano Estacado, a great level plateau in New Mexico and Texas. The Pecos flows into the Rio Grande in Texas, just 36 miles north of Del Rio. The river drains an area of more than 33,000 square miles. Reservoirs built along the river for irrigation include Alamogordo Reservoir and Lakes McMillan, Avalon, and Red Bluff. For location, see TEXAS (physical map).   FRANK D. REEVE

PÉCS, *paych* (pop. 130,600; alt. 525 ft.), is a rail, industrial, and wine center in Hungary. It is about 106 miles southwest of Budapest in Hungary's coal-mining region.

Pécs is built on the site of an ancient Roman settlement. For the location of the city, see HUNGARY (color map). The first university in Hungary was founded at Pécs in 1367.

PECTIN, *PECK tin,* is a white substance found in most fruits and some vegetables. It is neutral, neither acid nor alkaline. In foodstuffs, it belongs to the carbohydrate group. Pectin is used to thicken or stiffen a mixture with which it is cooked. It makes jelly "jell," instead of remaining thin and syrupy. The amount of pectin in fruit depends on the ripeness and kind of fruit. Some fruits are high in pectin. They include apples, blackberries, crab apples, cranberries, currants, gooseberries, grapes, loganberries, and plums. Other fruits lack sufficient pectin to make them jell. Among these are apricots, cherries, huckleberries, peaches, pears, pineapples, raspberries, and strawberries.

Commercial pectins can be made by concentrating certain fruit juices. These pectins are used in making jelly from fruits that do not have enough pectin to jell easily. Commercial pectin requires more sugar in jelly-making, but produces more jelly.   LENNA F. COOPER

See also LEMON; COLLOID; JELLY AND JAM.

PEDAGOGY, *PED uh GOH jih.* In ancient Greece and Rome boys were accompanied to school by a slave called a *pedagogue.* The pedagogue taught the children and often protected them. The word *pedagogue* means a *leader of children.* Pedagogy today means the science and art of teaching.

Modern pedagogy emphasizes systematized learning, or instruction, dealing with the aims, principles, and methods of teaching. Such instruction is provided by the Department of Education in a college, and by the School of Education in a university.   HOLLIS L. CASWELL

See also EDUCATION; EDUCATION, HISTORY OF; TEACHING.

PEDESTAL. See ARCHITECTURE (Architectural Terms).

PEDESTRIAN. See TRAFFIC (Traffic Control).

PEDIATRICS, *PEE dih AT ricks,* is a branch of medicine that deals with the care of babies and children. Doctors in this field are called *pediatricians.* They usually have had several years of study concentrated on child health and diseases. The American Academy of Pediatrics awards certificates in pediatrics.

See also DISEASE (Diseases of Children).

PEDICAB, *PED ih KAB,* is a type of three-wheeled vehicle used as a taxicab. It is built like a bicycle, but it has two rear wheels instead of one. The passenger carriage sits above the rear wheels. The carriage is often covered and partially enclosed. The driver sits on a bicycle seat and pushes pedals that turn the rear wheels. He guides the pedicab with bicycle handle bars. Pedicabs are used widely in the Orient, especially in China and Japan, where they have almost entirely replaced jinrikishas.

See also CHINA (picture: Pedicab School Buses); JINRIKISHA.

PEDICEL. See RACEME.

PEDIGREE is a record of the ancestors of an animal or plant. To be most useful, a pedigree should record *traits* (characteristics) of the ancestors as well as their names and their birth and death dates. Breeders use pedigree information to predict such traits as size, strength, and color of hair in offspring. This information is considered so important in the improvement of livestock that breeders' associations have been formed to record the pedigrees of animals used for breeding. These animals are then said to be *registered.*

Pedigrees of plants are also helpful. But they are usually made for groups rather than individual plants. Hybrid corn breeders are careful to select and preserve known *pedigree lines* (families) of corn. Records of human ancestry are sometimes called "family trees." The study of some family pedigrees enables scientists to predict the inheritance of certain diseases and physical defects. See GENEALOGY.   J. HERBERT TAYLOR

See also BREEDING; GENETICS; HEREDITY.

PEDIMENT. See ARCHITECTURE (Architectural Terms).

PEDODONTICS. See DENTISTRY (Fields in Dentistry).

PEDOMETER, *pee DAHM uh tur,* is a small instrument that measures the distance a person walks. The pedometer, which looks like a watch, is carried in the pocket. With each step, the motion of the body causes a small lever to move. This lever records the number of steps taken. To find out how far he has walked, the walker must find the average length of his step and multiply it by the number of steps recorded by the pedometer. In some pedometers, an adjustment is made in the mechanism to account for the length of the step, and then this instrument measures the distance walked and no multiplication is required. In other pedometers, a wheel rolls along the ground and gives a measurement of the distance covered.   E. A. FESSENDEN

PEDRO, *PAY throo,* was the name of two emperors of Brazil, father and son.

Pedro I (1798-1834), also **Pedro IV** of Portugal, was the son of King John VI of Portugal. He was born in Lisbon, but in 1807 fled to Brazil with the royal family to escape the invading French troops. In 1821, he was named regent of Brazil. The next year, Brazil declared its independence and Pedro became emperor under the new constitution. But he could not rule according to the constitution, and gave up

The Large, Foot-Powered Pedicab has been a popular and dependable taxicab in cities in the Orient for several years.

Three Lions

the throne in 1831 in favor of his son, Pedro II.

Pedro II (1825-1891) was crowned emperor of Brazil in 1841. Although only 15 years old, he soon controlled his country. He gained wide respect as a moderate and humane ruler. Under him, Brazil took part in the overthrow of the Argentine dictator, Juan Manuel de Rosas. In 1867, Pedro opened the Amazon River to world commerce.

Chicago Historical Society
Pedro II

Between 1871 and 1888, Pedro's government passed a series of acts abolishing slavery in Brazil. This action cost the emperor the support of the great landowners. In 1889, the army ousted him and formed a republic. Pedro was born in Rio de Janeiro. DONALD E. WORCESTER

See also ANDRADA E SILVA, JOSÉ BONIFÁCIO DE; BRAZIL (Independence and Empire).

PEDRO MIGUEL LOCKS. See PANAMA CANAL (The Pedro Miguel and Miraflores Locks).

PEDROLINO. See PIERROT.

PEDUNCLE. See RACEME.

PEE DEE, or **YADKIN, RIVER** rises as the Yadkin River in the Blue Ridge Mountains of North Carolina. It becomes the Pee Dee River after it passes through a series of lakes which form the western boundary of Uharie National Forest, and after flowing across the North Carolina Piedmont. The combined river flows 435 miles southeast to empty into Winyah Bay, on the South Carolina coast. The Little Pee Dee River of eastern South Carolina is a tributary. Electric-power plants on the Pee Dee and Yadkin rivers are a chief source of power in the Carolinas. For location, see NORTH CAROLINA (physical map).   HUGH T. LEFLER

PEEL, SIR ROBERT (1788-1850), was a famous British statesman. He founded the London police force in 1829. The police have been called "bobbies," after Peel's nickname, ever since.

Peel was born near Bury, the son of a wealthy textile manufacturer. He was educated at Harrow School and at Christ Church, Oxford University, where he won honors in classics and mathematics. When he was 21, he made his brilliant first speech in the House of Commons. This speech led to his appointment as under secretary for war and the colonies.

From 1812 to 1818, as chief secretary, Peel ruled Ireland with a firm hand. He maintained order by establishing an Irish police force, whose members were commonly called "Peelers." His strong opposition to a measure permitting Roman Catholics to vote kept that proposal from becoming law until 1829. Such personal bitterness over the measure grew up between Peel and Daniel O'Connell, the Irish leader, that the two nearly fought a duel.

In 1819 Peel headed a commission to study British currency. He recommended important reforms which gave Great Britain a sounder currency system. He became home secretary in 1822, but resigned in 1827 when George Canning became prime minister, because they disagreed on the Roman Catholic question. In 1828, Peel returned to office under the duke of Welling-

ton. Peel organized the London police force in 1829 to aid in enforcing the criminal code, which he helped revise and reform. In the same year the political situation caused him to change his mind on the Roman Catholic question. He helped prepare and pass the Catholic Emancipation Act, which gave voting rights to Roman Catholics.

Starts Conservative Party. Peel went out of office again in 1830 when the duke of Wellington's ministry fell. He opposed the Reform Bill, designed to give the vote to more persons and better representation to new industrial towns. As a member of the minority opposition in the House of Commons, he formed the Conservative party from the old Tory party. Although the party was conservative in regard to the British constitution, Peel labored to make the party concerned with the nation's welfare.

Chicago Historical Society
Sir Robert Peel

As leader of the Conservative party, Peel became prime minister for a short time in 1834. He became prime minister again in 1841, and remained in this office until 1846.

Prime Minister. Under his leadership, certain important tax reforms were made. Circumstances caused him to change his mind in regard to the Corn Laws, which worked to the advantage of landowners by keeping food prices high. In 1842, Peel caused the laws to be amended so that prices would be lower. Then a famine in Ireland, which also resulted in great hardship in England, led him to favor the complete repeal of the Corn Laws. He admitted that he could no longer answer the arguments of Richard Cobden of the Anti-Corn Law League, and he argued for free trade (see CORN LAWS). Soon after the Corn Laws were repealed in 1846, Peel went out of office.   JAMES L. GODFREY

PEEPER. See TREE FROG.

PEER GYNT. See GRIEG, EDVARD; IBSEN, HENRIK.

PEERAGE. See NOBILITY.

PEERCE, JAN (1904-   ), became one of the most successful American opera and concert tenors of his day. His faultless musicianship won praise from Arturo Toscanini and other leading conductors. Peerce was the tenor in several of the famous Toscanini-NBC opera radio broadcasts. The broadcasts were later transferred to commercial recordings. Peerce's excellent though not spectacular voice retained its power even when he was more than 60 years old.

Peerce was born in New York City. His real name was JACOB PINCUS PERELMUTH. Peerce played the violin in dance orchestras before he became a tenor at Radio City in 1933. He made his operatic debut in 1937 in Philadelphia as the duke in Giuseppe Verdi's *Rigoletto*. Peerce appeared in a New York recital in 1939, and made his debut with the Metropolitan Opera in 1941 in Verdi's *La Traviata*.   MAX DE SCHAUENSEE

PEEWEE. See WOOD PEEWEE.

PEEWIT. See LAPWING.

PEGASUS

Palazzo Spada, Rome (Anderson from Art Reference Bureau)

Pegasus, the Winged Horse, is watered by his master Bellerophon in this marble bas-relief by an unknown artist.

PEGASUS is a constellation of the Northern Celestial Hemisphere, found well up in the evening sky of autumn.

A large square called *The Great Square of Pegasus* marks it in the sky. A line drawn down the east side of the square and extended an equal distance south indicates the point where the sun stands on March 21, the day spring begins. The name *Pegasus* comes from the mythical Greek winged horse that was turned into a constellation by the god Zeus. I. M. LEVITT

See also ANDROMEDA.

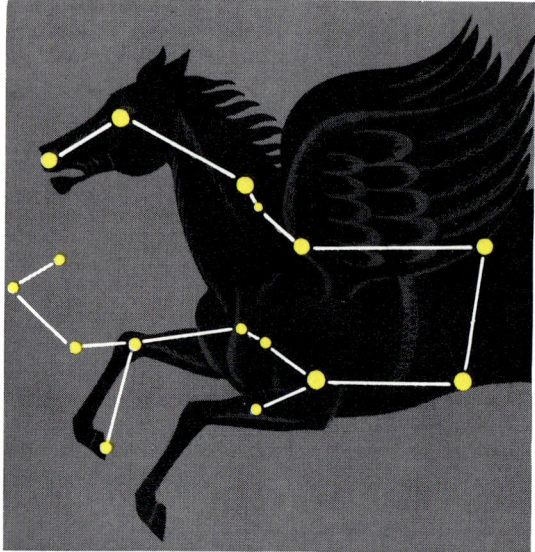

The Constellation Pegasus, the Winged Horse

PEGASUS, *PEG uh sus,* was a winged horse in Greek mythology. Perseus, a son of Zeus, cut off the head of the Gorgon Medusa, and Pegasus was born from the trickling blood. The horse flew up to join the gods, and was caught by the goddess Athena. Athena tamed the horse with a golden bridle.

Athena gave this bridle to Bellerophon before he started out to fight the Chimaera. Bellerophon also tamed Pegasus with it, and rode the winged horse to conquer the Chimaera and the Amazons. But Bellerophon became proud. Pegasus threw Bellerophon off and flew into the sky. Zeus made the horse into a constellation.

Another legend about Pegasus is that the Muses were holding a contest of song. The music charmed the streams and made Mount Helicon grow toward the heavens. The god Poseidon ordered Pegasus to make it stop growing by striking it with his hoof. Pegasus did this, and the fountain Hippocrene sprang forth. Its waters inspired people to write poetry. Two other fountains of inspiration, Aganippe and Pirene, were also made by the hoof of Pegasus. In this way, Pegasus is connected with poetry. A poet is said to *mount his Pegasus* when he begins to write. H. LLOYD STOW

See also CHIMAERA.

PEGMATITE. See BERYL; FELDSPAR.

PEIPING. See PEKING.

PEIPUS, LAKE. See LAKE PEIPUS.

PEIRCE, CHARLES SANDERS (1839-1914), an American philosopher, logician, and scientist, founded the philosophical system called *pragmatism*. This philosophy teaches that the meaning and value of ideas can be found only in their practical results.

Later, another philosopher, William James, adapted Peirce's theories to his own system of pragmatism, and Peirce changed the name of his original system to *pragmaticism*. James once called Peirce "the most original thinker of his generation" (see JAMES, WILLIAM; PRAGMATISM).

Peirce was born in Cambridge, Mass., the son of Benjamin Peirce, then considered one of America's leading mathematicians. The boy received his early education from his father, who trained him in the fundamental principles of mathematics and logical reasoning. When Peirce was 8, he began to study chemistry, and a few years later set up his own chemical laboratory. He was graduated from Harvard University when he was only 19. He later did graduate work at Harvard and received his master's degree there in 1862.

In 1861, Peirce joined the staff of the United States Coast Survey, and remained associated with it for 30 years. In addition to other duties, he was in charge of the coast survey's investigations of the earth's gravity. He did original work on the use of precise pendulums in gravity determinations. He also studied at the Harvard Observatory, where he collected material for his book *Photometric Researches* (1878). This was his only book published during his lifetime.

During these years, Peirce's interest in philosophy and logic continued to grow. He lectured at Harvard and Johns Hopkins universities and Bryn Mawr College on philosophy, the philosophy of science, and logic. In 1866, he became interested in Boolean algebra, a method of dealing with logical reasoning by means of algebraic symbols. He wrote many papers on this subject and other branches of logic. After Peirce's death, many unpublished papers were found in his study. A number of these papers were published as *Collected Papers* (1931-1934).　　　　　　　　G. Gamow

PEIXOTO, FLORIANO. See Brazil (The Republic).

PEKING, *PEA KING* (pop. 4,010,000; alt. 165 ft.), is one of the most beautiful cities in China. The original plan of the city has not changed since ancient times. The old walled cities that make up Peking still house some of the richest treasures of Chinese civilization. The city has been the capital of China most of the time since A.D. 1403. The word *Peking* means *northern capital*. In 1928, the Nationalist government was established in Nanking. Peking was renamed *Peiping*, which means *northern pacification*. In 1949, the Communists gained control of China and established their government in Peiping, once again named Peking. They introduced many modern ways of life to the city. But the people kept their love of Chinese ritual and tradition.

Description. Peking lies on a sandy plain, about 12 miles west of the Pei River and nearly 100 miles from the Gulf of Chihli. For location, see China (map).

Peking was originally divided into two parts—the *Inner City* (Manchu City) and the *Outer City* (Chinese City). The Inner City also included the Imperial and Forbidden cities. The Manchu emperors used the Inner City chiefly for their courts, and the Chinese people lived in the Outer City. The Communists have made many changes in the physical appearance of Peking since 1949. They have torn down some of the walls that divided the Inner and Outer cities. But people still use these old names when describing Peking.

The Inner City was built in a square, with each side about four miles long. Walls 50 feet high enclosed the city. They were broken by 10 huge gates and dotted with 10-story defense towers. One of the largest buildings in the Inner City is the Hall of Examinations. Scholars who wished to become government officials took examinations in the hall's 10,000 tiny rooms.

The Inner City still has many famous temples. The best known of these are the Confucius Temple and the Lama Temple. A statue of Buddha, about 70 feet high, stands near the Lama Temple. The Hall of Classics is nearby. Writings of old Chinese literature are carved on its walls.

Two other cities stood within the Inner City. One was the *Imperial City*, surrounded by its own wall 5 miles long. It now includes the offices of the government. The Imperial City also has three lakes, *Peihai* (North Sea), *Chunghai* (Central Sea), and *Nanhai* (South Sea). Coal Hill, a man-made hill 160 feet high, stands near the shore of Peihai. Trees and pagodas cover the hill.

The other part of the Inner City was the *Forbidden City*, which stood within the Imperial City. The Imperial Palace was in the Forbidden City. Only members

Ewing Galloway

Triple Arches form this delicately carved stone gate on the walk that leads to the Hall of Classics in Peking, China. For thousands of years, the Chinese have been skillful stone carvers. Stone carving is one of their most ancient arts.

of the imperial household could enter it. It is now open to the public, and part of it has been turned into the *Working People's Palace of Culture*. *Tien An Men* (Gate of Heavenly Peace), the entrance to the Imperial Palace, has been widened. Communist rallies and mass meetings are held in the square in front of the gate. Many impressive structures stand in this area, the Monument to the People's Heroes, the Working People's Palace of Culture, the Museum of the Chinese Revolution, the Museum of Chinese History, and the Peking Library. One of the grand new structures in the remodeled city is the Soviet Exhibition Center.

The Outer City stood outside of the Inner City's southern wall. The Outer City had its own walls, which measured about 10 miles around. The blue-domed Temple of Heaven stands in the Outer City. The emperor used to worship on New Year's Day at the altar within the Temple of Heaven.

Culture. Peking is the home of Tsinghua, Peking, Peking Normal, and the Chinese People's universities. The city also houses the Central College of Finance and Economics, the Peking College of Political Science and Law, the College of Diplomacy, and about 20 other institutions of higher learning.

Industry and Trade. The city has long been an intellectual and cultural center, rather than an industrial city. But the Communists have encouraged development of industry in Peking. Today, the city has machine shops, textile mills, and a nearby blast furnace. There are cotton and flour mills, and factories that produce agricultural machinery, electrical equipment, iron and steel, and machine tools. Workers in small shops make tapestries, porcelain, and tile. Glass, silk, and cigarettes are also produced.

Peking, a railroad and trading center, serves as the distributing point for the products of Manchuria, Mongolia, and all northern China. Five railroads lead from the city. One goes to Nanking and Shanghai, one to Hankow, one to Kalgan, and two to Manchuria.

History. Peking was a city as far back as 1000 B.C., and has been the capital of several Chinese kingdoms. It was the capital of the Chin dynasty in the A.D. 1100's. Its selection as capital was based on its strategic location. The city lies on a broad plain, and was easy to defend in old-style warfare. It is only 30 miles south of the Great Wall of China, and guarded the route by which China was often invaded.

In A.D. 1264, Kublai Khan and his Mongol hordes invaded China. Kublai Khan picked Peking as his capital, and laid out and built the city in its present design. Marco Polo told of the city in his stories about his trip to China. The Ming emperors used Peking as their capital after 1421, and added to the walls that surrounded it. It was also the capital of the Manchu emperors from 1644 until 1912.

Britain and France made war on China in 1860, and their troops occupied the city. In 1901, foreign troops fought their way from Tientsin to Peking to rescue the foreign embassies which were under siege during the Boxer Rebellion. After the Chinese Revolution in 1912, Peking was for a time the seat of several temporary governments, and war lords fought for control of the city. In 1928, Nanking became the capital of the Chi-

nese Republic. Peking's name was changed to Peiping. A clash between Chinese and Japanese troops on July 7, 1937, at Marco Polo Bridge, a few miles south of the city, started the Chinese-Japanese War. The Japanese quickly occupied Peking and held it until the end of World War II. It became the capital of Communist China on Oct. 1, 1949.

After the Communists took over Peking, they built many new homes, hotels, offices, and other buildings. The government is also enforcing a strict sanitation system. The city has a new railway station that can accommodate about 14,000 people.   THEODORE H. E. CHEN

See also CHINA (pictures).

PEKING MAN is the name of an ancient type of human being who lived in northern China about a million years ago. Scientists originally called him *Sinanthropus pekinensis* (Chinese man of Peking). But many now consider him to be *Homo erectus pekinensis* (erect man of Peking), the ancestor of the Mongoloid race. In 1927, Davidson Black, a Canadian anatomist, found a tooth near Peking, China. He found the top of a skull in 1929. Scientists later discovered more bones of the same kind. These bones are heavy, and indicate that Peking man was a little more than 5 feet tall, and stood upright. The skulls have heavy brow ridges. The brain was smaller than that of modern man. In 1941, the bones disappeared while being shipped out of China for safekeeping.   CARLETON S. COON

See also PREHISTORIC MAN (picture: Peking Man); CAVE DWELLERS.

PEKINGESE, *PEE king EEZ*, is a small dog with long hair, a broad flat face, and a tail that curls over its back. It is one of the three Chinese breeds of dogs with curled tails. The others are the chow chow and the pug.

The Pekingese has short legs, a long body, and a large head with long-fringed ears. Its front legs are bowed, and its tail is plumed. Its eyes are quite prominent. When the Pekingese trots, it sways from side to side somewhat as the bulldog does. It may be almost any color, but is usually tan or brown with light shadings. In size, it ranges from 6 pounds to 10 pounds. One kind of Pekingese, the *sleeve Pekingese*, was so named because ladies of the Chinese court carried the dogs in their balloonlike sleeves.

The Pekingese was the royal dog of China, and at one time only people of royal blood could own the dog. It was raised in China for many hundreds of years, but the outside world did not know of the dog until 1860, when the British Army seized Peking and Admiral Lord Hayes took two Pekingese to England. The Pekingese is a mischievous, intelligent animal. In spite of its small size, it is bold and brave.   JOSEPHINE Z. RINE

See also DOG (color picture: Toy Dogs).

PEKOE. See TEA.

PELAGIAN HERESY, *puh LAY juhn*, is the name given to theological doctrines proposed by the British monk Pelagius (who died after A.D. 418). Condemned by church councils in the 400's and 500's, it exaggerated the natural powers of man. Denying that God raised human nature to a *super*-natural level, it claimed that the grace of God is needed merely to help man do good more easily. Denying original sin, it held that the sin of Adam infected the human race only as bad example. The redemption of Jesus had value not in itself but only by way of good example. Semi-Pelagianism modified some of these doctrines to say that the grace of God is not necessary for man to begin a supernatural conversion to God. The chief opponents of these heresies were Saint Augustine and his followers.   FRANCIS L. FILAS

See also AUGUSTINE, SAINT.

PELAGIUS, *pea LAY jih us,* was the name of two popes of the Roman Catholic Church.

Pelagius I (?-A.D. 561), a Roman nobleman, was deacon of the Roman Church in the early part of the A.D. 500's. He cooperated closely with Pope Agapetus I and Pope Vigilius. During Vigilius' absence in Constantinople, Pelagius governed the Roman Church from 546 to 551. Pelagius also had to deal with Totila when that Gothic chieftain sacked Rome in 546. Pelagius succeeded Vigilius as pope in 556.

Pelagius II (?-A.D. 590) was elected to succeed Pope Benedict I in 578 or 579. He appealed to the Byzantine emperor for help against the invading Lombards, and also enlisted the aid of the Franks in the same cause. He built and restored many churches in the city of Rome, and lived to see the conversion of the Visigoths to Roman Catholicism in 589. Pelagius was born in Rome.   GUSTAVE WEIGEL and FULTON J. SHEEN

PELÉ (1941-   ) won fame in the 1960's as the world's greatest soccer player. He was the world's highest salaried athlete in the 1960's, earning over $200,000 a year. An inside left forward, Pelé electrified crowds with his daring dribbling, perfect passing, and accurate shooting. He holds every major scoring record in Brazil, and has averaged almost a goal a game in international competition.

Pelé was born EDSON ARANTES DO NASCIMENTO in Três Coracões, Brazil. Pelé joined the Santos (Brazil) Football Club in 1956. He led the Brazilian national team to World Soccer Cup championships in 1958 and 1962. He led Santos to world club titles in 1962 and 1963.   HERMAN WEISKOPF

PELECYPOD. See MOLLUSK (Bivalves).

PELÉE, MONT. See MONT PELÉE.

PELELIU, *PEL uh lyoo,* or, popularly, *PEL uh LEE oo,* is a narrow raised reef island in the Western Pacific. It is in the Palau group of the Western Caroline Islands, about 600 miles east of the Philippines. Both Germany, which owned the island from about 1899 until World War I, and Japan, which held it under a League of Nations mandate until World War II, mined phosphate on Peleliu.

The Japanese used Peleliu as a military base, and dug caves in the soft coral rock for use in defense. U.S. Marines landed on Peleliu on Sept. 15, 1944, expecting a short campaign. They captured the airfield within a week. But the defenders retreated into their caves on the main ridge of the island and fought on. Organized resistance on Peleliu ended by November 25. But the last soldiers on the island did not surrender until February, 1945.

Since the end of World War II, the United States has administered Peleliu as Pacific Islands Trust Territory. About 740 people live there. The island has an area of about 5 square miles.   EDWIN H. BRYAN, JR.

See also PALAU ISLANDS.

PELEUS. See ACHILLES.

PELIAS. See ARGONAUTS.

PELICAN, *PEHL ih kun,* is a large water bird with a naked pouch on the underside of its bill and the front of the upper neck. The pelican is almost voiceless. It is the world's largest web-footed bird. The Australian pelican lives in Australia, New Zealand, and New Guinea. North America has both white and brown pelicans.

The American white pelican weighs about 16 pounds, and is about 5 feet long. It has a wingspread of 8 to 10 feet. The feathers on its body are snowy white, and the tips of the wings are black.

This bird nests in colonies in the western states and Canada. Many breed on islands in the salt lakes of Utah and Nevada. In winter the white pelican is found along the coast in California and the Gulf Coast, and the marshy lakes of the South.

The enormous elastic pouch attached to the pelican's bill can hold several quarts of water. The bird does not store food in this pouch, as many persons believe. The pelican uses it as a scoop to catch small fish, which are then swallowed and carried in the stomach.

Both young and old pelicans have large appetites. The bird feeds its young by passing partly digested food from its stomach back up into the pouch. The young pelican puts its head deep into the parent's pouch to get this food.

Pelicans live in large colonies and often help each other catch fish. White pelicans swim together in a line, beating the water with their wings. They drive their prey ahead of them, while they scoop and capture the fish with open bills, sweeping them into the pouch.

During the breeding season of the white pelican, a horny triangle grows on the top of the bill of both male

The Pelican plunges with open bill into a school of small fish, scoops one up in his pouch, and swallows it immediately.

William LaVarre, Gendreau

Sawders

From Their Perch on Piling off the Florida Coast, These Expert Fishermen Watch the Water with Sharp Eyes.

and female. The birds usually build their nests on the shores of an island in an inland lake. The nest is made of earth, gravel, and sand, with twigs placed roughly on top. The female pelican lays from one to four dull white eggs.

The brown pelican fishes by diving from the air. Sometimes it plunges beneath the surface. Brown pelicans nest in colonies on the ground or in low trees. Pelicans are swift swimmers and strong, graceful fliers. Some kinds of pelicans can stay in the air for hours. They are awkward on land.

In 1903, the United States government set aside Pelican Island in Florida as a pelican refuge. The island is in the Indian River near Sebastian. There are several other bird reserves in the West with great flocks of these curious birds.

An old legend says that when there is no food, the pelican tears her breast and feeds her young with her own blood. This story made the bird a symbol of charity, mother love, and self-sacrifice as well as a religious symbol. Louisiana, nicknamed the Pelican State, uses a seal that pictures a pelican feeding its young.

Scientific Classification. The pelican belongs to the family *Pelecanidae*. The Australian pelican is genus *Pelecanus*, species *conspicillatus*. The American white pelican is *P. erythrorhynchos*. The European white pelican is *P. onocrotalus*. The eastern brown is *P. occidentalis*, subspecies *carolinensis*, and the California brown is *P. occidentalis californicus*.   ALEXANDER WETMORE

See also BIRD (color picture, Water Birds).

PELICAN FLOWER is a strange flowering vine that grows in the tropics. The flower may be 18 inches wide. It is made up of a large greenish-yellow tube that starts downward, then bends up and out. The edges flare out in the shape of a shield that has purple veins and spots. The shield ends in a long, dangling "tail" which may extend 3 feet or more. The flower bud looks something like a pelican.

Scientific Classification. The pelican flower is in the birthwort family, *Aristolochiaceae*. It is genus *Aristolochia*, species *grandiflora*.   H. D. HARRINGTON

PELICAN STATE. See LOUISIANA.

PELION, *PEE lih un*, is a mountain in Thessaly in Greece. In ancient times, it was thought to be the home of the centaur Chiron who lived in a cave near its top. The ship *Argo* was built from trees that grew on its sides. Pelion lies between Volo and the east coast, and rises 5,305 feet above the sea. According to Greek mythology, the Giants took Pelion and piled it on top of another mountain named Ossa. They were trying to climb to Olympus, home of the gods. See also ARGONAUTS; CENTAUR.   PADRAIC COLUM

PELLAGRA, *puh LAY gruh*, is a disease caused by a lack of niacin and the vitamin-B complex in the diet (see VITAMIN [Vitamin-B Complex]). These substances are found in fresh beef and yeast, as well as in many other protein foods. Persons who live mostly on corn, which has a high starch and sugar content, and do not eat much meat protein are likely to get pellagra. This disease was once common in the southern United

States. It now occurs in Italy, Egypt, parts of France and Spain, and in the Caribbean countries.

A person who has pellagra is tired and nervous. His skin is usually pale. After being in the sun, he usually has bright-red blotches on his skin. This leaves the skin thick and rough. The patient also suffers from indigestion, diarrhea, and constipation. The tongue becomes red and swollen, and the throat may burn. Cases of pellagra that are not treated can lead to insanity.

Pellagra is treated by changing the diet of the diseased person so that it includes certain portions of fresh lean beef and yeast. The new diet has enough of the important body-building foods and less sugar and starch. Sometimes niacin tablets are given. Joseph Goldberger of the United States Public Health Service proved that pellagra is caused by a dietary deficiency (see GOLDBERGER, JOSEPH). J. F. A. McMANUS

PELLEGRINA, LA. See GEM (Some Famous Gems).

PELOPIDAS, *pee LAHP ih dus,* was a general and statesman in ancient Thebes during the 300's B.C. In 382 B.C., the Spartans seized Thebes, and Pelopidas fled. Returning in 379 B.C., he drove the Spartans out and freed his homeland. With the aid of Epaminondas, another general, he trained the Thebans in military discipline and strategy. They formed a special group of 300 soldiers known as the *Sacred Band.* The two Theban generals defeated Sparta in the Battle of Leuctra in 371 B.C., and Thebes became the most powerful state in Greece. Pelopidas used his power to support democratic governments in other Greek cities. In 364 B.C., he was killed in battle. Epaminondas died in war two years later, and the Theban supremacy collapsed. THOMAS W. AFRICA

PELOPONNESIAN WAR, *PEHL oh puh NEE zhan,* was fought by the ancient Greek city-states of Athens and Sparta from 431 to 404 B.C. According to Thucydides, a Greek historian who lived during the war, the Peloponnesian League, consisting of Sparta and its allies, attacked the Athenian empire because it feared the growing power of Athens.

The war was divided into three parts: (1) *The Archidamian War* (431-421 B.C.) was named for Archidamus, the Spartan king who led annual attacks on Athens. Archidamus hoped to force the Athenians to surrender, but the Athenian navy and walls successfully defended the city. (2) *The Peace of Nicias* (421-413 B.C.) was named for the peace arranged by Nicias, an Athenian politician. The peace was broken when Athenian commander Alcibiades persuaded Athens to attack the Peloponnesian League in 418 B.C. and Sicily in 415 B.C. Both attacks failed. (3) *The Decelean or Ionian War* (413-404 B.C.) ended in victory for Sparta. Sparta gained the support of Persia, helped subjects of Athens revolt, and forced Athens to surrender. DONALD KAGAN

See also ALCIBIADES; ATHENS; PERICLES; SPARTA.

PELOPONNESUS, *PEHL oh puh NEE sus,* is the ancient name of the southern peninsula of Greece. In medieval times, the area became known as Morea, and it is sometimes still called by that name. Ancient Peloponnesus was divided into six districts: Messenia, Argolis, Laconia, Elis, Arcadia, and Achaea. NORMAN A. DOENGES

See also ACHAEAN; ARCADIA; LACONIA; MESSENIA.

PELOPS. See TANTALUS.

PELOTA. See JAI ALAI.

PELT. See FUR (pictures).

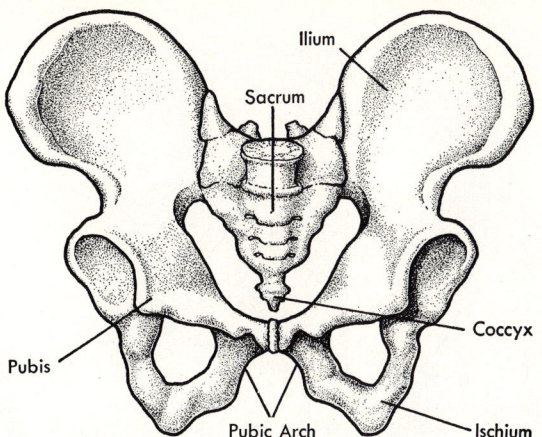

The Bones of the Pelvis Form a Basinlike Structure.

PELVIC GIRDLE. See SKELETON.

PELVIS is the framework of bones that supports the lower part of the abdomen. It surrounds the reproductive organs and those organs that eliminate body wastes, such as the urinary bladder and lower intestine. A female's pelvis is flatter and broader than a male's, and it has a larger central cavity. This central opening forms part of the birth canal in the female through which babies are born.

The spinal column extends upward from the top of the pelvis. The *femurs* (thigh bones) connect to the lower part of the pelvis in large ball-and-socket joints that allow the legs to move in many directions. When a person stands, these joints bear the entire weight of the trunk and upper body. Many large muscle masses lead from the pelvis to the femurs.

Two big, symmetrical hipbones form the pelvis. These bones join in front to form the *symphysis pubis.* In back, they form a strong union with the *sacrum* (five backbones joined to form a single bone). Each hipbone in an adult appears to be one solid bone. But it is formed by three bones, the *ilium, ischium,* and *pubis,* that unite as the body matures. The ilium is the broad, flat bone you feel when you rest your hand on the hip. When you sit down, much of your weight rests on the ischium. The pubis bones form two arches in front that join at the symphysis. GORDON FARRELL

PEMBINA. See NORTH DAKOTA (Exploration and Early Settlement).

PEMBROKE STATE COLLEGE. See UNIVERSITIES AND COLLEGES (table).

PEMMICAN, *PEHM ih kun,* was one of the first forms of concentrated food. The North American Indians made pemmican by drying buffalo or deer meat and pounding it into a powder. The powdered meat was then mixed with hot fat. When the mass of fat and meat cooled, it was cut into cakes. Sometimes berries were added to the mixture to give it flavor. Pemmican is tough and not too tasty, but it keeps almost indefinitely and does not take up much room. A small bag of it would keep a person alive for days.

Today, explorers, surveyors, hunters, and others who must make long trips into regions where there are no supplies, often take pemmican with them. Pemmican is now usually made of beef. The people of South America make *tasajo,* which is much like pemmican, as is the *biltong* of South Africa. LEONE RUTLEDGE CARROLL

207

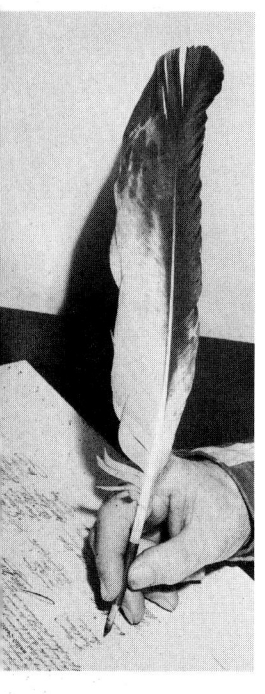

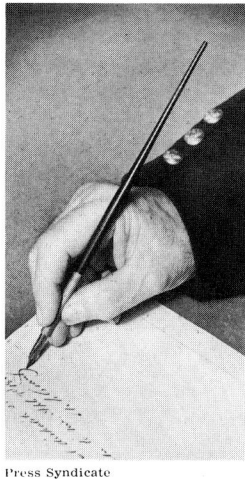

Press Syndicate

Pens of Long Ago. The quill pen, *left*, dates from the period of the American Revolution. The steel pen, *above*, was used by General Ulysses S. Grant to sign the treaty ending the Civil War.

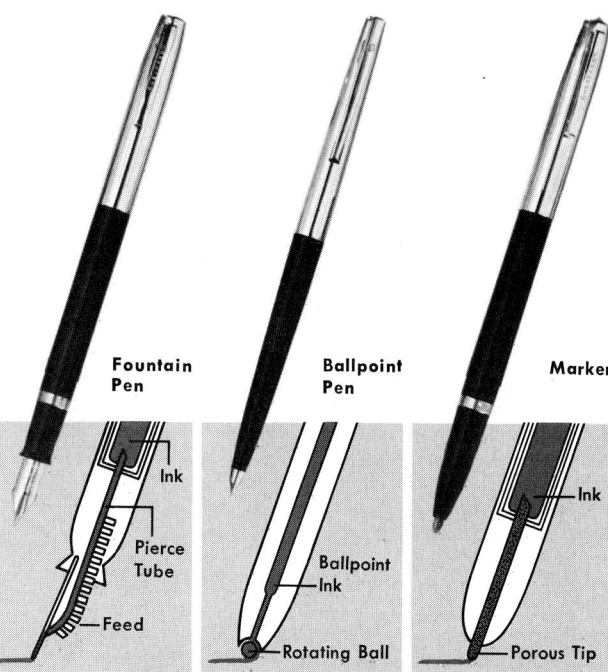

Fountain Pen   Ballpoint Pen   Marker

Ink · Pierce Tube · Feed · Ballpoint Ink · Rotating Ball · Ink · Porous Tip

W. A. Sheaffer Pen Co.

PEN is an instrument used to write or draw with ink or some other fluid. It is one of man's oldest and most important communication tools. Throughout history, people have used pens to carry on business and to record their ideas and the events of their time. Today, typewriters have replaced pens for most business correspondence, but pens are still widely used for personal writing and for signing business correspondence. In the United States alone, about $1\frac{1}{4}$ billion pens are sold every year.

All pens are instruments that allow ink to flow onto paper or other material in a controlled manner. Some old-fashioned pens must be continually dipped into ink. But most pens used today have a reservoir that holds a supply of ink. The three basic kinds of pens are (1) the slit *nib* (point), or fountain pen; (2) the ballpoint; and (3) the marker.

Fountain Pens. Any pen that carries its own ink supply is a fountain pen. But the term is usually used to refer only to such pens with slit nibs.

Most fountain pens hold their ink supply either in a disposable *cartridge* (container) made of plastic, or in a permanent container in the form of a rubber sac. These reservoirs are inside the pen's hollow *barrel* (frame). When a disposable cartridge runs dry, it can be removed and replaced with a new one. The rubber sac is filled by the vacuum method. The person filling the pen pulls on a lever in the barrel. This action presses the lever against the sac, forcing out most of the air. When the pen is dipped in ink and the lever is released, a vacuum forms and draws in the ink.

In all fountain pens, a system of tiny passages leads from the nib to the ink reservoir. These passages carry air into the space above the ink. The air permits ink to flow into a tube that leads to the writing point. Behind the point is a hard rubber or plastic part called a *feed*. If too much ink flows down, the ink will fill the comb-like slots of the feed rather than blot the paper. This extra ink is used up in writing before air will flow to the reservoir and release more ink. Most fountain pens have a cap that can be placed over the point when the pen is not in use. Capping helps reduce ink evaporation. It also protects the point from damage and prevents ink leakage.

Ballpoint Pens are the most widely used type of pen. Almost 85 per cent of all pens made in the United States are ballpoints. Ballpoints are convenient because they do not require frequent refilling, as some fountain pens do.

The ballpoint gets its name from the hard, tiny ball that is its writing tip. The ball is held in a socket below a tube leading from the ink supply. Slightly less than half of the ball sticks out below the socket. The ink wets the ball. As the pen moves across the paper, the ball rotates, thus transferring the ink from the ball to the paper.

The ball is made of a hard material, usually tungsten carbide or a metal. Some balls are made of ruby. Ballpoint ink is syrupy. It is stored in an open-ended tube or in a tube with a grease plug on top of the ink. The plug follows the ink down and keeps it from leaking out of the top of the reservoir.

Markers and Specialty Pens can be used to write on paper, metal, glass, plastic, and many other surfaces. The ink or other liquid flows from a cartridge or from an ink-soaked wick to a *porous tip* (one that soaks up liquid). The tip, often made of felt or plastic, is extremely flexible. The tip usually lets out a wider line of ink than ballpoints and fountain pens do. Markers work in much the same way as fountain pens. Marker ink is strongly colored and dries quickly.

Specialty pens are designed for specific purposes. Some specialty pens contain glue, watercolors, or invisible ink (see INK [Invisible Ink]).

History. The earliest writing tools probably included brushes and sharp pieces of metal or bone. As early as 300 B.C., the Greeks and Egyptians made pens from the hollow reeds of the calamus plant. They poured ink in the stem, and squeezed it onto a surface as needed.

About 50 B.C., men discovered that sharpened goose *quills* (large feathers) made excellent writing instruments. The word *pen* itself comes from the Latin *penna*, which means *feather*. Metal points, often called *nibs*, were later added to the quill. The nib tips did not wear out as fast as quill tips. Nib-tipped quill pens were widely used until the mid-1800's.

By 1650, some pens were made entirely of metal, sometimes with precious stones as the tip. By then, some pens held their own supply of ink. Steel nibs that could be inserted into a holder were invented about 1750. By 1850, pen manufacturers were using alloys of rhodium, osmium, and iridium to make very hard tips.

In 1884, Lewis Waterman, a U.S. inventor, introduced one of the first practical fountain pens. The pen was filled with ink squeezed from an eyedropper. In 1913, W. A. Sheaffer developed a lever-fill fountain pen. Disposable ink cartridges for fountain pens were developed in the 1920's.

John Loud of the United States invented a ballpoint pen during the 1880's. But the first commercially successful ballpoints were developed in the mid-1940's. Marker pens were introduced in 1951.   A. BRUCE CARLSON

PEN NAME is a fictitious name an author uses when he does not want to use his real name. Some authors use more than one pen name for different types of books. In early times, many writers used pen names because they feared their political writings might lead to punishment or death. Some writers use pen names to avoid publicity, as did Charles Dodgson, who wrote *Alice's Adventures in Wonderland* under the pen name of Lewis Carroll. See also PSEUDONYM.   ELSDON C. SMITH

PENAL COLONY. At one time, almost every country in the world sent its prisoners to colonies in other lands. Portugal had penal colonies throughout its colonial history. Most Portuguese criminals were sent to Ceuta, in North Africa. Criminals were sent to Hispaniola from Spain as early as 1497. Great Britain established penal colonies mostly as a substitute for galley labor. In spite of objections of the colonists, Britain sent many prisoners to Maryland and other American colonies. The Revolutionary War ended penal colonies in America. Then the British shipped criminals to Australia.

The best-known penal colony was Devil's Island in French Guiana. This French penal colony was started by Napoleon III in 1852. The prisoners at Devil's Island have been transferred or liberated, and this area is now being used as a housing project.

Penal colonies have been known for their brutal and inhuman treatment of prisoners. Men were chained together and brutally whipped. Today conditions have improved, but most penal colonies are still far from being modern institutions for punishment.   JOHN J. FLOHERTY

PENANCE. See ROMAN CATHOLIC CHURCH (The Sacraments).

PENANG. See MALAYA (History); MALAYSIA.

PENATES. See LARES AND PENATES.

PÉNAUD, ALPHONSE. See HELICOPTER (Early Experiments).

PENCE, plural of penny. See PENNY.

PENCIL is the most widely used tool for writing and drawing. It makes marks with *graphite* or some other material. The marking material is inside a wood, metal, or plastic case. Pencils are inexpensive and easy to carry, and their marks can be erased. The number of pencils sold each year is about double that of all other writing tools combined. More than 2 billion pencils are sold each year in the United States alone. This total equals about 10 pencils for each person in the country.

There are three main types of pencils: (1) wood-cased black *lead pencils;* (2) colored pencils; and (3) mechanical pencils.

Lead Pencils really contain no lead. The marking material is a mixture of the mineral graphite and fine clay combined with certain chemicals and wax. When graphite was first used in pencils, people thought it contained lead. Therefore, they called it *lead* or *black lead*. People still call the graphite mixture *lead* and the pencils *lead pencils*.

The amount of clay that pencil makers mix with graphite depends on how hard they wish to make the lead. The less clay they use, the softer and blacker the lead will be.

To make lead, workers blend the clay and graphite with water in a high-speed mixer. This mixture is placed in a machine and squeezed out of a narrow opening as one long black string of lead. The lead is cut into pieces about $7\frac{1}{4}$ inches long. The pieces are then hardened in firing ovens. Finally, the pieces of lead are treated with a wax so they will write smoothly.

The wood cases for most pencils are made of incense cedar. This wood has a soft, straight *grain* (pattern) that permits easy sharpening without splitting.

Workmen saw the cedar logs into *slats* (narrow strips) $7\frac{1}{4}$ inches long, $\frac{1}{4}$ inch thick, and $2\frac{3}{4}$ inches wide. The slats are heated in an oven to remove moisture. Then workers cut nine parallel grooves in each slat. Lead strips are laid in the grooves and another slat is glued on top, making a sort of "sandwich." The sandwich is then dried and cut into nine pieces, each in the shape of a pencil. Workers use machines to sand the pencils until they are smooth. Then they apply several coats of varnish to give the pencils a shiny finish. A machine then stamps the pencils with the name of the maker. Another machine cuts a small *shoulder* (rim) at one end of the pencil. Workers place a *ferrule* (brass ring) on the shoulder, put an eraser in the ferrule, and clamp the eraser in place.

Colored Pencils are made in much the same way as lead pencils. They also contain clay and wax, but the clay and wax are mixed with coloring materials called *pigments* and *dyes*, rather than with graphite. Colored leads made from dyes are widely used because their marks can be removed with soap and water.

Mechanical Pencils usually have a metal or plastic case. The leads used in mechanical pencils are similar to those used in wood-cased pencils. Mechanical pencils are convenient because they require no sharpening. A person forces lead out of the pointed end by turning the cap, or by some other mechanical method. The lead rests inside a *spiral* (round coil) inside the case and is held in place by a rod that has a stud (piece of metal)

HOW A LEAD PENCIL IS MADE

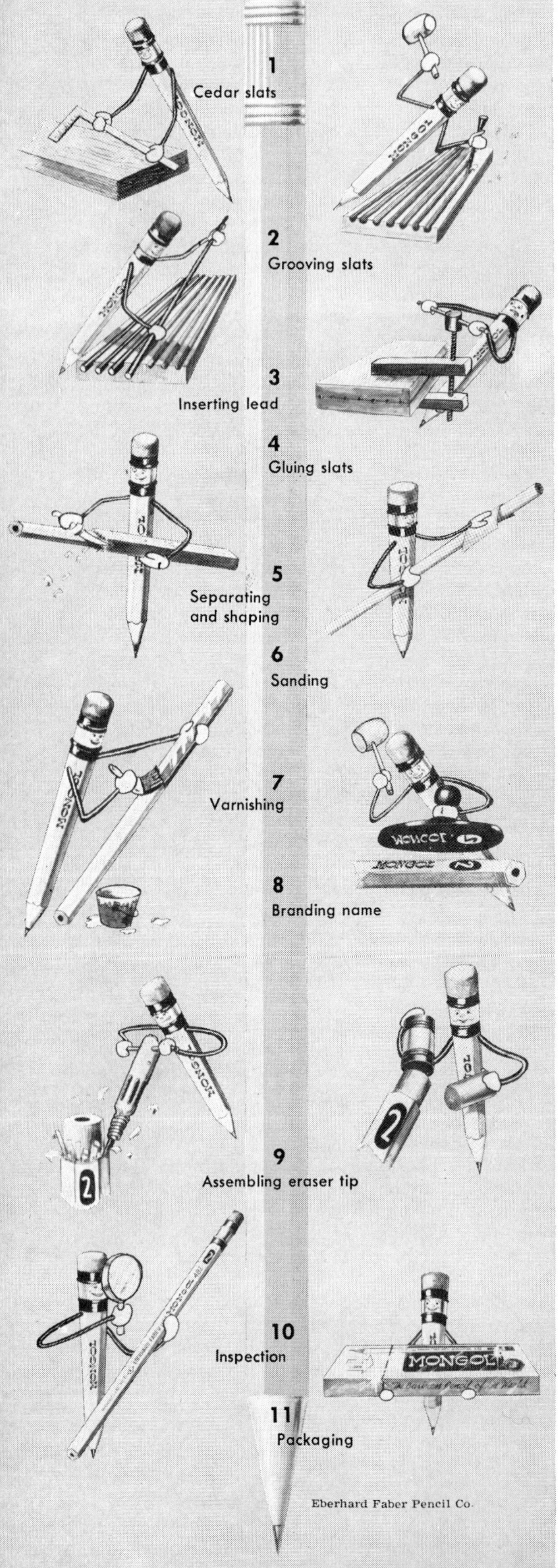

1 Cedar slats

2 Grooving slats

3 Inserting lead

4 Gluing slats

5 Separating and shaping

6 Sanding

7 Varnishing

8 Branding name

9 Assembling eraser tip

10 Inspection

11 Packaging

Eberhard Faber Pencil Co.

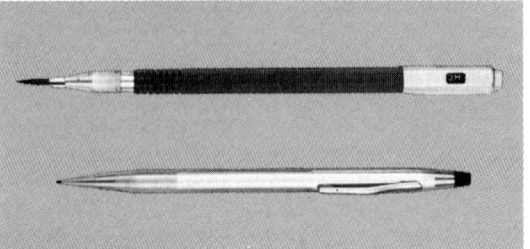

WORLD BOOK photo by E. F. Hoppe

Mechanical Pencils may hold a special drafting lead, *top*, or writing lead, *bottom*. Neither requires sharpening.

fastened to it. When one end of the pencil is twisted, the rod and stud move downward in the spiral. This action forces the lead toward the point. Some pencils are made so that the lead can be either pushed out or pulled back inside the frame.

History. The earliest writing tools probably included brushes made from plants. The word pencil itself comes from the Latin *pēnicillus*, which means *little tail* or *little brush*. The ancient Greeks and Romans first used pieces of lead as pencils shortly before the birth of Christ. These pencils made faint lines. The English made the first graphite pencils, in the mid-1500's. The Germans were the first to enclose the graphite in a wood case, about 1650. In 1795, Nicolas Jacques Conté of France developed a pencil-making process that is still used today. He discovered that he could bind powdered graphite together by mixing it with fine clay. He hardened the mixture by heating it to high temperatures.

In 1812, William Monroe of Concord, Mass., sold the first American-made pencils to a Boston hardware dealer. The first mechanical pencils were developed in the 1700's. The pencil industry became important in the United States during the Civil War (1861-1865). The demand for U.S.-made products—including pencils—increased after the Union navy blockaded Southern ports, preventing their import from Europe. Today, the United States is the world's leading manufacturer of pencils.   ERIC Q. BOHLIN and A. BRUCE CARLSON

See also ERASER; GRAPHITE.

PEND OREILLE LAKE, *PAHN duh RAY*, is the largest and deepest natural lake in Idaho. It lies in the northwestern part of the state. For location, see IDAHO (physical map). It covers 125 square miles, and is over 1,000 feet deep in several places. Albeni Falls Dam on the Pend Oreille River controls the lake's water level. Fishermen catch over a million fish a year in the lake, chiefly salmon.   HARRY H. CALDWELL

PENDENTIVE. See BYZANTINE ART (Architecture).

PENDERGAST, TOM. See TRUMAN, HARRY S. (Political Career).

PENDLETON, GEORGE HUNT (1825-1889), a United States senator, sponsored the Pendleton Act, which created the civil service system in 1883 (see CIVIL SERVICE [History]). A Democrat from Ohio, Pendleton served in the U.S. House of Representatives from 1857 to 1865, and in the U.S. Senate from 1879 to 1885. He was the Democratic party's candidate for Vice-President in 1864, but he lost the election. From 1885 to 1889, Pendleton served as minister to Germany. He was born in Cincinnati, Ohio.   JAMES H. RODABAUGH

PENDULUM, *PEN dyoo lum.* If an object that pivots around a fixed point is pulled aside and let go, gravity makes it swing back and forth at a regular rate. Such a body is called a *pendulum*. The simplest pendulum consists of a small weight hanging from a string. The path traveled by the weight is called the *arc*. The *period of vibration* is the time it takes the weight to pass back and forth once over this arc.

If a pendulum is taken from one place to another on the earth, the period will change slightly due to a change in the pull of gravity. The period increases if the pendulum is taken from sea level to the top of a mountain, because gravity becomes slightly weaker at greater heights. A simple pendulum about 9.78 inches long will have a period of 1 second at sea level. A pendulum 4 times as long will have a period of 2 seconds. One that is 9 times as long will have a period of 3 seconds, and so on.

The Italian physicist Galileo discovered the laws of the pendulum. He noticed that a hanging church lamp would swing with a constant period, whether the arc was large or small. He believed that a pendulum could be used to regulate the movements of clocks. The Dutch scientist Christian Huygens built the first pendulum clock in 1657.

Simple Pendulums, such as those used in clocks, usually consist of a rod with a heavy weight at one end and a hard bearing at the other. A screw at the end of the rod permits the weight, or *bob*, to be raised or lowered. When the bob is lowered, the pendulum swings slower, and the clock runs more slowly. When the bob is raised, the pendulum swings faster, and the clock runs faster. The bearing on which the pendulum swings must be as nearly frictionless as possible. It is often made of a knife edge of agate set in a grooved agate plate. The weight of the pendulum tends to make the bearing slip sideways as the pendulum swings. For this reason, pendulums are made long so that they beat slowly, and swing through a small arc.

Clock Pendulums. A device called an *escapement* is

PENDULUM

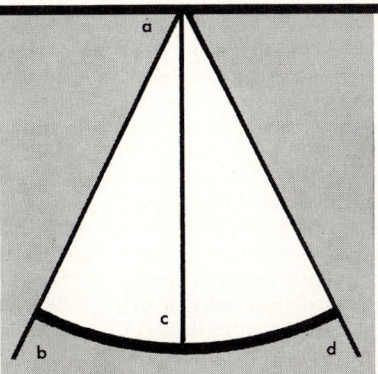

A **Simple Pendulum** swings back and forth on the fixed point *a*, and forms an arc between *b* and *d*. The time it takes to go from *b* to *d* and back to *b* is the pendulum's *period*.

Clock Pendulums have a weight at one end. Inside the clock, the *escapement* keeps the pendulum swinging by giving it small but regular pushes. Changes in temperature cause an ordinary pendulum to expand or contract, and can make a clock run faster or slower. Regulator clocks have gridiron pendulums, *lower right*, that consist of several brass and steel rods. Some rods expand upward and others downward to equalize the total length of the pendulum.

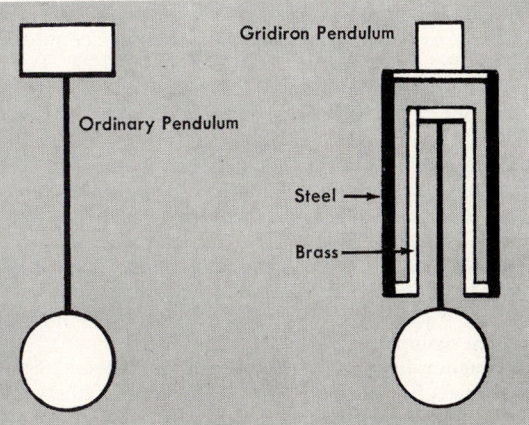

Newman-Schmidt

A **Foucault Pendulum,** *above,* shows the rotation of the earth. It swings in one direction in space. But the rotation of the earth makes the pendulum appear to change its direction of swing.

PENELOPE

fastened to the clock's mechanism. It gives small but regular pushes to the pendulum, and keeps it swinging. The escapement lets one tooth of a toothed-wheel turn past it at a time. It does this each time the pendulum swings aside. This action gives the familiar "tick-tock" sound to the clock.

The rod in a clock pendulum tends to expand when it is warm and to shorten when it is cold. This would make a clock run slower in warm weather than in cold. Clocks known as *regulators* come with so-called *gridiron* pendulums. These consist of several brass and steel rods so attached that some expand upward and some downward. This keeps the total length of the pendulum constant. In another device, the length is kept constant by the expansion and contraction of mercury in a cup which swings at the end of the rod.

Other Pendulums. A simple swinging pendulum is only one type of a much larger class of pendulums called *rotary pendulums*. When a pendulum going round and round is seen in the plane of its rotation, it seems to be swinging back and forth like an ordinary simple pendulum. The actions of rotary pendulums merge by imperceptible steps into ordinary wheel-like motions, or *revolutions. Torsion pendulums* are used in the so-called 400-day clocks. The pendulum is a vertical wire that becomes a spring when wound up. A weight attached to the wire creates a constant tension.

Another kind of pendulum is held up by two strings instead of by one. This is called a *bifilar* (pronounced *by FY lur) pendulum*. A form of bifilar pendulum was developed by Lord Kelvin as an excellent earthquake detector. A bifilar pendulum is very sensitive to variations of the *plumb line* (line toward the center of the earth). Bifilar pendulums show that the earth does not rotate on its axis smoothly, but speeds up and slows down very slightly. Such changes in rotation result from the pull of gravity exerted on the spinning earth by the sun and moon.

In 1851, the French scientist Jean Foucault hung a large iron ball on a wire about 200 feet long to show that the earth rotates. A Foucault pendulum swings in one direction in relation to space. But the earth turns under it, so the direction of the pendulum's movement in relation to the rotating earth changes at a regular rate. At the equator, a Foucault pendulum does not change its apparent direction at all. The change in apparent direction is fastest at the North Pole (see CORIOLIS FORCE).

One remarkable type of pendulum measures minute differences in the strength of gravity. It can detect a change of one part in a million. Geologists use it to detect underground mineral deposits.   IRA M. FREEMAN

See also CLOCK; FOUCAULT, JEAN B. L.; GALILEO; GRAVITATION; HUYGENS, CHRISTIAN.

PENELOPE, *pee NEL oh pee,* a legendary heroine of Greece, became famous for her faithfulness to her husband Ulysses (Odysseus). After the birth of their son Telemachus, Ulysses left on an expedition against Troy. He did not return for 20 years, but Penelope remained faithful to him.

Many suitors, hoping that Ulysses was dead, tried to persuade Penelope to marry again. For a time Penelope held the suitors off, giving the excuse that she must first

The Art Institute of Chicago
Penelope, the Wife of Ulysses, was considered a model of wifely virtue by the ancient Greeks because of her faithfulness.

weave a shroud for her father-in-law. Each day she worked on the shroud, and each night she unraveled the work she had accomplished during the day. When a maid servant revealed her trick, Penelope promised to select the suitor who could string Ulysses' great bow. Each suitor tried and failed.

A beggar, who came to the palace and was given shelter, asked to try. He easily strung the bow. The beggar was Ulysses in disguise. With the bow, he killed all the suitors. Ulysses then regained his palace and his kingdom.   O. M. PEARL

See also ODYSSEY; ULYSSES.

PENEPLAIN, *PEE nee PLAIN,* means *almost a plain.* A peneplain is the result of the leveling process that takes place between mountains and valleys through soil erosion. Waters that flow into rivers take soil from the hills and mountains and carry it into valleys. This raises the level of the valleys and lowers the height of the mountains. After many years of this process, the land becomes almost as flat as a plain. By the time the land has reached the peneplain stage, it has eroded as much as it can in this final stage in the cycle of erosion.

PENEUS. See AUGEAN STABLES; DAPHNE.

PENG TEH-HUAI (1900-   ) was Communist China's defense minister from 1954 to 1959. He served as commander in chief of the Chinese Communist forces in Korea in 1951, during the Korean War. In 1955, he became, by decree, a member of the Central Committee of the Politburo. However, in December, 1966, Peng was arrested and imprisoned in Peking. He was accused of opposing the ideas and policies of Mao Tse-tung, China's ruler.

Peng was born in Hsiangtan, in Hunan province. He rose through the ranks of the Kuomintang (Nationalist) army. But he deserted the army to join the Communists in 1928.   GEORGE E. TAYLOR

PENGUIN, *PEN gwin,* is an unusual bird that stands upright on very short legs and walks with an amusing, clumsy waddle. Penguins cannot fly, but they are excellent swimmers.

Penguins live in the southern half of the world. Several kinds live on the ice of the Antarctic. Others are found farther north in areas touched by cold sea currents that originate in Antarctica. There are penguin colonies in New Zealand, Australia, South Africa, and as far north as the Galapagos Islands, which lie almost on the equator. Penguins are not found in other areas of the world because they will not cross into warm ocean water from the cold Antarctic currents.

Penguins are popular attractions in zoos. But they are difficult to keep in captivity, because they catch diseases easily and die.

Appearance. All penguins have short, thick feathers on their stocky bodies. Their feathers are white on the belly and black or bluish black on the back. Some penguins have crests of long feathers on the sides of their heads and patches of brightly colored feathers on their short, thick necks.

Penguins lost the ability to fly millions of years ago. Their wings developed into flippers, which serve as paddles in the water. These flippers, and the webbed feet, make penguins marvelous swimmers and divers. Their short, dense feathers form a waterproof coat. Thick layers of fat keep them warm in cold water.

The largest penguin, the emperor penguin, stands about 4 feet high and weighs close to 100 pounds. The 17 other *species* (kinds) vary in size. The smallest species is only about 1 foot high.

Habits. Penguins eat fish. They spend much of their lives in water, but lay eggs and raise their young on land. While on land, they make their nests in enormous colonies called *rookeries*. A single rookery may contain as many as a million birds. Most species make their nests on bare ground or in grass. They lay their eggs in shallow hollows scraped in the dirt. A few species lay eggs in tunnels dug in the ground.

Emperor penguins have remarkable nesting habits.

Jean Rivolier

The Large Emperor Penguins hatch their eggs and raise their young on solid Antarctic ice fields during the long winter.

The female bird comes out of the ocean at the start of the Antarctic autumn. The female lays a single egg on bare ice, and immediately returns to the water. The male takes over the job of keeping the egg warm until it hatches. He rolls the egg onto his feet and covers it with the lower part of his belly, which has several rolls of fat.

Royal Penguins gather by the thousands on Macquarie Island every September to build nests and raise their young. The barren, rocky island, off the southeast coast of Australia, is a wild-life sanctuary for several kinds of penguins and seals.

Laird, Pix

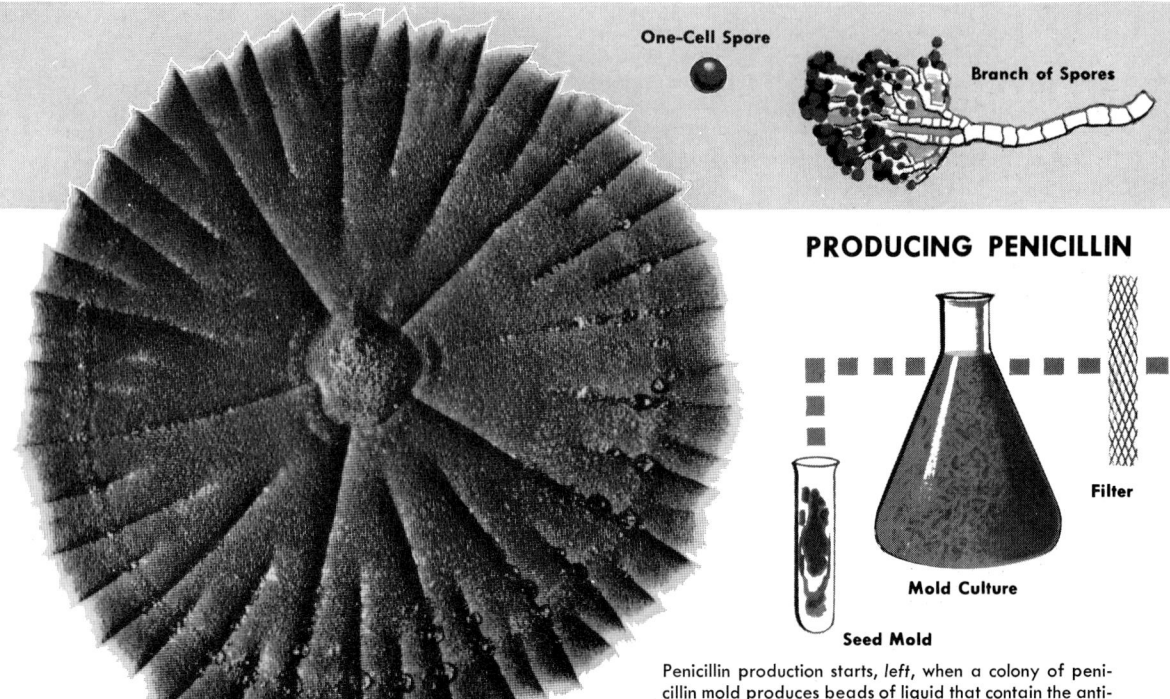

One-Cell Spore

Branch of Spores

PRODUCING PENICILLIN

Filter

Mold Culture

Seed Mold

Penicillin production starts, *left*, when a colony of penicillin mold produces beads of liquid that contain the antibiotic. The mold grows on a brothlike substance. Filters remove the mold and only liquid penicillin and broth remain. Further treatment removes all impurities. The substance that remains is dried to obtain pure penicillin powder.

Chas. Pfizer & Co., Inc.

Carrying the egg on his feet, the male penguin waddles into a large group with other males. The males huddle together to keep warm. For two months, during the worst part of the winter, the males keep the eggs warm. They do not eat during this period.

When the *chick* (young penguin) hatches, the male feeds it a milklike substance produced in his *crop* (throat). He feeds the chick through his mouth.

Soon after the chicks have hatched, the females return to the colony to care for them. The males then go to sea to get food for themselves and for the chicks. After three weeks, the males return to the colony with food. The chicks are herded together in tight groups. The adults form a circle around them to keep them warm. In six months, the young penguins are able to take care of themselves.

Scientific Classification. Penguins make up the penguin order, *Sphenisciformes* and the family *Spheniscidae*. The emperor penguin is genus *Aptenodytes*, species *A. forsteri*.   RAYMOND A. PAYNTER, JR.

See also ANIMAL (color picture: Animals of the Polar Regions); ANTARCTICA (Birds).

PENICILLIN, *PEN uh SILL in*, is a powerful *germicide* or germ killer, that is produced by molds belonging to the genus *Penicillium*.

Penicillin was the first substance from molds to be used for treating infectious diseases in man. Its success was so striking that it ushered in the "antibiotic age," for we now have many excellent similar drugs known as *antibiotics* (see ANTIBIOTIC).

What Penicillin Does. Many germicides can kill bacteria and other microorganisms. But nearly all kill equally well the cells that make up the body. This means they are poisonous and cannot be used in the body. But penicillin and other antibiotics are more harmful to certain germs than to body cells. Therefore, they can be used against these germs even while the germs are causing disease in the body. If penicillin can be applied directly to the infected part or conveyed there in the blood, it will kill the germs. The person then will be cured of his disease.

Not all harmful germs are affected by penicillin. It is not a "cure-all" for every infection. It is not at all effective against diseases that are not caused by germs, such as cancer. But most of the bacteria that cause common infections, such as those of the blood, are very sensitive to it.

How Penicillin Is Given. Doctors can put penicillin directly on an infection that occurs on the surface of the body. But when the disease is within the body, the drug must reach the infected part by way of the blood stream. Penicillin is destroyed in the stomach and intestine before it can reach the blood stream. Therefore, doctors usually inject a solution containing the drug into the muscles. But scientists have developed one form of penicillin, called penicillin V, that can be given by mouth.

Sensitivity. Although penicillin is the least poisonous antibiotic available, a few persons become sensitive, or *allergic*, to it. For these people, even tiny amounts of the drug cause great discomfort. Some persons are so sensitive to the drug that they would die if it were injected into their bodies. Persons who receive penicillin by mouth do not seem to develop a sensitivity to it.

Chas. Pfizer & Co., Inc.

Manufacturers place purified liquid penicillin in huge tanks, *right*, where it dries to a powder. To keep the penicillin free from impurities, workers wear masks and lint-free clothes.

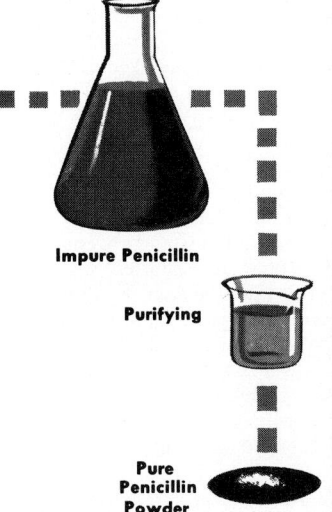

Impure Penicillin

Purifying

Pure
Penicillin
Powder

Resistance. Most bacteria can develop the capacity to grow even when an antibiotic is present. Doctors call these organisms *resistant*. The drug no longer affects them. Fortunately, this seldom happens with penicillin when it is given by a doctor. For he knows how much and how often the drug can be given safely. However, one bacterium, the staphylococcus, has many strains that naturally resist penicillin.

History. Penicillin was discovered in London in 1928 by Alexander Fleming. He found a mold growing on a culture of some common germs. Around the mold, these germs were dissolving. Fleming grew the mold on broth. Then he put drops of the broth in test tubes that contained some bacteria that cause disease. He found that the broth stopped the growth of these organisms. He called the broth *penicillin*. But later, the word was applied only to the active chemical substance that was formed in the broth. In 1940, Howard W. Florey of Australia and Ernst Chain of Great Britain reported on how penicillin could be purified for use.

Manufacture. Penicillin was first produced by growing *Penicillium notatum* on culture fluid or broth in bottles or pans, but the yield was small. Later, a better culture fluid was found. Then the mold was grown in the depths of the fluid, which was constantly stirred by a stream of air. This is called *deep culture*. Manufacturers use tanks that hold from 10,000 to 15,000 gallons for this process. Soon better strains of *Penicillium* were found. The *Penicillium* strains used by manufacturers produce about 5,000 times as much penicillin as the strain used originally by the researchers. In the United States alone, hundreds of tons of penicillin are made

every year. Although chemists have made penicillin in a laboratory without the mold, it is cheaper to let the mold do the work.   HOWARD WALTER FLOREY

See also CHAIN, ERNST B.; FLEMING, SIR ALEXANDER; FLOREY, LORD; MOLD.

PENINSULA, *pen IN syu luh*, is an area of land that is nearly surrounded by water. Some peninsulas, such as India, are joined to the mainland by a broad base. Others are connected by a narrow strip of land, called an *isthmus* (see ISTHMUS). The largest peninsula in the world is Arabia. It contains about 1,000,000 square miles.

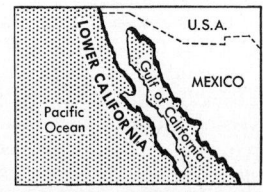

A Typical Peninsula, Lower California.

PENINSULA STATE. See FLORIDA.

PENINSULAR WAR. See NAPOLEON I (Dominates Europe); SPAIN (French Conquest).

PENITENTIARY. See PRISON (Kinds).

PENMANSHIP. See HANDWRITING.

PENN, JOHN (1740-1788), a North Carolina delegate to the Continental Congress from 1775 to 1780, was a signer of the Declaration of Independence. When Penn was 21, he received a license to practice law. He practiced successfully for about 12 years in Virginia. In 1774, he moved to North Carolina, where he became a Revolutionary leader and served as a member of the provincial congress. He returned to his law practice after the Revolutionary War. Penn was born in Caroline County, Virginia.   KENNETH R. ROSSMAN

Brown Bros.

William Penn Founded the Colony of Pennsylvania as a refuge from persecution for his fellow Quakers.

PENN, WILLIAM (1644-1718), was a famous English Quaker who founded Pennsylvania. The Quakers, or Friends, were treated very badly in England. They wanted to live in peace and freedom. Penn, one of their leaders, persuaded King Charles II to allow them to set up a colony in America. This colony became the state of Pennsylvania.

Youthful Rebel. Penn was born on Oct. 14, 1644, in London, the son of a naval officer later knighted as Admiral Sir William Penn. The boy went to school in Essex. He entered Christ Church College, Oxford University, in 1660. This was the year the Stuart family returned to the throne of England. The university students were becoming extravagant in dress and behavior, and Penn did not like this. He also opposed the university rule that everyone must attend the Church of England, because he believed in religious freedom and the individual's right to worship as he pleased. He met with other rebellious students, outside the university, and was expelled from school. His father then sent Penn to France and Italy, hoping that the fashionable life there would make the boy forget his religious beliefs, or at least change them.

After two years of travel and study, Penn returned as a fashionable gentleman. The signs of his religious zeal were gone. His father was glad for the change in him, and sent him to study law at Lincoln's Inn, London, a good place to train for statesmanship.

Penn went to Ireland in 1667 to manage his father's estates. There, he became acquainted with Thomas Loe, a Quaker preacher. Loe convinced him of the truth of the Quaker faith. Penn was then 22 years old.

He had a brilliant future ahead of him, but he put it aside to become a Quaker at a time when Quakers were scorned and ridiculed, imprisoned, and sometimes put to death. His father was heartbroken, and the struggle between the two caused them both much pain.

Persecution. Penn was imprisoned three times for writing and preaching about Quakerism. He was first imprisoned in the Tower of London. After eight months, his father managed to have him released. During this imprisonment, Penn wrote *No Cross, No Crown* (1668), a piece explaining Quaker beliefs and practices.

The next year, he was arrested at a Quaker meeting and was accused of rioting and conspiracy. During his trial at the Old Bailey court, Penn encouraged his jurors to stick to their original verdict, in spite of the judges' threats of fine and imprisonment. This established the power of the jury in trial by jury. Penn's third imprisonment came after his father's death in 1670.

In 1675, Penn was invited to settle a dispute between two owners of land in the West New Jersey colony. It was agreed that he and two other trustees would govern West New Jersey, for which he drew up a charter with rules for government. Two years later, he went to The Netherlands and Germany with George Fox and other Quaker leaders (see Fox, GEORGE). In these countries, Penn met other Quakers who were eager to settle in a free, new land. Some people in England also wanted to settle where they could worship in their own way without fear. Penn realized that the only hope for the Quakers was in America.

Founds Pennsylvania. Charles II owed Penn's father an unpaid debt, which with interest amounted to about $80,000. In 1680, Penn asked the king to repay the debt with wilderness land in America. On March 4, 1681, a charter was granted, giving Penn the territory west of the Delaware River between New York and Maryland. The charter also gave him almost unlimited ruling power over it. The king's council added *Penn* to the suggested name of *Sylvania*, making *Pennsylvania*, which means *Penn's Woods*. Penn opened the land to the

William Penn visited his colony of Pennsylvania for the first time in 1682. Quaker settlers welcomed him in Philadelphia.

Brown Bros.

Bettmann Archive

William Penn Inspected Deeds during the planning of Philadelphia. His wisdom and caution in matters such as these provided the harmony and good government which made the city in its early days truly "The City of Brotherly Love."

Quakers, and they moved in by the thousands from England, Germany, The Netherlands, and Wales. He drew up a Frame of Government for his colony which greatly influenced later charters. The influence of this document is noticeable even in the Constitution of the United States.

In October, 1682, Penn sailed up the Delaware River, and saw his colony for the first time. That same year he made his first treaty with the Indians. His dealings with the Indians were so just that they never attacked the colony. Penn returned to England in 1684, after the colony was well started. See PENNSYLVANIA (History); PHILADELPHIA (History).

Arrested Again. Penn was an old friend of King James II. He won from the king pardons for religious prisoners of many faiths. But the revolution of 1688 brought William and Mary to the throne, and James II was exiled. Penn came under suspicion as a friend of James II, and was arrested several times. Later he was allowed his freedom, but had to remain in London. He wrote two of his greatest works at this time. They were *Essay Towards the Present and Future Peace of Europe* (1693) and *Some Fruits of Solitude* (1693). Penn's *Essay* was a plan for a league of nations in Europe based on international justice. The other work was a short book of wise sayings.

In 1693, Penn was declared innocent of plotting against the government. In 1699, he returned to Pennsylvania, where there had been some troubles with government, slavery, and piracy. Penn settled the problems and rewrote the constitution to meet the new needs of the people who were rapidly coming to the colony.

Penn returned to London in 1701, when King William tried to make Penn's colony a royal province. The king died before he could carry out his plan, but fresh troubles came upon Penn. He was sent to prison for a year for false claims of debts. This imprisonment ruined his health, and in 1712 he had a stroke which paralyzed him. However, he lived for six more years.

At his death, Penn left his interests in Pennsylvania to his four sons. Thomas Penn (1702-1775) managed the interests until 1741. John Penn (1729-1795), a grandson, was lieutenant governor of Pennsylvania from 1763 to 1771 and from 1773 to 1776. Another grandson, Richard Penn (1735-1811), was lieutenant governor from 1771 to 1773. VIRGINIA HAVILAND

See also DELAWARE (English Rule); DOLL (Colonial Dolls; picture: Oldest American Doll); PAINTING (color picture: *Penn's Treaty with the Indians*).

PENN CENTRAL RAILROAD. See RAILROAD (Leading Railroad Companies).

PENNANT is a type of long, narrow flag. The edges of some pennants taper to a point. Others are split to appear swallow-tailed. Pennants may bear various colors and symbols. Sometimes ships' signal flags include pennants marked with numerals. Many colleges and universities have their own pennants. Pennants are also used as emblems of sports championships, especially in baseball. ARTHUR E. DuBois

PENNELL, *PEN'l*, **JOSEPH** (1860-1926), an American etcher, improved black and white art in the United States. Although influenced by James McNeill Whistler, Pennell developed his own style of sharp contrasts in light and shade. He made etchings of scenes in Philadelphia, Italy, and England, and wrote and illustrated many books. They include *Modern Illustration* (1895) and *Etchers and Etching* (1919). Pennell was born in Philadelphia, and attended the Pennsylvania Academy of the Fine Arts. S. W. HAYTER

PENNEY, JAMES CASH (1875-   ), an American merchant, established the J. C. Penney Company. Penney began his career as a clerk in a general store. He bought a partnership in a store in Wyoming, and later established new stores in partnership with men he trained. These stores were first called the *Golden Rule* stores. Penney headed 1,612 stores when he retired in 1946. After his retirement, he established the James C. Penney Foundation to aid religious, scientific, and educational projects. He wrote an autobiography, *Fifty Years with the Golden Rule* (1950). Penney was born in Hamilton, Mo. HAROLD F. WILLIAMSON

PENNINE CHAIN, *PEN ine*, is a series of uplands in northern England. The Pennines run through the central part of the country like a backbone, starting in Northumberland and Cumberland counties and extending south to Derbyshire and Staffordshire. The highest point in the chain is Cross Fell, which rises 2,930 feet. The Pennine Chain is rich in minerals, especially coal. GEORGE B. CRESSEY

PENNSYLVANIA

THE KEYSTONE STATE

Pennsylvania (blue) ranks 33rd in size among all the states, and is 2nd in size among the Middle Atlantic States (gray).

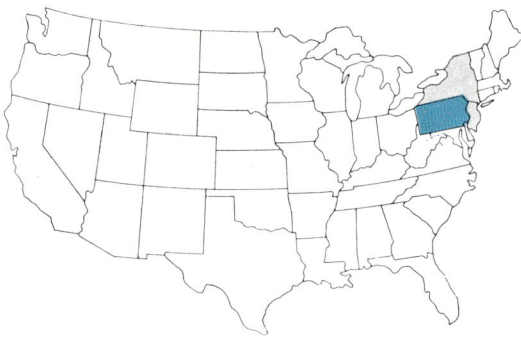

PENNSYLVANIA has the third largest population of all the states. Only California and New York have more people. Pennsylvania is one of four states officially called *commonwealths*. The other three are Kentucky, Massachusetts, and Virginia. Harrisburg is the capital of Pennsylvania, and Philadelphia is the largest city.

Pennsylvania ranks among the leading states in both manufacturing and mining. Northeastern Pennsylvania supplies all the *anthracite* (hard) coal that is produced in the United States. Mines in western Pennsylvania produce huge quantities of *bituminous* (soft) coal, which is used in making coke and in generating electricity. Pennsylvania supplies about one-fourth of the nation's coke, an important fuel used in the steel industry. Pennsylvania is the leading state in the production of pig iron and steel. It produces about a

Steel Mill Furnace in Monessen

WORLD BOOK photo by Three Lions

Independence Hall in Philadelphia

Hollyman, Photo Researchers

FACTS IN BRIEF

Capital: Harrisburg.

Government: *Congress*—U.S. Senators, 2; U.S. Representatives, 27. *Electoral Votes*—29. *State Legislature*—senators, 50; representatives, 203. *Counties*—67. *Voting Age*—21 years.

Area: 45,333 square miles (including 326 square miles of inland water), 33rd in size among the states. *Greatest Distances*—(east-west) 307 miles; (north-south) 169 miles. *Coastline*—51 miles (on Lake Erie).

Elevation: *Highest*—Mount Davis, 3,213 feet above sea level, in Somerset County. *Lowest*—sea level along the Delaware River.

Population: *1960 Census*—11,319,366, third among the states; density, 250 persons to the square mile; distribution, 72 per cent urban, 28 per cent rural. *Estimated 1965 Population*—11,860,000.

Chief Products: *Manufacturing*—chemicals, clothing, food products, machinery, metals and metal products, paper products, printing and publishing. *Agriculture*—dairy products, field crops, livestock, poultry and eggs, vegetables. *Mining*—coal, gas, petroleum, sand and gravel, stone.

Statehood: Dec. 12, 1787, the 2nd state.

State Motto: *Virtue, Liberty, and Independence.*

State Song: None.

Vannucci, Three Lions
Fertile Farmland near the Susquehanna River

fourth of all the pig iron and a fourth of all the steel manufactured in the United States. Pennsylvania also stands among the leading food-processing states.

Philadelphia, in southeast Pennsylvania, is the state's leading manufacturing city, and one of the nation's cultural, educational, and historical centers. It also is one of the world's chief port cities. Pittsburgh, on the Ohio River in western Pennsylvania, is the leading steel-producing city in the world. It is also the largest inland river port in the United States. The world's largest chocolate factory is in Hershey.

Most of Pennsylvania is made up of hills, plateaus, ridges, and valleys. The northwestern and southeastern corners of the state are low and flat. The lowest point in the state is sea level along the Delaware River. Mount Davis, in southern Pennsylvania, rises 3,213 feet above sea level and is the highest point in the state. Forests cover more than half of Pennsylvania. Much of the state has rich farmland. The southeastern section has some of the richest soil in the United States. Crop and poultry farming prosper there. Dairy farming thrives in the northeast, and cattle raising is important in the southwest. The soil along Lake Erie in the northwest is good for growing fruits and vegetables.

Many visitors to the state enjoy a trip through the section of southeastern Pennsylvania in which the Pennsylvania Dutch people live. Most of these people are descended from German immigrants. They are known for their fine cooking and for the colorful designs and decorations on their buildings and on many of their possessions. Some of the Pennsylvania Dutch groups, including the Amish and Mennonites, are called the *Plain People.* Many Amish people still live and dress as their ancestors did, and farm with old-fashioned tools.

King Charles II of England gave the Pennsylvania region to William Penn in 1681. The word *Pennsylvania* means *Penn's Woods.* Penn, a Quaker, established the Pennsylvania colony as a place where his fellow Quakers and persons of other faiths could have religious freedom.

The First and Second Continental Congresses met in Philadelphia before and during the Revolutionary War. On July 4, 1776, the Declaration of Independence was adopted in Pennsylvania's State House (now Independence Hall) in Philadelphia. British troops captured Philadelphia in September, 1777, and held the city until June, 1778. General George Washington and his troops spent the winter and spring of 1777-1778 in Valley Forge. Philadelphia was the site of the Constitutional Convention in 1787, and served as the nation's capital from 1790 to 1800. On Dec. 12, 1787, Pennsylvania *ratified* (approved) the U.S. Constitution and became the second state of the Union.

During the Civil War, the historic Battle of Gettysburg (July 1-3, 1863) marked a turning point in the fighting. In this battle, Union forces broke the strength of General Robert E. Lee's Confederate army. President Abraham Lincoln delivered his Gettysburg Address at the battlefield on Nov. 19, 1863.

Pennsylvania is nicknamed the *Keystone State* because it was the center, or keystone, of the "arch" formed by the original 13 American states. It is sometimes called the *Quaker State* because William Penn and many of his followers were Quakers. For the relationship of Pennsylvania to the other states in its region, see MIDDLE ATLANTIC STATES.

The contributors of this article are George F. Deasy, Professor of Geography at Pennsylvania State University; James R. Doran, Executive Editor of the Harrisburg Patriot-News; *and Sylvester K. Stevens, Executive Director of the Pennsylvania Historical and Museum Commission.*

Constitution. Pennsylvania has had the same constitution since 1873. The state had adopted earlier constitutions in 1776, 1790, and 1838.

Constitutional *amendments* (changes) may be proposed by the state legislature. An amendment must be approved by a majority of both houses of the state legislature. It must then be approved in a similar manner by the next legislature. Finally, it must be approved by a majority of the persons voting on the amendment.

Amendments also can be proposed by a constitutional convention. Before a constitutional convention can meet, it must be approved by a majority of both legislative houses and by the voters in a regular election.

Executive. Pennsylvania's governor serves a four-year term. He can serve more than one term, but not two terms in a row. The governor receives a yearly salary of $45,000. For a list of Pennsylvania's governors, see the *History* section of this article.

The governor appoints the secretary of the commonwealth (secretary of state), attorney general, adjutant general, and several other administrative officials. The people of Pennsylvania elect the lieutenant governor, the state treasurer, and the auditor general. Like the governor, these elected officials serve four-year terms. They may serve more than one term, but not in succession.

Legislature, called the *general assembly*, consists of a 50-member senate and a 203-member house of representatives. Voters in each of the state's 50 senatorial districts elect one senator. Voters in each of the 203 representative districts elect one representative. Senators serve four-year terms, and representatives serve two-year terms. Legislative sessions begin on the first Tuesday in January and last until all business is completed. In even-numbered years, the legislature can only consider state budget matters.

In 1964, the state supreme court ordered the legislature to *reapportion* (redivide) itself to provide equal representation based on population. The legislature failed to do so, and the supreme court reapportioned the legislature in 1966. In 1968, a constitutional amendment was approved providing for reapportionment by a five-member commission after each United States census.

Courts. Pennsylvania's highest court is the state supreme court. It has seven judges, elected to 21-year terms. These are the longest specified terms to which any state officials in the United States are elected. Supreme court justices cannot be re-elected. The justice with the shortest remaining time in office serves as chief justice.

Pennsylvania's superior court meets at fixed times each year in Harrisburg, Philadelphia, Pittsburgh, and Scranton. The superior court has seven judges, elected to 10-year terms. They can be re-elected. All judges in Pennsylvania must retire at the age of 70.

Pennsylvania is divided into 59 judicial districts. Philadelphia is a district by itself. Each judicial district has a court of common pleas, except Philadelphia, which has seven common pleas courts. Other courts in the state include probate courts; county courts; and justice of the peace, magistrate, or police courts.

Local Government. Pennsylvania has four kinds of local government units: (1) counties, (2) townships, (3) boroughs, and (4) cities. Each of the state's 67 *counties* is governed by a board of three commissioners, elected to four-year terms. Most rural communities operate as *townships*. Larger townships are called first-class townships. They are governed by boards made up of at least five commissioners who are elected to four-year terms. Smaller townships are called second-class townships. These townships are governed by boards made up of three supervisors elected to six-year terms.

Pennsylvania is one of the few states that has *boroughs*. These are incorporated units of municipal government that are smaller than cities. Most of Pennsylvania's boroughs are governed by a mayor and by councils that the people elect to four-year terms.

Pennsylvania has four classes of *cities*, based on population. First-class cities have a million or more persons. Second-class cities have between 500,000 and 999,999 persons. Second-class A cities have between 135,000 and 499,999 persons. Third-class cities have fewer than

The Governor's Mansion in Harrisburg was completed in 1968. It stands north of the Capitol. The mansion lawn and gardens overlook the Susquehanna River.

Commonwealth of Pennsylvania

The State Seal

Symbols of Pennsylvania. On the seal, the eagle represents speed, strength, bravery, and wisdom. The ship symbolizes commerce. The plow and sheaves of wheat stand for agricultural abundance. The stalk of corn and the olive branch represent peace and plenty. The seal was adopted in 1893. The state flag, adopted in 1907, shows the state's coat of arms supported by two horses. The flag bears the state motto—*Virtue, Liberty, and Independence.*

Seal, flag, flower, and bird illustrations courtesy Eli Lilly and Company

The State Flag

135,000 persons. Many cities use the commission form of government. Some use the mayor-council form.

Units of local government can adopt *home rule* (self-government) to the extent of selecting or changing their form of government. They can also merge with other units.

Taxation. A sales and use tax accounts for more than half the state government's income. A *use tax* is a tax on goods bought outside the state, but used in the state. Other sources of income include a corporate income tax, taxes on the transfer of stocks and other valuable documents, estate and gift taxes, licenses, and property taxes. About a fifth of the income comes from federal grants and other U.S. government programs.

Politics. Pennsylvania favored Republican candidates in most state and national elections between the Civil War and the 1930's. Democrats have gained strength since the early 1930's, especially in the larger cities. Since 1932, Republican presidential candidates have won the state's electoral votes only three times. For Pennsylvania's electoral votes and voting record in presidential elections, see ELECTORAL COLLEGE (table).

State Capitol in Harrisburg was completed in 1906. Harrisburg became the capital in 1812. Earlier capitals were Chester (1681-1683), Philadelphia (1683-1799), and Lancaster (1799-1812).

Ellis Sawyer, FPG

The State Bird
Ruffed Grouse

The State Flower
Mountain Laurel

The State Tree
Hemlock

PENNSYLVANIA

HIGHWAYS

- ⊛ State Capital
- ○ Cities and Towns
- ○ County Seat
- ▢ City Limits
- County Line

Expressways
Major Roads
Other Roads

U.S.   State   Nat. Interstate

1 inch = 25 Statute miles

Miles 0 5 10 20 30

Lambert Conformal Conic Projection

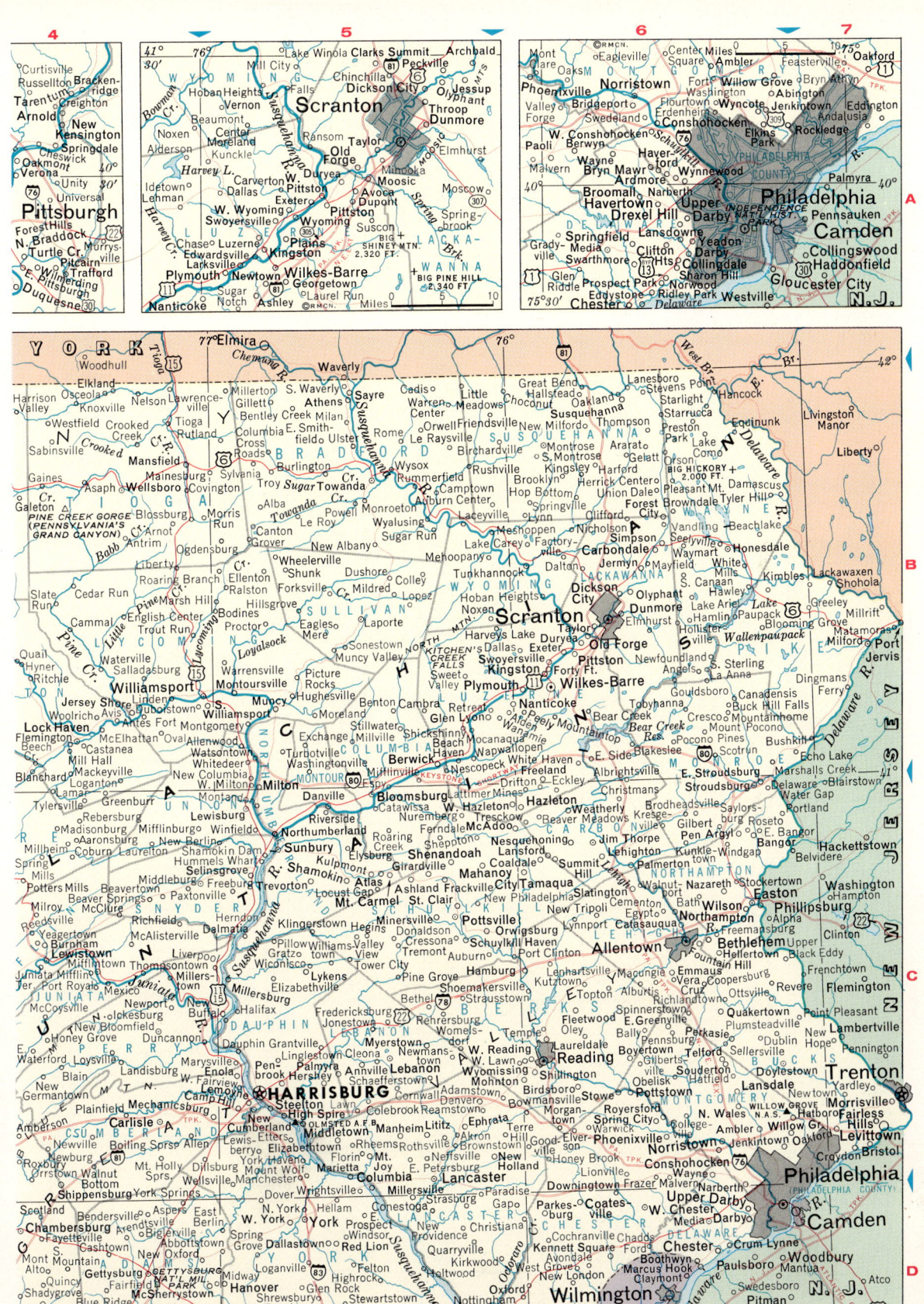

Population

11,860,000 Estimate 1965
11,319,366 1960
10,498,012 1950
9,900,180 1940
9,631,350 1930
8,720,017 1920
7,665,111 1910
6,302,115 1900
5,258,113 1890
4,282,891 1880
3,521,951 1870
2,906,215 1860
2,311,786 1850
1,724,033 1840
1,348,233 1830
1,049,458 1820
810,091 1810
602,365 1800
434,373 1790

Metropolitan Areas

Altoona 137,270
Bethlehem-Easton-Allentown ....492,168 (428,943 living in Pennsylvania)
Erie 250,682
Harrisburg 371,653
Johnstown 280,733
Lancaster 278,359
Philadelphia ..4,342,897
Pittsburgh 2,405,435
Reading 275,414
Scranton 234,531
Wilkes-Barre-Hazleton 346,972
York 290,242

Counties

Adams .....51,906..D 4
Allegheny 1,628,587..C 1
Armstrong .79,524..C 2
Beaver ...206,948..C 1
Bedford ....42,451..D 3
Berks .....275,414..C 5
Blair .....137,270..C 3
Bradford ..54,925..B 5
Bucks ....308,567..C 6
Butler ....114,639..C 1
Cambria ..203,283..C 3
Cameron ...7,586..B 3
Carbon ....52,889..C 6
Centre .....78,580..C 3
Chester ...210,608..D 6
Clarion ....37,408..B 2
Clearfield ..81,534..B 3
Clinton .....37,619..B 4
Columbia ..53,489..B 5
Crawford ..77,956..B 1
Cumberland ....124,816..C 4
Dauphin ..220,255..C 5
Delaware .553,154..D 6
Elk ....37,328..B 3
Erie ......250,682..B 1
Fayette ...169,340..D 2
Forest ....4,485..B 2
Franklin ...88,172..D 4
Fulton ......10,597..D 3
Greene .....39,424..D 1
Huntingdon 39,457..C 3
Indiana ....75,366..C 2
Jefferson ...46,792..B 2
Juniata ....15,874..C 4
Lackawanna ..234,531..B 6
Lancaster .278,359..D 5
Lawrence .112,965..B 1
Lebanon ...90,853..C 5
Lehigh ....227,536..C 6
Luzerne ...346,972..B 5
Lycoming .109,367..B 4
McKean ...54,517..B 3
Mercer ....127,519..B 1
Mifflin .....44,348..C 4
Monroe ....39,567..B 6
Montgomery .516,682..C 6
Montour ...16,730..B 5
Northampton .201,412..C 6
Northumberland ....104,138..B 5
Perry ....26,582..C 4
Philadelphia 2,002,512..D 6
Pike ....9,158..B 6
Potter .....16,483..B 3
Schuylkill 173,027..C 5
Snyder ....25,922..C 4
Somerset ...77,450..D 2
Sullivan ....6,251..B 5
Susquehanna ...33,137..B 5
Tioga .....36,614..B 4
Union .....25,646..C 4
Venango ...65,295..B 2
Warren ....45,582..B 2
Washington .....217,271..C 1
Wayne .....28,737..B 6
Westmoreland ....352,629..C 2
Wyoming ..16,813..B 5
York .....238,336..D 5

Cities and Towns

Abington ....8,000..A 6
Acosta ....975..C 2
Adamstown .1,190..C 5
Akron ......2,167..C 5
Albion ......1,630..B 1
Alburtis ....1,086..C 6
Aldan* .....4,998..D 6
Aliquippa ..26,369..A 3
Allentown 108,347.°C 6
Allison .....1,285..D 2
Allison Park 5,000..A 4
Altoona ....69,407..C 3
Ambler .....6,765..C 6
Ambridge ..13,865..C 1
Ambridge Heights* ...5,106..C 1
Annville ....4,264..C 5
Antes Fort ....390..B 4
Apollo ......2,694..C 2
Archbald ....5,471..A 5
Ardmore ...15,000..A 6
Arnold ......9,437..C 2
Ashland .....5,237..C 5
Ashley ......4,258..A 5
Aspinwall ...3,727..A 4
Athens ......4,515..B 5
Atlas ....1,574..C 5
Auburn ....936..C 5
Austin ....721..B 3
Avalon ......6,859..A 3
Avella ......1,310..C 1
Avis ....1,262..B 4
Avoca ....3,562..A 5
Avondale ....1,016..D 6
Avonmore ...1,351..C 2
Baden ......6,109..C 1
Bairdford ......950..A 4
Bala-Cynwyd* ..8,000..C 6
Baldwin ...24,489..A 4
Baldwin Township* 3,004..A 3
Bangor .....5,766..C 6
Barnesboro ..3,035..C 3
Bath ....1,736..C 6
Beaver .....6,160.°C 1
Beaver Falls ....16,240..C 1
Beaver Meadows ..1,392..C 6
Beaverdale ..1,000..C 3
Bedford ....3,696.°C 3
Belle Vernon 1,784..C 2
Bellefonte ...6,088.°C 4
Belleville ....1,539..C 4
Bellevue ...11,412..C 1
Bellwood ....2,330..C 3
Ben Avon* ..2,553..C 2
Bentleyville .3,160..C 1
Benton ....981..B 5
Berlin ......1,600..D 3
Berwick ....13,353..B 5
Berwyn ......5,000..A 6
Bessemer ....1,491..C 1
Bethayres-Huntingdon Valley* ...2,500..C 6
Bethel Park 23,650..A 3
Bethlehem .75,408..C 6
Big Run .....857..C 3
Biglerville ....923..D 4
Birdsboro ...3,025..C 6
Blairsville ..4,930..C 2
Bloomsburg 10,655.°C 5
Blossburg ...1,956..B 4
Blue Ridge Summit ....650..D 4
Bobtown ....1,167..D 2
Boiling Springs ...1,182..C 4
Bolivar ....716..C 2
Boothwyn ...5,000..D 6
Boston* .....2,300..C 2
Boswell .....1,508..C 2
Boyertown ...4,067..C 6
Boynton ......800..D 2
Brackenridge 5,697..A 4
Braddock ..12,337..A 4
Braddock Hills* .....2,414..C 2
Bradenville .1,000..C 2
Bradford ..15,061..B 3
Brentwood .13,706..A 4
Briarcliff* ..9,000..A 6
Bridgeport ..5,306..A 6
Bridgeville ..7,112..A 3
Bristol .....12,364..C 7
Brockway ...2,563..B 3
Brookhaven* 6,984..D 6
Brookville ...4,620.°B 2
Broomall ..19,722..A 6
Broughton* .3,500..C 1
Brownstown .1,379..C 3
Brownsville .6,055..C 2
Bryn Athyn .1,057..A 7
Bryn Mawr ..9,000..A 6
Burgettstown 2,383..C 1
Burnham ....2,755..C 4
Butler .....20,975.°C 2
Cairnbrook ..1,100..C 3
California ...5,978..C 2
Cambridge Springs ...2,031..B 1
Camp Hill ..8,559..C 5
Canonsburg 12,910..C 1
Canton .....2,102..B 5
Carbondale 13,595..B 6
Carlisle ....16,623.°C 4
Carmichaels ..788..D 2
Carnegie ...11,887..C 1
Carrolltown .1,525..C 3
Carverton .....970..A 5
Castle Shannon .11,836..A 3
Catasauqua .5,062..C 6
Catawissa ...1,824..C 5
Cementon ...1,800..C 6
Centerville ..5,088..C 2
Central City .1,604..C 3
Centre Hall .1,109..C 4
Chambersburg .....17,670.°D 4
Charleroi ....8,148..C 2
Chatwood* ..3,621..D 6
Cheltenham* 7,000..C 6
Chester ....63,658..D 6
Chester Township* 3,602..D 6
Cheswick ...2,734..A 4
Chicora .....1,156..C 2
Christiana ..1,069..D 5
Churchill* ..3,428..C 2
Clairton ...18,389..C 2
Claridge .....1,100..C 2
Clarion .....4,958.°B 2
Clarks Summit ...3,693..A 5
Claysburg ...1,439..C 3
Claysville ....986..C 1
Clearfield ...9,270.°B 3
Cleona ......1,988..C 5
Clifton Heights ...8,005..A 6
Clymer .....2,251..C 2
Coaldale ....3,949..C 6
Coalport ......821..C 3
Coatesville .12,971..D 6
Cochranton .1,139..B 1
Collegeville .2,254..C 6
Collingdale .10,268..A 6
Colonial Park* ....2,500..C 5
Columbia ..12,075..C 5
Colver .....1,261..C 3
Colwyn* ....3,074..D 6
Conemaugh .3,334..C 3
Conestoga ....D 5
Confluence ....938..D 2
Conneautville 1,100..B 1
Connellsville .....12,814..C 2
Conshohocken ....10,259..C 6
Conway .....1,926..C 1
Coopersburg .1,800..C 6
Coplay* .....3,701..C 6
Coraopolis ..9,643..C 1
Cornwall .....1,934..C 5
Cornwells Heights* .10,000..C 7
Corry ....7,744..B 2
Coudersport .2,889.°B 3
Crabtree ......950..C 2
Crafton .....8,418..A 3
Creighton ...2,865..A 4
Cresson .....2,659..C 3
Cressona ....1,854..C 5
Croydon ....9,000..C 7
Crucible .....1,064..D 2
Crum Lynne .3,500..D 6
Curtisville ..1,376..C 2
Curwensville 3,231..C 3
Dale* ....2,807..C 3
Dallas ......2,586..B 6
Dallastown ..3,615..D 5
Dalton .....1,227..B 6
Danville ....6,889.°C 5
Danville East* .....1,758..B 5
Darby ......14,059..D 6
Dayton ....769..C 2
Delaware Water Gap ..554..C 6
Delta ....822..D 5
Denver ......1,875..C 5
Derry ....3,426..C 2
Dickson City 7,738..B 6
Dillsburg ....1,322..C 4
Dixonville ....868..C 2
Donaldson .....637..C 5
Donora ....11,131..C 2
Dormont ...13,098..A 3
Dover ....975..D 5
Downingtown 7,248..D 6
Doylestown ..5,917.°C 6
Dravosburg ..3,458..A 4
Drexel Hill 39,000..A 6
Du Bois ...10,667..B 3
Duboistown .1,358..B 4
Duke Center ...800..B 3
Dunbar .....1,536..D 2
Duncannon .1,800..C 4
Duncansville 1,396..C 3
Dunlo ....982..C 3
Dunmore ...18,917..B 6
Dupont .....3,669..A 5
Duquesne ..15,019..C 2
Duryea .....5,626..B 6
East Bangor ..970..C 6
East Berlin .1,037..D 5
East Brady .1,282..C 2
East Faxon* 3,641..B 4
East Greenville ......1,931..C 6
East Lansdowne* ...3,224..D 6
East McKeesport* .....3,470..C 2
East Norriton Township* 10,273..C 6
East Petersburg ......2,053..C 5
East Pittsburgh ......4,122..A 4
East Stroudsburg ......7,674..C 6
East Uniontown* .....2,424..D 2
East Vandergrift* .....1,388..C 2
East Washington ....2,483..C 1
East Weissport* ....200..C 6
Easton .....31,955.°C 6
Ebensburg ...4,111.°C 3
Economy* ....5,925..C 1
Eddystone ...3,006..A 6
Edenborn .....800..D 2
Edgely* ......950..C 6
Edgewood ....5,124..A 4
Edgewood* ..3,399..C 5
Edgeworth ..2,030..A 3
Edinboro ....1,703..B 1
Edwardsville 5,711..A 5
Egypt ....1,500..C 6
Ehrenfeld .....566..C 3
Eldred ......1,107..B 3
Elizabeth ...2,597..C 2
Elizabethtown ......6,780..C 5
Elizabethville 1,455..C 5
Elkins Park 12,000..A 6
Elkland .....2,189..B 4
Ellport .....1,458..C 1
Ellsworth ....1,456..C 1
Ellwood City .....12,413..C 1
Elmora ......1,057..C 3
Elrama ....823..C 2
Elysburg ....1,100..C 5
Emlenton .....844..B 2
Emmaus ...10,262..C 6
Emporium ...3,397.°B 3
Emsworth ...3,341..A 3
Enhaut* ....2,000..C 5
Enola ....4,500..C 5
Ephrata ....7,688..C 5
Erdenheim ..3,700..A 6
Erie ......138,440.°A 1
Ernest ....950..C 2
Espy ....1,375..B 5
Essington* ..3,300..D 6
Etna ....5,519..A 4
Evans City ..1,825..C 1
Everett .....2,279..C 3
Everson .....1,304..C 2
Exeter ......4,747..B 6
Export ......1,518..C 2
Factoryville ...991..B 6
Fairbank* .....760..D 2
Fairchance ..2,120..D 2
Fairhope ....1,700..D 3
Fairless Hills 8,000..C 7
Fairoaks .....1,239..A 3
Fairview .....2,100..A 1
Falls Creek .1,344..B 3
Farmington ...800..D 2
Farrell ....13,793..B 1
Faxon* .....1,841..B 4
Fayette City 1,159..C 2
Fayetteville ...810..D 4
Feasterville .6,000..A 7
Ferndale ....2,717..C 3
Fleetwood ...2,647..C 6
Flemington ..1,608..B 4
Florin ......1,518..C 5
Flourtown ..4,000..A 6
Folcroft* ...9,008..D 6
Folsom* ....5,000..D 6
Ford City ...5,440..C 2
Forest City ..2,651..B 6
Forest Hills .8,796..A 4
Forestville* ...200..C 5
Fort Washington ....2,500..A 6
Forty Fort ..6,431..B 6
Fountain Hill .....5,428..C 6
Fox Chapel* 3,302..C 2
Frackville ...5,654..C 5
Franklin ....9,586.°B 2
Franklin* ...1,352..C 3
Fredericktown .....1,270..C 1
Freedom ....2,895..C 1
Freeland ....5,068..B 6
Freemansburg ......1,652..C 6
Freeport ....2,439..C 2
Frisco* ......900..C 2
Fullerton* ...5,500..C 6
Galeton .....1,646..B 4
Gallitzin ....2,783..C 3
Gap ....815..D 5
Garden City* 2,000..D 6
Garden View* ....2,418..B 4
Geistown ....3,186..C 3
Georgetown ..2,200..A 5
Gettysburg ..7,960.°D 4
Gibsonia ....1,150..A 4
Gilberton* ..1,712..C 5
Gipsy ....800..C 3
Girard ......2,451..A 1
Girardville ..2,958..C 5
Gladwyne* ..2,500..C 6
Glassport ...8,418..C 2
Glen Lyon ..4,173..B 5
Glen Rock ..1,546..D 5
Glenolden* ..8,229..A 6
Glenshaw ..30,471..A 4
Glenside* ..22,500..C 6
Grace Park* 2,000..A 6
Grandview Heights* ...3,800..C 5
Grapeville* ..1,600..C 2
Grassflat .....845..C 3
Green Ridge* 3,500..D 6
Green Tree* .6,275..C 1
Greencastle .2,988..D 4
Greenock ....1,500..C 2
Greensburg 17,383.°C 2
Greenville ...8,765..B 1
Greenwood ..1,500..C 3
Grindstone* .1,094..D 2
Grove City ..8,368..B 1
Halifax ....824..C 5
Hallstead ...1,580..B 6
Hamburg ....3,747..C 6
Hamilton Park* ....3,500..C 5
Hanover ...15,538..D 5
Harmarville .2,000..A 4
Harmony ....1,142..C 1
Harrisburg .79,697.°C 5
Harrison ...15,710..C 2
Hastings ....1,751..C 3
Hatboro .....7,315..C 6
Hatfield .....1,941..C 6
Haverford ...5,000..A 6
Havertown .35,000..A 6
Hawley ......1,433..B 6
Hazleton ...32,056..C 6
Heidelberg* .2,118..C 2
Hellam ......1,234..D 5
Hellertown ..6,716..C 6
Herminie ....1,571..C 2
Hershey ....6,851..C 5
Hickory Township* ....14,134..B 1
High Spire ..2,999..C 5
Hiller* ......1,746..D 2
Hillsville .....800..B 1
Hollidaysburg ......6,475.°C 3
Hollywood* .2,000..D 6
Holmes* ....3,000..D 6
Homeacre* ..3,508..C 2
Homer City .2,471..C 2
Homestead ..7,502..A 4
Honesdale ...5,569.°B 6
Honey Brook 1,023..C 6
Hooversville .1,120..C 3
Hopwood ....1,615..D 2
Horsham* ...3,500..C 6
Houston .....1,865..C 1
Houtzdale ...1,239..C 3
Hughestown* 1,615..B 5
Hughesville .2,218..B 5
Hummels Wharf .....900..C 5
Hummelstown* ....4,474..C 5
Huntingdon .7,234.°C 3
Hyde Park* .2,500..C 6
Hyndman ...1,124..D 3
Imperial ....2,000..A 3
Indiana ....13,005.°C 2
Industry* ...2,338..C 1
Ingram .....4,730..A 3
Irvona ....781..C 3
Irwin ....4,270..C 2
Isabella ......856..D 2
Jamestown ....897..B 1
Jeannette ..16,565..C 2
Jefferson* ..8,280..C 2
Jenkintown ..5,017..C 6
Jenners ......958..C 2
Jermyn .....2,568..B 6
Jerome .....1,241..C 3
Jersey Shore 5,613..B 4
Jessup ......5,456..A 5
Jim Thorpe .5,945.°C 6
Johnsonburg 4,966..B 3
Johnstown .53,949..C 3
Jonestown ....813..C 5
Juniata Terrace ...1,130..C 4
Kane ....5,380..B 3
Kenhorst* ...2,815..C 6
Kenmawr* ...3,000..C 1
Kennett Square ...4,355..D 6
King of Prussia* ..6,000..C 6
Kingston ...20,261..B 6
Kittanning ..6,793.°C 2
Knox ....1,247..B 2
Koppel ......1,389..C 1

*Does not appear on the map; key shows general location.

°County Seat.
Sources: 1960 Census and special censuses.

PENNSYLVANIA

Kulpmont ...4,288..C 5
Kutztown ...3,312..C 6
Lacey Park* 4,000..C 6
Lafayette Hill* .....3,500..C 6
Lake City ...1,722..A 1
Lakemont ...1,500..C 3
Lancaster ..61,055.°C 5
Langeloth ...1,112..C 1
Lansdale ..12,612..C 6
Lansdowne .21,601..A 6
Lansford ....5,958..C 6
Laporte ....195.°B 5
Larksville ...4,390..A 5
Latrobe ....11,932..C 2
Laurel Run ...855..A 5
Laureldale ..4,051..C 6
Lawnton* ...3,500..C 5
Lawrence ...1,048..C 1
Lawrence Park .....4,403..A 1
Lebanon ...30,045.°C 5
Lee Park* ..3,500..B 6
Leechburg ...3,545..C 2
Leetsdale ...2,153..A 3
Lehighton ...6,318..C 6
Leith* ......1,622..D 2
Lemoyne .....4,662..C 5
Lester* .....2,000..D 6
Levittown ..58,000..C 7
Lewisburg ...5,523.°C 5
Lewistown .12,640.°C 4
Lewistown Junction* ...300..C 4
Liberty* ....3,624..C 3
Library* ....3,000..C 3
Ligonier ....2,276..C 2
Lilly ....1,642..C 3
Linesville ...1,255..B 1
Linwood* ...4,460..D 6
Lititz ....5,987..C 5
Littlestown .2,756..D 4
Lock Haven 11,748.°B 4
Locust Gap ...700..C 5
Lorain* .....1,324..C 3
Loretto .....1,338..C 3
Lower Allen Township* 12,881..C 5
Lucernemines 1,524..C 2
Luzerne ....5,118..A 5
Lykens .....2,527..C 5
Lyndora ....5,700..C 2
Lynnwood* ..2,230..C 2
Macungie ...1,266..C 6
Madera ....808..C 3
Mahanoy City .....8,536..C 5
Malvern ....2,268..C 6
Manchester ..1,454..C 5
Manheim ....4,790..C 5
Manor* .....1,136..C 2
Mansfield ...2,678..B 4
Mapleton Depot ......666..C 4
Marcus Hook 3,299..D 6
Marienville ....844..B 2
Marietta ....2,385..C 5
Marion Hill* 2,278..C 1
Mars ....1,522..C 1
Marshallton* 2,316..B 5
Marsteller ....958..C 3
Martinsburg .1,772..C 3
Marysville ..2,580..C 5
Masontown ..4,730..D 2
Matamoras ..2,087..B 7
Mather .....1,033..D 1
Mayfield ....1,996..B 6
McAdoo .....3,560..C 5
McChesneytown* .....1,140..C 2
McClure ....1,001..C 4
McConnellsburg ....1,245.°D 3
McDonald ..3,141..A 3
McGrann* ....800..C 2
McKees Rocks ....13,185..C 1
McKeesport 45,489..C 2
McKnight* 15,000..C 1
McSherrystown ......2,839..D 4
Meadowlands 1,967..C 1
Meadville ..16,671.°B 1
Mechanicsburg ......8,123..C 4
Media ......5,803..D 6
Melrose Park* ....6,000..C 6
Mercer .....2,800.°B 1
Mercersburg 1,759..D 4
Meridian ....1,649..C 2
Meyersdale ..2,901..D 2
Middleburg ..1,366.°C 4
Middletown 11,182..C 5
Midland ....6,425..C 1
Midway .....1,012..D 4
Mifflin ....745..C 4
Mifflinburg .2,476..C 4
Mifflintown ...887.°C 4
Mifflinville ...1,027..B 5
Mildred ......800..B 5
Milford .....1,198.°B 7
Mill Hall ...1,891..B 4
Millcreek Township* 32,081..B 1
Millersburg .2,984..C 5
Millersville ..5,353..D 5
Millsboro ...1,179..D 1
Millvale .....6,624..A 4
Millville ......952..B 5
Milmont Park* .....2,000..D 6
Milroy ......1,666..C 4
Milton ......7,972..B 5
Minersville ..6,606..C 5
Mocanaqua ..1,104..B 5
Mohnton ....2,223..C 6
Monaca .....8,394..C 1
Monessen ...18,424..C 2
Monongahela 8,388..C 2
Monroeville* 22,446..C 2
Mont Alto ...1,039..D 4
Mont Clare ...1,124..A 6
Montgomery .2,150..B 5
Montoursville 5,211..B 5
Montrose ....2,363.°B 6
Montrose Hill* .....2,000..C 1
Moon Run ....650..A 3
Moosic ......4,243..A 5
Morrisville ..7,790..C 7
Morton* ....2,207..D 6
Moscow .....1,212..A 5
Mount Carmel ...10,760..C 5
Mount Holly Springs ....1,840..C 4
Mount Jewett 1,226..B 3
Mount Joy ...3,292..C 5
Mount Lebanon .35,361..C 1
Mount Oliver 5,980..A 4
Mount Penn* 3,574..C 6
Mount Pleasant ..6,107..C 2
Mount Union 4,091..C 4
Mount Wolf 1,514..C 5
Mountaintop 1,600..B 6
Muncy ......2,830..B 5
Munhall ...17,312..A 4
Murrysville ..1,200..A 4
Muse ....1,386..C 1
Myerstown ..3,268..C 5
Nanticoke ..15,601..B 6
Nanty Glo ...4,608..C 3
Narberth ....5,109..C 6
Nazareth ....6,209..C 6
Neffsville .....975..C 5
Nemacolin ...1,404..D 2
Nescopeck ...1,934..B 5
Nesquehoning 2,714..C 6
Neville Island* ...2,400..C 1
New Bethlehem .1,599..B 2
New Bloomfield .987.°C 4
New Brighton 8,397..C 1
New Castle .44,790.°B 1
New Castle Northwest* 2,007..B 1
New Cumberland ......9,257..C 5
New Eagle* .2,670..C 1
New Florence .958..C 2
New Freedom 1,395..D 5
New Holland 3,425..C 5
New Hope .....958..C 7
New Kensington ....23,485..C 2
New Milford 1,129..B 6
New Oxford 1,407..D 4
New Philadelphia ...1,702..C 5
New Salem ...860..D 2
New Wilmington ....2,203..B 1
Newmanstown ......1,200..C 5
Newport .....1,861..C 4
Newtown ....2,400..A 5
Newtown ....2,323..C 7
Newtown Square* ..10,585..D 6
Newville .....1,656..C 4
Nicholson .....942..B 6
Normalville ....900..D 2
Norristown .38,925.°C 6
North Apollo 1,741..C 2
North Belle Vernon* ...3,148..C 2
North Bend ...900..B 4
North Braddock 13,204..A 4
North Catasauqua* ...2,805..C 6
North Charleroi* .2,259..C 1
North East ..4,217..A 2
North Girard, see Lake City
North Vandergrift* ......1,827..C 2
North Versailles* ..13,583..C 2
North Wales 3,673..C 6
North Warren ...1,458..B 2
North York .2,290..D 5
Northampton 8,866..C 6
Northumberland ......4,156..C 5
Norwood ....6,729..A 6
Nottingham* 2,500..C 6
Oakdale .....1,695..A 3
Oakford .....2,000..C 7
Oakland* ...2,303..B 1
Oakland ......889..B 6
Oakmont ....7,504..C 2
Oberlin* ....2,500..C 5
Ohioville* ...3,050..C 1
Oil City ....17,692..B 2
Old Forge ...8,928..B 6
Oliver ....1,250..D 2
Olyphant ....5,864..B 6
Oreland* ....6,700..C 6
Orwigsburg ..2,131..C 5
Osceola Mills 1,777..C 3
Oxford ......3,376..D 5
Paint ....1,275..C 3
Palmer Heights* ..2,597..C 6
Palmerton ...5,942..C 6
Palmyra .....6,999..C 5
Paoli ....5,000..A 6
Parker ....945..B 2
Parkesburg ..2,759..D 6
Parkside* ...2,426..D 6
Parkville* ...1,300..D 5
Patterson Township* 2,930..C 1
Patton ......2,880..C 3
Paxtang* ....1,916..C 5
Peckville ....6,374..A 5
Peely ....833..B 6
Pen Argyl ...3,693..C 6
Penbrook ....3,671..C 5
Penn Hills* 59,317..C 1
Penn Valley* 3,500..C 6
Penn Wynne* 4,500..C 6
Penndel* ....2,158..C 7
Pennsburg ...1,698..C 6
Pennside* ...3,000..C 6
Perkasie ....4,650..C 6
Philadelphia 2,002,512.°D 6
Philipsburg .3,872..C 3
Phoenixville 13,797..C 6
Pilgrim Garden* ..5,000..D 6
Pine Grove ..2,267..C 5
Pitcairn ....5,383..A 4
Pittsburgh 604,332.°C 1
Pittston ...12,407..B 6
Plains ......8,500..A 5
Pleasant Gap 1,389..C 4
Pleasant Hills ......8,573..C 2
Plum* ......17,910..C 2
Plymouth ..10,401..B 6
Plymouth Meeting* ..4,000..C 6
Plymouth Valley* ...1,700..C 6
Plymptonville* .....1,220..B 3
Point Marion 1,853..D 2
Polk ....3,574..B 2
Port Allegany 2,742..B 3
Port Carbon* 2,775..C 5
Port Vue* ...6,635..C 2
Portage .....3,933..C 3
Pottstown ..26,144..C 6
Pottsville ..21,659.°C 5
Pringle* ....1,418..B 5
Prospect Park .....7,049..A 6
Punxsutawney ....8,805..C 3
Quakertown .6,305..C 6
Quarryville ..1,427..D 5
Rankin ......5,164..A 4
Reading ....98,177.°C 6
Reamstown ....950..C 5
Red Lion ....5,594..D 5
Reedsville .....950..C 4
Reno ....866..B 2
Renovo ......3,316..B 4
Republic .....1,921..D 2
Reserve Township* .4,230..C 2
Retreat ....890..B 5
Revloc ....900..C 3
Reynoldsville 3,158..B 3
Ridgway .....6,387.°B 3
Ridley Park .7,387..A 6
Rimersburg ..1,323..B 2
Riverside ....1,580..C 5
Roaring Spring ....2,937..C 3
Robertsdale ....975..C 3
Robesonia* ..1,579..C 5
Robinson .....875..C 2
Rochester ...5,952..C 1
Rochester Township* 3,863..C 1
Rockledge ...2,587..A 6
Rockwood ....1,101..D 2
Rocky Grove 3,168..B 2
Roscoe ......1,315..C 2
Rosemont* ..4,000..C 6
Roseto ......1,630..C 6
Roslyn* .....8,500..C 6
Rossiter ....950..C 3
Roulette ....850..B 3
Rouseville .....923..B 2
Royersford ..3,969..C 6
Saegertown ..1,131..B 1
Sagamore .....800..C 2
St. Clair .....5,159..C 5
St. Marys ...8,065..B 3
Salisbury .....862..D 2
Saltsburg ....1,054..C 2
Sandy* .....2,070..B 3
Saxton ....977..C 3
Sayre ....7,917..B 5
Scalp Level .1,445..C 3
Schuylkill Haven ....6,470..C 5
Scotland ......800..D 4
Scott Township* 20,328..C 1
Scottdale ...6,244..C 2
Scranton ..111,443.°B 6
Secane* .....2,000..D 6
Selinsgrove ..3,948..C 5
Sellersville ..2,497..C 6
Seneca ....800..B 2
Seward ....754..C 2
Sewickley ...6,157..C 1
Shadygrove ....800..D 4
Shamokin ..13,674..C 5
Sharon .....25,267..B 1
Sharon Hill .7,464..A 6
Sharpsburg ..6,096..A 4
Sharpsville ..6,061..B 1
Shavertown* .2,000..B 5
Sheffield ....1,971..B 2
Shenandoah 11,073..C 5
Shickshinny .1,843..B 5
Shillington ..5,639..C 6
Shinglehouse 1,298..B 3
Shippensburg 6,138..C 4
Shoemakersville ......1,464..C 6
Simpson .....1,800..B 6
Sinking Spring* ...2,244..C 5
Slatington ..4,316..C 6
Slickville .....950..C 2
Sligo ....814..B 2
Slippery Rock 2,563..B 1
Slovan ......1,018..C 1
Smethport ...1,725.°B 3
Smithfield* .2,547..C 3
Smithfield .....939..D 2
Smithmill .....880..C 3
Somerset ....6,347.°C 2
Souderton ...5,381..C 6
South Coatesville* 2,032..D 6
South Connellsville ....2,434..D 2
South Fork .2,053..C 3
South Greensburg ......3,058..C 2
South Renovo .777..B 4
South Uniontown* ....3,603..D 2
South Waverly ...1,382..B 5
South Williamsport ......6,972..B 4
Southampton* ..4,500..C 6
Southmont ...2,857..C 3
Southwest ....800..C 2
Southwest Greensburg* .....3,264..C 2
Spangler ....2,658..C 3
Spring City ..3,162..C 6
Spring Garden Township* 11,387..D 5
Spring Grove 1,675..D 5
Spring Mills ..800..C 4
Springdale ..5,602..C 2
Springfield 27,772..A 6
State College ...27,584..C 4
Steelton ....11,266..C 5
Stewartstown 1,164..D 5
Stoneboro ...1,267..B 1
Stowe ......11,730..A 3
Stowe ....3,501..C 6
Strabane ....1,940..C 1
Strafford* ...2,500..C 6
Strasburg ...1,416..D 5
Stroudsburg .6,070.°C 6
Sugar Notch 1,524..A 5
Summerville ....895..B 2
Summit Hill 4,386..C 6
Sunbury ...13,687.°C 5
Susquehanna 2,591..B 6
Swarthmore .5,753..A 6
Swedeland ....950..A 6
Swissvale ...15,089..A 4
Swoyersville 6,751..B 6
Sykesville ...1,479..B 3
Tamaqua ...10,173..C 6
Tarentum ...8,232..C 2
Taylor ....6,148..B 6
Telford .....2,763..C 6
Temple ......1,633..C 6
Templeton ....900..C 2
Terre Hill ...1,129..C 5
Throop ......4,732..A 5
Tidioute ......860..B 2
Tionesta ......778.°B 2
Titusville ...8,356..B 2
Tobyhanna ....900..B 6
Topton ......1,684..C 6
Torrance ....C 2
Towanda ....4,293.°B 5
Tower City ..1,968..C 5
Trafford ....4,330..A 4
Trainer* ....2,358..D 6
Tremont .....1,893..C 5
Tresckow ....1,145..C 6
Trevorton ...2,597..C 5
Trevose* ....6,000..C 7
Troy ....1,478..B 5
Trucksville* .2,300..B 5
Tullytown* ..2,452..C 7
Tuna ....900..B 3
Tunkhannock 2,297.°B 6
Turtle Creek 10,607..A 4
Twin Rocks ...900..C 3
Tyrone .....7,792..C 3
Union City ..3,819..B 2
Uniontown .17,942.°D 2
United ......2,044..C 2
Unity ....900..A 4
Upland* ....4,343..D 6
Upper Darby ...44,000..D 6
Valley Forge ..450..C 6
Valley View .1,540..C 5
Vanderbilt ....826..C 2
Vandergrift ..8,742..C 2
Vanport .....2,917..C 1
Verona .....4,032..A 4
Versailles* ..2,297..C 2
Vestaburg .....950..C 2
Villanova* ..4,000..C 6
Vintondale ....938..C 3
Wallingford* 3,000..D 6
Walnutport ..1,609..C 6
Wampum ....1,085..C 1
Wanamie .....950..B 5
Warminster* 3,000..C 6
Warren ....14,505.°B 2
Washington 23,545.°C 1
Washington North* ...2,077..C 1
Washington West* ....3,951..C 1
Waterford ...1,390..B 2
Watsontown .2,431..B 5
Waymart ....1,106..B 6
Wayne .....10,000..C 6
Waynesboro 10,427..D 4
Waynesburg .5,188.°D 1
Weatherly ..2,591..C 6
Webster ......898..C 2
Weedville .....600..B 3
Wellsboro ...4,369.°B 4
Wesleyville ..3,534..A 1
West Chester ..15,705.°D 6
West Conshohocken ....2,254..A 6
West Decatur .900..C 3
West Fairview ..1,718..C 5
West Grove ..1,607..D 6
West Hazleton ..6,278..C 5
West Homestead* .....4,155..C 2
West Lawn .2,059..C 5
West Mayfield* .2,201..C 1
West Middlesex .1,301..B 1
West Mifflin ..27,289..C 2
West Newton 3,982..C 2
West Norriton* .8,342..C 6
West Pittsburg 850..C 1
West Pittston 6,998..A 5
West Reading 4,938..C 6
West View ..8,079..A 3
West Wyoming ..3,166..A 5
West Wyomissing* ..2,500..C 6
West York ..5,526..D 5
Westbrook Park* .....5,000..A 6
Westfield ...1,333..B 4
Westmont ...6,573..C 3
Wheatland ..1,813..B 1
Whitaker* ..2,130..C 2
White Haven 1,778..B 6
White Oak* .9,047..C 2
Whitehall* .16,075..C 2
Whitney ......775..C 2
Wiconisco ...1,402..C 5
Wilkes-Barre ....63,551.°B 6
Wilkes-Barre Township* .4,319..B 6
Wilkins Township* 8,272..C 2
Wilkinsburg 30,066..C 2
Williamsburg ....1,792..C 3
Williamsport .....41,967.°B 4
Williamstown 2,097..C 5
Willow Grove ....10,000..C 6
Wilmerding ..4,349..A 4
Wilson ......8,465..C 6
Winburne ......800..C 3
Windber .....6,994..C 3
Windgap ....1,930..C 6
Windsor .....1,029..D 5
Womelsdorf .1,471..C 5
Wood ....800..C 3
Woodland .....900..C 3
Worthington ..772..C 2
Wrightsville 2,345..C 5
Wyncote ....6,000..A 6
Wynnewood .7,200..A 6
Wyoming ....4,127..A 5
Wyomissing .5,044..C 6
Yardley .....2,271..C 7
Yatesboro ....900..C 2
Yeadon ....11,610..A 6
Yeagertown ..1,349..C 4
York ....54,504.°D 5
York Haven ...736..C 5
Youngsville ..2,211..B 2
Youngwood ..2,813..C 2
Zelienople ...3,284..C 1

*Does not appear on the map; key shows general location.

°County Seat.
Sources: 1960 Census and special censuses.

Amish Boys ride a supermarket bronco. The Amish are one of several religious groups that are called the *Plain People.*

Tortora, Three Lions

PENNSYLVANIA / People

The 1960 United States census reported that Pennsylvania had a population of 11,319,366. This was an increase of about 8 per cent over the 1950 figure, 10,498,012. The U.S. Bureau of the Census estimated that by 1965, the state's population had grown to about 11,860,000.

Almost three-fourths of the people of Pennsylvania live in urban areas. That is, they live in or near cities and towns of 2,500 or more persons. Slightly more than a fourth of the people make their homes in rural areas. About four-fifths of the population live in one of the state's 12 Standard Metropolitan Statistical Areas as defined by the U.S. Bureau of the Budget (see METROPOLITAN AREA). These areas are Altoona, Bethlehem-Easton-Allentown, Erie, Harrisburg, Johnstown, Lancaster, Philadelphia, Pittsburgh, Reading, Scranton, Wilkes-Barre-Hazleton, and York. For the populations of these metropolitan areas, see the *Index* to the political map of Pennsylvania.

Philadelphia is the state's largest city, and the fourth largest in the United States. Other large Pennsylvania cities, in order of population, are Pittsburgh, Erie, Scranton, Allentown, Reading, and Harrisburg, the state capital. See the separate articles on the cities of Pennsylvania

listed in the *Related Articles* at the end of this article.

About 96 of every 100 Pennsylvanians were born in the United States. The largest group of persons born in other countries came from Italy. Other large groups, in order of size, include those from Poland, Russia, Germany, Austria, Czechoslovakia, and England.

Several groups are the descendants of Germans who came to Pennsylvania during the 1600's and 1700's. They are often called *Pennsylvania Dutch.* Some of these people still speak a mixture of German and English. Others speak English, but with an accent. The Pennsylvania Dutch include such religious groups as the Amish, Dunkers, and Mennonites. See PENNSYLVANIA DUTCH.

More than half the church members in Pennsylvania are Roman Catholics. Other large religious groups include Lutherans, Methodists, and Presbyterians.

POPULATION

This map shows the *population density* of Pennsylvania, and how it varies in different parts of the state. Population density is the average number of persons who live on each square mile.

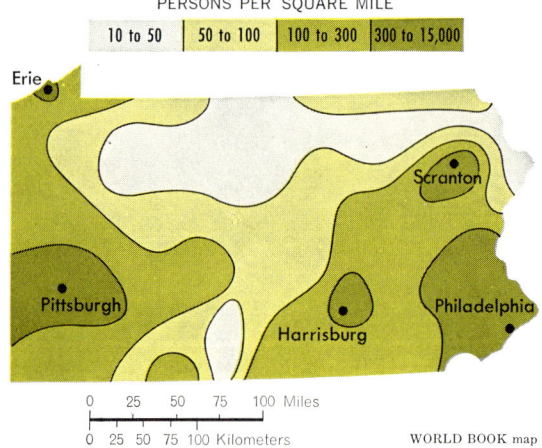

PERSONS PER SQUARE MILE

| 10 to 50 | 50 to 100 | 100 to 300 | 300 to 15,000 |

WORLD BOOK map

PENNSYLVANIA / Education

Schools. Most of the early teaching in Pennsylvania was controlled by churches. During the 1640's, Swedish Lutheran ministers taught in Tinicum, near what is now Essington. Pennsylvania's first colonial constitution, adopted in 1682, provided that children should know how to read and write by the age of 12. The Friends' public school, founded in Philadelphia by Quakers in 1689, still exists as the William Penn Charter School.

The state constitution of 1790 stated that the legislature should provide schools for the children of poor parents. In 1834, the legislature passed the Free School Act. This act provided for the establishment of school districts throughout the state. A law requiring children between 8 and 13 to attend school was passed in 1895.

Today, each city, township, and borough in Pennsylvania has, or is part of, a school district. A 17-member

council of education, appointed by the governor, establishes policies for the state's public school system. The superintendent of public instruction administers the policies. A state law requires children between 8 and 17 to attend school. For the number of students and teachers in Pennsylvania, see EDUCATION (table).

In the early 1960's, the state acted to provide a number of two-year community colleges. The first of these colleges, Harrisburg Area Community College, opened in 1964. It is sponsored by 62 school districts in three counties.

Libraries. Benjamin Franklin founded the Library Company of Philadelphia in 1731. It was the first subscription library in the American colonies. Members contributed money to buy books, which they could then use without charge. In 1876, more than a hundred

Pennsylvania has 92 universities and colleges accredited by the Middle States Association of Colleges and Secondary Schools. For enrollments and further information, see UNIVERSITIES AND COLLEGES (table).

Name	Location	Founded	Name	Location	Founded
Academy of the New Church	Bryn Athyn	1876	Lehigh University	Bethlehem	1865
Albright College	Reading	1856	Lincoln University	Lincoln University	1854
Allegheny College	Meadville	1815	Lock Haven State College	Lock Haven	1870
Alliance College	Cambridge Springs	1912	Lycoming College	Williamsport	1812
Alvernia College	Reading	1958	Mansfield State College	Mansfield	1854
Beaver College	Glenside	1853	Mary Immaculate Seminary		
Bloomsburg State College	Bloomsburg	1839	and College	Northampton	1939
Bryn Mawr College	Bryn Mawr	1880	Marywood College	Scranton	1915
Bucknell University	Lewisburg	1846	Mercyhurst College	Erie	1926
Cabrini College	Radnor	1957	Messiah College	Grantham	1909
California State College	California	1852	Millersville State College	Millersville	1855
Carnegie-Mellon University	Pittsburgh	1900	Moore College of Art	Philadelphia	1844
Cedar Crest College	Allentown	1867	Moravian College	Bethlehem	1858
Chatham College	Pittsburgh	1869	Mount Mercy College	Pittsburgh	1929
Chestnut Hill College	Philadelphia	1871	Muhlenberg College	Allentown	1848
Cheyney State College	Cheyney	1837	Pennsylvania, University of	Philadelphia	1756
Clarion State College	Clarion	1866	Pennsylvania College		
College Misericordia	Dallas	1924	of Optometry	Philadelphia	1919
Crozer Theological Seminary	Chester	1868	Pennsylvania State University	State College	1855
Delaware Valley College of			Philadelphia College of Art	Philadelphia	1876
Science and Agriculture	Doylestown	1896	Philadelphia College of Bible	Philadelphia	1958
Dickinson College	Carlisle	1773	Philadelphia College of		
Drexel Institute of Technology	Philadelphia	1891	Pharmacy and Science	Philadelphia	1821
Dropsie College for Hebrew			Philadelphia College of		
and Cognate Learning	Philadelphia	1907	Textiles and Science	Philadelphia	1884
Duquesne University	Pittsburgh	1878	Pittsburgh, University of	Pittsburgh	1787
East Stroudsburg State			PMC Colleges	Chester	1821
College	East Stroudsburg	1893	Point Park College	Pittsburgh	1966
Eastern Baptist College	St. Davids	1932	Rosemont College	Rosemont	1921
Eastern Baptist Theological			St. Francis College	Loretto	1847
Seminary	Philadelphia	1925	St. Joseph's College	Philadelphia	1851
Edinboro State College	Edinboro	1857	St. Vincent College	Latrobe	1846
Elizabethtown College	Elizabethtown	1899	Scranton, University of	Scranton	1888
Franklin and Marshall			Seton Hill College	Greensburg	1883
College	Lancaster	1787	Shippensburg State College	Shippensburg	1871
Gannon College	Erie	1944	Slippery Rock State College	Slippery Rock	1889
Geneva College	Beaver Falls	1848	Susquehanna University	Selinsgrove	1858
Gettysburg College	Gettysburg	1832	Swarthmore College	Swarthmore	1864
Gratz College	Philadelphia	1952	Temple University	Philadelphia	1888
Grove City College	Grove City	1876	Thiel College	Greenville	1870
Gwynedd-Mercy College	Gwynedd Valley	1948	Ursinus College	Collegeville	1869
Haverford College	Haverford	1833	Villa Maria College	Erie	1882
Holy Family College	Philadelphia	1954	Villanova University	Villanova	1842
Immaculata College	Immaculata	1920	Washington and Jefferson		
Indiana University of			College	Washington	1802
Pennsylvania	Indiana	1871	Waynesburg College	Waynesburg	1850
Juniata College	Huntingdon	1876	West Chester State College	West Chester	1871
King's College	Wilkes-Barre	1946	Westminster College	New Wilmington	1852
Kutztown State College	Kutztown	1860	Westminster Theological		
Lafayette College	Easton	1826	Seminary	Philadelphia	1929
La Salle College	Philadelphia	1863	Wilkes College	Wilkes-Barre	1933
Lebanon Valley College	Annville	1866	Wilson College	Chambersburg	1869

librarians gathered in Philadelphia for the first meeting of the American Library Association.

Today, Pennsylvania has about 430 public libraries and 40 bookmobiles. The Philadelphia Free Library has nearly 2½ million volumes. The Carnegie Library in Pittsburgh and the University of Pennsylvania library both have collections of almost 2 million volumes. Famous book collections in the state include the Haverford College Quaker books, and the Horace Howard Furness Memorial Library of Shakespearean literature at the University of Pennsylvania.

Museums. The Pennsylvania Academy of the Fine Arts in Philadelphia, founded in 1805, is the nation's oldest art school. The Academy of Natural Sciences of Philadelphia is the oldest institution of natural sciences

in the United States. It was founded in 1812. The nation's first institute of applied sciences and mechanical arts, the Franklin Institute, opened in Philadelphia in 1824. It houses the Fels Planetarium. The state museum and archives, called the William Penn Memorial Museum and Archives, opened in Harrisburg in 1964. The Carnegie Institute Museum in Pittsburgh includes the Museum of Science and the Gallery of Fine Arts. In 1965, Strasburg was picked as the site of the Pennsylvania State Railroad Museum. Other excellent Pennsylvania museums include the Bucks County Historical Museum in Doylestown, Drake Well Museum in Titusville, Hershey Museum in Hershey, Pennsylvania Farm Museum in Lancaster County, Philadelphia Museum of Art, and Rodin Museum in Philadelphia.

PENNSYLVANIA / *A Visitor's Guide*

Winter and summer sports and beautiful waterfalls attract visitors to the Pocono Mountains. The Delaware Water Gap, along the Pennsylvania-New Jersey border, is a popular summer resort area. The Pennsylvania Dutch region in southeastern Pennsylvania is another favorite of sightseers. Many tourists and historians visit the state's many historic sites and battlefields of the Revolutionary and Civil wars.

The Liberty Bell in Philadelphia

WORLD BOOK photo, by Three Lions

Tortora, Three Lions

A Pennsylvania Dutch Barn near New Smithville

——— PLACES TO VISIT ———

Following are brief descriptions of some of Pennsylvania's many interesting places to visit.

Ephrata Cloisters, in Ephrata, is a restored religious community built by German Seventh-Day Baptists in 1732. During the summer months, the famous Ephrata choir sings and a historical pageant is presented.

Flagship *Niagara*, restored in Erie, is the ship of Oliver Hazard Perry, who defeated the British navy on the Great Lakes during the War of 1812.

Hawk Mountain Bird Sanctuary, in the Kittatinny Mountains, is one of the world's few refuges for birds of prey, such as eagles and hawks.

Pennsylvania Farm Museum, a village near Lancaster, tells the story of Pennsylvania's village and farm life from the 1800's until modern times.

Philadelphia, the birthplace of the United States, served as the nation's capital during most of the Revolutionary War. Visitors can see many historic sites by visiting Independence National Historical Park. The U.S. Mint conducts four tours daily. See PHILADELPHIA (The City).

Pine Creek Gorge, near Wellsboro, is a beautiful 1,100-foot-deep canyon dug thousands of years ago by the Pine Creek River. It is known as the *Grand Canyon of Pennsylvania.*

Roadside America, near Hamburg, is an indoor miniature village that tells the story of American life from pioneer days to the present.

Mummer's Parade on New Year's Day in Philadelphia

R. R. Frame & Co.

Oliver Perry's Flagship in Erie

Grant Heilman

Naddeo, Three Lions
Cloisters in Ephrata

Osborne, Three Lions
Horse Show in Devon

Rockville Bridge, near Harrisburg, stretches 3,820 feet across the Susquehanna River. It is one of the world's largest stone arch bridges.

Strasburg Railroad, near Lancaster, still operates on old-time steam equipment. It is one of the oldest chartered short-line railroads in the United States.

National Forests, Shrines, and Historic Sites. Allegheny National Forest in central Pennsylvania is the state's only national forest. Gettysburg National Military Park was the scene of the historic Battle of Gettysburg during the Civil War. There, on Nov. 19, 1863, Abraham Lincoln delivered his immortal Gettysburg Address. Independence National Historical Park in Philadelphia includes Independence Hall, Congress Hall, and many other famous historic places. Other sites in the state include Fort Necessity National Battlefield in southwestern Pennsylvania, Gettysburg National Cemetery, Gloria Dei (Old Swedes') Church National Historic Site in Philadelphia, and Hopewell Village National Historic Site in southeastern Pennsylvania.

State Parks and Forests. Pennsylvania has more than 75 state parks, and 10 historical parks, 2 state forest monuments, 7 natural areas, and 47 state forest picnic areas. For information on the state parks of Pennsylvania, write to Director, Pennsylvania Department of Forests and Waters, Division of State Parks, Harrisburg, Pa. 17120.

Memorial Day Services at Gettysburg National Cemetery
Lane, Three Lions

ANNUAL EVENTS

One of Pennsylvania's most popular annual events is the Mummer's Parade, held on New Year's Day in Philadelphia. People celebrate the New Year by dressing in costumes and marching through the streets. Other annual events in Pennsylvania include the following.

January-March: State Farm Show in Harrisburg (January); Glass Manufacturers' Show in Pittsburgh (January); Exhibition of the Pennsylvania Academy of the Fine Arts in Philadelphia (last week in January); Winter Carnivals at Erie and Denton Hill (February); Iceboat Races at Harmony, Lake Naomi, Pocono, and Wallenpaupack (February); Annual Boy Scouts Pilgrimage at Valley Forge (February 22); Charter Day, honoring the granting of Pennsylvania's charter to William Penn, statewide (March 4); Sportsmen's Show in Philadelphia (February).

April-June: Oil Painting Exhibition in Philadelphia (April); Penn Relay Carnival in Philadelphia (last week in April); Apple Blossom Festival in York (May 15-30); Artists' Masked Ball in Philadelphia (May); Bach Festival in Bethlehem (third week in May); Memorial Day Celebration in Gettysburg (May 30); Pocono Mountain Music Festival in the Pocono Mountains (June); Horse Show and County Fair in Devon (June); Flag Day Celebration at the Betsy Ross House in Philadelphia (June 14); Pageant and Fete at Gloria Dei (Old Swedes') Church in Philadelphia (second week in June); Craft Festival at Pennsylvania Farm Museum near Lancaster (third week in June).

July-September: Pennsylvania German Folklore Festival in Kutztown (first week in July); Pocono Mountains Horse Show in Stroudsburg (July); Pennsylvania Dutch Days in Hershey (August); Farmfolk Festival in New Milford (August-September); Labor Day Pageant in Harrisburg (first week in September).

October-December: International Exhibition of Paintings at the Carnegie Institute Museum in Pittsburgh (October); Pennsylvania National Horse Show in Harrisburg (October); Pennsylvania Day, statewide (October 24); Navy Day and Open House at the Navy Yard in Philadelphia (October 27); Army-Navy football game in Philadelphia (November).

229

PENNSYLVANIA

State Capitals ⊛   Cities and Towns •

Rail Lines   City Limits

1 inch = 35.5 Statute Miles

Miles 0   10   20   30

Lambert Conformal Conic Projection

Mixed Evergreen and
Deciduous Trees

Deciduous Trees

230

Specially created for **World Book Encyclopedia** by Rand McNally and World Book editors

Grant Heilman

Coal Rolls into Railroad Cars from a coal breaker in Shamokin in the Appalachian Ridge and Valley Region. Pennsylvania's hard-coal fields lie in the eastern part of this region.

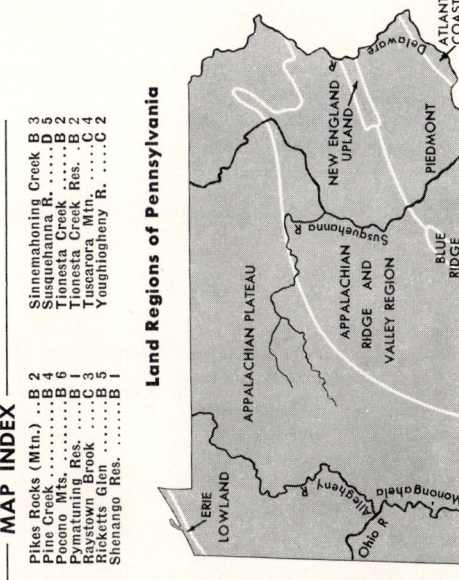

Land Regions of Pennsylvania

PENNSYLVANIA/The Land

Land Regions. Pennsylvania has seven main land regions. They are, from west to east: (1) the Erie Lowland, (2) the Appalachian Plateau, (3) the Appalachian Ridge and Valley Region, (4) the Blue Ridge, (5) the Piedmont, (6) the New England Upland, and (7) the Atlantic Coastal Plain.

The Erie Lowland covers parts of Pennsylvania and New York state. It is a narrow strip in the extreme northwestern corner of Pennsylvania, along the shores of Lake Erie. The flat land of the region was once part of the lake bed. Vegetables and fruits, especially grapes, thrive in its sandy soil.

The Appalachian Plateau extends from New York to Alabama. In Pennsylvania, it is also called the *Allegheny Plateau*. It covers the entire northern and western portions of Pennsylvania, except for the narrow Erie Lowland region. The Appalachian Plateau consists of deep, narrow valleys and broad-topped plateaulike *divides* (land ridges from which rivers flow in opposite directions). Glacial rocks and boulders dot the northern

part of the region. Plateaus rise to more than 2,000 feet in the north-central section, and slope gradually to the east, west, and southwest. Chestnut Ridge and the Laurel Hills, in southwestern Pennsylvania, form some of the higher and more rugged parts of the region. Mount Davis, the state's highest point, rises 3,213 feet in Somerset County near the southern boundary. The western Appalachian Plateau has many coal, gas, and oil fields. The Pocono Mountains are in the eastern part of the Appalachian Plateau.

The Appalachian Ridge and Valley Region extends from New York to Alabama. In Pennsylvania, it forms a wide strip of land that curves south and east of the Appalachian Plateau. The area where the ridge and valley region and the Appalachian Plateau come together is called the *Allegheny Front*.

An area called the Great Valley sweeps along the southern and eastern boundary of Pennsylvania's ridge and valley region. The Great Valley is divided into the Cumberland, Lebanon, and Lehigh valleys. All

these valleys are noted for fertile farmland. North and west of the Great Valley, the region consists of a series of long, parallel ridges and valleys that curve from southwest to northeast. The ridges include Blue, Jacks, and Tuscarora mountains, which belong to the Appalachian Mountain system. The ridges consist of folded layers of *sedimentary rock* (rock formed from deposits laid down by ancient rivers and lakes). Erosion has worn down the softer rock layers, forming the valleys that lie between the ridges. The Delaware Water Gap opens through the Kittatinny Mountains along the Pennsylvania-New Jersey boundary. Pennsylvania's hard-coal fields and slate formations are in the eastern part of the Appalachian Ridge and Valley Region.

The Blue Ridge, named for the Blue Ridge Mountains, stretches from southern Pennsylvania to Georgia. In Pennsylvania, it forms a narrow, finger-shaped region at the state's south-central border. Beautiful South Mountain, scenic Buchanan Valley, and part of Gettysburg National Park are in this region.

Scheller, Three Lions

Delaware River winds along the eastern border of Pennsylvania, and touches five of Pennsylvania's seven land regions. The river also helps drain the eastern and central parts of the state. A railroad bridge crosses the river near Stroudsburg.

Farmers Harvest Wheat near Lancaster in the Piedmont region. They use combines (machines that cut and thresh the grain). The Pennsylvania Dutch areas of Lancaster and York counties have some of the richest farmland in the country.

Grant Heilman, Alpha

The Piedmont extends from New Jersey to Alabama. In Pennsylvania, it covers most of the southeastern part of the state. The region has rolling plains, and low hills with irregular ridges and fertile valleys. The Pennsylvania Dutch areas of Lancaster and York counties have some of the richest farmland in the United States.

The New England Upland extends from Pennsylvania to Maine. In Pennsylvania, it forms a narrow rectangular region in the eastern part of the state. This region is a ridge that crosses parts of Berks, Bucks, Lehigh, and Northampton counties.

The Atlantic Coastal Plain stretches from New York to southern Florida. In Pennsylvania, it is a narrow strip of land that crosses the southeastern corner of the state. The coastal plain is low, level, and fertile. It drops to sea level along the Delaware River. Philadelphia is near the center of the region.

Rivers, Waterfalls, and Lakes. Eastern and central Pennsylvania are drained by the Delaware, Juniata, Lehigh, Schuylkill, and Susquehanna rivers. The Ohio River system drains western Pennsylvania. The Ohio begins where the Allegheny and Monongahela rivers meet at Pittsburgh. It flows to the Gulf of Mexico by way of the Mississippi River.

Some of the most spectacular waterfalls in the eastern United States plunge over cliffs in the Pocono Mountains. Falls include Bushkill, Raymondskill, and Winona falls. Other waterfalls in the state are Beaver, Buttermilk, Dingmans, and Silver Thread.

Lake Conneaut is the largest natural lake entirely within Pennsylvania. It covers about $1\frac{1}{2}$ square miles in the northwestern section. The largest body of water in the state is man-made Lake Wallenpaupack. It covers 9 square miles in northeastern Pennsylvania, and is used to provide hydroelectric power. Pymatuning Reservoir, also man-made, covers almost 26 square miles. It extends into Ohio. Many glacial lakes dot the northeastern Appalachian Plateau. Lake Erie touches the northwestern corner of Pennsylvania.

SEASONAL TEMPERATURES

JANUARY

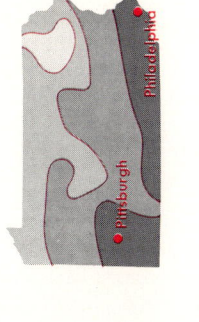
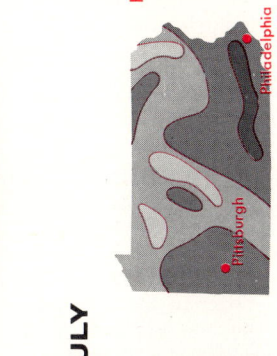

AVERAGE OF DAILY HIGH TEMPERATURES

Degrees Fahrenheit	Degrees Centigrade
40 to 44	4 to 7
36 to 40	2 to 4
32 to 36	0 to 2
28 to 32	-2 to 0

AVERAGE OF DAILY LOW TEMPERATURES

Degrees Centigrade	Degrees Fahrenheit
-4 to -2	24 to 28
-7 to -4	20 to 24
-9 to -7	16 to 20
-11 to -9	12 to 16

JULY

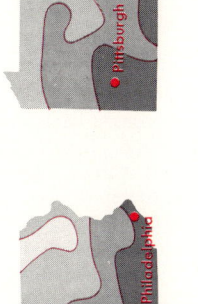

AVERAGE OF DAILY HIGH TEMPERATURES

Degrees Fahrenheit	Degrees Centigrade
88 to 92	31 to 33
84 to 88	29 to 31
80 to 84	27 to 29
76 to 80	24 to 27

AVERAGE OF DAILY LOW TEMPERATURES

Degrees Centigrade	Degrees Fahrenheit
19 to 21	66 to 70
17 to 19	62 to 66
14 to 17	58 to 62
12 to 14	54 to 58
10 to 12	50 to 54

AVERAGE YEARLY PRECIPITATION
(Rain, Melted Snow, and Other Moisture)

Inches	Centimeters
44 to 52	112 to 132
36 to 44	91 to 112
28 to 36	71 to 91

Scale: 0 50 100 200 Miles — 0 50 100 200 300 Kilometers

WORLD BOOK maps

MONTHLY WEATHER IN PHILADELPHIA AND PITTSBURGH

		JAN	FEB	MAR	APR	MAY	JUNE	JULY	AUG	SEPT	OCT	NOV	DEC
PHILADELPHIA	Average of: High Temperatures	41	42	52	62	74	83	87	84	78	67	55	44
	Low Temperatures	25	25	33	41	52	62	66	64	58	46	37	27
	Days of Rain or Snow	12	9	12	11	12	11	9	9	8	8	9	10
PITTSBURGH	Days of Rain or Snow	16	14	16	15	11	12	10	9	7	11	12	16
	High Temperatures	37	38	48	59	71	79	83	81	75	63	49	38
	Low Temperatures	21	21	29	38	49	58	62	59	55	43	33	24

Temperatures are given in degrees Fahrenheit.

Source: U.S. Weather Bureau

Fog and Haze often cover the mountains near Stevensville. Pennsylvania has a moist climate, ideal for agriculture.

Grant Heilman

PENNSYLVANIA/Climate

Pennsylvania has a moist climate with cold winters and warm summers. Temperatures are generally lower in the northern and western parts of the state than in the southern and eastern portions. January temperatures average 26° F. in northern Pennsylvania, 27° F. in the Erie Lowland, and 34° F. in the southeastern section. Average July temperatures range from 70° F. in the northwest to 75° F. in the southwest and 77° F. in the southeast. The state's record low temperature, −42° F., occurred in Smethport in McKean County on Jan. 5, 1904. Phoenixville, in southeastern Pennsylvania, recorded the state's highest temperature, 111° F., on July 9 and 10, 1936.

Pennsylvania's yearly *precipitation* (rain, melted snow, and other forms of moisture) averages about 42 inches. It ranges from 34 to 44 inches a year in the northwest, and from 42 to 47 inches a year in the southeast. Snowfall averages from 20 inches in the extreme southeast to 90 inches in McKean County in the northwest.

A Mushroom Farmer uses a miner's lamp to inspect his crop in a windowless barn. Mushrooms need darkness to start to grow. Chester County farmers produce most of the mushrooms in Pennsylvania.

WORLD BOOK photo by Three Lions

PENNSYLVANIA /*Economy*

Philadelphia is Pennsylvania's leading manufacturing center, followed by Pittsburgh. Other important manufacturing cities include Allentown, Bethlehem, Erie, Lancaster, Reading, Scranton, Wilkes-Barre, and York. Much of Pennsylvania has rich farmland. Dairy farming thrives in the northeast, poultry farming in the southeast, and cattle raising in the southwest. Some of the best farmland in the United States is in southeastern Pennsylvania. Coal is mined in the northeastern and western counties. Oil wells are found in the northwest. Limestone, natural gas, and many other minerals are also mined in the state. Pennsylvania's tourist industry flourishes in Philadelphia, on Lake Erie, in the Pocono Mountains, throughout the Pennsylvania Dutch area, and in many other sections.

Natural Resources of Pennsylvania include rich soils, great mineral wealth, and good water supplies. The state also has abundant forests and plant and animal life.

Soil. Pennsylvania has many kinds of soil. Much of the Piedmont, the New England Upland, and the Atlantic Coastal Plain regions are covered with well-drained, gray-brown to reddish-brown soils. These are some of the most fertile soils in the eastern United

States. Rich shale and limestone soils cover the valleys of the Appalachian Ridge and Valley Region. Stony soils cover much of the hard, sandstone-capped ridges. Gravelly and sandy loams, formed by glacial lake deposits, cover the Erie Lowland in extreme northwestern Pennsylvania. Infertile sandstone and shale soils cover much of the Appalachian Plateau.

Minerals. Large deposits of *anthracite* (hard) coal occur in Lackawanna, Luzerne, Northumberland, Schuylkill, and other counties in northeastern Pennsylvania. The western part of the state has huge deposits of *bituminous* (soft) coal. Deposits of limestone, sand and gravel, and slate are also common. Most of the western counties have small petroleum and natural gas fields. Morgantown and Cornwall have small deposits of iron ore. Other minerals found in Pennsylvania include cobalt, copper, gold, silver, and zinc.

Forests cover about 15 million acres, or more than half the state. Mixtures of hardwood and softwood trees are found in northern Pennsylvania and on the higher ridges in the south. They consist mainly of beeches, birches, hemlocks, maples, and pines. Hardwoods, including hickories, oaks, and walnuts, grow chiefly in the lowland sections of southeastern and southwestern Pennsylvania. These hardwood trees may also be found in some of the northern valleys of the Appalachian Ridge and Valley Region. Other common Pennsylvania trees include the ash, linden, poplar, sassafras, sycamore, and weeping willow.

PRODUCTION IN PENNSYLVANIA

Total yearly value of goods produced—$20,602,108,000

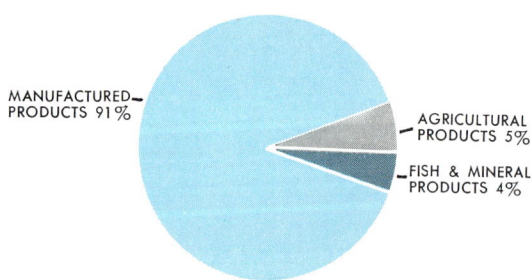

MANUFACTURED PRODUCTS 91%

AGRICULTURAL PRODUCTS 5%

FISH & MINERAL PRODUCTS 4%

Note: Manufacturing percentage based on value added by manufacture. Other percentages based on value of production. Fish Products are less than 1 per cent.

Source: Latest available U.S. Government statistics

EMPLOYMENT IN PENNSYLVANIA

Average yearly number of persons employed—3,906,003

		Number of Employees
Manufacturing	𝍖	1,406,000
Wholesale & Retail Trade	𝍖	680,500
Services	𝍖	545,300
Government	𝍖	456,600
Transportation & Public Utilities	𝍖	264,400
Agriculture	𝍖	171,000
Construction	𝍖	163,200
Finance, Insurance & Real Estate	𝍖	160,300
Fishing, Forestry & Mining	𝍖	58,703

Source: Employment statistics supplied by employers to government agencies

Plant Life. Rhododendrons, wild azaleas, wild berries, wild ginger, and wintergreen grow throughout Pennsylvania. Shrubbery of mountain laurel, the state flower, spreads over much of the countryside. Colorful clusters of bouncing Bet, hound's-tongue, milkweed, sundew, and viper's bugloss brighten the riverbanks. Greenbriers and ferns grow in the western valleys. Common spring flowers found in Pennsylvania include the anemone, bloodroot, dogtooth violet, hepatica, and wild honeysuckle.

Animal Life in Pennsylvania's fields and forests includes deer, moles, muskrats, opossums, rabbits, and skunks. Hunters search the mountains and wooded areas of northern Pennsylvania for black bears, the state's most prized game animals. The ruffed grouse, Pennsylvania's state bird, feeds along woodland streams. Wild turkeys live in some parts of the state. Other common game birds include gray partridges and ring-necked pheasants. More than 150 kinds of fishes are found in Pennsylvania's lakes, rivers, and streams. They include bass, brown trout, carp, chubs, and pickerels.

Manufacturing, including processing, accounts for more than 90 per cent of the value of goods produced in Pennsylvania. Manufactured goods have a *value added by manufacture* of about $18,752,000,000 yearly. This figure represents the value created in products by Pennsylvania's industries, not counting such costs as materials, supplies, and fuels. Pennsylvania ranks among the leading manufacturing states. Its chief manufacturing industries are, in order of importance, (1) primary metals, (2) electrical machinery, (3) machinery, and (4) food and related products.

Primary Metals industries produce products that have a value added of about $3,758,875,000 a year. Pittsburgh accounts for more than half this total. The primary metals industries smelt, refine, and roll metals. They also manufacture such items as nails, bolts, and basic metal products such as castings. Pennsylvania leads the United States in the production of pig iron and steel. It produces about a fourth of the nation's pig iron and about a fourth of its steel. It also manufactures about three-tenths of the nation's coke, a fuel used in smelting iron ore. Pennsylvania produces more than 32 million tons of steel annually. Huge furnaces are in Bethlehem, Coatesville, Johnstown, Lebanon, Morrisville, Pittsburgh, and Steelton. Much of the iron ore processed in Pennsylvania comes from northern Minnesota. Some iron ore comes from other countries.

Electrical Machinery has a yearly value added of about $1,856,971,000. Electrical machinery industries produce such products as electrical appliances, electronics instruments, measuring instruments, and turbines. Philadelphia is the state's leading producer of electrical machinery, followed by Pittsburgh and Lancaster.

Machinery, other than electrical, has a value added of about $1,832,812,000 annually. Factories in Philadelphia lead the state in the production of machinery. Pittsburgh plants rank second in the state. Other leading cities that manufacture machinery include Allentown, Lancaster, Reading, and York.

Food and Related Products have a value added of about $1,501,892,000 yearly. Pennsylvania is a leading food processing state. It leads the United States in mushroom canning, and ranks among the leaders in the

WORLD BOOK photo by Three Lions

Workers Make Glass Hurricane Lamps in a factory in Jeannette. Pennsylvania ranks among the most important industrial states, and is a leader in the manufacture of glass products.

manufacture of ice cream, potato chips, pretzels, and sausage. Hershey has the largest chocolate and cocoa factory in the world. Philadelphia is the state's principal food-processing center.

Other Leading Industries. Fabricated metal products, and chemicals and allied products rank fifth and sixth in Pennsylvania. Each of these industries has a value added of about $1\frac{1}{4}$ billion yearly. Philadelphia leads in the production of fabricated metal products, and produces most of the state's chemical products. Other important Pennsylvania industries include transportation equipment; the manufacture of clothing and related products; printing and publishing; stone, clay, and glass products; paper and allied products; and textile mill products.

Agriculture in Pennsylvania has a yearly gross income of about $1,055,000,000. Farmland covers more than a third of the state. Pennsylvania's more than 80,000 farms average 130 acres in size.

Livestock and Livestock Products have an annual value of about $677,166,000. Milk is Pennsylvania's leading farm product. It earns about $368 million a year—more than a third of the total farm income. Pennsylvania is among the leading milk producing states. It also ranks among the leaders in the production of eggs and dairy cattle, the second and third ranking farm products in the state. Dairy farming is especially important in northeastern Pennsylvania. Lancaster County,

235

in the southeast, has many poultry farms. Herds of livestock graze on the rolling hills of the southwest and on the land drained by the Susquehanna River.

Crops in Pennsylvania have an annual value of about $224,029,000. Greenhouse and nursery products are the leading cash crops, earning about $79,170,000 a year. Corn ranks second, followed by potatoes, wheat, and apples.

Southeastern Pennsylvania has some of the nation's richest farmland. Pennsylvania is the leading producer of mushrooms and cigar-filler tobacco, and is among the leading buckwheat producers. Mushrooms grow chiefly in Chester County, tobacco in Lancaster County, and buckwheat on the Appalachian Plateau. Large quantities of grapes are grown in the Erie Lowland. Southern and southeastern Pennsylvania have large apple and peach orchards. Vegetable farming thrives in the areas around Harrisburg, Philadelphia, Pittsburgh, and Reading.

Mining. Pennsylvania is one of the leading mining states. Mining in Pennsylvania has an annual value of about $795 million.

Pennsylvania ranks second only to West Virginia in coal production. The northeastern counties of Pennsylvania mine about 13 million tons of *anthracite* (hard) coal yearly. This production accounts for all the anthracite coal mined in the United States. Mines in the western counties and in other parts of the state produce about 80 million tons of *bituminous* (soft) coal a year. Bituminous coal is used to make coke for the steel industry. It is also burned to generate electricity.

Pennsylvania is one of the leading producers of crushed limestone. Limestone is used in the manufacture of cement and lime, and in smelting iron ore. Northwest Pennsylvania has about 60,000 producing oil wells. Oil refineries at Bradford, Franklin, Oil City, and Warren process the state's petroleum. The more than 17,800 gas wells in the state produce about 91 billion cubic feet of natural gas yearly. Iron ore is mined at Morgantown and at a pit in Cornwall that has operated since 1742. This Cornwall mine also provides cobalt, copper, silver, and sulfur. Other products mined in the state include gold, sand and gravel, slate, and zinc.

Electric Power. Coal is used to produce about nine-tenths of Pennsylvania's electric power. Hydroelectric plants provide much of the rest. In 1957, the nation's first large-scale, nuclear-power electric plant began operating in Shippingport. A second commercial nuclear-power station was scheduled to open in York County in the early 1970's. In 1965, 12 electric utility companies announced plans to build a giant power plant at the mouths of coal mines in Indiana County. The plant will send electricity to Delaware, Maryland, New Jersey, New York, Pennsylvania, Virginia, and Washington, D.C. It is scheduled for completion in the early 1970's. For Pennsylvania's kilowatt-hour production, see ELECTRIC POWER (table).

Transportation. Pennsylvania has been a transportation leader since colonial times. One famous early road, Queen's Road, linked Philadelphia and Chester. It was completed in 1706. The Old York Road was built between Philadelphia and New York City in the early 1700's. In the mid-1700's, the first Conestoga wagon was built in Conestoga, in what is now Lancaster County. The nation's first hard-surfaced road was opened between Philadelphia and Lancaster in 1795. The Pennsylvania Railroad (now part of the Penn Central Railroad), one of the nation's leading carriers, was chartered in 1846. The first section of the Pennsylvania Turnpike, between Middlesex and Irwin, was completed in 1940. It was later extended east to New Jersey, west to Ohio, and northward from Philadelphia to Scranton. The 313-mile Keystone Shortway, which will cross Pennsylvania from New Jersey to Ohio, was scheduled for completion in 1970.

Today, Pennsylvania has more than 100,000 miles of roads and highways, about 80 per cent of which are paved. The state ranks among the leaders in railroad mileage, with more than 8,800 miles of track. About 450 airports serve the state. All the major cities have municipal airports and also private landing fields.

Many Pennsylvania communities have water transportation. Pittsburgh is the largest inland river port in the United States, and the center of the state's inland waterway system. From Pittsburgh, boats can travel about 980 miles on the Ohio River, 80 miles on the Monongahela, and 66 miles on the Allegheny. Ocean-going ships can travel up the Delaware River as far as Philadelphia, and beyond to Morrisville. Philadelphia is one of the leading U.S. port cities. Other important ports in Pennsylvania include Chester, Clairton-Elizabeth, Erie, Marcus Hook, and Penn Manor.

Communication. Pennsylvania's first newspaper, the *American Weekly Mercury*, was established in Philadelphia in 1719. It was the fourth newspaper published in the American colonies, and the first outside Boston. Benjamin Franklin of Philadelphia published the *Pennsylvania Gazette* from 1729 until 1766, and *Poor Richard's Almanac* from 1733 until 1758. In 1741, Andrew Bradford established America's first magazine, in Philadelphia. He called it *The American Magazine, or A Monthly View of the Political State of the British Colonies.* Louis Godey founded *Godey's Lady's Book*, one of the first woman's magazines in the United States, in 1830 in Philadelphia.

In 1920, Frank Conrad, an engineer of the Westinghouse Electric Corporation, set up a broadcasting sta-

Steel Mill in Conshohocken manufactures products that help make Pennsylvania the leading U.S. producer of coke and pig iron.
WORLD BOOK photo by Three Lions

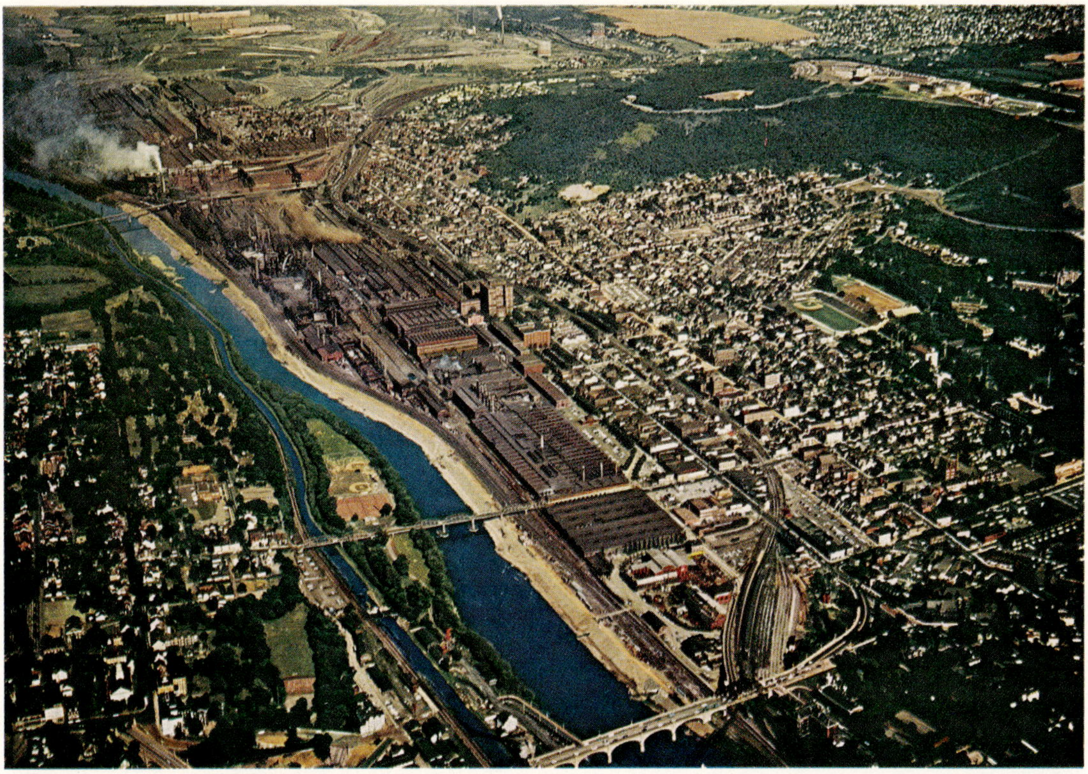

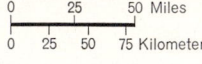

Bethlehem Steel Corp.

Bethlehem Steel Corporation Plant spreads across the city of Bethlehem in eastern Pennsylvania. The city is one of the largest steel-producing centers in the United States. Pennsylvania leads all the states in the production of steel.

tion, 8XK, in his Pittsburgh home. That same year, Conrad and some other Westinghouse engineers established radio station KDKA. It began broadcasting on Nov. 2, 1920. KDKA and Detroit's WWJ were the first regular commercial radio stations in the United States. Pennsylvania's first television station began broadcasting in Philadelphia in 1941. It still broadcasts as WRCV-TV.

Today, Pennsylvania has more than 500 newspapers, about 125 of which are dailies. Leading papers include the *Philadelphia Evening Bulletin*, the *Philadelphia Inquirer*, the *Post-Gazette* and *Sun-Telegraph* of Pittsburgh, and the *Pittsburgh Press*. The *Pittsburgh Courier* is one of the largest Negro newspapers in the United States. Over 550 periodicals are published in Pennsylvania. The state has about 225 radio stations and 20 TV stations.

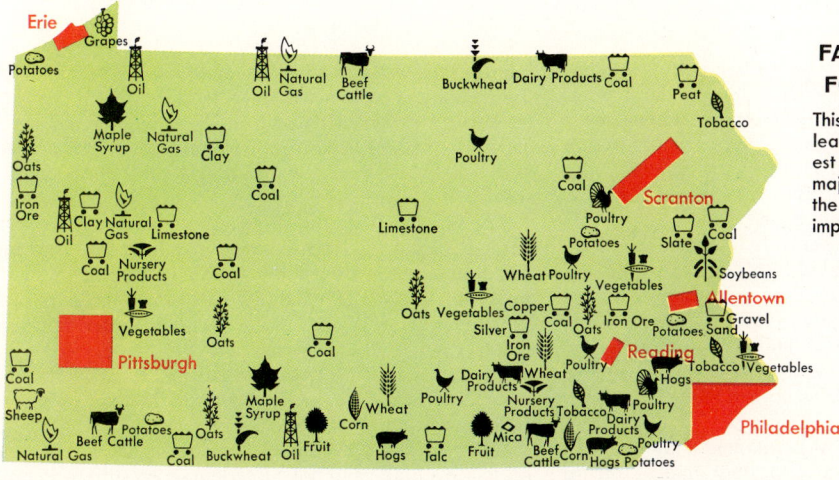

FARM, MINERAL, AND FOREST PRODUCTS

This map shows where the state's leading farm, mineral, and forest products are produced. The major urban areas (shown on the map in red) are the state's important manufacturing centers.

0 25 50 Miles
0 25 50 75 Kilometers

WORLD BOOK map

PENNSYLVANIA

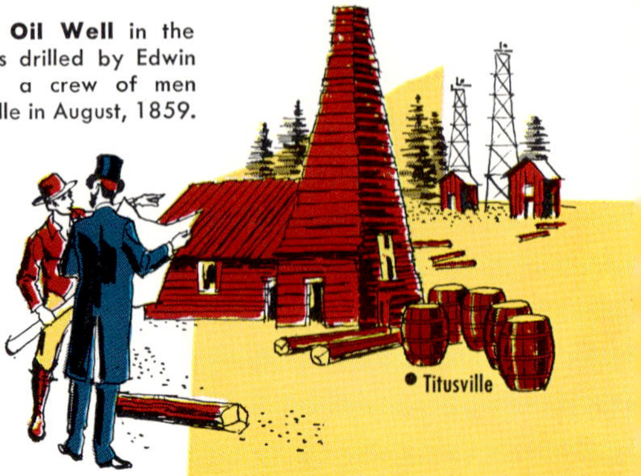

The First Oil Well in the country was drilled by Edwin Drake and a crew of men near Titusville in August, 1859.

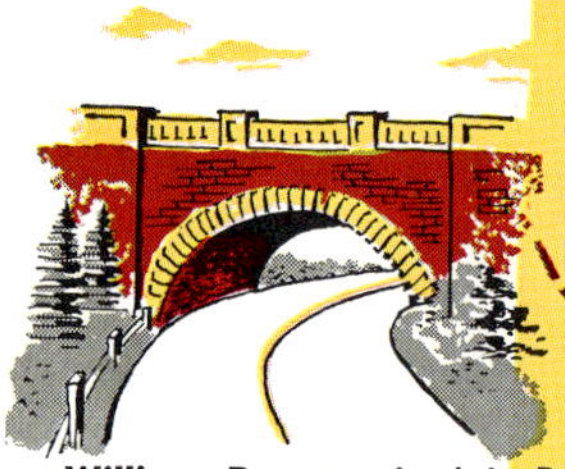

• Titusville

The Pennsylvania Turnpike covers 470 miles. The first turnpike, from Lancaster to Philadelphia, was completed in 1795. It was America's first paved road.

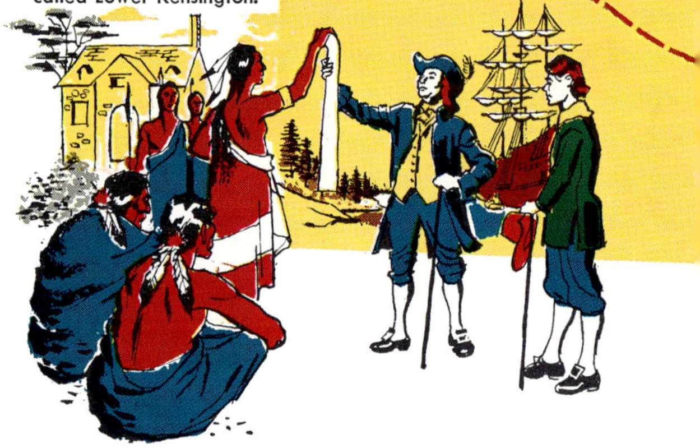

William Penn arrived in Pennsylvania in 1682. He arranged a treaty of friendship with the Indians in a section of Philadelphia now called Lower Kensington.

PENNSYLVANIA / History

Indian Days. Indians probably lived in the Pennsylvania region hundreds or even thousands of years before white men came. Early white explorers found Algonkian and Iroquoian Indians there. The Algonkian tribes included the Conoy, Delaware, Nanticoke, and Shawnee. The Iroquoian tribe, the Susquehannock, lived along the Susquehanna River.

Exploration and Settlement. In 1609, the British explorer Henry Hudson sailed into Delaware Bay. He was trying to find a trade route to the Far East for the Dutch East India Company. Hudson soon left the region, but his reports led the Dutch to send other explorers. In 1615, a Dutch explorer, Captain Cornelius Hendricksen, sailed up the Delaware River to what is now Philadelphia.

The Swedes made the first permanent settlements in the Pennsylvania region. In 1643, they made Tinicum Island, near what is now Philadelphia, the capital of their colony of New Sweden. In 1655, Dutch troops led by Peter Stuyvesant came from New Netherland and captured New Sweden (see STUYVESANT, PETER). The Dutch held the Pennsylvania region until 1664, when the English captured it.

The English Duke of York controlled the Pennsylvania region until 1681. That year, King Charles II of England granted the region to William Penn in payment of a debt to Penn's father. Penn wanted to name the region New Wales. But a Welsh member of England's Privy Council objected to the name. So Penn decided to call it *Sylvania*, which means *woods*. King Charles added *Penn* to the name in honor of Penn's father, an English admiral.

Colonial Days. William Penn, a Quaker, wanted his fellow Quakers to have freedom of worship in Penn-

HISTORIC PENNSYLVANIA

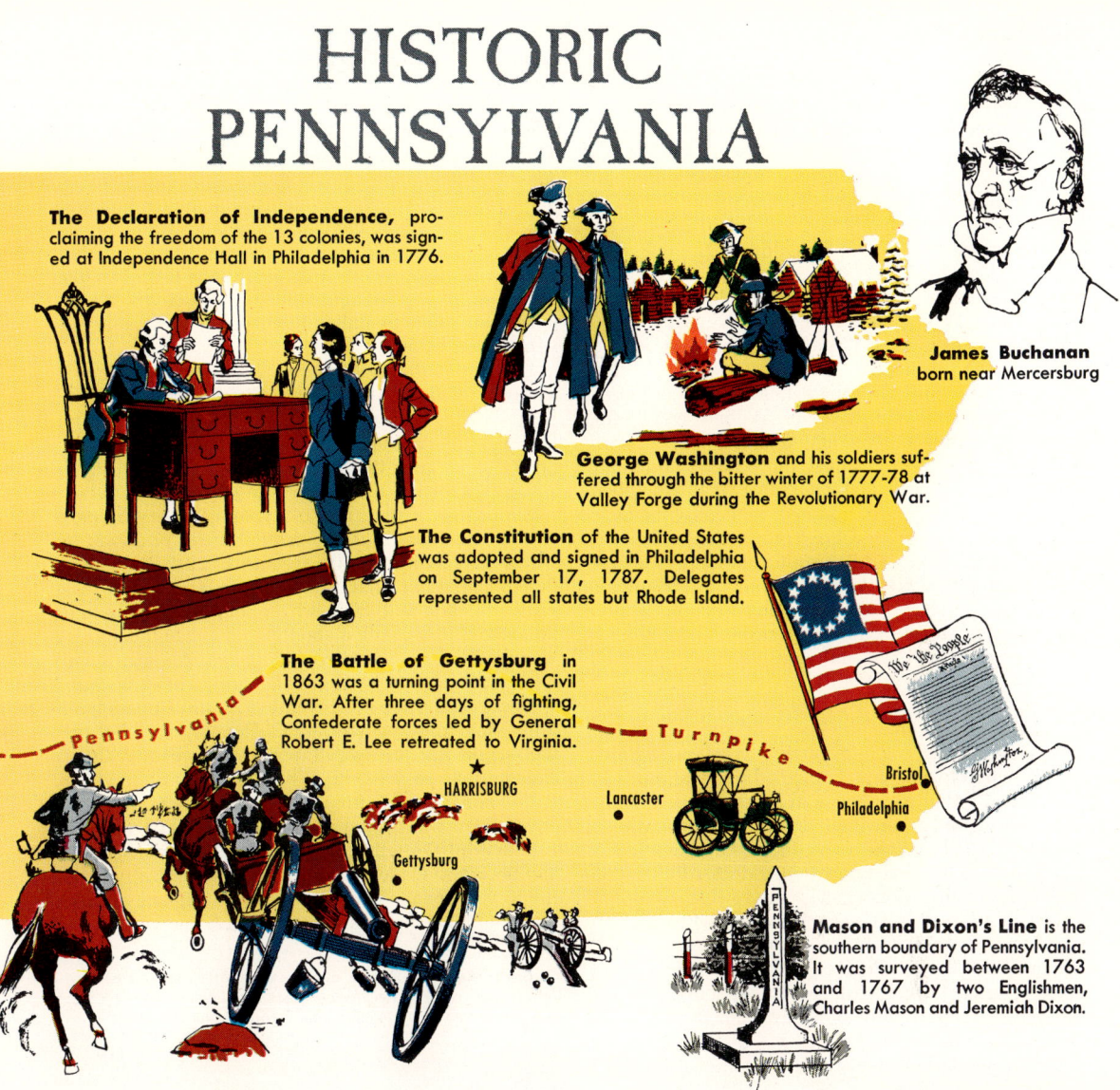

The Declaration of Independence, proclaiming the freedom of the 13 colonies, was signed at Independence Hall in Philadelphia in 1776.

James Buchanan born near Mercersburg

George Washington and his soldiers suffered through the bitter winter of 1777-78 at Valley Forge during the Revolutionary War.

The Constitution of the United States was adopted and signed in Philadelphia on September 17, 1787. Delegates represented all states but Rhode Island.

The Battle of Gettysburg in 1863 was a turning point in the Civil War. After three days of fighting, Confederate forces led by General Robert E. Lee retreated to Virginia.

Pennsylvania

Turnpike

HARRISBURG

Lancaster

Bristol

Philadelphia

Gettysburg

Mason and Dixon's Line is the southern boundary of Pennsylvania. It was surveyed between 1763 and 1767 by two Englishmen, Charles Mason and Jeremiah Dixon.

sylvania. He also desired religious freedom for persons of other faiths. Penn wanted Pennsylvanians to enjoy personal and property rights, and to have self-government.

Penn came to Pennsylvania in 1682. As governor, he brought with him the colony's first constitution, called the Frame of Government. This constitution was written by Penn. It provided for a deputy governor, and an elected legislature consisting of a provincial council (upper house) and a general assembly (lower house).

Penn made a treaty of friendship with the Indians shortly after he arrived in the region. He also paid the Indians for most of the land King Charles had given him, although he did not have to do so. According to legend, Penn and Tamenend, the chief of the Delaware Indians, exchanged wampum belts under the famous Shackamaxon elm near Philadelphia. Benjamin West's

painting *Penn's Treaty with the Indians* appears in color in the PAINTING article.

The general assembly did not fully approve of the Frame of Government. In 1683, the legislature drafted and adopted a second Frame of Government. This second constitution gave the people of Pennsylvania more voice in the government by reducing some of the powers of wealthy landowners.

Penn went to England in 1684, leaving control of the government in the hands of a deputy governor. Troubles developed in the legislature during Penn's absence. Members of the general assembly resented the provincial council's power to originate laws. The assembly rejected or delayed action on much legislation that had originated in the council. When Penn learned about the trouble, he placed most of the powers of government in the hands of the provincial council. But the council failed to restore order. In 1688, Penn appointed another deputy governor.

In 1688, King James II, a close friend of Penn's, was overthrown. King James' daughter Mary and her husband, Prince William of Orange, became joint rulers of England. William and Mary did not trust Penn because of his friendship with King James. In 1692, they deprived Penn of his right to govern Pennsylvania. The royal governor of New York was made governor of Pennsylvania as well. In 1693, Penn convinced William and Mary of his loyalty. They restored him as governor of Pennsylvania in 1694.

Troubles still existed in the Pennsylvania legislature. In 1696, Penn's deputy governor, William Markham, suggested some constitutional changes. He wanted both legislative houses to have the power to originate laws. But this change still did not satisfy many members of the legislature. Penn returned to Pennsylvania in 1699. In 1701, he wrote a new constitution, called the Charter of Privileges. This constitution made the general assembly the chief lawmaking body in the colony. It gave the provincial council an advisory role. It also gave greater control of the government to the people.

Penn returned to England again in 1701, and died there in 1718. Penn's family governed Pennsylvania until the Revolutionary War began in 1775.

Colonial Wars. From the late 1600's to the middle 1700's, the English colonists fought several wars against the French colonists and France's Indian allies. The French and Indian War began in western Pennsylvania in 1754. One of the most brutal battles of the war took place in 1755. The French and Indians ambushed and killed most of General Edward Braddock's soldiers on the banks of the Monongahela River. Fighting continued in Pennsylvania until 1758, when the French withdrew from the colony. The war ended in 1763, with a British victory. Pontiac, an Ottawa chief, led an uprising against the British settlers later in 1763. He was defeated in the Battle of Bushy Run. Pennsylvania bought land from the Indians in the Fort Stanwix Treaty of 1768. This treaty settled most of the Indian troubles in the colony.

The Revolutionary War. In the mid-1700's, Great Britain found itself in debt. To raise money, Britain imposed new taxes and trade restrictions on its colonies in America. The colonies united to oppose these measures. Colonial leaders met to discuss how to resist the British restrictions. The First Continental Congress met in Philadelphia on Sept. 5, 1774. The Congress voted to stop all trade with Great Britain.

The Revolutionary War began in April, 1775. That May, the Second Continental Congress met in Philadelphia. The delegates voted for independence from Britain. On July 4, 1776, Congress adopted the final draft of the Declaration of Independence in the Pennsylvania State House (now Independence Hall) in Philadelphia. Pennsylvania's first state convention was held in the State House at the same time.

British troops in New York and New Jersey threatened Philadelphia in December, 1776. Congress moved to Baltimore for safety. But the British were turned away, and Congress returned to Philadelphia in March, 1777. British troops marched into Pennsylvania in September, 1777. They defeated General George Washington's forces in the Battle of Brandywine on September 11. The British then marched toward Philadelphia. Congress moved first to Lancaster, and then to York. On September 20 and 21, the British killed many American soldiers in the *Paoli Massacre*, outside Philadelphia. On September 26, the British marched across the Schuylkill River and captured Philadelphia. Washington led a sudden attack against the British on October 4, hoping to force them out of the city. But the attack failed. Washington led his troops to Whitemarsh, and then to Valley Forge where they spent the winter and spring.

In spite of their victories in Pennsylvania, the war was beginning to go badly for the British. In June, 1778, they withdrew from Philadelphia. The Continental Congress returned to the city. While in York, the Congress had adopted the Articles of Confederation. Pennsylvania approved the Articles on July 9, 1778.

Meanwhile, settlers in the Wyoming Valley, in present-day Luzerne County, were in danger of attack by British and Indians. In the summer of 1778, the settlers fled to a fort near what is now Wilkes-Barre. That July, an army of about 800 British soldiers and Indians attacked the fort, killing about two-thirds of the settlers. Many of the survivors died while trying to escape. The incident became known as the *Wyoming Valley Massacre*.

The Constitutional Convention met in Philadelphia from May to September, 1787. Pennsylvania became the second state to *ratify* (approve) the United States Constitution, on Dec. 12, 1787. Philadelphia served as the nation's capital from 1790 until 1800, when the government was moved to Washington, D.C.

Industrial Growth. As early as 1750, Pennsylvania had become a leader in the colonial iron industry. After the Revolutionary War, Pennsylvania became a center

Quaker Meeting House of the early 1800's served as a religious and social center. Many Quakers, seeking religious freedom, moved to Pennsylvania from Europe in the late 1600's.

The Bettmann Archive

of the nation's industrial growth. In 1787, John Fitch launched the first workable steamboat on the Delaware River, near Philadelphia. In 1811, a steamboat built by Robert Fulton was launched at Pittsburgh. It became the first to travel on the Ohio and Mississippi rivers. The Schuylkill Canal connected Philadelphia and Reading in 1825. It was the first long canal in the United States. By 1840, the use of *anthracite* (hard) coal as a fuel led to improvements in Pennsylvania's iron-making industry. By the 1850's, many railroads carried coal from northeast Pennsylvania to Philadelphia. In 1859, Edwin Drake drilled the world's first oil well, near Titusville. By 1860, Pittsburgh had become a leading industrial city and was known as the *Gateway to the West*. Philadelphia was one of the nation's major manufacturing cities.

The Civil War. Many Pennsylvanians firmly opposed slavery. They were among the leaders of the *abolitionist* (antislavery) movement in the United States. The state gave strong support to the Union during the Civil War (1861-1865). Pennsylvania sent 340,000 troops to the Union army. Only New York sent more troops.

Several raids and one major Civil War battle took place on Pennsylvania soil. The Confederate cavalry generals James Ewell Brown "Jeb" Stuart and Wade Hampton led troops in raids through the Cumberland Valley in October, 1862. In June, 1863, General Robert E. Lee led his powerful Confederate army of about 75,000 men into Pennsylvania. On July 1, Union forces under General George G. Meade met the Confederates at Gettysburg, in southern Pennsylvania. The three-day battle that followed was one of the bloodiest in history. It broke the strength of the Confederacy, and Lee retreated to Virginia. On Nov. 19, 1863, President Abraham Lincoln dedicated part of the Gettysburg battlefield as a cemetery for those who had died there. The President delivered his famous Gettysburg Address at the ceremonies.

Confederate general John McCausland invaded Pennsylvania in July, 1864. His forces attacked and burned Chambersburg, and then quickly left the state.

Progress as a State. Pennsylvania prospered after the Civil War. Many new industries developed. Pennsylvania became a leading producer of oil and aluminum. Pittsburgh grew into one of the nation's largest steel producers. Thousands of immigrants poured into the state, and cities and towns grew. But industrial growth brought serious labor problems. Workers in many industries formed unions and demanded higher wages. Railroad workers went on strike in 1877. Riots broke out, and strikers destroyed valuable railroad property.

In 1889, Johnstown, in southern Pennsylvania, suffered one of the state's worst disasters—a flood that killed more than 2,000 persons (see JOHNSTOWN).

The Early 1900's brought continued industrial growth. For the first time, more than half the people of Pennsylvania lived in cities and towns. Pennsylvania mined most of the coal in the United States and manufactured about 60 per cent of its steel.

Manufacturing and mining in Pennsylvania achieved even greater growth after the United States entered World War I in 1917. In addition to production of military goods, the state contributed about 8 per cent of the manpower for the U.S. armed forces.

During the Great Depression of the 1930's, hundreds of thousands of Pennsylvania workers lost their jobs. Pennsylvania passed welfare laws in cooperation with the federal government to help ease the hardship. The state set up programs of highway building, reforestation, and conservation. The legislature passed bills that included a minimum wage for women and children, and a 44-hour workweek.

THE GOVERNORS OF PENNSYLVANIA

	Party	Term		Party	Term
Under Articles of Confederation			19. Henry Martyn Hoyt	Republican	1879-1883
			20. Robert Emory Pattison	Democratic	1883-1887
1. Joseph Reed	None	1778-1781	21. James Addams Beaver	Republican	1887-1891
2. William Moore	None	1781-1782	22. Robert Emory Pattison	Democratic	1891-1895
3. John Dickinson	None	1782-1785	23. Daniel Hartman Hastings	Republican	1895-1899
4. Benjamin Franklin	None	1785-1788	24. William Alexis Stone	Republican	1899-1903
			25. Samuel Whitaker Pennypacker	Republican	1903-1907
Under United States Constitution			26. Edwin Sydney Stuart	Republican	1907-1911
			27. John Kinley Tener	Republican	1911-1915
1. Benjamin Franklin	None	1785-1788	28. Martin Grove Brumbaugh	Republican	1915-1919
2. Thomas Mifflin	None	1788-1799	29. William Cameron Sproul	Republican	1919-1923
3. Thomas McKean	*Dem.-Rep.	1799-1808	30. Gifford Pinchot	Republican	1923-1927
4. Simon Snyder	Dem.-Rep.	1808-1817	31. John Stuchell Fisher	Republican	1927-1931
5. William Findlay	Dem.-Rep.	1817-1820	32. Gifford Pinchot	Republican	1931-1935
6. Joseph Hiester	Dem.-Rep.	1820-1823	33. George Howard Earle	Democratic	1935-1939
7. John Andrew Schulze	Dem.-Rep.	1823-1829	34. Arthur Horace James	Republican	1939-1943
8. George Wolf	Democratic	1829-1835	35. Edward Martin	Republican	1943-1947
9. Joseph Ritner	Anti-Masonic	1835-1839	36. John C. Bell, Jr.	Republican	1947
10. David Rittenhouse Porter	Democratic	1839-1845	37. James H. Duff	Republican	1947-1951
11. Francis Rawn Shunk	Democratic	1845-1848	38. John S. Fine	Republican	1951-1955
12. William Freame Johnston	Whig	1848-1852	39. George Michael Leader	Democratic	1955-1959
13. William Bigler	Democratic	1852-1855	40. David Leo Lawrence	Democratic	1959-1963
14. James Pollock	Whig	1855-1858	41. William W. Scranton	Republican	1963-1967
15. William Fisher Packer	Democratic	1858-1861	42. Raymond P. Shafer	Republican	1967-
16. Andrew Gregg Curtin	Republican	1861-1867			
17. John White Geary	Republican	1867-1873			
18. John Frederick Hartranft	Republican	1873-1879			

*Democratic-Republican

Pennsylvania Department of Highways

Golden Triangle in Pittsburgh is a fine example of urban renewal. The area has been almost completely rebuilt since the 1940's.

In 1936, floodwaters swept across many parts of the state. Pittsburgh and Johnstown were particularly hard hit. The floods killed more than a hundred persons and caused over $40 million in damage.

The 1940's and 1950's. During World War II (1939-1945), Pennsylvania's factories and shipyards again turned to military production. The state's economy continued to prosper after the war. In 1952, the United States Steel Corporation opened the huge Fairless Works in Fairless Hills near Morrisville. The first full-scale nuclear-power reactor for civilian purposes in the United States began producing electricity at Shippingport in 1957. In 1958, the first copper refinery built in the Eastern United States in more than 50 years started production near Reading.

Pennsylvania Today stands among the nation's leaders in both manufacturing and mining. But Pennsylvania's economy faces serious problems. After World War II, for example, the need for anthracite coal in the United States dropped sharply. The rich coal mines of northeastern Pennsylvania were forced to lower their production. Coal production continued to drop throughout the 1950's. Many mines closed, putting miners out

PENNSYLVANIA / Study Aids

Related Articles in WORLD BOOK include:

BIOGRAPHIES

Baldwin, Matthias W.	Kress, Samuel H.
Barry, John	Krol, John J. Cardinal
Biddle, Nicholas	Lorimer, George H.
Bok, Edward W.	Marshall, George C.
Bradford (family)	Meade, George G.
Buchanan, James	Mellon, Andrew W.
Carnegie, Andrew	Mifflin, Thomas
Clark, Joseph Sill	Morris, Robert
Clymer, George	Morton, John
Cornplanter	Muhlenberg (family)
Curtis, Cyrus H. K.	Palmer, A. Mitchell
Dallas, George M.	Pastorius, Francis D.
Davis, Richard H.	Peary, Robert E.
Drexel, Anthony J.	Penn, William
Eakins, Thomas	Pinchot, Gifford
Fels, Samuel S.	Pitcher, Molly
Fink, Mike	Rittenhouse, David
FitzSimons, Thomas	Ross, Betsy
Foster, Stephen C.	Ross, George
Franklin, Benjamin	Rush, Benjamin
Frick, Henry C.	Schwab, Charles M.
Fulton, Robert	Scranton, William W.
Gallatin, Albert	Smith, James
Girard, Stephen	Stetson, John B.
Girty, Simon	Taylor, George
Heinz, Henry J., II	Wanamaker, John
Hopkinson, Francis	Wayne, Anthony
Ingersoll, Jared	Wilmot, David
Kelly, Grace P.	Wilson, James
Knox, Philander C.	Wilson, William B.

CITIES

Allentown	Gettysburg	Pittsburgh
Altoona	Harrisburg	Reading
Bethlehem	Hershey	Scranton
Carlisle	Johnstown	Upper Darby
Chester	Lancaster	Washington
Easton	McKeesport	Wilkes-Barre
Ephrata	New Castle	Williamsport
Erie	Philadelphia	York

HISTORY

Civil War	Liberty Bell
Colonial Life in America	Mason and Dixon's Line
Conestoga Wagon	Revolutionary War in
Continental Congress	America
Fort Duquesne	Schwenkfelders
Fort Necessity	Trails of Early Days
French and Indian Wars	Underground Railroad
Gettysburg Address	Valley Forge
Independence Hall	Whiskey Rebellion
Lancaster Turnpike	Wyoming Valley Massacre

PHYSICAL FEATURES

Allegheny Mountains	Lehigh River
Allegheny River	Monongahela River
Appalachian Mountains	Ohio River
Blue Ridge Mountains	Pennsylvania Turnpike
Delaware River	Schuylkill River
Delaware Water Gap	Susquehanna River
Hog Island	Wyoming Valley
Lackawanna River	

PRODUCTS AND INDUSTRY

For Pennsylvania's rank among the states in production, see the following articles:

Apple	Clothing	Mining
Building Stone	Coal	Publishing
Cattle	Iron and Steel	Textile
Chemical Industry	Leather	Tobacco
Cherry	Manufacturing	Tomato
Chicken	Milk	

OTHER RELATED ARTICLES

Academy of Natural	Mennonites
Sciences of Philadelphia	Middle Atlantic States
Amish	Moravian Church
Brethren, Church of the	Pennsylvania Dutch
Centennial Exposition	Philadelphia Naval
Curtis Institute of Music	Base
Franklin Institute	Quakers
Knights of Labor	Safe Harbor Dam

236f

of work. By the early 1960's, Pennsylvania mines were producing only a fourth as much anthracite as they had in 1940. But production increased by the mid-1960's.

Pennsylvania's cities face problems similar to those of other American cities. Urban improvements are needed desperately. Slums must be cleared. New housing, schools, highways, and recreational facilities must be built. Pittsburgh and Philadelphia began modernization programs in the 1940's. By 1970, both cities had made great improvements. Today, most Pennsylvania cities are carrying out programs of redevelopment, with aid from the federal government.

Money is needed to solve Pennsylvania's problems. In 1953, the state put a 1 per cent sales tax into effect. In 1956, the tax became a sales and use tax, and the rate was raised to 3 per cent. By 1967, additional increases in the tax had raised the rate to 6 per cent—among the highest in the country. This tax brings in more than half the state government's income.

The state is spending large sums of money for research, education, conservation, and highways. A Council of Science and Technology was established in 1963 to study ways to bring more scientific industry into the state. That same year, Pennsylvania took steps to provide for the establishment of two-year community colleges throughout the state. The first of these colleges opened in Harrisburg in 1964. In 1963, Pennsylvania voters approved *Project 70*, an undertaking to add to park, recreational, and historical areas in the state. The Keystone Shortway, extending across the state from New Jersey to Ohio, was scheduled for completion in 1970.

In 1965, 12 large electric utility companies announced plans to build a giant electric power plant in Indiana County. The plant is scheduled for completion in the early 1970's. It will provide electric power for Delaware, Maryland, New Jersey, New York, Pennsylvania, Virginia, and Washington, D.C.

In 1967, Pennsylvania called its first constitutional convention in 94 years. In 1968, the voters approved several of the convention's proposals as constitutional amendments.

GEORGE F. DEASY, JAMES R. DORAN, and SYLVESTER K. STEVENS

Outline

I. **Government**
  A. Constitution
  B. Executive
  C. Legislature
  D. Courts
  E. Local Government
  F. Taxation
  G. Politics

II. **People**

III. **Education**
  A. Schools
  B. Libraries
  C. Museums

IV. **A Visitor's Guide**
  A. Places to Visit
  B. Annual Events

V. **The Land**
  A. Land Regions
  B. Rivers, Waterfalls, and Lakes

VI. **Climate**

VII. **Economy**
  A. Natural Resources
  B. Manufacturing
  C. Agriculture
  D. Mining
  E. Electric Power
  F. Transportation
  G. Communication

VIII. **History**

Questions

Why did William Penn lose control of Pennsylvania in 1692?

What rivers link Pittsburgh with the Gulf of Mexico?

During what years was Philadelphia the U.S. capital?

Where was the country's first oil well drilled?

Who founded America's first subscription library? What was it called? Where was it established?

Why did the Continental Congress leave Philadelphia in 1777?

From what region in Pennsylvania does all the hard coal in the United States come?

Which Pennsylvania officials serve the longest elective terms of state officials in the United States?

What major Civil War battle was fought in Pennsylvania? What important effect did this battle have on the outcome of the war?

Where is the world's largest chocolate factory?

Books for Young Readers

CARR, HARRIETT H. *Wheels for Conquest*. Macmillan, 1957. A story of the wagoners who hauled goods over the Allegheny Mountains. The story takes place in the early 1800's.

DE ANGELI, MARGUERITE L. *Henner's Lydia*. Doubleday, 1936. A picture storybook of the Pennsylvania Dutch country. *Thee, Hannah!* 1940. Hannah is the 9-year-old daughter of a large Quaker family.

FLORY, JANE. *Peddler's Summer*. Houghton, 1960. Country life in western Pennsylvania in the 1800's.

FRITZ, JEAN. *The Cabin Faced West*. Coward-McCann, 1958. A story about a pioneer girl.

MILHOUS, KATHERINE. *The Egg Tree*. Scribner, 1950. An Easter story. Caldecott medal winner. *With Bells On: A Christmas Story*. 1955.

SORENSEN, VIRGINIA. *Miracles on Maple Hill*. Harcourt, 1956. The story of a year in an old Pennsylvania farmhouse. Newbery medal winner.

STEVENS, SYLVESTER K., and others. *Exploring Pennsylvania: Its Geography, History, and Civics*. 2nd ed. Harcourt, 1963.

STRACHAN, MARGARET P. *Mennonite Martha*. Washburn, 1961. Twelve-year-old Martha learns to accept plain dress and work in the family group.

WALLOWER, LUCILLE. *Your Pennsylvania*. New ed. Penns Valley Publishers, 1959. *They Came to Pennsylvania*. 1960.

Books for Older Readers

BISSELL, RICHARD P. *The Monongahela*. Rinehart, 1952.

BRANNING, ROSALIND L. *Pennsylvania Constitutional Development*. Univ. of Pittsburgh Press, 1960.

DEATRICK, ELINOR S. *The Pennsylvania Citizen*. Rutgers Univ. Press, 1958.

Pennsylvania: A Guide to the Keystone State. Oxford, 1940.

STEVENS, SYLVESTER K. *Pennsylvania, Birthplace of a Nation*. Random House, 1964. *Pennsylvania: A Students' Guide to Localized History*. Teachers College Press, 1965.

WALLACE, PAUL A. W. *Pennsylvania: Seed of a Nation*. Harper, 1962.

University of Pennsylvania

University of Pennsylvania Dormitories, seen through the Memorial Tower Archway, were built in the early 1900's.

PENNSYLVANIA, UNIVERSITY OF, in Philadelphia, is one of the oldest universities in the United States. It is a privately controlled, coeducational school, but it receives state aid. Benjamin Franklin was one of the founders of the school. It started in 1740 as a Charity School, became an Academy in 1749, and was named the College and Academy of Philadelphia in 1756. The university adopted its present name in 1791.

The university offers undergraduate courses in liberal arts; finance and commerce; engineering; nursing; physical and occupational therapy; and medical microbiology. The Wharton School was the first collegiate business school in the U.S. The graduate and professional schools offer courses in arts and sciences; medicine; veterinary medicine; dental medicine; law; education; social work; fine arts; and communications. The Wharton School and nursing and engineering schools also have graduate divisions. Other academic divisions are the College of General Studies and the Evening School of Accounts and Finance. The University of Pennsylvania also has several noted research institutes.

The university library contains special collections on medieval history, Shakespeare, Sanskrit manuscripts, Italian Renaissance, and Walt Whitman, among others. The Union Library Catalogue lists 6,000,000 volumes owned by libraries in the Philadelphia area. The university museum contains noted collections of Babylonian material, Chinese sculpture, and Middle American, Pacific, and African art. It conducts archaeological field expeditions each year. For enrollment, see UNIVERSITIES AND COLLEGES (table).   GAYLORD P. HARNWELL

See also FRANKLIN, BENJAMIN (Civic Leader).

PENNSYLVANIA COLLEGE OF OPTOMETRY is a privately controlled coeducational school in Philadelphia. Courses in optometry lead to bachelor of science and doctor of optometry degrees. Students must have completed two years of college work before applying for admission. The college was founded in 1919. For enrollment, see UNIVERSITIES AND COLLEGES (table).

PENNSYLVANIA DUTCH refers to the people who came to Pennsylvania in the 1600's and 1700's from the German Rhineland, and their descendants. Some of these immigrants came from the German part of Switzerland, and others were French Huguenots. Actually none of them came from The Netherlands. They were called *Dutch* because the word *Deutsch*, which means *German*, was misinterpreted.

These settlers came to Pennsylvania mainly because of the promise of religious freedom there. They had suffered intolerance and persecution in Europe. They settled mainly in eastern Pennsylvania, in Berks, Lancaster, Lebanon, Lehigh, Northampton, and York counties. The broad valleys, gently flowing streams, and rich limestone soil reminded them of home. Their genius for farming made the region a garden spot. By 1750, they made up half the population of Pennsylvania.

Most of the original Pennsylvania Dutch belonged to the Lutheran or Reformed churches. They were called

Bettmann Archive

Pennsylvania Dutch made colorful, hand-drawn birth and baptismal certificates. This one dates from the early 1800's.

"the church people." Some of the settlers belonged to various groups that grew out of *pietism*, a religious movement which opposed all formal religious practices. The groups included the Amish and Mennonites, noted for their plain dress and distrust of formal church ways. Today they are called "the plain people," and live mainly in Lancaster County. Another early group, the Moravians, founded Bethlehem, Pa. See AMISH; MENNONITES; MORAVIANS.

Pennsylvania Dutch artisans invented the Conestoga wagon and the Pennsylvania rifle, which helped America win the West. The people still maintain their dialect and unique customs. Their distinctive art style is known for its colorful decorative motifs. Their love of music has resulted in beautiful church music, especially choirs such as the famed Bach choir. Characteristic dishes include *sauerkraut un schpeck* (sauerkraut and pork), *smearcase* (cottage cheese), and *schnitz un knepp* (dried apples and dumplings).   S. K. STEVENS

See also FLOWER (color picture: Flowers in Art).

PENNSYLVANIA STATE ROAD, also called FORBES' ROAD, was a route between Philadelphia and Pittsburgh. In 1758, General John Forbes marched west from Philadelphia to Fort Bedford. His men then cut a wagon road through the Allegheny Mountains to Fort Ligonier and on to Fort Duquesne (Pittsburgh). They established supply depots along the way. Many travelers and settlers moved west along the route. The Lincoln Highway, running through Bedford, Ligonier, and Greensburg, generally follows the Pennsylvania State Road.   W. TURRENTINE JACKSON

PENNSYLVANIA STATE UNIVERSITY is a state-affiliated coeducational land-grant school at State College, Pa. The school also has two-year undergraduate centers in Allentown, Altoona, Du Bois, Erie (Behrend), Hazleton, McKeesport, Mont Alto, New Kensington, Ogontz (near Philadelphia), Pottsville, Scranton, Wilkes-Barre, and Wyomissing. The university has colleges of agriculture, art and architecture, business administration, chemistry and physics, education, engineering, home economics, liberal arts, mineral industries, and physical education and athletics. Pennsylvania State University also has schools of forestry and journalism, and a graduate school. Courses at the university lead to bachelor's, master's, and doctor's degrees.

The university has cooperative programs in engineering with several liberal arts colleges. A research reactor for use in nuclear studies was completed in 1955. The university library maintains many important collections, including the Moody collection of Australian art and literature. The university library also operates branch libraries for the use of many of the departments of study.

The school colors are blue and white, and the athletic teams are called Nittany Lions. The university was founded in 1855 as Farmers' High School. After several changes, it adopted the name Pennsylvania State University in 1953. For enrollment, see UNIVERSITIES AND COLLEGES (table).   ERIC A. WALKER

PENNSYLVANIA TURNPIKE is a 470-mile, four-lane divided toll superhighway. It runs across the state between the Ohio state line and the New Jersey state line, and north from Philadelphia to Scranton. It was the first successful turnpike of any great length built for all types of motor vehicles. The original turnpike ran from Irwin to Middlesex (near Carlisle) and opened in 1940. The western extension, from Irwin to the Ohio border, opened in 1951. The highway was joined to the New Jersey turnpike in 1956. The northeastern extension, linking Philadelphia and Scranton, was completed in 1957. Construction of the Pennsylvania Turnpike cost about $538,750,000.

Critically reviewed by PENNSYLVANIA TURNPIKE COMMISSION

PENNSYLVANIAN EPOCH was one of the three geological periods in the Carboniferous Period, a part of the Paleozoic Era. The strata of the Pennsylvanian Epoch

Pennsylvania State University

Old Main, a Pennsylvania State University Landmark, is the administration building on the State College campus.

in North America, Asia, and Europe contain the world's largest supply of workable coal.

See also EARTH (table: Outline of Earth History).

PENNY is a bronze coin used in England and other countries. In the United States, the penny is a *cent* (see CENT).

The English penny and the U.S. cent have the same value. There are 240 pennies in an English pound sterling. The English penny was stamped with a cross until the reign of Edward I. It could easily be broken into four equal parts and was used in halves as a half-penny (pronounced *HAY pun ih*) and in fourths as a *farthing*. Its abbreviation is *d*. For the value of the pound, see MONEY (table).   LEWIS M. REAGAN

See also DENARIUS.

Chase Manhattan Bank Money Museum

The Penny of Great Britain, above, is stamped on one side with the head of Queen Elizabeth II.

PENNY PAPER. See NEWSPAPER (The Penny Papers); DAY, BENJAMIN H.

PENNYROYAL, *PEN ih ROI ul,* is the name of several herbs of the mint family. The leaves of these herbs have

239

a strongly pungent odor. The oil from various kinds of pennyroyal is used in medicine for its stimulating properties, in mosquito repellents, and in perfumes.

Scientific Classification. Pennyroyals belong to the mint family, *Labiatae*.   HAROLD NORMAN MOLDENKE

PENNYROYAL REGION. See KENTUCKY (Land Regions).

PENNYWEIGHT is a unit of measure in the troy system of weights. It is used to weigh gold, silver, platinum, and coins, as well as most jewels. The pennyweight was once the weight of a silver penny. Today it is standardized as one twentieth of an ounce, or 24 grains.

PENOBSCOT MARINE MUSEUM. See MAINE (Places to Visit).

PENOBSCOT RIVER, *puh NAHB skaht,* is the longest stream in Maine. It rises in a small lake near the Canadian border and flows eastward through great pine forests. It forms Chesuncook and Pamedumcook lakes. It then flows south for the rest of its 350 miles to empty into Penobscot Bay, on the Atlantic Ocean. Ocean vessels can sail up the Penobscot to Bangor, 60 miles from the sea. The name *Penobscot* comes from the Algonkian Indian words for *rocky river.* For the location of the river, see MAINE (physical map).   JOSEPH M. TREFETHEN

PENOLOGY. See CRIMINOLOGY (Rehabilitation).

PENSACOLA, Fla. (pop. 56,752; met. area 203,376; alt. 15 ft.), is the state's largest deepwater seaport. It lies on Pensacola Bay in the western corner of Florida (see FLORIDA [political map]). Its chief industries include pulp and paper mills, chemical plants, fishing, furniture and boat making, naval storage depots, and fertilizer. Maldonado, one of Hernando de Soto's captains, discovered Pensacola Bay, probably in 1540. In 1559, Tristan de Luna founded a settlement that lasted two years. Spain reoccupied Pensacola in 1698, when Don Andres d'Arriola established a fort where the city now stands. Pensacola has a council-manager form of government.   KATHRYN ABBEY HANNA

See also PENSACOLA NAVAL AIR STATION.

PENSACOLA DAM is a federal flood-control and electric-power project on the Neosho (Grand) River near Pensacola, Okla. The dam is the multiple-arch, hollow-buttress type. It is 145 feet high, has a length of 6,500 feet along the top, and can hold back 2 million acre-feet of water. The dam was completed in 1940 under the supervision of the Public Works Administration. The project cost $12,241,061.   T. W. MERMEL

PENSACOLA NAVAL AIR STATION, Fla., serves as the site of the United States Naval Air Training Command. The command trains naval aviators, air observers, and nonpilot aviation officers. It covers 11,386 acres and lies 9 miles west of Pensacola, near the Gulf of Mexico. Among major activities there are the Naval Air Basic Training Command, the Pre-Flight School, and the Naval School of Aviation Medicine. The Naval Aviation Museum is also there.

The Pensacola Naval Air Station was set up in 1914 on the site of an old naval shipyard. It reached a peak of activity during World War II, when 28,000 aviators were trained there. The station is known as the *Annapolis of the Air.*   JOHN A. OUDINE

PENSÉES. See PASCAL, BLAISE.

PENSION is a reward for past services, or a means of support for persons who have retired, been disabled, or are too old to work. Pensions are often called *annuities* or *benefit payments.* Survivors of workers who have died may also receive pensions. National, state, and local governments and business organizations pay pensions to their former employees.

The need for providing some kind of old-age security for workers became apparent in the 1850's. At this time, the factory system began to replace hand labor in manufacturing. It demanded vigorous young workers. As a result, many men and women who had worked at handicrafts despite advancing age had to leave their jobs. They were then forced to depend on their families or on public charity for support. Many workers were never able to earn enough to provide for their old age. Or else they found it impossible to save enough money for their retirement. The idea developed in many countries that industry or the government should provide financial help for the aged.

Most industrialized nations have pension plans for elderly workers. These plans may be supported in three ways: (1) by private industry, (2) by compulsory contributions of management and workers, or (3) wholly or in part by the government.

The United States has both government-sponsored and privately-managed pension programs. About 85 of every 100 persons in the United States who are 65 or older receive benefits from public or private pension plans. About $2\frac{1}{2}$ million persons receive private pensions. Almost all of those age 62 or over with private pensions also receive public pensions. Public programs provide about half the income for the aged in the U.S.

Government Pensions in the United States

Military Pensions to war veterans and their dependents are the oldest form of federal pensions. In 1792, Congress passed the first general U.S. military pension law. This law provided aid to disabled veterans of the Revolutionary War. Later it extended pensions to all those who had served in the war. In 1836, Congress granted pensions to widows of veterans.

The Revolutionary War cost the government about $70 million in pensions. The War of 1812 resulted in more than $46 million in pension payments. The Mexican War cost about $62 million in pensions, and payments to Civil War veterans and their dependents have exceeded $8,200,000,000. Pension payments from the Indian wars have totaled about $120 million.

By the mid-1960's, pensions to Spanish-American War veterans totaled over $4,600,000,000. The government had paid more than $24,800,000,000 to World War I veterans and their dependents, and more than $27,400,000,000 to veterans of World War II and their dependents. Korean War veterans and their dependents had received about $2,600,000,000 in pension payments.

A man or woman who makes the armed forces a career may retire with a pension after serving the required time. The federal social-security program also covers these personnel. Servicemen pay the same social-security contributions as other workers. The federal government pays the matching employer share.

Social Security provides pensions in both its social-insurance and public-assistance programs. The Social Security Act of 1935 includes social insurance for (1)

the aged, (2) survivors, and (3) disabled persons. It grants monthly benefits to retired persons who have reached the age of 62. When Congress passed the social-security law, about half the states had old-age assistance programs. But these programs often provided only small pensions and had strict residence requirements. The Social Security Act helps states make payments to needy persons in four categories: (1) the aged, (2) the blind, (3) the permanently and totally disabled, and (4) dependent children. See SOCIAL SECURITY.

Railroad workers have a social-security system of their own. Other government pensions include retirement plans established by the federal, state, and local governments for their civilian employees.

Private Pension Plans in the United States

Many businesses and industrial firms have pension plans for their employees. Pension amounts are usually based on a person's salary level and length of service. Other programs have resulted from collective bargaining between labor unions and management. These other programs are usually noncontributory. They often have pensions that are either a fixed amount, or a certain amount for every year of service.

Retirement pensions to employees supplement their social-security old-age benefits. The normal retirement age is almost always 65. Private pension plans with assets totaling about $77 billion cover about 25 million persons in the United States. One out of every 8 Americans aged 65 or over benefits from this.

Trust-Fund Plans are provided by some large business companies. The firm sets up a trust fund, and a bank or trust company administers it. The fund provides for pension payments. The company may start a fund for each employee on the day he begins work, and may add to it regularly, with no contributions from the worker. The employee receives a credit, perhaps 1 per cent of his salary, for each year of service. When he retires, the company multiplies his total percentage by his average yearly pay during, perhaps, his last 10 years on the job. For example, an employee with 40 years' service who earned an average of $8,000 during his last 10 years would receive a pension of $3,200 a year. This amounts to $266.66 a month, in addition to his social-security benefits. If a worker does not have to contribute to the pension fund, he may receive nothing if he leaves the company before the retirement age. Under other plans, he may receive a pension beginning at age 65, or a reduced pension starting at an earlier age.

Contributory Plans call for both the worker and company to contribute regularly to a pension fund. The worker receives his own money back, usually with interest, if he resigns or is discharged. Some pension plans give employees *vested rights*. That is, the employee receives a pension at the normal retirement age, based on what he and the company have contributed, even if he resigns or is discharged before retirement.

Group Annuity Plans involve contributions from a company and often from its employees as well. An insurance firm collects these payments and builds up a retirement income fund for each employee. It then pays a pension, usually a percentage such as 1 per cent, for each year of service, multiplied by the worker's average salary over the entire period of service.

Another form of this program is called the *money-purchase plan*. The worker and the company contribute a fixed percentage based on the employee's salary. The contributions accumulate with interest, and are used to buy whatever pension sum is available when the worker retires. Insurance firms also operate pension plans similar to trust-fund plans, called *deposit-administration plans*.

Profit-Sharing Plans are built from a percentage of a firm's profits each year. Each worker's share accumulates according to his length of service and earnings. Sometimes the employee contributes a certain amount to the fund each year.

Pension Plans in Other Lands

Voluntary Plans have been adopted in many countries to persuade workers to provide for their old age. As early as 1833, Great Britain sponsored a plan for selling government annuities. Belgium and France introduced savings funds for old-age pensions in 1850. Italy adopted a similar program in 1898. Canadian government annuities provided a voluntary method of saving for old age. They were first sold in 1908 under the Government Annuities Act of that year.

Contributory Systems. Compulsory payments into pension funds were started in 1854 in Prussia for certain occupations, such as miners, railroad workers, policemen, and firemen. In 1889, Germany adopted the first program of old-age pensions for all workers. It extended the plan in 1911 to cover survivors. France adopted a general compulsory insurance law in 1910, and combined it with other social insurance laws in 1928. In 1913, Sweden made insurance compulsory for all its citizens. In 1965, the Canadian parliament passed a compulsory National Pension Plan to supplement its "free" flat-pension system. This plan went into effect in 1966, and is financed by matching tax payments by workers and employers. Additional assistance payments are available to aged persons if they show need.

Most early systems requiring participation fixed the pension payments according to the contributions paid and the length of time paid. Most required plans now base payments chiefly on the level of earning, or make payments in standard amounts.

Free Pensions are also called *noncontributory pensions*. In 1891, Denmark became the first country to adopt a pension system financed entirely from general revenues. Persons 67 or over may receive pensions. They must be in need, of good character, and not be receiving public charity. New Zealand adopted a free pension system in 1898, and Australia in 1908. France introduced government payments for the needy aged in 1907, but changed to a contributory plan later.

British laws of the early 1900's granted old-age payments to the needy. Great Britain's program today is based on the Beveridge plan of social security "from the cradle to the grave" (see BEVERIDGE, WILLIAM). This plan calls for standard pensions, regardless of a person's previous earnings. Workers, employers, and the government contribute to the program. In 1961, Britain adopted a supplementary pension plan based on earnings on which contributions had been paid.

Canada pays $75 monthly payments to all aged persons. The minimum age for these pensions is 69, but will decrease gradually to 65 in 1970 and later years.

PENSION

Residence in Canada for 10 years is necessary to qualify. Payments stop when the pensioner leaves the country permanently, unless he had lived in Canada for 25 years after he was 21 years old. Pensions are also granted to needy widowed mothers, to disabled war veterans, and to dependents of servicemen who have died.

The government pension plans of some countries provide for automatic adjustment when the cost of living changes. These countries include Belgium, Denmark, France, Iceland, Israel, and The Netherlands. Canada started this plan in 1968. West Germany and Sweden have adopted pension plans based on the relative earnings of retired persons rather than on their actual money wages. This was done to keep pensions up to date with earnings.

All countries of Latin America have old-age pension plans of the contributory type. But these plans usually cover only industrial and commercial workers in the large cities. Few countries in Africa and Asia have pension plans, except for limited groups.

The communist-controlled nations do not require contributions in their pension systems. Otherwise, their plans resemble those of other countries that base the pensions on average earnings and length of service. It is not significant that there are no contributions, because the government fixes wages. It can have lower wages to make up for the lack of contributions.

Other Pension Plans. Private pension systems supplement government social insurance in some countries, such as Canada. These plans often apply only to higher-paid workers, who are covered entirely or partly by social security.

Canada had few pension plans before the 1900's. Early pension plans covered workers in a few manufacturing firms and those in the government civil service. Since the 1940's, the number of pension plans has increased. Contributory plans are more common in Canada than noncontributory types. These contributory plans may be administered by (1) the Annuities Branch of the Department of Labour, (2) private insurance companies, or (3) trust funds under the direction of trust companies or a group of trustees. ROBERT J. MYERS

Related Articles in WORLD BOOK include:

Aid to Dependent	Relief	Unemployment
Children	Social Security	Insurance
Annuity	Social Security	Veterans
Bonus	Administration	Administration
Civil Service	Townsend Plan	Workmen's
Insurance		Compensation

PENTAGON is a polygon having five sides. It is called *equilateral* if all sides have the same length. It is called *equiangular* if all its angles are equal. Like all polygons, except a triangle, a pentagon may be equilateral without being equiangular. Or it may be equiangular without being equilateral. A pentagon is *regular* if all the sides and interior angles are equal. Each angle equals 108°, and may be inscribed in a circle. A pentagon may be circumscribed around a circle by drawing tangents to the circle at the vertices of a regular inscribed pentagon. See also POLYGON.

PENTAGON BUILDING is the largest office building in the world. It houses the headquarters of the Department of Defense of the United States government. It lies on the west bank of the Potomac River in Arlington, Va., directly across from Washington, D.C.

Built in the form of a *pentagon*, or five-sided figure, the

The Pentagon, World's Largest Office Building, Stands Across the Potomac River from Washington, D.C.

U.S. Army

building's five concentric rings are connected by 10 spokelike corridors. It has five floors, a mezzanine, and a basement. The building covers 29 acres and has 3,705,397 square feet of office and other space. Its open center court occupies another 5 acres. The corridors cover 17½ miles. The perimeter, or outermost, wall of the concrete structure is faced with Indiana limestone. It stretches about a mile around.

The building is surrounded by 200 acres of lawn and terraces. Parking areas adjacent to it cover 67 acres, and can accommodate more than 9,000 vehicles. The lagoon in front of the river entrance to the building was formed by excavation and juncture with the river.

About 26,700 people work in the building. About half of them are civilians. Aside from the people who take care of the building, the officers, enlisted personnel, and civilians form part of four groups. These groups are the Departments of the Army, Navy, and Air Force, and the Office of the Secretary of Defense.

The Pentagon Building has the world's largest private telephone system, with 45,000 telephones and 160,000 miles of cable handling 280,000 calls a day. It also has the world's largest pneumatic tube system, comprising some 15 miles of tube. It also maintains what is probably the largest food service operation in the world. Restaurants and cafeterias there serve more than 17,500 meals each day. The building also has such facilities as a radio and television station, bank, dispensary, post office, shops, and a heliport.

Army engineers began building the Pentagon in September, 1941, and completed it in 16 months, by January, 1943. It was constructed originally to house the scattered offices of the War Department under one roof. The building cost $83,000,000. CHARLES B. MACDONALD

See also DEFENSE, DEPARTMENT OF (picture).

PENTAMETER. See METER (poetry).

PENTATEUCH, *PEN tuh tyook*, is the name of the first five books of the Bible—Genesis, Exodus, Leviticus, Numbers, and Deuteronomy. Its name comes from a Greek word meaning *five books*. According to tradition, Moses wrote the entire Pentateuch, and the work is often called the *Five Books of Moses*. Jews refer to the Pentateuch as the *Torah* or the *Law*.

Many scholars today, using textual data, believe that the Pentateuch actually came from five independent sources. They say that later editors, working at various periods, wove the sources into a unified work. They refer to these sources by the following symbols:

J and *E*, the two earliest documents, written about 1000 to 900 B.C. *J* uses the name *Jehovah*, or *Yahweh*, for God and *E* uses the name *Elohim*.

D, or *Deuteronomy*, a scroll found in Jerusalem in 621 B.C.

H, or *Holiness Code*, a short collection of laws.

P, or *Priestly Code*, probably completed during the Babylonian Exile of the Jews in the 500's B.C.

Other scholars, using archaeological data, do not accept this theory. They believe that, even if Moses did not write the Pentateuch, the work may be described as Mosaic, because its basic elements actually go back to his times and reflect his teachings. They also argue that these Biblical writings resemble writings of other peoples of the Fertile Crescent, and are at least as old (see FERTILE CRESCENT). They maintain that the books of the Bible had been passed on by word of mouth for

PENTECOSTAL CHURCHES

many generations before they were finally gathered and written down. ROBERT GORDIS

See also OLD TESTAMENT; BIBLE; TARGUM; and the separate article on each book mentioned.

PENTATHLON. See TRACK AND FIELD (The Pentathlon); OLYMPIC GAMES (History).

PENTATONIC SCALE. See MUSIC (History).

PENTECOST, *PEN tee kawst*, is an important springtime Jewish and Christian feast. Its name comes from the Greek word for fifty because Pentecost occurred on the fiftieth day after the first day of Passover. As a Jewish thanksgiving feast for the harvest, it was called the *Feast of Firstfruits* (Exodus 23: 16) and *Shabuot*, or the *Feast of Weeks* (Leviticus 23: 15-21). See SHABUOT.

From at least the 200's, Christians celebrated Pentecost on the seventh Sunday after Easter as one of their greatest feasts. It commemorated the descent of the Holy Spirit (called Holy Ghost in older English) upon the apostles on this day (Acts 2: 1-4). He had been promised by Jesus as "another Comforter" (John 14: 16) and came to strengthen the apostles after their nine days of prayer following the ascension of Jesus into heaven. They then showed themselves more courageous and zealous than they had been before. Pentecost was later called *Whitsunday*, or White Sunday, because the newly baptized wore their white baptismal robes on that day, marking the end of the joyous Easter season.

In masses of the Latin Rite of the Roman Catholic Church, red vestments are worn on Pentecost to symbolize the tongues of fire representing the Holy Spirit (Acts 2: 3). *Novena* prayers take their name from the nine (Latin, *novem*) days that the apostles had "continued with one accord in prayer" (Acts 1: 14). FRANCIS L. FILAS

See also EASTER; TRINITY.

PENTECOSTAL CHURCHES base their faith and practice on certain religious experiences that are recorded in the New Testament. Pentecostal churches teach that every Christian should seek to be "filled with the Holy Spirit." The proof of this occurrence comes when the person *speaks in tongues*. That is, the person will speak in a language he has never learned. The New Testament refers to the disciples speaking in tongues on the day of Pentecost (Acts 2), and mentions speaking in tongues elsewhere.

Pentecostals also believe that they can receive other supernatural gifts. For example, they believe they can be given the ability to prophesy, to heal, and to interpret what is said when someone speaks in an unknown tongue. The New Testament refers to these gifts in I Corinthians 12-14.

Aside from these distinctive qualities, however, individual Pentecostal denominations do not usually resemble each other. There are more than three dozen Pentecostal groups in the United States alone. They differ radically in size as well as in their interpretations of matters of faith and practice. The Assemblies of God, for example, has more than 8,000 churches with a membership of more than 500,000. The Fire Baptized Holiness Church has about 40 churches and less than 1,000 members. Some churches are controlled by the congregations, while others have bishops who govern.

Pentecostal churches trace their origins to revivals of tongue-speaking that occurred at Bethel Bible College in Topeka, Kans., in 1901, and at the Azusa Street Mission in Los Angeles in 1906. Similar revivals also took place in Great Britain and in Europe, Asia, and Latin America during the early 1900's. Since the 1930's, the Pentecostal denominations have grown rapidly. With a worldwide membership estimated at seven million, the Pentecostals are sometimes called Christianity's "Third Force," alongside Roman Catholicism and traditional Protestantism. JOHN THOMAS NICHOL

See also ASSEMBLIES OF GOD; RELIGION (table).

PENTHOUSE originally was a shed built onto a building. The word comes from the Latin words *pendere*, meaning *to hang*, and *ad*, meaning *to*. Today, *penthouse* usually refers to a dwelling unit on the roof of a high building.

PENTICTON, *pen TICK tun* (pop. 15,330; alt. 1,132 ft.), a city in south-central British Columbia, lies at the south end of Okanagan Lake. For location, see BRITISH COLUMBIA (political map). Tourism is the chief industry of the city, followed by fruit products (apples, apricots, cherries, peaches, pears, and prunes). Penticton serves as a distribution point for the products of the region. The city's Peach Festival in August is the high point of the civic year.

Founded in 1905, Penticton became a city in 1948. It has a mayor-council government. RODERICK HAIG-BROWN

PENTLAND FIRTH. See ORKNEY ISLANDS.

PENTODE. See ELECTRONICS (Multielectrode Tubes).

PENTOLITE. See EXPLOSIVE (High Explosives).

PENTOTHAL SODIUM, *PEN toh thal*, is a drug that has been called the "truth serum." It is not really a serum, but a *barbiturate* (a drug used as a sedative).

When Pentothal Sodium is injected into a person's veins, it brings on a state of hypnosis. Then the person may tell things he has forgotten or is trying to hide. Pentothal Sodium has been used on persons involved in criminal cases, but U.S. courts do not recognize statements made by drugged persons as legal evidence.

A more important use of the drug is as a general anesthetic, particularly in surgery. Pentothal Sodium is often used in treating mental conditions such as *amnesia* (loss of memory), schizophrenia, and combat neurosis. People with these conditions have thoughts locked in their subconscious minds. The "truth serum" loosens the restraints that keep these thoughts from coming into the open. In the treatment called *narcosynthesis*, the doctor talks to the half-sleeping person to draw out the buried thought.

Pentothal Sodium is a trade name for the drug *thiopental sodium*. It has also been called *sodium pentothal*. GEORGE L. BUSH

See also ANESTHESIA.

PENTSTEMON. See BEARDTONGUE.

PENUMBRA, *pee NUM bruh*, means *partial shadow*. When an opaque object cuts off the light from a luminous object, a shadow pattern results. Part of the shadow is almost totally dark, and is called the *umbra*. The rest of the shadow is only partially dark, and is the *penumbra*.

The earth's shadow is an example. Because the sun is larger than the earth, the earth casts a cone-shaped shadow that points away from the sun. This shadow is the umbra. At the same time, another diverging shadow

cone is formed. Here, the sun's rays are not completely cut off, and a penumbra forms. When the earth's umbra covers the face of the moon, a total lunar eclipse occurs. The penumbra portion of any shadow disappears when the source of light is a point rather than an area. Scientists also use the word *penumbra* to describe the grayish outer rim of a sunspot. R. WILLIAM SHAW

See also SHADOW; SUNSPOT.

PEONAGE, *PEE un ij*, is a system of forced labor in which the *peon* (laborer) is forced to work in payment of a debt. The word *peon* comes from the Spanish *peón*, meaning *day laborer*.

Peonage was common in most of the Spanish colonies of the Americas until the early 1900's, when nearly every civilized country of the world passed laws abolishing the practice. In Mexico, many Indians were forced to work out petty debts. The system was abolished in Mexico in 1917. But the term *peon* is still used to mean the impoverished Indian laborers of Latin America. These agricultural workers live on their employer's land and may receive a small payment for their work.

Peonage existed in the United States, particularly in the present states of New Mexico and Arizona, a short time after slavery was abolished. Negroes were arrested on false charges and fined. If they were not able to pay the fine, they were given to the highest bidder to work without wages for a period of time. At the end of this period, they could be arrested again and forced into service. In 1911, the Supreme Court declared all forms of peonage unconstitutional. ROBERT D. PATTON

PEONY, *PEE oh nih*, is the common name of a group of plants with large, handsome flowers. In early spring, peonies have shrubby or herblike stems. The clusters of leafy shoots, red and shiny green in appearance, make a striking effect a few weeks before the flowers appear in late spring or early summer.

The peonies belong to the crowfoot family. Many of the cultivated varieties common in America are the offspring of two species of the Eastern Hemisphere, the *common peony* of southern Europe and the *Chinese peony*. The large flowers of the common peony are red or crimson and are lovely to look at, although they do not have much fragrance. Many of the Chinese peonies, a large group of hybrids, bear double, sweet-scented blossoms. The peonies with woody stems are called *tree* or *moutan peonies*. This kind of peony is a native of western China. It has showy flowers which blossom in a wide range of white and rose-colored hues and grow on a stalk from 3 to 4 feet high. Tree peonies are slow-growing. In regions of late spring frosts, the buds are often injured. Once established, they bloom season

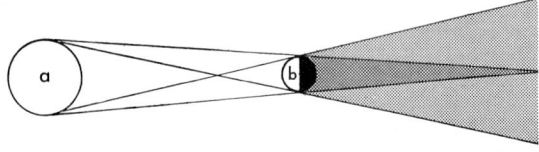

Diagram of the Penumbra. The sun, the source of light, is labeled (a), while (b) is a sphere on which the light falls. The heavily shaded cone behind (b) shows the umbra, where there is almost total darkness. The lightly shaded area shows the penumbra, which is in partial shadow.

J. C. Allen

Peony Blossoms Are Usually White, Pink, or Red.

after season. Ordinary bush peonies are planted by dividing the shoots.

Scientific Classification. Peonies are in the crow-foot family, *Ranunculaceae*. The common peony is genus *Paeonia*, species *P. officinalis;* the Chinese is *P. albiflora.* Most tree peonies in America are *P. suffruticosa.*   ALFRED C. HOTTES

See also FLOWER (color picture, Summer Garden Flowers).

PEOPLE'S PARTY. See POPULIST PARTY.

PEORIA, Ill. (pop. 103,162; met. area 313,412; alt. 470 ft.), is Illinois' third largest city. It is about 150 miles southwest of Chicago, at the foot of a broad basin of the Illinois River known as Peoria Lake. Business and manufacturing sections stand along the river. The residential districts are on the adjacent bluffs. Peoria is the home of Bradley University. For location, see ILLINOIS (color map).

Industry. Peoria is noted for the production of beer and whisky. Major industries are located along the Illinois River. The city produces earth-moving equipment, chemicals, and steel and wire products. Peoria also has large jobbing and wholesale businesses. Nearby mines provide large amounts of coal.

Excellent transportation is provided by 14 branch railroads, commercial airlines, and many bus and truck lines. The Illinois River is kept open for barge traffic the year around, and furnishes water transportation to Chicago and Mississippi River and Gulf ports.

History. The first white explorers found an Indian village on Peoria Lake. French settlers came to this region in the late 1600's. Frenchmen and half-breeds lived there almost continuously until 1812, when their village was destroyed by American militiamen who suspected them of being friendly with hostile Indians. The Americans built Fort Clark on the site of Peoria in 1813. A permanent settlement was made in 1819. Peoria became the county seat of Peoria County in 1825. It was incorporated as a town in 1835 and chartered as a city in 1845. Peoria has a council-manager form of government.   PAUL M. ANGLE

PEPIN THE SHORT, *PEP in* (714?-768), became king of the Franks and founded the Carolingian dynasty. Like his father, grandfather, and great-great-grandfather, Pepin served as mayor of the palace in the Merovingian kingdom in France and Germany. In each case, the mayor was the power behind the throne. In 751, an assembly of the Franks deposed Childeric, the last of the weak Merovingian kings, and proclaimed Pepin king. Pope Stephen II gave his approval when he anointed Pepin and his sons in 754.

When Pope Stephen II, who ruled Rome, asked Pepin for help against the Lombard king, Pepin sent his army to save Rome. The Lombards had captured Ravenna. Pepin recaptured the city and much of the nearby territory, and gave it all to the pope. The gift of the territory, known as "the Donation of Pepin," helped build the political power of the pope (see PAPAL STATES). Pepin added Aquitaine to his own kingdom, and began many important religious and educational reforms. His son, Charlemagne, carried on these reforms (see CHARLEMAGNE).   FRANKLIN D. SCOTT

PEPLOS. See GREECE, ANCIENT (Family Life).

PEPPER is a spice. The familiar black pepper known in every household is the product of a trailing or climbing shrub grown in Indonesia and other hot countries. The islands of Java and Madura furnish most of the pepper used in American homes. The United States buys almost 25,000 tons of this spice annually.

The pepper plant bears a small green berry about the size of a pea, which turns red as it ripens. The berries are gathered just when they begin to change color. They are then cleaned and dried. They are dried in the sun, or before a slow fire. In drying, the berries turn black. When the berries are ground and sifted, they form the black pepper which we know.

White pepper is made from the ripe berries of the same plant. These are bruised, and then washed until they are free from the pulpy matter and bits of stalk, and finally dried. White pepper has a finer flavor than black, but is not so strong. Red pepper is obtained from species of *Capsicum*, and the so-called Jamaica pepper is obtained from the pimiento tree. Jamaica pepper is also known as *allspice.*

The sharp, biting taste of ordinary pepper is due chiefly to an acrid resin and oil it contains. Pepper also has medicinal value.

Scientific Classification. The pepper makes up the pepper family, *Piperaceae.* Black pepper is classified as genus *Piper,* species *P. nigrum.* HAROLD NORMAN MOLDENKE

See also ALLSPICE; CAYENNE PEPPER; CUBEB; KAVA.

Pepper Plants grow 8 to 12 feet tall. The vines are trained to climb on tall poles.

American Spice Trade Assn.

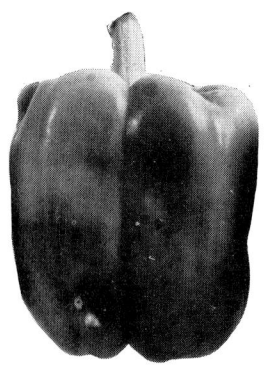

The Green Pepper, *above,* adds color and flavor to food. Chili peppers, *right,* are more spicy than green peppers. They are ground and mixed with other spices to make chili powder.

J. Horace McFarland; American Spice Trade Assn.

PEPPER is a shrubby perennial plant native to North and South America and grown primarily for its fruit. In areas where there is frost, peppers are grown as annuals. Botanists class the fruit of the garden pepper as a berry. Many seeds are contained within the fruit walls. The pungent flavor of peppers comes from *capsaicin,* a compound found in the walls of the fruit.

Most of the commercial garden peppers are grown in the warm regions of the United States. Farmers usually start the seeds in protected beds or flats. Sometimes they soak the seeds in a nutrient solution before sowing. When the tiny plants are strong enough, the farmer transplants them to the fields, setting them about 2 feet apart. The plants grow 3 to 4 feet high. The crop is grown like tomatoes, although the plants are never trained to stakes. The immature fruits are green, but change to red when they are fully ripe. Frost injures the plants when they are young. But in the fall, when they are mature, they can withstand severe frosts.

Although most varieties of peppers produce red fruits, there are some yellow-fruited varieties. There are also both mild and pungent types. The large-fruited salad peppers and those grown and dried for paprika are mild (see PAPRIKA). Pimiento, a thick-walled mild red pepper, is often canned. Chili peppers are very pungent.

Pepper plants are subject to a blight caused by bacteria. Farmers use streptomycin to control this disease. They make a solution of 500 parts of streptomycin to 1,000,000 parts of water and use it as a spray. Another disease, called *anthracnose,* causes soft spots that turn black or crack open, making the fruit useless. Proper irrigation has been found to be helpful in controlling this disease. Mulching also helps.

Scientific Classification. Garden peppers belong to the nightshade family, *Solanaceae.* They are genus *Capsicum,* species *C. frutescens.* JOHN H. MacGILLIVRAY

See also CAPSICUM.

PEPPER TREE gets its name from the strong-smelling berries that grow on it. It is not related to the familiar pepper plant. Pepper trees have drooping branches and bear yellowish-white flowers. The long feather-like leaves are filled with an oil that evaporates quickly. When the leaves are thrown into water, the oil escapes in jets with such force that the leaves jump as if alive.

The Pepper Tree has long, narrow leaves and red fruits.
Joseph Muench

Pepper trees are native to South America, but they are now grown in California, Arizona, and Texas because they make fine shade trees. Small and graceful, they reach a height of about 50 feet.

Scientific Classification. Pepper trees belong to the cashew family, *Anacardiaceae.* The species grown in the United States are genus *Schinus,* species *S. molle,* and *S. terebinthifolius.* T. EWALD MAKI

PEPPERDINE COLLEGE is a private, coeducational, liberal arts school in Los Angeles, Calif. Courses lead to bachelor's and master's degrees. The school was founded in 1937 as George Pepperdine College. For enrollment, see UNIVERSITIES AND COLLEGES (table).

PEPPERELL, WILLIAM. See LOUISBOURG (First Battle of Louisbourg).

246

PEPPERGRASS. See CRESS.

PEPPERIDGE. See BLACK TUPELO.

PEPPERMINT is a perennial herb of the mint family. It is grown widely for the fragrant oil found in glands of the leaves. This oil is the widely used peppermint of commerce, and is valuable in medicines as a flavoring. Medicines containing peppermint are used to relieve colic and toothache. Menthol, which is made from the peppermint oil, is a valued remedy for colds and croup. Peppermint is also used in manufacturing perfumes and soaps. The oil is probably the most popular of all flavorings used in candymaking. Probably about 60 times as much peppermint is used as wintergreen, and 4 times as much peppermint as spearmint. Peppermint oil is obtained by means of pressure and distillation.

Peppermint Leaves contain oil used in medicine and candy.

USDA

Oregon and Washington are the leading peppermint-producing states. They supply most of the peppermint oil produced in the United States.

The plant grows 1 to 3 feet high, and bears smooth, sharp-pointed oval leaves and small bluish-white flowers. Like all mints it has a square stem. It is raised in England and in various sections of continental Europe. In the United States the peppermint sections outside of Oregon are in Indiana, Washington, and Michigan. Peppermint is best grown in muck lands of reclaimed swamps.

Scientific Classification. Peppermint belongs to the mint family, *Labiatae*. It is classified as genus *Mentha*, species *M. piperita*.   HAROLD NORMAN MOLDENKE

See also MENTHOL; MINT.

PEPSI-COLA COMPANY. See SOFT DRINK.

PEPSIN is an enzyme found in the gastric juice. It changes proteins in food into substances called *peptones*. In chemical composition, pepsin is somewhat like the enzyme of saliva, called *ptyalin*, but its effects are entirely different. It acts in the presence of a weak acid. Pepsin has no effect on fats or carbohydrates. It is produced commercially by drying the mucous lining of the stomachs of pigs and calves. There are several commercial preparations of pepsin. They are given when it is necessary to aid digestion.   TERENCE A. ROGERS

See also DIGESTION; ENZYME.

PEPTONE. See PEPSIN.

PEPYS, *PEEPS* or *PEP iss,* **SAMUEL** (1633-1703), was an English government official. His famous *Diary* vividly pictured the age in which he lived. It overshadowed a notable career in the British navy.

His Diary. Pepys' *Diary* covers the period from 1660 to 1669. He recorded events in the reign of King Charles II, and personal incidents in his own life. He wrote the *Diary* in a code combination of shorthand, French, Spanish, Latin, Greek, and some characters that he invented. It covers only the early part of his career, when he served as the clerk of the navy.

Pepys often attended the gay affairs at the court of Charles II. He wrote frankly about the gossip and intrigues there, picturing famous actresses such as Nell Gwyn and other favorites of the king. The *Diary* includes anecdotes about music and the theater, thrilling accounts of the London fire, and domestic chitchat. Pepys humorously told of times when he kicked his cook, kissed his maid, or gave his wife a black eye. He pictured himself with greater honesty than he might have if he had known that millions of persons would later read his words. The six-volume work was translated between 1819 and 1822.

His Life. Pepys was born in London, and was graduated from Saint Paul's School and Cambridge University. Through the influence of Sir Edward Montagu, he received several official appointments. He became secretary to Montagu when the latter brought Charles II back to England in 1660. In the same year, Pepys became "clerk of the king's ships" and a member of the navy board. He mastered the navy's organizational and supply problems, although he had to employ a tutor to teach him multiplication when he took the post.

In 1673, when a commission to administer the navy replaced the Lord

Newberry Library
Samuel Pepys

High Admiral, Pepys became secretary for navy affairs. He became secretary of the Admiralty in 1686. Pepys served the British Navy with great devotion. On one occasion, when a parliamentary committee attacked the administration, he defended it so eloquently in a speech in the House of Commons that the charges were withdrawn. In 1679, he was accused of delivering naval information to French officials. The deathbed confession of a former servant cleared him. He remained on duty during the plague, and his quick, intelligent action during the London fire saved the navy office from destruction. In 1690, he published memoirs of the navy covering the period from 1678 to 1688.

Pepys served in parliament several times and as president of the Royal Society in 1684 and 1685. He was a friend of Sir Isaac Newton and Sir Christopher Wren. He remained in the admiralty until the fall of James II in 1689, and then retired.   ARNOLD WILLIAMS

See also BIOGRAPHY.

PEQUOD. See MELVILLE, HERMAN.

PEQUOT INDIANS. See CONNECTICUT (The Pequot War); INDIAN WARS (The Pequot War).

PERAK is the name of a state and a river in Malaysia. See MALAYSIA.

PERCALE, *pur KAYL,* is a closely woven cotton cloth used in making clothes, such as dresses, pajamas, and shirts. It usually has a colored *print* (design). It has a plain weave and a dull, smooth finish. Fine quality sheets are often called percale. Printed percale is often called *print.*   KENNETH R. FOX

PERCÉ ROCK. See QUEBEC (Places to Visit; color picture: Percé Village and Harbor on the Gaspé Peninsula).

Don Zeilstra

Percentage Attracts Shoppers because it shows how much a buyer can save on a store's regular prices. A sale at "25% off" means that regular prices have been reduced by $\frac{25}{100}$ or .25 or $\frac{1}{4}$ for a certain period of time.

PERCENTAGE refers to computing by hundredths. You often see numbers such as 2%, 30%, and 75%. The % symbol means *per cent*. You read the numbers "2 per cent," "30 per cent," and "75 per cent." *Per cent means hundredths:* 2% means 2 hundredths, 30% means 30 hundredths, and 75% means 75 hundredths. *Per cents are really common fractions:* 2% is $\frac{2}{100}$, 30% is $\frac{30}{100}$, and 75% is $\frac{75}{100}$. *Per cents are also decimal fractions:* 2% is .02, 30% is .30, and, 75% is .75. Suppose you want to find 25% of 60. You must find $\frac{25}{100}$, or .25, of 60. The term *per cent* is from the Latin words *per centum*, meaning by the hundreds.

We use percentage frequently in everyday life. Businessmen use percentage to compute profits, costs, and losses. Bankers use percentage to compute interest on savings and loans. Our taxes are percentages of income, prices, and other amounts. Scientists often show the results of their observations and experiments with percentages. In baseball, team standings and batting averages are based on percentages. On clothing labels, percentages often show the amounts of different fibers.

For hundreds of years, the business world has used the term *per cent*, and this custom has persisted to the present time. The custom may come from Roman taxes which were often stated as $\frac{1}{20}$, $\frac{1}{25}$, $\frac{1}{100}$, and so on. In the Middle Ages, merchants commonly used hundredths and per cent even before the appearance of the decimal number system (see DECIMAL NUMERAL SYSTEM). After the introduction of the decimal system, people no longer needed to use the term *per cent*. You can work with .25 just as easily as 25%. But percentage had become so deeply woven into business, professional, and everyday life that its use continued.

How to Change Per Cents to Fractions

Changing Per Cents to Decimal Fractions. Per cent, in English, means hundredths. To change a per cent to a decimal or a common fraction, you need only write the per cent as hundredths. To change a per cent to a decimal fraction, drop the % symbol and write in a decimal point two places to the left. Here are four examples:

$$25\% = .25 \qquad 37.5\% = .375$$
$$125\% = 1.25 \qquad 265\% = 2.65$$

Changing Per Cents to Common Fractions. To change a per cent to a common fraction, drop the % symbol and write in a denominator of 100. Here are four examples:

$$25\% = \frac{25}{100} = \frac{1}{4} \qquad 37.5\% = \frac{37.5}{100} = \frac{3}{8}$$
$$125\% = \frac{125}{100} = 1\frac{1}{4} \qquad 265\% = \frac{265}{100} = 2\frac{13}{20}$$

How to Change Fractions to Per Cents

Changing Decimal Fractions to Per Cents. To change a decimal fraction to a per cent, move the decimal point two places to the right and attach the % symbol. Here are four examples:

$$.07 \ (7\ hundredths) \quad = 7\%$$
$$.63 \ (63\ hundredths) \quad = 63\%$$
$$.625 \ (62.5\ hundredths) = 62.5\%$$
$$1.52 \ (152\ hundredths) \quad = 152\%$$

Changing Common Fractions to Per Cents. To change a common fraction to a per cent, divide the numerator by the denominator to get a decimal fraction. Then move the decimal point two places to the right and attach the % symbol. Here are four examples:

$$\tfrac{3}{5} = 3 \div 5 = \ .60 \ (60\ hundredths) \quad = \ 60\%$$
$$\tfrac{5}{8} = 5 \div 8 = \ .625 \ (62.5\ hundredths) = \ 62.5\%$$
$$\tfrac{2}{3} = 2 \div 3 = \ .66\tfrac{2}{3} \ (66\tfrac{2}{3}\ hundredths) = \ 66\tfrac{2}{3}\%$$
$$\tfrac{7}{4} = 7 \div 4 = \ 1.75 \ (175\ hundredths) = 175\%$$

Solving Percentage Problems

Because per cent means hundredths, you should re-state any per-cent problem in terms of decimal or common fractions. Then you can solve it fairly easily as a fraction problem.

How to Find a Per Cent of a Number. Suppose you want to find 4% of 50. This means you want to find 4 hundredths of 50. First, change 4% to a decimal or common fraction.

$$4\% = .04 \qquad\qquad 4\% = \tfrac{4}{100}$$

Second, multiply 50 by the fraction.

$$.04 \times 50 = 2 \qquad\qquad \tfrac{4}{100} \times 50 = 2$$

So 4% of 50 is 2.

Here are some more examples:

Find 30% of 72.

$$30\% = .30 \qquad\qquad 30\% = \tfrac{30}{100}$$

$$.30 \times 72 = 21.6 \qquad \tfrac{30}{100} \times 72 = \tfrac{2160}{100} = 21.6$$

$$30\% \text{ of } 72 \text{ is } 21.6$$

Find $66\tfrac{2}{3}\%$ of 915.

$$66\tfrac{2}{3}\% = .66\tfrac{2}{3} \qquad\qquad 66\tfrac{2}{3}\% = \tfrac{66\tfrac{2}{3}}{100} = \tfrac{200}{300}$$

$$.66\tfrac{2}{3} \times 915 = 610 \qquad \tfrac{2}{3} \times 915 = 610$$

$$66\tfrac{2}{3}\% \text{ of } 915 \text{ is } 610$$

Find 12.5% of 64.

$$12.5\% = .125 \qquad\qquad 12.5\% = \tfrac{12.5}{100} = \tfrac{25}{200}$$

$$.125 \times 64 = 8 \qquad\qquad \tfrac{1}{8} \times 64 = 8$$

$$12.5\% \text{ of } 64 \text{ is } 8$$

Find 250% of 32.

$$250\% = 2.5 \qquad\qquad 250\% = \tfrac{250}{100} = \tfrac{5}{2}$$

$$2.5 \times 32 = 80 \qquad\qquad \tfrac{5}{2} \times 32 = 80$$

$$250\% \text{ of } 32 \text{ is } 80$$

What Per Cent Is One Number of Another? Look at the statement $20 = 4 \times 5$. The numbers 4 and 5 are *factors* of 20. When you multiply these factors, you get the product 20. Suppose the factor 5 is missing: $20 = 4 \times ?$. You can find the missing factor by dividing 20 by 4: $20 \div 4 = 5$. Suppose the factor 4 is missing: $20 = ? \times 5$. You can find it the same way: $20 \div 5 = 4$. Now suppose one of the factors is a fraction. Look carefully at the problem $30 = ? \times \tfrac{1}{4}$. You can find the missing factor by dividing 30 by $\tfrac{1}{4}$:

$$30 \div \tfrac{1}{4} = 30 \times \tfrac{4}{1} = 120$$

So $30 = 120 \times \tfrac{1}{4}$. Per cents are hundredths, so you can use this process to find what per cent one number is of another.

Suppose you want to find what per cent of 30 the number 15 is. First, write the problem in the form $15 = ? \times 30$. You can find the missing factor by dividing 15 by 30:

$$15 \div 30 = .5 \qquad\qquad .5 = 50\%$$

So 15 is 50% of 30.

Here are two more examples:
17 is what per cent of 340?

$$17 = ? \times 340$$

$$17 \div 340 = .05 \qquad\qquad .05 = 5\%$$

$$17 \text{ is } 5\% \text{ of } 340$$

420 is what per cent of 70?

$$420 = ? \times 70$$

$$420 \div 70 = 6 \qquad\qquad 6 = 600\%$$

$$420 \text{ is } 600\% \text{ of } 70$$

Finding a Number When a Per Cent Is Known. Suppose you know that 6 is 25% of some number. What is the number? You can use the process of finding a missing factor to solve this problem. First, write the problem in the form $6 = 25\% \times ?$. Now 25% is .25, so the problem becomes $6 = .25 \times ?$. You can find the missing factor by dividing 6 by .25:

$$6 \div .25 = 24$$

So 6 is 25% of 24.

Here are some more examples:
17 is 40% of what number?

$$17 = .40 \times ? \qquad\qquad 17 \div .40 = 42.5$$

$$17 \text{ is } 40\% \text{ of } 42.5$$

46 is 115% of what number?

$$46 = 1.15 \times ? \qquad\qquad 46 \div 1.15 = 40$$

$$46 \text{ is } 115\% \text{ of } 40$$

Applications of Percentage

Commissions. Many companies pay their salesmen by giving them a *commission* (a certain amount for each article they sell). The commission is usually a certain

Percentage Protects Shoppers because it often shows the exact amount of a material that goes into a product. A clothing label shows amounts of different fibers that go into a fabric.
Don Zeilstra

PERCENTAGE

per cent of the price of the article that is sold.

Suppose a salesman receives a 15 per-cent commission on everything he sells. How much does he earn if he sells a refrigerator for $436? That is, what is 15 per cent of $436? First, remember that 15 per cent means 15 hundredths. You must find .15, or $\frac{15}{100}$, of 436.

$$15\% = .15 \qquad\qquad 15\% = \frac{15}{100}$$

$$.15 \times \$436 = \$65.40 \qquad \frac{15}{100} \times \$436 = \$65.40$$

So the salesman earns $65.40 on the sale.

Comparisons. Percentage gives us a method of comparing quantities. It helps to make a comparison where the relationship is not easy to see at once. For example, percentage helps people to compare volumes of sales on the stock market. Companies often use percentage to compare their business gains and losses. Engineers use percentage to compare production rates with their goals. Here is a more familiar example taken from the records of four baseball teams:

Chicago White Sox won 12 games and lost 8 games.
Cleveland Indians won 10 games and lost 7 games.
Kansas City Athletics won 14 games and lost 11 games.
New York Yankees won 11 games and lost 6 games.

What is the correct standing of the teams?

First, you can see that the Chicago White Sox played 20 games and won 12 of them. What per cent of 20 is 12? Remember the process of finding a missing factor.

$$12 = ? \times 20$$

$$12 \div 20 = .60 \qquad\qquad .60 = 60\%$$

So the Chicago team won 60 per cent of its games.

The Cleveland Indians played 17 games and won 10 of them. What per cent of 17 is 10?

$$10 = ? \times 17$$

$$10 \div 17 = .588 \qquad\qquad .588 = 58.8\%$$

The Cleveland team won 58.8 per cent of its games.

The Kansas City Athletics played 25 games and won 14 of them. What per cent of 25 is 14?

$$14 = ? \times 25$$

$$14 \div 25 = .56 \qquad\qquad .56 = 56\%$$

The Kansas City team won 56 per cent of its games.

The New York Yankees played 17 games and won 11 of them. What per cent of 17 is 11?

$$11 = ? \times 17$$

$$11 \div 17 = .647 \qquad\qquad .647 = 64.7\%$$

The New York team won 64.7% of its games.

Now you can arrange the teams on the basis of the per cent of games won:

New York Yankees.........................64.7
Chicago White Sox.........................60
Cleveland Indians.........................58.8
Kansas City Athletics.....................56

You can use percentage to compare other quantities.

Interest. When a person borrows money from a bank, the bank charges him *interest* on the loan. Paying interest is like paying rent for the use of the money. Bankers usually compute interest by percentage.

Suppose a businessman borrows $6,000 from the bank. The bank charges him 6 per-cent interest a year. How much interest does he have to pay every month? First, what is 6 per cent of $6,000?

$$6\% = .06$$

$$.06 \times \$6,000 = \$360 \qquad 6\% \text{ of } \$6,000 = \$360$$

So the businessman must pay the bank $360 on his loan for one year. To find how much he must pay for one month, divide $360 by 12:

$$\$360 \div 12 = \$30$$

So the businessman must pay the bank $30 every month as interest on his loan. See INTEREST.

Profits. A businessman usually charges a price for an article that includes the article's cost and his own profit. This price is the *selling price*. Businessmen usually compute their profits as percentages.

Suppose a dealer bought a bicycle from a manufacturer for $36. He wants to make a profit of 25 per cent on the price for which he sells the bicycle. How much must he charge for the bicycle and what will his profit be? If he wants to make a profit of 25 per cent, the cost of the bicycle from the manufacturer must be 75 per cent of the price he wants to ask. So the problem is to find the number of which $36 is 75 per cent. Remember the process of finding a missing factor.

$$75\% = .75$$

$$\$36 = ? \times .75$$

$$\$36 \div .75 = \$48 \qquad\qquad \$48 - \$36 = \$12$$

So the dealer must charge $48 for the bicycle. His profit will be $12. As a check, you can see that the profit, $12, is 25 per cent (or one fourth) of the selling price of $48.

Taxes. Many prices include taxes. For example, the price of a bracelet could include both federal and state tax charges. These taxes are usually computed as per cents of an article's price.

Suppose a college sells tickets for a football game. Each ticket costs $1.50. The $1.50 price includes a 10 per-cent federal tax on the college's income from the ticket. What is the income from each ticket? If the $1.50 price includes both income and the 10 per-cent tax, then the $1.50 must represent 110 per cent of the income. So the problem is to find the number of which $1.50 is 110 per cent.

$$110\% = 1.10$$

$$\$1.50 = ? \times 1.10$$

$$\$1.50 \div 1.10 = \$1.36 \text{ (to the nearest cent)}$$

So the income that the college earns from each ticket sold is $1.36. CLEON C. RICHTMEYER

See also DECIMAL NUMERAL SYSTEM; FRACTION; GRAPH; STATISTICS.

PERCEPTION. The world around us consists of various kinds and levels of physical energy. Our knowledge of the world comes through our sense organs, which react to these energies. Certain wavelengths of electromagnetic energy stimulate our eyes. Our ears sense certain kinds of mechanical vibrations in the air. Our noses and tongues are sensitive to certain chemical stimuli. Sense organs in our skin respond to pressure, temperature changes, and various stimuli related to pain. Sense organs in our joints, tendons, and muscles are sensitive to body movement and position.

The sense organs change the various environmental energies into nervous impulses, and these impulses then go to the brain. Through the psychological process of perception, the patterns of energies become known as objects, events, people, and other aspects of the world.

The process of perception does not reveal objects and events of the world. We see light and color, but there is no light or color in the electromagnetic waves that stimulate the eyes. In the same way, there is no music or noise in the vibrations that stimulate the ear. The brain organizes and interprets nervous impulses from the eyes as light and color, and impulses from the ears as sound. Together, the sense organs and the brain transform physical energy from environmental stimuli into information about the events around us.

When looking at the illustration on this page, you may first see only a complicated pattern of dark and light areas. As you study the pattern, your first perception may change, particularly if you are told that a bearded man is in the picture. After you have seen the man, it will be almost impossible not to see him when you look at the picture again. This picture emphasizes two important points about perception. First, stimulation of the sense organs alone does not determine the nature of what is perceived. Second, perception is a dynamic process of "working on" sensory data to produce perceptual objects and events. The "work" involves many physical, physiological, and psychological factors.

Factors Affecting Perception

Various factors influence what and how we perceive. Our perceptions are influenced by the ways our bodies are structured to receive and process stimuli from the environment. Our perceptions also reflect our emotions, needs, expectations, and learning.

Receptors. Each sensory system, such as vision, hearing, or touch, has its own specialized body parts. These parts are called *receptors*, and they change energies from the environment into nervous impulses. The human eye, for example, has two major kinds of receptors in the *retina* (the light-sensitive part of the eye). These receptors are called *rods* and *cones*. The rods respond to light, but not to color (different frequencies of light). The cones do respond to different frequencies of light, and are called color receptors. The rods allow us to see in dim light, and the cones enable us to see colors and sharp detail in bright light. Thus, the particular ways that receptors are structured and function help determine the perceptual effects related to them.

The Brain. Certain physical and functional features of the brain also determine some aspects of perception.

William M. Smith

Hidden Figure Designs show how we must "work on" sensory stimulation to perceive something recognizable. The face of a man with a beard and long hair appears in the top half of this design, in the center. It is a front view, cut off above the eyes. Do not look for such details as the eyes, but concentrate on getting an overall impression.

The part of the brain that serves vision has different kinds of cells that respond only under certain conditions of stimulation. Some of these cells respond only when a light goes off. Others respond when a light goes on, but they stop responding if the light stays on. Such cells also are arranged in special ways in the brain, and this fact is related to how we perceive. For example, some cells are arranged in columns or in clusters. Such arrangements are related to how we perceive edges and forms.

Learning, Emotion, and Motivation. Much evidence points to the conclusion that early experience, learning, emotion, and motivation are important in defining what and how we perceive. Part of this accumulating evidence comes from experiments that compare how persons in different cultures perceive things. The perception of such things as form, color, pain, and touch may differ from culture to culture, depending on habits and customs, and training of children.

A simple example of how learning can affect perception is provided by reading the phrases inside the two triangles in the illustration on the next page. Did you fail to see the duplicate word in each phrase? Most persons do, and some continue to do so even with many repeated readings. In learning to perceive words and sentences, we learn not to perceive each letter and word separately. Instead, we become able to scan the overall pattern and "fill in" the remainder. A poor reader is more likely than a good reader to see the duplicate word in each phrase.

Some illusions are related to learning and past experience. An illusion is not a false perception, as many

PERCEPTION

people believe, but one that is inconsistent with another perception. Since perception does not literally reveal the environment, no sensory system is closer to some absolute truth than any other. We tend to check visual illusions against touch, but touch can involve illusory effects, too. Look at the two triangular patches of gray containing black and white detail in the illustration on this page. If you see the patches as being different shades of gray, you are experiencing an illusion. The patches were made with the same paint.

Emotions and motivation can have an important effect on perception. Sometimes a severe emotional disturbance can prevent perception completely, as

PERCEPTUAL EFFECTS

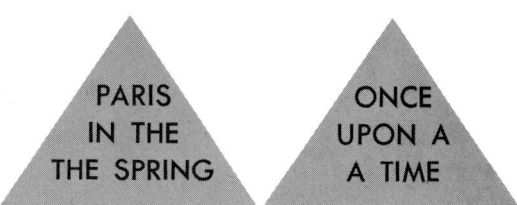

What are the two phrases printed in the two triangles above? Read them carefully. Did you read them correctly the first time?

How many complete cubes do you see in the drawing at the left? Three or five?

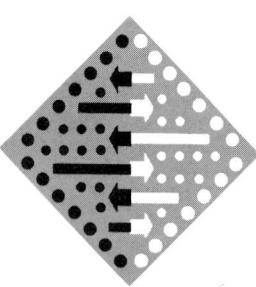

How do the two gray triangles at the left compare in brightness? In the drawings below, does the rectangle surrounded by black appear brighter than the rectangle surrounded by white? The text of this article discusses each of the perceptual effects shown here.

William M. Smith

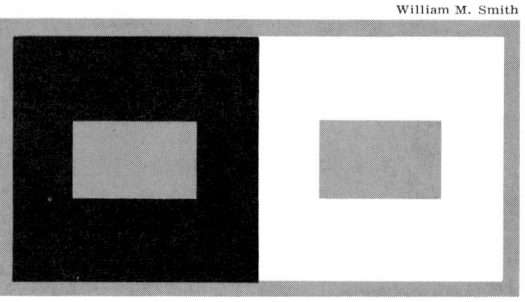

when emotional shock causes an individual to lose his hearing temporarily. We are more likely to perceive those aspects of our environment that are related to our motives. For example, motivation can affect the perceived characteristics of objects. To a hungry man, food may appear larger or more colorful than usual.

Understanding Perception

Types of Perception. Perception has three levels of complexity: (1) *detection*, (2) *recognition*, and (3) *discrimination*. Detection refers to whether a person can sense that he is being stimulated by some form of energy. For example, a light may be so dim that he can barely detect its presence. Recognition means being able to identify as well as detect a particular pattern of stimulation. Discrimination means being able to perceive patterns of stimulation as different. For example, a person may hear slight differences between two similar musical tones.

The field of study that deals with the levels of perception is called *psychophysics*. Experimental psychologists investigate the relationships between the physical properties of stimulus patterns and the perceived effects. They may try to find the relationship between sound frequency and the perceived pitch of the sound.

Principles of Perception. There are a number of general principles that help us understand the process of perception. One of the most important is the principle of *closure*. It tells us that we have the general tendency to perceive things as complete and unified. We tend to "fill in" parts that are missing, or parts that conform to an overall impression.

The principle of *constancy* states that despite changes that occur in stimulation, we have a strong tendency to perceive objects as constant in size, shape, color, and other qualities. For example, an orange will be perceived with its characteristic color under different kinds of light.

The opposite of the principle of constancy is also important. Sometimes an object or pattern of stimulation will remain constant, but the perceived effect will vary. Look at the gray and black cubes in the illustration on this page. At one moment you will see three complete cubes, and at another you may see five.

Another important principle relates to *perceptual context*. The perception of an object or event depends in part on the *context* (surrounding conditions). Look at the two gray rectangles in the illustration on this page. One rectangle is surrounded by a black area, and the other by a white area. Do the two gray rectangles seem identical? To most persons, gray surrounded by black appears brighter and somewhat larger. This effect is called *visual induction*. Notice, too, that the effect is opposite to that observed with the two gray triangles with black and white detail. In this case, the gray with black detail appears darker rather than brighter. But all four figures—rectangles and triangles—were made with the same paint.   WILLIAM M. SMITH

See Weights and Measures (table: Miscellaneous Weights and Measures).

PERCH is the name given to a family of about 100 different fresh-water fish that live in the cooler parts of the Northern Hemisphere. They all have rather long bodies, which may be either rounded or flattened. Their scales are small and tough. They are in the group of bony fishes, called *teleosts*, to which most of our common fishes belong. They grow from 6 to 18 inches long.

The name *perch* is most commonly given to the well-known *yellow perch* of North America. There are many yellow perch in the region of the Great Lakes, and in the lakes of New England, New York, and southern Canada.

The yellow perch usually grows between 6 and 15 inches long and weighs up to 4 pounds. Its name comes from its golden-yellow color. The sides are marked with several dark bars. It is sometimes called the *ringed perch*, as well as the *common perch*. A similar species is common in Europe.

Fishermen seek the yellow perch, and it is valued as food. It is easy to catch, and will bite on a simple pole and hook or a casting line any time of year. Almost any kind of bait can be used.

The *pike perch* is another member of the perch family that is well-known to American fishers. It is also called the *walleye*, *walleyed pike*, *pike*, *pickerel*, *dory*, *blowfish*, and *jack salmon*. This perch is common in the Great Lakes and the Mississippi Valley region. It likes clear water with rocky or sandy bottoms. Its size may be anywhere from 2 to 25 pounds. The usual length is 10 inches, but some pike perch reach a length of 3 feet. Pike perch may be caught with a simple pole and hook, by trolling, or by casting.

A small group of perch, called *darters*, has more members than any other group of fish in America. The darters are usually about 2½ inches long. The male is brilliantly colored. Darters are as agile as minnows.

Scientific Classification. Perch are in the fresh-water perch family, *Percidae*. The yellow perch is genus *Perca*, species *P. flavescens*. The pike perch is *Stizostedion vitreum*. Darters form the subfamily *Etheostominae*.   Carl L. Hubbs

See also Darter; Fish (color picture: Fresh-Water Fishes); Fishing (table: Game-Fishing World Records).

PERCHERON. See Horse (Draft Horses; color picture).

PERCIVALE, or Perceval. See Holy Grail.

PERCUSSION INSTRUMENT. See Music (Musical Instruments); Orchestra; Sound (Musical Sounds).

PERCY, CHARLES HARTING (1919-   ), an Illinois Republican, was elected to the United States Senate in 1966. He defeated his former college economics professor, Democrat Paul H. Douglas.

Before entering politics, Percy was a highly successful businessman. He worked his way through the University of Chicago by operating a cooperative purchasing association on campus. By the time he graduated in 1941, the company had annual sales of about $150,000. In 1949—at the age of 29—Percy became president and chief executive officer of the Bell & Howell Company, a manufacturer of photographic equipment. He ended all administrative ties with the company in 1966.

Percy served as chairman of the Ford Foundation's Fund for Adult Education from 1958 to 1961. In 1960, he was chairman of the platform committee for the Republican National Convention. In 1964, in his first try

for public office, he lost the race for governor of Illinois. Percy was born in Pensacola, Fla.

PERCY, THOMAS. See Ballad (Folk Ballads).

PEREKOP, ISTHMUS OF. See Crimea.

PERENNIAL, *pur EHN ih ul*, is a plant that lives for more than two years without replanting. Sometimes, as in the case of trees, perennials live for many years. Plants whose life span is two years, or two growing seasons, are called *biennials*. Those that live a single year, or one growing season, are called *annuals*. But this classification sometimes varies, because the above-ground parts of some plants are annual, while the parts below the ground are perennial. Some shrubs and herbs, such as the castor-oil plant, are perennials in the places they come from. But when grown in cold climates, they live only a year. For this reason, the term *perennial* is most commonly used to designate plants all of whose parts endure for more than two years.

There are two types of perennials. One type has *herbaceous stems* that die each year, but underground parts that live through the winter. New shoots come from the underground parts during the next growing season. Rhubarb and asparagus are examples of such perennials. The other type has *woody stems* that live for season after season. These stems increase their diameter by adding tissues (largely new wood) to those of previous seasons. Trees and shrubs are the main woody-stem perennials.   William C. Beaver

See also Annual; Biennial; Gardening (Kinds of Garden Plants).

PERFUME is a substance that gives off a pleasant odor. Many perfumes have odors similar to those of fresh flowers. Almost all perfumes are blended from a variety of natural and *synthetic* (man-made) substances. The most expensive perfumes contain oils from flowers and spices.

People use perfumes in many ways to create a pleasant odor. They apply paste and liquid perfumes to their bodies and clothing. They use lipsticks, face and body lotions and powders, and other cosmetics that contain perfume. By far the largest amount of perfume is used in soaps, especially bar soaps. Industrial *odorants* (low-priced, scented substances) are added to some products to hide unpleasant odors and make the products attractive to buyers. Paper, plastic, and rubber products are often treated with odorants. Since ancient times, plants and plant products with pleasing odors have been burned as incense during religious services.

All liquids used for body scenting, including colognes and toilet waters, are sometimes considered to be perfumes. But *true perfumes*—called *extracts* or *essences*—contain a greater amount of perfume oils and are more expensive than colognes and toilet waters. Most perfumes consist of 10 to 20 per cent perfume oils dissolved in alcohol. Colognes contain 3 to 5 per cent perfume oils dissolved in 80 to 90 per cent alcohol, with water making up the balance. Toilet waters have about 2 per cent of perfume oils in 60 to 80 per cent alcohol, and the balance consists of water.

How Perfumes Are Made

The composition of a perfume depends largely on its intended use. Most expensive body perfumes contain

SOURCE OF MATERIALS USED IN ONE FRENCH-TYPE PERFUME			
ODORS			**SOURCE**
FLORAL ODORS	Jasmine	Synthetic	Coal Tar
	Violet	Synthetic	Oil of Lemongrass
	Rose	Synthetic	Coal Tar and Alcohol
			Oil of Citronella
			Oil of Geranium
	Lily of the Valley	Synthetic	Oil of Citronella
	Carnation	Synthetic	Oil of Cloves
	Orange Blossom	Natural	Blossoms
	Mimosa	Natural	Flowers
ORIENTAL ODORS	Sandalwood	Natural	Wood
	Vetiver	Natural	Roots
	Styrax	Natural	Resin
	Patchouli	Natural	Leaves
ODORS ADDED TO MODIFY THE ODOR OF THE PERFUME	Coumarin	Synthetic	Coal Tar
	Oak Moss	Natural	Moss
	Ylang Ylang	Natural	Flowers
FIXATIVE AND DILUTING AGENT	Musk Ambrette	Synthetic	Coal Tar
	Alcohol	Natural	Molasses or Grain

Coty

A Perfumer accurately measures and combines various aromatic products and oils to create a new fragrance.

rare flower and spice oils from many parts of the world. Perfumes used in soapmaking come from low-cost, man-made materials. Industrial odorants consist of artificial fragrances or perfume by-products. Many perfumes are blends of flower and plant oils, animal substances, synthetics, alcohol, and water.

Plant Substances. Fragrant plants have tiny *sacs* (baglike parts) that make and store the substances that give them their pleasant odor. These substances are called *essential oils*. Essential oils taken from flower petals are used in the most delicate and expensive perfumes. Essential oils are also found in other parts of plants. They may come from the bark, buds, leaves, rinds, roots, wood, or from whole plants. Plants whose oils are used extensively in perfumes include the cinnamon, citronella, geranium, jasmine, lavender, patchouli, rose, rosemary, sandalwood, and tuberose.

Much essential oil is *extracted* (obtained) from plants by *steam distillation*. The first step in this process is to pass steam through the plant material. The essential oil quickly turns to gas, which is then passed through tubing and cooled to make it liquid again. The essential oil is obtained from some flowers by boiling the petals in water, rather than by passing steam through the petals.

Solvent extraction is an important way of obtaining essential oils from flowers. The petals are dissolved in a *solvent* (liquid that can dissolve other substances). The solvent is distilled from the solution, leaving a waxy material that contains the oil. This material is placed in ethyl alcohol. The essential oil dissolves in the alcohol and rises with it to the top of the wax. Heat is applied, and the alcohol evaporates, leaving a highly concentrated form of perfume oil.

Enfleurage is another method of extracting flower oils. Glass plates are covered with fat, and flower petals are spread over the fat. The fat absorbs the oil from the petals, forming a greasy *pomade*. The pomade is treated with alcohol to dissolve out the oil.

Animal Substances slow the evaporation of perfume oils, and make the fragrances long-lasting. For this rea-son, they are often called *fixatives*. Perfume ingredients from animals include castor, from the beaver; civet, a fatty substance from the civet; musk, from the male musk deer; and ambergris, from the sperm whale.

Synthetic Substances account for the largest amount of materials used in the perfume industry. The raw materials for these substances may be obtained from natural sources, petrochemicals, or coal tar. Some synthetic materials have the same chemical makeup as naturally occurring materials. Others are different from any material found in nature. Many synthetic odors have been developed in the United States to meet the increasing demand for perfumes. However, the United States still imports a variety of essential oils.

History

Ancient peoples burned fragrant resins, gums, and woods as incense at their religious ceremonies. They enjoyed the pleasant smell of the smoke from the burning incense. The word *perfume* itself comes from the Latin *per*, meaning *through*, and *fumus*, meaning *smoke*.

Perfumes have been found in the tombs of Egyptian *pharaohs* (rulers) who lived more than 3,000 years ago. The Egyptians soaked fragrant woods and resins in water and oil, and then rubbed their bodies with the liquid. They also *embalmed* (preserved) their dead with these liquids. The ancient Greeks and Romans learned about perfumes from the Egyptians.

For hundreds of years, perfume making was chiefly an Oriental art. In the early 1200's, the crusaders brought perfume from Palestine to England and France. By the 1500's, perfumes had become popular throughout Europe. Synthetic chemicals have been used extensively in perfumes since the late 1800's. Today, the perfume industry is a billion-dollar-a-year business in the United States.

PAUL Z. BEDOUKIAN

PERGAMUM, *PUR guh mum*, was a great Greek city in western Asia Minor. The kings of the Attalid dynasty, who ruled after 263 B.C., encouraged trade with other kingdoms and promoted the manufacture of brocade textiles and parchments. The Attalids were allied with Rome, and Pergamum came under Roman control in 133 B.C.

Aristonicus, a rebel, led a revolt of slaves to prevent Roman control. But he was defeated in 130 B.C. Under the Romans, Pergamum became a prosperous industrial and educational center. It had a medical school, a library, and many beautiful buildings. Galen, a great doctor, lived there in A.D. 100's. The city was also a center of early Christianity.   THOMAS W. AFRICA

See also LIBRARY (Libraries of Animal Skins).

PERGOLESI, *payr go LAY see*, **GIOVANNI BATTISTA** (1710-1736), an Italian composer of instrumental music, wrote for the stage and for the church. He won fame for two compositions that were quite different in character. The first of these works is *La Serva Padrona*, a musical farce which uses light, gay, and uncomplicated music as well as a simple plot taken from everyday life. The second work is the deeply moving *Stabat Mater*, Mary's lament on the death of Christ. Pergolesi was born in Jesi (Iesi), Italy.   KARL GEIRINGER

PERIANDER. See SEVEN WISE MEN OF GREECE.

PERIANTH is the outside covering, or envelope, of a flower. It includes both the calyx and the corolla. See also PLANT (Sexual Reproduction); FLOWER (The Parts).

PERICARDITIS is the inflammation of the *pericardium*, the sac of membrane that encloses the heart.

PERICARDIUM. See HEART (Parts of the Heart); MEMBRANE; PERICARDITIS.

PERICLES, *PEHR ih kleez* (490?-429 B.C.), was a Greek statesman whose name was given to the greatest period of Athenian history. He was the leader of the Athenian government for 30 years, and the "Age of Pericles" came to stand for all that was highest in the art and science of the ancient world.

Pericles was born in Athens, a member of a high-ranking noble family. He was educated by the greatest philosophers of his day. His mother was a niece of Cleisthenes, a statesman who had made many democratic reforms in the Athenian government (see CLEISTHENES). He had given the governing power to the assembly and popular courts. But because officials then received no pay, the poor could not afford to hold office. After Cleisthenes' death, the council of the Areopagus took back its power over the city.

Pericles was determined to continue the reforms of his great-uncle and entered politics with the democratic popular party. He and Ephialtes, the leader of this party, worked together to limit the power of the Areopagus. Pericles continued his reforms but found himself opposed by Cimon, the leader of the aristocratic party. Pericles managed to have his rival *ostracized* (banished) for favoring the Spartans.

Athenian Leader. In about 460 B.C., Ephialtes was killed. Pericles became leader of the popular party and the most powerful man in the state. He made many changes as head of the state. Public officials had never been paid before, but Pericles introduced salaries, first for the *archons*, and later for all officers. According to Aristotle's *Constitution of Athens*, as many as 20,000 persons were on the public payroll.

In 457 B.C., Pericles made his greatest reform. The common people were allowed to serve in any state office.

Pericles wanted to make Athens a democracy, but he also wanted to make it the most powerful state in Greece. His foreign policy was to expand the power of Athens by foreign conquest. He fought in Egypt, Boeotia, and the Aegean Islands. This angered Sparta, and the two states broke off friendly relations.

War with Sparta. Pericles' wars were not all successful and Cimon was allowed to return from exile to lead the armies. Cimon fought successfully against Persia and Athens made a favorable peace with that country in 449 B.C. Three years later, Athens signed a 30 years' peace treaty with Sparta allowing Athens to keep Aegina, Euboea, and the cities of the Delian League. But Pericles feared there could be no peace with Sparta, for the Spartans were jealous of Athenian power.

Pericles had moved the treasury of the Delian League from Delos to Athens during the war with Persia. After the war, he decided to keep it in Athens. He also decided to use this money and the money paid by the subject states to build up the Athenian navy and to beautify Athens. He built the temple of Athena Nike, the Propylaea, the Parthenon, and many other structures for the glory of Athens. The state enjoyed prosperity, and literature and philosophy flourished.

The Peloponnesian confederacy, headed by Sparta, declared war on Athens in 431 B.C. Pericles had been expecting this, and he called all the people of the surrounding districts into the city and allowed the Spartans and their allies to lay waste to the surrounding districts as they pleased. Pericles continued to build up the navy with the hope that Athens could defeat the Spartans with sea power. In 430 B.C., a plague broke out in the city, and many people died. The Athenians began to blame Pericles for all their troubles, and for a short while removed him from power. But he was soon recalled, and became even more powerful than before. He died of the plague during the war.   DONALD KAGAN

See also ATHENS (The Ancient City-State); PARTHENON; PELOPONNESIAN WAR; SPARTA.

PERIDINIAN. See PLANKTON.

PERIDOT, *PER ih doh*, one of the birthstones for August, is the transparent greenish variety of olivine. *Olivine*, a common rock-forming mineral, is a magnesium-iron silicate. See also GEM (color picture).

PERIGEE. See ORBIT; MOON (The Moon's Trip).

PERIHELION, *pehr ih HE lih un*, is the position of a planet or comet when it is closest to the sun. In the Northern Hemisphere, the earth is at perihelion at midwinter. At this time, the sun shows a larger diameter, but this difference is only 3 per cent of the sun's apparent size. A person cannot see the difference without instruments. When a planet or comet's distance from the sun is greatest, it is at *aphelion*.   MILES C. HARTLEY

PERILYMPH. See EAR (The Inner Ear).

PERIMETER. See ALGEBRA (Writing Formulas).

PERIOD, in geology. See EARTH (History).

PERIOD, in punctuation. See PUNCTUATION.

PERIODIC LAW. See CHEMISTRY (Development of Inorganic Chemistry); ELEMENT, CHEMICAL.

PERIODIC TABLE, or PERIODIC CHART. See ELEMENT, CHEMICAL; MENDELEEV, DMITRI I.

PERIODICAL

PERIODICAL is a publication that appears at regular intervals, especially a magazine. The interval between issues is more than one day. See also MAGAZINE; TRADE PUBLICATION.

PERIODICAL CICADA. See CICADA.

PERIODONTAL MEMBRANE. See TEETH (picture: The Parts of a Tooth).

PERIODONTICS. See DENTISTRY.

PERIOECI. See SPARTA (The People).

PERIOSTEUM. See BONE (Structure); MEMBRANE.

PERIPATETIC SCHOOL OF PHILOSOPHY, *PEHR ih puh TEHT ihk,* was established by the Greek philosopher Aristotle. The word *peripatetic* may be traced to either of two Greek words, one meaning *to walk* and the other meaning *a covered walk.* When Aristotle lectured to his followers, he walked about under the porticoes, or shaded walks, of the Lyceum at Athens. His school of philosophy got its name from this custom.

Aristotle was a pupil of Plato, who felt that a person could reach the truth only by logic and reason. Plato taught that the world of *appearances* (everyday life) falsified the *real* world of true ideas. Aristotle held that *reality* could not be separated from *appearance* in this way. He felt that to know reality, a person had to study appearances, and that appearances could lead to the truth about reality. He held that everything except pure form, or God, and pure matter was a combination of both form and matter. H. M. KALLEN

See also ARISTOTLE.

PERIQUE. See LOUISIANA (Agriculture).

PERISCOPE, *PEHR ih SKOHP,* is an optical instrument with which a person can make observations from a distance or around corners. It is built on the same basic principle as the telescope. In its simplest form, it consists of a long tube with a reflecting mirror or prism at each end. These reflecting surfaces are exactly parallel to one another, and are arranged at an angle of 45 degrees with the axis of the tube. Some periscopes have lenses to enlarge the image viewed through the tube.

Periscopes are important in weapons of war, such as submarines and tanks. Officers on a submerged submarine can observe events on the surface, looking for targets or navigating, by peering into their periscopes. Tank commanders can direct action in a battle and remain inside their tanks with the aid of periscopes.

The periscope on a submarine can move up and down, and can be rotated to look in a complete circle. Submarines often cruise at *periscope depth,* with only the periscope above the water.

Not all periscopes are used in warfare. The longest periscope in the world, 90 feet long, protects workers at the National Reactor Testing Station at Arco, Idaho. Scientists use the periscope to observe nuclear reactors in operation. D. SEGANISH

See also SUBMARINE; TANK, MILITARY.

PERISTALTIC WAVES. See STOMACH (The Stomach's Work).

PERISTYLE. See ARCHITECTURE (Architectural Terms).

PERITONEUM, *PEHR ih toh NEE um,* is the thin membrane that lines the abdominal cavity. It covers the organs in the abdomen and in the pelvis. The peritoneum is the most important of the serous membranes. Inflammation of this membrane, called *peritonitis,* is a serious condition. See also MEMBRANE; PERITONITIS.

PERITONITIS, *PEHR ih toh NYE tis,* is an inflammation of the *peritoneum,* the thin membrane that lines the abdominal cavity. It is a serious illness that can cause death. The peritoneum may become inflamed if it is attacked by bacteria, or if it is irritated by a foreign substance.

Peritonitis may be either *chronic* or *acute. Chronic peritonitis* lasts for a long time. It can cause inflamed tissues to grow together. As a result, the intestines may not be able to work properly. Persons suffering from tuberculosis sometimes develop chronic peritonitis.

Acute peritonitis occurs suddenly. The inflammation may affect a small part of the peritoneum, or it may involve a large area. It starts with fever, chills, vomiting, and severe abdominal pain. The abdomen becomes rigid and swells. The pulse becomes rapid, and the number of white blood cells increases.

Acute peritonitis is caused by bacteria that escape from some organ in the body, or by the presence of an irritating substance. Bacteria can escape from an organ such as the appendix if the organ is so badly infected that it tears open. This may follow such conditions as gangrene of the intestine, a damaged bowel, or an infected pancreas.

Peritonitis requires prompt medical care. Antibiotics and other drugs are used to treat any infection and control pain. If an organ breaks open, an operation is usually performed as soon as possible to close the opening and drain the infection. E. CLINTON TEXTER, JR.

PERIWINKLE, a plant. See MYRTLE.

PERIWINKLE is the common name for several species of small snails of the sea coast. The best known is the European periwinkle, which is common not only in northern Europe but also on the Atlantic coast of the northern United States. This periwinkle clings to rocks between high and low tide levels. Its thick, spiral shell is grayish-brown or nearly black. Europeans gather periwinkles for food, but Americans seldom eat them.

In the southern United States some kinds of freshwater snails are commonly referred to as periwinkles.

Scientific Classification. Periwinkles are in the periwinkle family, *Littorinidae.* The common European periwinkle is genus *Littorina,* species *L. littorea.* R. TUCKER ABBOTT

See also SNAIL.

A Periscope makes it possible for men in a submerged submarine, *below,* to see ships or other objects on the surface of the water, *right.*

U.S. Navy

PERJURY. A person commits perjury when he swears to tell the truth in a court of justice or some other judicial or legislative proceeding, and then deliberately tells a lie. In most states, the lie is perjury only if it has a direct bearing on the issue before the court, tribunal, or legislative body. An unintentional misstatement is not considered perjury. A person is guilty of *subornation of perjury* when he causes another person to commit perjury. Subornation of perjury is punishable by law. Perjury is usually considered a felony.   FRED E. INBAU

See also FELONY.

PERKIN, SIR WILLIAM HENRY (1838-1907), an English chemist, founded the aniline dye industry. At the age of 18, Perkin discovered a violet-colored dye while trying to make synthetic quinine. He and his father started a factory to make the dye commercially.

Perkin's other discoveries included synthetic tartaric acid, used in making effervescent beverages; cinnamic acid, used in medicine and perfume; and coumarin, used in the manufacture of perfume and food flavoring. Perkin also devised a method for the formation of unsaturated fatty acids, and worked on the polarization of light. Perkin was born in London, and attended the Royal College of Chemistry.   HENRY M. LEICESTER

See also ANILINE.

PERKINS, FRANCES (1882-1965), became the first woman Cabinet member in the United States. She served as secretary of labor under President Franklin D. Roosevelt from 1933 to 1945. In 1946, President Harry S. Truman appointed her a member of the U.S. Civil Service Commission. She served until 1953. Before entering government service, Miss Perkins served as director of investigations for the New York State Factory Commission (1912-1913) and chairman of the New York State Industrial Board (1926-1929). Miss Perkins was largely responsible for the 48-hour (in place of the 54-hour) workweek for women in her state. While serving in the Cabinet, she became chairman of the President's Committee on Economic Security.

United Press Int.
Frances Perkins

The report issued by this committee laid the basis for the Social Security Act.

Miss Perkins was born in Boston, and was graduated from Mt. Holyoke College. She wrote *People at Work* (1934) and *The Roosevelt I Knew* (1946).   HARVEY WISH

PERKINS, LUCY FITCH (1865-1937), an American writer and illustrator, became well known for her series of 25 "Twin" books for children. These stories tell either about children in other countries or about life in the United States. The unusual pencil drawings in the books are fascinating for children to copy. Mrs. Perkins' works include *The Dutch Twins* (1911), *The Japanese Twins* (1912), *The Irish Twins* (1913), *The Mexican Twins* (1915), *The Eskimo Twins* (1915), *The Swiss Twins* (1922), *The Colonial Twins of Virginia* (1924), and *The American Twins of 1812* (1925). Mrs. Perkins was born in Maples, Ind.   ROBERT K. LONG

PERMAFROST. See TUNDRA.

PERMUTATIONS AND COMBINATIONS

PERMALLOY, *PUR muh loy*, is a nickel-iron alloy that is easy to magnetize. It can be magnetized by wrapping an insulated wire around it and sending an electric current through the wire. Permalloy loses its magnetism when the current is turned off. Such a material is said to be *magnetically soft*. A weak alternating current sent through a coil wound around a permalloy bar produces a strong magnetic field in the material. For this reason, permalloy is an ideal material for use as the core of low-power inductors and transformers used in communication engineering. The term *permalloy* comes from the two words *permanent* and *alloy*. Permalloy was developed in 1916 by G. W. Elmen, an engineer for the Western Electric Company.   WILLIAM W. MULLINS

PERMANENT COURT OF INTERNATIONAL JUSTICE. See INTERNATIONAL COURT OF JUSTICE.

PERMANENT WAVE. See HAIRDRESSING.

PERMIAN PERIOD. See EARTH (table: Outline).

PERMIT. See POMPANO.

PERMUTATIONS AND COMBINATIONS are names that mathematicians use for certain groups of objects or symbols. *Permutations* are *ordered arrangements* of a set of objects. For example, ABC, ACB, and BAC are permutations of the set of symbols A, B, and C. *Combinations* are those permutations that include the same objects *regardless of the order in which they are arranged*. The sets ABC, ACB, and BAC are all examples of the same combination. Sets such as ABC, ABD, and ACD are examples of different combinations.

Understanding permutations and combinations helps solve certain problems in the fields of probability and statistics. These problems occur in science, engineering, business, economics, and insurance.

Solving Permutation Problems

The question, "How many sets of initials can be formed from the three letters A, B, and C?" is the same as the question, "How many permutations are there of 3 objects taken 3 at a time?" You can find the answer (1) by making a list of all the possibilities, (2) by reasoning, and (3) by using mathematical formulas.

By Listing. To find the answer by listing, you merely write down all the possibilities and count them. The list below shows there are 6 possibilities. Therefore there are 6 *permutations* of 3 objects taken 3 at a time.

ABC	BAC	CAB
ACB	BCA	CBA

You could also list the possibilities in the form of a diagram that shows the choices for each position:

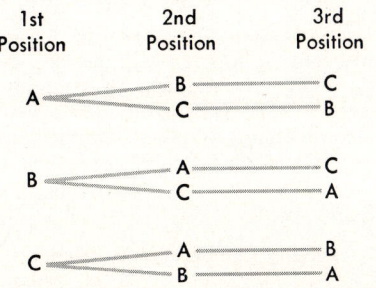

The diagram again shows that you can form 6 sets.

256a

PERMUTATIONS AND COMBINATIONS

By Reasoning. You could also find the number of permutations by reasoning. For the first initial, you have 3 possible choices, A or B or C. With each of these choices, you have only 2 possible choices left for the second position, and $3 \times 2 = 6$. With each of these 6, you have 1 possible choice for the third position, and $6 \times 1 = 6$. Therefore, the number of possible sets of initials is $3 \times 2 \times 1 = 6$.

Using reason is better than just listing the permutations because reasoning accounts for every possibility. In listing, you might forget to include some possibilities, especially if you had a large number of objects.

Suppose, for example, that you had 26 letters instead of only the letters A, B, and C, and that you were asked to find the total number of sets of *3 initials* that could be formed. Listing all the possibilities would be difficult and tedious. But finding the answer by reasoning would be easy. With every one of the 26 possible choices for the first initial, there would be 25 choices for the second initial. This makes a total of 650 possibilities ($26 \times 25 = 650$). With each of these 650 choices, there would be 24 letters remaining as possible choices for the third initial, making a total of 15,600 possible combinations ($650 \times 24 = 15,600$). The total number of permutations is therefore $26 \times 25 \times 24 = 15,600$.

The above example illustrates the *multiplication principle* for permutations: *If any position can be filled in* m *different ways, and if the next position can be filled in* n *different ways, there are* m *times* n *permutations possible.*

The multiplication principle helps you to find the answer to a slightly different problem. Suppose you had only A's, B's, and C's, but at least *3* of each. How many sets of 3 initials could you form? (The sets would include AAA, AAB, ABB, and so on.) Using the multiplication principle, you could calculate the answer: $3 \times 3 \times 3 = 27$ sets. With 26 letters and at least 3 of each, you could form $26 \times 26 \times 26 = 17,576$ sets.

By Using Symbols and Formulas. In mathematical terms, the number of permutations of n things taken r at a time is represented by the symbol P^n_r (sometimes written $_nP_r$). Using this symbol, you can express the answers to permutation problems as follows:

3 things (such as A, B, and C) taken 3 at a time
$$P^3_3 = 3 \times 2 \times 1 = 6$$

26 things taken 3 at a time
$$P^{26}_3 = 26 \times 25 \times 24 = 15,600$$

n things taken r at a time
$$P^n_r = n(n-1)(n-2) \ldots [n-(r-1)]$$

The last expression is the general formula. The bracketed quantity, $[n-(r-1)]$, means n minus the quantity $(r-1)$. Algebraically, this quantity is the same as $(n-r+1)$. This quantity tells you at what point to stop writing successive multipliers in the formula. For example, if n is 26 and r is 3, then $(n-r+1) = 26 - 3 + 1 = 24$ and so the multipliers for P^{26}_3 are $26 \times 25 \times 24$.

Solving Combination Problems

If you had 4 books, how many sets of 3 books could you form? This question is the same as the question,

"How many *combinations* are there of 4 things taken 3 at a time?" Suppose, for example, that the 4 books were written respectively by Adams, Beery, Cole, and Doe. If you chose books by Adams, Beery, and Cole, your reading material would be the same regardless of the order in which you read the books. In other words, there is only 1 *combination* of these 3 books taken 3 at a time. How many other 3-book combinations could you make from the 4 books? As in the permutation problem discussed above, you can find the answer (1) by listing the possibilities, (2) by reasoning, and (3) by using mathematical formulas.

By Listing. For simplicity, represent the 4 books by the letters A, B, C, and D. You could construct your list by writing down several groups of these 4 letters, and then crossing out one letter at a time, always leaving a group of 3. You would cross out a different letter each time so that the remaining group would always be a different combination.

$$
\begin{array}{ll}
\text{ABC}\!\!\!\diagup & \longrightarrow \text{ABC} \\
\text{AB}\!\!\!\diagup\text{D} & \longrightarrow \text{ABD} \\
\text{A}\!\!\!\diagup\text{CD} & \longrightarrow \text{ACD} \\
\!\!\!\diagup\!\text{BCD} & \longrightarrow \text{BCD}
\end{array}
$$

The list shows that there are 4 possible combinations.

By Reasoning. A knowledge of permutations enables you to arrive at the answer in the following way. You can select any 3 of the books in 6 different orders, for example, ABC, ACB, BAC, BCA, CAB, CBA. But these 6 *permutations* represent only a single *combination*. You can conclude that there are 6 permutations for *each* different combination of 3 books. Therefore, the total number of permutations must be equal to 6 times the number of possible combinations. Likewise, the number of possible combinations must be equal to the total number of permutations divided by 6.

The total number of permutations of 4 books taken 3 at a time is
$$P^4_3 = 4 \times 3 \times 2 = 24$$

The number of permutations for each combination of 3 books is
$$P^3_3 = 3 \times 2 \times 1 = 6$$

Therefore, the number of possible combinations is $24 \div 6 = 4$.

By Using Symbols and Formulas. The number of combinations of n objects taken r at a time is represented by the symbol C^n_r (sometimes written $\binom{n}{r}$ or $_nC_r$). In the example of the books, the number of possible combinations can be expressed and calculated as follows:

$$C^4_3 = \frac{P^4_3}{P^3_3} = \frac{4 \times 3 \times 2}{3 \times 2 \times 1} = \frac{24}{6} = 4$$

The general formula for combinations is
$$C^n_r = \frac{P^n_r}{P^r_r} = \frac{n(n-1)(n-2) \ldots (n-r+1)}{r(r-1)(r-2) \ldots 3 \times 2 \times 1}$$

For example, if $n = 6$ and $r = 4$,
$$C^6_4 = \frac{6 \times 5 \times 4 \times 3}{4 \times 3 \times 2 \times 1} = 15$$

Mathematicians simplify the formula for C^n_r by using *factorial notation* to represent the product of a positive whole number with all the positive whole numbers less than itself. *Factorial 3* means $3 \times 2 \times 1$, and it is written 3!. Likewise, 4! means $4 \times 3 \times 2 \times 1$. Permutation formulas can therefore be simplified as follows:

$$P_3^3 = 3! \qquad P_4^4 = 4! \qquad P_r^r = r!$$

The simplified combination formula is

$$C_r^n = \frac{n(n-1)(n-2) \ldots (n-r+1)}{r!}$$

Mathematicians simplify the above formula even more and write it as follows:

$$C_r^n = \frac{n!}{r!(n-r)!}$$

The last two formulas are the same because

$$\frac{n!}{r!(n-r)!} =$$

$$\frac{n(n-1)(n-2) \ldots (n-r+1)(n-r)(n-r-1)}{r!(n-r)(n-r-1)}$$

$$\frac{(n-r-2) \ldots 3 \times 2 \times 1}{(n-r-2) \ldots 3 \times 2 \times 1}$$

All factors in this expression can be divided out except for $n(n-1)(n-2) \ldots (n-r+1)$ in the numerator and $r!$ in the denominator. These are the same factors that appear in the original combination formula.

With the two forms of the combination formula, you can calculate the number of possible combinations in two ways. For example, if you had 5 books from which to choose a set of 3, you could find the number of combinations as follows:

$$C_3^5 = \frac{5 \times 4 \times 3}{3 \times 2 \times 1} = 10$$

$$C_3^5 = \frac{5 \times 4 \times 3 \times 2 \times 1}{(3 \times 2 \times 1)(2 \times 1)} = 10$$

If you divide out factors in the numerator and denominator of the above expressions, you will see that they are identical. See also FACTOR.

History

Early Greek works of the period 350-150 B.C. contain some mention of special cases of combinations. Some facts about permutations were noted by the Roman Boethius in 510, the Hindu Bhaskara in 1150, and by the Jewish scholars Rabbi ben Ezra and Levi ben Gerson in 1140 and 1321. A Chinese book, the *I-king*, treated permutations in the 1100's. The French monk Jean Borrel discussed permutations in connection with locks as early as 1559.

The real development of mathematical thought about permutations began in the 1600's with the development of the theory of probability. About this time, the French mathematician Blaise Pascal discovered an interesting device for computing combinations. The device, called the *Pascal triangle*, is shown in the illustration. Pascal constructed the triangle so that each number was the sum of the two numbers above it. Let us call each number in the triangle an *element*. The elements are arranged in *rows*. Each element has a certain *place* in a row determined by counting from left to right. Thus, 20 appears in the 4th place of the 7th row.

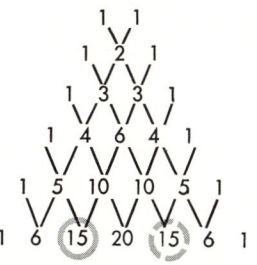

Pascal found that the element in the $(r+1)$th place of the $(n+1)$th row is the same as the number of combinations of n things taken r at a time (C_r^n). If n is 6 and r is 2, the number of combinations is given in the 7th row, the 3rd place (15, as circled). But 15 also appears in the 5th place of the 7th row (dashed circle). Because the triangle is symmetrical, the element in the $(r+1)$th place of the $(n+1)$th row is always the same as the element in the $(n-r+1)$th place of that row. This fact leads to the conclusion that $C_r^n = C_{n-r}^n$. Therefore, if n is 6 and r is 2, the same number of combinations is possible if the objects are taken 2 or 4 at a time. PHILLIP S. JONES

See also PROBABILITY.

PERNICIOUS ANEMIA. See ANEMIA.

PERÓN, *pay RAWN,* **JUAN DOMINGO** (1895-   ), was president of Argentina from 1946 to 1955. Then opposition to his regime became intense, and the army and navy forced his resignation after a three-day revolt.

Perón's governmental program was called *Justicialism,* supposedly a middle road between Communism and capitalism. Basically, Perón aimed to make Argentina the political, financial, and military power of Latin America. He geared Argentina's industry to support enlarged military forces. He used press censorship and other violations of civil rights to control his opposition. In 1955, the Roman Catholic Church broke with Perón after he challenged the authority of the church. Unrest appeared in the armed forces, and in September, 1955, Perón was ousted as president. He lived in exile in Spain, but his followers, called *Peronistas,* remained politically active in Argentina (see ARGENTINA [Years of Dictatorship; New Political Crises]).

Perón was born on Oct. 8, 1895, in southern Argentina. He first shared control of the government after a revolution in June, 1943. He held three cabinet posts in the government of President Pedro Ramírez. Perón's reform programs as secretary of labor and social welfare won him the enthusiastic support of labor. He gained strength from the backing of labor and the army. During World War II, Perón and his associates first favored Germany and Japan. After Argentina declared war on Germany and Japan in March, 1945, Perón was temporarily put out of his cabinet office. But he returned and became president of Argentina in 1946.

María Eva Duarte de Perón (1919-1952), the first wife of Juan Perón, helped him rise to power and became one of the most important women of her time. She was born in Los Toldos, Buenos Aires province, and married Perón in 1945. DONALD E. WORCESTER

Juan Perón
Larson, Black Star

PEROXIDE OF HYDROGEN

PEROXIDE OF HYDROGEN. See Hydrogen Peroxide.

PERPENDICULAR STYLE was a phase of English Gothic architecture in the 1400's and 1500's. Perpendicular lines distinguish it, as in the south and west cloisters of Westminster Abbey in London.

PERPETUAL CALENDAR. See Calendar.

PERPETUAL MOTION MACHINE is a device that can continuously produce work with no energy input, or that can continuously convert heat completely into work. No one has ever succeeded in building a perpetual motion machine and almost all scientists and engineers believe no one ever will. But experiments made in the hope of achieving perpetual motion have led scientists to develop two *laws of thermodynamics*. These laws summarize how all machines work. The first law says that energy cannot be created or destroyed. The second law says that heat, by itself, can flow only from a hot object to a colder object. See Thermodynamics.

Two kinds of perpetual motion machines have been suggested: (1) machines that would run forever without receiving energy from the outside, and (2) machines that would run forever and produce work by taking energy from the sea or from the atmosphere.

The first kind of perpetual motion machine could be made to run if it were possible to avoid resistance. However, the moving parts of all machines are subject to friction or some other kind of resistance, which slows down the machine. To keep running, the machine must use energy to overcome this resistance. Without energy input, all machines finally stop. Therefore, scientists have concluded that no machine creates energy.

The second kind of perpetual motion machine could be made to run continuously if it were possible to use up all the energy in a large source such as the sea or the atmosphere. This kind of machine would run only if all the energy of the randomly moving molecules in the source could be completely converted into useful work. No machine has been able to do this. As a result, scientists have concluded that no machine can convert all the heat supplied to it into work. The second law of thermodynamics is based on this conclusion.

The launching of space rockets and artificial satellites has given some persons the idea of obtaining perpetual motion with these devices. This is because the planets and their moons appear to have achieved perpetual motion. But they move in an almost perfect vacuum. The artificial satellites that orbit relatively close to the earth all have limited lifetimes because of atmospheric friction. The farther a satellite orbits from the earth, the longer its life expectancy. But scientists expect that even satellites that go into orbit around the sun may eventually hit the sun, perhaps in millions of years.

The release of atomic energy has also been considered a possible source of perpetual motion. Uranium and other atomic fuels do contain tremendous amounts of energy for their size. But after this energy is used up, the remaining matter must be replaced with fresh fuel. Devices that use atomic fuel cannot run forever. For example, atomic submarines must be refueled periodically. An advantage of atomic fuel is that it lasts longer than other fuels. See Atomic Energy. Charles L. Brown

See also Motion.

PERRAULT, *pair OH,* **CHARLES** (1628-1703), a French writer, is best known for a collection of fairy tales he wrote, *Mother Goose Tales*. The collection, published under his son's name in 1697, includes "The Sleeping Beauty," "Little Red Riding Hood," "Bluebeard," "Puss in Boots," "Cinderella," and "Tom Thumb." See Mother Goose.

Perrault was born in Paris. He became a high-ranking civil servant and a member of the French Academy under King Louis XIV. His older brother was the famous architect and scientist Claude Perrault. Charles was known for his progressive, evolutionary view of history. He helped start a famous literary battle called "The Quarrel of the Ancients and the Moderns." In *The Century of Louis the Great* (1687) and *Parallels Between the Ancients and the Moderns* (1688), he argued that the culture of his own time was superior to the culture of classical Greece and Rome. He felt that the "Moderns" would win the battle through science, the rational philosophy of René Descartes, and progress in knowledge, culture, and literature. Joel A. Hunt

See also Doré, Gustave (picture).

PERPETUAL-MOTION MACHINES

Perpetual-motion machines have long fascinated man. Many have been built, but all failed to work perpetually.

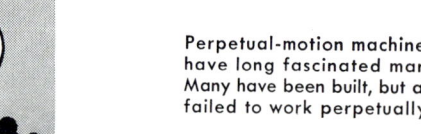

Endless-Chain Machine

Pivoting-Ball Machine

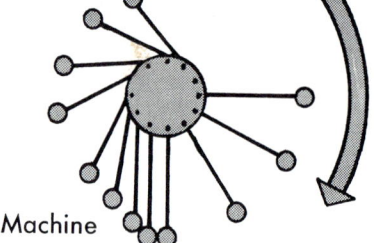

The right side of the endless-chain machine, *left*, is longer than its left side. The inventor believed this added weight would keep pulling the chain around. But the right side runs over idler wheels and these take up the extra weight, and the machine does not run.

Many inventors have experimented with the pivoting-ball machine, *above*. The balls swing out to the right and are supposed to keep the wheel turning. But the wheel stops moving because the dangling balls on the left balance the weight of those on the right side.

Chicago Historical Society

Commodore Matthew Perry Landed in Yokohama and was ushered into a tent, where he met the commissioners of the Emperor. By his stern manner and a firm display of armed might, Perry forced the Japanese to open their ports to world trade.

In his dealings with the Japanese, Perry deliberately used elaborate ceremony. He and his officers wore their finest uniforms and were always accompanied by a well-drilled honor guard to impress the Japanese.

PERRY is the family name of two brothers who became famous United States naval officers.

Oliver Hazard Perry (1785-1819) became noted for his heroism during the War of 1812. At the outbreak of the war, he was a naval lieutenant but had no sea command. He offered his services on the Great Lakes, and received command of the Lake Erie naval force.

Except for a brief period when he fought on Lake Ontario and helped capture Fort George in Canada, he spent the spring and summer of 1813 in Erie, Pa., outfitting his fleet for battle. In August, he left Erie, crossing the Erie bar. The water was so shallow that the guns had to be removed so the ships would not run aground. It is not known why Commander Robert H. Barclay of the British fleet did not take advantage of this occasion to attack.

Perry made his headquarters at Put-in-Bay, off the Ohio shore, and on Sept. 10, 1813, sailed from there to fight the British. His fleet included nine small ships, the largest of which were the *Lawrence*, commanded by Perry, and the *Niagara*, commanded by Jesse Duncan Elliott. The *Lawrence* flew a motto flag bearing James Lawrence's dying words, "Don't give up the ship." During the battle, the *Niagara* hung back and took very little part in the fighting. The *Lawrence* suffered many casualties, and finally was disabled. Perry then rowed to the *Niagara*. Under his command, the *Niagara* kept the British from boarding the *Lawrence*. Two British ships became entangled, and the *Niagara* raked them with broadsides. The British fleet of six vessels surrendered after about 15 minutes.

Perry then sent to General William Henry Harrison, the military commander in the West, the famous message, "We have met the enemy, and they are ours." As a reward, Perry was promoted to captain and received a gold medal and a vote of thanks and $7,500 from Congress. He also was awarded $5,000 in prize money. The victory gave control of Lake Erie to the Americans. General Harrison was able to cross the lake and take a large part of Upper Canada. Perry helped transport the troops. He later took part in the battle around Detroit and on the Thames River in Canada.

Perry was born in South Kingston, R.I., on Aug. 20, 1785, the son of a naval officer. At the age of 14, he became a midshipman, and served under his father in the West Indies during the naval war with France. During the war with Tripoli, he was twice stationed in the Mediterranean Sea, first, in 1802 and 1803, on board the *Adams*, and again, from 1804 to 1806, on board the *Constellation* and other ships.

In 1807, as a lieutenant, Perry directed the construction of gunboats at Newport, R.I. He next took command of the *Revenge*, which ran aground in a fog in 1811 and was lost. An inquiry cleared Perry of any blame for this loss because a pilot had at that time been in charge of the ship.

Perry commanded the *Java* in the Mediterranean Sea in 1816 and 1817. In 1819, he took a small fleet to Venezuela on a diplomatic mission for the government. While sailing homeward along the Orinoco River after this mission, he contracted yellow fever and died within a few days. He was buried at Port of Spain, Trinidad, but his body was later brought back to Newport, R.I.

See FLAG (color picture: Flags in American History); PERRY'S VICTORY AND INTERNATIONAL PEACE MEMORIAL NATIONAL MONUMENT; OHIO (color picture); PENNSYLVANIA (picture: Flagship); WAR OF 1812 (picture).

Matthew Calbraith Perry (1794-1858) opened Japanese ports to world trade. He sailed the first U.S. Navy ships into Tokyo Bay on July 8, 1853. He arranged a treaty with Japan in 1854, protecting American seamen and property in Japanese waters. Naval units sent from other countries to Japan for this same purpose had been fired upon. The Japanese distrusted other countries and had shut themselves off from the rest of the world.

But Perry impressed Japan with a show of force and dignity. He arrived in Tokyo Bay with his decks cleared for action and a letter from President Millard Fillmore. He refused to deal with anyone except the highest officials. Perry's boldness succeeded. He presented his documents to two Japanese princes, who were the emperor's representatives. Perry then went to China to give the Japanese time to study Fillmore's proposals.

Perry returned to Japan in February, 1854, and again made a show of force in Tokyo Bay. A few weeks later the Japanese signed a treaty in Yokohama, granting the United States trading rights in two Japanese ports, Hakodate and Shimoda. Perry then returned to Washington as a member of the naval efficiency board. He published his record of the expedition, *Narrative of the Expedition of an American Squadron to the China Seas and Japan*, in 1856.

The opening of Japan ranks as one of history's most significant diplomatic achievements. It not only changed American and European policy toward Japan, but brought about a change inside Japan itself. Within 50 years, Japan had become a great world power (see JAPAN [History]).

Perry was born on April 10, 1794, in Newport, R.I. At the age of 15, he enlisted as a midshipman on the *Revenge*, commanded by his brother, Oliver Hazard Perry. From 1810 to 1812, he served on the *President* under Commodore John Rodgers. As a lieutenant, he was an executive officer of the *Cyane*, which helped found an American Negro colony in Africa in 1820.

Perry's first independent command was the *Concord*, in which he took John Randolph to Russia as the United States envoy in 1830. During the next 10 years, Perry was active in naval affairs and originated the apprentice system for the education of seamen.

Perry became a captain in 1837, and later took command of the *Fulton II*, one of the first naval steamships. In 1839 and 1840, he directed the first school of naval gunnery, on board the *Fulton II*. In 1843, he commanded the African Squadron which aided in wiping out the slave trade, and helped protect the settlements of American Negroes in Africa.

In the Mexican War, Perry commanded the *Mississippi* and served as commander in chief of the squadron off the east coast of Mexico. His squadron, up to that time the largest under the United States flag, worked with army forces led by General Winfield Scott in the siege and capture of Veracruz. From 1848 to 1852, Perry served at the New York Navy Yard where he directed the building of mail steamships. In 1852, he again took command of the *Mississippi* to protect American fisheries off the coast of British provinces in America.   RICHARD S. WEST, JR.

PERRY, BLISS (1860-1954), an American author and educator, won recognition as general editor of the Cambridge Editions of the Poets (1905-1909). Perry also edited the *Atlantic Monthly* magazine from 1899 to 1909, and taught English literature at Harvard University from 1907 to 1930. His writings include *A Study of Prose Fiction* (1902) and his autobiography, *And Gladly Teach* (1935). He was born in Williamstown, Mass.   CLAUDE A. EGGERTSEN

PERRY'S VICTORY AND INTERNATIONAL PEACE MEMORIAL NATIONAL MONUMENT lies on an island in Lake Erie, in Ohio. The monument covers

Commodore Oliver Perry at the Battle of Lake Erie on September 10, 1813. Perry is ordering his gunners to fire at the British ship. Although his ships were outgunned, Perry's cool courage and daring seamanship won the battle.

about 22 acres. It was established in 1936 to preserve the memory of Oliver Hazard Perry's naval victory in the War of 1812, and the later years of peace between Great Britain and the United States.

See also OHIO (color picture: Perry's Victory Monument).

PERRYVILLE, BATTLE OF. See CIVIL WAR (Perryville).

PERSE, SAINT-JOHN (1887-   ), is the pen name of ALEXIS LÉGER, a French poet and diplomat. He received the Nobel prize for literature in 1960.

Perse was born in the West Indies. Until World War II, he led a dual existence. Under his real name, he became secretary-general of the French ministry of foreign affairs. Under his pen name, he published the epic poem *Anabase* (1924). The identity of "Saint-John Perse" was revealed only when he went into exile in the U.S., after the Germans occupied France in 1940.

Perse remained in Washington, D.C. until 1959 and wrote most of his works there—*Exil, Vents, Amers, Chronique,* and *Oiseaux.* This poetry sings of human experience, using a rich ceremonial style. Through the interplay of its abundant and varied images, the poet tries to convey the immediate presence of "man in the fullness of his being."   LeRoy C. Breunig

See also FRENCH LITERATURE (Poetry).

PERSEPHONE. See PROSERPINA.

PERSEPOLIS, *pur SEHP oh lis,* was a ceremonial center of the Persian Empire during the days of Darius I and his successors. The ruins of the once magnificent buildings lie in southwestern Iran, near the present city of Shiraz.

Archaeologists have uncovered remains of stairways, columns, and sculptured figures. King Cambyses may have started building Persepolis about 528 B.C. Persepolis flourished until Greeks, under Alexander the Great, destroyed it about 330 B.C.   RICHARD N. FRYE

See also DARIUS (picture); IRAN (picture); SCULPTURE (color picture: Lion Fighting a Bull).

PERSEUS, *PUR syoos,* or *PUR see us,* was the son of Zeus (Jupiter) and Danaë in Greek mythology. The evil king Polydectes tricked him into going after the head of the Gorgon Medusa. Perseus succeeded because Hermes (Mercury) and Athena (Minerva) came to his aid. Hermes led him to the Graeae, the hags of the sea. They told him how to obtain winged sandals, a magic case in which to carry Medusa's head, and Pluto's helmet, which would make him invisible. Hermes then gave him a sword, and Athena gave him a shiny shield.

Perseus did not dare look directly at Medusa's face, or he would have turned to stone. He used the shield as a mirror and cut off Medusa's head. He later rescued Andromeda and married her. When Perseus returned home, he turned Polydectes to stone.   PHILIP W. HARSH

Related Articles in WORLD BOOK include:

Andromeda	Mercury	Pegasus
Gorgon	Minerva	Pluto
Medusa		

PERSEUS is a constellation of the northern celestial hemisphere, west of the constellation Auriga. Perseus contains the binary star Algol (see ALGOL). The two stars of Algol periodically eclipse one another, so that Algol appears alternately fainter and brighter. In Greek mythology, Perseus, son of Zeus, won this place among the stars. See also CONSTELLATION.   I. M. LEVITT

Marble sculpture by Antonio Canova

Perseus Cut Off the Head of the Monster Medusa, *above.* The Greeks named the constellation Perseus, *below,* after him.

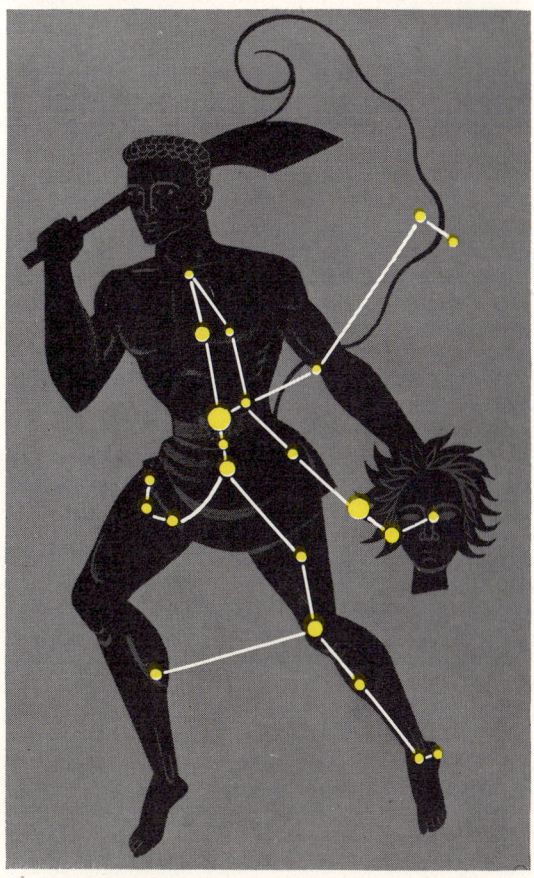

General John J. Pershing, *above*, led his troops under the Arch of Victory on New York's 5th Avenue, *left*, after World War I ended in 1918.

Brown Bros.; U&U

PERSHING, *PUR shing*, **JOHN JOSEPH** (1860-1948), commanded the American Expeditionary Forces (A.E.F.) in Europe during World War I. The A.E.F. was the first United States Army ever sent to Europe. Pershing trained and led in battle an army that grew within 18 months from a small group of regulars to almost two million men. After the war, he received the highest rank that had ever been given an American Army officer, general of the armies of the United States.

Teacher-Soldier. Pershing was born on Sept. 13, 1860, near Laclede, Mo. His father, a railway section foreman, gave him a good basic education. Pershing began to teach in a local Negro school at 17, and saved enough to enter the teacher-training school in Kirksville, Mo.

While in school, he saw a newspaper announcement of a United States Military Academy examination. He took the test in hope of receiving free education. He passed the examination, entered the academy, and was graduated in 1886. He began active service by fighting against the Apache. While serving as military instructor at the University of Nebraska, he earned a law degree.

Pershing was teaching tactics at the U.S. Military Academy when the Spanish-American War began in 1898. He fought with distinction as a first lieutenant with the 10th Cavalry in the Santiago campaign.

Promotion and Tragedy. Pershing served in the Philippines from 1899 to 1903, and directed the Mindanao Island campaign against the Moros, a fierce, rebellious tribe. He was still a first lieutenant at 40, and considered resigning from the Army because of slow promotion. But he became a captain while in the Philippines. His work in subduing the Moros, who had never before been conquered, won the admiration of President Theodore Roosevelt.

Pershing became military attaché to the United States Embassy in Japan after the outbreak of the Russo-Japanese War in 1904. He went with Japanese General Tamemoto Kuroki to Manchuria, where as military observer he studied modern warfare on a large scale. He returned to the Philippines after the war. In 1906, President Roosevelt promoted Pershing from captain to brigadier general over 862 officers.

Pershing next served in San Francisco as command-

ing officer of the 8th Brigade. Here, in 1915, tragedy struck. Pershing's wife and three daughters died in a fire at the Army post. Only his son Warren was saved.

Mexican Campaign. In 1916, Pershing took command of the army that entered Mexico in pursuit of Francisco (Pancho) Villa and his bandits. Villa had raided and burned the border town of Columbus, N.M. Pershing's long pursuit broke Villa's power. This made "Black Jack" Pershing (so called because he had once commanded an all-Negro troop) a public figure in the United States. When the United States entered World War I in 1917, Pershing was chosen to lead the A.E.F.

World War I. Upon arriving in France, Pershing laid a wreath on the tomb of the Marquis de Lafayette. One of his staff officers, Col. Charles E. Staunton, gave a short speech on Pershing's behalf. In the speech, Staunton announced: "Lafayette, we are here." This symbolized the repayment of aid that Lafayette and other Frenchmen had given America during the Revolutionary War.

Pershing's greatest work as commander of the A.E.F. was to preserve the unity of the American Army in combat and maintain the spirit of the offensive. The Allied generals wanted to use the American troops to fill the ranks of their battered armies, but Pershing insisted that, except in certain cases, the American Army should fight independently. He believed that the knowledge of a large, fresh American Army would hurt German morale. Also, the Americans had been trained for fast, driving warfare, which Pershing believed was needed to win. He opposed the slow trench warfare of the Allied armies. His theories proved to be correct.

Later Career. Pershing served as chief of staff of the U.S. Army from 1921 to 1924. After his retirement, he served as chairman of the American Battle Monuments Commission and in several honorary diplomatic assignments. Pershing was an early advocate of United States entry into World War II. He consulted with Chief of Staff George C. Marshall, but took no other active part in the war. He was buried in Arlington National Cemetery.   MAURICE MATLOFF

See also WORLD WAR I ("Lafayette, We are Here!").

PERSIA. See IRAN; PERSIA, ANCIENT.

The Oriental Institute, University of Chicago

Ruins of Persepolis, ancient Persia's greatest city, lie in southwestern Iran. Darius I built the city about 500 B.C. Parts of Darius' audience hall, *front*, and palace are still standing.

PERSIA, ANCIENT, was a land that included parts of what are now Iran and Afghanistan. Under Cyrus the Great, Darius I, Xerxes, and other leaders it became the home of a great civilization, and the center of a vast empire. The name *Persia* came from *Persis*, the Greek name for the region. The Persians themselves called the region the *land of the Aryans*, from which the name *Iran* comes. The Persians called their language *Aryan*.

The early Persians were nomads who came to the area from what is now southern Russia about 900 B.C. They were good organizers and administrators, and the empire they created lasted over 200 years. They made important contributions in government, law, and religion. The Persians developed an efficient "pony express" relay system of mail delivery, built an irrigation system, and introduced the first widespread system for using coins as money. They also tried to standardize weights and measures. For a quotation about the Persian postal system, see POST OFFICE (Early Years).

The Persians treated their subjects better than earlier rulers had, and they probably influenced the actions and policies of later governments. Alexander the Great built on Persian accomplishments to unify his empire. So did the Arabs in building their civilization.

In the 500's B.C., Persia became the center of the vast Achaemenid Empire, which included most of the known world. It extended from North Africa and southeastern Europe in the west to India in the east, and from the Gulf of Oman in the south to southern Russia in the north. The Persians ruled an area almost as large as the continental United States. Persians invaded Greece in the early 400's B.C. But the Greeks drove them from Europe, ending the empire's expansion. Alexander the Great conquered the empire in 331 B.C. Later, Parthians and Sassanians controlled Persia before it was conquered by Arabs in A.D. 641.

Way of Life

The People. Ancient sculptures show that the Persians were a handsome people with long, straight noses. Persians dressed in long robes, later called *caftans*, and wore jewelry and false hair.

Most of the common people lived in mud huts, much like the huts many of the country people of Iran live in today. Nobles and kings built large stone houses and palaces. The ruins of some of these still stand.

The Persians adopted many of the customs of the Elamites, the people they had conquered. But they kept

Richard N. Frye, the contributor of this article, is Aga Khan Professor of Iranian at Harvard University, and the author of The Heritage of Persia.

The Oriental Institute,
University of Chicago

Sculpture of Persian Head was found at Persepolis.

British Museum, London

Silver Drinking Cup was used by a king or nobleman.

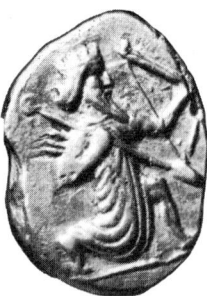

American Numismatic Society

Persian Coins served the entire empire. Achaemenid coin, *left*, was minted in the 400's B.C., Sassanian coin, *right*, about A.D. 400.

Zoroastrian Religious Symbol, a winged image of Ahura Mazda, "the wise spirit," watches over the ruins of Persepolis.

Inge Morath, Magnum

many traditions of the *nomadic* (wandering) peoples. For example, they taught their sons to ride horses, shoot bows, and speak the truth. The Persians considered it a disgrace to lie or to be in debt.

Early Persian families formed into clans, and clans into tribes. But as the empire grew, social units larger than the family began to disappear. Persian men could have several wives. A king could select his wives only from the six highest families. Rulers had large *harems*, where all the women in the family lived.

Language and Literature. The people of ancient Persia spoke a language much like the Sanskrit language of India, and Greek and Latin. The Persians developed a cuneiform system of writing (see CUNEIFORM). But the cuneiform system was used only for royal inscriptions, because few people could read it. The Persians used Aramaic as a written language throughout their empire. Aramaic was widely used in Syria, Palestine, and Mesopotamia then, and the Persians extended its use to India and central Asia. Local languages were used in various parts of the empire.

Little is known of the literature of ancient Persia. But stories of ancient heroes still survive, probably passed along by minstrels and folk tales.

Religion. The early Persians believed in gods of nature, such as the sun, sky, and fire. They believed these gods had social powers. Mithras, the sun god, for example, controlled contracts. The Persians had no temples. They prayed and offered sacrifices on mountains.

Zoroaster (or Zarathustra), a prophet who lived about 600 B.C., reformed the ancient religion. He preached a faith based on good thoughts, words, and deeds, emphasizing a supreme god called Ahura Mazda, "the wise spirit." Zoroaster's followers, called *Zoroastrians*, gradually spread his religion all over Persia. Zoroaster's teachings are found in the *Gathas*, part of the Zoroastrian holy book called the *Avesta*.

Art and Architecture in ancient Persia was a mixture of Greek, Egyptian, and other cultures. Remains of huge royal palaces have been found that stood at Persepolis and Susa, in what is now Iran. Goblets, plates, and other objects made of gold during the Persian Empire have been found. After Alexander the Great conquered Persia, silver became popular, and many silver art objects have been found. Ancient Persian textiles, rugs, and pottery are exhibited in many museums today.

Economy. Early Persians were farmers. They raised grain and livestock. Deserts covered much of the region, and the peasants developed irrigation to grow wheat, barley, oats, and vegetables. They used underground tunnels to avoid evaporation by the hot sun, and brought water as much as a hundred miles from the mountains to the valleys and plains. Persia had few large towns until Alexander the Great conquered it. Crafts developed after cities were founded. Pottery, weaving, and metal work in copper, iron, gold, and silver became important occupations. Pots and pans became more important than weapons, armor, and farming tools. Potters and weavers made clothing, pottery, and rugs for the people.

Caravans carried trade goods from many parts of the world through Persia to the Mediterranean Sea. Important articles of trade included precious and semiprecious stones, and spices. A silk route to central Asia and China was opened, probably during the 100's B.C. Trade routes from Mesopotamia to the Far East led across Persia, skirting the central desert.

Other routes led east to India, and north to the Caucasus Mountains and the Black Sea. The Persians built roads between cities in their empire. The most famous was the royal road that linked Sardis in western Asia Minor to Susa near the Persian Gulf. The Persians used the roads to deliver mail swiftly by relays of horsemen.

Government

Well-organized bureaus governed the Achaemenid Empire (549-331 B.C.). The empire was divided into provinces called *satrapies*, each governed by an official called a *satrap*. Satraps ruled and lived like minor kings. But the *king of kings*, who ruled the empire from Persia, had final and absolute authority. The kings *codified* (systematized) the laws in various parts of the empire. Troops in the satrapies were controlled by the central government. A secret service, sometimes called the *eyes and ears of the king*, informed the king of affairs throughout the empire.

Under the Parthians (155 B.C.-A.D. 225) and Sassanians (A.D. 225-641), Persians kept the title king of kings. Some of these Persian rulers were strong, but others were weak. Local lords exercised great powers during the Parthian period. A powerful state church existed under the Sassanians. Priests served in important civil posts, but church and state remained separate.

History

Early Civilization. The first known civilization in Persia was that of the Elamites, who settled the region

sometime before 1200 B.C. Tribes of Medes and Persians wandered into Persia beginning about 900 B.C. The Medes created the first state on the Persian plateau about 700 B.C., and reached the height of their power in the late 600's B.C. The Persians, led by Cyrus the Great, overthrew the Medes in 549 B.C.

The Achaemenid Empire. Cyrus enlarged the Median empire by seizing the kingdom of Lydia in 547 B.C. and gradually absorbing Greek colonies in Ionia, in western Asia Minor. He called this the Achaemenid Empire, after his ancestor, Achaemenes. He conquered Babylonia in 539 B.C. and freed the Jews in captivity there, allowing them to return to Palestine. Cyrus was killed in 529 B.C. He had created an empire that extended from the Mediterranean Sea and western Asia Minor to the Indus River in what is now Pakistan, and from the Gulf of Oman to the Caucasus Mountains.

Cambyses, Cyrus' son, conquered Egypt about 525 B.C., but died on his way back to Persia. A civil war for control of the empire followed, and Darius I, a relative of Cambyses, became king in 521 B.C.

Darius reorganized the government under the satrapy system, established the absolute power of the king of kings, and developed a regulated system of taxation. He also built palaces at Persepolis and Susa—his two capitals. Darius expanded the Persian Empire in all directions.

In 510 B.C., the Persians invaded what is now southern Russia and southeast Europe, but did not conquer much land. Darius sent an army into Greece in 490 B.C.,

PERSIAN EMPIRE-ABOUT 500 B.C.

■ Persia
■ Persian Empire
★ Capital
• City or Town

This map shows the Achaemenid Empire of ancient Persia at its peak in 500 B.C., during the reign of Darius I. Persis, later called *Persia*, was the center of an empire that stretched west to the central Mediterranean Sea, east to India, and from the Gulf of Oman in the south to southern Russia in the north. Darius ruled this vast empire from two capitals, Susa and Persepolis.

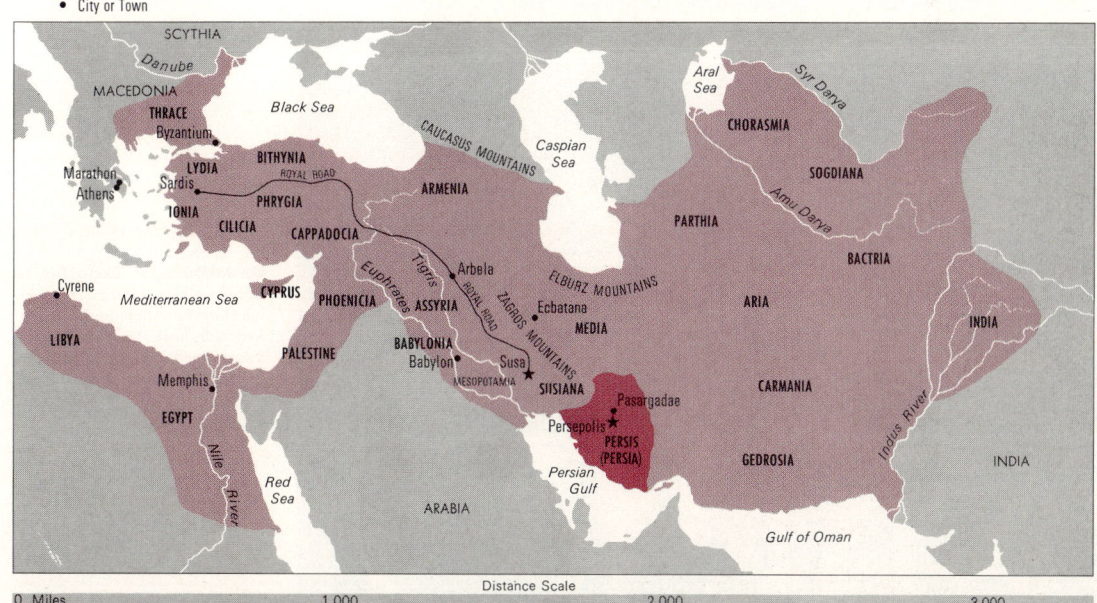

British Museum, London

An Achaemenid Cylinder Seal shows King Darius killing a lion. Impressions were made by rolling the seal across soft clay.

but it was defeated by Athenian forces at Marathon. Darius died in 486 B.C., while preparing for new attacks on Greece.

Xerxes, Darius' son, invaded Greece in 480 B.C., and defeated a Spartan force after a fierce battle at Thermopylae. But the Persians suffered crushing defeats at Salamis and Plataea, and were driven from Europe in 479 B.C. See GREECE, ANCIENT (The Persian Wars).

After Xerxes' death, Persia declined. But the empire continued to exist in spite of revolts until 331 B.C., when Greek forces under Alexander the Great defeated a huge Persian army at the Battle of Arbela (sometimes called the Battle of Gaugamela). This ended the Achaemenid Empire, and Persia became part of Alexander's empire.

Greek Rule of Persia lasted until about 155 B.C. The Greeks founded many new cities, and introduced Greek culture. They set up an independent kingdom in Bactria, from which they spread Greek ideas and culture to India and central Asia. In about 155 B.C., Mithridates I, king of the Parthians, captured Persia.

The Parthian Empire lasted until about A.D. 225. The Parthians built a large empire across eastern Asia Minor and southwest Asia. During the last 200 years of their rule, the Parthians had to fight the Romans in the west and the Kushans in what is now Afghanistan. Civil wars erupted in their empire. In about A.D. 225, a Persian named Ardashir overthrew the Parthians and seized control of the Parthian Empire. After more than 550 years under other rulers, Persians again ruled Persia.

The Sassanian Dynasty, named for Sassan, grandfather of Ardashir, ruled Persia until 641. Wars between Persians and Romans continued through much of the Sassanian reign, and the fighting helped to weaken both sides. After the Romans adopted Christianity in the 300's, the conflict seemed to become a religious struggle between Christianity and Zoroastrianism, the religion of the Persians.

The Sassanian civilization reached its high point in the mid-500's. Persians won several victories over the Romans, and reconquered land that had been part of the Achaemenid Empire. Persian troops advanced to the walls of Constantinople (now Istanbul, Turkey), then the capital of the Byzantine (East Roman) Empire. But they were defeated there and forced to withdraw from all the land they had conquered.

The rise of Islam, a new religion in Arabia, brought a sudden end to the Sassanian dynasty in the mid-600's. Arabs invaded Persia and defeated the Persians in 637 and 641. Islam spread across the Persian plateau. But the new Islamic rulers kept much of the Persian organization, art and architecture, and culture.

For the history of Persia after the Arab conquest, see IRAN (History). RICHARD N. FRYE

Naqsh-i-Rustam, Iran (Herzfeld Archives)

Investiture of Ardashir I, a rock relief sculpture at Naqsh-i-Rustam, near Persepolis, shows Ardashir, *left,* founder of the Sassanian Dynasty, taking the symbol of royalty from Ahura Mazda, the supreme Zoroastrian god.

PERSIAN CAT. See CAT (Longhair Cats).

PERSIAN GULF, *PUR zhun,* is an arm of the Arabian Sea that separates Iran from Arabia. It is connected with the Gulf of Oman by the Strait of Hormuz. The gulf is about 500 miles long and 230 miles wide at its greatest width. Including its islands, the gulf covers an area of 90,000 square miles.

The chief ports on the gulf are Bandar 'Abbās, Būshehr, Kuwait, and Manama. Ahvāz and Abadan are important river ports. The principal islands in the Persian Gulf are the Bahrain group, Hormuz, and Qeshm. The Persian Gulf is one of the largest and oldest sources of the world's pearl supply, and ranks as one of the principal oil-exporting areas. BOSTWICK H. KETCHUM

The Persian Gulf Separates Iran and Arabia.

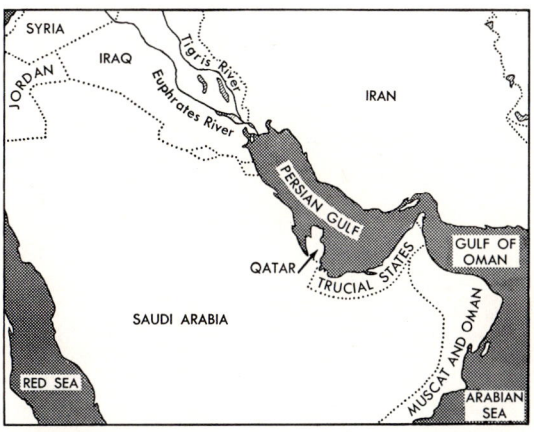

PERSIAN LAMB. See FUR (Lamb and Sheep); KARAKUL.

PERSIAN LYNX. See CARACAL.

PERSIAN WARS. See GREECE, ANCIENT (The Persian Wars).

PERSIMMON is any one of a group of small trees that belong to the ebony family. Two are grown for their pulpy, edible fruit, also called *persimmons.* The principal kinds of persimmons are the oriental or Japanese, the date-plum, and the American. The oriental and the date-plum persimmon are native to central and Northern China. The American is native to the Southeastern United States.

Both the American and the oriental persimmon are grown in the United States. The oriental persimmon or *kaki,* is grown commercially. It is ornamental, with large, shiny, dark-green leaves and yellowish-green flowers. The tree trunk is usually straight, but the branches twist and turn. The trees are favorite haunts of opossums.

Persimmon fruit is round

W. H. Hodge

Oriental Persimmons have a sweet taste after they have been frozen.

---

or egg-shaped and ranges from $\frac{1}{2}$ inch to 2 inches in diameter. It is usually yellowish or orange, but may be streaked with red. The fruit contains a strong astringent that causes a person's mouth to pucker. When the fruit is so dead-ripe and soft that it looks wrinkled and almost spoiled, it tastes the best. Then it tastes very sweet and has a rich, fruity flavor. Indians made a kind of bread by mixing mashed persimmon pulp with crushed corn.

Scientific Classification. Persimmons belong to the ebony family, *Ebenaceae.* The American persimmon is genus *Diospyros,* species *D. virginiana.* The Oriental or Japanese persimmon is *D. kaki.* JULIAN C. CRANE

PERSISTENCE OF VISION. See EYE (Persistence of Vision).

PERSON (in law). See BILL OF EXCHANGE.

PERSON, in grammar, is the feature of a language that shows the difference between the speaker, the person spoken to, and any other person or thing. If a word stands for the speaker, it is in the *first person.* If it stands for the person spoken to, it is in the *second person.* If it stands for any other person or thing (the person or thing spoken of), it is in the *third person.* English shows person by a change in the form or spelling of a personal pronoun or verb. Nouns do not have different forms to show person.

Different forms of personal pronouns show person. *I* and *we* are first person. *You* is second person. *He, she, it,* and *they* are third person.

Verbs change form to show person only in the third person, singular, of the present tense. An *-s* is added to the first (or second) person, singular, present tense, to form the third person. For example, I *drive* is first person, you *drive* is second person, but he *drives* is third person.

The word *be* changes form to show person in the singular, present tense as follows: I *am,* you *are,* he *is.* But plural forms of *be* in the present tense are the same: we *are,* you *are,* they *are.* First and third person forms of *be* in the singular, past tense, are alike but the second person is different. I *was* is first person, he *was* is third person, but you *were* is second person. PAUL ROBERTS

See also VERB.

PERSONAL LIBERTY. See CIVIL RIGHTS.

PERSONAL NAME. See NAME, PERSONAL.

PERSONAL PROPERTY is one of the two classes into which all property is divided. *Real* property refers to such immovable objects as land, houses, and trees. *Personal* property includes all other kinds of property, such as furniture, livestock, and harvested crops. It is much easier to transfer personal property than real property. Real property must be transferred in writing, but personal property may be transferred orally.

When a man dies, his heirs usually inherit his real property. But personal property generally passes into the hands of the estate administrator who sells it and divides the proceeds among the next of kin, unless a will makes other provisions for disposing of it. WILLIAM TUCKER DEAN

Related Articles in WORLD BOOK include:

Administrator	Heir
Bill of Sale	Next of Kin
Contract	Property Tax
Fixture	Real Estate

PERSONALITY

PERSONALITY is a term that has many general meanings. Sometimes the word refers to the ability to get along well socially. For example, we speak of glamor courses designed to give a person "more personality." The term also may refer to the most striking impression that an individual makes on other persons. We may say, "She has a shy personality" or "He has a disturbed personality."

To a psychologist, personality is an area of study that deals with complex human behavior, including emotions, actions, and *cognitive* (thought) processes. Personality psychologists study the enduring patterns of behavior that make individuals different from each other. They try to learn how these patterns develop, how they are organized, and how they change.

The Nature of Personality

Personality Types. For centuries, men have tried to group the vast differences among people into simple units. Some of the resulting groupings divide people into personality types based on certain characteristics.

The ancient Greek physician Hippocrates divided individuals into such types as *sanguine* (cheerful) and *melancholic* (depressed). He attributed their behavioral differences to a predominance of one of the body fluids. For example, a person was cheerful if blood (sanguis) was the dominant influence on his behavior.

Some of the more recent theories about personality types have tried to associate body build and temperament. Classifications based on body measurements were developed by two psychiatrists, Ernst Kretschmer of Germany and William Sheldon of the United States.

The Swiss psychologist Carl G. Jung, who studied psychological characteristics, classified people as introverts or extroverts (see EXTROVERT; INTROVERT).

The simplicity of personality-type theories is appealing, but it also limits their value. An individual's behavior is so complex, diverse, and variable that he cannot be sorted usefully into a simple category.

Personality Traits. Related to personality-type theories is the search for broad traits or dispositions to describe enduring differences among people. Personality traits are regarded as dimensions that range from high to low. For example, anxiety is a trait that varies from the greatest anxiety to the least anxiety. Most people have some degree of anxiety along the scale between the two extremes. Psychologists have studied such personality dimensions as aggressiveness, dependency, and extroversion-introversion. People differ greatly in the degree to which they show such traits.

Studies of personality traits help reveal the relationships between an individual's standing on different personality dimensions. For example, a group of children may be tested for intelligence and may also be given questionnaires about their attitudes. In addition, they may be asked to rate their own characteristics, and may be rated by their teachers. The results are then correlated statistically to discover the relationships among all this information.

Walter Mischel, the contributor of this article, is Professor of Psychology at Stanford University and author of Personality and Assessment.

Ratings and Self-Reports. Research on personality traits tends to rely heavily on broad ratings of personality. In self-ratings, a person indicates the degree to which he thinks he possesses certain personality characteristics. Ratings may also be obtained from teachers, friends, or others who know the person or who have watched him in special situations.

These judgments may be affected by many types of bias. A person may give the responses that he thinks are expected and socially desirable, even if they are not true. Moreover, his answers may reflect his preconceptions and *stereotypes* (fixed ways of thinking), rather than an accurate description of his behavior. Tests that ask a person to rate such attributes as friendliness or adjustment provide broad self-characterizations rather than detailed descriptions of behavior. Consequently, the findings of such tests may partly reveal the concepts and stereotypes that people apply to themselves and to others. These findings may not necessarily reflect the people's actual behavior outside the test.

Some techniques are designed to reduce the role of personal meanings and concepts. Other approaches deliberately seek to clarify the individual's concepts about himself. These personal concepts are especially important in theories that stress the role of the self and one's image of oneself. For example, in his theory of self-realization, the American psychologist Carl R. Rogers focuses on *phenomenology*—a person's private experiences and perceptions.

Projective Tests. Some investigators have tried to avoid the problems of relying on a person's ratings or reports about himself by creating indirect clinical techniques in the form of projective tests. These methods require the person to respond to a situation in which there are no clear guidelines and no right or wrong answers. He may, for example, be asked how inkblots appear to him on the Rorschach Test. Or he may be instructed to create a story about the characters in one of the series of pictures in the Thematic Apperception Test. Projective techniques rely on a trained clinician to interpret the person's attributes indirectly from his test behavior. The value of this approach for revealing aspects of personality is controversial and is still being studied.

Freud's Psychoanalytic Theory. According to the Austrian physician Sigmund Freud, the personality has three parts: (1) the *id*, which represents instinctive impulses of sex and aggression; (2) the *ego*, which represents the demands of the real world; and (3) the *superego*, or conscience, which represents standards of behavior incorporated into the personality during childhood.

According to Freud, mental life is characterized by internal conflicts that are largely unconscious. Impulses from the id seek immediate gratification, but they conflict with the ego and the superego. When unacceptable impulses threaten to emerge, a person experiences anxiety. To reduce this anxiety, he may use various personality defenses. He may, for example, *displace* (transfer) his emotions to less threatening objects. A child who is afraid to express aggression toward his father may become angry at his pet dog instead.

Freud's ideas have had great influence on the study

of personality, but they are highly controversial. Many of his ideas had to be modified severely by psychologists to take greater account of social and environmental variables. See DEVELOPMENTAL PSYCHOLOGY.

Personality and Environment

Trait theories and psychoanalytic theories both assume that broad internal personality dispositions determine an individual's behavior in many situations. However, research on the consistency of various personality traits indicates that what people do, think, and feel may depend greatly on the specific conditions in which their behavior occurs.

An individual may be honest in one situation and dishonest in another. He may be passive in some situations but aggressive in other situations or with different people. Many contemporary approaches to the study of personality therefore emphasize the role of specific social experiences and environmental events in the development and modification of behavior. Psychologists are gradually moving away from broad theorizing about the nature of personality. Instead, they are studying experimentally the conditions that determine complex behavior.

Personality Development. Some psychologists have examined the effects of early experiences on later personality development. Other investigators have studied the stability of particular patterns of personality over long periods of time. Their findings suggest that such tendencies as striving to achieve may persist to some degree from childhood into adulthood. However, research has also shown that personality continues to change as a result of new experiences and modifications in the environment.

Throughout his development, a person learns about himself and his world by observing people and events. He also learns by trying new kinds of behavior directly. The rewards and punishments he receives after trying various patterns of behavior affect his future behavior in similar situations. People also learn by observing the results of the behavior of such social models as their parents. Suppose a child repeatedly sees adults succeed in antisocial or criminal acts. If he sees such behavior rewarded, he is more likely to copy it than if it is punished or leads to no clear consequences. A child will more readily imitate a model who is powerful or who rewards or takes care of him.

As the child develops, he copies some of the behavior of many models, including his friends as well as his parents. He combines aspects of their behavior into new patterns. Through direct and observational learning and cognitive growth, he also acquires standards and values that help him regulate and evaluate his own behavior. Gradually, each individual develops an enormous set of potential behaviors. The particular behavior patterns he shows in specific situations depend on motivational factors. See MOTIVATION.

A person's cognitive and social learning experiences vary as a result of the particular social and cultural conditions to which he is exposed in the home, at school, and in other environments. Personality traits may predict many important aspects of behavior. But the setting in which behavior occurs often provides the best predictions about what people will do. Thus, although extensive differences among persons are found

in most human actions, considerable uniformity and regularity can occur when environmental conditions are very powerful. Strong success experiences in a new situation, for example, may override the effects of past failure experiences and of personality traits in determining an individual's future reactions to that new situation. Similarly, prolonged or intense environmental changes, such as lengthy hospitalization or imprisonment, may lead to major personality changes.

Emotional Reactions. During the course of development, we acquire intense emotional reactions to many stimuli. Events that once were neutral may become either pleasurable or painful as the result of conditioning (see LEARNING [How We Learn]).

Some reactions may involve strong anxiety and can have crippling effects. For example, a child who has a frightening experience with a dog may become afraid of all dogs. This fear may *generalize* (spread) even more widely to other animals and to such objects as fur coats, for example, or hair. Such fears are especially hard to unlearn because the frightened person tends to avoid all contact with situations that provoke his fear. Consequently, he prevents himself from having experiences that might eliminate his fear—petting harmless dogs, for example. Emotional upsets of this kind may also be acquired by observing the intense fear reactions of other persons.

As a result of social learning, we generalize from our experiences to new but similar or related situations. But we do not generalize indiscriminately. A young boy may learn to express physical aggression in many settings, including school, play, and home. But he also learns not to be aggressive in other situations, as when visiting his grandparents.

Personality Change. Research on cognitive and social learning processes is leading to new forms of psychotherapy to help persons who have psychological problems. Some of these problems are the result of learning deficits. For example, some persons lack fundamental academic and vocational skills, such as reading proficiency. Individuals who have inadequate relations with others need to learn essential interpersonal skills. Some persons have these basic skills, but they suffer because of emotional fears and strong inhibitions.

Psychoanalytic therapy to change personality tends to stress insight into the history through which the problems developed. Learning methods try to change the disturbing behavior itself by carefully planned relearning and conditioning techniques. Still other forms of personality change may be achieved by creating special environments for learning more adaptive personality patterns. See ABNORMAL PSYCHOLOGY (Treatment of Mental Disorders).   WALTER MISCHEL

PERSONIFICATION. See FIGURE OF SPEECH.

PERSONNEL RELATIONS

PERSONNEL RELATIONS refers to relationships that exist between those managing an organization and the people who work there. It includes hiring, training, and paying employees; developing programs of employee benefits; handling the personal problems of employees; maintaining pleasant, safe, and healthy working conditions; providing for adequate communication between workers and employers; keeping personnel records; and encouraging recreational and social activities. The term *personnel relations* stresses the individual employee. The field does not usually include *industrial relations* or *labor-management relations*. These fields deal with groups of employers and employees, and often work through organized unions. For a description of these fields, see INDUSTRIAL RELATIONS; LABOR-MANAGEMENT RELATIONS.

Personnel management is a specialized branch of management that is concerned with the effective and efficient utilization of employees. One of its basic responsibilities is to establish proper personnel relations so that maximum results can be achieved. Like other specialized functions in any organization, such as accounting or engineering, it provides the top management with guidance and assistance in handling problems in a specific field.

The over-all impact of personnel policies and the action of management in dealing with employees establish personnel relations for an organization. Good personnel policies attract and hold good employees, who will work to achieve the organization's goals. Good personnel policies also provide the basis for good employer-employee relations.

The Scope of Personnel Relations

Personnel relations programs are developed to create conditions most likely to produce a maximum contribution on the part of employees. Most authorities believe that an organization must provide conditions that will satisfy its employees' needs in order to obtain the maximum effort from them. People seek a variety of satisfactions from their work. Personnel programs utilize the knowledge of why people work, and what needs and desires they seek to satisfy.

In the past, personnel experts placed strong emphasis upon economic needs as a motivating factor. They felt that higher wages and incentive payments had the greatest influence on employee efforts. Research and study have modified this view. Experts now believe that many workers also seek noneconomic satisfactions involving personal and social needs. A major book that focused attention on these problems is *Management and the Worker* by F. J. Roethlisberger and W. J. Dickson.

Today, most personnel relations programs try to take into account both economic and noneconomic factors. Management often provides paid vacations, recreational and social programs, educational opportunities, safety measures for the protection of employees, and health and welfare benefits, including paid sick leave. Many organizations provide facilities for their workers to take short "coffee breaks" during the day. These breaks allow the employees to relax for a few minutes from the routine of their work.

Modern personnel relations programs also try to encourage among workers a sense of belonging and a sense of the importance of each job. Many organizations publish interoffice newspapers called *house organs*. They contain information about birthdays and weddings, sketches of individual employees, and other news items. Usually each worker receives some space in the office or factory for his personal belongings. This may be a locker, a desk, or an entire office. Awards for service to the organization indicate to workers management's interest in the caliber of work and length of service. The training programs in many organizations include some explanation of how a person's particular job fits into the total picture.

The personnel relations of an organization consists not only of the personnel policies and procedures, but also, and more importantly, of the way in which these policies are carried out. Wage policy must be so administered that people feel they are receiving fair and equitable treatment. Systems of rewards for good work and of penalties for poor work must be justly administered.

Development of Personnel Relations

Top management, with the assistance of personnel managers and other specialists, usually develops the personnel policies and procedures of an organization. Many organizations publish their policies and distribute them to management and employees. All management—from the head of the organization to the lowest level of supervision—is responsible for carrying out the policies.

The increasing complexities of personnel relations, together with the growth of specialized knowledge and techniques for dealing with them, has led to the development of a specialized staff. Personnel managers provide advice and consultation to other managers.

History

The field of personnel management is relatively new. Some phases of personnel relations—such as hiring, training, and establishing wage rates—have always been carried on in some way. Other activities—such as programs of health, safety, and employee benefits—have developed since the early 1900's.

The field of personnel management owes much to work done in the areas of scientific management and industrial psychology. The efforts of such men as Frank Gilbreth and F. W. Taylor, in the early 1900's, helped develop a scientific management approach. About the same time psychologists became interested in problems in industry. Hugo Munsterberg's book, *Psychology and Industrial Efficiency*, led to further interest and development of psychological studies in the industrial field. See INDUSTRIAL PSYCHOLOGY.

The need for more effective use of manpower during World War I stimulated interest in the study of problems in personnel relations. After the war, business and industry undertook broad personnel programs. Increased emphasis on personnel relations grew out of the rapid growth of unions during the 1930's and 1940's, the high level of employment and the difficulty of finding good employees during and after World War II, and the increase in federal and state legislation relating to employer-employee relations. This increased attention and the increased complexity of personnel problems firmly established personnel management as part of modern business management.   ROBERT F. RISLEY

PERSPECTIVE

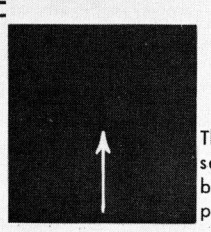

The arrow shows how the observer's line of sight would be directed in the one-point perspective figures below.

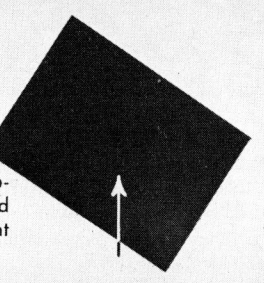

In this figure, the arrow points out the sight direction and object position in two-point perspective.

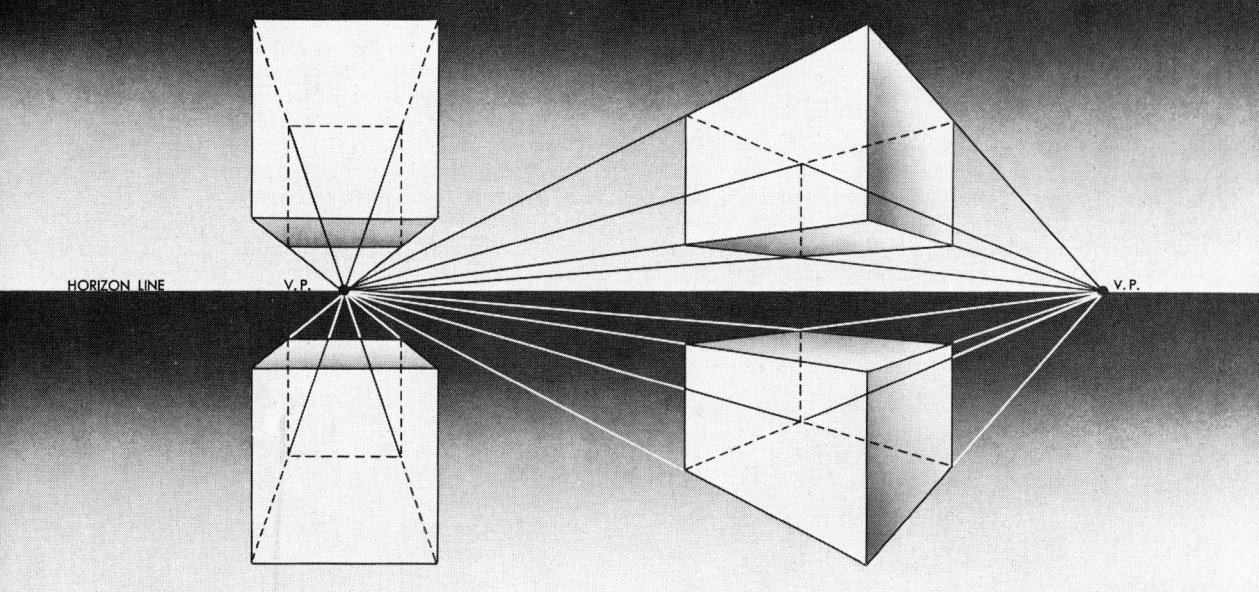

HORIZON LINE   V. P.   V. P.

When you look squarely at the ends of these rectangular blocks—one above and one below the line of vision, or horizon line—the lines of perspective meet at one vanishing point.

When you look at the blocks from this angle, the lines of perspective from the two sides and top (or bottom) meet at two different vanishing points, one on each side of the object.

PERSPECTIVE, *pur SPECK tiv,* is the art and science of representing objects on a flat surface as they appear to the eye from a distance. A *plane* (flat surface) has two dimensions—length and width. A realistic drawing or painting must represent a third dimension—depth. In order to create the illusion of depth, artists use *aerial perspective* and *linear perspective*.

Aerial Perspective is based on the fact that moisture and dust in the air obscure distant objects. An artist achieves the effect of distance by gradually changing the tones of color or the strength of lines. He draws objects nearest to the observer in sharp, heavy lines and bright colors. Fainter and lighter colors and lines make the objects seem to fade into the distance.

Linear Perspective is based on the idea that an object appears to grow smaller in size as the distance between it and the observer increases. It is called *foreshortening*. A ship seems to grow smaller and smaller as it sails away, until it can no longer be seen. This apparent decrease in size is gradual. If several objects of the same size stand at different distances from the observer, they will appear to be of different sizes. Linear perspective also uses the principle that, as parallel lines recede, they seem to *converge* (meet at one point). For example, in a view of a long, straight road, the sides and telegraph wires appear to meet at a point on the horizon.

An artist represents linear perspective by moving all lines on his canvas toward a *vanishing point* on the horizon line. The eye level of the observer determines the location of the horizon line. If all lines vanish to a single point, the picture is in *parallel* or *one-point* perspective. For an example, see Raphael's *The School of Athens*, reproduced in color in the PAINTING article. Lines that vanish in two directions produce *angular* or *two-point* perspective. For an example, see Breughel's *Return of the Hunters*, also in color in the PAINTING article. Some painters use *multiple* perspective, painting various areas of their canvas in different perspectives.

Perspective Drawing. The Egyptians did not use perspective at all. The Chinese mastered aerial perspective, but not linear perspective. The Greeks and Romans used perspective to some extent, but did not understand the mathematical laws on which it is based. Artists of the Middle Ages did not care for realistic perspective. In the 1400's, the architects Filippo Brunelleschi and Leon Battista Alberti, and the painter Masaccio, first used mathematical rules for perspective drawing. Fra Angelico, Paolo Uccello, Leonardo da Vinci, and other Renaissance artists perfected their techniques. But many artists of today have given up realistic perspective in their works.   HARRY MUIR KURTZWORTH

See also PAINTING (How Do Painters Paint?).

PERSPIRATION

PERSPIRATION, PUR *spuh* RAY *shun,* or *sweat,* consists of water and certain dissolved substances produced by glands in the skin. Sweat glands are distributed over the entire surface of the body. But in certain areas they are larger and more concentrated. For example, there are many large sweat glands in the armpits, on the palms of the hands, and soles of the feet. The sweat glands are of almost no importance in ridding the body of waste materials. Their primary importance is to produce perspiration when the body needs to lose heat. Sweating itself does not reduce body heat. But when the sweat evaporates, it has a cooling effect. See EVAPORATION; TEMPERATURE, BODY.

People perspire in cool weather as well as in warm, at night as well as during the day. When it is cool, the small amount of sweat produced evaporates almost as soon as it is formed. This is called *insensible* perspiration. When the weather is warm, or during strenuous exercise, the sweat glands increase their production of perspiration. Then drops of water accumulate on the skin surface and we say a person is sweating. This is *sensible* perspiration. The *hypothalamus* (part of the brain which has the heat-regulating center) keeps body temperature constant. It receives impulses from warm blood and from heat receptors in the skin. It sends signals by way of the nerves to the sweat glands, which then produce sweat. Nervous tension and excitement also activate the sweat glands, especially those in the hands and armpits.

When the water of perspiration evaporates, certain solids (urea and salts) are left on the skin. Frequent bathing will keep these solids from accumulating and clogging the pores. Excess sweating in the armpits can be counteracted by applying various substances sold for this purpose. Most of these contain aluminum chloride. See DEODORIZER.

Many animals do not reduce body heat in the way that human beings do. For example, a dog has sweat glands, but they are not important in reducing the body temperature. Many persons believe that a dog perspires through its mouth. But a healthy dog rarely perspires. Instead, it cools itself by panting.   W. B. YOUMANS

See also ELIMINATION; PORE; SKIN.

PERTH (pop. 96,217; met. area 499,494; alt. 25 ft.), capital of the state of Western Australia, lies on the wide Swan River. Mount Eliza towers above the city. Part of the hill is now the 1,000-acre King's Park. St. George's Terrace, a wide business street, runs along the Swan River. For the city's location, see AUSTRALIA (political map).

Perth has one of the best climates in Australia, averaging 73° F. in the summer and 55° F. in the winter. The pleasant weather encourages yachting on the Swan River, and swimming in the still-water and surf beaches along the coast. Another favorite pastime is hiking in the Darling Range, a woodland located about 15 miles east of Perth.

Captain James Stirling founded Perth in 1829. It was the first settlement on Australia's west coast. Gold discoveries at Kalgoorlie in the 1890's hastened the growth of Perth.

Man-made improvements have added to the natural beauty of Perth. Swampy river ground in the city has been turned into neat lawns and tree-lined drives. Old buildings have been cleared away to prevent the growth of slums. Modern buildings in Perth include the University of Western Australia, founded in 1911. Railroads have linked Perth with cities in eastern Australia since 1917.   C. M. H. CLARK

PERTH AMBOY, N.J. (pop. 38,007; alt. 55 ft.), is an industrial center located where the Raritan River meets Raritan Bay and Staten Island Sound. It has a fine natural harbor. A large oil-refinery installation, oil-terminal centers, and several metal-refining plants are among the chief industries located in the area. For the location of Perth Amboy, see NEW JERSEY (political map).

The city was first called *Amboy,* which came partly from the Indian word *Ompoge,* meaning *a large level piece of ground.* In the early 1680's it was named *New Perth* for the Earl of Perth. Later, the two names were combined. Perth Amboy was granted a charter in 1718. It served as one of the twin capitals of New Jersey, with Burlington, from 1683 to 1790. A commission governs the city.   RICHARD P. McCORMICK

PERSPIRATION

An Inactive Person may give off as much as a quart of perspiration during a day.

A Very Active Person may give off as much as five gallons, or twenty quarts a day.

A Dog Does Not Perspire By Panting. It pants in order to cool itself. Actually, a healthy dog rarely perspires at all.
Chicago Tribune

Tom Hollyman, Photo Researcher

Peru, Land of the Incas, hides many ancient Inca cities among its mountains. Machu Picchu stands on an 8,000-foot mountain about 50 miles northwest of Cusco. The map, *right,* shows Peru's location on the west coast of South America.

PERU, *puh ROO*, is a mountainous country with a 1,400-mile coastline on South America's Pacific Coast. It ranks as the third largest South American country. Its official name is REPÚBLICA DEL PERÚ (REPUBLIC OF PERU). Lima is the capital and largest city.

The jagged, snow-capped Andes Mountains stretch north and south across the entire length of Peru. Vast expanses of brown desert, broken by narrow, fertile river valleys, form a thin coastal area west of the Andes. Most of the country's important cities stand in this area. A region of heavily wooded highlands and plains begins on the eastern slopes of the Andes and spreads out around the headwaters of the Amazon River.

C. Langdon White, the contributor of this article, is Professor of Geography at Stanford University.

The United States Is Seven Times as Large as Peru.

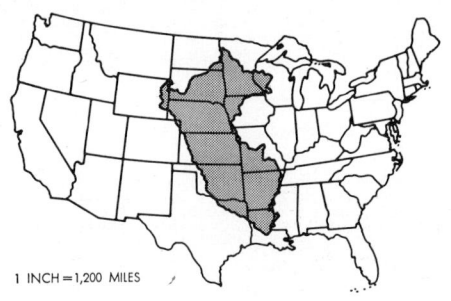

1 INCH = 1,200 MILES

FACTS IN BRIEF

Form of Government: Republic.
Capital: Lima.
Official Language: Spanish.
Area: 496,225 sq. mi. *Greatest Distances*—(north-south) 1,345 mi.; (east-west) 800 mi. *Coastline*—1,400 mi.
Population: *1961 Census*—10,420,357; distribution, 53 per cent rural, 47 per cent urban. *Estimated 1970 Population*—13,573,000; density, 27 persons to the square mile. *Estimated 1975 Population*—15,811,000.
Chief Products: *Agriculture*—barbasco, coffee, cotton, rice, sugar. *Fishing*—anchovies. *Manufacturing*—iron and steel, leather and rubber goods. *Mining*—coal, copper, gold, iron ore, lead, petroleum, zinc.
Flag: The *national flag,* flown by the people, has three vertical stripes, red, white, and red, from left to right. The colors are said to have been inspired by flamingoes seen by José de San Martín. The *state flag,* flown on public buildings, has the red, white, and red stripes and a coat of arms. The coat of arms shows a llama, cinchona tree, and cornucopia of coins, representing Peru's animal, vegetable, and mineral resources. The laurel and palm wreaths stand for patriotism and glory. See FLAG (color picture: Flags of the Americas).
National Anthem: "Himno Nacional del Perú."
Money: *Basic Unit*—sol. See MONEY (table). See also SOL.

269

PERU

Peru covers more than three times the area of California, but has only two-thirds as many people as that state. About 46 of every 100 Peruvians are of pure Indian descent and belong mainly to the Quechua or Aymara groups. Most of the rest are *mestizos* (people of mixed white and Indian ancestry).

A large part of the nation's wealth comes from deposits of copper, iron ore, petroleum, and other minerals. The Quechua Indians of Peru, whose ancestors founded the highly civilized Inca empire more than 700 years ago, cultivated potatoes and over 70 other plants long before white men began to raise them.

The Land and Its Resources

Land Regions. Peru has three land regions: (1) the coast, (2) the mountains, and (3) the plains.

The Coast extends from the Pacific Ocean to the Andes Mountains. It averages 40 miles in width and stretches almost 1,400 miles from north to south. The area is a desert, crossed by about 52 rivers that rise in the Andes.

The Mountains consist of parallel *cordilleras* (mountain ranges) separated by deep valleys. Seven peaks rise more than 19,000 feet above sea level. The country's highest mountain is 22,205-foot Huascarán in west-central Peru. Lake Titicaca, which lies 12,507 feet above sea level on the Peru-Bolivia border, is the most important inland body of water. Lake Titicaca covers 3,261 square miles, about three times the size of Rhode Island, and is

the world's highest navigable body of water. See LAKE TITICACA.

The Plains include the lower eastern slopes of the Andes and the vast, flat, wooded area east of the mountains. Here, the Marañon and Ucayali rivers form the beginning of the Amazon River.

Natural Resources. The mountains contain important mineral deposits, including bismuth, copper, gold, iron ore, lead, silver, sulfur, and zinc. The coast has petroleum, iron ore, copper, and phosphate. *Guano* (bird droppings) is found on the Chincha Islands. Exports of guano, used as fertilizer, helped pay for the nation's railroads in the 1880's. Most of the guano collected now is used by Peru's farmers. The eastern plains have petroleum and valuable forests.

Climate. The cold Peru (*Humboldt*) Current sweeps northward in the Pacific Ocean from Antarctica. With the help of cold water along Peru's shoreline, it keeps coastal temperatures cool—about 73° F. in summer and 61° F. in winter. The cold water also causes dry air along the coast. Lima, for example, gets less than two inches of rain per year. During winter—from May to October—a *garua* (heavy mist or fog) forms when clouds rest against the Coastal Range in the south. It is heavy enough to make the streets and sidewalks wet.

The latitude, altitude, and shape of the land all affect the climate in the mountains. The high mountains are cold and have snow on the peaks. The high basins are cool. The deep, sheltered valleys have warm, almost tropical, temperatures during the day. Rainfall ranges from very wet to very dry—50 to 10 inches. Dryness

---

PERU MAP INDEX

Departments*

Map Key	Name	Population	Area (sq. mi.)	Capital
A 2	Amazonas	157,500	15,945	Chachapoyas
B 2	Ancash	706,100	14,019	Huarás
C 3	Apurimac	324,000	7,975	Abancay
D 3	Arequipa	487,100	24,528	Arequipa
C 3	Ayacucho	462,800	17,058	Ayacucho
B 2	Cajamarca	944,600	13,675	Cajamarca
C 2	Callao (Constitutional Province)	301,500	29	Callao
C 3	Cusco	726,400	29,430	Cusco
C 2	Huancavelica	353,400	8,139	Huancavelica
B 2	Huánuco	406,700	13,635	Huánuco
C 2	Ica	333,400	8,205	Ica
C 2	Junin	653,300	16,751	Huancayo
B 2	La Libertad	735,200	8,973	Trujillo
B 2	Lambayeque	447,500	6,404	Chiclayo
C 2	Lima	2,845,000	13,087	Lima
A 2	Loreto	461,500	184,686	Iquitos
C 3	Madre de Dios	21,600	30,271	Puerto Maldonado
D 3	Moquegua	64,400	6,245	Moquegua
C 2	Pasco	176,000	8,438	Cerro de Pasco
B 1	Piura	856,600	12,767	Piura
D 3	Puno	815,700	27,947	Puno
B 2	San Martín	212,500	20,488	Moyobamba
D 3	Tacna	86,400	5,701	Tacna
A 1	Tumbes	76,300	1,827	Tumbes

Cities and Towns

Abancay	....9,053..	C 3
Arequipa	.135,358..	D 3
Ayacucho	..23,768..	C 3
Ayaviri	....7,553..	C 3
Barranca	.11,320..	C 2
Bellavista*	.43,128..	C 2
Bellavista	.15,670..	A 1
Cajabamba	..5,253..	B 2
Cajamarca	.22,705..	B 2
Callao	....155,953..	C 2
Camaná	....5,120..	D 3
Carabayllo	.37,837..	C 2
Castilla	...29,541..	B 1
Catacaos	...12,135..	B 1
Celendín	....5,646..	B 2
Cerro de Pasco	...21,363..	C 2
Chachapoyas	.6,860..	B 2
Chaclacayo*	.8,698..	C 2
Chancay	....6,145..	C 2
Chepén	...16,119..	B 2
Chiclayo	..95,667..	B 2
Chimbote	..59,990..	B 2
Chincha Alta	...20,817..	C 2
Chocope	...19,049..	B 2
Chosica	...25,248..	C 2
Chulucanas	19,714..	B 1
Cusco	...79,857..	C 3
El Alto	....8,496..	A 1
Ferreñafe	.12,112..	B 2
Guadalupe*	.6,882..	B 2
Huacho	...22,806..	C 2
Huamachuco	5,730..	B 2
Huancavelica	...11,039..	C 2
Huancayo	..64,153..	C 2
Huanta	....5,728..	C 3
Huánuco	...24,646..	B 2
Huaral	...11,481..	C 2
Huarás	...20,345..	B 2
Huarmey	...5,232..	C 2
Huarocondo*	2,921..	C 3
Ica	........49,097..	C 2
Ilabaya	...6,563..	D 3
Ilo	........9,986..	D 3
Imperial	...6,345..	C 2
Iquitos	...57,777..	A 3
Jauja	...12,751..	C 2
Juanjuí	...5,105..	B 2
Juliaca	...20,351..	D 3
Junin	........5,004..	C 2
La Libertad	.6,002..	D 3
Lamas	....7,139..	B 2
Lambayeque	10,629..	B 2
La Oroya	..24,724..	C 2
La Punta*	..5,909..	C 2
La Unión	...6,047..	B 2
Lima	....1,436,231..	C 2
Machu Picchu	....1,026..	C 3
Máncora	...7,943..	A 1
Mollendo	..19,049..	D 3
Monsefú	...11,141..	B 2
Moquegua	...7,795..	D 3
Morococha	..6,519..	C 2
Motupe	...5,864..	B 2
Moyobamba	.8,373..	B 2
Nazca	...13,587..	C 3
Negritos	...14,810..	A 1
Pacasmayo	.11,956..	B 2
Pachacamac	.8,475..	C 2
Paiján*	...5,815..	B 2
Paita	....9,615..	B 1
Pativilca	..15,325..	C 2
Paucarpata*	6,792..	D 3
Pimentel*	..6,252..	B 2
Pisco	......22,112..	C 2
Piura	....42,555..	B 1
Pucallpa	..26,391..	B 3
Pueblo Nuevo*	...6,646..	A 1
Puente Piedra*	..5,182..	C 2
Puno	...24,459..	D 3
Puquio	....8,144..	C 3
Querecotillo*	6,205..	A 1
Quillabamba	....8,644..	C 3
Quiruvilca	..5,060..	B 2
San Juan	...6,744..	D 3
San Pedro de Lloc	...7,497..	B 2
San Vicente de Cañete	.7,184..	C 2
Saña	......18,421..	B 2
Sechura	...5,157..	B 1
Sicuani	...10,664..	C 3
Sullana	...34,501..	A 1
Tabalosos	...5,344..	B 2
Tacna	...27,499..	D 3
Talara	...27,957..	A 1
Tarapoto	..13,907..	B 2
Tarma	...15,452..	C 2
Tingo María	5,208..	B 2
Trujillo	...100,130..	B 2
Tumbes	...20,885..	A 1
Villa Eten	..6,999..	B 2
Vitarte	...62,971..	C 2
Yanahuara	..8,535..	D 3
Yurimaguas	11,655..	B 2

Physical Features

Amazon River	......A 3	
Andes Mountains	..B 2	
Apurimac River	...C 3	
Bay of Sechura	....B 1	
Cerro Pumasillo (Mountain)	...C 3	
Cordillera Azul (Mountains)	.....B 2	
Cordillera de Vilcanota (Mountains)	.....C 3	
Cordillera Occidental o de la Costa (Mountains)	....C 2	
Corrientes River	...A 2	
Curaray River	...A 3	
El Boquerón (Pass)	..........B 2	
El Misti (Volcano)	.......D 3	
Ene River	........C 3	
Huallaga River	...B 2	
Huascarán (Mountain)	.....B 2	
Lake Junin	...C 2	
Lake Titicaca	...D 3	
Las Piedras River	C 3	
Madre de Dios River	...C 3	
Marañón River	...A 2	
Morona River	....A 2	
Napo River	......A 3	
Pastaza River	...A 2	
Paucartambo River	.........C 3	
Perené River	........C 3	
Point Chala	....D 3	
Point Coles	.....D 3	
Point Lachay	....C 2	
Point Negra	.....B 1	
Point Pariñas	...A 1	
Pongo de Manseriche (Gorge)	...A 2	
Purús River	......C 3	
Putumayo River	...A 3	
Santa River	........B 2	
Santiago River	....A 2	
Tambo River	......C 3	
Tigre River	........A 2	
Ucayali River	......B 3	
Urubamba River	...C 3	
Yavari River	......A 3	

*Does not appear on the map; key shows general location.

Sources: Departments, 1968 official estimates; cities, latest census (1961).

PERU

Legend:
- Barren Areas Above Timber
- Evergreen Trees
- Shrub
- Grass
- Barren Arid Areas

- ⊛ National Capital
- ★ Provincial Capitals
- • Cities and Towns
- — Rail Lines

1 inch = 145 Statute Miles

Miles 0 25 50 75 100 125 150

Oblique Conformal Conic Projection

COLOMBIA

BRAZIL

BOLIVIA

CHILE

ECUADOR

South Pacific Ocean

Longitude West of Greenwich

CM TERRAIN PERU
COPYRIGHT BY
RAND McNALLY & COMPANY
MADE IN U.S.A.

270a
FIA

Specially created for **World Book** Encyclopedia by Rand McNally and World Book editors

Equator

Napo
Caquetá
Putumayo
Japurá
Içá
Amazon
Leticia
Iquitos

Cape Pasado
Cape San Mateo
Portoviejo
Ambato
Quito
COTOPAXI 19,347 FT.
CAYAMBE 18,996 FT.
Ibarra
San Miguel
CHIMBORAZO 20,561 FT.
Riobamba
Bay of Santa Elena
LA PUNTILLA
Guayaquil
PUNÁ
Gulf of Guayaquil
Machala
Cuenca
Tumbes
El Alto
Máncora
Loja
Talara
Negritos
POINT PARIÑAS
Sullana
Bellavista
Paita
Piura
Castilla
Catacaos
Bay of Sechura
Sechura
Chulucanas
POINT NEGRA
Motupe
12,600 FT.
Chachapoyas
Moyobamba
Yurimaguas
Tabalosos
Tarapoto
Lamas
Ferreñafe
Lambayeque
Chiclayo
Monsefú
Villa Eten
Saña
Celendín
Juanjui
Chepén
Cajamarca
Pacasmayo
San Pedro de Lloc
Chocope
Cajabamba
Quiruvilca
Huamachuco
Trujillo
Chimbote
Santa
HUASCARÁN 22,205 FT.
La Unión
Huarás
Huánuco
21,765 FT.
Huarmey
Pativilca
Barranca
Huacho
POINT LACHAY
Chancay
Huaral
Morococha
Chosica
Carabayllo
Callao
Vitarte
LIMA
Pachacamac
San Vicente de Cañete
Chincha Alta
Pisco
Ica
Nazca
San Juan
POINT CHALA
Camaná
Mollendo
Moquegua
Ilo
POINT COLES
Tacna
Arica

Putumayo
Caquetá
Curaray
Napo
Tigre
Corrientes
Pastaza
Morona
Santiago
Marañón
PONGO DE MANSERICHE (GORGE)
Huallaga
Ucayali
Yavarí
Javarí
Itecoai
Tarauacá
Juruá
Pucallpa
EL BOQUERÓN
Tingo María
Perené
Cerro de Pasco
Lake Junín
Junín
Tarma
La Oroya
Jauja
Huancayo
Ene
Tambo
Apurímac
Huancavelica
Huanta
Ayacucho
Abancay
Quillabamba
Machu Picchu
CERRO PUMASILLO 20,492 FT.
Cusco
Sicuani
Ayaviri
Juliaca
Puno
Lake Titicaca
La Libertad
Yanahuara
EL MISTI 19,098 FT.
Arequipa
Ilabaya
VOLCÁN TACORA 19,521 FT.
SAJAMA 21,391 FT.
Purús
Las Piedras
Madre de Dios
Puerto Maldonado
Cobija
Embira
Iaco
Juruá
CORDILLERA DE VILCANOTA
CORDILLERA OCCIDENTAL DE LA COSTA
CORDILLERA AZUL
A N D E S
M T S.

increases from north to south and only the north and east sides of the mountains get enough rain to grow crops without irrigation. In Cusco, which lies 11,440 feet above sea level, the temperature varies from an average of 44° F. (winter) to about 51° F. (summer). But the range from day to night is much greater. At the higher elevations, there may be freezing temperatures any night in the year.

The plains have a rainy tropical climate and high temperatures. Many places in the plains average about 80° F. The rainfall varies from 50 to 100 inches per year.

Life of the People

More than half of the Peruvians live among the slopes, valleys, and plateaus of the Andes Mountains. About a fourth of the people live on the coast and only about a tenth live on the plains.

Language. All whites and most mestizos speak Spanish, Peru's official language. About one-fourth of the people speak only Spanish, and another fourth speak only one of the nation's Indian languages. About half the Peruvians speak both Spanish and an Indian tongue.

Way of Life. Most of the working people who live along the coast are farmers. Some own their own farms, but many work on big *haciendas* (plantations). More and more of those who live in or near cities work in factories, construction, and other industries. In the mountains, some Indians own tiny farms which yield barely enough food to live on. Both men and women tend crops and herd alpaca, llama, sheep, and occasionally cattle. Most Indians in the mountains are very poor and work as laborers. Some work on haciendas, and others work in the mines.

The plains population is scattered, averaging about one person per square mile. The way of life varies with each tribe. For example, the 1,000 Indians of the Yagua tribe are divided into 25 or 30 *clans* (family groups). All clan members live in one house. The women grow most of the crops. The men hunt, trap, and sometimes clear off patches of ground for crops. The entire clan moves to a new area when the supply of game becomes scarce.

Shelter. Most of the people in the coastal areas live in adobe houses. The better houses are covered with *stucco* (wall plaster). In the cities and towns, many of the home fronts meet the sidewalks, so that some streets look almost like alleys. Nearly all houses have skylights in their red-tile roofs, and the better ones have beautiful patios. Many of the houses in small villages have earthen floors and thatched roofs. A typical living room in many coastal houses has little more than a table and a few crude chairs or benches. Many people sleep on floor mats.

In the mountains, most Indians live in villages of adobe or straw huts. Each hut has one room, about 8 by 12 feet, with an earthen floor. Platforms covered with llama and sheep pelts serve as beds. Another small house serves as the kitchen. Travelers and their animals use temporary shelters that have stone walls and thatched roofs.

Many Indian tribes live in the plains region. The Yagua clans live in oval-shaped houses. The houses are made of bent poles covered with woven palm leaf

Peruvian Indians provide the chief source of farm labor on the country's large plantations. Many Indians including the boy, *above,* wear a bright blanket over their shoulders and a hat that resembles a derby. The Indians thresh wheat by driving horses across piles of the cut grain, *right.*

mats. The people sleep in hammocks that are hung in *tiers* (rows).

Food for people living on the coast includes such vegetables as rice, corn, and beans and such fruit as bananas, pineapples, oranges, and mangoes. These people eat a lot of seafood, but very little meat. They eat some chicken, turkey, duck, hog, and guinea pig. The mountain Indians eat potatoes, corn, barley, *quinoa* (an herb) seeds, *oca* (a root), and some wheat. The plains Indians kill anteater, armadillo, deer, monkey, *peccary* (wild pig), river turtle, sloth, and tapir for food. They also catch fish and grow corn and sweet manioc, a plant with a potatolike root.

Clothing. Most of the people living in the coastal region—especially those in the cities—dress much like people in the United States and Canada. People in the mountains wear woolen clothing because of the cold. Most of the men wear shirts, black trousers, vestlike jackets, and a *poncho,* a blanket with a hole in the middle that is worn over the shoulders. The men wear sandals made of leather or the rubber from old automobile tires. Women wear belts, hats, blouses, and several gaily colored skirts and petticoats. Many of the women also wear a bright blanket slung over the back and pinned in the front. In the plains, Yagua

Tom Hollyman, Photo Researchers; John Collier, Gamma

Indians wear a barkcloth skirt with a bark belt. The men wear a bark band around the neck and a woven palm crown on the head. Yagua women cover the upper body with palm fibers, but wear no headband. They wear bark bands around their arms and legs.

Recreation in the cities includes boxing, wrestling, fishing, swimming, dancing, golf, tennis, and soccer. Cockfights are popular throughout Peru, and bullfights attract large crowds to Lima's two bull rings.

On religious holidays, the people enjoy Roman Catholic *fiestas* (festivals). A fiesta often lasts several days. In the mountains, the people attend Mass and then celebrate the traditional festivals of their ancient religion, in which dancers wear masks and colorful costumes of skin and feathers.

Religion. More than 90 of every 100 Peruvians belong to the Roman Catholic Church, the state church. But in many parts of the country, mainly in the mountains, the people mix Catholicism with ancient Indian beliefs. Many Indians attend Catholic services, but also worship spirits of the Inca religion.

City Life. Peru has 10 cities with more than 50,000 persons each. But most towns have less than 10,000. Coastal cities have public squares, many parks, and gardens. Lima has many tall buildings. Lima also has large *barriadas* and *callejones* (slums) where thousands of poor and unemployed Indians live in misery.

In the mountains, most Indians live in villages. They go to open-air markets on Sunday to sell or trade items they produce. There are very few buildings more than one story high in the mountains, because there is always a threat of earthquakes. For generations, Iquitos was the only real city in the plains. But several settlements—especially Pucallpa—have grown rapidly in recent years because of improved transportation over the Andes.

Country Life. Farms in Peru range in size from huge plantations to tiny plots of ground farmed by the Indians. There also are many Indian *communes* (farms owned and run by many). Wealthy white people own the coastal plantations. Most of the work is done by Indians who come down from the mountains. Most large farms in the mountains are owned by mestizos. Most of the plantation owners do not live on their plantations. The plantations are not very productive.

Work of the People

Agriculture. The most productive farms lie along the coast, where rivers flowing from the Andes are used to irrigate the land. These farms produce cotton, sugar cane, rice, fruits, and vegetables. Farmers in the mountains produce just enough barley, corn, oca, and quinoa to feed their families. They also raise some wheat that they ship to coastal cities. Grazing llama, alpaca, and sheep are important in the *puna* (bunch grass country) at about 15,000 feet elevation.

Fishing Industry has grown greatly since 1940. The waters off the coast rank among the world's richest in marine life. The main food fishes that Peruvian fishermen catch are tuna, bonito, and swordfish. However, anchovettas—which are not considered fit to eat—have made Peru the world's leading exporter of fish products. Anchovettas, small fish related to the anchovy, are made into fishmeal that is used for stock feed.

Mining. Some of the world's richest mineral deposits are found in the mountains. These deposits include antimony, bismuth, copper, gold, silver, lead, zinc, and coal. Foreign companies control most of the mining industry. But the mining is done by Indians. Only they are able to work at such high altitudes. Labor in such thin air makes other men ill. Petroleum is produced along the northern coast area and a little is produced in the eastern plains.

Manufacturing and Processing. In the Lima-Callao area, factories produce cotton, wool, silk, and rayon textiles, chemicals, fertilizers, and rubber tires, and assemble automobiles and trucks. Other coastal cities

Peruvian Fishermen work on a pier in Callao. Peru now ranks as the world's leading exporter of fish products.

Carl Frank, Photo Researchers

that have manufacturing are Trujillo (sugar and paper) and Chimbote (iron, steel, and fishmeal). La Oroya, at more than 12,000 feet elevation, has the highest metal smelting and refining center in the world.

Electric Power. Some hydroelectric power has been developed. Most of it is in the Andes near the coast where the cities and industries are located. Most important projects are in the Santa River Valley of the north and in the Rimac Valley behind Lima.

Trade. Leading exports include fishmeal, sugar, cotton, and minerals. Imports consist mainly of manufactured goods such as machinery, clothing, and some food products. Peru trades mostly with the United States, but also with Argentina, Belgium, Chile, France, Great Britain, and West Germany. Peru is a member of the Latin-American Free Trade Association (LAFTA), which was formed in 1961 (see COMMON MARKET).

Transportation in Peru is best along the coast. Several railways run inland from major ports. The two principal lines are the Central Railway of Peru, which runs into the Andes from Callao, and the Southern Railway of Peru, from Mollendo. The Central is the highest standard gauge railroad in the world, reaching its greatest height at 15,865 feet above sea level. Rivers provide most of the transportation in the eastern plains.

Communication. Several television stations, about 60 radio stations, and more than 50 newspapers serve the people. Almost all Peru's 30 magazine- and 12 book-publishing firms are in Lima. The highest post office in the world stands in Cerro de Pasco at an altitude of 14,385 feet.

Education

The law requires Peruvian children between the ages of 7 and 16 to go to school. More than 1,100 elementary schools and over 300 high schools offer free education. Peru has about 130 technical schools, 20 teachers colleges, and 7 universities, the most famous of which is the University of San Marcos in Lima (see SAN MARCOS, UNIVERSITY OF). The Ministry of Education governs all the schools, but the Roman Catholic Church administers many of them.

Despite the government's efforts to spread education, about 40 of every 100 Peruvians cannot read or write. Many areas in the mountains and plains have no schools. Peru has few teachers, and most of them do not speak the Indian languages. But the government now trains teachers in these languages, and sends a government-paid teacher to any community that builds and maintains a schoolhouse. But most Indians receive no instruction in how to read or speak Spanish, so they cannot take part in political, social, and economic affairs. This means that approximately half the people of Peru do not take part in the national life.

The Arts

The Inca Indians became expert architects and stoneworkers hundreds of years before white men came to the Western Hemisphere (see SCULPTURE [American Indian]). They built large stone temples and other buildings, some of which still stand. Indians today practice the ancient arts of making pottery, metalwares, and colorful textiles.

Two Peruvian writers, Ricardo Palma (1833-1919)

and José Santos Chocano (1875-1934), have won international acclaim. Palma gained fame for his satires, and
Chocano for his poems. Artists such as José Sabogal
(1888-1956) and Camilo Blas (1903-   ) often paint
Indian life. The singer Yma Sumac (1927-   ) has performed in many countries. Composers frequently use
Indian melodies in their music, and theaters still present ancient Incan dramas.

What To See and Do in Peru

Visitors to Peru often travel into the Andes to see the
ancient Inca capital of Cusco, and the ruins of an Inca
city called Machu Picchu (see MACHU PICCHU). This
city, unknown for 400 years, was found in 1911.

The Spanish tradition appears in Lima more than in
almost any other Latin-American city. The center of
the city remains as its founder, the Spanish soldier Francisco Pizarro, planned it in the 1500's. Several buildings
constructed during his lifetime still stand. The National
Museum of Archaeology and Anthropology in Lima
has priceless pottery, textiles, and jewelry that tell the
story of the pre-Inca and Inca cultures.

Resort hotels on the coast attract thousands of tourists and vacationers each year. The Andes provide
some of the most impressive scenery in the world. Many
mountain resorts offer fishing, hunting, and skiing.

Government

Like the United States, Peru has a president, a two-
house congress, and a Supreme Court.

The President is elected by direct popular vote for a
six-year term. He may be re-elected for any number of
terms, but may not serve two terms in succession. The
president has a cabinet of 12 members and an Economic
Advisory Council to help him with his duties.

Congress includes a Senate of 50 members and a
Chamber of Deputies of 153 members. The people elect
members to both houses to serve six-year terms. Senators
and deputies may serve an indefinite number of terms,
which may be consecutive. The number elected from
each department depends on its population.

Courts. The Supreme Court consists of a president
and 10 judges appointed by congress. The president
appoints the members of the lower courts, including 19
superior courts and 251 courts of first instance. Every
town and village has at least one justice of the peace.
Peru's courts have no juries, and the judges alone decide
law cases. The nation's laws come from the constitution,
from court decisions, and from statutes passed by the
congress and the local governments. See LAW (Sources).

Local Government. Prefects, or governors, appointed
by the president administer Peru's 24 departments,
which are similar to states in the United States. The departments are divided into 140 provinces that resemble
counties in the United States. A subprefect, appointed
by the prefect of the department, governs each province.
Alcaldes, or mayors, elected by the people, administer
the cities and towns.

Taxation of imports provides most of the government's revenue. But much money comes from sales taxes
on products such as food and clothing.

Politics. The law requires qualified citizens between
the ages of 21 and 60 to vote in all national and local
elections. But the government does not enforce this law,
and few Peruvians take any interest in politics outside

Carl Frank, Photo Researchers
The University of San Marcos in Lima is the oldest university
in South America. The courtyard is a student meeting place.

their municipality or district. Besides, the law bars more
than half the people from voting, because it requires
voters to be able to read and write Spanish. As a result,
as few as 15 of every 100 persons vote in elections.

Important political parties are the American Popular
Revolutionary Alliance (APRA), the Christian Demo-
cratic Party, the Odria National Union Party, and the
Popular Action Party. There also are a few small
parties, including a Communist Party. Several parties
usually agree to support the same candidate in elections.
APRA is one of Peru's most influential political forces.
It favors dividing the large plantations among the small
farmers; control by Peru of foreign capital invested in
Peru; and government control of mining industries.

Armed Forces. All qualified men must serve two years
in the army, followed by 30 years in the reserve force.
There are about 30,000 men in the army, 6,000 in the
navy, and 7,000 in the air force.

History

The Inca Empire. Archaeologists believe that Indian
tribes lived in Peru as early as 2000 B.C. Cultures in-

cluding the Chavín, Chimu, and Nasca developed art, agriculture, governments, and religions hundreds of years before the white men came to South America. The Inca, an Indian society centered at Cusco, began expanding and conquering neighboring tribes between A.D. 1100 and 1200. At the height of the Inca empire's power, in the 1400's, it extended from northern Ecuador into northern Chile and Argentina, and from the Pacific Coast to the eastern slopes of the Andes. A small group of warlike leaders held tight control over the empire. See INCA.

The Spanish Conquest. In 1522, the Spanish explorer Pascual de Andagoya (1495?-1548) became the first white man to enter Peru. In 1532 and 1533, the forces of two Spanish soldiers, Francisco Pizarro and Diego de Almagro, seized most of Peru. The Spaniards enslaved many people of the Inca empire. But in 1542, Spain established the New Laws, which granted freedom to many Indian slaves. The Spanish settlers in Peru refused to recognize these laws, however, and the Indians' status remained unchanged. As a result of widespread discontent, the Indians rebelled unsuccessfully several times against their Spanish masters. In 1780, Tupac Amaru, a descendant of an Inca leader, led a widespread revolt. But the Spaniards captured and executed him in 1781, and crushed the uprising in 1782.

The Spaniards founded Lima in 1535, and made it the headquarters of their South American territories. For almost 300 years, Peru remained a center of Spanish power in South America.

The Republic. A force of Argentines and Chileans, led by the Argentine general José de San Martín, began the liberation of Peru in 1820. But the Peruvians had little desire to be free, and only a small group of nationalists aided San Martín. Most of the Indians did not want to be involved in the struggle. Business and political leaders wanted Spain to keep control of the country, because they held titles, property, and political offices granted by the Spanish king. But, in 1821, San Martín declared Peru an independent nation, although Spain still held much of the country. The Venezuelan revolutionary leader Simón Bolívar invaded Peru in 1823 with an army of Colombians and Venezuelans. Then in 1824, Antonio José de Sucre, a Bolívar general, defeated the Spaniards at Ayacucho in southern Peru. By the end of 1824, Spain held only the city of Callao. After a long siege, Bolívar subdued Callao in 1826.

When Bolívar left Peru in 1826, he gave control of the country to a council headed by Andrés Santa Cruz, one

--- RED-LETTER DATES IN PERU'S HISTORY ---

1100-1200 Peruvian Indians founded the Inca empire.
1522 Pascual de Andagoya discovered Peru.
1532-1533 Francisco Pizarro and Diego de Almagro conquered Peru.
1780 The Indians revolted unsuccessfully against Spain.
1820 General José de San Martín invaded Peru.
1821 Peru declared its independence from Spain.
1864 Spain seized the Chincha Islands from Peru.
1879 Spain recognized Peru's independence.
1883 Chile defeated Peru in the War of the Pacific.
1945 Peru became a charter member of the United Nations.
1956 Women voted in a Peruvian national election for the first time.

of his lieutenants (see BOLIVIA [Independence]). In 1827, Peruvian leaders forced Santa Cruz to call an assembly to write a constitution and elect a president. The assembly elected General José de la Mar (1788-1839) as the country's first president. Military rivals overthrew De la Mar in 1829. For the next few years, Peru had a series of dictatorships and armed uprisings among political rivals, all of whom were professional soldiers rather than political leaders. General Don Ramón Castilla (1797?-1867) seized the presidency in 1845, and held it until he retired in 1851. Peru enjoyed peace and prosperity during Castilla's reign. He developed the guano industry, and began trade with Europe and the United States. When Castilla retired, the people elected José Rufino Echenique (1808-1879) as president. But Echenique allowed corruption and extravagance to spread throughout the government. Castilla led an uprising in 1854, ousted Echenique, and ruled the country again from 1855 to 1862.

In 1864, Spain claimed that Peruvian laborers attacked Spanish immigrants who came to Peru to work on the plantations. Spain used this claim to seize the Chincha Islands. These islands lay off the coast of Peru and provided the nation's main source of guano. At that time, guano was Peru's most valuable natural resource. Spain demanded payment for the return of the islands. Bolivia, Chile, and Ecuador feared a return of Spanish power in South America, and joined Peru in declaring war on Spain in 1865. In 1866, the Spanish shelled the coast of Peru and tried to invade the country. But the Peruvians turned back the Spanish troops who tried to land at Callao, and the invading fleet withdrew. The United States wanted to keep peace in the Western Hemisphere, and immediately began negotiations to end the war. Through United States mediation, a truce was arranged in 1871, and a treaty of peace was signed in 1879. Spain formally recognized Peru's independence that year.

The War of the Pacific. The same year, Bolivia and Chile quarreled over rights to nitrate deposits in the Peruvian province of Tarapacá and the Bolivian province of Antofagasta. Peru and Bolivia became jealous of the Chileans, who had rights to develop the deposits. The two countries had agreed in 1873 that if one of them became involved in trouble with Chile, the other would come to its assistance. In 1878, Bolivia placed an export tax on the nitrate. Bolivia had promised Chile it would not do this, and the incident led to the outbreak of the War of the Pacific. But the Chileans routed both Peru and Bolivia and occupied Lima in 1881. Chile seized the provinces of Tacna, Arica, and Tarapacá from Peru, and the province of Atacama from Bolivia. Tacna was returned to Peru in 1929 through peaceful negotiations, but Chile kept the other provinces.

The people elected an army leader, Andrés Cáceres (1835?-1923), to the presidency in 1886. He improved the organization of the government, paid much of Peru's foreign debt, and expanded the nation's railroad system.

The 1900's. Augusto B. Leguía y Salcedo (1863-1932), a businessman and statesman, served as president from 1908 to 1912. He was re-elected in 1919, but soon became a dictator. In 1929 and 1930, the world economic depression caused an economic crisis in Peru and the people began to oppose his dictatorial methods.

Finally, in August, 1930, Colonel Luis M. Sánchez Cerro (1889-1933) overthrew Leguía and became president. Cerro was assassinated in 1933, and the people elected General Oscar Benavides (1876-1945), who served as president from 1933 until 1939.

Manuel Prado y Ugarteche (1889-1967) became president in 1939. He increased wages, abolished foreign-trade restrictions, and began other reforms. Peru broke relations with Germany, Italy, and Japan in World War II and finally declared war on Germany and Japan in 1945, but no Peruvian troops fought in the war.

Peru became a charter member of the United Nations in 1945. José Luis Bustamante y Rivero (1894-) was elected president that year. His support came from the powerful but outlawed party called APRA. General Manuel A. Odría (1897-) led a rebellion to oust Bustamante in 1948. He said Bustamante allowed too much U.S. investment, even though Bustamante and APRA had pledged to free Peru from foreign economic interference. Odría became president in 1950.

Women voted for the first time in 1956. The 1956 elections returned Prado (president from 1939 to 1945) to office. Odría had legalized APRA before the elections, and Prado won with APRA support. Peru's first important land-reform bill reached congress during Prado's term, but it never became law.

Recent Events. None of the three major candidates in the 1962 presidential election received one-third of the total votes—the amount needed to win. Peruvian military leaders charged election frauds, and formed a *junta* (military council) that took over the government. They feared APRA would gain control of the government if congress was allowed to choose the new president. Prado was arrested and deported. The junta authorized general elections in 1963, and Fernando Belaúnde Terry was elected president.

In 1964, Belaúnde announced Peru's first major land reform law. It authorized breaking up large estates and giving small plots of land to peasants. The government issued bonds to the former owners to pay for the land.

Peru began to have economic problems in the late 1960's, and the political parties that had supported Belaúnde disagreed over how to handle the problems. Belaúnde widened the split by signing an agreement with the International Petroleum Company (IPC), owned by Standard Oil of New Jersey. Under the agreement, IPC would turn over two of its oil fields to the Peruvian government and would buy the crude oil they produced. Belaúnde also canceled a $140-million government claim against the company for back taxes, and agreed to pay IPC for its plants and equipment at the two oil fields. The agreement was opposed even by members of Belaúnde's own party.

In 1968, a new military junta seized control and Belaúnde left the country. The junta feared that, with the other parties split, APRA would win the presidential election that had been scheduled for June, 1969. The junta canceled the oil agreement and seized the company's oil fields and the refinery at Talara. The United States did not end economic aid to the country because Peru offered to submit the case to Peruvian courts and pay the owners some money pending the court's decision.

Constitutional guarantees were restored for the people a month later and the junta said it would eventually

name civilians to the government. In 1969, Peru signed its first trade agreement with Russia. C. LANGDON WHITE

Related Articles in WORLD BOOK include:

BIOGRAPHIES

Atahualpa	Castilla, Ramón	San Martín,
Bolívar, Simón	Pizarro (family)	José de

CITIES

Arequipa	Chiclayo	Lima
Callao	Cusco	Trujillo

HISTORY

Aymara Indians	Latin America	Tacna-Arica Dispute
Inca	Machu Picchu	Trephining (picture)

PHYSICAL FEATURES

Amazon River	Huascarán	Purús River
Andes Mountains	Lake Titicaca	Sechura Desert
El Misti	Peru Current	

PRODUCTS

Alpaca	Fishing Industry	Llama	Zinc
Bismuth	Guano	Silver	
Copper	Lead	Vicuña	

Outline

I. **The Land and Its Resources**
   A. Land Regions   C. Climate
   B. Natural Resources
II. **Life of the People**
   A. Language   C. City Life
   B. Way of Life   D. Country Life
III. **Work of the People**
   A. Agriculture   E. Electric Power
   B. Fishing Industry   F. Trade
   C. Mining   G. Transportation
   D. Manufacturing and   H. Communication
       Processing
IV. **Education**   VII. **Government**
V. **The Arts**   VIII. **History**
VI. **What to See and Do in Peru**

Questions

What languages are spoken by most Peruvians?
How is Peru's government like that of the U.S.?
What were the results of the War of the Pacific?
How did guano help build the railroads of Peru?
What is the world's highest navigable body of water?
Why do Indians constantly leave the mountains?
When did Peruvian women first vote?

PERU CURRENT is a cool ocean current in the Pacific Ocean which flows northward along the west coast of South America. Along the coast of Peru, the temperature of its waters is 15° F. colder than is normal for the surface of the Pacific in that latitude. Most scientists believe that the cold waters of the Peru Current are due primarily to the winds which blow the warm surface waters away from the coast. This causes cooler waters from below to come to the surface. This current is also called *Humboldt Current*, for a German geographer (see HUMBOLDT, BARON VON). HENRY STOMMEL

PERU STATE COLLEGE. See UNIVERSITIES AND COLLEGES (table).

PERUTZ, MAX FERDINAND (1914-), a British-Austrian physicist, shared the Nobel prize in chemistry in 1962 with John C. Kendrew. Through X-ray techniques, they traced the structure of hemoglobin and myoglobin, two proteins found in blood and muscles. Perutz spent 22 years on his research, concentrating on hemoglobin. Born in Vienna, he fled to England in 1936 to escape Nazism. AARON J. IHDE

PESAH

PESAH. See PASSOVER.

PESCADORES ISLANDS, *pes kuh DOHR eez* (pop. 114,220), consist of 63 islands which cover a total area of 49 square miles in the Formosa Strait between Formosa and China. For location, see FORMOSA (map). A Chinese expedition discovered the islands in 1367. The islands were named *Pescadores* (fishermen's islands) in the 1500's by Portuguese sailors. They were occupied by the Dutch from 1622 to 1624, when China regained them. In the late 1600's, the Pescadores became a dependency of Formosa, and have belonged to Formosa since. Industries on the islands include fishing and fish processing. THEODORE H. E. CHEN

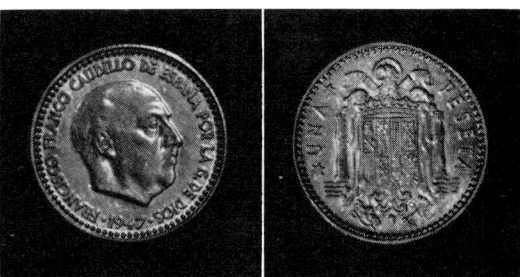

Chase Manhattan Bank Money Museum
The Peseta Is Spain's Monetary Unit.

PESETA, *peh SAY tah*, is the monetary unit of Spain and the Spanish dependencies, and of Andorra. It consists of 100 centimos. The early silver one-peseta piece showed the king's head and the Spanish coat of arms. Later coins showed such objects as a sheaf of wheat or a galleon. Silver coins have been issued in the value of one, two, and five pesetas. The peseta was issued in brass in 1937, and later in aluminum-bronze. For its value in dollars, see MONEY (table: Values of Monetary Units). BURTON HOBSON

PESHTIGO FIRE. See WISCONSIN (Statehood).

PESO, *PAY soh*, originally was the name of the old Spanish dollar. It was called the *peso de oro* when made of gold, and the *peso de plata* when made of silver. The peso is no longer the standard of value in Spain. Its place has been taken by the peseta. But the peso is still an important money unit in Spanish American countries, although its value varies in each country. The peso is the monetary unit of Argentina, Bolivia, Colombia, Cuba, the Dominican Republic, Mexico, the Philippines, and Uruguay. The name *peso* comes from the Latin word *pensum*, meaning weight. For the value of the peso in dollars, see MONEY (table: Values of Monetary Units). BURTON HOBSON

See also PIECE OF EIGHT.

PESSIMISM, *PEHS uh miz'm*, is the philosophy which holds that there is more bad than good in the world and more pain than pleasure. In its contention that the world is essentially evil, pessimism is the opposite of *optimism*, or the belief that this is the best possible world. There are many grades and variations of pessimists, including those who feel that the hereafter is uncertain and determine to enjoy the present fully. Strictly speaking, pessimism is more a personal attitude than a philosophy. Modern thought, being concerned with the intrinsic value of life, phrases the problem principally in the question of whether life is worth living. Arthur Schopenhauer, a German philosopher, was the most famous modern pessimist. FLOYD H. ROSS

PEST CONTROL. See FUMIGATION; INSECTICIDE; INSECT (Insect Control).

PESTALOZZI, *pes tuh LAHT see*, or *pes tah LAWT see*, **JOHANN HEINRICH** (1746-1827), a Swiss educator, contributed greatly to the development of educational practices and theory. Although he carried on his work in Switzerland, his ideas and influence spread throughout Europe and the United States.

He believed that education should be based on the natural development of the child. He felt education should stress moral and physical, as well as intellectual, development. Pestalozzi wrote that "the aim of all instruction is and can be nothing but the development of human nature by the harmonious cultivation of its powers and talents and the promotion of manliness of life." He believed a pupil learned best by using his own senses and by discovering things for himself. His book, *How Gertrude Teaches Her Children* (1801), is one of the great classics on education.

Pestalozzi was born in Zurich, Switzerland. He received his early education at schools in Zurich, and then attended the University of Zurich. He first studied for the ministry, but later changed to law. Poor health forced him to abandon law, and Pestalozzi settled on his farm near Zurich. There he carried on agricultural experiments.

When the experiments failed, he decided to convert the farm into a school for poor children. It was his first opportunity to test his educational theories. He taught all his pupils reading, writing, and arithmetic. The boys learned farming, and the girls were taught gardening, housekeeping, and sewing. The pupils were supposed to earn their keep and help pay the school's expenses by spinning cotton. But the plan failed, and Pestalozzi was forced to close the school. In the following years, he wrote several books explaining his ideas. His most famous book of this period is *Leonard and Gertrude* (1781-1787).

In 1798, Pestalozzi was appointed head of a school of orphans at Stans. The next year, he became a teacher at an elementary school in Burgdorf. He organized an institute for training teachers, because his methods were so successful. He later moved the institute to Münchenbuchsee (near Bern) and then to Yverdon on Lake Neuchâtel. Pestalozzi's most famous educational experiments were carried on at the institute. Statesmen and educators from all parts of the world came to study his methods and ideas. GALEN SAYLOR

This Silver Peso Is the Monetary Unit of Mexico.
Chase Manhattan Bank Money Museum

H. Armstrong Roberts

Children Enjoy Watching the Activities of Pets of All Kinds. Goldfish make particularly good pets for young children, because they are easy to care for.

PET. Animals have been kept as pets by people in all parts of the world for thousands of years. The most common pets are dogs, cats, parakeets, canaries, and fish. But many people keep unusual pets, such as raccoons, skunks, alligators, and monkeys. Mexican children sometimes keep insects such as fleas and cockroaches as pets. Many Japanese children tame mice and teach them to dance to music. Australian children sometimes make pets of kangaroos. Explorers in Antarctica have treated penguins as pets. The people of India make pets of mongooses. Cormorants are common pets in China.

Pets can make interesting, playful companions. People enjoy teaching them to do tricks and to obey commands. By caring for pets, children learn responsibility. They must see that their pets have food, exercise, and a proper place to live, so that they will be happy and healthy. In addition to providing companionship, many pets are useful. Dogs hunt, guard property, herd cattle and sheep, and lead the blind. Cats may earn their keep by catching mice or rats, and canaries fill the air with their happy, pleasing songs.

Kinds of Pets

Pets for the Home. The kind of home you live in, and where you live have much to do with the kind of pet you choose. Dogs, cats, birds, and fish are easy to care for in almost any kind of home.

Before choosing a dog as a pet, you should consider the size of both your home and the dog. For example, a collie needs a large home with a big yard for exercise. If you live in an apartment, you should be sure pets are allowed. Then choose a small dog, such as a spaniel. A small dog can get most of its exercise by playing around the house, and needs only short walks outside for fresh air.

Cats do not depend on their masters as much as dogs

277

Puppies make wonderful pets for children. They are not difficult to care for, particularly if there is a fenced yard in which they can run and play.

Ralston Purina Co.; H. Armstrong Roberts

Cats are usually independent, strong-willed animals. But they are also active, and love to play. Cats enjoy taking part in simple games, such as jumping in the air for a ball.

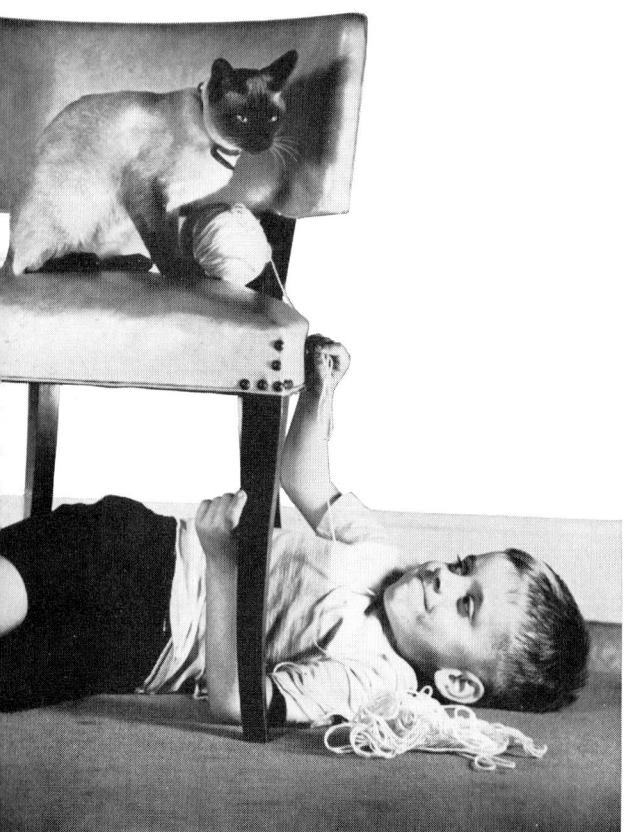

do. Many persons prefer them for this reason. They are quieter and gentler than dogs. But they, too, need outdoor exercise. On pleasant days, a cat can run around in a yard. A cat should always be brought inside to a warm, snug bed at night.

Various kinds of birds make fine pets for a small home or apartment. They live in cages that take little space, and their singing, beauty, and antics will please you by the hour. Canaries sing songs, and their pert, happy ways make them pleasing pets. Finches also have musical voices. Their bright colors and active ways are fun to watch. The parakeet, one of the most popular birds, can learn to talk, and is a great clown. A parakeet can walk a tightrope, go through a tunnel, push and pull toys, and ride in toy cars or trains.

Fish have one advantage over most other pets. They can be left alone for a day or two without being fed. Most fish need food only a few times a week. You can make what is often called a *balanced aquarium* by growing plants in the fish tank. The plants supply some oxygen for the fish. The water does not need to be changed, but occasionally more water must be added to replace that which evaporates. Some tropical fish need extra care, such as controlled temperature, special foods, or oxygen bubbled through the water (see AQUARIUM [A Home Aquarium]).

Other small animals, including white mice, guinea pigs, hamsters, turtles, and squirrels may be kept as pets in a home.

Farm Pets. Farm children usually have many kinds of pets. Almost every farm has one or more dogs, and cats to keep down the mice. The children also play with and care for the baby animals that live on the farm. They may make pets of lambs, rabbits, kids, and even pigs. Baby chickens and ducklings often follow children around the yard, hoping for food. The children may have a pony, or a gentle horse to ride. Many farm boys and girls raise calves to show at county fairs. They brush their calves to keep them clean and sleek. They make sure that the animals have clean straw for their beds.

Pets in School. Many school classes keep animals in the classroom as pets. Boys and girls learn how these animals eat, sleep, play, and take care of their young. They build houses or cages for their pets, and feed and care for them. Rabbits, guinea pigs, hamsters, mice, rats, turtles, fish, frogs, toads, and snakes are among the favorite schoolroom pets. Sometimes classes build glass ant houses or beehives. Then they can watch the activities of a whole group of insects.

Unusual Pets. Many kinds of wild animals may be caught and tamed. Even lions and bears may occasionally become household pets if they are trained while still young. Circus men often make pets of elephants. Even the savage grizzly bear has been tamed. Some persons keep pet skunks and other small wild animals. But most wild animals can be kept as pets only while they are young. They usually become short-tempered and dangerous when full grown.

Young raccoons make good pets. They will eat many kinds of food, including fruit, insects, and frogs. They like to wash their food before eating it. A pet "coon" can learn to walk on a leash like a dog. But if raccoons are allowed to run loose in the house, they may open drawers and throw everything out. Raccoons should be housed in wire cages, because they chew their way through wooden boxes or cages.

Monkeys and chimpanzees make amusing pets. They can learn to do many tricks. Monkeys are as mischievous as small children. But these playful animals may bite if they are teased.

Many boys keep pet snakes. They are clean animals, and can be kept in enclosures in a yard. Small snakes may live indoors in a *vivarium*, a large, glass-covered container with earth and a pan of water. Turtles, frogs, and toads may also live in vivariums.

Always check with your state conservation department before trapping a wild animal or bird to keep as a

Earle R. Edmiston

The Annual Jumping Frog Jubilee in Angels Camp, Calif., draws entrants from all over the world. Many youngsters train their pet frogs for the contest. Mark Twain first made Angels Camp famous in *The Celebrated Jumping Frog of Calaveras County.*

pet. Many states forbid trapping and caging certain wild birds and animals. For example, capturing blue jays is against the law in Illinois, Kansas, Maryland, Nebraska, Oregon, Pennsylvania, and Tennessee.

Choosing a Pet

Before buying a pet, learn as much as possible about all kinds of pets. Choose an animal that can live comfortably in the amount of space you have for it. Find out whether the pet needs outdoor exercise and, if so, how often. Will the pet need care during the day and will

N. Y. Zoological Society

Farm Animals make good pets. Many city zoos have children's sections, so that boys and girls who live in the city can get acquainted with geese, ducks, and other farm animals.

someone be at home to take care of it? How does the animal behave? Is it always friendly with strangers, or is it usually quiet? Does it like young children, or does it become easily upset and cross? What foods does it eat, and how much do these foods cost?

The only way to be certain what a pet will look like when it grows up, and how it will behave, is to buy a *purebred* animal. This is an animal whose parents were both of the same breed. But *mongrels*, or animals of mixed breeds, also make fine pets. You should buy your pet from someone who has raised that kind of animal for a long time, or from a well-kept pet shop. Then you can be sure that the animal has had good care, proper food, and all the necessary vaccinations against disease. You can expect your pet to enjoy a long, healthy, happy life, if it has been properly cared for when young.

Training Your Pet

Before you start to train any kind of pet, you must have its respect and affection. You must always treat it fairly. For example, the first time your dog jumps up at you, make it get down. If you let your dog jump on you when its paws are dry and clean, it probably will do so when they are wet and dirty. The dog does not know when it should not jump on you, so you should not let it form the habit. Say firmly, "No, no" or, "Get down" as you put your paws down. Do this every time, until it learns not to jump on you.

Always speak gently to your pet, and try not to make quick, unfamiliar movements. This does not mean you

Michael Rougier, *Life*, © 1955, Time, Inc.

Some Persons Enjoy Unusual Pets. ▲
Chimpanzees can learn many tricks. They are very lively and playful.

A Skunk may be an interesting pet for children in school. They can learn to feed and care for their unusual pet. ▶

Fluffy Baby Chicks make fine pets for children who live on farms. The chicks need fresh air and must be handled gently.
Vivienne

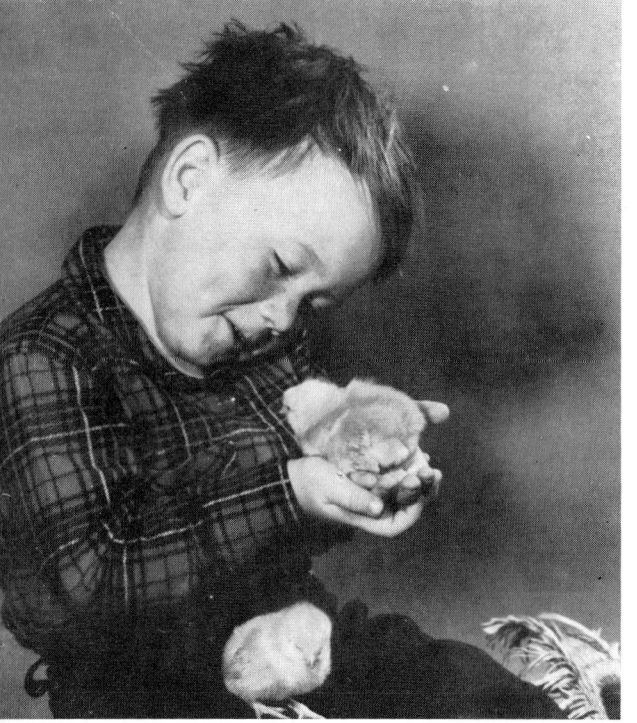

cannot scold your pet. If the animal misbehaves, scold it at once. Use simple words, such as *no, no* or *naughty*, and say them so that the pet knows you are unhappy with it. Do not shout or speak angrily. The pet will not remember for long why it is being scolded, so make the scolding short. Of course, this kind of training is useless for such pets as fish and turtles.

House Training. One of the first things you will want to do is to housebreak such a pet as a puppy or kitten. Use a newspaper if you are housebreaking a young puppy in cold weather, or if you have a small dog in an apartment where you cannot let it out. Keep the dog in the kitchen or in another room that can be easily cleaned. Always put the paper in the same place. If possible, pick a spot near an outside door. Then you can later train the dog to go outdoors. Take the puppy to its paper immediately after it eats, after it plays, after it naps, before it goes to sleep at night, and as soon as it gets up in the morning. If the puppy runs around in circles with its nose to the floor, rush it to the paper. Praise the pup whenever it performs where you want it to. If you find your pet in the act of dirtying the floor, rush it to the paper. Never rub the puppy's nose in its mistake. To train the dog to go outdoors, follow the same procedure. But take the dog outside instead of

Barbara Morgan

going to the newspaper when you think it needs to go.

Kittens are easily housebroken. Provide a box of sand or crumpled newspapers, show the cat the spot you have chosen, and put your pet inside the box to get used to it. Most kittens will return to the box. They are naturally clean and like to dig a hole and bury their droppings. Other cats can be trained to use newspaper like puppies.

Tricks. To teach an animal a trick, you must first make it understand what you want it to do. To teach a dog to sit, for example, push it down to a sitting position. As you do this, say the word *sit*. Praise your pet when it sits correctly. Soon you will find that whenever you say, "Sit," the dog will sit. To make it sit up, raise its front feet as you say, "Sit up." A dog can learn many commands, and such tricks as to fetch, to roll over, to beg, to "say prayers," and to "play dead."

Dogs tire quickly as you train them. You should not work with them more than 15 minutes at a time, and perhaps only once or twice a day. Stop at once if the dog is not paying attention, or if something else seems more interesting to it. You must have the dog's attention, and it must complete each command. Never allow your pet to perform a trick only halfway. And never become impatient when you try to teach it tricks.

Reward a dog with a pat on the head and a few words of praise when it has performed its lesson correctly. If you want to give the animal a special treat, feed it a dog biscuit or a piece of dog candy to exercise its teeth and gums. Ordinary cake, cookies, and candy are bad for a dog and should never be given to the pet.

A cat can be taught to do simple tricks, such as jumping in the air for a ball, leaping over a stick, or walking on its hind legs. You must be patient and gentle to interest the cat in the trick and gain its confidence. Cats should be rewarded with a piece of meat when they perform well. Parakeets usually learn tricks themselves when you put a ladder or toy car in their cages. Fish can learn to come to the side of the tank to receive their food, if you tap gently on the tank each time you feed them.

For Work. Most kinds of dogs can be trained to do certain types of work. Dogs can retrieve, or bring back, game for hunters. They can help herd livestock, pull carts or sleds, and perform many other tasks. Careful training will bring the dog to perfect responses. For example, start training retrievers when they are about six months old. To teach a puppy to return an object you have thrown, give a command such as *fetch* as you throw the object. As the dog learns to return the object, throw it farther and farther away. Training in retrieving from

281

the water starts by throwing an object a few feet into the water. Increase the distance until the dog retrieves the object perfectly.

Cats often keep homes and barns free from mice and rats. Pets such as frogs and toads help keep gardens free from certain kinds of insects.

Taking Care of Pets

Feeding. The first rule for feeding any pet is to keep its dishes clean. Wash them thoroughly every day. Never overfeed your pet. The animal should always have enough exercise and look sleek and slim. Give a dog only as much food as it will eat without leaving any food in the dish. If it leaves the dish before emptying it, take it away. Feed your pet less the next time. Feeding a dog the right food at regular times helps protect it against sickness.

A balanced diet is necessary if your pet is to be healthy. You can buy prepared food for most kinds of pets. Scientists plan these foods so that they contain the right amounts of vitamins, minerals, and proteins for each animal. By using these foods, you can be sure that your pet receives the right nourishment. Prepared foods usually do not need anything added to them. But you may want to give your pet a treat, such as a little horse meat for the dog or cat, or a piece of apple or some greens for the parakeet. Feed your pet at regular times, and be sure that it always has plenty of fresh water.

Housing. All pets must have good houses. Birds should live in cages suitable for their size and activity. For smaller birds, the cage bars should be close enough together so that the bird cannot push its head between the bars and strangle itself. The perches must be the correct size for the bird. They should be $\frac{1}{2}$ inch in diameter for canaries and parakeets, and 1 inch in diameter for mynas. Canaries, parakeets, and other flying birds should have room to fly inside the cage. Put their perches at the ends of the cage. Hopping birds, such as finches and mynas, should have the perches nearer to the bottom of the cage and closer together.

A dog or cat should have a warm, dry place for its bed. A basket, box, or pet bed will keep the pet off the floor and protect it from drafts. A dog living outdoors must have a house free from drafts. The door of the house should face away from the wind. It should be covered or sheltered against rain and snow. The house should be just large enough for the dog to stand up and turn around. A house that is too large will be cold.

Cleanliness. Most pets keep themselves clean. Cats sit for hours washing themselves. Birds preen themselves, or clean their feathers with their beaks. Canaries and mynas enjoy hopping in water and splashing around. Parakeets like to roll on wet lettuce leaves or to be sprayed with water from an atomizer.

Dogs and cats should not be bathed too often. Bathing removes the natural oils from their hair and skin. This makes them itch and scratch, and soon they may have open sores. They usually need baths only when they become very dirty. If your dog or cat becomes muddy, wipe off the loose mud, let its coat dry, then brush its coat well.

Treating Illness. Most pets will enjoy good health with proper food, housing, and grooming. If one should be hurt, swallow something harmful, or otherwise become ill, it should be taken to a *veterinarian*, or animal doctor. The veterinarian will make the pet comfortable and help it back to good health.

Don't try to treat your pet's illness yourself, unless you know exactly what is wrong and what to do for it. Home treatment may seriously delay finding out what is wrong, and may even harm the animal.

Pets in History

The ancient Egyptians tamed cats, hyenas, and baboons. They worshiped the cat and the baboon, and used the hyena as a hunting animal, much as hunters today use the dog. The ancient Assyrians used mastiffs as hunting dogs.

Wealthy Romans kept all sorts of wild animals, in addition to dogs and horses. The Roman emperor Caracalla had a pet lion named Scimitar that sat with him at the table, and slept at the foot of his bed. The Romans taught apes to ride dogs and to drive chariots. They also taught elephants to perform in circuses. In the Middle Ages, an English knight almost never went riding without his favorite falcon or hawk perched on his wrist (see FALCON AND FALCONRY).

Many famous people of the past kept and loved pets. Alexander the Great had his favorite horse, Bucephalus. George Washington kept foxhounds. Otto von Bismarck, a Prussian statesman, was fond of great Danes. Elizabeth Barrett Browning, the English poet, owned a cocker spaniel named Flush. Admiral Richard E. Byrd, the explorer, took his pet fox terrier Igloo with him to the Antarctic. President Franklin D. Roosevelt had a pet Scottish terrier named Fala. See DOG (Famous Dogs); HORSE (Famous Horses). F. E. DITTRICH

Related Articles in WORLD BOOK include:

Bird (Bird Pets)	Guinea Pig	Macaw	Rabbit
Canary	Guppy	Monkey	Raccoon
Cat	Hamster	Myna	Tropical
Dog	Horse	Parakeet	Fish
Goldfish	Lovebird	Parrot	

Outline

I. **Kinds of Pets**
   A. Pets for the Home   C. Pets in School
   B. Farm Pets   D. Unusual Pets
II. **Choosing a Pet**
III. **Training Your Pet**
   A. House Training   B. Tricks   C. For Work
IV. **Taking Care of Pets**
   A. Feeding   C. Cleanliness
   B. Housing   D. Treating Illness
V. **Pets in History**

Questions

Why do people keep pets?
What should you know about an animal before you buy it as a pet?
What kinds of homes should different pets have?
Where should you buy your pet? Why?
Why should you not try to treat a sick pet yourself?
How can you be sure your pet is getting a balanced diet?
Name several pets that are kept in other countries.
What animals can you keep in a vivarium?
What are the five most common pets?
What one advantage do fish have over many other pets?
What is a *purebred* animal? A *mongrel*?
What U.S. President had a famous pet?
What are some basic rules for taking care of pets?

282

PÉTAIN, *PAY TAN,* **HENRI PHILIPPE** (1856-1951), became a national hero of France because of his military leadership in World War I. Yet he was tried and imprisoned for treason in his old age because of his collaboration with the Germans in World War II.

Military Hero. Pétain was born at Cauchy-la-Tour. He was educated at the French military academy of Saint Cyr and served as an army officer. In 1916, during World War I, he commanded the French forces in the heroic defense of Verdun (see VERDUN, BATTLES OF). Here he spoke his famous words "They shall not pass." In April, 1917, Pétain was made chief of staff. He became commander in chief on the western front in May, 1917, and remained in that post until Marshal Ferdinand Foch assumed supreme command in March, 1918. Pétain was made a Marshal of France in 1918. He received the honor of being elected to the French Academy in 1929.

Political Career. Pétain served briefly as minister of war in 1934. His critics accused him of secret hostility to the French Republic and also of sympathy for the dictatorial government of Francisco Franco in Spain. He served as ambassador to Spain in 1939 and 1940. Pétain was called home to be Vice-Premier of France under Paul Reynaud in the

Pix

Henri Philippe Pétain

desperate World War II days of May, 1940, when France was unable to stop the German invasion. On June 16, 1940, Pétain became Premier, and, against the objections of some of his colleagues, arranged the armistice with Germany.

Collaborator. At the age of 84, Pétain became "chief of state" in the French government when its capital moved to Vichy. He accepted collaboration with Germany as an inescapable necessity. Before it dissolved, the French National Assembly voted to give Pétain full powers and authorized him to create a new constitution. He launched a "national revolution" that established political and economic institutions resembling those in fascist countries. His government undertook measures against Jews, paid heavy financial tribute to the Germans, and sent large numbers of French workers to Germany. He ordered French troops in North Africa to resist the Allied landings in November, 1942.

The Germans overran all of France in 1942, and Pétain became powerless. After the Allied troops landed in France in June, 1944, the Germans took him to Baden, where he remained until after the war.

In 1945, Pétain was returned to France. In an atmosphere of intense bitterness, he was tried for treason. At the age of 89, he was found guilty, deprived of all his honors, and sentenced to death. General Charles de Gaulle reduced his sentence to life imprisonment, and Pétain died in jail at 95.   E. J. KNAPTON

PETAL. See FLOWER (The Corolla).

PETALESHARO. See PAWNEE INDIANS.

PETATE, *pay TAH tay,* is a mat made of dried palm leaves or grass. The poorer people of Mexico and other Latin-American countries sleep on petates.

PETER I (1844-1921), a Serbian king, ruled from 1903 to 1921. After the death of his father, Prince Alexander, Peter became head of the Karageorgevic dynasty. He became king when the king of Serbia, also named Alexander, was assassinated. Upon assuming the throne, Peter sought help from Russia in acquiring the province of Bosnia. This province, ruled by Austria, was the home of many Slavs. Russia's support of Peter, together with the assassination of Archduke Francis Ferdinand of Austria by Serbs, helped produce World War I. After the war, Serbia and Bosnia became part of Yugoslavia. Peter retired from the throne in 1914, and his son Alexander served as regent. Peter was born in Belgrade. As a boy, he and his family lived in exile, and Peter was educated in Hungary and France.   R. V. BURKS

PETER I, THE GREAT (1672-1725), a Russian ruler, is famous for having gained access to the sea for Russia and for "westernizing" Russian customs and institutions. He raised Russia to the rank of a great power.

Early Life. Peter was born in Moscow. He came to the throne at the age of 10, together with his weak-minded half brother Ivan V (1666-1696). His sister Sophia seized the regency, but Peter deposed her in 1689 and assumed supreme power.

Through contacts with foreign artisans, soldiers, and merchants who lived in Moscow, Peter early in his life acquired an interest in western civilization. In 1697, he decided to extend his knowledge of the West, and sent a delegation on a tour through Germany, The Netherlands, England, and Austria. He included himself as a member. He used this famous trip not only for political negotiations, but also for studying military techniques, shipbuilding, and other western crafts, and for learning western habits.

A revolt of his royal guards made it necessary for Peter to return to Russia in 1698. He brutally suppressed the revolt and crushed all opposition, especially that of the nobility. This victory made Peter the unchallenged master of Russia. He then began his vast reform work.

Foreign Policy. Peter's first aims were to secure for Russia the rank of a great power and to gain access to the sea. To achieve the second purpose, he declared war on Turkey. He conquered the Turkish port of Azov on the Black Sea but later was forced to return it. Next, Peter engaged in a 20-year war with Sweden. After a bitter defeat at Narva in 1700 and a great victory at Poltava in 1709, he gained possession of most of Livonia and part of Finland, including the great ports of Riga, Reval, and Viborg on the Baltic Sea. Finally, he turned his attention eastward and made war on Persia, from which he acquired two ports on the Caspian Sea. He also ordered trips of discovery along the northern coast of Siberia and concluded trade negotiations with China.

Policies within Russia. Peter the Great strengthened his absolute power as czar, and forcibly introduced western habits. He demanded state service from all his nobility and abolished the old council of the nobility. He replaced it with a senate and various colleges, or ministries. He chose men of ability for high military and administrative offices, rather than merely hereditary nobles.

Culver

Czar Peter the Great, *right,* lashed out with his bare fist to fight off an armed assassin. Royal guards quickly disarmed the attacker, who was one of many noblemen in Russia unhappy over Peter's attempts to "westernize" the country.

Peter extended peasant serfdom, forced the serfs into industrial work, and harshly suppressed their rebellions (see SERF). He abolished the highest church office, the patriarchate, and introduced a system through which he controlled the church. He took land away from the monasteries and extended toleration to religious dissenters.

Peter paid careful attention to improving the Russian army and he also built a Russian navy. He introduced new industries, modernized mining in the Ural Mountains, built roads and canals, and improved the status of Russian merchants. He invited experts from other countries to direct new enterprises. To finance his reforms, he imposed high taxes and reserved profitable business monopolies for himself.

Peter founded schools and laid the basis for the Russian Academy of Sciences. He ordered children of the nobility to study abroad, encouraged the adoption of European manners, and called in foreign professors and scientists. He urged Russian women to take part in social life. He ordered the men to shave (the church favored beards) and to shorten their customary long coats. He founded the city of St. Petersburg (now Leningrad) as his "window to the West" and made it Russia's capital.

Peter the Great

Brown Bros.

Lasting Achievements. Peter truly transformed Russia, giving it a vigorous start on the path of modernization. But the haste with which he pushed reforms sometimes hindered progress. He brutally overrode all opposition. When his son Alexis opposed his reform work, Peter had him executed. He also drove his first wife from him when she opposed his reforms. Nevertheless, the influence of his constant work was lasting. His life ended prematurely at the age of 52, when he caught a cold while trying to save some soldiers from drowning. WALTHER KIRCHNER

See also CATHERINE (I); LENINGRAD; ROMANOV; RUSSIA (History).

PETER II (1923-   ), became king of Yugoslavia at the age of 11 when his father, King Alexander, was assassinated. During his childhood, Peter's cousin Prince Paul served as regent. Peter took the throne in 1941. During World War II, the German army invaded Yugoslavia and Peter set up an exile government in London. He never returned to his country. Communist partisans gained control of Yugoslavia during the war, and established a dictatorship in 1945. Peter was born in Belgrade. R. V. BURKS

See also ALEXANDER I.

PETER, EPISTLES OF, are the twenty-first and twenty-second books of the New Testament. The First Epistle was supposed to have been written by the Apostle Peter about A.D. 62 or 64. Some believe, however, that it was written about A.D. 95 by someone who used Peter's name. At this time the Christians were being persecuted by the Emperor Domitian. The Epistle recalls the teachings of Paul. Its purpose was to warn and strengthen the Christians who were facing death (I Peter 4: 12-14).

The Second Epistle is quite different in style from the First Epistle. The author's aim was to assure his readers that Christ would some day return (II Peter 3: 1-4). FREDERICK C. GRANT and FULTON J. SHEEN

PETER, SAINT, was the leading apostle of Jesus Christ. Jesus gave to him the name of Peter, which means *rock* (Matt. 16: 18). On the occasion when Peter affirmed his faith in Jesus as the Son of God, Jesus said to Peter:

"Thou art Peter; and upon this rock I will build my church, and the gates of hell shall not prevail against it. And I will give to thee the keys of the kingdom of heaven. And whatsoever thou shalt bind on earth, it shall be bound also in heaven; and whatsoever thou shalt loose on earth, it shall be loosed also in heaven."

Roman Catholics use this passage as the basis for their belief that Peter was appointed by Christ to be the first visible head of His Church on earth.

Until he met Jesus, Peter was an inconspicuous fisherman in Palestine. He was married and is believed to have had several children. He was a very human character, impulsive, generous, and not always too consistent. Sometimes he was given to blurting out statements which he later regretted. But, for all this, he was a natural spokesman for the apostles, and had qualities of leadership. Fear led him to deny that he knew Jesus at the time of His trial. But Peter's ardent love for Christ, and his enthusiastic faith in Christ as the Son of God, more than made up for his failings. When most of the other apostles were abandoning Christ, it was Peter who said: "Lord, to whom should we go? We believe and are sure that Thou art that Christ, the Son of the living God" (John 6: 69).

Early Life. Peter was born Simon, the son of Jona. His home was in Bethsaida, a town on Lake Gennesaret. The Apostle Andrew was Peter's brother, and the Apostle Philip also came from the same village. Simon later settled in Capernaum, where he lived with his mother-in-law and was a successful fisherman.

On one occasion, Jesus passed by and John the Baptist called Him "The Lamb of God." Andrew followed Jesus and spent the day with Him. He returned to tell Peter that he had found the Messiah. Andrew then took Peter to meet Jesus. At this first meeting, Jesus gave Peter his new name. Peter followed Jesus for some time as He preached in Galilee, Judea, and Jerusalem. But he returned to fishing, until one day Jesus called to him and his brother, "Come ye after me, and I will make you fishers of men" (Matt. 4:19). From that time on Peter remained with Christ.

Jesus singled out Peter on several occasions for special consideration. He sat in Peter's boat to preach to the multitude on the shores of Lake Gennesaret. When Jesus was walking on the water of the lake, He called to Peter to come to Him across the lake. He also took Peter along with two other apostles, James and John, up to Mount Tabor to witness the Transfiguration. He chose Peter to stay with Him in the Garden of Gethsemane the night before the Crucifixion.

The weak side of Peter's character is clearly revealed in the events leading up to the Crucifixion. Jesus asked Peter, along with James and John, to accompany Him to Gethsemane. But all three of them fell asleep during His agony. When Jesus predicted that Peter would deny Him, Peter was angry. Yet, when he was asked by those in the high priest's court whether he knew Jesus, fear made him say that he did not. Later, he was overcome with remorse over this incident. It may well have been a turning point in his character.

Ordered to Spread the Faith. The failings of Peter did not cause Jesus to lose His trust in him. The angel who appeared before the women at Christ's tomb on the morning of the resurrection gave a special message for Peter. Christ chose Peter of all the apostles as the one to whom He appeared on the day of the resurrection. Later He gave him special orders to spread the faith, at a meeting with all the apostles.

After the ascension, Peter began his mission, in which he did not falter until his death. He preached first in various cities of Palestine and made many converts. He met some opposition from the Jewish supreme council, but was not seriously persecuted until about A.D. 42, when King Herod Agrippa I had him thrown into prison to be executed. Peter escaped through a miracle and left Palestine.

It was Peter who first brought the Christian faith to the Gentiles when he baptized Cornelius, the Roman Centurion (Acts 10: 34-38).

Last Years. The record of Peter's life is not clear from this point on. Evidence shows that he traveled widely in the Middle East. Some scholars believe that he founded the Church in Corinth. His first Epistle was addressed to the Christians of Pontus, Galatia, Cappadocia, and Asia, and it is believed he had been to all these places.

At some time Peter came to Rome, where he preached for some time. Roman Catholics believe that Peter made Rome the center of the Christian Church. He may have been killed during the persecutions of the Emperor Nero between A.D. 64 and A.D. 68. According to tradition, he was crucified head downward at his own request, probably in the Neronian Gardens. The date of his death may have been June 29, celebrated as his feast day. June 29 is also the feast day of Saint Paul. Pope Pius XII in the Holy Year of 1950 announced that St. Peter's tomb had been found beneath his Basilica in Rome.　　FULTON J. SHEEN and MERRILL C. TENNEY

Saint Peter's Deliverance from Prison by an Angel Is One of Paul Gustave Doré's Many Biblical Illustrations.
Brown Bros.

PETER PAN, the hero of a play by Sir James Barrie, is a boy who refuses to grow up. Peter Pan persuades Wendy, John, and Michael Darling to fly with him and the fairy Tinker Bell to Never-Never Land. The Darling children and Peter Pan have adventures with the pirate Captain Hook, a crocodile, and an Indian princess. The play was first produced in 1904.

The character first appears in Barrie's story *The Little White Bird* (1902). Several chapters from the story were published in 1906 as *Peter Pan in Kensington Gardens.* In 1911, Barrie made the play into a story called *Peter Pan and Wendy.*   GEORGE ROBERT CARLSEN

See also BARRIE, SIR JAMES MATTHEW.

PETER RABBIT. See POTTER, BEATRIX.

PETER THE HERMIT (1050?-1115?) was a monk of Amiens who is famous as the preacher of the First Crusade. Little is known of his life from the time of his birth in Amiens until 1095. At that time he began to preach the necessity of a crusade to get back the Holy Land, which was in Moslem hands. He rode about

National Broadcasting Co.
The Story of Peter Pan became a musical hit in 1954, with Mary Martin playing the part of Peter. Actresses Maude Adams and Eva La Gallienne have also played the role on the stage.

The Peter Pan Statue in Kensington Gardens, London, was made by the British sculptor Sir George Frampton.
Martha E. Bonham

From the painting by Archer, Visual Education Service
Peter the Hermit preached to arouse interest in a crusade to regain the Holy Land from the Moslems.

France on muleback, dressed in a monk's cloak of rough cloth and bearing a crucifix. He hoped in this way to inspire men to join him. In 1096 he set out for Palestine with about 30,000 undisciplined followers. Most were from the poorer classes. After struggling through Europe and into Asia Minor, they became so unruly that Peter left them. He joined the army of Godfrey of Bouillon and helped capture Jerusalem.   FULTON J. SHEEN

See also CRUSADES.

PETERBOROUGH, Ont. (pop. 56,177; alt. 632 ft.), is a farming and resort center. The city straddles the Otonabee River. This river provides a convenient source of water power for Peterborough's industries. Peterborough is about 70 miles northeast of Toronto, the capital of Ontario. For the location of Peterborough, see ONTARIO (political map). Products made in Peterborough include canoes, motorboats, electrical equipment and generators, dairy equipment, clocks, tents, awnings, textiles, and cereals.

The nearby Trent Canal has one of the world's tallest hydraulic-lift locks. It is 65 feet high. Many summer resorts stand beside the nearby Kawartha Lakes. Founded about 1820, Peterborough became a city in 1905. It has a mayor-council government. D. M. L. FARR

PETERKIN, JULIA MOOD (1880-1961), an American author, won a Pulitzer prize in 1929 for her novel *Scarlet Sister Mary*. Mrs. Peterkin lived most of her life on a plantation, and her writings told of Negro customs and folklore.

She also wrote *Green Thursday* (1924), *Black April* (1927), *Bright Skin* (1932), and *Roll, Jordan, Roll* (1933). Ethel Barrymore, the famous actress, starred in the dramatization of *Scarlet Sister Mary*. Mrs. Peterkin was born in Laurens County, South Carolina. She lived most of her life in South Carolina. JOHN O. EIDSON

PETERS, SAMUEL. See BLUE LAWS.

PETER'S PENCE is the name applied in the Roman Catholic Church to voluntary offerings for the support of the pope. The custom is said to have originated in England in Saxon days. From there it probably spread to the continent of Europe, and became established by the middle of the 700's. Henry VIII abolished it in England.

The Seventh Provincial Council in 1849 approved its collection in the United States. FULTON J. SHEEN

PETERSBURG, Va. (pop. 36,750; alt. 15 ft.), is now a manufacturing center and tobacco and livestock market. It ranks as one of the most historic cities of the South.

Petersburg lies on the Appomattox River about 20 miles south of Richmond, the capital of Virginia. For location, see VIRGINIA (color map). The first settlement there was made in 1646. Petersburg citizens were active in Bacon's Rebellion in 1676. This was one of the towns attacked and burned in 1781 by British expeditions led by the American traitor, Benedict Arnold. During the War of 1812, Petersburg became known as the *cockade city* because of the jaunty feathered hats worn by its soldiers. The city was the "last ditch of the Confederacy" during the Civil War. When Petersburg fell in 1865, the Southern forces evacuated Richmond. Robert E. Lee's surrender at Appomattox, which ended the Civil War, followed soon afterward.

Today, Petersburg is an important center for the sale of leaf tobacco and the manufacture of tobacco products. Factories also make clothing, furniture, luggage, mechanical pencils, ball-point pens, optical lenses, and eyeglass frames. The city has a council-manager government. FRANCIS B. SIMKINS

See also FORT LEE.

PETERSBURG, SIEGE OF. See CIVIL WAR (Petersburg; table, Major Battles of the Civil War).

Poplar Grove National Cemetery in Petersburg, Va., holds over 6,000 Civil War graves. It was established in 1866.
Petersburg Chamber of Commerce

The Pennsylvania Monument on the site of Fort Mahone in Petersburg, Va., honors Pennsylvania volunteers of the Civil War.
Petersburg Chamber of Commerce

The Metropolitan Museum of Art

A Piece of Petit Point of the 1700's has a pattern embroidered in wool by fine stitches on a canvas base.

PETERSHAM is the family name of two American authors and illustrators of children's books, husband and wife. They won the 1946 Caldecott medal for *Rooster Crows*. Their book *Miki* (1929) pictured the life that Miska Petersham knew as a boy in Hungary. Other books include *The Christ Child* (1931), *Stories of the Presidents of the United States* (1953), *The Silver Mace* (1956), *David* (1958), and *Joseph and His Brothers* (1958).

Maud Fuller Petersham (1890-   ) was born in Kingston, N.Y., and attended the New York School of Fine Arts.

Miska Petersham (1889-1960) was born in Budapest, Hungary, and attended art schools in Budapest and in London.   RUTH HILL VIGUERS

PETIOLE. See LEAF (The Petiole).

PETIPA, MARIUS (1822-1910), was a great French *choreographer* (dance composer). Petipa joined the ballet of the Imperial Theatre in St. Petersburg (now Leningrad), Russia, in 1847. He served as its head from 1862 to 1903. He composed 57 evening-long ballets and many shorter ones. The best-known today include *Sleeping Beauty*, *Raymonda*, *Bayaderka*, and act three of *Swan Lake*.

Petipa's style is clear and grand. It demands highly-trained dancers with a dramatic yet cool and aristocratic quality. Under his leadership, the St. Petersburg ballet became the finest in the world and its school produced such great dancers as Nijinsky, Pavlova, and Fokine.

Petipa was born in Marseille. His family had been dancers since his great-grandfather's time. He danced as a boy in the United States and became a star at 19. But a leg injury in Russia slowed down his career and turned him toward choreography.   P. W. MANCHESTER

PETIT, *peh TEET*, **ROLAND** (1924-   ), is a French dancer and *choreographer* (dance composer). He created a popular, theatrical dance style, breaking away from the formal conventions of French ballet.

Petit was born in Villemomble. After dancing with the ballet of the Paris Opéra from 1939 to 1944, he cofounded the Ballets des Champs-Elysées in 1945.

Three years later, he formed his Ballets de Paris de Roland Petit. He choreographed his best-known work, *Carmen*, for this company. His wife Renée Jeannemaire appeared in the title role. Petit has also composed dances for England's Royal Ballet and for the Royal Danish Ballet. He choreographed and danced with his wife in the motion picture *Hans Christian Andersen* (1952).   SELMA JEANNE COHEN

PETIT JURY. See JURY AND TRIAL BY JURY.

PETIT MAL. See EPILEPSY.

PETIT POINT, *PEHT ih point*, is a type of needle point, or embroidery on a mesh material. The term is French and means *small dot*. The more common needle-point work is called *gros point*, meaning *large dot*. Petit point is preferred for working delicate designs. Many pieces of petit point have intricate, colorful patterns. It is done with yarn on a single-thread, or single-mesh, canvas that usually is made of linen. Most petit-point artists use the *tent stitch*, covering the canvas from right to left, using the left-to-right stitch.   HELEN MARLEY CALAWAY

See also EMBROIDERY; NEEDLE POINT.

PETIT TRIANON. See VERSAILLES.

PETITGRAIN OIL is a yellowish oil made from the leaves, twigs, and fruit of the bitter orange tree. It is used in many perfumes. Paraguay supplies about seven-tenths of the world's petitgrain oil. Petitgrain bigarade, a more valuable oil, is made from another variety of the bitter orange tree. This oil is produced in Mediterranean countries.   PAUL Z. BEDOUKIAN

See also ORANGE (The Bitter Orange).

PETITION is a written request submitted to a court, a public official, or a legislative body. Petitions are often used to influence the vote on certain bills in Congress. The right of petition is one of the fundamental privileges of a free people. There is no rule on how a petition shall be received. Officials to whom petitions are sent decide how to handle the requests.   THOMAS A. COWAN

PETITION OF RIGHT was drawn up in 1628 by the English Parliament and presented to King Charles I. It declared unconstitutional certain actions of the king, such as levying taxes without the consent of Parliament, billeting soldiers in private homes, setting up martial law, and imprisoning citizens illegally.

Charles did not like the Petition of Right, but he finally accepted it because he knew of no other way to persuade Parliament to vote the funds that he had demanded. But he had no intention of carrying out his part of the agreement. He continued his auto-cratic rule until his highhanded methods finally brought about his execution in 1649.

The Petition of Right had important results, even though it did not accomplish its immediate aims. It asserted, in effect, the supremacy of law over the personal wishes of the king. It was therefore a repudiation of the idea of absolute monarchy by divine right. The petition is a landmark in the history of constitutional government in England. Constitutional government was firmly established in 1689 by the passing of the famous Bill of Rights.   W. M. SOUTHGATE

See also BILL OF RIGHTS; CHARLES (I) of England.

PETN is short for *pentaerythritol tetranitrate*, an explosive more powerful than TNT. It is used as the core of detonating caps and fuses. The combination of PETN and TNT is called *Pentolite*. Doctors also use PETN in treating certain heart disorders.   JULIUS ROTH

PETRA, *PEE truh*, was an ancient city south of the Dead Sea in what is now Jordan. It was an important trading center from the late 400's B.C. to the early A.D. 200's. The city stood on the overland trade route that linked Arabia and the Mediterranean Sea. The Nabataeans, a group of Arabian people, settled in Petra in the 500's B.C. In A.D. 106, Roman forces conquered Petra and made it part of the Roman Empire. Petra prospered from A.D. 106 to the early 200's. The people built handsome temples on the small plain there, and they cut deeply into the cliffs to make their houses. Petra was often called the *rose-red city* because of its red stone buildings and the red cliffs that surrounded it.

About A.D. 235, Petra suddenly stopped making coins, and Palmyra, a city in Syria, took over most of Petra's trade. Petra then became chiefly a religious center. It became a Christian city by the A.D. 300's. Moslems controlled the city between A.D. 629 and 632. The Franks, a Germanic tribe, occupied it during the crusades, and held it until 1189. Soon after, the city was abandoned, and it fell to ruin (see JORDAN [picture: Ruins of Petra]).   MARY FRANCIS GYLES

PETRARCH (1304-1374) was a great Italian poet and scholar. His love poetry has had an unparalleled influence on world literature. He was also such a respected scholar that rulers and popes sought his services. Petrarch led in discovering the greatness of classical writers and helped start the movement later called *humanism*. Such Latin writers as Cicero and Livy might be almost unknown today if Petrarch had not found their lost works buried in monastery libraries.

In his own day, Petrarch's Latin writings were considered revivals of the Greek and Roman style of literature. His intimate knowledge of the classics led to his conviction that there is no essential conflict between classical and Christian thought. This conviction anticipated the spirit of the Renaissance.

Throughout his life, Petrarch composed poems of varying length in Italian to praise a beloved woman called Laura. Scholars are not certain that Laura really lived. At first, Petrarch saw in Laura a fleeting image of beauty which he never tired of describing. Eventually he added Christian dimensions to this image, reflecting implications of man's hopes, aspirations, and duties.

Petrarch wrote more than 400 poems in Italian. Of these, 366 form his *Canzoniere* (*Book of Songs*), on which his reputation rests. Petrarch divided the collection into two parts. The first contains poems presumably written during Laura's lifetime and the second written after her death. In the first part, the reader senses a parallel between the poet's attempts to define Laura and Apollo's pursuit of Daphne in the famous classical myth (see DAPHNE). In the second part, however, Laura assumes the role of a guide, leading her lover toward God and toward ultimate salvation.

The *Canzoniere* includes a roughly chronological history of the poet's overwhelming passion for Laura and ends with a hymn to the Virgin Mary. The work expresses a haunting sense of the passage of time and of the vanity of earthly endeavors. It also shows an intense awareness of the conflict between spiritual and earthly values. The tone of the collection alternates bodily pleasure with spiritual love and religious feeling. The poems thus mirror man's uneasy condition as being capable of both the lowest depths and the greatest heights. Technically, Petrarch achieved new perfection in writing the sonnet and the ode, the chief literary forms in the *Canzoniere*.

Petrarch was born FRANCESCO PETRACCO in Arezzo. He spent most of his productive years in France where his father was in political exile.   ALDO S. BERNARDO

PETREL, *PET rul*, is one of a large group of ocean birds. They range over all the oceans of the world. Petrels seldom come near land except during the breeding season, or when they are blown ashore by storms. They usually nest in protected ledges or in burrows along the shore. Petrels are colored black, gray, or white. They range from about 1 to 3 feet long. Some petrels feed by diving into the water. But most petrels fly close above the waves and pick up food from the surface. Small petrels are often called "Mother Carey's Chickens" by sailors. They have a "walking flight" as they course over the water. They seem to be walking on top of the ocean.

National Audubon Society

Petrels are shown flying over the water in this painting by the American artist John James Audubon. The painting is called *Petrels Over the Stormy Ocean.*

PETRIE, SIR FLINDERS

There are many kinds of petrels. Scientists have divided them into three groups. One group includes the *shearwaters*, *fulmars*, and *petrels*. Another is made up of the *storm petrels*, sometimes called *stormy petrels*, some of which breed along the Pacific Coast of North America. The third group is the *diving petrels*, which live only in the Southern Hemisphere.

Scientific Classification. Petrels make up three separate families of the order *Procellariiformes*. Shearwaters, fulmars, and petrels make up the family *Procellariidae*. Storm petrels are *Hydrobatidae*. Diving petrels are *Pelicanoididae*.   LEONARD W. WING

See also FULMAR; MOTHER CAREY'S CHICKEN; CAHOW; SHEARWATER.

PETRIE, *PEE trih,* **SIR FLINDERS** (1853-1942), an English archaeologist, served as professor of Egyptology at University College, London, from 1892 to 1933. In 1894, he founded the British School of Archaeology in Egypt. Petrie showed an early interest in archaeological research, and investigated the ancient British remains at Stonehenge. In 1880, he began a series of surveys and excavations in Egypt that resulted in important discoveries. He founded the *Journal of Egyptian Archaeology* in 1911. Petrie wrote many works, including *Stonehenge* (1880), *Pyramids and Temples of Gizeh* (1883), *Ten Years' Digging in Egypt* (1892), *Egypt and Israel* (1911). He was born WILLIAM MATTHEW FLINDERS PETRIE in Charlton, Kent, and was privately educated.   DAVID B. STOUT

See also ARCHAEOLOGY (The 1800's).

PETRIFICATION is the process by which an object becomes changed to stone, or *petrified*. See FOSSIL; PETRIFIED FOREST.

PETRIFIED FOREST is made up of tree trunks that were buried in mud, sand, or volcanic ash ages ago and have turned to stone. This action is caused by water that seeps through the mud and sand into the buried logs. There it fills the empty cells of the decaying wood with mineral matter until the whole structure has become solid stone. This stone, however, still shows every detail of the original wood structure, even under the microscope.

Petrified forests have been found in many states, especially in New York, Wyoming, and California. They date from different geologic periods and each has the types of trees that grew during its period.

In the United States, the most famous petrified forest lies in northern Arizona, near the town of Adamana. It covers about 40 square miles which have been set aside as the Petrified Forest National Park. In the park, thousands of petrified logs may be seen lying about on the surface where the rain has washed away the rock in which they had been buried. On the average, the logs measure 3 to 4 feet across and 60 to 80 feet long. Some are 125 feet long. Most of them have broken into many pieces that lie about like scattered gigantic cordwood. Others are still whole. None of them stands upright. Stripped of branches and leaves, they lie flat in the layers of rock that had been sand and mud carried there by a large river in Triassic times, perhaps more than 150 million years ago. The logs were nothing but driftwood like that which once made the Mississippi River and the tributaries of the Mississippi dangerous in flood time.

In life, they were the trunks of coniferous trees of the kind known as the Norfolk Island pine. Today they consist largely of the minerals chalcedony and agate, two forms of silica. Their grayish colors are made bright by streaks and spots of yellow, red, purple, and black. These streaks and spots were produced by the oxides of iron and manganese.

See also FOSSIL; PETRIFIED FOREST NATIONAL PARK.

PETRIFIED FOREST NATIONAL PARK lies in the Painted Desert in northern Arizona (see ARIZONA [physical map]). The park contains the greatest and most colorful concentration of petrified wood known in the world. Giant logs of agatized wood lie flat on the ground, surrounded by numerous broken sections and fragments. Six "forests" are within the

The *Old Faithful* Log in the Petrified Forest National Park Is Probably About 150,000,000 Years Old.

Lars Hedman

National Park Service

A Prehistoric Stone Carving of a Mountain Lion Was Found Near the Petrified Forest National Park.

area. The most colorful is called *Rainbow Forest*. The other forests are named *First, Second, Third, Black*, and *Blue*. The park covers almost 95,000 acres.

The trees in the area grew about 150 million years ago. Fragments of pottery found in the forest show that small groups of farming Indians lived there as early as A.D. 500 to 1400. The area became a national monument in 1906, and a national park in 1962.

PETRILLO, JAMES CAESAR (1892-   ), served as president of the American Federation of Musicians from 1940 to 1958. He continued as president of the Chicago branch of the union until 1963.

Petrillo's greatest victory as a labor leader came in 1942 when he forced recording companies to pay a royalty to the musicians for every record they sold. Petrillo fought the use of recorded music whenever it caused musicians unemployment. He barred many great artists from performing on the radio and making records until they became union members. Petrillo was born in Chicago.   JACK BARBASH

PETROCHEMICALS, *PET roh KEM uh kulz*, are chemicals made from crude oil and natural gas. They are among the most important materials used in industry. Petrochemicals are used in making plastics, detergents, synthetic fibers, synthetic rubber, paint, medicines, and fertilizer and other agricultural chemicals.

Making Petrochemicals. Crude oil and natural gas consist chiefly of compounds of the elements hydrogen and carbon, arranged in different ways. These compounds are called *hydrocarbons* (see HYDROCARBON). One of these hydrocarbons may be separated from the rest, purified, and sold as a petrochemical. In most cases, the chemical compounds in the oil or gas are first broken apart and then put together in another way to make chemicals that were not originally present in the oil or gas. Often, other chemicals are added. Chemicals produced this way are the most important petrochemicals.

Chemicals that are the same as petrochemicals can also be made from other raw materials. For example, they can be made from coal or farm products. Many chemicals even come partly from one and partly from another of these raw materials. Usually, when most of the supply of some chemical is believed to come from oil or gas, people call it a petrochemical.

Important Petrochemicals. Hundreds of petrochemicals have been accepted for commercial use. One important petrochemical is *ammonia*, which is produced from natural gas and finds its chief use in commercial fertilizers. *Methanol, ethanol*, and *propanol* are used as solvents for paint, as automobile antifreezes, in the manufacture of plastics, and to make still other chemicals. *Carbon black* is an important reinforcing material for automobile tires. Manufacturers use *ethylene glycol* and *glycerin* in antifreeze, dynamite, paint, and cellophane. *Butadiene* and *styrene* serve as important raw materials for synthetic rubber. *Dodecyl benzene* is the chief raw material for synthetic detergents used for washing clothes and dishes. Textile companies make synthetic fibers from *cyclohexane* and *paraxylene*.

History. Carbon black has been made from natural gas since the late 1800's. But the large-scale use of oil and gas as raw materials for making chemicals began in the 1920's. The use of petrochemicals spread rapidly. This was partly due to an increased demand for chemicals of all kinds, and because the supply of older chemicals could not meet the demand. Also, some of the newly invented chemicals enabled manufacturers to produce products that could not be made before. This resulted in a demand for these materials to make the things that people needed and wanted. Large numbers of research scientists and engineers invented and perfected efficient ways to make them. Today, experts estimate that at least one-fourth of all the chemicals used in industry, by weight, are made from petroleum and natural gas.   RICHARD C. McCURDY

Related Articles in WORLD BOOK include:

Ammonia	Hydrocarbon	Plastics
Chemical Industry	Petroleum	Rubber
Gas		

PETROGRAD. See LENINGRAD.

PETROL is the term used in Britain and other Commonwealth countries for gasoline. See GASOLINE.

PETROLATUM, *PET roh LAY tum*, or PETROLEUM JELLY, is a colorless to yellow, jellylike substance made from petroleum. Petrolatum is used as an ingredient in medicines and cosmetics. It is also sold in the jellylike state, often under the trade name *Vaseline*. See also MINERAL OIL.   CLARENCE KARR, JR.

PETROLEUM

PETROLEUM, *puh TROH lee um,* or *pea TROH lee um,* is often called *black gold* because it is so valuable to mankind. Petroleum comes from the earth as a dark liquid that contains hundreds of different materials. From these materials, men make thousands of useful products. Some of these products are gases so light and colorless that they are invisible. Other petroleum products are heavy, hard, and tough.

Petroleum provides man with many of his most useful fuels. Gasoline is the most important of these fuels. It powers the automobiles that families use for daily travel, and many of the trucks that rumble across the highways. Jet fuel made from petroleum sends airplanes streaking through the sky. Many railroad locomotives get their power from diesel oil made from petroleum. And millions of families heat their homes with petroleum fuels. Petroleum also provides the power for most

---

William B. Harper, the contributor of this article, is a petroleum specialist for the U.S. Bureau of Mines.

---

ships and boats. Farmers plant, cultivate, and harvest their crops with machines powered by gasoline, kerosene, and diesel fuel.

While petroleum fuels turn the wheels of industry and transportation, oils and greases made from petroleum help the wheels run smoothly. These oils and greases are called *lubricants*. Without them, the machines needed for modern mass production could not operate.

Petroleum also furnishes many special products used every day. The wax on the paper wrapper that keeps bread fresh comes from petroleum. The cleaning fluids used to freshen clothes are petroleum products, and so are the detergents used to wash clothes and dishes. The thousands of other petroleum products include such different things as plastics, explosives, rubber tires, printing ink, and paint.

The word *petroleum* comes from two Latin words, *petra*, meaning *rock*, and *oleum*, meaning *oil*. Men gave it this name because they first found it seeping up from the earth through cracks in rocks. Today, petroleum is usually called *oil*. Oilmen use the term *crude oil* for petroleum as it comes from the earth.

In the early days of the petroleum industry, finding oil was mostly a matter of luck. Early oilmen made and lost fortunes overnight. Locating oil is still a gamble. Scientists cannot pinpoint an underground storehouse of petroleum in advance. But the petroleum industry tries to reduce the risk by using modern scientific methods in its search.

Drilling an oil well may cost from $100,000 to $2,000,000, depending on its depth, location, and other conditions. If the well is found to be dry, this money is lost. Eight out of nine wells drilled in an

Bob Taylor

A Tall Oil Derrick provides the framework from which oil men drill deep into the earth in search of nature's storehouses of petroleum. Drilling is the only sure way to locate an oil pool.

American Petroleum Institute

A Petroleum Refinery at Twilight is a beehive of activity. The twinkling lights and setting sun outline the tall towers where the magic of chemistry turns crude oil into useful products. Refineries make the fuels that are essential to modern life.

area that has never before produced oil are dry.

The petroleum industry employs millions of workers. Some are geologists who search for oil in fields, in forests and jungles, in mountains, in deserts, and under the ocean floors. Oilmen drill wells in all parts of the world, from the Arctic regions to the Sahara. Many oil workers are needed to run refineries that turn petroleum into useful products. Other workers run pipelines, tank cars, ships, and trucks that carry these products where they are needed. The most familiar oil worker is the service-station attendant who fills the gasoline tank of the family car.

From Oil Well to Service Station

Oil Fields are the starting points of petroleum's long journey from deep in the earth to homes, farms, facto-

---

PETROLEUM TERMS

Barrel is the standard unit used to measure crude oil and most petroleum products. A barrel equals 42 gallons in the United States. In Canada, a barrel equals 35 imperial gallons, or 42 U.S. gallons.

Bringing in a Well means to reach oil and start a well flowing.

Derrick is a steel tower that holds the equipment used to drill an oil well.

Dry Hole is a well that fails to produce oil and gas in commercial quantities.

Exploratory Wells are drilled to find commercial deposits of oil or gas.

Gushers are wildly flowing wells. They may occur as the result of accidents called *blowouts*.

Horizon is an underground rock formation, usually one that contains oil or natural gas.

Lease is an arrangement by which an operator pays a landowner rent for the exclusive right to drill for, and produce, oil on his property.

Oil Pool is an underground reservoir or trap containing oil. It may be a collection of crude-oil droplets mixed through porous sandstone, sandy shale, or limestone formations.

Oil Traps are nonporous rock formations that contain oil pools.

Proration is a system of state rules that control the amount of oil that can be taken daily from wells or fields. Such conservation laws prevent waste of oil.

Roughneck is a general worker on a drilling rig.

Royalty is money paid to a landowner for oil produced on his land. Oil companies usually pay a royalty of one-eighth the value of each barrel of oil produced and sold. The landowner may also take his royalty in oil.

Secondary Recovery includes methods designed to take oil from a well that has nearly or completely stopped producing. Oilmen may inject gas or water into the reservoir to force the oil to a well where it is pumped to the surface.

Wildcat Well is a well drilled in an area where there is no production.

TRANSPORTING PETROLEUM

Railroads, ships, pipelines, and trucks all play a part in the vital job of moving petroleum from oil well to consumer. They transport crude oil from oil fields to refineries, and then move petroleum products to local distributors. Trucks form the final link in the transportation of petroleum.

Adapted courtesy Shell Oil Co.

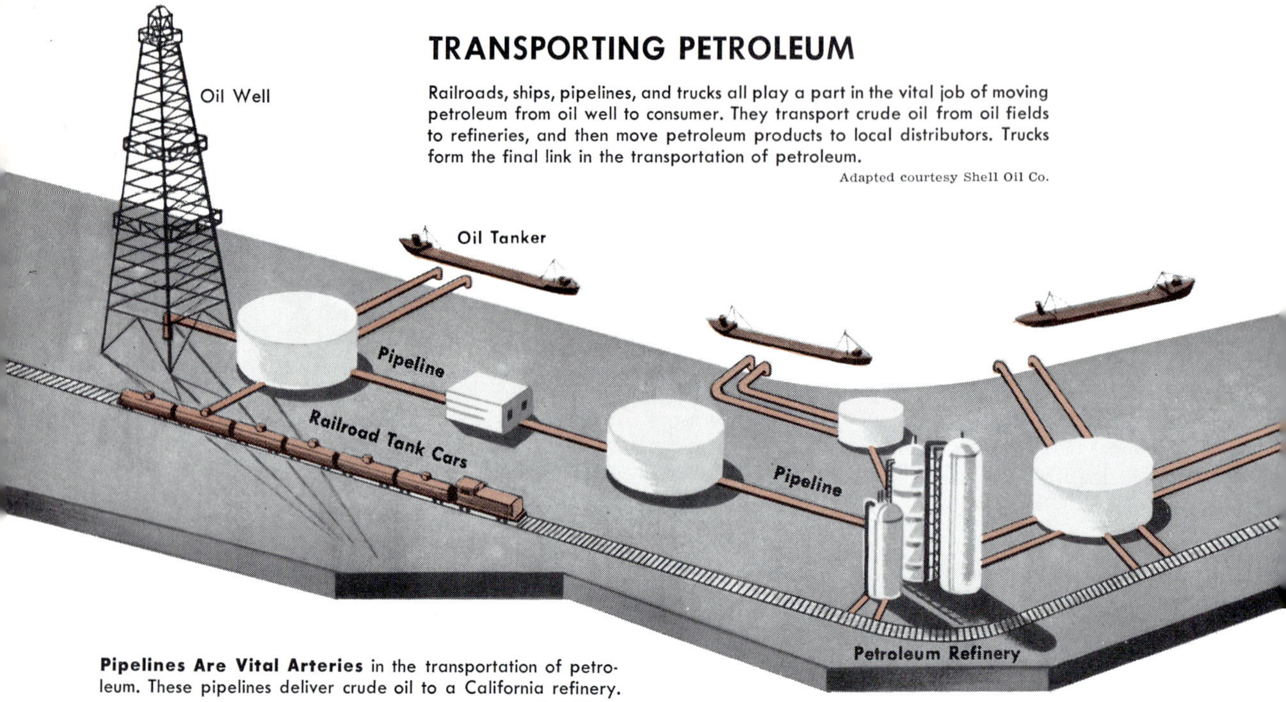

Oil Well

Oil Tanker

Pipeline

Railroad Tank Cars

Pipeline

Petroleum Refinery

Pipelines Are Vital Arteries in the transportation of petroleum. These pipelines deliver crude oil to a California refinery.

Shell Oil Co.

A Tanker Loads Petroleum at a Baton Rouge, La., refinery. Ships such as this carry oil across oceans and along coasts.

Standard Oil Co., N.J.

ries, and service stations. Only certain types of underground rock formations trap oil. These rock formations may be found in many parts of the world, under widely varying conditions of land and climate. Men pump oil from the earth below farm land, prairies, jungles, swamps, marshes, mountains, and ocean floors.

At first, an oil field may be a quiet section of farm land with only one or two tall steel derricks. These derricks mark the places where workers drill wells in their search for oil. They hold the equipment used to bore into the earth. The older derricks look like farm windmills with the blades removed. Some newer derricks, including portable ones, are more streamlined. See DERRICKS AND CRANES.

If a well brings in oil, a peaceful countryside can quickly change. Bulldozers, trucks, and cars swarm over the oil field. The roar of diesel engines, the cough of heavy-duty pumps, and the clang of steel fill the air. Drillers move in with heavy equipment to drill more wells. Soon drilling rigs dot the landscape. Pipes used to drill the wells, and casings to line the holes, are piled in stacks like logs for a fireplace. Skilled crews work

to bring up petroleum from the underground pools.

After oil begins to flow, workers may remove the rigs. Or, they may leave the derricks standing and remove only parts of the rig, such as the hoisting equipment. Oil continues to flow from the wells, but a quiet settles over the field. In some fields, clusters of valves and pipes mark the wells. In other fields, "walking" beams move up and down as they pump petroleum from the earth. The crude oil flows silently into storage tanks near the wells. Later, the oil is pumped through pipelines to storage tanks either at the refinery or at a terminal, from which the oil will be shipped by boat to a refinery.

Making Petroleum Products. An oil refinery turns crude oil into gasoline, diesel oil, lubricating oil, and other useful products. These industrial plants resemble giant chemical laboratories. Tall steel towers look like huge test tubes. Tanks shaped like baseballs crowd together amid miles of piping.

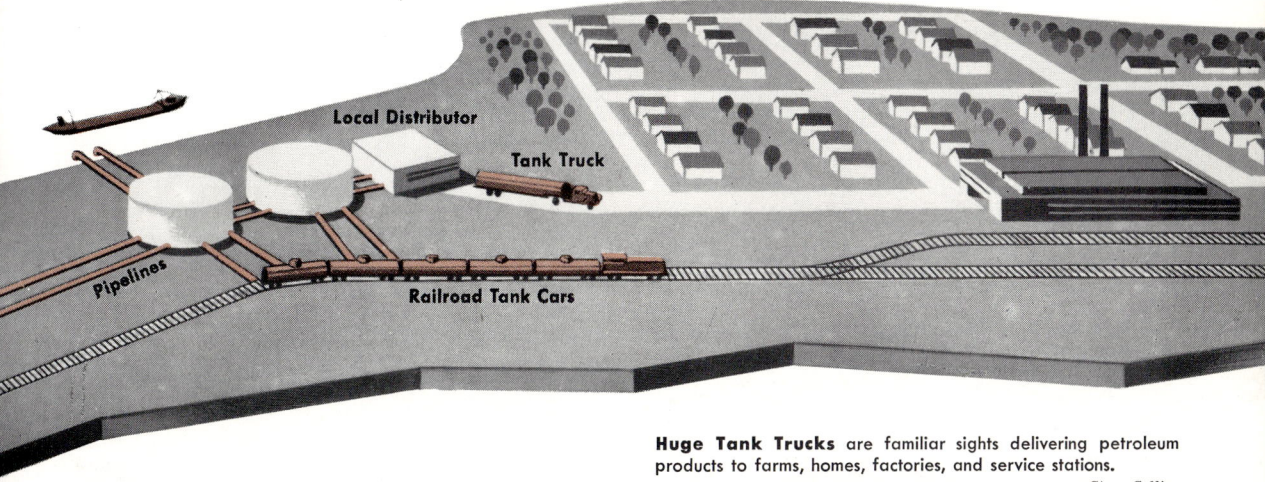

Consumers

Local Distributor

Tank Truck

Pipelines

Railroad Tank Cars

Huge Tank Trucks are familiar sights delivering petroleum products to farms, homes, factories, and service stations.

Steve Collins

Long Trains of Railroad Tank Cars rumble across country carrying their loads of crude oil and petroleum products.

General American Transportation Corp.

After crude oil comes to a refinery, it is stored in tanks until pumps force it through the plant and through the many kinds of equipment that change it into useful products. Refinery workers rarely see, or handle directly, the petroleum in this *continuous flow* process. They constantly check the dials and gauges of large control panels. These panels show the pressure, temperature, and rate of flow of the petroleum in every step of each manufacturing process. Samples are frequently taken at various steps. Chemists use these samples to check the quality of the product.

The location of an oil refinery depends on (1) the supply of crude oil, (2) an ample supply of water for use in the refinery, and (3) the nearness to a market. Some refineries have been built near oil fields to take advantage of a convenient supply of crude oil. Others depend on pipelines to bring crude oil to them over long distances. Most refineries are built near cities, and usually stand near a supply of water such as a river or lake.

Moving the Oil. Pipelines, railroad tank cars, trucks, barges, and large ships called *tankers* carry oil and oil products from producer to consumer quickly and economically. Pipelines carry more petroleum than do any other means of transportation.

In the United States, crude oil and petroleum products move through a network of about 211,000 miles of pipelines. Canada has about 15,000 miles of pipelines. The lines range in diameter from 2 to 36 inches. Pumping stations spaced up to 60 miles apart along a pipeline keep the oil moving at a speed of 2 to 3 miles an hour. See PIPELINE.

Tankers transport petroleum on the Great Lakes, along the coasts, and across the oceans. Barges move petroleum on lakes, rivers, and canals. About a fourth of all the vessels on the inland waterways of the United States are oil barges. Huge railroad tank cars carry oil over railways. Most of these cars can carry from 8,000 to 10,000 gallons of oil.

Trucks provide the final link in the oil-transportation chain. They carry products to local distributors, deliver gasoline and diesel fuel to filling stations and farms, and bring fuel oil to heat millions of homes. Tank trucks range in capacity from 500 to 12,000 gallons.

Service Stations, with their wide driveways, gasoline pumps, grease racks, and displays of oil and tires, are a familiar sight to everyone. Attendants provide many services in addition to putting gasoline and oil into automobiles and trucks. They clean windshields, check batteries and radiators, and supply road maps and travel directions. In the United States, more than 211,000

WHAT A BARREL OF CRUDE OIL PROVIDES

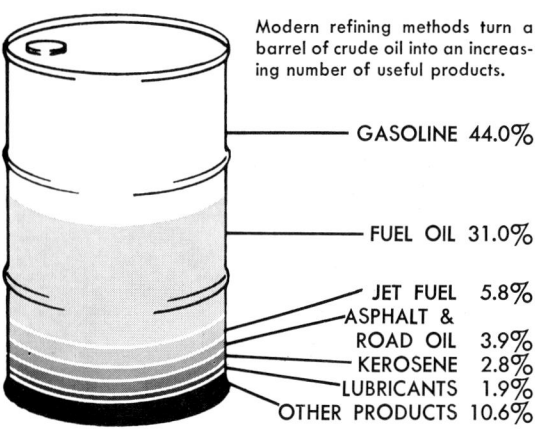

Modern refining methods turn a barrel of crude oil into an increasing number of useful products.

GASOLINE 44.0%

FUEL OIL 31.0%

JET FUEL 5.8%
ASPHALT &
ROAD OIL 3.9%
KEROSENE 2.8%
LUBRICANTS 1.9%
OTHER PRODUCTS 10.6%

Source: U.S. Bureau of Mines

Marathon Oil Co.

Gasoline Is the Chief Petroleum Product. Service-station attendants fill auto tanks from shiny pumps the world over.

service stations sell over $21 billion worth of products every year, including tires, batteries, and other automobile equipment. Independent businessmen own or operate about 95 of every 100 stations.

Petroleum Products

Gasoline is the chief product of petroleum. Automobiles, buses, trucks, and tractors use most of the gasoline in the United States. Motor vehicles use over $73\frac{1}{2}$ billion gallons of gasoline every year on U.S. roads and highways. Airplanes, excluding jets, use about $1\frac{1}{2}$ billion gallons of aviation gasoline each year. Other uses of gasoline bring the total consumption in the United States to over 77 billion gallons a year. The total rises each year. See GASOLINE.

Fuel Oils rank second to gasoline in importance. They provide a major source of heating and power. The United States uses about $60\frac{1}{4}$ billion gallons of fuel oils each year to heat homes and buildings, and to supply power for factories, railroads, ships, power plants, smelters, and trucks. See FUEL.

Lubricants, or oils and greases, are used to provide a slippery film between the moving parts of engines and machines. Without this film, friction would quickly wear them out. Close-fitting parts, such as those in airplane and automobile engines, would stick together or melt without lubricants. The United States uses more than $2\frac{1}{2}$ billion gallons of lubricants a year.

Jet Fuels can be a mixture of gasoline, kerosene, and oils with low freezing points, or straight kerosene used alone. United States commercial and military jet airplanes use more than $10\frac{1}{4}$ billion gallons of jet fuel each year.

Kerosene is used chiefly as a fuel. People in the United States use about $4\frac{1}{4}$ billion gallons of kerosene a year. See KEROSENE.

Asphalt and Road Oil are used chiefly to surface roads. Large amounts of asphalt are also used to cover roofs. In the United States, over nine-tenths of the paved roads and streets and about seven-tenths of the paved airport runways are made of asphalt. About 24 million tons of asphalt and over $1\frac{1}{4}$ million tons of road oil are used in the United States each year. See ASPHALT.

U.S. Air Force

Jet Fuel from Petroleum powers speedy airliners and military airplanes. Here, a jet tanker plane refuels a fighter before combat.

Black Ribbons of Asphalt Pave Streets and Highways. Asphalt was one of the first petroleum products put to use.

Natural Rubber Bureau

Other Petroleum Products include insect sprays, weed killers, rust preventives, LP (liquefied petroleum) gas, and petrochemicals. Some persons who live in rural areas heat their homes and power their refrigerators with LP gas, sometimes called *bottled gas* (see GAS [Liquefied Petroleum Gas]). *Petrochemicals* are chemicals made from petroleum. Industry uses petrochemicals to make such products as paint, detergents, synthetic rubber, plastics, antiseptics, cosmetics, drugs, anesthetics, fertilizers, and nylon and other synthetic fibers. Chemicals made from petroleum account for about a fourth of the *organic chemicals* (those that contain carbon) made in the United States. See PETROCHEMICALS.

Oil Regions of the World

Oil deposits that petroleum engineers believe can be removed from the ground profitably are called *reserves*. Petroleum experts estimate that almost 342 billion barrels of crude-oil reserves lie beneath the surface of the earth. The world uses over 10 billion barrels of oil a year, and the demand is rising. However, petroleum explorers continually find new oil fields. Experts believe there is little danger of running out of petroleum in the foreseeable future.

North America has almost 40 billion barrels of crude-oil reserves, or almost 12 per cent of the world total. The continent furnishes about one-third and uses over two-fifths of total world oil production.

The United States ranks as the leading oil-producing nation. The country has about 31 billion barrels of proved crude-oil reserves. The largest oil fields in the United States lie in Texas, Louisiana, California, and Oklahoma. These four states, together with Wyoming, New Mexico, Kansas, and Illinois, produce about nine-tenths of the nation's oil. A total of 31 states produce petroleum commercially.

Some of the nation's most important oil reserves lie off the coasts of Louisiana, Texas, and California. Oilmen drill wells beneath these waters from specially built platforms, barges, and man-made islands. They also drill from shore. U.S. *offshore wells* produce about 180 million barrels of oil annually.

Canada became a leading oil-producing nation in the 1950's. Alberta has the largest oil fields in the country, followed by Saskatchewan, British Columbia, and Manitoba. New Brunswick, Ontario, and the Northwest Territories also produce some oil. Geologists believe that the deposits of *bituminous sands* (sands saturated with oil) along the Athabasca River in Alberta are the largest known to man (see BITUMINOUS SANDS). These deposits may cover as much as 30,000 square miles and contain an estimated 300 billion to 600 billion barrels of petroleum. In 1964, construction began on the first plant to remove oil from this area. The plant began operating in 1966.

Mexico has several rich oil fields along the Pánuco River near Tampico, and on the Isthmus of Tehuantepec. The government owns the Mexican oil industry.

South America has over $22\frac{1}{2}$ billion barrels of petroleum reserves, nearly 7 per cent of the world's total. Venezuela alone has 17 billion barrels of reserves, and ranks third (after the United States and Russia) among the oil-producing nations of the world. Argentina, Bolivia, Brazil, Chile, Colombia, Ecuador, Peru, and Trinidad also have some petroleum.

Asia has the greatest oil reserves in the world, about 225 billion barrels. This is about two-thirds of the world total. But Asia produces only about 30 per cent of the world's oil. All but about 15 per cent of its oil lies in the Middle East nations of Iran, Iraq, Kuwait, and Saudi Arabia. Indonesia, in the Far East, has about $8\frac{1}{2}$ billion barrels, about 2.5 per cent of the world's total.

Europe. Western Europe has over $1\frac{1}{2}$ billion barrels of reserves, about 0.5 per cent of the world's total. It produces about 1 per cent of the world's oil. Eastern Europe, including Russia and its satellites, has an estimated 34 billion barrels of reserves.

Africa has oil in Algeria, Angola, Congo (Brazzaville), Egypt, Gabon, Libya, Morocco, Nigeria, and Tunisia. Africa's reserves have never been completely measured. Political difficulties in obtaining drilling and pipeline permits have slowed the development of Africa's petroleum industry.

How Petroleum Was Formed

Organic Theory. No one really knows how petroleum was formed. Most scientists accept the organic theory. According to this theory, petroleum was formed through millions of years in great oceans that covered many parts of the earth during prehistoric times. Tiny plants and animals lived in shallow water and along the coasts of the seas, just as they do today. As these plants and animals died, their remains settled on the muddy bottoms of the oceans. There, even smaller forms of life called *bacteria* caused them to decay.

Fine sand and mud, called *sediments*, drifted down

INTERESTING FACTS ABOUT PETROLEUM ———

Over 2,800,000,000 Barrels of Oil a Year are produced by the more than 588,000 oil wells in the United States. This is equal to about 609 gallons a year for each person in the country.

An Average Oil Well in the United States produces almost 13 barrels, or 542 gallons, a day.

Biggest User of Oil in the World is the United States.

Deepest Oil Well in the world was a dry hole drilled to a depth of 25,340 feet in Pecos County, Texas.

First Commercially Successful Oil Well in the United States was drilled by E. L. Drake near Titusville, Pa., in 1859. This well is generally considered to have launched the petroleum industry.

First Modern Oil Tanker was the *Gluckauf*, built in England for German owners. The vessel entered service in 1886.

First Petroleum Company in the United States was the Pennsylvania Rock Oil Company, incorporated in New York in 1854.

First Petroleum Pipeline in the United States was 5 miles long and ran from an oil field near Titusville, Pa., to a railroad. It was built in 1865.

First Petroleum Refinery in Canada was built by James Miller Williams in Ontario about 1857.

First Petroleum Refinery in the United States was a one-barrel still built in Pittsburgh by Samuel Kier in the early 1850's.

First Commercially Successful Oil Well in Canada was dug by James Miller Williams near Oil Springs, Ont., in 1857.

Oil Derricks have developed from 40-foot wooden structures to steel giants up to 200 feet high. Some can lift 1 million pounds and withstand winds up to 125 miles an hour.

WHERE PETROLEUM COMES FROM

This map shows the world's major petroleum-producing areas on land and off shore. The map also
locates areas of possible future production. These
are regions of sedimentary rock where oil is
usually found. About one-third of the world's
petroleum comes from North America, and most
of this oil comes from wells in the United States.

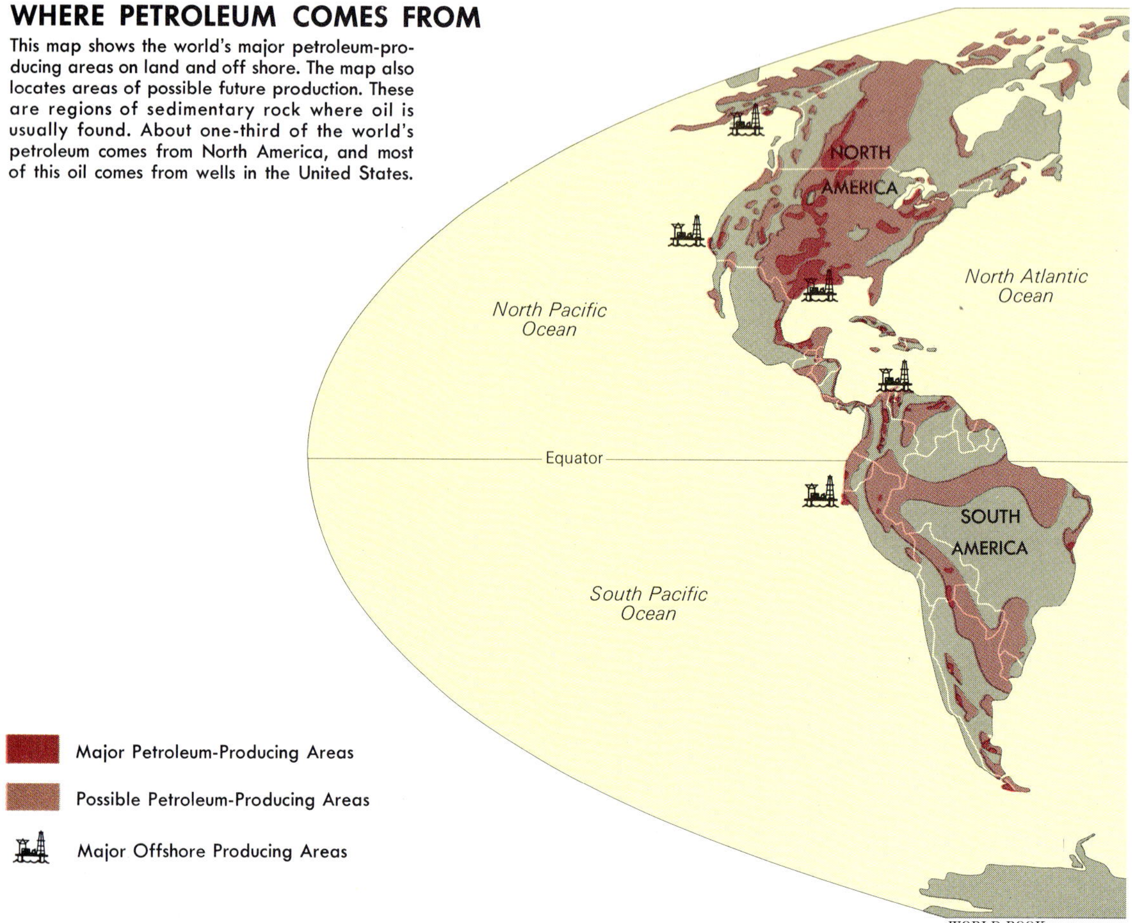

NORTH
AMERICA

North Atlantic
Ocean

North Pacific
Ocean

Equator

South Pacific
Ocean

SOUTH
AMERICA

■ Major Petroleum-Producing Areas

■ Possible Petroleum-Producing Areas

⚒ Major Offshore Producing Areas

WORLD BOOK map

On a Farm in Western Canada, a slender oil derrick overlooks a field of oats. Alberta leads all provinces in oil production.

Desert Oil from Arabia goes to all parts of the world. The
Middle East has over three-fifths of the world's oil reserves.

Photos, Standard Oil Co. (N.J.)

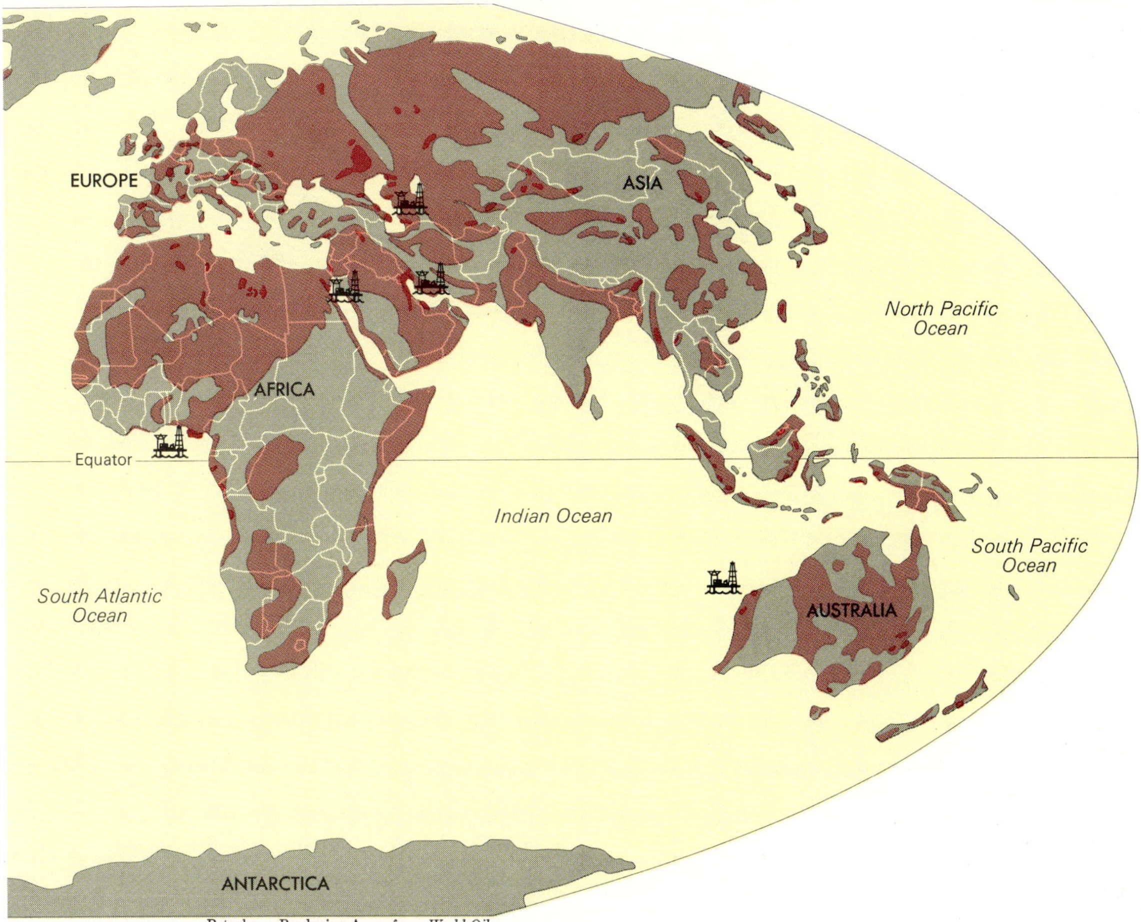

Petroleum-Producing Areas from *World Oil;*
Possible Petroleum-Producing Areas from American Petroleum Institute.

A Tropical Forest in Colombia grows above a rich oil deposit. South America has about 7 per cent of world oil reserves.

Offshore Wells in Venezuela, such as these in Lake Maracaibo, help make that country a leading producer of petroleum.

Photos, Standard Oil Co. (N.J.)

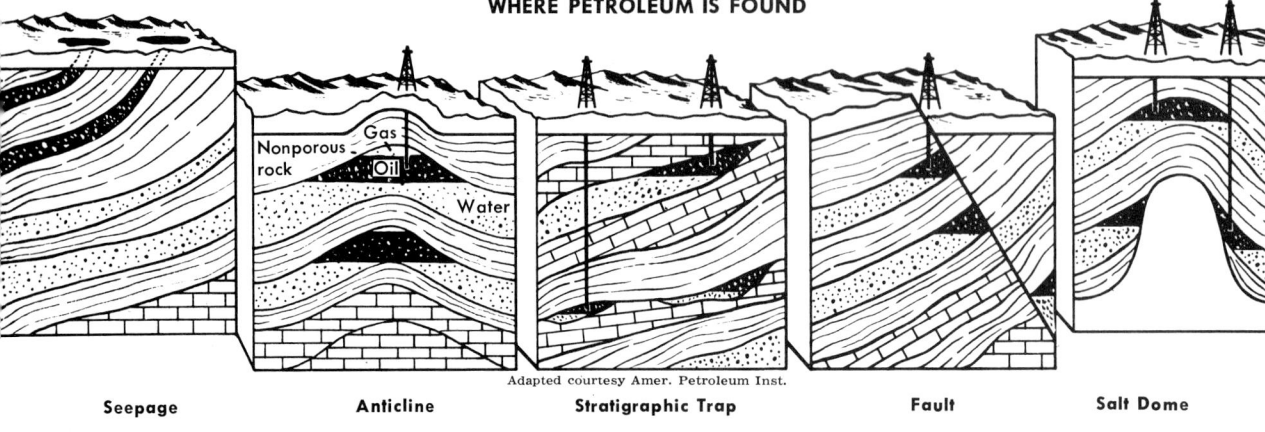

Adapted courtesy Amer. Petroleum Inst.

Seepage **Anticline** **Stratigraphic Trap** **Fault** **Salt Dome**

Petroleum Collects in various kinds of underground structures called *traps*. These were formed by changes in the earth crust.

Droplets of oil collected in the tiny spaces found in porous rocks. Layers of nonporous rocks sealed off the oil-bearing formations.

over the plant and animal matter. As these sediments piled up, their great weight pressed them into hard, compact *beds* (layers) of sedimentary rock (see ROCK [Sedimentary Rock]). During this process, bacteria, heat, pressure, and perhaps other natural forces changed the plant and animal remains into oil and natural gas.

Tiny drops of oil and bubbles of gas moved from the mud beds in which they were formed into other sedimentary rocks, usually sandstone or limestone. These *porous* rocks contained *pores* (small openings) through which the oil moved.

Through millions of years, layers of less porous sedimentary rock formed above the rock beds. This rock sealed the oil and gas into underground pools. Later, ancient seas drained away through movements of the earth's crust, and dry land appeared above the petroleum deposits.

Oil Shale. Not all the oil comes from underground pools. Some of it is obtained from *oil shale*, a rock made of compressed layers of clay, or silt and minerals. This shale does not contain oil, but a solid material called *kerogen*. Oil is obtained from the kerogen by heating crushed shale to about 900° F. At this temperature, kerogen molecules split to form molecules of *shale oil*. Oil shale is found in Colorado, Indiana, Kentucky, Pennsylvania, and West Virginia. It may provide an important source of oil when economical production methods are developed.

Oil Formation Today. No one knows whether oil is still being formed. Scientists have experimented with bacteria in an effort to learn more about the origin of petroleum. They have found that bacteria can change organic matter into material much like petroleum. They have also learned that bacteria can release petroleum from oil-bearing rocks.

How Men Find Petroleum

Scientists have no way of telling exactly where petroleum has formed underground. But oilmen know the kinds of *structures* (rock formations) that are likely to contain oil. The men who look for these underground structures are called *oil geologists* and *geophysicists*. See GEOPHYSICS.

Studying Rock Formations. The oil geologist begins the search for petroleum. He starts with a general knowledge of broad areas of the earth's surface, and pays special attention to regions that he knows have been the beds of ancient seas. The geologist selects an area he believes favorable to the formation of oil by using maps, surveys made from airplanes, and information about previous wells. He then studies the origin and character of the rock layers in the area. This information may tell him whether or not he is likely to find formations that may contain oil. The geologist also studies the layers of sandstone, limestone, sand, and shale in the earth's crust. He makes maps of the surface formations. He obtains *cores* (cylindrical samples) of the underground layers by drilling holes in the ground. From these cores, he tries to make a chart of the layers of rock and sand thousands of feet below the surface of the earth.

Geologists using skin-diving equipment explore the offshore ocean floor (see SKIN DIVING). They examine rock formations and collect rock samples. An instrument called the *marine sonoprobe* enables oil hunters to analyze subsurface formations by means of reflected sound waves. Waterproof cameras photograph the ocean floor.

Analyzing Earth Conditions. The geophysicist provides the geologist with information about the type and general characteristics of the rock structure below the surface in any area of the earth. The geologist uses this information to determine the possible location of oil reserves. The chief instruments used by the geophysicist include the gravimeter, seismograph, and magnetometer.

The Gravimeter (pronounced *gruh VIM uh tur*), or gravity meter, records the pull of gravity at the earth's surface. Different kinds of rock affect the pull of gravity in different ways. Rocks with greater densities, for example, increase the pull of gravity (see DENSITY). Many readings taken with a gravimeter over a large area furnish clues to the shape and depth of the underground rock layers.

The Seismograph (pronounced *SIZE moh graf*) measures the intensity of the earth's tremors, or vibrations,

Hunting for Petroleum. In the air, a streamlined magnetometer, *above*, helps locate oil by measuring the earth's magnetism. On the ground, geologists, *below*, chip samples of rock for study.

American Petroleum Institute

and the time it takes them to travel through the ground (see SEISMOGRAPH). An oil explorer uses a modified type of seismograph. He bores a shallow hole in the ground, lowers an explosive charge into the hole, and sets off an explosion. Shock waves from the explosion bounce off underground rocks, and reflect back to measuring instruments on the surface of the earth. The time it takes the shock waves to reach an underground rock layer and return to the surface shows how deep the layer lies. The time also furnishes clues to the type of rock formation.

The Magnetometer (pronounced MAG nuh TOM uh tur) records differences in the earth's magnetism. The magnetic pull of the earth varies with the type of rock structure below the ground. When the magnetic readings show a considerable difference from one area to another, they may indicate the presence of conditions favorable for the formation of oil. Geophysicists use a *flying magnetometer* to measure magnetic differences over large areas. The flying magnetometer is a small, bomb-shaped device contained in or suspended from an airplane. The magnetometer contains a magnetically sensitive unit that is only about as large as a cigarette. This unit measures variations in the strength of the earth's magnetic field.

Drilling an Oil Well

Drilling for oil is a tough, highly skilled, and often dangerous job. A drilling crew needs the strength and skill of a well-trained football team. At the base of the derrick, the oilmen guide long lengths of pipe in and out of the hole with the precision of a woman threading a needle. They are helped by a worker on a *monkey board*, a platform high in the derrick. Months of round-the-clock work may go into drilling a well. As the drill sinks deeper into the ground, the suspense gradually builds up. All the men are thinking the same thing: "Will we strike oil?" If they succeed, the excitement reaches a climax when the first drops of the black liquid flow from the well. When their work is finished, the drillers move on to a new location—and a new challenge.

Setting Up the Derrick. After the geologist has selected the best spot for drilling, huge trucks bring in heavy pieces of steel and drilling equipment. A crew

Humble Oil and Refining Company

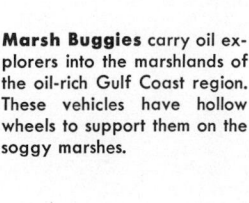

Marsh Buggies carry oil explorers into the marshlands of the oil-rich Gulf Coast region. These vehicles have hollow wheels to support them on the soggy marshes.

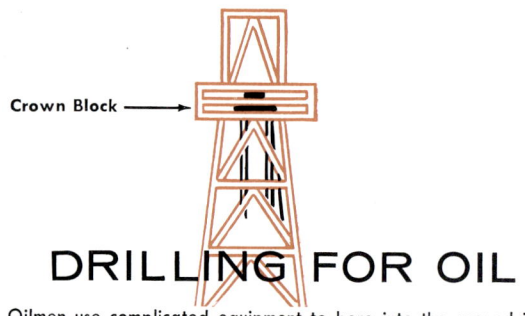

DRILLING FOR OIL

Crown Block

Oilmen use complicated equipment to bore into the ground in search of petroleum. The derrick and other equipment are called the *rig*. The most widely used rig has a tough *bit* that bores through the earth much as a carpenter's drill bores through wood. The bit is attached to the *drill pipe* which is lowered or lifted out of the well by means of hoisting machinery called the *draw works*.

of men called *rig builders* use steel beams to build a derrick over the spot where the well is to be drilled. Oilmen call the derrick and other drilling equipment a *rig*. The derrick usually stands between 80 and 200 feet high, depending on the depth of the well. It serves chiefly to help lift the drill pipe and casing in and out of the hole. The derrick supports a system of pulleys and blocks for lifting extremely heavy weights. The petroleum industry also uses portable *jackknife derricks*. These derricks have hinges in the middle, and are bent in half so they can be carried on trucks from well to well.

Methods of Drilling. After setting up the derrick and installing diesel engines or other power equipment, workers begin the job of drilling into the ground. Oilmen use two drilling methods: cable-tool and rotary.

Cable-Tool Drilling is a simple process. The men drill a hole in the ground much as a person might punch a hole in a piece of wood by hammering a nail through it. Cable-tool equipment consists of a heavy *bit* (cutting tool) attached to a long steel cable by means of an iron

Oil Drillers Pull the Pipe Out of the Hole to change the bit. During drilling, the rotary table (*arrows*) turns the drill pipe which provides the twisting motion to the bit.

API; Standard Oil Co.

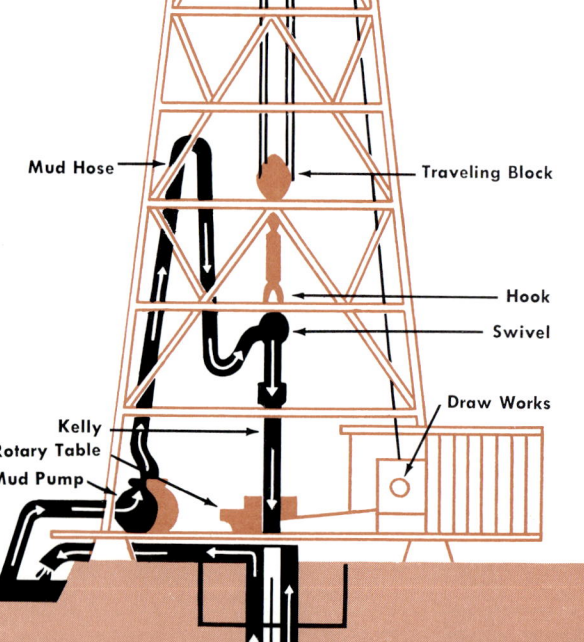

Mud Hose — Traveling Block

Hook

Swivel

Draw Works

Kelly
Rotary Table
Mud Pump

Casing

Drill Pipe

Bit

The Jagged Teeth of a Rock Bit cut through hard underground formations.

Ewing Galloway

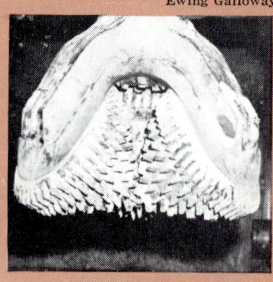

Bit

rod called a *stem*. The cable raises the bit, then drops it again and again. The dropping force drives the bit deeper and deeper into the earth. The jagged teeth of the bit crush soil and rock. From time to time, the workers raise the bit out of the hole and force water into the opening to flush out the soil and bits of rock. A long pipe called a *bailer* removes water, mud, and rock from the hole.

Drillers sank the first oil wells by means of the cable-tool method. Since the early 1900's, they have used this process largely to drill shallow holes through soft beds of rock.

Rotary Drilling is the most important method. It requires complicated equipment, but works on a simple principle. A rotary drill bores through the earth much as a carpenter's drill bores through wood. The main parts of a rotary drill are (1) the drill stem, (2) the rotary table, and (3) the draw works.

The *drill stem* includes the kelly, the drill pipe, the drill collar, and the bit. The *kelly* is the uppermost part of the drill stem. It is a hollow steel tube about 40 feet long with four or six sides. The *drill pipe* consists of 30-foot *lengths* (sections) of hollow steel tubing that screw together to form one long piece of pipe. The uppermost length of pipe is attached to the kelly, and the bottom end connects with the *drill collar*. This extra-heavy joint of hollow steel pipe fastens the drill pipe to the *bit*. Drillers use several types of bits to cut through different types of rock formations. A wedge-shaped piece of steel called a *fishtail bit* is used on soft formations. Drillers cut through hard formations with *rock bits*. The hard steel rock bit has a group of rotating teeth on its end. These teeth resemble gears. They grind and crush rock.

The *rotary table* is a heavy steel turntable, from 10 to 36 inches across. It rests on the floor of the derrick. An engine turns the rotary table, which turns the bit. A system of gears connects the rotary table to the power equipment. The square or hexagonal (six-sided) *bushing* (opening) in the rotary table holds the kelly.

The *draw works* is the heart of the equipment used to lower and raise the drill stem in and out of the hole. The main parts of the draw works are a hoisting drum, a hoisting cable, and two large *blocks* (sets of pulleys). The cable runs from the drum over the *crown block* at the top of the derrick to the *traveling block*, which hangs inside the derrick. When it is necessary to raise or lower the drill stem, the traveling block is attached to the kelly by means of a hook.

The Drilling Crew installs the drilling equipment and drills the well. A cable-tool drilling crew has two men. These are a *driller* who operates the equipment, and a *tool dresser* who sharpens the bits and does other jobs. In rotary drilling, the crew includes a driller and three to five workmen called *roughnecks*. A driller heads each crew and directs the work of the other men. Crews usually work 24 hours a day in three eight-hour shifts called *tours* (pronounced *towers*). The following sections describe rotary-drilling methods.

Starting to Drill. As soon as the crew *rigs up* (assembles) the rotary drill, the driller gives the order to begin *spudding in* (drilling). Diesel engines near the derrick turn the rotary table and kelly, and the bit digs into the earth. As the bit drives deeper, the top of the kelly sinks to the level of the rotary table. The crew then stops the

power, pulls up the kelly, disconnects it, and adds a section of drill pipe between the kelly and the drill collar. Then the men reattach the kelly and continue drilling. They repeat this process each time the top of the kelly approaches the rotary table. A well-trained crew can complete the entire operation in about 45 seconds. Drillers add a new section of pipe for about every 30 feet that the drill bites into the earth.

The Drilling Mud. As the bit bores into the ground, pumps force liquid mud down through the kelly and the drill pipe. The chief use of the mud is to carry *cuttings* (pieces of rock) out of the well through the space between the drill stem and the wall of the hole. The mud also plasters the walls of the well with a thick cake that helps prevent cave-ins, and helps cool and lubricate the bit.

Pulling the Pipe. Workers change the bit when it becomes dull, or when the rock formation changes. Each time they change the bit, they must pull all the pipe out of the hole. This is called *coming out of the hole*. Sometimes several thousand feet of drill pipe must be lifted out of the hole.

First the workers stop the pumps. Then they stop the rotary table and pull off the bushing that holds the kelly. The traveling block lifts the pipe out of the hole. The workers unscrew the drill stem into sections of three or four lengths each, depending on the height of the derrick. Then the workers stack the drill pipe upright in the derrick.

After pulling the bottom section of pipe, the men change the bit, reassemble the pipe, and lower it back into the hole. A worker climbs high in the derrick to a monkey board to help guide the pipe in and out of the well.

Whipstocking. Sometimes a bit or drill pipe breaks off inside the well and forms an obstruction. The men use special *fishing* tools to try to pull the obstruction out of the well. If this fails, they may use a method called *whipstocking* to drill around the obstruction. The driller pulls the pipe and fills the well with cement to a point just above the obstruction. Then he puts a large steel tool called a *whipstock* into the well. The whipstock is pointed at the top and has a groove in it like a shoehorn. When the drilling begins again, the bit passes through the whipstock and slides by the obstruction, making a new channel.

Oilmen also use whipstocks to drill a well at an angle. Many offshore wells are drilled from shore using this method. Several whipstocks gradually slant the well so that the pipe reaches far out under the ocean bottom. This process is called *directional drilling*.

Casing. To prevent the well from caving in, it is lined with steel pipe called *casing*. The casing also prevents substances in the well from contaminating fresh water in the ground. The casing is surrounded by cement to prevent gases and liquids from moving along the outside of the casing.

To install the casing, oilmen weld together 16- to 34-foot sections of pipe, and lower them into the hole. Then they pump wet cement into the casing, and cover the cement with a special plug that can be drilled through. Liquid mud is then pumped into the casing on top of this plug. The mud pushes the plug down the

Shell Oil Co.

Christmas Trees and Oil Pumps are familiar sights in oil fields. A Christmas tree, *left*, is a cluster of control valves used to cap a well. The "walking" beam of a pump, *above*, moves up and down to suck oil from a well that does not flow naturally.

casing, forcing the wet cement up around the outside. The plug goes to the bottom of the casing and holds the cement in place while it hardens. Then the men drill through the plug, and continue to drill the well.

Bringing Oil to the Surface

In the early days of the oil industry, many wells were wasteful *gushers* that shot oil and natural gas high into the air, sometimes for days. Today, oilmen work carefully to prevent gushers and to control the flow of oil. Scientific production methods have almost completely eliminated gushers.

A driller knows when the bit strikes oil. He examines the drilling mud for traces of it. He also studies the drill cuttings and makes special tests. The drilling crew becomes tense the moment that the bit hits oil. One mistake in bringing in the well may spoil the work of many weeks, and turn a producing well into a dry hole.

After determining that the bit has reached an oil-producing zone, the driller pulls the drill pipe from the hole. Only the casing remains. Usually drillers install an additional casing, called an *oil string* or *production string*, to protect the oil-producing zone from sand and other geological formations exposed during drilling. If the oil string ends above the production zone, drillers sometimes install a long piece of pipe called a *liner* that runs from the bottom of the casing to the production zone. The liner has many holes in it. Finally, a smaller pipe called the *tubing* is lowered into the well. The tubing extends from the liner to the surface of the ground. Oil travels through the holes in the liner and up the tubing to the surface.

Energy-Drive. Several different kinds of underground pressure force oil to the surface. Such pressure is called *energy-drive*. When a new field is opened, petroleum engineers want to know as quickly as possible which type of drive it has. The type of energy-drive influences the way the oil should be taken out of the ground in order to waste as little as possible. The three main kinds of drive are (1) water drive, (2) gas-cap drive, and (3) dissolved-gas drive.

Water-Drive fields have tremendous amounts of water under and at the edges of the oil deposits. The water pushes the oil toward the well and up to the surface.

Gas-Cap-Drive fields have a great cap of natural gas on top of the oil deposits. The gas pushes down on the oil and forces it up the well.

Dissolved-Gas-Drive fields do not have enough water to force up the oil, and most of the natural gas is dissolved in the oil. Because of this, it may be necessary to pump the oil from the time the well is brought in.

The Christmas Tree. Wells in water-drive and gas-cap-drive fields sometimes flow naturally. When the bit first strikes the production zone, the weight of the drilling mud usually controls the first flow until the workers install a *Christmas tree*. This is a group of control valves placed at the upper end of the tubing and casing. The valve system received its name because it slightly resembles a Christmas tree in shape. Pipes lead from the Christmas tree to a tank that separates the oil and natural gas. The oil goes to storage tanks in the field. Oilmen may pump some of the gas back into the field to maintain the underground pressure and keep the oil flowing. They also use the gas to run machinery at the oil field, or they may sell it to natural-gas companies for use in homes and factories.

Wells in dissolved-gas-drive fields almost never flow naturally. Most others stop flowing naturally after a time, unless the oilmen use special methods, such as injecting water or gas into an oil pool, to maintain the pressure. After a well stops flowing, the oilmen install pumps to suck the oil from underground. About nine-tenths of the wells in the United States are *pumpers*.

Refining Petroleum

The petroleum industry refines crude oil to obtain useful products. Refineries and chemical plants account for about a fifth of the industry's total investment in property and equipment. The United States has about 300 refineries that range in capacity from 40 to 365,000 barrels of oil a day. The world's largest refinery is in Abadan, Iran. It can process 412,000 barrels daily when running at full capacity.

Petroleum is composed of thousands of different combinations of just two elements—hydrogen and carbon. These combinations are called *hydrocarbons* (see HYDRO-CARBON). The hydrocarbons give special characteristics to the *fractions* (parts) of petroleum. Some of these fractions, such as gasoline and kerosene, are valuable products in themselves. Refineries must change other fractions before they can be used. Separating the fractions and converting them to useful products are the chief jobs of an oil refinery.

Distillation, or *fractionating*, is the first step in the refining process. It separates the various fractions of crude oil.

The fact that different hydrocarbons *vaporize* (boil) at different temperatures makes possible the process of distillation (see DISTILLATION [Fractional Distillation]). In a *pipe still*, oilmen start the distillation by running crude oil into pipes that pass through a furnace. As the oil is heated, gasoline is one of the first fractions to vaporize. Kerosene vaporizes next. At higher temperatures, such fractions as diesel oil and *lubricant stocks* (used in making lubricants) boil.

The mixture of hot vapors and liquid goes into a *fractionating tower*, or *bubble tower*. The vapor rises through the tower, which separates the fractions in a continuous process. Different fractions cool and condense at different levels in the tower and are drawn off.

For example, heavy fuel oils condense at the bottom of the tower, and gasoline condenses at the top.

Conversion. In the early days of the oil industry, the refining process consisted chiefly of distillation. Oilmen discarded the parts of crude petroleum that could not be distilled into kerosene or made into greases. The small quantities of gasoline needed in the early 1900's could be supplied by distillation. As the automobile became popular, the petroleum industry sought some way of increasing gasoline production. This was done by developing conversion processes that changed less useful fractions into gasoline and other valuable products. These processes change the molecules of the fractions by heating them under pressure, or by contact with a catalyst (see CATALYSIS).

The chief conversion methods include (1) thermal

DRILLING FOR OFFSHORE OIL

Rich petroleum deposits often lie beneath the water off seacoasts. To tap these offshore deposits, oilmen often use portable drilling platforms, *right*. A tugboat, *below*, tows the platform to the drilling site where the *spuds*, or legs, are lowered until they rest on the sea bottom. This platform can operate in water more than 100 feet deep, and drill to a depth of 20,000 feet. In addition to the derrick and drilling machinery, the platform has air-conditioned sleeping, eating, and recreation rooms for its 45-man crew.
R. G. LeTourneau Inc.

REFINING PETROLEUM

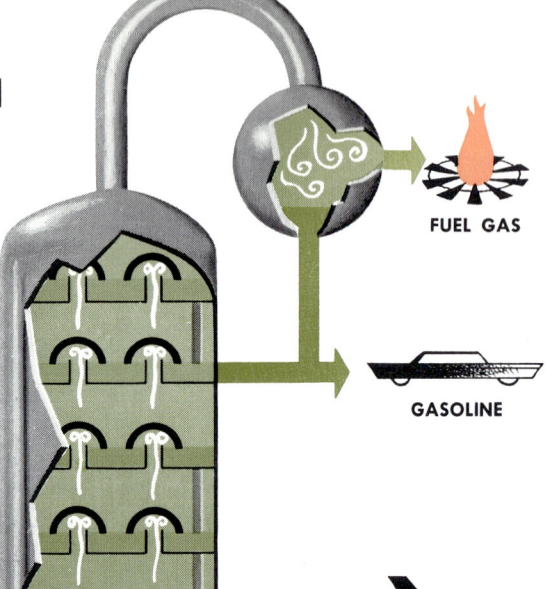

FUEL GAS

GASOLINE

Humble Oil and Refining Co.

Oil refineries break petroleum down into its various *fractions*, or parts, by means of fractional distillation. This takes place in tall fractionating towers, *above*. Crude oil, heated to a vapor, rises through the tower. Different fractions condense at different levels and are drawn off. The fractions, such as gasoline and kerosene, are further refined and processed.

KEROSENE—JET FUEL

HEATING OIL

LUBRICATING OIL

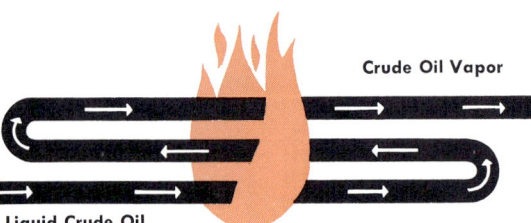

Crude Oil Vapor

Liquid Crude Oil

Crude Oil Is Heated to a Vapor in a furnace. The vapor leaves the furnace at a temperature of about 750° F. A pipe carries the vapor to the base of the fractionating tower.

Steam   Steam

**RESIDUAL PRODUCTS—
ASPHALT AND HEAVY FUEL OIL**

Live Steam is Fed into the Tower to speed up the process. The *residue*, or unvaporized oil, is drawn off from the tower and converted to heavy fuel oil, asphalt, and other products.

RESIDUE ▷

306

cracking, (2) catalytic cracking, (3) polymerization, (4) alkylation, (5) hydrogenation, and (6) reforming.

Thermal Cracking is the application of steady heat and pressure to *crack* (break down) heavier hydrocarbons into lighter ones such as gasoline. The first thermal-cracking method was called the Burton process, after its inventor, William M. Burton. The oil industry first used it in 1913. The thermal-cracking process increases the quantity and quality of gasoline obtained from crude oil. Gasoline produced by this process has a higher *octane number* than gasoline made by straight distillation. Octane number is a measure of the tendency of fuels to knock, or "ping," when used in high-compression, internal-combustion engines such as those in automobiles. The higher the octane number, the less knock. See GASOLINE (Kinds); OCTANE NUMBER.

Catalytic Cracking, sometimes called *cat cracking*, uses a catalyst to help break down petroleum fractions. This process produces more gasoline of higher octane number than thermal cracking does. Petroleum engineers pass petroleum vapor over alumina-silica mixtures, certain types of clay, or other catalysts (see ALUMINA; SILICA). Catalytic cracking came into use in 1936.

A newer type of catalytic cracking, called *fluid cat cracking*, is the most widely used process. Refineries use it to produce aviation gasoline, raw materials for synthetic rubber, and other petroleum products. In fluid cat cracking, a powdered catalyst flows through the petroleum like a fluid. Refineries began using this method in 1942.

Polymerization is the opposite of cracking. Instead of breaking down fractions, this process combines smaller fractions into larger ones. Refineries use controlled heat and pressure to convert natural gas and waste gases produced by cracking and other operations. The gases are condensed into high-octane liquids used in making gasoline. Polymerization came into general use in the mid-1930's. See POLYMERIZATION.

Alkylation does much the same job as polymerization. It combines gaseous hydrocarbons into a liquid suitable for gasoline. *Alkylate*, the product of alkylation, serves as an important ingredient in high-octane aviation gasoline. It is also an important part of most high-grade gasolines.

Hydrogenation is another way to obtain more useful products from crude oil. During the cracking process, refineries add hydrogen to heavier fractions, such as gas oil or fuel oil. The heavier fractions contain less hydrogen than do the lighter fractions. The addition of hydrogen makes heavier fractions lighter.

Reforming became important during World War II to obtain toluene for the explosive TNT, and to increase production of high-octane gasoline and other chemical products (see TNT). Reforming units in refineries produce important chemicals called *aromatics*. These include benzene, toluene, and xylene.

Chemical Treatment is given to gasoline, kerosene, lubricating oils, and other petroleum products to improve them and to remove sulfur, wax, sludge, and other unwanted materials. The oldest lubricating-oil process treats the oil with acid, caustic, and clay to take out heavy materials that would form sludge and cause engine parts to stick together (see CAUSTIC). Filters remove wax from oil to keep the oil from hardening in cold weather.

A newer method, the *solvent-refining* process, uses chemicals to dissolve one part of the oil from another. This also removes heavy materials and wax. Refineries blend lubricating oils of various *viscosities* (thicknesses) according to how the oil will be used. Synthetic materials added to the oil make it flow freely at low temperatures, protect engine parts from corrosion, and give the oil other special properties. Wax separated from lubricating oil is first purified. Then it is sold to make candles; as paraffin for kitchen use; for coating wax paper; and for other uses.

Petroleum Conservation

Petroleum, like other minerals, cannot be replaced once it is used. Industry and government have adopted many conservation measures to ensure that oil reserves will not be wasted.

Conservation Laws in petroleum-producing states aim to prevent the waste of oil. These regulations control methods and rates of production. They restrict the production of an oil field. They also regulate abandonment of wells that have ceased to produce. Abandoned wells can damage underground water resources if improperly plugged. Other conservation laws regulate the number of wells that can be drilled in a given area, so that the wells will not be drilled too close together. Most oil-conservation laws provide for a state commission to administer the laws. A major federal law was the Connally "Hot Oil" act of 1935. This law prohibits oil not produced in accordance with state conservation laws from being sold in interstate commerce. The provincial governments of Canada regulate oil production in ways similar to those used by the states.

Oil-Field Conservation includes three methods: secondary recovery, pressure maintenance, and plugging back.

Secondary-Recovery Methods are used to obtain crude oil from areas that can no longer produce oil economically. One secondary-recovery method uses either water or a gas to sweep oil from rock formations and into nearby wells. Oilmen pump the water or gas into the rock by means of *service* or *input* wells. In another secondary-recovery method, called *thermal recovery*, oilmen use heat to make thick oil flow more freely so it can be pumped out of the well. In one kind of thermal recovery, air is pumped into the formation, and the oil is set on fire. Although some of the oil burns, the heat permits most of the oil to be recovered. Hot water and steam are also used in thermal recovery.

Pressure Maintenance enables oilmen to get the maximum production from a well without using pumps. In this method, gas forced into oil-bearing formations produces enough pressure to force the oil to the surface without pumping. The gas used for this and the secondary-recovery processes is often separated from the petroleum produced in the field. After separation, the gas goes to a *gas conservation plant*, which removes such products as butane, propane, and natural gasoline. *Butane* and *propane* are used for liquefied petroleum gas. *Natural gasoline*, also called *casinghead gasoline*, is added to refinery-produced gasolines. The remaining gas is pumped back into the field or used as natural gas.

PETROLEUM

Plugging Back. Good oil-field practice requires drilling to the deepest oil-bearing formations. After pumping and secondary-recovery methods have drained the deepest pool, oilmen may plug back to shallower deposits if they exist. They cement off the bottom of the hole to the level of the next deepest deposits. Then they lower a *perforating gun* into the hole. This special type of gun shoots bullets of jet charges to make holes in the casing opposite the new producing zone. Oil then flows into the well through the holes.

Refinery Conservation. The miles of pipeline in refineries offer opportunities for oil to leak out. Large refineries often have conservation departments that check joints, pipes, and pumps for leaks. They take measurements to detect losses from pipes, processing units, and storage tanks. Refineries use millions of gallons of water a day in their coolers and condensers. After using the water, they run it through *settling basins*. In these basins, any oil in the water rises to the surface, and workers skim it off and return it to the tanks. Refineries paint the roofs of storage tanks a light color that reflects heat and reduces loss by evaporation.

The Petroleum Industry

The petroleum industry ranks as one of the largest in the world. In the United States, about $1\frac{1}{2}$ million persons earn their living from petroleum. The Canadian oil industry also provides jobs for thousands of workers. In the Middle East, petroleum furnishes the chief income of Iran, Iraq, Saudi Arabia, and other countries. Mexico and Venezuela are among the Latin-American nations with important petroleum industries. Some of these nations have used oil profits to pay for programs that raise the living standards of their people.

In the United States, the petroleum industry ranks as one of the giants of American business. The production and refining activities of the petroleum industry extend throughout most of the world. Its customers include almost everyone in the United States and millions of persons in other countries. Petroleum companies have an investment of over $64 billion in plants, property, and machinery. More than 42,000 companies, not including service stations, make up the petroleum industry in the United States.

In addition to providing jobs for thousands of workers, the industry pays dividends to about 3 million stockholders, and royalties to thousands of landowners. Taxes paid on petroleum products play an important part in supporting governmental operations. Some states build and maintain roads and provide other services with money collected from gasoline taxes.

The petroleum industry also ranks as one of the world's biggest customers for the products of other industries. It rents more tank cars and operates more tanker ships than any other industry. Oil companies are among the biggest buyers of steel, iron, motor vehicles, electric power, gasoline engines, cement, rubber, paint, and many other products.

The United States Department of the Interior aids the petroleum industry through the Office of Oil and Gas, and the Bureau of Mines. These serve primarily as research, fact-finding, and coordinating organizations. They work for adequate development, distribution, and use of oil and gas resources and facilities. The Department of the Interior is also aided by such advisory boards as the National Petroleum Council. The department also works closely with such industrial trade associations as the American Petroleum Institute, the American Gas Association, the National Petroleum Refiners Association, and the Independent Petroleum Association of America.

In Canada, the petroleum industry has expanded rapidly since prospectors made a great oil strike at Leduc, Alta., in 1947. It ranks as the fifth largest manufacturing industry in the country. The Department of Energy, Mines, and Resources is the chief federal agency that aids the petroleum industry. The provinces have similar government departments.

In Other Countries. Oil companies of the United States and Europe have discovered and developed most of the petroleum industries in Africa, the Middle East, and Latin America. In many countries in these areas, oil companies from other nations operate the petroleum industries and share the profits with the governments. Oil companies from the United States, Great Britain, France, and The Netherlands produce oil in Iran. The Arabian American Oil Company (Aramco) is the largest operator in Saudi Arabia. The joint British-American Kuwait Oil Company operates that country's petroleum industry. Iraq's petroleum is produced by the Iraq Petroleum Company owned by several companies in other countries. Companies from the United States and other countries operate in Algeria, Libya, and Venezuela. British and American oil companies developed

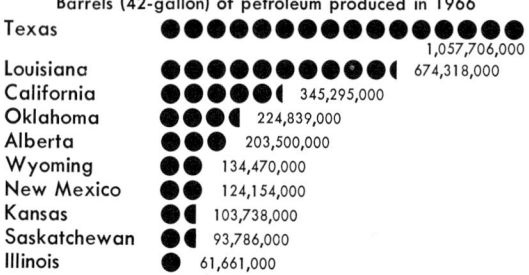

LEADING PETROLEUM PRODUCING STATES AND PROVINCES

Barrels (42-gallon) of petroleum produced in 1966

Texas	1,057,706,000
Louisiana	674,318,000
California	345,295,000
Oklahoma	224,839,000
Alberta	203,500,000
Wyoming	134,470,000
New Mexico	124,154,000
Kansas	103,738,000
Saskatchewan	93,786,000
Illinois	61,661,000

Sources: Bureau of Mines; Dominion Bureau of Statistics.

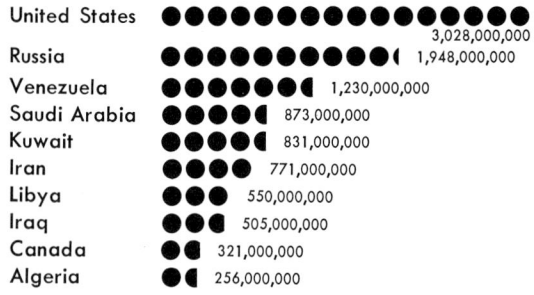

LEADING PETROLEUM PRODUCING COUNTRIES

Barrels (42-gallon) of petroleum produced in 1966

United States	3,028,000,000
Russia	1,948,000,000
Venezuela	1,230,000,000
Saudi Arabia	873,000,000
Kuwait	831,000,000
Iran	771,000,000
Libya	550,000,000
Iraq	505,000,000
Canada	321,000,000
Algeria	256,000,000

Source: Bureau of Mines.

the petroleum industry of Mexico. But the Mexican government seized the oil fields in 1938, and has operated the industry since that time.

History

In Early Times, man used petroleum that seeped to the surface from underground springs. The ancient Egyptians coated mummies with *pitch* (natural asphalt). The Old Testament tells how the mother of Moses coated his cradle with pitch so that it would float on the Nile River. The Chinese found natural gas while drilling for salt, and used natural gas for fuel as far back as 1000 B.C. About 600 B.C., King Nebuchadnezzar used asphalt to build the walls and pave the streets of Babylon. The Assyrians used asphalt to hold bricks together in the buildings of Nineveh, and the Persians also used it to build their cities. Boatmen on the Euphrates River made vessels of woven reeds smeared with asphalt. The people of Iraq still sail such boats on the Euphrates (see IRAQ [picture, Round Kufas]).

American Indians used petroleum hundreds of years before the white man came. The Toltec Indians of Mexico set mosaic tiles with bitumen (see BITUMEN). Remains of ancient oil wells have been found in the oil regions of Pennsylvania, Kentucky, and Ohio. No one knows how long ago the inhabitants dug these wells, but trees hundreds of years old grow over some of them. Jesuit missionaries in North America found Indians scooping up oil from *seepages* (surface pools) in the early 1600's. The Indians used the oil for fuel and medicine.

By 1750, many oil seepages had been found in New York, Pennsylvania, and West Virginia (then part of Virginia). Wells drilled for salt often produced oil as well. Saltmakers generally regarded oil as a nuisance that interfered with salt production. But some white men borrowed the Indian custom of using oil as medicine. About 1847, Samuel M. Kier of Pittsburgh began bottling petroleum for medicine as a side line of his salt business. The frontiersman Kit Carson collected oil from a seepage in Wyoming, and sold it to pioneers as axle grease for their wagons.

In 1852, the Canadian geologist Abraham Gesner (1797-1864) discovered kerosene, commonly called *coal oil*. It came into wide use for lighting lamps and lanterns. Some kerosene was distilled from coal, and some came from petroleum.

The Birth of the Oil Industry. Some historians believe that Romania may have had the first oil industry. Romania produced about 2,000 barrels of oil in 1857. Workmen used bags and buckets to bring up oil from hand-dug wells. Also in 1857, James Miller Williams (1818-1890) of Canada dug an oil well and established a refinery near present-day Oil Springs, Ont. He distilled and sold oil for lamps. But most historians trace the beginning of the oil industry on a large scale to 1859, when Edwin L. Drake (1819-1880) drilled his famous well near Titusville, Pa.

The story of Drake's well began in the early 1850's. George H. Bissel (1821-1884), a lawyer and businessman of New Haven, Conn., became interested in the possibilities of oil as a fuel and lubricant. In 1854, he and Jonathan G. Eveleth of New York City formed the Pennsylvania Rock Oil Company to produce oil on a farm Bissel had rented near Titusville.

Bissel spent the next four years searching for backers for his project and trying to develop a way to get the oil out of the ground. In 1857, he decided to drill for oil in the same way that saltmakers drilled for brine. But the company went bankrupt. In 1858, a group of businessmen formed the Seneca Oil Company. This firm hired Drake, a retired railroad conductor, to drill a well near Titusville.

Drake used a wooden rig and a steam-operated drill similar to the cable-tool drills of today. His crew consisted of a blacksmith named William A. ("Uncle Billy") Smith and Smith's two sons. Drake started drilling in June, 1859. When water and cave-ins threatened the well, Drake drove an iron pipe 39 feet into the ground to solid rock, and drilled inside the pipe. This pipe served as a casing.

Drake struck oil at a depth of $69\frac{1}{2}$ feet on Aug. 27, 1859. The oil bubbled to within a few feet of the surface. Drake put a pump on the well, which produced 10 to 35 barrels a day. The company sold the oil for $20 a barrel. Other men soon drilled wells nearby, after Drake showed them how to do it. As a result, the price of oil dropped to 10 cents a barrel in less than three years.

Growth of the Oil Industry. By the early 1860's, the Pennsylvania hills flowed with oil. Oilmen drilled thousands of wells. Bustling, crowded boom towns of tents and shacks sprang up almost overnight. At first, wagons and river barges carried the oil from the fields to refineries along the Atlantic Coast. Soon railroads built branch lines to the fields and also began carrying oil. In 1865, Samuel van Syckel built the first oil pipeline. It ran five miles from an oil field near Titusville to a railroad. A 60-mile line of 3-inch pipe was built from the oil regions to Pittsburgh in 1874. This line moved 3,500 barrels a day. Armed guards protected the early lines from wagon drivers and railroad men who considered pipelines a threat to their business.

Important oil-producing states of the 1880's included Pennsylvania, Kentucky, Ohio, Illinois, and Indiana. Prospectors found oil in Kansas in 1894, and in 1901 large-scale production began in Texas with the opening of the Spindletop field near Beaumont. Large-scale production started in Oklahoma in 1910. American production rose from 2,000 barrels in 1859 to 64 million barrels a year by 1900.

Commercial oil production spread rapidly throughout the world. Italy took its place as a small producer as early as 1860. After Italy, in order, production began in Canada, Russia, Poland, Japan, Germany, India, Indonesia, Peru, Mexico, Argentina, and Trinidad. The first important oil discoveries in the Middle East were made in Iran in 1908. Prospectors struck oil in commercial quantities in Iraq in 1927 and in Saudi Arabia in 1938. Commercial quantities of oil were later found in the small Arabian states of Kuwait and Qatar.

The United States has led in world oil production since 1860, except for the brief period from 1898 to 1901, when Russia took the lead.

Oil and the Automobile. In the 1800's, kerosene for lamps ranked as the chief product of the petroleum industry. Refineries also produced gasoline as a byproduct of kerosene. But gasoline exploded when burned in a kerosene lamp, and no practical use could

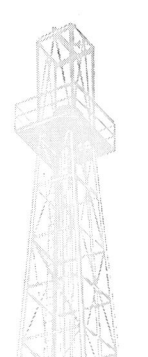

PETROLEUM THROUGH THE AGES

Man has used petroleum in one form or another for thousands of years. At first he found it seeping from the ground. Later, men learned to sink deep wells to tap underground pools of oil.

The Bible Says Noah Used Pitch, a natural form of asphalt, to seal the seams of the Ark before the Deluge covered the earth.

The Ancient Egyptians Greased Chariot Axles with petroleum that they found seeping from the ground.

Drake's Well launched the modern petroleum industry on Aug. 27, 1859, when it struck oil near Titusville, Pa. Edwin L. Drake, shown wearing a top hat, was a retired railroad conductor.

American Petroleum Institute

The Ancient Chinese Used Petroleum obtained from wells they drilled chiefly to find salt. They used oil and gas for fuel.

be found for it. Refineries often dumped gasoline into creeks and rivers to get rid of it.

Then, about 1900, gas and electric lights began replacing kerosene lamps, and the automobile rolled onto the American scene. The United States had only about 8,000 of the strange-looking, gasoline-powered horseless carriages in 1900. But, by 1910, more than 450,000 automobiles traveled on United States roads.

In those days, 100 gallons of crude oil produced only about 11 gallons of gasoline. Oilmen could not increase crude-oil production enough to meet the demand. Every increase in production resulted in making more kerosene and other products that could not be sold. The thermal-cracking process, introduced in 1913, helped solve the problem of making more gasoline from a barrel of petroleum. By 1918, oilmen could make 25 gallons of gasoline from 100 gallons of crude oil. Continued research and new methods increased this figure. By the mid-1960's, refineries produced nearly 45 gallons of gasoline from 100 gallons of crude oil.

Research also resulted in better oil products and many new ones. As engineers developed more powerful airplane and automobile engines, the oil industry provided better gasoline to run them. Improved gasoline, in turn, made possible even better engines.

After about 1920, oil caused great changes on farms. Gasoline taxes provided money to build good roads in country areas. Asphalt from petroleum provided an inexpensive way to pave highways, and road oil improved dusty farm roads. Farmers used more and more petroleum-powered tractors and other equipment to produce larger crops.

In World War II, petroleum supplied huge amounts of fuel and lubricants for airplanes, tanks, trucks, and ships, as well as fuel for flame throwers and fire bombs. It also provided raw materials for synthetic rubber, self-sealing gasoline tanks, and other products. Petroleum supplied toluene for TNT in bombs and shells, various compounds for waterproofing tents, asphalt for airfield runways, and ingredients for salves to treat the wounded. The United States government rationed gasoline and fuel oil from December, 1942, to August, 1945. Most other countries also rationed petroleum. During the war, the American petroleum industry supplied more than eight-tenths of the Allies' aviation gasoline. Petroleum products made up more than half of all United States shipments overseas.

The World Struggle for Oil became an important issue in national and international politics after World War II. Increased industrialization and rapidly growing populations heightened the need for this vital source of power.

In the United States, the search for new oil resources centered around the offshore deposits of Louisiana, Texas, California, and other states. These states claimed ownership of the *tidelands* (offshore areas within their traditional boundaries). The boundaries extended up to $10\frac{1}{2}$ miles from the coast. But, in 1945, President Harry S. Truman stated that these lands belonged to the United States and were "subject to its control and jurisdiction." In 1945 and 1951, he vetoed bills that would have granted ownership of these lands to the states.

The oil industry had been drilling offshore on a small scale since the mid-1930's. The tidelands dispute delayed development of new offshore wells, because oil companies did not know who legally owned the land, the states or the federal government. In 1953, President Dwight D. Eisenhower signed a law that granted states rights to offshore lands up to the ends of their historic boundaries. This law, known as the Submerged Lands Act, provides that states along the Gulf Coast must prove that their historic boundaries extend out up to $10\frac{1}{2}$ miles. The Submerged Lands Act paved the way for the states to lease offshore land to oil companies. Under the law, the federal government has title and jurisdiction to the land beyond the state boundaries.

On the international scene, the struggle for oil centered in the Middle East. In 1951, the government of Iran took over control of that country's British-owned oil industry. The British pulled their workers out of Iran. The lack of skilled Iranian technicians to run the industry resulted in an almost complete shutdown.

In 1954, after a change in government in Iran, a group of major oil companies reached an agreement with the Iranian government that settled the dispute. Under the agreement, a government corporation, the National Iranian Oil Company (N.I.O.C.), retained ownership of Iran's oil and the buildings and equipment of the country's petroleum industry. The oil companies formed an exploration and producing company and a refining company to operate the wells and the refinery at Abadan. The members of the group also formed 17 separate trading companies that bought the oil produced in Iran from the N.I.O.C. and sold it in other countries. Soon after the settlement, Iranian oil again began to flow to world markets.

Much oil from the Middle East is transported by ship westward around the Arabian Peninsula, north across the Red Sea, and through the Suez Canal to the Mediterranean Sea. From there, the oil is shipped to markets in Europe and the United States. In 1956, Egypt seized control of the Suez Canal. Britain and France then attacked Egypt, and tried to restore international control of the waterway. The United Nations settled the conflict, and the Suez Canal was reopened in 1957 under Egyptian control. The Arab-Israeli war of 1967 again closed the canal (see SUEZ CANAL). Arab countries stopped supplying petroleum to Western Europe for several months following the war.

After the Suez crisis, U.S. and European companies explored for oil in other areas to guard against any cutoff of Middle East supplies. As a result of this search, the African countries of Libya and Algeria have become leading producers of oil.

In the 1960's, oilmen increasingly directed their search for new petroleum deposits to offshore areas. They centered their exploration on submerged lands in the North Sea, between Great Britain and continental Europe. In the mid-1960's, offshore production accounted for about 16 per cent of the total petroleum output of the world's non-Communist countries.

Research and Development. In the 1950's, automobile manufacturers began producing cars with high-compression engines. These engines required gasoline of higher octanes than ever used before. Gasoline of up to 100 octane became available at service stations (see GASOLINE [Kinds of Gasoline]).

PETROLEUM

Automation in the petroleum industry reached new heights in 1957 when the Tidewater Oil Company opened the world's largest push-button refinery in Delaware. Automated refineries began operating in Mississippi and Alaska in 1963. See AUTOMATION.

Career Opportunities

The oil industry employs workers in more than 2,000 occupations, ranging from unskilled laborers to highly trained scientists and engineers.

Scientists and Engineers play a vital part in the petroleum industry. Geologists and geophysicists hunt for oil. Petroleum engineers supervise well drilling. Chemical engineers design and operate refineries. The oil industry also employs civil, mechanical, electrical, and electronic engineers. Chemists and other scientists test petroleum products and conduct research.

All these jobs require college training. High-school students interested in them should study such subjects as chemistry, physics, biology, and mathematics.

Oil-Field Workers include roughnecks, drillers, and rig builders. These men use large tools and mechanical equipment. They must have strong bodies and good physical coordination, and rank high in mechanical ability. High-school courses in industrial arts and science help train men for this field.

Machinists and Repairmen work throughout the oil industry. They include welders, painters, electricians, boilermakers, and carpenters. Such jobs require good mechanical judgment and the ability to do precision work. Most workers in this field learn their skills by on-the-job apprenticeship programs, or from experienced workers. Courses in such subjects as blueprint reading and drafting provide training for these jobs.

Checkers, Inspectors, and Equipment Operators read gauges, meters, and other instruments in oil fields and refineries, and along pipelines. They continually check all equipment to see that it runs properly, and make adjustments in the operation of machinery. Such jobs require good mechanical ability and keen perception. Workers in this group usually learn on the job, but high-school training in physics and mathematics helps prepare them.

Marketing Workers sell petroleum products and services to the public. They include salesmen, advertising personnel, and service-station attendants. These jobs require the personal qualities and business judgment to attract and retain customers. Mechanical aptitude often proves helpful.

Clerical and Administrative Workers find jobs in the offices of petroleum companies. They often advance to administrative positions. Workers in this field should be neat and be able to get along with people. They should have poise and good business ability. Clerical jobs require training in such subjects as shorthand, typing, and bookkeeping. Administrative jobs usually require college training in such fields as finance, business administration, and personnel administration.

Career Information on jobs in the petroleum industry can be obtained free from the American Petroleum Institute, 1271 Avenue of the Americas, New York, N.Y. 10020. Petroleum companies will also provide information on career opportunities.   WILLIAM B. HARPER

Related Articles. See the Mining sections of the various state, country, and province articles mentioned in the *Oil Regions of the World* section of this article. See also the following articles in WORLD BOOK:

PRODUCTS

Asphalt	Kerosene	Naphtha
Benzine	Lubricant	Paraffin
Butane and Propane	Microcrystalline	Petrochemicals
Fuel	Wax	Petrolatum
Gas (fuel)	Mineral Oil	Petroleum Coke
Gasoline	Napalm	Plastics

OTHER RELATED ARTICLES

Bituminous Sands	Distillation	Octane Number
Conservation	Hydrocarbon	Pipeline
(picture: Mineral	Hydrogenation	Tetraethyllead
Conservation)	Magnetometer	

Outline

I. From Oil Well to Service Station
  A. Oil Fields
  B. Making Petroleum Products
  C. Moving the Oil
  D. Service Stations
II. Petroleum Products
  A. Gasoline
  B. Fuel Oils
  C. Lubricants
  D. Jet Fuels
  E. Kerosene
  F. Asphalt and Road Oil
  G. Other Petroleum Products
III. Oil Regions of the World
  A. North America
  B. South America
  C. Asia
  D. Europe
  E. Africa
IV. How Petroleum Was Formed
  A. Organic Theory
  B. Oil Shale
  C. Oil Formation Today
V. How Men Find Petroleum
  A. Studying Rock Formations
  B. Analyzing Earth Conditions
VI. Drilling an Oil Well
  A. Setting Up the Derrick
  B. Methods of Drilling
  C. The Drilling Crew
  D. Starting to Drill
  E. The Drilling Mud
  F. Pulling the Pipe
  G. Whipstocking
  H. Casing
VII. Bringing Oil to the Surface
  A. Energy-Drive
  B. The Christmas Tree
VIII. Refining Petroleum
  A. Distillation
  B. Conversion
  C. Chemical Treatment
IX. Petroleum Conservation
  A. Conservation Laws
  B. Oil-Field Conservation
  C. Refinery Conservation
X. The Petroleum Industry
  A. In the United States
  B. In Canada
  C. In Other Countries
XI. History
XII. Career Opportunities

Questions

Where would you expect to find a "Christmas tree" in the oil industry? What is "fishing"?

How do oilmen prevent gushers?

What part did the automobile play in the development of the petroleum industry?

How do oilmen make sure that an area contains oil?

What common elements make up petroleum?

What part did a former railroad conductor play in the history of the petroleum industry?

What is offshore oil?

Why do refineries often paint the roofs of their storage tanks a light color?

Why did refineries at one time dump gasoline into creeks and rivers?

How do oilmen use skin-diving equipment?

What is a wildcat oil well?

On the average, how many dry oil wells are found in a new oil field?

What is the most important method of drilling for oil?

PETROLEUM COKE is a useful product obtained in refining crude oil (see PETROLEUM [Refining Petroleum]).

Production of Petroleum Coke begins after all the gasoline, kerosene, gas oils, lubricating oils, and other products have been distilled from crude oil. After this process is completed, pumps force the heavy *residual oil* that remains through tubes of a furnace. There, the oil is heated to a high temperature. It then stews in *coking drums* until it is converted into solid coke.

Coke cannot be melted. When it has to be molded into various shapes, it is first crushed to a fine powder and mixed with a *binder*, such as pitch. The resulting dough is pressed into molds or forced through dies. The forms are then baked to turn the binder into carbon.

Uses. Petroleum coke has many uses. Carbon or graphite electrodes are made from it. Petroleum coke in molded shapes is used for electrical and chemical purposes. Coke is a raw material for self-lubricating piston rings, bearings, and valve parts. It is also used in the refining of various metals and in the production of abrasives and heat-resisting materials.

The most common use for electrodes made from petroleum coke is in flashlight batteries and dry cells. They are also used to carry electric currents into electric furnaces, in electrochemical separation processes, in arc lamps, and in certain welding operations. Other electrical uses of molded carbon articles include the brushes used in electric motors and generators, resistor disks, parts for large radio-rectifier tubes, and electrodes.

Carbon made from petroleum coke is widely used in the chemical industry because of its resistance to chemicals. Petroleum coke is also important in the production of whetstones, abrasives for grinding wheels, and coated paper or cloth for sanding. It is used to make synthetic graphite for nuclear reactors. WILLIAM B. HARPER

PETROLEUM ENGINEERING. See ENGINEERING (table: Specialized Engineering Fields).

PETROLEUM JELLY. See PETROLATUM.

PETROLOGY, *pee TRAHL oh jih*, is the branch of the science of geology devoted to the study of rocks. It deals with the chemical composition, the formation, the breaking down, and the weathering of various rocks. A specialist in petrology is called a *petrologist*. See also ROCK.

PETRONIUS, *pee TROH nih us*, **GAIUS** (? -A.D. 66), was a Roman satirical novelist. Only part of his novel *Satyricon* has survived. An entertaining novel of Roman life, it is unrestrained, but still soundly critical of bad judgment in literature and art. The central portion of the book, "Trimalchio's Dinner," describes a lavish banquet at which every conceivable offense against good taste is committed. The Emperor Nero called Petronius his "arbiter of elegance." Petronius committed suicide when Nero ordered him arrested. MOSES HADAS

PETROPAVLOVSK. See KAMCHATKA PENINSULA.

PETTIT, ROBERT. See BASKETBALL (Great Basketball Players and Coaches).

PETTY, SIR WILLIAM (1623-1687), is best remembered as a political economist and a pioneer statistician. He stressed the importance of observation and of numerical measurement of economic matters. He wrote *Treatise of Taxes and Contributions* (1662-1685) and *Political Arithmetic* (1683). He was also active in medicine, music, and business. He served as surgeon-general with Oliver Cromwell's army in Ireland, where he became surveyor-

general. He was born in Romsey, England, and was graduated from Oxford University. H. W. SPIEGEL

PETTY OFFICER. See RANK IN ARMED SERVICES.

PETUNIA, *pea TYOO nih uh*, is any of a group of herblike plants native chiefly to Argentina and Brazil. In the United States, they are cultivated widely as annual garden flowers. The petunia plant is covered with tiny hairs. Gardeners value it for its beautiful funnel-shaped flowers, which are large and velvety.

Most petunias are perennials, but they are usually grown as annuals because they flower during their first year. Petunias may be grown from cuttings or from seeds. They thrive in a sunny location.

Scientific Classification. Petunias belong to the nightshade family, *Solanaceae*. They make up the genus *Petunia*. Cultivated petunias are *P. hybrida*. THEODOR JUST

See also FLOWER (color picture: Summer Garden Flowers); PAINTED-TONGUE.

PEVSNER, *PEVS ner*, **ANTOINE** (1886-1962), was a Russian-born painter and sculptor. He was influenced by the cubist painters and sculptor Alexander Archipenko, whom he met in Paris in 1911. He settled in Paris in 1923 and later became a French citizen.

Pevsner painted until 1923, when he turned to sculpture. One of his best-known early works is a portrait of artist Marcel Duchamp in 1926 made of blades of metal and transparent plastic. In his later work, Pevsner formed bronze, brass, and copper constructions with deep hollows that unite light and space. Two of his best-known works are *Construction in the Egg* (1948) and *Peace Column* (1954). Pevsner was born in Orël, Russia. Pevsner's brother is sculptor Naum Gabo (see GABO, NAUM). THEODORE E. KLITZKE

PEWEE. See WOOD PEWEE.

Antoine Pevsner's *The World* is one of the sculptor's brass and iron sculptures. This model was completed in 1946.
Musée National d'Art Moderne, Paris

The Art Institute of Chicago

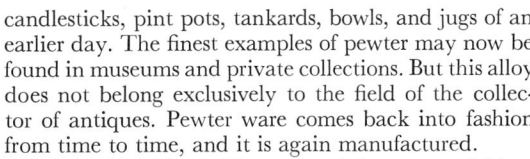

The Art Institute of Chicago

A Pewter Holy Water Font, *above,* with the Madonna and Child, dates from the 1700's.

Some Fine Pewter Pieces, *above right,* are several hundred years old.

Pewter Ware made today, *right,* follows the design of contemporary furnishings.

Reed & Barton

PEWTER, *PŸOO tur,* is a metal alloy whose principal element is tin. The chief metals used with the tin are copper, lead, antimony, and, occasionally, bismuth. The proportions of the various metals in the alloy vary. From 75 to 80 per cent of tin is combined with 20 to 25 per cent of the other metals. As a rule, the larger the proportion of tin, the better the pewter. The formula varies according to the kind of pewter desired.

During the 1600's and 1700's, people in England and the rest of Europe used pewter extensively for household utensils, and to some extent for church vessels. Craftsmen introduced pewter as a substitute for silver and gold. Pewter became popular with persons who could not afford the expensive metals. Many articles made of pewter are obvious copies of the work of goldsmiths and silversmiths. This happened because pewter craftsmen, like those working in precious metals, followed the general fashions of the times. However, pewterers did not attempt to copy the more elaborate pieces especially adapted to finer metals. They wisely chose the simple, finely designed, generally unornamented pieces with designs particularly adapted to pewter. The American colonists used many objects made of pewter. After 1800, china and glassware gradually replaced pewter.

There is much to interest collectors in the plates, candlesticks, pint pots, tankards, bowls, and jugs of an earlier day. The finest examples of pewter may now be found in museums and private collections. But this alloy does not belong exclusively to the field of the collector of antiques. Pewter ware comes back into fashion from time to time, and it is again manufactured.

Pewter tarnishes readily and needs frequent polishing. Pewter scratches easily and may be ruined by careless cleaning. It dents and breaks easily and does not stand heat well. But with reasonable care it can be kept in as good condition as silverware.   EUGENE F. BUNKER, JR.

See also COLONIAL LIFE IN AMERICA (Crafts).

PEYOTE. See MESCALINE; CACTUS.

PFEIFFER COLLEGE. See UNIVERSITIES AND COLLEGES (table).

PH is a number used by chemists to indicate the strength of an acid or a base. The number is usually on a scale ranging from 0 to 14. A pH below 7 indicates that a solution is acidic, and a pH above 7 indicates that a solution is basic. Strong acids have lower pH's than weak acids, and strong bases have higher pH's than weak bases. A *neutral* solution, such as pure water, is neither acidic nor basic. Its pH is 7.

Danish biochemist Søren Sørensen invented the pH system in 1909. The number indicates the concentration of hydrogen ions in a solution. A solution's pH is defined as the negative logarithm, to the base 10, of its hydrogen-ion concentration. This concentration is expressed in *moles* of hydrogen ions per liter of solution. One mole is 602,257,000,000,000,000,000,000 ions or other chemical particles. For example, a solution with a pH of 12 contains 10^{-12} (one million-millionth) of a mole of hydrogen ions per liter.

PH is measured with an electronic *pH meter* or with special dyes called *acid-base indicators.* The color of an indicator depends on the concentration of hydrogen ions. *pH paper* contains several indicators that change color at different pH's. When dipped into a solution, the paper's color indicates the approximate pH of the solution.   ESMARCH S. GILREATH

PHAEDRA, *FEE druh,* in Greek mythology, was the wife of Theseus, a great king of early Athens. She fell in love with Hippolytus, who was Theseus' son and her stepson. But he would have nothing to do with her. To get revenge, she told Theseus that Hippolytus had insulted her. Theseus banished his son and asked Poseidon to punish him. As Hippolytus drove his chariot along the shore, a monster appeared from the sea and caused the horses to bolt. Hippolytus was killed, and Phaedra hanged herself in remorse.

PHAËTHON, *FAY uh thahn,* in Greek mythology, was the son of the sun god Helios (Apollo) and the nymph Clymene. Clymene did not at first tell Phaëthon that his father was Helios. When she did tell him, the youth journeyed to the palace of the sun to ask Helios for proof of his birth. Helios promised to grant any wish

Phaëthon Disregarded His Father's Wishes and drove the steeds of the sun in a mad dash across the heavens.

his son made. Phaëthon asked to drive the chariot of the sun for one day. At first Helios denied him that wish, but he finally had to keep his promise. Phaëthon, a mortal, could not control the divine fiery steeds, and they tore up the heavens. They flew so high that the earth froze, and so low that it scorched. Rivers dried up, and rocks split. Earth called to the god Zeus for help, and he hurled a thunderbolt at Phaëthon. Phaëthon fell from the chariot to his death.   H. LLOYD STOW

PHAGE. See BACTERIOPHAGE.

PHAGOCYTE, *FAG oh site,* is a body cell that is part of the body's defense against disease. Phagocytes are special blood cells and cells from other body tissues. They move by flowing along with a wavelike motion, much as an ameba does (see AMEBA). Phagocytes surround and digest germs that enter the body. They also destroy worn-out and damaged blood cells in the bone marrow, spleen, and liver.   G. W. BEADLE

See also METCHNIKOFF, ÉLIE.

PHALANGE. See FOOT; HAND.

PHALANGER. See CUSCUS.

PHALANX, *FAY lanks,* was an ancient Greek offensive battle formation. A phalanx was made up of heavily armed infantry troops formed in tight ranks for the attack. The troops carried long spears and protected themselves with overlapping shields. The depth of each formation ranged from 8 to 12 ranks. The phalanx had great striking power, but no flexibility. It needed support from lighter troops. C. BRADFORD WELLES

PHALAROPE, *FAL uh rope,* is a small sandpiper-like bird that breeds in the Northern Hemisphere and winters in the Southern Hemisphere. Red and northern phalaropes breed in the arctic and subarctic. They winter on the high seas of the Atlantic, seldom coming ashore. The phalarope female is the "head of the family." She is larger and more brightly colored than the male. It is she who does the courting and establishes the nesting territory. The male builds the nest and incubates the eggs. But both the male and the female care for the young.

Allan D. Cruickshank, NAS

The Phalarope has thick, ducklike plumage. It is a prized game bird in many areas.

Scientific Classification. Phalaropes make up the phalarope family, *Phalaropodidae.*   LEONARD W. WING

PHANTASCOPE. See JENKINS, CHARLES FRANCIS.

PHARAOH, *FAIR oh,* was a title of the later kings of ancient Egypt. The Egyptians did not call their ruler pharaoh until the Eighteenth Dynasty (1570-1300 B.C.). Even then, pharaoh was not one of the king's most important titles. Writers of the Old Testament almost always used *pharaoh* as a title for the king of Egypt.

The word pharaoh comes from two Egyptian words, *peraa.* Per-aa means *great house,* and at first these words described the royal palace, not the king.

Ancient Egyptians considered the pharaoh a god and the son of a god. They thought he was the falcon god Horus in human form, and the son of Re, the sun god. In theory, the pharaoh owned all the land and people in Egypt. In reality, his power was limited by strong groups, including the priests and nobles. His actions were governed by rules of conduct which the Egyptians believed the gods had set down.   BARBARA MERTZ

See also EGYPT, ANCIENT (History); AKHENATON; RAMSES II.

PHARISEE, *FAR uh see,* was a member of a group of Jewish people who followed strict religious laws. The Pharisees lived in Judea in Palestine, in the time of Jesus. They did not have much to do with unbelievers or with Jews outside their own group. The Pharisees considered themselves more righteous and holy than ordinary men. The first five books of the Old Testament are called the *Pentateuch* (see PENTATEUCH). They contain all the basic Jewish laws. The Pharisees added their own interpretations to the Pentateuch, and developed many rules for daily living. Jesus said that the Pharisees added too many rules to the real law. He called them hypocrites, or pretenders (Matt. 23).

The Pharisees were a progressive party. They believed that religion must grow and not stand still. They were not like the Sadducees, who tried to set themselves up as the only interpreters of religion. The Pharisees insisted upon the rightful duty to interpret and explain the teachings of Judaism so they could be understood. They were the champions of the common people. The

PHARMACIST

Pharisees also believed in the resurrection of the dead and many things concerning angels and spirits. In all of this, their rivals, the Sadducees, bitterly disagreed.

After the Christian Church was organized, the Pharisees withdrew more than ever from the world. They worked with great care and for many years on the Talmud, which contains all Jewish civil laws. Many men of piety and learning, men such as Gamaliel and his famous pupil, Saul (Saint Paul), were among these Pharisees. LOUIS L. MANN and WILLIAM F. ROSENBLUM

See also GAMALIEL; PAUL, SAINT; SADDUCEE; TALMUD.

PHARMACIST. See PHARMACY.

PHARMACOLOGY, *FAHR muh KAHL oh jih,* is the study of the effects chemicals have on living things. It deals with how drugs modify tissue and organ functions. Pharmacology is linked with both biology and chemistry. It is a recent science, but it is closely connected with one of the oldest, the giving of remedies to relieve diseases. In a long history of trial and error, people found that some plants such as the poppy, belladonna, foxglove, and others produced certain results. Minerals such as Epsom salts, soda, or Glauber's salt were also found to give desired reactions.

Pharmacology really began during the 1900's with the rise of chemistry. For the first time the crude plant and mineral materials which act on living tissues could be analyzed. The active part of a material could be separated and used as a drug or medicine. Its composition and the exact effect it would have could be determined. Pharmacologists have developed new drugs.

The branch of pharmacology relating to poison is *toxicology.* Nearly all chemical agents are harmful to living tissue if enough of them is taken. When a physician knows how the chemicals act, he may use them for many different purposes. A. K. REYNOLDS

See also DRUG; PHARMACY.

PHARMACOPEIA, or PHARMACOPOEIA, *FAHR muh koh PE uh,* is a book containing tables of drugs. It includes a statement of their properties, the doses in which they may be safely taken, and the standards that determine their strength and purity. The volume is compiled usually under the highest professional, sometimes governmental, authority.

The first pharmacopeia was the *Nuremberg Pharmacopoeia.* It was published in Germany in 1542. From time to time, similar books were published. They varied in their accuracy and value. The necessity of standardizing such books became apparent. Today, almost all nations recognize the need for pharmacopeias. Pharmacopeias are continually revised and updated.

The first pharmacopeia published in the United States appeared in 1778. It was designed for use in the army. The earliest national pharmacopeia dates from 1820. This was the year in which the first convention of delegates of medical colleges and societies was assembled. Similar conventions were held every 10 years, to provide for new editions of the work. Now the United States Pharmacopeia is revised every five years. In 1907, under the provisions of the Food and Drugs Act, the pharmacopeia of the United States was made a legal standard. Laws of Congress enforce the requirements of the pharmacopeia. A. K. REYNOLDS

PHARMACY, *FAR muh sih,* is the science of preparing medicines. A person who prepares medicines for use is called a *druggist,* or *pharmacist.* He was once called an *apothecary.*

Duties of a Pharmacist. The chief duty of a pharmacist is filling and compounding prescriptions. A *prescription* is a list of the drugs in a medicine together with the amount of each drug to be used. Usually it also includes the directions that are to be written on the label for the patient as well as instructions to the pharmacist for making the medicine. Besides reading and filling prescriptions, a pharmacist must be able to prepare common ointments, antiseptic solutions, powders, and other common remedies. At one time he collected his own herbs and medicines. But in modern times these are supplied by pharmaceutical manufacturers. One of his duties is the sale of poisons and narcotics. Some of these drugs may be sold only on prescription.

Careers in Pharmacy. Pharmacists must be college graduates and must pass examinations before they are granted a license to practice. Practicing pharmacists must be *registered,* or licensed by the state. There are about 75 schools of pharmacy in the United States. Most of these are parts of large universities. These schools offer courses of study that prepare the pharmacist for his work. Such courses usually include physics, botany, zoology, organic and inorganic chemistry, and higher mathematics. They also include courses peculiar to the profession, such as *pharmacognosy,* which deals with the characteristics of crude drugs; and *materia medica,* which is the study of the nature and properties

The Pharmacist keeps a complete supply of drugs on hand with which to fill doctors' prescriptions for medicines.
American Druggist

of substances used to prepare remedies. Upon completion of study, the pharmacist is given a degree of Bachelor of Science in Pharmacy.

Registered pharmacists may work in drugstores, hospitals, industrial plants, research laboratories, for the federal or a state government, or the armed forces.

The American Pharmaceutical Association is the national organization of pharmacists. It was organized in 1852. Its primary purpose is to maintain a high level of standards for the profession. It publishes the *National Formulary*, one of the two books in the United States that establish the legal standards for drugs. The other is the *Pharmacopeia of the United States of America*. Headquarters of the organization are at 2215 Constitution Ave., Washington 7, D.C.   WALTER MODELL

See also DRUG; PHARMACOLOGY; PHARMACOPEIA; PRESCRIPTION; HOSPITAL (picture).

PHAROS. See ALEXANDRIA; LIGHTHOUSE; SEVEN WONDERS OF THE WORLD.

PHARSALUS, BATTLE OF. See CAESAR, GAIUS JULIUS (Civil War); POMPEY THE GREAT.

PHARYNX, *FAR ingks,* is a muscular cone-shaped tube that lies back of the nose, mouth, and larynx. It connects the mouth with the esophagus. The pharynx has openings from the nose and larynx. When a person is about to swallow, the muscles of the pharynx raise it so the food can pass easily into it. As soon as the food enters the pharynx, the muscles relax, allowing it to descend. Muscles then propel the food downward into the esophagus.

See also the Transvision three-dimensional color picture with HUMAN BODY.

PHASES OF THE MOON. See MOON (Phases).

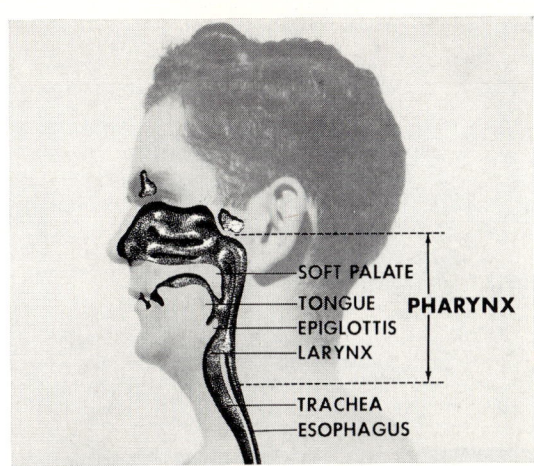

The Pharynx Connects the Mouth with the Esophagus.

PHEASANT, *FEZ unt,* is one of a group of birds that belong to the same family as the domestic fowl and the peacock. The word *pheasant* comes from *Phasis,* the name of a river in the ancient country of Colchis, on the eastern shore of the Black Sea. Pheasants have always lived in large numbers in this region. From here, according to legend, these birds were first exported to Europe.

Two of the best-known pheasants are the so-called *English pheasant,* which the Romans supposedly brought to England, and the Chinese *ring-necked pheasant.* The English pheasant first came from Asia Minor and the Chinese ring-necked pheasant from China. Large numbers of English pheasants are bred in English preserves as game birds. The males, or cocks, of this kind of pheasant are brilliantly colored. Their heads and necks are a bright green. The under parts of their bodies are bronze red. The sides of their bodies are reddish brown tipped with blue-black. Their long, tapering tails are gray, marked with bands of black. In different lights, their feathers reflect varying shades of black, green, purple, and gold. Female birds are of a yellowish-brown color, with markings of a darker brown. The cocks are about 3 feet long. The tail takes up at least half of this length. The females are about a foot shorter.

Ring-necked pheasants have a distinctive white ring about the neck. Their feathers show a similar brilliant combination of red, purple, green, and black. English and ring-necked pheasants have been bred together until purebred specimens have become rare.

English, Chinese ring-necked, and Mongolian pheasants have all been introduced into North America since 1881. These have interbred, and the ring-necked variety has been most successful. In the Dakotas and Manitoba they have helped to create a hunter's paradise. In many other states they are also an important game bird. The male ring-necked pheasant is a bird of brown, red, golden, buff, blue, and black plumage, usually with a white ring around the neck. It weighs from $2\frac{1}{2}$ to $4\frac{1}{2}$ pounds. The female is less brightly colored and smaller.

Pheasants nest on the ground. The female lays from six to 16 olive-buff eggs in a hollow among the leaves. The birds eat berries, seeds, and insects. In some localities they have become so numerous as to be a

The Reeve Pheasant of northern China has extremely long tail feathers which were once widely used to trim hats.

The Golden Pheasant gets its name from its golden yellow crest and breast. It may be seen in most large city zoos.

Arthur H. Fisher

menace to grainfields. But their insect-eating habits are helpful to farmers.

Among other well-known species are the *golden pheasant*, so called from its golden yellow crest and bright yellow breast; the *Chinese silver pheasant*, a beautiful bird whose white upper parts are delicately marked with black lines; and the *eared pheasant* of Central and Eastern Asia. The name refers to the long white tufts of feathers on the sides of the head. Their home is in central and southern Asia, where the demand for their beautiful feathers which have been used to trim hats has greatly reduced their numbers in some places.

Scientific Classification. Pheasants belong to the partridge, quail, and pheasant family, *Phasianidae*. The English pheasant is genus *Phasianus*, species *P. colchicus;* the ring-necked pheasant is *P. torquatus*.   JOSEPH J. HICKEY

See also BIRD (Bird Courtship; color pictures: Birds of Other Lands, Game Birds, Wings in Flight); GUINEA FOWL; POULTRY (Kinds); TRAGOPAN.

PHEIDIPPIDES. See MARATHON; GREECE, ANCIENT (Communication).

PHELPS, WILLIAM LYON (1865-1943), an American educator and literary critic, helped shape American literary tastes of his time. His course in modern fiction and drama was the first of its kind in American universities. Phelps acquainted many Americans with the works of Russian novelists. He received much criticism, but his books, lectures, and essays enjoyed national popularity. Phelps's many books include *Essays on Russian Novelists* (1911), *Reading the Bible* (1919), *What I Like in Prose* (1933), *What I Like in Poetry* (1934), *Marriage* (1940), and *The Mothers' Anthology* (1940).

Phelps was born in New Haven, Conn., and was graduated from Yale University. He joined the Yale faculty in 1892 as an English instructor, and taught English literature from 1901 to 1933. EDWIN H. CADY

United Press Int.
William Lyon Phelps

PHENACETIN, *fee NAS ee tin*, is a derivative of coal tar that is used in the treatment of fever and headache. It is often combined with aspirin in drug mixtures. The prolonged use of phenacetin can cause severe or even fatal damage to the kidneys. Phenacetin is also called ACETOPHENETIDIN. Its chemical formula is $C_{10}H_{13}O_2N$. See also COAL TAR.   SOLOMON GARB

PHENOL. See CARBOLIC ACID.

PHENOLIC RESIN. See BAKELITE; PLASTICS (The Invention of Bakelite; table: Kinds of Plastics).

PHENOLOGY is the study of when certain biological events take place. Phenologists study how these events are affected by seasonal weather changes. The events include the migration of birds, the hibernation of

318

animals, the changing of color in leaves, and the sprouting and flowering of plants. Farmers, ranchers, construction workers, and others whose work is affected by weather can use phenological information to plan their activities. For example, in some areas alfalfa is ready to be cut about 30 days after the common lilac blooms. A farmer can predict when he will have to cut his alfalfa by observing when lilacs bloom.

Scientific organizations in the United States and other countries have formed networks of persons who observe and report on certain phenological events. The organizations use the information these persons gather to make *phenological maps*. The maps have lines that connect the places in which living things reach a certain stage at the same time. JOSEPH M. CAPRIO

PHENOLPHTHALEIN, *FEE nohl THAL een* (chemical formula, $C_{20}H_{14}O_4$), is a chemical compound that is used as an indicator of alkalinity or acidity, and as a laxative. Phenolphthalein is also used in the manufacture of dyes. It is prepared by heating phenol and phthalic anhydride with sulfuric acid. Pure phenolphthalein forms small white crystals that dissolve in alcohol or ether. It turns red in the presence of an alkaline substance. As a laxative, phenolphthalein is part of many advertised medicines. It is one of the least poisonous of common laxatives, but some people are allergic to it. It must be used with care.

PHENOMENAL BERRY. See BURBANK, LUTHER.

PHENYLKETONURIA. See MENTAL RETARDATION.

PHI BETA KAPPA, *FI BAY tuh KAP uh*, is a college and university honor society that encourages scholarship in the liberal arts and sciences. It is the oldest American fraternity with a Greek-letter name. Both men and women can belong to Phi Beta Kappa.

Phi Beta Kappa was founded on Dec. 5, 1776, at the College of William and Mary, Williamsburg, Va. Fraternity members always encouraged scholarly endeavor, even though the organization was founded as a secret society. It became solely an honor society when secrecy was abandoned in the 1830's. Today, members are elected by vote of Phi Beta Kappa college faculty members. They select new members from seniors and juniors with high academic records. Membership is sometimes conferred for scholarship after graduation from college. The letters ΦΒΚ (Phi Beta Kappa) are the initials of the Greek words Φιλοσοφία Βίου Κυβερνήτης, meaning *Philosophy (is) the Guide of Life.*

Phi Beta Kappa members receive this gold key.

Phi Beta Kappa has active chapters at 184 colleges and universities in the United States, and a living membership of about 215,000. Its regular program includes scholarships and book awards, sponsored both by individual chapters and by the national organization. It publishes two magazines: *The Key Reporter*, for members, and *The American Scholar*, for all interested persons. The national organization, called the United Chapters of Phi Beta Kappa, has headquarters at 1811 Q Street NW, Washington, D.C. 20009.

Critically reviewed by UNITED CHAPTERS OF PHI BETA KAPPA

PHI BETA LAMBDA. See FUTURE BUSINESS LEADERS OF AMERICA.

Art Institute of Chicago

Phidias carved the frieze that runs above the columns of the Parthenon at Athens. The sculptures pictured the struggle of mythical Greeks with *centaurs*, which were half man, half horse.

PHIDIAS, *FIHD ih us* (490?-420? B.C.), was considered the greatest of Greek sculptors. He was renowned not for his statues of marble, but for those called *chryselephantine*. In these statues, the flesh parts were composed of ivory, and the drapery and accessories of gold. Three famous examples of this type, each about 40 feet high, were the *Lemnian Athena*, *Athena Parthenos*, and *Olympian Zeus*. The *Zeus* was considered one of the wonders of the ancient world (see SEVEN WONDERS OF THE WORLD).

Phidias made statues only of the gods, giving them nobility, dignity, and power. His style made a permanent impression upon Greek art. We can best judge his work by the sculptures of the Parthenon. These sculptures were designed by him and executed in his studio by his assistants, and perhaps in part by Phidias himself.

Phidias was born in Athens, and was trained there and at Argos. He became a friend and adviser to the Greek statesman Pericles. He helped Pericles beautify Athens. H. LLOYD STOW

See also ELGIN MARBLES; PARTHENON.

PHILADELPHIA was the name given to several cities by the ancient Greeks. The name means *brotherly love*. One was a small town in Lydia founded in the 100's B.C. by King Attalus II Philadelphus of Pergamum. It was a center of early Christianity. A pagan inscription found there indicates that its people followed a strict moral code. The town of Alaşehir, Turkey, stands on the site now.

Another ancient Philadelphia, in Palestine, began as a city called Rabbath-Ammon. But the Egyptian king Ptolemy II Philadelphus conquered it, renamed it, and introduced Greek customs and culture. The capital of Jordan, Amman, stands on this site. THOMAS W. AFRICA

PHILADELPHIA
The City of Brotherly Love

PHILADELPHIA is the birthplace of the United States and was the nation's capital during most of the Revolutionary War. It is the largest city in Pennsylvania and the fourth largest in the United States. Philadelphia ranks as a major center of commerce, industry, and culture, and is one of the world's leading ports.

William Penn, an English Quaker, founded Philadelphia in 1682. It quickly became the largest city in colonial America. Penn planned the town as a place of religious and racial freedom. He named it *Philadelphia*, which means *brotherly love* in Greek. As a result, Philadelphia was nicknamed the *City of Brotherly Love*. Because Penn and many of the first settlers were Quakers, it also became known as the *Quaker City*.

Throughout the 1700's, Philadelphia rivaled Boston as the political and cultural center of the American colonies. Visitors to the old sections of the city can see many historic shrines. Probably the most important place of interest is Independence Hall, where the Founding Fathers signed the Declaration of Independence and the United States Constitution. The Liberty Bell, which rang out the nation's freedom, rests in Independence Hall. Through this hall echoed the footsteps and words of George Washington, Thomas Jefferson, James Madison, John Jay, Benjamin Franklin, and other famous Americans.

Today, Philadelphia is a colorful blend of old and new. During the 1950's and 1960's, Philadelphia began far-reaching urban renewal programs. Large areas of old buildings were cleared away. New buildings took their places along the skyline. Industries built new factories along the Delaware and Schuylkill rivers. Wide highways were constructed to speed traffic through the metropolitan area. The city preserved historic sites as a part of the renewal program.

Downtown Philadelphia, *right*, spreads out on both sides of tree-lined Benjamin Franklin Parkway. The parkway ends at Rudolf Siemering's statue of George Washington at the entrance to Fairmount Park.

Elfreth's Alley, *below*, is one of the oldest streets in America where people still live. Its 33 brick houses were built during the early 1700's. This narrow cobblestone street near the river front is only one block long.

H. Armstrong Roberts

FACTS IN BRIEF

Population: 2,002,512; metropolitan area, 4,342,897.
Area: 130 sq. mi.; metropolitan area, 3,549 sq. mi.
Altitude: 100 ft.
Climate: For information on the monthly weather in Philadelphia, see PENNSYLVANIA (Climate).
Government: Mayor-council (4-year terms).
Founded: 1682. Chartered, 1701.
City Seal: A coat of arms is supported by two women. Above it, a right arm holds a pair of scales.
City Motto: "Philadelphia Maneto" ("Let Brotherly Love Continue").
City Flag: Two vertical blue stripes flank a yellow stripe bearing the city arms. See CITY (color picture, City Flags of the United States).

The City

Philadelphia lies at the southeastern tip of Pennsylvania. It is about 90 miles southwest of New York City and 135 miles northeast of Washington, D.C. The broad Delaware River runs along the eastern and southern sides of the city, separating Philadelphia from New Jersey. The river links the city to the Atlantic Ocean, about 100 miles to the south. The smaller Schuylkill River winds through central Philadelphia and flows into the Delaware River.

Philadelphia was built on a flat plain. It seems flatter than most other large American cities because it has no towering skyscrapers. By tradition, no building in the city rises higher than 548 feet. This is the height of the city hall, on top of which stands a 37-foot statue of William Penn looking out over the city he founded.

The Downtown Area lies between the Delaware River on the east and the Schuylkill River on the west. Vine Street forms the northern boundary and South Street is the southern boundary. This two-square-mile area once made up the entire city as laid out by William Penn. Here are Philadelphia's largest department stores and hotels, the business district, and the chief historical sites. The main downtown streets intersect at the city hall. They are Market Street, running east and west, and Broad Street, running north and south. Just west of the city hall, Penn Center has replaced the old Broad Street Station and an elevated section of railroad tracks. Penn Center includes office and apartment buildings and a hotel. To the north of the city hall on both sides of Broad Street is one of the poorer sections of the city. The row houses are old and run-down.

Independence Hall National Historic Park, one of the most historic areas, lies at the eastern end of Market and Chestnut streets. This park includes Independence Hall; Congress Hall, where Congress

321

PHILADELPHIA

Hinsey, Black Star

The Franklin Institute, founded in 1824, includes the Fels Planetarium, a library, a museum, and laboratories. The institute is devoted to scientific and educational work.

Philadelphia Museum of Art

The Philadelphia Museum of Art, rear, has many special rooms where art of different periods is featured. The present building opened in 1928. The old Fairmount Waterworks buildings, foreground, were built about 1822.

1 inch = 1.5 Statute Miles

0   ¼   ½   ¾   1

MILES

N
W   E
S

3
2

ROOSEVELT BLVD.

FRONT ST.

5TH ST.

GERMANTOWN AVE.

BROAD ST.

TEMPLE UNIVERSITY

HUNTING PARK AVE.

RIDGE AVE.

SCHUYLKILL EXP.

Fairmount Park

Cobbs Creek Park

H. Armstrong Roberts

The Chew House, or **Cliveden,** was held by British troops against an American attack in the Battle of Germantown during the Revolutionary War.

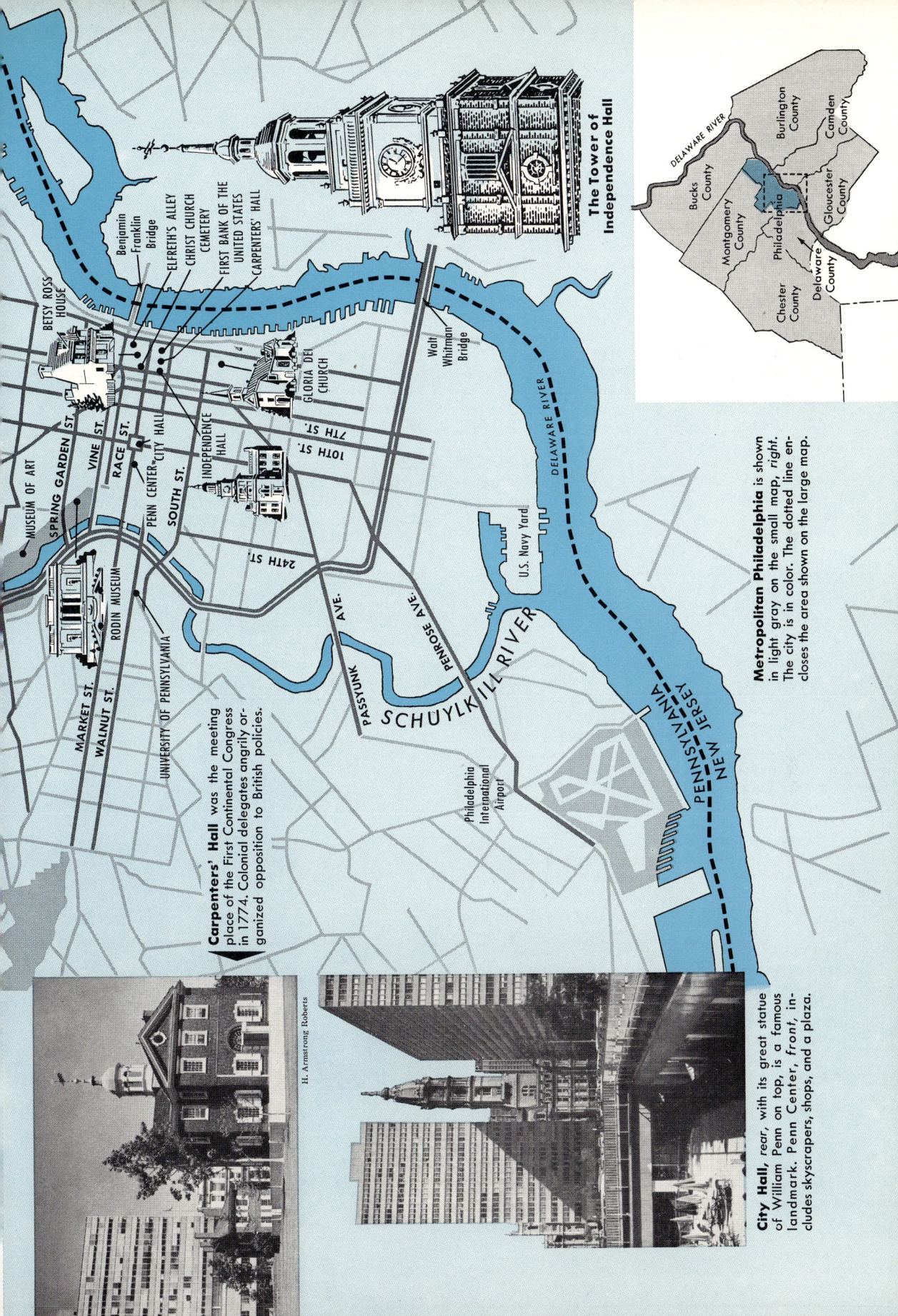

The Tower of
Independence Hall

BETSY ROSS
HOUSE

Benjamin
Franklin
Bridge
ELFRETH'S ALLEY
CHRIST CHURCH
CEMETERY
FIRST BANK OF THE
UNITED STATES
CARPENTERS' HALL

GLORIA DEI
CHURCH

MUSEUM OF ART

SPRING GARDEN ST.

VINE ST.

RACE ST.

Penn Center—CITY HALL

7TH ST.

10TH ST.

SOUTH ST.

INDEPENDENCE
HALL

Walt
Whitman
Bridge

RODIN MUSEUM

24TH ST.

UNIVERSITY OF PENNSYLVANIA

MARKET ST.

WALNUT ST.

PASSYUNK AVE.

PENROSE AVE.

SCHUYLKILL RIVER

U.S. Navy Yard

DELAWARE RIVER

PENNSYLVANIA
NEW JERSEY

Philadelphia
International
Airport

Metropolitan Philadelphia is shown in light gray on the small map, *right.* The city is in color. The dotted line encloses the area shown on the large map.

DELAWARE RIVER

Bucks
County

Montgomery
County

Burlington
County

Camden
County

Philadelphia

Gloucester
County

Chester
County

Delaware
County

Carpenters' Hall was the meeting place of the First Continental Congress in 1774. Colonial delegates angrily organized opposition to British policies.

H. Armstrong Roberts

City Hall, *rear,* with its great statue of William Penn on top, is a famous landmark. Penn Center, *front,* includes skyscrapers, shops, and a plaza.

PHILADELPHIA

met from 1790 to 1800; and Carpenters' Hall, where the First Continental Congress met. Nearby stands the Betsy Ross House, where the first American flag is said to have been made. Narrow, colorful Elfreth's Alley, one of the oldest streets in the country, runs north of the park. Some of its houses have been occupied continuously for more than 200 years.

Famous Churches add to the historic tradition of the city. One of the best known is old Christ Church (Episcopalian), built in 1727-1754. Famous Americans who had pews in this church include George Washington, Benjamin Franklin, and Betsy Ross. The tombs of Franklin and his wife are in the Christ Church Burial Ground. Gloria Dei Church (Swedish Lutheran), also known as Old Swedes' Church, is Philadelphia's oldest, having been completed in 1700. St. Joseph's Church stands on the site of the first Roman Catholic chapel in Philadelphia, built in 1733-1734. Other churches include Old St. George's Methodist Church, built in 1763, and "Old Pine" Presbyterian, begun in 1766. Mikveh Israel, established in 1740, is one of the oldest synagogues in the United States. The Friends' Meeting House, built in 1804, is the oldest Quaker meetinghouse in the city.

Fairmount Park, one of the largest city parks in the world, covers about 4,000 acres and extends about nine miles through the northwestern part of the city. Wissahickon Creek winds through the northern part of this huge park and the Schuylkill River cuts through the southern part. The Philadelphia Zoo stands in Fairmount Park. Established in 1859, the zoo was the first in the United States. During the summer, the park presents outdoor concerts and plays. The Japanese House also attracts many visitors to Fairmount Park.

Germantown, one of Philadelphia's most famous residential districts, lies east of Wissahickon Creek. A group of German settlers led by Francis Daniel Pastorius founded Germantown in 1683 (see PASTORIUS, FRANCIS DANIEL). In 1777, General George Washington fought the British here in the Battle of Germantown. Many fine old colonial houses still stand in the area.

The Waterfront extends for about 32 miles along the Delaware and Schuylkill rivers. It is lined with large industrial plants, refineries, shipyards, and warehouses. Ocean liners from all parts of the world dock at the Port of Philadelphia. This bustling port has almost 300 piers and wharves. The Pennsylvania, Reading, and Baltimore & Ohio railroads have large terminals in the port area. Farther south along the Delaware lies the Philadelphia Naval Base.

Highways. The Schuylkill Expressway, completed in 1958, is the first link in a vast 100-mile expressway system planned for the city. It connects Philadelphia with the Pennsylvania Turnpike, providing a continuous thruway to the Midwest. Other expressways in the plan include the Delaware, Vine Street, Crosstown, and Roosevelt. The expressways were scheduled to be completed by 1965. Three major toll bridges—the Tacony-Palmyra, the Walt Whitman, and the Benjamin Franklin—link Philadelphia to New Jersey.

The Metropolitan Area of Philadelphia includes Bucks, Montgomery, Chester, and Delaware counties in Pennsylvania, and Gloucester, Burlington, and Camden counties in New Jersey. To the west, Ardmore and the college towns of Bryn Mawr, Haverford, and Villanova lie along the "Main Line" of the Pennsylvania Railroad. The "Main Line" suburban area includes the homes of many of the area's oldest and wealthiest families. Large suburbs to the southwest include Upper Darby, Drexel Hill, Springfield, and Chester. The industrial suburbs of Conshohocken and Norristown lie along the Schuylkill to the northwest. Across the Delaware River, in New Jersey, the main suburbs include Camden, Pennsauken, Gloucester City, Westmont, and Collingswood. Mills, factories, and refineries stand in an almost unbroken line south of Philadelphia from Chester, Pa., to Wilmington, Del.

The People and Their Work

Philadelphia's people represent many nationality groups. William Penn's policy of religious freedom made Philadelphia the leading port of entry for Europeans escaping religious intolerance. English and Welsh Quakers first settled Philadelphia in 1682. The next year, German Mennonites and Quakers arrived and founded Germantown. Other European immigrants came from Italy, Poland, Russia, and other countries. The Quaker belief in equality for all men brought many Negroes to Philadelphia during the periods before and just after the Civil War. Today, about 25 per cent of the people of Philadelphia are Negroes.

Members of almost every religious faith live in Philadelphia. Roman Catholics make up the largest single religious group. Over a million persons belong to the more than 400 Roman Catholic churches in the city. Other major religious groups include Lutherans, Methodists, Presbyterians, Episcopalians, and Baptists. The city also has a large Jewish population. Founded by Quakers, Philadelphia is still a major headquarters of the Society of Friends in the United States.

The industries of the Philadelphia metropolitan area employ more than 1½ million persons. About a million of these people work in business offices, retail and wholesale trade, public administration, transportation, communications, construction, and service industries.

Manufacturing is Philadelphia's leading industry. Over 500,000 persons work in about 4,000 mills and factories. Of these workers, about 35,000 have jobs in industries that produce metals and nonelectrical machinery. Almost as many work in textile and clothing manufacturing plants. Philadelphia is a printing and publishing center, and a leading producer of electronics equipment. Other important products include processed foods, chemicals, leather, tools, scientific instruments, and drugs.

Commerce. Philadelphia has long been a leading financial center. The nation's first bank, the Bank of North America, was chartered there in 1781. Robert Morris, a Philadelphia merchant and a leading financier of the Revolutionary War, supervised this bank. The first national bank, the Bank of the United States, was founded in Philadelphia in 1791. In 1792, Congress established the first U.S. Mint in Philadelphia. The nation's first insurance companies were also set up here. Stephen Girard, a Philadelphia businessman, helped finance the War of 1812. Jay Cooke, a Philadelphia banker, was the Union's leading financial agent during the Civil War. Today, Philadelphia has 3 national banks and 20 state banks.

Shipping. The Delaware River, which links Philadelphia with the Atlantic Ocean, makes the city the largest fresh-water port in the world. The Port of Philadelphia extends about a hundred miles, from the city all the way to the ocean. The port handles about 50 million tons of cargo yearly, making it the fourth busiest port in the United States. The major imports include crude oil, iron ore, sugar, and wool. Coal and grain are among the leading exports. The Delaware River Port Authority maintains some bridges over the river and directs the improvement of shipping facilities on the river. But Philadelphia administers its own port. The Schuylkill River is navigable for about 8 miles above its mouth at Philadelphia.

Railroads. Philadelphia is the headquarters of two leading railroads, the Pennsylvania and the Reading. Manufacturers use both railroads to ship freight between Philadelphia and the Midwest. The Pennsylvania also provides passenger service to New York City, Washington, D.C., Chicago, and St. Louis. The Reading hauls coal from Pennsylvania mines to the port. Both railroads offer commuter service for suburban residents. The Baltimore & Ohio and the Pennsylvania-Reading Seashore Lines also provide freight service.

Aviation. The 2,500-acre Philadelphia International Airport lies in the southwestern corner of the city. It serves about two million passengers and handles about 39,000 tons of freight each year. North Philadelphia Airport serves as an auxiliary airport.

Publishing. Philadelphia has been a famous publishing center since the mid-1700's, when Benjamin Franklin published the *Pennsylvania Gazette* and *Poor Richard's Almanac*. The *Saturday Evening Post* was first published in Philadelphia in 1821. From 1897 until it ceased publication in 1969, the *Post* was owned by the Curtis Publishing Company, one of the world's largest magazine publishers. Many publishers of books in the field of education have headquarters in Philadelphia.

The nation's first daily newspaper, the *Pennsylvania Post and Daily Advertiser*, was published in Philadelphia in 1783. Today, the city has three major daily newspapers—the *Inquirer*, the *Evening Bulletin*, and the *Daily News*. Three television stations and 27 radio stations

H. Armstrong Roberts

Oil Refineries and factories spread along the banks of the Schuylkill River. Crude oil and other raw materials come into the Port of Philadelphia from all parts of the world. Many Philadelphia plants turn these raw materials into finished products. Skyscrapers rise in the business district, *rear.*

broadcast many types of programs from Philadelphia.

Sports. The annual Army-Navy football game and other major sports events take place at the John F. Kennedy Stadium. This stadium can seat about 100,-000 persons. The University of Pennsylvania's Franklin Field has a capacity of 80,000. The Philadelphia Eagles of the National Football League play there. The Philadelphia Phillies of the National League play baseball at Connie Mack Stadium. The Philadelphia 76ers of the National Basketball Association play at the Spectrum. Other stadiums include the Arena, Convention Hall, Municipal Auditorium, and the Palestra.

The lower Schuylkill River is a boating center. Crews of the University of Pennsylvania and other schools use the river for races. Fox hunting has been popular in the Philadelphia area since colonial days.

Education and the Arts

Schools. Philadelphia is known for many firsts in education. The city pioneered in establishing higher education for women. The Moore College of Art, founded in 1844, is the country's oldest school of art for women. The first U.S. medical school for women, the Woman's Medical College of Pennsylvania, was established in 1850. In 1885, Quakers founded Bryn Mawr College nearby. It was one of the nation's first colleges for women. The Pennsylvania Academy of the Fine Arts, established in 1805, was the first art school in the country. Spring Garden Institute, founded in 1850, was one of the first manual training schools.

The largest schools for higher education in the city include the University of Pennsylvania, Temple University, and the Drexel Institute of Technology. Chestnut Hill, Gratz, Holy Family, La Salle, and St. Joseph's colleges also have campuses in the city. Philadelphia has five leading medical schools. They are Jefferson Medical College; Hahnemann Medical College; Woman's Medical College of Pennsylvania; the Temple University and University of Pennsylvania schools of medicine. The Philadelphia College of Textiles and Science, and the Pennsylvania College of Optometry are specialized schools. Haverford and Swarthmore colleges and Villanova University are in the area.

The public schools of Philadelphia are noted for their progressive teaching methods. More than 230,000 students attend Philadelphia's 245 public schools. Other students go to more than 180 parochial schools.

Libraries. The Library Company of Philadelphia, founded by Benjamin Franklin in 1731, was the first subscription library in the United States. Members of the company contributed money to buy books, then used them free of charge. The library is now open to the public. It owns books that once belonged to William Penn, George Washington, and Thomas Jefferson. It also includes the entire library of James Logan, Penn's secretary and a former governor of the colony. The Free Library of Philadelphia has about 40 branches. It circulates about 5,000,000 books a year and has a large collection of rare books. The Historical Society of Pennsylvania ranks second only to the Library of Congress as the nation's largest center for manuscripts on American history. The American Philosophical Society houses a leading research library.

Museums. The Franklin Institute has one of the largest museums of applied science in the country. The Fels Planetarium is another of the institute's attractions. The Academy of Natural Sciences, founded in 1812, ranks as one of the oldest natural science museums in the world. The Atwater Kent Museum features exhibits that portray the history of Philadelphia. The Edgar Allan Poe House, where the poet lived from 1842 to 1844, is now a museum. It features first editions of Poe's works, including "The Raven" and "The Gold Bug." Other museums include the American Swedish Historical Foundation and the Commercial Museum.

The Philadelphia Museum of Art has one of the most famous collections in the nation. Its exhibits include Chinese, Japanese, and Indian temples. The Pennsylvania Academy of the Fine Arts displays some of the finest American paintings and sculpture, including a picture gallery of early Americans. The Rodin Museum has the largest collection outside of France by the noted French sculptor Auguste Rodin. Other well-known art galleries in the city include the Philadelphia Art Alliance and the Rosenbach Galleries.

Music and Theater. The world-famous Philadelphia Orchestra performs at the Academy of Music. The Philadelphia Grand Opera Company, the Philadelphia Lyric Opera Company, and the Metropolitan Opera Association of New York City also appear at the academy. Five professional theaters present plays.

Government

Philadelphia is both a city and a county. Until 1952, the city government and the Philadelphia County government operated separately within the same boundaries. That year, a new charter provided a "strong mayor" type of government. Under the charter, the city took over most county offices.

A mayor and a 17-member council govern the city. They are elected to four-year terms. The mayor may not serve more than two successive terms. He appoints a cabinet of four major officials: (1) a Managing Director, who ranks second to the mayor and appoints commissioners in charge of all city services; (2) a Director of Finance, who supervises the budget, revenue, and accounting; (3) a City Solicitor, who handles legal problems; and (4) a City Representative and Director of Commerce, who handles public relations for the city. More than half the city income comes from property taxes and a city income tax. Philadelphia administers its own water and sewerage systems.

History

Colonial Days. William Penn came up the Delaware River to the site of Philadelphia in 1682. He found pioneer English and Swedish settlers at Upland, which he renamed Chester. The year before, Penn had sent Thomas Holme, a surveyor, to lay out a site for what he called his "greene countrie towne." As a result, Philadelphia became one of the first cities in America built according to a plan.

Penn advertised his colony widely in Europe. His policy of religious freedom brought downtrodden and persecuted Europeans to Pennsylvania by the thousands. By 1700, Philadelphia had a population of 4,000. The next year it received its charter as a city.

Philadelphia, the capital of colonial Pennsylvania,

continued to grow rapidly. By 1760, it had about 19,000 persons and was the largest city in the American colonies. It also was the most important port and the largest manufacturing center.

Revolutionary War. Philadelphia provided two men who became leading voices of colonial protest before the Revolution. Benjamin Franklin was famous throughout the colonies for his *Poor Richard's Almanac* and for his newspaper, the *Pennsylvania Gazette*. The Pennsylvania legislature sent Franklin to England in 1757 to negotiate a fairer system of taxes. John Dickinson wrote colonial protests to England, including the "Declaration of Rights" and "Petition to the King" in 1765.

The First Continental Congress met in Carpenters' Hall in Philadelphia in 1774. It denounced many laws passed by England that violated the rights of the colonists. In 1775, the Second Continental Congress met in the State House, now Independence Hall. The next year, Benjamin Franklin helped Thomas Jefferson write the Declaration of Independence in Philadelphia.

Philadelphia became a battleground for a short time during the Revolutionary War. The British occupied the city from 1777 to 1778. General George Washington tried to recapture Philadelphia in the Battle of Germantown. But the British defeated his army.

Philadelphia was the seat of the national government throughout most of the war. In 1787, the Founding Fathers of the new nation met in Philadelphia and wrote the United States Constitution. New York City became the capital of the United States for a short time. Then the capital was moved back to Philadelphia from 1790 until 1800. In that year, Washington, D.C., became the capital. The state capital was moved from Philadelphia in 1799, first to Lancaster, then later to Harrisburg. At the time of the first United States census in 1790, Philadelphia with 29,500 persons ranked second to New York City in population.

Early 1800's. The development of coal fields west of Philadelphia in the early 1800's encouraged the growth of manufacturing industries. About 1830, Philadelphia lost first place as a port to New York City. But, between 1840 and 1860, Philadelphians built roads, canals, and railroads that brought greater trade with the Midwest. In 1854, the city extended its boundaries to include all Philadelphia County.

Civil War. Philadelphia Quakers helped lead the fight against Negro slavery. An abolition society had been founded in the city as early as 1775. Philadelphians formed the American Anti-Slavery Society in 1833. Throughout the Civil War, the Union depended on the city for industrial and financial support.

Late 1800's. In 1876, the Centennial Exposition held in the city displayed the story of a hundred years of the nation's growth (see CENTENNIAL EXPOSITION). But Philadelphia began to lose ground to New York City as a center of finance and commerce. The city government fell into the hands of political bosses and corrupt politicians. Older sections of the city became slums. Even the historic areas around Independence Hall became filled with run-down houses and shops.

Growth in 1900's. By 1910, immigration from Europe and migration from the southern states boosted Philadelphia's population over $1\frac{1}{2}$ million. Philadelphia was now the nation's third largest city, behind New York City and Chicago. The city began paving many

of its cobblestone streets. It also began building streetcar lines to connect all parts of Philadelphia.

During World Wars I and II, Philadelphia industries produced war materials. The shipyard at the Philadelphia Naval Base built and repaired warships.

A New Philadelphia. In 1951, Joseph S. Clark was elected mayor of Philadelphia and Richardson Dilworth was elected district attorney. Clark led the city in planning a vast urban renewal program. Prominent citizens committees, such as the Greater Philadelphia Movement, aided the city's efforts. Dilworth continued the program after he succeeded Clark as mayor in 1956.

The $150 million Penn Center became the first major project under Clark's leadership. Work also began in the 1950's on the $26 million Independence Mall project and the $100 million Food Distribution Center. From 1945 to 1960, manufacturers spent more than $2 billion on expansion in the area.

In the 1960's, the city started a $3\frac{1}{2}$ billion renewal program that will take almost 40 years to complete. The program includes improved highway and transportation systems, housing projects, elimination of slums, and separation of industrial and residential areas. It also calls for more libraries, parks, and shopping and recreation centers. S. K. STEVENS

Related Articles in WORLD BOOK include:

Feasts and Festivals (picture: The Mummer's Parade)	Liberty Bell
Franklin, Benjamin	Penn, William
Franklin Institute	Pennsylvania
Hog Island	Philadelphia Naval Base
Independence Hall	

Outline

I. **The City**
   A. The Downtown Area
   B. Independence Hall National Historical Park
   C. Famous Churches
   D. Fairmount Park
   E. Germantown
   F. The Waterfront
   G. Highways
   H. The Metropolitan Area

II. **The People and Their Work**
   A. Manufacturing
   B. Commerce
   C. Shipping
   D. Railroads
   E. Aviation
   F. Publishing
   G. Sports

III. **Education and the Arts**
   A. Schools
   B. Libraries
   C. Museums
   D. Music and Theater

IV. **Government**

V. **History**

Questions

Who founded and named Philadelphia?
What does the name *Philadelphia* mean?
Why is Philadelphia sometimes called the *Quaker City?*
What river connects Philadelphia to the Atlantic Ocean?
How did Philadelphia rank in population among American cities when the Revolutionary War began?
When was Philadelphia the nation's capital?
What two leading Philadelphians helped lead the colonial protest against English tax abuses?
What two famous documents were signed in Independence Hall?
What is unusual about the city government of Philadelphia?
What is the tallest building in Philadelphia? Why does the city have no taller buildings?

PHILADELPHIA COLLEGE OF ART

PHILADELPHIA COLLEGE OF ART is a private, coeducational school of art and art teacher education in Philadelphia, Pa. It stresses a creative application of art to industry. Courses lead to B.F.A. and B.S. degrees. The school was founded in 1876. For enrollment, see UNIVERSITIES AND COLLEGES (table).

PHILADELPHIA COLLEGE OF BIBLE. See UNIVERSITIES AND COLLEGES (table).

PHILADELPHIA COLLEGE OF PHARMACY AND SCIENCE. See UNIVERSITIES AND COLLEGES (table).

PHILADELPHIA COLLEGE OF TEXTILES AND SCIENCE. See UNIVERSITIES AND COLLEGES (table).

PHILADELPHIA NAVAL BASE, Pa., houses major United States naval activities in the Philadelphia area. It covers 1,275 acres along the banks of the Delaware River. Operations under the base's command include a damage control training center, a school for boilermen, an ammunition depot, and a shipyard, established in 1801. The naval base also serves as Fourth Naval District headquarters. The District operates an air engineering center and a home for aged and disabled navy veterans.   JOHN A. OUDINE

PHILAE is an island in the Nile River near Aswan in southern Egypt. See ASWAN.

PHILANDER SMITH COLLEGE. See UNIVERSITIES AND COLLEGES (table).

PHILANTHROPY, *fih LAN throh pih,* is the promotion of the well-being of mankind by individuals and groups who contribute their services or dedicate their property and money. Philanthropy differs from charity in that it usually helps a large group or an institution, rather than one or a few individuals.

Nearly all civilizations have practiced some type of philanthropy. The ancient Jews levied a *tithe* (tax) for the poor. In ancient Egypt and Greece, royal families gave gifts to establish libraries and universities. The medieval church supported hospitals and orphanages.

In Anglo-Saxon law, the legal basis of philanthropy rests on the Statute of Charitable Uses, passed in England in 1601. The statute approved governmental aid to poor, aged, and orphaned persons. It also provided for assistance to hospitals, schools, and universities.

In the United States, gifts from private donors helped establish many early churches, colleges, and hospitals. For example, gifts helped create and support Harvard College. In 1790, Benjamin Franklin established a fund to aid worthy young men. In 1829, James Smithson set aside money for the creation of the Smithsonian Institution (see SMITHSONIAN INSTITUTION).

Philanthropy has played an increasingly important role in American society since the Civil War. Men of large fortunes, such as John D. Rockefeller and Andrew Carnegie, established great foundations that have worked to better mankind nationally and internationally. The contributions of such men have set an example for the public, which voluntarily contributes about $10 billion annually through benevolent and civic agencies.   JOSEPH C. KIGER

Related Articles in WORLD BOOK include:

AMERICAN PHILANTHROPISTS

Armour, Philip D.	Baldwin, Matthias W.
Astor (William B.)	Carnegie, Andrew
Cooper, Peter	Kellogg, Will Keith
Corcoran, William W.	Mellon, Andrew
Cornell, Ezra	Morgan (John; John, Jr.;
Curtis, Cyrus H. K.	Junius)
Drexel, Anthony J.	Newberry, Walter L.
Duke, James B.	Peabody, George
Du Pont de Nemours	Pulitzer, Joseph
(Pierre [1870-1954])	Rockefeller (John D.;
Eastman, George	John D., Jr.)
Field (Marshall I;	Rosenwald, Julius
III; IV)	Sage, Russell
Ford (family)	Stanford, Leland
Girard, Stephen	Stetson, John B.
Gould (Helen M.)	Tilden, Samuel J.
Guggenheim (family)	Vanderbilt (Cornelius;
Harkness, Edward S.	William K.)
Harvard, John	Vassar, Matthew
Hopkins, Johns	Wanamaker, John
Juilliard, Augustus	

BRITISH PHILANTHROPISTS

Chalmers, Thomas	Shaftesbury
Rhodes, Cecil J.	(Anthony [1801-1885])
Rothschild (family)	Smithson, James
Selkirk, Earl of	Yale, Elihu

OTHER PHILANTHROPISTS

McGill, James	Nobel, Alfred B.
Medici (family)	

OTHER RELATED ARTICLES

Endowment	Foundation

PHILATELY. See STAMP COLLECTING.

PHILEMON. See BAUCIS AND PHILEMON.

PHILEMON, EPISTLE TO, is the eighteenth book of the New Testament. It is the shortest of the letters Paul wrote while he was a prisoner in Rome. He sent it to Philemon, one of his followers. Philemon was a rich man of Colossae, at whose house the Christians held their meetings. Paul was sending a runaway Christian slave back to his owner, and asked his friend to receive the slave kindly. The Epistle is considered one of the most beautiful letters ever written.   FREDERICK C. GRANT

PHILIDOR. See CHESS (History).

Culver
Philip II of France

Brown Bros.
Philip IV of France

PHILIP was the name of several French kings. Most important were Philip II, Philip IV, and Philip VI.

Philip II (1165-1223), known as Philip Augustus, was the first great king of the Capetian dynasty. A clever statesman, he not only expanded the kingdom of France, but also made the monarchy powerful.

Philip came to the throne when his father, Louis VII, died in 1180. His first triumph was adding Picardy to his kingdom. This region was promised him as a dowry, but he had to force his father-in-law to give it up.

Philip then determined to gain the English possessions in France for himself. To weaken England's power, he encouraged the sons of the English king, Henry II, to revolt against their father. Henry's oldest son, Richard the Lion-Hearted, took the English throne in 1189, and he and Philip went together on the Third Crusade. But Philip soon returned home and began to make trouble for the absent Richard.

In 1198 Richard returned and began a war against Philip, but was killed in battle the next year. Richard's brother, King John, went to war with Philip in 1202. Philip took advantage of John's mistakes and successfully conquered most of the English holdings in France. John kept only the southern part of Aquitaine, or Guienne. Philip's victory at the Battle of Bouvines in 1214 established his hold on the conquered regions.

Philip then held greater powers than any of his strongest barons, and he carried out a series of governmental reforms. These reforms laid the basis for the later rule of the French kings.

Philip IV (1268-1314) was called *the Fair* because he was considered the handsomest man of his time. He came to the throne in 1285. By his marriage, he added the region of Champagne to the kingdom of France. Then he began an unsuccessful war with England in 1294. A later war against Flanders resulted in a defeat at Courtrai in 1302.

That same year, Philip quarreled with Pope Boniface VIII, because he taxed Roman Catholic churches against the pope's orders. Philip had the pope arrested, but later released him. Three years later, in 1305, a French bishop became Pope Clement V. The new pope moved to Avignon, France, in 1309 and carried out the French king's orders, which included suppressing the Knights Templars (see KNIGHTS TEMPLARS).

Philip VI (1293-1350), a nephew of Philip IV, was the first king of the Valois dynasty. He came to the throne in 1328. That same year, he defeated the Flemish army at Cassel and gained the region of Guienne. But relations with England were unfriendly, and in 1337 the Hundred Years' War broke out. Philip was defeated several times, but succeeded in extending his rule throughout many more regions of France. He bought the rights of the last count of Vienne, who had the title of Dauphin (see DAUPHIN). This title was then passed to the eldest son of each French king until 1830. FRANKLIN D. SCOTT

Brown Bros.
Philip II of Spain

Brown Bros.
Philip V of Spain

quered Portugal in 1580. But his reign marked the beginning of the destruction of Spain as a world empire. In 1581, The Netherlands, one of the most valuable possessions of Spain, declared its independence. After Sir Francis Drake and other British captains attacked and plundered Spanish possessions in Mexico and South America, Philip sent the "Invincible Armada" against England in 1588. The British destroyed this great fleet, and shattered Spanish sea power. See ARMADA.

Philip regarded himself as the champion of the Roman Catholic faith, and supported the harsh measures of the Inquisition. He was born at Valladolid, Spain, and was married to Queen Mary I of England. See MARY (I); ESCORIAL; NETHERLANDS (History); SPAIN (History).

Philip V (1683-1746) became ruler of Spain in 1700. He was the first of the Spanish kings of the royal Bourbon family of France (see BOURBON). Other nations refused to recognize him as king, and the War of the Spanish Succession began. In 1713, Philip finally won recognition as king, but he lost many of his territories to Austria and England. Philip's second wife, Elizabeth Farnese of Parma, caused Philip much difficulty. He abdicated in 1724 in favor of his son, Louis, but returned in eight months when Louis died.

Philip was born in Versailles, France. He was the grandson of Louis XIV of France and of Maria Theresa of Spain. Philip inherited the throne through Charles II of Spain, Maria Theresa's brother. J. CARY DAVIS

See also SUCCESSION WARS (The War of the Spanish Succession).

PHILIP II (382-336 B.C.) was a great Macedonian king who became master of Greece. He was the father of

Historical Pictures Service

Philip II of Macedonia, the father of Alexander the Great, was fatally stabbed in 336 B.C. One of his guardsmen killed him while Philip was celebrating a daughter's marriage. Some ancient historians believed Philip's wife Olympias was behind the plot.

Brown Bros.
Philip VI of France

Related Articles in WORLD BOOK include:

Capetian Dynasty	France (History)	Salic Law
Crécy, Battle of	Hundred Years' War	Valois

PHILIP was the name of several kings of Spain. Two, Philip II and Philip V, became especially famous.

Philip II (1527-1598) ruled from 1556 until his death. He succeeded his father, Charles I of Spain. Charles ruled the Holy Roman Empire as Charles V, but Philip did not become emperor. Philip broke the power of the Turks in the Mediterranean Sea in 1571, and also con-

Alexander the Great, who carried out many of his father's dreams of conquest. See ALEXANDER THE GREAT.

Philip, the youngest son of Amyntas II, was born in Pella. In his early youth, he spent several years as a hostage in Thebes. There he learned much of military science from the foremost military leaders of the time. Philip was named regent for his nephew in 359 B.C. when his older brother died. But Philip soon made himself king. Within two years, he put down all opposition and established himself securely on the throne.

Philip immediately began to carry out his plans of conquest by attacking the Greek towns on his border. He had reorganized the Macedonian army so that it was far superior to the Greek armies. He used the heavy phalanx formation of infantry attack as a striking arm and heavy cavalry for the knockout blow (see PHALANX). He developed the light infantry and light cavalry and used them in an all-out pursuit which destroyed his opponents. Within a few years, he controlled most of the small states in Greece, and his power extended as far north as the Danube River.

In Athens, Demosthenes understood Philip's plans, and he thundered forth against Philip in his famous speeches, which came to be known as the *Philippics*. But the Athenians refused to listen to Demosthenes. They did not believe Philip was a threat to Athens, because he was at war with Thrace at the time. In 338 B.C., Demosthenes was finally able to rouse the Athenians, and they joined with Thebes in a defensive league against Philip. But the Macedonian king completely defeated the allied armies in the battle of Chaeronea that same year, and ended Greek independence.

Philip formed Greece into a political organization called the League of Corinth. All the cities were included except Sparta, which had never been conquered. The cities were represented in the *Synhedrion* (council) by population and by districts. Nations outside Greece were permitted to join.

Philip was chosen by the League to command the combined Greek forces to attack Persia. He was killed while preparing for this war.   THOMAS W. AFRICA

See also DEMOSTHENES; MACEDONIA; OLYMPIAS.

PHILIP, KING (? -1676), became chief of the Wampanoag Indians in 1662. His Indian name was Metacomet. He was the son of Massasoit, the Pilgrims' friend. Philip succeeded his older brother as chief.

As Philip saw the increasing amounts of land taken by the settlers, he grew concerned that the colonists would in time destroy his people. Soon after he became chief, he began preparations to massacre all the white settlers in New England. The great struggle known as King Philip's War began in 1675. Philip burned both white and Indian settlements. Men, women, and children were killed on both sides. King Philip almost succeeded in wiping out the English settlements in New England. But after the defeat of his forces by the English colonists, Philip was hunted down and killed in a swamp near present-day Mt. Hope, R.I. The war lasted about three years.   WILLIAM H. GILBERT

See also INDIAN WARS (King Philip's War); MASSASOIT.

Colonists Killed King Philip near present-day Mount Hope, R.I., after the Indian uprisings of 1676. ▶

PHILIP, PRINCE (1921-   ), DUKE OF EDINBURGH, married Princess Elizabeth of Great Britain in 1947. She became Queen Elizabeth II in 1952.

Philip was born on the Greek island of Corfu on June 10, 1921. His father, Prince Andrew of Greece, was the fourth son of King George I of Greece. Philip's mother, Princess Alice of Battenberg, was a great-granddaughter of Queen Victoria of Great Britain and sister to Admiral of the Fleet Lord Louis Mountbatten (see MOUNTBATTEN, LOUIS).

Philip received his education in England, at Cheam school and Gordonstoun school, and at the Royal Naval College in Dartmouth. During World War II, he served as a lieutenant in the British Navy with the Mediterranean Fleet and the British Pacific Fleet. In 1947, he renounced his title and rights of succession to the throne of Greece. He became a British citizen and took Mountbatten for his last name.

King George VI of Great Britain made Philip Duke of Edinburgh on the day of his wedding to Princess Elizabeth. In 1957, Elizabeth gave Philip the title of Prince of the United Kingdom.

Philip accompanied Queen Elizabeth on all her royal tours and official visits throughout the British Commonwealth of Nations. He made a world tour alone from October, 1956, to February, 1957, in connection with the Olympic Games in Melbourne, Australia, which he opened in November, 1956. On this tour he visited Antarctica, the first member of the British royal family to do so.

Prince Philip interested himself particularly in scientific research and education, and in industrial relations. He tirelessly visited factories, research institutions, colleges, and schools. He became a vigorous

Ayer Collection, Newberry Library

Associated Press Ltd.; Reuter Photos Ltd.

Prince Philip often represents Queen Elizabeth at affairs of state. He represented her at Kenya's independence ceremonies in Nairobi, *right*. He takes a personal interest in scientific research and education, and enjoys sailing and polo.

and popular public speaker, whose detailed knowledge of his subjects won the admiration of his hosts. Some of his talks were collected and published as *Selected Speeches*. Philip also became an enthusiastic yachtsman and polo player.　　　　　　　　　　C. L. MOWAT

See also ELIZABETH II.

PHILIP OF BETHSAIDA, SAINT, was one of the original company of the disciples of John the Baptist whom Jesus called at the beginning of His ministry (John 1: 44). His name is Greek, meaning *lover of horses*. He may have been of Greek descent, or he may have adopted the name because he lived in the Greek-speaking cities of Galilee.

Philip seems to have been a plain, practical, matter-of-fact person. At the feeding of the 5,000, he calculated how much the food for the crowd would have cost (John 6: 5-7). When the disciples questioned Jesus before His death, Philip asked Jesus to show them the Father. Jesus replied, "He that hath seen me hath seen the Father" (John 14: 8, 9). According to later tradition, Philip went to Phrygia as a missionary and died there as a martyr. His feast day is generally observed as the feast of Saints Philip and James (the Less) on May 1. But the Eastern Orthodox Church celebrates his feast day on November 14.　　FULTON J. SHEEN and MERRILL C. TENNEY

PHILIP THE EVANGELIST was one of the seven officers, or deacons, of the early Christian church in Jerusalem (Acts 6: 5). Philip was probably among the first to preach that Christianity was a religion for all peoples. In Samaria, Philip converted Simon Magus (Acts 8: 5). Later, he converted the treasurer of Ethiopia (Acts 8: 26-39).　　　　　　　FREDERICK C. GRANT

PHILIPPE. See ORLÉANS (family).

PHILIPPI, *fuh LIP eye*, was a city in western Thrace, about 8 miles from the Aegean coast. King Philip II of Macedon founded the city in 357 B.C. The city became an important gold-mining center. Mark Antony and Octavian (later Augustus) defeated two of Julius Caesar's assassins, Brutus and Cassius, at Philippi in 42 B.C. Octavian later made Philippi a colony for Antony's supporters who had been expelled from Italy. Philippi was the first city in Europe to be visited by St. Paul.　　　　　　　　　DONALD W. BRADEEN

See also PHILIPPIANS, EPISTLE TO THE.

PHILIPPIANS, EPISTLE TO THE, the 11th book of the New Testament, was written by the Apostle Paul about A.D. 60. In the *epistle* (letter), Paul urged Christians in Philippi (now a mass of ruins in northern Greece) to keep peace within the church and to guard against evil men. He thanked the Philippians for sending him money and a helper while he was ill and imprisoned in Rome. Paul told the Philippians that he had converted members of the Emperor's household to Christianity while he was in prison.　　W. W. SLOAN

PHILIPPICS. See CICERO, MARCUS TULLIUS; DEMOSTHENES.

331

The Carabao is a common beast of burden in the Philippines.

Northwest Orient Airlines

Volcanic Mount Mayon, the Philippines' most symmetrical mountain, rises 8,071 feet above the sheltered harbor of Legaspi in southern Luzon.

PHILIPPINES, *FIHL uh peenz,* an island country in the southwest Pacific Ocean, is one of the leading democracies of southeastern Asia. The country's full name is REPUBLIC OF THE PHILIPPINES. Quezon City is the official capital. Manila is the largest city and chief governmental center.

Rugged mountains rise above the thick jungles and green plains of the more than 7,000 tropical islands. The total area of the Philippines is a little larger than that of Wisconsin and Michigan combined. But the country has about three times as many people as those two states together. The brown-skinned, dark-haired people of the Philippines are called *Filipinos.* About 90 of every 100 Filipinos are Christians, making the Philippines the only Christian country in Asia.

The Philippines ranks among the world's leading producers of coconuts, rice, and sugar. Forests furnish mahogany and other fine lumber. Mines supply gold,

Carlos P. Romulo, the contributor of this article, is Secretary of Foreign Affairs of the Philippines. Jean Grossholtz, the critical reviewer, is Associate Professor of Political Science at Mount Holyoke College.

silver, and other minerals. The waters around the islands provide large catches of fish.

The United States governed the Philippines from the early 1900's to the mid-1940's. During this period, the Americans trained the Filipinos in self-government, introduced a public school system, and improved economic and social conditions. The United States granted the Philippines independence on July 4, 1946.

The Philippines often takes a leading part in the community of Asian countries. For the relationship of the Philippines to other Asian lands, see ASIA.

The Islands

The Philippines lies just north of the equator, stretching 1,152 miles from north to south, a distance about equal to that from Denver to Detroit. The northernmost islands are only about 330 miles from the mainland of Asia. The *Color Map* with this article shows that the islands face the Luzon Strait on the north, the Philippine Sea (a part of the Pacific Ocean) on the east, and the Celebes Sea on the south. The Sulu Sea lies southwest of the islands and the South China Sea lies to the west.

The islands range in size from 41,765-square-mile

Luzon to small patches of swampland or jagged rock. Only 463 of the more than 7,100 islands have an area of more than 1 square mile apiece. People live on only about 730 of the islands. About 4,300 islands do not even have names. Volcanic peaks rise steeply from the coasts of many of the islands. The few lowland areas include the large central plain of Luzon Island and the plain west of the city of Iloilo on Panay Island. Most of the people live on these plains and lowlands.

The country includes three main island groups. The Luzon group in the northern Philippines consists of Luzon, Mindoro, and other nearby islands. The Visayan group includes Bohol, Cebu, Leyte, Masbate, Negros, Palawan, Panay, Samar, and other small islands in the central Philippines. The Mindanao group consists of Mindanao and the islands of the Sulu Archipelago.

The chief Philippine islands are described below.

Bohol, *boh HAWL* (area 1,590 sq. mi.), lies in the Visayan group. Mountains rise to a height of 2,630 feet in the central part of this island. The people of Bohol raise rice, coconuts, corn, and abacá.

Cebu, *say BOO* (area 1,965 sq. mi.), in the Visayan group, is the most thickly populated Philippine island. About 700 persons live on every square mile. Cebu is only 20 miles from east to west, but it stretches 139 miles. Low mountains and hills cover this island. Corn is the chief agricultural product. Cebu also grows rice, sugar cane, coconuts, and tobacco. Large limestone deposits supply the island's cement factory with raw material. The people also mine some coal. Cebu, the island's chief city, is an important port.

Leyte, *LAY tee,* in Spanish, *LAY tay* (area 3,090 sq. mi.), became famous in World War II. It was the scene of the first landing of United States troops when they liberated the Philippines from the Japanese in 1944 and 1945. Leyte's mountains rise as high as 4,426 feet. Farmers raise abacá, rice, and tobacco. Copra is an important product. Tacloban is the chief city of Leyte.

Luzon, *loo ZAHN* (area 41,765 sq. mi.), in the northern group, is the largest and most important island. It is a little larger than Kentucky. Quezon City and

FACTS IN BRIEF

Capital: Quezon City.

Official Language: Pilipino.

Form of Government: Republic.

Area: 115,830 sq. mi. *Greatest Distances*—(north-south) 1,152 mi.; (east-west) 688 mi. *Coastline*—14,400 mi.

Population: *1960 Census*—27,087,685; distribution, 70 per cent rural, 30 per cent urban. *Estimated 1970 Population*—38,424,000; density, 332 persons to the square mile. *Estimated 1975 Population*—45,635,000.

Chief Products: *Agriculture*—abacá, coconuts, copra, corn, livestock, pineapples, rice, sugar, tobacco. *Manufacturing and Processing*—chemicals, clothing, foods, textiles, tobacco products. *Forestry*—kapok, mahogany. *Fishing Industry*—fish, mother-of-pearl, sponges. *Mining*—chromite, copper, gold, iron, manganese, silver.

Flag: The top half is blue, the bottom red. A white triangle at left has a gold sun (for liberty) and three gold stars (for the main island divisions). Red is for courage; white, purity; and blue, high political purpose. See FLAG (color picture: Flags of Asia and the Pacific).

National Anthem: "Lupang Hinirang" ("Land that I Love").

National Holiday: Independence Day, June 12.

Money: *Basic Unit*—Peso. One hundred centavos equal one peso. See MONEY (table: Values). See also PESO.

The Philippines lies off the coast of Southeast Asia, *right.* The map, *below,* compares its area with the United States.

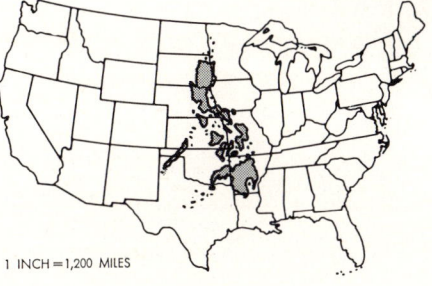

1 INCH = 1,200 MILES

Cities and Towns

Agoo 6,511
▲21,093..C 3
Alimodian* .6,732
▲18,121..F 4
Angeles ...75,900..K 8
Antipolo ..17,970
▲21,598..K 8
Aparri 13,167
▲33,424..B 3
Atimonan* .8,439
▲32,294..D 3
Baao* 6,764
▲22,724..E 4
Bacarra ...7,268
▲18,570..B 3
Bacolod ...142,000..F 4
Bago* ....58,834..F 4
Baguio ...50,436..C 3
Bais 5,058
▲433,653..G 4
Balangiga .5,343
▲8,215..F 5
Balayan ..5,693
▲23,745..E 3
Balingasag .5,502
▲19,715..G 5
Balintawak* 5,430..F 4
(Esca-
lante) .▲59,768..F 4
Bambang ..6,166
▲15,592..C 3
Bangued ..7,602
▲19,368..C 3
Bantayan ..7,920
▲30,623..F 4
Basey* 6,240
▲29,680..F 5
Basilan ..187,000..H 3
Batangas ..14,182
▲82,627..E 3
Bayambang .6,371
▲47,498..K 8
Bayawan ..6,204
▲30,429..G 4
Baybay ...10,021
▲51,799..F 5
Bayombong .8,312
▲17,499..C 3
Binalbagan 13,545
▲31,160..F 4
Binangonan* 6,932
▲31,274..D 3
Bogo 6,786
▲29,841..F 4
Bongabon .8,358
▲20,854..D 3
Buenavista* .5,770
▲17,927..G 5
Bulan 16,042
▲46,520..E 4
Bulusan* ..5,394
▲15,539..E 5
Burauen* ..8,677
31,807..F 5
Butuan ...82,485..G 5
Cabadbaran .5,954
▲26,216..G 5
Cabanatuan 69,580..D 3
Cadiz 15,514
▲88,542..F 4
Cagayan de
Oro ....68,274..G 5
Caibiran ..7,213
▲16,963..F 5
Calamba ..12,142
▲57,715..K 8
Calbayog ..77,832..E 5
Caloocan ..174,500..K 8
Camiling 9,799
▲40,536..D 3
Candelaria .6,132
▲29,928..L 8
Carcar ...6,657
▲36,304..F 4
Carigara ..8,299
▲26,761..F 5
Catarman ..8,248
▲39,434..E 5
Catbalogan .14,274
▲34,873..F 5
Cavite ...54,891..D 3
Cebu .....299,700..F 4
Cotabato .37,499..H 5
Cuyapo* ..7,617
▲30,634..D 3
Daet 19,726
▲35,434..D 4
Dagupan ..63,191..C 3
Danao* ...32,826..F 4
Dapitan ..27,517..G 4
Datu Piang 21,951
▲36,464..H 5
Davao ...269,300..H 5
Digos 8,725
▲31,174..H 5
Dipolog ..15,102
▲32,236..G 4
Donsol* ...5,509
▲23,703..E 4
Dulag* ...6,415
▲31,613..E 5
Dumaguete .35,282..G 4

Enrile 5,570
▲16,095..C 3
Gapan 6,741
▲32,514..K 8
General
Tinio 9,772
▲14,925..K 8
General
Trias 6,011
▲21,618..D 3
Gingoog ..52,677..G 5
Goa 5,087
▲24,663..E 4
Gubat 8,392
▲31,028..E 5
Guihulñgan* 6,401
▲42,993..F 4
Guimba ...8,280
▲38,148..D 3
Guinobatan* 7,935
▲48,157..E 4
Guiuan* ...5,865
▲22,881..F 5
Gumaca ...9,175
▲27,284..E 4
Himamaylan* 5,195
▲41,985..F 4
Hinigaran* 10,231
▲36,240..F 4
Iligan ...58,433..G 5
Iloilo ...180,900..F 4
Iriga 27,469
▲75,439..E 4
Irosin 6,631
▲23,134..E 5
Isabela* ..6,052
▲29,769..F 4
Itogon* ...7,466
▲32,742..C 3
Januiay* ..5,840
▲46,946..F 4
Jaro* 7,243
▲32,243..F 5
Jose Pañ-
ganiban ..5,291
▲27,144..D 4
Kabankalan .8,856
▲59,341..G 4
Kalibo ...6,025
▲21,303..F 4
Kidapawan* 5,727
▲61,675..H 5
Koronadal ..9,515
▲32,437..H 5
La Carlota 56,772..F 4
Laoag ...50,198..B 3
Laoang 8,557
▲41,158..E 5
Lapu-Lapu* 48,546..F 4
Legazpi ..60,593..E 4
Lemery 8,617
▲23,700..L 8
Lianga 5,772
▲17,182..G 6
Libmanan* .5,291
▲52,512..E 4
Ligao* ...10,547
▲53,376..E 4
Lilio* 6,697
▲11,064..D 3
Lingayen ..8,221
▲45,321..D 3
Lipa ....69,036..E 3
Lopez* 7,196
▲31,558..E 4
Lucban ...14,292
▲17,452..D 3
Lucena ...49,264..E 3
Lumban* ..7,206
▲9,719..D 3
Maasin 7,339
▲39,185..F 5
Magallanes .6,002
▲18,144..E 4
Magarao* ..5,811
▲8,501..E 4
Makati* ...12,869
▲114,540..D 3
Malabang ..7,884
▲27,152..H 5
Malalag Beach
(Malalag) .5,242
▲40,153..H 5
Malasiqui .5,314
▲50,730..K 8
Malaybalay .7,624
▲34,088..G 5
Malita 5,947
▲28,228..H 5
Manapla* ..8,044
▲46,809..F 4
Mandaluy-
ong* 16,757
▲71,619..D 3
Mandaon ..11,419
▲13,277..E 4
Mandaue* ..6,353
▲29,281..F 4
Manila ..1,356,000..D 3
Marawi ...27,049..G 5
Masbate ..11,647
▲31,613..E 5

Mati 7,870
▲23,479..H 6
Mauban ...6,293
▲18,703..D 3
Mendez-
Nuñez* ...5,908
▲11,427..D 3
Mercedes* ..5,081
▲13,983..D 4
Midsayap ..6,789
▲46,169..H 5
Miral*
(Bansalan) 6,602
▲45,360..H 5
Morong ...6,006
▲13,694..K 8
Muñoz 5,213
▲27,622..K 8
Nabua* ...14,146
▲66,657..E 4
Naga ....55,506..E 4
Nagcarlan* .8,214
▲18,227..D 3
Nasipit* ..7,531
▲14,996..G 5
Nasugbu ..8,468
▲34,845..D 3
Navotas* ..8,332
▲49,262..D 3
Olongapo ..5,034
▲45,330..D 3
Orion 7,663
▲14,672..K 8
Ormoc ...62,764..F 5
Oroquieta .5,331
▲29,477..G 4
Oton 5,511
▲27,246..F 4
Ozamiz ...44,091..G 4
Paete* ...7,443..K 8
Pagadian ..17,865
▲41,810..H 5
Pagbilao* .8,367
▲17,303..E 3
Palo 8,916
▲25,325..F 5
Palompon ..6,399
▲31,291..F 5
Panabo ...5,539
▲42,509..H 5
Paniqui ...6,492
▲35,416..K 8
Parañaque* 10,086
▲61,898..D 3
Parang* ...5,894
▲37,296..H 5
Pasay ...157,800..D 3
Pinama-
layan 6,236
▲39,240..E 3
Pontevedra* .6,476
▲22,751..F 4
Pototan ...5,475
▲37,231..F 4
Puerto
Princesa .7,551
▲23,125..G 2
Pulupandan* 7,990
▲14,844..F 4
Quezon
City ....482,400..D 3
Quintana ..4,422..K 8
Rajah
Buayan .84,988..H 5
Rizal 6,114
▲19,447..K 8
Robles*
(La Castel-
lana) ...14,011
▲35,630..F 4
Rosales ...5,477
▲24,347..K 8
Roxas ...49,326..F 4
Roxas 5,612
▲17,959..C 3
Sagay* ...5,110
▲71,335..F 4
Salaman
(Lebak) ..5,626
▲22,173..H 5
Sampaloc* .5,373
▲6,538..D 3
San
Antonio ..8,717
▲11,596..D 3
San Carlos 148,900..D 3
San Carlos .73,900..D 3
San Felipe .5,900
▲9,861..D 3
San Jacinto .5,120
▲17,330..E 4
San Jose ..6,364
▲17,124..F 3
San Jose ..10,353
▲38,078..K 8
San Juan del
Monte* ..12,743
▲56,861..D 3
San
Manuel ...5,993
▲20,959..C 3
San
Marcelino .6,841
▲13,914..D 3

San Mateo* .7,642
▲12,044..D 3
San Pablo .70,680..D 3
Santa
Barbara* .6,256
▲23,458..F 4
Santa Cruz .6,456
▲24,401..H 5
Santa Cruz .5,248
▲28,630..K 8
Santa
Magdalena 5,155
▲14,259..E 5
Santa Rosa .5,580
▲26,583..K 8
Santo
Domingo* .5,097
▲66,657..E 4
Sariaya* ...7,110
▲42,089..E 3
Silang ...7,407
▲28,631..K 8
Silay ...60,324..F 4
Sindangan .5,867
▲37,105..G 4
Sipocot ...5,914
▲32,650..K 8
Solano ...12,095
▲22,523..C 3
Sorsogon ..13,983
▲35,542..E 5
Surigao ...15,661
▲37,439..G 5
Tabaco ...11,599
▲46,416..E 4
Tacloban ..53,551..F 5
Tacurong ..6,413
▲27,695..H 5
Tagaytay ..7,203..K 8
Tagbilaran .7,206
▲20,250..G 4
Tagum 5,263
▲28,982..H 5
Talavera* .5,217
▲28,603..D 3

Talisay* ..20,254
▲46,380..F 4
Tanauan* ..7,145
▲44,975..K 8
Tanauan* ..7,355
▲23,421..F 5
Tanay* ...11,123
▲13,955..D 3
Tanjay ...12,355
▲39,547..G 4
Tañong*
(Malabon) 5,903
▲76,438..D 3
Tarlac ...1,764
▲98,285..D 3
Tayabas ...9,272
▲25,758..L 8
Tayug 5,629
▲20,755..J 8
Tibal-og
(Santo
Tomas)* ..9,450
▲16,687..H 5
Toboso* ...5,401
▲36,378..F 4
Toledo ...63,881..F 4
Tuguegarao 10,497
▲43,074..C 3
Urdaneta ..5,756
▲44,744..K 8
Victoria ..5,580
▲8,922..K 8
Victorias ..12,446
▲34,290..F 4
Vigan ...10,498
▲25,990..C 3
Villaba ...5,147
▲24,844..F 5
Virac 9,143
▲34,417..E 5
Wao 6,131
▲13,848..H 5
Wright 5,104
▲16,267..F 5
Zamboanga 158,000..H 4

Physical Features

Agno River ....K 8
Agusan River ......G 5
Aubarede Point ....C 4
Babuyan Channel ..B 3
Babuyan Islands ...B 3
Balabac Island ....H 1
Balabac Strait ....H 1
Balayan Bay ....L 8
Baler Bay ....D 3
Balintang Channel .B 3
Bancoran Island ...H 2
Basilan Island ....H 4
Basilan Strait ....H 4
Bataan Peninsula ..K 8
Batan Islands .....A 3
Bohol (Island) ....G 5
Bohol Strait ......G 5
Bugsuk Island .....G 1
Burias Island .....E 4
Busuanga Island ...E 2
Cagayan Islands ...G 3
Cagayan River .....C 3
Cagayan Sulu
Islands ....H 2
Calamian Group ...E 2
Calayan Island ....B 3
Camiguin Island ...F 4
Camiguin Island ...B 3
Camotes Sea ......F 5
Canlaon Volcano ...F 4
Cape Encanto ......D 3
Cape San Agustin ..H 6
Cape San Ildefonso C 4
Catanduanes Island E 5
Cebu (Island) .....F 4
Celebes Sea ......I 4
Corregidor (Island) .K 8
Culion Island .....E 2
Dalupiri Island ...B 3
Dasol Bay ....K 7
Davao Gulf ....H 5
Dinagat Island ....F 5
Dinagat Sound .....F 5
Dingalan Bay ......D 3
Dumaran Island ....F 2
Fuga Island ....B 3
Guimaras Island ...F 4
Honda Bay ....G 2
Iligan Bay ....G 4
Illana Bay ....H 4
Imuruan Bay ......F 2
Jolo Island ......I 3
Lagonoy Gulf .....E 4
Laguna de Bay
(lake) ....K 8
Lake Lanao ....H 5
Lake Mainit ......G 5
Lake Taal ....L 8
Lamon Bay ....D 3
Leyte Gulf ....F 5
Leyte (Island) ....F 5
Lianga Bay ....G 6
Linapacan Island ..F 2
Linapacan Strait ..F 2
Lingayen Gulf .....C 3
Lubang Island .....L 8

Lubang Islands ....E 2
Luzon (Island) ....C 3
Luzon Strait ......A 3
Magat River ....J 8
Manila Bay ....D 3
Marinduque
(Island) ....E 4
Masbate (Island) ..E 4
Mayon Volcano ....E 4
Mindanao Deep ....G 6
Mindanao (Island) .H 5
Mindanao Sea .....G 5
Mindoro (Island) ..E 3
Mindoro Strait ....E 3
Moro Gulf ....H 4
Mount Apo ....H 5
Mount Cauitan ....C 3
Mount Pulog ......C 3
Mount Sicapoo ....B 3
Negros (Island) ...G 4
Palawan (Island) ..E 2
Pampanga River ...K 8
Panay Gulf ....F 4
Panay (Island) ....F 4
Pangutaran Island .H 3
Philippine Sea ....E 5
Polillo Islands ...D 3
Polillo Strait ....D 3
Pulangi River .....H 5
Samar (Island) ....E 5
Samar Sea ....E 5
San Miguel Bay ...D 4
San Miguel
Islands ....A 3
Sarangani Bay .....I 5
Sarangani Islands ..I 5
Scarborough Shoal .D 1
Semirara Islands ..F 3
Siargao Island ....G 6
Sibuguey Bay .....H 4
Sibutu Island ....I 2
Sibutu Passage ...I 2
Sibuyan Island ...E 4
Sibuyan Sea ......E 4
Sierra Madre
(Mountains) .....C 4
Sindangan Bay ....G 4
Siquijor Island ...G 4
South China Sea ..F 1
Subic Bay ....K 8
Sulu Archipelago ..I 3
Sulu Sea ....G 2
Surigao Strait ....F 5
Tablas Island .....E 4
Tablas Strait .....E 3
Tawitawi Island ...I 2
Tayabas Bay ......E 4
Taytay Bay ....E 2
Ticao Island .....E 4
Tinaca Point .....I 5
Tolong Bay ....G 4
Tubbataha Reefs ...F 2
Verde Island .....L 8
Verde Island
Passage ....L 8
Visayan Sea ......F 4

*Does not appear on the map; key shows general location.
▲Population of entire municipality, including rural area.

Sources: 1960 census; 1965 official estimates for largest cities.

PHILIPPINES

Evergreen Trees

Mixed Evergreen and Deciduous Trees

Grass

★ National Capital

• Cities and Towns

Rail Lines

1 inch = 127 Statute Miles

Miles 0 10 20 40 60 80 100 120

Lambert Conformal Conic Projection

CM TERRAIN Philippines
COPYRIGHT BY
RAND McNALLY & COMPANY
MADE IN U.S.A.

Luzon Strait

BATAN ISLANDS

PRATAS ISLAND (CHINA)

South China Sea

SCARBOROUGH SHOAL

Lingayen Gulf

Baguio
Agoo
Dagupan
Lingayen
Santa Cruz
San Carlos
Camiling
Tarlac
Guimba
San Manuel
Bambang
Bayombong
Solano
Bangued
Enrile
Tuguegarao
Roxas
Vigan
Banguel
Laoag
Bacarra
Aparri

MT. SICAPPO 7,717 FT.
MT. CALITAN 8,510 FT.
MT. PULOG 9,626 FT.

Babuyan Channel
CALAYAN
DALUPIRI FUGA
CAMIGUIN
BABUYAN ISLANDS

Balintang Channel

CAGAYAN
SIERRA MADRE

AUBAREDE POINT
CAPE SAN ILDEFONSO
CAPE ENCANTO

LUZON

San Felipe
San Antonio
Olongapo
San Marcelino
San Jose
Cabanatuan
Bongabon
Camiling

QUEZON CITY
Manila
Pasay
Cavite
San Pablo
Nasugbu
Balayan
Lipa
Batangas

Lamon Bay
Mauban
Lucena
Gumaca
Daet
José Pañganiban

Tayabas Bay

POLILLO ISLANDS
Dingalan Bay

LUBANG ISLANDS

Manila Bay

MINDORO
Pinamalayan

Mindoro Strait

Tablas Strait

MARINDUQUE

Sibuyan Sea

BURIAS
TABLAS
MASBATE
Masbate
TICAO

San Miguel Bay
Goa
Naga
Iriga
Tabaco
Virac
CATANDUANES

Philippine Sea

MAYON VOLCANO 8,077 FT.
Legazpi
Magallanes
Bulan
San Jacinto
Mandaon
Sorsogon
Gubat
Irosin
Santa Magdalena
Laoang
Catarman
Calbayog
SAMAR
Wright
Catbalogan
Guiuan
Palapag

Samar Sea

Caibiran
Villaba
Carigara
Tacloban
Palo
Balangiga

Kalibo
Roxas
Bantayan
Bogo
PANAY
Pototan
Victorias
Cadiz
Iloilo
Oton
Silay
Bacolod
GUIMARAS
La Carlota
Binalbagan
Kabankalan
NEGROS
Bais
Bayawan
Dumaguete
SIQUIJOR

Visayan Sea

Palompon
Ormoc
LEYTE
Danao
Carcar
Maasin
Baybay
CEBU
San Carlos
Cebu
Toledo
BOHOL
Tagbilaran
Surigao
Camotes
LEYTE GULF
DINAGAT SOUND
SIARGAO

MINDANAO DEEP —34,440 FT.

Mindanao Sea

CALAMIAN GROUP
CULION
LINAPACAN
Linapacan Strait
SEMIRARA ISLANDS
BUSUANGA

PALAWAN

Taytay Bay
Imuruan Bay

DUMARAN

CAGAYAN ISLANDS
TUBBATAHA REEFS

Honda Bay
Puerto Princesa

6,839 FT. +5,948 FT.

Sulu Sea

BUGSUK
BALABAC
Balabac Strait
POLAU BANGGI

Marudu Bay
Kudat
MOUNT KINABALU 13,455 FT.
Sandakan
MALAYSIA

Darvel Bay
SIBUTU
TAWITAWI
TAWITAWI GROUP
SIASI
SIBUTU PASSAGE

Sulu Archipelago
JOLO

Zamboanga
Basilan
BASILAN
Basilan Strait
PANGUTARAN
SAN MIGUEL ISLANDS
BANCORAN
CAGAYAN SULU ISLANDS

Pagadian
MINDANAO
Illana Bay
Malabang
Cotabato
Datu Piang
Tacurong
Salaman
Koronadal
Rajah Buayan

Sibuguey Bay
Moro Gulf

Dipolog
Dapitan
Sindangan
Sindangan Bay
Ozamiz
Oroquieta
Iligan
Iligan Bay
Marawi
Balingasag
Cagayan de Oro
Malaybalay

Butuan
Cabadbaran
Gingoog
Lianga
Lianga Bay
CAMIGUIN

Lake Mainit

Waq
Midsayap
Lake Lanao
MT. APO 9,692 FT.
Davao
Digos
Malalag
Santa Cruz
Davao Gulf
MALITA
Mati
CAPE SAN AGUSTIN

Panabo
Tagum
Davao Beach

Sarangani Bay
TINACA POINT
SARANGANI ISLANDS

INDONESIA

Celebes Sea

Longitude East of Greenwich

335

Specially created for **World Book Encyclopedia** by Rand McNally and World Book editors

Luzon inset

Lingayen Gulf
Dagupan
San Carlos
Lingayen
Malasiqui
Dasol Bay
Camiling
Tarlac
San Manuel
Urdaneta
Rosales
Bayambang
Paniqui
Guimba
Tayug
Muñoz
Rizal
Bongabon
Cabanatuan

Magat
7,411 FT.
SIERRA MADRE

6,683 FT.
5,770 FT.
Gapan
General Tinio
Angeles
San Felipe
San Antonio
Olongapo
San Marcelino
San Jose

Baler Bay
CAPE ENCANTO
Dingalan Bay

QUEZON CITY
Caloocan
Manila
Orion
Antipolo
Cavite
Morong
General Trias
Santa Rosa
Paete
Silang
Santa Cruz
Tagaytay
Victoria
Mauban
Calamba
Nasugbu
Tanauan
San Pablo
Lucban
Balayan
Lipa
Tayabas
Lemery
Candelaria
Batangas
Lucena

Subic Bay
BATAAN PENINSULA
CORREGIDOR
Manila Bay
Laguna de Bay
Lake Taal
Balayan Bay
LUBANG ISLAND
Verde Island
Verde Passage
POLILLO
POLILLO ISLANDS
Lamon Bay

Miles 0 10 20 30

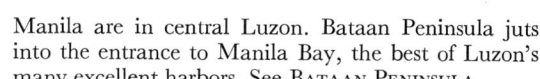

George Rodger, Magnum

Fishing Boats of the Moro Filipinos are called *vintas*. They dot the harbor of Zamboanga on Mindanao.

Fish of Many Varieties, both fresh and dried, rank second only to rice in importance in the Filipino diet.

Manila are in central Luzon. Bataan Peninsula juts into the entrance to Manila Bay, the best of Luzon's many excellent harbors. See BATAAN PENINSULA.

Rugged mountains cover most of Luzon. However, the largest lowland area of the Philippines lies between Manila Bay and Lingayen Gulf in central Luzon. Farmers grow two-fifths of the country's rice crop on this fertile plain. Rich forests grow along the coasts and in some inland sections. Mines in the mountains of northern Luzon provide gold, iron, and chromite.

Masbate, *mahs BAH tay* (area 1,563 sq. mi.), in the central Philippines, is one of the country's chief gold-producing areas. Low hills and mountains cover most of this island. Cattle graze on its grass-covered uplands. Farmers grow coconuts, rice, corn, tobacco, and other crops along the coast.

Mindanao, MIN *duh NAH oh*, in Spanish, MEEN *dah NAH oh* (area 38,344 sq. mi.), the second largest island, is a little larger than the state of Indiana. Mindanao lies at the extreme southeastern end of the Philippines. The country's highest mountains rise on this rugged island. Some are active volcanoes.

Mindanao has been called the *Philippine Land of Promise* because it has large areas of unused land and forests, and deposits of valuable minerals. Mindanao is one of the world's leading producers of abacá. Other products include copra, copper, corn, gold, iron, hardwood lumber, pineapples, and rice.

Mindoro, *mihn DOHR oh* (area 3,935 sq. mi.), lies 10 miles south of Luzon. Mindoro's mountains rise from coastal lowlands to heights of more than 8,000 feet. The island's chief products include mahogany lumber, livestock, rice, copra, and abacá.

Negros, *NAY grohs* (area 5,278 sq. mi.), ranks fourth in size among the Philippine Islands. It lies in the Visayan group. Several active volcanic peaks, including 8,071-foot Mount Canlaon, tower over L-shaped Negros. Sugar cane, the chief product, grows on the gentle slopes and plains of the coastal areas. Negros also has forests and grasslands. Bacolod, on the northwest coast, is a prosperous, fast-growing city.

Palawan, *pah LAH wahn* (area 5,751 sq. mi.), the third largest island, stretches far to the west of the other chief islands. Sliver-shaped Palawan is 275 miles long, but it has an average width of only 15 miles. Palawan has little flat ground, but the people raise corn, rice, and vegetables on the hillsides.

Panay, *pah NY* (area 4,748 sq. mi.), lies in the central Philippines. The island rises from fertile plains along the coast to high, rugged mountains in the interior. The Iloilo plain, in southeastern Panay, is one of the most fertile and thickly settled areas in the country. Farmers grow rice, sugar cane, corn, tobacco, and other crops. Weavers make fine textiles that are sold throughout the world. These textiles include *piña*, a cloth made of pineapple leaves, and *jusi*, a type of silk. Iloilo, the chief city, is an important port.

Samar, *SAH mahr* (area 5,185 sq. mi.), lies across the narrow San Juanico Strait from Leyte Island. Thick forests and low mountains cover most of this rugged island. Samar has developed slowly because of its wild countryside, and also because many destructive typhoons have hit it. Most of the people of Samar live on the narrow coastal lowlands. Abacá is an important product on Samar, but farmers also grow coconuts, rice, and corn.

Sulu Archipelago, *SOO loo* (area 1,038 sq. mi.), is a group of about 400 large and small islands and hundreds of rocks and reefs. These islands extend in a line from the southwestern Philippines almost to the northeast coast of Borneo. Moslem tribesmen called *Moros* live on the Sulu Archipelago. The Moros make their living chiefly by fishing and pearl diving. They also grow rice, and coconuts and other fruit.

The Land and Its Resources

Coastline, Bays, and Harbors. The jagged, 14,400-mile-long Philippine coastline has many excellent bays and harbors. The best is Manila Bay in west-central Luzon. In many places, especially in the central and southern Philippines, coral reefs make the harbors dangerous for ships. The water south of the Philippines and in the channels among most of the islands is shallow. But the water surrounding the islands to the north, east, and west reaches great depths. The Mindanao Deep, a 34,440-foot-deep chasm in the ocean floor, lies off the east coast of the Philippines.

Mountains. The tallest Philippine peak, 9,692-foot Mount Apo, looms over Mindanao Island. It is one of several active Philippine volcanoes. Beautiful Mount Mayon, one of the world's most perfectly shaped volcanic cones, stands near Legaspi in southern Luzon.

Rivers and Lakes. Rushing rivers rise in the mountains of the chief islands and flow to the sea. These rivers often flood the surrounding countryside during

the rainy season. Few Philippine rivers can be navigated by anything larger than rafts or small riverboats. The navigable, 220-mile-long Cagayan River flows through wide, fertile valleys in northeastern Luzon. Other important rivers include the Agno and Pampanga on Luzon, and the Agusan on Mindanao.

The largest Philippine lake is Laguna de Bay. It covers 344 square miles on Luzon Island. Mount Taal rises in the center of Lake Taal, 35 miles south of Manila. The volcanic cone of Mount Taal contains a small lake. Lakes Lanao and Mainit lie on Mindanao.

Natural Resources. The soil of the lowlands and mountain slopes is the chief natural resource of the Philippines. A large part of the country has fertile soil, but farmers cultivate only about 20 of every 100 acres.

Forests grow throughout the Philippines. They cover about three-fifths of the land. These forests contain more than 3,000 types of trees suitable for lumber. About three-fourths of the trees belong to a tall, tropical type called *Dipterocarpus*. Philippine mahogany, pine, ebony, cedar, banyan, and palm trees grow in the forests. Many of the trees grow from 5 to 7 feet thick. Thick groves of bamboo and about 10,000 kinds of flowering plants grow throughout the islands.

Minerals. The country has rich mineral deposits. Gold, the leading mineral, is found mostly on Luzon, Mindanao, and Masbate. The country also has deposits of silver, iron, copper, chromite, manganese, and limestone and other building rocks. Some islands have small coal beds. Geologists have found some petroleum deposits on Cebu, Leyte, and Luzon.

Animal Life. Monkeys chatter in the trees of the Philippines and bats make their homes in mountain caves. Wild hogs live on most of the islands, and deer roam some of the forests. The tiny *chevrotain* (mouse deer) lives on Palawan Island. This unusual mammal is about the size of a rabbit. It is neither a mouse nor a deer, but looks like a combination of both. It has no antlers. The 3-foot-high *tamarau* (pygmy buffalo) lives

Merchant Traders use a boat with double outriggers to transport small goods between the many islands.

Standard Oil Co. (N.J.)

PHILIPPINES

on Mindoro. The most important domestic animal is the patient, plodding *carabao* (water buffalo). The Filipinos use the carabao to pull plows in the rice fields and to haul heavy loads (see CARABAO).

Crocodiles, some as long as 18 feet, swim in some of the large rivers of Mindanao. Great snakes, many of them poisonous, live on the islands. Giant pythons, some as long as 30 feet, slither through the forests and jungles. Iguanas, geckos, monitors, and other lizards live in the country. More than 750 kinds of birds live in the Philippines. They include parrots, hornbills, eagles, and jungle fowl (see JUNGLE FOWL).

Sea Life. Whales, porpoises, dugongs, and about 2,000 kinds of fishes swim in the waters around the Philippines. They include the anchovy, sardine, herring, pompano, mackerel, squid, tuna, and mullet. Shrimps, crabs, and other shellfish also live in the Philippine waters. Sponges grow off the southern islands, and mother-of-pearl is found on the ocean bed near the Sulu Archipelago.

Climate. The Philippines has a warm, humid climate similar to that of Central America. There is little seasonal variation in temperature, because the country lies in the tropics. Temperatures seldom rise as high as 100° F. or drop below 70° F. Average monthly temperatures in Manila and Quezon City range from 75° F. in January to 82° F. in June.

Between 50 and 180 inches of rain falls every year. The lowland areas receive less rain than the uplands, because the mountains block the winds that carry rain-bearing clouds from the ocean. The country has wet and dry seasons, and most of the rain falls between June and November. About 80 inches of rain falls each year in the Manila area.

Fierce typhoons often hit the islands north of Panay between August and October. Three-fourths of the typhoons hit the parts of the Philippines north of Manila. They frequently cause great damage and loss of life. Violent earthquakes also occur in the Philippines. Mindanao has the most earthquakes.

Life of the People

The People. Most Filipinos belong to a race called the Filipino-Malaysian (see RACES OF MAN [Mongo-

loids]; MALAY). Their ancestors came to the islands from southeast Asia by way of the East Indies, beginning about 200 B.C. Pure-blooded Filipino-Malaysians have light brown skin, straight black hair, flat noses, and short, slender bodies. Scientists usually classify them into three groups, according to religion. These are: (1) Christians, (2) Moslems, and (3) pagans.

The Christian Filipino-Malaysians live throughout the country. The Moslems live chiefly on Mindanao and the islands of the Sulu Archipelago. The Spanish named these people *Moros*, or *Moors*, because they had the same religion, Islam, as the Moors of northwestern Africa (see MOOR). The Spanish and the Americans had difficulty subduing the Moro tribes. The Moros finally became peaceful in the early 1900's. The pagan Filipino-Malaysians make up several tribes in the mountains of northern Luzon (see IGOROT).

The second largest racial group is the country's 500,000 Chinese. The Philippines also has about 200,-000 Indonesians who live chiefly in the mountains of Luzon and Mindanao. These people are related to the Filipino-Malaysians. Their ancestors came to the Philippines from Malaya as early as 3000 B.C.

The 60,000 *Negritos* (little blacks) are descendants of the first people who lived in the Philippines. The early Negritos migrated to the islands long before 5000 B.C. Negritos are true pygmies (see PYGMY). Their average height (under 5 feet) is about that of an average 13-year-old American boy. Their small size, black skin, and kinky hair make the Negritos look entirely different from other Filipinos. Most Negritos live in scattered tribes that roam the forest-covered mountains and valleys of the larger islands.

The Philippines also has about 7,000 Americans and some Europeans. *Mestizos* (people of mixed Filipino and white or Mongoloid ancestry) make up an important part of the population. Many of the country's business and political leaders have been mestizos.

More than 20 million Filipinos belong to the Roman Catholic Church. Spanish priests converted many Filipinos to the Roman Catholic religion more than 400 years ago.

Bishop Gregorio Aglipay, a Filipino priest, left the Roman Catholic Church in 1902 and founded the Philippine Independent Church. The church's 1½ million members worship in a manner similar to Roman Catholics, but they do not believe in the authority of the pope. The country also has about 1½ million Moslems, 800,000 Protestants, and 40,000 Buddhists. The country has complete religious freedom.

Language. The people of the Philippines speak nine different languages of the Malayo-Polynesian family (see LANGUAGE [Other Language Families]). These languages are divided into about 90 local or tribe dialects. About 11 million Filipinos speak English in addition to their own local dialect.

About one-third of the people speak the Tagalog (pronounced *tah GAH lahg*) language of central Luzon. The national language, Pilipino, is based mainly on the Tagalog language. English and Spanish are the chief languages used by government officials and businessmen. English, Pilipino, and Spanish, the country's official languages, are taught in the schools.

Family Life in the Philippines is more like that in the United States or Canada than that of other Asian lands.

Roxas Boulevard (formerly Dewey Boulevard) in Manila follows the shore of Manila Bay to the port for ocean liners.
American President Lines

In many Asian countries, the man is the absolute head of the household and makes all important family decisions. But the Filipino husband treats his wife as an equal. She usually has charge of the family's money.

Shelter. Most of the people in rural areas live in small, one-room houses made of palm leaves and bamboo. The houses stand on sturdy bamboo poles that average about six feet in height. The houses are raised above the ground for protection against dampness. Some Filipinos keep animals and tools in the areas beneath the houses. The people use ladders or stairs to climb from the ground to their living quarters. They usually make the floors of their houses out of split bamboo logs. Mats woven from thin bamboo strips form all the walls. Roofs of palm leaves or corrugated iron cover the houses. Some city people live in bamboo houses built on poles. But the cities also have many brick and stone houses.

Food. Rice is the chief Philippine food. The people eat it with almost every meal, either alone or mixed with other foods. Fish ranks second in the Philippine diet. The milkfish is a favorite. The people also eat much pork, chicken, corn, vegetables, and fruit. A popular dish is *lechon* (a whole pig roasted over a charcoal fire). Other popular dishes include *adobo* (highly spiced chicken and pork mixed together) and *sugpo* (steamed shrimp). Filipinos drink *tuba*, an alcoholic beverage made from the sap of the blossoms of the coconut palm tree. See COCONUT PALM.

Clothing. Most of the people, especially those in cities and towns, wear clothing similar to that worn in the United States and Canada. The tribesmen may wear other types of clothing. For example, Moro men usually dress in tight trousers and loose shirts. They wrap brightly colored sashes around their waists and wind turbans around their heads. Sometimes they carry *krises* (beautiful swords decorated with gold and silver). The krise serves as a symbol of importance. Moro women wear loose, ankle-length trousers and short jackets. Many Indonesian tribesmen wear only *loincloths* (pieces of cloth wrapped around the hips and waist). Some Indonesian women wear tightly wrapped skirts and long-sleeved blouses. Others wear no blouses at all. The Negritos wear almost no clothing.

Recreation. Filipinos consider basketball their national game. They also enjoy baseball, boxing, volleyball, tennis, golf, and other games played in the United States and Canada. Cockfights are also popular.

Almost every community holds a yearly celebration in honor of its patron saint. The people celebrate the holiday with feasts, games, plays, fireworks, and a religious procession. One of the most important holidays is Rizal Day on December 30. The people celebrate this holiday to honor José Rizal, Philippine national hero. They parade through the streets with floats decorated with brightly colored flowers.

City Life. Eleven Philippine cities have populations over 100,000. The largest is Manila, with more than 1⅓ million persons. Most of the country's larger cities and towns lie along the coasts of the islands.

Most cities have public buildings similar to those in North America. These modern buildings usually stand along wide, tree-lined boulevards. The cities also have some Spanish-style buildings. Small shops and stalls huddle together in busy market places. Here, shoppers bargain with merchants over the price of goods. Every

James Sawders

Recoletos Church, a masterpiece of Spanish church architecture, stood in an area of Manila called *Intramuros* (the Walled City). World War II bombing raids destroyed the huge structure.

city has at least one church or cathedral whose spire rises above the low roofs of the houses and other buildings. Thatch-roofed houses line the narrow, twisting streets of the smaller cities. See the separate articles on Philippine cities listed in the *Related Articles* at the end of this article.

Country Life. Most Philippine farmers live in a *barrio* (small village). However, many also live along country roads, on the hillsides, or in the center of the fields. In the villages, the houses crowd together along narrow, dusty streets that spread out from the *plaza* (village square). A stone church usually stands on one side of the plaza. Next to it is the home of the village's Roman Catholic priest. The priest has a great influence on the lives of the villagers. They often come to him for advice. The people shop in markets along the sides of the plaza. Palm-leaf awnings in the markets provide shade. A statue of José Rizal usually stands in the plaza.

Work of the People

About 70 of every 100 persons make their living from agriculture, the country's chief industry. About 7 of every 100 are employed in manufacturing. The rest work at such occupations as mining, forestry, and fishing.

Agriculture. The Filipinos use about 20 of every 100 acres of land for farming. Most of the farms lie on lowland coastal plains or valleys, but farmers also raise crops on hillsides and mountain slopes. Most of the farms are small. About half the farmers own less than 5 acres of land apiece. (The average farm in the United States has about 300 acres.) Only about 60 of every 100 Filipino farmers own their land. The rest rent land.

Farming methods range from primitive hand tools to modern machinery. In the early 1950's, the government began an intensified program to introduce new agricultural methods. Experts taught farmers to use fertilizers, rotate their crops, and practice soil conservation.

Rice. The Philippines ranks among the leading rice-growing countries of the world. Farmers on all the large islands raise this valuable food crop, mostly for use

339

George Rodger, Magnum

Filipino Women weave a colorful rug from *abacá* (Manila hemp) fibers. The people are famed for their skill in weaving.

hemp, into the strongest type of fiber rope. Farmers on Mindanao and many other islands grow abacá.

Plantations on Mindanao raise pineapples. Sweet potatoes and bananas grow throughout the islands. Other important farm products include corn, tobacco, vegetables, and tropical fruits such as mangoes, papayas, and breadfruit. Many farmers raise goats, sheep, hogs, and carabaos. Filipinos raise few beef or dairy cattle because these animals do not thrive in the warm, humid climate. The country imports much of its milk in cans from the United States and Europe.

Manufacturing and Processing. The Philippines has little large-scale manufacturing, partly because of a scarcity of money and trained workers. This lack of heavy industry has been one of the country's major economic problems. In the 1950's, the government began to encourage manufacturing by lending money to new industries, reducing taxes on industries, and offering special inducements to investors from other countries. Since then, many factories have been established. The cement and textile industries now produce nearly enough to meet Philippine needs. Chemicals and drugs are also produced. An American oil firm built the first Philippine oil refinery at Batangas, in southwestern Luzon, in 1954. Other large American investments in the country include a tire factory and an aluminum plant. During the late 1940's and early 1950's, the manufacture of cigars, hats, mats, and fiber products grew from crafts carried on in homes or small shops to modern factory industries. Factories in many parts of the country make rope, refine sugar, and process copra to obtain coconut oil.

Forest Products. The forests provide more than 430 million board feet of lumber every year. Silk-cotton trees provide *kapok*, a silky material used in life belts,

within the country. Rice grows on about 50 of every 100 acres of cultivated land in the country. The best rice fields lie in central Luzon.

Farmers in lowland areas grow rice in water-soaked paddies. Low mud walls surround the paddies, and hold in rain and water brought from springs and streams. Farmers in upland areas raise hill, or dry, rice, that grows in fields similar to wheat fields. The rainfall in the upland regions provides enough water for dry rice. The Ifugao tribe lives in an area in northeastern Luzon that has almost no flat land. These people grow rice on terraces carved into the sides of steep mountains. The terraces are built as high as 4,000 feet above valley floors.

Other Crops. The Philippines ranks among the world's leading sugar growers. Sugar cane grows mainly on Negros, Luzon, and Panay.

Farmers raise coconut palms on plantations that cover large areas. Most of the plantations lie on the coastal lowlands of the larger islands. The chief coconut product is copra. Pressed, dried copra produces coconut oil, which people throughout the world use in making soap, candles, cooking fat, and margarine.

The country leads the world in production of abacá. Factories weave the tough fiber of the abacá, or Manila

A Young Woman wears the *balintawak*, a Filipino national costume. On holidays, the women dress up in fancy blouses called *camisas*, and long, brightly colored silk skirts.

Philippine Tourist & Travel Assoc.

Gay Filipino Dancers perform a rhythmic number for tourists in the Lake Taal region. Dance melodies reflect the influence of early Spanish music and culture.

American President Lines

upholstery, and mattresses. Groves of bamboo grow throughout the country. The Filipinos use bamboo to make houses, baskets, hats, pipes, furniture, and many other products. They eat the tender shoots of the bamboo plant. The forests also provide *rattan*, a tough, stringy material that comes from the reedy stems of certain types of palm trees. The Filipinos make furniture and other household articles from rattan.

Fishing Industry. Commercial fishermen sail to sea in small boats from the fishing villages that lie along the coasts. These fishermen catch anchovies, sardines, herring, bonito, pompano, mackerel, squid, tuna, mullet, swordfish, shrimps, and crabs. Divers gather mother-of-pearl off the Sulu Archipelago, and sponges from the waters off the southernmost islands.

Mining. Filipinos mine about 450,000 troy ounces of gold a year in the mountains of northern and southern Luzon, Masbate, and eastern Mindanao. The largest gold mines lie near the city of Baguio in northern Luzon. Other important mineral products include silver, iron, copper, manganese, chromite, and limestone.

Electric Power. Heavy rainfall and many rushing rivers and streams make the Philippines ideal for the development of hydroelectric power. However, few power projects have been built because of the lack of money and the difficulty of transporting construction equipment to the rugged mountain areas. The largest hydroelectric projects include one on the Caliraya River, southeast of Manila, and the Maria Cristina project near the town of Iligan on Mindanao Island. The Ambuklao project, near the city of Baguio on Luzon Island, was completed in 1956.

Trade. Copra, coconut oil, and other coconut products account for almost seven-tenths of the country's exports. The people sell about 85 per cent of their sugar to other countries. Other important exports include abacá fiber, gold, pineapples, rope, and lumber. Chief

imports include textiles, food, iron and steel products, and machinery. Most trade is with the United States.

Transportation. The rainy climate and rugged countryside make it difficult and expensive to construct roads and railroads. In spite of these conditions, the islands have one of the best transportation systems in Asia. Most of the roads and railroads were built when the United States governed the Philippines.

Aviation. Planes of the Philippine Air Lines (PAL) fly within the country and to several other countries including Australia, Japan, and the United States.

Railroads. The country has about 700 miles of railroads. The longest railroad, a government-owned line, links Manila to other cities on Luzon. Shorter, privately owned lines operate on the islands of Cebu and Panay.

Roads and Highways. Trucks, buses, and automobiles travel on the country's 18,000 miles of all-weather public roads. One of the most interesting buses is the *jeepney*, an American jeep enlarged to carry about 10 passengers. Ponies pulling light carriages called *carromatas* and *carretelas* can be seen in most parts of the country.

Shipping. The Philippine merchant fleet has more than 20 ships that sail to other countries. Many international shipping lines also serve the Philippines. Small steamboats, motor launches, and sailboats travel from one island to another. Manila ranks first among the Philippine ports. Other important ports include Cebu, Iloilo, Zamboanga, Jolo, Aparri, Davao, and Legaspi.

Communication. Most daily newspapers are published in Manila and Cebu. Many cities have weekly newspapers. Manila also has several book and magazine publishers. Telegraph and telephone systems link the major cities. The country has more than 1,000 government-owned and privately owned radio stations. The Philippines' first television station began broadcasting from Manila in 1945.

Education

The law requires all children between the ages of 7 and 10 to attend elementary school through the fourth grade. Many children complete the full six years of elementary school and then go on to the four-year high schools. Public elementary school education is free, but students pay a small tuition fee in the government-operated high schools. The government has also established more than 50 trade and agricultural schools. More than 5,200,000 children attend the 33,000 public elementary and high schools. More than 1,200,000 children go to private schools, most of which are Roman Catholic parochial schools.

The country has many institutions of higher learning. One of the most famous is the University of Santo Tomás in Manila. This Roman Catholic school was founded in 1611. It has almost 30,000 students. About 21,000 students attend the government-supported University of the Philippines. It was established in Manila in 1908 and moved to Quezon City in 1948.

The Arts

Some of the best Philippine architecture is found in the many churches built by the Spanish. These splendid buildings are built in a style called *baroque*. They have elaborate carvings and curved arches. Saint

George Rodger, Magnum

Coconuts Are a Major Crop in the Philippines. A skilled worker can husk as many as 1,000 coconuts in one day.

Augustin's Church in Manila was built during the 1500's. A bowl-shaped foundation gave it the strength to withstand the frequent earthquakes in the Philippines. It was the only major building left standing in Intramuros, the old walled city of Manila, after American bombings against the Japanese during World War II.

The country has produced many fine sculptors and painters. The most famous present-day sculptor, Guillermo Tolentino (1890-   ), carved statues of classical subjects. The paintings of Fabian de la Rosa (1869-1937), one of the best-known Philippine painters, show the life of the Filipinos.

Most Philippine literature is written in English. Some authors also write in Tagalog or other local languages, or in Spanish. José García Villa (1906-   ) has won fame for his abstract poetry. Nick Joaquin (1917-   ) and N. V. M. Gonzalez (1915-   ) are the best-known novelists. Carlos P. Romulo (1901-   ), a diplomat, general, and journalist, won the Pulitzer prize for general correspondence in 1942.

Government

The government of the Philippines resembles that of the United States. The Philippine constitution, adopted in 1935, outlines the duties and powers of the govern-ment. The president heads the executive branch of the government. The two-house Congress makes laws, and the courts interpret them. The Philippines has a system of checks and balances similar to that of the United States (see UNITED STATES, GOVERNMENT OF [Separation of Powers]). Philippine government differs from that in the United States because most political power is concentrated in the national government. Local governments in the Philippines have little power.

President. The people elect the president and vice-president for four-year terms. Neither official may serve more than eight years. The president appoints 10 secretaries to head the various executive departments. They, with six other officials, make up the Cabinet. The duties and powers of the president, vice-president, and Cabinet members are similar to those of these officials in the United States. But the Philippine president has much greater powers over Congress.

Congress. The Philippine Congress consists of a Senate and House of Representatives. The people elect the 24 senators for six-year terms. Eight senators are chosen every two years. The senators represent the entire country, not a particular state or province as in the United States and Canada. The people elect the 120 representatives for four-year terms. They represent districts similar to congressional districts in the U.S.

Courts. The 11 justices of the Supreme Court, the highest court in the country, have the power to declare laws unconstitutional by a two-thirds vote. The president appoints all judges with the approval of the Commission on Appointments, composed of several members of Congress. The judges of all courts can hold office until they reach the age of 70. Philippine law is a combination of civil law, common law, Moslem law, and tribal customs (see CIVIL LAW; COMMON LAW).

Local Government. The people elect the governors of the 65 provinces for four-year terms. A three-member board, also elected for four-year terms, helps decide local policies with the governor and other officials. Philippine provinces are divided into municipalities that usually consist of a large town and the surrounding villages and farming areas. The people elect the mayors and councils of the municipalities. The rural areas around the main towns of the municipalities are divided into barrios. The country also has 49 cities chartered directly by the government. These include the largest and most important cities in the country. The provincial governors have no power over these cities. In most chartered cities, the people elect mayors. The mayors of the other chartered cities are appointed by the president. Most of the mayors and city councils that are elected serve four-year terms.

Taxation. An income tax, license and business tax, and an excise tax provide the chief income of the government (see EXCISE). Other important taxes include those on imports and inheritances.

Politics. Persons 21 years of age and older who can read and write may vote in Philippine national elections. The country has two main political parties, the Liberal and the Nationalist. These parties have alternated in holding power.

Armed Forces. The Philippine army has about 50,000 men, all volunteers. The small air force and navy are also composed of volunteers. The Philippine and United States governments signed a 99-year military base agreement in 1947. It gave the United States the right to maintain military bases in the Philippines.

History

Early Days. Historians believe the Negritos were the first people to live in the Philippines. No one knows where they came from or when they arrived. Groups of Indonesians and Malaysians moved to the Philippines from parts of southern Asia after 3000 B.C. Japanese and Chinese traders reached the islands sometime after A.D. 700. Moslem Arab missionaries traveled to the Philippines in the 1300's and 1400's. They converted the Moros of Mindanao Island and the Sulu Archipelago to Islam, the Moslem religion. The Moros controlled most of the southern islands. Their warriors sailed in *vintas* (dugout canoes) to rob people on neighboring islands and the mainland of Asia.

Spanish Rule. The members of a Spanish expedition led by Ferdinand Magellan were the first Europeans to reach the Philippines. They anchored in what is now Cebu harbor in 1521, during the first round-the-world-voyage in history. Magellan was killed while helping one Filipino group fight another, and his fleet sailed for Spain soon after. Ruy Lopez de Villalobos (? -1546), a Spanish admiral, visited the islands in 1543. He named them *Las Felipinas* (The Philippines) in honor of the prince who became King Philip II of Spain. Miguel Lopez de Legaspi (1510?-1572), a Spanish general, established the first permanent Spanish settlement on Cebu Island in 1565. The Spaniards were attracted to the region by gold and spices. They also sought to expand Spain's colonial empire. Legaspi founded Manila in 1571. None of the Filipinos except the Moros opposed the Spaniards strongly.

The Spanish *friars* (priests) were the most powerful group in the Philippines. They converted most of the people from paganism to the Roman Catholic religion. They built a few schools and many churches. With the *caciques* (village chiefs), the friars ruled the people. The caciques were of Spanish-Filipino or Filipino an-

cestry. They became wealthy landowners. The friars and caciques ruled harshly.

Revolt Against the Spaniards. The Filipinos repeatedly tried to revolt against the Spaniards. But Spanish troops quickly put down all the rebellions. Changes began to take place during the 1800's. The Spaniards opened Manila to foreign trade in 1834, because they thought this would be profitable. The country's economy improved, and wealthy Filipinos began sending their children to universities in Manila and Europe. Before this, the children had gone only to small, local church schools. When these students returned to their homes, they tried to make the Spanish improve social and political conditions. One of the early leaders in the movement for freedom was José Rizal (1861-1896). Rizal worked for reform until 1896, when the Spaniards arrested him. They charged Rizal with trying to start a revolution. A firing squad executed him on Dec. 30, 1896.

In 1892, Andres Bonifacio formed a secret revolutionary society called the *Katipunan*. Its members revolted in 1896. Bonifacio was killed, and Emilio Aguinaldo, a Filipino municipal official, became the leader of the revolutionary forces. In 1897, the Spaniards promised political reforms if the rebel leaders would end the revolt and leave the Philippines. Aguinaldo and his chief aides agreed, and sailed to Hong Kong.

War with Spain and the United States. The United States declared war on Spain in April, 1898 (see SPANISH-AMERICAN WAR). Admiral George Dewey destroyed the Spanish fleet in Manila Bay on May 1, 1898. Two weeks later, Aguinaldo returned to the Philippines and formed a Filipino army, because the Spaniards had not kept their promises to him. His troops began fighting alongside the American forces. The Philippines declared its independence from Spain on June 12, 1898. On June 23, a group of Aguinaldo's supporters elected him president of the Philippine revolutionary government. American and Filipino soldiers captured Manila on Aug. 13, 1898, and the war ended.

The United States and Spain signed a peace treaty in Paris on Dec. 10, 1898. By the terms of the treaty, Spain ceded the Philippines to the United States. This angered Aguinaldo. He claimed that the United States had promised to make the Philippines independent immediately. Aguinaldo declared the establishment of the Philippine Republic on Jan. 23, 1899, and his troops began fighting the Americans on Feb. 4, 1899. American troops captured Aguinaldo in March, 1901, and he signed an oath of allegiance to the United States. The fighting ended soon afterwards, and the United States extended its rule throughout the islands.

Steps Toward Self-Government. Soon after the United States Senate approved the peace treaty with Spain, it adopted a resolution stating that the United States would eventually make the Philippines independent. However, the United States felt that the Filipinos were not ready for self-government at that time. President William McKinley appointed a five-man civilian commission to govern the Philippines. William Howard Taft, a federal judge who later became President of the United States, headed the commission. He was inaugurated as the first American governor of the Philippines on July 4, 1901.

RED-LETTER DATES IN THE PHILIPPINES

1300's and 1400's Moslem missionaries converted the Moros to the Islamic religion.

1521 Ferdinand Magellan landed in the Philippines.

1565 The Spanish established their first permanent settlement in the Philippines on Cebu Island.

1762-1764 The British occupied Manila.

1896 The Spanish executed José Rizal, a leader of the Philippine independence movement. Emilio Aguinaldo led a revolt against the Spanish.

1898 Spain ceded the Philippines to the United States after the Spanish-American War.

1901 William Howard Taft became the first American governor of the Philippines.

1935 The Commonwealth of the Philippines was established, with Manuel Quezon the first president.

1941-1944 The Japanese controlled the Philippines.

1945 The Philippines became a UN charter member.

1946 (July 4) The Republic of the Philippines was established.

1950-1954 The Philippine Army defeated the Communist-led Huk rebels.

1954 The Philippines joined the Southeast Asia Treaty Organization (SEATO).

1960 The Philippines asked the United States to store atomic weapons there.

1962 The Philippines claimed British North Borneo.

PHILIPPINES

For the next 40 years, the Filipinos made progress toward self-government. They elected their first legislature in 1907. The governor of the Philippines and the members of his commission served as the upper house. Elected representatives formed the lower house.

The United States Congress passed the Jones Act in 1916. This act replaced the commission with an elected senate. The Tydings-McDuffie Act of 1934 provided for independence 10 years after a constitution was drawn and adopted. This was done in 1936, and independence was scheduled for 1946. It also provided for the Commonwealth of the Philippines that was established in 1935. Under this, the Filipinos governed themselves almost completely. The United States controlled such matters as the islands' foreign affairs and defense. In 1935, the Filipinos elected Manuel Luis Quezon as the first president of the Commonwealth.

The United States helped the Philippines develop into a modern nation. Americans built roads, railroads, public buildings, and schools on the islands. American teachers trained Filipinos in the ways of democracy. Doctors from the United States taught the people public-health measures, and reduced the death rate from tropical diseases such as malaria and yellow fever.

Japan Strikes. The Japanese began to threaten the Philippines and other Asian countries during the late 1930's. The United States sent General Douglas MacArthur to act as military adviser to the Philippines in 1935. The Japanese attacked Pearl Harbor, Hawaii, on Dec. 7, 1941, and the Pacific phase of World War II began. Japanese troops landed on Luzon on December 10. MacArthur concentrated his outnumbered Filipino and American troops on Bataan Peninsula and Corregidor Island in Manila Bay. After a heroic resistance, they surrendered in April and May, 1942. However, small groups of Filipinos and Americans kept on fighting throughout the war. President Quezon escaped from Corregidor by submarine. He established a Philippine government-in-exile in Washington, D.C., on May 13,

A Social Center Library promotes the love of good books among the children in a crowded section of Manila. Volunteer workers help young readers select their books and magazines. The church-supported social center also sponsors recreational activities.
Three Lions

1942. Quezon died in 1944, and Sergio Osmeña (1878-1961), the vice-president, became president.

Liberation. When MacArthur left the Philippines in 1942, he promised the Filipinos, "I shall return." He made good his promise on October 20, 1944, when American troops landed on Leyte and began the bloody struggle to free the Philippines. The Americans controlled all of Leyte by December, and began landing on Luzon and the other large islands. They recaptured Manila in February, 1945, and most of the organized Japanese resistance ended soon afterward. The Philippines became a charter member of the United Nations later in 1945.

Independence. The Filipinos elected Manuel Roxas president in April, 1946. Three months later, on July 4, 1946, the United States granted the Philippines complete independence and the Republic of the Philippines was established. Roxas remained in office and became president of the Republic.

The war cost thousands of lives, caused much suffering, and damaged millions of dollars' worth of property. The Philippines began to rebuild, with aid from the United States. Roxas died in April, 1948. Elpidio Quirino, the vice-president, became president. He was elected to a full term as president in 1949.

In 1948, the government made Quezon City the official capital, because of the overcrowded conditions in Manila. However, Manila remained the chief governmental center. Quezon City is named for the first president of the Commonwealth of the Philippines.

The Huk Rebellion. A group of Communist-led rebels tried to seize power during the late 1940's and early 1950's. They won the support of many poor farmers, especially in central Luzon. The rebels belonged to a group called the *Hukbong Magpapalayang Bayan*, or *People's Liberation Army*. Its members were known as "Huks." The 20,000-man Huk army wanted the government to break up the large estates and give land to poor farmers. In 1949, the Huks declared their intention to seize the government. The Philippine Army waged a hard-fought campaign against the Huks for the next two years. The army began defeating the Huks in late 1950. Small-scale fighting continued until 1954.

Economic Problems. Serious economic problems faced the Philippines after independence. The United States sent the Philippines more than $800 million worth of economic aid between 1946 and 1951. Agricultural production suffered from the lack of modern farm machinery and methods. Most of the people were poor and the government was in debt. In 1950, the United States offered to give an additional $250 million in economic aid to the Philippines if the government would carry out certain reforms. These included a minimum-wage law and an increase in taxes. The Philippine Congress agreed, and the United States sent more money and technical experts to the Philippines. The country's economic condition began to improve. Modern methods of fertilization and cultivation were stressed. New industrial plants and hydroelectric stations were established. Between 1946 and 1955, average income per person increased from $120 to $175 a year.

The 1950's. The United States and the Philippines signed a mutual-defense treaty in 1951. The countries agreed to help each other if attacked. The Filipinos elected Ramón Magsaysay president in 1953. Magsaysay

344

The Philippine Congress meets in this imposing Legislative Building in Manila. The classical style structure was completely rebuilt after its total destruction by Japanese forces in World War II.

United Press Int.

had been secretary of defense under Quirino and played an important part in the war against the Huks. The Philippines signed the Southeast Asia Collective Defense Treaty with the United States, Great Britain, France, Australia, New Zealand, Pakistan, and Thailand in 1954. The purpose of this mutual-defense agreement was to guard against Communist aggression. The countries that signed this treaty were unofficially known as the Southeast Asia Treaty Organization (SEATO).

The Philippines and the United States signed a trade agreement in 1955 designed to improve trade relations and to encourage investment in the industries of the Philippines. Magsaysay died in an airplane crash in 1957, and Vice-President Carlos P. Garcia succeeded him. Garcia was elected president later that year.

Recent Developments. The Philippine government has passed various laws and development plans to try to help the farmers. Land-reform laws were passed in 1955 and 1963 to help the farmers buy land, to improve production, and to distribute wealth more evenly. But these programs have not been effective.

Vice-President Diosdado Macapagal defeated Garcia in the 1961 presidential election. In 1965, Ferdinand E. Marcos won the presidency. In 1966 and 1967, some farmers began to support the Huks. Marcos began a vigorous campaign to build roads and schoolhouses, and to increase rice production.   CARLOS P. ROMULO

Critically reviewed by JEAN GROSSHOLTZ

PRODUCTS

Abacá	Copra	Pineapple
Banana	Gold	Sugar
Coconut Palm	Kapok	

OTHER RELATED ARTICLES

Asia
Carabao
Christmas (Asia)
Clothing (color picture: The Orient)
Colombo Plan
Igorot
Mahogany (pictures)
Negrito
Southeast Asia Treaty Organization (SEATO)
Typhoon
Woman (In the Philippines)

Outline

I. **The Islands**
II. **The Land and Its Resources**
   A. Coastline, Bays, and Harbors
   B. Mountains
   C. Rivers and Lakes
   D. Natural Resources
   E. Climate
III. **Life of the People**
   A. The People
   B. Language
   C. Family Life
   D. City Life
   E. Country Life
IV. **Work of the People**
   A. Agriculture
   B. Manufacturing and Processing
   C. Forest Products
   D. Fishing Industry
   E. Mining
   F. Electric Power
   G. Trade
   H. Transportation
   I. Communication
V. **Education**
VI. **The Arts**
VII. **Government**
VIII. **History**

Questions

Who are the "Huks"?

Why is the coconut palm important to the economy of the Philippines?

Name two ways in which the Philippine government is similar to that of the United States. How is it different from the American government?

Which island is called the *Philippine Land of Promise?* Why?

When did the Philippines receive its independence from the United States?

What are the two most important foods in the Philippine diet?

What is the Philippine national game?

What is the largest island in the Philippines?

What are the two largest cities of the Philippines? Where are they located?

What part did Spain play in the history of the Philippines? What part did the United States play?

345

PHILISTIA

PHILISTIA, *fuh LIS tih uh,* was a region of ancient Palestine. It was in the southwestern part of Palestine, on the Mediterranean Coast. The Philistines of Bible times lived there. Philistia contained the five city-kingdoms of Gaza, Ashkelon, Ashdod, Ekron, and Gath.

The Philistines captured Samson, an Israelite. He broke his bonds and killed 1,000 men with the jawbone of an ass.

PHILISTINE, *fih LIHS tin,* or *FILL ihs tin,* was a member of the group of Aegean people who lived on Crete and other islands in the Aegean Sea. These people were driven from their homes by northern tribes who migrated into Greece. The Philistines plundered a number of coast towns along the eastern Mediterranean as they searched for a new home.

They tried to enter the north of Egypt but Pharaoh Ramses III defeated them. He stopped the Philistines, but could not throw them back. They settled along the coast of Canaan in what is now called the Gaza Strip. The Greeks called this territory and the land east of it *Palestine.*

As the Philistines attempted to conquer Canaan from the west, the Israelites made a similar attempt from the east. The two groups fought for the land. The Philistines usually controlled the land around the cities of Gaza, Gath, Ashkelon, Ashdod, and Ekron. The Philistines learned the art of smelting iron from the Hittites. This gave them a military and economic advantage over the Israelites. When David became king of Israel, he subdued the Philistines and forced them to pay tribute.

The word *Philistine* today means a person who is hostile to the arts.   W. W. SLOAN

See also AEGEAN CIVILIZATION; BEELZEBUB; DAVID; GATH; PALESTINE.

PHILLIP, ARTHUR. See AUSTRALIA (Early Settlement); NEW SOUTH WALES (History).

PHILLIPS, WENDELL (1811-1884), an orator and reformer, became famous as an advocate of abolition. In Faneuil Hall in Boston, Phillips delivered an address rebuking those who upheld the mob murder of Elijah P. Lovejoy, an antislavery leader, in Alton, Ill. Phillips' address became one of the most famous

Brown Bros.
Wendell Phillips

speeches in history for its protest against mob rule.

Uncompromising in his opposition to slavery, Phillips gave up his law practice in 1837 to join William Lloyd Garrison's group of abolitionists. He fought courageously against any individual, institution, or law that he thought prevented the abolition of slavery. He favored doing away with slavery even at the cost of breaking up the Union. Phillips severely criticized the administration of President Abraham Lincoln during the Civil War.

After the war, Phillips held together the American Anti-Slavery Society until Negroes were granted the vote through Amendment 15 to the U.S. Constitution. He also became interested in improving conditions for laborers. Many persons who did not agree with him admired his oratory. His best-known speeches include *Burial of John Brown, Toussaint L'Ouverture,* and *The Lost Arts.*

Phillips was born in Boston, and was graduated from Harvard University.   LOUIS FILLER

See also ABOLITIONIST.

PHILLIPS UNIVERSITY. See UNIVERSITIES AND COLLEGES (table).

PHILODENDRON, *FILL oh DEN drun,* is the name of various kinds of vinelike house plants grown for their beautiful foliage. The word *philodendron* means *lover of trees.* Many philodendrons are grown on "totem poles," or posts made of sphagnum moss, bark, and other materials. Philodendrons produce roots along their stems. For this reason, they will grow on poles if the stems are kept moist.

Philodendrons have handsome leaves that are thick and tough. But the leaves vary widely in size and shape on the different kinds of plants. The common name for some of these plants often suggests the form of their leaves. Among them are the *taper-tip, twice-cut, giant-leaf,* and *tri-leaf* philodendron.

Perhaps the most widely grown is the *heart-leaf* philodendron. This plant bears heart-shaped leaves about 1 to 2 inches long, and nearly as broad. The leaves are smooth and glossy. They have no indentations along their edges.

People like philodendrons as house plants because they are probably the easiest of all plants to grow. Philodendrons tolerate the changes in light, moisture, and temperature that are common in most houses. They need little care and do not fall prey to the usual plant pests. They grow best when they are not in direct sunlight. Often philodendrons will grow quite well in places too dark for other plants. They like almost any kind of soil. But they will also thrive in water.

Scientific Classification. Philodendrons belong to the arum family, *Araceae.* The heart-leaf philodendron is genus *Philodendron,* species *P. cordatum.*   GEORGE A. BEACH

PHILOLOGY. See LINGUISTICS.
PHILOSOPHER'S STONE. See ALCHEMY.

Ornamental Philodendron grows well outdoors in a tropical climate. It is often grown indoors as a house plant.
John Robinson

PHILOSOPHY has two important aims. First, it tries to give a person a unified view of the universe in which he lives. Second, it seeks to make a person a more critical thinker by sharpening his ability to think clearly and precisely. The American philosopher William James defined philosophy as "an unusually stubborn attempt to think clearly." A philosopher is an ordinary person who thinks more deeply and obstinately than other people. The word *philosophy* comes from two Greek words, *philo* and *sophia*, which together mean *love of wisdom*.

Philosophy has great value in our complicated world. Many persons have no real foundations or sets of beliefs. Philosophy can provide them with a reasoned framework within which to think. By accepting a particular philosophy, a person can begin to seek certain goals and to direct his life's behavior. For example, a Stoic tries to remain master of his emotions. An Epicurean seeks happiness through pleasure. A Rationalist attempts to gain knowledge through reason. A Christian strives for salvation through the grace and teachings of Jesus Christ. Each set of beliefs leads to a particular way of thinking and behaving.

Philosophy also examines the foundations of other studies. It asks the social scientist what he believes to be the nature of man. It asks the physical scientist why he uses the scientific method. Philosophy seeks to organize the results of the various sciences to show the many ways in which they are related.

Contributions of Philosophy

Philosophy and Science have always been related in some ways. Until about the 1700's, people made no distinction between the two fields. Both of them seek a knowledge of basic principles, and both try to be systematic in their investigations. But science tries to gain knowledge

Thinking Deeply is the philosopher's basic task. He tries to find consistent, logical answers to difficult problems. Sculptor Auguste Rodin expressed this task in his famous statue, *The Thinker*.

about a specific subject matter, and philosophy concerns itself with the laws and structure of all reality.

A natural scientist depends on his laboratory in solv-

--- **PHILOSOPHIC TERMS** ---

Atomism is a theory that all things are made up of small particles that cannot be further divided.

Axiology is the study of values. It involves such questions as "What is beautiful?" "What is good?" "What is holy?"

Being is a term that refers to anything that is, was, or can be. The most general thing that we can say about any object is that it has being. This means that the object exists or can be known in some way. A thought or a memory, as well as a table, has being.

Cause is an agent that brings about change. *Effect* is the immediate result of a cause. Philosophers speak of *cause-and-effect* relationships in the universe.

Concept is a thought or belief formed on the basis of experience.

Cosmology is the study of the universe as an orderly system.

Deduction is a method of reasoning from general statements to particular conclusions. *Induction* is a method of arriving at conclusions by examining particular facts. Induction depends on observation and experimentation.

Deism is a belief that God exists but has no present active relation to the world.

Dialectic is a process of change brought about by the conflict of two opposite forces. This conflict creates a new force, called a *synthesis*. The synthesis, in turn, becomes a new opposite in conflict with another force.

Empiricism is a theory that all knowledge comes from experience.

Epistemology is a branch of philosophy that studies the origins, nature, and limitations of knowledge.

Form is the structure, pattern, or plan of something.

For example, a statue may have the form of a man. *Matter* is the physical content of an object. Philosophers say that all objects are composed of form and matter.

Hedonism is a moral theory that emphasizes pleasure as the goal men should seek in order to be happy.

Idealism is a doctrine that considers mind or spirit as the basis of the universe. Many idealists maintain that things do not exist outside the mind, but only as the mind knows them.

Logic is a branch of philosophy that studies the rules and methods of correct thinking.

Materialism is a doctrine that all things are basically material.

Metaphysics is a branch of philosophy that seeks to understand reality, beyond what we know from our sense perceptions.

Monism is a belief that the entire universe is made of a single substance.

Naturalism is a theory that everything comes from nature and there is nothing beyond nature. A follower of naturalism rejects the supernatural and believes that all things are subject to scientific laws.

Pantheism is a doctrine that God is the whole world and all that is in it. Pantheists believe that God does not exist as a separate spirit.

Rationalism is a theory that knowledge can be derived only from logical or deductive procedures.

Realism is a doctrine that things exist in and of themselves, independent of the mind that knows them.

Theism is a belief that God exists as a distinct Being, and works through and in the world.

PHILOSOPHY

ing problems. A philosopher has no use for a laboratory. The physicist asks, "What is the law of falling bodies?" He tries to determine this law in his laboratory by measuring the way bodies fall. The philosopher accepts the physicist's findings and asks, "What kind of world is it in which bodies fall in this way?" He cannot answer this question by a laboratory experiment, but only by an intellectual one. He must try to decide what *cosmology*, or system of the universe, is consistent with laws of falling bodies.

Philosophy and Religion. When we speak of philosophy as a method of examining a body of knowledge, we must separate religion from it. Religion assumes that God can be known, and develops a ritual, a creed, and a moral code based on that assumption. Philosophy makes no such assumption. It examines the logic behind religious proofs, and tests the methods of investigation that religion uses. Philosophy questions the meanings of terms and sentences used in ritual, prayer, and talk about God. For example, a philosopher will examine the expression "God is all-powerful" to clarify its meaning and to judge the evidence offered for it.

When we speak of philosophy as a world-view, we must include religion in that world-view. Religion then becomes a part of philosophy or one philosophic position in a larger system. Both Aristotle and the German philosopher G. W. F. Hegel placed religion at the peak of their philosophic systems. Both accepted science and religion in their systems, but placed them at different levels. Aristotle considered religion superior to science, because religion is concerned with ultimate questions, such as those that apply to God. Hegel believed that religion embraces all aspects of science and therefore goes beyond science. See ARISTOTLE; HEGEL, G. W. F.

Philosophy and Government. Democracy, communism, and fascism are each based on a philosophic position.

Rational empiricism, the philosophic basis of democracy, believes that the world is both material and spiritual. It holds that change and progress occur by applying reason to experience, and human nature can be changed and improved by experience. On the basis of these principles, democracy stresses discussion and the use of reason as a way of arriving at conclusions. It emphasizes the importance of tolerance and freedom in developing intelligent, loyal citizens.

Dialectical materialism, the basis of communism, asserts that only material things are real. It believes that human nature, human beings, and society as a whole are products of the economic system. This philosophy states that all change occurs through a struggle of opposing forces in society, and comes to a climax by revolution. Accordingly, communism opposes religion because of its spiritual nature. It wishes to destroy the present capitalistic economic system, and to develop a new type of man and a new type of economic and social system.

Absolute idealism, on which fascism is based, stresses the existence of one *absolute reality*, a being or element that is complete in itself and does not depend on anything outside itself. It asserts that there is a principle of authority expressing the will of the absolute. As a political philosophy, absolute idealism considers the *state*, or the national government, as the absolute. According to this philosophy, everything in society is part of the state and subservient to it. From these doctrines follow dictatorship by an absolute ruler, rejection of parliamentary procedures, and submission of the individual to the state.

Philosophy and Education. For hundreds of years, education was based on the view that man is a rational being who learns only by using his reason. Education tried to offer facts from which reason could derive knowledge. Since the early 1900's, a new philosophical view of man and how he acquires knowledge has led to great changes in educational practice. Under the influence of the American philosopher John Dewey, man came to be viewed as a union of mind and body who learns by having experiences. Dewey's philosophy of *pragmatism* insisted that any experience was part of education (see PRAGMATISM). His arguments convinced many educators to change their methods. Today, such education tries to offer children positive experiences, and to develop their ability to learn from these experiences. See DEWEY, JOHN.

Problems of Philosophy

The problems philosophers study may be classified under four headings: (1) logic, (2) epistemology, (3) metaphysics, and (4) axiology.

Logic asks, "What are the rules of correct reasoning?" "How can we use scientific methods?"

Epistemology asks, "How do we know?" "What is truth?" "What do our terms mean?"

Metaphysics asks, "What is real?" "How does change come about?" "What is mind?"

Axiology asks, "What is the nature of the good?" "Of the beautiful?" "Of the religious?"

Philosophers are also concerned with questions involving the nature of man, of God, and of society.

What Is Real? We often use the expression "Seeing is believing" without thinking much about it. But sometimes we find that the expression is not quite true. You may be sure you see a puddle of water in the road, but when you come closer, the puddle may not be there at all. Or you may see a bent stick in a glass of water, but find that the stick is straight when you take it out. You then begin to wonder, "Was there a puddle in the road?" "Is the stick bent or straight?" These problems concern the question of deciding whether what we *perceive*, or sense, is real, and which of two perceptions is the true one (see PERCEPTION).

As you look at a stick, you might say, "I see a stick." But what you actually see is an image formed in your eye. If you compare the stick you now see with one you might have seen in a dream, you will find little difference. But you know that the one in the dream was a mental thing. This raises the question of the nature of what you perceive. Is the stick a real thing independent of your knowledge of it? Or is the stick simply what you know of it, or a purely mental thing? The philosophic theory called *realism* insists that objects exist independently of our knowledge of them. *Idealism* argues that they only exist in the mind. See IDEALISM; REALISM.

Another aspect of the problem of what is real is the philosophic discussion of universals and particulars. When you look at a set of books, you recognize that they are all books. All books are alike as books. This means that each book is an example of a "Book" in a general sense. Philosophers call this general "Book" a *universal*, and the individual books *particulars*. They ask, "Is the particular book or the universal 'Book' the real one?" Some philosophers say that only the universal is real. The particular book seems to change, but the universal remains unchanged.

The Nature of the Universe. The questions "What is the universe made of?" and "How does it operate?" have challenged philosophers since ancient times. Many early peoples believed that the universe was composed of only one element. Some ancient Greek philosophers claimed that it was all water, all air, or all fire. Others said it was made up of four elements—earth, air, fire, and water—and the principles of love and hate that caused the elements to combine and separate.

Later philosophers spoke of the universe as a gigantic machine that ran according to its own physical laws, with no particular purpose. Their philosophy is called *mechanism* (see MECHANIST). Others, called *teleologists*, believed that there is purpose in the universe. They argued that the material aspects of the universe run in a law-abiding, mechanical way, but that the processes are all going toward a goal God has in view. *Determinists* tried to show that events cause other events according to definite laws. But many contended that God's will, or some other nonmaterial element or being, is the source that originally determines these events.

Scientific findings of the 1900's have caused philosophers to modify many of their views. Science has found such a close relationship between matter and space that philosophers can no longer speak in terms of strict materialism. They must include space or energy in their theories. The change from using classical mathematics to using statistical mathematics makes scientists say not that things *are* a certain way, but that they *probably are* that way. As a result, some philosophers speak of probability rather than of determinism.

Is Man Free? The question of man's freedom is not a political one, but refers to his position in the universe. Some philosophers say that in a universe in which law reigns, men, as material bodies, are subject to the same laws as matter. These laws determine men's actions so that they *must* act the way they do. Other philosophers believe that men are free to change the course of events.

To be free means that a person can do (1) as he pleases, or (2) as he chooses. To do as he *pleases* means that he can act without any reason at all if he wishes. This is not freedom, but *caprice*, or whim. To do as he *chooses* means that he can select his course of action from among several courses open to him, then do what he has chosen to do. Both meanings imply that the future is not yet completely determined. This means that if man is free, he can somehow direct his own future and that of others.

Some philosophers believe that freedom to *do* or to *act* means going against the physical laws of nature. They say that man can choose or will to *think* freely, but he cannot act except as the laws of nature command him. Others, called *psychological determinists*, argue that even when a person thinks, he is subject to laws—those of the mind.

Some philosophers maintain that nobody can give a definite answer to the question, "Is man free?" There-fore, the question itself has no meaning. But others point out that the meaning of guilt and responsibility depends on how we try to answer this question. If we say that a person has some freedom, we can hold him responsible for his own actions. But if we say that a person is not free to choose his actions, can we ever consider him guilty of wrongdoing? See FREE WILL.

What Is Good and What Is Evil? Philosophy has always been concerned with judging human behavior. It tries to discover, through reason and observation, what is meant by good and evil and what a good life is.

We use the word *good* to mean *moral*, *useful*, or *pleasurable*. Usually *evil* means *immoral* or *bad*. Many persons think of a good life as one filled with pleasure. They believe that a person has a good life if he has enough money to live in luxury and to do whatever he wants. But, in this sense, a good life could easily be an evil life for someone who uses his money for evil purposes. Therefore, we must distinguish between a pleasurable life and a moral life. A person who lives righteously may be said to lead a good life in a moral sense.

Some people argue that even a moral life is based on pleasure. They say that we always do what we do for the pleasure in it. Therefore, if we are good, it is because we get pleasure from being good. But most people feel that if a person is moral for no other reason than to get pleasure, his act loses its moral character. For example, if someone returns something he found only because he knows he will be rewarded, we do not consider his act as moral.

Philosophers set up criteria, or standards, for judging moral goodness in terms of (1) man himself, (2) God, and (3) the world in which man lives.

Using *man himself* as a standard, philosophers believe that a person may be called morally good if he lives according to his true nature. But philosophers differ as to what man's true nature is. Aristotle said that man's true nature is to be rational. This means that the good man would live according to reason. The hedonists believed that men naturally seek happiness through pleasure (see HEDONIST). Therefore, the good man would always seek pleasure. The Epicureans maintained that man's nature is to seek a maximum of pleasure and a minimum of pain (see EPICURUS). The moral man, therefore, would try to get as much pleasure as possible with as little pain as possible. The Epicureans defined evil as that which gives pain.

If *God* is the standard of goodness, the moral man is one who lives according to God's will, and tries to imitate God. Evil would be defined as going against God's will. But man faces the problem of knowing what God wills.

Taking *the world* as the standard of goodness leads to defining a moral man as one who lives in accordance with the laws of nature. All civilization then becomes a source of evil. But nature itself may be viewed either as a struggle for existence or as a condition of childlike simplicity. Each of these views leads to a different kind of life.

Some philosophers say that morality has its own nature and is independent of anything outside itself. They say that the moral man lives according to the demands of morality as he understands them. The good is then like a color. It cannot be described or explained. It must be "seen" to be known.

The Tools of Philosophy

The philosopher uses certain standard methods of investigation, even though he does not go into a laboratory and set up experiments.

Reason is the chief tool of philosophy. Some philosophers begin with *axioms*, or general principles, and use reason to *deduce*, or arrive at, certain conclusions based on those principles. This is known as the *deductive method* (see DEDUCTIVE METHOD).

The French philosopher René Descartes and his followers believed that the deductive method was the only way to arrive at truth. Their fundamental rule was the *principle of consistency* which said that "nothing can be true which involves a contradiction." Starting with basic axioms, Descartes tried to deduce the structure of all reality. See DESCARTES, RENÉ.

The usefulness of deductive reasoning in all fields of knowledge depends on how true the original axioms are. Geometry is a good example of the use of deductive reasoning. See GEOMETRY; LOGIC.

Observation. Some philosophers insist that the only way to gain knowledge is through an empirical approach (see EMPIRICISM). Like scientists, they rely on sense observation and experimentation.

Empiricists use the *inductive method* of investigation (see INDUCTIVE METHOD). They begin by observing particular facts, then draw broad conclusions on the basis of these observations. For example, philosophers observe the information obtained by scientists about the physical nature of the universe. From this information, they try to formulate general principles that will explain scientific knowledge and make the universe intelligible. In ethics, philosophers observe the behavior called "moral," and try to find general laws of morality.

The inductive method involves four steps: (1) observation, (2) generalization, (3) deduction, and (4) testing conclusions. By *observation*, a philosopher gathers information relating to the problem he wishes to study. By *generalization*, he formulates a hypothetical, or tentative, answer to the problem. By *deduction*, he derives logical conclusions from his hypothesis. By *testing conclusions*, he seeks further observations to see whether the hypothesis can be proven.

Faith may be used in various ways. We speak of having faith and of knowing by faith. *Having faith* in God, for example, usually means trusting or relying on God. A person who has faith in the administration of justice feels that justice will be administered adequately. He relies on the administration of justice in critical situations.

We use the expression *having faith* in another way when we say of someone that "he truly has faith." Here we mean that the person truly believes and accepts. If a person has faith that God exists, he firmly believes that God exists, despite any arguments against this belief. He accepts the existence of God as a fact that cannot be denied. In this sense, faith is important in all our activities, not only in religion. The scientist has faith in his ability to find answers to meaningful questions. The citizen of a law-abiding country has faith in his

police officials. The philosopher has faith in the soundness of his approach to questions. Children have faith in their parents' love. To have faith in this sense means to have a set of beliefs that serve as a basis for living.

Knowing by faith means that faith is a way by which we come to know certain things. For example, a person knows by faith that he ought to be honest, or that God exists. Knowing by faith that God exists does not mean that a person knows that God exists because he believes it. Rather, he believes that God exists because, through the agency he calls faith, he has come to know God. Philosophers often accept knowledge on the basis of faith. The American philosopher George Santayana used the concept of knowing by faith in connection with the most fundamental knowledge that any person can have—that he, the person, exists.

Intuition is a method of observing. The word itself means a sort of *experience*. But it may be used in various senses. *To know intuitively* means to know in a mysterious, inexplicable, and direct fashion. For example, when a person says, "I knew intuitively that something was wrong," he means that he knew without any obvious reason for knowing. Or, when a person says, "I had an intuition," he means that he had a kind of mysterious revelation.

Intuition plays an important part in philosophy. Philosophers use the word to mean an experience that is direct and immediate. They believe that there are some things we can experience or know directly without reasoning about them or testing them. *Ethical intuitionism* says that we know what is good by intuition. We experience goodness directly, just as we experience colors directly. *Epistemological intuitionism* goes further and claims that all our knowledge is based on intuition. See INTUITION.

History

Ancient Times. The period of ancient philosophy extended from about 600 B.C. to the A.D. 500's. The earliest Greek philosophers included Thales, Heraclitus, Parmenides, and Democritus. They studied the nature of reality, and suggested various theories about the universe. Some said the universe was made of a single substance, such as water or fire. Others said that everything in the universe was alive. Heraclitus believed that the universe was in a constant state of flux, or change. Parmenides claimed that it was unchanging. The *Pythagorean* school maintained that numbers were the true realities, and all other things in the universe were imitations of numbers (see PYTHAGORAS).

Later philosophers studied problems of conduct. The *Sophists*, the professional teachers in Greece, discussed

ANCIENT PHILOSOPHERS

SOCRATES   PLATO   ARISTOTLE

questions of morality and the nature of the state. They wanted to develop clever debaters, and were more concerned with persuading people than with reaching the truth. Some even denied that there was any truth at all. They said that all knowledge is relative, and that things are correct or incorrect only as people consider them so. The Sophists also claimed that there are no absolute standards of morality. They declared that the will of those in power determines what people consider right or wrong. See SOPHIST.

Socrates' chief task was to combat the Sophists. He believed that truth can be attained, and he developed *the Socratic method* as a way of reaching it. Through a series of questions and answers and concrete examples, he tested statements that people had accepted as true. In morals, Socrates believed that knowledge was the highest virtue. His famous maxim was "Know thyself." Socrates was put to death in 399 B.C. He left no writings of his own, but his philosophy is known through the writings of Plato. *The Apology* describes Socrates' defense of his life and teachings. See SOCRATES.

Plato was Socrates' greatest pupil. He presented his philosophy in *The Republic* and various other *Dialogues*. Plato believed that the ideas we have of things are more real than the things themselves. He described two worlds: (1) the world of eternal, unchanging ideas, and (2) the world of change. Plato considered a knowledge of mathematics essential to knowing the world of ideas. He believed that an understanding of ideal forms in mathematics, such as the circle or the square, leads to an understanding of ideal forms in all aspects of life. Plato also spoke of the immortality of the soul. He believed that a *Demiurge*, which in Greek means *worker*, created the world and fashioned man's soul. See PLATO.

Aristotle, Plato's pupil, made valuable contributions to both deductive and inductive logic. His works ranged from biology to politics and psychology. Aristotle did not speak of a separate world of ideas. In his *Metaphysics*, he maintained that the world of senses, or the material world, is the real one. He tried to show that *forms*, or ideas, exist within all objects in the material world. By using the rules of logic, Aristotle sought to find cause-and-effect relationships between things in the world. He believed in a first "uncaused cause," or God, and considered theology the highest science (see THEOLOGY). Aristotle spoke of God as pure form, rather than as a personal Being who influences men's lives.

After Aristotle, the Stoics and Epicureans were concerned with rules of conduct (see STOIC). Roman philosophers followed Greek lines of thought.

Early Christian Philosophers tried to interpret Christianity and to relate it to the philosophy of the Greeks and Romans. They wanted to defend and bring into their philosophic systems such Christian doctrines as immortality; love; monotheism, or belief in one God; and the example of Christ as God and Man. Their works centered around discussions of (1) faith and reason, (2) the existence of God, (3) the relation of God to the world, (4) the relation of universals to particulars, (5) the nature of man and his immortality, and (6) the nature of Christ.

St. Augustine's *City of God*, written in the 400's, became one of the most important philosophic works of the Middle Ages. St. Augustine taught that all history is *teleological*, or purposeful, and is directed by God. God

RELIGIOUS PHILOSOPHERS

ST. AUGUSTINE

AQUINAS

is above everything, and man and the world are God's creatures. The supreme goal of man is mystical union with God. See AUGUSTINE, SAINT.

In the 1200's, St. Thomas Aquinas summed up scholastic philosophy in his *Summa Theologica*. St. Thomas was influenced by the philosophic theories of Aristotle. He argued that the universe was organized on the basis of reason, and that a knowledge of it leads to God. He said that a person should use both faith and reason in believing in God. See AQUINAS, SAINT THOMAS.

John Duns Scotus and William of Ockham opposed Aquinas' philosophic system. Johannes Eckhart, a mystic, claimed that belief in God is direct and inexplicable. He said that it cannot be proved or discussed in rational terms.

The Christian era in philosophy lasted until about the 1400's. Philosophy came to depend more and more on reason, and became separated from theology. Religious leaders did not accept reason as a proper criterion for religious truths.

During the Renaissance, in the 1400's, 1500's, and early 1600's, philosophers turned their attention to the way things happen on earth, and the way people could seek truth through reason. Scientists of the era were so successful in their methods of investigation that these methods became the criteria for all other fields. Mathematics grew in importance with the findings of Nicolaus Copernicus and Sir Isaac Newton.

Copernicus, Galileo, and Johannes Kepler laid the foundation on which Newton later built his great system of the world. Galileo made measurement and experiment the sources of all truth. Newton described the world as a giant machine. His great work *Philosophiae Naturalis Principia Mathematica* became the basis for the science of physics. See NEWTON, SIR ISAAC.

Niccolò Machiavelli, an Italian statesman, stressed reason rather than morality in politics (see MACHIAVELLI, NICCOLÒ). In *The Prince*, his most famous work, he urged rulers to use force, severity, and even deceit and immoral acts in order to achieve nationalistic goals.

RENAISSANCE PHILOSOPHERS

MACHIAVELLI **MONTAIGNE** **NEWTON**

PHILOSOPHY

In France, Jean Bodin (1530-1596) introduced the idea that the state is based on a social contract. Jean Jacques Rousseau developed this idea further during the 1700's (see ROUSSEAU, JEAN JACQUES).

But Michel de Montaigne, a French philosopher of the 1500's, expressed skepticism and doubt about the ability of reason to find truth. In his essays, he urged a return to simplicity and nature, away from the corruptions of civilization. See MONTAIGNE, MICHEL DE.

The Appeal to Reason. In the 1600's, human reason was elevated to a position of highest authority. Philosophic interest shifted radically from the supernatural to the natural. Philosophers used deductive reasoning to gain knowledge, with mathematics as their model. They believed that, just as mathematics starts from

and believed that experience and observation would give rise to fundamental ideas. All knowledge could then be built up from these ideas.

In England, John Locke rejected Descartes' philosophy of innate ideas or axioms. In his *Essay Concerning Human Understanding*, he spoke of the mind as a "blank tablet" upon which experience writes. He said that experience acts on the mind through sensation and reflection. Through *sensation*, the mind receives a picture of things in the world. Through *reflection*, the mind acts on what it has received. These two processes give man all his ideas. Our ideas themselves may be simple or complex. By comparing and combining simple ideas, our understanding builds complex ones. Knowledge is simply recognizing the connection and separation of ideas. See LOCKE, JOHN.

George Berkeley, an Irish bishop and philosopher,

THE APPEAL TO REASON (THE 1600's)

THE APPEAL TO EXPERIENCE (THE 1700's)

DESCARTES   SPINOZA

LOCKE   BERKELEY

axioms, philosophic thought could start from axioms that are native to reason and are true independently of experience. They called these *self-evident axioms*. On the basis of these axioms, they tried to build a system of truths that would be related logically.

Descartes wished to create a system of thought that would have the certainty of mathematics but would include metaphysics. He began by seeking a fundamental truth that could not be doubted, and came up with *Cogito, ergo sum*, or "I think, therefore I exist." He declared that the existence of God could be proved because man could not have the idea of God unless this idea had originally come from God. In a similar way, he proved the existence of the world. As a way of judging truth, he adopted the principle that anything men clearly and distinctly perceive must be true. Descartes also emphasized a basic dualism between the mind and the body. His *Discourse on the Method of Reasoning* and *Principles of Philosophy* exerted great influence on philosophic thought.

Baruch Spinoza, the Dutch philosopher, followed Descartes' methods and aims. He considered God a substance on which all other substances depend. God causes all other substances, but He is His own cause. Spinoza's book, *Ethics*, is written like a geometry problem. It starts with definitions and axioms, and proceeds to establish proofs. It ends with a strict determinism. Spinoza considered the intellectual love of God the highest good man can attain. See SPINOZA, BARUCH.

The Appeal to Experience. During the 1700's, epistemology, rather than metaphysics, became important. Philosophic speculation centered around the questions of how man acquires knowledge and knows truth. Physics and mechanics became models for knowledge, with Newton's book on physics the most important example. Philosophers adopted an empirical approach,

built upon Locke's theories. He accepted the axiom that ideas are the source of knowledge, and maintained that ideas alone are real. He stated his philosophy in the words "To be is to be perceived." Nothing exists in itself, but only as it is perceived. But perceptions are only ideas or mental images. Therefore, only ideas exist. And all ideas exist ultimately in God, the eternal mind. See BERKELEY, GEORGE.

David Hume drew the consequences of the empirical theory of knowledge in his *Treatise upon Human Nature*. He said that all our knowledge is limited to what we experience. The only things we can know are *phenomena*, or objects of sense perception. And even in the world of experience, all we can reach is probability, not truth. We can have no absolute or certain knowledge. See HUME, DAVID.

The Appeal to Humanism. Philosophers of the 1700's reduced all knowledge to individual experience. Philosophers of the 1800's turned their attention to various aspects of human experience. The human being became the center of philosophic attention.

In Germany, Immanuel Kant, disturbed by Hume's conclusions that we can know only what we have experienced, asked how experience was possible. He showed that through our senses we get impressions of things, but our minds shape and organize these impressions so that they become meaningful. In looking at a painting, for example, we *sense* color, but our minds distinguish between various colors and organize them into shapes and forms. The mind does this through *a priori*, or rational, judgments that do not depend on experience. These judgments also enable us to have knowledge even of those things which we have not experienced. Kant's *Critique of Pure Reason*, published in 1781, was one of the most influential philosophic works ever written. See KANT, IMMANUEL.

THE APPEAL TO HUMANISM (THE 1800'S)

KANT   **HEGEL**   **NIETZSCHE**

THE APPEAL TO ADJUSTMENT (THE 1900'S)

RUSSELL   **JAMES**   **DEWEY**

G. W. F. Hegel considered reason the absolute that directs the world. He said reason unfolds itself in history in a logical, evolutionary way. In all aspects of the universe, opposing elements work against each other to produce new elements. This *dialectical* process is repeated over and over until pure reason remains as the one element left in the world.

In *Das Kapital*, Karl Marx tried to frame a new way of life for men on earth. His philosophy of dialectical materialism was based on some of Hegel's views. But Marx's themes centered around economics instead of reason, a classless society instead of God, and revolution instead of logic. See MARX, KARL.

Friedrich Nietzsche rejected the dialectical approach of Hegel and Marx. He considered the desire for power to be a basic instinct for all men. He thought this *will to power* was the driving force of change, and felt reason was its instrument. He believed that the goal of history was the development of a society of supermen. He rejected Christianity because it emphasized meekness and humility. See NIETZSCHE, FRIEDRICH.

The Danish philosopher Søren A. Kierkegaard laid the foundation for *existentialism* (see EXISTENTIALISM). Kierkegaard taught that each person has complete inner freedom to direct his own life. Because man is aware of this freedom, he must assert it by acting as much as possible, and by being aware of his actions at all times. The goal of all human experience is knowledge of God. But, like everything else in life, spiritual progress is completely free. A person may advance or retreat, as he chooses. See KIERKEGAARD, SØREN AABYE.

The Appeal to Adjustment. In the 1900's, philosophy has taken two major directions. One is based on the development of logic, mathematics, and science; the other, on an increasing concern about man himself.

The British philosophers Bertrand Russell and Alfred North Whitehead and the American philosopher F. S. C. Northrop (1893-) turned their attention to the philosophy of science. They tried to build a systematic picture of physical reality based on scientific developments. Many of their writings discussed man's ability to know and to use scientific methods.

The British philosophers George Edward Moore (1873-1958), Ludwig Wittgenstein (1889-1951), and Gilbert Ryle (1900-) rejected traditional philosophic discussions about the nature of reality. They concentrated on analyzing the language that philosophy uses in speaking about the world.

Most philosophic works of the 1900's have been based on man's concern for himself. The philosophy of pragmatism, developed in the United States by Charles Sanders Peirce, William James, and John Dewey, made social adjustment and improvement the goals of life. Later philosophers have been concerned with human psychology and man's situation on earth. Such existentialists as Jean-Paul Sartre, Albert Camus, Karl Jaspers (1883-1969), and Martin Heidegger (1889-) have discussed the universe in terms of human emotions.

All these philosophies have turned away from the traditional philosophic approach to such fields as metaphysics, ethics, aesthetics, and axiology. They are concerned with how man can survive in, and adjust to, his changing world.   LOUIS O. KATTSOFF

Related Articles in WORLD BOOK include:

AMERICAN PHILOSOPHERS

Adams, Henry Brooks	James, William
Dewey, John	Mumford, Lewis
Durant, Will	Peirce, Charles S.
Emerson, Ralph W.	Royce, Josiah
Fiske, John	Santayana, George
Hoffer, Eric	Thoreau, Henry D.

BRITISH PHILOSOPHERS

Bacon, Francis	Locke, John
Bacon, Roger	Mill (family)
Bentham, Jeremy	Paley, William
Berkeley, George	Russell, Bertrand A. W.
Bradley, Francis H.	Spencer, Herbert
Erigena, Johannes S.	Tyndall, John
Hobbes, Thomas	Whitehead, Alfred North
Hume, David	

FRENCH PHILOSOPHERS

Abelard, Peter	Marcel, Gabriel
Bayle, Pierre	Pascal, Blaise
Bergson, Henri	Rousseau, Jean Jacques
Comte, Auguste	Sartre, Jean-Paul
Condillac, Étienne B. de	Tocqueville, Alexis de
Descartes, René	Voltaire
Diderot, Denis	

GERMAN PHILOSOPHERS

Feuerbach, Ludwig	Leibniz, Gottfried W.
Fichte, Johann G.	Marx, Karl
Harnack, Adolf von	Nietzsche, Friedrich
Hegel, Georg W. F.	Rosenberg, Alfred
Heidegger, Martin	Schelling, Friedrich von
Herbart, Johann F.	Schopenhauer, Arthur
Herder, Johann G. von	Schweitzer, Albert
Jaspers, Karl	Spengler, Oswald
Kant, Immanuel	Wundt, Wilhelm

GREEK PHILOSOPHERS

Anaxagoras	Empedocles	Pyrrho of Elis
Anaximander	Epictetus	Pythagoras
Anaximenes	Epicurus	Socrates
Aristotle	Heraclitus	Thales
Carneades	Parmenides	Zeno
Democritus	Plato	Zeno of Elea
Diogenes		

ROMAN PHILOSOPHERS

Lucretius	Plotinus
Marcus Aurelius	Seneca, Lucius A.

OTHER PHILOSOPHERS

Albertus Magnus, Saint	Kierkegaard, Søren A.
Aquinas, Saint Thomas	Maimonides
Arminius, Jacobus	Marsilius of Padua
Augustine, Saint	Nägeli, Karl W.
Averroës	Origen
Berdyaev, Nicolas	Ortega y Gasset, José
Boethius, Manlius S.	Porphyry
Confucius	Spinoza, Baruch
Croce, Benedetto	Tagore, Sir Rabindranath
Erasmus, Desiderius	Tolstoy, Leo N.
Iqbal, Sir Muhammad	Unamuno, Miguel de

PHILOSOPHIC IDEAS

Atomism	Materialism	Pre-Socratic
Cynic School	Mechanist	Philosophy
of Philosophy	Metaphysics	Rationalism
Deism	Neoplatonism	Realism
Existentialism	Pantheism	Scholasticism
Gnostic	Peripatetic	Skepticism
Hedonist	School of	Sophist Philosophy
Humanism	Philosophy	Stoic Philosophy
Idealism	Pragmatism	Supernaturalism
		Utilitarianism

TOOLS OF PHILOSOPHY

Deductive Method	Intuition
Empiricism	Perception
Inductive Method	Reason

OTHER RELATED ARTICLES

Aesthetics	Ethics	Science
Brook Farm	Logic	Theology
Education	Religion	

Outline

I. Contributions of Philosophy
  A. Philosophy and Science
  B. Philosophy and Religion
  C. Philosophy and Government
  D. Philosophy and Education

II. Problems of Philosophy
  A. What Is Real?
  B. The Nature of the Universe
  C. Is Man Free?
  D. What Is Good and What Is Evil?

III. The Tools of Philosophy
  A. Reason
  B. Observation
  C. Faith
  D. Intuition

IV. History

Questions

What are the aims of philosophy?
How has science influenced philosophy?
How did Aristotle's theory about the universe differ from Plato's?
Can we always depend on our sense perceptions? Why?
What steps does the inductive method involve?
What influence has philosophy had on education?
What do mechanists say about the nature of the universe? Teleologists?
How do we gain knowledge according to the theories of (1) René Descartes? (2) John Locke? (3) Immanuel Kant?
What problems did early Christian philosophers face?
How would you define a good life? Why?

PHIPS, SIR WILLIAM. See MASSACHUSETTS (Troubles with England).

PHLEBITIS, *flee BY tus,* is an inflammation of a vein, chiefly the veins in the legs. Injury or infection of the blood vessel damages the lining. A clot, called a *thrombus,* forms at the site of the damage. This condition is called *thrombophlebitis.* Blood cells, captured from the slow-moving venous blood, enlarge the clot until the vessel is blocked (see EMBOLISM). A loose clot may break off and be carried by the blood stream to the lungs. This complication is often fatal.   FRANK V. THEIS

PHLEGETHON. See TARTARUS.

PHLOEM, *FLOH em,* is a tissue in the stems, roots, and leaves of higher plants. It consists of cells whose function is conducting dissolved food. In woody stems, it is part of the inner bark, just outside the cambium. Phloem is called *hard bast* when it includes long cells that help make the stem stiff, and *soft bast* when it is made up mostly of *sieve tubes* through which pass foods manufactured by the leaves.   ARTHUR W. GALSTON

See also BARK; BAST.

PHLOGISTON THEORY. See CHEMISTRY (History).

PHLOX, *flocks,* is a common garden flower with brilliantly colored blossoms. The name *phlox* comes from the Greek word for *flame.* In spite of their range of showy colors, the phlox blossoms are never flame-colored.

These flowers first came from North America. They are favorite garden flowers because they are hardy and grow well in fertile soil. Many different varieties have been developed by breeding. All annual phlox are derived from *Drummond phlox,* a species that grows wild in Texas. The familiar wild *sweet William,* whose bluish or pale lilac flowers are among the early summer blossoms, also belongs to the phlox group. See SWEET WILLIAM.

The flowers grow in clusters on the tops of stems which may be two or three feet high. Annual varieties of phlox are grown from seeds.

Scientific Classification. Phlox belongs to the phlox family, *Polemoniaceae.* Annual phlox is genus *Phlox,* species *P. drummondii.* Wild sweet William is *P. divaricata.*   ALFRED C. HOTTES

PHNOM PENH, *P'NAWM PEN* (pop. 403,500; alt. 33 ft.), is the capital of Cambodia in Southeast Asia. It stands where the Tonle Sap and Bassac rivers join the Mekong River. See CAMBODIA (map). Phnom Penh is an industrial center, with rice mills, textile factories, distilleries, and sawmills. The city was founded in the 1300's and became the capital of the Khmer Empire in 1434. It was abandoned several times, but became the permanent capital of Cambodia in 1867.   THOMAS E. ENNIS

PHOBIA, *FOH bih uh,* is a recurrent, persistent, unrealistic, and often intense fear of some idea, situation, or external object. Persons suffering from the types of mental illness called *neuroses* often have phobias (see NEUROSIS). If the patient is forced to remain in a situation for which he has a phobia, he becomes agitated, and may even cry. Persons with phobias also often have tremors and become overwhelmed with panic. Doctors have found that reassuring the patient that his fear is unrealistic accomplishes little in easing the fear.

Some types of phobias are related to the patient's location. For example, *agoraphobia* is the fear of a large, open space, and *claustrophobia* is the fear of a confined space. Other types of phobias include *aichmophobia* (sharp instruments), *ailurophobia* (cats), *anthropophobia* (human society), *astraphobia* (thunderstorms), *erythrophobia* (blushing), *hydrophobia* (water), *microphobia* (germs), and *mysophobia* (dirt). *Zoophobia* is a fear of animals, *nyctophobia* is a fear of the dark, and *phobophobia* is a fear of fear.

Sigmund Freud, the founder of psychoanalysis, thought that in phobia the thing feared served as a symbol for some other fear. Usually, the other fear stemmed from an event that had occurred in early childhood, and had been *repressed*, or forgotten (see Subconscious). The person himself does not consciously know what the original fear is. But it produces feelings of anxiety which he attributes to the object for which he now has the phobia. In treating phobias, doctors help the patient recall the incident that originally produced the fear. Psychoanalysis is a common method used to treat phobias.   George A. Ulett

See also Emotion; Mental Illness; Psychoanalysis.

PHOBOS. See Mars (Satellites).

PHOCIS. See Delphi.

PHOEBE, *FEE bee,* a small, active bird, belongs to the flycatcher family. It has a grayish-olive back and a yellowish-white breast. The eastern phoebe is common throughout eastern North America in summer. The phoebe gets its name from its monotonous call, "fee-bee." It lives around farm buildings and bridges, where it plasters its nest to rafters and beams. It builds its nest from moss and mud, and lines it with grass and hair. The phoebe lays three to eight white eggs, which in rare cases are spotted with a cinnamon color. It eats insects caught on short flights from its perch.

Scientific Classification. The phoebe is in the tyrant flycatcher family, *Tyrannidae*. The eastern phoebe is genus *Sayornis*, species *S. phoebe.*   George J. Wallace

PHOENICIA, *fee NISH ih uh,* was the name the ancient Greeks gave to the region which is now roughly the coastal areas of Syria, Lebanon, and Israel. The Eleutherus River formed the northern boundary and Mount Carmel the southern. This region lay between the Lebanon Mountains to the east and the Mediterranean Sea on the west.

The origin of the word *Phoenicia* is not certain. It appears to have developed from the word *Canaan,* meaning *land of purple,* the name first used for ancient Palestine and Syria. Canaan was an important source of red-purple dyed goods. The Greeks probably used their word *phoinix,* which meant *red-purple,* when referring to the people who traded these red-purple goods to them. *Phoínike,* or *Phoenicia,* eventually became the name of Canaan's coastal strip.

The Phoenicians were one of the great peoples of the ancient world. They were great sailors, navigators, and traders. They became famous in history for two achievements. They were among the first to send out explorers and colonies throughout the Mediterranean Sea area, and even beyond the Strait of Gibraltar. And they left their alphabet to the western world. The Greek alphabet developed from that of the Phoenicians, and the Roman and all western alphabets have been taken from the Greek.

Way of Life

Phoenicians cannot be easily distinguished from other peoples who lived in Canaan before the Israelites

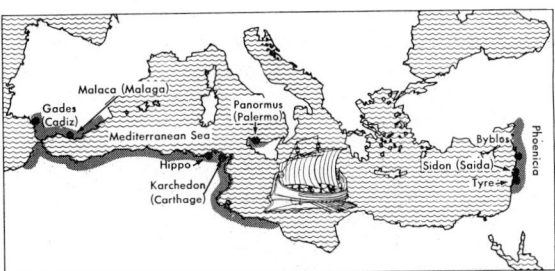

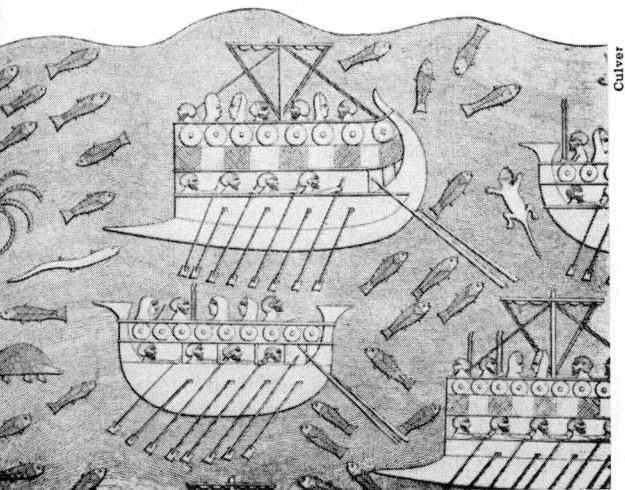

Bettmann Archive

Phoenician Traders carried their goods far and wide in ancient Europe. They traded cloth and costly goods for tin and other goods from southwestern England, *above.* Warships with pointed prows protected them, *left.* Phoenician colonies stretched around the Mediterranean Sea, map, *upper left.*

PHOENICIA

settled there. For this reason, the Phoenicians are sometimes called *Canaanites* in the Old Testament. More often, they are called *Sidonians*, from the name of the Phoenician city of Sidon. Scholars now know that the northern Phoenician city of Ugarit (now Ras Shamra in western Syria) was in contact with Cretan civilization as early as 1900 B.C. Between 1400 and 1100 B.C., a Mycenaean colony thrived at Ugarit.

Language. The Phoenicians spoke a dialect of the Semitic languages. The Phoenician language was closely related to Hebrew. It was more distantly related to Aramaic and to the Semitic languages of Mesopotamia, such as Assyrian and Babylonian. Scholars once believed that the Phoenicians had invented their alphabet independently. But later discoveries indicated that they had adapted it from earlier writing. The Phoenician alphabet consisted of 22 consonant signs. The Greeks added the vowel signs later.

By the beginning of the Christian Era, Aramaic had become the language of Phoenicia. But North Africans near the former Phoenician colony of Carthage continued to speak the Phoenician language until the A.D. 500's, using a dialect called *Punic*. Some names of places in southern Spain, colonized by the Phoenicians in the 700's B.C. or earlier, come from the Phoenician language. The name of *Gades* (now Cádiz, Spain) comes from the Phoenician word for *wall*. The word *bible* comes from the Greek word for *book*. The Greeks took this word from the Phoenician city of Byblos, a trading center for papyrus.

A few fragments of Phoenician literature have survived in Greek translation. Since 1929, important discoveries have been made at the site of ancient Ugarit. Religious inscriptions on clay tablets discovered there clarify some formerly obscure passages in the Old Testament. The tablets were written in cuneiform, in an alphabetical style that differs from the standard Phoenician.

Trade and Manufacturing. The Phoenicians were seagoing traders from the very beginning of their recorded history. The Egyptians knew about the "ships of Gebal" (Byblos) as early as 2900 B.C. But Phoenicia did not reach its peak as a great sea power until about 1000 B.C., and after.

The city of Sidon grew famous for its purple dye, and developed a well-known glass industry. Tyre also had a purple-dyeing industry, and became noted for the bad odor which the dye works caused. Phoenicia was one of the garden spots of the Roman Empire, and exported wine, oil, and laurel and cedar wood, as well as textiles and other manufactured goods.

The Phoenicians learned most of their methods of manufacturing from the Egyptians. They cast, hammered, and engraved metals, such as gold and silver. They carved many objects from ivory, including pieces of furniture. From early times, Phoenicians knew how to weave woolen and linen cloth. The craftsmen dyed the cloth and often sewed it into robes before they sold it. The Greeks later adopted the *keton*, a Phoenician shirtlike garment.

Religion. Phoenicians had many gods and goddesses called *baal* (lord) and *baalat* (lady). All Phoenicians worshipped the same major gods, although these gods sometimes were known by different names in different cities. For example, Melqart, god of Tyre, could also be thought of as the *Baal* of Tyre. The Phoenicians practiced sacrifices similar to those practiced by most other Semitic peoples. But they also offered human sacrifices in Phoenicia and in their colonies, which gained for them a reputation for cruelty.

The story of Astarte and her lover Adonis, well-known in Phoenicia, was carried from there to Greece, where Astarte became the Greek goddess Aphrodite. The Romans later knew her as Venus. The tragic death of her lover by the tusks of a wild boar and her lament for him comes down to us through Greek, Latin, and English literature in the story of Venus and Adonis.

Government. The ancient Phoenicians lived in a number of independent city-states. Like the Greeks, they never united their cities into a single country. These cities originally were aristocracies ruled by kings. Beginning in the 800's B.C., councils of elders ruled with the kings, and some of the councils were more powerful than the kings. Later, most cities were ruled by government officials called *shofets*. Most of the Phoenician mountains came down to the sea, and the ancient towns were originally built on islands, like Tyre and Arvad, or occupied a small harbor area on the mainland with hills in back of it. The most important of these coastal cities, from north to south, were Arvad, Byblos, Berytus (now Beirut), Sidon, Tyre, and Acco. Beirut the present-day capital and chief seaport of Lebanon, is the only city still important.

History

Foreign Control. Phoenicia was a natural meeting place for foreign cultures, because it lay on the main avenue of traffic between Egypt to the south and Asia Minor and Mesopotamia to the east. Egypt exerted the earliest influence on the Phoenicians. As early as the time of the Old Kingdom, from 2700 B.C. to 2200 B.C., Egypt was importing the famed cedars of Lebanon. By the time of the Middle Kingdom, from 2050 B.C. to 1780 B.C., the two countries had established regular trade. The Phoenicians exported timber and pitch, and imported gold and manufactured articles. In the 1400's

Brown Bros.

Phoenician Achievements included a well-developed alphabet, *left*, and beautiful buildings.

356

B.C., Phoenicia became a frontier province of Egypt, and remained one for about 100 years. During this period, the Phoenician cities influenced Egypt almost as much as Egypt influenced them. Phoenician nobles often visited the Egyptian court. Phoenician cults and religious ideas affected Egyptian thought.

Babylonian culture also influenced early Phoenicia. By the 1300's B.C., the princes of Phoenicia were writing in Babylonian cuneiform (see CUNEIFORM). The Phoenicians learned to seal their documents with Babylonian cylinders and seals. The Babylonians also taught the Phoenicians many of their mythological tales about the beginning of the world, the birth of the gods, and the creation of the first man. Some scholars believe that Phoenicia may have been the channel through which the Babylonian legends about the creation and the flood passed to the Hebrews farther south and to the Greeks.

For a short period in the 1200's B.C., Phoenicia came under the Hittite sphere of influence, but gained its freedom when the Hittite Empire collapsed.

The Spread of Phoenician Influence. The Phoenician cities gained their independence about 1100 B.C. For the next 400 years, they stood at the height of their power and prosperity. There were Phoenician settlements on the island of Cyprus even before 1200 B.C. After that date, Phoenician sailors opened up the entire Mediterranean to their ships and commerce. They established colonies along the southern coast of Spain, the northern coast of Africa, and the western coast of Sicily. It may be said that the western Mediterranean was a "Phoenician lake" before the coming of the Greeks. Phoenicians influenced Western culture through their colony of Carthage. This greatest of all Phoenician colonies in the west was founded by people from the city of Tyre about 750 B.C. Queen Dido was one of the legendary founders of Carthage (see DIDO). Phoenician colonies, including Carthage, resembled the cities of Phoenicia. Their residents included many manufacturers, industrial workers, merchants, and seamen.

The city of Tyre seems to have played the main part in the colonizing activity of the Phoenicians. A vivid description of Tyre's far-flung commerce appears in the Old Testament (Ezekiel 27: 3-25). When King David of Israel established his royal residence at Jerusalem, he built his palace with stone and cedars from Lebanon (II Samuel 5: 11). The first book of Kings tells that Hiram, king of Tyre in the 900's B.C., was a friend of David's successor, King Solomon. When Solomon built his famous Temple, he asked Hiram for firs and cedars from Lebanon, and for men to cut the timber. When Solomon built a navy, Hiram lent him certain workers who were "shipmen that had knowledge of the sea" (I Kings 9: 27). The base of this fleet was the Red Sea port of Ezion-Geber on the Gulf of Aqaba. This site, recently excavated, contains the remains of a once great smelting and mining center. Hiram and Solomon combined to send from this port great fleets of merchant vessels, which came back loaded with "gold and silver, ivory and apes and peacocks" (II Chronicles 9: 21). In return, Solomon traded grain, olive oil, wine, and other agricultural products with Hiram.

Some scholars believe that Phoenician influence and perhaps Phoenician colonists reached Corinth and Thebes on the mainland of Greece. This tradition of Phoenician colonization in Greece may be exaggerated. But the Phoenicians appear in the poems of Homer as skilled artisans, merchants, and sailors. The Phoenician alphabet also reached Greece before 800 B.C.

Control of both sides of the Strait of Gibraltar gave the Phoenicians access to the Atlantic Ocean. They established a trading monopoly along the coasts of northwestern Africa and western Europe. Some scholars believe that the Phoenicians may have sailed as far as Cornwall, in southwestern Britain, and worked the tin mines there. Phoenicians sailed around Africa in the 600's B.C., some 2,000 years before the Portuguese accomplished the same feat in A.D. 1497. The Greek historian Herodotus tells this story in the fourth book of his *History*.

Decline. The Assyrians captured the Phoenician cities in 842 B.C. For the next 200 years, Phoenicia was under the control of Assyria. This period was one of hardship, revolt, and suppression. After the downfall of the Assyrians in 612 B.C., Phoenicia was briefly controlled by the Babylonians. Later, the region became part of the Persian Empire created by King Cyrus I (see CYRUS THE GREAT). At this time, the city of Sidon seems to have surpassed Tyre in importance. Under Persian rule, Phoenician cities prospered and Phoenicians were still considered excellent shipbuilders and sailors. During the Persian Wars, from 498 B.C. to 479 B.C., the Phoenician fleet ranked as the strongest arm of the Persian Navy in its attack upon Greece. Herodotus says that in this fleet the king of Sidon ranked second to Xerxes, the Persian ruler (see XERXES [I]). The Phoenician fleet, however, was almost completely destroyed by the Greeks at the Battle of Salamis in 480 B.C.

Phoenicia came under Greco-Macedonian rule when Alexander the Great captured the city of Tyre in 332 B.C. His successors, the rulers of Egypt and Syria, fought among themselves for possession of the Phoenician cities and for control of their shipbuilding and commercial resources. During this period, the culture of Phoenicia changed. Greek gradually became the language of literature and learning. Aramaic, which had earlier replaced the Phoenician language, became the language of the marketplace and of the common people. Many philosophers of the time, including Zeno of Sidon and Diodorus of Tyre, were of Phoenician origin.

In 64 B.C., the Roman general Pompey the Great made Phoenicia part of the Roman province of Syria. The Romans established a famous law school at Beirut. Tyre and Sidon became important centers of learning, and continued to prosper commercially. Tyre became known for the manufacture of fine glass. Phoenicia, together with the rest of Syria, fell to Moslem invaders in the A.D. 600's.   LOUIS L. ORLIN

Related Articles in WORLD BOOK include:

CITIES

| Byblos | Carthage | Sidon | Tyre | Utica |

OTHER RELATED ARTICLES

Alphabet	Clothing (color picture:
Ancient Civilization	Costumes of Ancient Peoples)
Astarte	Mediterranean Sea (History)
Baal	

Bettmann Archive

The Phoenix was a mythological bird representing the sun. After living for 500 years, it burned itself on a funeral pyre.

PHOENIX, *FEE niks,* was a fabled bird in Greek mythology. Only one such bird existed at any time, and it was always male. It had brilliant gold and reddish-purple feathers, and was as large or larger than an eagle. According to some Greek writers, the phoenix lived exactly 500 years. Other writers believed its life cycle was as long as 97,200 years.

At the end of each life cycle, the phoenix burned itself on a funeral pyre. Another phoenix then rose from the ashes with renewed youth and beauty. The young phoenix, after rising from the ashes, carried the remains of its father to the altar of the sun god in the Egyptian city of *Heliopolis* (City of the Sun). The long life of the phoenix, and its dramatic rebirth from its own ashes, made it a symbol of immortality and spiritual rebirth.

The Greeks probably took their idea of the phoenix from the Egyptians, who worshiped the *benu,* a sacred bird similar to the stork. The benu, like the phoenix, was connected with the sun worship rites in Heliopolis. Both birds represented the sun, which dies in its flames each evening and emerges each morning.   I. J. GELB

PHOENIX, Ariz. (pop. 505,666; met. area 663,510; alt. 1,090 ft.), is the capital and largest city of the state. It is in the center of Salt River Valley (see ARIZONA [political map]). Citrus fruits, cotton, grain, hay, safflower, and vegetables are grown in the valley,

Central Avenue Cuts Through the Heart of Phoenix, Ariz., and leads to the scenic Phoenix Mountains nearby.

Phoenix Chamber of Commerce

a rich, irrigated area. Phoenix is a shipping center for the crops and beef cattle of the area. Canneries, cotton gins, and food-processing and milling plants stand in the city. Products include aluminum, iron, leather, steel, and wool. Aircraft, air-conditioning, and electronic and electrical equipment are also produced in Phoenix. The city's warm, dry climate has made it a winter resort area. For the monthly weather in Phoenix, see ARIZONA (Climate). Luke Air Force Base, Williams Air Force Base, and a naval air installation are located in the area. Two transcontinental railroads and two transcontinental airlines, as well as regional airlines and interstate trucking lines, serve the city.

Phoenix was named for the fabled bird of ancient Greece, which supposedly burned itself on a pyre every 500 years, and arose again. The name was suggested because pioneers found prehistoric ruins and irrigation canals used in farming.

The seat of Maricopa County, Phoenix has a council-manager type of government.   ALICE B. GOOD

See also ARIZONA (pictures).

PHOENIX ISLANDS is a group of eight small coral islands in the Pacific Ocean. They lie near the equator, about 500 miles north of Samoa. They rise less than 30 feet above sea level, and cover a total land area of 34 square miles. The islands are Canton, Enderbury, Phoenix, Sydney, Birnie, McKean, Gardner, and Hull. For location, see PACIFIC ISLANDS (color map).

Most of the islands are not fertile, and they have a population of about 1,300. Great Britain claimed the Phoenix Islands as a protectorate in 1892. The islands were annexed to the British colony of Gilbert and Ellice Islands in 1937. In 1938, the United States claimed sovereignty over Canton and Enderbury islands, and a dispute arose. In 1939, both were placed under joint British-American rule. Canton and Enderbury cover 27 square miles in the Phoenix Islands group, and have 320 inhabitants.   EDWIN H. BRYAN, JR.

See also CANTON AND ENDERBURY ISLANDS.

PHON, *fahn,* is a unit for measuring the loudness of sound. It is related to the decibel, the unit that measures sound intensity (see DECIBEL). By definition, sound waves vibrating at 1,000 *hertz* (cycles per second) have an equal number of phons and decibels. But a 60-decibel, 500-hertz tone does not sound so loud, and has fewer phons. See also SOUND (Measuring Sound).

PHONEME. See LINGUISTICS.

PHONETICS, *foh NET iks,* is the science of speech sounds, and the symbols by which they are shown in writing and printing. This science is based on a study of all the parts of the body concerned in making speech. It includes the positions of the parts of the body necessary for producing spoken words, and the effect of air from the lungs as it passes through the larynx, pharynx, vocal cords, nasal passages, and mouth.

The natural way of learning to speak is by imitating sounds made by others. Speech difficulties may sometimes be overcome if a person is shown where to place some part of the speech apparatus to make sounds.

The Phonetic Ideal is a language in which every spoken sound is represented by one letter and only one. No language has reached this ideal, but Spanish and Italian are close to it. German and Spanish add a few marks to letters, because there are not enough letters to cover all the sounds. Italian has only one silent letter,

Learning Phonics. Children practice listening carefully to hear the sounds in the words they use. They also learn to associate the sounds in the words with written letters.

Parade Magazine

h, which is used before *e* and *i* to make the preceding *g* or *c* hard, as in *spaghetti*. French is among the most complex in this respect. It has many spellings for the same sound; four accent marks; and a cedilla for words like *François* that have an *s* sound for *c*.

English Spelling is difficult because spelling was decided on by printers hundreds of years ago, but speech has continued to change sounds.

English is far from the phonetic ideal. "*Though* he pulled *through* a *cough* and *hiccough*, he still had a *rough* night on a *bough*," contains six different sounds spelled the same. Every vowel has several sounds as in c*a*ke, h*a*t, b*a*th, *a*rm, and in n*o*d, r*o*de, w*o*men. *A* and *e* each have about eight sounds. English-speaking people have tried in some ways to reproduce sounds phonetically. *Pin* and *pine*, and *pinning* and *pining*, mark the difference in the *i* sounds. But there is no reason for a spelling difference in *till* and *until*.

An International Phonetic Alphabet has been compiled by experts to represent the various sounds. These symbols can be applied to all languages. In English, they show clearly the difference between the *th* of *ether* (θ) and the *th* of *either* (ð), and between the *ssi* of *mission* (ʃ) and the *si* of *vision* (ʒ). Another symbol shows the *ng* sound of *sing* (ŋ). Phonetic symbols are especially useful for vowel sounds, as in the *a* of *father* (ɑ) and the *a* of one pronunciation of *ask* (a), or the *u* sound of *pull* (ʊ), the *oo* sound of *pool* (u), and the stressed *u* sound of *sun* (ʌ).

The commonest sound in English is that of *e* in ag*e*nt. It is so common that some experts have called it the "zero vowel." It appears in print as *a*round, mom*e*nt, charity, porp*oi*se, act*o*r and circ*u*s. The symbol for this sound is an inverted e (ə), called a *schwa*.

Reformed Spelling has been tried by many persons, to make spelling come closer to sound. Its value is doubtful, because pronunciation changes rapidly. A series of technical dictionaries would be necessary to explain the language if simplified spelling were widely adopted throughout the world.   Clarence Stratton

See also Alphabet; English Language; Laubach, Frank C.; Pronunciation.

PHONICS, *FAHN icks,* is the association of letters or combinations of letters with their appropriate speech sounds. Phonics also includes understanding the principles that govern the use of letters in words. In reading, phonics helps us understand the sound of a word that is unfamiliar. In spelling, phonics helps us write the appropriate letters for the sounds we hear.

Phonics can be taught synthetically or analytically. In the *synthetic* approach, the child learns the sounds of individual letters and letter combinations, usually before he learns to read. When the child meets an unfamiliar word, he *synthesizes*, or sounds out, the sounds that make up the word. In the *analytic* approach, the child develops a vocabulary of words he knows by sight. He does this while learning to read. The child eventually analyzes the words for their sounds. In this way, he understands both the sound of the letters and the reasons some letters are used instead of others. The child then applies these reasons, or *principles*, and learns to recognize the sounds of new words. Because of research in reading and psychology, most educators believe that the analytic approach produces better results than the synthetic approach.

In reading, phonics has both advantages and disadvantages. A knowledge of phonics makes it possible to reconstruct the sounds of many words that are not known by sight. But phonics has limitations, because many words are not spelled as they sound. Different letters may represent the same sound, as in *meet* and *meat;* or the same letter may have many sounds, as the *a* in *fall, fat,* and *watch.* Because of these and other irregularities in the language, phonics can never be the only technique used to teach word recognition and spelling.

Educators recognize phonics as a necessary part of any effective reading program, but they recommend the use of additional aids. For example, the reader is taught to recognize new words by picture clues, and by noting the likenesses and differences in words, and by recognizing prefixes, suffixes, roots, and syllables.   A. Sterl Artley

See also Phonetics; Pronunciation; Reading; Linguistics (Structural Linguistics).

Zenith Radio Corp.

PHONOGRAPH. The phonograph is the most familiar device for storing sound which can be later reproduced. It is a source of enjoyment and pleasure for millions. It also plays an important role in industry and communication.

The main use of the phonograph is as a source of enjoyment in the home. It has served to increase appreciation of fine music and great poetry. By listening to the compositions of the great composers performed by the greatest artists, the student learns to enjoy and appreciate great music.

Small children enjoy songs and stories which are especially recorded for them. But phonographs have many other important uses. Great actors have recorded readings from the plays of Shakespeare, and political works. Authors have read selections from their own works. Experts have read the poems of such masters as Chaucer and Dante.

History-making speeches have been preserved on phonograph records. Phonograph records also are used in teaching correct pronunciation of foreign languages. Recordings are made of great musical classics in which an important instrument or a solo voice has been left out, so that a singer or musician can play in company with the finest orchestras or string quartets. Many industrial firms record sales talks as a means of increasing the use of their product, or to train salesmen. Most large business offices use a dictating machine, which is really a type of phonograph.

The home recording devices permit an individual to record his favorite radio program and play it back, or to record home talent. By use of home recording devices, students of voice or an instrument are able to hear their performances as they really are. Speech defects can be corrected. Singers can learn to improve their singing. There are many stores in the United States where recordings can be made. Such records often are used as holiday and anniversary greetings.

Scientists have also found uses for the phonograph. They have recorded sounds of insects and birds. The folk songs of remote sections of the country or the speech of primitive tribes can also be recorded and preserved.

Radio broadcasting studios also use recordings for various purposes. They can record music and dramatic scenes and broadcast them at the most convenient times of the day. The radio also uses recording devices to take down descriptions of the exciting sports, political, or other news events. These can be broadcast later on. Such radio records are called *transcriptions*.

How the Phonograph Works

All sound is made up of vibrations. One scientist has pointed out that if you could hold your hand beside your ears, and wave your hands rapidly (as much as 5 to 15,000 times a second), you could re-create all the sounds produced by a great symphony orchestra. The phonograph stores a series of vibrations on a record in such a way that they can be transformed back into sound waves.

The four essential parts of the phonograph are: (1) the phonograph record, (2) the turntable which revolves, (3) the pickup which takes the sound from the record, and (4) the loudspeaker which reproduces the sound.

The phonograph stores vibrations in a tiny groove on the phonograph record. This groove consists of many tiny wavy lines which represent the vibrations that were made by the person who sang, played a musical instrument, or spoke into the microphone. The record is placed on the turntable of the phonograph, where it revolves. The needle on the pickup vibrates back and forth along the groove. This vibration twists a small crystal in the pickup. When the crystal is twisted, it gives off electrical charges or currents which vary according to the wave pattern on the record. Before they can be of any use, however, these electrical impulses must be amplified, or made stronger, by the electron tubes in the phonograph.

The amplified impulse is carried to a loudspeaker. The loudspeaker consists of a small electromagnet and a cone-shaped disk of cardboard in the center of which a piece of steel is attached. When the electrical impulses reach the loudspeaker, they cause the electromagnet to alternately attract and repel the steel on the disk. This causes the cardboard to vibrate and reproduce the electrical vibrations in the form of sound.

Phonograph Records

The ordinary phonograph record is usually a thin, flat disc ten or twelve inches in diameter, although children's records are smaller. It is the part of the phonograph upon which music and speech are stored. In making a phonograph record, the musician or speaker speaks into a microphone. The sound of his voice is converted into electrical impulses which are amplified a thousand or more times. These electrical impulses travel to a tiny magnet which influences a small tool. This tool cuts a grooved pattern onto the surface of a wax plate which is rotating below it on a turntable. The pattern begins on the outer part of the disc and spirals inside to within an inch or two of the center of the turntable.

For making an ordinary phonograph record, the tiny chisel vibrates sideways, often as much as ten thousand times a second. For making the kind of phonograph records used in radio studios, which are called transcriptions, the "hill and dale" method is often used. Here the

HOW PHONOGRAPH RECORDS ARE MADE

HOW SOUND IS RECORDED

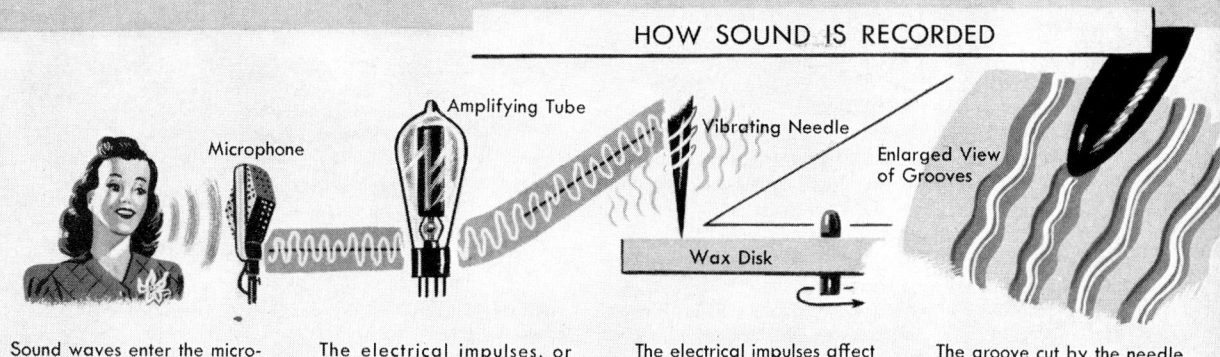

Microphone — Amplifying Tube — Vibrating Needle — Enlarged View of Grooves — Wax Disk

Sound waves enter the microphone where they are turned into electrical impulses.

The electrical impulses, or waves, are greatly increased in the amplifying tubes.

The electrical impulses affect a crystal which controls the vibrating needle.

The groove cut by the needle varies with the strength and type of electrical impulse.

FROM THIS ORIGINAL RECORD MANY DUPLICATES ARE MADE

From this original record a metal form is made. This form is then used to press thousands of duplicate records.

By a Process of Electroplating, a metal matrix is made. This matrix is used to press, or form, the many duplicate records.

HOW SOUND IS RELEASED

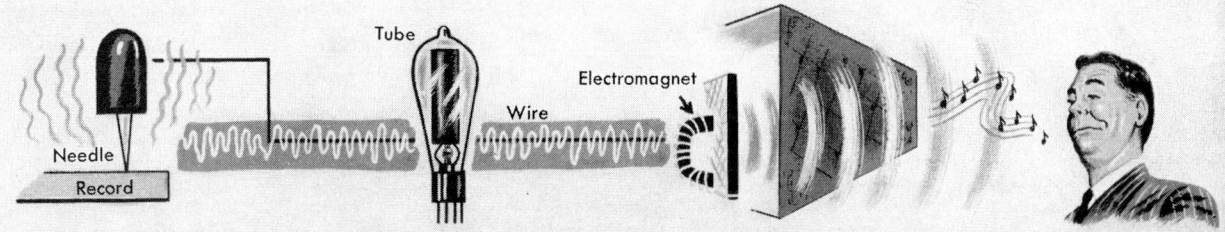

Needle — Record — Tube — Wire — Electromagnet

When the record revolves, the grooves move the needle in a series of vibrations.

Mechanical vibrations are turned into electrical impulses and amplified.

The electrical impulses vibrate the speaker diaphragm, producing sound.

Sounds produced by the phonograph diaphragm are exactly like those recorded on the original "plate."

TWO TYPES OF RECORDING GROOVES
(Greatly Magnified)

A Record is the mechanical medium of recording sound so that it may be reproduced over and over again.

LATERAL-CUT RECORD—TOP VIEW OF GROOVE
Tool moves from side to side to cut vibration impressions.

Cutting Tool, or Needle

HILL-AND-DALE RECORD—SIDE CROSS-SECTION VIEW
Tool moves up and down to cut vibration impressions.

chisel, instead of cutting sideways, cuts deeper and shallower into the phonograph record.

The disc on which the pattern is cut has a flat, wax-covered surface upon a metal base. After the pattern is cut it is electroplated, first with a thin layer of gold, which contains the pattern of the grooves, and then with chromium. This chromium is used as the master record.

The record itself is made in a large press. One arm of the press contains the chromium negative, as it is called, of one side of the record. The base of the press contains the negative of the other side. Warm shellac which contains other substances is placed between the two negatives, and they are brought together to press out the completed record. The record also contains clay, which makes it harder and less likely to be scratched by phonograph needles, and various waxes which improve the sound that is made. The clay, while it makes the record last longer, also tends to make it sound scratchy. Unbreakable records are now being made of a plastic. These records do not have the scratching effect (surface noise) produced by the clay.

Phonograph records are made to be played at various speeds. Some may make 78 revolutions, or turns, a minute. Others make 45, or as few as $33\frac{1}{3}$ turns a minute. The slower-playing ones were designed to give more music on a single record.

Phonographic Devices

Record Changing. Many phonographs have devices called *record changers* which play a series of records automatically. In most of these changers, the records are stacked over the turntable. A record-support arm drops one record at a time on the turntable.

Recordings of long selections played with record changers must be especially printed. The usual phonograph record has the first part of a selection printed on one side of the record, the second part printed on the other. In records for the ordinary automatic changer, the second part of the selection must be printed on a second record, the third part on a third record and so on. The last half of the selection will be printed in order on the backs of the records. To play the last half of the selection, the stack of records is turned over, and the records drop down on the turntable in proper order.

Other kinds of changers are able to turn each record over, playing both sides in order. Still other record-

Ewing Galloway

An Early Edison Phonograph recorded sound on a cylinder covered with a sheet of tin foil. Words spoken into the diaphragm moved a stylus that cut the soft metal. A hand crank operated the machine. Later, cylinders coated with wax were used.

changing devices have two pickups. One plays the top of the record, and the second then plays the bottom.

The crystal pickup of the phonograph weighs about two ounces. Lightness is a great advantage, for then there is less wear on the record. The pickup will reproduce sound vibrations usually in between three and ten thousand vibrations per second.

Needles. Many different kinds of needles are used. Some are permanent needles made of semiprecious jewels or alloys which permit the playing of a great number of records without changing the needle. Ordinary steel needles are often used and must be changed frequently. Cactus thorn needles do not scratch the surface of the record, but require frequent sharpening.

Home Recording Devices usually consist of a microphone, a cutting head on the phonograph, and cellulose acetate plastic records which receive the vibrations of the needle. Such records do not wear as long as the records which are made commercially.

Other Recorders which apply a different principle have been developed. These include the wire recorder and the tape recorder. On these the vibrations are preserved on wire or tape. See TAPE RECORDER.

High Fidelity and Stereophonic Phonographs

In the 1950's, manufacturers developed new and better phonographic equipment. Perhaps the most significant development was the introduction of Hi-Fi, or high fidelity sound systems. Hi-Fi uses specially constructed *components*, or parts, to reproduce sound almost exactly as it sounded originally. A Hi-Fi record player consists of a record changer, a needle cartridge, a sound amplifier, and loudspeakers. It usually has at least two speakers, one to reproduce high and the other low sounds. It sometimes uses four or five speakers. With such a complete sound system it becomes possible to regulate, and even blank out, the high or low sounds that come through the speakers.

Record manufacturers began production of stereophonic records for use on stereophonic phonographs in 1958. Stereophonic sound is a form of Hi-Fi, but it doubles most of the basic components. Stereophonic recordings make two simultaneous sound tracks with two separate microphones. One microphone stands on each side of the group that is making the recording. Stereophonic phonographs replay both sound tracks at the same time. To do this, they have two amplifiers in-

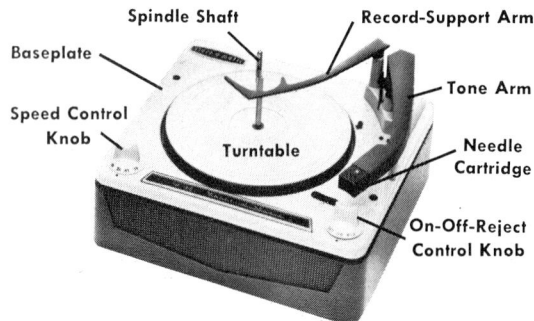

Spindle Shaft
Record-Support Arm
Baseplate
Tone Arm
Speed Control Knob
Turntable
Needle Cartridge
On-Off-Reject Control Knob

Voice of Music

A Record Changer plays records automatically. After one record plays, the support arm drops another on the turntable.

STEREOPHONIC SOUND

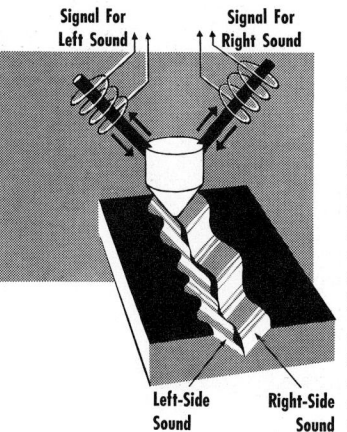

Signal For Left Sound   **Signal For Right Sound**

Left-Side Sound   **Right-Side Sound**

Stereophonic sound has greater depth and direction than ordinary sound. Music seems to come from instruments spread across the room instead of directly from a speaker. Recording stereo, *right*, requires two microphones, one on each side of the group making the recording. Each microphone picks up sound from one side of the group and records it on one side of the record groove. When a stereo record is played, *lower right*, each sound track is reproduced through a separate system of speakers and amplifiers. This produces a feeling of depth.

Stereo Record Grooves, *above*, have two sound tracks, one on each side. The needle touches both tracks. The tone arm has two generators that connect to the needle. Each generator picks up vibrations from one side of the groove.

Best Stereophonic Listening is obtained in the shaded area between the two speakers.

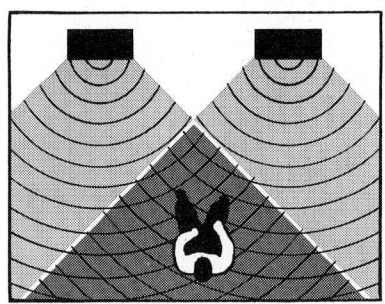

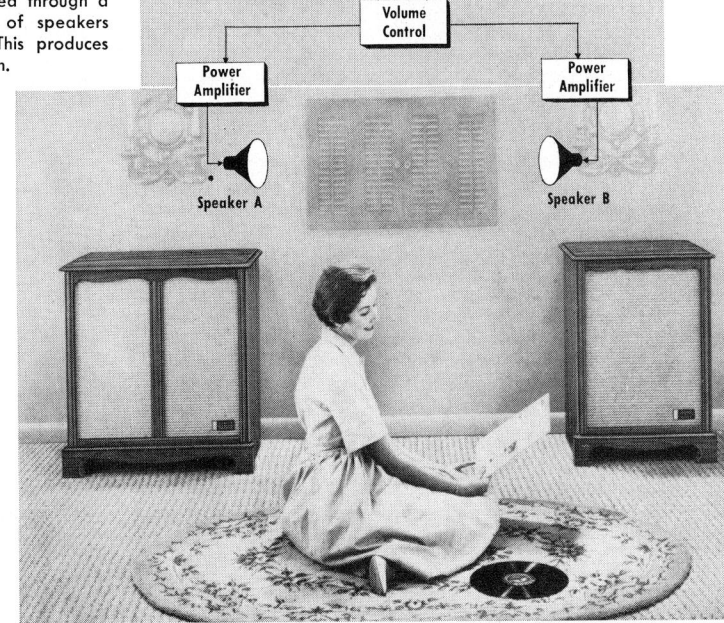

Microphone A   Microphone B

Amplifier   Amplifier

RECORDING STUDIO

YOUR HOME

Pre-Amplifier   Pre-Amplifier

Volume Control

Power Amplifier   Power Amplifier

Speaker A   Speaker B

Popular Science Monthly; Zenith Radio Corp.

stead of the one on ordinary Hi-Fi. The two loudspeakers are placed apart, and each speaker replays a separate sound track made by each microphone. As a result, the sound from the recording becomes almost identical with the sound as it was originally played. See HIGH FIDELITY.

History

The first practical phonograph was invented by Thomas A. Edison in 1877, although German experimenters had recorded sound on tin foil before this. Unlike the modern phonograph, it did not operate by the means of electricity. The record was a sheet of tin foil wrapped around a cylinder, which could be rotated. The first needle was placed in the center of a diaphragm which vibrated and traced a pattern on the foil when struck by sound waves. The first sounds ever recorded on a phonograph were the verse "Mary Had a Little Lamb." The first improvement of the phonograph was to coat the cylinder with wax, which was done in 1885 by Chichester A. Bell and Charles S. Tainter, who invented the Graphophone. In 1887 Emile Berliner developed the gramophone and the method by which the needle vibrates sideways rather than up and down. This

system came to be called the lateral-cut method.

All the early phonographs counted on the vibrations of the sound waves themselves to cut the grooves in the record. This method was not very efficient. Not all the different pitches of sound waves were transcribed. Only about three and one half octaves of notes could be reproduced. When recordings were made the musicians were compelled to huddle about a large megaphone which collected the sound. Some instruments had to be played extremely softly in order not to drown out others. In fact, most musical instruments reproduced very badly on the first records. Singers, however, fared better. Many of the early vocal recordings of such great artists are truly a monument to their memory.

In the middle 1920's an electrical method of recording was developed which is basically the one used at the present time. This was much more effective than the older method. Instruments sound almost as they do in the concert hall.   RAYMOND F. YATES

See also BERLINER, EMILE; EDISON, THOMAS A. (The Wizard of Menlo Park); HIGH FIDELITY; LIBRARY (In Recreation); TAPE RECORDER.

PHORCUS. See GORGON.

PHOSPHATES

PHOSPHATES, *FAHS fayts,* are chemical compounds that contain phosphorus and oxygen in the phosphate radical, $PO_4^{\equiv}$. There are large amounts of natural phosphates. They occur in phosphate rocks, mostly combined with the elements calcium and magnesium. They also occur in the remains of animals (bone ash) and of plants (vegetable mold). Phosphates are necessary to the growth of plants and animals, and have extensive use as fertilizers.

Beds of *guano* (bird manure) on certain islands of the Pacific have supplied great quantities of fertilizing phosphates. The principal producers of phosphate rock are the United States, Tunisia, Morocco, and Russia. The most extensive phosphate rock deposits in the United States are in North Carolina and Idaho. The largest American mines are in Florida and Tennessee. The United States produces about 21,700,000 tons a year. The United States has set aside about 2,307,000 acres of phosphate lands to conserve the supply.

When crops grow year after year on the same piece of soil, they gradually remove the natural supply of phosphates. Then the soil needs artificial fertilizers. Phosphate rock is the chief source of fertilizers containing phosphates. A soluble fertilizer known as superphosphate acts much more quickly than the pulverized rock. It is made by crushing the phosphate rock and treating it with sulfuric acid.

Calcium dihydrogen phosphate is used in phosphate baking powders. GEORGE L. BUSH

See also BAKING POWDER; FERTILIZER.

PHOSPHOR, *FAHS fur,* is a substance that absorbs certain types of energy and gives off part of that energy as visible light. The energy can be supplied by X rays, cathode rays, ultraviolet radiations, or alpha particles from radioactive substances. If luminescence stops im-

Glowing Phosphor Particles used in fluorescent light tubes absorb invisible ultraviolet rays and then radiate visible light.

Lamp Division, General Electric

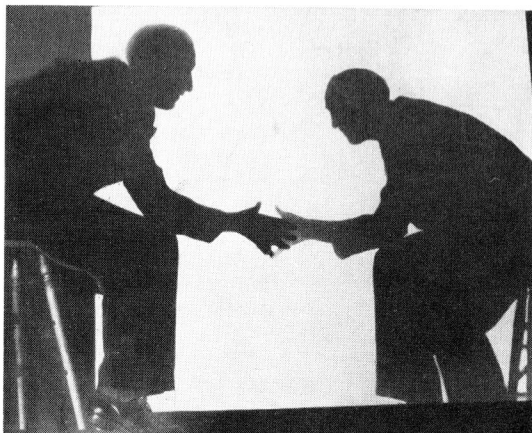

General Electric

Shaking Hands with His Own Shadow. This phosphorescent screen has absorbed light rays from the beam of a powerful spotlight which made the shadow of the seated man. The screen continues to glow with phosphorescent light, except where the man's shadow falls, after the light is turned off. This allows the man to appear to be shaking hands with his own shadow, seen at the right of the screen.

mediately after the energy supply is removed, the material is said to be *fluorescent.* If the light continues for some time, the material is *phosphorescent.* Phosphors are used in fluorescent lamps, television tubes, and other devices. See also FLUORESCENT LAMP; PHOSPHORESCENCE. JAMES S. FRITZ

PHOSPHORESCENCE, *FAHS foh RES uns,* is the giving off of light by a substance that has been exposed to certain forms of radiant energy, such as light or X rays. The light that is given off is called *phosphorescent light.* A phosphorescent substance may continue to glow for a long time after it has been exposed to radiation.

The phosphorescent light may be of any color. It may be green, yellow, blue, orange, red, or a mixture of these colors. The color depends upon the substance that has been exposed, and upon the radiation that has been acting on the substance.

Phosphorescent Materials. A substance that has the power to give off a phosphorescent light is said to be *phosphorescent.* Some common phosphorescent substances are gelatin, celluloid, ivory, paraffin, glue, and egg shells. Many minerals are phosphorescent. A group of minerals called *sulfides* are common examples. They include barium sulfide, calcium sulfide, and strontium sulfide. Other minerals called *calcites* are also phosphorescent.

Phosphorescent Light may last for a few days or for only a fraction of a second. Phosphorescence that lasts a very short time is known as *fluorescence.* The length of time the light will last depends upon the kind of substance that is used and on the temperature of the substance. For example, a phosphorescent substance which contains manganese or copper will give off a long-lasting bright light. The temperature of this substance must remain the same as the temperature of the room if the light is to last. If the temperature of the substance is raised, the light will become brighter, but it will not last as long.

Phosphorescence can also be found in the animal world, especially among the lower forms of animals.

Such animals as the firefly, glowworm, and jellyfish have the property of phosphorescence. The sea is filled with many tiny animals that glow in the dark. Phosphorescence in animal and plant substances is called *bioluminescence*.

Phosphorescence was first noticed in barium sulfate in about 1600. Credit for this discovery is usually given to a shoemaker in Bologna, Italy. He found that if barium sulfate was exposed to light it would give off a light of its own. Long before this time, ancient peoples noticed that diamonds and other gems would give off light in the darkness after they were exposed to light. Today, phosphorescence is used in such industries as radio, radar, and television.   E. A. Fessenden

See also Bioluminescence; Fluorescence.

PHOSPHORIC ACID, *fahs FOHR ik,* is the most common acid of phosphorus. Industry uses it to make inorganic phosphate compounds. It is also used in fertilizers, soft drinks, and flavoring syrups. Its normal sodium salt, Na_3PO_4, is an excellent water softener.

Most phosphoric acid is made by burning pure phosphorus to form phosphorus pentoxide, which is reacted with water. An older method, treating phosphate rock with sulfuric acid, produced an impure acid. Pure phosphoric acid forms colorless crystals that melt at about 41.5° C. It is very soluble in water. Technically, phosphoric acid is called *orthophosphoric acid.* Its chemical formula is H_3PO_4.   S. Young Tyree, Jr.

PHOSPHORUS (in astronomy). See Evening Star.

PHOSPHORUS, *FAHS foh rus,* is a chemical element that man, animals, and plants need for normal growth. Phosphorus is also used in the manufacture of many industrial products, such as plant fertilizers. Plants absorb phosphorus compounds from the soil, and human beings and animals eat the plants and other foods containing phosphorus. Foods that are rich in phosphorus include egg yolks, milk, fish, and peas. In the human body, phosphorus compounds are found chiefly in the bones, brain, and nerves. Phosphorus is an important part of *adenosine triphosphate*, a compound which supplies organisms with energy.

Phosphorus is found in minerals. Small amounts are also found in nerves, muscles, and other animal tissue. It is commercially produced in several solid forms.

One of the most important sources of phosphorus is *phosphate rock (phosphorite).* Phosphate rock consists of the mineral *apatite,* an impure tricalcium phosphate, mixed with clay and other elements. Large deposits are found in Russia, Morocco, and Florida. Phosphorus is also present in the mineral *hydroxyapatite.*

Phosphorus is made commercially in several different forms called *allotropes.* The white form is a soft, waxy solid that is made from one of the phosphorus minerals by various methods. White phosphorus combines readily with other elements, and ignites in air at about room temperature. For this reason, it is usually stored and shipped under water. Phosphorus is unsafe to handle out of water. White phosphorus is poisonous, and can cause serious burns. The white form is *phosphorescent.* That is, it glows in the dark when it is exposed to air. The name *phosphorus* comes from a Greek word meaning *light bearer.*

Red phosphorus is a brownish-red powder prepared by heating white phosphorus to a high temperature (250° C.) or by exposing it to sunlight. Red phosphorus

does not burn as readily as the white form, and is neither poisonous nor phosphorescent. But it should be handled carefully at certain temperatures because it can change to white phosphorus. Black (violet) phosphorus resembles the mineral graphite. It is prepared by heating white phosphorus under high pressure.

The red form of phosphorus is used in the manufacture of safety matches, pesticides, and smoke bombs. Phosphoric acid is a basic chemical used in drugs, animal feed, and fertilizers. Other phosphorus compounds are used by industry in the production of steel, china, and baking powder.

Phosphorus was discovered in 1669 by the German alchemist Hennig Brand. The chemical symbol for phosphorus is P. It has the atomic number 15 and atomic weight 30.9738. White phosphorus melts at 44.1° C. and boils at 280° C.   Frank C. Andrews

See also Allotropy; Phosphates; Phosphorescence; Phosphoric Acid.

PHOT. See Foot-Candle.

PHOTIUS, *FOE shih us* (A.D. 820?-892?), a noted Byzantine scholar and prelate, became patriarch of Constantinople (now Istanbul) in 858. He succeeded Patriarch Ignatius, who resigned because of disagreements in the church. Photius also became known for his digest of the writings of classic Greek authors. Photius had never been a clergyman, and his appointment was disputed. Pope Nicholas I denounced him. Under the leadership of Photius, a Council of Constantinople challenged the pope's right to rule in the East, and in 867 the council denounced the pope. This dispute began the great argument between the Greek and Roman Catholic churches that later ended in their separation. Although Photius was deposed in 867, he became patriarch again in 877. But in 886 he was once more deposed. Photius' chief literary works include the *Myriobiblion* and the *Amphilochia.* The first of these is a collection of extracts from, and abridgments of, 280 volumes by classical authors. Many of the originals of these works are now lost. The *Amphilochia* is a collection of questions and answers on difficult points in the Bible.

Photius, who was born in Constantinople, died in exile in a monastery in Armenia.   Franklin D. Scott

See also Eastern Orthodox Churches; Patriarch.

PHOTOCHEMISTRY deals with the chemical changes produced in substances by light. Only absorbed light can cause these changes; reflected or transmitted light cannot. The light may be infrared or ultraviolet, as well as from the visible rays of the spectrum. Important chemical reactions that result from light absorption are photosynthesis in plants and the production of an image on a photographic plate. The process of vision depends on photochemical change.   Walter J. Moore

See also Photography (Developing Film); Photosynthesis.

PHOTOCOMPOSITION. See Type (How Type Is Set).

PHOTOELECTRIC CELL. See Electric Eye; Electronics (Photoelectric Cells).

PHOTOELECTRIC EFFECT. See Light (Effects).

PHOTOELECTRIC LIGHT METER. See Light Meter.

PHOTOELECTRIC PHOTOMETER. See Astronomy (Optical Recording Equipment).

PHOTOENGRAVING

PHOTOENGRAVING AND PHOTOLITHOGRAPHY
are processes used to make printing plates or cylinders for the three major methods of printing. These methods are (1) letterpress, (2) offset lithography, and (3) gravure. On letterpress printing plates, the parts that print are above the nonprinting parts. On offset lithographic plates, the printing parts and the nonprinting parts are on the same level. On gravure cylinders and plates, the printing parts are below the nonprinting parts. For a discussion of the three printing methods, see PRINTING.

Photoengraving is used to make letterpress printing plates. Photolithography is used to make offset lithographic plates. Gravure cylinders and plates are made by a process similar to photoengraving. Many authorities call this process *gravure photoengraving*.

E. J. Triebe, the critical reviewer of this article, is President of Kingsport Press, Incorporated.

Letterpress Photoengraving

Letterpress photoengraving produces printing plates by means of photography and *etching* (engraving with acid). The process is used mostly to reproduce illustrations. It also can be used to create *relief* (raised) letters for printing words, but type is usually used. There are two chief kinds of photoengraved plates: (1) line engravings and (2) halftone engravings.

Line Engravings are made from *copy* (the original material to be reproduced) that consists only of solid lines or solid areas. Such copy includes diagrams and charts, pen-and-ink drawings, and proofs of type.

Making the Negative. The first step in making a line engraving is to photograph the copy to get a negative. A photoengraver places the copy before a large camera. He then floods the copy with intense white light from arc or fluorescent lamps. He adjusts the camera to get a negative the exact size needed for the printed reproduction. After the copy has been photographed, the

PHOTOGRAPHING THE ORIGINAL COPY

The first step in photoengraving and photolithography is to photograph the original copy to get a negative of it. The photographic work is similar in both processes.

A Process Camera is used to produce a negative of the exact size needed for the reproduction.

Original Line Drawing   Camera   Line Negative

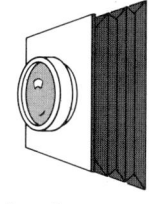 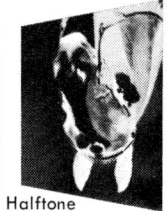

Original Photograph   Camera   Halftone Screen   Halftone Negative

WORLD BOOK photo

Line and Continuous Tone Copy are photographed separately. Tone copy is shot through a screen, which breaks up the image into tiny dots.

Halftone Screen Size depends on the paper used in printing. A coarse screen is best for rough paper, and a fine screen is best for smooth paper. The screen sizes, *below*, are 65, 120, and 150 lines, respectively. The enlargement, *right*, shows the halftone dot pattern.

South Carolina State Development Board

  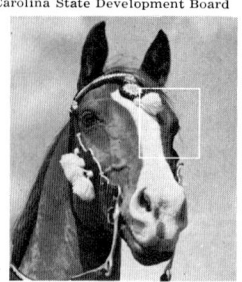 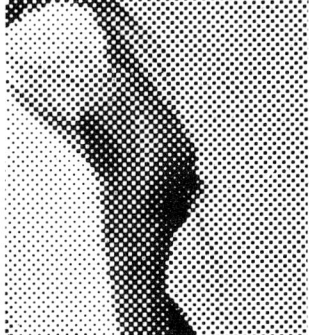

366

negative is developed. It is a reversal of the original copy. The solid lines and areas on the copy are transparent on the negative. The white background areas on the copy are opaque on the negative.

The photoengraver then prepares a *flat*. He fastens the negative, along with any other negatives he has made, to a sheet of glass or plastic. He places the flat—negative side down—on a metal plate that has been coated with a substance sensitive to light. Usually zinc, copper, or magnesium plates are used. The flat and plate are put in a *vacuum printing frame*. The vacuum creates airtight contact between the plate and flat. The negative now serves as a stencil. Light rays from powerful lamps pass through the transparent (image) parts of the negative. The rays harden the light-sensitive coating on the plate under these parts and make it insoluble. The opaque parts of the negative block the light, and the coating under them stays soft and soluble. The plate is then soaked in water to wash away the soft, unexposed parts of the coating. Only the hard image, which is acid resistant, remains on the developed plate.

Etching the Plate. The photoengraver next gives the plate several acid baths. Each dip into the acid is called a *bite*. With each bite, the acid etches away a little more of the background of the plate. After the first bite, and before each succeeding bite, the photoengraver brushes the sides of the image with an acid-resistant powder called *dragon's blood*. This powder protects the image from being undercut by the acid. The photoengraver gives the plate as many powderings and bites as are needed to make the image stand in sharp relief.

Many photoengravers use a process called *powderless etching*. It requires only one bite, eliminating the repeated powderings. The developed plate is placed face down in a machine that throws acid against the plate. The sides of the image are not undercut because the acid does not hit them directly. In addition, the acid contains special chemicals that form a protective film on the sides of the image during etching.

After the plate has been etched, the photoengraver mounts it on a wood, metal, or plastic block so that it is the same height as type (0.918 inch). The plate is then ready to be printed with the type.

Halftone Engravings are made from *continuous tone* copy. Such copy has a range of tones, and includes oil paintings, water colors, and black-and-white and color photographs. To reproduce the tones, the photoengraver creates an optical illusion on the printed page. If you were to look through a magnifying glass at a black-and-white photograph in a book, newspaper, or magazine, you would see that it is made up of many tiny dots. The areas with large dots close together are seen as dark gray or black shadows. The areas with small, widely spaced dots appear as highlights of light gray or white. The photoengraver creates the dots by photographing the copy through a halftone screen.

The Halftone Screen consists of two sheets of glass. Each sheet is ruled with parallel opaque lines. The sheets are cemented together so that the lines cross at right angles, forming squares. The number of lines to the inch determines the coarseness or fineness of the screen, which, in turn, determines the density of the dots. The lines may range from about 45 to 400 per

inch, but 60- to 150-line screens are the most common. The screen size is determined chiefly by the paper on which the illustration will be printed. If rough paper is to be used, a coarse screen does a better job of reproducing the illustration. For smooth paper, a fine screen is better. Most newspapers are printed on rough paper, and use a screen of about 65 lines. Most magazines are printed on smooth paper, and use a screen of about 120 lines.

Making the Negative. The photoengraver places the copy before the camera, illuminates the copy, and adjusts the camera for the size negative he wants. He then inserts a halftone screen between the film and the camera lens. The screen permits light reflected from the copy to pass through only the spaces between the lines onto the film. Thus, the screen breaks the light into tiny dots. The lightest areas in the copy reflect the most light and cast the biggest, most closely spaced dots on the

WORLD BOOK photo

Vacuum Printing Frame holds the negatives and metal plate in airtight contact. Light passes through the transparent (image) areas of the negatives, hardening the plate's acid-resistant coating under these areas. After development, the plate is etched.

Powderless Etching of the developed plate creates the relief image with one acid bite. In an etching machine, acid splashes directly against the face of the plate, and eats away the nonimage background. The sides of the image are not undercut because the acid strikes them indirectly. In addition, chemicals added to the acid build up a protective film along the sides.

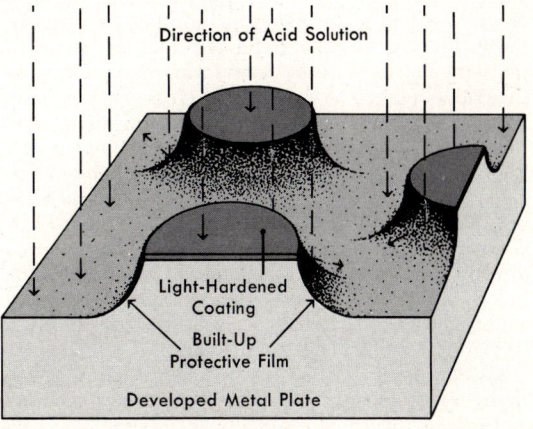

Direction of Acid Solution

Light-Hardened Coating

Built-Up Protective Film

Developed Metal Plate

366a

PHOTOENGRAVING

negative. The darkest areas reflect the least light and produce the smallest, most widely spaced dots. These sizes are reversed when the images are transferred from the negative to the metal plate. For example, the areas with the largest black dots on the negative block the most light and create the smallest, most widely spaced dots on the plate.

Etching the Plate. The halftone negative is handled in much the same way as the line negative. It is fastened to a flat and printed on a metal plate. The plate is developed, and the unexposed parts of the coating are washed away. Halftone etching also resembles line etching, but it is more delicate. The tones of the original copy must be reproduced, the spaces between the tiny dots must be etched to the right depth, and the sides of the dots must not be undercut.

Color Engravings. To reproduce full-color copy, such as paintings and color photographs, the photoengraver photographs the copy four times to get a separate negative of the red, yellow, blue, and black in the copy. Plates are made from the negatives. Each plate prints yellow, blue, red, or black ink. To learn more about color engravings, see PRINTING (Printing in Color).

Other Methods for making letterpress engravings include the use of electronic engraving machines and photopolymer plastic plates.

Electronic Engraving Machines use a tiny beam of light that scans the original copy. Light reflected from the copy creates impulses that activate a V-shaped tool called a *stylus.* The stylus cuts or burns lines or dots into a metal or plastic plate according to the strength of the impulses. Where the copy is whitest, the impulses are strongest and the stylus cuts deepest. In shadow areas, the stylus makes a shallow cut.

Photopolymer Plastic Plates have a layer of light-sensitive plastic on a metal base. To make a line or halftone engraving, the plastic is simply exposed to a negative under intense light. The plastic hardens according to how much light passes through the negative. The areas that receive the most light (the image areas) are the hardest. The plate is sprayed with a caustic soda solution, which washes away the soft, unhardened plastic. The hard image stands in sharp relief.

Photolithography

Photolithography is a photographic and chemical process used to make plates for printing by offset lithography. On these plates, the printing images are on the same flat level as the nonprinting parts. Offset lithography is based on the fact that grease and water do not mix. The flat printing images are chemically treated so that when the plate is on the press, they repel water from water rollers and accept greasy ink from ink rollers. The nonprinting parts, in turn, accept water and repel ink.

On the press, the inked images are not transferred directly from the plate to the paper to be printed. The images are first *offset* (transferred) to a rubber-covered cylinder, which then offsets them to the paper. Offset lithography is often called simply *offset.*

Making the Negative. The first step in photolithography is to photograph all the copy, including proofs of metal type. The photographic work is similar to that

used in photoengraving. The line copy, which includes type proofs, and the continuous tone copy are photographed separately. The continuous tone copy is shot through a halftone screen to get the dot pattern. After the negatives have been made, they are *stripped* (pieced) together on a flat exactly as the type and illustrations are to appear in print. After the flat has been prepared, the images on it are transferred to the offset plate.

Making the Plate. Many kinds of offset plates are used, but they fall into three main groups: (1) surface plates, (2) deep etch plates, and (3) bimetal plates.

Surface Plates are usually made of a thin sheet of aluminum covered with a light-sensitive coating. The platemaker can apply the coating himself, or he can use *presensitized plates.* Presensitized plates are coated when purchased, and can be stored in the dark and used when desired. If the printer coats the plates, they must be used shortly thereafter, because the coating hardens quickly. A hard coating will not take an image.

The negative flat is placed on the plate, and both are put in a vacuum printing frame. Light from high-intensity lamps shines through the negatives, hardening the coating under the transparent parts. The opaque parts of the negatives block the light, leaving the coating under them soft. *Developing ink* is spread over the exposed plate. The plate is rinsed with water, and the soft, nonprinting parts are washed away. Only the hard, ink-receptive, water-repellent images remain.

Deep Etch Plates are made in much the same way as surface plates. But a positive flat is used instead of a negative flat. Positives can be made by rephotographing

MAKING A DEEP ETCH OFFSET PLATE

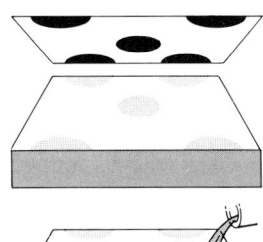

Exposure. The metal plate and film positives are exposed under bright light. The light hardens the coating on the plate under the transparent (nonprinting) parts of the positives.

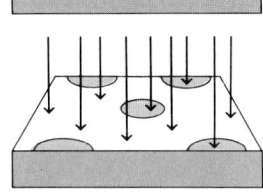

Development. The plate is washed to remove the soft parts of the coating, which are the image areas. The hard coating remains on the nonimage areas.

Etching. Acid bites slightly into the exposed metal that forms the image areas. The hard coating protects the nonimage areas from the bite of the acid.

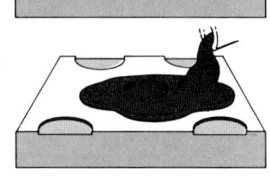

Lacquering. The etched plate is treated with lacquer to make the images attract greasy ink. The coating on the nonprinting parts is scrubbed off.

Finished Plate has slightly sunken images. On the press, they will repel water and accept ink. The nonprinting parts will accept water and repel ink.

the negatives or by printing them on film. By using a positive flat, the light-hardened areas become the non-printing areas. The image areas have the soft coating. The plates are washed after exposure, and the soft coating in the image areas is dissolved. Next, acid is applied to eat away a little of the exposed metal in the image areas. The slightly sunken images are then lacquered to make them attract ink. The coating on the nonprinting parts is scrubbed off.

Bimetal Plates are made of two metals, one on top of the other. One metal is copper, which has a natural attraction for ink. The second metal can be chromium, aluminum, or some other metal that has an attraction for water. Copper can be the top or bottom metal. Bimetal plates can use negative or positive flats. One type of widely used plate has chromium over copper. The chromium is exposed to a positive flat. After the plate has been washed, the chromium is exposed in the image areas. The images are then etched through the chromium to the ink-receptive copper. The coating is scrubbed off the nonimage areas, exposing the water-receptive chromium.

Gravure Photoengraving

Gravure photoengraving produces printing images that are below the nonprinting areas. Gravure printing is done from heavy engraved copper-plated cylinders that are placed on the press, or from thin engraved copper plates that are clamped around a cylinder on the press. In printing, the sunken images are filled with ink as the rotating cylinder dips into a trough of ink. A thin

MAKING A GRAVURE PLATE OR CYLINDER

Exposure. The screened carbon tissue is exposed to positives. The little squares of gelatin harden according to how much light passes through the light and dark areas of the film.

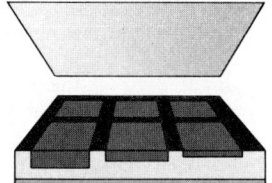

Transfer. The tissue is dampened, and then transferred gelatin side down to the plate or cylinder on which the printing images are to be etched.

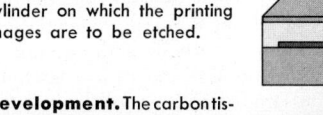

Development. The carbon tissue is developed in water, and the paper backing is stripped away. Squares of varying thickness are left on the metal.

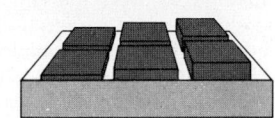

Etching. Acid quickly penetrates the thin squares and bites deep cells in the copper. It eats through the thick squares slowly and bites shallow cells.

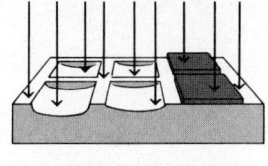

Finished Plate has thousands of cells. The deepest will hold the most ink and print the darkest tones. The shallowest will print the lightest tones.

blade wipes off the excess ink from the nonprinting surface. Paper is then pressed into the sunken images, and the ink is transferred to it.

Making the Negative. All copy to be reproduced by gravure printing must be photographed. The photographic work is much the same as for letterpress and offset, except that continuous tone copy is not photographed through a halftone screen. After the negatives have been made, film positives are made from them.

The positives are assembled exactly as the type and illustrations are to appear in print. But then, instead of exposing the positives directly onto a light-sensitive plate, they are exposed onto a sheet of *carbon tissue*. This is a sheet of paper covered with light-sensitive gelatin that has already been exposed to a *gravure screen*. The gravure screen is the opposite of the halftone screen. Instead of black lines crossing to form transparent squares, transparent lines cross to form opaque squares. After the carbon tissue has been exposed to the screen, the tissue has a *latent* (hidden) image on it of light-hardened crosslines.

The positives are then printed on the screened carbon tissue. Light passes through the positives, hardening the little squares of soft gelatin to varying degrees. The darkest parts of the positives allow the least light to pass through. The gelatin squares remain softest under these parts. The lightest parts of the positives allow the most light to strike the gelatin. The squares become hardest under these parts.

Etching the Plate or Cylinder. The carbon tissue is placed gelatin side down on the copper plate or cylinder, and developed in water. The water soaks through the paper backing and dissolves the soft gelatin next to the paper. The paper is removed. The tissue is further treated with water until all the soluble gelatin has been washed away. Thousands of little gelatin squares of varying thickness remain on the metal. The thickest squares were the whitest areas on the positives. The thinnest squares were the shadow areas.

The copper is now etched. The acid bites tiny *cells* (pits) into the metal according to the thickness of the gelatin. It quickly penetrates the thin gelatin squares and bites deeply into the copper. It penetrates the thick squares slowly and bites shallow cells. On the press, the deepest cells hold the most ink and print the darkest tones. The shallowest cells hold the least ink and print the lightest tones.

Several other processes are also used to make gravure engravings. The *News-Dultgen* process prints a continuous tone positive and a halftone positive made from the same negative on the carbon tissue. This creates cells that vary in size as well as in depth. Instead of carbon tissue, some processes use a light-sensitive coating applied directly to the metal. Electronic engravers are also used to cut intaglio images. These machines are similar to those used in making relief engravings for letterpress printing. Critically reviewed by E. J. TRIEBE

Related Articles in WORLD BOOK include:

Engraving	Offset
Etching	Photography
Intaglio	Printing
Lithography	Rotogravure

PHOTOGELATIN. See PRINTING (Collotype).

PHOTOGRAMMETRY

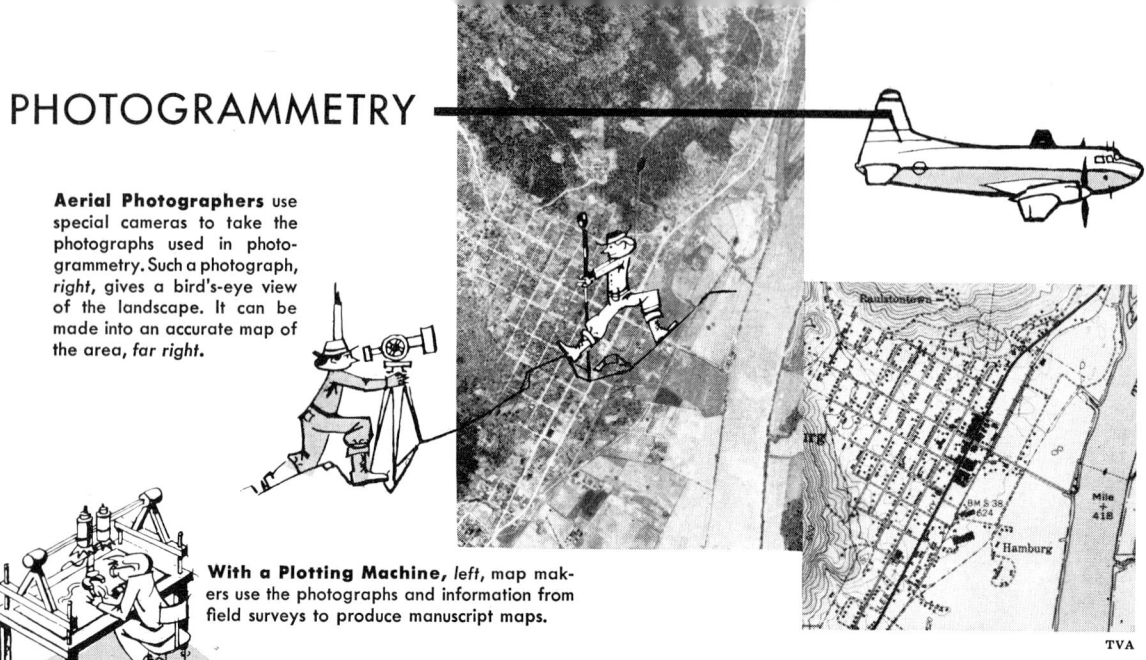

Aerial Photographers use special cameras to take the photographs used in photogrammetry. Such a photograph, *right*, gives a bird's-eye view of the landscape. It can be made into an accurate map of the area, *far right*.

TVA

With a Plotting Machine, *left*, map makers use the photographs and information from field surveys to produce manuscript maps.

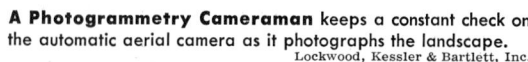

A Field Survey must then be made, *right*, to classify buildings, identify roads, and check the accuracy of the map.

A Photogrammetry Cameraman keeps a constant check on the automatic aerial camera as it photographs the landscape.
Lockwood, Kessler & Bartlett, Inc.

PHOTOGRAMMETRY, *FOH toh GRAM uh tree*, is the science of making maps by means of photography. The photographs used may be taken from the ground or from an airplane. When taken from the ground, the photographs are made with the camera in a horizontal position. Sometimes, when the photographs are taken from a high point looking down on an area, the camera is placed at an angle. Ground photogrammetry is used to show abrupt changes in contour, such as cliffs. It is also used when photographing from the air is difficult.

Aerial photographs taken from an airplane are most commonly used for map making, although they may also be used for aerial surveying. Successive photographs of small parts of the earth's surface are taken with special cameras that point straight down. Each photograph overlaps the next one. The series taken during the plane's flight is called a *strip*. Thus a given area can be covered with a series of strips that also overlap, giving a bird's-eye view of the landscape.

Groups of photographs can be matched together to make an *air mosaic* map. However, the pictures are distorted because of the tilt of the plane or variations in its altitude. Distortion also results if the ground is rugged. For example, mountains and valleys, because they do not have the same elevation, will look out of position and proportion on the aerial photographs. But accurate maps can be made if the position and altitude of a series of points that have been fixed by ground survey can be identified on the aerial photograph.

The actual details of the photograph are transferred to a map by a draftsman or with the use of automatic plotting machines. Pairs of photographs that overlap an area give a three-dimensional view that can be seen with a stereoscope.   E. B. ESPENSHADE, JR.

See also MAP; SURVEYING.

PHOTOGRAPHIC COPYING uses light-sensitive materials to make copies of typewritten, drawn, printed, or hand written documents. The documents themselves may even be photographed or duplicated copies. There are three main types of photographic copying: contact copying, projection copying, and electrostatic copying.

Contact Copying. The *photocopier* is a commonly used contact copying device. In it, the original is placed in contact with a piece of light-sensitive negative paper and exposed to light. After exposure, the negative paper is put in contact with a piece of positive paper. The two papers are then passed through a liquid photographic developer in the machine. The liquid develops the image on the negative paper and transfers it to the positive paper. The positive paper is then a copy of the original. A photocopier has no lens, so it cannot reduce or enlarge an original. Other contact copying machines use ammonia vapor, alkali solutions, heat, or water in place of a photographic developer (see BLUEPRINT).

Projection Copying machines use a lens and can make copies that are larger or smaller than the originals. In the *copy camera*, light reflected from the original is projected on light-sensitive film through the lens. The developed film produces a negative of the original in the form of a white-on-black image. To get a positive copy, the negative is *printed* (projected) on a piece of positive paper. One negative can be used to make any number of copies.

The *photostat* is another photographic copying machine which uses projection. It copies directly on photographic paper without first making a negative. Microfilm copies are made by projection copying (see MICROFILM).

Electrostatic Copying uses light from the original to produce an electric image on materials made light-sensitive by an electric charge. The *direct electrostatic process* forms the electric image, either by contact or projection, directly on zinc-oxide coated paper. Positively charged *toner* (ink) particles are attracted to, and stick to, the negatively charged image to make a permanent copy. The *electrostatic transfer method*, called *xerography*, uses a lens to form a positively charged image on a rotating selenium drum. Negatively charged toner powder is poured over the drum, and sticks to the electric image. The toner image is then transferred to positively charged paper and melted to its surface, making a permanent copy.   C. M. DICK, JR.

See also PRINTING (Electrostatic Printing).

PHOTOGRAPHIC SOCIETY OF AMERICA is an organization that promotes photography as an art and a science. Its seven divisions are concerned with color photography, black and white photography, motion pictures, nature photography, photo-journalism, stereo photography, and photographic techniques. It has about 10,000 members and 1,000 affiliated clubs in the United States and 65 other countries. The society was organized in 1934. Its headquarters are at 2005 Walnut Street, Philadelphia, Pa.

Critically reviewed by PHOTOGRAPHIC SOCIETY OF AMERICA

A Photostat Machine, *left,* copies documents directly on photographic paper. This process makes the writing on white paper appear on the copy as white writing on a black background.

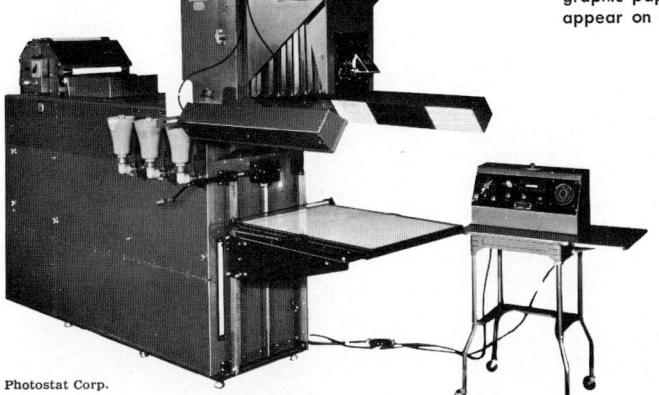

Photostat Corp.

The Photographic Copying Machine, *below left,* copies documents by first making a white-on-black image, called a *negative,* on photographic film. The negative is then used to make black-on-white prints which are the actual copies. The machine automatically develops and dries the prints.

Electrostatic Copying Machines work by making ink stick to an electric image of a document. Some machines form the image directly on specially coated paper. Others form the image on a drum that transfers the copy to ordinary paper. The machine, *below,* makes enlarged drawings from microfilm held in a punched card. Other electrostatic machines copy from full-size documents.

Xerox Corp.

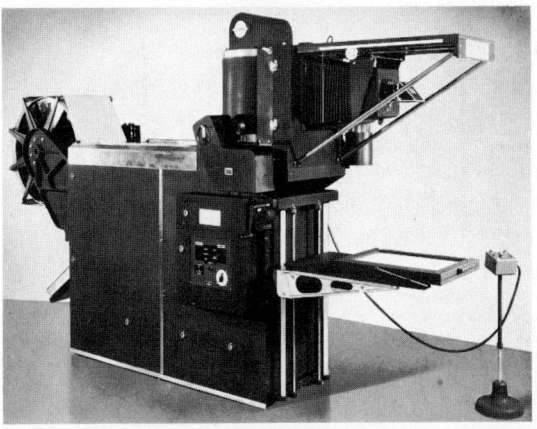

Xerox Corp.

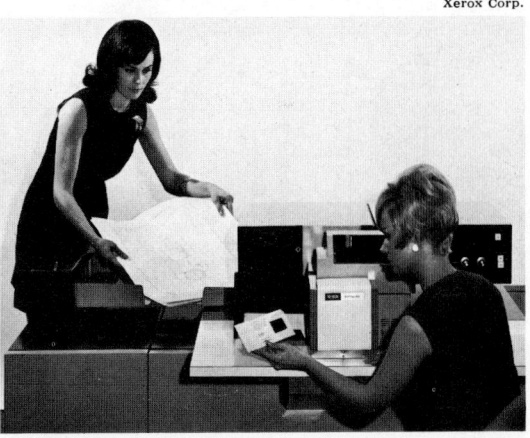

WORLD BOOK photo

PHOTOGRAPHY

PHOTOGRAPHY. A photograph is a picture made with a camera. The word *photography* means *writing* or *drawing with light*. A camera picture is a picture drawn with rays of light.

Photography enriches our lives in many ways. Most illustrations in newspapers, magazines, and books are photographs. Photography is important in advertising, business, industry, and science. Photography also helps man explore the earth, the oceans, and outer space.

Some photographs, like some paintings, have lasting value as great works of art. We admire such pictures because they are beautiful, or because they express ideas that we find worth-while.

Photography is one of the most popular hobbies in the world. Almost half the families in the United States own cameras. Amateur photographers take pictures that will remind them of their families and friends, their travels, and important events. Many persons become so interested in photography that they join camera clubs and meet with other enthusiasts. They sometimes enter their pictures in contests or display them at exhibits and in photographic galleries.

Motion pictures make up a special field of photography. This field includes hundreds of professional motion-picture photographers and thousands of amateurs. Most of the principles used in *still* photography are also used in making motion pictures. See MOTION PICTURE.

Clifton C. Edom, the contributor of this article, is Director of Photojournalism at the University of Missouri School of Journalism. WORLD BOOK photos by Don Stebbing.

Mathew Brady, Library of Congress

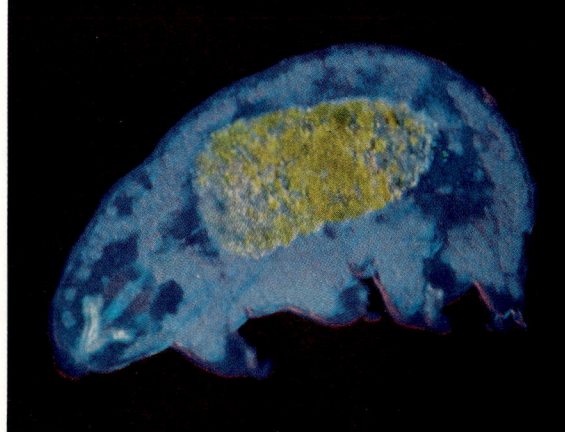

Roman Vishniac, Publix

Art Kane

PHOTOGRAPHY ✺ TAKING GOOD SNAPSHOTS

Flash Reflector

Flashbulb

Viewfinder

Shutter Release Button

Aperture

Lens

Camera Lock

Film Advancer

The Parts of a Camera. A camera, in the simplest terms, is a box with an *aperture* (small opening) at one end. It is like a room with a Venetian blind over the window. The aperture lets light into the camera just as a window lets light into a room. The inside of a camera must be dark so that light cannot reach the light-sensitive film until you take a picture. A *shutter* over the opening works like a Venetian blind. The shutter opens to let light enter the camera, and closes to keep light out. When you take a picture, you press the *shutter release button*. The shutter opens, lets light into the camera, and quickly closes.

Light passes through a glass *lens* when it enters the camera. The lens bends the light rays so that they form a sharp *image* (picture) on a piece of film. This image is the picture you photographed. The image appears on the film only after the film has gone through a complicated chemical process called *developing*.

Before taking a picture, you look through the *viewfinder* of the camera to make sure that all of your subject will appear in the picture. After taking a picture, you turn the *film advancer* to move the film forward through the camera and get the film set for the next picture. Most cameras are equipped with a holder for flashbulbs. The use of flashbulbs adds extra light to a scene, especially indoors.

Most cameras, regardless of their size, shape, or cost, have these basic parts. Cameras differ in the way that the parts can be controlled. The simplest cameras have *fixed controls*. The parts always work in the same way. More advanced cameras have *adjustable controls* which the photographer must set before taking a picture. This article explains how to use simple box cameras and ad-

COMMON MISTAKES AND HOW TO AVOID THEM

Poor Background. Check the viewfinder to see that trees or other objects do not "grow" from the subject's head, *right*.

Chopped-Off Head. Make sure all of the subject appears in the viewfinder at the exact moment that you snap the picture.

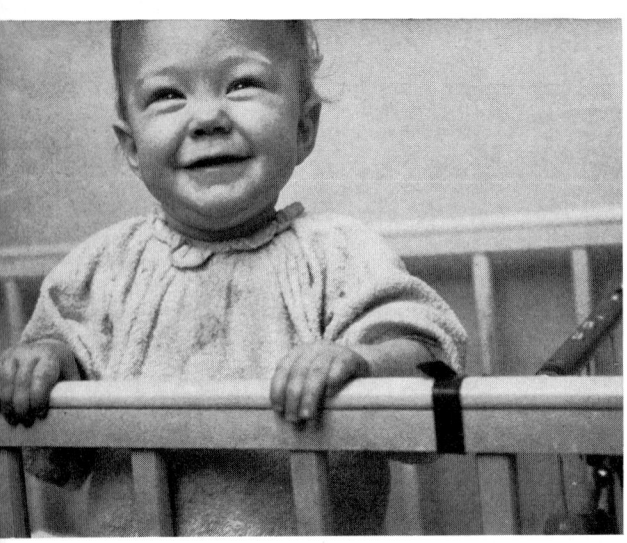

justable cameras. For a discussion of specific types of cameras, such as press cameras or reflex cameras, see CAMERA (Types of Cameras).

Using Box Cameras is easy because they are the simplest cameras. Many persons use them to learn how to take pictures. Some box cameras have fixed controls. Others have a few controls that must be set.

Before you use a box camera, study the instruction booklet that came with it. This booklet shows where the film advancer, viewfinder, and other parts of the camera are located. Do not put film in the camera until you have practiced how you will take a picture. Choose a subject and frame it in your viewfinder. Only what you see in the viewfinder will appear in the final picture. Practice loading and unloading your camera with an old roll of film. After you know how your camera works, you are ready to take pictures.

Whenever you load the camera with film, protect the film from strong light. If you are outdoors, load the camera in the shade of a tree or in the shadow of your body. This protection will prevent light streaks and glare spots from ruining the pictures.

Most box cameras will make a good picture of any subject that is about 6 feet or more away from the camera. If you stand closer, your subject will be out-of-focus and blurred in the picture.

The shutter of most box cameras opens and closes in about 1/50 of a second. Any movement of either the camera or the subject during that time will cause a blurred picture. Make sure that nothing is moving in the scene you photograph. Hold the camera steady, and press the shutter release button gently.

Many box cameras have two settings to control the shutter speed. These settings are marked *I* (for instantaneous) and *B* (for brief or bulb). The *I* setting makes the shutter work at its normal speed. Use this setting whenever you have enough light to take a picture. The *B* setting keeps the shutter open for as long as you press down the shutter release button. Use this setting at night when the light is dim. Because of the poor light, the shutter may have to stay open for several seconds so that enough light will reach the film. Put the camera on a *tripod* (three-legged stand) or some other sturdy support to keep it from moving while the shutter is open.

PHOTOGRAPHY TERMS

Cable Release is a cord that releases the shutter. It helps prevent camera movement because the photographer does not touch the camera.

Changing Bag is a lightproof bag made of dark cloth that serves as a darkroom. The photographer puts his hands into the bag to load film into a camera or a developing tank.

Fog is a dark, hazy covering over film or printing paper. Fog is caused by light that accidentally reaches the film or by development at temperatures that are too warm.

Latitude, in exposure, means the amount by which film can be overexposed or underexposed without losing too much quality in the image.

Lens Shade, or *lens hood*, is an attachment that keeps light from striking the lens directly and making glare spots appear in the picture.

Parallax is the difference between what the viewfinder shows and what the lens records on the film.

T (time) is a shutter setting used for long exposures. The shutter release button must be pressed twice—once to open the shutter, and again to close it.

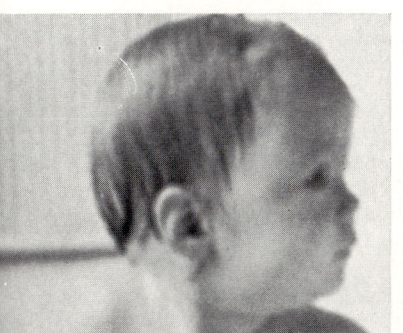

Out-Of-Focus. Stand at least six feet away from the subject.

Tilted Camera. Keep the camera level when you snap the picture.

Camera Movement. Hold the camera steady and press the shutter release button gently.

Obstructed Lens. Make sure that the camera strap or your finger does not cover part of the lens.

WORLD BOOK photos

373

Front Lighting is seldom useful for portraits. The sun shines directly into the subject's face, causing him to squint. The sun also casts harsh shadows under his eyebrows, nose, chin, and cheekbones.

Side Lighting produces dark shadows on one side of a person's face. Fill in the shadows by using a flashbulb. Or take the picture near an object that reflects light, such as a light-colored building.

Back Lighting forms bright highlights on the subject's hair and shoulders. But a dark shadow may cover his face. Light from a flashbulb will fill in the shadow area and improve the photograph.

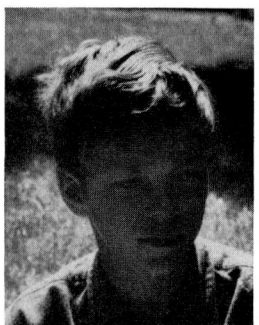

Flash Fill-In, used with back lighting, produces good detail and even lighting. For close-ups, cover the flash reflector with a white handkerchief to prevent overexposing the front of the subject.

WORLD BOOK photos

Lighting. The photographer's skill in using light helps determine whether his pictures are good or bad. On a dark, cloudy day, there may not be enough light to make a proper image on the film. The film will be *underexposed*, and the picture will turn out dark and uninteresting. On the other hand, you will probably *overexpose* the film if you photograph white snow or shining water in bright sunlight. Film will be overexposed if it receives more light than necessary. An overexposed picture is too bright and has no really dark tones. Different kinds of light are best for various types of photographs.

Hazy or Cloudy Sunlight is best for taking pictures of people. A thin layer of haze or clouds covering the sun breaks up the sunlight. Hazy or cloudy sunlight creates soft shadows and many shades of gray in a picture. This makes the picture of a person look natural because there are no deep shadows across his face.

Bright Sunlight produces the best pictures of landscape scenes. The sun makes each detail in the scene stand out sharply. The sun also casts deep shadows, creating dark areas and light areas in the picture. A picture with sharp details and strong contrasts between light and dark areas is both attractive and interesting.

If you must photograph a person in bright sunlight, control the shadows on his face. Before you take the picture, study the way in which the sunlight falls on the subject. Try to have him stand so that the sun does not cast deep shadows on his face. There are four ways in which the sun can fall on a subject.

Side Lighting is light that shines on one side of the subject. Shadows cover the other side of his face. You can lighten this shadowy area by photographing the person near the sunny side of a light-colored building. Or you can use a flashbulb to provide light to fill in the shadows. This technique is called *flash fill-in*. The extra light also adds detail to the dark side of the subject's face. If you stand closer than 8 feet from your subject, cover the flash reflector with a white handkerchief. The handkerchief will cut down the light from the flashbulb so that the subject receives an equal amount of light from the sun and the bulb.

Top Lighting is light that falls directly on the subject from the sun overhead. The sun casts dark, unattractive shadows under a person's eyebrows and nose. You can lighten these shadow areas with flash fill-in.

Front Lighting shines into the subject's face. It causes the same unattractive shadows as top lighting. Front lighting also makes the person squint because he is looking directly into the sun. Your picture will be better if you change your position slightly so that the sun shines on one side of the person.

Back Lighting comes from behind the subject. If the sunlight is strong, it will produce a dark shadow over the person's entire face. In this case, using flash fill-in would improve the photograph. If the sunlight is weak, it will produce a soft, pleasant shadow over the person's face. When taking a back-lighted picture, you must use a *lens shade* (a hood that protects the lens from direct sunlight) on your camera. Otherwise, the sun will shine directly into the camera lens and make bright streaks and glare spots in the picture.

COMPOSING YOUR PICTURES

Composition is the arrangement of objects in a photograph. Good composition produces a pleasing photograph. For good composition, have only one center of interest in a picture and use a plain background so that all interest will be focused on the subject. When photographing distant landscapes, include a large object in the foreground to give the picture depth. Balance light and dark tones to create dramatic contrast in the picture. Study the lines and shapes of your subject material. Certain lines and shapes suggest feelings of peace, dignity, or action. Use these lines and shapes to make your photograph story or create a mood.

Light and Dark Tones, used together, create striking photographs. Add emphasis by contrasting dark against light, *left*, or light against dark, *right*.

Horizontal Lines suggest peace and rest. A picture is more interesting if the horizontal line is off-center and does not cut the picture in half.

Vertical Lines emphasize height and create feelings of dignity and grandeur.

Diagonal Lines suggest action and movement. They may also suggest conflict.

Balanced Objects at the front, back, and sides create order in a photograph and give a feeling of depth.

Radiating Lines can be used by a creative photographer to form interesting patterns and abstract shapes.

Triangular Lines direct attention to the center of interest. Triangles can suggest rest or movement.

Photos by Frank Fenner

PHOTOGRAPHY ⬡ ADJUSTABLE CAMERAS

If you have an adjustable camera, you must take three basic steps before taking a picture. You must (1) set the shutter speed, (2) adjust the size of the lens aperture, and (3) focus the lens on your subject.

The Shutter on an adjustable camera works at different speeds. This is important for two reasons. First, it helps control the amount of light that reaches the film. A fast shutter admits less light than a slow shutter does. Second, the shutter helps prevent a picture from being blurred if the camera or the subject moves. A fast shutter will "stop" movement. The more rapidly a subject is moving, the faster must be the shutter speed.

The shutter speeds appear as numbers on the camera's shutter scale. Each number represents a fraction of a second. For example, 60 stands for 1/60th of a second, and 500 means 1/500th of a second. The higher the number, the faster the shutter speed.

Each number on the scale represents either half the speed or twice the speed of the next number. When set at 250, the shutter opens and closes twice as fast as when it is set at 125. When set at 250, the shutter works half as fast as when it is set at 500.

The Lens Aperture also controls the amount of light that reaches the film. A large aperture admits more light than a small one does. An adjustable camera has a circle of thin, overlapping metal leaves that changes the size of the aperture. This device is called an *iris diaphragm*. The diaphragm expands and contracts over the aperture to admit different amounts of light.

The various sizes of the aperture are called *f-stops*. The *f-stops* appear as *f-numbers* on a scale next to the shutter speeds. The *f*-numbers on some cameras include 2.8, 4, 5.6, 8, 11, 16, and 22. The smaller the number, the larger the aperture. The *f* stands for *fraction*. Just as 1/2 is larger than 1/4, *f*/8 is larger than *f*/16.

The *f*-stops are set up in the same way as the shutter speeds. Each *f*-stop lets in either half as much or twice as much light as the stop next to it. For example, when you change the setting from *f*/16 to *f*/11, the aperture opens up by one *f*-stop and admits twice as much light. In the same way, when you "stop down" from *f*/8 to *f*/11, the aperture closes down by one stop and admits half as much light.

The lens aperture also helps control the overall sharpness of the picture. As the aperture becomes smaller, the area of sharpness in front of and behind the subject becomes larger. This area of sharpness is called *depth of field*. Depth of field extends from the nearest part of the subject area in focus to the farthest part in focus. A small aperture, such as *f*/16, creates great depth of field. This means that a deep area in front of and behind the subject will be in sharp focus. As you increase the size of the aperture, the area in sharp focus becomes shallower. At a wide aperture, such as *f*/5.6, the subject will be in sharp focus, but objects in front of and behind the subject will be blurred.

Focusing determines whether your subject will appear sharp or blurred in the picture. When you focus, you adjust the lens so it forms a sharp image of your subject on the film.

Accurate focusing depends on (1) the distance between the camera lens and the subject, and (2) the distance between the lens and the film in the camera. When you turn the camera's focusing knob, the lens moves toward or away from the film. This adjustment enables you to take a sharp picture of most subjects, regardless of their distance from the camera. Focusing on *infinity* (a far-away scene) requires a short distance between lens and film. Focusing close up requires a longer distance.

There are several ways to know when your subject is in focus. Most cameras have a *focusing scale*. The numbers on the scale represent various distances in feet. The infinity symbol (∞) on the scale stands for any distance beyond the distances given in feet. To focus, you first measure or estimate the distance from the camera to the subject. Then set this distance at the corresponding number on the focusing scale. As you adjust the setting, the lens moves to its proper distance from the film.

Many cameras have a special viewing screen that lets you see an image of your subject while you are focusing. If the camera has a *ground-glass* screen, you focus by moving the lens back and forth until the image in the viewing screen becomes sharp. A camera with a *range finder* shows two images of the subject. One type of range finder shows two identical images of the same subject. You turn the focusing knob until the double image becomes one sharp image. The other type of range finder splits one image of the subject into two halves. You focus by bringing the two halves together.

Focusing also affects a picture's depth of field. The closer the lens is to the subject, the shallower the depth of field. When you focus close up, only your subject and a small surrounding area will be in focus. You gain greater depth of field when you focus on a subject that is farther from the camera.

Exposure refers to the total amount of light that reaches the film while you are taking a picture. The correct exposure depends upon the right combination of shutter speed and *f*-stop. To set these controls, you must first consider the amount of light on your subject.

On a cloudy day, more light must reach the film to make an image. You should use a large *f*-stop and a slow shutter speed to provide a greater exposure. Sunny days require less exposure. Set the *f*-stop so that

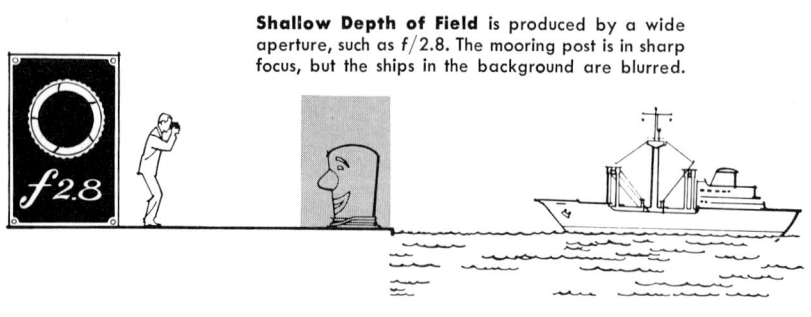

Shallow Depth of Field is produced by a wide aperture, such as *f*/2.8. The mooring post is in sharp focus, but the ships in the background are blurred.

Shutter Speeds can range from *B* to 1/500th of a second. The higher the number, the faster the shutter speed. These photographs show the type of action certain shutter speeds will stop. The *B* setting should be used for time exposures at night. Set at 1/60, the shutter will not stop action. Set at 1/125, it will stop a slow-moving bicycle. Set at 1/500, it will stop splashing water.

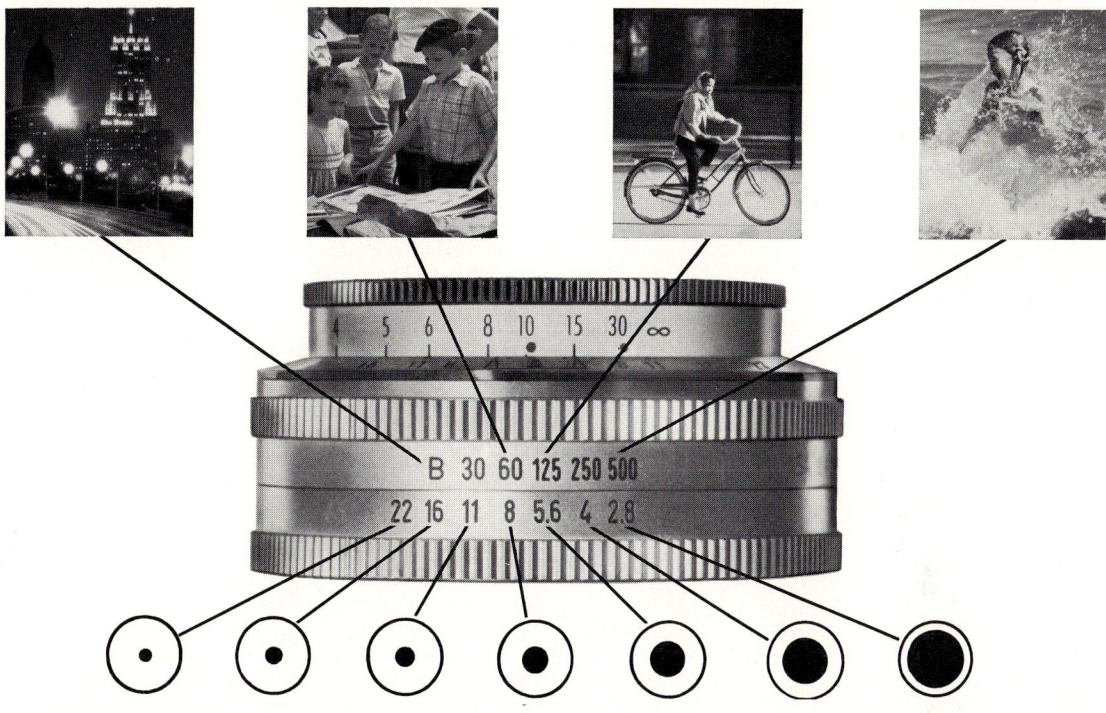

F-Numbers can range from *f*/22 to *f*/2.8. The larger the number, the smaller the lens opening and the less light admitted into the camera. The circles in the illustration show how the lens opening becomes larger as the *f*-numbers become smaller.

it is half-closed, and use a medium shutter speed. A particularly bright scene, such as white snow reflecting bright sunlight, requires the least exposure. Use a small *f*-stop and a fast shutter speed to prevent the bright light from overexposing the film.

Before taking a picture, you should also consider the movement of your subject and the depth of field that you want. If your subject is moving, you will need a fast shutter speed to prevent blurring. If you want a large area of your picture to be in sharp focus, you will need a small *f*-stop to provide greater depth of field. But if you change one control, you must also change the other. When you use a fast shutter speed to stop action, less light reaches the film. So you must increase the size of the *f*-stop. In the same way, when you use a small *f*-stop to provide greater depth of field, less light reaches the film. So you must use a slower shutter speed. By using these two controls together, you can make sure that the proper amount of light reaches the film.

Suppose you want to photograph some lions outdoor at the zoo on a bright sunny day. The correct settings for your camera would be *f*/11 at 1/60. If the lions are moving, you should use a faster shutter speed, such as 1/125. This speed is twice as fast as 1/60, so half as much light will reach the film. You then must make the aperture twice as large and set the *f*-stop at *f*/8. In the same way, if you change the shutter speed to 1/250— four times as fast—you must change the *f*-stop to *f*/5.6 —four times as large.

Now suppose you want to include the natural surroundings of the lions in your picture. You will want great depth of field so that the rocks behind the lions and the *moat* (ditch) in front will appear sharply. You should use a small aperture, such as *f*/16. The film will receive half as much light as it did when the *f*-stop was *f*/11. You must also change the shutter speed from 1/60 to 1/30 so that light will reach the film for twice as long a time.

WORLD BOOK photos

Great Depth of Field is produced by a small aperture, such as *f*/22. Both the mooring post and the ships in the background are in sharp focus.

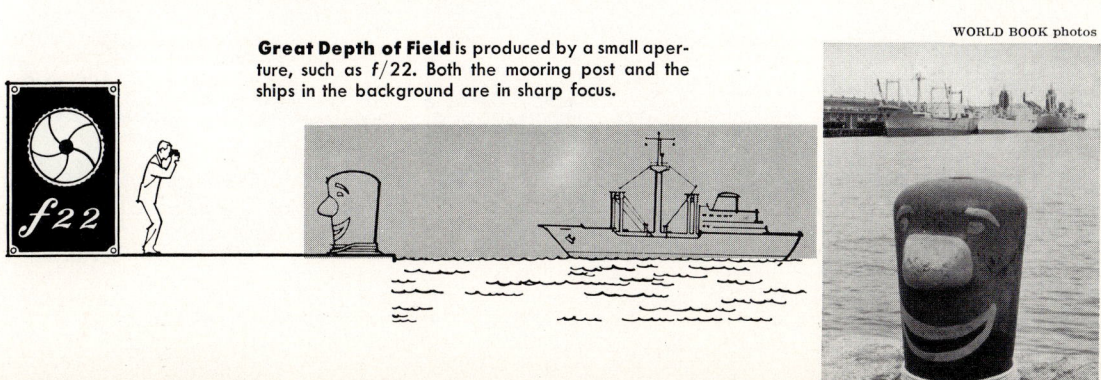

PHOTOGRAPHY ACCESSORIES

Filters. Colors photographed with black-and-white film become black, white, and various shades of gray in a picture. Photographers use filters to lighten or darken certain areas of a picture, and to increase the contrast between the different shades of gray.

A filter is a piece of colored, plasticlike gelatin or colored glass in a holder that fits over the lens of the camera. The filter allows light of its own color to pass through the lens to the film. It *filters* (holds back) light of certain other colors. Thus, a filter lightens its own color in a picture and darkens certain other colors.

Most photographers use yellow, red, and green filters in black-and-white photography. A *yellow filter* improves pictures of landscapes because it produces natural-looking skies. A blue sky photographed without a filter may appear completely white in a picture. A yellow filter deepens the sky tone, providing contrast between the dark sky and the white clouds.

A *red filter* makes a blue sky appear almost black. This filter creates a dramatic contrast between the sky and the clouds. It also cuts through haze in distant landscapes. However, a red filter does not make good photographs of persons because skin tones appear washed out.

A *green filter* provides much the same sky tones as a yellow filter, and produces normal skin tones. It also improves the tones of green leaves and grass, and makes flowers stand out from a green background.

A *polarizing filter* reduces the glare from shiny surfaces, such as water or glass. See POLARIZED LIGHT.

Most filters hold back some light from the film, and so you must increase the exposure when using them. The *filter factor* listed with the film's instruction sheet tells how much the exposure should be increased.

Exposure Meters, also called *light meters*, help assure correct exposures. The *photoelectric cell meter* is the most accurate kind. It measures the amount of light in a scene and shows the camera settings for the correct exposure. There are two types of photoelectric meters: (1) incident light meter, and (2) reflected light meter.

An *incident light meter* measures the amount of light on the subject. The meter must receive the same light as the subject to give an accurate reading. To take a reading, point the meter toward the sky. Or stand next to your subject and aim the meter toward the spot where you will stand to take the picture.

A *reflected light meter* measures the light that is reflected from the subject toward the camera. To take a reading, point the meter toward your subject. If you are photographing a person, hold the meter about 6 inches from his face. The meter will measure the light reflected from his face instead of light from the sky or the background. If the subject has light and shadow on his face, take separate readings of the light and dark areas. Base your settings on an average of the two readings. For scenic photographs, always point the reflected light meter slightly downward so it will not measure excess light from the sky. Be sure the meter does not measure the shadow of your body or hand. See LIGHT METER.

A Filter lightens its own color and darkens others. Colors, *left*, become black, white, and gray when photographed with black-and-white film, *below*. Compare these pictures with the bottom photographs. The *yellow* filter darkened the blue sky, bringing out the clouds. The *red* filter made the sky very dark, but lightened the red shirt. The *green* filter lightened the green jacket.

WORLD BOOK photos

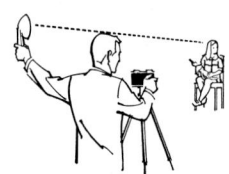

Flash On the Camera produces harsh front lighting and a shadow outline on one side of the subject.

Flash Off the Camera produces side lighting. It throws the shadow low and away from the subject.

Bounce Flash gives soft, even lighting when the light *bounces* (reflects) off a light-colored ceiling.

WORLD BOOK photos

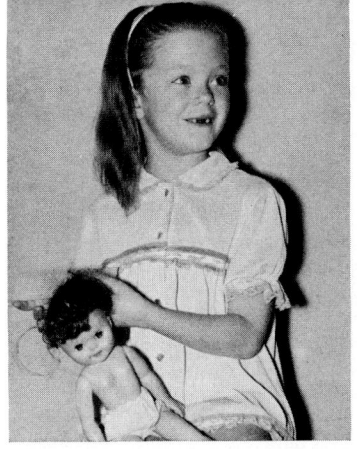
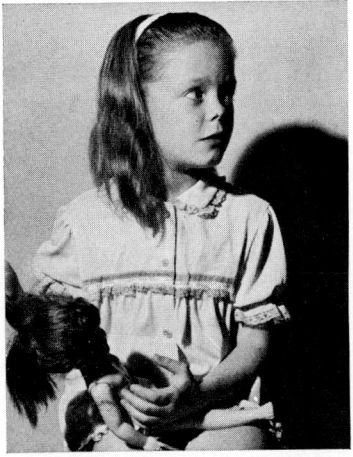
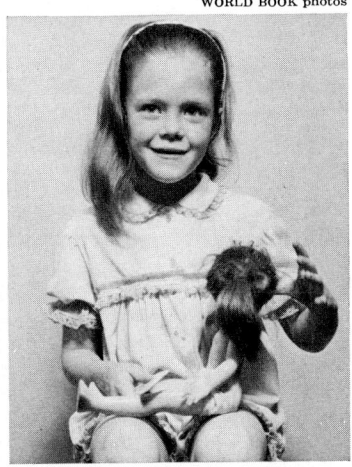

Artificial Lighting lets you shoot pictures that you could not take with *natural lighting* (daylight). The most common sources of artificial light are (1) photoflood lamps, (2) flashbulbs, and (3) electronic flash.

Photoflood Lamps must be plugged into an electrical outlet. They burn for at least three hours. The most convenient type is a small lamp with a built-in reflector that can be clamped onto a chair or tripod.

Flashbulbs operate on batteries and are easy to carry because of their light weight. They differ in the amount of light they produce. When choosing a bulb, you must be sure it can be used with the shutter on your camera. Most cameras have a built-in *flash synchronizer*. This device makes sure that the greatest brightness of the bulb's light occurs at the instant when the shutter reaches its full opening. Some bulbs work with all shutter speeds. Others work only with slow speeds.

It is easy to determine exposure when using flash. First, set the shutter speed for the scene. Then check the instruction sheet that comes with the film or the flashbulb to find the *guide number* for the bulb you are using. To determine the proper *f*-stop, divide the guide number by the number of feet between the flashbulb and the subject. If the guide number for a flashbulb is 160, and the bulb is 10 feet from the subject, the *f*-stop would be *f*/16. Most cameras must also be set on *M*, the setting for flash synchronization. See FLASHBULB.

Electronic Flash, also called *strobe light*, is produced by an electrical discharge in a gas-filled bulb. Electronic flash fires thousands of flashes before the bulb needs replacing. The flash from an electronic-flash unit lasts a much shorter time than that from a flashbulb. An electronic flash may last only from 1/500th to 1/2000th of a second. The burst of light is so great and intense

that the flash, not the shutter, stops the action in the picture. Because of the flash's speed, the shutter must be fully open before the flash occurs. This is called *X-synchronization*. Most cameras must be set on *X* for electronic flash. Portable electronic-flash units operate on batteries.

Special Lenses greatly increase the usefulness of a camera. These lenses allow you to take extreme closeups, to photograph unusually wide areas, or to photograph far-distant objects.

Closeup Lenses slip over the normal lens as filters do. With them you can take sharp pictures of subjects at a closer distance than with the normal lens. Focusing with a closeup lens must be exact because you have hardly any depth of field. Use a tape measure, and measure the exact distance from the front of the subject to the front of the lens.

At close distances, your viewfinder may not show exactly what will appear in the picture. If the viewfinder is above the lens of your camera, it will show a slightly different view of the subject from that "seen" by the lens. This difference in view is called *parallax*. It may cause the top of a person's head to appear chopped-off in the picture. You can avoid this fault by tilting the camera up slightly just before you take the picture.

Wide-angle and Telephoto Lenses are called *interchangeable lenses* because they replace a camera's normal lens. With a normal lens, size and depth relationships among the objects in a picture are the same as seen by the eye. A wide-angle lens includes a wider area of a scene than a normal lens does. But it makes all the objects seem smaller and farther away. A telephoto lens covers a narrower area of a scene, but it makes objects appear larger and closer.

PHOTOGRAPHY / DEVELOPING FILM

When you take a picture, the camera lens gathers in light reflected from objects in the scene. Light-colored objects reflect a great deal of light. Dark objects reflect little light, or none at all. The lights and darks reflected from the scene go through the lens onto the film.

Photographic film is a thin sheet of plastic with a thin coating called an *emulsion*. The emulsion consists of tiny grains of silver salts held together by gelatin, a jellylike substance. The silver salts used are silver bromide and silver iodide. Silver salts are *sensitive* to light. That is, they change when light hits them. When you take a picture, some salts in the emulsion are struck by a great deal of light. These salts undergo a great change. Other salts are struck by a small amount of light, and they change only slightly. Still other salts get no light, and they do not change at all. In this way, the lights and darks reflected from a scene make an image on the emulsion.

You cannot see the silver salts react to light. The image on the film remains invisible until the film is developed. The developing process has five steps: (1) developer, (2) stop bath, (3) fixing bath, (4) washing, and (5) drying. First, the salts that were struck by light are changed by the *developer* into metallic silver. The exposed areas of the film become dark. The *stop bath*, which is usually plain water, removes the developer so it will not make the exposed areas too dark. The unexposed salts must now be removed from the film, because they are still sensitive to light. The *fixing bath*, or *hypo*, dissolves the unexposed salts so they can be washed away. It also toughens the film (see HYPO). *Washing* the film in water removes the unexposed salts. These unexposed areas of the film become transparent. Washing also removes the chemicals of the fixing bath. After *drying* the film, you have a permanent, visible image.

The developed film is called a *negative*. What was white or bright in the scene you photographed is dark. This is because the bright areas reflected the most light and caused the greatest change in the silver salts. What was darkest in the scene is clear on the negative. The dark areas reflected no light and did not affect the silver salts.

Developing Your Own Film. To develop film at home, you will need three chemicals, several pieces of equipment, and running water. The instruction sheet

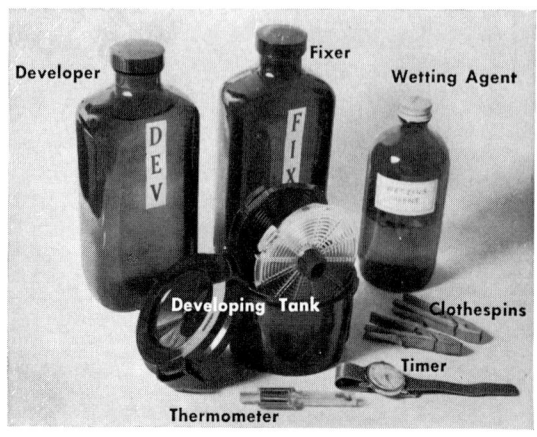

These Are the Basic Supplies Needed to Develop Film.

Developer · Fixer · Wetting Agent · Developing Tank · Clothespins · Timer · Thermometer

that comes with a roll of film lists the developer and fixing chemicals that should be used. You will also need a *wetting agent*. This liquid prevents negatives from being water-spotted, and speeds up the drying time.

Use an ordinary measuring cup or a *darkroom graduate* to measure the solutions. Wash the cup after each use to avoid ruining one chemical with another. Mix and store each solution in a bottle. The bottles should be amber-colored to keep light from harming the chemicals. Label each bottle with the name of its contents.

The *time-temperature* method of development produces the best results. Develop the film for the recommended time at the recommended temperature. You must keep all solutions at the same temperature, including the water used for the stop bath and the wash. Differences in temperature can cause the film emulsion to wrinkle and break up. Test the temperatures with a *darkroom thermometer*. Time each development process with a *darkroom timer* or a watch with a second hand.

Film must be developed in total darkness because the film is still sensitive to light. Many beginners use a darkened kitchen, bathroom, or closet as a temporary darkroom. A *developing tank* lets you develop film with the lights on. Wind the film onto a reel, put the reel into the tank, and pour the solutions in and out of the tank. The tank is designed to keep light away from the film. Some tanks, however, must be loaded with film in complete darkness. You can use a lightproof closet or a *changing*

HOW BLACK-AND-WHITE FILM WORKS

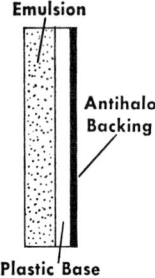

Emulsion

Antihalo Backing

Plastic Base

Black-and-white film consists of three layers: (1) an *emulsion* made up of light-sensitive silver salts in gelatin; (2) a *plastic base* that supports the emulsion; and (3) an *antihalo backing* containing a dye that absorbs light which has passed through the emulsion. When film is exposed, the light reflected from a subject strikes the emulsion. The lighter the subject, the more light it reflects. The silver salts hit by light undergo a change. The

greater the light, the greater the change. In this way, an invisible image of the subject forms on the emulsion. The image becomes visible when the film is developed and becomes a negative. The exposed silver salts turn dark. The unexposed areas of the film become transparent.

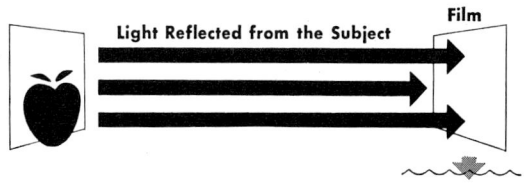

Light Reflected from the Subject

Film

Development Process

Negative

WORLD BOOK Diagrams

Load the Film onto the tank reel. Place the reel in the tank and fasten the cover. Do this in total darkness unless you use a daylight-loading tank. Prepare the three developing solutions and the wetting agent. Check their temperatures.

Add the Developer and begin timing the process. Agitate as directed. When the time is up, empty the developer into its bottle. Pour the stop bath in and out of the tank twice. Add the fixer and begin timing. Agitate properly. Empty the fixer into its bottle.

bag (a special lightproof bag) to protect the film from light while putting it into the tank.

During the development process, the developer and fixing solutions must be *agitated* (moved about). Agitation keeps a fresh supply of solution in contact with the film so that the image develops evenly. The instruction sheet tells how long and how often to agitate.

Problem Negatives. Even though you expose the film correctly, your negatives may be faulty because of mistakes in developing. If the developer is too warm or the film remains in the developer too long, the negative will be *overdeveloped*. It will appear quite *dense* (dark), with no detail in the highlight areas. The negative will be *underdeveloped* if the developer is too cold, or if the film is not developed long enough. An underdeveloped negative appears *thin* (almost transparent). If the entire negative appears gray, the film was not in the fixing bath long enough.

Careless handling can result in scratches on a negative. Do not touch the negative until it is dry. Then handle it by the edges only. Keep your negatives in special negative storage envelopes.

Streaks and spots on negatives indicate improper development. Light and dark streaks result from uneven development. Agitate the solutions properly so they cover all the film for the same amount of time. Air bubbles in the solutions cause spots on negatives. Proper agitation prevents these bubbles.

Wash the Film for 30 minutes. Let a thin stream of lukewarm water run into the middle of the open tank. Then place the reel in the wetting agent solution for 30 seconds. Remove the film from the reel. Clip a clothespin to one end of the filmstrip and hang it in a dust-free area to dry. Clip a clothespin to the lower end to prevent curling. Cut the dry filmstrip into sections convenient for printing.

Overdeveloped Negative is too dark, and has no detail in the highlight areas.

Perfect Negative has good tone contrast and detail in both shadow and highlight areas.

Underdeveloped Negative has no dark black areas and no detail in the shadow areas.

Spotted Negative is due to improper agitation. Careless handling causes scratches.

WORLD BOOK photos

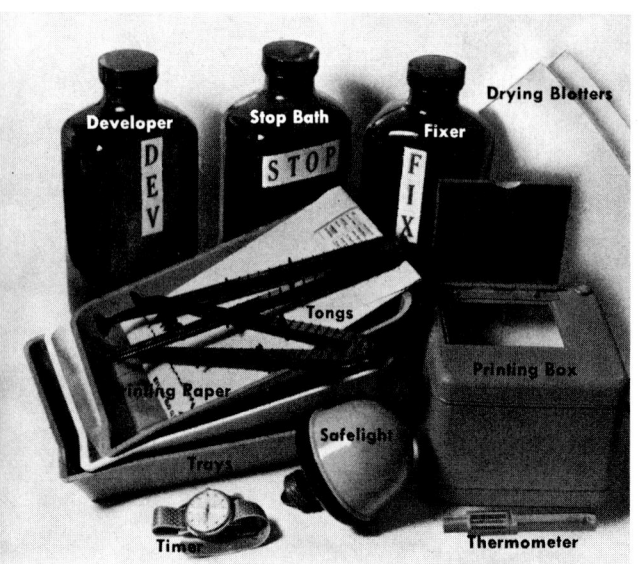

These Are the Supplies Needed to Make Contact Prints.

WORLD BOOK photos

Making A Contact Print. Prepare the three solutions first. Arrange the trays in front of you so that from left to right you have: (1) developer, (2) stop bath, and (3) fixer. Turn the room light off and the safelight on. Place the negative, dull side up, in the printing box. Place the paper, shiny side down, over the negative and close the lid. Turn on the exposing light for 3 seconds. Using one pair of tongs, slide the paper, shiny side up, completely into the developer. Agitate by rocking the tray gently. At the end of the development time, place the print in the stop bath for 30 seconds. Using the other pair of tongs, slide the print into the fixer and agitate immediately. After 30 seconds you can turn on the room light. At the end of the fixing time, wash the print for 1 hour in lukewarm running water. Let it dry between blotters.

PHOTOGRAPHY ⬡ CONTACT PRINTING

The process of printing photographs transfers the image on the negative to a piece of paper. Printing reverses the light and dark tones of the negative. As a result, the paper print shows the scene as you originally photographed it.

Prints are made in much the same way as negatives. Printing paper is coated with an emulsion that contains light-sensitive silver salts. Light passes through the negative and transfers the negative image to the paper. During the exposure, the dark areas of the negative hold back some of the light. These dark areas become light areas on the print. The clear areas of the negative let much light pass through to the paper. These clear areas become dark on the print. Thus, the tones of the print become the same as those in the scene you photographed. For this reason, a print is called a *positive.*

The exposed printing paper contains an invisible image. The paper must be developed before it will produce a visible image. To develop prints, you repeat the steps used to develop film: developer, stop bath, fixing bath, washing, and drying.

Contact printing is the simplest method of printing photographs. The dull side of the negative and the shiny side of the printing paper must be in direct contact during the exposure. Light shining through the negative makes an image directly on the paper. A contact print is always the same size as its negative because it is made directly from the negative. You can use either a printing frame or a printing box to hold the negative and paper together.

A *printing frame* consists of a wooden frame that holds a sheet of glass. Spring clamps on the frame hold the negative and paper tightly together against the glass. To expose the paper, place the negative and then the paper on the glass inside the frame. Place the frame, glass side up, about a foot under a 100-watt frosted light bulb.

When you turn on the light, it shines down through the glass and the negative, and makes a latent image on the paper. You must estimate the correct exposure time. It depends on the density of the negative, the strength of the light, and the distance between the printing paper and the light source. An exposure of 2 seconds is recommended for this type of printing frame.

You can easily make a printing frame. Buy a piece of window glass that is a little larger than the printing paper. Cover the edges of the glass with adhesive tape so they will not scratch the negative. Place the paper on a flat surface, such as a table top. Put the negative on top of the paper, and cover both with the glass.

A *printing box* is a box with a light at the bottom and glass at the top. To use it, place the negative and then the paper on top of the glass. Close the lid of the box to press the negative and the paper together. When you turn on the light, it shines up through the glass and the negative, making an image on the paper.

In addition to a printing device, you will need chemicals and equipment to develop the prints. The developer and fixing chemicals used in printing are different from those used in developing film. The stop bath used in printing is an acetic acid solution rather than water. Other necessary supplies include (1) three bottles for mixing and storing the chemical solutions, (2) three trays to hold the prints and solutions during the development process, and (3) two pairs of tongs to move the prints from one tray to another. Use the measuring cup, thermometer, and timing device that you used in developing the film.

You also will need a package of printing paper, a dim colored light called a *safelight*, and photographic drying blotters for drying the prints. Most printing papers cannot be handled under room lights. A safelight will not expose the paper, but it will let you see what you are doing. This light can be a specially-coated bulb or a low-wattage bulb covered with a filter. Be sure to cover the printing paper if you turn on the regular room lights.

PHOTOGRAPHY ⊕ ENLARGING

Enlarging, or *projection printing*, produces a print that is larger than its negative. The negative is not in contact with the printing paper during the exposure. A *photographic enlarger* holds the negative, and an *easel* holds the printing paper. The enlarger projects the negative image onto the paper somewhat as a slide projector throws an image onto a screen. The enlarger *blows up* (increases the size of) the negative image, and makes a larger image on the paper.

An enlarger has three basic parts: (1) a light bulb, (2) a negative carrier, and (3) a lens. The *enlarger head* contains these parts. The top of the enlarger head holds a light bulb that is turned on to expose the printing paper. The *negative carrier* is a frame that holds the negative when it is placed in the enlarger. The lens of the enlarger projects the negative image. The enlarger head can be raised or lowered. Its position determines the size of the enlargement. The higher the head, the larger the image produced.

The enlarger lens has a focusing device that controls the sharpness of the image it projects on the paper. The lens also has a diaphragm that can be opened up or closed down to control the exposure. The diaphragm sometimes will let you make a good print from a poor negative. If a negative is thin because of underexposure or underdevelopment, you can underexpose the print. Use a short exposure time and a small *f*-stop on the enlarger to provide a brief exposure. On the other hand, if you have a dense overexposed or overdeveloped negative, increase the exposure of the print. Use a long exposure time and a large *f*-stop.

An easel holds the printing paper flat during the exposure. Most easels can be made smaller or larger to hold different sizes of paper. Use a *camel's-hair brush* to remove dust from the negative before putting it into the negative carrier. Specks of dust on a negative will enlarge into white marks on a print.

In developing enlargements, you can use the same chemicals and equipment used to develop contact prints.

Negative Carrier holds the negative when it is placed in the enlarger.

Light Bulb, which exposes the printing paper, is at the top of the enlarger head.

Focusing Control raises or lowers the lens to bring the negative image into sharp focus.

Projection Control raises or lowers the enlarger head to control the size of the image projected by the lens.

Red Safety Filter swings under the lens to prevent the enlarger light from exposing the printing paper. A photographer uses the filter when he makes focusing adjustments or other changes.

Lens enlarges the negative image. The lens diaphragm controls the amount of light that exposes the printing paper.

Camel's-Hair Brush removes dust from negatives.

Burning-In Tool is a card with a hole in it. It lets extra light expose areas of a picture that print too light.

Dodging Tools are pieces of cardboard on wire. They hold back light from areas of a picture that print too dark.

Easel holds the printing paper flat during the exposure.

WORLD BOOK photo

ENLARGING TECHNIQUES

Focusing. Set the lens at its widest opening and turn on only the enlarger light. Focus a small detail of the negative on a piece of white cardboard.

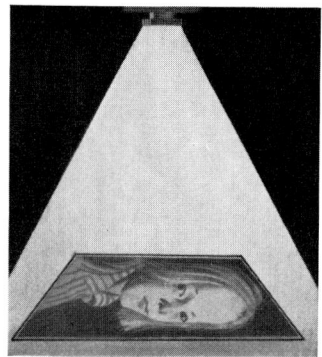

Exposing. Close the lens down to f/8. Turn the enlarger light off and the safelight on. Replace the cardboard with print paper and make the exposure.

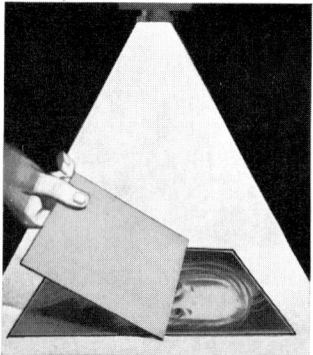

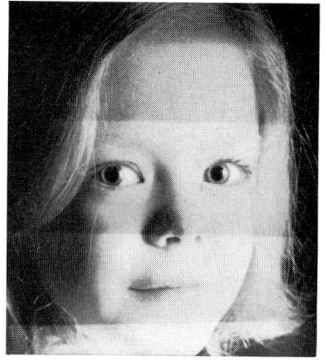

Test Strips help determine the correct exposure time. Cover all but a fifth of the print paper with cardboard. Expose for 10 seconds. Expose four more strips at 10 seconds each. After development, the paper will show exposures of 50, 40, 30, 20, and 10 seconds. Select the best time for the print.

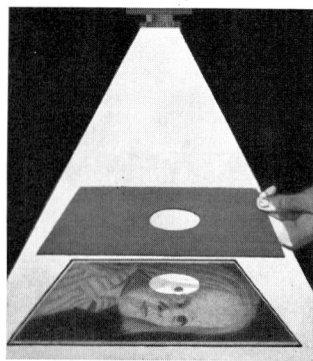

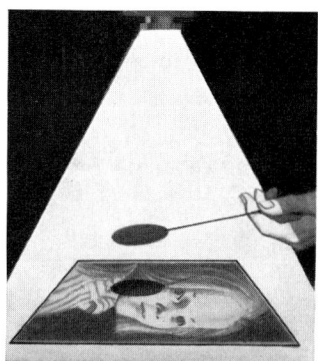

Burning In allows extra light to darken part of a print. Move the cardboard in quick circles about halfway between the lens and the print paper.

Dodging lightens part of a print by holding back light. Move the tool in small circles so that its edges will blend into the rest of the print.

Enlarging Controls can improve a poor photograph. This picture is dark, cluttered, and uninteresting. Compare it with the three photographs below.

Cropping, or rearranging, a picture focuses attention on the squirrel. Enlarging the squirrel to fill the entire print also removes unnecessary objects from the foreground and background.

Adding Detail and Contrast improves the print. Dodging the tree and squirrel lightens them and brings out detail, *above*. Burning in the snow darkens it and adds detail, *below*.

WORLD BOOK photos

380d

PHOTOGRAPHY  PRINTING PAPERS

Printing papers for contact printing and enlarging come in different weights, surfaces, and contrasts. A paper can be *single-weight* or *double-weight*. Most photographers use double-weight paper for portraits and other special types of photographs. Prints made on double-weight paper will not curl or damage easily. These prints must be washed longer than prints made on single-weight paper to remove the development chemicals.

A paper's surface can be *glossy* (shiny), *semi-matte* (slightly shiny), or *matte* (dull). Most photographers use glossy or semi-matte paper. Professional portrait photographers use matte paper.

A paper has *contrast* so that good prints can be made from many types of negatives. For example, a *flat* negative has few dark and light areas. It will produce a print that is gray and uninteresting. This kind of negative needs a *hard* (high-contrast) paper that will add contrast to the tones of the print. A *contrasty* negative has extreme contrast between dark and light areas. It should be printed on a *soft* (low-contrast) paper.

The number of a paper indicates its grade of contrast. Printing papers usually range from No. 1, which has the least contrast, to No. 5, which provides the greatest contrast. A No. 1 paper produces the widest range of tones, including black, white, and many shades of gray. Use this paper with very overexposed negatives that have extreme contrasts in tone. Use No. 2 or No. 3 paper to print properly exposed negatives. These papers produce fewer gray shades, but they give contrasting blacks and whites that add life to a picture. No. 4 and No. 5 papers produce the fewest shades of gray. They usually will make a good print from a flat negative.

Some papers have the different grades of contrast built into them. These *multiple-* or *variable-contrast* papers require a different color of light to produce each grade of contrast. Colored printing filters must be placed over the lens when the papers are exposed. Multiple-contrast papers are popular because the photographer can print any type of negative from them. He does not have to buy a box of each grade of paper.

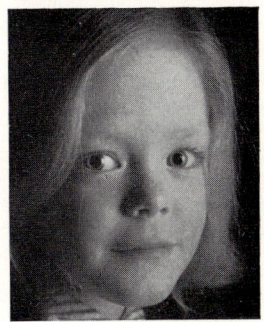 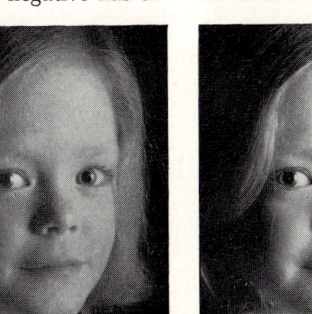 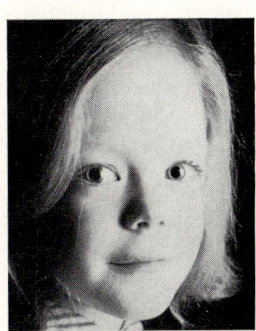

Printing Papers control the contrast of prints. These prints were made from a properly exposed negative. The print made on low-contrast paper, *left,* lacks highlights and contrast. The normal-contrast paper, *middle,* produced a print with good detail in shadow and highlight areas. The high-contrast paper, *right,* produced a print with harsh highlights.

WORLD BOOK photos

PHOTOGRAPHY CHOOSING BLACK-AND-WHITE FILM

There are many types of film for taking various kinds of black-and-white pictures. Some films can be used for snapshots and other general photographs. Other films are made for special uses. A good photographer chooses film that is best for the kind of picture he wants to take. Two basic points should be considered when choosing film: (1) color sensitivity and (2) film speed.

Color Sensitivity. The eye sees an object in terms of color and brightness. For example, a sweater may appear red, but it can also appear light red or dark red. Black-and-white film does not "see" color. The film makes a colored object appear gray in a picture. Film does see brightness. A bright color appears light gray in the picture, and a dark color appears dark gray. Film produces the most natural-looking picture when it makes the brightness of the grays correspond to the brightness of the original colors. The color sensitivity of a film determines whether the pictures will look natural.

There are two main types of black-and-white film, based on color sensitivity: (1) panchromatic and (2) orthochromatic. *Panchromatic* film is sensitive to all colors. It records them all as various shades of gray. The brightness of the grays corresponds to the brightness of the colors photographed. A picture made with "pan" film has contrasting light and dark tones that resemble the contrasting tones of the original scene. *Orthochromatic* film is sensitive to all colors except red. "Ortho" film records red objects as black. It is oversensitive to blue, and often makes blue skies appear white. Ortho film gives strong contrast between blacks and whites.

Film Speed is the speed with which a film reacts to light. This speed determines how much exposure the film needs to record an image of a subject. A *fast* film is highly sensitive to light. Its emulsion needs less exposure to record an image. *Medium-speed* and *slow-speed* film needs more exposure.

A film's instruction sheet tells the speed of the film. The speed usually is given in the form of an *ASA number*. *ASA* stands for the American Standards Association, which set up a standard method of determining film speeds. The speeds range from 1 to 200, or higher. The higher the ASA number, the faster the film. If you use an exposure meter, you must set the film speed number on the meter before it will show the correct exposure.

Fast films have several advantages. A fast film will record an image in dim light. It permits the use of a small *f*-stop or a fast shutter speed, or both. However, the negative of a fast film cannot be enlarged without some loss of quality. A fast film is more sensitive to light because its emulsion contains larger grains of silver salts. If the negative is enlarged, these grains will give the print a speckled, hazy appearance called *graininess*.

PHOTOGRAPHY ⬡ COLOR

To understand color photography, you need to know some of the basic principles of color. Color depends primarily on light. Light that looks white to our eyes is really a mixture of all the colors of the rainbow. Any color can be reproduced by blending only three basic colors—blue, green, and red. These colors are called the *primary colors* of light. In color photography, blue light, green light, and red light are blended in certain proportions to reproduce any color. The colors in a picture are matched with those in the scene that was photographed.

For a full discussion of the basic principles of color, see COLOR (Color in Light; How the Eye Sees Color).

Color Film. There are two types of color film: (1) negative and (2) reversal. *Negative* film produces color negatives, from which color prints are made. *Reversal* film produces color *transparencies* (slides). A slide is usually viewed by placing it in a slide viewer or a projector, which projects the colored picture onto a screen.

Negative and reversal films are made in almost the same way. Each consists of three layers of emulsion on a sheet of plastic. These emulsions are similar to a black-and-white film emulsion. But in color film, each emulsion is affected by only one of the primary colors of light. The first emulsion is affected only by blue light. The second emulsion is affected only by green light. The third emulsion is affected only by red light.

When color film is exposed, light passes through the first emulsion and records an image of the blue areas of a scene. Light then passes through a special yellow filter layer. The filter prevents any unused blue light from

entering the next two emulsions. Then light passes through the second emulsion. This layer records an image of only the green areas of the scene. Finally, light passes through the third emulsion, which records an image of the red areas of the scene. By this process, light forms three separate images on the film. The three images are not colored. The film is dyed during the development process. The images representing specific colors are necessary so that the right parts of the film can be dyed the correct colors.

Developing Color Film. Color film is developed in a special developer. The developer changes the exposed silver salts on the emulsions to metallic silver. A silver image forms on each emulsion layer. Each image represents the color of light that exposed the layer.

The developer causes colored dyes to form in each layer. Each layer contains a substance called a *coupler*. During the development process, this substance *couples* (joins) with a chemical in the developer to produce a colored dye. The couplers produce a different colored dye in each layer of the film.

These dyes are not blue, green, and red. The dyes are the *complementary* (opposite) colors of blue, green, and red. Yellow is the complement of blue. A yellow dye forms in the first layer, because this emulsion has recorded blue light. *Magenta* (bluish-red) is the complement of green. A magenta dye forms in the second layer, which has recorded green light. *Cyan* (bluish-green) is the complement of red. A cyan dye forms in the third layer, which has recorded red light. After development, each layer contains the color complementary to the color originally recorded.

Complementary colors are used as dyes because they

HOW COLOR FILM WORKS

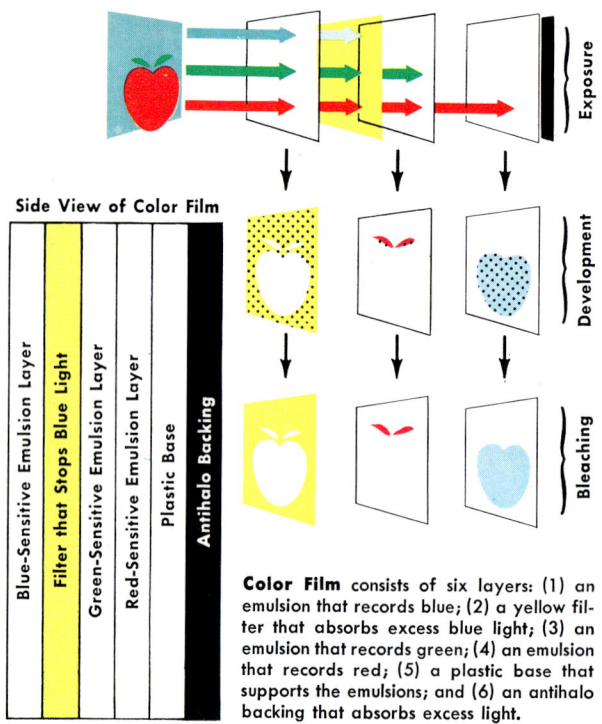

Side View of Color Film

Blue-Sensitive Emulsion Layer | Filter that Stops Blue Light | Green-Sensitive Emulsion Layer | Red-Sensitive Emulsion Layer | Plastic Base | Antihalo Backing

Exposure

Development

Bleaching

Color Film consists of six layers: (1) an emulsion that records blue; (2) a yellow filter that absorbs excess blue light; (3) an emulsion that records green; (4) an emulsion that records red; (5) a plastic base that supports the emulsions; and (6) an antihalo backing that absorbs excess light.

Color Negative Film produces color prints. After exposure, the film contains images of the blue, green, and red areas of the subject. When the film is developed, the exposed silver salts change to metallic silver. A negative silver image forms in each layer of the film. Then a colored dye forms over each image. The silver is then bleached out of each image, leaving the dye. In the developed color negative, a yellow dye covers the image made by blue light. A *magenta* (bluish-red) dye covers the image made by green light. A *cyan* (bluish-green) dye covers the image made by red light. These colors are difficult to see because the entire negative has an orange tint that improves the color quality of prints. When the negative is printed, each dye holds back light of its complementary color. The yellow dye absorbs blue light, and lets red and green pass through the negative. The magenta dye absorbs green light, and lets blue and red pass through. The cyan dye absorbs red light, and lets blue and green pass through. In this way, the original colors appear in the print.

COMMON MISTAKES IN USING COLOR FILM

Accurate Exposure of color film produces natural, lifelike colors. One type of color film is designed for use in daylight. Another type should be used only with artificial light.

Overexposed Color Picture

Properly Exposed Color Picture

Underexposed Color Picture

reproduce the original colors of the subject when white light is passed through the film. To make a color print of a picture, white light is passed through the color negative. To project a color slide onto a viewing screen, white light is passed through the slide. The white light is made up of the primary colors blue, green, and red.

When white light is passed through the film, each dye acts as a filter on a primary color. The yellow dye absorbs blue light. This dye lets red and green light pass through the film. The magenta dye absorbs green light. It lets red and blue light pass through the film. The cyan dye absorbs red, and lets blue and green pass through the film. In this way, the original colors of the subject appear in a print of a picture or on a screen.

WORLD BOOK photos

Daylight Exposure of artificial-light color film makes all colors bluish. Daylight color film exposed with clear flash produces an orange picture.

Color Reversal Film produces color slides. After exposure, the film contains images of the blue, green, and red areas of the subject. The film then goes through two development processes. The first development changes the exposed silver salts to metallic silver. A negative silver image forms in each layer of the film. Then the film is re-exposed so that the remaining silver salts can be developed. During the second development, colored dyes form around the silver images of the subject. The silver is then bleached out of each image, leaving transparent film in those areas. In the developed film, a yellow dye surrounds the image made by blue light. A *magenta* (bluish-red) dye surrounds the image made by green light. A *cyan* (bluish-green) dye surrounds the image made by red light. When the slide is projected onto a viewing screen, each dye holds back light of its complementary color, and the original colors of the subject appear on the screen.

First Exposure

First Development

WORLD BOOK diagrams

Second Exposure

Color Development and Bleaching

PHOTOGRAPHY 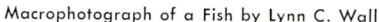 ART

Art in photography depends on the imagination of the photographer. A creative photographer selects and captures qualities in his subject that make the picture artistic rather than commonplace. His subjects can range from the stark, simple beauty of a portrait to the rich colors and fine detail of a scientific photograph of a fish. A creative photographer sees natural beauty such as the shadows, reflections, and colors of a fiord in Norway. He sees the striking pattern of vertical lines and shadows surrounding a boy fishing from a pier. The photographer can control his camera so that the picture blurs, conveying the idea of birds in flight. Or he can use his darkroom equipment creatively to produce a print from several negatives, as in "The Dream Boat." This photograph resembles a Japanese painting. Irving Penn's photograph of a couple in a canoe contains the blurred lines and patches of bright color found in an Impressionist painting.

"The Dream Boat" by Chin-San Long

Macrophotograph of a Fish by Lynn C. Wall

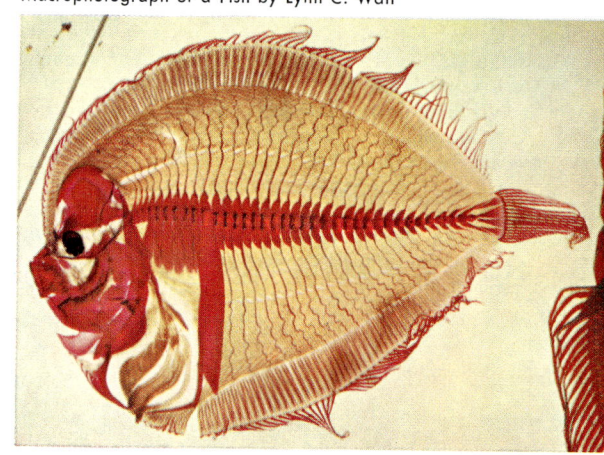

Birds in Flight by Dr. Pedro Galliker

Boy Fishing by Wynn Bullock

Couple in a Canoe by Irving Penn

Portrait by Richard Avedon

Norway Fiord by Ernst Haas

Magnum

PHOTOGRAPHY HISTORY

Beginnings. The camera was probably invented during the early 1500's. Historians have credited the invention to many persons, including the great Italian artist Leonardo da Vinci (1452-1519). The first crude camera was called the *camera obscura* (*dark chamber*). It was a darkened box with a tiny hole in one wall that admitted light. The light formed an image on the opposite wall. This image was an upside-down picture of the scene outside. Artists used the camera obscura as a sketching aid. They traced the lines and shapes of the image, and then colored the picture. See CAMERA OBSCURA.

The first camera obscura was large enough for a man to enter. By the early 1600's, the device was a sedan chair or a tent that artists carried into the countryside to sketch landscapes. During the 1660's, the camera obscura became a box about 2 feet long. A lens placed over the hole made the image larger and sharper. A mirror inside the camera reflected the image onto a piece of ground glass at the top of the camera. This form of the camera obscura resembled today's single-lens reflex camera.

The camera obscura provided a way to project an image onto a screen or a piece of paper. But scientists wanted to find a way to make the images permanent. In 1727, the German physicist Johann H. Schulze (1687-1744) discovered that silver salts are sensitive to light. He proved that light darkens silver salts. Schulze used sunlight to make images on silver salts, but he did not try to make these images permanent.

The first person to make a permanent image was Joseph Nicéphore Niépce (1765-1833), a French physicist. Niépce wanted light to form a permanent image in the camera obscura so that an artist would not have to trace the image. He exposed a light-sensitive metal plate in the camera, and then used an engraving process to "fix" the image. Niépce is credited with "the first photographs made by a camera." A photograph he made in 1826 still exists today.

In the 1830's, the French inventor Louis J. M. Daguerre (1787-1851) produced the first popular form of photography, the *daguerreotype*. Daguerre, who had been Niépce's partner for several years, based his process on Niépce's work. Daguerre exposed a light-sensitive metal plate, and developed the image with mercury vapor. He "fixed" the image with common salt. Daguerre announced his process in 1839, and this date is generally accepted as the beginning of photography. See DAGUERREOTYPE.

Also in 1839, the British scientist William H. F. Talbot (1800-1877) announced that he had invented a light-sensitive paper. This paper, coated with salt and silver nitrate, produced a negative from which positive prints could be made. Talbot's invention was the first negative-positive system of making photographs. His friend, the astronomer Sir John F. W. Herschel (1792-1871) named the invention *photography*. Herschel also suggested the use of sodium thiosulphate (hypo) as a fixing agent. Both Talbot and Daguerre then began using hypo in their processes.

In 1841, Talbot patented the *calotype*, an improved version of his process. He later called it the *talbotype*. Talbot's process was not widely used because the daguerreotype produced a much clearer picture. See TALBOTYPE.

Major Advancements. During the second half of the 1800's, scientists made great technical advances in photographic processes. With improved, easier techniques, more and more persons began to take pictures.

Technical Improvements. Many cameras made after 1840 had better lenses than those in the early camera obscuras. In 1840, a Hungarian scientist, Josef M. Petzval (1807-1891), designed a portrait lens and a landscape lens. The portrait lens transmitted 16 times as much light as previous lenses did. It made shorter

The Camera Obscura of the 1600's was a portable room mounted on poles. A lens covered the hole in each side. In this engraving, the top and front of the camera have been removed to show the artist inside. He is tracing an image cast on transparent paper hanging opposite one of the lenses.

George Eastman House; The Gernsheim Collection

The World's First Photograph, *right,* taken in 1826 by Nicéphore Niépce, shows a view from his window. He exposed a pewter plate 8 hours in a camera obscura. The photograph, lost for many years, was found in a trunk in London in 1952.

exposure times possible. Petzval's landscape lens produced sharper pictures of large areas than had been possible before.

In 1851, Frederick Scott Archer (1813-1857), a British photographer, introduced a new photographic process. He coated a glass plate with a sticky, wet substance called *collodion*. He then dipped the glass in light-sensitive silver salts. The collodion had to remain moist during the exposure and the development of the picture. For this reason, the process was called the *wet-collodion process*, or *wet-plate photography*. The photographer often carried his "darkroom" with him so he could develop the plates before they dried. His equipment usually included a tent that served as a darkroom, plus a camera, glass plates, chemicals, measuring utensils, and trays. He used a wagon to carry all this equipment. In 1856, photographers began using thin metal plates, instead of glass, to hold the collodion emulsion. These plates were called *ferrotypes*, but later became known as *tintypes*.

One of the greatest advancements in photography came in 1871 with the invention of the *dry-plate process*. A British physician, Richard L. Maddox (1816-1902), replaced collodion with gelatin. The gelatin could dry on the plate without harming the silver salts. A photographer no longer needed to carry a darkroom around with him.

In the late 1870's, scientists improved the light-sensitivity of the gelatin emulsion. Early daguerreotypes required an exposure of 10 minutes or more, and the camera had to be mounted on a tripod. Now the emulsion could record an image in 1/25th of a second. With the improved gelatin emulsion, a photographer could hold the camera in his hand and take snapshots.

New Types of Photography began to develop during the 1800's. One of the first photographers to use the camera creatively was Gaspard Felix Tournachon (1820-1910), a Frenchman who called himself Nadar. Nadar stressed the pose and gestures of the person he photographed because he wanted to show the subject's character. Nadar also took the first aerial photographs. In 1856, he photographed Paris from a balloon.

Another early art photographer was Julia M. Cameron (1815-1879), an American. She photographed such famous persons as Charles Darwin, Henry Wadsworth Longfellow, and Alfred, Lord Tennyson. Mrs. Cameron tried to record the spirit and character of each person she photographed. She insisted on taking close-up portraits, and most of her pictures were out of focus. But she captured feeling and character better than most other photographers of her time.

The first war photographs were made in 1855. Roger Fenton (1819-1869), a British photographer, covered the Crimean War for a London newspaper. One of the most famous war photographers of all time was Mathew B. Brady (1823?-1896), an American who covered the Civil War. Brady and his assistants traveled with the Union Army. Most of the Civil War pictures credited to Brady were taken by members of his staff. But Brady organized, directed, and financed the entire project.

In the late 1800's and early 1900's, some photographers tried to do more than just record an event. They used their photographs to persuade and convince. William Henry Jackson (1843-1942), an American, took some of the first pictures of the western United States. His photographs of the Yellowstone area helped persuade Congress to establish Yellowstone National Park.

Two other Americans, Jacob A. Riis (1849-1914) and Lewis W. Hine (1874-1940), used pictures to expose social evils. Riis, a newspaperman, used his photographs to illustrate his news stories about the slums of New York City. His picture stories led to the abolition of Mulberry Bend, one of the city's worst tenement sections (see RIIS, JACOB A.). Hine, a sociologist, exposed the working conditions of the poor. His pictures of children working in dimly-lighted factories and in coal mines led to the passage of child-labor laws.

George Eastman House

Aerial Photography began with Nadar's balloon flight over Paris in 1856. The French artist Honoré Daumier made fun of Nadar in this lithograph, called "Nadar Raising Photography to the Height of Art."

Early Art Photography included portraits by Julia Margaret Cameron. This portrait of Sir John Herschel, taken in 1867, is one of her most dramatic photographs.

Courtesy of The Art Institute of Chicago, Alfred Stieglitz Collection

Denver Public Library, Western Collection

Photographer of the West William Henry Jackson took pictures of yosemite Valley in 1873.

PHOTOGRAPHY ⊙ HISTORY

Photography for Everyone. In 1888, George Eastman (1854-1932), an American dry-plate manufacturer, revolutionized photography by marketing the Kodak camera. The Kodak was a simple snapshot camera that could be used by amateurs. It held a roll of film that made a hundred pictures. After a person had used up the film, he returned the camera with the film still inside to Eastman's company in Rochester, N.Y. The company developed the film and printed the pictures, and returned the camera with a new roll of film in it.

The first roll film consisted of light-sensitive gelatin coated onto a paper backing. After the film had been developed, the gelatin emulsion was transferred from the paper onto a piece of glass. Then prints were made. Transferring the emulsion was difficult, and required too much skill for amateur photographers.

In 1889, Eastman substituted a celluloid base for the paper. Printing photographs became much easier because the gelatin emulsion did not have to be removed from the base. Persons who wished to develop and print their own pictures could buy processing kits. Other persons followed Eastman's slogan: "You press the button, we do the rest." Photography became an international hobby.

During the late 1800's and early 1900's, scientists made other improvements in the tools and processes of photography. They introduced the time-temperature method of developing film, which greatly simplified the development process. They improved camera lenses, developed a precision enlarger, and increased the light-sensitivity of film and printing papers.

In 1924, the Leica camera was marketed in Germany. This miniature camera takes 35-millimeter film, the size used in making motion pictures. Many persons used the new type of camera to take *candid photographs* (pictures taken without the subject's knowledge). In

1929, the electric flashbulb was patented in Germany. Two years later, Harold E. Edgerton (1903-   ), an American engineer, invented electronic flash. Artificial lighting greatly increased the type of subjects that could be photographed.

As photography became more popular with amateurs, professional photographers advanced photography in new ways. A French photographer, Jean-Eugène-Auguste Atget (1856-1927), took photographs of Paris showing the city's people and its historic buildings and statues. In the United States, Alfred Stieglitz (1864-1946) worked to establish photography as a creative art. In 1902, he and some other photographers formed the Photo-Secession, a group active in promoting photography as an art form until about 1910. One member, Edward Steichen (1879-   ), carried on Stieglitz's ideas and sought recognition for photography as art. Steichen organized "The Family of Man" picture exhibit in 1955. It was one of the most popular exhibits ever held.

Lázló Moholy-Nagy (1895-1947), a Hungarian who moved to the United States, made abstract photographs called *photograms*. He placed objects on a piece of printing paper in the darkroom and exposed them with a flashlight. The American photographers Paul Strand (1890-   ) and Edward Weston (1886-1958) took detailed close-up photographs. Among Strand's photographs are large details of machines. Weston revealed the beauty of such natural shapes as peppers and cabbages. Walker Evans (1903-   ) and Dorothea Lange (1895-1965) photographed poverty-stricken farmers in the South during the 1930's.

Henri Cartier-Bresson (1908-   ), a French photographer, used a miniature camera to capture "decisive moments" in people's lives. His success in recording fleeting events and emotions has greatly influenced photo-journalism. Margaret Bourke-White (1906-   ), an American, also produced important works of photo-journalism. Ansel Adams (1902-   ), also of the United

George Eastman House

George Eastman holds one of the first Kodak cameras. The camera, identical with the one that took this picture in 1890, produced a hundred round negatives.

Courtesy of The Art Institute of Chicago, Alfred Stieglitz Collection

Alfred Stieglitz led the movement for creative photography in the early 1900's. He created the atmosphere of "Spring Showers" in this 1902 photograph.

Edward Weston in his "Halved Cabbage" shows his style of emphasizing textures and sharp, clean lines.

Edward Weston

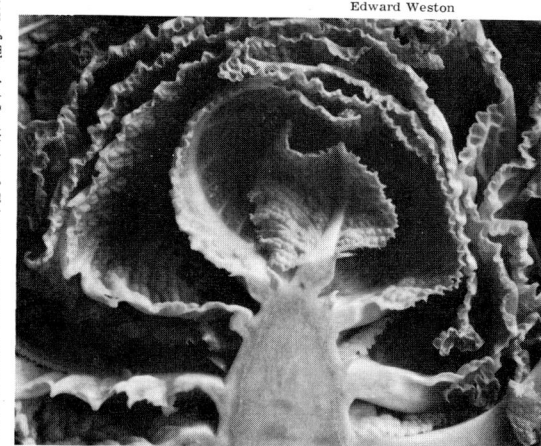

States, specialized in photographing scenes of nature, especially the mountains and deserts of the West.

Photography Today. Cameras and photographic equipment are both becoming more and more automatic. Many of today's cameras have built-in exposure meters that automatically set the camera's controls (see CAMERA [Recent Developments]). Many darkrooms also have automatic features. *Dry darkrooms* are equipped with machines that in 10 seconds can produce a print that is 80 per cent dry.

The Polaroid camera produces a print from black-and-white film in 10 seconds. This process, introduced in 1947, makes it possible for persons to make their own pictures without using a darkroom.

The number of photographers who use color increases every year. Manufacturers are developing simpler methods of processing color film so that amateur photographers can develop their own color pictures. A color processing machine, introduced in 1963, produces a color print in seven minutes. Also in 1963, the Polaroid Corporation produced a color film for the Polaroid camera that develops itself in about 60 seconds.

Photography is taking an increasingly important place in many fields of science. Special high-speed cameras can show the tiny hummingbird in flight. These cameras can also reveal information about the path of a bullet as it leaves a gun. Underwater cameras unlock the secrets of a sunken ship, or let scientists study the ocean floor. Infrared film that penetrates haze permits photography at high altitudes. When mounted on a telescope, the camera provides detailed and permanent records of the stars and planets (see PHYSICS [Science Project: Photographing The Vapor Trails]). A camera attached to a microscope can take enlarged pictures of many of the tiniest cells, atoms, and bacteria (see MICROSCOPE [Science Project: Making Photomicrographs]).

Photography has an important part in military and police work. Aerial photographs are necessary in the preparation of maps for any military action. These photographs are made with highly specialized cameras in airplanes. The use of aerial photography to make maps of ground areas is called *photogrammetry*. Police officials use photography when investigating almost any crime. They need photographic records of the place where the crime was committed. Pictures of a body, a broken window, or a damaged safe are used as evidence in many court trials. Pictures of fingerprints provide a valuable clue to the identity of criminals. Photographers use infrared and ultraviolet films to make burned documents readable, and to detect forgeries or illegal erasures on documents. These films record infrared or ultraviolet light that the eye cannot see.

FAMOUS FIRSTS IN PHOTOGRAPHY

1826 Joseph Nicéphore Niépce made the first permanent photograph with a camera.

1839 Louis J. M. Daguerre announced his daguerreotype process, the first practical photographic method.

1839 William H. F. Talbot announced his invention of a negative-positive process of making photographs.

1851 Frederick Scott Archer introduced the wet-collodion process, using glass plates to hold the emulsion.

1861 Mathew B. Brady produced the first of his famous photographs of the Civil War.

1871 Richard L. Maddox introduced the dry-plate process, replacing collodion with gelatin.

1888 George Eastman introduced the Kodak camera, which made photography available to millions of persons.

1924 The Leica camera went on the market, and started the candid camera craze.

1931 Harold E. Edgerton invented electronic flash.

1935 Eastman Kodak Company introduced Kodachrome film.

1942 Eastman Kodak introduced Kodacolor film.

1947 Edwin Land introduced his Polaroid Land Camera, beginning a new technique of 60-second photography.

1963 The Polaroid Corporation marketed a color film that develops itself in the camera in about 60 seconds.

Margaret Bourke-White, *Life* © 1946 Time Inc.

Margaret Bourke-White produces dynamic picture stories for major news magazines. Her subjects range from World War II battle scenes to a jet airplane breaking the sound barrier. She took this photograph of Mohandas Gandhi, the famous spiritual and political leader of India, in 1930.

Arthur Siegel

Arthur Siegel, an American free-lance photographer, specializes in picture stories for national business and picture magazines. He is also noted for his experimental work in color photography.

380m

PHOTOGRAPHY ⬡ CAREERS

Photography offers a wide variety of interesting careers. A young person interested in a career in photography should have a general academic education. His knowledge of photography should extend beyond the technical knowledge of taking pictures. Some colleges and universities offer courses in photography for students studying journalism, fine arts, science, or engineering. A few colleges, and some art and technical institutes, give courses that lead to a bachelor's degree in photography. Information about careers in photography can be obtained from Professional Photographers of America, Inc., 1090 Executive Way, Oakleaf Commons, Des Plaines, Ill. 60018.

Commercial Photography. The pictures taken by a commercial photographer are usually used for advertising. He photographs many different subjects, including machines, buildings, food, and persons performing various tasks.

Portraiture. A portrait photographer must understand and like people because he photographs important events in their lives. Some portrait photographers specialize in one type of portraiture, such as photographing weddings or children. A portrait photographer must know how to pose and light his subjects, and how to retouch negatives to correct unattractive blemishes.

Advertising Photograph by Les Tirschel

Scientific Photograph: Honey Ant by Ross E. Hutchins

News Photograph: "D-Day Invasion" from *Images of War* by Robert Capa

Magnum

Photojournalism. A photojournalist, or *press photographer*, takes pictures for newspapers and magazines. He must know how to seek out and record dramatic action in such activities as sports and politics. Some photojournalists take pictures that try to influence the public. These pictures may show the need for better homes in slum areas or for less crowded classrooms in schools. A photojournalist who works for a news magazine often prepares picture stories. He creates a story in his mind, and tells it with pictures.

Science Photography. Photographic careers in science are increasing in number and importance. *Photographic engineering* is a new branch of photography. A photographic engineer works closely with scientists and engineers. He may prepare a complete series of photographs on the launching of a guided missile so that scientists can study each step in the launching. Or he may photograph the parts of a machine to show how they work.

Other Careers. Photography offers careers for researchers in photographic materials, chemistry, and optics. Persons interested in darkroom work hold jobs in photofinishing laboratories. The industry also needs business administrators and persons to sell photographic supplies. Other careers are open to persons who can teach photography or write about it.   CLIFTON C. EDOM

PHOTOGRAPHY STUDY AIDS

Related Articles in WORLD BOOK include:

BIOGRAPHIES

Bourke-White, Margaret	Lumière (family)
Brady, Mathew B.	Niépce, Joseph N.
Daguerre, Louis J. M.	Riis, Jacob A.
Eastman, George	Stanley (family)
Edgerton, Harold E.	Steichen, Edward
Fairchild, Sherman M.	Stieglitz, Alfred
Herschel (Sir John F. W.)	Talbot, William H. F.
Land, Edwin H.	

PHOTOGRAPHIC APPLICATIONS

Blueprint	Microfilm	Photogrammetry
Daguerreotype	Motion Picture	Photographic
Filmstrip	Photoengraving	Copying
Halftone	and Photo-	Photomicrography
Hologram	lithography	Talbotype

PHOTOGRAPHIC EQUIPMENT

Airbrush	Light Meter
Camera	Projection
Camera Obscura	Machine
Flashbulb	Stereoscope

OTHER RELATED ARTICLES

Astronomy	Eastman Kodak	Modeling
Ballistics	Company	Photographic So-
(picture)	Infrared Rays	ciety of America

Outline

I. **Taking Good Snapshots**
  A. The Parts of a Camera
  B. Using Box Cameras
  C. Common Mistakes
  D. Lighting
  E. Composition
II. **Adjustable Cameras**
  A. The Shutter
  B. The Lens Aperture
  C. Focusing
  D. Exposure
III. **Accessories**
  A. Filters
  B. Exposure Meters
  C. Artificial Lighting
  D. Special Lenses
IV. **Developing Film**
  A. Developing Your Own Film
  B. Problem Negatives
V. **Contact Printing**
VI. **Enlarging**
VII. **Printing Papers**
VIII. **Choosing Black-and-White Film**
IX. **Color Photography**
  A. Color Film
  B. Developing Color Film
X. **Photography as Art**
XI. **History**
XII. **Careers**

Questions

How are filters used in photography?

In what two ways can you increase depth of field in taking a picture?

How does the emulsion of color film differ from the emulsion of black-and-white film?

What is a *filter factor?* an *ASA number?*

What is meant by *exposure?*

Why does the image on film become negative during development? Why does printing reverse the image?

Why was the dry-plate process easier than the wet-plate process?

What are the functions of the shutter? The diaphragm? When should *flash fill-in* be used?

In what two ways did George Eastman help make amateur photography possible?

Books for Beginning Photographers

Many inexpensive instruction booklets for the beginner are available at camera stores.

EASTMAN KODAK COMPANY. *How to Make Good Pictures.* 31st ed. The Company, Rochester, N.Y., 1965. The Eastman Kodak Company also publishes up-to-date booklets on specific aspects of photography, such as *How to Make and Use a Pin Hole Camera.* These booklets are available from the company or camera dealers.

KOHN, EUGENE. *Photography: A Manual for Shutterbugs.* Prentice-Hall, 1965.

MARSHALL, LUCILE R. *Photography for Teen-Agers.* 2nd ed. Prentice-Hall, 1957.

MILLER, THOMAS H., AND BRUMMITT, WYATT. *This Is Photography: Its Means and Ends.* Garden City, 1959.

SUSSMAN, AARON. *The Amateur Photographer's Handbook.* 7th ed. Crowell, 1965.

ZIM, HERBERT, AND BURNETT, R. W. *Photography: The Amateur's Guide to Better Pictures.* Rev. ed. Golden Press, 1964.

Books for Advanced Photographers

BOMBACK, EDWARD S. *Manual of Colour Photography.* Fountain Press, 1965.

BRUCE, HELEN F. *Your Guide to Photography.* Barnes, 1965.

DAUGHERTY, CHARLES M. *Mirror with a Memory: The Art of Photography.* Harcourt, 1959.

FEININGER, ANDREAS. *The Complete Photographer.* Prentice-Hall, 1965.

HIGHLAND, HAROLD J. *Audel's Guide to Creative Photography.* Audel, 1960.

LOOTENS, JOSEPH C. *On Photographic Enlarging and Print Quality.* 5th ed., rev. & enl. Garden City, 1958.

NEBLETTE, CARROLL B. *Photography: Its Materials and Processes.* 6th ed. Van Nostrand, 1962.

NEWHALL, BEAUMONT. *The History of Photography from 1839 to the Present Day.* Rev. ed. 1964. Museum of Modern Art, 1964.

PHOTOLITHOGRAPHY. See LITHOGRAPHY.

PHOTOMETER. See LIGHT METER.

PHOTOMICROGRAPHY

PHOTOMICROGRAPHY, *FOH toh my KRAHG ruh fih,* is the art of recording enlarged images by replacing the eyepiece of a microscope with a camera. A picture taken in this manner often reveals more than the eye can see. Color filters are used to emphasize particular structures. Ultraviolet light may bring out otherwise invisible details. See also SNOW (pictures).   PETER GRAY

PHOTON, *FOE tahn,* is a unit, or bundle, of electromagnetic radiation. In 1901, the German physicist Max Planck suggested that radiation consists of bundles of energy. He called these bundles *quanta.* They were later called photons. Planck suggested that the energy of each photon is proportional to the frequency of the radiation. In 1905, Albert Einstein used Planck's quantum theory to explain the *photoelectric effect,* the emission of electrons from a metal when it is struck by photons. See also QUANTUM THEORY. CLARENCE E. BENNETT

PHOTOPERIODISM, *foe toh PEER ee od iz'm,* is the response of a plant or animal to the relative length of light and darkness to which it is exposed. Variations in light and dark affect such activities as the migration of birds and the falling of leaves.

Plants are of three photoperiodic types. *Short-day plants* flower only if exposed to light for less than a certain length of time each day. *Long-day plants* need a daily light period that is longer than a certain minimum time. *Day-neutral plants* bloom in either short or long photoperiods. In short- and long-day plants, the length of the dark period seems to be more important than that of the light period. Light influences on *phytochrome,* a bluish pigment, apparently cause photoperiodic behavior in plants.   ARTHUR W. GALSTON

See also PLANT (How Plants Are Dependent on Light).

PHOTOSPHERE. See SUN (Parts of the Sun).

PHOTOSTAT. See PHOTOGRAPHIC COPYING.

PHOTOSYNTHESIS, *foe toe SIN thee siss,* is a food-making process that occurs in green plants. It is the chief function of leaves. It also occurs in certain bacteria called *photosynthetic bacteria.* The word *photosynthesis* means *putting together with light.* Green plants combine energy from light with water and carbon dioxide to make food. All our food comes from this important energy-converting activity of green plants. Food energy originally comes from light and is stored in food made by green plants. Animals eat the plants, and human beings eat animal products as well as plants.

The light used in photosynthesis is absorbed by a green pigment called *chlorophyll.* In plant cells, chlorophyll is contained in bodies called *chloroplasts.* In photosynthetic bacteria, chlorophyll is held in similar, but much smaller, bodies called *chromatophores.*

In chloroplasts, light causes carbon dioxide to combine with the hydrogen atoms of water to form sugar. Oxygen is given off in the process. From sugar, and with nitrogen, sulfur, and phosphorus, green plants make starch, fat, protein, and vitamins. In photosynthetic bacteria, carbon dioxide reacts with compounds other than water to form sugar. No oxygen is released.

Green plants convert carbon dioxide and water into food and oxygen. Both food and oxygen are essential for the life of human beings, animals, and nongreen plants such as fungi. Human beings and animals get energy by eating food and using oxygen in the air to "burn" food. In the process, carbon dioxide and water are returned to the atmosphere. Thus, the carbon and oxygen balance on earth is maintained.   MELVIN CALVIN

See also BIOCHEMISTRY; CARBON DIOXIDE; CHLOROPHYLL; LEAF (The Leaf as a Food "Factory").

PHOTOTROPISM. See PLANT (How Plants Are Dependent on Light).

PHOTOTYPESETTING. See PRINTING (Setting the Type).

PHRENIC NERVE. See DIAPHRAGM.

PHRENOLOGY, *free NAHL oh jih,* is a pseudoscience which attempts to read character from the shape of a person's head. It developed from the progress made in anatomy and physiology in the early 1800's. The founder of phrenology, Franz J. Gall, had learned the

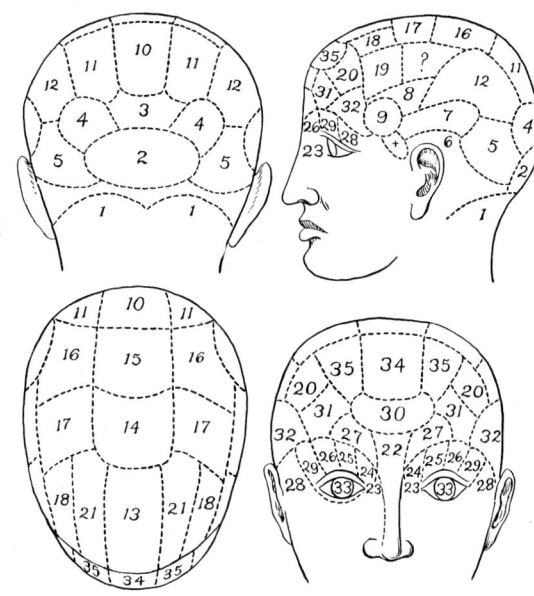

A Phrenological Chart shows the supposed relation of personal abilities, talents, and emotions to the shape of the head. Below is the key to the chart.

AFFECTIVE

(I) PROPENSITIES	(II) SENTIMENTS
(1) Amativeness	(10) Self-esteem
(2) Philoprogenitive- ness	(11) Love of approbation
(3) Inhabitativeness or concentrativeness	(12) Cautiousness
(4) Adhesiveness	(13) Benevolence
(5) Combativeness	(14) Veneration
(6) Destructiveness and alimentiveness	(15) Firmness
(7) Secretiveness	(16) Conscientiousness
(8) Acquisitiveness	(17) Hope
(9) Constructiveness	(18) Wonder
	(19) Ideality
	(20) Wit
	(21) Imitation

INTELLECTUAL

(I) PERCEPTIVE	
(22) Individuality	(30) Eventuality
(23) Form	(31) Time
(24) Size	(32) Tune
(25) Weight	(33) Language
(26) Coloring	
(27) Locality	
(28) Number	(II) REFLECTIVE
(29) Order	(34) Comparison
	(35) Causality

anatomy of the brain. Based on this knowledge, he claimed that mental qualities were associated with physical characteristics.

In phrenology the different parts of the brain are supposed to be the seats of certain qualities and functions. Gall first noticed that men with certain bumps, or prominences, on their heads had certain definite qualities. He observed the heads of students, and thought that he could feel the "organ" of *number* in mathematicians, the organ of *tune* in musicians, and the organ of *reverence* in devout churchgoers. He also decided that a certain bump gave poets their skill and that other bumps made men thieves or murderers. He claimed the insane had skulls of certain shapes.

Scientists say that this division of the brain into special areas is unscientific. The shape of the brain itself cannot even be determined from the shape of the skull. The sciences of physiology and psychology have shown that different portions of the brain do have certain functions, but these usually merely receive sensory stimuli and relate them to action. Man does not yet know enough about the brain to show what causes the differences between persons. The knowledge we have tends to disprove phrenology.   JOHN MULHOLLAND

See also GALL, FRANZ JOSEPH.

PHRIXUS. See HELLESPONT.

PHRYGIA, *FRIJ ih uh,* was an ancient country between the Mediterranean Sea and the Black Sea, in what is now central Turkey. The Phrygians were an Indo-European people who came from southeastern Europe after 1200 B.C. and settled in lands once ruled by the Hittites. Legends tell that the early Phrygian kings included Gordius and Midas, whose great rock tombs may still be seen in the mountains. See GORDIAN KNOT; MIDAS.

Cimmerians—invaders from around the Caucasus Mountains—conquered Phrygia about 700 B.C. Phrygian communities still existed to about 550 B.C. The Phrygians later came under Persian, Greek, and then Roman rule. The Phrygians were known for their art and ceramics, and skill in tomb-building. They contributed many Oriental ideas to the early Greeks, especially in music. The Romans adopted the Phrygian worship of the goddess Cybele, the Great Mother of the Gods.   LOUIS L. ORLIN

PHTHISIS. See TUBERCULOSIS.

PHYFE, *fife,* **DUNCAN** (1768-1854), an American cabinetmaker and furniture designer, won fame for the artistic beauty of his furniture. Gracefully proportioned, his furniture was also soundly constructed. Phyfe used reeding, and incorporated flat carvings of leaves, cornucopias, and wheat ears in his ornamentation. Lyre supports and brass ornaments distinguished his designs. His earliest designs came from the Sheraton and Hepplewhite styles, but later ones were influenced by the Empire style. Phyfe's favorite wood was mahogany, but he often used exotic woods for inlay. Phyfe was born in Scotland. He settled first in Albany, N.Y., and in 1790 moved to New York City.   OTTO V. HULA

See also FURNITURE (Duncan Phyfe).

PHYLLOXERA, *FILL AHK sir uh,* is any one of a group of small plant lice. They feed on trees and shrubs.

One of the most important kinds of phylloxera is the *grape phylloxera.* This insect sucks the sap from the leaves and roots of grapevines, causing *galls* (swellings). The damage to the root stunts and often kills the vine. The grape phylloxera is native to the eastern United States. The vines in this region resist them, but the insect does much damage in the western United States and in Europe. It is controlled by grafting the vines to rootstock from the eastern United States and by periodically flooding or fumigating the soil.

The life cycle of the grape phylloxera lasts two years. Fertilized eggs are laid under the bark of the vine in the fall. In the spring, these eggs hatch into wingless young that move to the leaves to feed. They lay unfertilized eggs which soon hatch. Several of these generations are produced during the summer. In the fall, the young insects move to the roots and hibernate there during the winter. During the next spring and summer they feed on the roots and produce young from unfertilized eggs. As fall approaches, winged insects are produced that lay eggs in other vines. After these eggs hatch, the insects mate, the females lay fertilized eggs, and the cycle repeats.

USDA

Tiny Phylloxera, a form of plant lice, attack the leaves and roots of grapevines.

Scientific Classification. Phylloxera are in the aphid family, *Aphidae.* The grape phylloxera is genus *Phylloxera,* species *P. vitifoliae.*   DONALD J. BORROR

PHYLUM, *FYE lum,* is a unit of scientific classification. Animals and plants are classified in seven major groups called kingdoms, phyla, classes, orders, families, genera, and species. Members of a phylum are more closely related than are members of a kingdom. But members of a phylum are not so closely related as are members of a class.   WILLIAM V. MAYER

See also CLASSIFICATION (table).

PHYSIATRICS. See MEDICINE (table: Kinds of Medical Specialty Fields); PHYSICAL THERAPY.

PHYSICAL CHANGE is a change of matter from one form to another without any change in its chemical structure, solubility, color, taste, or odor. When a piece of wood is made into sawdust, the change is a *physical change.* If the piece of wood were burned, the wood would turn into new substances, ash and gases, and the change would be chemical. Another example of a physical change is the melting of ice to water. Physical changes sometimes require energy, as when water is changed to steam by heat.   CLARENCE E. BENNETT

PHYSICAL CHEMISTRY is the study of the general rules and principles that govern the chemical properties of matter. Students of physical chemistry study such problems as how and why atoms join together in molecules; how atoms and molecules form gases, liquids, and solids; and how electricity is related to chemistry. Students usually study physical chemistry after getting a thorough background in physics, mathematics, and general chemistry.   WALTER J. MOORE

PHYSICAL DEFECT. See HANDICAPPED.

PHYSICAL EDUCATION

PHYSICAL EDUCATION forms an important part of the modern program of general education. It includes physical activities and sports of all kinds designed to improve posture, physical development, and general fitness and health. Physical education also provides fun and recreation. Programs in physical education cover a wide variety of activities. These include dancing, swimming, lifesaving, exercises, camping, and dozens of sports such as archery, golf, tennis, baseball, basketball, soccer, wrestling, and boxing.

School Programs

In Elementary Schools, physical-education programs usually include physical examinations, rhythmics (exercises done to music), a few simple tests of posture and physical ability, and games designed to improve physical coordination. Some elementary schools provide swimming instruction. Physical-education programs for grade-school students emphasize basic instruction. But some competitive games may be added after school hours. Elementary schools usually have few physical-education instructors and generally lack gymnasiums and other facilities. For this reason, their activities are limited to beginning essentials that can be taught to large groups. Elementary-school programs also give students an understanding of courtesy, cooperation, sportsmanship, and team play.

In High Schools, physical-education programs center on organized games, especially basketball, football, baseball, soccer, and field hockey. Physical-education instructors in high school consider participation in track and field and swimming basic for all students, boys and girls alike. Almost all high schools give some training in these sports.

Many high schools also include calisthenics, gymnastics, and various fitness tests in their physical-education programs. Instructors teach health and safety, including the principles of hygiene, nutrition, and general physical care. Sportsmanship is also emphasized, along with desirable personality traits and character qualities. Many high schools have organized intramural sports programs, as well as varsity competition between schools.

In Universities and Colleges, physical-education programs are divided into two main parts—basic instruction and intramural sports. *Basic instruction* includes classes in health, safety, first aid, and hygiene, as well as training in individual sports and activities. *Intramural sports* include competition among various campus groups in such sports as baseball and basketball.

College physical-education programs usually include a testing program to determine the physical fitness of each student. Instructors advise the students on their needs, and help them develop their fitness. Most colleges and universities require students to take two years of physical education. Grades are given on the basis of knowledge, attitude, sportsmanship, and general fitness.

Development of Physical Education

Physical education is one of the newest subjects in the modern educational program. But it is one of the oldest forms of education. Physical training has always been fashioned to the culture of the people and of the age. For example, the Spartans stressed physical training in order to make better soldiers. During the Renaissance, physical education was encouraged as a necessary part of developing a complete personality.

Early History. Primitive peoples taught their children only familiar activities. Instruction came mostly from friends and relatives, and was highly informal. Boys learned how to become better warriors and hunters. Girls learned domestic skills, such as gardening, weaving, and making pottery.

Programs for physical education became more formal as civilizations grew. The Greeks developed a complete and systematic program, and made it a part of their general educational system. They opened gymnasiums so that people could exercise. Greek physical education stressed athletics. The Greeks also sponsored festivals where citizens could display their physical strength to the public. The Olympic Games grew from this system (see OLYMPIC GAMES). Music and art accompanied all activities as a part of the sports festival.

For the Romans, physical education served only as training for war. It developed the bodies of soldiers for military purposes, but it made no attempt to develop the health of the general public.

Most organized physical education during the Middle Ages trained men for battle. From the 1000's to the 1500's, knights clashed in tournaments and jousts throughout Western Europe. These tests of fighting skill rank with the ancient Greek Olympic Games as being among the greatest athletic spectacles of all time.

The Renaissance and Reformation brought important changes in physical education. This age saw the change from the medieval to the modern world. Some educators combined physical with mental training. Schools gave instruction not only in classical subjects, but also in dancing, riding, fencing, swimming, wrestling, archery, running, jumping, and ball games.

In Modern Times, Germany became one of the first countries to develop a systematic program for physical education. Guts Muths (1759-1839) wrote about the health value of including gymnastics in every educational program. In Dessau, in 1774, Johann Basedow opened a school that combined physical exercise and mental education. About 1800, Friedrich Ludwig Jahn promoted a national movement for gymnastics. Later, Adolph Spiess introduced Jahn's teaching into the German school system. The German system of gymnastics featured much apparatus, including parallel bars, horizontal bars, climbing ladders, and the side and long horse. Activities that were added later included handball, soccer, track running, and cross-country running. Military men considered swimming instruction as a basic requirement.

Early in the 1800's, a similar movement began in Sweden under the influence of Per Henrik Ling and his son, Hjalmar. The Swedish system attempted to increase the physical development of young persons. This system of exercise stressed *postural* positions, or positions that were fixed and held by command and signals. The Swedish system spread throughout the world, and is recognized as the best method for developing weak muscles and correcting faulty posture among large groups of youths. Later, the stall bars, balance beam, the swinging pole, vaulting, the long horse, and the buck were added to the Swedish system.

Parade Magazine

High-School Physical Education Courses include such activities, *clockwise*, as: badminton, basketball, field hockey, modern
dancing, tennis, volleyball, softball, archery, tumbling, ballroom
dancing, and, on the mat in the center, wrestling.

Denmark later broke away from the stiff, postural
work of Ling and his followers. Niels Bukh developed
the Danish system, which stresses easy-flowing movement, continuous flexibility, grace, and stamina. The
Danish system became widely used for general conditioning and limbering-up exercises.

England had developed a physical-education program
during the 1800's. This system included some of the
methods used in Germany and Sweden, but it placed
great stress on sports and games, rather than on organized gymnastics. These activities developed a person
physically, as well as providing a source of enjoyment
and recreation.

The sports and games included swimming, cricket,
rugby, soccer, tennis, and rowing. The system seldom
employed instructors in physical education, and the
students organized their own activities. Many features
of the English system came to the United States in the
late 1800's.

Physical Education in the United States. Systematic
physical education in the United States began during
the 1870's, when colleges such as Amherst, Harvard,
and Yale developed programs that stressed the importance of physical development and personal hygiene.
Many activities centered around pulley weights, medicine balls, and strength tests. Later, colleges held
strength-test competitions. Similar competitions developed in high schools. As the system developed, games
and sports received the most emphasis, but students
were also given considerable instruction in the funda-

mentals of games, hygiene, and good sportsmanship.

During World War I, men in the armed forces of the
United States received instruction in recreational
games, boxing, wrestling, and swimming. A great demand for more physical education came after the war,
when the public learned that almost half of the nation's
young men were unfit for combat service. By the late
1930's, 44 states had passed laws requiring instruction
in physical education. Today, physical education plays
an important part in every school program. Adult
groups in many schools, industries, and professions
recognize the need for adult physical education programs. By 1960, more than 200 institutions offered
graduate work in the field.

Careers in Physical Education

Specialists in physical education have many career
opportunities, including positions as physical instructors, athletic directors, athletic coaches, directors of
playgrounds, and directors of youth and recreational
organizations. Specialists must have a bachelor's degree
in physical education.   T. K. Cureton, Jr.

Related Articles in World Book include:

Acrobatics	Health
Amusements	Isometric Contraction
Camping	Jahn, Friedrich Ludwig
Dumbbell	Play
Exercise	Recreation
Game	Safety
Gymnasium	Sports and Sportsmanship
Gymnastics	Tournament

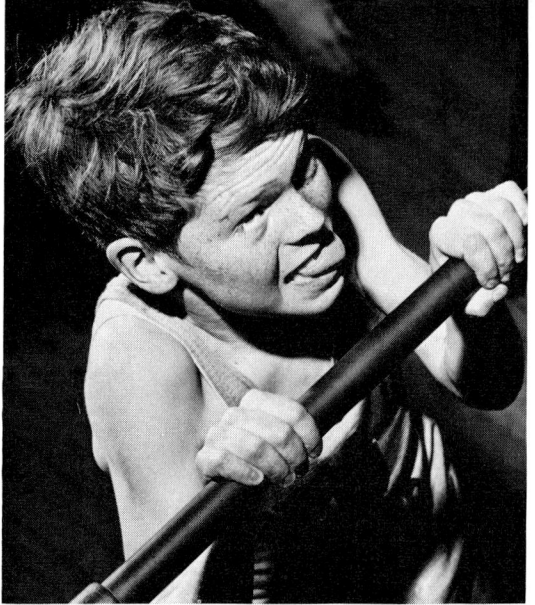

The Milwaukee Journal

PHYSICAL FITNESS is the ability to demonstrate vigorous physical action. It includes endurance, power, strength, and agility. A person who is physically fit has the ability to combine these traits into smooth, effective action both at work and in play.

Aspects of Physical Fitness

Physical fitness cannot always be measured accurately, because fitness includes mental as well as bodily activity, and varies according to age. Many professional persons have different views on physical fitness, and on the emphasis it should receive. But all these views regard physical fitness as desirable. To most physicians, physical fitness means the ability to resist infection and remain healthy. For many nutritionists, physical fitness means that the body receives proper and sufficient nourishment. Mental hygienists and religious leaders regard physical fitness as only one of the many roads leading to clean, righteous living. Physical educators emphasize actual physical ability in sports, work, and physical tests.

Physical Fitness and Body Build. Certain body types appear better suited for physical fitness than others.

For example, the best athletes are usually tall, lean, fast, and well muscled. Physical fitness is not easily developed in persons who tend to be extremely fat or thin, or in those who have poor muscular coordination. But persons of all body types can greatly improve their fitness with the proper training exercises. The actual degree of fitness depends largely on the kind and amount of physical training a person receives over a long period of time.

Physical Fitness and Age. The basic traits of physical fitness improve steadily after the age of 6. In girls, fitness begins to level off at 14. In boys, it levels off at 17. A person generally becomes less physically fit after the age of 25, but he can delay complete unfitness by exercising and by participating in various sports. Persons who do not have some type of daily exercise, whether at work or play, tend to lose their fitness before the age of 25. Lack of exercise often leads to poor posture and nervousness, and accounts for much of the muscular soreness that generally comes from bodily exertion.

Physical Fitness and Health. In general, there is a close relationship between a person's health and his physical fitness. For example, muscular activity aids bodily functions, such as digestion and removal of waste. Educators recognize that children need muscular activity if they are to grow properly. For this reason, most schools have a required program of physical education for students (see PHYSICAL EDUCATION [School Programs]).

Physical fitness also contributes to a person's mental health. Compared to physically unfit persons, physically fit persons tend to be more relaxed, more confident, and more determined to face difficult physical tasks. Physical educators regard sportsmanship, fair play, and social adjustment as necessary parts of any physical-fitness program.

Developing Physical Fitness

Activities for Physical Fitness include many types of exercises. The effectiveness of the exercises depends on how rigorously and regularly they are performed. In general, easy exercises do not develop physical fitness. Physical educators believe that fitness comes after a steady buildup from relatively easy to harder exercises. Activities that lead to physical fitness include swim-

U.S. Marine Corps

Group Drill Exercises, such as those used by the marines, are excellent for improving all-around physical condition.

ming, climbing, running, calisthenics, and acrobatics.

In general, an effective fitness program includes many activities, rather than stressing only one. Some exercises, such as skating, rowing, and skiing, are good for all-around flexibility and body building. Other exercises help develop strength and resistance by using pulley weights, medicine balls, treadmills, rowing machines, and specially built bicycles.

Some exercises are designed to increase stamina. In one program, for example, a person does three different exercises, one after the other. He rows, runs, and swims, each from 10 to 30 minutes, depending on the stage of training. For effective, all-around fitness, many persons participate in their favorite sport from three to five times a week.

Contrary to popular belief, many sports develop little or no fitness, either because they are not practiced often enough or because they are not strenuous enough. These sports include golf, bowling, volleyball, shuffleboard, and baseball. Also, different sports develop only certain parts of the body. Basketball and soccer develop the legs, but not the arms. Gymnastic exercises develop the arms and shoulders, but not the legs. Swimming makes little use of the weight-bearing muscles. In running, the legs bear almost the entire burden of the body's weight. See EXERCISE.

Causes of Unfitness. Physical unfitness has many causes. Some persons simply refuse to take part in any type of physical activity, even walking. Others become unfit at the dinner table, either by eating and drinking too much, or by not eating enough of the right kind of foods (see NUTRITION; WEIGHT CONTROL). Other persons believe they are too busy to be bothered with physical recreation. As a result, their physical and intellectual life lacks balance.

Goals for Physical Fitness. Most persons do not intentionally become physically unfit. They do not realize that at any age physical fitness needs a plan of some kind. Every person should have a definite plan for developing and maintaining his physical fitness. Keeping fit is one of the best ways to resist the strains of everyday life. A plan should involve several patterns of physical training, and should recognize that persons have different requirements at various ages. Teen-age children can participate in several vigorous sports and recreational activities. Older persons can combine calisthenics with exercises such as walking, rowing, and swimming.

Moderation in living habits is also important for physical fitness to be acquired and maintained. Exercise should be sufficient to keep the weight within reasonable limits. A physician can best recommend the most useful fitness program for older persons or persons who are ill.   T. K. CURETON, JR.

Related Articles in WORLD BOOK include:

Acrobatics	Isometric Contraction
Exercise	Physical Education
Game	Play
Gymnasium	Recreation
Gymnastics	Sports and Sportsmanship
Health	Weight Lifting
Hiking	

PHYSICAL GEOGRAPHY. See GEOGRAPHY (Divisions).

PHYSICAL SCIENCE. See ASTRONOMY; CHEMISTRY; PHYSICS.

PHYSICAL THERAPY, also known as *physiotherapy*, is the use of any physical agent to treat a disease or injury. It is part of the branch of medicine called physical medicine and rehabilitation. Doctors who specialize in this branch of medicine are called *physiatrists*. They usually direct and supervise all treatment. The treatments themselves are often given by specially trained persons called *physical therapists*.

Uses of Physical Therapy. Physical therapy is helpful in many kinds of diseases and disabilities. For example, it is often used in poliomyelitis, multiple sclerosis, heart diseases, and various types of paralysis and muscle weaknesses. It is also important in amputations, fractures and other injuries, and orthopedic conditions. With the aid of physical therapy, a disabled person can regain a constructive and creative life.

Aids in Physical Therapy. Many different kinds of physical equipment, exercises, and self-help devices are used to help the disabled person. Radiant heat lamps, electric heating pads, and paraffin baths are used to apply heat. When heat is applied to the body tissues, it relieves pain, improves circulation, and relaxes muscles. Cold, when used soon after injury, lessens pain, hemorrhage, and swelling. Ultraviolet radiation kills germs and promotes healing. Ultrasound is used to treat inflammatory conditions of the joints and nerves, and painful amputation stumps.

Exercise helps to maintain or improve body function and posture. It increases muscle tone, strength, and endurance. Some exercises can be done by the patient himself. For others, the patient might need the help of the doctor or therapist. Often mechanical devices are used. These include parallel bars, stationary bicycles, pulleys and weights, and dumbbells.

Self-help devices such as splints, braces, crutches, and wheel chairs help disabled persons perform their daily living activities. Doctors and therapists train persons to use these devices and to develop confidence in accomplishing daily tasks.

Careers in Physical Therapy. Persons who want to be physical therapists can take one of two kinds of educational programs. One program, for high-school graduates, leads to a bachelor's degree. Studies include courses in the humanities and sciences. It also includes professional subjects, such as the theory and practice of physical therapy. The other program is for college graduates. It consists of 12 to 18 months of intensive professional education.

Some states require that physical therapists be licensed or registered before they may practice. Physical therapists work in hospitals, schools for the handicapped, and clinics.

The American Physical Therapy Association is a national organization for physical therapists. Its aim is to maintain the professional standards. It publishes the official professional journal, *The Physical Therapy Review*, each month.   LOUIS B. NEWMAN

Related Articles in WORLD BOOK include:

Baths and Bathing	Hydrotherapy
(Medicinal Bathing)	Sound (Ultrasound)
Diathermy	Ultraviolet Rays
Exercise	

PHYSICIAN. See MEDICINE.

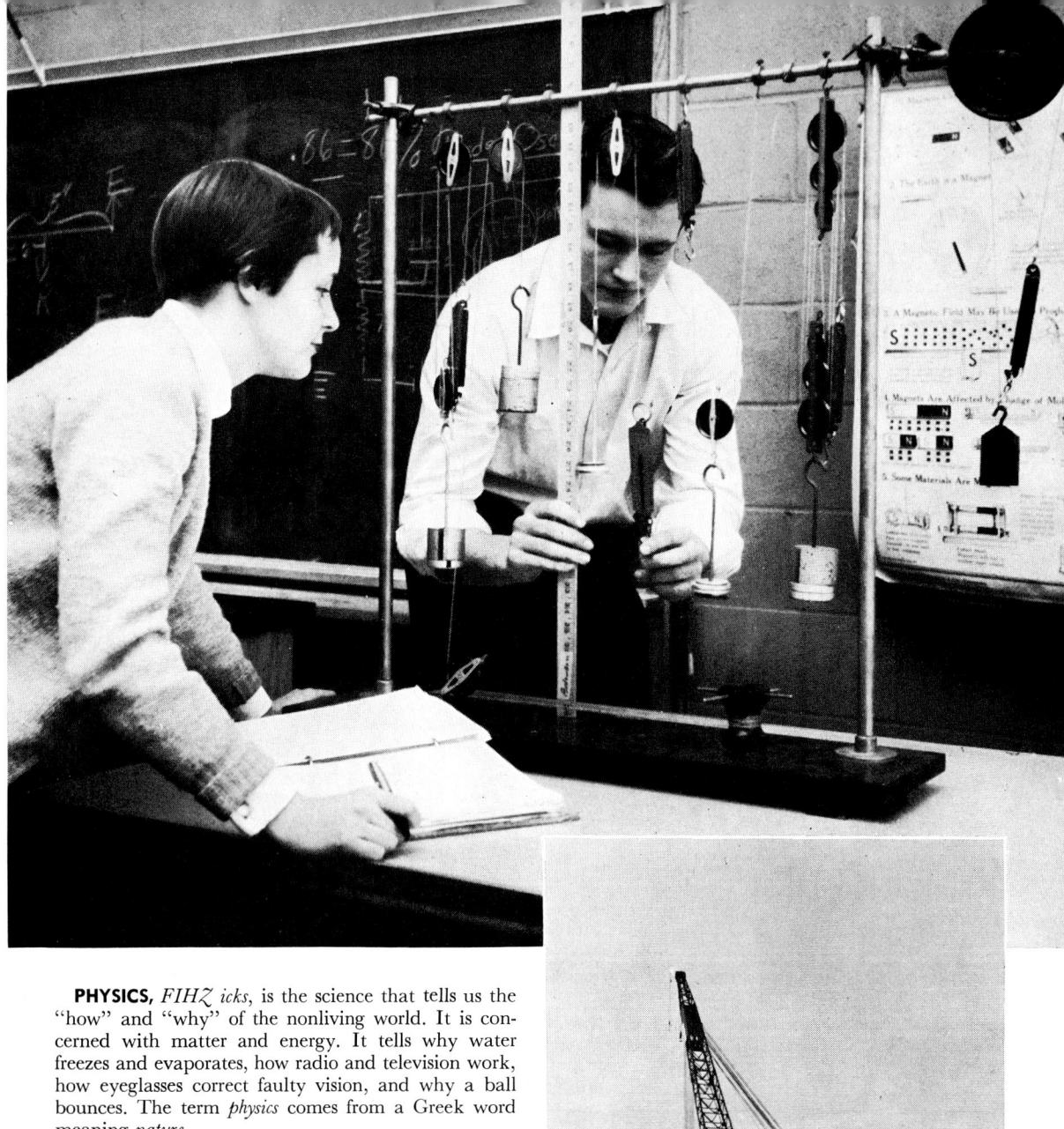

PHYSICS, *FIHZ icks,* is the science that tells us the "how" and "why" of the nonliving world. It is concerned with matter and energy. It tells why water freezes and evaporates, how radio and television work, how eyeglasses correct faulty vision, and why a ball bounces. The term *physics* comes from a Greek word meaning *nature.*

Physics covers such a great range of ideas that no simple definition of this fascinating science is satisfactory. The best way to understand physics is to try to break up the subject into smaller fields. These fields are not always clear-cut. Sometimes they overlap each other, and some gaps occur. But, by describing the main parts, we can form a more complete picture of physics.

How Physics Affects Our Lives

With a knowledge of physics, man can harness the forces of nature and put them to work. By using the

Physics Students Learn Basic Physical Principles in their school work. By experimenting in the laboratory with pulleys, they understand how these devices are used on a large scale in cranes and derricks to lift and move heavy objects.

Parade Magazine; American Hoist & Derrick Co.

388

principles of physics, he builds generators to produce electricity for homes and factories. He burns gasoline to drive automobile engines, and lifts tons of scrap iron with a magnet. Physicists have released energy from the atom and used it to propel a submarine beneath the North Pole. Using the principles of physics, engineers build airplanes that carry man far above the earth. High-speed rockets are sent even farther, soaring above the atmosphere to launch artificial satellites. These rockets carry instruments that measure the physical properties of space, adding to our knowledge of the world around us.

Physics enables man to harness other kinds of energy and put them to work. For example, an understanding of sound energy makes possible the musical instruments that combine to produce great symphonies. Knowledge of how light energy can be controlled enables photographers to take beautiful pictures.

The housewife comes in contact with the laws of physics when she uses a vacuum cleaner or an electric iron. At home, we also enjoy phonograph records and television programs—all made possible by an understanding of physics. Every time you pick up the telephone or send a telegram you are putting physics to work.

What Physicists Study

The subjects studied by physicists can be divided into seven main groups: (1) mechanics, (2) heat, (3) light, (4) electricity and magnetism, (5) sound, (6) atomic and nuclear physics, and (7) solid state physics. Each division covers a wide range of problems, and each has many uses. The science of physics changes continually, and some subjects studied today were undreamed of a hundred years ago.

Physics overlaps several other sciences. For example, *biophysics* applies principles of physics to living things. *Physical chemistry* applies physical principles to the reactions of chemical compounds. *Astronomy* and *geology* lean heavily on principles of physics. *Engineering* applies the principles of physics to products of many kinds that man can use. Physics itself depends on *mathematics* and *logic*.

Mechanics is the study of objects, forces, and motion, and such properties of matter as elasticity and weight. It deals with the forces that make an airplane fly and keep an automobile on a highway when speeding around a curve. Or it may study the forces that press on a deep-sea diver. Mechanics is also concerned with such varied problems as the efficiency of machines and the paths of bullets and other projectiles.

Mechanics is divided into two main fields, fluid mechanics and solid mechanics. *Fluid* mechanics is the study of the forces and motion of fluids and of gases. *Solid* mechanics includes *dynamics*, or the study of motion or change of motion of moving bodies, and *statics*, or the study of bodies at rest.

The principles of mechanics tell us the meaning of weight, mass, force, energy, space, time, and rotational motion. Through mechanics, scientists have studied the principles of a spinning top and have applied them to such practical inventions as the gyrocompass. See MECHANICS; DYNAMICS; STATICS.

Heat. The study of heat is called *thermodynamics*. Physicists study how heat can be changed into work,

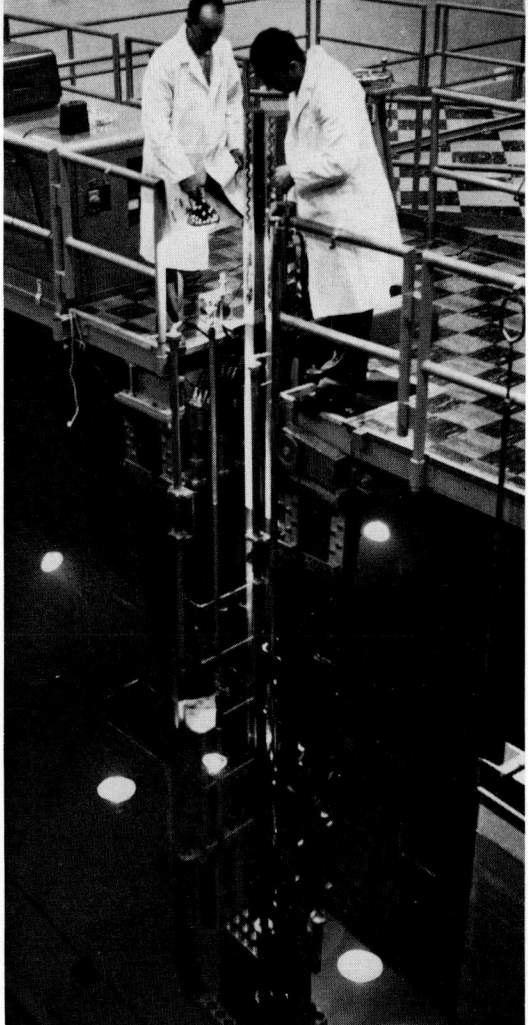

U. S. Navy

Nuclear Reactors are used in research in nuclear physics. The reactors help scientists study the properties of atoms and their particles, and develop more efficient ways to use reactors.

how it is produced, how it is transferred from one place to another, and how it changes matter. Heat ranks as one of the most important kinds of energy that man uses. Heat energy pushes the pistons of a steam engine, the blades of a steam turbine, and the pistons of a gasoline engine. It may be changed into electrical energy or mechanical energy. It may come from energy locked up inside conventional fuels, such as coal or gas, or from energy in the atoms of such elements as uranium and plutonium. The knowledge that physicists gain from the study of heat and how it acts aids in making use of heat energy to warm homes, cook foods, and run machines. See HEAT; THERMODYNAMICS.

Light. The study of light is called *optics*. It involves learning what light is, how it behaves, and how it can be used. A knowledge of how light behaves enabled man to develop such instruments as the microscope and the telescope. The study of the visible spectrum and of invisible electromagnetic waves also falls in the field of optics. These studies aid in many areas of science. For example, the study of the spectrum enables chemists to

MILESTONES IN PHYSICS

Galileo Was the First Great Experimenter and the father of modern astronomy. He was also an outstanding mathematician.

Newton Formulated the Laws of Gravitation and Motion and contributed greatly to the theories of light and optical science.

Faraday Was One of the Most Gifted Experimenters. His electrical discoveries made the present electrical age possible.

Edison Was the World's Most Productive Inventor. He invented the electric light, the phonograph, and many other devices.

Roentgen Opened a New World of Physical Science with his discovery of the penetrating and invisible Roentgen rays, or X rays.

Einstein Developed the Theory of Relativity which revised older theories of time and space, and led to the use of atomic power.

Rutherford Investigated the Structure of the Atom, and the behavior of radioactive substances.

Meitner   Bush   Fermi   Oppenheimer   Lawrence

Many of the World's Greatest Scientists contributed to the making of the atomic bomb, a milestone in the history of mankind.

analyze materials and determine what elements they contain. The properties of light as energy help in studying other forms of energy. See LIGHT; OPTICS.

Electricity and Magnetism are closely related. Electricity can produce magnetism, and magnetism can produce electricity. An understanding of this important relationship has led man to develop some of his most valuable servants. Huge generators provide the electric current that runs laborsaving devices in homes and powerful machines in industry. Electricity provides light and heat and runs air-conditioning machines.

One of the most important advances in science has been the development of *electronics*, the branch of physics that studies the behavior of electrons, especially in vacuum- or gas-filled tubes and in special materials known as *semiconductors*. Electronics has made possible most of the modern wonders of communication including radio, television, and the telephone. The study of electronics has also resulted in the development of radar, the electric eye, and computers. See ELECTRICITY; ELECTROMAGNETISM; ELECTRONICS; MAGNET AND MAGNETISM.

Sound. The study of sound is called *acoustics*. It explains how sound is produced, transmitted, and reflected; and why it changes. The study of sound enables engineers to build auditoriums that have little echo. It has helped doctors learn about deafness and develop hearing aids. Acoustics helps men design phonographs that can reproduce almost exactly the sound heard in a concert hall. *Ultrasonic* devices send out sound waves that vibrate at frequencies too high for humans to hear. See ACOUSTICS; SOUND.

Atomic and Nuclear Physics have revealed many of the secrets of matter. Knowledge gained from the study of nuclear physics has released the greatest energy known on earth, the energy of the atom. This energy has great possibilities as a source of tremendous amounts of power for peaceful uses. But it may also be a source of destructive power in time of war.

Atomic physics studies atoms and their physical properties. It also studies atomic structure, isotopes, and the properties and behavior of electrons in atoms. See ATOM.

Nuclear physics is concerned with the *nucleus* (the central core) of the atom and the various radiations that come from it. Physicists in this field study nuclear reactions, nuclear particles, and nuclear energy. See ATOMIC ENERGY; NUCLEAR PHYSICS.

Solid State Physics supplied information that led to such developments as the transistor and the solar battery. It involves the study of the physical properties and atomic structure of solids, particularly of crystals. Solid state physics studies elasticity, magnetism, specific heat, and the conduction of heat and electricity. It is also concerned with the relationship between the purity of a metal and its strength and ability to conduct electricity. See SOLID STATE PHYSICS; SOLAR ENERGY (Solar Batteries); TRANSISTOR.

History

When prehistoric man first began to observe things about him, his only laboratory was the world he saw. He put rollers under heavy loads and saw that he could pull them more easily. He tied a string to the ends of a slender branch and found that he could shoot a pointed stick farther than he could throw it. After hundreds of years of slow progress, the people of

---

RED-LETTER DATES IN PHYSICS

c. 400 B.C.	Democritus wrote that all matter consists of tiny bits of material called atoms.
300's B.C.	Aristotle, using deduction and logic, rather than experiments and observation, formed theories in many areas of physics.
200's B.C.	Archimedes discovered laws for the behavior of levers and of liquids.
A.D. 100's	Ptolemy pictured the earth as standing still, with the sun, moon, planets, and stars moving in circles around it.
1543	Copernicus wrote that the earth and planets move in circles around the sun.
c. 1600	Galileo discovered important laws in many fields of physics, especially mechanics.
	William Gilbert provided a foundation for the study of electricity and magnetism.
c. 1678	Christian Huygens formulated the wave theory of light.
1687	Sir Isaac Newton developed the basic laws of mechanics.
c. 1730	Daniel Bernoulli developed the kinetic theory of gases.
1799	Benjamin Thompson stated that motion of particles in a substance produces heat.
c. 1803	John Dalton first proposed his atomic theory about the structure of matter.
1831	Michael Faraday produced electricity with magnetism.
c. 1850	James P. Joule found that heat and energy are interchangeable at a fixed rate.
c. 1864	James Clerk Maxwell developed the electromagnetic theory of light.
1880	Albert Michelson accurately measured the speed of light.
c. 1887	The Michelson-Morley experiment disproved the existence of ether.
1895	Wilhelm K. Roentgen discovered X rays.
1896	Antoine Henri Becquerel discovered natural radioactivity.
c. 1897	Sir Joseph John Thomson discovered the electron.
1900	Max Planck proposed the quantum theory.
1905	Albert Einstein published his Special Theory of Relativity.
1915	Einstein announced his General Theory of Relativity.
1924	Louis de Broglie put forth the wave theory of the electron.
1926	Erwin Schrödinger developed principles of wave mechanics, or quantum mechanics.
1938	Otto Hahn and Fritz Strassmann achieved fission of uranium.
1939	Lise Meitner and Otto Frisch proposed an explanation of the fission experiment.
1942	Enrico Fermi and associates achieved the first controlled nuclear chain reaction.
1945	The United States exploded the first atomic bomb.
1952	The United States exploded the first large-size hydrogen bomb.
1956	The law of parity was proved not universally true by T. D. Lee and C. N. Yang.
1957-1958	In the International Geophysical Year, physicists and other scientists from 66 countries studied such subjects as the earth's magnetism, the ionosphere, and cosmic radiation.
1962	The Mariner II spacecraft discovered a "solar wind" in interplanetary space.

PHYSICS

ancient civilizations arrived at many practical methods of doing things. They also began to express general physical laws that described their ideas about nature.

The Greeks stressed the value of general ideas and laws. But they based most of their laws on logical arguments and "common sense," rather than on experiments or observation. They anticipated many ideas held by scientists in later years. During the 500's B.C. for example, Pythagoras thought the earth was a sphere. In the 400's B.C., Anaxagoras guessed that the moon shines by reflected sunlight, and that eclipses occur when the earth blocks the sun's rays. About 400 B.C., Democritus taught that matter is composed of small particles which he called atoms.

Aristotle, one of the greatest of the Greek philosophers, wrote extensively about physics and other sciences. But he did not often use experimental methods. Aristotle drew his conclusions mainly from logical argument. Many of his writings that came to future generations included mistaken ideas. For example, he believed that the earth is the center of the universe, with the rest of the universe moving around it. The Egyptian astronomer Ptolemy developed this same idea in more detail during the A.D. 100's.

But some Greeks performed scientific experiments to gain knowledge. During the 200's B.C., Archimedes discovered that the weight of a floating body equals the weight of the water it displaces. In other experiments, he learned the law of the lever, and laid important foundations for mechanics and the laws of liquids.

The Middle Ages and the Renaissance. After the achievements of the Greeks, progress in physics lagged for hundreds of years. In Europe during the Middle Ages, from A.D. 400 to 1400, only a few men had any interest in science or the physical world. The Arabs aided the study of science by translating and preserving many writings of the Greeks. They also performed experiments in some areas of physics, such as optics. They made great improvements in mathematics (see MATHEMATICS [The Middle Ages]).

Some revival of learning occurred in Europe about 1100. It resulted in the translation of Greek writings into Latin, the language of educated persons of that time. Scholars regarded the writings of Aristotle as their chief authority. To question these writings seemed heresy. Ptolemy's views of the universe were also considered unassailable truths.

But some men began to see the importance of observation and experiment to advance science. One of these was the English friar Roger Bacon, who lived in the 1200's. Bacon attempted to set forth a system of knowledge of nature based on observation and experiment.

During the 1300's and 1400's, the intellectual awakening called the Renaissance began in art and literature. Some of the Renaissance thinkers were also interested in science. For example, Leonardo da Vinci, the great Italian painter, was also a physicist and an engineer. He studied mechanics and even planned various types of flying machines. His drawings and designs were far ahead of his time. But, in spite of Da Vinci's many accomplishments, few persons of his day knew about his scientific ideas.

The Rebirth of Physics began in the mid-1500's. In 1543, the Polish astronomer Nicolaus Copernicus published his theory that the earth and planets move around the sun. This work marked an important step in the advance of physics. It helped develop laws of motion for the planets, and was a new interpretation of observed events based on physical principles.

The development of physics based on observation of designed experiments can be traced to three men, William Gilbert and Isaac Newton of England, and Galileo of Italy.

William Gilbert, the physician of Queen Elizabeth I, experimented in magnetism and static electricity. In 1600, he published the first real study of magnetism. He demonstrated his views by both arguments and experiments, but carefully separated his arguments from facts he had observed.

Galileo was one of the few men of the 1500's willing to defend the results of observation, even if they disagreed with the views of accepted authorities. Observations indicated to Galileo that some of Aristotle's principles of physics were wrong. So he designed experiments to demonstrate more accurate principles. For example, Aristotle thought that the heavier an object is, the faster it falls. But Galileo observed falling bodies of different weights. He found that bodies of different weights fall with about the same velocity. He then designed experiments to find the true laws of falling bodies. Galileo slowed the speed of fall by rolling the weights down inclined planes. He found that the speed of a falling body increases in proportion to the time of fall. Galileo stressed the importance of carefully controlled experiments. He based his conclusions on observations and the results of experiments, rather than on deductive logic. See FALLING BODIES, LAW OF.

Galileo found that the scientific instruments of his time were not exact enough for his measurements. He

Physicists of the 1950's investigated many different areas of physics. Yang and Lee studied basic properties of matter. Van Allen conducted research into conditions in space. Bardeen discovered principles of electrical conduction in solids.

| C. N. Yang | Tsung Dao Lee | J. A. Van Allen | John Bardeen |

improved measuring devices, including the clock and the telescope, and he invented the thermometer. With these instruments, he made exact measurements in his experiments. Many men of Galileo's time did not accept his ideas. They preferred to continue to believe the ancient Greek "authorities." But Galileo's discoveries laid the foundation for the work of Newton and later scientists.

Isaac Newton had one of the most brilliant and penetrating minds the world has ever known. During the late 1600's and early 1700's, he organized the scientific thought of his day into a few fundamental statements, or laws. For example, he formulated a law of gravitation and showed that both objects on earth and the celestial bodies such as the planets and stars obey this law. Newton also laid down the basic laws of mechanics much as we use them today.

Newton's studies of prisms and lenses laid the foundation for the modern study of optics. He also developed a theory of the nature of light. In the late 1600's, the Dutch physicist Christian Huygens proposed that light travels in waves. Newton found that certain properties of light not explained by Huygens' wave theory could be explained by a *corpuscular* theory. He taught that light consists of small particles moving in straight lines. Until the 1800's, most scientists accepted Newton's theory.

Newton and Gottfried Leibniz, a German philosopher, independently developed a new system of mathematics at about the same time. This system, which is now known as *calculus*, could solve certain problems in physics that previously had not been solvable (see MATHEMATICS [Calculus]).

The fundamental laws of physics expressed by Newton guided other scientists of the 1700's in their work. During this period, the various branches of physics began to develop separately. Scientists studied mechanics, heat, light, and electricity as if they were more or less independent phenomena. But the general principles of Newton united them.

The 1800's saw the rapid development of the physics founded by Galileo, Newton, and Gilbert. New experiments came thick and fast, and new and powerful instruments and machines were developed. Inventions resulting from research in the 1800's included the steam engine, electric motor, telegraph, and telephone.

During this period, scientific knowledge advanced in all branches of physics. In the area of heat, for example, scientists showed that heat is a form of energy. In 1824, the French engineer Nicolas Sadi Carnot dealt with the use of heat to do work. His idea that heat is interchangeable with work was the foundation for the science of thermodynamics. James P. Joule of England then showed that work and heat are interchangeable at a fixed rate of exchange.

From this study of heat, an idea emerged that eventually ruled the scientific world. This idea is the basic importance of energy. The concept of energy was not new. Men knew that a moving object, such as a falling weight or a stream of water, has energy of motion and can be harnessed to do work. But now they discovered that heat is a form of energy, produced by increased energy of motion of the particles that make up a substance. During the 1800's, light and sound were also recognized as forms of energy.

In 1801, Thomas Young (1773-1829) of England showed how a wave theory of light could explain many of the puzzles in optics. By the mid-1850's, the new wave theory replaced the corpuscular theory of Newton. But light traveling in waves must travel through a substance, as sound waves travel through air. Scientists knew light could travel through a vacuum, so they proposed that a material called *ether* exists throughout all space, including vacuums (see ETHER).

About 1820, observations by André Marie Ampère of France and Hans Christian Oersted of Denmark showed that electricity and magnetism are related. Based on this work, Michael Faraday of England tried to produce one from the other. In 1831, he found that a moving magnet would induce an electric current in a coil of wire. This discovery made possible the conversion of mechanical power into electrical power, and the operation of generators.

James Clerk Maxwell of Great Britain expressed the experimental discoveries of Faraday in mathematical form during the 1860's. He offered a theory that explained previous observations in electricity and magnetism. Maxwell's electromagnetic theory stated that light, electricity, and magnetism consist of waves of electric and magnetic forces. He predicted that electromagnetic waves could be produced by electrical means. In 1887, Heinrich Hertz of Germany produced waves from electrical sources that fitted Maxwell's predictions. Radio, radar, and television are based on this work.

The Beginning of Modern Physics. In the late 1800's, many physicists thought they had explained all the main principles of the universe and had discovered all the natural laws. They believed that nothing remained for future physicists to achieve except increased accuracy and the working out of a few minor inconsistencies. But, as work went on, the difficulties became magnified and new discoveries opened a whole new area of physics.

The existence of ether was necessary to the wave theory of light. In 1887, two American physicists, Albert A. Michelson and Edward W. Morley (1838-1923), designed an experiment to study ether. They tried to find out how fast the earth moves through it. But they could find no trace of movement of the earth through ether, or of ether itself.

During the 1700's, the idea that matter consists of small particles that cannot be divided began to gain acceptance. In 1808, the English chemist John Dalton used the concept of indivisible particles, or atoms, to explain the way elements combine to form compounds. Scientists accepted this idea until the 1890's. Then the picture of atoms as solid objects began to fade. Scientists discovered the electron, X rays, and natural radioactivity. These discoveries indicated that atoms have some kind of internal structure. See ATOM; ATOMIC ENERGY (Development).

Relativity and Quanta. The early 1900's were years of revolution in physics. Scientists continued to examine the inconsistencies in the classical physics of Newton and Maxwell, and discovered new interpretations of observed events.

Einstein and Relativity. Newton's theory of mechanics explained and predicted many ordinary events. But it was replaced by the Special Theory of Relativity,

A WORLD BOOK SCIENCE PROJECT
ATOMIC PHYSICS

The purpose of this project is to see the action of atomic particles by observing the trails they make in the vapor of a diffusion cloud chamber. Cloud chambers are a basic tool of modern physics.

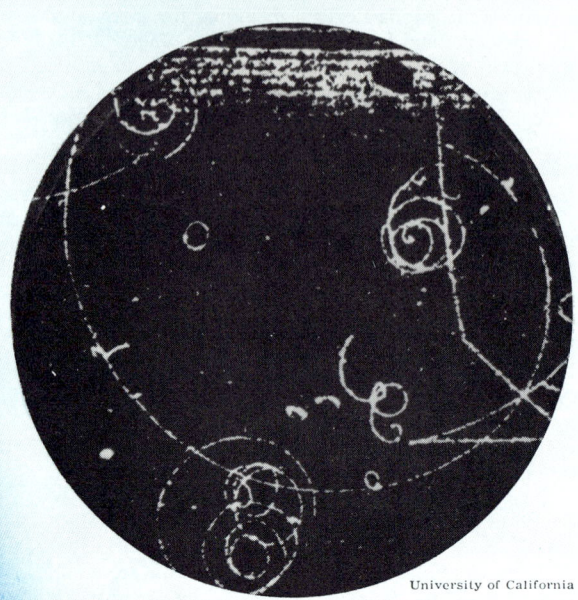

University of California

THE DIFFUSION CLOUD CHAMBER

A diffusion cloud chamber consists of a sealed transparent glass chamber as shown, *left*. The inside of the chamber is filled with alcohol vapor and contains a source of radioactivity, which gives off subatomic particles. When conditions are just right, the particles, such as alpha and beta particles, leave a visible trail, *above*, as they move through the vapor. These trails consist of droplets. The droplets form when the vapor in the chamber condenses on contact with free ions. Free ions are produced when the particles collide with air or vapor molecules as they move through the chamber, *below*. Certain particles can be recognized by the kinds of vapor trails they leave.

Alcohol vapor

Dry ice

VAPOR TRAIL

Charged particle   Free ions   Condensation droplets

MATERIALS

All the materials for this project can be easily obtained in your own neighborhood except for the radioactive pin. You can get the pin or a similar item from companies that sell laboratory supplies to schools. The pins are not dangerous.

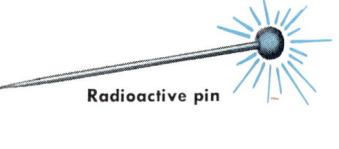

Radioactive pin

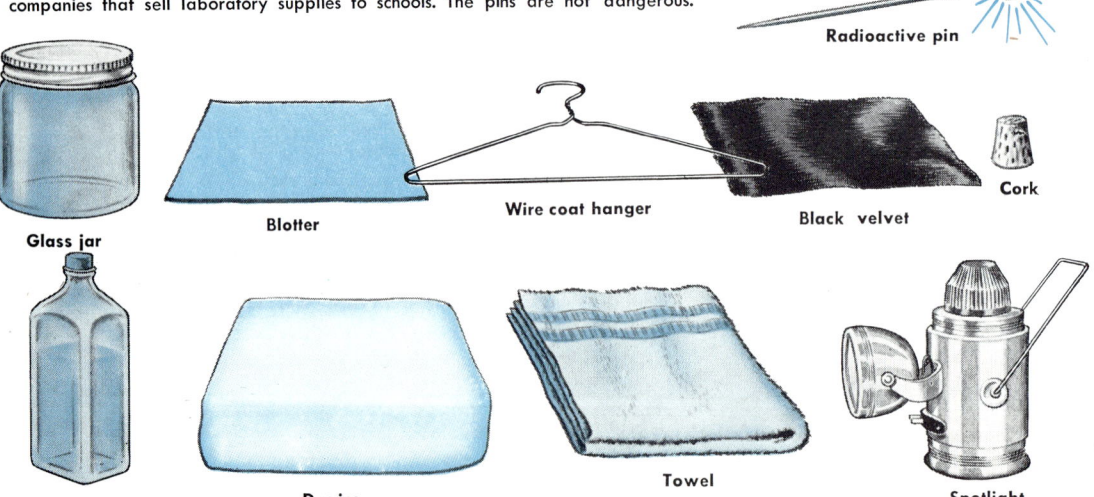

Glass jar

Blotter

Wire coat hanger

Black velvet

Cork

Alcohol

Dry ice

Towel

Spotlight

To make the cloud chamber, cut a circle from the blotter large enough to cover the bottom of the jar. Snip a piece of wire from the coat hanger and twist it into a clip to hold the blotter in place as shown, *right*. Cut a circle from the black velvet and place it in the jar lid. Stick the radioactive pin into the cork, and set the cork in the jar lid near the edge. Cut a circle the size of the jar lid in the towel. Wrap the dry ice in the towel so that the circle is centered on top.

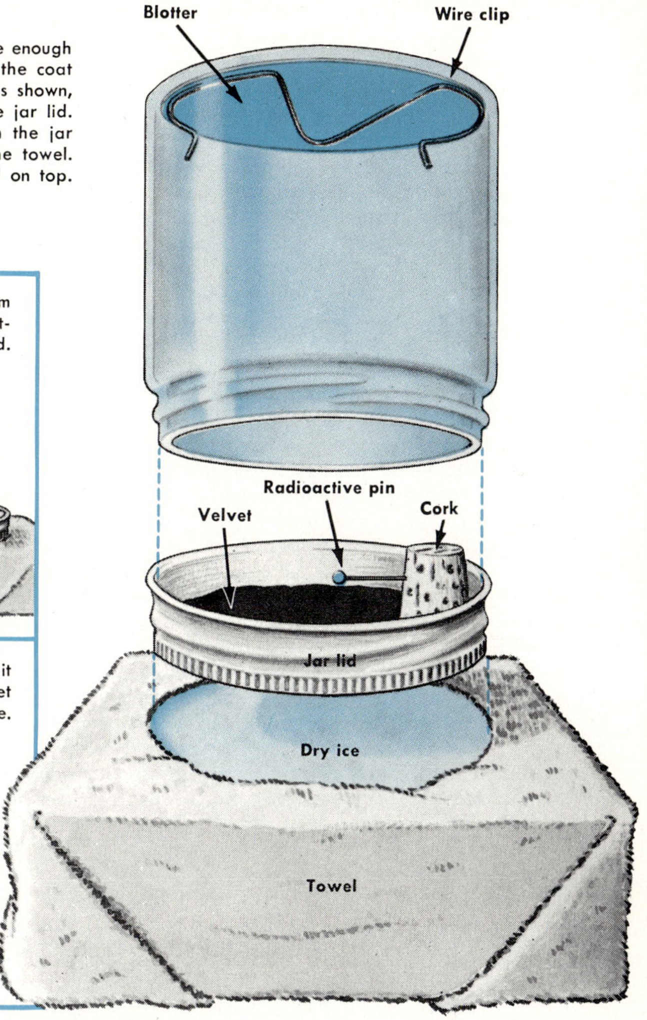

To Prepare the Chamber, rinse the jar with hot water to warm it. Swish alcohol around the sides of the jar and saturate the blotter. Pour off the excess alcohol, and screw the jar onto the lid.

To Operate the Chamber, position the spotlight so that it shines directly into the jar. Look into the jar at the black velvet lining in the lid. You should see vapor trails forming there.

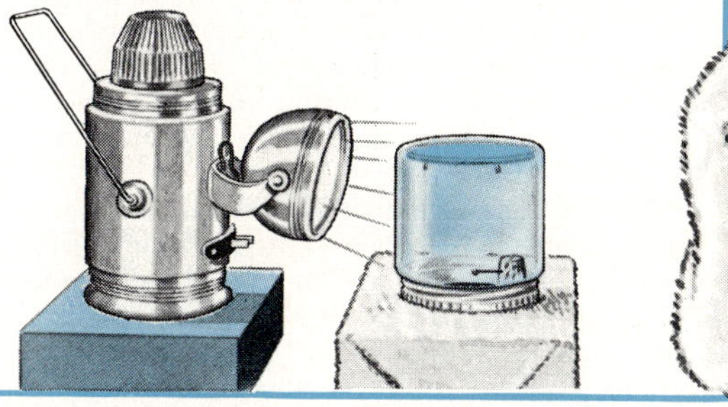

Blotter — Wire clip

Radioactive pin — Velvet — Cork

Jar lid

Dry ice

Towel

PHOTOGRAPHING THE VAPOR TRAILS

Illustrated by Art Lutz for WORLD BOOK

For further study, you can take photographs of vapor trails like those shown, *below.* Use a 35-mm. camera with a lens for close work. Try lens openings from f/3.5 to f/8, and shutter speeds from 1/10 to 1/100 second, using any film rated ASA 200.

Alpha Particles are helium nuclei. Because they are heavy, they leave straight, dense vapor trails that are easy to see.

Beta Particles are electrons. They are light and easily deflected by other particles, so they leave irregular trails.

Cosmic Radiation can also make vapor trails. Set up the cloud chamber without the radioactive pin to see these trails.

Physics—Physical Science Study Committee, courtesy, D. C. Heath & Co.

Brookhaven National Laboratory

E. W. Cowan, California Institute of Technology

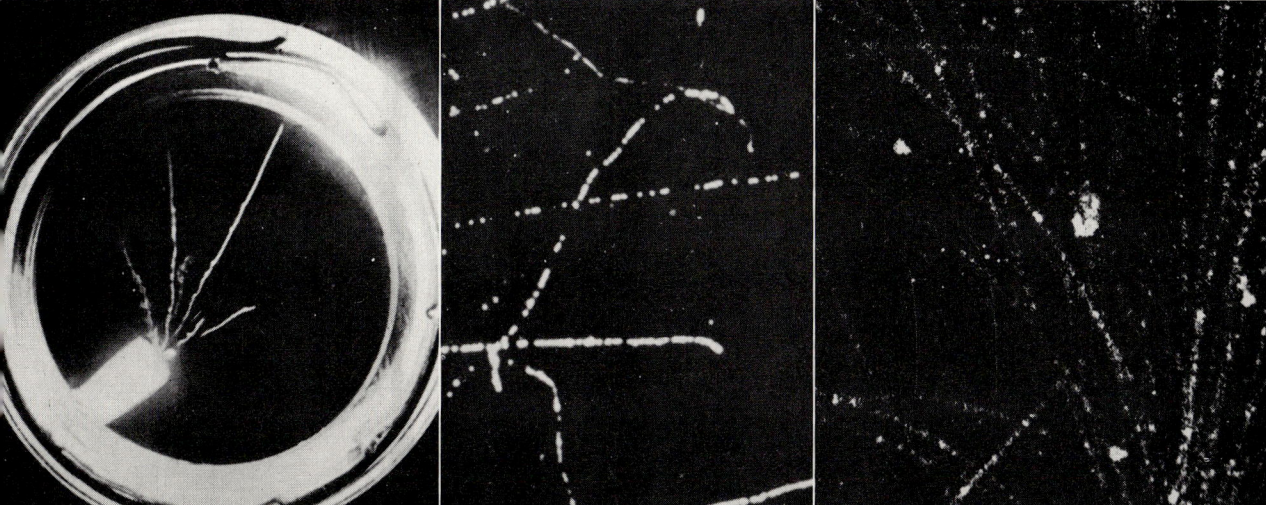

introduced by Albert Einstein of Germany in 1905. Einstein stated that man's ideas of space and time are not absolute. They are relative to the position of the observer. But he thought that the laws of physics should be the same for different observers, even if they are moving relative to one another with a constant velocity. He established that nothing can travel faster than the speed of light—186,282 miles a second. Einstein also found that mass is a form of energy, and that mass is related to energy by his famous equation $E=mc^2$. In this equation, E stands for energy, m stands for mass, and c^2 stands for the speed of light multiplied by itself. This equation later showed that atomic fission and fusion could release enormous amounts of energy.

The Michelson-Morley experiment had shown that the ether proposed by scientists after Newton did not exist. Without ether, the forces of gravity and waves of radiation had no medium through which to travel. Therefore, the theories of the classical physicists could not be right. Einstein tried to replace the gravitational theories of Newton with a more exact statement of the laws of gravitation. In his General Theory of Relativity, announced in 1915, he regarded gravity not as a property of all bodies as Newton had, but as a property of the space in which bodies exist. According to Einstein, what appears to us as a force might appear to someone else as a kind of curvature in space of which we are unaware.

After 1915, Einstein and other physicists developed a Unified Field Theory. This theory attempted to unite all the forces known in physics into a single physical principle. See RELATIVITY.

The Quantum Theory. In 1900, Max Planck of Germany published a theory about the way energy is transferred. He stated that energy is not given off in a continuous stream, but in a stream of separate units, or *quanta*. In 1905, Einstein extended this concept to light. He said that light, in spite of its wave nature, must be composed of energy particles called *photons*. See QUANTUM THEORY.

The idea that radiations combine the properties of waves and particles led Louis V. de Broglie of France to theorize in 1924 that a similar situation might exist for matter. Later experiments showed that, under certain conditions, electrons do behave like waves, rather than particles.

In 1926, the Austrian physicist Erwin Schrödinger developed *quantum mechanics*, or *wave mechanics*. This enables scientists to deal with small particles, such as the electron, that do not follow the rules of classical physics. In 1927, Werner Heisenberg of Germany put forth the "principle of indeterminacy." He stated that certain kinds of information about very small particles cannot be obtained. The methods that must be used to observe such small particles throw off quanta of energy that disturb the position or motion of the particles. Scientists would observe the "disturbed" particle rather than its natural position or motion.

Uncovering the Secrets of the Atom has led physicists on one of the most dramatic and important scientific searches in the history of man. This still-unfinished "detective story" has given man the destructive power of the atomic bomb and the lifesaving power of radioactive isotopes.

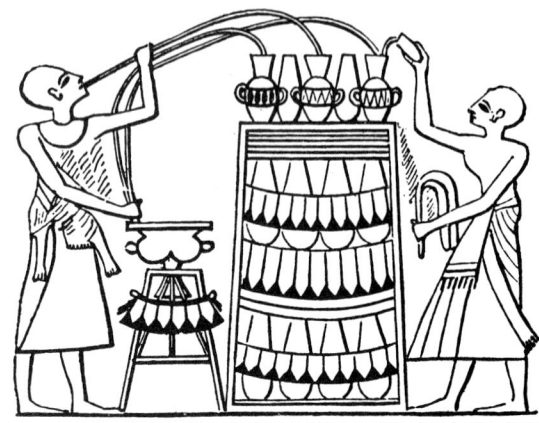

From *Manners & Customs of the Ancient Egyptians* by J. G. Wilkinson (London, 1837)

The Ancient Egyptians invented many practical devices that were based on principles of physics. One of these devices, the siphon, is illustrated in pictures painted earlier than 1100 B.C.

The discovery that atoms have an internal structure led physicists to search into the heart of these tiny units of matter. In 1911, Ernest Rutherford, in England, theorized that the mass of an atom lies in a *nucleus* (central core). In 1913, Niels Bohr of Denmark proposed a theory of the arrangement of electrons. Bohr pictured the atom as a miniature solar system, with electrons revolving around the nucleus in definite *orbits* (paths). The discovery of other atomic particles continued after this early work. James Chadwick of England found the neutron in 1932, and Hideki Yukawa of Japan proposed the existence of the meson in 1935.

One of the most important breakthroughs in atomic physics came in 1938, when Otto Hahn and Fritz Strassmann of Germany split the uranium atom. Two Austrian physicists, Lise Meitner and Otto Frisch, explained what happened during this *fission* (splitting) process. Other physicists combined the explanation with Einstein's $E=mc^2$ formula, and proposed that atomic fission could provide huge amounts of energy. In 1942, Enrico Fermi and his co-workers at the University of Chicago turned theory into reality when they achieved the first controlled fission chain reaction. This historic achievement marked the beginning of the Atomic Age. For additional information, see ATOMIC ENERGY (Development of Atomic Energy).

Physics Today is one of the most active and most important of all sciences. In laboratories throughout the world, physicists delve into the mysteries of nature to unearth the secrets of the universe. Endless questions and experiments lead them to discard old theories and propose new ones. For example, two Chinese-born American physicists, Tsung Dao Lee and Chen Ning Yang, startled the scientific world in 1956 when they disproved the 30-year-old law of the conservation of parity. This law states, in part, that matter would retain its same basic physical properties if the direction of motion of the particles within the atom were reversed. The work of Lee and Yang opened new fields of research in physics.

The International Geophysical Year (IGY) further increased the world-wide interest in physics that had been stirred by the development of atomic energy.

From July, 1957, to December, 1958, physicists and other scientists from 66 nations cooperated on world-wide research into the earth and its surroundings. This program brought such scientific advances as the launching of artificial earth satellites to investigate conditions in space. With newly developed tools, physicists extended their research into outer space.

Careers in Physics

Probably few fields offer the excitement and satisfaction to be found in a career devoted to physics. Whether a physicist works in the laboratory of a university or industrial company, or teaches in a high school or a college, he is taking part in one of man's greatest adventures—understanding the world. But few careers require the dedication and training needed by physics.

Training for a career in physics begins in the home when boys and girls learn to make things and to discover why things work. It continues with elementary- and high-school studies in science and mathematics. Here, the prospective physicist develops the alert, inquiring mind needed in his future work.

The chief training of a physicist takes place in college. He learns higher mathematics, the basic tool of physics. After a year or two of general courses in physics, the student may begin to specialize. He may take courses in electricity, optics, or nuclear physics. Most physicists continue their training after receiving a bachelor's degree. A position of responsibility in physics usually requires a doctorate.

Employment opportunities for physicists are almost unlimited. Since World War II, the demand for competent physicists has increased to the highest point in history. The need for physicists in industry, teaching, and research is much greater than the supply.

Some physicists conduct experiments and work with instruments and other equipment. Others, trained in mathematical analysis of physical problems, work with theories. These two sides of physics are closely related, and many physicists excel equally in both.

Many industries employ physicists in their research departments. These men usually work in *applied* physics, or fields directly related to improving a manufacturing process or the company's product. They may also work in *basic* physics, or the study of general physical principles that may or may not have practical applications. Many physicists work in government research laboratories. Others work in the laboratories of foundations and research institutions. Physicists in colleges and universities may conduct research and help train other physicists.   HARVEY E. WHITE

Related Articles in WORLD BOOK include:

AMERICAN PHYSICISTS

Anderson, Carl D.	Feynman, Richard P.
Bardeen, John	Gamow, George
Bloch, Felix	Gibbs, Josiah W.
Brattain, Walter H.	Glaser, Donald A.
Bridgman, Percy W.	Goddard, Robert H.
Chamberlain, Owen	Henry, Joseph
Compton (Karl; Arthur)	Hofstadter, Robert
Condon, Edward U.	Kerst, Donald W.
Davisson, Clinton J.	Lamb, Willis E., Jr.
Dempster, Arthur J.	Langley, Samuel P.
Dolbear, Amos E.	Lawrence, Ernest O.
Dunning, John R.	Lee, Tsung Dao
Einstein, Albert	Mayer, Maria G.

McMillan, Edwin M.	Stern, Otto
Michelson, Albert A.	Szilard, Leo
Millikan, Robert A.	Teller, Edward
Nier, Alfred O. C.	Thompson, Benjamin
Oppenheimer, J. Robert	Townes, Charles Hard
Pupin, Michael I.	Van Allen, James A.
Purcell, Edward M.	Von Békésy, Georg
Rabi, Isidor I.	Von Kármán, Theodore
Rowland, Henry A.	Wigner, Eugene Paul
Schwinger, Julian S.	Wood, Robert W.
Segrè, Emilio	Yang, Chen Ning
Shockley, William	Zworykin, Vladimir K.

BRITISH PHYSICISTS

Appleton, Sir Edward	Kendrew, John C.
Aston, Francis W.	Lodge, Sir Oliver J.
Blackett, Patrick M. S.	Low, Archibald M.
Boyle, Robert	Maxwell, James C.
Bragg, Sir William H.	Moseley, Henry G. J.
Cavendish, Henry	Newton, Sir Isaac
Chadwick, Sir James	Perutz, Max Ferdinand
Cockcroft, Sir John D.	Powell, Cecil F.
Crookes, Sir William	Rayleigh, Baron
Dalton, John	Rutherford, Ernest
Dirac, Paul A. M.	Thomson, Sir Joseph J.
Faraday, Michael	Tyndall, John
Hooke, Robert	Walton, Ernest T. S.
Jeans, Sir James H.	Watson-Watt, Sir Robert A.
Joule, James P.	Wheatstone, Sir Charles
Kelvin, Lord	Wilson, Charles T. R.

FRENCH PHYSICISTS

Ampère, André M.	Du Fay, Charles F.
Becquerel	Foucault, Jean B. L.
Broglie, Louis V. de	Gay-Lussac, Joseph L.
Coulomb, Charles A. de	Pascal, Blaise
Curie	

GERMAN PHYSICISTS

Boltzmann, Ludwig	Jensen, J. Hans
Born, Max	Kusch, Polykarp
Bothe, Walther	Laue, Max T. F. von
Clausius, Rudolf J.	Mayer, Julius R. von
Fahrenheit, Gabriel D.	Mössbauer, Rudolf L.
Franck, James	Nernst, Walther H.
Geiger, Hans	Ohm, Georg S.
Heisenberg, Werner	Planck, Max K. E. L.
Helmholtz, Herman	Roentgen, Wilhelm K.
Hertz, Gustav	Stark, Johannes
Hertz, Heinrich R.	

ITALIAN PHYSICISTS

Avogadro, Amedeo	Galileo	Torricelli, Evangelista
	Galvani, Luigi	
Fermi, Enrico	Marconi, Guglielmo	Volta, Count

OTHER PHYSICISTS

Arrhenius, Svante A.	Pauli, Wolfgang
Basov, Nikolai G.	Piccard (Auguste)
Bohr, Niels	Prokhorov, Alexander M.
Bose, Sir Jagadis C.	Raman, Sir Chandrasekhara V.
Cherenkov, Pavel A.	Schrödinger, Erwin
Debye, Peter J. W.	Siegbahn, Karl M. G.
Frank, Ilya M.	Tamm, Igor Y.
Huygens, Christian	Tomonaga, Shinichiro
Kapitza, Peter	Van der Waals, Johannes D.
Lorentz, Hendrik A.	Yukawa, Hideki
Mach, Ernst	Zeeman, Pieter
Meitner, Lise	Zernike, Frits
Oersted, Hans C.	

ATOMIC AND NUCLEAR PHYSICS

Alpha Ray	Atom	Atomic Reactor
Antineutron	Atomic Bomb	Beta Ray
Antiproton	Atomic Energy	Cosmic Rays

PHYSICS

Crookes Tube
Delta Ray
Electron
Fission
Fusion
Gamma Ray
Hydrogen Bomb
Ion and Ionization

Irradiation
Isotope
Meson
Neutron
Parity
Photon
Proton

Radiation
Radioactivity
Transmutation
  of Elements
Transuranium
  Elements
X Rays

ELECTRICITY

Ammeter
Ampere
Anode
Battery
Capacitor
Cathode
Converter
Coulomb
Electric
  Current
Electric
  Generator
Electric
  Measurement
Electric Meter
Electric Motor
Electric Switch
Electricity

Electrode
Electrolyte
Electromotive
  Force
Electromotive
  Series
Electroscope
Farad
Fuel Cell
Fuse, Electric
Galvanometer
Geissler Tube
Henry
Induction Coil
Induction,
  Electric
Insulator,
  Electric

Kilowatt
Lenz's Law
Leyden Jar
Magneto
Ohm
Ohm's Law
Potentiometer
Rheostat
Solenoid
Thermoelectricity
Transformer
Volt
Voltmeter
Watt
Wattmeter
Wheatstone Bridge

ELECTRONICS

Cathode Rays
Cryotron
Electric Eye
Electric Field
Electrocardiograph
Electroencephalograph
Electron Gun
Electron Microscope
Electronics
Frequency Modulation
Geiger Counter
Germicidal Lamp
Iconoscope
Kilohertz
Laser
Maser
Mass Spectroscopy
Megahertz
Microwave

Oscillograph
Oscilloscope
Radar
Radio
Radio Control
Radio Telescope
Semiconductor
Shoran
Short Wave
Sniperscope
Sonar
Stroboscope
Telephone
Teletypesetter
Television
Transistor
Ultrahigh Frequency Wave
Van de Graaff Generator
Very High Frequency Wave

HEAT

Absolute Zero
Boiling Point
British Thermal
  Unit
Calorie
Centigrade Scale
Combustion
Distillation
Dust Explosion
Entropy
Evaporation

Expansion
Fire
Freezing
Heat
Heating
Insulation
Melting Point
Pyrometry
Radiometer
Regelation
Specific Heat

Spontaneous
  Combustion
Steam
Sublimation
Temperature
Thermal Barrier
Thermocouple
Thermodynamics
Thermograph
Thermometer
Thermostat

LIGHT

Aberration
Angstrom
  Unit
Arc Light
Bioluminescence
Candela
Clavilux
Color
Diffraction
Electric Light
Eye

Fluorescence
Fluorescent Lamp
Foot-Candle
Illuminating Gas
Infrared Rays
Interferometer
Lamp
Lens
Light
Light Meter
Luminescence

Magnifying Glass
Microscope
Mirage
Mirror
Neon
Newton's Rings
Optics
Penumbra
Phosphorescence
Photosynthesis
Polarized Light

Reflection
Refraction
Refractometer

Shadow
Spectrograph
Spectroscope

Ultraviolet Rays
Vapor Lamp

MAGNETISM

Compass
Dipping Needle
Electromagnet
Electromagnetism
Gauss
Induction, Electromagnetic
Loadstone

Magnet and Magnetism
Magnetic Equator
Magnetic Storm
Magnetohydrodynamics
Magnetometer
Maxwell

MECHANICS

Acceleration
Aerodynamics
Adhesion
Ballistics
Bernoulli's
  Principle
Capillarity
Cohesion
Condensation
Dyne
Efficiency
Falling Bodies,
  Law of
Foot-Pound
Force
Friction

Gas
Gravity,
  Center of
Horsepower
Hydraulics
Hydrostatics
Inclined Plane
Inertia
Kilogram-Meter
Lever
Liquid
Manometer
Mechanical Unit
Mechanics
Momentum
Motion

Osmosis
Pascal's Law
Pendulum
Pneumatics
Power
Pressure
Pulley
Screw
Siphon
Surface Tension
Torque
Vacuum
Velocity
Viscosity
Wedge
Work

SOUND

Acoustics
Decibel
Echo
Harmonics

Noise
Phon
Pitch
Sound

Tone
Tuning Fork
Ultrasonic Wave
Vibration

OTHER RELATED ARTICLES

Doppler Effect
Gravitation
Interference
Machine
Matter

Nobel Prize
Quantum Theory
Solar Energy
Solid State Physics
Waves

Outline

I. How Physics Affects Our Lives
II. What Physicists Study
  A. Mechanics
  B. Heat
  C. Light
  D. Electricity and
    Magnetism
  E. Sound
  F. Atomic and Nuclear
    Physics
  G. Solid State Physics
III. History
IV. Careers in Physics
  A. Training
  B. Employment

Questions

When and by whom was the term "atom" first used to describe tiny particles of matter?

What are some examples of the application of physics in our daily lives?

What are the main divisions of physics? What areas of study overlap with other sciences?

How did the study of heat in the 1800's produce one of the most important ideas known to science?

When did physicists first split the atom?

What is the quantum theory? Who developed it?

When did physics begin to have separate branches?

How was the Michelson-Morley experiment important in revising theories of gravitation and waves of radiation in modern physics?

How did a theory in astronomy signal a renaissance in physics during the 1500's?

How does Einstein's simple formula, $E=mc^2$, explain the possibility of creating fantastic amounts of energy?

In what ways do applied physics and basic physics differ?

PHYSIOGNOMY, FIZ ih AHG no mih, is a pseudo science which tries to read character by bodily signs, such as color, hair, form, length of legs, voice, and so on. Aristotle was one of the first to write of it. According to physiognomy, timidity, courage, and anger are all dependent on physical characteristics. Persons with thick noses are supposed to be insensitive. Those with sharp noses are said to be quick-tempered.

In the late 1700's Johann Kaspar Lavater (1741-1801) brought physiognomy back to public attention. He noticed the most striking features of his friends and related them to their personalities. Then he studied the faces of great men. He concluded that every feature of Voltaire's face showed wit and satire. Lavater said the shape of the brows, nose, mouth, ears, and chin showed benevolence, stupidity, ambition, quick temper, firmness, and so on. But when he did not know the personality of the person he analyzed, his methods failed.

Sir Charles Bell began the true scientific study of features and expression in the early 1800's. His work was continued by Charles Darwin. According to Darwin, certain expressions were once useful but are now only habits. For example, we may sneer and raise the lip merely to express an emotion, while the dog snarls and shows his teeth in a real threat to bite. A tendency to anger or fear may give the face a habitual expression which in turn gives the face an angry or fearful appearance. Much can be learned about character from studying faces. But it cannot be done with the pseudoscientific methods of physiognomy.

PHYSIOGRAPHY. See GEOGRAPHY (Physical Geography).

PHYSIOLOGICAL CHEMISTRY. See BIOCHEMISTRY.

PHYSIOLOGICAL PSYCHOLOGY is the study of human and animal behavior through the combined methods of physiology and psychology. *Physiology* is the study of how the organs of the body perform their functions. Physiological psychologists try to find out how the functions of the nervous system and body organs are related to the way people and animals behave. Research of this kind draws heavily upon techniques developed in other sciences, especially physics, biology, and biochemistry.

Research in physiological psychology concentrates in three areas. Scientists study the eyes, ears, and other sensory receptors to learn how such stimuli as light and sound are translated into messages sent to the brain. Physiological psychologists also investigate the problem of how the structure and function of the brain relates to learning, memory, and motivation. A third area of research involves how the muscles of the arms, legs, and other parts of the body are linked together by nerve cells to provide adaptive responses to stimuli.

Studies of the eye have revealed that certain receptors of the retina are instrumental in *coding* (translating) movement, shape, contour, and other aspects of visual stimuli into nerve impulses. In hearing, research has uncovered nerve fibers leading from the ear that respond to specific frequencies of sound. Researchers who implanted electrodes into the brain have learned that structures deep within the brain have specific roles in behavior. For example, the hypothalamus is closely related to hunger and thirst. The temporal lobe plays an important part in sleeping, dreaming, and wakefulness. New insight into the chemistry of the *synapse*, the place where nerve cells meet, has led to new concepts about the integration of muscular activity.

See also BRAIN (illustration: Parts of the Brain); EAR (How We Hear); EYE (How We See); NERVOUS SYSTEM; PERCEPTION.

PHYSIOLOGY, FIZ ih AHL oh jih, is a branch of biology, the study of living things. In physiology the actions of the different parts of plants, animals, and man are studied. This includes how the work of one structure or organ fits in with the work of others; and how a structure or organ acts when it is healthy and how it acts when it is diseased.

Physiology, anatomy, and biochemistry are closely related. Anatomy includes the study of the shape and parts of the body as seen by the naked eye and through the microscope. Biochemistry is the study of the chemicals which make up the body, and the chemical changes that go on in living things. For example, the study of the stomach shows how these three sciences are connected. The anatomist studies the structure of the stomach muscles and glands. The biochemist studies the chemicals that make up stomach cells, and the chemical changes that occur when the cells pour gastric juice into the stomach. The physiologist is interested in discovering what body activities make the cells secrete gastric juices when food enters the stomach. He also studies the churning movements of the stomach. The anatomist tries to find out how the body starts these movements when it has food to digest.

These three studies are also closely allied to medicine, the study of disease. But of the three, physiology is most closely related to medicine. In most diseases, parts of the body are not acting the way they should. Doctors must depend on physiology to tell them how an organ acts when it is well before they can understand much about its diseases or how to keep it healthy.

The value of physiology to the human race has been great. It helps find the right way to solve public problems of hygiene, sanitation, and housing. A knowledge of the way the body works can help a person stay healthy and aid in curing disease when it appears.

The study of physiology shows that knowledge of health and disease should come from careful observation and experiment instead of unproved claims.

One of the outstanding benefits of physiology to mankind has been in the field of diabetes. This disease develops when certain parts of the pancreas do not act the way they should. Many young persons used to die from diabetes each year. Then, in 1922, physiologists completed a long series of experiments on animals. In the experiments, they first produced diabetes in the animals, and then controlled it in them. After this, doctors could use the same treatment for human beings. Many thousands of patients who would have died from diabetes now live long, active lives.   VICTOR JOHNSON

See also ANATOMY; BIOCHEMISTRY; HUMAN BODY; MEDICINE.

PHYSIOTHERAPY. See MENTAL ILLNESS (How Mental Illnesses Are Treated); PHYSICAL THERAPY.

PI. See CIRCLE (The Use of Pi).

PIA MATER. See BRAIN (Brain Membranes).

PIANISSIMO. See MUSIC (Terms Used in Music).

PIANKASHAW INDIANS. See MIAMI INDIANS.

Steinway & Sons

Long Hours of Practice, *above,* are required to become a good pianist. "Van" Cliburn, *below,* won international acclaim as a pianist in the late 1950's.

United Press Int.

Flemish Virginals Date from the Mid-1400's.

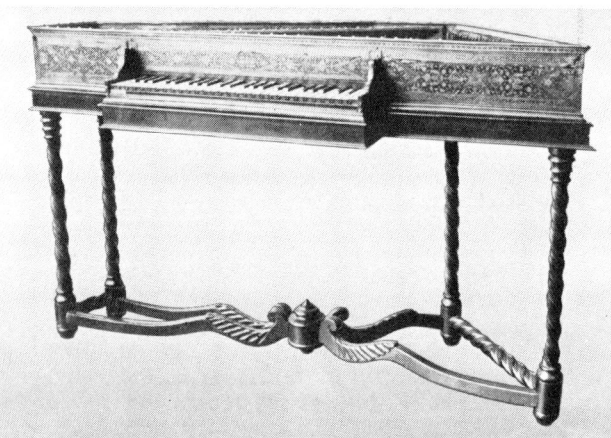

An Early Italian Spinet Produced Light Tinkling Tones.

PIANO, *pih AN oh,* is a keyboard instrument that makes a beautiful, extremely variable sound. It represents the most highly developed means of satisfying musical needs within a single instrument. It can produce both melody and harmony at the same time. Its range covers almost all the sounds used in music. And it can produce an extraordinary variety of soft and loud notes with great speed and beautiful tone-color effects.

To perform its unique functions, the piano makes use of strict scientific principles, such as those governing the vibration of stretched metal strings and those involving the behavior of sound. But a piano is more than a mechanical device, because it can express human emotions.

In an orchestra, a piano is sometimes grouped with the stringed instruments, because it has strings. It may also be classed as a percussion instrument, because the strings are struck. But it is not usually regarded as a member of any section of an orchestra. Pianists can play as soloists with an orchestra, as part of an orchestra, as part of smaller chamber-music groups, or as soloists.

Parts of a Piano

A piano has four essential elements: strings, action, soundboard, and framework. The *strings* generate sounds when struck by padded hammers. The player controls the hammers through the *action,* which includes a set of 88 keys. The *soundboard* amplifies the sound made by the vibrating strings. The *framework* holds the whole piano together.

The Strings. A piano has about 230 steel-wire strings, each tuned to one of the 88 notes of the equal-temperament musical scale. This scale is designed to modify the notes of the natural scale so they will be in tune with one another, no matter what key the pianist plays in. About 58 of the notes, called *unisons,* have three strings each, and almost all the rest have two strings.

The vibrating length of each string is calculated according to certain laws of physics to determine the piano's *scale,* or *stringing pattern.* The shortest string, in the *treble* or high section, is about 2 inches long. The longest string, in the *bass* or low section, may be as long as 80 inches in larger pianos.

The stringing pattern determines the tonal characteristics of the piano. But the strings also react differently in their harmonic content, or color, depending on how hard they are struck. This factor makes possible a great variation in the degree of expressiveness that can be drawn from the piano, depending on the artistry of the player.

The Action permits the pianist not only to obtain wide variations in tone color, but also to produce tones

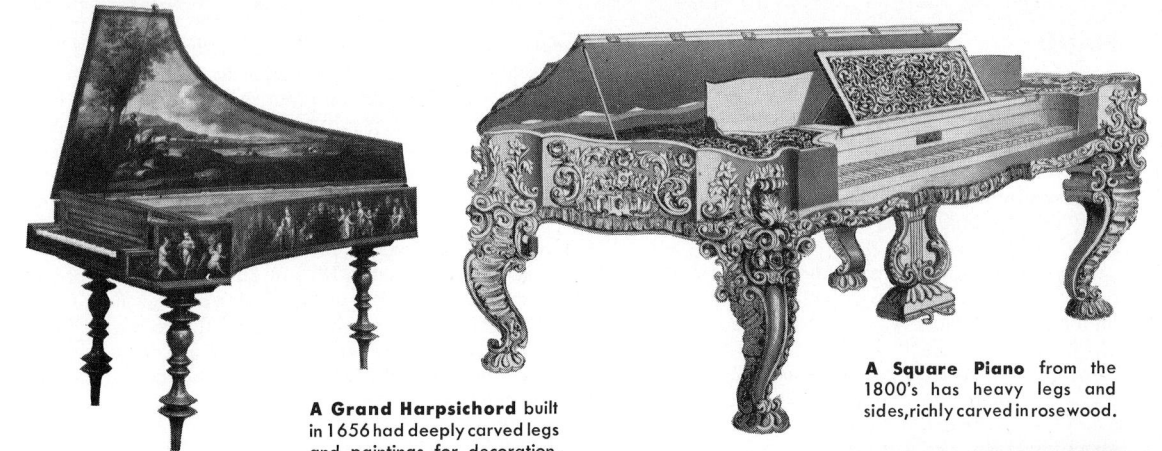

A Grand Harpsichord built
in 1656 had deeply carved legs
and paintings for decoration.

A Square Piano from the
1800's has heavy legs and
sides, richly carved in rosewood.

Art Institute of Chicago; Metropolitan Museum of Art
Bartolommeo Cristofori Made This Piano in 1720.

This Ornate Piano was called a
"harmonium" by its English makers.

both quickly and slowly, and either loudly or softly.

When the player presses down a key, it moves a system of levers that propels a hammer. The action is designed to send the hammer part of the way towards the string, then release it. The hammer hits the string of its own momentum, and instantly jumps away. When the player releases the key, a part of the action called the *damper* presses against the string, silencing it. But, as long as the pianist holds the key down, he holds the damper off the string, allowing it to vibrate. The player can also press a *pedal* with his foot to hold the dampers for all the notes away from the strings, allowing succeeding notes to enrich one another.

The hammer consists of a wooden head covered with a special kind of felt. It can be made hard or soft, producing further variations in tone. There are about 4,000 parts, mostly of wood, in the action of one piano.

The Soundboard, a sheet of wood about $\frac{3}{8}$ of an inch thick, has about 4,000 square inches of surface area exposed to the atmosphere. It vibrates when the strings do, greatly intensifying the power of their vibrations. The strings pass over *bridges*, strips of wood attached to the soundboard. They transmit their vibrations to the soundboard through the bridges.

The Framework. In the average piano, each string exerts a pull of about 150 pounds when it is in tune.

The total stress in a single piano with 230 strings is about 35,000 pounds, or $17\frac{1}{2}$ tons. The iron-plate and wooden supporting structure is specially designed to withstand this tremendous strain.

The development of the iron plate allowed piano-builders to take full musical advantage of the vibrating characteristics of highly stretched strings. But the plate also serves partly to reproduce and amplify some of the harmonics generated by the moving strings.

Sizes and Kinds

Pianos are classified by the way they are strung. A *grand* piano has strings that run horizontally. A *vertical* piano has strings running up and down.

Grand Pianos. If pianos were used only by professional concert artists, the *concert grand* would serve adequately. This 9-foot-long instrument has power suitable for a concert hall. From a scientific and artistic standpoint, it is ideal. But it is also the largest and most expensive piano. Smaller grand pianos, some as small as 5 feet, 1 inch in length, are more practical for the home.

Vertical Pianos take even less space. They are commonly classed as *spinet* (less than 39 inches high), *console* (39 to 41 inches), and *studio* (higher than 41 inches). The present-day vertical dates from 1935. About 97 of every 100 pianos sold each year are vertical.

PIANO

As a piece of furniture, a vertical piano outdates the bulky *upright*, which sometimes stood 60 inches tall. In its time and place, the upright was extremely popular. It played an important part in developing the piano as a home instrument. Another style that enjoyed popularity in the 1800's was the *square*, with horizontal stringing. See SPINET.

Player Pianos flourished from the late 1800's to the late 1920's. Inventors developed them while working on automatic devices to play music at home. The first player pianos were actually mechanical piano players. They were encased in cabinets that could be pushed up to any piano, so that wooden "fingers" extended over the keys. Seated in front of the cabinet, the operator pumped foot pedals to make the pneumatic mechanism work. A moving roll of paper, cut with patterns of holes, directed air pressure to the "fingers," making them play upon the keys.

Foot pumping, pneumatics, and air pressure were common to all mechanical players. The next step was to put the mechanism inside the case of the piano.

Reproducing players provide the expression automatically, copying exactly the playing of the person who made the roll. Many great pianists made reproducing player rolls before the advent of the phonograph. Some great early performances have been transferred to phonograph records by means of these rolls.

Electronic Pianos. Attempts to improve the conventional piano with electronic devices have not been successful. Many persons have worked on electronic instruments, but have not succeeded in producing any that are as good as conventional pianos.

History

The piano as we know it was the result of a gradual evolution, with many persons contributing to it. No one knows when man first discovered the musical beauty of the stretched string. Ancient peoples developed the *harp* and *lyre*, in which they plucked strings with their fingers (see HARP; LYRE). Later, peoples in the Middle East developed the *dulcimer*, in which they struck a set of strings with mallets (see DULCIMER). Europeans developed the *clavichord*, which had a keyboard to control the mallets (see CLAVICHORD). The *harpsichord* represented a still further development. It had quills to pluck the strings (see HARPSICHORD).

In 1709, an Italian named Bartolommeo Cristofori (1655-1731) worked out the principle of striking a hammer against strings to make a keyboard instrument that could be played loudly or softly by the touch of the fingers. He called his invention *gravicembalo col piano e forte*, or *harpsichord with soft and loud*. Cristofori's contribution fitted in with man's growing artistic ideals. But the harpsichord remained the dominant musical instrument of the 1700's. Johann Sebastian Bach did not like the piano of his time, and wrote for the harpsichord instead. In the late 1700's, John Broadwood discovered that a hammer striking the wrong point on the string would harm the harmonic content, or overtone richness, of the sound. Another important development was the invention of piano wire drawn from steel.

Cristofori's hammers were flat pieces of wood covered with leather. In the 1840's, felt was added, and a process for gluing it was developed in the 1870's. Other developments included Sebastian Erard's *double escapement*, a way to make the hammer fall back part of the way from the string while the key is held down. An American, Alpheus Babcock of Philadelphia, invented a cast-metal plate for square pianos about 1822. Another American, Jonas Chickering of Boston, made a grand piano in 1840 with a plate cast in one piece. Isaac Hawkins produced the first upright piano in 1800, and an action developed in 1826 by an Englishman, Robert Wornum, made this style practical. The New York City firm of Steinway & Sons developed the *overstrung bass*, with the longer bass strings stretched across the higher ones. The longer strings created more sound and better tone color.   JOHN B. CARLSON

Related Articles. WORLD BOOK includes the following biographies of famous pianists:

Albéniz, Isaac	Iturbi, José
Arrau, Claudio	Landowska, Wanda
Brahms, Johannes	Liszt, Franz
Bülow, Baron von	MacDowell, Edward
Busoni, Ferruccio B.	Moszkowski, Moritz
Chopin, Frédéric F.	Mozart, Wolfgang A.
Clementi, Muzio	Pachmann, Vladimir de
Cliburn, Van	Paderewski, Ignace J.
Cortot, Alfred	Rachmaninoff, Sergei V.
Czerny, Karl	Rosenthal, Moriz
Dohnányi, Ernst von	Rubinstein, Anton G.
Ganz, Rudolph	Rubinstein, Arthur
Gershwin, George	Saint-Saëns, Camille
Gieseking, Walter	Satie, Erik
Gould, Glenn	Schnabel, Artur
Grainger, Percy A.	Schumann, Clara
Granados, Enrique	Schumann, Robert
Hess, Dame Myra	Serkin, Rudolf
Horowitz, Vladimir	Tatum, Art

PIASTER, *pee AS tur*, or PIASTRE, is an old name for the Spanish dollar. Eight-*real* pieces (piasters) were the "pieces of eight" which were thought to be buried by the pirates of the Spanish Main. The term is no longer used in Spain. In Spanish-American countries, the peso is sometimes called a piaster.

The piaster was made a money unit in Turkey when the gold standard was set up in 1916. Nickel and silver piaster coins are in circulation. Ten- and five-piaster coins were made in aluminum bronze from 1924 to 1926. Piasters are also used in Egypt, Lebanon, Sudan, Syria, and Vietnam. See also PESO.   BURTON HOBSON

PIATIGORSKY, *pyuh tih GAWR skih,* **GREGOR** (1903-   ), is a famous Russian-born cellist. At the age of 15, he became first cellist of the Imperial Opera in Moscow. In 1921, after the Bolshevik Revolution, he fled from Russia. He played with the Berlin Philharmonic from 1924 to 1928. He made his first concert tour of the United States in 1929, and became an American citizen in 1942. Piatigorsky was born in Ekaterinoslav (now Dnepropetrovsk), and began to study the cello at the age of 8.   DOROTHY DELAY

PIAVE RIVER, *PYAH vay,* is a mountain stream that flows down from the Alps near the northern Italian border to the Adriatic Sea northeast of Venice. It is 134 miles long. The Piave River forms a beautiful and fertile valley across the province of Venezia. For location, see ITALY (physical map).

PICA. See TYPE (Sizes of Type).

PICADOR. See BULLFIGHTING.

PICARESQUE NOVEL. See SPANISH LITERATURE (Prose); NOVEL (Early Beginnings).

PICASSO, PABLO (1881-   ), is the most famous painter of the 1900's. He is also known for his sculpture, drawings, graphics, and ceramics. In some ways, he is the artist most characteristic of this century, because he has responded to changing conditions, moods, and challenges so intensely and so rapidly. His searching style has made him the leader in expressing the complexity of the 1900's.

Picasso's art challenges the viewer's traditional view of life. He appears drawn to tension and conflict. Picasso seems to explore the fantastic world of nightmare and deep imagination which modern psychology and modern art cite as great influences on our daily actions. He hopes to arouse and reveal unknown influences that lie hidden in the viewer's unconscious life. His images radiate the strangeness of dreams, yet have the appearance of fact. Perhaps Picasso was influenced by the art of his native Spain, which often seems fascinated by the visionary and the monstrous.

Early Career. Picasso was born in Málaga, Spain, but has lived in France since 1904. He was a child prodigy, painting realistic works when he was only 14. His first personal style, the *Blue Period* (1901-1904), focused on themes of loneliness and despair, and featured mainly shades of blue. This style gave way between 1904 and 1906 to one which stressed warmer colors and moods. Abandoning the thin, discouraged faces of the Blue Period, Picasso gave his subjects new flexibility and frequently included circus scenes. By 1906, he began painting great figures that are massive, as if to withstand potential shock or fear.

In 1907, Picasso painted *Les Demoiselles d'Avignon*,

Pablo Picasso, *left,* became one of the leading artists of the 1900's. *Guernica,* shown *below,* is considered one of his masterpieces. Picasso painted this symbolic work as a protest against the bombing of a Spanish town by the Nazis.

© Karsh, Ottawa

a landmark in art. This picture marked a decisive break with traditional notions of beauty and harmony. Five monstrous female figures with masks rather than faces pose in a convulsive, jagged array—distorted, shaken, and savagely transformed. Out of this disruptive image grew the style known as *cubism.* See CUBISM.

Early in 1912, Picasso began including newspaper clippings, bits of debris, and stenciled words in his paintings. In this way he hoped to break down the distinction between art and nonart and to make the viewer rethink his relationship to traditional art.

Later Career. After World War I, Picasso extended his explorations of form, placing special emphasis on brilliantly colored dreamlike images. From 1918 to 1924, he painted in a classical style, with huge and stately figures. In the 1920's and 1930's, Picasso portrayed figures as though from the inside out, and the lifeless objects in these works appear to have a life of their own. His *Guernica* (1937) was painted as a protest against the Nazi bombing of a Spanish town. The painting is Picasso's attempt to make a public statement using his personal symbols of rage and despair. The picture is an expression of crisis and disaster beyond individual control. In 1944, Picasso joined the Communist Party because he felt the Communists had been most effective in fighting the Nazis. But today Picasso's art is officially condemned as "decadent" and "unacceptable" in most Communist countries.

After 1945, Picasso's painting, sculpture, and ceramics developed a more relaxed and gentle feeling. He appeared to make peace with the emotions that had tormented him so often in the past. Some critics feel this new Picasso has outlived the best days of his art. Others feel this represents another advance in Picasso's visual and mental adventures in art.   LAWRENCE D. STEEFEL, JR.

For color reproductions of Picasso's paintings, see PAINTING (Modes of Composition); EUROPE (Art); ANIMAL (Man and the Animals). See also BRONZE (picture).

PICCADILLY CIRCUS. See LONDON (Piccadilly Circus).

PICCALILLI is a popular relish made from chopped and pickled cucumbers, other vegetables, and spices.

The Museum of Modern Art, New York

PICCARD

PICCARD, *pee KAHR,* is the name of a Swiss family of scientists, two of whom were twin brothers. The twins —Jean and Auguste—were born at Basel, Switzerland, and were educated in Zurich.

Auguste Piccard (1884-1962), a physicist, invented an airtight gondola which he attached to a huge balloon. With it, he ascended about 53,000 feet into the stratosphere in 1932. In 1953, he descended 10,300 feet into the sea in a steel sphere called a *bathyscaph* (see BATHYSCAPH). He and his son Jacques designed another bathyscaph in which Jacques and a companion descended 35,800 feet in the Pacific in 1960. Auguste Piccard was a professor of physics at the University of Brussels before and after World War II.

Jean Piccard (1884-1963), an aeronautical engineer and chemist, was a scientific observer on a stratospheric balloon ascent of more than 57,500 feet piloted by his wife Jeannette. He made a solo ascent in 1937 in an open gondola lifted by 100 six-foot balloons. The flight tested the idea of multiple balloons for stratospheric flights (see BALLOON [Balloon Explorations]).

Piccard taught at the University of Chicago from 1916 to 1919, and then taught in Switzerland for seven

Bowmar Educational Records

The Piccolo is smaller than a flute. A piccolo player makes music by blowing across a hole in the mouthpiece.

Mouthpiece

Tone Holes (Under Keys)

Keys

Auguste Piccard ascended to a height of about 53,000 feet in 1932 in the airtight aluminum gondola attached to his balloon.
Brown Bros.

years. He returned to the United States in 1926 and became an American citizen in 1931. CARL T. CHASE
Critically reviewed by DON PICCARD

PICCOLO, *PICK oh lo,* is the smallest of the wood-wind instruments and the highest in pitch. It is really a half-size flute. It is used to extend the upper range of the wood-wind instruments and to add a shrill, strongly heard effect. Its most important use is in military and

concert bands. Beethoven used it in his "Egmont Overture" and Wagner in *Die Meistersinger.* The C piccolo is a transposing instrument sounding an octave higher than the part is written. CHARLES B. RIGHTER

PICHINCHA, *pee CHEEN chah,* a twin-cratered volcano, rises 15,696 feet in the Andes Mountains in north-central Ecuador. For location, see ECUADOR (color map). The volcano last erupted in 1881. Climbers may ascend the peaks from Quito, which lies about 5 miles to the southeast. On Pichincha's lower slopes, patriot forces defeated the Spanish royalists in the Battle of Pichincha in 1822, thus liberating Ecuador.

PICKEREL, *PICK ur ul,* is the name given to three small members of the pike family. The pike perch is often wrongly called a pickerel. Like all pikes, true pickerels have large mouths and greedy appetites. They fight stubbornly when caught on a hook. All pickerels live in fresh water. They usually feed on much smaller fishes.

The three kinds of pickerel are the *bulldog pickerel,* which lives east of the Alleghenies from Massachusetts to Florida; the *mud pickerel,* found abundantly in the Mississippi Valley; and the *chain pickerel,* which lives in lakes and streams east and south of the Alleghenies, from Maine to Florida and west to Arkansas. The bulldog pickerel and the mud pickerel seldom grow more than a foot long, and are too small to be important

The Chain Pickerel Is a Popular Game Fish.
New York Zoological Society

food or game fishes. The chain pickerel is a game fish, popular with sportsmen. Its flesh is good to eat. It commonly reaches a length of about 2 feet and may even reach an extreme size of about 3 feet. Its greatest weight is about 10 pounds.

Scientific Classification. Pickerels are in the pike family, *Esocidae.* The bulldog pickerel is genus *Esox,* species *E. americanus;* mud pickerel, *E. vermiculatus;* and chain pickerel, *E. reticulatus.*   CARL L. HUBBS

See also MUSKELLUNGE; PIKE; FISHING (table: Game-Fishing World Records).

PICKERING is the family name of two American astronomers who were brothers. **Edward Charles Pickering** (1846-1919) invented a meridian photometer to measure the brightness of stars. He also directed a program of photographing stars and their spectra. He served as director of the Harvard Observatory for 42 years, from 1877 until his death. **William Henry Pickering** (1858-1938) discovered Phoebe, the faint ninth satellite of Saturn, in 1889. The Pickerings were born in Boston.   HELEN WRIGHT

PICKERING, JOHN. See IMPEACHMENT.

PICKERING, TIMOTHY (1745-1829), was a leading American statesman. He served as postmaster general from 1791 to 1795, secretary of war in 1795, and secretary of state from 1795 to 1800. A member of the Federalist party, he represented Massachusetts in the U.S. Senate from 1803 to 1811 and in the House of Representatives from 1813 to 1817. Pickering opposed the policies of Presidents Thomas Jefferson and James Madison. In 1804, he sponsored a plan to have New England secede from the Union. But the plan failed. Pickering was born in Salem, Mass. BENJAMIN W. LABAREE

PICKET. See LABOR (Strikes and Lockouts); STRIKE.

PICKETT, GEORGE EDWARD (1825-1875), was a Confederate general. His charge in the Battle of Gettysburg during the Civil War ranks as one of the great events in American history. On July 3, 1863, Cemetery Ridge was a key to the Union Army's positions. Pickett's division charged up the hill in the face of heavy fire, and his troops broke through a part of the Union lines. Soldiers fought hand to hand. No help came to Pickett from the main Confederate lines, and at last his men fell back, after suffering terrible losses.

The failure of Pickett's charge ended the Battle of Gettysburg, and General Robert E. Lee retreated the next day. The charge and the battle marked the "high tide" of the Confederate cause. The battle shattered the Army of Northern Virginia, and it never regained its former power. Although Pickett continued in command of his division, he was broken in spirit. He later served with General James Longstreet.

Pickett was born in Richmond, Va., and was graduated from the United States Military Academy in 1846. He served in the Mexican War and on the Indian frontier. Pickett became a major general in 1862, and fought in the Battle of Seven Pines and

General George Pickett
Chicago Historical Society

at Fredericksburg. After the Civil War, he returned to Richmond and headed the Virginia agency of a New York insurance company.   FRANK E. VANDIVER

PICKETT, JOSEPH (1848-1918), an American storekeeper, carpenter, and shipbuilder by trade, won fame as a folk artist. He had no lessons, and painted only as a hobby. Of his three paintings known to exist, the most noted is *Manchester Valley* in the Museum of Modern Art in New York City. Pickett used rich, harmonious colors, and had a feeling for line and textures rare in an untrained painter. He was born in New Hope, Pa., and found most of his subjects in this town, where he lived.   EDWIN L. FULWIDER

PICKFORD, MARY (1893-   ), a motion-picture actress and producer, won fame as "America's Sweetheart." Only five feet tall, she often played children's roles in such films as *Daddy Long Legs* and *Rebecca of Sunnybrook Farm.* Later she played adult roles, and co-starred in *The Taming of the Shrew* with her husband, Douglas Fairbanks. Miss Pickford was born Gladys Mary Smith in Toronto, Canada, on April 8, 1893. She wrote *My Rendezvous With Life* (1935) and *Sunshine and Shadow* (1955).   NARDI REEDER CAMPION

United Press Int.
Mary Pickford

See also MOTION PICTURE (The Silent Era; picture).

PICKLE is a fruit or vegetable preserved in vinegar and salt. Pickles are made with or without sugar, and are usually seasoned with spices. Meats preserved in brine and vinegar are called pickled meats. Pickled pigs' feet and corned beef are prepared in a pickling solution, or brine.

The most common vegetable for pickles is the cucumber. Other fruits and vegetables often used in making pickles or relishes are cauliflower, onions, tomatoes, beets, red and green peppers, cabbage, crab apples, peaches, pears, and watermelon.

In making most pickles, the fruits or vegetables are soaked in brine and vinegar. Then they are flavored with seasonings such as mustard, dill, horse-radish, cinnamon, allspice, cloves, celery seed, peppercorn, and pimiento. The pickle is then sealed tightly in jars. Some firms prepare a mixture of many spices especially for use in making certain types of pickles. They call this product "pickling spice."

Cucumber pickles may be either sweet or sour. Dill pickles are the most common type of sour pickles. Small cucumbers, or gherkins, are the best known of the sweet type. Gherkins are preserved whole or in slices.

The pickling industry has grown rapidly since the 1930's. About $160 million worth of pickles and pickle products is made each year.   LEONE RUTLEDGE CARROLL

See also CUCUMBER; DILL.

PICKTHALL, MARJORIE. See CANADIAN LITERATURE (Poetry of the 1900's).

PICKWICK PAPERS. See DICKENS, CHARLES (Literary Success).

403

PICRIC ACID

PICRIC ACID, *PIK rik,* is an important industrial chemical. Its name comes from the Greek word *pikros,* meaning *bitter,* which describes its taste. Peter Woulfe, a chemist, first isolated the acid in 1771.

Although best known as an explosive, picric acid is no longer used in shells because it corrodes the metal casings. It combines with metals to form salts called *picrates,* which are unstable and are used to set off more stable explosives. The acid is also used as a *mordant* (dye-fixative), and in ointments for burns.

Picric acid is a yellow crystalline solid, slightly soluble in water. It melts at 122° C. (252° F.), and its chemical formula is $C_6H_2(NO_2)_3OH$.   JOHN E. LEFFLER

PICT was the name of an ancient people of Scotland. The Picts were given this name by the Romans because they painted or tattooed their skins. The Latin word for *painter* is *pictor.* The first historical reference to the Picts occurs in a speech made by a Roman orator in A.D. 297. The Pictish tribes fought the Romans for many years. The Romans built a long wall on the English-Scottish border to keep them out of Britain. Later, the Picts fought the Teutonic conquerors of Britain, the Angles and Saxons. They disappeared as a race about A.D. 900. See also SCOTLAND (Early Years).   ROBERT S. HOYT

PICTOGRAPH is picture writing. Before the development of the alphabet, many ancient peoples conveyed messages by pictographs. The Egyptians carved or painted pictographs on tombs and monuments. Picture writing was also a means of communication for the Aztecs and for the early American Indians. Pictographs were of two kinds: those that represented objects, such as a drawing of the moon or of a star, and those that represented ideas, such as a drawing of a woman with a broom, to represent a wife. Modern pictographs use pictures and words to tell a story better than words alone could tell it.   DYNO LOWENSTEIN

See also GRAPH; HIEROGLYPHIC; ALPHABET; EASTER ISLAND.

PICTOU, *PICK too,* Nova Scotia (pop. 4,254; alt. 36 ft.), a port on Northumberland Strait, has the largest live-lobster industry in Canada. Pictou lies on a fine harbor formed by the meeting point of the East, West, and Middle rivers. For location, see NOVA SCOTIA (political map). Industries include shipbuilding and lumbering.

Pictou was first settled in 1767 by six families from Pennsylvania and Maryland. In 1773, a large ship brought nearly 200 settlers to Pictou from Scotland. During the early 1800's, thousands of Scots came to Nova Scotia through this port. Pictou has a mayor-council form of government.   THOMAS H. RADDALL

PICTURE. See ART MUSEUM; ETCHING; MOTION PICTURE; PAINTING; PHOTOGRAPHY; POSTER.

PICTURE WRITING. See HIEROGLYPHIC; ALPHABET; CUNEIFORM; PICTOGRAPH.

PIDGIN ENGLISH is one of several *bridge* or *minimum* dialects, based on English, used in Asia and the South Seas between Westerners and Asians, and among peoples who have no common tongue. Although usually deplored as a corruption of English, it serves the needs of millions who would be unable to communicate without it. The vernacular dialect of English spoken in Hawaii is also called *Pidgin.*   S. I. HAYAKAWA

Chase Manhattan Bank Money Museum

A Piece of Eight. Coins of this sort, known also as "Spanish milled dollars," were once widely used in the Americas, including the United States. They were called "pieces of eight" because they were worth eight reals, the real being valued at about 12½ cents. The coin pictured here was minted in Mexico during the reign of King Charles III of Spain.

PIECE OF EIGHT was a name for the Spanish *peso,* which corresponded to the American dollar (see PESO). It was so named because it was worth 8 *reals* and once had an *8* stamped on it. The piece of eight was sometimes cut into pie-shaped smaller denominations called *bits.* The most popular size was the quarter, called *two bits.* The United States quarter is sometimes called *two bits* today. The piece of eight was used when pirate activity was widespread. The coin figures in many pirate stories, including *Treasure Island.*   BURTON HOBSON

See also REAL.

PIECEWORK is a form of wage payment in which employers pay employees a specified amount for each unit of satisfactory output produced. This system contrasts with *time wages,* where an employee receives pay for the amount of time he works. Piecework rates are designed to encourage employees to produce more in a given period.

There are many types of specific piecework plans. Some pay a premium for time saved. Most pay a guaranteed minimum wage. Most plans have individual rates, but some pay for group output.   GERALD SOMERS

PIED PIPER OF HAMELIN is a mythical character who was made famous by Robert Browning in a poem based on a legend. According to the legend, the German town of Hamelin was infested by rats. One day, a strange man dressed in a suit of many colors walked into Hamelin and offered to rid the town of the pests for a certain sum of money. When the mayor agreed, the man drew out a pipe and walked along the streets playing a haunting tune. All the rats came tumbling out of the houses and followed the Piper to the Weser River, where they drowned. When the Piper claimed his reward, the mayor refused to pay him. The Piper swore vengeance. Once more he walked along the streets playing his strange melody. This time all the children ran from their homes and followed him to a cave in the nearby Köppen Hill. The cave closed upon them, and the children were never seen again.

This legend seems to be based at least in part on fact. Old writings on the walls of several houses in Hamelin say that on July 26, 1284, a Piper led 130 children out of town and that they were lost in Köppen Hill. Some believe that the Piper was an agent of the Bishop of Olmütz who in the late 1200's drew many Hamelin lads to Moravia, where they settled. Others

The Pied Piper Lured the Children of Hamelin by playing his magic pipe. According to an old legend, the Mayor of Hamelin broke his promise to give the Piper money for ridding the town of rats. The Piper then bewitched the children with his music, and led them out of town. The children were never seen again.

claim that the children were kidnaped by robbers. It is also possible that the Pied Piper legend came from the Children's Crusade of 1212.   ARTHUR M. SELVI

See also CRUSADES (The Children's Crusade).

PIEDMONT, *PEED mahnt*, is a territorial region of Italy in the upper valley of the Po River. For location, see ITALY (political map). The name *Piedmont* means *foot of the mountain*. It refers to the region's position at the base of the Alps. The region covers 9,807 square miles and has a population of about 4 million. It includes the provinces of Alessandria, Asti, Cuneo, Novara, Torino, and Vercelli. The Piedmont's capital is Turin. Farming is the chief industry in this fertile region. Piedmont was at one time part of the Sardinian kingdom (see SARDINIA, KINGDOM OF).   SHEPARD B. CLOUGH

PIEDMONT COLLEGE. See UNIVERSITIES AND COLLEGES (table).

PIEDMONT REGION is an area of gently rolling to hilly land lying between the Appalachian Mountains and the Atlantic Coastal Plain. It is sometimes called the Piedmont Plateau. It was named for the Piedmont region in Italy. It varies in width from about 50 miles in the north to more than 125 miles in the south.

The division between the Piedmont Region and the Coastal Plain is sharply marked by the fall line for the rivers flowing toward the sea. Along the fall line, streams from the west leave the harder, rocky ground near the mountains and drop to the softer Coastal Plain.

Many large cities have developed along the fall line, partly because of the available water power and the nearness to tidewater. They include Newark, N.J.; Philadelphia, Pa.; Wilmington, Del.; Baltimore, Md.; Washington, D.C.; Richmond, Va.; and Columbia, S.C.

The Piedmont Region covers about 80,000 square miles. It ranges in elevation from 300 feet above sea level on the east to 1,200 feet on the west.

Tobacco is widely grown in the Piedmont Region. The Piedmont cities of Durham and Winston-Salem, N.C.; and Richmond, Va., account for half of the total production of manufactured tobacco in the United States. The Piedmont section of Virginia and Pennsylvania is fine apple-growing country. The dairy industry is an important source of income in the northern Piedmont. The southern Piedmont ranks as the leading cotton-textile producing area in the country. Birmingham, Ala., is the leading iron and steel center of the South.   E. WILLARD MILLER

See also FALL LINE; PLATEAU.

PIEPLANT. See RHUBARB.

PIEPOUDRE, *PI pou der*, **COURT OF**, or PIEPOWDER, was the name of an English court during the Middle Ages. Local disputes among peddlers and tradesmen were settled in the Court of Piepoudre. See also FAIRS AND EXPOSITIONS (Scottish and Irish Fairs).

PIER has two meanings. One kind of pier is a pillar or post supporting a heavy weight. Such piers may form the end of a span of a bridge, the foundation posts of a large building, or the support from which an arch springs. Another kind is a platform on posts or piles extending into a body of water. This kind is used as a breakwater and for such activities as loading ships.

In building construction, piers are used when it is necessary to extend the foundation to a great depth to find suitable support.   R. G. HENNES

See also ARCHITECTURE (Architectural Terms); BRIDGE (The Pier Principle); COFFERDAM; HARBOR; DOCK (picture).

The Piedmont Region Borders the Appalachian Mountains.

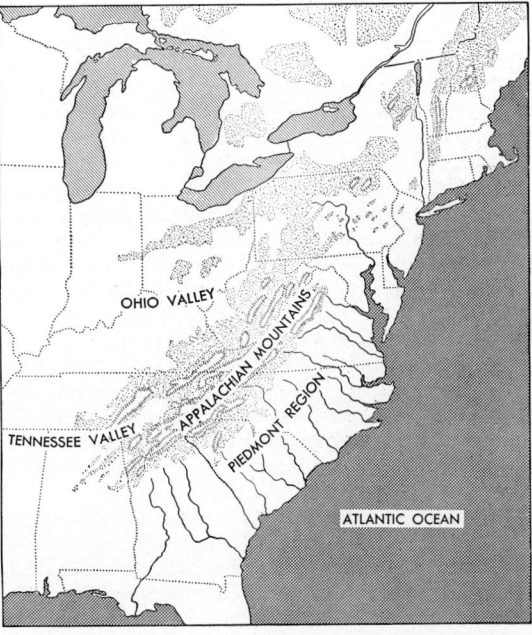

FRANKLIN PIERCE

The United States Flag had 31 stars throughout Pierce's term of office.

TAYLOR
12th President
1849 — 1850

FILLMORE
13th President
1850 — 1853

BUCHANAN
15th President
1857 — 1861

LINCOLN
16th President
1861 — 1865

Painting by George P. A. Healy; Mellon
Collection, National Gallery of Art

14TH PRESIDENT OF THE UNITED STATES 1853-1857

PIERCE, FRANKLIN (1804-1869), served as President during a period of increasing bitterness between North and South that later led to the Civil War. He won the Democratic nomination for President in 1852 after the four strongest candidates had fought to a stalemate. Pierce gained support because he strongly favored the Compromise of 1850, which sought to settle the slavery dispute. "If the compromise measures are not . . . firmly maintained," he said, "the Constitution will be trampled in the dust." At 48, Pierce became the youngest President up to that time.

The personal good looks of Pierce and his brilliant speaking manner impressed all who met him. People in New Hampshire respected his service as a U.S. Representative and Senator, and as a brigadier general in the Mexican War. But few persons outside his home state had heard of Pierce until he ran for President.

As President, Pierce faced two difficult problems: (1) growing Northern opposition to any expansion of slavery, and (2) rising prejudice against immigrants. He angered Northerners by supporting the Kansas-Nebraska Act, which made slavery possible in a large area of the West. This act provided the issue that created the Republican party. Pierce stirred up further opposition when he protected the rights of immigrants. Those opposed to granting rights to immigrants also formed a new party, called the Know-Nothing, or American, party. By the time Pierce's term ended, the Democratic party had lost much of its strength. Few Democrats favored Pierce for re-election.

The years of Pierce's administration marked one of the most prosperous periods in American history. The California gold rush still attracted men westward. Federal grants of land spurred railroads to extend their lines westward. And the Gadsden Purchase added land from Mexico to the Territory of New Mexico. The literary world discussed such new works as Thoreau's *Walden*, Longfellow's *The Song of Hiawatha*, and Whitman's *Leaves of Grass*. People hummed Stephen Foster's "My Old Kentucky Home, Good Night." At Christmastime in 1855, carolers sang "Hark! The Herald Angels Sing" for the first time.

Early Life

Franklin Pierce was born in Hillsboro, N.H., on Nov. 23, 1804. His father, Benjamin Pierce, had served in the Revolutionary War, and later became a brigadier general in the state militia. The elder Pierce served two terms as governor of New Hampshire. Franklin spent a happy childhood with his six older and two younger brothers and sisters.

At the age of 11, the boy was sent to the academy in nearby Hancock. Friends recalled that just after Franklin entered the school, he became homesick and returned home on foot. His father put the runaway into a wagon, drove him halfway back to the academy, and dropped him at the roadside, never saying a word. The boy trudged the remaining seven miles back to school. A year later, he transferred to the academy at Francestown, N.H., and later to Phillips Exeter Academy. In 1820, Pierce entered Bowdoin College, where he became a close friend of classmate Nathaniel Hawthorne.

─── **IMPORTANT DATES IN PIERCE'S LIFE** ───

1804 (Nov. 23) Born in Hillsboro, N.H.
1833 Elected to the U.S. House of Representatives.
1834 (Nov. 10) Married Jane Means Appleton.
1837 Elected to the United States Senate.
1847 Served as brigadier general in the Mexican War.
1852 Elected President of the United States.
1869 (Oct. 8) Died in Concord, N.H.

Pierce spent much of his college life in social activities. He joined literary and political clubs, and became active in debating groups. At the end of his second year, Pierce's marks were the lowest in his class. He then settled down to study, and ranked third in his class when he was graduated in 1824.

Political and Public Career

Pierce began studying law under Governor Levi Woodbury of New Hampshire. He later studied under Judge Samuel Howe and Judge Edmund Parker. In 1827, Pierce opened his own law office in Concord, N.H.

Entry into Politics. Pierce supported Andrew Jackson's campaign for the presidency. In 1829, he won election to the New Hampshire House of Representatives. He was re-elected two years later and became speaker of the house. In 1833, Pierce won a seat in the United States House of Representatives. After serving two terms he was elected to the United States Senate. At 33, he became the youngest Senator.

Pierce's Family. Pierce's years in Congress were not happy. In 1834, he had married Jane Means Appleton (March 12, 1806-Dec. 2, 1863), the daughter of a former president of Bowdoin College. Mrs. Pierce suffered from tuberculosis. She disliked Washington, and seldom accompanied her husband to the capital. Her natural shyness deepened to melancholy after two of their three sons died in early childhood. Pierce finally agreed to his wife's wishes and resigned from the Senate in 1842, shortly before his term ended.

Soldier. Soon after the Mexican War began in 1846, President James K. Polk commissioned Pierce a colonel in the U.S. Army. A few months later, Pierce was promoted to brigadier general. He served under General Winfield Scott on the expedition to Mexico City. Pierce commanded a brigade in the attack on Churubusco, and suffered a leg injury when thrown from his horse. He returned to the assault the next day. When

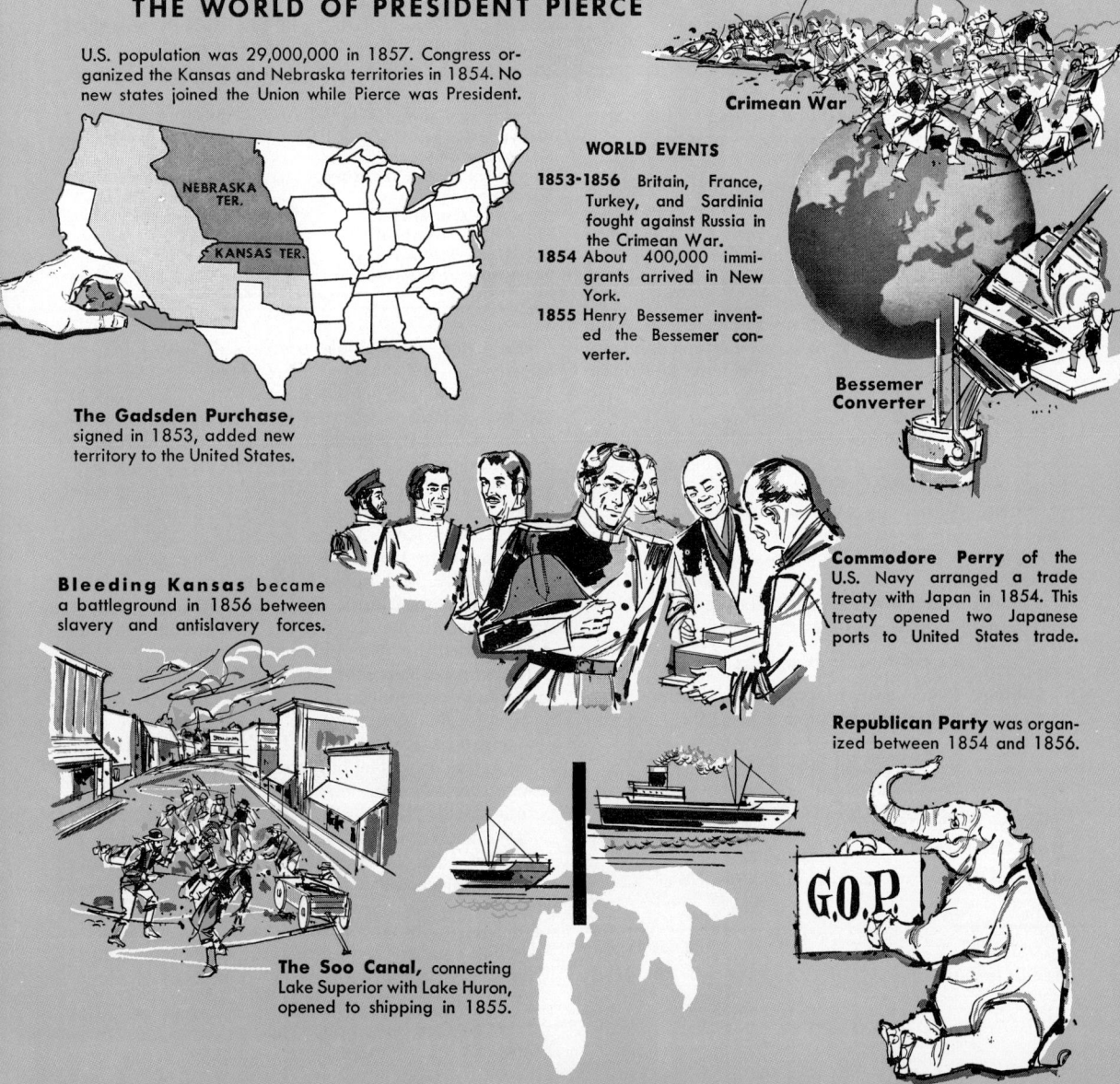

THE WORLD OF PRESIDENT PIERCE

U.S. population was 29,000,000 in 1857. Congress organized the Kansas and Nebraska territories in 1854. No new states joined the Union while Pierce was President.

Crimean War

WORLD EVENTS

1853-1856 Britain, France, Turkey, and Sardinia fought against Russia in the Crimean War.

1854 About 400,000 immigrants arrived in New York.

1855 Henry Bessemer invented the Bessemer converter.

Bessemer Converter

The Gadsden Purchase, signed in 1853, added new territory to the United States.

Bleeding Kansas became a battleground in 1856 between slavery and antislavery forces.

Commodore Perry of the U.S. Navy arranged a trade treaty with Japan in 1854. This treaty opened two Japanese ports to United States trade.

Republican Party was organized between 1854 and 1856.

The Soo Canal, connecting Lake Superior with Lake Huron, opened to shipping in 1855.

G.O.P.

Franklin Pierce Was Born in Hillsboro, N.H. The house in which he was born fell into ruin, and nothing remains of it today. The Pierce family moved to the handsome clapboard home, above, also in Hillsboro, when Franklin was only three weeks old.

Brown Bros.

Maine Historical Society

Jane Pierce, overcome by the death of her son in 1853, remained in seclusion for nearly half her husband's term.

close to the enemy lines, he wrenched his injured leg, fainted from pain, and lay helpless under fire until the end of the battle. For this, political enemies later accused Pierce of cowardice.

Election of 1852. Pierce resumed his law practice in Concord after the war. He had become one of New Hampshire's leading Democrats by the time his party's national convention met in 1852. The delegates faced a difficult job in choosing a candidate for President who would be acceptable to all factions of the party. The four strongest candidates were Senator Stephen A. Douglas of Illinois and three former Cabinet members —James Buchanan, William L. Marcy, and Lewis Cass.

After 34 ballots, it began to appear that none of the favored candidates could win the nomination. Delegates from Virginia then nominated Pierce. The New Englander expected some Northern support, and the South trusted him because he had supported the Compromise of 1850 and endorsed strict enforcement of the Fugitive Slave Law. As the balloting continued, several Buchanan delegations swung to Pierce, and he won on the 49th ballot. The convention chose Senator William R. D. King of Alabama for Vice-President.

The Whigs nominated General Winfield Scott for President and Secretary of the Navy William A. Graham for Vice-President. The Compromise of 1850 had temporarily settled the slavery problem, and no real issues appeared to separate the two parties (see COMPROMISE OF 1850). But the campaign disclosed that Scott really opposed slavery, causing opposition to him in the South. Pierce won a majority of the popular vote, and carried many more states than did Scott.

Pierce's Administration (1853-1857)

Cabinet. Pierce tried to promote harmony in the Democratic party by choosing men from all factions for

```
————— PIERCE'S ELECTION —————
Place of Nominating Convention....Baltimore

Ballot on Which Nominated.......49th

Whig Opponent...................Winfield Scott

Electoral Vote....................254 (Pierce) to
                                      42 (Scott)

Popular Vote.....................1,601,117 (Pierce) to
                                   1,385,453 (Scott)

Age at Inauguration..............48
```

his Cabinet. His appointments consisted of two conservative Southerners (Guthrie and Dobbin), two conservative Northerners (Marcy and Campbell), an antislavery Northerner (McClelland), a states' rights Southerner (Davis), and a New England Whig (Cushing). Vice-President King, who had been ill for several months, died in April, 1853, without ever performing the duties of his office (see KING, WILLIAM R. D.).

```
————— VICE-PRESIDENT AND CABINET —————
Vice-President......................*William R. D. King
Secretary of State..................William L. Marcy
Secretary of the Treasury...........James Guthrie
Secretary of War....................*Jefferson Davis
Attorney General....................Caleb Cushing
Postmaster General..................James Campbell
Secretary of the Navy...............James C. Dobbin
Secretary of the Interior...........Robert McClelland
             *Has a separate biography in WORLD BOOK.
```

Life in the White House began in an atmosphere of tragedy and grief for the Pierces. They had seen their 11-year-old son Benjamin die in a railroad accident just two months before the inauguration. Mrs. Pierce collapsed from grief, and did not attend her husband's inauguration. She secluded herself in an upstairs bedroom for nearly half of his term. Washington gossips called her "the shadow in the White House."

Mrs. Abby Kent Means, an aunt of Mrs. Pierce, served as White House hostess during Pierce's first two years in office. Mrs. Pierce finally appeared at a White House function on Jan. 1, 1855, and thereafter attended state dinners frequently. But one visitor remarked that she remained the "very picture of melancholy."

The Kansas-Nebraska Act. In January, 1854, Senator Douglas introduced a bill which he hoped would hasten frontier settlement. It proposed to carve two new territories, Kansas and Nebraska, out of the Indian lands in the West. The bill provided that settlers in the new territories would decide for themselves whether to permit slavery. Douglas' bill threatened to upset the uneasy slavery truce established by the compromises of 1820 and 1850. A farsighted statesman would have seen the danger in such a law. But Pierce, acting on the advice of his party leaders, supported the bill. It became law on May 30, 1854 (see KANSAS-NEBRASKA ACT). Both slavery and antislavery people poured into Kansas. Each group sought to control the territory.

Their rivalry soon developed into armed clashes (see KANSAS ["Bleeding Kansas"]).

The Kansas-Nebraska Act created a violent realignment of political parties. The Democrats defended the existing laws on slavery. The Whigs, already weakened by sectionalism, disintegrated. This hastened the birth of the new Republican party and the Know-Nothing party (see KNOW-NOTHING; REPUBLICAN PARTY).

Foreign Affairs. In his inaugural address, Pierce had boldly summarized his attitude toward foreign policy by saying: "My administration will not be controlled by any timid forebodings of evil from expansion." In 1853, he advocated the annexation of Hawaii. This plan fell through, partly because King Kamehameha died. The Gadsden Purchase of 1853 provided the country with a southern railroad route to the Pacific Coast and settled the boundary question with Mexico (see GADSDEN PURCHASE). At Pierce's insistence, the Senate ratified a trade treaty with Japan in 1854. This treaty opened Japan to American trading interests.

Acts of this kind fitted well with the attitude of the American people, who believed in national expansion. But when three of Pierce's diplomats claimed in 1854 that the United States had the right to seize Cuba from Spain, the public reacted against the President. See OSTEND MANIFESTO.

Later Years

Pierce's handling of the slavery issue destroyed his political usefulness. After the inauguration of James Buchanan, Pierce and his wife went abroad in a futile attempt to improve her health. They spent two years on Madeira, visited Europe, then returned home. Mrs. Pierce died in Andover, Mass., on Dec. 2, 1863.

Pierce became a bitter critic of President Abraham Lincoln during the Civil War. He charged that Lincoln could have avoided the conflict by proper leadership. Pierce died on Oct. 8, 1869, and was buried next to his wife in the Old North Cemetery at Concord. The Pierce home at Hillsboro, N.H., has been preserved as a state historic site. An authoritative book on Pierce is *Franklin Pierce* by Roy F. Nichols.　　PHILIP S. KLEIN

Related Articles in WORLD BOOK include:

Gadsden Purchase　　King, William R. D.
Kansas-Nebraska Act　　President of the United States

Outline

I. Early Life
II. Political and Public Career
　A. Entry into Politics　　C. Soldier
　B. Pierce's Family　　D. Election of 1852
III. Pierce's Administration (1853-1857)
　A. Cabinet
　B. Life in the White House
　C. The Kansas-Nebraska Act
　D. Foreign Affairs
IV. Later Years

Questions

Why did Pierce's position on the Kansas-Nebraska Act turn Northerners against him?

What tragedy influenced Pierce's life in the White House? Who was "the shadow in the White House"?

Why did Pierce win the Democratic presidential nomination over better-known candidates?

Why was Pierce later accused of cowardice during the Mexican War?

Why was Pierce rejected for renomination?

PIERO DELLA FRANCESCA, *PYEH roh* DELL *uh frahn* CHAYS *kah* (1416?-1492), was a great Italian painter in the early Renaissance. Piero della Francesca combined the clear design of the Florentine painters with the colorful light of many painters in The Netherlands. He wrote on the laws of perspective drawing. Piero's frescoes include the series *The Legend of the Cross.* A detail from a scene in the series, *The Queen of Sheba at the Sacred Bridge,* appears in color in the PAINTING article. His portraits of the Duke and Duchess of Urbino are in the Uffizi Gallery in Florence.

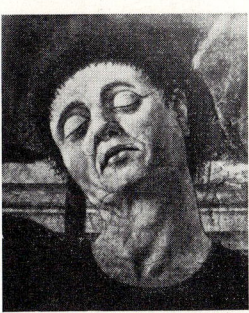
Historical Pictures Service
Piero della Francesca

Adoration and *Baptism of Christ* are in the National Gallery of London. Piero was born in Borgo San Sepolcro, Italy.　　WOLFGANG LOTZ

PIERPONT, FRANCIS HARRISON (1814-1899), served as governor of the "Restored Government of Virginia" during the Civil War. After Virginia withdrew from the Union, 34 counties in the western part of the state organized the "Restored Government" in 1861 and remained loyal to the Union. In 1863, West Virginia was admitted to the Union. Arthur I. Boreman was appointed governor. But Pierpont remained governor of the few Virginia counties that stayed loyal to the North. After Union forces captured Richmond in 1865, Pierpont returned there and governed Virginia until 1868. He was born near Morgantown, Virginia (now West Virginia). Pierpont represents West Virginia in Statuary Hall in Washington, D.C.　　W. B. HESSELTINE

PIERRE, *peer,* S. Dak. (pop. 10,088; alt. 1,440 ft.), is the capital of the state. It also serves as the chief trading center of a large agricultural region. Pierre lies on the east bank of the Missouri River, near the center of South Dakota (see SOUTH DAKOTA [political map]).

The state capitol has a central rotunda, flanked by the legislative wings. The capitol was completed in 1910. Many of Pierre's residents work in the city's federal and state government offices. The livestock industry is another important source of income in Pierre.

Pierre was named for Pierre Chouteau, an early fur trader. The first permanent settlers arrived in 1878, and the Chicago and North Western Railway reached the settlement in 1880. The town prospered as the railroad terminus. Pierre became the state capital in 1889, shortly after South Dakota was made a state.

The seat of Hughes County, Pierre has a mayor-council type of government.　　EVERETT W. STERLING

PIERROT, *PYEH* ROH, a character in French pantomime, was descended from the Italian character, Pedrolino. Costumed in a white blouse and pantaloons, and with a white face, Pierrot usually appeared as an honest and outspoken servant. In English pantomime, Pierrot is more of a clown. Some ballets represent him as a poet in love with Columbine (see COLUMBINE).　　RICHARD MOODY

PIETÁ. See MICHELANGELO (with color pictures); JESUS CHRIST (color picture); BRONZE (picture).

PIETERMARITZBURG

PIETERMARITZBURG, *PEE ter MAR its burg* (pop. 91,-988; met. area 128,598; alt. 2,360 ft.), is the capital and a major trading center of Natal Province in South Africa. It lies about 45 miles northwest of Durban. For location, see SOUTH AFRICA (color map).

Pietermaritzburg serves as a trading center for southwestern Natal. Its factories make metal products, rubber, bricks, tile, furniture, leather, and canvas. The city has a university, a teachers college, and many beautiful parks and gardens. Dutch Boers founded Pietermaritzburg in 1838.   HIBBERD V. B. KLINE, JR.

PIEZOELECTRICITY, *py EE zoh ee LECK TRISS uh tih.* Certain nonmetallic minerals, such as quartz, Rochelle salt, tourmaline, and some other crystals, conduct electricity. In 1880, Pierre and Jacques Curie, two French scientists, found that certain crystals develop an electric charge on the surface when they are stretched or compressed along an axis. Scientists later found that such crystals also vibrate when they are placed in an alternating electrical field. This phenomenon is called *piezoelectricity.* Crystals that have these properties are called *piezoelectric crystals.*

Piezoelectric crystals have many important uses. Thin, carefully cut slices of crystals control the frequency of electric current in radio transmitters. They are cut so that only currents of a certain frequency can pass through. Radio receivers use piezoelectric crystals to filter sounds. They are also used in microphones, hearing aids, and telephone receivers.   SAMUEL SEELY

See also QUARTZ; CRYSTAL AND CRYSTALLIZATION.

PIG. See HOG.

PIG IRON. See IRON AND STEEL (Pig Iron).

PIGAFETTA, ANTONIO. See EXPLORATION AND DISCOVERY (table: Famous Explorers).

PIGEON, *PIHJ un,* is the name given to some birds in the dove family. Larger members of the family are usually called *pigeons,* and the smaller ones *doves.* Scientists have identified about 290 species of these birds. Some kinds live in almost every part of the world except the very cold regions. They are most abundant in or near the tropics, but many make their homes in the temperate zones.

Pigeons are noted for the soft cooing sounds they make during the mating season. They are usually considered gentle and may often be a symbol of peace. However, pigeons can fight viciously.

Scientists believe that all tame or domestic pigeons are descended from the wild *rock dove.* This bird nests on cliffs in Europe, Asia, and Africa. It is slate blue, with two black wing bars, a white rump, a black band on its tail, and a green and purple gloss on its neck. Many modern domestic types differ greatly from their wild relatives. But when domestic pigeons run wild, many revert to this ancestral color type. For example, this coloring is common among flocks that live in and around large cities.

Many persons enjoy feeding pigeons in city parks and squares. Perhaps the most famous pigeons in the world are those that flutter down each day to be fed in Saint Mark's Square in Venice, Italy.

Pigeon Raising has been popular for thousands of years. Many people enjoy the brilliant colors and delightful antics of these birds. Pigeons should be kept in special houses called *lofts* or *cotes.* These can be simple and inexpensive. Even a packing crate will do.

Pigeons eat peas and whole grains such as wheat and corn. But they must also eat sand or some other kind of grit. The gritty material helps break up the food in the pigeons' powerful, muscular gizzards. Pigeons eat a great deal and often their *crops* (gullets)

David Preston

White Jacobin Pigeons are prized as show birds in America and Europe. Their neck feathers flare to form a fluffy white hood or ruff.

410

The Big Victoria Crown Pigeon of Australia is now extinct there, but may still be seen on Santa Catalina Island near Los Angeles.

The Swiss Mondaine Pigeon is a large bird bred mainly for its fine squabs.

The Picturesque Fantail has long been a favorite with breeders.

The Tumbler is the stunt flier and acrobat of the pigeon world.

Pouters are both the aristocrats and the clowns among pigeons.

Santa Catalina Island Co.; "The Pigeon" by Wendell M. Levi; Ylla, Guillumette; James Ruzek

The Racing Homing Pigeon is a bird which has rare speed, courage, and intelligence, and an accurate homing instinct.

The Ptarmigan Pigeon takes its name from the feathers that cover its feet like those of the ptarmigan.

are stretched with food. When pigeons drink, they do not tip their heads up with each sip as most birds do. Instead, they thrust their beaks into the water and pump the liquid down their throats in much the same way that horses drink.

Some persons believe that pigeons mate for life. They appear to be affectionate, and mated pairs spend much time billing and cooing. The males and females are so similar in color and appearance that it is hard to tell them apart.

A pair can raise as many as 11 broods a year, but the average is about 6 or 7. Many pigeon breeders do not allow the birds to nest all year. They separate the males and females during the winter months. This keeps the adults in better physical condition and improves the vigor of the young.

The female usually lays two white eggs. The nest is a simple, clumsily made structure of coarse twigs and grass. Both birds take turns sitting on the eggs, which hatch in about 17 days. The young, called *squabs*, are almost naked and blind when hatched. But they develop rapidly and are soon covered with spiny pinfeathers. They are very ugly. Newly hatched young are fed a whitish liquid called *pigeon's milk*, formed in the parents' crops. Both parents feed the young by pumping this "milk" down their gullets.

Domestic Breeds. There are more than 150 different breeds of domestic pigeons. Many of these include various strains. Some may be raised for food, others for racing, carrying messages, or recreation and show. Popular types raised for food include the *homer*, the *carneaux*, the *dragoon*, the *white maltese*, and the *white king*. These large birds produce big squabs that are considered a delicacy. They are marketed when they are about a month old.

The *homer*, or *homing pigeon*, is used for racing and for carrying messages. These pigeons are noted for their ability to find their way home from great distances.

The *fantail* is one of the fanciest breeds of show pigeons. This bird dances on its toes, holding its head far back and spreading its enormous fan-shaped tail. Most pigeons have 12 tail feathers, but the fantail may have as many as 30. The vain, pompous *pouter pigeon* struts about with its neck puffed out like a balloon. It can fill special sacs in its neck with air to puff them up. The popular *tumbler* performs acrobatics in the air, sometimes doing backward loops. Another acrobat, the *roller*, flies in a circle for a long time, then "rolls" about a hundred feet while throwing its head and neck backward. The *jacobin* has luxurious plumage. A dense ruff of long neck feathers hangs over its head like a hood. The *barbs* and *carrier pigeons* have large, fleshy *wattles*, or skin growths, at the base of their beaks, and fleshy rosettes around their eyes. The feet of most pigeons are covered with scales, but some types have a thick growth of feathers on their feet.

Other Pigeons. The *crowned pigeon* of New Guinea, one of the most beautiful species, is also the largest—about the size of a large chicken. Tufts of thin, lacy feathers form a crest on its head. Brightly colored *fruit pigeons* live in Asia and on the South Pacific islands. These birds build such poor nests that the female must hold her eggs, as well as the nest, in place every time

the wind blows. The *band-tailed pigeon*, a native of the western United States, is about the size of a large domestic pigeon. It has a black band across its tail. Hunters find this a favorite game bird. They shoot large numbers of band-tailed pigeons every fall when the birds gather to eat wild fruits.

The *passenger pigeon*, also native to North America, once numbered in the millions. But hunters killed these birds in such great numbers that they became extinct. Scientists believe the last passenger pigeon died in 1914 in the Zoological Gardens in Cincinnati. In 1813, John James Audubon, the naturalist, reported seeing a flock of passenger pigeons that took many hours to fly past him.

The *bleeding-heart pigeon* is native to the Philippines. Its under parts are completely white except for a great splash of red over its chest and lower neck.

Scientific Classification. Pigeons belong to the order *Columbiformes*. Pigeons and doves make up the pigeon and dove family, *Columbidae*. The rock dove is genus *Columba*, species *C. livia*. The band-tailed pigeon is *C. fasciata*. The crowned pigeon is genus *Goura*, species *G. victoria*. The fruit pigeon is genus *Ptilinopus*, species *P. superbus*. The bleeding-heart pigeon is genus *Gallicolumba*, species *G. luzonica*. The passenger pigeon (extinct) is genus *Ectopistes*, species *E. migratorius*.   GEORGE E. HUDSON

Related Articles in WORLD BOOK include:

Bird (Other Bird Noises)	Dove	Passenger Pigeon
Brain (picture: Animal Brains)	Ear (picture: Inner Ears)	Poultry
Carrier Pigeon	Homing Pigeon	Rock Pigeon
	Mourning Dove	Turtledove

PIGEON GUILLEMOT. See GUILLEMOT.

PIGEON HAWK. See FALCON AND FALCONRY.

PIGFISH. See GRUNT.

PIGGYBACK SERVICE. See RAILROAD (Freight Cars).

PIGMENT is a finely powdered, colored substance that gives its color to another material. It does this when it is mixed with the material or applied over its surface in a thin layer. Pigment does not dissolve, but remains suspended in the liquid when it is mixed or ground in a liquid to form paint. Colored substances that dissolve in liquids and give their color effects by staining are called dyes. The various methods of painting differ from one another in the material with which the color is applied. But the pigments used are the same in all types. See also PAINT; ALBINO; COLOR; HAIR (The Color of Hair); SKIN.

PIGMY. See PYGMY.

PIGSKIN. See HOG (Other Uses).

PIGWEED is a common annual weed. Its strong, hardy root thrives in any cultivable soil. This persistent weed sometimes grows 2 or 3 feet high. It produces large coarse leaves and small greenish flowers that grow in a densely crowded head. The leaves are sometimes covered with stiff hairs. Pigweed is best killed by uprooting the plant completely, or by a 2,4-D spray. The goosefoot is also called pigweed.

Scientific Classification. Pigweed belongs to the amaranth family, *Amaranthaceae*. Redroot pigweed is genus *Amaranthus*, species *A. retroflexus*. Rough pigweed is classified as *A. hybridus*. The goosefoot belongs to the goosefoot family, *Chenopodiaceae*. The goosefoot makes up the genus *Chenopodium*.   LOUIS PYENSON

See also AMARANTH; LAMB'S-QUARTERS.

U.S. Fish and Wildlife Service

The Pika, or Cony, Is a Small Relative of the Rabbit.

PIKA, *PIE kuh,* is a small, furry animal that lives in Asia, Europe, and western North America. Pikas belong to the same animal order as hares and rabbits, but they look much more like guinea pigs.

The *American pika,* also called a *cony, conie, little chief hare,* or *calling hare,* is about 7 inches long. Its tail measures less than 1 inch long. Its coat is grayish-brown on the back, and white or light-brown on the underside.

American pikas live among loose rock on mountainsides, beyond the point where trees can grow. Pikas eat plants, and spend much of their time collecting food for winter. Pikas often live in large groups called *colonies.* Their loud, squeaking calls warn other pikas of approaching enemies.

Scientific Classification. Pikas are in the pika family, *Ochotonidae.* American pikas are genus *Ochotona,* species *O. princeps* and *O. collaris.* CHARLES M. KIRKPATRICK

See also RABBIT.

PIKE is the common name of a fresh-water fish noted for its greedy appetite and fighting quality. The names *pike* and *pickerel* are often confused. Three members of the pike family are called pickerel: the *bulldog, mud,* and *chain* pickerels. The three forms of muskellunge also are in the pike family. The so-called *pike perch,* more accurately called *walleye,* is a perch. The *gar pike* (gar-fish) is a gar.

The *northern pike* is the most important member of the family. It lives in the northern fresh waters of Europe and Asia, and in the Great Lakes and smaller

The Northern Pike delights fishermen with the fierce fight it puts up when hooked. Its flesh is excellent for eating.

Frank R. Martin, U.S. Fish and Wildlife Service

lakes in Canada and the upper Mississippi Valley of North America. The northern pike may grow to be four feet long and weigh more than 40 pounds. It commonly weighs from 2 to 10 pounds. It is bluish- or greenish-gray, with irregular rows of whitish or yellowish spots. The northern pike is a fine game fish and its flesh is good to eat.

Scientific Classification. The northern pike belongs to the pike family, *Esocidae.* It is classified as genus *Esox,* species *E. lucius.* CARL L. HUBBS

See also FISH (color picture: Fresh-Water Fishes); FISHING (table: Game-Fishing World Records); MUSKELLUNGE; PICKEREL.

PIKE, ALBERT. See OKLAHOMA (The Civil War).

PIKE, ZEBULON MONTGOMERY (1779-1813), an American general and explorer, won fame for his discovery of Pikes Peak in 1806. While Meriwether Lewis and William Clark explored the Northwest, Pike explored the upper Mississippi River. Later, he explored the Southwest to obtain information about the land and its resources, especially south from the upper reaches of the Arkansas River, which rises in central Colorado.

Pike first sighted the peak which now bears his name from at least 150 miles out on the plains. Searching further for the

Brown Bros.

Zebulon Pike

headwaters of the Red River, Pike crossed the Sangre de Cristo Range of mountains into New Mexico. A detachment of Spanish troops met Pike and escorted him and his men to Santa Fe. He and his men were released several months later. Pike returned from his trip with valuable information for the government. An accusation that Pike was involved in the Aaron Burr-James Wilkinson scheme for conquest and empire in the Southwest was proved false.

Pike was born in Lamberton, N.J., Jan. 5, 1779. He began his military career at the age of 15. In the War of 1812, he led a successful advance on York (Toronto), Canada, in which he lost his life. RICHARD A. BARTLETT

PIKE PERCH. See PERCH.

PIKES PEAK is probably the best known of the Rocky Mountain peaks in Colorado. It is the first one seen as travelers approach from the east. It lifts its snow-capped peak 14,110 feet above sea level, in the Front Range. Pine and spruce forests grow to a height of 11,700 feet on the slopes of Pikes Peak. The mountain was named for Lieutenant Zebulon Montgomery Pike. In November, 1806, Pike climbed partway up the mountain, but lack of supplies forced him to turn back. The ascent was later made by an exploring party led by Major Stephen Harriman Long in 1820. Today the top of Pikes Peak can be reached on horseback or by a nine-mile cog railway. A 30-mile automobile highway leads to the top from Colorado Springs, six miles to the east. The famous Pikes Peak Auto Race is held there every summer. A huge searchlight was placed on top of the moun-

Pontius Pilate, the Roman governor of Judea, presided at the trial of Jesus. Pilate believed that Jesus was innocent, but let Him be put to death because he feared losing his job.

Brown Bros.

tain in 1905. The United States Weather Bureau maintains one of the highest meteorological stations in the world on Pikes Peak. For location, see COLORADO (color map). Pikes Peak is the center of one of the most popular mountain-resort areas in America. Denver lies 65 miles north of the peak.   TIM K. KELLEY

See also COLORADO (color picture); MOUNTAIN (table; color picture, Mountains of the World); PIKE, ZEBULON MONTGOMERY.

PIKES PEAK OR BUST. See WESTERN FRONTIER LIFE (The Search for Gold and Silver).

PIKEVILLE COLLEGE is a coeducational Presbyterian school at Pikeville, Ky. It was founded in 1889, as Pikeville Collegiate Institute, a junior college. It assumed its present name in 1909. Pikeville College awarded its first bachelor's degree in 1957. For enrollment, see UNIVERSITIES AND COLLEGES (table).

PILASTER. See ARCHITECTURE (Architectural Terms).

PILATE, *PIE lut,* **PONTIUS,** was the Roman procurator, or governor, of Judea at the time of the Crucifixion. He ruled from A.D. 26 to 36. He exercised complete power over the people who lived in Judea, Samaria, and part of Idumea, except persons who were Roman citizens. Pilate was considered an unfit ruler and never could understand the religious feelings of the Jews or their national pride.

When Jesus Christ came to trial before Pilate, the Roman ruler tried to release Him. He believed Jesus innocent. But the priests and the enemies of Jesus demanded His death. Pilate would have freed Him if he had not been afraid of losing his own office. All four of the Gospels in the Bible give full accounts of Christ's trial.

Little is known about the last years of Pilate's life. History tells us that he was called to Rome to defend himself against charges of cruelty to the Jewish people. A legend says that he was sent to Gaul as an exile and committed suicide there. According to another story,

Pilate's body was thrown first into the Tiber River, then into the Rhône. Neither river would receive it. Finally, his body was plunged into a lake near Lucerne, Switzerland. A mountain near this lake is now called Mount Pilatus.

Pilate was made a saint by the Abyssinian Church, because, according to belief, he was converted to Christianity and died a martyr. Anatole France wrote a story, *The Procurator of Judea*, about Pilate as an exile in Gaul.   FREDERICK C. GRANT

See also BARABBAS; JESUS CHRIST.

PILCHARD. See FISH (color picture, Salt-Water Fishes); SARDINE.

PILCHER, PERCY. See GLIDER (Pioneer Gliders).

PILE is a long piece of timber, steel, or concrete used to support a building, bridge, pier, or wharf. Piles may be driven into the ground by a pile driver, a type of drop hammer that batters the pile into position with a weight. Hydraulic jacks and jetting, a method of shooting a jet of water to make an opening in the ground, are also used to place piles. Concrete piles may be cast in the position in which they are to be used. Timber piles are usually made of long, tapered tree trunks. They are sometimes protected by an iron band to keep them from shattering under the heavy blows of a pile driver.

Piles are also used to retain water and soil. Chicago's lake front is protected by steel piling. Bulkheads and cofferdams are constructed with this type of piling. Cofferdams are temporary enclosures in water that consist of lines of piles driven close together and packed with soil or rock.   R. G. HENNES

See also BUILDING AND WRECKING MACHINES (Pile-Driving Machinery; picture, Construction Machines); BUILDING CONSTRUCTION (Foundations); COFFERDAM.

PILE, ATOMIC, is a device that produces atomic energy. See ATOMIC REACTOR.

PILES. See HEMORRHOID.

414

Visual Education Service

The Pilgrims Pray in Gratitude That They Have Finally Reached the New Land After a Long, Stormy Voyage.

PILGRIM is one of a band of English settlers who landed at what is now Plymouth, Mass., in 1620. The Pilgrims established Plymouth Colony on the shore of Cape Cod Bay. They came to America seeking freedom to worship as they thought proper.

In England, they were part of a body of Protestants called *Puritans* because they wished to *purify* the Church of England. Before 1600, some of the Puritans decided

that they could not reform the Church from within. They separated from the Church of England and set up congregations of their own. These persons who separated from the Church became known as *Separatists*. One group of Separatists, under the leadership of William Brewster, met in the village of Scrooby. English officials persecuted them, and in 1608 they fled from England and settled in Leiden, Holland.

Pilgrims Going to Church, painted by George H. Broughton in 1867, shows how the pilgrims traveled in bands for self-protection.

The men carried muskets to church and placed them on gun racks. The preacher with his Bible is in the center of the picture.

Courtesy of The New-York Historical Society, N.Y.C.

Bettmann Archive

A Pillory locked the arms and head of a person between two wooden boards. Another device, the *stocks*, held a person's legs. The pillory and stocks were used in the American colonies to punish persons who committed minor offenses.

But the Separatists preferred farming to city life. They were afraid their children would be more Dutch than English. And they feared a war between Holland and Spain. They longed to return to their English way of life, yet to keep their own kind of worship. The new land of America appealed to them, and some English merchants agreed to finance a trip to America. In July, 1620, Brewster led a group of Separatists back to England. In September, they set sail for America in the *Mayflower*. They dropped anchor in what is now Provincetown harbor on Nov. 21, 1620.

The term *Pilgrim* may come from William Bradford's history. He wrote that "they knew they were pilgrims" when they left Holland. MARSHALL SMELSER

See also PLYMOUTH COLONY; BRADFORD, WILLIAM; MAYFLOWER; MAYFLOWER COMPACT.

PILGRIM'S PROGRESS is a famous novel written by John Bunyan (see BUNYAN, JOHN). This book is one of the great religious classics of the world. It is an *allegory*, because the characters and incidents suggest deeper meanings than they represent on the surface. Part I was published in 1678 and Part II in 1684.

The Pilgrim's Progress tells the story of the life of man. The hero's name is Christian. Every character, location, or incident in the story bears a picture-creating name. There is the Giant Despair, Mr. By-Ends, Ignorance, the Slough of Despond, the River of Death, and the Celestial City. *The Pilgrim's Progress* has been translated into a great many languages. ARNOLD WILLIAMS

PILLARS OF HERCULES was the name ancient Greeks gave to two rocks on either side of the Strait of Gibraltar. They called the rock which stands on the European (Gibraltar) side *Calpe*. The Greeks called the rock on the opposite side of the narrow strait *Abyla*. Greek legend told that Hercules placed the rocks there when he went to the kingdom of Geryon. Later both rocks were pictured as pillars bound together by a scroll bearing the Latin words *ne plus ultra* (*no more beyond*). This was a warning to sailors not to enter the Atlantic. See also GIBRALTAR, STRAIT OF. WILLIAM F. MCDONALD

PILLORY, *PILL oh ree,* was an instrument once used to punish people for minor offenses. It consisted of a wooden framework with holes cut in it for the arms and head of the victims. They were locked into these holes for a certain length of time. The pillory stood on a platform in the public square. Men and women suffered not only because of their uncomfortable position, but also because passers-by jeered and often threw stones and rotten eggs at them. Often the prisoners' heads were shaved to increase their shame.

The English government used the pillory in the 1600's to punish certain writers and publishers. Daniel Defoe was subjected to the pillory for publishing a libelous essay. The Puritans brought the pillory with them to New England, and used it to punish "notorious drunkards, scolds, and bawds." MARVIN E. WOLFGANG

See also STOCKS.

PILLSBURY, HARRY NELSON. See CHESS (Famous Chess Players).

PILLSBURY, JOHN SARGENT (1828-1901), was a Minnesota industrialist and Republican politician. He served as governor of Minnesota from 1876 to 1882. He was a state senator from 1863 to 1875. With members of his family, Pillsbury established the Pillsbury Mills in 1872. By the early 1900's the mills had become the world's largest flour mills. For his contributions to the University of Minnesota, he was made a life regent. He was born in Sutton, N.H. HAROLD T. HAGG

PILOT can refer to an aircraft pilot, who is a person in charge of *piloting* (guiding) an aircraft. He is responsible for the safety of his craft, crew, passengers, and cargo. He must be educated in navigation, aerodynamics, meteorology, radio, air regulations, and flying.

A harbor or river pilot guides ships or boats through hazardous waters close to shore, in bays, harbors, or rivers. While the pilot is aboard, he is responsible for the ship's safety. He must know the currents, tides, and depths of the water through which he guides the ship. Also, the pilot must always be on the lookout for other ships.

See also AIRPLANE PILOT; AIRPLANE (A Trip in an Airliner); NAVIGATION.

PILOT, AUTOMATIC. See GYROPILOT.

PILOT BREAD is an unleavened bread that used to be carried on ships that had to make long voyages. It was like oldtime hardtack, and would keep for a long time.

416

PILOT CLUB INTERNATIONAL is a service and civic organization for executive business and professional women. It promotes international peace and cultural relations, high standards in business, and active participation in movements to improve the civic, social, industrial, and commercial welfare of communities. The organization was founded in Macon, Ga., in 1921. It has over 430 clubs and 12,500 members in the United States, Canada, and other countries. Headquarters are in the Persons Building, Macon, Ga.   WILDA RICHARDSON

PILOT FISH is a kind of fish found in most tropical seas and the warmer temperate seas. It also lives off the coasts of the Americas from Cape Cod to Brazil. The pilot fish is about a foot long. It is bluish in color with five or six dark vertical bands. The fish has delicate flesh that tastes somewhat like mackerel. This fish gets its name because it follows ships and sharks. Ancient peoples regarded the pilot fish as sacred. They thought it directed lost sailors to land.

Scientific Classification. The pilot fish is a member of the pompano family, *Carangidae*. It is classified as genus *Naucrates*, species *N. ductor*.   LEONARD P. SCHULTZ

New York Zoological Society

The Pilot Fish was once believed to help sharks by warning them of danger or leading them to food. Scientists now believe it follows the shark only to eat food the shark leaves.

PILOT SNAKE. See COPPERHEAD.

PILOT WHALE is a large porpoise that swims in *schools* (groups). Sometimes hundreds follow one or more *leaders* (pilots).

The pilot whale is black, with a white streak down the middle of its underside. It grows from 14 to 21 feet long and weighs from $\frac{3}{4}$ to $2\frac{1}{2}$ tons. Its head has a "cushion" of fat that contains an oil valuable for lubrication.

Pilot whales are sometimes called blackfish. The name *blackfish* also refers to various kinds of true fish. Along the north Pacific Coast, the killer whale is known as the blackfish (see KILLER WHALE).

Scientific Classification. Pilot whales belong to the dolphin family, *Delphinidae*. They make up the genus *Globicephala*.   RAYMOND M. GILMORE

PILOTING. See NAVIGATION (Methods).

PILOTWEED. See COMPASS PLANT.

PILSEN. See PLZEŇ.

PILSUDSKI, *peel SOOT skee*, **JÓZEF** (1867-1935), a Polish patriot, led the movement to liberate Poland from Russia, and helped unite his country. Pilsudski served as first Chief of State and Minister of War in Poland after it became a republic in 1918.

The new democratic constitution provided for a weak presidency, so Pilsudski refused to be a candidate for the office. He quit politics temporarily in

1922, and in 1926 used military force to overthrow the government. Professor Ignacy Mościcki became the new president. Pilsudski became the premier, and served until 1928. In 1930, he became premier again. From 1926 until his death, however, Pilsudski kept the real power of the government in his own hands.

U&U

Józef Pilsudski

Pilsudski became a professional revolutionary in his youth. He took part in the plot to kill Czar Alexander III of Russia in 1887, and was exiled to Siberia. After his release in 1892, Pilsudski joined the new Polish Socialist party and continued to work for the independence of Poland. The Russians again arrested him for his activities. He was sent to an asylum when he feigned insanity, but he escaped.

During World War I, Pilsudski fought at the head of the Polish Legions he had organized and allied with Germany and Austria-Hungary. But he refused to take an oath of allegiance to Germany, and was imprisoned at Magdeburg, Germany, in the last months of the war.

After the collapse of Germany and Austria-Hungary, Pilsudski became a national hero and headed the Polish provisional government. Later, as Chief of State and First Marshal of Poland, he led his armies against the Lithuanians, Ukrainians, and Russians. During his last years, Pilsudski increased the presidential powers and limited the power of parliament.

Pilsudski was born near the city of Vilnius, now in Lithuania. He spent one year at Kharkov University in the Russian Ukraine.   CHARLES MORLEY

PILTDOWN MAN. In 1911, part of a human skull was found in a gravel pit at Piltdown in Sussex, England. Several years later other parts were found. Some scientists believed that the skull represented an ancient form of man who lived as long as a million years ago. They called this early form the Piltdown Man. The jawbone indicated that Piltdown Man had a jaw like an ape.

In 1953, British scientists announced that they had tested the fluorine content of the bones, and found that the jawbone with the skull was that of a modern ape. They believed that the skull was less than 50,000 years old, and that there had been a "deliberate fake" in adding the jaw to the skull.   CARLETON S. COON

PILUM. See SPEAR.

PIMA. See COTTON (Egyptian Cotton).

PIMA INDIANS, *PEE mah*, live along the Gila and Salt rivers near Phoenix, Ariz. They gave their name to the *Piman* language, also spoken by the Papago of Arizona and the Yaqui of Mexico. The Pima have lived with the Maricopa Indians since the early 1800's. Both groups follow the same customs.

The ancestors of the Pima, members of the *Hohokam* (pronounced *hoh HOH kum*) culture, developed an advanced way of life around A.D. 1000. They built substantial villages of adobe pit houses, and farmed with the aid of irrigation canals. They made beautiful objects

PIMENTO

of stone and shell. The Hohokam culture declined about 1400, possibly because of raiding Apache Indians. Tribal traditions say that many Pima were killed or enslaved, and others fled to the mountains. When white men came to the area in the 1600's, they found the Pima living in simple dome-shaped houses of poles covered with thatch and mud. These houses clustered together in small farming settlements called *rancherías*. Because of this loose grouping, the Pima chief had little power. Religious leadership also remained weak. But the Pima had a highly developed mythology. They were a peaceful people, but they fought well when attacked. They made fine baskets.

The Pima now live in houses like those of their white neighbors. They still make a living as farmers. An elected council, governing under a constitution and bylaws, now rules the tribe.　　　BERTHA P. DUTTON

PIMENTO, *peh MEN toh,* is the popular name of a small evergreen tree of the myrtle family. A spice known as *allspice, Jamaica pepper,* or *pimento* comes from this tree. The name of the tree comes from *pimienta,* the Spanish word for peppercorns. The tree is native to the West Indies. Most commercial pimento spice comes from Jamaica.

The pimento usually grows to a height of 20 to 30 feet. Occasionally it is as tall as 40 feet. The slender, upright trunk has many branches at the top and is covered with smooth gray bark. The shining green leaves are pointed and narrow. They have an essential oil, and have a pleasant odor when fresh. The fruit is a small berry that is black, glossy, sweet, and juicy when ripe, and about the size of a black currant. The unripe berry is used for the spice of commerce. The fruit loses much of its pleasant odor when it matures. The red fleshy condiment called pimento is the fruit of the paprika plant and is a *capsicum* (see CAPSICUM). It is used for stuffing green olives.

West Indian Pimento bears small berries which are used to make the spice called *allspice, or Jamaica pepper.* N.Y. Botanical Garden

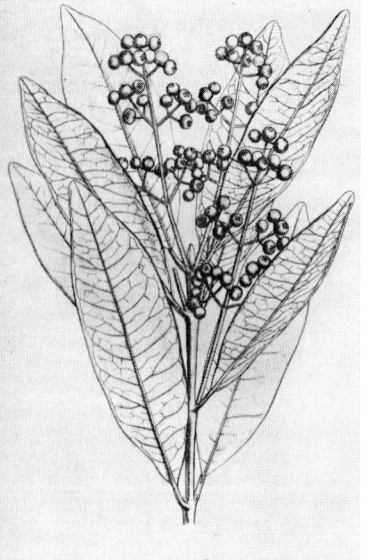

Scientific Classification. The pimento belongs to the myrtle family, *Myrtaceae.* It is classified as genus *Pimenta,* species *P. dioica.*
　　　HAROLD NORMAN MOLDENKE

See also ALLSPICE.

PIMPERNEL is a small annual plant that grows wild in Europe and Asia. It is sometimes planted in flower gardens of North America and often runs wild. The plant is low and spreading, with oval leaves in pairs on the stem. The small, bell-shaped flowers grow along the stem singly rather than in clusters. There are several varieties, with red, scarlet, blue, or white flowers. Another name for the pimpernel is *poor-man's-weatherglass.*

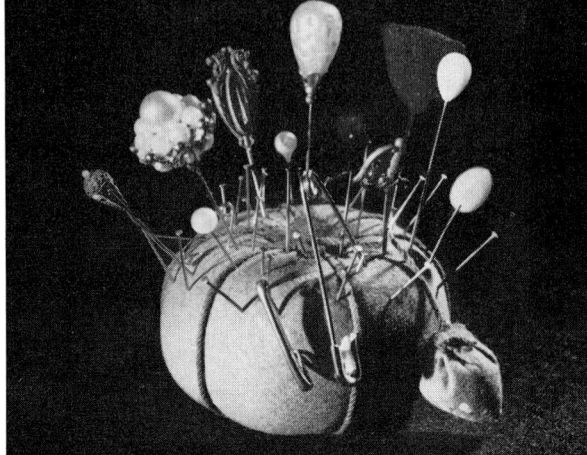
Frank Fenner
Decorative Pins were used to fasten clothing hundreds of years before ordinary safety and straight pins came into use.

This name refers to the flowers' habit of closing at the approach of cloudy or rainy weather.

Scientific Classification. The pimpernel belongs to the primrose family, *Primulaceae.* It is classified as genus *Anagallis,* species *A. arvensis.*　　　JULIAN A. STEYERMARK

PIMPLE is a sharp, raised area on the skin. When the skin's fat glands become overactive, the oil they produce plugs the pores. These plugs collect waste material from the cells and dirt from the air. The dirt and wastes may collect on top of the plugs, forming *blackheads.* As a plug grows, it causes irritation. To rid itself of the unwanted substances, the body causes pus to form around the plug, producing a pimple. When the pimple breaks, the grease plug and waste are forced out with the pus. Pimples should not be squeezed as that harms tissues of the skin and scars may form. See also ACNE.

PIN. The first pins were thorns and sharp fishbones. Early peoples used them to hold together their garments of animal skins. During the Bronze Age, men began to make pins from bronze wire which they pointed at one end and bent at the other to form a crude head. Highly ornamented pins of bronze have been found in Egyptian tombs that are more than 3,000 years old. The Romans also used bronze pins, with decorated and jeweled heads, to fasten their robes. In the 1100's, pins were so scarce and valuable in England that the Parliament adopted a law allowing pins to be sold on two days of the year only, January 1 and 2.

Pins were probably handmade articles until 1824. Then Lemuel Wright, an American, patented a machine to make pins from single pieces of wire. Wright's machine, which he took to England, was the first step in the modern manufacture of pins.

Straight pins are often called *common pins.* Many straight pins are used in dressmaking establishments, clothing factories, laundries, and retail stores.

Safety pins are so called because their pointed ends can be slipped into a protecting cap. They are used chiefly for pinning clothing. They prevent injuries because the point is protected when the pin is closed. Some men and women who lived during ancient times used safety pins. These pins were made of gold and bronze. In 1849, Walter Hunt of New York patented a design for a modern safety pin.

Pins are manufactured with great speed. Iron, brass,

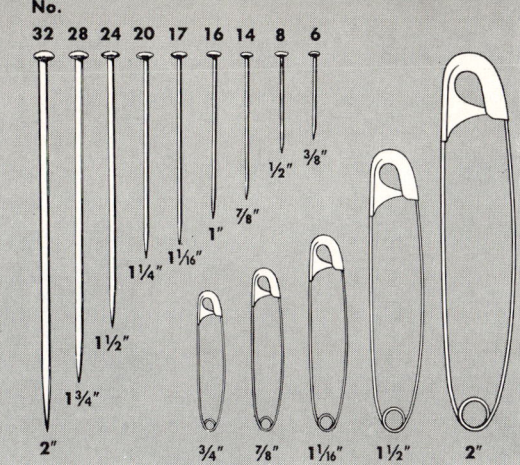

No.

32 28 24 20 17 16 14 8 6

½" 3/8"
7/8"
1"
1 1/16"
1¼"
1½"
1¾"
2"
¾" 7/8" 1 1/16" 1½" 2"

Straight Pins and Safety Pins come in standard size lengths. Pin manufacturers also make a 3-inch blanket safety pin.

or steel wire is fed to a machine from a reel. The wire is straightened, and cut into proper lengths. It is held by lateral jaws, and just enough of the wire sticks out to form a head. A blow from a die flattens and shapes this end into a head. The pins are then carried forward until the lower end touches revolving files. These grind and shape the point. The pins are boiled for several hours in a tin preparation, and are washed and polished.

Another machine sticks the pins into the papers in which they are sold. It crimps the paper and thrusts the pins in place at the same time.   WALTER R. WILLIAMS, JR.

See also INVENTION (picture, The Story of an Invention); BROOCH; ETRUSCAN (picture).

PIÑA CLOTH. See FIBER (Vegetable Fiber).

PIÑATA. See CHRISTMAS (Latin America); EASTER (In Mexico).

PINBALL MACHINE. See SLOT MACHINE.

PINCHING BUG. See STAG BEETLE.

PINCHOT, *PIN shoh,* **GIFFORD** (1865-1946), served as governor of Pennsylvania from 1923 to 1927 and from 1931 to 1935. As governor, Pinchot proposed the measures that settled the great coal strike of 1923. He also became known as one of the first persons to favor planned conservation of United States forests.

Pinchot became a member of the National Forest Commission in 1896 and was appointed chief of the Division of Forestry in 1898. This bureau became the Forest Service of the U.S. Department of Agriculture in

Gifford Pinchot
Chandler

1905. Pinchot served as its chief until 1910, when he became president of the National Conservation Committee. He wrote *The Fight for Conservation* (1910).

Pinchot was born in Simsbury, Conn., and was graduated from Yale University in 1889. He studied forestry in France, Germany, Switzerland, and Austria. He taught forestry at Yale from 1903 to 1906. During World War I, he served as a member of the

PINCKNEY

United States Food Administration Bureau. He died in New York City on Oct. 4, 1946.   C. B. BAKER

See also TAFT, WILLIAM HOWARD (Legislative Defeats).

PINCKNEY, *PINK nih,* is the name of a southern colonial family of patriots in the American Revolutionary period.

Elizabeth Lucas Pinckney (1722-1793), a colonial planter of South Carolina, developed and successfully grew indigo plants on her father's plantation near Charleston in the early 1740's. Because of the demand in Europe for the blue dye produced from this plant, indigo became a leading export throughout colonial times. Elizabeth Pinckney taught other farmers her knowledge of the crop. Her experience with flax, hemp, and silk culture also helped to promote the economic development of South Carolina.

At the age of sixteen, Elizabeth Lucas took charge of her father's three plantations in South Carolina. Later, she married Charles Pinckney. The couple went to London in 1753, where Pinckney served as a colonial agent. In 1758, soon after their return to America, Pinckney died. For the remaining thirty-five years of her life, Elizabeth Pinckney successfully managed her large plantation holdings.

Elizabeth Pinckney did so much to promote independence in the colonies that upon her death in Philadelphia, President George Washington, at his own request, served as a pallbearer. Her *Journal and Letters* (1739-1762) tells of her interesting life.

Elizabeth Lucas Pinckney was probably born in Antigua, British West Indies.   J. CARLYLE SITTERSON

Charles Cotesworth Pinckney (1746-1825), son of Elizabeth Lucas Pinckney, served the United States as statesman and soldier. After the Revolutionary War, Pinckney became a member of the Constitutional Convention in Philadelphia.

Brown Bros.
Charles Pinckney

In 1796, Pinckney was appointed United States Minister to France. He took part in the negotiations with agents of Prince Talleyrand, the famous French statesman, concerning relations between France and the United States. These negotiations came to be known as the XYZ Affair. The agents demanded a loan to France and money as a gift, or bribe, for Talleyrand. When Pinckney was asked for his reply to their demands, he said, "It is No! No! Not a sixpence." The slogan, "Millions for defense, but not one cent for tribute" is often credited to Pinckney, but it actually originated with Robert Goodloe Harper, a Federalist politician and leader (see XYZ AFFAIR).

Pinckney returned to the United States after the failure of the mission, and served two years in the army. In 1800, he was the Federalist candidate for Vice-President, and, in 1804 and 1808, he ran for President against Thomas Jefferson and against James Madison.

Pinckney was born in Charleston, S.C., and was educated in England and France. He practiced law in Charleston at the beginning of the Revolutionary War.

Thomas Pinckney (1750-1828), son of Elizabeth Lucas Pinckney, also served the United States as a statesman and soldier. He arranged the Treaty of San Lorenzo el Real, or Pinckney Treaty, with Spain in 1795 (see PINCKNEY TREATY). Largely as a result of this work, he became a Federalist candidate for Vice-President in 1796, but lost to Thomas Jefferson.

Pinckney was born in Charleston, S.C., and was educated in England and France. He served as governor of South Carolina from 1787 to 1789, and as U.S. Representative from 1797 to 1801.   ROBERT J. TAYLOR

PINCKNEY, CHARLES (1757-1824), an American political leader, wrote the *Pinckney Draught*, a plan for a United States constitution. He submitted his plan to the Constitutional Convention of 1787. More than 30 of its provisions were incorporated into the U.S. Constitution, which Pinckney signed as a delegate from South Carolina. From 1784 to 1787, Pinckney was a delegate to the Congress of the Confederation, the governing body which preceded the Congress of the United States. He served as governor of South Carolina four times, in the U.S. Senate from 1798 to 1801, and in the U.S. House of Representatives from 1819 to 1821. He was minister to Spain from 1801 to 1805. He was born in Charleston, S.C.   KENNETH R. ROSSMAN

PINCKNEY TREATY ended disputes between the United States and Spain over possession of the Floridas and the mouth of the Mississippi River. It was signed on Oct. 27, 1795. Spain recognized the 31st parallel as the southern boundary of the United States, and agreed to let Americans land their goods tax-free at New Orleans for three years. Both the United States and Spain gained free use of the Mississippi. See also PINCKNEY (Thomas).   MERRILL JENSEN

PINDAR, *PIN der* (522?-443 B.C.), was the greatest lyric poet of ancient Greece. He is generally credited with inventing the Pindaric ode. This type of ode is built of three stanzas—the *strophe, antistrophe,* and *epode*—repeated in series. Pindar wrote these stately, intricate poems in praise of some event, such as an athletic victory at the great national games. The games came in four-year cycles, in turn at Olympia, Delphi, Nemea, and Corinth. Pindar's odes were intended for elaborate performance, with music and dance, when the victor returned to his native city.

Pindar's odes are unlike any other poetry, except for some of the choral lyrics in the tragedies of the dramatist Aeschylus. They are perfect in form and beautiful in language. But they lose much of their beauty in translation. His other poetry was lost.

Pindar was a deeply religious man, the first Greek writer to speak of the immortality of the soul and judgment by the gods after death. In politics, he was conservative and antidemocratic. Pindar's fame was so great that when Alexander the Great burned Thebes to the ground, Pindar's house was the only one spared. Pindar was born at Cynoscephalae, near Thebes, a member of a noble family.   MOSES HADAS

PINDUS MOUNTAINS. See GREECE (The Central Pindus).

PINE

PINE is the common name of the largest and most important group of *conifers,* or cone-bearing trees. Other trees also have cones and belong to the pine family. Among these are the larch, spruce, hemlock, and fir. But they all differ from trees of the pine genus, which comprises about 80 different kinds of pines. They are scattered throughout the Northern Hemisphere. Of these, 35 are native to the United States.

Pines are evergreen trees. They have needle-shaped leaves that grow in bundles of two to five each. These leaves stay on the tree for two years or more. At the base of each bundle is a scaly covering, called a *sheath,* which holds the leaf buds. The fruit of the pine is a woody cone. It takes two years to mature.

Soft, or White, Pines

All soft pines except the piñon have five needles in each bundle of leaves. The soft pines have light-colored wood with a soft, uniform texture.

Eastern White Pine was the most important forest tree in North America until about 1890. Then the last virgin stands were cut. This tree is still widely planted for

The Long Needles of the Loblolly Pine look like the end of a witch's broom. The longest ones on this twig measure 16 inches. The large cones have spiny tips. Loblolly pines grow in the southern United States. They furnish good lumber.

U.S. Forest Service

timber and as an ornamental. It is the largest of the northeastern conifers. Some trees reach a height of more than 200 feet. White pine grows from Minnesota to Maine, northward into Canada, and southward to the mountains of Georgia. Its slender, blue-green needles grow in bundles of five. White pines can be easily identified by their slender, thin-scaled cones, which are about five inches long. The white pine is the state tree of Maine and Michigan. Another similar tree, the *western white pine*, grows from British Columbia to California, extending eastward to western Montana. It is the state tree of Idaho.

Sugar Pine is the largest of the pines. It reaches a maximum height of 246 feet and has a trunk 10 feet in diameter. This tree is native to the mountains of California and Oregon. Sugar pine cones range from 10 to 26 inches long and are frequently used for decorations.

Foxtail and Bristlecone Pine are found in the mountain areas of the southwestern United States. These trees are small and have short, stout needles, which remain on the tree for about 10 to 17 years. Bristlecone pine are among the world's oldest trees. A small stand

Josef Muench

A Famous Old Jeffrey Pine, growing from the top of Sentinel Dome in Yosemite National Park, shows the marks of its struggle with high winds and barren soil.

The Austrian Pine has stiff, dark green needles about 6 inches long, and 3-inch oval cones. This hardy tree often grows 90 feet high.

U.S. Forest Service

The Longleaf Pine has needles 12 to 18 inches long, and spiny, dull brown cones. Its scaly bark is an orange-brown color.

U.S. Forest Service

Sugar Pine Cones grow 15 inches or more, and are the longest cones known. The tree has a straight, tapering trunk, topped by a flattened crown. Its blue-green needles have a white tinge.

Rutherford Platt

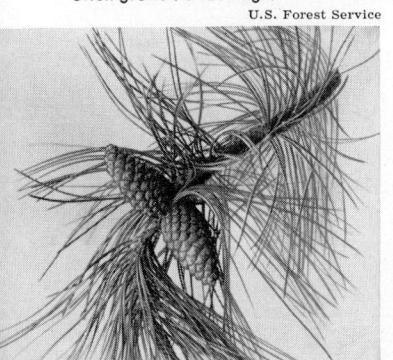

U.S. Forest Service

The Furrowed Trunk of a ponderosa pine is a dark brown color. This mighty tree is prized for its fine lumber.

A Ponderosa Pine lifts its great crown nearly 200 feet in the air, *right*. Ponderosas grow in western North America.

of these timber-line trees contains some that are more than 4,600 years old.

Limber Pine and Whitebark Pine are found in the mountains of the western United States. Their stout needles grow about three inches long. Their cones have thick scales and large, wingless, thick-shelled seeds, for which the trees are often called the "stone" pines.

Piñon, or **Nut Pines,** are native to southwestern United States. They produce edible nuts.

Hard, or Yellow, Pines

Hard pines have harder and darker wood than soft pines. Also, there is a sharp distinction between the wood that forms in the spring of the year and that formed in the summer. Hard pines do not lose their scaly bud sheaths when their needles mature. Their cone scales have thickened tips and sharp prickles.

Northeastern Hard Pines are important sources of wood for lumber and for pulp. The red pine, jack pine, and pitch pine are important members of this group.

Red Pine, also called *Norway Pine*, is a large, straight tree much prized for its lumber. It grows best in the Great Lakes regions, extending northward into Canada and eastward through New York and the New England states. It can be identified by its slender, brittle needles. They grow about five inches long in clusters of two.

Jack Pine is a medium-sized tree used chiefly for paper pulp. It is essentially a Canadian tree, extending farther north than most other pines. Its needles grow in clusters of two, but are short and twisted.

Pitch Pine grows from Maine to Georgia. Its sharp,

Resinous Sap Flows into Pans that girdle this Georgia pine. Longleaf and slash pines are the chief sources of the resin used in making turpentine.

Mydans, F.S.A.

The Jeffrey Pine has extremely gnarled bark. It is also commonly called the western yellow pine. The Jeffrey grows along the Pacific Coast.

Josef Muench

The White Pine has a dark brown trunk with deep cracks. It has soft, blue-green needles. White pines furnish much of the lumber used in construction work.

Rutherford Platt

stiff needles form clusters of three. A forest of pitch pine in New Jersey is called the "pine barrens."

Southern Hard Pines, or Yellow Pines, are highly valued for pulp and lumber. Two species are important sources of turpentine and resin.

Longleaf Pine ranges from North Carolina to Louisiana. It has flexible, dark green needles that may be 18 inches long. Timber from this tree has been used in such construction as ships, bridges, and railroad cars.

Shortleaf Pine is found from New York to Texas. It has short needles and small cones. Its light seeds are easily carried by the wind. Shortleaf pine lumber is used for boxes, crates, and paper pulp.

Loblolly Pine grows from New Jersey to Texas. It has a deeply furrowed bark with cinnamon-red flat ridges between the furrows. It is the most important of the southern pines.

Slash Pine extends from South Carolina to Louisiana. It is tapped for turpentine and resin, and is also an important source of lumber and paper pulp.

Western Hard Pines are among the most important lumber trees in the United States. Three of the 12 species are particularly prized commercially.

Ponderosa Pine, the most important western pine, is found through the mountain regions of the West. Its needles may be 10 inches long; they grow in groups of twos or threes. It is the state tree of Montana.

Jeffrey Pine is native of the Sierra Nevada Mountains of California. It resembles the ponderosa pine but its cones are much larger. The bark smells like pineapple.

Lodgepole Pine is found in the high mountains of the West. It is common in Yellowstone National Park. Indians used small lodgepole pines to support their tepees. Today, the lodgepole pine is used for railroad ties and poles.

Scientific Classification. Pine trees belong to the pine family, *Pinaceae.* They make up the genus *Pinus.* Eastern white pine is *P. strobus.* Sugar pine is *P. lambertiana.* Jack pine is *P. banksiana.* Longleaf pine is *P. palustris.* Ponderosa pine is *P. ponderosa.*   RICHARD J. PRESTON, JR.

Related Articles in WORLD BOOK include:

THE PINE FAMILY

Bristlecone Pine	Evergreen	Larch
Cedar	Fir	Piñon
Currant	Hemlock	Spruce
Douglas Fir		

PRODUCTS FROM PINE

Paper (How Paper	Rayon	Rosin	Turpentine
Is Made)	Resin	Tar	

OTHER RELATED ARTICLES

Arkansas (color picture:	Beefwood
The State Tree)	Cone-Bearing Trees

PINE BLUFF, Ark. (pop. 57,108; met. area 81,373; alt. 230 ft.), is the state's fourth largest city. Standing on a bluff near large pine forests, it overlooks the Arkansas River. It is 42 miles southeast of Little Rock (see ARKANSAS [political map]). Pine Bluff has the state's leading cotton market. About 40 cotton gins produce a yearly average of 75,000 bales of cotton from crops grown nearby. More than 140 manufacturing plants produce such products as caskets, electric transformers, furniture, mechanical cotton pickers, sheets and pillow cases, textile products, and wood pulp and paper. Pine Bluff received its charter in 1839. It has a mayor-council government.   WALTER L. BROWN

PINE FLAT DAM is part of a flood-control project in the rich agricultural area of central California. It stands on the Kings River near Fresno. It is a 430-foot-high concrete gravity-type structure with a crest length of 1,820 feet. It has a volume content of 2,200,000 cubic yards of concrete. The reservoir has a 1 million acre-foot capacity. The project retains flood flows and provides a method of regulating the normal water supply. It was completed in 1954.   T. W. MERMEL

See also DAM (Masonry Dams).

PINE SISKIN is a small finch of North America. It eats the seeds from the cones of evergreen trees. It is about 4 or 5 inches long, and is colored gray and brown. The yellow spots on its wings and tail can be easily seen when the bird is flying. The pine siskin breeds in mountain regions of Canada and the northeastern United States. It migrates, but not to any constant places. It may spend the winter almost anywhere in the United States or Mexico. The bird usually nests in evergreen trees, and makes its nest of twigs, roots, plant bark, and hair. It lays three or four pale green or bluish eggs marked with reddish-brown spots.

G. Blake Johnson, NAS

Pine Siskins eat seeds from the cones of evergreens.

Scientific Classification. The pine siskin belongs to the New World seedeaters family, *Fringillidae.* It is classified as genus *Spinus,* species *S. pinus.*   HERBERT FRIEDMANN

PINE-TREE SHILLING was a silver coin minted in Massachusetts Bay from 1652 to 1682. A pine tree encircled by *Masathusets* appeared on one side of the coin. *In New England An Dom, 1652, XII* was on the other side. Some pine-tree shillings were about as large as a half dollar.

Pine-tree shillings were called *Boston shillings,* or *Bay shillings,* until 1680. Then they became known as pine-tree shillings. Three-penny and six-penny pieces were made in the same period. All pine-tree coins were dated 1652.   ELSTON G. BRADFIELD

The Pine-Tree Shilling was a silver coin of the New England colonies. Note the quaint spelling "Masathusets."

Chase Manhattan Bank Money Museum

Large Pineapple Fields in the Hawaiian Islands are terraced and contour-planted to prevent soil erosion.

Packers at a Pineapple Factory canning table, *right*, carefully inspect and grade the yellow slices before placing the fruit in the cans.

The Pineapple Plants must be sprayed with fertilizer solutions at various times throughout the growing season. Another spray used on the fields destroys insects.

PINE TREE STATE. See MAINE.

PINEAL, *PIN ee ul*, **GLAND** is a structure about the size of a pea located just above the base of the brain. This gland has interested scientists and philosophers for many years. For example, according to René Descartes, the French philosopher, the pineal is "the seat of the soul." However, the function of the gland remains as much a mystery in modern times as it was in the past. Rarely, tumors of the pineal gland develop. Some of these are associated with early sexual development. See also GLAND (The Pineal Gland).   T. B. SCHWARTZ

PINEAPPLE is a delicious and fragrant fruit that grew first in tropical America. It received its name because it looks like a pine cone. It is usually about the size of a coconut, though the very large varieties may be much larger, weighing from 16 to 20 pounds. It has a yellowish or reddish skin. Under the skin is a firm, pale yellow or white meat. A hard covering protects the fruit. The pineapple will stand more rough handling and keep longer than most other tropical fruits. Its excellent and distinctive flavor makes the pineapple a favorite dessert and salad fruit.

The pineapple plant bears a single thick stalk with stout, toothed leaves. The ripe head results from a thickened spine of the plant. Outside, the solid fruit is covered with the tips of the thick, hard floral bracts, or leaf-like petals. At the top it has a tuft of smaller leaves. Only one fruit grows on any one stalk, but the same root may produce more than one fruiting stem.

The Spaniards brought the pineapple to Europe after their explorations in South America. The earliest mention of the pineapple in England was made by John Evelyn in his *Diary*, in which he speaks of having tasted a pineapple from Barbados at the table of Charles II. For many years pineapples grew in private gardens in England and on the Continent. The European markets are largely supplied by the plantations of northern Africa, the Canaries, the Azores, and the West Indies. Queensland supplies pineapples for Australia. Florida also produces pineapples for market, but the crop is much lighter than it once was. Most of the American supply of canned pineapple comes from Hawaii. Considerable pineapple shipments also come from Puerto Rico, Cuba, the Bahamas, Jamaica, Trinidad, and the Philippines.

Pineapples do not ordinarily produce seed. For commercial production they may be propagated by plantings of *crowns* (the tufts of leaves at the top of the fruits), by the use of *suckers* (from near the base of the stalks), from *slips* (at the base of the fruits), and from *ratoons* (bud roots). Suckers are most commonly used. Plantations bear fruit for several years before they have to be reset,

The Ginaca Machine peels, cores, and end-cuts about 100 pineapples a minute. The fruit then passes to trimming tables.

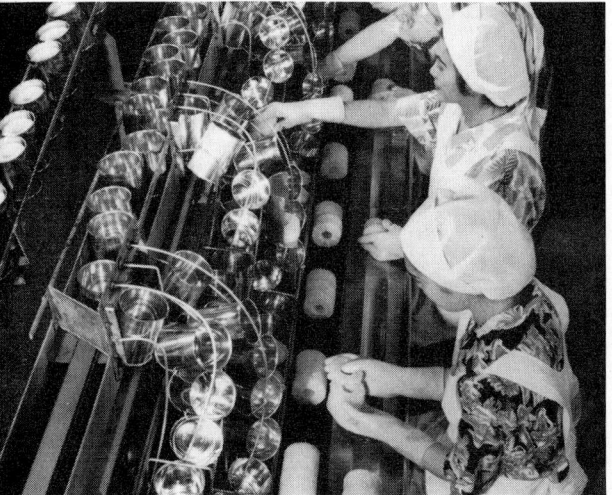

Dole

as the old plants are replaced by suckers. The fruits are harvested by hand. The workers wear heavy canvas gloves and leggings to avoid injury from the spines, and do the cutting with hooked knives. Pineapples for markets a long distance away are harvested before they are ripe and allowed to ripen on the way to market. The main harvest season extends from May to July. The first crop of pineapple matures in its second year after planting. The piña cloth of the Philippines, a delicate fabric, is woven from the fiber of the larger leaves.

Scientific Classification. Pineapples make up the pineapple family, *Bromeliaceae*. They are classified as genus *Ananas*, species *A. comosus*.   JULIAN C. CRANE

See also HAWAII (Agriculture; pictures).

PINEL, PHILIPPE. See MENTAL ILLNESS (Humane Treatment).

PINERO, SIR ARTHUR WING (1855-1934), ranks second to George Bernard Shaw as the most successful and productive English playwright of the period around 1900. Pinero's work can be divided broadly into two categories: early farces and sentimental comedies such as *The Magistrate* (1885) and *Dandy Dick* (1887); and serious social plays of his mature years, notably *The Second Mrs. Tanqueray* (1893) and *Mid-Channel* (1909).

Pinero and the critics of his time believed his social plays were his most important works. These plays dealt

with controversial subjects, but they usually confirmed, rather than attacked, conventional attitudes and prejudices. Today, only Pinero's lighter works have retained their appeal. His serious plays now seem to owe their success to the commercial "well-made play" formula that emphasized plot complications over ideas. Pinero was born in London.   RALPH G. ALLEN

PIÑERO, JESÚS TORIBIO. See PUERTO RICO (Building a Democracy).

PINES, ISLE OF. See ISLE OF PINES.

PING-PONG. See TABLE TENNIS.

PINK is a group of flowering plants that botanists have named *Dianthus*, the Greek word for *Jove's flower*. The blossoms are often seen in shades of pink, but the name *pink*, according to many authorities, is used in the sense of *pierce*, or *puncture*, and refers to the crinkled edges of the petals. The group includes several favorite garden flowers that are admired for their beauty and delicate scent. The spicy fragrance of many old-fashioned gardens comes from beds of clove pinks, clustered in their grasslike leaves, and showing combinations of pink, white, and red. The cultivated pinks include the *carnation;* derivatives of the *common,* or *feather, pink; clove pinks; rainbow pinks;* small-flowered *maiden pinks;* and *sweet Williams,* or *bunch pinks.* Pinks are grown from seeds and cuttings.

Inter-State Nurseries
The Little Joe Pink adds beauty and a delicate spicy fragrance to flower gardens.

Scientific Classification. The pink belongs to the pink family, *Caryophyllaceae.* The parent of the cultivated carnation is genus *Dianthus,* species *D. caryophyllus;* the common pink is *D. plumarius;* the rainbow, *D. chinensis;* the maiden, *D. deltoides;* the sweet William, *D. barbatus.*   DONALD WYMAN

See also BABIES'-BREATH; CARNATION; SWEET WILLIAM.

PINK BOLLWORM is an insect that attacks cotton plants in many parts of the world. The feeding of this insect reduces the yield and quality of cotton lint and the oil content of the seeds. Experts believe the insect was imported from Egypt into Mexico in 1911 in shipments of cotton seed. It was first discovered in the United States in Texas in 1917. Large sums of money have been spent in an effort to kill the insect in the United States.

The adult is a small grayish-brown moth, with a wingspread of about three fifths of an inch. The larva is about a half inch long. The eggs are laid on all parts of the cotton plant. When the larvae hatch, they feed on the pollen and fleshy parts of the flower. The infested flowers do not open normally, and many of them fall off. Later, the larvae enter the growing cotton bolls, eat the

425

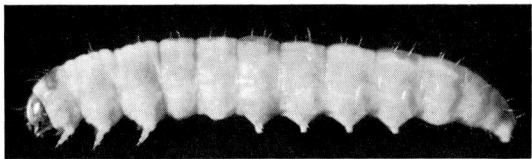

USDA

The Pink Bollworm in the caterpillar stage may seriously damage the blossoms and bolls of the cotton plant.

USDA

The Pink Bollworm Moth is the adult form of the pink bollworm. These harmful insects attack cotton crops in six states.

seeds, burrow through the lint, and check the growth of the bolls. This causes the growing cotton to rot.

In spring and summer the larvae mature in from 8 to 16 days. Those hatched in fall and winter may remain as larvae from a few months to two years or more. When the summer larvae are grown, they leave the bolls. They spend the third, or pupal, stage of their lives under trash or two or three inches beneath the surface of the soil. The pupal period lasts from 6 to 20 days. The resting larvae mature in the ground or in the seed and lint inside the boll. The insect may be easily carried to any distance while in this resting larval stage. Breeding begins early in spring and continues until frost, with several generations produced in a season.

Scientific Classification. The pink cotton bollworm belongs to the gelechiid moth family, *Gelechiidae*. It is genus *Pectinophora*, species *P. gossypiella*.   E. GORTON LINSLEY

PINKERTON, ALLAN (1819-1884), an American detective, in 1850 established one of the first detective agencies in the United States. He first won fame for exposing the activities of a band of counterfeiters. In 1861, Pinkerton guarded Abraham Lincoln as he journeyed from Springfield, Ill., to Washington, D.C., to be inaugurated as President. Soon after the outbreak of the Civil War, Pinkerton helped organize a federal secret service, of which he became chief. During this time, he operated his own organization in Chicago, and established branches in several cities. After the Civil War,

Allan Pinkerton
Pinkerton Natl. Detective Agency

Pinkerton organized groups of armed men known as "Pinkerton Men," whose services were available to employers at a daily fee. These forces broke labor strikes that occurred during the Reconstruction period. Members of labor unions hated the "Pinkerton Men" because these men were employed on the side of management against the unions.

Pinkerton also smashed several Western gangs. His earliest "Wild West" case ended with the capture of the Reno brothers, a gang of train robbers, in 1868.

Pinkerton was born in Glasgow, Scotland, and moved to the United States about 1842. In Illinois, he became deputy sheriff of Kane County and later of Cook County. Pinkerton wrote several books from an autobiographical point of view. His writings included *Criminal Reminiscences and Detective Sketches* (1879), *The Spy of the Rebellion* (1883), and *Thirty Years a Detective* (1884).   O. W. WILSON

See also LINCOLN, ABRAHAM (picture: President-Elect Lincoln).

PINKEYE. See CONJUNCTIVITIS.

PINNA. See EAR (The Outer Ear).

PINNACLES NATIONAL MONUMENT is located in western California, about 75 miles west of Fresno. This area has many spirelike rock formations that tower from 500 to 1,200 feet high. They can be seen for many miles. The monument also has many caves and canyons, and a variety of colorful volcanic formations. The Pinnacles National Monument covers about 14,500 acres. It was established in 1908. For location, see CALIFORNIA (physical map).   C. LANGDON WHITE

PINOCCHIO. See COLLODI, CARLO.

PINOCHLE, *PEA nuck'l*, is one of the most popular card games in the United States. A pinochle deck consists of 48 cards. Each of the four suits has 12 cards, two each of every card from the nines through the aces. The aces are the highest cards, followed by the tens, kings, queens, jacks, and nines.

The object of the game is to bid a certain number and then to reach that score. Players make points in two ways. The winner of the bid *melds*. That is, he shows certain combinations of his cards and adds the points they represent. After the hand has been played, the bidder receives specified points for the cards in the tricks he has taken.

There are many variations of pinochle, but one of the most popular forms of the game is *auction pinochle*. It is played by three persons, with a fourth acting as dealer. The dealer gives 15 cards to each player, and sets three to one side. These three cards are called the *widow*. The player to his left is the first to bid on the strength of his hand. The minimum bid is usually set at 300. Every overbid must be a multiple of 10 (300, 310, 320, 330). The player who bids highest names his trump suit and then melds. He may use the widow cards in his meld and then substitute them for cards in his hand. The three he discards count in his scoring later.

The bidder's opponents play as partners. The bidder plays the first card, and the other two play on it in turn. Each trick of three cards is taken by the person who plays the highest card in the suit led, or who trumps highest. If the two highest cards are alike, the one that was played first wins the trick.

A winning bidder collects the amount, or twice the amount, of his bid from each opponent. If he has lost, the bidder pays each opponent the amount, or twice the amount, of his bid. LILLIAN FRANKEL

PIÑON, *PEA nyahn,* is the name of four varieties of small, scrubby pine trees that grow in the semiarid regions of the southwestern United States. The small cones of the piñon contain seeds, called *pine nuts,* that have a delicate nutty flavor. Pine nuts form an important part of the diet of Indians of the Southwest.

Piñons have short needles that grow singly or in clusters of two, three, or four, depending on the species. The trees often grow as sprawling shrubs, but a few may reach a height of 40 feet. They grow either in pure stands or mixed with junipers and scrub oaks. Piñon wood is fine textured and fairly hard. The wood may be used for fence posts, railroad ties, or fuel.

Scientific Classification. Piñons belong to the pine family, *Pinaceae.* They are varieties of genus *Pinus,* species *P. cembroides; P. quadrifolia; P. edulis;* and *P. monophylla.* RICHARD J. PRESTON, JR.

See also CONE-BEARING TREES; NEW MEXICO (color picture: The State Tree); NEVADA (color picture).

PINSCHER. See DOBERMAN PINSCHER; TOY DOG.

PINT is a unit of capacity measure in the English system. It is used for both liquid and dry measure. The pint is equal to one-half of a quart and one-eighth of a gallon. In the United States, it contains 16 fluid ounces.

PINTA. See CARAVEL; COLUMBUS, CHRISTOPHER (First Voyage to America).

PINTADO. See KINGFISH.

PINTAIL, a long-tailed fresh-water duck, is found from Alaska to Florida, and also in Cuba, Puerto Rico, and the Bahamas. The pintail is one of the river ducks, along with the teal, the black ducks, and others. This important game bird has a brown head and neck, with a white line on each side of the neck. Its breast is white, and its body is covered with dark gray, white, purple, and green. The bird usually nests in Alaska and the Yukon, but it also breeds as far south as Utah.

Scientific Classification. The pintail belongs to the family of surface ducks, *Anatidae.* It is classified as genus *Anas,* species *A. acuta.* JOSEPH J. HICKEY

See also BIRD (color pictures: Wild Ducks and Wild Geese, Along the Flyways [Central Flyway]).

The Pintail Duck of North America is named for the long, pointed middle feathers of its tail.
C. J. Albrecht

PINTER, HAROLD (1930-   ), is an English playwright who gained fame for dramas that show modern man being attacked by terrifying forces surrounding him. Pinter's plays are called "comedies of menace" because they blend humor and realistic dialogue with undefined tensions that seem to lurk just below the surface of the action. His plots usually become cat-and-mouse games between an aggressor and a victim. Many of his plays are set in a bare room in a mysterious house.

Pinter sustains much of his sinister atmosphere by using pauses and silences. "Language is a highly ambiguous commerce," he once said. "So often below the words spoken is the thing known but unspoken. I think we communicate only too well in our silences."

Pinter was born in London. He began his career writing plays for radio and television. His one-act plays include *The Room* (1957), *The Dumb Waiter* (1957), *A Slight Ache* (1959), *The Dwarfs* (1961), *The Collection* (1961), and *The Lover* (1963). His longer plays include *The Birthday Party* (1958), *The Caretaker* (1960), and *The Homecoming* (1965). THOMAS A. ERHARD

PINTO. See HORSE (Color; color picture).

PINWORM, or THREADWORM, is a small roundworm. Pinworms are *parasites.* That is, they live in the body of other animals. They are about $\frac{1}{4}$ inch long and have white bodies and pointed tails. Several kinds of pinworms infect horses and rabbits. Only one kind, *Enterobius vermicularius,* commonly infects human beings.

The young worms live in the upper part of the large intestine. When the females are ready to lay eggs, they crawl down the rectum and out the intestinal opening called the *anus,* usually at night. They lay eggs on the surrounding skin. This movement causes skin swellings and severe itching. The eggs fall off onto the bedding or clothing, or may be picked up under fingernails in scratching. If the eggs are swallowed, they reach the intestine and become adult pinworms.

Pinworms are not very harmful unless they are present in large numbers. But eggs are often stirred up in the air and may infect new animals or reinfect the original carrier. In some cities, 10 to 60 per cent of the children may have pinworms at some time. Doctors use various drugs to treat pinworm infection.

Scientific Classification. Pinworms belong to the family *Oxyuridae.* J. A. MCLEOD

PINZA, *PEEN tsah,* or *PEEN zah,* **EZIO** (1892-1957), an Italian bass singer, became famous for his deep, melodious voice and his skillful acting. He sang with the Metropolitan Opera Company of New York City from 1926 to 1948. He received special acclaim for his performances in the title roles of the operas *Don Giovanni* and *Boris Godunov,* and as Mephistopheles in the opera *Faust.* In 1948, he turned from opera and won new recognition in the musical show *South Pacific,* and again in *Fanny* in 1954. He also appeared in several motion pictures.

Pinza was born in Rome. He studied engineering before turning to a musical career. DANIEL A. HARRIS

PINZÓN, VICENTI. See AMAZON RIVER; CABRAL, PEDRO ALVARES.

PION. See MESON.

PIONEER, space probe. See SPACE TRAVEL (table: Space Probes).

WORLD BOOK illustration by H. Charles McBarron

Facing Danger at Each Turn of the Trail, America's pioneers struggled westward and tamed a wilderness. The story of their courage and achievements still thrills Americans today.

PIONEER LIFE IN AMERICA

PIONEER LIFE IN AMERICA. The story of the pioneers is a thrilling tale of men and women who pushed America's frontier from the Appalachian Mountains to the Pacific Ocean. There were many famous frontiersmen, among them Daniel Boone, Kit Carson, and Davy Crockett. But the real heroes of the frontier were thousands of pioneers who never became famous. Their courage and hard work tamed a wilderness, and made way for the rise of a great nation.

This article tells about the people who followed the westward trails that had been blazed by explorers or fur traders. It describes life in an early pioneer settlement just west of the Appalachians. It also tells about the long, dangerous journey by wagon train across the Great Plains and the Rocky Mountains.

From about 1760 to 1850, the settlers moved westward in two big migrations. The first migration pushed the frontier as far west as the Mississippi Valley. During the second migration, settlers from the East and Midwest reached California and Oregon.

For the story of the first European colonists in America, see the WORLD BOOK article COLONIAL LIFE IN AMERICA. For the history of the settlements that developed in the West after 1850, see WESTERN FRONTIER LIFE. See also WESTWARD MOVEMENT.

The contributor of this article is Ruby Price Henderson of the Crow Island School, Winnetka, Ill., author of Pioneer Living. *The article was critically reviewed by Robert G. Athearn, Professor of History at the University of Colorado.*

The men and women who pushed the frontier westward across America probably never thought of themselves as brave pioneers. Many of them simply loved adventure and enjoyed facing danger. But most of them faced danger and hardship because they were not content with what they had. They wanted a chance to improve their lives. They had heard about the great forests and farmlands of the West, still untouched by ax or plow. They were eager to use the fine timber and rich soil, and to build new homes for their families.

Conquering the Wilderness. The men and women who pioneered needed many skills to make their hopes come true. Most frontiersmen were farmers. But a pioneer also had to be a clever hunter and trapper. He had to know how to build a shelter, a boat, a wagon, or a sled. Using only an ax, he cleared land for a farm. He planted seeds and harvested crops with homemade tools. If his plow broke, he either fixed it or made a new one.

A pioneer woman worked as hard as her husband. She did much of the heavy farm work, and still found time to care for the children. She also nursed any member of the family who became ill. The frontier housewife knew how to cook wild fowl and other game on an open fire. She spun yarn from flax or wool, and wove the yarn into cloth.

Getting along on the frontier meant being a good neighbor. Most families, when they set out on the westward trail, joined several others who were making the same journey. On the trail, the pioneers were always ready to help each other. If food became scarce, they shared their supplies. At the end of the journey, the pioneers continued to help each other. Families got together to build houses, plow fields, or harvest crops.

Establishing the Frontier. The pioneers usually traveled on trails that had been blazed by explorers or fur traders. The trail blazers kept moving west, sometimes setting up forts or trading posts as they went. After a few years, cattle raisers were driving herds along the trails, heading for the western pastures. Like the explorers and fur traders, most cattlemen kept moving.

The first settlers followed the cattlemen to the frontier. They made clearings in the wilderness for small farms. After raising a crop or two, many became restless and moved farther west. Their places were taken by pioneers who wanted to build permanent communities. These newcomers bought land that could be developed into large farms. They built churches and schools, and organized local governments. Soon these frontier communities attracted blacksmiths, millers, teachers, doctors, merchants, and freight handlers.

In some places, the growth of frontier communities gave free Negroes a chance to start a new life. Some of these Negroes had been freed from slavery by their masters or by state legislatures. Others had bought their freedom or had simply run away. Most of the free Negroes headed for towns in the Northwest Territory, where the law forbade slavery. The Northwest Territory was a huge region that later became the states of Ohio, Indiana, Illinois, Michigan, Wisconsin, and part of Minnesota. See NORTHWEST TERRITORY.

PIONEER LIFE IN AMERICA/*Moving Westward*

Thousands of pioneers struggled through the rugged Appalachian Mountains during the late 1700's and early 1800's. These pioneers established frontier settlements in Kentucky, Tennessee, Ohio, Illinois, and other lands as far west as the Mississippi Valley.

This section of the article tells how the early pioneers traveled across the Appalachians. The next section describes a typical settlement west of the mountains. For the story of America's second big migration, west of the Mississippi Valley, see the section *Crossing the Plains*.

Crossing the Appalachians

The first pioneers hacked their way through the Appalachians along steep, narrow trails. They swam or waded across streams, and floated down rivers in canoes or on clumsy rafts. As pioneer travel increased, the trails became wide enough for wagons, and large boats carried groups of pioneers and their livestock on the rivers. After 1811, steamboats operated on the Ohio and Mississippi rivers. About the same time, roads linked some frontier settlements with Eastern cities.

The pioneers followed several main routes on their way west. One route went through Cumberland Gap, a natural pass in the mountains. In 1775, a band of woodsmen led by Daniel Boone cut the Wilderness Road through the gap. Thousands of pioneers used the road to reach the rich farmlands of Kentucky. Another route followed the Pennsylvania river valleys to Pittsburgh. There, many pioneers boarded river craft and floated down the Ohio. In 1811, work began on a road that later led from Cumberland, Md., to Vandalia, Ill. It became known as the National Road or the Cumberland Road. Many pioneers from New England traveled west on the Mohawk Trail across New York. Then they followed the southern shores of the Great Lakes. The Erie Canal, completed in 1825, provided a water route between the East and the West. It was the first important national waterway built in the United States.

How the Pioneers Traveled

The first test of pioneering skill came even before the journey west began. A pioneer had to know what to take on the long, hard trip, and what to leave behind. He needed certain equipment for the journey, and other supplies to start life on the frontier.

No pioneer could be without a rifle and an ax. They were more important than anything else he owned. With his rifle, a pioneer could shoot game for food, or fight off wild animals. With his ax, he could cut logs to make a raft or a shelter, or clear land for a farm.

Many pioneers set off on foot, carrying little more than rifle and ax. But most pioneer families had one or two pack animals, and a wagon or a cart. Some took along a cow to provide milk and to serve as a pack animal. If a family owned sheep, they were herded by a dog that also helped the men and boys hunt game.

TRAILS OF THE PIONEERS

This map shows the major routes of the pioneers during the two big westward migrations. The eastern region (yellow) was settled during the first migration, in the late 1700's and early 1800's. The western region (green) was crossed during the second migration by the pioneers of the 1840's.

Astoria

Fort Vancouver

Whitman Mission

CASCADE RANGE

BLUE MOUNTAINS

Columbia River

Snake River

Fort Boise

Fort Hall

OREGON TRAIL

ROCKY

SOUTH PASS

INDEPENDENCE ROCK

GREAT   PLAINS

Missouri River

CALIFORNIA TRAIL

Great Salt Lake

MORMON TRAIL

Salt Lake City

Fort Bridger

Fort Laramie

North Platte River

OREGON TRAIL

Fort Kearny

Platte River

MORMON TRAIL

Nauvoo

SIERRA NEVADA

DONNER PASS

Sutter's Fort (Sacramento)

San Francisco

Sacramento River

San Joaquin R.

Green River

MOUNTAINS

South Platte River

Bent's Fort

Cimarron Crossing

SANTA FE TRAIL

Council Grove

Independence

Vandalia

St. Louis

Mississippi River

Los Angeles

MOJAVE DESERT

OLD SPANISH TRAIL

RATON PASS

CIMARRON CUTOFF

Santa Fe

Colorado River

Arkansas River

Cimarron River

Canadian River

Red River

Rio Grande

NATCHEZ TRACE

Natchez

The Long Westward Journey was generally made by several families traveling to-gether. The pioneers helped one another on the trail, and often shared their supplies.

430

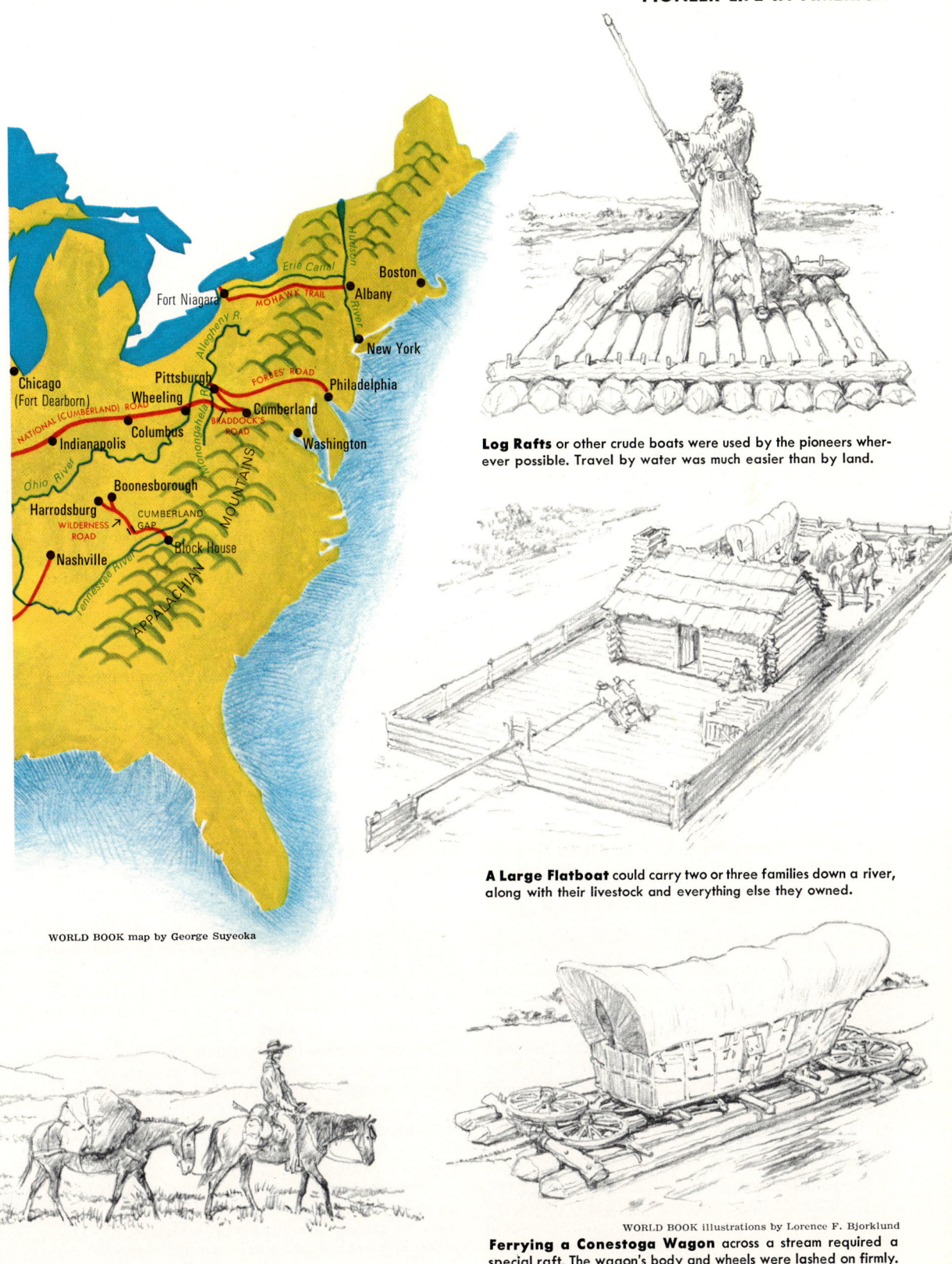

Log Rafts or other crude boats were used by the pioneers wherever possible. Travel by water was much easier than by land.

A Large Flatboat could carry two or three families down a river, along with their livestock and everything else they owned.

WORLD BOOK map by George Suyeoka

WORLD BOOK illustrations by Lorence F. Bjorklund

Ferrying a Conestoga Wagon across a stream required a special raft. The wagon's body and wheels were lashed on firmly.

Map labels: Boston, Albany, Fort Niagara, New York, Erie Canal, Hudson River, Mohawk Trail, Chicago (Fort Dearborn), Pittsburgh, Wheeling, Forbes' Road, Philadelphia, Cumberland, Washington, Allegheny R., National (Cumberland) Road, Indianapolis, Columbus, Braddock's Road, Ohio River, Monongahela R., Boonesborough, Harrodsburg, Wilderness Road, Cumberland Gap, Block House, Appalachian Mountains, Nashville, Tennessee River

431

Any tool or household utensil that could be made on the frontier was left behind. Most pioneers took along an adz, an auger, a hammer, a saw, a hoe, and a plowshare. Household goods consisted of a few pots and pans, an iron kettle, and perhaps a spinning wheel. The women found room for a little extra clothing, a few blankets, and such prized possessions as a clock and a family Bible.

Hunting and fishing provided most of the food along the way. The pioneers also carried some corn meal, salt pork, and dried beef. Johnnycake, a kind of corn bread, was a favorite because it did not spoil on a long trip.

Most of the pioneers walked, but some rode horseback. The settlers drove their pack animals and livestock ahead of them. They could travel only a few miles a day, and most trips took several weeks. Later, after roads had been built, the Conestoga wagon became the favorite vehicle for pioneer travel. It was named for the Pennsylvania valley where it was first built. A Conestoga had broad-rimmed wheels, high curved sides, and a rounded, white canvas roof. It could carry a family and everyone's possessions. See CONESTOGA WAGON.

For river travel, most pioneers used a large barge called a flatboat. It could carry several families with all their supplies and livestock. A boxlike house stood in the center of the flatboat. The pioneers used it for shelter and protection. The house became a floating fort in case of attack by Indians or river pirates. Perhaps, at the end of the journey, some of the pioneers settled near the river. They took apart the house and flatboat, and used the lumber to build shelters ashore.

PIONEER LIFE IN AMERICA /*A Pioneer Settlement*

The frontier often became a battleground for savage warfare between the pioneers and the Indians. When the pioneers moved westward, they invaded lands that had been Indian hunting grounds for thousands of years. Some tribes gave up their lands under treaties with the British, French, or colonial governments. But the Indians or the settlers often broke the treaties and fought for the land. During the Revolutionary War, the English armed some tribes and encouraged them to attack the settlers. Bands of Indians frequently raided the frontier settlements. In the late 1770's, Indian attacks drove most of the pioneers back east of the mountains. But in a short time, thousands of pioneers again turned westward.

During the War of 1812, some tribes again helped the British fight the Americans. After the Americans won the war, the tribes surrendered most of their lands east of the Mississippi River. For accounts of the major battles between the Indians and the pioneers, see INDIAN WARS.

A Pioneer Home

In some settlements, a pioneer bought his homesite from a company that owned a big tract and divided it for sale. In other places, public lands had been *surveyed* (measured), and homesites could be bought from a government agent. Many pioneers settled on public lands before the land had been surveyed. These settlers, who became known as *squatters*, did not have title to the land. After the land had been surveyed, a squatter could buy it under rights of ownership called *squatter's rights* (see SQUATTER'S RIGHTS).

Clearing the Land was the first task of a pioneer family. Most pioneers arrived at a settlement in spring, the planting season. A spring arrival gave them time to prepare for the next winter. The settlers wanted to have a snug home before cold weather began. Even more important, they wanted to raise enough crops to provide a supply of food for winter.

The pioneer family picked a place that seemed best for farming, and started clearing the land so they could plow the soil and plant seeds. No time could be spared to build a home. The family put up a temporary shelter called a *half-camp*. Twisted bark and branches formed the roof and three sides of the half-camp. The fourth side was open, and faced a fire that burned day and night. During the day, the fire was used to cook food. At night, the crackling blaze warmed the shelter and kept away wild animals.

A pioneer had no machines to clear the land. He swung his ax to cut away the brush, chop down trees, and trim logs. Neighbors lent a hand removing rocks and stumps. Every member of the family pitched in to help with the work of starting life on the frontier.

Building a Home. A log cabin was the typical pioneer home in Kentucky, Tennessee, and many other wooded regions. The men and boys cut trees into logs from 12 to 15 feet long. Then they chopped notches close to the ends. The notches held the logs to each other when they were fitted together to form the sides of the cabin. Four thick logs made up the foundation.

The sides of a log cabin were seven or eight feet high. No man could lift the heavy logs by himself, so his neighbors gathered to help him. The job was called a *house-raising*, and the women and children helped. Their chief task was to plug the spaces between the logs, using clay, moss, or mud. Filling the spaces was called *chinking*.

Roofing began after the cabin sides had been completed. First the men fitted logs together on top of the sides to form the frame of the roof. Then they fastened *clapboards* (thin boards) to the frame. They overlapped the clapboards so that rain would run off. Few of the early pioneers had building nails. They used wooden pins to hold the parts of the roof together. The boys had the important job of whittling the pins.

The ground served as the cabin floor until the pioneer found time to build a wooden floor. He split logs into slabs called *puncheons*. Then he pushed them lengthwise into the earth, split side up, and wedged them together. A puncheon floor was much smoother and warmer than the ground, and it also improved the looks of the cabin.

A fireplace stood at one end of the cabin. It had a log chimney, chinked and lined with clay. The hearth, made of stones, was the family's favorite gathering place. The mother kept a fire burning most of the time for cooking, and to provide light and warmth.

432

Frontier cabins had only small windows, covered with animal skins or greased paper. Greased paper let light into the cabin. Glass later replaced these window coverings when storekeepers brought it from the East.

The cabin door was made of thick pieces of wood fastened to crosspieces. The door swung on hinges made of leather. A deerskin string was tied to the latch and hung outside. When someone pulled the latchstring, it drew up the latch and the door opened. At night, the latchstring hung inside, and the family put strong bars across the door to keep it shut. The latchstring hanging outside a cabin door became a symbol of pioneer hospitality. Even today, many people tell friends that "the latchstring is always out."

Furnishings. A family started life on the frontier with a few pieces of handmade furniture and some household utensils. After getting settled, the pioneers bought other things from a peddler or a frontier store. Every growing settlement had a blacksmith, a cabinetmaker, and other craftsmen.

The family's table was made of several split log slabs with four sturdy legs. Benches and stools were made of smaller slabs. A pole, stuck into a wall, formed the outside rail of the bedstead. A notched log held up the free end. Crosspoles were laid from the pole to a side wall. The crosspoles held a mattress stuffed with dried grass or leaves. Quilts, blankets, or animal skins served as bed coverings. Many pioneers had no beds. They simply rolled up in buffalo robes and slept on the floor. Some cabins had a loft where the boys slept. A steep ladder, built onto one side of the cabin, led to the loft.

The boys of pioneer families made many of the household utensils. Most of the boys were skillful whittlers, and carved wooden spoons, ladles, bowls, and platters. They also whittled long pegs that were driven into the cabin walls to hold the family's clothing. Deer antlers, hung over the door, made a good rack for the pioneer's rifle, bullet pouch, and powder horn.

Most pioneer families brought a few pieces of china or pewter to the frontier. These cherished possessions were put on shelves as reminders of bygone days in the East. In a year or two, a successful pioneer might buy a cupboard to hold such treasures. Or he might add a room to the cabin.

Food. Corn and meat were the basic foods of a pioneer family. The family ate corn in some form at almost every meal. The pioneers raised corn as their chief crop because it kept well in any season, and could be used in many ways. After the corn had been husked, the kernels could be ground into corn meal. The settlers used the meal to make mush, porridge, or various kinds of corn bread—ashcake, hoecake, johnnycake, or corn pone. For a special treat, ears of corn were roasted.

The pioneers raised cattle, hogs, sheep, and chickens. They also hunted wild fowl and other game for much of their meat supply. Many meals consisted of wild duck, pigeon, or turkey; or bear, buffalo, deer, opossum, rabbit, or squirrel. Wild pigs were hunted in many areas.

The pioneers had no refrigeration, but they knew how to keep meat from spoiling. They cut some kinds of meat into strips and dried them in the sun. They also smoked the strips over a fire. Other meat, especially pork, kept well after being salted or soaked in *brine* (very salty water).

Salt was in great demand on the frontier for preserving and seasoning food. It brought a high price when traders from the East sold it by the barrel. Instead of paying the high price, some settlers banded together once a year and traveled to a salt lick, where natural salt formed on the ground. Wild animals came there to lick the salt. A trip to a salt lick, no matter what the distance, was worthwhile for the settlers. There was good hunting at the salt lick, and the men took home enough salt to supply the community for a year.

Raising vegetables and herbs was a job of the women

A Half-Camp had to be built by each new family at a pioneer settlement. There was no time to build a cabin until the family's homesite had been cleared and seeds planted for the first crop.

WORLD BOOK illustration by Lorence F. Bjorklund

LIFE ON THE FRONTIER

In a typical settlement, men, women, and children worked at farm and household tasks from dawn to dusk. The boys at a corner of the cabin are grinding corn. Near the stream, a woman washes clothes, and a man makes soap. Not far from the stockade, *upper right*, men are building a schoolhouse.

Splitting Logs with a mallet and several wedges, a frontiersman made thick slabs called *puncheons*. He used the puncheons for his cabin floor, or to build tables, benches, or stools.

Grinding Corn was often the job of pioneer boys. One type of mill consisted of two stones. When the top stone was turned, corn poured between the stones was ground into a coarse meal.

434

WORLD BOOK illustrations by Lorence F. Bjorklund

A Corn Husking Party brightened settlement life at harvest time. The ears of corn were divided into equal piles. Neighbors formed teams that competed to see which could husk a pile first. A settler used a husking pin, *left*, to tear the husks from the corn.

435

A FRONTIER HOME

The pioneer cabin was a workshop as well as a home. By the light from the fireplace, the mother is grating corn while the father repairs a farm tool. All furnishings of this typical log cabin are homemade. Near the door, long pegs in the wall form a ladder leading to a loft where the boys slept.

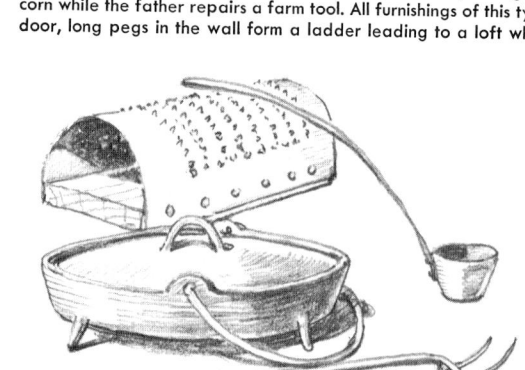

Iron Cooking Utensils were prized by pioneer women. Most housewives brought a tight-lidded baking kettle, *center*, from the East. Also shown are a corn grater, a ladle, and a toasting fork.

Molding Rifle Bullets required skillful handling of hot lead. A frontiersman liked to mold his own bullets, so he could be sure they would fit exactly into the barrel of his rifle.

436

Making Candles was a job for the women and girls. They twisted string or strips of cloth into wicks, dipped them repeatedly into hot animal fat, then hung them to cool and harden.

WORLD BOOK illustrations by Lorence F. Bjorklund

A Spinning Wheel, brought from the East, became a treasure on the frontier. The lucky housewife who had one could spin yarn, weave cloth, and make her family's clothing.

437

and girls. Most of the vegetables planted by the pioneers could be cooked into hearty meals—beans, cabbages, potatoes, squash, and turnips. Herbs included dill and sage.

Milk from the family cow was the chief mealtime drink. Coffee and tea were too expensive for the frontier. Whiskey, made from corn, was a popular drink of the men. The pioneers sometimes mixed corn whiskey with milk, added some sweetening, and served it to the entire family. Common sweetenings included honey, molasses, and maple sugar or maple syrup.

Clothing was harder to provide on the frontier than either food or shelter. Clothing materials were expensive, and making clothes was a long, difficult process. A pioneer housewife spun linen yarn from flax, and wool yarn from the wool of sheep. She wove the yarn into cloth, which she used to make shirts, trousers, dresses, and shawls. Spinning and weaving took a long time, but even more time was needed to grow flax or raise sheep. Most pioneers, for their first year or two on the frontier, wore the clothes they had brought with them. After this clothing wore out, they made garments of deerskin, like those worn by the Indians.

Many frontiersmen wore a deerskin hunting shirt and deerskin trousers. The shirt fitted loosely and hung to the thighs. It had no buttons, and was held in place by a belt. Instead of a collar, the shirt had a cape, perhaps trimmed with fringe. Deerskin clothing became cold and stiff when wet, and felt uncomfortable next to the skin. A man in deerskin usually wore underclothes of linsey-woolsey, a homemade material of part linen and part wool.

Linsey-woolsey was the favorite material of the pioneer housewife for making clothes for herself and the children. She used deerskin only if she had no cloth. Most pioneer women wore a petticoat and a dress that resembled a smock. The petticoat was worn as a skirt, not as an undergarment. In cold weather, women wore a shawl of wool or linsey-woolsey. Pioneer boys and girls wore the same kind of clothing as their parents.

The children and many adults went barefoot much of the time. Few pioneers had boots or shoes. They wore homemade moccasins or *shoepacks* made of hide. Shoepacks resembled moccasins, but they covered the ankles and had sturdy soles. For warmth and comfort, the pioneers stuffed their moccasins or shoepacks with deer hair or dry leaves.

In summer, the women and girls wore sunbonnets large enough to shield the face and neck. In winter, they covered their heads with shawls or wore woolen bonnets. Men and boys wore coonskin caps or fur hats in cold weather. In summer, they had hats made of loosely woven straw or corn husks.

Tools. A pioneer started farming with the hoe, plow, and other tools that he brought with him to the frontier. His cabin soon became a workshop as well as a home. The pioneers made most of their own farm tools, including flails, harrows, and rakes. Sometimes they made pitchforks by attaching long handles to deer antlers. The settlers also made many household items. They whittled wooden spoons, bowls, and platters, and used gourds and animal horns for cups and containers.

The pioneers made several kinds of mills to grind corn into meal. Some made a hand mill of two large, flat stones, one on top of the other. Corn was placed between the stones. The top stone had a wooden handle attached. When the handle was turned, the corn was ground into meal. Another type of mill consisted of a heavy log and a hollowed tree stump. Corn was put into the hollow and pounded into meal with the log. Some housewives simply grated the corn into a coarse meal. They made a grater by punching holes in a piece of sheet iron and fastening it to a block of wood. The corn was rubbed against the sharp, raised edges of the holes in the metal.

Some pioneers used homemade mills even after a miller settled in the community. Many brought their corn to the miller, giving him some in payment for grinding it into meal. They also used corn or corn meal instead of money to buy iron tools or iron bars from a blacksmith. They used the iron bars to make or repair many farm and household tools.

The pioneers usually molded their own rifle bullets from lumps of lead sold by the settlement storekeeper. He also sold gunpowder. A newcomer could get these vital supplies by promising to pay for them later with farm products. If a settlement had no store, a few settlers traveled together to the nearest town or trading post. There they could find lead, gunpowder, and other supplies from the East. They paid for these supplies with furs, corn, or homemade corn whiskey.

Caring for the Sick was the responsibility of the pioneer housewife. The early settlements had no doctors, but every woman could count on her neighbors for help when she needed it.

The pioneers made medicines from such plants as ginseng and jack-in-the-pulpit. They used the medicines to treat colds, pneumonia, and ague, an illness similar to malaria. Many pioneers believed some objects had magic powers that cured or prevented illness. A rattlesnake's heart was supposed to cure epilepsy. A dead spider, hung on the neck, was thought to prevent ague. A bag of asafetida, an herb that smells like garlic, was worn around the neck to keep a person healthy.

Serious diseases that spread rapidly, including cholera, smallpox, and yellow fever, often caused great problems in the Eastern cities. Most of the early settlers escaped these contagious diseases because they lived far from the cities. During the early 1800's, some newcomers from the East arrived in frontier settlements after catching a contagious disease. Many people then died because they did not know how to prevent the disease from spreading.

Education and Religion

Education. During the early years of a settlement, every home served as a school. Parents were the only teachers, but they spent little time on spelling or arithmetic. They taught boys and girls the skills needed to live on the frontier. A boy learned to use an ax and a rifle, to farm and to care for livestock, and to repair tools. A girl learned to cook, sew, spin, and weave. Parents also taught children to obey older persons and to behave politely.

In time, a schoolteacher arrived at most pioneer settlements. The settlers then built a one-room log schoolhouse. In most communities, the teacher was "boarded around" in payment for his services. He lived for a few months with one family and then with another, and received his food and lodging free. Some communities paid their teacher a small salary.

A settlement school had few books, and no blackboards, charts, or maps. The children learned by repeating lessons read by the teacher. He taught them reading, writing, and arithmetic. They wrote on boards, and used pieces of charcoal as pencils. Some had pens, made of goose quills, and ink made from bark or berries. Slates came into use about 1825. Most children attended school only during the winter. At other times they were needed at home to help with the farm and household tasks.

Religion. Almost every large pioneer settlement had a church. In small settlements, services were held in one of the homes. Parents taught prayers and hymns to their children, and kept Sunday as a day of rest and worship.

A traveling preacher visited many settlements regularly. He conducted church services and funerals, and performed marriages and baptisms. The preacher was called a "circuit rider" because he rode horseback from one settlement to another on a route known as a circuit.

Sometimes a preacher organized an outdoor religious meeting, or "camp service," which lasted several days and nights. It attracted families from many settlements on the frontier. The people brought food and other supplies, and camped in a large clearing where the meeting was held. The preacher led the pioneers in reciting prayers and singing hymns. Everyone enjoyed a camp service, especially the unmarried girls and men. It gave them a chance to make friendships that could lead to courtship and marriage.

Law and Order

The pioneers made and enforced their own rules of behavior. There were no courts or law officers in the early settlements. If men quarreled, they fought with their fists, or even with knives or guns. The settlers would have nothing to do with a bully or his family. A man could not stay long in a frontier community without the help of neighbors. He either stayed out of trouble, or left in disgrace.

Most of the pioneers wanted to live peacefully and earn their living by hard work. But the frontier also attracted robbers and other outlaws. Sometimes outlaws raided a settlement and stole horses and cattle. The settlers then armed themselves and rode after the bandits. Horse thieves or cattle rustlers could expect to be hanged or shot if they were captured.

During the late 1700's and early 1800's, court systems were established in Kentucky, Ohio, Tennessee, and other frontier states. The courts decided many disputes between settlers who quarreled over debts or land claims. Some of the lawyers who argued cases in these courts became famous political leaders. They included two future Presidents of the United States—Andrew Jackson and James K. Polk.

Social Activities

The pioneers brightened life on the frontier with many parties. They mixed work with fun and sports whenever possible. In autumn, they held corn husking contests and nutting parties. In spring, they gathered in a maple grove to make sugar and syrup. The women

often got together for a quilting party. The quilts were much in demand as bed coverings.

The settlers always enjoyed a house-raising for newcomers or newlyweds. The men stopped working on the house now and then to drink whiskey, run races, or hold wrestling bouts or shooting contests. After the job was finished, everyone celebrated with a gay feast. The women prepared plenty of food, and after eating, the settlers sat around telling stories. As a rule, someone brought along a fiddle, and dancing and singing went on until late in the night.

A wedding was a special time of fun and celebration. The pioneers liked to play tricks on a couple about to be married. Perhaps the women "kidnaped" the bride while the men rode off with the groom. Of course, both managed to escape in time to be married. The wedding feast, provided by the groom's parents, lasted all night. Daily tasks were set aside. Some wedding parties continued for as long as three days and nights.

Indian Attacks

The early settlers lived in constant fear of an attack by Indians. Most bands of raiding Indians consisted of 5 or 6 warriors, but some had as many as 20. After picking a home to attack, the Indians hid all night and struck at dawn. Some had guns, and others swung tomahawks or knives. In most attacks, the Indians killed and scalped everyone in the family except teenage boys and girls, who were taken prisoner.

The Indians gathered up clothing and household articles and took them along. If the settler had horses, the raiders loaded their loot on the animals. Otherwise, the Indians forced their captives to carry it. The raiders also killed the livestock, and burned the cabin and other buildings.

Even the bravest settler had little chance to save himself or his family in a surprise attack. Every man kept careful watch for Indians, and warned his nearest neighbor at the first sign of danger. Messengers spread the alarm throughout the settlement, and the settlers joined forces to fight the Indians.

A fort called a *stockade* was the main defense of a frontier settlement. A typical stockade was rectangular, with walls of sharply pointed logs at least 10 feet high. At each of two corners of the stockade stood a *blockhouse*, a two-story tower built of thick timber. Each blockhouse held at least 25 men. Small sheds or cabins provided living quarters in the stockade. Every man and boy who could handle a rifle stood guard at a firing post in one of the blockhouses. A firing post was a slit in a wall, just wide enough to shoot through. The women and girls kept the riflemen supplied with ammunition, food, and water.

The Indians seldom attacked a stockade, because they did not want to face the heavy rifle fire. If the warriors realized that they could not make a surprise attack, they usually moved on to another settlement.

The stockade also sheltered new arrivals at a settlement. All newcomers headed for the stockade, where they learned what to do in case of an alarm. Most of the new arrivals stayed in the stockade until they began the task of settling on their own land.

WORLD BOOK illustration by H. Charles McBarron

A Backbreaking Climb up a steep riverbank was just part of a day's work for the pioneers of the 1840's. Sometimes friendly Plains Indians helped the settlers along the trail to the West.

PIONEER LIFE IN AMERICA / *Crossing the Plains*

By the 1830's, the first big westward migration had pushed the frontier to the Mississippi Valley. Pioneers were rapidly settling Arkansas, Missouri, and Iowa—states just west of the Mississippi River. Explorers, missionaries, traders, and fur trappers had gone even farther west and southwest. They told of great forests and fertile valleys in the Oregon region and other lands west of the Rocky Mountains, 2,000 miles away.

The stories of the trailblazers made exciting news for many midwestern settlers who, by the 1840's, were ready for new adventures. The news also stirred hundreds of families arriving from the East seeking places to settle. In 1846, the Mormons, fleeing persecution in Illinois because of their religious beliefs, began their journey to the valley of the Great Salt Lake in Utah.

After gold was discovered in California in 1848, thousands of fortune seekers joined the migration. See MORMONS; GOLD RUSH.

The westward trails led over hundreds of miles of dusty, treeless plains and waterless deserts. They wound through dangerous mountain passes, and crossed and recrossed rushing streams and wide, muddy rivers. The travelers had to be on guard every moment against an Indian attack. But the first settlers of the Far West, like the earlier pioneers who had crossed the Appalachians, were eager for new opportunities. They were willing to risk their lives to reach the distant lands.

Some who set out on the westward trails died on the way, but few turned back. The men and women who succeeded became heroes of an important chapter in the history of America. By the end of the 1840's, they had pushed the nation's frontier to the Pacific Coast.

The Wagon Train

A family going to Oregon or California in the 1840's had to plan on a journey of four or five months. During most of the trip, the family lived in a canvas-covered wagon pulled by several teams of oxen or mules. The wagon was called a *prairie schooner* because, from a distance, its white top looked like the sails of a ship. It resembled the Conestoga, used by the pioneers who traveled the early roads in the East.

As many as a hundred families banded together for the long trip. Their wagons formed a caravan called a *wagon train.* Most men with families drove their own wagons. Single men rode horseback. They herded the group's livestock or rode alongside of the wagons, helping the drivers stay on the trail.

Each wagon train was guided by a scout who knew the route and the best places to camp. A wagon train also had a leader. He was elected by the people in the wagon train, and they agreed to obey his orders. Several men became famous as scouts or leaders of the Far West migration, including Jim Bridger, Kit Carson, and William L. Sublette. For their contributions to the settlement of the Far West, see the WORLD BOOK biographies of these men.

Most wagon trains started from Independence, Mo., and followed the Oregon Trail across the Great Plains. Settlers bound for California left the Oregon Trail after following it across the Rocky Mountains by way of South Pass. They turned south near Fort Hall, and used trails through what is now Nevada to the Sacramento Valley. Settlers bound for Oregon stayed on the Oregon Trail, heading northwest to the Columbia River and on to the Willamette Valley. In the Rockies, most large wagon trains were divided into small groups. The small groups were better suited for travel on the steep mountain trails. Another route to California from Independence was the Santa Fe Trail. It led southwest to Santa Fe, in present-day New Mexico. From there, the Old Spanish Trail led to Los Angeles.

Life on the Trail

On the long journey west, the pioneers had one main rule: "Keep moving." They stopped for a day or two at such places as Fort Laramie or Fort Bridger to repair equipment and buy supplies. But usually the wagons halted only at noon and nightfall. By keeping on the move, a wagon train could travel 15 or 20 miles a day. If the oxen hauling the wagons became exhausted, they were shot or simply left to die where they fell. They were replaced by animals herded behind the wagon train.

The "keep moving" rule killed many animals, but it saved many human lives. Almost all westward journeys started in spring. A spring departure gave the settlers time—if they kept moving—to get through the western mountains before snow blocked the passes. In 1846, a group led by George Donner was late reaching the Sierra Nevada. They became snowbound for two months. After their supplies gave out, they killed their animals for food. The group even boiled and ate the

bones and hides. Later, some of the Donner party kept from starving by eating the flesh of companions who had died. Only 47 of the 82 men, women, and children who became snowbound survived the horrible suffering. See DONNER PASS.

As long as the pioneers of the 1840's kept moving westward, the Plains Indians allowed them to pass through their hunting grounds. Some tribes guided the early pioneers, or helped them at difficult river crossings. The Indians even supplied some wagon trains with vegetables and buffalo meat in exchange for tobacco, whiskey, or pieces of iron. During the late 1850's and early 1860's, farmers and cattlemen began to settle on the plains. Then the tribes defended their hunting grounds by attacking the settlers.

Even in the early days, the pioneers usually defended themselves against a possible Indian attack at night. They formed the wagons into a circle called a *night ring,* and slept in the area inside. The night ring, like the stockade of the early settlers in the East, became a famous pioneer defense against Indians. Probably the best description of a night ring was written by Jesse Applegate, one of the leaders of a wagon train bound for Oregon in 1843. He wrote:

"... the sun is now getting low in the west, and at length the painstaking pilot is standing ready to conduct the train in the circle which he has previously measured and marked out, which is to form the invariable fortification for the night. The leading wagons follow him so nearly round the circle, that but a wagon length separates them. Each wagon follows in its track, the rear closing on the front, until its tongue and ox chains will perfectly reach from one to the other. And so accurate the measurement and perfect the practice, that the hindmost wagon of the train always precisely closes the gateway.... Within ten minutes from the time the leading wagon halted, the barricade is formed, the teams unyoked and driven out to pasture."

Some pastured animals might be stolen during the night, and sometimes a guard was killed by Indian raiders. But the Indians usually stayed away from the night ring, fearing the gunfire that would come from the wagons if they attacked.

The diaries kept by many pioneers of the 1840's tell mostly of hardships and tragedies on the trail. But not all memories of the westward journey were sad. Octavius T. Howe, describing the migration of the 1840's, wrote:

"... Those who crossed the plains, though they lived beyond the age allotted to man, never forgot the ungratified thirst, the intense heat and bitter cold, the craving hunger and utter physical exhaustion of the trail, and the rude crosses which marked the last resting places of loved companions. But there was another side. Neither would they ever forget the level prairie, covered with lush grass and dotted with larkspur, verbena, lupin, and geranium; the glorious sunrise in the mountains; the camp fire of buffalo chips at night, the last pipe before bedtime and the pure, sweet air of the desert. True they had suffered, but the satisfaction of deeds accomplished and difficulties overcome more than compensated and made the overland passage a thing never to be forgotten and a life-long pleasure in remembrance."

From *Argonauts of '49,* courtesy of Harvard University Press.

Ernst Peterson, Publix

Ruts of Pioneer Wagons on Oregon Trail at South Pass, Wyo.

PIONEER LIFE IN AMERICA / *A Visitor's Guide to Pioneer America*

Americans take great pride in their pioneer ancestors. Monuments, parks, and historic sites from coast to coast honor the first settlers of almost every community. Entire frontier settlements have been reconstructed. Museums exhibit pioneer tools, clothing, furniture, and crafts.

A traveler may follow several routes of the pioneers. For example, the National Road is now U.S. Highway 40. It links Washington, D.C., and St. Louis, and is called the National Old Trail Road. The Natchez Trace National Parkway, between Nashville, Tenn., and Natchez, Miss., follows the ancient Indian trail used by the early settlers of the Gulf States. U.S. Highway 30, westward from Kearney, Nebr., closely follows the Oregon Trail. At several points, travelers can clearly see ruts made in the ground by the wagon trains.

PLACES TO VISIT

Following are brief descriptions of some especially interesting places to visit. See also the Places to Visit section of the WORLD BOOK article on each state.

Andrew Jackson Historical State Park, in Lancaster, S.C., has a museum of pioneer objects and several reconstructed shops of the pioneer period.

Cades Cove, part of Great Smoky Mountains National Park on the Tennessee-North Carolina border, is an entire frontier community whose buildings have been preserved. They include barns, churches, mills, and many log cabins.

Campus Martius Museum, in Marietta, Ohio, stands on the site of a stockade built by the first settlers of Ohio.

Its exhibits include a pioneer kitchen, and displays of pioneer clothing, furniture, and tools.

Cumberland Gap National Historical Park, at the meeting point of Kentucky, Tennessee, and Virginia, includes the natural pass through the Appalachian Mountains used by many pioneers traveling the Wilderness Road.

Davy Crockett Cabin, in Rutherford, Tenn., is a log cabin of the pioneer period. Crockett lived in it during the early 1800's. The homemade furnishings include a rocking chair made by the famous frontiersman.

Emigrant Spring, in downtown Independence, Mo., is the well where pioneers bound for the Far West filled their water kegs before heading across the Great Plains.

Fort Bridger, a trading post on the Oregon Trail in the 1840's, is a state park near the town of Fort Bridger, Wyo. Many of the fort's original buildings have been restored. The park has a museum.

Fort Laramie National Historical Site, near Fort Laramie, Wyo., is a restoration of an important stopping place for wagon trains on the Oregon Trail.

Fort Recovery, in the village of Fort Recovery, Ohio, is a reproduction of part of a fort built in 1793.

Independence Rock, a huge block of granite on the north bank of the Sweetwater River near Alcova, Wyo., is a landmark of the Oregon Trail. Hundreds of settlers bound for the Far West scratched their names on the rock.

Lincoln Pioneer Village, in Rockport, Ind., has 17 log buildings with pioneer furnishings. A stockade encloses the village.

Ellis-Sawyer, F.P.G.

Mill at Cades Cove in Tennessee

Jack Zhert

Lincoln's New Salem State Park near Springfield, Ill.

Reconstruction of Sutter's Fort in Sacramento, Calif.

Fort Harrod in Harrodsburg, Ky.

Jack Zhert   Department of Public Information, Kentucky

Lincoln's New Salem State Park, near Springfield, Ill., has a reproduction of the pioneer settlement in which Abraham Lincoln lived from 1831 to 1837.

Marshall Gold Discovery Historic State Park, in Coloma, Calif., marks the site where gold was discovered in 1848. Nearby is a museum with relics of the gold rush days.

Pennsylvania Farm Museum, near Lancaster, Pa., is a reproduction of a pioneer village. The farming methods of the settlers, and many of their crafts, may be seen.

Pioneer Memorial State Park, in Harrodsburg, Ky., is a reconstruction of Fort Harrod, Kentucky's first permanent settlement.

Pioneer Monument State Park, in Salt Lake City, Utah, has a monument marking the spot where Brigham Young, the famous Mormon leader, first viewed the area. **Pioneer Memorial Museum,** in Salt Lake City, has exhibits of the early Mormon settlement.

Roadside America, near Hamburg, Pa., is a miniature indoor village that tells the story of American life from pioneer days to the present.

South Pass, near South Pass City, Wyo., is a valley along the Oregon Trail through the Rocky Mountains. Ruts made by the settlers' wagons may still be seen.

Sutter's Fort State Historical Monument, in Sacramento, Calif., is a reconstruction of the fort built in 1839 by John A. Sutter, a famous trader.

Watters Smith Memorial State Park, near Clarksburg, W.Va., has a museum with many articles used by pioneers, and reconstructed shops of an early West Virginia settlement.

RUBY PRICE HENDERSON

Critically reviewed by ROBERT G. ATHEARN

Related Articles. For the history of pioneering in the various states, see the History section of the WORLD BOOK state articles, such as OHIO (History). See also the following articles:

BIOGRAPHIES

Anza, Juan Bautista de	Fink, Mike
Appleseed, Johnny	Frémont, John Charles
Ashley, William H.	Girty, Simon
Astor (John Jacob)	Gist, Christopher
Austin (Moses; Stephen)	Goodyear, Miles
Boone, Daniel	Jemison, Mary
Bowie, James	Lewis, Meriwether
Bridger, James	Marshall, James W.
Carson, Kit	Maverick, Samuel A.
Chouteau (family)	McLoughlin, John
Clark, George Rogers	Rice, Henry M.
Clark, William	Sevier, John
Colter, John	Smith, Jedediah S.
Crockett, David	Sublette, William L.
Dubuque, Julien	Whitman, Marcus

PIONEER TRAVEL

Braddock's Road	Natchez Trace	Santa Fe Trail
Conestoga Wagon	National Road	Trails of Early
Erie Canal	Oregon Trail	Days
Lancaster Turnpike	Pennsylvania	Wilderness
Mohawk Trail	State Road	Road

OTHER RELATED ARTICLES

Blockhouse	Scout
Boom Town	Trading Post
Circuit Rider	United States, History
Clothing (color picture:	of (America in the
North America)	Early 1800's)
Colonial Life in America	Vigilante
Forty-Niner	Watauga Association
Gold Rush	Western Frontier Life
Indian Wars	Westward Movement
Log Cabin	

Outline

I. The Pioneers
  A. Conquering the Wilderness
  B. Establishing the Frontier
II. Moving Westward
  A. Crossing the Appalachians
  B. How the Pioneers Traveled
III. A Pioneer Settlement
  A. A Pioneer Home
  B. Education and Religion
  C. Law and Order
  D. Social Activities
  E. Indian Attacks
IV. Crossing the Plains
  A. The Wagon Train
  B. Life on the Trail
V. A Visitor's Guide to Pioneer America

Questions

How did pioneer families help each other?
What was the main defense of a frontier settlement?
Why was the "keep moving" so important for pioneers crossing the Great Plains?
Why was corn the chief crop of the frontier farmer?
How did a pioneer make a puncheon floor?
How did some settlers avoid paying high prices for salt?
How did the pioneers use the house of a flatboat?
What were a pioneer's two most important possessions?
What were two main routes followed by the early pioneers across the Appalachian Mountains?
Why was the latchstring a symbol of hospitality among the pioneers?

Books for Young Readers

ADAMS, SAMUEL HOPKINS. *The Santa Fe Trail.* Random House, 1951.
AMERICAN HERITAGE. *The Erie Canal.* American Heritage, 1964.
CARR, MARY JANE. *Children of the Covered Wagon: A Story of the Old Oregon Trail.* Crowell, 1957.
DAUGHERTY, JAMES H. *Daniel Boone.* Viking, 1939. Newbery Medal winner. *Trappers and Traders of the Far West.* Random House, 1952. *Marcus and Narcissa Whitman, Pioneers of Oregon.* Viking, 1953.
DORIAN, EDITH M., and WILSON, W. N. *Trails West and Men Who Made Them.* McGraw, 1955.
GARST, DORIS S. *Kit Carson, Trail Blazer and Scout.* Messner, 1942. *Big Foot Wallace of the Texas Rangers.* 1951. *Jim Bridger, Greatest of the Mountain Men.* Houghton, 1952.
MIERS, EARL S. *The Wild and Woolly West.* Rand McNally, 1964.
NEUBERGER, RICHARD L. *The Lewis and Clark Expedition.* Random House, 1951.
ROSS, NANCY W. *Heroines of the Early West.* Random House, 1960.
ROURKE, CONSTANCE M. *Davy Crockett.* Harcourt, 1955.
STEELE, WILLIAM O. *Buffalo Knife.* Harcourt, 1952. *Westward Adventure: The True Stories of Six Pioneers.* 1962. *The Year of the Bloody Sevens.* 1963.
TUNIS, EDWIN. *Frontier Living.* World Publishing Co., 1961.

Books for Older Readers

AMERICAN HERITAGE. *The American Heritage Book of the Pioneer Spirit.* Simon & Schuster, 1959. *The American Heritage History of the Great West.* American Heritage, 1965.
BAKELESS, JOHN E. *The Adventures of Lewis and Clark.* Houghton, 1962.
BILLINGTON, RAY A. *The Far Western Frontier, 1830-1860.* Harper, 1956. *Westward Expansion: A History of the American Frontier.* 2nd ed. Macmillan, 1960.
CLARK, THOMAS D. *Frontier America: The Story of the Westward Movement.* Scribner, 1955.
DE VOTO, BERNARD A. *Year of Decision: 1846.* Houghton, 1943. *The Course of Empire,* 1952.
GUTHRIE, ALFRED B., JR. *The Way West.* Houghton, 1949. A historical novel.
LAVENDER, DAVID. *Westward Vision: The Story of the Oregon Trail.* McGraw-Hill, 1963.
LEWIS, MERIWETHER. *The Journals of Lewis and Clark.* Numerous editions.
PARKMAN, FRANCIS. *The Oregon Trail.* Numerous editions.
RIEGEL, ROBERT E., and ATHEARN, ROBERT G. *America Moves West.* 4th ed. Holt, Rinehart and Winston, 1964.
VAN EVERY, DALE. *The Final Challenge: The American Frontier, 1804-1845.* Morrow, 1964.

PIPAL, or BO TREE. See BO TREE.

PIPE is a musical instrument that is the ancestor of our present pipe organ and all other wind instruments. It is probably the oldest of musical instruments. According to Greek legend, it was invented by Pan (see PAN). Cave men fashioned bones into rude pipes. The flute is a pipe of the *whistle* type, in which air blown against a sharp edge sets in motion the air in a hollow tube. The oboe and clarinet are *reed whistles,* in which the movements of a thin piece of wood or other material set the air in motion. The trumpet operates on the principle of setting the air in motion through vibrations of the player's lips. WORLD BOOK has an article on each wind instrument mentioned. CHARLES B. RIGHTER

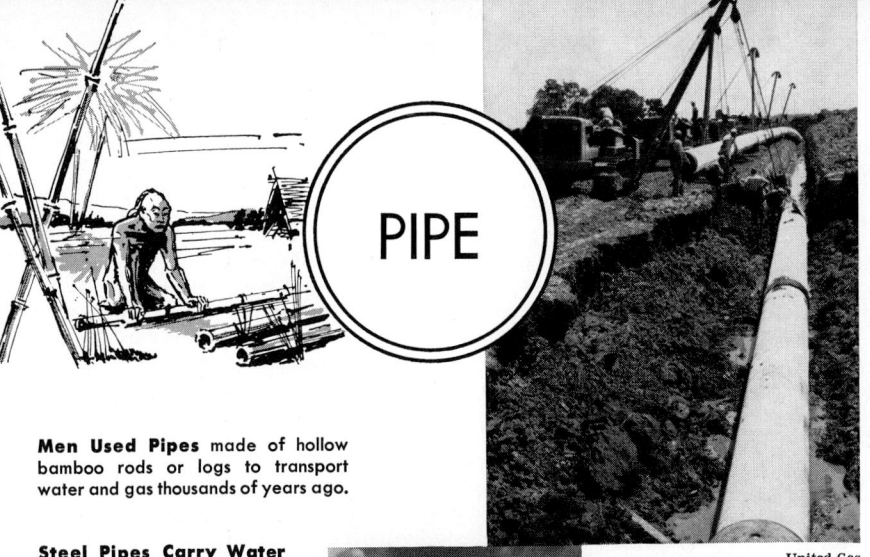

PIPE

Natural Gas Pipelines branch out in a great network over the United States and Canada. Some of this pipe measures 36 inches in diameter.

United Gas

Men Used Pipes made of hollow bamboo rods or logs to transport water and gas thousands of years ago.

Steel Pipes Carry Water to water towers, *right,* and then distribute it to thousands of outlets in a single industry or throughout an entire town.

GM Photographic; Pillsbury Mills Inc.

Nuclear Power Reactors that produce electricity, *right,* require pipes of many different sizes and made of many different kinds of materials.

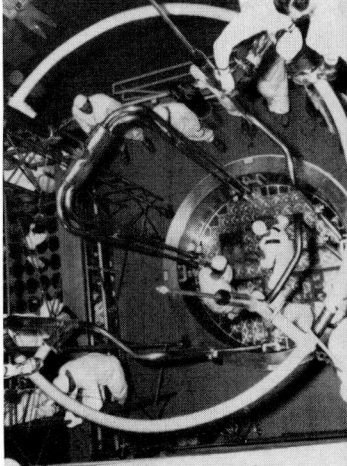

Westinghouse Atomic Power Division

Flour Mills Use Pipes. Metal pipes feed wheat into the "break" rolls, *left,* for the first of 17 grinding operations in making flour.

The walls, floors, and basements of modern office buildings and hotels have a maze of pipes. The pipes carry hot and cold water for general use, steam for heating, and refrigerants for air conditioning. Chemical factories, refineries, and similar industries depend almost entirely on pipes to move their products about within the manufacturing plant. Warships often have such a maze of pipes that sailors on the ships find it difficult to move about.

Pipes also serve other purposes than to carry fluids. Pneumatic pipes transport containers carrying messages. Much of our electrical and telephone wiring runs through pipes known as conduits, which protect the wires from water and breakage (see CONDUIT).

Kinds of Pipe. Most water pipe larger than 3 inches in diameter is made of cast iron, reinforced concrete, steel, or a mixture of asbestos and cement. Smaller water pipes in buildings may be made of galvanized steel, copper, wrought iron, or plastic. Gas and oil pipelines are built of steel pipe. Cast iron, glazed tile, and concrete are among the materials used for drain and sewer pipe. Irrigation systems may have light aluminum pipe that can be easily moved. Atomic-power plants have stainless steel piping. Pipe may be made in several ways, depending on the material and type of pipe desired. These ways include molding, casting, welding, and drawing or pushing the material over a sharp point to make a center hole.

History. People made pipe of clay thousands of years ago to carry water. The Romans used lead pipe to connect their public fountains to aqueducts. American pioneers made water systems from logs with holes bored through their centers. Later, they made pipes from hoops and wooden staves in much the same way barrels are made.

JOHN C. GEYER

PIPE is a tube used to transport liquids and gases from one place to another. Pipelines compare in importance with highways and railroads as a means of transporting materials useful to man. Each day the average home uses about a ton of water. Huge pipes bring this water to the city from wells, lakes, or other sources of supply. A vast network of pipes then distributes the water to every home, and to each sink, toilet, and other water fixtures in the house. Another network of pipes carries the waste water away from these fixtures through drains and sewer pipes (see SEWAGE). Long pipelines buried in the ground transport and distribute natural gas in the United States and Canada in the same way water is distributed (see PIPELINE). Similar pipelines transport crude oil from wells to refineries.

PIPE

Most Pipe Bowls today are made from the seasoned roots of the brier plant, which grows near the Mediterranean coast.

TYPES OF PIPES

SQUAT BULLDOG SHAPE
(QUARTER BENT BIT)

PEAR SHAPE

BULLDOG SHAPE

APPLE SHAPE

POT SHAPE (SHORT STEM)

Kaywoodie Pipes, Inc.

PIPE (tobacco). A tobacco pipe usually has two parts. These are a *bowl*, which holds the tobacco, and a *stem*, which conducts the smoke to the smoker. The most common pipes today have bowls made from brier root. These roots are very hard, and often have a beautiful grain. The stem of the brier pipe is usually made from hard rubber or some plastic material. A popular pipe in the United States has a bowl made from a hollowed-out corncob, and a wooden stem. Another pipe has a bowl of clay, porcelain, or the claylike mineral, *meerschaum*. Some pipes with unusual curved shapes are made from calabash gourd stems.

Pleasure smoking began with the American Indians, who introduced pipes to the white men. The Indians

smoked a ceremonial pipe called a *peace pipe*, or *calumet*. It had a bowl made of red sandstone. It is believed that pipes had been used in Europe for smoking medicinal herbs for many years before Europeans learned about smoking tobacco. The tobacco pipe was introduced to Europe in 1586 by Sir Ralph Lane, the commander of a group of colonists in Virginia. He sent a pipe to Sir Walter Raleigh. Pipe smoking soon became popular. There is a legend that Raleigh's servant threw a bucket of water on him when he first saw his master smoking a pipe. He thought Sir Walter was on fire. The Europeans at first used silver pipes, or walnut shells.

Among the most curious pipes are the *hookahs*, which are smoked in various parts of the Near East. The bowl of the hookah fits into an airtight vase which is partly filled with water. A tube from the bowl passes downward below the surface of the water. Another flexible tube with a mouthpiece is fitted into the side of the vase above the water. Thus the smoke passes through the water before it enters the mouth. In this way it is cooled and loses much of its "bite."　　　ROY FLANNAGAN

See also BRIER; MEERSCHAUM; PEACE PIPE; TOBACCO.

PIPE CLAY. See CLAY.

PIPE OF PEACE. See PEACE PIPE; INDIAN, AMERICAN (color picture, Hunters of the Plains).

PIPE ORGAN. See ORGAN.

PIPE SPRING NATIONAL MONUMENT is in northwestern Arizona on the Kaibab Indian reservation. A memorial to western pioneer life, it has an historic stone fort and other structures built by Mormon pioneers. The monument covers 40 acres. It was established in 1923.　　　C. LANGDON WHITE

PIPEFISH gets its name from its long snout, which looks like a tube or pipe. The pipefishes form a group of fishes that live in temperate and warm seas. They are relatives of the sea horse, or *hippocampus*. The pipefish has a long slim body like that of a snake The body is covered with bony plates. Certain kinds of pipefishes may grow 18 inches long. The long snout ends in a small, narrow, toothless mouth.

Male pipefishes have an unusual pouch on the abdomen in which they carry the eggs. The female fish places the eggs in this pouch, where they hatch. The young pipefishes remain in the pouch until they can care for themselves and are able to leave.

Scientific Classification. The pipefish belongs to the family *Syngnathidae*. A common pipefish is genus *Oostethes*, species *brachyurus*.　　　LEONARD P. SCHULTZ

See also FISH (picture, Unusual Breeding Habits).

Long, Slender Pipefishes Look Almost Like Snakes.
Gene Wolfsheimer

Gardner-Denver Co., Quincy, Ill.

Laying a Cross-Country Pipeline is a highly mechanized operation. Machines dig trenches at least 30 inches deep, hoist 16- to 42-inch pipes into place, wrap them to protect against corrosion, and test them for leaks.

PIPELINE is a system of pipe used to carry materials such as natural gas, crude oil, water, gasoline, and fuel oils. Pipelines also carry industrial waste, crushed coal, and sewage. Most are buried underground at depths greater than 2 feet. But they may be laid on the surface of the ground or under water. They run across deserts, over mountains, and under rivers.

Pipelines are an economical way of transporting a product from where it is produced to where it is used. Some petroleum pipelines supply refineries hundreds of miles away from oil fields. Other pipelines run equally great distances from refineries to market areas. Natural-gas pipelines extend over large sections of North America. In the United States, they deliver about a third of the nation's energy.

Most pipelines are made of steel. But some are made of plastic, aluminum, or various alloys. A coat of coal-tar enamel, asphalt, or plastic protects most steel pipes. The pipes may also be wrapped with kraft paper, asbestos felt, or fiberglass to strengthen and protect this coat.

Pipeline Systems

In many ways, pipeline systems resemble a railroad. They have trunk lines, feeders, terminals, switch systems, dispatchers, and telegraph, telephone, and radio systems. For example, crude oil is stored in tanks near the well. *Gathering* lines pick up the oil from the tanks and move it to *trunk* pipelines that make up the long-distance arteries of the system. Trunk lines, in turn, either move the oil directly to refineries or take it to

H. F. Steen, the contributor of this article, is President of the El Paso Natural Gas Company.

shipping points from which it is taken to the refineries by tanker ships, barges, rail, or truck. *Product* pipelines carry refined petroleum products to the market area.

Huge pumps, placed from 35 to 150 miles apart, push petroleum through the pipelines. The pumps are powered by diesel engines or electric motors. They exert pressure of about 1,000 to 1,500 pounds per square inch on pipes up to 12 inches in diameter. They keep pressure of from 550 to 900 pounds in 24- to 36-inch pipes.

A pipeline system delivers a batch of oil to a tanker or to a refinery in much the same way that a railroad train delivers goods to market. The dispatcher can calculate the exact amount of oil that reaches any point, because he knows how fast the oil is being pumped through the lines. Sometimes, engineers inject a radioactive material at the head of a batch. A Geiger counter or some other recording device then tells when the oil has arrived at its destination.

Observers patrol modern high-pressure pipelines from the ground and from airplanes. They look for leaks and for such conditions as soil erosion and floods that might cause future damage.

Pipelines in the United States

The American pipeline industry developed in the late 1920's, when seamless and electrically welded steel pipe became available. Pipeline networks were built from the oil and gas producing regions to the industrialized

445

MAJOR PIPELINES IN THE UNITED STATES AND CANADA

About a million miles of pipeline carry natural gas, crude oil, and petroleum products across the U.S. and Canada. This map shows major crude oil and petroleum product pipelines, red, and major natural gas pipelines, blue. Texas and Louisiana are the leading petroleum and natural gas producing states. Alberta is Canada's top petroleum and natural gas producer.

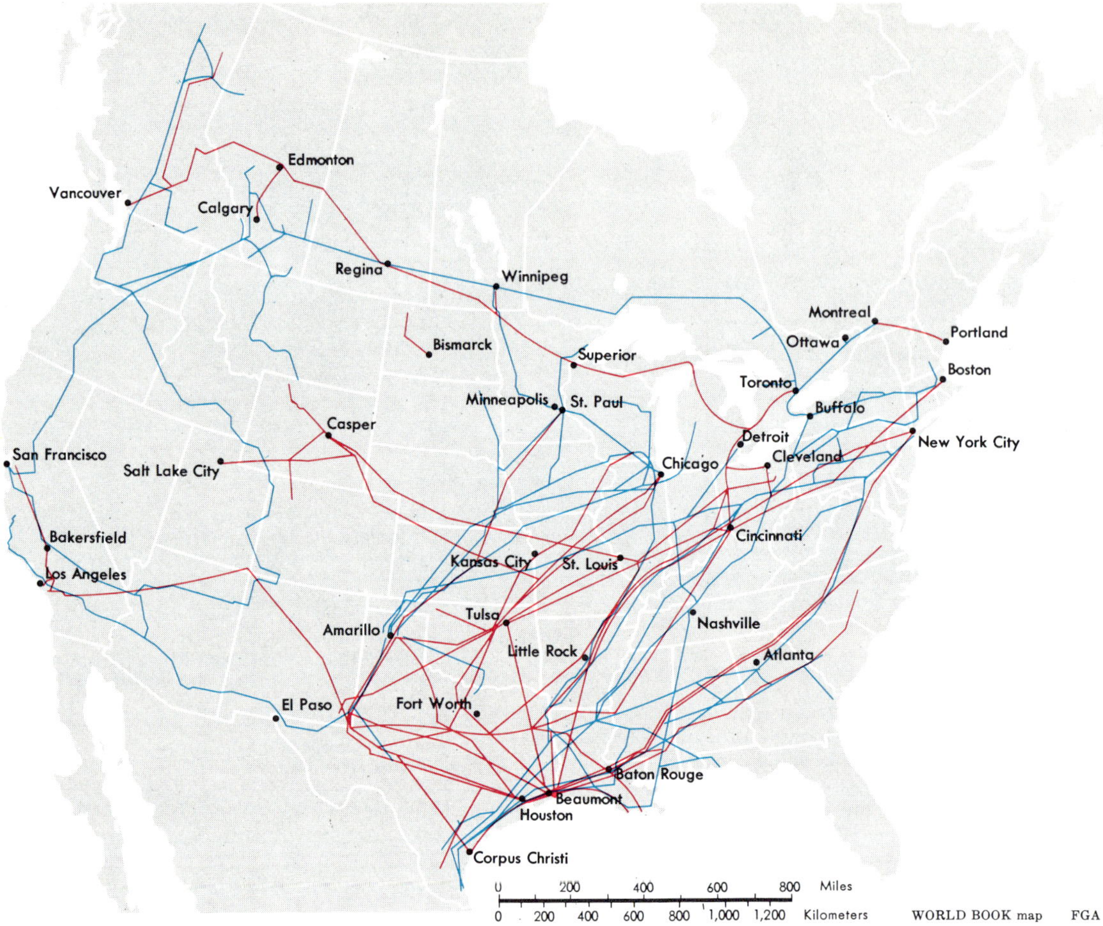

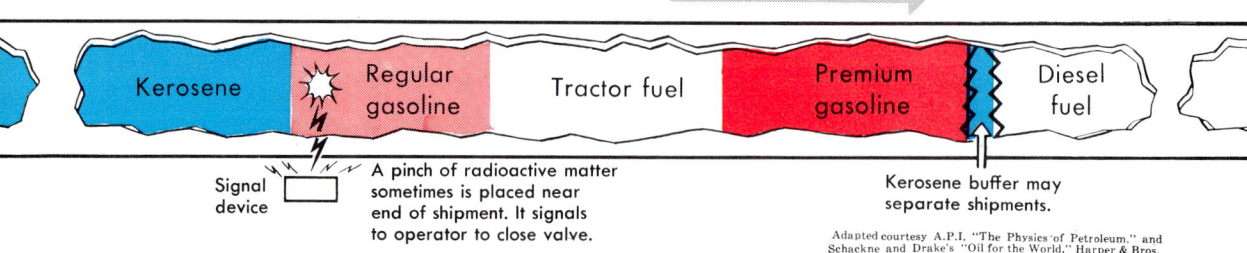

WORLD BOOK map   FGA

sections of the South, Midwest, and West. Few pipelines, however, were more than 200 miles long. The pipes were seldom larger than 14 to 16 inches.

Long pipelines, extending from 950 to 1,200 miles, developed in the 1930's. In 1931, a 1,000-mile pipeline ran from the Texas Panhandle to Chicago, Ill. In 1942, the United States government constructed two oil pipelines to provide safe, economical transportation for oil during World War II. These lines extended from Texas to Pennsylvania, with a branch going to Linden, N.J. They are called the *Big Inch* and the *Little Big Inch*. The Big Inch runs 1,341 miles, and the Little Big Inch runs 1,475 miles. In 1946, both lines were converted to carry natural gas. In 1958, the Little Big Inch was reconverted to carry both liquid natural gas and refined petroleum products (see Big Inch).

PIPELINE CARRIES PETROLEUM "SANDWICH"

Direction of Flow

Kerosene · Regular gasoline · Tractor fuel · Premium gasoline · Diesel fuel

Signal device

A pinch of radioactive matter sometimes is placed near end of shipment. It signals to operator to close valve.

Kerosene buffer may separate shipments.

Adapted courtesy A.P.I. "The Physics of Petroleum," and Schackne and Drake's "Oil for the World," Harper & Bros.

A pipeline network of 4,300 miles brings natural gas from Texas to New York City. This line also supplies gas to cities in North Carolina, Delaware, and New Jersey. Since 1955, new line was laid parallel to part of the Texas-New York line. The 36-inch section of pipe in the line covers 1,643 miles. This was the first long-distance use of 36-inch pipe. A series of pipelines from 24 to 36 inches in diameter connects California to natural-gas sources in Texas, New Mexico, Colorado, and Canada. In 1955, a 626-mile Alaskan pipeline opened between Haines and Fairbanks to carry engine fuels. The largest undersea pipeline, 48 miles long, carries gas and oil from wells off the Louisiana coast.

Pipelines in Other Countries

Canada has one of the longest gas pipelines in the world, the *Trans-Canada Pipeline*. It carries natural gas from the Alberta-Saskatchewan border to Montreal, Que., a distance of almost 2,300 miles. The *Interprovincial Pipeline*, an oil pipeline, runs about 2,000 miles from Redwater, Alta., to Port Credit, Ont.

The Middle East has several long pipelines. Since 1916, pipelines have become essential to the Middle East oil industry. The *Trans-Arabian Pipeline*, completed in 1950, consists of 30- and 31-inch pipe and runs from oil fields in Saudi Arabia to Sidon (Ṣaydā), Lebanon.

Europe has built a network of oil pipelines since the 1950's. The 242-mile *Nord-West Ölleitung* links Wilhelmshaven and Rotterdam with Cologne and Frankfurt. The 478-mile *South European Pipeline* runs between Lavéra, France, and Karlsruhe, West Germany. The *Central European Pipeline* links Genoa, Italy, with Aigle, Switzerland, and Ingolstadt, West Germany. Russia's *Comecon* oil pipeline, one of the world's longest, extends from the Urals into East Europe. With its branches, it is about 3,800 miles long.

North African pipelines run north from oil- and gas-producing areas in central Algeria and Libya to ports along the Mediterranean Sea.

History

About 2,500 years ago, the Chinese used hollow bamboo to pipe natural gas and water. A stone tube carried water to the pool of Siloam near Jerusalem. Archaeologists discovered lead water pipes at Pompeii.

Natural Gas. The first pipeline in the United States consisted of hollow logs used to transport natural gas at Fredonia, N.Y. The first long-distance pipeline, built in 1870, carried gas 25 miles from West Bloomfield, N.Y., to Rochester, N.Y. It consisted of white pine logs bored with 8-inch holes. The first iron pipeline, built in 1872, carried gas 5½ miles from a well to Titusville, Pa. By the mid-1960's, U.S. natural gas pipelines totaled more than 787,000 miles in length.

Crude-Oil Pipelines date back to the discovery of oil in Titusville, Pa., in 1859. In 1865, Samuel van Syckel laid the first successful crude-oil pipeline. It consisted of 2-inch wrought iron pipe that was screwed together. It was 5 miles long, and moved 800 barrels of oil a day from an oil field near Titusville to a railroad. The first major pipeline for moving crude oil was completed in 1879. It used 6-inch pipe, and ran 110 miles from Coryville, Pa., to Williamsport, Pa. It moved 10,000 barrels of oil a day. Early pipelines depended

The pipelines of the United States are long enough to reach the moon four times or to go around the earth about 41 times.

chiefly on gravity and natural pressures to move fuels.

Construction of pipelines increased sharply between 1880 and 1900, when many new oil fields were discovered in Ohio, West Virginia, Indiana, and Illinois. In 1903, California constructed its first major oil pipeline between the San Joaquin Valley and San Francisco. The demand for longer pipelines increased as a result of oil discoveries along the Gulf of Mexico in Texas. Between 1907 and 1910, lines were completed between the Gulf Coast and Oklahoma and between the Texas Gulf Coast and Baton Rouge, La. In the early 1920's, a line linked the Teapot Dome oil field in Wyoming to refineries in the Middle West. By 1929, the discovery of oil in east Texas led to the construction of 10 pipelines. In 1939, a pipeline was built across the Rocky Mountains from Wyoming to Salt Lake City, Utah.

After World War II, many 6- to 12-inch pipes were replaced with larger pipes ranging from 16 to 26 inches. By the mid-1960's, the length of crude-oil pipelines in the United States totaled more than 149,000 miles.

Product Pipelines also developed in the oil regions of Pennsylvania. In 1893, a 4-inch pipeline carried kerosene from Bradford, Pa., to Wilkes-Barre, Pa.

Product pipelines had their greatest development as a result of the increased cost of shipping products by rail. In the late 1920's, a crude-oil line that ran from Pennsylvania to New York was converted to move petroleum products from refineries to marketing areas.

Engineers first thought that a pipeline could carry only one product at a time because different products would mix together. But they found that they could use pressure to control the flow of several materials. Today, a pipeline can carry diesel oil, furnace oil, kerosene, and gasoline at one time.

Product pipelines have grown rapidly since about 1930. They now extend about 61,000 miles, and move about 20 per cent of all petroleum products in the United States. Today, one product system consists of about 6,000 miles, and delivers up to 250,000 barrels of petroleum products a day. The system links the refining centers in Oklahoma and Kansas to markets in Kansas, Iowa, North Dakota, South Dakota, Wisconsin, and Minnesota.   H. F. STEEN

Related Articles in WORLD BOOK include:

447

PIPESTONE NATIONAL MONUMENT

PIPESTONE NATIONAL MONUMENT is in southwestern Minnesota. It has a quarry of red pipestone that Indians used to make peace pipes. The stone was first described by George Catlin, in whose honor it is called *catlinite*. The monument covers an area of over 280 acres. It was established in 1937.   C. LANGDON WHITE

PIPIL INDIANS. See EL SALVADOR (Early Days).

PIPIT, *PIP it,* or WATER PIPIT, is a small American songbird, about 7 inches long. Its feathers are brownish-gray above, but paler on the lower part of its body. The white outer tail feathers show when the bird flies. It has a characteristic graceful walk and a habit of

Hugh M. Halliday, NAS

The Water Pipit may be seen almost anywhere in the United States while it is migrating in the spring and fall.

wagging its tail. The pipit, like the lark, has the delightful habit of singing while flying.

The pipit lives in most of North America. It spends the winter in the Gulf States and south to Mexico and Central America. It nests far to the north, and on high mountains in the United States. Its nest is built of grasses and is placed on the ground. The female lays five to seven eggs. The eggs are grayish-white or bluish-white, thickly speckled with dark brown. The pipit eats harmful insects, as well as seeds, small shellfish, and animals such as snails and slugs.

Scientific Classification. The water pipit belongs to the pipit and wagtail family, *Motacillidae*. It is classified as genus *Anthus*, species *A. spinoletta*.   GEORGE J. WALLACE

PIPPIN. See APPLE (Varieties).

PIQUÉ, *pee KAY,* is a fabric of cotton, rayon, or silk, with raised cords. The cords usually run the length of the material. Piqué may be plain or have a printed design. The fabric is used for neckwear, trimmings, vests, dresses, and infants' coats.

PIRAEUS, *pie REE us,* or, in Greek, PIRAIÉVS (pop. 183,877; alt. 30 ft.), the port of Athens, is the third largest city in Greece. It lies on the Gulf of Aegina, five miles southwest of Athens (see GREECE [color map]). More than half the trade of Greece passes through the city's three harbors. Piraeus also manufactures leather, alcoholic drinks, macaroni, and cotton and woolen goods.

Ancient Piraeus was built in 493 B.C., and was famed as one of the masterpieces of the Age of Pericles

(see PERICLES). Long walls connected the city with nearby Athens. The walls protected Athens from attacks by land or sea. In 86 B.C., the Roman general Sulla destroyed Piraeus. In 1834, the government chose the fishing village of Monte Leone as the port for the modern city of Athens. Monte Leone was renamed Piraeus because it stood on the site of the ancient city. Allied and German bombings destroyed part of the city during World War II. Piraeus was restored after the war, with United States aid.   HARRY N. HOWARD

See also ATHENS (picture: Ancient Athens; map).

PIRANDELLO, *pihr un DELL oh,* **LUIGI** (1867-1936), was an Italian writer noted for his philosophic plays. Most of Pirandello's works reflect a pessimistic view of life because they show the difficulty of knowing what is true about human beings. In his ironic plays, novels, and stories, the truth is often the opposite of what his characters believe. Pirandello received the 1934 Nobel prize for literature.

Most of Pirandello's dramas ask: What is real? What is the truth? *Six Characters in Search of an Author* (1921) is a fantasy about six people who claim to be characters in a play but have no author to guide their actions. *Henry IV* (1922) concerns the identity of a man who pretends madness. It questions our ideas about what is insanity and what is normal. In *Each in His Own Way* (1925), a man deceives people around him to avoid feeling guilt for his conduct. *As You Desire Me* (1930) is about a dancer who wishes to live the life of a beautiful woman whom she resembles.

Pirandello first achieved literary recognition with his novel *The Late Mattia Pascal* (1904), which deals with the contrast between appearance and reality. His other novels include *The Outcast* (1893) and *Shoot* (1916). Many of Pirandello's short stories were collected in *The Naked Truth* (1933) and *Better Think Twice About It* (1934).

Pirandello was born in Agrigento, Sicily. In 1925, he formed a theater company to perform his plays and the works of younger writers.   FREDERICK J. HUNTER

See also ITALIAN LITERATURE (The 1900's).

PIRANESI, *pee rah NAY see,* **GIOVANNI BATTISTA** (1720-1778), was an Italian etcher, architect, and archaeologist. His prints had a wide influence on later etchers such as James Whistler, as well as on stage sets, for more than 100 years. Although he made some 1,300 large etchings of Roman buildings and coins, his series of etchings called *Carceri d' Invenzione,* or imaginary prisons, remained more popular than his architectural illustrations. Piranesi claimed he saw them in the delirium of a fever.

Piranesi was born in Venice, the son of a stonemason. He studied architecture in Rome, and became passionately interested in Roman antiquities. The ancient buildings provided the subjects for the greater number of his etchings (see ROMAN EMPIRE [picture: The Roman Forum]). Piranesi also became a leading authority on Roman archaeology.   S. W. HAYTER

PIRANHA, *pih RAHN yuh,* or CARIBE, is a bloodthirsty fish of the Amazon river. Some scientists consider it more dangerous than a shark. Piranhas range from only about 4 to 18 inches long but attack in great numbers. Thousands of them sometimes travel in a group, and they have been known to tear all the flesh off the skeleton of an animal or a human being in

Field Museum of Natural History

The Bloodthirsty Piranha fish has razor-sharp teeth. Sometimes thousands of these fierce little fish travel in one group.

only a few minutes. There are about 20 different kinds of piranha, colored bluish-gray, yellow, or green, and spotted with red or gold. Closely related species eat plants. See ANIMAL (picture: The Piranha's Teeth).

Scientific Classification. The best-known piranhas belong to the characid family, *Characidae*, and are in the genera *Pygocentrus* and *Serrasalmo*. Plant-eating species are in the genera *Metynnis* and *Myleus*.   CARL L. HUBBS

PIRATE, *PIE rut*, is a sea robber. Since ancient times, pirates have harassed merchant ships on all the oceans of the world. Occasionally, acts of piracy still occur, especially in the Mediterranean Sea and the Far East. The great age of piracy lasted from the 1500's through the 1700's. Pirates seized ships for cargo, plundered coastal towns for riches, and organized powerful gangs to exact tribute and demand ransom for prisoners.

The crime of piracy, defined as armed robbery on the high seas or assaults on land by ships, is against the laws of all nations. Pirates may be tried in all countries. Therefore pirates fly the flag of no nation, except to deceive others. In the past, pirates have defiantly flown their own flag, the skull and crossbones on a black field, which has become the well-known symbol of piracy. The flag was called the *Jolly Roger*.

Pirates have been called by a variety of other names: buccaneers, corsairs, filibusters, freebooters, ladrones, picaroons, and rovers. Privateers were not really pirates, but legally licensed naval aids in time of war.

How Pirates Lived. Through the influence of motion pictures and of such fiction as Robert Louis Stevenson's

Treasure Island, Sir James Barrie's *Peter Pan*, and Rafael Sabatini's *Captain Blood*, the pirate of imagination is a romantic blend of many details. He is pictured as a swarthy ruffian with a black beard or a fierce mustache. He wears gold earrings and a turban or large hat, and carries a sword or dagger in his hand and a brace of pistols in his belt. He may be directing his men to bury treasure or ordering a victim to walk the plank. He is often depicted as a cavalier, in high boots and elegant brocaded waistcoat.

Actually, pirates were more often desperate, drunken men who dressed in tatters and wasted food and money as soon as they got either. Most pirates rarely lived long. They often turned to piracy in protest against admittedly oppressive conditions at home or on board merchant vessels, yet they could seldom control themselves when they had chosen the alluring life of a free, unrestrained outlaw.

But there were certain exceptions to these conditions. A rough form of democracy often existed. The buccaneers chose their own captains by majority vote, and drew up rules and regulations called "pirate articles." These articles contained basic rules of conduct and determined the shares of treasure each man might claim, as well as setting down compensations for injury or for the loss in action of an eye, arm, finger, or leg.

Sometimes pirates voiced their protests against the

Drawing by Harve Stein from *Pirate Quest* by Nancy Faulkner, Doubleday & Co., Inc. © 1955 Anne I. Faulkner

Pirates of Long Ago swarmed over merchant ships on the high seas to rob them of their treasure. Blackbeard, *left*, became one of the most feared pirates operating in the West Indies.

449

PIRE, DOMINIQUE GEORGES

injustices of society by setting up free colonies of their own. The most striking example of this was Libertatia, a pirate community on the island of Madagascar in the late 1600's. Piracy was an organized business, but the motto of the pirates there was "For God and Liberty." These pirates held all their money and goods in a common treasury. Libertatia was a kind of communistic utopia, under "Misson the Good," a Frenchman.

Periods of widespread pirate activity appear to be related to times of intense commercial rivalry or bitter religious hostility among the great nations. Moslem-Christian warfare in the 1500's and 1600's nourished the fleets of Mediterranean corsairs. Pirates were known as *Barbary corsairs*. They sailed from ports and hiding places along Africa's Barbary Coast, and menaced shipping for 300 years.

In 1830, the French occupied Algiers, ending pirate attacks and making the Mediterranean safe for navigation. Contests between Spain and other European nations led to increased piracy in the West Indies and along the American coasts in the 1600's and 1700's. Every buccaneer dreamed of capturing one of the great galleons of the Spanish plate fleet. Pirates of New York and New England during colonial times had close connections with smuggling and other illegal trading, in defiance of British laws. Their activities grew out of the fierce spirit of independence that finally resulted in the complete break with England.

Famous Pirates. The most active corsairs of the 1500's included Uruj Barbarossa, named this because of his red beard. His pirates plundered the fleets that sailed between ports in Italy and Spain and the European colonies in the Western Hemisphere. Barbarossa's brother, Khair-ed-Din, succeeded him as the leading pirate. The Sultan Selim of Constantinople appointed him governor general of Algiers.

Khair-ed-Din and his men were the most feared pirates in the Mediterranean. In the 1600's, Ali Pichinin became the greatest Barbary corsair. His huge fleet roamed the Mediterranean.

Some pirates were national heroes and patriots. For example, Sir Henry Morgan became commander of English forces in Jamaica. The pirate Jean Laffite helped American forces defend New Orleans in the War of 1812. Famous navigators and explorers, like Sir Francis Drake and William Dampier, also committed acts of piracy. Notorious pirates included Captain Jack Rackham, or "Calico Jack"; Bartholomew Roberts, or "Black Bart"; Captain Kidd; Edward Teach, or "Blackbeard"; Stede Bonnet; Captain Greaves; Anne Bonney; and Mary Read.   WILLARD H. BONNER

Related Articles in WORLD BOOK include:

Barbarossa	Filibuster	Privateer
Barbary States	Greaves, Captain	Sea Dog
Blackbeard	Kidd, William	Verrazano,
Bonnet, Stede	Laffite, Jean	Giovanni da
Buccaneer	Morgan, Sir Henry	

PIRE, *peer,* **DOMINIQUE GEORGES** (1910-1969), a Belgian priest, was awarded the Nobel peace prize in 1958 for his work in aiding persons who had to flee their homelands after World War II. His organization, "Aid to Displaced Persons," finds sponsors and builds villages for persons who have no homes. Father Pire founded many other international relief organizations. He was born in Dinant.   ALAN KEITH-LUCAS

PIRENE. See PEGASUS (mythology).

PIRENNE, *pee rehn,* **HENRI** (1862-1935), was a Belgian historian. He is best known for his seven-volume *History of Belgium* (1900-1932), considered the standard work on the subject. Pirenne specialized in studying medieval economic history, and especially medieval cities. Pirenne's works are noted for their scholarship and bold interpretations, often challenging traditional views. His *Medieval Cities* (1925) and *Mohammed and Charlemagne* (published in 1937, after his death) became classics of historical interpretation, and are still widely read. Pirenne theorized in *Mohammed and Charlemagne* that the Moslem conquests, rather than Germanic invasions, ended the Roman Empire and the ancient world. Many scholars dispute this theory today, however.

Pirenne was born in Verviers, Belgium. He was a professor of history at the University of Ghent from 1886 to 1930. While imprisoned by the Germans during World War I, Pirenne wrote a *History of Europe* without using books or notes.   ROLAND N. STROMBERG

PIROGUE, *pih ROHG,* is a special kind of dugout canoe. The Louisiana pirogue is a flat-bottomed boat made from a cypress log. People use these boats for fishing and transportation in the swamps and bayous of southern Louisiana. The boats may be from 6 to 20 feet long. They have round, flaring sides and a sharp bow. Either paddles or poles are used to propel pirogues.   ROBERT H. BURGESS

PISA, *PEE zuh* (pop. 90,928; alt. 16 ft.), is an old city of Italy famed for its marble bell tower (see LEANING TOWER OF PISA). It lies on both banks of the River Arno. For location, see ITALY (political map). Pisa has a university founded in 1343 and an academy of fine arts established by Napoleon. The town also has valuable art treasures, and the house where the scientist Galileo was born. The town is an important manufacturing center.   SHEPARD B. CLOUGH

PISA, COUNCIL OF, met in 1409 to end the division of the Roman Catholic Church called *the Great Schism of the West*. This division had disturbed the church for 30 years. At the time, two popes, Gregory XII and Benedict XIII, claimed the allegiance of the church. At the Council of Pisa, the two rival popes agreed to give up their claims so that a new pope could be chosen. But, at the appointed time, they both failed to do so, and both were deposed.

The council elected Alexander V, but Gregory and Benedict refused to lay aside their rights. The schism continued for eight more years. It finally ended in 1417, when another council met at Constance and elected Martin V as the new pope.   FULTON J. SHEEN

See also POPE (The Troubles of the Papacy).

PISA, LEANING TOWER OF. See LEANING TOWER OF PISA.

PISANO, GIOVANNI. See SCULPTURE (Italian Renaissance; picture: The Massacre of the Innocents).

PISCATAQUA RIVER. See NEW HAMPSHIRE (Rivers and Lakes).

PISCES, *PIS eez,* THE FISHES, is a *constellation* (group of stars) and a sign of the zodiac. It is a large constellation, but it is hard to see because it has no bright stars. Pisces is located southeast of the great square of Pegasus. The early Romans named the constellation *Pisces*, or *fishes*,

The Constellation Pisces, the Fishes

because they thought these stars looked like two fishes with a ribbon connecting their tails.

The twelfth sign of the *zodiac* (an imaginary path in which the moon and planets travel) was named for the constellation Pisces in ancient times. But the position of the stars in relation to the sun has changed since then. Today, Pisces is not in the same section of the zodiac. The stars of Pisces are in the area originally occupied by Aries. The sun appears to enter this area on March 21, the first day of spring. The stars of the constellation Aquarius are now in the area originally occupied by Pisces. I. M. LEVITT

See also ASTRONOMY (How to Use a Star Map); ZODIAC.

PISGAH, MOUNT. See MOUNT PISGAH.

PISISTRATUS, *pye SIS tra tus* (? -527 B.C.), was a ruler of ancient Athens. He was a war hero and leader of the poor people of Athens. He employed the poor in such public works programs as building temples and fountains. Later Athenians called Pisistratus' reign "an age of gold," because of his mild rule. Pisistratus gained power in 560 B.C., but the powerful Alcmeonid family took control of the city in 556 B.C. Pisistratus went to nearby Macedon, made a fortune in mining, and formed an army of hired soldiers. His troops took Athens in 546 B.C., and he ruled the government until his death.

Pisistratus encouraged writers and artists, and ordered one of the first collections of Homer's poems to be made. THOMAS W. AFRICA

PISSARRO, *pih SAHR oh*, **CAMILLE** (1830-1903), was the oldest member of the French Impressionist group of painters (see IMPRESSIONISM). He tended to be the group's theorist and teacher. Paul Cézanne and Vincent van Gogh considered him their master. His association with Cézanne gave Pissarro's work a more solid structure than that of other Impressionists. Eye trouble forced him indoors during his old age, and he painted views of the Paris boulevards.

Pissarro was born on St. Thomas Island in the West Indies. ROBERT GOLDWATER

PISSIS, *PEE sees*, is a high peak in the Andes Mountains of South America, and the fourth highest mountain in the Western Hemisphere. It stands on the border between the provinces of Catamarca and La Rioja, Argentina, about 70 miles west of the city of Fiambalá. The peak is 22,546 feet high.

PISTACHIO NUT, *pihs TASH ih oh*, sometimes called GREEN ALMOND, is the small seed of the pistachio tree. This tree grows in the eastern Mediterranean region, in southwestern Asia, and, to some extent, in California and the southern United States. The pistachio nut may be an inch long. It has a smooth, thin, and hard shell that tends to open at the edge much like the shell of an oyster. Its thin, smooth husk, or skin, is pale red to yellow. The husk is removed before the kernel is processed. The kernel may either be eaten as a nut, or be ground and used as a flavoring and coloring for such foods as ice cream and candy. The kernel's texture is very fine, and it has a mild and agreeable flavor. Pistachio kernels can be salted in brine while still in the shell. In southwestern Asia and the eastern Mediterranean region, pistachio kernels are sometimes pressed for the oil that they yield.

The pistachio tree grows well in dry regions. It seldom rises more than 30 feet high, but its branches spread out widely. Its thick, resinous leaves drop off during the winter.

Every pistachio tree is either male or female. In order to produce nuts, the female trees must have a male tree nearby to provide pollen for their flowers.

Scientific Classification. The pistachio tree belongs to the cashew family, *Anacardiaceae*. It is genus *Pistacia*, species *P. vera*. REID M. BROOKS

PISTIL. See FLOWER (The Parts of a Flower).

Arthur H. Fisher

The Pistachio Nut has a thin, crinkly outer husk when ripe, *above left*. The husk has been removed, *center*, and one-half the shell pried away. The edible green kernel, *right*, has a mild flavor. Pistachio nuts grow in great clusters on the twigs, *below*.

PISTOL

ENGLISH WHEEL LOCK
1640

"HALL" BREECH-
LOADING FLINTLOCK
1800

DERRINGER
1855

Winchester Gun Museum, Olin Mathieson Chemical Corp.; Harry C. Knode & Co.

A Pistol Duel with Aaron Burr ended the life of the famous American statesman Alexander Hamilton, *left*.

In Pistol Shooting Matches, *below*, the gun must be held in one hand without support. The common outdoor distances to the target are 25 and 50 yards.

Courtesy *Guns* Magazine

PISTOL, *PIHS t'l*, is any small firearm that can be fired with one hand. It has a short barrel with an open muzzle at one end and a breech at the other. A firing mechanism, often called a *lock*, sets off the charge in the firing chamber. Pistols are inaccurate but deadly weapons, and can be made more deadly by rapid-firing mechanisms. Many pistols are designed to fire several shots in succession. In an *automatic*, the pistol contains a magazine of new shells that feed automatically into the breech. In a *revolver*, five or six firing chambers are mounted in a revolving drum. After one is emptied, the drum revolves, moving a new chamber into place (see REVOLVER). There are many other kinds of pistols.

Machine pistols have removable stocks, and are fired like machine guns. *Dueling* and *target* pistols have long barrels for accuracy. *Very* pistols shoot colored flares.

Early Pistols. Firearms held in the hands did not become practical before the invention of the *wheel lock* about 1515. The wheel lock had a serrated metal wheel that struck a spark when it revolved against a flint. With the wheel lock, soldiers no longer had to carry live flames to ignite the powder in their guns. Wheel-lock guns became the main firearms of cavalry under Henry VIII of England and Francis I of France.

During the middle 1500's, *snaphaunce* and *flintlock* pistols appeared. They were less tricky than the wheel

SINGLE ACTION FRONTIER 1873-1940

GERMAN LUGER WORLD WAR I 1914

.44 MAGNUM REVOLVER

Winchester Gun Museum; Olin Mathieson Chemical Corp.; Harry C. Knode & Co.; Sturm, Ruger & Co., Inc.

How the Colt .45 Automatic Works

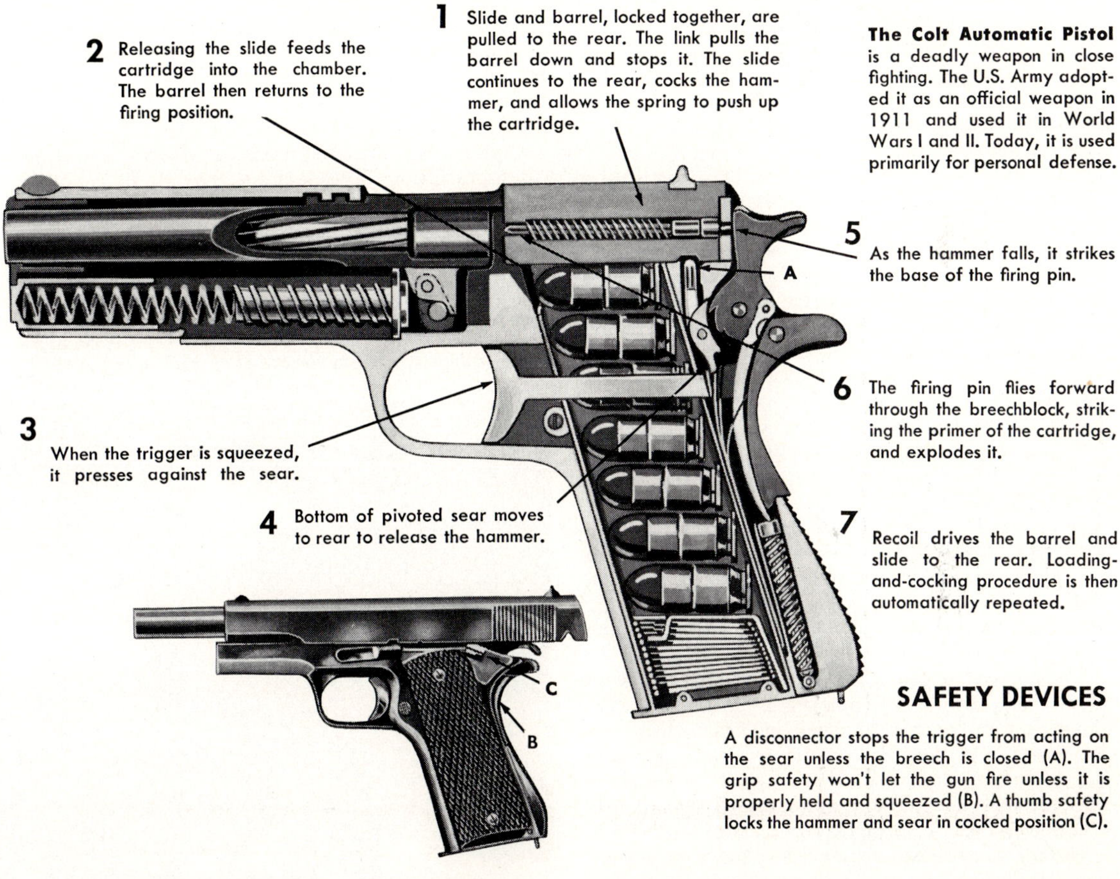

2 Releasing the slide feeds the cartridge into the chamber. The barrel then returns to the firing position.

1 Slide and barrel, locked together, are pulled to the rear. The link pulls the barrel down and stops it. The slide continues to the rear, cocks the hammer, and allows the spring to push up the cartridge.

The Colt Automatic Pistol is a deadly weapon in close fighting. The U.S. Army adopted it as an official weapon in 1911 and used it in World Wars I and II. Today, it is used primarily for personal defense.

5 As the hammer falls, it strikes the base of the firing pin.

A

3 When the trigger is squeezed, it presses against the sear.

6 The firing pin flies forward through the breechblock, striking the primer of the cartridge, and explodes it.

4 Bottom of pivoted sear moves to rear to release the hammer.

C

B

7 Recoil drives the barrel and slide to the rear. Loading-and-cocking procedure is then automatically repeated.

SAFETY DEVICES

A disconnector stops the trigger from acting on the sear unless the breech is closed (A). The grip safety won't let the gun fire unless it is properly held and squeezed (B). A thumb safety locks the hammer and sear in cocked position (C).

lock, and came into widespread use. The screw or cannon barrel pistol, invented before 1660, was loaded from the breech end. After putting in a bullet and a powder charge, the gunner closed the breech by twisting a metal sleeve. See FLINTLOCK.

In the 1600's and 1700's, many variations of gun locks were developed, including flintlock revolvers. Alexander Forsyth (1769-1843) invented the percussion cap in 1807. Pistols using his principle were loaded from the muzzle, with a sliding can of priming powder on the breech. *Derringers* are descended from percussion-cap pistols, but are breech-loaded. They are named for Henry Deringer, Jr. (1786-1868), a pistol-maker.

Rapid-Fire Pistols. Guns that could be fired more than once were used as early as the 1500's, but one of the first practical revolvers was produced by Samuel Colt in 1836. Breech-loading did not become safe until 1856, when Smith and Wesson developed a brass cartridge that kept hot gases away from the gunner.

The Borchardt, the first automatic pistol, was produced in 1893. It followed Hiram Maxim's automatic rifle of 1883, and was loaded and locked by a knee-action joint, a device also used in the German Luger-Parabellum. The Browning automatic appeared in 1898. JAMES B. HODGSON, JR.

See also WESTERN FRONTIER LIFE (picture).

453

PISTON

PISTON, *PIS tun*, is a device that slides back and forth inside a cylinder. A piston is used in pumps, compressors, and engines.

In engines it is attached to a *connecting rod* that passes to the outside of the cylinder and is fastened to the crankshaft. When the gases inside the cylinder expand, the piston is forced outward and turns the crankshaft. The *compression rings* prevent gases from leaking past the piston during the compression and power strokes of the engine. The *oil ring* scrapes excess lubricating oil from the cylinder walls. The *piston pin* (wrist pin) fastens the piston to the connecting rod outside the cylinder.

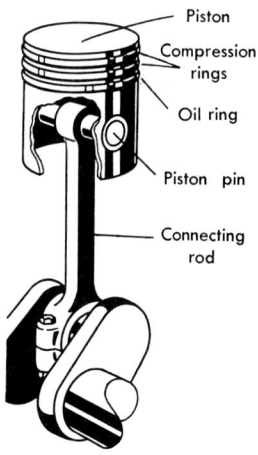

Piston

Compression rings

Oil ring

Piston pin

Connecting rod

FRANKLIN M. RECK

See also DIESEL ENGINE; FREE-PISTON ENGINE; GASOLINE ENGINE; PUMP; STEAM ENGINE.

PISTON, WALTER (1894-   ), is an American composer. His music, written mainly for orchestra, includes several symphonies and the ballet *The Incredible Flutist*. He also wrote chamber music, and books on harmony, counterpoint, and orchestration. Piston was born in Rockland, Me. He attended art school in Boston, and later studied music at Harvard University and in Paris. He joined the Harvard faculty in 1926 and served as professor of music from 1944 to 1960. He received Pulitzer prizes in 1948 and 1961.   HALSEY STEVENS

PIT VIPER. See SNAKE (Poisonous Snakes; color picture: The Mouth of a Pit Viper); VIPER.

PITCAIRN ISLAND, *PIT kairn*, is a remote island in the South Pacific Ocean. It is just south of the Tropic of Capricorn and almost 5,000 miles east of Australia. Pitcairn is famous as the home of the mutineers of the sailing ship *Bounty*.

Pitcairn Island belongs to Great Britain. It has an area of only two square miles, but the soil is fertile. Potatoes, yams, melons, bananas, coffee, and arrowroot are grown in gardens and on tiny farms. In the early days of the whaling industry (1840's), ships stopped there for fresh vegetables. Today, ships stop at Pitcairn several times a year. The population is about 90.

History. Pitcairn was discovered by the English navigator Philip Carteret in 1767, but nobody lived there until 1790. In that year nine mutineers from the British ship *Bounty* landed on the island. They brought with them six men and 12 women who were natives of Tahiti. Because the proportion of men to women was unequal, there was vicious fighting among the colonists. After several years, all the 15 men were dead except the English mutineer John Adams. In 1808, an American ship visited the island and found a peaceful and contented colony ruled by the elderly John Adams. A British vessel visited the island seven years later, but no action was ever taken against Adams.

In 1831, a drought threatened Pitcairn, and the islanders were removed to Tahiti. They returned the following year. Great Britain took formal possession of the island in 1838. The descendants of the original settlers became too numerous for the little island, and in 1856 the entire colony was moved to Norfolk Island. But several families returned to the island later.

Pitcairn Today is under British administration by the governor of the Fiji Islands, but local affairs are carried on by an all-Pitcairn council. Pitcairn has no taxes or customs duties, and the sale of special-issue Pitcairn stamps provides the only revenue. The uninhabited islands of Oeno, Henderson, and Ducie are administered as part of the Pitcairn District.

The people of Pitcairn live in wooden homes in Adamstown, the island's only village. They farm their tiny fields without mechanical farming aids. There are no cattle or pigs on Pitcairn. The domestic meat supply is limited to chickens, fish, and goats. Pitcairn residents sell hand-carved wooden figures to passengers on ships that stop at the island. Many people have left Pitcairn in recent years because few ships stop there now, and because of the danger of fallout from a proposed French nuclear testing site nearby.

Children on Pitcairn attend a modern school in Adamstown from 5 years of age through 12. Some of the residents of the island go to New Zealand to continue their education.   EDWIN H. BRYAN, JR.

See also BLIGH, WILLIAM; NORDHOFF, CHARLES B.

Relics from the *Bounty* are examined by Fletcher and Fred Christian, descendants of the Fletcher Christian who led the ship's crew in mutiny in 1789. The ocean off Pitcairn Island in the South Pacific yielded the ghostly remains of the scuttled ship in 1957.

Luis Marden, © National Geographic Society

PITCH. The pitch of a screw is the distance from crest to crest of the thread. As a screw rotates one full turn, the object in contact with the screw moves along the axis of the screw the distance of the pitch. In airplane and ship propellers, the pitch is the distance the propeller would advance with each revolution if it were cutting through a solid in the same way that a screw cuts through wood. The word pitch also refers to the angle at which the propeller blades of an airplane meet the air.

See also PROPELLER; SCREW.

PITCH is a black, gluelike substance that is left behind when coal tar or petroleum is distilled. In its natural form, it is called *asphalt*. Pitch is highly adhesive and water repellent. It is used for roofing materials, road pavings, and waterproofing applications. It is also used in making the carbon *electrodes* (electrical poles) for the electrolytic cells that produce aluminum.   CLARENCE KARR, JR.

See also ASPHALT; COAL TAR.

PITCH is the characteristic of a sound determined by the *frequency of vibration* of the sound waves. High-pitched sounds have higher frequencies than low-pitched sounds. To the ear, pure high pitches sound shrill, and pure low pitches sound bass. When a violin player tunes his instrument, he adjusts each string so that it will vibrate a certain number of times a second.

The pitch of most sounds we hear is actually due to a blend of various frequencies. The sounds produced by a musical instrument, a whistle, or a siren have several frequencies at the same time. The lowest frequency, called the *fundamental frequency*, is produced by an object vibrating as a whole. The higher frequencies, called *harmonics* or *overtones*, are produced by an object vibrating in parts. For example, a violin string vibrates as a whole, and in halves, thirds, and so on at the same time. The overtones are whole number multiples of the fundamental frequency. A tuning fork produces a sound wave of a single frequency. So do pitch pipes, which are used to get the correct number of vibrations for certain notes.

The notes we play and sing today did not always have the same pitch. Handel tuned the A above middle C as low as 422.5 vibrations a second. Today, the standard for pitch is the Stuttgart, or concert, pitch. It places A at 440 vibrations a second.   ROBERT LINDSAY

See also MUSIC (Sound in Music); SOUND (Quality of Sound); HARMONICS; VIBRATION.

PITCH LAKE. See ASPHALT.

PITCHBLENDE, *PITCH blend,* is a brown to black or green mineral. It is the most important source of radium and uranium. Pitchblende's name comes from its pitchlike luster. The composition of pitchblende varies, but it always contains uranium in combination with oxygen. Oxides of other metals are also found in pitchblende. *Uraninite* is a crystallized form of pitchblende. Radium was first obtained from pitchblende found in Bohemia. Today the richest deposits of pitchblende are found in the Congo and in the Great Bear Lake region of Canada. Other sources include Saxony, Hungary, Norway, Sweden, Cornwall in England, and Connecticut, Texas, and North Carolina in the United States. Polonium and actinium are also obtained from pitchblende. See also ACTINIUM; POLONIUM; RADIUM; URANIUM.   A. PABST

Chicago Historical Society

Molly Pitcher Took the Place of Her Fallen Husband during the Battle of Monmouth in the American Revolution.

PITCHER, MOLLY (1754-1832), was a heroine of the Battle of Monmouth in the Revolutionary War. She was born near Trenton, N.J. Her real name was Mary Ludwig. At an early age she went to Carlisle, Pa., as a servant in the home of Colonel William Irvine. In 1769 she was married to John Casper Hays, a young barber who lived in the village. Her husband enlisted as a gunner in the First Pennsylvania Artillery in 1775. He spent the winter of 1777 and 1778 at Valley Forge. Like many other soldiers' wives, Molly Pitcher joined her husband in camp and made herself useful by cooking, washing, and doing other work around the camp.

The Battle of Monmouth occurred on Sunday, June 28, 1778. This was one of the hottest days of a hot summer. The great heat and the efforts and excitement of battle made the soldiers very thirsty. Molly had followed the troops to battle, and she busied herself carrying water in a pitcher to the thirsty soldiers from a nearby spring. From this episode she got her nickname of Molly Pitcher. Her husband fell from a heat stroke while firing his gun. She promptly took his place and fought the rest of the battle.

After the war, she and her husband returned to Carlisle. Several years after Hays' death in 1789, she married George McCauley (McKolly). He had been a soldier in the Revolutionary War and a friend of her first husband. The marriage proved an unhappy one. In 1822, the Pennsylvania state legislature awarded Molly Pitcher a yearly pension of $40.   CLARENCE L. VER STEEG

PITCHER PLANT is the name of a family of plants with pitcher-shaped leaves that form traps for insects. Pitcher plants are called *carnivorous plants* because they feed on animal life (see CARNIVOROUS PLANT). These unusual plants have many local names. Among them are *sidesaddle flower, huntsman's-cup,* and *Indian dipper.*

The common *northern* pitcher plant grows in marshes and swamps east of the Rocky Mountains from Labrador south to Florida. The lower edges of its leaves are folded together to form a tube, or pitcher. The top edges are left open to form the lid, or spout. Rain water collects in these pitchers. Thick, bristly hairs grow at the mouth of each pitcher. These hairs all point downward and inward. Tiny honey glands cover the inner surface of the lid. The smell of the sweet juice attracts insects. Once the insect alights, the hairs prevent its leaving. It slides down to the base of the tube, where it drowns. After a while, the plant digests the insect.

455

J. Horace McFarland

The Pitcher Plant traps insects in its trumpet-shaped leaves.
A liquid inside the leaves drowns them and helps digest them.

The globe-shaped flower of the pitcher plant grows singly on a long, slender stem. It is a deep reddish-purple color. The people of Newfoundland chose the pitcher plant as their provincial flower (see NEWFOUND-LAND [color picture: The Floral Emblem]).

A pitcher plant with yellow flowers grows in the Southern States. It has tall, erect, trumpet-shaped leaves. Another species, called the *cobra plant*, is native to California. Most of the insects caught by this plant are killed, but a certain moth makes its home in the pitcher.

Scientific Classification. Pitcher plants belong to the sarracenia family, *Sarraceniaceae*. The northern pitcher plant is genus *Sarracenia*, species *S. purpurea*. The southern plant is *S. flava*. The California pitcher plant is classified as *Darlingtonia californica*.　　GEORGE H. M. LAWRENCE

PITHECANTHROPUS ERECTUS. See JAVA MAN.

PITMAN, SIR ISAAC (1813-1897), a British school-master, invented phonetic shorthand. He used 38 symbols to represent the sounds of vowels and consonants. This method proved much superior to older systems. It was used widely in England and the United States, and revisions of it are still taught in many schools. Pitman published his first shorthand manual in 1837. He also published many practice books, and founded a school at Bath, England, to teach his system. He was born at Trowbridge, England.　　GALEN SAYLOR

See also SHORTHAND.

PITOT TUBE is an instrument which measures certain pressures of a fluid. The instrument was named for the man who invented it, Henri Pitot (1695-1771), a French physicist. See also AIRCRAFT INSTRUMENTS (Air Speed and Machmeter Instruments).

PITT is the family name of two British statesmen. They form one of the most illustrious father-son combinations in British political history.

William Pitt, (1708-1778), EARL OF CHATHAM is chiefly remembered as the *organizer of victory* and empire builder during the Seven Years' War, and for his powerful defense of the rights of American colonists. His grandfather, Thomas Pitt, had helped to build British trade in India.

Born in Westminster, the son of a member of Parliament, William Pitt attended Eton College and Oxford University. Because of poor health, he was not graduated from Oxford. In 1735, he entered Parliament. From the first, he distinguished himself by his fiery attacks on Sir Robert Walpole and on the practice of subsidizing troops from the German province of Hanover with British money.

Pitt enjoyed great popularity, but he had little power for several years. He did, however, study the French military and economic structure, and in time gained a full knowledge of France.

In 1746, Pitt became paymaster-general of the forces. In this office, he showed great ability and unusual honesty. As the years went by, however, his position did not improve. In despair and frustration, he bitterly denounced both the government's war policy and the weakness of the House of Commons. This action led directly to Pitt's dismissal in 1755. But with the renewal of the war with France the following year, he returned to office as secretary of state. Again he criticized his colleagues, again he left office, and again he returned. "I know," he said, "that I can save the country, and that I alone can."

His task seemed insurmountable, for on every side he found defeat and confusion. But in five years, he gained great success. Pitt strengthened the British fleet and blocked French ports; he sent supplies to Frederick the Great of Prussia, and attacked France on all fronts. Great victories, especially in 1759, marked his policy everywhere. The French were defeated in India, America, Europe, the West Indies, and on the sea. But in spite of these victories, other ministers opposed his demand that the war be continued until France was completely defeated. He resigned in 1761.

During the next five years, Pitt resumed his opposition to the government. He denounced the Peace of Paris (1763) as far too lenient and aroused the British people to criticize the House of Commons. He denounced British policy toward the American colonists. This made him popular on both sides of the Atlantic.

Pitt was too powerful and too popular to remain out of office for long. In July, 1766, he became prime minister and had his first opportunity at full control of the government. His ministry lacked unity, and he did both Great Britain and himself great damage by entering the House of Lords as the Earl of Chatham. He and his ministers proved incapable of solving troubles in America and India, and of governing Britain itself. Within a few months, Pitt became greatly depressed. After the resignation of his more dependable ministers, he let the direction of affairs fall into the hands of Charles Townshend. Pitt resigned in October, 1768.

During the next 10 years, he had occasional periods of prominence. He supported parliamentary reform. He also studied the American situation, protested

Bettmann Archive; Brown Bros.

William Pitt, the Earl of Chatham, *center,* appeared in the House of Lords, *left,* to denounce harsh British measures against the American colonies. His son, William Pitt the Younger, *right,* became one of England's greatest prime ministers.

against British policy there, and rejoiced when America resisted that policy. At no time, however, did he gain much of a following. But he always remained capable of dominating his listeners, and his last speeches on the American war were among his best.

Pitt was most outstanding as a wartime leader. He had neither the patience nor the temperament for political manipulation, and he did not deal successfully with financial problems. At the time that he achieved his greatest fame, however, the ability to inspire generals and arouse people was more important than skill in making political deals and balancing the budget.

William Pitt the Younger (1759-1806), the son of William Pitt, Earl of Chatham, became Britain's chancellor of the exchequer at the age of 23 and prime minister at 24. He was the youngest man ever to hold either post. He served as prime minister from 1783 to 1801 and from 1804 to 1806. He dominated British politics during the interval between these two terms.

Pitt was born in Kent, and entered Cambridge University at the age of 14. Because of poor health and his cold manner, he took no pleasure in his university experience. After graduation in 1780, he studied law. He was admitted to the bar, but his main interest lay in politics.

In January, 1781, Pitt entered parliament. His amazing abilities quickly made him outstanding. His first speech, always one of the most difficult tests in politics, was remarkable. Many observers believed that Pitt showed ability equal to that of his father. In committee work, he was informed, penetrating, and self-possessed.

Almost immediately, Pitt began to press for parliamentary reform and the reduction of the influence of the king. He quickly gained favor with older politicians. In 1782 and 1783, he served as chancellor of the exchequer under Lord Shelburne.

In December, 1783, Pitt became prime minister. He held this office for the next 17 years. During the first three months, he experienced great difficulty in the House of Commons because he singlehandedly had to meet the attacks of the opposition, led by Charles James Fox, Edmund Burke, Richard Brinsley Sheridan, and Lord North. Pitt's fellow cabinet members were all in the House of Lords. In March, 1784, however, he called for a new election and scored a great triumph. This provided him with a majority in the House of Commons.

Pitt then turned his attention to improving the economic situation in Great Britain. He increased the revenue, funded the debt, improved credit, and negotiated a free-trade treaty with France. He extended the authority of the British government over India. But Pitt also had troubles. Late in 1787, King George III became insane, and Pitt had to struggle against a Whig party campaign to name the Prince of Wales as regent. Pitt feared that, if the campaign succeeded, the Whigs would take over the government. George's recovery in 1789 relieved the situation.

A more important problem soon challenged Pitt—the French Revolution. At first, he failed to sense its significance. But his attitude changed when France declared war on Britain in February, 1793. Pitt organized a vast coalition of European countries, both large and small, to fight France. After some successes, the alliance suffered military defeats. Several of the member nations seceded from the alliance. After the rise of Napoleon Bonaparte in France, the situation steadily grew worse. Pitt entered into peace negotiations with the French government, but was unsuccessful. The coalition came to a dismal end when Napoleon's smashing triumphs over Austria brought about the latter's withdrawal.

Because Britain was still at war with France, Napoleon sought to end his struggle by striking through Egypt and the Near East. Although defeated in this attempt and immediately faced by a second coalition, Napoleon soon scored a decisive victory. Pitt's strategy had failed again. British successes on the sea did not offset Napoleon's victories on land.

Pitt had resigned office a few months earlier over his failure to persuade George III to include voting rights for Roman Catholics in the Act of Union (1801), forming the Kingdom of Great Britain and Ireland. Pitt returned to office in 1804 to organize a third coalition of nations against Napoleon.

This coalition also fell before the French, and its failure proved disastrous to Pitt. He was sadly troubled already because of the king's increasing mental disorder and his own poor health and disorganized finances. He could not survive the military defeats of Britain's allies. Even Admiral Horatio Nelson's astounding victory could not make up for the losses. Though Pitt could say "England has saved herself by her exertions, and will, I trust, save Europe by her example," he also rec-

457

ognized the significance of Napoleon's victory at Austerlitz. "Roll up that map," he said of a map of Europe, "it will not be wanted these ten years."

Pitt died on Jan. 23, 1806. He was buried in Westminster Abbey.   CHARLES F. MULLETT

PITT DIAMOND. See DIAMOND (Famous Diamonds).

PITTACUS. See SEVEN WISE MEN OF GREECE.

PITTI PALACE is the largest palace in Florence, Italy. It was once a home of the Italian kings. The palace houses one of the finest collections of paintings in the world. This collection includes works by such famous artists as Raphael, Titian, Andrea del Sarto, Dürer, Rubens, and Rembrandt.

The palace was begun in 1458 for Luca Pitti. Filippo Brunelleschi designed the center section. Cosimo de' Medici (Cosimo I, Duke of Tuscany) bought the palace in 1549, when only the first floor had been built. His architect, Bartolommeo Ammanati, carried the work to its first complete stage between 1559 and 1570. Other additions to the palace were made later.

The most striking feature of the Pitti Palace is its

Italian State Tourist Office
The Pitti Palace Was Once the Home of Italian Kings.

impressive and enormous front and its powerful masonry of great stones. The Boboli Gardens, behind the palace, are considered among the most beautiful formal gardens in Italy.   TALBOT HAMLIN

PITTMAN, KEY (1872-1940), a Nevada Democrat, served in the U.S. Senate from 1913 until his death. Pittman sponsored the Pittman Act of 1918, which provided for the sale of silver coin to Great Britain. In 1933, he became president *pro tempore* of the Senate and chairman of the Senate Committee on Foreign Relations. He sponsored the Pittman Resolution of 1935, which forbade the sale of arms to nations at war. In 1939, Pittman helped write the Neutrality Act, which permitted the sale of war goods on a cash-and-carry basis. He was born in Vicksburg, Miss.   JAMES W. HULSE

PITTSBURG LANDING, BATTLE OF. See CIVIL WAR (Shiloh, or Pittsburg Landing).

PITTSBURGH, Pa., produces more steel than any other city in the world. Flames from its great steel furnaces cast a red glow across the sky that may be seen miles away. The sight is especially spectacular at night, and has given Pittsburgh the nickname of the *Hearth of the Nation.* Pittsburgh is the second largest city in Pennsylvania, and the 16th largest in the United States.

About a fifth of the nation's steel comes from Pittsburgh. This is about 5 per cent of the world's supply. The bustling city also produces a third of the plate glass used in the United States, a fifth of the nation's window glass, and a sixth of its bottles and jars.

Location, Size, and Description. Pittsburgh lies in southwestern Pennsylvania, where the Monongahela and Allegheny rivers join to form the Ohio River. The original town lay within the fork of the Allegheny and Monongahela. Pittsburgh has spread in all directions until it now covers about 55 square miles. For location, see PENNSYLVANIA (political map).

The city's steel mills and other manufacturing plants line the banks of the Allegheny, Monongahela, and Ohio rivers for more than 20 miles. The area between the Allegheny and Monongahela, near the fork, is called the *Golden Triangle.* Almost every Pittsburgh company has its headquarters in this wedge-shaped downtown business district. Stainless steel skyscrapers rise in the 23-acre Gateway Center. The center faces 36-acre Point State Park at the western tip of the triangle. Other downtown skyscrapers include the 30-story aluminum Alcoa Building, and the Gulf and U.S. Steel buildings, both over 40 stories high.

Attractive residential sections lie on the rolling hills

FACTS IN BRIEF

Population: 604,332; metropolitan area, 2,405,435.
Area: 55 sq. mi.; metropolitan area, 3,053 sq. mi.
Altitude: 745 feet above sea level.
Climate: For information on Pittsburgh's monthly temperatures and rainfall, see PENNSYLVANIA (Climate).
Government: Mayor-council (four-year terms).
Founded: As a fort, 1754; as a town, 1764. Incorporated as a borough, 1794; as a city, 1816.
Motto: *Benigno Numine* (With divine providence).
Flag: Two vertical black stripes flank a gold stripe bearing the city coat of arms. See CITY (picture).

Pittsburgh Chamber of Commerce

The Red Glow from Pittsburgh's Great Steel Furnaces Lights Up the Sky Over the City at Night.

beyond the business and manufacturing districts. These communities include Oakland, East End, and Squirrel Hill.

Pittsburgh has more than 150 bridges, and numerous viaducts, because of its rivers and its many hills and valleys. The bridges include the two-level Fort Pitt, built in the 1950's, and the George Westinghouse (see BRIDGE [picture]).

The metropolitan area of Pittsburgh includes four counties, and covers 3,053 square miles. Residential and manufacturing communities in this area include Braddock, Homestead, McKeesport, and Wilkinsburg.

Manufacturing. The importance of Pittsburgh as a manufacturing center is closely related to the rich natural resources of the region around the city. About a fourth of the coal mined in the United States comes from the nearby Allegheny district. Much of the coal is used in Pittsburgh steel mills. These mills make about 25 million tons of steel a year. See also PENNSYLVANIA (color picture, Bethlehem Steel).

The city manufactures nearly a fourth of the nation's pig iron, and about half its coke and coke by-products.

The Golden Triangle is Pittsburgh's business district. Two rivers, the Allegheny, *left*, and the Monongahela, *right*, meet here to form the Ohio River. Bridges link the Golden Triangle and the areas of the city across the Allegheny and Monongahela. Early Pittsburgh, *inset*, grew up near the point. Pioneers traveling west on the Ohio River started from Pittsburgh.

Pittsburgh Chamber of Commerce

PITTSBURGH

The world's largest coke-making plant is in Pittsburgh. The region's petroleum wells produce almost 2 million barrels of oil a month.

Glass has been a leading Pittsburgh product since 1797. The city also makes air brakes, aluminum, bakery goods, brass and bronze products, chemical explosives, clay products, and cordage. Other products include electrical machinery, meat and other food products, paints and varnishes, pipe, printed materials, and tobacco products.

Transportation and Communication. Pittsburgh is the nation's largest inland river port. It handles 54 million tons of freight a year along its 27 miles of water front. Much of the coal, iron ore, and other heavy freight comes on long boat tows, usually made up of a dozen flat barges.

Seven railroads serve Pittsburgh. Nine airlines use the Greater Pittsburgh Airport, 14 miles west of the downtown area. A system of highways and boulevards, double-decked along the river front, keeps traffic flowing through the city. Inclined railways carry passengers and freight up some of the city's hills. Probably the best known of these railways is the Mount Washington Incline, which lifts passengers 400 feet up from downtown Pittsburgh to residential sections.

Major daily newspapers in Pittsburgh are the *Post-Gazette and Sun-Telegraph* and the *Press.* The city has 18 radio and 4 television stations. Radio station KDKA, a pioneer in broadcasting, began operations in Pittsburgh in November, 1920.

Education. About 65,000 students attend more than a hundred public schools in Pittsburgh. Another 50,000 pupils go to private and parochial schools. The University of Pittsburgh holds classes in the Cathedral of Learning, a 42-story skyscraper. Other institutions of higher education include the Carnegie-Mellon University, Duquesne University, and Chatham and Mount Mercy colleges.

The Carnegie Institute Museum and Library was established in 1896 by a gift of more than $25 million from Andrew Carnegie. It includes the Museum of Science and the Gallery of Fine Arts. The gallery is famed for its annual exhibit of contemporary paintings. Pittsburgh's Carnegie Library owns more than a million books and maintains 16 branches. The Mellon Institute, part of Carnegie-Mellon University, conducts scientific and industrial studies. Andrew W. Mellon and his brother, Richard B. Mellon, founded it in 1913.

Recreation. Pittsburgh has more than 2,500 acres of parks. Schenley Park covers 422 acres and includes the Phipps Conservatory, famed for its flower shows. The city zoo is in 366-acre Highland Park. Trails lead through more than 300 acres of wilderness in Frick Park. Mellon Park lies on top of a six-story underground garage. The park covers a city block in downtown Pittsburgh. The waters of a fountain plunge over a series of terraces to street level.

The Pittsburgh Pirates play baseball in the National League. The city is also the home of the Pittsburgh Steelers of the National Football League. The Pittsburgh Symphony Orchestra performs at Syria Mosque. Musical programs are also presented at Carnegie Hall. During the summer, musical events are held at Pitt Stadium.

Other Interesting Places to Visit include:

Buhl Planetarium. The movements of stars and planets are reproduced on the ceiling.

Conservatory Aviary, in West Park. Many kinds of tropical birds fly freely amid a natural setting of plants, waterfalls, and pools.

Fort Pitt Blockhouse, in Point State Park. It was built in 1764 just outside the fort, and is the city's only pre-Revolutionary War building. It is now a museum.

Grandview Observation Deck, on Mount Washington. This large pavilion overlooks the Golden Triangle.

Stephen Collins Foster Memorial Building, honoring Pittsburgh's famous composer. A collection of original Foster manuscripts is on display.

History. In 1753, 21-year-old George Washington was sent to the Pittsburgh region to report on its military possibilities. He wrote in his journal: "I spent some time viewing the Rivers and the Land in the Fork; which I think well suited for a Fort."

Virginia militiamen started to build a fort, but the French drove them away. In 1754, French troops built Fort Duquesne on the site. British troops under General John Forbes occupied the area in 1758. Forbes built a new fort, and named it Fort Pitt after the English statesman, William Pitt. A town was founded near the fort in 1764, and the settlers named it Pittsburgh.

After the Revolutionary War, Pittsburgh became a starting point for pioneers traveling west. It was called the *Gateway to the West.* Allegheny County was formed in 1788, with Pittsburgh as its seat.

Many Pittsburgh industries, notably glass and iron, began around 1800. Transportation developments in the 1800's helped the growth of industry and the city. The first steamboat on western rivers was launched at Pittsburgh in 1811. The Pennsylvania Canal System opened its main line in 1834. A railroad entered the city in 1851.

During the Civil War, Pittsburgh's iron and steel production increased with the demand for arms and ammunition. The Pittsburgh aluminum industry began in 1888. Steady industrial growth brought thousands of persons to work in the city's factories during the late 1800's and early 1900's. Many came from southern and central Europe. In World War II, Pittsburgh produced more steel than Germany and Japan together. The city's industrial leadership has given it the nicknames of *Iron City, Steel City,* and *Arsenal of the World.*

Smoke from the steel mills and other factories resulted in the nickname of the *Smoky City.* A smoke-control program began in 1941. By the 1950's, Pittsburgh had changed from a smoggy, grimy city to a clean, pleasant community. In 1947, the city started an urban renewal program. Skyscrapers replaced old buildings, especially in the Golden Triangle. Many slums were cleared away, and highways and bridges were built.

In 1957, Pittsburgh became the first American city to use electricity generated by atomic energy. The nuclear-power plant in nearby Shippingport supplies part of Pittsburgh's electricity. Civic plans for the 1960's included construction of an auditorium, a new symphony hall, a cross-town boulevard, and more highways and bridges. The city's new sports arena has a roof that can be slid back and forth, so events may be held indoors or in the open.   LAURA C. FREY

See also ALLEGHENY RIVER; GLASS; IRON AND STEEL; MONONGAHELA RIVER.

Sawders; University of Pittsburgh

The University of Pittsburgh occupies a tree-studded campus in the eastern part of the city. The imposing Cathedral of Learning, *left*, a 42-story skyscraper in Gothic design, houses many of the university's undergraduate classes. The graceful shaft rises from a terraced lawn.

PITTSBURGH, UNIVERSITY OF, is a private, state-related, coeducational university in Pittsburgh, Pa. Many of its undergraduate classes meet in a 42-story skyscraper called the Cathedral of Learning. The university has undergraduate schools of liberal arts, engineering and mines, and nursing. It also has graduate schools of business, dentistry, education, engineering and mines, law, library and information science, medicine, pharmacy, public health, public and international affairs, and social work. The university houses a large space center and one of the nation's leading health centers. It has two-year campuses at Johnstown, Bradford, Titusville, and Greensburg. It was founded in 1787. For enrollment, see UNIVERSITIES AND COLLEGES (table).   E. H. LITCHFIELD

PITTSBURGH AGREEMENT. See CZECHOSLOVAKIA (Independence).

PITTSFIELD, Mass. (pop. 57,879; met. area 76,772; alt. 1,015 ft.), is an important industrial and resort city in hilly western Massachusetts (see MASSACHUSETTS [political map]). It is the seat of Berkshire County. Textiles, paper, chemicals, ordnance supplies, and electric machinery are made in the city. Pittsfield became a city in 1889. It has a mayor-council type of government. For the monthly weather in Pittsfield, see MASSACHUSETTS (Climate).   WILLIAM J. REID

PITUITARY GLAND, *pih TYOO ih TAIR ih*, is the master gland of the human body. It controls the activity of other glands. The pituitary gland makes and releases the hormones that stimulate the sex glands, the thyroid gland, and the adrenal glands (see HORMONE). It regulates growth and other body functions.

The pituitary gland is also known as the *hypophysis*. It is located almost at the center of the skull and hangs from the base of the brain. There are three important parts to the pituitary gland. They are the front part, or *anterior lobe;* the middle, or *intermediate* part; and the rear, or *posterior lobe.*

One of the most important tasks of the anterior lobe is to stimulate growth. If the lobe is diseased or removed in youth, a child will not grow properly. The bones of the body do not become longer as in normal growth, and there is little increase in body weight.

If the anterior lobe is too active in youth, an individual will grow too much and become a giant. If the gland becomes too active in later life, the jaw, nose, and hands become enlarged.

When the posterior lobe is injured, the kidneys cannot keep back the proper amount of water, and excessive urine is formed. This results in a disease called *diabetes insipidus.* The individual becomes very thirsty. He finds it necessary to drink a great deal of water.

Doctors treat diseases and abnormalities caused by the pituitary by giving the patient an extract of the gland, or by lowering the activity of the gland through surgery or X-ray treatments.   T. B. SCHWARTZ

See also ACTH; DWARF; GIANT; GLAND; Trans-Vision three-dimensional color picture in HUMAN BODY.

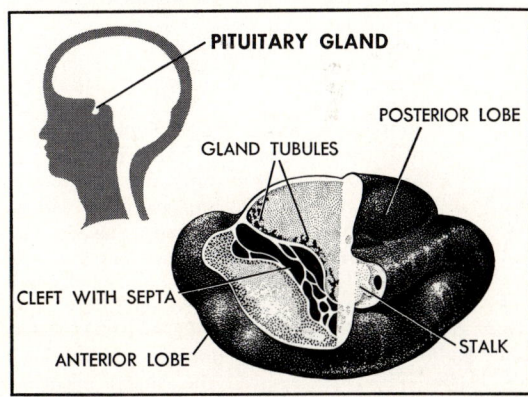

The Pituitary Gland Is Attached to the Brain.

PITZ, HENRY CLARENCE (1895-   ), an American painter and illustrator, won recognition for his murals, prints, and illustrations in books and magazines. He illustrated more than 140 books, most of them for children. Books that he wrote and illustrated include *The Practice of Illustration* (1946), *A Treasury of American Book Illustration* (1947), *Drawing Trees* (1956), and *Ink Drawing Technique* (1957). Pitz was born in Philadelphia, and attended the Museum School of Art and Spring Garden Institute.   RUTH HILL VIGUERS

PITZER COLLEGE. See UNIVERSITIES AND COLLEGES (table).

PIUS

PIUS, *PIE us,* was the name of 12 popes of the Roman Catholic Church, all of them important historically. Their reigns were:

Pius I, Saint	(140?-155?)	Pius VII	(1800-1823)
Pius II	(1458-1464)	Pius VIII	(1829-1830)
Pius III	(1503)	Pius IX	(1846-1878)
Pius IV	(1559-1565)	Pius X, Saint	(1903-1914)
Pius V, Saint	(1566-1572)	Pius XI	(1922-1939)
Pius VI	(1775-1799)	Pius XII	(1939-1958)

Saint Pius V (1504-1572) enforced the reform decrees of the Council of Trent. He published a new breviary, a new missal, and the Tridentine Catechism. His greatest political triumph was the formation of the Holy League against the Turks. Spain and Venice joined the Papal States to form a navy which, under Don Juan of Austria, defeated the Turks at Lepanto in 1571. This defeat ended Turkish control of the Mediterranean Sea. Pius also led the reformation within the Roman Catholic Church. He worked to reform the clergy. He obliged his bishops to live in their dioceses, and the cardinals to live simply and piously.

Pius was born MICHELE GHISLERI in Lombardy. At the age of 15 he entered the Dominican order, and distinguished himself by his austerity and piety. He was made a cardinal in 1557. He succeeded Pope Pius IV in 1566. He was *canonized* (made a saint) in 1712.

Pius VII (1740-1823) was pope through the difficult years of Napoleon's rule and the European settlement that followed Napoleon's defeat in 1815. At first, Pius followed a conciliatory policy with Napoleon. He concluded an agreement with Napoleon that settled the confused French religious problem. The agreement guided church-state relations in France for over 100 years. In 1804, Pius went to Paris to crown Napoleon emperor.

However, as Napoleon increased his demands, Pius stiffened his resistance. He refused to join the continental blockade against England, and he refused to grant Napoleon a divorce from Josephine. In 1809, Napoleon annexed the Papal States. Pius excommunicated all who took part in this action. He was arrested and held at Fontainebleau until 1814. Pius' strong stand against Napoleon won him the admiration of the European powers. They supported his bid to reclaim the Papal States after Napoleon's defeat.

Pius was born GREGORIO LUIGI BARNABA CHIARAMONTI at Cesena. He became a Benedictine monk, and in 1785 was made a cardinal. He succeeded Pius VI as pope in 1800. The election took place in Venice, because Rome was under French control.

Pius IX (1792-1878) enjoyed the longest reign in papal history. His early acts as pope promised a liberal and popular government for the Papal States. He pardoned political prisoners, admitted laymen to the government, and promised a constitution. He fled Rome in 1848 when revolutionists made the city a republic. After his restoration in 1850, Pius followed a highly conservative policy in government matters.

In 1854, Pius defined the doctrine of the Immaculate Conception of the Virgin Mary as an article of Roman Catholic dogma (see IMMACULATE CONCEPTION). Ten years later, he issued the Syllabus of Errors, a collection of propositions that gave the impression that Pius was opposed to all progress and to modern civilization.

The outstanding event of Pius IX's reign was the

Tomczak, Pix

Pope Pius XII blessed millions of people from all parts of the world in private and public audiences during his 19-year reign. He is remembered for his strong appeals for world peace.

assembling of the First Vatican Council in 1869, the first general council since the 1500's. The council defined matters of doctrine and supported the doctrine of papal infallibility. To Roman Catholics, this placed the final teaching authority of the pope within the Church beyond all possible dispute.

Italy took the Papal States and Rome by force during the unification in the 1860's and 1870's. Pius became a voluntary prisoner in the Vatican. He refused any accord that did not recognize him as a sovereign ruler. He believed that he would be looked on as "the Italian king's chaplain" if he settled for anything less. See ITALY (Italy United).

Pius was born COUNT GIOVANNI MARIA MASTAI-FERRETTI at Sinigaglia. He was ordained a priest in 1819, created an archbishop in 1827, and made a cardinal in 1840. As archbishop of Imola, he was noted for his liberal sympathies and his criticism of the conservative Pope Gregory XVI.

Saint Pius X (1835-1914) removed the Roman Catholic Church of the United States from a mission status, and created two new American cardinals, Farley and O'Connell. Pius is remembered for his interest in the reform of church music, his codification of canon law, and his promotion of frequent communion for the people. Pius condemned Modernism, the belief that doctrine is subjective and that the essence of religion is a subjective religious experience. He grieved at the coming of World War I, which he was powerless to prevent. Many people believe that his death was hastened by the outbreak of this war. Pius was born GIUSEPPE SARTO in Riese, and became pope in 1903. He was beatified in 1951, and canonized in 1954.

Pius XI (1857-1939) settled the so-called "Roman Question" with Italy. As a result of this settlement, the pope received temporal sovereignty over Vatican City. Pius condemned Communism, Naziism, and Fascism. He set forth principles on labor, education, and marriage.

Pius was born ACHILLE RATTI, in Desio. He became a priest at the age of 22, and was appointed Ambrosian Librarian at Milan. He later served many years in the Vatican Library. He was papal nuncio to the Polish republic in 1918, and became archbishop of Milan and a cardinal in 1921. Elected pope in 1922, he proved to be democratic, frank, and courageous. In 1924, he created the American cardinals Hayes and Mundelein.

Pius XII (1876-1958) sought to save Rome from destruction during World War II. He also promoted relief for war-stricken areas, and set up a remarkable information service for prisoners of war. His Christmas messages constituted one of history's most thorough analyses on the subject of peace. Pius also promoted many church reforms, such as evening masses and use of the vernacular in church services. His speeches and writings covered many points of doctrine and morals.

Pius was born EUGENIO PACELLI in Rome. He served with distinction in the papal diplomatic service and in codifying canon law. He toured the United States, South America, and Europe as cardinal secretary of state during the reign of Pius XI, and was remembered for his distinguished appearance, scholarship, and wide human interests. He became pope in 1939, after one of the shortest conclaves by the College of Cardinals in papal history.   THOMAS P. NEILL and FULTON J. SHEEN

See also POPE (pictures: Pius IX, X, XI, XII).

PIXIE, or PIXY. See FAIRY (Household Fairies).

PIZARRO, *pih ZAHR oh*, is the name of a Spanish family of explorers and adventurers. Two brothers, Francisco and Gonzalo, became famous.

Francisco Pizarro (1478?-1541) became famous for his conquest of Peru. He was born in Trujillo, Spain. He sailed to the Americas, and lived for some years on the island of Hispaniola. Pizarro joined Vasco Núñez de Balboa's colony of Darién, in what is now Panama. Pizarro accompanied Balboa on his march to the sea in 1513 (see BALBOA, VASCO NÚÑEZ DE).

After Balboa's death in 1519, Pizarro received a grant of land in Panama and became a cattle rancher. But he soon became interested in reports of the rich Inca Indian empire. With an illiterate adventurer, Diego de Almagro (1475?-1538), and a priest, Fernando de Luque, he started searching for this empire.

Their first expedition, in 1524 and 1525, failed to reach Peru. In 1526, Pizarro and Almagro again set out from Panama. This voyage also failed. On the island of Gallo off the coast of Ecuador, Pizarro could persuade only 13 men to remain with him, while the rest returned to Panama. Almagro brought Pizarro reinforcements, and they reached a Peruvian city before turning back.

The explorers then decided that Pizarro should go to Spain and try to obtain the king's permission for the conquest of Peru. He went in 1528, and received the king's consent. Pizarro sailed from Panama in 1531, with his three brothers and about 180 men, and started his campaign from the Inca city of Tumbes.

He found the Inca empire in confusion. Atahualpa had recently rebelled against his brother, Huáscar (1495?-1533), the ruler of the empire. Atahualpa had seized the throne, but had not ended all resistance to his rule. Pizarro advanced to Cajamarca, where Atahualpa was staying. He massacred Atahualpa's followers, and took him prisoner. Atahualpa offered a huge treasure in return for his freedom. Pizarro collected the treasure and then strangled Atahualpa (see ATAHUALPA).

With reinforcements brought by Almagro, Pizarro advanced to Cusco, the Inca capital. He placed a relative of Huáscar on the throne there as a puppet. Pizarro founded the city of Lima, now the capital of Peru.

In 1536, Pizarro had to put down an Inca rebellion. Almagro gained followers and revolted in 1538 because he believed that the Pizarro family had treated him unfairly. In this civil war, Almagro was defeated and put to death by Pizarro's brother Hernando.

The Spanish king rewarded Francisco Pizarro with the title of marquis. Pizarro ruled Peru from Lima until June 26, 1541. On that day a group of former followers of Almagro burst into his house and killed him, as he entertained guests at dinner.   CHARLES E. NOWELL

Gonzalo Pizarro (1506?-1548) accompanied his older brother Francisco in the conquest of Peru. He also explored much of northwestern South America.

He was colorful and ruthless, and grew popular among Spaniards who enriched themselves by exploiting the Indians. In 1544, Pizarro joined a group of these Spaniards to oppose laws that were intended to protect the Indians. He refused to accept the laws. Without authority from Spain, he set himself up as governor and captain-general of Peru.

For three years, Pizarro held off the Spanish authorities, but they gradually undermined his forces. Finally, he surrendered and was beheaded as a traitor. Pizarro was born in Trujillo, Spain.   FRANK GOODWYN

See also INCA; LIMA; PERU (The Spanish Conquest).

Historical Pictures Service

Francisco Pizarro and his band of men spent five months on the small, desolate island of Gallo off the coast of Ecuador in 1526. They suffered greatly from lack of food while waiting for Pizarro's partner, Almagro, to return with supplies and reinforcements.

The Grassy Plains of Central and Western North America Once Supported Great Herds of Wild Buffaloes.

Charles Herbert, Western Ways

PKU. See MENTAL RETARDATION.

PLACE VALUE. See DECIMAL NUMERAL SYSTEM; NUMERATION SYSTEMS.

PLACEBO, *pluh SEE boh,* is a Latin word meaning *I shall please.* In the Roman Catholic Church it is sometimes used to denote the Vespers for the Dead. In medicine, a placebo is a substance that contains no drugs, but is given to satisfy a patient.

PLACENTA. See EMBRYO.

PLACENTIA, *pluh SEN shuh,* Newfoundland (pop. 1,847; alt. 50 ft.), is the site of the first French settlement in North America. It lies in the southeast corner of Newfoundland, about 63 miles southwest of the capital, St. John's. For location, see NEWFOUNDLAND (political map). Placentia was the headquarters of the French from 1662 until Newfoundland was given to Great Britain by the Peace of Utrecht in 1713. The town has ruins of the old French forts, and French and Basque tombstones dating back to the 1600's. Placentia is a popular tourist resort because of its historical interest and the excellent salmon fishing in nearby streams. During World War II, Fort McAndrew, a United States naval base, was established at Argentia, a small town near Placentia.   FRED W. ROWE

PLACER. See GOLD; MINING (Kinds); SAND.

PLACID, LAKE. See LAKE PLACID.

PLAGIOCLASE. See FELDSPAR.

PLAGUE, BUBONIC. See BUBONIC PLAGUE.

PLAID. See TARTAN.

PLAIN, *playn,* is a broad, nearly level stretch of land with no abrupt changes in elevation. Plains are generally lower than the land around them. They may be found along the coast or inland. Coastal plains generally rise from sea level until they meet higher land forms, such as mountains or plateaus. Inland plains may be found at high altitudes. The Great Plains in the United States slope eastward from the foot of the Rocky Mountains at about 10 feet a mile. They range in height from 2,000 to 5,000 feet above sea level.

Many plains, such as the Great Plains, have few trees because of dry or cold climates. Thick forests usually thrive on plains in humid climates. Plains are usually well populated because the soils are often rich, and buildings and roads are easy to build on the level terrain.

Coastal Plain is a stretch of lowland along a seacoast, which slopes gently toward the sea. In many cases such a plain may once have been below sea level. It is made of material washed down from mountain streams. This material gradually piles up and builds a plain on the sea floor. This may become pushed up to become part of the land area of the continent.

The *Atlantic Coastal Plain* is a good example of a fertile and well-populated coastal plain. It lies along the eastern shore of North America from Canada to Mexico. Many coastal plains have few and poor harbors, but the rising sea level has produced some fine bay harbors in parts of the Atlantic Coastal Plain. The sharp slope which marks the line between the other land and the coastal plain is called the *Fall Line.*

Flood Plain is a plain formed of mud and sand left by the overflow of a river. Floods in high regions carry off quantities of earth and other matter. They leave this material lower down on the plains when they flood the river valley. The overflow waters lie still on the surface of the land and a natural deposit occurs. The flood plains of the Mississippi River cover an area of 50,000 square miles. There the deposits are so light that the river is constantly washing out new channels.

The Rhine, the Po, and the Ganges rivers have remarkable flood plains. The Nile shows most clearly the action of the river in forming plains.   SAMUEL N. DICKEN

Related Articles in WORLD BOOK include:

Fall Line	Pampa	Plateau	Selva
Great Plains	Peneplain	Prairie	Steppe
Llanos			

PLAIN SONG. See MUSIC (The Middle Ages).

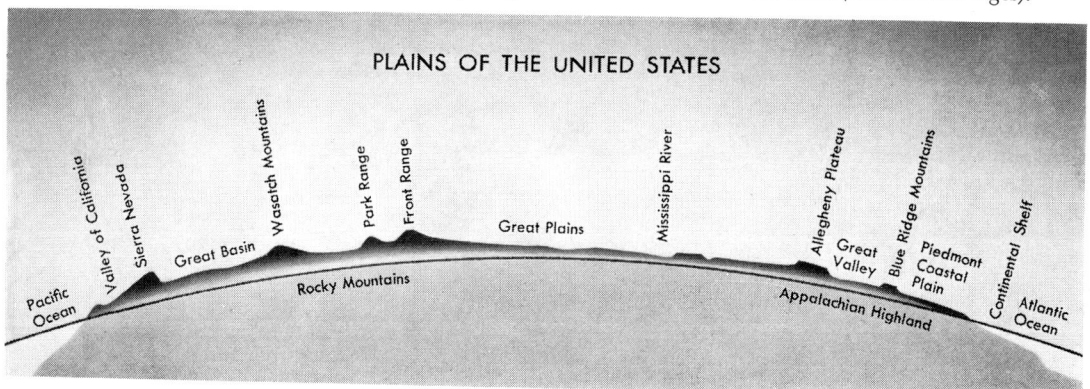

PLAINS OF THE UNITED STATES

Pacific Ocean · Valley of California · Sierra Nevada · Great Basin · Wasatch Mountains · Rocky Mountains · Park Range · Front Range · Great Plains · Mississippi River · Allegheny Plateau · Great Valley · Blue Ridge Mountains · Piedmont Coastal Plain · Continental Shelf · Atlantic Ocean · Appalachian Highland

PLAINFIELD, N.J. (pop. 45,330; alt. 100 ft.), is a residential and commercial city in northeastern New Jersey. For location, see NEW JERSEY (political map).

Plainfield's factory products include building materials, clothing, drugs and medicines, furniture, machinery, precision instruments, printing equipment, and canvas, lumber, paper, and steel products.

Originally called *Milltown*, the town received the name of Plainfield about 1800. In 1867, Plainfield received its city charter. The city has a mayor-council type of government. RICHARD P. McCORMICK

PLAINS INDIANS. See INDIAN, AMERICAN (Plains Indians; color picture: Hunters of the Plains).

PLAINS OF ABRAHAM is a level plateau on tableland southwest of the city of Quebec, Canada. There the English and French fought the Battle of Quebec on Sept. 13, 1759 (see QUEBEC, BATTLE OF). General James Wolfe commanded the English, and the Marquis de Montcalm led the French. The English victory marked the downfall of French power in North America. The plains were named for Abraham Martin, a riverboat pilot who once owned part of the area. In 1908, the plains were the scene of the Quebec Tercentenary Celebration, marking the 300th anniversary of the founding of Quebec. Canada set the site apart then as National Battlefields Park. JEAN-CHARLES BONENFANT

PLAINTIFF. See COURT (How a Court Works).

PLAN OF IGUALA. See ITURBIDE, AGUSTÍN DE.

PLANARIAN is a small flatworm that lives in water or damp soil. Its soft, thin body is about a half-inch long. Its triangular-shaped head has a pair of colored spots that react to light. But these "eyes" do not form images as true eyes do. The worm feeds on other small animals or on dead animal material.

A planarian can *regenerate* (grow again) missing body parts. If the body is cut into two or three pieces, each piece can grow into a whole planarian. Scientists can "train" planarians to do simple things. For example, they can be taught to look for water in certain places in a *maze* (system of paths). When the trained worms are cut in half, the regenerated planarians learn more quickly than untrained planarians.

Scientific Classification. Planarians belong to the order *Tricladida* of the class *Turbellaria* in the flatworm phylum, *Platyhelminthes*. J. A. McLEOD

See also FLATWORM (pictures); REGENERATION.

A Microscopic View of a Planarian shows that the worm's body is transparent. Its "eyes," *right,* are on top. The underside contains the worm's *proboscis* (feeding tube), *center.*
WORLD BOOK photo

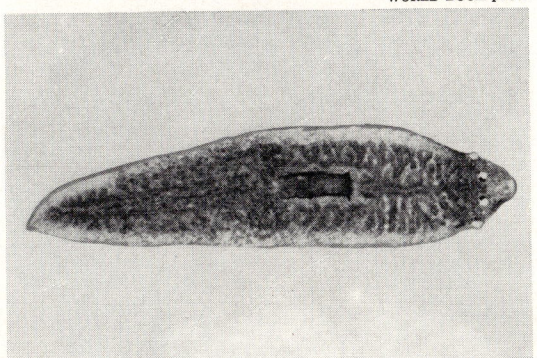

PLANCK, *plahnk,* **MAX KARL ERNST LUDWIG** (1858-1947), a German theoretical physicist, concentrated on the study of thermodynamics. The phenomena of absorption and emission of radiant energy concerned him deeply. In 1901 he published his law of radiation, which laid the foundations for the development of the *quantum theory*. This new theory revolutionized physics. In 1918, Planck was awarded the Nobel prize for physics.

The major concept involved in Planck's radiation theory was that radiant energy, such as light, is composed basically of tiny irreducible bits of energy, called *quanta*. The energy

Wide World
Max Planck

associated with each quantum is measured by multiplying the frequency of the radiation, v, by a universal constant, h. Thus, energy (E) equals hv. For example, a quantum of red light carries less energy than ultraviolet light because it has a lower frequency. The constant, h, is known as *Planck's constant*. Planck's radiation theory applies to all forms of electromagnetic radiation, including radio waves and X rays.

Planck's concept that radiant energy is composed of tiny packets of quanta disagreed completely with former ideas about the nature of radiation. Scientists had thought that radiation was a continuous stream of energy that had a wavelike or vibratory motion. But these previous theories had not explained the absorption and emission of energy by matter. Planck's theory, on the other hand, accounted for the red, green, and ultraviolet light emitted by a glowing object.

Albert Einstein and Niels Bohr applied Planck's quantum theory to the problems of photoelectric emission and atomic structure. The new theory succeeded in explaining the structure of the outer part of the atom (see BOHR, NIELS).

Planck was born in Kiel, Germany. He studied at the universities of Munich and Berlin, and taught physics at the universities of Kiel and Berlin. RALPH E. LAPP

See also LIGHT (The Nature of Light); QUANTUM THEORY; RADIATION (Laws and Theories).

PLANE. See AIRPLANE.

PLANE GEOMETRY. See GEOMETRY.

PLANE TABLE is an instrument used in surveying and map making. It consists of a drawing board mounted on a *tripod* (three-legged stand). The drawing board is leveled, and a map is placed on it. An *alidade* (telescope fastened to a straightedge) is set up on the map. The telescope and straightedge move parallel with one another. When the mapmaker sights an object through the telescope, he can use the straightedge to draw a line on the map parallel to his line of sight. By sighting an object from two different positions, he can locate a point on a map. The point is located where the two lines intersect. B. AUSTIN BARRY

PLANE TREE. See SYCAMORE.

PLANER. See MACHINE TOOL (Kinds; picture).

465

PLANET is any of the nine largest objects that travel around the sun. The earth is a planet that travels around the sun once a year. Going outward from the sun, the planets are Mercury, Venus, Earth, Mars, Jupiter, Saturn, Uranus, Neptune, and Pluto. The sun, the planets and their *satellites* (moons), and smaller objects called asteroids, meteors, and comets make up the *solar system.*

The sun and the stars are giant, shining balls of hot gases. The planets are dark, solid bodies, much smaller than the sun and stars. The main difference between the stars and the planets is that the stars produce their own heat and light, but the planets do not. All light and nearly all heat on the planets comes to them from the sun. The planets can be seen only because they reflect the light of the sun. Six of the planets—Mercury, Venus, Mars, Jupiter, Saturn, and Uranus—are bright enough to be seen from the earth without a telescope.

Planets and stars look much alike in the night sky, but there are two ways to tell them apart. First, the planets shine with a steady light, but the stars seem to twinkle. Second, the planets change their positions in relation to the stars. This movement was first noted by the ancient Greeks, who called the moving objects *planetae,* meaning *wanderers.*

The planets differ greatly in size and in distance from the sun. All of them together weigh less than a hundredth as much as the sun. The diameter of Jupiter, the largest planet, is about a tenth of the sun's diameter. Yet Jupiter is almost 30 times as large as Mercury, the smallest planet. Earth and the three other planets nearest the sun are somewhat similar in size. They are called the *terrestrial* (earthlike) planets. The four largest planets are much farther from the sun and are called *major* planets. Astronomers know little about Pluto, and do not put it in either group.

Suppose the solar system could be shrunk so that the sun were the size of a half dollar. If you placed the sun at home plate on a baseball diamond, all the terrestrial

The contributor of this article is Hyron Spinrad, Associate Professor of Astronomy at the University of California in Berkeley.

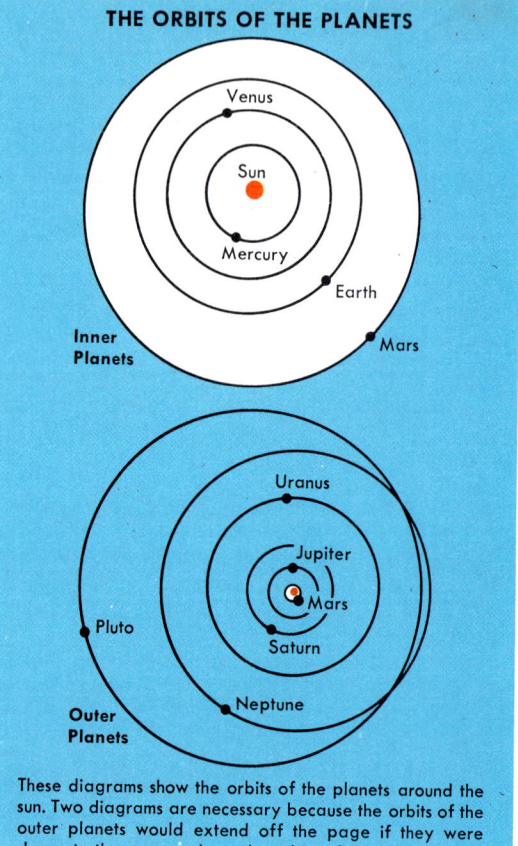

THE ORBITS OF THE PLANETS

Venus
Sun
Mercury
Earth
Mars
Inner Planets

Uranus
Jupiter
Mars
Pluto
Saturn
Neptune
Outer Planets

These diagrams show the orbits of the planets around the sun. Two diagrams are necessary because the orbits of the outer planets would extend off the page if they were drawn to the same scale as the orbits of the inner planets.

planets would be within 16 feet of home. The major planets would begin near the pitcher's mound, and would extend far into the outfield. Pluto, the most distant planet, would be about 420 feet from home plate.

Astronomers do not think there are any planets in the solar system beyond Pluto. But they are almost certain that most of the stars in the universe have planets travel-

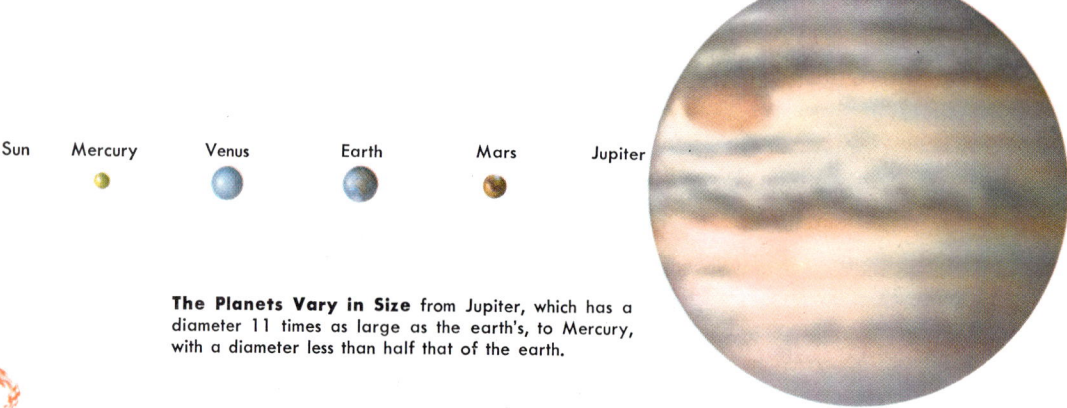

Sun   Mercury   Venus   Earth   Mars   Jupiter

The Planets Vary in Size from Jupiter, which has a diameter 11 times as large as the earth's, to Mercury, with a diameter less than half that of the earth.

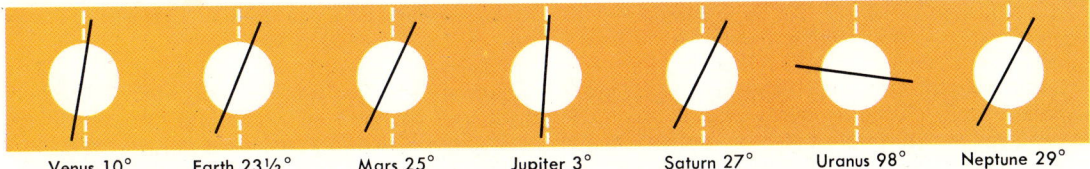

Venus 10°   Earth 23½°   Mars 25°   Jupiter 3°   Saturn 27°   Uranus 98°   Neptune 29°

The Axes of the Planets, *solid lines,* are imaginary lines on which the planets rotate. A planet's axis is not perpendicular to its path around the sun, but tilts in relation to the perpendicular position, *broken lines.* The tilts of Mercury and Pluto are not known.

ing around them. There are more than 100 billion stars in the *galaxy* (family of stars) that includes the sun, and over 100 billion other galaxies can be seen in the universe. Suppose one star in every galaxy had a planet like the earth, and intelligent life existed on one of every million of these planets. There would be a hundred thousand planets with intelligent life.

How the Planets Move

As seen from the earth, the planets and the stars move westward across the sky. A person using a telescope to observe a planet must turn it constantly to keep the planet in view. From night to night, in addition to its motion across the sky, each planet shifts its position slightly eastward in relation to the stars. At certain times, a planet's position may temporarily shift westward, but it always returns to its regular eastward shift.

Orbiting the Sun. All the planets move around the sun in the same direction. Three laws of planetary motion describing their orbits were published in the 1600's by the German astronomer Johannes Kepler.

Kepler's First Law says that the planets move in *elliptical* (oval-shaped) orbits. As a result, the planets are a little closer to the sun at some points in their orbits than at others. For example, the earth comes within 91,400,-000 miles of the sun at its *perihelion* (point of the orbit nearest the sun). It goes 94,500,000 miles from the sun at its *aphelion* (point farthest from the sun).

Kepler's Second Law is also called the *law of areas.* It says that an imaginary line between the sun and a planet sweeps across equal areas in equal periods of time. When a planet is nearest the sun, the line sweeps across a wide, but short, wedge-shaped area, because

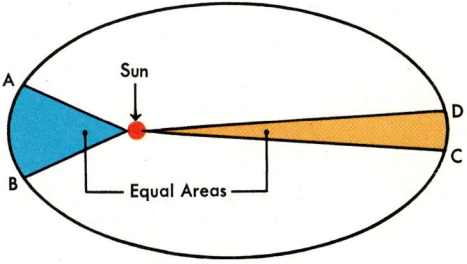

Kepler's Second Law shows how a planet covers equal areas of its orbit in equal periods of time. The planet travels at a higher speed near the sun, from *A* to *B,* than far from the sun, *C* to *D.*

the planet moves fastest there. When the planet is farthest from the sun, the line sweeps across a narrow, but long, area in an equal period of time, because the planet moves slowest there.

Kepler's Third Law says that a planet's *orbital period* (the time required to go around the sun) depends on its average distance from the sun. According to this law, the square of the period (the period multiplied once by itself) divided by the cube of the distance (the distance multiplied twice by itself) is the same for all the planets. For example, a planet that is four times as far from the sun as another planet takes eight times as long to go around the sun. This law was once used to find a planet's average distance from the sun after its orbital period had been measured.

Rotation. Each planet rotates as it revolves around the sun. The planets' *rotation periods* (the time required to spin around once) range from less than 10 hours for

Saturn   Uranus   Neptune   Pluto

WORLD BOOK illustration by Alex Ebel

PLANET

Jupiter to 243 days for Venus. The earth rotates once every 24 hours, or one day. For an illustration of the earth's rotation and revolution, see the article EARTH (illustration: Three Motions of the Earth).

Each planet spins around its *rotational axis*, an imaginary line through its center. The rotational axis is not *perpendicular* (at an angle of 90°) to the path of the planet's orbit. It tilts at an angle from the perpendicular position. The earth's axis, for example, tilts about $23\frac{1}{2}°$. Because of the tilt, the equators of the planets do not always face the sun directly. As a result, the northern and southern halves of the planets are not heated evenly throughout the year. This uneven heating produces the changes on the earth that cause the spring, summer, autumn, and winter seasons (see SEASON).

Conditions on the Planets

The temperature, atmosphere, surface features, length of days and nights, and other conditions on the planets vary widely. They depend on three things: (1) the planet's distance from the sun, (2) the planet's atmosphere, and (3) the planet's rotation.

Temperature. The planets nearest the sun receive more heat than those far away from it. The temperature on the closest planet, Mercury, rises to about 625° F. (329° C.) during the day. On Earth, which is about $2\frac{1}{2}$ times as far from the sun as Mercury, the daytime temperature averages only about 60° F. (16° C.). Pluto is more than 100 times as far from the sun as Mercury. The temperature there is probably more than 300° F. below zero (−184° C.).

The temperature on a planet is estimated from measurements of *infrared radiation* (heat waves) and radio waves that the planet sends out. These measurements

are difficult to make for objects with low temperatures. For this reason, temperature estimates for cold planets are less reliable than those for warm planets.

Atmosphere is the mixture of gases that surrounds a planet. The atmospheres of the terrestrial planets consist chiefly of carbon dioxide and nitrogen. The atmospheres of the major planets consist mostly of helium, hydrogen, methane, and ammonia. The earth is the only planet with a large amount of oxygen in its atmosphere.

Astronomers determine the kinds of gases in a planet's atmosphere by studying the light, radio waves, and other radiation coming from the planet.

The *atmospheric pressure* (force exerted by the weight of gases) on the surface of a planet depends on the amount of gas in the atmosphere. The atmosphere of Mars contains so little gas that the surface pressure is less than one-fifth of a pound per square inch. The earth's atmosphere contains more gas and produces a pressure of 14.7 pounds per square inch at sea level. The atmosphere of Venus has so much gas that its surface pressure is about 294 pounds per square inch.

Astronomers can estimate the amount of gas in a planet's atmosphere by measuring how the temperature varies throughout the atmosphere. A much more accurate, but more difficult, method is to measure changes in radio waves sent through the planet's atmosphere by a passing spacecraft.

Surface Features of a planet like the earth include mountains, valleys, lakes, rivers, flat areas, and craters. A planet's surface is shaped partly by conditions on the planet itself, and partly by collisions with meteors.

Studying the Planets

Men began studying the planets thousands of years ago. They kept records of how the planets moved and

THE PLANETS AT A GLANCE*

	MERCURY ☿	VENUS ♀	EARTH ⊕	MARS ♂
Distance from the Sun (Miles):				
At Perihelion	29,000,000	66,800,000	91,400,000	128,000,000
At Aphelion	43,000,000	67,700,000	94,500,000	155,000,000
Closest Approach to Earth (Miles)	53,000,000	25,000,000	——	35,000,000
Length of Year (Earth-days)	88	225	365	687
Average Orbital Speed (Miles per Second)	30	22	19	15
Diameter at Equator (Miles)	3,100	7,570	7,930	4,200
Rotation Period	59 earth-days	243 earth-days	23 hrs. 56 min.	24 hrs. 37 min.
Tilt of Axis (Degrees)	?	10	$23\frac{1}{2}$	25
Temperature: Day	625° F.	980° F.	60° F.	−10° F.
	(329° C.)	(527° C.)	(16° C.)	(−23° C.)
Temperature: Night	80° F.	620° F.	40° F.	−150° F.
	(27° C.)(?)	(327° C.)	(4° C.)	(−101° C.)(?)
Atmosphere:				
Pressure (Pounds per Square Inch)	?	294(?)	14.7	0.15
Gases	Carbon dioxide(?)	Carbon dioxide, Nitrogen, Hydrogen, Water vapor	Nitrogen, Oxygen, Carbon dioxide, Water vapor	Carbon dioxide, Nitrogen(?), Argon(?), Water vapor
Mass (Earth = 1)	0.06	0.82	1	0.11
Density (Water = 1)	5.1	5.2	5.5	4
Weight of 100 lb. Object (Pounds)	37	90	100	38
Number of Satellites	0	0	1	2

*All figures are approximate.

how they changed in brightness. The motion of the planets was not well understood until the 1600's. Today, there are still many unanswered questions about conditions on the planets. See also EXOBIOLOGY.

Explaining the Motion of the Planets brought about one of the most interesting disputes in the history of science. The dispute involved two important theories.

One theory of planetary motion was suggested in A.D. 150 by Ptolemy, a Greek astronomer and philosopher. Ptolemy believed the earth was the center of the universe. He thought the sun and the planets traveled around the earth once a day. Ptolemy's theory explained what men saw in the sky. It guided people's thinking about the universe for over a thousand years.

The dispute began in 1543, when the Polish astronomer Nicolaus Copernicus suggested that the earth and the other planets traveled around the sun. This theory made it easier to describe the motions of the planets, and astronomers soon began to use it. But religious leaders called Copernicus a fool for saying that the earth was just another planet. They forbade the use of his writings until 1757.

Discoveries by other astronomers gradually convinced people that the Copernican theory was correct. The Copernican theory gained support after Sir Isaac Newton of England discovered his law of universal gravitation about 1665. This law described the sun's pull on the planets.

For more information about how early astronomers solved the puzzle of planetary motions, see ASTRONOMY (History).

Improved Observations. After the motions of the planets became understood, astronomers began detailed studies of the individual planets. With better telescopes that had greater magnifying power, they measured the size, colors, and other characteristics of the planets. They also discovered the most distant planets—Uranus, Neptune, and Pluto.

The discovery that planets send out radio waves, and the study of these waves, led to greater understanding of conditions on each planet. During the space age, man has made more accurate measurements and has photographed some of the planets from space.

Unanswered Questions. Astronomers still have many questions about the planets. For example, they would like to know if any form of life exists on Mars. They wonder if Jupiter is as cold as is suggested by its distance from the sun, or whether it gives off heat in some way. They also would like to know why Venus has an average surface temperature of 800° F. (427° C.), when it is surrounded by clouds that should reflect much of the sun's heat.

HYRON SPINRAD

Related Articles in WORLD BOOK include:

PLANETS

Earth	Mercury	Saturn
Jupiter	Neptune	Uranus
Mars	Pluto	Venus

BIOGRAPHIES

Brahe, Tycho	Herschel (Sir	Newton, Sir Isaac
Copernicus,	William)	Ptolemy (astronomer)
Nicolaus	Kepler, Johannes	Tombaugh, Clyde W.
Galileo	Lowell, Percival	

OTHER RELATED ARTICLES

Asteroid	Meteor	Solar System
Astrology	Moon	Space Travel
Astronomy	Observatory	Sun
Day	Orbit	Telescope
Evening Star	Radio Telescope	Year
Gravitation	Satellite	Zodiac

JUPITER ♃	SATURN ♄	URANUS ♅	NEPTUNE ♆	PLUTO ♇
460,000,000	838,000,000	1,700,000,000	2,771,000,000	2,770,000,000
507,000,000	937,000,000	1,870,000,000	2,819,000,000	4,580,000,000
390,000,000	793,000,000	1,700,000,000	2,678,000,000	2,700,000,000
4,333	10,759	30,685	60,188	90,700
8	6	4	3	3
88,700	75,100	29,000	27,600	4,000(?)
9 hrs. 55 min.	10 hrs. 14 min.	10 hrs. 49 min.	15 hrs. 40 min.	6 earth-days
3	27	98	29	?
−170° F.	−240° F.	−240° F.	−280° F.	−300° F.
(−112° C.)	(−151° C.)	(−151° C.)	(−173° C.)	(−184° C.)
−170° F.	−240° F.	?	?	?
(−112° C.)	(−151° C.)			
15(?)	15(?)	?	?	?
Hydrogen,	Hydrogen,	Hydrogen,	Hydrogen,	None known
Helium,	Helium,	Helium,	Methane,	
Methane,	Methane,	Methane	Helium,	
Ammonia	Ammonia(?)		Ammonia	
318	95	14.6	17.3	Less than 1
1.33	0.68	1.7	2.2	?
260	116	97	143	?
12	10	5	2	0

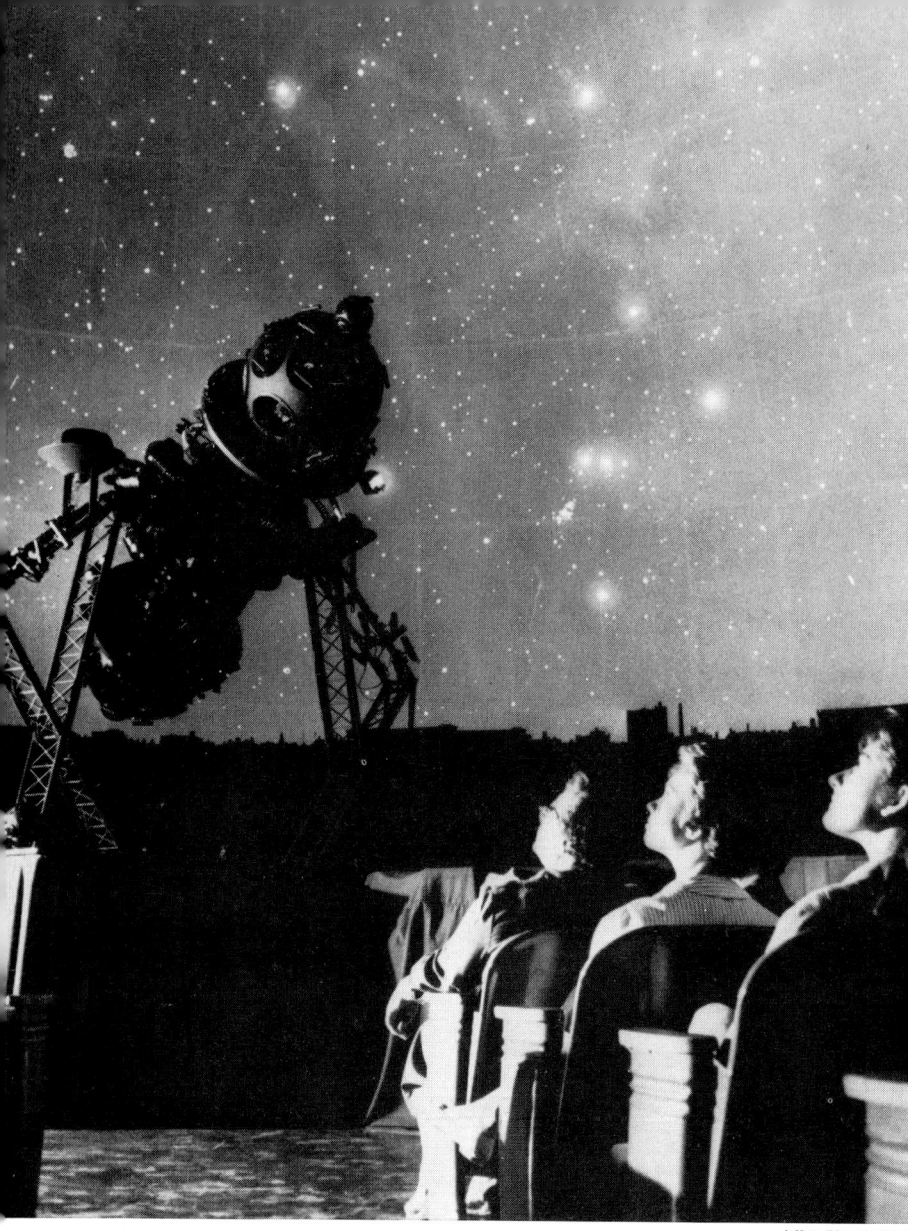

The Adler Planetarium in Chicago can show the movement of the sun, moon, and planets, as well as all of the stars visible to the unaided eye. A giant projector reproduces part of the heavens on the inside of a huge dome. Using the planetarium, astronomers give lectures about the solar system and universe.

Adler Planetarium

PLANETARIUM, *PLAN ee TAIR ih um.* A planetarium is a device for showing the movements of the planets. It is an almanac set to mechanical terms. The motions of the moon and the planets are very complicated. It requires ingenious machinery to show all the peculiarities of their orbits, or paths.

The simplest form of planetarium is called an *orrery.* It consists of a central ball that represents the sun, and a series of gears. The gears have arms that carry lesser globes, which represent the motions of earth, moon, and planets. When the device is set in motion by clockwork, an orrery gives a rough idea of how the earth, moon, and planets revolve about the sun.

Mathematical computations of the motions of the heavenly bodies can be made with great accuracy. Such computations are generally presented in the form of mathematical tables which the ordinary person finds difficult to understand. These tables, however, can be translated into geometrical shapes that look like wavy lines, and these shapes can be further translated into the action of trains of gear wheels. The point in the gear train that represents the actual position of a heavenly body moves a little searchlight or magic lantern. This projects light and portrays all that body's motions in the sky.

A modern planetarium consists of a dome with an inside that is whitened like a motion-picture screen. In the center of this dome is a machine that contains a great many cog wheels, projectors, lanterns, and electrical devices. When the room is darkened, and the projectors are illuminated and set in motion, a representation of the sky in action appears. It takes 119 optical projectors to illustrate each motion of a heavenly object.

At a typical planetarium, a lecturer stands in a control booth in a large aluminum-domed circular room. The audience sits before him, while overhead is a representation of the heavenly bodies. The projectors can make this picture of the sky go slow or very fast, cut-

468

ting years into minutes and days into seconds. At such speeds, the moon flits through its phases, and the complicated motions of the planets can be clearly seen. The stars can be turned on or shut off at will. The whole dome of the sky moves to represent the appearance of the heavens at any place.

The first modern planetarium, the Deutsches Museum in Munich, Germany, was built in 1923. Today, planetariums add to the educational resources of many of the world's major cities. Important planetariums outside the United States include those in Brussels, Belgium; Caracas, Venezuela; Chorzów, Poland; Edmonton, Alberta, Canada; The Hague, The Netherlands; Hamburg, Jena, and Nuremberg, Germany; Johannesburg, South Africa; London, England; Milan and Rome, Italy; Montevideo, Uruguay; Moscow, Russia; Osaka and Tokyo, Japan; Paris, France; Peking, China; and São Paulo, Brazil.

Major United States planetariums include those in Boston; Chapel Hill, N.C.; Chicago; Denver; Flint, Mich.; Los Angeles; New York City; Philadelphia; Pittsburgh; St. Louis; and San Francisco. Some planetariums are connected with observatories or astronomical museums.　　　　　　　　　　　　E. C. Slipher

PLANETESIMAL THEORY. See Earth (How the Earth Began).

PLANETOID. See Asteroid.

PLANING MACHINE. See Machine Tool (Kinds; picture).

PLANKTON, *PLANK tun*, is the mass of small, drifting animal and plant life that lives in bodies of water. The name *plankton* comes from the Greek word for *wandering*. The plankton consists mainly of small animals, such as protozoans, larval fishes, and crustaceans, but

Plankton drifts quietly with the currents and tides of the sea. These tiny plants and animals provide food for many fish.
From *The Open Sea* by Alister C. Hardy, Courtesy William Collins Son & Co. Ltd.

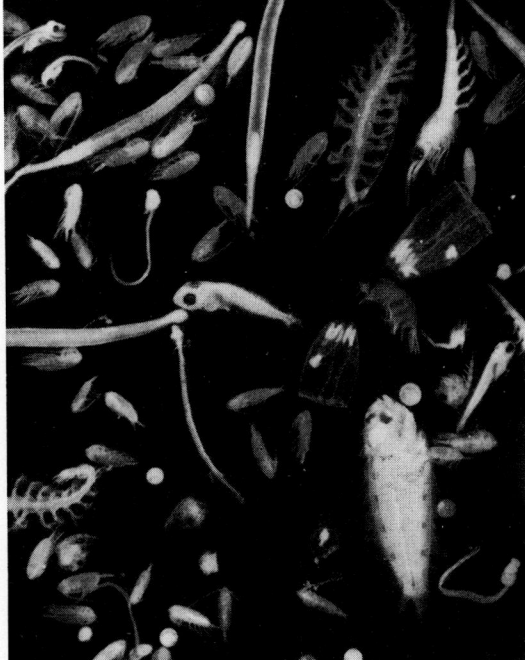

also includes some larger ones, such as jellyfish. During the day, the plankton animals usually swim hundreds of feet below the surface. But at night, they rise to the upper levels of the water.

The plankton also consists of tiny plants, such as algae. There are three groups of drifting plant life: the diatoms, the peridinians, and the coccospheres. Plankton is important as food for larger animals, such as herring, mackerel, and whales.

The life in or on the bottom of bodies of water is called *benthos*. The animals of larger size that swim freely, and independently determine their movements in the body of water, are called *nekton*.　　Leonard P. Schultz

Related Articles in World Book include:

Algae	Diatom	Ocean (Life	Ooze
Copepod	Jellyfish	in the Ocean)	Protozoan

PLANNED PARENTHOOD is a name given to the birth control movement. An international organization and private and government organizations around the world promote planned parenthood. These organizations distribute information on birth control methods, and make *contraceptive* (birth control) devices available. They urge couples to space the birth of children and to have only the number of children they want and can care for properly. They also urge the use of birth control devices for women whose health might be endangered by childbirth.

This article discusses organizations devoted to planned parenthood. For more information on birth control and the arguments for and against its use, see the article on Birth Control.

Planned Parenthood-World Population (PPWP) is the major planned parenthood organization in the United States. It works to make birth control information and devices available wherever they are wanted in the country. PPWP was founded as the American Birth Control League in 1914 by Margaret Sanger (see Sanger, Margaret). It was called the Planned Parenthood Federation of America from 1941 to 1963, when the organization took its present name.

PPWP affiliates (organizations associated with PPWP) operate about 400 clinics in more than 150 United States cities. They serve more than 350,000 women each year. PPWP's funds come from donations by corporations, foundations, and individuals. Its headquarters are at 515 Madison Avenue, New York, N.Y. 10022.

International Planned Parenthood Federation (IPPF) is made up of planned parenthood groups from more than 50 nations. It includes PPWP. IPPF was organized in 1952 to promote individual and political acceptance of birth control and family planning in order to slow the growth of world population. It works mainly in the developing countries of Africa, Asia, and Latin America. Its funds come from PPWP, which gives half of the money it collects to IPPF; from individuals, corporations, and foundations; and from governments, including those of Great Britain, Sweden, and the United States. Its headquarters are at 18/20 Lower Regent Street, London, England.

Critically reviewed by Planned Parenthood-World Population

PLANNING, CITY. See City Planning.

PLANOGRAPHIC PRINTING. See Lithography; Offset; Printing (Printing by Offset Lithography).

PLANT

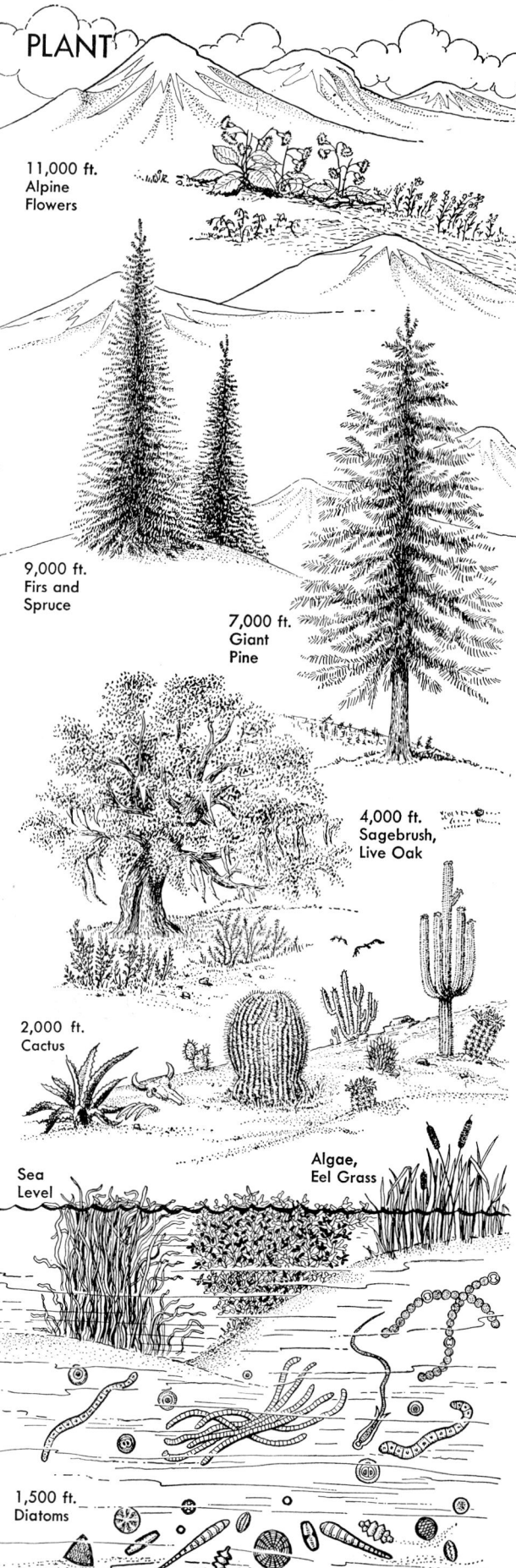

11,000 ft.
Alpine
Flowers

9,000 ft.
Firs and
Spruce

7,000 ft.
Giant
Pine

4,000 ft.
Sagebrush,
Live Oak

2,000 ft.
Cactus

Sea
Level

Algae,
Eel Grass

1,500 ft.
Diatoms

PLANT. Many of us take plants for granted. We think that they are the special concern of the farmer, or gardener, or florist. But without plants there could be no life on earth. Most of the food we eat comes from plants. Plants create the food that all the animals eat, so we are using the food that plants made even when we eat a steak or drink a glass of milk. Sometimes we eat plants directly, as when we eat potatoes or beans.

As well as being eaten, plants enter into almost every one of our daily activities. We build most of our houses of wood which comes from plants. Much of our clothing comes from plants. Many men make their living by raising certain kinds of plants and selling their products. We all enjoy the sight of a forest, and the beautiful colors and fragrance of the flowers. Plants keep rivers from flooding and keep soil from being washed away.

Not all plants are helpful to man, however. The annoying diseases called hay fever and rose fever are caused by tiny particles produced by plants. Some plants grow in fields and gardens as weeds and choke out the useful plants that provide food and beauty. Still other plants, so tiny they can not be seen except under a powerful microscope, cause many human diseases. These tiny plants are called bacteria. However, some bacteria are so useful that it is safe to say that we could not possibly live without them.

Kinds of Plants

Scientists know that there are more than 335,000 different species of plants. Actually, if we traveled all over the world we could see more different kinds of plants than these, but some of these are merely varieties, much as all dogs are merely different breeds of one basic kind of animal.

The plant kingdom has the scientific name *Plantae*. The kingdom has two main divisions, or *subkingdoms*, called *Thallophyta* and *Embryophyta*. See THALLOPHYTE; EMBRYOPHYTE.

The simplest plants are found in the subkingdom *Thallophyta*, which includes one-celled bacteria and algae, and fungi that are like the molds often seen growing on bread and cheese. Certain seaweeds in this subkingdom probably live longer than any other kinds of plants.

Within the subkingdom *Embryophyta* are two groups, or *phyla*, called the *Bryophyta* and *Tracheophyta*. The *Bryophytes* are also relatively simple plants and include the mosses and liverworts that are found in forests, on bare rocks, on rooftops, and elsewhere. Some of these plants have stems and leaves, but no roots. The phylum *Tracheophyta* includes the ferns, club mosses, and quillworts. Most of the plants we know belong to a division, or *subphylum*, of *Tracheophyta* called *Pteropsida*. This subphylum includes seed-bearing plants. Such plants include our common grasses and vegetables, and most trees, shrubs, and flowers.

Difference Between Plants and Animals

It might seem easy to tell plants and animals apart, but sometimes it is very difficult. Most of the animals that we can see move about freely, while the plants seem fixed. There are few plants, however, that do not move from place to place at some time in their lives. And animals often cannot move about. Sea squirts are fixed animals at one stage in their lives but at another stage they are somewhat like little tadpoles and move about as tadpoles do. Millions of plants float freely in streams and ocean currents, though many of them do not move through their own efforts.

We might say that plants are green and animals are not, but this difference is not a dependable way to tell one from the other. Few of the plants called fungi ever show any green color, while many fish, birds, and insects are green. We would not think of calling a fish or bird a plant, or a fungus an animal because of its color. Some green things have characteristics which might lead us to consider them either as plants or animals. Nobody knows whether some of these borderland living things are plants or animals. The zoologists claim them as animals and the botanists consider them plants.

Yet there are differences in living organisms that distinguish most plants from most animals. Among these are the following:

An adult living thing able to move about freely under its own power is more likely to be an animal than a plant.

The ability of a living thing to take solid food into its body through a mouth and to discharge wastes after the food has been digested is much more common in animals than it is in plants.

Most plants possess green coloring matter that can use the sun's energy to help in the manufacture of food. Such a substance is rarely found in living things that are considered animals.

If you burn a piece of cotton cloth and a piece of wool cloth, you can tell from the smell of the smoke that the materials burned are different. The cotton cloth, which is made from the slender hairs of plant seeds, is made up almost entirely of a material known as cellulose. The cell walls of most plants are largely cellulose. Wool, on the other hand, is hair from an animal. Animal cells do not have cellulose walls. The presence of cellulose in the cell walls of a living thing leads us to assume that it is a plant. Absence of cellulose helps us to say that it is an animal.

If size, or long life, or ability to live in unusual places are measures of success, then plants are more successful than animals. No animals can approach in size or age the giant sequoia trees of the Pacific Coast of the United States. It is doubtful if animals can manage to live in the great variety of places where plants succeed.

In plants, as in animals, there are definite life cycles in which individuals are young or old, and an old individual can never become a young individual.

Appearance and Structure of Plants

Plants may be almost any imaginable color. They may be huge, or so small that you cannot see them with the naked eye. A giant seaweed is just as much a plant as is a pine tree, or a yeast plant, or a bacterium too small to see.

Stems. Probably most of the plants that we know are flowering plants. Take a rose bush, for example. We know that it has woody stems with thorns on them. We know that if you cut this stem, the flower and the leaves above the cut will wither and die. We know that if you put the end of the stem in water, the rose and its leaves that have been removed from the parent plant will not wither so quickly. This is because the stem is able to get water to the leaves and to the flower and keep them supplied with at least some of their needs.

IMPORTANCE OF PLANTS TO MAN

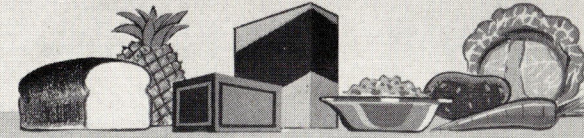

Plants Are Used for Food

Plants Are Made into Drinks

Fibers Used for Making Clothes Are Made from Plants

Plant Products Are Made into Shelter

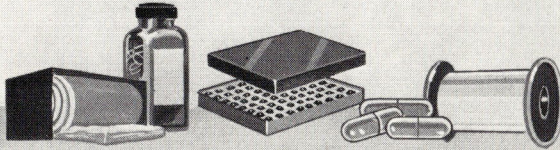

Drugs Are Manufactured from Plants

Plants Aid Communication and Distribution

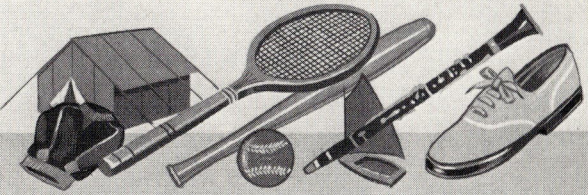

Sporting Goods Are Made from Plants

Plants Furnish Raw Materials for Manufacturing

SOME MEMBERS OF THE LILY FAMILY

Solomon's-Seal

Aloe

Hyacinth

Tulip

Mariposa Lily

Orville Logan Snider, Shostal

The Easter Lily, one of the best-known members of the lily family, has become a symbol of Easter.

Dogtooth Violet

Asparagus

Trillium

Tiger Lily

SOME MEMBERS OF THE ROSE FAMILY

Blackberry

Apricot

Strawberry

Apple

Spiraea

Fred Bond, Publix

The Rose, one of the most beautiful and fragrant flowers, is often used by poets as a symbol of beauty.

Raspberry

Plum

Pear

Peach

Cherry

PLANT

From this, we know that one of the uses a plant finds in stems is that of moving liquids from one part of the plant to another. But roots, leaves, and other parts of plants also move liquids from one part of the plant to another.

For the most part, botanists do not recognize that true stems are found in plants lower than the group to which the ferns belong. If you look at the twigs of almost any woody plant in late summer or fall, you will find that they bear buds near the tip. If you search at the base of the leaf of your rose, you may find what appears to be a very small bud tucked between the leaf and the stem. This bearing of buds is one of the things that helps a botanist decide whether a plant part is a stem or not. Structures that bear buds and leaves are normally considered as stems.

Stems may or may not be easy to see. In the average tree, the trunk, branches, and twigs are stems. They are, in trees, the most conspicuous part of the plant in winter. In the summer, the leaves that are borne on the stem may be the most conspicuous.

The potato that we eat is merely an underground stem bearing buds that we call "eyes." This stem is used by the plant chiefly for storing food rather than for conducting liquids from one part to another. In an ordinary head of celery, the stem is merely the very heart of the head to which the leaves are attached. In fact, the stem may be so small and short in some plants such as cabbage, lettuce, celery and spinach that the plants may be considered as stemless at that stage when they are most commonly eaten by us.

We cannot distinguish between stems and leaves by saying that leaves are green and stems are not, because many plants have green stems, some of which look much like leaves. On the other hand, we all know that many leaves are not green. Many ornamental house plants have leaves that are red, yellow, brown, or blue. Neither can we say that stems and leaves are the parts of a plant aboveground while the underground parts are the roots. Look at an onion. It grows underground like the bulbs of tulips and hyacinths in a flower garden. These bulbs are underground buds and in many cases, as in the onion, the leaves of the bulb supply us with food.

Stems, then, are plant parts that may be organs of food storage or of reproduction that may be useful in moving liquids from one part of the plant to another, or they may merely hold certain parts high in the air if necessary, or merely bear buds.

The tissue of stems may be soft and weak or very hard and woody. *Woody* stems are usually able to survive more severe conditions that are bad for plants than are nonwoody, or *herbaceous*, stems. We cannot say that woody plants are large and herbs small and let it go at that. Banana plants that look like trees are not trees because they do not have woody stems. Strawberry plants that sprawl on the ground are not herbs because their stems are truly woody. We recognize different groupings of woody plants as vines, trees, and shrubs.

Vines are rarely erect. They climb, wind, or sprawl over some support. They are not necessarily woody. *Trees*, in a strict sense, have a single trunk, or *bole*, with a branching head and are, when mature, normally over ten feet tall. *Shrubs*, on the other hand, usually have many trunks. They usually branch close to the ground and are not commonly over ten feet tall.

Herbs are frequently classified as annuals, biennials, and perennials. An *annual* goes through its life cycle from seed to seed in a year. A *biennial* requires two seasons to complete the cycle. A *perennial* may live many seasons, producing seeds year after year once the plant has become mature. In many plants such as the orchids, many years are required to reach maturity.

Roots. Stems bear buds and leaves and often flowers, but roots do none of these things. Roots are important to plants in many ways. They absorb liquids, though they are not the only plant parts capable of doing this. They store food, as in such root crops as radishes, carrots, and turnips. They hold plants erect, as in the prop roots of corn, or hold plants to supports, as in the clinging roots of some vines. They absorb water from the air and hold it, as in some of the hanging roots of some orchids. They serve as hosts for the bacteria that take nitrogen from the air, as in most of the clovers and related groups of leguminous plants.

We might think that the root system of a beet plant, for example, may be considered as only the part that we pull and eat. As a matter of fact, the beet that we eat is a relatively small part of the beet's root system. A beet's root system may penetrate the earth to a depth of ten feet or more if conditions are suitable. When we pull the beet, most of this root system is left in the ground. The root system of a single cabbage plant may spread through as much as two hundred cubic feet of soil. That of a common tomato plant may be even larger. A common field-corn plant may have roots that spread out over an area of four square feet and go down in the earth eight feet or more. A squash plant may spread its roots over an area of twenty square feet through the upper foot of good garden soil. The total length of the roots of a winter rye plant, excluding the root hairs, may be more than 375 miles.

Normally, grass roots grow at the rate of about one half inch a day but, under vigorous growing conditions, the growth may be as much as two and one-half inches a day for some weeks. Such elaborate root systems make it possible for plants to draw on the resources available over a considerable volume of soil. Hybrid corn, for example, has a deep root system. It can prosper in a dry season where corn with ordinary roots would be destroyed or at best would make only a poor yield for the farmer's efforts.

Probably the most interesting part of a plant's root system is the active region where there are many fine root hairs. Generally these are the places where water and food are absorbed from the soil. Plants whose root systems are constantly covered by water, as in the water lily, do not have root hairs. One of the strangest relationships between plants is found on the roots of certain evergreens where the plant itself does not grow root hairs. Instead, the work of root hairs is taken over by certain fungi that grow in the roots. The fungi gain some food from the plants on which they grow. At the same time these plants receive liquids from the soil through the fungi. In this way both are able to exist.

True roots are recognized as being found only in those plant groups which include the ferns and flowering plants. Many of the same functions are to be found in lower plants where they are performed by structures known as *rhizoids*. Other structures that perform the functions of roots but are not considered as roots are to be found in many of the parasitic plants, such as dodder and many of the fungi. Some of these structures penetrate the tissues of host organisms and absorb from them some of the materials the parasite needs. Some of these structures are known as *haustoria*.

Leaves. If you look at almost any bud you will find that it is made up of scales that may look somewhat like the small leaves they are. The most common kinds of leaves are more or less broad and thin, and are arranged along the stems, usually near the tips. They are most commonly the greenest part of a flowering plant. They vary in size from tiny invisible scales to enormous fronds such as you see on palms. Probably their most common job is that of exposing green tissue to the sun. Many of them are also used in storing food, in attracting insects, in holding water, in preventing water loss, or for other purposes.

To most persons, leaves are the broad green parts of a plant. They are borne on parts of the stem. In general, their function is to expose a generous amount of green matter to the sun in such a way that food will be manufactured. Some stems are also green, so this food manufacturing activity is not limited to leaves.

Leaves, like stems and roots, are of many different kinds. Some are juicy and crisp like those of lettuce. Others are tough and wiry like pine needles.

Leaves like those of the pines have a fairly small surface. The surfaces of the needles are of such a nature that water does not readily pass through them. This limits the amount of water lost through them. The pine can live where usable water is scarce even in winter, when much of it is frozen and not available for use. On the other hand, plants like the common water lily have broad leaves that quickly lose whatever water they have if exposed long to dry air. The water lily therefore must live where there is an abundance of water.

If you wipe any drinking glass so that it is clean and dry on the inside and place it in the sun for a few minutes over a common green leaf, such as you find on a house plant, you will soon notice that the inside of the glass becomes clouded with moisture. This loss of water

is part of the normal activities of this part of the plant. The water that leaves the plant in this vapor form is almost free of many of the salts that were in the water that entered the roots. The loss of this water through the leaves permits more water to enter the plant and bring with it some of the materials the plant needs to live. Fortunately, plants seem to be able to select, to some extent, what they need from what may be available to them.

Frequently in dry seasons you may see corn leaves curled much more tightly than they are when water is plentiful. In bitter cold weather, you may see the broad waxy leaves of rhododendrons curled in somewhat the same way. In each of these cases, the curled leaves are likely to use less water than those that are expanded.

Leaves sometimes can be used to help the plants reproduce. Cut off a piece of begonia leaf. Press it firmly into some moist soil in a flowerpot and leave it in this position for some time. It may form roots and stems and eventually resemble the parent plant from which you took it.

How Plants Make and Use Their Food

The green part of most plants is one of the most important things in nature. It is called *chlorophyll*, a name that means *light green leaf*. This chlorophyll may be found not only in leaves but in stems and flowers as well. If the sun falls on it and the temperature is right, chlorophyll can combine water and carbon dioxide to start a strain of compounds that yield starches and sugars. For the most part the plants get the carbon dioxide from the air. They usually get the water through the roots from the ground, though this is not always true. The carbon dioxide is freed into the air by the breathing of animals, by fires, by processes of decay, and even by some activities of plants themselves. In combining this gas with water, the plant gives off some oxygen that is useful to all animals. The process by which the green matter in plants combines water and carbon dioxide to form starches or sugars and to free oxygen is known as *photosynthesis*, which means the use

SOME PLANTS CANNOT MAKE THEIR OWN FOOD—THEY MUST DEPEND ON FOOD MADE AND STORED BY OTHER PLANTS

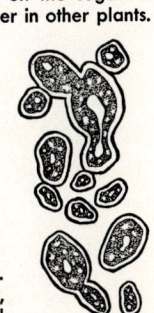

Yeast Plants are very valuable to man. They live on the sugar and water in other plants.

Bacteria live on both living and dead substances—on plants as well as animals.

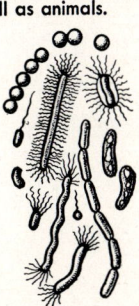

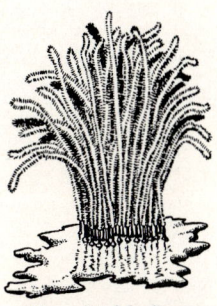

Molds grow in many places. They live on bread, fruit, paper, meat, leather, and many other substances.

Mushrooms live both in the soil and on dead plants; particularly on decayed stumps or trunks of trees.

Slime Molds live on dead plants, and, like mushrooms, particularly on decaying logs.

FRUITS UNKNOWN
TO OUR FOREFATHERS

Persimmon

Loganberry

Guava

Avocado

Casaba Melon

Mango

Banana

Grapefruit

Kumquat

Papaya

Jean McEllwein

VEGETABLES UNKNOWN TO OUR FOREFATHERS

Artichoke

Soybean

Swiss Chard

Chinese Cabbage

Zucchini or Italian Squash

Cowpea or Black-Eyed Pea

Kohlrabi

French Endive

Broccoli

of light in putting things together. Water brings the plant dissolved food materials. See PHOTOSYNTHESIS.

Possibly you have heard over the radio or read in the newspapers of *hydroponics*. Through the use of hydroponics, men have been able to grow plants without soil. The minerals that the plants need are supplied in solutions, and the sun and air do the rest. Most of the experiments in this field have been carried on in improving the combinations of minerals in solution that are needed by different plants. As yet, little has been done to see that the carbon dioxide needs of the leaves are available in the most useful amounts. See HYDROPONICS.

Small amounts of zinc, with which iron is galvanized, have an effect on the growth of plants. Water that has been carried only a short distance in a galvanized iron pail may take up enough zinc to upset the usefulness of that water to some plants.

Little differences in the minerals that get to plants may affect the usefulness of the plants to man and to other animals. Alkali disease, or "blind staggers," in some domestic animals can frequently be traced to the fact that the animals have fed on certain plants that have grown in soils in which the chemical selenium was available. Strangely enough, some plants grown in these soils will take up the selenium while others will not. Among some of the plants that do take up selenium are gunweed, snow-on-the-mountain, saltbush, and a number of milk vetches. When these same plants grow on soils in which selenium is not present, they may be perfectly harmless to the cattle and the horses that eat them.

We must remember that when light is not available to green plants they give off carbon dioxide much as do animals. In the winter we frequently find ponds where the water is fairly warm but where the ice becomes covered with a deep blanket of snow. This means that the water plants in the pond have an abundance of water and a suitable temperature but they lack the necessary light to keep their chlorophyll at work. As a result, the water may become heavily charged with carbon dioxide and unsuitable for fish. If the fish are present, they may crowd around air holes in the ice trying to get their oxygen needs direct from the air. If the ice should be free of snow, light can get through, and the plants will release oxygen and keep the water in good condition for the fish.

Plants can not have light available to them at all times, and so they must store up food to provide for their needs when it is not present. This they do in many ways. Plants store food in roots, stems, and leaves. Seeds and fruits are particularly important food-storage areas. For this reason they are often the parts that we harvest for our own use.

Because the mineral and other needs of plants vary, it is only reasonable that the natural environment determines, to a considerable extent, the kinds of plants found in any particular place. If a plant can exist in a region where the water in the soil is well supplied with salt, and another cannot live there, it is only natural that the first will be found in such a place and the second will not.

Some plants, for example, need much light and others need little. Some need much moisture that contains certain minerals, and others need water that has other kinds of minerals. Some need much air and others need none. A plant that needs no air to live must get the food ordinarily supplied by air from some other source. Many plants that cause diseases in humans are *anaerobic*. They do not need air to live. Such plants may enter wounds and grow rapidly. Anaerobic bacteria often cause infections in deep and narrow wounds such as those made by nails or bullets. Among such bacteria are the ones that cause tetanus (lockjaw).

How Plants Reproduce

Vegetative Reproduction. The simplest kind of plant, like the simplest kind of animal, is a single cell. The simplest way for this cell to reproduce is to first increase in size. Then it may break into two pieces to make two little individuals. These may then again grow to be the size of the parent cell. This method of reproduction is spoken of as one type of *vegetative reproduction*. It is very important to plants and to man.

It is true that potatoes, peonies, cannas, and seedless oranges have flowers. But for the most part, we do not get new crops of potatoes, cannas, and seedless oranges from the seeds of those flowers. When we want new potatoes for the year, we cut up some of last year's crop and plant the pieces. To be sure, we take care to have an eye, or bud, in each part, but these are not flowers. With the cannas, we cut up the underground parts. If we have house plants in our home, it is quite probable that our neighbors borrow slips or leaves, root these in water and get new plants in that way. In all of these cases, these new plants are just like the old ones. They could not be different. Some plants have no flowers, and many of these form new individuals by the vegetative method.

When an orchardist finds a fruit tree that bears exceptionally good fruit, he may take a slip from that tree and root it or graft it to one of his other trees. The fruit that this slip bears will be that of the parent tree. You may have seen an apple tree in which different branches bore different kinds of apples. A single apple tree once bore thirty different kinds of apples.

Many of our ornamental shrubs, such as roses, are made to produce new individuals by bending the branches down so that they touch the ground. The branches may develop roots where they touch the moist earth. When the roots are well enough developed, the new plant may be cut free from the old one. Many of the weeds in a garden are not destroyed when they are cut with a hoe. We may merely make two or more plants by cutting them up in this way. In fact, many of the bulbs and similar plants in our spring flower gardens must be taken up every few years and "separated" if they are to do their best.

Some of the larger plants whose fruits we eat frequently are reproduced almost wholly by this vegetative method. Bananas, asparagus, and pineapples are a few of the most common of these.

Many plants have special parts of their bodies suitable for the production of tiny one-celled structures. These cells are called *spores*. Each of these structures may alone, or combined with another cell, produce a new plant. One of the greatest marvels of nature is the fact that a single cell, so small that it cannot be seen with the naked eye, may be capable of producing an

478

Some Plants, like potatoes, will grow from pieces cut from them and planted. Each piece must have an eye or bud.

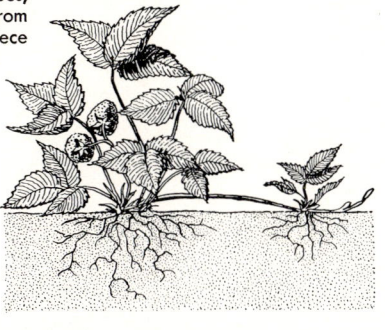

Other Plants, Like Strawberries, send out trailing ground stems, which take root to produce new plants.

Grafting of various kinds will result in the growth of new plants on old stems.

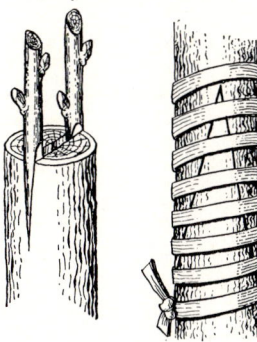

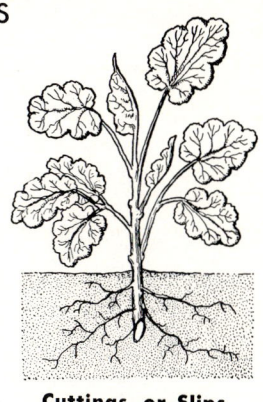

Cuttings, or Slips, develop roots. These become new plants when they are planted.

enormous plant like the one from which it came.

In spring you may find moss plants producing little slender cups on tall stems. If these are tapped, they may yield a little cloud of spores. In the same way, the horsetails that grow commonly along railroad embankments in early spring bear conelike structures that yield clouds of spores. Pine trees may shed clouds of spores in early summer when birds alight on them or when the wind blows. Sometimes you can see clouds of spores shed from many grasses.

All of these spores are not alike. In some cases, as in the moss spores, or in some of the fern spores, a single spore could be enough to produce a new plant. But in the pine this is not so. As a matter of fact, the dust shed from the pine is usually not a single spore but a spore that has developed into a small few-celled plant part that we call *pollen*. This pollen produces still smaller cells that must unite with other cells before the life cycle can be continued.

The production of plants by means of spores that do not need to unite with others to continue the cycle is a type of nonsexual, or *asexual, reproduction*. It is common in the lower plants such as the algae and fungi. Such plants as bread mold, for example, can reproduce themselves by getting a single spore to a suitable food supply. We commonly hear that the pollen or dust that one finds on certain parts of common flowers is the male cell of a plant. This is not quite true even though the pollen does produce the male cells.

Sexual Reproduction. Most of us know what a hollyhock looks like. In the typical flower like a hollyhock there are a number of parts that we can recognize easily. In the bud, the outer part of the flower is composed of a group of greenish leaflike structures. Taken together, these make up the *calyx*, the function of which may be to protect the young flower in the bud. The parts of the calyx are the *sepals*. The sepals may be separated or joined. They may be small and plain or large and showy. Sometimes, they are the most conspicuous part of the flower.

Inside the calyx in a hollyhock we find a group of large showy structures, the *petals*. Taken together, the petals make up the *corolla*. In different flowers these may be colored and shaped variously and may be separate or united one with the other. In some flowers, they are united also with the calyx.

The calyx and corolla are sometimes spoken of as the *floral envelope*, or *perianth*. The parts inside the perianth are necessary for the production of good seeds, and they are called the *essential organs*.

In many common flowers, such as the hollyhock, the outer set of essential organs is made up of *stamens*. In the hollyhock, these are fastened together at their bases into a tube, but at the end they appear as little sacs which contain yellow dust, the pollen. The sac in which the pollen is contained is called the *anther*. The stem on which the anther is borne is the *filament*. The anther and filament together make the stamen. All the stamens together make up the *androecium*.

The stamens of some flowers toss their pollen dust freely into the air in great quantities. Some keep it as a sticky mass that they free only under certain circumstances. If you poke the flower of a barberry plant, you will see that these stamens behave like little springs. Many clovers have stamens which move suddenly when they are properly irritated, as by the visit of a bee.

Inside the hollyhock flower, when it is young, we find a tube of stamens. If you tear one side of this tube with your fingernail or with a pin, you will find that inside it are still other structures. In some flowers these structures are numerous and separate. In others they are more or less united. These structures are the *pistils*. Taken all together, the pistils make up the *gynoecium*. You will see that the pistils are usually made up of one or more sections fastened together lengthwise. These are really modified leaves just as the sepals, petals, and filaments. The pistil is composed of one or more *carpels*. Like the filament, the carpels bear spore cases, though it is not common for these cases to contain more than one spore, and usually this is too small to be seen with the naked eye.

The egg develops inside this spore. Most of the elaborate structures that you see in a flower are designed to assist in bringing the sperm from the pollen

479

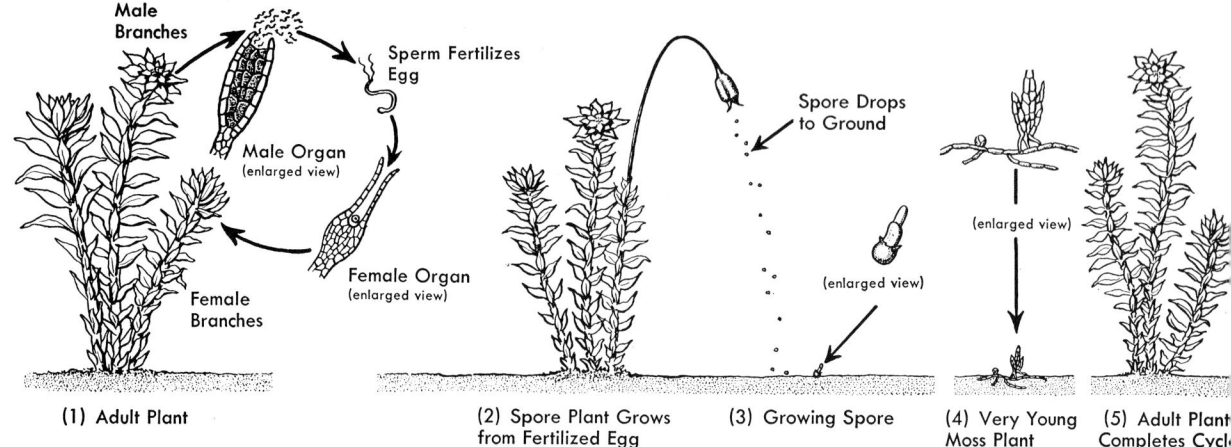

Male
Branches

Sperm Fertilizes
Egg

Male Organ
(enlarged view)

Female Organ
(enlarged view)

Female
Branches

Spore Drops
to Ground

(enlarged view)

(enlarged view)

(1) Adult Plant

(2) Spore Plant Grows
from Fertilized Egg

(3) Growing Spore

(4) Very Young
Moss Plant

(5) Adult Plant
Completes Cycle

to the egg inside the spore borne by the carpel. When this union has taken place, development begins in which an *ovule*, or immature seed, eventually becomes a mature *seed*. When the whole pistil has matured, it is known as the *fruit*. Frequently, other parts of the plant may join the pistil to make a mature fruit.

In the hollyhock, the pistil was swollen at the base. From this base arose a number of slender, threadlike structures, the ends of which finally burst through the tube of stamens and eventually bent back and mixed with the stamens. The base of a pistil such as this is called the *ovary*. This is topped by the *styles*, the ends of which are the *stigmas*.

There are a number of general ways in which the pollen gets from the stamen to where it can develop a tube to carry the sperms to the egg down inside the pistil.

A simple way for the pollen to get to the pistil is for the stamen to reach over and touch the pistil. Possibly still simpler is for the flower never to open at all but just let the pollen on the stamen in the flower reach the pistil in that same flower. We speak of this general sort of pollination as *self-pollination*. It is an almost certain method if the pollen happens to mature at a time when the flower can use it. Plants that can be pollinated in this way might be expected to produce fertile seeds easily, and many of them are among our worst weeds. It also happens that many of our most important plants are of this type. Our small grains, like wheat, are self-pollinating. About all a wheat plant needs in order to develop a good head of fruits is the necessary vigor, and freedom from its natural enemies.

In general, plants that are self-pollinated do not have flowers that are brilliantly colored or highly fragrant. They do not need to attract visitors to help them in their work. Neither do they possess great quantities of pollen, since this is not necessary.

Many plants may pollinate themselves if other kinds of pollination fail. In the hollyhock, for example, we may find that old maturing styles of the pistil bend back and mix with the stamens, though at first they are held erect free from those of the same flower in which they are borne.

When the styles of a hollyhock remain thrust straight up through the stamen tube of their parent flower, they stand a good chance of being visited by a bee that has come immediately from another hollyhock flower. On the bee's body, there will probably be an abundance of pollen from those other flowers. Some of this may be rubbed onto the ready stigmas of the flower.

In this way, the pollen of one flower pollinates the stigma of another. This is what we call *cross-pollination*.

Cross-pollination is brought about in various ways. We have already mentioned that a bee might bring pollen from another flower of the same kind. But there are many other animals that help in this work. Butterflies, flies, moths, wasps, birds, mammals, and other creatures help. The creatures that serve flowers best in this way commonly have scales, hairs, or other structures on their bodies in which the pollen becomes entangled. Flowers that rely on animals to bring about cross-pollination frequently possess qualities likely to attract the needed visitors to the vicinity. Color, food value, fragrance, or shape lure the needed guest.

Among the important commercial plants that rely on animals to bring about cross-pollination are the orchard trees, and the clovers, including alfalfa. Peas, beans, pumpkins, tomatoes, and hundreds of garden flowers are also pollinated in this way. Since many insects are enemies of important food plants, we have developed poison sprays to keep these in control. Unfortunately, these same sprays may be fatal to the insects that pollinate the plants. Because of this, the fruits cannot grow.

Another common method by which plants get cross-pollination is by the wind. Since such plants merely free their pollen into the moving air, there is much likelihood that there will be a tremendous waste of pollen. Plants that produce pollen in enormous amounts can meet this situation. Pines, many grasses, ragweed, cattail, and such plants are usually wind-pollinated. Since much of this pollen affects the health of some persons by giving them hay fever, these plants may have a direct influence on the health of persons who live among them. It is probable that wind pollination has existed

SOME SEEDLESS PLANTS, LIKE FERNS, GROW INDIRECTLY FROM A SPORE

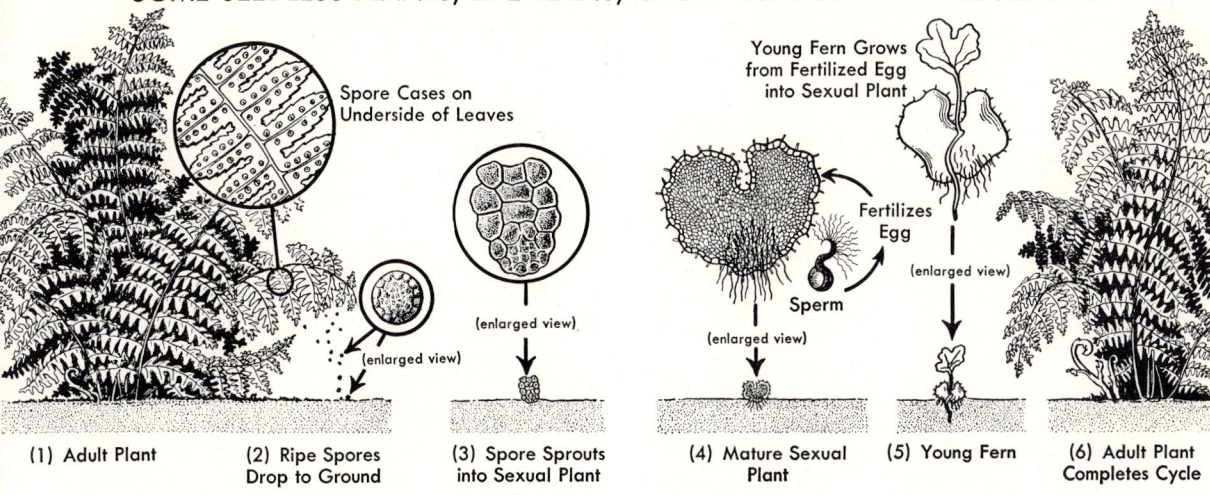

Spore Cases on Underside of Leaves

(enlarged view)

(enlarged view)

Young Fern Grows from Fertilized Egg into Sexual Plant

Fertilizes Egg

(enlarged view)

Sperm

(enlarged view)

(1) Adult Plant   (2) Ripe Spores Drop to Ground   (3) Spore Sprouts into Sexual Plant   (4) Mature Sexual Plant   (5) Young Fern   (6) Adult Plant Completes Cycle

longer on the earth than has pollination by insects or by other animals. One of the interesting things about plants that use the wind to carry their pollen is that many of them release their pollen only when the air is moving.

Corn is a wind-pollinated plant. That is why it is important that different kinds of corn be grown reasonable distances apart unless we wish to grow corn representing mixtures of the types present. Usually, corn to be grown as seed is protected against unwanted pollen.

Obviously, there is more chance of a plant's failing to receive pollen if it is of the wind-pollinated type than if it is of the insect-pollinated type, and more chance of failure in the insect-pollinated type than in the self-pollinated type. It happens that in some of our weeds there is an even surer way of producing fertile seeds than is to be found in the self-pollinated type.

A surprising number of plants, like the dandelion, for example, produce showy flowers with pollen that is eaten by insects. One would think that such plants use insects to bring about cross-pollination. We know, however, that in the dandelion the pollen does not function at all. Fertile seeds or fruits are produced without any pollination. This means that these plants do not even need to open their flowers to produce seeds that will grow. Many plants are known to be able to produce fertile seeds by this method. Many of them are weeds.

If a plant is naturally cross-pollinated, we will not know what the next generation will be like unless we make it impossible for unwanted pollens to reach the plants. One way to control such crosses is to put bags around the parts of the plants that would receive the pollen and then remove the bags and dust the desired pollen on with a brush or by hand. This may be a slow process, but it often pays. If we let wind-pollinated plants have their own way, they would soon lose many of the qualities we have built up in them by selecting their parents carefully over the years.

TYPICAL SEED PLANTS GROW FROM POLLINATED SEEDS

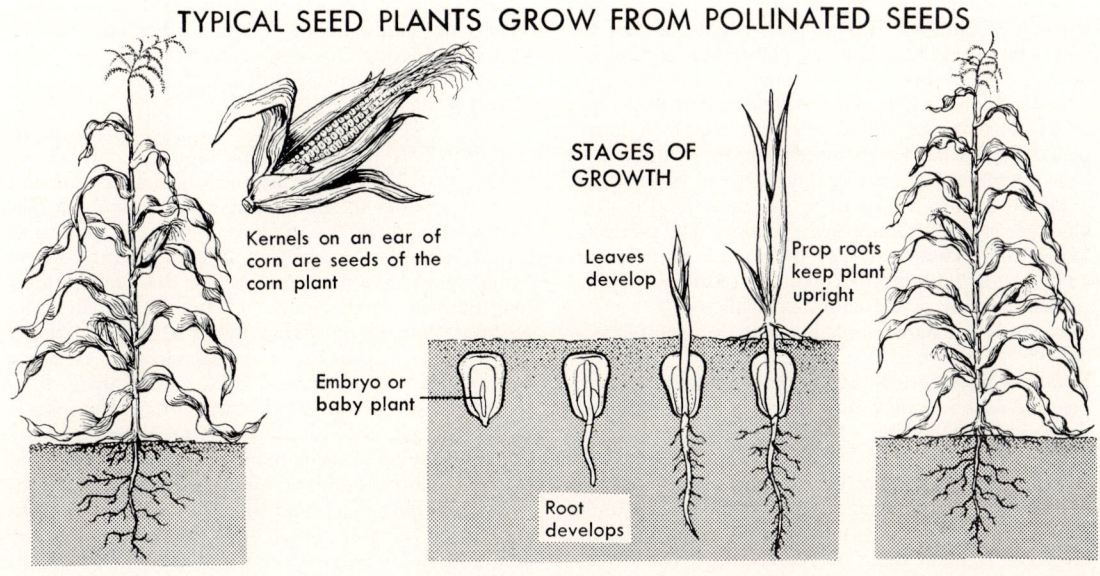

Kernels on an ear of corn are seeds of the corn plant

STAGES OF GROWTH

Leaves develop

Prop roots keep plant upright

Embryo or baby plant

Root develops

481

PLANT

We might think that self-pollination would be undesirable in plants. But with most of our small grains, where this is the common thing, it really is most fortunate. Imagine having to go over a field of wheat each year and seeing to it that the pollen that reached each flower was of a particular sort. Once a strain of a self-pollinated plant has become established it is likely to continue for a long time with the same characteristics. The difficulty in these plants is to get new kinds. This is commonly done by removing the pollen-producing part of the flower before it has time to free its pollen and then introducing pollen that we wish to use in making the cross.

Because men have learned how to make these crosses, however, we are now able to grow wheat in great areas that formerly could not support it. This has meant the difference between prosperity and starvation in many places in the world such as the Soviet Union, China, and western parts of the United States. It has improved the yield of these plants wherever they may be grown. A few discoveries like this made in some of our agricultural colleges may return many times in a year the cost of carrying on the investigations and of developing the new grain.

Where Plants Live

Some plants are found in abundance in hot springs, while others live equally successfully on snow and ice. Some are found carrying on their life processes in total darkness, while others are at their best in intense sunlight.

Waters in which much lime is dissolved are liked by some plants while others favor those with an acid content. Still others do best in waters in which much iron, salt, sulfur, or other minerals are dissolved. Few, if any, plants can exist in all the extremes suggested. A plant that does well in cold salt water is not likely to thrive in a hot sulfur spring.

Some plants are so sensitive to minor differences of light, heat, moisture, or chemical nature that even a slight difference may increase the number of places where they can live. Another slight difference may bar them completely from a given place. This is most important to man. For example, some kinds of corn must have ten more days to mature their kernels than other kinds. This means that kinds that require a longer period can not be grown successfully in a climate that lacks the number of suitable days between killing frosts.

Prolonged hot, dry weather may be as fatal to some kinds of corn as a short growing season. The successful farmer must know not only the nature of the plants he is growing but also the conditions of soil, water, and climate that are available in his locality.

For the most part, plants live wherever the physical conditions they need are present at the right time. Scientists have sorted plants into various groups depending on where they grow. Among the commoner of these are the following:

Plants that live, for the most part, in water, are called *hydrophytes*. They may extend certain portions of their bodies into the air but most of the plant is under water. Since water under motion is more powerful than air under motion, these plants have developed weak, pliable stems. These stems give and take with the currents rather than standing erect against them. Since water is buoyant, most of these plants can not remain erect when not supported by the water.

Plants found where there is little or no water, at least for some period of the year, are called *xerophytes*. Such plants usually are able to make the best use of the water available and to hold what they can get until such time as it is needed. Spongy stems, wax coverings, and hidden reservoirs are some of the structures we find in these plants that are common on deserts or in other dry places.

Mesophyte is a general name applied to plants that are more or less between the hydrophytes and the xerophytes. Most of the plants grown on farms or in gardens are mesophytes. They would be drowned by too much water and would die with too little.

A whole science known as *ecology* has been developed to help us understand the relationships between the surroundings and the living things there. Plant ecology refers to how plants get along in their environment. Agriculture, forestry, and horticulture are merely the sciences of learning how to make certain living things do what we want them to do in a given place.

Only comparatively recently have persons recognized the importance of studying little areas. We speak of *microclimates*, meaning little climates. If we could control the little climates in our back yard, we would need to have little worry about the big ones elsewhere, and when we make a garden we make a piece of ground suitable for the growth of certain plants that would be useful to us. In doing this, we are working with microclimates or with *microecology*.

How Plants Are Dependent on Soil

One of the most important places in which little climates are constantly at work is in the soil. When a woodchuck makes a hole in the ground, he mixes the soil and he lets in air, water, and organic material. The mixing of the soil brings together new combinations of minerals from which plants may select what they need. When air enters, it acts on some of the minerals and breaks some of them down. This makes other new combinations. Water further changes the mixture and dissolves some minerals, leaving others exposed to the air. All this is like stirring a soup of foods that plants may need.

When a plant is growing in this soil, it thrusts its roots into new regions, making new holes which are smaller than those made by the woodchuck. Air and water may enter these holes, and when the plant dies its tissue may be useful to other plants. The making of topsoil is simply the exploring of earthy matter where living things have not grown before, and creating new conditions in which plants and animals can live successfully. Not all the living things at work in doing this are as conspicuous as the woodchuck. A single gram of loam or surface soil may contain up to fifty-eight million bacteria. Some of these may in part serve as food for up to two million protozoa. Some of the bacteria may be nitrogen-fixing and capable of adding as much as forty pounds of nitrogen to an acre in a year.

We are doing much and should do more to prevent the loss of valuable topsoil. But, more than this, we should be doing what we can to develop new topsoils

HOW PLANTS BREATHE, EAT, AND DRINK

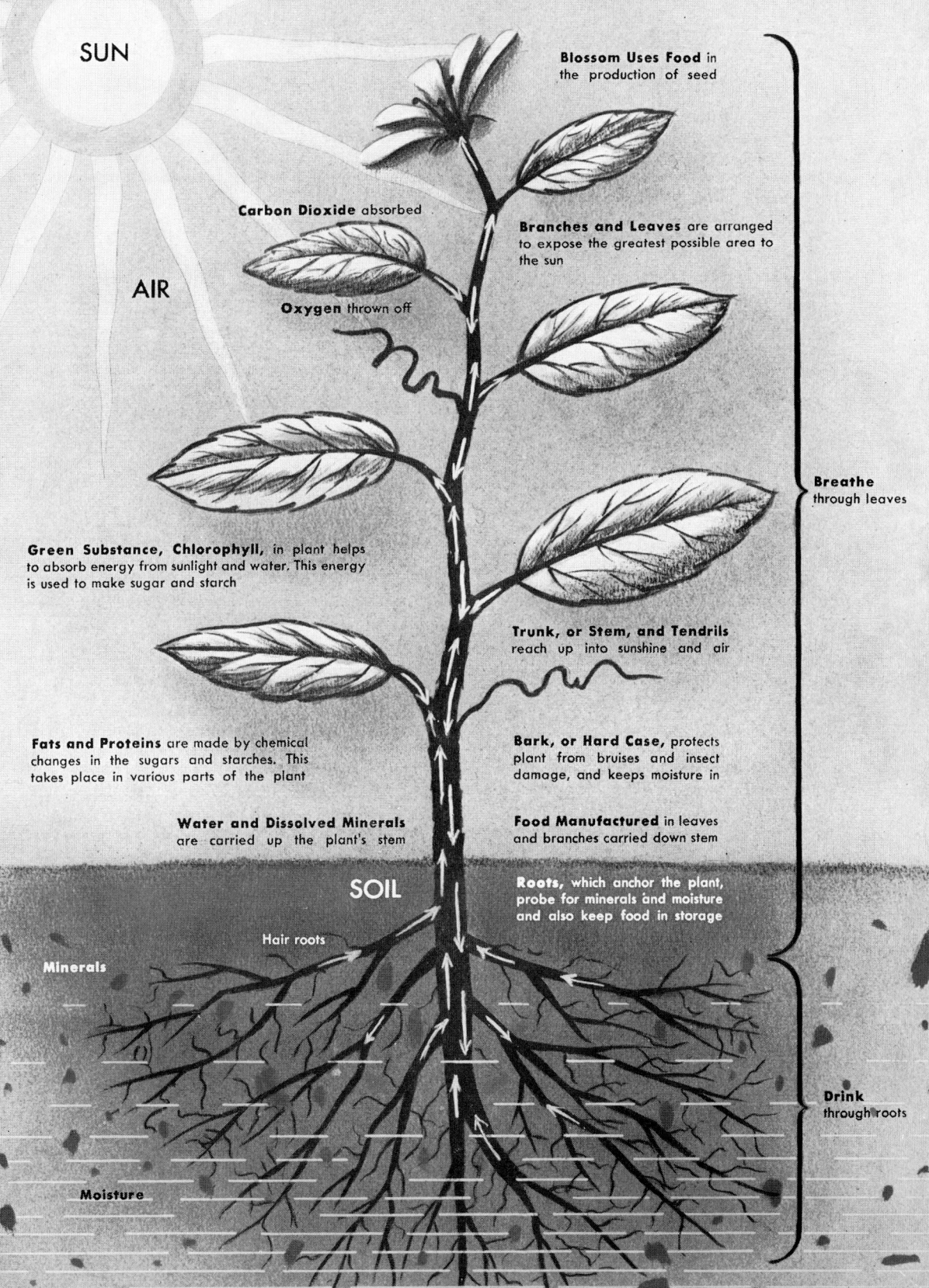

SUN

Blossom Uses Food in the production of seed

Carbon Dioxide absorbed

AIR

Branches and Leaves are arranged to expose the greatest possible area to the sun

Oxygen thrown off

Green Substance, Chlorophyll, in plant helps to absorb energy from sunlight and water. This energy is used to make sugar and starch

Breathe through leaves

Trunk, or Stem, and Tendrils reach up into sunshine and air

Fats and Proteins are made by chemical changes in the sugars and starches. This takes place in various parts of the plant

Bark, or Hard Case, protects plant from bruises and insect damage, and keeps moisture in

Water and Dissolved Minerals are carried up the plant's stem

Food Manufactured in leaves and branches carried down stem

SOIL

Roots, which anchor the plant, probe for minerals and moisture and also keep food in storage

Hair roots

Minerals

Drink through roots

Moisture

Feeler roots

WHAT PLANTS DO IN ORDER TO SURVIVE

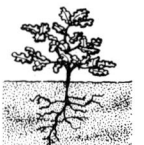   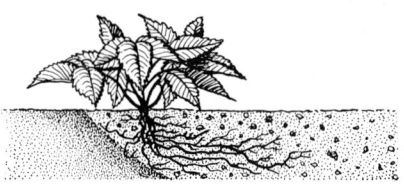

Roots Penetrate deep into the soil, and stems rise into the light and air. Even when disturbed, they follow this pattern.

Roots Will Turn toward soil that is loose and properly drained, if it contains the needed minerals.

 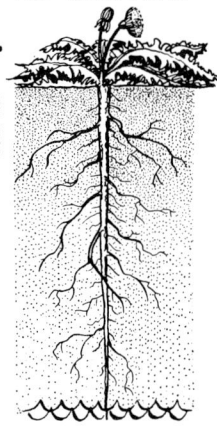  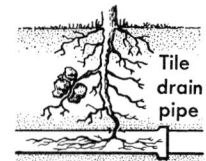

Tile drain pipe

Leaves Turn to the source of sunlight to present the greatest possible amount of surface and absorb the most rays.

Roots will grow to great depths to reach stores of moisture.

Stems Will Develop great strength to support branches. Roots will often penetrate obstacles they meet.

to replace those that have been lost. In nature it may take as much as five hundred years to form an inch of topsoil, but soil students tell us that as much as an inch can be restored from subsoil in two years' time. This means that the organisms which do this work must be well-fed and vigorous. We cannot dump a bushel of earthworms on a clay garden and expect them to make rich loam before the end of the season. Properly fed plants can do much to improve the soil. They do this in part by regulating the temperatures underground, by holding and using the available rainfall, and by letting air into previously inaccessible areas. They also serve as food for other living things that come in to use the soil to whose richness they may have added.

How Plants Are Dependent on Light

We have already outlined the story of photosynthesis in general. We know that most plants need light to develop some of their fundamental foods.

Did you ever think why there is likely to be such an abundance of showy flowers in the woods in spring? To be sure there are some flowers to be found there all summer, but in the spring they seem to be most conspicuous. The reason for this, of course, is that in summer the leaves of the taller plants shut the light out from the ground. This may help you to understand one possible reason why we go to the woods in spring for flowers. The spring flowers that we collect in the woods are making the most of the time of the year when an abundance of light is available to them. Most of them have a reserve of food stored underground a previous season and they draw on this. They develop leaves and flowers and fruits quickly. By the time the treetops have leafed out and formed a shade, many of the flowering plants have done most of their work for the year.

Cattails in swamps have leaves that point directly upward. Someone has suggested that this is ideal for a plant that needs a uniform amount of light through the day. In the morning and evening, the leaves expose a broad surface to the sun. At noon, when the sun is most intense, they expose a small surface. In this way they have a more or less uniform amount of light through the day. The movements of plants caused by light are called *phototropism*. The stems of plants tend to turn toward the source of light.

Probably you have seen a place where a board had been left on the lawn in summer for only a day or two. When the board was removed, the plants beneath may have turned yellow and may even have died. Light was shut from them by the board and they could not manufacture new food. The temperature was high, however, and the plants continued to *respire*, or to use up their tissue at a rapid rate. The result was that they died. These same plants might remain in darkness for months on end and never be any the worse for it. In winter, they may lie buried under snow banks where little, if any, light can penetrate. In spite of this, the plant does not die as it did in darkness in the summer. The reason is that in winter the temperature is down to such a point that respiration is cut down and the plant does not use up its resources as it did in the summer.

One of the most common experiments performed by young botanists is to pin some corks to opposite sides of a leaf that is exposed to the sun and leave them for a few days. When they are removed, the chances are that the leaves have lost their green color where light has not been able to reach them. Unless a plant is a parasite on another plant, it must have light to continue its existence.

One other important aspect of light involves many of our well-known crop plants. These plants depend upon the length of the day for their ripening. Some ripen when the days become longer, some ripen when the days become shorter.

How Plants Compete with Each Other

If all the seeds produced by one plant were to start growing, there would not be room enough for all young plants. Some must be crowded out even by their own kind. Competition among plants is not limited to close relatives. There are all sorts of other plants trying to make their own way and to get what they need, regardless of whether they affect other plants.

Possibly the simplest way to get this idea is to think of two seeds planted side by side. If the ground is dry so that neither seed can get the water it needs, they may lie idle but ready to grow possibly for as much as forty years or more. Suppose now that a small amount of moisture becomes available. One of the seeds has a seed coat that is mucilagelike and quickly takes up the water that is available. The other with a hard, dry coat is not affected. The first seed with the water it has may begin to grow. This gives it an advantage over its neighbor. It can develop a root system that will take water from its competitor or it may develop leaves that may shade its neighbor and thus prevent its getting the light it needs.

Fortunately no one plant possesses all the things that make it succeed in competing with other plants in all places. If this were the case, we might possibly have only one kind of plant on the earth after a while. But the plant that got a good start in spring may not be able to survive the conditions of summer. Then the plant that got a late start may step in and crowd out its earlier neighbor.

Plants and Animals

Most plants could get along better without animals than animals could get along without plants. But animals are very useful to certain plants. Some animals help some plants pollinate their flowers. Some experts believe that most oak trees and many nut trees are planted by squirrels that bury the nuts in such a manner that they are able to germinate successfully. When beavers build their dams, they flood considerable areas of lowlands. Eventually these mud flats become excellent stretches of rich earth in which plants can grow exceptionally well. But in the process the flood may kill many trees that originally grew in the area flooded.

The mere fact that many animals eat plants helps other plants, strange as that may seem. We have already noted that plants commonly compete with each other. It is easy to see that when an animal removes a competing plant by eating it, the animal helps make things easier for rival plants. It may even let light reach the ground, thus permitting plants to grow that otherwise would have had no chance.

Man helps many plants survive by storing the seeds and bulbs during times of the year when they might otherwise be destroyed. In addition, he plants, waters, and otherwise cares for the plants that are useful to him, with the result that many are able to grow in parts of the world where they could not otherwise survive.

Many animals are destructive to plants. Mammals, birds, insects, and other animals feed upon them, and in so doing may kill the plants. Generally, if man keeps out of the picture, natural checks keep most animal enemies of plants from multiplying too greatly.

Possibly the greatest use of plants to animals is that of supplying them with food. Experts in wildlife say that the cover plants provide for animals is fully as important as the food supplied. Of what value is it to any animal to be able to fill its own stomach, if, when it has had a good meal, it cannot prevent other animals from using it as a meal?

How Plants Have Developed

The plants that we now see on the earth have not always existed. Many of the plants that covered the earth in great abundance in the earlier history of the earth are now known only from their fossil remains. Some few plants are "living fossils."

In general, the simpler plants appeared on the earth before those that are more complicated in structure. The flowering plants have been found on the earth only since about the beginning of the Cenozoic era, or for probably not more than a hundred million years. For the preceding one hundred and twenty-five million years, the most highly developed plants were represented by plants that are now seen as pines and their relatives. This was known as the Age of Reptiles. Before this was the Age of Fishes, which included the earlier members of the phylum *Tracheophyta*, such as club mosses and horsetails. This age lasted for some one hundred and fifty million years. It began with the Silurian period and ended with the Pennsylvanian. During this period, the major coal beds were laid down. Before that, the only plants to be found were those such as liverworts, mosses, algae, fungi, and bacteria. Probably the earliest plants were somewhat like bacteria. But they left no fossil remains, as did the more highly developed plants of more recent times.

Importance of Plants

It is quite probable that in the history of the world, plants influenced man before man influenced plants. Man took things as he found them before he began to make them as he wanted them to be. And to some extent this is true today in man's relationships with plants. On a hike, or on an exploring expedition, we take and use the plants as we find them. At home on the farms and gardens, and in the greenhouses and factories, we make them do what we wish them to do.

Probably plants are of most importance to man because of their food value. Early men undoubtedly moved into different parts of their world in part because of the kind and amount of food available to them in the different areas. Some remained in particular areas and developed habits and customs based largely on the conditions necessary for collecting the plant food available there. Even today seaweeds provide considerable food for some Oriental peoples.

Early peoples who lived near fresh-water marshes in temperate climates fed largely on rice and similar plants of these wet lands. It was not until later that men learned how to put marshes where dry land had been and grow their rice there. Even today in the Great Lakes region near Michigan, there are Indians who use wild rice extensively as food. Among the beliefs of some of these Indians is the conviction that one must not try to plant wild rice where it does not grow naturally. They believe that if the Great Spirit had wished it to grow elsewhere it would have grown there anyway. It is quite possible that the Indians tried to plant rice fields by sowing dried grains and found that it did not succeed. Only fairly recently have plant physiologists discovered that wild rice loses its vitality if it is dried in the same way that we dry wheat, corn, oats, rye, and similar cereals. The Indians were not in position to make this discovery and so merely developed a rule that one should not try to plant dry rice, since this was obviously a waste of time and of good food.

HOW PLANTS PROTECT THEMSELVES

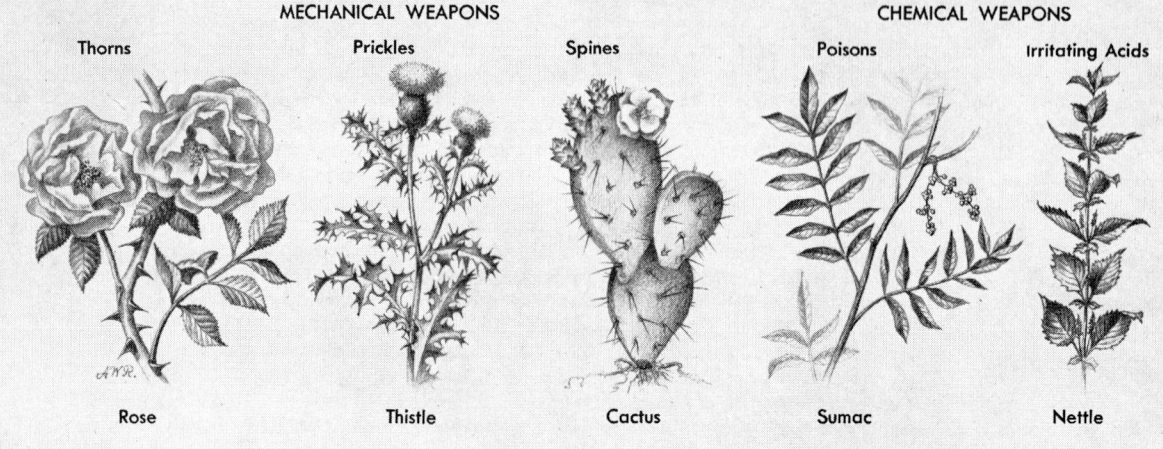

MECHANICAL WEAPONS			CHEMICAL WEAPONS	
Thorns	Prickles	Spines	Poisons	Irritating Acids
Rose	Thistle	Cactus	Sumac	Nettle

Similar customs of peoples have developed all over the world. The Bitterroot Indians of our Northwest were named after the plant whose roots supplied them with much of their food. In the Southwest there were other Indians whose life centered around the growing of other root crops. Still farther west there were tribes that depended more on acorns. Corn growing affected the customs of most of the Indians who lived east of the upper Mississippi from Virginia through New England.

Plants have figured in the civilization of man because of the role they have played in providing him with shelter from the elements. This is true whether it refers to the shelter gained through clothing or the shelter gained by using plants to make dwellings. The use of plants in this connection changed as man developed the necessary skills in weaving, spinning, beating, and otherwise treating fibers for use as shelter.

Some of the earliest records of man in America show that early Americans used plants considerably. The earlier cave dwellers who found their way underground with the help of torches of burning reeds, wore grass sandals. The sandals and torches of some of these early peoples are still to be seen in some of our museums. Whether man used plant materials in the making of garments before he used them for fuel seems doubtful, but it is probable that plants were used as food before they had either of these uses.

Plants supplied early man with weapons in the form of clubs, spears, arrows and bows, with equipment such as boats and pack-carrying outfits, with dyes, trinkets, and medicines. Some were even used as measures of wealth. And from each of these early beginnings have sprung greater and greater uses as knowledge of plants and their uses has increased.

Early man used plants as he found them or merely carved, bent, and shaped them to his needs. Modern man is more concerned with plant materials that may serve as raw substances from which better materials may be produced than are found in nature. From inferior grades of trees we now make plastic woods that are lighter and stronger than any natural woods. Instead of feeding mulberry leaves to silkworms, we now feed slash pine and many small woody plants into machines that chew them to a pulp. This pulp we treat with chemicals until we finally have a rayon fiber superior in many

ways to the silk we got from the silkworm. And there is relatively little human labor involved in its manufacture.

The system of breaking plant materials down into raw substances and combining them into more useful substances has solved many problems. It also has created problems. Through the use of machines, we can get a superior fiber from inferior plants. But, at the same time, we may throw out of work persons who once earned a livelihood by doing relatively simple jobs.

The vast stores of oil that have supplied us with fuel are rapidly disappearing from the earth, and new substitutes must be found. Undoubtedly plants will be considered as fuel sources.

What goes on before your eyes at the surface of the earth is going to be increasingly important. As minerals in mines become exhausted, we are going to get substitutes from plants dependent on the topsoil. We can not replace the minerals, so we must develop new topsoil to support new plants in greater abundance to meet increased demands. There is nothing to be distressed about in the situation. Rather, there is a wholesome challenge to us to help make better use of the resources of the world. A newer and greater responsibility will come to the raiser of plants when we have to get fuel from plants instead of from oil wells, when plastics from plants replace minerals from mines, and when modern means of transportation open to settlement vast parts of the earth that have been unpopulated by man because they could not supply some one or few elements that are essential to man's survival.

How Man Has Changed Plants

Man can improve his use of plants in two ways. One way is by breeding plants and improving each kind of plant individually. The other way is by discovering new kinds of plants and developing them for his own use. The second method is called *plant exploration*.

At first man was content to eat the plants where he found them. Later he noticed that some kinds of plants were better than others. He saved the seed from these plants to grow new ones. In this way the basic food crops of the world were developed.

With the development of the science of genetics, new ways have been found of improving plants. Man has changed plants greatly from their original forms. A

486

PLANT ODDITIES

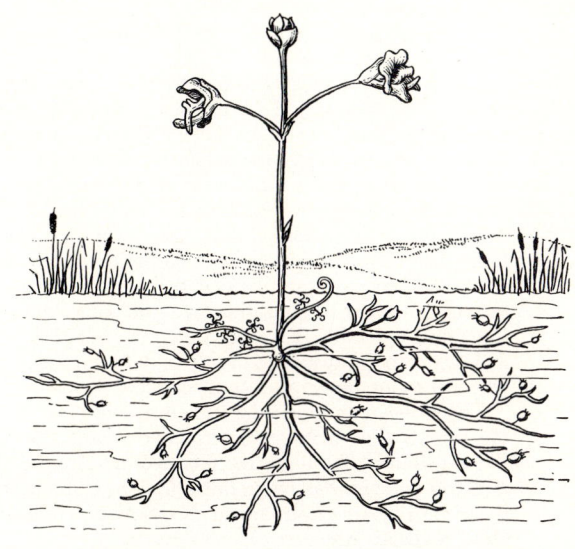

The Sundew feeds on insects which are trapped by its sticky leaves. The leaves curl in about the entangled insects, and the plant absorbs them.

The Bladderwort has pouches, or bladders, on its roots which trap insects that enter them. Although the plant lives under water most of the year, at blossoming time the bladders fill with air and the plant rises to the surface.

Victoria Regia, the giant water lily, grows leaves as much as four feet across. Some are strong enough to support a man. The huge water plant blossoms at night.

Duckweeds are so tiny that 7,000,000 of them could be placed side by side on a Victoria regia leaf.

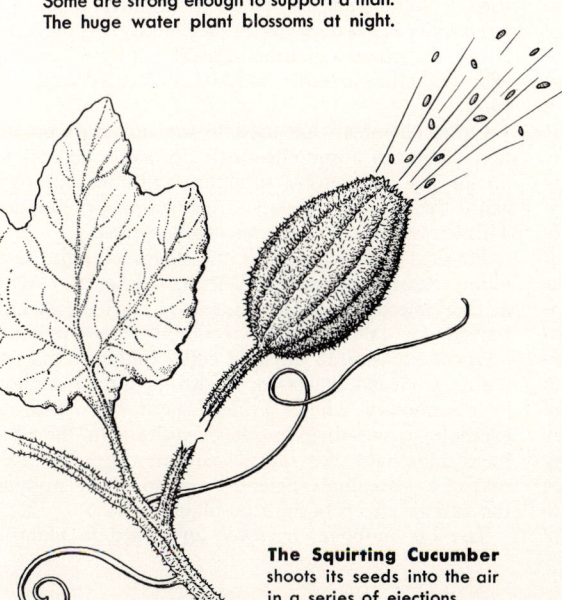

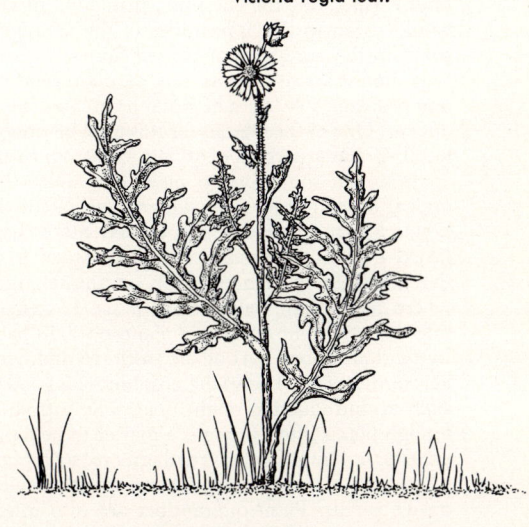

The Squirting Cucumber shoots its seeds into the air in a series of ejections.

The Compass Plant deserves its name. Its leaves and branches point in the directions of the cardinal points of the compass.

PLANT

Russian scientist, N. I. Vavilov, cultivated more than 35,000 different strains of wheat.

Plants are bred for a great many different purposes. Some are changed in order to improve the quality of the food they produce. The tomatoes we grow in our garden, for example, are quite different from the original tomato and taste much better. Other plants are bred so that they can grow in places where little rain falls. Still others resist the attacks of different diseases or insects. Special kinds of corn are grown that have strong roots and do not fall over easily in a high wind. Still other plants will produce food earlier in the growing season. Others have been bred so that they will require less human labor in their growing. And some kinds of fruits and vegetables have been bred so that they will look better to the customer, or ship better from the place where they are grown to distant markets.

The soybean and the tung tree are among the important plants that plant explorers have brought to the United States. The tung tree produces a valuable oil, and the soybean has by-products that have increased the income of American farmers. See SOYBEAN (picture: How Soybeans Are Used).

Among the most remarkable developments in plant breeding has been the discovery of new plants which offer a better food supply to the human race. Plants are now being bred for an increased supply of vitamins, as well as for many other important food elements.

In 1900, the chestnut was abundant throughout the northeastern part of the United States. It has now practically disappeared, chiefly because of the attack of a chestnut blight disease. Men are now working to develop a cross between the survivors of this native chestnut with some foreign chestnut that can resist the disease. This is done in the hope that the resultant cross between the two kinds may have the good qualities of both.

There are other trees that might possibly die out should diseases known to them get out of control. The Dutch elm disease, for example, might eventually wipe out all our American elms, much as the chestnut blight wiped out the chestnut. Just think of what this would mean to the appearance of the average village street in the northeastern United States.

It almost seems that as soon as plant workers solve one problem, new ones of equal or greater importance appear. One of the reasons for this may be traced to the habit of many persons of trying to introduce into any environment some foreign plant or animal that may appeal to their fancy. The danger associated with such practice is so great that the United States has established a plant quarantine system designed to prevent the introduction of new plants or animals into areas where they might well become pests. In general, it is safe to say that the sending of plants or plant parts, even by mail, from one part of the world to another is dangerous unless one knows the possibility for good or harm such an introduction might hold. The introduction of foreign plants into an area is a matter to be handled by experts, not by amateurs. Furthermore, such plants may often carry diseases or animal parasites that will ravage native plants. Plant quarantines are also intended to prevent exceptionally useful plants from getting out of an area. Such a quarantine was once tried in Brazil to keep the valuable rubber trees from being shipped to other countries.

Science Studies Plant Life

Man's knowledge about plants has greatly increased since a hundred years ago, when Justus von Liebig, the German scientist, discovered what elements in the soil were necessary for the successful growth of plants. Yet, as thoroughly as plants and their habits have been studied, there are probably a great many plants that might be useful to man still waiting to be discovered. This is particularly true in tropical lands. Some of these plants may prove to be as important to our civilization as the potato, corn, or the tobacco plant, none of which was known in the Old World before Columbus discovered America.

Important research in genetics and breeding has been carried on by means of X rays and a drug called *colchicine* (see COLCHICUM). Both the X rays and the drug seem to affect the central units of heredity, called *genes*, in the plant cells. Sometimes the number of genes in the cell is doubled. Then the offspring will be much larger than the parents. Seeds have been exposed to the explosions of atomic bombs under a great variety of conditions. Few persons question that the use of atomic energy may affect greatly the plants exposed to it. We do not know what the eventual results of such exposure may turn out to be.

Chemicals are being used to change the way plants grow. Some chemicals can make roots grow on plants where formerly they did not grow. Other chemicals called *auxins* affect the growth of plants and increase it markedly.

Fruit is often stored in atmosphere which contains much carbon dioxide so that the fruit will not decay too rapidly. As a result, many fruits and vegetables may be made to last longer and cost less. On the other hand, if an orange, for example, is placed in an atmosphere containing much of the gas *ethylene* it will ripen more quickly. Other chemicals, both vitamins and hormones, have been used to stimulate the growth of plants. In recent years such hormones have been used to kill plants as well as to improve them. The weed killer 2,4-D depends for its effectiveness on stimulating the growth of broad-leaved plants to such an extent that the plants die. See AUXIN; WEED (Weed Control).

Other chemicals are used to increase fruit production of plants. Some chemicals, for example, sprayed on the first blossoms of tomatoes and cucumbers will cause the fruit to develop earlier without pollination. This leads to more or less seedless varieties.

Physical effects, such as the effect of light upon plants, have been studied. Doctors Garner and Allard of the United States Department of Agriculture have proved, for example, that regulating the number of hours of exposure to daylight could influence the way plants produced flowers or foodstuffs. Growing plants in greenhouses where artificial light was used, for example, made them produce earlier. On the other hand, blue light seems to slow up plant growth in the case of oat seedlings. Scientists are still busy studying the various effects of light on plant growth.

The big problem, however, in regard to plants is

488

the intense study of the process of photosynthesis. Scientists are studying how plants produce food by means of photosynthesis and are trying to duplicate the way chlorophyll works.　　　　E. Laurence Palmer

Related Articles. See Botany with its list of Related Articles. See also the following:

KINDS OF PLANTS

Algae	Grass	Poisonous	Vegetable
Carnivorous	Herb	Plant	Vine
Plant	Legume	Shrub	Water
Fern	Lichen	Teasel	Plant
Fungi	Moss	Tree	Weed
Gourd	Mushroom		

PARTS OF PLANTS

Bark	Cellulose	Fruit	Root
Bud	Chlorophyll	Grain	Sap
Bulb	Chloroplast	Leaf	Seed
Catkin	Cotyledon	Nut	Stem
Cell	Flower	Phloem	Wood

PLANT BREEDING AND GROWING

Adaptation	Gardening	Photoperiodism
Agriculture	Grafting	Photosynthesis
Auxin	Growth	Pollen and
Breeding	(Plant Growth)	Pollination
Dwarf (Dwarf	Herbarium	Reproduction
Plants)	Hybrid	(Plant)
Farm and	Hydroponics	Soil
Farming	Nursery	Terrarium
Gametophyte		

PLANT DISEASES AND PESTS

Aphid	Dutch Elm Disease	Phylloxera
Apple Maggot	Ergot	Pink Bollworm
Army Worm	Fungus Disease	Potato Bug
Bean Beetle	Gall	Rose Chafer
Blight	Grain Weevil	Rot
Boll Weevil	Gypsy Moth	Rust
Brown-Tail Moth	Japanese Beetle	San Jose Scale
Cankerworm	Leafhopper	Scale Insect
Chafer	Measuring Worm	Smut
Codling Moth	Mediterranean	Tent Caterpillar
Corn Borer	Fruit Fly	Thrips
Corn Ear Worm	Mildew	Tussock Moth
Cutworm	Mosaic Disease	Weevil
Damping Off	Parasite	Wilt
Disease (Plant	Peach Moth	Wireworm
Diseases)		

PLANT PRODUCTS

Bay Rum	Fiber	Perfume	Tar
Cattail	Food	Resin	Tobacco
Drug	Gutta-Percha	Rosin	Turpentine
Dyes and	Humus	Rubber	Veneer
Dyeing	Lumber	Snuff	

OTHER RELATED ARTICLES

Agronomy	Classification	Plant Quarantine
Animal (The Impor-	Embryophyte	Pteridophyte
tance of Animals)	Fossil	Thallophyte
Biological Clock	Habitat	Topiary Work
Botanical Garden	Horticulture	

Outline

Questions

About how many different kinds of plants do scientists know?

How would you explain the statement "All the food we eat comes from plants?"

In what ways do we use plants besides for food?

How may plants be harmful to man?

How can we tell plants from animals?

How are trees different from shrubs?

What is a biennial plant? A perennial? An annual?

How did plants supply early man with weapons?

How do plants make their food?

What is cross-pollination? In what ways does cross-pollination take place?

Books for Young Readers

Blough, Glenn O. *Discovering Plants.* McGraw, 1966.

Fenton, Carroll L., and Kitchen, H. B. *Plants That Feed Us.* Day, 1956. An account of 36 familiar grains and vegetables.

Frisch, Rose E. *Plants That Feed the World.* Van Nostrand, 1966.

Selsam, Millicent. *Play with Plants.* Morrow, 1949. *Plants We Eat.* 1955. *Plants that Heal.* 1959. *How to Grow House Plants.* 1960. *Plants that Move.* 1962.

Sterling, Dorothy. *The Story of Mosses, Ferns and Mushrooms.* Doubleday, 1955.

Webber, Irma E. *Up Above and Down Below.* W. R. Scott, 1943. An easy text about plants above and below ground. *Travelers All: The Story of How Plants Go Places.* 1944. *Bits That Grow Big: Where Plants Come From.* 1949.

Zim, Herbert S. *Plants: A Guide to Plant Hobbies.* Harcourt, 1947. *What's Inside of Plants?* Morrow, 1952.

Books for Older Readers

Bold, Harold C. *The Plant Kingdom.* 2nd ed. Prentice-Hall, 1964.

Dodge, Bertha S. *Plants That Changed the World.* Little, Brown, 1959.

Gray, Asa. *Manual of Botany: A Handbook of the Flowering Plants and Ferns of the Central and Northeastern United States and Adjacent Canada.* 8th centennial ed. American Book Co., 1950.

Hylander, Clarence J. *The World of Plant Life.* 2nd ed. Macmillan, 1956.

Jaques, Harry E. *Plant Families: How to Know Them.* 2nd ed. 1948.

Lehner, Ernst and Johanna. *Folklore and Odysseys of Food and Medicinal Plants.* Tudor, 1962.

Nelson, Kennard S. *Flower and Plant Production in the Greenhouse.* Interstate, 1966.

Stefferud, Alfred. *The Wonders of Seeds.* Harcourt, 1956.

PLANT, AQUATIC. See Water Plant.

PLANT BREEDING. See Breeding.

PLANT COMMUNITY. See Ecology; Plant (Where Plants Live).

PLANT LOUSE. See Aphid.

PLANT QUARANTINE laws regulate the movement both of plants and of other materials that may carry a plant disease or insect pest. The reason for the quarantine is to keep the disease or insect from spreading from infested areas. Some laws list plants which may not be shipped in and out of a locality. They may also give directions for moving, packing, and labeling.

In a quarantine, officials may examine all plants at the border of the quarantined area and keep out the dangerous types. Other laws merely require an inspection of the plants or the place where they were grown.

Foreign plant quarantines control the shipping of plants from other countries. Foreign quarantines include those intended to keep out white-pine blister rust, Dutch elm disease, and the European pine-shoot moth. Domestic quarantines control plant movements from place to place within the country. They protect against stem rust, gypsy moth, Japanese beetle, white-pine blister rust, and the white-fringed beetle.

In the United States, local, state, and federal governments may quarantine plants. The Agriculture Research Service in the Department of Agriculture helps enforce federal quarantines of plants that may carry diseases or insect pests.   WILLIAM R. VAN DERSAL

See also INSECT (The Importance of Insects).

PLANTAGENET, *plan TAJ uh net,* was the family name of a line of kings that ruled England from 1154 to 1399. The kings descended from the marriage of Matilda, daughter of King Henry I, to Geoffrey, count of Anjou, France. Geoffrey was nicknamed *Plantagenet* because he wore a sprig of the broom (*genet*) plant in his cap. Many historians call these kings *Angevins.*

The Plantagenet dynasty began with Henry II, son of Matilda and Geoffrey. Henry ruled from 1154 to 1189 over England and vast possessions in France. He centralized the English government, established peace and order, and founded the English common law system. His son, Richard the Lion-Hearted, led the Third Crusade and ruled from 1189 to 1199. Richard's younger brother John succeeded him and ruled from 1199 to 1216. King John lost most of England's French possessions, and was forced to grant the Magna Carta in 1215 (see MAGNA CARTA).

John's son, Henry III, ruled ineffectively from 1216 to 1272. Henry's son, Edward I, ruled from 1272 to 1307, conquered Wales and most of Scotland, and improved the English government and legal system. Edward's son, Edward II, lost Scotland, was deposed by Parliament, and then murdered by barons in 1327. His son, Edward III, ruled from 1327 to 1377 and began the *Hundred Years' War* with France. After Edward III's grandson, Richard II, was deposed in 1399, the Plantagenets split into the houses of Lancaster and York. These two houses then ruled England until 1485 (see LANCASTER; YORK).   BRYCE LYON

See also the separate biographies in WORLD BOOK for each ruler mentioned, such as HENRY (II) of England.

PLANTAIN, *PLAN tin,* is the common name of a group of low-growing herbs, several of which are common weeds. The *common,* or *broad-leaf,* plantain which gardeners find so troublesome may be recognized in spring by its rosette of broad light-green leaves that grow from the roots. Tall, slender spikes grow up from the center of the leaf clusters. These spikes are thickly

Broad, Shiny Green Leaves and the tall spikes of tiny flowers make it easy to identify the common plantain. ▶

covered with tiny green flowers all summer. The common plantain is spread by birds, which eagerly eat the seeds and help scatter them about. Plantain seeds are also fed to cage birds. Other plantains include the *narrow-leaf plantain,* or *rib grass,* which has narrow leaves and short, thick spikes; and the *seaside plantain* with leaves used in medicine to lessen inflammation.

A tropical plant called the plantain is a kind of banana. The fruit of this plant looks much like the banana, but is not so sweet or so pleasing in flavor. This fruit forms one of the chief articles of food in tropical countries. A type of flour is made from the fruit.

Scientific Classification. Plantains belong to the plantain family, *Plantaginaceae.* The broad-leaf plantain is genus *Plantago,* species *P. major.* The narrow-leaf is *P. lanceolata.* The seaside plantain is *P. maritima.*   ARTHUR CRONQUIST

PLANTAIN LILY. See DAY LILY.

PLANTATION is a large land area where workmen usually grow a single crop. The most common plantation crops are cocoa, coffee, cotton, rice, rubber, sugar cane, bananas, pineapple, and other kinds of tropical fruit. Most plantations are found in rich, level land areas in the tropical and subtropical regions of the world.

Plantations vary widely, depending largely upon their stage in development. Three separate types of plantations may be characterized as those that use slave labor, "free" labor, and skilled labor.

Slave-Labor Plantations were established by western Europeans in the colonies they established throughout the world. The Europeans furnished money and management for plantation development and also the market for what was produced. Most of the plantation workers were slaves or *indentured servants* who were bound by contract to serve a landowner. They usually worked long hours in large gangs, and received barely

Nature Magazine

United Press Int.

Bomblike Containers, *left,* are used to freeze a plasma-and-alcohol mixture at −70°C. This process is the final step in producing gamma globulin.

Jars of Whole Blood, *right,* are assembled in a laboratory for separation of plasma. Plasma remains when red and white cells are removed from the blood. The plasma then can be broken down into other parts, such as gamma globulin.

Wide World

enough food to live on. They enjoyed few of the comforts of life. Few forms of near slavery still exist. Plantation owners were the ruling class in society then. Plantations were operated with slave labor in America from the colonial period until slavery was abolished in 1863. After that date, plantations operated with free labor.

"Free"-Labor Plantations came into use when slavery fell into disrepute. These large farming units produced single crops and paid low wages to hired hands. Laborers who worked for wages and *sharecroppers* (farmers who worked for a share of the crop) did most of the work. But they usually depended on the plantation owner for food and the necessities of daily living and soon became indebted to him. Various degrees of semislavery developed, including *peonage*. Peons are forced to work to pay off debts. Each sharecropper received a share of the crop from a specific piece of land on which he usually did all the work. Wage laborers worked in gangs and received wages or had an open account at the plantation *commissary* (supply store). Many such plantations still exist today, and their owners form the ruling class in the regions in which they are located.

Skilled-Labor Plantations are now developing in some areas. Sharecroppers and wage hands are disappearing. Since World War II, plantation agriculture in the United States has changed rapidly. Machines and skilled workmen are now being used instead of mule power and hand labor. Laborers receive higher wages and live better than plantation workers did in earlier days. Plantations no longer use gangs of slaves or peons. A more democratic society has replaced the rule by plantation owners. In many areas, plantations are being broken up, and the land is being distributed among the former plantation workers.   MARSHALL HARRIS

See also COLONIAL LIFE IN AMERICA (color picture: Southern Plantation); MISSISSIPPI (Places to Visit).

PLANTATION OF IRELAND. See NORTHERN IRELAND (How Northern Ireland Became a Country).

PLANTING. See FARM AND FARMING.

PLANTS, DISEASES OF. See DISEASE (Plant Diseases).

PLASMA, *PLAZ muh,* is the straw-colored liquid part of blood. It is the part that remains when the red and

white blood cells are removed. Plasma contains water, salts, proteins, and other materials.

Plasma carries dissolved food materials to all parts of the body. It picks up waste materials, produced by the body cells, and carries them to the organs that remove wastes from the body. Plasma also carries secretions from certain glands in the body.

Proteins. One of the proteins found in plasma is called *fibrinogen*. If it were not for this remarkable substance, you would bleed to death from the slightest cut. Fibrinogen makes it possible for the blood to clot and seal off the wound.

Another protein contained in plasma is called *globulin*. Globulin carries disease-fighting substances known as *antibodies* (see ANTIBODY). These are produced by your body when you have a disease. The antibodies help destroy germs, and, in addition, help prevent you from getting the disease again. When this occurs, you have developed an *immunity* to the disease. Most antibodies are concentrated in a portion of the globulin protein called *gamma globulin*. Doctors use gamma globulin to help prevent infectious jaundice, measles, and other diseases.

A third protein that is found in plasma is called *albumin*. It is the same kind of substance that makes up the white of an egg. Albumin helps keep the blood volume and blood pressure normal.

Preparation. During the 1930's, researchers found that plasma could be separated from whole blood. Plasma is obtained by separating out the blood cells in a machine called a *centrifuge* (see CENTRIFUGE). The liquid plasma can be kept for a much longer time than whole blood. Plasma can also be frozen or dried. In these forms it can be kept indefinitely.

Uses of Plasma. Plasma is used for blood transfusions when whole blood is not needed or cannot be obtained. It is also used commonly to restore blood volume lost during severe bleeding. It has saved the lives of millions of soldiers injured in battle, and of persons injured in accidents. Plasma often is used during operations to combat the condition known as shock. It works almost as well as whole blood in treating shock and in replacing blood depleted during bleeding.

In certain diseases, the body is literally starved for a protein which has been broken down into a form that can be used. Scientists have learned how to produce

491

such substances from plasma and from other materials.

Artificial Plasmas. Scientists have tried to find safe substitutes for plasma. But substitutes are not as effective as whole blood or plasma. AUSTIN EDWARD SMITH

See also ALBUMIN; BLOOD; GLOBULIN; SERUM; TRANSFUSION, BLOOD.

PLASMA, in physics, is a gas that contains nearly equal numbers of positively- and negatively-charged particles, usually positive ions and electrons. Plasma is generated by ionizing a gas, either by heating it to a high temperature or by passing high-energy electrons through it. The atmosphere of a star is a plasma generated by heat. The glowing gas in a neon sign is a plasma generated by electrons passing through neon gas.

Plasma may provide the means to harness a *thermonuclear reaction*, the same reaction that causes an H-bomb explosion. Scientists control plasma with electric or magnetic fields. If they can create a thermonuclear reaction within a hydrogen plasma, they may be able to control the reaction so that the energy it releases may be used to produce power. Scientists could start a thermonuclear reaction within a hydrogen plasma if they could raise the temperature of the plasma to about 100,000,-000° C. They hope to attain this temperature by delivering energy to a plasma while it is held away from container walls by a magnetic field. This energy may be delivered as electromagnetic energy or as the kinetic energy of particles externally accelerated. Heat from the reaction could then be used to generate steam, which in turn could be used to produce electric power. See ATOMIC ENERGY (Nuclear Fusion).

Another possible use of plasma is for electrical rockets. In this application a very high exhaust velocity could be created by utilizing electrical power generated on the spaceship to accelerate a plasma. While only small vehicle accelerations can be produced with engines of this type, they can operate for very long periods of time. These engines would be more effective than chemical reaction engines for interplanetary travel. See ROCKET (Rockets of the Future). A. THEODORE FORRESTER

PLASMODIUM. See MALARIA; SLIME MOLD.

PLASSEY, BATTLE OF. See CLIVE, ROBERT.

PLASTER OF PARIS is a white powder that, when mixed with water to form a paste, will turn hard in a few minutes. This substance is used for casting small statuary, for surgical casts, for enveloping the wax impressions of teeth made by dentists, and for many other purposes. Plaster of Paris is made by heating gypsum, a stone that is composed of calcium sulfate and water. When the water is driven off, the gypsum becomes a powder. When water is added again, the mass hardens to a stonelike substance which is similar to the original gypsum.

See also GYPSUM.

PLASTERING. Plaster is a mortar coating that is applied to the inside wall surfaces and ceilings of buildings to make them more airtight and to provide a finished surface. Plastering is putting the plaster on these inside walls. When plaster is put on outside walls, it is called stuccoing (see STUCCO).

Plasterers use a plaster that is made of sand and a cementing agent, such as gypsum, lime, or Portland cement. The ingredients are mixed with water. Hair or fiber is mixed with the first and second coats to strengthen the plaster. The hair is goat or cattle hair, and the fiber is Manila, jute, or wood fiber.

Lightweight materials such as *perlite* or *vermiculite* may be used instead of sand. These materials absorb sound and are fire resistant.

Plaster Bases. Plaster can be put directly on a masonry wall, but it cannot be put directly on a solid wood wall. The surfaces to which plaster can be applied are called plaster bases. Bases may be of various kinds of building blocks, or brick or stone. Bases may also be made with *laths*. Laths are metal sheets, pieces of gypsum or fiberboard, or wooden strips that are put on the surface to be plastered to provide a better grip for the plaster.

Wood laths are laid parallel, with narrow spaces between them. The plaster enters the spaces and forms wedges, called *keys*. The wedges hold the plaster to the laths. In most modern buildings, gypsum-board or metal laths are used. Metal laths are metal sheets about 2 feet wide and 8 feet long. Open spaces in the sheets allow plaster to penetrate and in this way obtain a firm grip. Gypsum-board has a gypsum plaster core between surfaces of heavy paper. The paper and the core are pressed together to form a plastering surface.

Plastering. The plaster is put on the plaster base with a special tool called a *trowel*. It is smoothed with a tool called a *darby* and may be made more even with a long straightedge called the *rod*. Wood or metal strips, called *grounds*, are placed around openings and along the top of the baseboard as guides for finishing the plaster-

Plasterers Apply the Mortar Coating in two or three coats to finish off the inside walls and ceilings of buildings.

Contracting Plasterers' & Lathers' Int. Assn. and *Plastering Industries* Mag.

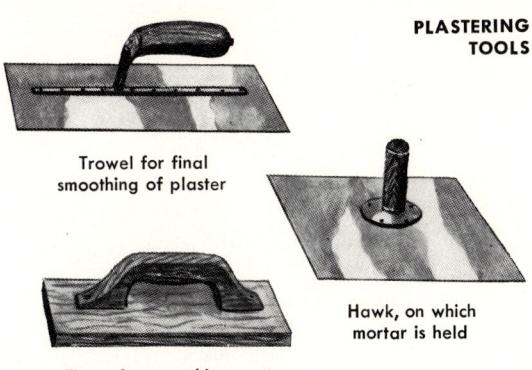

Trowel for final
smoothing of plaster

Hawk, on which
mortar is held

Float, for smoothing mortar

Plastering Tools, *above,* include the trowel, hawk, and float.
The finished wall surfaces, *below,* show two plaster textures.
From *Plasterers' Manual,* Courtesy Portland Cement Assn.

Modern American

English Cottage

ing. If the plastered wall is large, plaster guides called
screeds are made on the scratch coat.

Three coats of plaster should be used if the plaster
is placed on wood or metal lath. But only two coats are
necessary if the plaster is put on a brick or tile surface.

The surface finish of the plaster may be a *white coat*
of lime putty, which has a thick, puttylike consistency
when applied. Gypsum gauging plaster is added
to the putty coat to avoid hair cracking by reducing
shrinkage. The material is formed into a smooth finish
with a steel trowel. The sand-float finish is a rough finish
that is made by going over the last coat of gypsum plaster and sand with a special kind of wood or cork trowel,
called the *float.* The sand-float finish looks like rough
sandpaper. Plasters of special kinds may be applied in
different ways to look like natural stones. The most
common of these are *scagliola,* which is an imitation
marble; imitation *caen* stone; and imitation *travertine*
stone.   GEORGE W. WASHA

See also BUILDING TRADE (Career Opportunities);
CEMENT AND CONCRETE; PLASTER OF PARIS; STAFF.

PLASTIC BOMB is a puttylike explosive that can
be hidden easily because it can be molded into any
shape. The bomb is a mixture of TNT and RDX (also
called hexogen or cyclonite). Only a powerful detonator
can set it off. The U.S. Army developed plastic bombs
during World War II. The bombs became famous in
the early 1960's when a French terrorist group, the
Secret Army Organization (OAS), used them to try to
prevent Algerian independence.

See also RDX.

PLASTIC EYEGLASS. See LENS, CONTACT.

PLASTIC SURGERY is the branch of surgery which has
to do with restoring lost parts of the body, repairing
parts that do not work properly, or improving appearance. It depends upon transplanting living tissue. The
word *plastic* comes from a Greek word meaning to mold
or shape. The two major fields in plastic surgery are
reconstructive surgery and cosmetic surgery.

Reconstructive Surgery repairs and sometimes entirely cures injury sustained in war or in industrial or
traffic accidents. Injured muscles, bones, blood vessels,
and nerves can be restored by surgical means. Sometimes these operations are performed in several stages.

Operations to improve harelip and cleft palate are
outstanding examples of reconstructive surgery. Many
such operations are highly successful. Injuries to the
face involving loss of tissue can often be repaired by
operations. In these operations, flaps of skin and underlying tissue may be transplanted in one step from
thigh to arm. In the second step they are transplanted
from arm to face. Such operations are useful following
gunshot injuries, automobile crash wounds, severe
burns, or other mutilations. The use of tinted, rubber-
like plastics has permitted doctors to restore noses and
ears by fashioning lifelike artificial substitutes.

Following injury or a disease, the course of nerves
may be altered by transplantation. Muscles which remain intact after paralyzing diseases, such as infantile
paralysis, may be used by transplanting their tendons to
replace paralyzed muscles. Unequal limbs can be lengthened or shortened. This is accomplished by taking out
or putting in lengths of bone and by stretching muscles
or permitting them to take up slack.

Plastic artificial eyes have been produced that can
be stitched to the eye muscles so that they may move
exactly as does a normal eye.

Cosmetic Surgery consists in remodeling the nose,
mouth, or ears. One operation is commonly known as
face lifting. This involves taking up the slack of
wrinkled skin by means of incisions concealed within
the hairy area of the scalp. Unless there are good professional reasons for doing face lifting, many surgeons
prefer to avoid it. It is particularly difficult and prone
to failure through infection. But features that are really
repulsive to the extent of interfering with earning a livelihood, or features that make the individual excessively
unhappy, can often be improved through use of cosmetic surgery.

Plastic surgeons may qualify for a diploma from a
board of specialists known as the American Board of
Plastic Surgery, which certifies to their experience and
good repute. Plastic surgery has been a fruitful field for
quacks and unqualified practitioners who make promises they cannot fulfill. The qualifications of a plastic
surgeon should always be checked through the local
medical society or by writing to the American Medical
Association at Chicago.   W. W. BAUER

See also GRAFTING (surgery); SKIN GRAFTING.

PLASTICINE, *PLAS tuh seen,* is an artificial substitute
for modeling clay used by a sculptor. Ordinary modeling clay sometimes dries faster than the sculptor can
work. This forces him to keep moistening it as he
works. But plasticine is an oily type of clay that never
dries or hardens, thus lightening the sculptor's work.

493

PLASTICS

PLASTICS are man-made materials that can be shaped in almost any form. They may be any color of the rainbow, or as clear and colorless as crystal. Plastics may have the hardness of steel or the softness of silk. Manufacturers can shape them into long-wearing machine parts or into women's stockings. The word *plastics* comes from the Greek word *plastikos*, which means *able to be molded*.

Manufacturers make plastics from chemicals. They get these chemicals from basic raw materials such as coal, limestone, petroleum, salt, and water. Solid plastics can be made to look and act like glass, wood, metal, and many other materials. But they usually can be manufactured more cheaply than these materials. Liquid plastics may be used as adhesives and paints.

Products made from plastics are attractive, easy to use, and long-lasting. They brighten homes, schools, offices, and factories. They make our lives more comfortable and our work lighter.

The plastics industry uses the word *plastics* in the plural form to refer to such things as plastics products and plastics materials. Such usage avoids confusion with the term *plastic*. This term describes any material, such as clay, that can be pressed into various shapes.

Types of Plastics

Scientists and engineers have developed hundreds of plastics. These man-made materials have a wide variety of *properties* (characteristics) such as hardness, softness, and transparency. Hard plastics are used in some products, and soft plastics are used in others. Vinyl alloys, for example, can be used in many products because they have a wide range of properties. Some vinyls are hard and others are soft. Some are transparent and others are not. The properties of plastics depend on the chemicals and the methods used to make them.

Hard Plastics, or rigid plastics, are used to make such products as dinnerware, football helmets, and cases for clocks, radios, cameras, and flashlights. The surfaces of

J. Harry DuBois, the contributor of this article, is a plastics company executive and author of the books Plastics *and* Plastics Mold Engineering.

PLASTICS ARE USED THROUGHOUT THE HOME

Many kinds of plastics may be found in furniture, appliances, decorations, toys, and special materials that protect the home from wear and the weather.

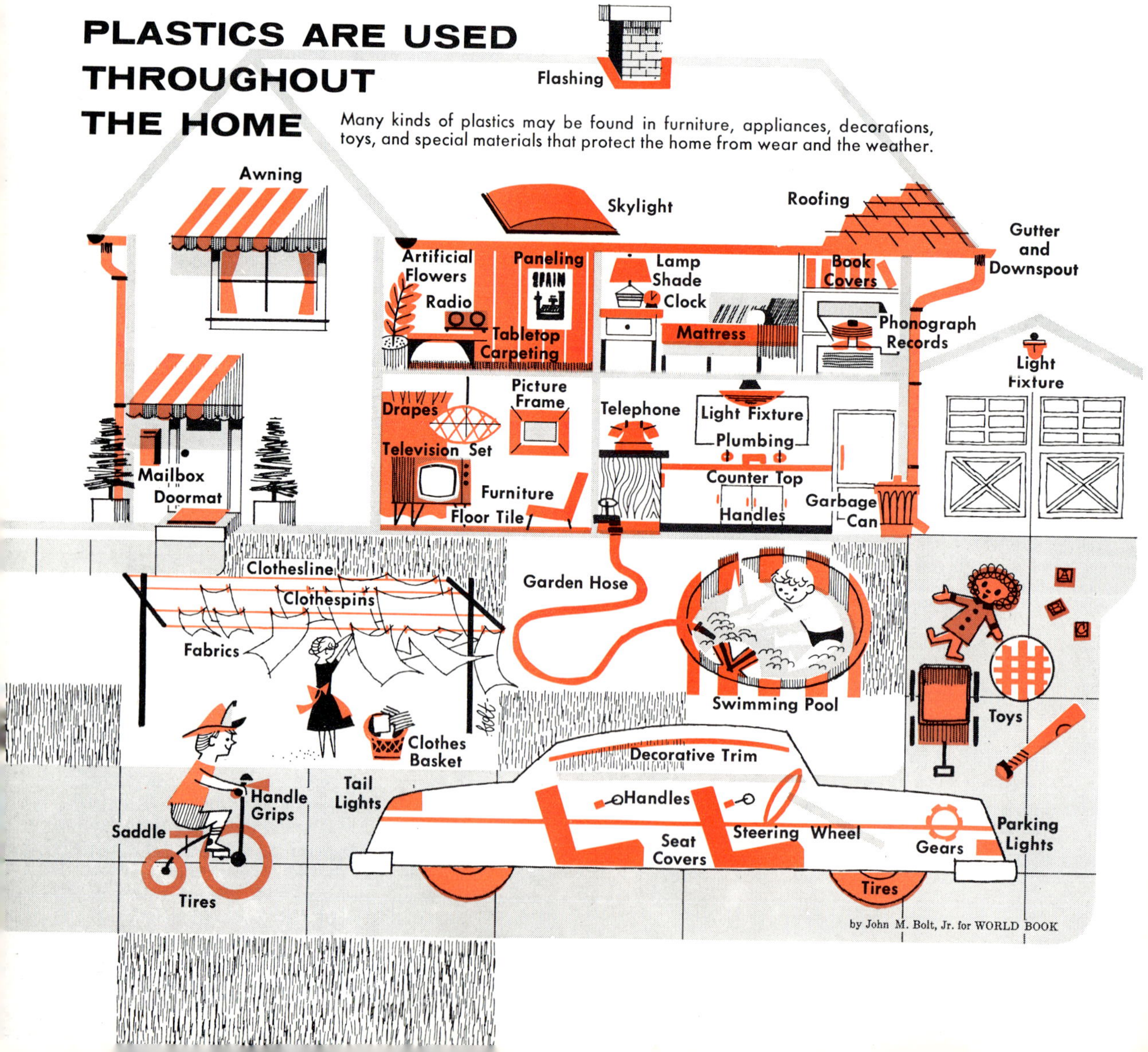

Flashing

Awning

Skylight

Roofing

Gutter and Downspout

Artificial Flowers

Paneling

Radio

Lamp Shade

Clock

Book Covers

Tabletop

Carpeting

Mattress

Phonograph Records

Light Fixture

Picture Frame

Drapes

Telephone

Light Fixture

Plumbing

Television Set

Counter Top

Mailbox

Doormat

Furniture

Handles

Garbage Can

Floor Tile

Clothesline

Garden Hose

Clothespins

Fabrics

Swimming Pool

Toys

Clothes Basket

Decorative Trim

Handle Grips

Tail Lights

Handles

Seat Covers

Steering Wheel

Gears

Parking Lights

Saddle

Tires

Tires

by John M. Bolt, Jr. for WORLD BOOK

these products resist wear and scratching. Examples of hard plastics include *melamines, phenolics, epoxy,* and *alkyds.* Many plastics become stronger and harder when mixed with substances such as finely ground wood, metallic compounds, glass fibers, and asbestos. These substances are called *fillers.* When mixed with fillers, epoxy compounds become so hard and strong that they can be used to make dies for shaping metal. Plastics strengthened by sheets or mats of glass fibers, cloth, or paper are called *reinforced plastics.*

Fabrics woven from plastics fibers feel soft, but the fibers are made from hard plastics. *Nylon* is hard enough to be used to make gears for machinery. But when drawn into fine threads, nylon can be used to weave delicate stockings and lingerie.

Soft Plastics, or flexible plastics, include *polyethylenes, silicones, soft vinyls,* and *urethanes.* These plastics are used to make flexible products such as toys, squeeze bottles, dishpans, and laundry baskets.

Some plastics are *foamed* to make soft spongelike materials used in cushions for furniture and automobiles. Plastics engineers can increase the softness of some plastics by combining them with other plastics, or by adding chemicals called *plasticizers.*

Transparent Plastics may be either hard or soft. Some are colored, and others are as clear as glass. Common transparent plastics include *polystyrenes, vinyls, acrylics,* and *polyethylenes.* These plastics are widely used as envelopes to package food, medicines, toys,

---

PLASTICS TERMS

Accelerator is a chemical that speeds up the hardening of liquid resins.

Ceramoplastics are heat-resistant inorganic plastics made by combining synthetic mica and glass.

Cold Mold is a name for resins that are pressed into an unheated mold, then hardened by heat or steam.

Filler, when added to a synthetic resin, gives it extra hardness and strength. Common fillers include ground wood, metallic compounds, glass fibers, and asbestos.

Monofilament is a plastics material that has been forced through a small hole to form a single fiber.

Oleoresinous refers to plastics that contain drying oils or resins.

Organosol is a plastisol containing chemicals that control its "pastiness."

Plasticizer, when added to certain synthetic resins, makes them softer and more flexible.

Plastisol is a pasty liquid made of particles of resin in a chemical softener. It is used as a molding and casting compound or as a fabric coating.

Postforming is a process used to bend or shape a hardened thermosetting laminate.

Reinforced Plastics are strong, lightweight combinations of plastics with glass fibers, cloth, or paper.

Resinoid is a thermosetting synthetic resin.

Scintillation Plastics give off flashes of light when exposed to radioactive energy. They are used to detect nuclear and cosmic radiation.

Shell Molding or **Solvent Molding** is a method of forming thin, shell-like plastics products. The surface of a mold is coated with a resin dissolved in a chemical called a *solvent.* As the solvent evaporates, the resin hardens on the mold surface and forms a thin shell.

Stereochemistry is the science of making plastics with special properties by "building" molecules with definite arrangements of atoms.

ADVANTAGES OF PLASTICS

Hard Plastics are lightweight protectors that can take rugged treatment without losing their shape or beauty.

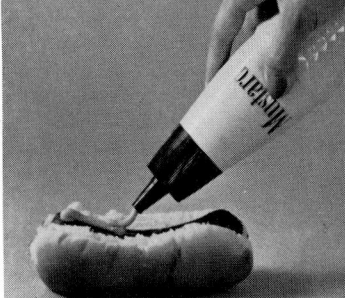

Soft Plastics that bend at the touch of a finger make colorful containers for a variety of household products.

Transparent Plastics keep food and other products fresh and clean, and allow the customer to see what he buys.

Decorative Plastics capture the beauty of flowers and of materials such as polished marble and fine wood.

Resistant Plastics make attractive handles and other parts that withstand the heat produced by appliances.

Plastics Fibers and Fabrics range from delicate thread in women's stockings to durable materials for drapes and rugs.

by Martin-Trlak Inc.
for WORLD BOOK

clothing, and many other products. Soft transparent plastics slipcovers protect furniture without hiding its beauty. Hard clear plastics take the place of glass in watch crystals and optical lenses. Contact lenses made of acrylic are more transparent and less fragile than lenses made of glass.

Decorative Plastics often look like gold, silver, marble, wood, or leather. Manufacturers create these effects (1) by coloring the plastics, (2) by giving them special coatings or surface textures, or (3) by combining them with other materials. Plastics wall and floor tiles brighten many homes, stores, and offices. Plastics with special textures are used to make shoes, belts, and luggage. Toys, novelties, and jewelry are made from plastics coated with thin metal films. Layers of plastics joined together or combined with other materials form hard-wearing tabletops and wall coverings. These layered combinations are called *laminates*. In some laminates, the plastics are joined to paper that has been printed with the natural grain of marble or wood.

Resistant Plastics withstand heat and chemicals. Engineers use asbestos-filled *phenolics* to make rocket nose cones that must withstand high temperatures. Chemists use containers and pipes made of plastics to store chemicals and to move them from one place to another. Laminated phenolics, used in homes for tables and counters, resist burns and stains.

Plastics Fibers and Fabrics have special properties that make them suitable for clothing and other textile products. Plastics used to make textiles can be drawn into fine threads, then woven or knitted into fabrics. These fabrics are strong, light, and stain-resistant. Examples of plastics fibers include *nylon*, *Orlon*, *Dacron*, and *Dynel*. See FIBER (Synthetic Fibers).

Special Uses of Plastics

Each kind of plastics has many properties. By studying these properties, scientists and engineers can choose the best plastics for any job. Because plastics have many special properties, they can do certain jobs better than other materials. In some cases, only plastics can be used at a reasonable cost.

In Industry. Tough, long-wearing plastics make excellent machine parts. Plastics gears and bearings run silently and need little or no oiling. Plastics adhesives, such as epoxy resins, can permanently join metals. Such "welding" is used in making some aluminum bicycle frames. Silicone plastics serve as lubricants.

In various industries, plastics do highly specialized jobs. Laminated phenolic boards form a thin base for circuits in television sets and other electronic devices. Metallic strips on the surface of these boards take the place of wires in the circuit. In the petroleum industry, microscopic plastics spheres are used to prevent evaporation from huge storage tanks. Millions of these tiny spheres float on the oil and seal it against evaporation.

In Architecture and Home Building, reinforced polyester plastics can be made to look like marble, old stone, and many other materials. Colorful panels of *translucent* (partly transparent) plastics beautify many buildings, both inside and outside. Cement blocks can be made to look like glazed tile by coating them with layers of hard glossy plastics.

Plastics finishes provide protection against the weather. Builders use alkyd paints made from plastics resins. They also use siding material and roof coverings made of plastics. Spongelike foamed plastics make excellent insulators against heat and cold. The foam does not rot, and it is vermin-proof.

In Medicine, certain plastics have important uses for two main reasons. (1) They do not harm the body. (2) They are not affected by chemicals in the body.

Doctors use plastics rivets, screws, and plates to join broken bones. They sew up wounds and surgical incisions with plastics thread. Surgeons can replace parts of the intestines with sections made of plastics. They insert plastics devices into the heart to take the place of faulty valves. Medical specialists use strong lightweight plastics to make artificial arms, legs, and other body parts. The plastics parts are made to match the skin color of the patient. Some artificial hands have a plastics "skin," complete with fingerprints.

Dentists use plastics adhesives to cement inlays in place. Dentures can be made quickly and easily when shaped in plastics molds. The molds reproduce the tiniest details, and do not shrink as they harden. As a result, the dentures fit properly and comfortably. Many dentures themselves are made of plastics.

In Science. Polyethylene plastics make good shields for *nuclear reactors* (atomic power plants). They absorb neutrons better than an equally thick shield of concrete or water, yet are much lighter. Because of its low weight, polyethylene shielding is especially valuable in atomic submarines and merchant ships. Other plastics, called *scintillation plastics*, can detect radioactivity. They are used to detect nuclear explosions and to study cosmic radiation. The action of these plastics resembles that of a Geiger counter. When they absorb radioactive energy, they give off light waves that can be recorded by electronic equipment.

How Plastics Are Made

The substances used to make plastics are called *synthetic resins*. These synthetic resins are made from chemicals that come from such natural resources as coal, limestone, petroleum, salt, and water. Chemical manufacturers make the resins and sell them to companies that make plastics products. These firms shape the resins into toys, dinnerware, rocket parts, and many other items.

Making Synthetic Resins. To understand how synthetic resins are made, it is helpful to know something about the chemistry of plastics. Synthetic resins consist of billions of tiny invisible particles called *molecules*. Each molecule contains even tinier particles called *atoms*—chiefly of carbon, hydrogen, oxygen, and nitrogen. Chemists often picture a molecule of synthetic resin as a long chain. Each "link" of the chain is a group of atoms called a *monomer*. The chainlike molecule is called a *polymer*. Making synthetic resins can be thought of as "building" polymers.

Resin manufacturers build polymers by combining chemical compounds. These compounds range from *ammonia* and *benzene* to chemicals with tongue-twisting names such as *hexamethylenetetramine*. When the manufacturer combines the compounds, various chemical reactions take place. The reactions cause certain atoms to cluster together and form the monomer "links." The monomers are then "connected" into a chainlike molecule by a process called *polymerization*. This process changes the substance into a synthetic resin.

The steps in polymer-building can be illustrated by the production of *polystyrene* resin. To make polystyrene, the chemical manufacturer starts with the liquid *benzene* and the gas *ethylene*. (Both chemicals come from petroleum.)

First, the manufacturer bubbles the ethylene through the benzene. During this process, the two compounds react to form the liquid *ethylbenzene*.

Next, the chemical maker uses the ethylbenzene to make the liquid *styrene*. He does this by heating ethylbenzene gas to a high temperature, and bringing it into contact with certain metal oxides. This process removes some hydrogen atoms from the ethylbenzene. The remaining atoms form molecules of styrene.

Finally, the manufacturer *polymerizes* the styrene to make solid *polystyrene*. To do this, he adds chemicals to the styrene, heats it, and puts it under pressure. A chemical reaction causes the styrene monomers to link together and form chainlike molecules of polystyrene. The manufacturer then grinds the solid polystyrene into grainlike particles. These particles are the raw material used to mold polystyrene products.

Manufacturers sell polystyrene resin in a variety of forms. They can strengthen it by adding glass fibers as a filler. Or they can make the resin soft and flexible by combining it with another polymer. Normally, polystyrene is hard, clear, and colorless. Resin makers can add *pigments* (coloring matter) to produce unlimited varieties of transparency and color.

Making Plastics Products. Manufacturers use synthetic resins to make many types of products. These products include paints, lubricants, adhesives, and molded items such as bottle caps, artificial limbs, and hulls for small boats. Manufacturers use various methods to make each type of product. The most important methods are (1) molding, (2) casting, (3) laminating, (4) extrusion, and (5) calendering.

Molding usually involves three basic operations. (1) The manufacturer starts with a solid resin in pellet or powder form. He heats the resin until it melts into a thick sirupy liquid. (2) The manufacturer then forces the melted resin into a mold under great pressure. (3) Finally, the manufacturer *cures* (hardens) the resin so that it keeps its shape when removed from the mold. He cures *thermoplastic* resins merely by allowing them to cool. Products made from such resins melt when heated, and can even be molded into new shapes. Manufacturers cure *thermosetting* resins by adding heat and applying pressure while the resin is in the mold. The heat and pressure cause chemical changes that make the resin hard. Thermosetting plastics cannot be remelted.

Casting resembles molding, but the cast product hardens without the use of pressure. The manufacturer merely pours a liquid or melted resin into a mold. He then adds chemicals to harden the plastics. Manufacturers use casting to shape both thermoplastic and thermosetting resins.

Laminating makes "sandwiches" from sheets of paper, cloth, or metal foil. The manufacturer first treats the sheets with a plastics resin. Then he places the sheets one on top of the other. A machine squeezes the sheets together and heats them until the resin has joined them

firmly. Laminating produces strong materials with a wide range of thicknesses for such products as electrical insulation, gears, and tabletops.

Extrusion machines form products by squeezing melted plastics through a specially shaped die in a continuous stream. This process is used to make plastics fibers, pipes, moldings, sheets, and other products that have the same shape everywhere along their length.

Calendering gives paper, cloth, wood, and other materials a thin plastics coating. The material to be coated is fed between two rollers. The rollers spread an even layer of melted resin over the material. They squeeze the resin and the material together to join them firmly. Calendering produces thin sheets of plastics in a similar way. As the resin is squeezed between rollers, it forms a thin layer on one of the rollers. This layer is pulled off in the form of a sheet.

Development of Plastics

The commercial molding of plastics-like natural substances in the United States began about 1845. It continued through the early 1900's. The natural molding materials used in this period were the forerunners of man-made plastics. They included *lac* (from which *shellac* is made), *gutta-percha*, and *cemented asbestos* (a mixture of asbestos fibers and an adhesive). These substances come directly from animal, vegetable, or mineral sources. See LAC; GUTTA-PERCHA; ASBESTOS.

Products made from these natural "plastics" included brush handles, knobs, electrical insulation, early phonograph records, and novelty items. Museums and collectors treasure many beautifully molded products of this period.

The natural molding materials had several disadvantages. Manufacturers sometimes had trouble getting raw materials. Some materials could not be molded easily. And many molded articles broke easily because they were not strong enough.

The Invention of Celluloid. In 1869, John W. Hyatt (1837-1920), a printer of Albany, N.Y., invented *Celluloid*, the first synthetic plastics material to receive wide commercial use. Hyatt was seeking a substitute for ivory to make billiard balls.

Hyatt made Celluloid by combining camphor with *pyroxylin* (cellulose nitrate, a substance obtained by treating cotton fibers with certain acids). Celluloid closely resembled two less successful pyroxylin plastics called *Parkesine* and *Xylonite*. Alexander Parkes (1813-1890), an English chemist, had introduced Parkesine in 1862. His associate, Daniel Spill (1832-1887), invented Xylonite in 1867.

Celluloid could be sawed, carved, and made into sheets. As a result, new plastics products appeared on the market. Common Celluloid articles included combs, collars, dentures, carriage curtains, clock cases, and the first photographic roll film. But Celluloid was hard to mold and it caught fire easily.

Soon after the invention of Celluloid, chemists developed other products made from plant fibers. In 1884, the French chemist Hilaire Chardonnet (1839-1924) invented *viscose rayon*, the first man-made fiber. Jacques E. Brandenberger (1872-1954), a Swiss chemist, invented *cellophane* in 1908. See RAYON; CELLOPHANE.

HOW PLASTICS PRODUCTS ARE MADE

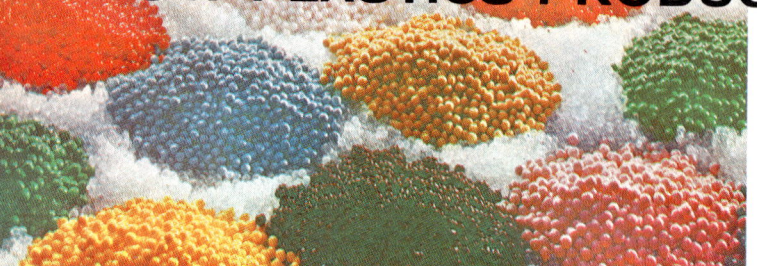

Manufacturers make many kinds of products from colorful synthetic resins. These resins consist of thousands of small particles that melt into a sirupy liquid when heated. The resins are then shaped into products by several methods as shown by the illustrations on these pages.

Eastman Chemical Products, Inc.

MOLDING
is like making waffles

Machines squeeze the resin between two halves of a mold to shape both sides of the product. Compression molding is used for thermosetting resins, and injection molding for thermoplastic resins. Blow molding makes bottles and other hollow items.

Ashtrays

COMPRESSION MOLDING

Casters

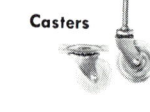

Dinnerware

Switch Plates

Telephone Parts

INJECTION MOLDING

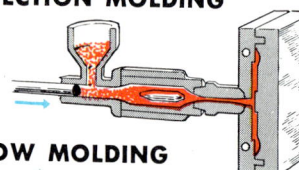

Toys

Plumbing Fixtures

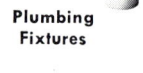

Toothbrushes

BLOW MOLDING

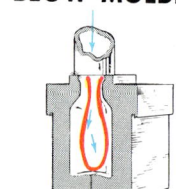

Toys

Bottles

Lamp Shades

CASTING
is like baking a cake

The resin is simply poured—not squeezed—into a mold. The casting mold may be only one piece, like a cake pan, or it may have two halves that fit together. Manufacturers use casting to shape thermosetting and thermoplastic resins.

The Marblette Corp.

Brush Handles

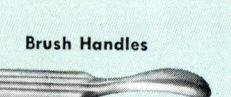
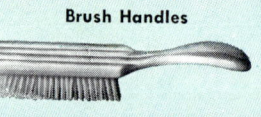

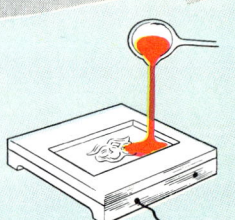

Cutlery Handles

Knobs

Jewelry

LAMINATING
is like making a sandwich

Sheets of paper, cloth, or metal foil pass between rollers and are coated with melted resin. The sheets are stacked one on top of the other and squeezed together in a press. When the sticky resin hardens, it holds the layers tightly together.

Paneling

Gears

Electronic Circuits

Tabletops

EXTRUSION
is like squeezing toothpaste

Workers place solid resin into the extrusion machine. The resin melts as a large screw pushes it through a heating chamber. The screw forces a continuous stream of melted resin through an opening. Various openings are used to shape tubes, fibers, moldings, and similar products.

Rope

Decorative Moldings

Drinking Straws

Insulation for Wire

Tubing

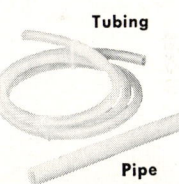

Garden Hose

Pipe

CALENDERING
is like spreading butter

Rollers spread melted resin over sheets of paper or cloth to form a protective finish or a strong "backing." Calendering machines also produce thin plastics films and sheets by squeezing resin between a pair of rollers.

Wallet Cards

Playing Cards

Tape

Wallpaper

Rainwear

Diagrams by Art Lutz, art and photography by Martin-Trlak Inc. for WORLD BOOK.

PLASTICS

The Invention of Bakelite. During the late 1800's, English and American chemists experimented with combinations of carbolic acid (also called phenol) and formaldehyde. This combination produced a resin. But the scientists could not control the violent reaction that occurred when the chemicals were mixed. In 1909, Leo H. Baekeland (1863-1944), a New York City chemist, succeeded in controlling the reaction. He invented the first completely synthetic resin, *Bakelite*.

Baekeland produced his resin while trying to make a better kind of varnish. At first, he did not recognize the value of Bakelite as a plastics material. Richard W. Seabury (1883-   ), a Boonton, N.J., rubber manufacturer, showed that the new resin could be molded. Seabury mixed Bakelite with asbestos fibers, and molded a part for an electrical instrument.

Baekeland also invented special phenolic compounds for making molded, cast, and laminated products. Bakelite became widely used to make telephones and handles for pots and irons. The electrical and automotive industries used Bakelite for many products.

The Plastics Industry Grows. During the 1920's and 1930's, the plastics industry kept pace with the expanding chemical industry. Chemists learned to produce three plastics in commercial quantities: (1) cellulose acetate, (2) acrylics, and (3) polystyrene. Scientists had known how to make these resins in the laboratory for almost a hundred years, but only in small quantities.

During World War I, airplane manufacturers used *cellulose acetate* lacquer to protect and tighten fabric wing coverings. In 1929, chemical companies first produced cellulose acetate as a molding compound.

Chemical firms began producing *acrylics*, such as Lucite and Plexiglas, in the 1930's. The acrylics are now standard materials for airplane windows.

The Dow Chemical Company first marketed *polystyrene* plastics in 1937. Manufacturers use these plastics to make radio and clock cases, electrical equipment, and wall tile.

The shortage of some raw materials during World War II led to further advances in plastics. New plastics of the 1940's included *polyethylene*, used for electrical insulation and food packaging; *silicones*, important in lubricants, protective coatings, and high-temperature electrical insulation; and *epoxy*, noted for its great strength and adhesive qualities.

Developments in the 1950's and 1960's progressed rapidly. Scientists, engineers, and craftsmen found new uses for plastics in medicine, nuclear and space research, industry, and architecture.

An important field of research in the 1960's was the development of *refractory* plastics. These plastics have special heat-resistant properties that make them ideal for precision electronics equipment in missiles. For

KINDS OF PLASTICS

All plastics are classified as *thermosetting* or *thermoplastic*, depending on the way they act when heated. This table lists 21 common thermosetting and thermoplastic materials according to their chemical names. Each kind includes hundreds of *alloys* (mixtures) formed by adding chemicals to the basic material.

THERMOSETTING MATERIALS

Thermosetting materials can be melted only once. After melting, they harden as heat is added, much as an egg hardens when cooked.

Phenolic: inexpensive, resists heat and cold. Used for paints, adhesives, printing plates, electrical devices.

Polyester: strong, hardens quickly, molds under low pressure. Used for boats, luggage, swimming pools, automobile bodies, chairs.

Silicone: resists weather, has high elasticity and good electrical qualities. Used for oven gaskets, electrical insulation, oils, greases, waterproof materials.

Urethane: tough, resists chemicals. Used for electrical insulation, structural parts, plastics foams.

Alkyd: resists heat, has good electrical qualities. Used for paints, enamels, electronic tube bases, electrical parts.

Allylic: strong, resists heat and weather. Used for electronics parts, coatings for moisture protection.

Epoxy: resists water and weather, hardens quickly, has high bonding strength. Used for adhesives, casting compounds, reinforced plastics, protective coatings, tools.

Melamine and Urea: easily colored, resists heat, odorless, tasteless. Used for dinnerware, lamp shades, adhesives, buttons, tabletops, electrical parts.

by Martin-Trlak Inc. for WORLD BOOK

example, chemists produced refractory *ceramoplastics* by combining synthetic mica with glass (see MICA). Other areas of research included the improvement of adhesives and of plastics that resist chemicals.

The Plastics Industry

The United States leads the world in the production of plastics, supplying more than half the total output. West Germany ranks second, followed by Great Britain, Russia, and Japan. The plastics industry is growing rapidly in Canada, Mexico, and South America. The growth of the industry in any country depends on plentiful supplies of coal and petroleum.

Pennsylvania leads all the states in the manufacture of raw plastics. Other leading states are Illinois, New Jersey, New York, North Carolina, Ohio, Massachusetts, and Texas. Quebec manufactures more raw plastics than any other province in Canada.

Plastics companies may be divided into three general groups: (1) *material makers* (mostly chemical companies) who manufacture resins; (2) *processors* who shape the resins into products; and (3) *fabricators and finishers* who make products by cutting, drilling, and assembling plastics parts. The plastics industry in the United States includes about 5,800 companies. About 200 of these companies are material-making firms, about 2,600 are processors, and about 3,000 are fabricators and finishers. Most material makers are located in coal and petroleum

A Teflon Coating on Kitchenware provides a slippery surface that makes it easy to wash off grease and sticky foods.

Du Pont

regions. Most of the processors, fabricators, and finishers operate in industrial areas where they can easily serve many industries.

Career Opportunities

The plastics industry offers a variety of job opportunities. Careers in research and development attract

THERMOPLASTIC MATERIALS

Thermoplastic materials can be melted again and again, much like the wax in a candle. They melt when heated to a certain temperature, but harden again as they cool.

ABS (Acrylonitrile-Butadiene-Styrene): strong, long wearing, resists stains and weather. Used for telephones, wheels, handles, appliance parts, luggage, electric switch housings.

Acetal: tough, stiff, springy, has high melting point. Used for refrigerator and washing machine parts, cams, wheels.

Acrylic: resists weather and chemicals, easily colored, has high impact strength. Used for optical lenses, shoe heels, airplane canopies, signs, displays, automobile tail lights, fabrics.

Cellulose Acetate: tough, has high melting point. Used for toys, novelties, knobs, handles, packaging, electrical parts.

Cellulose Acetate Butyrate: tough, resists water. Used for steering wheels, pipe, tool handles, industrial parts.

Nylon: strong, springy, resists abrasion, has good electrical qualities. Used for fabrics, gears, bearings, hardware, brush bristles, electrical appliances.

Polycarbonate: resists heat and weather, has high impact strength. Used for business machine parts, electrical connectors, coil forms, light diffusers.

Polyethylene: lightweight, flexible, has waxlike feel. Used for squeeze bottles, packaging, electrical insulation.

Polypropylene: lightweight, flexible, resists heat and chemicals. Used for rope, packaging, wire insulation, pipe and fittings, baby bottles, appliance parts.

Polystyrene: lightweight, inexpensive, tasteless, odorless. Used for housewares, toys, electrical insulation, radio cabinets.

Polyvinyl Chloride: strong, easily colored, flexible, resists abrasion. Used for imitation leather, phonograph records, packaging, pipe, paper coatings.

Tetrafluoroethylene: resists heat and chemicals, slides easily. Used for cable insulation, bearings, valve seats, gaskets, frypan coatings, slides and cams.

Vinylidene Chloride: crystal clear, tough. Used for bristles, window screens, packages for meat and other foods.

by Martin-Trlak Inc. for WORLD BOOK

PLASTICS

chemists, physicists, and engineers. Machine designers develop plastics processing equipment. Tool engineers design molds and dies, and develop new production methods. Other opportunities are open to sales engineers, buyers, and management personnel. Skilled workers may be employed in quality control, testing, inspecting, and scheduling. They also operate machines such as evaporators, mills, mixers, and stills.

Engineering students interested in careers in plastics should take special college courses that emphasize polymer chemistry. In these courses, students study the properties of plastics, methods of producing resins, and the design and fabrication of plastics products.

Further information about engineering careers in plastics may be obtained from the Society of Plastics Engineers, Inc., 65 Prospect St., Stamford, Conn. In Canada, students may write to the Society of Plastics Engineers, Inc., R.R. 1, West Hill, Ont.

Plastics Hobbies

Plastics offer a challenge to the home craftsman or hobbyist. He can buy clear or colored plastics in sheets, rods, tubes, and films, or as compounds for molding and casting. He needs only simple tools to work with most plastics materials. Many plastics can easily be sawed, drilled, polished, and cemented. Some cut like soft brass and can be carved.

The home craftsman can use thermoplastic film to make protective coverings for furniture and other household items. He joins the seams of these coverings merely by heating the edges of the film and pressing them together. The hobbyist can make vases and Halloween masks by molding a heated plastics sheet in a form made of wood or plaster.

Craftsmen also can buy many kinds of plastics kits. Some kits contain detailed plastics parts for making models of cars, planes, and ships. Other kits include resins and molds for making chessmen, checkers, toy soldiers, and other items. Similar kits can be used to preserve flowers and insects in blocks or sheets of crystal-clear plastics.   J. HARRY DuBois

Related Articles in WORLD BOOK include:

Acetate	Dynel	Rayon
Artificial Limbs	Furfural	Resin, Synthetic
Baekeland, Leo H.	Glass (Kinds)	Rubber (Synthetic
Bakelite	Lignin	Rubber)
Casein	Lucite	Saran
Cellophane	Mylar	Silicone
Celluloid	Nylon	Synthetics
Chemical Industry	Orlon	Teflon
Chemurgy	Plexiglas	Vinyl
Dacron	Polymerization	

Outline

I. **Types of Plastics**
   A. Hard Plastics
   B. Soft Plastics
   C. Transparent Plastics
   D. Decorative Plastics
   E. Resistant Plastics
   F. Plastics Fibers and Fabrics
II. **Special Uses of Plastics**
   A. In Industry
   B. In Architecture and Home Building
   C. In Medicine
   D. In Science

III. **How Plastics Are Made**
   A. Making Synthetic Resins
   B. Making Plastics Products
IV. **Development of Plastics**
V. **The Plastics Industry**
VI. **Career Opportunities**
VII. **Plastics Hobbies**

Questions

What plastics material is used for both delicate stockings and rugged machine parts?

What are the leading plastics producing countries?

What are some uses of plastics in medicine? In architecture and home building?

How does *casting* differ from *molding?*

What is a *filler? A plasticizer?*

What are the chief natural sources of synthetic plastics?

Who invented the first synthetic plastics material to receive wide commercial use?

What plastics material is a good shield against nuclear radiation?

What are *ceramoplastics?*

How does a manufacturer harden thermoplastic resins? Thermosetting resins?

PLASTRON. See TURTLE.

PLATA, RÍO DE LA. See RÍO DE LA PLATA.

PLATAEA, BATTLE OF. See GREECE, ANCIENT (The Persian Wars); THEBES.

PLATE. See PORCELAIN; POTTERY.

PLATE GLASS. See GLASS (Flat Glass).

PLATEAU, *pluh TOH,* is a raised section of land that covers a considerable area. It is always distinctly higher than the surrounding territory. Plateaus vary from a few hundred to several thousand feet in height. A *tableland* is similar to a plateau. A *plain* is lower than either a plateau or tableland. Streams on plateaus often cut deep valleys. These valleys sometimes form huge canyons, such as the famous Grand Canyon in Arizona. Sometimes a plateau is so carved by erosion that it looks like a range of mountains. This is true of the Catskill Mountains in New York. This deeply eroded range is really part of the Allegheny Plateau.

In North and South America, the higher plateaus, such as the Columbia Plateau, are in the western parts of the continents. The lower ones are in the eastern parts. A high plateau lies between the Rockies and the Sierra Nevada in North America. A plateau in Bolivia, South America, is bordered by the giant peaks of the Andes. The loftiest plateaus on earth are found in the Himalaya regions of Central Asia, often called "the roof of the world." Some of the high plateaus are of little value to mankind because they are so rugged that exchanging goods over them is difficult or impossible. The climate is not favorable enough to support a large population. Plateaus of a lower altitude are often excellent grazing grounds for sheep and cattle. Such plateaus are found in the western United States and in western Australia. The plateaus of the Appalachian regions in the eastern United States have valuable deposits of coal.   ELDRED D. WILSON

See also BUTTE (hill); MESA; PAMIRS; PLAIN; PLAINS OF ABRAHAM.

PLATELET. See BLOOD (Parts of the Blood; Blood Clotting; pictures); SEROTONIN.

PLATFORM, POLITICAL. See POLITICAL CONVENTION (Convention Machinery).

PLATFORM SCALE. See SCALE, WEIGHING.

PLATINA FOX. See FUR (Names of Furs).

PLATINUM, *PLAT ih num* (chemical symbol, Pt), is a precious, silver-white metal that is even more valuable than gold. Its atomic number is 78, and its atomic weight is 195.09. Platinum is one of the heaviest substances known. One cubic foot of platinum weighs about 21 times as much as one cubic foot of water.

Properties. Platinum has many special characteristics that make it valuable. Only gold and silver are easier to shape than platinum. It can be shaped and worked in almost every possible way. It can be drawn into fine wire, or it can be hammered into thin sheets. It does not corrode or tarnish when exposed to air, because it does not combine readily with oxygen or sulfur compounds found in air. Strong acids that dissolve most metals do not attack platinum. Platinum can best be dissolved in a mixture of nitric and hydrochloric acid called *aqua regia* (see AQUA REGIA). It has a relatively high melting point of 1769° C., and is easy to shape. It combines readily with arsenic, phosphorus, and silicon. Platinum also forms alloys with most metals. Its most useful alloys are formed with iridium, nickel, osmium, palladium, rhodium, ruthenium, and tungsten.

Uses. Chemical laboratories often use platinum containers, because platinum resists heat and chemicals. For the same reason, platinum parts are sometimes used in large-scale production equipment. Certain gases, such as hydrogen, diffuse through hot platinum, but other gases will not. Platinum is often used to separate certain gases and is especially useful in chemical experiments to trap nitrogen in the atmosphere. It is also used as a catalyst in manufacturing certain chemicals, such as acetic acid and nitric acid (see CATALYSIS). As a catalyst, platinum speeds up necessary chemical reactions. The glass industry uses platinum to make dies for fiber glass. Platinum has become a favorite material for use in expensive jewelry. Its strength, hardness, color, and freedom from tarnish

South American Gold & Platinum Co.

Platinum in Colombia usually occurs in fine particles that are scattered throughout the gravel in alluvial deposits.

make it ideal for gem settings. Delicate designs can be made in platinum settings. It is also used on the best surgical instruments.

An alloy of platinum with iridium makes an excellent surface for fine engravings. The same alloy makes standards of weights and measures, contact points with electrical equipment, and the tips of fountain pens. The salts of platinum are used in certain types of photographic prints.

Production. The Italian scientist Julius Scaliger discovered platinum in 1557. But fairly large quantities were not discovered until about 1750, when the Spaniards found it in Peru. They named the metal *platinum*, from their word *plata*, meaning *silver*. The ore, called *native*, or crude, platinum, usually occurs in beds of gold-bearing sand. Miners call it *white gold*. Native platinum contains from 60 to 85 per cent pure platinum. The small, irregular grains that contain the ore also contain other rare metals, such as iridium, osmium, palladium, rhodium, and ruthenium. The grains also contain small amounts of iron, copper, chromium, and titanium. Occasionally, a large nugget of native platinum will be found. In 1843, a lump weighing over 21 pounds was found in Russia.

Russia produces the largest share of the world's platinum-group metals. Other important sources of platinum are in the Transvaal province in South Africa and in Sudbury, Ont. Colombia and the United States also have sources of platinum.

The United States consumes about 691,000 troy ounces of platinum a year. About one-tenth of this comes from its own mines and from scrap. The rest is imported largely from Canada, which recovers large quantities as a by-product of the nickel industry.

In the United States, platinum occurs in the gold-bearing deposits in California, Nevada, and Oregon. A large amount also comes from the process of refining gold and copper. ALBERT J. PHILLIPS

See also DUCTILITY; ELEMENT, CHEMICAL (table); IRIDIUM.

PLATINUM FOX. See FUR (Fox).

LEADING PLATINUM-GROUP METALS PRODUCING COUNTRIES

Troy ounces of platinum-group metals produced in 1966*

Russia
1,700,000 ounces
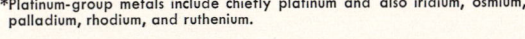

South Africa
784,000 ounces

Canada
386,000 ounces

United States
51,000 ounces

Colombia
18,000 ounces

*Platinum-group metals include chiefly platinum and also iridium, osmium, palladium, rhodium, and ruthenium.

Source: U.S. Bureau of Mines.

The Greek Philosophers, Plato, *left,* **and Aristotle,** *right,* as they are pictured by the painter Raphael, in a wall fresco at the Vatican in Rome. The younger man, Aristotle, was greatly influenced by the philosophy of the older.

PLATO, *PLAY toh* (427?-347 B.C.), was one of the greatest philosophers of Western culture. He has exerted a tremendous influence over all subsequent philosophical thought.

About the age of 21, Plato came under the influence of Socrates and devoted himself to philosophy (see SOCRATES). In 397 B.C. he opened a school called *the Academy,* because it was located in the Grove of Academus. The Academy soon became the intellectual center of Greece and the first university in the history of Europe.

Plato never allowed his Academy lectures to be written down. He believed that readers outside the Academy might misunderstand his doctrines and would not be adequately prepared to grasp their meaning. He also felt that the written words could not answer questions or defend themselves against misconceptions, as a living teacher could. But Plato expressed his philosophic thinking in a number of written dialogues which rank among the greatest literary and philosophic masterpieces of all times.

His Philosophy. From his teacher Socrates, Plato accepted both the distinction between opinion and knowledge and an interest in the problems of a good life for man. He believed that the realm of nature and of human experience was in a constant flux, with nothing really permanent. Even if a person made a true statement about some existing fact, the fact would soon change and the statement would no longer be true. So he concluded that men could never gain knowledge, but only opinions, from their sense perceptions and im-

mediate experiences. But if man's mind could ascend from specific objects and ideas to universal ones, then he could have an unchanging formal object of knowledge. For example, if he could go from the many visible and changeable circles in nature to the idea of the Circle as it appears in geometry, he could grasp a firm reality.

Plato believed that these formal structures, grasped by the mind alone, were more knowable and more real than the changeable material objects that we grasp through our senses.

By using such mathematical forms as the circle as models, he went on to discover such universal ideas as temperance, justice, and the nature of the ideal statesman. For example, to tune a musical instrument, a player adjusts the strings according to arithmetical ratios that define particular notes. These arithmetical relations express harmonic intervals, and never get out of tune. The harmonic relations cannot be heard, but are understood by the mind. In the material world, the strings of the musical instrument produce audible harmonies, and constantly go out of tune. Therefore Plato said that only the universal ratios or ideas of harmony have true being. This is an *idealistic* theory, because Plato argues that man must penetrate beyond the material world grasped by his senses, and discover the intelligible world of ideas and forms.

This view is expressed in *The Republic,* where Plato outlines the nature of the just man and the ideal state. Both the just man and the ideal state must develop wisdom in their actions, courage in their decisions and difficulties, and temperance in their desires and appetites.

Plato believed that these virtues—temperance, courage, and wisdom—will make their possessors just. He also worked out a theory of education, which was planned to develop these virtues in the individual and in the state. Plato knew that this ideal state could only be realized imperfectly in this world, but he held it up as a goal toward which people should work.

His Life. Plato was born in Athens. He belonged to an aristocratic and influential family, and was reported to be descended from the great Athenian statesman and lawgiver, Solon. The word *Plato* was a nickname, meaning *broad-shouldered.* His real name was Aristocles. The unjust execution of his teacher, Socrates, embittered him, so he left Athens to travel and study in Greece, Italy, Sicily, and probably North Africa and Egypt. Plato did not take part in the active political life of Athens, but preferred to try to enlighten the people through his teachings and writings on government and statesmanship.

He went to Sicily in 368 B.C. to educate the young prince, Dionysius II, in the virtues necessary for a just and good ruler. Plato could not resist this opportunity to try to develop the kind of wise ruler he later described in *The Republic.* But there were enemies who opposed his plan, and Plato barely escaped from Sicily with his life. He returned to Athens in 366 B.C. Except for another futile visit to Dionysius, Plato remained in Athens until his death.

Plato's writings were made widely available to English readers in the translations of the dialogues by Benjamin Jowett (1817-1893), an outstanding classical scholar of Oxford University.   LEWIS M. HAMMOND

PLATOON, *pluh TOON,* is the basic tactical unit of the United States Army. It is formed by two or more squads, with an average of 30 or 40 men, and is commanded by a lieutenant. Two or more platoons usually make up a company. The U.S. Navy uses platoons primarily in training units. In the Navy, an ensign commands a platoon.

PLATOON SCHOOL is a plan of organization used in elementary schools. It is called platoon school because the entire enrollment of the school is divided by classes into two groups, or platoons. The two platoons take turns attending classes in the so-called *home rooms,* where standard subjects are taught, and in *special rooms* for activities such as music, drawing, manual training, sewing, and cooking.

The platoon plan is designed to provide pupil instruction by teachers with special skills in subjects such as music. The plan is also designed to get the greatest use from a school building. The first school of the platoon type, organized by William Wirt, was adopted in Bluffton, Ind., in 1900. The plan, once widely used, has been largely discontinued.   HOLLIS L. CASWELL

PLATT, THOMAS C. See ROOSEVELT, THEODORE (Governor of New York; Vice-President).

PLATT AMENDMENT. See CUBA (United States Control; Independence).

PLATT NATIONAL PARK is the smallest national park in the United States. It covers 911.97 acres in southern Oklahoma, just outside the town of Sulphur. The park has fresh-water springs, cold mineral-water springs, sparkling streams, wooded valleys, and gently rolling grass-covered hills. Visitors may picnic, camp, swim, and hike there.

Small animals, birds, and plant life may be seen throughout Platt National Park. Huge buffalo herds once roamed this section of the country. But the herds shrank after the white man came. Today, a small herd of buffaloes still lives in the park.

The springs in the park were used by the Indians as healing waters long before the white man came. No one

Water from Mineral Springs in Platt National Park flows over a small waterfall in rocky Travertine Creek.

National Park Service

knows who was the first white man to enter the area. But Thomas Nuttal, a famous botanist, made the first record of such a visit when he explored the region in 1819. In 1902 the federal government set aside the area as Sulphur Springs Reservation. In 1906 the territory became Platt National Park. It was named after Senator Orville Platt of Connecticut, long a friend of the Oklahoma Indians.   JAMES J. CULLINANE

PLATTDEUTSCH. See GERMAN LANGUAGE.

PLATTE RIVER, *plat,* is the most important river in Nebraska and one of the largest branches of the Missouri River. It is formed by the union of the North and South Platte rivers, both of which begin in the mountains of northern Colorado. The two rivers join in western Nebraska. For location, see NEBRASKA (physical map). From this junction, the river flows in a general easterly direction and empties into the Missouri at Plattsmouth. The North Platte is the longer of the two branches. It flows 618 miles, and the South Platte is 424 miles long. The main stream is about 310 miles long. The Platte and its branches drain a region of about 90,200 square miles. This area includes some of the best irrigated sections of Colorado, Nebraska, and Wyoming. The Platte is too shallow for navigation. However, its valley provides an excellent roadbed. Many pioneers traveled along it.   JAMES C. OLSON

PLATTSBURGH, N.Y. (pop. 21,090; alt. 120 ft.), is an industrial center and the largest city in northeastern New York. It lies on Lake Champlain about 20 miles south of the Canadian border (see NEW YORK [map]). The city was named for Zephaniah Platt, one of its founders. Factories in Plattsburgh make wood and paper products, candy, ice cream, soda pop, optical goods, razor blades, and dairy products.

Plattsburgh lay on the invasion route of the British in both the Revolutionary War and the War of 1812. The Battle of Plattsburgh and the naval battle on Lake Champlain occurred in 1814. State University College at Plattsburgh is located in the city. Plattsburgh was incorporated as a village in 1795, and became a city in 1902. It has a mayor-council form of government.   WILLIAM E. YOUNG

PLATY. See FISH (color picture: Tropical Fresh-Water Fishes).

PLATYHELMINTH. See FLATWORM.

PLATYPUS, *PLAT ih pus,* is an animal that lives along streams in Australia and Tasmania. It has a bill like that of a duck, and is often called a *duckbill.* Although it lays eggs instead of bearing its young alive, the platypus is a true mammal, not a bird. It nurses its young with milk as do other mammals.

The leathery bill of the platypus is at the front of the head, where most other mammals have noses and lips. The platypus uses its bill to find shellfish, worms, and certain water insects at the bottom of streams. These are its principal foods. The platypus chews its food with horny plates on both sides of its jaw. Adults have no teeth. The body of the platypus is about 18 to 20 inches long, including the tail. The paddle-shaped tail helps the animal swim. The soft, thick fur that covers its body protects the platypus under water.

Both the front and hind feet have claws. The female uses its claws to dig a long tunnel in the bank of a stream, where it builds a nest. There it lays from one to three eggs, each less than an inch long. The eggs have soft, leathery shells, like those of snakes and turtles. When the eggs hatch, the female uses its tail to hold the young close to its body and nurse them. The young have no fur when hatched. They stay hidden in the nest until they are several months old.

The male platypus has a hollow claw, or spur, on each hind leg. The spurs are connected with poison glands. The platypus scratches and poisons its enemies with the spurs.

Webs of skin grow between the toes on all four of the platypus's feet. The webs of the front feet grow far out beyond the toes as thick flaps of skin. Its webbed feet and its tail make the platypus an expert swimmer and diver. When it needs to use its front claws for digging, the platypus folds the flaps back out of the way.

N.Y. Zoological Society

The Platypus, or Duckbill, has a strange, skin-covered bill where most other mammals have their noses and lips.

Platypuses were once killed in large numbers for their fur. Australian law now forbids hunting them.

Scientific Classification. The platypus makes up the platypus family, *Ornithorhynchidae*. It is genus *Ornithorhynchus*, species *O. anatinus*. FRANK B. GOLLEY

See also AUSTRALIA (color picture: The Platypus).

PLAUTUS (254 B.C.?-184 B.C.) was an important Roman writer of comedy. His plays are versions of Greek New Comedy, which emphasized young men in love with slave girls, mistaken identities, cunning servants, and deceived masters. Plautus added earthy Italian comic elements and his own boisterous wit. Subtle techniques of plot construction and characterization did not concern him as much as producing laughter. He was a master of dialogue, writing a lively stream of puns, love talk, and abuse.

Plautus wrote 21 plays. *Amphitruo* is a mythological story about the god Jupiter fathering Hercules with a human man's wife. In *Menaechmi*, two long-separated brothers find each other after great confusion. In *Casina*, father and son are rivals for the same girl.

TITUS MACCIUS PLAUTUS was born in Sarsina, Italy. He worked as a stagehand with a traveling acting troupe before turning to playwriting. NORMAN T. PRATT

PLAY. See DRAMA; THEATER.

PLAY is recreation, or what we do for fun. Play activities range from running and skipping to sports such as golf and swimming.

Adult play generally takes place during leisure hours. It fulfills a deep need for relaxation after a routine or trying day of work. To a child, play is almost the same as life. It is the child's response to the world about him. He acts out what he observes, and learns about himself and the world. In doing so, he may express emotions that indicate whether he is happy or sad.

Types of Play Activities fall into three groups: (1) *motor play*, or doing, as in skating and baseball; (2) *sensory play*, or observing games and sports; and (3) *intellectual play*, as in playing chess or solving puzzles.

People have different tastes in play. In fact, play is usually a form of self-expression. Some persons enjoy sports. Others prefer to develop a hobby such as woodworking or painting. Children like to sing, pound a wooden hammer, make nonsense rhymes, or pretend they are someone else. Girls skip rope and cut out dolls. Boys like to fix things and play marbles. Generally, men prefer active, strenuous activities. Even many adults over 65 participate in active sports, such as tennis and volleyball. Many activities are popular with all age groups.

The Importance of Play. There have always been many attitudes toward play. Some persons once believed it sinful. Others regarded it as a waste of time. But now, play is considered a necessary part of growing up. Sound play activities help children develop healthy attitudes and bodies. Recreational activities teach them to get along with others. The personality of a child grows as he learns a new skill and develops confidence in a sport. In competitive games, he learns how to lose gracefully.

History. Play is as old as history itself. Toys have been found in the ruins of ancient Egypt, Babylonia, China, and among the remains of the Aztec civilization.

The modern play movement in the United States began in 1886, when Boston, Mass., opened sandgardens for small children. The movement spread rapidly, because play and recreational areas offered a practical answer to the crowded conditions of city life. The public in general came to recognize that health and social development were important to a child's education. Many cities developed vast playground systems once the modern play movement got underway. Child-labor laws and a long summer vacation from school made it necessary to provide more recreational facilities. Adults took a more active part in recreational activities as a result of a shorter work week and a higher income.

As a result of the modern play movement, boating, golfing, and tennis have become everyday sports. People take a greater interest in music, painting, and books. National and local youth agencies have developed planned recreational activities, and employ trained personnel to conduct them. LILLIAN FRANKEL

Related Articles in WORLD BOOK include:

Amusements	Recreation
Doll	Safety (Recreation)
Game	Sports and Sportsmanship
Kindergarten	Storytelling
Leisure	Toy
Physical Education	Tricks and
Playground	Puzzles

Children at a Playground in California climb on a weird-looking "fun tree," built especially for that purpose. The modernistic tree has a framework of steel pipe and metal lath that is covered with cement.

Oakland, Calif., Park Dept.

PLAYGROUND is an outdoor area set aside for play. Playgrounds were first started for children. But persons of all ages enjoy the many different playground activities offered today. Small children can play informally in sand piles, and on seesaws and swings. Older boys and girls may play or practice games and sports on the playground. Adults may participate in such games as tennis, badminton, and horseshoes. Many playgrounds have space for basketball, baseball, and even football. Some playgrounds have outdoor swimming pools.

Playgrounds often become a center of community activity. Parents come to watch competitive contests and other special events. Holiday celebrations, such as those on the Fourth of July and Labor Day, are often held in playgrounds. Many schools hold yearly play days on playgrounds.

Before 1900, children played on the lawns of their homes, in vacant lots, and in the streets. The movement for public playgrounds was started shortly before 1900 by Jacob Riis, a New York City newspaperman. Riis and others recognized the great need for play space and recreation activities in the growing cities. The slum areas had no lawns or vacant lots for play. Most of the early schools did not have land around them that could be used for play. By 1899, Boston had 21 sand lots for small children. Other Eastern cities followed Boston's example, and soon sand gardens and playgrounds were being organized in several cities. In 1889, the Charlesbank Outdoor Gymnasium opened in Boston. It provided apparatus for gymnastics, a running track, and space for games for older boys and men. A section was added to this playground two years later for women and girls.

Today, practically all schools have playgrounds. Cities have several playgrounds located in various community districts. City playgrounds are usually under the direction of park and recreation boards. Sometimes they are developed and controlled jointly by park districts, school boards, and recreation commissions. Playgrounds are usually provided for in modern city planning. Building ordinances often require that new communities include space for parks and playgrounds.

Playground programs are planned and conducted by trained playground leaders who usually have majored in physical education and recreation in college. They learn how to plan and conduct playground activities according to the educational, growth, and developmental needs of boys and girls. Good playground leaders know how to perform in all kinds of games, sports, and dances, and how to interest others in them. They also know how to organize adults so they too may enjoy all types of playground activities. WALTER H. GREGG

See also GAME (recreation); GYMNASIUM; PARK (City Parks); PLAY; RECREATION; SAFETY (School).

Playgrounds Are Safe Places for children to use up extra energy. Many playgrounds employ trained recreation leaders.
Roy Pinney, Photo-library

507

PLAYING CARDS

PLAYING CARDS. See CARD GAME.

PLAZA MÉXICO. See MEXICO CITY (Sports: color picture).

PLEBEIAN, *plee BEE yun,* was a commoner in the early Roman Republic. The plebeians included freed slaves, peasant farmers, and dependents of *patricians* (aristocrats). It is not known how the difference between plebeians and patricians first arose, but it existed by the early 500's B.C.

Plebeians had to serve in the army, but were denied many rights. For many years, they could not hold public office, vote on laws, or become priests. They were forbidden to marry persons not of their class. Judges often treated the plebeians unfairly.

Early in the 400's B.C., the plebeians threatened to refuse to fight unless they were allowed to choose their own *tribunes* (officials). The plebeians were given the right to elect tribunes who could *veto* (reject) unfair acts of judges and lawmakers. Later, in 445 B.C., the plebeians received the right to marry patricians. In 367 B.C. they were allowed to run for the office of *consul* (chief government official). By 300 B.C. they had been declared eligible for the priesthoods and other offices. In 287 B.C., the *comitia tributa* (assembly of all the people— plebeians and patricians alike) was given the power to make laws that bound everyone.

Wealthy plebeians then began joining the patricians to form a new upper class. But tribunes and the *comitia* remained to protect the poor classes of Rome until the end of the republic, in 27 B.C.   HERBERT M. HOWE

See also PATRICIAN; PRAETOR; TRIBUNE.

PLEBISCITE, *PLEB ih site,* is a vote of the people on any question. But the term has come to mean the vote of inhabitants in a territory to choose the nation that will govern them. The plebiscite was first used during the 1790's when the citizens of Nice and Savoy voted for or against union with France.

Modern plebiscites are almost always under international control. On May 9, 1956, for example, the United Nations supervised a plebiscite in British Togoland, West Africa. It was to decide whether the people wished to unite with the Gold Coast or continue under trusteeship rule. The people in British Togoland favored union with the Gold Coast (now Ghana). Plebiscites have also been held to decide the status of the Saar in Europe.

Plebiscites are intended to give territories freedom of choice, but interested nations sometimes try to influence the vote by military pressure. In any case, plebiscites have marked a long step forward in permitting people of certain territories some freedom in choosing their form of government.   PAYSON S. WILD, JR.

PLECOPTERA is an order of insects that lay their eggs in water. The young live in streams or along the rocky shallows of ponds and lakes. They form a large part of the diet of trout and other fish. The adults have wings but do not fly well and seldom wander far from their breeding place. They often can be seen clinging to rocks at the water's edge. For this reason, they are commonly called *stone flies.*

See also STONE FLY.

PLECTRUM. See BANJO; MANDOLIN; SPINET.

PLEDGE. See OATH.

PLEDGE TO THE FLAG is a solemn promise of allegiance to the United States. It reads:

> I pledge allegiance to the flag of the United States of America and to the Republic for which it stands, one Nation under God, indivisible, with liberty and justice for all.

Public-school children first recited the pledge as they saluted the flag during the National School Celebration held in 1892. President Benjamin Harrison had called for patriotic exercises in schools to mark the 400th anniversary of the discovery of America. Francis Bellamy (1855-1931) of Boston, an associate editor of *The Youth's Companion,* wrote the original pledge. The National Flag Conferences of the American Legion expanded the original wording in 1923 and 1924. In 1942, Congress made the pledge part of its code for the use of the flag. In 1954, it added the words "under God."   WHITNEY SMITH, JR.

PLÉIADE, a group of French poets. See FRENCH LITERATURE (The Pléiade); BELLAY, JOACHIM DU; RONSARD, PIERRE DE.

PLEIADES, *PLEA yuh deez,* or the SEVEN SISTERS, is a loose cluster of stars in the constellation Taurus (see TAURUS). Astronomers estimate that the Pleiades is

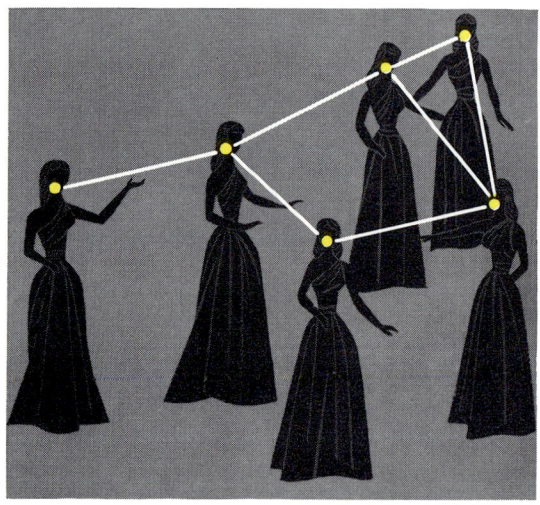

The Star Cluster Pleiades, or the Seven Sisters, has six clearly visible stars and one faint star not shown here.

490 light-years away from the earth. Six stars can easily be seen without a telescope. About 200 stars in the Pleiades may be seen with a telescope. Photographs of the cluster have revealed knots of nebulous material composed mainly of dust that reflects the light of the stars in the Pleiades. Many persons mistake the Pleiades for the Little Dipper.

In Greek myths, the Pleiades represented the seven daughters of Atlas and the nymph Pleione. According to one version, Zeus first transformed the sisters into doves, and then into stars to enable them to escape the attention of Orion. The sisters are Alcyone, Merope, Celaeno, Taygeta, Maia, Electra, and Sterope.

According to one legend, only six of the stars can be seen because Merope hid herself in shame over marrying a mortal.   I. M. LEVITT

PLEISTOCENE EPOCH. See ICE AGE.

PLEKHANOV, *pleh KAH nawf,* **GEORGI VALENTINOVICH** (1857-1918), was a Russian political writer, social thinker, and a theorist of Marxism. He wrote many works, usually from a Marxian point of view, on political, economic, and philosophical subjects, and developed an early Marxian literary theory.

He shared the leadership of the Russian revolutionists for a time with Lenin. But the two quarreled over doctrine. Plekhanov opposed the Bolsheviks before and after they took power. ERNEST J. SIMMONS

PLENIPOTENTIARY. See DIPLOMACY.

PLESIOSAUR, *PLEE sih oh SAWR,* was a prehistoric marine animal that lived about 200,000,000 years ago. This huge sea serpent had paddle-like legs. See PREHISTORIC ANIMAL (The Age of Dinosaurs).

PLESSY VS. FERGUSON. See EDUCATION, HISTORY OF (Recent Developments).

PLEURA, *PLOOR uh,* is a thin membrane that lines the *thoracic cavity,* or chest cavity, and covers the lungs. The part covering the lungs is called the *pulmonary pleura.* The remaining part, called the *parietal pleura,* lines the chest wall and covers the diaphragm. The two parts of the pleura unite at the root of the lung.

In a healthy person, the two parts of the pleura touch. They secrete a trace of watery fluid that lubricates their surfaces. If the pleura fills with liquid, as in one kind of *pleurisy,* or if it fills with air, as when the lung collapses, the space between the two parts becomes a *pleural cavity.* WILLIAM V. MAYER

See also LUNG; MEMBRANE; PLEURISY.

PLEURISY, *PLOOR uh sih,* is inflammation of the pleura, a membrane that lines the inside of the chest and covers the lungs (see PLEURA). The two surfaces of the membrane are moist and allow the lungs to move smoothly over the chest wall when a person breathes. When the pleura is inflamed, the surfaces become dry and rough, and rub together. This condition, called *dry pleurisy,* causes intense pain, made worse by coughing and deep breathing. Sometime later, a small amount of fluid may pass from blood vessels into the pleural cavity. This fluid relieves the pain and is eventually absorbed. But sometimes so much fluid collects in the cavity that the lung becomes compressed. This condition is called *wet pleurisy,* or *pleurisy with effusion.*

Chills and fever, difficult breathing, and a short, dry cough are symptoms of pleurisy. Dry pleurisy is treated by rest in bed, and by strapping the chest to limit movement. Pleurisy with effusion sometimes requires tapping the chest to draw off the fluid. In all cases, a physician should be called at once. Pleurisy usually occurs as a complication of pneumonia, tuberculosis, and other infectious diseases. If pleurisy occurs with pneumonia, doctors often give the patient antibiotic drugs. MARK D. ALTSCHULE

PLEXIGLAS is the trademark of a type of plastic made by the Rohm & Haas Company of Philadelphia. In spite of its name, Plexiglas is not glass, but is an acrylic plastic (see PLASTICS [The Plastics Industry Grows]). It is manufactured in clear, colorless form, and in transparent, translucent, and opaque colors. Plexiglas is used in aircraft windows, because it is almost unbreakable. Other uses include lighting fixtures, electric signs, automobile tail lights, and control panels on household appliances. BURNAP POST

PLEXUS means an intertwining or interweaving, as in a network. In a nerve plexus, such as the *brachial plexus* which supplies the arm, there is a complex interweaving of nerve fibers. In a *vascular plexus,* made up of arteries, veins, or lymphatics, the vessels have many openings into each other. See also SOLAR PLEXUS.

PLIMSOLL, *PLIM sahl,* **MARK** is a load-line marking on the side of a ship's hull. It shows how much cargo the ship can carry safely under different conditions. The position of the marking depends on the type and size of the vessel. The name came from the load-line markings on British merchant ships owned by Samuel Plimsoll. It was through Plimsoll's efforts that an act of parliament to prevent overloading was passed. A ship loaded "down to the Plimsoll Mark" carries capacity cargo. Any more cargo would lessen its chances of a safe voyage.

Load lines on American ships have been established by the American Bureau of Shipping as provided under the Load Line Act of 1929. These rules apply to deep-sea vessels of 150 gross tons or more.

The distance between the Plimsoll Mark and the deck is the ship's "freeboard." Special markings were established in 1935 for Great Lakes and Atlantic and Pacific coast voyages. ALEXANDER LAING

PLINY, *PLIHN ih,* is the family name of an uncle and a nephew who were Roman writers.

Pliny the Elder (A.D. 23-79), or GAIUS PLINIUS SECUNDUS, wrote many historical and technical works. Only his 37-volume *Natural History* has survived. Although this work was used during the Middle Ages, its only value now is to show the state of scientific knowledge during Pliny's time.

Pliny was born at Novum Comum (now Como) in northern Italy. As a lawyer, he held important public offices. He was admiral of the fleet near Pompeii when Mount Vesuvius erupted in A.D. 79, and he died there trying to help the refugees.

Pliny the Younger (A.D. 61-113?), or GAIUS PLINIUS CAECILIUS SECUNDUS, was the nephew of Pliny the Elder. His most important works are his *Letters,* collected in 10 books. They show the life and interests of a Roman gentleman, scholar, and philanthropist. Some of the letters, addressed to the historian Tacitus, give a de-

Pliny the Elder held many discussions with the Roman emperor Vespasian, who was one of his close friends.

Bettmann Archive

tailed account of the eruption of Vesuvius, and describe his uncle, Pliny the Elder. Pliny served as governor of Bithynia, and wrote letters to the Emperor Trajan describing the Christians and asking what to do about them. These letters are the earliest accounts of Christians written by a pagan. Pliny the Younger was born in Novum Comum. He was well educated, and by the time he was 20 was considered one of the most learned men of his time. Pliny studied under Quintilian and was a good orator. MOSES HADAS

PLIOCENE EPOCH. See EARTH (table: Outline of Earth History).

PLIQUE-À-JOUR, PLEEK a ZHOOR, is a delicate type of enameling. The enamel is put in openings in the object to be enameled, so that it looks like a miniature stained-glass window. The art of plique-à-jour lies in keeping the enamel together until it has been permanently fused by heat. Plique-à-jour enamels are the most translucent enamels, because they have no background to stop the light. The glittering of plique-à-jour enamels often gives the effect of small jewels. See also ENAMEL (Decorative Enameling). EUGENE F. BUNKER, JR.

PLOEŞTI, plaw YESHT (pop. 147,695; met. area 191,-663; alt. 490 ft.), is the center of Romania's rich oil region in the south-central part of the country (see ROMANIA [color map]). Railroads and pipelines connect Ploeşti with the Black Sea coast. The city was heavily bombed by Allied forces during World War II.

PLOT. See DRAMA (The Structure of Drama); LITERATURE (Plot); NOVEL (Technique of the Novel).

PLOTINUS, ploh TY nus (205?-270?), was the leader of a school of Greek philosophy known as *Neoplatonism.* Plotinus said that the material world is unreal, politics trivial, the body a temporary prison for the soul, and life a journey through a landscape of illusion. Reality lay "yonder" in a solitary perfect being, *The One,* the source of all truth, goodness, and beauty. He said that pure souls may hope to "return" there. Sometimes this return occurred as a mystical vision. Plotinus believed he had experienced such a vision. See NEOPLATONISM.

Plotinus may have been born in Egypt. He joined a military campaign to the East to try to learn more about Indian philosophy. He planned to found a city of philosophers, but never did so. Plotinus spent the last years of his life teaching in Rome. He disliked writing but dictated six sets of nine lectures called the *Enneads.* Plotinus' pessimism catches only one side of Plato's philosophy—that in which philosophy is a consolation or escape from the world—but this was the side most appealing to Romans of his time. ROBERT BRUMBAUGH

PLOTTER. See NAVIGATION (Instruments).

PLOVDIV, PLAWV diff (pop. 222,737; alt. 320 ft.), Bulgaria's second largest city, lies on the Maritsa River, about 100 miles southeast of Sofia. For location, see BULGARIA (color map). Plovdiv is an important railway and trading center for the products of southern Bulgaria. The city has metal, textile, and food-processing industries. Its trade fair is well known. Plovdiv is also an educational center with a medical institute, higher institutes of agriculture and food industry, and an archaeological museum. IRWIN T. SANDERS

See also BULGARIA (pictures).

PLOVER, *PLUHV* er, is the name for a group of small, stout shore birds. The plover has a short body and a short bill. It secures its food from the surface of the ground rather than by probing. Most plovers have only three toes, but the black-bellied plover has a small hind toe in addition to the usual three. The plover has a short, thick neck. Its wings are pointed and reach beyond the end of its tail.

The plover builds its nest on the ground. The female usually lays four eggs. The eggs are so spotted that they are hard to distinguish from the pebbles around them. When the bird hatches, it is usually covered with light-brown or gray feathers marked with dark spots.

There are many kinds of plover throughout the world. Twelve species have been recorded in North America. Two common species in North America are the *black-bellied plover* and the *golden plover.* Both birds make their nests in arctic Alaska and Canada. In the winter, the golden plover flies thousands of miles to Hawaii and to Central and South America. The smallest plover found in North America is the *snowy plover.* This bird is light-colored and makes its home along the Gulf Coast from Florida into the Mississippi Valley, in Utah, and along the Pacific Coast. The *semipalmated* or *ringnecked plover* nests in Alaska and Canada. It has a black band across its neck. Other common North American plovers include the *piping plover,* the *Wilson's plover,* the *mountain plover,* and the *killdeer.*

Scientific Classification. Plovers belong to the plover and lapwing family, *Charadriidae.* The black-bellied plover is genus *Squatarola,* species *S. squatarola;* the golden is *Pluvialis dominica;* the snowy is *Charadrius alexandrinus;* the semipalmated is *C. semipalmatus;* the piping is *C. melodus;* the Wilson's is *C. wilsonia;* the mountain is *Eupoda montana;* and the killdeer is *C. vociferus.* ALFRED M. BAILEY

Related Articles in WORLD BOOK include:

Animal (color picture: Animals of the Polar Regions)	Crocodile Bird Jaçana
Bird (color pictures: Birds' Eggs, Water Birds)	Killdeer Lapwing
Bustard	Turnstone

PLOW is an implement used to prepare the earth for planting. Early man used a stick to turn up the soil. Later, he realized that more soil could be broken up with a better tool. He broke off a forked branch from a tree, and sharpened one prong to turn the soil. He hitched his wife to the other end of the fork, and used the main branch as a handle as she pulled the implement over the ground. This was the first plow. Later, oxen were used to pull the plow. In some parts of the world today, implements almost as crude as the tree branch are still used, drawn by human beings, oxen, or camels.

Parts of a Plow. The modern plow is quite different from the forked stick. The *beam,* usually made of iron, is the part by which the plow is drawn. The handles attached to it are sometimes made of wood. The *frog* of the plow is the frame of the working part, or *bottom,* of the plow, and is usually of steel. Attached to the plow bottom are the share, moldboard, and landside. The plow bottom lifts, turns, and breaks up the soil.

The *share* is the cutting edge that tears the furrow slice loose from the ground. The plowshare receives most of the power needed to operate a plow bottom in the ground. Plowshares are made of steel or iron.

The *moldboard* is made of chilled iron or soft steel.

The Plow of Prehistoric Times was merely a stick that hoed the ground.

Oxen Pulled the Roman Farmer's Plow. Like all ancient plows, it did little more than hoe and scratch the surface of the land.

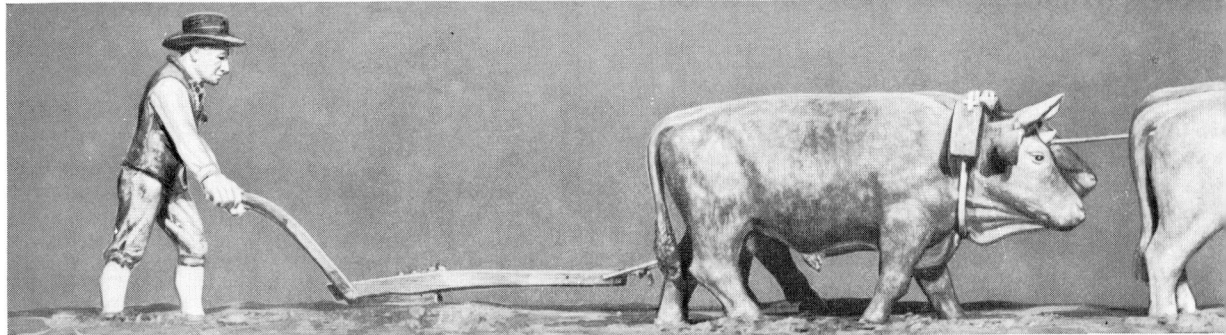

The Early American Plow was still a wooden tool. It was clumsy to use and required great power to pull, but it did tend to turn the ground over and pulverize it to some extent. In heavy soil, less than an acre a day could be plowed.

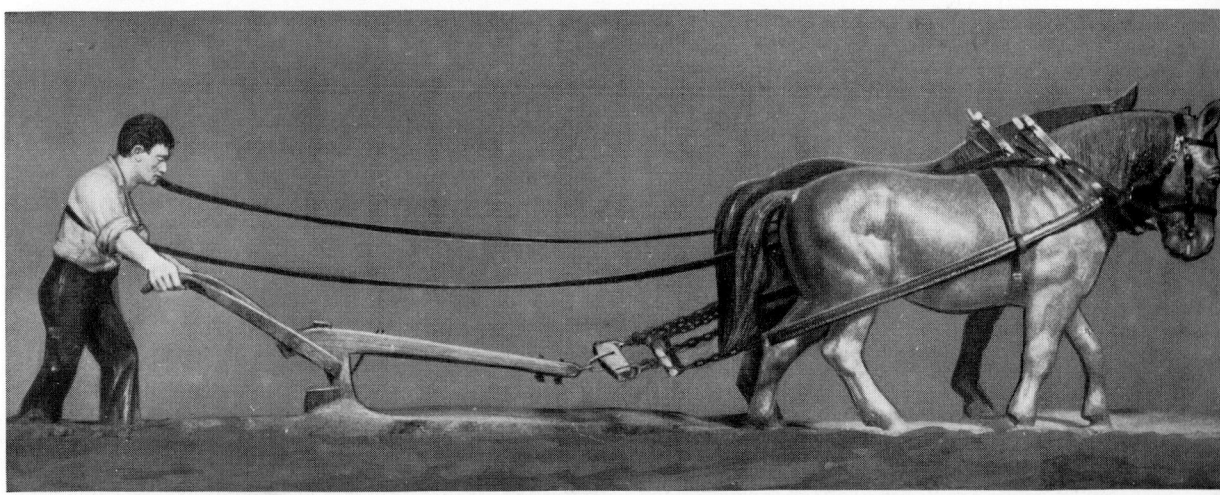

Cast-Iron Plows Followed those made of wood and sheathed with metal surfaces. In 1797, a patent was granted to Charles Newbold for such a cast-iron plow with a moldboard, share, and landside all in one casting. Plowing was speeded up as a result.

N.Y. Museum of Science and Industry

Blacksmith John Deere Is Credited with having made the first steel plow from old saws in 1837. It was capable of turning the tough soil of the prairies. Sticky soil which had clung to cast iron slid off the shiny steel.

International Harvester Co.

A Large Gang Plow can turn over many acres of land in a day. Plows of this type, drawn by diesel tractors, are used by many wheat farmers on the Great Plains to prepare the land for planting.

It is attached to the plow bottom at the upper edge of the share. It turns the soil and breaks it up. There are three general types of moldboards: the *stubble*, the *general-purpose*, and the *sod*, or *breaker*. The stubble moldboard is short and steep, and has a sharp curve for use in land that needs to be broken up fine. The general-purpose moldboard has a longer curve than the stubble moldboard, and does a good job on the soil under average conditions. The breaker, or sod, type of moldboard is used for turning heavy earth, or prairie earth that has never been plowed. It has a long, gradual turn, and is used for plowing shallow furrows.

The *landside* is a sidepiece opposite the moldboard. This piece presses against the side of the ground, and offsets the side pressure exerted on the moldboard. It eases the strain, and helps steady the motion of the plow. Landsides also are made of chilled iron or soft steel.

Coulters and *jointers* are cutting attachments that cut a sharp, clean furrow. They are attached to the beam and cut the earth ahead of the share. The coulter is a knife or blade, and the jointer is a small, shovel-like plow. The jointer is necessary on plows that must cut stubborn ground.

Kinds of Plows. The *walking plow* is especially useful in tilling a small plot of ground. It turns only one furrow, and can be drawn by a team of horses or a yoke of oxen. It is called a walking plow because the plowman walks behind the implement and keeps it in position by grasping the handles.

The *sulky* is a riding plow. It is horse-drawn, and turns only one furrow. The *gang plow* can also be ridden. It has two or more moldboards. Gang plows usually have three wheels. One runs in the open furrow just ahead of the first plow bottom, another turns in the furrow just back of the last bottom, and the third rolls on the unplowed land. The depth of the furrow is regulated by levers which the driver operates.

Tractor Plows have replaced horse-drawn plows on more level farm lands. They have from one to five bottoms. The bottoms of tractor plows are mounted on frames, so that each bottom stays in place. The parts of the tractor plow bottoms are about the same as on horse-drawn bottoms.

The *disk plow* is constructed differently from the moldboard types. It turns the furrow with a rolling blade, 2 feet or more in diameter. The disk plow cuts a furrow 8 to 12 inches wide, and is used in plowing hard, sticky, or stony land. A. D. LONGHOUSE

See also DEERE, JOHN; FARM AND FARMING; WOOD, JETHRO.

PLUM is a fruit that contains a stonelike seed. The plum may be as small as a cherry or as large as a small peach. It may be round or oval. The thin skin may be green, yellow, red, blue, or purple. The thick, juicy flesh surrounds a flattened, hard pit that contains the seed. Botanists call the plum a *drupe* (see DRUPE).

Plums have many uses as food. Many are eaten fresh. Others are used to make jelly, preserves, plum butter, and jam. Some are dried to make *prunes* (see PRUNE).

The plum tree grows in temperate regions of the world. It may be low and shrubby, but sometimes it grows 30 feet high. It has white flowers that usually appear before the leaves do.

Almost 2,000 varieties of plums are known, but only about 150 are important. The important varieties come from five main types of plums, all with different characteristics: European, Japanese, American, damson, and ornamental.

European Plums, also called *garden*, or *common*, *plums*, are blue or red, medium to very large fruits. Although they can be eaten fresh and canned, most of them are dried as prunes. Prunes have a high sugar content. The *French*, or *Agen*, variety of plum is the most important kind used to produce prunes. European plums grown in the United States include *President*, *Tragedy*, *Green Gage*, *Reine Claude*, and *Grand Duke*.

Garden plum trees have been grown in Europe since the beginning of the Christian Era. Plum trees were first brought to America from Europe about 1620, but not until the late 1700's were these trees planted in any

Western Fruit Grower

Duarte Plums, *above, are a popular breakfast fruit.*

Flowers of the Plum Tree, *left, bloom before the late summer fruit crop.*

Wickson, Redheart, Duarte, Red Rosa, Kelsey, and *Burbank.* Most of the commercial orchards of Japanese plum are located on the Pacific Coast, especially in California.

American Plums include several varieties, of which the most important is the cold-resistant *Prunus americana.* It grows wild east of the Rocky Mountains. The skin and flesh are amber and have a good flavor. *Hortulan* plums are bushy and thorny, but less resistant to cold than *P. americana.* The *sand cherry* plum grows in the Middle West and Canada.

Damson Plums, which are tart and blue, are favorites for jellies and jams. The trees resemble the European types, but are smaller and more resistant to cold. The several types include bullaces, St. Juliens, and mirabelles.

Ornamental Plums, such as *myrobalan,* produce red foliage and fruit that is suitable for jellies and jams. The myrobalan plum has greater value as a rootstock for other stone fruits, such as the apricot.

Scientific Classification. Plums belong to the rose family, *Rosaceae.* They are genus *Prunus.* European plums, including prunes, are *P. domestica.* Japanese or salicina plums are *P. salicina.* The native American plum is *P. americana.* Hortulan plums are *P. hortulana,* and sand cherry plums are *P. besseyi.* Damson plums are *P. insititia.* Ornamental plums include the myrobalan plum, which is classified as *P. cerasifera.*   REID M. BROOKS

See also DRUPE; GRAFTING; PLANT (color picture: Some Members of the Rose Family); PRUNE.

PLUM CURCULIO. See CURCULIO.

PLUMB LINE, or PLUMMET, is a string or line with a weight fastened to one end. The weight, called a *plumb bob,* keeps the line straight up and down. Plumb lines are used by bricklayers and stonemasons as vertical guides in building walls. Surveyors and engineers use plumb lines to set sighting instruments called *transits* over a specific point.

Plumb lines are also used to determine the depth of water or of excavations. But today, most ships use instruments called *fathometers* and *sonars* to measure the depth of the water.   B. AUSTIN BARRY

See also LEAD, SOUNDING; SURVEYING (Surveying Tools); TRANSIT.

PLUMBAGO, *plum BAY goh,* or LEADWORT, is the name of several garden plants and shrubs that are grown for their handsome clusters of blue, white, or reddish-purple flowers. Each flower is shaped much like a phlox blossom. The flaring petals are joined at the center to form a long tube. The leaves are also somewhat like those of the phlox. They are oval, shiny, and dark green. An annual form of plumbago that is often used in northern gardens grows up to $1\frac{1}{2}$ feet high and has spikes of rich blue flowers. One of the handsomest shrubs in southern California and the Gulf States is a plumbago that forms large bushes or vines. Pale blue or white flowers cover it for much of the year. This plumbago can be grown in northern states only in greenhouses.

Scientific Classification. Plumbagos belong to the leadwort family, *Plumbaginaceae.* Annual plumbagos are genus *Plumbago,* species *P. caerulea;* the bushy plumbago is species *P. capensis.*   J. J. LEVISON

number. European plum trees must be planted in cool, dry areas, where the *brown-rot fungus* and the *plum curculio* insect do not spread easily. For example, they grow on the northeastern Atlantic Coast and on the Pacific Coast.

Japanese, or **Salicina, Plums** are eaten fresh, cooked, and canned. Some make fine jelly. Prunes are never made from these plums. These yellow, crimson, and purple fruits range from small to large. All are very juicy and sweet. The Japanese plum grew originally in China as a wild tree. The Japanese cultivated it for many years before it was brought to the United States in 1870. Varieties include *Beauty, Burmosa, Santa Rosa,*

LEADING PLUM GROWING STATES AND PROVINCES

Tons of fresh plums and prunes grown in 1967

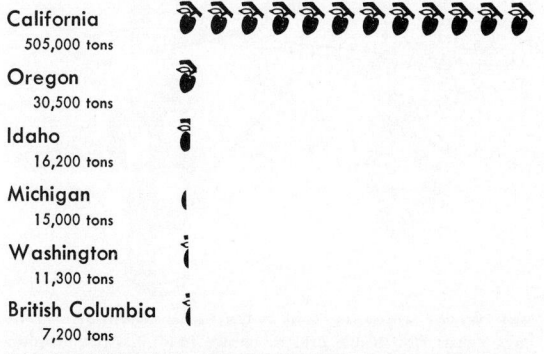

California	505,000 tons
Oregon	30,500 tons
Idaho	16,200 tons
Michigan	15,000 tons
Washington	11,300 tons
British Columbia	7,200 tons

Sources: U.S. Department of Agriculture; Dominion Bureau of Statistics

PLUMBING

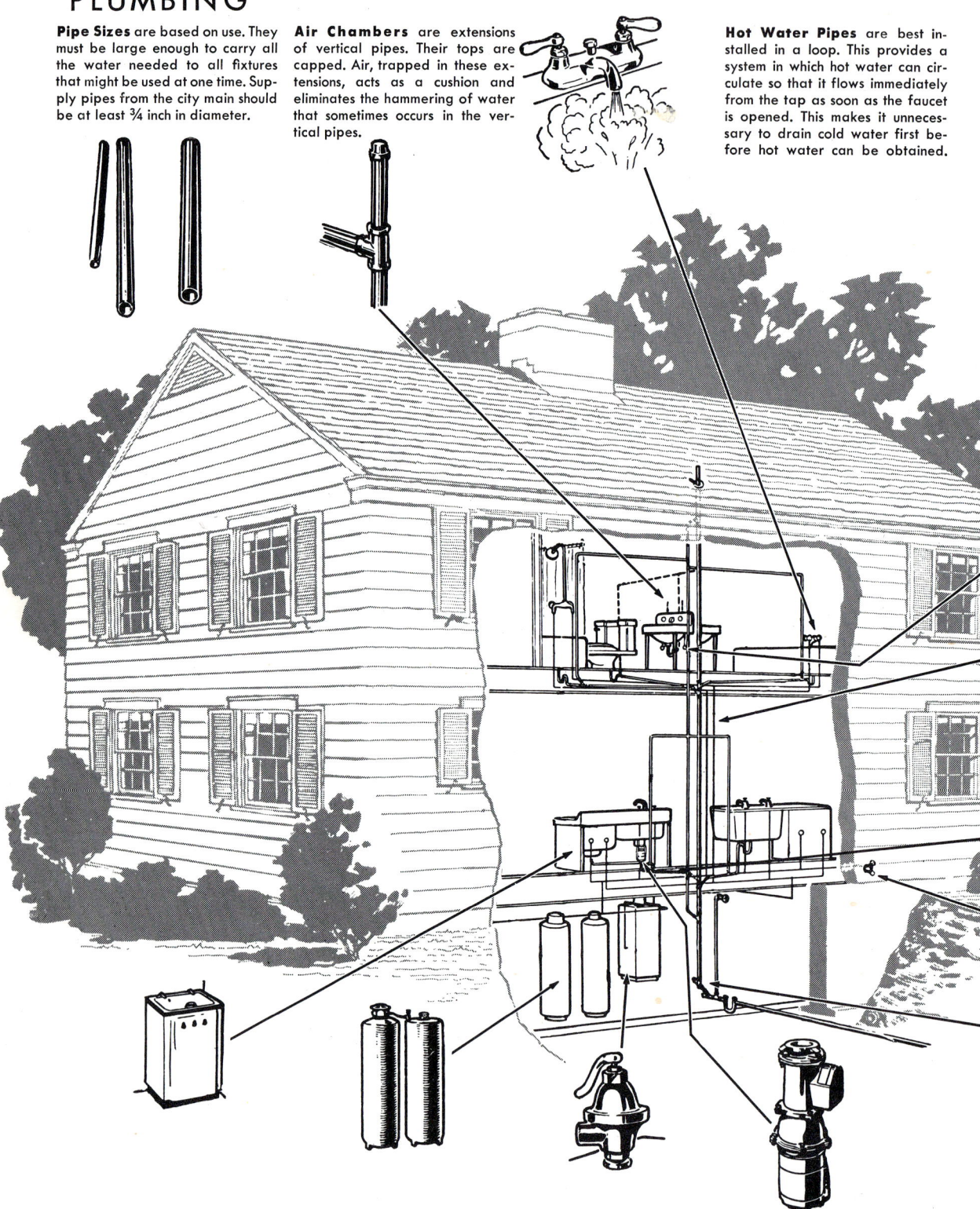

Pipe Sizes are based on use. They must be large enough to carry all the water needed to all fixtures that might be used at one time. Supply pipes from the city main should be at least ¾ inch in diameter.

Air Chambers are extensions of vertical pipes. Their tops are capped. Air, trapped in these extensions, acts as a cushion and eliminates the hammering of water that sometimes occurs in the vertical pipes.

Hot Water Pipes are best installed in a loop. This provides a system in which hot water can circulate so that it flows immediately from the tap as soon as the faucet is opened. This makes it unnecessary to drain cold water first before hot water can be obtained.

Special Equipment often needs specifically designed plumbing. Installation of some machines such as dishwashers may be governed by local laws.

Water Softeners remove the minerals that make water "hard." Soft water makes washing easier and prolongs the usefulness of pipes.

Hot Water Heaters must have valves that relieve pressure created by steam. They must also have thermostats to control water temperature.

Garbage Grinder shreds waste food. It is connected to the kitchen sink drain, and discharges the waste into the sewage system.

Pipe Corrosion can be lessened if the pipe materials are carefully chosen. Some kinds of water contain more corrosive substances than do other kinds. Careful analysis of the water helps determine the kind of pipe needed.

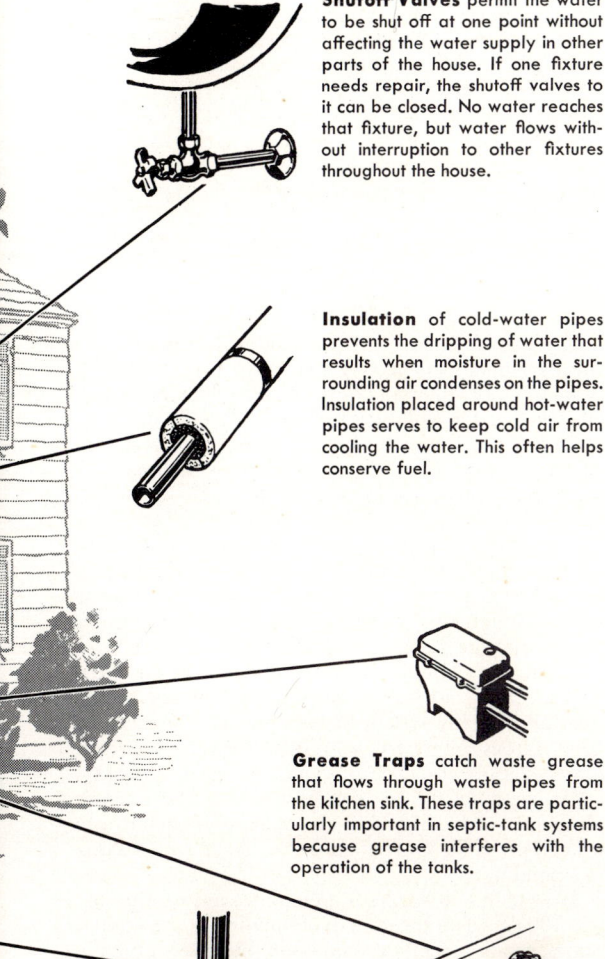

Shutoff Valves permit the water to be shut off at one point without affecting the water supply in other parts of the house. If one fixture needs repair, the shutoff valves to it can be closed. No water reaches that fixture, but water flows without interruption to other fixtures throughout the house.

Insulation of cold-water pipes prevents the dripping of water that results when moisture in the surrounding air condenses on the pipes. Insulation placed around hot-water pipes serves to keep cold air from cooling the water. This often helps conserve fuel.

Grease Traps catch waste grease that flows through waste pipes from the kitchen sink. These traps are particularly important in septic-tank systems because grease interferes with the operation of the tanks.

Cleanouts provide an opening into the drainage system. When the system becomes clogged, these outlets can be opened to clean the pipe.

Hose Outlets and other connections that supply water outside the house should have stop and drain valves inside the house to prevent freezing.

PLUMBING, *PLUM ing.* In Roman times, water was carried to houses through lead pipes. The Latin word for lead is *plumbum*, and from this comes our word *plumbing*.

A plumbing system consists of two sets of pipes. One set brings in clean water. The other set carries away dirty water. Sewer water and sewer gas smell bad and carry germs. This makes it important to keep clean water and dirty water completely separated.

Plumbing Problems

Cross Connections. Poorly designed plumbing fixtures allow dirty water to enter the clean water system. Sanitary engineers call these cross connections. About 95 per cent of the typhoid fever cases reported in the United States in the 1930's resulted from cross connections between the water supply and the drain pipe system. The amebic dysentery epidemic in Chicago during the Century of Progress Exposition in 1933 was traced to a faulty plumbing system in a large hotel. Because of the poor design of the plumbing, sewage had entered the drinking water.

To avoid cross connections, faucets or supply lines to washbowls, tubs, or toilets should discharge well above the point where the water in this equipment will overflow. Otherwise, dirty water may siphon into the drinking water supply when a sudden drop in pressure occurs in the water system. Such pressure drops often take place in tall buildings, but they may occur at ground level when there is a heavy use of water to fight a large fire. Many persons use a hose screwed to a faucet to fill washing machines and tubs. If one of these open hoses dips into the dirty water in a tub, and if the pressure of water in the clean water pipes is suddenly lowered, dirty water will be drawn into the clean-water pipes. It will contaminate them and may spread sickness. City waterworks take care to maintain good water pressure in the clean water pipes at all times.

Sewer Gas is an unpleasant substance. To prevent it from entering houses, every sink, bowl, tub, and toilet that discharges into the sewer must have a water trap. A *water trap* is a loop of pipe placed lower than the drain but higher than the sewer. It catches and holds enough water to form a gastight valve between the fixture and the sewer.

A special *vent* pipe must lead from each trap into an air pipe that goes through the roof. Sewer gas escapes through this pipe. A *screw plug* in the bottom of each water trap permits the pipe to be opened for cleaning out heavy solids that may collect there. Sometimes people clean clogged water traps with chemicals sold in stores. These products contain strong alkalies or strong acids that can cause burns and damage pipes. The directions for handling and using them should be followed carefully.

Soap and Grease that collect in the pipes also cause trouble. If the water in a locality is *hard*, or contains much lime, the lime will combine with soapy water and grease in sewer water. Then a sticky and insoluble *lime soap* forms. This material is troublesome in sewers, because there is no easy way to get it out. Many plumbing systems, especially those in hotels and restaurants, have separate drains for the sinks. Toilet waste goes straight to the sewer. Kitchen pipes discharge into a *catch basin* that traps the lime soap and waste grease, and lets grease-free water drain off from beneath. From time to time, this slime must be cleaned out of the catch basin. If slime gets into the sewer it may collect in such large amounts that the sewer will not be able to carry flood water adequately in a heavy storm. Synthetic detergents do not form insoluble slime with hard water. To prevent trouble, waste grease should be disposed of in the garbage instead of in the sink.

Flooding. As long as the water level in the sewer is lower than the level in any part of the house, the sewer will discharge normally. If the sewer becomes stopped up or filled with flood water, sewage may flow back into the house. Most basements have a floor drain that contains a hollow ball. If flood water comes up from the sewer, the ball floats and rises against a ring. This seals the drain and prevents sewer water from rising into the basement.

Waste-Water Systems. Pipes for waste water are larger than those that supply fresh water, and are seldom completely full. Water flowing in partly filled pipes acts like an air pump. It compresses the air in some parts of the system and produces a partial vacuum in others. The compressed air may force bad air back into plumbing fixtures on lower floors; or the vacuum may suck water out of traps, thus breaking the seal and allowing bad air and gases to escape.

Waste pipes must be large enough to carry away the used water as fast as it is discharged. The system also must include a secondary system of vent pipes that open to the outside air. These pipes connect with the discharge side of each fixture trap where air might be compressed or where a vacuum might form. Most cities have laws that state the requirements to be met. A plumbing inspector must approve each installation before it is used.

Because each set of fixtures must be provided with drain and vent pipe, it is economical to arrange the plumbing so that the laundry is in the basement directly below the kitchen fixtures and the bathroom is above the kitchen. All fixtures then connect to one "stack" of drain and vent pipes. In one-story houses, the kitchen and bathroom may be built with all fixtures attached to the same wall.

Leaks and Corrosion. The amount of water wasted because of small leaks is astonishing. A hole the size of a pencil lead may waste 500 gallons of water each day. A small, continuous drip or a toilet fixture that does not shut off completely after flushing may double the monthly water bill. A hot water system leak wastes water and fuel.

Water has a tendency to attack metals. In the case of iron, this is called *rusting*. A more general term is *corrosion*. Manufacturers often coat iron pipe with zinc to protect it from corrosion. This *galvanized* pipe is used in water supply lines. Sometimes copper or brass pipe is used because it resists corrosion.

Frozen Pipes are one of the most serious difficulties that can occur in a plumbing system. Water starts to turn to ice at 32° F. But usually the pipes in a plumbing system do not freeze until the air temperature has remained below freezing for several hours. The speed at which plumbing pipes freeze depends on the location of the pipes and how much water flows through them. Even a moderate trickle of water can keep pipes from freezing except in the coldest weather.

Freezing water expands, and the expanding water exerts tremendous pressure on a material that confines it. It bursts plumbing pipes at their weakest places. Therefore, breakage often occurs at joints and elbows where the threads make the pipes a little thinner. Whenever possible, plumbers avoid placing pipes along outside walls where they would be subjected to sustained low temperatures during cold weather.

Frozen water pipes should be thawed with care. Burning matches or torches applied to the pipes, or the use of any kind of open flame, are dangerous. Setting fire to oil-soaked rags wrapped around the frozen pipes can be disastrous. Even if the walls of the building do not catch fire, the sudden heat can cause the pipes to burst and flood the area with water.

A portable electric heater can be used to warm the surrounding area and the pipes themselves. If this does not work, the pipes can be wrapped with cloth, and hot water poured on them until the ice in the pipes melts. Rags placed on the floor under the pipe will absorb the spilled water. If the pipes freeze so hard that neither of these methods works, a plumber should be called.

History

Plumbing is an ancient occupation. Historians credit the Egyptians with having made the first crude lead pipes to carry water and drainage. But Roman plumbers developed a plumbing system. They built drainage systems of tile, brick, stone, and lead sewers. These conveyed drainage from houses and public buildings to three main streams. Stone channels under the streets carried the drainage into the Tiber River. Water from the aqueducts ran through the underground channels to clean them. Plumbers also kept busy maintaining the public baths in Rome. One of their duties was to carve the elaborate water spouts from which the water flowed into the pools.

During the Middle Ages, interest in sanitation declined. Only castles, monasteries, and houses of the wealthy had any system for sewage and drainage. In these places plumbers were called upon to fashion ornate washbowls and tubs, and to make elaborate water spouts of fish or implike creatures. These early plumbers established drainage systems so that waste water ran through pipes into the moats surrounding the buildings.

The greatest advances in plumbing came during the late 1800's, when the growth of building in the United States made adequate sanitation necessary. Steam-powered pumps raised water to the top floors of buildings. New heating systems using water and steam were invented. Soon the demand for plumbers increased. They were needed to install the equipment and keep it in working order. In large cities, the demand for plumbers became so great that two new groups were formed to divide the work. One group, the *steam fitters*, was responsible for installing and maintaining steam pipes. The other group, called *pipe fitters*, installed and repaired all other kinds of pipe.   C. Fred Gurnham

See also BLOWTORCH; FAUCET; PIPE; SEWAGE; STEAM FITTER.

PLUMCOT. See Burbank, Luther.

PLUMMER, HENRY. See Montana (The Gold Rush).

PLUMULE. See Cotyledon; Germination.

PLUNKETT, EDWARD JOHN MORETON DRAX. See Dunsany, Lord.

PLURAL. See Number (in grammar).

PLURALISM. See Government (How Much Government?); Metaphysics (Doctrines).

PLUSH. See Velvet.

PLUTARCH, *PLOO tahrk* (A.D. 46? - A.D. 120?), a Greek biographer and essayist, became famous for his work, *Parallel Lives of Illustrious Greeks and Romans.* Plutarch wrote the *Lives,* or biographies, in pairs of one Greek and one Roman statesman or general. The comparisons are often forced, but the *Lives* constitute an important source of historical information. *Plutarch's Lives* became the basis of many stories and poems of the Middle Ages. William Shakespeare and other Elizabethan dramatists used a brilliant translation by Sir Thomas North (1535?-1601?) as a source of material for many of their historical plays. The *Lives* contains sharply drawn character sketches and lively historical descriptions of Greece and Rome.

Among Plutarch's other writings are his *Morals.* They include essays on historical, religious, and philosophical topics. Among them is a curious account of *The Face on the Moon.*

Plutarch was born at Chaeronea, in Boeotia, Greece, near the homes of Hesiod and Pindar. He studied philosophy in Athens and later lectured on this subject in Rome. In travels through Greece, Italy, and Egypt, he spent much time studying and collecting facts on the men of whom he wrote. He returned to Chaeronea as a priest of Apollo, and it is believed that he wrote his great works there.   C. Bradford Welles

PLUTO is the most distant planet from the sun. Pluto and Neptune are the only planets that cannot be seen without a telescope. Astronomers "discovered" both these planets by using mathematics.

Pluto is about 39 times as far from the sun as the earth is. Its mean distance from the sun is about 3,675,000,000 miles. Pluto travels around the sun in an *elliptical* (oval-shaped) orbit. At some points in its orbit, it comes closer to the sun than Neptune, the second farthest planet. Pluto travels around the sun once about every 248 years, compared to once a year for the earth.

As it orbits the sun, Pluto spins on its axis, an imaginary line through its center. The planet spins around once in about six earth-days, compared to one day for the earth.

Astronomers know little about Pluto's size or surface

--- PLUTO AT A GLANCE ---

Distance from the Sun: *Shortest*—2,770,000,000 miles; *Greatest*—4,580,000,000 miles; *Mean*—3,675,000,000 miles.

Distance from the Earth: *Shortest*—2,700,000,000 miles; *Greatest*—4,670,000,000 miles.

Diameter: About 4,000 miles.

Length of Year: About 248 earth-years.

Rotation Period: About 6 earth-days.

Average Temperature: About −300° F. (−184° C.)

Atmosphere: None.

Satellites: None.

conditions, because the planet is so far from the earth. Pluto has an estimated diameter of 4,000 miles, about half that of the earth. The temperature on Pluto may be as low as −360° F. (−218° C.). The planet does not appear to have any atmosphere. No one knows whether it has any form of life.

In 1905, Percival Lowell, an American astronomer, found that the force of gravity of some unknown planet seemed to be affecting the orbits of Neptune and Uranus. He predicted the location of a new planet, and began searching for it from his observatory in Flagstaff, Ariz. Lowell used a telescope to photograph the area of the sky where he thought the planet would be found. He died in 1916 without finding it.

In 1929, Clyde W. Tombaugh, an assistant at the Lowell Observatory, used predictions made by Lowell and other astronomers and photographed the sky with a more powerful telescope. On March 13, 1930, Tombaugh found Pluto's image on three photographs. The planet was named after the Greek and Roman god of the lower world.   Hyron Spinrad

See also Astronomy (A Trip Through the Universe [color picture]); Lowell, Percival; Planet; Solar System; Tombaugh, Clyde W.

Brown Bros.

Pluto, the God of the Lower World, is shown with his wife, Proserpina, whom he kidnaped from the Upper World. At his feet is his three-headed watchdog, Cerberus.

PLUTO, in Greek and Roman mythology, ruled the Lower World, or abode of the dead. He was also called *Hades* by the Greeks, and *Dis* and *Orcus* by the Romans. His symbol, a helmet, made its wearer invisible. It was believed that all men visited his dreary palace sooner or later. Men worshiped Pluto, but did not like him. They feared him, and turned their faces away from his altar as they sacrificed black sheep to him. They built very few temples to this unpopular god. Although the people considered Pluto cold and without mercy, they also thought him to be a just god.

According to belief, Pluto was not really cruel, but he wanted no other god to interfere with his rights. He had some human feelings. He fell in love with Proser-

PLUTONIUM

pina (Persephone) and carried her off to his kingdom.

Pluto was sometimes considered a god of riches and wealth, since gold and silver came from the earth. Usually, however, the Greek god of wealth was the blind Plutus, son of Demeter. The word *plutocrat* comes from the Greek word for wealth. PHILIP W. HARSH

See also HADES; PLUTUS; PROSERPINA.

PLUTONIUM, *ploo TOH nih um* (chemical symbol, Pu), is a man-made, radioactive element. Its atomic number is 94. Its most stable isotope has a mass number of 244. Four American scientists, G. T. Seaborg, J. W. Kennedy, E. M. McMillan, and A. C. Wahl, discovered plutonium in 1940 (see MCMILLAN, EDWIN M.; SEABORG, GLENN T.).

Certain uranium ores contain plutonium, but the amount is too small to make its extraction practical. Plutonium is formed when neptunium, element 93, loses a beta particle from its nucleus. The beta particle is given off from a neutron in the nucleus, which then changes into a proton. This change creates plutonium, element 94. Since the discovery of plutonium, about 15 isotopes have been produced. They have mass numbers ranging from 232 to 246.

The most important isotope is Pu-239, because it is fissionable. It is manufactured in quantities in uranium chain reactors by bombarding uranium with neutrons. It serves as a source of energy in nuclear explosions and nuclear reactors (see ATOMIC BOMB; HYDROGEN BOMB). Pu-239 has a half-life of 24,000 years (see RADIOACTIVITY [Half-Life]). It is extremely poisonous.

The metal is silvery-white, and has a melting point of 639.5° C. (±2° C.). It undergoes five changes between room temperature and melting point. It therefore has six different *allotropic* (physical) forms (see ALLOTROPY). It boils at 3235° C. (±19° C.). GLENN T. SEABORG

See also ATOMIC ENERGY (Chain Reactions); TRANSURANIUM ELEMENTS; URANIUM.

PLUTUS, *PLOO tus*, was a god of wealth in Greek mythology. He was the son of Demeter and Iasion. Zeus (Jupiter) blinded him so that he would give riches to good and bad people alike. He is often shown lame, because wealth comes slowly, or with wings, to show that money flies away fast. See also PLUTO.

PLYMOUTH, *PLIM uth*, England (pop. 247,400; alt. 30 ft.), is a seaport and naval base on the Channel coast, about 195 miles southwest of London. It lies on Plymouth Sound, where the River Tamar flows into the sea (see GREAT BRITAIN [political map]). The center of the city was rebuilt after World War II bombings. Sir Francis Drake and other explorers sailed from Plymouth. The city was the last European port touched by the *Mayflower*. JOHN W. WEBB

PLYMOUTH, Mass. (pop. 11,000; alt. 50 ft.), is often called *America's Home Town*. In 1620, colonists from England sailed across the Atlantic in the *Mayflower* and settled at Plymouth. The town lies on a shallow harbor, about 40 miles south of Boston (see MASSACHUSETTS [political map]). Plimoth Plantation, a reconstruction of the original settlement, features *Mayflower II*, built the way the original *Mayflower* is believed to have looked (see MAYFLOWER [picture: *Mayflower II*]). Plymouth has one of the world's largest rope-making plants. It has a limited town meeting government. WILLIAM J. REID

PLYMOUTH COLONY was the second permanent English settlement in America. The colonists who settled there called themselves *Pilgrims* because of their wanderings in search of religious freedom. In 1620, they established their colony on the rocky western shore of Cape Cod Bay in southeastern Massachusetts. This region had been called *Plimouth* on John Smith's map of New England, drawn in 1614. Plymouth Colony remained independent until 1691, when it became part of Massachusetts Bay Colony.

Plymouth Colony and the Pilgrims have become for all Americans a lesson of how a people with little more than courage, perseverance, and hard work could build themselves a home in a hostile world. Their bravery set an example for future generations of Americans. They established the town meeting form of government and the Congregational Church in America.

Many tourists visit modern Plymouth with its memorials to the Pilgrim forefathers. Just south of town there is a model of the original Pilgrim village. Plimoth Plantation, Inc., a nonprofit organization dedicated to the preservation of the Pilgrim heritage, also maintains a replica of the first Pilgrim house and of the *Mayflower*.

The Founding of Plymouth Colony

Most of the Pilgrims were *Separatists* (Puritans who had separated from the Church of England). The government of England arrested and tried the Separatists because of their *nonconformity* (refusal to belong to the Church of England). In 1608, a group of Separatists moved to The Netherlands. After a few years, some of them became dissatisfied, and felt that things would be better in a new land. They secured financial backing in London, and, in 1620, left The Netherlands in a small ship called the *Speedwell*. The ship stopped in England, and the expedition was joined by some additional Separatists and by a few other Englishmen who hoped to better their lives. The group left England in the *Speedwell* and a larger ship, the *Mayflower*. The *Speedwell* proved unseaworthy, and the little fleet returned to England twice. Finally, in September, 1620, the *Mayflower* sailed alone from Plymouth, England, with 102 passengers, including women and children.

A rough passage of 65 days brought the *Mayflower* to Cape Cod. The Pilgrims had expected to settle somewhere within the limits of the original grant of the Virginia Company. But errors in navigation led them to the New England region. Adverse winds and the shoals off Cape Cod forced the *Mayflower* to stay north. The ship anchored in Provincetown harbor inside the tip of Cape Cod on November 21 (November 11, according to the calendar then in use).

The Pilgrim leaders were uncertain of their legal position because they were in the area without authority. They also knew they would need discipline among themselves. To solve these problems, the 41 men aboard met and signed the Mayflower Compact, the first agreement for self-government in America. They also elected John Carver as their first governor.

The Landing at Plymouth. The sea-weary Pilgrims were anxious to learn more about the country. For almost a month, they explored the coast around Cape Cod Bay. They had to take refuge on an island in Plymouth harbor during a blinding snowstorm. On Dec. 21 (Dec. 11), 1620, they landed at Plymouth.

PLYMOUTH COLONY

Atlantic Ocean

PLYMOUTH

Cape Cod Bay

The *Mayflower* anchored in Plymouth Bay in December, 1620, after the Pilgrims had chosen a settlement site.

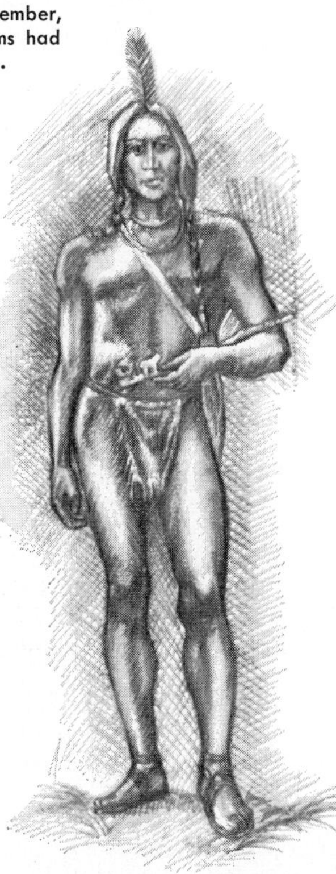

Chief Massasoit met the Pilgrims in a treaty council soon after they landed at Plymouth. Governor Carver and the Indian chieftain made a treaty of friendship that lasted until Massasoit died in 1661.

There they found a stream with clear pure water, some cleared land, and a high hill that could be fortified. This site was once an Indian village, but a smallpox plague had wiped out all the Indians in 1617. The Pilgrims decided that this would be their new home. The *Mayflower* sailed across Cape Cod Bay and anchored in Plymouth harbor on December 26 (December 16).

The First Year in the New Land was a difficult one for the Pilgrims. Poor and inadequate food, strenuous work, and changeable weather made the settlers susceptible to sickness. The colony lost almost half its members during that first winter.

But help came to the Pilgrims. One spring morning, an Indian walked into the little village and introduced himself to the startled people as Samoset. Two weeks later he returned with Squanto. The two Indians introduced the Pilgrims to Massasoit, the *sachem* (chief) of the Wampanoag tribe that controlled all southeastern Massachusetts. Governor Carver and the chief exchanged gifts and arranged a treaty of peace. Shortly afterward, the *Mayflower* sailed for England, leaving the Pilgrims on their own. Then Carver died, and William Bradford became governor of the colony.

The Pilgrims, under Squanto's direction, caught *ale-wives* (a fish in the herring family) and used them as fertilizer in planting corn, pumpkins, and beans. They hunted and fished for food. The bountiful harvest that year led Governor Bradford to declare a celebration. Sometime in the autumn of 1621, the Pilgrims invited

The Pilgrims Who Stayed at Plymouth Colony gazed sadly after the distant *Mayflower* as it sailed back to England.
Visual Education Service

519

Plymouth Colony had snug, sturdy houses built with thick planks the Pilgrims sawed out of trees from nearby forests. Each house was built around a huge chimney. This picture shows a replica of Plymouth Colony as it looked in 1627, built at Plimoth Plantation in Plymouth, Mass.

Courtesy of Plimoth Plantation

their Indian friends to join them in a three-day festival which we now call the first Thanksgiving.

Life in Plymouth Colony

The Pilgrims received legal rights to settle at Plymouth under a patent granted by the Council for New England in 1621. Governor Bradford received a new patent, the Warwick Patent, in 1630. It granted him all the land south of a line between Narragansett Bay and Cohasset. Under this patent, Bradford could have claimed ownership of the entire colony, but he shared control with the other settlers. He turned the patent over to all the *freemen* (voters) of the colony in 1640. A few years later, surveyors marked off an area corresponding to the present counties of Bristol, Barnstable, and Plymouth as the colony of Plymouth.

Expansion of the Colony. In November, 1621, the ship *Fortune* arrived with 35 new colonists. Other ships brought additional settlers but the population grew to only 300 settlers in 10 years. Some of the colonists decided to move from Plymouth to better lands. Some went north and established the towns of Duxbury, Marshfield, and Scituate. Others moved west to Rehoboth, or farther east on Cape Cod to settle Sandwich, Barnstable, Yarmouth, and Eastham.

Government. The men who signed the Mayflower Compact were the freemen of the colony. They, along with any newly chosen freemen, met once a year to discuss the problems of the colony. This body, called the General Court, elected the governor and his assistants, made laws, and levied taxes. In outlying towns, the freemen gathered in a town meeting to elect their own officers and settle town matters. Beginning in 1639, these individual towns sent representatives to the General Court at Plymouth.

Economic Life. The Pilgrims organized a joint-stock company with some London merchants to finance the voyage. The partnership was to last for seven years. The Pilgrims agreed to put the results of their labor into a common fund, which would provide the necessities of life for the settlers. At the end of seven years, all the profits and property were to be divided among the financiers and the settlers. This experiment did not work out, and in 1623 individual ownership replaced corporation ownership. The London merchants in 1627 agreed to sell their interest in the company to the Pilgrims, who finished paying off the debt in 1648.

The Pilgrims at first expected to make a profit from fishing. But they were never very successful at this. They turned to farming for their existence and to fur trading for profit. When other Puritans settled Massachusetts Bay Colony in 1628, the Pilgrims developed a prosperous trade in corn and cattle with them. Through steady and hard work, the colony was able to live moderately well without extremes of wealth or poverty.

The Honored Ones. William Bradford, second governor of Plymouth, wrote a history of the *Mayflower* adventure. He listed the passengers as follows:

Mr. John Carver; Kathrine, his wife; Desire Minter; & 2. man-servants, John Howland, Roger Wilder; William Latham, a boy; & a maid servant, & a child yt was put to him, called Jasper More.

Mr. William Brewster; Mary, his wife; with 2. sons, whose names were Love & Wrasling; and a boy was put to him called Richard More; and another of his brothers. The rest of his childeren were left behind, & came over afterwards.

Mr. Edward Winslow; Elizabeth, his wife; & 2. men servants, caled Georg Sowle and Elias Story; also a litle girle was put to him, caled Ellen, the sister of Richard More.

William Bradford, and Dorothy, his wife; having but one child, a sone, left behind, who came afterward.

Mr. Isaack Allerton, and Mary, his wife; with 3. children, Bartholmew, Remember, & Mary; and a servant boy, John Hooke.

Mr. Samuell Fuller, and a servant, caled William Butten. His wife was [left] behind, & a child, which came afterwards.

John Crakston, and his sone, John Crakston.

Captin Myles Standish, and Rose, his wife.

Mr. Christopher Martin, and his wife, and 2. servants, who were Salamon Prower and John Langemore.

Mr. William Mullines, and his wife, and 2. children, Joseph & Priscila; and a servant, Robart Carter.

Mr. William White, and Susana, his wife, and one sone, caled Resolved, and one borne a ship-board caled Perigriene; & 2. servants, named William Holbeck & Edward Thomson.

Mr. Steven Hopkins, & Elizabeth, his wife, and 2. children, caled Giles, and Constanta, a doughter, both by a former wife; and 2. more by this wife, caled Damaris & Oceanus; the last was borne at sea; and 2. servants, called Edward Doty and Edward Litster.

Mr. Richard Warren; but his wife and childeren were lefte behind, and came afterwards.

John Billinton, and Elen, his wife; and 2. sones, John & Francis.

Edward Tillie, and Ann, his wife; and 2. children that were their cossens, Henery Samson and Humillity Coper.

John Tillie, and his wife; and Eelizabeth, their doughter.

Francis Cooke, and his sone John. But his wife & other children came afterwards.

Thomas Rogers, and Joseph, his sone. His other children came afterwards.

Thomas Tinker, and his wife, and a sone.

John Rigdale, and Alice, his wife.

James Chilton, and his wife, and Mary, their dougter. They had an other doughter, yt was maried, came afterward.

Edward Fuller, and his wife, and Samuell, their sonne.

John Turner, and 2. sones. He had a doughter came some years after to Salem, wher she is now living.

Francis Eaton, and Sarah, his wife, and Samuell, their sone, a yong child.

Moyses Fletcher, John Goodman, Thomas Williams, Digerie Preist, Edmond Margeson, Peter Browne, Richard Britterige, Richard Clarke, Richard Gardenar, Gilbart Winslow.

John Alden was hired for a cooper, at South-Hampton, wher the ship victuled; and being a hopefull yong man, was much desired, but left to his owne liking to go or stay when he came here; but he stayed, and maryed here.

John Allerton and Thomas Enlish were both hired, the later to goe mr [master] of a shalop here, and ye other was reputed as one of ye company, but was to go back (being a seaman) for the help of others behind. But they both dyed here, before the shipe returned.

Ther were also other 2. seamen hired to stay a year here in the country, William Trevore, and one Ely. But when their time was out, they both returned.

These, bening aboute a hundred sowls, came over in this first ship; and began this worke, which God of his goodnes hath hithertoo blessed; let his holy name have ye praise.

Although 102 Pilgrims sailed from England, one died and another was born during the voyage. So 102 reached the harbor at Provincetown, Mass. Four more died and one was born there. The group that landed at Plymouth consisted of 99 Pilgrims. MARSHALL SMELSER

Related Articles in WORLD BOOK include:

Alden	Mayflower
Bradford (family)	Mayflower Compact
Brewster, William	Mayflower Descendants,
Carver, John	General Society of
Colonial Life in America	Pilgrim
Courtship of Miles	Plymouth Company
Standish, The	Plymouth Rock
Massachusetts (color	Puritan
picture: A Pilgrim House)	Samoset
Massachusetts Bay Colony	Squanto
Massasoit	Standish, Miles

PLYMOUTH COMPANY was formed by English merchants in 1606. Its full title was *The Virginia Company of Plymouth*. The object of the company was to increase English trade by settling colonists in North America. The organization received permission from King James I to colonize territory on the northeastern shore of America between the parallels of 38° and 45° north latitude.

In 1607, the Plymouth Company attempted to set up a colony. The site for the settlement was on Sabino Peninsula, in what is now the state of Maine. From the beginning, the colony seemed doomed to failure. A great fire destroyed many of the settlers' buildings, and violent quarrels arose among the colonists. Spain also was interested in acquiring land in North America, and threatened the new settlement. Some of the company's leaders died before the colony was fairly started. In addition, a severe winter brought more hardships to the discouraged colonists. The settlement was abandoned after about a year.

A. S. Burbank

The Granite Canopy Built over Plymouth Rock, *above,* bears the inscription "Erected by the National Society of the Colonial Dames of America to Commemorate the Three Hundredth Anniversary of the Landing of the Pilgrims." Plymouth Rock, *below,* stands near the spot where the Pilgrims are believed to have first set foot when they landed at Plymouth Bay in 1620.

In 1620, some members of the Old Plymouth Company formed an organization known as the New England Council, or the Corporation for New England, and received a charter from the king. This organization leased lands to the Pilgrims in 1621, and to the Massachusetts Bay Company in 1628. But the council never became a profitable organization, and in 1635 its promoters returned their charter to the king. G. G. DODDS

See also MASSACHUSETTS BAY COLONY; PLYMOUTH COLONY.

PLYMOUTH ROCK, a granite boulder with the date 1620 carved on it, lies near the sea at Plymouth, Mass. According to a popular story, the Pilgrims on the *Mayflower* stepped ashore on this rock when they landed in America on Dec. 21, 1620. Many historians, however, doubt that the Pilgrims actually stepped on the rock. It is more likely that the rock was near the spot where the Pilgrims landed.

In 1920, Plymouth Rock was moved from the beach to its present location. There it stands under a large granite canopy, a memorial to the courage of the Pilgrims. MARSHALL SMELSER

See also MAYFLOWER.

PLYMOUTH STATE COLLEGE. See NEW HAMPSHIRE, UNIVERSITY OF.

PLYWOOD

PLYWOOD is a building material made of an odd number of thin layers of wood glued together. The layers, called *plies* or *veneers*, are arranged so that the *grain direction* (direction of the wood fibers) of each layer is at right angles to that of the layer next to it. The outside plies are called *faces* and *backs*, and the center ply or plies are called the *core*. The plies immediately below the faces and backs are called *crossbands*. The simplest plywood is made of three plies of veneer. However, five, seven, nine, or more plies may be used. Lumbermen also use the term *plywood* for panels that have a solid lumber core up to 3 inches thick in place of a veneer core. These are used for doors.

Use of Plywood. The chief advantage of plywood is that by gluing together an odd number of plies of veneer, greater strength can be obtained than with ordinary wood. Plywood can also be cut to exact sizes and produced in large panels for ease of application, strength, and smooth surfaces. It shrinks and swells less than ordinary wood, and has greater resistance to splitting at the ends. This permits carpenters to fasten plywood sheets with nails or screws close to the edges. Plywood also has little or no tendency to warp or twist. In addi-

tion, expensive woods can be used for the faces because they are only needed in thin sheets. Plywood can also be made in curved shapes.

Construction men use plywood chiefly for floors, to line roofs and walls, and for wall paneling. It is particularly suited for the forms used for shaping concrete for home, building, bridge, and dam foundations. Carpenters and cabinetmakers find wide use for plywood in furniture, cabinets, counters, and millwork. Manufacturers use it in truck bodies, boats, freight and passenger train cars, house trailers, office equipment, sporting goods, highway signs, and many other products.

Kinds of Plywood. Lumbermen classify plywood in two ways—by material and by use. The materials used for plywood are classified as hardwood and softwood. Most *softwood* plywood is made of Douglas fir. But western hemlock, white fir, ponderosa pine, redwood, and many other types of trees are used. *Hardwood* plywood is available in more than 80 kinds of wood. These include domestic woods such as oak, red gum, poplar, birch, cherry, and walnut. Imported woods include mahogany and attractive tropical woods.

Interior plywood is usually made with glues that are moisture-resistant. *Exterior* plywood is designed to withstand severe conditions resulting from moisture and

Plywood Is Made from thin sheets of wood that are peeled off big logs, *above*. The logs go from storage ponds, *left*, to lathes that peel them into veneer, *center*. After rollers put on glue, *right*, workmen stack the sheets with the wood grains at right angles.

Douglas Fir Plywood Assn.

A Giant Press Squeezes the Sheets Together, *left*. It also heats the plywood. The combination of heat, pressure, and glue binds the plies of wood together permanently. Finished plywood, *above*, is then sanded, cut, inspected, and stacked for shipment.

humidity. It is always made with waterproof glues.

The most commonly available types of plywood panels are 4 feet wide, 8 feet long, and from $\frac{1}{4}$ to $\frac{3}{4}$ of an inch thick. Dimensions of plywood panels usually range from 3 to 5 feet wide, 5 to 12 feet long, and $\frac{3}{16}$ to $1\frac{3}{16}$ inches thick. Three, five, or seven plies are normally used.

Making Plywood is done in three steps. These are (1) the log, (2) the veneer, and (3) the lay-up.

Logs used for plywood are selected for straightness, roundness, and freedom from knots and decay. After the bark is removed and the logs cut to the desired lengths, they are steam-heated. This softens their surfaces, and they are placed into the lathe or slicer to be converted to veneer (see VENEER).

Veneer is made in one of three ways. These are (1) sawing, (2) slicing, or (3) rotary cutting. *Sawing* is used only for fine finishing woods, such as ebony or knotty pine, which are too brittle or unsuitable for slicing. *Slicing* is used chiefly for fine-figured woods for furniture or wall-panel faces. Slicing is done by moving the log, called a *flitch*, against a heavy, stationary knife. About nine-tenths of veneer is *rotary cut* by means of a lathe. The log is placed in a lathe and then revolved against a stationary knife extending across its length. The veneer is unwound in a long, continuous ribbon.

The Lay-Up takes place after the plies are dried, trimmed, and matched. A thin layer of glue is applied to each ply. Workers then *lay-up*, or place, the plies with the grain in each ply opposite to that in the adjacent ply. Giant hydraulic presses squeeze the plies together with heat and pressure, or pressure only. Then the finished plywood is again dried, trimmed, sanded, or otherwise finished into sheets.   GEORGE W. WASHA

PLZEŇ, *PUL zen y'*, or PILSEN, *PILL zun* (pop. 141,736; alt. 995 ft.), is one of the most important cities in Bohemia. Plzeň stands at the junction of two rivers, the Mies and the Radbusa. For location, see CZECHOSLOVAKIA (color map). It was a great Roman Catholic stronghold in the days of the religious wars, and withstood many sieges. The famous Skoda iron and steel works were established there. Plzeň lies in the great hop-growing region of Bohemia. Its Pilsener beer is known throughout the world.   S. HARRISON THOMSON

P.M. stands for the Latin words *post meridiem*, which mean *after noon*. See DAY.

PMC COLLEGES. See UNIVERSITIES AND COLLEGES (table).

PNEUMATIC TIRE. See TIRE.

PNEUMATIC TOOL is a power implement operated by compressed air. Such tools are used extensively for work in foundries, quarries, steel mills, and manufacturing plants, and on all types of construction projects. These powerful tools are usually operated with a pressure of 90 pounds to the square inch. Because of their simple, sturdy design, and the safety of compressed air power, pneumatic tools can be operated safely and easily. Often, they are small and weigh only a few pounds.

There are two main types of pneumatic tools, those that deliver a forward striking blow and those that deliver rotative power.

The Striking Principle is used in riveting, calking, scaling, chipping, ramming, and digging tools. An example is the pneumatic hammer, used mainly for riveting. It has a piston that moves back and forth in

a barrel to deliver blows to the hammer tool. Power is supplied by compressed air generally fed into the handle of the tool through a flexible hose, which enables the hammer to be used in all positions. A pneumatic hammer can deliver as many as 6,000 strokes every minute.

The Rotative Power Principle is used for torque wrenches, standard and torque control impact wrenches, drills, grinders, screwdrivers, wire wrappers, and saws. The impact wrench, typical of this type of tool, is powered by an air motor. Air enters the motor and is forced against enclosed vanes or blades, which are attached to a cylinder. The cylinder rotates and produces a powerful force. This force passes into an impact mechanism, a device that automatically converts the motor's turning force into powerful rotary impacts when

A Paving Breaker Is a Pneumatic Tool that construction workers can use to break up concrete roads and brick walls.

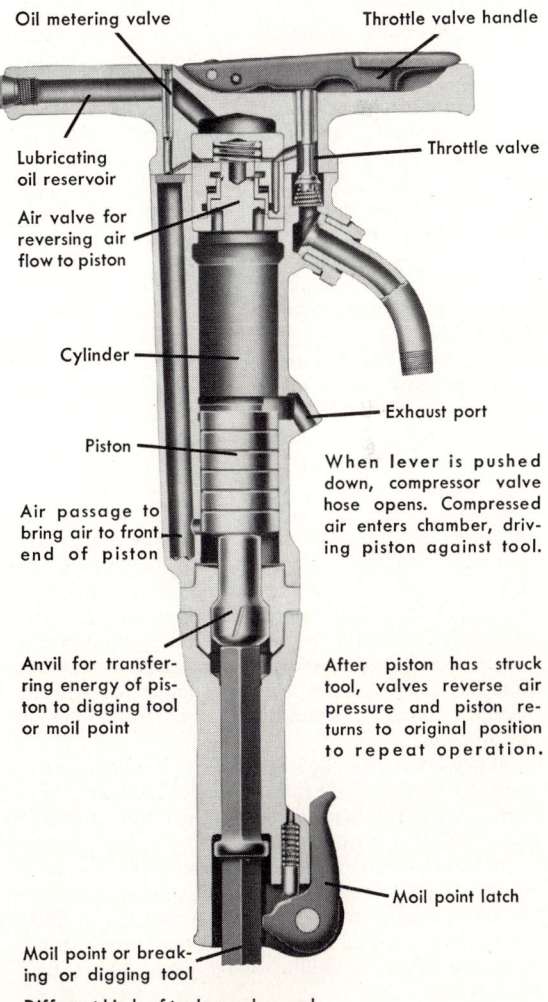

Oil metering valve

Throttle valve handle

Lubricating oil reservoir

Throttle valve

Air valve for reversing air flow to piston

Cylinder

Exhaust port

Piston

When lever is pushed down, compressor valve hose opens. Compressed air enters chamber, driving piston against tool.

Air passage to bring air to front end of piston

Anvil for transferring energy of piston to digging tool or moil point

After piston has struck tool, valves reverse air pressure and piston returns to original position to repeat operation.

Moil point latch

Moil point or breaking or digging tool

Different kinds of tools may be used in the paving breaker, depending on the job to be performed.
Ingersoll-Rand Company

there is sufficient resistance to the turning. These rotary impacts may be produced as often as 2,900 times every minute.

Both the striking and rotative principles are used in the rock drill. It delivers a striking blow, and then turns the drill steel as it draws back to make another forward blow.　　　　　　　　　　　　HERBERT D. KYNOR, JR.

See also DRILLING TOOLS (Rock Drills).

PNEUMATIC TUBE. See COMMUNICATION (picture: Pneumatic Tubes).

PNEUMATICS is the branch of physics that studies the properties of gases, either at rest or in motion. Numerous tools and machines used in industry have been developed as a result of the knowledge acquired about the laws of pressure and elasticity of the air. See also GAS (matter); PNEUMATIC TOOL; PUMP.

PNEUMOCOCCUS. See PNEUMONIA.

PNEUMONIA, *noo MOH nih uh,* is an infectious disease of the lungs. There are several types, which vary with the location and extent of the diseased lung tissue. Persons under 5 years of age and those over 65 are most often afflicted by pneumonia. In children the disease usually attacks the small bronchi and their branches, causing the type known as *bronchopneumonia.* Pneumonia in both lungs is called *double pneumonia.*

Several different germs cause pneumonia. The *pneumococcus* group is responsible for most cases of *lobar pneumonia.* In this common form, the air sacs of an entire lobe or several lobes of the lungs fill first with clotted blood, then with *leucocytes* (white blood cells). *Virus pneumonia* is another form of pneumonia. It is caused by viruses, which are germs so tiny that only the largest can be seen under a powerful microscope (see VIRUS).

Symptoms and Treatment. Pneumonia sometimes begins suddenly. But it may follow a bad cold, or occur as a complication of influenza, measles, and some other diseases. It may also follow surgery.

The first symptoms are chills, a pain in the chest, a hard dry cough, and a high fever. The patient soon begins to cough up brownish-red phlegm, and his breathing becomes more difficult. Fever and inflammation may last 5 to 11 days. The turning point in the disease is reached when the patient seems to be at his worst. His fever falls rapidly and breathing becomes easier. He awakens feeling weak but fairly comfortable.

It is especially important to keep a patient in bed from the first day of illness until he has recovered completely. A physician should treat every person who has pneumonia.

Physicians center their efforts on keeping up the patient's strength, nutrition, and fluid intake. Pneumonia patients must have plenty of fresh air. If breathing is difficult, doctors often give the patient oxygen by means of a mask or an oxygen tent. Serums may be helpful in occasional cases in which bacteria invade the blood stream (see SERUM). However, serums sometimes cause harmful reactions. Doctors often use sulfonamide drugs, penicillin, and other drugs to treat pneumonia.

Transmission and Prevention. Pneumonia is transmitted from one person to another. The germs leave the body in discharges from the nose and mouth, and infect other persons through the nose and mouth. Spitting, coughing, and sneezing spread the germs. When persons with the disease cough or sneeze, they spray droplets that contain the germs into the air. If another person breathes the air with these germs, he may get the disease.

Physicians and health officers urge that all patients be kept away from other persons. It is very important to disinfect discharges and any articles used by the patient. A person with pneumonia should protect others by destroying all sputum during the attack and for several weeks after.

Pneumonia may attack at all seasons of the year. It is especially prevalent in winter and spring. A person can guard against pneumonia by avoiding exposure to severe cold and to rain and snow. He should stay away from crowds during epidemics. Anyone suffering from a cold or measles should stay quietly in bed in a well-ventilated room and should eat food that is easily digested.

Pneumonia is often fatal to persons who have low vitality, who are overweight, or who drink too much alcoholic liquor. A person should keep his body resistance high and get plenty of rest, particularly when epidemics of pneumonia are prevalent. He should eat well-balanced meals.　　　　　　MARK D. ALTSCHULE

See also DISEASE (table).

PNEUMOTHORAX, *NEW moh THOH racks,* is air in the space between the lungs and the chest wall. A thin membrane, called the *pleura,* covers the outside of the lungs and the inside of the chest wall, forming a cavity (see PLEURA). Air entering this cavity compresses the lung. The lung then cannot expand completely. Pneumothorax caused by a wound is called *traumatic pneumothorax.* A tear in the lung itself causes *spontaneous pneumothorax.* Doctors sometimes induce pneumothorax in one lung during the treatment of tuberculosis. This procedure allows the treated lung to rest and speeds healing.　　　　　　　　　　　MARK D. ALTSCHULE

PNOM PENH. See PHNOM PENH.

PO RIVER is the largest waterway in Italy. It is important for the volume of water it carries from the mountains to the sea, and for the fertile valley it has created along its course. The Po begins near Monte Viso, in the Cottian Alps, and flows in an easterly direction about 405 miles to a large delta in the Adriatic Sea. Almost every river in northern Italy is a branch of the Po. Lakes Maggiore, Como, Lecco, Iseo, and Garda also empty their waters into the Po. The river is rapid in its upper courses, but becomes a sluggish stream long before it reaches the sea. The Po River has often caused disastrous floods. About 300 B.C. the Etruscans built artificial embankments in an effort to control the waters. The river's continual deposits of silt raise the level of the water. From time to time, the embankments have been raised to heights above the river. For location, see ITALY (physical map).

Some of Italy's large cities lie on the banks of the Po, including Turin, Piacenza, and Cremona. Large electric power plants operate along the upper sections of the river. Large ships can sail up the Po as far as Turin, and much freight is carried along this section of the river.　　　　　　　　　SHEPARD B. CLOUGH

See also ITALY (Natural Resources).

POACHING. See GAME (Private Game Preserves).

POCAHONTAS, *POH kuh HAHN tus* (1595?-1617), was the daughter of the American Indian chief, Powhatan. Captain John Smith, the leader of the settlers in Jamestown, Va., claimed that she saved his life. He wrote in his book *True Relation of Virginia* that her father was about to kill him with a stone war club. But Pocahontas, he claimed, placed her head upon his and begged her father to spare Smith's life. It is not certain that this is a true story, because Smith, in the earliest edition of his book, failed to include an account of the incident with Pocahontas and her father.

National Gallery of Art, Washington, D.C.

Pocahontas died shortly after this portrait of her was painted in England in 1616.

The name *Pocahontas* meant *playful one*. She was a child of about 12 at the time of the incident. She is mentioned in William Strachey's *The Histories of Travell into Virginia Britania* (1612). Strachey, the first secretary of the Virginia colony, said Pocahontas married an Indian chief from her tribe when she was about 14 years old. She was not seen in the Jamestown area for about three years after that.

In the meantime, fighting broke out between the white settlers and the Indians. Pocahontas was lured on board an English ship in the spring of 1613 and temporarily held captive. During this time, she and the English settler, John Rolfe, fell in love. Pocahontas was converted to Christianity and baptized with the English name Rebecca. She and Rolfe were married in 1614.

Pocahontas went with her husband to London in 1616. The English thought of her as an Indian "princess." While waiting to sail back to America, she died of smallpox.

Her son, Thomas, was educated in England. He later went to America and became an important person in Virginia. A number of noted Virginia families claim to be descended from him. E. ADAMSON HOEBEL

See also POWHATAN; ROLFE, JOHN; SMITH, JOHN.

Pocahontas Saved the Life of Captain John Smith. Smith said that Pocahontas' father, Powhatan, was about to kill him with a club when she threw herself between them.

Library of Congress

POCATELLO, *POH kuh TELL oh*, Idaho (pop. 39,194; alt. 4,460 ft.), is an air, highway, and rail gateway to the Pacific Northwest. Greater Pocatello also includes Chubbuck and North Pocatello. For location, see IDAHO (political map).

Pocatello lies in the center of a rich farming region. It serves as a market place and shipping point for crops and livestock. Its factories and mills make cement, dairy products, elemental phosphorus, feed products, flour, phosphate fertilizers, steel, and venetian blinds. Heavy guns are relined at a naval ordnance plant in Pocatello.

The city is the home of Idaho State College. Tourists visit Caribou National Forest, the Pocatello Game Preserve, the Fort Hall Indian Agency, and Ross Park. Other parks are nearby, including Yellowstone National Park.

Pocatello was founded in 1882. Land did not become available to settlers until 1891, because the area was part of the Fort Hall Indian Reservation. Pocatello received its city charter in 1893, and was named after a Bannock Indian chief. It grew steadily with the progress of the Union Pacific Railroad, which maintains large yards there. Pocatello has a council-manager form of government. WILLIAM S. GREEVER and JANET GROFF GREEVER

POCKET BOROUGH. See BOROUGH.

POCKET-CHAMBER. See RADIATION (Protecting Ourselves from High-Energy Radiation).

POCKET VETO. See VETO.

POCO. See MUSIC (Terms).

PODGORNY, *pod GOHR nee*, **NIKOLAI VIKTOROVICH** (1903-   ), is a Russian government official and Communist Party leader. Podgorny became chairman of the Presidium of the Supreme Soviet in 1965. The Presidium handles legislative matters between sessions of the Supreme Soviet, Russia's legislature.

Podgorny was born in Karlovka, the Ukraine. He became a member of the Communist Party in 1930. The following year, he graduated from a food institute in Kiev. He worked in various administrative posts in the food industry from 1931 to 1946. The Kharkov regional party committee in the Ukraine appointed him first secretary in 1950. Podgorny also served as first secretary of the Ukrainian Communist Party from 1957 to 1963. WALTER C. CLEMENS, JR.

PODIATRY, *poh DY uh trih*, is the branch of medicine concerned with the diagnosis and treatment of foot diseases and deformities. It is sometimes called *chiropody*. The podiatrist treats conditions such as calluses, corns, bunions, and dislocated bones. He may prescribe drugs, perform minor surgery, or use various physical therapy devices. He is a specialist in preventive foot hygiene. He prescribes correct shoes and fits corrective devices.

There are six accredited schools of podiatry in the United States. A person entering one of these schools must meet certain requirements. He must be a high school graduate and have one or two years of college work. The schools offer a four-year course leading to a degree of Doctor of Surgical Chiropody (D.S.C.) or Doctor of Podiatry (Pod.D). The American Podiatry Association has headquarters at 3301 Sixteenth Street NW, Washington, D.C. 20010. A. RUBIN

POE, EDGAR ALLAN

POE, EDGAR ALLAN (1809-1849), was one of America's greatest poets, short-story writers, and literary critics. "The Raven" is one of the best-known poems in American literature, and an example of the haunting quality of many of Poe's works. With "The Murders in the Rue Morgue" and other short stories, Poe became the father of modern mystery and detective fiction. "The Fall of the House of Usher," "The Masque of the Red Death," and other such tales made him a fore-runner of symbolism, impressionism, and the grotesque in modern literature. "The Poetic Principle," the "Marginalia," and his reviews contain important principles of literary criticism, which, together with his poetry and fiction, influenced many later writers, including T. S. Eliot, André Gide, James Joyce, Algernon Charles Swinburne, and three generations of French poets.

For many years, critics disagreed on Poe's place in literature. Up to World War I, he was admired mainly for his romantic lyric poems, his tales of terror, and his clever detective stories. Since that time, scholars have become more concerned with Poe's symbolic poems and tales—those in which mystery, atmosphere, and extraordinary events and characters represent the interplay of conflicting feelings and values.

Poe's Life

Since his death, more books have been published on Poe than on any other American author. The mystery of Poe the man and the artist has fascinated biographers. Poe was hounded by economic troubles, hurt by his enemies, and haunted by nightmares and visions. Yet out of the very frustrations and failures of his personal life came his artistic successes.

Early Life. Poe was born in Boston on Jan. 19, 1809. His father deserted the family and his mother died before Poe was three years old. John Allan, a tobacco exporter in Richmond, Va., and his wife Frances raised Poe as a foster child, but never legally adopted him. From 1815 to 1820, the family lived in England, and Poe attended a private school near London, where he did well in his studies.

In 1826, Poe entered the University of Virginia, where he was an excellent student. But because his foster father sent him barely enough money to live, Poe gambled to try to win money for books and clothing. His resulting debts caused Allan to withdraw him from the university. Allan then wanted Poe to study law, but Poe determined to follow a literary career. After the two quarreled in March, 1827, Poe left home for Boston, where he later enlisted in the Army as "Edgar A. Perry."

By the time he was honorably discharged in 1829, he had attained the rank of sergeant major. He then moved to Baltimore to live with his aunt, Mrs. Maria Clemm, and her daughter, Virginia. In 1830, Poe entered the U.S. Military Academy in a final effort to gain Allan's good will. But Frances Allan had died in 1829 and when Allan decided to remarry in 1830, Poe concluded he would never be reconciled with Allan or receive an inheritance. So he deliberately broke regulations to force his dismissal from West Point.

Early Literary Career. Poe's career began with two volumes of poetry, *Tamerlane and Other Poems* (1827) and *Al Aaraaf, Tamerlane, and Minor Poems* (1829).

Poems (1831), included three of his best works—"To Helen," "The City in the Sea," and "Israfel." But, discouraged by lack of recognition, he started writing short stories. The first five were published in 1832.

In 1833, Poe's story "MS. Found in a Bottle" won a $50 prize and the friendship of John P. Kennedy, a novelist and lawyer. Kennedy helped Poe get a job with the *Southern Literary Messenger*, which Poe edited so well that subscriptions increased from 500 to over 3,500. On May 16, 1836, Poe married his cousin Virginia Clemm, who was then not quite 14 years old. As he could not support his wife and aunt on a salary of $10 a week, he resigned from the magazine and moved to New York City early in 1837.

Midcareer. Poe's most productive period as a fiction writer and critic extended from 1837 to 1845. He spent 18 months in New York City, and published his only novel *The Narrative of Arthur Gordon Pym* (1838) during that time. Poe moved to Philadelphia in 1838, and edited two magazines there. Despite his success as an editor and writer, however, he was so underpaid that he and his family often went without enough food.

In Philadelphia, Poe wrote significant reviews of the works of Longfellow and Hawthorne. Some of his greatest tales appeared in a collection of his first 25 stories, *Tales of the Grotesque and Arabesque* (1840). But they brought him neither important recognition nor money.

From 1844 until his death, Poe lived in New York City. During the mid-1840's, he wrote and edited as much as 15 hours a day and enjoyed a growing reputation as a short-story writer. His tale "The Gold-Bug" (1843) sold 300,000 copies. In many ways, 1845 was his best year—12 stories published in *Tales* and 30 poems in *The Raven and Other Poems*. "The Raven" brought him his greatest recognition. Also in 1845, James Russell Lowell wrote the first essay-length appreciation of Poe as a writer. He praised Poe as "the most discriminating, philosophical and fearless critic upon imaginative works who has written in America."

The Tragic Period. The last years of Poe's life were marked by tragedy. His wife died of tuberculosis in 1847 after five years of illness. This "intolerable sorrow" led Poe to occasional drinking to ease his despair. His drinking, or gossip about it, sometimes spoiled his chances to get or hold a job. But according to his business associates, Poe was usually sober, responsible, courteous, and hard-working. His drinking troubles were largely due to a low tolerance for any kind of alcohol. Contrary to what some persons believe, he was neither a habitual drunkard nor a drug addict.

Edgar Allan Poe
Brown University Press

In 1849, Poe became engaged to marry the widowed Mrs. Sarah Royster Shelton, his boyhood sweetheart. On his way to bring Mrs. Clemm to the wedding, Poe stopped in Baltimore, probably on September 28. There are various theories about the events of the next few days. All that is known is that Poe was found lying outside a voting place on October 3. He died in a hospital four days later, without regaining consciousness. The cause of his death remains unknown.

Poe's Works

Fiction. Poe's most popular tales are filled with an atmosphere of the strange, the bizarre, and the terrible. He insisted that these tales of terror were an expression of psychological and moral realities, rather than of sensation for its own sake. Many of Poe's stories are called "moral allegories" because the theme of moral responsibility prevails in them.

For example, "The Fall of the House of Usher," perhaps Poe's best story, concerns the twins Roderick and Madeline Usher. When Madeline falls into a trance, Roderick buries her in a deep vault, thinking she is dead. He represents the overrefined intellect and his twin sister the suppressed moral self. In this story and others, such as "Morella" and "Ligeia," Poe means that man cannot separate his moral self from his intellect without destroying himself. In "William Wilson," the hero, by killing his double, his conscience, destroys himself.

In "The Tell-Tale Heart," "The Black Cat," and "The Imp of the Perverse," the narrator has a compulsion to kill and later to confess his murder. "The Cask of Amontillado" and "Hop-Frog" deal with murder as revenge. Poe wrote of the inhumanity of man in "The Pit and the Pendulum," the dark and silent indifference of the universe in "Shadow" and "Silence," and the triumph of time and death over human folly and pride in "The Masque of the Red Death."

Poe's character C. Auguste Dupin, a private detective, became the model for many later fictional detectives. Dupin appeared in three stories. "The Purloined Letter" is a suspenseful story noted for its characterizations and its economy of plot and style. In "The Murders in the Rue Morgue" and "The Mystery of Marie Rogêt," Dupin's imagination as well as his powers of careful observation enable him to solve the crimes.

Poetry. Despite its theatrical effects and stylistic flaws, "The Raven" is Poe's best-known poem and one of the most famous works in American literature. The theme of "The Raven"—the narrator's grief over the loss of an ideal love—recurs in other of Poe's works. This poem has a dramatic intensity that makes the hypnotic monotony of rhythm and tone a realistic reflection of the speaker's state of mind.

"To Helen," "Ulalume," and "For Annie" also dramatize deep-felt loyalty to a woman who symbolizes an ideal, spiritual value. These poems are noted for their subtle use of rhyme, rhythm, symbols, and psychology. They show Poe's ability to use rhythmic and tonal qualities that reinforce ideas and subconscious feelings.

In "The Valley of Unrest" and "Sonnet—To Science," Poe described man's loss of innocence and sense of wonder and beauty. In "Lenore," "Annabel Lee," and "Eldorado," Poe implies that only love, beauty, or aspiration can save man from despair.

Essays and Criticism. Poe's critical thought was influenced by his career as a magazine journalist. He felt the magazine article to be the literary form most responsive to the need for "the curt, the condensed, the pointed, the readily diffused." From 1844 to 1849, Poe published a number of jottings and short essays in various journals. These "Marginalia," as well as

scattered reviews and letters, contain some of Poe's basic ideas on the nature of man, society, democracy, reform, and literature. His long essay *Eureka* (1848) tries to explain the riddle of the universe—its origin, expansion, and ultimate destiny. This work is a primary source for understanding his poetic view of matter, spirit, space, and the interrelationship of God and man.

"The Poetic Principle," first a lecture and then an essay published in 1850, best states Poe's ideas of poetry. His reviews of Hawthorne's *Twice-Told Tales* express Poe's finest insights into the nature of originality, allegory, and the short story.

Poe believed that the ideal critic should be objective, analytical, and, if necessary, unhesitatingly negative. He insisted that criticism should deal with qualities of beauty, not with history, biography, or philosophy. By the "Didactic Heresy," Poe meant that beauty was incompatible with any deliberate moralizing or instruction. He believed that truth and fact should have only a hidden or submerged place in a poem, indirectly suggested rather than explicitly stated. In "The Philosophy of Composition," in order to offset the notion that all poetry is composed by pure inspiration, a "species of fine frenzy," Poe exaggerated the role of the poet's conscious control of his creative process.

Introduction to Poe: A Thematic Reader (1967) by Eric W. Carlson is one of the many books on Poe's life and works.

ERIC W. CARLSON

POET LAUREATE, *LAW ree ayt*, is the title given to the outstanding or official poet of a state or nation. The name usually refers to the poet laureate of Great Britain. The United States does not have a poet laureate, but about half of the states do.

The British poet laureate is the official poet of the king or queen. He is expected to write odes praising persons or events on special occasions. He belongs to the royal household, and receives a modest income.

In England during the Middle Ages, universities gave the title to poets. Early English court poets such as Geoffrey Chaucer (1340?-1400) and Edmund Spenser (1552?-1599) were also called *laureates*. But Ben Jonson (1573?-1637) is considered the first poet laureate in the modern sense. His successor, William Davenant (1606-1668), was the first poet laureate officially appointed by the king.

CHARLES W. COOPER

─── POETS LAUREATE ───

Name	Born	Appointed	Died
*Sir William Davenant	1606	1638	1668
*John Dryden	1631	1668	1700
Thomas Shadwell	1642?	1688	1692
Nahum Tate	1652	1692	1715
Nicholas Rowe	1674	1715	1718
Laurence Eusden	1688	1718	1730
Colley Cibber	1671	1730	1757
William Whitehead	1715	1758	1785
Thomas Warton	1728	1785	1790
Henry James Pye	1745	1790	1813
*Robert Southey	1774	1813	1843
*William Wordsworth	1770	1843	1850
*Alfred, Lord Tennyson	1809	1850	1892
Alfred Austin	1835	1896	1913
*Robert Bridges	1844	1913	1930
*John Masefield	1878	1930	1967
Cecil Day-Lewis	1904	1968	

*Has a separate biography in WORLD BOOK.

POETRY

POETRY is language used in a special way. Its words form patterns of verse, of sound, and of thought that appeal strongly to the imagination. Here is *Who Has Seen the Wind?* by Christina Rossetti:

> Who has seen the wind?
>   Neither I nor you;
> But when the leaves hang trembling,
>   The wind is passing through.
>
> Who has seen the wind?
>   Neither you nor I;
> But when the trees bow down their heads,
>   The wind is passing by.

You can tell that this is poetry by the way it looks and by the way it sounds when read aloud. Your eye sees the pattern of the lines, and your ear catches the rhythm and the rhyme. But these words also suggest much more than they say. They stir your imagination and bring to your mind the feeling of a windy day.

Poetry is one of the oldest and most important branches of literature. From earliest times, people have enjoyed songs as they worked and played. Poets have recited stories of gods and heroes. They have won great honor in every civilization, and today such names as Robert Frost and Carl Sandburg command great respect. Millions of persons read poetry and many even write their own verse once in a while.

Enjoying Poetry

If you are interested in life and in people, you will probably like poetry—at least some poetry. Walt Whitman expressed in *Beginning My Studies* the great joy and excitement he felt in being alive and active:

> Beginning my studies, the first step pleased me so much,
> The mere fact, consciousness—these forms—the power of motion,
> The least insect or animal—the senses—eyesight—love;
> The first step, I say, awed me and pleased me so much,
> I have hardly gone, and hardly wished to go, any farther,
> But stop and loiter all the time, to sing it in ecstatic songs.

Whitman was struck with wonder as he looked about him and thought of such things as the power of motion, an insect, or eyesight. He was bursting to share his experiences, and his poem may bring you something of his excitement and joy.

For greater enjoyment, you will do well to begin by reading poetry aloud. Without giving much attention to the verse as such, try to get the feel of the language as a pattern of sound. It is a good idea to read a poem rather slowly—again and again—with an alert mind full of questions about life itself. If you are really curious about words and things, you will often turn to your dictionary or encyclopedia. The language of poetry is packed under pressure, and the meaning of a single word may trigger the thought, letting the entire poem explode in your imagination.

Writing Poetry

The enjoyment of reading poetry often leads to the enjoyment of writing verse. An American poet, John Holmes, writes of "the satisfaction of springing at last the obstinate words into the stubborn line." Many persons find rich rewards in the magic of words that capture thought, the startling image or metaphor, and the sheer fun of rhyming.

All life, all things seen and felt, all joys and sorrows—all these belong to poetry. Your themes need not be sweet or somber. They may be bitter or gay. What you write need not be conventional. It may be experimental. You may begin by writing limericks or jingles, then try the sonnet or the triolet. Or you may begin with free verse, then try the ballad.

Persons who write verse often find encouragement in clubs, classes, writers' groups, and poetry contests. They use the dictionary, thesaurus, vocabulary of rhymes, and writers' manuals. They find hints in books by poets, such as Robert Hillyer's *The First Principles of Verse* and Richard Armour's *Writing Light Verse*.

Most poets hope to see their verse in print—to share their experience, as they recorded it in poetry. Verse is published in hundreds of magazines and newspapers—regional, religious, juvenile, general, and special-interest. Some of these publications even pay for their verses. One book, *Writer's Market*, provides an up-to-date list in its yearly edition, and magazines such as *The Writer* announce contests. But, as most poets know, being a poet is not a career. It is instead an enriching avocation.

Types of Poetry

Poets have written many kinds of poetry. There are two main types, *lyric* and *narrative*. Some persons regard *dramatic* poetry as a third main type.

$\mathcal{G}$reat $\mathcal{P}$oets

Masters of Poetry from 1550 to the present are listed in chronological order. Great poets who wrote before 1550 include Homer of Greece, Virgil of Rome, Dante Alighieri of Italy, and Geoffrey Chaucer of England. Outstanding early poems by unknown authors include *Beowulf, Song of Roland,* and *El Cid.*
Each poet has a separate biography in WORLD BOOK.

GRAY (1716-1771) BRIT.

POPE (1688-1744) BRIT.

DRYDEN (1631-1700) BRIT.

MILTON (1608-1674) BRIT.

DONNE (1571?-1631) BRIT.

SHAKESPEARE (1564-1616) BRIT.

SPENSER (1552?-1599) BRIT.

1550   1600   1650   1700   1750

Lyric poems are usually short, and many have a songlike quality. The poet expresses his personal reactions to things—what he sees, hears, thinks, and feels. The two poems quoted earlier in this article are lyrics. For information on the various kinds of lyrics, see the separate articles on BALLADE; ELEGY; EPIGRAM; HYMN; IDYL; ODE; SONG; SONNET.

Narrative poems tell a story and are usually rather long. The poet suggests the setting, characters, and events, and gives them meaning. Epics and ballads are among the foremost kinds of narrative poetry. We think of fables and romances as prose works, but many early examples were written as narrative poems. For information on these forms, see the separate articles on BALLAD; EPIC; FABLE; ROMANCE.

Dramatic poems resemble narrative poems because they tell a story and are fairly long. But the poet tells the story through the speech of one or more of the characters in the story. "My Last Duchess," a dramatic monologue by Robert Browning, is a famous example. Through what the duke says in his monologue, while supposedly speaking to a visitor, Browning shows the duke's character and reveals much about the duchess.

How a Poet Writes

A poet, as an artist, creates something with his imagination that did not exist before, and gives it permanent form. Unlike other artists, he works with language. Unlike other writers, he writes in verse.

In *verse*, lines of words extend as far as the poet wishes to make them. In *prose*, they are as wide as the page or column in which they appear. More important, the reader of verse usually feels a more-or-less regular

Homer

THOMAS (1914-1953) BRIT.
ELIOT (1888-1965) BRIT.
POUND (1885-   ) AMER.
JIMÉNEZ (1881-1958) SP.
SANDBURG (1878-1967) AMER.
FROST (1874-1963) AMER.
HOFMANNSTHAL (1874-1929) GER.
CLAUDEL (1868-1955) FR.
YEATS (1865-1939) IR.
KIPLING (1865-1936) BRIT.
RIMBAUD (1854-1891) FR.
DICKINSON (1830-1886) AMER.
BAUDELAIRE (1821-1867) FR.
WHITMAN (1819-1892) AMER.
BROWNING (1812-1889) BRIT.
TENNYSON (1809-1892) BRIT.
POE (1809-1849) AMER.
LONGFELLOW (1807-1882) AMER.
PUSHKIN (1799-1837) RUSS.
HEINE (1797-1856) GER.
KEATS (1795-1821) BRIT.
SHELLEY (1792-1822) BRIT.
BYRON (1788-1824) BRIT.
COLERIDGE (1772-1834) BRIT.
WORDSWORTH (1770-1850) BRIT.
BURNS (1759-1796) BRIT.
GOETHE (1749-1832) GER.

T. S. Eliot

William Shakespeare

Dante Alighieri

1800   1850   1900   1950   2000

rhythm. The reader of prose is rarely aware of any strong rhythmical effects. See PROSE.

Verse and Melody. Poets who write in modern English can use either *bound verse* or *free verse*. Bound verse, as in the poem by Christina Rossetti, is the older and more common form. It is *bound to*, or based on, a metrical pattern. A poem in free verse, such as the one by Walt Whitman, has no regular metrical pattern.

You can usually tell easily which verse system the poet has used. By reading a few lines aloud, you will discover "how the poem goes." If you become conscious of a fairly regular beat, the poem has a metrical pattern and is therefore in bound verse. If not, it is in free verse. Try reading aloud the opening lines of Browning's "My Last Duchess":

> That's my last Duchess painted on the wall,
> Looking as if she were alive. I call
> That piece a wonder, now: Fra Pandolf's hands
> Worked busily a day, and there she stands.
> Will 't please you sit and look at her? I said
> "Fra Pandolf" by design, for never read
> Strangers like you that pictured countenance,
> The depth and passion of its earnest glance,
> But to myself they turned . . .

You may have read a few lines before realizing that this is bound verse. It has a metrical pattern (it goes *de-DUMM de-DUMM de-DUMM de-DUMM de-DUMM*), and its lines rhyme in pairs. Once you become aware of such a pattern, you expect the poem to continue following it fairly closely.

But the *melody* of a poem does not consist of the metrical pattern as such. It lies in the use the poet makes of his pattern, and the freedom he allows himself. He has bound himself to a form, but he is not a slave to it. As you read or listen to his poem, your ear expects regularity, but is happily surprised with variations. As you read Browning's lines, you find that the

accents and stresses do not always fall where they "belong." Also, the poet's thought often runs on from line to line, instead of pausing at the end of each line. By making subtle variations in the rhythm, the poet gives his lines melody—like a free-flowing song with a steady beat in the accompaniment.

Image and Picture. The poet works not only with the melody of language, but also with the pictures it flashes to the reader's mind. Sometimes he develops a single picture, as Lord Tennyson did in "The Eagle":

> He clasps the crag with crooked hands;
> Close to the sun in lonely lands,
> Ringed with the azure world, he stands.
>
> The wrinkled sea beneath him crawls;
> He watches from his mountain walls,
> And like a thunderbolt he falls.

The poet does not have to limit himself to things that can be seen. He often suggests sound and movement. Alfred Noyes begins "The Highwayman" with these lines:

> The wind was a torrent of darkness among the gusty trees,
> The moon was a ghostly galleon tossed upon cloudy seas,
> The road was a ribbon of moonlight over the purple moor . . .

Then, with the night scene pictured, "The highwayman came riding, up to the old inn-door." Here the poet has used language that is both *sensory* and *figurative*: it appeals to our senses and creates powerful images. The metaphors suggest striking comparisons: the wind and the torrent, the moon and the ship, the sky and the sea, and the road and the ribbon (see METAPHOR). There are also strong images of things seen (darkness, moon, and moor), of things heard (wind and riding), and of things in motion (wind, tossing galleon, and riding). These words stir the imagination far more than a simple statement that a highwayman rode to an inn one night. See FIGURE OF SPEECH; IMAGINATION.

TERMS USED IN POETRY

Alexandrine is a line of iambic hexameter, a common line in French poetry.

*****Alliteration** uses words beginning with the same sounds.

Amphibrach is a three-syllable foot, *de-DUMM-de*.

Amphimacer is a three-syllable foot, *DUMM-de-DUMM*.

Anacrusis is an unexpected unstressed syllable at the beginning of a trochaic or dactylic line.

Anapest is a basic foot in rising triple rhythm, *de-de-DUMM*.

Assonance uses repeated vowel sounds with varying consonant sounds at the ends of lines, as in "mine" and "night."

Ballad Meter is a four-line stanza, usually $a^4b^3c^4b^3$.

*****Ballade**, a French form, has three stanzas rhymed *ababbcbC* and an *envoy* of *bcbC*, the *C* line repeated.

*****Blank Verse** is poetry in unrhymed iambic pentameter.

Bound Verse is verse based on a metrical pattern.

Cadence is rhythmical flow and phrasing in language.

Caesura is a thought-pause or stop within a line.

Catalexis is the omission of an expected unstressed syllable at the end of a trochaic or dactylic line.

Common Measure resembles ballad meter. It is often used in hymns, and may be called *hymnal stanza*.

*****Couplet** is a pair of rhyming lines. *Closed* couplets complete the thought within two lines. *Open* couplets continue the thought from one pair of lines to another. *Heroic* couplets are in iambic pentameter.

Dactyl is a basic foot in falling triple rhythm, *DUMM-de-de*.

Dimeter is a line of two feet.

Double Rhyme has two rhyming syllables, as in "dreary" and "weary" or "market" and "park it."

*****Elegy** usually laments a death or meditates on a solemn subject. In ancient poetry, it was written in *elegiacs*, paired lines of hexameter and pentameter.

End-Stopped Line ends with a thought-pause or stop.

Feminine Ending is the addition of an unstressed syllable at the end of an iambic or anapestic line. A rhyme-word with a feminine ending is often called a *feminine rhyme*.

Foot is a rhythmic unit of two or three syllables.

*****Free Verse** is verse without metrical pattern. Its lines are divided according to *cadences*, or natural patterns of speech. French poets originated it as *vers libre*, a term sometimes used in English.

Heptameter is a line of seven feet.

Heroic Line is iambic pentameter, whether in blank verse, the *heroic couplet*, or the four-line *heroic stanza*, rhyming $abab^5$.

Hexameter is a line of six feet.

Iamb is a basic foot in rising duple rhythm, *de-DUMM*.

Initial Truncation is the omission of an expected unstressed syllable at the beginning of an iambic or anapestic line.

*Has a separate article in WORLD BOOK.

Thought and Feeling. Sometimes the poet deals with complicated ideas and emotions, even with themes that may seem simple, such as nature or war. These ideas may be difficult to communicate, but they are rewarding after we have grasped and felt them. William Blake wrote in his "Auguries of Innocence":

> To see a world in a grain of sand,
> And a heaven in a wild flower;
> Hold infinity in the palm of your hand,
> And eternity in an hour.

In the light of what we now know of atomic science and outer space, these lines mean more today than when they were written, in the early 1800's. The thought at first seems simple, but it opens up like a flower when we reflect on it. This kind of poem may mean somewhat different things to different persons.

In developing his thought, the poet often makes literary and personal allusions, uses striking metaphors, or treats his theme with irony. Archibald MacLeish based his poem "The Too-Late Born" on an allusion to the famous *Song of Roland* (see ROLAND). "We too, we too," he says, heard the distant horn—Roland's signal of distress—and returned through the mountain passes to Roncevaux, only to find

> upon the darkening plain
> The dead against the dead and on the silent ground
> The silent slain—

The poet knew war. He had lost a brother in battle. He is "too-late born," he suggests ironically, to feel any romance in the slaughter of war. See IRONY.

Metrical Patterns

Feet, Meter, and Rhyme Scheme. Each poem in bound verse is based on a *metrical pattern* that can be described in terms of (1) its basic foot, (2) its meter, and (3) its rhyme scheme. These terms are explained below. After reading this section, try to determine the metrical

patterns of the lines of poetry quoted in the *Questions* at the end of this article.

Feet. We tend to hear the syllables of a line in groups of twos or threes. Each of these rhythmic units is called a *foot*. In English poetry, the rhythm is based on the natural accents we place on words. For example, we stress the first syllable of the word *heavily*, but not the last two syllables. Its rhythm goes *DUMM-de-de*, and, in a line of poetry, we could mark it ′ ˇ ˇ. The four basic feet in English verse are *iambic* (*de-DUMM*), *anapestic* (*de-de-DUMM*), *trochaic* (*DUMM-de*), and *dactylic* (*DUMM-de-de*). We call the first two *rising* rhythms and the last two *falling* rhythms. We also distinguish *duple* rhythms (iambic and trochaic) from *triple* rhythms (anapestic and dactylic). The *amphibrach* (*de-DUMM-de*) is less common. Four even rarer feet are the *amphimacer* (*DUMM-de-DUMM*), *spondee* (*DUMM-DUMM*), *pyrrhic* (*de-de*), and *tribrach* (*de-de-de*).

English metrical patterns are called *accentual*, because they are based on the natural accents of the words themselves. There are other kinds of meter: *quantitative*, as in Greek, and *syllabic*, as in French. The Greeks based their meter on the long and short vowel sounds in their words. The word *anthropos* (ahn throh poss, meaning *man*) would have to fit into a line so that the rhythm would emphasize its long *o* sound (*throh*), not its short one (*poss*). The French developed syllabic meter because their language does not have heavy stresses or long and short vowels. Instead, French poets often count the number of syllables in each line.

Meter. The number of feet in a line sets its meter:

monometer, one foot	pentameter, five feet
dimeter, two feet	hexameter, six feet
trimeter, three feet	heptameter, seven feet
tetrameter, four feet	octameter, eight feet

Rhyme Scheme. When the ends of words at the ends of two or more lines of poetry sound alike, they are

---

TERMS USED IN POETRY (continued)

*Limerick is a popular form of light verse, written in anapestic rhythm, $aa^3bb^2a^3$.

*Meter is either the number of feet in a line, or the combination of the number and the kind of feet.

Metrical Pattern, the basis of bound verse, consists of a basic foot, a meter, and a rhyme-scheme.

Monometer is a line with only one foot.

Octameter is a line of eight feet.

Octave is an eight-line stanza, or the first part of an Italian sonnet.

*Ode, a poem of moderate length, usually expresses exalted praise, suggesting one of the classical forms.

Ottava Rima is an eight-line stanza form, $abab_abcc^5$.

Pentameter, a line of five feet, is common in English verse.

Pyrrhic, an unusual foot, has two unstressed syllables, *de-de*.

Quatrain is a four-line stanza or four-line poem.

*Rhyme is the repetition of a sound at the ends of two or more lines, or within lines.

Rhyme Royal is a seven-line stanza form, $ababbcc^5$.

Rhyme Scheme is the pattern of rhymes in a stanza or poem.

*Rhythm is the feeling of a recurring beat or accent.

Rondeau, a French form, repeats the opening phrase (R) as a refrain: (R)aabba aabR aabbaR.

Run-On Line carries the thought on to the next line,

*Has a separate article in WORLD BOOK

without an expected pause or stop at the end of the line.

Sestet is the six-line part of an Italian sonnet.

*Sonnet is a 14-line form with several possible basic rhyme-schemes, the *Italian* rhyming *abbaabba cdecde* or *cdcdcd*, and the *Elizabethan* rhyming *ababcdcdefefgg*.

Sonnet Sequence is a long poem made up of sonnets.

Spenserian Stanza has nine lines, $ababbcbc^5c^6$.

Spondee is a foot with two stressed syllables, *DUMM-DUMM*.

Stanza is a repeated pattern of lines with a rhyme-scheme.

Terza Rima is a three-line continuing stanza form, with rhymes running *aba bcb cdc ded*, and so on.

Tetrameter is a line of four feet.

Tribrach is a foot with three unstressed syllables, *de-de-de*.

Trimeter is a line of three feet.

Triolet, a complicated French form, repeats several of its eight lines: *ABaAabAB*.

Triplet is a three-line stanza or three-line poem.

Trochee is a basic foot in falling duple rhythm, *DUMM-de*.

Verse is a line or stanza of poetry, or language in verses.

Villanelle, an elaborate French form, repeats two rhyming lines, *A* and *A′*, in an intricate form: *AbA′ abA abA′ abA abA′ abAA′*.

said to rhyme, as in "lore" and "door." "Napping" and "tapping" form *double* rhymes, and "mournfully" and "scornfully" are *triple* rhymes. The arrangement of rhymed lines forms the rhyme-scheme of the poem. A *stanza* is a repeated pattern of lines with a fixed rhyme-scheme, such as the four-line stanza of a ballad. In some poetic forms, such as the ballade, a rhyme-scheme dominates the poem as a whole. Other poems have a continuing sequence of rhymes, as in couplets.

To summarize a rhyme-scheme, you can use one letter for the first rhyme-sound, another for the second, and so on. In Blake's poem on page P—528c, the words "sand," "flower," "hand," and "hour" would be indicated as *a*, *b*, *a*, and *b*. If one line of the poem is repeated entirely, as in some complicated French forms, it is shown with a capital letter. A small number shows the number of feet in a line or a group of lines. The first and third lines of Blake's poem have four feet each, and the second and fourth have three. The full description of his rhyme-scheme would be $a^4b^3a^4b^3$.

Scansion. To scan verses and find their metrical pattern either (1) tap your fingers to count stresses as you read, or (2) mark the stressed syllables with accents (′) and the unstressed syllables with breves (˘). In this way, you find not only the basic metrical pattern, but also the variations the poet has allowed himself. English verse does not always scan easily, and two readers may scan the same line in quite different ways. Most scholars agree that the melody of a poem is far more important than purely mechanical scansion. It is wise not to try to force on a poem a pattern that the poet may not have intended.

Metrical Variations. The poet may depart from his strict metrical pattern in several ways. He can (1) substitute some other foot for the expected basic one, (2)

add or omit an unstressed syllable at the beginning or end of a line, or (3) pause in his thought within a line or continue his thought from line to line.

Substitution. Iambic lines prevail in Shakespeare's "Sonnet CXVI" (on this page), with a number of substitutions. For example, many persons read the phrase in the second line, "Love is not love," as a trochee followed by a spondee, *DUMM-de DUMM-DUMM.*

Addition or Omission. In the same sonnet, two lines end with two-syllable words, "shaken" and "taken." The extra syllables of these two words are called *feminine endings.* A poet can also add extra unstressed syllables at the beginnings of lines that would normally begin with stressed syllables. This unusual device is called *anacrusis.* The poet may omit the first syllable of an iambic or anapestic line. This device, *initial truncation,* appears in the third line of A. E. Housman's "To an Athlete Dying Young." Truncation of the final syllable, called *catalexis,* appears in the second and fourth lines of Edgar Allan Poe's "The Raven." The lines from Housman and Poe mentioned above are quoted in the *Questions* at the end of this article.

Pause or Continuance. The ideas expressed in a poem often affect its meter. If an idea (or a sentence) ends at the end of a line, we call the line *end-stopped,* as in the quotation from Cowper in the *Questions.* Many poets use *run-on lines,* where the thought carries on without pause from line to line. Browning did this in the lines quoted from "My Last Duchess" (on page P—528b). A thought-pause or stop within a line is a *caesura.* It is common in poems with long lines. Each line quoted from "The Highwayman" (on page P—528b) has one.

The Development of Poetry

Throughout history, various systems of verse-writing have developed because of variations in culture and language. The bound verse and free verse we know in

---

What Makes a Poem Great?

Sonnet CXVI
by William Shakespeare

Let me not to the marriage of true minds
Admit impediments. Love is not love
Which alters when it alteration finds,
Or bends with the remover to remove.
Oh, no! It is an ever-fixèd mark
That looks on tempests and is never shaken;
It is the star to every wandering bark,
Whose worth's unknown, although his height be taken.
Love's not Time's fool, though rosy lips and cheeks
Within his bending sickle's compass come;
Love alters not with his brief hours and weeks,
But bears it out even to the edge of doom.
   If this be error and upon me proved,
   I never writ, nor no man ever loved.

Any poem is a "good" poem for you if you like it or if it seems worth while. And you might say that a poem is "bad" for you if it "leaves you cold." But there are some poems that we may reasonably call "great," whether or not they appeal to everyone. We can learn something about the nature of great poetry by examining two great poems: a sonnet by Shakespeare and a poem by Emily Dickinson.

These poets and poems could hardly be more different. Shakespeare was a famous dramatist when he died in 1616. Emily Dickinson, America's greatest woman poet, died unknown in 1886. Shakespeare put his ideas into a strict form, the sonnet. The other poem, in common measure, rhymes more loosely. The poems differ in form, in theme, and in feeling. Yet both are great.

We can hardly understand Shakespeare's sonnet without giving special attention to a number of words that he uses in slightly unusual senses or with enriching overtones. At first glance, the poem looks like a lyric on love and marriage, and we may read it that way if we wish. But when we consider all the clues, this sonnet becomes a poem on enduring friendship. It would be a shame to miss the navigation metaphor—the landmark and the seaman sighting the position of his ship. The

English are only two of these systems. The early Hebrews wrote in phrase-patterns somewhat like English free verse. The ancient Greeks developed quantitative meters to formalize the rhythm of their language. The Anglo-Saxons wrote four-stress lines with *alliteration*, or words beginning with the same consonant sounds, as in this modernized example from *Beowulf:*

> Of men he was mildest   and most beloved,
> To his kin the kindest,   keenest for praise.

Medieval French poets counted syllables as the basis of their verse, and used *assonance*, repeated vowel sounds at the ends of lines with varying consonants. Later French poets invented elaborate rhyme-schemes. Other peoples developed various systems, as in Persia, India, and Japan. One famous Japanese form, the *haiku*, has only 3 lines, with a total of 17 syllables. It has no rhyme or rhythm in the way that Western poetry has, but it follows strict rules (see JAPANESE LITERATURE). Here is a famous example:

> Snail, my little man,
> Slowly—ah, very slowly—
> Climb up Mount Fuji!

Poetry of the People. Poetry is not only world-wide, but also is older than other forms of literature. No one knows the origin of many nursery rhymes that children have enjoyed for hundreds of years. When European settlers came to North America in the 1600's and 1700's, they brought folk songs and poems with them. Different versions survived, some in Canada and others in the Appalachian Mountains, and were finally put in writing. Folk poetry includes the words to folk songs, spirituals, cowboy songs, and sea chanteys. Folk poets composed ballads about the railroad engineer "Casey" Jones and the outlaw Jesse James. In the same tradition, the Canadian poet Robert Service wrote "The Shooting of Dan McGrew." The poetry of the people includes much that is certainly not great, but it has continuing appeal.

The Three Traditions. We can trace the development of poetry in the history of the literature of each national culture. Such WORLD BOOK articles as AMERICAN LITERATURE, CANADIAN LITERATURE, and ENGLISH LITERATURE give details of these developments. It is also important to trace the development of poetry in terms of three major traditions—classical, romantic, and realistic. These traditions cut across national boundaries and extend through long periods of time.

The *classical* tradition stems from the poetry and poetic theories of the ancient Greeks. They originated many forms, including the epic, ode, elegy, idyl, and epigram. Latin poets based their work largely on Greek forms. Here is an epigram by a Roman poet:

> Mycilla dyes her locks, 'tis said,
> But 'tis a foul aspersion.
> She buys them black; they therefore need
> No subsequent immersion.

The spirit of classical poetry is often formal, urbane, rational, and, as in this case, satiric. This tradition began in early Greek poetry, in the 700's B.C., and lasted through the A.D. 400's. Scholars rediscovered ancient literature about a thousand years later in one of the most important developments of the Renaissance. In English poetry, the works of Ben Jonson and, quite differently, those of John Milton show classical influences. A stricter imitation of ancient models developed in French and English poetry during the later 1600's and the 1700's. John Dryden and Alexander Pope were *neoclassic* poets of the period. Traces of this tradition survive today.

The *romantic* tradition comes from the poetry in the familiar image of Father Time with his scythe also appears. The idea that "love alters not" echoes through the lines from first to last, and the poem is woven together with a melody at once simple and elaborate.

Emily Dickinson's poem differs from the sonnet in almost every way. The poet has not used any words with unusual *denotations*, or specific meanings, although her simplest words are rich in *connotations*, or associations. Even a limited knowledge of Emily Dickinson and the New England of her time will help the poem "catch fire" in the reader's mind. In this brief allegory, Death stops by in his carriage on a wintry afternoon. With an air of gentility, he takes the "I" of the poem for a drive through the town and into the country, past the strange house, the horses heading toward eternity. But, in the common measure of the poetic form, and with the simplest of images, the poet touches her somber lyric with irony and light.

Both these poems achieve greatness, because the poets have used language with skill and imagination. In each case, the poet has created a unified form that is both moving and pleasing. The words, packed with meaning, express ideas that expand in the reader's mind, and each poem becomes a memorable experience.

"Because I Could Not Stop for Death"
by Emily Dickinson

> Because I could not stop for Death,
> He kindly stopped for me;
> The carriage held but just ourselves
> And Immortality.
>
> We slowly drove, he knew no haste,
> And I had put away
> My labor, and my leisure too,
> For his civility.
>
> We passed the school where children played
> At wrestling in a ring;
> We passed the fields of gazing grain,
> We passed the setting sun.
>
> We paused before a house that seemed
> A swelling of the ground;
> The roof was scarcely visible,
> The cornice but a mound.
>
> Since then 'tis centuries; but each
> Feels shorter than the day
> I first surmised the horses' heads
> Were toward eternity.

POETRY

Romance languages, which spread from France to England during the Middle Ages (see ROMANCE LANGUAGE). Minstrels recited the deeds of Charlemagne and King Arthur. In France, troubadours composed intricate love songs. Poets in Italy developed the sonnet as a rich and expressive form. In England, Edmund Spenser revived such medieval techniques as allegory, elaborate versification, and pageantry in his romantic epic *The Faerie Queene*. The poetry of Shakespeare shows some other aspects of the romantic spirit, especially looseness of form and imaginative richness. Romanticism gave way to revived classicism in the later 1600's and the 1700's. Then it burst forth again during the late 1700's in the mystical writings of William Blake and in the love and nature poetry of Robert Burns. The romantic poets of the early 1800's—William Wordsworth, Samuel Taylor Coleridge, Lord Byron, Percy Bysshe Shelley, and John Keats—produced one of the richest periods in English literature. Somewhat modified, the romantic tradition was carried on by Tennyson and Browning in England, and by Edgar Allan Poe, Henry Wadsworth Longfellow, John Greenleaf Whittier, and Sidney Lanier in America. John Masefield, Bliss Carman, and Stephen Vincent Benét have written romantic poetry in our time, but with greater realism.

The *realistic* tradition has become important only since the 1800's. It breaks with classical forms and the romantic spirit. Realism treats candidly the outward details of daily life and the inward thoughts and feelings of personal life. Walt Whitman led in the development of free verse and psychological realism. Robert Frost and T. S. Eliot also belong to this tradition.

The Rich Heritage. Few English-speaking persons can read Homer in ancient Greek, Horace in Latin, François Villon in French, Petrarch or Dante in Italian, Alexander Pushkin in Russian, or Heinrich Heine in German. Yet we can catch something of these poets from English translations, many of which are masterpieces in their own right.　　CHARLES W. COOPER

Related Articles. See the articles on national literatures, such as AMERICAN LITERATURE. See the Arts sections of the country articles. See also the following:

AMERICAN POETS

Aiken, Conrad P.
Benét (family)
Bishop, Elizabeth
Bradstreet, Anne D.
Brooks, Gwendolyn
Bryant, William Cullen
Ciardi, John
Coffin, Robert P. T.
Crane, Hart
Cummings, E. E.
Dickinson, Emily
Dillon, George
Doolittle, Hilda
Dunbar, Paul L.
Eberhart, Richard
Emerson, Ralph Waldo
Ferlinghetti, Lawrence
Field, Eugene
Freneau, Philip
Frost, Robert L.
Ginsberg, Allen
Guest, Edgar A.
Hillyer, Robert S.
Holmes, Oliver Wendell
Hughes, Langston
Jeffers, Robinson
Johnson, James Weldon
Kilmer, Joyce
Lanier, Sidney
Lindbergh, Charles A.
　(Anne Morrow)
Lindsay, Vachel
Longfellow, Henry W.
Lowell, Amy
Lowell, James Russell
Lowell, Robert
MacLeish, Archibald
Markham, Edwin
Masters, Edgar Lee
McGinley, Phyllis
Millay, Edna St. Vincent
Miller, Joaquin
Monroe, Harriet
Moore, Marianne C.
Morley, Christopher
Nash, Ogden

Nathan, Robert
Parker, Dorothy
Poe, Edgar Allan
Pound, Ezra L.
Ransom, John Crowe
Rexroth, Kenneth
Riley, James Whitcomb
Robinson, Edwin A.
Roethke, Theodore
Sandburg, Carl
Santayana, George
Seeger, Alan
Shapiro, Karl J.
Stedman, Edmund C.
Stevens, Wallace
Tate, Allen
Taylor, Edward
Teasdale, Sara
Untermeyer, Louis
Updike, John
Van Doren (Mark)
Viereck, Peter
Warren, Robert Penn
Wheatley, Phillis
Whitman, Walt
Whittier, John Greenleaf
Wilbur, Richard
Williams, William Carlos
Wylie, Elinor

BRITISH POETS

Addison, Joseph
Arnold, Matthew
Auden, W. H.
Betjeman, John
Blake, William
Bridges, Robert S.
Brooke, Rupert
Browning, Elizabeth B.
Browning, Robert
Burns, Robert
Butler, Samuel (1612)
Byron, Lord
Caedmon
Chapman, George
Chaucer, Geoffrey
Chesterton, G. K.
Coleridge, Samuel Taylor
Cowley, Abraham
Cowper, William
De la Mare, Walter
Donne, John
Dryden, John
Eliot, T. S.
FitzGerald, Edward
Goldsmith, Oliver
Graves, Robert
Gray, Thomas
Hardy, Thomas
Herbert, George
Herrick, Robert
Hood, Thomas
Hopkins, Gerard Manley
Housman, A. E.
Hunt, Leigh
Jonson, Ben
Keats, John
Kipling, Rudyard
Landor, Walter Savage
Langland, William
Lear, Edward
Lovelace, Richard
Macaulay, Thomas B.
Marlowe, Christopher
Marvell, Andrew
Masefield, John
Meredith, George
Milne, Alan A.
Milton, John
Morris, William
Noyes, Alfred
Pope, Alexander
Rossetti, Christina G.
Rossetti, Dante G.
Scott, Sir Walter
Shakespeare, William
Shelley, Percy Bysshe
Sidney, Sir Philip
Sitwell (family)
Skelton, John
Southey, Robert
Spender, Stephen
Spenser, Edmund
Stevenson, Robert Louis
Suckling, Sir John
Surrey, Earl of
Swinburne, Algernon C.
Tennyson, Lord
Thomas, Dylan
Thompson, Francis
Thomson, James
Vaughan, Henry
Waller, Edmund
Wilde, Oscar
Wordsworth, William
Wyatt, Sir Thomas
Young, Edward

CANADIAN POETS

Carman, Bliss
Lampman, Archibald
Mair, Charles
McCrae, John
Moodie, Susanna
Roberts, Sir Charles G. D.
Sangster, Charles
Scott, Duncan C.
Service, Robert W.

FRENCH POETS

Apollinaire, Guillaume
Baudelaire, Charles
Bellay, Joachim du
Boileau-Despréaux, Nicolas
Breton, André
Chrétien de Troyes
Claudel, Paul
Froissart, Jean
Gautier, Théophile
Hugo, Victor M.
La Fontaine, Jean de
Lamartine, Alphonse de
Malherbe, François de
Mallarmé, Stéphane
Marot, Clément
Mauriac, François
Mistral, Frédéric
Musset, Alfred de
Nerval, Gerard de
Perrault, Charles
Perse, Saint-John
Prévert, Jacques
Rimbaud, Arthur
Ronsard, Pierre de
Rostand, Edmond
Sainte-Beuve, Charles A.

Sully-Prudhomme, René F. A.
Valéry, Paul
Verlaine, Paul

Vigny, Alfred de
Villon, François
Voltaire

German Language Poets

George, Stefan
Goethe, Johann W. von
Gottfried von Strassbourg
Hartmann von Aue
Heine, Heinrich
Hofmannsthal, Hugo von
Mörike, Eduard
Novalis
Rilke, Rainer Maria

Sachs, Hans
Sachs, Nelly
Schiller, Johann
C. F. von
Walther von der
Vogelweide
Werfel, Franz
Wolfram von
Eschenbach

Greek Poets

Anacreon
Epimenides
Hesiod

Homer
Pindar
Sappho

Simonides of Ceos
Theocritus
Thespis

Irish Poets

Colum, Padraic
Moore, Thomas
Russell, George W.

Stephens, James
Wilde, Oscar
Yeats, William Butler

Italian Poets

Alfieri, Vittorio
Ariosto, Ludovico
Carducci, Giosuè
D'Annunzio, Gabriele
Dante Alighieri

Leopardi, Giacomo
Petrarch
Quasimodo, Salvatore
Tasso, Torquato

Latin-American Poets

Darío, Rubén   Mistral, Gabriela   Neruda, Pablo

Persian Poets

Firdausi
Hafiz

Omar Khayyám
Saadi

Roman Poets

Catullus, Gaius V.
Horace
Juvenal

Lucretius
Martial

Ovid
Virgil

Russian Poets

Bunin, Ivan A.
Pasternak, Boris L.

Pushkin, Alexander S.
Yevtushenko, Yevgeni

Scandinavian Poets

Bjørnson, Bjørnstjerne
Karlfeldt, Erik A.

Lagerkvist, Pär F.
Wergeland, Henrik A.

Spanish Poets

García Lorca, Federico
Góngora, Luis de

Jiménez, Juan Ramón
Unamuno, Miguel de

Other Poets

Bialik, Chaim N.
Gibran, Kahlil
Halevi, Judah
Iqbal, Sir Muhammad

Li Po
Shevchenko, Taras
Tagore, Sir Rabindranath
Topelius, Zachris

Famous Poems

Aeneid
Beowulf
Canterbury Tales
Courtship of Miles
Standish
Divine Comedy
Evangeline

Frietchie,
Barbara
Gilgamesh,
Epic of
Hiawatha
Iliad
King-Horn

Lochinvar
Mahabharata
Nibelungenlied
Odyssey
Ramayana
Roland
Rubáiyát

Forms of Poetry

Ballad
Blank Verse
Elegy

Epic
Epigram
Epitaph

Free Verse
Idyl
Limerick

Ode
Psalms
Sonnet

Poets and Minstrels

Bard
Mastersinger

Minnesinger
Minstrel

Poet Laureate
Troubadour

Trouvère

Other Related Articles

Anthology
Choral Speaking
Elision

Meter (poetry)
Pulitzer Prizes

Rhyme
Rhythm

Outline

I. Enjoying Poetry
II. Writing Poetry
III. Types of Poetry
  A. Lyric   B. Narrative   C. Dramatic
IV. How a Poet Writes
  A. Verse and Melody   C. Thought and Feeling
  B. Image and Picture
V. Metrical Patterns
  A. Feet, Meter, and Rhyme-Scheme
  B. Scansion
  C. Metrical Variations
VI. The Development of Poetry
  A. Poetry of the People   C. The Rich
  B. The Three Traditions   Heritage

Questions

The answers to the first question below follow after the question. The answers to the other questions appear throughout the article.

What is the metrical pattern of each of the following?

(1)   The time you won your town the race
       We chaired you through the market-place;
       Man and boy stood cheering by,
       And home we brought you shoulder-high.

(2)   I am monarch of all I survey;
       My right there is none to dispute;
       From the center all round to the sea
       I am lord of the fowl and the brute.

(3)   Cannon to right of them,
           Cannon to left of them,
           Cannon in front of them
             Volleyed and thundered . . .

(4)
Once upon a midnight dreary, while I pondered, weak and weary,
Over many a quaint and curious volume of forgotten lore,
While I nodded, nearly napping, suddenly there came a tapping,
As of someone gently rapping, rapping at my chamber door . . .

Answers to metrical pattern problems:
(1) These lines from A. E. Housman's "To an Athlete Dying Young" are *iambic tetrameter* (four *de-DUMM* feet per line), rhyming *aabb*[4].
(2) These lines from William Cowper's "Verses Supposed to be Written by Alexander Selkirk" are *anapestic trimeter* (three *de-de-DUMM* feet per line), rhyming *abab*[3].
(3) These lines from Lord Tennyson's "The Charge of the Light Brigade" are *dactylic dimeter* (two *DUMM-de-de* feet per line), rhyming *aaab*[2].
(4) These lines from Edgar Allan Poe's "The Raven" are *trochaic octameter* (eight *DUMM-de* feet per line), rhyming *abcb*[8], but with many rhyme-words within the lines.

What is the best way to discover a poem's meaning?
Why is rhythm important to poetry?
Where did the major 14-line poetic form develop?
What can you gain from reading poetry aloud?
How would you explain the melody of a poem?
Which language has poetry based on an *accentual* meter?
How does narrative poetry differ from lyric poetry?
What are three metrical variations in poetry?
How can you learn to judge a poem?
What are the three main types of poetry?

POETS' CORNER. See Westminster Abbey.

POGROM, *poh GRAHM,* is a massacre of helpless people, particularly Jews. Many pogroms took place in Russia during the 1800's. See also GENOCIDE.

POGY. See MENHADEN.

POHAI, GULF OF. See YELLOW SEA.

POI. See HAWAII (Food).

POINCARÉ, *PWAN KAH RAY,* **JULES HENRI** (1854-1912), a French scientist, was one of the greatest mathematicians of modern times. Using mathematics as his tool, Poincaré also investigated the tides, electricity, light, and the motions of the planets. He wrote several essays and books on the philosophy of science. He was elected to the French Academy, the highest honor a French writer can receive, because of the literary quality of his writing. Many of Poincaré's books have been translated into English. The most famous include *Science and Hypothesis* (1902), *The Value of Science* (1906), and *Science and Method* (1909).

Poincaré was born in Nancy. He attended the Polytechnique school, where he won many prizes in mathematics. From 1881 until his death, he taught at the University of Paris. PHILLIP S. JONES

POINCARÉ, *PWAN KAH RAY,* **RAYMOND** (1860-1934), served four times as premier of France, and was president of France from 1913 to 1920. He gained a reputation as a financier and an ardent nationalist.

Poincaré first became premier in 1912 and tried to maintain and strengthen French alliances. In 1922, after his term as president, he became premier again. The Treaty of Versailles required Germany to pay huge reparations to France, and Poincaré demanded prompt payments. In 1923, after the Reparations Commission declared Germany in default, Poincaré ordered French troops into the Ruhr to force Germany to pay (see RUHR [History]). Poincaré was defeated in the 1924 elections, and resigned his premiership.

He served as premier again from 1926 to 1928, during a financial and political crisis. His measures to stabilize the French economy won him the title "savior of the franc." After a fourth premiership from 1928 to 1929, he resigned. Poincaré was born on Aug. 20, 1860, in Bar-le-Duc, France. E. J. KNAPTON

POINCIANA, *POYN sih AN uh,* is one of the most beautiful flowering trees. It is a native of Madagascar, but has been widely planted in warm climates because of its immense clusters of brilliant flowers. Each flower is from 3 to 4 inches across, with 5 widely spreading red petals. One of these petals is streaked and dotted with yellow. There are 10 long stamens that stand well above the flower and add to its beauty. The blossoms are followed by the seed pods, which are 2 feet long or more, and look like great purplish-brown Lima bean pods. The pods contain hard, oblong beans. In some of the poorer countries where the royal poinciana grows, people knock the pods from the trees and burn them as fuel.

Royal poincianas are commonly found in southern Florida and the West Indies. During their long summer season of bloom, they turn the roads along which they grow into lines of fiery red. At other seasons of the year they are beautiful because of their lacy, fernlike foliage of soft green leaves, divided and subdivided into many tiny leaflets. The trees grow rapidly, soon developing strong, gnarled trunks and spreading branches that may reach 40 feet above the ground.

Scientific Classification. Poincianas are classified in the pea family, *Leguminosae.* They make up the genus *Poinciana.* Royal poincianas belong to the genus *Delonix,* species *D. regia.* K. A. ARMSON

POINSETTIA, *poyn SET ih uh,* is a plant of the spurge family. It has tiny flowers surrounded by large, colored *bracts* (special leaves). The bracts are usually bright red, but may also be yellowish or white. The brilliant red bracts contrast with the green leaves and make the poinsettia popular for decoration during the Christmas season. In tropical and subtropical regions, the poinsettia thrives outdoors. It may grow 2 to 10 feet tall. It is a popular garden shrub in the southern states and California. In cold climates, the poinsettia must be grown indoors. As a potted plant, it grows from 1 to 4 feet tall.

Scientific Classification. The poinsettia belongs to the spurge family, *Euphorbiaceae.* It is genus *Euphorbia,* species *E. pulcherrima.* H. D. HARRINGTON

See also FLOWER (color picture: Flowers in Festivals).

POINT, in type. See TYPE (Sizes).

POINT BARROW. See ALASKA (introduction).

POINT FOUR PROGRAM, also called TECHNICAL ASSISTANCE PROGRAM, was authorized in 1949 by the United States Congress through the Act for International Development. The Point Four Program received its name because it was the fourth point in President Harry S. Truman's inaugural address in January, 1949. He called for "a bold new program for making the benefits of our scientific advances and industrial progress available for the improvement and growth of underdeveloped areas." Congress appropriated $25 million for the initial technical assistance program. Part of this amount was given to the United Nations. The International Cooperation Agency (ICA) was responsible for the technical assistance program from 1955 until the agency was dissolved in 1961. Then the Agency for International Development (AID) became responsible for all nonmilitary foreign assistance programs. See also FOREIGN AID. CHARLES P. SCHLEICHER

POINT OF DEPARTURE. See NAVIGATION (Leaving Port).

POINT OF ORDER. See PARLIAMENTARY PROCEDURE (table: Terms).

POINT PELEE NATIONAL PARK. See CANADA (National Parks).

POINTER is a dog used to hunt quail and other game birds. The dog is called *pointer* because it stops as still as a statue when it smells a bird, and *points* by facing the direction of the bird, often with one front paw lifted and its tail held out stiffly behind. The pointer is classed as a sporting dog and as a field dog, along with setters, spaniels, and retrievers. Setters, spaniels, and retrievers usually have long hair, but the pointer has a short coat like a hound, and houndlike ears, head, and body. It weighs about 45 to 60 pounds, and is white with spots of lemon, *liver* (reddish-brown), or black.

The pointer has speed and a keen sense of smell. Pointers are popular in America and England for hunting and field trials. MAXWELL RIDDLE

See also DOG (color picture: Sporting Dogs).

POINTILLISM. See SEURAT, GEORGES; PAINTING (Color).

POISON GAS

POISON is a substance that kills living things or makes them ill. Poisons may be swallowed, inhaled, injected, or absorbed by the skin or body membranes. The study of poisons is called *toxicology*, and many poisons are called *toxins*.

The strongest poisons are usually found only in laboratories. They cause few deaths because they seldom occur in everyday surroundings. Most deaths are caused by weaker poisons that are contained in common household products. About a million to two million human beings suffer from poisoning each year in the United States, and about 8,000 deaths result. Poisons found in farm and household products cause most of the U.S. poisonings and deaths. These products include insect sprays, rat poisons, cleaning and polishing compounds, and such fuels as gasoline. Even detergents have caused fatal poisonings when swallowed. Medications taken in large amounts can also cause poisoning.

To prevent poisonings, never eat untested foods, such as wild mushrooms or berries, or foods in unlabeled containers. Keep all medicines and chemicals out of the reach of small children. Children are more sensitive to poison than adults and a smaller amount may cause a child's death. Also, young children may swallow large portions of bad-tasting chemicals that an adult would avoid, such as lye, kerosene, and gasoline.

Poison control centers have been set up in many U.S. hospitals to give emergency information to doctors and the public. They furnish first aid information and the location of the nearest hospital. Some centers advise only doctors on the appropriate *antidote*. An antidote is a drug that relieves the harmful effects of poisons. For detailed information, see FIRST AID (chart: Antidotes for Some Common Poisons).

Poisons can be useful and even life-saving. Useful medicines, such as *curare* and *ouabain*, were discovered because they were used first as poisons on arrows. Ouabain is similar to the drug *digitalis* (see DIGITALIS).

─────────── TREATMENT FOR POISONING ───────────

For emergency treatment of poisoning, call your hospital or physician immediately. If possible, tell the doctor the name of the poison. These emergency steps may be taken if no other advice has been given:

Swallowed Poison. If the poison is a corrosive poison, such as lye and rust remover, or a petroleum product, such as gasoline, DO NOT make the patient vomit. If the patient can swallow and is conscious, give him water and milk and wait for the doctor. If the poison is not a corrosive or petroleum product, try to make the patient vomit by touching the back of his throat with the blunt end of a spoon or your finger. When vomiting begins, place the patient face down with his head lower than his hips. Save the poison container and the patient's urine and vomit for the doctor to analyze.

Inhaled Poison. Carry the patient to fresh air. Do not let him walk. Loosen all the patient's tight clothing and wrap him in a blanket to prevent chills. Apply artificial respiration if breathing stops or becomes irregular. Do not give alcohol in any form.

Poison in the Eye. Hold eyes open and keep washing them with running water until the doctor arrives. Do not apply any chemicals.

Poison on the Skin and Chemical Burns. Remove the patient's clothing if necessary. Drench and wash the skin with water. When the poison is removed, cover the patient with loose, clean cloth. Do not use ointments or other first aid treatment for burns.

Plant and Animal Poisoning. When organisms, such as certain bacteria, produce a poison, the poison is called a *toxin* (see TOXIN). Some *fungi* (simple plants) produce toxins that are dangerous to human beings when swallowed in infested food. For example, some mushrooms have a toxic effect when eaten.

Many plants, such as larkspur and poison ivy, produce poisons that can be dangerous for human beings and livestock. Plant roots, stems, leaves, seeds, and fruits may contain poison.

Many animals have poisonous bites or stings. These include bees, wasps, scorpions, snakes, spiders, octopuses, and snails. Most animals use their poison to defend themselves or to attack other organisms. Some fish, such as sting rays, have poisonous spines. Some salamanders, frogs, and toads have poison in their skin. For more information, see the WORLD BOOK articles on SNAKE BITE and each of the above animals.

Kinds of Poisons. Scientists classify poisons in many different ways. A common classification lists five kinds: (1) corrosive poisons, (2) irritant poisons, (3) systemic poisons, (4) poisonous gases, and (5) poisonous foods.

Corrosive poisons destroy living tissue that they touch. Hydrochloric acid, nitric acid, and *sodium hydroxide* (lye) are corrosive poisons. A person who swallows this type of poison may destroy the lining of his mouth and throat.

Irritant poisons cause *inflammation* (swelling and soreness) of the mucous membranes. These membranes line many air passages of the body, such as the nose. Irritants also affect the stomach, intestines, and nerve centers. Arsenic, lead, and most of the metallic poisons are irritant poisons. Arsenic causes vomiting and may affect the heart, kidneys, and other organs.

Systemic poisons attack the nervous system and other important organs, such as the kidneys, liver, and heart. Strychnine, a common rat poison, causes convulsions and difficulty in swallowing (see STRYCHNINE). Hydrocyanic acid and overdoses of heroin and opium may cause death. The belladonna plant's poisonous berries produce hot flashes, thirst, and *delirium* (disorder of the mind). Many *barbiturates* (sedatives) are systemic poisons when taken in large doses.

Poisonous gases make breathing difficult and can cause death. Some poisonous gases, such as carbon monoxide from automobiles and gas heaters, are especially dangerous because they are difficult to notice at first. Some gases irritate the lungs, eyes, nose, or skin.

Food poisoning can come from eating certain chemicals or organisms and their toxins. Chemicals, such as insecticides, and plants and animals, such as hemlock and certain shellfish, can cause food poisoning.

Botulism, poisoning caused by a toxin produced by bacteria, can cause paralysis and death.   SOLOMON GARB

Critically reviewed by the AMERICAN MEDICAL ASSOCIATION

Related Articles in WORLD BOOK include:

Alkaloid	Barbiturate	Food Poisoning
Antidote	Belladonna	Lead Poisoning
Arsenic	Botulism	Poisonous Plant
Asphyxiation	First Aid	

POISON GAS. See CHEMICAL-BIOLOGICAL-RADIOLOGICAL WARFARE; GAS MASK; FUMIGATION.

531

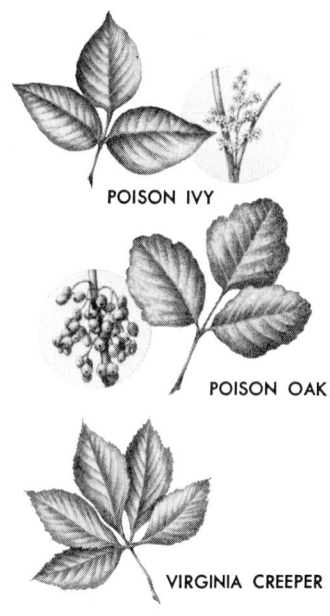

POISON IVY

POISON OAK

VIRGINIA CREEPER

Poison Ivy and Poison Oak have only three leaflets and can be easily distinguished from nonpoisonous Virginia Creeper, which has five. Poison ivy vines, *right*, often twine around tree trunks.

J. Horace McFarland

POISON IVY is the common name for several kinds of harmful vines or shrubs related to sumac. Poison ivy grows plentifully in nearly all parts of the United States and southern Canada. Some kinds usually grow as vines twining on tree trunks or straggling over the ground. But these often form upright bushes if they have no support to climb upon. Other species, particularly in the Southern States and on the Pacific Coast, are more inclined to form bushes than to twine. These are usually known as *poison oak*, but are often hard to distinguish from the others.

The tissues of all these plants contain a poisonous oil somewhat like carbolic acid. This oil is extremely irritating to the skin. It may be brushed onto the clothing or skins of persons coming in contact with the plants. Many persons have been poisoned merely by taking off their shoes after walking through poison ivy. People can get poisoned from other people, but only if the oil remains on their skin. The eruptions themselves are not a source of infection.

Appearance. Because these poisonous plants are very common, everyone who goes into the woods and fields should learn to recognize them. The leaves of both the bushy and the climbing kinds are shiny green, turning red and orange in the autumn. Each leaf is made up of three leaflets more or less notched at the edges. Two of the leaflets form a pair on opposite sides of the stalk, while the third leaflet stands by itself at the tip of the leaf. Small greenish flowers grow in bunches attached to the main stem close to the point where each leaf joins it. Later in the season clusters of poisonous, berrylike drupes form. These drupes are a dirty yellowish white, and have a waxy look like the berries of mistletoe.

Control and Treatment. Some efforts have been made to destroy these plants by uprooting them or by spraying them with plant-killing chemicals. But poison ivy and poison oak are so common that such methods have not been very effective. Contact with the plants should be avoided as far as possible.

After the oil has touched the skin, it usually takes some time for it to penetrate and do its damage. Before this happens, it is wise to wash the skin thoroughly several times with plenty of soap and water. Care should be taken not to touch the face or any other part of the body, for even tiny amounts of the oil will cause irritation.

If poisoning develops, the itching reddened skin and the blisters may be treated with soothing dressings of calamine lotion, Epsom salts, or bicarbonate of soda. Scientists have developed a vaccine that can be injected or taken by mouth. However, this is effective only if taken before exposure.

Scientific Classification. The several species of poison ivy and poison oak belong to the cashew family, *Anacardiaceae*. The commonest kind in the northeastern and north-central parts of the United States is classified as genus *Rhus*, species *R. radicans*. The plant of the Pacific Coast is *R. diversiloba*. HAROLD NORMAN MOLDENKE

See also POISON OAK; SUMAC; VIRGINIA CREEPER.

POISON OAK is another name for poison ivy, but is used especially for the bushy forms of that plant. Like poison ivy, species of poison oak have leaves composed of three leaflets, and sometimes grow as vines.

Scientific Classification. Poison oak belongs to the cashew family, *Anacardiaceae*. Two common kinds of poison oak are classified as genus *Rhus*, species *R. radicans*, and *R. diversiloba*. J. J. LEVISON

See also POISON IVY; SUMAC.

POISON SUMAC. See SUMAC.

POISONOUS PLANT is any plant that is injurious to human beings or to animals. There are many kinds of poisonous plants. Some kinds are merely unwholesome, or are only moderately poisonous. Others contain substances that are among the deadliest poisons known. One well-known example of such a substance is nicotine, which is found in the tobacco plant. Nicotine is so deadly that a very small quantity can kill a human being quickly.

Fortunately, many of the most dangerous plants are shunned because they look, smell, or taste disagreeable. Some grow in places where few men or domestic animals come in contact with them. Even so, poisonous plants cause a great deal of harm each year in almost every part of the world. Many persons have died from eating poisonous mushrooms, which may be hard to distinguish from the wholesome kinds. Farm animals have been killed by grazing on poisonous plants.

Bacteria, which are actually one-celled plants, also cause suffering and death. Many diseases result from the *toxins* (poisons) that bacteria pour into the blood as they multiply in the body. *Botulism*, a form of food poisoning that is often fatal to people, is caused by bacteria.

Not all poisonous plants do their harm by being eaten. Some, such as poison ivy, poison sumac, and manchineel, irritate the skin or eyes. Certain others, known as *allergens*, are harmful only to persons who are sensitive, or allergic, to them. A well-known allergen is the pollen of ragweed, which causes hay fever and asthma. See ALLERGY.

Some families of flowering plants contain many very poisonous species. For example, the spurge family, *Euphorbiaceae*, includes the cassava, croton, and the castor-oil plant, all poisonous. Another group is the nightshade family, *Solanaceae*. Besides such wholesome vegetables as tomato, potato, and eggplant, it contains such deadly members as belladonna and deadly nightshade, henbane, Jimson weed, and tobacco. Several exceedingly poisonous plants, including monkshood, larkspur, and hellebore, belong to the buttercup family, *Ranunculaceae*.

Some poisonous plants are not wholly bad. Some are useful for destroying insect pests. Many of the most valuable drugs used in medicine are poisons extracted from plants and given in controlled doses. Among these are aconite, atropine, cocaine, digitalis, hyoscine, morphine, quinine, and strychnine.   HAROLD NORMAN MOLDENKE

Related Articles in WORLD BOOK include:

Aconite	Gelsemium	Nicotine
Alkaloid	Hellebore	Nightshade
Antidote	Hemlock	Oleander
Bacteria	Henbane	Poison Ivy
Belladonna	Jimson Weed	Poison Oak
Cassava	Larkspur	Pokeweed
Castor Oil	Locoweed	Prussic Acid
Croton	Manchineel	Ragweed
Datura	Mushroom (Poisonous	Rhubarb
Digitalis	Mushrooms; color pic-	Spurge Family
Dogbane	ture; Deadly Amanitas)	Sumac

POITIERS, *pwah TYAY*, **BATTLE OF,** was fought in 1356, near the present French town of Poitiers. A famous English victory in the Hundred Years' War resulted from the Battle of Poitiers. The English forces were led by Edward, "the Black Prince" of England. King John of France led the French troops.

The English were greatly outnumbered, but the Black Prince fought skillfully. At the height of the battle the English horsemen suddenly appeared behind the French lines. The French fled, leaving King John and his son Philip to be captured.   ROBERT S. HOYT

See also EDWARD (The Black Prince).

POKER is a card game in which players make bets on the cards they hold, or hope to hold. There are countless types of poker games, but all come under either of two general classifications.

In *draw poker*, each player is dealt five cards, face down. After placing a bet, he is entitled to discard not more than three of his cards and draw the same number from the deck in an attempt to improve his hand. After all players have filled out their hands, the betting proceeds. In regular *stud poker*, each player receives one card *in the hole* (face down). This is followed by one card face up. Bets are made on the two cards. After bets are placed, a second face-up card is dealt. This continues until each player has five cards. Many groups play seven-card stud, in which two hole cards are followed by four face-up cards, and then a final hole card.

Although poker games differ, the card combinations they bet on are the same everywhere. Following is a list of hands, with examples and in order of rank:

Royal flush	A-K-Q-J-10	(one suit)
Straight flush	2-3-4-5-6	(one suit)
Four-of-a-kind	8-8-8-8	
Full house	J-J-J-4-4	
Flush	2-5-6-J-K	(one suit)
Straight	2-3-4-5-6	(any suits)
Three-of-a-kind	7-7-7-2-3	
Two pairs	K-K-4-4-5	
One pair	J-J-7-9-Q	
Highest card	A-K-7-6-2 wins over A-K-7-5-3	

Where two hands are of the same rank, the one with the higher cards wins.   JOHN SCARNE

POKEWEED is a tall, branching perennial herb with greenish-white flowers and deep purple, juicy berries. It flourishes in waste places and along roadsides and fencerows from Ontario to Florida, and west to Texas and Minnesota. The stem of the pokeweed grows 4 to 10 feet high. The plant has a brilliant appearance in fall, when the leaves become red and the berries ripen. It is known locally by such common names as *poke*, *scoke*, *pigeonberry*, *pokeberry*, *inkberry*, and *red nightshade*.

The berries, together with the poisonous roots, are used in medicines that treat skin and blood disease, and relieve pain and inflammation. Pokeweed seeds are poisonous, and the leaves are frequently mottled by a virus disease that may be carried to flowers and vegetables by insects. Pokeweed plants must be cut off below ground level in order to kill them.

Pokeweed Berries grow on graceful, arched spikes. The ripe berries contrast strikingly with the red leaves in fall.

J. C. Allen

Scientific Classification. The pokeweed is in the pokeweed family *Phytolaccaceae*. It is genus *Phytolacca*, species *P. americana*.   LOUIS PYENSON

Embassy of the Polish People's Republic

The Beautiful Carpathian Mountains in Southeastern Poland are a popular resort area. Their forests, lakes, mineral springs, and wildlife attract tourists throughout the year.

POLAND is a Communist-controlled country in central Europe. A land of plains and gently rolling hills, it has fertile soil and important mineral deposits. Poland has a long history and a rich cultural heritage. In 1966, Poland celebrated a thousand years of Christianity.

Poland's fortunes have varied greatly. At times, the

M. Kamil Dziewanowski, the contributor of this article, is Professor of History at Boston University and author of Communist Party of Poland: An Outline of History, *and* Joseph Pilsudski and Eastern Europe, 1918-1922.

Poles have had a large country, at times they had a small country, and at times, no country at all. Their bigger, more powerful neighbors have often fought over Poland. But the Polish people have always kept a strong national loyalty and patriotism. Two Polish patriots also played a part in early American history. Thaddeus Kosciusko built the United States Military Academy at West Point, and Casimir Pulaski founded the United States cavalry.

Poland is named for a Slavic tribe, the *Polians*

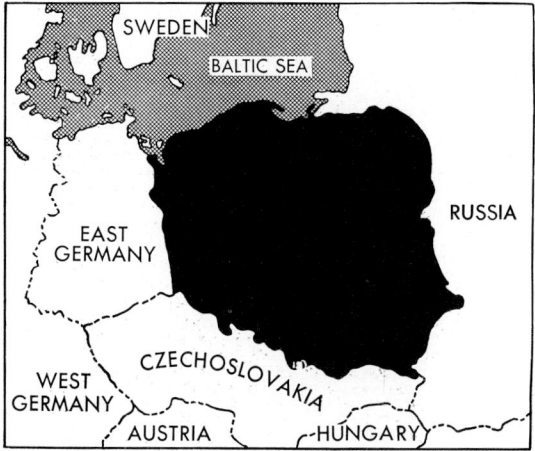

Poland Lies Between East Germany and Russia.

———— FACTS IN BRIEF ————

Capital: Warsaw.

Official Language: Polish.

Form of Government: People's Republic (Communist dictatorship).

Parliament: 459 members, serving four-year terms.

Political Divisions: 17 voivodships (provinces) and 5 cities of voivodship status. Each voivodship is divided into districts.

Area: 120,665 sq. mi. *Greatest Distances*—(east-west) 400 miles; (north-south) 360 miles. *Coastline*—310 miles.

Elevation: *Highest*—Rysy Peak, 8,212 feet; *Lowest*—sea level.

Population: *1960 Census*—29,775,508; distribution, 51 per cent rural, 49 per cent urban. *Estimated 1970 Population*—32,912,000; density, 273 persons to the square mile. *Estimated 1975 Population*—34,591,000.

Chief Products: *Agriculture*—barley, cattle, flax, horses, oats, potatoes, rye, sheep, sugar beets. *Manufacturing*—cement, chemicals, machinery, textiles, transportation equipment. *Mining*—coal, copper, iron, lead, potassium salt, rock salt, zinc.

National Anthem: "Jeszcze Polska nie Zginęla" ("Poland Has Not Yet Perished").

Flag: The top half is white, the bottom red. These colors were used in the 1200's on the Polish coat of arms. Adopted 1919. See FLAG (color picture: Flags of Europe).

Money: *Basic Unit*—zloty. 100 groszy equal 1 zloty. For its value in dollars, see MONEY (table: Values).

(dwellers of the field), who once lived there. The country's official name in Polish is POLSKA RZECZPOSPOLITA LUDOWA (POLISH PEOPLE'S REPUBLIC). Warsaw is the capital and largest city.

Poland (black) is smaller in size than New Mexico.

The Land

Most of Poland is flat or gently rolling. The coastline is low and sandy. Several hooks of land enclose shallow lagoons. Northern Poland has many small lakes.

The countryside rises gradually toward the Carpathian and Sudetes mountains in the south. The Carpathian Mountains in the southeast contain 8,212-foot Rysy Peak, the highest point in Poland.

Poland's chief river is the Vistula, which rises in the interior of the country and flows northward to Danzig (Gdańsk). It drains four-fifths of Poland. The Bug, Narew, and Pilica rivers flow into the Vistula. The Warta River empties into the Oder, which flows into the Baltic Sea. Canals link Poland's main river systems.

Natural Resources. Poland has a large supply of good timber, largely pine and spruce, in its northern forests. Its mineral wealth includes coal, rock salt, potassium salt, iron, zinc, sulfur, copper, and lead. Its coal and zinc deposits are among the world's most valuable.

Climate. Most of Poland has fairly mild winters and moderate summers. January temperatures average

C. A. F., Warsaw

Warsaw, Poland's Capital, is a center of Polish art, education, and industry. Constitution Square, *right*, stands near the center of the city.

*Does not appear on map; key shows general location.

Source: Official estimates.

Polish Tourist Office

The Folk Music and Dancing of the Tatra mountaineers are lively and rhythmic. The Tatra range is part of the Carpathian Mountains. Many of the people wear colorful regional costumes on special holidays.

30° F., and July temperatures average 70° F. Most of Poland has from 20 to 40 inches of rain a year.

The People

Most Poles are descended from the Slavic tribes that occupied the region in the 400's. The largest minority group is Ukrainian. Germans, Byelorussians, and Jews make up small minority groups.

The Polish language is of Slavic origin. Polish is written, however, in the Roman alphabet.

Way of Life. Most Poles live in small cities or on farms. Most of them live in brick or stone houses. The government built many new apartment buildings after World War II. However, the country still suffers from a housing shortage because of the enormous destruction Polish cities suffered during World War II.

Most Poles dress in regular European fashions, but everyday clothing tends to be rather drab. On special holidays, the people in some districts such as Kraków dress up in brightly colored national costumes. The men wear white shirts with small, neat bow ties; vests or waistcoats; loose, baggy trousers; and high boots. The women wear long, full skirts; white blouses; and decorated boots or black pumps. Most Polish holidays are associated with religion.

The national drink is *wodka* (vodka). Favorite foods include *bigos* (meat and cabbage); *krupnik* (barley soup); *pierogi*, a dumpling; *kielbasa*, a sausage; and hams.

Poles are high spirited. Many of their songs are gay. Dances such as the *mazurka* and *oberek* resemble American square dances. Great emphasis is placed on sports. Over 2 million persons belong to organized sports groups. Favorite sports include soccer, basketball, boxing, cycling, fencing, track, skiing, and swimming.

Cities. Warsaw is the capital and largest city of Poland. Danzig, at the mouth of the Vistula, is the chief port. Kraków, which lies in the heart of a rich salt-mining region, has Jagiellonian University. Jagiellonian, founded in 1364, is one of the oldest universities in Europe. International fairs are held in Poznań each June. See the separate articles on Polish cities listed in the *Related Articles* section of this article.

The Center of Danzig (Gdańsk) was almost completely destroyed during World War II. But it has been rebuilt as it was before the war. The city is the hub of the Polish shipping industry.

Guy Gravett

Agriculture. About five out of every ten persons in Poland earn their living from agriculture. Most of them own their own farms, but about 30,000 families work on the 1,200 *collective farms* (huge, government-owned farms). The government once tried to develop a system of collective farming, but since the late 1950's there has been a gradual return to private ownership of farms.

Poland grows more rye and potatoes than any other country in the world except Russia. Other important crops include sugar beets, oats, wheat, barley, and flax.

Manufacturing. Most Polish industries were *nationalized* (put under state control) after World War II. Steel mills produce about 10 million tons of steel a year. Cotton, wool, and silk textile mills are important in the Polish economic life. About $10\frac{1}{2}$ million tons of cement are made annually. Other industries manufacture heavy machinery, locomotives, and farm equipment. The chemical industries have developed steadily in recent years. The Poles have built a number of dams to provide hydroelectric power for industry.

Mining. The large coal reserves near Poland's southern border make the country one of the world's largest coal-producing nations. Over 160 million tons of coal are mined every year. Southwest Poland has the leading lead and zinc mines in Europe. Copper, iron ore, potassium salt, rock salt, and sulfur are also mined in Poland.

Trade. Most of Poland's trade is with the Communist countries of eastern Europe. However, Poland conducts more trade with Western nations than any other Communist nation except Yugoslavia and Czechoslovakia. Coal; foodstuffs, especially ham; and ships are Poland's leading exports. Poland imports heavy machinery, precision instruments, high grade iron ore, and petroleum.

Transportation and Communication. The Vistula and Oder rivers are Poland's most important transportation routes. Several ocean liners sail from Danzig, Gdynia, and Stettin, Poland's Baltic ports. About 17,000 miles of railways and 12,000 miles of highways serve Poland. Airlines link Warsaw with other Polish cities and the capitals of other countries.

The country has several radio stations and television stations. Telephone and telegraph lines connect the main cities of Poland.

Social and Cultural Achievements

Education. Poland's educational system is set up to provide free education from elementary school through college. Children may go to nursery school and kindergarten from the time they are three until they reach the age of seven. Then they may attend an eight-year elementary school, followed by four years in a general or vocational high school. Those who continue may take four to five years of college to complete their education. Both public and parochial schools are largely controlled by the government. There are universities in Warsaw, Kraków, Poznań, Wrocław, Łódź, Toruń, and Lublin. Lublin has two universities. One of them, The Catholic University of Lublin, is the only private university in a Communist country.

Religion. More than 94 of every 100 Poles belong to the Roman Catholic Church. Protestants make up the next largest religious group.

The Arts. The best-known Polish poet is Adam Mickiewicz (1798-1855), who wrote the epic poem, *Pan Tadeusz*. Henryk Sienkiewicz (1846-1916) won the

C. A. F., Warsaw

Poland Produces Fine Porcelain and Chinaware. Some of the best pieces are decorated with hand-painted designs.

1905 Nobel prize for literature for his novel, *Quo Vadis?* Władysław S. Reymont (1868-1925) won the 1924 Nobel prize for literature for his novel, *The Peasants*.

Frédéric Chopin (1810?-1849) immortalized the folk culture of his country in his preludes, mazurkas, sonatas, and polonaises. Ignace Paderewski (1860-1941) and Arthur Rubinstein (1889-   ) are also famous. Warsaw's new Teatr Wielki ranks as the largest opera house in Europe and one of the largest in the world.

Government

National Government. Poland is ruled by the country's Communist Party, the Polish United Worker's

Most Poles are Roman Catholics, and religion is important in their lives. Poland has been a Christian country for 1,000 years.

Gerald Howson

PARTITION OF 1772

First Partition. Russia, Prussia, and Austria each took some of the Polish land nearest to its own territory.

PARTITION OF 1793

Second Partition reduced Poland to half its 1772 size as Russia and Prussia each took more land.

PARTITION OF 1795

Third Partition. Poland ceased to exist as a nation after Russia, Prussia, and Austria took the rest of the land.

Party. The first secretary of the party central committee is actually the country's most powerful leader. The premier serves as chairman of the council of ministers, the highest administrative body. The *Sejm* (parliament), a one-house legislature, has one member for each 60,000 persons. Members are elected to four-year terms by the people.

A 15-man council of state acts for the Sejm when it is not in session. Both the council of ministers and the council of state are largely made up of carefully selected members of the Communist Party who are then approved by the Sejm.

All citizens over the age of 18 may vote in national elections, but they can vote only for candidates acceptable to the Communists. There are three parties, all Communist or Communist dominated. They are the United Workers' Party, the United Peasant Party, and the Democratic Party.

Local Government. Each of the voivodships and districts is governed by a local people's council. Council members are chosen for three-year terms.

History

Early History. Polish history began in the 900's, when the Polians united the other tribes of the region under them. The Poles were converted to Christianity in 966, and Western culture came to Poland. Boleslav the Brave (992-1025) was one of the first rulers of the Piast dynasty. He made Poland an independent kingdom, and was crowned its first king in 1025.

When Boleslav III died in 1138, the country was divided among his sons. The resulting principalities warred among themselves for many years. This weakened all, and, in 1241, the Asian Mongols invaded Poland.

At about the same time, Conrad, one of the local rulers, invited the Order of Teutonic Knights to help him fight the heathen tribe of Prussians. The Prussians

---
IMPORTANT DATES IN POLAND

900's The Polians united the tribes of their region.
1025 Poland became an independent kingdom.
1241 Mongolian invasions devastated much of Poland.
1410 Poland defeated the Teutonic Knights at the Battle of Grunwald.
1569 Poland and Lithuania were officially united.
1683 Sobieski defeated the Turks at Vienna.
1772 Poland was partitioned the first time, among Russia, Prussia, and Austria.
1793 Poland was partitioned the second time, between Russia and Prussia.
1795 Poland was partitioned the third time, among Russia, Prussia, and Austria. The country disappeared as a separate nation.
1830 The Poles revolted against Russian rule, but were defeated in the following year.
1863 The Poles again revolted against, and were beaten by, the Russians.
1918 Poland proclaimed itself an independent republic.
1926 Józef Pilsudski made himself a semidictator.
1939 Poland was partitioned the fourth time, between Germany and Russia.
1945 A Russian-controlled government was set up, and new boundaries were established.
1952 A new constitution, similar to that of Russia, was adopted.
1956 After anti-Russian riots, Polish Communist Władysław Gomułka became head of the government.
1961 Poland started a five-year program aimed at increasing industrial production by 50 per cent.
1966 Poland celebrated 1,000 years of Christianity.

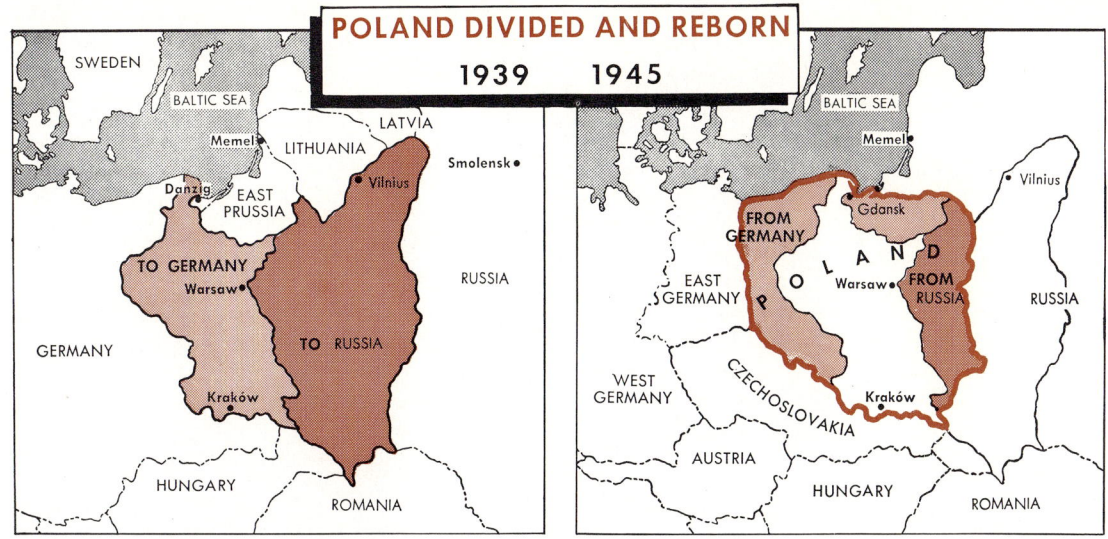

POLAND DIVIDED AND REBORN
1939   1945

At the Beginning of World War II, Germany and Russia split Poland almost in half along a north-south line.

At the End of World War II, a new Poland arose. Germany lost land to Poland. Russia kept land taken in the east.

were almost wiped out after fifty years of conflict. The Knights then founded their state near the mouth of the Vistula, which cut off Polish access to the Baltic.

Władysław I (1260-1333) united most of the warring principalities. His son, Casimir the Great (1309-1370), gave law, prosperity, and culture to Poland. In 1347, he established the first statute of laws in Europe. He founded Jagiellonian University in 1364. Casimir also gave refuge to the Jews who were being driven from most European countries at that time.

Union with Lithuania. Queen Jadwiga (1370-1399) married Władysław Jagello, duke of Lithuania, in the late 1300's. This marriage established the Jagellon dynasty and united Lithuania and Poland in a federal union. To break up this union, the Teutonic Knights declared war on Poland. Poland defeated them in 1410, and took most of their land. In 1569, Lithuania and Poland were united under one king and parliament.

Poland prospered under the Jagellon dynasty. When the last of the Jagellon dynasty died in 1572, Poland extended from the Baltic Sea almost to the Black Sea.

Decline of Polish Power. After 1572, the kings were chosen by the nobility, who took over much of the power.

The *szlachta* (gentry) were jealous of each other, so the Polish king usually was chosen from some other nation. Stephen Bathory of Transylvania (Hungary) became king in 1575. Three members of Swedish royalty ruled Poland from 1587 to 1668. During this period, Poland fought wars with the Turks, Swedes, and Russians. It lost most of its Baltic territories to Sweden, and the eastern Ukraine to Russia. General John Sobieski (1624-1696) became King John III in 1674, and defeated the Turks in 1683. See JOHN III SOBIESKI.

Partitioning of Poland. Through Russian pressure, Stanislaw Poniatowski (1732-1798) was elected king in 1764. A strong reform party among the Polish nobles disliked the choice and Russia's growing interference in Poland's domestic affairs. Russia, Prussia, and Austria took advantage of the resulting unrest and partitioned Poland in 1772. Russia took some of the eastern

provinces, Austria took the southern province that became known as Galicia, and Prussia took Polish Pomerania, except for Danzig. Poland lost about one-third of its territory and half its population.

The Polish diet then began a program of internal reforms. The world's first ministry of education was formed in 1773. On May 3, 1791, the diet proclaimed a new constitution. It called for a hereditary limited monarchy, a cabinet of ministers, and social reform, such as limiting serfdom. The constitution alarmed the powers which had partitioned Poland, and set the stage for the second partition in 1793. Russia took most of Lithuania and the Ukraine. Prussia took Danzig and most of the country west of Warsaw.

In 1794 and 1795, Thaddeus Kosciusko (1746-1817) led a patriotic movement that opposed the breaking up of Poland. But his forces were defeated, and the third partition took place in October, 1795. Russia took the rest of Lithuania and the Ukraine, Prussia took central Poland, and Austria took the remainder of the south.

In 1807, Napoleon I united much of the Polish territory of Austria and Prussia, and set up the Grand Duchy of Warsaw. The Congress of Vienna, held in 1814 and 1815 after Napoleon's defeat, gave part of the Grand Duchy to Prussia and Galicia to Austria. The largest part went to Russia, which organized it as a separate Polish constitutional monarchy under the rule of the czar.

The Rise of Liberalism and Nationalism. In 1830, the Poles attempted to overthrow Russian rule. They drove the Russians out of Warsaw, but the Russians recaptured the city in 1831. Poland lost its constitutional rights, then became part of Russia. Another revolution took place in 1863, but it also failed. Russia then set out to make Poland as Russian as possible. Russian was made the official language of Poland.

World War I. Poland became a chief battleground of central Europe in World War I. Poles were drafted to fight in the German, Austrian, and Russian armies. In 1915, the Germans drove the Russians out of most of

Shipbuilding has become a leading industry in Poland since World War II. The shipyards at Danzig (Gdańsk) are among the busiest in Europe. They produce large ocean-going vessels.

Centralna Agencja Fotograficzna

Poland. On Nov. 5, 1916, an "independent" kingdom of Poland was proclaimed under German and Austrian protection. After the Allied victory in 1918, the country made itself an independent republic. Józef Pilsudski (1867-1935) became Poland's first head of state.

The Peace Settlement. The Treaty of Versailles gave Poland free access to the Baltic Sea through what became known as the *Polish Corridor*. This was a strip of land with an area of 6,327 square miles that separated East Prussia from the rest of Germany. The port city of Danzig was made a free state under League of Nations supervision, with special harbor privileges given to Poland. Poland received most of Galicia in the south from Austria, and most of the Poznań and Upper Silesia regions from Germany.

In 1920, Polish and Russian troops clashed over the location of the border between the two countries. The Polish Army advanced as far as Kiev before it was defeated by the Russians. The Curzon Line was then proposed as the boundary between Poland and Russia, but both countries rejected it (see CURZON LINE). The Russian troops advanced into Poland, but, with Allied help, the Poles beat them back near Warsaw. The Treaty of Riga, signed in 1921, returned to Poland almost all its eastern frontier of 1793.

In October, 1920, an unofficial Polish force took possession of the region around the Lithuanian city of Vilnius (Wilno). In 1923, the Allies recognized Poland's claim to the Vilnius district.

Between World Wars I and II. In 1921, Poland adopted a new democratic constitution. Gradually, the country was rebuilt.

About one-third of the population consisted of minorities. Chief among these were Ukrainians, White Russians, Germans, and Lithuanians. They opposed the increased efforts of the Polish government to "Polonize" some of them. Poland also had the highest percentage of Jews of any European country. The dissatisfaction of these minorities contributed to the instability of Poland between World Wars I and II.

There was much instability in the Polish government, because of the more than 30 political parties. In May,

1926, Pilsudski seized power after a two-day military revolt. He made himself practically a dictator.

In 1921, Poland made alliances with France and Romania. Poland signed a nonaggression pact with Russia in 1932. Then in 1934, Poland signed a nonaggression pact with Germany to keep Germany from pressing claims to Polish territory.

A new constitution was adopted in 1935, shortly before Pilsudski's death. It was designed to preserve the dictatorial government. After Pilsudski died, Marshal Edward Smigly-Rydz, Josef Beck, and a group of Pilsudski's colonels retained absolute rule.

In 1938, Germany received part of Czechoslovakia under the Munich Agreement. The following year, Hitler turned against Poland.

The Fourth Partition. After Hitler took the rest of Czechoslovakia, Great Britain realized that Poland would be the next country attacked. On March 31, 1939, Prime Minister Chamberlain declared that if the Polish government resisted any threat to its independence, the British would help. Hitler forced a crisis by demanding Danzig, new German transport rights in the Polish Corridor, and new privileges for the German minority in Poland.

The Poles considered the German demands a threat to their independence. They made a defensive alliance with Great Britain which Germany declared was an "unfriendly act" and a policy of "encirclement." In April, 1939, Hitler ended the German-Polish nonaggression pact made in 1934.

During the summer of 1939, there were many acts of violence by Nazis against Poles in Danzig. The Nazis brought in arms and organized a Danzig "Free Corps." On August 23, Germany and Russia signed a friendship and nonaggression pact and a political agreement about the partition of Poland.

On the morning of Sept. 1, 1939, Germany attacked Poland, without a declaration of war. Great Britain and France declared war on Germany. Russia invaded Poland on September 17. The Poles fought stubbornly, but they were no match for their enemies. On September 28, Germany and Russia signed an agreement dividing Poland. Germany took the western 72,000 square miles, and Russia the eastern 78,000.

During World War II. Germany attacked Russia in June, 1941, and all Poland came under German control. During the occupation, over 3 million Jews and about as many Poles were killed in concentration camps.

Many Poles were active in the war outside Poland. The Polish government-in-exile established itself in London. In July, 1941, this government signed an agreement with Russia, voiding the 1939 Russian-German partitioning of Poland. Thousands of Polish servicemen escaped from Poland and fought against Germany by fighting for the Polish government-in-exile. Many fought on the Italian front, and there was a Polish air force and a Polish navy in Great Britain.

The Russian army invaded German-controlled Poland in 1944. Polish underground forces helped the Reds drive out the Germans. A Russian-dominated government was set up in Lublin in opposition to the Polish government in London. In January, 1945, Russia recognized the Lublin Committee as the provisional government of Poland. In February at Yalta, the United States and Great Britain agreed to recognize a new provisional government formed chiefly by the Lublin Communist group (see YALTA CONFERENCE). Also at Yalta, it was agreed to recognize the Curzon Line as Poland's eastern boundary. Thus nearly half of Poland's prewar territory was transferred to Russia. To compensate Poland for this loss, the country was given most of the Polish land east of the Oder and Neisse rivers, which Germany had held. In effect, the new boundaries shifted the country westward, and gave Poland the rich industrial area that had formerly been German. The new boundary between Poland and Germany is still a problem today. West Germany refuses to recognize the line and wants the territory east of the Oder and Neisse returned. Russia has upheld the boundary. Poland joined the United Nations in 1945.

Communist Rule. The Communist-dominated government crushed all resistance in 1945 and began to nationalize industry, agriculture, and trade. In 1947, a three-year plan started to repair war damage and raise the economy above prewar levels. By 1949, the government claimed national income had risen 25 per cent and production 75 per cent. Poland's six-year plan to develop production of all kinds began in 1950.

A new constitution, similar to that of Russia, was adopted in 1952. It abolished the office of president, and substituted for it a council of state.

In 1953, the council of state ordered Catholic priests and bishops to take a loyalty oath to the state. The government dismissed clergy members accused of government opposition. Stefan Cardinal Wyszyński, leader of Poland's Roman Catholics, was arrested for failure to punish a bishop accused of antigovernment practices.

Polish workers, angered by political terror and low living standards, rioted in 1956 in anti-Russian demonstrations in Poznań, Stettin, and other cities. The Polish Communist Party named Władysław Gomułka as first secretary of the party, despite opposition from Russia. Gomułka removed Konstantin K. Rokossovsky, a Russian marshal who had been made Poland's defense minister by Moscow. Cardinal Wyszyński was reinstated at the head of Poland's Roman Catholic Church. The government approved voluntary religious education in the schools. Gomułka also announced that collective farms were no longer compulsory. Most collective farms were dissolved. Intellectual freedom increased. Schools gained more authority to teach their own program of study. The government also began to allow some foreign books, movies, and music.

After the 1957 elections, the Communists allowed a few independent and Roman Catholic deputies to be elected. The Communists have canceled some of the concessions they made after the 1956 riots. Poland follows Russia's foreign policies, but has some freedom from Russia in its internal affairs. In 1968, students rioted in nine Polish cities demanding greater civil liberties. The Communists blamed Jews and intellectuals for the student unrest. M. KAMIL DZIEWANOWSKI

Related Articles in WORLD BOOK include:

BIOGRAPHIES

Chopin, Frédéric F.	Landowska, Wanda
Conrad, Joseph	Malinowski, Bronislaw
Copernicus, Nicolaus	Paderewski, Ignace J.
Curie (Marie S.)	Pilsudski, Józef
Dubinsky, David	Pulaski, Casimir
Gomułka, Władysław	Rubinstein, Arthur
John III Sobieski	Sienkiewicz, Henryk
Kosciusko, Thaddeus	Wieniawski, Henri

CITIES

Bydgoszcz	Kraków	Poznań	Warsaw
Danzig (Gdańsk)	Łódź	Stettin	Wrocław
Katowice	Lublin		

HISTORY

Curzon Line	Russia	World War II
Polish Corridor	Warsaw Pact	

PHYSICAL FEATURES AND REGIONS

Carpathian Mountains	Masurian Lakes	Silesia
	Oder River	Sudetes Mountains
Galicia	Poznań	Vistula River

PRODUCTS AND INDUSTRY

For Poland's rank among other countries in production, see the following articles:

Agriculture	Horse	Potato
Coal	Lumber	Rye
Flax	Oats	Sugar Beet

OTHER RELATED ARTICLES

Christmas (In Poland)	Ruthenian
Easter (In Poland)	Slav

Outline

I. The Land
    A. Natural Resources   B. Climate

II. The People
    A. Way of Life   E. Mining
    B. Cities   F. Trade
    C. Agriculture   G. Transportation and
    D. Manufacturing   Communication

III. Social and Cultural Achievements

IV. Government

V. History

Questions

What was the Polish Corridor? Its purpose?
Why is the Oder-Neisse boundary important?
What is Poland's most important river?
What is the chief mineral resource of Poland?
Who is considered Poland's greatest composer?
What are some products Poland imports and exports?
To what church do most Polish people belong?
What countries partitioned Poland in the 1700's?

Chicago Daily News

The Polar Bear Looks Meek in a Zoo, but it is one of the fiercest of all bears. Polar bears are very active in their native Arctic home, and have a speed of movement that has astonished those who watch them. They live on walrus, seal, and fish.

POLAR BEAR is a great, flesh-eating bear of the Far North that lives on the ice floes and in the cold waters of the Arctic Ocean. Some polar bears spend part of their time on the arctic shores of Alaska, northern Canada, Greenland, and Siberia. Many, however, live on or near the islands of the Arctic Ocean, and never come within hundreds of miles of the mainland. The favorite hunting ground of this bear is the edge of the pack ice, where icebergs and broken pan ice alternate with areas of open water. Occasionally, polar bears are seen in the Atlantic Ocean as far south as the Gulf of St. Lawrence.

A full-grown polar bear may be as much as nine and a half feet long, and weigh about 1,000 pounds, with an extreme of 1,600 pounds. Its warm, dense coat of fur is white, with a tinge of yellow. Besides keeping the bear warm, this coat makes the bear hard to see against the white background of snow and ice. It can creep unseen over the ice toward the seals which it kills for food. The polar bear has a smaller head, a longer neck, and a more slender body than other bears. This build helps to make it a powerful swimmer with great agility in the water. The soles of its feet have a dense pad of fur, which keeps the bear from slipping on the surface of melting ice.

In winter the she-bear enters a hollow or cave in the icebergs. She gives birth to one or two cubs there.

Scientific Classification. The polar bear belongs to the family *Ursidae*. It is classified as genus *Thalarctos*, species *T. maritimus.*   THEODORE H. EATON, JR.

See also ANIMAL (color picture, Animals of the Polar Regions).

A Huge Mother Polar Bear Stands Guard over her woolly little cub. Polar bear cubs weigh about one pound at birth.

Milwaukee Journal

POLAR EXPLORATION. See Exploration and Discovery (Polar Exploration; table); Antarctica (Exploration); Arctic.

POLAR PROJECTION MAP. See Aviation (color map: Air Age).

POLARIS, a ballistic missile. See Guided Missile (Recent Developments).

POLARIS is a name for the North Star. See North Star.

POLARIZATION. See Polarized Light; Battery.

POLARIZED LIGHT consists of light waves that have a simple, orderly arrangement. The waves of ordinary light are arranged in a complex, disorderly manner. Ordinary light from the sun or a lamp is composed of disorderly waves that vibrate in *all* directions perpendicular to the light beam. But polarized light consists of orderly waves that vibrate in only *one* direction.

Because of its orderly structure, polarized light can be used in ways that would be impossible with ordinary light. For example, the internal physical structure of many transparent materials can be seen with the aid of polarized light. Light polarizers are powerful tools that are used in science, industry, and everyday life.

How Light Is Polarized. To understand polarization, think of a light beam as a train of electromagnetic waves. The electromagnetic forces making up these waves vibrate in a crosswise direction, perpendicular to the path of the beam. A rough example of these waves can be made by attaching a rope to a wall and shaking the other end. A train of waves will move along the

length of the rope. Each part of the rope will vibrate not lengthwise, however, but crosswise. Waves that vibrate in this way are called *transverse waves*. See Waves (Wave Forms).

Polarized light does not vibrate in all directions crosswise to its path. Ordinary light can be polarized by passing it through a special *light polarizing filter*. This filter allows only the waves that vibrate in one crosswise direction to pass through. The structure of the filter prevents the passage of light waves that vibrate in other crosswise directions. In scientific terms, the polarizing filter passes the *components* (parts) of the light waves that vibrate in one *vibration-direction*. The components of waves that vibrate in all other directions are held back. The light that passes through is called *polarized light*.

All the vibrations that pass through a polarizing filter vibrate in one *transverse* (crosswise) direction parallel to the optical grain of the filter. The *optical grain* is the transmission axis of the filter. Polarized light can pass completely through a second polarizing filter whose transmission axis is parallel to that of the first. But if the second polarizer is rotated like a wheel, it will gradually dim the light that comes through it. It will cut off the light entirely when its axis is "crossed" at 90° to the axis of the first filter. This occurs because each polarizing filter absorbs all components of the light that do not vibrate parallel to the filter's axis. As a result, the brightness of the light beam is gradually reduced as the axis

HOW LIGHT IS POLARIZED

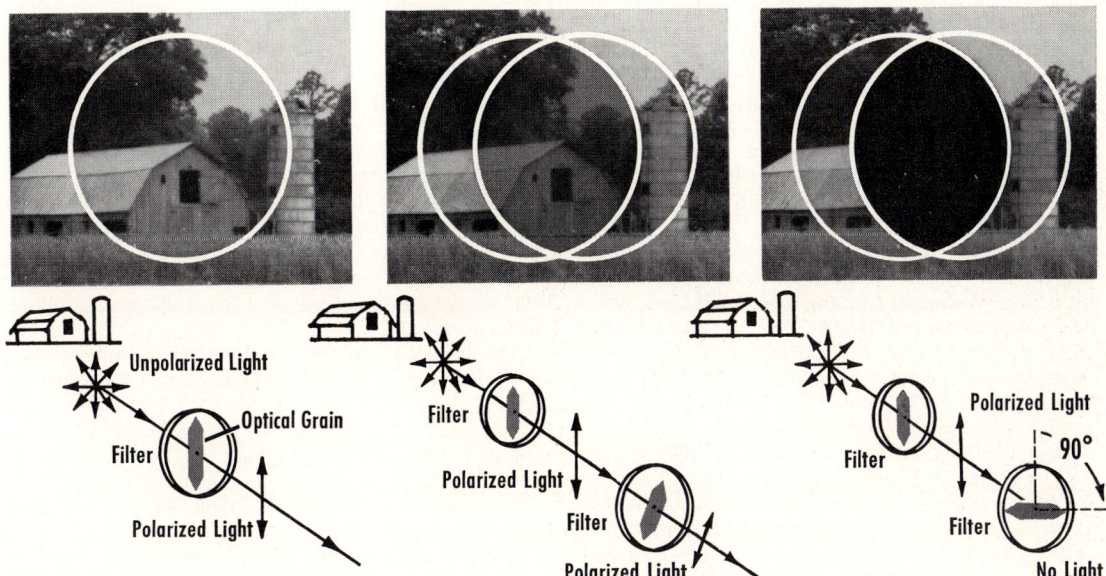

A polarizing filter absorbs some of the light that falls on it and transmits the rest. The transmitted light waves vibrate in a direction parallel to the optical grain of the polarizing filter.

Second filter absorbs some of the light coming from the first filter if the optical grains of the two filters are not aligned. The greater the angle between the optical grains, the more light is absorbed.

Light is completely absorbed when the optical grain of the second filter is set at 90 degrees to the grain of the first. Then, none of the light coming from the first filter can get through the second one.

Without a Polarizing Filter. This photograph looks like a double exposure because the camera sees reflections.

Press Syndicate

With a Polarizing Filter. This photograph is clear because a filter placed over the camera lens absorbs the reflections.

of the second polarizer cuts across the transmission axis of the first.

Many applications of polarized light are based on this phenomenon. For example, much of the light around us is already polarized. Mirrorlike reflections from shiny horizontal surfaces, such as pavement and water, consist largely of light that has been horizontally polarized in the process of reflection. Polarized sunglasses, with their transmission axis set vertically, block the horizontally polarized light making up the bright reflections. Photographers use polarizing filters to cut down glare and reflections from shiny surfaces such as windows and water.

Polarizing Materials. The most widely used light polarizers consist of thin plastic sheets. A typical plastic sheet contains millions of long, slender, carefully aligned chains of iodine molecules. Each of these chains acts like an individual polarizing filter. Sheet polarizers have greatly extended the uses of polarized light because of their low cost and convenient size. Edwin H. Land, inventor of the Polaroid Land camera, invented the first sheet polarizer in 1928, when he was only 19 years old.

Some natural crystals, such as *tourmaline*, can polarize light. Tourmaline transmits the components that lie in one vibration-direction, and holds back others by absorbing them internally. Another natural polarizing crystal is *calcite*, or *Iceland spar*. It divides the light into two polarized beams that are at right angles to each other. *Nicol* prisms are cut from Iceland spar so that one of these beams is eliminated.

Uses of Polarized Light. There are many practical uses of polarized light in addition to sunglasses and photography. Scientists have suggested that polarized glass be used for car headlights and windshields to prevent driving glare from lights of approaching cars.

Scientists can study the structure of many transparent materials with the aid of crossed polarizing filters. Microscopes equipped with polarizers show many colorless crystals and biology specimens in brilliant color. A *polariscope*, an instrument equipped with polarizers, is used to find *strains* (weak spots) in glass

objects such as eyeglasses and laboratory glassware. Chemists can tell the type and amount of sugar in a solution by using a *saccharimeter*, a type of polariscope. Special polarizing filters that produce circularly polarized light are used on radarscopes to trap unwanted reflections. RICHARD T. KRIEBEL

See also HUYGENS, CHRISTIAN; LAND, EDWIN H.

POLAROGRAPHY. See HEYROVSKÝ, JAROSLAV.

POLAROID LAND CAMERA. See CAMERA (picture: Kinds); PHOTOGRAPHY (Photography Today).

POLDER, *POHL der*, is an area of land that was once under water, but is now protected by dikes, dams, and other structures. The term is a Dutch word and refers to land that the Dutch reclaimed from swamps, lakes, and the North Sea. See also NETHERLANDS (introduction).

POLE. The earth is constantly *rotating* (spinning) on an imaginary line called an *axis*. The axis passes through the center of the earth and ends at either *pole*. The north end of the axis is the North Pole, 90 degrees north of the equator. The South Pole is the south end of the axis, 90 degrees south of the equator.

The term *pole* may be used to describe such a point on any kind of sphere that revolves like the earth. For example, the term *celestial pole* refers to a point in the heavens about which the stars seem to revolve. A bright star nearest this point is called the *North Star*, or sometimes *polestar*.

In addition to the north and south geographic poles, the earth has the north and south magnetic poles, which attract the north and south needles of compasses. The north magnetic pole is near Prince of Wales Island in Canada, about 1,000 miles from the north geographic pole. The south magnetic pole is near the edge of Antarctica, about 1,500 miles from the south geographic pole.

In physics, the word *pole* means the point where magnetic lines of force appear to originate. Unlike magnetic poles attract one another, and like magnetic poles repel each other. W. ELMER EKBLAW

See also EARTH (The Earth's Shape and Size); MAGNET AND MAGNETISM; NORTH POLE; NORTH STAR; SOUTH POLE.

POLE VAULT is an event in track and field competition in which an athlete uses a pole to propel his body over a crossbar set at a certain height. The equipment needed for pole vaulting includes the pole, a crossbar, and two upright standards to support the crossbar. The pole can be made of bamboo, steel alloy, aluminum, or fiber glass. It is from 12 to 16 feet in length. The fundamentals of pole vaulting include (1) the grip, (2) the run, (3) the take-off, (4) the swing, (5) the push-off, (6) over the bar, and (7) the landing.

The Grip is important in pole vaulting. The athlete must position his hands properly and place them at the ideal height on the pole. The vaulter stands the pole next to the crossbar to see where the crossbar meets the pole. He grips the pole with his right hand at about this point. He places his left hand 2 to 3 feet below the right hand, and holds the pole parallel to the ground. The thumb of the left hand is toward the body and the thumb of the right hand is away from the body.

The Run down the runway toward the crossbar is made almost at top speed, but the vaulter controls the run carefully. Markers along the runway allow him to gauge his stride and take-off position so that he takes off from the same foot in every vault. The vaulter holds the pole parallel to the ground as he runs, and keeps his eye fixed on the box that is set in the ground beneath the crossbar.

The Take-Off. The vaulter places the end of the pole in the box and slides his left hand up to meet his right hand. As the speed obtained down the runway is transformed into upward motion, the pole pulls the vaulter's hands above his head and is ready to catapult the vaulter up and over the bar.

The Swing and Pull-Up. As the vaulter holds onto the rising pole and swings his body through the air, he pulls his knees up toward his chest and then shoots his feet up toward the bar. As the vaulter continues to pull his feet upward, the right leg crosses over the left leg. The swing and pull-up produce a handstand effect with the vaulter's chest next to the crossbar.

Over the Bar. While the vaulter is in the handstand position, his feet start down on the other side of the crossbar. This jackknife position of the body is essential for maximum height. The vaulter then pushes the pole away from him so it will not hit the crossbar and knock it down. As the vaulter releases the pole, he turns his thumbs inward to help prevent his elbows from hitting the crossbar. The vaulter rolls as he lands, to prevent injury.   BOB MATHIAS

See also TRACK AND FIELD (table, World Track and Field Records; Famous Track and Field Champions [Richards, "Bob," Robert; Uelses, John]; picture); WARMERDAM, CORNELIUS.

POLECAT is an animal that belongs to the weasel family. It is closely related to the skunk of North America. It once lived in many places throughout Europe, including the British Isles. Now it is being killed off because it eats some domestic fowl and game birds. Its principal food is rabbit. It also eats rats, mice, eels, fish, frogs, toads, snakes, eggs, and wild birds. The polecat lives in a hole in the ground or in a tree.

The polecat hunts at night, and usually stores surplus food in a special room in the burrow. The four or five young are born in April or May, 40 days after mating. They are light-colored, but darken like the parents in

Neil Leifer, courtesy *The Saturday Evening Post*, © 1963, Curtis Publishing Co.

A Pole Vaulter uses a flexible fiber glass pole to raise himself over a high crossbar balanced on two uprights. This picture series shows how the pole bends under the vaulter's weight. As the pole unbends, the spring helps to propel the vaulter over the crossbar. A vault is successful if the vaulter soars over the crossbar without knocking it off the uprights.

about eight months. Like the skunk, the polecat secretes, and can discharge at will, a liquid of a most disagreeable odor. The common male polecat is about 22 inches long, with a tail 8 inches in length. The female is about 4 inches shorter. Its long, loose, nearly black fur with a purplish gloss is marketed under the name of *fitch*. The skunk is sometimes incorrectly called polecat.

Scientific Classification. The polecat belongs to the family *Mustelidae*. It is classified as genus *Mustela*, species *M. putorius*.   E. LENDELL COCKRUM

See also SKUNK.

POLESTAR. See NORTH STAR; STAR (color picture, Why the North Star Does Not Rise or Set).

POLICE

Modern Communications are vital to the smooth and efficient coordination of all police operations.

Chicago Police Dept.

Sympathy and Tact are as important to police work as guns and handcuffs. This policewoman is calming a lost child.

Chicago Police Dept.

Los Angeles Police Dept.

POLICE are community helpers who keep us safe on the streets and in our homes. A policeman is trained to care for lost children and to give first aid. He knows how to quiet crowds, control traffic, and comfort accident victims. He is an expert at handling weapons, and knows how to capture dangerous criminals. In all his work, the policeman stands ready to give his life if necessary to protect and help the community.

Every country in the world has a police system. Each level of government, from village to national, has a police force. These forces work together to enforce laws, prevent crime, and protect lives and property.

What a Policeman Does

The patrolman who guards the streets and the neigh-

borhood policeman who directs traffic both belong to the *municipal* (local) police force. The term *police department* usually refers to such a force. A police department may be supported by a village, town, city, or special district. All police departments have three main duties: (1) general policing, carried out by uniformed patrolmen; (2) detective work; and (3) traffic control.

A local police department usually has authority only within the limits of its community. A policeman may arrest anyone he sees committing a crime. If he does not see the person committing the crime, but has reason to suspect him, he must get a court order called a *warrant* before he can make the arrest. A prisoner must be released if no charges are brought against him within a certain period after his arrest. A police officer

Los Angeles Police Dept.

Being Ready for Instant Action is essential for all policemen, including motorcycle officers who patrol busy highways.

Police Dept., City of New York

Emergency Rescue Operations are an everyday activity for policemen. Helicopters give police speed and maneuverability.

Chicago Police Dept.

Policemen Work Wherever They Are Needed on land, on sea, and in the air. Here, divers are searching for evidence.

Los Angeles Police Dept.

Scientific Knowledge gives policemen modern tools to fight crime. This inspector is checking out a dangerous explosive.

Chicago Police Dept.

Fighting Crime Requires Special Aids, including dogs that are specially trained to track down and help capture criminals.

must have a special search warrant before he can search a citizen's home. See ARREST; WARRANT.

The Patrol Division is the largest group in most police departments. Patrolmen may travel over their *beats* (routes) on foot, in squad cars, or on motorcycles. They are prepared to handle accidents, crimes, or disturbances of any sort. Police cars are equipped with two-way radios, so that policemen can be sent anywhere at a moment's notice in an emergency. Foot patrolmen get in touch with headquarters through *call boxes* (special police telephones) along their beats. In some cities, they carry two-way pocket radios.

Patrolmen are often organized into squads that are headed by sergeants. A lieutenant may have charge of several squads.

The Detective Division in some cities is divided into various bureaus or squads that investigate special kinds of crime. The *homicide squad* investigates murder and suicide. The *narcotics squad* fights the illegal use of drugs. The *vice squad* tries to stop gambling and other kinds of vice. Often, when detectives investigate crimes, they wear ordinary street clothes so they will not be recognized as policemen. That is why detectives are called *plain-clothes men*. Fingerprint experts, firearms identification authorities, laboratory researchers, photographers, and other specialists help detectives.

Most large police departments also have a *juvenile*, or *youth*, *division*. In smaller departments, one or two officers in the detective division are often assigned to work with youngsters.

POLICE IN MANY LANDS

Policemen Have the Same Duties in many countries. They direct traffic, answer questions, give tickets, stand guard, and watch for danger.

France

Canada

Photo Researchers, Susan McCartney; Malak, Miller Services Ltd.; Central Office of Information

Great Britain

The Traffic Division has special duties that include directing traffic; protecting children on their way to and from school; enforcing parking, speed, and other traffic safety laws; and inspecting vehicles to see that they meet various safety and license requirements. Policemen on horseback and on motorcycles help control crowds on special occasions. Policemen use helicopters and airplanes to watch traffic. In many cities, river and harbor police use speedboats to patrol waterways.

Kinds of Police

There are local, district, county, state and provincial, and federal police agencies in the United States and Canada. Each agency is responsible only to the officials of its division of the government. No central agency controls the police system. But all police agencies cooperate, and use nationwide radio and teletype facilities to work with each other. They also exchange information on criminals and report crime statistics.

In addition to public police agencies supported by taxes, private police and private detective agencies also do special police work in most cities. For example, privately hired industrial policemen guard factories and railroads. Other private police forces may protect hotels, stores, office buildings, and private estates.

Local Police forces vary in size, depending on the type and size of the community they serve, and the number of people in it. A police department may consist of one town marshal, or it may have more than 24,000 men and women, as in New York City. An average police force has about 2 policemen for every 1,000 persons in the community. Large cities are usually divided into *precincts* (districts), each with its own police station. Police in smaller cities or towns operate from a single station called *police headquarters*.

Most police departments are organized along the same general lines. The head of the department may be known as the *chief, commissioner, director, superintendent,* or *captain commanding*. Commissioned officers ranking below him are, in order of importance, the *deputy, inspector, captain, lieutenant,* and *sergeant*. Non-ranking officers are called *patrolmen, officers,* or *privates*.

County Police powers extend throughout the county, except in incorporated towns and cities that have their own police forces (see COUNTY). The *sheriff* is usually the chief law-enforcement officer in the county. He has charge of the county jail and its prisoners. A sheriff may have one deputy or hundreds. In southern and western areas of the United States, the sheriff's office conducts full-scale police operations. Most northeastern states limit the sheriff's duties to civil matters (see CIVIL LAW). Some counties have regular police forces headed by a chief of police, rather than a sheriff.

State Police. All states have either state police or state highway patrol forces. *State police* have full police powers throughout the state. *State highway patrols* may have full police powers, or they may have authority to enforce only traffic laws. A commissioner or superintendent appointed by the governor heads the state law-enforcement agency. State police are often called *troopers,* because, in early days, they were organized along military lines. Many rode horses.

Federal Police agencies track down violators of various federal laws. They usually work closely with local, county, and state police.

In the United States, nine major federal law-enforcement agencies have full-scale police powers. They are the Federal Bureau of Investigation (FBI), the Border Patrol, and the Bureau of Narcotics and Dangerous Drugs in the Department of Justice; the Bureau of the Chief Postal Inspector in the Post Office Department; and the United States Secret Service, the Internal Revenue Service, the Alcohol Tax Unit, the Bureau of Customs, and the United States Coast Guard.

Federal laws define the duties of each agency to prevent overlapping in authority or operations. All have power to enforce only national laws. A federal officer may make arrests within a state only for counterfeiting, kidnaping, evasion of federal taxes, or other violations of federal law.

In addition to the major federal agencies, several departments or bureaus have limited powers to enforce laws. They include the Department of State (passport and extradition laws), the National Park Service (forest

548

San Marino   India

Almasy, Three Lions; United Press Int.
Austria

preservation), the Public Health Service (laws concerning epidemic diseases), and the Department of Agriculture (laws concerning animal and plant quarantine).

In Canada, the Royal Canadian Mounted Police enforces federal laws. This force, organized in 1873, is one of the most famous in the world. It is the only police force in unsettled areas and in the Northwest and Yukon territories. Besides acting as federal police, the "mounties" may also serve as local or provincial police. Any community or province can hire their services by paying the government a certain sum for each trooper stationed in the area. Ontario and Quebec are the only provinces that have provincial police forces. The mounties have been contracted for the police work in all the other provinces. Today, most mounties use motor vehicles instead of horses. See ROYAL CANADIAN MOUNTED POLICE.

Police of Other Lands

In most European countries, the national governments have more control over the police forces than they have in the United States or Canada.

In France, *la Sûreté nationale* is the national law-enforcement agency. District prefects of police administer the system in various regions. Individual policemen are called *agents*. The *gendarmerie* (military police) have charge of police affairs in small cities and rural areas. A military policeman is called a *gendarme*. Italian police work is carried out by *la pubblica sicurezza*, the plain-clothes police, and by the *carabinieri* (uniformed military police). *La police judiciare* is the national police organization of Belgium.

Great Britain has about 150 local police forces, each responsible to a local government authority. The national government provides financial aid to local forces. The British Home Office maintains a staff of Inspectors of Constabulary who check on the local agencies. The government stops its subsidy for any agency that receives a bad report. The head of a British police department is called the *chief constable*. In difficult investigations, provincial police may request help from the London Metropolitan Police, which has headquarters in New Scotland Yard. *Scotland Yard* is a name used for the Criminal Investigation Department (C.I.D.) of the Metropolitan police. See SCOTLAND YARD.

Some countries maintain national secret-police systems with networks of agents and counterspies who watch for signs of disloyalty. The Russian czars had a secret-police force called the Cheka. Under the communists, this force was called OGPU, NKVD, and MVD. The State Security Committee (KGB) is the secret police today. Before and during World War II, the Nazis used the dreaded Gestapo. See GESTAPO; MVD.

Police organizations in many countries exchange information and cooperate in locating criminals through *Interpol*, the International Criminal Police Organization. This agency has its headquarters in Paris.

History

In England. The Anglo-Saxons of the A.D. 800's organized the people for military purposes into tens, tithings, and hundreds. In each community, 10 families made up a *tithing*, and chose a *tithing man* as their representative. Ten tithings made up a *hundred*, and elected a *reeve* as their spokesman and leader. Several hundreds made up a *shire* (county). The word *sheriff* is a shortened form of *shire reeve*. When the Normans conquered England in 1066, they used this system for public protection and safety. Men over 16 had to stand *watch and ward* duty in their community. On such duty, the men questioned travelers after dark, held all suspicious persons, and watched for any disturbances. All able-bodied men would join in a *hue and cry* (a chase to capture a suspect).

As cities grew, the police system became larger and more organized. By 1800, London had its own night watch, and also many special police to guard docks, markets, and other places. Special police, called "Bow Street runners," served notices and warrants for city courts. In 1829, Sir Robert Peel organized the Metropolitan Police of London, a body of paid and trained policemen for day and night duty. The public called these policemen "bobbies" or "peelers," after Sir Robert, and the name bobbies is still used today.

549

POLICE

In the United States. The English colonists brought the watch and ward system to America. The men who stood watch served without pay, and wealthy citizens often hired others to serve for them.

In 1838, Boston set up a paid police force of six men to stand watch during the day. In 1844, the New York legislature passed a law establishing an 800-man police force in New York City for day and night duty. By 1870, cities throughout the United States had police departments organized like that of New York City. The Boston police strike of 1919 gained nationwide attention. Members of the Policeman's Union went on strike when the police commissioner refused to allow them to join national labor unions. For almost a day, Boston had no police protection. Calvin Coolidge, then governor of Massachusetts, called out the state guard and ended the strike.

Texas had the first state police system in the United States. The Texas Rangers, organized in 1835, at first served as a border patrol, but later took over general police work (see TEXAS RANGERS). Massachusetts appointed a number of state constables in 1865, and Connecticut established a similar force in 1903.

In the late 1800's, policemen were called constables. The name *cop*, a slang word for policeman, may have come from the initials *C.O.P.*, which stood for *constable on patrol*. But some authorities say that *cop* is a shortened form of *copper*, a name that referred to the star-shaped copper badges policemen wore.

The growth of industries, the increasing population, and the widespread use of the automobile brought many changes in police work. The police adopted new methods, including mobile patrols, air patrols, radio communications, training programs, and the use of laboratory techniques in crime investigations.

Careers in Police Work

Improvement in its efficiency and scope has made police work attractive to many young people. Applicants must pass civil-service tests to join most police forces. Once accepted, a policeman may be dismissed only after a proper hearing. Retirement and pension systems are offered to policemen. Disadvantages of a police career include long hours, relatively low pay, and sometimes great danger. But police officers can find satisfaction in devoting themselves to public service.

Qualifications for police work vary, but all departments expect members to have a good character and reputation. A high-school diploma is usually a requirement. Most federal agencies and many local departments require some college training. Police standards for physical fitness, height, and weight resemble those of the armed forces. Age limits are usually between 21 and 32. Many colleges and universities offer law enforcement and criminology courses. Some have special training schools for police. Several cities offer police cadet training to qualified high-school graduates.

Information about a police career can be obtained from the chief of the local or state law enforcement agency. Information about careers with a federal agency can be obtained from the agency's headquarters in Washington, D.C.   Critically reviewed by the INTERNATIONAL ASSOCIATION OF CHIEFS OF POLICE

Related Articles in WORLD BOOK include:

BIOGRAPHIES

Beria, Lavrenti P.
Burns, William J.
Garrett, Patrick F.
Hoover, J. Edgar
Peel, Sir Robert
Pinkerton, Allan
Vollmer, August

KINDS OF POLICE

Border Patrol, United States
Constable
Federal Bureau of Investigation
Gendarme
Marshal
Royal Canadian Mounted Police
Scotland Yard
Secret Police
Secret Service, United States
Sheriff
Texas Rangers

PICTURES OF POLICEMEN

The following articles have pictures of policemen:
Australia
Bolivia
Canada
Fiji Islands
Hungary

OTHER RELATED ARTICLES

Ballistics
Court
Crime
Criminology
Detective Agency
Fingerprinting
Footprinting
Helicopter (In Public Service)
Interpol
Justice of the Peace
Law Enforcement
Lie Detector
Parking Meter
Search Warrant
Traffic
Western Frontier Life (Law Enforcement)
Wiretapping

Outline

I. **What a Policeman Does**
  A. The Patrol Division
  B. The Detective Division
  C. The Traffic Division

II. **Kinds of Police**
  A. Local Police
  B. County Police
  C. State Police
  D. Federal Police

III. **Police of Other Lands**
IV. **History**
V. **Careers in Police Work**

Questions

Why are policemen called "cops"? Why are British policemen often called "bobbies"?

What public services do the police perform?

What is the relationship between federal, state, and local police forces in the United States?

What is the work of the patrol division of a police force? The homicide squad? The narcotics squad?

What was the first state to have a police force?

How was the Anglo-Saxon police system organized?

How does the Royal Canadian Mounted Police serve individual communities in Canada?

What are the duties of a sheriff?

May a policeman arrest anyone he wants to? When may he search a private house?

POLICE DOG is the common but incorrect name for the German shepherd dog. This name is not correct because many other breeds of dogs, such as the Airedale terrier and Doberman pinscher, are trained to help the police. Such dogs receive special training in tracking down criminals, in guard duty, and in other types of work. See also GERMAN SHEPHERD DOG.   OLGA DAKAN

POLICE STATE is a state in which the authority of the police dominates the people. The methods of a police state include arbitrary imprisonment and execution. A police state is the opposite of constitutional government, under which people are protected from abusive acts by the government. In ancient times, Sparta had the most developed form of police state. During the 1900's, fascist and communist countries have been dependent upon the police state to maintain their power. See also SECRET POLICE.   WILLIAM EBENSTEIN

POLICY. See INSURANCE (How Insurance Works).

POLIOMYELITIS, *POH li oh MY uh LY tis,* or *polio,* is an inflammation of the brain and spinal cord. The disease is sometimes called *infantile paralysis* because scientists once thought that only children got it, and that it always caused paralysis. Doctors now know that poliomyelitis may affect persons of any age. It does not always leave the victim paralyzed. The name poliomyelitis comes from two Greek words—*polios,* meaning *gray,* and *myelos,* meaning *marrow.* The disease is caused by tiny virus particles that attack the gray matter of the brain and spinal cord.

Although other communicable diseases strike more persons each year, few have such drastic and lasting effects as poliomyelitis. No part of the world is free from it, and it may occur as an epidemic or in scattered cases.

Scientists have fought a long battle against polio. The disease was known in ancient times, but it was not until 1955 that doctors found a way to control it. In that year, a vaccine developed by Jonas E. Salk of the University of Pittsburgh was declared safe and effective. One of the largest medical field trials in American history was carried on to prove the usefulness of the vaccine. About 1,830,000 school children took part in the tests.

Later, an *oral vaccine* (one that can be taken by mouth) was developed by Albert Sabin of the University of Cincinnati. Two strains of the virus in the vaccine were approved for use in the United States in 1961. Researchers still seek ways to fight poliomyelitis after the virus attacks the nerves.

Cause of Poliomyelitis. The viruses that cause polio are small even when compared with other known viruses. If our red blood cells were 2 feet in diameter, a polio virus would be only about the size of a pinhead. In comparison, a smallpox virus would be about as big as a dime.

Polio viruses can grow only in living cells. They get into the body through the nose and mouth, and are carried to the intestines. Then they travel along the nerve fibers or are carried by the blood stream to the central nervous system. There, they enter a nerve cell and make it work for them rather than for the body. The viruses multiply so rapidly that they damage or kill the cell. Paralysis results when many cells are destroyed. Accurate records of paralysis have been kept only since 1954. They show that paralysis develops in from 47 to 75 per cent of the cases. This paralysis may be in the leg, arm, and trunk muscles.

Scientists usually call the three kinds of polio viruses types I, II, and III. Because each type can cause the disease, it might be possible to have polio more than once. But experts consider this possibility remote. Records show that only a few persons have had polio twice. Both Salk and Sabin vaccines protect against all three types.

How Polio Starts. Scientists do not know exactly how polio spreads or why epidemics occur. Most authorities believe that the virus spreads from the nose, throat, and intestines of infected persons. The polio virus does not always cause disease. The virus has been found in the bodies of apparently healthy persons, especially during epidemics.

American doctors reported 57,879 cases of polio in 1952, the highest number ever recorded. Since polio

The National Foundation

Polio Patients with severe muscle damage learn to walk again by wearing specially designed braces and using crutches.

vaccine came into widespread use in 1955, the number of cases has declined.

Kinds of Poliomyelitis. Infection by a polio virus does not always result in severe illness. Some persons show symptoms of infection, such as fever, headache, sore throat, and vomiting. These symptoms may last for only about 24 hours and then disappear. The symptoms are common in many kinds of ailments, and the doctor may not be able to diagnose the illness definitely as polio. Public health officers have estimated that there may be about 100 cases of this mild form for every recognized case of polio. The vague illness occurs most often during polio epidemics and is more common in children than in adults.

Severe polio attacks start with the same symptoms as the mild attacks. But the symptoms do not disappear. Stiffness of the neck and back develops. The muscles may become weak, and movement is difficult. Pain may occur in the back and legs, especially when these parts are stretched or straightened. The muscles may be tender to touch or pressure. If paralysis develops the person may not be able to stand or walk.

Most persons who have polio do not become permanently paralyzed. But paralysis can occur in many degrees and combinations. Doctors have special names for certain kinds of paralysis.

Spinal Paralytic Poliomyelitis is probably the most common form. It occurs when the viruses attack the nerve cells that control the muscles of the legs, arms, trunk, diaphragm, abdomen, and pelvis.

Bulbar Paralysis is the most serious form of polio. It results from damage to the nerve cells of the brain stem. Certain of these nerves control the muscles for swallowing and for moving the eyes, tongue, face, and neck. The nerves that control breathing and the circulation of body fluids may also be affected.

Treatment. No drug has yet been found that can kill the polio virus or control its spread in the body. But the

551

POLIOMYELITIS

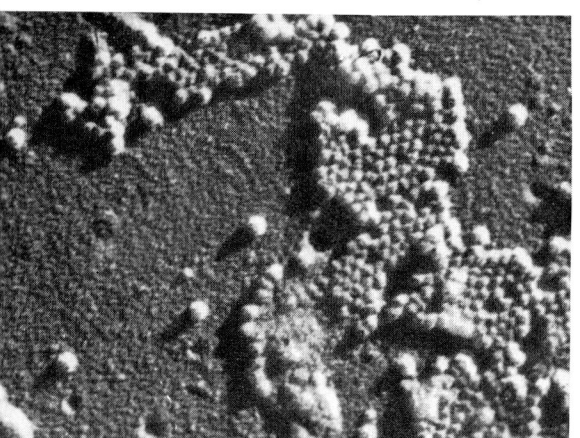

The Isolation of Polio Virus in its pure form came in the late 1940's. This virus is magnified 77,000 times.

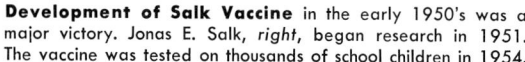

Development of Salk Vaccine in the early 1950's was a major victory. Jonas E. Salk, *right*, began research in 1951. The vaccine was tested on thousands of school children in 1954.

Wide World

degree of recovery often depends upon immediate medical attention and good nursing care.

Complete rest in bed is perhaps the most important treatment. Doctors believe that fatigue may make the disease more severe. They use simple treatments, such as hot, moist bandages, to relieve pain. Soon after the fever subsides, nurses and physical therapists may gently move the patient's limbs to prevent deformities and painful tightening of the muscles. Later, more intensive exercises help strengthen and retrain the muscles. Sometimes patients exercise in pools, because the warmth and buoyancy of the water helps them.

When breathing muscles are paralyzed, doctors may use mechanical devices such as an *iron lung* (respirator) to help the patient breathe. Most patients need these machines only temporarily. Studies show that about two thirds of these patients recover their natural breathing. See IRON LUNG.

Doctors prescribe treatments that help the patient regain as much use of his body as possible. Even those who have been extensively paralyzed can often develop enough movement to carry on many activities. Less severely paralyzed persons usually resume most of their previous activities. But some may need splints, braces, or crutches.

Immunity. Doctors believe that many persons may have a natural immunity against the disease. The body develops polio *antibodies* (substances that fight disease). Antibodies form when a person has had polio or has come in contact with the virus. A newborn baby may get antibodies from its mother, but these last only about six months. Then the child must develop its own. Mild attacks also help develop immunity.

Prevention. The Salk and Sabin vaccines help to prevent polio. These vaccines contain polio viruses

that have been killed or those that have been stripped of their ability to paralyze. They challenge the body to make antibodies. The vaccines do not cure polio. Doctors urge their patients to have polio vaccinations early. The vaccinations usually are given in four doses spread over a period of time. A person must have all four for full protection.

Other precautions also are helpful, particularly when there are polio cases in the community. It is best not to become chilled or overtired. Rest gives the body a chance to fight off the disease and helps check the spread of the virus in the body. If symptoms of the disease should develop, a person should call a doctor promptly and go to bed at once.

History. Scientists believe that people have suffered from poliomyelitis since ancient times. An Egyptian carving of about 1400 B.C. shows a young man with a withered leg that may have resulted from polio. But it was not until 1840 that Jacob Heine, a German bone doctor, gave the first complete medical description of poliomyelitis. In 1902, Karl Landsteiner, an Austrian immunologist, proved that a virus caused the disease.

Franklin D. Roosevelt, himself partially paralyzed by polio, founded the Georgia Warm Springs Foundation in 1927. It was the first institution devoted exclusively to caring for polio patients. His efforts also led to the establishment of the National Foundation for Infantile Paralysis (now called the National Foundation) in 1938. This organization provided the financing for the research that led to development of the Salk and Sabin vaccines.

In the 1930's, Sister Elizabeth Kenny, an Australian nurse, developed a method for treating polio victims. She used hot woolen packs to relieve the muscle spasms and pain.

In 1949, three Harvard University bacteriologists, John F. Enders, Frederick C. Robbins, and Thomas H. Weller, developed and applied a practical way to grow polio viruses outside the body. Their work made it possible to produce the large quantities of viruses needed to make vaccines. Four years later, Salk developed the first successful polio vaccine. In 1955, Sabin began testing a polio vaccine that could be taken by mouth. Two of the virus strains in the vaccine were approved for use in 1961.

In the United States, most cases of poliomyelitis occur in children between 4 and 15 years of age. But recent statistics show that polio also affects many young adults.   WILLIAM A. SPENCER

Related Articles in WORLD BOOK include:

Disease (table)	Sabin, Albert B.
Enders, John F.	Salk, Jonas E.
Kenny, Elizabeth	Vaccination
National Foundation	Virus
Physical Therapy	Warm Springs Foundation,
Robbins, Frederick C.	Georgia
Roosevelt, Franklin D.	Weller, Thomas H.
(The Warm Springs	
Foundation)	

POLISH is a preparation which may be used on wood, metal, and other surfaces to produce a glossy finish. Most polishes are made of waxes mixed into liquid or salve. After the polish is spread over a surface, everything evaporates but the wax. It forms a protective coating. Some polishes for metals remove tarnish. They act as cleaners as well as polishers. Some shoe polishes, such as shoe blacking, contain a dye that restores color and provides a coating.   GEORGE L. BUSH

See also WAX.

POLISH CORRIDOR is a historic strip of land that was once the ancient Polish province of Pomorze. Poland lost the province to Prussia in 1772. When Prussia became a German state in 1871, the area fell into German control.

After World War I, the Versailles Treaty established the corridor of land to give Poland free access to the Baltic Sea. The corridor separated East Prussia and the port city of Danzig from the rest of Germany. In 1939, Germany regained control of the area when Nazi troops invaded Poland. After World War II, the corridor was returned to Poland.   WILLIAM A. JENKS

See also DANZIG; POLAND (History).

The Polish Corridor Before World War II Is in Black.

POLISH NATIONAL CATHOLIC CHURCH OF AMERICA is a religious group which resulted from friction between Polish immigrants in the United States and the Roman Catholic Church. A congregation in Scranton, Pa., under the leadership of a Catholic priest, Francis Hodur, split from the Roman Catholic Church and formed the Polish National Catholic Church in 1897. Other congregations soon followed. In the 1920's, the group founded a branch in Poland. For membership in the United States, see RELIGION (table). LEON GROCHOWSKI

POLISH SUCCESSION WAR. See SUCCESSION WARS.

POLISHING. See GRINDING AND POLISHING.

POLISTES. See WASP.

POLITBURO, *poh LIT byoo roh,* is the political bureau of the Central Committee that controls the Communist Party in Russia. The Central Committee also had an organizational bureau, the *Orgburo*. These two bureaus were set up in 1919. They were merged in 1952 to form the *Presidium* of the Central Committee. In 1966, the Presidium was renamed the Politburo.

In the early days of the Politburo, members were outstanding Bolshevik leaders. Lenin dominated the group until his death. Stalin gained control of the Politburo, and gradually removed his political and party adversaries from it. He replaced them with hand-picked associates. After Stalin's death, Nikita Khrushchev handled the Presidium in the same way. Now, members of the Politburo are men who have worked their way up in the party hierarchy, rather than starting as professional revolutionaries as earlier members did. The first Politburo had five members. The Politburo now has 11 full members and 9 alternates.

The Politburo keeps no public minutes and makes no reports. But all important decisions need its approval. It is the only body in Russia where government, party, army, and police direction coincide. WILLIAM B. BALLIS

POLITENESS. See ETIQUETTE.

POLITI, LEO (1908-   ), is an American artist and author-illustrator of books for children. In 1950, he received the Caldecott medal for his book, *Song of the Swallows.* He won the Regina medal in 1966. Politi was born in Fresno, Calif., of Italian parents. He grew up in Italy. After his graduation from art school, Politi returned to California. There, he became interested in drawing and writing about Mexican children. He wrote and illustrated *Pedro, the Angel of Olvera Street* (1946), *A Boat for Peppe* (1950), *Little Leo* (1951), *Rosa* (1963), and *Piccolo's Prank* (1965). RUTH HILL VIGUERS

See also LITERATURE FOR CHILDREN (picture: Juan Greets the Swallows).

POLITICAL CONVENTION is the means by which political parties in the United States select their nominees for President and Vice-President. Political conventions formerly were widely used to choose party nominees for congressional and state offices. But now states select most party nominees by using the direct primary. See PRIMARY ELECTION.

National political conventions are held every four years, preceding the November presidential elections. By television and radio, people throughout the United States watch and listen to the proceedings of the Democratic and Republican conventions. The national convention gives all citizens an opportunity to observe one

United Press Int.

Demonstrations at a Political Convention burst out frequently. Political parties nominate their candidates for President and Vice-President at conventions. The delegates wave state banners, cheer, sing, march about the hall, then assemble before the speaker's platform, *left,* in support of their candidate. They seek to demonstrate that their candidate has the strongest backing.

of the processes of representative government. And when two strong candidates seek nomination, a national convention is more exciting than a World Series.

How Delegates Are Chosen. Each presidential election year, the national party committees select the time and place of the conventions and notify their state and territorial committees of the number of convention votes allotted to each. The Republican and Democratic conventions have about 1,350 delegates each.

Each party has its own method of deciding how many votes each state shall have in the convention. There are usually more delegates than votes, and therefore some of the delegates can cast only a fraction of a vote.

Sometimes states are *overrepresented* in the convention. For example, in a Republican convention, a Southern state having few Republicans may be given as many convention votes as a heavily Republican Northern state. Various reforms have been undertaken from time to time to bring about fairer representation in the conventions.

In 19 states, delegates may be elected directly by voters in primary elections. In Alabama, Arkansas, and Rhode Island, primaries are optional. In New York, only district delegates are picked by primary election. In the rest, delegates are chosen by district or state conventions. All methods must conform to state law.

Sixteen states have *presidential preference primary* laws, by which the voters of each major party indicate their choice for the presidential nomination. They usually mark this choice on the same ballot on which they elect delegates to the national convention. On the whole, however, convention delegates are not required to abide by the choice which voters have indicated in the primary.

Convention delegates are chosen not only from the states and Washington, D.C., but also from various possessions such as the Virgin Islands, even though the citizens of these governmental units cannot vote in presidential elections.

For each delegate an alternate is chosen, ready to take the place of a delegate who may be called away or struck down by accident or illness.

Among the convention delegates are large numbers of United States Senators, Representatives, former ambassadors, governors, and local officeholders or party leaders. Federal employees once were permitted to take part in the conventions as delegates or in other ways, but the Hatch Acts now forbid this. See HATCH POLITICAL ACTIVITY ACTS.

Preconvention Campaigns. The instructions or pledges of the various delegates may indicate the relative strength of prospective candidates. It is becoming increasingly the custom for avowed candidates to tour the nation months in advance of nominating conventions in efforts to win the support of the electorate and of the party's local, district, and state organizations. Days in advance of the actual opening of the convention, backers of the various candidates, with other party leaders, arrive in the convention city. Each group talks with other factions in efforts to win increased support for its candidate. These efforts continue, on and off the convention floor, up to and during the actual balloting.

The Convention Opens. The party's permanent national committee has previously chosen a temporary chairman, who opens the convention with a *keynote speech*. The purpose of this speech is to raise the enthusiasm of the delegates to a high pitch, and to call for party harmony. After this speech, the convention committees are chosen.

Convention Machinery. Four convention committees are chosen, with each state and territorial delegation entitled to one member on each. They are the committees on permanent organization; credentials; rules and order of business; and platform and resolutions.

The *committee on permanent organization* nominates the permanent chairman of the convention, who customarily has been selected by party leaders before the convention. It also nominates the other permanent officers of the convention, and the delegates usually accept its recommendations. The *committee on rules and procedure* sets up the machinery under which the convention will operate, and usually recommends that the convention follow the rules of the U.S. House of Representatives. It may also set up rules for the makeup and powers of future national committees, and for methods of selecting future delegates. The *credentials committee* decides which one of two or more groups of delegates from a state is entitled to vote, in case there is a dispute. The *platform and resolutions committee* draws up a statement of principles and policies which the party is pledged to advocate and promote—the *platform* on which the party and its candidates will stand.

Convention Procedure. The chairman of the national committee calls the convention to order. Throughout the convention, party leaders deliver rousing speeches. Most of these speeches are designed to help one or another candidate win the nomination.

The climax of the convention is the nomination of a candidate for President. It begins when the secretary of the convention calls the roll of the states alphabetically. Each state has the right to propose a candidate. The proposal is usually made with a long and elaborate speech, followed by several shorter seconding speeches. In practice, however, most states *pass* (decline to propose a candidate) until the states having the several leading contenders rise to put their favorite sons before the convention.

As each presidential contender is placed in nomination, his supporters rise, wave banners, parade around the hall, and cheer and sing while the band plays. Each group strives for the longest and loudest demonstration to show that its man has strong backing.

Balloting then begins, again by roll call of states. The process is repeated until one candidate receives a majority of votes. Frequently, as when a President in office is being renominated by his party, the nomination is assured on the first ballot. But the balloting also can stretch out into many roll calls, and may require two or three days to complete. The same process of balloting is used to nominate for Vice-President, but this contest is rarely long or bitter.

When the candidates have been chosen, the presidential and vice-presidential nominees deliver acceptance speeches—sometimes a weary hour or two before sunrise. Then the delegates go back to their home states to begin the campaign.

Nominations in Early Days. In the early years of the Republic, candidates were chosen by the parties' members in Congress. This was called the *caucus* method, and continued until 1824, when it began to fall into disfavor. From then until 1840, nominations were made more or less informally by state legislatures and mass meetings. Out of that developed the idea of regular party conventions of delegates from the whole nation.

The first nominating convention believed to be really national in scope was held by the Anti-Masonic party in Baltimore in 1831. The Democrats date as their first national convention the parley in Baltimore in 1832 that nominated Andrew Jackson for his second term.

A Whig convention "of young men" in 1832 adopted ten resolutions, and these were considered to be the first national party platform. The Republican party, organized in 1854-1856, is often described as a successor to the Federalist and the Whig parties.

The early method of having Congressmen nominate presidential candidates had to be discarded because, as the historian Viscount James Bryce noted, the Congressmen "had not been chosen for any such purpose, and the President was not constitutionally responsible to them, but rather set up to check them . . . There was therefore need for a method of selecting the candidate which the whole of a party would recognize as fair and entitled to respect . . . The elaborate nominating scheme of primaries and conventions which was being constructed for the purpose of city, state, and congressional elections was applied to the election of the President, and the national convention was the result."

National Conventions Today. Both major political parties often meet in the same convention city, and in the same hall, but a few weeks apart. This custom results in some economies in the tremendous expense of holding the conventions, and simplifies the process of seeking gifts toward convention expenses from the businesses of the host city. Cities compete for the honor of playing host to national conventions because of the business and publicity that such a meeting brings. The city selected is usually one that has good railroad connections and hotel and convention-hall accommodations. Sometimes a particular city is chosen because of the need to whip up party enthusiasm there. Chicago has had more major national political conventions than any other city.

The first television coverage of the Republican and Democratic national conventions was from Philadelphia to principal cities of the East in 1948. A huge television audience estimated at 70 million persons in 34 states viewed the 1952 conventions. Today, nearly everyone in the United States watches the national conventions on television.

The parties do not bear the expense of television and radio coverage. The sponsors of the television and radio broadcasts of the major conventions pay the networks to air their advertising messages. The networks pay the difference between the total cost and the amount of income from advertising. WALTER F. MORSE

Related Articles in WORLD BOOK include:

Campaign	Democratic Party	Republican Party
Delegate	Political Party	Unit Rule

POLITICAL ECONOMY is economics. See ECONOMICS.

Arthur Settel

Political Party campaign buttons bring back memories of once-burning election issues, great political rivalries, and hard-fought campaigns. Names, pictures, and slogans on the buttons help bring a candidate or party before the voters.

POLITICAL PARTY. In modern democracies, political parties are groups of citizens who seek to win control of the government in a legal manner, by means of the popular vote in elections. They frequently draft *party platforms*, or programs for legislative and administrative action. Their candidates, if elected to office, are morally bound to follow these programs.

Political parties are as much a part of the government of modern democracies as are the legislature, the executive, or the courts. In the United States, the President is always considered to be the leader of the political party that nominated him. In Congress, the practice of both houses provides for a *majority leader*, or chairman of the majority party in each house, and a *minority leader*, or chairman of the minority party in each house. Each committee in the Senate and the House of Representatives is divided into a majority and a minority on the basis of party membership.

Political parties are important also because the moral standards of any modern government reflect those of the political party in office.

Political parties are absolutely necessary to modern democratic government. In a representative democracy, where all the people are permitted to vote and to take part in the government, there must be some arrangement for nominating candidates for public office and for selecting the issues for public debate and determination. Political parties perform this function. They offer the means for forming tickets of candidates to present to the voters at the polls. They also present issues to the people.

Political parties are so intimately a part of modern government that every citizen should be familiar with the organization and practices of parties.

Politics as a Career

Political parties are no better and no worse than their leaders. Political leaders, or *politicians*, commonly reflect the political morality of the rank and file of the party membership. At the same time, they have the opportunity to raise public moral standards.

At various times, people have tended to condemn politics and politicians as corrupt and immoral. This is a foolish and dangerous attitude to take in a democracy. It is true that some political leaders, in both local and national politics, have engaged in corrupt practices. It is also true that there have been unfortunate alliances between various "political machines" and organized crime. But such occasions are the exception rather than the rule in American politics. When such irregularities occur, it is largely because the citizens have neglected their civic duty of watching their representatives, and of voting for good government.

Opportunity for Service. The Greek philosophers Socrates, Plato, and Aristotle taught the youth of Athens that politics is the most useful and honorable of all the professions. Good government requires good leadership, and this leadership depends upon the character of the politicians. This situation is just as true of modern democracies as it was of the Greek city-state. Some of the most famous statesmen in British history have been professional politicians. The list includes men like the elder and the younger Pitt, Palmerston, Disraeli, Gladstone, Ramsay MacDonald, and Winston Churchill. The American roll of honor includes such revered names as those of the politicians Benjamin Franklin, George Washington, Alexander Hamilton, Thomas Jefferson, James Madison, Daniel Webster, Abraham Lincoln, Theodore Roosevelt, and Woodrow Wilson.

To have good government in every democracy, the most competent and promising young men should be attracted into political careers. Industry and science can flourish only under stable government, while freedom

556

can be maintained only under a government devoted to justice. Government of this sort is determined in large measure by the personal integrity of the men who serve as executives and legislators.

Combined Careers. Most young men and women who aspire to political leadership find it necessary to combine their political careers with a profession such as law, teaching, journalism, or public relations, or some business such as insurance or farming. Most of the members of state legislatures are lawyers, businessmen, or farmers. They continue their practice or business during the months when the legislature is not in session. Many men and women serve as party officers such as precinct captains, ward chairmen, county or state committeemen, without any thought of ever running for public office. Frequently, these men and women are more important in party councils than is the average Senator or Representative, particularly if they become members of the national committee of their party.

Preparation for a Political Career. A boy or girl who has some thought of entering politics can start preparing for a political career in high school, or even in grade school. He should study English composition and literature to improve his speaking and writing ability. He may gain greater mastery of language through study of some foreign language. He should not neglect mathematics as a means of understanding economic problems. His study of history should include ancient, modern, and American history. Naturally, he will take courses in *civics* (government). He should study at least one science like physics, chemistry, or biology to help him understand the significance of modern scientific issues. If economics and psychology are available, the student should take both courses.

Outside the classroom, the young man or woman should attend political meetings, and visit the city council, the state legislature, or Congress. He should seek to talk with local and state politicians. It would be well to begin active service by offering to assist the precinct captain of his party in the precinct in which he lives. In time, he may find that the ward chairman has such confidence in him that he may be offered the post of precinct captain. By means of such service, he will observe and take part in politics at the grass roots. With this intimate experience with actual politics, he will be better prepared to take his place in politics and to combat corruption wherever he finds it. He will also be able to seek election to some local office. Too frequently, young men in college assume that they can win nomination to some important office soon after graduation without serving any apprenticeship in practical politics. The road to nomination and election is not that smooth.

Party Systems

The Two-Party System. Great Britain, the United States, and some other countries have the two-party system. There are two major parties. These parties alternate in the control of the government for varying periods of time. Generally, one party tends to be conservative and to resist governmental control or ownership of the production and distribution of economic goods. The other party tends to be radical or progressive and to call for governmental controls.

The two-party system is in accord with the tradition of Western democracy. This tradition looks upon democracy not only as government by the majority but also as a fair attitude toward opposition to the prevailing government. It cannot tolerate efforts to overthrow the constitutional government by force, but it must recognize freedom of speech and freedom of the press, as well as the right of political parties to oppose the party that happens to have control of the government.

The One-Party System. In dictatorships, only one political party is permitted to exist and operate. In Russia, for example, only the Communist party is tolerated. The membership of this one and only party includes only a small fraction of the people. The party, in turn, is ruthlessly governed by a small group of party leaders. The people themselves have little or no voice in political decisions.

Multiple-Party System. In some parliamentary governments, there are more than two major parties. In France, the National Assembly contains five major parties and several *splinter parties* (offshoots of the major parties). In the Italian Chamber of Deputies, there are six major parties and a dozen minor parties. The Japanese House of Representatives shows four major parties and four minor parties, while about 5 per cent of the members describe themselves as independents. In West Germany, there are three major parties and a dozen splinter parties.

The two-party system tends to produce a more stable government than the multiple-party system, where upsets are common. In Great Britain, under the two-party system, there were only two changes in the cabinet from 1945 to 1953. In France, in the same period, twenty-one cabinets resigned.

Parliamentary governments having the multiple-party system frequently change their cabinets because it is necessary for the cabinet to win and hold the support of a bloc of parties in the legislature. The cabinet in Great Britain generally is responsible to only one party, but in France the cabinet must conform to the programs of the three or four parties which make up the bloc in support of the ministers. It is difficult to please so many groups of people. Any one of the parties in the bloc behind the cabinet may withdraw its support at any time, and thus bring about the fall of the ministers. Where there are many parties, government may be almost paralyzed by crisis after crisis. The dictator Adolf Hitler took advantage of such a series of crises to rise to power in Germany.

Single-Member Constituencies. American as well as British tradition insists that representatives in the lower house of the legislature be elected from *single-member constituencies*. One representative in Congress, for example, is elected from each congressional district. This method tends to promote the two-party system. The contest over one seat tends to draw the voters into two opposing sides. The French electoral system assigns an average of seven deputies for the National Assembly to every election district. This method invites small parties to concentrate their votes on one candidate in an effort to capture at least one out of seven seats. They would have no such opportunity in a single-member constituency.

The reduction of districts from larger to smaller units,

such as occurred in Japan after World War II, has always tended to reduce the number of political parties. The Communist party, wherever it has appeared as a minority party, has always approved the large electoral district as a means of obtaining a foothold in a national legislature which it could not obtain with smaller districts.

Pressure Groups. We must not confuse political parties with pressure groups. Pressure groups are associations of persons organized for the purpose of influencing public opinion and of persuading executives and legislators to take certain action. Labor unions, chambers of commerce, and industrial and professional groups almost continuously engage in propaganda in favor of their programs. This propaganda, if truthful and good for public welfare, is not dangerous. Rather, it is helpful to good government. Examples of permanent associations that act as pressure groups include the American Federation of Labor and Congress of Industrial Organizations, the National Association of Manufacturers, the Chamber of Commerce of the United States, the American Legion, and the American Farm Bureau Federation.

Frequently, citizens form temporary associations to promote a particular policy or program, either local or national. While these groups offer programs of action, they usually do not take part in the nomination and election of governmental officers, as political parties do.

Party Organization

All political parties tend to become highly organized. In the United States, both major parties and some of the minor parties are organized on the national, state, and local government levels.

The National Leader. The President of the United States is the leader of his party. The defeated presidential candidate of a major party is generally accepted as leader of his party until the national convention of the party, four years later, renominates him or else nominates another candidate. There are frequent exceptions, however.

The National Committee. The top committee in both the Democratic and Republican parties is the national committee. In each party, the national committee consists of one committeeman and one committeewoman from each state in the United States, and from the District of Columbia and the Commonwealth of Puerto Rico. The Democratic National Committee includes also representatives from the Virgin Islands and the Panama Canal Zone. The members of the national committee in each party are formally named by the national convention, but actually the national convention merely ratifies the selection made by the party in each state. In some states, the election of party officers is governed by state laws. In others, the party follows its own rules. The committeemen are frequently businessmen or lawyers. The national committee makes the arrangements for the national convention which nominates the candidates for President and Vice-President. The chairman plays a leading role in the presidential campaign. He directs the campaign strategy, collects funds for campaign expenses, and publishes propaganda on behalf of the candidate. Each party has permanent national headquarters in Washington, D.C. In addition to the national committee, each party has a congressional campaign committee to support the election of its candidates as Representatives and Senators.

State Committees. Each major party has a state committee or state central committee within each one of the states. The number of members of the state committee varies. In some states, these members are elected by the direct primaries. In other states, they are appointed by state or county conventions or by committees in the counties or congressional districts. The state chairman generally has great influence. He supervises the presidential campaign in his state, as well as the campaign of his party's candidate for governor. He collects and distributes campaign funds and controls publicity. He has considerable *patronage* (power to name appointees to government jobs).

County Committees. Almost every county in the United States has both a Democratic and a Republican county committee. In some states, the county committee is chosen by county conventions. In other states, the county committee consists of ward chairmen. The county chairman is frequently the "boss" of a city or county political machine. He has extensive control over appointments in the city or county administration.

Precinct Committeemen. There are more than 146,300 election precincts in the United States. In most of them, either one or both major parties have a precinct captain or committeeman. In some states, these party officers are elected in the party primary; in others, they are appointed by the county committee. The precinct committeeman prepares the party poll book showing the names of the five or six hundred voters in the district, and indicating which ones are Republicans, Democrats, or members of some other party. He and his assistants check on registration of voters, urging those of his party to register on the proper days. He distributes promotional literature and urges voters to vote on election day. He may even provide automobile transportation for sick or indifferent voters.

Most precinct committeemen undertake the hard duties of their office because of a genuine interest in politics. In order to win the gratitude of voters, the precinct committeeman frequently assists them in various ways. He helps immigrants to become citizens, bails out prisoners under arrest, finds positions for unemployed persons, and sometimes gives out charity. These activities often bring more votes on election day than persuasion, argument, or the issues being voted on.

The precinct committeeman operates at the "grass roots" of American democracy. James A. Farley, who managed the presidential campaign of Franklin D. Roosevelt in 1932, was unusually successful in winning the loyalty and enthusiasm of the precinct committeemen of the Democratic party. Farley believed that the endeavors of the precinct committeemen were equal in importance with the character of the candidate and the party platform. In the final analysis, it is the precinct committeeman who must get the voters to the polls. And votes win elections.

Development of Parties in the United States

Beginnings. Political parties appeared in colonial times in what is now the United States. The opponents of the British Crown and Parliament became known as *Whigs*, while the citizens who supported the British

Beginnings of Political Parties in the United States

The present Republican and Democratic parties can trace their **origins** to the time when constitutional government was founded in the United States. For later development, see DEMOCRATIC PARTY; REPUBLICAN PARTY.

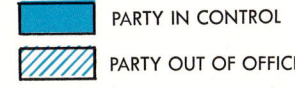

PARTY IN CONTROL

PARTY OUT OF OFFICE

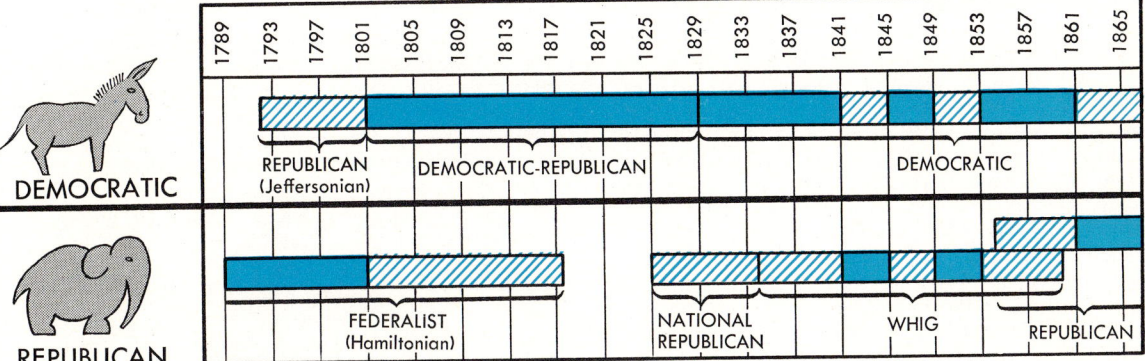

1789	1793	1797	1801	1805	1809	1813	1817	1821	1825	1829	1833	1837	1841	1845	1849	1853	1857	1861	1865

DEMOCRATIC

REPUBLICAN (Jeffersonian) · DEMOCRATIC-REPUBLICAN · DEMOCRATIC

REPUBLICAN

FEDERALIST (Hamiltonian) · NATIONAL REPUBLICAN · WHIG · REPUBLICAN

Government were called *Tories.* After 1765, during the struggle over separation from Great Britain, many of the Tories stood steadfastly with the British Empire, and were called *Loyalists.* After the United States had won the Revolutionary War, sharp differences in economic and political interests again gave rise to two groups. The farmers, especially in the western districts, desired to weaken the already weak Confederation, so that the thirteen states would remain as almost independent nations. These were the *Anti-Federalists.* The merchants and planters of the Atlantic seaboard desired to introduce more order and uniformity by increasing the powers of the central government. It was this *Federalist* party that succeeded in calling the constitutional convention in 1787 in Philadelphia.

The Federalist Party. The contest over ratifying the United States Constitution, which was adopted by the Philadelphia convention, placed the Anti-Federalists in opposition to the Federalists. The Federalists supported the achievement of George Washington, Alexander Hamilton, and James Madison in winning the adoption of a Constitution which retained the federal system of states, but also greatly strengthened the central government. Ratification was carried in all the thirteen states only after leading Federalists had promised that a Bill of Rights would be adopted as soon as the new federal government was established.

Washington, Madison, and Hamilton had hoped that the new federal government could operate without political parties. The Constitution contained no provision on parties, but it did not prohibit them. In the course of a few years, the Fathers of the Republic revised their views on political parties.

In 1789, George Washington, who had been elected the first President of the United States, appointed both Federalists and Anti-Federalists as members of his Cabinet. His Cabinet included Alexander Hamilton, the leader of the Federalists, and Thomas Jefferson, to whom the Anti-Federalists now looked for leadership. Washington's attempt to govern with a Cabinet of two parties proved to be a failure. After the split-up of his Cabinet in 1793, Washington carried on his administration with Federalist support alone. In the meantime,

Thomas Jefferson had built a new party on more positive principles than anti-federalism; his program emphasized democratic progress as well as states' rights. His new party was first called Republican, then Democratic-Republican, and finally merely Democratic party.

The control of the central government by the Federalist party came to an end in 1801 when Jefferson defeated John Adams for the Presidency. By this time, however, the Federalist party had made its remarkable contribution to American progress. It had created an admirable national government under which the American people were to prosper and achieve peace within their vast territory.

The Democratic Party dominated the federal government from 1801 to 1861. It lost the Presidential elections of 1840 and 1848. However, it recovered its control after both of these temporary defeats. Under Thomas Jefferson as President (1801-1809), the party still maintained its principle of states' rights and strict interpretation of the Constitution. But even Jefferson violated these principles when his patriotism led him to acquire the Louisiana Territory without a constitutional amendment. Again, President Andrew Jackson trampled on states' rights when he threatened to use military force to prevent South Carolina from nullifying federal law.

Under Thomas Jefferson, the Democratic party stressed the development of the democratic process. The party was indeed largely responsible for removing restrictions on the ballot and for the extension of manhood suffrage. President Jackson also introduced into the central government much of the pioneer freedom of the West, frequently called Jacksonian democracy. At the same time, aristocratic slaveowners supported the Democratic party in the Southern States. The clash between Southern and Northern Democrats, however, led to the defeat of the Democratic party in the Presidential election of 1860.

During the period of supremacy of the Democratic party, the principal opposition party had been the Whig party, the successor of the Federalists. This party, to which both Daniel Webster and Henry Clay belonged, split over the issue of slavery into the Northern and

Southern Whigs. The party succeeded in electing its candidates for the Presidency in 1840 and 1848, only to lose again to the Democratic party.

The Republican Party. In the meantime, the growing public opinion against slavery in the North surged far beyond Whig compromises and tended toward the spirit of the new Republican party, founded in 1854-1856. By the Presidential election of 1860, the Whig party had gone to pieces, while the Democratic party had broken into two parties, one in the South and the other in the North. The candidate of the Republican party, Abraham Lincoln, failed to win a majority of the popular vote. But he had the largest popular plurality, as well as a majority of the Electoral College, and thus became President.

The period of 1801-1861 saw many minor parties such as the Anti-Masons; the Free Soil party; and the Native-American, or Know-Nothing, party.

For the later history of the two leading political parties in the United States, see DEMOCRATIC PARTY; REPUBLICAN PARTY.

The Two-Party System Today. During the 1940's and 1950's, some political scientists have urged that the two major parties *realign*. This would mean, for instance, that all conservatives would move into the Republican party and all liberals would be driven into the Democratic party. Advocates of realignment have pointed

out that some Southern Democratic leaders have views much like those of the conservative Republicans, while many Republican leaders see eye to eye with liberal Democrats on social and economic issues.

Opponents of realignment in both parties contend that such a movement might divide the parties along class lines, and lead to head-on collisions between the "haves" and the "have-nots." In this respect, the history of American political parties is significant. Before 1854, every major party in the United States contained both slavery and antislavery leaders. Compromise kept the peace. But after 1854 the Republican party captured most of the antislavery voters and the Democratic party became the party of slavery leaders. The result was a violent showdown, leading to civil war.

The Fathers of the Republic intended Congress to serve as a representative body where all sections, interests, and groups could adjust differences and make compromises that would preserve the peace and promote the general welfare. Today, the principal agency for such compromises is the two-party system. Compromises of conflicting interests within each political party lead to statesmanlike compromises in Congress.

Political Parties in Canada

The Canadian system of party organization is much like that of Great Britain. The chief executive is always a member of the majority party in Parliament. In Canada political parties need only be interested in gain-

Political Party Rallies usually feature fiery speeches praising the party, criticizing the opposition, and inspiring party members to greater effort. Canadian Prime Minister Lester Pearson, *below*, addresses a Liberal Party rally.

United Press Int.

ing control of Parliament, which controls all political appointments.

It is customary for each party to elect its leader in both the Canadian and the Provincial parliaments. The leader of the majority party is the prime minister and the leader of the minority becomes the head of the opposition. The Cabinet really becomes a committee of the party in power, although it is never called by that name.

In some respects, the party system works better in Canada than it does in the United States, because a party division in government is not so likely to occur.

Origin and Development of Parties. Political parties first appeared in Canada after the War of 1812. A small group of aristocratic Tories, known as the *Family Compact*, ruled Canada at that time. An opposition group appeared and demanded a more democratic government. The members of this group felt that the adoption of the English type of government would create a more democratic government. William Lyon Mackenzie and Robert Baldwin were well-known leaders of the reform group. In Lower Canada, too, there was a demand for greater popular rights. There, the leader of the reform was Louis J. Papineau.

The reform movement led to the Rebellion of 1837, which resulted in certain reforms. But the rebellion turned many persons against the reform group. Some of the less radical of the reformers, including Baldwin and Sir Louis H. Lafontaine, gradually withdrew from the group. By 1849, new parties were beginning to take shape. The Liberal-Conservative party (known since the early 1940's as the Progressive Conservative party) was formed with Sir John A. Macdonald as leader. The less radical of the reform group, and some of the most conservative among the Tories, joined this party.

The more radical reformers formed two powerful minor parties between 1850 and 1867. In Upper Canada, they were known as the *Clear Grits*. In Lower Canada, they were known as the *Rouges* (Reds). These parties were finally absorbed into the Liberal party.

For a long time after 1867 there were only two great parties, the Conservative and Liberal. During the 1930's, the Liberals increased greatly in strength. Except for a period from 1957 to 1963, the Liberals have controlled the Canadian government since 1935.

It has not always been easy to find much difference between the ideas of the Conservatives and those of the Liberals. The Liberals have stood for more rights for the provinces and for lower tariffs. The Conservatives have believed in a stronger central government and a tariff favoring all parts of the British Commonwealth.

Minor Political Parties have developed in Canada during recent times. The French Nationalist party was powerful in Quebec and had considerable influence for a time in Canadian affairs. The Farmers' (Progressive), party developed great strength in the western provinces after World War I. The Social Credit party won government control in Alberta and gained several seats in the Canadian Parliament. This party believed that depressions are caused by a shortage of purchasing power, and proposed that the government take steps to increase purchasing power. The Labour party in Canada has a small membership, but makes its influence felt by joining with the Liberals on some issues.

The most important political movement of recent years has been the rise of the Cooperative Common-

wealth Federation (CCF). The CCF followed the principles of democratic socialism. It began to gain strength in the late 1930's, mainly from the minor parties and the Liberals. Many members of these parties felt that more radical social reform was needed. The CCF won nine seats in Parliament in 1940. By 1944, it had gained control of the government of Saskatchewan. Many persons thought for a time that the CCF would gain a majority in Parliament and control the Canadian government. But it lost most of its membership in 1961 when the CCF joined the newly organized New Democratic party.   KENNETH COLEGROVE and FREDERICK F. BLACHLY

Related Articles in WORLD BOOK include:

POLITICAL PARTIES

Anti-Federalist	Dixiecrat Party	Liberty Party
Anti-Masonic Party	Farmer-Labor	Loco-Foco
Anti-Monopoly	Party	National Republican Party
Party	Federalist Party	lican Party
Conservative Party	Free Soil Party	Populist Party
Constitutional	Greenback Party	Progressive
Union Party	Know-Nothing	Party
Democratic Party	Labour Party	Prohibition Party
Democratic-	Liberal Party	Republican Party
Republican	Liberal Republi-	Tory
Party	can Party	Whig

OTHER RELATED ARTICLES

Abolitionist	Conservatism	Political
Barnburner	Delegate	Convention
Bucktail	Gerrymander	Primary Election
Caucus	Government	Proportional
Coalition	Left Wing	Representation
Communism	Liberalism	Right Wing
(Main Features)	Mugwump	Socialism
Congress of the	Nonpartisan	Spoils System
United States	League	Woman Suffrage

Outline

I. Politics as a Career
  A. Opportunity for Service
  B. Combined Careers
  C. Preparation for a Political Career
II. Party Systems
  A. The Two-Party System
  B. The One-Party System
  C. Multiple-Party System
  D. Single-Member Constituencies
  E. Pressure Groups
III. Party Organization
  A. The National Leader
  B. The National Committee
  C. State Committees
  D. County Committees
  E. Precinct Committeemen
IV. Development of Parties in the United States
  A. Beginnings
  B. The Federalist Party
  C. The Democratic Party
  D. The Republican Party
  E. The Two-Party System Today
V. Political Parties in Canada
  A. Origin and Development of Parties
  B. Minor Political Parties

Questions

Why are political parties necessary to modern democratic government?

How can a student prepare for a career in politics?

What were the first political parties in the United States? In Canada?

What is the two-party system? How did it develop?

How did the debate over ratifying the United States Constitution affect political parties?

What are the national committees of the Democratic and Republican parties? How is each organized?

What are *splinter parties?* Precinct committeemen?

Why may there be more than two major political parties in some parliamentary governments?

POLITICAL RIGHTS. See CITIZENSHIP.

POLITICAL SCIENCE

POLITICAL SCIENCE is the systematic study of political life. Political scientists study government, political parties, pressure groups, international relations, and public administration. All these are activities of individuals and groups, and involve basic human relationships. Political science deals with such fundamental values as equality, freedom, justice, and power.

Political science is closely related to history, law, philosophy, and sociology. History provides much of the raw material with which the political scientist works. Law, especially public law, supplies a framework of formal ideas for the political scientist. Philosophy relates political science to the other sciences, and sociology provides the social setting for the facts of political life.

The importance of political science has increased greatly with the growth and spread of democracy during modern times. In every democratic country, political science is essential in the processes of government. The political scientist studies these processes and the operations of government agencies and departments. His work provides a factual basis for criticism and reform—probably the most important elements of democratic government. Political scientists also develop useful materials for the education of young persons. Without that kind of training for future citizens, a democratic society could not prosper.

The field of political science is growing rapidly. Many research specialists and teachers choose careers in political science. They often participate in government programs as advisers. They also act as consultants to legislators or other public officials.

Fields of Political Science

In the United States, political science is generally divided into six main fields: (1) political theory and philosophy, (2) comparative government, (3) American government and politics, (4) public administration, (5) international relations, and (6) political behavior.

Political Theory and Philosophy are usually dealt with historically. Most political scientists believe that the history of political thought forms the basis of all political studies. They consider the reading of great books on political theory and philosophy to be essential for a broad education in politics. The writers of these works include Plato, Aristotle, Cicero, Saint Augustine, Saint Thomas Aquinas, Niccolò Machiavelli, Thomas Hobbes, John Locke, Montesquieu, Immanuel Kant, Georg Wilhelm Friedrich Hegel, and Karl Marx. Careful attention is also given to the writings of Jeremy Bentham and John Stuart Mill.

The classic political and philosophical works help the political scientist explore and understand many issues of *empirical politics* (politics based on experience). With this understanding, he can establish correct generalizations based on verified facts. Generalizations of this kind deal with such broad subjects as how power is

The contributor of this article is Carl J. Friedrich, Eaton Professor of the Science of Government at Harvard University and author of Constitutional Government and Democracy, *and* Man and His Government.

gained or lost, and the problems of representative government.

Comparative Government. An understanding of political reality may be achieved by comparing the political institutions and practices of two or more countries. Some scholars in comparative government specialize by studying the countries of a particular area of the world. Among these area specialists, the best known are probably the political scientists who study Russia and its satellites. The Communist dictatorships make all activities of the people a concern of the government. In these countries, a sound interpretation of any general activity, such as the economy, can be made only as part of a political study.

American Government and Politics is a field of political science only in the United States. In Great Britain, the study of British government and politics would take its place. Political scientists generally give special study to their own country's government. They feel it is necessary to study its development more deeply than that of other governments.

The U.S. government has a federal system. Study of the American government considers (1) national government and politics, (2) state government and politics, and (3) local government and politics.

American political scientists have made notable progress in arriving at realistic understandings of Congress, the presidency, and the Supreme Court. They have also gained important insight into many agencies and departments of the U.S. government. This understanding and insight help shape programs for reforming governmental processes or operations.

Public Administration is actually part of comparative government and of American government and politics. It is separated from those fields because of the range and complications of modern administrative activities. Public administration deals with such tasks of public officials as accounting, budgets, and personnel management. Public officials often work closely with political scientists who are experts in administration.

International Relations include diplomacy, international law, and international organization. Since 1945, much emphasis has been placed on the study of the United Nations. Vital aspects of the modern world, including imperialism and nationalism, are important segments of international relations. This field of political science also deals with defense policies and a wide range of problems connected with peace and war.

Political Behavior is the field that explores the way people respond to certain political conditions or influences. For example, the political scientist may take note of how many women voters favor a candidate who looks handsome on television. Behavioral studies are the most recent trend in political science. They have been influenced by developments in such behavioral sciences as anthropology, psychology, and sociology. Political scientists have developed ways to study certain key behavior patterns in politics. Studies have been made in communications, propaganda, voting behavior, and other activities.

The Development of Political Science

The ancient Greek philosopher Aristotle called political science the "master science." He considered politics the highest science because he thought all other sciences depended on it. For many years, most scientists laughed at this idea. But today, many scientists share Aristotle's opinion because they realize that a nuclear war could wipe out mankind. They are convinced that the knowledge of how to control the results of scientific work politically—in other words, how to maintain peace—is probably the most important of all human endeavors.

Aristotle and his teacher, Plato, believed that the main task of political science was to work out a model political order. This political order would establish maximum justice while remaining completely stable. Plato was primarily a philosopher of ideas. He derived his insight chiefly from *abstract speculation* (thinking about non-concrete things). Aristotle, on the other hand, insisted on *empirical studies* (investigation based on experience) to construct his political theories. See ARISTOTLE; PLATO.

Scholasticism was the philosophy of the Middle Ages. Its followers, often called *scholastics*, undertook to fit the Greek tradition of political science into the religious framework of Christianity. Their main concern was with ethics and moral laws. The greatest scholastic was Saint Thomas Aquinas, who ranked all other political subjects below law. In one of his most important works, *Summa Theologica*, Aquinas elaborated Aristotle's theories and adapted them to Christian purposes. Aquinas emphasized certain rights and duties of individuals in the processes of government. In doing so, he laid the foundations for modern constitutional government. See AQUINAS, SAINT THOMAS; SCHOLASTICISM.

Secularism. The theories of the medieval philosophers were challenged in the 1500's and early 1600's. Niccolò Machiavelli, a famous Florentine politician, pushed aside Christian idealism in favor of realistic power politics. Machiavelli's ideas were generalized by Thomas Hobbes, an English philosopher. Hobbes claimed that man's entire life was a "ceaseless search for power." This approach became known as *secularism* because it separated politics from religion. Three writers who put those ideas into legalistic form were Jean Bodin, a French jurist; Johannes Althusius, a German political scientist; and Hugo Grotius, a Dutch lawyer who founded the science of international law.

Constitutionalism developed during the mid-1600's. It was a reaction to *absolutism* (absolute rule by one person). The reaction was especially strong in England where it was climaxed by the "Glorious Revolution" of 1688 (see ENGLAND [The Restoration]). Several English writers influenced the basic theories of Western constitutionalism. They included Richard Hooker, John Milton, and James Harrington. Constitutionalism emphasized basic human rights and the separation of governing powers. These ideas were given their classical form by John Locke, an English philosopher. Locke was probably the most influential political writer of his time. His *Two Treatises on Civil Government*, published in 1689, helped shape the United States Constitution.

Liberalism developed as a political philosophy largely from the theories of Locke. Liberalism represents a willingness to change ideas, proposals, and policies to meet current problems. Locke's theories were given a broader base by Montesquieu, one of a group of French writers called the *philosophes*. Liberal theories were reinforced by the radical *individualism* of Jean Jacques Rousseau and the *utilitarian* theories of David Hume,

a Scotsman, and Jeremy Bentham, an Englishman. Individualists believe that freedom for the individual is as important as the welfare of any community. Utilitarians believe that the goal of politics is "the greatest happiness of the greatest number." John Stuart Mill, the English philosopher and economist, summarized most of the liberal ideas that had developed up to that time.

Three great German philosophers contributed liberal ideas that were somewhat different from classic liberalism. They were Immanuel Kant, Johann Gottlieb Fichte, and Georg Wilhelm Friedrich Hegel. The liberalism of Fichte and Hegel included ideas of socialism and nationalism. Kant's liberalism included a theory of universal peace through world organization. Kant explained his theory in a brief classic, *On Eternal Peace*, published in 1795. See LIBERALISM.

Democracy and Socialism. Some of Rousseau's writings carried his political theories beyond radical individualism. In *The Social Contract*, published in 1762, Rousseau became the theorist of democracy. His emphasis on the *collective*—the general will, as Rousseau described it—gave rise to socialism. Eventually, the theories about democracy became divided. Liberal, constitutional, democratic ideas were followed in America. Socialist democratic ideas became predominant in Europe. Karl Marx, a German philosopher and economist, carried socialist ideas to extremes and founded present-day Communism. With the help of Friedrich Engels, another German economist, Marx wrote the *Communist Manifesto*, published in 1848. Basic Marxist doctrines were used by Lenin, leader of the Russian revolution, to formulate his totalitarian theory of Communist dictatorship. See COMMUNISM; DEMOCRACY; SOCIALISM.

Contemporary Ideas. Since about 1900, most political scientists have sought increasingly to strengthen the empirical basis of their work. They have been returning to Aristotle's view of basing political theories and methods on man's experiences. As a result, much progress has been made in descriptive and analytical work, and in quantitative studies.

Today, political scientists make practical improvement and political reform their major concerns. The modern approach of using empirical methods in political science is being taken up in one country after another. Many political studies consider most nations of the world. Such global interests find expression in the International Political Science Association. About 40 national political science associations work together in this organization.   CARL J. FRIEDRICH

See also GOVERNMENT and its Related Articles.

POLITICIAN, *PAHL uh TISH un*, is a person who works in party politics. He organizes the members of his party to win nomination for party-endorsed candidates. Then he works to persuade the people of both parties to vote for his candidates in general elections. Politicians are necessary for the success of democratic government. Between elections, they help form a link between officeholders and the people. During campaigns, they help define issues. See also POLITICAL PARTY; STATESMAN.   ROBERT A. DAHL

POLIZIANO, ANGELO. See ITALIAN LITERATURE (The 1400's).

JAMES K. POLK

L. C. Handy

The United States Flag had 26 stars when Polk took office.

W. H. HARRISON
9th President
1841

TYLER
10th President
1841 — 1845

TAYLOR
12th President
1849 — 1850

FILLMORE
13th President
1850 — 1853

11TH PRESIDENT OF THE UNITED STATES 1845-1849

POLK, JAMES KNOX (1795-1849), was President when the United States achieved its greatest territorial growth. During his presidency, the American Flag was raised over most of the area now forming nine Western States, and Texas became a member of the Union. Polk successfully directed the Mexican War, which won much of this territory. He carried out every item of his political program. Of all American Presidents, only George Washington had such a clear record of success.

Polk's era was the "Fabulous 40's." The country seethed with excitement, energy, and prosperity. Covered wagons were beating out the Oregon Trail across the prairies and mountains to the Pacific Coast. The telegraph, a new wonder, carried news of Polk's nomination. The discovery of gold in California started one of the greatest movements of people in American history. On their way west, the "forty-niners" sang such songs as "Be Kind to the Loved Ones at Home" and Stephen Foster's "Oh! Susanna." Such authors and poets as Emerson, Thoreau, Hawthorne, Longfellow, Lowell, Whittier, and Poe produced the "Golden Age of American letters."

The national scene had its unpleasant side, too. Reformers called attention to the hardships of children working in factories and to the poverty of immigrants. Slavery rested uneasily in the thoughts of many Americans.

A lack of concern by Polk for these social problems made reformers dislike him. They regarded him as a tool of the slaveowners. Their unfriendly writings outlived Polk's reputation for success. This explains why, for a time, history held Polk in low regard.

Although Polk was a close friend and follower of Andrew Jackson, he lacked Jackson's personal attraction. He was cold, silent, narrow, and ungenerous. He

did not seek a second term, and few people regretted it.

The nomination of Polk by the Democratic party surprised the nation. But he defeated the Whig candidate, the famous Henry Clay, because he understood the desire of Americans to see the United States become more powerful. Like most Americans of his day, Polk believed it was the "manifest destiny" of the United States to expand across North America. In this sense he appears to deserve the tribute of George Bancroft, the great historian who served as his Secretary of the Navy. Bancroft called Polk "prudent, farsighted . . . one of the very foremost of our public men, and one of the very best and most honest and most successful Presidents the country ever had."

Early Life

Childhood. James K. Polk, the son of Samuel Polk and Jane Knox Polk, was born on Nov. 2, 1795, on a farm near Pineville, N.C. His mother, a great-grand-niece of the Scottish religious leader John Knox, was a devout Presbyterian. She outlived her son. The Polks emigrated from Ireland to America. The family name was originally *Pollock* or *Pollok*. In time it became *Polk*, after being slurringly pronounced *Poll'k*.

In 1806, Samuel Polk moved his large and growing family across the mountains to the fertile Duck River valley in central Tennessee. He combined farming and

--- **IMPORTANT DATES IN POLK'S LIFE** ---

1795	(Nov. 2) Born near Pineville, N.C.
1806	Moved to Tennessee.
1824	(Jan. 1) Married Sarah Childress.
1825	Elected to the U.S. House of Representatives.
1835	Elected Speaker of the House.
1839	Elected Governor of Tennessee.
1844	Elected President of the United States.
1849	(June 15) Died in Nashville, Tenn.

surveying with land speculation, and became one of the wealthiest men of his region.

James, the oldest of 10 children, was a small and sickly boy. His parents spared him many of the chores done by most farm boys. But James learned to help his father survey and manage the large farms. He later worked briefly as a clerk in a general store.

Education. Polk studied for a year in the Zion Church in Maury, then entered the Murfreesboro Academy. In 1815, he entered the sophomore class of the University of North Carolina. He was graduated at the top of his class in 1818.

After graduation, Polk returned home and entered the law office of Felix Grundy, one of the foremost lawyers and politicians in Tennessee. Grundy introduced him to the great Andrew Jackson. After a year of study, Polk was admitted to the bar in 1820. He began to practice in Columbia, and soon had all the cases he could handle.

Political and Public Activities

Lawyer and Legislator. Local politics proved more attractive than law. Polk's short height and his speeches on behalf of the Democratic party won him the nickname of "Napoleon of the Stump." In 1819, while still practicing law, he became chief clerk of the Tennessee Senate. He was elected to the Tennessee House of Representatives in 1823. There he worked to improve the state school system and to reduce taxes. More important to his future, he decided to support Andrew Jackson's presidential ambitions. "Old Hickory" took a keen interest in Polk's political career. Jackson and Polk became so close that Polk received the nickname of "Young Hickory."

Polk's Family. At nearby Murfreesboro, Polk met and courted Sarah Childress (Sept. 4, 1803-Aug. 14, 1891). She was the daughter of a well-to-do country merchant. She had been brought up in a strict religious environment, and attended the Salem Female Academy, founded by the Moravians. A friend said that Mrs. Polk's black hair, dark eyes, and dark complexion made her look like "one of the Spanish donnas." She and Polk were married in a large country wedding on New Year's Day in 1824. Mrs. Polk encouraged her

THE WORLD OF PRESIDENT POLK

Texas became a state in 1845, Iowa in 1846, and Wisconsin in 1848. Oregon became a territory in 1848, and Minnesota in the following year. U.S. population was 22,700,000 in 1849.

Liberia

WORLD EVENTS

1845-47 A potato famine swept through Ireland.
1847 Liberia became the first Negro republic in Africa.
1848 Marx and Engels issued *The Communist Manifesto*.
1848 Revolutions flared in France, Germany, and Italy.

The Discovery of Gold in California in 1848 drew thousands of prospectors west.

The Mexican War (1846-48) ended in a U.S. victory and annexation of land from Mexico.

First U.S. Postage Stamps, issued in 1847, pictured George Washington and Benjamin Franklin.

The U.S. Naval Academy was founded in 1845 by Congress on George Bancroft's proposal.

The Sewing Machine, patented by Elias Howe in 1846, aided in the mass production of clothes.

Department of the Interior was established in 1849 on Polk's last day as President.

Portrait by George Dury, Photograph by Frick Art Reference Library

Sarah Childress Polk served as the official secretary to the President, the first First Lady to do so. Devoutly religious, Mrs. Polk banned card-playing, dancing, and alcoholic beverages from the White House. The Polks had no children.

Polk's Birthplace, shown in this artist's sketch, was a log cabin that lay in ruins by the late 1840's. A stone marks the site, near Pineville in Mecklenburg County, North Carolina.

husband's political career and was devoted to Jackson, whom she called "Uncle Andrew." In turn, Jackson called her "Sally." The Polks had no children.

Congressman. In 1825, Polk was elected to the first of seven consecutive terms in the United States House of Representatives. He was one of its youngest members, and quickly established himself as a loyal Democratic party man. He attracted attention by his bitter opposition to the policies of President John Quincy Adams, who had defeated Jackson in 1824.

In 1835, during Jackson's presidency, Polk became Speaker of the House. He rode to the Capitol in a coach "built after the latest style," with Venetian blinds in the windows. He worked hard, and in 14 years as a Congressman was absent only once. During his three years as Speaker, Polk claimed that he had "to decide more questions of parliamentary law and order" than all his predecessors combined. No other Speaker ever became President.

Governor. In 1839, Jackson persuaded Polk to run for governor of Tennessee. He felt that only Polk could unite the state Democratic party, which had been torn by internal strife and by Whig victories of the previous four years. Polk won the election. In his inaugural address, he announced that he supported states' rights and slavery, and opposed the centralization of powers in Washington.

The businesslike Polk shunned the social life of the state capital. He complained to his wife that he "could not lose half a day just to go and dine." He lost his bid for re-election in the Whig landslide of 1841. He ran again in 1843, but lost.

Meanwhile, Polk's interests had shifted back to the national scene. He felt he had Jackson's support for the vice-presidency. He probably toyed with the idea of the presidency, but neither he nor anyone else took his chances for that office seriously in 1843.

Election of 1844. A combination of circumstances now played into Polk's hand. Former President Martin Van Buren was again the leading candidate for the

Democratic nomination. The annexation of Texas was the chief political issue of the day. Van Buren opposed immediate annexation because it might lead to war with Mexico. This position cost Van Buren the support of the West and of the South, which sought to expand slave territory. Polk cleverly argued that Texas and Oregon had always belonged to the United States by right. He called for "the immediate reannexation of Texas" and for the "reoccupation" of the disputed Oregon Territory.

At the Democratic presidential convention of 1844, Van Buren failed to win the two-thirds vote then required for nomination. The delegates could not agree on Van Buren or his chief rival, Lewis Cass of Michigan, a former U.S. minister to France. On the eighth ballot, the historian George Bancroft, a delegate from Massachusetts, proposed Polk as a compromise candidate. On the next roll call, the convention unanimously accepted Polk, who became the first "dark horse," or little-known, presidential candidate. The delegates selected Senator Silas Wright of New York for Vice-President. But Wright, an admirer of Van Buren, rejected the nomination. This was the only time a man actually nominated for Vice-President refused to run. The Democrats then nominated George M. Dallas, a Pennsylvania lawyer.

Polk was not well known nationally, and many persons asked: "Who is James K. Polk?" This question became a Whig campaign slogan. The Democrats countered with their slogan of "54-40 or Fight!" They meant that the United States should have the entire Oregon Territory, north to the latitude of 54° 40', even if the country had to go to war with Britain for it.

The Whigs nominated former Senator Henry Clay of Kentucky for President and Senator Theodore Frelinghuysen of New Jersey for Vice-President. Polk, a relative unknown, was opposing a man who twice had run for the presidency and lost. Clay tried to keep the Texas issue out of the campaign, because he feared he would lose the northern antislavery vote if he supported annexation. Polk took a forthright position for annexa-

———————— POLK'S ELECTION ————————	
Place of Nominating Convention	Baltimore
Ballot on Which Nominated	9th
Whig Opponent	Henry Clay
Electoral Vote	170 (Polk) to 105 (Clay)
Popular Vote	1,338,464 (Polk) to 1,300,097 (Clay)
Age at Inauguration	49

tion. He won the election by about 40,000 votes.

Polk's Administration (1845-1849)

A cold, steady rain swept the unpaved streets of Washington during Polk's inauguration. The new President confided to Bancroft, whom he had appointed Secretary of the Navy, that "there are four great measures which are to be measures of my administration." Polk's four goals were to: (1) reduce the tariff, (2) reestablish an independent treasury, (3) settle the Oregon boundary dispute with Great Britain, and (4) acquire California. He was to achieve all these objectives.

Life in the White House changed greatly during Polk's administration. The Polks held informal evening receptions twice a month in the Executive Mansion, where gas lights for the first time replaced oil lamps and candles.

Mrs. Polk became the first wife of a President to serve as her husband's secretary. Throughout his public career, she looked over and approved his writings. She read the leading newspapers and clipped items for her husband to see.

Because of Mrs. Polk's strict Moravian beliefs, she and the President refused to attend the theater or the horse races. Mrs. Polk banned dancing, card-playing, and alcoholic drinks from the White House. She also refused to permit visitors in the White House on the Sabbath. Polk even declined to accept the credentials of the Austrian minister who called on him at the White House on a Sunday. The Polks attended the First Presbyterian Church regularly, although Polk himself joined no church until shortly before he died.

Tariff Reduction. Polk had long favored a tariff for revenue only, with "protection being incident and not the object." The Tariff Act passed by Congress in 1846 included some protective features. But it admitted tea and coffee duty-free, and also generally lowered rates. This law was the first tariff to be drafted by the executive branch of the government, and the first to be based on the value, rather than on the quantity, of imported goods.

An Independent Treasury. Less than a week after passing the tariff bill, Congress set up an independent treasury to hold and disburse federal funds. Subtreasuries were established in several major cities. President Van Buren had persuaded Congress to create such federal depositories, independent of private business and state banks. But the Whigs had repealed the law in 1841. The Independent Treasury Act of 1846 formed the basis of the nation's fiscal system until Congress passed a law that established the Federal Reserve System in 1913 (see FEDERAL RESERVE SYSTEM).

"Oregon Fever" swept the country in the early

VICE-PRESIDENT AND CABINET

Vice-President	*George M. Dallas
Secretary of State	*James Buchanan
Secretary of the Treasury	Robert J. Walker
Secretary of War	William L. Marcy
Attorney General	John Y. Mason
	Nathan Clifford (1846)
	Isaac Toucey (1848)
Postmaster General	Cave Johnson
Secretary of the Navy	*George Bancroft
	John Y. Mason (1846)

*Has a separate biography in WORLD BOOK.

1840's. Beginning in 1843, thousands of pioneers plodded along the Oregon Trail and settled along the banks of the Willamette and Columbia rivers in the Oregon Territory. The British, who were strongly established north of the Columbia, claimed the entire territory. The dispute between the United States and Britain had been "settled" in 1818 by an agreement for joint occupation. Now many Congressmen demanded an end to that agreement. They clamored for American possession of the territory, all the way north to the latitude of 54° 40′.

During the 1844 presidential campaign, Polk maintained that title to the Oregon Territory was "clear and unquestionable" because of American settlements there. As President, he modified his position. He did not want to fight Britain over the disputed territory, particularly because war with Mexico appeared near. But he confided in his diary that "the only way to treat John Bull is to look him straight in the eye." First, Polk renewed an earlier offer to compromise on the 49th parallel. Britain rejected the offer, but later made the same proposal, which became the basis of the Oregon Treaty of 1846. See OREGON TERRITORY.

The Mexican War achieved the fourth of Polk's goals, the acquisition of California. Earlier he had offered to buy California from Mexico. But Mexico had no intention of selling, particularly because it was then engaged in a dispute with the United States over Texas, a former Mexican possession. The United States had annexed Texas, but Mexico refused to give up its claims or agree to a boundary for the new state. The two countries also argued over unpaid money claims. Negotiations broke down. Polk then ordered American troops to occupy disputed territory on the Mexican side of the Nueces River. American General Zachary Taylor advanced to the bank of the Rio Grande. On April 25, 1846, American and Mexican soldiers clashed at Matamoros, on the Rio Grande. On May 11, Polk asked Congress to declare war, saying that "Mexico has passed the boundary of the United States, has invaded our territory, and shed American blood on American soil."

The Mexican War ended in an American victory. Under the peace treaty signed in 1848, Mexico gave up all claims to Texas, and also ceded land forming all or part of present-day Arizona, California, Colorado, Nevada, New Mexico, Utah, and Wyoming.

"The Polk Doctrine." A few months after the Mexican War, Polk reaffirmed and extended the Monroe Doctrine in a special message to Congress (see MONROE DOCTRINE). He said the doctrine was "our settled policy, that no further European colony or dominion shall, with our consent, be planted or established on any part of the North American Continent." Polk extended the doctrine to cover any European interference with the relations of the American countries to each other.

Retirement. When Polk had accepted the nomination for President in 1844, he declared that he would "enter upon the discharge of the high and solemn duties of the office with the settled purpose of not being a candidate for re-election." He was the first President not to seek re-election. Polk left the nation not only his record of political accomplishment and territory acquired, but also a diary that is an invaluable record of his presidency.

After his successor, Zachary Taylor, was inaugurated, the white-haired Polk returned to his home in Nashville, Tenn., worn out by four years of hard work. He became ill with cholera and died on June 15, 1849. Polk was buried in the city cemetery, and later in the garden tomb east of his estate, "Polk Place." For a time, Mrs. Polk managed a plantation on the Yalobusha River. She died in 1891, and was buried beside her husband. In 1893, their tombs were moved to the grounds of the Tennessee Capitol in Nashville.

Authoritative works on the life of Polk include *James K. Polk* by Eugene I. McCormac and *James K. Polk* by Charles G. Sellers.   HENRY STEELE COMMAGER

Related Articles in WORLD BOOK include:

Clay, Henry	President of the United
Dallas, George Mifflin	States
Fifty-Four Forty or Fight	Tennessee (picture, Three
Manifest Destiny	U.S. Presidents)
Mexican War	Wilmot Proviso
Mexico (History)	

Outline

I. Early Life
   A. Childhood   B. Education
II. Political and Public Activities
   A. Lawyer and Legislator   D. Governor
   B. Polk's Family   E. Election of 1844
   C. Congressman
III. Polk's Administration (1845-1849)
   A. Life in the White House E. The Mexican War
   B. Tariff Reduction   F. "The Polk Doctrine"
   C. An Independent   G. Retirement
      Treasury
   D. "Oregon Fever"

Questions

What were the four major goals of Polk's administration? How were they accomplished?

How did life in the White House change under the Polks? Why?

Why did he refuse to run for re-election?

What regions did the United States acquire during his administration?

Why is Polk considered one of the most successful Presidents?

Why was he nicknamed "Young Hickory"?

What happened to make Polk the first "dark horse" presidential candidate?

What was the meaning of "54-40 or Fight!"?

POLK, LEONIDAS (1806-1864), an Episcopal bishop, was a Confederate general in the Civil War. He commanded the defense of the Mississippi River in 1861. He fought in the battles at Belmont, Mo.; Shiloh, Tenn.; Perryville, Mo.; and Murfreesboro, Tenn. He led a corps at Chickamauga, Ga., and served in the Atlanta campaign. Polk was killed in action at Pine Mountain, Ga.

He was born in Raleigh, N.C., and was graduated from the United States Military Academy in 1827. That same year, he left the army to study for the ministry. In 1841, he became the first Protestant Episcopal bishop of Louisiana. Polk helped found the University of the South in Sewanee, Tenn.   FRANK E. VANDIVER

POLKA. See DANCING (The 1800's).

POLL. See POLL OF PUBLIC OPINION; VOTING.

POLL OF PUBLIC OPINION is a method of learning what people think about current problems. A poll can find out what millions of people think by asking a small number of those millions how *they* feel about it, provided that this small number is properly selected. The process of selection is called *sampling*.

How Polls Are Conducted

If a poll is to be reliable, it must be carefully planned and carried out. The six steps in polling are (1) defining the objectives, (2) formulating the questions, (3) pretesting them, (4) selecting the sample, (5) interviewing it, and (6) tabulating and analyzing results.

Defining the Objectives. A poll-taker must decide exactly what he wants to know. He may start with what people think, why they think as they do, how intensely they feel, how well-informed they are, and how their views affect their actions.

Formulating the Questions is a delicate task. The questions must be worded so that everyone can understand them correctly. They should contain no unfamiliar words, or words with two or more meanings. They should seek one answer at a time. And they should be unbiased.

The form of the question is as important as its wording. Some questions ask simply for one of two answers. In others, the person is asked to pick from several statements the one that comes closest to expressing his own view. Or the person may be asked for his general opinion in an open or free-answer question. The form of question used depends on the nature of the subject, how widely it has been discussed, how clear the issues may be, and other factors.

Pretesting the Questions. Interviewers try questions out with the various types of people who will be included in the poll. The order in which they are asked may affect the answers people give.

Selecting the Sample may be done in either of two ways: *quota* or *judgment* sampling and *random* or *probability* sampling. In either case, the poll-takers must first determine the large group (called a *population* or a *universe*) that the sample is to represent. Persons who have no interest in the problem studied would be excluded from the population polled. Then the poll-takers must make sure that the small group really represents the larger population.

Quota Sampling divides the population into subgroups, and assigns each subgroup a proportion in the final sample. The subgroups are analyzed on the basis of (1) geographic location, (2) community size, (3) economic level, (4) sex, and (5) age. These five *controls* are generally used in sampling political issues in the United States. The final sample must have the right proportion of persons who live in various parts of the country. It must have the right proportion of persons who live in large cities, suburbs, small towns, and rural areas. It must have the right proportion of persons in various income levels. It must have the right proportion of men and women, and of older and younger adults. Most polls include about half the sample in the over 40 group, and the other half in the 21 to 40 group. The resulting sample will be representative in terms of these five controls, but it may not be representative in other respects.

Random or Probability Sampling tries to overcome

Public Opinion Polls try to find out what people think about various issues. Personal interviews are considered the most reliable polling method. A trained interviewer, *right*, asks people questions and writes down their answers.

American Institute of Public Opinion

this defect in the quota method by selecting the sample at random. If the sample is completely random and is large enough, all the subgroups in the population will be represented in approximately correct proportions within it. The technique is especially easy to use in polling special groups. It has the advantage of assuring a high degree of representativeness in all respects.

Size can affect the value of the sample. Relatively small samples will yield accurate results if they are carefully drawn. Nationwide samples in the U.S. usually include from 1,500 to 5,000 persons.

Interviewing the Sample. Some early polls were conducted by printing questions in a newspaper or magazine and asking readers to send in their answers by mail. Others were conducted by mailing questionnaires to a sample group and asking the people to return them. But many people did not mail in their answers.

A third method of polling, the one generally considered most reliable, is personal interviewing. It has obvious advantages. Everyone in the sample can express his views. The interviewer can make sure that the question is understood and that the answer is adequate and relevant. But there is some slight chance that the interviewer may prejudice the answers by the way he asks the questions.

Tabulating and Analyzing the Results is the final step. Answers to questions calling for a simple *yes* or *no* response, or those calling for a choice of predetermined answers, can be tabulated easily. But when the question is of the free-answer type, the answers must be grouped before they can be counted. This process is called *coding*. It is one of the most difficult phases of polling. The answers can be tabulated by hand if the number of interviews is small and the questions fairly direct. But if several hundred questionnaires must be analyzed, card-punching and card-sorting machines will provide accurate counts quickly.

Uses for Polls

Public-opinion polls can be used in many ways. The most important are as public reports, confidential commercial reports, and research reports.

Public Reports. Most persons who know about public-opinion polls have heard of them through newspapers or magazines. Some polling organizations report in news releases sold or distributed to newspapers or magazines. Some publications operate their own polls.

Confidential Reports often aid businesses, political candidates, organizations connected with public welfare, and government agencies. The results of many polls are never made public, because they are designed to answer questions only for certain organizations that pay for the research and use it in making policy and planning programs.

Research Reports aid social scientists. Beginning about 1940, when the Office of Public Opinion Research was established at Princeton University, many schools developed laboratory facilities in connection with courses in attitude and opinion theory. They offer opportunities for research and professional training in sampling theory and practice, interviewing, analytical procedures, and other aspects of polling methods. Chief among these are the National Opinion Research Center at the University of Chicago, the Bureau of Applied Social Research at Columbia University, and the Survey Research Center at the University of Michigan.

History

The First Poll of public opinion that was at all like those of today was conducted in July, 1824. The Harrisburg *Pennsylvanian* reported a "straw vote" in Dela-

567

ware that predicted the election of Andrew Jackson as President. But Jackson lost to John Quincy Adams.

Newspapers and magazines continued taking most of the polls until well into the 1900's. The *Farm Journal* began its series of presidential election polls in 1912.

The *Literary Digest* poll became famous, and made the polling system well known. But in the presidential election of 1936, when it sent out more than 10 million ballots, it incorrectly predicted that Alfred M. Landon would defeat Franklin D. Roosevelt. One reason for this error was that names for the sample were taken chiefly from telephone books and lists of automobile owners. As a result, families with no telephones or cars, about one-third of all families, were overlooked.

The Modern Poll was developing at the time of the *Literary Digest* error. In 1930, the Psychological Corporation launched a periodic market survey, called the *Psychological Barometer*, which interviewed consumers in their homes in 15 American cities and towns.

In 1934 and 1935, Paul Cherrington, Elmo Roper, George Gallup, and Archibald M. Crossley began experimental nationwide opinion surveys based on carefully designed quota samples and personal interviewing. Their polls correctly forecast Roosevelt's re-election in 1936. Since then, polling organizations have started in many countries.

Increasing Accuracy. Modern scientific polls have usually proved to be very accurate. In hundreds of local, state, and national elections, one of the leading polling organizations had an average error of less than 3 per cent over a 25-year period. But, in the presidential election of 1948, the leading polls incorrectly predicted that Thomas E. Dewey would defeat Harry S. Truman. Scholars later claimed that the mistake did not arise from inherent weaknesses in methods or techniques. Instead, they pointed to mistakes in the selection and application of methods, to poor timing in the final round of interviewing, and to faulty assumptions in making forecasts based on the poll data. The polls modified their procedures, and correctly predicted the 1952, 1956, 1960, and 1964 presidential elections. In 1968, the polls declared the election too close to call.   HADLEY CANTRIL and CLYDE W. HART

See also GALLUP, GEORGE H.; MOTIVATION RESEARCH; PROPAGANDA; PUBLIC OPINION; STATISTICS.

POLL TAX is a tax levied equally on all the citizens of a community. The amount of the tax is the same for a poor man as it is for a rich man. The term *poll tax* comes from the English word *poll*, which means *head*. Many persons refer to it as a *head tax*. It is sometimes called a *capitation* tax, from the Latin *caput*, meaning *head*. Some persons object to poll taxes because they feel that taxes should be based only on income and property.

The United States has never levied a national poll tax. But in the past, laws in several states required that a citizen who did not pay the poll tax could not vote. Amendment 24 to the U.S. Constitution, ratified in 1964, made it illegal for a state to use payment of taxes as a voting requirement in national elections.

In 1966, the Supreme Court of the United States declared poll taxes unconstitutional if they are used as a prerequisite for voting in state and local elections. The court held that such taxes violated the equal protection of the law guaranteed by Amendment 14 to the U.S. Constitution.   CHARLES J. GAA

See also TAXATION.

POLLACK, *PAHL uck*, is a food fish that is related to the cod. It grows about 2 or 3 feet long and has a projecting lower jaw. Pollacks travel in schools. They always seem to be hungry and often prey on young fish. Pollacks are caught along the east coast of North America in seine nets. They are also caught along the Atlantic coast of Europe.

Scientific Classification. Pollacks belong to the codfish family, *Gadidae*. The pollack of the United States Atlantic coast is genus *Pollachius*, species *P. virens*. That of Europe is *P. pollachius*.   CARL L. HUBBS

POLLAIUOLO, *pohl lah YWOH loh*, **ANTONIO DEL** (1431? or 1432?-1498), was an Italian sculptor and painter. The ways in which he portrayed the human body in his sculpture and painting greatly influenced the work of the Renaissance artists Andrea del Verrocchio, Leonardo da Vinci, and Michelangelo.

Pollaiuolo was born in Florence. About 1460, he completed three large paintings of the deeds of Hercules. These paintings have not survived, but two small versions show figures struggling furiously. He reworked the subject of *Hercules and Antaeus* in a small bronze group that is so powerful in its expressive use of anatomy that the viewer feels he is participating in the action. This work is reproduced in the SCULPTURE article. Pollaiuolo lived in Rome from about 1483 until his death, designing and casting the bronze tombs of Popes Sixtus IV and Innocent VIII.   G. HAYDN HUNTLEY

POLLED CATTLE. See CATTLE (Horns; Beef Cattle).

POLLEN AND POLLINATION. The tiny yellow grains that can be seen in most flowers are pollen. They are used to form seeds. Plants make the pollen in the saclike *anthers* of their flowers. The anthers are considered the male organs of reproduction. The female organs include the pollen-receiving *stigma* leading to the *ovary*, which is the egg-bearing part of the plant. Pollination is simply the transfer of pollen from the anther to the stigma. Pollen that reaches the stigma grows down through pollen tubes to the *ovules* (tiny egg cells) inside the ovary. When the pollen reaches an egg cell, it causes the cell to divide. Each cell then becomes a seed embryo and develops all the structures of the seed. This process is called *fertilization*, and is necessary for the reproduction of some plants. See REPRODUCTION (Plant Reproduction).

Pollen Grains have different shapes in different kinds of plants. But they are all exactly alike in the same plant. Some kinds are smooth, and other kinds of pollen are covered with spines or knobs. Usually, plants form pollen while the flower buds are growing.

Size and Number. Pollen grains vary in size as well as shape. For example, the pollen of an iris blossom is about $\frac{1}{100}$ of an inch in diameter. But saxifrage pollen is often less than $\frac{1}{3,000}$ of an inch in diameter. Because so many of the grains are wasted, plants that depend on wind for pollination usually produce many thousands of pollen grains. Scientists have estimated that the male flowers of a corn plant produce more than 50 million grains of pollen.

Length of Life. Some pollen grains live longer than others. Pollen from grasses usually lives only 1 or 2 days. But corn and tobacco pollen can germinate after several

POLLEN AND POLLINATION

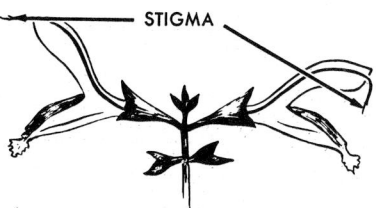

STIGMA

Older Flower, *right*, is ready to receive pollen. The stigma droops, so a bee entering the flower will touch it. The younger flower, *left*, is shedding pollen. Its stigma sticks straight out. A bee can enter without touching it.

Hermann Eisenbeiss

Stigma | Upper lip of petals

Position of style

Pair of anthers

Pollen

Pollination of the European Sage is a complicated operation. When the entering bee's head hits the stamen lever (1), a hinge (2) causes the anthers to move downward (3). When the anthers hit the bee's back, they deposit pollen on it. When the bee goes on to a flower that is ready to receive pollen, the pollen brushes off onto the drooping stigma.

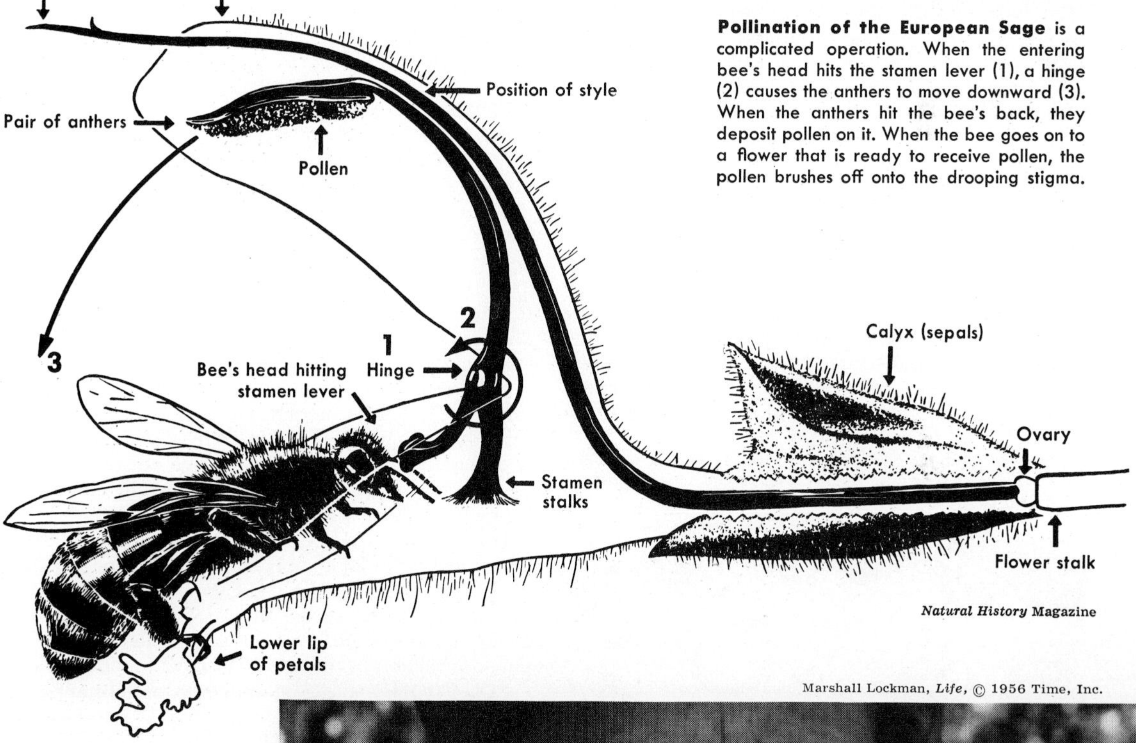

3

1   2

Bee's head hitting stamen lever   Hinge

Calyx (sepals)

Ovary

Stamen stalks

Flower stalk

Natural History Magazine

Lower lip of petals

Marshall Lockman, *Life*, © 1956 Time, Inc.

Artificial Pollination is a painstaking job. The plant breeder or horticulturist takes up pollen from one plant on a special brush. Then she carefully transfers it to the stigma of another flower.

POLLEN AND POLLINATION

years. Properly stored date pollen has been kept for 10 years.

Self-Pollination occurs in flowers that can transfer pollen from their own anthers to their own stigmas. Sometimes the pollination occurs before the blossom opens. For example, certain kinds of milkweed produce pollen and allow it to grow down the pollen tube to the stigma before the petals open. Several kinds of flowers are so constructed that pollen from other blossoms cannot enter them. Peas, beans, and snapdragons grow a trap door for protection against other pollens. Only heavy insects such as bees are able to open the flap and enter the flower. Flowers that have no odor are usually self-pollinating.

Cross-Pollination. Many flowers must depend on wind, insects, birds, or some other means to carry their pollen from one flower to another. These are the *cross-pollinating* flowers. Often the things we consider beautiful in flowers are aids for cross-pollination. The blossoms, fragrant scent, and sweet nectar attract various insects, which carry the pollen from plant to plant.

By Insects. The most important carriers of pollen are honeybees. They gather nectar for honey and pollen for food. They have small cavities on their hind legs to carry pollen to the hive. But some pollen clings to their bodies and is carried to other flowers. Some people believe that red, blue, or pink flowers attract bees by their color. Yellow or white flowers usually attract them with nectar.

Ants, beetles, moths, and butterflies are also pollen carriers. Flowers that give off their fragrance at night, like some honeysuckles, are pollinated by night-flying moths. Those that are most fragrant in the daytime attract bees and butterflies. Sometimes specific insects are necessary to pollinate certain flowers. The fig cannot produce seeds that will grow unless it is pollinated by

Pollen Grains are so small that they look like tiny specks to the unaided eye. But they have definite shapes and surface patterns depending on the kind of plant that produced them.

Brooklyn Botanic Garden

a certain small wasp. The yucca flower is pollinated only by the yucca, or *Pronuba*, moth.

Wind. Almost all common trees and shrubs are pollinated by the wind. Wind may carry pollen grains as high as 3 miles into the air and deposit them 100 miles from their original plant. Some pollens carried by the wind are very irritating to a person's nose and throat. Certain people develop hay fever during the pollination period of some grasses, weeds, and trees (see HAY FEVER).

Birds. Hummingbirds, sundews, and honeysuckers pollinate trumpet- and tubular-shaped flowers. The necks of these flowers are so narrow, only the long, thin beaks of these birds can reach the pollen.

Artificial Pollination. Sometimes scientists want to grow pure breeds of certain plants or develop new types. They cannot depend on the chance pollination of wind, birds, or insects. In these cases, scientists will transfer carefully selected pollen from plant to plant with special brushes.   WILLIAM C. BEAVER

Related Articles in WORLD BOOK include:

Bee	Fig
Breeding (Plant Breeding)	Flower (color pic-
Burbank, Luther	ture: From Pollen
Corn (The Corn Plant)	to Seed)
Cross-Pollination	Seed

POLLEN INDEX. See HAY FEVER.

POLLINOSIS. See HAY FEVER.

POLLIWOG. See TADPOLE.

POLLOCK, JACKSON (1912-1956), was an American artist who had an important influence on modern painting as a main figure in the abstract expressionist movement. Pollock devised a painting technique in which he dripped paint onto his huge canvases. The drippings formed sweeping, rhythmic patterns of line that seem to weave across the surface. Pollock's painting *Number 27* is an example of this technique. It is reproduced in color in the PAINTING article.

Pollock painted with his canvas on the floor. He said "I feel nearer, more a part of the painting, since this way I can walk around it, work from the four sides, and literally be *in* the painting." The attitude that the working artist is *in* the painting is generally considered characteristic of abstract expressionism.

Pollock was born in Cody, Wyo. From 1929 to 1931, he studied with Thomas Hart Benton at the Art Students' League in New York City. He worked in the Federal Art Project from 1938 to 1942. Pollock painted in an expressionistic symbolic style before moving to pure abstraction in the late 1940's.   DORE ASHTON

POLLUTION is the contamination of substances so that they are unfit for an intended use. Waste materials from human beings, animals, and some industries pollute water. Water contaminated by bacteria is unfit for drinking even though it can be used for certain industrial purposes. Water for industry can be contaminated by dissolved minerals. Air can become polluted from smoke, dust, and exhaust gases from automobiles. Air pollution is often a serious problem in large cities.   W. NORTON JONES, JR.

For more detailed information on pollution, see AIR POLLUTION; WATER (How Man Poisons Water).

POLLUX, *PAHL uks,* is the brightest star in the constellation Gemini. Together with Castor, it makes up the twin stars that identify Gemini. Pollux is about 33 light-years away from earth, and is 16 times the sun's diameter. See also CASTOR AND POLLUX; GEMINI.

POLO

Polo Horses crash together in a thrilling moment during a polo game. Such spirited action occurs when players fight for possession of the ball.

United Press Int.

POLO, *POH loh*, is a ball game played by men on horseback on an outdoor or indoor field. Its rules resemble the rules that are used in hockey (see HOCKEY). Two teams of four men each try to drive the ball through their opponents' goal posts.

Outdoor Polo

The Field and Equipment. A regulation polo field is a grass-covered strip 300 yards long and 200 yards wide. The field is only 160 yards wide if the sidelines are boarded. The sideboards are 11 inches high. The goal posts are made of light wood or papier-mâché so that they will break easily if a horse runs into them. The posts are spaced 24 feet apart at opposite ends of the field. The players use white-painted willow balls that are $3\frac{1}{4}$ inches in diameter. The balls weigh between $4\frac{1}{4}$ and $4\frac{3}{4}$ ounces. The players carry cane or rattan mallets from 48 to 54 inches long. At one end of the mallet is a horizontal piece of hardwood, and at the other end, a lightweight strap made of *web* (a strong cloth material). The strap fastens to the thumb. A polo player's equipment usually consists of boots, white breeches, knee guards, whip, spurs, mallet, and a jersey.

The Horses. Polo horses are not of any special breed or of any definite size. Thoroughbreds and three-quarter thoroughbreds are generally considered the most acceptable. They range from 60 to 64 inches in height, and weigh from 850 to 1,000 pounds. Once called *ponies*, they are now properly called *horses*. It takes from six months to a year to train a polo horse. The horse must get used to having clubs swung near its head. It must also be able to stop quickly, and to turn, twist, and

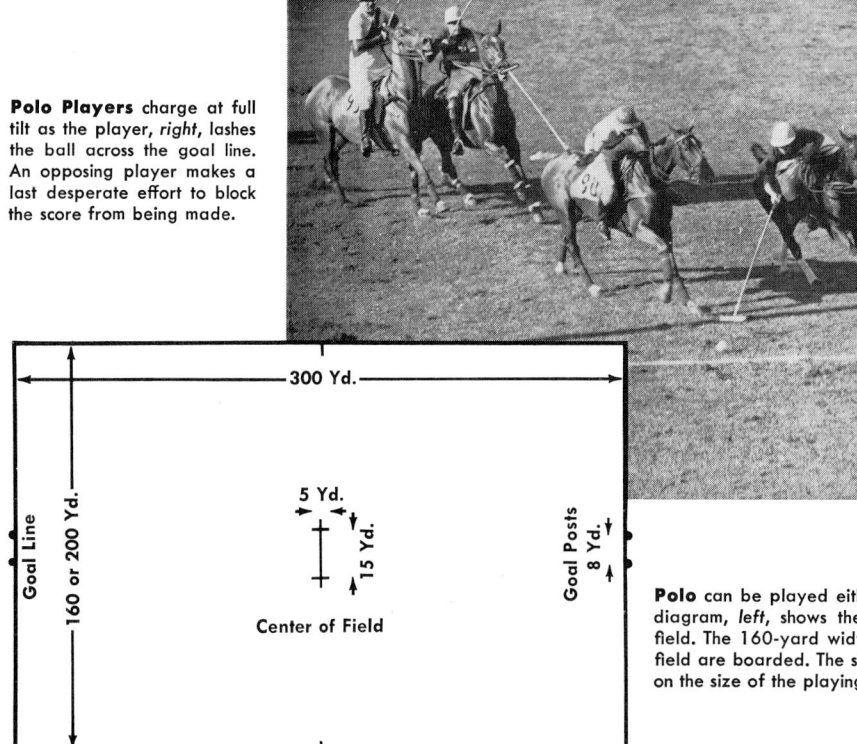

Polo Players charge at full tilt as the player, *right*, lashes the ball across the goal line. An opposing player makes a last desperate effort to block the score from being made.

Wide World

300 Yd.

Goal Line

160 or 200 Yd.

5 Yd.

15 Yd.

Center of Field

Goal Posts
8 Yd.

Polo can be played either indoors or outdoors. The diagram, *left*, shows the dimensions of an outdoor field. The 160-yard width is used if the sides of the field are boarded. The size of indoor fields depends on the size of the playing arena.

resume stride with little loss of speed. Most difficult of all, the horse must have the courage to bump into another horse, at angles up to 45 degrees, upon the command of its rider. The horse's equipment consists of saddle, bridle, bit, and leg boots or bandages.

The Game. At the start, each team is stationed to defend its respective goal. The first two men play *forward* (offensively) while the third and fourth play *back* (defensively). Tournament rules dictate whether there are six or eight *chukkers* (periods). Each chukker is $7\frac{1}{2}$ minutes long. Three-minute intervals are allowed between chukkers for the players to change horses. The half-time intermission is five to seven minutes.

Most games are played on the *flat basis*. But they may also be played on the *handicap basis*. Polo players have handicaps ranging from 0 to 10. The best players have the highest handicaps. On the flat basis, the handicaps of each team's members are added to make sure the team's total handicap does not exceed the limit set for the tournament. If it does, the team cannot play in the tournament. On the handicap basis, the total team handicaps may count in the scoring. If team *A* has a handicap of 20 and team *B* of 17, the game starts with a score of 3-0 in favor of team *B*.

Other Kinds of Polo

Arena Polo is played on indoor fields of sand, clay, or dirt, with teams of three men each. The playing rules are basically the same as for the outdoor game except for the size of the playing field, the type of ball used, and the length of the game. The indoor playing field is limited by the size of the playing arena. The two

major indoor polo arenas in New York and Chicago are 100 yards long and 50 yards wide, with 10-foot-wide goals painted on opposite ends. The arena game has four periods of $7\frac{1}{2}$ minutes each. The ball used has a leather cover and is inflated with air. It is $4\frac{1}{4}$ to $4\frac{1}{2}$ inches in diameter, and weighs 6 ounces.

Indoor-Outdoor Polo has won increased popularity in recent years. It is played outdoors, but the players use the same rules that they do in arena polo. The field is 100 yards long and 50 yards wide, and is enclosed by a board fence 4 to $4\frac{1}{2}$ feet high. The indoor-outdoor version of polo is popular wherever there is warm weather and a dry climate. This type of polo has the same advantage as arena polo in that fewer horses are needed than for outdoor polo.

History

Polo may have originated in Persia, now Iran, about 4,000 years ago. The modern game had its beginning in 1862 at Punjab, India, when a group of British officers copied the sport from some tribal horsemen. The game was introduced in England in 1869. In Egypt, India, and England, polo was an outdoor sport. But the first polo game in America was played indoors at Dickel's Riding Academy in New York City in 1876. It remained an indoor sport in the United States until 1880, when it became equally popular as an outdoor game. In 1886, teams from England and the United States played the first international polo series at Newport, R.I. Tommy Hitchcock, Jr., is generally considered the greatest player of all time.   PATRICK CONNORS

See also WATER POLO.

MARCO POLO

Marco Polo, *center below,* left for the Orient with his father and uncle in 1271. Their journey from Venice to China was one of the longest overland trips made during the Middle Ages. The solid black line on the map, *right,* shows their overland route to China. The broken line marks their return trip, which lasted from 1292 to 1295.

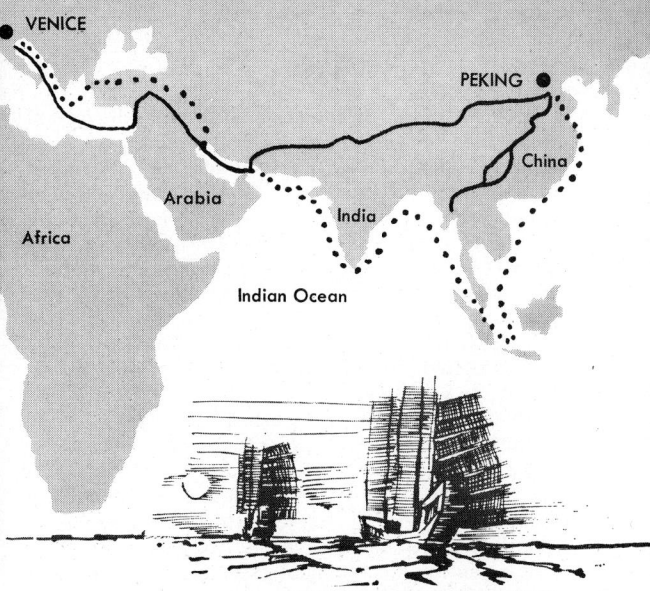

Greenlee Collection, Newberry Library

POLO, MARCO (1254?-1324?), an Italian traveler, became famous for his journeys in central Asia and China. His stories of his trips gave Europe the first real information about the Orient.

Polo was born in Venice. His father, Nicolò Polo, and his uncle, Maffeo Polo, were Venetian merchants. The brothers were not poor, but they could not afford to hire other men to do their buying and selling. So they became experienced travelers. They sailed throughout the eastern Mediterranean Sea area, and traded in Constantinople long before Marco was born. Once they traveled overland to *Cathay,* the name they gave to China. When they returned from a trip in 1269, they prepared for a much longer visit to Cathay. They decided to take Marco with them.

The Great Journey. In 1271, the three Polos set out by boat for Palestine. From there they traveled by caravan across Asia. Nicolò and Maffeo had been presented to the Mongol conqueror Kublai Khan on their earlier trip. This time, Kublai Khan was even more cordial when they reached his court at Peking. He had many tasks for men trained in Venetian commerce. He sent Marco on missions to many parts of China. Finally, in 1292, two years before Kublai Khan died, the Polos started on the trip home.

They reached Venice after being away for 24 years, and even their relatives scarcely recognized them. The Polos gave a great banquet. Many guests wondered if these men really had visited Cathay, and hoped there would be strange and wonderful gifts. All evening, the Polos kept changing from one set of silk robes to another. Then they proved their wealth by opening bags of jewels upon the table. Kublai Khan had given them gifts, but the Polos had exchanged them in Peking for rubies and emeralds, which were easier to carry.

The Book of Marco Polo. In 1298, Marco Polo was taken prisoner in a sea battle between Venice and Genoa. As a captive, he dictated to a French friend the story of his journey, published later as *The Book of Marco Polo.* He mentioned many strange customs of Cathay, such as the use of paper money. He told of wars that Kublai Khan fought against neighboring

islanders. These were the Japanese. The book became very popular in later years, and was translated into many languages. It inspired later explorers and discoverers, including Christopher Columbus. Many persons did not believe all the stories in the book. But historians have found that when Marco Polo described far-off places he had actually seen, he was a sharp observer with a good memory. FRANKLIN L. FORD

See also CATHAY; FAIRS AND EXPOSITIONS (Chinese Fairs); KUBLAI KHAN.

POLONAISE, POH *loh* NAYZ, is a dignified national dance of Poland which developed from the promenade.

POLONIUM, *poh* LOH *nee uhm,* is a radioactive metallic element belonging to the uranium decay series. Marie and Pierre Curie of France discovered the element in 1898. Polonium occurs naturally in pitchblende, as a decay product of radium. It is also produced artificially by bombarding bismuth with neutrons.

Polonium has the chemical symbol Po. Its atomic number is 84, and its most stable isotope has a mass number of 210. Polonium decays into an isotope of lead by giving off alpha rays. Polonium's half-life is about 138 days. J. GORDON PARR

POLTAVA, BATTLE OF. See ARMY (Famous Land Battles of History); CHARLES (XII).

POLTERGEIST. See FAIRY.

POLYANDRY. See MARRIAGE (Marriage Customs).

POLYBIUS, *poh* LIHB *ih us* (204?-122? B.C.), was a Greek historian. He is best known for his *Histories* which deal with the growth of the Roman Republic from 266 to 146 B.C. He pictured Rome sympathetically, and tried to make his fellow Greeks accept Roman rule. Of his 40 books, only five complete ones and selections from others remain in existence today.

Polybius was born in Megalopolis, Arcadia. As a young man, he held important political positions in his home city. After Rome conquered Macedonia in 168 B.C., he was taken as a prisoner to Rome. He later went on expeditions to Spain and Africa. Polybius helped Greece obtain favorable terms in a treaty with the Romans. C. BRADFORD WELLES

POLYBUS. See OEDIPUS.

POLYCARP, SAINT (A.D. 69?-155?), a disciple of John the Evangelist, became Bishop of Smyrna (now İzmir), Turkey. He was an important link between the Apostles and the Christian writers who came after him. An account of his martyrdom tells that when the proconsul directed him to curse Christ, Polycarp replied, "For 86 years I have been serving Him, and He has done no wrong to me. How then dare I blaspheme my King who has saved me?" WALTER J. BURGHARDT

POLYCLITUS. See GREECE, ANCIENT (Arts).

POLYCONIC PROJECTION. See MAP (Conic Projections).

POLYCOTYLEDON. See SEED (Kinds of Seeds).

POLYCRATES, *poh LICK ruh teez* (? -522 B.C.?), ruled the Greek island of Samos from about 540 to 520 B.C. He made Samos a center of the arts and built many public works, including an aqueduct and a temple to the goddess Hera. Polycrates built the strongest navy of that time and controlled the Aegean Sea. He made an alliance with King Amasis of Egypt. According to the Greek historian Herodotus, Amasis broke the alliance because he feared that jealousy over Polycrates' good fortune would anger the gods. To avoid the anger of the gods, Polycrates threw his most prized possession, a ring, into the sea. However, it came back to him inside a fish.

Polycrates survived a revolt by part of his navy, but the Persian governor lured him to the mainland of Asia Minor where he was murdered. DONALD W. BRADEEN

POLYCYTHEMIA. See BLOODLETTING.

POLYETHYLENE. See PLASTICS (Transparent Plastics).

POLYGAMY, *poh LIG uh mih*, can refer either to a system in which a man has more than one wife at a time, or, less commonly, to a system in which a woman has more than one husband at a time. The word *polygamy* comes from two Greek words meaning *many marriages*. Scholars use the term *polygyny* for the taking of more than one wife, and *polyandry* for the taking of more than one husband.

Polygyny is much more common than polyandry. Many peoples have practiced polygyny, and some still do, especially in Asia and Africa. The Moslem religion allows a man to have as many as four wives, and the Hindu religion sets no limit on the number of wives a man may have. The taking of many wives was once customary in China and Turkey, but those countries now have laws against the practice. In the United States, the Mormons practiced polygyny until 1890. Congress passed the first law forbidding polygyny in 1862.

The taking of more than one husband is common among primitive groups. It was permitted among the Todas of India and the Eskimos. Some groups in Tibet still practice it. JOHN W. WADE

See also MARRIAGE; MORMONS (Church Doctrines).

POLYGNOTUS, *pohl ihg NO tus* (475?-447? B.C.), a famous Greek artist, introduced many realistic elements of art in his paintings. His works were mainly tinted outlines traced upon a colored background, without shading or perspective. Among his paintings were *The Capture of Troy* and *The Descent of Odysseus into Hades*. Polygnotus was born on the island of Thasos.

POLYGON, *PAHL ih gahn*, is a plane figure bounded by straight lines.

The lines are called *sides*. The sum of the sides is the *perimeter*. The angles formed by the sides are the *angles* of the polygon, and the meeting points of the sides are the *vertices* of the polygon. A polygon with three sides is a triangle; with four sides, a quadrilateral; with five sides, a pentagon; with six, a hexagon; with eight, an octagon, and so on. See the separate articles in WORLD BOOK for each polygon, such as TRIANGLE.

If all the sides are equal, the polygon is *equilateral*. The polygon is *equiangular* if all the inside angles are equal. A polygon is *convex* if no side, when extended, enters the polygon.

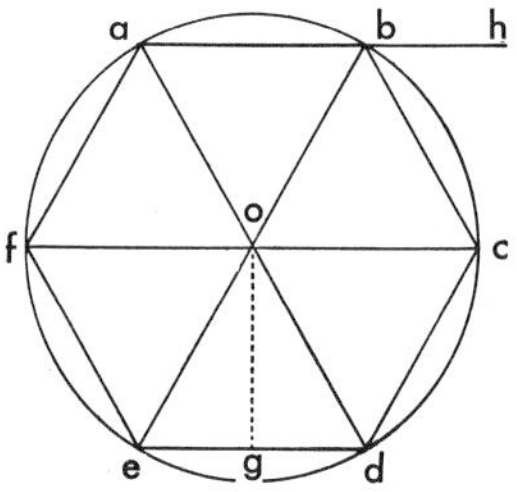

The angles inside the perimeter are called the *interior* angles. If the sides are extended, they form other angles outside the polygon that are called the *exterior* angles.

In the figure, the angle *abc* is an interior angle, and the angle *hbc* is an exterior angle.

The sum of the interior angles of a triangle is 180°, or two right angles. The sum of the interior angles of a quadrilateral is 360°, or four right angles. *The sum of the interior angles of any convex polygon is the number of sides minus 2, times two right angles.* Let n stand for the number of sides of any polygon, and s for the sum of its interior angles. Then

$$s = (n-2)\ 180°$$

The sum of the exterior angles of a polygon, taking one at each vertex, is four right angles, or 360°.

A regular polygon is both equilateral and equiangular. A regular polygon may be divided into congruent isosceles triangles. The area of each triangle is the product of its base and half its altitude. In the figure, the area of triangle *eod* is equal to

$$\frac{ed \times og}{2}$$

The area of the polygon equals the number of triangles times the area of each triangle. HARRY C. BARBER

POLYGRAPH. See LIE DETECTOR.

POLYGYNY. See POLYGAMY; MARRIAGE (Customs).

POLYHYMNIA. See MUSE.

POLYMER is a type of molecule formed when two or more molecules called *monomers* combine with each other. A polymer may contain thousands of monomers.

For example, the molecules of the gas ethylene are monomers. If these monomers are compressed, heated, and exposed to oxygen or peroxide, they *polymerize* (combine and form polymers). When this happens, the ethylene changes into *polyethylene*, a tough solid used in making many plastic articles. DAVID R. LIDE, JR.

See also MONOMER; POLYMERIZATION.

POLYMERIZATION, *PAHL ih mer ih ZAY shun*, is a chemical process important in the production of synthetic rubber, plastics, paints, and artificial fibers. In this process, molecules called *monomers* combine with each other to form larger molecules called *polymers*. If the monomers are alike, the process is called *homopolymerization*. If they are different, it is called *copolymerization*. Polystyrene is a solid plastic that results

polymerization

Polymerization takes place when single molecules called *monomers* combine to form chainlike molecules called *polymers*. Heat, pressure, or chemical treatment may be used to polymerize various substances, such as plastics, synthetic rubber, and petroleum products.

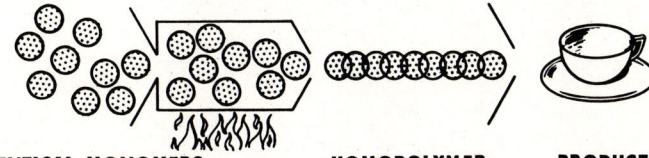

Homopolymerization occurs when identical monomers combine.

IDENTICAL MONOMERS   HOMOPOLYMER   PRODUCT

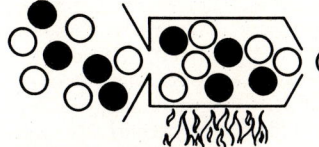 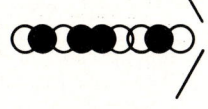 

DIFFERENT MONOMERS   COPOLYMER   PRODUCT

Copolymerization occurs when different monomers combine.

from the homopolymerization of the liquid hydrocarbon styrene. Styrene-butadiene rubber is made by copolymerizing styrene and butadiene.

Polymerization processes are also classified according to the way the chemical changes take place. In one kind, called *addition polymerization*, the process occurs in three steps. First, heat or light is used to break up a catalyst, such as a peroxide, into fragments called *free radicals*. Then the free radicals cause the monomers to add on to each other in long chains. Finally, the free radicals are destroyed, stopping the growth of the polymers.   JAMES S. FRITZ

See also MONOMER; PETROLEUM (Conversion).

POLYMORPHISM, *PAHL ih MAWR fiz'm*, is the occurrence of three or more distinct types of adults in a single species. *Polymorphism* means *many forms*. The honeybee is an example. There are three types of adults—queen, worker, and drone. Polymorphism is common among insects, jellyfish, bacteria, molds, and protozoa. Breeds and varieties of domesticated animals and plants are not examples of polymorphism.   NEAL D. BUFFALOE

POLYMYXIN. See ANTIBIOTIC (Kinds).

POLYNESIA. See PACIFIC ISLANDS.

POLYNICES. See ANTIGONE.

POLYNOMIAL. See ALGEBRA (Other Definitions).

POLYP, *PAHL ihp*, is the name for any coelenterate that lives attached to the stream or sea bottom. Examples of simple polyps are the fresh-water hydra and the sea anemone. The coral is a compound form of polyp.

Most polyps look like a hollow cylinder. The free end has a mouth surrounded by a circle of tentacles which reach out for food. Polyps most often form new animals by growing buds that break free. They also reproduce by dividing in half and by eggs. Some coelenterates develop in two different stages. In one stage they are polyps. The polyp stage produces a swimming stage called a *medusa*, or jellyfish. This stage produces polyps.   ROY WALDO MINER

See also COELENTERATE with its list of Related Articles.

POLYPHEMUS, *PAHL ih FEE mus*, was a one-eyed giant cannibal called a *Cyclops* in Homer's *Odyssey*. Ulysses and his men wandered into his cave. Polyphemus imprisoned the men and ate six of them. But Ulysses and the others made Polyphemus drunk on wine and put out his eye. Then they escaped from the cave. Polyphemus loved the nymph Galatea, but she ignored him because he was so ugly. He killed Acis, the boy whom Galatea loved.   JOSEPH FONTENROSE

See also CYCLOPS; GALATEA; ODYSSEY; ULYSSES.

POLYPHONY, *poh LIHF oh nih*, is a musical term. A polyphonic composition has several simultaneous, harmonizing parts. The parts are independent of each other and equally important. Although polyphonic music is mainly vocal, the term may also refer to instrumental works. The word *polyphony* comes from the Greek language and means *many-voiced*.

See also COUNTERPOINT.

POLYSTYRENE. See PLASTICS (Making Synthetic Resins; table, Kinds of Plastics).

POLYTECHNIC INSTITUTE OF BROOKLYN. See BROOKLYN, POLYTECHNIC INSTITUTE OF.

POLYTHEISM, *PAHL ih thee iz'm*, is a belief and worship of several gods, instead of belief in one God, which is called *monotheism*. Man very early learned to fear or to welcome the powers of nature. He regarded the sun, the moon, storms, seasons, and other forces as personal beings. Later he worshiped them as spirits and gods. One god usually became more important than the others. In time this led to monotheism. The Greeks and Romans developed an elaborate form of polytheism. Christianity and Islam followed Judaism in insisting that there is only one God.   A. EUSTACE HAYDON

POLYTONALITY. See MUSIC (The 1900's).

POMATO. See BURBANK, LUTHER.

POME, *pohm*, is the fleshy fruit of any plant of the rose family that has several leathery walled seed cases, or *carpels*. Apples, pears, and quince have five carpels. The calyx and stamens of pomes start above the carpels and are quite noticeable on mature fruits. The fleshy portion of the fruit that surrounds the core is called the *receptacle*. See also FRUIT.   ROY E. MARSHALL

POMEGRANATE, *PAHM GRAN it*, is the fruit of a plant that is raised in warm climates. The plant grows wild in western Asia and northwestern India. The pomegranate cannot stand low temperatures, so it is grown commercially in the United States only in the southern part of the country. The plant is bushlike when wild, but under cultivation it is trained to grow as a small tree. It reaches a height of 15 to 20 feet and bears many slender branches. Large scarlet flowers grow at the ends of the

USDA

Fruit of the Pomegranate is full of seeds, but the pulp has a refreshing taste and makes excellent cooling drinks.

branches. The fruit has a hard rind and looks somewhat like an orange. It is of a deep gold-red color. The fruit has many seeds. Each seed is inside a layer of crimson pulp which has a pleasant, refreshing taste.

The pulp of the fruit is used to make cooling drinks. The rind contains a large amount of tannic acid, which is used as medicine for contracting the skin, and is also valuable in tanning leather. The pomegranate was familiar to the Hebrews in Biblical times. A picture of the fruit appeared on the pillars of Solomon's Temple. In classic mythology, Proserpina was forced to spend six months of each year in Hades because she had eaten six seeds of the pomegranate while living with Pluto (see PROSERPINA).

Scientific Classification. Pomegranates make up the pomegranate family, *Punicaceae*. The cultivated pomegranate is genus *Punica*, species *P. granatum*. JULIAN C. CRANE

POMERANIA, *PAHM er AYN yuh,* or *PAHM er AY nih uh,* called POMMERN in German, was an old Prussian province in northern Germany. It was located south of the Baltic Sea and west of Poland. The area was 11,654 square miles.

Most of the land formerly occupied by Pomerania is flat, but there are low hills in the eastern part of the region. The low coast line is cut by many inlets, and there are several harbors along the Baltic Sea. The Oder River divided the country into two parts, called *Hither Pomerania* and *Farther Pomerania*. Stettin was the capital city. It lies in Poland on the banks of the Oder River.

After the Germanic Vandals, the Slavic Wends occupied Pomerania. They intermarried with the Germans and by the 1600's had lost their identity. Most of Farther Pomerania became part of Brandenburg after the Treaty of Westphalia in 1648, and the rest of Pomerania went to Sweden. In 1720, Prussia regained some parts of Swedish Pomerania. In 1815, all Pomerania came under Prussian control. After World War II, the eastern and central parts of the province became Polish territory, and western Pomerania was taken into Russian-dominated East Germany. JAMES K. POLLOCK

POMERANIAN is the name of a small dog related to the chow, the spitz dog, and the Siberian husky. It is a member of the *lupine* family, whose members are closer relatives of the wolf than other dogs. The Pomeranian weighs between 3 and 7 pounds, and has a sharp-nosed foxlike face, and small pointed ears. It may be almost any color from black to white, or even orange. It has a soft, fluffy undercoat and a long, thick topcoat with a frill around its neck. Its tail is also thickly covered with hair, and curls up over its back. The dog has a sharp bark. JOSEPHINE Z. RINE

See also DOG (color picture, Toy Dogs).

POMO INDIANS were a group of tribes famous for their excellent basketry. The Pomo differed from other tribes of the California area where they lived, because men as well as women worked on these baskets. The Pomo surpassed other Indians in their use of feathers and shell beads to decorate their baskets, and in the variety of their design patterns.

The Pomo once occupied almost all the Russian River valley of what is now northwestern California. Their simple way of life resembled that of other tribes of the area (see INDIAN, AMERICAN [California-Intermountain Indians]). In addition to their homes, the Pomo built dance houses for religious ceremonies. They also built small sweat houses of reeds and bark. Inside, the Indians sprinkled water over a pile of hot stones to produce steam. Here the men took daily steam baths, slept, and often spent much of the winter.

Today, most Pomo live as farmers on or near their reservation at Clear Lake, Calif. CHARLES E. DIBBLE

POMOLOGY. See HORTICULTURE.

POMONA, *poh MOH nuh,* was a goddess of fruit and trees in Roman mythology. Vertumnus loved her, but she would not accept him. He dressed like an old woman, went into her garden, and talked to her about love. When Pomona admitted she loved Vertumnus, he threw off his disguise and she consented to marry him.

POMONA, Calif. (pop. 67,157; alt. 855 ft.), is an industrial city 28 miles east of Los Angeles. Its factories produce aircraft and aircraft parts, light machine goods, missiles, pumps, and tile. The Los Angeles County Fair is held in Pomona each September. The city was incorporated in 1888. It has a council-manager government. For location, see CALIFORNIA (political map). GEORGE SHAFTEL

POMONA COLLEGE is a private, coeducational school at Claremont, Calif. Courses in arts and sciences lead to the bachelor's degree. Pomona, founded in 1887, is noted for its large herbarium. There is an ROTC unit on campus. For enrollment, see UNIVERSITIES AND COLLEGES (table).

POMONA GLASS. See GLASSWARE.

POMPADOUR. See HAIRDRESSING.

POMPADOUR, MARQUISE DE (1721-1764), JEANNE ANTOINETTE POISSON, was a mistress of King Louis XV of France. Madame de Pompadour played an important part in the politics of Louis' reign. She probably was responsible for the alliance between France and Austria in the Seven Years' War in 1756. Madame de Pompadour kept her influence over the king long after his love for her had cooled. She entertained him and held her political power by serving as his secretary.

She was born in Paris, a

Madame de Pompadour
Brown Bros.

member of a middle-class family. She received an excellent education and was introduced to high society at the home of a wealthy financier. In 1741, she married Lenormand d'Étoiles, the nephew of this financier. Five years later, she met King Louis at a masked ball. Louis fell in love with her, and she went to live in Versailles as his mistress. She received the title of the Marquise de Pompadour. She lived in Versailles for the rest of her life.   RICHARD M. BRACE

See also LOUIS (XV).

POMPANO, *PAHM puh no*, is the name of a group of valuable food fishes. Several kinds of pompanos are found in the salt waters around North and South America. The *common pompano*, or *butterfish*, lives in the oceans along the Atlantic coast of the United States. It

The Jack Pompano is the game fish of the pompano family. It often reaches a weight of 20 pounds.

is also found in the seas from the West Indies to Brazil. This fish is about a foot and a half long. The average weight is 7 or 8 pounds. It is colored bluish above and silvery or slightly golden underneath. The breast is yellowish. The body is oblong and flattened. The flesh of the pompano is highly prized for its rich and delicate flavor. Large numbers are caught in nets. Many of these are taken on the Florida coasts. The pompano rarely takes a hook.

Another species is the *round pompano*, which lives as

far north as Cape Cod. It reaches a foot or more in length, and weighs about 3 pounds. It is a good food fish. The largest of the pompano group is the *great pompano*, or *permit*. The great pompano often grows 3 feet long, and weighs about 30 pounds. It lives in the seas from Florida to the West Indies. The great pompano also is an excellent food fish.

Scientific Classification. The pompanos belong to the family *Carangidae*. The common pompano is genus *Trachinotus*, species *T. carolinus*. The round pompano is *T. falcatus*. The great pompano is *T. goodei*. LEONARD P. SCHULTZ

POMPEII, *pahm PA ye*, was an ancient city in Italy which disappeared after the eruption of Mount Vesuvius in A.D. 79. For hundreds of years the city lay buried under cinders, ashes, and stone. Since Pompeii was rediscovered, much has been learned about its history. Each year excavations bring forth additional bits of ancient art and architecture. Much also has been learned about the everyday life of the ancient Romans, and about their manners and customs.

Early Days. Pompeii was not a remarkable city. But it has become better known than many of the wealthier Roman towns because its ruins were so well preserved. Pompeii lay on a plateau of ancient lava near the Bay of Naples, less than a mile from the foot of Mount Vesuvius. For location, see ITALY (physical map). The city was closely connected with the ancient history of Campania, a region below Rome along the gulfs of Naples and Salerno. Scholars believe that the original inhabitants of Pompeii belonged to an Italic tribe from the region. They founded the city during the 700's B.C. The area later came under the influence of Greek colonies along the coast, and the primitive village developed into a town with paved streets and public buildings constructed in the Greek style. Etruscan influence appears in temples, in some private houses, and in the street-plan of the town. Pompeii became a Roman community in 91 B.C.

Pompeii was built in the form of an oval about two miles around. A great wall with eight gates surrounded the city. The streets crossed each other at right angles,

Sawders

The Ruins of Pompeii include the remains of the home of a nobleman, Cornelius Rufus. The rooms are grouped around an *atrium*, or reception hall. A pool lies in its center. Other visible portions of the house include a statue, columns, and parts of the walls.

Mount Vesuvius looms in the background over the once-thriving city of Pompeii. The cinders and hot, wet ashes which buried the city aided in preserving its ruins intact for almost 2,000 years.

More than half of the city has been uncovered. Visitors may see remains of the amphitheater, several temples, streets, public baths, villas, and the ancient public square, or forum.

and were paved with blocks of lava. Ancient wheel ruts may still be seen in the pavements. In the center of the city was the open square, or forum. It was surrounded by a group of important buildings. There were also two theaters, a gladiators' court, many temples, and several large public baths. The fair blue skies of Pompeii attracted many wealthy Romans. They built great *villas* (homes) near the shore of the Mediterranean, where they might enjoy the mild, sunny climate. The Pompeians built their villas with all the conveniences of a town in country surroundings. The large dwellings often consisted of two parts, the master's house and gardens, and the farmer's house with stables, barns, orchards, and fields. Most dwellings were constructed along the lines of a typical Roman house, with rooms grouped around the *atrium* (reception room). Town houses in Pompeii often had shops bordering the street. Archaeologists believe that most of the buildings had more than one story. The upper parts may have been constructed partly of wood. They projected out over the street, like French and English houses of the Middle Ages. See ROMAN EMPIRE (color picture: A Roman House).

Pompeii carried on a prosperous trade in wine, oil, and breadstuffs. It was a market for the produce of a rich countryside, and its port had wide connections in the Mediterranean area. Pompeii was also an industrial center, and produced certain specialties, such as millstones, fish sauce, perfumes, and cloth. Its inhabitants

included wealthy landowners, prosperous merchants and manufacturers, tradesmen, craftsmen, artisans, and slaves.

The Eruption of Mount Vesuvius in A.D. 63 damaged Pompeii, Naples, and Herculaneum. Statues fell, columns were broken, and some buildings collapsed. However, the people did not believe there would be more danger, and they repaired their cities and continued plowing and planting the rich soil formed from lava. In the summer of A.D. 79, Vesuvius erupted suddenly and with great violence. Streams of lava and mud poured into Herculaneum, and filled the town and its harbor. But the people had time to escape.

Hot ashes, stones, and cinders rained down on Pompeii. The darkened air was filled with poisonous gas and fumes. The Roman writer Pliny the Younger told in a letter how he led his mother to safety through the deadly fumes and falling stones. Pliny the Elder, another Roman writer, commanded a fleet that rescued some people. He landed to view the eruption, and died on the shore.

About 2,000 persons out of a population of some 20,000 were killed in Pompeii. Some were trapped in their homes and killed by hot ashes. Others breathed the poisonous fumes and died as they fled. Archaeologists find the *shells* (molds) of the bodies preserved in the hardened ash. By carefully pouring plaster into the shells, they can make a detailed copy of the individual, even to the expression of agony on his face.

A Bronze Bathtub excavated from the ruins of Pompeii is surprisingly modern in its design. The tub shows skilled Pompeiian craftsmanship.

Highly Polished Metal served as a mirror.

A Bronze Pitcher illustrates the Pompeiians' artistic skill.

"Beware the Dog" says the legend on this ancient floor mosaic.

Oil Was Burned in this old Pompeiian bronze lantern.

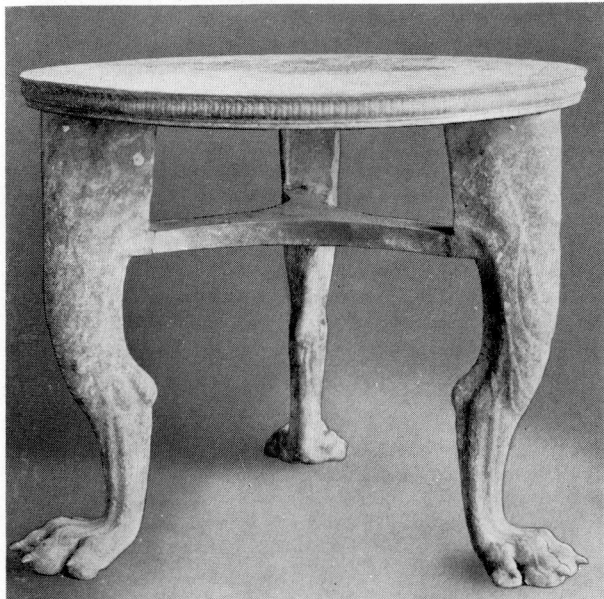

Because Bronze Was Easy to Mold it was used for many purposes in ancient times. This is a 3-legged lion-footed bronze table.

Field Museum of Natural History

A Blue Glass Wine Vessel found in Pompeii shows that glass blowing was a well-developed art in the ancient city.

POMPEII

Rather than the lava, showers of hot, wet ashes and cinders sprayed Pompeii. When these dried, they covered and sealed up much of the city. Only the tops of walls and columns emerged above the waste. Survivors dug out valuables they had left behind, and even took statues, marbles, and bronzes. But later eruptions and erosion erased the last traces of the city.

The eruption of Vesuvius destroyed not only Pompeii but also the nearby cities of Stabiae and Herculaneum (see HERCULANEUM). It changed the entire geography of the Campania region around Pompeii. It turned the Sarno River back from its course, and raised the sea beach so that there was no way of locating the site of the buried city. Pompeii lay beneath the ash deposits for almost 1,700 years.

Excavations. The buried city was not completely forgotten. Peasants living in the area searched for hidden treasure. They did not excavate openly, but they tunneled into the deposits, and reached houses. In the 1500's, workers digging an underground tunnel to change the course of the Sarno River discovered parts of the amphitheater, forum, and a temple. But no one paid much attention to these finds.

In 1748, a peasant was digging in a vineyard and struck a buried wall. His discovery came to the attention of authorities in Italy, and soon men began to carry on excavations in the region. At first, the diggers hoped to recover objects to enrich the museums of the kings of the Two Sicilies. For about 100 years, the search concentrated on important buildings, such as the forum, theaters, and larger houses.

After 1860, Giuseppe Fiorelli served as director of the excavations. He instituted the first systematic uncovering of the whole city block by block. About 50 years ago, archaeologists decided not to remove treasures from the city, but to keep them and to restore buildings as much as possible to their original condition. The Italian government has given money for this work.

Remains. More than half of the buried city of Pompeii has now been uncovered. A visitor may see buildings as they stood almost 2,000 years ago. He may walk in and out of houses and up and down narrow lanes, just as the Pompeians did in their day. He may see the ruins of the ancient public square, with many of the surrounding buildings. He may see the famous old Temple of Jupiter, which was an ancient ruin at the time of the eruption. He may wander through the old Roman public halls, and admire the beautiful temples of Apollo and Fortuna Augusta.

Workers have uncovered a large part of the city wall. The disaster occurred during a local election campaign. Election slogans can still be seen on the walls of houses. Not many valuables have been found. Historians believe that the Pompeians carried many of their possessions with them as they fled from the city. Workmen have found bracelets, earrings, gems, and coins. They have also discovered household statues of silver, bronze, and ivory, as well as utensils of metal and glass. Many domestic treasures came to light near Boscoreale, a town near Naples. Thousands of Pompeian objects are on display in the National Museum at Naples, about 13 miles from Pompeii. MARY FRANCIS GYLES

See also VESUVIUS.

POMPEY THE GREAT (106-48 B.C.) was an outstanding Roman general and statesman. He was the last obstacle in Julius Caesar's rise to power.

Pompey was born in Rome, the son of a prominent nobleman. He grew up during the war between Gaius Marius and Lucius Sulla, and in 83 B.C. raised his own army of three legions to help the aristocrat Sulla against the forces of Marius in Italy. Then he wiped out the supporters of Marius in Sicily and Italy.

When Sulla died in 78 B.C., the consul Marcus Lepidus tried to repeal his conservative reforms. But Pompey opposed him and drove him out of Italy. The senate then sent Pompey to Spain to put down an army of Marius' supporters led by Sertorius. After Sertorius was murdered by his own men, Pompey won an easy victory and returned to Rome in 71 B.C.

The conservative group in Rome did not wish to see Pompey gain further glory, but he was elected consul in 70 B.C. He broke with the conservatives and restored the powers of the tribunes that Sulla had taken away. Through popular support, Pompey was given the task, in 67 B.C., of clearing the Mediterranean Sea of pirates. In 66 B.C., he fought Mithridates of Pontus. Pompey defeated him and conquered eastern Asia Minor, Syria, and Palestine.

Visual Education Service

Pompey the Great

The senate refused to approve his acts in Asia and his promises of land to his troops. So Pompey, Julius Caesar, and Marcus Crassus formed the First Triumvirate in 60 B.C. (see TRIUMVIRATE). They worked together against the senate for several years. But Pompey became fearful of Caesar's ever-increasing power, and turned back to the conservatives. In the resulting civil war, Pompey was defeated in Italy and again at Pharsalus in Thessaly in 48 B.C. He escaped to Egypt, but was killed there by order of the Roman-dominated Egyptian government. CHESTER G. STARR

See also CAESAR, GAIUS JULIUS; CRASSUS, MARCUS LICINIUS; MITHRIDATES; SULLA, LUCIUS CORNELIUS.

PONAPE, *POH nuh PAY* (pop. 11,998), is the largest island of the eastern Caroline Islands. It lies in the western Pacific Ocean, 750 miles southeast of Guam. Ponape has an area of 129 square miles. The island is volcanic rock surrounded by coral reefs. For location, see PACIFIC ISLANDS (color map).

The shores of Ponape are mangrove swamps. Firm ground with rich vegetation lies inland. Mountains rise over 2,300 feet. Crops raised on the island include coconuts, taros, bananas, breadfruit, and limes. Ponape is famous for its fine yams. The climate is moist and hot, with heavy rainfall between June and September.

Germany bought Ponape from Spain in 1899. Japan, an enemy of Germany during World War I, occupied Ponape in 1914. The Treaty of Versailles gave it to Japan in 1920. During World War II, Japan used the island as an air base. After the war, Japan surrendered it to the Allies. The United States now controls Ponape under a United Nations trusteeship. EDWIN H. BRYAN, JR.

PONCE, *PAWN say* (pop. 114,286; met. area 145,586; alt. 18 ft.), is the second largest city in Puerto Rico. It lies near the south coast, a little west of the middle of the island. For location, see PUERTO RICO (political map). The docks of Ponce take care of a large part of the island's exports and imports. They are at Playa Ponce, nearly four miles from Ponce.   JAIME BENÍTEZ

PONCE DE LEÓN, *PAWN thay day lay AWN,* **JUAN** (1460?-1521), was a Spanish explorer and conqueror. He conquered Puerto Rico and explored Florida, which he claimed for the Spanish government.

Ponce de León was born in San Servos, Spain. After serving in the final Spanish war against the Moors, he sailed in 1493 on Christopher Columbus' second voyage to America. He conquered Puerto Rico in 1508 and 1509, and became governor of the island in 1509.

But his ambitions were not satisfied. Indians told Ponce de León of an island named Bimini, where there was a marvelous fountain that could restore youth to old persons. The Indians were actually repeating a European legend that they had heard from the white men. In the medieval lore of Europe, this fountain was the Water of Life, found in the Garden of Eden, which was supposed to be in the Far East. The early Spaniards in America thought America was the Far East.

Ponce de León went with a sea expedition to find Bimini. On March 27, 1513, he sighted an island, and on April 2, he reached the North American mainland. He named the area *Florida,* which in Spanish means *full of flowers,* because of the many flowers he saw there. He explored much of the Florida coast, but he did not find a fountain. He then returned to Puerto Rico.

Eight years later, he led an expedition to colonize Florida. He failed in his effort to found a colony, and received a severe wound in a battle with Indians. He died of his injury in Cuba.   CHARLES E. NOWELL

See also FLORIDA (Exploration and Spanish Settlement); FOUNTAIN OF YOUTH.

Ponce de León drank water from every spring he came upon while exploring Florida, hoping that he would discover the legendary Fountain of Youth.
Brown Bros.

PONCHO. See LATIN AMERICA (Clothing); BOLIVIA (Way of Life); CAMPING (Clothing); ECUADOR (Way of Life); PERU (Way of Life).

POND. See LAKE. For plant and animal life found in and around ponds see ALGAE; BEAVER; CRAYFISH; DRAGONFLY; FROG; MOSQUITO; SALAMANDER; SNAIL; WATER BEETLE; WATER BUG; WATER FLEA; WATER PLANT.

POND LILY. See WATER LILY.

PONDICHERRY. See INDIA (The New Republic; political map).

PONDWEED is a plant that grows in water, especially calm water. Pondweeds have small, hard-to-see flowers that stand above the water. They often have two kinds of leaves. Firm, broad leaves float on top of the water; soft, narrow leaves are under the surface of the water. Pondweeds are found throughout the world.

Scientific Classification. Pondweeds belong to the pondweed family, *Potamogetonaceae.* They make up the genus *Potamogeton.*   ARTHUR CRONQUIST

PONIARD. See DAGGER.

PONS, *pahnz,* or *pawns,* **LILY** (1904-   ), a coloratura soprano, started her career as a pianist but became a singer instead. She made her American operatic debut in 1931 in Gaetano Donizetti's *Lucia di Lammermoor* at the Metropolitan Opera House in New York City. She also sang leading roles in such operas as *Lakmé, Rigoletto, Mignon,* and *The Magic Flute.* In 1956, the Metropolitan Opera held a special celebration to honor her 25th season with that company.

Lily Pons was born at Cannes, in southern France. She entered the Paris Conservatory at the age of 13 to study piano. She did not begin to study voice until she was 21. In 1940, she became a citizen of the United States.   MARTIAL SINGHER

PONSELLE, ROSA MELBA (1897-   ), is an American dramatic soprano. Her singing won acclaim for its outstanding beauty and richness of tone. She made her debut with the Metropolitan Opera in New York City in 1918, singing the role of Leonora in Giuseppe Verdi's *La Forza del Destino.* She remained a leading soprano with the Metropolitan until 1936. Miss Ponselle also sang at Covent Garden in London and in the principal opera houses of Italy. She became famous for her recital and orchestra appearances. Many of her recordings have become collectors' items. Miss Ponselle was born in Meriden, Conn. Enrico Caruso sponsored her Metropolitan Opera debut.   DANIEL A. HARRIS

PONT DU GARD. See AQUEDUCT (Ancient Aqueducts).

PONTA DELGADA (pop. 22,316; alt. 118 ft.) is the most important city and port of the Portuguese Azores. Volcanic craters, gardens, and lakes make Ponta Delgada attractive. Beet-sugar manufacturing is an important industry. The city is on São Miguel Island. See also AZORES; SÃO MIGUEL ISLAND.

PONTCHARTRAIN, LAKE. See LAKE PONTCHARTRAIN.

PONTIAC, *PAHN tih ack* (1720?-1769), an American Indian chief, helped the French troops against the English in the French and Indian War of 1754. Pontiac is considered one of the best organizers of American Indian tribes.

The American historian, Francis Parkman, wrote

that Pontiac's mother was a Chippewa Indian. Pontiac was born in northern Ohio. He became leader of the united tribes of the Chippewa, Potawatomi, and Ottawa Indians. Parkman's famous classic, *History of the Conspiracy of Pontiac*, deals with the struggle between England and France for control of North America.

Although Pontiac was friendly toward the English at first, he became angry in 1760 when they advanced into his territory. During the next two years, he organized "The Conspiracy of Pontiac" among the Indians. It is said that the conspiracy included all the Indian tribes in the Mississippi Valley.

In May, 1763, Pontiac struck. He captured eight frontier forts and killed several hundred settlers and soldiers. He laid siege to Detroit until November, 1763, but he could not capture it. The French and English declared peace late in 1763, and the French stopped helping the Indians. Pontiac, defeated and discredited, was forced to withdraw to Ohio, and his conspiracy came to an end.

Facts about Pontiac's death are obscure. He was killed in Illinois, supposedly by an Indian of the Kaskaskia tribe.   WILLIAM H. GILBERT

PONTIAC, Mich. (pop. 82,233; alt. 930 ft.), once was an important center for the manufacture of wagons and buggies. Today, thousands of automobiles roll off the assembly lines of Pontiac's large automobile fac-

Chief Pontiac greeted the British Major Robert Rogers with friendship in the early 1760's, but later organized and led a great Indian movement against the British settlers in America.

From a mural by Charles Yardley Turner, Bettmann Archive

tories. The city was named for the famous American Indian chief, Pontiac.

The city lies on the Clinton River in southeastern Michigan, about 26 miles northwest of Detroit. These two automobile cities are connected by the Wider Woodward Highway. For location, see MICHIGAN (political map).

Pontiac covers about 20 square miles of wooded hills. Around the city, fine hunting areas and many spring-water lakes provide good fishing. Eleven state parks are nearby. Large country estates have been built in the vicinity of Pontiac.

Cranbrook Institutions in nearby Bloomfield Hills include Cranbrook School for Boys, Kingswood School for Girls, Brookside Day School, the Academy of Arts, the Institute of Sciences, and Christ Church. Saint Mary's College, a theological school for men, is at Orchard Lake, five miles to the west. Oakland University is also nearby.

Several plants of the General Motors Corporation provide the chief industry of Pontiac. They make automobiles and automobile parts, trucks, buses, and airplanes. Rubber goods, paints and varnishes, brick and clay products, iron products and machine shop tools, and industrial police equipment are also made there.

The region was settled in 1818. It was incorporated as a village in 1837, and received a city charter in 1861. The city of Pontiac has a commission-manager form of government.   WILLIS F. DUNBAR

PONTIFEX, *PON tih feks,* was a member of the board of officials that supervised the religious activities of ancient Rome. The board determined when religious holidays and ceremonies would take place. Romans consulted the board to learn whether planned activities followed sacred law. The *pontifex maximus,* the highest religious authority, headed the board. The emperor later held this position.

Pontifices were appointed for life. The king appointed them in early Rome. In the later years of the republic, members were nominated by the board and elected by an assembly. The board originally had four members. By the 40's B.C., it had 16.   FRANK C. BOURNE

PONTIFF. See POPE.

PONTINE MARSHES is a swamp area in Italy that covers about 175,000 acres below Rome between Cisterna and Terracina. For centuries, the Pontine Marshes were responsible for widespread malaria epidemics in central Italy. The early Roman emperors, and later Pope Sixtus V, drained the parts above sea level by digging drainage canals. In the 1930's, Benito Mussolini had the rest of the marshes drained by a system of dikes and pumps. In addition to getting rid of the malaria menace, drainage of this area made available many acres of rich farm land. Grain and various other agricultural products now are grown in the Pontine region. Cattle and sheep are also raised in this area. Towns built on this reclaimed land include Latina, Aprilia, Pomezia, Pontinia, and Sabaudia. GEORGE KISH

PONTIUS PILATE. See PILATE, PONTIUS.

PONTOON BRIDGE is a bridge supported by *pontoons* (flat-bottomed boats), metal cylinders, or other portable floats. A pontoon bridge is sometimes called a *ponton* bridge. A flooring of timber is usually laid across a pontoon bridge. Pontoon bridges are especially important during wartime. These bridges are built to replace

U.S. Signal Corps

Army Engineers Construct a Pontoon Bridge across the Moselle River in France. By placing the boatlike floats very close together, engineers make the bridge strong enough to support heavy loads such as tanks and big guns.

those that have been destroyed by enemy forces. Special pontoon-laying troops bridge streams with mechanical exactness, even under fire. The soldiers lay the flooring, section by section, fastening it securely to the pontoons. Pontoon bridges are usually of limited strength, although sufficient to carry ordinary road vehicles. Soldiers must break step in crossing them to prevent the swaying of the bridge caused by marching in time.

The importance of pontoon-bridge building was shown on all European fronts during World War II. Retreating troops blew up many bridges across important rivers. Engineers of pursuing armies built pontoon bridges, permitting troops and mechanized equipment to cross. In the United States, pontoons have been used for permanent bridges in places where deep water makes pier construction too expensive. Three large concrete floating bridges have been built in Washington. One of these has the longest floating span in North America. This span stretches 7,758 feet across Lake Washington. R. G. Hennes

See also BRIDGE (picture: Pontoon Bridge); ROMAN EMPIRE (color picture: The Roman Army).

PONTOPPIDAN, *pawn TAWP ee dahn,* **HENRIK** (1857-1943), a Danish novelist and short-story writer, shared the 1917 Nobel prize in literature. The long novels *The Promised Land* (1891-1895), *Lucky Per* (1898-1904), and *The Realm of the Dead* (1912-1916) are among his masterpieces. These novels are realistic, giving a penetrating, unflattering, and often somber picture of contemporary Danish society. Pontoppidan was concerned with the problems of individual honesty and of finding one's own personality. He was born in Fredericia, Jutland. EINAR HAUGEN

PONTUS was the name of an ancient area on the south shore of the Black Sea in Asia Minor. Pontus reached its greatest importance under King Mithridates VI (120?-63 B.C.). At that time, it included other nearby areas in what is now Turkey, and lands north of the Black Sea in what is now southern Russia. Mithridates fought three wars against Rome. After the last one, in 63 B.C., the victorious Roman general Pompey divided Pontus into two parts. One part was combined with the Roman province of Bithynia. The other became the Roman province of Pontus. HENRY C. BOREN

See also MITHRIDATES VI.

PONTUS EUXINUS. See BLACK SEA.

PONY. See HORSE (Ponies); SHETLAND PONY.

PONY EXPRESS. Daring horseback riders of the pony express once carried United States mail between St. Joseph, Mo., and Sacramento, Calif. The mail then was taken by steamer to San Francisco, Calif. The service began on April 3, 1860. Its promoters meant to prove that the central route followed by the pony express was better than the longer southern route used by the stagecoaches of the Butterfield Overland Mail. Senator William M. Gwin of California was the chief promoter of the pony express. A freight firm, known as Russell, Majors, and Waddell, backed the project.

The pony express route followed the well-known Oregon-California Trail, along the Platte River in Nebraska, through South Pass in Wyoming. At Fort Bridger, Wyo., the riders left the emigrant trail, swung to the south of the Great Salt Lake, and then headed due west across the salt desert to the Sierra Nevada mountains at Carson City, Nev. This route saved over 100 miles. Relay stations stood 10 to 15 miles apart along the route. Lonely keepers watched the stations and took care of the ponies.

Young pony express riders rode at top speed from one station to the next. As the rider approached the station, the keeper brought out a fresh horse, which was saddled and ready to travel. The rider jumped from his horse,

583

A **Pony Express Rider** switches to a fresh mount and begins to carry the mail on another step of his dangerous dash across the West.

Detail of a painting by Frederic Remington, Gilcrease Museum, Tulsa, Okla.

grabbed the mail bags, and was on his way again in two minutes' time. Usually each man rode 75 miles. But if a rider could not carry the mail, the first rider kept going. There were about 190 stations, 400 station keepers and assistants, over 400 horses, and 80 riders.

Pony express riders earned from $100 to $150 a month, high wages for the time. Riders usually carried only two revolvers and a knife to defend themselves against attacks by Indians and bandits. They rode day and night in all kinds of weather. The mail was lost only once in all the 650,000 miles ridden by the pony express.

Riders carried the mail in leather, rainproof pouches, strapped to the front and back of the saddle. The postage rate, at first $5 a half ounce, was later changed to $1. The mail never weighed over 20 pounds.

The first pony express trip took 10 days to cover the distance of 1,966 miles. Later trips were made in eight or nine days. This was 12 or 14 days shorter than the time required by the Overland Mail. Once the mail was carried from Fort Kearny, Nebr., to Fort Churchill, Nev., in six days, a record. The rider on this trip carried the news of Abraham Lincoln's election in November, 1860. On short stretches, riders occasionally made a speed of 25 miles an hour. Nearly 250 miles a day was the normal speed.

The pony express ended on Oct. 24, 1861. There was no need for it, because the telegraph now stretched from coast to coast. The promoters of the pony express were ruined financially. W. TURRENTINE JACKSON

See also WESTERN FRONTIER LIFE (Communication).

POODLE, *POO d'l,* is one of a breed of smart, friendly house dogs. The poodle was once used as a hunter and retriever, but it is no longer classed as a field dog. The poodle originated in Germany in the 1500's. Today, it is found throughout Europe and North America. Poodles may be colored white, black, gray, blue, brown, or apricot. Their hair is curly or frizzy, with a topknot on the head and a pompon on the tail. The three varieties of poodles are classified by shoulder height. The *toy* is 10 inches or under; the *miniature* is from 10 to 15 inches; and the *standard* is over 15 inches. Poodles range in weight from 3 to 60 pounds. JOSEPHINE Z. RINE

See also DOG (color picture: Nonsporting Dogs).

POOL. See BILLIARDS (How to Play Pocket Billiards).
POOL. See TRUST.
POOLE, ERNEST (1880-1950), was an American novelist, playwright, and short-story writer. He won a Pulitzer prize in 1918 for *His Family,* a novel set in New York City. He also wrote the best seller *The Harbor* (1915) about labor-management conflicts on the New York City docks. His plays include *None So Blind* and *A Man's Friends.* Poole was born in Chicago, and was graduated from Princeton University. HARRY H. CLARK

POONA, *POO nuh* (pop. 806,351; met. area 824,243; alt. 1,720 ft.) is the second largest city in the state of Mahārāshtra, India. See INDIA (political map). Poona, which lies in the hills, is the summer headquarters of the Mahārāshtra government. It is the site of Deccan University, Fergusson College, the Bhandarkar Oriental Research Institute, and the Deccan Education Society. Cotton, penicillin, and sugar are chief industries. Dairying is important to the area. ROBERT I. CRANE

POOR CLARES, ORDER OF. See FRANCISCAN.
POOR PEOPLE'S CAMPAIGN. See NEGRO (Continuing Problems).
POOR RELIEF. See RELIEF (in economics); POVERTY.

Curly Coated Poodles Are Intelligent, Friendly Dogs.
Marcellia Harris

584

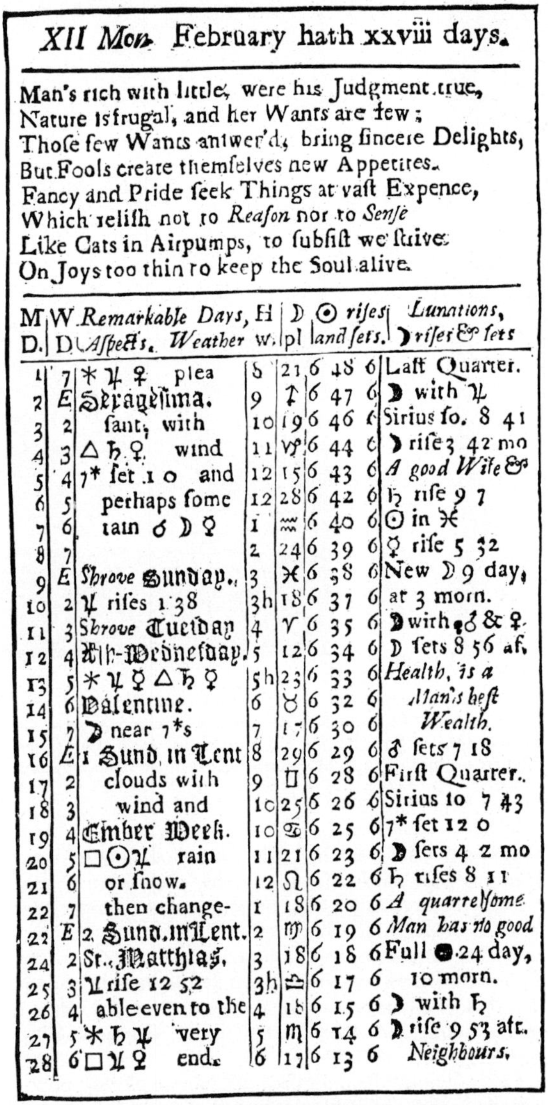

XII Mon. February hath xxviii days.

Man's rich with little, were his Judgment true,
Nature is frugal, and her Wants are few;
Thoſe few Wants anſwer'd, bring ſincere Delights,
But Fools create themſelves new Appetites.
Fancy and Pride ſeek Things at vaſt Expence,
Which relish not to *Reaſon* nor to *Senſe*
Like Cats in Airpumps, to ſubſiſt we ſtrive
On Joys too thin to keep the Soul alive.

M. D.	W. D.	*Remarkable Days, Aſpects, Weather*	H w.	☽ pl	☉ *riſes and ſets.*		*Lunations,* ☽ *riſes & ſets*
1	7	✱ ♃ ♀ plea	8	21	6 48	6	Laſt Quarter.
2	E	Sexageſima.	9	♐	6 47	6	☽ with ♃
3	2	ſant, with	10	19	6 46	6	Sirius ſo. 8 41
4	3	△ ♄ ♀ wind	11	♑	6 44	6	☽ riſe 3 42 mo
5	4	7* ſet 1 0 and	12	15	6 43	6	*A good Wife &*
6	5	perhaps ſome	12	28	6 42	6	♄ riſe 9 7
7	6	rain ☌ ☽ ☿	1	♒	6 40	6	☉ in ♓
8	7		2	24	6 39	6	☿ riſe 5 32
9	E	*Shrove* Sunday.	3	♓	6 38	6	New ☽ 9 day,
10	2	♃ riſes 1 38	3h	18	6 37	6	at 3 morn.
11	3	*Shrove* Tueſday	4	♈	6 35	6	☽ with ♂ & ♀
12	4	Aſh-Wedneſday.	5	12	6 34	6	☽ ſets 8 56 af.
13	5	✱ ♃ ☿ △ ♄ ♀	5h	23	6 33	6	*Health, is a*
14	6	Valentine.	6	♉	6 32	6	*Man's beſt*
15	7	☽ near 7*s	7	17	6 30	6	*Wealth.*
16	E	1 Sund. in Lent	8	29	6 29	6	♂ ſets 7 18
17	2	clouds with	9	♊	6 28	6	Firſt Quarter.
18	3	wind and	10	25	6 26	6	Sirius ſo 7 43
19	4	Ember Week.	10	♋	6 25	6	7* ſet 12 0
20	5	□ ☉ ♃ rain	11	21	6 23	6	☽ ſets 4 2 mo
21	6	or ſnow.	12	♌	6 22	6	♄ riſes 8 11
22	7	then change-	1	18	6 20	6	*A quarrelſome*
23	E	2 Sund. in Lent.	2	♍	6 19	6	*Man has no good*
24	2	St. Matthias.	3	18	6 18	6	Full ☽ 24 day,
25	3	♃ riſe 12 52	3h	♎	6 17	6	10 morn.
26	4	able even to the	4	18	6 15	6	☽ with ♄
27	5	✱ ♄ ♃ very	5	♏	6 14	6	☽ riſe 9 53 aft.
28	6	□ ♃ ♀ end.	6	17	6 13	6	*Neighbours.*

This Page from *Poor Richard's Almanac* opens with the moral saying that "Man's rich with little, were his Judgment true; Nature is frugal, and her Wants are few."

POOR RICHARD'S ALMANAC is the name given to the almanac that Benjamin Franklin published for 26 years. The first edition was dated 1733. The almanac was called *Poor Richard* until 1748, when it was enlarged from 24 to 36 pages. It was then called *Poor Richard Improved.* Franklin wrote it under the pseudonym Richard Saunders, but published it under his own name.

Franklin's print shop originally printed the almanacs of other people. But Franklin decided to save money and to propagate his religious and political ideas through an almanac of his own. Franklin sold about 10,000 copies of his almanac a year.

Poor Richard had all the usual features of almanacs including astrological predictions, jokes, and verses. The account of Richard's experiences with his wife made Richard the first character in American fiction.

The almanac was most famous for its sayings. Franklin himself said he "assembled" the "wisdom of many ages and nations" into these proverbs. Franklin rewrote these proverbs whenever he chose. He used them to fill in "all the little spaces that occurred between the remarkable days in the calendar."

In the 1758 edition, Franklin brought a collection of proverbs together in the front of the book as "the harangue of a wise old man" on "The Way to Wealth." This section was very widely reprinted in America, Great Britain, and France. The proverbs in this section are moral and prudential. Some examples include:

"A penny saved is a penny earned."

"Early to bed and early to rise,
Makes a man healthy, wealthy, and wise."

"God helps them that help themselves."

But "The Way to Wealth" alone gives a misleading impression of Franklin's proverbial wisdom in general. Many of the less frequently reprinted sayings have quite a different character. They are much more witty and cynical observations on life than are found in "The Way to Wealth."

EDWARD WAGENKNECHT

POORWILL. See WHIPPOORWILL.

POP ART. See PAINTING (After 1900); UNITED STATES (The Arts in the United States [Painting]).

POPCORN is a type of corn with small, hard kernels. Under heat, the kernels "pop" (burst) into a tasty white food that is a favorite of young and old alike. A popcorn plant is smaller than most varieties of field corn, but it has the same food value. Each kernel has a tough covering and contains much starch.

A popcorn kernel "pops" when it contains about 13.5 per cent moisture and is heated to about 400° F. Scientists say the heat changes the moisture into steam. The hard covering keeps the steam from escaping, causing pressure to build up inside the kernel. The pressure finally bursts the kernel. Good popcorn kernels expand from 30 to 35 times their size when popped.

Farmers grow popcorn in much the same way as field corn. But rows of popcorn are planted closer together. The ears are carefully harvested after they have matured and dried. Most U.S. commercial popcorn is grown in Indiana, Iowa, Illinois, and Ohio.

J. C. Allen

These Hard, Shiny Kernels of Popcorn will turn into a delightful refreshment when they explode in the corn popper.

Scientific Classification. Popcorn belongs to the grass family, *Gramineae.* It is genus *Zea,* species *Z. mays,* variety *everta.*

GUY W. MCKEE

POPÉ. See INDIAN WARS (The Pueblo Revolt).

Wide World

The Pope is both head of the Roman Catholic Church and Bishop of Rome. Pope Paul VI, just after his coronation, gave the blessing *Urbi et Orbi* (to the city and to the world) before the huge crowd that came to St. Peter's Square to see him crowned.

POPE is the title of the spiritual ruler of the Roman Catholic Church. The church regards the pope as its visible head and Jesus Christ as its invisible head. Roman Catholics believe that Christ established the office of pope when he said to Simon, who was also called *Peter,* or *the Rock:*

"And I say also unto thee, That thou art Peter, and upon this rock I will build my Church; and the gates of hell shall not prevail against it." Matt. 16: 18.

The word *pope* comes from the Latin word *papa,* which means *father.* One of the pope's most important titles is that of *Bishop of Rome.* The pope is also called *pontiff.* The Latin word *pontifex,* or pontiff, was used for a member of the council of priests in ancient Rome (see PONTIFEX).

Unlike other positions of authority and leadership, the office of the pope has continued in an unbroken line throughout the years. During this time, every other European institution that existed when it began has fallen. Roman Catholics believe that this is an indication of the divine foundation of their church, enabling it to rise above the human weaknesses of its members.

The Papacy

The system of government of the Roman Catholic Church with the pope as supreme head is called *the papacy.* The word papacy also refers to *the office of the pope.* The congregations, tribunals, and offices in Rome through which the pope governs the church make up *the curia.* The pope's seat of authority is in Rome. It is called *the Apostolic See* or *the Holy See.* The pope lives in the Vatican palace, located in the independent state of Vatican City. Vatican City lies within the city of Rome.

The *hierarchy,* or governing body of the church, is organized somewhat like a pyramid. The pope stands alone at the head of the entire church. Below him are a number of cardinals, patriarchs, archbishops, and bishops. A large number of abbots, prelates, and vicars form the base of the hierarchy. Members of the hierarchy inform the pope of their activities through written reports and personal visits. As a result, he has a continual flow of information about all areas of church government. See ROMAN CATHOLIC CHURCH (The Hierarchy).

Officially, any Roman Catholic can be elected pope. But, since the 1300's, the pope has always been chosen from among the cardinals. For hundreds of years, only Italians have been chosen to wear the papal crown. Possibly this is because of the geographic position of Rome in Italy, and because most cardinals have come from Italy. The last non-Italian pope was Adrian VI (born Adrian Florensz in Utrecht, Holland), who was elected in 1522.

The Powers of the Pope extend to all aspects of church affairs. They are divided into two basic groups: (1) *spiritual,* or those concerned with matters of faith, morals, religious practices, and church government; and (2) *temporal,* or those concerned with the civil administration of the Vatican.

Spiritual Powers. Roman Catholics believe that the pope is *infallible* in matters of faith and morals. This means they believe that the pope cannot possibly commit an error when he speaks *ex cathedra,* or by virtue of his office, on matters concerning faith and morals. He claims divine assistance as the successor of St. Peter when he speaks in this manner.

The pope does not have infallibility in connection

Wide World

with other aspects of church affairs. But he does have absolute authority. He is considered the highest teacher, judge, and governing power of the church. He has the power to *canonize* saints, or to declare that they may be venerated. He can absolve persons from certain sins, and inflict punishment, such as excommunication, on persons who disobey his orders on certain matters or the precepts of the church. He can also make laws for the entire church, and dispense with church laws. He appoints cardinals, appoints or deposes bishops, establishes and divides dioceses, and approves new religious orders. Whenever he wishes, the pope can call an *ecumenical council*, or general conference of the church, to help him decide church policies.

Temporal Powers. The pope is the ruler of Vatican City, which has an area of 108.7 acres and a population of about 1,000. It has its own flag, coins, stamps, public works, and telephone and broadcasting systems. As an independent state, Vatican City has diplomatic status. The pope sends representatives to other countries, and receives diplomats from them. Ambassadors and envoys from Vatican City are called *nuncios* and *internuncios*. In Roman Catholic countries, these messengers take precedence over all other members of the diplomatic corps. The pope relies on voluntary contributions from members of the church for money to pay for his living expenses, his household, and his many charities. These contributions are collected in an annual gift called *Peter's pence.* See VATICAN CITY.

Papal Swiss Guards protect the Vatican. These guards are recruited in Switzerland, and wear colorful uniforms designed by Michelangelo in the 1500's. See SWISS GUARDS.

Titles and Insignia. The pope's full title is Bishop of Rome, Vicar of Jesus Christ, Successor of the Prince of the Apostles, Supreme Pontiff of the Universal Church, Patriarch of the West, Primate of Italy, Archbishop and Metropolitan of the Roman Province, and Sovereign of the State of Vatican City. The pope is addressed as "Your Holiness." He speaks of himself in official documents as "Servant of the Servants of God." Each man who is elected pope takes a new name to use during his reign. He usually chooses the name of an earlier pope whom he admires.

The pope's clothes, always white in color, are the same style as those a bishop wears. The pope wears low, open, red shoes with a cross embroidered on the front of each shoe. His liturgical vestments also resemble those of other bishops, but his cope has a clasp ornamented with precious jewels. The pope wears a low broadbrimmed hat when he goes outside. In processions, he wears the *tiara*, or triple crown, that symbolizes his office. The pope's *pallium*, a band of wool embroidered with crosses, shows his rank as an archbishop. The pope wears a cross of gold which is said to contain a relic of the true Cross. His jewelry also includes a pontifical ring, called *the fisherman's ring*. St. Peter had been a fisherman. Christ said to him and his brother: "Follow me and I will make you fishers of men." Matt. 4: 19.

The Sacred College, also called the College of Cardinals, acts as an advisory group to the pope. The pope usually asks the opinion of the college on all important church matters.

Meetings of the Sacred College are called *consistories*. A consistory may be secret, semipublic, or public. Only the pope and the cardinals attend a *secret consistory*. At such a meeting, the pope announces the names of men he wishes to make cardinals and the college votes on each name. He gives new cardinals their sapphire rings as a symbol of their offices. If a cardinal comes from another part of the world, the pope assigns him an honorary position as the head of a diocese in Italy. All cardinals have honorary positions as pastors

587

Alinari from Art Reference Bureau

Saint Peter Is Called the First Pope by Roman Catholics. This statue of Saint Peter may have been done in the 1200's. It is located in Saint Peter's Church in Vatican City.

Leo I

Gregory I

of churches in Rome. The pope also appoints the *Cardinal Camerlengo* (Chancellor of the Roman Catholic Church) at a secret consistory. Bishops as well as cardinals attend a *semipublic consistory*. These meetings are usually held to discuss candidates for beatification and canonization. Churchmen and laymen may be invited to a *public consistory*. Here, the pope performs the ceremony of giving new cardinals their red hats.

The most important function of the Sacred College is the election of a new pope. When a pope dies, a member of the college must verify his death. The car-

THE POPES

Name	Start of Reign	Name	Start of Reign	Name	Start of Reign	Name	Start of Reign
*St. Peter (the Apostle)	A.D. 42	*St. Julius I	337	*Honorius I	625	Anastasius	855
St. Linus	67	Liberius	352	(See vacant 1 year and 6 months.)		*St. Nicholas I	858
St. Anacletus (Cletus)	76	Felix II	355	Severinus	640	Adrian II	867
*St. Clement I	88	*St. Damasus I	366	John IV.	640	John VIII	872
St. Evaristus	97	Ursinus	366	*Theodore I	642	Marinus I	882
St. Alexander I	105	St. Siricius	384	St. Martin I	649	St. Adrian III	884
St. Sixtus I	115	*St. Anastasius I	399	St. Eugenius I	654	†Stephen V (VI)	885
St. Telesphorus	125	St. Innocent I	401	St. Vitalianus	657	Formosus	891
St. Hyginus	136	St. Zosimus	417	Adeodatus	672	Boniface VI	896
St. Pius I	140	St. Boniface I	418	*Donus	676	†Stephen VI (VII)	896
St. Anicetus	155	Eulalius	418	St. Agatho	678	Romanus	897
St. Soterus	166	St. Celestine I	422	St. Leo II	682	*Theodore II	897
St. Eleutherius	175	St. Sixtus III	432	St. Benedict II	684	John IX	898
*St. Victor I	189	*St. Leo I, the Great.	440	John V	685	Benedict IV	900
St. Zephirinus	199	St. Hilary	461	Conon	686	Leo V	903
*St. Calixtus I	217	St. Simplicius	468	Theodore; Paschal.	687	Christopher	903
Hippolytus	217	St. Felix III	483	*St. Sergius I	687	*Sergius III	904
St. Urban I	222	St. Gelasius I	492	John VI	701	*Anastasius III	911
St. Pontianus	230	*Anastasius II	496	John VII	705	Lando	913
St. Anterus	235	St. Symmachus	498	Sisinnius	708	John X	914
St. Fabian	236	Laurentius	498	*Constantine	708	Leo VI	928
St. Cornelius	251	St. Hormisdas	514	St. Gregory II	715	†Stephen VII (VIII)	928
Novatianus	251	*St. John I	523	St. Gregory III	731	John XI	931
*St. Lucius I	253	St. Felix IV	526	St. Zachary	741	Leo VII	936
*St. Stephen I	254	Dioscorus	530	*†Stephen II (III)	752	†Stephen VIII (IX)	939
St. Sixtus II	257	Boniface II	530	St. Paul I	757	Marinus II	942
St. Dionysius	259	John II	533	Constantine	767	*Agapetus II	946
St. Felix I	269	*St. Agapetus I	535	Philip	768	*John XII	955
St. Eutychianus	275	St. Sylverius	536	*†Stephen III (IV)	768	Leo VIII	963
St. Caius	283	Vigilius	537	Adrian I	772	Benedict V	964
St. Marcellinus	296	*Pelagius I	556	*St. Leo III	795	John XIII	965
(See vacant about 4 years.)		John III	561	†Stephen IV (V)	816	Benedict VI	973
St. Marcellus I	308	Benedict I	575	*St. Paschal I	817	Boniface VII	974
St. Eusebius	309	*Pelagius II	579	Eugenius II	824	Benedict VII	974
St. Melchiades or Miltiades	311	*St. Gregory I, the Great	590	Valentinus	827	John XIV	983
		Sabinianus	604	Gregory IV	827	John XV	985
*St. Sylvester I	314	Boniface III	607	John	844	Gregory V	996
St. Marcus	336	St. Boniface IV	608	*Sergius II	844	John XVI	997
		St. Deusdedit	615	St. Leo IV	847	*Sylvester II	999
		Boniface V	619	Benedict III	855	John XVII	1003
						John XVIII	1004

Antipopes in *italics*.
Source: *Pontifical Yearbook*

588

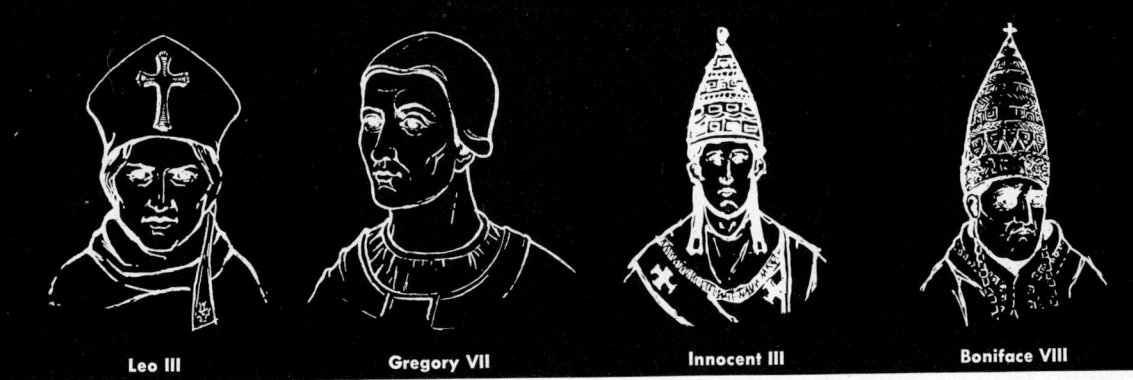

Leo III **Gregory VII** **Innocent III** **Boniface VIII**

dinal dean touches the forehead of the dead pope three times with a silver mallet and calls the pope by his baptismal name. He then announces that "the pope is truly dead." The Sacred College takes over the administration of the church until a new pope is chosen, but it lacks some of the powers of the pope.

How the Pope Is Elected

The Conclave is the name given to the Sacred College when it meets to elect a new pope. The conclave begins between the 15th and 18th day after the death of the pope. The word *conclave* also refers to the walled-off area in the Vatican where the cardinals stay during the election period. They remain in the conclave, completely shut off from the outside world, until they have chosen a pope. In 1945, Pope Pius XII issued detailed instructions on the election of a new pope. In 1962, Pope John XXIII revised these instructions slightly.

The cardinals assemble from all parts of the world to elect the pope. On the appointed day, they attend a Mass of the Holy Ghost and ask for guidance in their difficult task. Later, they form a procession to the con-

THE POPES

Name	Start of Reign	Name	Start of Reign	Name	Start of Reign	Name	Start of Reign
*Sergius IV	1009	Eugenius III	1145	removed to Avi-		*St. Pius V	1566
Benedict VIII	1012	*Anastasius IV	1153	gnon, France)	1305	*Gregory XIII	1572
Gregory	1012	*Adrian IV (Nicho-		(See vacant 11 months.)		*Sixtus V	1585
*John XIX	1024	las Brekespear, an		John XXII	1316	Urban VII	1590
Benedict IX (de-		Englishman)	1154	*Nicholas V at Rome*	1328	Gregory XIV	1590
posed)	1032	Alexander III	1159	Benedict XII	1334	Innocent IX	1591
Sylvester III	1045	*Victor IV*	1159	Clement VI	1342	*Clement VIII	1592
Benedict IX (2nd		*Paschal III*	1164	Innocent VI	1352	Leo XI	1605
time)	1045	*Calixtus III*	1168	Urban V	1362	*Paul V	1605
Gregory VI	1045	*Innocent III*	1179	Gregory XI (throne		Gregory XV	1621
Clement II	1046	*Lucius III	1181	restored to Rome)	1370	*Urban VIII	1623
Benedict IX (3rd		Urban III	1185	Urban VI	1378	Innocent X	1644
time)	1047	Gregory VIII	1187	Boniface IX	1389	Alexander VII	1655
*Damasus II	1048	Clement III	1187	*Benedict XIII*	1394	Clement IX	1667
St. Leo IX	1049	*Celestine III	1191	Innocent VII	1404	Clement X	1670
*Victor II	1055	*Innocent III	1198	Gregory XII	1406	Innocent XI	1676
*†Stephen IX (X)	1057	Honorius III	1216	*Clement VII*	1378	Alexander VIII	1689
Benedict X	1058	Gregory IX	1227	*Alexander V*	1409	Innocent XII	1691
Nicholas II	1059	Celestine IV	1241	*John XXIII*	1410	Clement XI	1700
Alexander II	1061	(See vacant 1 year		Martin V	1417	Innocent XIII	1721
Honorius II	1061	and 8 months.)		Eugenius IV	1431	Benedict XIII	1724
*St. Gregory VII		Innocent IV	1243	*Felix V*	1439	Clement XII	1730
(Hildebrand)	1073	Alexander IV	1254	Nicholas V	1447	*Benedict XIV	1740
Clement III	1080	Urban IV	1261	Calixtus III	1455	Clement XIII	1758
(See vacant 1		Clement IV	1265	Pius II	1458	Clement XIV	1769
year.)		(See vacant 2 years		Paul II	1464	Pius VI	1775
*Victor III	1086	and 9 months.)		*Sixtus IV	1471	*Pius VII	1800
*Urban II	1088	Gregory X	1271	Innocent VIII	1484	Leo XII	1823
*Paschal II	1099	Innocent V	1276	*Alexander VI	1492	Pius VIII	1829
Theodore	1100	Adrian V	1276	Pius III	1503	Gregory XVI	1831
Albert	1102	John XXI	1276	*Julius II	1503	*Pius IX	1846
Sylvester IV	1105	Nicholas III	1277	*Leo X	1513	*Leo XIII	1878
*Gelasius II	1118	Martin IV	1281	*Adrian VI	1522	*St. Pius X	1903
Gregory VIII	1118	Honorius IV	1285	*Clement VII	1523	*Benedict XV	1914
*Calixtus II	1119	Nicholas IV	1288	*Paul III	1534	*Pius XI	1922
Honorius II	1124	(See vacant 2 years		Julius III	1550	*Pius XII	1939
Celestine II	1124	and 3 months.)		Marcellus II	1555	*John XXIII	1958
Innocent II	1130	*St. Celestine V	1294	*Paul IV	1555	*Paul VI	1963
Anacletus II	1130	*Boniface VIII	1294	Pius IV	1559		
Victor IV	1138	Benedict XI	1303				
*Lucius II	1144	Clement V (Papacy					

*Has a biography in WORLD BOOK.
†In 1961, the church dropped Stephen II, who died in 752, from the list of popes. The numbers of the others named Stephen were moved up.

589

Pius IX

Leo XIII

Pius X

Historical Pictures Service; United Press Int.; Wide World

clave. They pray and take oaths of secrecy and loyalty. Each cardinal may bring one or two *conclavists* (assistants) into the conclave. No other outsider is allowed inside. A search party inspects the conclave to make sure that no unauthorized persons are present. Then the doors are locked. Two persons inside and two outside keep the keys until the doors are opened after the election. Each cardinal is assigned to his own room. All meet to vote in the Sistine Chapel.

The Balloting. If the number of cardinals voting can be divided evenly by three, the balloting to elect a pope takes place until one man receives at least two-thirds of the votes. If the number cannot be divided evenly by three, the balloting continues until one man receives at least two-thirds of the votes plus one. All the cardinals sit on special canopied thrones around the walls of the chapel. They fill out their *scrutinies* (ballots) in disguised handwriting, and fold them lengthwise. Each cardinal walks to the altar at one end of the chapel and prays. He drops his ballot into a large gold cup placed on a table in front of the altar. The votes are then counted and checked.

The cardinals vote again immediately if no one is elected on the first ballot. If the second ballot also fails, the scrutinies are burned with a mixture of straw, so that the smoke escaping from the chimney will be black. Voting sessions are held each day in the morning and evening, until a new pope is elected. When a pope has been chosen, the scrutinies are burned alone, so that the smoke will be white. Outside, thousands of people crowd into St. Peter's Square to watch the *fumata* (smoke signal). Tension mounts each time the smoke begins to rise from the chimney. The crowds burst into loud cheers of "*Viva il papa*" ("Long live the pope") when the thin white stream of smoke announces to the world that a new pope has been elected.

After a successful balloting, the dean of the Sacred College asks the elected candidate whether he accepts the office, and what name he wishes to use as pope. He is pope as soon as he accepts, even before his coronation. All the cardinals, except the one chosen as pope, lower the canopies over their thrones. The new pope remains seated on what is now his first papal throne, and receives homage from the cardinals. Then he dresses in his white papal robes. Vatican officials have three sets of robes ready, to fit a small, medium, or large man. The senior cardinal deacon steps out on the balcony of St. Peter's Church and announces to the people in Latin, "*Habemus papam*" ("We have a pope"). Then

the pope appears and gives his first blessing, "*Urbi et Orbi*" ("to the city and to the world"). This blessing shows his concern, as pope, with all Roman Catholics, and, as Bishop of Rome, with the people of the city.

The Coronation of the pope usually takes place several weeks after his election. The pope may choose the site of his coronation. In the 1900's, most popes have been crowned in St. Peter's Church. The pope wears full papal dress. He sits on a portable throne and is carried in a procession from the Vatican to the place of his coronation. A church official stops the procession three times. Each time, he burns some flax at the end of a reed and says in Latin, "Holy Father, thus passes the glory of the world." At the coronation site, the cardinals pay homage to the pope by bowing before him and kissing his foot. The pope then says Mass. The coronation takes place after Mass. The senior cardinal deacon places the three-tiered crown on the pope's head. He announces that the pope is now "Father of princes and kings, Ruler of the world on earth, and Vicar of our Saviour Jesus Christ." The coronation ends with a blessing given by the pope to his flock.

History

Beginnings. Leading Roman Catholic scholars agree that St. Peter visited the Christian community in Rome in A.D. 64. Tradition says that he presided over the church in Rome, and was martyred there during the reign of Nero. Roman Catholics date the beginning of the papacy with Peter.

Christianity became the chief religion of the Roman Empire under Constantine the Great in the 300's. The Bishop of Rome, as bishop of the capital city of the empire in the West, gained great power. In the 400's, conflicts arose among the various churches in the East. Pope Leo the Great tried to restore order to the Eastern churches at the Council of Chalcedon in 451. Six hundred and thirty bishops and four papal legates assembled to hear Leo's decree. According to tradition, they exclaimed unanimously, "What Leo believes we all believe; anathema to him who believes anything else. Peter has spoken through the mouth of Leo."

Many people in the East did not accept Leo's decrees. Egypt and Syria broke away and formed separate churches. But the spiritual *primacy* (control) of the church at Rome had been strengthened. All Italy turned to Leo when Attila, King of the Huns, ravaged central and western Europe (see ATTILA). He invaded Italy in 452 and threatened Rome, but withdrew with-

Benedict XV   Pius XI   Pius XII   John XXIII

U&U; United Press Int.; © Karsh, Pix

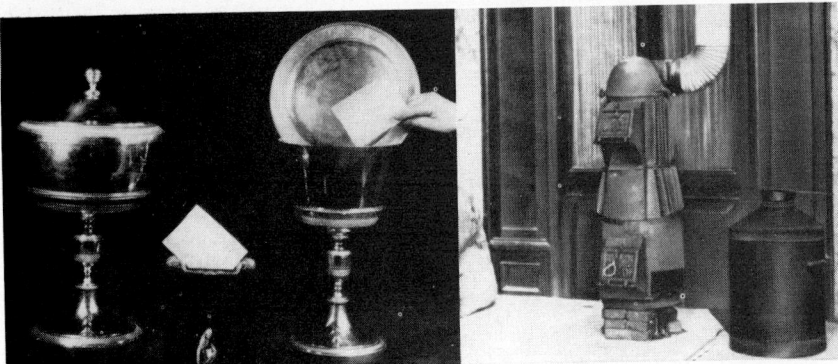

Black Star; Wide World

out attacking when Leo came to meet him and spoke with him. Leo also intervened and saved Rome in 455 when Genseric, leader of the Vandals, threatened to destroy the city (see GENSERIC).

The Growth of the Papacy. During the next 300 years, the papacy carried out one of the greatest tasks ever undertaken by an institution. It spread the Christian faith among the Anglo-Saxons, Visigoths, Franks, Lombards, and other tribes that had gained control of western Europe. In the 500's, St. Benedict founded the Benedictine order of monks. These monks played an important part in teaching Christian doctrines to the peoples of Europe. See BENEDICTINE.

The *pontificate*, or reign, of Pope Gregory I, from 590 to 604, was a great period in papal history. Gregory brought about many reforms in the papacy. He insisted that the clergy not marry. He suppressed *simony*, or the

Electing a New Pope, the cardinals place *scrutinies*, or ballots, in a cup, *above left*. The scrutinies are counted and then burned, *above*. If a pope has not been elected, straw is burned with them, and black smoke appears. If a pope is elected, the scrutinies are burned alone, and the waiting crowd sees white smoke, *right*.

During the Coronation, the pope is carried in procession through the throngs to an altar where he says Mass.

practice of buying and selling church offices instead of earning them through ability. His reforms did much to elevate the papacy spiritually.

Pope Leo III crowned Charlemagne Emperor of the West on Christmas Day, 800, in St. Peter's Church (see CHARLEMAGNE). This action established a new concept of a united Christendom. The popes now claimed the right to crown the emperors. But the emperors, in turn, had the right to confirm the election of popes.

Religious conflicts developed between Rome and Constantinople during the 800's. Pope Nicholas I denounced Photius, the Patriarch of Constantinople. But Photius declared himself no longer a member of the church. This *Photian Schism* began a great argument between the East and the West. It resulted in a final break in 1054. See EASTERN ORTHODOX CHURCHES; PHOTIUS.

The powers of the papacy gradually increased during the Middle Ages. The church acquired control of several provinces and cities in the central part of Italy. These possessions were known as *the Papal States* (see PAPAL STATES). The church revived literature and learning, and helped bring about great advances in art and science. But the civil wars and disorders of the times affected the condition of the papacy. Corrupt administration weakened it spiritually. Church officials sold bishoprics and church property for personal gain. Emperors and rulers gained control of the papacy, and appointed their own supporters as popes.

Otto the Great brought some order to the papacy when he was crowned Holy Roman Emperor in 962 (see HOLY ROMAN EMPIRE). But he kept strict control of papal elections. In the mid-1000's, Pope Nicholas II instituted many reforms in the papacy. He took the power to choose the pope away from the court and returned it to the church. Nicholas established the Sacred College to choose the pope. The emperors could no longer interfere in papal elections. But they kept the right to confirm the choice of the college. The choice also had to be approved by the clergymen and members of the church at Rome. During the pontificate of Innocent III, from 1198 to 1216, nearly every European ruler submitted to the power and authority of the church.

The Troubles of the Papacy often stemmed from its struggles with emperors, kings, and other rulers. In the days when the papacy had great temporal powers, political considerations played an important part in the selection of a pope. Emperors and rulers tried to control or influence the papacy in order to further their own ambitions. In some cases, they appointed antipopes to support them. An *antipope* is a man who has been improperly elected pope. He sets himself up in opposition to the pope who has been regularly chosen in accordance with canon law. Some emperors even used military force to displace popes and set up antipopes. The kings of France and Sicily often interfered in the selection of the pope. Sometimes factions within the church itself opposed the authority of the pope and supported an antipope. The first antipope usually noted was Hippolytus, who was elected in 217. The last antipope was Felix V, a Duke of Savoy, who was elected in the 1400's.

The period of the 1300's saw great conflicts within the church. In 1305, under the influence of King Philip of France, a French archbishop was elected and crowned at Lyon as Pope Clement V. Clement moved the papal court from Rome to Avignon in 1309, and appointed only French cardinals. The papacy remained in France during the reigns of seven popes. This period is often called "the seventy years' captivity." All the popes of the period were French. The French court exerted much influence on the popes, and greatly reduced the prestige of the papacy. The period of "captivity" ended in 1377 when Pope Gregory XI returned the papal throne from Avignon to Rome. But the troubles were not over.

After Gregory's death in 1378, the cardinals chose Pope Urban VI, an Italian. They later claimed that the election had not been valid, because they were forced into it. They then elected a French cardinal as Pope Clement VII. France and Spain recognized Clement. Italy, Germany, and all northern Europe except Scotland supported Urban. This rivalry caused the *Great Schism of the West* that divided the church for almost 40 years. Both Urban and Clement appointed their own cardinals. Each group of cardinals continued to elect its own rulers. The general Council of Pisa that met in 1409 to unite the church ended by creating a third claimant to the papal throne, Alexander V (see PISA, COUNCIL OF). The Council of Constance deposed John XXIII, an antipope who succeeded Alexander, in 1415, and elected Pope Martin V in 1417. All sides accepted Martin, and the Great Schism ended.

Some historians consider the lines stemming from Clement and from the Council of Pisa as antipopes. Others say that these men were popes in their own parts of the church, although none of them can be considered the single pope for the whole church. The problem causes some confusion in numbering the popes.

The Protestant Reformation started within the church in the 1500's. The Protestants did not accept the authority of the pope, and broke away from the Roman Catholic Church. The church carried on its own Counter Reformation. The Council of Trent, which met from 1545 to 1563, outlined and reaffirmed Roman Catholic doctrines. See COUNTER REFORMATION; REFORMATION; TRENT, COUNCIL OF.

The temporal powers of the pope suffered a severe blow when Napoleon Bonaparte annexed the Papal States in 1809. The Congress of Vienna restored the states to the papacy in 1815 under the protection of Austria. But, during the struggle for unification in Italy, from 1848 to 1870, all the papal provinces were confiscated by the state. To show their resistance, Pope Pius IX and the three popes who followed him during the next 60 years made themselves voluntary prisoners in the Vatican.

In the 1900's, the papacy has enjoyed high prestige and influence. Pope Leo XIII and his successors followed a policy of more detailed papal teaching on the moral and social issues of the day. This increased the spiritual influence of the papacy. Pius X, who became pope in 1903, worked hard to keep peace in Europe. The shock and horror of the outbreak of World War I hastened his death in 1914. Pope Benedict XV, who succeeded him, continued the papal policy of strict neutrality and impartiality during the war.

In 1929, Pope Pius XI and the Italian government settled the 60-year dispute between church and state with two documents—the Lateran Treaty and the Concordat. The treaty had international importance. It gave the pope full sovereignty over Vatican City. The Concordat dealt with relations between the Vatican and Italy. By the terms of the treaty, canon law is recognized in Italy (see CANON LAW). Italian courts consider marriage by the church as legal. Italian schools have compulsory religious education. Religious communities and ecclesiastics in Italy have the right to own property. Also, the treaty provided that the papacy be paid by the government for the loss of the Papal States.

On July 25, 1929, Pius XI emerged from the Vatican and entered St. Peter's Square in a huge procession witnessed by about 250,000 persons. His appearance signaled the return of the papacy's temporal power and the end of the controversy with the state in Italy.

Pope Pius XII succeeded Pius XI in 1939. His work for peace during World War II, and the help he gave to victims of the war, won him worldwide acclaim. He also made important changes in church doctrine and ritual. Pius died in 1958, and Pope John XXIII succeeded him. John increased the number of cardinals in the Sacred College, and made many other administrative changes. In January, 1959, John called the Second Vatican Council. The council began in 1962. Pope Paul VI succeeded John in 1963, and continued the council (see VATICAN COUNCIL). Paul traveled widely. He was the first pope to visit the Holy Land, the United States, and South America.

In a 1968 *encyclical* (letter to his bishops), Paul reaffirmed the church's stand against artificial birth control. The encyclical stirred some opposition within the church.   FULTON J. SHEEN

Related Articles. See the separate biographies of popes listed with asterisks in the *table* with this article. See also the following articles:

Outline

I. The Papacy
   A. The Powers of the Pope C. The Sacred College
   B. Titles and Insignia
II. How the Pope Is Elected
   A. The Conclave
   B. The Balloting   C. The Coronation
III. History

Questions

How is the hierarchy of the church organized?
Under what circumstances is the pope considered infallible?
What temporal powers does the pope have?
During a papal election, how do people outside the Vatican learn that a new pope has been chosen?
What is (1) an ecumenical council? (2) a consistory? (3) a conclave?
What are the functions of the Sacred College?
How is the pope addressed?
How was the papacy important during the Middle Ages?
How did the Great Schism of the West come about?
Why did the popes shut themselves up as prisoners in the Vatican for 60 years?

POPE, ALEXANDER (1688-1744), was the greatest English poet and satirist of the early 1700's. His main purpose in life was to "write well, lastingly well, immortally well." He fulfilled his purpose. Pope's works are probably quoted more than those of any other English writer except Shakespeare. Many of his lines are familiar, everyday sayings, such as "Fools rush in where angels fear to tread," "A little learning is a dangerous thing," "To err is human, to forgive divine," and "Hope springs eternal in the human breast."

Pope excelled as a poet in a period known as the *Classical Age.* English writers of this period used such forms of poetry as the *heroic couplet.* The heroic couplet consists of two rhymed lines of 10 syllables each. Every second syllable is accented. Pope polished the heroic couplet until it sparkled with brilliance.

Early Life. Pope was born in London. He was educated in private schools and by tutors. But he acquired much of his learning by studying languages and literature by himself. His constant studying brought on a serious illness when he was 12 years old. As a result of this illness, he was a hunchback for the rest of his life. His bad health prevented him from entering business, so he devoted his time to writing.

His Works. When Pope was young, perhaps only 16, he wrote *Pastorals* (verses with pastoral, or rural, themes). He showed great metrical ability in these. Recognition of his skill as a poet came in 1711,

Alexander Pope

when he published *Essay on Criticism.* In polished couplets, Pope set forth in this work his own literary standards, as well as some of those of his time. The next year, he published *The Rape of the Lock,* a mock-heroic poem that poked fun at epic poetry. By the age of 23, he had become famous. He soon became a member of the "Scriblerus Club," which included among its members Jonathan Swift, John Gay, and John Arbuthnot.

Pope translated Homer's *Iliad* into heroic couplets. The first volume appeared in 1715, but Pope did not complete the project until five years later. This translation and one of Homer's *Odyssey* in 1725 and 1726 brought him a considerable amount of money. In 1719, he bought the lease of a house in Twickenham, where he spent the rest of his life.

Pope published an edition of Shakespeare in 1725. Lewis Theobald, another author of the time, pointed out some errors in the edition. Pope then selected Theobald as the first hero of his *Dunciad,* a satire on dullness. Many years later, when Pope expanded *The Dunciad,* he made the hero Colley Cibber, then poet laureate of England. Pope's acid pen satirized these two men unmercifully. But not all Pope's work was satirical. His *Essay on Man* (1733-1734) and his *Moral Essays* (1731-1735) show a profound understanding of human nature and of philosophy.   GEORGE F. SENSABAUGH

POPISH PLOT. See OATES, TITUS.

Tall, Graceful Lombardy Poplars make excellent windbreaks in open areas. They grow much faster than most other trees.

POPLAR is any one of a group of fast-growing trees found throughout the Northern Hemisphere. Aspens and cottonwoods are poplars. About 10 of the 35 species in the group are native to North America. These trees have pointed leaves with wavy, toothed edges. Many kinds of poplars have such flat leafstalks that even a slight breeze will cause the leaves to flutter. Early in spring, before the leaves appear, small greenish flowers form in drooping clusters called *catkins*. Tiny seeds are hidden in fluffy cottony hairs that make it easy for the wind to carry them through the air.

Poplars grow best in moist places. They grow easily from *cuttings*, or cut twigs. People often plant poplars for shade trees because they grow fast. But they do not live long. Also, their roots tend to clog underground drainpipes and sewers. For this reason, some cities forbid planting poplars along streets. Poplar wood is whitish or light brown. It is also soft, light, and weak. Manufacturers use it to make boxes and crates. Papermakers use it for paper pulp and excelsior.

Balsam poplar, or *tacamahac*, is widely distributed across Canada. It lives as far north as trees will grow and south to the northern United States. The sticky buds and young leaves have an odor of balsam. Honeybees use the fragrant gummy substance to waterproof their hives. *Balm of Gilead* is a cultivated variety with heart-shaped leaves.

The *white poplar* has leaves that are silvery white beneath and have three or five lobes like a maple leaf. The bark on the branches is white. The *Lombardy poplar* looks like an exclamation point. It has diamond-shaped leaves and a tall, narrow shape. Its upright branches press toward the trunk. People often plant these poplars in rows in formal gardens, for roadside landscaping, and to shelter other plants from winds. These trees do not produce seeds.

The *Carolina poplar* is a hybrid derived from the native eastern cottonwood and the black poplar from Europe (see HYBRID). It has triangle-shaped leaves. This tree probably originated first in France about 1750. It can endure city smoke and dust and often is seen growing in large cities. All Carolina poplar trees are male and do not produce the cottony seeds.

Scientific Classification. Poplar trees belong to the willow family, *Salicaceae*. Balsam poplar is genus *Populus*, species *balsamifera*; white poplar is *P. alba*, Lombardy poplar is *P. nigra*, var. *italica*. Carolina poplar is *P. canadensis*. ELBERT L. LITTLE, JR.

See also ASPEN; BALM OF GILEAD; COTTONWOOD; TREE (color picture, Autumn Colors).

Lombardy Poplar Leaves flutter with a clattering sound in the faintest breeze. The triangular leaves are light green.

The Bark of Lombardy and other black poplars is darker and much rougher than that of white poplar varieties.

William M. Harlow

Omar Marcus

Snow-Capped Popocatepetl stands out boldly above the plateau of central Mexico. Many old fortresses and historic churches and cathedrals lie in view of the majestic sleeping volcano. Popocatepetl is one of the highest peaks in North America.

POPLIN is a ribbed fabric. It can be made of wool, cotton, rayon, silk, synthetics, or a mixture of these. The ribs run across the fabric. They are formed by using coarse filling yarns in a plain weave. The name *poplin* comes from *papeline*, a fabric woven of silk at Avignon, France, in the 1400's. The new fabric was named in honor of the papal residence at Avignon. The first poplin was made from silk.   KENNETH R. FOX

POPOCATEPETL, *poh* POH *kah* TAY *pet'l,* is a volcano about 40 miles southeast of Mexico City. For location, see MEXICO (physical map). It is one of the highest peaks in North America. Its altitude (17,887 feet) is only 2,433 feet less than that of Mount McKinley, the highest peak on the continent. Its Aztec name means *smoking mountain.* Popocatepetl is often called simply "Popo." The top of Popocatepetl is always covered with snow. Banana, palm, and orange trees grow at its base. In the clear Mexican air, the mountain appears closer to Mexico City than it really is. Popocatepetl has not erupted violently in years, but clouds of smoke and gas, and sometimes stones and ashes, pour from its mouth. A small eruption of ash took place in the crater in 1943. The last major eruption of Popocatepetl occurred in 1702. Sulfur inside the crater has been mined from time to time, although transportation is difficult in the region.

The mountain can be climbed fairly easily. A member of Hernando Cortes' group which conquered Mexico in the 1520's was probably the first white man to climb it.   GORDON A. MACDONALD

POPOVICH, PAVEL R. See ASTRONAUT.

POPPAEA SABINA. See NERO.

POPPY is the common name for several related groups of flowers. The most important member is the white opium poppy of China, India, and Iran. It has been raised in the Orient since ancient times.

The flowers of poppies are admired for their delicate beauty and gracefulness. Breeders have produced many variations in the size and form of the blossom. The plants are hardy and easy to cultivate. The tiny seeds have no narcotic properties, and are sold for bird food. They also yield an oil used in preparing some foods. The oil cake remaining is a valuable cattle food. Poppy seeds are also used as flavoring. They may be sprinkled on bread and rolls, or used in filling for cakes.

The common corn poppy grows wild in the grain fields and grassy meadows of Europe. Many varieties of the poppy, including the *Shirley poppy,* are grown from seed in flower gardens. The *Iceland poppy* grows as far south as Colorado. Its long-lasting flowers are various shades of yellow, rose-pink, and scarlet. The California poppy, or "cup of gold," grows wild in the "Golden State." The most showy of all poppies is the large-flowered Oriental poppy, whose red, orange, white, or salmon blossoms often have blackish-purple centers.

Many poppies are annual plants that can be grown from seed. But the Oriental poppy is a perennial, best transplanted by root sections in late summer. The poppy is one of the flowers of the month of August.

Opium comes from the young capsule of the poppy

595

where the seeds develop. To obtain it, workers slit the capsules late in the day. The milky juice that seeps out solidifies overnight, and is collected by hand next day. It takes about 120,000 seed capsules to yield 25 to 40 pounds of opium per acre.

Scientific Classification. The poppy family is *Papaveraceae*. The opium poppy is genus *Papaver*, species *somniferum;* the corn, *P. rhoeas;* the Iceland, *P. nudicaule;* the Oriental, *P. orientale.* The California poppy is *Eschscholtzia californica.*   ROBERT W. SCHERY

See also CELANDINE; DUTCHMAN'S-BREECHES; FLOWER (color picture, Flowers of Roadside, Field, and Prairie [California Poppies]); OPIUM.

Shirley Poppies are an annual species of poppy, with flowers in many delicate shades of pink, red, and white.

W. Atlee Burpee Co.

POPPY WEEK honors the men and women who have served in the United States armed services. It is usually celebrated as the week which ends on the Saturday before Memorial Day (see MEMORIAL DAY). During this week, local communities choose one day as Poppy Day. Volunteers, sponsored by several veterans groups, sell poppies to the public for the benefit of disabled and needy veterans. The money collected is used for medical and educational services.

After World War I, the poppy became the symbol of the tragedy of war and of the renewal of life, because many of the battlefields of France bloomed with poppies. Artificial poppies were sold in the United States for the benefit of children in France and Belgium who were victims of the war. The Veterans of Foreign Wars in the United States conducted the first nationwide poppy sale for the benefit of war veterans in 1922. After that, other groups working for and with war veterans joined the campaign.   RAYMOND HOYT JAHN

POPULAR MUSIC is written for dancing, listening, and singing. Popular songs have melodies and words that are easy to remember. Many of these songs, often called *pops*, become popular quickly, then fade out just as rapidly. Songs that enjoy great popularity are called *hits*. A few, such as "Sweet Genevieve" (1869), "Let Me Call You Sweetheart" (1910), "Star Dust" (1929), and "White Christmas" (1942), remain popular year after year. These are called *standards*.

Popular music comes into our homes on phonograph records, on radio, and on television. Music stores sell sheet music of popular songs that can be played on the piano. Motion pictures often help make a song popular, or "bring back" songs that were popular years ago. Many popular songs are written for musical plays.

Recorded popular music helps create a pleasant atmosphere in many offices and factories. *Jukeboxes* (coin machines that play phonograph records) provide popular music in public places, such as restaurants.

The first popular song of the United States was probably "Yankee Doodle," which became widely sung and played in colonial times (see YANKEE DOODLE). "Dixie" swept to popularity in 1860, and became the fighting song of Southern troops during the Civil War (see DIXIE). "Casey Jones," "Home on the Range," "I've Been Working On the Railroad," and "Down By the Old Mill Stream" are other popular songs that have been enjoyed for many years.

Kinds of Popular Music

Dance Music is written for many styles of dancing. Boleros, polkas, mazurkas, and reels are played to accompany these folk dances. "Turkey in the Straw," a square-dance tune, and "On the Beautiful Blue Danube," a world-famous waltz, have been favorites for many generations. New dance styles started to appear in the United States during the early 1900's. Many of them lasted only briefly, but some, such as the fox trot, are still popular. In fact, most popular songs now are written to be played as fox trots. The titles of some songs are also the names of the dances that originally went with them, such as "Charleston," "The Big Apple," and "Lambeth Walk."

The popularity of dance music reached its height during the 1930's and early 1940's. During this period, outstanding dance-band leaders included Tommy Dorsey, Benny Goodman, Guy Lombardo, Glenn Miller, and Artie Shaw. These bands played both romantic, *sweet* music, such as "Deep Purple" and "Embraceable You," and peppy, *swing* tunes, such as "One O'Clock Jump" and "Jersey Bounce."

Singers worked with many bands. Mildred Bailey sang with Paul Whiteman's orchestra, Marion Hutton with Glenn Miller, Frank Sinatra with Harry James, and Tommy and Jimmy Dorsey, and Doris Day with Les Brown. Often, the singers had only small parts—they added variety to the orchestral arrangements, but were not the featured items on the program. The big bands declined in importance and popularity in the 1940's, and many singers became the star attractions. In the 1950's, such singers as Dinah Shore and Perry Como starred on television and made hit recordings, with orchestras to accompany them.

Many tunes, such as "Honeysuckle Rose" and "Way Down Yonder in New Orleans," were written as popular songs, but are played mostly as *jazz* rather than as dance music (see JAZZ). Some *blues* songs, such as "St. Louis Blues," are heard as both jazz and dance music. Other types of popular music include Hawaiian songs, calypso music, folk ballads, and Negro songs such as spirituals (see CALYPSO; FOLK MUSIC; SPIRITUAL).

Hillbilly and Cowboy Songs are imitations of the folk music popular in the Southern and Western United States. These songs usually have a guitar accompaniment, and often include yodeling (see YODEL). Roy Acuff, Eddy Arnold, Gene Autry, Tennessee Ernie Ford, Roy Rogers, and other singers have gained fame with such songs as "San Antonio Rose," "Tennessee Waltz," and "Back in the Saddle Again."

Some persons consider the rock-and-roll music of the 1950's as an offshoot of hillbilly songs. The twanging guitar accompaniment, simple lyrics, and choice of subject matter may be derived from the same sources.

Latin-American Music uses rhythms that are more complicated than most other popular music. People dance the tango, conga, rhumba, samba, and mambo to such popular songs as "I Yi Yi Yi Yi (I Like You Very Much)," "Jealousie," "Lady of Spain," and "La Paloma." The orchestras of Xavier Cugat, Perez Prado, and Tito Puente feature Latin-American music.

Writing Popular Music

Writing words and composing music for them has become a big business. Sometimes the words and music of a popular song are written by one person. For example, Irving Berlin wrote both the music and *lyrics* (words) of "White Christmas," "Easter Parade," and many other songs. Cole Porter composed such songs as "Begin the Beguine" and "Night and Day." Carrie Jacobs Bond's songs included "I Love You Truly."

Usually one person writes the music and another writes the words. Hoagland H. (Hoagy) Carmichael composed the music of "Star Dust," and Mitchell Parish wrote the words. John H. (Johnny) Mercer wrote the words of Carmichael's "Lazybones." George Gershwin composed the music and his brother Ira wrote the lyrics of such songs as "The Man I Love" and "I Got Rhythm." The team of Richard Rodgers and Lorenz Hart produced many tunes, including "Manhattan" and "Blue Moon." Rodgers composed the music and Oscar Hammerstein II wrote the words of "Some Enchanted Evening," "People Will Say We're in Love," and many other songs. Hammerstein also wrote the lyrics of such Jerome Kern songs as "Ol' Man River" and "All the Things You Are."

The term *Tin Pan Alley* refers to the entire popular-music industry. It is also an area in New York City where offices of popular-music publishers are located.

Famous Popular Musicians

Dorsey Brothers were musicians and orchestra leaders during the 1930's, 1940's, and 1950's. Jimmy (1904-1957) and Tommy (1905-1956) formed the Dorsey Brothers Orchestra in 1934, but they parted in 1935 because of differences in style. Each brother led his own band until 1953 when they formed one band called the *Fabulous Dorseys*. Jimmy played the clarinet and alto saxophone. Tommy's trombone playing and his excellent arrangements won him the title *Sentimental Gentleman of Swing*. JAMES FRANCIS DORSEY and THOMAS FRANCIS

DORSEY, JR., were born in Shenandoah, Pa.

Kostelanetz, André (1901-), was born in St. Petersburg (now Leningrad), Russia. He moved to the United States in 1922, and began conducting orchestras over radio in 1928. He won fame for his smooth style and sweet arrangements, and for his concert versions of many classical works.

Lombardo, Guy (1902-), was born in London, Ont. He and his brothers began playing in the early 1920's, and developed a distinctively slow, romantic style about 1924. His "Royal Canadians" won wide popularity on radio and television shows and on tour.

Miller, Glenn (1904-1944), was born in Clarinda, Ia. He worked with big bands, including those of Red Nichols and Tommy and Jimmy Dorsey, before he had enough money to form his own group in the late 1930's. He was killed while in the air corps in World War II.

Waring, Fred (1900-), was born in Tyrone, Pa. He began playing in 1921, and soon turned to radio and motion pictures. His "Pennsylvanians" featured smooth styling and orchestral effects. He also used choral arrangements. Critically reviewed by OSCAR HAMMERSTEIN II

Related Articles in WORLD BOOK include:

Beatles	Dancing	Jazz
Berlin, Irving	Dixie	Kern, Jerome D.
Bond, Carrie J.	Folk Music	Porter, Cole
Calypso	Friml, Rudolf	Rodgers, Richard
Carmichael,	Gershwin, George	Romberg, Sigmund
Hoagy	Goodman, Benny	Tin Pan Alley
Cohan,	Hammerstein	Yankee Doodle
George M.	Herbert, Victor	

POPULAR SOVEREIGNTY. See SQUATTER SOVEREIGNTY.

POPULATION of a country or other area is the total number of people who live in it. Populations change as a result of *natural increase* and *migration*. Natural increase is the difference between births and deaths. Most countries have more births than deaths, so their population increases, unless a net loss results from migration. If persons leaving an area are more numerous than persons moving in, migration contributes to population *decreases*. If immigrants are more numerous than emigrants, migration contributes to population *increases*.

World Population rose to about 3,616,000,000 in 1970. The population increases about 65 million yearly, an annual rate of increase of 1.9 per cent. In recent times, the rate of growth has been increasing, and the total population has been growing larger. World population totaled about 500 million in 1650. It doubled in the period from 1650 to 1850, and has more than doubled in the last 100 years. See WORLD.

Several great redistributions in world population have occurred in the last few hundred years. These included (1) the occupation of the Americas and Oceania by Europeans and their descendants, (2) the movement of the Russians across Asia to the Pacific Ocean, and (3) the movement of Chinese to Manchuria. In these and all other areas, the rate of natural increase grew.

European populations in Europe and overseas increased rapidly in the early period of the Industrial Revolution as death rates dropped. But later declines in birth rates reduced rates of increase and even changed them to rates of decrease for brief periods in France and Austria prior to World War II. Several European

TEN MOST DENSELY POPULATED STATES

Number of persons to the square mile

New Jersey
774 persons
𝕏𝕏𝕏𝕏𝕏𝕏𝕏𝕏𝕏𝕏𝕏𝕏𝕏𝕏𝕏𝕏

Rhode Island
708 persons
𝕏𝕏𝕏𝕏𝕏𝕏𝕏𝕏𝕏𝕏𝕏𝕏𝕏𝕏𝕏

Massachusetts
624 persons
𝕏𝕏𝕏𝕏𝕏𝕏𝕏𝕏𝕏𝕏𝕏𝕏

Connecticut
506 persons
𝕏𝕏𝕏𝕏𝕏𝕏𝕏𝕏𝕏𝕏

New York
339 persons
𝕏𝕏𝕏𝕏𝕏𝕏𝕏

Maryland
293 persons
𝕏𝕏𝕏𝕏𝕏𝕏

Pennsylvania
250 persons
𝕏𝕏𝕏𝕏𝕏

Ohio
235 persons
𝕏𝕏𝕏𝕏𝕏

Delaware
217 persons
𝕏𝕏𝕏𝕏

Illinois
179 persons
𝕏𝕏𝕏𝕏

Based on 1960 census figures.

countries, such as Belgium and The Netherlands, rank among those with the highest population *density* (the average number of persons living on each square mile).

Asia's population has increased because of reduced death rates brought about first by the reduction of famine and epidemic, and, later, by more comprehensive health measures. Increase in Africa's population has come more recently. It is also associated with reductions in death rates. Rapid rates of population increase are also occurring in the Latin-American countries, where birth rates have remained high while death rates have been greatly reduced.

The populations of continents show the effects of differing rates of natural increase and migration on the populations living there since the mid-1600's. The past 300 years have been the great period of expansion. Asia has had relatively few emigrants, and it now has more than half of the world's population, just as

— WORLD POPULATION AND YEARLY GROWTH —

Major Area	Population (1970 estimate)	Yearly Growth (1963-1967)
World	3,616,000,000	1.9%
Africa	353,000,000	2.5
Asia	2,081,000,000	2.0
Australia	13,000,000	1.9
Europe	649,000,000	0.9
North America	323,000,000	1.9
Oceania (including Australia and New Zealand)	20,000,000	1.9
South America	190,000,000	2.8

Source: *Demographic Yearbook, 1967,* UN

it did in the mid-1600's. Mass migration from Europe has contributed greatly to the huge population gains of the Americas. The most populous country is Communist China, which has 751 million people. The next three are India with 548,806,000; Russia with 243,722,-000; and the United States with 208,615,000. See the color maps on population with the articles on states, provinces, regions, and continents.

Overpopulation. No one knows how many persons the earth can support. As populations grew in areas with limited resources, experts feared that food production would not keep pace with population increases. Thomas R. Malthus, the English economist, developed a theory that, because population tended to grow more rapidly than the food supply, it caused continual pressure on available resources. He saw war, famine, and other disasters as the usual limitations to population growth. Many scholars have agreed with Malthus, but many have not. In the great period of European expansion, and in the Western countries with declining birth rates, some persons argued that Malthus had been proved wrong. Food and facilities had improved more rapidly than population. But, in recent years, rapid increases in population in underdeveloped areas have led to renewed discussions of Malthus' theories. International organizations and national governments have sought to increase food production and to foster economic development generally, in order to raise the level of living for the growing populations.

Births, Deaths, and Migrations. Before the Industrial Revolution, birth and death rates were high in all countries. With the industrial developments in Western countries and in Japan, death rates gradually declined before birth rates did. But eventually birth rates also declined, and rates of population increase again became relatively low. In agricultural regions where incomes were low and illiteracy high, declines in death rates have occurred without corresponding declines in birth rates. This lag in the decline of birth rates has produced the high rates of population increase in most of Asia, Africa, and Latin America.

The mass migration from Europe to the Americas helped in the development of the countries that sent migrants as well as those that received them. But today, there are no major areas of undeveloped land requiring large numbers of immigrants. Governments desiring some immigrants often do not want to accept persons from the countries that might want to send them.

Urban and Rural Population. The movement from the rural areas to the cities grew with industrialization in Western countries and Japan. Today, it is occurring in most of the countries of the world, even in those that remain agricultural. In 1800, only 5 of every 100 persons in the United States lived in places of 2,500 or more population. In 1960, about 2 of every 3 persons lived in places of this size or larger. In 1800, about 20 per cent of the population of England and Wales lived in cities. Today, about 20 per cent of the population lives in rural areas.

Census. Most governments conduct *censuses* (regular counts of the population) to learn the numbers, the places of residence, and the characteristics of their peoples. The statistical study of these *vital statistics* (characteristics) is called *demography.* The United States government has taken a census of the American population once each 10 years since 1790. Many countries took censuses of population in 1950, and even more took them in 1960. See Census; Demography.

Age. A rapidly growing population usually has a high proportion of children. A slowly growing population usually has a lower proportion of children. Statistics on the proportions of various age groups help society prepare in advance for more schoolchildren, workers, or aged persons. Current estimates of these proportions for the population of the world indicate that 1 person in 3 is below 15 years of age. About 3 of every 5 persons are between the ages of 15 and 60, and fewer than 1 in 10 are over 60 years of age. In the United States, 31 per cent are less than 15 years old, 56 per cent between 15 and 60, and 13 per cent over 60. In some Central American countries, more than 40 per cent of the population is below 15 years of age, while only 4 per cent is over 60.

In the United States, the first federal census in 1790 determined that nearly 4 million people lived in the country. By 1970, the U.S. population had increased to about 208,615,000—about 53 times as great as it had been just 180 years before. The rate of increase during each 10-year period remained high in the colonial and early national periods. But it declined until it stood only slightly over 7 per cent between 1930 and 1940. With reduced death rates, the population is now growing about 1.6 per cent each year. About 3,304,000 persons are added each year. About 79 per cent of the growth is due to natural increase, and about 21 per cent to net immigration.

The growth of the various regions of the United States is influenced greatly by migrations within the country. In recent decades, the West has grown most rapidly and the Northeast least rapidly. The center of population, which was located near Baltimore in 1790, moved steadily west, and was in Clinton County, Ill., in 1960. Most of the increase has occurred in urban areas, where increasing proportions of the population live.

Men have outnumbered women throughout most of the history of the United States, because most of the immigrants were men. But death rates at most ages are higher for men than for women. Therefore, as immigra-

tion has declined, the proportion of women has increased. By 1950, there were more women than men living in the United States.

The United States population is made up of people from many races and nationalities. About 7 per cent of the people were born in other countries. About 8 of every 9 are white, and about 1 in 10 is Negro. Indians, Chinese, Japanese, and other nonwhite groups make up less than 1 per cent of the total.

The future growth of the population depends on many factors, and it is not possible to forecast what will happen. But if the rate of growth continues as in recent years, the population will be about 228 million in 1975, and 250 million in 1980. CONRAD TAEUBER

Related Articles in WORLD BOOK include:

Birth Control	Malthus,	Vital Statistics
Immigration and	Thomas R.	World
Emigration	Migration	

POPULIST PARTY was a political party that took a prominent part in United States politics during the 1890's. The party resulted from a variety of unsolved abuses, especially the continuing decline in prices of such crops as wheat and cotton. Several small groups of people seeking reforms united to form the party.

A long and severe depression had struck the farmers of the nation after the Civil War. To protect themselves, the farmers had united in the Grange movement of 1867 and the Farmers' Alliances of the 1870's and 1880's. These groups, together with the Knights of Labor, sent delegates to Cincinnati in 1891 to form a new political party. They adopted the name *People's Party*, but were usually called the *Populist Party*. In 1892, the Populists nominated James B. Weaver of Iowa for President.

The Populist Party stood for social reform that would help the farmers and the workers. It wanted the government to increase the amount of money in circulation by the unlimited coinage of silver and by printing paper notes. Many persons believed that this would relieve unemployment and raise farm prices. The party also supported the eight-hour work day, the direct election of senators, the initiative and referendum, the use of the *Australian* (secret) ballot, and other reforms. Many easterners considered the Populists dangerous radicals.

In the election of 1892, the new party showed its strength. Its presidential candidate polled over 1 million votes, and many Populist candidates won state offices. In the congressional election of 1894, the Populist Party polled almost 1½ million votes.

By 1896, many Democrats had also come to favor the Populist program. These Democrats gained control of their party, so that it now stood for many of the things the Populists favored. In 1896, the Democrats nominated William Jennings Bryan for President. The Populists decided to join the Democrats in supporting Bryan. But Bryan lost the election to Republican William McKinley by about 600,000 votes out of 13½ million.

The strength of the Populist Party dropped rapidly after 1896. This decline was partly because national prosperity was returning, and partly because the major parties gradually took over many of the points in the reform platform of the Populists. RICHARD HOFSTADTER

See also DONNELLY, IGNATIUS.

POQUELIN, JEAN BAPTISTE. See MOLIÈRE.

POPULATION DENSITY OF THE CONTINENTS

Estimated number of persons per square mile in 1970

Europe
160 persons

Asia
122 persons

North America
34 persons

Africa
30 persons

South America
28 persons

Australia
4 persons

Antarctica has no permanent population.

Source: *Demographic Yearbook, 1967,* UN

PORCELAIN

Theodore Haviland & Co.

Beautiful Porcelain used in many homes today first came from China. Its whiteness and translucence make it one of the homemaker's proudest possessions.

PORCELAIN, *POHR seh lin,* is often called chinaware because it first came from China. Porcelain first developed from ordinary pottery, but it is a thing beyond and apart from it. It is a most precious and most highly organized product of the potter's art. All chinaware or porcelain is *pottery,* in the sense that it is one of the highest members of the great pottery family. But not all pottery is chinaware by any means. One might say that all dollars are money, but not all moneys are dollars. A silver dollar is minted by the same processes as pennies and nickels. But the silver dollar differs from pennies and nickels not only in its higher value but also in its material. In much the same way porcelain or chinaware is wholly different from all other pottery in materials and in its characteristics.

The material of which chinaware is made is called the *body* or *paste.* Chinaware differs from other pottery because of its whiteness. It is white not merely on the surface, but all the way through. It appears white when broken. Also, it is more or less *translucent,* which means that it lets light through. The edges of thin china plates or saucers should let light through, if they are held toward the light. Bowls, cups, and often all the body of entire plates and saucers are translucent, unless they are unusually thick.

The glaze is the glassy substance with which the body or paste of the object is coated. When the body has been baked, or *fired,* but not glazed, it is spoken of as *biscuit.* Medallions, busts, or small pieces of sculpture are often made of *biscuit.* There was usually no biscuit stage in the making of Chinese porcelain. The fluid glaze was applied directly to the air-dried object. Glaze and body were fired at the same time in a furnace or *kiln* at great heat (from 1350° to 1500° centigrade).

Kinds of Porcelain

There are three main kinds of porcelain, or chinaware: *hard-paste porcelain, soft-paste porcelain* (which was produced in earlier attempts to make hard-paste), and a so-called artificial porcelain which is known as *bone china.* Bone china was developed in trying to make hard-paste porcelain like that from China, which has always been the model and the ideal of porcelain makers.

Hard-Paste Porcelain. The materials used in making hard-paste porcelain are kaolin, or China clay, and petuntse, or China stone.

Kaolin comes from the weathering, or decomposition,

of feldspar in granitelike rock. Kaolin does not melt together, even at the greatest heat to which the oven or kiln can be brought. *Petuntse,* or China stone, contains feldspar, silicate of alumina, and potash, or sometimes soda. Petuntse melts, or is fusible, in great heat. The melting of the fusible petuntse in the kiln produces a glassy substance. This substance holds the nonfusible China clay or kaolin in *suspension,* which means that it holds it together. This makes hard-paste porcelain translucent and *vitreous,* or glasslike. The kaolin might be called the bone of the porcelain body. The fusible petuntse is like the flesh, and the glaze may be compared to the skin.

The term *glaze* is only another form of the word *glass.* Chemically, there is not much difference between the glaze on the surface of china and ordinary glass. The glaze is transparent, and usually colorless or almost so. The white body or paste beneath the glaze can be easily seen. In China, the glaze was made of pure petuntse or China stone, which was sometimes softened with a little lime. In Western, European, and Japanese porcelain, the hard-paste body was usually fired or baked first. A heat of from 600° to 900° centigrade was used for this. Afterwards, the biscuit body was covered with a coating of glaze and fired at the full temperature of 1350° to 1500° centigrade. The firing made the molten glaze an actual part of the porcelain body.

When the edge of a hard-paste porcelain bowl or plate is struck sharply with a pencil or similar light object it will give forth a clear, ringing bell-like note. When a piece of hard-paste porcelain is chipped or broken the break or fracture is shell-like, or *conchoidal.* It is very much like the chipping or fracture of a piece of flint.

The paste of hard-paste porcelain does not always have exactly the same composition. The proportions of kaolin and petuntse may vary. As much as 65 per cent of kaolin can be used in the mixture. The porcelain is said to be of *severe* type if the percentage of kaolin is high. The porcelain is said to be *mild* if the percentage of kaolin is low. The earlier hard-paste porcelain of Sèvres belongs to the severe type, and so does most German porcelain. China of this type may be very useful, but it is likely to be harsh to the sight and cold to the touch. Chinese china belongs to the mild type as does much of the porcelain made at Sèvres in later years. The mild porcelain is much more pleasant to see and to touch. It is usually decorated more beautifully. The comparison of a piece of German severe porcelain with a piece of mild Chinese porcelain shows that the Chinese is mellow and satiny but the German is rough, hard, and unsympathetic. Severe china does not take decoration so well as the milder kind does.

Soft-Paste Porcelain was made from combinations of a white-firing clay with a fusible silicate, such as a pulverized *frit,* or mass of glass, sand, or broken china. Soft-paste china was first used after kaolin had been found in Europe. It is sometimes called *artificial,* because the materials in it were substituted for those used in making Oriental china. European pioneers in porcelain used these materials in trying to reproduce the qualities of Chinese china. Soft-paste china differs from hard-paste china in the softer whiteness of its body. The whiteness is sometimes creamy in tone, and usually is more translucent than hard-paste china. When soft-paste china is chipped or broken, the break is likely to be straight and not shell-like as in hard porcelain. The unglazed portion thus exposed is grainy and chalky. Most of the early European china was soft-paste, and nearly always had a mellow quality about it. The most highly prized old Sèvres china was soft-paste.

Bone China is another artificial type of china. It is made from kaolin, petuntse, and a quantity of bone ash. This combination was discovered about 1750 and the process developed in England from that time onward. The body is a true porcelain paste that has been made more fusible by adding a large proportion of calcium phosphate in the form of bone ash. Bone china holds a middle place between hard-paste and soft-paste porcelain. It is generally not so white as the hard paste, but it is whiter than the soft paste.

The Making of Chinaware

In making china, all the materials are first finely ground up, or pulverized, and washed and filtered. Then they are mixed in the proper proportions, and the resulting clay is thoroughly worked and kneaded. A lump of this plastic clay may be thrown on the potter's wheel and gradually shaped by the potter's thumbs and fingers as the wheel revolves. Or pieces may be molded by pressing the moist clay firmly into molds of the desired shape. Among the articles which must be molded are fluted articles, pieces with raised patterns or holes, cup handles, teapot spouts, dish covers, vegetable dishes, lids, most plates, and all platters of other than circular shape. Such things as spouts and cup handles are separately molded and then attached in their proper places with *slip*, or a thick, creamy fluid mixture of the clay. They are then set away to dry until they are ready to be fired. Porcelain may also be cast by pouring thick slips into plaster-of-Paris molds. The mold is removed after the water drains off or evaporates and the clay is dry and hard enough to hold its shape.

Decoration of China. The body of the piece may be ornamented by engraving, embossing, or by perforations. Reliefs may be applied before the piece is fired or before glazing. The decoration may also be made with colors or gilding, or both. Two sorts of colors are used, *underglaze* and *enamel*. Underglaze colors are applied before glazing and firing. A process of transfer of printed decorations for designs in one underglaze color came into use about 1757. Enamel colors and gold colors require a second firing to make them fuse with the glaze and become permanent. The most reliable underglaze color is blue made from cobalt. It is often seen in the old blue and white ware of China. Other underglaze colors have been tried, but none is so satisfactory as blue. The widest variety of enamel colors was perfected at an early period. Some china painters became very famous. They used an almost unlimited palette of colors. A third way of applying color decoration is by colored glazes, as in the old Chinese celadon ware.

Markings on Chinaware. The European china factories usually marked much of their china to show who had manufactured it. But often some of their finest products were unmarked. Even after the pieces were marked, sometimes the marks differed widely. The two well-

Lenox, Inc.
Ingredients for Porcelain Are Poured into Molds.

known interlaced L's of Vincennes were often different from other L's of the same manufacture. Other marks also never looked twice the same. The royal cipher (which later became the recognized mark of Sèvres), the crossed swords of Dresden, the three wavy lines of Copenhagen, the anchor of Chelsea, the crescent of Worcester, or the crowned D of Derby all were differently done at times. The marks of chinaware in some cases are trustworthy. But there are many other instances when they are completely false.

The Ware Is "Jiggered" to a Fine Smoothness.
Lenox, Inc.

DECORATIVE PORCELAIN

Chinese Blue and White Porcelain Bowl of the Wan Li period has English silvergilt mounts. Handles are delicately worked figurines.

Royal Copenhagen Porcelain of a Javanese dancing girl

Royal Sèvres Porcelain vases made in the 1780's

Exquisite Workmanship makes this little snuffbox almost jewel-like. It is German Meissen of the early 1800's.

Covered Urn of jasper ware made by Wedgwood in the 1700's

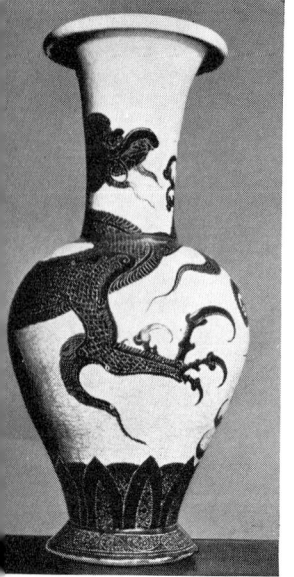

Chinese Porcelain Vase of the Sung dynasty period

A Young Woman Holding a Basket. The delicate decoration of this Meissen porcelain is typical of German work during the 1700's.

Chinese beaker-shaped vase of the Ming dynasty

Lenox Imperial

Crown Derby

Plain Edme-Wedgwood

English Lustre

German Meissen

English Worcester

Lenox, Inc.; Metropolitan Museum of Art; Josiah Wedgwood & Sons; Art Institute of Chicago; William S. Pitcairn Corp.

Chelsea Rose

Chinese Lowestoft

Lenox, Inc.

A Worker Attaches the Base to a Soup Cup.

Very little trust can be placed on the marks of Chinese porcelain. They have often been forged and misapplied. False marks have been made time and again to the order of exporters. This practice has been going on for hundreds of years. The average person usually considers a mark on a piece of Chinese porcelain as merely an interesting item of decoration, and nothing more. The mark may tell the truth, but more probably it is a forgery.

Chinese Chinaware. Most of the old Chinese chinaware was made in the factories of Kingtehchen. Sometimes the articles made there were decorated at other places, such as Nanking. They were then exported to the china-loving West. One Kingtehchen product is that large and varied group called Lowestoft. This was made to the order of foreign merchants and decorated for individual customers in England and America. Often coats of arms and monograms were put on the Lowestoft china. The name Lowestoft is not correct. The greatest part of this kind of china never came within miles of the little town in East Anglia which is named Lowestoft.

Japanese China. All the Japanese know about china making came from the country of China itself. Their most famous factory, Arita, was founded in 1605. It has produced the well-known Kakiyemon and Imari types. These have been much copied by European factories.

China Factories in Europe are numerous and well-known. In England there are the Worcester, Derby, Bow, Chelsea, Spode (now Copeland's), Bristol, Caughley, Minton, and Wedgwood. In France there are the factories at Limoges and in Paris. In Italy are the Capo di Monte and Ginori (Doccia) factories. In Denmark is the Copenhagen factory, and in Germany the famous Dresden (Meissen) plant. The Wedgwood factory in England was established very early, but it did not make much porcelain until years later. Many other factories in England produced quite admirable porcelain. But they generally did not exist for very long. The Lowestoft factory started about 1757 and closed about 1802. Nothing but soft-paste china was ever made there. It was decorated very well and was quite beautiful. But it is now very rare and hardly ever to be seen outside a museum. A very little of the Chinese porcelain called Lowestoft may possibly have been decorated there. But there is some question even about

that. The name seems to have been given to the Chinese porcelain from certain types of decoration that were popular at Lowestoft. But these types had been largely stolen or copied from other factories. The Lowestoft concern appears to have been mainly a china-selling business.

American China Factories have made full use of the many technical advances, experience, and traditions in decoration which were part of the ancient porcelain industry. They are putting forth modern wares which compare favorably with the products of a great past. England, France, and America carry on extensive china making. Large quantities are also made in Czechoslovakia, Germany, and Japan.

In the study of chinaware it is always necessary to distinguish what is porcelain and what is not. Charm and beauty of outside appearance sometimes tempt us to include such members of the pottery family as Delft, the various Staffordshires, the finer Italian faïence, or the fascinating pottery of Quimper in Brittany. But these are not china. They belong to the earthenware side of the pottery family.

History of Chinaware

It is said that the Chinese began to make porcelain before the Christian Era, but there are no genuine specimens of earlier dates than those of the Sung dynasty (A.D. 960-1279).

Introduction into Europe. At an early period, articles of precious Chinese porcelain were occasionally brought to Europe. Trade with the Orient and diplomatic relations with the Far East made this introduction of chinaware possible. Perhaps the returning Crusaders may now and then have brought back from the East a bit of porcelain, just as they brought spices, plants and furlined night clothes. But there is no definite proof that they did.

The first really known instance of Europe's concern with porcelain was in 1447. A letter was written in that year to the Sultan of "Babylon." It asked the Sultan to look kindly on French commerce in the seaports of

After Firing, the Ware Is Inspected for Flaws.

Lenox, Inc.

Lenox, Inc.
Decorations on Cups Are Added by Skilled Artists.

the Near East. The letter ended with a request for a present of porcelain to be brought back to the King, Charles VII of France, by his ambassador. But it is quite probable that the Medici in Florence as well as the merchant princes in Venice had specimens of Chinese porcelain as early as this or earlier. The Italians had carried on a great trade with the East.

Chinese porcelain or chinaware was very rare for a long time. Only the very great and wealthy could hope to own a few pieces of it. In 1567 Queen Elizabeth had a "porringer of white porselyn and a cup of green porselyn." Francis I of France had among his treasures "vases and dishes of porcelain, curiously wrought."

From 1600 on, there was a great increase in trade with the Orient. This trade made the people of Europe better acquainted with porcelain and its fine quality. After 1650, ships of the English, French, and Dutch East India companies brought the elegance and charms of chinaware within the reach of the average person. By 1660 there were merchants in Paris who had a thriving business in fine porcelain. After about 1655 in England, the habit of drinking tea, coffee, and chocolate made chinaware popular among the general public. Much of the chinaware brought to England at that time consisted of thin teacups without handles, and the teapots, sugar bowls, and pitchers that went with them.

It is said that Nell Gwyn used to go down to the London docks and poke around among the newly arrived cargoes from East India, so that she could have the first pick of anything she liked, such as fine articles of porcelain. It needed only the example of Queen Mary, a few years later, to encourage the demand for chinaware. Through the 1700's the love of chinaware and the desire to own it affected all ranks of society.

China Factories Built. There was as much demand for china on the continent of Europe as there was in England. Everybody wanted to buy it. It was only natural that enterprising persons in England and on the continent should try to make china themselves. There was much demand for it and a good market in which to sell it. But the Chinese were not giving away the secret of a precious product. There were many attempts to make porcelain in Europe before the secret was discovered. Some of the results of the experiments then made are exceedingly beautiful and much prized. But they are not true porcelain. Francesco de' Medici, the Grand

PORCH is often the roof-covered entrance to a building. The roof extends from the main wall of the building. It can also be a screen- or glass-enclosed extension on a house, which is often used to sleep in.

PORCUPINE, *PAWR kyoo pine*, is an animal that has strong, stiff quills on its back, sides, and tail. Porcupine quills are long, sharp bristles of hairs that are *fused* (grown together). Porcupines defend themselves by striking attackers with their quilled tails. The quills come out easily and stick into the attacker's flesh. Porcupines cannot shoot quills at their enemies, as some persons believe. In some kinds of porcupines, the tip of each quill is covered with tiny, backward-pointing projections called *barbs*. The barbs hook into the flesh, and the quills are almost impossible to remove. Porcupine victims may die from infections caused by germs on the quills, or from damage to a vital organ. Quills may even stick in an attacker's jaw, making the animal unable to open its mouth and causing starvation. Only *pumas* (North American mountain lions) seem able to attack porcupines successfully.

Porcupines are *rodents* (gnawing animals). Biologists classify them as *Old World porcupines* and *New World porcupines*. Old World porcupines live in Africa, southeastern Asia, India, and southern Europe. Most kinds of Old World porcupines grow about 3 feet long, including the tail. They make their homes in tunnels in the ground, and do not climb trees.

New World porcupines live in North and South America. Only one kind, the *North American porcupine*, lives in North America. North American porcupines are about 3 feet long and weigh about 20 pounds. Their yellowish-white quills are 2 to 3 inches long. Their fur is brownish-black. North American porcupines live chiefly in pine forests. They make their homes in trees, stumps, hollow logs, and rock slides. They eat green vegetation and tree bark. They often climb trees to strip the bark from the upper part of the tree. They may kill a tree in this way.

This European Porcupine is well protected by sharp quills.

Ylla, Guillumette

Female North American porcupines give birth to a single offspring in the spring. The babies have quills at birth. North American porcupines are often incorrectly called *hedgehogs*. True hedgehogs live only in the Eastern Hemisphere. The flesh of the North American porcupine is edible, but most persons do not consider it tasty.

Scientific Classification. Old World porcupines make up the family *Hystricidae*. New World porcupines make up the family *Erethizontidae*. North American porcupines are genus *Erethizon*, species *E. dorsatum*.   DANIEL H. BRANT

PORCUPINE FISH is a kind of puffer that has a short, rounded body with long spines. These spines protect the fish against its enemies, just as quills protect a porcupine. The jaw teeth are joined to form a beak.

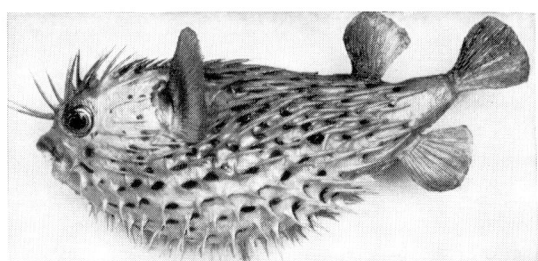

Field Museum of Natural History

The Porcupine Fish has strong, sharp spines on its body, and teeth grown together so that they form a beak.

These fish can also inflate their bodies with water. Most porcupine fish live in warm or tropical waters.

Scientific Classification. The porcupine fish belongs to the porcupine fish and burrfish family, *Diodontidae*. It is genus *Diodon*, species *D. hystrix*.   CARL L. HUBBS

PORCUPINE MOUNTAINS. See MICHIGAN (Land Regions).

PORE is the tiny opening of a skin gland. The glands are like little sacks set deep in the skin. The cells inside the sacks produce sweat if the gland is a sweat gland, and oil if it is an oil gland. The face has many oil glands. The oil that these glands produce is normally a liquid. *Blackheads* form if the oil *cakes* (becomes solid) within the pores. If the skin festers about these blackheads, acne pimples result. If certain kinds of bacteria get into the pores, they cause boils. When sweat glands are blocked up, prickly heat develops. See also ACNE; PERSPIRATION; SKIN.   RICHARD L. SUTTON, JR.

PORGY, *PAWR gih*, is a red fish with blue patches that lives in the Mediterranean Sea and North Atlantic Ocean. The porgy has an oval body about 8 or 10 inches long.

Scientific Classification. The porgy belongs to the porgy and sea bream family, *Sparidae*. It is genus *Pagrus*, species *P. pagrus*.   CARL L. HUBBS

The Grass Porgy is named for its habit of living among grasslike seaweeds along the coast of Florida.

N.Y. Zoological Society

PORGY AND BESS. See OPERA (Some of the Famous Operas).

PORIFERA. See SPONGE.

PORK is the meat from hogs. About three of every four pounds of meat on a hog are made into fresh, cured, or smoked pork *cuts* (pieces). The rest is used in making lard and sausage. Some pork is *cured* (covered with a special liquid mixture) and *smoked* (baked) to give the meat more flavor and to keep it from spoiling too quickly. Americans eat about 58 pounds of pork per person in a year.

PORK CUTS AND HOW TO COOK THEM

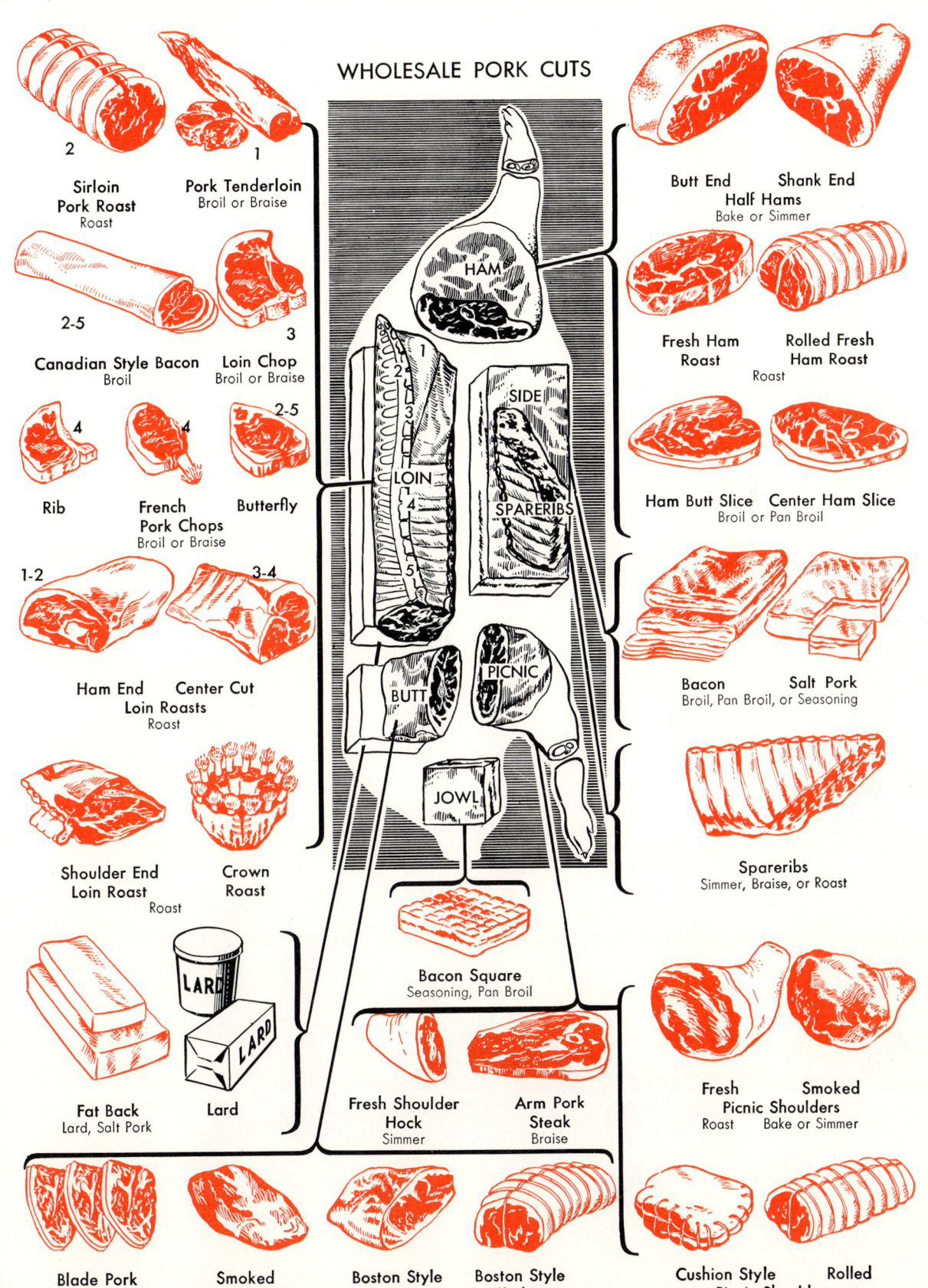

WHOLESALE PORK CUTS

2
Sirloin Pork Roast
Roast

1
Pork Tenderloin
Broil or Braise

2-5
Canadian Style Bacon
Broil

3
Loin Chop
Broil or Braise

4
Rib

4
French Pork Chops
Broil or Braise

2-5
Butterfly

1-2 **3-4**
Ham End **Center Cut**
Loin Roasts
Roast

Shoulder End Loin Roast
Roast

Crown Roast

LARD
LARD

Fat Back
Lard, Salt Pork

Lard

Blade Pork Steaks
Braise

Smoked Cottage Roll
Bake or Pan Broil

Boston Style Butt

Boston Style Rolled Butt
Roast

Butt End **Shank End**
Half Hams
Bake or Simmer

Fresh Ham Roast

Rolled Fresh Ham Roast
Roast

Ham Butt Slice **Center Ham Slice**
Broil or Pan Broil

Bacon **Salt Pork**
Broil, Pan Broil, or Seasoning

Spareribs
Simmer, Braise, or Roast

Bacon Square
Seasoning, Pan Broil

Fresh Shoulder Hock
Simmer

Arm Pork Steak
Braise

Fresh **Smoked**
Picnic Shoulders
Roast   Bake or Simmer

Cushion Style **Rolled**
Picnic Shoulders
Roast

Prepared in co-operation with National Live Stock & Meat Board

PORK BARREL

Pork is divided into six classes for sale. *Butcher carcasses* are the best quality. They are cut at the packing house into fresh pork, hams, and bacon. *Bacon carcasses* are thinner hogs with less fat covering than butcher carcasses. *Packing carcasses* do not have enough quality to be sold as fresh pork. They are usually smoked or salt-dried. *Shipper carcasses* are good-quality pork bodies that are sold whole to retail butcher shops that prefer to cut up their own pork. *Roasting* and *suckling pigs* also are sold whole, mainly to hotels and restaurants.

Official U.S. grades of pork are *No. 1, No. 2, No. 3, Medium,* and *Cull.* No. 1 has a firm covering of fat and smooth skin that is free of wrinkles and hair roots. No. 2 and No. 3 grades are fatter than No. 1 and not quite as good. Medium grade has less fat than the top three grades, and Cull has little *finish* (fat). Most pork sold comes from hogs that are 7 to 12 months old. The younger hogs produce the highest quality pork.

Fresh pork should be cooked well, because the meat sometimes contains a worm that causes a disease called *trichinosis.*   JOHN C. AYRES

Related Articles in WORLD BOOK include:

Bacon	Meat	Sausage
Ham	Meat Packing	Trichina
Lard		

PORK BARREL. Legislators usually seek as many government projects and improvements for their districts as they can. Bills appropriating money for such projects are usually called "the pork barrel." A legislator customarily votes for expenditures in other districts, even though he may think them unnecessary or extravagant, in order to have legislators from those districts vote for projects in his district (see LOGROLLING). Excessive pork-barrel practices have led to movements to give the President the power to veto individual items in an appropriation bill without killing the whole bill. Such movements have failed. However, defenders of this system point out that pork-barrel projects such as river and harbor improvements increase the country's wealth by providing more public facilities.   WILLIAM G. CARLETON

PORKFISH. See GRUNT.

POROSITY, *poh RAHS uh tee,* is the existence of many small holes or spaces in a material. In some porous materials, such as charcoal, earthenware pottery, and sponges, these holes connect together. Gases and liquids can pass through the connected holes. In other porous materials, the small spaces inside are separated from each other by solid material. Bricks and certain types of foam rubber are examples of this kind of porous material. These materials can usually absorb liquids and gases.

Porosity is desirable in some materials and undesirable in others. For example, porous filters of charcoal can remove impurities from the air. But porosity in iron castings is a defect which reduces the strength of the metal.

On the atomic scale, every material is considered porous because there is much free space between their atoms or molecules. For example, the spaces between the atoms of the metal palladium are large enough for hydrogen atoms to move about.

See also DIFFUSION; MOLECULE.

PORPHYRY, *PAWR fih rih,* is the name of any igneous rock in which one kind of crystal is much larger than the rest. An ordinary granite, for instance, consists of a solid mass of small crystals of quartz, feldspar, and some dark-colored mineral. Some granites also contain large crystals of feldspar, one inch to several inches long, scattered through the rock. They are then called "granite porphyry." The mass of smaller crystals in which the large ones lie is called the "groundmass." See also GRANITE.   RICHARD M. PEARL

PORPHYRY, *PAWR fih rih* (233-304), a philosopher in the Neo-Platonic group, described how all the qualities persons attribute to things may be classified. This subject, put forth in his book *Introduction to the Categories,* had great influence on medieval philosophy. It raised the problem of the status of universal propositions which occupied logicians for hundreds of years. Porphyry was born in Tyre. He studied in Athens. Porphyry then traveled to Rome, where he joined Plotinus (see PLOTINUS).   LEWIS M. HAMMOND

PORPOISE, *PAWR pus,* is a small whalelike mammal that is often confused with the dolphin. The two animals can be told apart by their snouts. The snout of the dolphin forms a "beak," but that of the porpoise does not. Almost all the trained "porpoises" that perform in aquariums are really dolphins.

The common porpoise grows about 5 feet long and weighs up to 100 pounds. It has a gray back and a white underside. This porpoise is found in the coastal

The Common Porpoise Has a Gray Back and a White Underside.

by Tom Dolan for WORLD BOOK

608

waters of North America, South America, Europe, Asia, and Africa. Several hundred years ago, porpoise meat was a favorite food in England and France.

Common porpoises travel in small groups, ranging from two to five animals. They eat herring, mackerel, and other fish, and also feed on crustaceans and squids. When the porpoise comes to the surface of the water to breathe, it swims with a slow rolling motion. Other porpoises include the killer whale, the white-vented porpoise, the finless porpoise, and the grampus porpoise.

Scientific Classification. Porpoises belong in the whale order, *Cetacea*. The common porpoise is in the dolphin and porpoise family, *Delphinidae*. It is genus *Phocaena*, species *P. phocaena*.   RAYMOND M. GILMORE

See also DOLPHIN; KILLER WHALE; WHALE.

PORT. See WINE (Types).

PORT is a place where ships and boats load and unload passengers and cargoes. Large, bustling ports have buildings and equipment for receiving, storing, and reshipping goods. Such facilities include wharves, warehouses, tugs, ferries, mechanical loaders and unloaders, and railroad and truck transportation.

Some ports, such as Cherbourg, France, and Rio de Janeiro, Brazil, stand on natural harbors formed by bays and inlets. Others, such as Los Angeles and Genoa, Italy, are built on artificial harbors protected by breakwaters and jetties. Many great ports lie on rivers far from the sea. Inland ports include London, Montreal, New Orleans, and Bordeaux, France.

Ports may also be classified by their purpose or function. For example, Gibraltar is a naval, or strategic, port. Concarneau, France, is a fishing port. Cape Town, South Africa, serves as a fuel-storage port for ships sailing around the tip of Africa. Kuwait, on the Persian Gulf, is a leading petroleum port.

Much United States and Canadian commerce passes through ports on the Great Lakes. Inland waterways make it possible for all but the largest ocean ships to sail to Chicago, Toronto, and other Great Lakes ports.

Among the chief ports in the United States, besides those listed on the pictograph, are San Francisco; Toledo, Ohio; Baltimore; Norfolk, Va.; and Los Angeles—Long Beach. The main ports in Canada include Montreal; Vancouver, B.C.; Sept Îles, Que.; and Port Arthur and Fort William, Ont. Public port authorities, such as the Port of New York Authority, may direct the operation of major ports.   J. ROWLAND ILLICK

See also FREE PORT; HARBOR; PORT OF ENTRY.

PORT ARTHUR lies near the tip of the Liaotung Peninsula in Northern China (see CHINA [political map]). Port Arthur and Dairen form a municipality with a population of about 1½ million. The Chinese name for Port Arthur is *Lü-shun-k'ou*. The Japanese called it *Ryojun*. There are two sections in Port Arthur, the old Chinese city and the new town built by the Russians after they took Port Arthur in 1898. During their occupation of Manchuria, the Japanese made many improvements in the Chinese quarter of Port Arthur. The city is about 50 feet above sea level.

The British gave Port Arthur its name when they used the city as a base to fight China in 1857. Later, the city became a Chinese naval base. Port Arthur fell to Russia in 1898. Japan took the city in 1905, after an important battle of the Russo-Japanese War. After World War II, China and Russia made an agreement to share the port as a naval base.   THEODORE H. E. CHEN

PORT ARTHUR, Ontario (pop. 48,340; alt. 616 ft.), is an important Canadian port on the Great Lakes. It lies on the north shore of Lake Superior at the mouth of the Kaministiquia River (see ONTARIO [political map]). With its twin city, Fort William, it forms a metropolitan area with a population of over 96,500. Port Arthur has foundries, grain elevators, lumber mills, machine shops, pulp and paper mills, and woodworking plants. It is an important dry-dock and shipbuilding center. The base for an early road to the Red River settlement, Port Arthur was founded in 1869 as Dawson's Landing. In 1870, it was named Prince Arthur's Landing, and later Port Arthur. Both names honored Prince Arthur, Duke of Connaught, who later became governor general of Canada. The city was chartered in 1906.   D. M. L. FARR

PORT ARTHUR, Tex. (pop. 66,676; alt. 10 ft.), is an important port and manufacturing center in southeastern Texas (see TEXAS [political map]). With Beaumont and Orange, it forms a metropolitan area with a population of about 306,000. Highly industrialized, Port Arthur is the center of one of the world's largest oil-refining districts. The Port Arthur-Orange Bridge, over the Neches River, is the tallest highway bridge in the South. The city's chief industries include oil refining, chemicals, shipbuilding, and fishing. It has a council-manager government.   H. BAILEY CARROLL

LEADING PORTS OF THE WORLD
Tons of cargo handled in 1966

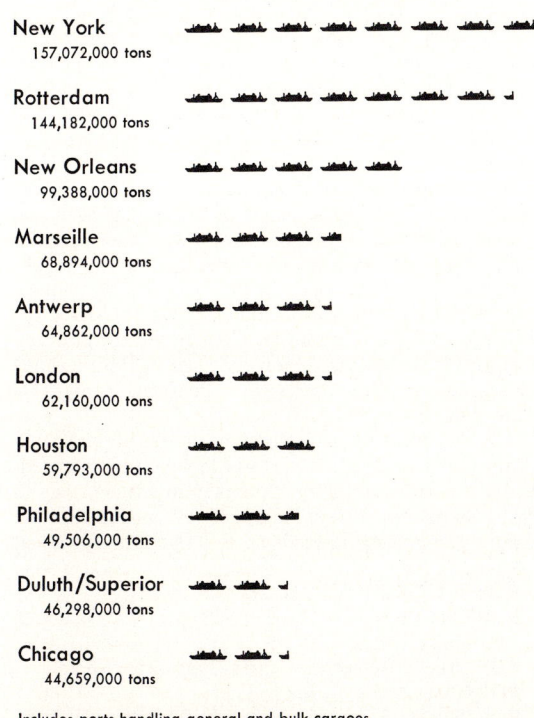

New York 157,072,000 tons	
Rotterdam 144,182,000 tons	
New Orleans 99,388,000 tons	
Marseille 68,894,000 tons	
Antwerp 64,862,000 tons	
London 62,160,000 tons	
Houston 59,793,000 tons	
Philadelphia 49,506,000 tons	
Duluth/Superior 46,298,000 tons	
Chicago 44,659,000 tons	

Includes ports handling general and bulk cargoes.
Excludes ports of Communist countries.

Sources: Corps of Engineers; *Norwegian Shipping News*, May, 1967

PORT-AU-PRINCE, PORT-oh-*PRINCE* (pop. 240,000; alt. 25 ft.), is the capital, largest city, and chief port of Haiti. Two peninsulas which project westward from the city protect its harbor. Government buildings, the cathedral, the University of Haiti, and the business buildings which line the broad, sunny streets help to make Port-au-Prince the center of Haitian life. Its industries include sugar mills and rice mills. For location, see HAITI (map).   OTIS P. STARKEY

PORT BORDEN. See BORDEN.

PORT ELIZABETH (pop. 249,211; met. area 290,693; alt. 225 ft.) is a leading seaport and manufacturing city in South Africa. Port Elizabeth lies 450 miles east of Cape Town. See SOUTH AFRICA (color map).

Because of its importance as a trading center, the city is often called the *Liverpool of South Africa.* Several American companies have automobile assembly plants and rubber factories near the city. In the city's Feather Market Hall, farmers sell ostrich feathers. The first large group of English settlers to reach South Africa settled in Port Elizabeth in 1820.   HIBBERD V. B. KLINE, JR.

PORT LOUIS (pop. 134,900; alt. 30 ft.) is the capital and chief port of Mauritius, an independent island country in the Indian Ocean. The city lies on the northwestern coast of the island in a cove surrounded by mountains. The architecture in the city shows French influence. See also MAURITIUS.   BURTON BENEDICT

PORT MORESBY (pop. about 42,000; alt. 50 ft.) is the capital of the Territory of Papua and New Guinea. The city is in southeastern New Guinea. During World War II, it was an important Allied naval base. Its harbor was discovered by Captain John Moresby in 1873. For location, see AUSTRALIA (political map).

PORT OF ENTRY is any place established by a government to receive aliens, imported goods, and customs duties. Customs officers admit all imported goods, collect duties, and enforce the provisions of the customs and navigation laws. When any person unloads goods of another country at a port that does not have a custom house, he is guilty of smuggling.

Ports of entry may include seaports, lakeports, and airports situated at the borders or throughout the country. A custom house may be located wherever goods of other countries are held until they are distributed to local trade.   PAYSON S. WILD, JR.

PORT OF NEW YORK AUTHORITY is a self-supporting corporate agency of the states of New Jersey and New York. It was established in 1921 to plan and develop terminal and transportation facilities, and to improve and protect the commerce of the port district. Six commissioners from each state serve without pay for terms of six years. The Port Authority appears before the Interstate Commerce Commission, the Civil Aeronautics Board, and the Federal Maritime Commission in the interest of the port area. It has trade development offices in Chicago; Cleveland; London; New York; Pittsburgh; Rio de Janeiro; Washington; Zurich, Switzerland; and San Juan, Puerto Rico. These offices promote commerce through the port of New York. The Authority's 23 terminal and transportation facilities include bridges, tunnels, marine and inland terminals, airports, heliports, and an interstate rail rapid transit system.

Critically reviewed by the PORT OF NEW YORK AUTHORITY

PORT-OF-SPAIN (pop. 93,954; alt. 50 ft.) is the capital and trade center of Trinidad and Tobago. It served as the temporary capital of the West Indies Federation from 1958 until 1962. The Port-of-Spain harbor accommodates large ships and serves as a naval base. For location, see VENEZUELA (color map).

PORT ROYAL. See ANNAPOLIS ROYAL; CANADA (National Parks).

PORT SAID, port *SIDE,* or PORT sah *EED* (pop. 256,-100; alt. 3 ft.), is an Egyptian port at the Mediterranean end of the Suez Canal. It is one of the busiest ports in the world. In Arabic its name is BŪR SA'ID. For the location of Port Said, see EGYPT (political map). The administrative headquarters for the Suez Canal are located in Port Said.

Industries include cotton ginning, trading, wool spinning, leather tanning, salt processing, fishing, and oil refining. Men building the canal founded Port Said in 1859. For many years, it was a fueling station for ships passing through the canal.   GEORGE H. T. KIMBLE

PORT SUDAN (pop. 110,000; alt. 10 ft.), the main port of Sudan, lies on the Red Sea, 250 miles northeast of Atbara. For location, see SUDAN (map). Port Sudan was founded in 1906, and has become a major commercial and shipping center, with an excellent harbor and modern docking facilities. Eighty-five per cent of Sudan's trade with other countries moves through the port. Exports from Port Sudan include cotton and cottonseed, gum arabic, oilseeds, beans, hides, and cattle and sheep.   GEORGE H. T. KIMBLE

PORTAGE is the carrying of goods or boats overland between two bodies of water, or around some obstacle such as a waterfall or river rapids. The term *portage* is also used for the land route over which the goods are carried.

The North American Indians traveled thousands of miles by portaging between rivers and lakes. The Indians traveled as far upstream as their boats could go. Then they carried their canoes and goods overland to the next stream or lake, and continued their journey by water.

At one time, the term *portage* meant the part of the ship's cargo that was set aside as all or part of a seaman's wages. It could also mean the space set aside for such cargo, the tonnage of a vessel, and the freight charges or fees for carrying freight.   R. E. GREGG

PORTAGE LA PRAIRIE, Manitoba (pop. 13,012; alt. 857 ft.), serves as the market city for the surrounding *Portage Plains* farming region. Portage la Prairie ranks as Manitoba's fifth largest manufacturing center. Its main industry is food processing.

The city received its name from an old portage used by fur traders. It dates back to 1738, when French traders built Fort La Reine near the present site. Portage la Prairie has a mayor-council form of government. For the location of Portage la Prairie, see MANITOBA (political map).   W. L. MORTON

PORTAL CIRCULATION. See CIRCULATION.

PORTAL VEIN. See LIVER; HUMAN BODY (Trans-Vision illustration).

PORTALES, DIEGO. See CHILE (Formative Years).

PORTCULLIS. See CASTLE.

PORTEÑOS. See BUENOS AIRES (The People); ARGENTINA (Colonial Years).

PORTER. See BEER.

Chicago Historical Society

David Porter

Brown Bros.

David Dixon Porter

PORTER is the family name of two United States naval officers, father and son.

David Porter (1780-1843), as a captain, commanded the *Essex* during the War of 1812. The *Essex* operated in the Pacific Ocean, and was the first warship to fly the United States flag in those waters. Porter almost entirely destroyed the English whaling industry in the Pacific. Porter's adopted son, David G. Farragut, who later became the navy's first admiral, also made the voyage (see FARRAGUT, DAVID GLASGOW). Later, Porter surrendered to the English ships *Cherub* and *Phoebe*. He returned home as a hero, and in 1815 became one of three navy commissioners.

In 1823, Porter resigned this post to lead an expedition against pirates in the West Indies. He was insulted at Fajardo, Puerto Rico, and he forced the Puerto Rican officials to apologize. A court-martial in 1825 found him guilty of acting beyond his orders and suspended him for six months. He resigned and served with the Mexican Navy in 1826 and helped reorganize the country's naval forces.

Returning to the United States in 1829, Porter was appointed United States consul general to Algiers. He served as chargé d'affaires in Turkey from 1831 to 1839, and as minister to Turkey from 1839 until his death.

He was born in Boston, Mass., on Feb. 1, 1780. As a boy, he served on merchant ships. At the age of 18, he joined the U.S. Navy as a midshipman.

David Dixon Porter (1813-1891) became noted for his Civil War service. In the attack on New Orleans in 1862, he directed a mortar squadron under the command of his adopted brother, David Farragut. Porter fired mortar shells at Fort Jackson and Fort Saint Philip for four days. Then Farragut went past the forts and destroyed the Confederate fleet. The forts surrendered to Porter a few days later.

Later in 1862, Porter commanded the upper Mississippi squadron. In 1863, he helped the army capture the Arkansas Post. He also aided in the siege of Vicksburg, Miss., and became a rear admiral for this action. In 1865, as commander of 60 naval vessels, the largest fleet assembled during the war, he took part in the capture of Fort Fisher, N.C. He became a vice-admiral in 1866, and served as superintendent of the United States Naval Academy from 1866 to 1869. In 1870, he succeeded Farragut as an admiral, becoming the second person in the history of the navy to hold that rank. In 1877, Porter became head of the Board of Inspection. He maintained an office in the Department of the Navy,

making annual reports and influencing naval affairs.

Porter was born in Chester, Pa., on June 8, 1813. At the age of 10, he went with his father to fight pirates in the West Indies. He also served with his father as a midshipman in the Mexican Navy. He fought under his cousin, Captain Henry Porter, in a fierce battle with a Spanish vessel off Cuba, and was captured there. At the age of 16, Porter joined the U.S. Navy as a midshipman. He became a lieutenant in 1841, and commanded the vessel *Spitfire* during the Mexican War, 1846 to 1848. RICHARD S. WEST, JR.

PORTER, COLE (1893-1964), was an American composer of popular music. His songs include "Begin the Beguine," "Night and Day," "So in Love Am I," and "What Is This Thing Called Love?" He wrote many successful musical comedies, including *Anything Goes* (1934), *Red, Hot, and Blue* (1936), *Leave It to Me* (1938), *Something for the Boys* (1942), *Mexican Hayride* (1943), *Kiss Me, Kate* (1948), *Can-Can* (1953), and *Silk Stockings* (1954). He also composed the music for the motion pictures *Born to Dance* (1936), *Rosalie* (1937), *Something to Shout About* (1942), and *High Society* (1956). He wrote the words for the songs in most of his shows.

Porter was born in Peru, Ind. After his graduation from Yale University, he enrolled in Harvard Law School. But he turned from

Graphic House, Inc.

Cole Porter

law to music, and studied composition at Harvard and in Paris. He wrote his first musical comedy, *See America First* (1916), in Paris. His first major success was *Fifty Million Frenchmen* in 1929. GILBERT CHASE

PORTER, FITZ-JOHN (1822-1891), an American soldier, became the central figure in a celebrated military inquiry. In the Civil War, he became a corps commander in the Army of the Potomac. He fought under General George B. McClellan in the Peninsula and at the battles of the Seven Days. At the second battle of Bull Run, Porter commanded a corps under General John Pope. Later, Pope charged him with disobedience and misconduct. A court-martial found him guilty, and he was dismissed from the army. In 1879, a board of officers reviewed his case and reported in his favor. He was restored to his rank in 1886. Porter was born in Portsmouth, N.H., and was graduated from the United States Military Academy. T. HARRY WILLIAMS

PORTER, GENE STRATTON (1868-1924), was an American writer of sentimental outdoor stories. Her novel *Freckles* (1904) enjoyed a sale of nearly 2 million

Gene Stratton Porter

Brown Bros.

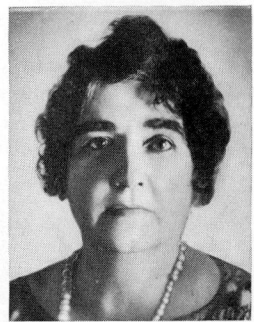

copies. Other novels, such as *A Girl of the Limberlost* (1909), *The Harvester* (1911), and *Laddie* (1913), became almost as popular. Mrs. Porter said that she owed her success to her belief in "the love and joy of life." She was born in Wabash County, Indiana, which she used as the setting for *Freckles*.   HERBERT R. BROWN

PORTER, GEORGE. See NOBEL PRIZES (table [1967]).

PORTER, KATHERINE ANNE (1890-   ), is an American novelist and short-story writer. She has written comparatively little, but her work is finished and impeccable. Her stories often deal with sensitive adolescent girls and young women, and her themes are frequently disillusionment and suffering. Her subtle and fastidious style strongly influenced such writers as Eudora Welty, whom Miss Porter was one of the first to encourage (see WELTY, EUDORA).

Miss Porter was born at Indian Creek, Tex., and she often set her stories in Texas, Louisiana, and Mexico. Many of her best stories were published in *Flowering Judas* (1930); *Pale Horse, Pale Rider* (1939); *The Leaning Tower* (1944); and *Collected Short Stories* (1965), which earned her the fiction Pulitzer prize in 1966. *Ship of Fools* (1962) was her first novel.   RICHARD ELLMANN

PORTER, WILLIAM SYDNEY. See HENRY, O.

PORTHOLE. See SHIP AND SHIPPING (Nautical Terms).

PORTICO. See ARCHITECTURE (Architectural Terms).

PORTINARI, *pohr tee NAH ree*, **CÂNDIDO** (1903-1962), a Brazilian painter, became famous for his paintings of laborers and historical figures. They are powerfully drawn, colorful, and dramatic. Portinari's best-known works include murals in the Ministry of Education in Rio de Janeiro, the Library of Congress in Washington, D.C., and the United Nations General Assembly Hall in New York City. Portinari was born in the Brazilian state of São Paulo, the son of Italian parents.   ROBERT C. SMITH

See also MURAL PAINTING (color picture).

PORTLAND, Me. (pop. 72,566; met. area 139,122; alt. 25 ft.), has one of the finest harbors on the Atlantic Coast, and is closer to Europe than any other transatlantic port in the United States. It is the largest city in Maine and a leading industrial and commercial center. During World War II, Portland was the base for the North Atlantic Fleet of the U.S. Navy.

Location, Size, and Description. Portland lies on the southwest coast of Maine, about 60 miles southwest of Augusta, the state capital. The city of Portland covers nearly 22 square miles. It is built on a narrow peninsula with a maximum height of 187 feet above sea level, and overlooks island-studded Casco Bay to the east. Mount Washington and the other mountains of the Presidential Range, to the northwest, tower in the distance. Between these peaks and the coast is a network of lakes and valleys to which Portland is the eastern gateway. To the south is famous Old Orchard Beach, a long stretch of smooth, hard sand. For location, see MAINE (political map). For information on Portland's monthly weather, see MAINE (Climate).

Cultural Life. Portland is the home of a branch of the University of Maine, Westbrook Junior College, schools for the deaf and blind, and the Sweat Museum. The city hall contains the Kotzchmar organ, one of the largest organs in the world. It was a gift from publisher Cyrus H. K. Curtis, who was born in Portland.

Recreation. The city has 33 parks. Deering's Oaks, once a part of Deering's Woods, is mentioned in Henry Wadsworth Longfellow's poem, "My Lost Youth." Lincoln Park is a civic center surrounded by government buildings. The old home of Longfellow, who was born in Portland, is next to the Historical Society Museum.

Industry and Trade. Portland has many small manufacturing plants. Pulpwood and potatoes are among the leading products shipped from the port. Large tankers unload at the docks, bringing oil for the Portland-Montreal pipeline to Canada.

Transportation. Over 4 million tons of products are shipped in and out of the harbor of Portland yearly, making it one of the chief Atlantic ports. Steamers connect Portland with many ports in other countries.

History. Portland was founded in 1632. It was first called *Machigonne*, and later *Falmouth*. The settlement was destroyed twice by Indians. During the Revolutionary War, the British bombarded the port. In 1791, a lighthouse was erected at what is now the adjacent city of South Portland. The lighthouse, called Portland Head Light, is standing today. A great fire in 1866 ruined a large part of Portland, but the city was soon rebuilt. In 1899 the city of Deering was annexed. Portland is the seat of Cumberland County, and has a council-manager type of government.   ROBERT M. YORK

PORTLAND, Ore. (pop. 372,676; met. area 821,897; alt. 77 ft.), is a fresh-water port on the Willamette River. It is the largest city in Oregon. Ocean ships reach Portland by way of the Columbia River. Portland was named by the toss of a coin. In 1845, two of the city's founders, Asa L. Lovejoy and Francis W. Pettygrove, used that method to pick the name. Lovejoy, who wanted to call it Boston, lost. Portland is called the *City of Roses* because of its many rose gardens. Every June, the famous Rose Festival is celebrated.

Location, Size, and Description. Portland lies near the meeting point of the Willamette and Columbia rivers. The city covers more than 60 square miles of gentle slopes on both banks of the Willamette. Mount Hood, in the Cascade Range to the east, can be seen from the city. The Oregon Coast Range rises in the west. The Columbia River Highway, Mount Hood Loop Drive, and Roosevelt Highway lead to scenic areas. For location, see OREGON (political map). For information on Portland's monthly weather, see OREGON (Climate).

Cultural Life. Portland is the home of the Medical School and the School of Dentistry of the University of Oregon. Reed College, Lewis and Clark College, the University of Portland, Portland State College, and the Oregon Historical Society are in the city. Multnomah College, a nonprofit, coeducational, independent junior college, also is in Portland. The city has an art museum.

Recreation. In Portland's Washington Park are the statues of *The Coming of the White Man*, and of Sacagawea, the Indian woman who guided the Lewis and Clark expedition. Portland is the home of the famous International Rose Test Gardens and Peninsula Park with its sunken rose gardens. Mount Tabor Park covers an ancient cinder cone. Council Crest Park lies about 1,100 feet above the business district of the city.

Industries. The chief products of Portland factories include wood products, flour, furniture, knitted goods, woolen textiles, chemicals, plastics, canned fruits and vegetables, aluminum, and other metal materials. Great quantities of lumber, wheat, and fruit are shipped from Portland's harbor. During World War II, Portland was an important shipbuilding center. There is an Air Force base at Portland International Airport.

Portland was founded in 1845 and chartered in 1851. It has a commission plan of government. Portland is the seat of Multnomah County.   RICHARD M. HIGHSMITH, JR.

See also OREGON (pictures).

PORTLAND, UNIVERSITY OF. See UNIVERSITIES AND COLLEGES (table).

PORTLAND CEMENT. See CEMENT AND CONCRETE.

PORTLAND STATE COLLEGE is a coeducational liberal arts college in Portland, Ore. Courses lead to bachelor's degrees in liberal arts and sciences, business administration, applied science, and elementary and secondary education. It awards master's degrees in liberal arts. It was founded in 1946. For enrollment, see UNIVERSITIES AND COLLEGES (table).

PORTLAND VASE. See VASE; GLASSWARE (picture).

PORTO, *POHR toh,* or Oporto (pop. 319,250; alt. 25 ft.), is Portugal's second largest city. It lies on the Douro River, three miles inland from the ocean (see PORTUGAL [color map]). The city has become famous for its excellent port wines. Porto is one of Portugal's chief seaports. It has distilleries, food-processing plants, sugar refineries, textile mills, and other industries. Porto has many churches and monasteries which date from the Middle Ages. The University of Porto was founded in 1911.   CHARLES E. NOWELL

PÔRTO ALEGRE, *POHR too uh LEH gree* (pop. 889,000; alt. 10 ft.), is the capital of the state of Rio Grande do Sul, Brazil. Pôrto Alegre stands at the junction of five rivers, 190 miles north of Rio Grande. For its location, see BRAZIL (political map). It is a modern city, and an important industrial center. Pôrto Alegre serves as the outlet for the export of the bountiful agricultural products of the interior. Coal is mined near the city. The city has a state university and a Roman Catholic university. The earliest settlers in Pôrto Alegre were Portuguese from the Azores. They came in the early 1700's.   MANOEL CARDOZO

PORTO-NOVO *POHR tuh NOH voh* (pop. 69,500; alt. 10 ft.) is the capital of Dahomey, a republic in western Africa. The city lies 7 miles north of the Gulf of Guinea (see DAHOMEY [map]). Porto-Novo exports palm oil, palm kernels, cotton, and kapok. It was founded in the 1600's.

PORTO RICO, officially changed to *Puerto Rico* in 1932. See PUERTO RICO.

PORTO SANTO ISLAND. See MADEIRA.

PORTOBELO, *PAWR toh VAY loh,* or *POHR toh BELL oh* (pop. 591; alt. 20 ft.), a village on the Atlantic Coast of Panama, was often attacked by Henry Morgan and other English pirates of the 1600's and 1700's. The town was one of the chief Spanish trading centers in Latin America. Spanish ships sailed from Portobelo to Spain with treasures of Latin America.

Christopher Columbus anchored in the village's fine harbor in 1502. The name in Spanish means *beautiful harbor.* The Spaniards founded the town in 1597. But pirate attacks frightened away the Spanish ships and merchants, and Portobelo lost importance as a seaport after the early 1700's.   JOHN BIESANZ and MAVIS BIESANZ

PORTOLÁ, GASPAR DE. See CALIFORNIA (Spanish and Russian Settlement).

PORTOLANO. See MAP (Map Making in Europe).

PORTRAIT. See PAINTING (Portraits); PHOTOGRAPHY.

PORTSMOUTH, *PORTS muth* (pop. 219,110; alt. 25 ft.), is Great Britain's chief naval station and arsenal. It lies on Portsea Island in Portsmouth Bay, 95 miles southwest of London (see GREAT BRITAIN [political map]). It has fine harbor facilities, dry docks, and repair yards. A famous warship, the *Victory,* rests there. Lord Horatio Nelson was killed on the decks of the *Victory* when he won the Battle of Trafalgar in 1805. Charles Dickens' birthplace is now a museum in Portsmouth.   JOHN W. WEBB

PORTSMOUTH, N.H. (pop. 25,833; alt. 15 ft.), is the chief seaport on New Hampshire's 13-mile coastline. Portsmouth was founded as Strawberry Bank in 1630, and was incorporated as a city in 1849. The city lies at the mouth of the Piscataqua River, 47 miles southeast of Concord (see NEW HAMPSHIRE [political map]). The Portsmouth Naval Shipyard and Pease Air Force Base of the Strategic Air Command are nearby. The city has a council-manager government. See also PORTSMOUTH NAVAL SHIPYARD.   J. DUANE SQUIRES

PORTSMOUTH, Ohio (pop. 33,637; alt. 533 ft.), is a transportation and industrial center for a rich farming and mining region. It lies at the meeting point of the Ohio and Scioto rivers (see OHIO [political map]). Portsmouth has steel mills, iron foundries, shoe factories, and brickmaking and woodworking plants. The Atomic Energy Commission operates a large plant nearby. Portsmouth has a council-manager government.

PORTSMOUTH, Va. (pop. 114,773; alt. 10 ft.), is one of three cities that make up the port of Hampton Roads. The city lies across the Elizabeth River from Norfolk (see VIRGINIA [political map]). It has Norfolk Naval Shipyard, and a naval hospital and ammunition depot. With Norfolk, Portsmouth forms a metropolitan area that has a population of 578,507.

Products of Portsmouth factories include baskets, chemicals, vegetable oils, fats, brass, iron and steel, fertilizer, transportation equipment, veneer and lumber goods, seafood and meats, dairy products, and foam-rubber products. The city was chartered in 1752. It has a council-manager government.   FRANCIS B. SIMKINS

See also HAMPTON ROADS; NORFOLK NAVAL BASE.

PORTSMOUTH, TREATY OF. See RUSSO-JAPANESE WAR; JAPAN (Increasing World Power).

PORTSMOUTH NAVAL SHIPYARD, N.H., occupies over 200 acres on a group of connected islands in the Piscataqua River. The islands are physically within Maine, but the naval base uses nearby Portsmouth, N.H., as its post office address. Major commands located at the base include a naval hospital, marine barracks, and naval disciplinary command. Shipbuilding on the Piscataqua River dates from 1645, but the first ship built at the navy yard, established in 1800, was not launched until 1815. In 1905, Russia and Japan signed the Treaty of Portsmouth, which ended the Russo-Japanese War. After World War I, the base specialized in submarine construction. In 1964, the U.S. Department of Defense ordered a gradual closing of the base to be completed by 1975.   JOHN A. OUDINE

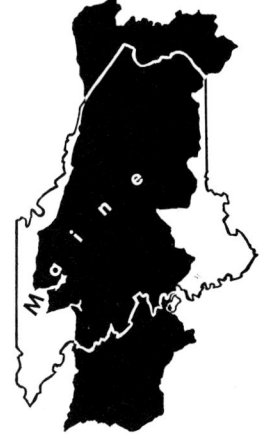

Portuguese Fishermen have braved the sea for hundreds of years. Their families often wait for them at the shore to help them bring in the catch.

George Holton, Photo Researchers

PORTUGAL, *PAWR chuh guhl,* is the westernmost country of continental Europe. It is a small republic to the west of Spain. The Portuguese call their country República Portuguesa, which means Republic of Portugal. The capital and largest city of Portugal is Lisbon.

Portugal covers an area a little larger than the state of Maine. It is a narrow country with a long Atlantic coastline. Portugal owns large areas in Asia and Africa. Its overseas provinces have an area more than 20 times as large as Portugal itself.

Portugal has an area only a little larger than that of the state of Maine.

Charles E. Nowell, the contributor of this article, is Professor of History at the University of Illinois and author of A History of Portugal; The Great Discoveries.

Most Portuguese earn their living as farmers, fishermen, and foresters. Their country is famous for its port and Madeira wines, its sardines, its cork, and its citrus fruits.

The Portuguese became sailors and seafarers in early times. Portuguese traders founded the first European colonies in many parts of the world. The golden age of Portuguese history in the 1400's and 1500's is full of great names and events. Bartolomeu Dias sailed

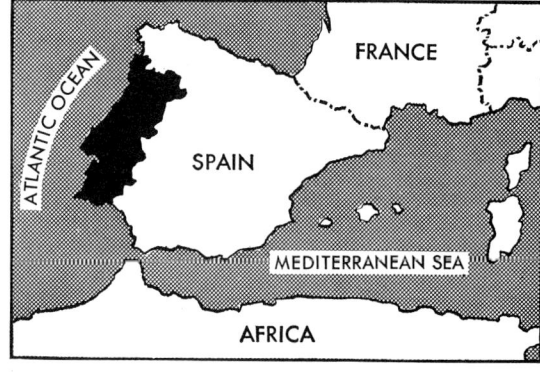

FACTS IN BRIEF

Form of Government: Corporative republic.
Capital: Lisbon.
Divisions: 22 districts; 7 overseas provinces.
Parliament: *Assembleia Nacional* (National Assembly), made up of 130 members elected by direct vote for four-year terms.
Official Language: Portuguese.
Area: *Mainland*—34,309 sq. mi. (including the Azores and Madeira islands, 35,510 sq. mi.); *Total* (including overseas provinces)—840,840 sq. mi. *Greatest distances*—(north-south) 350 miles; (east-west) 125 miles. *Coastline*—on the Atlantic Ocean, about 500 miles.
Elevation: *Highest*—Malhão, in Serra da Estrela, 6,532 feet; *Lowest*—sea level along the coast.
Population: *1960 Census*—8,851,289 (including Azores and Madeira islands); distribution, 77 per cent rural,

23 per cent urban. *Estimated 1970 Population*—9,755,000; density, 275 persons to the square mile. *Estimated 1975 Population*—10,303,000.
Chief Products: *Agriculture*—barley, beans, citrus fruits, grapes, maize, oats, potatoes, rice, rye, wheat. *Fishing*—cod, sardines, tuna. *Forestry*—cork, lumber, resin. *Manufacturing and Processing*—canned fish, embroidery, lace, olive oil, pottery, textiles, tiles, wine. *Mining*—coal, copper, kaolin, pyrites, slate, sulfur, tungsten.
Flag: The two vertical stripes are green (for hope) and red (for the blood of heroes). The coat of arms in the center stands for the Christian faith and the search for knowledge. See Flag (picture: Flags of Europe).
National Anthem: "A Portuguesa" ("The Portuguese").
National Holiday: Day of Portugal, June 10.
Money: *Basic Unit*—escudo. See Money (table); Escudo.

Cork from the Oak Forests of Portugal is carried on oxcarts. Portugal furnishes more than half the world's supply of cork.

Pix

Pottery Jugs and Pitchers are for sale at this market. The large building is one of Portugal's many religious structures.

De Dienes, Rapho-Guillumette

around the Cape of Good Hope, and Vasco da Gama discovered the sea route to India.

The Land and Its Resources

Location, Size, and Surface Features. The Atlantic Ocean forms the southern and western boundaries of Portugal. Spain lies on the north and east. Mainland Portugal covers 34,309 square miles.

The country is divided into three geographic regions. In the northeast corner there is a highland region, which is a continuation of the great central plateau of Spain. Many river valleys cut through the highlands. The second region is the lowland plain along the coast. In the southwest corner of the country, the lowland region extends far inland in the great river valleys. Rivers have made some of the coastal areas into rich delta land. The third region is the central highland, which covers the rest of Portugal.

Portugal has three important rivers. They all rise in Spain and flow westward and southward. The Douro drains northern Portugal. It flows through the highland region and empties into the Atlantic near the city of Porto. The Tagus, called *Tejo* in Portugal, drains a large part of central Portugal. Its mouth forms the wide bay at Lisbon. The Guadiana forms part of the frontier with Spain.

Natural Resources. Portugal has some mineral wealth, but most of its mineral deposits have not been developed. There are coal deposits in the north, and copper deposits in the southeast. Portugal also has deposits of pyrites, kaolin, sulfur, and uranium. In the Serra da Estrela there are deposits of wolframite, a tungsten ore. These are the largest wolframite deposits in Europe.

Forests cover many of Portugal's hills. Pine trees grow in large areas, and there are vast cork oak forests. The forests produce two of Portugal's important resources, cork and resin. The country has many green plants and flowers.

The Atlantic Ocean near Portugal teems with sardines and tuna fish. Fishing is an important industry.

Climate. Temperatures in Portugal average 50° F. in January and 70° F. in July. Between 20 and 40 inches of rain falls annually over most of Portugal.

The People and Their Work

The People who first lived in Portugal were the Iberians. But many peoples invaded the country and mixed with the original Iberians. These invaders included the Phoenicians, Celts, Carthaginians, Romans, Greeks, Goths, and Moors. Portugal has no minority problem, because almost all the people of the mainland and the two island groups are Portuguese. The Portuguese language is a great deal like Spanish. See PORTU-GUESE LANGUAGE.

Way of Life. The Portuguese people are skilled fishermen and good farmers. They have a deep love for their country, and take pride in its place in history. Seafood is used in almost every meal in Portugal. Portuguese cooks prepare famous chowders and other seafood dishes.

Cities. Lisbon is the capital and largest city of Portugal. Funchal is the capital of the Madeira Island group. Braga lies in the heart of the fertile coastland in the northwestern part of Portugal. Porto is an important seaport. See the separate articles on cities listed in the *Related Articles* section of this article.

Agriculture. About two out of five of the Portuguese people earn their living by farming. Most of the farmers use the same tools and primitive methods that their ancestors used. For example, Portuguese wine makers press a large part of the grape crop by treading the grapes with their bare feet. The chief farming region

615

is the central highland. A leading product is the wine grape, which is grown in the river valleys that cut across the highland. The vineyards of the Douro Valley yield grapes for port wine, named for the city of Porto. Grapes from Madeira are used for Madeira wine. The vineyards of southern Portugal grow grapes to eat, either fresh or dried as raisins. Oranges, lemons, tangerines, figs, and almonds are plentiful in southern Portugal. Olive groves are found throughout the country. Farmers grow rice on the easily flooded plains of the Tagus River. Cattle find good grazing in the central highlands. Sheep and hogs are raised in the south.

Cork. Oak forests produce one of Portugal's most important products. The bark of the cork oak provides cork which is used throughout the world. Portugal supplies more than half the world's cork. Cork oak trees can grow on hillsides that are otherwise worthless.

Fisheries. Fishing is second only to grape growing among Portuguese industries. The country has about 16,600 fishing boats. Portuguese fishermen catch sardines and tuna for food. The country's fishing fleets bring back cod from the sea off Newfoundland.

Mining. Portugal's most important mineral product is wolframite, which is mined in the northeastern part of Portugal. It is the raw form of tungsten, which has the highest melting point of all metals. This mineral became especially valuable during World War II, when both Germany and the Allies bought it from Portugal. The country produces some coal and some pyrites. Lead is found at Coimbra, copper at São Domingos (near Sines) and elsewhere, and antimony near Porto. Kaolin, a pure white clay, is mined.

Manufactures. Portugal's two most important manufacturing industries are wine making and sardine packing. The country's first heavy industry was a steel mill built at Seixal, a few miles southeast of Lisbon. It began operations in 1961. Portugal also has textile mills and tobacco factories. Other products include olive oil, flour, finished cork, and tile. The chief tilemaking center is Sácavem, just outside Lisbon. The Portuguese people also show great skill in making pottery and lace. Women on Madeira Island make fine embroidery.

Transportation. Portugal has railroads totaling only about 2,230 miles. The Portuguese often use boats to travel. Portugal has about 18,000 miles of highways, many of them built in the 1900's. Farmers usually travel by oxcart or muleback.

Trade. Portugal has always had close trade relations with Great Britain. Generally, Great Britain is Portugal's best customer. Portugal also trades with the United States and with countries of western Europe. Among the chief imports are machinery, coal, cotton, wheat, and iron and steel. Exports include cork, tungsten, sardines, wines, wool, and resin.

Social and Cultural Achievements

Education. Portuguese law requires that all children between the ages of seven and twelve must go to school.

PORTUGAL MAP INDEX

Districts*

Angra do Heroísmo (Azores)**	96,174	**
Aveiro	524,592	B 3
Beja	276,895	D 4
Braga	596,768	A 3
Bragança	233,441	A 4
Castelo Branco	316,536	B 3
Coimbra	433,656	B 3
Évora	219,916	D 4
Faro	314,841	E 3
Funchal (Madeira)**	268,937	**
Guarda	282,606	B 3
Horta (Azores)**	49,382	**
Leiria	404,500	B 3
Lisboa	1,382,959	D 3
Ponta Delgada (Azores)**	181,924	**
Portalegre	188,482	D 4
Porto	1,193,368	A 3
Santarém	461,707	D 3
Setúbal	377,186	D 3
Viana do Castelo	277,748	A 3
Vila Real	325,358	A 4
Viseu	482,416	B 3

Cities and Towns

Abrantes	8,172	C 3
Águeda	8,345	B 3
Albufeira	8,416	E 3
Alcácer do Sal	14,733	D 3
Alcobaça	5,166	C 3
Alcochete	7,447	D 3
Alenquer	8,273	C 2
Algés	14,353	D 2
Aljezur	5,333	E 3
Aljustrel	9,913	E 3
Almada	31,523	D 2
Almeirim	8,902	C 3
Almodôvar	5,453	E 3
Alpiarça	7,856	C 3
Alportel	9,058	E 4
Alter do Chão	4,838	C 4
Amadora	36,319	D 2
Amarante	4,513	A 3
Arraiolos	4,510	D 4
Aveiro	24,067	B 3
Barcelos	5,420	A 3
Barreiro	23,433	D 2
Batalha	7,053	C 3
Beja	18,040	D 4
Benavente	6,223	D 3
Bombarral	4,662	C 2
Borba	5,258	D 4
Braga	34,085	A 3
Bragança	8,662	A 5
Caldas da Rainha	11,185	C 2
Campo Maior	8,807	C 4
Cantanhede	6,630	B 3
Cartaxo	6,665	C 3
Cascais	13,352	D 2
Castanheira de Pêra	5,385	B 3
Castelo Branco	17,616	C 4
Castelo de Vide	4,900	C 4
Castro Marim	5,347	E 4
Castro Verde	5,538	E 3
Chaves	12,490	A 4
Coimbra	28,788	B 3
Coruche	21,945	D 3
Cova da Piedade	15,448	D 2
Covilhã	23,595	B 4
Elvas	14,548	D 4
Entron-camento	7,355	C 3
Ermezinde	11,020	A 3
Espinho	8,799	A 3
Estarreja	6,211	B 3
Estremoz	10,122	D 4
Évora	34.145	D 4
Fafe	7,126	A 3
Faro	24,877	E 4
Fatima	5,852	C 3
Ferreira do Alentejo	8,108	D 3
Figueira da Foz	10,568	B 3
Figueiró dos Vinhos	5,781	C 3
Fundão	5,651	B 4
Gondomar	11,182	A 3
Grândola	12,028	D 3
Guarda	12,787	B 4
Guimarães	11,909	A 3
Idanha-a-Nova	4,567	C 4
Ílhavo	12,646	B 3
Lagoa	5,915	E 3
Lagos	10,008	E 3
Lamego	10,236	A 4
Leiria	7,477	C 3
Lisbon (Lisboa)	822,000	D 2
Loulé	16,152	E 3
Loures	7,623	D 2
Lourinhã	8,677	C 2
Lousã	8,191	B 3
Mafra	7,032	D 2
Mangualde	6,972	B 4
Manteigas	4,528	B 4
Marinha Grande	15,699	C 3
Matozinhos	24,804	A 3
Mértola	5,682	E 4
Mira	13,384	B 3
Miranda do Corvo	5,103	B 3
Miranda do Douro	5,687	A 5
Mirandela	5,979	A 4
Moita	9,504	D 3
Monchique	9,371	E 3
Montemor-o-Novo	13,115	D 3
Montijo	21,947	D 3
Moscavide	22,065	D 2
Moura	12,126	D 4
Murtosa	5,779	B 3
Nazaré	9,189	C 2
Niza	5,262	C 4
Óbidos	4.599	C 2
Odemira	7,727	E 3
Oeiras	6,857	D 2
Olhão	12,654	E 4
Oliveira de Azemeis	5,953	B 3
Ourique	6,189	E 3
Ovar	14,128	B 3
Palmela	6,487	D 3
Pedrógão Grande	4,659	C 3
Penafiel	6,022	A 3
Penela	4,548	B 3
Peniche	11,388	C 2
Peso da Régua	5,563	A 4
Pombal	9,973	C 3
Ponte de Sor	13,010	C 3
Portalegre	13,374	C 4
Portimão	17,145	E 3
Porto	319,250	A 3
Póvoa de Varzim	17,696	A 3
Proença-a-Nova	6,060	C 4
Redondo	8,925	D 4
Reguengos	7,107	D 4
Rio Maior	9,032	C 3
Salvaterra de Magos	6,867	C 3
Santarém	20,457	C 3
Santiago do Cacém	6,939	D 3
Santo Tirso	10,428	A 3
São João da Madeira	11,921	B 3
Serpa	10,967	E 4
Sertã	6,909	C 3
Setúbal	50,966	D 3
Sezimbra	16,837	D 2
Silves	9,014	E 3
Sines	8,866	E 3
Soure	9,655	B 3
Tavira	12,046	E 4
Tomar	12,974	C 3
Torres Novas	11,974	C 3
Torres Vedras	13,091	C 2
Vagos	8,281	B 3
Valbom	11,182	A 3
Viana do Alentejo	4,923	D 3
Viana do Castelo	14,371	A 3
Vila de Rei	5,462	C 3
Vila do Conde	12,771	A 3
Vila Franca de Xira	13,404	C 2
Vila Nova de Gaia	41,424	A 3
Vila Real	10,672	A 4
Vila Real de Santo António	11,096	E 4
Vila Viçosa	4,585	D 4
Viseu	16,961	B 4

Physical Features

Águeda River	B 5
Aldeadávila Dam	A 5
Ardila River	D 4
Bay of Lagos	E 3
Bay of Setúbal	D 3
Berlengas Is.	C 2
Caia River	C 4
Canha River	D 3
Cape Espichel	D 2
Cape Mondego	B 3
Cape St. Vincent	E 3
Cávado River	A 3
Chança River	E 4
Côa River	B 5
Douro River	A 3
Estrela (Mt.)	B 4
Guadiana River	E 4
Gulf of Cadiz	E 4
Lima River	A 3
Minho River	A 3
Mira River	E 3
Mondego River	B 3
Ponsul River	C 4
Sabor River	A 5
Sado River	D 3
Serra da Estrela (Mts.)	B 4
Serra de Alvelos (Mts.)	C 3
Serra de Monchique (Mts.)	E 3
Serra de Montemuro (Mts.)	A 4
Serra de Nogueira (Mts.)	A 5
Serra de Ossa (Mts.)	D 4
Serra de São Mamede (Mts.)	C 4
Serra do Alvão (Mts.)	A 4
Serra do Reboredo (Mts.)	A 5
Sor River	C 3
Sorraia River	D 3
Tagus River	C 3
Tâmega River	A 3
Tua River	A 4
Vouga River	B 4
Zêzere River	B 4

*Does not appear on map; key shows general location.

**Azores and Madeira Islands appear on the map of Africa.

PORTUGAL

Legend	
	Evergreen Trees
	Mixed Evergreen and Deciduous Trees
	Shrub
	Grass
⊛	National Capital
•	Cities and Towns
—	Rail Lines

1 inch = 39.5 Statute Miles

Miles 0 5 10 20 30 40

Conic Projection

Longitude West of Greenwich

North Atlantic Ocean

SPAIN

LISBON

Bay of Lagos

Gulf of Cadiz

CM TERRAIN PORTUGAL
COPYRIGHT BY
RAND MCNALLY & COMPANY
MADE IN U.S.A.

616a

FIA

Specially created for World Book Encyclopedia by Rand McNally and World Book editors

PORTUGAL

About 800,000 students attend Portugal's 14,000 elementary schools. The more than 120 secondary schools provide education for 87,000 pupils. There are two types of secondary schools. One offers classical courses, and the other specializes in technical subjects.

The oldest educational institution in Portugal is Coimbra University. It was founded at Lisbon in 1290, and has been at Coimbra since 1537. New universities were founded at Lisbon and Pôrto in 1911.

The Arts. In early times, nearly all the art was religious. In the 1400's, Nuno Gonsalves painted pictures of saints, and, in the 1500's, Vasco Fernandes painted beautiful scenes from the Bible to adorn the walls of Portugal's greatest cathedrals. As time passed, religious art gave way to art based on everyday life. The greatest Portuguese painter of the 1800's was Miguel Lupi, whose best works are portraits. Churches and other old buildings, such as the Tower of Belem, are built in styles that the Portuguese learned in Africa and Asia.

Portugal has a wealth of folk music. The people sing songs which range from lively dancing songs, called *chulas* and *viras*, to the famous *fados*, which are sad songs sung to the accompaniment of a guitar. Pottery, tiles, lace, and handmade furniture are made for sale and export. See PORTUGUESE LITERATURE AND BRAZILIAN LITERATURE.

Religion. Freedom of worship is permitted in Portugal. The Church and government have been separate

De Dienes, Rapho-Guillumette

Stair-Step Streets run up the steep hills in many parts of old Lisbon. The people of this old section have no parks or playgrounds near by, so they use the streets for baby-sitting, washing clothes, and sunning. Some houses in this area are nearly a thousand years old.

Portuguese Grape Pickers work in a sunny vineyard in the Douro Valley. These grapes are used to make port wine. Grape growing is one of the leading industries in Portugal.

E. A. Weber, Photo Researchers

since 1910, although the government is Roman Catholic in its sympathies. Most Portuguese are Roman Catholics. The shrine of Our Lady of Fatima is in Portugal.

Government

National Government. The constitution of 1933 provides what the Portuguese call a *corporative republic*. In this system, various groups of the population, such as labor organizations and cultural groups, have a voice in the government. The president appoints both the prime minister and his cabinet, and they are responsible only to him. The prime minister is the real head of the government. The National Assembly has certain powers to levy taxes and to pass laws. An advisory group, called the Corporative Chamber, is made up of representatives chosen by local authorities and commercial, industrial, religious, and cultural groups.

Only those men who can read and write, or who pay certain property taxes, may vote in elections. Women may vote only if they have gone through secondary school, or when they act as the head of a family.

The government nominates candidates for offices. Others may run, but they seldom win because the government controls publicity and ballot distribution. This system allowed Prime Minister Salazar to rule as a dictator for over 35 years in the 1900's.

The Azores and Madeira islands are governed as part of the mainland. They are electoral districts of the country, and send representatives to the National Assembly.

Overseas Provinces of Portugal have the same rights and obligations as the administrative districts of the mother country. Each has a governor and is locally self-governing. However, the budgets of the provinces must be approved by the minister for overseas provinces in Lisbon. The overseas provinces are listed below.

Overseas Province	Area (sq. mi.)	Population
Angola	481,354	5,518,000
Cape Verde Islands	1,557	245,000
Macao	6	280,000
Mozambique	302,330	7,384,000
Portuguese Guinea	13,948	531,000
Portuguese Timor	5,763	596,000
São Tomé and Príncipe	372	62,000

History

Early Years. When Phoenician and Carthaginian sailors came to Portugal in the 800's B.C., they found people called *Iberians* living there. Tradition says that the Greeks founded colonies at the mouth of the Tagus River, where Lisbon now stands, in the 500's and 400's B.C. The Romans founded settlements in Portugal after they conquered it in the 100's B.C. They called the area *Lusitania*. In the A.D. 400's, the whole Iberian Peninsula was invaded by the Visigoths, a warlike Germanic tribe. The Visigoths lived peacefully until the Moslem Arabs and Moors conquered the peninsula in the 700's.

The Middle Ages. The Moorish rulers were able men, and Portugal prospered under their rule. In the 1000's, Moorish power grew weaker. Spanish Christians began to reconquer the peninsula. The region of Porto, also called Oporto, was the first area regained by the Christians. The Latin name for Porto was *Portus*,

617

PORTUGAL

and from this area the country took its present name.

In the late 1000's, Henry of Burgundy was one of the French knights who fought against the Moslems. In 1094, the Spanish king, Alfonso VI, rewarded Henry with the counties of Porto and Coimbra, giving him the title of Count of Portugal. Henry's son, Afonso Henriques, won many victories over the Moors. In 1143 he took the title of King of Portugal. Four years later, he captured Lisbon and made it his capital. By the middle 1200's, all the land of Portugal on the Iberian Peninsula had been won from the Moors. King John I of the House of Avis came to the throne in 1385. Portugal prospered during his reign. He made a permanent alliance with England in 1386. This alliance, still in force,

RED-LETTER DATES IN PORTUGAL

800's B.C. Phoenician sailors visited the coast of what is now Portugal.

218-133 B.C. Romans conquered the area of Portugal.

A.D. 711 Moslem Moors invaded the Iberian Peninsula.

1143 Afonso Henriques made Portugal an independent kingdom.

1415 Portugal began its first overseas expansion in Morocco.

1497-1498 Portuguese navigator Vasco da Gama sailed around Africa to India.

1500 Pedro Álvares Cabral discovered Brazil for Portugal.

1580 King Philip II of Spain seized the Portuguese throne.

1640 John, Duke of Braganza, restored Portugal's independence.

1822 Portugal lost Brazil in a bloodless revolution.

1910 Patriots established the Republic of Portugal.

1949 Portugal joined the North Atlantic Treaty Organization.

1955 Portugal joined the United Nations.

1957 The government set up corporations to regulate sources of revenue.

1961 India seized the Portuguese provinces of Goa, Damão, and Diu in India.

is considered the oldest political alliance in Europe.

Voyages of Discovery. King John's son Henry, called Prince Henry the Navigator, encouraged navigation, and offered prizes for discoveries. Portuguese sailors followed the west coast of Africa into unknown seas, looking for new countries. By 1419, the island of Madeira, which probably had been discovered earlier by the Italians, was discovered again. Before King John I died in 1433, Portuguese ships had reached the Azores.

Exploration continued in the later 1400's. In 1488 a Portuguese captain, Bartolomeu Dias, discovered the Cape of Good Hope at the southern end of Africa.

King Manuel I, who is called the Fortunate, came to the throne in 1495. Two years later, Vasco da Gama sailed around the Cape of Good Hope and reached India in 1498. In 1500, another Portuguese captain, Pedro Álvares Cabral, discovered Brazil.

Years of Decline in Portugal's power began under the next ruler, John III, who became king in 1521. Many Jews had been forced to leave the country, and their banking and commercial power went with them. The Inquisition hurt the cultural and commercial development of the country. See INQUISITION.

In 1580, King Philip II of Spain seized the Portuguese throne. During the period of Spanish rule, English, Dutch, and French forces attacked the Portuguese colonies. But a Portuguese nobleman, John, duke of Braganza, succeeded in pushing out the Spanish rulers in 1640. He was crowned as John IV, and became the first king of the House of Braganza.

In the 1600's, Portuguese power and influence continued to weaken. In 1703 Portugal made an important trade agreement with England, called the Methuen Treaty. It allowed Portugal to sell wine to England at special prices. The country also admitted English woolen goods without duty. This improved Portugal's economy by setting up its wine trade. An earthquake at Lisbon in 1755 destroyed most of the city's buildings and killed about 60,000 persons.

The 1800's and 1900's. French forces seized Lisbon in 1807, during the Napoleonic Wars, and many young Portuguese were forced to join the French army. England sent an army to Portugal commanded by Arthur Wellesley, who later became the duke of Wellington. With Portuguese help, Wellesley drove out the French. Meanwhile, the ruler of the country, John VI, had fled to Brazil. When he returned in 1821, he found the people demanding a constitutional government. A liberal constitution was written in 1822, providing for freedom of speech and religion, abolition of class privileges, and only a restricted veto power for the king. But the constitution granted few privileges to the Brazilians, who declared their independence in 1822 (see BRAZIL [Independence and Empire]). Soon after, the king discarded the constitution of 1822.

In the later 1800's, Portugal made great progress. Sanitary reforms were made in Lisbon after the plague of 1861, which killed King Pedro V and many of his subjects. Slavery was done away with in Portugal's colonies in 1878. But long years of extravagance and poor government followed. On Feb. 1, 1908, King Carlos and Crown Prince Luis were assassinated on the streets of Lisbon by revolutionists.

King Carlos was followed by 19-year-old Manuel II, who was too young to govern. Manuel fled the country in 1910. Portuguese leaders founded a republic, with Manuel de Arriaga as the first president. In the 16 years after the republic was founded, there were 18 revolutions. During World War I, Portugal lived up to its alliance with England and fought against Germany.

After World War I, Portugal had a period of great disorder. The country's finances were in a bad state when General Antonio Oscar de Fragoso Carmona became president in 1926. Carmona was formally elected in 1928. He appointed Antonio de Oliveira Salazar as finance minister, with a free hand to end the country's financial troubles. Salazar became prime minister in 1932 and soon assumed the powers of a dictator. His government sympathized with the cause of Francisco Franco during the Spanish Civil War (1936-1939).

World War II. Portugal remained neutral during World War II, although Japanese forces occupied Portuguese Timor in 1942. European refugees poured into Lisbon, hoping for passage to the Americas. Lisbon was an important listening post for both Axis and Allied intelligence agents. In 1943 Portugal leased bases in the Azores to Great Britain. These bases were returned three years later. Portugal also gave the United States rights to bases in the Azores. This agreement is still in force.

After World War II, Portugal applied for admission to the United Nations, but the request was blocked by

Russia until 1955, when Portugal was admitted. In 1949, Portugal joined the North Atlantic Treaty Organization (see NORTH ATLANTIC TREATY ORGANIZATION). It also made new trade agreements with Great Britain and other countries to improve its economic outlook.

In April, 1951, President Carmona died, after being in office for 25 years. In July, 1951, Francisco Higino Craveiro Lopes was elected president. But opponents charged the election was not free.

The Portuguese government announced in 1953 a six-year program to develop the country's economy. Work was started on projects to build oil-refining plants, iron and steel foundries, and tin-plate factories. The government also began modernizing Portugal's agriculture, as well as its transportation and electric-power systems. In 1957, the government set up corporations to control agriculture, credit and insurance, fishing and canning, and transportation and tourism. Portugal and six other nations formed the European Free Trade Association (Outer Seven) in 1959.

Américo Tomaz was elected president in 1958 and again in 1965. Salazar remained as prime minister. In 1968 Salazar suffered a stroke and was not expected to live. He was replaced as prime minister by Marcello Caetano. Caetano had served in the Finance Ministry under Salazar and had held many other government posts. He had left the government in the 1950's to teach law at the University of Lisbon.

Colonial Problems troubled Portugal during the 1960's. In 1961, Indian troops seized Portugal's provinces of Goa, Damão, and Diu in India. The occupation ended 451 years of Portuguese rule. In 1961, a rebellion began in Angola, a Portuguese colony in Africa. The Angolans charged Portugal with using forced labor and providing poor medical care. Portugal refused a UN investigation, and the trouble continued in the late 1960's. Portugal faced rebellion in Portuguese Guinea and Mozambique, other African colonies. Macao, a Portuguese colony in southern China, became the scene of anti-Portuguese riots in 1967.　CHARLES E. NOWELL

Related Articles in WORLD BOOK include:

BIOGRAPHIES

Cabral, Pedro Á.	Magellan, Ferdinand
Da Gama, Vasco	Moniz, Antônio C.
Dias, Bartolomeu	Pedro (I)
Henry the Navigator	Queirós, Pedro F. de
John VI	Salazar, Antonio de Oliveira

CITIES

Braga	Funchal	Lisbon	Porto

HISTORY

Exploration and Discovery	Line of Demarcation
Iberia	World War I

PHYSICAL FEATURES AND PROVINCES

Angola	Macao	São Tomé and
Azores	Madeira	Príncipe
Cape Saint Vincent	Mozambique	Tagus River
Douro River	Portuguese Guinea	Timor

OTHER RELATED ARTICLES

Centavo	Portuguese Language
Clothing (color picture)	Portuguese Literature and
Cork	Brazilian Literature
European Monetary	Rice (picture: Farmers
Agreement	Winnow Rice)
Olive (table)	Wine (table)
Our Lady of Fatima	

Questions

What country is Portugal's nearest neighbor? In what ways are the two countries alike?
What are Portugal's chief natural resources?
Where did the name *Portugal* come from?
What are Portugal's most important industries?
What country is Portugal's oldest ally?
How are Portugal's overseas provinces governed?
What is a *corporative republic* form of government?
What state is about the same size as Portugal?
Who were the first settlers in Portugal?
Which famous explorers were Portuguese?

PORTUGUESE EAST AFRICA. See MOZAMBIQUE.

PORTUGUESE GUINEA, *GIHN ih,* is an overseas province of Portugal on the west coast of Africa. The *map* shows that it faces the Atlantic Ocean between Senegal, a member of the French Community, and the Republic of Guinea. The Bijagós (Bissagos) Islands, which lie just off the coast, form a part of the province. Portuguese Guinea covers an area of 13,948 square miles, and has a population of 531,000. Bissau is the capital and largest city.

Rolling grasslands, called *savannas,* spread across the northern parts of Portuguese Guinea (see SAVANNA). Tropical rain forests cover the southern regions, and

PORTUGUESE GUINEA

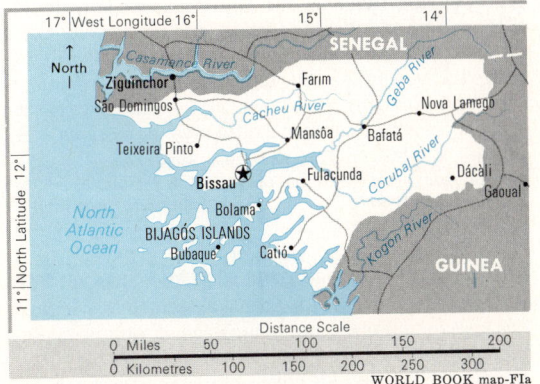

WORLD BOOK map-FIa

619

swamps stretch across the coastal areas. Yearly temperatures average 81° F., and rainfall totals about 50 inches. The heaviest rains fall between May and November.

Agriculture provides the chief source of income in Portuguese Guinea. Important farm products include almonds, animal hides, beeswax, coconuts, copra, corn, millet, palm oil, peanuts, rice, and rubber.

Bissau (pop. about 25,000) is the chief port in Portuguese Guinea, and has served as its capital since 1942 (see BISSAU). Another important port, Bolama (pop. about 5,000), stands on Bolama Island, the easternmost of the Bijagós Islands. The city of Bolama has a safe harbor, and handles much trade.

Portuguese sailors discovered Bolama Island in 1446. For many years, Great Britain and Portugal quarreled over ownership of the area. In 1870, the United States was asked to judge the claims of the two disputing powers. The American decision awarded the territory to Portugal. The region became a separate colony in 1879, and its boundaries were set in 1886. A Portuguese governor and council control the area. African nationalist leaders have been calling for independence since neighboring Guinea became an independent country in 1958. Strong rebel forces have been trying to seize control of the province, and Portugal has sent thousands of troops there to battle the rebels.   L. GRAY COWAN

PORTUGUESE INDIA was a Portuguese overseas province in India from the 1500's until 1961. After the 1600's, it consisted of the districts of Goa, on the west-central coast of India, and Damão and Diu, on India's Gulf of Cambay. See also GOA.   ROBERT I. CRANE

PORTUGUESE LANGUAGE is the official language of Portugal and of Brazil. Portuguese is a Romance language and is much like Spanish. But the Portuguese language is softer and less emphatic than Spanish.

The Portuguese language is spoken by more than 75 million persons in Brazil. Portuguese colonizers brought the language into the country in the 1500's. In time, Brazilian Portuguese came to have somewhat the same relation to the language of central Portugal that American English has to British English. The Brazilians took words from the Tupi Indians of the region and from African slaves. In Brazil, unstressed syllables are spoken more clearly than in Portugal. Galician is a dialect of Portuguese.

Since the early 1900's, many persons in Portugal and Brazil have wanted to simplify and standardize Portuguese spelling. Scholars wished to take out many double consonants and other old-fashioned letter combinations. In 1943, the governments of Portugal and Brazil approved a new system, in which *f* is substituted for *ph*, *t* for *th*, and *i* for *y*.   HARVEY L. JOHNSON

Here are some common Portuguese expressions:

bom dia, *BOHNG DEE uh,* good day   **mãe,** *mahng,* mother
perdão, *puhr DAHNG oh,* pardon me   **pai,** *py,* father
se faz favor, *seh fahz*   **obrigado,** *oo brae GAH*
  fuh VOHR, please   *doo,* thank you

See also ROMANCE LANGUAGE.

PORTUGUESE LITERATURE AND BRAZILIAN LITERATURE for hundreds of years have been closely related, because they use the same language, Portuguese. Portuguese literature is especially noted for charming poetry; Brazilian literature, for novels of social criticism.

Portuguese Literature. The first known Portuguese text is a love poem published in 1189. The poet Sá de Miranda (1485-1558) founded the classical school of writing. Gil Vicente (1469?-1536?) brought drama to Portugal. He wrote plays in Portuguese, Spanish, and a combination of the two.

Portugal's greatest writer is Luiz de Camões (1524-1580). In 1572, he published the greatest piece in all Portuguese literature, *Os Lusíadas* (*The Lusitanians*). This is a long epic poem celebrating Portugal's history and heroes. The poem is tied in with the story of Vasco da Gama's historic voyage to India. Camões inserted much Greek mythology into his poem. In the hundred years after Camões' time, Portuguese authors wrote poetry in sonnet form and romantic prose tales.

Almeida Garrett (1799-1854) revived the art of drama in Portugal. He is considered the chief lyric poet of the early 1800's, and the most important dramatist since Gil Vicente. José Maria de Eça de Queiroz (1843-1900) is considered the leading realistic novelist of Portugal. His novels and short stories contain delightful descriptions.

Brazilian Literature. The first important Brazilian literary figure was Gregório de Matos, who wrote in the 1600's. He drew bitter poetic caricatures of political leaders sent from Portugal. He was the first writer to paint a true picture of Brazilian life. The greatest figure in Brazilian letters, Joaquim Maria Machado de Assis (1839-1908), was a mulatto born of humble parents. His chief novels, *Bras Cubas, Quincas Borba,* and *Dom Casmurro,* show his keen irony and acute observation.

Euclydes da Cunha (1866-1909) wrote *Os Sertões,* probably the outstanding single book by a Brazilian. It tells of a revolt against the government. *Canaan,* by José Pereira da Graça Aranha (1868-1931), presents the problems confronting German immigrants in a new land. Monteiro Lobato (1883-1948) won lasting fame with his hillbilly character, Jeca Tatú, or Joe Armadillo. José Lins do Rego (1901-1957) traced the decay of the old plantation system. Jorge Amado (1912-   ) wrote stories of the slums of Bahia. Erico Verissimo (1905-   ), the most popular present-day author, is a master of character and plot. His novels deal with life in the district of Rio Grande do Sul.   HARVEY L. JOHNSON

PORTUGUESE MAN-OF-WAR is a jellyfish that floats on the surface of tropical seas and the Gulf Stream. The Portuguese man-of-war is not really a single animal, but a group of animals attached to a hollow float that looks like a bladder. The full-grown float is about 8 inches long. It is filled with gas that allows it to float on the water. Hanging from the float are long stringlike filaments called *tentacles.* They may be 100 feet long. These tentacles act as arms and are used to grasp food. They contain a poison that seems to paralyze fish on contact. These tentacles are also dangerous to man. Swimmers touching them will suffer painful welts, or even shock and prostration that could be fatal.

All the animals that are a part of one float make up what is called a *colony.* Each animal in the colony has a different job to do. Some of them reproduce their kind. Others find food, while still others protect the colony against enemies.

Scientific Classification. The Portuguese man-of-war is in the phylum *Coelenterata.* It is genus *Physalia,* species *P. pelagica.*   RALPH BUCHSBAUM

See also COELENTERATE.

N.Y. Zoological Society

The Portuguese Man-of-War is a pretty sight on the surface. But just below water, it has a fish clutched in its long tentacles, ready to eat as it floats about.

PORTUGUESE WEST AFRICA. See ANGOLA.

PORTULACA, *POHR tyoo LAY kuh,* is the name of a group of herbs with dainty red, yellow, pink, white, or purple flowers. The *rose moss* of Brazil, grown as a garden flower, grows flat or to about 1 foot in height, with narrow, fleshy leaves about an inch long. The *kitchen garden portulaca* grows to 1½ feet tall, with bright yellow flowers, about a half inch wide, and broad leaves. It is sometimes used as an herb in cooking.

Portulacas make beautiful plants for a border or a rock garden. They grow best in poor, rather light soil, and should be given a sunny, exposed position. The flowers open only in full sun. Several species make charming potted plants, and are especially suited for summer flowering in a greenhouse. But they are not satisfactory as cut flowers.

Scientific Classification. Portulacas belong to the purslane family, *Portulacaceae.* Rose moss is genus *Portulaca,* species *P. grandiflora.* The kitchen garden portulaca is *P. oleracea.*

HAROLD NORMAN MOLDENKE

See also HERB.

Portulaca is a colorful flower that thrives in hot weather.

J. Horace McFarland

POSADA. See CHRISTMAS (Latin America).

POSEIDON. See NEPTUNE (god).

POSITION. See NAVIGATION (Methods).

POSITIVE ELECTRICITY. See ELECTRICITY.

POSITIVE NUMBER. See ALGEBRA (Positive and Negative Numbers).

POSITIVISM. See COMTE, AUGUSTE.

POSITRON. See ATOM (Antiparticles); ANDERSON, CARL DAVID.

POSSESSIVE CASE. See CASE.

POSSUM. See OPOSSUM.

POST, EMILY PRICE (1873?-1960), made a career out of good manners. Her book *Etiquette* tells people how to behave properly in all types of social situations. After its publication in 1922, Mrs. Post became established as an authority on proper behavior. She emphasized that good manners are based on common sense and a regard for the feelings of others. She revised her book frequently to take into account changing social conditions and new patterns of social behavior.

Emily Post was born in Baltimore, Md., the daughter of a wealthy architect. Her first book, *The Flight of the Moth* (1904), was a fictional story of life among socially gracious people in the early 1900's. Her other books include *How to Behave Though a Debutante* (1928), *The Personality of a House* (1930), *Children Are People* (1940), and *Motor Manners* (1950). She also wrote newspaper columns and made radio broadcasts.   CARL NIEMEYER

See also ETIQUETTE.

POST, WILEY (1899-1935), was a pioneer American high-altitude pilot, and the first man to fly around the world alone. He was born on a farm near Grand Saline, Tex., and at 16 went to Kansas City to learn how to be a mechanic. He occasionally worked in oil fields, and in 1924 lost an eye in an oil-field accident.

Post used the money he received as compensation to buy his first airplane. He became a pilot and set many intercity speed records in the *Winnie Mae,* an advanced airplane for its time. He also helped prove that high-altitude flight was possible. Post lost his life in

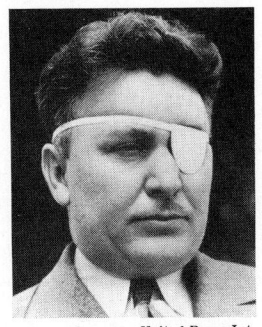

United Press Int.

Wiley Post

an air crash with Will Rogers in Alaska. ROBERT B. HOTZ

See also AIRPLANE (color picture: Airplanes That Made History); GYROPILOT.

POST EXCHANGE is a store or shop that the United States Army operates for its personnel at military camps. It is usually called the "PX." The Air Force calls it a *base exchange.* In the Navy it is a *Navy exchange* ashore or a *ship's store* afloat.

A post exchange sells not only personal items such as toilet articles and cigarettes, but also gift items and luxuries. Some have facilities such as bowling alleys and snack bars. Profits are usually spent on post recreational activities.   CHARLES B. MACDONALD

POST-IMPRESSIONISM. See PAINTING (In the 1800's).

POST MORTEM is the Latin for *after death.* The term *post mortem* has come to mean the medical examination of a dead human body. Its purpose is to learn the cause of death. Generally, a post-mortem examination of a body may not be made without consent of the surviving spouse or next of kin, except in cases where murder or another crime is suspected.   FRED E. INBAU

See also AUTOPSY.

WHAT HAPPENS TO YOUR LETTER

Mailed. You drop the properly addressed letter into the mailbox near your home.

Picked Up. A postal employee picks up your letter at the mailbox and carries it to the post office. Pick-up schedules are printed on all mailboxes.

U.S. Post Office Dept.

POST OFFICE. You may have found several pieces of mail in your mailbox this morning. There may have been letters from your Aunt Jane in Philadelphia and your Uncle Karl in Germany. Perhaps there was a seed catalogue from Iowa for your father. How was this mail gathered from places thousands of miles apart and delivered to your home? It came to you through the *post office* and the *postal system*.

How Your Letter Travels

Have you ever wondered what happens to a letter after you drop it into a corner mailbox? Let's take an imaginary trip with such a letter and find out how the post office carries the letter on its way. First of all, you address the letter to a friend of yours:

Miss Barbara Lynch
7 Jordan Avenue
Chicago, Illinois 60618

Then you put a stamp in the upper righthand corner of the envelope and drop it into the corner mailbox. A short time later, a truck drives up to the box and a post-office worker takes out all the mail and puts it in the truck to be taken to the post office.

In the Post Office, postal clerks sort the letters according to envelope size, and stack them, face up, with the stamps in the same position. They put the letters into a machine that *cancels* (marks) the stamps so they cannot be used again. The canceling machine prints on the envelope the date, city, state, and whether the letter was canceled in the A.M. or P.M. In large post offices, automatic machines prepare letters for cancellation, and cancel the stamps.

Next, clerks separate the mail according to its destinations. Out-of-town mail is sorted according to states. Thus your letter is put in a pigeonhole marked "Illinois."

Other clerks separate letters according to the cities they are addressed to within each state. Your letter then goes in the "Chicago" pigeonhole.

Your Letter Goes on Its Way. All out-of-town mail is bundled carefully, placed in mail sacks, and taken to a truck, a train, or an airplane. Your letter and others are put on the first transportation to Chicago.

When the mail arrives in Chicago, it is rushed to the post office and sorted according to local ZIP-code areas. Your letter is handled faster if you put the proper ZIP-code number, such as "60618," on the envelope. The last two numbers of the ZIP code indicate the local area. Postal clerks again sort the mail so that every letter carrier, or postman, will get all the mail for the people living along his route.

The Postman. When the carrier gets his own bundle of mail, he separates it according to the house numbers on the streets he serves. Your letter to Barbara is popped into a pigeonhole marked "7 Jordan Avenue."

The mail is then carefully tied up. Trucks take it to *relay boxes* along the postman's route. These are big green boxes that have "Not for the deposit of mail" printed on them. The mail is left in them because most

U.S. Post Office Dept.

Stacked and Cancelled. In the post office, all letters are stacked face up, according to envelope size. Then a machine cancels the stamps so that they cannot be used again.

Sorted. Letters for local delivery are sorted out first. Then your letter and others going out of town are sorted, first by states, and then by cities in the states.

Bundled. All letters going out of town by regular mail are bundled and placed in mail sacks. Then the mail sacks are taken to the railroad station.

Put on Train. Carts at the station haul mail sacks to the train. There they are put aboard a railway mail car.

Traveling Post Office. Clerks in railway mail cars sort and distribute mail as the train speeds across country.

United Press Int.

Sorted Again. When your letter reaches its destination, it is sorted with the other mail according to the ZIP code, and according to the specific mail routes.

Stored. A truck takes your letter to a relay box along the postman's route. He picks it up from this box when he is ready to deliver his load of mail.

carriers couldn't possibly carry at one time all the letters and magazines they must deliver every day. The postal rules say the postman cannot carry more than 35 pounds at one time. Postmen who deliver mail from vehicles carry the whole day's delivery in the vehicle.

Your letter is put in the relay box near Barbara's house. The postman takes the mail from this box and starts down the block. When he comes to Barbara's house, he drops your letter to Barbara into her mailbox.

Importance of the Post Office

Human progress and the postal system developed together. For centuries, man has used the postal system as his chief means of exchanging ideas with persons in distant places. Until the telegraph, telephone, radio, and television were invented, the postal system was about the only safe way of getting news from and giving news to persons in faraway places.

Just imagine your community without postal service! You would not often hear from your friends or relatives who live outside the community, because it would cost too much to send messages. No other means of communication is as inexpensive as the postal system. You would not be able to exchange news with pen pals in other countries. There would be little to read but local books, magazines, and newspapers which you would buy at newsstands. It would be difficult to operate most businesses and industries.

Furthermore, there might not even be a United States. This country probably could not have grown and remained united without postal communications.

Post-Office Services

Postage Stamps. The post office sells postage stamps to put on letters or packages. These stamps are proof that the sender has paid for sending his mail. About three out of every ten dollars of post-office income come from the sale of stamps. About 23 billion stamps are issued every year in the United States. Placed end

Delivered. The postman delivers your letter to your friend.

U.S. Post Office Dept.

to end, they would encircle the world 14 times.

Stamps for ordinary surface mail are printed in the following denominations: 1¢ through 6¢, 8¢, 10¢, 12¢, 13¢, 15¢, 20¢, 25¢, 30¢, 40¢, 50¢, $1, and $5. There also are airmail stamps of various denominations, such as 10¢ and 20¢, and 30¢ special-delivery stamps.

At various times during the year, the post office issues special stamps called *commemorative stamps*. Some such stamps honor distinguished persons who are dead. No living person may be shown on a United States postage stamp, although this is not true of stamps in other countries. Other commemorative stamps pay tribute to great historical events, to places of scenic beauty, or to particular industries or organizations. These commemorative stamps have the same values, and are used in the same way, as regular postage stamps.

Stamped Envelopes. The post office sells envelopes with postage printed on them for a small fee. Persons

624

who use the mails often use stamped envelopes to save the time and labor of sticking stamps to envelopes.

Postal Cards also are sold by post offices. Postal cards have the postage printed on them, but cost only the value of the postage. Private companies make *post cards*. But these cards do not have a stamp on them.

Metered Postage. Companies that send out many pieces of mail often use a postage meter to speed up mailing. They lease a meter from an authorized manufacturer, and get a postal permit to use it. The company brings the meter to the post office and buys a certain amount of postage. A post-office employee sets the meter for this amount. The meter contains printing dies which stamp the envelopes used by the company. It also contains counters that show the company how much postage it has used and how much it has left.

Precanceled Stamps are used to reduce the time and labor cost of handling mail. They are canceled by the post office before the user puts them on envelopes for mailing. They can be purchased only at post offices where the user has a precancel permit.

Parcel Post is the postal service for sending packages of certain sizes and weights through the mails. To qualify for parcel-post service, a package must fall within certain size and weight limits. These vary according to the class of post office and the distance the parcel is being sent. See PARCEL POST.

City Delivery. The post office delivers mail free of charge to persons in most cities of the United States. Any town with at least 2,500 persons and $10,000 or more in annual postal receipts may have city delivery if it meets certain conditions. For example, the town must have sidewalks, house numbers, and street signs.

Rural Delivery. People who live in the country receive mail without additional charges. There are about 33,000 rural carriers who serve over 9 million families. These carriers not only deliver mail, but also collect it. sell postage stamps, issue money orders, and register mail. See RURAL DELIVERY.

Star-Route Service. This service was set up primarily to carry mail by truck between post offices where train service is not available. Star-route carriers are not government employees. They work under contract with the postal transportation service. There are about 12,000 star-route contractors. See STAR ROUTE.

General Delivery. A person can have his mail directed to General Delivery, if he is not sure what his address will be in a city. The post office will hold the mail for 10 days in most cases.

Post-Office Boxes may be rented in post offices. They are located in post-office lobbies. Individuals and companies often use them because they provide fast, convenient mail delivery. They also make mail available after regular post-office hours.

Collect on Delivery (C.O.D.) permits a person to order something of value through the mail and pay for it when it arrives. Any mailable package or sealed letter may be sent C.O.D. if it has been ordered by the addressee. The person receiving the mail pays the price of the enclosure plus a money order fee and possibly the postage. The money is returned to the sender by postal money order.

Registry. When a person wants special protection for a letter or package, he can pay a small fee to the post office and have it registered. The person to whom the registered mail is sent must sign a postal receipt before the mail is delivered to him.

Insurance. Persons may insure packages for full value up to $200. If the package is lost or damaged in the mails, the sender is paid the actual value of the item up to the amount of the insurance.

Certificate of Mailing. If a person wants proof that he mailed a letter or package, he can pay a small fee at the time of mailing. He fills out a certificate which the post office then certifies as legal proof that he mailed the letter or package.

Certified Service. When a person wants proof of delivery for items not having actual monetary value, he may pay 30 cents in addition to regular postage and receive certified service. The sender must fill out the certified coupon before mailing, as well as the return receipt card if one is desired. Post offices keep a record of certified-mail delivery for two years.

Special Delivery. For a fee of 30 cents added to regular postage, mail sent first class and weighing less than two pounds will receive special treatment in the

Moving Trains Receive Mail. The mail sack is attached to a crane along the tracks, *above*. A steel catcher arm on the train, *below*, grabs the mail sack as the train passes by.

Marks

Roman Post Roads had horses and couriers placed, or *posted*, along them. Our word *post* is from a Latin word, *positum*, meaning *to place.*

mails. It also will be delivered by a special messenger as soon as it arrives at a post office, instead of being held for ordinary delivery by a regular postman. Other classes of mail may also be sent special delivery.

Special Handling. A person may pay a small fee to have fourth-class mail sent by special handling. This means that a package will be transported between post offices along with first-class mail.

Dead-Mail Office. Mail that cannot be delivered, or returned, goes to one of the branches of the Dead-Mail Office. Money sent in letters that cannot be delivered is turned over to the post office. At regular intervals there is a sale of the contents of "dead" packages. Funds from such sales also go to the Post Office. See DEAD-MAIL OFFICE.

Money Order. Post offices sell money orders to provide a safe, convenient way to send money through the mails. See MONEY ORDER.

Nonpostal Stamps. Stamps other than those used for postage may be bought in post offices. Nonpostal stamps include documentary internal-revenue stamps that go on legal documents, migratory-bird stamps attached to hunting licenses, and United States Savings Stamps.

Other Services. Post offices serve as headquarters for the registration of aliens. They also give information to the public regarding civil service employment.

Postal Inspection. Over 900 postal inspectors safeguard and improve postal services. Some solve administrative problems. They investigate post-office personnel and routines, and suggest ways of improving services. Other inspectors deal with crimes involving the mails. They investigate the mailing of explosives, firearms, and poisons; mail thefts; post-office burglaries; the use of the mails to defraud; and forged money orders.

Classes of Post Offices

United States post offices are divided into four classes by *revenue units.* A revenue unit is the average amount of revenue, or income from postal fees, a post office receives annually for each 1,000 pieces of mail mailed there. A revenue unit also includes income from special service transactions. *First class* post offices have 950 or more revenue units. Post offices having 190 to 949 revenue units are *second class.* Those with 36 to 189 are *third class.* *Fourth class* post offices have less than 36 revenue units. In the mid-1960's, there were more than 4,400 first class post offices in the United States.

Postmasters are civil-service employees. Normally, they serve until they reach retirement age (in most cases, 70 years). First-, second-, and third-class postmasters are appointed by the President of the United States and approved by the Senate. Fourth-class postmasters are appointed by the U.S. postmaster general.

Post-Office Careers

The Post Office Department offers careers that may be divided into two groups. The larger group includes jobs that deal directly with the gathering, distribution, and delivery of mail. This group covers about 525,000 workers. The second group includes about 75,000 persons. They perform jobs that are similar to jobs found in many other businesses.

Postal workers are not required to meet any specific educational requirements, although persons with at least a high-school education are preferred. Postal workers must pass a Civil Service examination before being hired. See CIVIL SERVICE.

Careers in Positions Handling Direct Mail. More than half of all postal employees hold positions as regular *full-time mail carriers,* and *post-office clerks.* Carriers deliver mail everywhere. Postal clerks handle a variety of jobs. Many deal directly with the public at stamp, parcel-post, delivery, money-order, and postal-savings windows. Others serve behind the scenes, sorting and routing mail, keeping records of postal-savings accounts, and tabulating money-order receipts.

Substitute mail carriers and *substitute post-office clerks* replace absent workers or take on extra duties, often on short notice. *Postal transportation clerks* sort and distribute mail in railway and highway post offices (trains and trucks). *Postal inspectors* investigate violations of postal regulations, and improve post-office services. *Foremen* and *superintendents* supervise and direct workers. *Postmasters* are in charge of all personnel and operations in their post offices.

Careers in Supplementary Mail-Service Jobs. *Mechanics* keep mail trucks in good running condition. *Engineers* and *janitors* care for post-office buildings. *Watchmen* protect postal buildings and properties. *Typists, accountants, auditors,* and *machine operators* help to keep records of postal operations. *Drivers, dispatchers,* and *route supervisors* handle motor-unit transfers of mail. *Mail handlers* in large post offices do much of the heavy work involved in handling mailbags.

History

Early Years. As long ago as 3000 B.C., fast couriers, or runners, memorized messages and carried them for their rulers. Only rulers used this early postal system. There was no demand for a general postal service, because few people could read or write. Early "letters" were carved on clay or bronze. Later, they were carved on bone or wood, and protected by a wax coating. Still later, they were written on the skins of animals (parchment), or on materials that were made from vegetable matter (papyrus).

Herodotus, the Greek historian (484?-424? B.C.), wrote about the Persian postal system of 500 B.C. in these words: **"There is no mortal thing faster than these messengers . . . neither snow nor rain nor heat nor gloom of night stays these couriers from the swift completion of their appointed rounds."** The last part of

First Class. Letters, postal cards, and all other material that is wholly or partly in writing, or sealed against inspection. In 1963, the Post Office Department banned odd-shaped letters and envelopes less than $4\frac{1}{4}$ inches long and 3 inches wide to standardize mail for handling by machines.

Within United States and possessions, Canada, and Mexico:
- Letters (per ounce or fraction thereof)........6¢
- Postal cards (each)...........................5¢

To all other countries:
- Letters (first ounce or fraction thereof).......13¢
- Letters (each additional ounce or fraction thereof).8¢
- Postal cards (each)...........................8¢

Air mail within United States and possessions, Canada, and Mexico:
- Letters and packages (per ounce or fraction thereof up to 7 ounces)...................10¢
- Letters and packages over 7 ounces up to 70 pounds vary in cost, according to size and weight, from 80¢ to $56.08.
- Postal cards.................................8¢

Air mail to other countries:
- Air-letter sheet (each)......................13¢
- Postal cards (each)..........................13¢
- Other air mail varies in cost according to the weight of the piece of mail and the location of the country to which it is sent.

Second Class. Newspapers and periodicals.

For the general public: 5¢ for the first 2 ounces or fraction thereof, and 1¢ for each additional ounce or fraction thereof. Fourth-class rates apply if lower.

For publishers: the rates vary according to (1) whether the item is printed in or out of the county it is mailed in; (2) the percentage of reading and advertising matter in the publication; (3) the weight of the publication; and (4) the other countries to which the magazine or newspaper may be sent. Certain religious and educational publications may be mailed anywhere in the country at 1.9¢ per pound.

Third Class. Any mail that weighs less than 16 ounces that is not included in first or second class.

Single piece rates:
- First 2 ounces or fraction thereof............6¢
- Each additional ounce or fraction thereof......2¢

Bulk rates:
- Books and catalogs having at least 24 pages, 22 of which are printed; seeds; plants; etc. (per pound or fraction thereof)............16¢
- All other printed matter and merchandise (per pound or fraction thereof).................22¢
- Minimum rate per piece...................3.6¢
- Lower rates apply to bulk mailings by authorized nonprofit organizations.

Rate for keys and identification cards without cover:
- First 2 ounces or fraction thereof............14¢
- Each additional 2 ounces or fraction thereof....7¢

Fourth Class. Any matter that weighs 16 ounces or more that is not included in first or second class. For rates, see PARCEL POST.

---

this quotation is inscribed on the front of the General Post Office in New York City.

Caesar Augustus (63 B.C.–A.D. 14), the first Roman emperor, created the first "modern" postal system. He needed swift communications to hold his empire together, and built fine roads for his messengers.

When the Roman Empire was destroyed, the postal system it created was destroyed also. There was not much communication, on an organized scale, between peoples in Europe until the early 1300's.

The writings of Marco Polo (1254?-1324) about

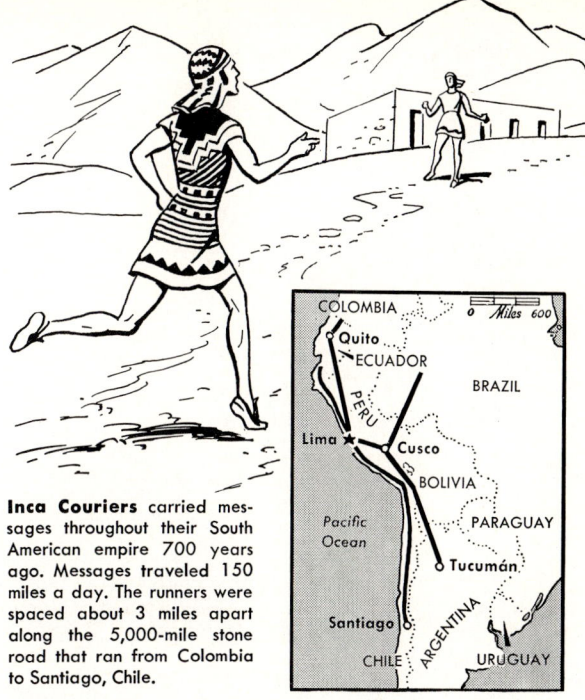

Inca Couriers carried messages throughout their South American empire 700 years ago. Messages traveled 150 miles a day. The runners were spaced about 3 miles apart along the 5,000-mile stone road that ran from Colombia to Santiago, Chile.

the China of Kublai Khan (1216-1294) describe a postal system of messengers and horses. China then had 10,000 postal stations. The Aztec in Mexico and Central America had a parcel-post system to distribute fresh fish among their villages in the 1200's.

The Beginnings of Public Mails. During the 1400's, King Edward IV of England (1442-1483) set up a system of post houses which were primarily for carrying official mail. There is convincing evidence that private persons also used the early posts. Under Henry VIII (1491-1547), an Englishman named Sir Brian Tuke was made the first "Master of the Posts." Under Tuke, the service became more available to ordinary citizens.

In 1683, Charles II of Great Britain (1630-1685) started the London Penny Post. Letters could be mailed anywhere within London for a penny. Outside the city, bad roads, slow horses, and indifferent messengers delayed mail delivery. The post office eventually overcame these difficulties.

In Great Britain in 1836, Rowland Hill (1795-1879) wrote a pamphlet suggesting a cheap, uniform rate for letters, the present-day envelope, and adhesive postage stamps. Previously, postmasters had written "Paid" on the outside of a sealed letter before it was sent. Or, if payment had not been made in advance, the money was collected from the person receiving the mail. Hill's reforms were, for the most part, adopted in Great Britain in 1840. The first postage stamps in the world were issued in Britain on May 6, 1840.

American Colonial Days. The first indication of an official American postal system appeared in 1639. In that year, the Massachusetts colony gave Richard Fairbanks permission to receive and dispatch ship mail at his home in Boston. He was paid one cent for every letter he handled. The Boston Post Road was so named because of the postal system begun on it in 1672.

In 1692, King William III of Great Britain gave Thomas Neale the monopoly on all postal services in

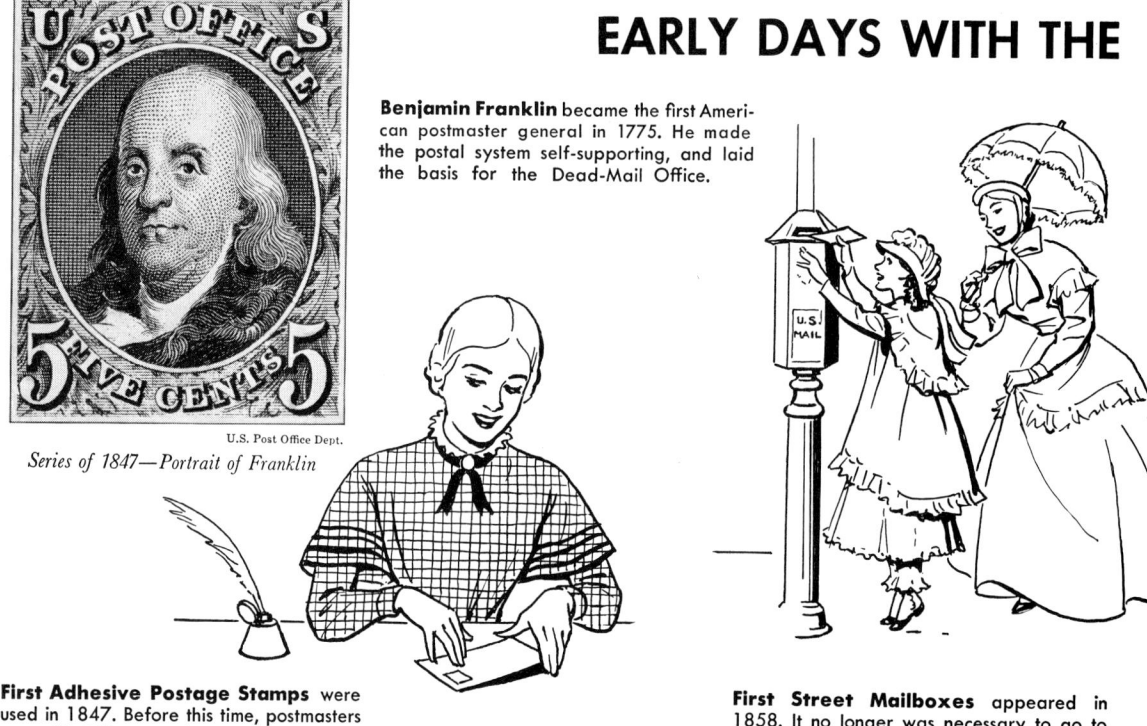

EARLY DAYS WITH THE

U.S. Post Office Dept.

Series of 1847—Portrait of Franklin

Benjamin Franklin became the first American postmaster general in 1775. He made the postal system self-supporting, and laid the basis for the Dead-Mail Office.

First Adhesive Postage Stamps were used in 1847. Before this time, postmasters wrote "Paid" on envelopes.

First Street Mailboxes appeared in 1858. It no longer was necessary to go to the post office to mail letters.

the colonies. The colonists disliked this postal system, because the authorities could open their mail to see if it contained evidence of disloyalty to the king. Postage was high, and, to the colonists, it represented a tax.

Benjamin Franklin (1706-1790) was the first great name in American postal service. He served as co-deputy postmaster general of the colonies from 1753 to 1774. The Second Continental Congress appointed him the first American postmaster general in 1775. See FRANKLIN, BENJAMIN (Civic Leader).

In the 1700's and 1800's. When the United States was being formed, George Washington insisted on developing an efficient mail service, and personally helped in surveying post routes to speed the mails.

In 1782, the Continental Congress guaranteed the mail service as a symbol of freedom by decreeing that private letters could not be opened or delayed by postal authorities. This was a milestone in the advance of human liberty. Before this time, the mail service had been primarily for the use of the government, and private citizens who used it ran the risk of having their mail opened and read.

In 1789, Samuel Osgood (1748-1813) became the first postmaster general to serve under the United States Constitution. At that time, there were 75 post offices in the country and fewer than 2,000 miles of post roads.

The postmaster general became a member of the President's Cabinet in 1829. Adhesive postage stamps were introduced in the United States in 1847. Registry service began in 1855.

--------- **RED-LETTER DATES IN POSTAL HISTORY** ---------

1516 First successful public postal system was established between Vienna and Berlin.
1683 London Penny Post began operating in England.
1692 Andrew Hamilton was appointed deputy postmaster general to help Thomas Neale establish a colonial postal system.
1775 Benjamin Franklin was appointed the first postmaster general under the Continental Congress.
1789 Samuel Osgood was appointed the first postmaster general under the United States Constitution.
1829 Postmaster general became a Cabinet post.
1840 Great Britain issued the first postage stamps.
1847 United States introduced postage stamps.
1855 Registry service was established.
1858 Street letter boxes were introduced.
1860 Pony express service was established between St. Joseph, Mo., and Sacramento, Calif.
1863 Free city delivery was begun, and a uniform letter rate was set up.
1864 Railway post-office service was begun, and the money-order system was established.

1873 Postal cards were first used.
1874 Universal Postal Union was formed in Bern, Switzerland, to help in the exchange of mail between countries.
1885 Special-delivery service became available.
1896 Rural Free Delivery service began.
1910 Post office started Postal Savings System.
1913 Parcel-post, postal-insurance, and collect-on-delivery services were established.
1918 First regular continuous air-mail route was established—between New York City and Washington, D.C.
1941 Highway post-office service began.
1943 Postal-delivery zone system was introduced.
1947 Helicopter shuttle service started in several cities to speed mail from airports to post offices.
1953 Post office began carrying some ordinary first-class mail by airplane.
1955 Certified service established.
1963 Zone Improvement Plan (*ZIP*) service began operation.

UNITED STATES MAIL

Pony Express Commemorative Stamp—Issue of 1940

Overland Mail traveled by stage-coach from Missouri to California. It followed a southern route via Texas. The trip took 25 days.

Pony Express Riders followed the Oregon-California trail from Missouri to California. Their time for the trip usually was about 8 days.

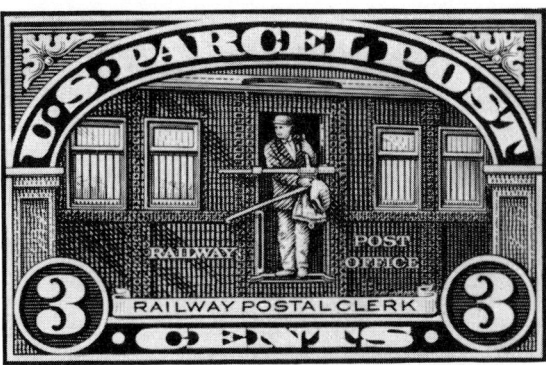

Parcel-Post Stamp—Issue of 1912–13

First Railway Mail Cars began operating in 1864. The first official test run was made August 28, between Chicago and Clinton, Iowa.

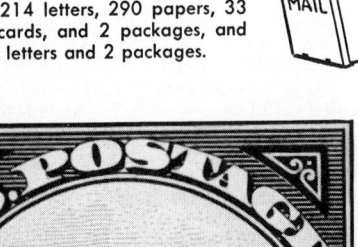

Rural Free Delivery started in 1896. In the first week, patrons received 214 letters, 290 papers, 33 postal cards, and 2 packages, and sent 18 letters and 2 packages.

Parcel-Post Stamp—Issue of 1912–13

U.S. Post Office Dept.

Air-Mail Stamp—Issue of 1918

First Regular Air-Mail Service in the world was inaugurated in 1918. The flight was between Washington, D.C., and New York City.

POST OFFICE

The pony express was perhaps the most colorful development in the history of United States mail. For 18 months in 1860 and 1861, pony express riders carried mail from St. Joseph, Mo., to Sacramento, Calif. These daring riders reduced the time for delivering mail from the East Coast to the West Coast from 24 days to about 10 days. The pony express service ended with completion of the transcontinental telegraph in 1861. See PONY EXPRESS.

In 1863, letters were first carried free of charge to homes and businesses. The service started in 49 cities, and soon spread throughout the nation. In 1864, railway post offices started operating. They speed delivery time on mail, because clerks can sort some of the mail in special mail cars as the train moves across country. In small towns, mail sacks are picked up by catcher arms on the cars while the train is moving. The mail sacks are delivered by tossing them from the moving train to the station platform. In 1864, the post office began selling money orders, mainly to help soldiers send money home during the Civil War.

The post office began selling postal cards in 1873. The Universal Postal Union was founded in 1874 to improve international service. In 1885, special-delivery service was begun in America. The first Rural Free Delivery routes began in 1896 in West Virginia.

In the Early 1900's. The Postal-Savings System was begun in 1910. In 1913, parcel-post and C.O.D. services were introduced. By 1918, airplanes carried mail regularly (see AIRMAIL AND AIR PARCEL POST). In 1925, special-handling service was made available.

Recent Developments. The first highway post-office route was established in 1941, between Washington, D.C., and Harrisonburg, Va. The highway service uses buses to distribute mail to post offices in rural areas that are not served by railways or other transportation facilities. Clerks sort mail in the buses on the way.

In 1947, the post office introduced the *air-letter sheet*. Messages are written on the inside of the sheet, which is then folded and sealed. In several U.S. cities, helicopters shuttle mail from the airport to the main post office, and from there to suburbs. The first such flight was in Los Angeles in 1947. Air parcel-post service began in 1948. In 1953, the post office began flying regular first class mail between certain cities when plane space was available.

Since 1900, the number of post offices in the United States has decreased. Modern rural-carrier service, traveling on improved roads, has reduced the need for post offices in many small communities. In 1901, there were 76,945 post offices in the United States. Today there are about 33,000 United States post offices. They handle about 72 billion pieces of mail a year. This is over half the total handled by all the rest of the world's post offices. In 1958, some postage rates were increased for the first time since 1932. In the 1960's, many post offices began using automated mail-handling equipment.

In 1963, postal rates increased again. The post office also began the *Zone Improvement Plan* (*ZIP*), a fast, new system of mail sorting and distribution. Mailers use five-number *ZIP codes* in addresses on letters and packages. The numbers stand for postal

regions, cities, and sections of large cities. In 1966, the Postal-Savings System was discontinued. Postal rates were again increased in 1968.

Canadian Postal System

The Canada Post Office operates more than 11,000 post offices and employs more than 41,000 persons. About 9,000 letter carriers deliver the mail in Canadian cities and towns. The post office also operates a 145,000-mile network of rural mail delivery routes. Its services include a post office savings bank and a world-wide money order system.

Benjamin Franklin organized Canada's first regular postal service in 1763, before the American Revolution. Until 1851, the British Post Office directed Canada's postal system from London. Each province operated its own post offices from 1851 to 1867. The federal government has operated the Canada Post Office since 1867.

Critically reviewed by the CANADA POST OFFICE and the U.S. POST OFFICE DEPARTMENT

Related Articles in WORLD BOOK include:

Airmail and Air Parcel Post
Dead-Mail Office
Engraving and Printing, Bureau of
Franking and Penalty Privileges
Franklin, Benjamin
Mail-Order Business
Money Order
Parcel Post

Post Office Department
Postal Card
Postal Union, Universal
Railroad (Mails; picture: Types of Passenger-Train Cars)
Rural Delivery
Stamp
Stamp Collecting
Star Route

Outline

I. How Your Letter Travels
  A. In the Post Office
  B. Your Letter Goes on Its Way
  C. The Postman

II. Importance of the Post Office

III. Post-Office Services
  A. Postage Stamps
  B. Stamped Envelopes
  C. Postal Cards
  D. Metered Postage
  E. Precanceled Stamps
  F. Parcel Post
  G. City Delivery
  H. Rural Free Delivery
  I. Star-Route Service
  J. General Delivery
  K. Post-Office Boxes
  L. Collect on Delivery (C.O.D.)
  M. Registry
  N. Insurance
  O. Certificate of Mailing
  P. Certified Service
  Q. Special Delivery
  R. Special Handling
  S. Dead-Mail Office
  T. Money Order
  U. Nonpostal Stamps
  V. Postal Savings
  W. Other Services
  X. Postal Inspection

IV. Classes of Post Offices

V. Post-Office Careers
  A. Careers in Positions Handling Direct Mail
  B. Careers in Supplementary Mail-Service Jobs

VI. History

VII. Canadian Postal System

Questions

How can the postal act of 1782 be considered an advance of human freedom?

What is postage?

When did regular airmail service go into operation?

Why should ZIP codes be given in addresses?

What is the difference between a *post card* and a *postal card?*

What are two requirements a town must meet to have city delivery?

What are the four classes of mail? Give an example of each class.

What did Franklin do for early American postal service?

How many pounds of mail is a postman allowed to carry at one time?

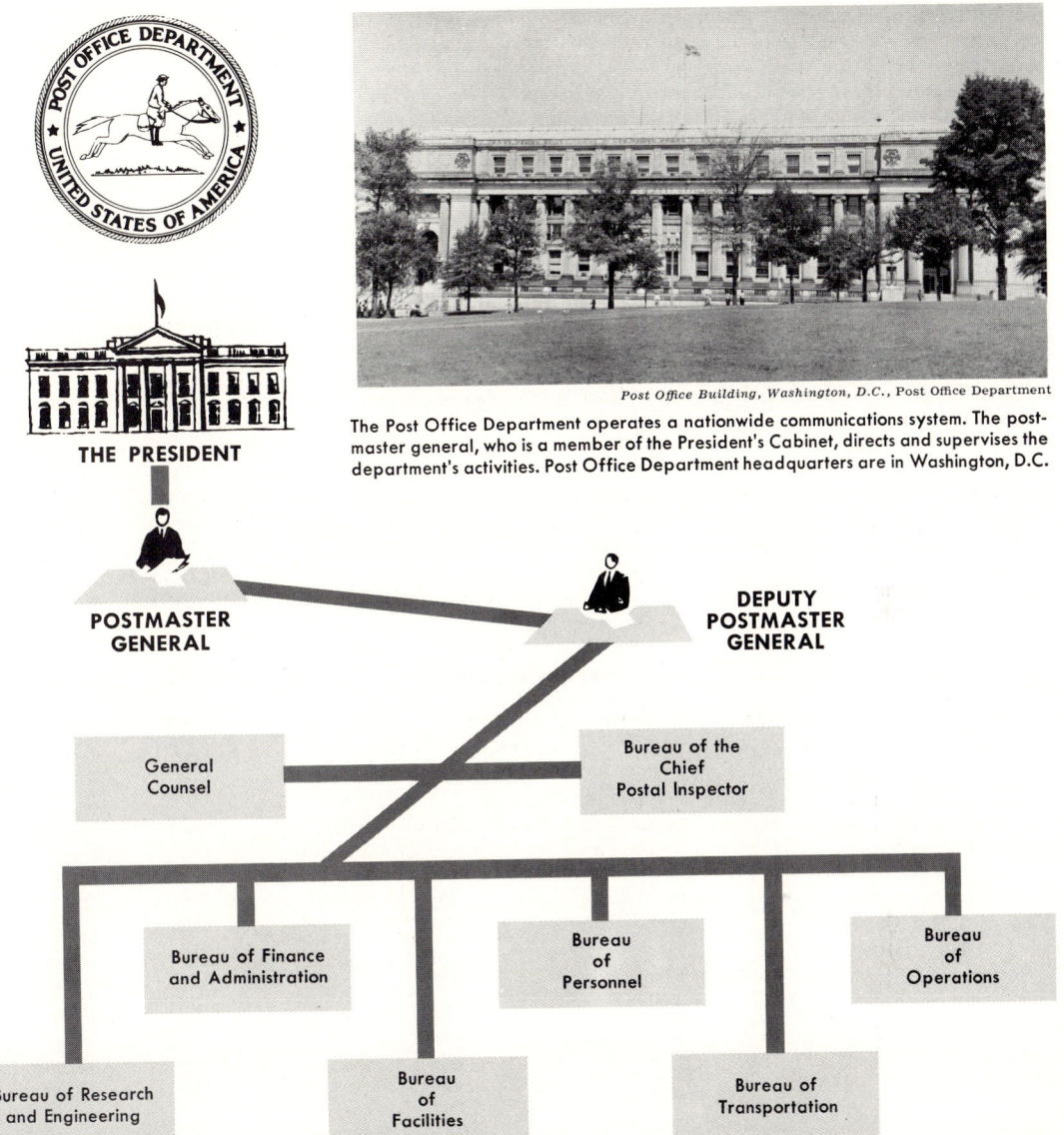

Post Office Building, Washington, D.C., Post Office Department

The Post Office Department operates a nationwide communications system. The postmaster general, who is a member of the President's Cabinet, directs and supervises the department's activities. Post Office Department headquarters are in Washington, D.C.

POST OFFICE DEPARTMENT is an executive department of the United States government. The postmaster general, a member of the President's Cabinet, heads the department. The Post Office Department provides mail services, including pickup and delivery, and the sale of postage stamps and money orders. It has headquarters in Washington, D.C.

Functions. The Post Office Department is one of the world's largest businesses. It has annual gross receipts of over $5½ billion. It has the responsibility of delivering letters and other mail sent through the post offices. Its delivery services include city, rural, village, special, and collect-on-delivery, or C.O.D. It sells postage stamps, postal money orders, and foreign money orders. Other mail services include registered mail, insurance, air mail, and certified mail. The department

publishes the *Postal Manual*, which provides complete postal information. The *Directory of Post Offices*, also published by the Post Office Department, lists all U.S. post offices.

The Postmaster General is appointed by the President with the Senate's approval. The President also appoints other high officials of the department, and postmasters of the first, second, and third classes. The deputy postmaster general is the chief assistant of the postmaster general. He has authority to act for the postmaster general on department matters. The Office of the Postmaster General also includes a judicial officer, an Office of Regional Administration, and special aides. An advisory board recommends improvements in postal services. It consists of the postmaster general and deputy postmaster general and seven members representing the public. The Citizens Stamp Advisory Committee advises the postmaster general on subjects to be honored by commemorative stamps.

Organization. The department has a chief postal inspector, a general counsel, and six bureaus headed by assistant postmasters general. The bureaus are: Transportation, Operations, Finance and Administration, Facilities, Personnel, and Research and Engineering. The Post Office Department also operates 15 regional offices and 6 postal data centers.

History. The Continental Congress created the Postal Service in 1775 and appointed Benjamin Franklin the first postmaster general. The U.S. Congress passed the first postal act in 1789. The postmaster general became a member of the President's Cabinet in 1829. The department became an executive department in 1872. The postmaster general received complete administrative authority over the department in 1949.

The Post Office Department operates about 33,000 post offices in the United States and its possessions. The department employs more than 700,000 workers.

Critically reviewed by the POST OFFICE DEPARTMENT

See also FLAG (color picture: Flags of the United States Government); POST OFFICE with its list of Related Articles.

POSTAGE AND POSTAGE STAMP. See POST OFFICE (Postage Stamps); STAMP; STAMP COLLECTING.

POSTAL CARD is a card with a printed postage stamp sold by a post office for forwarding through the mails. Austria issued the first postal cards in 1869. The United States first issued postal cards in 1873. See also POST OFFICE (Post-Office Services).

POSTAL UNION, UNIVERSAL (UPU) is a specialized agency of the United Nations that sets rules for the free flow of mail between countries. By the late 1960's, about 125 countries were members of the union. Postal authorities in these countries have pledged to handle all mail with equal care, no matter where the mail comes from or where it is going.

The UPU operates under an international agreement called the Universal Postal Convention. The convention lists uniform postal rates and procedures for member countries to follow in transporting *ordinary mail*. Ordinary mail includes letters, post cards, and small packages. Separate rules govern the transportation of other mail, such as parcel post, newspaper and magazine subscriptions, insured letters and packages, and postal money orders.

Under the convention, each country keeps the postage it collects on international mail. But each must repay other members for the cost of transporting mail across their borders. Transportation charges are calcu-

---

POSTMASTERS GENERAL

Name	Year Appointed	Under President	Name	Year Appointed	Under President
†*Benjamin Franklin	1775		Horace Maynard	1880	Hayes
†Richard Bache	1776		Thomas L. James	1881	Garfield,
†Ebenezer Hazard	1782				Arthur
Samuel Osgood	1789	Washington	Timothy O. Howe	1881	Arthur
*Timothy Pickering	1791	Washington	Walter Q. Gresham	1883	Arthur
Joseph Habersham	1795	Washington	Frank Hatton	1884	Arthur
	1797	J. Adams	William F. Vilas	1885	Cleveland
	1801	Jefferson	Don M. Dickinson	1888	Cleveland
Gideon Granger	1801	Jefferson	*John Wanamaker	1889	B. Harrison
	1809	Madison	Wilson S. Bissell	1893	Cleveland
Return Meigs, Jr.	1814	Madison	William L. Wilson	1895	Cleveland
	1817	Monroe	James Gary	1897	McKinley
John McLean	1823	Monroe	Charles E. Smith	1898	McKinley,
	1825	J. Q. Adams			T. Roosevelt
William T. Barry	1829	Jackson	Henry C. Payne	1902	T. Roosevelt
*Amos Kendall	1835	Jackson	Robert J. Wynne	1904	T. Roosevelt
	1837	Van Buren	George B. Cortelyou	1905	T. Roosevelt
John M. Niles	1840	Van Buren	George von L. Meyer	1907	T. Roosevelt
Francis Granger	1841	W. H. Harrison,	Frank H. Hitchcock	1909	Taft
		Tyler	Albert S. Burleson	1913	Wilson
Charles A. Wickliffe	1841	Tyler	*Will H. Hayes	1921	Harding
Cave Johnson	1845	Polk	Hubert Work	1922	Harding
*Jacob Collamer	1849	Taylor	Harry S. New	1923	Harding,
Nathan K. Hall	1850	Fillmore			Coolidge
Sam D. Hubbard	1852	Fillmore	Walter F. Brown	1929	Hoover
*James Campbell	1853	Pierce	*James A. Farley	1933	F. D. Roosevelt
Aaron V. Brown	1857	Buchanan	Frank C. Walker	1940	F. D. Roosevelt,
Joseph Holt	1859	Buchanan			Truman
Horatio King	1861	Lincoln	Robert E. Hannegan	1945	Truman
*Montgomery Blair	1861	Lincoln	Jesse M. Donaldson	1947	Truman
William Dennison	1864	Lincoln,	Arthur E. Summerfield	1953	Eisenhower
		A. Johnson	J. Edward Day	1961	Kennedy
Alexander W. Randall	1866	A. Johnson	*John A. Gronouski	1963	Kennedy,
John A. J. Creswell	1869	Grant			L. B. Johnson
James W. Marshall	1874	Grant	*Lawrence F. O'Brien	1965	L. B. Johnson
Marshall Jewell	1874	Grant	W. Marvin Watson	1968	L. B. Johnson
James N. Tyner	1876	Grant	Winton M. Blount	1969	Nixon
David M. Key	1877	Hayes			

†Served under the Continental Congress.   *Has a separate biography in WORLD BOOK.

Swiss Federal Railroads

The Universal Postal Union is symbolized at Bern, Switzerland, by a statue showing messengers circling the world.

lated by the UPU, based on samplings of international mail usually taken every three years.

The *Universal Postal Congress* is the main legislative body of the UPU. It usually meets every five years in a member country to review and amend the convention. If a congress changes a convention, all UPU members must abide by the changes, even if members must alter their national laws.

The *Executive Council* is a permanent body that handles UPU affairs between congresses. It consists of 27 members, elected on the basis of geographical representation. The *Consultative Commission on Postal Studies* conducts technical research in international postal matters. The *International Bureau* is the UPU's permanent secretariat. It also acts as an information center and clearinghouse for settling the UPU's financial accounts.

The first international postal congress was held by 22 countries in 1874 in Bern, Switzerland. The first postal convention went into effect in 1875. The UPU received its present name in 1878 at the second postal congress. It became a specialized agency of the United Nations in 1947. The UPU's permanent headquarters is in Bern.   Critically reviewed by the UNIVERSAL POSTAL UNION

POSTAL ZONE. See PARCEL POST (Parcel Post Rates).

POSTER is a simple, bold advertisement. It is designed to promote a product, a service, a name, or an idea. Most posters are large sheets of printed paper displayed where many people are likely to see them.

The success of a poster depends on its simplicity. Most people are either riding or walking when they see a poster, so it must catch their attention and get its message across quickly. Some of the most successful posters, such as *billboards*, have used as little as one word or one picture to relay their message. Some posters serve simply as a reminder of a well-known product. Other advertising messages in magazines, newspapers, or on television offer the reader or viewer more de-

tailed information on the product being advertised.

The poster has been a means of communication for hundreds of years. It started with handbills and signboards in Europe. In the late 1800's, such painters as Henri de Toulouse-Lautrec and Alphonse Mucha created posters and supervised their reproduction on lithograph stones. Surviving copies of these posters are now highly valued by art collectors and museums.

Designing posters has proven to be a helpful tool in training art students to express ideas clearly and forcefully.   RICHARD S. COYNE

See also ADVERTISING; COMMERCIAL ART; LETTERING; FLAGG, JAMES MONTGOMERY.

POSTMASTER GENERAL. See POST OFFICE DEPARTMENT.

POSTULATE. See GEOMETRY (Assumptions).

POSTURE is the position of a person's body and the way he sits or stands. It is judged to be *good*, *normal*, or *bad* by the position of the head, chest, trunk, pelvis, knees, and feet.

In standing posture, a person should:

1. Hold the head erect but balanced without tension.
2. Hold the chest up and slightly forward, but free to breathe.
3. Hold the shoulders well back, but not hunched or strained backward.

Posters Attract Attention, and are designed to communicate a simple message quickly. Types of poster design vary greatly.
Courtesy Poster Originals, Ltd.

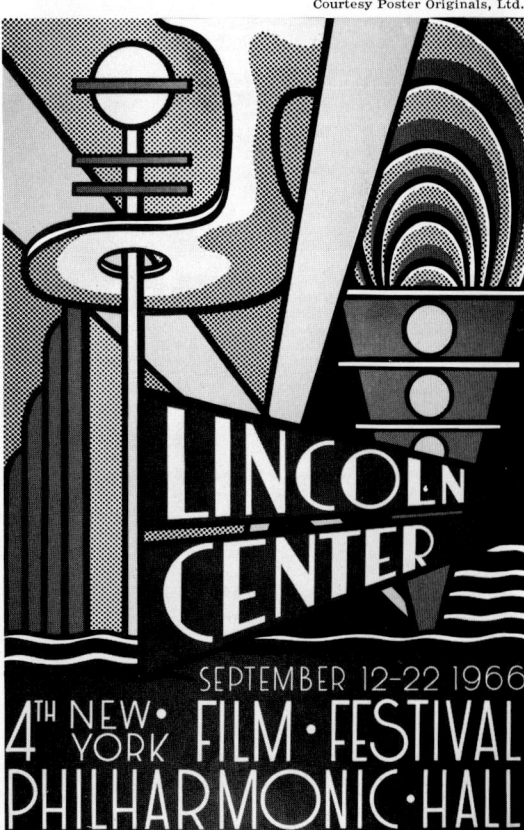

POSTURE

RIGHT

Back bent; knees stiff; the head and chest low; abdomen relaxed.

WRONG

In dusting, bend the knees, and put weight on balls of the feet. Keep back as straight as possible. To balance weight, place one foot ahead of the other.

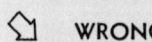

Chest low; abdomen relaxed; shoulders drooping; back curved.

WRONG

RIGHT

In walking, the body should be held erect, with chin up; abdomen in; and shoulders square but "easy." To get best exercise, swing both arms vigorously.

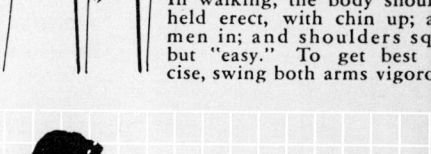

GOOD POSTURE. Head erect. Shoulders and chest high. Abdomen flat. Normal spinal curve and body in proper balance.

FAULTY POSTURE. Head forward. Shoulders rounded. Chest, abdomen relaxed. Abnormal spinal curve. Organs may suffer.

UNBALANCED BODY due to poor posture may result in sway-back, round shoulders, spinal curvature, strain, and backache.

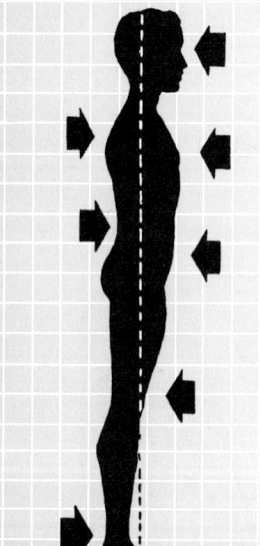

A   B

GOOD POSTURE

Correct posture, *left* (A), is ensured by holding the body in a balanced position; faulty posture makes a person seem shorter, *left* (B). To test posture, stand with back to wall as shown, *center.* Space at back of waist should be about thickness of the hand.

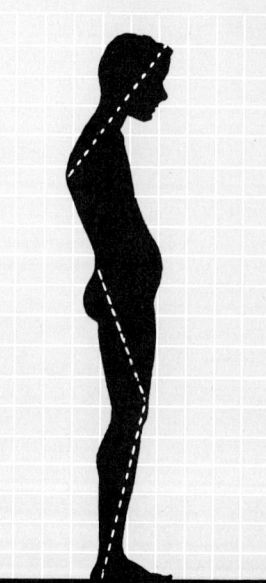

NECK

SPINE

PELVIC BONE
CENTER OF WEIGHT

KNEES

LINE OF BALANCE

TRUNK

TESTING POSTURE

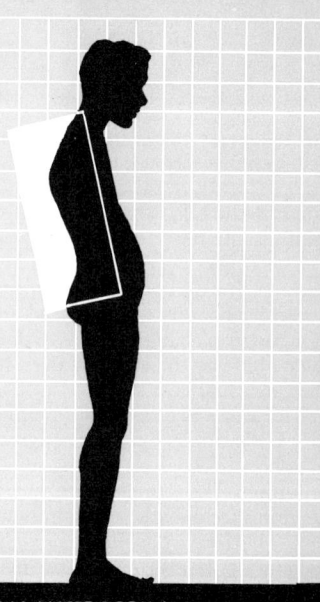

HOW TO RELAX

To stand at ease, *right,* place one foot slightly ahead of other; relax abdomen; keep chest high and shoulders back. To relax in a chair, *above,* sit well back. Place one foot forward on the floor and keep head as high as comfort will permit.

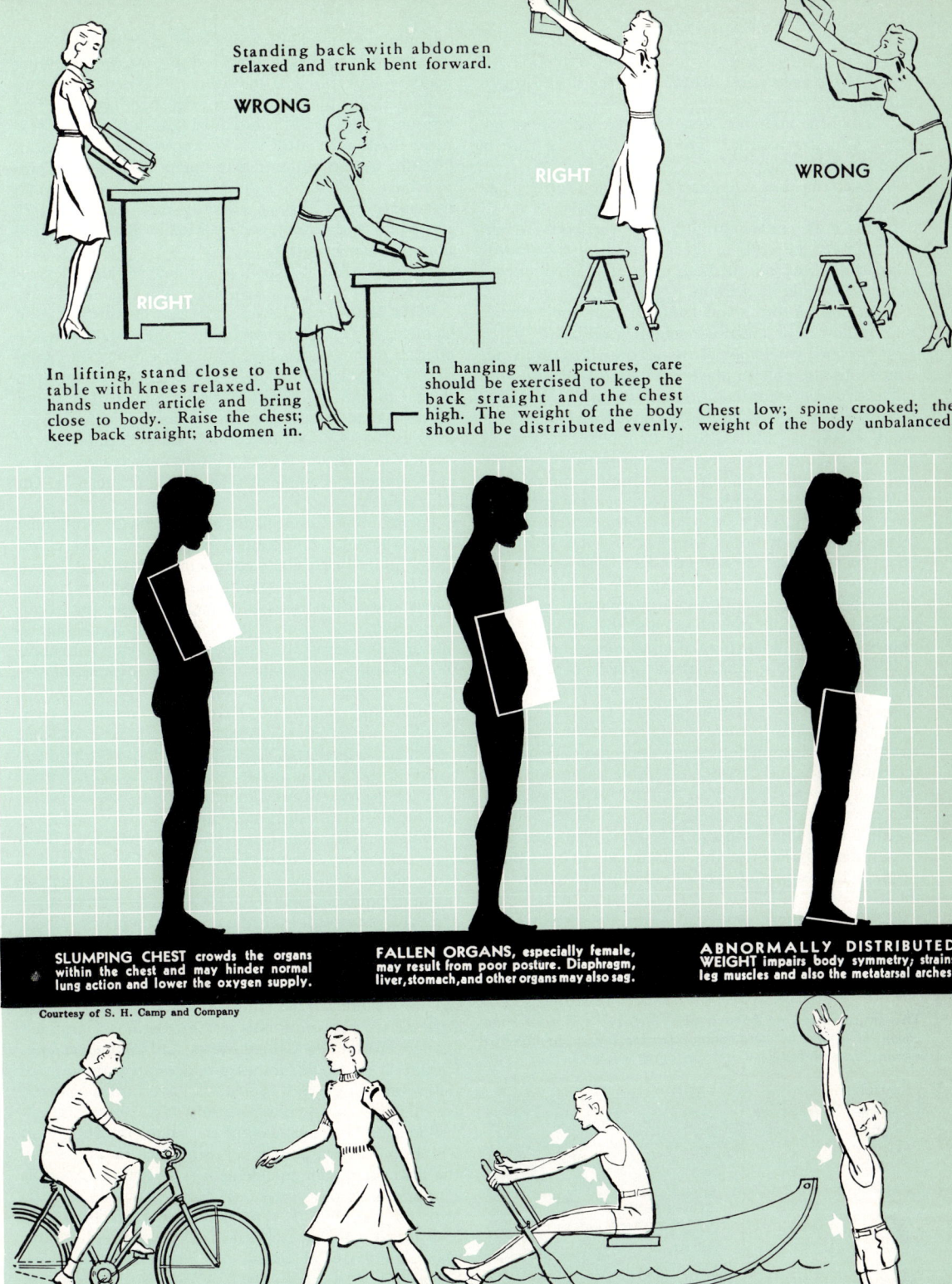

Standing back with abdomen relaxed and trunk bent forward.

WRONG

RIGHT

RIGHT

WRONG

In lifting, stand close to the table with knees relaxed. Put hands under article and bring close to body. Raise the chest; keep back straight; abdomen in.

In hanging wall pictures, care should be exercised to keep the back straight and the chest high. The weight of the body should be distributed evenly.

Chest low; spine crooked; the weight of the body unbalanced.

SLUMPING CHEST crowds the organs within the chest and may hinder normal lung action and lower the oxygen supply.

FALLEN ORGANS, especially female, may result from poor posture. Diaphragm, liver, stomach, and other organs may also sag.

ABNORMALLY DISTRIBUTED WEIGHT impairs body symmetry; strains leg muscles and also the metatarsal arches.

Courtesy of S. H. Camp and Company

EXERCISES THAT IMPROVE POSTURE

Bicycling, walking, rowing, and various sports like basketball are types of exercise which help to lay the foundation for good posture. In these sports, it is necessary to keep a straight back, with chest held high. The arrows serve to show the muscles that are strengthened by each type of exercise. Walking needs no equipment of any kind, but to get the most out of it, the walker should swing both arms —left arm forward with right leg and vice versa. Bicycling is excellent for athletes in training.

4. Let the arms hang naturally by the sides without tension.

5. Hold the abdomen somewhat flat, or at least not allow it to sag forward. The back will take care of itself if this is done.

6. Hold the knees balanced, neither overstretched nor bent.

7. Place the feet naturally, with the body weight slightly over the balls of the feet and on the outside edges of the feet, not toed out or in. The inside arches of the feet should be held up.

As a posture test, stand facing a wall and "stretch tall." Allow your toes to touch the baseboard. Then lean forward, with your chest just touching the wall. You should be able to place both hands, one over the other, between your abdomen and the wall. Now turn around. Put your heels to the baseboard, and allow your head, shoulders, and buttocks to touch the wall. If you can put your fist between the lower back and the wall, your standing posture needs improvement.

Posture can be measured. A *conformateur* (a series of rods that fit the back or front) measures *static posture* (a person's posture when standing still). A *pedograph* (footprint machine) measures the feet. The whole body can be photographed to show front, side, and rear views. Then the picture can be marked to show the exact position of the head, shoulders, chest, pelvis, knees, abdomen, spine, and feet in relation to each other.

Posture can be a guide to the way a person feels. If he is tired, his posture may be poorer than usual. Posture can also reflect mental attitude. Changes in posture may affect a person's appearance, gait, and personality. Good posture gives an impression of poise and self-confidence, and creates a favorable impression with others. It allows the body to function at its best. The best posture is always *moving*, because holding a single position for a long time affects the circulation and respiration. Physical training, learning about body functions, and learning to relax, all aid in posture improvement.   T. K. Cureton, Jr.

POTASH is the commercial name for certain compounds of the element potassium. The word *potash* generally is used to mean potassium carbonate (K_2CO_3)

The Importance of Potash as a fertilizer is shown by the comparative sizes of these cotton bolls. The one at the left was grown in potash-fertilized soil; the other was not.

American Potash Institute

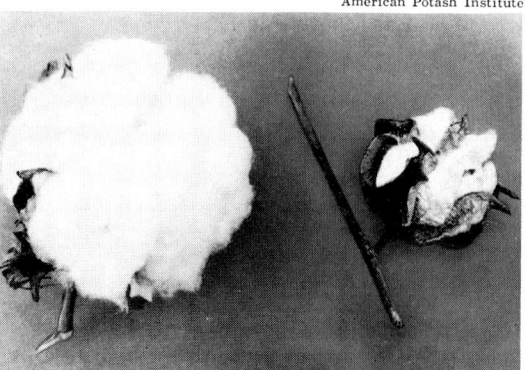

which may be used in place of soda ash in making glass. Potash was originally obtained by *leaching* (running water slowly through) the ashes of burned wood and boiling down the solution in large open kettles. The residue, a white solid, was called potash because it was made from *ashes* in *pots*. The potash obtained from leaching is used in the preparation of crude soap. Commercially, potassium carbonate is prepared from the mineral *sylvite*. This is a nearly pure compound of potassium and chlorine. New Mexico is the principal potash-producing state.   George L. Bush

See also Mining (Room and Pillar Mining); Potassium.

POTASSIUM, *poh TAS ih um,* is a silver-white metallic element. A piece of potassium dropped in water quickly releases hydrogen gas and ignites it, causing an explosion. Pure potassium rapidly combines with oxygen in the air to form an *oxide* film on its surface. The metal must be stored under a petroleum liquid such as kerosene to keep it from combining with the moisture or oxygen in the air. Next to lithium, potassium is the lightest metal. Potassium is so soft that it can be cut with a knife.

Potassium is essential for plant growth. Soil must have potassium compounds to produce good crops. Large quantities of these compounds are used in fertilizers to increase crop production. Muriate of potash (potassium chloride) is the most common potassium compound used in fertilizers. However, some plants, including tobacco and citrus fruits, cannot withstand much chloride, so sulfate of potash (potassium sulfate) is used instead.

Potassium compounds have many industrial uses. Caustic potash (potassium hydroxide) is used in making ceramics, detergents, glass, soaps, and textile dyes. Saltpeter (potassium nitrate) is used in the manufacture of black gunpowder and matches. Potassium bromides and iodides are used in medicine.

Potassium is never found as a pure metal. It is always combined with other substances. The pure metal is obtained by passing an electric current through a *fused* (melted) potassium *salt* (compound). The current separates the potassium from the other elements combined with it.

Potassium salts exist in large deposits near Carlsbad, N.Mex., in the Canadian province of Saskatchewan and in Stassfurt, East Germany. The world's leading producers of potassium salts are Canada, East Germany, France, Russia, the United States, and West Germany. California and Utah mines produce large amounts of potassium compounds. Scientists have also developed methods of taking potassium salts from sea water.

Potassium is a member of the alkali metals group. The chemical symbol for potassium is K, from *kalium*, the Latin name for the element. Its atomic number is 19 and its atomic weight is 39.102. Potassium melts at 63.65° C. (146.6° F.) and boils at 774° C. (1425° F.). The metal was first isolated in 1807 by Sir Humphry Davy, the English chemist.   Warren S. Peterson

See also Alkali; Fertilizer; Potash; Saltpeter.

POTASSIUM BITARTRATE. See Cream of Tartar.

POTASSIUM BROMIDE. See Bromide.

POTASSIUM CYANIDE. See Cyanide.

POTASSIUM HYDROXIDE. See Caustic.

POTASSIUM NITRATE. See Saltpeter.

POTATO

A Potato Plant in full bloom shows partially grown tubers. These potatoes will be ready for harvest in 4 to 6 weeks. A potato plant usually produces 3 to 6 marketable potatoes.

POTATO, *puh TAY toh,* is one of the world's most valued and most widely grown vegetables. The edible part of a potato is a *tuber,* which grows in the ground. Tubers are not part of the roots of the plant, but are formed from underground stems. Potatoes are usually round or oval, and rather hard. Their skin is thin and usually brown, but some have red or rosy skins. The common potato is called the *white potato* or *Irish potato.*

About 11 billion bushels of potatoes are grown each year throughout the world. They are most widely used as a table food—baked, boiled, or fried. Potatoes have a smooth, bland flavor, and are often served with other vegetables and with meats. Manufacturers use millions of bushels of potatoes each year to make potato

Harold W. Gausman, the contributor of this article, is Research Plant Physiologist, U.S. Department of Agriculture, Weslaco, Tex.

chips and packaged French-fried potatoes. Frozen French-fried potatoes and baked potatoes can also be bought. Canners prepare potatoes either alone or with other vegetables and meat. Dehydrated potato powder is also sold. Mashed potatoes can be made from this powder by adding water or milk. In Europe, potato starch is commonly used to thicken soups and puddings.

Manufacturers use millions of bushels of potatoes a year to make alcohol, flour, and starch. European farmers use large quantities of potatoes as cattle feed.

Food Value

The potato is about 80 per cent water and 20 per cent solid matter. Starch accounts for about 85 per cent of the potato's solid matter. About 10 per cent of the solid matter is protein. Potatoes also contain the vitamins thiamine, riboflavin, niacin (nicotinic acid), ascorbic acid, and a small trace of vitamin A. Many

other elements, including calcium, iron, magnesium, phosphorus, potassium, and sodium are also present in potatoes. Contrary to a common belief, potatoes are not especially fattening. A medium-size raw potato contains only about 70 calories.

Growing Potatoes

The Potato Plant must be replanted each year. The plants die when the tubers mature or when frost occurs.

The part of the plant growing above the ground has spreading stalks and coarse, dark green leaves, much like those of the tomato plant. The flowers are white, purple, or yellow, and rather small. On certain varieties of potato plants, the flowers develop into seed balls that contain 200 or more seeds.

The potato tubers develop at the ends or on the branches of *stolons* (shoots) which grow from the underground parts of the plant's main stem. The tubers range in size from that of a pea to more than 6 inches in length. A tuber may weigh as much as 2 or 3 pounds. Usually from three to six marketable potatoes develop on a plant. Occasionally there may be as many as 10 to 20 potatoes, depending upon the variety, weather, and soil conditions.

The leaves and stolons develop alternately around the plant's main stem. Mature plants vary greatly in size. They may range in height from 18 inches to as much as 5 or 6 feet when the plants are held up. The spread of the plant varies from 18 to 24 inches.

Potato plants usually are grown from the *eyes* (bud

Food Value of the Potato

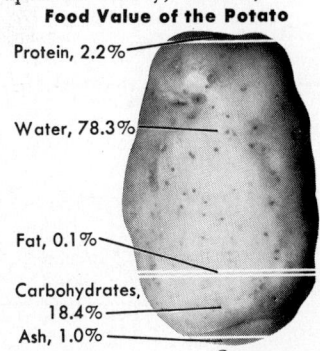

Protein, 2.2%

Water, 78.3%

Fat, 0.1%

Carbohydrates, 18.4%

Ash, 1.0%

POTATO

parts) of the tubers. But they can also be grown from seeds. Plant breeders often use seeds to develop new varieties of potatoes.

There are many varieties of potatoes. In the United States, the most widely grown varieties of certified seed potatoes are, in order of production, *Katahdin, Russet Burbank, Kennebec, Red Pontiac, Cobbler, White Rose,* and *Red Lasoda.* The *Katahdin, Russet Burbank,* and *Kennebec* are good baking potatoes. The others are best for boiling and other cooking methods.

The potato is a member of the nightshade family and a close relative of the tomato, red pepper, tobacco plant, and eggplant. However, it is not related to the sweet potato or yam.

Potato Planting. The potato, a cool-weather plant, requires about 90 to 120 days to mature. In the United States, potatoes grow best in the Northern and Western states, where the average growing temperature ranges between 60° and 70° F. Farmers in the South grow them as winter and early spring crops. In the northernmost states, potatoes are planted in May and June and harvested in September and October. In the middle states, they are planted in March, April, and May, and are harvested in July, August, and September.

The best potatoes to use for planting have been grown especially for this purpose. These potatoes are *certified* for trueness to type and freedom from disease.

Seed potatoes may be cut into sections weighing from 1 to 2 ounces, or they may be planted whole. Each piece must contain at least one *eye* (bud). The potato pieces are planted from 2 to 5 inches deep and spaced from 6 to 16 inches apart in a row. Rows usually are 30 to 36 inches apart. Commercial potato growers use machines that plant two to four rows at a time.

Each acre of ground planted requires from 7 to 50 bushels of seed potatoes, depending on the size of the seed pieces and the distance at which they are spaced. Commercial growers generally use from 20 to 30 bushels to each acre.

Fertilizer usually is placed in the soil at each side of the seed pieces. Fertilizer requirements vary, depending on the natural soil reserves, rainfall, soil structure, and crop rotation.

Potatoes can grow in relatively poor soil with little attention. But potatoes grow best in loamy, well-aerated soil that is carefully cultivated and supplied with plenty of water.

Insect Pests and Diseases. The most serious insect pests that attack potato plants are the *potato bug,* or *Colorado beetle, leafhopper, flea beetle, aphid,* and the *potato psyllid.* Insects that damage potato tubers include the *white grub, wireworm, potato tuber worm,* and *scab gnat.* Insects that feed on the plants may be controlled by such insecticides as DDT, Parathion, Endosulfan, Carbaryl, Di-Syston, or Phorate. Other insects can be partly controlled by planting potatoes in soil without sod in it. Wireworms also may be controlled by working Diazinon or Parathion into the soil. Tuber worms that attack the foliage are controlled with DDT, Endosulfan, or Guthion.

Potatoes are subject to several diseases that vary in severity. The most important fungous and bacterial diseases include late blight, rhizoctonia, scab, and ring rot. Important virus diseases include mosaic, leafroll, and spindle tuber.

Late blight is controlled by planting disease-free seed potatoes, and by spraying or dusting the plants with such organic fungicides as Maneb or Zineb.

Rhizoctonia and *scab* may be partially controlled by treating the seeds with certain mercurials, and by plant-

---

LEADING POTATO GROWING STATES

Bags (100 pounds) of potatoes grown in 1967

Idaho
63,900,000 bags

Maine
37,604,000 bags

California
33,331,000 bags

Washington
22,090,000 bags

New York
17,764,000 bags

North Dakota
14,280,000 bags

Minnesota
13,488,000 bags

Oregon
13,252,000 bags

Wisconsin
13,251,000 bags

Colorado
11,608,000 bags

Source: U.S. Department of Agriculture

LEADING POTATO GROWING COUNTRIES

Bags (100 pounds) of potatoes grown in 1967

Russia
1,807,800,000 bags

Poland
975,700,000 bags

Germany (West)
469,600,000 bags

China (Mainland)
*462,970,000 bags

United States
303,200,000 bags

Germany (East)
266,700,000 bags

France
224,300,000 bags

Great Britain
153,400,000 bags

Czechoslovakia
111,100,000 bags

Spain
92,400,000 bags

*1965 estimate, latest available production figure

Source: U.S. Department of Agriculture

ing disease-free seed potatoes. Scab may also be controlled by making the soil acid with sulfur. *Ring rot* is best controlled by the use of disease-free seed potatoes.

The *virus* diseases can be controlled by removing the diseased plants and tubers from the field, by controlling insects that carry the virus, and by using certified seed potatoes.

Harvesting Potatoes. Home gardeners often dig only enough potatoes for a few days' cooking needs. They leave the remainder in the ground, if the weather is not too cold. Commercial potato growers use tractor-drawn potato diggers or combines to harvest potatoes. These machines dig one or two rows at a time and separate the potato tubers from the soil and vines. When a combine is used, the machine digs the potatoes and loads them into trucks, boxes, or bags.

After the potatoes have been gathered, the trucks haul them to a mechanical grader. The potatoes are washed under jet sprays. The bad potatoes are removed, and the good ones are graded for size, then packed in bags for shipment to market.

Production in the United States. Potatoes are grown commercially in every state. A large percentage of the potatoes come from large farms where growing conditions are best and the potato is the main crop. The United States produces over 300 million bags, or more than 15 million tons, of potatoes a year.

The United States ranks fifth in world potato production, and produces about 200 bushels per acre. California, Idaho, and Maine lead in potato growing. See IDAHO (color picture).

Most of the potatoes are grown in the North. Farmers harvest these potatoes in the late summer and early fall. They store them for use in the winter and early spring.

The winter and spring crop of potatoes comes mainly from Arizona, California, Florida, North Carolina, and Texas. The summer crop is grown chiefly in New Jersey, Virginia, Washington, and Wisconsin. Most of these early and mid-season potatoes are sold as soon as they are harvested.

World Potato Production. Russia grows more potatoes than any other country. Its estimated annual production totals more than 1¾ billion bags. This is about six times the production of the United States. China (Mainland), Germany (West), and Poland also rank ahead of the United States. Other leading growers of potatoes include Czechoslovakia, Germany (East), Great Britain, France, and Spain.

History

The potato originated in South America. Most botanists and plant breeders agree that the white potato comes from a species found in the high plateaus of Peru and Bolivia. The first mention of the potato in a book was probably by Cieza de León in *Cornica de Peru*, published in Seville, Spain, in 1553. He recorded that potatoes were grown in Colombia and Peru in 1538.

More than 400 years ago, the Inca Indians of Peru and Bolivia grew potatoes high in the Andes Mountains, where it was too cold for corn or wheat to grow. These people harvested the potatoes, walked on them to break them into pieces, and dried them in the sun. From the dried potatoes, the Indians made a light, floury substance called *chuño*. Chuño did not spoil, and the

Deere and Co.

A Mechanical Potato Digger separates potatoes from soil, vines, and roots, and drops the tubers on top of the ground.

Indians used it instead of wheat to make their bread.

Spanish explorers introduced potatoes into Europe, possibly as early as 1550. Potatoes appear in the records of two hospitals in Seville in 1573. From Spain, potatoes were taken to Italy, then to England and Ireland. People grew potatoes in England in 1586.

The potato grew so well in Ireland, and had such great food value, that the Irish adopted it as their main food. They became economically dependent upon potatoes. In 1845 and 1846 the Irish potato crop failed because of a late-blight plant disease. As a result, thousands of Irish died of starvation or migrated to the United States.

White potatoes were probably introduced into North America in 1621. They may have been brought to Virginia from England by way of Bermuda. The white potato became known as the *Irish potato*, because Irish immigrants brought potatoes with them when they settled in Londonderry, N.H., in 1719.

Scientific Classification. The white potato belongs to the nightshade family, *Solanaceae*. It is genus *Solanum*, species *S. tuberosum*.   HAROLD W. GAUSMAN

Related Articles in WORLD BOOK include:

Alcohol	Corn Borer	Solanum
Belladonna	Fungicide	Starch
Burbank, Luther	Nightshade	Sweet Potato
Chemurgy	Potato Bug	

USDA

The Potato Bug deposits eggs on potato vines in the spring. The larvae then feed on the tender leaves, and damage them.

POTATO BUG, or **COLORADO BEETLE,** is a stout yellow beetle and the most destructive of the insect pests that attack the potato plant. This beetle is about half an inch long. It may be recognized by its wing covers, each of which has five black stripes. The insect is said to have originated in Mexico. When potatoes were first raised in the western part of the United States, the beetle spread from its original food plant, the buffalo bur, and traveled from field to field, living on potato vines. By 1860 it had become troublesome in Nebraska, and by 1875 it had spread to the Atlantic.

The beetles come out of the ground in spring and lay their yellow eggs in clusters on the underside of the leaves of the potato plant. The soft-bodied, orange-red larvae feed on the tender leaves. After three weeks of greedy eating, they drop off, burrow into the ground, and emerge as full-grown insects about 10 days later. There are two or three broods a season. This pest can be controlled by sprays or dusts. The enemies of potato beetles include stinkbugs, toads, snakes, and birds.

Scientific Classification. The potato bug belongs to the leaf beetle family, *Chrysomelidae*, and the order *Coleoptera*. It is genus *Leptinotarsa*, species *L. decemlineata*.   H. H. Ross

See also BEETLE (color picture); BIRD (How Birds Help the Farmer).

POTATO FAMINE. See IRELAND (Potato Famine).

POTAWATOMI, *paht uh WAHT oh mih*, **INDIANS** belonged to the Algonkian language group of eastern forest tribes. They were closely allied with the Chippewa and Ottawa. From early times, these three tribes formed a confederacy known as "the three fires." In early days, the Potawatomi lived near the eastern end of Lake Superior. They had been driven there by their enemies. Later, they lived on the shores of Green Bay, Wisconsin, and elsewhere around Lake Michigan. They lived in the Chicago region after the Miami Indians left there about 1700.

The Potawatomi raised corn, made maple sugar, and hunted buffaloes. They lived in cone-shaped lodges covered with bark. Early travelers described the Potawatomi as being polite and more humane than other tribes of the area. Many Potawatomi became Christians.

The Potawatomi sided with the French until the end of the French and Indian Wars. They took a prominent part in the Indian rebellion under Pontiac (see INDIAN WARS [Along the Frontier]; PONTIAC). They fought with the British against the Americans in the Revolutionary War and the War of 1812. A group of Potawatomi and their Chippewa and Ottawa allies ambushed the retreating garrison of Fort Dearborn in Chicago in August, 1812 (see FORT DEARBORN). After the war, the Potawatomi and their allies became friendly with American settlers. They ceded their lands in Illinois to the United States government in the 1830's. The tribe then moved to new lands west of the Mississippi River. They were the last Indians, along with the Chippewa and Ottawa, to leave Illinois.

A few Potawatomi still live in Wisconsin and Michigan, but most of them now make their homes on reservations in Oklahoma and Kansas, in the United States, and Ontario, Canada.   WAYNE C. TEMPLE

POTENTIAL, ELECTRIC. See ELECTRIC CURRENT.

POTENTIAL ENERGY. See ENERGY.

POTENTIOMETER, *poh TEN shih AHM ee tur*, is a device that measures electric current, voltage, and resistance precisely. It shows drops in voltage or differences in potentials by comparing an unknown electromotive force with a known one. It is used to calibrate voltmeters or ammeters, and to control radio volume. See also AMMETER; ELECTRIC CURRENT; VOLTMETER.

POTHOLE is a hole gouged or dug out in the bed of a swift river or stream by the sand and fine stones that the water carries with it. Potholes are usually circular. The river or stream acts as a huge, whirling, scouring brush in carving them out.

POTIPHAR. See JOSEPH (A Slave in Egypt).

POTLATCH. See INDIAN, AMERICAN (Northwest Coast Indians).

POTOMAC, *poh TOE muck*, **RIVER** is a beautiful and historic stream that forms the boundary between Maryland, West Virginia, and Virginia. The Potomac flows 287 miles in a winding southeast course from its source in the Allegheny Mountains to its mouth in the Chesapeake Bay. Large ships can sail inland for

The Potomac River flows past the majestic Lincoln Memorial, foreground, as it forms the southwestern border of Washington, D.C.

H. Armstrong Roberts

115 miles to Washington, D.C. The Potomac is from 2 to 7 miles wide for its last 100 miles. It drains an area of 14,500 square miles. For location, see VIRGINIA (physical map).

The Potomac is associated with American history. It breaks through the Blue Ridge Mountains at Harpers Ferry, the scene of John Brown's Raid. Mount Vernon, the home of George Washington, overlooks the river 17 miles below the nation's capital. RAUS M. HANSON

See also CHESAPEAKE AND OHIO CANAL; HARPERS FERRY; WASHINGTON, D.C. (color map).

POTOSÍ, *POH toh SEE* (pop. 58,501), lies about 13,600 feet above sea level in southwestern Bolivia. For location, see BOLIVIA (color map).

Potosí was founded in 1546, after Spanish explorers discovered one of the world's richest deposits of silver nearby. Potosí's population dropped from 160,000 in the 1600's to about 8,000 in the 1800's when silver deposits were exhausted. But tin mining became a large industry in the 1900's, and Potosí again grew. The same mines used by the Spanish to dig silver ore were used for tin. HAROLD OSBORNE

POTSDAM (pop. 110,790; alt. 105 ft.) stands on the Havel River, 16 miles southwest of Berlin in East Germany. For location, see GERMANY (political map). Flower growing is one of the important industries in Potsdam, especially the cultivation of winter violets. Broad squares and public gardens add to the city's beauty. See also POTSDAM CONFERENCE. JAMES K. POLLOCK

POTSDAM CONFERENCE was a meeting of Allied leaders following Germany's defeat in World War II. It was held at Potsdam, near Berlin. President Harry S. Truman of the United States, Marshal Joseph Stalin of Russia, and Prime Minister Winston Churchill of Great Britain started the meeting on July 17, 1945. Clement Attlee succeeded Churchill as prime minister on July 26. Attlee represented Britain during the rest of the conference, which ended on August 2.

The main task at Potsdam was to approve earlier agreements on occupation zones and administrations for German territory. Russia secured control of Eastern Europe at Potsdam, pending final peace treaty settlements, and repeated its willingness to go to war against Japan. The British and Americans also drew up an ultimatum to Japan at Potsdam. ROBERT HUGH FERRELL

POTSHERD. See ARCHAEOLOGY (Finding and Gathering Materials).

POTTER, BEATRIX (1866-1943), was a British author and illustrator. Her *Peter Rabbit* books became known in all parts of the world. She also wrote *Two Bad Mice, Jemima Puddleduck, Jeremy Fisher, Roly Poly Pudding,*

Frederick Warne & Co., Inc.

Peter Rabbit was the hero of many children's books written and illustrated by Beatrix Potter. Her first Peter Rabbit book grew out of letters she wrote in 1893 to a friend's invalid son.

The Tale of Tom Kitten, The Tailor of Gloucester, and *Wag by Wall.*

She was born in London, but lived most of her life in a country cottage in Sawrey, Westmoreland County. There she had as pets many of the small animals that appeared as characters in her stories. The water-color drawings in her books are the result of her close observations of the countryside about her. NORMAN RICE

POTTER'S CLAY. See CLAY (Uses).

POTTER'S FIELD is a free burial ground for strangers, criminals, and persons who are too poor to pay the expense of a funeral.

The Bible story of Judas Iscariot tells of the first plot of ground known as a potter's field. When Judas betrayed Jesus Christ to the high priests of Jerusalem for 30 pieces of silver, the priests would not use the money for their temple. Instead they bought "the potter's field to bury strangers in" (Matt. 27:7). The field has been located in the Valley of Hinnom because this has an ancient long-used cemetery, and clay for the making of pottery. The version of St. Matthew gives to potter's field the significance it has now. CHARLES L. WALLIS

CNS, Guillumette

Pottery is made throughout the world. Today, craftsmen everywhere still use processes that date back thousands of years.

POTTERY includes all tiles, dishes, and other articles that are made of baked clay. The finest type of pottery is called *porcelain*. All other pottery is called *earthenware* or *stoneware*. Man made earthenware long before he discovered how to make porcelain.

It is usually easy to tell the difference between earthenware and porcelain. Earthenware is *opaque*. That is, no light will show through it. Thin porcelain is *translucent*. That is, light will show through it. Some very fine and thin earthenware, which is made almost like porcelain, is fairly translucent. The clay of which earthenware is made may be red, brown, yellow, gray, bluish, or white. The mixture of which porcelain is made is white all the way through.

Pottery making is one of the oldest of human crafts. Prehistoric savages shaped crude bowls and other pottery. One of the first inventions made by man was the potter's wheel. Prehistoric man shaped all his pottery in his hands. Then one day someone had the idea of shaping it on a moving disk, very much like the turntable of a phonograph. The early potter's wheel turned as the potter worked a foot pedal. The modern wheel is not much different. Indeed, all the processes used in making pottery—molding, casting, modeling, glazing, and firing—are almost the same today as they were hundreds of years ago. The only difference is that the machines, ovens, and other devices have changed.

Making Pottery

Molding. Pottery making begins with the choice of suitable clay, and careful preparation of the clay. The potter removes all grit, pebbles, and other substances so that the clay will be perfectly smooth. Then he adds just enough water so that the clay can be kneaded into a tough "dough," somewhat like bread dough. He throws a lump of clay on the center of the disk of the potter's wheel. Before he starts molding his clay, the potter dips his hands into water. This keeps the clay from sticking to his hands. Suppose the potter wants to make a jar. He will plunge both thumbs into the middle of the clay mass. He does not have to move his fingers around the piece of clay. The clay moves around instead. By working his thumbs and fingers in certain ways and gradually drawing up the sides, or walls, he brings the clay to the finished shape of a jar. Then he sets it away to dry and harden.

Suppose he is making a flat plate. He first rolls out the kneaded clay "dough" with a rolling pin, just as a cook rolls out a piecrust dough. Then he presses the flat dough over a mold of a plate, just as the cook presses dough in the pie pan, and trims the edges. Some pieces cannot be molded by hand or pressed over a mold. To make these pieces, the potter presses the moist clay firmly *into* a mold and leaves it to dry. When the clay is dry enough to hold its shape, he removes the parts of the mold, one at a time.

Spouts, handles, knobs, and the like are often modeled by hand. When a pitcher is still moist and sticky enough, the potter attaches the handle in its proper place with *slip*. Slip is a creamy "batter" of clay which acts as cement when the pieces are baked, or *fired*.

Pottery is always dried before it is fired. This is to make sure that it is holding its desired shape. The firing is done in an oven called a *kiln*. The firing takes several days. The fires are allowed to die down and the kiln is cooled off for some days before it is opened.

Glazing puts a shiny coating on pottery. Sometimes glaze is put on the air-dried pottery before the pottery is fired. In such cases the glaze fuses (melts) at the same time that the clay is baked. Often the glaze is applied after the pottery is fired. Then the pottery must be fired a second time, so that the glaze is fused. Glaze must be fused so that it will attach itself firmly to the clay body.

Earthenware may be divided into two great classes—glazed and unglazed. Unglazed pottery is not necessarily cheap or unfinished. Some of the finest Wedgwood pottery is unglazed. And some of the best ancient pottery—including the highly decorative terra cotta work—is unglazed.

Sometimes a glaze is applied for practical reasons. Glazing the inside of a bowl, jar, or pitcher will keep it from absorbing any of the liquid it is meant to contain. Also, a coating of glaze will give a perfectly smooth, hard surface to a body of coarse or rough texture. Sometimes glaze is applied merely to decorate a piece or to make it appear more finished.

Glazes are of various sorts and have different properties. *Lead glaze* is made chiefly of a finely ground mixture of silicates or sand and oxide of lead. It is trans-

HOW POTTERY IS MADE

Pottery Making by "Building" was one of the earliest methods. After the base of the vessel had been cut, the clay was rolled into ropes or coils. One was laid on top of the other and the potter shaped the work as the vessel was built up. The method was very slow and the work was not particularly even, but the products were quite satisfactory.

A Variation of Building consists in cutting the flattened clay into slabs. These are then placed one on the other as in coil work and the shaping is done with the fingers or bits of wood or stone. For making vessels with more or less straight sides the method was faster than using coils, but for forming more graceful rounded shapes it was not as good.

"Throwing" on the Potter's Wheel has been the chief method of pottery making in all countries from early times. As the wheel spun—moved at first by the foot, later by mechanical power—the potter drew the revolving clay up with his thumbs and fingers to the desired shape. Skilled "throwers" are able to fashion beautiful and sturdy ware.

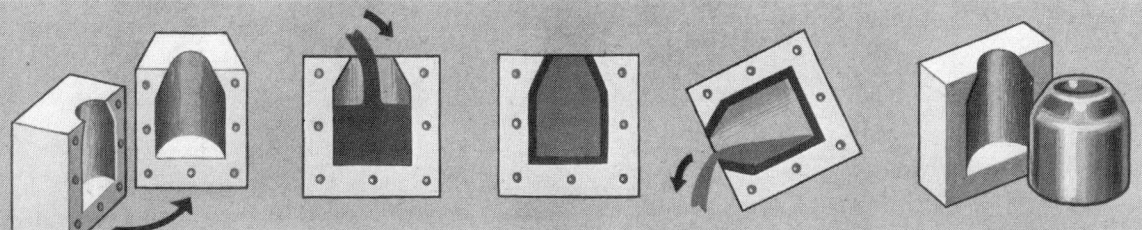

Molding Is the Commercial Method of making pottery. Liquid clay, or slip, is poured into the mold. The slip first hardens next to the mold. When the wall has hardened to the necessary thickness, the surplus slip is poured off. The remaining part is allowed to set until it is hard. Then the cast is opened and the piece is removed, ready for the firing operation.

Heat in Kilns was once tested with Seger cones which melted at different temperatures within the furnace.

"Green" Pottery is fired twice. The first firing removes the remaining moisture from the clay. The vessel is then dipped into the liquid glaze-and-color and is returned to the firing furnace for a second heating. This firing hardens the piece and brings out the color of the glaze applied to its surface. When it is removed, after cooling, the ware is complete.

POTTERY

parent. Uncolored lead glaze shows the color of the earthenware body underneath. But sometimes coloring matter is added to the glaze to make it green, brown, or some other color. *Tin glaze*, or *stanniferous glaze*, is made of silicates and tin oxide finely ground together. It is opaque white. In other words, the color of the clay body will not show through, and the glaze will produce a smooth, pure-white surface. Tin glaze may be colored. The metallic lusters—gold, silver, copper—of some of the beautiful old Persian and Moorish, or Hispano-Moresque, tiles and pottery were produced by adding certain colorings to the glaze. *Salt glaze* is made of salt and is transparent.

The lead and tin glazes are applied in a liquid state to a piece that has been air-dried or previously fired. Sometimes they are painted on with a brush. At other times the piece of pottery is dipped into the glazing mixture. The article is then allowed to dry before it is fired to fuse the glaze. As the glaze melts, it blends with the clay body to give a smooth, nonporous glassy surface. Some vases and jars show streaks or blobs of different-colored glazes down their sides. This effect is produced by brushing or dabbing on one colored glaze after another, over the first coat of glaze. The firing blends the different-colored glazes. Salt glaze is applied

by throwing salt into the top of the kiln just before the end of the firing. The intense heat turns the salt to vapor. The salt vapor settles on all the exposed pottery surfaces inside the kiln.

Decorating is done by several methods. *Incised* ornaments are cut on the piece with a pointed stick or other sharp tool. *Impressed* ornaments are made by pressing a design-mold on the piece. Both are done before the unglazed body has completely dried.

Slip tracing and *slip coating* make use of the same thin clay mixture that is used to stick handles to pitchers. Slip is so thin that it flows easily. In slip tracing, yellow or white slip might be traced or painted on a red body, or red slip on a white body. In slip coating, a red body might be dipped in white or yellow slip. Then, when the thin slip coating (called *engobe*) has nearly dried, part of it is cut or scraped away from the red body. This leaves the design showing in red. *Sgraffito*, or scratch decoration, is done by scratching designs in outline through a coating of slip. Different-colored glazes are sometimes used to heighten the effects of this process. Sometimes flat or modeled designs are *applied*, or attached to pottery.

Painting may be done *underglaze* or *overglaze*. This means that painting may be done either before or after the glaze is applied. Blue is the best and most popular color for underglaze painting. Enamel colors are used

Handmade Pottery Is Piled High on a boat in the harbor of Salvador (Bahia) on the coast of Brazil. The clay vessels are made by skilled potters in the more distant parts of the country and brought to the port by boats such as these.

Office of Inter-American Affairs

A Chinese Pottery Horse

Art Institute of Chicago
A Painted Pottery Jar

for overglaze painting. When the piece is fired, the enamel colors blend with the glaze. *Transfer printing* was invented about 1750. Engraved designs are printed from copper plates on paper. The design on paper is then transferred to the surface of the pottery. Transfer printing may be done either underglaze or overglaze.

Quality of Pottery depends upon both the technical skill and the good taste of the potter. Skill includes choosing the right kind of clay and preparing it carefully. The potter must know how much of other ingredients to add to the raw clay—such as ground flint which gives the piece extra hardness. Skill also includes knowing how to fire and glaze a piece correctly. The good taste of the potter determines the shape of the piece, the type of glazing or lack of glazing, and the decoration used. If an article is shaped to suit exactly the use for which it is intended, the chances are that it will be graceful and beautiful. The pitcher that does not pour right and the bowl that is unhandy to use are poorly shaped. The ancient Greek, Etruscan, and other vessels are simple, vigorous, and graceful. Their forms were the result of carefully studied adaptation to purpose.

History of Pottery

Early Pottery. Many examples of pottery of the finer types are found in most large museums. The ancient Greek and Etruscan pottery and terra cottas have a grace of form and elegance of decoration that are still a source of inspiration. Early Chinese pottery and clay figures have very simple and pure lines. Persian tiles and pottery show an amazing wealth of imagination and intricate decoration. The Persians used gorgeous and dazzling color effects in the glazed tiles that they used to decorate both the inside and outside walls of their buildings. Whole fronts of palaces and mosques were often encrusted with brilliant, many-colored tiles. Some of these tiles were eight-sided. Others were shaped like a cross, with equal arms and pointed ends. These

were made to set between the eight-sided tiles to give an unbroken expanse of tile-covered surface. A good many of these tiles are now in museums. But they need to be seen in their original setting to be fully appreciated.

The Moors in Spain also used brilliantly colored glazed tiles, especially in their gardens. The Moors taught the Spaniards much about the art of pottery and tilemaking. And the Spaniards carried the art to the Americas. As early as the middle of the 1500's some of the Aztec in Mexico had become excellent potters. Especially excellent were their *maiolica* (majolica) pottery and gaily hued glazed tiles. The fronts of some of the old Mexican churches and palaces are completely covered with these tiles. Often the early Aztec-Spanish pottery shows strong Chinese influence, in both shape and decoration. The reason for this is that from the end of the 1500's there was much direct trade between Mexico and China. The Chinese porcelain that was imported had a strong effect on native Mexican potters.

European Pottery. The Chinese porcelain brought to Holland in the 1600's and early 1700's by the Dutch East India Company greatly influenced the Delft potters. Some of the finest and most prized blue and white Delft ware owes its charm mainly to the decorations adapted from the designs on the Chinese blue and white plates, platters, bowls, and teapots.

Italy, during the Renaissance, produced a great quantity of rich *faïence* and *maiolica*. Fine faïence is still made at Gubbio, Deruta, Florence, and several other factories. Italy is also known for the glazed floor tiles of the Renaissance. The many-colored floor tiles in the Raphael *stanze* of the Vatican are more modern copies. But some of the finest original floor tiling may be seen in the Chapel of the Noble Guard and in the Villa Pia, in the Vatican garden, and also at the Villa d'Este at Tivoli.

The beauty of Italian faïence and maiolica had a strong effect on the pottery of France and Spain. The tradition has continued in France, where work of the highest quality has been produced. One of the best-

645

Pix

The Potto is a small animal that lives in the forests of Africa. It is about the size of a squirrel. Pottos usually sleep during the day, and hunt for food at night. The picture shows a baby potto.

known modern French earthenware products is the peasant ware of Quimper, in the province of Brittany.

Among fine English earthenware are the Staffordshire dishes which were transfer-printed with American views, usually in blue. They were made for the American market and were exported in large quantities. The best artists of the day prepared the sketches and engraved the copperplates from which the designs were printed. Other well-known types of English earthenware are Queensware (first made by Wedgwood); Rockingham; the salt-glaze white ware of Bristol, Leeds, and Liverpool; and the so-called *stone china* made by the Spode factory. Ever since the 1700's the Wedgwood black "basalt" and "jasper" pieces have been among the most beautiful and highly esteemed kinds of earthenware. Another product designed especially for the American market was the so-called *gaudy Dutch.*

American Pottery includes old Pennsylvania-German *tulip ware,* so named because tulips were often used in the decoration. The Pennsylvania-German tiles and pottery have not been made since the middle of the 1800's. But recently there has been a revival of this craft.

Stoneware is made in both America and Europe. It has a very hard gray body. It is salt-glazed and slightly decorated with underglaze blue. It occurs usually in the form of beer mugs, butter crocks, pickle jars, and the like.   HAROLD DONALDSON EBERLEIN

Related Articles in WORLD BOOK include:

Australia (picture: An
  Australian Craftsman)
Ceramics
Clay
Delft
Enamel
Faïence
Geometric Style

Greece, Ancient
  (color pictures)
Indian, American
  (Arts and Crafts)
Kaolin
Kiln
Latin America (picture:
  Useful Pottery Objects)

Majolica
Palissy, Bernard
Porcelain
Portugal (picture: Pottery)
Pyrometry
Rookwood Pottery

Spode (family)
Stoneware
Terra Cotta
Tile
Wedgwood, Josiah
Wedgwood Ware

Outline

I. Making Pottery
  A. Molding
  B. Glazing
  C. Decorating
  D. Quality of Pottery

II. History of Pottery
  A. Early Pottery
  B. European Pottery
  C. American Pottery

Questions

What qualities go into good pottery?
What is *slip?* How is it used?
How does pottery differ from porcelain?
Why does Aztec-Spanish pottery show Chinese influence?
Why is glaze applied? Is all fine pottery glazed?
Why is pottery dried before firing?
How do craftsmen decorate pottery?
How does a potter use a potter's wheel?

POTTO is a small animal that lives in western Africa. It belongs to the order of animals that includes monkeys, apes, and man. But the potto looks more like a sloth than a monkey or ape. It is a member of a group of animals called *slow lemurs* or *lorises.* The potto has a short tail, and the tips of several neck *vertebrae* (spine bones) project through the skin. The animal may use this partially exposed backbone as a defense. The potto is a slow-moving animal that spends its time in trees. It can grip branches firmly because its thumb faces the other fingers. The index finger is a mere stub, and has no nails or joints.

Pottos live alone or in pairs, and are most active at night. They eat insects, fruits, and eggs. In captivity, the potto requires careful treatment. It is delicate and must be kept in a warm cage.

Scientific Classification. Pottos belong to the loris family, *Lorisidae,* and make up the genus *Perodicticus.* The only species is *P. potto.*   THEODORE H. EATON, JR.

POUCHED MAMMAL. See MARSUPIAL.

POUGHKEEPSIE, *poh KIP sih,* N.Y. (pop. 38,330; alt. 155 ft.), is an educational and industrial center on the east bank of the Hudson River halfway between New York and Albany (see NEW YORK [political map]). The name Poughkeepsie comes from Indian words meaning *the reed-covered lodge by the little water place.* It is the home of Vassar College, Oakwood School, Marist College, and Poughkeepsie Day School. Industries in Poughkeepsie make cream separators, business machines, printing type, bearings, and cough drops. Poughkeepsie was founded by the Dutch in 1687. On July 26, 1788, New York state ratified the United States Constitution there. Poughkeepsie was incorporated as a village in 1799, and as a city in 1854. It is the county seat of Dutchess County, and has a council-manager government.   WILLIAM E. YOUNG

POULENC, *POO LAHNK,* **FRANCIS** (1899-1963), was one of *Les Six,* a group of French composers in the 1920's that rejected romanticism and impressionism. Poulenc composed such light works as *Rapsodie Nègre* (1917), *Mouvements Perpétuels* (1918), and *Les Mamelles de Tirésias* (1944). He showed sincere religious feeling in his *Mass* (1937), and *Dialogue of the Carmelites* (1956). He was born in Paris.   WILLIAM FLEMING

646

POULTRY

POULTRY is a term used for all fowl that are raised for meat and eggs. Chickens cackling in barnyards, ducks paddling in ponds, and geese parading through fields are common sights on farms. Turkey raising alone is a large business in the United States. Poultry also includes guinea fowl, ostriches, partridge, peacocks, pheasant, pigeons, quail, and swans.

On the average, each American eats almost 40 pounds of chicken meat, nearly 10 pounds of turkey, and over 320 eggs every year. All poultry produces meat, but chickens lay most of the eggs we eat. Poultry meat and eggs provide proteins, vitamins, and minerals.

Poultry raising became an important industry in the United States during the 1930's. In the late 1960's, farmers earned about $3¾ billion a year from poultry. Chicken eggs accounted for about half of this amount. Scientific care and breeding have produced poultry that provides tender meat and large eggs.

John W. West, the contributor of this article, is Head of the Poultry Science Department at Oklahoma State University.

Poultry Farms in the United States raise more chickens than any other kind of bird. Of every 100 farm birds, about 95 are chickens, 4 are turkeys, and 1 is a duck, goose, or other kind of poultry.

H. Armstrong Roberts

POULTRY AND EGGS PROVIDE A BIG SLICE OF LIVESTOCK INCOME

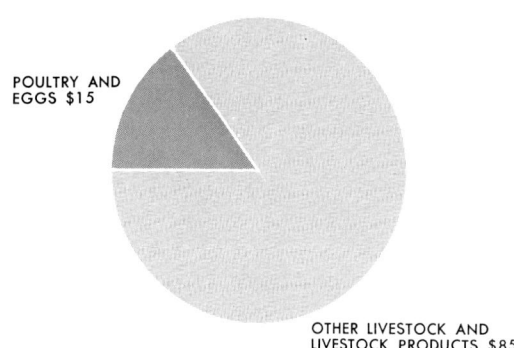

POULTRY AND EGGS $15

OTHER LIVESTOCK AND LIVESTOCK PRODUCTS $85

Source: U.S. Department of Agriculture

Poultry and eggs bring in about $15 out of every $100 of farm income from livestock and livestock products in the United States. Chicken eggs produce about one-half of this $15.

Young people often raise poultry as part of their activities in 4-H Clubs or the Future Farmers of America. Poultry raising is popular among boys and girls because only a little cash is needed to start and because the birds and eggs can be sold within a few weeks.

Kinds of Poultry. Chickens, turkeys, ducks, and geese are the most important kinds of poultry. Farmers in the United States produce 20 times as many chickens as all other poultry combined. Chicken eggs and meat account for about $85 of every $100 earned by American poultry farmers. Turkeys bring in about $13, and ducks, geese, pigeons, and guinea fowl about $2 of every $100. Duck production is more important in the mid-Atlantic

states and the Midwest than in other parts of the United States. Most geese are raised in the Midwest, and most guinea fowl in the Midwest and South.

Other kinds of poultry have little importance in the United States. These fowl include peacocks and ostriches, and such game birds as quail, partridge, pheasant, and grouse. Many people regard the meat of game birds as a delicacy. Government-operated farms raise large numbers of game birds every year to replace those shot by hunters. These birds are released in wildlife areas. Peacocks are raised mainly for show purposes, although people in some countries eat peacock meat. Farmers raise ostriches chiefly for their long feathers, which are used to decorate hats and other clothing.

Raising Poultry. About half of the farmers in the United States raise poultry. Some farms specialize in raising only egg-laying or meat-producing chickens, or only turkeys, ducks, or geese. Each of these poultry farms may raise thousands of birds every year. But many farmers who raise poultry also do other kinds of farming. The farmer's wife and children usually feed and care for the poultry raised on these farms.

Farmers who specialize in raising poultry usually buy baby chickens, turkeys, and ducks from a *hatchery*, which specializes in hatching poultry from eggs. Hatcheries use *incubators* (egg-hatching machines heated by electricity). Eggs must be kept at a constant temperature for a certain period in order to hatch. Turkey and duck eggs, for example, take about 28 days to hatch. Chicken eggs take 21 days. Turkey, duck, and chicken eggs must be kept at temperatures from 99½° F. to 100° F.

Farmers sometimes use incubators to hatch other kinds of poultry. Farmers who raise only small flocks

GROWTH OF THE U.S. POULTRY INDUSTRY

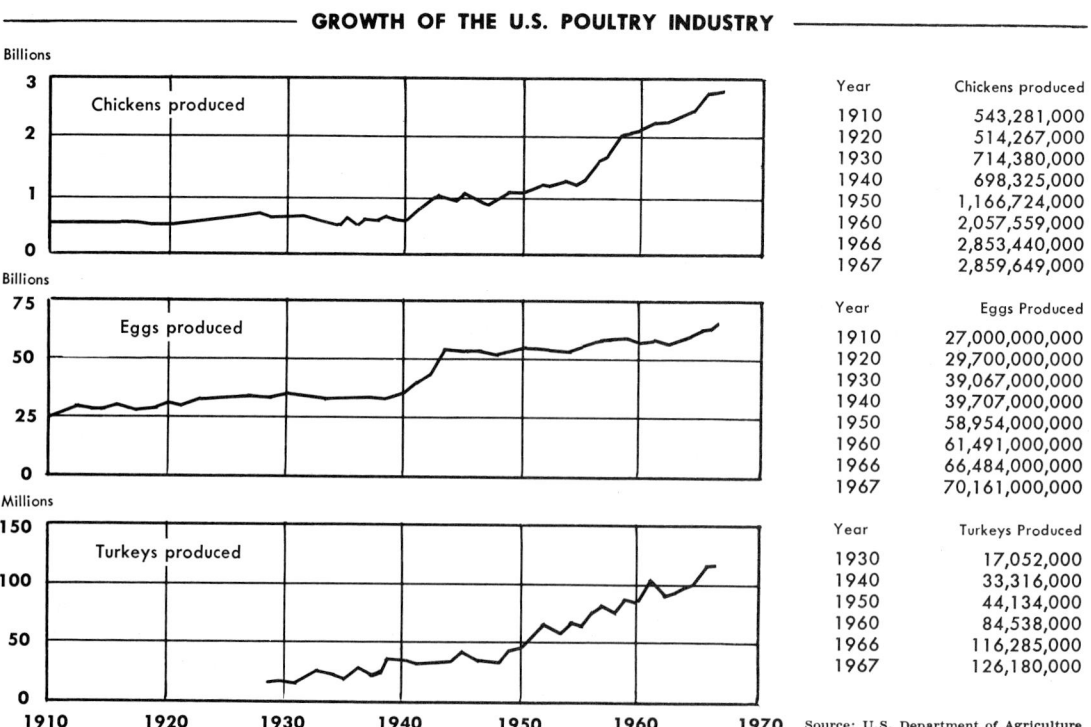

Year	Chickens produced
1910	543,281,000
1920	514,267,000
1930	714,380,000
1940	698,325,000
1950	1,166,724,000
1960	2,057,559,000
1966	2,853,440,000
1967	2,859,649,000

Year	Eggs Produced
1910	27,000,000,000
1920	29,700,000,000
1930	39,067,000,000
1940	39,707,000,000
1950	58,954,000,000
1960	61,491,000,000
1966	66,484,000,000
1967	70,161,000,000

Year	Turkeys Produced
1930	17,052,000
1940	33,316,000
1950	44,134,000
1960	84,538,000
1966	116,285,000
1967	126,180,000

Source: U.S. Department of Agriculture

Each person in the United States eats more than 6 eggs a week, or over 320 eggs a year.

THE IMPORTANCE OF EGGS AND POULTRY AS FOOD

Poultry ranks behind beef and pork as the third most important meat in the United States. Each person eats an average of 46 pounds of poultry a year.

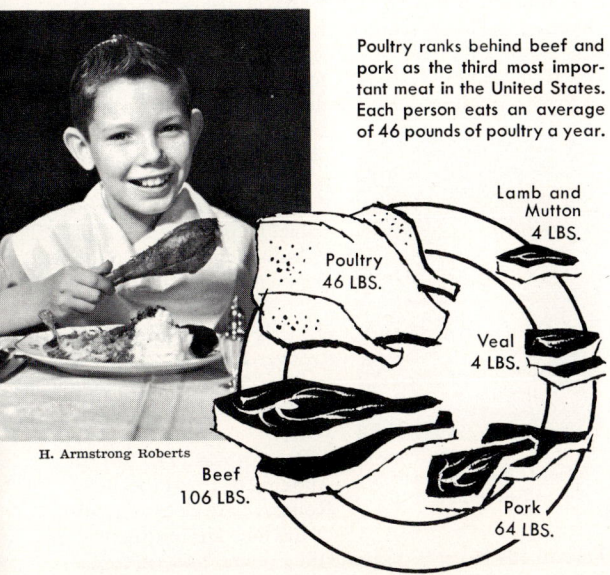

H. Armstrong Roberts

Poultry 46 LBS.

Lamb and Mutton 4 LBS.

Veal 4 LBS.

Beef 106 LBS.

Pork 64 LBS.

Source: *National Food Situation*, Aug., 1968, Economic Research Service, U.S. Department of Agriculture

of these birds usually let the parent birds hatch the eggs rather than placing the eggs in an incubator. Some farmers use chickens to hatch and raise small numbers of less important poultry. Pigeons hatch and care for their own young.

Most farmers keep their baby birds in heated *brooder houses* until the birds are 8 weeks old and are fully feathered. Baby chickens and turkeys require extra care because they are weak and subject to many diseases. Ducks and geese are hardier, and do not need as much attention. Turkeys must have more vitamins in their feed than chickens. Otherwise, the care and feeding of most poultry is about the same as that for chickens. See CHICKEN (Chicken Farming).

On farms that specialize in raising chickens, the farmer often keeps the birds in chicken houses from the time they are hatched until they are killed for meat. Turkeys, ducks, and geese can also be raised in this manner. But these larger birds need more room, and are usually raised in a fenced field after they become 8 weeks old.

Marketing Poultry. Most meat chickens are sold as broilers and fryers when they are 9 to 12 weeks old. Scientific care has made it possible to raise chickens weighing more than 4 pounds at this age. Turkeys are usually marketed when 5 to 6 months old. The average female turkey weighs 16 pounds and the male 26 pounds at this age. Many housewives prefer turkeys that weigh less than 12 pounds, because the heavier birds provide too much meat for the average family. Since the 1930's, turkey raisers have produced large flocks of smaller turkeys. Most turkeys raised in the United States are sold at Thanksgiving and Christmas. But turkeys are sold throughout the year.

Ducks are usually sold when they are about 11 weeks old and weigh 5 to 6 pounds. Ducks are called *ducklings* at this age. Geese are often marketed when they are 10 weeks old and weigh about 14 pounds. Most geese are also sold at Thanksgiving and Christmas time. Pigeons sold for meat are usually marketed as *squabs* when they are 4 weeks old and weigh less than 1 pound.   JOHN W. WEST

Related Articles in WORLD BOOK include:

Agriculture	Grouse	Partridge
Chicken	Guinea Fowl	Peacock
Duck	Incubator	Pheasant
Egg	Jungle Fowl	Pigeon
Farm and Farming	Livestock	Quail
Feather	Nutrition	Turkey
Goose	Ostrich	

POUND is a common unit of weight for measuring many things. There are three kinds of pounds—*apothecaries'*, *avoirdupois*, and *troy*. The pound avoirdupois has 16 ounces. This is equal to 7,000 grains, or 0.45359237 kilograms. Troy and apothecaries' pounds have 12 ounces, and have 5,760 grains, or 0.3732 kilograms each. The grain is the basis of computation in all three denominations, and does not vary. The troy pound is used for weighing precious metals. The avoirdupois pound is used for measuring heavier and cheaper merchandise such as meat, cheese, and butter. Druggists use the apothecaries' pound in preparing drugs and medicines. Pound is abbreviated as *lb*.   E. G. STRAUS

See also APOTHECARIES' WEIGHT; AVOIRDUPOIS; TROY WEIGHT.

POUND, EZRA LOOMIS (1885-   ), is an American poet and critic. He became one of the most influential and controversial literary figures of his time. Pound's admirers regard his *Cantos* as the most important long poem in modern literature. His detractors find the *Cantos* confused and filled with malice.

Pound left the United States, which he called "a half-savage country," in 1908 to live in Venice and London. He published his first poetry in Europe, and he became the friend and critic of writers William Butler Yeats and James Joyce. He also helped such then unknown writers as T. S. Eliot and Robert Frost.

Pound's early work, collected in *Personae* (1909), reflects his deep conviction that the poet plays a vital role in maintaining the standards of his society. In 1920, Pound published *Hugh Selwyn Mauberley*, a despairing poem describing his struggles in what he considered a morally decaying culture. Pound then began examining what he felt had gone wrong with the world.

In the first of his *Cantos*, written from about 1915 to 1925, Pound tries to "tell the tale of the tribe" in a highly personal manner. He traces the rise and fall of Eastern and Western empires, emphasizing the destructive role of materialism and greed. The *Cantos* written during the late 1920's and early 1930's deal with the corruption Pound

Wide World
Ezra Pound

saw developing in American life since the time of two of his heroes, Thomas Jefferson and Martin Van Buren. Pound's indignation finally turned to anti-Semitism and opposition to capitalism.

Pound became an admirer of the Fascist rule of Italian dictator Benito Mussolini. During World War II, Pound broadcast Fascist propaganda to the United States. After the war, the United States arrested Pound on a charge of treason. He was judged insane in 1946 and spent 12 years in a Washington, D.C., mental hospital. He was released in 1958 and returned to Italy.

Pound was born in Hailey, Ida., and attended Hamilton College and the University of Pennsylvania. He taught briefly before moving to Europe. ELMER W. BORKLUND

POUND, ROSCOE (1870-1964), was an American educator and authority on law. He introduced to the United States a view of the nature and purpose of law which came to be known as "sociological jurisprudence." This view treats law as a system of social engineering.

Pound wrote widely on legal history, legal philosophy, and law reform. He became, perhaps, the best-known figure in American legal education. His books include *The Spirit of the Common Law* (1921), *Law and Morals* (1924), *The Formative Era of American Law* (1938), and, in addition, *Social Control Through Law* (1942). Pound was born in Lincoln, Nebr., and was graduated from Harvard Law School. He became a professor of law at Harvard in 1910, and served as dean of the Harvard Law School from 1916 to 1936. H. G. REUSCHLEIN

POUND STERLING is the monetary unit of Great Britain and some other countries. The British pound (£) is equal to 20 shillings (s) or 240 pence (d). There are paper bills for 10 shillings, £1, £5, and £10. Great Britain formerly issued notes of higher denominations up to £1,000. A £1 gold coin is a *sovereign*.

Sovereigns were first made in 1489, during the time of Henry VII. The sovereign was called a *unite*, in honor of the uniting of England and Scotland in 1707. George III chose the sovereign as the monetary unit, and it was first issued regularly in 1817. Half sovereigns, two-pound, and five-pound pieces were coined. Sovereigns were made for circulation until 1931, when Great

Chase Manhattan Bank Money Museum
The Pound Sterling is the monetary unit of Great Britain. Queen Elizabeth II is shown on the face of the bill.

Britain left the gold standard. They are now made for dealings with nations that require payment in gold.

When a nation buys more from other countries than it sells to them, it usually must pay the difference in an *international money* (widely accepted currency). The British pound sterling has often been used as international money. But gold and United States dollars are the major forms of international money. BURTON HOBSON

See also MONEY (table).

POUNDAGE. See TARIFF (The Middle Ages).

POUNDAL. See DYNE.

POUSSIN, *POO SAN*, **NICOLAS** (1594-1665), one of the leading French painters of the 1600's, was one of the last important artists to paint in the classic manner of the Renaissance. His art is marked by a strong sense of form and order, which seems to control the appear-

Louvre, Paris (detail)
Nicolas Poussin painted this self-portrait in 1650.

ance of all objects in his pictures. He subordinated color to form, and felt that subject matter should be as noble as possible. One of Poussin's paintings, *Saint John on Patmos*, appears in color in the PAINTING article. His art and principles strongly affected the work of the French Academy when it was founded in 1635.

Poussin was born in Les Andelys. In 1624 he went to Rome, where he lived most of his life. He returned to Paris in 1640 to help decorate the Louvre. JOSEPH C. SLOANE

See also MIDAS (picture); SABINE (picture: Early Romans Kidnaped the Sabine Women).

POUTRINCOURT, *poo tran KOOR*, **JEAN DE BIENCOURT DE** (1557-1615), BARON DE ST. JUST, a French colonizer, helped found Acadia, a region in eastern Canada (see ACADIA). He went to Canada in 1604 with Sieur de Monts (see MONTS, SIEUR DE). Poutrincourt was given a grant of land and established a colony at Port Royal.

In 1606, Poutrincourt accompanied Samuel de Champlain in his exploration of the Bay of Fundy. In 1607, Poutrincourt went back to France. He returned to Acadia in 1610, and lived at Port Royal until 1613, when the settlement was wiped out by the English settlers from Virginia. He then went back to France. He was born in Picardy, France. IAN C. C. GRAHAM

POVERTY is the lack of enough income or resources to satisfy a person's minimum needs. Although poverty can be found in all countries and regions, the minimum needs of people are not everywhere the same. Minimum needs vary according to place and time.

For example, minimum needs vary from country to country. Many things that most Americans consider basic—such as refrigerators and indoor plumbing—would be regarded as luxuries in countries with little industry, such as Albania and Haiti. That is because most of the people in a country or region with little industry have fewer choices available to them.

Minimum needs vary within a country from one time to another. For example, colonial Americans would have regarded as luxuries what most Americans today regard as minimum needs. Today, some poor people have better household goods, medical care, and transportation than even the wealthy had 200 years ago.

Most nations of the world recognize poverty as a major social problem. But this was not always true. For a long time, men accepted the idea that poverty was something certain unfortunate people had to endure. Resources were scarce, and workers could do little to increase production. The most poor people could hope for was a rich man's charity.

Poverty in the United States and other industrialized nations is far different from poverty in much of the rest of the world. In underdeveloped countries such as India, society as a whole is poor. In industrialized countries, poverty is not as widespread. Only certain persons, families, groups, and areas are poverty-stricken.

This article deals with poverty in the United States. For a discussion of poverty in underdeveloped countries, see WORLD (Economy of the World); and UNDERDEVELOPED COUNTRY.

Poverty As a Social Problem

Who Are the Poor? There is no single, generally accepted way to measure poverty. The U.S. government uses income as its yardstick, and identifies the poor as those whose yearly incomes fall below certain levels. In the late 1960's, for example, it classified as poor any nonfarm family of seven or more persons whose annual income was $5,430 or less. A family of four was considered poor if its income was $3,335 or less, and a family of two if its income did not exceed $2,115.

In general, farm families can live on less income than city families. Many rural families have their own gardens and raise some animals for food. Also, they do not have certain expenses—such as transportation to work—which city families have. As a result, the poverty level is somewhat lower for farm families.

According to the government's yardstick for poverty, in the late 1960's, one of every seven persons was poor. Although over 90 per cent of all poor families lived in cities, only one out of every seven city persons was poor. In rural areas, one out of every four persons was poor. About half of the poor families lived in the South. One of every four children under 18 years of age lived in poverty or near-poverty. Two out of five persons 65 and over were poor or near-poor. Two of every three poor Americans were white. About 12 per cent of all white

Lawrence Senesh, the contributor of this article, is Professor of Economic Education at Purdue University.

persons were poor as compared with about 41 per cent of nonwhites. The nonwhite classification includes Negroes, American Indians, Chinese, Japanese, and Filipinos. About half of all families headed by a woman were poor or near-poor. The heads of about 60 per cent of all poor families had only a grade school education, and many had no specialized skills. These numbers do not express the misery of poverty—crowded rooms and no privacy, the ache of hunger, lack of heat in the winter, no doctor for the sick, and no hope of jobs for those wanting employment.

What Causes Poverty? Poverty in the United States and most industrially developed countries is usually related to difficulty in getting and holding a job. Ability, education, and skills help determine the kind of job an individual gets. For example, all people do not have the same physical and mental abilities. Some are born with limitations that prevent them from performing certain jobs. Poor health and physical disabilities prevent some persons from holding jobs.

Scientific and technological advancement have made education and training more important. This has increased the demand for professional and skilled workers, and lessened demand for the unskilled. Workers with

---

POVERTY IN THE UNITED STATES

This table shows the "poverty line" for families of various sizes in the late 1960's. For example, the government classified a nonfarm family of three as poor if its annual money income was $2,600 or less.

Family Size	Nonfarm	Farm
1	$1,635	$1,145
2	2,115	1,475
3	2,600	1,815
4	3,335	2,345
5	3,930	2,755
6	4,410	3,090
7 or more	5,430	3,790

Source: *Social Security Bulletin*, March, 1968

---

little education and job training earn little income.

Economic slumps and changes in manpower requirements often bring poverty. When business drops off, production also declines. If the downturn continues, many persons are laid off. Unemployment also can result if consumers turn to new kinds of products, if machines can do a job more efficiently than workers, or if an industry moves out of a community. See MANPOWER (How Manpower Requirements Change).

Poverty is also caused by social conditions, such as discrimination against minority groups. Whites frequently discriminate against nonwhites. There has been discrimination against nonwhites in educational institutions. Some discrimination makes it difficult for nonwhites to go into business for themselves. Qualified Negroes and other nonwhites are often passed over when good jobs are available. Unemployment is highest among nonwhites, and their income is about half that of whites with similar education.

In the United States, some employers discriminate against older workers. Most job openings are for workers 45 years of age and younger. Persons 65 and over are the most poverty-stricken age group in the nation. Medical science and better health services enable people to live longer than they did in the past. Yet most companies require workers to retire at 65. Social security and other programs for the aged are often insufficient to permit retired persons to live comfortably.

The Effects of Poverty. Social scientists who study poverty give various reasons why society should be concerned with the problems of the poor. For example, economists argue that persons who are poorly housed, poorly fed, and poorly educated cannot produce to the fullest extent in business and industry. As a result, the economy produces fewer goods and services. Goods and services not produced are lost forever.

Political scientists claim that poverty can create hostility against the political system. The poor often blame the government for their predicament. Especially bitter persons may turn to radical political ideas or movements that threaten the existing political system.

"Poverty breeds poverty," according to many sociologists and anthropologists. Children of the poor, they claim, have a good chance of remaining poor all their lives. Poor parents cannot give their children the economic, educational, and social opportunities that would help them improve their position in life. Because the poor cannot afford good food, housing, and medical care, illness comes more often and stays longer. Many poor adults become discouraged with their plight. Unable to get and hold good jobs, they lose all sense of dignity and self-respect. With loss of hope, some become resigned to poverty as a way of life. In time, many children of the poor acquire the same feelings of helplessness and hopelessness.

Poverty also may make other social problems worse. Some poor persons, discouraged with their lives, turn to drink to escape their frustrations. Crime and delinquency rates are high in slum areas. Also, low-income families in cities have the highest divorce rate in the United States.

Measures to Eliminate Poverty

The United States, which is the richest country in the world, could eliminate most poverty with relatively little sacrifice of resources. However, Americans are divided over the question of whether poverty is a matter of individual or national responsibility. Some persons still believe that the poor are responsible for their condition, and should help themselves. Others argue that the problem is too big and complex for individuals or groups to solve. They believe it is morally wrong to allow poverty to ruin the lives of some, while most persons enjoy prosperity.

Improving Job Opportunities. Probably the most acceptable way to eliminate poverty is to make sure that there are enough jobs, and that people are helped to qualify for them.

The Employment Act of 1946 charges the federal government with the responsibility for maintaining economic stability. The President's Council of Economic Advisers studies the amount of unemployment each year, and recommends to the President ways to achieve high levels of employment. The U.S. government is also committed to the promotion of economic growth. Such growth results from increasing production of goods and services. The normal growth rate since the mid-1940's has reduced poverty by about one per cent a year.

Elementary and secondary schools provide young people with the basic skills they need to qualify for many jobs. However, a college education is needed for an increasing number of the economy's jobs. Many persons believe it is wasteful to let students drop out of school because they lack the money to continue their education. Private and government scholarships and loans assist many needy and deserving students.

Vocational training programs help to reduce poverty. The federal antipoverty programs based on the Economic Opportunity Act of 1964 stress vocational education and training for young adults. Some employers provide on-the-job training. Labor unions and private industry often jointly sponsor apprenticeship programs.

Some government programs are designed to improve job opportunities in certain areas. Under one such program, the federal and state governments try to create jobs in *depressed areas* by encouraging industries to locate there. Most depressed areas have many unemployed people, and few industries and businesses.

The Civil Rights Act of 1964 bans discrimination in employment. The act established the Equal Employment Opportunity Commission to ensure that all job applicants receive the same consideration. But much discrimination in employment persists.

State and federal minimum wage laws are designed to guarantee workers a respectable income. But some persons oppose minimum wages. They argue that small firms that make little profit may have to close if they are forced to increase wages to the legal minimum. This would eliminate some jobs and create more unemployment.

Social Welfare Assistance. Poverty is a complex problem and cannot be solved by any single approach. For example, simply creating jobs will not help everyone escape poverty, because some persons are unable to work.

The government's social welfare programs provide or add to the incomes of many persons. These programs provide cash payments and medical and other assistance to the retired, the unemployed, the disabled and handicapped, widows, dependent children, and others in need. For detailed information on various social security and public assistance programs, see SOCIAL SECURITY; MEDICARE; RELIEF; and UNEMPLOYMENT INSURANCE.

Social insurance benefits—such as old-age, survivors, and disability payments—are financed by taxes paid by workers and employers. But most public assistance programs—such as aid to dependent children—are financed by general taxes. Through taxes, some income is taken from high-income workers, and the funds are transferred to low-income workers. There is much criticism of existing programs. Many Americans argue that the cost of collecting and distributing these funds is extremely high, and that the system is too complicated and humiliating. Others point out that many of the poor are not included in the existing welfare programs. Many claim that politicians have too much control over the present welfare programs.

Some persons favor unifying most welfare programs into a single program for all needy people. One such proposal is for a guaranteed income in the form of a *negative income tax*. Under this plan, families whose incomes fall below the poverty level would receive an income supplement from the government. Once the poverty level income is set, no proof of need would be required.

The idea of the negative income tax has been widely

accepted by members of both major political parties, by economists, and by business, labor, and civil rights leaders. Disagreement centers on the question: How high could the poverty level be set without discouraging the poor from seeking jobs and doing productive work?

Economists point out that the guaranteed annual income, together with other measures for fighting poverty, would have both a short-run and long-run effect. In the short run, it would lessen the misery of the poor. In the long run, it would break the vicious cycle in which the children of the poor are trapped.   LAWRENCE SENESH

Related Articles in WORLD BOOK include:

Appalachia	Housing (Low-Income Housing)
City	Minimum Wage
Cultural Deprivation	Social Work
Food Stamp Program	Standard of Living
Head Start	Urban Renewal

POWDER. See COSMETICS; GUNPOWDER.

POWDER HORN was an instrument for carrying the gunpowder used in muzzle-loading muskets. It was usually made from the horn of an ox or cow. The hollow horn was cut at the ends. Then caps, usually metal, were placed on the ends of the horn to hold the powder in. To load a musket, the cap on the small end of the powder horn was removed, and the powder poured into the muzzle of the gun. Powder horns were usually slung over the wearer's shoulder. The pouch contained a bullet mold, bullets, and a flax wad for swabbing the gun barrel. See also FLINTLOCK (picture). JACK O'CONNOR

POWDER KEG OF EUROPE. See BALKANS.

POWDER METALLURGY is a process that reduces metals to powdered form and presses the powder into certain somewhat restricted shapes. A single metal or a mixture of metals may be used in powder metallurgy. Usually a heating and cooling process, called *annealing*, follows the pressing operation. This adds strength to the finished product (see ANNEALING).

Powder metallurgy has many advantages over other methods of mixing metals. Some metals will not mix (alloy) when they are heated to the melting, or *fusion*, point. But these metals can be made to form valuable compounds by powdering them, and then mixing the powders together. Graphite will not fuse with metals by heat alone. But it can be powdered and mixed with powdered metals, pressed into shape, and heated to make a bearing. Such a bearing does not need frequent oiling, because the graphite acts as a self-lubricant. Other advantages of powder metallurgy include rapid production, high dimensional accuracy, low scrap loss, and, except for the diemaking, use of unskilled labor.

Metals are made into powders in many ways. The simplest is to break up solid metals in crushing machines. Another is by electrolysis (see ELECTROLYSIS). A third way is to heat the oxide compound of the metal in contact with hydrogen.   HARRISON ASHLEY SCHMITT

POWDER RIVER rises in the southern foothills of the Bighorn Mountains in central Wyoming. It flows 486 miles to southeast Montana. The Powder River joins the Yellowstone River near Terry, Mont. Its main tributaries include the Little Powder River in Wyoming and Montana, and Crazy Woman Creek in Wyoming. The sluggish, muddy, shallow river is put to little use. For location, see WYOMING (physical map).

POWDERLY, TERENCE V. See LABOR (The Knights of Labor).

POWELL, ADAM CLAYTON, JR. (1908-   ), is a political and religious leader of New York City's Harlem area. From 1945 to 1955, he and William Dawson of Chicago were the only Negroes in the United States Congress. Powell strongly condemned all forms of segregation and discrimination, especially in his early years in Congress. Later, his absenteeism, his boastful attitude,

Wide World
Adam Clayton Powell, Jr.

and his colorful private life disappointed many reformers and offended many congressmen. However, he remained popular in his own congressional district.

Powell has been pastor of the Abyssinian Baptist Church in Harlem since 1937, and has represented the Harlem district in the House of Representatives since 1945. In 1960, he became chairman of the House Committee on Education and Labor. Powell was denied his seat in Congress by the House in 1967 on grounds he misused public funds. He won a special election to fill the vacancy, but he did not claim his seat. He won the regular election in 1968 and returned to Congress in January, 1969. In 1969, the U.S. Supreme Court ruled that Congress had acted unconstitutionally when it excluded Powell in 1967.

Powell was born in New Haven, Conn. He graduated from Colgate University and received graduate degrees from Columbia and Shaw universities. RICHARD BARDOLPH

POWELL, ANTHONY (1905-   ), an English writer, is best known for his series of related novels *A Dance to the Music of Time*. The series began with *A Question of Upbringing* (1951), and includes *The Acceptance World* (1953), *The Kindly Ones* (1962), and *The Military Philosophers* (1969). Powell describes the changing nature of the English upper-middle class and upper class which he felt occurred following World War II. The novels are all told in the first person by Nicholas Jenkins, who speaks for the author.

Powell was born in London. His first novels were satiric and partly autobiographical. They include *Afternoon Men* (1931), *Agents and Patrons* (1936), and *What's Become of Waring?* (1939).   JOHN ESPEY

POWELL, CECIL FRANK (1903-   ), a British physicist, won the 1950 Nobel prize in physics for developing a simple technique to photograph the action of high-speed particles. With this technique, now used everywhere in nuclear research, he and his coworkers discovered the existence of two types of mesons, and showed how they disintegrate (see MESON). Powell was born in Tonbridge, England. In 1928 he became a professor of physics at the University of Bristol.

POWELL, JOHN WESLEY (1834-1902), was an American geologist, an authority on irrigation, and a student of Indians. In 1869, he led the first expedition down the canyons of the Green and Colorado rivers. He became director of the Bureau of American Ethnology in 1879, and of the U.S. Geological Survey in 1881. He was born in Mount Morris, N.Y.   CARROLL LANE FENTON

651

POWER

POWER, in physics, means the rate of doing work. The idea of power involves three factors: (1) force, (2) distance, and (3) time. Physicists consider that work is done whenever a force moves a body a certain distance (see WORK). Work is measured by multiplying the size of the force by the distance the object moves in the direction in which the force is acting. Thus, in the English system, work is measured in *foot-pounds* or some other convenient unit (see FOOT-POUND). When an object is moved 1 foot against a resisting force of 1 pound, 1 foot-pound of work has been done. Power is measured by dividing the work done by the time required to do the work. The English unit of work is the *horsepower* which equals 550 foot-pounds per second or 33,000 foot-pounds per minute.

The finding of new sources of power has been one of the key reasons for the progress of civilization. A man using hand tools produces relatively little power. In modern times, hand tools could not produce enough food and other materials to meet even a part of the many human needs. To increase his output, man has developed machines that use the energy released by coal, gasoline, water, steam, electricity, and atomic reactions. Machines convert this energy to useful work, and produce more goods at a faster rate than one person could ever hope to produce.

The Importance of Power

Modern civilization has developed because man has harnessed other forces to add to the power of his own muscles. Man put animals to work for him, and learned to make the wind move his boats. The energy from flowing streams turned a mill wheel that ground flour. For thousands of years, man knew only the power in his own muscles and those of animals, and the power found in wind and water. Not until the invention of the steam engine did a new source of power become available. The steam engine provided power for machines in factories and speeded land and ocean transportation.

Since 1800, man has developed many new sources of power, and many ways to transmit power to machines where they do work. Man discovered that coal is excellent fuel for steam engines. In the late 1800's, he discovered that electricity could light homes and run machines. The use of petroleum fuels for engines was also developed. The 1930's and 1940's saw the development of the most powerful known kind of energy—atomic energy.

The discovery of new sources of power has greatly changed the history of the world. For example, in the 1800's, nations that had good supplies of coal, such as Great Britain, Germany, France, and the United States, were able to develop large manufacturing industries. Their political strength depended partly on their control of coal to supply power.

In more recent times, the development of new sources of power has changed the life of entire communities. For example, since the 1930's, the Tennessee Valley Authority (TVA) has constructed power dams on the Tennessee River and its branches. This project has greatly increased the prosperity of the Tennessee Valley and made the region a major industrial area. In the 1950's, a power development in British Columbia trans-

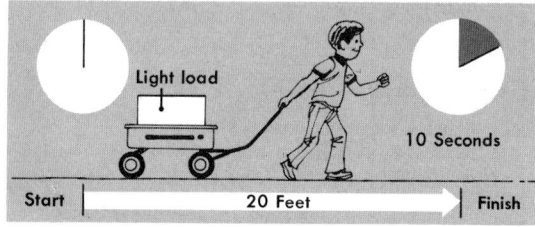

The Power Needed to Pull a Wagon depends on its weight, and how far and fast it is pulled. A child uses less power to pull a light load 20 feet in 10 seconds, *above*, than he does to pull a heavy load the same distance in the same time, *below*.

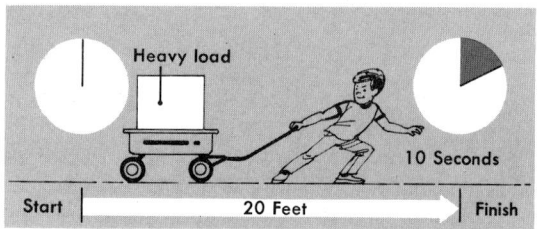

formed a remote Indian village, Kitimat, into one of the largest aluminum-producing centers in the world.

Underdeveloped nations throughout the world look for new sources of power to replace man and animals. Large-scale power developments have brought increased industrialization to India, Mexico, and several other nations. The rapid growth of Russian industry can be partly traced to the development of water power.

The sources of power have done more than aid man to produce goods. They have made possible new means of transportation and communication. Automobiles, airplanes, and rockets depend on power, as do radio, telephone, and television.

Sources of Power

The demand for power almost always exceeds the supply. Man continually seeks ways to keep pace with the need for additional power. Usually, he adapts old, well-known sources to make them more efficient. The chief sources of power include (1) men and animals, (2) water, (3) wind, (4) steam, (5) internal-combustion engines, (6) electricity, and (7) atomic energy.

Men and Animals have been important sources of power since the earliest times. The horse was once the chief source of power for agriculture, and still is in some countries. But horses and other work animals cannot compete with machines. They tire easily and require large amounts of food. Because of this, machines have largely replaced horses in the United States, Canada, and other highly developed nations. The number of farm horses in the United States has dropped from 21 million in 1910 to about 3 million today.

Man has the same limitations as animals as a source of power. Also, the use of machines to replace human labor helps advance civilization. In areas where most men must spend their time in physical labor, progress is usually slow. Machines give men the time and energy to devote to government, art, literature, and invention.

Water is an excellent source of power. By harnessing the energy in moving water, man can generate huge amounts of electrical energy to run factories and to provide light and heat. But water also has serious limitations as a source of power. There is no danger that water supplies are being exhausted. But rivers, waterfalls, lakes, and other large supplies of water are not evenly distributed throughout the world. Some communities have little or no water to produce the power they need.

Wind was once a major source of power. Men used it to turn windmills and to move ships. But other power sources have gradually replaced it. Today, wind is used only in scattered areas of the world. The chief disadvantage of wind is that it is not dependable.

However, man has not completely given up wind as a source of power. In Great Britain, engineers have developed an experimental wind turbine. They plan to build a practical wind turbine designed to produce 2,000 kilowatts of electricity. If successful, the wind turbine may become an inexpensive source of power in areas that have low supplies of fuels and water.

Steam became an important source of power in the 1700's. The development of the steam engine played an important part in the industrial revolution (see INDUSTRIAL REVOLUTION). One of the chief uses of steam was to power railroad locomotives. Diesel and electric locomotives have largely replaced steam locomotives in the United States and Canada. But steam engines are still used to generate electricity and to power ships. See STEAM ENGINE.

Internal-Combustion Engines power automobiles, airplanes, and many other vehicles. The development of the gasoline engine in the late 1800's gave man a compact source of power ideally suited to transportation needs. The diesel engine, developed in the late 1890's, provided a low-cost source of power that has been adopted for locomotives, trucks, and industrial uses. See DIESEL ENGINE; GASOLINE ENGINE.

Electricity is one of man's chief sources of power. Electric current produced by huge generators flows through transmission lines to homes and industries. Industry uses it to run motors that range from the tiny devices that operate electric clocks to huge motors that drive giant cranes. See ELECTRIC POWER.

Atomic Energy may become man's greatest source of power. Man has learned to convert to useful work the tremendous amounts of heat produced by splitting atoms. Atomic reactors run ships and generators. In future years, atomic energy may become a substitute for coal and oil.

Thermonuclear reactions that produce energy by combining atoms rather than splitting them hold some promise for the future. But scientists have found no way to harness this power to produce electricity. See ATOMIC ENERGY; ATOMIC REACTOR.

Measuring Power

When James Watt of England offered to sell his steam engines to farmers and miners, he was probably asked how many horses they would replace. Watt measured the rate at which a horse could do work. He concluded that an average draft horse could exert steadily a 150-pound force while walking at a speed of $2\frac{1}{2}$ miles an hour. The horse thus performed work at the rate of 33,000 foot-pounds per minute, or 550 foot-pounds per second. Watt defined this rate as 1 *horsepower*. See HORSEPOWER.

The formula for power is $P=\frac{W}{t}$, where P stands for power, W for work, and t for time. Work is equal to force multiplied by displacement in the direction of the force. For example, suppose a man who weighs 220 pounds runs up a 10-foot flight of stairs in 4 seconds. He has worked at the rate of 1 horsepower:

$$P=\frac{220 \text{ pounds} \times 10 \text{ feet}}{4 \text{ seconds}} = \frac{550 \text{ foot-pounds}}{1 \text{ second}}$$

In this example, only the vertical height (10 feet) is important in calculating the work done. The horizontal distance has no effect, because the man does work only against the force of gravity, which is vertical.

Scientists use other units to measure power. In the metric system, the unit of power is the *erg per second*. An *erg* is the amount of work done when a force of 1 dyne moves an object a distance of 1 centimeter. One erg is about the amount of work a fly would do in stepping up on a dime. Because the erg is such a small unit of work, the metric system also uses a larger unit called the *joule*. One joule equals 10 million ergs (see JOULE). The unit of power in the metric system is the *watt*. One watt equals one joule of work per second (see WATT). And one horsepower equals 746 watts.   ROBERT L. WEBER

Related Articles in WORLD BOOK include:

Atomic Energy	Fuel	Solar Energy
Diesel Engine	Gasoline	Turbine
Electric Power	Engine	Water Power
Energy	Power Plant	Work
Force		

POWER, in the social sciences, is the ability of persons or groups to impose their will on others. Persons with power can enforce their decisions by applying, or threatening to apply, penalties against those who disobey their orders or demands. Power is present in almost all human relationships. Teachers have power over students, employers over employees, parents over children, bullies over weaklings, and militarily strong nations over weak nations.

Forms of Power include *coercion*, *influence*, and *authority*. Coercion is the use of physical force to enforce decisions. Influence is the ability to produce an effect through example, persuasion, or some other means without using force.

Authority is power that is based on agreement by a majority of the members of a society or group. For example, teachers have power (authority) over their students because it is widely recognized and agreed that they must have it to keep order and teach effectively. In democracies, the authority of government is based on the consent of the governed. Leaders chosen by the voters in free elections have authority to make decisions for the people. See AUTHORITY.

Main Sources of Power include (1) superior resources, (2) superior numbers, and (3) superior organization.

Resources may be physical or human. Physical resources include money, goods, and property. They give a person the power to buy what he wants, and enable him to command the services of others. Human resources that give power include intelligence, knowledge, skill, prestige, social position, bravery, and personal charm or beauty. Such qualities become a source of power when they enable a person to lead, influence, or control other persons.

Power in numbers can be seen in elections which give the winners the authority to make decisions for the group. But numbers are not all-important. Inferior numbers can exercise power when they have control of important resources, such as the military.

Superior numbers and resources do not by themselves give a person a high degree of power over others. People must know how to use their resources effectively. They do this through organization. Individuals alone have relatively little power to affect important decisions. But by joining together in some kind of organization, they can become powerful. Political parties, pressure groups, and other associations attempt to gain power through social organization. Countries also join together to consolidate power. International power groups include the European Economic Community (EEC) and the Organization of American States (OAS).

Systems of Power. Power relationships occur in all societies and organized groups. There are important differences in how private and public power systems enforce their decisions. The leaders of private groups—such as businesses and clubs—can fine, suspend, and even expel dissenting members. But only public power systems—that is, governments—can legally use physical force, including imprisonment. Governments control the police and the military, the chief agents of force. This monopoly of force makes control of the state an important source of power.

The social organization that enables certain people to govern in all the organized groups of a community or society makes up the *power structure.* Sometimes, the most powerful persons are referred to as *the Establishment,* or the *power elite.*   WOLF HEYDEBRAND

POWER, in arithmetic, is the product of a number multiplied by itself a specified number of times. For example, $3 \times 3 \times 3 \times 3 \times 3$ is called the fifth power of 3, and is written 3^5. In 3^5, the number 3 is called the *base* and 5 is called the *exponent.* The second and third powers of a number are called its *square* and its *cube* (see CUBE; SQUARE). The first power of a number is the number itself. For example, 3^1 is 3. The operation of finding the power of a number is known as *involution* in mathematics (see INVOLUTION).   HOWARD W. EVES

POWER OF ATTORNEY is a legal, written document. The signer of the document appoints an agent or attorney who has the power to act for the signer. When a power of attorney is officially recorded, it must generally be certified by a notary public.

The power of attorney is especially useful to persons who are ill and unable to conduct their own affairs, or to persons who must be away from home for a long time. In times of war, many members of the armed forces make out a power of attorney to someone at home. This is especially true of those who leave civilian business to the management of friends and relatives.

A *general* power of attorney permits the agent to act for the signer in all circumstances. A *special* power of attorney permits the agent to do only those things which the signer lists in the document. The death of the signer usually voids the power of attorney.   THOMAS A. COWAN

POWER PLANT is any system that generates power. Many systems and fuels can be used. The systems may be divided into two main groups—transportation power plants and stationary power plants.

Transportation Power Plants run automobiles, buses, trucks, airplanes, locomotives, and other vehicles. The internal-combustion engine ranks as the most widely used transportation power plant. Automobiles use gasoline engines. But most large trucks and buses, and many modern locomotives, use diesel engines that burn oil as a fuel. Many airplanes are powered by internal-combustion engines similar to those used in automobiles. But the gas-turbine jet engine is rapidly replacing the piston engine in commercial and military aircraft. The power plants of ships are divided between steam turbines and diesel engines.

Stationary Power Plants, or *power stations,* are used chiefly to generate large amounts of power, such as electricity. Plants that produce electric power are usually operated by either steam turbines or water turbines. Steam-turbine plants burn coal or oil as fuel to change water into steam. But internal-combustion engines are also used. Atomic power plants have also come into use to produce electricity and to power submarines and other vehicles. Atomic power plants use nuclear fuel to generate high-pressure steam.   SAMUEL SEELY

Related Articles in WORLD BOOK include:

Airplane (Engines)	Electric Power	Power
Atomic Energy	Gasoline Engine	Rocket
Atomic Reactor	Horsepower	Solar Energy
Automobile	Hydraulic Engine	Steam Engine
(The Engine)	Jet Propulsion	Turbine
Diesel Engine	Locomotive	Water Power

POWER SHOVEL. See BUILDING AND WRECKING MACHINES; MINING (picture: A Giant Power Shovel).

POWER STATION. See POWER PLANT (Stationary Power Plants).

POWERS, HIRAM (1805-1873), an American sculptor, became noted for his statues of many famous Americans, including Benjamin Franklin, George Washington, and Daniel Webster. His most famous work probably is the *Greek Slave,* because of its purity of treatment and beauty of form. His works also include *Eve Repentant* and *Proserpine.* Powers was born in Woodstock, Vt. He worked for years in a wax-works museum. In 1837 he moved to Florence, Italy. See also EVERETT, EDWARD (picture).   JEAN LIPMAN

POWHATAN, *POW huh TAN* (?-1618), was the Indian chief in the romantic story about John Smith and Pocahontas. Powhatan was ready to kill Smith when Pocahontas, the Indian's daughter, stopped him and saved Smith's life. No one knows if this story is true. Powhatan is also famous for building the Powhatan Confederacy of Indian tribes (see POWHATAN INDIANS).

Powhatan was at first friendly toward the English settlers of Virginia at Jamestown. But the settlers' demands finally angered him, and he became hostile. He fought the white men until 1614, when Pocahontas married John Rolfe, an Englishman. He then became friendly and helped the settlers until his death.

His real name was *Wahunsonacock,* but he was called Powhatan after his favorite village. This village stood on the north bank of the James River just east of present-day Richmond, Va.   E. ADAMSON HOEBEL

See also POCAHONTAS; SMITH, JOHN.

POWHATAN INDIANS formed a small but important tribe of eastern North America. They controlled the Powhatan Confederacy of Virginia, which once included 30 different tribes totaling about 9,000 persons. The confederacy occupied much of what became the colony and state of Virginia. The chief of the Powhatan tribe headed the confederacy. A famous chief, Wahunsonacock, was also known as Powhatan (see POWHATAN). The first permanent English settlement in North America was made among these Indians.

The customs of the Powhatan resembled those of other tribes along the eastern coast (see INDIAN, AMERICAN [Eastern Forests Indians]). They worshiped animal spirits, especially the Great Hare (creator).

The Powhatan often clashed with the settlers, particularly under Opechancanough, who was believed to be Chief Powhatan's brother (see INDIAN WARS [Colonial Days]). The tribe died out, but during the middle 1900's several hundred Indians in Virginia and Delaware formed a revived Confederacy.   WILLIAM H. GILBERT

POZNAŃ, *PAWZ nahn* (pop. 429,300; alt. 292 ft.), is a Polish city on the Warta River, about 175 miles

Eastfoto

Poznań's City Hall, with its fine council chamber, is considered one of the most beautiful Renaissance buildings in Europe.

west of Warsaw (see POLAND [map]). Located in the rich farmlands of western Poland, Poznań is a leading producer of agricultural implements. It also manufactures aircraft, automobile bodies, and furniture. International fairs are held in Poznań every year in June. The city is also an important educational center. Anti-Communist riots in Poznań made world headlines in June, 1956.   M. KAMIL DZIEWANOWSKI

POZNAŃ is a political division of Poland that extends over a fertile agricultural area. Poznań has a population of over 2 million and covers an area of about 10,000 square miles. Its chief cities, Gniezno and Pila, produce farm implements, wood products, and textiles. The city of Poznań forms a separate political division.

Poznań was a part of the kingdom of Poland, established in the 900's. Taken by Prussia in the Polish partition of 1793, it became the grand duchy of Posen. Napoleon conquered the grand duchy in 1807. The Congress of Vienna returned the area to Prussia after Napoleon's defeat in 1814. Poznań remained under Prussian control until the Russians invaded it during World War I. At the close of the war, Poznań became part of the new Polish republic. In World War II, first German troops and then Russian troops invaded and occupied Poznań. Since World War II, Poznań has been a part of Poland.   M. KAMIL DZIEWANOWSKI

PPG INDUSTRIES. See GLASS (Leading Companies).

PRADO. See MADRID (Famous Buildings).

PRADO Y UGARTECHE, MANUEL. See PERU (The 1900's).

PRAETOR, *PREE tur*, was a law official in ancient Rome. Citizens brought complaints before the praetor. He decided which complaints were justified, and assigned them to judges for trial. When a praetor took office, he issued an *edict* (public order) stating how he would interpret the law in granting trials. Each new praetor generally copied or improved upon the successful edicts of earlier praetors. In that way, praetors helped to build the Roman legal system, which in turn influenced many of the legal systems used today. Praetors also served as governors of Roman provinces, and later they presided over criminal courts.

The office of praetor was created in 367 B.C. The number of praetors was increased to two in 242 B.C., and eventually increased to 16.   FRANK C. BOURNE

See also LAW (Law in Ancient Rome).

PRAETORIAN GUARD, *pre TOH rih un*, was the personal guard of the Roman emperors. Until the reign of Septimius Severus (A.D. 193-211), only soldiers recruited in Italy could serve in the guard. Septimius opened the guard to soldiers from all the Roman legions throughout the empire.

Emperor Augustus made the praetorians a standing army. He divided them into nine *cohorts* (groups) of a thousand men each. Three cohorts remained in Rome, and the others were stationed in nearby cities. Members received much higher pay than other soldiers. They became so powerful they could overthrow emperors whenever they chose. Emperor Constantine finally abolished the guard in A.D. 312.   FRANK C. BOURNE

See also ROMAN EMPIRE (The Army).

PRAETORIUS, MICHAEL (1571-1621), a German composer of church music, became known also as a music historian. Praetorius wrote *Syntagma Musicum* (1615-1620), in which he named and described musical instruments known to the 1600's, and gave a historical account of church music of the period. His compositions include many motets, madrigals, dance pieces, and two books of hymns. Praetorius was born in Kreuzberg, Thuringia, Germany.   WARREN S. FREEMAN

PRAGMATIC SANCTION

PRAGMATIC SANCTION. The emperor of the Holy Roman Empire could issue two kinds of decrees that had the force of law. If anyone asked the emperor to say the final word on a disputed point of law, he issued an *imperial rescript*. If the emperor, without being asked, wished to set forth a law in the interest of the state, he issued a decree called *pragmatica sanctio*. These two Latin words mean *a decree based on wise statecraft*.

The most important pragmatic sanction was issued by Emperor Charles VI in 1713. At that time, German law required rulers to pass their property on to their oldest male heirs. But Charles had no male heirs. By issuing a pragmatic sanction, he gave himself permission to settle his estates on his oldest daughter. In this way, Charles hoped to prevent other powers from dividing the empire. Several countries agreed to observe his pragmatic sanction. But they broke their pledges after Charles died, beginning the War of the Austrian Succession. ROBERT G. L. WAITE

See also MARIA THERESA; SUCCESSION WARS.

PRAGMATISM is the philosophy that an idea must be judged by how it works, rather than by how it looks or sounds. William James, who is often called the founder of pragmatism, once said that it was "a new name for old ways of thinking." The pragmatist believes that nothing is "self-evident." To him, an idea is true if it works and false if it does not work. Pragmatism has been called a peculiarly American philosophy.

According to pragmatism, we cannot judge any idea true or false simply by looking at it. We consider a proposition true so long as it proves effective in linking the past and future, and in organizing present experience to our satisfaction. An idea may thus be true under certain circumstances but false under others.

For example, astronomers have always had to explain the apparent motions of the sun and the planets. For more than 2,000 years, the ideas of the Ptolemaic system explained these apparent motions in ways that seemed satisfactory. But, as observation continued, the earth-centered universe of the Ptolemaic system became clumsy and complicated. The Copernican idea that the earth and the planets revolved around the sun seemed more promising. Kepler and Newton worked this idea into a system that explained the movements more simply. Later, astronomers made observations that could not be explained by Newton's ideas. The theory of relativity was found to be more satisfactory.

Most persons would say that the theories of Ptolemy were proved false and replaced by the Copernican view, which later proved false in its turn. But a pragmatist would say that both the Ptolemaic and the Copernican theories were *true* until they failed to work.

Pragmatism is often misunderstood to mean that any idea is true if it enables a person to get what he wants. Thus, a delusion of grandeur might give a person great confidence in himself, and enable him to dominate others and accomplish his purposes. Benito Mussolini seems to have had some such conception. But the American philosophers who gave form to the doctrines of pragmatism—William James, Charles Peirce, and John Dewey—said nothing to justify this interpretation. They claimed that an idea could be said to "work" only when actions based upon it resulted in the predicted results.

Pragmatism may be considered as the logic that lies behind scientific method. When the emphasis is laid not upon *how* we think, but on the fact that all the thinking we know of is done by many different human beings, pragmatism is known as *humanism*. The humanism of the philosopher F. C. S. Schiller may be considered the English version of pragmatism. GOODWIN WATSON

See also DEWEY, JOHN; JAMES, WILLIAM; PEIRCE, CHARLES SANDERS.

PRAGUE, *prahg* (pop. 1,014,254; alt. 575 ft.), is the capital of Czechoslovakia. It is called PRAHA (pronounced *PRAH hah*) in the Czech and Slovak languages. The city lies along both banks of the Vltava (Moldau) River, about 150 miles northwest of Vienna. Many bridges span the river. For location, see CZECHOSLOVAKIA (color map).

Palaces and public buildings line the banks of the Vltava. Their colorful towers make the city look like one great cathedral. The Old Town square, on the east bank of the Vltava, is the historic center of Prague. Some of Prague's most historic monuments stand in this square. The Old Town Hall, built in 1381, is at one side. On another side stands the famous Tyn Church. Its ancient spires can be seen from every part of the city. The Powder Tower, built about 1475, re-

Owen, Black Star

Prague's Charles Bridge, with its fortress tower, was built in the 1300's. The statues lining the bridge were added later.

mains an entrance gate to the old city. A monument to John Huss, a religious reformer and former rector of Charles (Prague) University, stands in Old Town square (see HUSS, JOHN). The royal tombs of 1589 are in the St. Vitus Cathedral, founded in 1344. The center of the modern city of Prague is Wenceslaus Square.

Its Institutions. Prague has been an important cultural center since the 1300's. The city is the home of Charles University, founded by Emperor Charles IV in 1348. It also has two polytechnic institutes, a famous music conservatory, and an academy of art. Prague also has many industrial plants. Factories and mills produce railway cars, leather goods, textiles, chemicals, flour, and beer. Czechoslovakia is a rich sugar country, and many sugar products are sold in Prague.

Prague is one of the oldest cities in central Europe. Relics of Roman times, and a Jewish graveyard dating from the 600's, are within its limits. Italian architects were brought to Prague in the 1600's. They built many elaborate castles and churches, some of which still stand. The Waldstein Palace is perhaps the best known of these buildings. Among the many other famous buildings in Prague are Czernin Palace and St. Nicholas Church.

History. The city was founded by German settlers in 759, and Princess Libussa ruled the inhabitants for many years. In the 900's, the city took on new importance under the rule of the Duke of Bohemia, Saint Wenceslaus.

In 1424, the followers of John Huss, or Hussites, conquered Prague. After the Thirty Years' War (1618-1648), the city fell under the control of Hapsburg emperors. The Hapsburgs ruled Prague for almost 300 years, until the end of World War I. Prague became largely a German city. In 1848, Prague was the scene of an unsuccessful revolt against the Hapsburgs. During the last half of the 1800's and the early 1900's, many rural people moved to Prague. They restored the original Slavic character of the city. After World War I, Prague became the capital of the independent Republic of Czechoslovakia.

When the Nazis annexed the republic in 1939, Prague became the capital of the German protectorate of Bohemia and Moravia. After World War II, Prague was made the capital of the communist-dominated Czechoslovak People's Republic.   M. KAMIL DZIEWANOWSKI

See also CZECHOSLOVAKIA (picture, Prague).

PRAGUE, TREATY OF. See SEVEN WEEKS' WAR.

PRAIA, *PRI uh* (pop. 9,880), is the capital and chief city of Portugal's Cape Verde Islands. It is a seaport on the southeastern coast of Santiago, the largest of the Cape Verde Islands. Praia serves as a trading center for the islands.

See also CAPE VERDE ISLANDS.

PRAIRIE, *PRAIR ih*, is the term for any broad stretch of flat land covered with grass. It comes from the French word meaning *extensive meadow*. Prairies are sometimes called *grasslands*. The surface of prairie regions is not so level as that of plains. Low hills and shallow river valleys often relieve the flatness of prairies. Prairie regions commonly lie 300 to 1,500 feet above sea level. Prairie land is usually fertile. It is usually covered by coarse grass, with few trees except where it is cultivated. Most of the soil is suited to the growing of grain and hay.

The Mississippi and Ohio river valleys are prairies.

Illinois is often called the "Prairie State." But most of the land in western Ohio, Indiana, Missouri, Iowa, Wisconsin, and part of Minnesota is also prairie. In Canada, Alberta, Manitoba, and Saskatchewan are called the "Prairie Provinces."   ERNEST L. THURSTON

See also PLAIN.

PRAIRIE CHICKEN is a member of the grouse family. It lives on central and western plains of the United States. It is about 18 inches long and weighs about two pounds. Its feathers are yellowish brown and white above, crossed with black bars, and white and brown barred below. The head of the prairie chicken is deep buff with brown stripes.

This grouse is famous for its unusual courtship habits. The male bird erects the feather tufts on his neck, spreads and raises his tail, and stretches out his wings and allows them to droop. He inflates two pouches on the side of his throat with air and makes a hollow booming noise. He also leaps about and dances during the courtship period. It is an excellent game bird.

Several races or subspecies of this bird are recognized by scientists. The greater prairie chicken, described above, now lives from Michigan and Indiana westward to the Great Plains. It once lived as far east as Pennsylvania but is now greatly reduced in numbers. The lesser prairie chicken lives in the southern part of the Central Plains area, from Kansas to Texas. Atwater's prairie chicken on the coast of Texas is now nearing extinction. A fourth race, called the heath hen, has already become extinct.

Scientific Classification. The prairie chicken belongs to the family *Tetraonidae*. It is genus *Tympanuchus*, species *T. cupido*.   JOSEPH J. HICKEY

See also BIRD (color picture, Game Birds); GROUSE.

PRAIRIE DOG is a member of the ground-squirrel family. It received its name because it has a shrill bark much like that of a dog. It lives in the western part of North America, from Canada to Mexico.

The prairie dog is a sturdy animal, about a foot long. Its short, coarse fur is grayish brown in color. It has small beady eyes, short legs, pouched cheeks, and a short, flat tail. The prairie dog is strong and makes a good pet.

A Watchful Prairie Dog, *left,* keeps guard at the entrance to its burrow. If an enemy approaches, it barks loudly to warn other prairie dogs, and then rushes to safety in its home, *right,* deep in the ground. A mound of dirt at the entrance keeps out rain water.
James Simon, Western Ways

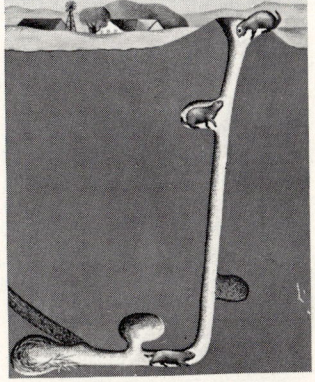

PRAIRIE PIGEON

The prairie dog lives in a community with other prairie dogs. It builds its home by digging a tunnel straight downward for 12 feet or more. At the bottom of the tunnel it hollows out several rooms—a sleeping room, a room for storing food, and other rooms. At the entrance to the hole, the prairie dog makes a mound of earth that keeps water from entering its home. The prairie dog spends the winter in its home, but often comes out on sunny days when the wind is not blowing. If an enemy, such as a coyote, should come into sight, the prairie dogs warn each other with loud chirps or barks. Then they rush into their homes deep underground, where they are out of danger. The prairie dog has enemies such as the rattlesnake and burrowing owl that live in vacant burrows in the ground.

The prairie dog is a serious pest to farmers and cattle raisers in the West, because it eats grasses and roots, and because it digs open burrows. A running horse or cow that steps into one of these holes may break a leg. The prairie dog is especially fond of alfalfa and grain. At one time, large numbers of prairie dogs lived in the western part of the United States but the prairie dog population has been reduced greatly. Millions of these animals are killed through poisoned food and poison gases.

Scientific Classification. Prairie dogs belong to the squirrel family, *Sciuridae*. The black-tailed prairie dog is genus *Cynomys*, species *C. ludovicianus*. The white-tailed prairie dog is *C. leucurus*.   THEODORE H. EATON, JR.

See also ANIMAL (color picture: Animals of the Grasslands); GOPHER; RODENT; SQUIRREL.

PRAIRIE PIGEON. See FRANKLIN'S GULL.

PRAIRIE PROVINCES is the name given to the three Canadian provinces of Alberta, Saskatchewan, and Manitoba. These prairie lands form the most northern section of the Great Plains region of North America.

The Prairie Provinces cover a total of 757,985 square miles between British Columbia and Ontario in western Canada. They contain the only large tracts of prairie land in Canada.

See also ALBERTA; MANITOBA; SASKATCHEWAN.

PRAIRIE SCHOONER. See PIONEER LIFE IN AMERICA (The Wagon Train).

PRAIRIE STATE. See ILLINOIS.

PRAIRIE VIEW AGRICULTURAL AND MECHANICAL COLLEGE is a state-controlled, coeducational land-grant college at Prairie View, Tex., founded in 1876. It is a part of Texas A&M University System. Courses in arts and science, agriculture, and mechanics lead to bachelor's and master's degrees. For enrollment, see UNIVERSITIES AND COLLEGES (table [Texas A&M University System]).

PRAJADHIPOK. See THAILAND (After World War I).

PRASAD, RAJENDRA (1884-1963), became president of the Republic of India in 1950. As a follower of Mohandas Gandhi, Prasad served four times as president of the Indian National Congress. He joined the non-cooperation movement in 1920, and served several prison terms for his nationalist activities. A believer in the simple life, he encouraged the revival of village handicrafts.

Prasad was born in the province of Bihar, India, and was graduated from Presidency College, Calcutta. Prasad was a college professor and judge, and also wrote books on Indian history and studies of Mohandas Gandhi.   RICHARD L. PARK

PRASEODYMIUM, *PRAY zee oh DIM ih um* (chemical symbol, Pr), is one of the rare-earth elements. Its atomic number is 59, and its atomic weight is 140.907. German chemist C. F. Auer von Welsbach first discovered praseodymium in 1885, when he separated salts of the so-called element didymium into praseodymium and neodymium. The name *praseodymium* comes from the Greek word *prasios*, meaning *leek-green*, since the element occurred in the green fraction, or part, of didymium. Praseodymium is best separated from the other rare earths by ion-exchange processes (see RARE EARTH).

Praseodymium melts at 935° C., and boils at 3127° C. It makes a useful alloy, especially in *misch metal* (a mixture of rare earths). Praseodymium oxide is a black powder that dissolves in acid to form green solutions or green salts. These praseodymium salts are used in the ceramics industry for coloring glasses and for glazing.   FRANK H. SPEDDING

See also ELEMENT, CHEMICAL (table).

PRATIQUE. See BILL OF HEALTH.

PRATT, EDWIN JOHN. See CANADIAN LITERATURE (Poetry of the 1900's).

PRATT INSTITUTE is a privately controlled, professional school in New York City. It is coeducational and nonsectarian. Pratt Institute offers programs in art, architecture, engineering, fashion, food science and management, humanities, science, and social science. Pratt Institute also has a graduate library school. Courses lead to bachelor's and master's degrees. Pratt Institute was founded in 1887. For its enrollment, see UNIVERSITIES AND COLLEGES (table).

PRAVDA. See RUSSIA (Communication).

PRAWN. See SHRIMP.

PRAXITELES, *praks IT uh leez*, was the greatest Greek sculptor of the 300's B.C. He worked in marble, and excelled in portraying the human form. His statues show youthful gods full of grace and the joy of life. Their bodies are relaxed and beautiful. The figures stand with one hip thrust out, a pose that became known as "the S-curve of Praxiteles." The faces have a dreamy look.

The Satyr by Praxiteles shows the lifelike style of the ancient Greek sculptor.

The Art Institute of Chicago

Several original works of Praxiteles are still in existence. The most famous of these is the statue at Olympia of the god Hermes carrying the infant Dionysus (see HERMES OF PRAXITELES).

Praxiteles' special skill lay in his mastery of surface finish, so that it suggested actual flesh, hair, or cloth. A photographer once mistook the marble robe of Hermes for a dust-cloth, and asked that it be removed before he took the picture.   H. LLOYD STOW

PRAYER is a form of worship in which a person may offer devotion, thanks, confession, or supplication to his God. Some persons kneel while they pray. Others sit, stand, or lie on the ground. Prayers differ according to the faith. Roman Catholics may pray to saints or the Virgin Mary as well as to God.

See also ISLAM (pictures); LORD'S PRAYER.

PRAYER BOOK is a collection of prayers in printed form for use at private devotions or public services. A well-known prayer book is the *Book of Common Prayer* used by the Church of England. It contains church doctrine, ordinances, and forms for the sacraments, as well as prayers. It first appeared during the Reformation. The Episcopal Church in America uses the prayer book in a revised form. Prayers and devotions of the Roman Catholic Church are contained in books called the *breviary* and the *missal*.   BERNARD RAMM

See also BREVIARY; MISSAL.

PRAYER RUG. See RUGS AND CARPETS (Prayer Rugs).

PRAYER WHEEL is a wheel or cylinder hung in a place of worship and turned by the worshiper in making his prayer. The type found today in some Tibetan Buddhist temples is a cylinder with a prayer or other sacred writing inscribed on it. Turning the wheel is supposed to have the effect of repeating the prayer. Similar wheels were used in ancient Egyptian and Greek temples and some early Christian churches.

PRAYING MANTIS. See MANTID.

PREACHER BIRD. See VIREO.

PREACHING FRIARS. See DOMINICAN.

PREAMBLE. See GOVERNMENT (The U.S. Constitution); UNITED NATIONS (The Preamble to the United Nations Charter).

PREBLE, EDWARD (1761-1807), an American naval officer, bombarded the Barbary pirates at Tripoli (now in Libya) in 1804. He was assigned in 1803 to command a squadron sent to the Mediterranean Sea to protect American ships and seamen from the pirates. After the pirates captured the frigate *Philadelphia* at Tripoli, he sent Stephen Decatur on a spectacular sneak mission to destroy it (see DECATUR, STEPHEN). Preble obtained light gunboats at Naples, Italy, and conducted a spirited bombardment of Tripoli.

Preble was born in Portland, Maine. He ran away to sea at 16, and served with the Massachusetts state navy during the Revolutionary War. He trained many officers who later became famous in the War of 1812, including Stephen Decatur, Thomas MacDonough and David Porter.   RICHARD S. WEST, JR.

PRE-CAMBRIAN TIME is the term for all geological time before the Cambrian period. See ICE AGE.

PRECEDENT. See LAW (Common Law).

PRECEPTORIAL SYSTEM. See WILSON, WOODROW (University President).

PRECESSION. See GYROSCOPE (Gyroscopic Forces).

PRECESSION OF THE EQUINOXES. See EQUINOX.

PRECINCT. See POLITICAL PARTY (Precinct Committeemen); VOTING (Voting Districts).

PRECIOUS METALS are those metals that jewelers consider most valuable, such as gold, silver, platinum, and palladium. See JEWELRY.

PRECIOUS STONE. See GEM.

PRECIPITATION. See HAIL; RAIN; SLEET; SNOW; WEATHER.

PRECIPITATOR. See AIR CLEANER.

PRÉCIS, *PRAY see,* or *pray SEE,* is a kind of brief and pointed summary of a book, article, or legal case, covering the essential points.

PREDESTINATION, in Christian theology, is a doctrine which sets forth the belief that the eternal destiny of man is determined by God. The word comes from the Latin, and means *determined beforehand*. Belief in predestination is based on Paul's words (Rom. 8:28-30). Saint Augustine (A.D. 354-430) and Saint Thomas Aquinas led in developing the doctrine. John Calvin later emphasized it.

A belief in some form of predestination is found also in the ancient religions of Greece, China, India, and Egypt. Islam teaches that men are predestined to goodness and happiness, also to evil and misery.

See also CALVIN, JOHN; FOREORDINATION.

PREDICATE. See SENTENCE (Parts of a Sentence).

PRE-EMPTION is the act of buying something ahead of other persons, or the right to do so. The term comes from two Latin words, *emptio*, which means *buying*, and *pre*, which means *before*.

Pre-emption had special meaning in the United States during the 1800's. People called *squatters* moved into unsettled areas and built on land they did not own. Real-estate speculators called *claim-jumpers* often worked with lawyers to take away the squatters' land.

Beginning about 1800, Congress granted the right of pre-emption to some squatters. In 1841, Congress passed a pre-emption law that applied to all squatters. A squatter who lived on surveyed government land and made improvements on it had the right to buy that land before anyone else could do so. When the land he occupied was offered for sale, he could buy up to 160 acres of it for $1.25 an acre.

A person who already owned as much as 320 acres of land could not get more by pre-emption. A married woman living with her husband could not get any land by pre-emption, and neither could a person who moved from his residence to another part of the same state.

After the Civil War, big land companies sent out "dummy" settlers, who filed applications for land which they did not intend to keep as their own. In return for a cash payment from a land company, a dummy settler would file his claim, live on it for six months, buy it for an absurdly low price, and hand it over to his employer. Then he would file another claim.

Congress finally abolished the system of pre-emption in 1891. During the years in which pre-emption was in force, about 200 million acres of land passed from the government to private owners.   RICHARD HOFSTADTER

See also HOMESTEAD ACT; PUBLIC LANDS; SQUATTER'S RIGHTS; TYLER, JOHN (Tyler's Accomplishments).

PREFABRICATION. See BUILDING CONSTRUCTION; HOUSE (picture, Building a Prefabricated House).

PREFACE. See BOOK (Parts of a Book).

PREFECT, *PRE feckt,* is the chief civil administrator of a French department (see DEPARTMENT). His duties are similar to those of a state governor in the United States. But French prefects are not elected. They are appointed by the Minister of the Interior.

PREFERRED STOCK. See STOCK, CAPITAL.

PREFIX. See SPELLING (Spelling Rules).

PREGNANCY. See GESTATION; EMBRYO.

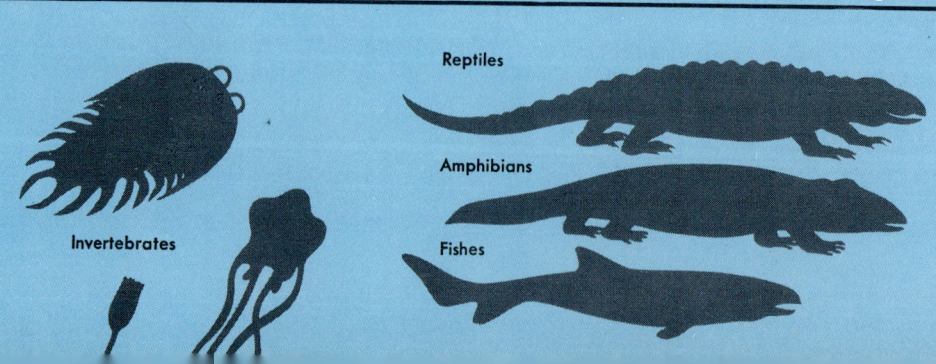

Huge Dinosaurs Battled to the Death in prehistoric swamps. The meat-eating *Allosaurus*, right, preyed on the huge, plant-eating *Brontosaurus*, left, millions of years before man appeared.

PREHISTORIC ANIMAL

	PALEOZOIC						
ERAS	Began 600,000,000 years ago			375,000,000 years long			
PERIODS	CAMBRIAN	ORDOVICIAN	SILURIAN	DEVONIAN	MISSISSIPPIAN	PENNSYLVANIAN	PERMIAN
	Began 600,000,000 years ago	Began 480,000,000 years ago	Began 435,000,000 years ago	Began 405,000,000 years ago	Began 345,000,000 years ago	Began 310,000,000 years ago	Began 275,000,000 years ago
	120,000,000 years long	45,000,000 years long	30,000,000 years long	60,000,000 years long	35,000,000 years long	35,000,000 years long	50,000,000 years long

EPOCHS

Reptiles

Amphibians

Invertebrates

Fishes

PREHISTORIC ANIMAL is any animal that lived before man learned to write, about 5,000 years ago. Prehistoric animals ranged in size from tiny, one-celled animals called protozoans to huge, awkward dinosaurs. Some prehistoric animals looked much like the animals of today. Others were completely different from any animals now alive. All prehistoric animals did not live at the same time.

Scientists who study prehistoric animals are called *paleontologists*. They learn about ancient animals from *fossils*. Fossils are shells, bones, and other traces of animals and plants buried in rocks. Fossils of prehistoric animals tell scientists where the animals lived and what they were like. Scientists believe animals have lived on earth more than 600 million years.

Animals Through the Ages

The farther back we go in time, the dimmer the record of fossils becomes. It quickly fades about 600 million years ago, at the beginning of what geologists call the Cambrian Period. Paleontologists know that life existed 3,100,000,000 years ago. But fossils found in rocks formed before the Cambrian Period are mostly *algae* (simple plants). See ALGAE.

The fossil record shows that animals changed slowly through the ages. The record has many gaps, but scientists can set up series of related animals showing the way they developed. The evidence from fossils supports the theory of evolution. This theory states that animals and plants changed through time, and that living things are the much-changed descendants of ancestors that lived long ago. See EVOLUTION.

The Earliest Animals. The oldest known fossils of animals were formed by *invertebrates*, or animals without backbones. Some of these animals resembled jellyfish, sponges, snails, clams, worms, and other invertebrates that live today. The prehistoric invertebrates

Samuel Paul Welles, the contributor of this article, is Lecturer and Principal Museum Paleontologist at the University of California, Berkeley; and the coauthor of From Bones to Bodies.

lived in the ocean waters. They left fossils in rocks formed in the Cambrian Period. The most common animals of this period were flat shellfish called *trilobites* (see TRILOBITE). They were the first *arthropods*, animals with jointed legs, to become common.

Animals with Backbones are called *vertebrates* (see VERTEBRATE). They probably first appeared about 450 million years ago. The oldest forms were small armored animals called *ostracoderms* (shell-skinned). They resembled fish, but lacked jaws. Their mouths were only small holes or slits that could not open wide. The early vertebrates swam in the water and fed on soft decaying material or on tiny plants and animals. They breathed through gills, as do present-day fish (see GILL).

Gradually, fish developed jaws. By the Devonian Period, which began about 405 million years ago, fish with jaws were fairly numerous. They had a great advantage over their jawless ancestors. They could bite and eat other animals. Many Devonian fish developed

— INTERESTING FACTS ABOUT PREHISTORIC ANIMALS —

Dinosaur Eggs were first discovered in Mongolia in 1923 by scientists of the American Museum of Natural History.

Earliest Known Bird, *Archaeopteryx*, looked like a dinosaur with feathers. It had teeth and a long tail.

Earliest Known Horse, *Hyracotherium*, was about the size of a small dog. It is also called *Eohippus*.

Largest Flesh-Eating Animal that ever lived was the dinosaur *Tyrannosaurus*. It stood almost 20 feet high and grew 45 feet long.

Largest Four-Footed Animal that ever lived was the dinosaur *Brachiosaurus*. It held its head 38 feet in the air, grew about 70 feet long, and weighed about 85 tons.

Largest Flying Reptile, *Pteranodon*, had a wingspread of 40 feet, about the length of a trailer truck.

Longest Neck of any animal was that of the dinosaur *Brachiosaurus*. This animal's neck had 13 bones, and measured 28 feet, 8 inches long.

Oldest Known Egg, laid about 270 million years ago, is that of a primitive mammal-like reptile.

Smallest Dinosaur, *Compsognathus*, was about the size of a chicken. Its skull was only 3 inches long.

MESOZOIC			CENOZOIC		
Began 225,000,000 years ago 160,000,000 years long			Began 65,000,000 years ago		65,000,000 years long
TRIASSIC	JURASSIC	CRETACEOUS	TERTIARY		QUATERNARY
Began 225,000,000 years ago 45,000,000 years long	Began 180,000,000 years ago 50,000,000 years long	Began 130,000,000 years ago 65,000,000 years long	Began 65,000,000 years ago 61,500,000 years long		Began 3,500,000 years ago 3,500,000 years long

Dinosaurs

PALEOCENE	EOCENE	OLIGOCENE	MIOCENE	PLIOCENE	PLEISTOCENE	RECENT
Began 65,000,000 years ago 10,000,000 years long	Began 55,000,000 years ago 15,000,000 years long	Began 40,000,000 years ago 14,000,000 years long	Began 26,000,000 years ago 12,000,000 years long	Began 14,000,000 years ago 10,500,000 years long	Began 3,500,000 years ago 3,500,000 years long	Began 10-25,000 years ago 10-25,000 years long

Mammals

PREHISTORIC ANIMALS

Archaeopteryx
1½ feet long
wingspread 2 feet

Rhamphorhynchus
wingspread 2 feet

Dimetrodon
10 feet long

Diplodocus
87 feet long

Eryops
5 feet long

Trilobite
2 inches long

Allosaurus
34 feet long

Eurypterus
8 to 10 inches long

Ammonite
2 inches to 6 feet across

Crossopterygian
2 feet long

Pteranodon
wingspread 40 feet

Hyaenodon
4 feet long

Ichthyornis
8 inches long

Mammoth
9 feet high at the shoulder

Smilodon
6 feet long

Teleoceras
10 feet long

Hyracotherium (Eohippus)
1 foot high at the shoulder

Ichthyosaurus
6 to 30 feet long

Archelon
12 feet long

Elasmosaurus
40 feet long

Walter Ferguson

bony armor for protection. Ancestors of sharks and ray-finned fish also appeared during this period.

Some Devonian fishes had lungs as well as gills. A few fishes developed such efficient lungs that they could breathe air. These early *lungfish* closely resembled the lungfish of today (see LUNGFISH).

The ancestors of the first land animals also appeared during the Devonian Period. Certain fish with lungs, called *crossopterygians*, or *lobe-fins*, developed fins that had muscles supported by bones. These fish could use their fins as legs to move about on the bottoms of pools, or to come out on land for a short time. Scientists believe that, through time, fins with muscles and bones developed into the legs of land animals.

The First Land Animals were *amphibians*, the ancestors of present-day frogs, toads, and salamanders (see AMPHIBIAN). The earliest known amphibians lived near the end of the Devonian Period. They had heads and tails much like the crossopterygians. But the early amphibians had legs and feet instead of fins.

The Mississippian Period (about 345 million years ago) and the Pennsylvanian Period came next in the earth's history. Outside the United States these two periods are combined as the Carboniferous Period. Many kinds of amphibians developed during this time. They lived along the shores of steaming swamps. The largest known amphibians were about 15 feet long.

Some of the early amphibians developed into reptiles —the ancestors of modern snakes, lizards, crocodiles, and turtles (see REPTILE). The reptiles of the Pennsylvanian Period (about 310 million years ago) resembled the amphibians in many ways. But they had scaly skin that protected their bodies from drying up, so they could live in dry places. The early reptiles were the first animals to lay eggs with shells. Because of the shell, the reptiles could lay their eggs on land, and the eggs would not dry up.

New kinds of invertebrates appeared at the same time that the first land animals developed. Some of them were *arachnids* like present-day spiders and scorpions (see ARACHNID). These arachnids lived on land. Insects became widespread in the Pennsylvanian Period and reached enormous sizes. Some dragonflies had wingspreads of 2 feet.

During the Permian Period (about 275 million years ago), reptiles developed until they became larger and more powerful than the amphibians, and became rulers of the land. During this period, reptiles called *therapsids* developed. These reptiles resembled mammals in some ways, and scientists believe the therapsids were ancestors of the mammals.

The Age of Dinosaurs began about 200 million years ago, toward the end of the Triassic Period. For about the next 140 million years, dinosaurs dominated the earth. Other animals living at the same time as dinosaurs included invertebrates, fish, amphibians, sea reptiles, flying reptiles, birds, and mammals.

Dinosaurs were the most spectacular land animals that ever lived. Huge plant-eating dinosaurs lived in swamps and along seashores. The largest of these great reptiles, *Brachiosaurus*, weighed as much as 85 tons and grew about 70 feet long. Tender plants provided the huge amount of food needed by the plant-eating dinosaurs. Their worst enemies were large *carnivorous*, or flesh-eating, dinosaurs. *Duck-billed* dinosaurs with wide mouths and webbed feet lived near the water. *Stegosaurs* were protected by armored plates. *Ankylosaurs* had heavy armor that made them look like living tanks. *Ceratopsians* had up to five horns on their heads. For a more complete description of the dinosaurs, see DINOSAUR.

Invertebrates lived mainly in the oceans. They included protozoans, jellyfish, corals, sponges, worms, snails, and clams. *Ammonites*, or shellfish related to the pearly nautilus, were the most common Mesozoic invertebrates (see NAUTILUS). They had coiled shells. Many different kinds of insects lived on the land.

Fish. The most common fishes in the Age of Dinosaurs were *ray-finned* fish, related to the present-day bowfin and gar (see BOWFIN; GAR). Modern bony fish appeared at the end of the Mesozoic Era.

Amphibians. At the end of the Triassic Period, the more ancient and larger types of amphibians died out. But smaller amphibians, such as frogs, toads, and salamanders, continued through the rest of the Mesozoic Era and into modern times.

Sea Reptiles were of several kinds. *Ichthyosaurs* had fishlike bodies. *Mosasaurs* were gigantic marine lizards, some of which grew 40 feet long. *Plesiosaurs* were huge, broad sea serpents with paddlelike legs. They reached lengths of about 40 feet. Some had short necks, but their skulls measured as much as 9 feet long. Others had short heads, but necks twice as long as their bodies.

Flying Reptiles, called *pterosaurs* or *pterodactyls*, appeared in the Jurassic Period. Some had wings 40 feet across. Others were no larger than robins. Pterosaurs had no feathers. A thin web of skin formed each wing.

Birds appeared at about the same time as the pterosaurs. They looked like small dinosaurs, but their fossils show clear impressions, or prints, of feathers. These ancient birds had teeth and long tails. See ARCHAEOPTERYX.

Mammals lived late in the Mesozoic Era. Scientists know little about the early mammals. They have discovered only a few fossil skulls and jaws of these animals. But they have found thousands of teeth. Most Mesozoic mammals were tiny animals, no bigger than rats, with furry bodies and pointed snouts. The largest grew as big as woodchucks. They were warm-blooded.

The Age of Mammals, or the Cenozoic Era, began at the end of the Mesozoic Era, about 65 million years ago. It continues to the present day. The surface of the earth changed greatly toward the end of the Mesozoic. Mountain ranges rose, and the climate became colder and drier. Shallow oceans drained away and great swamplands dried up. The mammals could adjust to these conditions. But most reptiles could not, and many kinds died out.

The rise of the mountains created new living places. During the Cenozoic Era, many types of mammals developed from the early, small, primitive kinds.

Some plant-eating mammals of the early Cenozoic Era grew almost as large as elephants. The *uintatheres* were clumsy creatures with heavy legs and small brains. They had three pairs of bony projections along the tops of their skulls. Early flesh-eating mammals called *creodonts* had long bodies and short legs.

The small ancestors of many modern mammals, including horses, camels, and *carnivores* (flesh eaters), lived in the early Cenozoic Era. The first horse, *Hyracotherium* (also called *Eohippus*, or *dawn horse*), had four toes on its front feet and three toes on its hind feet. It was about the size of a fox. The first camel, *Protylopus*, was about the same size as *Eohippus*. *Miacis*, a carnivore about as big as a weasel, was an ancestor of such modern carnivores as the dog and cat.

In the middle of the Cenozoic Era, the carnivores began to develop into doglike and catlike animals. Some catlike animals, called *saber-toothed cats*, had a pair of long, strong upper teeth (see SABER-TOOTHED CAT).

About 20 million years ago, the mountains began to wear down and large areas of grassland appeared. Long-faced giant pigs and hornless rhinoceroses roamed the plains. A three-toed horse called *Merychippus*, or *chewing horse*, appeared. It was about the size of a donkey. *Merychippus* had long teeth to grind coarse grasses. Ancestors of the deer first appeared, and mastodons entered America.

Later in the Cenozoic Era, the climate became drier and colder. Relatives of the elephant were numerous. Some of them had long lower jaws and downward-curving tusks. Others, called *shovel-tuskers*, had two flat teeth that stuck straight outward from their lower jaws and broadened into a "scoop shovel" nearly 2 feet wide. Some camels grew about 10 feet tall, or slightly larger than modern camels. They had long legs and long necks. The Pleistocene Epoch, which began about $3\frac{1}{2}$ million years ago and ended in the Ice Age, was the time in which scientists believe prehistoric man developed (see PREHISTORIC MAN). Mammoths and mastodons that looked like hairy elephants lived on the North American plains together with camels, llamas, and one-toed horses (see MAMMOTH; MASTODON). Other animals included giant ground sloths the size of small elephants, and *glyptodonts* with solid shells of bony armor that resembled the armadillo (see GROUND SLOTH). *Smilodon*, the last and largest of the saber-toothed cats, probably terrorized the slow-moving mastodons and sloths. The woolly *coelodont*, a relative of the rhinoceros, lived in the vast prairies of Europe and Asia during the Ice Age. Cave men hunted the giant cave bear, an ancestor of the European brown bear, and drew pictures of it. Many kinds of mammals of the Ice Age still exist today. See ICE AGE.

Determining When Prehistoric Animals Lived

Paleontologists use several methods to learn when prehistoric animals lived. Most fossils form in *sedimentary* rocks, or rocks built up in layers (see ROCK [Organic Sediments]). The oldest fossils usually lie in the deepest layers. The order of the rock layers indicates the order in which the animals developed.

But the rock layers do not tell how long ago an animal lived. To learn this, scientists must find the age of the rocks. In one method, they study the amount of radioactive elements in the rocks (see RADIOGEOLOGY). The rocks containing the oldest fossils known are about 3,100,000,000 years old.

Why Prehistoric Animals Disappeared

Animals became *extinct* (died out) chiefly because the earth changed. Their bodies and habits often could not change fast enough to keep up with the changing conditions. For example, when mountains rose up or seas drained away, the climate and conditions on the earth changed. Animals that could not adapt themselves to the new conditions died out.

Evolutionary changes in other animals appear to have been often responsible for extinction. A plant-eating form may disappear if more efficient competitors for the same food supply have appeared. A flesh-eating animal may become extinct if the animals that it eats become fast enough to escape, or if they die out.

All the animals of one kind did not die out at once. One kind may have disappeared on one continent, but left related survivors on other continents. For example, rhinoceroses vanished from North America, but other rhinoceroses still exist in Africa and Asia. All kinds of animals did not die when conditions changed. Some animals moved to new areas with better conditions. Others adapted themselves to the changes.

Living Fossils

Some large groups of animals have died out, leaving only a few survivors. These survivors have not changed much from their remote ancestors. Scientists call them *living fossils*. They include the king crab, a relative of the scorpion; the *coelacanth*, a kind of crossopterygian; and a lizardlike reptile called the tuatara (see COELACANTH; KING CRAB). These creatures give scientists an opportunity to study the bodies and habits of living animals that closely resemble animals of prehistoric times.

SAMUEL PAUL WELLES

Critically reviewed by ROY CHAPMAN ANDREWS and ALFRED S. ROMER

Related Articles in WORLD BOOK include:

PREHISTORIC ANIMALS

Outline

I. **Animals Through the Ages**
    A. The Earliest Animals C. The First Land Animals
    B. Animals with   D. The Age of Dinosaurs
       Backbones   E. The Age of Mammals
II. **Determining When Prehistoric Animals Lived**
III. **Why Prehistoric Animals Disappeared**
IV. **Living Fossils**

Questions

Why did many prehistoric animals become extinct?

How do we know what prehistoric animals were like?

What kinds of reptiles lived in the Age of Dinosaurs besides the dinosaurs?

When did birds first appear? What were they like?

Why were the crossopterygians important to the development of the vertebrates?

What were the earliest mammals like?

What is a living fossil? Why are living fossils helpful to paleontologists in studying prehistoric animals?

What were the first land animals?

What common animal did the first vertebrate resemble?

Why were bony plates valuable to early fish?

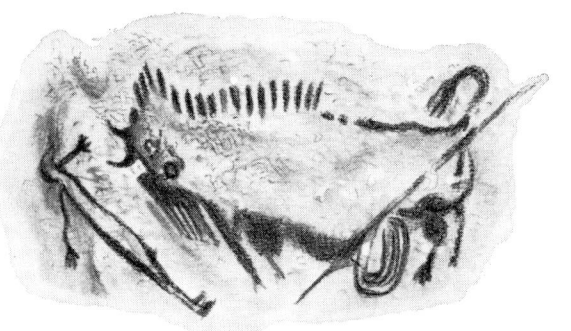

PREHISTORIC MAN

PREHISTORIC MAN. Most scientists believe that man has lived on earth for about one million years. But we have written records of man's history only since about 3000 B.C. The period before man learned to write is called *prehistory*. This prehistoric period was at least 100 times as long as the period of man's recorded history, which began about 5,000 years ago.

Compared with the length of time that life has existed on earth, man is a recent arrival. For a description of early animal life and earth history, see PREHISTORIC ANIMAL; EARTH.

Prehistoric men did not have cities or writing, but they were not apelike creatures without intelligence. They learned to communicate with language; to hunt efficiently; to live in groups; to make fire; and to create useful and beautiful arts and crafts. In time, they cultivated crops, *domesticated* (tamed) animals, and lived in permanent dwellings in villages.

The study of prehistoric men forms part of the science of *anthropology*. Anthropologists work with the skeletal remains of ancient man. They also study primitive men of today whose ways of life resemble those of prehistoric men. Archaeologists try to find things that ancient peoples left behind. These scientists have found comparatively few remains. Their work is like assembling a jigsaw puzzle that lacks many pieces. For this reason, they differ about some details, although they agree on the main points. See ANTHROPOLOGY; ARCHAEOLOGY.

Carleton S. Coon, the contributor of this article, is Research Curator of Anthropology, University Museum, University of Pennsylvania.

Scientists classify the periods of prehistoric cultures on the basis of toolmaking techniques. Early men made their tools of stone, so the entire prehistoric period is usually called the *Stone Age*. Most scholars divide the Stone Age into three main periods: (1) the *Old Stone Age*, or *Paleolithic* period; (2) the *Middle Stone Age*, or *Mesolithic* period; and (3) the *New Stone Age*, or *Neolithic* period. In some isolated parts of the world, almost every stone-toolmaking technique known in the past continued in use into the A.D. 1900's.

The Old Stone Age

The Old Stone Age, or Paleolithic period, corresponds roughly to the Ice Age, which began about a million years ago and ended about 8000 B.C. (see ICE AGE). Men lived in Europe, Africa, and Asia. In late Ice-Age times, they also lived in North America. Scientists divide the Old Stone Age into three eras: the Lower, Middle, and Upper Paleolithic periods.

The *Lower Paleolithic* period began about $1\frac{3}{4}$ million years ago and lasted until about 300,000 years ago. Archaeologists have found three main kinds of tools that are characteristic of this period. *Pebble tools*, the earliest tools known, are oval, water-worn stones with one end split off. *Choppers* are heavy scrapers flaked on one side. Chopping tools, a form of the chopper, are flaked on both sides. *Hand axes*, or *core-biface tools*, are almond-

Cro-Magnon Man lived by hunting. He dressed in animal skins and painted pictures of animals deep within caves. A scene from a cave at Lascaux, France, above, shows a wounded bison charging a hunter. Other animals include a mammoth and a woolly rhinoceros.

Alton S. Tobey

shaped, pointed at one end, and *flaked* (chipped) on both sides.

The *Middle Paleolithic* period, which began about 300,000 years ago, lasted until about 30,000 years ago. People of this period made *flake tools* by striking thin, sharp flakes from large stones.

The *Upper Paleolithic* period began about 30,000 years ago and lasted until the end of the Ice Age. *Blade tools* characterized this period. Craftsmen used stone hammers and punches to strike long, sharp flakes from carefully prepared cores of flint. They shaped the blades into chisels, scrapers, and drills.

Hunting and Gathering. Throughout the Old Stone Age, men got their food by hunting animals and gathering wild plants. Wooden spears were the main weapons. Several men hunted together, some driving the animals forward and others killing the prey from ambush. The women collected berries and seeds, and searched for roots with pointed digging sticks.

Food, Shelter, and Clothing. The first evidence of fire comes from Lower Paleolithic remains in China. People of Middle Paleolithic times probably cooked their food lightly. Animal bones found in sites of this period had been split to get out the marrow, because they had been heated too little for it to separate naturally. Upper Paleolithic people may have boiled their food in bark or skin containers. Animal bones show that the people sucked out the cooked marrow.

Remains from Old Stone Age times indicate that the people lived in small groups. Many must have lived as *nomads*, wandering in search of game. It was probably during such wanderings that Upper Paleolithic hunters from Asia crossed the then existing land bridge into America and became the first Indians (see INDIAN, AMERICAN [History]). Other groups lived in semipermanent settlements if game was plentiful nearby. Many prehistoric men lived in rock shelters or caves, and are called *cave men* or *cave dwellers* (see CAVE DWELLERS). Others built pit houses or brush shelters.

Archaeologists have found scrapers for cleaning hides, and needles for sewing them, in Upper Paleolithic sites. These remains indicate that people made skins into robes or even fitted garments.

The First Artists were men of Upper Paleolithic times. Caves in France, Spain, and Italy reveal wall engravings and paintings, sculpture, clay modeling, and carvings on bones, antlers, and ivory. Most subjects are animals, but early artists also represented people. Cave artists used four colors: white, made from pipe clay; black, made with charcoal; and red and yellow, made from ocher, a kind of iron ore. They mixed pigment with grease to form a kind of crayon, or sprayed it as a powder by blowing it through bone tubes. Artists worked in the dark inner chambers of caves by the light of oil lamps or torches.

Much cave art is of superb quality. The artists may well have been full-time specialists who did not need to hunt. Animal pictures are so faithful in body details that the artists must have cut up many of the beasts they painted in order to study them. A color photograph of cave paintings on the left wall of The Hall of the Bulls at Lascaux appears in the PAINTING article.

Sorcerers and Magic. Various peoples of the later Old Stone Age placed tools and other objects in graves where they buried their dead. This custom may indi-

cate a belief in some kind of afterlife. Most scholars believe that cave art had a religious function. Most of the paintings lie far within the caves, and are difficult to reach. Artists often painted new figures on top of old ones. For these reasons, some archaeologists believe that the paintings, especially those of animals, probably had something to do with magical rites to increase the food supply. Some of the humanlike forms disguised as animals may represent spirits.

The Middle Stone Age

The Middle Stone Age, or *Mesolithic* period, began about 10,000 B.C. It lasted about 2,000 years in some parts of the world, but was longer in other parts. The stone tools that distinguish this period from earlier and later ones are tiny flints called *microliths*. Many were attached to pieces of wood or bone to make larger tools.

Scientists believe that the Middle Stone Age is important, not because of the tools used, but because it bridged the gap between the Old and New Stone ages. In many areas, the climate became warmer after the last glaciers of the Ice Age had retreated. Forests replaced the open plains of the Old Stone Age. The great herds of reindeer, bison, and mammoths gave way to smaller groups of deer and boars. Hunting probably became more difficult for the people of the Middle Stone Age, sometimes called "forest folk." But two innovations helped them. One, the bow and arrow, may have originated in Upper Paleolithic times. The other, the domestication of the dog, probably occurred when wild dogs began living in human settlements.

The New Stone Age

The New Stone Age, or *Neolithic* period, began about 8000 B.C. in a belt between what is now Turkey and Afghanistan. It lasted until the people learned to smelt metals, about 3000 B.C. Archaeologists once described this period as one in which men ground and polished their stone tools, instead of chipping them. Scientists now claim that the New Stone Age is important mainly because the people grew crops and *domesticated* (tamed) animals they could use for food.

Farming and Herding. Some scholars believe that agriculture began when people discovered defective grains and legumes (pod-bearing plants) that failed to open when ripe. Men may have cultivated such plants because they could take their time harvesting them, instead of gathering them as they split open. The earliest domesticated food animals may also have been defective, because the wild ancestors of many domestic animals were too large and fierce to tame.

Farming and herding did not begin in a single place or at one time. Important centers included the Middle East from Palestine to Afghanistan, Southeast Asia, and South and Middle America. Farming and herding spread from these centers. The first farmers in the Middle East probably grew wheat, barley, peas, and beans. Those in Southeast Asia raised rice, coconuts, taro, bananas, and citrus fruits. In America, the early Indians raised corn, squash, potatoes, manioc, and beans.

Farming and herding allowed people to store food for winter and times of scarcity. These practices also made it possible to accumulate wealth.

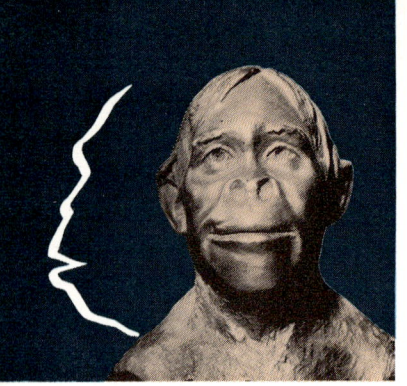

Courtesy Dr. Raymond A. Dart,
Univ. of The Witwatersrand, Johannesburg

Australopithecus

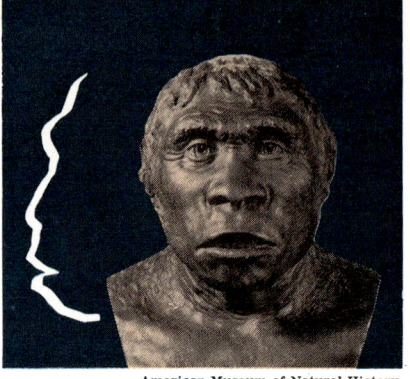

American Museum of Natural History

Java Man

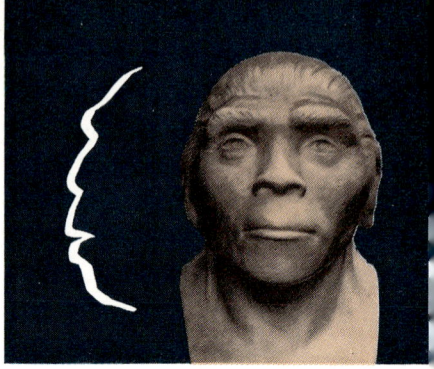

Field Museum of Natural History

Peking Man

DATE	1,000,000 B.C.	700,000 B.C.	150,000 B.C.
GEOLOGIC PERIOD	PLEISTOCENE		
FOSSIL MEN	Pithecanthropus Heidelberg Australopithecines Sinanthropus	Steinheim Swanscombe Fontéchevade	Neanderthal
CULTURAL STAGE	STONE AGE PALEOLITHIC LOWER MIDDLE		
ELEMENTS OF CULTURE	pebble tools, hand axes, choppers fire	flake tools	men buried their dead

Sculptures Made by Anthropologists, *top,* show how prehistoric men may have looked. White lines indicate profiles.

Building Villages. When people could raise a steady food supply, they stopped wandering and settled in villages. They built houses of poles, straw, bricks, or stone, and erected stockades to protect their settlements. They built fences to guard their fields from wild animals. Some European peoples built houses on piles driven into lake bottoms (see LAKE DWELLING).

New Arts and Crafts of the Neolithic period included pottery, basketry, and weaving. Women made pottery by the *coiling* technique, building up jars and bowls with long ropes of clay. They often painted or scratched designs on the pottery before baking it in fire. The earliest baskets probably consisted of woven reed mats and fishing nets. Craftsmen spun wool, flax, and cotton, and wove cloth on upright hand looms.

Religion in the New Stone Age centered around agricultural life. Good crops depended on the weather, so the earth was often thought of as a mother goddess who brought vegetation. Other gods represented the rain and the sun. These beliefs led to a yearly series of rituals. In regions of scarce rainfall, these rituals included rainmaking ceremonies. In many tropical regions with plenty of rain, people had to know when the rainy season would come, so they could prepare the ground and plant seeds at the right times. Some priests learned to count the days before rainfall by measuring the length of the shadow cast by a stick called a *gnomon*. Others worked out elaborate calendars.

Many European peoples of this period built various structures with large stones called *megaliths*. Some of these served as tombstones, and others probably had religious significance. See MEGALITHIC MONUMENTS.

The Beginnings of History

Recorded history began about 3000 B.C. By this time, certain villages in Mesopotamia (present-day Iraq) and Egypt had become cities. The city dwellers invented writing. According to many scholars, civilization began with cities and writing. See CIVILIZATION.

At the same time, people discovered how to smelt and cast copper, silver, and gold into ornaments, weapons, and tools. The Bronze Age began in Mesopotamia shortly after 3000 B.C., when metalworkers learned to mix tin with copper to produce bronze. They also began using wheeled chariots and invented sailing ships. The Iron Age followed the Bronze Age in many areas. It began in Asia Minor (now Turkey) about 1100 B.C., when people first smelted and forged iron.

Early Forms of Man

Scientists have found most of the remains of prehistoric man in Europe, Africa, and Asia. The few specimens found in America come from fairly recent times, about 10,000 years ago.

The earliest people left their dead lying on the ground, and the oldest remains come from geologic deposits. Some bones were washed into streams, and glaciers "bulldozed" others into gravel banks. Later human remains are often found in caves or mounds, to-

668

From *The Story of Man* by Dr. Carleton S. Coon; Alfred A. Knopf, Inc.

Neanderthal Man

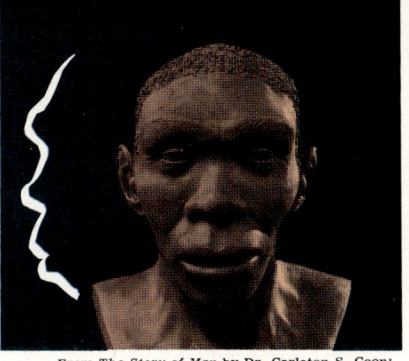

From *The Story of Man* by Dr. Carleton S. Coon; Alfred A. Knopf, Inc.

Rhodesian Man

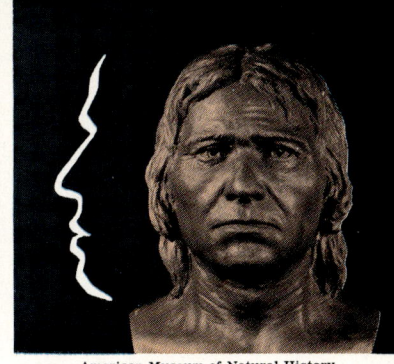

American Museum of Natural History

Cro-Magnon Man

30,000 B.C.	25,000 B.C.	8,000 B.C.	6,000 B.C.	3,000 B.C.	1,000 B.C.

HOLOCENE

Solo	Cro-Magnon	Grimaldi	All Modern Races
Rhodesian	Combe-Capelle	Chancelade	

	MESOLITHIC	NEOLITHIC	BRONZE AGE	IRON AGE
UPPER				

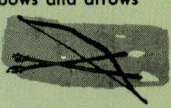

cave paintings, sewing, spear throwers

dogs, bows and arrows

farming, villages, pottery, weaving

wheels, cities, writing, nonferrous metals

iron alphabets empires

---

gether with tools and other objects. Most of the bones have been *fossilized*, or hardened like stone. For this reason, skeletal remains of prehistoric men are sometimes called *fossil men*. See FOSSIL.

All the remains of early forms of man fall within the Pleistocene period, or Ice Age. The variations in climate and vegetation caused by the movements of the glaciers help scientists determine the age of fossil men. Experts also compare human bones with those of animals found at the same time. They can tell whether human and animal bones are of equal age by comparing the amount of fluorine in each (see FLUORINE). This fluorine test exposed the famous Piltdown hoax by showing that the skullcap and the jaw belonged to different periods (see PILTDOWN MAN). Dates can also be determined by measuring the radiocarbon in an object (see RADIOCARBON).

Scientists use several methods to compare and classify fossil men. The most common involves skull measurement. Scientists may compare various proportions of the skull. Or they may determine the size of the brain by measuring the capacity of the cranium.

Australopithecines. The fossil skull of a creature with a human-shaped *cranium* (brain case) and an apelike face was discovered in 1924 in Bechuanaland (now Botswana). Since then, other specimens have been discovered in South Africa and Tanzania. Scientists have identified them as *Australopithecines* (southern apes). They believe that the Australopithecines lived from about 1,750,000 to 500,000 years ago.

The Australopithecines had flat faces and could stand erect. Their brains measured between 435 and 635 cubic centimeters in volume. This brain volume is similar to that of apes. But the Australopithecines' large teeth were less apelike than modern man's teeth.

There were two *species* (groups) of Australopithecines in both South Africa and Tanzania. One species was smaller, more slender, and more human-looking. The other was more rugged and less human-looking. In South Africa, the smaller species is called *Australopithecus africanus*, and the larger is called *Australopithecus robustus*. In Tanzania, the smaller species was named *Homo habilis* (skillful man) because its teeth were more like human teeth and because scientists believe it made stone tools. The larger species in Tanzania is called *Zinjanthropus*. Only *Homo habilis* has been proposed as a possible human ancestor.

Homo Erectus, or *erect man*, is the name many scientists give to all fossil races with a human body and a brain ranging between 700 and 1,100 cc. *Homo erectus* ranks a step above Australopithecus and one below *Homo sapiens*, or modern man. Three varieties, or subspecies, have been clearly identified. The first, Java Man, or *Homo erectus javensis* (also called *Pithecanthropus erectus*), may be about 1½ million years old. The second, Peking Man, or *Homo erectus pekinensis* (also called *Sinanthropus pekinensis*), dates from about one million years ago. The third, Chellean Man, was found in Tanganyika (now Tanzania), in a layer above Zinjanthropus in 1960. It is about 500,000 years old. The remains of Peking Man come from a cave. They show that he was the first man who we know used fire. Both Java

669

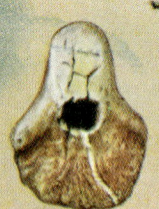

Barbed spear point

Bark fishing float

Flint ax mounted in antler

Middle Stone Age men enjoyed a warmer climate. New techniques, including the bow and arrow, helped them adjust to changed conditions. Maglemosian peoples, shown *at right*, lived along the shores of northern Europe. A woman smokes fish to preserve it. One man shapes a fishing spear and another casts a net into the water. In the distance archers aim at flying birds.

Mattock head made from antler

Blunt wooden arrow

Microlithic arrowheads

Bone fishhooks

Wooden bow

Old Stone Age families often lived in caves. The drawing *at left* shows Neanderthal people of Europe. A man twirls a stick to kindle fire. One woman scrapes a skin while another prepares a spear shaft. Tools, *right* and *below*, range in date from a crude pebble tool of Lower Paleolithic times, found in South Africa, to a carved Upper Paleolithic spearhead from Europe.

Chisel-like burin

Scraper

Bone needle

Hand Ax   Scraper   Pebble tool   Flint knife

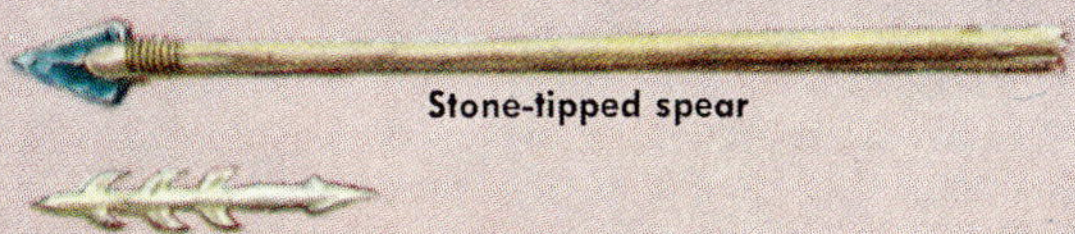

Stone-tipped spear

Antler spearhead

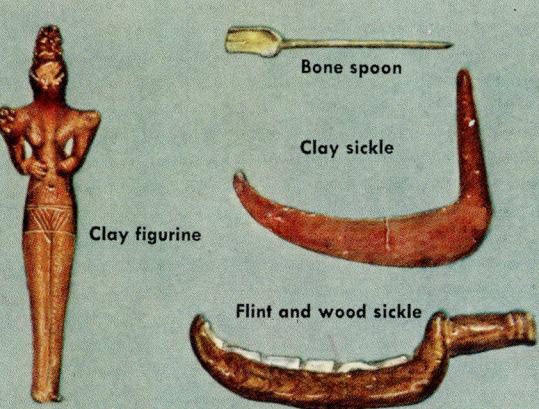

Alton S. Tobey

New Stone Age people were the world's first farmers. The busy scene *at left* represents a Mesopotamian village of about 4500 B.C. Using a sickle, one man harvests grain and collects it in a basket. A herder guards his flock of goats, and a hunter has just returned with an antelope over his shoulder. In front of the mud huts, women mold pottery, spin, bake, and weave.

Bone spoon

Clay sickle

Stone mortar and pestle

Pottery jar

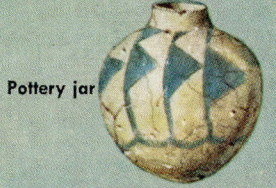

Clay figurine

Flint and wood sickle

Alton S. Tobey

The Massive Sandstone Blocks of Stonehenge were probably moved by hundreds of workers using ropes and log sledges.

modern man. Neanderthal people had long faces, heavy brow ridges, and long, protruding noses.

Other Early Sapiens Forms come from Asia and Africa. Solo Man, or *Homo sapiens soloensis* (formerly *Homo soloensis*), is represented by several skullcaps found near the Solo River in Java. They date back to the late Ice Age, about 50,000 years ago. Solo Man had heavier brow ridges than Neanderthal Man and a smaller cranium. Solo people might have been the ancestors of the Australian Aborigines. Rhodesian Man, *Homo sapiens rhodesiensis* (formerly *Homo rhodesiensis*), comes from central and southern Africa. Rhodesian Man resembled Solo Man closely, as far as scientists can tell. This form had a long face, and may have been the ancestor of some of the African races of today.

Late Ice-Age Men date from between 30,000 and 8000 B.C. One important group, the Cro-Magnons, is represented by more than 100 skeletons. Cro-Magnon people were the first known artists, and created the famous cave paintings. They resembled modern man in all important features, except that their jaws, faces, and teeth, like those of the Eskimos, were enlarged by heavy chewing. Specimens found in Europe and Africa include remains from Combe-Capelle and Chancelade, France; and Grimaldi, Italy.   CARLETON S. COON

Related Articles. See the articles on various peoples of prehistoric times, such as INDIAN, AMERICAN. See also the following articles in WORLD BOOK:

EARLY FORMS OF MAN

Cro-Magnon Man	Java Man	Peking Man
Heidelberg Man	Neanderthal Man	

OTHER RELATED ARTICLES

Anthropology	Iron Age	Piltdown Man
Archaeology	Kitchen Midden	Prehistoric
Bronze Age	Lake Dwelling	Animal
Cave Dwellers	Megalithic Monuments	Stone Age
Family (picture)		

Outline

I. **The Old Stone Age**
  A. Hunting and Gathering   C. The First Artists
  B. Food, Shelter, and   D. Sorcerers and Magic
     Clothing
II. **The Middle Stone Age**
III. **The New Stone Age**
  A. Farming and Herding   C. New Arts and Crafts
  B. Building Villages   D. Religion
IV. **The Beginnings of History**
V. **Early Forms of Man**
  A. Australopithecus   C. Homo Sapiens
  B. Homo Erectus

Questions

What form of prehistoric man was probably the first to use fire?

How did early religious rites depend on man's ways of getting food?

What improvements helped men hunt in the Middle Stone Age?

What do animal bones tell us about the way prehistoric men cooked their food?

What type of prehistoric man was the first known artist?

On what basis do scientists classify the periods of man's prehistoric cultures?

What does cave art indicate about man's early religion?

How did men's lives change in the New Stone Age?

What custom of Neanderthal Man resulted in his skeleton being the first complete human one found?

What two developments are considered to mark the beginnings of civilization?

Man and Peking Man had large teeth, chinless jaws, and sloping foreheads.

Archaeologists have found several fragments comparable to Peking Man in other parts of the world. One form, Heidelberg Man, is represented by a jaw, found near Heidelberg, Germany. Three jaws and one parietal bone from North Africa were identified as *Homo erectus*.

Homo Sapiens, or *wise man*, is the name usually given to all races with a human body and a brain measuring from 1,100 cc. upward, and averaging between 1,350 and 1,500 cc. This group includes all modern men.

Pre-Neanderthals are the earliest examples of *Homo sapiens*. They date from about 300,000 B.C. Archaeologists have found skull fragments near Swanscombe, England, and Steinheim, Germany. Neither skull is complete, but the corresponding parts are almost identical. Steinheim Man had a modern-sized face with projecting ridges above the eyebrows. No facial bones of Swanscombe Man have been discovered.

Neanderthals were the first human fossils to be recognized as such. The first Neanderthal Man to receive the name was discovered by quarry workmen in 1856 near Düsseldorf, Germany. Since then, scientists have found about 30 skeletons of Neanderthal Man in Europe, the Middle East, and central Asia. Neanderthal people probably lived between 75,000 and 30,000 years ago. These people provide the earliest complete skeletons known, because they buried their dead. At first, scientists thought that Neanderthal Man was a squat, stooping, brutish, somewhat apelike creature. But later research showed that the bodies of Neanderthal men and women were completely human, fully erect, and very muscular. Their brains were as large as those of

PREJUDICE, *PREHJ oo dis*, is a form of thinking in which a person reaches conclusions that are in conflict with the facts, because he prejudges them. For example, if he is prejudiced against Englishmen, he may dislike one particular Englishman even though he has no reason for his dislike. Prejudice can exist with respect to almost anything, and varies in intensity from moderate distortion to complete delusion. Prejudices may be either favorable or unfavorable, but most persons use the word for negative judgments. The results of prejudice are often harmful. Psychologists and sociologists have devoted much study to the subject, seeking ways to control, reduce, or prevent prejudice. If it could be controlled, people could make judgments only on the basis of facts. See also BIAS.   JOHN F. CUBER

PRELATE, *PREL it*, is the title of a high-ranking church official. In the Church of England, the only prelates are bishops and archbishops. In the Roman Catholic Church, the term is also applied to popes, cardinals, abbots, and other monastic officials, as well as to honorary prelates. See also ABBOT; ARCHBISHOP; BISHOP; CARDINAL; POPE.

PRELUDE. See OVERTURE.

PREMIER, *PRE mih er*, or *pre MEER*, is the head of the cabinet in France and various other countries throughout the world. Such a leader is known as the *prime minister* in Great Britain and in other countries of the Commonwealth of Nations.

The premier is a member of the majority party, or one of the leading parties of the legislative body, or parliament. He is responsible to the parliament and to the people. A premier generally appoints the ministers who make up his cabinet. He and his cabinet generally resign when a majority of the members of parliament disagree with him on any important matter. A new premier is then appointed by the president or ruler of the country. The new premier is often one of the leaders of the party which opposed the old premier. Sometimes a premier may not resign when he is opposed, but may ask for a new parliamentary election instead. This election shows whether the people themselves agree with the premier's policies or those of the parliament. If the people support the premier, they elect a new parliament and the premier keeps his post as leader. In Russia, the chairman of the Council of Ministers usually assumes the title of premier. There he is the real head of the government, and has dictatorial powers.

The United States government has no premier. The President himself is head of the Cabinet. PAYSON S. WILD, JR.

See also CABINET; PARLIAMENT.

PREMIUM. See INSURANCE (How Insurance Works).

PRENDERGAST, MAURICE BRAZIL (1859-1924), was an American painter and illustrator. His paintings capture the life and movement of crowds in city parks and at the seaside. His paintings show his familiarity with European postimpressionist experiments in the handling of form, color, and light.

Prendergast was born in St. John's, Nfld., and grew up in Boston. He was attracted by Robert Henri's philosophy of independent and spontaneous expression in art. In 1908, he joined Henri's group of realistic painters called *The Eight* (later the *Ashcan School*). For more information on the group, see HENRI, ROBERT. In 1913, Prendergast exhibited in the famous Armory Show of modern art in New York City. E. MAURICE BLOCH

PREPARATORY SCHOOL, in the United States, is a private secondary school that prepares students for college. In Great Britain, a preparatory school corresponds to a private elementary school in the United States. It prepares students for the so-called public schools, such as Eton and Harrow.

In the United States, public secondary education expanded slowly until the 1890's and 1900's. Private secondary schools called *academies* remained popular until the mid-1800's (see ACADEMY). But as the public high school increased its scope, the number of academies declined. Many academies became preparatory schools. The older preparatory schools are usually boarding schools (see BOARDING SCHOOL). Those preparatory schools established more recently usually serve students who live at home.

Formerly, preparatory schools taught only boys. But the number of preparatory schools for girls has grown, because many colleges now accept women on the same basis as men.

The group of colleges to which preparatory schools send most of their students influences the course of studies. Preparatory schools usually emphasize work in English, foreign languages, history, mathematics, and science. They generally admit those students who have the capacity to study these subjects profitably. Most preparatory schools maintain a high standard of achievement for their students.

Some preparatory schools have substantial endowments that help to support the school. Others gain financial support from tuition.   HOLLIS L. CASWELL

PREPOSITION, *PREP oh ZISH un*, is a part of speech that shows the relation between its object and some other word in the sentence. It is "a word that looks backward as well as forward." Common prepositions include *at, by, against, above, on, upon, from, without, under, over, in, through, during*. The phrasal prepositions include *according to, on account of, corresponding to, by means of, by way of*, and *instead of*.

The Object of a Preposition is in the objective, or accusative, case. This is true except in the case of the "double possessive," where the possessive form follows the preposition *of*, as in, "Our Art Institute boasts several paintings *of Millet's*," and, "I have a strong admiration for that cousin *of yours*."

The object of a preposition may be an adjective or an adverb used as a noun, in such phrases as *on high* and *from afar*. It may be an infinitive, a participle, a phrase (as, *from of old*), or a clause. All these units are here used as nouns.

The Appropriate Preposition must be used to complete the meaning intended. Every preposition gives a different shade of meaning to the word which precedes it. A man may be impatient *with* his secretary, or he may grow impatient *at* a delay in trains, or become increasingly impatient *under* the disappointment, because he is impatient *for* the arrival of a friend.

The Question of Order is not now considered so important as it once was. It used to be said that a preposition was a word that one should *never* end a sentence with. One reason for this was that it ought to precede its object. Following this rule closely may create stilted sentences. It turns the vigorous idiom, "*What* did you

PRE-RAPHAELITE BROTHERHOOD

come *for?*" into the stilted "*For what* did you come?"

Rules to Watch include use of the objective case after the preposition. Many persons say "between you and *I*" for "between you and *me.*" One must always remember also that *between* refers to only two persons or objects. *Among* is used when there are more than two. Avoid such statements as "between each act." *Each* is singular, and *between* implies two objects. The phrase should be "between acts" or "between each two acts."

Prepositions should not be repeated, as in, "For what town are you bound *for* now?" One *for* must be omitted.

In "He went *for* to find his sister," the *for* is *redundant*, or considered unnecessary, and should be omitted.

In and *into* have different meanings. A boy jumps *into* a lake, but he jumps up and down *in* the lake. *Into* implies movement from one place to another.

Without is a preposition and must not be used for the conjunction *unless*. "I cannot come *without* my sister is invited also," should be "*unless* my sister is invited also."

Of is superfluous after *off*. "We picked these cherries *off of* the tree," should be, "*off* the tree." The preposition is likewise unnecessary in the commonly heard phrases *follow after, ponder over, add on, crave for,* and *want for.*

From, not *than*, follows the adjective *different* in "The house looks different *from* what I expected." One would never say, "*This differs than that.*" If you remember that "different" comes from "differ," you will always say: "This is different *from* that."

Beside expresses position. "The oak is *beside* the garage," not "*besides* the garage."   CLARENCE STRATTON

PRE-RAPHAELITE BROTHERHOOD. See ENGLISH LITERATURE (The Victorian Age); ROSSETTI, DANTE G.

PRESBYOPIA. See EYE (Changes in the Eye).

PRESBYTERIAN CHURCH IN THE UNITED STATES was formed by a group of Southern churches that broke away from the Presbyterian Church in the U.S.A. The break took place shortly after the start of the Civil War in 1861. Members of the church are often called *Southern Presbyterians.*

The Presbyterian Church in the United States has 15 *synods* (church councils) and 74 *presbyteries* (divisions of synods). The offices of the General Assembly, General Council, and the Boards of Annuities and Relief, National Ministries, and Women's Work are in Atlanta, Ga. Headquarters for World Missions are in Nashville, Tenn., and for Christian Education in Richmond, Va. The church has missions in Brazil, Ecuador, Iraq, Japan, Korea, Mexico, Portugal, Taiwan, and the Congo. For membership, see RELIGION (table).

Critically reviewed by PRESBYTERIAN CHURCH IN THE UNITED STATES

See also PRESBYTERIANS.

PRESBYTERIAN COLLEGE is a coeducational liberal arts school in Clinton, S.C. It was founded in 1880. For enrollment, see UNIVERSITIES AND COLLEGES (table).

PRESBYTERIAN SCHOOL OF CHRISTIAN EDUCATION is a coeducational school located in Richmond, Va., that prepares laymen and women for full-time church vocations. It is owned and controlled by the Presbyterian Church in the United States. The school grants the bachelor of Christian education, master of arts in English Bible, and master of Christian education degrees. It was founded in 1914. For enrollment, see UNIVERSITIES (table).   CHARLES E. S. KRAEMER

Painting by Sir George Harvey, from Culver

Early Presbyterians in Scotland, called Covenanters, strove to uphold their faith when the Church of England tried to force its views on Scotland in the 1600's.

PRESBYTERIANS form a large group of Protestant denominations in the English-speaking world. Outside the English-speaking countries, most churches of this tradition are called *Reformed*—for example, the French Reformed Church. The term *Reformed* refers to a church reformed according to the Biblical Gospel. A favorite motto of the Presbyterian and Reformed churches is *semper reformanda* (ever being reformed). About 100 denominations belong to the World Alliance of Reformed Churches.

The term *presbyterian* refers to a distinctive pattern of church government. *Presbyter* is the New Testament term for *elder*. Presbyterian congregations are governed by boards, called *sessions* or *consistories*, composed of the minister and lay elders. The sessions send representatives to church councils, called *presbyteries* or *classes*, which oversee the congregations of the district. The presbyteries are represented in regional *synods* or *assemblies*. A system of representative government operates at all levels, with lay elders participating equally with ministers. All ministers have equal rank.

Teaching and Worship. The Presbyterian and Reformed tradition has always referred to the Bible as the final authority in religious matters. The churches have produced a series of official statements expressing their understanding of Biblical truth. Of these basic documents of Reformed theology, the two best-loved and most influential are the *Heidelberg Catechism* (1566) and the *Westminster Shorter Catechism* (1647). The earlier catechism is most widely used in Europe, and the later one is more popular in English-speaking countries. The American Presbyterian *Confession of 1967* is another official statement.

The most influential theologian in the developing years of the Reformed tradition was John Calvin. He was more a commentator on the Bible than a systematic thinker, and scholars debate whether Calvin's thought can be summed up under any single theme. One central point in Calvin's thinking is the conviction that God is the actual present ruler over all creation. This belief is basic to the Reformed tradition generally.

Predestination is another important theme. It is less central in Calvin, but more important in the thought of some later Reformed theologians. Predestination is a doctrine which states that God determines the eternal destiny of man. The conception is illustrated by Jesus' saying "You have not chosen me, it is I who have chosen you" (John 15:16). Predestination is no longer a characteristic theme of Reformed preaching or teaching. See PREDESTINATION.

In worship, the Reformed churches have always stressed preaching, along with the Biblical sacraments of baptism and the Lord's Supper. The Reformed churches have produced many great preachers. Congregational worship was once characterized by the singing of psalms translated into the *vernacular* (local languages) and arranged in meter. Within the last 100 or 200 years, hymns have generally replaced psalms. The formal *liturgies* (church services) during the Reformation of the 1500's were largely abandoned in favor of *free prayer* beginning in the 1600's. During the last 100 years, churches have partially returned to set forms of worship.

History. The Reformed tradition has always been the most international of the main Protestant bodies. Unlike Anglicanism and Lutheranism, Reformed churches often had to organize without government support, and sometimes under persecution. Many of their leaders, including Calvin and John Knox, were exiles or refugees from France, England, Scotland, The Netherlands, Germany, Italy, Poland, or Hungary. Geneva, Switzerland, was a notable international refugee center. From Geneva, Reformed ideas and leaders spread throughout Europe. Reformed churches were organized in nearly all European countries, each with its statement of faith, its liturgy, and its own form of government.

The term *presbyterian* was not generally used for Reformed churches until the English Civil War of the 1640's. During that war, Parliament summoned the Westminster Assembly, a council of clergymen, to advise the government on church affairs. The assembly devised a plan of presbyterian organization for the Churches of England, of Scotland, and of Ireland. It also drafted the Westminster Confession, the Larger and Shorter catechisms, and a manual for worship. This program did not survive the restoration of the monarchy in 1660. But the theology of the Westminster documents remained influential for Presbyterians, Congregationalists, and most Baptists throughout the English-speaking world.

The Presbyterian and Reformed churches played an important part in the great missionary movement of the 1800's. About half the member churches of the present World Alliance are "younger" churches formed in Asia, Africa, and Latin America. In several cases, the Presbyterian and Reformed churches have played an important role in forming united churches with other denominations. This has been the case in China, Japan, south India, and the Philippines. The Reformed churches have also made notable contributions of personnel and funds for national and international organizations dedicated to Christian unity, including the World Council of Churches.

For the membership of major Presbyterian bodies in the United States, see RELIGION (table).   J. H. NICHOLS

See also UNITED PRESBYTERIAN CHURCH IN THE U.S.A.; PRESBYTERIAN CHURCH IN THE UNITED STATES; UNITED CHURCH OF CANADA; CALVIN, JOHN; KNOX, JOHN.

PRESBYTERY. See PRESBYTERIANS.

PRESCHOOL EDUCATION refers to organized teaching and caring for young children before they go to the first grade. In general, the term *preschool education* includes all the informal education and guidance provided

by families and parents from the time of the child's birth. In the United States, however, it usually refers to nursery schools and kindergartens.

Nursery schools deal mainly with children who are two, three, or four years old. The children learn to care for themselves physically. They learn how to dress, keep clean, and play with other children. See NURSERY SCHOOL.

Children who are five years old may attend kindergarten. There they engage in music, art, and group activities which are appropriate to their age. See KINDERGARTEN.

Nursery schools spread rapidly during the depression of the 1930's to help care for children of employed mothers. The trend slowed down by the 1950's. Kindergartens have spread much more widely with greater public and private support.   R. FREEMAN BUTTS

PRESCOTT, WILLIAM (1726-1795), an American colonel, served in three wars, including the Revolutionary War in America. He built the fortifications on Breed's Hill, and led the militia in the Battle of Bunker Hill. It was once believed that Prescott said to his troops, "Don't fire until you see the whites of their eyes," although it is now thought that probably this order was never given. Prescott was born in Groton, Mass.   JOHN R. ALDEN

PRESCOTT, WILLIAM HICKLING (1796-1859), an American historian, wrote chiefly about Spain and its relations with the New World and with the Protestant Reformation. His work became noted for its factual accuracy, and many of his writings rank as classics in the study and writing of history.

Prescott's first historical study, *The History of the Reign of Ferdinand and Isabella the Catholic*, was published in 1838. Two of his greatest works are *The History of the Conquest of Mexico* (1843) and *The History of the Conquest of Peru* (1847). His articles and reviews began to appear in the *North American Review* in 1821.

Prescott lost the sight of one eye through an accident, and his other eye became weakened. Because of his poor eyesight, he employed specially trained readers to read to him. Prescott wrote with the aid of a *noctograph*, a special frame with brass wires that kept him from running lines together. Prescott was born in Salem, Mass., and attended Harvard University.   MERLE CURTI

PRESCRIPTION is a written order given by a physician or dentist directing another person to supply medication or treatment to a patient. Best known are the prescriptions given to pharmacists for medicine. Prescriptions may also be written to opticians for grinding eyeglass lenses, to brace shops for special shoes or braces, or to physical therapists for special exercises. Doctors once wrote all prescriptions in Latin, but now they usually write them in English. The symbol ℞, which means *take*, usually begins a prescription. See ℞.   SOLOMON GARB

PRESERVATION, FOOD. See FOOD PRESERVATION; CANNING; PURE FOOD AND DRUG LAWS.

PRESIDENT is the title of the chief executive officer in a number of republics. It usually also is the title of the heads of business companies, corporations, colleges, institutions, and societies. See also ADDRESS, FORM OF; CABINET; PRESIDENT OF THE UNITED STATES.

PRESIDENT *of the* UNITED STATES

Seal of the President of the United States

PRESIDENT OF THE UNITED STATES. Every four years, on a day late in January, a solemn ceremony takes place on the steps of the Capitol in Washington, D.C. A new President of the United States is being inaugurated. With his left hand on an open Bible and his right hand upraised, he takes the presidential oath of office from the Chief Justice of the United States.

★ ★ ★ ★ ★

PRESIDENTIAL OATH OF OFFICE

"I do solemnly swear (or affirm) that I will faithfully execute the office of President of the United States, and will, to the best of my ability, preserve, protect, and defend the Constitution of the United States."

★ ★ ★ ★ ★

Witnessing the ceremony on the Capitol grounds are hundreds of dignitaries and as many as 100,000 spectators. Millions of other Americans across the nation listen to the ceremony on radio and watch it on television. The United States Marine Band plays. Churchmen of the principal religious faiths offer prayers.

The new President delivers his inaugural address, which may set the theme of his administration. The Voice of America broadcasts his words throughout the world in nearly 50 languages and dialects.

The presidential office is unique because it blends

1
GEORGE WASHINGTON

2 JOHN ADAMS **3** THOMAS JEFFERSON **4** JAMES MADISON **5** JAMES MONROE **6** JOHN QUINCY ADAMS

7 ANDREW JACKSON **8** MARTIN VAN BUREN **9** WILLIAM H. HARRISON **10** JOHN TYLER **11** JAMES K. POLK

Bettmann Archive, 12, 14; Brown Bros., 22; Chicago Historical Society, 17, 18; Corcoran Gallery of Art, Washington, D.C., 13; Culver, 15; Ewing Galloway, 11; L. C. Handy, 8, 9, 16, 25, 29; Harris & Ewing, 27, 31; Keystone View, 30; Library of Congress, 2, 6, 19, 20, 21, 23;

12 ZACHARY TAYLOR
13 MILLARD FILLMORE
14 FRANKLIN PIERCE
15 JAMES BUCHANAN
16 ABRAHAM LINCOLN

17 ANDREW JOHNSON
18 ULYSSES S. GRANT
19 RUTHERFORD B. HAYES
20 JAMES A. GARFIELD
21 CHESTER A. ARTHUR

22, 24 GROVER CLEVELAND
23 BENJAMIN HARRISON
25 WILLIAM McKINLEY
26 THEODORE ROOSEVELT
27 WILLIAM H. TAFT

28 WOODROW WILSON
29 WARREN G. HARDING
30 CALVIN COOLIDGE
31 HERBERT C. HOOVER
32 FRANKLIN D. ROOSEVELT

33 HARRY S. TRUMAN
34 DWIGHT D. EISENHOWER
35 JOHN F. KENNEDY
36 LYNDON B. JOHNSON
37 RICHARD M. NIXON

Museum of Fine Arts, Boston, 4, 5; National Gallery of Art, Washington, D.C., Mellon Coll., 1; New-York Historical Society, 7; George Tames © N.Y. Times, 34; U & U, 26, 28; The White House, Courtesy National Park Service, 3, 10, 33; Wide World, 32; U. S. News & W.R., 35; The White House, 36, 37.

PRESIDENT OF THE UNITED STATES

enormous power with effective responsibility. The presidency is the most powerful elective office in the world. The President is powerful because the United States is strong, and because the office he holds has a tradition of success. The Presidents have constructively shaped many important developments in American history.

Roles of the President

The President has so many different and important duties that he may be described as "many men in one." In other countries, his duties would be performed by more than one official, perhaps a king and a prime minister. As chief of state, the President conducts many ceremonial affairs. As chief executive, he makes sure that federal laws are enforced. As commander in chief of the armed forces, he is responsible for national defense in peace or war. He directs United States foreign policy and plays an important role in world affairs. As leader of his political party, he helps shape the party's stand on domestic and foreign issues. He urges Congress to act on his legislative proposals.

The President and Vice-President are the only executives of the federal government elected to office. The President appoints most other high officials of the executive branch of the government. He also appoints members of the Supreme Court. But he has no direct control over the separate judicial or legislative branches of the government.

THE PRESIDENTS OF THE UNITED STATES

	Born	Birthplace	College or University	Religion	Occupation or Profession
1. George Washington...	Feb. 22, 1732	Wakefield, Va.		Episcopalian	Planter
2. John Adams.........	Oct. 30, 1735	Braintree, Mass.	Harvard	Unitarian	Lawyer
3. Thomas Jefferson....	Apr. 13, 1743	Albemarle County, Va.	William and Mary	Unitarian*	Planter, lawyer
4. James Madison.......	Mar. 16, 1751	Port Conway, Va.	Princeton	Episcopalian	Lawyer
5. James Monroe.......	Apr. 28, 1758	Westmoreland County, Va.	William and Mary	Episcopalian	Lawyer
6. John Quincy Adams..	July 11, 1767	Braintree, Mass.	Harvard	Unitarian	Lawyer
7. Andrew Jackson......	Mar. 15, 1767	Waxhaw settlement, S.C.		Presbyterian	Lawyer
8. Martin Van Buren....	Dec. 5, 1782	Kinderhook, N.Y.		Dutch Reformed	Lawyer
9. William H. Harrison...	Feb. 9, 1773	Berkeley, Va.	Hampden-Sydney	Episcopalian	Soldier
10. John Tyler..........	Mar. 29, 1790	Greenway, Va.	William and Mary	Episcopalian	Lawyer
11. James K. Polk.......	Nov. 2, 1795	near Pineville, N.C.	U. of N. Carolina	Methodist	Lawyer
12. Zachary Taylor......	Nov. 24, 1784	Orange County, Va.		Episcopalian	Soldier
13. Millard Fillmore......	Jan. 7, 1800	Locke, N.Y.		Unitarian	Lawyer
14. Franklin Pierce.......	Nov. 23, 1804	Hillsboro, N.H.	Bowdoin	Episcopalian	Lawyer
15. James Buchanan.....	Apr. 23, 1791	near Mercersburg, Pa.	Dickinson	Presbyterian	Lawyer
16. Abraham Lincoln.....	Feb. 12, 1809	Hardin County, Ky.		Presbyterian*	Lawyer
17. Andrew Johnson.....	Dec. 29, 1808	Raleigh, N.C.		Methodist*	Tailor
18. Ulysses S. Grant.....	Apr. 27, 1822	Point Pleasant, Ohio	U.S. Military Academy	Methodist	Soldier
19. Rutherford B. Hayes..	Oct. 4, 1822	Delaware, Ohio	Kenyon	Methodist*	Lawyer
20. James A. Garfield....	Nov. 19, 1831	Orange, Ohio	Williams	Disciples of Christ	Lawyer
21. Chester A. Arthur....	Oct. 5, 1830	Fairfield, Vt.	Union	Episcopalian	Lawyer
22. Grover Cleveland.....	Mar. 18, 1837	Caldwell, N.J.		Presbyterian	Lawyer
23. Benjamin Harrison....	Aug. 20, 1833	North Bend, Ohio	Miami	Presbyterian	Lawyer
24. Grover Cleveland.....	Mar. 18, 1837	Caldwell, N.J.		Presbyterian	Lawyer
25. William McKinley.....	Jan. 29, 1843	Niles, Ohio	Allegheny College	Methodist	Lawyer
26. Theodore Roosevelt...	Oct. 27, 1858	New York, N.Y.	Harvard	Dutch Reformed	Author
27. William H. Taft.......	Sept. 15, 1857	Cincinnati, Ohio	Yale	Unitarian	Lawyer
28. Woodrow Wilson.....	Dec. 29, 1856	Staunton, Va.	Princeton	Presbyterian	Educator
29. Warren G. Harding...	Nov. 2, 1865	Blooming Grove, Ohio	Ohio Central	Baptist	Editor
30. Calvin Coolidge......	July 4, 1872	Plymouth Notch, Vt.	Amherst	Congregationalist	Lawyer
31. Herbert C. Hoover....	Aug. 10, 1874	West Branch, Iowa	Stanford	Friend (Quaker)	Engineer
32. Franklin D. Roosevelt.	Jan. 30, 1882	Hyde Park, N.Y.	Harvard	Episcopalian	Lawyer
33. Harry S. Truman.....	May 8, 1884	Lamar, Mo.		Baptist	Businessman
34. Dwight D. Eisenhower.	Oct. 14, 1890	Denison, Tex.	U.S. Military Academy	Presbyterian	Soldier
35. John F. Kennedy.....	May 29, 1917	Brookline, Mass.	Harvard	Roman Catholic	Author
36. Lyndon B. Johnson...	Aug. 27, 1908	near Stonewall, Tex.	Southwest Texas State Teachers	Christian Church	Teacher
37. Richard M. Nixon....	Jan. 9, 1913	Yorba Linda, Calif.	Whittier	Friend (Quaker)	Lawyer

Each President has a separate biography and picture in WORLD BOOK.

*Church preference; never joined any church.

678

Chief of State. The President is the ceremonial head of the United States government. He symbolizes, said President William Howard Taft, "the dignity and majesty" of the American people. The President's duties in this regard compare with those of the kings or queens of other nations. For example, he decorates war heroes, dedicates parks and post offices, launches charity drives, usually throws out the first ball to open the baseball season, and even greets high school essay prize winners who visit the White House. The President sometimes travels to other countries on official state visits. He receives visiting chiefs of state of other countries at the White House.

Chief Executive. The Constitution provides that the President "shall take care that the laws be faithfully executed." He enforces acts of Congress, judgments of federal courts, and treaties with other countries. He interprets laws in applying them to specific situations. Congress, if dissatisfied with his interpretation of a law, may amend the law. The Supreme Court may declare that the President's interpretation of a law was illegal.

The Constitution gives the President power "to grant reprieves and pardons for offenses against the United States except in cases of impeachment." As chief executive, the President also has emergency powers. For example, the Taft-Hartley Act authorizes him to take emergency measures when he believes a labor-management conflict threatens the "national health or safety."

	Political Party	Age at Inauguration	Served	Died		Age at Death	Place of Burial	Runner-up	Vice-President
1.	Federalist	57	1789-1797	Dec.	14, 1799	67	Mount Vernon, Va.	None	John Adams
2.	Federalist	61	1797-1801	July	4, 1826	90	Quincy, Mass.	Thomas Jefferson	Thomas Jefferson
3.	Democratic-Republican	57	1801-1809	July	4, 1826	83	Monticello, Va.	Aaron Burr	Aaron Burr
								Charles C. Pinckney	George Clinton
4.	Democratic-Republican	57	1809-1817	June	28, 1836	85	Montpelier, Va.	Charles C. Pinckney	George Clinton
								De Witt Clinton	Elbridge Gerry
5.	Democratic-Republican	58	1817-1825	July	4, 1831	73	Richmond, Va.	Rufus King	Daniel D. Tompkins
								No opposition	
6.	Democratic-Republican	57	1825-1829	Feb.	23, 1848	80	Quincy, Mass.	Andrew Jackson	John C. Calhoun
7.	Democrat	61	1829-1837	June	8, 1845	78	Hermitage, Tenn.	John Quincy Adams	John C. Calhoun
								Henry Clay	Martin Van Buren
8.	Democrat	54	1837-1841	July	24, 1862	79	Kinderhook, N.Y.	William H. Harrison	Richard M. Johnson
9.	Whig	68	1841	Apr.	4, 1841	68	North Bend, Ohio	Martin Van Buren	John Tyler
10.	Whig	51	1841-1845	Jan.	18, 1862	71	Richmond, Va.		
11.	Democrat	49	1845-1849	June	15, 1849	53	Nashville, Tenn.	Henry Clay	George M. Dallas
12.	Whig	64	1849-1850	July	9, 1850	65	Louisville, Ky.	Lewis Cass	Millard Fillmore
13.	Whig	50	1850-1853	Mar.	8, 1874	74	Buffalo, N.Y.		
14.	Democrat	48	1853-1857	Oct.	8, 1869	64	Concord, N.H.	Winfield Scott	William R. King
15.	Democrat	65	1857-1861	June	1, 1868	77	Lancaster, Pa.	John C. Frémont	John C. Breckinridge
16.	Republican	52	1861-1865	Apr.	15, 1865	56	Springfield, Ill.	Stephen A. Douglas	Hannibal Hamlin
								Geo. B. McClellan	Andrew Johnson
17.	National Union†	56	1865-1869	July	31, 1875	66	Greeneville, Tenn.		
18.	Republican	46	1869-1877	July	23, 1885	63	New York City	Horatio Seymour	Schuyler Colfax
								Horace Greeley	Henry Wilson
19.	Republican	54	1877-1881	Jan.	17, 1893	70	Fremont, Ohio	Samuel J. Tilden	William A. Wheeler
20.	Republican	49	1881	Sept.	19, 1881	49	Cleveland, Ohio	Winfield S. Hancock	Chester A. Arthur
21.	Republican	50	1881-1885	Nov.	18, 1886	56	Albany, N.Y.		
22.	Democrat	47	1885-1889	June	24, 1908	71	Princeton, N.J.	James G. Blaine	Thomas A. Hendricks
23.	Republican	55	1889-1893	Mar.	13, 1901	67	Indianapolis, Ind.	Grover Cleveland	Levi P. Morton
24.	Democrat	55	1893-1897	June	24, 1908	71	Princeton, N.J.	Benjamin Harrison	Adlai E. Stevenson
25.	Republican	54	1897-1901	Sept.	14, 1901	58	Canton, Ohio	William J. Bryan	Garret A. Hobart
								William J. Bryan	Theodore Roosevelt
26.	Republican	42	1901-1909	Jan.	6, 1919	60	Oyster Bay, N.Y.	Alton B. Parker	Charles W. Fairbanks
27.	Republican	51	1909-1913	Mar.	8, 1930	72	Arlington, Va.	William J. Bryan	James S. Sherman
28.	Democrat	56	1913-1921	Feb.	3, 1924	67	Washington, D.C.	Theodore Roosevelt	Thomas R. Marshall
								Charles E. Hughes	
29.	Republican	55	1921-1923	Aug.	2, 1923	57	Marion, Ohio	James M. Cox	Calvin Coolidge
30.	Republican	51	1923-1929	Jan.	5, 1933	60	Plymouth Notch, Vt.	John W. Davis	Charles G. Dawes
31.	Republican	54	1929-1933	Oct.	20, 1964	90	West Branch, Ia.	Alfred E. Smith	Charles Curtis
32.	Democrat	51	1933-1945	Apr.	12, 1945	63	Hyde Park, N.Y.	Herbert Hoover	John N. Garner
								Alfred M. Landon	
								Wendell L. Willkie	Henry A. Wallace
								Thomas E. Dewey	Harry S. Truman
33.	Democrat	60	1945-1953					Thomas E. Dewey	Alben W. Barkley
34.	Republican	62	1953-1961	Mar.	28, 1969	78	Abilene, Kans.	Adlai E. Stevenson	Richard M. Nixon
35.	Democrat	43	1961-1963	Nov.	22, 1963	46	Arlington, Va.	Richard M. Nixon	Lyndon B. Johnson
36.	Democrat	55	1963-1969					Barry M. Goldwater	Hubert H. Humphrey
37.	Republican	56	1969-					Hubert H. Humphrey	Spiro T. Agnew

†The National Union party consisted of Republicans and War Democrats. Johnson was a Democrat.

PRESIDENT OF THE UNITED STATES

The President nominates members of the Cabinet, justices of the Supreme Court, ambassadors, and other high officials such as the heads of boards, agencies, and commissions. These nominations must be approved by a majority vote of the Senate. The President can fill thousands of lesser offices without Senate approval.

He shapes and determines policy, delegates functions and authority, coordinates and reorganizes agencies, and issues *executive orders*. Such orders are issued solely by the President under authority given him directly by the Constitution or under statutes enacted by Congress. For example, the President may issue an executive order to reorganize an administrative agency. The Supreme Court has ruled that the President's power to remove high officials is implied by his power to appoint these officials. But this power has been restricted by other Supreme Court decisions. For example, the Court has held that the President cannot remove an officer engaging in quasi-legislative and quasi-judicial duties, except for reasons provided in statutes passed by Congress.

Foreign Policy Director. The President shares foreign-policy making with Congress, but he holds the most important position in international relations. His capacity for speed, unity, continuity, secrecy, and flexibility of method are qualities of utmost importance in foreign affairs. The President makes treaties and appoints ambassadors and ministers subject to the approval of the Senate. He makes executive agreements with other nations. These agreements do not have to be approved by the Senate. The President appoints special agents, takes part in international conferences, and receives the diplomatic representatives of other nations. He proposes legislation dealing with foreign aid, the tariff, international monetary policy, and other subjects.

The secretary of state is the President's chief adviser and assistant in foreign relations. Such secretaries of state as John Quincy Adams, Hamilton Fish, Daniel Webster, Charles Evans Hughes, and John Foster Dulles often made policy. In contrast, Presidents Woodrow Wilson and Franklin D. Roosevelt acted largely as their own secretaries of state. They did much of the major diplomatic negotiating, relied on such personal assistants as Colonel Edward M. House and Harry Hopkins, and often ignored their secretaries of state.

Commander in Chief. The Constitution designates the President as commander in chief of the armed forces. This post symbolizes the supremacy of civilian authority over military authority in the United States. The President decides disputes among the branches of the armed forces. He serves as the guiding spirit of military alliances with other countries. The people depend primarily on the President to keep the nation's defenses strong enough for any emergency.

The Constitution gives Congress the sole power to declare war. But the President may send the armed forces into situations that are equal to war. For example, President William McKinley sent troops into the Boxer Rebellion in 1900, and President Harry S. Truman sent them to Korea in a "police action" in 1950.

The President serves as custodian of the nation's nuclear weapons. The armed forces may not use these weapons without his approval. President Dwight D. Eisenhower threatened to use nuclear weapons against Communist China if that country did not end the Korean conflict. President John F. Kennedy ordered that nuclear weapons be made ready for action when Russian missiles in Cuba threatened U.S. security.

As commander in chief, the President can exercise much authority over domestic affairs in time of war. During World War II, Franklin D. Roosevelt created many emergency agencies, seized scores of strike-bound industrial plants, and moved thousands of American citizens of Japanese descent from the West Coast.

Legislative Leader. Almost all Presidents have taken some active role in influencing legislation. They have had varied success. President John Tyler, for example, was almost powerless before Congress. But Andrew Jackson, Lyndon B. Johnson, the Roosevelts, and Wilson won the adoption of ambitious legislative programs.

The President cannot force Congress to approve his program. If the opposing political party controls Congress, or either house of Congress, a legislative deadlock can develop. The Constitution does not provide for the deadlock to be resolved by new elections, as happens with most parliamentary systems of government.

Yet the President has powerful tools with which he can influence Congress. He can veto bills, knowing that, historically, vetoes have seldom been overridden. A threatened veto often deters Congress from action he opposes (see VETO).

The President exerts legislative leadership in his annual State of the Union message, in special messages,

---

FACTS IN BRIEF ABOUT THE PRESIDENT

Qualifications: The United States Constitution provides that a candidate for the presidency must be a "natural-born" U.S. citizen. He must also be at least 35 years old, and must have lived in the United States for at least 14 years. No law or court decision has yet defined the exact meaning of the term *natural-born*. Authorities assume that the term applies to all citizens born in the United States and its territories. But they are not sure if the term also includes children born to U.S. citizens in other countries.

How Nominated: By a national political party convention.

How Elected: By a majority vote of the Electoral College, held in December following the general election held on the first Tuesday after the first Monday in November of every fourth year.

Inauguration: Held at noon on January 20 after election. If January 20 is a Sunday, the ceremony may be held privately that day and again in public on January 21.

Term: The President is elected for four years and is eligible for a second term of four years. He may not be elected to more than two terms.

Income: $200,000 a year salary, a $50,000 annual allowance for expenses, and an annual travel allowance of $40,000. After the President leaves office, he is eligible for a $25,000-a-year pension, clerical assistants, office space, and free mailing privileges. The widow of a former President is entitled to receive a pension of $10,000 per year.

Succession: If a President dies or is disabled, the Vice-President assumes the office. See PRESIDENTIAL SUCCESSION.

Removal from Office: Impeachment by a majority vote of the House of Representatives, and trial and conviction by a two-thirds vote of those present in the Senate.

WORLD BOOK photo

The President's Desk stands in his White House office. It is often covered with important letters and documents. Decisions made here may affect the lives of people in all parts of the world.

Abbie Rowe, courtesy National Park Service

The Cabinet Room in the executive wing of the White House is the scene of meetings of government leaders. The President confers here with the Cabinet and the National Security Council.

and in actual drafts of bills submitted through his party's congressional leaders. He also issues an annual budget message and an annual economic report.

To further the progress of legislation, the President may write, telephone, or meet with leaders of the Senate and the House of Representatives. He may go directly to the people, asking for their support in statements to the newspapers or by broadcasts over radio and television. But he exercises legislative leadership perhaps most effectively through his role as head of his political party.

Political Leader. As the leader of his political party, the President chooses the national committee chairman. The committee then formally elects the man he has selected. The President usually has enough control of his party to ensure his own renomination or to hand-pick his successor.

The President can exert various pressures on the legislators of his party. He can apply his *patronage* power, or his power to make appointments to thousands of federal jobs. He may discreetly threaten that a congressman must support his legislative program or run the risk of losing the President's favor in the appointment of judges, postmasters, port collectors, and other officials. The President may also reward faithful legislators by helping them in their campaigns for re-election. Except in times of emergency, however, one of the troublesome problems of the President has been the difficulty of rallying Congress behind his program. Legislators, even in the President's own party, owe their first loyalty to their state and local party organizations, and to the voters who will either re-elect them or vote them out of office.

Popular Leader. The President has a unique claim upon the nation's attention, because he and the Vice-President are the only public officials elected by all the people. He exploits his advantageous position by telling the people in periodic radio and television addresses what he has done, or wants to do. Franklin D. Roosevelt's "fireside chats" were persuasive radio reports on the progress of his administration.

Television provides the President with an especially effective means for reaching the people. It gives him immediate access to homes throughout the nation and, with the aid of communications satellites, throughout western Europe also. President Eisenhower discussed foreign policy with his secretary of state and staged a "Cabinet meeting" before television cameras. President Kennedy often held press conferences on television. He asked for the nation's support in televised speeches during such events as the 1962 Cuban missile crisis. President Johnson appeared on national television to explain his actions when North Vietnamese torpedo boats attacked U.S. ships in 1964.

Newsmen constantly report on the activities of the President and his family. Newspapers and magazines carry articles on where the President goes to church, how his wife wears her hair, and the activities of his children. Such publicity keeps the nation's attention focused on the White House. It gives the President a great advantage over his political opponents, whose speeches and other activities usually receive far less newspaper, radio, and television coverage.

As the President has become more and more exposed to public view, concern over his "image" has grown. Modern Presidents depend heavily on their press secretaries, speechwriters, and other public relations aides who help them increase their popular appeal and "sell" their policies to the people.

Presidents watch the incoming White House mail as an indication of public sentiment. The mail averages 6,000 pieces a day. It has reached peaks of about 19,000 in one day. A large staff reads, summarizes, and answers this mail.

ROADS TO THE WHITE HOUSE

PRESIDENTIAL ELECTION

The chief road to the White House
is the presidential election,
which is held every four years.

Political Parties nominate their candidates for President and Vice-President at national conventions.

The Nation's Voters select a President and Vice-President by casting ballots for presidential electors.

The Electoral College, made up of electors chosen by all the states and the District of Columbia, elects the President and Vice-President.

SELECTION BY CONGRESS

If the Electoral College fails to
give any candidate a majority,
these steps can follow:

The House of Representatives chooses the President from among the top three candidates. Each state's House delegation has only one vote, and the winner must receive a majority of the votes that are cast.

If the House Fails to choose a President, the Vice-President, chosen by the Electoral College or the Senate, becomes President.

If Both Houses Fail to choose a President or Vice-President, Congress shall by law deal with the situation. Congress would probably make the terms of the Presidential Succession Act applicable in this case. The Speaker of the House would then become President.

PRESIDENTIAL SUCCESSION

If the President dies or
is unable to perform his duties,
he is replaced by the Vice-President.

The Vice-President, upon succeeding to the presidency, may then nominate a new Vice-President who takes office after being approved by Congress.

Next in Line to the Presidency after the Vice-President are the following government officials:

1. Speaker of the House
2. President *Pro Tempore* of the Senate
3. Secretary of State
4. Secretary of the Treasury
5. Secretary of Defense
6. Attorney General
7. Postmaster General
8. Secretary of the Interior
9. Secretary of Agriculture
10. Secretary of Commerce
11. Secretary of Labor
12. Secretary of Health, Education, and Welfare
13. Secretary of Housing and Urban Development
14. Secretary of Transportation

The Executive Office. The President is personally responsible for so many duties that he cannot possibly handle each without assistance. The staff of the Executive Office cares for many of these duties. It includes more than 1,000 persons who work in the White House and the adjacent Executive Office Building. The White House Office includes the President's physician; military aide; press, personal, and social secretaries; and special assistants and advisers. The Executive Office also includes the Bureau of the Budget, Council of Economic Advisers, National Security Council, Office of Economic Opportunity, National Aeronautics and Space Council, Office of Emergency Planning, Office of Science and Technology, Office of the Special Representative for Trade Negotiations, and National Council on Marine Resources and Engineering Development. Executive departments, such as the Department of State, are not part of the Executive Office, although they are part of the *executive branch* of the government.

Before 1967, the role of the Executive Office was important in running the government when the President became ill. After President Wilson's stroke, the White House was run by Mrs. Wilson; Joseph Tumulty, his secretary; and Rear Admiral Cary T. Grayson, his doctor. When President Eisenhower was ill, Sherman Adams, his aide, ran internal White House operations. Vice-President Nixon performed other of his tasks.

Amendment 25 to the United States Constitution, proclaimed in 1967, stipulates that if the President is disabled, the Vice-President becomes Acting President. If a disabled President refuses to yield his power, the Vice-President, with the approval of a majority of the Cabinet or a special commission, may relieve him of his duties temporarily. When the President declares he is again fit for office, he resumes his duties. But if the Vice-President and a majority of the Cabinet or the commission believe he is still disabled, Congress then decides the issue.

How a President Is Elected

The Nomination. History has proved that anyone wanting to become President will have a better chance if he lives in a populous industrial state. He must be physically capable of going through a strenuous political campaign and assuming the burdens of the presidency. He must be acceptable to the professional organization of his party. He must demonstrate that his views and talents are what the people feel they need and want. He must appear to be a winner.

A candidate may find it more difficult to capture his party's nomination than to win the election. Normally, he must build personal organizations in as many states as possible. He must get to know many voters, party workers, and potential delegates to the national convention, and offer a platform of wide appeal to voters.

Some candidates take part in primary elections. Voters in the primaries select delegates to the national party convention who have announced their support of a particular candidate.

The convention itself is a political spectacle of extravagant oratory, wild cheering, and marching delegates. But what really counts is not the fanfare, but the behind-the-scenes appeals of the candidates and their managers for delegate support. Deals may be made, patronage promised, a platform altered. Even the vice-

EXECUTIVE OFFICE OF THE PRESIDENT

William R. Wilson

WHITE HOUSE OFFICE
Includes the President's press, personal, and social secretaries; physician; military aide; and special assistants and advisers who help him make policies and present his ideas to Congress and to the people. The White House Office also includes the First Lady's press secretary and staff.

BUREAU OF THE BUDGET
Prepares the federal budget that the President presents to Congress each year. The Bureau also acts as a "watchdog" to supervise the administration of the budget, and suggests ways to make the work of federal government agencies more efficient and economical. A director is in charge of the Bureau.

NATIONAL COUNCIL ON MARINE RESOURCES AND ENGINEERING DEVELOPMENT
Works to assure that marine science activities are used to promote the nation's security and welfare. The office includes the Vice-President; Secretaries of State, the Navy, the Interior, Commerce, Transportation, and Health, Education, and Welfare; and other officials.

COUNCIL OF ECONOMIC ADVISERS
Studies the national economy, evaluates federal economic policies and programs, and recommends ways to promote economic growth and stability. The Council helps the President prepare the annual economic report to Congress. A chairman and two other members form the Council.

NATIONAL AERONAUTICS AND SPACE COUNCIL
Includes the Vice-President, Secretaries of State and Defense, Administrator of the National Aeronautics and Space Council, and Chairman of the Atomic Energy Commission. It plans the aeronautics and space program, and helps assign space responsibilities to U.S. government agencies.

OFFICE OF ECONOMIC OPPORTUNITY
Manages the United States antipoverty program, often called the War on Poverty. The Office administers the Job Corps, Volunteers in Service to America (VISTA), and the Community Action Program. A director is in charge of the Office.

NATIONAL SECURITY COUNCIL
Includes the President, Vice-President, Secretaries of State and Defense, Director of the Office of Emergency Planning, and other officials. It coordinates federal programs that affect U.S. security. The Central Intelligence Agency informs the Council about U.S. intelligence operations.

OFFICE OF EMERGENCY PLANNING
Advises the President on using the nation's resources, stabilizing the civilian economy, and organizing the federal government after an enemy attack or other emergency. The Office also studies the U.S. civil defense program, and assigns radio frequencies to government agencies.

SPECIAL REPRESENTATIVE FOR TRADE NEGOTIATIONS
Works to increase United States trade with other countries. The Special Representative and two Deputies make agreements with other countries for reducing tariffs. These officials also advise the President on many international trade matters.

OFFICE OF SCIENCE AND TECHNOLOGY
Works to assure that science is used effectively to promote the nation's security and welfare. The Office evaluates the scientific and technological programs of the federal government, and works to improve the relationship between the government and the nation's scientists and engineers.

presidency may be bargained away for votes. If support of the major candidates becomes deadlocked, the nomination may go to a "dark horse" such as Warren G. Harding in 1920. See POLITICAL CONVENTION.

The Campaign usually begins in earnest on Labor Day. Many presidential campaigns have been highlighted with slogans and catchwords. The Whigs campaigned on "Tippecanoe and Tyler, Too" in 1840. "Turn the Rascals Out," Liberal Republicans demanded in 1872. "You Never Had It So Good," claimed the Democrats in 1952.

Candidates may "barnstorm" the country in tours or conduct "front-porch" campaigns at home. In 1896, William Jennings Bryan toured the country. His opponent William McKinley stayed at home in Canton, Ohio, and read carefully written statements to delegations assembled on his front steps. In 1948, Harry S. Truman made a folksy "whistle-stop" tour by train, hammering the theme of "the plain people's President against the privileged people's Congress."

Presidential candidates usually travel with a large staff of speech writers, researchers, secretaries, and policy advisers. They are also accompanied by reporters and photographers "covering" the campaign. Candidates usually travel by airplane, especially if they are concentrating on the votes of large cities. The candidates use television for speeches and informal statements. In 1960, televised debates between the two candidates were held for the first time.

The Election is held every four years, on the first Tuesday after the first Monday in November. Technically, the voters choose the Electoral College, which later elects the President. Actually, the public knows who the next President will be a few hours after the polls close. See ELECTORAL COLLEGE.

Life of the President

The President can never escape from his job. He may spend his evenings reading reports, and his sleep may be broken by a sudden crisis in the United States or in some faraway corner of the world. When the President leaves Washington, his official problems go with him. The White House mail pouch arrives daily, bringing papers for him to read and sign. He keeps in close touch with his aides in Washington by private telephone lines and by secret radio channels.

In the White House. The nature of the President's workday depends on the man and on the times. President Chester A. Arthur, who loved leisure, worked only a four-day week. He began each day at 10 A.M. and took three hours off for lunch. Today, the President usually puts in a long work week that revolves around a series of meetings and appointments. He meets with the secretary of state, the secretary of defense, the chairman of the Joint Chiefs of Staff, and the chairman of the Council of Economic Advisers. He also presides over meetings of the Cabinet, the National Security Council, his legislative leaders from Congress, and a press conference. Before each meeting, members of his staff brief him on the subjects to be discussed. He also receives daily briefings on security matters from his assistant for national security affairs and from the director of the Central Intelligence Agency.

Wide World

Presidential Nominating Conventions began in the 1830's. Previously, candidates had been nominated by congressional caucuses, state legislatures, state conventions, or local meetings.

The first official seen by the President each morning at his office is usually the presidential assistant. With his assistant, the President makes assignments for the day and goes over reports. The assistant may be in and out of the President's office six or seven times a day, bringing him reports or receiving instructions for other staff members.

When the President is not presiding over meetings or preparing for them, he sees many visitors from all walks of life. President Truman received visitors from 10 or 11 A.M. to 1 P.M., and resumed at 3 P.M. for another hour or more. Most calls are limited to 15 minutes. To save the President's time, visitors must give the appointments secretary a memorandum of subjects to be discussed long before the meeting. The President receives this memorandum just before the conference.

In a typical day, President Eisenhower had 15 appointments during which he saw perhaps 40 persons. Sometimes the chief executive has appointments with whole delegations, such as labor leaders, political workers, or 4-H Club boys and girls. They file through his office or, weather permitting, meet the President briefly in the rose garden of the White House.

The President's Travels. "I am much pleased," wrote President George Washington after a tour of the South, "to see with my own eyes the situation of the country . . . and to learn more accurately the disposition of the people . . ." Most Presidents have been seasoned travelers. They travel to learn "the disposition of the people," to carry important issues to the public, or to campaign for re-election. They may also go outside the United States in performing the duties of their office.

During his 12 years in office, President Franklin D. Roosevelt traveled about 364,000 miles. President Eisenhower made many trips abroad, including one journey of 22,370 miles in which he visited 11 countries in 19 days. The President has a special yacht, several aircraft, and a private railroad car. He may also use a naval ship. During prolonged visits, he may set up a "temporary White House," as did President Truman at Key West, Fla.; Franklin D. Roosevelt at Warm

68od

ELECTION CAMPAIGNS

Brown Bros.

The Front-Porch Campaign of Warren G. Harding, *right*, in 1920, resembled the tactics which William McKinley used so successfully in the elections of 1896 and 1900.

The Whistle-Stop Campaign reached a high point in 1948. President Harry S. Truman, *above*, toured the United States in a special railroad car during his battle for election.

Springs, Ga.; and Theodore Roosevelt at Sagamore Hill in Oyster Bay, N.Y. A staff of assistants accompanies the President to the temporary White House.

Guarding the President. The Secret Service maintains a 24-hour guard in the White House and accompanies the President wherever he goes. If he takes a walk, plays golf, or goes to the theater, Secret Service men always accompany him. When the President is driven in his limousine, Secret Service agents precede and follow him, alert for danger. If the President stays in a hotel, he usually takes over an entire floor. An elevator is reserved for the presidential party.

When the President travels by train, the switches en route are spiked and guarded. The train crew is specially selected, and the locomotive and coaches are checked. An advance train tests the safety of the route. When the President crosses the ocean by air, naval vessels are stationed at various points along the way. See SECRET SERVICE, UNITED STATES.

Social Responsibilities. The President's duties take up much of his social life. As chief of state, he gives official dinners in the White House for the diplomatic corps, the Supreme Court, and the Vice-President. He holds a half-dozen formal receptions a year, as well as special dinners and receptions for visiting dignitaries. Presidents Martin Van Buren and Arthur were among the heaviest entertainers. Calvin Coolidge always insisted that his formal dinners reflect the wealth of the country and the dignity of the presidency.

Theodore Roosevelt liked to have three or four luncheon guests of varying backgrounds to provide lively conversation. President Eisenhower introduced the White House "stag dinner," with a dozen or more male guests from public and private life. President Kennedy invited leading artists to perform at White House social affairs.

Recreation. In their free time, Presidents have turned to various forms of recreation. Grover Cleveland, Herbert Hoover, and others preferred fishing. Franklin D. Roosevelt swam and collected stamps. Theodore Roosevelt hiked, boxed, and hunted big game. Warren G. Harding played poker, Woodrow Wilson liked billiards, and Dwight D. Eisenhower played golf.

Salary. A 1969 law fixed the President's salary at $200,000 a year. The President also has a $50,000 annual expense allowance and a $40,000 travel allowance. Increases in the President's salary reflect the rising cost of maintaining his office and the White House. In 1789, the first Congress fixed the President's salary at $25,000 a year. In 1873, it was raised to $50,000. A 1906 law authorized travel expenses up to $25,000 a year. In 1909, the salary was raised to $75,000 a year. The travel allowance was raised to $40,000 in 1948. In 1949, the President's salary was set at $100,000 a year, and he was given a $50,000 expense allowance.

Retirement. As he leaves office, a President carries with him great prestige and sometimes great influence. He may retire to private life, but his responsibilities as a party leader and national figure often continue. Popular ex-Presidents, such as Dwight D. Eisenhower, have been called upon by their parties to campaign for the party nominees in congressional and presidential elections.

Ex-Presidents Grover Cleveland and Theodore Roosevelt ran again for the presidency. Cleveland won a second term in 1892, after serving his first term from 1885 to 1889. Some ex-Presidents served in other important government positions. John Quincy Adams was elected to the House of Representatives. William Howard Taft became chief justice of the Supreme Court. Some ex-Presidents served as advisers to succeeding Presidents. For example, Thomas Jefferson advised Presidents Madison and Monroe, and influenced the development of the Monroe Doctrine. In 1963, the Senate added to the stature of ex-Presidents by approving a proposal that permits them to speak on the Senate floor.

Development of the Presidency

The Constitutional Convention that met in 1787 did not have an exact working model to follow in creating the presidency. The convention delegates consulted the examples of the British monarch and of the governors of the royal provinces. They studied the writings of John Locke, Montesquieu, and Sir William Blackstone. Above all, they examined the New York governorship, easily the strongest governorship of the day.

680e

Association of American Railroads

Andrew Jackson was the first President to ride on a railroad train. In 1833, he rode from Ellicott's Mill, Md., to Baltimore.

Wide World

Theodore Roosevelt met with Russian and Japanese delegates in 1905 and helped end the Russo-Japanese War. In 1906, he became the first American to win the Nobel prize for peace.

INTERESTING FACTS

Who is the only President buried in Washington, D.C.? Wilson.

Who was the only President who had served as speaker of the house? Polk.

Who was the largest President? Taft, who stood about 6 feet tall and weighed more than 300 pounds.

Who was the only President to serve two nonconsecutive terms? Cleveland.

Who held the first regular presidential press conferences? Wilson.

Who was the first President to be sworn into office on an airplane? Lyndon B. Johnson.

Who was the only man to serve as both President and chief justice? Taft.

Who was the first President sworn into office by a woman? Lyndon B. Johnson by Judge Sarah T. Hughes.

Who was the only President to be married in the White House? Cleveland.

Who was the first President to visit a foreign country while in office? Theodore Roosevelt.

Which Presidents are buried in Arlington National Cemetery? Taft and Kennedy.

Who was the only man whose father and son both became President? John Scott Harrison.

Who were the only Presidents to be sworn into office by a former President? Coolidge and Hoover (by Taft).

Which President never married? Buchanan.

Who were the only father and son who both served as President? John Adams and John Quincy Adams.

What two former Presidents died on the same day? John Adams and Jefferson.

Which Presidents lived past the age of 90? John Adams and Hoover.

What President lived the shortest time? Kennedy, 46.

Which President was elected by the widest margin? Lyndon B. Johnson, by almost 16 million votes.

Who was the first President nominated by a national political convention? Jackson.

Who was the first President to live in the White House? John Adams.

James Madison in 1809 gave the first inaugural ball ever held in Washington, D.C.

Some Founding Fathers favored a weak, even a plural, executive, largely the creature of the legislature. The majority, dissatisfied with the weak executive of the Articles of Confederation, supported a strong executive. Mindful of the popular fear of monarchy, the delegates, for practical reasons, rejected Alexander Hamilton's proposal for an executive having the powers and tenure of the British monarch. The title *President* had been used to designate the chief executive officer of Congress under the Articles of Confederation.

Growth of Presidential Powers. In the years since the Founding Fathers established the presidency, the President's powers and responsibilities have grown tremendously. Power, personality, and circumstance have contributed to the development of the presidency. The legal powers granted to the President have not changed greatly since 1789. But the use of these powers has differed strikingly among Presidents. The Presidents have varied in imagination, energy, political know-how, speaking skills, and other qualities. Presidents with strong personalities often excelled at "selling" their policies to the public or to Congress. The nature of the times may greatly affect what the President can do with his legal powers. During periods of peace, the power of the presidency may decline. In time of war, economic depression, or social reform, its powers may greatly increase.

Strong and weak Presidents have appeared in almost regular cycles. President George Washington, aided by the skillful Alexander Hamilton, truly led the country and Congress. Thomas Jefferson, more a party leader than a chief executive, was a highly successful President, although he tended to defer to Congress. Under his weaker successors, the office declined.

Andrew Jackson restored the presidency to its original vigor with his extraordinary personality. He regarded his powers as autonomous, declaring that "The Executive must . . . itself be guided by its own opinion of the Constitution." During the Civil War, Abraham Lincoln exercised the "war power" entirely on his own

ABOUT PRESIDENTS

Which President had the most children? Tyler, 15.

Who was the first President to be married while in office? Tyler.

Who was the first President to be inaugurated in Washington, D.C.? Jefferson.

Who was the first President to speak on radio? Wilson.

Who was the first President to speak on television? F. D. Roosevelt.

What two Presidents died in the White House? W. H. Harrison and Taylor.

Which President served the shortest time in office? W. H. Harrison, one month, 1841.

Which President served the longest? F. D. Roosevelt, twelve years, one month, eight days.

Which Presidents were born in log cabins? Jackson, Polk, Fillmore, Buchanan, Lincoln, Garfield.

Which President received the greatest number of electoral votes? F. D. Roosevelt in 1936, 523.

Which President was elected unanimously by the Electoral College? Washington, 1789, 1792.

Which President ran for office without an opponent? Monroe, 1820.

Beginning in 1840, all Presidents elected at 20-year intervals have died in office. Who are they? W. H. Harrison, Lincoln, Garfield, McKinley, Harding, Franklin Roosevelt, and Kennedy.

Which Presidents signed the Constitution? Washington, Madison.

Who was the only child of a President to be born in the White House? Esther Cleveland, 1893.

Which Presidents were assassinated? Lincoln, Garfield, McKinley, Kennedy.

What other Presidents died in office? W. H. Harrison, Taylor, Harding, Franklin D. Roosevelt.

How many U.S. Military Academy graduates became President? Two, Grant and Eisenhower.

How many Presidents died on the Fourth of July? Three: Jefferson, 1826; John Adams, 1826; Monroe, 1831.

Who was the first President born after the adoption of the U.S. Constitution? Tyler.

United Press Int.

Dwight D. Eisenhower was the first President to travel in a jet airplane when he flew to conferences in Bonn, Germany, in 1959.

Woodrow Wilson, the first President to use radio, spoke to American troops in 1919.

Wide World

Franklin D. Roosevelt in 1939 became the first President to appear on television. He also spoke in radio "fireside chats."

authority. He instituted a manpower draft, blockaded the South, and took other strong measures. Congress's ultimate reaction against Lincoln's presidency fell on Andrew Johnson. The presidential office then went into general decline except for the administrations of Rutherford B. Hayes and Grover Cleveland.

Theodore Roosevelt, with a dynamic personality and a "stewardship theory," scored a popular success with his "Square Deal" program. He believed that the President is "bound actively and affirmatively to do all he could for the people." Roosevelt's successor, William Howard Taft, interpreted presidential power conservatively. He contended that the chief executive could do only that which can "be fairly and reasonably traced to some specific grant of power or justly implied."

Woodrow Wilson and Franklin D. Roosevelt, in leading the nation through periods of crisis, revived and extended Theodore Roosevelt's stewardship theory. Franklin Roosevelt took office during the severe economic depression of the 1930's. A master of public

relations, he radiated confidence at press conferences and in "fireside chats" on the radio. He pushed through Congress an unprecedented number of laws to support and stabilize the economy. By personal diplomacy, he led the nations that fought against Germany and Japan in World War II, and laid the basis for the United Nations. Roosevelt's actions during the war committed succeeding U.S. Presidents to a continuing role of leadership in world affairs.

President Harry S. Truman faced the beginnings of the Cold War between the East and the West. He helped expand and regularize the role of the U.S. President as leader of the Free World. He used aid to Greece and Turkey, the European Recovery Program, and the "Point Four" program of help to underdeveloped nations to meet the threat of Communism. Acting under the United Nations charter, and on his own authority as commander in chief, Truman sent U.S. troops to fight in Korea without a declaration of war from Congress.

Dwight D. Eisenhower's administration faced few

HOW TO PREPARE FOR THE PRESIDENCY

BY PRESIDENT JOHN F. KENNEDY
1961-1963

Fred Blumenthal, Washington correspondent of Parade Magazine, *asked President Kennedy this question: "Somewhere in our land today there is a high school or college student who will one day be sitting in your chair. If you could now speak to this future President, what advice and guidance would you give him or her?" This was the President's answer:*

The first lesson of the presidency is that it is impossible to foretell the precise nature of the problems that will confront you or the specific skills and capacities which those problems will demand. It is an office which called upon a man of peace, Lincoln, to become a great leader in a bloody war; which required a profound believer in limiting the scope of federal government, Jefferson, to expand dramatically the powers and range of that government; which challenged a man dedicated to domestic social reform, Franklin Roosevelt, to lead this nation into a deep and irrevocable involvement in world affairs. And when you assume the presidency you too will face problems, difficulties, crises and challenges which no one can now foresee.

In 1645, John Winthrop, Deputy Governor of Massachusetts Bay Colony after a long and stormy trial acquitting him of impeachment for exceeding his authority, reminded his fellow citizens that "when you call one to be a magistrate, he doth not profess nor undertake to have sufficient skill for that office, nor can you furnish him with gifts. . . therefore you must run the hazard of his skill and ability."

This insight into the nature of governing affirms the lesson of our history that there is no program of vocational training for the presidency; no specific area of knowledge that is peculiarly relevant. Nor are qualities of great leadership drawn from any particular section of the country or section of society. Nine of our Presidents, among them some of the most brilliant in office, did not attend college; whereas Thomas Jefferson was one of the great scholars of the age and Woodrow Wilson the president of Princeton University. We have had Presidents who were lawyers and soldiers and teachers. One was an engineer and another a journalist. They have been drawn from the wealthiest and most distinguished families of the nation, and have come from poor and anonymous beginnings. Some, seemingly well endowed with great abilities and fine qualities, were unable to cope with the demands of the office, while others rose to a greatness far beyond any expectation.

Thus I cannot counsel you about what subjects to study or what vocation to follow. But whatever you do you would be well advised to practice stern discipline and vigorous, unremitting effort. For high qualities and great achievements are not merely matters of chance or birth. They are the product of long and disciplined toil.

Yet, in a more general way, there are experiences which you can pursue, experiences which will support you in the conduct of your great office.

It will help you to know the country you seek to lead. It was one of the great strengths of a President such as Theodore Roosevelt that he knew and loved the diverse magnificence of our fields and mountain ranges, deserts and great rivers, our abundant farmlands and the thousand voices of our cities. No revolution in communication or transportation can destroy the fact that this continent is, as Whitman said, "a nation of nations," which you must see and know before you can govern.

Nor is it accidental that many of our outstanding Presidents, men such as Jefferson or Wilson or Truman, have had a deep sense of history. For of all the disciplines, the study of the folly and achievements of man is best calculated to help develop the critical sense of what is permanent and meaningful amid the mass of superficial and transient events and decisions which engulf the presidency. And it is on this sense, more than any other, that great leadership depends.

Most important of all, and most difficult to consciously pursue, is an understanding of the people you will lead. You, and at times you alone, will be the spokesman for the great and often silent majority. And the final measure of your administration will, in large measure, rest on how well you respond to their inward hopes while leading them toward new horizons of ambition and achievement. Perhaps you will derive this quality from your origins, as did Lincoln; or from the application of understanding and compassion to the problems of government, as did Franklin Roosevelt. Yet, although the possible sources of this understanding are many, if you find the opportunity to know and work with Americans of diverse backgrounds, occupations and beliefs, then I would urge you to take eagerly that opportunity to enrich yourself.

As a great world leader you will have problems and responsibilities which were not faced by Presidents throughout much of our history. As President of the United States you are a focus of the attention, ambitions and desires of people and nations throughout the world. It will help you to travel and to learn about these other lands. For the welfare and security of the United States, the future of your own country, is bound to your capacity to exercise leadership and judgment on a global scale.

The most important human qualities of leadership are best embodied in that most towering of American Presidents, Lincoln: a combination of humility and self-confidence, inner resolution and energy, which gives a President the capacity to listen to others, to be aware of his own limitations, but also to follow the command of John Adams that "In all great and essential measures the President is bound by honor and his conscience. . . to act his own mature and unbiased judgment." I can advise you to be aware of the importance of these qualities, but no one can tell you how to develop them. I only hope, for the welfare of our country, that you will possess them when you come to office.

No one can guarantee that if you follow this or any other advice you will become a great President. For the presidency is peculiarly an office which is shaped by the individual who holds it. And greatness depends on the times as well as the man. But if you work toward your goal, practice discipline and unremitting effort, wish Godspeed to those who will hold and protect the great office of the Republic so that it may pass unimpaired to you and those who will follow you, then, if some chance keeps you from the presidency, you will still know that you are prepared to serve well your nation as a citizen.

© 1962, Parade Publications, Inc., 733 Third Ave., New York 17, N.Y.

major crises. The mood of the American people favored a moderately conservative presidency. Eisenhower helped end the conflict in Korea, and proposed to make atomic energy available to all nations for peaceful purposes. Eisenhower used a new technique of presidential power to meet Communist threats in Lebanon and Quemoy. He received permission from Congress, in advance of actual conflict, to use United States military forces when he thought it necessary to do so.

President John F. Kennedy's worst setback and his strongest achievement occurred during crisis. Kennedy was blamed for not supplying air support to an invasion attempt against Castro's Cuba in 1961. But in 1962, Kennedy's naval blockade of Cuba forced Soviet Premier Nikita Khrushchev to remove Russian missiles from the island. Kennedy used a wide variety of presidential powers in support of civil rights for Negroes. He sent federal troops to the University of Mississippi when a mob threatened to prevent James Meredith, a Negro, from enrolling in the school. He also used personal persuasion, provisions in government contracts, and civil service procedures to promote civil rights. But Kennedy had only limited success in getting Congress to act on his civil rights bill and other domestic legislation.

President Lyndon B. Johnson, a former Senate Democratic leader, was highly successful in his role as legislative leader. Johnson persuaded Congress to pass the civil rights and tax cut bills proposed by Kennedy. He also won congressional approval of his own *War on Poverty* program. In 1964, Congress approved the Gulf of Tonkin resolution, which gave Johnson power to take "all necessary steps" to help South Vietnam defend itself. By late 1968 Johnson had authorized the use of over 540,000 U.S. troops in Vietnam.

The repeated success of U.S. Presidents in leading the nation in periods of challenge and change has produced much of the office's enormous prestige. The presidency is always an accumulation of the triumphs, failures, and practices of the past. And the office is always bigger than the man.

Challenges to the Presidency are built into the U.S. system of government. The legislative and judicial branches of the government sometimes act to prohibit or limit presidential action that might lead to an expansion of the President's powers.

Congress presents a never-ending challenge to the presidency. The most serious conflict between Congress and the executive branch resulted in the impeachment of President Andrew Johnson. If the Senate had convicted Johnson, the presidency might have been doomed to weakness for years afterward.

The Supreme Court may also limit the President. In the case of *ex parte Milligan* (1866), for example, the Court ruled that the President had unlawfully authorized the trial of civilians by military commissions in an area far removed from the theater of war. Union forces had arrested a civilian and tried him before a military commission. He was found guilty of treasonable practices and sentenced to be hanged.

In *Schechter Brothers vs. United States* (1935), the Supreme Court declared unconstitutional the executive orders regulating the economy under broad authority delegated by Congress. Under the National Recovery Act of 1933, the President had approved a code regulating trade practices, wages, and working hours in the live-poultry industry of New York City. This decision did much to end the National Recovery Administration (see NATIONAL RECOVERY ADMINISTRATION).

In *Youngstown Sheet and Tube Company vs. Sawyer* (1952), the Court held that the President's seizure and operation of the country's steel mills on his own authority, rather than on the authority of Congress, was unconstitutional. The seizure had occurred shortly before a nationwide steel strike was to take place.

But such challenges from Congress and the Supreme Court have never been great enough to bring about a lasting halt in the trend toward expansion of the President's importance and responsibility. The continuing atmosphere of international crisis, the tendency to choose Presidents with dynamic personalities, and the communications advances that aid the President in appealing for popular support all suggest that the impact and prestige of the office will continue to grow.　　　　　　　　　　　　　LOUIS W. KOENIG

Related Articles. See the separate biographies of each President. Other articles in WORLD BOOK include:

Address, Form of	Franking and	United States,
Budget,	Penalty Privileges	History of
Bureau of the	Hail to the Chief	United States
Cabinet	Hot Line	Constitution
Central Intel-	Impeachment	Vice-President
ligence Agency	National Security	of the United
Economic Advisers,	Council	States
Council of	Political	White House
Election	Convention	White House
Electoral College	Political Party	Conferences
Flag (color pic-	Presidential	White House
ture: Flags of	Succession	Hostess
the United States	United States,	
Government)	Government of	

Outline

I. Roles of the President
　A. Chief of State
　B. Chief Executive
　C. Foreign Policy
　　　Director
　D. Commander in Chief
　E. Legislative Leader
　F. Political Leader
　G. Popular Leader
　H. The Executive Office

II. How a President Is Elected
　A. The Nomination
　B. The Campaign
　C. The Election

III. Life of the President
　A. In the White House
　B. The President's
　　　Travels
　C. Guarding the
　　　President
　D. Social Responsibilities
　E. Recreation
　F. Salary
　G. Retirement

IV. Development of the Presidency
　A. Growth of Presi-
　　　dential Powers
　B. Challenges to
　　　the Presidency

Questions

What are the qualifications of a presidential candidate?
Who succeeds a President if he dies in office?
Who elects the President? When?
How may a President be removed from office?
In what ways is the President "many men in one"?
How does the President lead his political party?
How does he exercise legislative leadership?
Where does the President receive his authority to delegate duties to subordinates?
How do the responsibilities of the President affect his private life?
What is the role of the Executive Office?
What forms of recreation have Presidents favored?

PRESIDENTIAL DISABILITY. See UNITED STATES CONSTITUTION (Amendment 25).

PRESIDENTIAL MEDAL OF FREEDOM. See DECORATIONS AND MEDALS (Civilian Awards; table).

PRESIDENTIAL RANGE. See WHITE MOUNTAINS.

PRESIDENTIAL SUCCESSION is provided for by Article II of the United States Constitution. It states that the Vice-President shall assume the duties and powers of the President if the President dies or is unable to carry out the duties of his office. Amendment 20 of the United States Constitution, adopted in 1933, provides that the Vice-President-elect becomes President if the President-elect dies before his term begins. If both the President and Vice-President should die or become disqualified, succession to the presidency is determined by the Presidential Succession Act of 1886, amended in 1947. This law states that the speaker of the House, and then the president *pro tempore* of the Senate, are next in succession to the presidency. The Cabinet follows in this order:

1. Secretary of State
2. Secretary of the Treasury
3. Secretary of Defense
4. Attorney General
5. Postmaster General
6. Secretary of the Interior
7. Secretary of Agriculture
8. Secretary of Commerce
9. Secretary of Labor
10. Secretary of Health, Education, and Welfare
11. Secretary of Housing and Urban Development
12. Secretary of Transportation

The Agriculture, Commerce, and Labor departments were not in existence when the law was passed in 1886. They were included in the Presidential Succession Act of 1947. Also that year, the secretary of defense was given the place formerly held by the secretary of war. In 1965, Congress added the secretaries of health, education, and welfare; and housing and urban development to presidential succession. The secretary of transportation was added in 1966. No Cabinet member may become acting President unless he is a citizen and at least 35 years old. If the Cabinet member who would logically succeed to the presidency is less than 35, the presidency passes to the next eligible Cabinet member.

Under the terms of Amendment 25, proclaimed in 1967, it is unlikely that anyone other than the Vice-President would ever succeed to the presidency. The amendment permits the President to nominate a Vice-President whenever a vacancy exists in that office. The nominee would take office when confirmed by a majority vote of both houses of Congress. Therefore, the office of Vice-President would almost always be filled. The amendment also establishes procedures for temporarily relieving the President if he becomes unable to perform his duties because of illness or for any other reason. The Vice-President would become acting President at such times. MURRAY S. STEDMAN, JR.

See also CABINET; UNITED STATES CONSTITUTION (Amendments 20 and 25).

PRESIDIO. See MONTEREY.

PRESIDIO OF SAN FRANCISCO. See SAN FRANCISCO (The Presidio; map).

PRESIDIUM. See RUSSIA (Government [table]); POLITBURO.

PRE-SOCRATIC PHILOSOPHY is the earliest stage of Western philosophy. The name refers to philosophy before Socrates. The pre-Socratic philosophers were the first to seek knowledge to satisfy their curiosity about natural processes, rather than for practical advantage or for religious purposes.

Pre-Socratic philosophy began in the 500's B.C. in Ionia, on the coast of Asia across the Aegean Sea from Greece. The Ionian wise men were impressed by the constant change they observed—changes of seasons, changes from day to night, transition from life to death. They felt that something must be permanent that endures through change.

Early Pre-Socratic Philosophers were chiefly concerned with discovering the nature of this underlying permanence. They held different views, but all believed that this permanence was material. Thales, the first known Ionian philosopher, said it was water; Heraclitus, fire; and Anaximenes, air. But the main importance of these philosophers lies in the fact that they first raised the question of the basic nature of things, and that they believed the permanent has a unity or order that can be known by the human mind.

The followers of the mathematician Pythagoras distinguished between the world of change and the world of number. They discovered the principle of musical harmony and believed this principle could be explained in terms of number. From this, they decided that all things are capable of number, and that number gives order and harmony to the whole world. The harmony in man's body is his soul.

Parmenides differed from the other pre-Socratic philosophers by believing that change is an illusion. For him, the only reality was *that which is* rather than *that which changes* or *only seems*. Parmenides thus introduced the important distinction between reason and the senses, between truth and appearance.

Later Pre-Socratic Philosophers tried to answer Parmenides' logical arguments against change. Empedocles gave up the earlier notion that only one substance exists. Everything, he said, is a mixture of four elements—earth, water, air, and fire—set in motion by the forces of Love and Strife. Anaxagoras kept the idea of many kinds of "stuffs," but introduced the principle of Mind as the organizing element. He thus abandoned the emphasis on physical and material forces.

The pre-Socratics were primarily concerned with the nature of the *cosmos* (world) and its objects. They examined the problem of the one and the many, unity and multiplicity. They failed to solve the problem, but they made important contributions to later thought by the gradual introduction of so many distinctions and new concepts. These were later taken up by Plato and Aristotle in their brilliant attempts to solve the same problem. JASON L. SAUNDERS

Related Articles in WORLD BOOK include:

Anaxagoras	Empedocles	Pythagoras
Anaximenes	Heraclitus	Socrates
Atomism	Parmenides	Thales

PRESQUE ISLE, *PRESK ILE,* Me. (pop. 12,886; alt. 446 ft.), is the largest city in Aroostook County. It lies in the center of the large Aroostook potato-producing region in northeastern Maine (see MAINE [political map]). The area was settled in the 1820's, but Presque Isle was not incorporated until 1859. ROBERT M. YORK

PRESS. See NEWSPAPER; PRINTING; FREEDOM OF THE PRESS.

PRESS AGENT. See PUBLIC RELATIONS.

PRESS ASSOCIATION. See NEWS SERVICE.

PRESS CLIPPING BUREAU, or *Clipping Bureau,* is an organization set up to furnish customers with clippings of articles that have appeared in various publications. Authors, actors, politicians, and organizations often subscribe to clipping services. The first clipping bureau was started by Count de Chambure in Paris in 1876. It was called *L'Argus de la Presse* (*The All-seeing Eye of the Newspapers*). EARL FRANKLIN ENGLISH

PRESSBURG. See BRATISLAVA.

PRESSBURG, TREATY OF, was signed on Dec. 26, 1805. Napoleon Bonaparte, the French emperor, forced Austria to sign the treaty after a brilliant victory in the Battle of Austerlitz (see AUSTERLITZ, BATTLE OF).

Under the terms of the treaty, Austria had to give Venice, Istria, and the Dalmatian coast to Italy, and to recognize Napoleon as king of Italy. Austria also ceded important areas to three of Napoleon's satellites: Bavaria, Baden, and Württemberg. ROBERT G. L. WAITE

PRESSEY, SIDNEY L. See TEACHING MACHINE.

PRESSURE is often defined as force per unit area. In physics, the term is usually applied to *fluids* (gases or liquids). If a fluid is exposed to suitable forces, pressure is produced in it. The greater the force, the greater the pressure. Pressure is measured in such units as pounds per square inch or grams per square centimeter.

Atmospheric pressure is one of the most common examples of pressure. It is produced by the weight of the air from the top of the atmosphere as it presses down upon the layers of air below it. At sea level, the average atmospheric pressure is 14.7 pounds per square inch. This decreases with altitude because of less air pressing from above. See AIR (Weight and Pressure).

If a fluid is at rest, pressure is transmitted equally to all its parts and, at any one point, is the same in all directions. The fluid acts this way because the molecules in it move freely. The molecules are far apart in a gas and comparatively close together in a liquid.

The French scientist Blaise Pascal discovered the fact that pressure in a fluid is transmitted equally to all distances and in all directions. He formulated *Pascal's Law* to describe the effects of pressure within a liquid (see HYDROSTATICS; PASCAL'S LAW). This law has many practical applications. For example, it controls the action of hydraulic brakes and presses. See HYDRAULICS.

The greater the pressure in a gas, the smaller its volume. This decrease in volume occurs because the molecules are pushed closer together. Under ordinary conditions, the volume of a gas decreases by half when the pressure doubles. The law that describes how the volume of a gas changes when the pressure changes is called *Boyle's Law,* after Robert Boyle, the Irish scientist who discovered it (see GAS [Gas Laws]). The volume of liquids and solids also decreases when pressure increases, but by very much smaller amounts than for gases.

The ability of a gas to compress and expand has many practical uses. Air tires, air cushions, and air brakes are based on this elasticity of air.

Pressure changes the boiling point of water. The boiling point is that temperature at which the pressure of the steam is equal to the atmospheric pressure. At sea level, the two pressures are equal at 100°C. or 212°F. At places above sea level, the pressure is less and the temperature of the boiling point is lower. It has been found that the boiling point decreases 5°C. for every mile above sea level, or about 1°F. for every 500 feet in increase. This makes cooking at high altitudes difficult, because the cooking of food depends upon the temperature to which the food is heated, not on whether the surrounding water is boiling. See BOILING POINT.

Atmospheric pressure plays an important part in our daily lives. For example, wind is the movement of air from a point of high pressure to a point of low pressure. Pressure changes precede storms. Barometers detect storms by measuring such changes. P. W. BRIDGMAN

Related Articles in WORLD BOOK include:

Air (Science Project: The Effects of Air Pressure)	Barometer Gas Gauge	Manometer Pascal's Law

PRESSURE COOKER. See COOKING (Steaming).

PRESSURE GAUGE. See GAUGE.

PRESSURE GROUPS. See POLITICAL PARTY (Pressure Groups); GOVERNMENT (Democratic and Communist Governments); PROPAGANDA.

PRESSURE SUIT. See AVIATION MEDICINE (Hazards from Motions of Airplanes).

PRESTER JOHN (meaning *Priest John*) was a legendary Christian priest and king. He is supposed to have lived in the 1100's. Many travelers of the Middle Ages, including Marco Polo, claimed that he ruled over a vast kingdom in central Asia. Later reports, especially by Portuguese explorers, made him the emperor of Ethiopia. Prester John was said to be a direct descendant of the Magi (see MAGI). Pope Alexander III sent a messenger to look for him in 1177, but the messenger never returned. ARTHUR M. SELVI

PRETORIA, *pree TOHR ee uh* (pop. 303,684; met. area 422,590; alt. 4,472 ft.), is one of the two capitals of South Africa. The president directs the administrative affairs of the country from Pretoria, and Parliament meets in Cape Town, about 830 miles to the southwest. The city lies on a plateau in the province of Transvaal. See SOUTH AFRICA (color map; picture).

Many residents of Pretoria hold government jobs. Others work in railroad workshops, and in factories that make steel, cement, chemicals, paint, glassware, pottery, and metal products. Pretoria also has a university, a zoo, several museums, and an observatory.

The Boers founded Pretoria in 1855. When the Union of South Africa was formed in 1910, Pretoria became the administrative capital. HIBBERD V. B. KLINE, JR.

PRETORIUS, *pree TOE ree us,* was the family name of two pioneer *Boer,* or Dutch, leaders in South Africa, father and son. Both were born in Graaff-Reinet, Cape Colony. The people of South Africa named their capital city *Pretoria* in honor of these two patriots.

Andries Wilhelmus Jacobus Pretorius (1799-1853) was selected by his fellow Boers to lead them on the *Great Trek,* a migration from the British-held Cape Colony to free territory farther north. As commandant of the Boer forces, he won an important victory over the Zulu chief, Dingaan, in 1838. He opposed British rule in South Africa, and helped establish the South African Republic (now Transvaal Province) in 1852.

Marthinus Wessels Pretorius (1819-1901) succeeded his father as leader of the Transvaal Boers. He served as president of the Orange Free State and the South African Republic. In 1880, Pretorius aided in the successful revolt against the British annexation of the Transvaal.   T. WALTER WALLBANK

PRETZEL is a type of German biscuit. It is brittle and twisted, with a glazed, salted surface. *Pretzel* comes from the Latin word *pretiola*, meaning *a small reward*. The pretzel was first made by monks in southern Europe as a reward for children who learned their prayers. It was shaped to represent the crossed arms of a child praying. The first commercial pretzel bakery in the United States opened in Lititz, Pa., in 1861. This bakery is still in operation.

PREVAILING WESTERLY is a wind that blows over the North and South middle latitudes in an easterly direction. Prevailing westerlies over the South Pacific Ocean blow with such great force that seamen call this region the "roaring forties." Over the great land masses of the Northern Hemisphere, the westerlies are often turned from their course by mountain ranges. They are also interrupted by great cyclonic storms common over land and sea along the polar front.

The United States and the southern half of Canada lie within the path of the westerlies. The direction of these winds may change near the surface, but it is usually steady in the upper air. The prevailing westerlies make flying from west to east faster than flying in the opposite direction.   VANCE E. MOYER

PREVENTION OF CRUELTY TO ANIMALS, SO-CIETY FOR THE. See SOCIETY FOR THE PREVENTION OF CRUELTY TO ANIMALS.

PREVENTIVE MEDICINE. See MEDICINE (table: Kinds of Medical Specialty Fields).

PRÉVERT, JACQUES (1900-   ), is probably the most popular French poet of the mid-1900's. His popularity resulted almost entirely from one volume, *Paroles (Spoken Words)*, which became an immediate best seller when it appeared in 1946. Prévert's poems are rich in the clever use of words and humor. They declare the need for individual happiness and love, and attack with playful mockery the most respected human institutions. The simple sentence structure of many of Prévert's poems makes them favorites in beginning French courses.

Prévert was born in Neuilly-sur-Seine. He joined the surrealist movement during the 1920's, and his poems reflect the fantasy and freedom of expression typical of surrealism. Prévert also wrote the scripts for several films directed by Marcel Carné.   LeROY C. BREUNIG

PREVIOUS QUESTION. See PARLIAMENTARY PROCEDURE (table: Terms).

PRÉVOST'S THEORY OF EXCHANGE. See HEAT (Radiation).

PRIAM, *PRY um*, in Greek mythology, was the last king of Troy. His father was Laomedon. Priam had 50 sons, of whom two were Hector and Paris, and 50 daughters, of whom one was Cassandra.

When Paris eloped with Helen of Troy, the Trojan War began. Priam lost most of his sons during the war. Achilles killed his son Hector, and Priam went alone at night to Achilles' tent to beg Hector's body so that he might bury it properly. Achilles pitied the old man and gave him the body. Later, as Priam clung to the altar of Zeus on the night that Troy fell, Achilles' son Pyrrhus, or Neoptolemus, killed him. Priam's remain-

ing sons were also killed that night, and the royal line of Troy came to an end.   JOSEPH FONTENROSE

See also HECUBA; ILIAD; PARIS (legend).

PRIBILOF ISLANDS, *PRIHB uh lawf,* are a group of four hilly islands in the Bering Sea. They rank as the largest fur sanctuary in the world. The Pribilof Islands include the two large islands of Saint Paul and Saint George, and the two smaller islands of Otter and Walrus. They cover 76 square miles and have about 700 people. Gerasim Pribilof, a Russian, discovered the islands in 1786. The United States obtained the Pribilofs when it bought Alaska in 1867. For location, see ALASKA (physical map).

The Pribilofs are the breeding grounds for about $1\frac{1}{2}$ million fur seals which go there each spring. For many years, there were no restrictions on hunting the seals. As a result, they almost became extinct. In 1911, several countries agreed to protect the seals, and the United States received charge of the herd. In 1957, the United States, Canada, Russia, and Japan agreed to restrict seal hunting to the Pribilofs and two Russian islands. The treaty was extended for six years in 1963.

About 60,000 fur-seal skins are permitted to be taken each year. A year's quota of skins averages more than $3\frac{1}{2}$ million in value.   NEAL M. BOWERS

See also BERING SEA CONTROVERSY; SEAL.

PRICE is the amount of money for which something can be bought or sold. The price states the worth in money of each unit of a good or service. The price of a bus ride, for example, might be 50 cents, while the price of a dozen eggs might also be 50 cents. This article discusses how prices are determined and why they are important in *free enterprise economies*, including the United States and Canada. In *planned economies*, such as those of the Communist nations, prices are often set by the government.

How Price Is Determined. The economic forces of *supply* and *demand* are the basic determiners of price. Consumers are the buyers, or *demanders*, of most products, and producers and other businessmen are the *suppliers*. Consumers try to buy at the lowest possible prices, while producers sell their goods for the highest prices they can get. The *market price* depends on the demand for the product in relation to its supply.

Demand (quantity wanted for purchase) varies according to price changes. As the price of an article falls, the quantity demanded generally rises. As the price increases, the quantity demanded usually decreases. For example, buyers will probably purchase more ice cream cones at 15 cents a cone than at 20 cents, and still more at 10 cents than at 15 cents. Some persons would not buy more ice cream cones at 10 cents than at 15 cents. But some new purchasers would buy at the lower price, and thus increase total demand.

Demand behaves like this for three main reasons: (1) A person's income is limited, and he cannot buy everything he wants. (2) However, a person can satisfy his desire for a specific good. (3) An increase in the price of a product will encourage consumers to substitute less expensive goods for it.

Sellers react to price changes exactly opposite to the way buyers react. As the market price increases, the amount that sellers will *supply* (offer for sale) generally rises. This is especially true when prices increase faster than production costs. As a greater quantity is offered for sale, supply eventually exceeds demand at the higher market price, and the price goes down. The amount supplied at the lower prices also tends to fall.

The amount of a good that buyers and sellers are willing to purchase or supply varies as prices go up or down. But at a certain price, buyers are willing to purchase the exact amount that sellers are willing to offer for sale. The price at this level is called the *equilibrium price*. Demand and supply rarely stay constant for long, because consumer tastes, income, and prices of other goods change as do production costs. Thus as demand or supply conditions change, the price moves up or down to a new equilibrium level.

The government plays a limited part in determining prices in a free enterprise system. In the United States, for example, the national and state legislatures have passed some laws that change the normal working of supply and demand. In times of war, for instance, the government has set *ceiling prices* (maximum prices) on scarce consumer goods to control inflation. It has then rationed the available supply among the people. For further information on the government's role in setting prices, see PRICE CONTROL; AGRICULTURE (Surpluses); PUBLIC UTILITY; and MINIMUM WAGE.

What Prices Do. Prices work through supply and demand to determine (1) what goods and services will be produced, and (2) for whom they will be produced.

Consumers influence what will be produced by the prices they are willing to pay for goods and services. They will spend more money on and pay higher prices for those things they want most. Businessmen can earn profits only by producing what persons are willing and able to buy. Their desire to earn profits prompts them to produce the things that are demanded by consumers.

The price system also helps determine who will get the available goods and services. Generally, these products will go to those persons who want them and are able to pay for them. The quality and amount of goods and services a person can afford depend largely on the size of his income. A person's income, in turn, is influenced by supply and demand. A worker with marketable skills will usually receive higher wages—a higher price for his services—than an unskilled worker. This is true because there is a greater demand for skilled than unskilled workers, and a smaller supply of skilled workers. In addition, a skilled worker generally contributes more to the market value of his company's product. ROBERT F. LANZILLOTTI

Related Articles in WORLD BOOK include:

Discount	Inflation and	Monopoly and
Distribution	Deflation	Competition
Free Enterprise	Market	Supply and Demand
System		Value

PRICE, LEONTYNE (1927-   ), became one of the most celebrated sopranos of her time. She excelled in the operas of Giuseppe Verdi, and Aïda is probably her most praised role. Her brilliant voice has an exciting vibrating quality and excellent range.

Miss Price was born in Laurel, Miss., and studied at the Juilliard School of Music in New York City. In 1952, she toured the United States playing Bess in

George Gershwin's *Porgy and Bess*. Her singing of Aïda at the La Scala Opera in Milan in 1960 made her an international star. She made her Metropolitan Opera debut in 1961 in Verdi's *Il Trovatore*.   MAX DE SCHAUENSEE

PRICE CONTROL. Governments sometimes introduce controls to keep prices from skyrocketing, especially in time of war or emergency. In price control, prices are not allowed to rise above certain levels, in an attempt to fight inflation and establish a stable economy.

During World War II, the price control program of the United States was carried on by the Office of Price Administration (OPA). It could place *ceilings* (top prices) on rents and many commodities. By fall of 1946, most federal price controls (except rent) had been lifted. In 1950, the government revived price controls because of threatened inflation. It set up the Office of Price Stabilization in 1951. Controls were removed and the office abolished in 1953.   JOHN H. FREDERICK

See also DEPRESSION; INFLATION AND DEFLATION; PARITY; RATIONING; WORLD WAR II (Government Controls).

PRICE TOWER. See OKLAHOMA (Places to Visit).

PRICKLY ASH is one of a group of trees or shrubs belonging to the *rue* family. The name refers to the sharp prickles on the twigs. It is also based on the similarity between the leaves of the prickly ash and those of the true ash (see ASH). The *southern prickly ash* is a small tree with a warty trunk. It grows on the sandy coast of Virginia and southward. It is called *toothache tree* because the bark produces a cooling sensation when chewed, and acts as an anesthetic for toothache. The *northern prickly ash* is an aromatic shrub with yellowish-green flowers, found in rocky woods and riverbanks.

Scientific Classification. The prickly ash belongs to the rue family, *Rutaceae*. The southern prickly ash is genus *Zanthoxylum*, species *Z. clava herculis;* the northern is *Z. americanum*.   THEODORE W. BRETZ

PRICKLY HEAT is a skin rash of tiny, red pimples that itch. It is also called *heat rash*. It may appear often when the weather is warm and moist. The rash occurs where the skin would normally be sweaty. It is common among infants. Prickly heat is due to blocking of sweat pores so that sweat cannot reach the surface in the usual way. It is relieved by keeping the skin cool with cool poultices and mild dusting powders. The disorder is annoying, but not harmful.   RICHARD L. SUTTON, JR.

PRICKLY PEAR, also called NOPAL, or INDIAN FIG, is a type of cactus with prickly fruits which are shaped somewhat like a pear or fig. Many species grow in dry parts of the southwestern United States and northern Mexico. They can stand long periods with little water, but they grow better with moderate rainfall, as in parts of Florida, southern Brazil, and northern Argentina.

The prickly fruit grows on the edge of the flat leaflike joints. In Mexico and Central America, the kinds that are good to eat are called *tuna*. Luther Burbank developed spineless varieties, which are raised as food for people and livestock.

Prickly pears have been introduced into Mediterranean countries, India, Ceylon, South Africa, the Canary Islands, and the Malagasy Republic. The chief reason for their wide spread is their food value and their use in the cochineal dye industry. The cochineal insect, which gives a red dye, feeds on prickly pears.

The prickly pear is often planted in the lava seams

of Mount Vesuvius as soon as the flow has cooled. The roots readily grow into the cracks in the rock.

One species of prickly pear was brought to Australia in 1788 for a cochineal dye industry that was never established. Later, two other species were brought there as curiosities. After 1900, they spread so quickly that they soon became dangerous pests. By 1925, they had grown so dense that about 30 million acres were useless for crops or grazing. The Australian government then brought in an Argentine moth, *Cactoblastis cactorum*. The larvae of this insect live within the so-called leaves and destroy them. Within seven years, the heavy growth of prickly pears had been almost destroyed.

Scientific Classification. Prickly pears belong to the cactus family, *Cactaceae*. They are members of the flat-stemmed group of genus *Opuntia*. The common species in the Southwest is *O. ficus-indica*. EDMUND C. JAEGER

See also FLOWER (color picture: Flowers of the Desert).

PRIDE AND PREJUDICE. See AUSTEN, JANE.

PRIDE'S PURGE. See RUMP PARLIAMENT.

PRIEST is the title used by various religions for the person who officiates at worship. The name comes from the Greek *presbyter*, meaning *elder*. Christian churches that have a priesthood are the Roman Catholic, Eastern Orthodox, Anglican, Episcopal, Mormon, and Scandinavian Lutheran churches. Roman Catholic priests of the Latin rite vow never to marry. Priests in Eastern Orthodox Churches may enter into marriage before they are ordained, unless they are monks. Priests who belong to religious orders take vows of poverty and self-sacrifice. Other religions, including Shintoism and Mahayana Buddhism in Japan, also have priests. Judaism today has no priesthood, but in ancient times it had a class of priests, headed by the high priest. R. PIERCE BEAVER

See also HIGH PRIEST; MINISTER; RABBI.

PRIESTLEY, JOHN BOYNTON (1894-　　), is an English novelist, playwright, and journalist who writes his novels in the realistic tradition of the 1800's. His best-known novel is *The Good Companions* (1929), an amusing story of a wandering music-hall troupe. His nostalgic novel *Lost Empires* (1965) also concerns the music-hall world. *Angel Pavement* (1930) is a more serious novel about the business world in London. Priestley wrote many nonfiction works, including *Literature and Western Man* (1960).

Priestley's most popular plays include *Dangerous Corner* (1932) and *An Inspector Calls* (1945), both satires on middle-class life. *Time and the Conways* (1937) is a science-fiction play about time.

Priestley was born in Bradford, Yorkshire. After graduating from Cambridge University, he became a journalist in London in 1922. HARRY T. MOORE

PRIESTLEY, JOSEPH (1733-1804), an English clergyman and chemist, shares the credit for the discovery of oxygen with Carl Wilhelm Scheele of Sweden (see OXYGEN). Priestley called the gas "dephlogisticated air." The great French chemist Antoine Lavoisier gave it the name *oxygen*.

Priestley was born near Leeds, and studied for the ministry. He lectured in Suffolk for several years on history and the sciences. Finally he became a *dissenting* (nonconformist) minister in Leeds and Birmingham.

Through his friendship with Benjamin Franklin, Priestley became interested in electricity, with which he performed many brilliant experiments. Priestley turned to chemistry in 1772, and discovered hydrochloric acid and *laughing gas* (nitrous oxide). In 1774, he discovered sulfur dioxide.

Priestley's sympathies for the cause of the French Revolution made him unpopular in England. In 1791, an angry mob burned his home and chapel in Birmingham. Priestley left England and moved to the United States in 1794. He settled permanently in Northumberland, Pa. HENRY M. LEICESTER

PRIESTLY CODE. See PENTATEUCH.

PRIETO QUINTUPLETS. See QUINTUPLETS.

PRIMARY COLORS. See COLOR.

PRIMARY ELECTION is a method of selecting candidates to run for public office. In a primary election, a political party, in effect, holds an election among its own members to select the party members who will represent it in the coming general election. In the primary, any number of party members can run as candidates for a particular public office. But only the winning candidate or candidates can represent the party in the general election. Parties use the primary to screen their candidates for office. They can find out from the primary votes which candidates the members of their parties prefer.

Direct and Indirect. The *direct primary* is the most common form of primary election. In the direct primary, party members who want to run for office file petitions to have their names placed on the ballot. Voters then vote directly for the candidates of their choice. In an *indirect primary*, party members vote for delegates to party conventions, where candidates are chosen.

Open and Closed. A primary election is considered *closed* when each voter must declare his party choice, either when he registers to vote or when he actually votes. He can vote only for the candidates on his party's primary ballot, and his party contest is closed to members of other parties. In an *open primary*, the voter receives ballots for all the parties in the election, and chooses both his party and his candidates in the voting booth.

Non-Partisan Primaries are often used for judicial, school board, and local elections. Candidates are listed on the ballot with no indication of political affiliation. The voters choose the best candidates on the basis of their individual merits, not their party membership. The candidates with the greatest numbers of votes become the opposing candidates in the general election.

The Presidential Primary is used in a number of states to choose delegates to the national party conventions. Each candidate who enters the election lists a slate of delegates who have promised to support him at the convention. The party members show their choice for the presidential nomination by voting for the slate of delegates committed to him. In a *presidential preferential primary*, the voters choose delegates to the convention, but the delegates are not bound to support the candidates they represent.

History. Before primary elections were used, political parties nominated candidates for office at party conventions and caucuses. Political bosses often handpicked candidates, making shady deals to win enough votes. People gradually turned against the caucus-convention system as being undemocratic and open to corruption. Reform movements urged "No More Boss Rule" and "Down with King Caucus!"

In 1903, Wisconsin passed the first state-wide primary law. Within 10 years, most states did likewise. Today, every state uses primary elections.   WILLIAM A. HAMBLEY, JR.

See also CAUCUS; ELECTION.

PRIMARY SCHOOL. See ELEMENTARY SCHOOL.

PRIMATE is a member of the highest order in the animal kingdom. The name *primate* comes from the Latin *primus*, meaning *first*. The order of primates includes man as well as the apes, monkeys, lemurs, and others whose physical characteristics are most like man's. Primates usually have a relatively large brain, nails rather than claws, and the ability to grasp objects well with their hands. They live mainly in tropical climates, although one type of monkey lives as far north as Japan. Most primates are *arboreal* (tree dwellers). But some, such as the baboon and gorilla, also spend much time on the ground. Primates are members of the class *Mammalia*.   GEORGE B. SCHALLER

See also APE; LEMUR; MAN; MONKEY; TARSIER.

PRIME MERIDIAN. See GREENWICH MERIDIAN; MERIDIAN.

PRIME MINISTER is the head of the government in Great Britain and many other countries. The head of the state—the king or queen of a monarchy or the president of a republic—appoints him. In most countries, the head of state can appoint only the leader of the majority party in the legislature or of a coalition. The prime minister and his cabinet are responsible to the legislature. This is known as the *cabinet system* of government (see CABINET).

In Great Britain, the prime minister is the leader of the party that wins an election. The king or queen must abide by his advice. If he resigns, the whole government falls with him, and the people must elect a new parliament. The prime minister has considerable freedom in choosing members of his cabinet, but he cannot easily ignore important leaders of his party. He is the unquestioned leader of his party, even though other ministers may be stronger personalities. The cabinet must agree on most government actions, but the prime minister has certain rights alone, such as dissolving parliament and calling an election. In some respects, the prime minister of Great Britain is considered more powerful than the President of the United States, because he is the real leader of the majority party. Thus, he need not fear parliamentary checks and balances.

Cabinet government developed in Great Britain during the reign of George I, who spoke no English and took little interest in the government. Sir Robert Walpole, First Lord of the Treasury, came to be known as the *prime* (first) minister. The title did not become official until 1905. The English prime minister also holds the title First Lord of the Treasury.

Under the French constitution of 1958, the head of the French cabinet is now also called *premier* (prime minister). His powers are not as great as those of the British prime minister, because the president of the republic overshadows his authority.   ROBERT G. NEUMANN

PRIME NUMBER. See FACTOR.

PRIMER. See AMMUNITION (The Explosive Train).

PRIMITIVE MAN. Peoples who obtain all their food by hunting and fishing, and by gathering wild fruits, nuts, and seeds, are often called *primitive men*. Their bodies and brains are as well developed as those of the rest of mankind. They may know many skills and have much knowledge about their environment. They often have rich stores of legends, music, and poetry. But their *cultures* (ways of life) are usually simpler than those of our own Western civilization.

These peoples have not yet shared in man's great inventions and discoveries, on which our civilization is based. Most of them do not know how to grow their own food, or work with metals. They do not know how to read or write because they have no need for these skills. They often live in tribal units which have no knowledge of the outside world, except for their own near neighbors. For this reason, scientists call such peoples *nonliterate*, or *preliterate*. Primitive men are sometimes also called *uncivilized*, because they do not have writing or cities, which characterize civilization. But all primitive peoples share with civilized men the basic activities that make up human culture. See CIVILIZATION; CULTURE.

Primitive Peoples of Today live in remote areas of the world. In many cases, the small bands in which they live are all that remain of once-large groups. Some primitive peoples, such as the Tasmanians, have died out completely. Others, like many Indians of North America, have abandoned their former cultures, and have adopted new ways of life.

Primitive hunting peoples include the Bushmen of the southern deserts and the pygmies of the deep forests of Africa; Indians and Eskimos in the far northlands of Canada; the Australian Aborigines; Indians in the jungles of South America; and pygmies on some Pacific islands.

Primitive *pastoral* (herding) peoples include the Bedouins of Africa and the Mongols of Asia. They live on the meat or milk of their herds, and scoff at the humdrum lives of farmers. See NOMAD.

Primitive Cultures vary a great deal. For example, the Eskimos make excellent warm fur clothing and snow houses, and carve delightful figures in ivory and stone. The Australian Aborigines wear no clothes and own very few possessions, but they have elaborate religious ceremonies, with dramatic legends and dance festivals. Many hunting groups live in small, wandering bands that must keep moving to be near their food and water supplies. But the Indians of the Pacific Northwest had many possessions and built permanent villages, because good runs of fish provided a reliable supply of food. The Iroquois Indians organized a great intertribal federation. In parts of Africa and Polynesia, wealthy chiefs and rulers had great power.   MAY EDEL

Related Articles in WORLD BOOK include:

Africa (Ways of Life)	Eskimo
Australia (The	Hottentot
Aborigines)	Indian, American
Bedouin	Pygmy
Bushman	

PRIMO DE RIVERA, MIGUEL (1870-1930), MARQUES DE ESTELLA, was a Spanish army general. He overthrew Spain's constitutional government in 1923, and ruled as dictator from 1923 to 1930, during the reign of King Alfonso XIII. He withdrew Spain from the League of

Nations, and he ended a rebellion in Spanish Morocco. Political and social unrest eventually forced him to resign in 1930.

Primo was born in Cádiz. He was a member of an important military family, and served as an officer in Morocco, Cuba, and the Philippines. In 1922, he became captain general of Barcelona. Primo was dissatisfied with Spain's constitutional government. In 1923, with the king's approval, he led a bloodless overthrow of the government. But he had no distinct philosophy, program, or following. Soon after his resignation, he died in exile in Paris.   STANLEY G. PAYNE

See also SPAIN (The Reign of Alfonso XIII).

PRIMOGENITURE, *PRY moh JEHN ih tyoor,* is a system of inheritance widely used in Europe for hundreds of years. Under this system, the oldest child in a family, and often the oldest son, has the sole right to inherit land and other possessions from his parents. Primogeniture first developed under the feudal system (see FEUDALISM). In England and other countries, the oldest child in the royal family became the successor to the throne. The system kept a nobleman's large landholdings from being broken up among his children into many small estates. It preserved not only the large estates, but the social position and prestige of the families as well. Peasants and other landholders also practiced primogeniture.

Primogeniture gradually disappeared in Europe, except among ruling families, as the feudal system died out. It came to an end in England in 1925, except for the royal family. The United States abolished primogeniture by law.   BRYCE LYON

See also JEFFERSON, THOMAS (Virginia Lawmaker).

PRIMROSE is the common name of a group of early-blooming plants. Cultivated primroses are among the loveliest of ornamental garden flowers. Many of these have been derived from the *common primrose,* which grows wild in woods and meadows of Europe.

This primrose has deeply veined leaves and yellowish-white blossoms. A single blossom grows on one flower stalk. In the garden and greenhouse, one sees flowers of pure yellow, pink, lilac, and various shades of red, and single and double varieties. Some primroses make excellent potted plants for the window garden. The primrose is the flower for the month of February.

Primroses grown in the garden need shade and rich, moist loam. They may be started from seed, which is planted in February in shallow pans or boxes in a mix-

The Delicate Primrose Is a Popular Ornamental Flower.
J. Horace McFarland

ture of sand, loam, and leaf mold. The young plants should be set out in the open in May, then placed in the permanent bed in September and protected over winter. They will flower the following spring.

Scientific Classification. Primroses belong to the primrose family, *Primulaceae.* The common primrose is genus *Primula,* species *P. vulgaris.* Among the greenhouse and window forms are the Chinese primrose, *P. sinensis,* and the Japanese, *P. japonica.*   DONALD WYMAN

See also COWSLIP; CYCLAMEN; FLOWER (color picture: Flowers of the Desert).

PRIMROSE, WILLIAM (1903-   ), a Scottish violist, became known for his outstanding performances in solo concert. He made his debut as a violinist at Albert Hall, London, in 1923. From 1930 to 1935, he toured Europe and the Americas as violist of the London String Quartet, and, later, as a solo violist. In 1937, he became a violist with the National Broadcasting Company Symphony Orchestra, and later served as soloist. In 1938, he founded his own quartet. He taught viola at the Curtis Institute of Music and the Juilliard School of Music. Primrose was born in Glasgow, Scotland, and studied with Eugène Ysaÿe.   DOROTHY DeLAY

PRIMUS BERRY. See BURBANK, LUTHER.

PRINCE is a title of the highest rank of the nobility. The word comes from the Latin *princeps,* meaning *first. Princeps* was used as a title for civil and military officials among the ancient Romans. The German Visigoth and Lombard tribes that settled in the Roman Empire used *prince* to mean independent authority. The crusaders followed this practice when they set up governments in the Near East.

In modern times, the title *prince* or *princess* can be used in many ways. It is the title of the ruler of the principality of Liechtenstein. In Great Britain, only the eldest son of the ruler has a legal right to the title of prince, and only after the ruler has created him Prince of Wales. The eldest daughter of the ruler is called Princess Royal. As a mark of courtesy, other members of the royal family, and they alone, are called prince or princess. In France, male members of the former royal Bourbon family are called prince. In Italy the title is commonly used by the heads of many of the great Italian families.   I. J. SANDERS

See also PRINCIPALITY.

PRINCE ALBERT, Sask. (pop. 26,269; alt. 1,413 ft.), is an important commercial trading center. It lies in the center of the province, about 100 miles north of Saskatoon. Prince Albert is on the North Saskatchewan River near the Prince Albert National Park (see SASKATCHEWAN [political map]). Industries include the manufacture of wood products, meat packing, brewing, bottling, and oil refining. Air and rail lines serve Prince Albert. Founded in 1886, Prince Albert was incorporated as a city in 1904. It has a council-mayor form of government.   JEAN BRUCHESI

PRINCE ALBERT NATIONAL PARK. See CANADA (National Parks).

PRINCE CONSORT is the husband of a reigning queen. In countries where the daughter of a king may inherit the throne, her husband does not have the title of king. Denmark, Great Britain, and The Netherlands allow a woman to rule as monarch.

689

The contributors of this article are Frank MacKinnon, Principal of Prince of Wales College and author of The Government of Prince Edward Island; *Clive H. Stewart, Professor of Geology at St. Dunstan's University; and Wallace Ward, Managing Editor of* The Guardian *and* The Evening Patriot.

Chris Lund, National Film Board of Canada

Charlottetown, Prince Edward Island's Only City

PRINCE EDWARD ISLAND

PRINCE EDWARD ISLAND is the smallest but most thickly populated province of Canada. Its people usually call their province "The Island" or simply use its initials, "P.E.I." The people of Prince Edward Island live in small, scattered communities. But the average number of persons to the square mile is greater than in any other province. Charlottetown is the capital and only city of Prince Edward Island.

Prince Edward Island is the only province that is entirely separated from the North American mainland. It lies in the Gulf of St. Lawrence, a rich fishing area off Canada's Atlantic coast. Lobsters are the most valuable catch of the island's fishing industry. Oysters from Prince Edward Island are known for their delicious flavor. The province ranks among the leading oyster producers of Canada and the United States. Fishermen also catch cod, herring, and mackerel in the gulf waters.

But agriculture is Prince Edward Island's chief source of income. The island's fertile red soil is its greatest natural resource, and farms cover a greater percentage of the land than in any other province. Each year, Prince Edward Island exports thousands of bushels of potatoes, its chief crop. Other important crops include fruits, grains, and vegetables. The Canadian fur-farming industry started on Prince Edward Island during the 1880's, and thrived there for many years.

The island lacks valuable minerals and cheap sources of power. And transportation to and from the mainland

is expensive. For these reasons, manufacturing has never been too important in the province's economy. But the island, helped by federal funds, is attracting new industries. The greatest expansion has been in the quick-freezing and packaging of farm products and seafood.

Prince Edward Island has miles of red or white sandy beaches along its coasts, with warm ocean currents offshore. Few of the people live far from a good beach. The island's streams are well stocked with fish. Almost every boy, wherever he lives on the island, learns at an early age to fish for trout. The island also offers exciting sailing, and has several fine golf courses. All these attractions bring hundreds of thousands of tourists to Prince Edward Island every year.

Micmac Indians lived on the island before white men first arrived. The Indians called the island *Abegweit* (cradled on the waves). A Micmac legend tells how the god Glooscap finished painting the beauties of the world. Then he dipped his brush into a mixture of all the colors and created Abegweit, his favorite island. The British named the island in honor of a son of King George III. The province's fertile red soil and its location in the Gulf of St. Lawrence have given it two nicknames—the *Garden of the Gulf* and the *Million Acre Farm.*

Prince Edward Island is one of the Atlantic Provinces. For its relationship to the other Canadian provinces, see the articles on ATLANTIC PROVINCES; CANADA; CANADA, GOVERNMENT OF; CANADA, HISTORY OF.

Capital: Charlottetown.

Government: *Parliament*—Senators, 4; Members of the House of Commons, 4. *Provincial Legislature*—Members of the Legislative Assembly, 32. *Counties*—3. *Voting Age*—18 years.

Area: 2,184 square miles, 10th and smallest in size among the provinces. *Greatest Distances*—(east-west) 120 miles; (north-south) 35 miles. *Coastline*—500 miles.

Elevation: *Highest*—450 feet above sea level in Queens County. *Lowest*—sea level along the coasts.

Population: *1966 Census*—108,535, 10th and smallest among the provinces; density, 50 persons to the square mile; distribution, 63 per cent rural, 37 per cent urban. *Estimated 1971 Population*—112,000.

Chief Products: *Agriculture*—dairy products, fruits, hay, oats, vegetables. *Manufacturing*—food products, wood products. *Fishing Industry*—clams, cod, herring, lobsters, mackerel, oysters.

Entered the Dominion: July 1, 1873; the 7th province.

Provincial Motto: *Parva sub ingenti* (The small under the large).

Prince Edward Island (blue) is the smallest province in Canada, and the smallest of the four Atlantic Provinces.

Inner and Outer Harbors at Tignish

George Hunter, Publix

The Provincial Coat of Arms

The Provincial Flag

Symbols of Prince Edward Island. The three oak saplings on the provincial coat of arms stand for the three counties of Prince Edward Island. The oak tree symbolizes Canada and England. The British lion stretches across the top of the shield. The coat of arms was adopted in 1905. The provincial flag, adopted in 1964, bears an adaptation of the coat of arms.

The Floral Emblem
Lady's-Slipper

PRINCE EDWARD ISLAND/*Government*

Lieutenant-Governor of Prince Edward Island represents Queen Elizabeth in the province. He is appointed by the governor-general-in-council of Canada. The lieutenant-governor's position is largely honorary, like that of the governor-general.

Premier of Prince Edward Island is the actual head of the provincial government. The province, like the other provinces and Canada itself, has a *parliamentary* form of government. The premier is a member of the legislative assembly, where he is the leader of the majority party. The voters elect the premier as they do the other members of the legislative assembly. The premier receives a salary of $9,000 a year in addition to the allowances he gets as an assembly member. For a list of all the premiers of Prince Edward Island, see the *History* section of this article.

The premier presides over the executive council, or cabinet. The council includes nine ministers appointed by the premier from among his party's members in the legislative assembly. Each council member directs one or more departments of the provincial government. The executive council resigns if it loses the support of a majority of the assembly.

Legislative Assembly is a one-house legislature that makes the provincial laws. It has 32 members, who are elected from 16 electoral districts. The members of the legislature are elected to terms that may last up to five years. However, the lieutenant-governor, on the advice of the premier, may call for an election before the end of the five-year period. If he does so, all members of the assembly must run again for office.

Courts. The highest court on Prince Edward Island is the supreme court, made up of a chief justice and three assistant justices. A county court judge presides in each of the province's three counties. These jus-

Prince Edward Island Travel Bureau

Provincial Building in Charlottetown is often called the "birthplace of Canada." Colonial statesmen met here in 1864 to lay the plans that led to the confederation of Canada. In front of the building is a memorial to Jacques Cartier, who discovered the island in 1534. Charlottetown has been the provincial capital since 1769.

tices and judges are appointed by the governor-general-in-council. They serve until the age of 75. The province also has five magistrate's courts.

Local Government. None of the island's three counties has a county government. Charlottetown, the only city, and most towns have a mayor-council form of government. Only Summerside has a council-manager government. The villages are governed by boards of three village commissioners.

Taxation. Taxes levied by the provincial government account for about a third of its income. The most important ones are a general sales tax and a gasoline tax. About two-thirds of the province's income comes from federal-provincial tax-sharing arrangements and federal grants. License fees and governmental liquor sales are other sources of income.

Politics. The island has two political parties—the Liberal party and the Progressive Conservative party, usually called simply the Conservative party. The Liberals have controlled more than half the administrations of Prince Edward Island.

Mackenzie, Miller Services

Government House in Charlottetown stands on beautifully landscaped grounds. It is the home of the lieutenant-governor, Queen Elizabeth's official representative in Prince Edward Island.

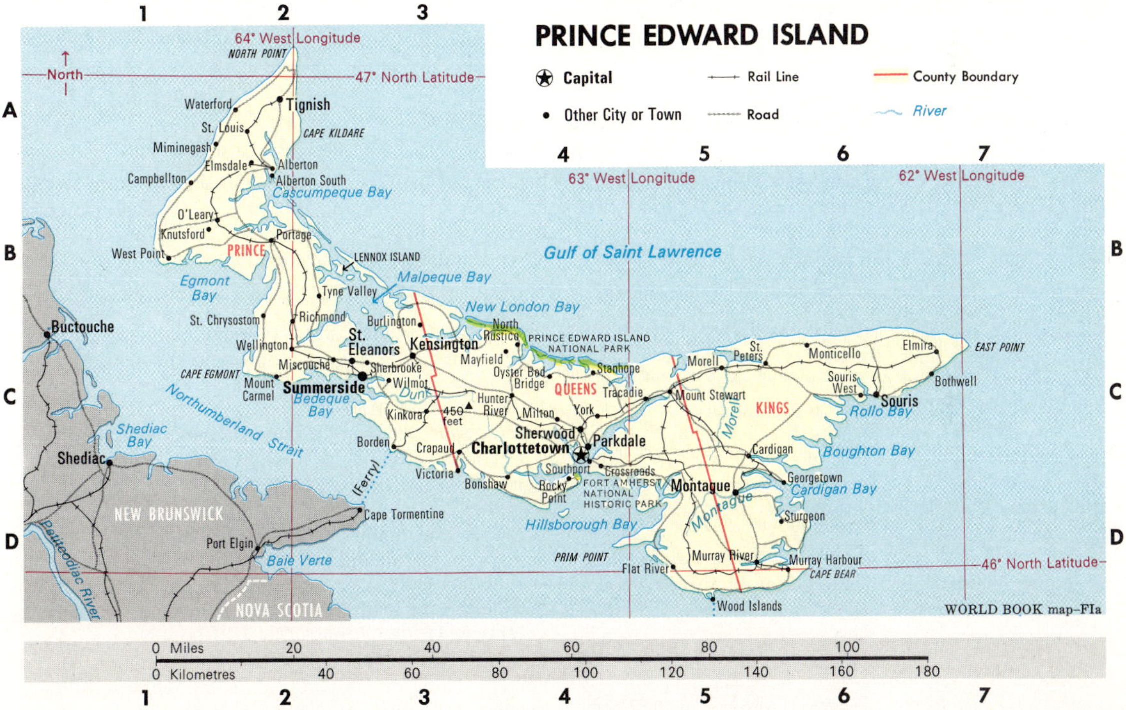

PRINCE EDWARD ISLAND

★ **Capital** ⊢ Rail Line — County Boundary
• **Other City or Town** ---- Road ∿ River

WORLD BOOK map–FIa

| 0 Miles | 20 | 40 | 60 | 80 | 100 |
| 0 Kilometres | 40 | 60 | 80 | 100 | 120 | 140 | 160 | 180 |

Population

112,000	..Estimate..1971	
108,535	...Census..1966	
104,629	.....".....1961	
98,429	.....".....1951	
95,047	.....".....1941	
88,038	.....".....1931	
88,615	.....".....1921	
93,728	.....".....1911	
103,259	.....".....1901	
109,078	.....".....1891	
108,891	.....".....1881	
94,021	.....".....1871	

Counties

Kings	......18,015..C 5	
Prince	....42,688..B 2	
Queens	...47,832..C 4	

Physical Features

Bedeque Bay	.......C 2	
Boughton' Bay	.....C 6	
Cape Bear	.........D 6	
Cape Egmont	.......C 2	
Cape Kildare	.....A 2	
Cardigan Bay	.....D 6	
Cascumpeque Bay	..B 2	
Dunk River	........C 3	
East Point	.........C 7	
Egmont Bay	.......B 1	
Hillsborough Bay	..D 4	
Lennox Island	...B 2	
Malpeque Bay	.....B 3	
Morell River	.....C 5	
Montague River	..D 5	
New London		
Bay	.........B 4	
North Point	.......A 2	
Prim Point	........D 4	
Rollo Bay	.........C 6	

Cities and Towns

Alberton	......796..A 2	
Alberton South	262..A 2	
Bonshaw	.....184..C 3	
Borden	......714..C 3	
Bothwell	.....72..C 7	
Burlington	...59..C 3	
Campbellton	.148..B 1	
Cardigan	...263..C 5	
Charlotte-		
town	.....18,427..C 4	
Crapaud	.....239..C 3	
Crossroads	..245..D 4	
Elmira	......128..C 7	
Elmsdale	....395..A 2	
Flat River	...126..D 5	
Georgetown	..826..D 6	
Hunter River	.325..C 4	
Kensington	1,022..C 3	
Kinkora	....268..C 3	
Knutsford	...244..B 1	

Mayfield	.....232..C 4	
Milton	......158..C 4	
Miminegash	..269..A 1	
Miscouche	...729..C 2	
Montague	...1,289..D 5	
Monticello	...92..C 6	
Morell	......393..C 5	
Mount Carmel	293..C 2	
Mount Stewart	429..C 5	
Murray		
Harbour	...397..D 6	
Murray River	.522..D 5	
North Rustico	874..C 4	
O'Leary	....738..B 1	
Oyster Bed		
Bridge	...236..C 4	
Parkdale	..2,071..C 4	
Portage	......49..B 2	
Richmond	...235..B 2	
Rocky Point	..60..D 4	
St. Chrysostom	230..B 2	
St. Eleanors	.1,419..C 3	

St. Louis	.....140..A 2	
St. Peters	...289..C 5	
Sherbrooke	..247..C 3	
Sherwood	..2,407..C 4	
Souris	....1,443..C 6	
Souris West	.240..C 6	
Southport	...259..C 4	
Stanhope	...236..C 4	
Sturgeon	...266..D 6	
Summer-		
side	...10,042..C 3	
Tignish	.....982..A 2	
Tracadie	...139..C 5	
Tyne Valley	.149..B 2	
Victoria	....169..D 3	
Waterford	...99..A 2	
Wellington	..330..C 2	
West Point	...44..B 1	
Wilmot	.....619..C 3	
Wood Islands	.142..D 5	
York	........242..C 4	

Source: 1966 Census

693

The 1966 Canadian census reported that Prince Edward Island had 108,535 persons. The population had increased almost 4 per cent over the 1961 figure of 104,629. If the annual growth rate continues, the population will be about 112,000 by 1971.

About a third of Prince Edward Island's people live in urban areas. About a sixth—18,427 persons—live in Charlottetown, the capital and only city of the province. The island has about 25 incorporated towns and villages, ranging in population from about 200 to 10,000. See CHARLOTTETOWN; BORDEN; SUMMERSIDE.

Almost all the province's people were born in Canada. About 80 per cent have English, Irish, or Scottish ancestors, and nearly all the islanders speak English. Seventeen per cent are of French descent, and French is spoken in a few small communities. About 300 Micmac Indians live on a reservation on Lennox Island.

Roman Catholics form the largest single religious group—almost half the total population. Other religious groups include members of the United Church of Canada, and Presbyterians, Anglicans, and Baptists.

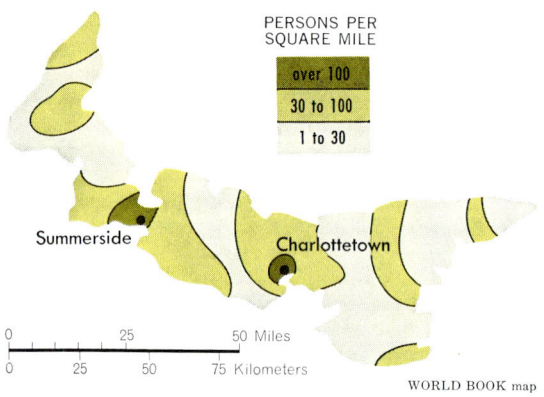

This map shows the *population density* of Prince Edward Island, and how it varies in parts of the province. Population density is the average number of persons who live on each square mile.

PERSONS PER SQUARE MILE
over 100
30 to 100
1 to 30

Summerside   Charlottetown

0   25   50 Miles
0   25   50   75 Kilometers

WORLD BOOK map

About 300,000 vacationers visit Prince Edward Island every summer. They enjoy a pleasant outdoor life, with its sunny days and cool nights. Many visitors go sailing and swim off the island's red or white sandy beaches. Fishermen catch trout in the streams and cast for ocean fish in the surf. Motorboats take sportsmen to the deep-sea fishing grounds near Prince Edward Island for cod, halibut, and mackerel.

PLACES TO VISIT

Following are brief descriptions of some of Prince Edward Island's many interesting places to visit.

Cardigan, the site of federal trout-raising grounds, has man-made pools with thousands of fish.

Confederation Chamber, in the Provincial Building in Charlottetown, is called the *Birthplace of Canada*. This room remains furnished as it was in 1864 when the Fathers of Confederation first met there and planned the union of Canada.

Fathers of Confederation Memorial Centre, in Charlottetown, was built in 1964 to honor the meeting of the Fathers of Confederation. It includes an art gallery, library, memorial hall, museum, and theater.

Lennox Island, in Malpeque Bay, has a Micmac Indian reservation.

Malpeque Bay has the island's chief oyster farms.

Micmac Village, near Rocky Point, is a reproduction of an Indian settlement of the 1700's.

North Rustico is a major lobster-fishing center.

Souris, the home port of many commercial fishing boats, provides facilities for deep-sea fishing.

Woodleigh Replicas, near Burlington, has many reproductions of British castles, churches, and inns.

National Parks. Prince Edward Island National Park includes one of Canada's best golf courses, Green Gables. Along one fairway stands the white farmhouse believed to be the scene of the story *Anne of Green Gables* by Lucy Maud Montgomery. Every year, about 50,000 persons visit this house, where the author is supposed to have lived. For the area and chief features of the park, see CANADA (National Parks).

Fort Amherst National Historic Park, near Charlottetown, is believed to be the site of a British fort built in 1758 and an earlier French settlement. It includes a small historical museum.

Provincial Parks. Prince Edward Island established its park system in 1958. Today, the province has about 20 provincial parks. For information on them, write to Director, Parks Division, Department of Tourist Development, Provincial Building, Charlottetown, P.E.I.

Fathers of Confederation Memorial Centre
Jowett, Miller Services

Schools. The first schools on Prince Edward Island were established during the early 1800's. In 1852, the provincial Free Education Act created a property tax to provide funds for school costs. The province established its department of education in 1877. Since 1945, the provincial minister of education has headed this agency. Provincial law requires children between the ages of 7 and 15 to attend school. Most elementary schools have classes through the 10th grade. For information on the number of students and teachers on Prince Edward Island, see EDUCATION (table).

The province has one university and one college. St. Dunstan's University, a private institution near Charlottetown, was founded in 1855. Prince of Wales College in Charlottetown was established in 1834. Both of these schools have separate articles in WORLD BOOK. For their enrollments, see CANADA (table: Universities and Colleges). Charlottetown and Summerside have vocational schools.

Libraries and Museums. In 1933, Prince Edward Island established Canada's first provincial library system.

The Fathers of Confederation Memorial Centre, built in 1964, includes the main provincial library, an art gallery, a historical museum, and a theater. The province has 24 branch libraries. Miscouche and Montague also have historical museums.

Prince Edward Island Travel Bureau
Highland Games and Gathering of the Clans

ANNUAL EVENTS

The most important annual events are the Lobster Carnival and Livestock Exhibition in Summerside in July, and Old Home Week in Charlottetown in mid-August. Pacing and trotting horse races are held every day and night of Old Home Week. An arts festival runs from June to September in the Fathers of Confederation Memorial Centre. Other annual events on Prince Edward Island include the following.

July: Dominion Day on July 1; Fisherman's Regatta in North Rustico; Fisheries Exhibition and Regatta in Souris; Regatta and Strawberry Festival in Montague; Northumberland Strait Swim in Borden.

August: Highland Games and Gathering of the Clans at some scenic spot; Prince County Exhibition in Alberton; Prince County Plowing Match in O'Leary.

September: Provincial Plowing Match in Dundas; Egmont Bay and Mont Carmel Exhibition in Abrams Village.

October: Provincial Fur Show in Charlottetown.

Fishing Harbor in Malpeque
George Hunter, Publix

Mackenzie, Miller Services
Green Gables Farm

George Hunter, Publix

Malak, Miller Services

Seaside Beaches stretch for miles along the coast. In summer, the water temperature may reach 70° F.

Quiet Farms cover most of Prince Edward Island. The rich, red soil of this farm near Malpeque produces excellent crops.

PRINCE EDWARD ISLAND/The Land

Almost all the land of Prince Edward Island is a gently rolling plain. Only a few hilly areas rise more than 200 feet above sea level. The tallest point, in Queens County, is 450 feet high. Many tidal inlets (called *rivers* locally) and deep bays indent the 500-mile coastline. Two of the bays, Hillsborough and Malpeque, nearly cut the island into three parts. Some low cliffs rise along the eastern and southern coasts. Near the shores lie Lennox Island and several other small islands that belong to the province.

PRINCE EDWARD ISLAND/Climate

Prince Edward Island, surrounded by warm ocean currents, has a milder climate than that of the Canadian mainland. It has an average January temperature of 19° F., and an average July temperature of 67° F. The province's lowest temperature on record, −27° F., occurred on Jan. 29, 1877. The highest reading was 98° F. on Aug. 19, 1935. Both temperatures were recorded in Charlottetown. The province has an annual average of 40 inches of *precipitation*. It has an average yearly snowfall of 113 inches.

SEASONAL TEMPERATURES

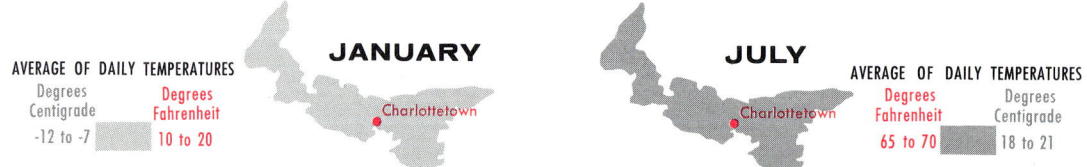

AVERAGE OF DAILY TEMPERATURES

Degrees Centigrade	Degrees Fahrenheit
-12 to -7	10 to 20

JANUARY

Charlottetown

JULY

Charlottetown

AVERAGE OF DAILY TEMPERATURES

Degrees Fahrenheit	Degrees Centigrade
65 to 70	18 to 21

AVERAGE YEARLY PRECIPITATION
(Rain, Melted Snow, and Other Moisture)

Charlottetown

Inches	Centimeters
40 to 45	102 to 114
35 to 40	89 to 102

0   25   50   75   100 Miles
0   25   50   75   100 125 150 Kilometers

WORLD BOOK maps

MONTHLY WEATHER IN CHARLOTTETOWN												
	JAN	FEB	MAR	APR	MAY	JUNE	JULY	AUG	SEPT	OCT	NOV	DEC	Average of:
	26	25	34	44	57	67	74	74	66	55	43	31	High Temperatures
	11	10	20	30	40	50	59	58	57	42	32	19	Low Temperatures
	15	13	13	13	13	13	10	10	13	13	15	16	Days of Rain or Snow

Temperatures are given in degrees Fahrenheit.

Source: Meteorological Branch, Canadian Department of Transport

Farming and fishing are among the most important industries of Prince Edward Island. The tourist industry also ranks high. Manufacturing is limited almost entirely to processing farm products and seafood.

All values given in this section are in Canadian dollars. For their value in U.S. money, see MONEY (table).

Natural Resources. Rich red soil is the province's chief resource. This *loam* (mixture of clay, decayed matter, and sand) lies on beds of soft red or brown sandstones and shales. The island has no minerals of commercial value. Even much of the rock used in building roads must be imported.

Plant Life. Northern grasses and wild flowers thrive in the red soil. Most of the forests that once covered the island have been cut down, and the land is used for farming. Small wood lots of beech, birch, evergreen, and maple trees dot the land.

Animal Life. The island has small game animals such as ducks, geese, Hungarian partridges, ring-necked pheasants, snipes, and snowshoe rabbits. Game fishes include brook and sea trout. Clams, cod, lobsters, mackerel, and oysters live in the offshore waters.

Agriculture. Farm production on Prince Edward Island has an annual value of about $12,333,000. Farmland makes up over 66 per cent of the land area, more than in any other province. The island has about 6,350 farms, averaging about 145 acres. About 90 per cent of the farmers own their farms.

Potatoes, grown for table use and for seed, are the chief crop. The province exports thousands of bushels of potatoes yearly to South America, the United States, and the West Indies. Other important crops include barley, fruits, oats, vegetables, and wheat. Broad fields produce hay for the dairy industry. In addition to dairy

PRODUCTION IN PRINCE EDWARD ISLAND
Total yearly value of goods produced—$25,801,000

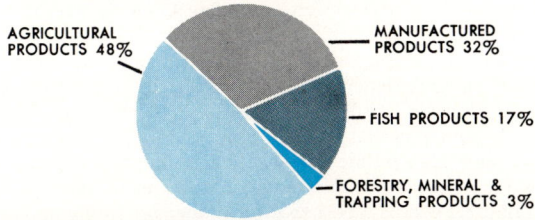

AGRICULTURAL PRODUCTS 48%

MANUFACTURED PRODUCTS 32%

FISH PRODUCTS 17%

FORESTRY, MINERAL & TRAPPING PRODUCTS 3%

Note: Percentages based on net value of production (total value of shipments less such costs as materials, fuel, electricity, and supplies). Mineral and Trapping Products are each less than 1 per cent.
Source: Dominion Bureau of Statistics

EMPLOYMENT IN PRINCE EDWARD ISLAND
Average yearly number of persons employed—22,305

	Number of Employees
Services	4,953
Wholesale & Retail Trade	3,715
Government & Defense	2,981
Manufacturing	2,769
Transportation, Communications & Utilities	2,523
Construction	1,869
Agriculture, Fishing & Other	3,495

Source: 1961 Census of Canada

cattle, livestock raised on the island includes beef cattle, hogs, poultry, and sheep.

Manufacturing. Goods manufactured on Prince Edward Island have a *value added by manufacture* of about $8,131,000 a year. This figure represents the value created in products by the province's industries, not counting such costs as materials, supplies, and fuel.

The cost of transportation to and from the Canadian mainland makes manufacturing expensive. Also, the island lacks cheap sources of power. Manufacturers depend chiefly on diesel and electric power developed from oil imported in tankers. For the province's kilowatt-hour production, see ELECTRIC POWER (table).

The processing of agricultural and fishing products accounts for most of the manufacturing activity. Shipyards in Alberton and Georgetown produce fishing craft and other small vessels.

Fishing Industry. The province's fish catch has an annual value of about $4,489,000. Lobsters are the most valuable catch. Prince Edward Island ranks among the leading Canadian provinces and states of the United States in oyster production. The federal government controls the oyster beds and operates an oyster research center and hatchery at Ellerslie. Fishermen catch cod, halibut, herring, and mackerel in the deeper waters of the Gulf of St. Lawrence. Much of the catch is exported.

Transportation. Two ferryboat lines carry passengers and motor vehicles across Northumberland Strait between Prince Edward Island and the Canadian mainland. One line, connecting Borden with Cape Tormentine, N.B., nine miles away, also carries railroad cars. It has powerful icebreakers that smash through the ice in winter. The other ferryboat line, operating from April to November, connects Wood Islands with Caribou, N.S., 14 miles away. The federal government is considering plans for either a bridge or *causeway* (raised highway) between the island and the mainland.

The Canadian National Railways operates about 280 miles of track along the length of the island. In 1951, this division became the first system in Canada to be completely equipped with diesel engines. An airline provides regularly scheduled service from Charlottetown and Summerside to cities in nearby provinces. It also provides this service to the Magdalen Islands in the Gulf of St. Lawrence.

Sheltered bays provide good harbors at Alberton, Charlottetown, Georgetown, Montague, Murray Harbour, Souris, and Summerside. Most of the harbors remain free of ice about eight months of the year.

The province has about 3,360 miles of roads, of which about a third are paved. In proportion to population, it has more miles of roads than any province.

Communication. Prince Edward Island has three daily newspapers. The *Patriot* was founded in Charlottetown in 1864, and the *Guardian* appeared in the capital in 1887. The *Journal-Pioneer* was established in Summerside in 1865.

Two radio stations serve the province. Station CFCY, the first one on the island, began broadcasting from Charlottetown in 1924. Station CJRW operates in Summerside. The island's first and only television station, CFCY-TV, began operating in Charlottetown in 1956.

Exploration and Early History. The Indians of what is now Prince Edward Island belonged to the Micmac tribe. The first white man to land on the island was the French explorer Jacques Cartier, on June 30, 1534. Another French explorer, Samuel de Champlain, claimed the island for France in 1603. He named it *Ile St. Jean* (Isle St. John).

French colonists began to settle on the island about 1720. British troops took over the area in 1758, during the French and Indian War (1754-1763). In the Treaty of Paris of 1763, France gave the island to Great Britain. The British changed its name to St. John's Island and made it a part of Nova Scotia.

The island's location apart from the Canadian mainland made it too difficult to govern. The British depended on landlords living in England to develop the area. Few of these landlords kept their promises to improve their property, and the land-ownership question led to bitter political disputes.

In 1769, St. John's Island became a separate British colony. The British changed its name to Prince Edward Island in 1799.

Self-Government. The British gave the colonists control of their local affairs in 1851. In 1864, delegates from Prince Edward Island, New Brunswick, and Nova Scotia met in Charlottetown to discuss forming a *Maritime union* (union of these Maritime colonies). Delegates from present-day Ontario and Quebec joined them and proposed a federal union of all the provinces. The delegates met again later in 1864 in Quebec. This conference drew up a plan for Canadian union that led to the creation of the Dominion of Canada on July 1, 1867.

Prince Edward Island refused to join the Dominion. The people were enjoying a period of great economic prosperity, and did not feel they needed union. In addition, they feared that the larger provinces would control their small island in the new government.

Member of the Union. An economic depression soon developed, and the people realized that they needed help. On July 1, 1873, Prince Edward Island entered the Dominion as the seventh province. James C. Pope, a Conservative who was born on the island, became the first provincial premier in the confederation.

The problem of absentee land ownership continued until 1875, when the Canadian government passed the Land Purchase Act. This act gave the province funds to buy out the landlords. The people bought the land from the province and improved their own farms.

By the Treaty of Paris, signed in 1763, France transferred control of Prince Edward Island to Great Britain.

The Land Purchase Act of 1875 provided funds which allowed the province to buy land held by absentee landlords.

Union with Canada made emigration from the island to the rest of the country a simple matter. During the 1890's, thousands of islanders began moving away. They sought greater job opportunities in the larger, more developed provinces.

The island was chiefly a farming region, with no important industrial activity and few large personal incomes. The province's limited income from taxes decreased as the population grew smaller, and the island became more dependent on federal aid.

During the 1920's and 1930's, the province expanded such governmental services as education, health and welfare, and public works. The high costs of these services increased the province's financial problems. The 1941 census report showed an increase in the population, and Premier J. Walter Jones obtained important increases in federal aid.

IMPORTANT DATES ON PRINCE EDWARD ISLAND

1534 The French explorer Jacques Cartier landed on what is now Prince Edward Island.

1603 The French explorer Samuel de Champlain claimed the island for France and named it Ile St. Jean.

c. 1720 France established colonies near present-day Charlottetown and Georgetown.

1758 British troops took over the island during the French and Indian War.

1763 France ceded the island to Great Britain in the Treaty of Paris. Britain renamed the area St. John's Island and annexed it to Nova Scotia.

1769 The island became a separate British colony.

1799 The colony was renamed Prince Edward Island.

1851 The colony was granted self-government.

1864 The first Confederation Conference was held in Charlottetown to discuss a federal union.

1873 The island entered the Dominion of Canada on July 1.

1875 Absentee land ownership on the island was ended.

1890's Thousands of islanders began moving to the mainland in search of greater job opportunities.

1941 The federal census reported the first increase in the provincial population since 1891.

1964 Queen Elizabeth officially opened the Fathers of Confederation Memorial Centre in Charlottetown.

HISTORICAL PRINCE EDWARD ISLAND

The Fishing Industry of the province grew from commercial fishing experiments first carried on in 1719.

Samuel de Champlain claimed the island for France in 1603. Champlain named it Isle St. Jean (Isle St. John).

The Federal Union of Canadian provinces grew from the conferences first held at Charlottetown in 1864.

The Fur-Farming Industry began on Prince Edward Island in the 1880's.

Charlottetown ★

Georgetown

First Settlements were established by French colonists in the early 1700's near Charlottetown and Georgetown.

Jacques Cartier discovered Prince Edward Island in 1534, during a voyage of exploration to North America.

Prince Edward Island Today. In spite of some industrial expansion during the 1960's, the province still depends heavily on federal assistance. Premier Alex B. Campbell arranged still more increases in this aid. Today, about two-thirds of the income of Prince Edward Island comes from the federal government.

With this increased help, the province built 15 regional high schools and 2 technical schools, and many new highways. The provincial government also began providing free hospital insurance for all the people.

In 1964, the Fathers of Confederation Memorial Centre opened in Charlottetown. Queen Elizabeth officially opened the $5,600,000 memorial.

FRANK MACKINNON, CLIVE H. STEWART, and WALLACE WARD

THE PREMIERS OF PRINCE EDWARD ISLAND

	Party	Term		Party	Term
1. James C. Pope	Conservative	1873	14. John H. Bell	Liberal	1919-1923
2. Lemuel C. Owen	Conservative	1873-1876	15. James Stewart	Conservative	1923-1927
3. Louis H. Davies	Liberal	1876-1879	16. Albert C. Saunders	Liberal	1927-1930
4. William W. Sullivan	Conservative	1879-1889	17. Walter M. Lea	Liberal	1930-1931
5. Neil McLeod	Conservative	1889-1891	18. James Stewart	Conservative	1931-1933
6. Frederick Peters	Liberal	1891-1897	19. W. J. P. MacMillan	Conservative	1933-1935
7. Alexander B. Warburton	Liberal	1897-1898	20. Walter M. Lea	Liberal	1935-1936
8. Donald Farquharson	Liberal	1898-1901	21. Thane A. Campbell	Liberal	1936-1943
9. Arthur Peters	Liberal	1901-1908	22. J. Walter Jones	Liberal	1943-1953
10. Francis L. Haszard	Liberal	1908-1911	23. Alexander W. Matheson	Liberal	1953-1959
11. Herbert J. Palmer	Liberal	1911	24. Walter R. Shaw	Progressive Conservative	1959-1966
12. John A. Mathieson	Conservative	1911-1917			
13. Aubin E. Arsenault	Conservative	1917-1919	25. Alex B. Campbell	Liberal	1966-

Related Articles in WORLD BOOK include:

Acadia
Atlantic Provinces
Borden
Canada, Government of
Canada, History of
Charlottetown

Davies, Sir Louis H.
Gulf of Saint Lawrence
Harris, Robert
Saint Dunstan's University
Summerside

Outline

I. Government
  A. Lieutenant-Governor
  B. Premier
  C. Legislative Assembly
  D. Courts
  E. Local Government
  F. Taxation
  G. Politics
II. People
III. Education
  A. Schools
  B. Libraries and Museums
IV. A Visitor's Guide
  A. Places to Visit
  B. Annual Events
V. The Land
VI. Climate
VII. Economy
  A. Natural Resources
  B. Agriculture
  C. Manufacturing
  D. Fishing Industry
  E. Transportation
  F. Communication
VIII. History

Questions

How does Prince Edward Island rank among the provinces in size? In population to the square mile?

Why has the island's manufacturing developed slowly?

How do railroad cars get to the island?

Which nationally important conference took place on Prince Edward Island? When was it held?

How is the island nearly cut into three parts?

What is the province's chief crop?

What is Prince Edward Island's only city?

Why did Prince Edward Island refuse at first to join the Dominion of Canada?

Books for Young Readers

BLAKELEY, PHYLLIS R. *The Story of Prince Edward Island.* Dent (Toronto), 1963.

STIRLING, LILLA. *Jockie: A Story of Prince Edward Island.* Scribner, 1951. A story of a boy and his horse.

Books for Older Readers

BOLGER, FRANCIS W. P. *Prince Edward Island and Confederation, 1863-1873.* St. Dunstan's Univ. Press (Charlottetown), 1964.

CALLBECK, LORNE C. *The Cradle of Confederation: A Brief History of Prince Edward Island from Its Discovery in 1534 to the Present Time.* Brunswick Press (Fredericton), 1964.

CLARK, ANDREW H. *Three Centuries and the Island: A Historical Geography of Settlement and Agriculture in Prince Edward Island, Canada.* Univ. of Toronto Press, 1959.

MACKINNON, FRANK. *The Government of Prince Edward Island.* Univ. of Toronto Press, 1951.

MACMILLAN, CYRUS. *Glooskap's Country and Other Indian Tales.* Oxford Univ. Press, 1956.

MONTGOMERY, LUCY M. *Anne of Green Gables.* Ryerson (Toronto), 1964. *Anne of the Island.* 1956.

PRINCE EDWARD ISLAND NATIONAL PARK. See CANADA (National Parks).

PRINCE GEORGE, B.C. (pop. 24,471; alt. 1,867 ft.), is the leading lumber producer in the interior of the province. It also serves as a farming and supply center. It is the commercial and transportation gateway to the province's North Country (see BRITISH COLUMBIA [political map]). The city was incorporated in 1916. It has a mayor-council government. RODERICK HAIG-BROWN

PRINCE OF WALES is the title given to the first male heir to the throne of Great Britain. He is always the oldest son of the sovereign, unless that son has died or given up the title. Edward I, the English king who conquered Wales in 1282, defeated and killed the last Welsh Prince of Wales. In 1301, he gave the title to his oldest son. Later, this son became king as Edward II. His son, who later became Edward III, was not given the title, but all later male heirs have received it.

The title *Prince of Wales* is purely honorary. Sons of British monarchs do not inherit the title. It is newly created for each prince. The monarch's oldest son becomes *Duke of Cornwall.* Even after he is named Prince of Wales, he receives his income from the Duchy of Cornwall, not from Wales. Queen Elizabeth II's son, Prince Charles, became Duke of Cornwall when his mother took the throne in 1952. He was named Prince of Wales by his mother in 1958. MARION F. LANSING

See also CHARLES, PRINCE; EDWARD (II).

PRINCE OF WALES COLLEGE is a coeducational college in Charlottetown, P.E.I. It is supported by the province. The college grants bachelor's degrees in agriculture, arts and science, education, and home economics. It was established in 1834. For enrollment, see CANADA (table: Universities and Colleges).

PRINCE RUPERT, British Columbia (pop. 14,677; alt. 18 ft.), lies on Kaien Island north of the mouth of the Skeena River. Bridges connect it to the mainland. Prince Rupert is a fishing, logging, and pulp-producing center, with one of the world's largest cold-storage plants for fish. It is the terminus for the northern line of the Canadian National Railways. A 490-mile ferry route along the scenic Inside Passage to Skagway, Alaska, begins in Prince Rupert. The city has a mayor-council government. For location, see BRITISH COLUMBIA (political map). RODERICK HAIG-BROWN

PRINCE'S FEATHER. See AMARANTH.

PRINCESS. See PRINCE.

PRINCESS OF CLÈVES. See LA FAYETTE, MADAME DE.

PRINCETON, N.J. (pop. 11,890; alt. 210 ft.), the home of Princeton University and Princeton Theological Seminary, lies in central New Jersey (see NEW JERSEY [political map]). During the Revolutionary War, George Washington defeated a British division at Princeton, after it had taken refuge in Nassau Hall at Princeton University. The Continental Congress met in Princeton in 1783, and received the Treaty of Peace ending the Revolutionary War. Princeton has a mayor-council government. RICHARD P. McCORMICK

PRINCETON, BATTLE OF. See REVOLUTIONARY WAR IN AMERICA (Princeton and Trenton; table: Major Battles of the Revolutionary War).

PRINCETON THEOLOGICAL SEMINARY. See UNIVERSITIES AND COLLEGES (table).

PRINCETON UNIVERSITY is the fourth oldest university in the United States. Only Harvard, William and Mary, and Yale are older. This school for men is located in Princeton, N.J., a small community in the center of the state. It provides undergraduate and graduate instruction primarily in architecture, engineering, liberal arts, and the sciences.

Princeton graduates and faculty members have played an important role in United States political history. Richard Stockton, a member of the first Princeton graduating class, and John Witherspoon, an early

Orren Jack Turner

Ivy-Covered Nassau Hall, completed in 1756, was the first building constructed on the present Princeton University campus.

president of the university, were signers of the Declaration of Independence. One-sixth of the members of the Constitutional Convention studied at Princeton. Presidents James Madison and Woodrow Wilson were graduated from Princeton. Wilson headed the university from 1902 to 1910. Vice-Presidents Aaron Burr and George M. Dallas; eight associate justices of the Supreme Court of the United States; and 28 Cabinet members have been graduated from the university. Statesmen John Foster Dulles, James Forrestal, and Adlai E. Stevenson were Princeton graduates.

Campus Buildings. The Princeton campus covers about 2,500 acres. There are over 150 buildings, not including about 600 faculty homes. The school's administrative offices are located in Nassau Hall. Completed in 1756, this famous building is the oldest on the campus. It was occupied by British and colonial forces during the Revolutionary War. General George Washington captured the building on Jan. 3, 1777, to end the Battle of Princeton, a turning point in the war. Nassau Hall was the national capitol for five months in 1783, when the Continental Congress met there. George Washington received congressional thanks in Nassau Hall's prayer room for his conduct of the war.

The University Chapel has stained glass windows that portray the life, teachings, and influence of Christ. Grover Cleveland Memorial Tower honors the U.S. President who served as a Princeton trustee. The university has 12 libraries. The main one is the Harvey S. Firestone Memorial Library. The 12 libraries hold two million volumes and have collections that range from Egyptian papyri and Babylonian cylinder seals to the papers of Woodrow Wilson, Secretary of State John Foster Dulles, and Secretary of Defense James Forrestal.

Research plays an important role at Princeton. Two of the university's largest research facilities are the Plasma Physics Laboratory and a three billion electron-volt accelerator. They are located on the James Forrestal campus, about three miles from the main campus. Also on the Forrestal campus are the auditory research laboratories, the Daniel and Florence Guggenheim Laboratories for the Aerospace Propulsion Sciences, and most of the other laboratories for the aerospace and mechanical sciences department.

Educational Program. The undergraduate plan of study includes the preceptorial method, which brings teacher and student together and fosters individualism. The four-course plan of study is a program designed to encourage self-education. Under this plan, the student receives a broad coverage of knowledge in his underclass years. In his upperclass years, he engages in a specific field or interdepartmental program.

Princeton has 27 departments and 29 interdepartmental programs. The graduate school offers courses in architecture, engineering and applied science, liberal arts and sciences, and public and international affairs. The Woodrow Wilson School prepares students for careers in public service. The Graduate College buildings, dedicated in 1913, were the first residence halls for graduate students in the United States.

History. Princeton University was founded in 1746 as the College of New Jersey. The college received its charter from George II of England. It was originally sponsored by the Presbyterian Church, but it was one of the first colleges in the United States to admit students of all faiths. The first classes were held in 1747 in Elizabeth, N.J. The students met in the home of the college's first president, Rev. Jonathan Dickinson. The college moved to Newark in 1748, and to Princeton in 1756. It was renamed Princeton University in 1896.

During the 1960's, the university expanded its building program. It built an art museum; five engineering buildings; the Woolworth Center of Musical Studies; an architecture building; the Woodrow Wilson School of Public and International Affairs; the William Charles Peyton Hall for the Astrophysical Sciences; the George M. Moffett Biological Laboratory; mathematics, physics, and statistics buildings; the Stockwell Jadwin Gymnasium; 10 dormitories for undergraduates; two quadrangles at the graduate college; and a student center. For enrollment, see UNIVERSITIES AND COLLEGES (table). DAN D. COYLE

See also ATOMIC ENERGY (Nuclear Fusion); DODDS, HAROLD W.; WILSON, WOODROW (University President); WITHERSPOON, JOHN.

PRINCIPAL, in crime. See ACCOMPLICE.

PRINCIPAL, in economics. See INTEREST.

PRINCIPAL, in law. See AGENT.

PRINCIPALITY is a territory ruled by a prince. Andorra, Liechtenstein, and Monaco are three European principalities. All are small, independent countries. For more information on these principalities, see the separate articles in WORLD BOOK.

PRÍNCIPE ISLAND, *PRIHN suh pea,* together with São Tomé Island, forms the Portuguese overseas province of São Tomé and Príncipe. The islands lie in the Gulf of Guinea (see AFRICA [political map]). Príncipe covers 54 square miles, and has a population of 4,605. Its only sizable settlement is Santo Antonio, on the eastern coast. Chief products include bananas, cacao, coconuts, coffee, palm oil, and sugar. CHARLES E. NOWELL

PRINCIPIA COLLEGE. See UNIVERSITIES AND COLLEGES (table).

PRING, MARTIN. See NEW HAMPSHIRE (Exploration).

PRINT. See ENGRAVING; JAPANESE PRINT; PERCALE; PHOTOGRAPHY (Contact Printing); PRINTING.

699

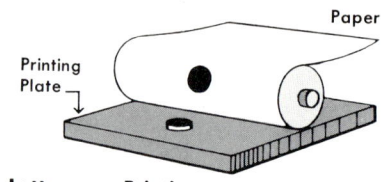

Letterpress Printing
is done from a raised surface.

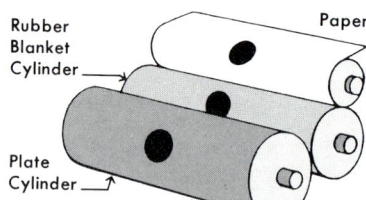

Offset Lithographic Printing
is done from a flat surface.

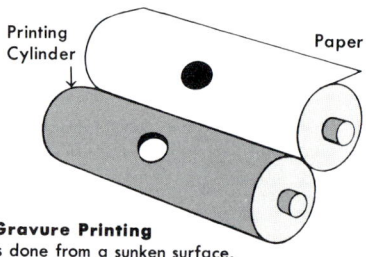

Gravure Printing
is done from a sunken surface.

WORLD BOOK photo

PRINTING

An Amazing Variety of Printed Items—from books, magazines, and newspapers to packages, textiles, and wallpaper—rolls off printing presses every day. Almost all these items are printed by one of the three processes diagramed above.

PRINTING is one of our most important means of mass communication, along with radio, television, and motion pictures. Printing forms the basis of our whole educational system. Modern business depends on printing for everything from sales slips to money and stock certificates. Advertising depends chiefly on printing to sell goods and services.

The printing and publishing industry is a big business in many countries throughout the world. It is the eighth largest industry in both the United States and Canada. In addition to books, newspapers, and magazines, thousands of other items roll off printing presses every day. These items include billboard signs, candy bar wrappers, beverage cans, calendars, ruled writing tablets, wallpaper, textiles, post cards, playing cards, street banners, mail order catalogs, comic books, and reproductions of great works of art.

Printing as we know it today began only about 500 years ago. Before that time, everything people read had to be copied by hand or printed from wood blocks carved by hand. Then one of the greatest events in history took place. About 1440, Johannes Gutenberg of Germany invented *printing with movable type*. Gutenberg made separate pieces of metal type for each letter to be printed. The same pieces of metal type could be used over and over again—to print many different books. A printer could quickly make any number of copies of a book, each exactly the same as all the others.

Printing soon became the first means of mass communication. It put more knowledge in the hands of more people faster and cheaper than ever before. As a result, reading and writing spread widely and rapidly. Printing became man's most powerful weapon against his worst enemy—ignorance.

Almost all printing today is done by one of three major processes: (1) letterpress, (2) offset lithography, or (3) gravure. Each of these processes uses a different kind of *printing surface* (the letters, pictures, or designs on a printing plate that do the printing). In *letterpress*, the printing surface is raised. In *offset lithography*, the printing surface and the nonprinting surface are on the same flat level. In *gravure*, the printing surface is below the nonprinting surface.

This article describes each of the three major printing processes—from setting the type to running the presses. It also discusses other printing processes and color printing. It traces the history of printing, and describes career opportunities in printing. Separate WORLD BOOK articles, such as BOOKBINDING and PHOTOENGRAVING AND PHOTOLITHOGRAPHY, provide details on the steps in printing. Other articles, including COMMUNICATION and LIBRARY, give information on the importance of printing in communication and education.

E. J. Triebe, the critical reviewer of this article, is President of Kingsport Press, Incorporated. The illustrations were prepared for WORLD BOOK *by Dick Larson, unless otherwise credited.*

Letterpress is the oldest and most widely used printing process. More than a thousand years ago, the Chinese printed by letterpress. They cut *relief* (raised) characters and designs out of wood blocks. Then they inked the relief surfaces and pressed them against paper. This basic principle of letterpress printing remains unchanged today.

Letterpress accounts for at least half the dollar value of all printing in the United States. It is used to print most newspapers and magazines, and many books. Letterpress is also used to print stationery, packages, advertising matter, and many other items.

Setting the Type. Printing begins in the *composing room* of a printing plant. Here, the written *copy* (the words to be printed) is *set* (put into type). Ever since Gutenberg invented movable type, type has traditionally been in the form of raised metal letters. Today, most metal type is set by machine, but some is still set by hand. In addition, much type today is in the form of filmed images of letters, rather than raised metal letters. Typesetting can be classified as (1) hot metal typesetting or (2) cold type typesetting.

Hot Metal Typesetting includes all typesetting methods that use metal type. Most metal typesetting is done on two machines—the *Linotype* or the *Monotype*.

The Linotype casts full lines of metal type. All the letters are joined in one piece, called a *slug*. The Linotype operator sits at a typewriterlike keyboard. When he strikes a key, he releases a *matrix* (a mold for a specific letter). After a line of matrices has been released, the machine pours molten metal into the molds. The metal hardens quickly, and the finished slug drops into a tray called a *galley*. The *Intertype* is a similar line-casting machine. See LINOTYPE.

The Monotype casts separate letters instead of whole lines of type. The Monotype consists of two machines—a *keyboard* machine and a *caster*. When the operator strikes a key on the keyboard, he punches a set of holes in a paper tape. Each different arrangement of holes represents a different letter, number, or some other character to be printed. The tape is fed into the caster, which has matrices corresponding to the keyboard characters. The tape selects the proper matrix, and molten metal is poured into it. The letters are assembled side by side. After a line has been completed, it drops into a galley. See MONOTYPE.

Some type, such as that used for newspaper headlines, is too large to be set by machine, and must be set by hand. Other type is set by hand because the Linotype or Monotype does not set every available style of type. The typesetter, who is called a *compositor*, takes the type from a shallow drawer called a *case*. He assembles it, letter by letter, in a small tray called a *composing stick*. After the tray is full, he transfers the type to a galley. See TYPE.

Cold Type Typesetting, also called *photocomposition*, includes all typesetting methods that do not use metal type. Most cold type is produced on high-speed *phototypesetting machines*. These machines produce "galleys" of photographic images of letters, instead of galleys of actual type. Instead of a mold for each letter, they have a negative film for each letter. When the operator strikes

the keys of his machine, a beam of light projects through the proper negatives onto photographic film. The film is then developed, and the images on it are transferred to the printing plates.

There are several kinds of phototypesetters. Some produce type on photographic paper as well as on film. Several types of phototypesetters have two units. One unit contains the keyboard and produces punched tape. The second unit produces images on film or paper according to the coded tape. Both the Intertype and Monotype have been adapted to produce cold type.

Electronic Computers simplify the preparation of the tapes that operate typesetting machines. Normally, the operator of a typesetting machine must *justify* the type. That is, he determines the spacing between letters and words so that each line looks pleasing, and the right-hand margins are aligned. He also decides how to hyphenate words that are continued on the next line.

In a computerized typesetting system, the operator types the copy on a special keyboard and produces a punched tape. He ignores justification and hyphenation. The tape is fed into a computer that justifies lines and hyphenates words. The computer turns out the final tape for the typesetting machines. See COMPUTER.

Proofing. All set type must be checked for errors. Metal type is placed on a small press and inked. Paper is laid on the inked type, and a cylinder is rolled over the paper. A *proof* (trial impression) is then *pulled* (stripped off). To proofread photographic type, a proof is produced from the film by making a photographic print.

A *proofreader* checks all proofs for accuracy. If any errors have been made, the type goes back to the typesetter to be corrected. See PROOFREADING.

Reproducing Illustrations. To reproduce illustrations for letterpress printing, relief plates called *engravings* must be made. Engravings are made by a process called *photoengraving*. There are two chief kinds of engravings: (1) line engravings and (2) halftone engravings.

Line Engravings are made from copy consisting of solid areas or lines, such as diagrams, pen-and-ink drawings, and proofs of type. A *photoengraver* photographs the copy to get a negative. He places the negative on a metal plate coated with a light-sensitive substance. He then passes light through the negative to transfer the image to the plate. The photoengraver develops the plate and puts it in an acid bath. The acid eats away the background, leaving the image in relief.

Halftone Engravings are made from photographs, paintings, or other copy that has tones or shades. To reproduce the tones, the photoengraver photographs the copy through a *halftone screen*. This screen looks like a window screen, but is much finer. The screen breaks up the image on the negative into tiny dots of different sizes. The halftone negative is then printed on a metal plate. After the plate has been developed, it is bathed in acid. The acid eats away the background, leaving the dots in relief. When the illustration is printed, the viewer's eye blends the dots into duplicates of the original tones. To learn how color illustrations are reproduced, see the section *Printing in Color*.

Printers also use *photopolymer plates* to reproduce

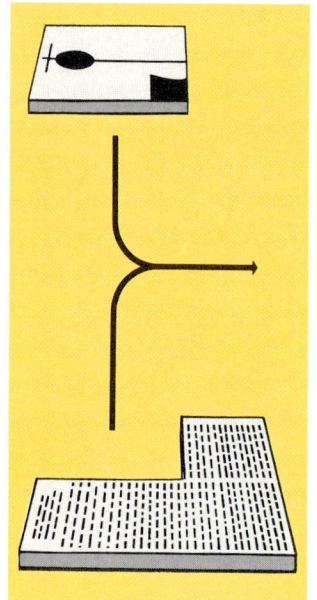

WORLD BOOK photo

Raised Metal Type and an Engraving are assembled to make up a page for letterpress printing, *left.* They are locked up tightly, *right,* in a metal frame called a *chase.* On a platen or flat-bed cylinder press, printing can be done directly from the locked-up page, called a *type form.*

illustrations. These plates have a layer of light-sensitive plastic on a metal base. When a negative is exposed to the plastic, the plastic hardens in the image areas. The plate is then sprayed with a caustic soda solution. The solution washes away the soft background, leaving the hard image in relief. For more information on photoengraving, see PHOTOENGRAVING AND PHOTOLITHOGRAPHY.

Making Up the Pages. The galleys of type and the engravings go to a *makeup man.* He puts the engravings and the type for each page into a frame called a *chase.* Page proofs are pulled and proofread. The type and engravings are then *locked up* tightly in the chase with wood or metal blocks called *furniture* and metal wedges called *quoins.* The locked-up page is called a *type form.*

Making Duplicate Plates. Letterpress printing can be done directly from type forms. But printers often use *duplicate plates* made from the forms. One reason for making duplicate plates is that type is soft, and wears down quickly on the press. Another reason is that one type of printing press, the rotary press, cannot use a flat chase. This press requires the printing surfaces to be fastened to cylinders. Duplicate plates can be curved to fit the cylinders.

Letterpress uses four kinds of duplicate plates: (1) electrotypes, (2) stereotypes, (3) plastic plates, and (4) rubber plates.

Electrotypes reproduce the finest details of the original type and engravings. An *electrotyper* makes a mold, usually of plastic, of the type form. He puts the mold in a copper-plating bath, and a copper shell forms on the mold. The electrotyper then strips off the shell, and has a perfect duplicate of the page form. See ELECTROTYPING.

Stereotypes can be made quickly, but they do not reproduce details well. They are used mostly to print newspapers. A *stereotyper* makes a mold of the type form, using a sheet of cardboardlike paper called a *mat.* He places the molded mat in a *casting box* and pours molten metal into the mat. The metal hardens quickly, and the plate is formed. See STEREOTYPING.

Plastic Plates are strong and easy to make. The materials used are *thermosetting plastics* and *thermoplastic plastics.* Thermosetting plastics soften only once when heated, and then harden permanently. Heat cannot soften them again. Thermoplastic plastics can be softened again and again with heat.

The platemaker presses a sheet of thermosetting plastic on the type form under heat and pressure to get a mold. He fills the hardened mold with powdered or liquid thermoplastic plastic, and again applies heat and pressure. He then strips the finished plastic plate from the mold. The photopolymer plates used for making engravings can also be used to make original plates of type and illustrations.

Rubber Plates are made in much the same way as plastic plates. The platemaker makes a thermosetting plastic mold of the type form. He then places a sheet of rubber on the mold. Next, he forms the plate by pressing the rubber into the mold under heat and pressure.

Running the Presses. The duplicate plates or type forms go to the *pressroom* of the printing plant. Here, amid the thumping and whirring of the presses and the smell of ink, the actual printing is done. The main job of a press is to transfer ink from the printing plates to the paper. But some presses can do much more. They can pick up the blank paper, move it through the press, print on both sides of the paper in one or more colors,

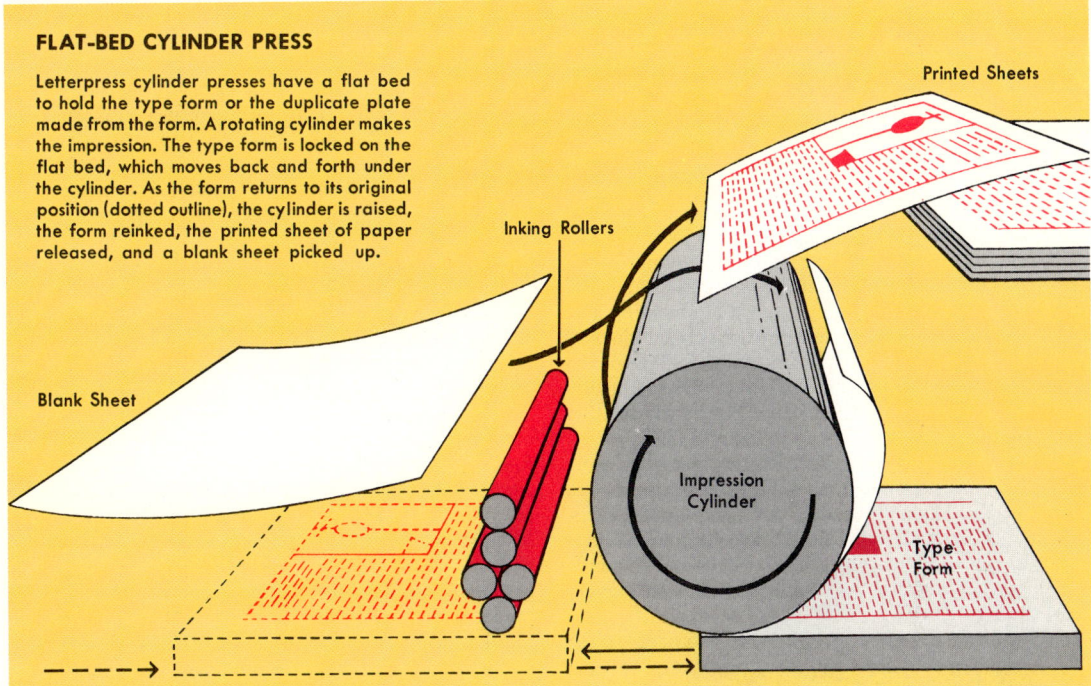

FLAT-BED CYLINDER PRESS

Letterpress cylinder presses have a flat bed to hold the type form or the duplicate plate made from the form. A rotating cylinder makes the impression. The type form is locked on the flat bed, which moves back and forth under the cylinder. As the form returns to its original position (dotted outline), the cylinder is raised, the form reinked, the printed sheet of paper released, and a blank sheet picked up.

Printed Sheets

Inking Rollers

Blank Sheet

Impression Cylinder

Type Form

and cut the printed paper and fold it into pages.

The presses used for letterpress printing vary in size and design. They are usually divided into three groups: (1) platen presses, (2) flat-bed cylinder presses, and (3) rotary presses.

Platen Presses use two flat surfaces to print. One surface is the *bed*. It holds the type form or duplicate plate. The other surface is a metal plate called the *platen*. It holds the paper or other material to be printed. Most platen presses run automatically. Rollers ink the form as a sheet of paper is fed to the platen. The platen then swings against the form and prints the sheet as the rollers roll back to an inking plate. As the platen swings back, the printed sheet is released.

Platen presses are widely used for printing handbills, programs, and similar items. Such printing is called *job printing*. Most print shops that do general work have a platen press. Platen presses have long been used in high school printing classes.

Flat-Bed Cylinder Presses, or *Cylinder Presses*, have a flat bed to hold the duplicate plate or type form. A heavy rotating cylinder makes the impression. The bed moves back and forth under the impression cylinder. As the cylinder turns, it picks up a sheet of paper. The cylinder rolls the paper over the form as the bed passes under it. Then, as the bed returns to its original position, the cylinder lifts, rollers ink the form, and the printed sheet is released.

Cylinder presses can be *vertical* or *horizontal*. That is, the bed can move up and down against the cylinder or back and forth under it. A *perfecting* cylinder press prints both sides of the paper. It has two flat beds and two cylinders. Flat-bed presses are used to print books, cartons, pamphlets, and many other items.

Rotary Presses are used for the mass production of newspapers, magazines, and books. These presses have cylinders both to make the impression and to hold the duplicate plates. The paper is printed as it passes between the impression cylinder and the plate cylinder.

A rotary press operates with a *unit system* or a *common impression system*. In a unit system, each plate cylinder has its own impression cylinder. Each of these units has a separate inking system. The number of units determines the number of colors to be printed. For example, two units print two colors, and four units print four colors. A common impression system uses only one impression cylinder, but up to five plate cylinders may be grouped around it. Each plate cylinder has its own inking system.

Rotary presses can be either *sheet-fed* or *web-fed*. Sheet-fed presses print single sheets of paper. Web-fed presses print from a huge roll of paper. The paper passes between the cylinders in a continuous stream called a *web*. A device on the press cuts the printed paper into sheets and folds them into pages for a newspaper, magazine, or book. Most web-fed rotaries are perfecting presses.

A *pressman* operates the presses. After he has set up his press, he prints some sample copies. Then, in a process called *makeready*, he makes various adjustments to get the best possible impression. He pastes pieces of paper on the impression surface or under the printing plate to build up areas that print too lightly. In places where the impression is too heavy, he cuts away some of the layers of paper, called *packing*, that cover the impression surface.

For the story of how pages are bound into books, see the article on BOOKBINDING.

Lithography is a method of printing from a flat surface. It is based on the fact that grease and water do not mix. Alois Senefelder, a German, discovered lithography in 1798. He drew a design on a stone with a greasy crayon. Then he dampened the stone, and the water stuck only to the parts not covered by the design. Next, he inked the stone, and the greasy ink stuck only to the design. Senefelder then pressed paper against the stone, and transferred the image to the paper.

Today, the same principle is used in commercial printing. Thin metal plates have replaced the stone, and the images are put on the plates photographically. The printing press does not transfer the inked images directly from the plates to the paper. Instead, the press first *offsets* (transfers) the images onto a rubber-covered cylinder, which then offsets them onto the paper or other material to be printed.

Offset lithography is the fastest-growing printing process. It ranks second in use to letterpress. It is used to print books, magazines, stationery, metal containers, cartons, labels, and many other items. The process is often called simply *offset* or *lithography*. It is also known as *planography*, because the printing is done from a *plane* (flat) surface.

Offset Printing Plates are made by a process called *photolithography*. The first step is to photograph all the copy, including sharp, clean *reproduction proofs* of raised metal type. The photographic work is much like that used in letterpress photoengraving. After the negatives have been made, they are *stripped* (pieced) together exactly as the type and illustrations are to appear in print. The stripped negatives are exposed on a metal plate that has a light-sensitive coating. Light from powerful lamps shines through the negatives and hardens the images on the plate. The plate is developed and then chemically treated so that when it is on the press, only the images will accept ink.

Many types of offset plates are used. They are made of different metals and have various light-sensitive coatings. Some plates use positive films rather than negative films. For more information on offset plate-making, see PHOTOENGRAVING AND PHOTOLITHOGRAPHY.

Offset Presses are rotary presses. The printing plate is clamped to the plate cylinder. As the cylinder rotates, it presses against water rollers, which wet the plate so the nonprinting areas will repel ink. The cylinder next passes against ink rollers. The greasy ink sticks only to the image areas. The turning plate cylinder then offsets the inked images onto a rubber *blanket* cylinder. The rotating blanket cylinder, in turn, offsets the images onto the paper carried by the impression cylinder.

Offset presses have a unit system. Some presses print only black or any other single color. Other presses print four or more colors. Most sheet-fed offset presses print a single color on one side of the paper only. A few sheet-fed presses are perfecting presses.

Most web-fed offset presses are multicolor perfecting presses. The most popular web offset press is the perfecting *blanket-to-blanket* press. This press has no impression cylinders. The web passes between the two blanket cylinders of two units. The blanket cylinder of one unit serves as the impression cylinder for the other. The paper is printed on both sides as it goes between the blankets. The printed paper can be delivered on another roll. Or the paper can be cut into sheets and piled, or it can be cut and folded into groups of pages called *signatures*.

WORLD BOOK is printed on web offset presses. These presses can produce 17,000 WORLD BOOK signatures an hour. The presses can use a 5½-mile roll of paper every 30 minutes as the web speeds through at about 1,000 feet per minute. For more information on offset printing, see OFFSET.

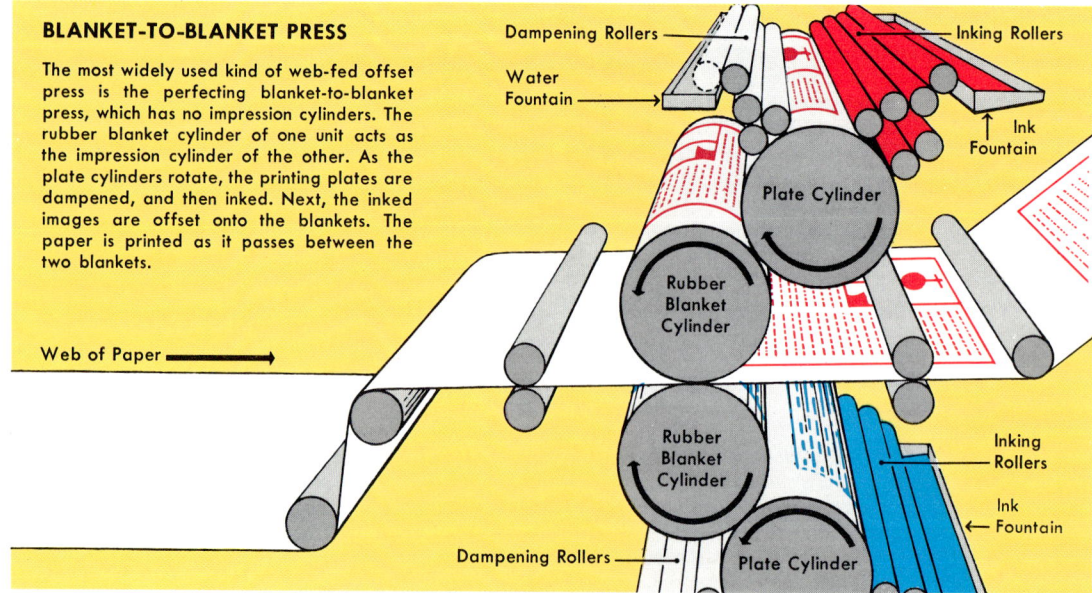

BLANKET-TO-BLANKET PRESS

The most widely used kind of web-fed offset press is the perfecting blanket-to-blanket press, which has no impression cylinders. The rubber blanket cylinder of one unit acts as the impression cylinder of the other. As the plate cylinders rotate, the printing plates are dampened, and then inked. Next, the inked images are offset onto the blankets. The paper is printed as it passes between the two blankets.

Dampening Rollers

Water Fountain

Inking Rollers

Ink Fountain

Plate Cylinder

Rubber Blanket Cylinder

Web of Paper

Rubber Blanket Cylinder

Inking Rollers

Ink Fountain

Dampening Rollers

Plate Cylinder

Gravure is an *intaglio* (*in TAL yoh*) method of printing. That is, the words, pictures, or designs to be printed are sunk into the printing plate or printing cylinder. For hundreds of years, artists have used the intaglio principle to make engravings. The artist uses a sharp-pointed tool to cut a picture into a metal plate. He then covers the plate with ink and wipes it clean. The ink remains only in the sunken lines of the picture. Next, the artist presses paper against the plate and into the sunken lines, transferring the inked image to the paper. Commercial gravure works in a similar way, but the images are put on the printing plate or cylinder photographically. Then acid is used to cut the images into the plate.

Gravure ranks third in use among the major printing processes. It is used to print the magazine sections of newspapers, and also wedding invitations, calling cards, mail order catalogs, food and candy wrappers, paper money, postage stamps, stock certificates and bonds, wallpaper, and many other items.

Gravure Printing Plates and Cylinders. Gravure printing is done from engraved plates or cylinders. They are made by a process similar to photoengraving. All the copy, including reproduction proofs of metal type, is photographed. But tone copy, such as photographs and paintings, is not photographed through a screen, as it is for letterpress and offset printing. After the negatives have been made, film positives are made from them. The positives of the type and illustrations are then stripped together as they are to appear in print. Next, the images on the positives are transferred to the printing surface through the use of *carbon tissue*, a sheet of paper covered with light-sensitive gelatin. The carbon tissue is first exposed under bright light to a screen. Then it is exposed to the film positives. The gelatin hardens according to how much light passes through the positives. For example, the darkest areas on the positives

allow the least light to pass through. The gelatin is softest in these areas.

The exposed tissue is placed gelatin side down on a thin, flexible copper plate or heavy copper-plated cylinder. The tissue is developed in water, and the paper backing is stripped off. Thousands of little gelatin squares of varying thickness are left standing on the copper. The plate or cylinder is then bathed in acid. The acid eats through the gelatin squares, and bites thousands of little *cells* (pits) into the copper. It penetrates the thinnest squares fastest, and bites deepest in these areas. On the printing press, the deepest cells hold the most ink and print the darkest tones. The shallowest ones hold the least ink and print the lightest tones.

There are also several other gravure platemaking processes. Some processes do not use carbon tissue. Instead, a light-sensitive coating is applied directly to the printing plate or cylinder. Other processes produce cells that vary in size as well as in depth in order to create clearer, sharper tones. For more information on gravure platemaking, see PHOTOENGRAVING AND PHOTOLITHOGRAPHY.

Gravure Presses are either sheet-fed or web-fed rotary presses. Sheet-fed presses print from engraved copper plates, which are clamped around the plate cylinder. Web-fed presses print from engraved copper-plated cylinders, which are positioned on the press. Web-fed gravure presses are called *rotogravure* presses. They can run at speeds of over 1,000 feet per minute.

On a gravure press, several methods can be used to ink the printing cylinder. Most presses use a trough of ink. As the cylinder rotates, it dips into the trough, filling the cells with ink. A *doctor blade* wipes the surface clean, so that ink remains only in the cells. The impression roller then presses paper against the printing cylinder and into the cells. The pressure transfers the ink in each cell to the paper.

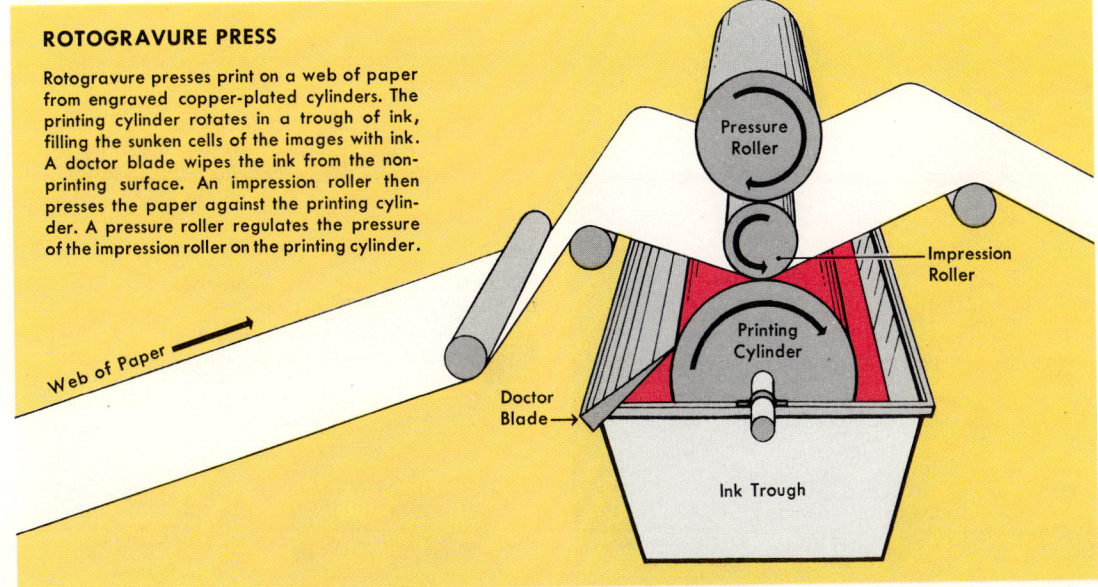

ROTOGRAVURE PRESS

Rotogravure presses print on a web of paper from engraved copper-plated cylinders. The printing cylinder rotates in a trough of ink, filling the sunken cells of the images with ink. A doctor blade wipes the ink from the non-printing surface. An impression roller then presses the paper against the printing cylinder. A pressure roller regulates the pressure of the impression roller on the printing cylinder.

Pressure Roller

Impression Roller

Printing Cylinder

Web of Paper

Doctor Blade →

Ink Trough

Letterpress, lithography, and gravure can reproduce anything in color—from comic strips to masterworks of art. There are two chief kinds of color printing: (1) *process color printing* and (2) *flat color printing.*

Process Color Printing is used mainly to reproduce color copy that contains shades or tones. Such copy includes oil paintings, water colors, and color photographs. By using only tiny dots of transparent red, blue, and yellow ink, process color printing can reproduce copy containing almost all the colors and tones of the rainbow.

Three printing plates must be made—one each to print red, blue, and yellow ink. Usually, a black plate is also made, because black ink adds sharpness to the printed illustration.

The first step in making color plates is to photographically separate the colors in the copy. A cameraman photographs the copy four times to get a *separation negative* of the red, yellow, blue, and black in the copy. Each time, he uses a different colored filter to block out all colors from each negative except the desired color. *Electronic color scanners* can also be used. They scan the copy with a small light beam, and produce color separation negatives quickly and automatically.

For letterpress and offset printing, the cameraman also shoots the copy through a halftone screen to get the dot pattern. He turns the screen at a different angle for each color so that the dots will fall side by side, not on top of one another, in printing. The eye mixes the colors of the dots on the printed page into all the colors and shades of the original copy. For example, what the eye sees as green is really an area of tiny blue and yellow dots.

An *indirect screening* process is also used. In this method, the cameraman shoots the copy through the different colored filters, but not through a halftone screen. He then rephotographs the unscreened negatives to produce positives. Finally, he shoots the positives through a screen to make the halftone negatives. Gravure process color printing also uses a screen, but it is printed on the carbon tissue.

After the separation negatives have been made, the steps follow the regular procedures for making letterpress photoengravings, offset plates, or gravure plates and cylinders. On a four-color rotary press, each plate has its own supply of red, blue, yellow, or black ink. The paper passes from one set of cylinders to the next, picking up the different colors and emerging fully printed. Usually, only red, blue, yellow, and black inks are used on the presses. Other colors are sometimes added to achieve special effects.

Flat Color Printing is used chiefly to print *line copy* in solid colors. Such copy includes diagrams, headlines and other type matter, cartoons and comic strips, and trademarks on stationery. Flat color printing is simpler than process color printing. Separate plates must be made for each color of opaque ink, but halftone dots are not used to create tones or other colors.

PRINTING WITH PROCESS COLORS

To reproduce the picture of the apple, *below left,* four printing plates were used —one each for the yellow, red, blue, and black in the original copy. The plates were made from negatives. To make the negatives, the copy was photographed four times through a halftone screen and through filters that eliminated all colors from each negative except the color desired. The pictures, *below right,* show the plates. The circle, *right,* is a magnified area of the full-color reproduction, showing how the dots on the plates reproduced the colors and tones of the copy.

WORLD BOOK photo

Yellow Plate

Red Plate

Blue Plate

Black Plate

In addition to letterpress, offset lithography, and gravure, there are many other printing processes. The most important ones include *screen process, collotype,* and *electrostatic* printing.

Screen Process Printing requires a stencil and a fine cloth or wire screen. The stencil carries the design to be printed. It can be made simply by cutting the design out of paper. The stencil is mounted against the screen. Ink is squeezed through the stencil onto the surface to be printed. The design can also be traced directly on the screen, and the nonprinting parts painted out. Or the screen can be given a light-sensitive coating and the design put on it photographically.

Screen process can be used to print on paper, glass, cloth, wood, or almost any other material. It is used to print on objects of almost all sizes and shapes, including draperies, banners, bottles, toys, and furniture. Most screen process printing is done on automatic or hand-operated presses. Screen process is also called *silk screen printing* or *serigraphy*, especially in the fine arts (see SILK SCREEN PRINTING).

Collotype Printing is similar to lithography. A light-sensitive coating of gelatin is put on a metal or glass plate. The gelatin is exposed to light under an un-screened negative that carries the image to be printed. The light passes through the negative, hardening the gelatin to varying degrees. The plate is then soaked in a solution of water and glycerin. The hardest parts of the gelatin absorb the least solution, and the softest parts absorb the most. On the printing press, the hardest, driest parts accept the most ink and print the darkest tones. The softest, wettest parts accept the least ink and print the lightest tones.

Collotype is used to print post cards, greeting cards, posters, and reproductions of paintings. The process is sometimes called *photogelatin printing*.

Electrostatic Printing reproduces original material without ink or pressure. There are several electrostatic processes, of which the best known is *xerography*. This process uses a plate coated with selenium, a substance that conducts electricity when exposed to light. The plate is first given an electrostatic charge. Then the copy is projected through a lens, and a positively charged *latent* (hidden) image forms on the plate. The plate is dusted with negatively charged black powder, which clings only to the image. Paper is placed on the plate and given a positive charge, which attracts the powder image to the paper. The paper is heated briefly. The heat melts the powder, and the permanent print is formed. Other electrostatic processes work in a similar way. But they use specially coated, electrically charged paper instead of a selenium plate.

Electrostatic printing is widely used for making copies of office records. The process is relatively new, and its uses are being expanded and developed rapidly. One new electrostatic technique, developed for the U.S. Army, makes it possible to print a map in five colors within 30 minutes.

On the Printing Press, the yellow plate is usually printed first, then the red, blue, and black plates. The diagram shows a unit type web offset press similar to those that print WORLD BOOK.

Yellow

Yellow and Red

Yellow, Red, and Blue

Yellow, Red, Blue, and Black

Paper-Feeding Unit

Yellow Printing Unit

Red Printing Unit

Blue Printing Unit

Black Printing Unit

Ink-Drying Unit

The history of printing can be traced back thousands of years, to when man first learned to press carved designs into wet clay. Yet printing as we know it today has a short history. Modern printing began only about 500 years ago with the invention of movable type by Johannes Gutenberg of Germany.

Printing in the Orient. About A.D. 105, Ts'ai Lun, a Chinese, invented paper. The Chinese probably also invented *block printing.* They carved characters and pictures on wood blocks, inked the raised images, and transferred the ink to paper.

About 1045, a Chinese printer named Pi Sheng made the first movable type. He made a separate piece of clay type for each character. The use of movable type did not develop in China because the Chinese language has thousands of different characters. Printers would have had to make too many pieces of type. They found it easier to print from wood blocks.

The Invention of Movable Type. While the people of the Orient were printing from wood blocks, the people of Europe were still producing handwritten books. Many monks spent their lives laboriously copying books with quills and reeds. In the early 1400's, Europeans finally discovered block printing. The earliest dated European wood block print is a picture of Saint Christopher, printed in 1423. About this same time, Europeans began to produce *block books* by binding prints together.

Meanwhile, the Renaissance was sweeping through Europe. The great desire for learning created a huge demand for books that hand copying and block printing could not satisfy. Movable type solved the problem.

Most historians consider Johannes Gutenberg the inventor of movable type in Europe. Gutenberg began using separate pieces of raised metal type about 1440. He adapted his printing press from a machine used to press grapes or cheese. Gutenberg assembled his pieces of type in a form, and then inked the type. Next, he placed paper on the type. Then, by turning a huge wood screw on the press, he brought down a wood block against the paper. The Gutenberg press could print about 300 copies a day. By 1456, Gutenberg's famous 42-line Bible was completed. Each column had 42 lines of type. See GUTENBERG, JOHANNES.

Many people feared that the new art of printing was a "black" art that came from Satan. They could not understand how books could be produced so quickly, or how all copies could look exactly alike. In spite of people's fears, printing spread rapidly. By 1500, there were more than 1,000 print shops in Europe, and several million books had been produced.

Early Printing in North America. In 1539, an Italian printer, Juan Pablos (Giovanni Paoli), set up a print shop in Mexico City. Most historians believe his was the first print shop in North America. In 1639, Stephen Daye and his son Matthew set up the first press in the American Colonies, in Cambridge, Mass. (see DAYE, STEPHEN).

Printing spread quickly through the colonies, though the colonial authorities often placed strict controls on printers. The early printers were more than operators of print shops. They were also America's first publishers of newspapers, books, and magazines. In 1704, John

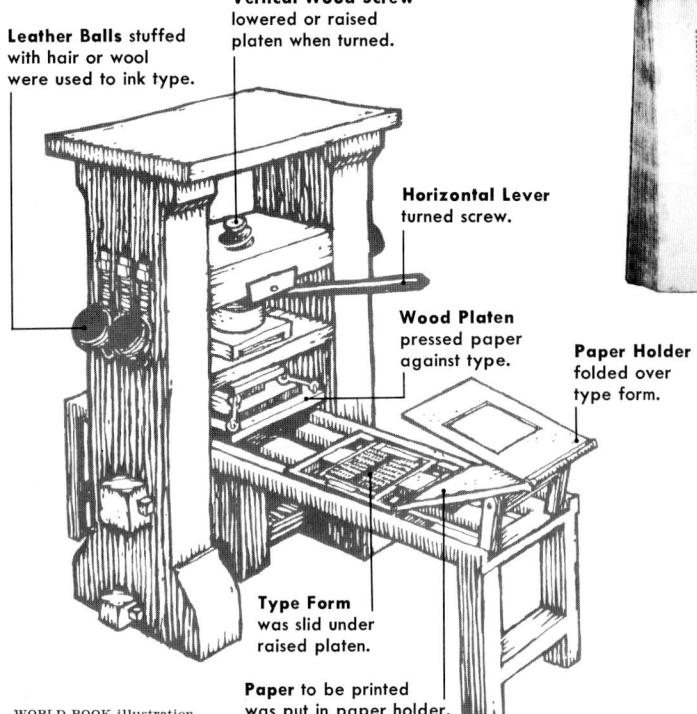

Leather Balls stuffed with hair or wool were used to ink type.

Vertical Wood Screw lowered or raised platen when turned.

Horizontal Lever turned screw.

Wood Platen pressed paper against type.

Type Form was slid under raised platen.

Paper to be printed was put in paper holder.

WORLD BOOK illustration by Tom Dunnington

Paper Holder folded over type form.

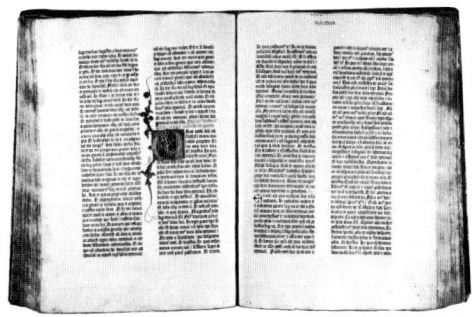

WORLD BOOK photo

Gutenberg's Press probably looked like this drawing, *left.* It was adapted from a cheese or wine press, and could print about 300 sheets a day. Although the press was exceedingly crude, it produced what is still one of the most magnificent examples of the art of printing—the Gutenberg Bible, *above.*

Modern Web Offset Press, *right,* is one of the giant presses used to print WORLD BOOK. The three-story, 110-foot-long press can print a $5\frac{1}{2}$-mile roll of paper every 30 minutes. The press's delivery unit, shown here, cuts the printed web into sheets and folds the sheets into groups of pages.

Campbell established the *Boston News-Letter*, the first regularly published paper in the colonies. In 1751, Bartholomew Green of Boston set up Canada's first print shop, in Halifax, N.S. Green died that same year, and his former assistant, John Bushell, took over the shop. In 1752, Bushell began publishing the *Halifax Gazette*, Canada's first newspaper.

Printers accompanied or soon followed the pioneers westward. During the 1780's and 1790's, printers set up shops and began publishing papers in Kentucky, Tennessee, and Ohio. In 1808, newspaper publishing crossed the Mississippi River when the *Missouri Gazette* came off the press in St. Louis.

New Presses and Typecasting Machines. The printing press changed little from Gutenberg's time until the 1800's. An English nobleman, the earl of Stanhope, built the first all-iron press about 1800. In 1811, Friedrich Koenig of Germany invented a steam-powered cylinder press. This press used a revolving cylinder that pressed the paper against a flat bed of type. *The Times of London* used the press for the first time in 1814. It could print 1,100 sheets per hour.

In 1846, Richard Hoe, an American, invented the rotary press. He attached type to a revolving cylinder, and used another cylinder to make the impression. The first Hoe presses printed 8,000 sheets per hour. Later models turned out 20,000 sheets per hour. In 1865, William Bullock, an American, found a way to print from a continuous roll of paper, and invented the high-speed web-fed rotary press.

Until the 1880's, printers set all type by hand, just

WORLD BOOK photo

as Gutenberg had done over 400 years before. In 1884, Ottmar Mergenthaler, a German living in the United States, patented the Linotype (see MERGENTHALER, OTTMAR). This machine, which casts a full line of type in one piece of metal, made typesetting more efficient. In 1887, Tolbert Lanston, an American, invented the Monotype, which casts separate pieces of type.

Developments in Platemaking. In 1826, Joseph Nicéphore Niépce, a French physicist, produced the world's first photograph. This achievement, and further developments in photography, made possible photoengraving, the halftone process, and photolithography and modern offset printing.

In 1852, William Fox Talbot of England patented photoengraving. Two Americans, Max and Louis Levy, perfected the halftone screen in the 1880's. Alphonse Louis Poitevin of France invented photolithography in 1855. By the late 1800's, offset presses appeared in Europe. These early presses were used to print tin sheets for making cans and boxes.

About 1905, Ira Rubel, an American papermaker and printer, accidentally discovered the offset method for printing on paper. While running his press, Rubel unintentionally transferred the inked images onto the rubber-covered impression cylinder, instead of onto paper. Then, when he ran paper through the press, the impression cylinder offset the images onto the paper. Rubel noticed that the offset images were unusually sharp. Improvements in the offset press followed, and offset printing quickly came into general use.

Since the 1930's, more advances have been made in printing than in all the years since Gutenberg. The printing industry today is being changed through such developments as phototypesetting, computerized typesetting, electrostatic printing, and optical scanning equipment. Another new development is *three-dimensional printing* of pictures. This process creates the appearance of three dimensions on a flat surface, giving a viewer the impression that he can reach into a picture.

U.S. and Canadian Printing Industries. Printing is the eighth largest industry in the United States, and one of the fastest growing. In the mid-1960's, the industry's yearly sales totaled about $18 billion.

More than 38,000 firms make up the American printing industry. These firms include book, newspaper, and magazine publishers, because publishing is so closely connected with printing. The U.S. printing industry employs about a million persons. Most printing firms are small, and more than 30,000 companies have fewer than 20 employees. Only about 1,500 printing and publishing firms employ over 100 persons. The five largest private printing and publishing firms in the United States, in order of sales, are R. R. Donnelley & Sons Company; McCall Corporation; Western Publishing Company, Incorporated; W. F. Hall Printing Company; and Cuneo Press, Incorporated. The U.S. Government Printing Office is the largest printing establishment in the country (see GOVERNMENT PRINTING OFFICE).

Printing is also Canada's eighth largest industry. In the mid-1960's, sales totaled more than $950 million a year. Canada has about 3,500 printing and publishing firms. They employ about 75,000 persons.

PRINTING / Careers in Printing

The printing industry offers career opportunities for men and women with many kinds of skills and interests. The industry needs people with ability in photography, electronics, or chemistry. It looks for people who like to work with their hands or enjoy operating machines. The industry needs layout and design artists. It seeks people with skills in English to be proofreaders, or with skills in mathematics to be cost estimators. According to the U.S. government, job opportunities in printing will expand faster than in most other industries during the years ahead.

Wages and salaries in printing are among the highest in the United States. The industry also offers stable employment, because economic slumps affect printing less than most other businesses. Experienced printing personnel can find jobs almost anywhere in the country. A person also has a good chance to start his own business in the printing field.

Skilled Occupations include typesetting, photoengraving, electrotyping and stereotyping, lithographic platemaking, press work, and bookbinding. Advancing technology is rapidly changing these jobs and creating a need for more technically capable people. As a result, more and more printing firms prefer to hire high school graduates, especially those who have had courses in chemistry, physics, and mathematics. Many firms also prefer young people who have taken high school or vocational school printing courses. Students who work in print shops during summer vacations or after school hours improve their chances of getting a full-time job after graduation.

After being hired full time, most young men must work as *apprentices* (helpers) from three to six years, depending on the type of job. The apprentice then becomes a *journeyman* (fully qualified craftsman). Many journeymen become foremen and supervisors, and some go into business for themselves.

Professional Occupations in the printing industry are plentiful for college graduates. Many colleges offer special courses in printing and other graphic arts. Carnegie-Mellon University is famous for its program of management education in graphic arts. Many journalism schools have courses in the mechanics of printing. College graduates in business administration, accounting, and liberal arts can find opportunities in management, production, cost estimating, and sales. The industry also needs engineers, scientists, and technicians to develop and design the machines and to improve the inks, paper, and other materials used in printing. Many large printing plants employ art school graduates in their design departments.

For more information about printing as a career, write to the Education Council of the Graphic Arts Industry, 4615 Forbes Avenue, Pittsburgh, Pa. 15213; or to the Bureau of Apprenticeship, United States Department of Labor, Washington, D.C. 20025.

Critically reviewed by E. J. TRIEBE

PRINTING / Study Aids

Related Articles in WORLD BOOK include:

BIOGRAPHIES

Outline

Questions

Why was the invention of movable type one of the most important events in all history?

What are the three major printing processes? How do they differ?

What is the difference between hot type and cold type?

Why are duplicate plates often made for letterpress printing?

What printing process does not use ink or pressure?

What is the difference between the Linotype and the Monotype?

Why is water used in printing by offset lithography?

Why was the development of photography so important in the history of printing?

Although the Chinese made the first movable type, they did not develop its use. Why?

How are *separation negatives* made for process color printing?

Why do more and more printing firms prefer to hire high school graduates?

How did Ira Rubel discover the offset method for printing on paper?

PRINTING, BUREAU OF ENGRAVING AND. See
ENGRAVING AND PRINTING, BUREAU OF.

PRIORITY, *pry AHR uh tih,* is the first chance to get
goods or services. The term is based on the word *prior,*
which means *preceding.* In rationing of materials essential to war, priority is given to the persons or firms
whose work is most important to the war effort. In public relief, families most seriously in need usually are
given benefits first.   ROBERT D. PATTON

PRIORY, *PRY oh rih,* is a monastic house. It ranks
second in importance below an abbey. Its director is
called a prior if a man, and a prioress if a woman. See
also ABBEY; MONASTICISM.

PRISCILLA MULLENS. See ALDEN; COURTSHIP OF
MILES STANDISH.

PRISM, *priz'm,* is a solid bounded by two congruent
polygons, and three or more parallelograms. The polygons, which are in parallel planes, are the bases, and the
parallelograms are the lateral faces. The solid is a *right
prism* if the lateral edges of the parallelogram are perpendicular to the base. Otherwise it is called an *oblique
prism.*

Prisms used in binoculars, periscopes, and many
scientific optical instruments are made of glass or quartz.
They vary in size and shape. They are transparent, and
can be used to reflect light rays, *refract* (bend) them, or
separate their colors.

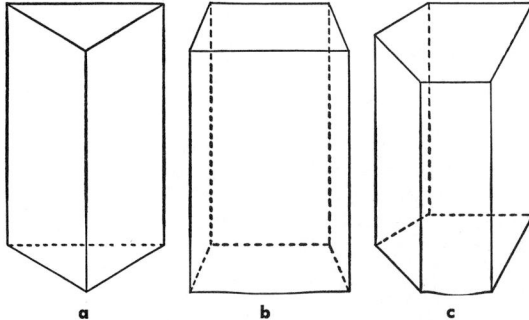

a   b   c

Prisms are named according to the shape of their
bases. For example, prism *a* is a triangular prism, *b* is
rectangular, and *c* is pentagonal. The surface area of a
prism is found by adding together the areas of all its
lateral faces and its two bases. The volume of a prism is
found by multiplying the area of one base by the *altitude* (perpendicular distance between bases). The formula for this multiplication is $V = Bh.$

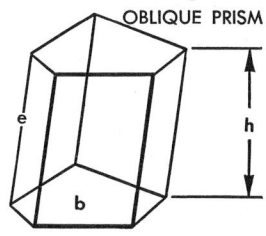
OBLIQUE PRISM

In this oblique prism, *b*
is the base, *h* is the altitude,
and *e* is a lateral edge. The
lateral edge is oblique to
the base. As a result, it is
longer than *h.*

Problems. (1) What is the
entire surface of a right
prism whose base is 2 inches
square and whose altitude is 6 inches?

Lateral area in sq. in. $=(4 \times 2) \times 6 = 48$
Area of bases in sq. in. $=2 \times (2 \times 2) = 8$
Entire surface in sq. in. $= 56$

(2) What is the volume of a triangular prism 20 inches
high, whose base is a right triangle with a base of
12 inches and an altitude of 8 inches?

Area of base in sq. in. $= 12 \times \frac{8}{2} = 48$
Volume in cu. in. $= 48 \times 20 = 960$

(3) For this barn, find
(1) the number of square
feet of surface to paint; (2)
the number of square feet
of roof to shingle; and (3)
the number of cubic feet of
storage space.

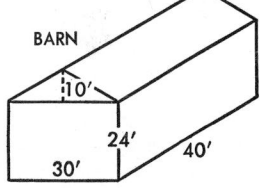
BARN

Solution. First find the
areas as usual (see TRIAN-
GLE; RECTANGLE). To find
the volume of the barn, think of the top of the barn as
made up of a triangular prism with base 30′ wide and
10′ high. See that the rest of the barn also is a rectangular prism with base 30′ × 24′ and altitude 40′.

For the top, or triangular, prism
$V = Bh$
$V = \frac{1}{2}(10 \times 30) \times 40 = 6,000$
For the lower, or rectangular, prism
$V = Bh$
$V = (30 \times 24) \times 40 = 28,800$
The total volume
$6,000 + 28,800 = 34,800$ cu. ft.   MILES C. HARTLEY

See also LIGHT; POLYGON; QUADRILATERAL.

Bausch & Lomb

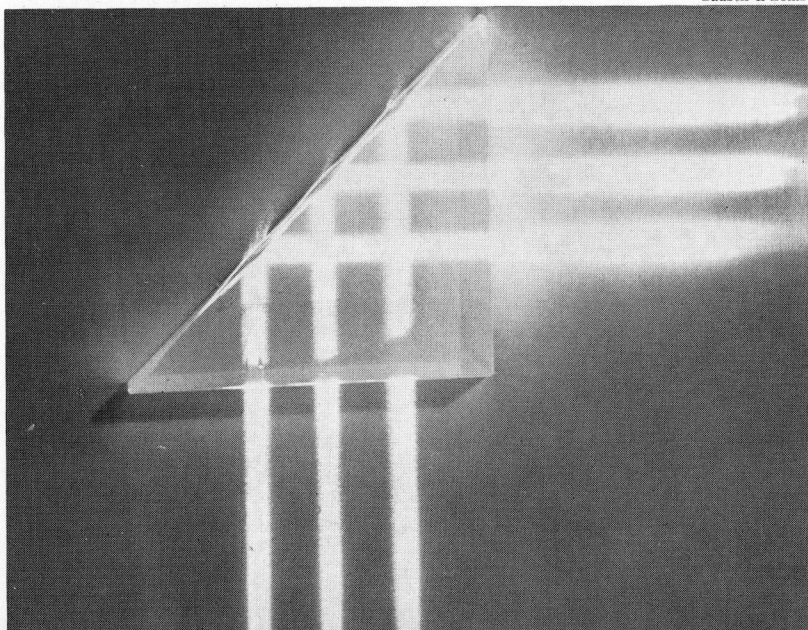

A Right-Angle Prism is able
to change the direction of three
parallel rays of light by means
of internal reflection.

PRISON

PRISON is a place of confinement for criminals or persons accused of breaking the law. In a broad sense, all penitentiaries, jails, houses of correction, workhouses, bridewells, and police lockups are prisons. In the United States, the term *prison* usually refers to institutions for confining persons convicted of serious crimes and sentenced to terms of more than one year. In other countries, the term also refers to institutions for confining accused persons awaiting trial, and to institutions for confining persons sentenced to terms of less than a year.

Kinds of American Prisons

Prisons in the United States may be classed generally as (1) jails and lockups, (2) federal prisons, and (3) state prisons.

Jails and Lockups. Most American institutions used for the detention and safekeeping of persons awaiting trial are maintained by cities or counties. But the federal government maintains one such institution in New York. The four principal types of detention institutions are: (1) the station lockup, (2) the small town municipal jail or lockup, (3) the county jail, and (4) special detention facilities for children.

Station Lockups are maintained by the police departments of large cities. Each police precinct may have its own lockup. Persons arrested in the precinct are held in the lockup for a few hours until arrangements for a hearing or a trial can be made. Criminals rarely serve sentences in these institutions.

Small Town Municipal Jails resemble the police lockups of large cities. But they house criminals serving sentences, as well as accused persons awaiting trials and hearings. Frequently, persons who cannot pay fines "work off" their fines at rates varying from 50 cents to five dollars a day. The United States has about 15,000 station lockups and small-town municipal jails. Less than half the persons held in them are subsequently convicted of crimes.

County Jails are usually under control of county sheriffs. They are used as (1) lockups for persons arrested by the sheriff or his staff, (2) penal institutions for convicted criminals serving sentences of less than one year, and (3) detention institutions for persons accused of serious crimes who have been ordered by lower courts to await a hearing by a grand jury or a higher court. There are about 3,800 county jails in the United States.

Special Detention Institutions are used for children accused of crime or delinquency who are not allowed to remain at home until the time of the hearing. Sometimes it is necessary to keep the child in an institution because the home is inadequate, because he might run away, because the offense is serious, or for some other reason. In some states, children in such cases are kept in jails and lockups. But the laws of most states restrict the use of such institutions. As a result, special institutions, often called *juvenile halls* or *juvenile homes*, have been created. However, about 100,000 children are detained in police lockups and county jails each year.

Federal Prisons. The U.S. government maintains institutions for persons convicted of violating federal laws dealing with drugs, liquor, income tax, immigration, the mails, national security, and interstate crimes.

Robert J. Smith, Black Star

Prisoners at the California Institution for Women can go to school, receive vocational training, and get professional counseling as part of the program for rehabilitation.

The Bureau of Prisons operates 33 institutions housing about 25,000 prisoners (see PRISONS, BUREAU OF). There are federal *penitentiaries* at Atlanta, Ga.; Leavenworth, Kans.; Lewisburg, Pa.; Marion, Ill.; McNeil Island, Wash.; and Terre Haute, Ind. *Reformatories* include a women's reformatory at Alderson, W.Va.; and men's reformatories at Chillicothe, Ohio; El Reno, Okla.; Lompoc, Calif.; and Petersburg, Va. *Juvenile and youth institutions* are located at Ashland, Ky.; Englewood, Colo.; Greenlee, Va.; Tucson, Ariz.; and Washington, D.C. *Correctional institutions* are located at Danbury, Conn.; La Tuna, Tex.; Milan, Mich.; Sandstone, Minn.; Seagoville, Tex.; Tallahassee, Fla.; Terminal Island, Calif.; and Texarkana, Tex. The bureau operates *camps* at Allenwood, Pa.; Eglin Air Force Base, Fla.; Florence, Ariz.; Greenville, S.C.; McNeil Island, Wash.; Montgomery, Ala.; and Safford, Ariz. The bureau maintains a detention headquarters in New York City and a medical center at Springfield, Mo.

The government closed its maximum-security prison on Alcatraz Island in San Francisco Bay in 1963. It opened the $12,000,000 maximum-security prison at Marion, Ill., to replace Alcatraz.

State Prisons. Each state maintains at least one institution for persons who have committed acts punishable by imprisonment for more than one year. These institutions resemble federal prisons in the way they are administered, and in the handling of the inmates. Some of the larger states, such as California, have a series of institutions for men. They range from a secure prison for hardened criminals to open camps and honor farms for men who can be trusted. States with smaller populations have only one institution for older male offenders, one institution for adult male offenders under a specified age such as 30, an institution for women, and two or three institutions for youths. These prisons, like those maintained by the federal government, protect society from criminals and, at the same time, punish and rehabilitate persons who have been convicted of crimes.

Modern Prisons

Most state and federal prisons are walled enclosures. They contain a number of cell-blocks, industrial build-

Men in Federal Reformatories receive training in vocations suited to their interests and abilities. Education and training help prepare these men for future employment.

U.S. Prisons

Group Participation in Sports and other recreational activities makes up an important part of American prison rehabilitation programs. Sports are under professional supervision.

U.S. Prisons

ings, a chapel, a laundry, an administration building, a gymnasium, a large dining room, and other buildings. An open space within the enclosure, called *the yard*, is used for recreation. Baseball and football are popular.

Cell-Blocks are prisons within prisons. A visitor must pass through three or four gates to get inside the wall. He must pass through more gates to get inside a cell-block. Most cell-blocks are rectangular. Tiers of cells face outward toward the two long sides of the cell-block, but they are separated from the walls, windows, and gates by a wide aisle. Even if a prisoner were to escape from his cell, he would be inside the cell-block. If he then were able to go through a cell-block gate or window, he still would have to get over the prison wall.

In some cell-blocks, the tiers of cells stand along two walls, like the rooms on each side of a hotel corridor. Each cell gets sunlight and air from a barred window, rather than through the door. In two or three prisons, the cell-blocks are circular. Tiers of cells surround a watchtower that stands in the center of the cell-block. The English philosopher Jeremy Bentham developed this design in the 1700's. He felt that the guard in the center tower would be able to see into each cell. This would make it possible for one guard to supervise a large number of prisoners. But officials found that this construction also enabled prisoners to watch the guard and misbehave when he turned his back.

Rehabilitation. In most prisons, men with good records may leave their cells during the day. Some work in prison factories or do maintenance tasks such as garden work and equipment repairing. Others work as clerks and typists, or attend the prison school. If there is enough work to do, the prisoners work an eight-hour day unless they are in school or some other kind of training program. Men with outstanding conduct records may be made *trusties* and permitted to work outside the walls. Some trusties drive trucks or act as chauffeurs for officials, but most of them work in gardens or on farms. Some may be allowed to live in special camps outside the walls. They enter the prison only for medical attention and special events. In these camps, prisoners often act as night watchmen. Records show that these privileged inmates seldom escape or take ad-

vantage of the trust placed in them by prison officials.

Several institutions allow prisoners to work on their hobbies at the end of the regular work period. If the warden gives his permission, inmates may sell the articles they make. Some prisons maintain small stores nearby to sell these goods to the public.

Punishment. Men with bad records may be confined in their cells at all times. Or they may be removed to special punishment cells where they are isolated from the rest of the inmates. Prisoners call these punishment cells *the hole*, although they are above ground and do not differ much from other cells. When confined in a punishment cell, a prisoner usually receives a restricted diet. Only a few prisons feed these men a diet of bread and water. If a prisoner commits a crime in prison, he is tried in an outside court. If convicted, his sentence begins when the old one has been served.

Personnel. Each prison is under the direct supervision of a *warden*. At one time almost all wardens were appointed as a reward for political activity, without regard for their fitness. This practice still exists in some parts of the United States. But in most areas, wardens either rise through the ranks or obtain their jobs on a merit basis. Each warden has three separate staffs under him. The *custodial staff* consists of the guards and their officers, who use military titles such as *sergeant* and *captain*. Usually a deputy warden is in charge of the custodial staff. The industrial foremen and tradesmen, such as the managers of prison factories, chefs, and machinists, make up the *industrial staff*. It is often directed by a superintendent of industries. The third staff is called the *professional*, or *care and treatment*, *staff*, and may be headed by a second deputy warden. It includes the physicians, dentists, nurses, teachers, chaplains, social workers, sociologists, psychologists, psychiatrists, and other personnel directly concerned with the treatment and training of prisoners. The warden has authority over all employees. His duty is to maintain order and prevent escapes. But he also has the responsibility of maintaining a rehabilitation program, including a school, work activities, and recreation. Guards who do not come in direct contact with the prisoners are the only ones who carry guns, except in cases of emergency.

PRISON

Classification. When a person enters a prison, he is interviewed by a committee made up of representatives from each of the three staffs. On the basis of these interviews and other information, the inmate is classified according to likelihood of escape; vocational aptitude and interest; need for medical, dental, religious, and psychiatric attention; need for education; and other requirements. Within the limitations of the facilities and personnel available, the prison assigns him to a program that will help rehabilitate him. He receives periodic examinations to make sure the program is being followed and to determine if progress is being made. If a prison gives care to its classification and rehabilitation programs, the whole period of imprisonment can be considered as a period of preparing the prisoner for parole.

The Parole System entitles a prisoner to have his criminal and prison records studied by a board of responsible citizens, some of whom may be prison officials. If the record shows that he is becoming rehabilitated and is not likely to commit another crime, and if he has served a specified part of his sentence, the board may place him under the supervision and guidance of a parole officer in his home community. During this period he is considered as "in custody." See PAROLE.

History

People in ancient and medieval times rarely used imprisonment as a penalty. Until the late 1200's in England and later in the rest of Europe, only special groups of offenders were imprisoned. Early church authorities imprisoned persons, partly because the death penalty was forbidden. From about 1500 to the early 1700's, galleys were used as places of confinement for criminals in England and France. When these ships could no longer be sailed, prisoners were held in them on shore.

The House of Correction appeared about the middle 1500's. Prisoners were forced to work, on the theory that this would reform them. These institutions used corporal punishment (see CORPORAL PUNISHMENT). But, until the late 1700's, the primary use of imprisonment was for persons awaiting trial. One of the first prison-reform movements reached its peak at about the time of the American and French revolutions. This movement popularized the use of prisons for punishing and reforming criminals, rather than for detaining them while they awaited trial. In about 1780, John Howard, an English sheriff, wrote a shocking account of conditions in English jails and houses of correction. He favored separate cells and useful occupations for all prisoners.

The early American colonists established jails and houses of correction. At first, these buildings were used principally as places of detention for persons awaiting trial, but before long they became places for punishment after conviction. By present-day standards, the conditions of these institutions were horrible. Prisoners suffered inhumane treatment and were neglected, whether convicted or awaiting trial. Jails provided no religious services. Drunkenness and vice were common.

Early Reforms. The Quakers of Philadelphia were the first to bring about reforms in these institutions. They believed that imprisonment should be substituted for the death penalty, and that prisoners should not suffer physically. They introduced more humane systems of prison management. Prisoners were not considered outcasts, but human beings who could be returned to society.

The new system of prison administration was so successful that its fame spread. Opposition to the death penalty meant that prisons would have many men with long sentences. The states built prisons to hold them. These new prisons were called *penitentiaries* because they were to produce *penitence* among the inmates, and reform as well as punish them. At first, the prisons were administered under the *separate and silent system*, which kept all prisoners in solitary confinement and prevented them from talking with each other. The prisoners could work in their cells, but their most important task was to remain silent and reflect on their crimes. The Western Penitentiary of Pennsylvania, which opened in 1828, used this system, and it was adopted by many countries. Each prisoner lived in a cell with two compartments. One section served as living quarters. In the other, the prisoner worked at his lathe, loom, or cobbler's bench. A narrow slit in the outer wall provided light and air. Once a prisoner entered his cell, he stayed there for the term of his sentence.

A new type of prison administration, called the *congregate and silent system*, began in 1816. Prisoners were kept in their cells only at night. During the day they worked in large shops, where they maintained complete silence. The prison at Auburn, N.Y., first adopted this system. It is sometimes called the *Auburn system*. Until the 1930's, many prisons required that inmates be silent at all times. Almost all have abolished this requirement. A few continue to require silence at certain times and places, such as during meals.

Later Reforms. Most prison reforms can be traced to the ideas of an Australian, Captain Alexander Maconochie (1787-1860), and to the Declaration of Principles passed in 1870 by the National Prison Association (now the American Correctional Association).

Maconochie devised a *mark system* enabling prisoners to gain their freedom after earning a certain number of "marks." This method spread to England and Ireland in the 1850's and to the U.S. in 1863. By that time, it was known as the *Irish system*. It combined the goal of reform with rewards for good conduct and privileges for prisoners who showed signs of rehabilitation.

The 37 principles passed by the Cincinnati Prison Congress in 1870 included classification of prisoners, graded prisons for different types of prisoners, and emphasis on reform rather than punishment. The principles led to vocational and educational training for prisoners, and modification of cruel forms of punishment and the silent system. Many of the principles were incorporated into the *Elmira system*. This system was named for the Elmira (N.Y.) Reformatory, which started the parole system in 1876.   HANS W. MATTICK

Related Articles in WORLD BOOK include:

PRISONER OF CHILLON. See CHILLON.

PRISONER OF WAR is any member of the armed forces who has been captured by an enemy in wartime, except doctors and chaplains, who are exempt.

The Hague Convention of 1907 and the Geneva Convention of 1929 stated that captors should treat prisoners in the same way their own soldiers were treated. Prisoners could work voluntarily but they should be paid. Captured officers were to receive at least as much salary as that given to officers of the same rank in the captor's army. Prisoners could send and receive mail, but the captors could censor all correspondence.

Some nations, including Germany and Japan, have violated the rules for the treatment of prisoners. During the Korean War, the Chinese communists and the North Koreans were charged with subjecting prisoners to cruel forms of emotional pressure, called *brainwashing*.

After the Korean War, the United States reviewed its code of conduct for American men taken prisoner. This code states that a prisoner is "bound to give only name, rank, service number, and date of birth." It assumes that each soldier is ready to die in defense of his country, and that he will neither cause injury to his fellow prisoners, nor say or write anything disloyal to his country. The code says that each soldier is responsible for his actions while a prisoner.   TELFORD TAYLOR

See also GENEVA CONVENTIONS; KOREAN WAR (Truce Talks).

PRISONS, BUREAU OF, is the division of the U.S. Department of Justice that supervises the care of all federal prisoners. Violators of federal laws are often held in state, county, and city jails. The bureau inspects these institutions to see that they meet federal specifications. It also pays for the support of federal prisoners kept in them.

A prisoner in a federal prison is under the direct supervision of the Bureau of Prisons. Federal penal institutions include six penitentiaries, five reformatories, five juvenile and youth institutions, eight correctional institutions, seven camps, a detention headquarters, and a medical center. These institutions can handle about 25,000 prisoners. The Director of the Bureau of Prisons acts as administrator of the federal prison system.   JAMES V. BENNETT

See also PRISON.

PRIVACY, RIGHT OF. Whether the law should recognize and protect the right of privacy of an individual depends upon a weighing of conflicting interests. Most American courts will give some protection to privacy. Laws forbid wire tapping and entering living quarters without the owner's permission or a warrant. A person has a right not to have his picture used for advertising without his consent. Some courts recognize a right not to have private information disclosed which would be clearly more embarrassing than newsworthy.

Improper publicity may cause a person a great deal of worry and mental suffering. Unreasonable restraints on publicity may infringe upon freedom of the press. But persons who seek the limelight, such as actors, athletes, public officials, and other celebrities, are in no position to object to fair publicity. Neither are persons whose conduct makes them newsworthy, such as those involved in court proceedings, even though they do not desire publicity.   EDWARD W. CLEARY

PRIVATE. See RANK IN ARMED SERVICES.

PRIVATE SCHOOL refers loosely to any school which is not managed by public authorities, and which does not receive public funds or tax support. Private schools are usually operated by individuals, by independent boards of trustees, or by religious groups. Some of them, such as business schools and music schools, make money for their owners. But most are nonprofit institutions, such as religious schools.

Private schools are principally supported by tuition fees, gifts and contributions, grants from sponsors (such as a church), or by endowments. Private schools do not have to pay taxes on their property if they are primarily charitable, philanthropic, or nonprofit.

In the United States, private schools declined in importance when the public-school systems were built up in the 1800's. Today, nearly one-fifth of all U.S. schoolchildren attend private schools. Roman Catholic schools enroll about 85 per cent of the private school students (see PAROCHIAL SCHOOL).

Private schools must operate under the general authority and regulations of the states with respect to minimum standards of health, safety, and quality of education. The Oregon case decided by the Supreme Court of the United States in 1925 asserted the right of private schools to exist. This case also reasserted the right of the states to general supervision over private schools. But the states cannot require all children to attend public schools.   R. FREEMAN BUTTS

See also EDUCATION, HISTORY OF; SCHOOL (Private and Parochial Schools); SEMINARY.

PRIVATEER, *PRY vuh TEER,* is a privately owned armed vessel. Before the development of strong navies, many nations commissioned privately owned ships to assist them in time of war. Such commissions, first used in the 1400's, were known as *letters of marque,* and ships and crews acting under them were called privateers. The privateers attacked merchant ships of the enemy nation and sank or robbed them.

Privateers helped the colonies against Great Britain in the Revolutionary War. On March 18, 1776, the Second Continental Congress authorized privateers. This action was taken after the British Parliament had prohibited all trade with the colonies and authorized seizure of their ships. George Washington was part owner of at least one privateer. Colonial privateers captured about 600 British ships.

From 1798 to 1801 the United States authorized privateers to seize French vessels, because many American ships were being taken by warships of republican France. In the War of 1812, American privateers captured 1,345 British ships. Some privateers became pirates after the war.

In 1856, the United States refused to sign the Declaration of Paris outlawing privateering because it feared it might need privateers to support its weak navy. See PARIS, TREATIES OF (Treaty of 1856).

During the Civil War, the Confederate Government issued letters of marque, but after the first year of war a volunteer naval system was substituted for privateering. The federal government tried privateering in 1863, and Chile used it against Spain in 1865. These were the last known instances of privateering.   THEODORE ROPP

See also MARQUE AND REPRISAL.

PRIVET, *PRIV et,* is a popular shrub planted in parks and gardens of North America. It is usually pruned and trained as a close-growing hedge, but is sometimes allowed to grow tall. It then forms a large bush about the size of its close relative, the lilac. The white flowers of privets are much smaller and less showy than those of the lilac, but are similar in general shape. Their odor is less sweet than that of the lilac. The privet is also related to the olive tree, and its smooth, dark-skinned fruit resembles a tiny ripe olive. The common privet is native to southern Europe and northern Africa. Other species grow wild in Asia and Australia.

Scientific Classification. The privets belong to the olive family, *Oleaceae.* The common privet is genus *Ligustrum,* species *L. vulgare.*   J. J. LEVISON

PRIVILEGED QUESTION. See PARLIAMENTARY PROCEDURE (table: Terms).

PRIVY COUNCIL is an honorary council appointed by the Crown of Great Britain. Members of the Privy Council include Cabinet members, as well as statesmen, judges, and scholars. Privy councilors are selected from all parts of the British Empire. The title of councilor is honorary in most cases. A member of the council becomes a salaried official only when he is given a place in the Cabinet. The lord president of the council is a member of the British Cabinet.

Council members serve during the life of the sovereign who appointed them, and for six months after his or her death. The full council meets on rare occasions, such as the beginning of a reign, or when the reigning sovereign announces his or her marriage. The administrative work of the council is carried on through state departments. Each department is headed by a minister responsible to Parliament. The Judicial Committee is the highest judicial authority in the British Commonwealth. A member of the Privy Council uses the title *Right Honorable* before his name, and letters *P.C.* (privy councilor) after his name.

The beginning of the Privy Council can be traced to the council of William the Conqueror. The council advised the king on matters of state, and set the laws for the kingdom. The importance of the Privy Council declined as Parliament increased in power.

The British North America Act of 1867 established the King's (or Queen's) Privy Council for Canada. The Cabinet of the Dominion of Canada sits as a committee of the Canadian Privy Council.   J. SALWYN SCHAPIRO

PRIVY SEAL is an official stamp that was once used on public documents in Great Britain. The privy seal authorized the issue of money from the Treasury, and was the stamp of approval for documents passing to the keeper of the great seal. Use of the privy seal was discontinued in 1884, but the office of keeper of the privy seal still exists. Today the keeper's official title is lord privy seal and leader of the House of Lords. The holder of the title is the third minister of the Cabinet of the British government.   J. SALWYN SCHAPIRO

PRIX DE ROME, GRAND. See ÉCOLE DES BEAUX-ARTS.

PRIZE FIGHTING. See BOXING.

PROBABILITY. When we say that one event is more probable than another, we mean it is more likely to happen. The branch of mathematics called *probability*

tries to express in numbers, statements of the form: An event *A* is more (or less) probable than an event *B*.

If a person tosses up a coin, there are only two ways it can fall—heads or tails. It is as likely to fall one way as the other, so we say that the probability of falling heads is $\frac{1}{2}$. But in tossing three coins, there are *eight* possibilities: hhh, hht, hth, htt, thh, tht, tth, and ttt. Only *three* of these combinations have two heads, so the probability of throwing exactly two heads is $\frac{3}{8}$.

Now suppose a person throws two dice. There are 36 different possible combinations. But there is only one combination that will give two "ones," so the probability of throwing two "ones" is $\frac{1}{36}$. There are two ways to throw a "one" and a "two," so the probability of this throw is $\frac{2}{36}$, or $\frac{1}{18}$.

There is a mathematical statement for all situations of this kind. Let *M* stand for any number of events that are equally likely to happen. Let *N* stand for the number of these events that would be favorable. Then the probability that a favorable event will happen is $\frac{N}{M}$.

Life insurance companies use probability rules. When a person takes out a life insurance policy, the company must be able to estimate how long he will probably live. Each age has a different probability, called *life expectancy.* Mathematicians have prepared tables of life expectancy. Scientists use rules of probability in interpreting statistics and estimating true values from experimental data.   T. H. HILDEBRANDT

See also FERMAT, PIERRE DE; PASCAL, BLAISE; STATISTICS; PERMUTATIONS AND COMBINATIONS.

PROBATE refers to official proof. When a person dies, his will must be *probated* (proved to be genuine). The person's executors bring the will before a court where wills and estates are handled. This court is called the *probate,* or *surrogate's, court.* The executors present the will to the court and show proof that it is the true will of the deceased. A will should be offered for probate as soon as possible after the death of the person who made it. After the will is presented, the court issues a notice to all heirs who would have shared the property if no will had been made. This notice is called a *citation.*

A hearing is held in the probate court, and any possible heir is given a chance to object to the probate of the will. The probate judge hears all claims and witnesses are examined just as they are in a civil suit. The judge then makes his decision as to whether or not the will is genuine. If all requirements have been met, the will is approved and registered and the executors carry out its provisions.   WILLIAM TUCKER DEAN

See also EXECUTOR; WILL.

PROBATION. See PAROLE.

PROBLEM SOLVING, in psychology. See THOUGHT AND JUDGMENT.

PROBOSCIS. See BUTTERFLY (Head; picture); FLY (The Body of a Fly); MOTH (Head; pictures).

PROBOSCIS MONKEY. See MONKEY (Old World).

PROCAINE. See NOVOCAIN.

PROCLAMATION is an executive notice issued under the authority of the head of a state or country. It announces some order or regulation that is important to the people. A proclamation that grants a pardon to rebels is a *proclamation of amnesty.* A proclamation may declare a public holiday. Usually a proclamation appears in printed form. See also EMANCIPATION PROCLAMATION.   THOMAS A. COWAN

PROCLAMATION OF 1763. See REVOLUTIONARY WAR IN AMERICA (Acts of 1763; map: Political Conflicts).

PROCTOLOGY. See MEDICINE (table: Kinds of Medical Specialty Fields).

PROCTOR, Vt. (pop. 1,978; alt. 475 ft.), is one of the largest marble-quarrying and marble-manufacturing centers in the United States. For location, see VERMONT (political map). The city was named after the Proctor family, which was prominent in Vermont.

Proctor lies in southwestern Vermont, near Rutland. Marble is brought to the mills from quarries in Vermont, other parts of the United States, and from many other countries. The Marble Exhibit attracts many visitors each summer.   WALTER R. HARD, JR.

PROCYON, *PROH sih on*, is a star in the constellation Canis Minor. It is sometimes called the *little dog star*. Procyon, a first-magnitude star, forms a triangle with Betelgeuse in Orion and Sirius in Canis Major. It is about 10 light-years from earth. See also CANIS MAJOR.

PRODUCER. See MOTION PICTURE (People Who Make Motion Pictures); THEATER (Careers).

PRODUCER GAS. See GAS (Coke Oven Gas).

PRODUCTION is the first step in the series of economic processes that bring goods and services to people. The other steps include *distribution* (getting the goods to persons who use them) and *consumption* (the final use of the goods). For example, the producers of a loaf of bread include the people who raise the grain, those who make flour, and those who bake the loaves. The bakery salesmen and the truck drivers who deliver the bread are distributors. Consumers buy and eat the bread. In a balanced economy, production and consumption are about equal and goods flow smoothly from maker to user.

Most economists agree that in the United States, enough goods could be produced to satisfy the needs and wants of all the people, if factories, mills, and mines worked to capacity, and if all farmlands were cultivated properly. When a lack of balance exists, some blame can be placed on consumption, because many persons do not have money to buy goods they want. Other factors, such as technological change, overextension of credit, and improper distribution of goods can unbalance the economy.   ROBERT D. PATTON

See also CONSUMPTION; DISTRIBUTION; ECONOMICS; FACTORY; MASS PRODUCTION; NATIONAL INCOME.

PRODUCTION, MASS. See MASS PRODUCTION.

PRODUCTION CREDIT ASSOCIATION. See FARM CREDIT ADMINISTRATION.

PROFESSION, CHOICE OF. See VOCATIONAL GUIDANCE.

PROFILE MOUNTAIN. See NEW HAMPSHIRE (Places to Visit); WHITE MOUNTAINS (picture).

PROFIT is the amount of money a company has left over from the sale of its products after it has paid for all the expenses of production. These expenses include money paid for such things as raw materials, workers' salaries, and machinery. They also include a reasonable return on the owner's investment, a salary for the labor he supplies to the firm, and other costs that are hard to calculate. A main task of accounting is to define and measure profits accurately.

Profits are vital to the economic system of the United States, Canada, and other countries where private enterprise is encouraged. In such countries, profits belong to the owners of companies or the stockholders of corpora-

tions. One of the chief reasons for operating a business is to make a profit. The desire for profits motivates firms to produce their goods as efficiently as possible. This is because the lower a firm's costs are, the greater its profits will be.

A business can earn a profit only by producing goods and services whose selling price is greater than the cost of producing them. Therefore, businessmen seek to use labor and raw materials to produce those things that people want and are willing to buy at relatively high prices. They try to avoid producing goods that have to be sold cheaply, because consumers are not eager to buy them. Thus, the search for profits is also the search for the uses of a country's labor and raw materials that will satisfy consumers most completely.

Some businessmen constantly lower prices to capture sales and profits from their competitors. However, there are several reasons why competition does not eliminate profits. For one thing, at any one time, there will be many firms that have discovered profitable opportunities their competitors cannot yet match. Sometimes, new firms cannot duplicate a profitable product because of patents or trademarks, or for other reasons. Sometimes, new firms cannot produce goods as cheaply as established ones. The bother and risk of entering an unfamiliar industry also keeps some new firms from competing with a product that is not especially profitable. The established firms can then enjoy reasonable profits without fear of new competition.   ROBERT DORFMAN

See also FREE ENTERPRISE SYSTEM (The Role of Profits); PRICE; ACCOUNTING; BUSINESS; CORPORATION.

PROFIT SHARING. Many employers share part of their profits with their employees. They do this to encourage productive work and to induce the employees to remain with the company.

Profit-sharing plans are usually based on the net profit of the firm, after all interest, taxes, and other charges against the gross profits have been paid. A certain percentage of the profit is set aside for the employees, and each worker is paid according to his salary or his length of service with the company.

Some industrialists object to profit-sharing plans, because workers do not share the responsibilities and risks of the business. Some labor leaders also oppose such plans, believing that workers should concentrate their efforts on obtaining higher wages. But other industrialists and labor leaders believe that properly administered profit-sharing plans promote better understanding between employer and employees, and stimulate efficiency, since both employer and employees share in any gains achieved by joint effort.   ROBERT D. PATTON

PROGERIA, *proh JEE rih uh*, is premature old age. It usually attacks children. The skin becomes wrinkled, the hair turns gray, and the body tissues become like those of old people. A disease of the pituitary gland is thought to cause progeria.

PROGESTERONE. See GLAND (The Sex Glands).

PROGRAM MUSIC is composed to tell a specific story, usually describing fairly obvious actions or moods. Composers of all periods have written program music. It became especially popular with composers of the romantic style. Ludwig van Beethoven's *Symphony No. 6*, often called "Pastorale," greatly influenced program music. Many composers call their programmatic works *tone poems* or *symphonic poems*. Grant Fletcher

PROGRAMMED LEARNING. See Teaching Machine.

PROGRAMMING is the planning of operations to be performed by computers or other automatic machines. See Computer.

PROGRESS, THEORY OF SOCIAL. Progress is a movement toward desirable goals. Social progress implies that human nature is improving, and that mankind is becoming better. But this idea is not always supported by factual evidence. As material gains are made, other problems arise—often as a result of the "gains." Social scientists prefer to discuss social *change*, rather than social *progress*. They can describe, measure, and analyze it, without implying that the truths discovered are good or bad. Lloyd Allen Cook

See also Sociology.

PROGRESSION, in mathematics, is a sequence of related numbers or symbols called *terms*. The following examples illustrate three common kinds of progressions:

Arithmetic progression: 1,2,3,4,5,6, . . . and so on;
Geometric progression: 2,4,8,16,32, . . . and so on;
Harmonic progression: $\frac{1}{2}, \frac{1}{4}, \frac{1}{6}, \frac{1}{8}$, . . . and so on.

In each of these progressions, the terms after the first are formed in different ways. Each term of an arithmetic progression is formed by *adding* a quantity called the *common difference* to the previous term. In the example, the common difference is 1. Each term of a geometric progression is formed by *multiplying* the previous term by a quantity called the *common ratio*. In the example, the common ratio is 2. Each term of a harmonic progression is a fraction. The numerators are all 1's and the denominators are formed like the terms of an arithmetic progression. In the example, the common difference of the denominators is 2.

Progressions are useful in solving many problems in science and business. For example, they simplify the calculation of compound interest (see Interest). Mathematicians have developed formulas for finding the value of any term of a progression and for finding the sum of any number of terms.

Arithmetic Progressions may have various first terms and common differences, as shown below:

	First Term	Common Difference	Arithmetic Progression
A	2	3	2, 5, 8, 11, 14, 17, . . .
B	3	−2	3, 1, −1, −3, −5, . . .
C	1	$\frac{1}{2}$	1, $1\frac{1}{2}$, 2, $2\frac{1}{2}$, 3, . . .
D	a	d	$a, a + d, a + 2d, a + 3d,$ . . .

In example A, the 4th term (11) is equal to $2 + 3 + 3 + 3$, which can also be written $2 + (4 - 1)3$. The value of *any* term can be found by adding to the first term the product of the common difference times one less than the number of the term. In general, a can be used to represent the first term, and d the common difference. The formula for the nth term (U_n) is

$$U_n = a + (n - 1)d$$

The sum of the first 6 terms of example A is $2 + 5 + 8 + 11 + 14 + 17 = 57$. Note that the sum of the

first and last terms (2,17) is 19. Likewise, the sums of the 2nd and 5th terms (5,14) and the 3rd and 4th terms (8,11) are also 19. The sum of all 6 terms (57) is equal to 3 times 19, or 3 times the sum of the first and last terms. In general, the sum of any number of terms of an arithmetic progression is one-half the number of terms times the sum of the first and last terms. If we use the symbol S_n to represent the sum, the formula is

$$S_n = \frac{n}{2}(a + U_n)$$

Geometric Progressions may have various first terms and common ratios as shown below:

	First Term	Common Ratio	Geometric Progression
A	2	3	2, 6, 18, 54, 162, . . .
B	1	$\frac{1}{2}$	1, $\frac{1}{2}, \frac{1}{4}, \frac{1}{8}, \frac{1}{16}$, . . .
C	a	r	$a, ar, ar^2, ar^3, \ldots ar^{n-1},$ . . .

Example C indicates that the value of the nth term (U_n) is ar^{n-1}. The exponent $(n - 1)$ means that r is to be used as a factor $(n - 1)$ times. Using this formula, the 6th term in example A can be calculated:

$$U_6 = 2(3)^5 = 2 \times 3 \times 3 \times 3 \times 3 \times 3 = 486$$

The sum of n terms can be calculated by the formula

$$S_n = \frac{a - ar^n}{1 - r}$$

For example, the sum of the first 4 terms of example A is calculated as follows:

$$S_4 = \frac{2 - 2(3)^4}{1 - 3} = \frac{2 - 162}{-2} = 80$$

If r is less than 1, the sum of an *infinite* number of terms approaches the limit $a/(1 - r)$. See Series (Working with Infinite Series). Phillip S. Jones

PROGRESSIVE EDUCATION was a revolt against the traditional schools of the United States of the 1800's. It grew from the belief that schools had failed to keep pace with rapid changes in American life.

The Traditional School usually stressed the teaching of specific subjects—reading, writing, arithmetic, geography, history, and grammar. The teacher lectured or dictated a lesson and the students copied it in their notebooks. The students then learned by heart what was in their notebooks and recited what they learned from their textbooks. The teacher enforced order and quiet among students except for recitation periods. Students sat at rows of desks fastened to the floor, and could not move or talk except with permission.

Progressive Educators thought that traditional education should be reformed. Famous progressive educators of the 1800's included Horace Mann, Francis Parker, and G. Stanley Hall. In the early 1900's, John Dewey and William H. Kilpatrick became well-known spokesmen for progressive education. See the separate articles in World Book on each of these men.

Progressive educators tried to reform elementary school methods in several ways. They thought teachers should pay more attention to the individual child and not treat all children alike. Progressive educators believed that children learn best when they are genuinely interested in the material, and not when they are forced to memorize facts that seem useless to them. Children should learn by direct contact with things, places, and people, as well as by reading and hearing about them. Thus, schools should not only have classrooms, but also science laboratories, work shops, art studios, kitchens, gymnasiums, and gardens. Progressive educators believed that this procedure would develop the child's physical, social, and emotional nature as well as his mind.

Progressive educators also stressed greater freedom, activity, and informality in the classroom. They believed that children learn better when they can move about and work at their own pace. The children should gather materials from many sources rather than from just one textbook, and should work in groups with other students. Discussion, dramatics, music, and art activities became a larger part of classroom procedures along with lecturing and recitation.

Progressive education spread more widely through elementary schools than it did in high schools or colleges. Teachers planned individual instruction, and centered it around projects, units, or activities rather than the usual courses or subjects. They taught students of different abilities in separate groups. Rapid learners studied together and slower learners studied together.

Criticism of Progressive Education. Many writers and some educators began increasingly to criticize progressive education during the 1940's and 1950's. They charged students did not learn fundamental subjects well enough. Other educators said that students learned as well under progressive education as under traditional methods. But by the early 1960's, many schools had begun to experiment with different teaching methods. Many experiments used "progressive" principles, but they did not use the term.

More difficult courses were introduced into elementary and secondary schools. More stress was placed on training gifted students, and on guiding and testing as means of identifying gifted students. National committees of scholars and teachers began to develop courses of study that stressed physical and biological sciences, mathematics, and other subjects. See EDUCATION (Various Views on Education).   R. FREEMAN BUTTS

PROGRESSIVE EDUCATION ASSOCIATION was an organization founded in the United States to encourage new and progressive ideas in public and private schools of all grade levels. The organization was founded in 1919. It was dissolved in 1955.

PROGRESSIVE PARTY is a name given to several political parties that have been organized in the United States. The earlier Progressive parties protested against the conservative policies of the major parties. In general, the Progressives stood for liberal social, political, and economic reform.

The "Bull Moose" Party. Shortly after the renomination of William Howard Taft in 1912, a group of Republicans left their party to found a new group called the *Progressive party*. It was nicknamed the "Bull Moose" party. The Progressives nominated Theodore Roosevelt and Hiram Johnson for President and Vice-President. They polled more votes in the election than the Republicans, but not as many as the Democrats. The Progressives nominated Roosevelt again in 1916 but he refused to run, and most of the Progressive leaders went back to the Republican party.

The La Follette Progressives. In 1924, a group of farm, labor, and religious leaders formed a new Progressive movement. Senators Robert M. La Follette and Burton K. Wheeler were nominated to run for President and Vice-President. The Progressives polled nearly 5,000,000 votes, but carried only La Follette's home state, Wisconsin. His sons, Governor Philip La Follette and Senator Robert M. La Follette, Jr., led the Wisconsin Progressive party, which had considerable success from 1934 to 1938. During the 1940's, this party lost strength steadily. It voted to merge with the Republicans in 1946.

The Progressive Party of 1948 was formed by various left-wing groups, including the Communists. Henry A. Wallace, former Democratic Vice-President of the United States, was the Progressive party's unsuccessful candidate for President in the 1948 election.   DONALD R. McCOY

See also BEVERIDGE, ALBERT JEREMIAH; LA FOLLETTE; ROOSEVELT, THEODORE ("Bull Moose" Candidate); WALLACE, HENRY AGARD.

PROHIBITION, *PROH uh BISH un*, or *PROH hih BISH un*, is the forbidding by law of the sale, and sometimes the manufacture, of alcoholic beverages. Such beverages include beer, gin, rum, whiskey, and wine.

The question of prohibition has been one of great public interest, particularly in Canada and the United States, for more than 100 years.

Prohibition in the United States

During the 15 years just before the Civil War, Maine and 12 other states passed statewide prohibition laws. But they were either repealed later or declared unconstitutional in all states except Maine. After the war the liquor business developed rapidly, and there was a strong movement again for prohibition.

Both the Democratic and the Republican parties had refused to consider prohibition in their platforms. That was the reason why the Prohibition party was organized in 1869. This party tried to make prohibition a political issue. In 1874 the Woman's Christian Temperance Union was organized. Both groups, as well as other smaller bodies, did much to bring about prohibition. The Anti-Saloon League, organized in Ohio in 1893, was very effective. Leaders of this group worked locally, getting cities, townships, and counties to go "dry." This was done where state-wide prohibition seemed impossible. On July 1, 1919, 31 states were "dry" or had voted for state-wide prohibition on a definite date. Local action by cities, townships and counties had been chiefly responsible for this increase in prohibition.

National Action was also taken. In 1913, the United States Congress passed the Webb-Kenyon law. This stopped the shipping of liquor from a "wet" to a "dry" state. In addition, in 1917 the Jones-Randall Bill was passed. This act made it unlawful to use the United States mails to send liquor advertisements or circulars addressed to people in "dry" territory.

In 1913, the Anti-Saloon League started a national campaign for a prohibition amendment to the Constitution. This amendment was to prohibit the manufacture and sale of alcoholic beverages throughout the United States. But the amendment did not receive the necessary two-thirds vote in the House of Representatives when it was submitted in 1914.

During World War I, the prohibition leaders strengthened their cause through the food-control bill. This bill carried a section prohibiting the manufacture of distilled liquor, beer, and wine. No whiskey was manufactured after Sept. 8, 1917. No beer was manufactured after May 1, 1919. On July 1, 1919, under the wartime act, no more intoxicants were sold. No saloon in America could operate legally after that date. And still there was no national amendment to the Constitution in effect.

Amendment 18. In 1917, Congress provided for an amendment that would make the entire country prohibition territory. The amendment was as follows:

Section 1. After one year from the ratification of this article the manufacture, sale, or transportation of intoxicating liquors within, the importation thereof into, or the exportation thereof from the United States and all territory subject to the jurisdiction thereof for beverage purposes is hereby prohibited.

Section 2. The Congress and the several States shall have concurrent power to enforce this article by appropriate legislation.

Section 3. This article shall be inoperative unless it shall have been ratified as an amendment to the Constitution by the legislatures of the several States, as provided in the Constitution, within seven years from the date of the submission hereof to the States by the Congress.

This was Amendment 18. It went into effect on Jan. 16, 1920. To help enforce it, the Volstead Act was passed in 1919. This measure carefully defined alcoholic drinks. In 1929 the Jones Law was passed. This law provided fines up to $10,000 for offenses against the Prohibition law, or imprisonment up to five years, or both. The Jones Law was amended by Congress in certain respects in 1931.

Repeal of Amendment 18. In 1932, the Republican and Democratic party platforms worked to have the question of repeal submitted to the people. Congress passed a resolution proposing the repeal in February, 1933. It read:

Section 1. The eighteenth article of amendment to the Constitution of the United States is hereby repealed.

Section 2. The transportation or importation into any State, Territory, or possession of the United States for delivery or use therein of intoxicating liquors, in violation of the laws thereof, is hereby prohibited.

Section 3. This article shall be inoperative unless it shall have been ratified as an amendment to the Constitution by convention in the several States, as provided in the Constitution, within seven years from the date of the submission hereof to the States by the Congress.

This was Amendment 21. By December 5, 1933, 36 states had ratified or approved it. National prohibition was repealed. This turned the problem of controlling liquor traffic back to the states. By 1936 all but eight states again permitted the manufacture and sale of liquors. By 1966, all states permitted the sale of liquor. However, parts of many states remained dry through local option.

Prohibition in Canada

The Canada Temperance Act, passed in 1878, left the problem of prohibition up to counties and municipalities. Some of them did put the law into force. But prohibition's greatest progress in Canada came after World War I started. Saskatchewan began by closing every bar, and finally closed every package liquor store. Eventually every province except Quebec had declared for prohibition.

By 1924, a reaction began. The prohibition laws were gradually changed. All the provinces eventually returned to some plan of liquor sale under government control. Several provinces required a purchaser of liquor to have a permit. These permits limit the amounts that may be purchased within a certain time. Spirituous or alcoholic liquors are not sold in many parts of Canada by the glass.　　　　　JOHN A. KROUT

Related Articles in WORLD BOOK include:

American Council on Alcohol Problems	Temperance
Good Templars	Volstead Act
Local Option	Woman's Christian
Prohibition Party	Temperance Union

PROHIBITION PARTY is a political organization of the United States. Its major purpose is to prevent the use of alcoholic beverages in the country. The party was organized in 1869. It began immediately to present candidates for state and local elections, and in 1872 it nominated candidates for President and Vice-President.

The party reached its greatest strength in 1892, when 271,000 votes were cast for its candidates. The party has declined in strength since then. In 1968, about 14,700 persons voted the Prohibition ticket.

The Prohibition Party has worked closely with the Anti-Saloon League. Their greatest triumph was passage of Amendment 18 to the Constitution, which forbade the production of intoxicants. See also PROHIBITION.　　　　　DONALD R. McCOY

PROJECT APOLLO. See SPACE TRAVEL.

PROJECT GEMINI. See SPACE TRAVEL.

PROJECT MERCURY. See ASTRONAUT.

PROJECT MOHOLE. See MOHOLE.

PROJECTILE. See AMMUNITION; GUIDED MISSILE (Ballistic Missiles); ROCKET; TORPEDO.

PROJECTION. See MAP (Map Projections).

PROJECTION MACHINE is a device for throwing pictures on a screen. The technical name for a projection machine is a *stereopticon*. In its simplest form, the stereopticon consists of a source of light, a film or slide that holds the picture to be projected, a lens for focusing the picture on the screen, and a reflector for concentrating the light on the picture.

A toy magic lantern that uses photographic slides is one form of projection machine. A home projector for candid camera films is a familiar kind of stereopticon. Here the light consists of a small but powerful electric light, the picture is a transparent photograph, often in color, and the lens is generally double. The lenses in front of the picture enlarge it on the screen. The picture must be inserted upside down, because the lens also reverses the picture. There is a concave mirror behind the light filament, and a thick, *plano-convex* lens (a lens with one flat and one rounded side) between the light and the film.

Schools generally use larger slide projection machines. Here the light source may be a carbon arc. The pictures come on glass slides of a standard size, $3\frac{1}{2} \times 4$ inches.

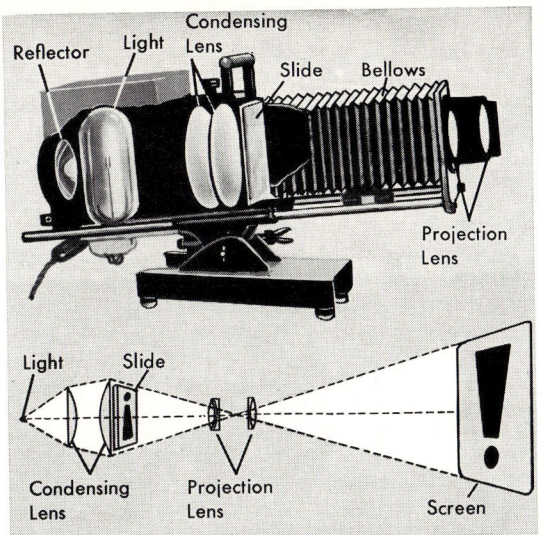

The Stereopticon projects the image of a slide onto a screen. A reflector and a condensing-lens system concentrate the rays from a powerful light, and beam them through the transparent slide. A projection-lens system focuses the rays to produce a clear image. The slide must be upside down, because the projection lens reverses the image. Some stereopticons have a mechanism that automatically changes the slides. A recording may be synchronized with this mechanism to provide sound.

There are two plano-convex lenses between the light and the glass slide. Usually there are four projector lenses.

A combination of stereopticon and phonograph is a popular way of teaching certain subjects, such as mathematics, because the student can see the pictures and also hear the lecture. EDITH LILLIAN SMITH WEBSTER

See also FILMSTRIP; MOTION PICTURE (Projector; Wide-Screen Processes).

PROKHOROV, *prawk HOR off,* or *PRO ho roff,* **ALEXANDER MIKHAILOVICH** (1916-   ), is a noted Russian physicist. In 1953, he and Russian physicist Nikolai Basov stated principles for using the energy of molecules to amplify radio waves. They published an improved method of operating these amplifiers, called *masers,* in 1955 (see MASER). For their work, Prokhorov and Basov shared the 1964 Nobel prize in physics with physicist Charles H. Townes of the United States.

Prokhorov was born in Atherton, Australia, and was graduated from Leningrad State University. In 1946, he became a research physicist at the Lebedev Physics Institute of Moscow. He became chief of the institute's Oscillation Laboratory in 1954. R. T. ELLICKSON

PROKOFIEV, *pro KOHF yehf,* **SERGEI SERGEYE-VICH** (1891-1953), was an important Russian composer. His symphonic fairy tale *Peter and the Wolf* (1936) is perhaps his best-known work. But Prokofiev also wrote seven symphonies, six operas, and many other compositions.

Prokofiev's music has a strong element of the grotesque, which he alternates with a lyrical quality. His harmonies are bold, and his rhythms dynamic. His *Classical Symphony* (1917) was one of the earliest works of the neoclassical movement. His ballets include *The Age of Steel, Romeo and Juliet,* and *Cinderella.*

His opera, *War and Peace,* is based on Tolstoy's novel.

Born in Sontsovka, Russia, Prokofiev began his musical training under his mother's guidance. He wrote his first compositions when he was five years old. Later, he studied at the St. Petersburg Conservatory with Nicholas Rimsky-Korsakov. From 1919 to 1922, he lived in America. He spent the next 10 years in Paris, and returned to Moscow in 1932. HALSEY STEVENS

PROLETARIAT. See COMMUNISM (Origins of Communism).

PROLOGUE, *PRO log,* is an introduction to a play or other writing. The term comes from the Greek *pro,* meaning *before,* and *logos,* meaning *speech.* The prologue explains the situation at the time the first scene of the play opens, or tells in general what the play is about. The prologue to Shakespeare's *Romeo and Juliet* informs the audience that the play concerns "a pair of star-cross'd lovers." Chaucer wrote a prologue to introduce his *Canterbury Tales.* His prologue describes pilgrims going to Canterbury. J. N. HOOK

PROMETHEUS, *proh ME thyoos,* in Greek mythology, was an immortal member of a group of giant gods called Titans. Prometheus (*forethought*) and his brother Epimetheus (*afterthought*) were assigned by the gods to give the animals the powers they needed. Epimetheus worked hard at this task, but when it was man's turn, there was no gift left.

Prometheus, a son of the Titan Iapetus, took pity on the helplessness of primitive man. He stole fire from the gods and gave it to man. Zeus (Jupiter) was so angered that he caused Prometheus to be chained to Mount Caucasus. A vulture came every day to tear at his liver, and every night the liver grew again. Prometheus suffered for thousands of years. At last Hercules killed the vulture and set Prometheus free. G. M. KIRKWOOD

See also DEUCALION; PANDORA.

PROMETHIUM, *proh ME thih um* (chemical symbol, Pm), is one of the rare-earth metals. Its atomic number is 61, its most stable isotope has a mass number of 145, and its most abundant isotope has a mass number of 147. The element is named for the Greek hero Prometheus, the fire giver. Three American chemists, J. A. Marinsky, Lawrence E. Glendenin, and Charles D. Coryell, first isolated promethium in 1945. The element exists as radioactive isotopes among the fission products of uranium, thorium, and plutonium. It does not occur naturally. See also ELEMENT, CHEMICAL (table); RARE EARTH; ATOMIC ENERGY (picture: A Tiny Atomic Battery). FRANK H. SPEDDING

PROMISSORY NOTE. See NOTE.

PROMONTORY. See CAPE.

PRONGHORN is sometimes called the American antelope. It is probably the fastest large mammal of North America. It can sprint for a short distance at a mile a minute. It can run at a rate of 40 miles an hour for about two miles. The pronghorn is not a true antelope. It has no close relatives anywhere. It has changed little from its ancestor which lived in the early American Pleistocene Age, between one and two million years ago.

A graceful hoofed animal, the pronghorn has a rather chunky body, large ears, slender legs, and short tail. Its general color varies from light tan to reddish brown. The pronghorn has some white fur on its under parts,

American Museum of Natural History
Speedy Pronghorns Live in Western North America.

its rump, the sides of its face, and on its throat.

The buck pronghorn stands 35 to 41 inches high at the shoulder and weighs 100 to 140 pounds. Its horns are about 12 to 15 inches long and consist of a bony core on which a black horny covering grows. This covering is shed and renewed every year. The pronghorn is the only animal in the world that regularly sheds its horn covers.

The pronghorn lives on open grassland. It has remarkably keen sight. It depends on its eyes to detect its principal enemies—wolves and coyotes—and on its speed to escape from danger.

Pronghorns mate in September and October. Each buck tries to collect several mates. He seldom keeps more than three or four at a time, but an occasional buck may have as many as eight. The *does* (females) generally bear twins in May, or as early as March in the south. Pronghorns feed on grasses and the tender twigs of sagebrush, atriplex, rabbit brush, and other shrubs.

Pronghorns are social creatures. In winter, the bands of pronghorns gather into herds. The animals are estimated to have numbered as many as a hundred million at one time. They occupied a vast range from central Saskatchewan to central Mexico, and from western Iowa almost to the Pacific Coast. In 1908, only 20,000 remained. Under strict protection, pronghorns now number at least 250,000. Some states and provinces permit seasonal hunting of the pronghorn.

Scientific Classification. The pronghorn is the sole representative of the family *Antilocapridae*. It is genus *Antilocapra*, species *A. americana*. VICTOR H. CAHALANE

See also ANIMAL (color picture, Animals of the Grasslands).

PRONOUN is the part of speech used in place of a noun to avoid repetition of the noun. The term comes from the Latin *pro* and *nomen*, meaning *for name*. The following sentence is awkward. "Mrs. Allen warned Richard not to soil Mrs. Allen's new rug with the mud Richard was bringing in on Richard's shoes." The use of pronouns makes the sentence easier to read and understand. "Mrs. Allen warned Richard not to soil *her* new rug with the mud *he* was bringing in on *his* shoes."

A pronoun mentions a person or thing without naming it. The word to which it refers is its *antecedent*. The antecedent may be either expressed or understood. A pronoun must agree with its antecedent in person, number, and gender. Its case depends upon its use in the sentence. The case is determined in a sentence in the same way the case of a noun is determined.

Pronouns are classified as personal, intensive, reflexive, interrogative, relative, demonstrative, and indefinite. The possessive forms are called *pronominal adjectives*, or *possessive adjectives*, when they modify nouns.

Personal Pronouns are those which represent the speaker, the person spoken to, or the person or thing spoken of. Those which stand for the speaker (I, we, me, etc.) are the *first personal pronouns*. Those which refer to the person spoken to (thou, you, etc.) are the *second personal pronouns*. Those which refer to the person or thing spoken of (he, she, it, they, etc.) are *third personal pronouns*.

Personal pronouns have various forms to express all the different uses and changes because of number, person, gender, and case. Other pronouns have fewer forms. The declension of the simple personal pronouns is given in the table with this article.

The forms *thou, thy, thine, thee,* and *ye* are found in sacred and older English writings and in Quaker speech. Modern speech uses *you, your,* and *yours* for both singular and plural.

Intensive and Reflexive Pronouns are formed by the addition of *self* or *selves* to the personal pronouns. They have the same form for the nominative and objective, or accusative, cases. They have no possessive use.

The *reflexive* pronoun is used in "He washed *himself*"; "She saw *herself* reflected in her child." The *intensive* pronoun is used in "I did it *myself*"; "You *yourself* once expressed the same opinion."

	SINGULAR	PLURAL
First person	myself	ourselves
Second person	thyself, yourself	yourselves
Third person	himself, herself, itself	themselves

It is wrong to use these pronouns instead of personal pronouns, as in "My mother and *myself* shall leave for the East tomorrow." The sentence should be "My mother and *I* shall leave for the East tomorrow."

Interrogative Pronouns, *who, which,* and *what,* are used to ask questions.

Who refers only to human beings or personified objects. Its three forms are the same for both singular and plural. "*Who* came?" "*Whose* writing is this?" "To *whom* are you telephoning?"

Which refers to human beings, animals, and inanimate objects. It has the same form for the nominative and the objective cases and has no possessive use. "*Which* of these men in the photograph is your father?"

What refers principally to animals, objects, and abstract ideas, as in "*What* are you looking for?"

Relative Pronouns not only "relate" to an antecedent in a preceding clause but also connect a clause with the clause containing the antecedent. The relative pronouns are *who, which, that,* and *what.* "That boy *who* is sitting at the desk is my son. He has a volume of history, *which* seems to be interesting. The chapter *that* he is reading is an account of World War II. Let us ask him *what* it says about the battle of Okinawa." *That* has only one form. The nominatives of the others are *who, which;* the possessive, *whose;* the objectives, *whom, which.*

The compound relative pronouns in common use are *whoever, whichever,* and *whatever. Whoso, whosoever, whichsoever,* and *whatsoever* are gradually disappearing.

Who is used for persons, the higher animals, and objects personified. The relative *which* is used for animals and things only. *That* refers to both persons and things. *What* is used only in the neuter sense. The antecedent is embodied in the meaning of *what* as *that which* and *the thing which.*

The possessive *whose* may be used for things when *of which* sounds awkward. "The pages *whose* edges you have trimmed should be placed in your notebooks" is used rather than "The pages the edges *of which* you have trimmed should be placed in your notebooks."

Which introduces "nonrestrictive" clauses and *that* introduces "restrictive" clauses. "The bombs, *which* were made in this country, exploded prematurely." The subordinate clause, *which were made in this country,* is nonrestrictive because it simply adds a new thought and suggests that all the bombs referred to exploded prematurely. "The bombs *that* were made in this country exploded prematurely." The clause is restrictive because it limits the meaning and suggests that only some of the bombs (those made in this country) exploded.

The sound of the sentence may determine the choice between *that* and *which.* "That electric fan *which* you sold me." This is because of the repetition of *that. That* is always preferred when the antecedent refers to both persons and things. "Porters look after all travelers and baggage *that* arrive by steamer."

Demonstrative Pronouns are those which point out some particular person or thing, answering the question "Which?" Demonstrative pronouns are *this* and its plural *these,* referring to persons and objects near by; and *that* and its plural *those,* referring to persons and objects more distant. "*These* look fresher than *those.*" These words are *demonstrative adjectives* when they modify nouns. "*These* peaches look fresher than *those* apricots."

Indefinite Pronouns are those which have the same double use as demonstratives but do not refer to definite persons or things. They include *one, each, other, any, some, either, neither, both, many, sundry, several,* and *certain;* and their compounds, such as *anyone, anybody, each one, someone, somebody, no one, everyone, either one, anybody else, nobody else. None* is also an indefinite pronoun, but it cannot be used as an adjective. The pronoun *it* is called an indefinite pronoun in a use like "*It* is storming."

Either and *neither* should not be used in connection with more than two persons or things. *Each, every, either,* and *neither* are singular in meaning. They must be followed by singular pronouns. "*Every* boy and girl should bring *his* contribution tomorrow." The masculine *his* is used because there is no singular pronoun which covers both sexes.

Common Errors are noted in the following examples: "Margaret, too, was naturally curious, but *it* never tormented her as it did her sister." The pronoun *it* has no antecedent. The clause should be, "but *her curiosity* never tormented her."

The case of a relative pronoun depends upon its use in the sentence, not upon the case of its antecedent. "He is a faithful employee, *whom* I know will prove a valuable worker," should be "*who* I know will prove a valuable worker." *Who* is the subject of *will prove,* not the object of *know.*

One is likely to lose *their* head when an accident occurs," should be "One is likely to lose *his* head." *One* is singular and cannot be followed by the plural.

"He handles a racket better than *her,*" should be "better than *she.*" Expand the sentence to read, "He handles a racket better *than she does.*" *She* is the subject of *does* and must be in the nominative case.

"It was *her* we wanted," should be "It was *she* we wanted." The verb *to be* cannot take an object. It requires the same case after it as before it. We say "I knew it to be *him,*" because the subject of *to be* is in the objective case; but "It is *I*" instead of "It is *me,*" because *it* is in the nominative.

"That canary of *her's* is molting *it's* feathers," should be "That canary of *hers* is molting *its* feathers." The forms *hers* and *its* are already possessive. *It's* is not a pronoun but a contraction of *it is* and therefore a pronoun subject and a verb together. CLARENCE STRATTON

See also ANTECEDENT; CASE; DECLENSION; GENDER.

PRONTOSIL. See SULFA DRUGS.

	SINGULAR			PLURAL		
	NOM.	POSS.	OBJ. OR ACC.	NOM.	POSS.	OBJ. OR ACC.
First person......	I	my, mine	me	we	our, ours	us
Second person....	you, thou	your, yours, thy, thine	you, thee	you, ye	your, yours	you, ye
Third person.....	he	his	him	they	their, theirs	them
	she	her, hers	her			
	it	its	it			

PRONUNCIATION

PRONUNCIATION means saying a word aloud. The term comes from the Latin word *pronuntiare*, meaning *to proclaim*. The degree of distinctness in pronunciation is called *enunciation*.

The English language is the hardest language of all to pronounce. Boys and girls who have spoken English all their lives may think French and German and other foreign tongues are much harder to pronounce. The reason for this is that some of the sounds common in foreign pronunciation are not found in English pronunciation. Before a student can pronounce French, he must learn how to place his mouth and tongue into position to make the new sounds. He must learn how to articulate properly before he can pronounce correctly. The German *a*, the French *u*, the *r* in either language—all are new to one who has spoken only English. To the Frenchman the *u* in *tu* is automatic but the *u* in the English *tube* is perhaps difficult. Perhaps you have noticed how hard it is for French and German people to pronounce the sound of *th* in English words. They pronounce it as *t*. The reason is that the *th* in French and German spelling is actually pronounced *t*.

The words of foreign languages are easier to pronounce than those in English because they follow regular rules. The words of English follow no set rules. The unmarked German *a* is always pronounced *ah*. The English *a* has many different pronunciations in different words. The French diphthong *ou* is always pronounced *oo*. The same diphthong in English is pronounced differently in each of the following words: *thought, thousand, through, though, thorough, could, rough*. The consonant combination *gh* in English is silent in such words as *though*, but pronounced as a hard *g* in *ghoul*, as *f* in *rough*, and as *p* in *hiccough*.

One of the reasons that rules do not apply to pronunciation of English is that the language has borrowed so much from other languages. For example, in most cases an *e* added to the end of a word is silent. Its only purpose is to make the vowel before it long. Thus, in *cape* (pronounced *cayp*) the *e* is silent, while the *a* is long. But in the word *cafe* the *e* is pronounced *ay*, while the *a* is short and almost slurred over. *Cafe* is one of the words that we have taken from the French. The final *e* of the French word *café* has an acute accent over it, which gives it the sound of a long *a*. In English we usually drop the accent marks of other languages, but keep much the same pronunciation.

A second reason that rules do not apply to English pronunciations is that over a period of years we have changed our ideas about correct pronunciations. In the 1700's the word *soot* was pronounced *sut* (as in *but*). By the end of the century, speakers had changed the pronunciation so that the word rhymed with *boot*. And at the same time the present pronunciation became popular — with the vowel sound the same as that in *pull*. The word *cement* is both a noun and a verb. In former times the noun was accented on the first syllable, and the verb on the second. Today the noun and the verb are pronounced with the accent on the second syllable.

The common word *been* has had several spellings and pronunciations in the history of the English language. It has been pronounced at times as *bin, ben,* and *bean*. At the time America was being colonized, the first pronunciation was the more common. That is the pronunciation brought to America and kept today, although the second pronunciation is sometimes heard. The last pronunciation — like the word *bean* — is the accepted pronunciation in England.

Regional Differences are found in English, just as in other languages. In England it may be difficult for a cockney Englishman and an Oxford-educated Englishman to understand each other.

American English has some distinct dialects. The English language had already grown up before the American colonies were settled. There was no reason for strong dialects to grow in different areas.

Most Americans speak what is called by scholars "Western English." Even the New England states in time have given up their dialect in favor of Western English. The dialect formerly spoken throughout New England is now heard only around Boston, Mass. It is often called the "Hah-vahd accent," because it features a broad *a*, skips over the *r* before consonants, and has been common at Harvard University, near Boston. Another main dialect is that of the southeastern United States. This so-called "Southern accent" also omits the *r* before consonants (*su-thun* for *southern*) and adds a *y* sound before some vowels (*cyard* for *card*). Many Southerners also pronounce a short *a* sound before the *ow* sound (*da-own* for *down*) and use a broad *a* sound where spelling calls for a long *i* (*trahd* for *tried*).

The United States also has some minor dialects which are heard in very limited areas. Certain groups in New York City reverse the *oi* and *er* sounds, and say *t* and *d* when they mean *th*. *Oil* is pronounced *erl*, and *girl* is pronounced *goil; there* becomes *dere*, and *with* becomes *wit*.

One of the most interesting local dialects is that of the southern Appalachian and the Ozark mountains. It is a slow drawl having some of the peculiarities of the Southern dialect. In addition, the mountaineers often substitute the broad *a* sound for the short *e* sound (*bahr* for *bear*), and the *u* sound for the broad *a* (*fur* for *far*). Sometimes a final unstressed *a* becomes *y* (*Sary* for *Sarah*), and a final *d* becomes *t* (*holt* for *hold*). The short *u* is pronounced as any other vowel but *u*. Often too, the accent is placed on the wrong syllable (*GEE tahr* for *gui TAR*).

Pronunciation of American English is growing more unified, especially since television, radio, and motion picture have come within everyone's reach. Announcers and actors use accepted pronunciations.

Learning Pronunciation must start with learning about syllables. Syllables are the natural divisions of a word according to pronunciation. A new syllable is formed around each new vowel sound. Each syllable stands by itself in pronunciation. There are some rules which will help in breaking a word into syllables.

Where two vowels are separated by a consonant, the consonant is usually pronounced with the second vowel. *Genus* is broken up as *GE-nus*, the *n* belonging to the second syllable. The consonant is pronounced with the first vowel when that vowel is short, but stressed. Thus, *general* becomes *GEN-er-al*.

Two consonants that come together in a word are pronounced separately, and belong in separate syllables. *Garden* is broken up as *GAR-den*. Among the consonants which cannot be separated are *ph, th, sh, ch,* and others that are pronounced as a single sound.

Learning pronunciation also means learning how to pronounce the simple combinations of letters. Most difficult-to-pronounce article titles in THE WORLD BOOK ENCYCLOPEDIA are followed by their pronunciations. Instead of using a complicated set of marks, THE WORLD BOOK ENCYCLOPEDIA indicates sound by using unmarked combinations of letters which show clearly the sounds. Accents are indicated by syllables set in capital letters (main or primary accent) and small capitals (secondary accent).

Any long word can be broken up into parts that are already familiar. The word *decantation* is long and looks hard. But it can be broken up into familiar parts—*de-can-ta-tion*. The first part is the same as the first syllable of *demon*. The second part is the same as a tin *can*. The third and fourth parts look like *nation*, beginning with *t* instead of *n*. Thus, decantation is pronounced *dee-kan-TAY-shun*. Many persons already know the word plantation, and find it easy to substitute *dec* for *pl* in learning to say decantation. There are many such shortcuts in learning pronunciation.

PAUL R. HANNA

Related Articles in WORLD BOOK include:

Accent	Homonym
Consonant	Phonetics
Diacritical Mark	Vowel
Diphthong	

FREQUENTLY MISPRONOUNCED WORDS

Some words that are often pronounced incorrectly are listed in this table. Correct pronunciations are listed for each word. When there are two accepted pronunciations for a word, both pronunciations are given.

Word	Pronunciation	Word	Pronunciation	Word	Pronunciation
abysmal	*uh BIZ muhl*	comparable	*KAHM puh ruh buhl*	indisputable	IN *dis PYOO tuh buhl*
abyss	*uh BIS*	comptroller	*kuhn TROHL uhr*		*in DIS pyuh tuh buhl*
accelerate	*ak SEL uh rayt*	connoisseur	*kahn uh SUR*	inexplicable	*in EK spluh kuh buhl*
access	*AK sehs*	contemplative	*KAHN tuhm play tiv*	infamous	*IN fuh muhs*
accouterment	*uh KOO tuhr muhnt*		*kuhn TEM pluh tiv*	influence	*IN floo uhns*
accurate	*AK yuh rit*	corps	*kor*	irrelevant	*ih REL uh vunt*
across	*uh KRAWS*	credence	*KREE duhns*	juvenile	*JOO vuh nuhl*
actual	*AK chuh wuhl*	crochet	*kroh SHAY*		*JOO vuh nyl*
acumen	*uh KYOO muhn*	curriculum	*kuh RIK yuh luhm*	lamentable	*LAM uhn tuh buhl*
admirable	*AD muh ruh buhl*	debenture	*duh BEN chuhr*	larynx	*LAR ingks*
advocacy	*AD vuh kuh see*	decathlon	*duh KATH luhn*	lichen	*LY kuhn*
aggrandizement	*uh GRAN diz muhnt*	demoniacal	*dee muh NY uh kuhl*	magnate	*MAG nayt*
ague	*AY gyoo*	demonstrate	*DEM uhn strayt*	maintenance	*MAYN tuh nuhns*
albino	*al BY noh*	demonstrative	*dih MAHN struh tihv*	mezzo	*MET soh*
albumen	*al BYOO muhn*	derisive	*dih RY sihv*		*MEZ oh*
alias	*AY lee uhs*	despicable	*DES pih kuh buhl*	mischievous	*MIS chuh vuhs*
amalgamate	*uh MAL guh mayt*	desultory	*DES uhl taw ree*	nonchalant	*NAHN shuh luhnt*
amicable	*AM uh kuh buhl*	deteriorate	*dee TIHR ee uh rayt*		NAHN *shuh LAHNT*
anonymity	*an uh NIM uh tee*	disreputable	*dis REP yuh tuh buhl*	ogre	*OH guhr*
apostate	*uh PAHS tayt*	docile	*DAHS uhl*	orgy	*AWR jee*
	uh PAHS tit	draught	*draft*	oyster	*OIS tuhr*
athlete	*ATH leet*	drowned	*drownd*	paradise	*PAIR uh dys*
avoirdupois	*av uhr duh POYZ*	dynasty	*DY nuh stee*	parliament	*PAR luh munt*
because	*bih KAWZ*	dysentery	*DIS uhn tair ee*	pharynx	*FAR ingks*
bicycle	*BY suh kuhl*	ecumenical	*ek yoo MEN uh kuhl*	physique	*fuh ZEEK*
	BY SIK *uhl*	ensemble	*ahn SAHM buhl*	picture	*PIK chuhr*
blackguard	*BLAG ahrd*	envelope	*EN vuh lohp*	poem	*POH uhm*
	BLAG uhrd		*AHN vuh lohp*	preferable	*PREF ur uh buhl*
boatswain	*BOH suhn*	error	*AIR uhr*		*PREF ruh buhl*
burial	*BAIR ee uhl*	exponent	*ek SPOH nunt*	ptomaine	*TOH mayn*
cache	*kash*	February	*FEB roo* AIR *ee*		*toh MAYN*
calumny	*KAL uhm nee*	figure	*FIG yuhr*	pueblo	*PWEB loh*
camellia	*kuh MEEL yuh*	forbade	*fuhr BAD*	radiator	*RAY dee ay tuhr*
	kuh MEE lee uh	formidable	*FOR muh duh buhl*	recognize	*REK uhg nyz*
candidate	*KAN duh dayt*	fuel	*FYOO uhl*	salivary	*SAL uh* VAIR *ee*
	KAN duh dit	garage	*guh RAHZH*	salmon	*SAM uhn*
carouse	*kuh ROWZ*		*guh RAHJ*	schedule	*SKEJ ool*
centrifugal	*sen TRIF yuh guhl*	genuine	*JEN yoo uhn*	schism	*SIZ uhm*
	sen TRIF uh guhl	gesture	*JES chur*	scion	*SY uhn*
ceramics	*suh RAM iks*	grievous	*GREEV uhs*	secretive	*sih KREE tihv*
chagrin	*shuh GRIN*	hearth	*hahrth*	silhouette	*sil oo ET*
chamois	*SHAM ee*	heroine	*HAIR oh in*	status	*STAY tuhs*
charade	*shuh RAYD*	hospitable	*HOS pih tuh buhl*		*STAT uhs*
chasten	*CHAY suhn*		*hos PIT uh buhl*	subtle	*SUHT uhl*
chastise	*chas TYZ*	hypocrisy	*hih PAHK ruh see*	superfluous	*soo PUHR floo uhs*
chef	*shef*	impious	*IM pee uhs*	suede	*SWAYD*
clandestine	*klan DES tuhn*	impotent	*IM puh tuhnt*	vehement	*VEE uh muhnt*
clientele	*kly uhn TEL*	incomparable	*in KOM puhr uh buhl*	victual	*VIHT uhl*
column	*KAHL uhm*		*in KOM pruh buhl*		

PROOFREADING

PROOFREADING means reading printed copy and marking any errors found in it. Everything that is printed—newspapers, magazines, books, advertising matter, and even such a small item as a calling card—must be proofread before it goes to press. If a newspaper ran an advertisement saying that a store had dresses for $1.95, when the true price was $21.95, it could easily cause a stampede to the store. Newspapers and magazines can be forced to pay any losses an advertiser suffers as the result of such an error.

How Proofreading Works. When a body of type is set, the typesetter prints a *proof* (trial copy) from it. The proofreader then compares the printed proof with the original manuscript, marking any errors with a set of symbols called *proofreaders' marks*. Every proofreader and every typesetter knows these marks. The proofreader reads mechanically, looking for any misspellings, mistakes, or broken type, and also with an awareness of content, questioning anything inconsistent.

After the proof is read, the typesetter "reads" the marks and makes all corrections. He also makes any other changes called for by the author, editor, or client. When no more corrections need to be made, the type is ready for printing.

Proofreaders' Marks are shown in the table with this article. Some of the most common include:

The *delete* sign (𝔤) got its name from the Latin word *delere*, meaning *to destroy*. Another Latin word, *stet*, means *let it stand*. It is used to restore words or letters crossed out.

Italic letters (ital) are slanting letters generally used for titles and for stressed words. *Roman* letters (rom) are straight up-and-down. *Boldface* type (bf) is heavier than ordinary type. It is often used for headings.

Lower case (lc) means small letters. Old handset type was kept in sectioned boxes called *cases*. Small letters were kept in the case below capital letters. Most type is set mechanically today, but capitals and small letters are still referred to as upper case and lower case. *Wrong font* (wf) means that the wrong kind of type has been used. A complete set of one design of type is called a *font*.

PROOFREADERS' MARKS

In Margin	In Copy	Meaning
m	autun	Insert
𝔤	autumn,	Delete
tr	the in autumn	Transpose
sp	for 8 months	Spell out
ital	Autumn's Reveries	Use italics
rom	Autumn's Reveries	Use roman type
bf	Autumn's Reveries	Use boldface type
lc	AUTUMN'S REVERIES	Use lower case
uc	Autumn's Reveries	Use upper case
caps	autumn's reveries	Use capital letters
sc	Autumn's Reveries	Use small capitals
wf	autumn	Wrong font
x	Reveries	Broken letter
9	Vutumn	Inverted letter
⌒	Au tumn's Reveries	Close up
#	Autumn'sReveries	More space
stet	autumn	Let it stand
⑦	Mrs. Smith⊙	Is this correct?
out: see copy	2416 Road	Something left out
⊏	[Autumn's	Move left
⊐	Autumn's]	Move right
¶	autumn. Until	New paragraph
═	autumn's reveries	Straighten line
⊙	autumn Until	Insert period
⋀	in autumn he	Insert comma
⋁	Autumns Reveries	Insert apostrophe
⋎ ⋎	Autumn's Reveries	Insert quotes
⹀/	reelect	Insert hyphen
⊙	as follows grain	Insert colon
⊐	Autumn's	Indent one em
‖	12 / 13	Align type

Accidental errors that occur in typesetting are called *typographical errors* or *typos*. Many typos are difficult to find because they are psychological, rather than due to misspelling.

Proofreaders' Marks on the printed proof show corrections that must be made in typeset matter, *left*. The corrected version, or revised proof, *right*, shows the same material after the typesetter has made all the proofreader's corrections.

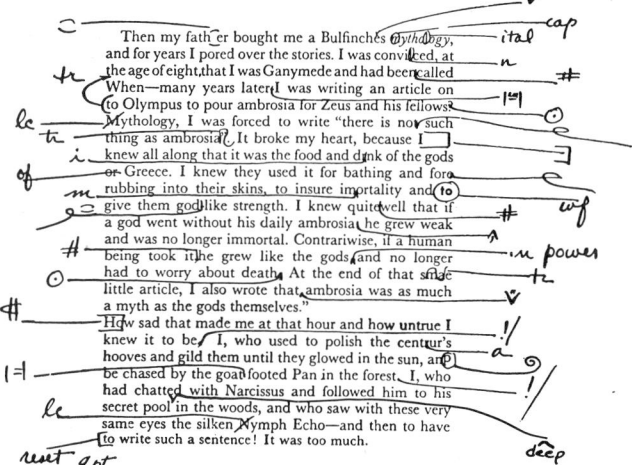

Then my father bought me a Bulfinch's *Mythology*, and for years I pored over the stories. I was convinced, at the age of eight, that I was Ganymede and had been called to Olympus to pour ambrosia for Zeus and his fellows. When—many years later—I was writing an article on mythology, I was forced to write "there is no such thing as ambrosia." It broke my heart, because I knew all along that it was the food and drink of the gods of Greece. I knew they used it for bathing and for rubbing into their skins, to insure immortality and to give them godlike strength. I knew quite well that if a god went without his daily ambrosia, he grew weak and was no longer immortal. Contrariwise, if a human being took it, he grew like the gods in power and no longer had to worry about death. At the end of that same little article, I also wrote that "ambrosia was as much a myth as the gods themselves."

How sad that made me at that hour and how untrue I knew it to be! I, who used to polish the centaur's hooves and gild them until they glowed in the sun, and be chased by the goat-footed Pan in the forest! I, who had chatted with Narcissus and followed him to his secret pool deep in the woods, and who saw with these very same eyes the silken nymph Echo—and then to have to write such a sentence! It was too much.

PROPAGANDA is a method used to influence people to believe certain ideas or to follow certain courses of action. Propaganda has sold everything from toothpaste to war. Nearly everyone everyday does something or thinks something partly because propaganda has urged him to do so. The list of propagandists includes preachers, teachers, politicians, editors, advertisers, salesmen, reformers, authors, artists, parents—as well as our friends and ourselves.

The word *propaganda* comes from the Latin phrase, *Congregatio de Propaganda Fide*, or *Congregation for the Propagation of the Faith*. This committee of the Roman Catholic Church works to *propagate* or spread the doctrines of the church in other countries. Its workers might be called missionaries. All propagandists, in a sense, are missionaries. They are missionaries for an idea, an attitude, or a plan of action.

There is a common impression that we should be suspicious of anything called propaganda because it is a bit shady. The word is often connected with the activities of selfish or dishonest persons who conceal their real purposes and perhaps even their identity. But propaganda can be either good or bad. Whether we consider it good or bad depends upon what we think of the propagandist's aim. Most persons would agree that organized attempts to raise money for charity are good forms of propaganda. Yet such efforts are propaganda just as much as the efforts of communist organizations to influence us in ways we call bad.

How Propaganda Works

The methods which propagandists use are simple and age-old. One of the basic rules of the propagandist is to connect the idea or thing he is propagandizing with words about which everyone feels strongly in one way or another. These words are symbols. Each one stands not only for its specific dictionary meaning, but also for experiences, emotions, and attitudes that have come to be bound up with the word in a vague but extremely important way. Some of these symbols to which most Americans respond favorably are: mother, home, justice, health, beauty, love, money, security, and education. A propagandist will pick out one or two of these symbols and try to build up a firm association between these symbols and the idea or product in which he is especially interested. And there are, of course, just as powerful symbols which arouse unfavorable attitudes. Examples, of these are: murder, cruelty, barbarity, and death. The propagandist appeals to these symbols to get people to reject a program or fight against something which he himself opposes.

There are two characteristics of effective propaganda which the expert in the field always bears in mind. Any attempt to influence people's thought or action must be reasonable: arguments must make sense and must not be too farfetched. Any good propagandist remembers that his propaganda is competing with other propaganda and that people's memories are likely to be short. He must repeat his themes over and over again in many ways to attract and hold attention.

Why Is Propaganda Successful?

Some persons have claimed that most human beings are unthinking, like sheep, and can be led around by those who use propaganda skillfully. There is basically little reason for such a claim. Everyone is affected by propaganda, because human beings have common characteristics upon which the propagandist can capitalize. Love, hate, and fear are emotions which every person has. Combined with these basic emotions are the common desires that most persons have come to have as members of a social community.

One important common characteristic is language. Few persons realize the extent to which language actually molds thinking. Most words are loaded with emotion of some kind or other, and people react not only to the dictionary meaning of a word but to a maze of feelings which the word arouses.

A second important characteristic is complexity. We have to take other persons' word for things. For example, when a person buys a certain product in the drugstore and finds the bottle has been marked "poison" by the druggist, he takes the druggist's word for it, though he may not understand at all why this particular thing actually is a poison. In the same way, he is likely to take other persons' judgments concerning politics, music, or the best kind of automobiles.

A third common characteristic is our desire to gain and hold the respect of others. Peoples of one race tend to think they are superior to other races. People who live under one form of government usually think it is better than others. Students who go to one school tend to think their school is better than others.

Everyone is inclined to believe that what he would like to have true is actually true. This tendency is especially strong in his beliefs about himself. It is always more comforting for a person to feel that he is more intelligent, attractive, and virtuous than perhaps he actually is. For this reason propaganda that encourages our desire to flatter ourselves is much more successful than the kind that discourages complacency and damages self-confidence.

Vehicles of Propaganda

Person-to-Person. A great deal of propaganda passes from person to person in private conversations. Some of the most effective work for social, civic, or political causes is done through personal contacts. But *whispering campaigns* are often used by propagandists who wish not to be held responsible for ideas they start.

Printed Matter. Almost any person or group with money can publish printed matter to sell a product, promote a cause, or engage in any other form of propaganda. Even the fairest and most impartial newspaper is a medium of propaganda. Every daily newspaper has an editorial page on which it expresses opinion on events and personalities in the news. Editorial judgment is persuasively presented, and it often forms the basis on which many persons interpret the news. Good journalists uphold a code of ethics which distinguishes between news and editorial opinion. This code holds that in an editorial column the publisher is entitled to advocate any cause he chooses. But in the news columns, the complete and unbiased facts should be reported.

Schools. Pressure groups often attempt to influence school and college teachers and officials because the pressure groups want instruction material shaped to spread among young people opinions favorable to certain interests. Efforts are constantly made to introduce propaganda matter into the schools through such means as free pamphlets, films, and various contests.

Churches. While churches seldom take sides directly in political and economic controversies, they are in a position to exercise great influence on questions of moral and social importance. Churches help in public efforts to control vice, in slum clearance, and in other public-welfare movements.

Organizations. There are more than 800 national associations in the United States. They include learned societies; professional, business, and trade associations; labor unions, fraternal orders, and college fraternities; women's clubs; civic and reform bodies; and patriotic orders. Their membership ranges from a few hundred up to several million. Many publish their own periodicals, both to unite their members and to gain the support of the general public.

Lobbying. Between four and five hundred organizations maintain offices with salaried officers in Washington, D.C., to meet members of Congress and persuade them to vote for laws favorable to their organization's interests, or to kill unfavorable laws. These people are called *lobbyists*. They range from large organizations to individuals who are so deeply interested in some cause that they spend their own time and money to advance it. Lobbies are also active in state capitals.

Some lobbyists work openly and use only legitimate methods to convince legislators. Others have given lobbying a corrupt reputation by using such means as bribery, luxurious entertainment, and threats.

Publicity. For many years theatrical producers, circuses, lecturers, and musicians employed press agents to secure favorable publicity in towns where they appeared. The public relations counselor has largely replaced the old-fashioned press agent. Most large organizations now have departments of public relations. Their business is to cultivate the good will of the public. Because of the important part the consumer plays in the prosperity of industry, large sums are spent to spread favorable opinions of a company's policies.

Advertising. The usual aim of advertising is to influence people to buy certain goods. The advertiser tries to make the consumer want his own firm's product more than the product of a rival. Most businessmen insist on truth in advertising, and work to improve its standards.

People are influenced to buy certain products by something they have seen or heard, in newspapers and magazines, on radio or television, on cards displayed in buses, on billboards, in direct-mail letters, or even in a trail of smoke written across the sky by an airplane. The number of people reached by these methods, and the strength of their buying power, are carefully studied by market research firms and others. The results determine which advertising media are most used.

Art. When we realize that millions of dollars are spent for commercial art work and for illustrations in printed matter, we can see how powerful art can be as propaganda. The comic strips, which are favorite reading matter of many adults as well as children, are so popular that many advertisements are now composed entirely of them. Artists may even use the standard

TYPES OF PROPAGANDA

"funnies" to promote certain opinions and prejudices. The influence of cartoons in crystallizing public opinion for or against politicians is well known.

Motion Pictures have become one of the most powerful influences on the public mind. Because motion pictures cost so much to produce, and must appeal to the largest possible "box office," they are likely to represent the most common popular prejudices.

In judging the value of a motion picture, such questions as the following arise: Does it make the audience more tolerant of other races and religions? Does it expose injustice, snobbery, greed, or jingoism? Does it put an unnatural emphasis on crime, drunkenness, or sex? Does it convey a favorable or unfavorable attitude toward any special group? Motion pictures can do all these things, or their opposites.

Radio and Television are rapidly becoming powerful instruments of propaganda because they can reach millions of persons of all classes. In recent years, an increasing percentage of advertising money has been spent for radio and television time and talent. Political leaders and public officials use these means of communication to explain their policies to large numbers of people.

Detecting Propaganda

Fact and Fiction. Propaganda is so widespread in the modern world that it is important that the citizen be able to distinguish propaganda from facts. In the long run, the ability to detect propaganda depends largely on the intelligence of the individual citizen. He must learn to ask himself questions about everything he reads, sees, and hears. For example, when he is reading a newspaper he should ask: Where does this dispatch or story come from? What news agency or correspondent wrote it? Is some person or organization trying to influence me for its own selfish ends? Is the story backed up by firsthand evidence, or does it contain only vague assertions? When a person is watching a broadcast, he should ask himself: Who sponsors this program? Apart from the advertising announcements which are usually plainly indicated, are there any evidences that someone is trying to influence my opinion? Does this news commentator seem to be sticking to the

Outdoor Advertising Assn.; General Electric

Propaganda Is All Around Us, urging us to believe an idea, accept a fact, or buy a product. We often think of propaganda only in terms of political speeches, *far left*, but advertisements on television and radio also try to sell us something. Billboards use few words to carry their impact. Newspapers present editorial views on a special editorial page.

actual news sources, or is he inserting unwarranted opinions and colored words?

Propaganda Analysis. Various agencies have been established to study propaganda and to assist the public in analyzing it scientifically. Consumer's movements examine the conflicting claims of advertisers and carry on laboratory research to determine the value of various products. Many schools have established consumer courses to train students to get their money's worth in buying.

In general, the citizens of a democracy do not want to be duped into thinking only what the propagandist wants them to think. But if they are not trained to be wary of propaganda devices, they are likely to follow movements and ideas which would not seem reasonable to them if they knew how to separate the facts from the tricks of propaganda. For this reason, there is a great need for education on detecting propaganda. A number of years ago, the Institute for Propaganda Analysis listed seven propaganda devices in common use. They are:

Name Calling. This means applying some label that people generally dislike or fear to a person, or organization, or an idea. Such words as "warmonger," "isolationist," "imperialist," "pacifist," "red," "fascist," "fifth columnist," or "alien" may be used to tag persons whom the propagandist wants to discredit rather than to describe accurately. The terms he uses will depend on his purposes and the prejudices of his audience.

Glittering Generality. A propagandist likes to connect a high-sounding word to what he is advocating, so that people will accept what he wants them to accept without examining his arguments.

Transfer. This is a propagandist's device to carry over the reputation of some organization which is respected to some program the propagandist wants accepted.

Testimonial. Quoting some well-known person in favor of a given product or policy is another propaganda practice.

Plain Folks. Propagandists sometimes make an effort to win public confidence on the basis that a man's ideas are good because he belongs to the common people.

Card Stacking. Selecting and using facts to give a false or misleading idea is a common trick. The propagandist tries to make out the best case possible for his side and the worst for his opponent by carefully using only those facts which back up his point of view.

Band Wagon. The public is often urged to follow the crowd and accept the propagandist's program because "everybody's doing it."

Government and Propaganda

In the last analysis, all governments depend for their survival upon public opinion. The difference in the line of propaganda followed is determined by the different aims of each type of government.

In a dictatorship, whether it is fascist or communist in type, all propaganda drives into people's minds the single, official point of view. Newspapers and radios are strictly controlled by the government, and criticism of government policy is punished. Dictators try to eliminate any ideas which might question or challenge the official point of view.

Democratic governments work on the opposite principle. They believe that everyone should be permitted to think, speak, and write what he believes. Democracies carefully protect freedom of expression.

The Limitations of Propaganda

The scope of the propagandists—no matter how clever they are or how much power they have—is limited by certain basic ideals, fundamental needs, or highly cherished values which the people of their group possess. The cleverest propagandist in the world, even with complete control over communications, could not destroy the place of the family in American life, because it is too permanent.   HADLEY CANTRIL and CLYDE W. HART

Related Articles in WORLD BOOK include:

Advertising	Magazine
Cartoon	Motion Picture
Censorship	Newspaper
Consumer Education	Poll of Public Opinion
Democracy	Public Opinion
Freedom	Television
Goebbels, Paul J.	World War II (Psychological
Lobbying	Warfare)

Todd Shipyard; American Airlines

The Broad-Bladed Propeller of an Ocean Liner in dry dock is swung into position to be fitted onto the propeller shaft.

PROPAGATION, in botany, is the growing of new plants. See PLANT (How Plants Reproduce); REPRODUCTION.

PROPANE. See BUTANE AND PROPANE.

PROPELLANT. See SPACE TRAVEL (Getting into Space and Back); AMMUNITION.

PROPELLER has blades mounted on a power-driven shaft. It produces a forward thrust by its action on air or water. The best-known types of propellers are those that drive ships and airplanes.

The first screw propeller for ships was developed by John Fitch in 1796. His propeller was in the form of a spiral around a cylindrical rod. John Ericsson, a Swedish-American inventor, perfected the first successful propeller with blades in 1837 (see ERICSSON, JOHN).

Marine Propellers range in diameter from 10 inches for small boats, to 96 inches for the average motorship. They are usually made of manganese and bronze.

The propeller bites into the water in the same way a screw bites into wood. The *pitch* is the distance a propeller would advance with each revolution if it were cutting into a solid medium, like a screw into wood. Actually, the propeller does not advance this full distance, since the water does not offer as much resistance as wood. The difference between the pitch and the actual distance the propeller does advance in the water is called the *slip*. The slip is usually about 15 per cent with the most efficient marine propeller. The number of revolutions varies, depending on the type of ship and the kind of engine driving it.

Navy ships most often have three-blade propellers, while merchant ships usually have four blades. Propellers on single-screw ships turn to the right, or clockwise, when viewed from the stern when the ship is going ahead. Twin-screw vessels usually have out-turning propellers. The starboard screw turns clockwise, and the port screw counterclockwise, for ahead motion. Twin-screw ships are easily steered by reversing one of the engines while the other goes full ahead. Destroyers and

Controllable-Pitch Propellers provide the thrust for turbo-prop airliners. The blade angles can be adjusted in flight.

other small craft can make very sharp turns in this way. Conventional propellers are slowed by *cavitation*, a vacuum that forms as the propeller turns. United States Navy ships hope to increase their speed by using *supercavitating propellers* that are designed to utilize the cavitation (see SCREW [picture: A Supercavitating Propeller]).

The Airplane Propeller is also known as an *air screw*. It changes the power of the engine into a thrust that pulls or pushes the airplane through the air. The propeller has two or more blades, each shaped like an airplane wing. The cross sections of the blade are *airfoil sections* similar to those used in wings. The efficiency of a propeller drops off and the noise it makes increases rapidly as the speed of the tips of its blades increases beyond the speed of sound.

A *Fixed-Pitch Propeller* is one in which the angle at which the blades are set is fixed. Such propellers are efficient only at one speed of flight, and for a definite horsepower output.

A *Controllable-Pitch Propeller* is one in which the angle of the blades can be adjusted while the propeller is spinning. This adjustment can be controlled either manually or automatically to give the most efficient blade angle at various air speeds and under different kinds of operating conditions, such as in climbing.

A *Constant-Speed Propeller* automatically keeps turning at the same number of revolutions per minute under all conditions of flight. It does not gain speed in dives or lose speed in climbs.

A *Feathering Propeller* is one in which the blade angle can be increased enough to streamline the blades with the engine stopped. In case of an engine failure, the pilot can *feather*, or rotate, the blades so that their leading and trailing edges parallel the path of flight. This decreases the propeller's air resistance, and prevents possible damage to the engine.

A *Reversible-Pitch Propeller* can have the pitch reversed so that the direction of thrust is reversed. This acts as a brake and reduces the landing run on the ground. It is of great value for large airplanes, particularly if the runways are covered with ice or snow so that wheel brakes are not effective. C. B. SMITH

See also AIRPLANE (Propellers); MOTORBOAT; SCREW; SHIP AND SHIPPING (The Propellers).

PROPER MOTION. See ASTRONOMY (Measuring the Motion of the Stars).

PROPERTY, in law, means ownership. It may refer to a car, a farm, a watch, or anything else that is owned. Property also may refer to an interest in something that is owned by someone else, such as stock in a corporation. The corporation owns the machinery, the raw materials, and the finished products. But the stockholder is entitled to share in the corporation's profits. There are two ways to classify property. *Real property* includes land and the things permanently attached to it, such as buildings and trees. All other things are called *personal property.*

Various types of interest in property exist in American and English law. For example, an owner of land has *absolute* property interest if he is the only person with an interest in the land. The owner may allow another person to occupy it as a farm for 10 years. During that time, the owner is entitled to be paid for the use of the land, but he cannot use it himself. In this case, he has a *qualified nonpossessory* property interest. The farmer is entitled to possess the land and he can prevent anyone from interfering with his use of the property. He has a *qualified possessory* interest. During the 10 years, the farmer can provide for an *easement* by permitting a neighbor to walk through the land to reach a road or other piece of land. The easement gives the neighbor a *qualified nonpossessory* interest. These types of interest also apply to personal property.

Property interests may be acquired in several ways. A person may buy property, find it, or receive it as a gift. He also may get property by a court order, as in the distribution of the estate of a person who has died without leaving a will. Not all nations permit the type of private ownership allowed in the United States. In Russia, for example, the government has taken much land from private owners. ROBERT E. SULLIVAN

Related Articles in WORLD BOOK include:

Abstract	Arson	Assignment
Appraisal	Assessment	Attachment

Attainder	Estate	Public Domain
Deed	Fee	Real Estate
Depreciation	Joint Tenancy	Receiver
Domesday Book	Mortgage	Riparian Rights
Easement	Personal Property	Title
Eminent Domain	Property Tax	Trustee

PROPERTY, PERSONAL. See PERSONAL PROPERTY.

PROPERTY INSURANCE. See INSURANCE.

PROPERTY TAX is levied by governments on owners of property. This property includes real estate, such as homes, buildings, and vacant land. It also includes personal property, such as home furnishings, stocks and bonds, and automobiles.

In the United States and Canada, only provincial, state, and local governments levy property taxes. The federal governments of the two countries do not use this type of tax. Since the early 1930's, states have relied less and less on property taxes. But the tax continues to be an important source of revenue for local governments.

The property tax rate varies, depending on the tax revenue needs of the government. The rate is usually based on the property's *assessed valuation.* This is a certain percentage of the property's total value as determined by the government. Property is rarely taxed at its full market value. CHARLES J. GAA

See also PERSONAL PROPERTY.

PROPHET, *PRAHF et,* is a word taken from the Greek, where it means *one who proclaims.* The Biblical prophets spoke out most about the evils of their own time. But Biblical prophecy also described what would happen if people did or did not do certain things, and what the prophet hoped for in his people's future. The great age of Hebrew prophecy began in the 700's B.C., with the so-called "writing" prophets, Amos, Micah, Hosea, and Isaiah. Hebrew prophecy is distinctive in its lofty poetry and its plea for social justice. CYRUS H. GORDON

Related Articles in WORLD BOOK include:

Amos	Haggai	Jonah	Obadiah
Elijah	Hosea	Malachi	Samuel
Elisha	Isaiah	Micah	Zechariah
Ezekiel	Jeremiah	Nahum	Zephaniah
Habakkuk	Joel		

PROPHYLAXIS, *PRO fuh LACK sis,* means any treatment that protects a person from a disease. Prophylaxis is also called *preventive* treatment. Treatment is called

Boston Public Library

Micah, Haggai, Malachi, and Zechariah are the prophets shown in this panel from *Frieze of the Prophets,* by John Singer Sargent. The frieze is part of the famous murals, *Pageant of Religion,* in the Boston Public Library.

corrective when the patient already has a disease or unhealthful condition.

Preventive treatment has become more and more important in modern medicine. Methods pioneered by Louis Pasteur, Robert Koch, and others proved it is possible to strengthen the body so it will be immune to certain diseases. This branch of medicine is called *immunology*. *Collective prophylaxis* is preventive medicine in the field of public health. Sanitation, group vaccination, and insecticides can protect whole communities. Dental prophylaxis specializes in preventing tooth decay and crooked teeth. W. W. BAUER

See also IMMUNITY.

PROPJET. See JET PROPULSION (Turboprop).

PROPOLIS. See BEE (Bee Glue).

PROPONTIS, an old name for the Sea of Marmara. See MARMARA, SEA OF.

PROPORTION, in mathematics, means an equality of ratios. The ratio of one number *a* to another number *b* is the quotient obtained by dividing the first by the second. Thus, the ratio of *a* to *b* may be written $\frac{a}{b}$ and the ratio of *c* to *d* may be written $\frac{c}{d}$. These ratios may also be written *a:b* and *c:d*. The colon means *divided by*. See RATIO.

The four numbers *a*, *b*, *c*, and *d* are said to be in proportion if the ratio of *a* to *b* equals the ratio of *c* to *d*. The proportion is written in either of two ways: $\frac{a}{b}=\frac{c}{d}$ or *a:b=c:d*. The first way is preferred, because it gives proportion in the usual form of an algebraic equation.

The first term *a* and the last, or fourth, term *d* are called the *extremes of the proportion*. The second term *b* and the third term *c* are called the *means*. The product of the extremes equals the product of the means, or $ad=bc$. In the proportion $\frac{a}{b}=\frac{b}{c}$, *b* is called the *mean proportional* between *a* and *c*, and *c* is the *third proportional* to *a* and *b*. In the proportion $\frac{a}{b}=\frac{c}{d}$, *d* is the *fourth proportional* to *a*, *b*, and *c*.

Problems. (1) Find a third proportional to 3 and 6.

Solution: $\frac{3}{6}=\frac{6}{x}$

Multiply by 6*x*. $3x=36$ and $x=12$

Check: $\frac{3}{6}=\frac{6}{12}$ Or, $3:6=6:x$

Product of extremes equals product of means: $3x=36$ and $x=12$.

(2) Find a mean proportional between 8 and 18.

Plan: $\frac{8}{x}=\frac{x}{18}$ Or, $8:x=x:18$

Now multiply by 18*x*, and continue as in the first problem. MILES C. HARTLEY

PROPORTIONAL REPRESENTATION, often called **PR,** is a system of electing members of a legislature. It is designed to give a political party a share of the seats in the legislature in proportion to its share of the total vote cast in an election. PR has three basic features: (1) three or more legislators are chosen from each district at the same time; (2) the ballots are counted in a special way to give each political party its share of the vote; and (3) there are usually more than two active political parties. These elements are present in both kinds of PR, the *List System* and the *Hare System*.

The List System. Each political party offers a list of candidates for the legislature, and the voter marks his ballot for the party he chooses, not the individual candidates. If a party wins 40 per cent of the vote, it receives 40 per cent of the available seats in the legislature. In a campaign to fill 100 seats, the first 40 candidates on the party's list would be elected. If another party wins 20 per cent of the vote, its top 20 candidates receive seats in the legislature.

The Hare System is much more complicated. Each voter numbers the candidates on his ballot in the order of his choice. After counting the total number of ballots, election officials determine a mathematical *election quota*, the minimum needed for election. Then they count all the first choices. A candidate who wins the quota of first choices is declared elected. All of his ballots above the quota are redistributed to the candidates chosen second by the voters. Next, the candidate with the fewest number of ballots is eliminated. His ballots are redistributed to the second-choice candidates listed. If the second-choice candidate has already been elected, the ballot is passed on to the third choice, and so on. This process continues until enough candidates have reached the election quota to fill all the seats. An English lawyer, Thomas Hare, described the system in 1859. WILLIAM A. HAMBLEY, JR.

PROPRIETARY COLONY. See COLONIAL LIFE IN AMERICA (Types of Colonies).

PROPRIETARY MEDICINE. See PATENT MEDICINE.

PROPRIOCEPTOR. See SENSES.

PROPULSION, JET. See JET PROPULSION.

PROPYLAEA. See ACROPOLIS.

PROSCENIUM. See THEATER (The Stage).

PROSE is man's usual way of expressing himself in speech or in writing. It is basically any written or spoken language that is not poetry. It includes novels, plays, short stories, articles, newspaper stories, essays, and everyday conversation. Poetry is chiefly a matter of artificial form. The poet fits his words into a common rhythm or meter. He breaks his poems into lines and often groups the lines into stanzas. The prose writer is also concerned with form, but less so than the poet. His words may have rhythm, but it is generally uneven.

Much prose is so musical that it is almost poetry. The prose writings of John Donne and Anglican writers of the 1600's are so poetical that they may be called *poetical prose*. Their prose was strongly influenced by the fact that they followed the rhythmic pattern of the King James Version of the Bible. About 1920, a group of American poets wrote what they called *polyphonic prose*, which was a prose form with rhythm and irregular rhymes.

But prose can be distinguished from poetry by more than its form. The Latin word from which the word *prose* comes means *straightforward* or *matter-of-fact*. Good prose writers try to write in a lively and vivid style. But, at the same time, their main purpose is to tell their story straightforwardly, in a clear and simple way. The poet, however, often conveys his ideas by suggestion and figures of speech.

There are various kinds of prose. Roughly, they are classed under *narration* (storytelling), *description*, *exposition* (explanation), and *argumentation*. Most prose combines two or more of these. Stories, which are narrative, include description and exposition. An oration, which is mainly argumentative, may contain exposition, description, and narration.   J. N. Hook

Related Articles in WORLD BOOK include:

Biography	Essay	Orators and
Conversation	Fable	Oratory
Diary	Fiction	Short Story
Drama	Novel	Storytelling

PROSE EDDA. See EDDA.

PROSERPINA, *proh SUR pih nuh,* or PERSEPHONE, *pur SEHF oh nee,* was the lovely daughter of Ceres (Demeter) in Roman and Greek mythology. Ceres was the goddess of agriculture. Proserpina was gathering flowers in a meadow one day when the earth opened. Pluto dashed up in his black chariot and seized her. Then he took her to his kingdom of the Lower World.

Ceres wandered over the earth looking for Proserpina. The crops died because Ceres neglected her duties. Jupiter finally ordered Pluto to release Proserpina, if she

Proserpina Struggles with Pluto in this beautiful statue, made in the 1600's by the Italian sculptor Giovanni Bernini.
Art Institute of Chicago

had not eaten while she was in the Lower World. But Proserpina had eaten some seeds of a pomegranate. This meant that she would have to spend part of each year with Pluto. It is winter when Proserpina is underground, and summer when she is on the earth. In summer, the happy Ceres makes the crops grow. This legend helped explain the changes in the seasons.   VAN JOHNSON

See also MYTHOLOGY (The Underground Queen).

PROSLAVERY MOVEMENT was an attempt by Southerners to justify and expand slavery in America between the 1830's and 1860. Southerners argued that both the Bible and history endorsed slavery, that *emancipation* (freeing the slaves) was impractical, and that slavery was necessary to save the Southern economy. John C. Calhoun and other well-known Americans defended slavery. They called it "the law of nature," "a positive good," and "the greatest and most admirable agent of civilization."

The proslavery movement wanted to extend slavery into the Western territories and wanted to add Texas to the Union. Former President John Quincy Adams called the Mexican War (1846-1848) "a slave-power conspiracy," a means to gain more slave territory. Abolitionists condemned efforts to acquire Cuba as an attempt to add another slave state. In the late 1850's, some Southerners wanted the foreign slave trade reopened. The Civil War destroyed slavery in the nation and ended the proslavery movement.   FRANK L. KLEMENT

See also CIVIL WAR ("An Irrepressible Conflict").

PROSPECTING means searching for valuable mineral deposits. Prospectors have found the supplies of coal, petroleum, uranium, and other fuels that are so important to industry. They have also discovered deposits of copper, diamonds, gold, iron, and other minerals.

Early Prospectors in the United States were lured by the promise of rich discoveries of gold, silver, and other precious metals. They traveled across the mountains in the West carrying picks, shovels, gold pans, and other supplies. Early petroleum prospectors drilled holes in rocks looking for signs of underground oil reservoirs. Other prospectors explored deep canyons and high mountains. Most early prospectors had no scientific training, and relied chiefly on experience and luck to discover deposits. Most of them found only hardship and disappointment.

Today's Prospector must rely on the instruments and methods of the geological sciences to be successful. He must have a thorough training in mining geology. He must be able to analyze the results obtained from many types of prospecting instruments. Continued extraction of mineral wealth has been possible only by digging deeper into the earth, or by finding additional hidden deposits near areas mined earlier.

Studies of known deposits help to determine the conditions under which undiscovered deposits may occur. This knowledge helps the geologist locate areas that may yield significant ore deposits. Once the prospector finds such an area, he has to determine the location, value, and size of the buried mineral deposit. He examines surface rocks that may indicate deposits. The prospector may also drill holes and take out specimens of rocks and fragments that can be studied to determine the value of the deposit.

Uranium Prospectors often use portable Geiger counters to check the amount of radioactivity in rocks and mineral deposits.

Wide World

Prospectors today need geological training and use geophysical instruments in discovering valuable ores.

Instruments also aid the prospector. Gravity meters measure variations in the force of gravity in the deposit area. Magnetometers check the amount of magnetism in an area. Geiger counters measure the amounts of radioactive minerals in rocks (see GEIGER COUNTER). Ultraviolet lamps cause certain minerals to give off definite colors. In the *seismic* method of prospecting, geologists use explosives to create small earthquakes or waves in the rock. The path of these waves through the rock may indicate the conditions beneath the earth's surface (see SEISMOGRAPH).

Chemistry also helps the prospector locate valuable deposits of coal, copper, lead, oil, zinc, and other minerals. The presence of *trace elements* (chemical elements in very small amounts) at the ground surface may indicate large deposits under the ground. Chemical examination of rocks, plants, and water in an area may also indicate mineral deposits.

Today, most searching is done for deeply buried deposits, because most surface deposits have been discovered. Large-scale prospecting is undertaken only after careful study, because of the expensive equipment and personnel required. GEORGE B. CLARK

See also GOLD RUSH; PETROLEUM (How Men Find Petroleum); URANIUM (with picture).

PROSPERITY. See INFLATION AND DEFLATION.

PROSTATE GLAND is a structure composed of muscular and glandular tissue. It is present only in males. It secretes a substance used to transport sperm cells. The gland is about the size of a large walnut, and lies just below the urinary bladder. The *urethra*, which is the tube that empties the bladder, passes through it. In later life, the prostate tends to become larger. It may press upon the urethral tube, interfering with the passage of urine. Surgeons may then have to remove either all, or part of, the gland. ROBERTO F. ESCAMILLA

PROSTHETICS, *prahs THET iks*, is a branch of medicine, particularly surgery or dentistry, that supplies artificial parts for the body. For example, a person may lose an arm or leg in an accident. Artificial limbs can be made to take the place of the lost part. The artificial part is called a *prosthesis*. The replacing of lost teeth is called *prosthodontics*. Manufacturers make artificial body parts of wood, plastic, or stainless steel. See also ARTIFICIAL LIMBS; DENTISTRY (Prosthodontics); HANDICAPPED (The Crippled).

PROTACTINIUM, *proh tak TIN ee uhm*, is a radioactive metal belonging to the actinide series of elements. Two teams of scientists independently isolated the element in 1917. These were Otto Hahn and Lise Meitner of Germany, and Frederick Soddy and John Cranston of Great Britain. Protactinium occurs naturally in all uranium ores. It is also produced artificially by bombarding thorium with alpha particles.

Protactinium has the symbol Pa. Its atomic number is 91, and its most stable isotope has a mass number of 231. Protactinium is the link between the actinide decay series and the uranium decay series. It decays into actinium by giving off alpha rays. J. GORDON PARR

PROTAGORAS. See ORATORS AND ORATORY.

PROTECTION. Early man was a fairly helpless creature. Stones and crude clubs were his only protection against animals or other men that might attack him. Rough skins and rude huts were his only protection against cold until he discovered fire. The cave man had no protection against disease. His only protection against hunger was his skill as a hunter. His death usually came as soon as he was too old or weak to defend himself against his many enemies.

Today, man faces many more threats to his life, property, and general security than the cave man did. Early man did not have to face perils such as traffic accidents, fires, and the dangers of atomic warfare.

Yet modern man lives much longer, and many times more comfortably, than early man did, because he has learned better ways to protect himself against life's dangers. Science has provided him with medicines and surgery for the prevention and treatment of disease. Community, state, and national laws have established many forms of protection for all citizens against crime, accidents, disease, fire, and other dangers. Through insurance, man has learned to protect himself or his family against want, even if some of these forms of protection fail. Man's greatest protective force, both collective and individual, is the simple use of caution. Most human misfortunes, other than such natural disturbances as storms, floods, and earthquakes, result from a lack of caution.

Personal Security

Civil Liberty is the highest form of protection given the individual citizen in a civilized nation. Civil liberty guarantees his right as a free man to pursue happiness in whatever manner he chooses so long as he breaks no laws. Civil liberty guarantees the right to vote, the right of personal privacy in the home, the right to a fair trial, the right to worship, and other freedoms. The courts and such organizations as the American Civil Liberties Union guard against violations of civil liberties.

Protection Against Want is a problem that mankind has met in many different ways. When food was scarce, early man merely moved on to a place where food was more plentiful. But in our modern society, both the individual and the government take measures to prevent want.

The individual may protect himself and his family against want through savings, life insurance, old-age annuities, endowment funds, or similar means. His employer may also set up a pension fund to protect him against want after he is too old to work. The employer, the employee, or both may contribute to the fund.

In the United States, federal unemployment insurance and social security laws supplement the individual means of protection against want. The states also have many laws that assist the needy, such as aid to dependent children, assistance to the aged and physically handicapped, and relief.

Protection Against Loss is a security function that is carried almost entirely by insurance. Dependent families are protected to some extent against the death of the wage earner who provides for them through insurance. Losses suffered through theft, fire, traffic accidents, storms, shipwrecks, and many other hazards can be redeemed through insurance. The United States government protects the individual against some types of loss.

For example, the Federal Deposit Insurance Corporation, a government agency, insures bank deposits.

Protection of Achievement is important to the inventor, the composer of music, the artist, the writer, and the publisher of creative works. Patents, copyrights, and trademarks protect these people from having their "brain children" stolen by dishonest persons.

Community Security

Protection of Life and Property concerns the whole community, although each individual receives his share of the security provided.

Fire insurance provides some protection against damage from fires. But insurance companies could not underwrite the huge losses nor the deaths that would result from fires if there were no fire departments maintained by small and large communities.

Crime could make life as dangerous as it was in the Middle Ages. But the community gives protection by such law enforcement agencies as the Federal Bureau of Investigation, United States Secret Service, and police departments. There are also the various courts, and the prisons in which convicted criminals can be kept. Crime prevention organizations and parole systems, which check released criminals, are also part of this kind of protection.

Protection of Health is also a community problem as well as an individual one. The personal physician could not take care of his patients properly if it were not for the various hospitals, clinics, and laboratories set up in the community. States, counties, and cities protect their citizens against plagues and epidemics through health departments and the operation of sanitary engineering systems.

National and International Security

Protecting a nation against attack by enemies is a double task—that of providing adequate national defense and also that of keeping the peace. Such protection is the duty of the national government.

National Defense is the responsibility of the armed forces of the United States. These forces are the army, navy, air force, marine corps, and, in wartime, the coast guard. During wartime, the nation rallies to this form of protection.

Means of Maintaining Peace are the joint responsibility of the legislative and executive branches of the United States government. The President, through the Department of State, makes treaties that go into effect only if approved by a two-thirds majority vote of the Senate. The Congress also sometimes adopts laws directing the Chief Executive to take certain courses of action designed to maintain peace between the United States and other countries.   John J. Floherty

Related Articles. See SAFETY with its list of Related Articles. See also the following articles:

Civil Defense	National Defense	Public Health
Civil Rights	Patent	Service
Fire Fighting	Police	Pure Food and
Insurance	Public Health	Drug Laws
Law Enforcement		Social Security

PROTECTION OF WILDLIFE. See WILDLIFE CONSERVATION; GAME; BIRD (How We Protect Birds).

PROTECTIVE COLORATION

PROTECTIVE COLORATION is coloring that helps to protect plants and animals from enemies. The color of the individual may blend with its surroundings, so that the plant or animal cannot be discovered easily by its enemies. For example, some frogs and snakes that live in green grass and weeds are colored green. Birds, reptiles, and other animals that live in the desert may be either gray or sand colored. Some hares, rabbits, and weasels have earth-colored coats during the warm months, and white fur during the winter. The kallima butterfly has the coloring of a dead leaf, and the walking stick insect has the coloring of a twig.

Color is sometimes useful not only to protect the individual, but also to help it get what it needs. The petals of brightly-colored flowers attract insects and hummingbirds which feed on nectar and, at the same time, carry pollen from one flower to another.

One form of protective coloration is called *mimicry*. This coloring makes animals that are defenseless against their enemies look like other animals which are feared or avoided. For example, some moths and flies look like bees and wasps. The viceroy butterfly, an insect that birds like to eat, has a color pattern similar to that of the monarch butterfly, which birds do not like to eat.

Another form of protective coloration is called *warning coloration*. Many brightly colored insects, such as ladybugs, milkweed bugs, bumblebees, and wasps, are unpleasant tasting and bristly textured. Their warning coloration reminds predatory creatures of previous experiences with similar insects, and frightens them away.

Protective coloration has developed over tens of thousands of years. Plants and animals that were not properly protected against enemies were destroyed. Those individuals protected by color continued to live and reproduce their kind. This process in nature is known as *natural selection*.   C. BROOKE WORTH

Related Articles in WORLD BOOK include:

Animal (Animal Defenses; color picture, Animal Camouflage)
Bird (How Birds Protect Themselves; color picture, Color Protects Them)
Butterfly (Disguises; color picture, Kallima)
Flounder (picture)
Mimicry
Walking Stick

PROTECTIVE TARIFF. See TARIFF.

PROTECTORATE, *proh TECK tur it,* is a weak country that is controlled by a stronger country. Protectorates usually have a certain amount of self-government, but the "protecting" nation has the final voice in important matters. The protecting power conducts all foreign relations for the protectorate, and also handles its defense and finances.   PAYSON S. WILD, JR.

PROTEIN, *PRO teen,* is a chemical compound that is an essential part of every cell. All living things must have proteins to stay alive. Proteins repair damaged cells, build new tissues, and do many other vital jobs. All proteins contain the chemical elements carbon, hydrogen, nitrogen, and oxygen. Some proteins also contain sulfur or phosphorus. Men and animals make proteins from food. Plants make proteins from simple substances, using energy that came originally from sunlight (see PHOTOSYNTHESIS).

Importance of Proteins. Most of the flesh of animals and most of the living matter in plants are proteins. All *enzymes* (substances that speed up chemical reactions in the body) and most hormones are proteins (see HORMONE). So are all antigens and antibodies. *Antigens* are proteins from other organisms that may make a person ill when present in the body. The body fights them by producing *antibodies*, which neutralize the antigens. See ANTIBODY; ENZYME.

People become seriously ill if they do not get enough proteins. For example, some children in Africa and Central and South America suffer from a disease called *kwashiorkor* because their food is low in proteins. They grow slowly and have little resistance to diseases. Some babies are born lacking an enzyme needed to make best use of the food they eat. As a result, certain by-products from the proteins may build up in the body in sufficient amounts to harm the brain (see MENTAL RETARDATION [Causes]).

Some persons suffer from a disease called *sickle-cell anemia* because their blood cells contain a kind of protein not exactly suited to its job. Blood cells containing such faulty protein frequently collapse, causing anemia (see ANEMIA).

THE FOOD VALUE OF PROTEINS

The food value of a protein depends on the kind and amount of amino acids it contains, not on the total amount of protein in each serving. Peanuts are high in total protein, but the *biological value* of the protein (percentage of useful amino acids) is low. Eggs have a much lower percentage of protein, but the percentage of useful amino acids in an egg is three times that in a peanut.

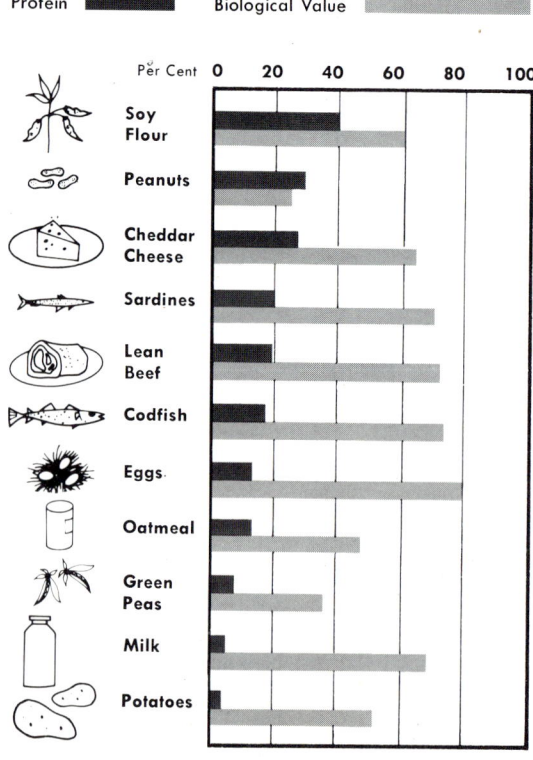

734

Structure of Proteins. Proteins consist of many units called *amino acids* linked together in long chains. Amino acids are organic acids that contain nitrogen (see AMINO ACID). The individual chains, called *peptides*, either lie straight, or coiled like a spring. At intervals along their lengths, they are linked to other peptide chains to form the complex network of peptides that makes up a protein.

Proteins in Food. The protein value of foods depends on the amounts and proportions of amino acids in them. Foods of high protein value include lean meat, fish, cheese, eggs, and milk. These foods are not only rich in proteins, but also contain all the amino acids needed by the body. *Gelatin* is a protein with little food value because it lacks two kinds of amino acids that the body needs.

Proteins are digested in the stomach and small intestine, and are absorbed into the blood as amino acids. The amino acids are carried to all organs and tissues, where they are used to build new cells.

Making Proteins. Living things make proteins from amino acids in their cells. Scientists have found more than 20 kinds of amino acids in plant and animal cells.

A single protein molecule may contain many hundreds of each of about 20 kinds of amino acids. The total number of amino acids, the number of each kind of amino acid, and the order in which the acids are arranged vary from protein to protein. For these reasons, the possible number of proteins a cell could make from its amino acids is vast. But most cells make only the kinds of proteins they need.

Most scientists believe the job of making proteins is controlled by a kind of nucleic acid called *DNA* (see NUCLEIC ACID). DNA is present in the cell nucleus. Scientists believe DNA directs the making of a compound called *messenger RNA*. Messenger RNA carries information for combining amino acids in the proper order to make the kinds of proteins the cell needs. Messenger RNA molecules leave the nucleus and travel to the *cytoplasm* (part of the cell outside the nucleus). In the cytoplasm, they attach themselves to tiny particles called *microsomes*. The cytoplasm already contains a group of compounds called *soluble RNA* that are different from messenger RNA compounds. There is a soluble RNA compound for each kind of amino acid. Amino acids combine with their soluble RNA partners and travel to the microsomes. There, under the direction of messenger RNA, they are assembled into proteins (see CELL [Producing Proteins; The Code of Life]).   D. RALPH STRENGTH

Related Articles in WORLD BOOK include:

Albumin	Enzyme	Milk (Proteins)
Amino Acid	Gelatin	Nucleic Acid
Cheese	Gluten	Nutrition (Proteins;
Eggs	Life	tables)

PROTEROZOIC ERA. See EARTH (The Earth's Earliest History).

PROTESILAUS, *proh TESS uh LAY us,* was a Greek chief who fought in the Trojan War. An oracle said that the first Greek to set foot on Trojan soil would die at once. Protesilaus saw that the other chiefs did not want to land. He jumped ashore and was instantly killed by the Trojans.

See also TROY.

PROTEST. See NOTE.

PROTESTANT, *PRAHT us tunt,* is the general name for all Christian denominations outside the Roman Catholic or Eastern Orthodox churches. Protestants number about 316 million. This total includes official church members, as well as persons not formally connected with special denominations. For membership of the various Protestant denominations in the United States, see RELIGION (table).

Protestantism resulted from a great religious and political movement, the Reformation, which began in Europe in the 1500's. The word *protestant* comes from the Latin *protestans, one who protests.* It was first used in Germany in 1529. At that time a *Diet* (special assembly) at Speyer decreed that the Bible should be taught only along the lines authorized by the Roman Catholic Church. The assembly also decreed that the Mass should be restored in the German states where it had been discontinued. Several princes and 14 imperial cities made a formal protest against the decrees. Because of their protest, they became known as *Protestants.* The name soon came to mean all those who separated from the Catholic Church.

Characteristics. There are hundreds of Protestant denominations and sects that differ slightly or greatly from each other. But certain features characterize almost all Protestants.

Protestants accept the Bible as the reliable and final source of information about God and the salvation of man. They prefer the Bible, rather than church authority, as the final rule of faith, because they believe it is closer to anything else to the original events in the life of Jesus Christ.

The meaning of key Biblical passages is usually open to dispute and subject to several interpretations. Protestants believe that each person should rely on his own judgment in religious matters. In accepting the Bible as the authority for his beliefs, a Protestant sets himself up as the judge and interpreter of the Bible. This principle of "private judgment" accounts for the great variety of sects that characterize Protestantism.

Protestants teach "the priesthood of all believers." They encourage each person to rely on his own conscience and to listen to his own judgment as God speaks to him. Protestants do not dispense with all authority, but place themselves under what they consider the true authority, that of God addressing the individual directly.

Protestantism teaches the doctrine of *callings* (vocations). This means that God calls each person to do a certain job in life. Because God assigns this work, it is sacred and important no matter how humble it may seem to be. It does not have to be a religious vocation.

Many Protestants also hold a special view of original sin. They believe that all men are lost by Adam's fall, but that some persons, through no merit of their own, are saved by God's grace.

Protestantism has tended, among certain churches, to stress the transcendence of God and to minimize the liturgical aspects of Christianity, stressing simple church services, decorations, and organization. Protestants stress preaching and hearing of *the Word* (Bible teachings) rather than practice of the sacraments. Many Protestants believe in the doctrine of "justification by faith." This is the act by which a sinner is freed through faith

PROTESTANT

from the penalty of his sin, and is accepted by God as worthy of being saved.

Main Branches. Protestantism may be said to have expressed itself in two main forms, *classical Protestantism* and *radical Protestantism*. Classical Protestantism includes the original groups which first revolted against the Roman Catholic Church, especially Lutherans, Calvinists, and Anglicans. Lutheranism, founded by Martin Luther, was the earliest expression of Protestantism. Lutherans live mainly in Germany, the United States, and the Scandinavian countries. Calvinism, or Reformed Christianity, came second in historical order, and forms one of the largest Protestant denominations in the world. It originated in the teachings of John Calvin. Protestant denominations which follow Calvinistic teachings include the Presbyterians, and various Reformed churches in America and Europe. Anglicanism grew out of Henry VIII's break with the Roman Catholic Church. It includes the Church of England and related groups such as the Protestant Episcopal Church in the United States.

Radical Protestantism designates religious groups that broke away from classical Protestantism, or grew up independently. Many such sects were formed around some particular doctrine which members of the group felt to be expressive of the essential core of Christianity. Several radical Protestant denominations stress *evangelicalism* (salvation through repentance and faith in Christ). Members often exhibit an intensely personal religious commitment, and may view the church as essentially a voluntary association. The main groups include Baptists, Congregationalists, and Methodists.

Unity Movements. Protestant denominations have shown an increasing desire to overcome the old divisions. The *ecumenical movement* seeks to unite not only various Protestant denominations and sects, but also Catholic, Protestant, and Eastern Orthodox churches.

In 1846, a group in London formed the Evangelical Alliance to provide individual Christians with an opportunity to unite in friendship and discussion. About the same time, the YMCA and YWCA were organized in England. In 1895, the World Student Christian Federation brought together U.S. and European students to seek ways of extending the Christian faith to all students.

In the early 1900's, churchmen held conventions of Protestant denominations, as well as meetings between Protestants and representatives of the Eastern Orthodox Churches. In 1948, church leaders founded the World Council of Churches, made up of Protestant and Eastern Orthodox groups.　　　　　HOWARD R. BURKLE

Related Articles in WORLD BOOK include:

PROTESTANT LEADERS

Abbott, Lyman	Channing, William E.
Asbury, Francis	Cotton, John
Barth, Karl	Coverdale, Miles
Beecher (family)	Cranmer, Thomas
Booth (family)	Donne, John
Brewster, William	Dowie, John A.
Brooks, Phillips	Drummond, Henry
Buchman, Frank	Dyer, Mary
Bunyan, John	Eddy, Mary Baker
Bushnell, Horace	Edwards, Jonathan
Calvin, John	Finney, Charles G.
Chalmers, Thomas	Fosdick, Harry E.

Fox, George	Raikes, Robert
Fry, Franklin C	Ridley, Nicholas
Graham, Billy	Ritschl, Albrecht
Hooker, Richard	Seabury, Samuel
Hooker, Thomas	Smith, Joseph
Huss, John	Smith, Joseph F.
Hutchinson, Anne M.	Smith, Samuel F.
Kagawa, Toyohiko	Söderblom, Nathan
Kierkegaard, Søren A.	Spurgeon, Charles H.
Knox, John	Sunday, Billy
Latimer, Hugh	Swedenborg, Emanuel
Laud, William	Talmage, Thomas D.
Luther, Martin	Taylor, Jeremy
Makemie, Francis	Tennent (brothers)
Manning, William T.	Tillich, Paul
Marshall, Peter	Trench, Richard
Mather (family)	Tyndale, William
McPherson, Aimee S.	Watts, Isaac
Melanchthon, Philipp	Wesley (family)
Moody, Dwight L.	Whitefield, George
Mott, John R.	Wilberforce (Samuel)
Muhlenberg (family)	Williams, Roger
Niebuhr (family)	Wycliffe, John
Oxnam, Garfield Bromley	Young, Brigham
Peale, Norman Vincent	Zwingli, Huldreich
Penn, William	

PROTESTANT CHURCHES AND GROUPS

See ANGLICANS; BAPTISTS; LUTHERANS; METHODISTS; PRESBYTERIANS; and the articles on specific churches listed in these articles. See also the following:

Adventists	Jehovah's Witnesses
Amanites	Latter Day Saints, Re-
Amish	organized Church of
Assemblies of God	Jesus Christ of
Brethren	Mennonites
Christian Church (Disciples	Moravian Church
of Christ)	Mormons
Christian Reformed Church	Pentecostal Churches
Christian Scientists	Quakers
Church of God in Christ	Reformed Churches in
Church of the Nazarene	America
Churches of Christ	Schwenkfelders
Churches of God	Seventh-day Adventists
Congregational Christian	Shakers
Church	Swedenborgians
Doukhobors	Unitarian Universalist
Evangelical United	Association
Brethren Church	Unitarians
House of David	United Church of Canada
Hutterites	United Church of Christ

PROTESTANT ORGANIZATIONS

Baptist Training Union	Unity School of
Baptist Youth Fellowships	Christianity
Bible Society, American	Volunteers of America
Christian Endeavor	Walther League
Evangelical Alliance	World Council of Churches
Gideons International	Young Men's Christian
Luther League	Association
Moody Bible Institute	Young Women's Christian
National Council of	Association
Churches	Youth for Christ
Salvation Army, The	International
United Methodist	
Youth Fellowship	

OTHER RELATED ARTICLES

Anabaptists	Nonconformist
Augsburg Confession	Oneida Community
Camp Meeting	Oxford Movement
Covenanters	Predestination
Fundamentalism	Puritan
Great Awakening	Reformation
Huguenots	Thirty-Nine Articles
Hussites	Tractarians
Lollards	Waldenses

PROTEUS, *PRO tyoos,* or *PRO tee us,* was a minor Greek god of the sea. He served as herdsman for the flocks of seals and other creatures of the sea. His greatest power was his ability to change his shape instantly. He could become a savage animal, fire, or water whenever he wanted to. He also was noted for his wisdom and knowledge of future events. The person who wished to have Proteus answer a question had to catch him and hold him fast in spite of all his changing forms. Only then would he answer.   O. M. PEARL

PROTISTA is a group of one-celled organisms. Members of this group are called *protists.* Most protists are so small they can only be seen under a microscope. Protists may have characteristics of both animals and plants. Some scientists classify them in a *kingdom* (group) called *Protista* in the system of scientific classification. Other scientists classify these organisms in two kingdoms, Protista and *Monera.* When separated in two kingdoms, Protista includes organisms called *protozoans.* Monera includes bacteria and blue-green *algae* (seaweed). See also CLASSIFICATION; MONERA.

PROTISTS. See EVOLUTION (The Theory of Evolution).

PROTIUM. See HYDROGEN (Properties).

PROTOCOL, *PRO toh kahl,* is a document containing a record of talks carried on by diplomatic representatives. The document shows that the diplomats have agreed on important issues. A protocol is an official government paper, but it does not have the force of a treaty until ratified by the governments concerned (see TREATY). The term *protocol* also means the elaborate official etiquette of state ceremonies.   PAYSON S. WILD

See also DIPLOMACY.

PROTON, *PRO tahn,* is a positively charged particle found in the nucleus of an atom. Protons, with neutrons and electrons, are the units from which atoms are built (see ELECTRON; NEUTRON). A proton has a mass 1,836 times that of an electron. A hydrogen atom has one proton. Heavier atoms have more. See also ATOM; BARYON; ELECTRICITY (Basic Principles).

PROTON ACCELERATOR. See ATOM SMASHER.

PROTOPLASM is usually a colorless, jellylike substance. It is found in all living matter, both plant and animal. Protoplasm has been called the "physical basis of life," because it is the substance in which all the vital processes center. All plants and animals are made up of cells. A cell is simply a tiny bit of protoplasm enclosed by a thin tissue called the *cell membrane.* Most cells have two parts. A bit of protoplasm in the center of the cell, called the *nucleus,* controls the metabolism and reproduction of the cell. The protoplasm outside the nucleus is called the *cytoplasm.* Neither the nucleus nor the cytoplasm can function without the other.

The chemical structure of both the nucleus and the cytoplasm is very complex. Protoplasm is not one particular substance with a definite chemical composition. Rather, it is a mixture of several different chemical compounds. The composition of these compounds differs from cell to cell, and from one group of body tissues to another. The most important chemical compounds found in protoplasm are proteins, which are compounds of carbon, hydrogen, oxygen, and nitrogen. Sulfur, phosphorus, and other elements are also present. Protoplasm usually contains fats and carbohydrates.

These two substances have no nitrogen. In all the compounds present, carbon is the essential element.

Chemists can analyze the composition of protoplasm, but they do not know why it lives. The same elements that are found in protoplasm are found in nonliving things. But in living matter, these elements are so arranged that certain chemical reactions take place, because life is a continual rebuilding of matter.

Some properties of protoplasm may be readily seen in the activities of a one-celled animal such as the ameba. This tiny creature is a mass of protoplasm that moves and responds to changes in temperature and touch. The protoplasm can take in food and throw off waste matter. It breathes, and it can reproduce itself by cell division. The problem of duplicating the chemical structure and activities of protoplasm has been studied by chemists for many years. But protoplasm has not yet been duplicated in a laboratory.   E. V. COWDRY

See also AMEBA; CELL; CILIA; COLLOID; LIFE (The Structure of Living Things).

PROTOZOAN, *PROH toh ZO un,* is a one-celled animal that is a member of the phylum *Protozoa.* Protozoans are the simplest kind of animals, and therefore the lowest group in the animal kingdom. The term *protozoan* comes from Greek, and means *first animal.* All other animals, called *metazoa,* consist of many cells.

Characteristics of Protozoa

There are about 20,000 kinds of protozoa, most of them so small that they can be seen only through a microscope. Therefore, they are sometimes called *microzoa.* Nearly all protozoans live in water.

Structure. The *ameba* is one of the simplest protozoans. The single cell that makes up its body carries on all the necessary life processes by itself. The cell eats, breathes, and responds to its surroundings. There are no special organs for any of the ameba's activities. When the ameba moves, it thrusts a part of the cell in one direction and draws the rest of the cell after the thrust-out part.

Other protozoans are more complicated in structure. Some of them, called *ciliates,* have tiny hairlike projections that help them move about. The *paramecium* has a definite groove on one side that serves as a mouth.

Some one-celled animals have a bright red spot called the *eyespot.* This spot may be sensitive to light.

The bodies of some protozoans contain chlorophyll, the green substance also found in plants. This enables them to make their own food (see PHOTOSYNTHESIS).

Reproduction. Some protozoans reproduce by splitting in two. Each half of the original cell becomes a separate animal. In other protozoans, the parent cell suddenly swells in one direction. The swollen part breaks off and forms a new animal. This process is called *budding.* A third form of reproduction occurs among protozoa that are parasites, such as the tiny animal that causes malaria. These protozoans reproduce by dividing into many smaller cells called *spores.* The paramecium shows the beginnings of sexual reproduction. In all these methods of reproduction, the nucleus of the cell is divided among the new animals. See REPRODUCTION.

Usefulness. In spite of their small size, protozoans

PROTOZOA

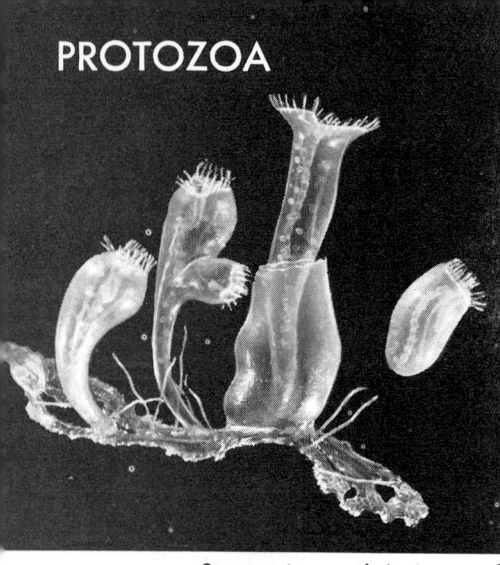

Stentor is one of the largest of the protozoa. It assumes many forms.

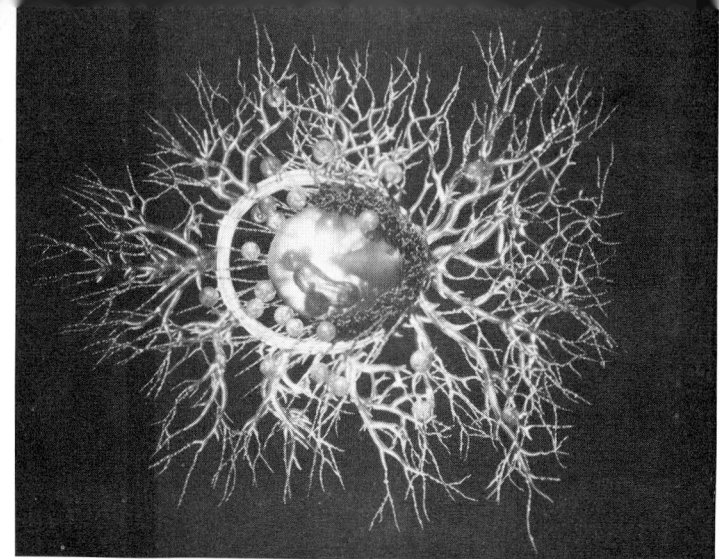

Radiolaria Have Complex Skeletons of unusual beauty. One of the most remarkable of these one-celled animals is this Lithocircus magnificus.

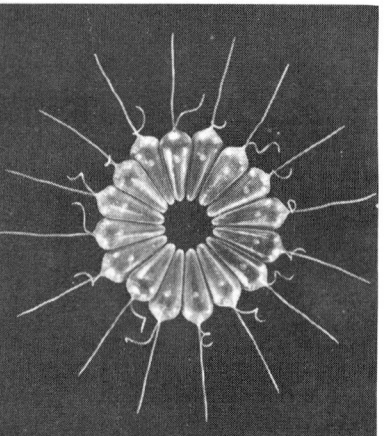

Cyclonexus Annularis forms this balanced, simple ring colony.

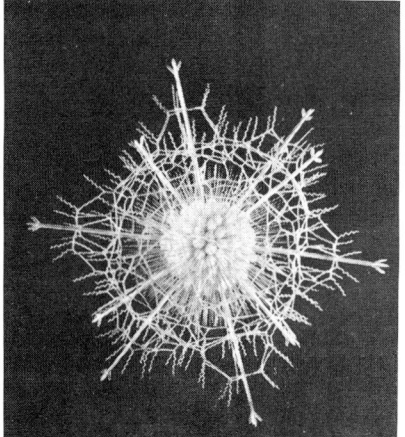

Lychonosphaera Regina is a tiny protozoan from Pacific surface waters.

Globigerina is covered with spines radiating from its limestone shell

Photos of Glass Models from Bausch & Lomb; American Museum of Natural History

Arcella Is Enclosed by Its Hemispherical Shell. The pseudopods, or "feet," extend from a hole on the under side. When the animal divides, one "daughter" retains the shell. The other has to construct a new one by its secretions.

are very important for both human beings and animals. Millions of protozoans swim in the sea. Other sea animals eat them, and even whales depend partly on these one-celled creatures for food. Some protozoans, such as the foraminifers, are covered with stony shells. When the animals die, they settle to the bottom of the ocean and contribute to the formation of limestone. The fossil shells of these and other protozoans are largely responsible for the chalk cliffs in southern England.

Many one-celled animals are serious enemies of human beings and animals. Malaria and African sleeping sickness are among the diseases they cause.

Kinds of Protozoans

There are four basic divisions among the protozoans: (1) the flagellates, (2) the Sarcodina, (3) the Sporozoa, and (4) the ciliates. They are divided according to the ways they move about.

Flagellates have one or more long hairlike projections from their bodies called *flagella*. These flagella whip about rapidly to move the flagellate through the water. Flagellates are usually oval in shape, and many have chlorophyll in their bodies. The green *euglena* is shaped much like a submarine. It is common in fresh water. The *volvox* is a green ball of flagellated cells that live together. This ball moves about when the flagella of the individual members which make it up are whipped in the water. The *trypanosomes*, which cause African sleeping sickness, are also flagellates.

The Sarcodina group includes various protozoans that resemble ameba. Many of these amebalike protozoans live in the bodies of human beings and animals. Some cause disease and others do not. For example, the harmless mouth ameba is found in the mouths of about three of every four persons.

Radiolaria are among this group of amebalike protozoans. Radiolarians have a tiny skeleton that is made of silica. After a radiolarian dies this skeleton sinks to the ocean floor. Millions of shells have accumulated in parts of the ocean, forming thick layers of ooze. The *foraminifers* have shells made of chalklike material. Some of the ancient foraminifers were almost as large as a quarter. Geologists seeking oil study foraminifer fossil shells in rocks found below the surface. They indicate how the earth layers are arranged.

The Sporozoa, a special group of protozoans, reproduce by means of spores. They live as parasites. The malarial parasite is the best known of the Sporozoa.

The Ciliates are the most complex one-celled animals. They are also known in zoology as *infusoria*. All of them have, at one time or another, fine hairlike projections called *cilia*. These cilia help them move about to capture food. The *stentors*, which are shaped something like a horn or trumpet, rank among the largest of all single-celled animals. Another kind of ciliate, the *vorticella*, looks something like a funnel with a long tube. The vorticella creates a little whirlpool around the top of the funnel to draw in food.   RALPH BUCHSBAUM

Related Articles in WORLD BOOK include:

Ameba	Euglena	Paramecium
Cell	Fission	Trypanosome
Cilia	Nummulite	

PROTOZOOLOGY, PROH *toh zoh AHL oh jih*, is the branch of the zoological sciences that deals with the study of protozoa (see PROTOZOAN). Persons who special-

PROUDHON, PIERRE JOSEPH

ize in this field are called *protozoologists*. These scientists usually have completed extensive study in invertebrate zoology. They then limit their work to the protozoa.

PROTRACTOR is a device for measuring the size of angles. Protractors are made of plastic, paper, or metal. They are usually a semicircle. The angles from 0 to 180 degrees (or, occasionally, from 0 to 3200 mils) are printed or cut on them. The bottom edge is placed along one line of the angle. The reading is made where the other line crosses the scale.

Plane protractors lie flat on the work on the drafting board. One plane protractor can measure all the angles on any size of drafting board. A spherical protractor, used in astronomy and navigation, indicates measure-

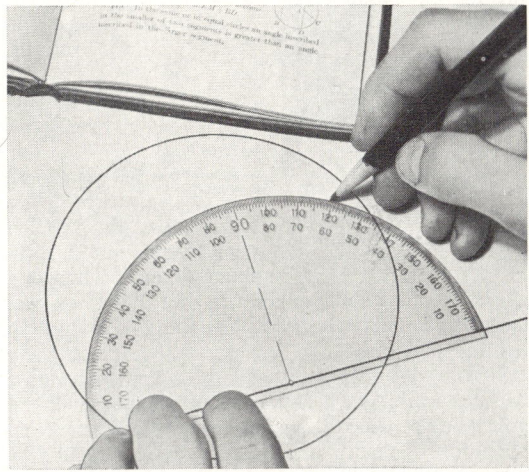

Press Syndicate
A Student Measures Angles by Use of a Protractor.

ments of spherical angles and is made of paper or plastic bent into the arc of a sphere. Only one size of sphere can be used with a spherical protractor.   PHILLIP S. JONES

See also MECHANICAL DRAWING.

PROTURA, a small order of primitive insects, is made up of about 90 species. All Protura are very small, and none have antennae or wings. They live in damp places, such as between decaying leaves or in moss.

PROUD FLESH. See GRANULATION.

PROUDHON, PROO *DAWN*, **PIERRE JOSEPH** (1809-1865), was a French socialist and reformer. In 1837, he published his *Essai de Grammaire Générale*. This work won him a three-year pension from the Academy of Besançon. But three years later, his *What Is Property?* lost him the academy's approval. This book revealed his socialistic ideas, and stated that "property is theft."

Proudhon wrote many other works. His literary and political activities often led to trouble with the French government. He spent a number of years in prison and in exile. His work is not always consistent and is sometimes difficult to interpret, because of his love for paradoxical and extreme phrases. He condemned owning property, for example, but did not condemn peasant proprietors who neither abused their land nor used it as a source of revenue from others.

Political Ideas. Proudhon was enthusiastic about the ideas of liberty, justice, and equality. His idea of liberty implied the rejection of all authority, except for that in the family. Unlike many other socialist writers, he had little use for the powers of government. He had contempt for representative government and democracy. He was an *anarchist*, or a believer in a social order without government (see ANARCHISM).

Proudhon argued that society should operate by means of contracts. These contracts should be voluntary agreements among free and equal peoples. He believed that the voluntary agreements would establish a system of mutual rights and duties, which would result in justice.

Proudhon urged equality, but was inconsistent in this. He believed in the existence of inferior races, and was a firm opponent of giving greater political and social rights to women.

Brown Bros.
Pierre Joseph Proudhon

Economic Beliefs. Proudhon advocated free credit, and founded the People's Bank to carry out his ideas about finance. The bank gained about 27,000 subscribers, but Proudhon was forced to liquidate it after a few months, because of political difficulties.

In some of his works, Proudhon favored cooperation between workingmen and small proprietors. Such cooperation, he believed, would be more likely to bring about liberty, justice, and equality than any action by the government.

Early Life. Proudhon was born at Besançon, and studied at the College of Besançon. From 1843 to 1847, he worked in a printing plant in Lyon. He moved to Paris in 1848.   H. W. SPIEGEL

PROUST, *proost,* **MARCEL** (1871-1922), was one of the greatest French novelists of the 1900's. His work first seemed to be obscure because of his complex literary style. Critics charged that his subject matter was immoral and decadent. But the lapse of several decades has increased his appeal and revealed to modern readers the striking originality of his technique.

Proust's great work is a fictional autobiography in several volumes that has been translated as *Remembrance of Things Past.* It is a novel of manners, a succession of love stories that end sadly, and a recording of the hero's efforts to become a writer and thereby give significance to his experience. Proust created a colorful series of characters and reflected extensively on art and on society in this complex novel.

Random House, Inc.
Marcel Proust

He was born into a well-to-do family in Paris. He was deeply attached to his cultured and beautiful mother. Proust suffered from asthma and was a semi-invalid for most of his life. After 1900, he wrote constantly in spite of his illness.   HENRI PEYRE

See also FRENCH LITERATURE (The Novel).

PROVENÇAL. See ROMANCE LANGUAGE; TROUBADOUR; MISTRAL, FRÉDÉRIC.

PROVENCE, *praw VAHNS,* was the early name of a former province in southeastern France. The name is still used to refer to that region. The people of Provence spoke Provençal. This was the language of the literature of southern France during the Middle Ages.

PROVERB, *PRAHV urb,* tells a truth or some bit of useful wisdom in a short sentence. The language is generally picturesque and simple. Only those sayings which many people have used for a long time are called proverbs. A man may compose a proverb that becomes a part of everyday speech. But most proverbs have been created through common usage.

Every language has its proverbs. Often the same proverb occurs among several different peoples. In some cases similar proverbs come from the same source. But in other cases they probably have no connection. Lawrence Sterne's "God tempers the wind to the shorn lamb" means the same as the old Turkish proverb "God makes a nest for the blind bird."

The Bible contains an entire book of Proverbs (see PROVERBS). Many of our most common proverbs come from that book. Some of them are:

Hope deferred maketh the heart sick.

A soft answer turneth away wrath.

Pride goeth before destruction.

Miguel de Cervantes' novel *Don Quixote* contains many proverbs. Cervantes collected the proverbs from the Spanish peasants, who supposedly could carry on a sensible conversation for a whole evening in nothing but proverbs (see DON QUIXOTE).

Benjamin Franklin used many proverbial expressions in his *Poor Richard's Almanac.* He wrote many of them himself, and took the rest from other sources. Many are still quoted (see POOR RICHARD'S ALMANAC).

Most real proverbs trace their origins to the early days of a people's history. Today, books and newspapers contain many pointed statements. But few of them become proverbs.   J. N. HOOK

See also EPIGRAM.

PROVERBS is a book in the Old Testament, or Hebrew Bible. It is often called *the Proverbs of Solomon* because, according to tradition, King Solomon wrote it.

The book opens with several poems in praise of wisdom, but most of it consists of shorter epigrams and proverbs. They urge men to develop such virtues as responsibility, honesty, loyalty, and faithfulness. Many of the sayings in Proverbs have become part of everyday speech. Chapter 31, praising a virtuous woman, is one of the best-known passages.

The book of Proverbs is part of the Wisdom literature common to the ancient Egyptians, Syrians, and Mesopotamians. The purpose of this literature was to train young men for the responsibilities of adult life. Proverbs 22: 17 to 24: 22 resembles the Egyptian Wisdom book of *Amenemope.* Many of the Hebrew proverbs are ancient. Scholars believe that they were probably assembled during the period of the Second Temple, in the 300's and 200's B.C.   ROBERT GORDIS

See also PROVERB.

Greater Providence Chamber of Commerce

Office Buildings in the Business District of Providence, R.I., Overlook Narragansett Bay, *background.*

PROVIDENCE, R.I. (pop. 187,061; alt. 80 ft.), is the capital of Rhode Island and the second largest city in New England. Providence is an important Atlantic Coast port. Roger Williams, the founder of Providence, gave the town this name because he believed Divine guidance had brought him there. He is buried in the city (see WILLIAMS, ROGER).

Location, Size, and Description. Providence lies at the head of Narragansett Bay, about 25 miles north of the Atlantic Ocean, and about 45 miles southwest of Boston. The city is laid out on seven hills, and covers an area of nearly 20 square miles. The oldest part of Providence lies on the slope of a stretch of high land, between the Blackstone-Seekonk River on the east and the Moshassuck-Providence River on the west. The present business section, west of the Providence River, was built on land raised from low river banks. With Pawtucket and surrounding parts of Rhode Island and Massachusetts, Providence forms a metropolitan area with a population of 821,101. See RHODE ISLAND (map).

Cultural Life. Brown University is the oldest and most famous of Providence's many educational institutions. Colleges in Providence include Bryant College, Catholic Teachers College, Providence College, Providence-Barrington Bible College, and Rhode Island College.

The Rhode Island School of Design in Providence is one of the greatest textile and jewelry schools in the world. The city has several galleries devoted to sculpture, painting, pottery, and Chinese art. The Pendleton House is noted for its collection of American furniture. The city is the home of the Athenaeum and the John Hay and John Carter Brown libraries. The Rhode Island Historical, the Annmary Brown, and the Audubon Society libraries are also in Providence.

There are many old churches in Providence. The Unitarian Church, built in 1816, has a bell cast by Paul Revere and his son. Saint John's Church was founded in 1722. The present building dates from 1810. The First Baptist Church was founded by Roger Williams. Historic buildings in the city include the Stephen Hop-

kins House, whose owner was governor of the state ten times, and the Esek Hopkins House, the home of the first commander in chief of the American navy. John Brown House, built by a famous merchant in 1786, is an outstanding example of Georgian architecture. Another historic building is the Old Colony House, or State House, built in 1763. The state Capitol, officially opened in 1901, is made of white Georgia marble (see RHODE ISLAND [color picture]). Homes dating from the 1700's stand on the city's east side.

Recreation. Roger Williams Park covers more than 400 acres. Park attractions include a statue in memory of Roger Williams, a natural history museum, a temple of music, and many fountains and rose gardens. Lincoln Woods Park near the city covers 627 acres. Most of the park is heavily wooded. It provides fresh-water swimming, bridle paths, and picnic areas.

Industry and Trade. Factories in Providence make cotton and woolen goods, jewelry, and machines and tools. Much gold, silver, and bronze work is done in the city. Other products include screws, files, knives, artificial flowers, and rubber goods. The first fully automated U.S. Post Office operates in Providence.

History. Providence was founded in 1636 by Roger Williams after he was exiled from Massachusetts. It was the first settlement in Rhode Island. Providence received a city charter in 1832. For many years both Newport and Providence were capitals of Rhode Island. In 1900, Providence became the only capital.

The seat of Providence County, the city has a mayor-council type of government. CLARKSON A. COLLINS III

PROVIDENCE COLLEGE is a private liberal arts school for men at Providence, R.I. It is controlled and conducted by the Roman Catholic Dominican Fathers, but is open to students of all faiths. The college grants bachelor's degrees in arts, science, and business administration. It was founded in 1917. For enrollment, see UNIVERSITIES AND COLLEGES (table).

PROVIDENCE PLANTATIONS. See RHODE ISLAND (Settlement).

PROVINCE, *PRAHV ins,* in Roman times, was a conquered district ruled by an official from Rome. Later, independent countries that united to form a state frequently called themselves provinces. An example is the United Provinces of Holland. Still later, independent countries were divided into provinces. Today, many countries have provinces.

In North America, the term *province* usually refers to one of the political divisions of Canada. There are 10 of these provinces. Each has its own local government. Canadian provinces perform much the same functions as American states.   JOHN R. ALDEN

See also CANADA, GOVERNMENT OF (Provincial and Territorial Governments); CHARTER.

PROVINCETOWN. See MAYFLOWER.

PROVISIONAL GOVERNMENT is a temporary government set up because of an emergency such as war, revolution, or other disorder. Provisional governments are usually not established according to constitutional patterns. Instead, rebels may seize power, hoping to establish a new order.   ROBERT G. NEUMANN

PROVO, Utah (pop. 36,047), is the third largest city in the state. It was named for Étienne Provot, an early fur trapper. The city lies at the foot of the Wasatch Range, at an altitude of 4,549 feet, and overlooks Utah Lake to the west. Provo is about 40 miles south of Salt Lake City (see UTAH [political map]). Provo and nearby Orem form a metropolitan area with a population of 106,991. Provo is known as the *Steel Center of the West,* because the Geneva Steel Company is nearby.

Provo is in Utah County, an agricultural region. The city is the home of Brigham Young University. The region was first visited in September, 1776, by a party of exploring missionaries led by Father Silvestre Escalante, a Spanish priest. Provo was founded in 1849 by Mormon pioneers. The city has a commission form of government.   A. R. MORTENSEN

PROVOST is a superintendent or ruling head. He is an administrative officer in some universities and colleges. The term *provost* also applies to a church or cathedral dignitary, and a military police officer.

PROVOST MARSHAL GENERAL directs the United States Army Military Police Corps. He supervises activities relating to prisoners of war, crime investigations, desertions and absences without leave, and security clearances. The chief military police officer of an army field unit or post is called the *provost marshal.* See also MILITARY POLICE.

PROW is the name sometimes given to the *bow* (front end) of a boat.

PROXIMA CENTAURI. See CENTAURUS.

PROXY is a substitute. Suppose you have been assigned to deliver an important report before a meeting of your club. On the day of the meeting you are too ill to attend. You therefore call upon another club member to act for you. This club member becomes your *proxy* and delivers your report to the club meeting.

The use of a proxy is limited almost entirely to business meetings. A stockholder in a corporation may be unable to attend a meeting of the organization. He may then request another stockholder to vote for him on any issue. This must be a formal request. The person who casts the vote is known as a proxy. The paper which authorizes him to vote is also known as a proxy. Stockholders of national banks may vote by proxy, but bank clerks and tellers may not be proxies for the stockholders.

Voting by proxy is forbidden at political elections, but during political conventions many delegates vote by proxy. In past years, marriage by proxy was common, especially among royalty. Some states in the United States permit such marriages.   JOHN ALAN APPLEMAN

PRUDENTIAL INSURANCE COMPANY OF AMERICA. See INSURANCE (table, 25 Largest Life Insurance Companies).

PRUNE is a sweet plum that has been dried. The drying gives prunes their wrinkled appearance. Plums that are especially well suited to drying are called *prune plums.* The prune is healthful because of its high iron and vitamin content.

Prune plums were first grown in western Asia, near the Caucasus Mountains and the Caspian Sea. Today they are a leading crop in California, where about 150,-000 tons of the dried fruit are produced each year. The warm, dry climate of the fertile California valleys provides ideal growing conditions. Prunes are also grown in central Europe and South America.

The French prune plum (Prune d'Agen) makes up 90 per cent of the prune production in California. It was brought to the United States from France by Louis Pellier, a fruit grower, in 1856. Other prune plums include the Imperial, the Sugar, and the Robe de Sergeant.

Prune plum trees usually produce a large crop seven years after planting. The trees sprout white blossoms in spring. The fruit develops in summer. In August or September, the fully developed fruit either falls to the ground or is gently shaken from the tree. It is then taken to a dehydrator in lug boxes or portable bins, where it is washed. The dehydrator dries the plums with a forced draft of hot air. The drying lasts from 14 to 24 hours. This drying process reduces $2\frac{1}{2}$ pounds of fresh plums to about one pound of prunes.

The prunes are placed in bins, where they are *cured* for at least two weeks. Curing gives the prunes a uniform moisture content of between 18 and 20 per cent. The prunes are then graded according to size. Before the prunes are packed to be sold, they are given a hot water or steam bath to pasteurize them and to bring their moisture content to between 26 and 32 per cent.

Critically reviewed by the CALIFORNIA PRUNE ADVISORY BOARD

See also PLUM.

Prunes come from special varieties of plums that can be dried without spoiling the fruit. Prune plums require a warm climate.

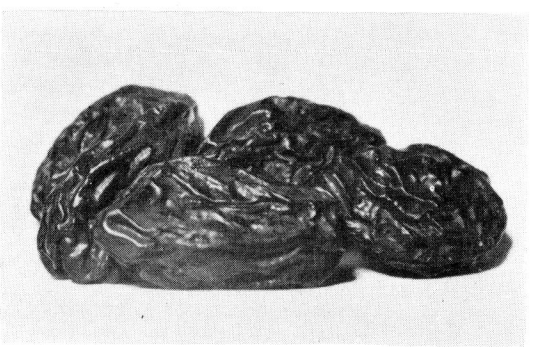

Dead Branches should be removed immediately

Obstructing Branches should be taken off

Splits in the crotch should be cabled

Pruning makes trees more symmetrical

The Top should not be cut off

PRINCIPLES OF PRUNING

Correct Pruning is shown in Figure 1. The cut is at a sharp angle just above the bud. In (2) the cut is too long. In (3) it is too high above the bud. In (4) it is too close to the top bud.

CUTTING OFF A BRANCH

To Remove a Limb, cut at (1) first. Follow with cut (2). Then cut off the stub (3) as close to the trunk as possible.

PRUNING

TOOLS USED IN PRUNING

(1) Pole saw; (2) pole pruner; (3) mallet; (4) cross-cut saw; (5) heavy-duty saw; (6) pruning saw; (7) pruning knife; (8) two-hand pruner, or lopper; (9) hedge shears; (10) ax; (11) pruning shears; (12) wedge; (13) chisel; (14) gouge.

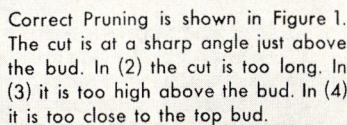
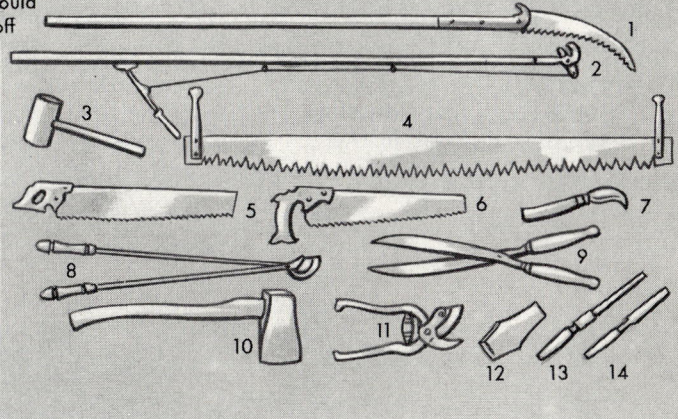

PRUNING is the cutting away of plant parts, such as branches, shoots, buds, or roots. Pruning helps plants recover from the shock of being moved. It controls the shape and beauty of ornamental plants. Pruning also helps improve the quantity and quality of fruit.

Transplanted trees and shrubs are pruned to prevent water loss through the leaves. Usually about a third of the leaf-producing area is removed. Whole branches may be removed or the top third of each branch may be cut.

However, the top of a shade tree should not be pruned, for that would destroy the shape of the tree. Spruce, pine, and similar evergreens usually are not cut. They develop naturally into their characteristic shapes. But junipers and cedars used for foundation plantings are often sheared to a desired form.

Gardeners remove weak stems from shrubs at ground level. The diseased and broken branches are also removed. People prune shrubs that flower early in the spring, such as lilacs, just after they flower. Shrubs that flower in the summer, like hybrid tea roses, are pruned in the spring. Gardeners shear hedges periodically to encourage dense and compact growth and to maintain a desired shape.

Fruitgrowers keep their fruit trees well pruned. By cutting out undesirable parts, they obtain low trees with open tops. This allows light to reach all parts of the tree. It also makes spraying the trees and picking the ripe fruit easier. Well-pruned trees produce high-quality fruit. Trees pruned so that the limbs are well spaced will not break when the heavy fruit loads down their branches.

Training of a fruit tree begins when the tree is about a year old. At that time, the grower cuts the top from the tree. This stimulates the development of branches. When the new branches are about a month old, the grower selects the strongest and best ones to remain on the tree. He cuts the others off. During their early years, fruit trees require only a little pruning. Old trees are usually pruned heavily to increase their vigor and production.

HENRY T. NORTHEN

See FRUIT.

PRUSSIA

PRUSSIA, *PRUSH ah,* was a powerful military nation in north-central Europe, for hundreds of years. When the Prussian king became emperor of a united Germany, in 1871, Prussia became the largest state in the German Empire. After World War II, Prussia was broken up into small districts and ceased to exist as a German state. Much of the land once called Prussia now lies in Communist East Germany, Poland, and Russia.

Prussia was more than the name of a country, however. It also represented a military way of life. Prussian armies were among the most rigidly drilled and disciplined in the world. The generals, from the aristocratic class called *Junkers,* owned huge estates.

The Land and Its Resources. At the height of its power in the late 1800's, Prussia occupied the northern two thirds of Germany. It extended from Belgium and The Netherlands on the west to Russia on the east. The North Sea and the Baltic Sea bordered Prussia on the north. Austria-Hungary lay to the south.

Prussia had a low, sandy coast, bordered by many lagoons. The coast was separated from the central plain of Prussia by a belt of lakes and tree-covered hills. The central plain contained many lakes and waterways. Highlands to the south contained deposits of coal, iron, silver, copper, nickel, and lead. The most fertile land for farming lay in the valleys of the Oder, Elbe, and Rhine rivers.

The People and Their Work. The rulers of Prussia, headed by the royal family of Hohenzollern, controlled lands originally peopled by Slavs, and conquered and colonized by Germans in the Middle Ages. There were about 200 families of hereditary aristocrats, or Junkers, who owned most of the land. Men who worked the farms had no land of their own, and served in the Prussian army about eight or nine months each year.

The main cities of Prussia were Berlin, the capital, and Königsberg (now Kaliningrad) in East Prussia.

Early History. The story of the rise of the Hohenzollern family is the story of Prussia. The Hohenzollerns were a family of German counts. In 1415, the Hohenzollerns became rulers, or *margraves,* of the large district, or *mark,* of Brandenburg. When they came to take part in the election of the Holy Roman Emperor, they received the title of *Elector of Brandenburg.* In the 1600's, the Hohenzollerns won the districts of West Prussia and East Prussia from Poland.

Prussia was greatly strengthened during the rule of the Great Elector, Frederick William, from 1640 to 1688. His son, Frederick I, was crowned the first King of Prussia in 1701. He built a strong army.

Frederick the Great, or **Frederick II,** came to the throne of Prussia in 1740. He helped form the Prussian theory of government based on discipline and authority. He believed in the idea "might makes right." His tax collectors were called *war commissars,* and all the members of his cabinet were called *war ministers.*

Using the strong army his father had organized, he seized Silesia from Austria in 1740. During the Seven Years' War, he gained additional land. In the late 1700's, he partitioned Poland with Russia and Austria.

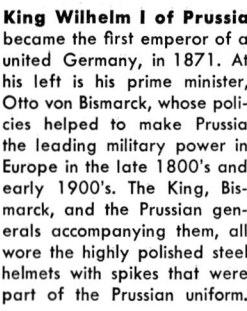

King Wilhelm I of Prussia became the first emperor of a united Germany, in 1871. At his left is his prime minister, Otto von Bismarck, whose policies helped to make Prussia the leading military power in Europe in the late 1800's and early 1900's. The King, Bismarck, and the Prussian generals accompanying them, all wore the highly polished steel helmets with spikes that were part of the Prussian uniform.

Napoleonic Period. Less skillful rulers followed Frederick the Great, and Napoleon easily defeated the Prussians in 1806. To restore Prussia's power, Gerhard von Scharnhorst and August von Gneisenau set up universal military training. The schools were designed to make the people better soldiers. As a result, more people learned to read and write in Prussia than in any other country of Europe in the 1800's. A new Prussian army under the command of Gebhard von Blücher helped to defeat Napoleon at Leipzig in 1813 and at Waterloo in 1815.

German Empire. Prussia reached the peak of its power after King Wilhelm I came to the throne in 1861 and chose Otto von Bismarck as prime minister. Bismarck greatly strengthened the Prussian army, and set out to unify Germany. In 1864, Prussia and Austria gained the Danish provinces of Schleswig and Holstein. When Austria quarreled with Prussia, Bismarck formed the North German Confederation, including the states north of the Main River. King Wilhelm headed the confederation. Bismarck next maneuvered France into war in 1870, and took Alsace and part of Lorraine as the price of peace. This victory enabled him to persuade the southern states of Germany to join the confederation. In 1871, the North German Confederation became the German Empire. Wilhelm then became the first emperor of the new German Empire.

Decline of Prussia. The Prussian desire for more land was one cause of World War I, but Germany lost. In the peace settlement, a large strip of land was given to Poland. This strip, called *the Polish Corridor*, separated West Prussia from East Prussia. In the new German republic, Prussia and the other states became administrative districts. Hitler started World War II in Europe by invading Poland to take back the land lost in World War I. Prussian generals commanded many of Hitler's armies. The war brought heavy destruction to most of Prussia. At the end of the war, Russia seized the northern half of East Prussia. Poland took the rest of Prussia east of the Oder River, as well as the city of Stettin (now Szczecin) west of the river. The district of Brandenburg was placed in the Russian zone of occupation, or East Germany. In 1947, the state of Prussia was legally abolished by the Allied Control Council. In 1952, Communist East Germany also abolished the province of Brandenburg, dividing it into administrative districts.   JAMES K. POLLOCK

Related Articles in WORLD BOOK include:

Berlin	Hohenzollern
Bismarck	Junker
Blücher, Gebhard von	Krupp
Brandenburg	Louise of Mecklenburg-
Danzig	Strelitz
Franco-Prussian War	Polish Corridor
Frederick of Prussia	Seven Years' War
Frederick William	Succession Wars (War of the
of Brandenburg	Austrian Succession)
Frederick William	Wilhelm
of Prussia	World War I
Germany	World War II
Hindenburg, Paul von	

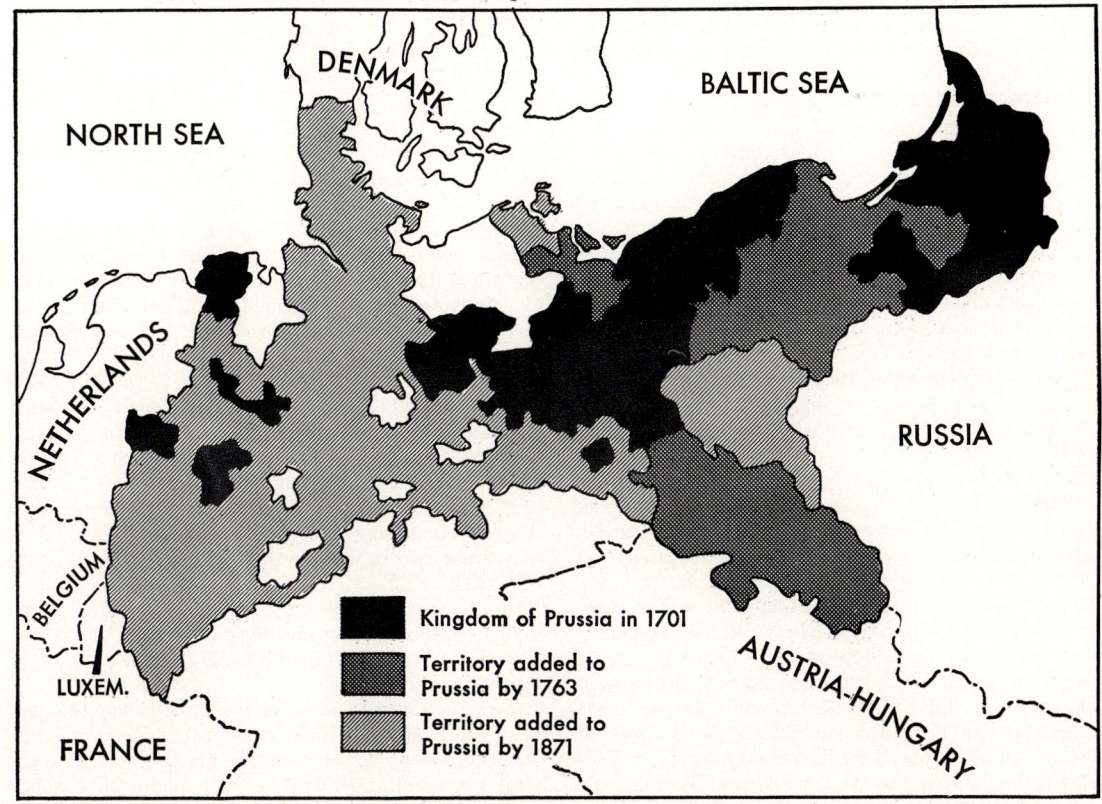

Prussia Grew in Size from a Small Kingdom to the Greatest Military Power in Europe.

Kingdom of Prussia in 1701

Territory added to Prussia by 1763

Territory added to Prussia by 1871

PRUSSIAN BLUE (chemical formula, $Fe_4[Fe(CN)_6]_3$) is a dark blue solid substance with a coppery luster. It was formerly used in the manufacture of laundry bluing, paint, and blue ink. Aniline products, however, are replacing Prussian blue for these purposes (see ANILINE). The chemical is prepared commercially by mixing ferrous sulfate and potassium ferrocyanide, and combining the product with oxygen. Prussian blue does not crystallize or dissolve in water. But alkalies will decompose it. A color used in oil painting is also called Prussian blue. See also PRUSSIC ACID. GEORGE L. BUSH

PRUSSIC ACID, or HYDROCYANIC ACID, *HY droh sy AN ick* (chemical formula, HCN), is called *prussic acid* because it was first obtained from Prussian blue. The pure acid is a clear liquid. It evaporates so quickly that if a drop of it is placed on glass, part of the drop will be frozen by the cold produced by the rapid evaporation of the rest. The acid has a faint odor of peach blossoms or bitter almonds. It is one of the most poisonous substances known, either as a liquid or a gas. A few states use the gas HCN in executing criminals. The gas is created when lumps of sodium or potassium cyanide are dropped into sulfuric acid. Hydrocyanic acid is also used to control the scale insect on orange trees. Sodium cyanide (NaCN) is used in extracting gold and silver from ores. Potassium cyanide is used in casehardening steel. See also METALLURGY (Leaching).

PRUT RIVER, *proot*, is an important waterway in south-central Europe. It rises in the Carpathian Mountains in the southwestern Ukraine, and flows north and southeast to form part of the Russian-Romanian border. For location, see ROMANIA (color map). It meets the Danube River north of the city of Reni in the Ukraine. The Prut is over 500 miles long, but is navigable only for 70 miles south of Leovo, Romania.

PRZHEVALSKI'S HORSE, *puhr zhuh VAHL skeez*, is one of the first wild horses to be discovered. The Russian explorer Nikolai M. Przhevalski found the skin and skull of one of these horses in central Asia in 1881. About 20 years later, animal collectors captured 32 colts. The horse resembles a donkey, but is related to the domestic horse. It has a grayish-brown coat and a brown mane. It has a black streak along its back, and sometimes there are black streaks on its shoulders. The lower parts of its legs are black and there are faint bars on the upper parts. This wild horse stands about 53 inches high at the shoulders.

Scientific Classification. Przhevalski's horse belongs to the family *Equidae*. It is classified as genus *Equus*, species *E. przewalskii*. E. LENDELL COCKRUM

See also HORSE (Wild Horses; picture); TARPAN.

PSALMS, *sahmz*, is the name of a collection of about 150 Hebrew religious poems in the Old Testament. They are much like hymns. The ancient Egyptians and Babylonians also wrote beautiful psalms, but the Hebrew psalms are considered the most outstanding.

King David is supposed to have written some psalms. As hundreds of years went by, other psalm writers added to his collection. The book of Psalms contains songs of David, Asaph, the Korahites, the "choir director," and others. It can be called an *anthology* (collection) of Hebrew religious poetry for the period from the days of David through the period of the Second Temple.

The book of Psalms is one of the best-known books in the Bible. For more than 2,000 years it has been considered one of the finest pieces of writing about the inner life of man. It tells of his spiritual thoughts and longings, and his feeling toward God. The words and ideas of these poems are beautiful and inspiring. They describe man's sorrows and joys, loves and hates, gentleness and anger, faith and fear. They are like a mirror in which man sees his thoughts.

There are also some psalms that might be called *nature poetry*. They speak of the mountains and valleys, the streams and hillsides, and all nature, with deep religious feeling. Psalm 45 is a celebration of a royal marriage. Psalms 120 to 134 are called the *Songs of the Ascents*, which is supposed to mean songs sung by pilgrims as they went up to Jerusalem. Some of the greater Psalms are 8, 19, 23, 24, 27, 46, 51, 65, 72, 90, 103, 107, 121, 139, and 145. Perhaps the best known of all the psalms is the twenty-third, which begins, "The Lord is my Shepherd, I shall not want." This and many other psalms have been set to music and are a basic element in Christian and Jewish worship. ROBERT GORDIS

PSEUDONYM, *SYOO doh nihm*, is a fictitious name that a person may use to avoid responsibility or to help win fame. Criminals may use pseudonyms to conceal their identity even from their friends. Almost all actors and actresses adopt a short and pleasant sounding *stage name*. Musicians, artists, and writers also use pseudonyms sometimes. A famous pseudonym, *Mark Twain*, was used by Samuel Clemens. See also ALIAS; NAME, PERSONAL (Other Names). ELSDON C. SMITH

PSEUDOPOD. See AMEBA.

PSEUDOSCIENCES. See ALCHEMY; ASTROLOGY; FORTUNETELLING; GRAPHOLOGY; NUMEROLOGY; PALMISTRY; PHRENOLOGY; PHYSIOGNOMY.

PSILOMELANE. See MANGANESE (Sources).

PSITTACOSIS, *sit uh KO sis*, is a contagious disease that is carried by some birds. It is also called *parrot fever* or *ornithosis*. Psittacosis occurs mostly in members of the parrot family, but is also found in pigeons and some poultry. Human beings can contract this disease by handling sick birds or infectious articles.

Psittacosis is caused by a virus. The symptoms of the disease include nausea, diarrhea, chills, and high fever. Certain antibiotics will cure some cases, but serious infections can cause pneumonia or death. Because of this disease, the government forbids the importation of parrots into the United States without rigid inspection. JOHN L. LAVAN

PSORIASIS, *so RYE uh sis*, is a skin disease. Its cause is unknown. Psoriasis appears most often on the back of a person's legs and arms. Tiny red eruptions group together to form great red patches of skin. These patches heal from the center, leaving thick, silver-white scales. A drug containing *lipase*, a fat-splitting enzyme, is sometimes used in treating this disease.

PSYCHE, *SYE kee*, was a lovely princess in classical literature. Her beauty was so great that the goddess Venus (Aphrodite) became jealous of her. Venus ordered her son Cupid (Eros) to make Psyche fall in love with some ugly person.

Cupid was so startled at the loveliness of Psyche that he pricked himself with one of his own arrows. The wound made him love her, and he married her. He kept her in his palace and visited her every night. But Psyche

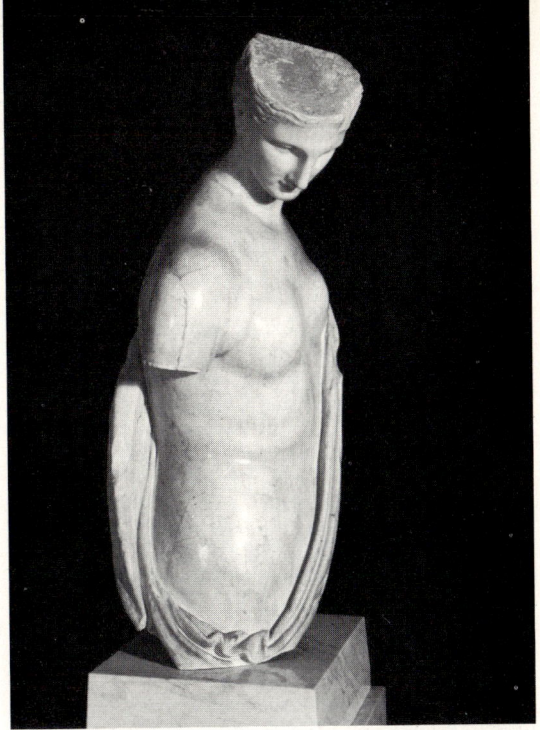

Museo Nazionale, Naples, Italy

Psyche of Capua is a Greek statue of the beautiful princess of classical mythology. It was probably carved in the 300's B.C.

never saw her husband. Cupid had told her that he would have to leave her if she looked at him.

One night, Psyche crept to his room with a lighted lamp. The beauty of the handsome young god surprised her, and she spilled a drop of hot oil on his shoulder. Cupid awakened, and vanished.

In her grief, Psyche went to Venus and begged to see her husband again. Venus compelled her to perform three hard tasks. The last of these caused Psyche's death. Cupid brought her back to life again. Then he begged Jupiter (Zeus) to make Venus forgive both of them. Jupiter did, and also gave immortality to Psyche.

Cupid represents the heart, and Psyche was thought to be the human soul. Her tasks and sorrows stand for the struggles of the human soul. The Greek word *psyche* means *soul*, *mind*, or *life*. VAN JOHNSON

PSYCHEDELICS. See HALLUCINATORY DRUG.

PSYCHIATRY, *sigh KYE uh trih*, is the branch of medicine concerned with investigating and treating mental illness. It has become an increasingly important part of modern medicine. Mental patients occupy about half of the hospital beds in the United States. Doctors estimate that 10 of every 100 adults will seek psychiatric help at some time.

Psychiatry differs from psychology because it is a medical specialty practiced by physicians who treat mentally ill persons. Psychologists are not physicians, and deal with the study of the behavior and mental activities of both humans and animals. They often administer tests to help psychiatrists discover a patient's troubles. Clinical psychologists help by giving patients special treatment. See PSYCHOLOGY.

There are more than 100 kinds of psychiatric disease. Some persons are so ill that they must be hospitalized. Other persons may be anxious and worried, but the doctor can treat them in his office or in a clinic. Most people are at some time depressed, worried, or extremely angry. But unless these conditions last a long time, or become so severe that they interfere with the person's own daily life or that of the people about him, doctors do not consider them symptoms of mental illness.

Cause. Physicians do not know all the causes of mental illness. Sometimes mental illness results from changes in the brain itself as a result of injury, infection, or old age. But the cause of many important illnesses, such as manic-depressive psychosis and schizophrenia, remain unknown. Some psychiatrists believe that physical changes produce such conditions as these. They also think that people may inherit the tendency to develop these diseases. Other psychiatrists believe that past experiences and conflicts in the person's life have been so emotionally upsetting that mental illness results. Most doctors agree that the mild emotional disorders known as *neuroses* probably are caused by emotional disturbances. Sigmund Freud, an Austrian physician who founded psychoanalysis, stressed the importance of past experience in mental illness. He emphasized the function of the unconscious mind as a storehouse for *repressed* (forgotten) unpleasant memories, which produce anxiety and other symptoms of mental disease.

Treatment. Psychiatrists direct the treatment of all mentally ill patients who are hospitalized. Specially trained nurses, psychiatric social workers, psychologists, ward attendants, and occupational therapists assist the doctors. The patient participates in the daily activities of the hospital, which plays an important part in his recovery. The doctor talks with the patient, asking him about his past, his relationships with people, and his thoughts and dreams. Sometimes during this exploration of his unconscious mind, the patient relaxes on a couch and says aloud whatever comes into his mind. Occasionally the doctor may use hypnosis or special drugs to help patients relax more. Sedative drugs are particularly important in treating excited patients.

The patient also often enters group discussions or acts out different life roles in a play. These activities help him to learn more about his own difficulties and to see them in relation to the problems of others.

Restlessness, agitation, and overactivity characterize some mental illnesses. For patients with these symptoms, doctors often prescribe soothing baths and wet sheet packs, which serve to calm the person. Sometimes tranquilizing drugs such as chlorpromazine and reserpine help quiet the patient so that he responds to other forms of treatment. Restraints and strait jackets are rarely used in modern mental hospitals.

Psychiatrists use several other methods to treat patients with mental illness. Shock treatment has been effective in treating some conditions (see SHOCK TREATMENT). The doctor can inject insulin, which lowers the concentration of sugar in the patient's blood and produces a physical shock. Or he can use an electric current, which causes convulsions. This treatment has saved the lives of many patients with depression.

Brain operations were once performed to relieve the symptoms of certain mental illnesses. In these operations, the surgeon destroyed small parts of the brain. But doctors believe they can obtain better and more lasting results with other forms of treatment now. Therefore, they recommend surgery only rarely.

Careers in Psychiatry. A psychiatrist must have many years of training to prepare him for the wide range of activity necessary in his profession. After graduation from high school, the student enters college where he completes a premedical course that often includes elective studies in psychology. He then attends a medical school for four years and works as an intern in a medical hospital for at least one year. He must take examinations given by a state board of examiners to obtain a license to practice. Only then can he begin the special five-year study of psychiatry. This includes three years in mental hospitals as a resident doctor in training, as well as courses of study in his chosen field. When he has finished the five-year course, the doctor is eligible to take a specialty examination. Upon passing this examination, he may practice psychiatry. A psychoanalyst must have additional training. GEORGE A. ULETT

Related Articles in WORLD BOOK include:

Abnormal Psychology	Jung, Carl G.	Psychoanalysis
Adler, Alfred	Menninger (family)	Psychology
Ambivalence	Menninger Foundation	Psychosomatic Medicine
Freud, Sigmund	Mental Illness	Psychotherapy

PSYCHICAL RESEARCH, *SI kih kul,* is the study of supernatural things. It is the investigation of all things which indicate that mind and matter have powers beyond those which are known. The term *psychical research* appeared in 1882, when the Society for Psychical Research was established in England. The founders of this society studied cases of premonition, haunted houses, the claims of spiritual mediums, trances, hypnosis, and the existence of apparently supernatural forces.

Other societies have been organized throughout the world and have made their own investigations. Although thousands of cases of premonitions have been collected, investigators do not believe that there is any reliable evidence to support the claims of persons who believe that the spirits of the dead return to earth or that there is such a thing as mind reading. There is a general opinion, however, that many examples of special abilities exist which should be studied by scientifically trained psychologists.

See also EXTRASENSORY PERCEPTION; SPIRITUALISTS.

PSYCHOANALYSIS, *sy koh uh NAL ih sis,* is a method of *psychotherapy,* the treatment of persons with mental problems. The Austrian physician Sigmund Freud developed psychoanalysis in the late 1800's and early 1900's. Psychoanalysis has also come to mean the facts and theories about the way the mind works which Freud and other psychoanalysts who followed him discovered by psychoanalyzing patients. Thus, psychoanalysis is both a method and a branch of science.

The Psychoanalytic Method depends on cooperation between the psychoanalyst and his patient. The patient tries to tell the psychoanalyst what he is thinking and feeling without consciously controlling his thoughts. Psychiatrists often call this procedure *free association.* The psychoanalyst listens and draws conclusions from what the patient says about what is going on in his mind. At the appropriate time, the doctor tells his conclusions to the patient. In this way, the doctor helps the patient solve problems by bringing to the surface past experiences that may lie at the bottom of his difficulties.

Many years of training are needed to qualify a person to practice psychoanalysis. In the United States, nearly all psychoanalysts are physicians with an average of seven or eight years of special training in psychiatry and psychoanalysis after medical school.

Psychoanalytic Theory is a part of psychology. The most important new discovery of psychoanalysis had to do with consciousness. Until Freud's time, scientists generally agreed that a person knew what he was thinking. In other words, a person was conscious of everything of any importance that was going on in his mind. Freud showed that this was far from true. Many important things go on in a person's mind without his knowing about them. These *unconscious* activities of the mind include thoughts, feelings, and wishes.

This fact explains many things about the mind. For example, it explains why the psychoanalytic method works. When a patient stops consciously controlling his thoughts, his mind comes under control of his unconscious activities. By listening to what the patient says, the psychoanalyst can discover what his unconscious thoughts, feelings, and wishes are.

The discovery of unconscious mental activity also led to the explanation of the nature and causes of certain mental illnesses. These include particularly the *neuroses* and, to some extent, the *functional psychoses.* In these illnesses, the patients' complaints proved to be caused by unconscious conflicts over desires they had in childhood. As children, the patients feared that their parents or other persons would hurt or punish them for these desires.

Freud and other psychoanalysts discovered that unconscious conflicts of this sort play an important part in everyone's mental life. The discovery of the importance of conflict in mental life is one of the basic discoveries made by Freud. CHARLES BRENNER

Related Articles in WORLD BOOK include:

Abnormal Psychology	Libido	Psychology
Catharsis	Mental Illness	Psychosis
Ego	Mood	Psychotherapy
Freud, Sigmund	Neurosis	Subconscious
Hysteria	Psychiatry	

PSYCHODRAMA. See MENTAL ILLNESS (Special Techniques); ROLE PLAYING.

PSYCHOLOGICAL BLOCK. See BLOCK, PSYCHOLOGICAL.

PSYCHOLOGICAL WARFARE uses propaganda to reach certain goals. It can be used before a war to deter fighting, or during a war to win it. A nation uses psychological warfare to convince its potential enemy that he cannot possibly win, and that he should not start to fight. During a war, it uses psychological warfare to convince enemy troops that their cause is unjust and hopeless. It persuades enemy civilians that they can end their suffering by ending the war. Its goal is to destroy the enemy's will to fight.

Psychological warfare can take many forms. Before fighting breaks out, one nation may issue "news" releases and make broadcasts to convince its opponent that it cannot be defeated. It may spread rumors to make the opposing people ready to accept defeat. During war, propaganda units broadcast to enemy troops.

See also PROPAGANDA; WORLD WAR II (Secret War).

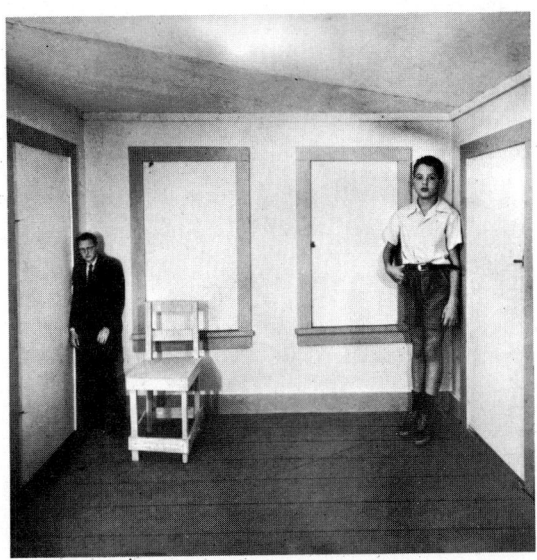

Eric Schaal, *Life* © 1957 Time, Inc.

A Psychologist's Study of Perception shows that we often see what we expect to see. In this room, the boy and man seem distorted. The boy is much taller than the man, *left*, and much shorter than the man when they switch places, *right*. Actually, slanting walls and floor distort the room. But experience makes us assume that the room is normal, so we distort the man and boy.

PSYCHOLOGY is the science that studies why human beings and animals behave as they do. Psychologists are interested in understanding the whole range of human experience, including the reasons for people's motives, thoughts, feelings, and emotions. These problems have puzzled man for centuries. But the scientific study of such problems began only in the mid-1800's.

Psychologists have learned much about behavior and experience, but they have made only a beginning. There is a great deal they know little about, and a lot to be discovered. Suppose you ask yourself: "How does my brain function as a mind?" You would be asking a question that has baffled investigators for hundreds of years. The question is still largely unanswered, but it is being studied by many psychologists collaborating with neurophysiologists and other scientists.

An understanding of why we behave as we do, and why we experience things as we do, has great importance in our daily lives. People want to know how to make better adjustments to situations, and how to learn about themselves so they can reduce their worries and anxieties. They want to discover their skills and aptitudes so they can select a career in which they are likely to be happy and successful. People also want to know how to teach children, both at home and in school, and how to get along better with each other and achieve lasting peace among nations. Psychologists investigate these problems through careful experimentation and trained observation.

Psychology is sometimes classed with biology, sociology, and anthropology as one of the behavioral sciences. Psychology is also closely related to psychiatry. However, psychiatry is a medical science that deals almost entirely with mental illness. Psychology studies all kinds of human behavior, normal and abnormal. Psychiatrists are physicians with special training in the field of mental illness. Most psychologists have a Ph.D. or M.A. degree, rather than medical-school training.

Major Fields of Psychology

Psychology is a broad science and includes many areas of inquiry. Psychological studies range from the causes of international tensions to the ability of earthworms to learn the path through a maze. WORLD BOOK has an article on every major field of psychology. Each of these fields is briefly described here as a guide to the separate articles.

Abnormal Psychology studies all forms of abnormal behavior in man.

Clinical Psychology deals with normal and abnormal behavior, and with the individual's psychological adjustment to himself and his environment.

Comparative Psychology studies the behavior and abilities of different animal species.

Developmental Psychology is the study of changes in human behavior from birth to old age.

Educational Psychology applies principles of psychology to the educational process.

Industrial Psychology applies psychological principles and techniques to the needs and problems of industry.

Learning deals with the process of acquiring and modifying behavior through experience and practice.

Motivation concerns the basic forces that impel people or animals to act and to do what they do.

Perception studies the complex process by which patterns of environmental energies become known as objects, events, people, and other aspects of the world.

Personality studies the different characteristics of people, how these characteristics develop, and how they can be measured.

Physiological Psychology is concerned with the relationship between behavior and the function of the nerv-

749

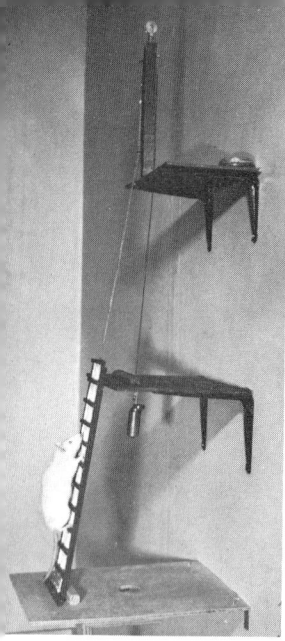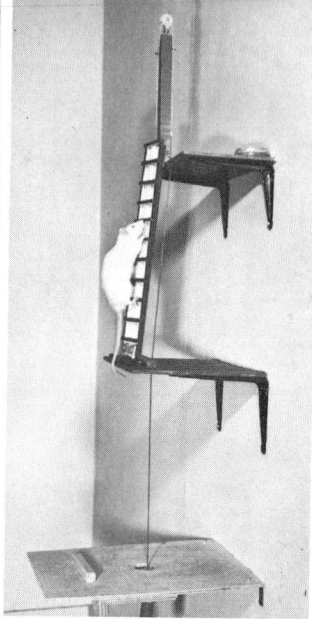

Animal Experiments enable psychologists to study behavior and learning. This experiment is designed to test the ability of rats to solve problems. The rat's problem here is to get a piece of cheese which is on a shelf out of the animal's reach. To solve the problem, the rat climbs the ladder to the lower shelf, *far left.* Then the rat pulls a string to haul up the ladder, *middle,* and climbs the ladder to the top shelf, *right.*

Robert W. Kelley, *Life* © 1952 Time, Inc.

ous system, including the various organs of the body.

Social Psychology studies relationships among people in groups; the roles of language, communication, and propaganda; and the formation of public opinion.

Testing considers the many methods of measuring a person's intelligence, abilities, aptitudes, and personality characteristics.

Thought concerns the many factors that affect the nature, quality, range, and accuracy of our thinking.

Methods of Psychology

Psychologists try to establish principles that can be used to explain, predict, and control or change behavior. They follow the general scientific method used by physicists, chemists, and other physical scientists. Psychologists use four main techniques to gather information about behavior: (1) experiments, (2) natural observation, (3) case histories, and (4) surveys.

Experiments. Many interacting conditions and events affect human and animal behavior. To understand behavior, psychologists must discover how these factors influence behavior. The experimental method enables a psychologist to control all the conditions that determine the aspect of behavior he is studying. He can change one condition and observe the effect on another condition while all other factors remain constant.

Natural Observation is the direct observation of human or animal behavior in its natural environment. Psychologists using this method do not attempt to control any conditions of behavior. They must observe and record their observations accurately to avoid basing conclusions on their own prejudices.

Case Histories. When compiling a case history, the psychologist carefully collects information about an individual's past and present life. He might observe the person's actions, or interview the individual to gather information about his thoughts and feelings. A case history may give a psychologist insight into causes of behavior that cannot be discovered by experiments. For example, the detailed study of a criminal might reveal some causes of various types of behavior.

Surveys are often conducted in studies of group behavior or opinions. The psychologist interviews members of a group orally or by written questionnaires. After the data have been analyzed statistically, the psychologist can draw conclusions about average attitudes or behavior. He must be careful to select a *representative group* (persons from different areas of life), so that many shades of opinion can be faithfully gathered.

History

Beginnings. For hundreds of years, man has wondered about the reasons for his thoughts and actions. The word *psychology* comes from the Greek words *psyche* (mind or soul) and *logos* (study of). Until the late 1800's, psychology was an area of study within philosophy.

Plato, Aristotle, and other ancient philosophers developed theories about the causes of behavior and the relationship between mind and body. They believed that the mind was a separate, identifiable thing, located in a specific part of the body.

In the 1600's and 1700's, some philosophers believed the mind was divided into several inborn *faculties,* including thought, will, and reason, which accounted for different kinds of behavior. During this same period, such philosophers as Thomas Hobbes and John Locke rejected the idea of inborn faculties of the mind. They believed the mind is empty at birth and that a person must have experiences in order to develop ideas. According to these theorists, we get ideas by *associating* (relating) our experiences. See ASSOCIATION; MIND.

The establishment of psychology as a science based on careful observation and experimentation is generally considered to have taken place in 1879. That year, Wilhelm Wundt, a German philosopher who had studied medicine and physiology, founded what was probably the first psychological laboratory, in Leipzig.

From the late 1800's until the 1930's, four important schools of psychology greatly influenced the development of psychology. These schools were (1) structuralism, (2) behaviorism, (3) gestalt psychology, and (4) psychoanalysis.

Structuralism. Wundt and his students thought psychology's main purpose was to describe and analyze *conscious experience*—experiences including sensations, images, and feelings of which only the person himself is aware. They regarded conscious experience in the same way as chemists think of such compounds as water. Chemists break water down into hydrogen and oxygen, combined in a certain proportion. Wundt and his students, often called *structuralists*, tried to do the same for conscious experience. For example, they analyzed the sensation of wetness as the simultaneous experiencing of something cool and the touch of something smooth. This combination of two experiences—temperature and touch—results in the more complex experience of wetness. The primary method of study used by the structuralists was *introspection*, whereby a person described his own experience when stimulated by some object or event.

Behaviorism was introduced into psychology in 1913 by the American psychologist John B. Watson. It was a reaction against structuralism and the introspective study of conscious experience. Watson called for the study of the observable behavior of men and animals, not of their experiences.

The behaviorists began laboratory studies of stimulus-response relationships in behavior. Their theories and methods were strongly influenced by the experiments of the Russian physiologist Ivan P. Pavlov. He discovered that animals could be trained to respond to stimuli by association (see REFLEX ACTION [Conditioned Reflex]).

Most psychologists agree that their science should study behavior, and rely chiefly on experimental methods. But many think the behaviorists neglected some important questions because they ignored such problems as thought processes and personality development.

Gestalt Psychology was concerned with the organization of mental processes. Like behaviorism, it was also a reaction against structuralism. The German word *gestalt* (pronounced *guh SHTAHLT*) means *pattern* or *form*. Gestalt psychologists believed that human beings and animals tend to perceive organized patterns, not individual parts that are merely added together. According to them, the relationship between different parts of a stimulus, which we perceive as a whole or a pattern, gives us our meanings. The gestaltists attacked the structuralist view that experience could be broken down into its parts, such as seeing, hearing, and feeling. Gestaltists believed that all these factors must be studied together in order to understand their relationships.

Max Wertheimer founded gestaltism in Germany about 1912. In the 1930's, Wertheimer and his associates—Wolfgang Köhler, Kurt Koffka, and Kurt Lewin—moved to the United States, where they headed the gestalt movement.

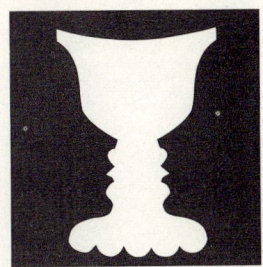

Figure-Ground Patterns demonstrate the gestalt idea that we tend to organize visual stimuli into perceptions. This pattern can be organized in two ways: (1) as a white vase on a black background, or (2) as two black faces on a white background.

Psychoanalysis began in Europe in the early 1900's under the leadership of Sigmund Freud, an Austrian physician. Freud treated persons who were unable to adjust to the world about them. He developed a theory of personality to explain why people became emotionally disturbed.

According to psychoanalytic theory, a person *represses* (removes from awareness) the needs and desires that are unacceptable to himself or society. Freud believed that these unconscious mental processes strongly influence conscious behavior and personality.

Many psychologists today disagree with Freud's theory. But most of them credit him with demonstrating how unconscious events can influence behavior.

Psychology Today is a rapidly growing field in which many investigators work on a variety of problems. Some psychologists, influenced by behaviorism, prefer to study observable behavior. They are sometimes called *stimulus-response psychologists* because they believe all behavior results from stimuli. Other psychologists, sometimes called *cognitive theorists*, base their ideas on gestalt psychology. They study thought processes such as perceiving, learning, and problem-solving. Many psychologists do not follow any one theory or school of thought. They prefer to establish specific relationships in behavior, rather than broad theories. These psychologists deal with such topics as how we see, how we learn, and how we form attitudes.

Careers in Psychology

Most future psychologists major in psychology while studying for a bachelor's degree at a college or university. They can earn a master's degree in about a year. In about five more years of postgraduate study, they can earn a doctor's degree in psychology. Most graduate students in clinical psychology intern for one school year in a psychological clinic, just as a medical student interns in a hospital.

Further career information in psychology can be obtained from the American Psychological Association, 1200 17th St. NW, Washington, D.C. 20036.   HADLEY CANTRIL

Related Articles in WORLD BOOK include:

FIELDS OF PSYCHOLOGY

See the following articles with their lists of Related Articles:

Abnormal Psychology	Motivation
Clinical Psychology	Perception
Comparative Psychology	Personality
Developmental Psychology	Physiological Psychology
Educational Psychology	Social Psychology
Industrial Psychology	Testing
Learning	Thought and Judgment

BIOGRAPHIES

Adler, Alfred	Hall, G. Stanley	Terman, Lewis M.
Binet, Alfred	James, William	Thorndike,
Boring, Edwin G.	Jung, Carl G.	Edward L.
Ebbinghaus,	Koffka, Kurt	Thurstone,
Hermann	Köhler, Wolfgang	Louis L.
Ellis, Havelock	Lewin, Kurt	Watson, John B.
Freud, Sigmund	Pavlov, Ivan P.	Wundt, Wilhelm
Gesell, Arnold L.	Seashore, Carl E.	Yerkes, Robert M.

PSYCHONEUROSIS. See NEUROSIS.

PSYCHOPATHOLOGY. See ABNORMAL PSYCHOLOGY.

PSYCHOPHYSICS. See PERCEPTION (Understanding Perception).

PSYCHOSIS

PSYCHOSIS, *sy KOH sis.* Psychiatrists usually divide mental illnesses into two groups—the *neuroses* and the *psychoses.* The psychoses include the more severe illnesses that usually require care in a hospital.

Some psychoses have physical causes. For example, the brain may be diseased as the result of an infection such as *general paresis,* which is caused by syphilis. Or, a physical illness of another part of the body may affect the brain, as in delirium due to pneumonia. These are called *organic psychoses.* In *toxic psychoses,* a harmful or poisonous substance (toxin) affects the brain. An example of this is a psychosis caused by lead poisoning.

Most psychoses have no known physical cause. Doctors call these *functional psychoses.* The most common of these include manic-depressive psychosis and schizophrenia. CHARLES BRENNER

See also MENTAL ILLNESS (Kinds of Mental Illnesses); NEUROSIS.

PSYCHOSOMATIC MEDICINE, *sy koh soh MAT ik,* is the use of the methods and principles of psychology in the treatment of physical ailments. The term is taken from the Greek words *psyche,* which means *mind,* and *soma,* which refers to the body.

Doctors have long known that emotional disturbances affect a person's body. For example, when a person is afraid or angry, adrenalin flows into the blood, increasing the action of the heart. Certain mental conflicts may make a person more susceptible to disease, or cause what appears to be a disease. Bodily disorders that appear to be related to emotional disturbances include asthma, *peptic ulcer* (stomach ulcer), *rheumatoid arthritis* (inflammation and stiffness of the joints), *neurodermatitis* (chronic skin disorders), and *hypertension* (high blood pressure).

Ordinary medical treatment alone seldom cures psychosomatic disorders. For instance, much of the treatment for peptic ulcer involves rest and *psychotherapy* (treatment by psychological means). Psychotherapy includes giving support, encouragement, and reassurance to the patient. A doctor often finds that, if he explores and corrects a patient's emotional conflicts, in addition to giving him medical treatment, the symptoms of a disorder disappear.

Psychosomatic medicine usually is not considered a special field of medicine. Most medical doctors have had some training in psychology and psychiatry. They often use psychological methods along with other methods of treatment. Some patients need help from doctors who specialize in psychiatry. GEORGE A. ULETT

PSYCHOTHERAPY, *sy koh THER uh pih,* is any treatment that tries to cure a patient by psychological rather than physical means. In psychotherapy, the doctor and the patient talk with one another. In other forms of treatment, the doctor prescribes some medicine, performs a surgical operation, or treats the patient with an X-ray machine or some other medical device.

A psychotherapist is usually a *psychiatrist,* a physician who, after graduating from medical school, spends several years studying about the care of mentally ill persons (see PSYCHIATRY). Some psychotherapy is also done by psychologists. Psychologists are not physicians. But they have had special training in psychology both in college and after graduation. Often a psychologist may have an M.A. or a Ph.D. degree in psychology.

Psychotherapy may be used alone or in combination with other types of medical treatment. The illnesses that are best treated by psychotherapy are those with mental causes, such as neuroses. Psychotherapy may be used with a single patient, or with a small group of patients (group psychotherapy). A particular method of psychotherapy, developed by Sigmund Freud, is called *psychoanalysis.* CHARLES BRENNER

See also MENTAL ILLNESS; NEUROSIS; PSYCHOANALYSIS; SHOCK TREATMENT; TRAUMA.

PSYCHROMETER. See HYGROMETER.

PSYLLIUM, *SIL ih um,* is an herb grown in southern Europe and India. It bears a seed that is used as a drug. The seed of the psyllium has laxative qualities and is used in medicines. When the seed is moistened, it looks like gelatin.

The psyllium is an annual herb and grows as high as 20 inches. Its leaves resemble grass and are from 1 to 2½ inches long. It has tiny flowers that are arranged in spikes, about half an inch long.

Scientific Classification. Psyllium belongs to the plantain family, *Plantaginaceae.* It is classified as genus *Plantago,* species *P. psyllium.* HAROLD NORMAN MOLDENKE

PT BOAT was one of the smallest, fastest, and most maneuverable fighting ships of the United States Navy. The letters PT stood for *patrol torpedo,* which meant that the craft carried out patrol duties and also carried torpedoes for combat. PT boats were often called *mosquito boats,* because they "stung" the enemy with great speed, and were most deadly in the dark.

PT boats made a remarkable record in World War II, and destroyed over 250,000 tons of Japanese shipping. General Douglas MacArthur, his wife and child, and various officers and statesmen fled from the Bataan Peninsula to the island of Mindanao in PT boats in March, 1942, on their journey from the Philippines to Australia. PT boats were taken from the active list in 1959. But in 1962, two boats had their torpedo tubes removed to increase their speed, and were put back on the list as *PTF boats* (patrol torpedo boats, fast). Since 1962, a number of other PTF boats have been acquired from Norway.

The PT boat was about 70 to 90 feet long and over 50 tons in displacement. The largest boats were made of aluminum and were capable of speeds of more than 50 knots (about 57 mph). They had about 10,000 horsepower in their four high-speed, supercharged gasoline engines of about 2,500 horsepower each. Some experi-

U.S. Navy PT Boats were fast-moving patrol craft. They won fame during World War II for attacks against Japanese shipping.
U.S. Navy

mental PT boats had gas turbines of comparable power.

PT boat hulls were basically different from those of other warships. They were called *planing* hulls because they skimmed or planed on the water surface. Larger ships cut through the water and will not rise up on the surface. They have *displacement* hulls.

PT boats, although much larger than high-speed, outboard-motor runabouts, had similar hulls. They were broad beamed, with a shallow *V*-shaped bottom. This design made PT boats of little use in rough or choppy water. The high rate of fuel consumption by their powerful engines also limited their range of operation. PT boats carried small, multipurpose guns, and sometimes rockets, in addition to torpedoes. Their most efficient use was restricted and the Navy kept few on active duty in peacetime.   RAYMOND V. B. BLACKMAN

See also TORPEDO; TORPEDO BOAT.

P.T.A. See PARENTS AND TEACHERS, NATIONAL CONGRESS OF.

PTARMIGAN, *TAR muh gan,* is the name for a group of birds that resemble the grouse. The ptarmigan is found in northern parts of the Northern Hemisphere, such as Alaska, the Aleutian Islands, and Greenland. Every ptarmigan can be recognized by the covering of short feathers on its feet. These help the bird to travel across the snow in the winter. In winter the feathers of the ptarmigan are white, like the snow. In summer the plumage is reddish brown and black.

The ptarmigan builds its nest on the ground. The nest is lined with grass or leaves. A female ptarmigan may lay from 4 to 15 eggs. The eggs may be cream colored or red, covered with black or dark brown spots. In winter, the ptarmigan hides in snowbanks for safety.

Three kinds of ptarmigan live in North America. They are the white-tailed ptarmigan, the rock ptarmigan, and the willow ptarmigan. The white-tailed ptarmigan lives in the Rocky Mountains. Its home may be anywhere from central Alaska south to New Mexico. The rock ptarmigan lives in the Arctic region. It may live anywhere from the Aleutian Islands to Greenland. The willow ptarmigan makes its home in the Arctic region, Newfoundland, British Columbia, and northern Europe and Siberia. The willow ptarmigan is the state bird of Alaska (see ALASKA [color picture]).

Scientific Classification. Ptarmigans are in the grouse family, *Tetraonidae.* Willow ptarmigans are genus *Lagopus,* species *L. lagopus;* rock ptarmigans are *L. mutus;* white-tailed ptarmigans are *L. leucurus.*   JOSEPH J. HICKEY

See also BIRD (color picture: Color Protects Them).

PTERANODON. See PTERODACTYL.

PTERIDOPHYTE, *TEHR ih doh FITE,* or FERN PLANT, is one of a large and important group of plants that are simpler in their structures than flowering plants. The name *pteridophyte* means *fern plant.* Not all the pteridophytes are ferns, but ferns are the best known of the group, and many of the others look more or less like ferns.

The pteridophytes lack flowers but they have many of the same organs and habits that flowering plants have. Their tissues are distinctly divided into roots, stems, and leaves, as those of flowering plants are.

Instead of reproducing by seeds as flowering plants do, the pteridophytes multiply by means of very small bodies called *spores* (see SPORE). These spores do not result from flowers, but grow on special parts of the plant in little cases. The spore cases of ferns are the

roundish brown specks appearing on the back of certain of the fern leaves. When the spores drift away and start to grow, they produce small plants quite different from the ferns. After a time these small plants give rise to young ferns, which grow and produce another generation of spores. Other plants in the pteridophyte group, such as horsetails, club mosses, and ground pines, have a life history similar to that of the ferns.

Millions of years ago the pteridophytes were among the largest and most common kinds of plants. Many of the world's coal deposits are formed largely by the remains of pteridophytes. Fossil records show that many pteridophytes reached the size of large trees. But present-day kinds, except the tree ferns of the tropics, are small, non-woody herbs.   ROLLA M. TRYON

See also CLUB MOSS; FERN; HORSETAIL.

PTERODACTYL, *TAIR oh DACK til,* was a reptile that could fly. It is also called a PTEROSAUR. Pterodactyls lived during the last part of the Mesozoic era,

Painting by Charles R. Knight,
from American Museum of Natural History
The Pterodactyl Was a Prehistoric Flying Reptile.

from about 150 million years ago to about 65 million years ago. They were true reptiles, not the ancestors of birds. Pterodactyls ranged from about the size of sparrows to about 4 feet long. Their wingspreads ranged from a foot to about 35 feet. They had large heads, and noses that looked like birds' beaks with teeth. The short body and tail were covered with hairless, wrinkled skin. The front legs ended in "fingers." The fourth "finger" had long bones. Strong membranes connected these bones to the body and hind legs, forming wings somewhat like bats' wings. Most experts believe pterodactyls flew poorly, and used their wings only for gliding. Scientists have found fossils of many pterodactyls. They believe there were about 20 *genera* (related groups). Two kinds were *Rhamphorhynchus,* which had a long, paddlelike tail, and *Pteranodon,* which had a large crest on the back of its head. The *Pteranodon* had no teeth and no tail.   SAMUEL PAUL WELLES

PTOLEMY, *TAHL ee mih,* was the family name of the Macedonian kings of ancient Egypt. They ruled from 323 to 30 B.C.

Ptolemy I, called SOTER or SAVIOR (367?-283 B.C.), was one of Alexander the Great's favorite generals. He was a shrewd ruler. After Alexander's death in 323 B.C., he seized Egypt as his share of the divided empire. He assumed the title of king of Egypt.

Ptolemy made Alexandria his capital. He encouraged

PTOLEMY

Greek and other foreign soldiers to settle in Egypt. They helped him to extend his rule to Cyrene, Crete, and Cyprus. He developed Egypt into a great commercial nation. He fostered learning and established the museum

Ptolemy I
Culver

and library in Alexandria (see ALEXANDRIAN LIBRARY). He also founded the famous religious cult of Serapis (see SERAPIS). He was considered the greatest king of the Macedonian line.

Ptolemy II, called PHILADELPHUS (308-246 B.C.), son of Ptolemy I, married his sister Arsinoe. He carried on wars in Syria and the Aegean Sea, and he established Egyptian power in Nubia. He developed the capital at Alexandria. He continued the library and completed the lighthouse begun by his father on the island of Pharos (see SEVEN WONDERS OF THE WORLD). Ptolemy II was fond of natural science and natural history. He developed a well organized and efficient government in Egypt.

Ptolemy III, called EUERGETES or BENEFACTOR (280?-221 B.C.), the son of Ptolemy II, successfully led his armies deep into western Asia. From there, he brought back to Egypt the statues of the gods that had been carried off by the Persians. Later in his reign his power weakened and he lost some of Egypt's foreign provinces. He was a great builder of temples.

Ptolemy V, called EPIPHANES or ILLUSTRIOUS (210-181 B.C.), was only an infant when his father, Ptolemy IV, died in 203 B.C. He was long dominated by evil and plotting regents. Antiochus III, a Seleucid king, hoped to gain power in Egypt through the marriage of his daughter to Ptolemy V. The Rosetta Stone contained a decree of Ptolemy V in 196 B.C. granting important concessions to the priests (see ROSETTA STONE).

Ptolemy XI, called AULETES or the FLUTE PLAYER (?-51 B.C.), was the son of Ptolemy VIII. He was a weakling who owed his throne to support of the Roman Empire. He lived in Rome as an exile for part of his unpopular reign. After he died, Egypt was ruled by his younger daughter, Cleopatra, and her brothers, Ptolemy XII and XIII (see CLEOPATRA). THOMAS W. AFRICA

PTOLEMY was one of the greatest astronomers and geographers of ancient times. He was born CLAUDIUS PTOLEMY, but almost nothing is known about the events of his life. However, his astronomical observations were made at Alexandria, Egypt, about A.D. 150. Ptolemy's observations and theories are preserved in a 13-volume work which he entitled *Mathematike Syntaxis*, or *Mathematical Composition*. Because of the admiration this work won, it became known as the *Almagest*, a combination Greek-Arabic term meaning *the greatest*.

In the *Syntaxis*, Ptolemy rejected the idea that the earth moves. He pointed out that the earth is round and that gravity is directed toward the center of the earth. Ptolemy placed the motionless earth at the center of the universe. Around it went the moon, sun, and

planets at various rates of speed. Ptolemy believed that the stars were brilliant spots of light in a concave dome that arched over everything. Against this stellar background, Ptolemy traced the motions of the planets and worked out a theory for each of them. He stated that the planets are much closer to the earth than the stars, but are farther away than the moon. Ptolemy developed his system of astronomy largely from the ideas of the Greek astronomer HIPPARCHUS (see HIPPARCHUS). This system was accepted as authoritative throughout Europe until 1543, when the Polish astronomer Nicolaus Copernicus proved that it was wrong (see COPERNICUS, NICOLAUS).

Ayer Collection, Newberry Library
Ptolemy

Ptolemy devoted two volumes of the *Syntaxis* to a catalog of the stars. He described a mathematical arrangement of the stars, and gave a celestial latitude and longitude for each of them. This catalog included 1,022 stars, found in 48 constellations. Ptolemy also discovered the irregularity of the moon in its orbit. This irregularity is known as *evection*.

Ptolemy dealt with certain technical aspects of astronomy in his other writings. His serious treatment of astrology helped to spread that superstition. In a book entitled *Optics*, Ptolemy discussed the refraction of light as it passes from one medium into another medium of different density. This book also included a table of refractions.

Ptolemy's *Geography* opens with an excellent theory of map projection. The rest of the book contains a list of places with their longitudes and latitudes, as well as 26 color maps and a map of the world. He exaggerated the land mass from Spain to China, and underestimated the size of the ocean. This mistake later encouraged Columbus to undertake his famous voyage of discovery in 1492. EDWARD ROSEN

PTOMAINE POISONING, *TOH main*, is a common name for certain kinds of stomach and intestinal irritations. *Ptomaines* are chemical compounds produced when foods decay. Doctors no longer believe that ptomaines cause food poisoning or infection. Some ptomaines are poisonous when injected into animals. But no one has proven that they are poisonous when taken in edible foods. Doctors believe that attacks once called ptomaine poisoning are due to bacterial infection, poisoning, or other causes. MARTIN FROBISHER

PTOMAINES are chemical compounds related to ammonia. They are produced as waste products by bacteria that cause decay or decomposition of organic plant or animal matter. They bear some resemblance to the alkaloids that are found in poisonous plants and animals.

In 1870, the Italian investigator Francesco Selmi introduced the word ptomaine (from the Greek *ptoma, a corpse*) to describe these waste products. Further interest in ptomaines was stimulated by researches of the French chemist Armand Gautier, in 1872, and of the German chemist Ludwig Brieger in Berlin, in 1882. See also PTOMAINE POISONING. MARTIN FROBISHER

PTYALIN. See Enzyme; Digestion (From Mouth to Stomach); Saliva.

PU-YI, *poo YEE* (1906-1967), often called Henry Pu-Yi, was the last emperor of China. In 1911 and 1912, while he was still a child, a revolution overthrew his Manchu government and replaced it with a republic. Pu-Yi was allowed to remain in Peking, the capital. But in 1924 he fled from warlords to Japanese protection in the nearby city of Tientsin. In 1931, the Japanese seized a large part of northeastern China and made it a puppet state called *Manchukuo*. In 1934, they made Pu-Yi ruler of Manchukuo. He ruled until the end of World War II. He was captured by the Russians and transferred to the Communist Chinese, who pardoned him in 1959. Pu-Yi was born in Peking. Marius B. Jansen

PUBERTY. See Teen Age.

PUBIS. See Pelvis; Human Body (Trans-Vision).

PUBLIC ACCOUNTANT. See Accounting; Certified Public Accountant.

PUBLIC ADDRESS SYSTEM is a system of a microphone, amplifier, and one or more loudspeakers that are connected to amplify and carry sound to several places at once. It is used where many persons are to hear the same speech or music at the same time.

A public address system may consist of a microphone and amplifier, located in a central place such as in the principal's office of a school, and one or more loudspeakers, sometimes located in each of the classrooms and assembly halls. A central switchboard enables the principal at the microphone to turn electric current into any or all of the receivers. Then, as he speaks, his words are transmitted to all the receivers on that circuit.

A modified form of public address system is used where a lecturer wishes his words to reach farther than they might carry by his voice alone. A microphone is placed on a table where an experiment is being conducted and loudspeakers are placed about the room. The lecturer, using an ordinary tone of voice, is able to talk to the entire class. His voice can also carry to groups outside the room via a loudspeaker. Palmer H. Craig

See also Loudspeaker.

PUBLIC DEFENDER is an official paid by the state to defend persons who are too poor to have their own lawyers when they are accused of a crime. Most public defenders have only criminal jurisdiction, and usually do not handle civil cases.

The first public defender was appointed in Los Angeles County, California, in 1914. His duties also included helping workers to collect wages, and representing citizens in small lawsuits, although today most public defenders do not perform such tasks. Public defenders are fairly common today, but many courts appoint private attorneys, who usually must serve without pay, to defend the poor. Erwin N. Griswold

PUBLIC DOMAIN means that the right to possession or ownership of property belongs to the public rather than to an individual. Public lands are called public domain (see Public Lands). Creative works whose copyright or patent has expired are said to be in the public domain (see Copyright; Patent). So are processes that have been generally known for many years.

PUBLIC EDUCATION. See Education; Democracy (Education and Democracy).

PUBLIC FINANCE. See City and Local Governments (Finances); National Budget; Taxation.

PUBLIC HEALTH means the health of everyone in a community. It is one of the basic concerns of government, along with police, fire, and military protection. Public health agencies at all levels of government, from local to international, work together to keep people healthy. Doctors, nurses, sanitary engineers, and other public health workers help protect the community against conditions that threaten the lives and health of citizens.

Public health is generally taken for granted in the United States, Canada, and other countries of Western civilization. We can drink from a public water fountain and not worry about getting typhoid fever. We know that the milk we buy does not contain tuberculosis germs. We sit in a crowded theater or train without fear of getting smallpox. Our streets are kept free from filth in which disease germs thrive.

But in many parts of the world, disease and poor living conditions are severe problems. About 700 million persons in Africa, Asia, and Central and South America suffer from malaria. Diseases that result from poor food or starvation occur in many regions of the world. Solving public health problems throughout the world is important to everyone. An epidemic that starts in a distant place may quickly spread around the world if public health workers cannot control it.

Public Health in the Community

Disease Prevention and Control are important problems in public health. The local community usually is best able to prevent and control the spread of disease. It provides proper sanitation, enforces quarantines, and sponsors immunization programs.

Sanitation is important because many disease germs breed in filth. Some, such as the germs of typhoid fever, may enter drinking water or food and infect countless persons. Every community provides for the disposal of garbage and other wastes. The community also makes sure that its drinking water is pure.

Contagious diseases such as diphtheria, whooping cough, and smallpox spread rapidly from person to person. Public health officers *quarantine* (isolate) any person with a contagious disease.

Many communities have immunization programs that help protect people against disease. *Immunity* is the ability to resist and overcome a disease. To make sure that everyone in the community is protected against certain diseases, health departments may provide immunizing drugs. In many areas, for example, health department doctors give vaccinations against such diseases as smallpox, diphtheria, polio, tetanus, and whooping cough. See Immunity.

Health Laws help ensure healthful living and working conditions for everyone. Housing codes, for example, require all dwellings to have proper exits, heat, light, and ventilation. These codes set standards for toilet facilities and for garbage disposal. They also require that owners keep the buildings clean, in good repair, and free of insects and rats. Other health laws require factories to have adequate lighting and ventilation. Machines must be equipped with safety devices to protect the workers. Mines must have proper ventilation to get rid of poisonous gases.

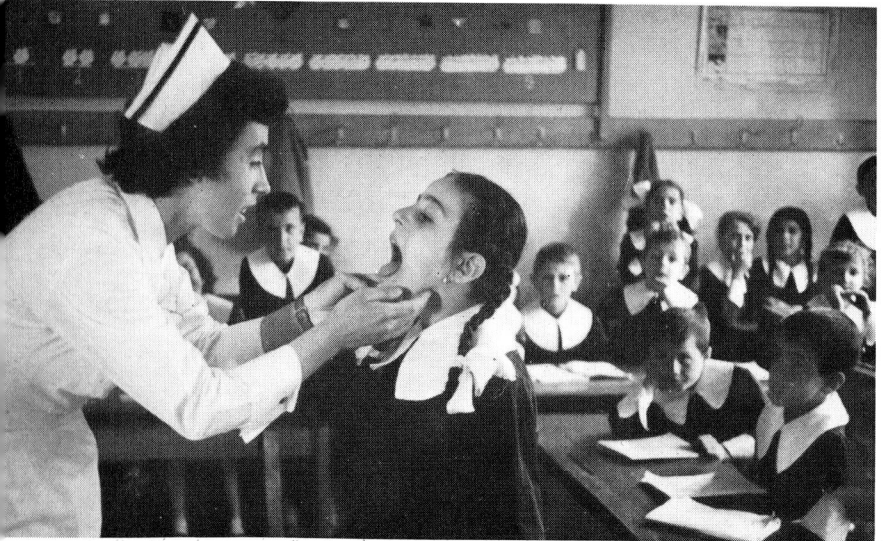

Teaching Health is an important part of public health. School children in Ankara, Turkey, *left*, learn about hygiene from public health nurses.

United Nations; Chas. Pfizer & Co., Inc.

Tuberculosis Institute of Chicago and Cook County

Mobile X-Ray Units form part of the public health service of many communities. These units make it possible for millions of persons to have free chest X rays, which help detect tuberculosis.

Testing Drugs makes sure they meet public health standards set by federal laws. A machine, *right*, separates the contents of each drug. Every ingredient is then tested thoroughly by chemists.

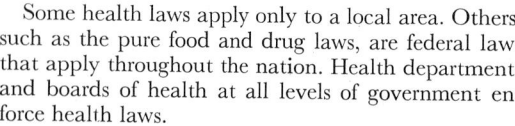

Some health laws apply only to a local area. Others, such as the pure food and drug laws, are federal laws that apply throughout the nation. Health departments and boards of health at all levels of government enforce health laws.

Food and Drug Control protects the public against foods and drugs that are impure or otherwise harmful. In the United States and Canada, the government establishes and enforces standards for many products that could endanger health. For example, federal agents inspect meat before and after the animals are slaughtered. They make sure the meat is processed under sanitary conditions, and is labeled and packaged correctly. Local governments set minimum standards of cleanliness for groceries, butcher shops, dairies, and restaurants. Federal laws also regulate the contents of

drugs and cosmetics, and how these products are advertised. Drugs and cosmetics must pass tests to show that they do not contain harmful ingredients, and that all claims made about them are true. See PURE FOOD AND DRUG LAWS.

Vital Statistics are records that give information about health, diseases, accidents, and disabilities. They also include birth and death records. Doctors must report certain diseases. If a person has whooping cough, for example, the doctor must report it to the board of health. When a patient dies, the doctor reports the cause of death, along with the person's age, sex, and race. See VITAL STATISTICS.

Public health officials use these reports to plan effective programs to prevent and control disease. For example, many cases of polio might be reported in a certain area of a city. The board of health would probably recommend that polio vaccine be given to every person in the city. Such widespread action could help prevent a polio epidemic (see EPIDEMIC).

Health Education helps the public understand and prevent disease. A person who knows what causes a disease can take steps to protect himself against it. Many schools offer courses that teach students the rules of good physical and mental health. Health departments and voluntary health agencies teach people how to guard against disease. As part of their education programs, they encourage everyone to have an annual chest X ray. These examinations make it possible to detect tuberculosis in its early stages. Mobile X-ray units, supplied by the National Tuberculosis and Respiratory Disease Association, give free X rays.

Health Agencies and Organizations. In the United States and Canada, government agencies and voluntary organizations work for public health. These groups are active from national to local levels.

Federal agencies control international and interstate quarantine. They also check the quality of food and drugs. The United States Public Health Service and the Canadian Department of National Health and Welfare are federal agencies.

State and provincial agencies often give financial and technical help to local health units. Local agencies may operate clinics, hospitals, public health nursing services, and school health services.

Voluntary health organizations depend on contributions from private citizens for their support. These organizations help educate the public to protect itself against disease. They also promote laws to improve health protection. Many of these agencies support research projects. National voluntary agencies include the American National and Canadian Red Cross, the Health League of Canada, and the National Foundation. Other groups such as civic clubs and parent-teacher associations help voluntary agencies.

World Health Problems

Contagious Diseases are one of the chief threats to world health. Modern transportation lets people travel easily and quickly. But diseases can also spread more easily and quickly than they once could. For example, smallpox is rare in the United States. But several cases of this dread disease occurred after World War II. The smallpox germ was brought into the country by U.S. troops returning from China.

Most nations try to prevent diseases from spreading from one country to another. When ships enter a port of another country, they are inspected for disease. Planes are also inspected after international flights. Most governments require international travelers to show certificates of vaccination and inoculation before allowing them to return to their homelands.

Malnutrition results from eating poor and insufficient food. It is widespread in all underdeveloped countries. Persons who do not eat adequate food can get such diseases as rickets, scurvy, and beriberi. Malnutrition lowers the body's resistance to disease. As a result, many contagious diseases start in places where malnutrition flourishes. Diseases also spread rapidly among undernourished people, often causing widespread epidemics. International organizations help countries

get and distribute food to raise the standards of nutrition. These agencies include the Food and Agriculture Organization of the United Nations, and the UN Children's Fund.

Other Health Problems. Many diseases flourish in tropical countries. Tropical diseases include heatstroke and sunstroke, various ailments that result from poor nutrition, and many sicknesses caused by parasites. Other diseases are widespread in such regions as Asia, Africa, and parts of southern Europe. These diseases include yellow fever and sleeping sickness. The diseases not only kill and disable people who live in these regions, but also may spread to other countries. Persons traveling for business or pleasure, or officials on government business, may become *carriers* who spread disease.

The governments of most countries work constantly to raise the health standards of their people. The World Health Organization (WHO), an agency of the United Nations, helps governments plan and coordinate health programs. It also provides funds to help fight disease throughout the world.   LEROY E. BURNEY

Related Articles in WORLD BOOK include:

Air Pollution	Medicine
Bill of Health	Nursing (Public Health
Disease (Preventing	Nurses)
Disease)	Public Health Service
Garbage Disposal	Pure Food and Drug Laws
Health	Quarantine
Health, Board of	Red Cross
Health Council, National	Sanitation
Health, Education, and	Sewage
Welfare, Department of	Smoke Prevention
Housing	Water (City Water Systems)
Malnutrition	World Health Organization

PUBLIC HEALTH SERVICE (PHS) is a division of the United States government's Department of Health, Education, and Welfare. It consists of three operating agencies: the Consumer Protection and Environmental Health Service, the Health Services and Mental Health Administration, and the National Institutes of Health. These agencies work with state and local agencies, educational and research institutions, and private industry to conduct health research, control disease, and provide health information, education, and services. The PHS also cooperates with foreign governments and international organizations in carrying on studies and activities that improve health throughout the world.

The assistant secretary for health and scientific affairs directs the Public Health Service. The surgeon general is his principal deputy. An earlier health agency, the Marine Hospital Service, was established in the Department of the Treasury in 1798. It became the Public Health Service in 1912.

Critically reviewed by the PUBLIC HEALTH SERVICE

Related Articles. For more information on agencies of the Public Health Service, see HEALTH, EDUCATION, AND WELFARE, DEPARTMENT OF, and NATIONAL INSTITUTES OF HEALTH. See also the following:

Food and Drug Adminis-	Pure Food and Drug Laws
tration	Quarantine
Health, Board of	Sanitation

PUBLIC HOUSING. See HOUSING (Low-Income Housing); HOUSING AND URBAN DEVELOPMENT, DEPARTMENT OF.

PUBLIC LANDS

PUBLIC LANDS include all the territory owned by a national government. The United States government owns about 707,000,000 acres of land. Congress may use or dispose of it in whatever way it feels will best serve the public interest.

The government reserves some of the public lands for Indian reservations, military and naval installations, reclamation projects, wildlife refuges, federal buildings, and national cemeteries, forests, monuments, and parks. For information on the use of public lands reserved by the government, see the following articles: CONSERVATION (Conservation in the United States); INDIAN, AMERICAN (Canada and the United States); NATIONAL CEMETERY; NATIONAL FOREST; NATIONAL MONUMENT; NATIONAL PARK.

The term *public lands*, however, commonly applies to land which the government is willing to sell or lease to private sources for development and settlement. Before 1934, the government sold over 1,000,000,000 acres of land in the continental United States. Since then, the government does not normally sell public lands, but leases them for purposes specified by law.

Management of Public Lands

The federal government owns and controls about 500,000,000 acres of land in the continental United States. Most of this land is located in the Western States and Alaska. This land is under the jurisdiction of 28 different federal agencies and bureaus, most of them within the Department of the Interior, the Department of Agriculture, and the Department of Defense.

In surveying public lands, the government divides an area into units of 36 square miles, called *townships*. Each township is further divided in a checkerboard fashion into 36 sections of 1 square mile. Each section, containing 640 acres, is divided into quarter sections of 160 acres each. In order to help locate and describe any particular piece of land, surveyors use certain meridians of longitude (north-south lines), called *principal meridians*, and certain parallels of latitude (east-west lines), called *base lines*. All townships lying in a line from north to south are described as a *range*. See WESTWARD MOVEMENT (picture, The Land Ordinance of 1785).

History

Acquisition of Public Lands. Between 1781 and 1786, the federal government gained control over a large area west of the Allegheny Mountains and north of the Ohio River. Four eastern states had claimed this region during the colonial period. By 1802, other seaboard states ceded what is now the states of Alabama and Mississippi. After 1802, additions to the public lands came as a result of the expansion of the national boundaries.

The purchase of Louisiana in 1803 almost doubled the size of the United States. Other important additions of territory include: the acquisition of Florida in 1819, the annexation of Texas in 1845 and Oregon in 1846, the cession by Mexico of a vast territory between Texas and the Pacific Ocean in 1848, the Gadsden Purchase in 1853, the purchase of Alaska in 1867, and the annexation of Hawaii in 1898. Almost all this land became part of the public lands of the United States. Texas and Hawaii retained control of the public lands within their boundaries, because they had been independent nations.

Disposal of Public Lands. As early as 1783, land companies tried to purchase public lands for the purpose of establishing settlements in the area north of the Ohio River. Their actions forced Congress to formulate a policy for the disposition of public lands. In the Ordinance of 1785, Congress adopted policies intended to produce revenue and encourage compact settlement. The ordinance also established a permanent method for surveying. The land policies expressed in this law represented the views of Easterners, and soon proved unpopular in the West. Under pressure from Western Congressmen, later land laws permitted purchasers to buy a specified minimum amount of land at a low price. The laws encouraged settlers to buy public lands and to settle wherever they wanted to. A law of 1820 set 80 acres as the minimum amount of land that could be purchased, and established the cost at $1.25 an acre.

An important development in land policy came in 1862, with the passage of the Homestead Act. It provided that persons who lived on public lands for five years and made certain improvements might acquire title to 160 acres through the payment of very small fees. This law made it possible for workers in Eastern cities to move West and own farms of their own. See HOMESTEAD ACT; PRE-EMPTION; SQUATTER.

Individual settlers were not the only persons interested in obtaining grants of public land. Land companies and speculators bought large tracts of land to sell to people who wanted new homes in the West. Land companies proved unprofitable because individuals could purchase land for themselves with little trouble. But speculators continued to have a large and unpopular role in the purchase of public lands until the 1900's.

After 1850, corporations and individual promoters tried to gain control of large acreages for such purposes as grazing, mining, logging, or control of other natural resources. Much of the public land in the Far West passed into the hands of such groups.

The government also used the public lands to promote certain of its own objectives. It offered free land to veterans of every war from the American Revolutionary War through the Mexican War. It granted land to the states for the support of public education. The Morrill Act of 1862 gave to each state an amount of land in proportion to its population for the establishment of agricultural colleges (see LAND-GRANT COLLEGE OR UNIVERSITY). The government also gave generous grants of land to railroads along proposed rights of way to encourage railroad building west of the Mississippi River.

Close of the Public Lands. By 1890, nearly all the good farming land had been sold. Many Americans began to fear that large business corporations would ruthlessly exploit the resources of the West. The government began a positive conservation program in the early 1900's, while Theodore Roosevelt was President. The Taylor Grazing Act of 1934 provided for lease of some public lands for grazing. In 1935, President Franklin D. Roosevelt withdrew remaining public lands, excepting those in Alaska, from sale or homesteading. He also authorized programs for the wise use of these lands through leasing.   HAROLD W. BRADLEY

See also LAND MANAGEMENT, BUREAU OF; PUBLIC DOMAIN.

PUBLIC LIBRARY. See LIBRARY.

Public Opinion develops from many individual opinions. Citizens in a democracy are encouraged to express their views on such subjects as politics and foreign policy. Public opinion polls conduct door-to-door surveys to find out the opinions of people.

H. Armstrong Roberts

PUBLIC OPINION. Like many widely used terms, *public opinion* means different things to different persons, and in different situations. Any kind of opinion, whether individual or group, private or public, has to do with matters about which people are doubtful and undecided. It is no longer considered to be merely a matter of opinion that the earth is a sphere rotating on an axis and revolving in an orbit around the sun. It is a matter of *fact* which can be demonstrated, and about which "reasonable men do not differ." But it is a matter of *opinion* whether the nations of the earth should attempt to cooperate in some sort of international organization, and, if so, what form this organization should take. In matters of opinion, reasonable men may hold widely different viewpoints.

When a problem affects a number of people, they will discuss it and argue about it. These activities help to develop a common opinion, or *consensus*. Thus, a family which has to move from its present home may be uncertain whether to stay in the same neighborhood, and whether to rent, buy, or build a house. Family members may have differing views on these questions. These various views will have to be reconciled in some way before the family can reach a satisfactory decision. At first, therefore, the group cannot be said to have an opinion, although it is in the process of forming one. When a decision is worked out, it may be said to be group opinion in the sense that it is taken as a basis for group action.

In this illustration the opinion of the group differs from public opinion only because the family is a closed group and generally carries on such discussion in private. When discussion is open or public, then the matters involved are public and the opinions about these matters are public opinions. Public opinion, in

this sense, varies widely in its character and content. Public opinion may be merely a hodgepodge of individual opinions in the early stages of discussion, when issues are not sharply defined and people are not well informed about them. At other times, the opinions of many individuals may become similar enough to form a *majority opinion* or even a consensus which determines the kind of action a group will take.

Never before in the history of the world has there been such widespread discussion of public issues as there is today. This is extremely important because the spread of democracy as a form of government depends upon enlightened and responsible citizens.

There Is No One "Public"

A *public* is any group of people within which a controversy arises. They are the people who take part in the controversy and who are, or may be, affected by the way in which it is finally resolved. This group may be a fairly stable, organized one such as the residents of a local community or the citizens of the United States. A public also may be made up of a number of individuals who are unorganized and hard to identify, but who for widely varied reasons have a common interest in the matter at issue. Sometimes a public may be small and compact so that discussion takes place almost wholly through conversation and speech making in face-to-face situations. Nowadays, however, when modern means of communication make vast numbers of people aware of common interests, publics tend to be large and impersonal and to involve people who are not known to one another and are widely distributed over the country, or even among a number of countries. The members of such publics rarely meet each other face to face or have much direct communica-

759

tion. They are held together by the press, radio, television, motion pictures, and other means of communication. These impersonal but powerful publics are numerous in the highly complex society of today. Many of them even have their own specialized means of communication—their own newspapers and magazines, their own sponsored radio and television programs, their own local and national organizations representing opposing sides in controversies about issues.

The same person may be a member of several of these publics at one time. He may thus take part in discussions on a number of different problems and even develop opinions in one area that conflict with those he holds in other areas. His opinion about some economic issue, for example, may not be wholly in agreement with his opinion about some moral, religious, or political issue. Intense public controversies sometimes arise out of efforts to reconcile opinions about problems in one field with opinions in others.

The Process of Forming Opinion

Many factors affect the position people will take on any public issue. Some people are well informed or make an effort to become so; others make snap judgments on the basis of casual impressions. Some act quite independently, insisting on making up their own minds; others are influenced mainly by the views of their friends and associates. Equally well-informed persons often form differing opinions because they interpret facts differently, or because they have different interests, desires, anxieties, and prejudices.

Some individuals frequently have much more influence than others in the process of opinion formation. A Jean Jacques Rousseau, a Tom Paine, or a Thomas Jefferson appears to know all the facts and to have outstanding ability to determine how they should be dealt with. Therefore he may boldly and aggressively urge people to support a particular idea or a course of action. Leadership may be taken, too, by unknown or ordinary persons who, either as individuals or as small groups, spread their ideas slowly by word of mouth. In time they make a deep impression on the opinion of the masses of people.

Events also may have a great effect on the forming of opinion if they are dramatic enough, near enough, or personal enough to attract the attention of large numbers of individuals. The economic depression in the United States in the early 1930's focused public attention sharply on the need for economic reforms. Unemployment and widespread need changed more opinions than hundreds of lectures, radio talks, editorials, or sermons ever would have done.

Agencies of Public Opinion

An agency of public opinion is simply the carrier of information about public issues, and of views about these issues. The agency may be an individual, a group of individuals, or a mechanical device which helps them to communicate with other people. An agency of public opinion is not necessarily its originator or maker, but it may be so.

The Oldest Agency of public opinion is what Walter Bagehot, an English publicist of the 1800's, called *common talk*. Ordinary conversation among friends and acquaintances on the street, in public meeting places, in homes, or elsewhere, is still a powerful agency in forming public opinion. In early times, word of mouth was almost the only carrier of public opinion. It was but a step from friendly group discussions to the oration or the sermon, in which one person more apt at thought and expression than the rest undertakes to organize and state the prevailing opinion on some particular issue or problem for the group as a whole.

The Press. Speeches, books, and pamphlets were the principal means of expressing opinion until the 1800's. Then newspapers appeared in large numbers and soon developed wide circulations. The newspaper became more powerful than any other agency as a carrier of public opinion. Each newspaper usually builds up its own group of readers who depend on it for news and opinion about public affairs. Its power within the public is great, but this power is limited by rival newspapers with other points of view. Magazines are also powerful in making public opinion.

The cartoon is a powerful tool for expressing and molding opinion in the press. The cartoonist can caricature prominent persons and ideas, and thus can often express a point of view more bluntly and much more vigorously than it could be expressed in writing.

The Motion Picture is another important agency of public opinion. It has the advantage of giving people a vivid and concrete presentation of persons and events that otherwise could be known only through oral or printed reports. Audiences are introduced intimately to manners, customs, ideas, and ways of life that may be much different from their own. Many screen plays also express a point of view toward issues. Newsreels, travel pictures, documentary films, and other special kinds of motion pictures have been widely used to spread news and propaganda.

Radio and Television carry the voices and words of newscasters and commentators—and of newsworthy people themselves—directly into millions of homes. They also bring into the living room pictures of events as they occur. Radio and television have supplemented rather than replaced the newspaper and the motion picture as carriers of news and opinion. The older means of communication have time to give a more studied, fuller version of events than can the immediate reporting to which radio and television are best adapted.

Educational Agencies. Schools and other educational institutions have great importance among the agencies of opinion. Their importance lies partly in their ability to develop basic attitudes and points of view that have a great bearing on the opinions people will form about the issues that arise from day to day. They provide knowledge about social, economic, political, and other aspects of life, and equip people with the skills necessary to interpret information about current developments.

Other Agencies. The making of public opinion by special propaganda groups has by no means disappeared from modern society. The most important of these groups are those with political, economic, or religious interests. There are also similar groups of less power and importance busy creating ethical, nationalistic, racial, literary, artistic, and other types of public opinion. See PROPAGANDA.

Political opinion is made for the most part by or

for the political parties. Every large political party has an elaborate propaganda machine. Even the government in power, whether local or national, feels obliged to create a public opinion favorable to itself so that its program may be carried out.

The making of public opinion by economic groups is also important in modern society. Business and economic institutions constantly seek to create and maintain a public opinion favorable to their interests. Business, especially, is active in an endeavor to sell more goods and services. In doing so it uses advertising, salesmanship, and public relations to create favorable public opinion toward its products and business itself. Labor groups, farmer groups, and even consumers themselves are often organized for the purpose of making public opinion.

Public Opinion and Government

If people are going to live together in society, they must set up certain rules, regulations, and controls to give that society some permanent form, so that the society can carry on its life with little conflict or disorder. In a dictatorship, the controls set up are forced on the majority of the people by a small group who control the instruments of power. The people have little or no voice in deciding what kinds of controls are to be used. But in a democracy the controls rest on the voluntary consent of at least a majority of the members of society.

In many early societies, and in some countries today, leaders have used force or violence to make the people accept the rules. In some cases, the mere threat of violence is enough. Some leaders have used fraud to deceive the people. To protect their peoples from fraud, governments have extended laws against it to include unethical practices in medicine, advertising, selling, and other fields. See FRAUD.

Propaganda and censorship are the most widespread governmental controls over public opinion. With propaganda, the government seeks to make people accept its program and policies by persuading them that only such a program will keep them out of danger, or win a war, or meet some other emergency. Propaganda is actually a means of creating public opinion, rather than simply controlling it. Censorship, which seeks to eliminate ideas and attitudes, is a negative control over public opinion. It is often coupled with *counterpropaganda*, designed to meet the threat of one particular idea with one more favorable to the government. See CENSORSHIP; PROPAGANDA.

Democratic society requires the abandonment of the older, cruder, and less reasonable controls. Instead, an informed and intelligent public opinion is regarded as the best means of securing orderly conduct and cooperation among people. Public opinion becomes the ultimate controller of social goals, laws, and ways of life. Democracy as an ideal is government by an enlightened public opinion. The average man in any society soon learns to recognize that there are certain rules and regulations which he and everyone else in his society must live up to if he himself is to live in peace and freedom. Otherwise there will be no order, justice, or equality of opportunity.

When an individual has this point of view, he sooner or later resists any individual or group which seems to

be trying to gain more than its share of control in the whole society. The spread of education and the development of the newspaper, radio, and television have made it possible for more persons to learn more of what goes on in their society.

Controlling Public Opinion

There is little doubt that public opinion is the most powerful of all social controls in our modern world. Every group that is ambitious to rule or to exploit the masses of the people bends every effort to capture and control public opinion.

Democracy depends upon a balance of power of different groups rather than upon the power held by any one or few groups. Its basic controls will therefore be designed to secure for its citizens freedom to know the facts about public matters, to secure full and free public discussion, and to make public decisions effective. In the United States a number of such controls exist. First of all, the Constitution provides for a careful system of checks and balances. The President is balanced by Congress and the Supreme Court. Congress is balanced by the President and the Supreme Court. The Supreme Court is balanced by the President and Congress. In addition to this, the framers of the Constitution saw that they would have to provide further safeguards for the individual against any single group that might seize power. The first 10 amendments, or Bill of Rights, were added to the Constitution as a further protection of the opinions, privileges, and opportunities of citizens (see BILL OF RIGHTS).

One of these amendments assures freedom of speech, and this freedom has been jealously guarded throughout the history of the nation. The American Civil Liberties Union tries to help anyone, regardless of his views, if he feels that he has not obtained a fair hearing before the courts of justice or before the public itself. The machinery of Congress provides for congressional hearings where individuals are free to air their views.

An effective and progressive democracy depends on an enlightened public opinion. The surest, safest, and most constructive control of public opinion is education. The freedoms and liberties that a democratic society provides also impose a number of responsibilities upon citizens in a democracy. If they are to discharge these responsibilities capably and in their own interests, it is obvious that people must be sufficiently informed to know where their interests lie. They must be able to see the relationships among their own individual welfare, the proposals of the government, and the interests of various special groups.

Extensive and accurate education is democracy's greatest ally, just as it is the greatest enemy of antidemocratic forms of government. When people learn clearly the meaning of current events in their individual lives, they will make sound and sensible judgments. They will find it easier to see through the aims and devices of those who attempt to manipulate public opinion for narrowly selfish interests rather than the public good. HADLEY CANTRIL and CLYDE W. HART

See also ADVERTISING; CENSORSHIP; POLL OF PUBLIC OPINION; PROPAGANDA; PUBLIC RELATIONS.

PUBLIC OWNERSHIP. See GOVERNMENT OWNERSHIP.

PUBLIC RELATIONS

PUBLIC RELATIONS is the art of winning public favor for an organization or a person. In its simplest form, it is an extension of human relations. Evidence of efforts to create public opinion can be found in almost all periods of history. In its present form, public relations is a complex profession or business that is world-wide in scope.

Its Meaning. Despite the widespread influence of the profession, the term *public relations* is still rather widely misunderstood. Part of the misunderstanding arises from the combination of the two common words. When used together, they convey a meaning that is not explained by the definition of either *public* or *relations*. Public relations is more than merely relations with the public.

Another reason for the misunderstanding is that public relations is confused with *publicity*, which is but one of the devices, or methods, used by the profession. The same may be said about the work of a *press agent*, who often uses questionable methods to gain public favor that is not merited by the person or organization represented.

Authors of the many good books in the field stress the point that public relations attempts to gain public favor for an organization or a person only when the organization or person has ethical policies and practices, and strives to provide acceptable services to the public.

Methods of public relations communication include all the various devices and media of communications used in informing the public about any organization or person. In considering the public, the experts usually choose to reach many special groups as well as the general public. The devices and means of communication are carefully selected to accomplish this purpose. The devices are numerous. They include news stories; features; pictures; advertising; public addresses; letters and other mailing pieces; booklets and brochures; house organs and employee magazines; motion pictures, film strips, and picture exhibits; open houses and tours of the plant; personal visits of company representatives; pageants; and parades.

Public relations experts use research and opinion surveys to obtain information from the public for use by management in setting up policies and practices. Special groups that the experts contact include employees, stockholders, consumers, suppliers, creditors, government officials, other businesses, and educational institutions. These groups differ for each kind of organization. They may include agricultural groups, organized labor, young persons, older persons, alumni, parents, religious and national groups, veterans, men, or women. The experts contact these groups through the telephone, telegraph, radio, television, postal service, messenger, and conversation. The media used include newspapers, magazines, trade journals, radio stations, and television stations.

Early Days. Public relations as it is known today began to take form in the United States immediately after World War I. Rapid expansion in industry in the late 1800's had brought widespread corruption in business. This corruption led to widespread criticism of business in the early 1900's. Corporation leaders saw that their battle for bigger profits had strengthened this ill-feeling. They felt that the good will of the public would be more profitable to them. They had also seen the successful public relations campaigns carried out by the federal government, and by welfare agencies in winning approval for their various aims. Corporations began to set up programs designed to win the public's favor.

Recent Development. Professional public relations representatives have been employed to create a new idea of corporations in the public thinking. They combined the best features of earlier public relations programs. Most earlier programs had put more reliance on free publicity, good or bad, than upon more ethical and effective practices. But the new group adopted principles and procedures that were in the public interest. Improvements in such communications facilities as the telephone, telegraph, wireless telegraph, and newspapers and other periodicals aided the efforts of the public relations representatives.

Businesses employing public relations have continued to increase in number. Nonprofit organizations such as schools and hospitals began to see the need for organized attempts to gain public support. But public relations developed gradually until the close of World War II. Since then, it has had a large growth and has spread to nearly every large commercial and nonprofit organization. Today, public relations requires the efforts of tens of thousands of experts and demands the attention of millions of persons.

Careers in Public Relations. Organizations in nearly all fields of modern society use the services of public relations representatives. They may employ them as members of their staffs, or they may use the services of the many public relations counsels and consultants. The field of public relations has many well-established professional organizations on the international, national, regional, and local level. Such organizations make it easy to exchange new ideas and methods. They seek to maintain the standards of the profession.

Work in public relations is open to both men and women. The necessary qualifications have not been standardized, but are well established in the profession. Special talents and skills are called for in certain areas of public relations. Many representatives come from newspapers and advertising.

Formal courses in public relations have been available for about 40 years. But most large universities have only recently added training in this field to their programs. Such courses are usually offered in a school of journalism. Many good books and articles on public relations have become available.   EARL FRANKLIN ENGLISH

Related Articles in WORLD BOOK include:

Advertising	Press Clipping Bureau
Consumer Education	Propaganda
Motion Picture (Importance	Public Opinion
of Motion Pictures)	Salesmanship
Poll of Public Opinion	

PUBLIC REVENUE is funds raised through taxation to pay the expenses of government. See CITY AND LOCAL GOVERNMENTS (Finances); NATIONAL BUDGET; TAXATION.

PUBLIC ROADS, BUREAU OF. See ROADS, BUREAU OF PUBLIC.

PUBLIC SCHOOL. See EDUCATION; EDUCATION, HISTORY OF (The 1600's and 1700's; Public Schools); SCHOOL.

PUBLIC SPEAKING. Almost everyone belongs to an organization of some kind, and many persons belong to more than one. In group and club meetings, there are many opportunities to make speeches. Persons who speak effectively are likely to become the leaders of the group. Those who let others do all the talking seem likely to be the followers. Training in effective public speaking is an essential part of training for leadership in any field of activity.

A speaker who has a good purpose and is successful in attaining it is said to be *effective*. If he tries to make factual information clear, he is effective when the members of his audience understand the facts. If he tries to persuade members of the audience to agree to do something or to change their opinions, he is effective when they decide to take the action or when they do change their minds. If he tries to amuse the audience, he is effective when they show by applause or laughter that he is entertaining them.

Approach to a Speech

Every speaker must consider four points: (1) his subject, (2) his audience, (3) himself as a speaker, and (4) his occasion.

Subjects. The speaker's direct and indirect experiences are the two general sources of speech subjects. *Direct experience* is knowledge obtained by actual participation in events, through personally seeing, hearing, feeling, tasting, and smelling. *Indirect experience* is knowledge obtained through listening to the experiences of others and through reading what others have written. A speaker can usually make a more effective presentation with a subject from his direct experience than with a subject taken from someone else.

Subjects should stimulate speakers to their best efforts. At the same time, they must appeal to the audience and be keyed to the knowledge and experience of the listeners.

Subjects may be divided into three types: those which *inform*, those which *persuade*, and those which *entertain*. All are important.

Some examples of *informative* subjects are:
How to play chess
How designs are woven into cloth
The habits of snakes
How milk is pasteurized

Some examples of *persuasive* subjects are:
The thirteen-month calendar should be adopted.
The United States should adopt a uniform voting age of 18.
Capital punishment should be abolished.

Some examples of *entertaining* subjects are:
The private lives of our teachers
Inventions that never worked
Are women people?

Audiences. Speakers who talk about their subjects in terms of their own knowledge and their own wants, without regard for the knowledge and the wants of their audiences, are almost sure to fail. As a first step, the speaker should find out what the members of his audience already know about his subject. The problem of explaining the operation of a new fireless and heatless electric stove to a group of electrical engineers is very different from explaining it to an audience of people who know little about electricity.

M. E. Warren, Photo Researchers

Public Speakers should stand erect and speak loudly enough to be heard comfortably by every member of their audience.

The speaker who attempts to persuade an audience of high-school students to study economics should know their attitudes or opinions about studying economics. If he knows beforehand that his audience is strongly opposed to believing or doing what he proposes, then he recognizes that he faces a different and much more difficult problem from that of persuading a neutral or slightly favorable audience.

A speaker should also know whether the members of his audience want to hear about his subject. People usually listen only when they think the speaker's ideas will be of some benefit to them through satisfying one or more of their wants in whole or in part.

Speakers. The speaker's personality is probably the most important single factor in influencing audiences. Speakers should give some consideration to themselves.

Occasions. The speaker should think carefully about the time and place of his speech. Is the occasion appropriate for the subject he has chosen? The meeting of a businessmen's club would hardly be an appropriate occasion for a speech designed to sell household appliances. But such a meeting would be appropriate for a speech designed to raise money for community welfare.

Planning the Speech

When a speaker has given careful thought to his subject, his audience, his own personality, and the occasion, he is ready to plan the speech itself.

Purpose. A speaker's first step should be to select his general purpose. Does he wish to present factual information only, or *inform?* Does he wish to change beliefs or actions, or *persuade?* Or does he wish to amuse, or *entertain?* With his general purpose in mind, he should prepare a brief statement of his specific purpose. Examples of specific purposes are:

Informative. Tell a class how modern dairy operators pasteurize milk.

Persuasive. Convince an audience that Congress should propose an amendment to the Constitution providing for a uniform voting age of 18.

Entertaining. Amuse a school assembly with a discussion of the habits of teachers.

The Main Ideas. The next step should be to select the main ideas, or main divisions of the subject, as stated in the specific purpose. In informative speeches, the main ideas should define the specific purpose by answering the questions *who? what? where? when? why?* and *how?* In persuasive speeches, the main ideas ought to be the principal reasons for the desired belief or action. In entertaining speeches, the main ideas should be the divisions of the subject that can be amusing.

Supporting Material. After selecting the main ideas, the speaker should choose supporting material. This includes such things as *description, narration, comparisons, examples, testimony, statistics, visual aids* (charts, diagrams, demonstrations, slides, maps, motion pictures, photographs, samples, or working models), and *repetition* (restatement of important ideas to increase the chance that they will be remembered).

The selection of main ideas and supporting material completes the *body* (main part) of the speech.

Introduction. The speaker should next plan the introduction. This usually has two parts, the opening and the statement of the specific purpose. In the *opening*, the speaker catches the attention of his audience and arouses interest in his subject. In his *statement of specific purpose*, he tells the audience precisely what he intends to do in his speech.

Conclusion. Next comes the preparation of a conclusion. In informative speeches, this part should be a summary of the main ideas and specific purpose. In persuasive speeches, it should combine a summary with a final appeal to the audience to accept the arguments offered. Entertaining speeches usually end on a point of great amusement, without a formal conclusion.

Outline. After all these steps are completed, the speaker should prepare an outline. Here is a sample outline for the subject, Congress should propose an amendment providing for a uniform voting age of 18.

Introduction

Opening:

I. The issue, should 18-year-olds have the right to vote, is a common one to each generation, but the issue is especially pertinent when teen-age American war veterans return from combat. Because voting requirements are not found in the United States Constitution, each state establishes its own. These requirements vary in different states. A Constitutional amendment should be proposed to provide for a specific age at which citizens of the United States would have the right to vote.

Purpose:

II. Young men are required to register for selective service at age 18, and, at the same age, young women are considered to be of legal age in many states. It is time that we give proper consideration to the idea that if women are of legal age and men are considered mature enough to defend this country in armed combat at 18, they should also be allowed to vote at 18.

Body

I. The Constitution of the United States does not specify voter qualifications. The powers not specifically granted to the federal government are reserved for the states.

   A. Thus, the right to establish voter qualifi-

cations, including voting age, is left to the individual states.

   1. Twenty-one has come to be traditionally regarded as the age of maturity, and consequently many states consider 21 the legal voting age.
   2. Yet there are legal exceptions to this.
      a. In Georgia and Kentucky, a person is eligible to vote at age 18.
      b. In Alaska, a person is eligible to vote at age 19.
      c. In Hawaii, a person is eligible to vote at age 20.

   B. A Constitutional amendment could provide a consistent age for voter eligibility.
   1. At present, a person living in Georgia, Kentucky, Alaska, or Hawaii is allowed to vote before he is 21.
   2. A move to another state may nullify a person's right to vote.

II. Rights should be equal to the duties imposed on 18-year-olds.

   A. Young men at 18 risk their lives defending this country, but they are not able, in most cases, to vote until they are 21.
   B. Young women at 18 are considered to be of legal age in some states, but in most of the states, they are not able to vote until they are 21.

III. As life expectancy continues to increase, the proportion of elderly in the electorate increases.

   A. Since 1900, the average length of life has increased by more than 20 years.
   B. Enfranchising the 18-year-olds would offset the preponderance of the elderly in the electorate.

Conclusion

Men were given the right to vote by the states. The 19th Amendment was necessary in order to give women the right to vote. However, it has not been specified in either case at what age men and women become eligible to vote. Congress should propose a Constitutional amendment to provide for a uniform voting age of 18.

A speaker may deliver his talk directly from the outline, or he may use the outline as the basis for a written speech. Skilled speakers usually prefer to speak from the outline, without writing the whole speech down. A speech delivered from an outline, without being memorized, is said to be delivered *extempore*, or *extemporaneously*. Extempore speeches should not be confused with *impromptu* speeches which are made without any previous preparation, often without notice.

When preparing a speech for delivery, speakers should be careful to develop habits that will be helpful when the speech is presented. They should learn to walk gracefully and stand erect. They should talk directly to individual members of their audiences, speak loudly enough to be heard with ease, and vary the pitch and volume of their voices and their rate of speech to avoid being singsong or dull.   W. HAYES YEAGER

For the history of public speaking, see the article ORATORS AND ORATORY. See also DEBATE; SPEECH.

PUBLIC UTILITY is a business that performs an essential service to the public. Public utilities include telephone, telegraph, electricity, gas, water, and garbage disposal services. Public transportation systems such as airlines, bus lines, pipelines, railroads, and city transit systems are also public utilities. Many public utilities have a monopoly on their particular service within a given area. Most public utilities operate under government regulation or ownership.

Public utilities make up a major group of industries in the U.S. economy. They account for almost 30 per cent of the total assets of *nonfinancial businesses* (all firms except banks, insurance companies, and similar institutions). Among nonfinancial businesses, public utilities rank second only to the manufacturing group in total assets.

As the United States economy has become industrialized, urbanized, and interdependent, public-utility services have become necessary for the smooth functioning of economic activity. Interruption of any public utility service is considered a crisis.

Ownership. Most public utilities in the United States are privately owned. But in Canada and most other countries of the Free World, most are owned by the government. Government ownership in the United States exists chiefly at the local level. *Municipal* (city and town) governments own most airports, incinerators, transit systems, sewage-disposal systems, and water supply and distribution systems. Federal ownership is limited chiefly to electric generation and transmission facilities. Federally owned power plants account for about 13 per cent of the total electric generation capacity in the U.S. The electric generating and transmission facilities of the Tennessee Valley Authority are a well-known federal public-utility project.

Public utilities are often called *natural monopolies*. In a given area, one company can often provide certain services more efficiently and at lower cost than could several competing companies. Competition in the telephone industry, for example, would be costly and inefficient, because it would require several sets of telephone poles in a town instead of a single set. The nature of the service provided by a public utility makes a monopoly desirable.

Certain features of public utilities save money for the public. Many public-utility services are supplied under conditions of *decreasing cost*. That is, the unit cost of the service to the individual goes down as the service or number of customers increases. Also, the prices of services are regulated by government agencies.

Regulation. Government regulation of public utilities is necessary because they are given a legal monopoly on a service. The aim of utility regulation is to make sure that consumers have adequate supplies of high-quality service at the lowest prices that will still permit the utility company to make a reasonable profit. Most utility regulations are set down in a permit, certificate, or franchise granted by a governmental unit. The company receives the exclusive right to serve a given market. The company also usually must get permission from the regulating authority to reduce, withdraw, or change its service.

Public-utility regulations can be established at any level of government. Courts have ruled that the legislative branch has power to name activities that should be under utility regulation. Most states have *public-service commissions* or similar agencies that oversee the regulation of state utility activities. In some states, certain utility activities are regulated at the local level. Federal commissions regulate public-utility companies that provide service across state boundaries. The Interstate Commerce Commission regulates transportation other than airlines, natural-gas pipelines, and coastal shipping. The Federal Power Commission controls the transmission and sale of natural gas and electricity. The Federal Communications Commission has authority over interstate telecommunications and radio and television licensing. The Civil Aeronautics Board regulates the economic affairs of interstate airlines. The Federal Maritime Commission controls coastal shipping in U.S. vessels.

History. Public utilities in the modern sense can be traced to early English *common law*. Common law designated certain activities as "peculiarly affected with the public interest." Included were docks, inns, warehouses, ferries, and canal companies. These activities were regulated by court decision, and not by legislation or public-service commissions.

In the United States, regulations of public utilities by state legislation began in 1877. That year, the Supreme Court of the United States ruled that states could pass laws to regulate the prices charged by railroads and other companies. Laws setting forth specific regulations of price, profit, and quality of service soon proved unmanageable. Public-service commissions were developed to perform these functions. Federal regulation began in 1887, when the Interstate Commerce Act established the Interstate Commerce Commission. All the other federal utility commissions were established during or after the 1930's.　　　WALLACE F. LOVEJOY

Related Articles in WORLD BOOK include:

City and Local Governments	Federal Power Commission
Civil Aeronautics Board	Franchise
Federal Aviation Administration	Interstate Commerce Commission
Federal Communications Commission	Monopoly and Competition
Federal Maritime Commission	

PUBLIC WELFARE ASSOCIATION, AMERICAN, was founded in 1930. It serves as a clearing house for information, and seeks to raise the standards of public welfare administration. More than 5,200 agencies and individuals are members. The association has headquarters at 1313 E. 60th St., Chicago, Ill. 60637.

PUBLIC WORKS ADMINISTRATION. See NEW DEAL (Leading New Deal Agencies).

PUBLICITY. See ADVERTISING; BARNUM, PHINEAS TAYLOR; PUBLIC RELATIONS.

PUBLISHERS-HALL SYNDICATE is a news and feature syndicate that serves more than 2,000 daily and weekly newspapers throughout the world. Its services include over a hundred columns, cartoons, and other features. Publishers-Hall Syndicate was formed in June, 1967. It is owned by Field Enterprises, Inc., publisher of the *Chicago Sun-Times* and the *Chicago Daily News*. Headquarters are at 30 East 42nd Street, New York, N.Y. 10017.　　　ROBERT M. HALL

PUBLISHING

PUBLISHING means making public the words and pictures that creative minds have produced, that editors have selected and prepared for the printers, and that printers have reproduced.

The *publisher* of a book, newspaper, or magazine is the person or group who directs the business and general policies of the publication. A book publisher, or the publisher of a small magazine or newspaper, may also help edit or sell the publication. *Editors* have the responsibility of obtaining, choosing, revising, and preparing what is to be published. They often originate ideas for what is to be published. They must be sure that the rights to what they publish are protected (see COPYRIGHT). They work with writers, reporters, photographers, and illustrators. Other persons in a publishing house are responsible for mechanical production, and for advertising, promotion, and selling.

An important part of publishing is arranging for distribution to the consumers. Publishers of all kinds advertise and sell their publications by mail. Book publishers must also arrange for wholesalers, booksellers, or traveling representatives to sell their products to libraries, schools, colleges, and the public. Newspaper publishers must provide for newsstand distribution and home delivery. Magazine publishers sell by subscription and through wholesalers who distribute copies to local newsstands. Export agents handle the distribution of publications in other countries.

Types of Publishing

Books. Book publishers in the United States sell $1\frac{1}{2}$ billion copies of books each year. Buyers pay over $2 billion for these books. More than 20,000 new books appear in the United States annually. Over 8,000 reprints or revised editions of older books also appear. About 550 book firms issue five or more titles a year, and about 3,000 companies publish at least some books. About 25,000 persons work in book publishing, not counting production employees. See BOOK.

Trade-Book Publishing is the term used for issuing books of a general nature to be sold mainly through bookstores or the book departments of other stores. These books include many for children and young people, and adult books on biography, history, current affairs, travel, religion, cooking, and "how-to-do-it." A trade book must usually sell several thousand copies if it is to make a profit—8,000 copies is often quoted as the "break-even point." Many titles do not meet this figure. But the book may nevertheless earn the publisher a profit, because he may receive other income from it. For example, he may sell a book club the right to print extra quantities for its subscribers. He may sell reprint rights to a publisher of low-cost paper-covered reprints. He also may sell to newspapers or magazines the right to print parts of the book. Proceeds of such sales are shared with authors on varying terms. Authors usually get the larger share of film, drama, radio, and television rights. Trade-book sales total about 160 million books a year, with the publishers receiving almost $250 million.

Paper-Covered Book Publishing includes the production of small-sized, brightly covered paper-bound editions. These are usually reprints of higher-priced, hard-cover

Chandler B. Grannis, the contributor of this article, is Senior Associate Editor, Publishers' Weekly.

books, but include many new books. Two main factors make this kind of publishing possible. High-speed presses and binding machines make possible the mass production of 100,000 or more copies of each title. In the United States, about 800 magazine wholesalers and 120,000 newsstands provide the mass distribution of these books. Thousands of these books are also sold in schools. Sales of lower priced paper-bound books exceed 245 million copies a year, with the publishers receiving over $65 million. Higher-priced paperbacks are sold by general bookstores and college stores. About 50 million copies of them are sold each year. Publishers receive about $35 million annually for them.

Paper-covered book publishing also includes certain low-cost books for children. These are sold largely in supermarkets and in variety, candy, drug, and department stores. The publishers sell more than 120 million of these books a year, receiving around $35 million.

Book Clubs are a form of publishing in which readers agree to buy a certain number of books every year from among those selected by the club's editors. These books are sold by mail to the subscribers, usually at reduced prices. Club sales total 76 million books a year, for which members pay about $145 million.

Textbook Publishing, the largest branch of the book industry, each year accounts for more than 305 million copies of school and college books and workbooks. It brings in about $508 million a year to the publishers. This field of publishing is growing rapidly, with the increased school population, and support from government funds. The publishers work closely with educational leaders. Most elementary and high-school books are produced by carefully organized teams of editors, authors, illustrators, designers, and educational advisers. They are sold, mainly by traveling representatives, to schools, school systems, and state agencies. The college texts are usually prepared by scholars, and sold by salesmen to the colleges.

Subscription-Book Publishing involves the distribution of books through salesmen who call on buyers in homes, libraries, schools, colleges, or other places. These books include encyclopedias, sets of the classics, and sets of works by famous authors. Permanent staffs of editors keep the major encyclopedias, such as THE WORLD BOOK ENCYCLOPEDIA, up to date. They enlist the aid of outside contributors who are specialists in different fields of knowledge. About 90 million volumes of encyclopedias are sold every year, with the publishers' receipts amounting to over $410 million.

Other Book Publishing includes the highly specialized production of business, technical, scientific, medical, and law books. These books account for more than 33 million volumes sold each year, and bring in about $192 million to the publishers. Bibles, hymnals, and other religious books total about 70 million volumes a year, worth about $86 million to the publishers. *Subsidized publishing* is publishing at the expense of a professional, religious, or academic body, not primarily to make a profit but to meet some special need. *University presses* are publishers owned by universities. They do some subsidized publishing in addition to some technical and trade-book publishing. The total sales by uni-

LEADING PRINTING AND PUBLISHING COUNTRIES
Value added by manufacture in 1965

United States	$10,684,000,000
Great Britain	$1,363,000,000
Japan	*$991,000,000
Germany (West)	$940,000,000
Canada	$662,000,000
France	$590,000,000
Australia	$396,000,000
Italy	$343,000,000
Netherlands	$261,000,000
Sweden	$242,000,000

*1963, latest available information.
Figures for Russia and China (Mainland) are not available.

Source: Statistical Office of the UN

LEADING PRINTING AND PUBLISHING STATES AND PROVINCES
Value added by manufacture in 1965

State/Province	Value
New York	$2,878,830,000
Illinois	$1,379,718,000
California	$924,920,000
Pennsylvania	$796,808,000
Ohio	$758,667,000
Massachusetts	$515,576,000
New Jersey	$428,283,000
Ontario	$366,206,000
Michigan	$365,264,000
Missouri	$341,059,000

Sources: Bureau of the Census; Dominion Bureau of Statistics

versity presses amount to about $20 million each year.

Magazines. More than 8,600 magazines and periodicals of all kinds are published in the United States each year. The leading 700 magazines have a combined circulation of over 275 million copies a year. Magazines appear weekly, monthly, or quarterly (every three months). Some have general reading appeal. Others, such as trade journals and religious periodicals, cover special interests. One magazine has a circulation of over 15 million copies an issue. Several have circulations of more than 7 million copies. See MAGAZINE.

Newspapers. Newspaper publishing is one of the principal industries in the United States. There are about 1,750 daily newspapers; 560 Sunday newspapers; and 8,190 weekly newspapers. Daily newspapers have a combined circulation of about $60\frac{1}{2}$ million copies a day. Sunday newspapers have a total circulation of over $48\frac{1}{2}$ million copies each Sunday. Weekly newspapers have a combined circulation of about 24 million copies each week. In the mid-1960's, newspapers had an income of about $4\frac{1}{4}$ billion a year. See NEWSPAPER.

Careers in Publishing

Success in publishing depends to a great degree on the ability, originality, and luck of persons who choose this field for a career. One of the most successful magazines in the United States was begun in a garage with an original investment of only a few thousand dollars. In most cases, however, the publisher must invest a great deal more money, and a profit comes only after he has spent large sums for editorial work, printing, binding, and other phases of publishing.

The publishing industry affords opportunities for young men and women in many kinds of jobs. It needs writers, editors, researchers, artists, and proofreaders. Mechanical production requires printers, engravers, pressmen, and binders. The distribution and circulation of published works is carried on by salesmen, and by advertising and promotion workers. Other office workers assist them.

Literary agents are an important part of publishing. They assist writers in preparing manuscripts for publishing, and in finding publishers for their works.

Librarians perform an important role in publishing. Publishers often consult them about the types of books, magazines, and papers to be published. Librarians assist publishers and editors in editorial research by helping them assemble facts and other material for work to be published.

History

In ancient civilizations, scribes prepared copies of a poem, a play, a work of philosophy or religion, or a book of laws. Such manuscripts were written on sheets of paper-like *papyrus*, or of *parchment* (animal skin). The sheets were usually put together and rolled up to form scrolls. These books were for only a few persons in ancient Egypt, Greece, and other countries. Rich men could buy them and educated men could read them. When the Roman Empire was established about 400 years later, this kind of publishing had become a vital element in the civilized world. The Romans may be said to have begun newspaper publishing by posting bulletins of current events and official notices in public places. During the Middle Ages, beautiful manuscript books helped scholars, monks, and a few princes keep learning alive in Europe. Publishing in the modern sense was not possible until the development of movable type and the printing press in Europe about 1440. Printing had to be developed further before the written word could be made easily available in printed form to everyone (see PRINTING).

CHANDLER B. GRANNIS

Related Articles. See JOURNALISM with its list of related articles on publishers. See also:

Bibliography	Encyclopedia	Manuscript
Book	Illustration	Map
Bookbinding	Library	Newspaper
Copyright	Magazine	Type

PUCCINI, GIACOMO

United Press Int.

Giacomo Puccini

PUCCINI, *poo CHEE nee,* **GIACOMO** (1858-1924), an Italian operatic composer, became famous for his fluent, melodic writing and bold, dramatic harmonies. His talent and originality were outstanding in his school of Italian composers. Although Puccini won recognition for his first opera, *Le Villi* (1884), his real success began with the production of *Manon Lescaut* (1893). He attained greater heights with *La Bohème* (1896), which Arturo Toscanini, then a young man, conducted in Turin. *Tosca* (1900), *Madame Butterfly* (1904), and *The Girl of the Golden West* (1910) showed new sides of Puccini's ability. Puccini died before he could finish his opera *Turandot*, based on an Oriental fantasy, but Franco Alfano completed it for him. It was produced in 1926, after Puccini's death.

Puccini was born in Lucca, Italy, of a musical family. He studied piano with his uncle, and, later, was educated at Milan Conservatory under Amilcare Ponchielli and Antonio Bazzini. While a student at Milan, Puccini composed *Capriccio Sinfonico*, a work for orchestra.   JOYCE MICHELL

See also OPERA (Some of the Famous Operas [La Bohème; Madame Butterfly; Tosca]).

PUCCOON is a name applied to many different kinds of wild flowers. See BLOODROOT; GOLDENSEAL.

PUCK, or ROBIN GOODFELLOW, a mischievous spirit or elf in English folklore, tormented people, usually in fun. He was also called HOBGOBLIN, and in 1595, Edmund Spenser, in one of his poems, included *the Pouke* among evil spirits. In *A Midsummer-Night's Dream*, William Shakespeare presented him as a good-hearted elf. Enjoying his pranks on human beings, Puck exclaimed, "Lord, what fools these mortals be!"

Fairies Dancing Around Puck, who is seated on a mushroom. Puck was active at night and the people of old England believed that he did many things to annoy them. If freezing water had broken a pitcher or if the fire died out before morning, that was said to be the work of mischievous Puck.

Culver

Puck figures prominently in Rudyard Kipling's *Puck of Pook's Hill* and *Rewards and Fairies.*   KNOX WILSON

PUDDING STONE is a type of *conglomerate stone* that has a number of small pebbles cemented together with lime, silica, iron oxide, or clay. It received its name because of its appearance.

PUDU. See DEER (Kinds of Deer).

PUEBLA, *PWEB luh,* or *pyoo EB luh,* is a state in east-central Mexico between Mexico City and the Gulf of Mexico (see MEXICO [political map]). Puebla has a population of 2,307,852 and an area of 13,096 square miles. Mexico's three highest mountains, Orizaba (Citlaltépetl), Popocatepetl, and Ixtacihuatl, stand on Puebla's borders. Farmers grow barley, corn, green peppers, peanuts, potatoes, rice, sugar cane, and wheat. Puebla also produces apples, peaches, plums, and other fruits. It is also an important textile center. The city of Puebla is the capital.   CHARLES C. CUMBERLAND

PUEBLA (pop. 349,459; alt. 7,150 ft.), officially PUEBLA DE ZARAGOZA, *thah SAH rah GO sah,* one of the largest cities in Mexico, stands 65 miles southeast of Mexico City. It is the capital of the state of Puebla. For location, see MEXICO (political map). Puebla has many beautiful Spanish-style churches and other buildings. The city's chief products include cotton textiles, glass, fine pottery, and beautifully colored tiles. Founded about 1535, Puebla is one of the oldest Spanish settlements in Mexico.   CHARLES C. CUMBERLAND

PUEBLO, ship. See COLD WAR (Unrest in Southeast Asia); KOREAN WAR (Peace Negotiations).

PUEBLO, *pyoo EHB loh,* Colo. (pop. 91,181; met. area 118,707; alt. 4,690 ft.), is Colorado's chief industrial center. The city lies in a large farming and coal-mining district, and ranks as the state's second largest city. For location, see COLORADO (political map). For the weather in Pueblo, see COLORADO (Climate).

Pueblo has the largest steel mill west of the Mississippi River. Other industries include meat packing, flour milling, and the manufacture of brooms, brick, and tile. Pueblo has one of the largest piston-manufacturing plants in the country. Pueblo Ordnance Depot is one of the nation's largest ordnance installations.

The city was founded in 1840 as Fort Pueblo. However, Ute Indians destroyed the settlement in 1854. Gold seekers came upon the fort later the same year, and began another settlement called Fountain City. The town was formally laid out in 1860, and named Pueblo in honor of the old fort. The city was incorporated in 1870. It has a council-manager government. Pueblo is the seat of Pueblo County.   HAROLD H. DUNHAM

PUEBLO INDIANS, *PWEB loh.* Pueblo is the Spanish word for *village.* When Spanish explorers first arrived in New Mexico and Arizona in the 1500's, they found people living in compact, terraced structures. The Spanish called these settlements *pueblos,* and their occupants *Pueblo Indians.* These Indians were one of the most civilized groups of North American Indians.

Way of Life. Pueblo Indians lived as farmers, and grew corn, pumpkins, and beans. Because they stayed in one place, they were able to develop complex ways of living that included their famous apartment-house villages. They built their large buildings of boulders or adobe set in mud mortar. They made the rooms in terraces, so that the roofs of the lower rows of rooms formed the porches for those above. The houses, some-

Santa Fe Railway

Pueblo Indians of Taos, N. Mex., Have Lived in Adobe Houses With Windows and Doors Since the 1500's.

times four or five stories high, had few windows and no doors. People entered a room by climbing up a ladder to the roof, then down another ladder through a roof hole into the room below. In time of war, the Indians pulled up all the ladders and turned the village into a fort. They kept supplies of dried corn, beans, and squash inside the great buildings. Each pueblo contained at least one *kiva*, a ceremonial chamber for men.

Although many changes have occurred among the Pueblo Indians, most of them continue to live in their villages and farm their small fields. Many Indians work in nearby towns. The Pueblo Indians have always been excellent craftsmen. Some villages are known for their beautiful pottery, others for their fine baskets. Many Indians make jewelry of silver with turquoise or shell. In recent years, several artists have gained fame for their paintings of traditional subjects. Men and women in colorful costumes hold dramatic dances throughout the year in the old rituals.

Pueblo Villages

The following list of Pueblo villages is grouped according to the language spoken in each:

KERESAN FAMILY

Acoma	Laguna	Santa Ana	Zía
Cochiti	San Felipe	Santo Domingo	

SHOSHONEAN FAMILY (Hopi Villages)

Bakabi	Mishongnovi	Shungopavy, or
Hotevilla	Moenkopi	Shungopovi
Kiakotsmovi, or	Oraibi	Sichomovi
New Oraibi	Shipaulovi	Walpi

TANOAN FAMILY

Jemez Dialect
Jemez

Tigua Dialect
Isleta
Picurís
Sandía
Taos

Tewa Dialect
Hano (in "Hopiland")
Nambé
Pojoaque
San Ildefonso
San Juan
Santa Clara
Tesuque

ZUÑIAN FAMILY
Zuñi

History. The Pueblo way of life, part of the so-called *Anasazi* culture, is very old. (For the story of its earliest days, see CLIFF DWELLERS [History].) The first white man to see the Pueblo villages, Fray Marcos de Niza, traveled in what is now New Mexico in 1539. His reports inspired an expedition of explorers under Francisco Coronado in 1540. The Spanish did not find the gold they were looking for, but they did begin to subdue the Indian villages.

In the years that followed, they sent priests to convert the Indians, and built churches that still stand. In 1680 the Indians revolted under their leader, Popé, but the Spanish put down the uprising (see INDIAN WARS [The Pueblo Revolt]). The United States received the Pueblo country from Mexico in 1848, but the government guaranteed that the Indians could keep all their old customs and ceremonies.

Today about 23,000 Pueblo Indians live in 30 villages in New Mexico and Arizona. They do not make up one tribe. Each independent group has its own complete organization and its own officials, although different groups meet in councils to discuss common problems. Because of the various languages spoken by the people, the residents in one pueblo may not be able to talk to people in a nearby pueblo, unless they speak English. Most of the pueblos are in the Rio Grande valley of New Mexico, and are found between Taos and Albuquerque. Laguna and Acoma stand about 50 miles to the west. Zuni lies close to the Arizona border. The Hopi villages are located on three *mesas*, or tablelands, in Arizona.   BERTHA P. DUTTON

See also CIBOLA, SEVEN CITIES OF; HOPI INDIANS; NEW MEXICO (picture: Pueblo Ruins); ZUÑI INDIANS.

PUERTO BELLO. See PORTOBELO.

PUERTO PLATA, *PWER toe PLAH tah* (pop. 19,073; alt. 50 ft.), is the main seaport on the northern coast of the Dominican Republic. For location, see DOMINICAN REPUBLIC (map).

Puerto Plata exports coffee, cacao, sugar, and tobacco. The city produces chocolate, matches, dairy products, and liquor.   THOMAS G. MATHEWS

769

PUERTO RICO

Hills Surround Aguas Buenas in the Caguas Valley

Tom Hollyman, Photo Researchers

Fritz Henle, Photo Researchers

Church of San José, the Oldest Church in San Juan

Hannau

Modern Hotels Line the Beaches of San Juan

The contributors of this article are Thomas G. Mathews, Director of the Institute of Caribbean Studies of the University of Puerto Rico; Rafael Picó, Vice-Chairman, Board of Directors of the Banco Popular de Puerto Rico; and Pablo Vargas Badillo, Editor Emeritus of El Mundo.

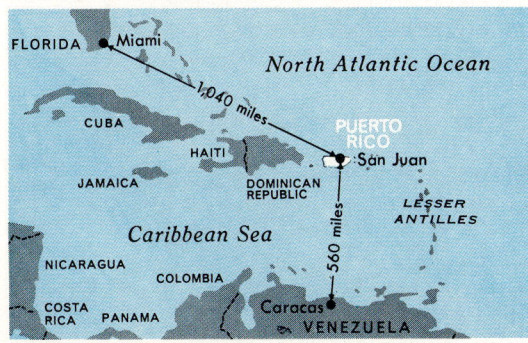

Puerto Rico, if it were a state, would rank 49th in size. Only Delaware and Rhode Island would have smaller areas.

PUERTO RICO is a beautiful, fertile island about a thousand miles southeast of Florida. It forms part of the boundary between the Atlantic Ocean and the Caribbean Sea. Puerto Rico's pleasant climate, sandy beaches, and resort hotels make the island a favorite vacation place for tourists from the U.S. mainland. Puerto Rico's official name is COMMONWEALTH OF PUERTO RICO.

Puerto Ricans are U.S. citizens, and can move to the mainland without immigration restrictions. But when living on the island, they cannot vote in presidential elections and do not pay federal income taxes. The commonwealth receives assistance and protection from the U.S. government. But the Puerto Rican government has authority in all local matters.

Puerto Rico is the only part of the United States where Christopher Columbus is believed to have landed. Columbus discovered the island in 1493 and claimed it for Spain. Spain surrendered Puerto Rico to the United States in 1898 at the end of the Spanish-American War.

The name *Puerto Rico* is Spanish. In English, it means *Rich Port*. In early colonial days, it was the name for San Juan, Puerto Rico's capital and largest city. The name gradually came to be used for the entire island.

Puerto Rico's Spanish heritage is reflected in the language and customs of its people. Spanish is the main language of Puerto Rico, although many Puerto Ricans speak English. The people celebrate religious holidays with colorful festivals. Churches and forts from Spanish colonial days still stand on the island.

Puerto Rico also reflects its ties with the United States. The island's large cities have freeways, housing projects, and shopping centers like those in many cities on the United States mainland. Puerto Rico also has about 2,000 factories owned by both United States and Puerto Rican investors.

FACTS IN BRIEF

Capital: San Juan.

Government: *Congress*—Resident Commissioner, who has no vote. *Commonwealth Legislature*—senators, 26; representatives, 51. *Local Government*—76 municipalities. *Voting Age*—21 years.

Area: 3,435 square miles (including Culebra, Mona, and Vieques islands). *Greatest Distances*—(east-west) 111 miles; (north-south) 39 miles. *Coastline*—311 miles.

Elevation: *Highest*—Cerro de Punta, 4,389 feet above sea level. *Lowest*—sea level along the coast.

Population: *1960 Census*—2,349,544; density, 684 persons to the square mile; distribution, 56 per cent rural, 44 per cent urban. *1965 Estimate*—2,641,000.

Chief Products: *Agriculture*—bananas, beef, coffee, eggs, livestock, milk, pineapples, plantains, poultry, sugar cane, tobacco. *Manufacturing*—candy; cement; chemicals; cigars; clothing; furniture; machinery and metal products; pottery and china; rum; stone, clay, and glass products; sugar; textiles.

Became a Commonwealth: July 25, 1952.

Commonwealth Motto: *Joannes Est Nomen Ejus* (John Is His Name).

Commonwealth Song: "La Borinqueña." Words by Lola Rodríguez de Tío; music by Felix Astol y Artés.

771

PUERTO RICO / Government

Puerto Rico is a self-governing commonwealth associated with the United States by its own desire and consent. Most federal laws apply to Puerto Rico as though it were a state. Puerto Rico is represented in the U.S. Congress by a resident commissioner. He is elected to a four-year term, but has no vote in Congress.

Commonwealth Government operates under its own constitution, adopted in 1952. The governor is the chief executive officer. He is elected to a four-year term and may be re-elected an unlimited number of times. The governor receives a yearly salary of $25,000. He appoints the other top executive officers.

The legislature of Puerto Rico consists of a senate and a house of representatives. Members of both houses serve four-year terms. The commonwealth is divided into 8 senatorial districts and 40 representative districts. The total number of senators and representatives varies from election to election, according to a complicated formula. Under this formula, if one political party controls more than two-thirds of the seats of either house, but does not have two-thirds of the popular vote, the minority parties receive extra *senators-at-large* or *representatives-at-large*.

Courts. The supreme court is the highest court in Puerto Rico. It has seven justices appointed by the governor for life. Puerto Rico's 30 superior court judges are appointed to 12-year terms. The 55 district court judges are appointed to 8-year terms.

Local Government. Puerto Rico has no counties. Its basic unit of local government is the *municipio* (*municipality*). The commonwealth is divided into 76 municipalities. The voters in each municipality elect a mayor and an assembly. The mayor appoints a secretary-auditor and a treasurer. Cities and towns within the municipalities operate under the municipal governments, and do not have separate governments.

Politics. Political parties that receive at least 5 per cent of the vote cast in Puerto Rican elections receive financial support from an electoral fund set up by the government. The commonwealth's leading political parties are the New Progressive Party, which wants Puerto Rico to

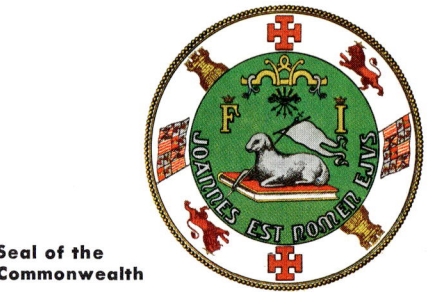

Seal of the Commonwealth

become a state, and the Popular Democratic Party, which favors continuing the island's commonwealth status. Other political parties in Puerto Rico include the Peoples Party, the Statehood Republican Party, and the Independence Party.

PUERTO RICO / People

Puerto Rico is a crowded island. New Jersey and Rhode Island are the only states that have more people per square mile. The 1960 United States census reported that Puerto Rico had 2,349,544 persons. The population had increased about 6 per cent over the 1950 figure, 2,210,703. The U.S. Bureau of the Census estimated that by 1965 the island's population had reached about 2,641,000.

More than two-thirds of Puerto Rico's people live in the metropolitan areas of San Juan, Ponce, and Mayagüez. These three areas are Standard Metropolitan Statistical Areas as defined by the U.S. Bureau of the Budget (see METROPOLITAN AREA). For their populations, see the *Index* to the political map of Puerto Rico.

San Juan, Puerto Rico's capital and largest city, is a seaport on the north coast. Ponce, the second largest city, is a commercial and cultural center on the south coast. Mayagüez, on the west coast, is the third largest city. It is becoming a major industrial center.

The first inhabitants of Puerto Rico were the Arawak Indians. Most of them were killed or died of disease after the Spanish settlers came. No full-blooded Indians are now known to live in Puerto Rico. But some Puerto Ricans are descended from Indians who intermarried with Spanish settlers. Beginning in 1510, Negroes were brought from Africa to work on the plantations and in the small gold mines. Today, their descendants live chiefly in the lowlands near the coast.

By far the largest part of the present population is of Spanish descent. There are smaller numbers of Portuguese, Italians, and French. About four of every five Puerto Ricans are Roman Catholics. Members of the Assemblies of God, Baptist, Methodist, and Presbyterian churches make up the largest Protestant groups.

Flag of the Commonwealth

Carl Levin Associates, Inc.

Symbols of Puerto Rico. On the seal, the lamb symbolizes peace and brotherhood. King Ferdinand of Spain granted the seal to Spanish settlers in 1511. The initials stand for Ferdinand and his queen, Isabella. The symbols in the border are taken from Spanish coats of arms. The flag was designed about 1895 and was officially adopted in 1952. It resembles the Cuban flag, recalling the 1890's, when both countries opposed Spanish rule.

Puerto Rico's Capitol, in San Juan, was first used in 1929. San Juan has been the capital since 1521. The first capital, established in 1508, was Caparra, across the bay from San Juan.

PUERTO RICO MAP INDEX

PUERTO RICO

★ COMMONWEALTH CAPITAL
● CITIES AND TOWNS
— MAJOR ROADS
— MUNICIPAL BOUNDARIES

WORLD BOOK map

0 5 10 Miles
0 5 10 15 Kilometers

PUERTO RICO / Education

When Puerto Rico became a territory of the United States in 1898, only 20 per cent of its people could read and write. One of the first things the U.S. government did was to set up a public school system similar to those in the states. Today, over 90 per cent of the people can read and write.

Education is a major concern of the commonwealth government. Nearly a third of Puerto Rico's budget is spent for education. The commonwealth has over 20,000 teachers, and about 750,000 students. Spanish is the main language used in the schools, but all students are taught English as a second language. Many adults who did not finish school when they were young attend evening classes.

Puerto Rico has four universities. The largest is the University of Puerto Rico, founded in 1903. Its oldest campus is in the Río Piedras district of San Juan. The university's colleges of agriculture, arts and sciences, and engineering are in Mayagüez, and its schools of medicine and dentistry are also in San Juan. The three other universities are the Inter American University, with campuses in San Germán and San Juan; the Catholic University of Puerto Rico, in Ponce; and the College of the Sacred Heart, in San Juan.

University of Puerto Rico, founded in 1903, is the largest of the commonwealth's four universities. Its oldest campus, below, is in San Juan.

Fritz Henle, Photo Researchers

PUERTO RICO / A Visitor's Guide

Puerto Rico is famous for its sandy beaches and resort hotels. The island offers deep-sea fishing, skin diving, and other water sports. Cockfighting, a popular Latin American sport, takes place in *galleras* (cockpits) on weekends. Many visitors explore the historic buildings and colorful shops of Old San Juan. U.S. citizens do not need passports to travel to Puerto Rico.

PLACES TO VISIT

Following are brief descriptions of some of Puerto Rico's many interesting places to visit.

El Morro Fortress, built by the Spaniards between 1539 and 1787, guards the Bay of San Juan.

Luquillo Beach, in the northeast corner of the island, is one of Puerto Rico's most beautiful beaches. It has public lockers and picnic tables.

Phosphorescent Bay, at La Parguera on the southwest coast, is a breath-taking sight on moonless nights. Large numbers of phosphorescent *plankton* (tiny water animals and plants) make flashes of light on the water.

San Germán, a town in the southwest, dates from early Spanish colonial days. It has one of the oldest churches in the Western Hemisphere.

El Yunque, "the anvil," is a mountain with a rain forest on its slopes. Wild parrots fly among the trees, and wild orchids grow on the forest floor. El Yunque is the most popular part of the Caribbean National Forest, Puerto Rico's only national forest. For the forest's area and other features, see NATIONAL FOREST (table).

ANNUAL EVENTS

Puerto Rico has yearly drama festivals, music festivals, sports tournaments, fishing contests, and flower shows. One of the leading annual events is the Casals Festival in San Juan, from late May through early June. Musicians from many lands take part in an orchestra and chamber music program under the direction of Pablo Casals, the world-famous cellist.

Puerto Ricans have many holidays that are not generally celebrated on the United States mainland. Three Kings' Day, January 6, marks the end of the Christmas season. Puerto Rican children receive gifts on that day, as well as at Christmas. Each town has a patron saint, and celebrates the saint's day with a colorful festival. Other annual events include the following.

January-June: Birthday of the Puerto Rican educator and essayist Eugenio María de Hostos (January 11); Drama Festival in San Juan (mid-January to March); Puerto Rican Theater Festival in Old San Juan (mid-March to May); Emancipation Day, marking the abolition of slavery in 1873 (March 22); Birthday of José de Diego, Puerto Rican patriot (April 16); Tropical Flower Show in San Juan (April); Eve of San Juan Bautista Day (June 23).

July-December: Birthday of Luis Muñoz Rivera, Puerto Rican patriot (July 17); Commonwealth Day, marking the adoption of the Puerto Rican Constitution in 1952 (July 25); Birthday of the Puerto Rican statesman, José Celso Barbosa (July 27); Columbus Day, called *Día de la Raza,* or Day of the Race (October 12); Discovery Day, marking Columbus' discovery of Puerto Rico in 1493 (November 19).

El Morro Fortress in San Juan

Tom Hollyman, Photo Researchers

Dan Page, Photo Researchers

Watching a Cockfight in Mayagüez

Photo by Hannau

Resort Beach in San Juan

Snorkel Divers off the Coast of Palominos Island

Tom Hollyman, Photo Researchers

Tom Hollyman, Photo Researchers

Carnival Crowd in San Juan

A ─ 18°30'

North Atlantic Ocean

PT. AGUIJEREADA

PT. PUERTO NUEVO · PT. CERRO GORDO

PT. PICÚA

SAN JUAN · C. SAN JUAN · San Juan / Juan Passage

ICACOS

Fajardo + EL YUNQUE 3,493 FT.

CULEBRA (P.R.)

Vieques Sound

PALOMINOS

PIÑEROS

PT. PUERCA · PT. MULAS

Pasaje (Passage) de Vieques

VIEQUES (P.R.)

PT. VACA

Longitude West of Greenwich

PT. MALDONADO

SIERRA DE LUQUILLO · EL TORO 3,524 FT.

Gurabo

SAN JUAN ★

Bayamón

Caguas

Loíza

Guaynabo

Bayamón

La Plata

Cayey

L. Carite

Guayama

SIERRA DE CAYEY

CERRO LA SANTA 2,953 FT.

L. Patillas

PT. FIGURAS

PT. TUNA

CARIBES IS.

BARCA IS.

PETRONA RATONES IS.

PT. YEGUAS · 18°

PT. CANDELERO

Arecibo

Cibuco

Manatí

Río Negro

Yanés

CORDILLERA CENTRAL

Caonillas

L. Guayabal

Coamo

Rincón Bay

CAJA DE MUERTOS

Camuy

Guajataca

L. Guajataca

Andsco

Culebrinas

CERRO DE PUNTA 4,389 FT.

MONTAÑAS DE UROYAN

Rosario

Blanco

Yauco

L. Yauco

L. Guayabal

Ponce

PT. CUCHARA

CAÑA GORDA IS.

BERBERIA · 66°30'

Caribbean Sea

PT. JIGÜERO

PT. CADENA

Mayagüez Bay

Mayagüez

LA CADENA 1,214 FT.

Guajataca

L. Cartagena

L. Guajataca

L. Guánica

Salinas Bay · Sucia Bay

C. ROJO · Phosphorescent Bay

C ─ 18°

Especially created for **World Book Encyclopedia** by Rand McNally and World Book editors

PUERTO RICO / The Land

Puerto Rico is the fourth largest of the islands that lie between Florida and the north coast of South America. It covers 3,435 square miles. Puerto Rico includes many smaller islands. The largest of these, in order of size, are Vieques, Mona, and Culebra.

Land Regions. Puerto Rico has four main land regions: (1) the Coastal Lowlands, (2) the Coastal Valleys, (3) the Foothills, and (4) the Central Mountains.

The *Coastal Lowlands* border the coast on the north and the south. The northern lowlands are from about 8 to 12 miles wide. Their climate is generally humid. The southern lowlands

Map Index

Aguadilla Bay	B 1
Añasco River	B 2
Arecibo River	C 3
Barca Island	C 3
Bayamón River	C 3
Berberia (Island)	C 3
Blanco River	B 2
Caja de Muertos (Island)	C 2
Camuy River	B 2
Caña Gorda Island	C 2
Caonillas River	B 2
Cape Rojo	C 1
Cape San Juan	B 4
Caribes Island	C 3
Cerro de Punta (Mtn.)	C 3
Highest Point in Puerto Rico	B 2
Cerro la Santa (Mtn.)	B 3
Cibuco River	B 3
Cordillera Central	B 3
Culebra (Island)	B 5
Culebrinas River	B 1
El Toro (Mtn.)	B 4
El Yunque (Mtn.)	B 4
Guajataca River	B 2
Guaynabo River	B 3
Gurabo River	B 4
Icacos (Island)	C 4
La Cadena (Mtn.)	B 1
Lake Carite	B 3
Lake Cartagena	C 2
Lake Guajataca	B 2
Lake Guánica	C 2

Lake Guayabal	B 3
Lake Patillas	B 3
La Plata River	C 3
Lake Yauco	B 2
Limón River	B 2
Loíza River	B 4
Manatí River	B 2
Mayagüez Bay	B 1
Montañas de Uroyan (Mts.)	B 1
Palominos (Island)	B 4
Pasaje (Passage) de Vieques	C 4
Phosphorescent Bay	C 1
Piñeros (Island)	B 4
Pt. Aguijereada	A 1
Pt. Cadena	B 1
Pt. Candelero	C 4
Pt. Cerro Gordo	B 3
Pt. Cuchara	C 2
Pt. Figuras	C 4
Pt. Jigüero	B 1
Pt. Maldonado	B 4
Pt. Mulas	B 5
Pt. Petrona	C 3
Pt. Picúa	B 4
Pt. Puerca	B 4
Pt. Puerto Nuevo	A 3
Pt. Tuna	C 4
Pt. Vaca	C 4
Pt. Yeguas	C 4
Ratones Island	B 3
Rincón Bay	B 1
Rosario River	B 2
Salinas Bay	C 1

San Juan Passage	B 4
Sierra de Cayey	B 3
Sierra de Luquillo	C 4
Sucia Bay	C 1
Toro Negro River	B 2
Vieques (Island)	B 5
Vieques Sound	B 5
Yauco River	B 2
Yunes River	B 2

CM TERRAIN PUERTO RICO · COPYRIGHT BY RAND McNALLY & COMPANY · MADE IN U.S.A.

18°30'

PUERTO RICO

★ Commonwealth Capital
● Cities

Evergreen Trees
Mixed Evergreen and Deciduous Trees
Deciduous Trees
Grass

1 inch = 16 Statute Miles
0 1 2 3 4 5 ... 10 ... 15 Statute Miles
0 1 2 3 4 5 ... 10 ... 15 Miles
Lambert Conformal Conic Projection

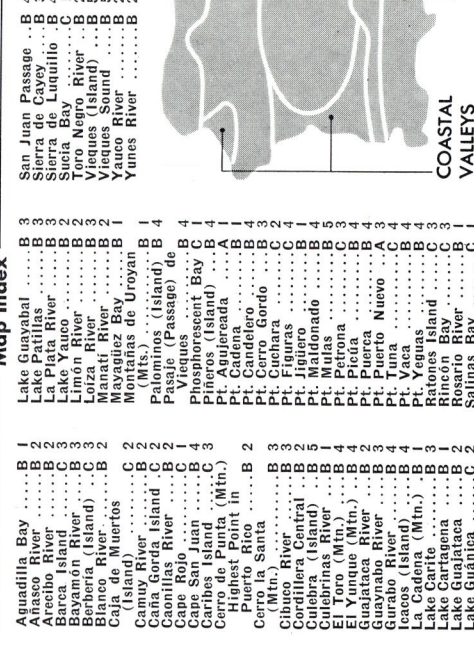

Land Regions of Puerto Rico

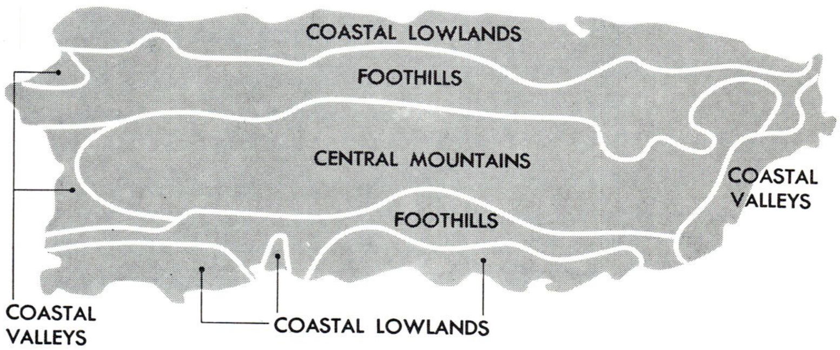

COASTAL LOWLANDS

FOOTHILLS

CENTRAL MOUNTAINS

FOOTHILLS

COASTAL LOWLANDS

COASTAL VALLEYS

COASTAL VALLEYS

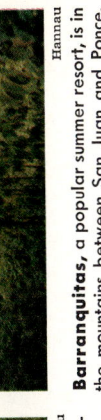

Hannau

Quiet Fishing Village of Las Croa-bas nestles in a coastal valley.

Barranquitas, a popular summer resort, is in the mountains between San Juan and Ponce.

Cutters Harvest Sugar Cane near Fajardo. Sugar cane, Puerto Rico's most important crop, is grown in the coastal lowlands and coastal valleys.

Tom Hollyman, Photo Researchers

Tom Hollyman, Photo Researchers

Lake Yauco lies in the hills of southwestern Puerto Rico. The lake was created by a dam on the Yauco River.

cover a narrower area, and have a much drier climate. Sugar cane is an important crop in both areas. Puerto Rico's largest cities, San Juan and Ponce, are in the coastal lowlands. Most industries are also in the lowlands.

The Coastal Valleys extend inland from the coast on the east and the west. Most of the land is used for sugar cane. Coconuts and other fruits also grow in these areas.

The Foothills rise in two long east-west chains, just inland from the north-ern and southern coastal lowlands. Much of the hilly area has jagged peaks and round basins. The basins were formed when water wore away the limestone that underlies the hills, and the ground sank.

The Central Mountains run east and west across the south-central part of the island. The main range is the Cor-dillera Central. The Sierra de Luquillo is a northeastern extension. The highest peak in Puerto Rico, Cerro de Punta, rises 4,389 feet in the Cordillera Cen-tral. Coffee is the main crop of the western part of the region. Citrus fruits are also grown there. Tobacco is grown in the mountain valleys and on the lower slopes in the east.

Coastline. Puerto Rico's general coastline measures 311 miles. The *tidal shoreline,* which includes small bays and inlets, is 700 miles long. The island has many sheltered beaches and harbors along the coast.

Rivers. Puerto Rico's longest rivers, such as the Arecibo, flow northward from the mountains into the Atlantic Ocean. None of the rivers can be used by large boats. But they are important sources of water for hydroelectric power, industries, and irrigation.

Puerto Rico's pleasant climate makes the island a popular vacation spot. The climate also provides good conditions for growing crops. Temperatures in Puerto Rico average about 73° F. in January and 80° F. in July. Frost and snow never occur, and even hail is rare. Sea breezes make the climate much more comfortable in summer than it is in the central United States.

In many parts of the island, some rain falls nearly every day. The rainfall is usually heavy, but it lasts only a short time. Rainfall varies greatly from one part of the island to another. The drier sections of the southern coast receive an average of 37 inches of rain a year. In some years, they have less than 20 inches. Rainfall in the north averages 70 inches a year. El Yunque, a mountain, gets over 200 inches of rain in some years.

Puerto Rico must be alert for hurricanes from June through November. But severe hurricanes occur only once every 10 years, on the average. These storms are predicted hours or even days in advance by the U.S. Weather Bureau. The storm warnings are announced by newspapers, radio, and television so that people have time to take shelter in strong buildings.

The highest temperature ever recorded in Puerto Rico, 103° F., occurred at San Lorenzo on Aug. 22, 1906. The lowest temperature, 40° F., was recorded at Aibonito on March 9, 1911.

Showers Drench El Yunque Rain Forest. El Yunque mountain and the surrounding valleys may get over 200 inches of rain a year.

Tom Hollyman, Photo Researchers

Tobacco Terraces form stripes on mountains near Gurabo in eastern Puerto Rico. Tobacco grown in this area makes fine cigars.

Tom Hollyman, Photo Researchers

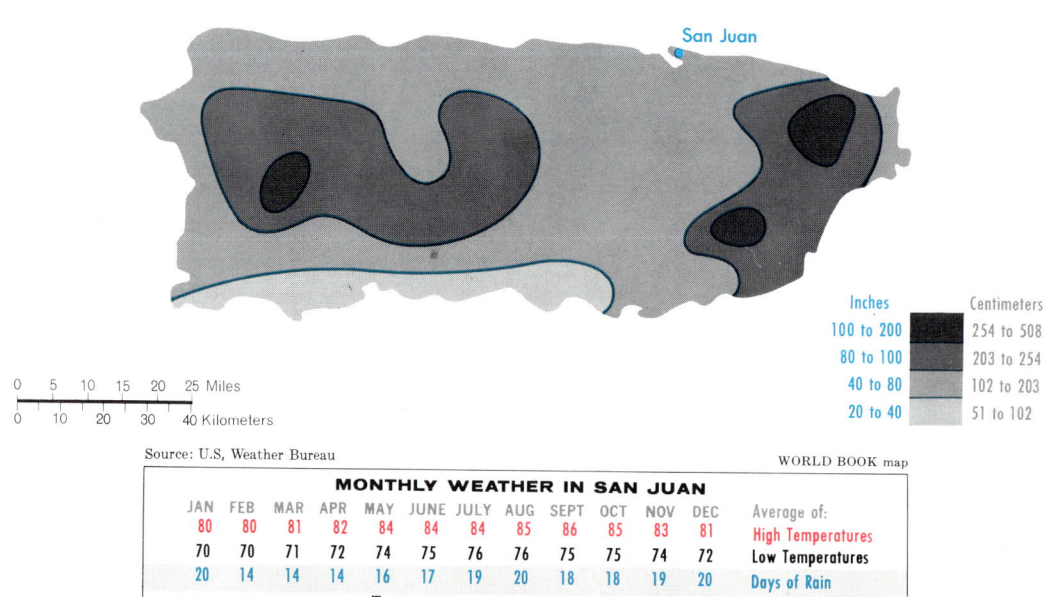

AVERAGE YEARLY PRECIPITATION
(Rain and Other Moisture)

San Juan

Inches	Centimeters
100 to 200	254 to 508
80 to 100	203 to 254
40 to 80	102 to 203
20 to 40	51 to 102

0 5 10 15 20 25 Miles
0 10 20 30 40 Kilometers

Source: U.S. Weather Bureau

WORLD BOOK map

MONTHLY WEATHER IN SAN JUAN												
	JAN	FEB	MAR	APR	MAY	JUNE	JULY	AUG	SEPT	OCT	NOV	DEC	Average of:
	80	80	81	82	84	84	84	85	86	85	83	81	High Temperatures
	70	70	71	72	74	75	76	76	75	75	74	72	Low Temperatures
	20	14	14	14	16	17	19	20	18	18	19	20	Days of Rain

Temperatures are given in degrees Fahrenheit.

In the past, Puerto Rico's economy was based on farm products, especially plantation crops such as coffee and sugar cane. Today, farming is still an important part of the island's economy. But manufacturing contributes more money to the economy of Puerto Rico than does farming.

More than 700,000 tourists visit Puerto Rico every year. Most of them come from the United States mainland. They spend over $200 million annually in Puerto Rico.

Natural Resources. One of Puerto Rico's most important natural resources is its climate. The year-round balmy weather not only attracts many tourists, but also helps make Puerto Rico a desirable location for industries. The warm, moist climate also allows Puerto Ricans to grow tropical crops that do not thrive in most parts of the U.S. mainland.

Soil is an important resource in Puerto Rico. The island has more than 350 types of soil. Soil erosion is a serious problem in the commonwealth. But it is being reduced by such conservation methods as contour planting of crops.

Minerals. Lime, sand and gravel, and stone account for almost all of Puerto Rico's mineral production. Spanish settlers washed gold out of Puerto Rican streams, but the gold supply was soon used up. Small deposits of cobalt and nickel and two large copper deposits have been found on the island. Salt is evaporated from sea water.

Plant Life. Much of the tropical forest that formerly covered Puerto Rico is gone. But the commonwealth and the U.S. government have established 14 forest reserves that cover about 86,000 acres.

More than 3,000 kinds of plants grow in Puerto Rico. Many Puerto Rican trees are valued for their beauty. These include the *flamboyan*, with flaming red blossoms; the African tulip; and the huge *ceiba* (kapok). Some trees bear delicious fruits and nuts which are little known elsewhere in the United States. Among these are breadfruit, guanábanas, papayas, sea grapes, and star apples. Many beautiful flowers, including orchids and poinsettias, grow on the island.

Animal Life. Like most heavily populated areas, Puerto Rico has few wild animals. Bats and mongooses are perhaps the only wild mammals. The island has few snakes of any kind, and no poisonous ones. However, it has iguanas and other lizards. It also has many kinds of birds. The coquí, a small frog, sounds a clear, musical note during the evening hours. The island's many kinds of insects include the cucubano, a large tropical relative of the common firefly. Some insects, such as mole crickets and termites, may damage buildings and crops.

The sea around the island contains many food and game fishes. They include barracuda, herring, marlin, mullet, pompano, sharks, snappers, Spanish mackerel, and tuna. Fishermen also catch lobsters and oysters.

Manufacturing accounts for about 67 per cent of the value of goods produced in Puerto Rico annually. Products manufactured and processed in the commonwealth have a *value added by manufacture* of about $621 million a year. This figure represents the value added to products by Puerto Rico's industries, not counting such costs of manufacturing as fuels, materials, and supplies.

More than 2,000 factories operate in Puerto Rico. They employ nearly 100,000 workers. Many of the factories were set up under Puerto Rico's *Operation Bootstrap* program for economic development. The commonwealth government helped the factory owners find factory locations, finance construction, and train workers.

Factories in Puerto Rico manufacture and process a great variety of products. These products include candy, cement, chemicals, cigars, clothing and textiles, electrical appliances, foods, furniture, leather goods, machinery, metals, molasses, paper products, pottery and china, and rum. Puerto Rico also refines petroleum, most of which is imported from Venezuela. The island has 18 *centrales* (sugar mills) that produce raw sugar from sugar cane.

Agriculture accounts for about $268 million a year, or about 29 per cent of the value of goods produced in Puerto Rico. More than 75 per cent of Puerto Rico's total land area is farmland. But less than 40 per cent of the land is of average or better than average fertility for growing crops. Much fertilizer must be used to enrich the fields, because the land has been worked hard for

PRODUCTION IN PUERTO RICO

Total yearly value of goods produced—$931,248,000

FISH AND MINERAL PRODUCTS 4%

AGRICULTURAL PRODUCTS 29%

MANUFACTURED PRODUCTS 67%

Note: Manufacturing percentage based on value added by manufacture. Other percentages based on value of production. Fish products are less than 1 per cent.

Source: Latest available government statistics

EMPLOYMENT IN PUERTO RICO

Average yearly number of persons employed—585,300

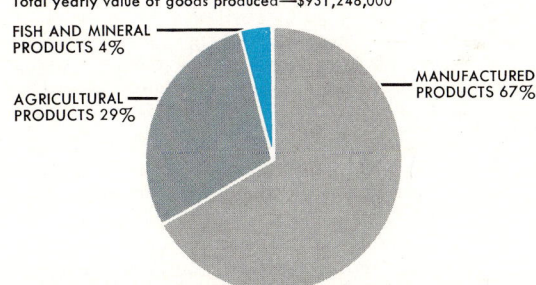

	Number of Employees
Agriculture, Forestry & Fishing	138,500
Wholesale & Retail Trade	100,300
Manufacturing	91,400
Government	83,800
Services	70,400
Construction & Mining	46,700
Transportation, Communications & Public Utilities	39,100
Home Needlework	8,300
Finance, Insurance & Real Estate	6,800

Source: Latest available government statistics

hundreds of years. Irrigation provides water for farms in the drier southern parts of the island. Irrigation is also used along the northwest coast in an area extending from Aguadilla to Arecibo.

Sugar cane is Puerto Rico's leading crop. About two-fifths of the cropland on the island is planted in sugar cane. About 40 per cent of the farm workers are employed in sugar cane farming. Most of the cane is grown in the coastal lowlands.

Coffee is Puerto Rico's second most valuable crop. It is grown in the western part of the central mountains. Farmers grow tobacco in the mountain valleys and on the lower slopes in the east-central mountains. Most of the tobacco is used to make cigars.

Pineapples are Puerto Rico's most important commercial fruit. They are grown in the coastal lowlands, especially in the north. Other fruits grown on the island include avocados, bananas, coconuts, grapefruit, oranges, and *plantains* (starchy fruits similar to bananas).

Puerto Rico's production of dairy products, livestock, and poultry is increasing rapidly to meet the needs of growing city populations. Vegetable production is also increasing.

Trade between Puerto Rico and the United States is similar to commerce between the states of the United States. Puerto Ricans do not pay customs duties on United States goods, as they do on goods imported from other countries.

In the past, Puerto Rico's most important exports to the United States were sugar, molasses, and rum. These products are still exported in large quantities. But Puerto Rico's most valuable exports today are clothing and textiles, petroleum, and other manufactured products.

Mayagüez has a *foreign trade zone* where owners can display, process, store, and reship their goods without paying customs duties on them. See FOREIGN TRADE ZONE.

Electric Power is produced and sold on the island by the Puerto Rico Water Resources Authority, a public corporation. The Water Resources Authority was created in 1941. Power is produced by plants that burn coal and other fuels, and also by hydroelectric plants.

The island also has a nuclear power plant at Rincón. This plant was built in cooperation with the United States Atomic Energy Commission.

Transportation. Puerto Rico has more than 3,000 miles of paved roads. These roads provide good transportation by automobile, bus, and truck throughout the island. Puerto Rico's four chief seaports are San Juan in the north, Guánica and Ponce in the south, and Mayagüez in the west.

The largest airport is San Juan International Airport, which opened in 1955. It handles more than 3 million passengers a year. Twelve scheduled airlines use this airport. Mayagüez and Ponce also have commercial airports.

Communication. Puerto Rico's oldest newspaper is *El Día*, which was established at Ponce in 1909. Other leading newspapers of Puerto Rico include *El Imparcial*, *El Mundo*, and the *San Juan Star*, all published in San Juan.

Puerto Rico's first radio station, WKAQ, began broadcasting from San Juan in 1922. WKAQ built Puerto Rico's first television station in 1954 in San Juan. Today, the commonwealth has 42 radio stations and 10 television stations.

Bethlehem Steel Co.

Giant Radio Telescope studies outer space from the hills south of Arecibo. Steel cables support the antenna 500 feet above the bowl-shaped reflector, which is 1,000 feet in diameter.

FARM AND MINERAL PRODUCTS

This map shows where the leading farm and mineral products are produced. The major urban areas (shown in red) are the important manufacturing centers.

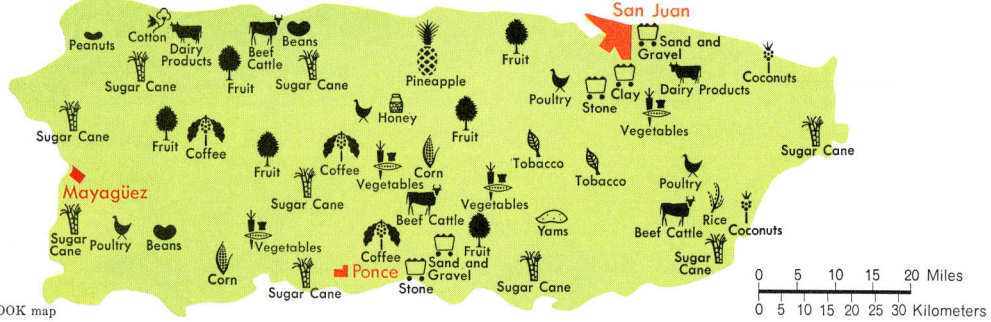

HISTORIC PUERTO RICO

First Settlement on Puerto Rico was begun in 1508 by Ponce de León and 50 of his men at Caparra, across the bay from present-day San Juan.

Columbus Discovered Puerto Rico during his second voyage. He probably landed on the island on Nov. 19, 1493, and named it San Juan Bautista.

The Commonwealth of Puerto Rico was established on July 25, 1952, when a constitution making the island a self-governing territory was approved by the United States.

Sugar Cane, brought from Santo Domingo by followers of Columbus, was first planted in 1515.

WORLD BOOK photo

"Operation Bootstrap," begun in the 1940's, encouraged Puerto Rico's industrial growth and raised the people's standard of living.

The End of Spanish Rule came in 1898, when Spain signed the Treaty of Paris, ending the Spanish-American War and ceding Puerto Rico to the United States.

PUERTO RICO / *History*

Spanish Rule. Christopher Columbus discovered Puerto Rico in 1493 during his second voyage to the Western Hemisphere. Spaniards, led by Juan Ponce de León, began to settle the island in 1508. The Borinquen, or Arawak, Indians who lived there rose against the settlers, but all their revolts failed. By the mid-1500's, nearly all the Indians had been killed or enslaved, or had died of disease.

The island colony suffered for hundreds of years from hurricanes and plagues. It was attacked by the Caribs, who lived on neighboring islands, and by the Dutch, English, and French. Nevertheless, the Spanish population slowly grew, fortifications and towns were built, and agriculture increased. After about 1850, the desire for greater freedom from Spain increased among Puerto Ricans. In 1897, Spain provided for a large amount of local rule and a new Puerto Rican government was set up in 1898 shortly before the Spanish-American War began.

U.S. Rule. On July 25, 1898, U.S. forces began to land in Puerto Rico after bombarding San Juan. Spain surrendered Puerto Rico to the United States in the Treaty of Paris, signed on Dec. 10, 1898.

Under the temporary U.S. military government, the use of U.S. money and postage stamps on the island was made official. The first U.S. civil governor was appointed by President William McKinley under the terms of the Organic Act of 1900, known as the *Foraker Act.*

The United States built dams, hospitals, roads, and schools. But the economy depended on agriculture, and U.S. firms owned and received much of the profits from the best plantations and largest sugar mills.

PUERTO RICO/*History*

The second Organic Act, or *Jones Act*, gave U.S. citizenship to Puerto Ricans. The island contributed troops to the U.S. armed forces during World Wars I and II. During the Korean War, the U.S. Army's 65th Infantry Regiment, made up of Puerto Ricans, won fame for its courage and daring.

Building a Democracy. In the early 1940's, Puerto Rican leaders, with aid from the United States, began a program to improve living conditions on the island. The program became known as *Operation Bootstrap*. Large farms were broken up, and land was redistributed among farm workers. An improved educational program rapidly reduced the number of Puerto Ricans who could not read and write. Thousands of old slum dwellings were torn down and replaced by modern housing.

On July 25, 1946, President Harry S. Truman appointed Jesús Toribio Piñero as the first island-born governor of Puerto Rico. One year later, Congress expanded Puerto Rican self-government by permitting the islanders to elect their own governor. Luis Muñoz Marín was elected governor in 1948. His Popular Democratic Party favored a commonwealth linked to the United States. Muñoz Marín overwhelmingly defeated candidates of parties that favored statehood or independence.

In 1950, Congress passed Public Law 600, which gave Puerto Rico the power to write its own constitution. Puerto Ricans approved the law in a referendum vote in 1951. A Puerto Rican convention then wrote a constitution modeled on that of the United States, and the Puerto Rican people approved it. The U.S. Congress approved the constitution on July 1, 1952, and on July 25 Puerto Rico became a self-governing commonwealth.

During the 1950's, a sharp rise occurred in Puerto Rican migration to the U.S. mainland. Thousands of islanders moved to New York City and other large mainland cities in search of jobs. Many could not speak English, and had difficulty adjusting to their new life.

Puerto Rico Today is in a period of rapid industrial growth. The commonwealth's Economic Development Association, known in Spanish as *Fomento*, has helped businessmen establish more than 2,000 factories on

the island. Industrial growth has reduced unemployment. But the unemployment rate is still about three times as high as it is in the United States.

Puerto Rico's leaders also stress the importance of cultural development. Through a program called *Operation Serenity*, Puerto Ricans work to preserve their Spanish traditions, and to promote the arts.

In 1964, Governor Muñoz Marín announced he would not run for a fifth term. Another Popular Democrat, Roberto Sánchez Vilella, became governor in January, 1965. In 1968, Luis A. Ferré, of the New Progressive Party, was elected governor. He defeated Luis Negrón Lopez, the Popular Democratic candidate.

In 1967, a majority of Puerto Rican voters chose commonwealth status, rather than statehood or independence. Ferré supports statehood for Puerto Rico, but he did not stress this issue in his campaign.

THOMAS G. MATHEWS, RAFAEL PICÓ, and PABLO VARGAS BADILLO

PUERTO RICO/*Study Aids*

Related Articles in WORLD BOOK include:

Inter American University of Puerto Rico
Mayagüez
Muñoz Marín, Luis
Pineapple
Ponce
Ponce de León, Juan
Puerto Rico, University of San Juan
Sánchez Vilella, Roberto
Spanish-American War
West Indies

Outline

I. Government
  A. Commonwealth Government
  B. Courts
  C. Local Government
  D. Politics

II. People

III. Education

IV. A Visitor's Guide
  A. Places to Visit
  B. Annual Events

V. The Land
  A. Land Regions
  B. Coastline
  C. Rivers

VI. Climate

VII. Economy
  A. Natural Resources
  B. Manufacturing
  C. Agriculture
  D. Trade
  E. Electric Power
  F. Transportation
  G. Communication

VIII. History

Questions

What are the three largest cities in Puerto Rico?

Who discovered Puerto Rico? When?

What is *Operation Bootstrap? Operation Serenity?*

On what days do Puerto Rican children receive their Christmas gifts?

Why is Puerto Rico's climate an important natural resource?

What is Puerto Rico's most valuable crop?

How did Puerto Rico become a territory of the United States? How did it become a commonwealth?

778d

What is the *coquí? El Yunque?*
Who is Luis Muñoz Marín?
What are Puerto Rico's chief exports?

Books for Young Readers

COLMAN, HILA. *The Girl from Puerto Rico.* Morrow, 1961. A teen-age girl from Puerto Rico faces the problems of adjustment to life in New York City.

MATHEWS, THOMAS G. *Luis Muñoz Marín: A Concise Biography.* American R. D. M. Corp., 1967.

PLENN, DORIS T. *The Green Song.* McKay, 1954. Story of the coquí, a tiny Puerto Rican frog with a chirping voice, that went to New York City.

ROLLINS, FRANCES. *Getting to Know Puerto Rico.* Coward-McCann, 1967.

Books for Older Readers

ANDERSON, ROBERT W. *Party Politics in Puerto Rico.* Stanford Univ. Press, 1965.

HANSON, EARL P. *Puerto Rico: Ally for Progress.* Van Nostrand, 1962.

LEWIS, GORDON K. *Puerto Rico: Freedom and Power in the Caribbean.* Monthly Review Press, 1963. A study of the island's history, progress, and problems.

PAGE, HOMER. *Puerto Rico: The Quiet Revolution.* Viking, 1963.

ROSSKAM, EDWIN. *The Alien.* Grossman, 1964. A novel set in La Perla, a San Juan slum.

PUERTO RICO, CATHOLIC UNIVERSITY OF. See UNIVERSITIES AND COLLEGES (table).

PUERTO RICO, UNIVERSITY OF, is a government-supported coeducational school. The Río Piedras Campus covers 288 acres in San Juan. It has divisions of business administration, education, general studies, humanities, law, natural sciences, pharmacy, and social sciences. Schools of dentistry and of medicine and tropical medicine are also in San Juan. A four-year branch campus in Mayagüez has colleges of agriculture, arts and sciences, and engineering. The agricultural experiment station has several outlying divisions. The university was founded in 1903. For enrollment, see UNIVERSITIES AND COLLEGES (table). JAIME BENÍTEZ

See also PUERTO RICO (Education [color picture]).

PUERTO RICO TROUGH. See ATLANTIC OCEAN (The Ocean Bed).

PUFF ADDER. See ADDER.

Hugh Spencer

Young Puffballs are considered a delicacy by some people. They are flavorful until they darken in color and shrink.

PUFFBALL is a mushroom that produces a ball-shaped fruit with spores completely enclosed. Many puffballs have white flesh. They are edible until the flesh begins to become colored, or corky in texture. As the puffballs mature, the inside becomes a mass of powdery spores, yellowish or purplish or olive-colored. Sometimes an

opening, or crater, develops in the top, through which puffs of "smoke," a cloud of tiny spores, may come out when the fruit is touched or squeezed. That is why one of the puffballs is called *devil's-snuffbox.*

Scientific Classification. The puffballs belong to the puffball family, *Lycoperdaceae.* The devil's-snuffbox is genus *Lycoperdon,* species *L. gemmatum.* WILLIAM F. HANNA

See also MUSHROOM (color picture: Puffball).

PUFFER is the common name of fishes that inflate their bodies like balloons. They are sometimes called *swellfish* or *globefish.* A common kind is the northern puffer of the Atlantic Coast. Related species live in tropical waters. Most of the time, the puffer looks like an ordinary fish, with a large head and protruding teeth. When disturbed, it inflates its stomach with air. It then floats belly upward on the water's surface until the danger has passed. See also PORCUPINE FISH.

Scientific Classification. The puffer belongs to the puffer family, *Tetraodontidae.* The northern puffer is genus *Sphaeroides,* species *S. maculatus.* CARL L. HUBBS

The Puffer, above, becomes twice its normal size and floats on the surface of the water when it inflates its stomach, below.

Marine Studios

PUFFIN, or SEA PARROT, is an odd-looking bird that lives in the Arctic waters of both hemispheres. It has a thick body, a large head, and a remarkable high, flattened bill. During the breeding season, colored growths form on the male puffin's beak. On the Atlantic and horned puffins, the breast and underparts are white. The wings, tail, and forepart of the neck are blackish, and the sides of the head and throat are white. The tufted puffin is dark underneath, with a white streaked plume on the side of the head. Puffins are expert swimmers and divers, and come to land mainly in June and July, during the breeding season. These birds nest in large colonies on rocky coasts. One white egg is laid in a burrow or crevice in the rocks.

Scientific Classification. Puffins belong to the auk family, *Alcidae.* The Atlantic puffin is genus *Fratercula,* species *F. arctica;* the horned puffin, *F. corniculata,* and the tufted, *Lunda cirrhata.* ALEXANDER WETMORE

See also BIRD (color picture: Birds of Other Lands).

PUG is a small dog with a short nose and a tail that curls tightly over its back. It is the largest of the toy-size dogs and weighs between 14 and 18 pounds. Its face is deeply wrinkled. Its hair is short and smooth. The pug originally came from China. JOSEPHINE Z. RINE

See also Dog (color picture: Toy Dogs); Toy Dog.

PUGACHEV, *poo guh CHAWF,* **EMELIAN IVANO-VICH** (1742?-1775), a Russian soldier, led a revolt against Russian landowners in 1773 and 1774. Pugachev's followers killed thousands of persons before the revolt was crushed.

Pugachev was born in southern Russia. He served with distinction in the Seven Years' War and the Russo-Turkish War of 1768 to 1774. But he was arrested several times for resisting authority. In 1773, he convinced peasants in the Ural Mountains that he was Czar Peter III. Peter had been dead more than 10 years, but many peasants believed he was still alive. Posing as the czar, Pugachev promised to free the peasants, who were forced to work much like slaves. He called for a peasant war against the landowners. With more than 20,000 followers, he swept westward across the Volga River and seized several cities. Government forces captured him in 1774. He was executed in Moscow. ALFRED ERICH SENN

PUGET, *PYOO jet,* **PETER** (1762?-1822), a British naval officer and explorer, played an important part in the exploration of the north Pacific Coast of North America. Puget Sound, in the state of Washington, Cape Puget in Alaska, and Puget Island in the Columbia River were named for him. From 1791 to 1795, Puget sailed as a lieutenant with Captain George Vancouver on a four-year voyage around the world. This voyage included a trip to Nootka Sound, near what is now Vancouver Island, to regain English territory from the Spaniards. See VANCOUVER, GEORGE.

In 1792, they discovered, and Puget explored, the sound, or arm of the Pacific Ocean, which Vancouver named for Puget. Puget surveyed the Yakutat Bay area on the southern Alaska coast, and helped to a large extent in the exploration of Cook Inlet and Prince William Sound, which lie farther north.

Puget became a captain in the British Navy in 1797. He served at Madras, India, from 1810 to 1818. In 1821, he became a rear admiral. WILLIAM P. BRANDON

Puget Sound Connects With the Pacific Ocean.

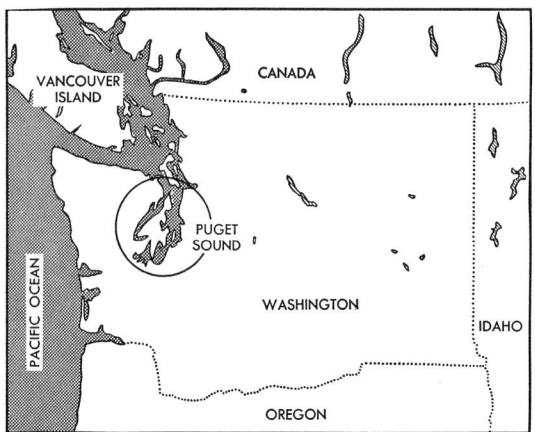

PUGET SOUND, *PYOO jet,* is a large, irregular inlet in the northwest corner of the state of Washington. Puget Sound is a leading American shipping center. The ports of Seattle, Tacoma, Bremerton, Olympia, and Everett stand on its banks. The sound is 80 miles long, and covers an area of about 2,000 square miles. The largest ships can steam into any part of the sound, as its depth is from 180 to 925 feet.

The Strait of Juan de Fuca links Puget Sound and the Pacific Ocean. From the meeting point of this strait and the Strait of Georgia, Puget Sound extends southward for about 35 miles before it divides into two main branches. These are Admiralty Inlet and the Hood Canal. The Lake Washington Canal extends from the sound to Lake Washington at Seattle.

Most of the sound's shores are high and wooded. The sound has many islands. Whidbey Island, over 40 miles long, is one of the largest islands in the United States.

The sound is noted for the fisheries and lumber mills along its shores. Fish packing and canning are among the most important industries of the region. Puget Sound is the center of Washington's great lumber industry. BOSTWICK H. KETCHUM

See also JUAN DE FUCA, STRAIT OF; PUGET, PETER; PUGET SOUND NAVAL SHIPYARD; WASHINGTON (picture: The Capitol Group at Olympia).

PUGET SOUND, UNIVERSITY OF. See UNIVERSITIES AND COLLEGES (table).

PUGET SOUND NAVAL SHIPYARD, Wash., forms a major part of United States naval activities at Bremerton. Base facilities include an 11,244-acre ammunition depot, hospital, marine barracks, and ships of the Pacific Reserve Fleet. The naval shipyard lies on an inlet off Puget Sound, about 16 miles by ferry from Seattle. It covers 820 acres, and was established in 1891 on land bought for $9,512. The shipyard has built almost every type of warship from aircraft carriers to guided-missile-equipped frigates. JOHN A. OUDINE

PUISNE, *PYOO nih,* is a term that refers to an associate judge or justice, to distinguish him from a chief justice. It is used in Great Britain and in many British countries. The word *puisne* comes from the Old French word *puisné,* which means *junior.*

PULASKI, *pu LAS kee,* **CASIMIR** (1748-1779), a Polish soldier, joined George Washington's forces and distinguished himself in the Battle of Brandywine. As a reward, Congress appointed him brigadier general in charge of cavalry. The following year, he organized an independent corps of cavalry and light infantry which became known as Pulaski's Legion. The legion participated in the siege of Savannah where Pulaski was wounded on Oct. 9, 1779. He died two days later.

In his twenties, Pulaski led an unsuccessful revolt of Polish forces against Russia, which controlled Poland at that time. Arrested and condemned to death, Pulaski fled to Turkey, and eventually he reached France. He learned of the American cause

Casimir Pulaski
Brown Bros.

Culver

Count Pulaski was fatally wounded leading French and American cavalry at the siege of Savannah in the American Revolution.

herd. It captures a runaway sheep by jumping on its back and riding there until the animal becomes too tired to run farther. Then the puli herds it back to the flock. The puli is about 17 inches tall at the shoulder. See also Dog (color picture: Working Dogs). OLGA DAKAN

PULITZER, *POOL it sir,* or *PYOO lit sir,* **JOSEPH** (1847-1911), was a Hungarian immigrant who became one of the greatest American newspaper publishers. He established the Pulitzer prizes for achievements in journalism, literature, music, and art (see PULITZER PRIZES).

Pulitzer was born in Mako, Hungary, on April 10, 1847. His family moved to Budapest when he was young. He left home at 17 in search of military adventure, but the armed forces of Austria, France, and Great Britain rejected him because of his poor health and bad eyesight. A United States recruiter enlisted Pulitzer in Hamburg, Germany, to fight with the Union Army in the Civil War. After brief service in the war, he settled in St. Louis, Mo., became a United States citizen, and worked as a laborer.

His Career. In 1868, Pulitzer became a reporter on a German-language newspaper in St. Louis. Within four years, he became managing editor and part owner of the paper. He won a seat in the Missouri House of Representatives in 1869. He became a powerful leader among the people of German descent in St. Louis, and helped Horace Greeley in his campaign for the presidency in 1872. But three years later, Pulitzer became a Democrat and sold his interest in the paper, which was Republican.

In 1876 and 1877, Pulitzer served as a correspondent in Washington, D.C., for the *New York Sun.* He bought the *St. Louis Dispatch* and *Evening Post* in 1878, and combined them into the *St. Louis Post-Dispatch.* Within four years, this newspaper made him a fortune.

In 1883, Pulitzer bought the *New York World.* This paper was then so poor that many persons believed he had made a mistake. But he soon transformed the *World* into a vigorous, crusading newspaper with the largest circulation in the nation. This paper was one of the first to use the color comics and sensationalism that gave rise to "yellow journalism" (see NEWSPAPER [Consolidation and Expansion]).

Pulitzer was almost totally blind after 1887, and also extremely sensitive to noise. From then until his death, he directed his newspapers from a yacht.

His Bequests. Pulitzer left $2 million to establish a graduate school of journalism at Columbia University. The Pulitzer prizes were created with part of this money. He left $500,-000 each to the New York Philharmonic Society and to the Metropolitan Museum of Art.

Pulitzer's will provided that the *World* should never be sold. But a court permitted the sale in 1931 because of financial losses. The family retained the *Post-Dispatch.* JOHN E. DREWRY

through Benjamin Franklin in France, and sailed for America, arriving in July, 1777.

Pulaski was born in the province of Podolia, Poland, and entered upon a military career at an early age. By an act of the United States Congress, October 11 is observed as Pulaski Day. CHARLES MORLEY

PULASKI SKYWAY, a part of U.S. Highway No. 1 in northern New Jersey, is an elevated four-lane highway leading west from Jersey City to the city limits of Newark. The steel and concrete viaduct extends $3\frac{1}{2}$ miles over the Newark Meadows. The skyway rises 145 feet above the Hackensack and Passaic rivers on two high cantilever bridges. An average of more than 41,000 vehicles use it daily.

The total cost of the project was over $21 million. This highway is a brilliant engineering feat, because of the difficult job of building it over marshy land. The completion of the project in 1932 improved one of the worst traffic-jam areas in the East. The road is named for Count Pulaski, a Polish hero who lost his life fighting for the colonies in the Revolutionary War in America (see PULASKI, CASIMIR). RICHARD P. MCCORMICK

PULI, *POO lih,* is a medium-sized dog used by Hungarian shepherds as a sheep dog. The origin of the word *puli* is unknown. The puli's coat is black, white, or gray and may have either a curly or corded texture. The dog is intelligent, easily trained, and a good shep-

Joseph Pulitzer
Brown Bros.

781

PULITZER PRIZES

PULITZER PRIZES are awards given in the United States each year for distinguished achievements in journalism, literature, and music. The newspaper that wins the prize for meritorious public service receives a $500 gold medal. Each of the other eight journalism prizes is a cash award of $1,000, and the seven in literature and music are $500 each. The Pulitzer prizes also include three scholarships worth $1,500 each, awarded to journalism students.

Joseph Pulitzer, an American newspaper publisher, left $2 million to Columbia University. He specified that the university should use the money to establish prizes for the advancement of education, public service, public morals, and American literature. Pulitzer also directed that the funds be used to organize a school of journalism. The trustees of Columbia University awarded the first Pulitzer prizes in 1917. See PULITZER, JOSEPH.

Journalism Awards cover the following categories:

(1) For disinterested and meritorious public service rendered by an American newspaper published daily or at least once a week: gold medal.

(2) For a distinguished example of local general or spot news reporting: $1,000. To be eligible for this or any of the following awards, the material must have appeared in an American newspaper published daily or at least once a week.

(3) For a distinguished example of local investigative or other specialized reporting: $1,000.

(4) For a distinguished example of reporting on national affairs: $1,000.

(5) For a distinguished example of reporting on international affairs, including United Nations correspondence: $1,000.

(6) For distinguished editorial writing. The writer must show clearness of style, moral purpose, sound reasoning, and power to influence public opinion in what he conceives to be the right direction. Due account is given to all the editorial writer's work during the year: $1,000.

(7) For a distinguished example of a cartoonist's work. The cartoon must embody an idea made clearly apparent, show good drawing and striking pictorial effect, and be intended to help some commendable cause of public importance. Due account is given to all the artist's work during the year: $1,000.

(8) For an outstanding example of spot news photography as exemplified by a news photograph or photographs. This prize is open to amateurs as well as to photographers regularly employed by newspapers, press associations, or press syndicates: $1,000.

(9) For an outstanding example of feature news photography. The photograph or photographs, sequence, or album may be black and white or color: $1,000.

Literature and Music Awards. The prizes in literature and music cover the following categories:

(1) For distinguished fiction published in book form by an American author, preferably dealing with American life: $500.

(2) For an American play, preferably original in source and dealing with American life, which shall represent in marked fashion the educational value and power of the stage: $500.

(3) For a distinguished book of the year on the history of the United States: $500.

(4) For a distinguished biography or autobiography by an American author, preferably on an American subject: $500.

(5) For a distinguished volume of verse published by an American poet: $500.

(6) For a distinguished work of general nonfiction by an American author: $500.

(7) For distinguished musical composition in the larger forms of chamber, orchestral, or choral music; or for an operatic work (including ballet), performed or published by a composer of established residence in the United States: $500.

Scholarship Awards are made annually to three graduates of the Columbia University Graduate School of Journalism who have passed their examinations with the highest honor and are otherwise most deserving. The awards are traveling scholarships each having a value of $1,500. They are made to allow winners to spend a year abroad studying the social, political, and moral conditions of the people, and the character and principles of the press of other lands.

The Advisory Board on Pulitzer prizes recommends award winners to the trustees of Columbia University. The board consists of the president of the university and publishers or editorial executives elected by the trustees for four-year terms. A faculty member of the Graduate School of Journalism serves as secretary of the board.

Nominations for prizes, except those in drama and music, must be in writing and sent to the board secretary by February 1. For the drama and music prizes, the board considers works produced during the 12 months ending March 31. Supporting material, such as a biography and photograph of the nominee, must accompany all nominations.

Columbia University selects juries in each category to survey the nominations. Jurors come from all walks of life. At some times, editors named by the American Society of Newspaper Editors have acted as jurors for the journalism prizes. University professors who are authorities on literature or music have served as jurors for the other awards.

Each jury usually makes from two to five recommendations to the advisory board. The board has full responsibility for selecting, accepting, or rejecting these suggestions. The university trustees make the final decisions. Names of winners are announced in May.

The advisory board may withhold prizes if it believes that any competition has failed to meet its standards.

In 1918, the advisory board awarded a Newspaper History Award to Minna Lewinson and Harry B. Hough for their history of public services by the American press in 1917. This was the only year that such an award was given. The board established the poetry prize in 1922. Previous awards in this category had been made from gifts of the Poetry Society.

The General Reporting category originally covered local, national, and international reporting. In 1929, the advisory board created a separate category of Correspondence, but discontinued it after the 1947 award. In 1942, it created the separate categories of Telegraphic Reporting (National) and Telegraphic Reporting (International). The board in 1948 merged these two awards with the Correspondence category to form the present categories of National Reporting and International Reporting. General Reporting became known as Local Reporting. In 1953, the board divided it into Local Reporting (1) under the pressure of edition time, and (2) not under the pressure of edition time. In 1964, the award was again changed to cover (1) Local General or Spot News Reporting and (2) Local Investigative or Other Specialized Reporting. The general nonfiction prize was first awarded in 1962. In 1968, the news photography category was divided into two categories: spot news photography and feature news photography.

Special Citations have been awarded occasionally by the board. The winners:

1938 *Edmonton* (Alberta) *Journal*, for its defense of the freedom of the press in Alberta.

1941 *The New York Times*, for the public educational value of its foreign news reports.

1944 Byron Price, Director of the United States Office of Censorship, for creating and administering newspaper and radio codes during World War II.

1944 Mrs. William Allen White, for her services as a member of the Advisory Board on Pulitzer prizes.

1944 *Richard Rodgers and *Oscar Hammerstein II, for their musical play *Oklahoma!*

1945 The cartographers of the American press, for their war maps that helped increase public information on the progress of armed forces in World War II.

1947 Columbia University and its Graduate School of Journalism, for efforts to maintain and advance the high standards governing the Pulitzer prizes.

1947 *St. Louis Post-Dispatch*, for unswerving adherence to the ideals of its founder and its constructive leadership in American journalism.

1948 Frank D. Fackenthal, Provost of Columbia University, for his interest in and service to the advisory board.

1951 Cyrus L. Sulzberger, *The New York Times*, for his exclusive interview with Archbishop Aloysius Stepinac.

1952 Max Kase, *New York Journal-American*, for his exclusive exposure of bribery in basketball.

1952 *The Kansas City* (Mo.) *Star*, for its news coverage of the 1951 flood in Kansas and Missouri.

1953 *The New York Times*, for the "Review of the Week" section in its Sunday edition.

1957 *Kenneth Roberts, for his historical novels that have helped create greater interest in early American history.

1958 *Walter Lippmann, syndicated columnist, for the wisdom and sense of responsibility in his comments on national and international affairs.

1960 Garrett Mattingly, for his book *The Armada*.

1961 *American Heritage Picture History of the Civil War*.

1964 The Gannett newspaper chain, for its special series *The Road to Integration*.

The New York Times and its staff have won the most journalism awards.

PULITZER PRIZES IN JOURNALISM
MERITORIOUS PUBLIC SERVICE

1917 No Award.
1918 *The New York Times*.
1919 *The Milwaukee Journal*.
1920 No Award.
1921 *Boston Post*.
1922 *The World* (New York).
1923 *Memphis Commercial Appeal*.
1924 *The World* (New York).
1925 No Award.
1926 *The Enquirer Sun* (Columbus, Ga.).
1927 *Canton* (Ohio) *Daily News*.
1928 *Indianapolis Times*.
1929 *The Evening World* (New York).
1930 No Award.
1931 *Atlanta Constitution*.
1932 *Indianapolis News*.
1933 *New York World-Telegram*.
1934 *Medford* (Ore.) *Mail Tribune*.
1935 *The Sacramento* (Calif.) *Bee*.
1936 *The Cedar Rapids* (Iowa) *Gazette*.
1937 *St. Louis Post-Dispatch*.
1938 *The Bismarck* (N.Dak.) *Tribune*.
1939 *The Miami* (Fla.) *Daily News*.
1940 *Waterbury* (Conn.) *Republican and American*.
1941 *St. Louis Post-Dispatch*.
1942 *Los Angeles Times*.
1943 *The World-Herald* (Omaha).
1944 *The New York Times*.

1945 *The Detroit Free Press*.
1946 *The Scranton* (Pa.) *Times*.
1947 *The Sun* (Baltimore).
1948 *St. Louis Post-Dispatch*.
1949 *Nebraska State Journal* (Lincoln).
1950 *Chicago Daily News; St. Louis Post-Dispatch*.
1951 *Miami* (Fla.) *Herald; Brooklyn Daily Eagle*.
1952 *St. Louis Post-Dispatch*.
1953 *The News Reporter* (Whiteville, N.C.); *Tabor City* (N.C.) *Tribune*.
1954 *Newsday* (Garden City, N.Y.).
1955 *Columbus* (Ga.) *Ledger* and *Sunday Ledger-Enquirer*.
1956 *Watsonville* (Calif.) *Register-Pajaronian*.
1957 *Chicago Daily News*.
1958 *Arkansas Gazette* (Little Rock).
1959 *Utica* (N.Y.) *Observer-Dispatch; Utica Daily Press*.
1960 *Los Angeles Times*.
1961 *Amarillo* (Tex.) *Globe-Times*.
1962 *The Panama City* (Fla.) *News-Herald*.
1963 *Chicago Daily News*.
1964 *The St. Petersburg* (Fla.) *Times*.
1965 *Hutchinson* (Kans.) *News*.
1966 *The Boston Globe*.
1967 *Courier-Journal* (Louisville); *Milwaukee Journal*.
1968 *The Riverside* (Calif.) *Press-Enterprise*.
1969 *Los Angeles Times*.

*Has a biography in THE WORLD BOOK ENCYCLOPEDIA

AN ORPHAN AT 8 IS NOW ONE OF THE WORLD'S GREATEST MINING ENGINEERS AND ECONOMISTS WHOSE AMBITION IS TO ELIMINATE THE CYCLE OF DEPRESSION AND UNEMPLOYMENT

THE SON OF A PLASTERER IS NOW THE WORLD'S GREATEST NEUROLOGIST AND HIS HOBBY IS GOOD HEALTH FOR POOR CHILDREN

A PRINTER'S APPRENTICE IS NOW CHIEF EXECUTIVE OF THE UNITED STATES

BUT THEY DIDN'T GET THERE BY HANGING AROUND THE CORNER DRUG STORE

The Des Moines Register

Darling's prize cartoon, 1924, left

Mauldin's prize cartoon, 1959, right

"I WON THE NOBEL PRIZE FOR LITERATURE. WHAT WAS YOUR CRIME?"
St. Louis Post-Dispatch

CARTOON

1922 Rollin Kirby, *The World* (New York).
1923 No Award.
1924 *Ding Darling, *New York Tribune*.
1925 Rollin Kirby, *The World* (New York).
1926 D. R. Fitzpatrick, *St. Louis Post-Dispatch*.
1927 Nelson Harding, *Brooklyn Daily Eagle*.
1928 Nelson Harding, *Brooklyn Daily Eagle*.
1929 Rollin Kirby, *The World* (New York).
1930 Charles R. Macauley, *Brooklyn Daily Eagle*.
1931 Edmund Duffy, *The Sun* (Baltimore).
1932 John T. McCutcheon, *Chicago Tribune*.
1933 Harold M. Talburt, *Washington* (D.C.) *Daily News*.
1934 Edmund Duffy, *The Sun* (Baltimore).
1935 Ross A. Lewis, *The Milwaukee Journal*.
1936 No Award.
1937 Clarence D. Batchelor, *Daily News* (New York).
1938 Vaughn Shoemaker, *Chicago Daily News*.
1939 Charles G. Werner, *The Daily Oklahoman* (Oklahoma City).
1940 Edmund Duffy, *The Sun* (Baltimore).
1941 Jacob Burck, *The Times* (Chicago).
1942 Herbert L. Block, Newspaper Enterprise Assn.
1943 *Ding Darling, *New York Herald Tribune*.
1944 Clifford K. Berryman, *The Washington* (D.C.) *Evening Star*.
1945 *Bill Mauldin, United Feature Syndicate, Inc.
1946 Bruce A. Russell, *Los Angeles Times*.
1947 Vaughn Shoemaker, *Chicago Daily News*.
1948 Reuben L. (Rube) Goldberg, *The Sun* (New York).
1949 Lute Pease, *Newark* (N.J.) *Evening News*.
1950 James T. Berryman, *The Washington* (D.C.) *Evening Star*.
1951 Reginald W. Manning, *Arizona Republic* (Phoenix).
1952 Fred L. Packer, *New York Mirror*.
1953 Edward D. Kuekes, *Cleveland Plain Dealer*.
1954 Herbert L. Block, *Washington* (D.C.) *Post*.
1955 Daniel R. Fitzpatrick, *St. Louis Post-Dispatch*.
1956 Robert York, *Louisville* (Ky.) *Times*.
1957 Tom Little, *Nashville Tennessean*.
1958 Bruce M. Shanks, *Buffalo* (N.Y.) *Evening News*.
1959 *Bill Mauldin, *St. Louis Post-Dispatch*.
1960 No Award

1961 Carey Orr, *Chicago Tribune*.
1962 Edmund S. Valtman, *The Hartford* (Conn.) *Times*.
1963 Frank Miller, *The Des Moines* (Iowa) *Register*.
1964 Paul Conrad, *The Denver Post*.
1965 No Award.
1966 Don Wright, *Miami News*.
1967 Patrick B. Oliphant, *The Denver Post*.
1968 Eugene G. Payne, *The Charlotte* (N.C.) *Observer*.
1969 John Fischetti, *Chicago Daily News*.

EDITORIAL WRITING

1917 *New York Tribune*.
1918 *The Courier-Journal* (Louisville).
1919 No Award.
1920 Harvey E. Newbranch, *Evening World-Herald* (Omaha).
1921 No Award.
1922 Frank M. O'Brien, *The New York Herald*.
1923 *William Allen White, *The Emporia* (Kans.) *Gazette*.
1924 *The Boston Herald*. Special prize to Frank I. Cobb, *The World* (New York).
1925 *Charleston* (S.C.) *News and Courier*.
1926 Edward M. Kingsbury, *The New York Times*.
1927 F. Lauriston Bullard, *The Boston Herald*.
1928 Grover C. Hall, *Montgomery* (Ala.) *Advertiser*.
1929 Louis I. Jaffe, *Norfolk* (Va.) *Virginian-Pilot*.
1930 No Award.
1931 Charles S. Ryckman, *Fremont* (Nebr.) *Tribune*.
1932 No Award.
1933 *The Kansas City* (Mo.) *Star*.
1934 E. P. Chase, *Atlantic* (Iowa) *News Telegraph*.
1935 No Award.
1936 Felix Morley, *The Washington* (D.C.) *Post;* George B. Parker, The Scripps-Howard Newspapers.
1937 John W. Owens, *The Sun* (Baltimore).
1938 W. W. Waymack, *The Register and Tribune* (Des Moines, Iowa).
1939 Ronald G. Callvert, *The Oregonian* (Portland).
1940 Bart Howard, *St. Louis Post-Dispatch*.
1941 Reuben Maury, *Daily News* (New York).
1942 Geoffrey Parson, *New York Herald Tribune*.
1943 Forrest W. Seymour, *The Register & Tribune* (Des Moines, Iowa).
1944 Henry J. Haskell, *The Kansas City* (Mo.) *Star*.
1945 George W. Potter, *The Providence* (R.I.) *Journal-Bulletin*.
1946 Hodding Carter, *The Delta Democrat-Times* (Greenville, Miss.).
1947 William H. Grimes, *The Wall Street Journal*.
1948 Virginius Dabney, *Richmond* (Va.) *Times-Dispatch*.
1949 John H. Crider, *The Boston Herald;* Herbert Elliston, *The Washington* (D.C.) *Post*.

*Has a biography in THE WORLD BOOK ENCYCLOPEDIA

1950 Carl M. Saunders, *Jackson* (Mich.) *Citizen Patriot*.
1951 William H. Fitzpatrick, *New Orleans States*.
1952 Louis LaCoss, *St. Louis Globe-Democrat*.
1953 Vermont C. Royster, *The Wall Street Journal*.
1954 Donald M. Murray, *The Boston Herald*.
1955 Royce Howes, *The Detroit Free Press*.
1956 Lauren K. Soth, *The Register & Tribune* (Des Moines, Iowa).
1957 Buford Boone, *Tuscaloosa* (Ala.) *News*.
1958 Harry S. Ashmore, *Arkansas Gazette* (Little Rock).
1959 Ralph McGill, *The Constitution* (Atlanta).
1960 Lenoir Chambers, *The Virginian-Pilot* (Norfolk, Va.).
1961 William J. Dorvillier, *San Juan* (P.R.) *Star*.
1962 Thomas M. Storke, *Santa Barbara News-Press*.
1963 Ira B. Harkey, Jr., *Pascagoula* (Miss.) *Chronicle*.
1964 Hazel Brannon Smith, *The Lexington* (Miss.) *Advertiser*.
1965 John R. Harrison, *The Gainesville* (Fla.) *Sun*.
1966 Robert Lasch, *St. Louis Post-Dispatch*.
1967 Eugene Patterson, *The Atlanta Constitution*.
1968 John S. Knight, Knight Newspapers.
1969 Paul Greenberg, *Pine Bluff* (Ark.) *Commercial*.

NATIONAL REPORTING

1942 Louis Stark, *The New York Times*.
1943 No Award.
1944 Dewey L. Fleming, *The Sun* (Baltimore).
1945 James B. Reston, *The New York Times*.
1946 Edward A. Harris, *St. Louis Post-Dispatch*.
1947 Edward T. Folliard, *The Washington* (D.C.) *Post*.
1948 Bert Andrews, *New York Herald Tribune;* Nat S. Finney, *The Minneapolis Tribune*.
1949 Charles P. Trussell, *The New York Times*.
1950 Edwin O. Guthman, *The Seattle Times*.
1951 No Award.
1952 Anthony Leviero, *The New York Times*.
1953 Don Whitehead, The Associated Press.
1954 Richard L. Wilson, The Cowles Newspapers.
1955 Anthony Lewis, *Washington* (D.C.) *Daily News*.
1956 Charles L. Bartlett, *Chattanooga* (Tenn.) *Times*.
1957 James B. Reston, *The New York Times*.
1958 Relman Morin, Associated Press; Clark Mollenhoff, *The Register & Tribune* (Des Moines, Iowa).
1959 Howard Van Smith, *Miami* (Fla.) *News*.
1960 Vance Trimble, Scripps-Howard Newspaper Alliance.
1961 Edward R. Cony, *The Wall Street Journal*.
1962 Nathan G. Caldwell and Gene S. Graham, *Nashville Tennessean*.
1963 Anthony Lewis, *The New York Times*.
1964 Merriman Smith, United Press International.
1965 Louis M. Kohlmeier, *The Wall Street Journal*.
1966 Haynes Johnson, *The Evening Star* (Washington).
1967 Monroe W. Karmin and Stanley W. Penn, *The Wall Street Journal*.
1968 Howard James, *The Christian Science Monitor;* Nathan K. Kotz, *The Des Moines* (Iowa) *Register*.
1969 Robert Kahn, *The Christian Science Monitor*.

GENERAL AND LOCAL REPORTING

1917 Herbert B. Swope, *The World* (New York).
1918 Harold A. Littledale, *New York Evening Post*.
1919 No Award.
1920 John J. Leary, Jr., *The World* (New York).
1921 Louis Seibold, *The World* (New York).
1922 Kirke L. Simpson, The Associated Press.
1923 Alva Johnston, *The New York Times*.
1924 Magner White, *San Diego* (Calif.) *Sun*.
1925 James W. Mulroy, Alvin H. Goldstein, *Chicago Daily News*.
1926 William B. Miller, *The Courier-Journal* (Louisville).
1927 John T. Rogers, *St. Louis Post-Dispatch*.
1928 No Award.
1929 Paul Y. Anderson, *St. Louis Post-Dispatch*.
1930 Russell D. Owen, *The New York Times*. Special award to W. O. Dapping, *Auburn* (N.Y.) *Citizen*.
1931 A. B. MacDonald, *The Kansas City* (Mo.) *Star*.
1932 W. C. Richards, D. D. Martin, J. S. Pooler, F. D.

Webb, J. N. W. Sloan, *The Detroit Free Press*.
1933 Francis A. Jamieson, The Associated Press.
1934 Royce Brier, *San Francisco Chronicle*.
1935 William H. Taylor, *New York Herald Tribune*.
1936 Lauren D. Lyman, *The New York Times*.
1937 John J. O'Neill, *New York Herald Tribune;* William L. Laurence, *The New York Times;* Howard W. Blakeslee, The Associated Press; Gobind Behari Lal, Universal Service; David Dietz, The Scripps-Howard Newspapers.
1938 Raymond Sprigle, *Pittsburgh Post-Gazette*.
1939 Thomas L. Stokes, *New York World-Telegram*.
1940 S. Burton Heath, *New York World-Telegram*.
1941 Westbrook Pegler, *New York World-Telegram*.
1942 Stanton Delaplane, *San Francisco Chronicle*.
1943 George Weller, *Chicago Daily News*.
1944 Paul Schoenstein and associates, *New York Journal-American*.
1945 Jack S. McDowell, *The Call-Bulletin* (San Francisco).
1946 William L. Laurence, *The New York Times*.
1947 Frederick Woltman, *New York World-Telegram*.
1948 George E. Goodwin, *The Atlanta Journal*.
1949 Malcolm Johnson, *The Sun* (New York).
1950 Meyer Berger, *The New York Times*.
1951 Edward S. Montgomery, *San Francisco Examiner*.
1952 George de Carvalho, *San Francisco Chronicle*.
1953 Award divided into two groups, *below*.

LOCAL REPORTING

(Under Pressure of Edition Time)

1953 *The Providence* (R.I.) *Journal and Evening Bulletin*.
1954 *Vicksburg* (Miss.) *Sunday Post-Herald*.
1955 Caro Brown, *Alice* (Tex.) *Daily Echo*.
1956 Lee Hills, *Detroit Free Press*.
1957 *Salt Lake* (Utah) *Tribune*.
1958 *Fargo* (N.Dak.) *Forum*.
1959 Mary Lou Werner, *The Evening Star* (Washington).
1960 Jack Nelson, *The Constitution* (Atlanta, Ga.).
1961 Sanche de Gramont, *New York Herald Tribune*.
1962 Robert D. Mullins, *Salt Lake City Deseret News*.
1963 Sylvan Fox, William Longgood, and Anthony Shannon, *The New York World-Telegram & Sun*.
1964 Award discontinued.

LOCAL REPORTING

(Not Under Pressure of Edition Time)

1953 Edward J. Mowery, *The New York World-Telegram & Sun*.
1954 Alvin S. McCoy, *The Kansas City* (Mo.) *Star*.
1955 Roland K. Towery, *Cuero* (Tex.) *Record*.
1956 Arthur Daley, *The New York Times*.
1957 Wallace Turner, William Lambert, *Portland* (Ore.) *Oregonian*.
1958 George Beveridge, *The Evening Star* (Washington).
1959 John H. Brislin, *Scranton Tribune* and *Sunday Scrantonian*.
1960 Miriam Ottenberg, *The Evening Star* (Washington).
1961 Edgar May, *Buffalo* (N.Y.) *Evening News*.
1962 George Bliss, *Chicago Tribune*.
1963 Oscar O. Griffin, Jr., *Pecos* (Tex.) *Independent Enterprise*.
1964 Award discontinued.

LOCAL GENERAL OR SPOT NEWS REPORTING

1964 Norman C. Miller, *The Wall Street Journal*.
1965 Melvin H. Ruder, *Hungry Horse News* (Columbia Falls, Mont.).
1966 The staff of the *Los Angeles Times*.
1967 Robert V. Cox, *The Chambersburg* (Pa.) *Public Opinion*.
1968 The staff of *The Detroit Free Press*.
1969 John Fetterman, *Louisville Courier-Journal*.

LOCAL SPECIALIZED REPORTING

1964 Albert V. Gaudiosi, James V. Magee, and Frederick A. Meyer, *The Philadelphia Bulletin*.

*Has a biography in THE WORLD BOOK ENCYCLOPEDIA

PULITZER PRIZES IN JOURNALISM

Photo by Toshio Sakai of UPI

Photo by Nathaniel Fein of the *New York Herald Tribune*

Pulitzer Prize Picture of 1949, *above,* shows Babe Ruth's dramatic farewell to baseball at Yankee Stadium.

A Pulitzer Prize Picture of 1968, *left,* shows American soldiers during a monsoon downpour in South Vietnam.

1965 Gene Goltz, *The Houston Post.*
1966 John A. Frasca, *The Tampa Tribune.*
1967 Gene Miller, *The Miami Herald.*
1968 J. Anthony Lukas, *The New York Times.*
1969 Albert L. Delugach, Denny Walsh, *St. Louis Globe-Democrat.*

NEWS PHOTOGRAPHY

1942 Milton Brooks, *The Detroit News.*
1943 Frank Noel, The Associated Press.
1944 Frank Filan, The Associated Press; Earle L. Bunker, *The World-Herald* (Omaha).
1945 Joe Rosenthal, The Associated Press.
1946 No Award.
1947 Arnold Hardy.
1948 Frank Cushing, *Boston Traveler.*
1949 Nathaniel Fein, *New York Herald Tribune.*
1950 Bill Crouch, *Oakland Tribune* (Calif.).
1951 Max Desfor, The Associated Press.
1952 John Robinson, Don Ultang, *The Register & Tribune* (Des Moines, Iowa).
1953 William M. Gallagher, *The Flint* (Mich.) *Journal.*
1954 Mrs. Walter M. Schau.
1955 John L. Gaunt, Jr., *Los Angeles Times.*
1956 *New York Daily News.*
1957 Harry A. Trask, *Boston Traveler.*
1958 William C. Beall, *Washington* (D.C.) *Daily News.*
1959 William Seaman, *The Minneapolis Star-Tribune.*
1960 Andrew Lopez, United Press International.
1961 Yasushi Nagao, *Mainichi* (Tokyo).
1962 Paul Vathis, The Associated Press.
1963 Hector Rondon, *La República* (Caracas, Venezuela).
1964 Robert H. Jackson, *The Dallas Times Herald.*
1965 Horst Faas, The Associated Press.
1966 Kyoichi Sawada, United Press International.
1967 Jack R. Thornell, The Associated Press.
1968 Award divided into two groups, *below.*

SPOT NEWS PHOTOGRAPHY

1968 Rocco Morabito, *The Jacksonville* (Fla.) *Journal.*
1969 Edward T. Adams, The Associated Press.

FEATURE NEWS PHOTOGRAPHY

1968 Toshio Sakai, United Press International.
1969 Moneta Sleet, Jr., *Ebony.*

GENERAL CORRESPONDENCE

1929 Paul S. Mowrer, *Chicago Daily News.*
1930 Leland Stowe, *New York Herald Tribune.*
1931 H. R. Knickerbocker, *Philadelphia Public Ledger* and *New York Evening Post.*

1932 Walter Duranty, *The New York Times;* Charles G. Ross, *St. Louis Post-Dispatch.*
1933 Edgar A. Mowrer, *Chicago Daily News.*
1934 Frederick T. Birchall, *The New York Times.*
1935 Arthur Krock, *The New York Times.*
1936 Wilfred C. Barber, *Chicago Tribune.*
1937 Anne O'Hare McCormick, *The New York Times.*
1938 Arthur Krock, *The New York Times.*
1939 Louis P. Lochner, The Associated Press.
1940 Otto D. Tolischus, *The New York Times.*
1941 Bronze plaque honoring American reporters in the war zones of Asia, Africa, and Europe.
1942 *Carlos P. Romulo, *The Philippines Herald.*
1943 Hanson W. Baldwin, *The New York Times.*
1944 *Ernie Pyle, Scripps-Howard Newspaper Alliance.
1945 Harold V. Boyle, The Associated Press.
1946 Arnaldo Cortesi, *The New York Times.*
1947 Brooks Atkinson, *The New York Times.*
1948 Award discontinued.

INTERNATIONAL REPORTING

1942 Laurence E. Allen, The Associated Press.
1943 Ira Wolfert, North American Newspaper Alliance.
1944 Daniel DeLuce, The Associated Press.
1945 Mark S. Watson, *The Sun* (Baltimore).
1946 Homer W. Bigart, *New York Herald Tribune.*
1947 Eddy Gilmore, The Associated Press.
1948 Paul W. Ward, *The Sun* (Baltimore).
1949 Price Day, *The Sun* (Baltimore).
1950 Edmund Stevens, *The Christian Science Monitor.*
1951 Keyes Beech, Fred Sparks, *Chicago Daily News;* Homer Bigart, Marguerite Higgins, *New York Herald Tribune;* Relman Morin, Don Whitehead, The Associated Press.
1952 John M. Hightower, The Associated Press.
1953 Austin C. Wehrwein, *The Milwaukee Journal.*
1954 Jim G. Lucas, The Scripps-Howard Newspapers.
1955 Harrison E. Salisbury, *The New York Times.*
1956 *William R. Hearst, Jr., Frank Conniff, Kingsbury Smith, International News Service.
1957 Russell Jones, The United Press.
1958 *The New York Times.*
1959 Joseph Martin, Philip Santora, *Daily News* (N.Y.).
1960 A. M. Rosenthal, *The New York Times.*
1961 Lynn Louis Heinzerling, The Associated Press.
1962 *Walter Lippmann, *New York Herald Tribune.*
1963 Hal Hendrix, *Miami* (Fla.) *News.*
1964 Malcolm W. Browne, The Associated Press, and David Halberstam, *The New York Times.*
1965 J. A. Livingston, *The Philadelphia Bulletin.*
1966 Peter Arnett, The Associated Press.
1967 R. John Hughes, *The Christian Science Monitor.*
1968 Alfred Friendly, *The Washington Post.*
1969 William Tuohy, *Los Angeles Times.*
*Has a biography in THE WORLD BOOK ENCYCLOPEDIA

FICTION

1918 *Ernest Poole, *His Family.*
1919 *Booth Tarkington, *The Magnificent Ambersons.*
1920 No Award.
1921 *Edith Wharton, *The Age of Innocence.*
1922 *Booth Tarkington, *Alice Adams.*
1923 *Willa Cather, *One of Ours.*
1924 Margaret Wilson, *The Able McLaughlins.*
1925 *Edna Ferber, *So Big.*
1926 *Sinclair Lewis, *Arrowsmith* (declined).
1927 *Louis Bromfield, *Early Autumn.*
1928 *Thornton Wilder, *The Bridge of San Luis Rey.*
1929 *Julia M. Peterkin, *Scarlet Sister Mary.*
1930 *Oliver H. P. La Farge, *Laughing Boy.*
1931 Margaret A. Barnes, *Years of Grace.*
1932 *Pearl S. Buck, *The Good Earth.*
1933 T. S. Stribling, *The Store.*
1934 Caroline Miller, *Lamb in His Bosom.*
1935 Josephine W. Johnson, *Now in November.*
1936 Harold L. Davis, *Honey in the Horn.*
1937 *Margaret Mitchell, *Gone with the Wind.*
1938 *John P. Marquand, *The Late George Apley.*
1939 *Marjorie Kinnan Rawlings, *The Yearling.*
1940 *John Steinbeck, *The Grapes of Wrath.*
1941 No Award.
1942 Ellen Glasgow, *In This Our Life.*
1943 *Upton B. Sinclair, *Dragon's Teeth.*
1944 Martin Flavin, *Journey in the Dark.*
1945 *John Hersey, *A Bell for Adano.*
1946 No Award.
1947 *Robert Penn Warren, *All the King's Men.*
1948 *James A. Michener, *Tales of the South Pacific.*
1949 *James G. Cozzens, *Guard of Honor.*
1950 *A. B. Guthrie, Jr., *The Way West.*
1951 Conrad Richter, *The Town.*
1952 *Herman Wouk, *The Caine Mutiny.*
1953 *Ernest Hemingway, *The Old Man and the Sea.*
1954 No Award.
1955 *William Faulkner, *A Fable.*
1956 *MacKinlay Kantor, *Andersonville.*
1957 No Award.
1958 James Agee, *A Death in the Family.*
1959 Robert L. Taylor, *The Travels of Jaimie McPheeters.*

1960 *Allen Drury, *Advise and Consent.*
1961 Harper Lee, *To Kill a Mockingbird.*
1962 Edwin O'Connor, *The Edge of Sadness.*
1963 *William Faulkner, *The Reivers.*
1964 No Award.
1965 Shirley Ann Grau, *The Keepers of the House.*
1966 *Katherine Ann Porter, *Collected Short Stories.*
1967 *Bernard Malamud, *The Fixer.*
1968 *William Styron, *The Confessions of Nat Turner.*
1969 N. Scott Momaday, *House Made of Dawn.*

MUSIC

1943 *William Schuman, *Secular Cantata No. 2.*
1944 *Howard Hanson, *Symphony No. 4, opus 34.*
1945 *Aaron Copland, *Appalachian Spring.*
1946 Leo Sowerby, *The Canticle of the Sun.*
1947 *Charles Ives, *Symphony No. 3.*
1948 *Walter Piston, *Symphony No. 3.*
1949 *Virgil Thomson, *Louisiana Story.*
1950 *Gian Carlo Menotti, *The Consul.*
1951 *Douglas Moore, *Giants in the Earth.*
1952 Gail Kubick, *Symphony Concertante.*
1953 No Award.
1954 Quincy Porter, *Concerto for Two Pianos and Orchestra.*
1955 *Gian Carlo Menotti, *The Saint of Bleecker Street.*
1956 Ernst Toch, *Symphony No. 3.*
1957 *Norman Dello Joio, *Meditations on Ecclesiastes.*
1958 *Samuel Barber, *Vanessa.*
1959 John La Montaine, *Concerto for Piano and Orchestra.*
1960 Elliot Carter, *Second String Quartet.*
1961 *Walter Piston, *Symphony No. 7.*
1962 Robert Ward, *The Crucible.*
1963 *Samuel Barber, *Piano Concerto No. 1.*
1964 No Award.
1965 No Award.
1966 Leslie Basset, *Variations for Orchestra.*
1967 Leon Kirchner, *String Quartet No. 3.*
1968 George Crumb, *Echoes of Time and the River,* orchestral suite.
1969 Karel Husa, *String Quartet No. 3.*

HISTORY

1917 J. J. Jusserand, *With Americans of Past and Present Days.*
1918 *James Rhodes, *A History of the Civil War, 1861-1865.*
1919 No Award.
1920 Justin H. Smith, *The War with Mexico.*
1921 *William S. Sims, *The Victory at Sea.*
1922 *James T. Adams, *The Founding of New England.*
1923 *Charles Warren, *The Supreme Court in United States History.*
1924 Charles H. McIlwain, *The American Revolution—A Constitutional Interpretation.*

*Has a biography in THE WORLD BOOK ENCYCLOPEDIA

Ben Stahl, courtesy The World Publishing Co.

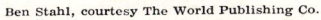

MacKinlay Kantor's 1956 Prize Novel, *Andersonville.*

Samuel Barber's 1958 Prize Opera, **Vanessa,** with libretto by Gian Carlo Menotti.

Louis Mélançon

1925 Frederic Paxson, *A History of the American Frontier.*
1926 *Edward Channing, *The War for Southern Independence,* volume 6 of *The History of the United States.*
1927 *Samuel F. Bemis, *Pinckney's Treaty.*
1928 *Vernon L. Parrington, *Main Currents in American Thought.*
1929 Fred A. Shannon, *The Organization and Administration of the Union Army, 1861-1865.*
1930 Claude H. Van Tyne, *The War of Independence.*
1931 Bernadotte E. Schmitt, *The Coming of the War: 1914.*
1932 *John J. Pershing, *My Experiences in the World War.*
1933 *Frederick J. Turner, *The Significance of Sections in American History.*
1934 Herbert Agar, *The People's Choice.*
1935 *Charles M. Andrews, *The Colonial Period of American History.*
1936 Andrew C. McLaughlin, *The Constitutional History of the United States.*
1937 *Van Wyck Brooks, *The Flowering of New England.*
1938 Paul H. Buck, *The Road to Reunion, 1865-1900.*
1939 Frank L. Mott, *A History of American Magazines.*
1940 *Carl Sandburg, *Abraham Lincoln: The War Years.*
1941 Marcus Hansen, *The Atlantic Migration, 1607-1860.*
1942 *Margaret Leech, *Reveille in Washington.*
1943 *Esther Forbes, *Paul Revere and the World He Lived In.*
1944 Merle Curti, *The Growth of American Thought.*
1945 Stephen Bonsal, *Unfinished Business.*
1946 *Arthur M. Schlesinger, Jr., *The Age of Jackson.*
1947 James P. Baxter III, *Scientists Against Time.*
1948 *Bernard DeVoto, *Across the Wide Missouri.*
1949 Roy F. Nichols, *The Disruption of American Democracy.*
1950 Oliver W. Larkin, *Art and Life in America.*
1951 R. Carlyle Buley, *The Old Northwest, Pioneer Period 1815-1840.*
1952 Oscar Handlin, *The Uprooted.*
1953 George Dangerfield, *The Era of Good Feelings.*
1954 *Bruce Catton, *A Stillness at Appomattox.*
1955 Paul Horgan, *Great River: The Rio Grande in North American History.*
1956 Richard Hofstadter, *The Age of Reform.*
1957 *George F. Kennan, *Russia Leaves the War: Soviet-American Relations, 1917-1920.*
1958 Bray Hammond, *Banks and Politics in America: From the Revolution to the Civil War.*
1959 Leonard D. White and Jean Schneider, *The Republican Era: 1869-1901.*
1960 *Margaret Leech, *In the Days of McKinley.*
1961 Herbert Feis, *Between War and Peace: The Potsdam Conference.*
1962 Lawrence Henry Gipson, *The Triumphant Empire: Thunder-Clouds Gather in the West, 1763-1766.*
1963 Constance McLaughlin Green, *Washington, Village and Capital, 1800-1878.*
1964 Sumner Chilton Powell, *Puritan Village: The Formation of a New England Town.*
1965 Irwin Unger, *The Greenback Era.*
1966 Perry Miller, *The Life of the Mind in America: From the Revolution to the Civil War.*
1967 William H. Goetzmann, *Exploration and Empire.*
1968 Bernard Bailyn, *The Ideological Origins of The American Revolution.*
1969 Leonard W. Levy, *Origins of the Fifth Amendment.*

BIOGRAPHY OR AUTOBIOGRAPHY

1917 *Laura E. H. Richards, Maude H. Elliott, Florence H. Hall, *Julia Ward Howe.*
1918 William C. Bruce, *Benjamin Franklin, Self-Revealed.*
1919 *Henry Adams, *The Education of Henry Adams.*
1920 *Albert J. Beveridge, *The Life of John Marshall.*
1921 *Edward W. Bok, *The Americanization of Edward Bok.*
1922 *Hamlin Garland, *A Daughter of the Middle Border.*
1923 Burton J. Hendrick, *The Life and Letters of Walter H. Page.*
1924 *Michael I. Pupin, *From Immigrant to Inventor.*

1925 M. A. DeWolfe Howe, *Barrett Wendell and His Letters.*
1926 *Harvey Cushing, *The Life of Sir William Osler.*
1927 Emory Holloway, *Whitman.*
1928 Charles E. Russell, *The American Orchestra and Theodore Thomas.*
1929 Burton J. Hendrick, *The Training of An American: The Earlier Life and Letters of Walter H. Page.*
1930 *Marquis James, *The Raven.*
1931 *Henry James, *Charles W. Eliot.*
1932 Henry F. Pringle, *Theodore Roosevelt.*
1933 *Allan Nevins, *Grover Cleveland.*
1934 Tyler Dennett, *John Hay.*
1935 *Douglas Southall Freeman, *R. E. Lee.*
1936 Ralph B. Perry, *The Thought and Character of William James.*
1937 *Allan Nevins, *Hamilton Fish.*
1938 Odell Shepard, *Pedlar's Progress;* *Marquis James, *Andrew Jackson.*
1939 *Carl Van Doren, *Benjamin Franklin.*
1940 *Ray S. Baker, *Woodrow Wilson, Life and Letters.*
1941 Ola E. Winslow, *Jonathan Edwards.*
1942 Forrest Wilson, *Crusader in Crinoline.*
1943 *Samuel E. Morison, *Admiral of the Ocean Sea.*
1944 Carlton Mabee, *The American Leonardo: The Life of Samuel F. B. Morse.*
1945 Russell B. Nye, *George Bancroft: Brahmin Rebel.*
1946 Linnie M. Wolfe, *Son of the Wilderness.*
1947 *William Allen White, *The Autobiography of William Allen White.*
1948 Margaret Clapp, *Forgotten First Citizen: John Bigelow.*
1949 *Robert E. Sherwood, *Roosevelt and Hopkins.*
1950 *Samuel F. Bemis, *John Quincy Adams and the Foundations of American Foreign Policy.*
1951 Margaret L. Coit, *John C. Calhoun: American Portrait.*
1952 Merlo J. Pusey, *Charles Evans Hughes.*
1953 David J. Mays, *Edmund Pendleton, 1721-1803.*
1954 *Charles A. Lindbergh, *The Spirit of St. Louis.*
1955 William S. White, *The Taft Story.*
1956 Talbot F. Hamlin, *Benjamin Henry Latrobe.*
1957 *John F. Kennedy, *Profiles in Courage.*
1958 *Douglas Southall Freeman, Mary W. Ashworth, John A. Carroll, *George Washington.*
1959 Arthur Walworth, *Woodrow Wilson, American Prophet.*
1960 *Samuel E. Morison, *John Paul Jones.*
1961 David Donald, *Charles Sumner and the Coming of the Civil War.*
1962 No Award.
1963 Leon Edel, *The Conquest of London* and *The Middle Years,* volumes II and III of *Henry James.*
1964 Walter Jackson Bates, *John Keats.*
1965 Ernest Samuels, *Henry Adams.*
1966 *Arthur M. Schlesinger, Jr., *A Thousand Days.*
1967 Justin Kaplan, *Mr. Clemens and Mark Twain.*
1968 George F. Kennan, *Memoirs (1925-1950).*
1969 Benjamin Lawrence Reid, *The Man from New York: John Quinn and His Friends.*

DRAMA

1918 Jesse L. Williams, *Why Marry?*
1919 No Award.
1920 *Eugene O'Neill, *Beyond the Horizon.*
1921 *Zona Gale, *Miss Lulu Bett.*
1922 *Eugene O'Neill, *Anna Christie.*
1923 *Owen Davis, *Icebound.*
1924 Hatcher Hughes, *Hell-Bent fer Heaven.*
1925 *Sidney Howard, *They Knew What They Wanted.*
1926 *George E. Kelly, *Craig's Wife.*
1927 *Paul Green, *In Abraham's Bosom.*
1928 *Eugene O'Neill, *Strange Interlude.*
1929 *Elmer Rice, *Street Scene.*
1930 *Marc Connelly, *The Green Pastures.*
1931 *Susan Glaspell, *Alison's House.*
1932 *George S. Kaufman, Morrie Ryskind, George and Ira Gershwin, *Of Thee I Sing.*
1933 *Maxwell Anderson, *Both Your Houses.*
*Has a biography in THE WORLD BOOK ENCYCLOPEDIA

1934 *Sidney Kingsley, *Men in White.*
1935 Zoe Akins, *The Old Maid.*
1936 *Robert E. Sherwood, *Idiot's Delight.*
1937 *George S. Kaufman, *Moss Hart, *You Can't Take It With You.*
1938 *Thornton Wilder, *Our Town.*
1939 *Robert E. Sherwood, *Abe Lincoln in Illinois.*
1940 *William Saroyan, *The Time of Your Life* (declined).
1941 *Robert E. Sherwood, *There Shall Be No Night.*
1942 No Award.
1943 *Thornton Wilder, *The Skin of Our Teeth.*
1944 No Award.
1945 Mary Chase, *Harvey.*
1946 *Howard Lindsay, *Russel Crouse, *State of the Union.*
1947 No Award.
1948 *Tennessee Williams, *A Streetcar Named Desire.*
1949 *Arthur Miller, *Death of a Salesman.*
1950 *Richard Rodgers, *Oscar Hammerstein II, and *Joshua Logan, *South Pacific.*
1951 No Award.
1952 Joseph Kramm, *The Shrike.*
1953 *William Inge, *Picnic.*
1954 John Patrick, *The Teahouse of the August Moon.*
1955 *Tennessee Williams, *Cat on a Hot Tin Roof.*
1956 Frances Goodrich, Albert Hackett, *The Diary of Anne Frank.*
1957 *Eugene O'Neill, *Long Day's Journey into Night.*
1958 Ketti Frings, *Look Homeward, Angel.*
1959 *Archibald MacLeish, *J.B.*
1960 George Abbott, Jerry Bock, Sheldon Harnick, and Jerome Weidman, *Fiorello.*
1961 Tad Mosel, *All the Way Home.*
1962 Abe Burrows and Frank Loesser, *How to Succeed in Business Without Really Trying.*
1963 No Award.
1964 No Award.
1965 Frank D. Gilroy, *The Subject Was Roses.*
1966 No award.
1967 *Edward Albee, *A Delicate Balance.*
1968 No Award.
1969 Howard Sackler, *The Great White Hope.*

J.B., Archibald MacLeish's prize play of 1959

Friedman-Abeles

POETRY

1918 *Sara Teasdale, *Love Songs.*
1919 Margaret Widdemer, *Old Road to Paradise;* *Carl Sandburg, *Corn Huskers.*
1920 No Award.
1921 No Award.
1922 *Edwin Arlington Robinson, *Collected Poems.*
1923 *Edna St. Vincent Millay, *The Ballad of the Harp-Weaver; A Few Figs from Thistles;* eight sonnets in *American Poetry, 1922: A Miscellany.*
1924 *Robert Frost, *New Hampshire: A Poem with Notes and Grace Notes.*
1925 *Edwin Arlington Robinson, *The Man Who Died Twice.*
1926 *Amy Lowell, *What's O'Clock.*
1927 Leonora Speyer, *Fiddler's Farewell.*
1928 *Edwin Arlington Robinson, *Tristram.*
1929 *Stephen Vincent Benét, *John Brown's Body.*
1930 *Conrad Aiken, *Selected Poems.*
1931 *Robert Frost, *Collected Poems.*
1932 *George Dillon, *The Flowering Stone.*
1933 *Archibald MacLeish, *Conquistador.*
1934 *Robert Hillyer, *Collected Verse.*
1935 Audrey Wurdemann, *Bright Ambush.*
1936 *Robert P. Tristram Coffin, *Strange Holiness.*
1937 *Robert Frost, *A Further Range.*
1938 Marya Zaturenska, *Cold Morning Sky.*
1939 John Gould Fletcher, *Selected Poems.*
1940 *Mark Van Doren, *Collected Poems.*
1941 Leonard Bacon, *Sunderland Capture.*
1942 *William Rose Benét, *The Dust Which Is God.*
1943 *Robert Frost, *A Witness Tree.*
1944 *Stephen Vincent Benét, *Western Star.*
1945 *Karl Shapiro, *V-Letter and Other Poems.*
1946 No Award.
1947 *Robert Lowell, *Lord Weary's Castle.*
1948 *W. H. Auden, *The Age of Anxiety.*
1949 *Peter Viereck, *Terror and Decorum.*
1950 *Gwendolyn Brooks, *Annie Allen.*
1951 *Carl Sandburg, *Complete Poems.*
1952 *Marianne Moore, *Collected Poems.*
1953 *Archibald MacLeish, *Collected Poems 1917-1952.*
1954 Theodore Roethke, *The Waking: Poems 1933-1953.*
1955 *Wallace Stevens, *Collected Poems.*
1956 *Elizabeth Bishop, *Poems: North and South.*
1957 *Richard Wilbur, *Things of This World.*
1958 *Robert Penn Warren, *Promises: Poems 1954-1956.*
1959 Stanley Kunitz, *Selected Poems, 1928-1958.*
1960 William DeWitt Snodgrass, *Heart's Needle.*
1961 Phyllis McGinley, *Times Three: Selected Verse from Three Decades.*
1962 Alan Dugan, *Poems.*
1963 *William Carlos Williams, *Pictures from Breughel.*
1964 Louis Simpson, *At the End of the Open Road.*
1965 John Berryman, *Seventy-Seven Dream Songs.*
1966 Richard Eberhart, *Selected Poems (1930-1965).*
1967 Anne Sexton, *Live or Die.*
1968 Anthony Hecht, *The Hard Hours.*
1969 George Oppen, *Of Being Numerous.*

GENERAL NONFICTION

1962 Theodore H. White, *The Making of the President, 1960.*
1963 Barbara W. Tuchman, *The Guns of August.*
1964 Richard Hofstadter, *Anti-Intellectualism in American Life.*
1965 Howard Mumford Jones, *O Strange New World.*
1966 Edwin Way Teale, *Wandering Through Winter.*
1967 David Brion Davis, *The Problem of Slavery in Western Culture.*
1968 *Will and Ariel Durant, *Rousseau and Revolution.*
1969 *Norman Mailer, *The Armies of the Night.* René Jules Dubos, *So Human An Animal: How We Are Shaped by Surroundings and Events.*

*Has a biography in THE WORLD BOOK ENCYCLOPEDIA

PULLEY

PULLEY is a wheel over which a rope or belt is passed for the purpose of transmitting energy and doing work. When the pulley carries a rope, its rim is grooved, but if it is to carry a belt the rim is barrel-shaped and the belt rides on the highest part of the rim.

The simplest pulley is a grooved wheel on a fixed axle. A rope passing over this wheel is tied to the load to be lifted, and a pull is applied to the other end of the rope. This pulley gives no mechanical advantage of lift, but changes the direction of the force applied to the load. This is important when the space directly under the

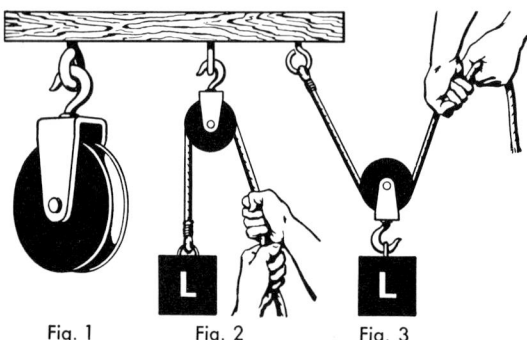

| Fig. 1 | Fig. 2 | Fig. 3 |

A Simple Pulley is shown in Figure 1. Figure 2 shows a fixed pulley which merely changes the direction of the force applied to the load (L). It has a mechanical advantage of 1. Figure 3 is a movable pulley from which the load is suspended.

load is hard to get at, as when the load is in a boat, a pit, or where footing is slippery.

When the task of the pulley is to carry a continuous turning motion, the two ends of the rope or belt are laced together. A second pulley, which is connected to the source of energy, transmits a steady rotation to the first pulley. If driver and driven pulleys are of the same size, the only advantage is a choice of directions from which the energy may come. If the pulleys are of different sizes, an advantage either of speed or of force may be obtained. When the belt between the two pulleys is crossed, the direction of turn of the driven pulley is reversed.

The second basic type of pulley is a *movable pulley*. The load is attached to the axle of this pulley. One end of the rope that passes through the pulley is attached to a fixed support above the load. A pull is applied to the free end of the rope in the same direction that the load is to move. The mechanical advantage of a movable pulley is 2. This means that the pull that is applied to the free end of the rope need be only half the weight of the load. The rope that is attached to the fixed support also carries half the load.   ROBERT F. PATON

See also BLOCK AND TACKLE; MACHINE.

PULLMAN, GEORGE MORTIMER (1831-1897), was an American inventor and businessman. He is remembered chiefly in connection with the railway sleeping car, which he improved and brought into general use.

Pullman was born in Brocton, N.Y. He learned the trade of a cabinetmaker and then branched out into work as a construction contractor. Moving to Chicago

Brown Bros.
George Pullman

in 1855, he became interested in improving the crude railway sleeping cars then in operation. In 1859, he remodeled two coaches into sleeping cars for the Chicago & Alton Railroad. He and his friend, Ben Field, then designed a larger and more elaborate car which they named *Pioneer*. It entered service in 1865, and was used in Abraham Lincoln's funeral train from Washington, D.C., to Springfield, Ill. It could be converted from day to night use by folding down the upper berths, making the seats into lower berths, and in the evening separating the berths by curtains.

Pullman introduced a dining car that had its own kitchen in 1868. He also introduced the parlor car in 1875 and the vestibule for direct connection between cars in 1887. He organized the Pullman Palace Car Company (later called the Pullman Company) in 1867. This firm built, staffed, and operated sleeping cars on all major railways. By 1890, Pullman had a virtual monopoly on the sleeping-car business in the United States. His company headquarters were in Pullman, Ill., a town built and owned by the company. The town became part of Chicago in 1889.   JOHN H. KEMBLE

PULLMAN COMPANY. See PULLMAN, GEORGE M.; PULLMAN STRIKE; CLEVELAND, GROVER (Labor Unrest).

PULLMAN SLEEPING CAR. See RAILROAD (picture: Beds on Wheels).

PULLMAN STRIKE of 1894 demonstrated the power of the United States courts to issue orders and injunctions in labor disputes affecting the public interest. Members of the American Railway Union struck the Great Northern Railway in a sympathy strike in Chicago to help Pullman Company employees in a wage dispute with their company. Violence followed, with damages estimated at $80 million.

The courts ordered Eugene Debs and other union officers to quit their strike activities. Debs then called upon all union members to strike, but the AFL refused to endorse such sympathy strikes. Debs was held in contempt of court and jailed. President Grover Cleveland sent federal troops to Illinois to protect the mails and company property.   GERALD G. SOMERS

See also DEBS, EUGENE VICTOR.

PULMONARY ARTERY. See ARTERY; HEART (How the Heart Works).

PULMONARY CIRCULATION. See CIRCULATION.

PULMONARY TUBERCULOSIS. See TUBERCULOSIS.

PULMONARY VEIN. See HEART (Left Side).

PULMOTOR. See RESUSCITATOR.

PULPIT is a raised structure, or platform, in a church, from which clergymen conduct services or deliver sermons. *Pulpit* comes from the Latin word *pulpitum*, which means *platform*. Any stage or rostrum used for public speaking used to be called a pulpit.

PULPWOOD. See PAPER (How Paper Is Made).

PULQUE. See ALCOHOLIC DRINK (Other Fermented Drinks); CENTURY PLANT.

PULSAR is a celestial object that sends out short bursts of radio waves at regular intervals. Astronomers named these objects pulsars because of the great regularity of the *pulsating* (on and off) radio waves coming from them. Pulsars were discovered in late 1967. At first, astronomers could detect only radio waves from pulsars. But in 1969, flashing light waves and X rays from one pulsar were observed.

Astronomers have many unanswered questions about pulsars. They do not know for certain how pulsars produce such regular radiation. However, many astronomers think that pulsars are small but dense stars composed mainly of neutrons. They believe the rapid spinning of these neutron stars produces the regular bursts of radio and light waves.

The *period* (interval between bursts) of some pulsars is slowly becoming longer. Different pulsars have different periods. The pulsars discovered so far have periods ranging from about $\frac{3}{100}$ of a second to about 4 seconds. A. G. W. CAMERON

PULSE is caused by a stretching of the arteries that takes place after each heartbeat. It can be felt by placing the fingers on the wrist above the thumb at a point over the *radial artery*. The pulse also can be felt by touching the temples where the *temporal artery* is located, and at other places on the body where an artery is near the surface. The wrists and temples are convenient points for feeling the pulse.

Each heartbeat consists of a contraction of the muscles of the heart that propels the blood into the arterial system, followed by a period of relaxation during which the heart refills. As the heart contracts, the blood is pumped into the *aorta* and *pulmonary arteries*. The aorta, the largest artery in the body, carries the blood aerated in the lungs from the left side of the heart to the rest of the body. As the blood rushes into the aorta its elastic walls are stretched and it expands to make room for the blood. As the blood moves on to enter the arteries that branch off from the aorta, the walls relax and it contracts to normal size. The walls of these arteries and of their branches also expand and contract as the blood passes through them. The expansion of these arteries causes the pulsation known as the *pulse*.

The pulse rate of children is faster, and that of old people often is slower than that of the average healthy adult. While pulse rates between 50 and 85 per minute are considered within normal limits, the normal rate for the average man is about 72. The pulse of the average woman is a little faster—76 to 80 per minute. The pulse rate of a newborn child may be as high as 140 per minute. The normal rate for a seven-year-old child is about 90 per minute. Slower rates of from 50 to 65 per minute are not unusual in old age. But regardless of a person's age, the pulse and heart rhythm should be regular.

A doctor feels a patient's pulse to find out if the heart is beating normally. If the pulse is too fast or too slow or irregular, the doctor examines the patient to diagnose the cause of the abnormal pulse. JOHN B. MIALE

See also ARTERY; HEART.

PULSEJET. See JET PROPULSION (Types).

PULTOWA, or POLTAVA, BATTLE OF. See ARMY (Famous Land Battles).

PULVILLUS. See FLY (The Body of a Fly).

PUMA. See MOUNTAIN LION.

PUMICE, *PUM ihs,* is a kind of white natural glass. It is a valuable scouring, scrubbing, and polishing material in both lump and powdered form. Lump pumice is the familiar *pumice stone.* Pumice is full of air bubbles, and is really a solid foam. Natural glass forms when red-hot lava flows from a volcano and cools very quickly. If the lava is full of volcanic gases, the gases escape and turn the lava into a foam.

Pumice floats on water. It is no lighter than any other natural glass, but it contains so many air chambers that it is light enough to float. Sailors reportedly walked two miles on floating pumice from their ships to the shore after the explosion of Krakatoa volcano in Indonesia in 1883. RICHARD M. PEARL

See also ABRASIVE; IGNEOUS ROCK.

PUMMELO. See GRAPEFRUIT.

Ewing Galloway

Feeling a Patient's Pulse, a doctor consults his watch to learn how many times the patient's heart beats each minute.

PUMP

PUMP is a device for moving liquids and gases. Gas pumps are often called *compressors* or *fans*. Pumps have hundreds of uses in the home and in industry. They are used in mining, irrigation, boilers, atomic engines, air conditioners, automobiles, wells, home-heating systems, and city water plants.

Reciprocating Pumps

In a typical reciprocating pump, a piston slides back and forth in a cylinder. With each movement, it traps part of the fluid to be moved. The fluid is then moved toward the discharge side of the pump. The pressure there rises as the fluid is squeezed by the moving piston. The pressure finally becomes high enough to force the fluid out. Reciprocating pumps differ from one another mainly in their valve arrangements. They are used as well-water pumps, tire pumps, air and gas compressors, and vacuum pumps.

The Lift Pump is the simplest reciprocating pump. It is used to pump water from wells. Lift pumps are often called *suction pumps*, because they create a partial vacuum that lifts the water from the well. The piston in the cylinder has a valve that opens as the piston moves down, but closes as the piston moves up. The bottom of the cylinder also has a valve that connects it to a pipe that extends to the water. The first downstroke of the piston presses against the air beneath it, and forces the air upward and out through the valve. A partial vacuum is formed when the piston rises. The water from the well then flows into the cylinder. The water cannot sink back into the well, because the cylinder valve closes when the water tries to run downward. After a few strokes, the piston sinks below the rising water in the cylinder. The water then flows through the valve to the top of the piston. The next upstroke of the piston lifts the water and discharges it from the spout.

The piston valve will not work unless it is airtight. This is usually done by *priming the pump*, or wetting the valve to keep it sealed tightly. A lift pump operates in a shallow well, usually at depths less than 27 feet.

Force Pumps are used in water wells and fire engines. They resemble lift pumps, but they discharge the water at high pressure, rather than merely lifting the water out. The force of the downstroke of the piston is applied directly to the water leaving the pump. As the piston moves upward, it creates a partial vacuum behind it, and water flows upward into the cylinder. The valve between the cylinder and the well closes as the piston moves downward. The downward-moving piston increases the water pressure in the cylinder. This forces the outlet valve open, and the water flows out. On the next upward piston stroke, the outlet valve closes.

Force pumps are generally run by mechanical power, rather than by hand. An air chamber is usually placed between the exit valve and the exit pipe to keep a steady stream of water going out the discharge pipe. The air chamber traps air in its upper portion. The downward stroke of the piston forces water into the air chamber, and compresses the air at the top. Then, while the piston draws in more water on the upstroke, the compressed air in the chamber forces a steady stream of water out of the discharge pipe.

A Tire Pump is a simple air-compressor pump. It operates much like a lift pump, except that the piston flap valve closes on the downstroke of the piston, and opens on the upstroke.

Mercury Vacuum Pumps produce a vacuum by using mercury as a piston. The pressure of the atmosphere can balance a column of mercury about $29\frac{1}{2}$ inches high. In a simple vacuum pump, a tube longer than this is connected to a reservoir of mercury by a rubber hose. The mercury in the tube will rise if the reservoir is elevated. The rising mercury forces the air from the tube. The top of the tube is then capped tight, and the reservoir is lowered. This leaves a vacuum at the top of the tube. The tube can then be sealed at the bottom to form a glass bulb in which there is almost no air. The vacuum of the original light bulb made by Thomas A. Edison was produced with a mercury pump of this kind.

Gear Pumps are usually used to pump thick fluids such as oil. Lubricating oil pumps of automobile engines are usually gear pumps. A gear pump consists mainly of a pair of meshing gears that rotate in a housing. As the fluid moves into the inlet region, it is trapped between the gear teeth, and carried around to the outlet side. The pressure in the outlet region builds up quickly, until it is high enough to discharge the fluid. Until the pressure is high enough, the fluid remains inside the housing near the outlet. The meshing teeth of the gears keep the fluid from passing back into the inlet region.

Centrifugal Pumps

Centrifugal pumps pump water by means of centrifugal force (see CENTRIFUGAL FORCE). For example, if you swing a pail of water around your head, the water does not spill out, because centrifugal force presses it toward the bottom of the bucket. If a number of bottomless buckets were whirled around inside a pipe, and there was only one hole where water could leave the pipe, each pail would throw some of its water out as it passed this hole. It would also suck up more water at the center. This is exactly how a centrifugal pump works. Instead of buckets, however, a centrifugal pump has several ribs or vanes mounted on a revolving disk. The water takes up the space between the vanes.

Centrifugal pumps are used as gas compressors as well as for pumping liquids for water-supply systems, mines, irrigation, dredging, and sewage disposal.

Other Pumps

Axial-Flow Pumps pump air as well as liquids. They supply large quantities of air needed to run jet airplane engines. A single engine may require 100 pounds of air each second, or enough air to fill an average room in a house. Axial-flow pumps consist of several propeller-like blades attached to a single shaft. At the inlet, the first set of rotating blades speeds up the air in a direction parallel to the shaft of the pump. Pressure builds up in the areas between the rows of blades as the blades continue to rotate. Like the centrifugal pump, the axial-flow pump rotates at high speed.

Air-Lift Pumps are widely used in oil wells and mines. They consist of an air pipe and a long drop pipe that is submerged below the liquid. The air pipe delivers air to the bottom of the drop pipe. This forms a mixture of air and liquid that is lighter than the liquid outside the drop pipe. As a result, the liquid in the drop pipe rises above the liquid on the outside.

HOW THE AIR PUMP WORKS

FIRST STROKE

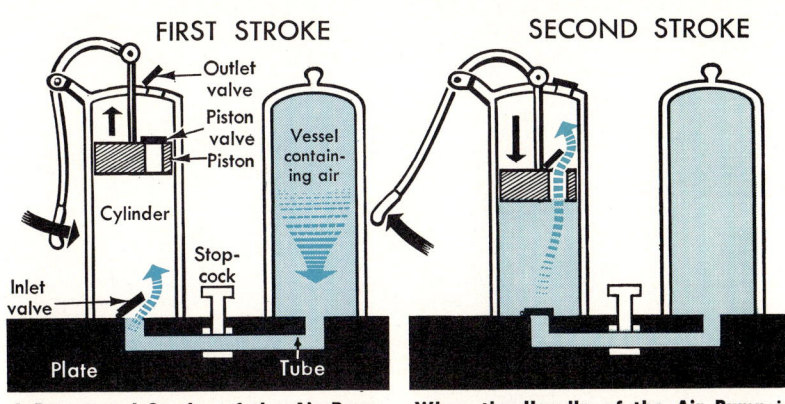

SECOND STROKE

THIRD STROKE

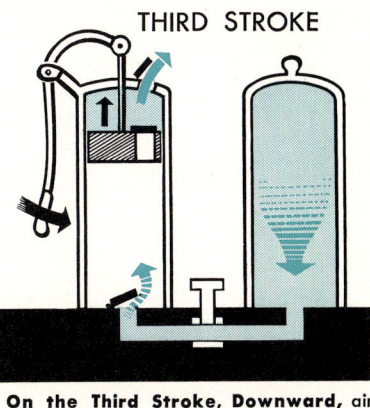

A Downward Stroke of the Air Pump Handle pulls the cylinder up, allowing air from the vessel at right to rush through the intake valve into the cylinder chamber. Air above the cylinder is forced out through the outlet valve at the top.

When the Handle of the Air Pump is pulled up, the cylinder piston is forced down. The outlet valve closes. Air in the bottom of the cylinder chamber is forced through the valve on the piston, closing the inlet valve leading to the air vessel.

On the Third Stroke, Downward, air again is sucked out of the vessel into the cylinder chamber. The valve on the piston is closed, and the air trapped in the top of the cylinder chamber by the previous stroke is forced outward.

Jet Pumps use the principle that the pressure of a fluid decreases if the fluid speeds up as a result of passing through a smaller passage. A steam-jet ejector uses this principle to pump air from a tank. Steam comes to the pump from an outside source, and moves faster as it moves into a narrow chamber inside the pump. This low-pressure area creates suction that draws the air into the chamber through another opening. The mixture of air and steam then flows into a wider chamber, where the mixture loses its velocity and gains enough pressure to be discharged. Aerators for water faucets use the same principle when they pump air into the water. See HYDRAULICS (Laws of Flowing Liquids).

Hydraulic Rams use large amounts of flowing water as a piston. They are often used to pump the water that flows from a reservoir. When the water reaches a certain speed inside the ram, a valve suddenly closes and stops the forward flow of the water. The oncoming water builds up considerable pressure and strikes against the closed valve like a battering ram. But the water has nowhere to go, except into an air chamber, where it is trapped. The compressed air in the chamber forces some of the water out. WILLARD L. ROGERS

See also HYDRAULICS; MILKING MACHINE; SIPHON.

HOW THE FORCE PUMP WORKS

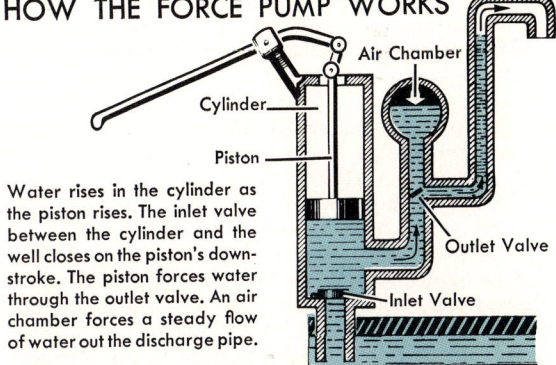

Water rises in the cylinder as the piston rises. The inlet valve between the cylinder and the well closes on the piston's down-stroke. The piston forces water through the outlet valve. An air chamber forces a steady flow of water out the discharge pipe.

HOW THE CENTRIFUGAL PUMP WORKS

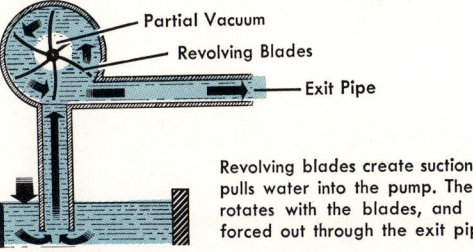

Revolving blades create suction, which pulls water into the pump. The water rotates with the blades, and is then forced out through the exit pipe.

HOW THE LIFT PUMP WORKS

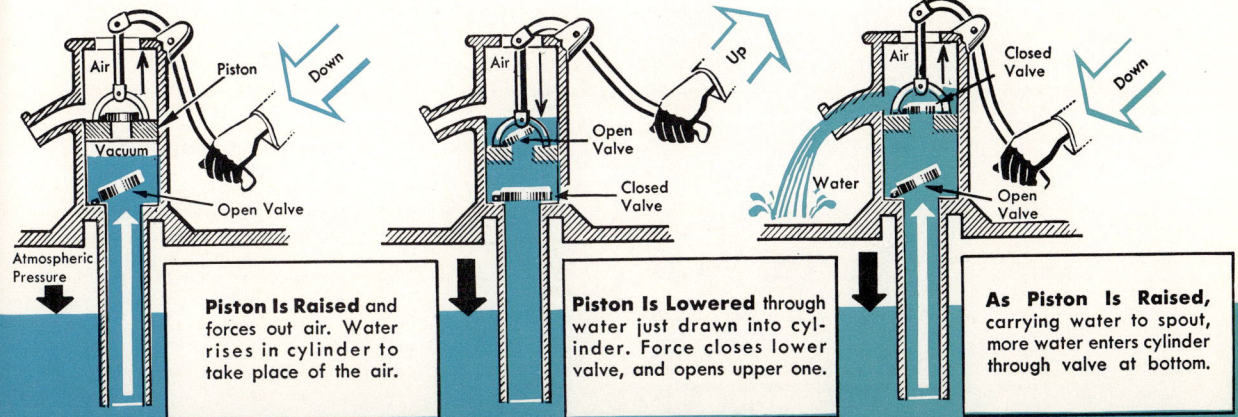

Piston Is Raised and forces out air. Water rises in cylinder to take place of the air.

Piston Is Lowered through water just drawn into cylinder. Force closes lower valve, and opens upper one.

As Piston Is Raised, carrying water to spout, more water enters cylinder through valve at bottom.

Pumpkins grow on trailing vines, often along old-fashioned rail fences, *above*. Children use the large orange field pumpkins, *right*, to carve jack-o'-lanterns for Halloween.

J. Horace McFarland; FPG

PUMPERNICKEL is a variety of heavy, dark bread. It is usually made from whole, coarse rye. One variety is made with wheat flour added to the rye. Pumpernickel is eaten in all parts of the world. It is made in much the same way as other kinds of bread. See also BREAD.

PUMPKIN, *PUMP kin*, is the fruit of the pumpkin plant, a trailing vine with broad, prickly leaves. There are two groups of pumpkins. These are the big orange-colored stock pumpkin and the finer textured straw-colored cheese pumpkin. The cheese pumpkin is used for commercial canned pumpkin. The big orange-colored pumpkin was brought to a high degree of perfection by the Indians. The cheese pumpkins are the result of controlled plant breeding.

Pumpkins often have been mentioned in songs and stories. John Greenleaf Whittier, in his poem "The Pumpkin," refers to their use as jack-o'-lanterns (see JACK-O'-LANTERN). James Whitcomb Riley mentions them in his poem "When the Frost Is on the Punkin."

The pumpkin is a good source of vitamin A and a fair source of vitamin C. It is also a fair source of energy. Pumpkins are cultivated in the same way as squashes.

Scientific Classification. Pumpkins belong to the gourd family, *Cucurbitaceae*. The large orange pumpkin is genus *Cucurbita*, species *C. pepo*. The cheese type is *C. moschata*.   ERVIN L. DENISEN

See also SQUASH; INDIANA (color picture: Roadside Market).

PUMPKIN SEED, the fish. See SUNFISH.

PUN is a play upon words that have the same or similar sounds, but different meanings. An example is: "Two coin collectors got together for old *dimes*' sake."

The pun is an old form of humor. The ancient Greeks and Romans showed their appreciation of a pun by groaning. This is still a traditional response. The pun has been called "the lowest form of wit." But considerable intelligence is needed to make up a good pun and to appreciate one.   J. N. HOOK

See also HUMOR (Puns).

PUNAKHA, *POON uk kuh* (pop. about 7,900; alt. 6,000 ft.), was the capital of Bhutan until the late 1950's, when Thimbu became the capital. Punakha lies on the upper Sankosh River, about 100 miles northeast of Darjeeling, India. It was founded in 1577. See also BHUTAN; THIMBU.

PUNCH AND JUDY are two famous characters in an English puppet show. The show originated in Italy, and the name *Punch* comes from the Italian character, *Pulcinella* or *Punchinello*. Punch became popular in England in the 1660's. The puppet show starring Punch shows him fighting his opponents and knocking them out. At the end of the show he either defeats the devil or is swallowed by a crocodile-like creature. This type of ending provided a "moral" for the show.   MARJORIE B. McPHARLIN

See also PUPPET (Later European Puppets; picture: The Punch and Judy Show).

PUNCHEON. See PIONEER LIFE IN AMERICA (A Pioneer Home).

Bettmann Archive

Punch-and-Judy Shows have delighted audiences for more than 300 years. The ill-tempered Punch, who continually quarrels with his wife, Judy, and other people, is said to represent the spirit of revolt that exists in human beings.

PUNCTUATION, PUNK *tyoo AY shun,* is the use of certain marks in writing and printing to make the writer's meaning clear.

Early writing and early printing had marks to show punctuation. But the signs were used according to the wish of the writer and to the marks which the printer had in his type cases. Ancient Greek, for example, often used a semicolon in place of our modern question mark. Printing and punctuation improved rapidly in Italy. Finally Aldus Manutius, a maker of books, began to use the various marks more systematically. Manutius is considered the father of our modern punctuation.

Marks were used more frequently some years ago. Today the trend is to use fewer and fewer marks, and in many places to use none at all. Writers today are less bound by the old rules. Some use *closed punctuation,* with a number of marks. Others use *open punctuation,* with few marks. The difference is best shown by entries in letter writing.

CLOSED	OPEN
3962 East Page Avenue,	1864 South Elm Road
Ashland, Ohio,	Clinton, Iowa
October 27, 1960.	December 10, 1960

It is easy to learn the rules of punctuation and to use them correctly. Punctuation is used merely to help the reader understand what is meant.

The Period (.) is a dot on the line of writing. It is used at the end of a statement or command and after an abbreviation. A period follows the sentence you have just read. If there are quotation marks at the end of a sentence, the period is placed inside these marks. Roman numerals (clxvi, CXXVI) are not followed by periods. Periods are not placed after page numbers in books, but they are placed after numbers in an outline or list. There are no periods after call letters for radio stations, some government bureaus, and some signals sent by code letters, as *WCFL, AAA, SOS.* Some persons, such as printers, call the period the "full stop."

The Question Mark (?) is used after a question. It is also called the *interrogation mark* or *point.* Every direct question should be followed by a question mark, as *Do you understand this rule?* An indirect question is only part of a sentence. It is followed by a period, as *I asked whether you understood this rule.* Plainly such a sentence does not ask a question.

The Exclamation Point (!) is used after a sentence which expresses strong feeling. *How cold it is!* Single words, phrases, or clauses of the same sort are followed by the exclamation mark. *Listen! You, over there! Trying to hide!* There are few occasions for using this mark, except in reporting speech. See EXCLAMATION POINT.

Quotation Marks (" ") enclose the exact words of a speaker. The first two marks are inverted commas placed above the line of writing. The second marks are apostrophes. They are sometimes called *double quotation marks,* or *double quotes.* They enclose only the spoken words, as in *"I'm going to telephone to Martha,"* said Bill, and *"Do you think,"* Mother asked, *"that she has come back from the shore?"* When one writer "quotes" another (that is, reproduces his exact words) he marks his borrowing by quotation marks. When several paragraphs are quoted, double quotation marks are placed at the beginning of every paragraph and at the end of the last one. Quotations within quotations are enclosed in single quotation marks, as "He answered, 'I will not,' when I

asked him," she reported. Quotation marks may enclose titles of poems, lectures, sermons, and the like. Sometimes titles are italicized instead.

The Colon (:) is one dot above another and has two uses. It is most frequently used after the salutation in a business letter, as *Dear Mr. Miller:, Gentlemen:, My dear Doctor:, Dear Sir:.* The other use is after such expressions as *to the following:, as follows:.* Often the colon in this use is followed by a list. *The chief national groups are as follows: English, French, Italian.* See COLON.

The Semicolon (;) is a dot above a comma. It is used in a compound sentence between two principal clauses which are not joined by a conjunction. *He struggled to land the bass; it flipped its tail as it vanished.* If principal clauses of a compound sentence contain commas, a semicolon is placed between the clauses even if the conjunction is used. *We rounded the corner yelling, swaying, and grinding; but having used the brakes too late, we skidded against the opposite wall.* The semicolon is also used instead of the comma after items in a series when these items are long or complicated.

The Dash (—) is used in informal writing to mark a sudden break in thought. *I considered her—it was a foolish opinion—too young to take care of herself.* Letter writers in a careless manner often use dashes instead of commas, semicolons, and periods.

Parentheses () enclose parts of the sentence which might easily have been omitted. The material between them is not connected grammatically with the rest of the sentence. *I explained to you (you don't remember when) why I cannot take a long trip.* One mark is called a *parenthesis.* The entire group of words enclosed by the marks is also called a *parenthesis.* See PARENTHESIS.

Brackets [] in quoted remarks enclose explanations not in the actual speech. *"I am a simple man." [Laughter].* Directions in plays may be in parentheses or in brackets. *Duke Morris [Seriously] But I need money. [He turns away.]*

The Comma (,) is the most commonly used mark. It has more uses than any other mark of punctuation. Most of the principal ones are here set down.

It follows the words, phrases, or clauses in a series. *We ate crabs, lobster, shrimp, and fish.*

It follows items in addresses and dates. *He was born at 611 East Minnesota Street, Indianapolis, Indiana, on November 24, 1911.*

It is placed around certain conjunctions, adverbs, and phrases, such as *now, however, nevertheless, for instance,* when it indicates a break in the construction. *Try, for instance, to borrow money without giving security.*

It is used after words, phrases, and clauses at the beginning of sentences unless there is a close connection. *If you perform that experiment again, I shall help you.*

It is used between the principal clauses of a compound sentence unless the sentence is short. *We stood terrified by the swollen stream, but one of us discovered a safe bridge along a huge fallen tree.*

It separates nonrestrictive subordinate clauses from the rest of the sentence. *The listening lad, who had been intently silent, suddenly let out a bloodcurdling yell.*

It is used to set off any unit which is not closely related to the rest of the sentence. Such expressions are described as *parenthetical,* and some writers would place parentheses around them. *Now that you have brought that box, not needed yet, put it in that dark corner.*

It sets off a word or phrase which explains some term. The second term is said to be an *appositive* of the first. *Radar, an electronic device, is of value in warfare.*

It sets off words like *well, yes, no,* and all nouns of address. *Yes, we saw the eclipse. Mr. Emerson, may I speak with Jane?*

It sets off quotations, especially in conversation. *"May I,"* he began shyly, *"have the next dance?" "Surely,"* she answered.

It is often used to avoid misunderstanding. *Some weeks before she arrived from Canada* is not clear. *Some weeks before, she arrived from Canada* is clear. See COMMA.

The Hyphen (-) is most commonly used to link compound words. It is also used at the end of a line when a word is broken and part of it is put on the next line.

The Apostrophe (') is used in the place of omitted letters in elisions (see ELISION). It is also used to show the possessive case in nouns. CLARENCE STRATTON

PUNCTURE WOUND. See WOUND.

PUNIC WARS, *PYOO nick,* were three struggles between ancient Rome and Carthage. Rome won all three wars. The wars made Rome the supreme power of the Western world, and helped Rome control all of the Mediterranean Sea. *Punic,* the Latin word for *Phoenician,* is used for the wars because Carthage had been founded by the Phoenicians.

The First Punic War (264-241 B.C.) began when Rome intervened to prevent Carthaginian control of the straits of Messina, between Sicily and Italy. Rome became a naval power in order to meet Carthage on equal terms. Both sides lost several fleets and many men. The war was decided when Rome conquered Sicily, and won a final naval battle there.

The Second Punic War (218-201 B.C.) developed from the first war, and was also caused by territorial rivalry in Spain between Rome and Carthage. Hannibal, a great Carthaginian general, crossed the Alps and invaded Italy (see HANNIBAL). The Romans finally stopped him from getting extra men and supplies, and defeated Hannibal in 202 B.C. Carthage then paid Rome a large sum and gave up Spain.

The Third Punic War (149-146 B.C.) resulted when Carthage rebelled against the restrictions of the Roman peace treaty of 201 B.C. Carthage was completely destroyed in this war. Rome won because it had better resources and more men. Carthage was richer in the beginning, but it had to rely on mercenaries (hired troops). Hannibal had proved that these troops could fight well, but there were never enough men. HENRY C. BOREN

Related Articles in WORLD BOOK include:

Army (Famous	Carthage	Roman Empire
Land Battles	Hamilcar Barca	(Overseas
[Metaurus; Zama])	Regulus,	Expansion)
Cannae	Marcus A.	Scipio

PUNISHMENT. See CAPITAL PUNISHMENT; CRIME; CRIMINOLOGY; PENAL COLONY; PRISON; REFORMATORY.

PUNJAB, *PUN jahb,* or *pun JAHB,* is a region lying in the northwestern section of India, and in West Pakistan. Punjab comes from a Sanskrit word meaning *five rivers.* The area is mostly flat, and is drained by the Indus River and its five tributaries. For location, see INDIA (political map).

Punjab (Pakistan) (pop. 23,007,577; area 62,034 sq. mi.) is part of the province of West Pakistan. Lahore, the largest city, has a number of cotton gins and presses, as well as plants making textiles, cement, glass, and surgical goods. Islāmābād serves as the capital of Pakistan. The leading industry of the province is farming. This is the leading wheat-producing area of the Indian subcontinent. Millet, maize (corn), sugar cane, oilseeds, rice, citrus fruit, mangoes, pomegranates, dates, and cotton also are grown. Widespread irrigation has made much of the land fertile. From 1950 to 1953 alone, 2 million acres of desert land were reclaimed by irrigation. Minerals such as coal, gypsum, and limestone are found in the northwestern part of the province.

Punjab (India) (pop. 20,186,931; area 47,065 sq. mi.) is a region that consists of two states—Punjab, where Punjabi is spoken, and Haryana, where Hindi is spoken. These states were created from the single state of Punjab in 1966. Part of Punjab was also included in the territory of Himachal Pradesh.

Indian Punjab is largely a farming region. Timber is found in the northeast part, in the Himalaya. Cities of Indian Punjab include Amritsar, the holy city of the Sikhs; and Chandigarh, the capital of Punjab and Haryana states. Chandigarh is also a Union Territory of India. Indian Punjab has cotton mills, small engineering plants, metalworks, and glassworks. It also produces cement, sporting goods, and fine handicrafts such as woolen carpets and muslin turbans.

Part of the Punjab region was once within the empire of Alexander the Great. Later, Mogul rulers held the area. In the early 1800's, it became a Sikh kingdom under Ranjit Singh. Great Britain annexed it in 1849. When India was partitioned in 1947, Punjab also was divided. The eastern section became an Indian state, while the western area, dominated by the Moslems, went to Pakistan. Thousands died as Moslems fled from eastern Punjab, and Hindus and Sikhs moved from Pakistan to India. ROBERT I. CRANE

See also AMRITSAR; CHANDIGARH; INDUS RIVER; LAHORE; NEW DELHI.

PUNKIE. See GNAT.

PUNT. See BOATS AND BOATING (Unusual Boats).

PUNT. See FOOTBALL (Plays).

PUNTARENAS, *POON tah RAY nahs* (pop. 19,582; alt. 6 ft.), is the chief seaport of Costa Rica on the Pacific Coast. For location, see COSTA RICA (color map). The city stands on a tongue of land that reaches out into the Gulf of Nicoya. It is a resort city. Gold, silver, cacao, and sugar are shipped from there. See also COSTA RICA (picture).

PUPA, *PYOO puh,* is the relatively motionless stage in the *metamorphosis* (development) of many kinds of insects. In complete metamorphosis, the larva of the insect changes into a pupa, which, in turn, develops into an adult insect (see LARVA).

Most pupae breathe and move very little. They do not eat at all. But during the pupal stage, the insect's body structures change greatly. They develop from larval structures into adult structures, which are usually very different.

The pupa looks different in different kinds of insects. In some insects, including butterflies and most moths, the pupa's antennae, legs, and wings are folded closely to its body. In others, including lace-

L. W. Brownell

The Cocoon of This Moth has been cut open to show the pupa within. An adult moth develops from a pupa.

wings and beetles, the antennae, legs, and wings are free. The pupa resembles somewhat the adult insect. In many groups of insects, the pupae are encased in cocoons of silk or other substances. Silk fiber comes from the cocoon of the silkworm moth. The pupa of the fly is encased in a *puparium*, the skin of the last larval stage.   ALEXANDER B. KLOTS

See also BUTTERFLY (Pupa); CHRYSALIS; COCOON; FLY (The Life of a Fly); METAMORPHOSIS; MOTH.

PUPIL. See EYE (The Eyeball; color diagram: Parts of the Eye).

PUPIN, *pyoo PEEN,* **MICHAEL IDVORSKY** (1858-1935), a Hungarian-born American physicist, won fame in many fields. His inventions led to great advances in long-distance telephone systems, telegraphy, and radio transmission networks. He held 34 patents. For his autobiography, *From Immigrant to Inventor* (1923), Pupin received the 1924 Pulitzer prize. Pupin was born in Idvor, Hungary (now Yugoslavia).   G. GAMOW

PUPPET. Puppets are figures usually in imitation of life, under an operator's control. They are used for dramatic presentations.

Types of Puppets. There are many different kinds of puppets. Some are worked by strings. Others are worked by rods or held over the hand and fingers, and there are combinations of these types. String puppets are often called *marionettes,* a word of French origin. It comes from the religious puppet plays of the Middle Ages in which one of the puppet characters represented the Virgin Mary. The name *Little Mary,* or *marionette,* came to be given the other puppets.

Types of puppets are the *hand puppet,* the *rod puppet,* the *hand-and-rod puppet,* and the *finger puppet.* There are also flat puppets known as *shadow figures,* used to cast black or colored shadows on a screen. Puppets may be moved by strings, wires, rods, hands, fingers, or magnetic attraction. They can be controlled from above, below, at a level with the operator, or from the back or sides of the stage, depending on the type of puppet.

A dummy, such as Charlie McCarthy, used in combination with ventriloquism, or "voice throwing," is operated from the back and held level with the ventriloquist. There are strings and rods inside such dummies and these work the head and the features. The ventriloquist's arm, which supports the dummy, also gives some movement to the body. The limbs of the dummy are usually moved only as they swing with the body. See VENTRILOQUISM.

Hand puppets are one of the easiest types to make, though not to operate. The hand puppet, in its simplest form, needs only a head on a tubelike costume. It is drawn over the hand, like a glove. The forefinger works the head, and the thumb and middle finger the two arms. Such puppets are often sold as toys, because even a child's hand can produce entertaining movements of the figure. Puppets made of paper bags are a popular variety of hand puppet among amateur *puppeteers,* or operators of puppet shows.

Rod puppets and shadow figures may be made simply, of everyday materials, and they also can be worked easily, even by young children. Varieties of these types are sometimes found in toy stores. String puppets are the most popular type in the United States.

Freida Zylstra

Staging a Puppet Show gives youngsters a chance to try their skill at a dramatic presentation with simple, inexpensive equipment. The string puppets, which are often called *marionettes,* can be made by hand. The stage set is handpainted cardboard.

MAKING A
HAND PUPPET

Using papier-mâché pulp, mold head and features onto a cardboard tube, rolled to fit the index finger. Decorate when dry.

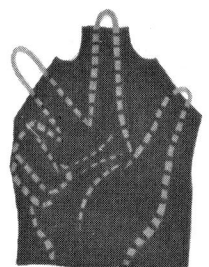

For the body, sew two identical pieces of cloth together, leaving the neck and armholes open. Sleeves may be attached.

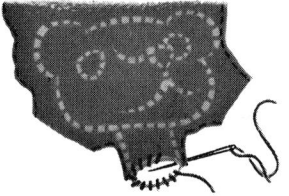

Turn body inside out over head. Sew cloth neck to paper tube.

American Broadcasting Co.

Kukla, Fran, and Ollie Shows featured puppets Kukla, a bald boy, and Ollie, a one-toothed dragon, with witty Fran Allison.

Puppeteers Bil and Cora Baird designed a wildly assorted family of hand puppets and marionettes for their delightful TV shows.

The Punch-and-Judy Show became popular in London in the 1660's. A man hid inside the box to work these famous puppets.

Bettmann Archive

Early Puppets. Greek literature of about 300 B.C. refers to "string-pullers," possibly puppeteers. Small jointed puppets or dolls with a wire attached to the head have been found in children's graves in Greece and Italy, and date back to about A.D. 100. After the break-up of the Roman Empire, the puppet theater kept alive some of the traditions of the Roman theater. It is thought that string-operated solid puppets originated in the Western World, then went eastward to China, and over the Bering Strait to the Americas. American Indians were using them before the coming of the white man. The flat shadow figures probably originated in Asia and made their way westward, reaching Europe and America during the 1700's as opaque silhouettes. There was then a vogue for black cut-paper figures.

Later European Puppets. In the Middle Ages, people used puppets to act out religious plays and morality plays. The popular puppet *Punchinello* came to France from Italy in the 1640's and became known as *Polichinelle*. He reached England about 1660, and his name was soon shortened to *Punch*. The first text of a Punch-and-Judy play was published in England in 1828 and was illustrated by the famous artist, George Cruikshank.

Many parts of Europe developed puppet heroes who spoke and acted like the people of the region. Certain places were also known for special types of puppets. The people of Barcelona, Spain, liked hand puppets of a special type. The people of Cologne, Germany, were fond of rod puppets. Flanders and Sicily used puppets of knights in armor. In the palaces and castles of the 1700's there were richly appointed private puppet theaters. Voltaire, the French philosopher and playwright, helped with puppet shows in such theaters.

Goethe, the great German poet, received a puppet theater on his twelfth birthday, and wrote his own plays for it. Toy puppet theaters and small hand puppets were favorites in the 1800's. Lewis Carroll, Hans Christian Andersen, and Tad Lincoln made their own. In Paris there were artistic groups of people who were fascinated by the hand puppets of the satirist, Lemercier de Neuville, and by rod puppet shows at the Petit-Théâtre and shadows at the Black Cat cabaret.

Puppets in America brought the theater to many people. Both children and grownups who could not afford the regular theater or who lived too far away from it, attended puppet shows until the movies took over the low-priced field. Around 1900 puppets were popular at fairs and circuses, in town halls and schoolhouses, and in parks and streets. Puppeteers presented popular versions of old-fashioned dramas. *Noah's Ark* and *Jephtha's Rash Vow* appeared for many years after such Biblical plays had ceased to be done by living actors.

Gradually in the 1900's, a new kind of puppet show developed. More skill and artistry were displayed. Most

798

MAKING A STRING PUPPET

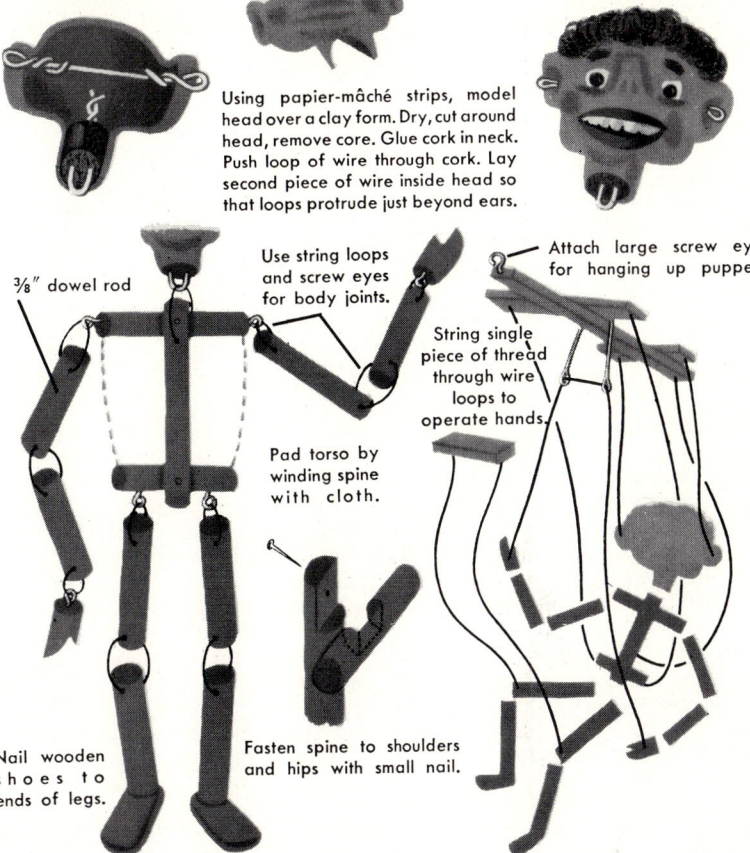

Join halves, paint head.

Using papier-mâché strips, model head over a clay form. Dry, cut around head, remove core. Glue cork in neck. Push loop of wire through cork. Lay second piece of wire inside head so that loops protrude just beyond ears.

⅜" dowel rod

Use string loops and screw eyes for body joints.

Attach large screw eye for hanging up puppet.

String single piece of thread through wire loops to operate hands.

Pad torso by winding spine with cloth.

Nail wooden shoes to ends of legs.

Fasten spine to shoulders and hips with small nail.

Eliot Elisofon, *Life*, © 1959 Time, Inc.

puppet theaters today are small and easy to travel with. Artists and writers who wanted to produce plays for small audiences of friends used puppets. They wrote plays especially for puppets and used puppet actors that were works of art. The professional puppet theater of today grew out of this type of sophisticated artistry.

In 1915, full-length plays with string puppets were produced by Ellen Van Volkenburg and the Chicago Little Theater. Tony Sarg gave his first public shows in 1916 in New York, and Ellen Van Volkenburg directed his famous production of *The Rose and The Ring*. Sarg's work helped to revive puppetry in the United States.

Many men and women contributed to this revival. Remo Bufano used all types of puppets in New York City. He had a little hand puppet, Orlando Furioso, and a huge thirty-five-foot telescoping string-puppet clown, used in the stage show, *Jumbo*. Forman Brown and Harry Burnett have done string-puppet musical comedies, and had their own Turnabout Theater in Los Angeles. George Pal and Lou Bunin have made films with puppet actors. Puppets are used widely in television programs. Burr Tillstrom's Kukla and Ollie, of *Kukla, Fran, and Ollie*, Howdy Doody, and Paul Winchell's Jerry Mahoney are among the best known. Puppets are also used in television advertising.

Publications and Societies. As a result of the puppet revival, many people became interested in producing

puppet shows. Puppetry became popular with school and civic groups. Many of these amateurs had no idea how to make a puppet. Puppeteers had always kept secret the mechanics of their trade, and they were reluctant to give assistance to newcomers. Gradually, writers published technical information.

One of the first books was *The Tony Sarg Marionette Book*, published in 1921 by F. J. McIsaac. In 1930, Paul McPharlin first issued *Puppetry, A Yearbook of Puppets and Marionettes*. During its 16 years, it recorded important events in puppetry throughout the world. Other books and pamphlets on puppets also appeared.

The Union Internationale des Marionnettes was founded in Prague in the 1930's, and held congresses. People interested in puppetry established national societies in many countries, notably England, France, and the United States. Periodicals on puppetry also appeared. The first one was *The Marionette*, in 1918. These publications contained historical articles, plays, and construction details for puppets and stages.

In May, 1958, the first International Festival of Puppet Theatres took place in Bucharest, Romania. More than 300 delegates came from 27 countries. More than 30 companies participated.   MARJORIE B. McPHARLIN

See also PUNCH AND JUDY; ROMAN NUMERALS (pictures).

PUPPY. See DOG (How to Care for Your Dog).

799

PURCELL, EDWARD MILLS (1912-   ), an American physicist, shared the 1952 Nobel prize for physics. He received the award for developing and applying a simple but precise method for determining the magnetic properties of nuclei. He did this by studying the energy they absorbed from radio waves of properly chosen wave lengths. Purcell also made important contributions to radio astronomy. He was born in Taylorville, Ill. In 1949, he became a professor of physics at Harvard University.   GERALD HOLTON

PURCELL, *PUR s'l,* **HENRY** (1659?-1695), an English composer, wrote *Dido and Aeneas* (1680), the first important English opera. Purcell evolved a new choral style that was clearly the product of Italian opera, rather than Elizabethan motet traditions. Melody was founded on rhythmic regularity, and modulation techniques showed a definite trend toward modern conceptions of harmony. In *Dido and Aeneas,* "Dido's Lament," or "When I Am Laid in Earth," is considered one of the most beautiful songs of sorrow to be found in opera.

At the age of ten, Purcell became a chorister at the Chapel Royal, where he composed his first anthems. Four years later, he became assistant keeper of the king's instruments. He served as organist in Westminster Abbey, and in 1682 became organist at the Chapel Royal. Purcell wrote six operas, incidental music to 54 plays, and music for the organ. *Te Deum and Jubilate in D* is considered one of his greatest compositions.

Purcell was probably born in London. He was buried in Westminster Abbey.   WARREN S. FREEMAN

PURCHASING POWER. See INFLATION AND DEFLATION.

PURDUE UNIVERSITY is a publicly controlled coeducational land-grant college at Lafayette, Ind. It is supported mostly by the state of Indiana, but receives some aid from the federal government.

Purdue is well known as an engineering school, having schools of civil, electrical, chemical, metallurgical, mechanical, and aeronautical engineering. In addition, there are schools of agriculture, home economics, pharmacy, science education, humanities, industrial management, and veterinary science and medicine. Purdue also has a graduate school and a research foundation. Courses lead to the bachelor's and master's degrees in science and the degree of doctor of philosophy. The university has army, navy, and air force ROTC units.

University extension centers are in Fort Wayne, Hammond, Indianapolis, and Michigan City.

Purdue's Hall of Music is the largest college auditorium in the world, seating over 6,100 people. The Ross-Ade stadium is named in honor of David Ross, a Lafayette manufacturer, and George Ade, novelist and playwright. The library contains an extensive collection of books on agriculture. The university owns and operates a daily radio station. School colors are old gold and black. The athletic team nickname is Boilermakers, and the best-known song is "Hail, Hail to Old Purdue." Purdue was founded in 1869, and is named for John Purdue, one of the school's early benefactors.

For Purdue's enrollment, see UNIVERSITIES AND COLLEGES (table).   JOHN W. HICKS

Purdue University Occupies a Large, Parklike Campus in West Lafayette, Ind.

Purdue University

Food and Drug Administration

Pure Food and Drug Laws require truthful and informative labeling and advertising. Biochemists of the Food and Drug Administration measure the amount of vitamins in foods by feeding test doses to laboratory animals and checking the results.

PURE FOOD AND DRUG LAWS seek to protect the public health from the sale of harmful, spoiled, impure, infected, cheapened, or otherwise adulterated foods, drugs, and cosmetics. They also seek to prevent false or misleading labeling or improper packaging of foods, drugs, cosmetics, and related products.

In the United States, the Federal Food and Drugs Act of 1906 and the Food, Drug, and Cosmetic Act of 1938, with its amendments, have been the most inclusive pure food and drug laws. The Food, Drug, and Cosmetic Act provides for seizures, injunctions, and penalties of from $1,000 to $10,000 for violations of the law. Manufacturers or shippers found guilty of breaking the law may also be imprisoned for from one to three years. The Food and Drug Administration (FDA) of the Department of Health, Education, and Welfare enforces the act.

In Canada, the Food and Drug Directorate of the Department of National Health and Welfare administers the Food and Drugs Act. It also enforces the Pro-

prietary or Patent Medicine Act. Other government agencies administer laws on the inspection and grading of canned foods, dairy products, fish, fruits, grain, livestock, meats, and vegetables. The food and drugs laws apply to the provinces, and to all types of commerce.

Foods

Food as defined in American pure-food laws includes (1) articles used for the normal nourishment of man or animals, including beverages, condiments, and the like; (2) chewing gum; and (3) materials used as a part of such articles.

Illegal Foods. The Food, Drug, and Cosmetic Act of 1938 prohibits the sale of adulterated foods. A food is considered illegal, if (1) any essential part of it has been removed, such as butterfat from "whole milk"; (2) it contains filthy or decomposed material or other injurious substances; or (3) it has been prepared, packaged, or stored under unsanitary conditions.

Food damaged by insects, rodents, or any other means is rejected. Foods produced from diseased animals are also illegal. No substance may be added to foods to make them appear deceptively bulky, heavy, more valuable, or better than they are.

Coal-tar dyes used in foods, drugs, or cosmetics must be harmless and from batches certified by the government for such use. Chemical additives in processed foods and pesticides used in growing crops must be proved safe beforehand. The amount used must not exceed the safe tolerance set by the FDA.

Legal Additions. A manufacturer may use food additives and pesticide residues, but he must first prove to the FDA that they are safe. The FDA then issues regulations stating the amount that may remain in or on the food.

Labeling. The Food, Drug, and Cosmetic Act provides a procedure for setting standards of identity, quality, and fill of container for foods. Both consumers and manufacturers may take part in the process.

A *Standard of Identity* fixes the legal composition or ingredients of the food. A *Standard of Fill of Container* states how much must be in the package. The *Standard of Quality* specifies a *minimum* level of quality. If a food does not meet these standards, it must be labeled by a statement, such as "Below Standard in Quality" or "Good Food—Not High Grade" in a certain style and size of type. Such food standards are not the same as "standards for grades" set up by the Department of Agriculture.

Labels on foods must state (1) the name and address of the manufacturer and distributor; (2) the net weight or volume in understandable and commonly used terms; (3) the common name of the food; (4) the name of each ingredient (unless there is a standard of identity for the food); (5) the addition of any chemical preservative, artificial flavor, or artificial colors except in certain dairy products; and (6) whether or not the product is an imitation of another product.

Inspection. FDA inspectors and analysts are stationed at 17 districts in all parts of the United States. The inspectors make sanitary inspections at factories and warehouses and check on adequate processing controls. They collect samples for analysis in the district laboratories.

PURE FOOD AND DRUG LAWS

The government may bring action in federal courts when goods that violate laws are shipped in interstate commerce. Foods, drugs, and cosmetics offered for import are refused admission if they do not meet the requirements for American products.

Related Food Laws. The Federal Meat Inspection Act of 1906 and the Poultry and Poultry Products Inspection Act of 1957 require that meats and poultry be processed under the continuous supervision of a Department of Agriculture inspector. Animals and poultry are inspected for disease before and after slaughter, and must be processed under sanitary conditions and properly labeled and packaged. Other laws regulate the purity of imported meats and poultry.

Drugs

Drugs are defined as (1) articles recognized, defined, and described in such official compilations as the *U.S. Pharmacopeia,* the *Homeopathic Pharmacopoeia of the U.S.,* or the *National Formulary;* (2) articles intended for use in the diagnosis, cure, lessening, treatment, or prevention of disease in man or animals; (3) articles, other than food, intended to affect the structure or any function of the body of man or animals; and (4) articles intended for use as a part of any of the articles listed above. The term *drugs* does not include *devices.*

"Devices" are defined as instruments, apparatus, and contrivances intended for the diagnosis or treatment of disease in man or animals or to affect any structure or bodily function in man or animals. The Food, Drug, and Cosmetic Act controls devices as well as drugs. The term "devices" includes such objects as ultra violet lamps, vibrators, and clinical thermometers. Some devices, called *prescription devices,* may be obtained only with a doctor's prescription.

New Drugs must be proved safe before they can be marketed. The FDA may refuse to permit marketing if the manufacturer does not show that the drug will be safe if the directions for use are followed.

Antibiotics and Insulin. Every batch of five major antibiotic drugs, and every batch of insulin, must be tested in FDA laboratories for purity and potency before it may be sold.

Prescription Drugs. For the safety of the public, certain drugs also may be sold only on the prescription of a physician. This regulation applies to drugs that are dangerous to use except under medical supervision. Such drugs are called *prescription drugs,* and must be labeled "Caution: Federal law prohibits dispensing without prescription." The Bureau of Narcotics and Dangerous Drugs of the Department of Justice controls most narcotics.

Over-the-Counter Drugs are drugs which may be used safely without medical supervision, and may be sold without prescription. The packages of such products must contain adequate directions for use and adequate warnings to protect uninformed persons. For example, most laxatives must contain a warning that they are not to be used when abdominal pain is present. This warning is intended to prevent use of the laxative when appendicitis is present.

Biological Drugs. The National Institutes of Health at Bethesda, Md., a branch of the Public Health Service, controls the potency and safety of biological products, such as vaccines and serums for use in man.

Biological products for veterinary use are subject to the same sort of control as to potency, sterility, and safety, as are those for use in man. But the veterinary products are under the control of the Biological Products Licensing Section of the Department of Agriculture.

Cosmetics

The term *cosmetics,* as defined in the Pure Food, Drug, and Cosmetic Act, includes such aids to beauty and grooming as lipstick, eye shadow, permanent-wave preparations, pomades, and tooth paste. The law requires that cosmetics not be injurious under recommended conditions of use. They may contain only approved coal-tar dyes, except for hair dyes, which must have special warning statements on their labels. Cosmetics are subject to the same general regulations as foods and drugs, except that clearance of ingredients for safety and listing them on the label are not required. But the labeling must not be false or misleading.

History

In the United States, the Federal Food and Drugs Act of 1906 and the Meat Inspection Act went into effect in 1907. They dealt only with interstate and foreign commerce in food and drugs, with no control over cosmetics or devices. But they were a turning point in the fight for protection of consumers. Harvey W. Wiley, then chief of the Bureau of Chemistry of the Department of Agriculture, had fought for this protection for many years. Public indignation caused by the use of impure beef during the Spanish-American War helped Wiley in the early 1900's. Upton Sinclair's book *The Jungle* revealed scandalous conditions in the meat-packing industry. European countries had reached the point of making laws barring imports of American meat. Samuel Hopkins Adams' articles on patent medicines in *Collier's Weekly* also aided Wiley's efforts for consumer protection. The Narcotic Act of 1914, amended in 1922 and thereafter, regulated traffic in opium and cocaine.

These laws cured many evils, but they had defects. Among the defects were the lack of authority to inspect factories and warehouses, the absence of a check on statements made in food and drug advertising, and the lack of premarketing safety clearance of drugs. Some of these defects were remedied by the Food, Drug, and Cosmetic Act of 1938, and later amendments have corrected still more. In 1938, Congress also extended the power of the Federal Trade Commission to forbid false advertising in the sale of food, drugs, and cosmetics. Nearly all states and many cities now have their own pure food and drug laws.

Canada passed its first pure food and drug law in 1874, barring the adulteration of drink, drugs, and food. It was one of the first countries to pass a law providing for grading and labeling of canned foods. Its Food and Drugs Act of 1920 forms the basis of the laws now in force throughout the country.   MARTIN FROBISHER

Critically reviewed by the FOOD AND DRUG ADMINISTRATION

Related Articles in WORLD BOOK include:

The Feast of Purim celebrates the Jews' rescue from a threatened massacre by King Ahasuerus. Esther, *kneeling*, the Jewish wife of Ahasuerus, successfully pleaded with her husband to save the Jews. This French diorama with wax figures was made in the 1700's.

Frank Darmstaedter, The Jewish Museum, N.Y.

PURGATORY is a state, according to Roman Catholic belief, in which persons who die in the friendship of God but without having fully made amends for their failings must atone for them by suffering before being admitted into heaven. Catholics believe that these sufferings are lessened by the offering of prayers and masses. The doctrine was defined by the Council of Trent. The Douay Bible indicates it in II Maccabees 12: 43-46 and Matthew 12: 32. FULTON J. SHEEN

PURIM, *POO rim,* is a joyous Jewish festival celebrated on the 14th day of the Hebrew month of Adar. It honors the delivery of the Jews of Persia (now Iran) from an evil plot to destroy them.

The name *Purim* comes from the Persian word *pur,* which means *lot.* Lots had been drawn to fix a day for the massacre of the Jews.

The scroll of Esther in the Hebrew Bible tells the story of Purim. Esther was the beautiful Jewish queen of King Ahasuerus. Haman, the king's wicked minister, persuaded Ahasuerus to destroy all the Jews in his kingdom. Urged by her cousin Mordecai, Esther pleaded with the king, and saved her people. Jews celebrate Purim with great merriment. Some fast on *Taanit Esther,* the day before Purim, to remember Esther's fast before she spoke to Ahasuerus. LEONARD C. MISHKIN

PURITAN is a name that is often misunderstood and, in consequence, badly misused. It was applied to any person who was numbered among a great body of Protestants in England. Puritan religious beliefs were first expressed in England in the late 1500's. The name *Puritan* was first used about 1566.

Basic Beliefs. Although Puritans differed greatly among themselves, they all had one common idea. They held to a simple religious belief, a simple manner of worship, and a simple method of church organization. Differences among Puritans were differences of degree. Most of the Puritans wanted to *purify* churches of priestly vestments and elaborate ceremonies. Some wanted to do away with statues and colored windows in churches, and with religious music.

Some of the Puritans followed many of the religious principles of the French religious leader and reformer, John Calvin. They said their views on church organization and government came from the Bible itself and from the practices of the early Christians. Most of the Puritans

firmly believed that all clergymen should be of equal rank.

They were equally firm in their belief that no bishop or other high church official should have any control over pastors of lower rank. Some Puritans said that each congregation should be independent of all others, and free to choose its own pastor.

History. For a long time, beginning in the late 1500's, all Puritans were opposed by officials of the Church of England and also by the English government which had supervision of religious affairs. Some of the democratic ideas of the Puritans finally won a place for themselves after many years of oppression, persecution, a civil war, and a period of political and religious dictatorship. But even after all these events took place, the Church of England continued to have a system of church government that was controlled by clergymen of differing rank.

King Henry VIII started to take away power from the Roman Catholic Church in England about 1536. He made various changes in church government, but many of the changes did not satisfy any of the Puritans. Some

Puritan Militia in Early New England, dressed in the traditional Puritan costume, stood for a review by its officers.

The Travelers

Library of Congress

Puritan Settlers Fought Off Indian Attacks in Salem, Massachusetts Bay Colony. The soldier nails a board which will secure the door. The man at the window protects the children from danger, and his son stands ready with a musket.

of the Puritans wanted to abolish the priesthood as well as do away with bishops. Others believed that any member of a congregation had the right to preach. Groups of Puritans began to disagree among themselves because some held stricter views than others. Some small groups completely broke away from the practices of the Church of England during the reign of King James I. These independent groups were called *Separatists*, or *Brownists*, after Robert Browne (1550?-1633?), one of their early leaders.

Some of these Separatists were among the Pilgrims who traveled across the Atlantic in 1620 and settled Plymouth Colony in New England. Other Puritans, less radical in their religious views, later established settlements elsewhere along the shore of Massachusetts Bay. The early Separatist colonists influenced later Puritan settlers who held different ideas, and who, before the influence of the Separatists, thought of themselves as faithful members of the Church of England.

For a time in the 1600's, the Puritans played an important part in English politics. Their influence lasted during the struggle between Charles I and his Parliament over the question of the divine right of kings. Parliament executed Charles I in 1649 and the Commonwealth was established under the devoted Puritan Oliver Cromwell. The Puritans at this time were called *Roundheads* because they cut their hair short. The political power of the Puritans came to an end in 1660, with the return of the Stuart dynasty. But the influence of the Puritans in strengthening Protestantism, and in increasing political freedom in England, has lasted until the present day.　　　　　　W. M. SOUTHGATE

Related Articles in WORLD BOOK include:

PURPLE is a color produced by mixing red and blue coloring matter. Different shades are produced by mixing different amounts of red and blue. Tyrian purple, which is a deep crimson, was used in ancient civilizations. The name came from the city of Tyre in Phoenicia. The dye came from a shellfish found in the Mediterranean Sea. The Romans called this shellfish *Purpura murex*. That is where we get the name *purple*. Since each shellfish yielded only a small quantity of the dye, the color was expensive. In the time of Cicero (106-43 B.C.), a pound of wool dyed with Tyrian purple was very expensive. Because of the high cost, purple was the symbol of rulers and of wealth. The Roman emperor wore a purple toga, the royal decrees of the Byzantine Empire are said to have been written with purple ink, and we still use the expression "the purple" to convey the idea of rank or authority.

Besides Tyrian purple, the ancients used a purple dye called *orseille* that was made from a lichen. It was brought from the Middle East, and was later used in the cities of Italy.

Kermes, a dyestuff made from an Oriental shield louse, later took the place of Tyrian purple. The Sanskrit word *kermes*, meaning *little worm*, is the origin of *crimson*. In Latin, *vermiculus* means *little worm*, and is the origin of our modern word *vermilion*. Today, purple dyes are made from coal-tar products.　　　　　　GEORG MANN

See also COLOR.

PURPLE FINCH. See BIRD (color picture: Other Bird Favorites).

PURPLE HEART. See DECORATIONS AND MEDALS (United States Decorations and Medals).

PURPLE MARTIN. See MARTIN.

PURPURA, *PUHR pyoor uh*, is a term used for various purple spots appearing in the body. *Purpura* is the Latin word for *purple*. These spots may be of many sizes and shapes. They may appear in the skin, in mucous membranes, or in the organs of the body. The spots are caused by blood escaping from small blood vessels into the surrounding tissue.　　　　　　OSCAR A. THORUP, JR.

PURSLANE, *PURS lane,* is a matting annual weed. One of the most common kinds is known as *pusley* or *pursley.* It is one of the worst pests in American gardens and cultivated fields. The plant covers a sizable area of ground, and is also a home for insects that feed on corn and melons. It has thick, fleshy leaves and stems, and little yellow flowers that open only on sunny mornings. The purslane bears many seeds, and it is important to destroy the plant before the seeds ripen. The young shoots of the purslane are sometimes eaten in salads.

Scientific Classification. Purslanes make up the purslane family, *Portulacaceae.* Pusley is classified as genus *Portulaca,* species *P. oleracea.* LOUIS PYENSON

PURÚS RIVER, *poo ROOS,* is one of the chief tributaries of the Amazon River. For location, see BRAZIL (physical map). It ranks as the fourth longest river in South America and the tenth longest in the Americas. The Purús drains an important rubber-producing region. It rises in the Andes Mountains of Peru and flows 1,850 miles before entering the Amazon in northwestern Brazil. See also RIVER (chart, Longest Rivers).

PUS is a yellow-white liquid that the body produces during infection. It has lymph and white blood cells. At one time doctors spoke of *laudable* pus, which was supposed to indicate a desirable condition in a wound. They no longer believe that pus is "laudable," but they do recognize its formation as one method by which the body is able to fight infection. See also ABSCESS; INFLAMMATION. JOHN B. MIALE

PUSAN, *poo sahn* (pop. 1,419,808; alt. 25 ft.), is the chief port of Korea. Pusan lies on the southeast coast, with a good harbor on the Korea Strait. It is Korea's nearest port to Japan. See KOREA (color map). The city is a center of Korea's fishing industry. It was the temporary capital of the Republic of Korea when North Korean troops occupied Seoul in 1950. The United States has Pusan Air Base there. CHARLES Y. HU

See also KOREAN WAR (The Pusan Perimeter).

PUSEY, EDWARD B. See OXFORD MOVEMENT.

PUSEY, *PYOO zih,* **NATHAN MARSH** (1907-   ), an American educator, became president of Harvard University in 1953. He was the first non-New Englander to hold that position. From 1944 to 1953, Pusey served as president of Lawrence College (now Lawrence University) in Appleton, Wis., and on the Wisconsin Governor's Commission on Human Rights. Pusey was born in Council Bluffs, Iowa, and was graduated *magna cum laude* from Harvard University. After study at the American School of Classical Studies in Athens, Greece, he received a doctorate at Harvard. Pusey published his observations on education in his book *The Age of the Scholar* (1963). JOHN S. BRUBACHER

PUSHKIN, *POOSH kin,* **ALEXANDER SERGEEVICH** (1799-1837), Russia's most celebrated poet, wrote long poems, lyrics, and prose. His work brought him fame as the founder of modern Russian literature. Pushkin's most famous work, *Eugene Onegin* (1823-1831), a long, narrative poem, and *The Bronze Horseman* (1833), reveal him as a master of realistic description and characterization. His best-known play, *Boris Godunov* (1825), shows the influence of William Shakespeare. He also wrote prose, including *Tales of Belkin* (1830), and a novel, *The Captain's Daughter* (1836).

Pushkin was born in Moscow. His father was de-

Grant Heilman

The Pusley Purslane has thick, dull green leaves and a fleshy stem that trails along the ground. This plant bears small, yellow flowers that develop many black, oval-shaped seeds.

scended from an old aristocratic family. His great-grandfather on his mother's side was a Negro who had been presented to Peter the Great by the Sultan of Turkey. Pushkin grew up in a cultured atmosphere. At school, he astonished his classmates and teachers by the ease with which he wrote verse. After he was graduated in 1817, he accepted a position in the civil service, but spent most of his time in the gay social whirl of St. Petersburg (now Leningrad). The czar's secret police watched Pushkin because he expressed ardent liberal views in political poems. Manuscript copies of these poems circulated widely and illegally. In 1820, Pushkin was exiled to southern Russia. That same year, he published *Ruslan and Lyudmila,* a charming, sophisticated fairy tale in verse.

He received impressions from exotic scenes of nature and from interesting persons he met during his wanderings through southern Russia. He wrote the series of "Southern Verse Tales" during this period, works that were influenced by Lord Byron (see BYRON, LORD). The best known of these are *The Prisoner of the Caucasus* (1822) and *The Fountain of Bakhchisarai* (1822).

Alexander Pushkin
Sovfoto

Pushkin was called back to Moscow in 1832, and Czar Nicholas I summoned him to a personal interview. Nicholas pardoned Pushkin, and became the censor of his writings. Pushkin lived the rest of his life under the close watch of the Russian secret police. He and his wife became the victims of intrigue in high society. As a consequence, Pushkin was killed in a duel in defense of his wife's honor. ERNEST J. SIMMONS

PUSHMATAHA. See CHOCTAW INDIANS.

PUSHTU, a variation of PASHTO. See AFGHANISTAN (Language); PAKISTAN (Language).

PUSSY. See CAT.

PUSSY WILLOW is a shrub or small tree of the willow family. It grows wild in the eastern part of North America from Nova Scotia south to Virginia and west to Missouri. The pussy willow thrives either in moist places or in dry ground, but seldom grows taller than 20 feet. It has many long, straight twigs without side branches. The twigs of the pussy willow have many flower buds on them.

J. Horace McFarland

The Pussy Willow Flowers are furry and soft, like the coat of a kitten. They appear in early spring, and it seems that nature has provided a fur coat to ward off the cold.

Early in the spring before the leaves unfold, the flower clusters break out of the hard buds. These clusters are called *catkins*. They are long and round, and are covered with a dense coat of silky, grayish-white hair. These catkins are thought to resemble tiny kittens climbing up the twig. Later the catkins develop into larger, loose masses covered with yellow pollen, before they form seeds or are shed by the tree.

Scientific Classification. The pussy willow belongs to the willow family, *Salicaceae.* It is genus *Salix,* species *S. discolor.* Several other species of willow with silky catkins are also known as pussy willows.   J. J. LEVISON

See also CATKIN; WILLOW.

PUT-IN-BAY, Ohio (pop. 357; alt. 10 ft.), is a small town on South Bass Island, in western Lake Erie. In the War of 1812, Oliver H. Perry won a great naval battle off Put-In-Bay (see PERRY [Oliver Hazard]).

PUTNAM, GEORGE. See EARHART, AMELIA.

PUTNAM, HERBERT (1861-1955), an American librarian, served as Librarian of Congress from 1899 to 1939. He held the position longer than any of the seven men who preceded him as Librarian of Congress. When he took over the work, the library had developed little beyond its original purpose as a legislative reference library. During Putnam's 40 years of service, the library grew into one of the greatest treasurehouses of books and manuscripts in the world. Putnam was born in New York City.   R. B. DOWNS

PUTNAM, ISRAEL (1718-1790), an American patriot, served as a general in the Revolutionary War in America. Putnam, one of the few experienced soldiers at the beginning of the war, rose from second lieutenant to lieutenant colonel in the French and Indian War. He became a major general in the Continental Army. During the difficult years before the war, Putnam was a stout opponent of the British government. He became a leader in the Sons of Liberty, and served as chairman of the Brooklyn (Conn.) Committee of Correspondence. When Putnam heard about the Battle of Lexington, he hurried to Cambridge, where he joined the colonial soldiers. Later, he fought in the Battle of Bunker Hill.

Putnam was born in Old Salem (now Danvers), Mass. During the French and Indian War, the Indians captured him, but he escaped from death through a dramatic rescue. In 1762, Putnam led a Connecticut regiment in an unsuccessful expedition against the French in the West Indies.   CLINTON ROSSITER

Israel Putnam, *left,* stopped his plowing to join the Revolutionary Army. Neighbors had just brought him word of the Battle of Lexington, and the news stirred him to action, *below.* He became a general.

Brown Bros.; Bettmann Archive

PUTNAM, RUFUS (1738-1824), a general in the Revolutionary War in America, became known as the founder and father of Ohio. Putnam and others organized the Ohio Company in 1786 to colonize the territory northwest of the Ohio River. Putnam was in charge of the first colony of settlers, and, in 1788, he established the first permanent white settlement at Marietta, Ohio.

After three years as a soldier in the French and Indian War, Putnam settled in New Braintree, Mass., in 1760, as a millwright and surveyor. He became a lieutenant colonel in the Continental Army when the Revolutionary War began in 1775. He planned and built the fortifications around Boston so successfully that, in 1776, he became chief engineer of the army, with the rank of colonel. Putnam served in numerous engagements, and became a brigadier general in 1783. In March, 1790, Putnam was appointed a judge of the Northwest Territory. In 1796, he became Surveyor General of the United States. Putnam was born in Sutton, Mass.   JOHN R. ALDEN

See also OHIO COMPANY.

PUTREFACTION. See DECAY; DECOMPOSITION; FERMENTATION; CANNING (Bacteria).

PUTSCH. See HITLER, ADOLF (The Beer Hall Putsch).

PUTTY is a filler material that is soft when applied, but slowly hardens. It is used to fill knotholes, cracks, and other defects in wood surfaces, before the surfaces are painted. Putty is also placed around the edges of panes of glass to hold them in window sash and doors. The most common form of putty is a mixture of powdered natural chalk, called whiting, and linseed oil to which a small proportion of white lead may be added. Putty hardens because linseed oil combines with oxygen from the air and soaks into the wood the putty fills.

Special putty is available for use in steel sash. Putty that is used around window and door frames to keep out air and water is usually made of asbestos fiber, drying oil, and pigment.   GEORGE W. WASHA

See also CALKING.

PUVIS DE CHAVANNES, PIERRE. See MURAL PAINTING.

PUYE CLIFF DWELLINGS. See NEW MEXICO (Places to Visit).

PUYSÉGUR, MARQUIS DE. See HYPNOTISM (History).

PUZZLE. See TRICKS AND PUZZLES.

PWA. See NEW DEAL (table).

PX. See POST EXCHANGE.

PYE, HENRY JAMES. See POET LAUREATE.

PYGMALION, *pig MAY lih uhn,* a sculptor in Greek legend, ruled as king of the island of Cyprus, famous for its worship of Aphrodite (Venus). Disgusted by the wicked women of his day, Pygmalion carved a beautiful ivory statue of a woman and then fell in love with it. In answer to his prayer, Aphrodite made the statue a living woman, Galatea. Pygmalion married her, and they had a son, Paphos.

In *Pygmalion,* a play by George Bernard Shaw, a gentleman of culture creates an elegant lady out of an ignorant girl. He then falls in love with her. The reactions of the lady he creates are somewhat more complicated than those of the legendary statue. *My Fair Lady,* a highly successful Broadway musical, was based on Shaw's *Pygmalion. My Fair Lady* was later made into a motion picture.   PHILIP W. HARSH

PYGMY, *PIHG mee,* is a general term for small people. It refers to the *Negrillos* (African pygmies) and the *Negritos* (pygmies of Asia, Malaysia, and the lands of the central and south Pacific Ocean). Scientists sometimes refer to the African pygmies as *Twides.* Some anthropologists consider pygmies to be Negroids, but others regard them as a separate race (see RACES OF MAN [Negroids]). For information on the pygmies of Asia, see NEGRITO. The term *pygmy* is often used to refer to anything that is small or tiny.

Pygmies in Africa live in parts of Burundi, Cameroon, Congo (Brazzaville), Congo (Léopoldville), Gabon, and Rwanda. They have many local names, such as Akka, Bambuti, Batwa, Babinga, and Efe.

Some scholars believe that at one time pygmies lived throughout Equatorial Africa. Most pygmies now live in the denser rain forest areas. There are about 180,000 pygmies in Africa.

Characteristics. African pygmies are usually about 4 feet 5 inches to 4 feet 8 inches tall. They have yellow-brown skin and round heads, with tightly curled, reddish-brown hair.

The legs of pygmies are short, but their arms are relatively long. Their abdomens swell out like those of small children. Pygmies have broad, flat noses and prominent eyeballs.

Pygmies usually speak the language of neighboring Negro tribes. It is not known whether they have languages of their own.

Pygmies in the Congo wear little clothing because of the hot, moist climate of the equatorial regions. They get much of their food by hunting and fishing in the tropical forests.

Three Lions

Attilio Gatti, Pix

Pygmy Dancers perform in a small clearing carved out of the dense jungle. Each African tribe has its own symbolic and traditional dances that are passed on from generation to generation. The dances may seem meaningless to observers, but each one tells a story.

Way of Life. African pygmies hunt and fish, and gather food from the surrounding forests. They have no domestic animals, and do not farm. The pygmy bow is small and has a limited range. The arrows usually have a deadly poison on the tip. Some groups have spears obtained from Negro tribes. The pygmies kill antelopes, monkeys, birds, elephants, and buffaloes with these weapons and with various forms of traps. They trade meat to the Negroes for iron goods and agricultural products. Pygmies wear few clothes and build only simple huts, which they abandon when they move. They also make baskets, bags, and pottery.

Pygmies live in small nomadic bands, each of which migrates throughout its own territory. The eldest male member of a band serves as its leader. He makes decisions with the help of a council of adult males. A pygmy marries someone outside his or her band. A wife resides with her husband's group, and her children belong to this group.

Pygmies believe in a supreme being who created the earth and sky. They pray and offer sacrifices of game and honey to this deity. They believe that life after death is very similar to this life. They use charms and other magical devices. VERNON R. DORJAHN

PYLE, ERNIE (1900-1945), an American newspaperman, won a Pulitzer prize in 1944 for his reporting. His syndicated columns during World War II told millions of Americans how their boys lived and fought as soldiers. Writing with humor and sensitivity, Pyle became one of the best-loved reporters. He traveled with American troops on nearly every front in Africa and Europe before he went to the Pacific war theater. A Japanese machine-gunner killed him on Ie Shima island during the battle for Okinawa.

ERNEST TAYLOR PYLE was born near Dana, Ind., and studied at Indiana University. He worked on newspapers in Indiana, Washington, D.C., and New York City before he became a columnist in 1935. The writing he did during the war was published as *Ernie Pyle in England, Here Is Your War*, and *Brave Men*. JOHN TEBBEL

PYLE, HOWARD (1853-1911), an American painter, became one of the most influential illustrators of his time. As a teacher, he helped develop the talents of such well-known artists as Maxfield Parrish, Edward A. Wilson, and N. C. Wyeth.

Pyle combined vigorous draftsmanship with a rich imagination. His sense of pictorial design and his firm, expressive style of drawing has been compared with that of Dürer. His energy and creativity enriched the tradition of American illustration. The books that Pyle wrote and illustrated continue to attract young readers. They include *The Merry Adventures of Robin Hood* (1883), *Pepper and Salt* (1885), *Twilight Land* (1895), and *The Story of King Arthur and His Knights* (1903). For many years, he illustrated pages in *Harper's Monthly* and drew illustrations for books written by other authors.

Pyle was born in Wilmington, Del., and studied at the Art Students' League in New York City. He taught at Drexel Institute in Philadelphia. NORMAN RICE

See also LITERATURE FOR CHILDREN (picture: Robin Hood).

PYLORUS. See STOMACH.

PYM, JOHN (1584-1643), an English leader in Parliament, opposed the attempts of King Charles I to rule England as an absolute monarch. Pym declared that

Ernie Pyle
United Press Int.

Howard Pyle
Harper & Bros.

"a parliament is that to the commonwealth, which the soul is to the body."

Pym became so influential in Parliament that his enemies nicknamed him *King Pym*. In January, 1642, the king entered Parliament with 400 guards to arrest Pym and four others. But Pym and the others had fled moments before. When the English Civil War broke out in August, 1642, Pym formed an alliance with Scotland which brought Scottish troops to fight against the king.

Pym was born in Somersetshire, England. He entered Parliament in 1621. Pym died of cancer during the second year of the civil war.   Lacey Baldwin Smith

PYNCHON, WILLIAM. See Meat Packing (Growth of the Industry); Springfield (History).

PYONGYANG, *PYAWNG yang* (pop. 653,100; alt. 60 ft.), is the capital of Communist North Korea. It lies on bluffs which rise above the Taedong River, 160 miles northwest of Seoul (see Korea [color map]). It was founded 3,000 years ago, and for many years was the capital of all Korea. When the Japanese ruled Korea they named the city *Heijō*.   Charles Y. Hu

PYORRHEA, *PY uh REE uh*, is a disease of the gums and bones surrounding the teeth. It is more properly called *pyorrhea alveolaris*. Pyorrhea usually begins with *gingivitis*, an inflammation of the gums (see Teeth [Gingivitis]). If this is not treated the gums become flabby, bleed easily, and soon recede from the teeth at the "gum line." Then pus forms in the crevices between the teeth. If pyorrhea continues, the teeth loosen and fall out. Even more serious than this effect is the spread of bacteria through the body. Rheumatism, arthritis, heart trouble, and other ailments are believed to result at times from pyorrhea.

Pyorrhea arises from infection of the membrane that lines the sockets in which the teeth lie. This membrane becomes diseased through injuries from the pressure of crooked teeth and poor dental work, through deposits of fermenting food particles, and through irritation from tartar or scale which forms on the teeth. Pyorrhea is curable in the early stages. A dentist should be consulted if the gums are red, soft, and bleed easily. Treatment consists in removal of tartar, antiseptic cleansing of the gums, grinding off rough surfaces of the teeth, and surgical cutting away of diseased gum tissue. Massage helps stimulate the gums. Proper care of the teeth will help to prevent the disease.   Paul R. Cannon

See also Dentistry (Periodontics).

PYRAMID is the name of a solid whose base is a polygon and whose lateral, or side, faces are triangles which meet at a common point. In a *regular pyramid* the lateral faces are all congruent isosceles triangles and the base is a regular polygon. The slant height of a regular pyramid is the altitude of one of these congruent isosceles triangles. The facts about pyramids are the same as those about cones, except that cones have circles for bases.

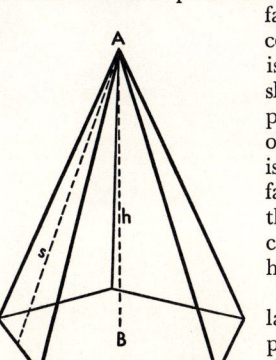

Area and Volume. The lateral area of a regular pyramid equals the sum of the areas of the isosceles

triangles. The volume of a pyramid is one third the volume of a prism of the same base and altitude.
$$V = \tfrac{1}{3} Bh$$

Problems. (1) How many square feet of sheeting will cover the sides of a steeple, a square pyramid in shape, with a base 12 feet square, and slant height 20 feet?
Area of one triangle $= \tfrac{1}{2}$ (20) 12 = 120
Four triangles = 480 square feet.
(2) What is the volume of a pyramid with a base 10 feet square and an altitude of 15 feet?
$V = \tfrac{1}{3} Bh$
$V = \tfrac{1}{3}$ (100) 15 = 500 cubic feet.
(3) At \$.45 a square foot, what will it cost to gild a five-sided pyramidal steeple with base 10 feet square and a slant height of 15 feet?

The Frustum of a Pyramid is the part of a pyramid between the base and a plane which cuts the pyramid parallel to the base.

To find the *lateral area of a frustum*, add together the trapezoids of which it is made. See Quadrilateral.

To find the *volume of a frustum*, complete the pyramid, find its altitude by proportion, and subtract the added pyramid from the whole pyramid.

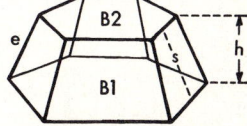

Frustum of a Pyramid
B_1—lower base
B_2—upper base
e —lateral edge
s —slant height
h —altitude

Problems. (1) How many square inches of sheet iron are needed to make a cake pan 8 inches by 5 inches at the bottom, and 9 inches by 6 inches at the top, with the slant height of $2\tfrac{1}{2}$ inches?

Two trapezoids $= 2 (\tfrac{1}{2})(2\tfrac{1}{2})(9+8) = 42\tfrac{1}{2}$
Two trapezoids $= 2 (\tfrac{1}{2})(2\tfrac{1}{2})(6+5) = 27\tfrac{1}{2}$
Bottom $= 5 \times 8$ $= 40$
Square inches of sheet iron $= 110$

(2) How many cubic inches will a box contain if its lower base is 10 inches square, its upper base 6 inches square, and its altitude 8 inches?

The altitude x of a pyramid, added in order to make the frustum into a large pyramid, is 12. This is found by solving the proportion $\dfrac{10}{6} = \dfrac{x+8}{x}$

The altitude of the whole pyramid is $8 + 12 = 20$. The volume of the whole pyramid is $\tfrac{1}{3}$ (20) 100 = $666\tfrac{2}{3}$ or 667.

The volume of the bottom pyramid is $\tfrac{1}{3}$ (12) 36 = 144.
The volume of the frustum in cubic inches is 667 − 144 = 523.

(3) Find the lateral surface of the frustum of a regular pyramid whose lower base is 10 feet square, upper base 5 feet square, and slant height 10 feet.

(4) Two frustums have the same shape, and each line in one is five times the corresponding line in the other. How do their volumes compare?   Miles C. Hartley

See also Cone; Triangle.

PYRAMID LAKE. See Nevada (Rivers and Lakes).

Harrison Forman; WORLD BOOK illustration

**THE EGYPTIAN
PYRAMID BUILDERS**

The Great Pyramid Near Cairo, *above,* ranks as one of man's most spectacular achievements. Its base covers an area large enough to hold 10 football fields. Workers cut huge blocks for the pyramid from limestone formations, *below.*

PYRAMIDS are big structures with square bases and four smooth, triangular-shaped sides that come to a point at the top. Many ancient peoples used pyramids as tombs or temples. The most famous pyramids are those built about 4,500 years ago as tombs for Egyptian kings. These Egyptian pyramids are considered among the Seven Wonders of the Ancient World.

Egyptian Pyramids

The ruins of 35 pyramids still stand near the Nile River in Egypt. Each was built to protect the body of an Egyptian king. The Egyptians thought that a man's body had to be preserved and protected so his soul could live forever. The Egyptians *mummified* (dried and wrapped) their dead and hid the mummies in large tombs. They buried the king's body inside or beneath a pyramid in a secret chamber that was filled with treas-

Barbara Mertz, the contributor of this article, is an authority on Egyptology and Near Eastern archaeology, and the author of Temples, Tombs, and Hieroglyphs.

ures of gold and precious objects. Many scholars believe that the pyramid shape had a religious meaning to the Egyptians. The sloping sides may have reminded the Egyptians of the slanting rays of the sun, by which the king's soul could climb to the sky and join the gods.

Funeral ceremonies were performed in temples that were attached to the pyramids. Most pyramids had two temples connected by a long stone passageway. One temple stood next to the pyramid and the other stood beside the river. Sometimes a smaller pyramid for the body of the queen stood next to the king's pyramid. The king's relatives and servants were buried in smaller rectangular tombs called *mastabas*, which had sloping sides and flat roofs.

The First Pyramids. Imhotep, a great physician, architect, and statesman, built the first known pyramid for King Zoser about 2650 B.C. Zoser's tomb did not have smooth sides. It rose in a series of giant steps, or terraces, and is called the *Step Pyramid*. It still stands south of Cairo at the site of the ancient city of Saqqārah. See ARCHITECTURE (Beginnings [picture]).

Preparing a Pyramid Site. Egyptian workers used a string device as a guideline. They stretched the string between two sticks that touched the surface of water in a trench dug around the base, *right*. Workers dug out or filled in the ground until other sticks of equal length fit in between the string and the ground.

Gangs of Workers dragged the blocks to the pyramid site on sledges and pulled them up ramps on the pyramid. They laid planks on the ramps to provide a firm roadway for the sledges.

WORLD BOOK illustrations

PYRAMIDS

The first smooth-sided pyramid was built about 2600 B.C. It still stands at Medum. It began as a stepped pyramid, and then the steps were filled in with casing stones to give the building smooth, sloping sides. Other early pyramids can be seen at Abusir and Dahshūr. Later pyramids were built at Hawara, Illahun, and Dahshūr—near what is now Cairo. Little of them remains.

The Three Pyramids at Giza (Al Jīzah) stand on the west bank of the Nile River outside Cairo (see EGYPT [physical map]). They are the largest and best preserved of all Egyptian pyramids. They were built about 2600 to 2500 B.C. The largest of the three was built for King Khufu (called Cheops by the Greeks). The second was the tomb of King Khafre (Chephren), and the third belonged to King Menkaure (Mycerinus). The huge Sphinx at Giza was also built for Khafre. It stands near his pyramid.

The pyramid of Khufu, called the *Great Pyramid*, is a marvel of building skill. It contains more than 2 million stone blocks that average $2\frac{1}{2}$ tons each. The pyramid was originally 481 feet tall, but some of its upper stones are gone now and it stands about 450 feet high. Its base covers about 13 acres.

A study of the Great Pyramid shows how these gigantic structures were built. The ancient Egyptians had no machinery or iron tools. They cut big limestone blocks with copper chisels and saws. Most of the stones came from quarries nearby. But some came from across the Nile River, and others came by boat from distant quarries. Gangs of men dragged the blocks to the pyramid site and pushed the first layer of stones into place. Then they built long ramps of earth and brick, and dragged the huge stones up the ramps to form the next layer. As they finished each layer, the workers raised and lengthened the ramps. Finally, when the topmost stone had been shoved into place, they covered the pyramid with an outer coating of white casing stones. They laid these outer stones so exactly that from a distance the finished pyramid appeared to have been cut out of a single white stone. Most of the casing stones are gone now, but a few are still in place at the bottom of the Great Pyramid. For pictures showing how the pyramids may have been built, see EGYPT, ANCIENT (pictures: Building the Pyramids).

The burial chamber is inside the Great Pyramid. A corridor leads from an entrance in one side to several rooms within the pyramid. One of the rooms is called the *Queen's Chamber*, although the queen is not buried there. The room was planned as the king's burial chamber. But Khufu changed the plan and built another burial chamber, called the *King's Chamber*. The *Grand Gallery*, a corridor 153 feet long and 28 feet high, leads to Khufu's chamber. It is considered one of the marvels of ancient architecture.

The ancient Greek historian Herodotus said that 400,000 men worked each year for 20 years to build the

Cross Section of the Great Pyramid shows the Grand Gallery, the King's Chamber, and the Queen's Chamber. After the burial, sealing plugs were allowed to slide down the passageway from the Grand Gallery to seal off the tomb. Workers left the tomb through an escape passageway.

WORLD BOOK diagram

WORLD BOOK photo

The Pyramid of the Sun at Teotihuacán, Mexico, had a larger base than the largest pyramid in Egypt.

Great Pyramid. Archaeologists now doubt these figures, but the true figures cannot be determined. Peasants built the pyramids. They worked on the tombs during periods when floodwaters of the Nile covered the fields and made farming impossible.

Thieves broke into most of the pyramids, stole the gold, and sometimes destroyed the bodies. Later Egyptian kings stopped using pyramids, and built secret tombs in cliffs. But some kings of the Cushite kingdom in Nubia, south of Egypt, built pyramids long after they were no longer used in Egypt.

American Pyramids

Indians of Central and South America also built pyramids. They built stepped pyramids that had flat tops which they used as platforms for their temples.

The Mochica Indians of Peru built big brick pyramids. *The Temple of the Sun*, near what is now Trujillo, on Peru's northern coast, has a terraced brick pyramid on top of a stepped platform. The Mayas of Central America built pyramid-shaped mounds of earth with temples on top (see MAYA [picture: El Castillo]).

The Toltec Indians of central Mexico also built big stepped pyramids. One of these pyramids, at Cholula, is one of the largest structures in the world. Peoples related to the Toltecs built the great pyramids of the Sun and Moon that still stand at Teotihuacán, near Mexico City. The Spanish conquerors destroyed most pyramids of the later Aztec Empire in Mexico. These pyramids were built in steps or terraces like the other American pyramids, and had temples on top. Two of the greatest were at Tenochtitlán (now Mexico City). Mound building Indians of North America built some pyramid-shaped mounds, but they were not true pyramids (see MOUND BUILDERS). BARBARA MERTZ

See also EGYPT (color picture: The Nile Valley).

PYRAMUS AND THISBE, *PIHR uh mus* and *THIZ bee*, are characters in an ancient legend. The Roman poet Ovid told their story in verse. Pyramus and Thisbe were two young lovers who lived next door to each other in Babylon. Their parents opposed the idea of their marriage and prevented them from keeping company. They had to carry on their courtship through a small opening in the wall between their houses.

Finally, they planned to meet by moonlight beneath a mulberry tree outside the city. Thisbe arrived first, but

was frightened by a lion and fled. She dropped her veil and the lion caught it and tore it with his bloody mouth. When Pyramus reached the spot some time later, he saw the lion and the blood-stained veil. He thought that Thisbe had been killed, and stabbed himself. Thisbe soon returned to the scene and found Pyramus dead. She seized his dagger and plunged it into her own breast. To commemorate the tragedy, the fruit of the mulberry tree changed from white to blood red.   THOMAS A. BRADY

PYRENEES, *PIR uh neez*, is the name of a mountain chain that forms a natural barrier between France and Spain. For location, see SPAIN (color map). The mountains extend from the Bay of Biscay to the Mediterranean Sea, a distance of about 270 miles. They cover an area of over 20,000 square miles. Their average height is only 3,500 feet, but many peaks in the central ranges rise over 10,000 feet above sea level. The highest point is Pico de Aneto (11,169 feet).

Glacier fields are found on the northern slopes of the Pyrenees. Minerals in the Pyrenees include iron, lead, silver, and cobalt. The iron mines near Bilbao, Spain, at the Biscay end of the Pyrenees, are a prosperous industry. There are forests of fir, pine, and oak.

The Pyrenees chain is a barrier to overland commerce, and France and Spain have had to trade with each other chiefly by sea for many years. Several roads cut through the mountains. Two railways cross them. The first, opened in 1928, runs between Pau, France, and Saragossa, Spain, by way of the Canfranc Tunnel. The second, opened in 1929, runs between Toulouse, France, and Barcelona, Spain. This line climbs to a height of 5,200 feet in crossing the mountains. There are more than 40 tunnels in a 57-mile central section of the Pyrenees. Several vacation resorts are on the northern slopes of the mountains. The small republic of Andorra is on the south slope of the eastern Pyrenees. The Basques live in the western Pyrenees.   WALTER C. LANGSAM

See also ANDORRA; BASQUE.

PYRETHRUM, *pie RETH rum*, or *pie REE thrum*, is a name applied to a group of flowers that give us an insect powder and medicine. Other names for it are *painted lady* and *painted daisy*. The flower heads grow singly or in small clusters on erect stems that are 1 or 2 feet high. They look like large daisies with pink, white, crimson, or lilac rays. Pyrethrums bloom in spring or early summer, and are grown as garden flowers or for cutting.

The insecticide is made from the dried and powdered flowers. There are two types, Persian powder and Dalmatian powder, made from different pyrethrums. Pyrethrum, in its pure form or in a mixture, is the least poisonous insecticide to animals and man. It is used in liquids, powders, and sprays for insect control on animals, in the garden, and in the home.

A pyrethrum known as feverfew is used as a tonic. A sedative for neuralgia, toothache, and headaches is also called pyrethrum. It is made from the root of a different kind of plant.

Scientific Classification. Pyrethrums belong to the composite family, *Compositae*. Persian powder is made from genus *Chrysanthemum*, species *C. coccineum*. Dalmatian powder is made from *C. cinerariaefolium*. Feverfew is *C. parthenium*. The sedative comes from *Anacyclus pyrethrum* of the same botanical family.   W. V. MILLER

See also FEVERFEW.

PYREX. See GLASS (Borosilicate Glass).

PYRIDINE. See COAL (table: What We Get from a Ton of Coal [Coal Tar]).

PYRIDOXINE. See VITAMIN (Vitamin B Complex); MILK (Vitamins).

PYRITE, or "fool's gold," as it is sometimes called, is a compound of iron and sulfur, FeS_2. Another name for it is iron pyrites. It is found in many places and looks like gold. Many a person has thought he has discovered gold, only to find it is pyrite. Real gold may be heated over a hot stove without injury, but fool's gold will sizzle, smoke, and smell bad. Pyrite is used in making sulfuric acid and in refrigerator fluid. Some Indians use it to make fire.   CECIL J. SCHNEER

See also MINERAL (color picture).

PYROCERAM, *PIE roh see RAM*, is a trademark of the Corning Glass Works for products made from hard, strong, crystalline materials called *glass-ceramics*. An entire family of glass-ceramics exists.

Some glass-ceramics are harder than steel, lighter than aluminum, and as strong as cast iron. They can withstand high temperatures and chemical attack. Some varieties are transparent, others opaque. Some glass-ceramics have the valuable property of staying the same size even at high temperatures. This means that sudden temperature changes cannot break them down.

S. D. Stookey of the Corning Glass Works invented these materials, which were first announced in 1957. Glass-ceramics were first used commercially in *radomes* (the nose sections of missiles), and as heat-resistant cooking utensils sold under the name Corning Ware. Other uses may be found in electronic and chemical equipment, turbines, and in the walls of buildings.

To make glass-ceramics, manufacturers melt a batch of glass-making chemicals containing a special *nucleating agent* at white heat. The molten glass is formed into the final shape required, and allowed to cool. As it cools, the nucleating agent forms billions of tiny crystal *nuclei* (centers). The glass is reheated to red heat. This causes crystals to grow on the nuclei, thus forming glass-ceramics.   S. D. STOOKEY

PYROGRAPHY, *pie RAHG ruh fih*, is the art of ornamenting the surface of wood or leather with designs made with a heated point or a fine flame. Sometimes the design is reproduced by hot plates under pressure. Velvet and even glass may be ornamented in this way.

PYROLIGNEOUS ACID. See ACETIC ACID.

PYROLUSITE. See MANGANESE (Sources).

PYROMANIA, *PYE roh MAY nih uh*, refers to a compulsion, or morbid impulse, to set fires. Psychiatrists believe that many pyromaniacs feel sexual excitement from setting a fire. Such emotions are thought to relate to a child's normal pleasure and excitement from playing with or watching a fire. A pyromaniac may want to commit *arson*, the criminal act of burning a house or building, in order to relieve his hostile and destructive feelings.   GEORGE A. ULETT

See also ARSON.

PYROMETRY, *py RAHM uh tree*, is a system of measuring temperatures. It usually refers to temperatures that are too high to be measured by ordinary thermometers. In pottery kilns, where it is necessary to measure not only the temperature, but also the effect

of the heat, *pyrometric*, or *Seger*, *cones* are sometimes used. These small pyramid-shaped cones are made of clay and salt, and will melt after being at a certain temperature for a given length of time. Unfired rings of clay are also used in kilns to measure the work done by heat.

Pyrometers are used when it is necessary to measure only the high temperature. One kind matches the color in the furnace against known temperatures of red-hot wires. A thermoelectric pyrometer is used when the temperature is to be recorded graphically, and for automatic temperature control. Pyrometry is important in heat-treating metals and in making glass.   RALPH G. OWENS

PYROPE. See GARNET.

PYROSIS. See HEARTBURN.

PYROTECHNICS is a term used to mean fireworks, or the art of making fireworks. See FIREWORKS.

PYROXENE, *PIH rock seen*, is a group of minerals often found with other minerals called feldspar. The pyroxene group of minerals is composed of iron, magnesium, and silica. These minerals, together with feldspar minerals, make up the darker igneous rocks and lavas. See also BASALT.   CECIL J. SCHNEER

PYROXYLIN. See CELLULOSE; PLASTICS (The Invention of Celluloid).

PYRRHA. See DEUCALION.

PYRRHIC. See DANCING (Greek Dancing).

PYRRHIC VICTORY. See PYRRHUS.

PYRRHO OF ELIS, *PIHR oh* (361?-270? B.C.), was one of a group of ancient Greek philosophers known as Skeptics. He traveled widely and learned many different philosophic viewpoints, each one claiming to be the truth. Because they could not all be right, Pyrrho decided to suspend judgment about truth, right, and wrong. Custom and convention, he felt, were the only guides to what is just or unjust. Even our senses tell us only how things *appear*, not what they really are. Pyrrho was born at Elis, Greece.   LEWIS M. HAMMOND

See also SKEPTICISM.

PYRRHUS, *PIHR us* (318?-272 B.C.), was a king of Epirus in Greece. His name has lived in the expression "Pyrrhic victory." It is used to refer to a victory which has cost more than it is worth. The expression arose from a remark Pyrrhus used after the battle of Asculum in which he lost almost all his men. He exclaimed, "Another such victory and I shall be ruined."

Pyrrhus, a second cousin of Alexander the Great, was born in Epirus. His father was king of Epirus. But he lost his throne and

Pyrrhus, the Greek General, has become the symbol of victories that have been gained at too great a cost.

Brown Bros.

was killed when his son was two years old. Pyrrhus was put on the throne at the age of 12, but at 17 he lost it. Later Pyrrhus went to Egypt where he served King Ptolemy.

Pyrrhus raised an army and returned to his native country. He recovered his throne, and then tried to conquer Macedonia. In 287 B.C., Pyrrhus became king of Macedonia, but lost his throne again the following year.

Tarentum, a Greek colony in lower Italy, and its neighbors appealed to Pyrrhus in 281 B.C. for aid against the Romans. Pyrrhus sent 25,000 men and 20 elephants. His forces conquered the Romans, chiefly because of the use of elephants in the battle.

Pyrrhus later helped the Greeks of Sicily against the Carthaginians. In this war he was successful at first. But he soon began to lose, and finally he was driven out of Sicily in 276 B.C. Two years later the Romans defeated him and forced him to return to Epirus. The next year he invaded Macedonia again, and once more was hailed as king. In 272 B.C., he marched south and made an unsuccessful attack on Sparta. He was killed in a battle with Antigonus Gonatus while trying to capture Argos.   THOMAS W. AFRICA

PYTHAGORAS, *pih THAG oh rus* (580 B.C.?–?), was a Greek philosopher and mathematician. He was famous for formulating the *Pythagorean Theorem*, but its principles were known earlier. The theorem states that the square of the hypotenuse of a right-angled triangle is equal to the sum of the squares of the other two sides.

As a philosopher, Pythagoras taught that number was the essence of all things. He mystically associated numbers with virtues, colors, and many other ideas. He also taught that the human soul is immortal and that after death it moves into another living body, sometimes that of an animal. This idea, called *transmigration of the soul*, appears in many early religions. It is still the belief of many of the Hindu sects of India. Pythagoras may have obtained some of his ideas during travels in the East.

Pythagoras believed that the earth was spherical and that the sun, moon, and planets have movements of their own. His successors developed the idea that the earth revolved about a central fire. This belief anticipated the Copernican theory of the universe (see COPERNICUS, NICOLAUS).

Little is known of Pythagoras' early life, but scholars believe that he was born on the island of Samos. In about 529 B.C., he settled in Crotona, Italy, and founded a *school* (brotherhood) among the aristocrats of that city. The people were suspicious of the Pythagorean brotherhood because its members were aristocrats, and killed most of them in a political uprising. Historians do not know whether Pythagoras left the city some time before the outbreak of violence and escaped death there, or was killed in it. The brotherhood of aristocrats was finally destroyed in the 400's B.C.   PHILLIP S. JONES

See also TRIANGLE.

Pythagoras
Brown Bros.

PYTHAGOREAN THEOREM

PYTHAGOREAN THEOREM, *pih THAG oh REE un THEE oh rum*, in geometry, states that in a right triangle the square of the hypotenuse equals the sum of the squares of the other two sides. A right triangle is one in which one angle equals 90°. The hypotenuse is the side opposite the right angle. Here is the theorem as a formula:
$$c^2 = a^2 + b^2$$

In this formula, c is the length of the hypotenuse and a and b are the lengths of the other two sides. If you know two sides of a right triangle, you can substitute these values in the formula and find the missing side.

Origins

The ancient Egyptians wanted to lay out square (90°) corners for their fields. They had few of the tools we have today. How could they make a 90° angle? About 2000 B.C., they discovered a "magic 3–4—5" triangle. Workmen took a loop of rope knotted into 12 equal spaces. They took three stakes and stretched the rope to form a triangle around the stakes. They placed the stakes so the triangle had sides of 3, 4, and 5 units. The side of 5 units was what we would call the hypotenuse, and the angle opposite it equaled 90°.

The ancient Greeks learned this trick from the Egyptians. Between 500 and 350 B.C., a group of Greek philosophers called the Pythagoreans explored the 3—4—5 triangle. *They learned to think of the triangle's sides as the sides of three squares.* The area of a square is a side multiplied by itself. In the 3—4—5 triangle, the area of a square of which the hypotenuse is a side equals the sum of the areas of the squares of the other two sides: $5\times5=3\times3 + 4\times4$. Then the Pythagoreans generalized this rule about the 3—4—5 triangle to apply to *all* right triangles. This general statement became the Pythagorean Theorem.

Euclid's Proof

In formal geometry, the Pythagorean Theorem has had many proofs. One of the most famous proofs belongs to the Greek mathematician Euclid (c. 300 B.C.). In this drawing, *ABC* is the original right triangle:

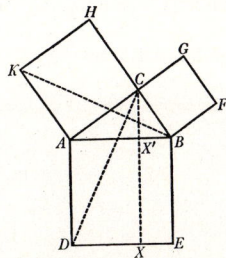

The squares are drawn for each side, and the right angle is at *C*. How can we prove that the square on the hypotenuse equals the other two squares?

Here are the steps in Euclid's proof. The reasons for each step come from axioms, postulates, and other theorems in geometry. First, by a series of statements, you show that the area of the square on side *AC* is twice the area of triangle *ABK*. Next, you show that triangles *ABK* and *ACD* are congruent (corresponding). Third, you show that the area of rectangle *ADXX'*

813

equals twice the area of triangle *ACD*. So the area of the square on side *AC* equals the area of rectangle *ADXX′*. In the same way, you show that the area of the square on side *BC* equals the area of rectangle *BX′XE*. Finally, because the square on the side *AB* is equal to the sum of its parts (*ADXX′* and *BX′XE*), it is equal to the sum of the squares on the other two sides.

PYTHEAS, *PITH ee us*, was a Greek explorer who lived in the late 300's B.C. Pytheas slipped by a blockade set up by the Carthaginian navy at Gibraltar in order to explore the northern coasts of Europe. He sailed around Britain, and explored there. He heard stories of a mysterious land called Thule, which was probably Norway.

Pytheas was a great navigator. He knew that the north star is not directly above the North Pole. He also realized that the moon had something to do with ocean tides. Many Greek scientists doubted his honesty. However, later discoveries showed that he was telling the truth about the things he had seen. Pytheas was born in Massilia (now Marseilles, France).   THOMAS W. AFRICA

See also EXPLORATION AND DISCOVERY (Greeks).

PYTHIA. See DELPHI.

PYTHIAN GAMES, *PITH ih un*, were popular national contests held by the ancient Greeks. The festivals honored the god Apollo. They were held at Delphi, near Apollo's shrine. The games were named for the monstrous serpent Python, which, according to legend, Apollo killed with his arrows when he was five days old.

The early Pythian games were held every eight years, and were contests between singers. A new series was begun about 586 B.C. and continued until about A.D. 300. The games were celebrated every four years during this time. Athletic contests and horse racing were added to the song contests. Later, dramatists, historians, poets, and artists competed for honors. Laurel wreaths and palm branches were given as prizes. C. BRADFORD WELLES

See also DELPHI; PYTHON (myth).

PYTHIAS. See DAMON AND PYTHIAS.

PYTHIAS, KNIGHTS OF. See KNIGHTS OF PYTHIAS.

PYTHON, *PY thahn*, is a large snake that lives in southeastern Asia, the East Indies, Africa, and Australia. Some pythons are among the world's largest snakes. The *reticulate python* of southeastern Asia and the East Indies and the *African rock python* may grow 30 feet long. Only the giant anaconda of South America is longer. The *amethystine python* of Australia and the East Indies and the *Indian python* of southeastern Asia and the East Indies grow about 20 feet long.

Pythons are also called *constrictors* because they squeeze their prey to death. They wind themselves around the victim and tighten their coils. To kill their prey, they do not have to squeeze hard enough to break the victim's bones or to change its shape. They squeeze just enough to stop the victim's breathing and blood circulation. Large pythons usually eat small animals about the size of a house cat. But they may kill larger animals such as wild pigs that weigh about a hundred pounds. Pythons swallow their prey whole, without chewing. It may take a python several days to digest a large victim.

Pythons live in rugged tropical regions that have heavy rainfall and forests, or some type of low, dense growth. Almost all pythons swim and climb well.

Like most snakes, pythons hatch from eggs. The number of eggs in the nest varies greatly. Some may have about a hundred eggs. The female python coils about her eggs until they hatch. The Indian python *incubates* her eggs, or keeps them warm with heat from her body. Incubation, very unusual in snakes, helps the eggs hatch more quickly.

The large pythons have beautiful, tough skins that can be made into valuable leather. Hunting pythons is not considered dangerous because these snakes are not poisonous and they do not attack man.

Scientific Classification. Pythons belong to the python and boa family, *Boidae*. The reticulate python is classified as genus *Python*, species *P. reticulatus*. The African rock python is *P. sebae*, the Indian, *P. molurus*, and the amethystine, *P. amethystinus*.   CLIFFORD H. POPE

See also ANACONDA; BOA CONSTRICTOR; SNAKE (color picture: Reticulate Python).

PYTHON was the name of a serpent in Greek mythology. He attacked the people and cattle around Delphi. Apollo killed Python with his arrows. He gave the name of Python to his oracle at Delphi, and founded the Pythian games to celebrate his victory.   PADRAIC COLUM

See also DELPHI; PYTHIAN GAMES.

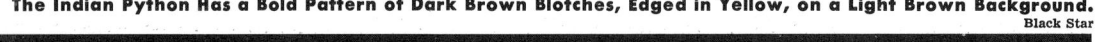

The Indian Python Has a Bold Pattern of Dark Brown Blotches, Edged in Yellow, on a Light Brown Background.
Black Star

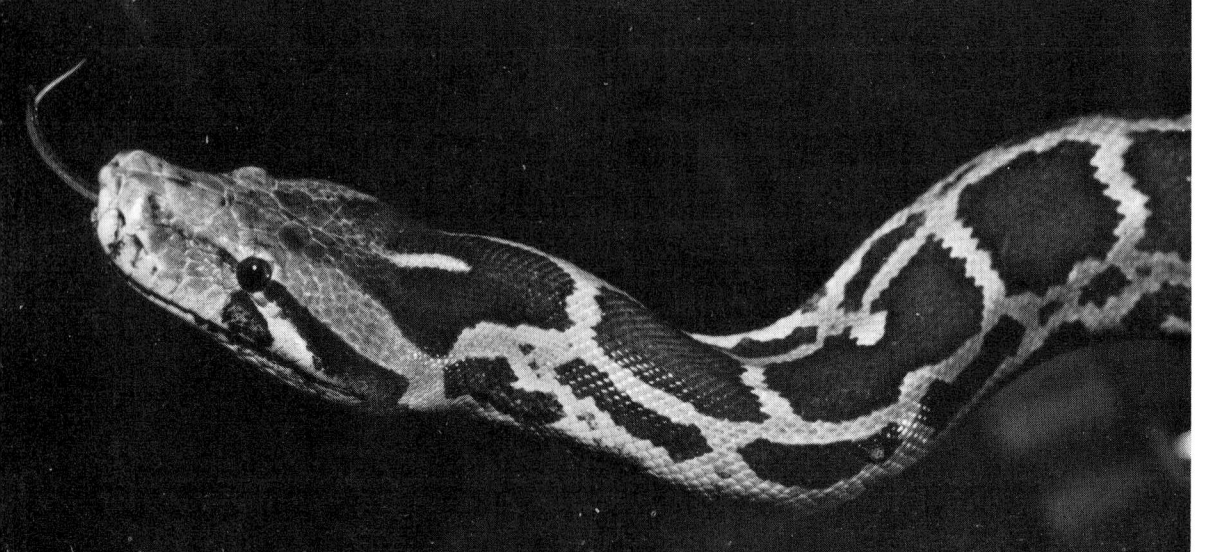